THE

BOOK of DAYS

A MISCELLANY

OF

POPULAR ANTIQUITIES

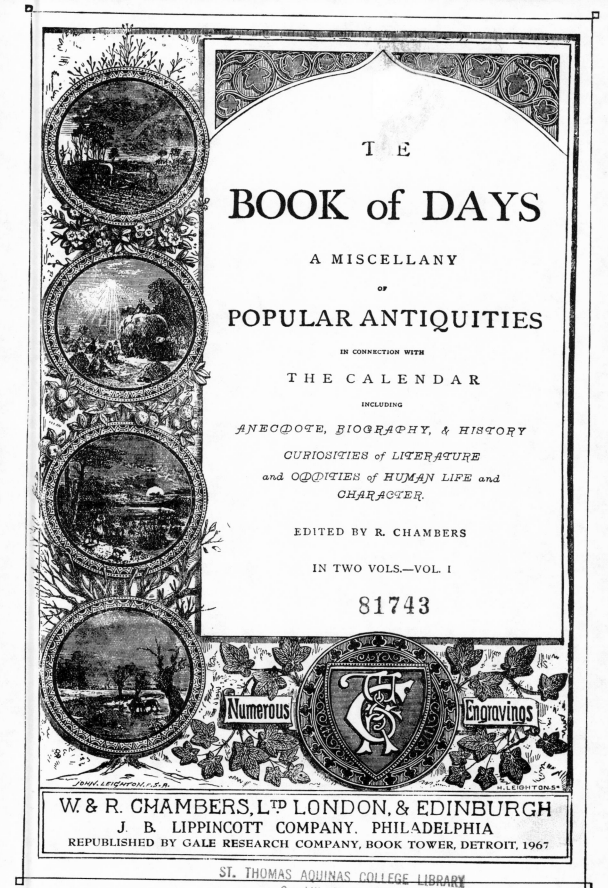

THE

BOOK of DAYS

A MISCELLANY

OF

POPULAR ANTIQUITIES

IN CONNECTION WITH

THE CALENDAR

INCLUDING

ANECDOTE, BIOGRAPHY, & HISTORY

CURIOSITIES of LITERATURE

and ODDITIES of HUMAN LIFE and

CHARACTER.

EDITED BY R. CHAMBERS

IN TWO VOLS.—VOL. I

81743

Numerous Engravings

JOHN. LEIGHTON. F.S.A.   H. LEIGHTON. S.

W. & R. CHAMBERS, Lᵀᴰ LONDON, & EDINBURGH
J. B. LIPPINCOTT COMPANY. PHILADELPHIA
REPUBLISHED BY GALE RESEARCH COMPANY, BOOK TOWER, DETROIT, 1967

ISBN 0-8103-3002-4

Library of Congress Catalog Card Number 67-13009

PREFACE

THE BOOK OF DAYS consists of—1. Matters connected with the Church Calendar, including the Popular Festivals, Saints' Days, and other Holidays, with illustrations of Christian Antiquities in general; 2. Phenomena connected with the Seasonal Changes; 3. Folk-Lore of the United Kingdom—namely, Popular Notions and Observances connected with Times and Seasons; 4. Notable Events, Biographies, and Anecdotes connected with the Days of the Year; 5. Articles of Popular Archæology, of an entertaining character, tending to illustrate the progress of Civilisation, Manners, Literature, and Ideas in these kingdoms; 6. Curious, Fugitive, and Inedited Pieces.

It has been the desire of the Editor—while not discouraging the progressive spirit of the age, to temper it with affectionate feelings towards what is poetical and elevated, honest and of good report, in the old national life; while in no way discountenancing great material interests, to evoke an equal activity in those feelings beyond self, on which depend remoter but infinitely greater interests; to kindle and sustain a spirit of patriotism tending to unity, peace, and prosperity in our own state, while not exclusive of feelings of benevolence as well as justice, towards others. It was desired that these volumes should be a repertory of old fireside ideas in general, as well as a means of improving the fireside wisdom of the present day.

List of Illustrations.

LIST OF ILLUSTRATIONS.

CORRIGENDA TO VOL. I.

Page 126: the article on the Legal Prosecutions of the Lower Animals, ought to have been placed in connection with St Anthony of Padua, under June 13.

TIME AND ITS NATURAL MEASURERS.

TIME is one of those things which cannot be defined. We only know or become sensible of it through certain processes of nature which require it for their being carried on and perfected, and towards which it may therefore be said to bear a relation. We only appreciate it as a fact in the universal frame of things, when we are enabled by these means to measure it. Thus, the rotation of the earth on its axis, the process by which we obtain the alternation of day and night, takes a certain space of time. This, multiplied by 366, gives the time required for the revolution of the earth around the sun, the process by which we enjoy the alternations of the seasons. The life of a well-constituted man will, under fair conditions, last during about seventy such spaces of time or years; very rarely to a hundred. The cluster of individuals termed a nation, or constituting a state, will pass through certain changes, inferring moral, social, and political improvement, in the course of still larger spaces of time; say several centuries: also certain processes of decay, requiring, perhaps, equal spaces of time. With such matters it is the province of history to deal; and actually from this source we learn pretty clearly what has been going on upon the surface of the earth during about four thousand years. We have also reason, however, to conclude, that our planet has existed for a prodigiously longer space of time than that. The sculptures of Egypt are held by scholars to imply that there was a political fabric of the monarchical kind in that country thirty-four centuries before the commencement of our present era. Rude weapons and implements of stone, flint, and bone, found interred in countries now occupied by civilised people, point, in like manner, to the existence of savage nations in those regions at a time long before the commencement of history. Geology, or the examination of the crust of the earth, still further prolongs our backward view of time. It shews that the earth has passed through a succession of physical changes, extending over a great series of ages; that during the same time vegetable and animal life underwent great changes; changes of one set of species for others; an advancement from invertebrate to vertebrate animals, from fishes to reptiles, from reptiles to birds and mammifers; of these man coming in the last. Thus it has happened that we could now give a biography of our little world, in which the four thousand years of written history would be multiplied many times over; and yet this vastly extended period must, after all, be regarded as but a point in that stretch of duration which we call time. All beyond, where related facts fail us—above all, a beginning or an end to time—are inconceivable; so entirely dependent is our idea of it upon measurement, or so purely, rather, may it be said to consist of measurement.

What we are more immediately concerned with at present is the YEAR, the space of time required for a revolution of the earth around the sun, being about one-seventieth of the ordinary duration of a healthy human life. It is a period very interesting to us in a natural point of view, because within it are included all seasonal changes, and of it nearly everything else in our experience of the appearances of the earth and sky is merely a repetition. Standing in this relation to us, the year has very reasonably become the unit of our ordinary reckonings of time when any larger space is concerned; above all, in the statement of the progress and completion of human life. An old man is said to die *full of years*. *His years have been few*, is the affecting expression we use regarding one who has died in youth. The *anniversary* of an event makes an appeal to our feelings. We also speak of the history of a nation as its *annals*—the transactions of its succession of years. There must have been a sense of the value and importance of the year as a space of time from a very early period in the history of humanity, for even the simplest and rudest people would be sensible of 'the seasons' difference,' and of the cycle which the seasons formed, and would soon begin, by observations of the rising of the stars, to ascertain roughly the space of time which that cycle occupied.

Striking, however, as the year is, and must always have been, to the senses of mankind, we can readily see that its value and character were not so liable to be appreciated as were those of the minor space of time during which the earth performed its rotation on its own axis. That space, within which the simple fathers of our

race saw light and darkness exchange possession of the earth—which gave themselves a waking and a sleeping time, and periodicised many others of their personal needs, powers, and sensations, as well as a vast variety of the obvious processes of external nature—must have impressed them as soon as reflection dawned in their minds; and the DAY, we may be very sure, therefore, was amongst the first of human ideas.

While thus obvious and thus important, the Day, to man's experience, is a space of time too frequently repeated, and amounting consequently to too large numbers, to be readily available in any sort of historic reckoning or reference. It is equally evident that, for such purposes, the year is a period too large to be in any great degree available, until mankind have advanced considerably in mental culture. We accordingly find that, amongst rude nations, the intermediate space of time marked by a revolution of the moon—the MONTH—has always been first employed for historical indications. This completes the series of natural periods or denominations of time, unless we are to agree with those who deem the *Week* to be also such, one determined by the observation of the principal aspects of the moon, as half in increase, full, half in decrease, and change, or simply by an arithmetical division of the month into four parts. All other denominations, as hours, minutes, &c., are unquestionably arbitrary, and some of them comparatively modern; in fact, deduced from clockwork, without which they could never have been measured or made sensible to us.

On Time.

Why sit'st thou by that ruined hall,
Thou aged carle, so stern and gray?
Dost thou its former pride recall,
Or ponder how it passed away?

Know'st thou not me? the Deep Voice cried.
So long enjoyed, so oft misused—
Alternate, in thy fickle pride,
Desired, neglected, and accused?

Before my breath, like blazing flax,
Man and his marvels pass away;
And changing empires wane and wax,
Are founded, flourish, and decay.

Redeem mine hours—the space is brief—
While in my glass the sand-grains shiver,
And measureless thy joy or grief,
When Time and thou shalt part for ever!

The Antiquary.

LONDON LEGEND OF THE CLOCK WHICH STRUCK THIRTEEN, AND SAVED A MAN'S LIFE.

There is a traditionary story very widely diffused over the country, to the effect that St Paul's clock on one occasion struck thirteen at midnight, with the extraordinary result of saving the life of a sentinel accused of sleeping at his post. It is not much less than half a century since the writer heard the tale related in a remote part of Scotland. In later times, the question has been put, Is there any historic basis for this tradition? followed by another still more pertinent, Is the alleged fact mechanically possible? and to both an affirmative answer has been given.

An obituary notice of John Hatfield, who died at his house in Glasshouse-yard, Aldersgate, on the 18th of June 1770, at the age of 102—which notice appeared in the *Public Advertiser* a few days afterwards—states that, when a soldier in the time of William and Mary, he was tried by a court-martial, on a charge of having fallen asleep when on duty upon the terrace at Windsor. It goes on to state—'He absolutely denied the charge against him, and solemnly declared [as a proof of his having been awake at the time], that he heard St Paul's clock strike thirteen, the truth of which was much doubted by the court because of the great distance. But while he was under sentence of death, an affidavit was made by several persons that the clock actually did strike thirteen instead of twelve; whereupon he received his majesty's pardon.' It is added, that a recital of these circumstances was engraved on the coffin-plate of the old soldier, 'to satisfy the world of the truth of a story which has been much doubted, though he had often confirmed it to many gentlemen, and a few days before his death told it to several of his acquaintances.'

An allusion to the story occurs in a poem styled A Trip to Windsor, one of a volume published in 1774 under the title of *Weeds of Parnassus, by Timothy Scribble:*

' The terrace walk we with surprise behold,
Of which the guides have oft the story told:
Hatfield, accused of sleeping on his post,
Heard Paul's bell sounding, or his life had lost.'

A correction, however, must here be applied—namely, that the clock which struck on this important occasion was Tom of Westminster, which was afterwards removed to St Paul's. It seems a long way for the sound to travel, and when we think of the noises which fill this bustling city even at midnight, the possibility of its being heard even in the suburbs seems faint. Yet we must recollect that London was a much quieter town a hundred and fifty years ago than now, and the fact that the tolling of St Paul's has often been heard at Windsor, is undoubted. There might, moreover, be a favourable state of the atmosphere.

As to the query, Is the striking of thirteen mechanically possible? a correspondent of the *Notes and Queries* has given it a satisfactory answer.* 'All striking clocks have two spindles for winding: one of these is for the *going* part, which turns the hands, and is connected with and regulated by the pendulum or balance-spring. Every time that the minute hand comes to twelve, it raises a catch connected with the *striking* part (which has been standing still for the previous sixty minutes), and the striking work then makes as many strokes on the bell (or spring gong) as the space between the notch which the catch has left and the next notch allows. When the catch falls into the next notch,

* Second Series, vii. 14.

it again stops the striking work till the minute hand reaches twelve again an hour afterwards. Now, if the catch be stiff, so as not to fall into the notch, or the notch be worn so as not to hold it, the clock will strike on till the catch does hold. . . . If a clock strike midnight and the succeeding hour together, there is thirteen at once, and very simply. . . . If the story of St Paul's clock be true, and it only happened once, it must have been from stiffness or some mechanical obstacles.'

In connection with the above London legend, it is worthy of remark that, on the morning of Thursday the 14th of March 1861, ' the inhabitants of the metropolis were roused by repeated strokes of the new great bell of Westminster, and most persons supposed it was for a death in the royal family. It proved, however, to be due to some derangement of the clock, for at four and five o'clock, ten or twelve strokes were struck instead of the proper number.' The gentleman who communicated this fact through the medium of the *Notes and Queries*, added: ' On mentioning this in the morning to a friend, who is deep in London antiquities, he observed that there is an opinion in the city that anything the matter with St Paul's great bell is an omen of ill to the royal family; and he added: "I hope the opinion will not extend to the Westminster bell." This was at 11 on Friday morning. I see this morning that it was not till 1 A.M. the lamented Duchess of Kent was considered in the least danger, and, as you are aware, she expired in less than twenty-four hours.'

DIFFERENCE BETWEEN A WATCH AND A CLOCK.

A watch differs from a clock in its having a vibrating wheel instead of a vibrating pendulum; and, as in a clock, gravity is always pulling the pendulum down to the bottom of its arc, which is its natural place of rest, but does not fix it there, because the momentum acquired during its fall from one side carries it up to an equal height on the other—so in a watch a spring, generally spiral, surrounding the axis of the balance-wheel, is always pulling this towards a middle position of rest, but does not fix it there, because the momentum acquired during its approach to the middle position from either side carries it just as far past on the other side, and the spring has to begin its work again. The balance-wheel at each vibration allows one tooth of the adjoining wheel to pass, as the pendulum does in a clock; and the record of the beats is preserved by the wheel which follows. A main-spring is used to keep up the motion of the watch, instead of the weight used in a clock; and as a spring acts equally well whatever be its position, a watch keeps time though carried in the pocket, or in a moving ship. In winding up a watch, one turn of the axle on which the key is fixed is rendered equivalent, by the train of wheels, to about 400 turns or beats of the balance-wheel; and thus the exertion, during a few seconds, of the hand which winds up, gives motion for twenty-four or thirty hours.—*Dr. Arnott.*

3

The Year.

The length of the year is strictly expressed by the space of time required for the revolution of the earth round the sun—namely, 365 days, 5 hours, 48 minutes, 49 seconds, and 7 tenths of a second, for to such a nicety has this time been ascertained. But for convenience in reckoning, it has been found necessary to make the year terminate with a day instead of a fraction of one, lumping the fractions together so as to make up a day among themselves. About forty-five years before Christ, Julius Cæsar, having, by the help of Sosigenes, an Alexandrian philosopher, come to a tolerably clear understanding of the length of the year, decreed that every fourth year should be held to consist of 366 days for the purpose of absorbing the odd hours. The arrangement he dictated was a rather clumsy one. A day in February, the sixth before the calends of March (*sextilis*), was to be repeated in that fourth year; and each fourth year was thus to be *bissextile*. It was as if we were to reckon the 23d of February twice over. Seeing that, in reality, a day every fourth year is too much by 11 minutes, 10 seconds, and 3 tenths of a second, it inevitably followed that the beginning of the year moved onward ahead of the point at which it was in the days of Cæsar; in other words, the natural time fell behind the reckoning. From the time of the Council of Nice, in 325, when the vernal equinox fell correctly on the 21st of March, Pope Gregory found in 1582 that there had been an over-reckoning to the extent of ten days, and now the vernal equinox fell on the 11th of March. To correct the past error, he decreed that the 5th of October that year should be reckoned as the 15th, and to keep the year right in future, the overplus being 18 hours, 37 minutes, and 10

seconds in a century, he ordered that every centurial year that could not be divided by 4, (1700, 1800, 1900, 2100, 2200, &c.) should *not* be bissextile, as it otherwise would be; thus, in short, dropping the extra day three times every four hundred years. The Gregorian style, as it was called, readily obtained sway in Catholic, but not in Protestant countries. It was not adopted in Britain till the year 1752, by which time the discrepancy between the Julian and Gregorian periods amounted to *eleven* days. An act of parliament was passed, dictating that the 3d of September that year should be reckoned the 14th, and that three of every four of the centurial years should, as in Pope Gregory's arrangement, not be bissextile or leap-years. It has consequently arisen—1800 not having been a leap-year—that the new and old styles now differ by *twelve* days, the 1st of January old style being the 13th of the month new style. In Russia and Greece the old style is still retained; wherefore it becomes necessary for one writing in these countries to any foreign correspondent, to set down his date thus: $\frac{12\text{th}}{24\text{th}}$ March, or $\frac{25\text{th September}}{7\text{th October}}$; or, it may be $\frac{28\text{th December 1880}}{9\text{th January 1881}}$.

'The old style is still retained in the accounts of Her Majesty's Treasury. This is why the Christmas dividends are not considered due till Twelfth Day, nor the midsummer dividends till the 5th of July; and in the same way it is not until the 5th of April that Lady Day is supposed to arrive. There is another piece of antiquity visible in the public accounts. In old times, the year was held to begin on the 25th of March, and this usage is also still observed in the computations over which the Chancellor of the Exchequer presides. The consequence is, that the first day of the financial year is the 5th of April, being old Lady Day, and with that day the reckonings of our annual budgets begin and end.' —*Times, February* 16, 1861.

The Day.

——There came the Day and Night,
Riding together both with equal pace;
The one on palfrey black, the other white;
But Night had covered her uncomely face
With a black veil, and held in hand a mace,
On top whereof the moon and stars were pight,
And sleep and darkness round about did trace:
But Day did bear upon his sceptre's height
The goodly sun encompassed with beames bright.
        Spenser.

The day of nature, being strictly the time required for one rotation of the earth on its axis,

is 23 hours, 56 minutes, 4 seconds, and 1 tenth of a second. In that time, a star comes round to appear in the same place where we had formerly seen it. But the earth, having an additional motion on its orbit round the sun, requires about 3 minutes, 56 seconds more, or 24 hours in all, to have the sun brought round to appear at the same place; in other words, for any place on the surface of the earth to come to the meridian. Thus arises the difference between a *sidereal* day and a *solar* day, between *apparent* and *mean* time, as will be more particularly explained elsewhere.

Fixing our attention for the present upon the solar day, or day of mean time, let us remark in the first place that, amongst the nations of antiquity, there were no divisions of the day beyond what were indicated by sun-rise and sun-set. Even among the Romans for many ages, the only point in the earth's daily revolution of which any public notice was taken was mid-day, which they used to announce by the sound of trumpet, whenever the sun was observed shining straight along between the Forum and a place called Græcostasis. To divide the day into a certain number of parts was, as has been remarked, an arbitrary arrangement, which only could be adopted when means had been invented of mechanically measuring time. We accordingly find no allusion to hours in the course of the Scriptural histories till we come to the Book of Daniel, who lived 552 years before Christ. 'Then Daniel, whose name was Belteshazzar, was astonished for *one hour*, and his thoughts troubled him.' The Jews and the Romans alike, on introducing a division of the day into twenty-four hours, assigned equal numbers to day and night, without regard to the varying length of these portions of the solar day; consequently, an hour was with them a varying quantity of time, according to the seasons and the latitude. Afterwards, the plan of an equal division was adopted, as was also that of dividing an hour into 60 minutes, and a minute into 60 seconds.

Before the hour division was adopted, men could only speak of such vague natural divisions as morning and evening, forenoon and afternoon, or make a reference to their meal-times. And these indications of time have still a certain hold upon us, partly because they are so natural and obvious, and partly through the effect of tradition. All before dinner is, with us, still morning—notwithstanding that the meal has nominally been postponed to an evening hour. The Scotch, long ago, had some terms of an original and poetical nature for certain periods of the day Besides the *dawin'* for the dawn, they spoke of the *skreigh o' day*, q. d., the cry of the coming day. Their term for the dusk, the *gloaming*, has been much admired, and is making its way into use in England.

Intimately connected with the day is the Week, a division of time which, whatever trace of a natural origin some may find in it, is certainly in a great measure arbitrary, since it does not consist in all countries of the same number of days. The week of Christian Europe, and of the Christian world generally, is, as is well known, a period of seven days, derived from the Jews, whose sacred scriptures represent it as a commemoration of the world having been created by God in six days, with one more on which he rested from his work, and which he therefore sanctified as a day of rest.

Of weeks there are 52, and one day over, in ordinary years, or two days over in leap-years; and hence the recurrence of a particular day of the month never falls in an immediately succeeding year on the same day of the week, but on one a day in advance in the one case, and two in the other. Every twenty-eight years, however, the days of the month and the days of the week once more coincide.

The week, with its terminal day among the Jews, and its initial day among the Christians, observed as a day of rest and of devotion, is to be regarded as in the main a religious institution. Considering, however, that the days have only various names within the range of one week, and that by this period many of the ordinary operations of life are determined and arranged, it must be deemed, independently of its connection with religion, a time-division of the highest importance.

While the Romans have directly given us the names of the months, we have immediately derived those of the days of the week from the Saxons. Both among the Romans, however, and the Saxons, the several days were dedicated to the chief national deities, and in the characters of these several sets of national deities there is, in nearly every instance, an obvious analogy and correspondence; so that the Roman names of the days have undergone little more than a translation in the Saxon and consequently English names. Thus, the first day of the week is *Sunnandaeg* with the Saxons; *Dies Solis* with the Romans. Monday is *Monan-daeg* with the Saxons; *Dies Lunæ* with the Romans. Tuesday is, among the Saxons, *Tues-daeg*—that is, Tuesco's Day—from Tuesco, a mythic person, supposed to have been the first warlike leader of the Teutonic nations: among the Romans it was *Dies Martis*, the day of Mars, their god of war. The fourth day of the week was, among the Saxons, *Woden's-daeg*, the day of Woden, or Oden, another mythical being of high warlike reputation among the northern nations, and the nearest in character to the Roman god of war. Amongst the Romans, however, this day was *Dies Mercurii*, Mercury's Day. The fifth day of the week, *Thors-daeg* of the Saxons, was dedicated to their god Thor, who, in his supremacy over other gods, and his attribute of the Thunderer, corresponds very exactly with Jupiter, whose day this was (*Dies Jovis*) among the Romans. Friday, dedicated to Venus among the Romans (*Dies Veneris*), was named by the Saxons, in honour of their corresponding deity (Friga), *Frigedaeg*. The last day of the week took its Roman name of *Dies Saturni*, and its Saxon appellative of *Seater-daeg*, respectively from deities who approach each other in character.

It may be remarked, that the modern German names of the days of the week correspond tolerably well with the ancient Saxon: *Sonntag*, Sunday; *Montag*, Monday; *Dienstag*, Tuesday; *Mittwoche*, mid-week day [this does not correspond, but Godenstag, which is less used, is Woden's Day]; *Donnerstag*, Thursday [this term, meaning the Thunderer's day, obviously corresponds with Thors-daeg]; *Freitag*, Friday; *Samstag* or *Sonnabend*, Saturday [the latter term means eve of Sunday]. The French names of the days of the week, on the other hand, as befits a language so largely framed on a Latin basis, are like those of ancient Rome: Dimanche [the Lord's Day], Lundi, Mardi, Mercrédi, Jeudi, Vendredi, Samedi.

With reference to the transference of honour

5

from Roman to Saxon deities in our names of the days of the week, a quaint poet of the last century thus expresses himself:

'The Sun still rules the week's initial day,
The Moon o'er Monday yet retains the sway;
But Tuesday, which to Mars was whilom given,
Is Tuesco's subject in the northern heaven;
And Woden hath the charge of Wednesday,
Which did belong of old to Mercury;
And Jove himself surrenders his own day
To Thor, a barbarous god of Saxon clay:
Friday, who under Venus once did wield
Love's balmy spells, must now to Frea yield;
While Saturn still holds fast his day, but loses
The Sabbath, which the central Sun abuses.
Just like the days do persons change their masters,
Those gods who them protect against disasters;
And souls which were to natal genii given,
Belong to guardian angels up in heaven:
And now each popish patron saint disgraces
The ancient local Genius's strong places.
Mutamus et mutamur—what's the odds
If men do sometimes change their plaything gods!
The final Jupiter will e'er remain
Unchanged, and always send us wind and rain,
And warmth and cold, and day and shady night,
Whose starry pole will shine with Cynthia's light:
Nor does it matter much, where Prudence reign,
What other gods their empire shall retain.'

THE DAY ABSOLUTE AND THE DAY PRACTICAL.

While the day absolute is readily seen to be measured by a single rotation of our globe on its axis, the day practical is a very different affair. Every meridian has its own practical day, differing from the practical day of every other meridian. That is to say, take any line of places extending between the poles; at the absolute moment of noon to them, it is midnight to the line of places on the antipodes, and some other hour of the day to each similar line of places between. Consequently, the denomination of a day—say the 1st of January—reigns over the earth during *two* of its rotations, or forty-eight hours. Another result is, that in a circumnavigation of the globe, you gain a day in reckoning by going eastward, and lose one by going westward—a fact that first was revealed to mankind at the conclusion of Magellan's voyage in September 1522, when the surviving mariners, finding themselves a day behind their countrymen, accused each other of sleeping or negligence, and thought such must have been the cause until the true one was explained.

The mariners of enlightened European nations, in pursuing their explorations some centuries ago, everywhere carried with them their own nominal day, without regard to the slide which it performed in absolute time by their easterly and westerly movements. As they went eastward, they found the expressed time always moving onward; as they moved westwards, they found it falling backwards. Where the two lines of exploration met, there, of course, it was certain that the nominal days of the two parties would come to a decided discrepancy. The meeting was between Asia and America, and accordingly in that part of the world, the day is (say) Thurs-

day in one place, and Wednesday in another not very far distant. Very oddly, the territory of Alaska, now belonging to the United States, having been first settled by Russians who had come from the west, while the rest was colonised by Europeans from the opposite direction, a different expression of the day prevails there; while, again, Manilla, in Asia, having been taken possession of by Spaniards coming from the east, differs from the day of our own East Indies. Thus the discrepancy overlaps a not inconsiderable space of the earth's surface.

It arises as a natural consequence of these facts, that throughout the earth there is not a simultaneous but a consecutive keeping of the Sabbath. 'The inhabitants of Great Britain at eight o'clock on Sabbath morning, may realise the idea that at that hour there is a general Sabbath over the earth from the furthest east to the furthest west. The Russians in America are finishing their latest *vespers*; the Christians in our own colony of British Columbia are commencing their earliest *matins*. Among Christians throughout the world, the Sabbath is more or less advanced, except at Manilla, where it is commenced at about four o'clock P.M. on our Sabbath. At the first institution of the Sabbath in the Garden of Eden, it was finished in the space of twenty-four hours; but now, since Christians are found in every meridian under the sun, the Sabbath, from its very commencement to its final close, extends to forty-eight, or rather to fifty-six hours, by taking the abnormal state of Manilla into account.'[*]

DAY AND NIGHT, AS CONNECTED WITH ANIMAL LIFE.

'Every animal, after a period of activity, becomes exhausted or fatigued, and a period of repose is necessary to recruit the weakened energies and qualify the system for renewed exertion. . . . . In the animals which are denominated *Diurnal*, including man, daylight is requisite for enabling them to provide their food, protection, and comfort, and to maintain that correspondence with one another which, in general, is requisite for the preservation of the social compact. Such animals rest during the night; and in order to guard the system from the influence of a cold connected with the descending branch of the curve,[†] and peculiarly injurious to an exhausted frame, they retire to places of shelter, or assume particular positions, until the rising sun restores the requisite warmth, and enables the renovated body to renew the ordinary labours of life.

'With the *Nocturnal* animals, on the other hand, the case is widely different. The daytime is the period of their repose; their eyes are

[*] John Husband, in *Notes and Queries*, 2nd Series, vii. 51.
[†] By the curve, the writer means a formula for expressing in one wavy line the rises and falls of the thermometer in the course of a certain space of time.

adapted for a scanty light, hearing and smelling co-operate, and the objects of their prey are most accessible. Even among diurnal animals, a cessation of labour frequently takes place during the day. Some retire to the shade; others seek for the coolness of a marsh or river, while many birds indulge in the pleasure of dusting themselves.

'*Crowing of the Cock.* The time-marking propensities of the common cock during the night-season have long been the subject of remark, and conjectures as to the cause very freely indulged in. The bird, in ordinary circumstances, begins to crow after midnight, and [he also crows] about daybreak, with usually one intermediate effort. It seems impossible to overlook the connection between the times of crowing and the minimum temperature of the night; nor can the latter be viewed apart from the state of the dew-point, or maximum degree of dampness. Other circumstances, however, exercise an influence, for it cannot be disputed that the times of crowing of different individuals are by no means similar, and that in certain states of the weather, especially before rain, the crowing is continued nearly all day.

'*Paroxysms of Disease.* The attendants on a sick-bed are well aware, that the objects of their anxiety experience, in ordinary circumstances, the greatest amount of suffering between midnight and daybreak, or the usual period of the crowing of the cock. If we contemplate a frame, at this period of the curve, weakened by disease, we shall see it exposed to a cold temperature against which it is ill qualified to contend. Nor is this all; for, while dry air accelerates evaporation, and usually induces a degree of chilliness on the skin, moist air never fails to produce the effect by its increased conducting power. The depressed temperature and the air approaching to saturation, at the lowest point of the curve, in their combined influences, act with painful energy, and require from an intelligent sick-nurse a due amount of counteracting arrangements.' —*Dr. John Fleming on the Temperature of the Seasons.* Edinburgh, 1852.

THE MONTHS.

Our arbitrary division of the year into twelve months, has manifestly taken its origin in the natural division determined by the moon's revolutions.

The month of nature, or lunar revolution, is strictly 29 days, 12 hours, 44 minutes, 3 seconds; and there are, of course, twelve such periods, and rather less than 11 days over, in a year. From an early period, there were efforts among some of the civilised nations to arrange the year in a division accordant with the revolutions of the moon; but they were all strangely irregular till Julius Cæsar reformed the Calendar, by establishing the system of three years of 365 followed by one (bissextile) of 366 days, and decreed that the latter should be divided as follows:

Januarius,	31	days.
Februarius,	30	„
Martius,	31	„
Aprilis,	30	„
Maius,	31	,
Junius,	30	„
Quintilis (altered to Julius),	31	„
Sextilis,	30	„
September,	31	„
October,	30	„
November,	31	„
December,	30	„
	366	„

The general idea of Cæsar was, that the months should consist of 31 and 30 days alternately; and this was effected in the bissextile or leap-year, consisting, as it did, of twelve times thirty with six over. In ordinary years, consisting of one day less, his arrangement gave 29 days to Februarius. Afterwards, his successor Augustus had the eighth of the series called after himself, and from vanity broke up the regularity of Cæsar's arrangement by taking another day from February to add to his own month, that it might not be shorter than July; a change which led to a shift of October and December for September and November as months of 31 days. In this arrangement, the year has since stood in all Christian countries.

The Roman names of the months, as settled by Augustus, have also been used in all Christian countries excepting Holland, where the following set of names prevails:

January,	Lauwmaand,	chilly month.
February,	Sprokelmaand,	vegetation month.
March,	Lentmaand,	spring month.
April,	Grasmaand,	grass month.
May,	Blowmaand,	flower month.
June,	Zomermaand,	summer month.
July,	Hooymaand,	hay month.
August,	Oostmaand,	harvest month.
September,	Herstmaand,	autumn month.
October,	Wynmaand,	wine month.
November,	Slagtmaand,	slaughter month.
December,	Wintermaand,	winter month.

'These characteristic names of the months are the remains of the ancient Gaulish titles, which were also used by our Anglo-Saxon ancestors.'—*Brady.**

Amidst the heats of the Revolution, the French Convention, in October 1793, adopted a set of names for the months, somewhat like that kept up in Holland, their year standing thus:

	French Months.	Signification.	English Months.
Autumn.	1. Vendémaire,	Vintage,	Sept. 22.
	2. Brumaire,	Foggy,	Oct. 22.
	3. Frimaire,	Frosty or Sleety,	Nov. 21.
Winter.	4. Nivose,	Snowy,	Dec. 21.
	5. Pluviose,	Rainy,	Jan. 20.
	6. Ventose,	Windy,	Feb. 19.
Spring.	7. Germinal,	Springing or Budding,	Mar. 21.
	8. Floréal,	Flowery,	Apr. 20.
	9. Prairial,	Hay Harvest,	May 20.
Summer.	10. Messidor,	Corn Harvest,	June 19.
	11. Thermidor,	Hot,	July 19.
	12. Fructidor,	Fruit,	Aug. 18.

* *Analysis of the Calendar.*

7

Five days at the end, corresponding to our 17th, 18th, 19th, 20th, and 21st of September, were supplementary, and named *sans-culottides*, in honour of the half-naked populace who took so prominent a part in the affairs of the Revolution. At the same time, to extinguish all traces of religion in the calendar, each month was divided into three decades, or periods of ten days, whereof the last was to be a holiday, the names of the days being merely expressive of numbers—Primidi, Duodi, Tredi, &c. And this arrangement was actually maintained for several years, with only this peculiarity, that many of the people preferred holding the Christian Sunday as a weekly holiday. The plan was ridiculed by an English wit in the following professed translation of the new French Calendar:

'Autumn—wheezy, sneezy, freezy.
Winter—slippy, drippy, nippy.
Spring—showery, flowery, bowery.
Summer—hoppy, croppy, poppy.'

'Thirty days hath September,
April, June, and November;
All the rest have thirty-one,
But February twenty-eight alone,
Except in leap-year, once in four,
When February has one day more.'

Sir Walter Scott, in conversation with a friend, adverted jocularly to 'that ancient and respectable, but unknown poet who had given us the invaluable formula, Thirty days hath September, &c.' It is truly a composition of considerable age, for it appears in a play entitled *The Return from Parnassus*, published in 1606, as well as in Winter's *Cambridge Almanac* for 1635.

From what has here been stated introductorily, the reader will be, in some measure, prepared to enter on a treatment of the individual days of the year. Knowing how the length of the year has been determined, how it has been divided into months, and how many days have been assigned to each of these minor periods, he will understand on what grounds men have proceeded in various seasonal observations, as well as in various civil and religious arrangements. He has seen the basis, in short, of both the Calendar and the Almanac.

THE CALENDAR—PRIMITIVE ALMANACS.

It was a custom in ancient Rome, one which came down from a very early period, to proclaim the first of the month, and affix a notice of its occurrence on a public place, that the people might be apprised of the religious festivals in which they would have to bear a part. From the Greek verb καλεω, I *call* or *proclaim*, this first of the month came to be styled the *Kalendæ* or Kalends, and *Fasti Calendares* became a name for the placard. Subsequently, by a very natural process of ideas, a book for accounts referring to days was called *Calendarium*, a calendar; and from this we have derived our word, applicable to an exposition of time arrangements generally.

At Pompeii there has been found an ancient calendar, cut upon a square block of marble, upon each side of which three months are registered in perpendicular columns, each headed by the proper sign of the zodiac. The information given is astronomical, agricultural, and religious. —*Lib. Ent. Knowl.*—*Pompeii*, vol. ii. pp. 287-8.

'The calendar, strictly speaking, refers to time in general—the almanac to only that portion of time which is comprehended in the annual revolution of the earth round the sun, and marking, by previous computation, numerous particulars of general interest and utility; religious feasts; public holidays; the days of the week, corresponding with those of the month; the increasing and decreasing length of the day; the variations between true and solar time; tables of the tides; the sun's passage through the zodiac; eclipses; conjunctions and other motions of the planets, &c., all calculated for that portion of duration comprehended within the year. . . The *calendar* denotes the *settled and national mode* of registering the course of time by the sun's progress: an *almanac* is a subsidiary manual formed out of that instrument. . . . . The etymology of the word *almanac* has been, perhaps, the subject of more dispute than that of any term admitted into our language. With the single exception of Verstegan, all our lexicographers derive the first syllable *al* from the article definite of the Arabic, which signifies *the;* but the roots of the remaining syllables are variously accounted for, some taking it from the Greek μανακος, a lunary circle; others from the Hebrew *manach*, to count; Johnson derives it from the Greek μην, a month; but why the first syllable should be in one language, which these authorities agree in, and the two last in any other language, it is not easy to comprehend. Whether, therefore, the Saxons originally took their term from the Arabic, either wholly or in part, Verstegan seems the most to be relied on. "They," he says, alluding to our ancient Saxon ancestors, "used to engrave upon certaine squared sticks, about a foot in length, or shorter, or longer as they pleased, the courses of the moones of the whole yeere, whereby they could alwaies certainely tell when the new moones, full moones, and changes should happen, as also their festivall daies; and such a carved stick they called an *al-mon-aght;* that is to say, al-mon-heed, to wit, the regard or observation of all the moones; and hence is derived the name of almanac." An instrument of this kind, of a very ancient date, is to be seen in St John's College at Cambridge, and there are still in the midland counties several remains of them.'—*Brady.**

The Clog Almanac.

The simple-minded, yet for his time intelligent and inquiring Dr Robert Plot, in his *Natural History of Staffordshire* (folio, 1686), gives an account of what he calls the *Clog Almanac*, which he found in popular use in that and other northern counties, but unknown further south, and which, from its being also used in Denmark, he conceived to

* *Analysis of the Calendar*, i. 143.

have come into England with our Danish invaders and settlers many centuries before. The clog bore the same relation to a printed almanac which the Exchequer tallies bore to a set of account books. It is a square stick of box, or any other hard wood, about eight inches long, fitted to be hung up in the family parlour for common reference, but sometimes carried as part of a walking-cane. Properly it was a perpetual almanac, designed mainly to shew the Sundays and other fixed holidays of the year, each person being content, for use of the instrument, to observe on what day the year actually began, as compared

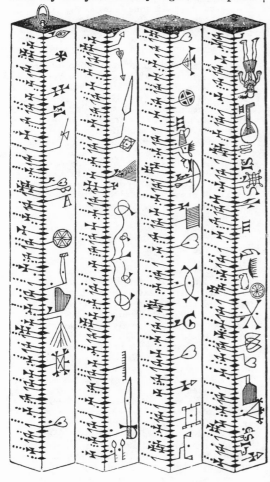

CLOG ALMANAC.

with that represented on the clog; so that, if they were various, a brief mental calculation of addition or subtraction was sufficient to enable him to attain what he desired to know.

The entire series of days constituting the year was represented by notches running along the angles of the square block, each side and angle thus presenting three months; the first day of a month was marked by a notch having a patulous stroke turned up from it, and each Sunday was dis-

tinguished by a notch somewhat broader than usual. There were indications—but they are not easily described—for the Golden Number and the cycle of the moon. The feasts were denoted by symbols resembling hieroglyphics, in a manner which will be best understood by examples. Thus, a peculiarly shaped emblem referred to the Circumcisio Domini on the 1st of January. From the notch on the 13th of that month proceeded a cross, as indicative of the episcopal rank of St Hilary : from that on the 25th, an axe for St Paul, such being the instrument of his martyrdom. Against St Valentine's Day was a true lover's knot, and against St David's Day (March 1), a harp, because the Welsh saint was accustomed on that instrument to praise God. The notch for the 2d of March (St Ceadda's Day) ended in a bough, indicating the hermit's life which Ceadda led in the woods near Lichfield. The 1st of May had a similar object with reference to the popular fête of *bringing home the May.* A rake on St Barnaby's Day (11th June) denoted hay harvest. St John the Baptist having been beheaded with a sword, his day (June 24) was graced with that implement. St Lawrence had his gridiron on the 10th of August, St Catherine her wheel on the 25th of the same month, and St Andrew his peculiar cross on the last of November. The 23d of November (St Clement's Day) was marked with a pot, in reference to the custom of going about that night begging drink to make merry with. For the Purification, Annunciation, and all other feasts of the Virgin, there was a heart, though 'what it should import, relating to Mary, unless because upon the shepherds' relation of their vision, Mary is said to have kept all these things and pondered them in her heart, I cannot imagine,' says our author. For Christmas there was a horn, 'the ancient vessel in which the Danes used to wassail or drink healths, signifying to us that this is the time we ought to make merry, *cornua exhaurienda notans,* as Wormius will have it.' The learned writer adds : 'The marks for the greater feasts observed in the church have a large point set in the middle of them, and another over against the preceding day, if vigils or fasts were observed before them.'

Written and Printed Almanacs.

The history of written almanacs has not been traced further back than the second century of the Christian era. All that is known is, that the Greeks of Alexandria, in or soon after the time of Ptolemy (100-150 A.D.), constructed almanacs ; and the evidence for this fact is an account of Theon the commentator on Ptolemy, in a manuscript found by Delambre at Paris, in which the method of arranging them is explained, and the materials necessary for them pointed out. The Greek astronomers were not astrologers. That pretended science appears to have been introduced into Europe from the East, where it has prevailed from time immemorial. Lalande, an assiduous inquirer after early astronomical works, has stated that the most ancient almanacs of which he could find any express mention were those of Solomon Jarchus, published about 1150. Petrus de Dacia,

THE BOOK OF DAYS.

about the year 1300, published an almanac, of which there is a manuscript copy in the Savilian Library at Oxford. In this almanac the influence of the planets is thus stated:

> 'Jupiter atque Venus boni, Saturnusque malignus;
> Sol et Mercurius cum Luna sunt mediocres.'

The 'homo signorum' (man of the signs), so common in later almanacs, is conjectured to have had its origin from Peter of Dacia.

During the middle ages, Oxford was the seat of British science, mixed as that science occasionally was with astrology, alchemy, and other kinds of false learning; and from Oxford the standard almanacs emanated; for instance, that of John Somers, written in 1380, of Nicolas de Lynna, published in 1386, and others.

An almanac for 1386 was printed as a literary curiosity in 1812. It is a small 8vo, and is thus introduced: '*Almanac for the Year* 1386. *Transcribed verbatim from the Original Antique Illuminated Manuscript in the Black Letter; omitting only the Monthly Calendars and some Tables. Containing many Curious Particulars illustrative of the Astronomy, Astrology, Chronology, History, Religious Tenets, and Theory and Practice of Medicine of the Age.* Printed for the Proprietor by C. Stower, Hackney, 1812. The Manuscript to be disposed of. Apply to the printer. Entered at Stationers' Hall.' The contents are—1. The Houses of the Planets and their Properties; 2. The Exposition of the Signs; 3. Chronicle of Events from the Birth of Cain; 4. To find the Prime Numbers; 5. Short Notes on Medicine; 6. On Blood-letting; 7. A Description of the Table of Signs and Movable Feasts; 8. Quantitates Diei Artificialis. Of the information given under the head, 'Exposycion of the Synes,' the following extract may serve as a specimen: 'Aquarius es a syne in the whilk the son es in Jan', and in that moneth are 7 plyos [pluviose] dayes, the 1, 2, 4, 5, 6, 15, 19, and if thoner is heard in that moneth, it betokens grete wynde, mykel fruite. and batel. Aquarius is hote, moyste, sanguyne, and of that ayre it es gode to byg castellis, or hous, or to wed.' The clumsy method of expressing numbers of more than two figures, shews that the Arabic notation had been but recently introduced, and was then imperfectly understood; for instance, 52mcc20 is put for 52.220.

Almanacs in manuscript of the fifteenth century are not uncommon. In the library at Lambeth Palace there is one dated 1460, at the end of which is a table of eclipses from 1460 to 1481. There is a very beautiful calendar in the library of the University of Cambridge, with the date of 1482.

The first almanac printed in Europe was probably the *Kalendarium Novum*, by Regiomontanus, calculated for the three years 1475, 1494, and 1513. It was published at Buda, in Hungary. Though it simply contained the eclipses and the places of the planets for the respective years, it was sold, it is said, for ten crowns of gold, and the whole impression was soon disposed of in Hungary, Germany, Italy, France, and England.

The first almanac known to have been printed in England was the *Sheapheards Kalendar*, translated from the French, and printed by Richard Pynson in 1497. It contains a large quantity of extraneous matter. As to the general influence of the celestial bodies, the reader is informed that

> 'Saturne is hyest and coldest, being full old,
> And Mars with his bluddy swerde ever ready to kyll.
> Sol and Luna is half good and half ill.'

Each month introduces itself with a description in verse. January may be given as an example:

> 'Called I am Januyere the colde.
> In Christmas season good fyre I love.
> Yonge Jesu, that sometime Judas solde,
> In me was circumcised for man's behove.
> Three kinges sought the sonne of God above;
> They kneeled downe, and dyd him homage, with love
> To God their Lorde that is mans own brother.'

Another very early printed almanac, of unusually small size, was exhibited to the Society of Antiquaries on the 16th of June 1842. Dr Bliss brought it with him from Oxford. It had been found by a friend of Dr Bliss at Edinburgh, in an old chest, and had been transmitted to him as a present to the Bodleian Library. Its dimensions were 2½ inches by 2 inches, and it consisted of fifteen leaves. The title in black letter, was *Almanacke for XII. Yere.* On the third leaf, 'Lately corrected and emprynted in the Fletestrete by Wynkyn de Worde. In the yere of the reyne of our most redoubted sovereayne Lorde Kinge Henry the VII.'

Almanacs became common on the continent before the end of the fifteenth century, but were not in general use in England till about the middle of the sixteenth. Skilful mathematicians were employed in constructing the astronomical part of the almanacs, but the astrologers supplied the supposed planetary influences and the predictions as to the weather and other interesting matters, which were required to render them attractive to the popular mind. The title-pages of two or three of these early almanacs will sufficiently indicate the nature of their contents.

A Prognossicacion and an Almanack fastened together, declaring the Dispocission of the People and also of the Wether, with certain Electyons and Tymes chosen both for Phisike and Surgerye, and for the husbandman. And also for Hawekyng, Huntyng, Fishyng, and Foulynge, according to the Science of Astronomy, made for the Yeare of our Lord God M.D.L., Calculated for the Merydyan of Yorke, and practiced by Anthony Askham. At the end, 'Imprynted at London, in Flete Strete, at the Signe of the George, next to Saynt Dunstan's Church, by Wyllyam Powell, cum privilegio ad imprimendum solum.' Then follows the Prognostication, the title-page to which is as follows: *A Prognossicacion for the Yere of our Lord M.CCCCC.L., Calculated upon the Merydyan of the Towne of Anwarpe and the Country thereabout, by Master Peter of Moorbeeke, Doctour in Physicke of the same Towne, whereunto is added the Judgment of M. Cornelius Schute, Doctour in Physicke of the Towne of Bruges in Flanders, upon and concerning the Disposicion, Estate, and Condicion of certaine Prynces, Contreys, and Regions, for the present Yere, gathered oute of his Prognossicacion for the same Yere. Translated*

10

oute of Duch into Englyshe by William Harrys. At the end, 'Imprynted at London by John Daye, dwellyne over Aldersgate, and Wyllyam Seres, dwellyne in Peter Colledge. These Bokes are to be sold at the Newe Shop by the Lytle Conduyte in Chepesyde.'

'*An Almanacke and Prognosticatyon for the Yeare of our Lorde MDLI., practysed by Simon Henringius and Lodowyke Boyard, Doctors in Physike and Astronomye, &c.* At Worcester in the Hygh Strete.'

'*A Newe Almanacke and Prognostication, Collected for the Yere of our Lord MDLVIII., wherein is expressed the Change and Full of the Moone, with their Quarters. The Varietie of the Ayre, and also of the Windes throughout the whole Yere, with Infortunate Times to Bie and Sell, take Medicine, Sowe, Plant, and Journey, &c. Made for the Meridian of Norwich and Pole Arcticke LII. Degrees, and serving for all England. By William Kenningham, Physician.* Imprynted at London by John Daye, dwelling over Aldersgate.'

Leonard Digges, a mathematician of some eminence, and the author of two or three practical treatises on geometry and mensuration, was also the author of a *Prognostication,* which was several times reprinted under his own superintendence, and that of his son, Thomas Digges.* It is not properly an almanac, but a sort of companion to the almanac, a collection of astrological materials, to be used by almanac-makers, or by the public generally. It is entitled '*A Prognostication everlasting of Right Good Effect, fructfully augmented by the Author, containing Plaine, Briefe, Pleasant, Chosen Rules to judge the Weather by the Sunne, Moon, Starres, Comets, Rainbow, Thunder, Clowdes, with other Extraordinary Tokens, not omitting the Aspects of Planets, with a Briefe Judgement for ever, of Plentie, Lacke, Sicknes, Dearth, Warres, &c., opening also many naturall causes worthie to be knowne. To these and other now at the last are joined divers generall pleasant Tables, with many compendious Rules, easie to be had in memorie, manifolde wayes profitable to all men of understanding.* Published by Leonard Digges. Lately Corrected and Augmented by Thomas Digges, his sonne. London, 1605.' The first edition was published in 1553; the second edition, in 1555, was 'fructfully augmented,' and was 'imprynted at London within the Blacke Fryars.' In his preface he thus discourses concerning the influence of the stars (the spelling modernised): 'What meteoroscoper, yea, who, learned in matters astronomical, noteth the great effects at the rising of the star called the Little Dog? Truly, the consent of the most learned do agree of his force. Yea, Pliny, in his *History of Nature,* affirms the seas to be then most fierce, wines to flow in cellars, standing waters to move, dogs inclined to madness. Further, these constellations rising—Orion, Arcturus, Corona—provoke tempestuous weather; the Kid and Goat, winds; Hyades, rain. What meteorologer consenteth not to the great alteration and mutation of air at the conjunction, opposition, or

* L. Digges's *Prognostication* was published 1553, 1555, 1556, 1567, 1576, 1578, 1605.

quadrant aspect of Saturn with either two lights? Who is ignorant, though poorly skilled in astronomy, that Jupiter, with Mercury or with the sun, enforces rage of winds? What is he that perceives not the fearful thunders, lightnings, and rains at the meeting of Mars and Venus, or Jupiter and Mars? Desist, for shame, to oppugn these judgments so strongly authorised. All truth, all experience, a multitude of infallible grounded rules, are against him.'

In France, a decree of Henry III., in 1579, forbade all makers of almanacs to prophesy, directly or indirectly, concerning affairs either of the state or of individuals. No such law was ever enacted in England. On the contrary, James I., allowing the liberty of prophesying to continue as before, granted a monopoly of the publication of almanacs to the two Universities and the Company of Stationers. The Universities, however, accepted an annuity from their colleagues, and relinquished any active exercise of their privilege. Under the patronage of the Stationers' Company, astrology continued to flourish.

Almanac-making, before this time, had become a profession, the members of which generally styled themselves Philomaths, by which they probably meant that they were fond of mathematical science; and the astrologers had formed themselves into a company, who had an annual dinner, which Ashmole, in his *Diary,* mentions having attended during several successive years. The Stationers' Company were not absolutely exclusive in their preference for astrological almanacs. Whilst they furnished an ample supply for the credulous, they were willing also to sell what would suit the taste of the sceptical; for Allstree's Almanac in 1624 calls the supposed influence of the planets and stars on the human body 'heathenish,' and dissuades from astrology in the following doggrel lines:

> 'Let every philomathy
> Leave lying astrology;
> And write true astronomy,
> And I'll bear you company.'

Thomas Decker, at a somewhat earlier period, evidently intending to ridicule the predictions of the almanac-makers, published *The Raven's Almanacke, foretelling of a Plague, Famine, and Civill Warr, that shall happen this present yere, 1609. With certaine Remedies, Rules and Receipts,* &c. It is dedicated 'To the Lyons of the Wood, to the Wilde Buckes of the Forrest, to the Harts of the Field, and to the whole country that are brought up wisely to prove Guls, and are born rich to dye Beggars.' By the Lyons, Buckes, and Harts, are meant the courtiers and gallants, or 'fast young men' of the time.

There was perhaps no period in which the prophetic almanacs were more eagerly purchased than during the civil wars of Charles I. and the parliament. The notorious William Lilly was one of the most influential of the astrologers and almanac-makers at that time, and in his autobiography not only exhibits a picture of himself little creditable to him, but furnishes portraits of several other almanac-makers of the seventeenth century, Dr Dee, Dr Forman, Booker, Winder, Kelly, Evans, &c. The character of

Sidrophel in *Hudibras* has been supposed to represent Lilly, but probably Butler merely meant to hold up to ridicule and scorn the class of persons of whom Lilly may be regarded as a type. He was evidently a crafty, time-serving knave, who made a good living out of the credulity of his countrymen. He was consulted as an astrologer about the affairs of the king, but afterwards, in 1645, when the royal cause began to decline, he became one of the parliamentary party. He was born in 1602, was educated at the grammar-school of Ashby-de-la-Zouch, came to London when he was about eighteen years of age, and spent the latter part of his life at Hersham, near Walton-on-Thames, where he died in 1681. In the chapter of his autobiography, *Of the Manner how I came to London*, he states that he was engaged as a servant in the house of Mr Gilbert Wright, who could neither read nor write, lived upon his annual rents, and was of no calling or profession. He states : 'My work was to go before my master to church ; to attend my master when he went abroad ; to make clean his shoes ; sweep the street ; help to drive bucks when he washed ; fetch water in a tub from the Thames (I have helped to carry eighteen tubs of water in one morning) ; weed the garden. All manner of drudgeries I performed, scraped trenchers,' &c. . . . . 'In 1644, I published *Merlinus Anglicus Junior* about April. In that year I published *Prophetical Merlin*, and had eight pounds for the copy.' Alluding to the comet which appeared in 1677, Lilly says : 'All comets signify wars, terrors, and strange events in the world.' He gives a curious explanation of the prophetic nature of these bodies : 'The spirits, well knowing what accidents shall come to pass, do form a star or comet, and give it what figure or shape they please, and cause its motion through the air, that people might behold it, and thence draw a signification of its events.' Further, a comet appearing in the sign Taurus portends 'mortality to the greater part of cattle, as horses, oxen, cows, &c.,' and also 'prodigious shipwrecks, damage in fisheries, monstrous floods, and destruction of fruit by caterpillars and other vermine.' Lilly, in his autobiography, appears on one occasion to have acted in one of the meanest of capacities. There is no doubt that he was employed as a spy ; but the chief source of income to Lilly, and to most of the other astrologers, was probably what was called casting nativities, and foretelling, or rather foreshadowing, the future events of the lives of individuals ; in fact, fortune-telling.

It has been mentioned before that the Stationers' Company had no objection to supply an almanac to the sceptics and scoffers who treated the celestial science with ridicule and contempt. Such an almanac was '*Poor Robin*, 1664: *an Almanack after a New Fashion, wherein the Reader may see (if he be not blinde) many Remarkable Things worthy of Observation, containing a Two-fold Kalender—viz., the Julian or English, and the Roundheads or Fanatics, with their several Saints' Daies, and Observations upon every Month*. Written by Poor Robin, Knight of the Burnt Island, a well-wisher to the Mathematics ; calculated for the Meridian of Saffron Walden, where the Pole is elevated 52 degrees and 6 minutes

above the Horizon. Printed for the Company of Stationers.'

Poor Robin has four lines of verse at the head of each of the odd pages of the Calendar. For instance, under January, we have

'Now blustering Boreas sends out of his quiver
Arrows of snow and hail, which makes men shiver ;
And though we hate sects and their vile partakers,
Yet those who want fires must now turn Quakers.'

As a specimen of his humour in prose, under January we are told that 'there will be much frost and cold weather in Greenland.' Under February, 'We may expect some showers of rain this month, or the next, or the next after that, or else we shall have a very dry spring.' *Poor Robin* first appeared in 1663. Robert Herrick, the poet, is said to have assisted in the compilation of the early numbers. It was not discontinued till 1828. The humour of the whole series was generally coarse, with little of originality, and a great deal of indecency.

In 1664, John Evelyn published his *Kalendarium Hortense*, the first Gardener's Almanac, containing directions for the employment of each month. This was dedicated to the poet Cowley, who acknowledged the compliment in one of his best pieces, entitled 'The Garden.' It was perhaps in this almanac that there appeared a sage counsel, to which Sir Walter Scott somewhere alludes, as being presented in an almanac of Charles II.'s time—namely, that every man ought for his health's sake to take a country walk of a mile, every morning before breakfast—'and, if possible, *let it be upon your own ground*.'

The next almanac-maker to whom the attention of the public was particularly directed was John Partridge, chiefly in consequence of Swift's pretended prophecy of his death. Partridge was born in 1644, and died in 1714. He was brought up to the trade of a shoemaker, which he practised in Covent Garden in 1680; but having acquired some knowledge of Latin, astronomy, and astrology, he at length published an almanac. Swift began his humorous attacks by *Predictions for the Year 1708, wherein the Month and the Day of the Month are set down, the Persons named, and the Great Actions and Events of Next Year particularly related as they will come to pass. Written to prevent the People of England from being further imposed upon by the Vulgar Almanac-makers.* After discussing with much gravity the subject of almanac-making, and censuring the almanac-makers for their methods of proceeding, he continues as follows : 'But now it is time to proceed to my predictions, which I have begun to calculate from the time the sun enters Aries, and this I take to be properly the beginning of the natural year. I pursue them to the time when he enters Libra, or somewhat more, which is the busy time of the year ; the remainder I have not yet adjusted,' &c. . . . 'My first prediction is but a trifle, yet I will mention it to shew how ignorant those sottish pretenders to astronomy are in their own concerns. It relates to Partridge the almanac-maker. I have consulted the star of his nativity by my own rules, and find he will infallibly die on the 29th of March next, about eleven at night, of a raging fever ; therefore, I advise him to consider of it, and settle his affairs in time.' Partridge, after the 29th of March, publicly denied that he had died, which increased the fun, and the game was kept up in *The Tatler*. Swift wrote *An Elegy on the Supposed Death of Partridge, the Almanac-maker,* followed by

'THE EPITAPH.

Here, five foot deep, lies on his back
A cobbler, starmonger, and quack,
Who to the stars, in pure good-will,
Does to his best look upward still.
Weep, all ye customers, that use
His pills, his almanacs, or shoes;
And you that did your fortunes seek,
Step to his grave but once a week.
This earth, which bears his body's print,
You 'll find has so much virtue in 't,
That I durst pawn my ears 'twill tell
Whate'er concerns you full as well
In physic, stolen goods, or love,
As he himself could when above.'

Partridge, having studied physic as well as astrology, in 1682 styled himself 'Physician to his Majesty,' and was one of the sworn physicians of the court, but never attended nor received any salary. His real epitaph, and a list of some of his works, are printed by Granger in his *Biographical History*. Partridge wrote a life of his contemporary almanac-maker, John Gadbury.

The *Vox Stellarum* of Francis Moore was the most successful of the predicting almanacs. There has been much doubt as to whether Francis Moore was a real person, or only a pseudonym. A communication to *Notes and Queries*, vol. iii. p. 466, states that 'Francis Moore, physician, was one of the many quack doctors who duped the credulous in the latter period of the seventeenth century. He practised in Westminster.* In all probability, then, as in our own time, the publication of an almanac was to act as an advertisement of his healing powers, &c. Cookson, Salmon, Gadbury, Andrews, Tanner, Coley, Partridge, &c., were all predecessors, and were students in physic and astrology. Moore's *Almanac* appears to be a perfect copy of Tanner's, which appeared in 1656, forty-two years prior to the appearance of Moore's. The portrait in Knight's *London* is certainly imaginary. There is a genuine and certainly very characteristic portrait, now of considerable rarity, representing him as a fat-faced man, in a wig and large neckcloth, inscribed "Francis Moore, born in Bridgenorth, in the county of Salop, the 29th of January 1656-7. John Drapentier, *delin. et sculp.*" Moore appears to have been succeeded as compiler of the *Almanac* by Mr Henry Andrews, who was born in 1744, and died at Royston, Herts, in 1820. "Andrews was astronomical calculator to the Board of Longitude, and for many years corresponded with Maskelyne

* Francis Moore, in his Almanac for 1711, dates 'from the Sign of the Old Lilly, near the Old Barge House, in Christ Church Parish, Southwark, July 19, 1710.' Then follows an advertisement in which he undertakes to cure diseases. Lysons mentions him as one of the remarkable men who, at different periods, resided at Lambeth, and says that his house was in Calcott's Alley, High Street, then called Back Lane, where he practised as astrologer, physician, and schoolmaster.

and other eminent men." '—*Notes and Queries*, vol. iv. p. 74. Mr Robert Cole, in a subsequent communication to *Notes and Queries*, vol. iv p. 162, states that he had purchased from Mr William Henry Andrews of Royston, son of Henry Andrews, the whole of the father's manuscripts, consisting of astronomical and astrological calculations, with a mass of very curious letters from persons desirous of having their nativities cast. Mr W. H. Andrews, in a letter addressed to Mr Cole, says: 'My father's calculations, &c., for Moore's *Almanac* continued during a period of forty-three years, and although, through his great talent and management, he increased the sale of that work from 100,000 to 500,000, yet, strange to say, all he received for his services was £25 per annum.'

The *Ladies' Diary*, one of the most respectable of the English almanacs of the eighteenth century, was commenced in 1704. Disclaiming astrology, prognostications, and quackery, the editor undertook to introduce the fair sex to the study of mathematics as a source of entertainment as well as instruction. Success was hardly to have been expected from such a speculation; but, by presenting mathematical questions as versified enigmas, with the answers in a similar form, by giving receipts for cookery and preserving, biographies of celebrated women, and other 'entertaining particulars peculiarly adapted for the use and diversion of the fair sex,' the success of the work was secured; so that, though the *Gentleman's Diary* was brought out in 1741 as a rival publication, the *Ladies' Diary* continued to circulate independently till 1841, when it was incorporated with the *Gentleman's Diary*. The projector and first editor of the *Ladies' Diary*, was John Tipper, a schoolmaster at Coventry.

In 1733, Benjamin Franklin published in the city of Philadelphia the first number of his almanac under the fictitious name of Richard Saunders. It was commonly called *Poor Richard's Almanac*, and was continued by Franklin about twenty-five years. It contained the usual astronomical information, 'besides many pleasant and witty verses, jests, and sayings.' The little spaces that occurred between the remarkable days of the calendar he filled with proverbial sentences inculcating industry and frugality. In 1757, he made a selection from these proverbial sentences, which he formed into a connected discourse, and prefixed to the almanac, as the address of a prudent old man to the people attending an auction. This discourse was afterwards published as a small tract, under the title of *The Way to Wealth*, and had an immense circulation in America and England. At the sale of the Ingraham Library, in Philadelphia, an original *Poor Richard's Almanac* sold for fifty-two dollars. —*Notes and Queries*, vol. xii. p. 143.

In 1775, the legal monopoly of the Stationers' Company was destroyed by a decision of the Court of Common Pleas, in the case of Thomas Carnan, a bookseller, who had invaded their exclusive right. Lord North, in 1779, brought in a bill to renew and legalise the Company's privilege, but, after an able argument by Erskine in favour of the public, the minister's bill was rejected. The defeated monopolists, however, still kept possession of the trade, by bribing their competitors, and by their influence over the book-market. In 1828, *The British Almanac* of the Society for the Diffusion of Useful Knowledge was published, and in the course of a few years the astrological portions disappeared from the other almanacs. Several new ones, containing valuable information, have since been presented to the public. But the measure which led to the improvement and great increase of almanacs, was the entire repeal of the stamp-duties thereon, by 3 and 4 Will. IV. c. 37, 13th August 1834. Hitherto, the stamp-duty upon each Moore's Almanac was 15*d*.

In a letter from Robert Heath, of Upnor Castle, date about 1753, the sheet almanac of the Stationers' Company is stated to sell ' 175,000, and they give three guineas for the copy; Moore's sells 75,000, and they give five guineas for the copy; the *Lady* sells above 30,000, and they give ten guineas, the most copy-money of any other. The *Gentleman's* copy is three guineas, sells 7000. Here are a fine company to write for.' In 1751, he describes White, who computes an ephemeris for the Stationers' Company, as living at Grantham, in Lincolnshire.

The Stationers' Company present annually to the Archbishop of Canterbury copies of their almanacs, which custom originated as follows: When Tenison was archbishop, a near relation of his, who was master of the Stationers' Company, thought it a compliment to call at Lambeth Palace in the Company's stately barge, on the morning of Lord Mayor's Day, when the archbishop sent out a pint of wine for each liveryman, with bread and cheese and hot-spiced ale for the watermen and attendants; and this grew into a settled custom; the Stationers' Company acknowledging the hospitality by presenting to the archbishop a copy of the several almanacs which they publish. The wine was served in small two-handled wooden bowls, or small cups, which were provided yearly by the Company. But since the abolition of the procession by water on Lord Mayor's Day, this custom has been discontinued.

Southey, in the *Doctor*, relates the following legal anecdote, to exemplify how necessary it is upon any important occasion to scrutinise the accuracy of a statement before it is taken on trust. A fellow was tried at the Old Bailey for highway robbery, and the prosecutor swore positively to him, saying he had seen his face distinctly, for it was a bright moonlight night. The counsel for the prisoner cross-questioned the man so as to make him repeat that assertion, and insist upon it. He then affirmed that this was a most important circumstance, and a most fortunate one for the prisoner at the bar: because the night on which the alleged robbery was said to have been committed was one in which there had been no moon: it was then during the dark quarter! In proof of this he handed an almanac to the bench, and the prisoner was acquitted accordingly. The prosecutor, however, had stated everything truly; and it was known afterwards that the almanac with which the counsel came provided, had been prepared and printed for the occasion.

14

The same writer remembers when a countryman had walked to the nearest large town, thirty miles distant, for the express purpose of seeing an almanac, the first that had been heard of in those parts. His inquiring neighbours crowded round the man on his return. ' Well, well,' said he, ' I know not; it maffles and talks. But all I could make out is, that Collop Monday falls on a Tuesday next year.'

THE RIDDLE OF THE YEAR.

There is a father with twice six sons; these sons have thirty daughters a piece, party-coloured, having one cheek white and the other black, who never see each other's face, nor live above twenty-four hours.

IMPROVEMENT OF SMALL PORTIONS OF TIME.

Among those who have contributed to the advancement of learning, many have risen to eminence in opposition to all the obstacles which external circumstances could place in their way, amidst the tumults of business, the distresses of poverty, or the dissipation of a wandering and unsettled state. A great part of the life of Erasmus was one continued peregrination: ill supplied with the gifts of fortune, and led from city to city, and from kingdom to kingdom, by the hopes of patrons and preferment—hopes which always flattered and always deceived him—he yet found means, by unshaken constancy and a vigilant improvement of those hours which, in the midst of the most restless activity, will remain unengaged, to write more than another in the same condition could have hoped to read. Compelled by want to attendance and solicitation, and so much versed in common life that he has transmitted to us the most perfect delineation of the manners of his age, he joined to his knowledge of the world such application to books, that he will stand for ever in the first rank of literary heroes. Now, this proficiency he sufficiently discovers by informing us that the *Praise of Folly*, one of his most celebrated performances, was composed by him on the road to Italy, lest the hours which he was obliged to spend on horseback should be tattled away, without regard to literature.—*Johnson.*

The Chancellor D'Aguesseau, finding that his wife always kept him waiting a quarter of an hour after the dinner-bell had rung, resolved to devote the time to writing a book on jurisprudence, and, putting the project in execution, in course of time produced a work in four quarto volumes.

Many persons thoughtlessly waste their own time simultaneously with that of others. Lord Sandwich, when he presided at the Board of Admiralty, paid no attention to any memorial that extended beyond a single page. 'If any man,' he said, ' will draw up his case, and will put his name to the bottom of the first page, I will give him an immediate reply; where he compels me to turn over the page, he must wait my pleasure.'

JOHN L. LEIGHTON

JANUARY

——— came old January, wrapped well
In many weeds to keep the cold away;
Yet did he quake and quiver like to quell,
And blowe his nayles to warm them if he may;
For they were numbed with holding all the day
An hatchet keene, with which he felled wood,
And from the trees did lop the needlesse spray;
Upon an huge great Earth-pot Steane he stood,
From whose wide mouth there flowed forth the Romane flood.

SPENSER.

(DESCRIPTIVE.)

JANUARY is the open gate of the year, shut until the shortest day passed, but now open to let in the lengthening daylight, which will soon fall upon dim patches of pale green, that shew where spring is still sleeping. Sometimes between the hoary pillars—when the winter is mild—a few wan snowdrops will peep out and catch the faint sunlight which streams in coldly through the opening gateway, like timid messengers sent to see if spring has yet stirred from her long sleep. But it is yet too early for the hardy crocus to throw its banded gold along the pathway; and as for the 'rathe primrose,' it sits huddled up in its little cloak of green, or is seen peeping through its half-closed yellow eye, as if watching the snow-flakes as they fall. Only the red-breasted robin —his heart filled with hope—sings his cheerful song on the naked hawthorn spray, through which the tiny buds are striving to break forth, like a

15

herald proclaiming glad tidings, and making known, far and wide, that erelong 'the winter will be over and gone,' and the moonlight-coloured May-blossoms once again appear.

All around, as yet, the landscape is barren and dreary. In the early morning, the withered sedge by the water-courses is silvered over with hoary rime; and if you handle the frosted flag-rushes, they seem to cut like swords. Huddled up like balls of feathers, the fieldfares sit in the leafless hedges, as if they had no heart to breakfast off the few hard, black, withered berries which still dangle in the wintry wind. Amid the cold frozen turnips, the hungry sheep look up and bleat pitifully; and if the cry of an early lamb falls on your ear, it makes the heart sorrowful only to listen to it. You pass the village churchyard, and almost shiver to think that the very dead who lie there must be pierced by the cold, for there is not even a crimson hip or haw to give a look of warmth to the stark hedges, through which the bleak wind whistles. Around the frozen pond the cattle assemble, lowing every now and then, as if impatient, and looking backward for the coming of the herdsman to break the ice. Even the nose of cherry-cheeked Patty looks blue, as she issues from the snow-covered cowshed with the smoking milk-pail on her head. There is no sound of the voices of village children in the winding lanes—nothing but the creaking of the old carrier's cart along the frost-bound road, and you pity the old wife who sits peeping out between the opening of the tilt, on her way to the neighbouring market-town. The very dog walks under the cart in silence, as if to avail himself of the little shelter it affords, instead of frisking and barking beside his master, as he does when 'the leaves are green and long.' There is a dull, leaden look about the sky, and you have no wish to climb the hill-top on which those gray clouds hang gloomily. You feel sorry for the poor donkey that stands hanging his head under the guide-post, and wish there were flies about to make him whisk his ears, and not leave him altogether motionless. The 'Jolly Farmer' swings on his creaking sign before the road-side alehouse, like the bones of a murderer in his gibbet-irons; and instead of entering the house, you hurry past the closed door, resolved to warm yourself by walking quicker, for you think a glass of ale must be but cold drink on such a morning. The old ostler seems bent double through cold, as he stands with his hands in his pockets, and his pitchfork thrust into the smoking manure-heap that litters the stable-yard.

A walk in the country on a fine frosty morning in January gives the blood a healthy circulation, and sets a man wondering why so many sit 'croodleing' over the fire at such a season. The trees, covered with hoar-frost, are beautiful to look upon, and the grass bending beneath its weight seems laden with crystal; while in the distance the hedges seem sheeted with May blossoms, so thickly, that you might fancy there was not room enough for a green leaf to peep out between the bloom. Sometimes a freezing shower comes down, and that is not quite so pleasant to be out in, for in a few moments everything around is covered with ice—the boughs seem as if cased in glass, the plumage of birds is stiffened by it, and they have to give their wings a brisk shaking before they are able to fly; as for a bunch of red holly-berries, could they but retain their icy covering, they would make the prettiest ornaments that could be placed on a mantel-piece. This is the time of year to see the beautiful ramification of the trees, for the branches are no longer hidden by leaves, and all the interlacings and crossings of exquisite network are visible—those pencilling of the sprays which too few of our artists study. Looking nearer at the hedges, we already see the tiny buds forming, mere specks on the stem, that do but little more than raise the bark; yet by the aid of a glass we can uncoil the future leaves which summer weaves in her loom into broad green curtains. The snails are asleep; they have glued up the doorways of their moveable habitations; and you may see a dozen of their houses fastened together if you probe among the dead leaves under the hedges with your walking-stick; while the worms have delved deep down into the earth, beyond the reach of the frost, and thither the mole has followed them, for he has not much choice of food in severe frosty weather. The woodman looks cold, though he wears his thick hedging gloves, for at this season he clears the thick underwood, and weaves into hurdles the smooth hazel-wands, or any long limber twigs that form the low thicket beneath the trees. He knows where the primroses are peeping out, and can tell of little bowery and sheltered hollows, where the wood-violets will erelong appear. The ditcher looks as thoughtful as a man digging his own grave, and takes no heed of the pretty robin that is piping its winter song on the withered gorse bushes with which he has just stopped up a gap in the hedge. Poor fellow, it is hard work for him, for the ground rings like iron when he strikes it with his spade, yet you would rather be the ditcher than the old man you passed a while ago, sitting on a pad of straw and breaking stones by the wayside, looking as if his legs were frozen. That was the golden-crested wren which darted across the road, and though the very smallest of our British birds, it never leaves us, no matter how severe the winter may be, but may be seen among the fir-trees, or pecking about where the holly and ivy are still green. If there is a spring-head or water-course unfrozen, there you are pretty sure to meet with the wag-tail—the smallest of all our walking birds, for he marches along like a soldier, instead of jumping, as if tied up in a sack, as most of our birds do when on the ground. Now the blue titmouse may be seen hanging by his claws, with his back downward, hunting for insects in some decaying bough, or peeping about the thatched eaves of the cottages and outhouses, where it will pull out the straw to stir up the insects that lie snug within the thatch. In the hollows of trees, caverns, old buildings, and dark out-of-the-way places, the bats hibernate, holding on by their claws, while asleep, head downwards, one over another, dozens together, there to await the coming of spring, along with the insects which will then come out of their hiding-places.

But unsightly as the bat appears to some eyes, there is no cleaner animal living, in spite of all our poets have written against it; for it makes a brush of its droll-looking little head, which it pokes under its umbrella-like wings, not leaving a cranny unswept, and parts its hair as carefully as a ringletted beauty. As for the insects it feeds upon, they are now in a state of torpor; most of the butterflies and moths are dead; those summer beauties that used to sit like folded pea-blossoms swinging on the flowers, have secured their eggs from the cold, to be hatched when the primrose-coloured sky of spring throws its warm light over the landscape. None of our clever warehouse packers can do their work so neatly as these insects; for, after laying their eggs in beautiful and regular order, they fill up the interstices with a gum that hardens like glue, and protects them in the severest weather. Those who wish for a good crop of fruit now hunt among the naked branches for these eggs, which are easily found through the dead leaves, to which they adhere; when these are destroyed, there is no fear of young grubs gnawing and piercing the bloom, nor can there be a better time to hunt for these destroyers of melting plums and juicy apples than in January. No doubt, the soft-billed birds that remain with us all the year round devour myriads of these eggs, and they serve to eke out the scanty subsistence these hardy choristers find strewn so sparingly in severe winters. How these birds manage to live through the killing frosts has long been a puzzle to our ablest naturalists, and after all their research, He alone knoweth without whose permission not a sparrow falls to the ground.

There is no better time than during a walk in January to get a good view of the mosses that grow on and around the trees, for at this season they stand boldly out in all their beautiful colourings, falling on the eye in masses of rich red, silver-gray, umbered brown, and gaudy orange; while the yellow moss is almost as dazzling as sunshine, and the green the most beautiful that gladdens the earth. In some places, we see it fitted together like exquisite mosaic work, in others it hangs down like graceful fringe, while the green looks like fairy trees, springing from a cushion of yielding satin. The screw moss is very curiously formed; it grows plentifully on old walls, and looks like dark-green flossy velvet. Now, if closely examined, a number of slender stems will be found springing from this soft bed, crowned with what botanists call the fruit. On this is a cap, just like that found on the unblown and well-known eschscholtzia; when this extinguisher-shaped cap is thrown off (it may be lifted off) a beautiful tuft of twisted hairs will be found beneath, compressed at the neck, and forming just such a brush as one can imagine the fairies use to sweep out the pollen from the flowers. Place this beautiful moss in water, and this brush will uncoil itself, if left above the surface, and release the seed within. Another of the scale mosses is equally curious, and if brought into a warm room, with a drop of water applied to the seed-vessel, it will burst open and throw out a little puff of dust; and this dust, when examined by a powerful glass, will be found to consist of links of little chains, not unlike the spring of a watch. But the most beautiful of all is the 'siller' cup moss, the silvery cup of which

is shaped like a nest—while the sporules inside look like eggs—such as a bird no larger than a gnat might build to breed in. This moss is commonly found on decayed wood. Sometimes, while hunting for curious mosses, at the stems of aged trees, we have aroused the little dormouse from his wintry sleep, as he lay coiled up, like a ball, in his snug burrow, where his store of provision was hoarded; for, unlike the fabled ant, he does lay in a stock for this dark season, which the ant does not.

Snow in the streets is very different from snow in the country, for there it no sooner falls than it begins to make more dirt, and is at once trampled into mud by a thousand passing feet on the pavement, while in the roadway the horses and vehicles work it into 'slush,' which only a brisk shower of rain can clear away. In the country snow is really white; there is none of that gray dirty look about it, which is seen in localities that neighbour upon town, but it lies on the fields, as Milton says, like

' A wintry veil of maiden white.'

The embankments look like stately terraces formed of the purest marble, and the hills in the distance are scarcely distinguishable from the fleecy clouds that crown their summits; while the wild open moors and hedgeless commons look like a sea of foam, whose waves were suddenly frozen into ridgy rest, the buried bushes only shewing like loftier crests. Vehicles pass along the scarcely distinguishable road with a strange, dull, muffled sound, like objects moving before the eye in a dream, so much do we miss the gritty and grinding noise which the wheels make in the dust of summer. What a different aspect the landscape presents when viewed from some neighbouring eminence! But for a few prominent landmarks, we should hardly know it was the same scene that we looked upon in summer; where the hedges then stretched like green walls across the country, we see but whitened barriers; for the only dark object that now catches the eye is the river that goes rolling between its powdered banks. The appearance of the village, too, is altered; the picturesque thatched roofs of the cottages have vanished, and but for the smoke that curls above the scene, you might fancy that all the inhabitants had fled, for neither flocks nor herds are seen or heard bleating and lowing from the fields, and all out-of-door employment has ceased. You hear the ringing of the blacksmith's hammer, and as you return when the day darkens, will see the light of his forge fall with a crimson glare across the snow-covered road. Even the striking of the church clock falls upon the ear with a deadened sound, and the report of the sportsman's gun dies away as soon as heard, leaving no prolonged echo behind.

While watching the snow fall, you can almost fancy that the flakes are white blossoms shaken from a land of flowers that lies somewhere above the sky; those that touch the river are gone in an instant, while some, as they fall slantways, unite together before they touch the earth. Science has seized upon and pictured the fantastic shapes the falling snow-flakes assume, and they are 'beautiful exceedingly.' Not less so is frost-work, which may be seen without stirring abroad on the window-panes; what a mingling of fern leaves and foliage of every shape, rare network and elfin embroidery, does this silent worker place before the eye, such as no pattern-drawer ever yet seized upon, although

'A thing of beauty is a joy for ever.'—*Keats.*

The farmer must attend to his cattle during this 'dead season,' for they require feeding early and late; and it is his business to put all the meat he can on their backs, so that they may weigh heavy, and realise a good price in the market. For this purpose, he must be active in cutting swedes and mangel-wurzel. Without this care, the farmer cannot keep pace with his neighbours. He gets rid of his saleable stock as soon as he can; he says, he 'likes to see fresh faces in his fields.' It is a pleasant sight to see the well-fed, clean-looking cattle in the straw-yard, or sniffing about the great barn-doors, where the thresher is at work, waiting for the straw he will throw out. It is a marvel that the poultry escape from those great heavy hoofs; as for a game-cock, he will make a dash at the head of an ox, as if he cared not a straw for his horns; and as for sucking pigs, they are farrowed to be killed.

The teams are also now busy taking the farm produce to market, for this is the season when corn, hay, and straw realise a good price; and a wagon piled high with clean white turnips, or laden with greens or carrots, has a pleasant look moving through the wintry landscape, as it conjures up before the hungry pedestrian visions of boiled beef and mutton, which a walk in frosty weather gives a hearty man a good appetite to enjoy. Manure can also be carted better to the fields during a frost than at any other time, for the ground is hard, and the wheels make but little impression on rough fallow lands. Let a thaw come, and few persons, unless they have lived in the country, can know the state of the roads that lead to some of our out-of-the-way villages in the clayey districts. A foot-passenger, to get on at all, must scramble through some gap in the hedge, and make his way by trespassing on the fields. In the lane, the horses are knee-deep in mire every step they take; and as for the wain, it is nearly buried up to the axles in places where the water has lodged. In vain does the wagoner keep whipping or patting his strong well-fed horses, or clapping his broad shoulder to the miry wheels: all is of no avail; he must either go home for more horses, or bring half-a-dozen men from the farm to dig out his wagon. It's of no use grumbling, for perhaps his master is one of the surveyors of the highways.

The gorse, furze, whin, or 'fuzz'—country people sometimes calling it by the last name—is often in flower all the year round, though the great golden-bellied baskets it hangs out in summer are now nearly closed, and of a pale yellowish green. Although its spikes are as sharp as spears, and there is no cutting out a golden branch without wearing thick gloves, still it is one of the most beautiful of our wayside shrubs, and we hardly wonder at Linnæus falling on his knees in admiration the first time he saw it. Many a time have

we cut a branch in January, put it in water, and placed it in a warm room, when in two or three days all its golden lamps have lighted up, and where it stood it seemed to 'make sunshine in the shady place.'

Where gorse grows abundantly, and bees have ready access to the bloom, there the finest-coloured and sweetest honey is produced. In a very mild season, we have seen, under sheltered hedges that face the south, the celandine in flower in January. Even when not in bloom, its large bright green leaves give a spring look to the barren embankments; but when out, its clear yellow star-shaped flowers catch the eye sooner than the primrose, through their deep golden hue. Country children call it the hedge buttercup, and their little hearts leap with delight when they see it springing up from among the dead leaves of winter. The common red or dead nettle may also occasionally be found in flower. Let those who would throw it aside as an unsightly weed, examine the bloom through a glass, and they will be amazed at its extreme loveliness; such ruby tints as it shews, imbedded in the softest bloom, never graced the rounded arm of beauty. The blue periwinkle is another beautiful flower that diadems the brow of January when the season is warm. It must be looked for in sheltered situations, for it is not at all a common wild-flower: once seen, it can never be mistaken, for the twisted bud before opening resembles the blue convolvulus. Nor must the common chickweed be overlooked, with its chaste white star-shaped flowers, which shew as early as the snowdrops. The large broad-leaved mouse-ear chickweed flowers later, and will be sought for in vain in January, though it sheds its seed and flowers frequently six times during the summer. Many other flowers we might name, though they are more likely to be found in bloom next month.

Many rare birds visit us occasionally in winter, which never make their appearance on our island at any other season. Some are only seen once now and then in the course of several years, and how they find their way hither at all, so far from their natural haunts, is somewhat of a mystery. Many birds come late in the autumn, and take their departure early in spring. Others remain with us all the year round, as the thrush and blackbird, which often commence singing in January. Wrens, larks, and many other small birds never leave our country. Flocks of wild-geese and other water-fowl, also visit our reedy marshes and sheltered lakes in winter; far up the sky their wild cries may be heard in the silence of midnight, as they arrive. Rooks now return from the neighbouring woods, where they have mostly wintered, to their nest-trees; while the smaller birds, which drew near to our habitation during the depth of winter, begin to disappear. Those that require insect food, go and forage among the grass and bushes; others retreat to the sides of stagnant pools, where, during the brief intervals of sunshine, gnats are now found. Others hunt in old walls, or among decayed trees, where insects are hidden in a dormant state, or are snugly ensconced in their warm cocoons, awaiting the first warm touch of spring, when, in the words of Solomon, 'the flowers appear on the earth . . . . and the voice of the turtle is heard in our land.'

HISTORY OF JANUARY.

It is very appropriate that this should be the first month of the year, as far as the northern hemisphere is concerned; since, its beginning being near the winter solstice, the year is thus made to present a complete series of the seasonal changes and operations, including equally the first movements of spring, and the death of all annual vegetation in the frozen arms of winter. Yet the earliest calendars, as the Jewish, the Egyptian, and Greek, did not place the commencement of the year at this point. It was not done till the formation of the Roman calendar, usually attributed to the second king, Numa Pompilius, whose reign is set down as terminating anno 672 B.C. Numa, it is said, having decreed that the year should commence now, added two new months to the ten into which the year had previously been divided, calling the first Januarius, in honour of Janus, the deity supposed to preside over doors (Lat. *janua*, a door), who might very naturally be presumed also to have something to do with the opening of the year.

Although, however, there was a general popular regard to the 1st of January as the beginning of the year, the ancient Jewish year, which opened with the 25th of March, continued long to have a legal position in Christian countries. In England, it was not till 1752 that the 1st of January became the initial day of the legal, as it had long been of the popular year. Before that time, it was customary to set down dates between the 1st of January and the 24th of March inclusive, thus: January 30, 1648-9: meaning, that popularly the year was 1649, but legally 1648. In Scotland, this desirable change was made by a decree of James VI. in privy council, in the year 1600. It was effected in France in 1564; in Holland, Protestant Germany, and Russia, in 1700; and in Sweden in 1753.

According to Verstegan, in his curious book *The Restitution of Decayed Intelligence* (4to, 1628), our Saxon ancestors originally called this month *Wolf-monat*— that is, Wolf-month—' because people were wont always in that month to be more in danger to be devoured of wolves than in any season else of the year, for that, through the extremity of cold and snow, those ravenous creatures could not find beasts sufficient to feed upon.' Subsequently, the month was named by the same people *Aefter-Yule*—that is, After Christmas. It is rather odd that we should have abandoned the Saxon names of the months, while retaining those of the days of the week.

CHARACTERISTICS OF JANUARY.

The deity Janus was represented by the Romans as a man with two faces, one looking backwards, the other forwards, implying that he stood between the old and the new year, with a regard to both. To this circumstance the English poet Cotton alludes in the following lines:

'Hark, the cock crows, and yon bright star
Tells us, the day himself's not far;
And see where, breaking from the night,
He gilds the western hills with light.
With him old Janus doth appear,
Peeping into the future year,
With such a look as seems to say,
The prospect is not good that way.
Thus do we rise ill sights to see,
And 'gainst ourselves to prophesy;
When the prophetic fear of things
A more tormenting mischief brings,
More full of soul-tormenting gall
Than direst mischiefs can befall.
But stay! but stay! Methinks my sight,
Better informed by clearer light,
Discerns sereneness in that brow,
That all contracted seemed but now.
His reversed face may shew distaste,
And frown upon the ills are past;
But that which this way looks is clear,
And smiles upon the new-born year.'

In the quaint drawings which illuminate the Catholic missals in the middle ages, January is represented by 'the figure of a man clad in white, as the type of the snow usually on the ground at that season, and blowing on his fingers as descriptive of the cold; under his left arm he holds a billet of wood, and near him stands the figure of the sign Aquarius, into which watery emblem in the zodiac the sun enters on the 19th of this month.'—*Brady*.

January is notedly, in our northern hemisphere, the coldest month in the year. The country people in England state the fact in their usual strong way:

'Janiveer—
Freeze the pot upon the fier.'

They even insist that the cold rather increases than decreases during the course of the month, notwithstanding the return of the sun from the Tropic of Capricorn, remarking:

'As the day lengthens,
The cold strengthens:'

or, as it is given in Germany, where the same idea prevails:

'Wenn die Tage beginnen zu langen,
Dann komm erst der Winter gegangen'—

the fact being, we suppose, that it only does so in some instances, while those of an opposite character pass unnoticed.

In the middle of the month, the sun at London is only 8h. 20m., at Edinburgh, 7h. 34m., above the horizon. There is a liability to severe and lasting frosts, and to heavy falls of snow. Vegetation lies dead, and it is usually 'sore times' for the animal creation; the farmer has his bestial, including the sheep, if he keeps any, much upon his hands for artificial supplies. The birds of the field and wood, reduced to great extremities, come nearer to the residences of men, in the hope of picking up a little food. The robin is especially remarkable for this forced familiarity. In unusually severe seasons, many birds perish of cold and hunger, and consequently, when the spring comes on, there is a marked diminution of that burst of sylvan song which usually makes the season so cheerful.

When frost occurs without a snow-fall—what is called in the north a *black frost*—the ground, wholly without protection, becomes hard for several inches deep. In Canada, it is sometimes frozen three feet down, so that any sort of building not founded considerably deeper, is sure to be dislodged at the next thaw. Even a macadamised road will be broken up and wholly ruined from this cause. In our country, and on the continent of Europe, a snowless frost gives the means of several amusements, which the rural people are enabled with good conscience to indulge in, as being thrown off from all more serious employments by the state of the ground.

> ' Now in the Netherlands, and where the Rhine
> Branched out in many a long canal, extends,
> From every province swarming, void of care,
> Batavia rushes forth; and as they sweep,
> On sounding skates, a thousand different ways
> In circling poise, swift as the winds along,
> The then gay land is maddened all to joy.
> Nor less the northern courts, wide o'er the snow,
> Pour a new pomp. Eager, on rapid sleds,
> Their vigorous youth in bold contention wheel
> The long-resounding course. Meantime to raise
> The manly strife, with highly blooming charms
> Flushed by the season, Scandinavia's dames,
> Or Russia's buxom daughters, glow around.'
> *Thomson.*

In Holland, the peasantry, male and female, take advantage of the state of the waters to come to market on skates, often bearing most part of a hundredweight on their heads; yet proceeding at the rate of ten miles an hour for two or three hours at a stretch.

In England, skating is on such occasions a favourite amusement; nor do the boys fail to improve the time by forming slides on lake, on pond, yea, even on the public highways, notwithstanding the frowns of old gentlemen and the threatenings of policemen. All of these amusements prevail during dry frost in Scotland, with one more, as yet little known in the south. It bears the name of *Curling*, and very much resembles bowls in its general arrangements, only with the specialty of flat stones to slide along the ice, instead of bowls to roll along the grass. Two parties are ranged in contention against each other, each man provided with a pair of handled stones and a broom, and having crampets on his feet to enable him to take a firm hold of the glassy surface. They play against each other, to have as many stones as possible lying near a fixed point, or *tee*, at the end of the course. When a player happens to impel his stone weakly, his associates sweep before it to favour its advance. A *skip*, or leader, stands at the tee, broom in hand, to guide the players of his party as to what they should attempt; whether to try to get through a certain open channel amongst the cluster of stones guarding the tee, or perhaps to come smashing among them, in the hope of producing rearrangements more favourable to his side. Incessant vociferation, frequent changes of fortune, the excitation of a healthy physical exercise, and the general feeling of sociality evoked, all contribute to render curl-

CURLING (FROM HARVEY'S WELL-KNOWN PICTURE).

ing one of the most delightful of amusements. It is further remarkable that, in a small community, the curling *rink* is usually surrounded by persons of all classes—the laird, the minister, and the provost, being all hail-fellow-well-met on this occasion with the tailors, shoemakers, and weavers, who at other times never meet them without a reverent vailing of the beaver. Very often a plain dinner of boiled beef with *greens* concludes the merry-meeting. There is a *Caledonian Curling Club* in Scotland, embracing the highest names in the land, and having scores of provincial societies affiliated to it. They possess an artificial pond in Strathallan, near the line of the Scottish Central Railway, and thither sometimes converge for one day's contention representatives from clubs scattered over fully a hundred and fifty miles of country.

When the low temperature of January is attended with a heavy snow-fall, as it often is, the ground receives a certain degree of protection, and is so far benefited for tillage in spring. But a load of snow is also productive of many serious inconveniences and dangers, and to none more than to the farmer, especially if he be at all concerned in *store-farming*. In Scotland, once every few years, there is a snow-fall of considerable depth, threatening entire destruction to sheep-stock. On one such occasion, in 1795, the snow was drifted in some hollows of the hills to the depth of a hundred feet. In 1772, there was a similar fall. At such times, the shepherd is exposed to frightful hardships and dangers, in trying to rescue some part of his charge. James Hogg tells us that, in the first-mentioned of these storms, seventeen shepherds perished in the southern district of Scotland, besides about thirty who, carried home insensible, were with difficulty recovered. At the same time, many farmers lost hundreds of their sheep.

SNOW CRYSTALS.

For the uninstructed mind, the fall of snow is a very common-place affair. To the thoughtless schoolboy, making up a handful of it into a missile, wherewith to surprise his friend passing on the other side of the way; to the labouring man plodding his way through it with pain and difficulty; to the agriculturist, who hails it as a comfortable wrappage for the ground during a portion of the dead season of the year, it is but a white cold substance, and nothing more. Even the eye of weather-wisdom could but distinguish that snow sometimes fell in broad flakes, and sometimes was of a powdery consistence; peculiarities from which certain inferences were drawn as to the severity and probable length of the storm. In the view of modern science, under favour of the microscope, snow is one of the most beautiful things in the museum of nature; each particle, when duly magnified, shewing a surprising regularity of figure, but various according to the degree of frost by which the snow has been produced. In the Book of Job, 'the treasures of the snow' are spoken of; and after one has seen the particles in this way, he is fully disposed to allow the justice of the expression.

The indefatigable Arctic voyager, Scoresby, was the first to observe the forms of snow particles, and for a time it was supposed that they assumed these remarkable figures in the polar regions alone. It was, however, ascertained by Mr

VARIOUS FORMS OF SNOW CRYSTALS.

James Glaisher, secretary of the British Meteorological Society, that, in the cold weather which marked the beginning of 1855, the same and even more complicated figures were presented in England.

In consistence, a snow particle is laminar, or flaky, and it is when we look at it in its breadth that the figure appears. With certain exceptions, which probably will be in time explained away, the figure is *stellar*—a star of six arms or points, forming of course angles of 60 degrees. And sometimes the figure is composed merely of six *spiculæ* meeting at a point in this regular way. It more frequently happens, however, that the spicular arms of the figure are feathered with other and smaller spiculæ, all meeting their respective stems at an angle of 60 degrees, or loaded with hexagonal prisms, all of which have of course the same angles. It is in obedience to a law governing the crystallisation of water, that this angle of 60 degrees everywhere prevails in the figures of snow particles, with the slight and probably only apparent exceptions which have been alluded to. But while there is thus a unity in the presiding law, the results are of infinite variety, probably no two particles being ever precisely alike. It is to be observed that there is a tendency to one *style of figure* at any particular time of a snowfall, in obedience to the degree of the temperature or some other condition of the atmosphere; yet within the range of this *style*, or general character, the minute differences may be described as endless. A very complicated form will even go through a series of minor changes as it melts on the object-glass of the observer; passing from the more complicated to the less, till it ends, perhaps, as a simple star of six points, just before becoming water.

The engraving on the preceding page represents a selection of figures from ninety-six given by Dr Scoresby in his work on the Arctic Regions.[*] It includes, as will be observed, certain triangular and other figures of apparently exceptional character. In a brochure issued by Mr Glaisher, and quoted below,[†] a hundred and fifty-one figures are presented, many of them paragons of geometrical beauty, and all calculated further to illustrate this interesting subject.[‡]

PROVERBS REGARDING JANUARY.

If the grass grows in Janiveer,
It grows the worse for 't all the year.

A January spring
Is worth naething.

Under water dearth,
Under snow bread.

March in Janiveer,
January in March, I fear.

If January calends be summerly gay,
'Twill be winterly weather till the calends of May.

The blackest month in all the year
Is the month of Janiveer.

[*] Published in 1820, 2 vols., 8vo.
[†] Report of Council of Brit. Meteor. Society, May 1855.
[‡] It has been found by Mr J. Spencer, and confirmed by observations of Mr Glaisher, that a weak solution of camphor produces, when rapidly dried, crystals resembling those of snow, of the more elementary forms.

SLEDGE-TRAVELLING ON SNOW IN THE NORTH OF EUROPE.

walt heil

Drinc heile

First of January.

'A massy bowl, to deck the jovial day,
Flash'd from its ample round a sunlike ray.
Full many a cent'ry it shone forth to grace
The festive spirit of th' Andarton race,
As, to the sons of sacred union dear,
It welcom'd with *lamb's-wool* the rising year.'

Polwhole.

HELD in the Roman Catholic Church as the festival of *Circumcisio Domini;* observed as a feast in the Church of England on the same account. In the Roman Church, the following saints are honoured on this day: St Fulgentius, bishop and confessor; St Odilo or Olou, sixth abbot of Cluni; St Almachus, martyr; St Eugendus, abbot; St Faine or Fanchea, virgin, of Ireland; St Mochua or Moncain, *alias* Claunus, abbot in Ireland; and St Mochua, *alias* Cronan, of Balla, abbot in Ireland.

Born.—Soame Jenyns, 1704, *London;* Baron Franz von Trenck, 1710; Edmund Burke, 1730, *Dublin;* G. A. Bürger, 1748, *Walmerswemde;* Miss Maria Edgeworth, 1767; Edward Stanley, Bishop of Norwich, 1779; Francis Earl of Ellesmere, 1800.

Died.—Louis XII. of France, 1515; W. Wycherley, 1716; C. A. Helvetius, 1772, *Paris;* Silvio Pellico, 1854; John Britton, antiquary and topographer, 1857.

EDMUND BURKE.

In the oratorical era of the House of Commons —the eighteenth century—who greater in that arena than Edmund Burke? A wonderful basis of knowledge was crowned in his case by the play of the most brilliant imagination. It is an example of 'inconsistency in expectations,' to look for life-long solidity of opinion in such a man. His early friend, *Single-speech Hamilton,* hit off his character as a politician in a single sentence: 'Whatever opinion Burke, from any motive, supports, so ductile is his imagination, that he soon conceives it to be right.' Goldsmith's epitaph upon him, in the poem *Retaliation,* is not less true:

'Here lies our good Edmund, whose genius was such,
We scarcely can praise it or blame it too much;
Who, born for the universe, narrowed his mind,
And to party gave up what was meant for mankind.
Though fraught with all learning, yet straining his throat
To persuade Tommy Townsend to lend him a vote;
Who, too deep for his hearers, still went on refining,
And thought of convincing, while they thought of dining;
Though equal to all things, for all things unfit;
Too nice for a statesman, too proud for a wit;
For a patriot too cool; for a drudge disobedient,
And too fond of the *right* to pursue the *expedient.*
In short, 'twas his fate, unemployed or in place, sir,
To eat mutton cold, and cut blocks with a razor.'

Turning away from the inconstancy of Mr Burke as a politician, let us contemplate him as a private friend in a day's journey, as delineated by Mr Hardy in his *Memoirs of Lord Charlemont.* 'One of the most satisfactory days, perhaps, that I ever passed in my life was going with him, *tête-à-tête,* from London to Beaconsfield. He stopped at Uxbridge whilst the horses were feeding, and happening to meet some gentlemen, of I know not what militia, who appeared to be perfect strangers to him, he entered into discourse with them at the gateway of the inn. His conversation at that moment completely exemplified what Johnson said of him: "That you could not meet Burke for half an hour under a shed, without saying he was an extraordinary man." He was on that day altogether uncommonly instructive and agreeable. Every object of the slightest notoriety, as we passed along, whether of natural or local history, furnished him with abundant materials for conversation. The house at Uxbridge, where the Treaty was held during Charles the First's time; the beautiful and undulating grounds of Bulstrode, formerly the residence of Chancellor Jeffreys ; and Waller's tomb, in Beaconsfield Churchyard, which, before we went home, we visited, and whose character—as a gentleman, a poet, and an orator—he shortly delineated, but with exquisite felicity of genius, altogether gave an uncommon interest to his eloquence ; and, although one-and-twenty years have now passed since that day, I entertain the most vivid and pleasing recollection of it.'

G. A. BÜRGER.

To the poet Bürger belongs the honour of having, by two ballads, impressed the poetical mind of England, and conduced in some measure to its being turned into new channels. A translation of these ballads, which appeared in 1796, was the first publication of Scott. The ride of the spectre bridegroom with his mistress, in Scott's version of *Lenore*, is a splendid piece of painting :

'Strong love prevailed ; she busks, she bounes,
　She mounts the barb behind,
And round her darling William's waist
　Her lily arms she twined.

And hurry ! hurry ! off they rode,
　As fast as fast might be ;
Spurned from the courser's thundering heels,
　The flashing pebbles flee.

And on the right, and on the left,
　Ere they could snatch a view,
Fast, fast, each mountain, mead and plain,
　And cot and castle, flew.

"Sit fast—dost fear ?　The moon shines clear—
　Fleet goes my barb—keep hold !
Fear'st thou ?"　"O no," she faintly said ;
　"But why so stern and cold ?

What yonder rings ? what yonder sings ?
　Why shrieks the owlet gray ?"
"'Tis death bells' clang, 'tis funeral song,
　The body to the clay.

With song and clang, at morrow's dawn,
　Ye may inter the dead :
To-night I ride, with my young bride,
　To deck our bridal bed.

Come with thy choir, thou coffined guest,
　To swell our nuptial song !
Come, priest, to bless our marriage feast,
　Come all, come all along !"

Ceased clang and song ; down sunk the bier ;
　The shrouded corpse arose :
And hurry ! hurry ! all the train
　The thundering steed pursues.

And forward ! forward ! on they go ;
　High snorts the straining steed ;
Thick pants the riders' labouring breath,
　As headlong on they speed.

"O William, why this savage haste ?
　And where thy bridal bed ?"
"'Tis distant far, low, damp, and chill,
　And narrow, trustless maid."

"No room for me ?"　"Enough for both ;
　Speed, speed, my barb, thy course !"
O'er thundering bridge, through boiling surge,
　He drove the furious horse.

Tramp ! tramp ! along the land they rode,
　Splash ! splash ! along the sea ;
The scourge is wight, the spur is bright,
　The flashing pebbles flee.

Fled past on right and left how fast,
　Each forest, grove, and bower !
On right and left fled past how fast
　Each city, town, and tower !

"Dost fear ? dost fear ?　The moon shines clear.
　Dost fear to ride with me ?
Hurrah ! hurrah ! the dead can ride !"
　"O William, let them be !

See there! see there! What yonder swings
And creaks 'mid whistling rain?"
"Gibbet and steel, the accursed wheel;
A murderer in his chain.

Hollo! thou felon, follow here:
To bridal bed we ride;
And thou shalt prance a fetter dance
Before me and my bride."

And hurry! hurry! clash, clash, clash!
The wasted form descends;
And fleet as wind through hazel bush
The wild career attends.

Tramp! tramp! along the land they rode,
Splash! splash! along the sea;
The scourge is red, the spur drops blood,
The flashing pebbles flee.

How fled what moonshine faintly shewed!
How fled what darkness hid!
How fled the earth beneath their feet,
The heaven above their head!

"Dost fear? dost fear? The moon shines clear,
And well the dead can ride;
Does faithful Helen fear for them?"
"O leave in peace the dead!"

"Barb! barb! methinks I hear the cock;
The sand will soon be run:
Barb! barb! I smell the morning air;
The race is well-nigh done."

Tramp! tramp! along the land they rode,
Splash! splash! along the sea;
The scourge is red, the spur drops blood,
The flashing pebbles flee.

"Hurrah! hurrah! well ride the dead;
The bride, the bride is come;
And soon we reach the bridal-bed,
For, Helen, here's my home."'

In his latter days, as a professor in the university of Göttingen, Bürger was inefficient, yet still much respected as the writer of the immortal *Lenore*. 'When Tieck became acquainted with him, he had been lately separated from his third wife. He was lean, pale, shrunken—misery was written in his features. His voice had lost its force; he could only make himself intelligible with difficulty; and yet he was obliged to speak. Now and then he would ride out, and there was something spectral about the pale man as he trotted through the streets of Göttingen on his lean white horse. One was reminded of the Ride of Death, which he had so forcibly described. Sometimes a ray of sunshine would fall on his gloomy soul, when any one succeeded in drawing him against his will into his old circle of good friends, whom he now anxiously avoided—shunning, indeed, all intercourse with mankind . . . . In *unconstrained* moments, Bürger could appear *unconstrained*, sympathetic, and even cheerful. He had something amiable and child-like in his nature.'—KÖPKE's *Reminiscences of Ludwig Tieck*, 1856.

FRANCIS, EARL OF ELLESMERE.

There is something in Johnson's remark, that personal merits in a man of high rank deserve to be 'handsomely acknowledged.' Sure of homage on account of birth and means, it must be unusually good impulses which lead him to study, to useful arts, or to administrative business. The second son of the Duke and Duchess of Sutherland, destined to an immense collateral inheritance, the Earl of Ellesmere devoted himself to elegant literature—in which his own efforts were far above mediocrity—to the patronage of the ennobling arts, and to disinterested duty in the public service. The benevolence of his nature led him in early life, as a member of the House of Commons, to lean to a liberal class of measures which were then little patronised, but the benefits of which were afterwards realised. At a time, moreover, when few were thinking much of the tastes and gratifications of the great body of the people, Lord Ellesmere prepared a splendid picture gallery which he made easily accessible to the public. This amiable nobleman died on the 18th February 1857.

WILLIAM WYCHERLEY.

While a literary man has his natural life, like other men, his fame has another and distinct life, which grows to maturity, flourishes a greater or less space of time, decays, and comes to an end, or in rare cases perseveres in a sort of immortality. Wycherley is one of the larger class of poets whose fame-life may be said to have died. First, his poems dropped out of notice; finally, his plays. Yet his name has still a place in literary biography, if only for one or two anecdotes which it includes, and for his having as a veteran patronised the youthful Pope.

One of Wycherley's most successful plays was entitled *The Plain Dealer;* and thereby hangs one of the anecdotes: 'Wycherley went down to Tunbridge, to take either the benefit of the waters or the diversions of the place; when walking one day upon the Wells Walk, with his friend Mr Fairbeard of Gray's Inn, just as he came up to the bookseller's, the Countess of Drogheda, a young widow, rich and beautiful, came to the bookseller and inquired for *The Plain Dealer*.

"Madam," says Mr Fairbeard, "since you are for the Plain Dealer, there he is for you," pushing Mr Wycherley towards her.

"Yes," says Mr Wycherley, "this lady can bear plain dealing, for she appears to be so accomplished, that what would be a compliment to others, when said to her would be plain dealing."

"No, truly, sir," said the lady, "I am not without my faults more than the rest of my sex: and yet, notwithstanding all my faults, I love plain dealing, and never am more fond of it than when it tells me of a fault."

"Then, madam," says Mr Fairbeard, "you and the Plain Dealer seem designed by heaven for each other."

'In short, Mr Wycherley accompanied her on her walks, waited upon her home, visited her daily at her lodgings whilst she stayed at Tunbridge, and after she went to London, at her lodgings in Hatton Garden, where in a little time he obtained her consent to marry her.'[*]

The story unfortunately does not end so

---

[*] Cibber's *Lives of the Poets*, 5 vols. 1753; vol. iii. p. 252.

pleasantly. The lady proved unreasonably jealous, and led her husband a rather sad life. After her death, her bequest to him was disputed at law, and, drowned in debt, he was immured in a jail for seven years!—such frightful penalties being then exigible by creditors.

LOUIS XII. OF FRANCE.

He was one of the few sovereigns of France who were entirely estimable. He was sober, sweet-natured, modest, laborious, loved knowledge, was filled with sentiments of honour, religion, and benevolence. He strove by economy to keep down the amount of the public burdens, and when his frugal habits were ridiculed in the theatre, he said laughingly that he would rather have the people to be amused by his stinginess than groan under his prodigality. He held as a principle that the justice of a prince obliged him to owe nothing, rather than his greatness to give much. It was rare indeed to find such correct ideas regarding the use and value of money in those days.

The first wife of Louis XII. being dead, he married, at fifty-three, a second and youthful spouse, the Princess Mary, sister of Henry VIII., and did not outlive the event three months. His widow returned to her own country, and married her first lover, Charles Brandon, Duke of Suffolk.

CORONATION OF CHARLES II. AT SCONE, 1651.

On the 1st of January 1651, the son of Charles I. was crowned as Charles II. by the Scots at Scone, the southern part of the country being occupied at the time by Cromwell with a hostile army. The extreme measure of cutting off the late king and extinguishing the monarchy was generally disapproved of in Scotland; but in taking up the young king, the Scots were chiefly animated by a desire of preserving and advancing their favourite Presbyterian church arrangements, according to the spirit of the famous Solemn League and Covenant. Charles, who was then only twenty, being anxious to get a footing in his father's lost dominions, consented, much against his will, to accept this Covenant, which inferred an active persecution of both popery and prelacy; and the Scots accordingly received him amongst them, fought a battle for him against Cromwell at Dunbar, and now crowned him. A sermon was preached on the occasion by Mr Robert Douglas, who had the reputation (but upon no just grounds) of being a descendant of Mary queen of Scots. The crown was put upon the young king's head by the Marquis of Argyle, whom ten years after he sent to the scaffold for compliances with Cromwell. The defeat of the Scots and their young king at Worcester on the 3d September of this year put an end to Charles's adventure, and he with difficulty escaped out of the country. How he subsequently treated the Covenant and its adherents need not here be particularised.

MARCH OF GENERAL MONK FROM COLDSTREAM.

On the 1st of January 1660, General Monk commenced that march from Scotland to London which was so instrumental in effecting the Restor-

ation. He started with his little army of six or seven thousand men from the town of Coldstream, in Berwickshire—a name which has been commemorated in the title of a regiment which he is believed to have embodied at the place, or soon after. Monk had spent about three weeks at Coldstream, which was a favourable spot for his purpose, as the Tweed was there fordable; but he seems to have found it a dismal place to quarter in. On his first arrival, he could get no provisions for his own dinner, and was obliged to content himself with a quid of tobacco. His chaplains, less easily satisfied, roamed about till they obtained a meal at the house of the Earl of Hume near by.—*Monk, a Historical Study, by M. Guizot, translated by J. Stuart Wortley,* 1838.

UNION OF IRELAND WITH GREAT BRITAIN, 1801.

On the 1st of January 1801—the initial day of the nineteenth century—Ireland passed into an incorporating union with Great Britain, and the three kingdoms were thenceforth styled the United Kingdom of Great Britain and Ireland.

The expression, 'initial day of the nineteenth century,' requires something to be said in its defence, for many persons regard the year 1800 as the beginning of the present century. The year 1801 is, in reality, entitled to this honour, because then only had the previous century been completed. To make this plain, let the reader reflect that it required the year 100 to complete the first century, the year 200 to complete the second century, and so on through all that followed. To say, then, that the year 1800 was the first of a new century, is to be led by sound, instead of fact.

DISCOVERY OF THE PLANETOIDS.

On the 1st of January 1801, the Sicilian astronomer, M. Piazzi, discovered a new planet, to which he gave the name of Ceres, in honour of a goddess formerly in much esteem in Sicily. It was the first discovered of a number of such bodies of small size, which occupy the place due to one such body of large size, between the orbits of Mars and Jupiter. [At present (1883), the number is over 235.]

'It was noted that between the orbits of Mercury and Venus there is an interval of thirty-one millions of miles; between those of Venus and the Earth, twenty-seven millions; and between those of the Earth and Mars, fifty millions; but between the orbits of Mars and Jupiter there intervenes the tremendous gap of three hundred and forty-nine millions of miles, to the apparent interruption of the general order, which, however, is again resumed beyond Jupiter.' This wide interval, and some other considerations, having raised the suspicion of an unknown planet between Mars and Jupiter, a combination of twenty-four practical observers was formed to search for the missing link. 'On New-Year's Day 1801, ere they had well got into harness, Piazzi, one of their number [at Palermo], made an observation on a small star in Taurus, which he took for one of Mayer's. On the 2d of January, he found that the supposed star had retrograded no less than 4′ in ÆR., and 3½′ in north declination. This retrogradation continued till about the 12th, when the movement became direct, and he followed the body till it was lost in the solar rays. Illness, however, prevented his getting observations enough to establish its nature, and he considered it to be cometary. Meantime, he had written to Bode and Oriani on the subject, but the delays of the post in that comparatively recent day, by keeping back the intelligence, precluded its being examined during that apparition. Curiosity and zeal were, however, on the alert; Bode immediately suspected the real nature of the stranger; and Olbers, Burckhardt, and Gauss computed its orbit from the slender data thus afforded. The knowledge of its having been stationary on the 12th of January, with an elongation from the sun of 4ˢ 2° 37′ 48″ aided the computation, and proved it to be a superior planet. . . . . Thus was Ceres discovered on the 1st of January 1801. Its diameter, according to Sir William Herschel, is only 163 miles.'—SMYTHE'S *Cycle of Celestial Objects*, i. 154.

New-Year's Day Festivities.

'Long ere the lingering dawn of that blithe morn
Which ushers in the year, the roosting cock,
Flapping his wings, repeats his larum shrill;
But on that morn no busy flail obeys
His rousing call; no sounds but sounds of joy
Salute the year—the first-foot's entering step,
That sudden on the floor is welcome heard,
Ere blushing maids have braided up their hair;
The laugh, the hearty kiss, the *good new year*
Pronounced with honest warmth. In village, grange,
And borough town, the steaming flagon, borne
From house to house, elates the poor man's heart,
And makes him feel that life has still its joys.
The aged and the young, man, woman, child,
Unite in social glee; even stranger dogs,
Meeting with bristling back, soon lay aside
Their snarling aspect, and in sportive chase,
Excursive scour, or wallow in the snow.
With sober cheerfulness, the grandam eyes
Her offspring round her, all in health and peace;
And, thankful that she's spared to see this day
Return once more, breathes low a secret prayer,
That God would shed a blessing on their heads.'
　　　　　　　　　　　　　　　Grahame.

As New-Year's Day, the first of January bears a prominent place in the popular calendar. It has ever been a custom among northern nations to see the old year out and the new one in, with the highest demonstrations of merriment and conviviality. To but a few does it seem to occur that the day is a memorandum of the subtraction of another year from the little sum of life; with the multitude, the top feeling is a desire to express good wishes for the next twelvemonths' experience of their friends, and be the subject of similar benevolence on the part of others, and to see this interchange of cordial feeling take place, as far as possible, in festive circumstances. It is seldom that an English family fails to sit up on the last night of the year till twelve o'clock, along with a few friends, to drink a happy New Year to each other over a cheerful glass. Very frequently,

too, persons nearly related but living apart, dine with each other on this day, to keep alive and cultivate mutual good feeling. It cannot be doubted that a custom of this kind must tend to obliterate any shades of dissatisfaction or jealous anger, that may have arisen during the previous year, and send the kindred onward through the next with renewed esteem and regard. To the same good purpose works the old custom of giving little presents among friends on this day:

'The King of Light, father of aged Time,
Hath brought about that day which is the prime,
To the slow-gliding months, when every eye
Wears symptoms of a sober jollity.'

Charles Lamb had a strong appreciation of the social character of New-Year's Day. He remarks that no one of whatever rank can regard it with indifference. 'Of all sounds of all bells,' says he, 'most solemn and touching is the peal which rings out the old year. I never hear it without a gathering up of my mind to a concentration of all the images that have been diffused over the past twelvemonth; all I have done or suffered, performed or neglected, in that regretted time. I begin to know its worth as when a person dies. It takes a personal colour; nor was it a poetical flight in a contemporary, when he exclaimed:

"I saw the skirts of the departing year."'

One could wish that the genial Elia had added something in recommendation of resolutions of improvement of the year to come, for which New-Year's Day is surely a most appropriate time. 'Every first of January that we arrive at, is an imaginary milestone on the turnpike track of human life: at once a resting-place for thought and meditation, and a starting point for fresh exertion in the performance of our journey. The man who does not at least *propose to himself* to be better *this* year than he was last, must be either very good or very bad indeed! And only to *propose* to be better, is something; if nothing else, it is an acknowledgment of our *need* to be so, which is the first step towards amendment. But, in fact, to propose to oneself to do well, is in some sort to *do* well, positively; for there is no such thing as a stationary point in human endeavours; he who is not worse to-day than he was yesterday, is better; and he who is not better, is worse.' *

The merrymakings of New-Year's Eve and New-Year's Day are of very ancient date in England. The head of the house assembled his family around a bowl of spiced ale, comically called *lamb's wool*, from which he drank their healths; then passed it to the rest, that they might drink too. The word that passed amongst them was the ancient Saxon phrase, *Wass hael;* that is, To your health. Hence this came to be recognised as the Wassail or Wassel Bowl. The poorer class of people carried a bowl adorned with ribbons round the neighbourhood, begging for something wherewith to obtain the means of filling it, that they too might enjoy wassail as well as the rich. In their compotations, they had songs suitable to the occasion, of which a Gloucestershire example has been preserved:

* *Mirror of the Months.*

' Wassail! wassail! over the town,
Our toast it is white, our ale it is brown :
Our bowl it is made of the maplin tree,
We be good fellows all ; I drink to thee.

Here's to ——,* and to his right ear,
God send our maister a happy New Year ;
A happy New Year as e'er he did see—
With my wassailing bowl I drink to thee.

Here's to ——,† and to his right eye,
God send our mistress a good Christmas pie :
A good Christmas pie as e'er I did see—
With my wassailing bowl I drink to thee.

Here's to Filpail,‡ and her long tail,
God send our measter us never may fail
Of a cup of good beer ; I pray you draw near,
And then you shall hear our jolly wassail.

Be here any maids, I suppose here be some ;
Sure they will not let young men stand on the
    cold stone ;
Sing hey O maids, come troll back the pin,
And the fairest maid in the house, let us all in.

Come, butler, come bring us a bowl of the best :
I hope your soul in heaven may rest :
But if you do bring us a bowl of the small,
Then down fall butler, bowl, and all.'

What follows is an example apparently in use
amongst children :

    ' Here we come a wassailing,
      Among the leaves so green,
    Here we come a wandering,
      So fair to be seen.

Chorus. Love and joy come to you,
      And to your wassel too,
    And God send you a happy New Year,
        A New Year,
    And God send you a happy New Year !
    Our wassel cup is made of rosemary-tree,
    So is your beer of the best barley.

We are not daily beggars,
    That beg from door to door ;
But we are neighbours' children,
    Whom you have seen before.

Call up the butler of this house,
    Put on his golden ring,
Let him bring us up a glass of beer
    And the better we shall sing.

We have got a little purse,
    Made of stretching leather skin,
We want a little of your money
    To line it well within.

Bring us out a table,
    And spread it with a cloth ;
Bring us out a mouldy cheese,
    And some of your Christmas loaf.

God bless the master of this house,
    Likewise the mistress too,
And all the little children,
    That round the table go !

Good master and mistress,
    While you're sitting by the fire,
Pray think of us poor children,
    Who are wandering in the mire.

Chorus. Love and joy come to you,' &c. §

   * The name of some horse.
   † The name of another horse.
   ‡ The name of a cow.
   § *Notes and Queries*, i. 137.

The custom of wassail at the New Year was
kept up in the monasteries as well as in private
houses. In front of the abbot, at the upper end
of the refectory table, was placed the mighty
bowl styled in their language *Poculum Caritatis,*
and from it the superior drank to all, and all
drank in succession to each other.* The corporation feasts of London still preserve a custom that
affords a reflex of that of the wassail bowl. A
double-handled flagon full of sweetened and
spiced wine being handed to the master, or other
person presiding, he drinks standing to the
general health, as announced by the toastmaster ;
then passes it to his neighbour on the left hand,
who drinks standing to his next neighbour, also
standing, and so on it goes, till all have drunk.
Such is the well-known ceremony of the *Loving
Cup.*

Till very few years ago in Scotland, the custom
of the wassail bowl at the passing away of the old
year might be said to be still in comparative
vigour. On the approach of twelve o'clock, a *hot
pint* was prepared—that is, a kettle or flagon full
of warm, spiced, and sweetened ale, with an infusion of spirits.† When the clock had struck the
knell of the departed year, each member of the
family drank of this mixture ' A good health and
a happy New Year and many of them ' to all the
rest, with a general hand-shaking, and perhaps a
dance round the table, with the addition of a song
to the tune of *Hey tuttie taitie :*

    ' Weel may we a' be,
    Ill may we never see,
    Here's to the king
    And the gude companie !' &c.

The elders of the family would then most probably sally out, with the hot kettle, and bearing
also a competent provision of buns and short-
bread, or bread and cheese, with the design of
visiting their neighbours, and interchanging with
them the same cordial greetings. If they met by
the way another party similarly bent, whom they
knew, they would stop and give and take sips from
their respective kettles. Reaching the friend's
house, they would enter with vociferous good
wishes, and soon send the kettle a-circulating.
If they were the first to enter the house since
twelve o'clock, they were deemed as the *first-
foot ;* and, as such, it was most important, for

   * *Archæologia,* xi. 420.
   † *Receipt for Making the Wassail Bowl.*—Simmer a small
quantity of the following spices in a teacupful of water,
viz. :—Cardamums, cloves, nutmeg, mace, ginger, cinnamon, and coriander. When done, put the spice to two,
four, or six bottles of port, sherry, or madeira, with one
pound and a half of fine loaf sugar (pounded) to four bottles, and set all on the fire in a clean bright saucepan ;
meanwhile, have yolks of 12 and the whites of 6 eggs well
whisked up in it. Then, when the spiced and sugared
wine is a little warm, take out one teacupful ; and so on
for three or four cups ; after which, when it boils, add
the whole of the remainder, pouring it in gradually, and
stirring it briskly all the time, so as to froth it. The
moment a fine froth is obtained, toss in 12 fine soft
roasted apples, and send it up hot. Spices for each bottle
of wine :—10 grains of mace, 46 grains of cloves, 37 grains
of cardamums, 28 grains of cinnamon, 12 grains of nutmeg,
48 grains of ginger, 49 grains of coriander seeds.—*Mark
Lane Express.*

luck to the family in the coming year, that they should make their entry, not empty-handed, but with their hands full of cakes and bread and cheese; of which, on the other hand, civility demanded that each individual in the house should partake.

To such an extent did this custom prevail in Edinburgh in the recollection of persons still living, that, according to their account, the principal streets were more thronged between twelve

FIRST-FOOTING IN EDINBURGH.

and one in the morning than they usually were at midday. Much innocent mirth prevailed, and mutual good feelings were largely promoted. An unlucky circumstance, which took place on the 1st January of 1812, proved the means of nearly extinguishing the custom. A small party of reckless boys formed the design of turning the innocent festivities of *first-footing* to account for purposes of plunder. They kept their counsel well. No sooner had the people come abroad on the principal thoroughfares of the Old Town, than these youths sallied out in small bands, and commenced the business which they had undertaken. Their previous agreement was, to *look out for the white neckcloths,*—such being the best mark by which they could distinguish in the dark individuals likely to carry any property worthy of being taken. A great number of gentlemen were thus spoiled of their watches and other valuables. The least resistance was resented by the most brutal maltreatment. A policeman, and a young man of the rank of a clerk in Leith, died of the injuries they had received. An affair so singular, so uncharacteristic of the people among whom it happened,

produced a widespread and lasting feeling of surprise. The outrage was expiated by the execution of three of the youthful rioters on the chief scene of their wickedness; but from that time, it was observed that the old custom of going about with the *hot pint*—the ancient wassail —fell off.

A gentleman of Preston has communicated to a popular publication,* that for many years past he has been in the habit of calling on a friend, an aged lady, at an early hour of New-Year's Day, being by her own desire, as he is a fair-complexioned person, and therefore assumed to be of good omen for the events of the year. On one occasion, he was prevented from attending to his old friend's request, and her first caller proved to be a dark-complexioned man; in consequence of which there came that year sickness, trouble, and commercial disaster.

In the parish of Berlen, near Snodland, in the county of Kent, are the remains of the old mansion of Groves, originally the property of a family named Hawks. On part of this house being pulled down in the latter part of the eighteenth century, there was found an oak beam supporting the chimney, which presented an antique carving exactly represented in the engraving at the head of this article. The words *Wass heil* and *Drinc heile* leave no doubt that the bowl in the centre was a representation of the wassail bowl of the time when the house was built, probably the sixteenth century. The two birds on the bowl are hawks—an allusion to the name of the family which originally possessed the mansion.

'The wassail bowle,' says Warton, 'is Shakspeare's Gossip's Bowl in the *Midsummer Night's Dream.* The composition was ale, nutmeg, sugar, toast, and roasted crabs or apples.' The word is interpreted by Verstegan as *wase hale*—that is, grow or become well. It came in time to signify festivity in general, and that of rather an intemperate kind. A wassail candle was a large candle used at feasts.

There was in Scotland a *first-footing* independent of the *hot-pint*. It was a time for some youthful friend of the family to steal to the door, in the hope of meeting there the young maiden of his fancy, and obtaining the privilege of a kiss, as her *first-foot*. Great was the disappointment on his part, and great the joking among the family, if through accident or plan, some half-withered aunt or ancient grand-dame came to receive him instead of the blooming Jenny.

It may safely be said that New-Year's Day has hitherto been observed in Scotland with a heartiness nowhere surpassed. It almost appears as if, by a sort of antagonism to the general gravity of the people, they were impelled to break out in a half-mad merriment on this day. Every face was bright with smiles; every hand ready with the grasp of friendship. All stiffness arising from age, profession, and rank, gave way. The soberest felt entitled to take a licence on that special day. Reunions of relatives very generally took place over the festive board, and thus many little family differences were obliterated. At the present time, the ancient practices are somewhat

* *Notes and Queries*, 2d Series, ii. 325.

decayed; yet the First of January is far from being reduced to the level of other days.

A grotesque manorial custom is described as being kept up in the reign of Charles II., in connection with Hilton in Staffordshire. There existed in that house a hollow brass image, about a foot high, representing a man kneeling in an indecorous posture. It was known all over the country as Jack of Hilton. There were two apertures, one very small at the mouth, another about two-thirds of an inch in diameter at the back, and the interior would hold rather more than four pints of water, 'which, when set to a strong fire, evaporates after the same manner as in an Æolipile, and vents itself at the mouth in a constant blast, blowing the fire so strongly that it is very audible, and makes a sensible impression in that part of the fire where the blast lights.'

Now the custom was this. An obligation lay upon the lord of the adjacent manor of Essington, every New-Year's Day, to bring a goose to Hilton, and drive it three times round the hall fire, which Jack of Hilton was all the time blowing by the discharge of his steam. He was then to carry the bird into the kitchen and deliver it to the cook; and when it was dressed, he was further to carry it in a dish to the table of his lord paramount, the lord of Hilton, receiving in return a dish of meat for his own mess.*

At Coventry, if not in other places throughout England, it was customary to eat what are called God-cakes on New-Year's Day. They were of a triangular shape, of about half an inch thick, and filled with a kind of mince-meat. There were halfpenny ones cried through the street; but others of much greater price—even it is said to the value of a pound—were used by the upper classes.†

A Happy New Year—Happiness.

Sir John Sinclair, visiting Lord Melville at Wimbledon on the last day of the year 1795, remained all night, and next morning entered his host's room at an early hour to wish him a happy New Year. Melville, who had been reading a long paper on the importance of conquering the Cape of Good Hope, as an additional security to our Indian possessions, said, as he received the shake of his friend's hand: 'I hope this year will be happier than the last, for I scarcely recollect having spent one happy day in the whole of it.' 'This confession, coming from an individual whose whole life hitherto had been a series of triumphs, and who appeared to stand secure upon the summit of political ambition, was often dwelt upon by my father, as exemplifying the vanity of human wishes.'—*Memoirs of Sir John Sinclair by his Son,* 1837, i. 275.

This anecdote recalls one which Gibbon extracts from the pages of Cardonne. He states that in the Closet of the Kaliph Abdalrahman the following confession was found after his decease: 'I have now reigned fifty years in victory or peace; beloved by my subjects, dreaded by my enemies,

and respected by my allies. Riches and honours, power and pleasure, have waited on my call, nor does any earthly blessing appear to have been wanting to my felicity. In this situation I have numbered the days of pure and genuine happiness which have fallen to my lot: they amount to *fourteen.* O man! place not thy confidence in this present world!'—*Decline and Fall of the Roman Empire.* x. p. 40.

An actual millionaire of our time, a respected member of parliament on the liberal side, conversing confidentially some years ago with a popular authoress, stated that he had once been a clerk in Liverpool, with forty pounds a year, living in a house of four small apartments; and he was fully of belief that he enjoyed greater happiness then, than he has since done in what must appear to the outer world as the most superbly fortunate and luxurious circumstances.

Much has been said, first and last, by sages, preachers, and poets, about happiness and its unattainableness here below; but, after all, there remains something to be done—a summing up for the jury, as it were. God certainly has not arranged that any such highly intelligent being as man should be perfectly happy; we have so many faculties to be exercised, so many desires and tastes calling for their several gratifications, and so many and so critical are the circumstances of relation in which these stand towards the outer world, that such a state never can be *fully* attained. But that approaches may be made to happiness, that by certain conduct we may secure many innocent gratifications, and avoid many painful experiences, is just as true. A harmonious exercise of the faculties in subjection to conscientiousness and benevolence—something to be always working at, something to be always hoping for—under the guidance of reason, so as to avoid over-carefulness on the one hand and over-sanguineness on the other—these, attended by a regard to the preservation of that health of body on which health of mind so much depends, will assuredly bring us as near to happiness as Providence, for the keeping of us in activity, has intended we should ever go; and that is all but up to the ideal point. Where, after an active life, the apparently successful man proclaims his having altogether failed to secure happiness, we may be very sure there has been some strange inconsistency in his expectations, some undue straining in a wrong direction, some want of stimulus to the needful activity, some pervading jar between him and his life relations, or that he has been tempted into acts and positions which leave a sting in the mind.

Solemn Thoughts for New-Year's Day, by Southey.

Come, melancholy Moraliser, come!
Gather with me the dark and wintry wreath;
   With me engarland now
   The Sepulchre of Time;

Come, Moraliser, to the funeral song!
I pour the dirge of the Departed Days;
   For well the funeral song
   Befits this solemn hour.

* Plot's *Natural History of Staffordshire,* p. 433.
† *Notes and Queries,* Sep. 20, 1856.

But hark ! even now the merry bells ring round
With clamorous joy to welcome in this day,
    This consecrated day,
    To mirth and indolence.

Mortal ! whilst Fortune with benignant hand
Fills to the brim thy cup of happiness,
    Whilst her unclouded sun
    Illumes thy summer day,

Canst thou rejoice—rejoice that Time flies fast ?
That night shall shadow soon thy summer sun ?
    That swift the stream of Years
    Rolls to eternity ?

If thou hast *wealth* to gratify each wish,
If pow'r be thine, remember what thou art—
    Remember thou art Man,
    And Death thine heritage !

Hast thou known *Love?* does beauty's better sun
Cheer thy fond heart with no capricious smile,
    Her eye all eloquence,
    Her voice all harmony ?

Oh ! state of happiness ! hark how the gale
Moans deep and hollow o'er the leafless grove :
    Winter is dark and cold—
    Where now the charms of spring ?

Sayst thou that Fancy paints the future scene
In hues too sombrous ? that the dark-stoled Maid
    With stern and frowning front
    Appals the shuddering soul?

And wouldst thou bid me court her fairy form,
When, as she sports her in some happier mood,
    Her many-coloured robes
    Dance varying to the sun ?

Ah ! vainly does the Pilgrim, whose long road
Leads o'er the barren mountain's storm-vexed
      height,
    With anxious gaze survey
    The fruitful far-off vale.

Oh ! there are those who love the pensive song,
To whom all sounds of mirth are dissonant !
    There are who at this hour
    Will love to contemplate !

For hopeless sorrow hail the lapse of Time,
Rejoicing when the fading orb of day
    Is sunk again in night,
    That one day more is gone !

And he who bears Affliction's heavy load
With patient piety, well pleased he knows
    The World a pilgrimage,
    The Grave the inn of rest !

New-Year's Gifts.

The custom of making presents on New-Year's Day has, as far as regards the intercourse of the adult population, become almost if not entirely obsolete. Presents are generally pleasant to the receiver on any day of the year, and are still made, but not on this day especially. The practice on New-Year's Day is now limited to gifts made by parents to their children, or by the elder collateral members of a family to the younger ; but the old custom, which has been gradually, like the drinking of healths, falling into disuse in England, is still in full force in France, as will presently be more particularly adverted to.

The practice of making presents on New-Year's Day was, no doubt, derived from the Romans. Suetonius and Tacitus both mention it. Claudius prohibited demanding presents except on this day. Brand, in his *Popular Antiquities*, observes, on the authority of Bishop Stillingfleet, that the Saxons kept the festival of the New Year with more than ordinary feasting and jollity, and with the presenting of New-Year's gifts to each other. Fosbroke notices the continuation of the practice during the middle ages ; and Ellis, in his additions to Brand, quotes Matthew Paris to shew that Henry III. extorted New-Year's gifts from his subjects.

The New-Year's gifts presented by individuals to each other were suited to sex, rank, situation, and circumstances. From Bishop Hall's *Satires* (1598), it appears that the usual gifts of tenants in the country to their landlords was a capon ; and Cowley, addressing the same class of society, says :

    'When with low legs and in an humble guise
    Ye offered up a capon-sacrifice
    Unto his worship at the New-Year's tide.'

Ben Jonson, in his *Masque of Christmas*, among other characters introduces ' New-Year's Gift in a blue coat, serving-man like, with an orange, and a sprig of rosemary on his head, his hat full of brooches, with a collar of gingerbread, his torch-bearer carrying a marchpane, with a bottle of wine on either arm.' An orange stuck with cloves was a common present, and is explained by Lupton, who says that the flavour of wine is improved, and the wine itself preserved from mouldiness, by an orange or lemon stuck with cloves being hung within the vessel, so as not to touch the liquor.

Gloves were customary New-Year's gifts. They were formerly a more expensive article than they are at present, and occasionally a sum of money was given instead, which was called 'glove-money.' Presents were of course made to persons in authority to secure favour, and too often were accepted by magistrates and judges. Sir Thomas More having, as lord chancellor, decided a cause in favour of a lady with the unattractive name of Croaker, on the ensuing New-Year's Day she sent him a pair of gloves with forty of the gold coins called an angel in them. Sir Thomas returned the gold with the following note : ' Mistress, since it were against good manners to refuse your New-Year's gift, I am content to take your gloves, but as for the *lining* I utterly refuse it.'

When pins were first invented and brought into use about the beginning of the sixteenth century, they were a New-Year's gift very acceptable to ladies, and money given for the purchase of them was called ' pin-money,' an expression which has been extended to a sum of money secured by a husband on his marriage for the private expenses of his wife. Pins made of metal, in their present form, must have been in use some time previous to 1543, in which year a statute was passed (35 Hen. VIII. c. 6), entitled ' An Acte for the true making of Pynnes,' in which it was enacted that the price charged should not exceed 6s. 8d. a thousand. Pins were previously made of boxwood, bone, and silver, for the richer classes ; those used by the poor were of common wood—in fact, skewers.

The custom of presenting New-Year's gifts to

the sovereigns of England may be traced back to the time of Henry VI. In Rymer's *Fœdera*, vol. x. p. 387, a list is given of gifts received by the king between Christmas Day and February 4, 1428, consisting of sums of 40s., 20s., 13s. 4d., 10s., 6s. 8d., and 3s. 4d.

A manuscript roll of the public revenue of the fifth year of Edward VI. has an entry of rewards given on New-Year's Day to the king's officers and servants, amounting to £155, 5s., and also of sums given to the servants of those who presented New-Year's gifts to the king.

A similar roll has been preserved of the reign of Philip and Mary. The Lord Cardinal Pole gave a 'saulte,' with a cover of silver and gilt, having a stone therein much enamelled of the story of Job; and received a pair of gilt silver pots, weighing 143¾ ounces. The queen's sister, the Lady Elizabeth, gave the fore part of a kyrtell, with a pair of sleeves of cloth of silver, richly embroidered over with Venice silver, and rayed with silver and black silk; and received three gilt silver bowls, weighing 132 ounces. Other gifts were—a sacrament cloth; a cup of crystal; a lute in a case, covered with black silk and gold, with two little round tables, the one of the *phisnamy* of the emperor and the king's majesty, the other of the king of Bohemia and his wife. Other gifts consisted of hosen of Garnsey-making, fruits, sugar-loaves, gloves, Turkey hens, a fat goose and capon, two swans, two fat oxen, conserves, rose-water, and other articles.

During the reign of Queen Elizabeth, the custom of presenting New-Year's gifts to the sovereign was carried to an extravagant height. The queen delighted in gorgeous dresses, in jewellery, in all kinds of ornaments for her person and palaces, and in purses filled with gold coin. The gifts regularly presented to her were of great value. An exact and descriptive inventory of them was made every year on a roll, which was signed by the queen herself, and by the proper officers. Nichols, in his *Progresses of Queen Elizabeth*, has given an accurate transcript of five of these rolls. The presents were made by the great officers of state, peers and peeresses, bishops, knights and their ladies, gentlemen and gentlewomen, physicians, apothecaries, and others of lower grade, down to her majesty's dustman. The presents consisted of sums of money, costly articles of ornament for the queen's person or apartments, caskets studded with precious stones, valuable necklaces, bracelets, gowns, embroidered mantles, smocks, petticoats, looking-glasses, fans, silk stockings, and a great variety of other articles. Howell, in his *History of the World*, mentions that 'Queen Elizabeth, in 1561, was presented with a pair of black silk knit stockings by her silk-woman, Mrs Montague, and thenceforth she never wore cloth hose any more.' The value of the gifts in each year cannot be ascertained, but some estimate may be made of it from the presents of gilt plate which were in all instances given in return by the queen; an exact account having been entered on the roll of the weight of the plate which each individual received in return for his gift. The total weight in 1577-8 amounted to 5882 ounces. The largest sum of

money given by any temporal lord was £20; but the Archbishop of Canterbury gave £40, the Archbishop of York £30, and other spiritual lords £20 or £10. The total amount in the year 1561-2 of money gifts was £1262, 11s. 8d. The queen's wardrobe and jewellery must have been principally supplied from her New-Year's gifts.

The Earl of Leicester's New-Year's gifts exceeded those of any other nobleman in costliness and elaborate workmanship. The description of the gift of 1571-2 may be given as a specimen: 'One armlet, or shakell of gold, all over fairely garnished with rubyes and dyamondes, haveing in the closing thearof a clocke, and in the fore part of the same a fayre lozengie dyamonde without a foyle, hanging thearat a round juell fully garnished with dyamondes, and perle pendant, weying 11 oz. qu. dim., and farthing golde weight: in a case of purple vellate all over embranderid with Venice golde, and lyned with greene vellat.'

In the reign of James I. the money gifts seem to have been continued for some time, but the ornamental articles presented appear to have been few and of small value. In January 1604, Sir Dudley Carleton, in a letter to Mr Winwood, observes: 'New-Year's Day passed without any solemnity, and the accustomed present of the purse and gold was hard to be had without asking.' Mr Nichols, in a note on this passage, observes: 'During the reigns of King Edward VI., Queen Mary, and Queen Elizabeth, the ceremony of giving and receiving New-Year's gifts at Court, which had long before been customary, was never omitted, and it was continued at least in the early years of King James; but I have never met with a roll of those gifts similar to the several specimens of them in the *Progresses of Queen Elizabeth*.' He afterwards, however, met with such a roll, which he has copied, and in a note attached to the commencement of the roll, he makes the following remarks: 'Since the note in that page [471 of vol. i., *Progresses of James I.*] was printed, the roll here accurately transcribed has been purchased by the trustees of the British Museum, from Mr Rodd, bookseller of Great Newport Street, in whose catalogue for 1824 it is mentioned. It is above ten feet in length; and, like the five printed in Queen Elizabeth's "Progresses," exhibits the gifts to the king on one side, and those from his majesty on the other, both sides being signed by the royal hand at top and bottom. The gifts certainly cannot compete in point of curiosity with those of either Queen Mary's or Queen Elizabeth's reign. Instead of curious articles of dress, rich jewels, &c., nothing was given by the nobility but gold coin.' The gifts from the nobility and prelates amounted altogether to £1293, 13s. 4d. The remainder were from persons who held some office about the king or court, and were generally articles of small value. The Duke of Lennox and the Archbishop of Canterbury gave each £40; all other temporal lords, £20 or £10; and the other spiritual lords, £30, £20, £13, 6s. 8d., or £10. The Duke of Lennox received 50 ounces of plate, the Archbishop of Canterbury 55 ounces; those who gave £20 received about 30 ounces, and for smaller sums the return-gift was in a similar proportion.

No rolls, nor indeed any notices, seem to have been preserved of New-Year's gifts presented to Charles I., though probably there were such. The custom, no doubt, ceased entirely during the Commonwealth, and was never afterwards revived, at least to any extent worthy of notice. Mr Nichols mentions that the last remains of the custom at court consisted in placing a crown-piece under the plate of each of the chaplains in waiting on New-Year's Day, and that this custom had ceased early in the nineteenth century.

There is a pleasant story of a New-Year's gift in the reign of King Charles I., in which the court jester, Archy Armstrong, figures as for once not the maker, but the victim of a jest. Coming on that morn to a nobleman to bid him good-morrow, Archy received a few gold pieces; which, however, falling short of his expectations in amount, he shook discontentedly in his hand, muttering that they were too light. The donor said: 'Prithee, then, Archy, let me see them again; and, by the way, there is one of them which I would be loth to part with.' Archy, expecting to get a larger gift, returned the pieces to his lordship, who put them in his pocket, with the remark: 'I once gave my money into the hands of a fool, who had not the wit to keep it.'—*Banquet of Jests*, 1634.

It cannot be said that the custom of giving presents to superiors was a very rational one: one can even imagine it to have been something rather oppressive—'a custom more honoured in the breach than the observance.' Yet Robert Herrick seems to have found no difficulty in bringing the smiles of his cheerful muse to bear upon it. It must be admitted, indeed, that the author of the *Hesperides* made his poem the gift. Thus it is he addresses Sir Simon Steward in

                   'A jolly
Verse, crowned with ivy and with holly;
That tells of winter's tales and mirth,
That milkmaids make about the hearth;
Of Christmas' sports, the wassail bowl,
That's tost up after fox-i'-th'-hole;
Of blind-man-buff, and of the care
That young men have to shoe the mare;
Of twelfth-tide cakes, of pease and beans,
Wherewith ye make those merry scenes;
Of crackling laurel, which fore-sounds
A plenteous harvest to your grounds;
Of those, and such like things, for shift,
We send, *instead of New-Year's gift*.
Read then, and when your faces shine
With buxom meat and cap'ring wine,
Remember us in cups full crown'd,
And let our city-health go round.
Then, as ye sit about your embers,
Call not to mind the fled Decembers;
But think on these, that are t' appear
As daughters to the instant year;
And to the bagpipes all address,
Till sleep take place of weariness.
And thus throughout, with Christmas plays,
Frolic the full twelve holidays.'

The custom of giving of presents among relatives and friends is much declined in England, but is still kept up with surprising

vigour in Paris, where the day is especially recognised from this circumstance as *Le Jour d'Etrennes*. Parents then bestow portions on their children, brothers on their sisters, and husbands make settlements on their wives. The mere externals of the day, as observed in Paris, are of a striking character: they were described as follows in an English journal, as observed in the year 1824, while as yet the restored Bourbon reigned in France: 'Carriages,' says this writer, 'may be seen rolling through the streets with cargoes of bon-bons, souvenirs, and the variety of etceteras with which little children and grown-up children are bribed into good humour; and here and there pastrycooks are to be met with, carrying upon boards enormous temples, pagodas, churches, and playhouses, made of fine flour and sugar, and the embellishments which render French pastry so inviting. But there is one street in Paris to which a New-Year's Day is a whole year's fortune—this is the Rue des Lombards, where the wholesale confectioners reside; for in Paris every trade and profession has its peculiar quarter. For several days preceding the 1st of January, this street is completely blocked up by carts and wagons laden with cases of sweetmeats for the provinces. These are of every form and description which the most singular fancy could imagine; bunches of carrots, green peas, boots and shoes, lobsters and crabs, hats, books, musical instruments, gridirons, frying-pans, and sauce-pans; all made of sugar, and coloured to imitate reality, and all made with a hollow within to hold the bon-bons. The most prevailing device is what is called a *cornet;* that is, a little cone ornamented in different ways, with a bag to draw over the large end, and close it up. In these things, the prices of which vary from one franc (tenpence) to fifty, the bon-bons are presented by those who choose to be at the expense of them, and by those who do not, they are only wrapped in a piece of paper; but bon-bons, in some way or other, must be presented. It would not, perhaps, be an exaggeration to state that the amount expended for presents on New-Year's Day in Paris, for sweetmeats alone, exceeds 500,000 francs, or £20,000 sterling. Jewellery is also sold to a very large amount, and the fancy articles exported in the first week of the year to England and other countries, is computed at one-fourth of the sale during the twelve months. In Paris, it is by no means uncommon for a man of 8000 or 10,000 francs a year, to make presents on New-Year's Day which cost him a fifteenth part of his income. No person able to give must on this day pay a visit empty-handed. Everybody accepts, and every man gives according to the means which he possesses. Females alone are excepted from the charge of giving. A pretty woman, respectably connected, may reckon her New-Year's presents at something considerable. Gowns, jewellery, gloves, stockings, and artificial flowers fill her drawing-room: for in Paris it is a custom to display all the gifts, in order to excite emulation, and to obtain as much as possible. At the palace, the New-Year's Day is a complete *jour de fête*. Every branch of the royal family is then expected to make handsome presents to the king. For the six months preceding January 1824, the female branches were busily occupied in preparing presents of their own manufacture, which would fill at least two common-sized wagons. The Duchess de Berri painted an entire room of japanned panels, to be set up in the palace, and the Duchess of Orleans prepared an elegant screen. An English gentleman, who was admitted suddenly into the presence of the Duchess de Berri two months before, found her and three of her maids of honour, lying on the carpet, painting the legs of a set of chairs, which were intended for the king. The day commences with the Parisians, at an early hour, by the interchange of their visits and bon-bons. The nearest relations are visited first, until the furthest in blood have had their calls; then friends and acquaintances. The conflict to anticipate each other's calls, occasions the most agreeable and whimsical scenes among these proficients in polite attentions. In these visits, and in gossiping at the confectioners' shops, which are the great lounge for the occasion, the morning of New-Year's Day is passed; a dinner is given by some member of the family to all the rest, and the evening concludes, like Christmas Day, with cards, dancing, or any other amusement that may be preferred.'

HOBSON, THE CAMBRIDGE CARRIER.

Died, January 1, 1630-1, Thomas Hobson, of Cambridge, the celebrated University carrier, who had the honour of two epitaphs written upon him by Milton. He was born in or about 1544; his father was a carrier, and he bequeathed to him 'the team ware, with which he now goeth, that is to say, the cart and eight horses,' harness, nag, &c. After his father's death, he continued the business of a carrier with great success; a considerable profit was then made by carrying letters, which the University of Cambridge licensed persons to do, before and after the introduction of the post-office system. The old man for many years passed monthly with his team between his own home in Cambridge, and the Bull Inn in Bishopsgate-street, and back again, conveying both packages and human beings. He is also said to have been the first person in the kingdom who let horses for hire, and the scrupulous pertinacity with which he refused to allow any horse to be taken from his stables except in its proper turn, has given him a kind of celebrity. If the horse he offered to his customer was objected to, he curtly replied, 'This or none;' and 'Hobson's choice—this or none,' became a proverb, which it is to this day. Steele, in the *Spectator*, No. 509, however, considers the proverb to be 'by vulgar error taken and used when a man is reduced to an extremity, whereas the propriety of the maxim is to use it when you would say, There is plenty, but you must make such a choice as not to hurt another who is to come after you.' 'He lived in Cambridge, and observing that the scholars rid hard, his manner was to keep a large stable of horses, with boots, bridles, and whips, to furnish the gentlemen at once, without going from college to college to borrow.' He used to tell the scholars they would 'come time enough to London if they

did not ride too 'fast.' By his rule of taking the horse which stood next the stable-door, 'every customer,' says Steele, 'was alike well served according to his chance, and every horse ridden with the same justice. This memorable man stands drawn in fresco at an inn (which he used) in Bishopsgate-street, with an hundred pound bag under his arm.'

Hobson grew rich by his business: in 1604, he contributed £50 to the loan to King James I. In 1626, he gave a large Bible to the church of St Benedict, in which parish he resided. He became possessed of several manors, and, in 1628, gave to the University and town the site of the Spinning House, or 'Hobson's Workhouse.' In 1630, Hobson's visits to London were suspended by order of the authorities, on account of the plague being in London; and it was during this cessation from business that he died. Milton, in one of his epitaphs on him, quaintly adverts to this fact, remarking that Death would never have hit him had he continued dodging it backwards and forwards between Cambridge and the Bull.

Hobson was twice married. By his first wife he had eight children, and he survived his second wife. He bequeathed considerable property to his family; money to the corporation, and the profits of certain pasture-land (now the site of Downing College) towards the maintenance and heightening of the conduit in Cambridge. He also left money to the poor of Cambridge, Chesterton, Waterbeach, Cottenham, and Buntingford, of which latter place he is believed to have been a native. He was buried in the chancel of Benedict's church, but no monument or inscription marks the spot. In one of Milton's humorous epitaphs on him, reference is made to his cart and wain, which proves that there is no foundation for the popular opinion that Hobson carried on his business by means of packhorses. In the second epitaph it is amusing to hear the author of England's solemn epic indulging in drolleries and puns regarding poor Hobson, the carrier:

' Rest, that gives all men life, gave him his death,
  And too much breathing put him out of breath;
  Nor were it contradiction to affirm
  Too long vacation hastened on his term.
  Merely to drive the time away he sickened,
  Fainted, and died, nor would with all be quickened
  Ease was his chief disease; and, to judge right,
  He died for weariness that his cart went light:
  His leisure told him that his time was come,
  And lack of load made his life burdensome:
  Obedient to the Moon, he spent his date
  In course reciprocal, and had his fate
  Linked to the mutual flowing of the seas:
  Yet, strange to think, his *wain* was his *increase.*
  His letters are delivered all and gone,
  Only remains this superscription.'

Several memorials of the benevolent old carrier, who is believed to have reached his eighty-fifth year, are preserved. There was formerly a picture of him at Anglesey Abbey; and Roger Yorke had another, supposed to have belonged to Mrs Katherine Pepys, who, in her will dated 1700, bequeathed 'old Mr Hobson's picture.' His saddle and bridle were preserved in the town-hall at Cambridge during the present century. A public-house in the town was called 'Old Hobson,' and another 'Hobson's House;' but he is traditionally said to have resided at the south-west corner of Pears Hill, and on the site of the two adjoining houses were his stables. Even in his life-time his popularity must have been great, as in 1617 was published a quarto tract, entitled 'Hobson's Horseload of Letters, or Precedent for Epistles of Business, &c.'

The name of Hobson has been given to a street in Cambridge, 'in which have long resided Messrs Swann and Sons, carriers, who possess a curious portrait of Hobson, mounted on a stately black nag. This was preserved for many years at Hobson's London inn, the Bull, in Bishopsgate Street.'—Cooper's *Annals of Cambridge*, vol. iii. p. 236.

There are several engraved portraits of Hobson: that by John Payne, who died about 1648, represents Hobson in a cloak, grasping a bag of money, and has these lines underneath:

'Laugh not to see so plaine a man in print,
The shadow's homely, yet there's something in't.
Witness the Bagg he wears (though seeming poore),
The fertile Mother of a thousand more:
He was a thriving Man, through lawful gain,
And wealthy grew by warrantable faime.
Men laugh at them that spend, not them that gather,
Like thriving sonnes of such a thrifty Father.'

HOBSON, THE CAMBRIDGE CARRIER.
From the Print by Payne.

This print is, most probably, from the fresco figure at the Bull Inn, which, in Chalmers's *English Poets*, 1810, is stated as 'lately to be seen,' but it has long since disappeared; and the Bull is more modernised than either the Green Dragon or the Four Swans inns, at a few houses distant: the Green Dragon has its outer galleries remaining, but modernised and inclosed with glass; the Four Swans is still more perfect, and is, perhaps, the most entire galleried inn

which remains in the metropolis, and shews how well adapted were the inns of old for the representation of stage plays. That the Bull was indeed for this purpose, we have evidence—the yard having supplied a stage to our early actors before James Burbage and his fellows obtained a patent from Queen Elizabeth for erecting a permanent building for theatrical entertainments. Tarlton often played here.—Collier's *Annals*, vol. iii. p. 291, and Tarlton's *Jests*, by Halliwell, pp. 13, 14. Anthony Bacon (the brother of Francis) lived in Bishopsgate Street, not far from the Bull Inn, to the great annoyance of his mother, who dreaded that the plays and interludes acted at the Bull might corrupt his servants.

On the whole, we obtain a pleasing idea of Hobson, as an honest, painstaking man; a little arbitrary perhaps, but full of sound principle, and essentially a well-wisher to his species.

JANUARY 2.

St Macarius of Alexandria, anchoret. St Concordius, martyr. St Adelard, abbot.

[It is not possible in this work to give special notices of all the saints of the Romish calendar; nor is it desirable that such should be done. There are, however, several of them who make a prominent figure in history; some have been remarkable as active and self-devoted missionaries of civilisation; while others supply curious examples of the singularities of which men are capable under what are now very generally regarded as morbid views of religion. Of such persons it does not seem improper that notices of a dispassionate nature should be given, among other memorable matters connected with the days of the year.]

ST MACARIUS.

St Macarius was a notable example of those early Christians who, for the sake of heavenly meditation, forsook the world and retired to live in savage wildernesses. Originally a confectioner in Alexandria, he withdrew, about the year 325, into the Thebais in Upper Egypt, and devoted himself wholly to religious thoughts. Afterwards, he took up his abode in still remoter deserts, bordering on Lybia, where there were indeed other hermits, but all out of sight of each other. He exceeded his neighbours in the practice of those austerities which were then thought the highest qualification for the blessed abodes of the future. 'For seven years together,' says Alban Butler, 'he lived only on raw herbs and pulse, and for the three following years contented himself with four or five ounces of bread a day;' not a fifth part of the diet required to keep the inmates of modern gaols in good health. Hearing great things of the self-denial of the monks of Tabenna, he went there in disguise, and astonished them all by passing through Lent on the aliment furnished by a few green cabbage leaves eaten on Sundays. He it was of whom the striking story is told, that, having once killed a gnat which bit him, he immediately hastened in a penitent and self-mortifying humour to the marshes of Sceté, which abound with great flies, a torment even to the wild boar, and exposed himself to these ravaging insects for six months; at the end of which time his body was a mass of putrid sores, and he only could be recognised by his voice.*

The self-devoting, self-denying, self-tormenting anchoret is an eccentricity of human nature now much out of fashion; which, however, we may still contemplate with some degree of interest, for the basis of the character is connected with both true religion and true virtue. We are told of Macarius that he was exposed to many temptations. 'One,' says Butler, 'was a suggestion to quit his desert and go to Rome, to serve the sick in the hospitals; which, by due reflection, he discovered to be a secret artifice of vain-glory inciting him to attract the eyes and esteem of the world. True humility alone could discover the snare which lurked under the specious gloss of holy charity. Finding this enemy extremely importunate, he threw himself on the ground in his cell, and cried out to the fiends, "Drag me hence, if you can, by force, for I will not stir." Thus he lay till night, and by this vigorous resistance they were quite disarmed. As soon as he arose they renewed the assault; and he, to stand firm against them, filled two great baskets with sand, and laying them on his shoulders, travelled along the wilderness. A person of his acquaintance meeting him, asked him what he meant, and made an offer of easing him of his burden; but the saint made no other reply than this: "I am tormenting my tormentor." He returned home in the evening, much fatigued in body, but freed from the temptation. St Macarius once saw in a vision, devils closing the eyes of the monks to drowsiness, and tempting them by divers methods to distractions, during the time of public prayer. Some, as often as they approached, chased them away by a secret supernatural force, whilst others were in dalliance with their suggestions. The saint burst into sighs and tears; and, when prayer was ended, admonished every one of his distractions, and of the snares of the enemy, with an earnest exhortation to employ, in that sacred duty, a more than ordinary watchfulness against his attacks. St Jerome and others relate, that, a certain anchoret in Nitria having left one hundred crowns at his death, which he had acquired by weaving cloth, the monks of that desert met to deliberate what should be done with the money. Some were for having it given to the poor, others to the church; but Macarius, Pambo, Isidore, and others, who were called the fathers, ordained that the one hundred crowns should be thrown into the grave and buried with the corpse of the deceased, and that at the same time the following words should be pronounced: *May thy money be with thee to perdition.*† This example struck such a terror into all the monks, that no one durst lay up any money by him.'

Butler quotes the definition of an anchoret given by the Abbot Rancé de la Trappe, as a lively portraiture of the great Macarius: 'When,'

says he, 'a soul relishes God in solitude, she thinks no more of anything but heaven, and forgets the earth, which has nothing in it that can now please her; she burns with the fire of divine love, and sighs only after God, regarding death as her greatest advantage: nevertheless they will find themselves much mistaken, who, leaving the world, imagine they shall go to God by straight paths, by roads sown with lilies and roses, in which they will have no difficulties to conquer, but that the hand of God will turn aside whatever could raise any in their way, or disturb the tranquillity of their retreat: on the contrary, they must be persuaded that temptations will everywhere follow them, that there is neither state nor place in which they can be exempt, that the peace which God promises is procured amidst tribulations, as the rose buds amidst thorns; God has not promised his servants that they shall not meet with trials, but that with the temptation he will give them grace to be able to bear it: heaven is offered to us on no other conditions; it is a kingdom of conquest, the prize of victory—but, O God, what a prize!'

Born.—John, Marquis of Granby, 1721; General Wolfe, Westerham, Kent, 1727.

Died. — Publius Ovidius Naso, the Roman poet, 18; Titus Livius, the Roman historian, 18, *Padua;* Alexander, Earl of Rosslyn, Lord Chancellor of England, 1805; Dr John Mason Good, 1827; Dr Andrew Ure, chemist, 1857.

GENERAL WOLFE.

When, in 1759, Pitt entrusted General Wolfe with the expedition against Quebec, on the day preceding his embarkation, Pitt, desirous of giving his last verbal instructions, invited him to dinner at Hayes, Lord Temple being the only other guest. As the evening advanced, Wolfe, heated, perhaps by his own aspiring thoughts, and the unwonted society of statesmen, broke forth in a strain of gasconade and bravado. He drew his sword and rapped the table with it, he flourished it round the room, and he talked of the mighty things which that sword was to achieve. The two Ministers sat aghast at an exhibition so unusual from any man of real sense and spirit. And when, at last, Wolfe had taken his leave, and his carriage was heard to roll from the door, Pitt seemed for the moment shaken in the right opinion which his deliberate judgment had formed of Wolfe: he lifted up his eyes and arms, and exclaimed to Lord Temple: 'Good God! that I should have entrusted the fate of the country and of the administration to such hands!' This story was told by Lord Temple himself to the Rt. Hon. Thomas Grenville, the friend of Lord Mahon, who has inserted the anecdote in his *History of England*, vol. iv. Lord Temple also told Mr Grenville, that on the evening in question, Wolfe had partaken most sparingly of wine, so that this ebullition could not have been the effect of any excess. The incident affords a striking proof how much a fault of manner may obscure and disparage high excellence of mind. Lord Mahon adds: 'It confirms Wolfe's own avowal, that he was not seen to advantage in the common occur-

---

* Butler's *Lives of the Saints.*   † Acts viii. 20.

rences of life, and shews how shyness may, at intervals, rush, as it were, for refuge, into the opposite extreme; but it should also lead us to view such defects of manner with indulgence, as proving that they may co-exist with the highest ability and the purest virtue.'

The death of General Wolfe was a kind of military martyrdom. He had failed in several attempts against the French power in Canada, dreaded a court martial, and resolved by a bold and original stroke to justify the confidence of Pitt, or die. Thence the singularity of his movement to get upon the plain of Abram behind Quebec. The French came out of their fortress, fought him, and were beaten; but a stray shot brought down the young hero in the moment of victory. The genius of West has depicted very successfully a scene which remains engraved in the national heart. Wolfe died on the 13th of September 1759, in the 33d year of his age. His body was brought to England, and interred at Greenwich.

The want of a *Life* of General Wolfe,—a strange want, considering the glory which rests on the name,—has caused some points regarding him to remain in doubt. It is doubtful, for example, if he was in service in the campaign of the Duke of Cumberland in the north of Scotland in 1746.

In *Jacobite Memoirs of the Rebellion of* 1745-6, a collection of original papers edited by Mr

THE DEATH OF GENERAL WOLFE.   (FROM THE PAINTING BY WEST.)

Robert Chambers in 1834, there are evidences of a gentleman's house at Aberdeen having been forcibly taken possession of by the Duke of Cumberland and General Hawley; who, not content with leaving no requital behind them, took away many articles of value, which are afterwards found to have been sold in London. In this unpleasant story, a 'Major Wolfe,' described as aide-de-camp to Hawley, figures as a bearer of rough messages. A painful question arises, 'Could this be the future hero of Quebec?' One fact is gratifying by contradiction, that this hero was not a major till 1749. Could it be his father? This is equally or more unlikely, for he was then a brigadier-general. It is to be observed that James Wolfe, though only nineteen at this time, was a captain in Barrell's regiment (having received that commission in June 1744), and Barrell's regiment, we know, stood in the left of the front line of the royal army at Culloden: a mistake of major for captain is easily conceivable. In the hope of getting conclusive evidence that the admired Wolfe was not involved in the personal barbarisms of Cumberland and Hawley, the editor of the *Jacobite Memoirs* wrote to Mr Southey, who, he understood, was prepared to compile a memoir of

General Wolfe from original materials; and he received the following answer:

'*Keswick, 11th August*, 1833.

'Sir,—Immediately upon receiving your obliging letter, I referred to my own notes and extracts from the correspondence of Wolfe with his family, the whole of which has been in my possession.

'There I find that his father was with the Duke of Cumberland's army in 1745, and that he himself was at Newcastle in the November of that year. His father was a general at that time; and Wolfe, I think, was not yet a major (though I cannot immediately ascertain this), for he only received his lieutenant's[*] commission in June 1744. My present impression is that he was not in the Scotch campaign, and that the Major Wolfe of whom your papers speak must have been some other person. His earliest letter from Scotland is dated January 1749.

'Throughout his letters Wolfe appears to have been a considerate, kind-hearted man, as much distinguished from most of his contemporary officers by humane and gentlemanly feeling as by the zeal with which he devoted himself to his profession. All that has hitherto been known of him tends to confirm this view of his character.

'I am much obliged to you for your offer of the volume in which the paper is printed, and shall thankfully receive it when it is published. Meantime, Sir, I have the honour to remain, &c.'

If, after all, there is nothing but character to plead against the conclusion that Wolfe was the harsh message-bearer of the brutal Hawley, it is to be feared that the defence is a weak one. In the army which marched into Scotland in 1746, and put down the rebellion, there was a general indignation and contempt for the Scottish nation, disposing men otherwise humane to take very harsh measures. The ordinary laws were trampled on; worthy friends of the government, who pleaded for mercy to the vanquished, were treated with contumely; some of the English officers were guilty of extreme cruelty towards the Highland peasantry. No one is remembered with more horror for his savage doings than a certain Captain Caroline Scott; and yet this is the same man whom Mallet introduces in his poem of the *Wedding Day* as a paragon of amiableness. The verses are as follows:

'A second see! of special note,
Plump Comus in a Colonel's coat;
Whom we this day expect from far,
A jolly first-rate man of war;
On whom we boldly dare repose,
To meet our friends, or meet our foes.'

To which the poet appends a prose note:

'The late Col. Caroline Scott, who, though extremely corpulent, was uncommonly active; and who, to much skill, spirit, and bravery, as an officer, joined *the greatest gentleness of manners as a companion and friend*. He died a sacrifice to the public, in the service of the East India Company, at Bengal, in the year 1755.'

If the Caroline Scott who tortured the poor Highlanders was really this gentle-natured man, the future hero of Quebec can be imagined as carrying rough messages to the lady at Aberdeen.

[*] Mistake for 'captain's.'

In the National Portrait Gallery, Westminster, there is a bust portrait of General Wolfe, representing him in profile, and with a boyish cast of countenance.

OVID.

Ovid died at about the age of sixty-one. We have only imperfect accounts of the Roman bards; but we know pretty clearly that Ovid lived as a gay and luxurious gentleman in Rome through the greater part of the reign of Augustus, and when past fifty was banished by that emperor, probably in consequence of his concern in some scandalous amour of a female member of the imperial family. Let us  think of what it would be for a darling of London society like the late Thomas Moore to have been condemned to spend his days at a fishing-village in Friesland or Lapland, and we shall have some idea of the pangs of the unfortunate Naso on taking up his forced abode at Tomi on the Black Sea. His epistles thence are full of complaints of the severity of the climate, the wildness of the scenery, and the savage nature of the surrounding people. How much we find expressed in that well-known line addressed to a book which he sent from Tomi to be published in Rome:—'Sine me, liber, ibis in urbem!' Yet it appears that the inhabitants appreciated his literary reputation, and treated him with due respect; also that he tried to accommodate himself to his new circumstances by learning their language. Death brought the only true relief which he could experience, after he had endured his exile at least eight years. It is an interesting instance of the respect which brilliant talents extort even from the rudest, that a local monument was reared to Ovid, and that Tomi is now called Ovidiopol, or Ovid's City.

'I have a veneration for Virgil,' says Dr King; 'I admire Horace; but I love Ovid. . . . Neither of these great poets knew how to move the passions so well as Ovid; witness some of the tales of his Metamorphoses, particularly the story of Ceyx and Halcyone, which I never read without weeping. No judicious critic hath ever yet denied that Ovid has more wit than any other poet of the Augustan age. That he has too much, and that his fancy is too luxuriant, is the fault generally imputed to him. All the imperfections of Ovid are really pleasing. But who would not excuse all his faults on account of his many excellencies, particularly his descriptions, which have never been equalled.'[*]

LORD CHANCELLOR ROSSLYN.

Alexander Wedderburn, Earl of Rosslyn, Lord Chancellor of England from 1793 to 1801, entered in his youth at the Scottish bar, but had from

[*] Political and Literary Anecdotes of his own Times, by Dr William King, Principal of St Mary Hall, Oxon. 1819, p. 30.

the first an inclination to try the English, as a higher field of ambition. After going through the usual drudgeries of a young Scotch counsel for three years, he was determined into that career which ended in the English chancellorship by an accident. There flourished at that time at the northern bar a veteran advocate named Lockhart, the Dean of the body, realising the highest income that had ever been known there, namely, a thousand a year, and only prevented from attaining the bench through the mean spite of the government, in consequence of his having gallantly gone to defend the otherwise helpless Scotch rebels at Carlisle in 1746.* Lockhart, with many merits, wanted that of a pleasant temper. He was habitually harsh and overbearing towards his juniors, four of whom (including Wedderburn) at length agreed that, on the first occasion of his shewing any insolence towards one of them, he should publicly insult him, for which object it was highly convenient that the Dean had been once threatened with a caning, and that his wife did not bear a perfectly pure character. In the summer of 1757, Wedderburn chanced to be opposed to Lockhart, who, nettled probably by the cogency of his arguments, hesitated not to apply to him the appellation of 'a presumptuous boy.' The young advocate, rising afterwards to reply, poured out upon Lockhart a torrent of invective such as no one in that place had ever heard before. 'The learned Dean,' said he, 'has confined himself on this occasion to vituperation; I do not say that he is capable of *reasoning*, but if *tears* would have answered his purpose, I am sure tears would not have been wanting.' Lockhart started up and threatened him with vengeance. 'I care little, my lords,' said Wedderburn, 'for what may be said or done by a man who has been disgraced in his person and dishonoured in his bed.' The judges felt their flesh creep at the words, and Lord President Craigie could with difficulty summon energy to tell the young pleader that this was language unbecoming an advocate and unbecoming a gentleman. According to Lord Campbell, 'Wedderburn, now in a state of such excitement as to have lost all sense of decorum and propriety, exclaimed that "his lordship had said as a judge what he could not justify as a gentleman." The President appealed to his brethren as to what was fit to be done, who unanimously resolved that Mr Wedderburn should retract his words and make an humble apology, on pain of deprivation. All of a sudden Wedderburn seemed to have subdued his passion, and put on an air of deliberate coolness; when, instead of the expected retractation and apology, he stripped off his gown, and holding it in his hands before the judges, he said: "My lords, I neither retract nor apologise, but I will save you the trouble of deprivation; there is my gown, and I will never wear it more; *virtute me involvo*." He then coolly laid his gown upon the bar, made a low bow to the judges, and, before they had reco-

* These particulars regarding Lockhart are stated from the writer's recollection of a conversation in 1833 with Sir William Macleod Bannatyne, who had entered at the Scotch bar *exactly seventy years before*, while Lockhart was still flourishing.

vered from their amazement, he left the court, which he never again entered.' *

It is said that he started that very day for London, where, thirty-six years afterwards, he attained the highest place which it is in the power of a barrister to reach. It is generally stated that he never revisited his native country till near the close of his life, after his resignation of the chancellorship.

There is something spirited, and which one admires and sympathises with, in the fact of a retort and reproof administered by a young barrister to an elderly one presuming upon his acquired reputation to be insolent and oppressive; but the violence of Wedderburn's language cannot be justified, and such merit as there was in the case one would have wished to see in connection with a name more noted for the social virtues, and less for a selfish ambition, than that of Alexander Wedderburn.

CAPTURE OF GRANADA, 1492.

The long resistance of the Moors to the Spanish troops of King Ferdinand and Isabella being at length overcome, arrangements were made for the surrender of their capital to the Spaniards. As the Bishop of Avila passed in to take possession of the Alhambra—the magnificent palace of the Moorish king—its former master mournfully passed out, saying only, 'Go in, and occupy the fortress which Allah has bestowed upon your powerful land, in punishment of the sins of the Moors!' The Catholic sovereigns meanwhile waited in the vega below, to see the silver cross mounted on the tower of the Alhambra, the appointed symbol of possession. As it appeared, a shout of joy rose from the assembled troops, and the choristers of the royal chapel broke forth with the anthem, *Te Deum laudamus*.

Boabdil, king of the Moors, accompanied by about fifty horsemen, here met the Spanish sovereigns, who generously refused to allow him to pay any outward homage to them, and delivered up to him, with expressions of kindness, his son who had been for some time in their hands as a hostage. Boabdil handed them the keys of the city, saying, 'Thine, O king, are our trophies, our kingdom, and our person; such is the will of God!' After some further conversation, the Moorish king passed on in gloomy silence, to avoid witnessing the entrance of the Spaniards into the city. Coming at about two leagues' distance to an elevated point, from which the last view of Granada was to be obtained, he could not restrain himself from turning round to take a parting look of that beautiful city which was lost to him and his for ever. 'God is great!' was all he could say; but a flood of tears burst from his eyes. His mother upbraided him for his softness; but his vizier endeavoured to console him by remarking that even great misfortunes served to confer a certain distinction. 'Allah Achbar!' said he; 'when did misfortunes ever equal mine?'

'From this circumstance,' says Mr Irving, in his *Chronicle of the Conquest of Granada*, 'the hill, which is not far from Padul, took the name

* *Lives of the Chancellors.*

of *Fez Allah Achbar ;* but the point of view commanding the last prospect of Granada is known among Spaniards by the name of *El ultimo suspiro del Moro*, or the Last Sigh of the Moor.'

EXECUTION OF JOHN OF LEYDEN, 'THE PROPHET.' 1536.

It was in 1523 that the sect of the Anabaptists rose in Germany, so named because they wished that people should re-baptize their children, so as to imitate Jesus Christ, who had been baptized when grown up. Two fanatics named Storck and Muncer were the leaders of this sect, the most horrible that had ever desolated Germany.

As Luther had raised princes, lords, and magistrates against the Pope and the bishops, Muncer raised the peasants against the princes, lords, and magistrates. He and his disciples addressed themselves to the inhabitants of Swabia, Misnia, Thuringia, and Franconia, preaching to them the doctrine of an equality of conditions among men. Germany became the theatre of bloody doings. The peasantry rose in Saxony, even as far as Alsace ; they massacred all the gentlemen they met, including in the slaughter a daughter of the Emperor Maximilian I.; they ravaged every district to which they penetrated ; and it was not till after they had carried on these frightful proceedings for three years, that the regular troops got the better of them. Muncer, who had aimed at being a second Mahomet, perished on the scaffold at Mulhausen.

The chiefs, however, did not perish with him. The peasants were raised anew, and acquiring additional strength in Westphalia, they made themselves masters of the city of Munster, the bishop of which fled at their approach. They here endeavoured to establish a theocracy like that of the Jews, to be governed by God alone ; but one named Matthew their principal prophet being killed, a tailor lad, called John of Leyden, assured them that God had appeared to him and named him king ; and what he said the people believed.

The pomp of his coronation was magnificent. One can yet see the money which he struck ; he took as his armorial bearings two swords placed the same way as the keys of the Pope. Monarch and prophet in one, he sent forth twelve apostles to announce his reign throughout all Low Germany. After the example of the Hebrew sovereigns, he wished to have a number of wives, and he espoused twelve at one time. One having spoken disrespectfully of him, he cut off her head in the presence of the rest, who, whether from fear or fanaticism, danced with him round the dead body of their companion.

This prophet-king had one virtue—courage. He defended Munster against its bishop with unfaltering resolution during a whole year. Notwithstanding the extremities to which he was reduced, he refused all offers of accommodation. At length he was taken, with arms in his hands, through treason among his own people ; and the bishop, after causing him to be carried about for some time from place to place as a monster, consigned him to the death reserved for all kings of his order.

40

EXTRAORDINARY LIGHT.

On the 2d of January 1756, at four in the afternoon, at Tuam, in Ireland, an unusual light, far above that of the brightest day, struck all the beholders with amazement. It then faded away by invisible degrees ; but at seven, from west to east, 'a sun of streamers' appeared across the sky, undulating like the waters of a rippling stream. A general feeling of alarm was excited by this singular phenomenon. The streamers gradually became discoloured, and flashed away to the north, attended by a shock, which all felt, but which did no damage.—*Gentleman's Magazine,* xxvi. 39. The affair seems to have been an example of the aurora borealis, only singular in its being bright enough to tell upon the daylight.

Unfounded but Persevering Popular Notions.

Under this head may be ranked a belief amongst book-collectors, that certain books of uncommon elegance were, by a peculiar dilettanteism of the typographer, printed from silver types. In reality, types of silver would not print a book more elegantly than types of the usual composite metal. The absurdity of the idea is also shewn by the circumstances under which books are for the most part *composed ;* some one has asked, very pertinently, if a set of thirsty compositors would not have quickly discovered 'how many ems, long primer, would purchase a gallon of beer.' It is surmised that the notion took its rise in a mistake of *silver* for *Elzevir* type, such being the term applied early in the last century to types of a small size, similar to those which had been used in the celebrated miniature editions of the Amsterdam printers, the Elzevirs.*

Another of these popular notions has a respectability about it, because, though not true, it proceeds on a conception of what is just and fitting. It represents all persons who have ever had anything to do with the invention or improvement of instruments of death, as suffering by them, generally as the first to suffer by them. Many cases are cited, but on strict examination scarcely one would be found to be true. It has been asserted, for example, that Dr Guillotin of Paris, who caused the introduction into France of the instrument bearing his name, was himself the first of its many victims ; whereas he in reality outlived the Revolution, and died peaceably in 1814. Nor is it irrelevant to keep in mind regarding Guillotin, that he was a man of gentle and amiable character, and proposed this instrument for execution as calculated to lessen the sufferings of criminals. So has it been said that the Regent Morton of Scotland introduced the similar instrument called the *Maiden* into his country, having adopted it from an instrument for beheading which long stood in terror of the wicked at one of the gates of the town of Halifax in Yorkshire. But it is ascertained that, whether Morton introduced it or not —and there is no proof that he did—it was in operation at Edinburgh some years before his death ; first under the name of the *Maiden*, and afterwards under that of the *Widow*—a change

* *Notes and Queries*, Mar. 16, 1861.

of appellation to which it would be entitled after the death of its first bridegroom.

It has likewise been represented that the *drop* used in hanging was an improvement effected by an eminent joiner and town-councillor of Edinburgh, the famous Deacon Brodie, and that when he was hanged in October 1788 for housebreaking, he was the first to put the utility of the plan to the proof. But it is quite certain that, whether Brodie made this improvement or not, he was not the first person to test its serviceableness, as it appears to have been in operation at least three years before his death.* Even his title to the improvement must be denied, except, perhaps, as far as regards the introduction of it into practice in Edinburgh, as some such contrivance was used at the execution of Earl Ferrers in 1760, being part of a scaffold which the family of the unfortunate nobleman caused their undertaker to prepare on that occasion, that his lordship might not swing off from a cart like a plebeian culprit. 'There was,' says Horace Walpole, 'a new contrivance for sinking the stage under him, which did not play well; and he suffered a little by the delay, but was dead in four minutes.'

It is much to be feared that there is no belief of any kind more extensively diffused in England, or more heartily entertained, than that which represents a Queen Anne's farthing as the greatest and most valuable of rarities. The story everywhere told and accepted is, that only three farthings were struck in her reign: that two are in public keeping; and that the third is still going about, and if it could be recovered would bring a prodigious price.

In point of fact, there were eight coinings of farthings in the reign of Queen Anne, besides a medal or token of similar size, and these coins are no greater rarities than any other product of the Mint issued a hundred and fifty years ago. Every now and then a poor person comes up from a remote place in the country to London, to sell *the* Queen Anne's farthing, of which he has become the fortunate possessor; and great, of course, is the disappointment when the numismatist offers him perhaps a shilling for the curiosity, justifying the lowness of the price by pulling out a drawer and shewing him eight or ten other examples of the same coin. On one occasion, a labourer and his wife came all the way from Yorkshire on foot to dispose of one of these provoking coins in the metropolis. It is related that a rural publican, having obtained one of the tokens, put it up in his window as a curiosity, and people came from far and near to see it, doubtless not a little to the alleviation of his beer barrels; nor did a statement of its real value by a numismatist, who happened to come to his house, induce him to put it away. About 1814, a confectioner's shopman in Dublin, having taken a Queen Anne's farthing, substituted an ordinary farthing for it in his master's till, and endeavoured to make a good thing for himself by selling it to the best advantage. The master, hearing of the trans-

* The *Scots Magazine*, in relating the execution of one William Mills for housebreaking, 21st September 1785, says, that 'part of the platform on which he stood dropped a few minutes before three.

action, had the man apprehended and tried in the Recorder's Court, when he was actually condemned to a twelvemonth's imprisonment for the offence.

Numismatists have set forth, as a possible reason for the universal belief in the rarity of Queen Anne's farthings, that there are several *pattern-pieces* of farthings of her reign in silver, and of beautiful execution, by Croker, which are rare and in request. But it is very unlikely that the appreciation of such an article amongst men of *vertu* would ever impress the bulk of the people in such a manner or to such results. A more plausible story is, that a lady in the north of England, having lost a Queen Anne's farthing or patternpiece, which she valued as a keepsake, advertised a reward for its recovery. In that case, the popular imagination would easily devise the remainder of the tale.

Unlucky Days.

That peculiar phase of superstition which has regard to lucky or unlucky, good or evil days, is to be found in all ages and climes, wherever the mystery-man of a tribe, or the sacerdotal caste of a nation, has acquired rule or authority over the minds of the people. All over the East, among the populations of antiquity, are to be found traces of this almost universal worship of Luck. It is one form of that culture of the beneficent and the maleficent principles, which marks the belief in good and evil, as an antagonistic duality of gods. From ancient Egypt the evil or unlucky days have received the name of 'Egyptian days.' Nor is it only in pagan, but in Christian times, that this superstition has held its potent sway. No season of year, no month, no week, is free from those untoward days on which it is dangerous, if not fatal, to begin any enterprise, work, or travel. They begin with New-Year's Day, and they only end with the last day of December. Passing over the heathen augurs, who predicted fortunate days for sacrifice or trade, wedding or war, let us see what our Anglo-Saxon forefathers believed in this matter of days. A Saxon MS. (*Cott. MS. Vitell.*, C. viii. fo. 20) gives the following account of these *Dies Mali:*—'Three days there are in the year, which we call Egyptian days; that is, in our language, dangerous days, on any occasion whatever, to the blood of man or beast. In the month which we call April, the last Monday; and then is the second, at the coming in of the month we call August; then is the third, which is the first Monday of the going out* of the month of December. He who on these three days reduces blood, be it of man, be it of beast, this we have heard say, that speedily on the first or seventh day, his life he will end. Or if his life be longer, so that he come not to the seventh day, or if he drink some time in these three days, he will end his life; and he that tastes of goose-flesh, within forty days' space his life he will end.'

In the ancient Exeter Calendar, a MS. said to

* The coming in of a month consisted of the first 15 days in the month (or 16 if it had 31 days); the going out, of the last 15 days of any month.

41

be of the age of Henry II., the first or Calends of January is set down as 'Dies Mala.'

These Saxon Calendars give us a total of about 24 evil days in the 365; or about one such in every fifteen. But the superstition 'lengthened its cords and strengthened its stakes;' it seems to have been felt or feared that the black days had but too small a hold on their regarders; so they were multiplied.

'Astronomers say that six days of the year are perilous of death; and therefore they forbid men to let blood on them, or take any drink; that is to say, January 3, July 1, October 2, the last of April, August 1, the last day going out of December. These six days with great diligence ought to be kept, but namely [mainly?] the latter three, for all the veins are then full. For then, whether man or beast be knit in them within 7 days, or certainly within 14 days, he shall die. And if they take any drinks within 15 days, they shall die; and if they eat any goose in these 3 days, within 40 days they shall die; and if any child be born in these 3 latter days, they shall die a wicked death. Astronomers and astrologers say that in the beginning of March, the seventh night, or the fourteenth day, let the blood of the right arm; and in the beginning of April, the 11th day, of the left arm; and in the end of May, 3d or 5th day, on whether arm thou wilt; and thus, of all the year, thou shalt orderly be kept from the fever, the falling gout, the sister gout, and loss of thy sight.'—*Book of Knowledge*, b. l. p. 19.

Those who may be inclined to pursue this subject more fully, will find an essay on 'Day-Fatality,' in John Aubrey's *Miscellanies*, in which he notes the days lucky and unlucky, of the Jews, Greeks, Romans, and of various distinguished individuals of later times.

In a comparatively modern MS. Calendar, of the time of Henry VI., in the writer's possession, one page of vellum is filled with the following, of which we modernise the spelling:—

'These underwritten be the perilous days, for to take any sickness in, or to be hurt in, or to be wedded in, or to take any journey upon, or to begin any work on, that he would well speed. The number of these days be in the year 32; they be these:—

In January there be 7:—1st, 2d, 4th, 5th, 7th, 10th, and 15th.
In February be 3:—6th, 7th, and 18th.
In March be 3:—1st, 6th, and 8th.
In April be 2:—6th and 11th.
In May be 3:—5th, 6th, and 7th.
In June be 2:—7th and 15th.
In July be 2:—5th and 19th.
In August be 2:—15th and 19th.
In September be 2:—6th and 7th.
In October is 1:—6th.
In November be 2:—15th and 16th.
In December be 3:—15th, 16th, and 17th.'

The copyist of this dread list of evil days, while apparently giving the superstition a qualified credence, manifests a higher and nobler faith, lifting his aspiration above days and seasons; for he has appended to the catalogue, in a bold firm hand of the time—'Sed tamen in Domino confido.' (But, notwithstanding, I will trust in the Lord.) Neither in this Calendar, nor in another of the same owner, prefixed to a small MS. volume containing a copy of *Magna Charta*, &c., is there inserted in the body of the Calendar anything to denote a 'Dies Mala.' After the Reformation, the old evil days appear to have abated much of the ancient malevolent influences, and to have left behind them only a general superstition against fishermen setting out to fish, or seamen to take a voyage, or landsmen a journey, or domestic servants to enter on a new place—on a Friday. In many country districts, especially in the north of England, no weddings take place on Friday, from this cause. According to a rhyming proverb, 'Friday's moon, come when it will, comes too soon.' Sir Thomas Overbury, in his charming sketch of a milkmaid, says, 'Her dreams are so chaste, that she dare tell them; only a Friday's dream is all her superstition; and she consents for fear of anger.' Erasmus dwells on the 'extraordinary inconsistency' of the English of his day, in eating flesh in Lent, yet holding it a heinous offence to eat any on a Friday out of Lent. The Friday superstitions cannot be wholly explained by the fact that it was ordained to be held as a fast by the Christians of Rome. Some portion of its maleficent character is probably due to the character of the Scandinavian Venus Freya, the wife of Odin, and goddess of fecundity. But we are met on the other hand by the fact that amongst the Brahmins of India a like superstitious aversion to Friday prevails. They say that 'on this day no business must be commenced.'[*] And herein is the fate foreshadowed of any antiquary who seeks to trace one of our still lingering superstitions to its source. Like the bewildered traveller at the cross roads, he knows not which to take. One leads him into the ancient Teuton forests; a second amongst the wilds of Scandinavia; a third to papal, and thence to pagan Rome; and a fourth carries him to the far east, and there he is left with the conviction that much of what is old and quaint and strange among us, of the superstitious relics of our fore-elders, has its root deep in the soil of one of the ancient homes of the race.

JANUARY 3.

St Peter Balsam, martyr, 311; St Anterus, pope, 235; St Gordius, martyr; Ste Geneviève, virgin.

STE GENEVIÈVE.

Sainte Geneviève, who has occupied, from the time of her death to the present day, the distinguished position of Patroness Saint of the city of Paris, lived in the fifth century, when Christianity, under corrupted forms, was contending with paganism for domination over the minds of rude and warlike races of men. Credible facts of this early period are few, obscure, and not easily separated from the fictions with which they have been combined; but the following principal events of the life of Ste Geneviève may be taken as probably authentic:—She was born in the year 422, at Nanterre, a village about four miles from Paris. At the early age of seven years she was consecrated to the service of religion by St Germanus, bishop of Auxerre, who happened to pass through the village, and was

[*] Dr Buchanan, *Asiat. Res.*, vol. vi. p. 172.

struck with her devotional manners. At the age of fifteen years she received the veil from the hands of the Archbishop of Paris, in which city she afterwards resided. By strict observance of the services of the Church, and by the practice of those austerities which were then regarded as the surest means of obtaining the blessedness of a future state, she acquired a reputation for sanctity which gave her considerable influence over the rulers and leaders of the people. When the Franks under Clovis had subdued the city of Paris, her solicitations are said to have moved the conqueror to acts of clemency and generosity. The miracles ascribed to Ste Geneviève may be passed over as hardly likely to obtain much credence in the present age. The date of her death has been fixed on January 3d, 512, five months after the decease of king Clovis. She was buried near him in the church of St Peter and St Paul, since named the church of Sainte Geneviève. The present handsome structure was completed in 1764. During the revolutionary period it was withdrawn from the services of religion, and named the Pantheon, but has since been restored to ecclesiastical uses and to its former name of Sainte Geneviève. Details of her life are given in Bollandus's 'Acta Sanctorum,' and in Butler's 'Lives of the Saints.'

Born. — Marcus Tullius Cicero, B.C. 107; Douglas Jerrold, 1803.
Died.—Jeremiah Horrox, mathematician, 1641; George Monk, Duke of Albemarle, 1670; Josiah Wedgwood, 1795; Charles Robert Maturin, novelist, 1842; Eliot Warburton, historical novelist, 1852.

MARCUS TULLIUS CICERO.

Cicero, like nearly every other great man, gives in his life a testimony to the value and necessity of diligent culture of the mind for the attainment of eminence. His education for oratory was most laborious. He himself declared that no man ought to pretend to the character of an orator without being previously acquainted with everything worth knowing in nature and art, as eloquence unbased upon knowledge is no better than the prattle of a child. He was six-and-twenty before he considered himself properly accomplished for his profession. 'He had learned the rudiments of grammar and languages from the ablest teachers; gone through the studies of humanity and the politer letters with the poet Archias; been instructed in philosophy by the principal professors of each sect—Phædrus the Epicurean, Philo the Academic, and Diodotus the Stoic; acquired a perfect knowledge of the law from the greatest lawyers as well as the greatest statesmen of Rome, the two Scævolas; all which accomplishments were but ministerial and subservient to that on which his hopes and ambition were singly placed, the reputation of an orator. To qualify himself therefore for this, he attended the pleadings of all the speakers of his time; heard the daily lectures of the most eminent orators of Greece, and was perpetually composing somewhat at home, and declaiming under their correction; and, that he might neglect nothing which might in any degree help to improve and polish his style, *he spent the inter-*

vals *of his leisure in the company of the ladies;* especially of those who were remarkable for a politeness of language, and whose fathers had been distinguished by a fame and reputation for eloquence. While he studied the law, therefore, under Scævola the augur, he frequently conversed with his wife Lælia, whose discourse, he says, was tinctured with all the elegance of her father Lælius, the politest speaker of his age: he was acquainted likewise with her daughter Mucia, who married the great orator Lucius Crassus; and with her granddaughters the two Liciniæ, ... who all excelled in that delicacy of the Latin tongue which was peculiar to their families, and valued themselves on preserving and propagating it to their posterity.'—Melmoth's *Life of Cicero.*

GENERAL MONK.

The most curious portion of Monk's private history is his marriage to Anne, daughter of John Clarges, a farrier in the Savoy in the Strand. She was first married to Thomas Radford, late farrier: they lived at the Three Spanish Gipsies in the New Exchange, Strand, and sold wash-balls, powder, gloves, &c., and she taught plain work to girls. In 1647 she became sempstress to Monk, and used to carry him linen. In 1649 she and her husband fell out and parted; but no certificate of any parish-register appears recording his burial. In 1652 she was married at the Church of St George, Southwark, to General Monk, though it is said her first husband was living at the time. In the following year she was delivered of a son, Christopher, who 'was suckled by Honour Mills, who sold apples, herbs, oysters, &c.' The father of 'Nan Clarges,' according to Aubrey's *Lives* (written about 1680), had his forge upon the site of No. 317, on the north side of the Strand. 'The shop is still of that trade,' says Aubrey; 'the corner shop, the first turning, on yᵉ right hand, as you come out the Strand into Drury Lane: the house is now built of brick.' The house alluded to is believed to be that at the right-hand corner of Drury Court, now a butcher's. The adjoining house, in the court, is now a whitesmith's, with a forge, &c. Nan's mother was one of *Five Women Barbers,* celebrated in her time. Nan is described by Clarendon as a person 'of the lowest extraction, without either wit or beauty;' and Aubrey says 'she was not at all handsome nor cleanly,' and that she was seamstress to Monk, when he was imprisoned in the Tower. She is known to have had great control and authority over him. Upon his being raised to a dukedom, and her becoming Duchess of Albemarle, her father, the farrier, is said to have raised a Maypole in the Strand, nearly opposite his forge, to commemorate his daughter's good fortune. She died a few days after the Duke, and is interred by his side in Henry the Seventh's Chapel, Westminster Abbey. The Duke was succeeded by his son, Christopher, who married Lady Elizabeth Cavendish, granddaughter of the Duke of Newcastle, and died childless. The Duchess' brother, Thomas Clarges, was a physician of note; was created a baronet in 1674, and was ancestor to the baronets; whence is named Clarges Street, Piccadilly.

JOSIAH WEDGWOOD.

Josiah Wedgwood, celebrated for his valuable improvements in the manufacture of earthenware, was born July 12th 1730, at Burslem, in Staffordshire, where his father and others of the family had for many years been employed in the potteries. At the early age of eleven years, his father being then dead, he worked as a thrower in a pottery belonging to his elder brother; and he continued to be thus employed till disease in his right leg

JOSIAH WEDGWOOD.

compelled him to relinquish the potter's wheel, and ultimately to have the limb cut off below the knee. He then began to occupy himself in making imitations of agates, jaspers, and other coloured stones, by combining metallic oxides with different clays, which he formed into knife-handles, small boxes, and ornaments for the mantelpiece. After various movements in business, he finally settled in a pottery of his own, at Burslem, where he continued for a time to make the small ornamental articles which had first brought him into notice, but by degrees began to manufacture fine earthenware for the table. He was successful, and took a second manufactory, where he made white stoneware; and then a third, where he produced a delicate cream-coloured ware, of which he presented some articles to Queen Charlotte, who was so well pleased with them and with a complete service which he executed by order, that she appointed him her potter. The new kind of earthenware, under the name of Queen's ware, became fashionable, and orders from the nobility and gentry flowed in upon him. He took into partnership Mr Bentley, son of the celebrated Dr Bentley, and opened a warehouse in London, where the goods were exhibited and sold. Mr Bentley, who was a man of learning and taste, and had a large circle of acquaintance among men of rank and science, superintended the business in the metropolis. Wedgwood's operations in earthenware and stoneware included the production of various articles of ornament for the cabinet, the drawing-room, and the boudoir. To facilitate the conveyance of his goods, as well as of materials required for the manufacture, he contributed a large sum towards the formation of the Trent and Mersey Canal, which was completed in 1770. On the bank of this canal,

while it was in progress, he erected, near Stoke, a large manufactory and a handsome mansion for his own residence, and there he built the village of Etruria, consisting chiefly of the habitations of his workmen. He died there on the 3d of January 1795, in the 65th year of his age. He was married, and had several children.

To Wedgwood originally, and to him almost exclusively during a period of more than thirty years, Great Britain was indebted for the rapid improvement and vast extension of the earthenware manufacture. During the early part of his life England produced only brown pottery and common articles of white earthenware for domestic use. The finer wares for the opulent classes of society, as well as porcelain, were imported from Holland, Germany, and France. He did not extend his operations to the manufacture of porcelain—the kaolin, or china-clay, not having been discovered in Cornwall till he was far advanced in life; but his earthenwares were of such excellence in quality, in form, and in beauty of ornamentation, as in a great degree to supersede the foreign china-wares, not only in this country, but in the markets of the civilised world. Wedgwood's success was the result of experiments and trials, conducted with persevering industry on scientific principles. He studied the chemistry of the aluminous, silicious, and alkaline earths, colouring substances, and glazes, which he employed. He engaged the most skilful artisans and artists, and superintended assiduously the operations of the workshop and the kiln. In order to ascertain and regulate the heat of his furnaces, he invented a pyrometer, by which the higher degrees of temperature might be accurately measured: it consisted of small cylinders of pure white clay, with an apparatus which showed the degrees of diminution in length which the cylinders underwent from the action of the fire. Besides the manufacture of the superior kinds of earthenware for the table and domestic purposes, he produced a great variety of works of fine art, such as imitations of cameos, intaglios, and other antique gems, vases, urns, busts, medallions, and other objects of curiosity and beauty. His imitations of the Etruscan vases gained him great celebrity, and were purchased largely. He also executed fifty copies of the Portland vase, which were sold for fifty guineas each.

DOUGLAS JERROLD.

No one that has seen Douglas Jerrold can ever forget him—a tiny round-shouldered man, with a pale aquiline visage, keen bright grey eyes, and a profusion of iron-brown hair; usually rather taciturn (though with a never-ceasing play of eye and lips) till an opportunity occurred for shooting forth one of those flashes of wit which made him the conversational chief of his day. The son of a poor manager haunting Sheerness, Jerrold owed little to education or early connection. He entered life as a midshipman, but early gravitated into a London literary career His first productions were plays, whereof one, based on the ballad of 'Black-eyed Susan' (written when the author was scarce twenty), obtained such success as redeemed theatres and made theatrical reputations, and yet Jerrold never realised from it above seventy pounds. He also wrote novels, but his chief productions were contributions to periodicals. In this walk he had for a long course of years no superior. His 'Caudle Lectures,' contributed to *Punch*, were perhaps the most attractive series of articles that ever appeared in any periodical work.

DOUGLAS JERROLD.

The drollery of his writings, though acknowledged to be great, would not perhaps have made Douglas Jerrold the remarkable power he was, if he had not also possessed such a singular strain of colloquial repartee. In his day, no man in the metropolis was one half so noted for the brilliancy and originality of his sayings. Jerrold's wit proved itself to be, unlike Sheridan's, unpremeditated, for his best sayings were answers to remarks of others; often, indeed, they consisted of clauses or single words deriving their significancy from their connection with what another person had said. Seldom or never did it consist of a pun or quibble. Generally, it derived its value from the sense lying under it. Always sharp, often caustic, it was never morose or truly ill-natured. Jerrold was, in reality, a kind-hearted man, full of feeling and tenderness; and of true goodness and worth, talent and accomplishment, he was ever the hearty admirer.

Specimens of conversational wit apart from the circumstances which produced them, are manifestly placed at a great disadvantage; yet some of Jerrold's good things bear repetition in print. His definition of dogmatism as 'puppyism come to maturity,' might be printed by itself in large type and put upon a church-door, without suffering any loss of point. What he said on passing the flamingly uxorious epitaph put up by a famous cook on his wife's tomb—'Mock Turtle!'—might equally have been placed on the tomb itself with perfect preservation of its poignancy. Similarly independent of all external aid is the keenness of his answer to a fussy clergyman, who was expressing opinions very revolting to Jerrold,—to the effect that the real evil of modern times was

the surplus population—'Yes, the *surplice* population.' It is related that a prosy old gentleman, meeting him as he was passing at his usual quick pace along Regent Street, poised himself into an attitude, and began: 'Well, Jerrold, my dear boy, what is going on?' 'I am,' said the wit, instantly shooting off. Such is an example of the brief fragmentary character of the wit of Jerrold. On another occasion it consisted of but a mono-syllable. It was at a dinner of artists, that a barrister present, having his health drunk in connection with the law, began an embarrassed answer by saying he did not see how the law could be considered as one of the arts, when Jerrold jerked in the word 'black,' and threw the company into convulsions. A bore in company remarking how charmed he was with the *Prodigue*, and that there was one particular song which always quite carried him away,—'Would that I could sing it!' ejaculated the wit.

What a profound rebuke to the *inner consciousness* school of modern poets there is in a little occurrence of Jerrold's life connected with a volume of the writings of Robert Browning! When recovering from a violent fit of sickness, he had been ordered to refrain from all reading and writing, which he had obeyed wonderfully well, although he found the monotony of a seaside life very trying to his active mind. One morning he had been left by Mrs Jerrold alone, while she had gone shopping, and during her absence a parcel of books from London arrived. Among them was Browning's 'Sordello,' which he commenced to read. Line after line, and page after page was devoured by the convalescent wit, but not a consecutive idea could he get from that mystic production. The thought then struck him that he had lost his reason during his illness, and that he was so imbecile that he did not know it. A perspiration burst from his brow, and he sat silent and thoughtful. When his wife returned, he thrust the mysterious volume into her hands, crying out, 'Read this, my dear!' After several attempts to make any sense out of the first page or so, she returned it, saying, 'Bother the gibberish! I don't understand a word of it!' 'Thank Heaven,' cried the delighted wit; 'then I am not an idiot!'

His winding up a review of Wordsworth's poems was equally good. 'He reminds me,' said Jerrold, 'of the Beadle of Parnassus, strutting about in a cocked hat, or, to be more poetical, of a modern Moses, who sits on Pisgah with his back obstinately turned to that promised land the Future; he is only fit for those old maid tabbies, the Muses! His Pegasus is a broken-winded hack, with a grammatical bridle, and a monosyllabic bit between his teeth!'

Mr Blanchard Jerrold, in his *Life* of his father, groups a few additional good things which will not here be considered superfluous. 'A dinner is discussed. Douglas Jerrold listens quietly, possibly tired of dinners, and declining pressing invitations to be present. In a few minutes he will chime in, "If an earthquake were to engulf England to-morrow, the English would manage to meet and dine somewhere among the rubbish, just to celebrate the event." A friend drops in, and walks across the smoking-room to Douglas

Jerrold's chair. The friend wants to rouse Mr Jerrold's sympathies in behalf of a mutual acquaintance who is in want of a round sum of money. But this mutual friend has already sent his hat about among his literary brethren on more than one occasion. Mr ——'s hat is becoming an institution, and friends were grieved at the indelicacy of the proceeding. On the occasion to which I now refer, the bearer of the hat was received by my father with evident dissatisfaction. "Well," said Douglas Jerrold, "how much does —— want this time?" "Why, just a four and two noughts will, I think, put him straight," the bearer of the hat replied. *Jerrold*—"Well, put me down for one of the noughts." "The Chain of Events," playing at the Lyceum Theatre, is mentioned. "Humph!" says Douglas Jerrold. "I'm afraid the manager will find it a door chain, strong enough to keep everybody out of the house." Then some somewhat lackadaisical young members drop in. They assume that the Club is not sufficiently west; they hint at something near Pall-Mall, and a little more style. Douglas Jerrold rebukes them. "No, no, gentlemen; not near Pall-Mall: we might catch coronets." A stormy discussion ensues, during which a gentleman rises to settle the matter in dispute. Waving his hands majestically over the excited disputants, he begins: "Gentlemen, all I want is common sense." "Exactly," says Douglas Jerrold, "that is precisely what you *do* want." The discussion is lost in a burst of laughter. The talk lightly passes to the writings of a certain Scot. A member holds that the Scot's name should be handed down to a grateful posterity. *Douglas Jerrold*—"I quite agree with you that he should have an itch in the Temple of Fame." Brown drops in. Brown is said by all his friends to be the toady of Jones. The assurance of Jones in a room is the proof that Brown is in the passage. When Jones has the influenza, Brown dutifully catches a cold in the head. *Douglas Jerrold to Brown*—"Have you heard the rumour that's flying about town?" "No." "Well, they say Jones pays the dog-tax for you." Douglas Jerrold is seriously disappointed with a certain book written by one of his friends, and has expressed his disappointment. *Friend*—"I have heard you said —— was the worst book I ever wrote." *Jerrold*—"No, I didn't. I said it was the worst book anybody ever wrote." A supper of sheep's-heads is proposed, and presently served. One gentleman present is particularly enthusiastic on the excellence of the dish, and, as he throws down his knife and fork, exclaims, "Well, sheep's-head for ever, say I!" *Jerrold*—"There's egotism!"'

It is worth while to note the succession of the prime jokers of London before Jerrold. The series begins with King Charles II., to whom succeeded the Earl of Dorset, after whom came the Earl of Chesterfield, who left his mantle to George Selwyn, whose successor was a man he detested, Richard Brinsley Sheridan; after whom was Jekyl, then Theodore Hook, whose successor was Jerrold: eight in all during a term of nearly two hundred years.

46

INTRODUCTION OF FEMALE ACTORS.

Pepys relates, in that singular chronicle of gossip, his Diary, under January 3, 1661, that he went to the theatre and saw the *Beggar's Bush* well performed; 'the first time,' says he, 'that ever I saw women come upon the stage.'

This was a theatre in Gibbon's Tennis Court, Vere Street, Clare Market, which had been opened at the recent restoration of the monarchy, after the long theatrical blank under the reign of the Puritans. It had heretofore been customary for young men to act the female parts. All Shakspeare's heroines were thus awkwardly enacted for the first sixty years. At length, on the restoration of the stage, it was thought that the public might perhaps endure the indecorum of female acting, and the venture is believed to have been first made at this theatre on the 8th of December 1660, when a lady acted Desdemona for the first time.

Colley Cibber gives a comic traditional story regarding the time when this fashion was coming in. 'Though women,' says he, 'were not admitted to the stage till the return of King Charles, yet it could not be so suddenly supplied with them, but that there was still a necessity, for some time, to put the handsomest young men into petticoats, which Kynaston was said to have then worn with success; particularly in the part of Evadne in the *Maid's Tragedy*, which I have heard him speak of, and which calls to my mind a ridiculous distress that arose from that sort of shifts which the stage was then put to. The king, coming before his usual time to a tragedy, found the actors not ready to begin; when his Majesty, not choosing to have as much patience as his good subjects, sent to them to know the meaning of it; upon which the master of the company came to the box, and rightly judging that the best excuse for their default would be the true one, fairly told his Majesty that the queen was not *shaved* yet. The king, whose good humour loved to laugh at a jest as well as make one, accepted the excuse, which served to divert him till the male queen could be effeminated. Kynaston was at that time so beautiful a youth, that the ladies of quality prided themselves in taking him with them in their coaches to Hyde Park in his theatrical habit, after the play, which in those days they might have sufficient time to do, because plays then were used to begin at four o'clock.' *

The Horn Book.

In the manuscript account books of the Archer family, quoted by Mr Halliwell in his elaborate notes on Shakspeare, occurs this entry: 'Jan. 3, 1715-16, one horn-book for Mr Eyres, 00 : 00 : 02.' The article referred to as thus purchased at twopence was one once most familiar, but now known only as a piece of antiquity, and that rather obscurely. The remark has been very justly made, that many books, at one time enjoying a more than usually great circulation, are precisely those likely to become the scarcest in a succeed-

* Cibber's *Apology for his Own Life.*

ing age; for example, nearly all school-books, and, above all, a Horn-Book. Down to the time of George II., there was perhaps no kind of book so largely and universally diffused as this said horn-book; at present, there is perhaps no book of that reign, of which it would be more difficult to procure a copy.

The annexed representation is copied from one given by Mr Halliwell, as taken from a black-letter example which was found some years ago in pulling down an old farm-house at Middleton, in Derbyshire. A portrait of King Charles I. in armour on horseback was upon the reverse, affording us an approximation to the date.

HORN BOOK.—17TH CENTURY.

The horn-book was the Primer of our ancestors —their established means of learning the elements of English literature. It consisted of a single leaf, containing on one side the alphabet large and small—in black-letter or in Roman—with perhaps a small regiment of monosyllables, and a copy of the Lord's Prayer; and this leaf was usually set in a frame of wood, with a slice of diaphanous horn in front — hence the name *horn*-book. Generally there was a handle to hold it by, and this handle had usually a hole for a string, whereby the apparatus was slung to the girdle of the scholar. In a *View of the Beau Monde*, 1731, p. 52, a lady is described as 'dressed like a child, in a bodice coat and leading-strings, with a horn-book tied to her side.' A various

kind of horn-book gave the leaf simply pasted against a slice of horn; but the one more generally in use was that above described. It is to it that Shenstone alludes in his beautiful cabinet-picture-poem, *The Schoolmistress*, where he tells of the children, how

'Their books of stature small they take in hand,
  Which with pellucid horn secured are,
  To save from fingers wet the letters fair.'

It ought not to be forgotten that the alphabet on the horn-book was invariably prefaced with a Cross: whence it came to be called the Christ Cross Row, or by corruption the Criss Cross Row, a term which was often used instead of horn-book.

In earlier times, it is thought that a cast-leaden plate, containing the alphabet in raised letters, was used for the instruction of the youth of England, as Sir George Musgrave of Eden-hall possesses two carved stones which appear to have been moulds for such a production.

MIGRATORY BOGS.

On a bitter winter's night, when rain had softened the ground, and loosened such soil as was deficient in cohesiveness, a whole mass of Irish bog or peat-moss shifted from its place. It was on the 3d of January 1853; and the spot was in a wild region called Enagh Monmore. The mass was nearly a mile in circumference, and several feet deep. On it moved, urged apparently by the force of gravity, over sloping ground, and continuing its strange march for twenty-four hours, when a change in the contour of the ground brought it to rest. Its extent of movement averaged about a quarter of a mile.

Such phenomena as these, although not frequent in occurrence, are sufficiently numerous to deserve notice. There are in many, if not most countries, patches of ground covered with soft boggy masses, too insecure to build upon, and not very useful in any other way. Bogs, mosses, quagmires, marshes, fens—all have certain points of resemblance: they are all masses of vegetable matter, more or less mixed with earth, and moistened with streams running through them, springs rising beneath them, or rains falling upon them. Some are masses almost as solid as wood, fibrous, and nearly dry; some are liquid black mud; others are soft, green, vegetable, spongy accumulations; while the rest present intermediate characters. Peat-bogs of the hardest kind are believed to be the result of decayed forests, acted upon by long-continued heat, moisture, and pressure; mosses and marshes are probably of more recent formation, and are more thoroughly saturated with water. In most cases they fill hollows in the ground; and if the edges of those hollows are not well defined and sufficiently elevated, we are very likely to hear of the occurrence of *quaking bogs* and *flow-mosses*.

In the year 1697, at Charleville, near Limerick, a peat-bog burst its bounds. There was heard for some time underground a noise like thunder at a great distance or when nearly spent. Soon afterwards, the partially-dried crust of a large bog began to move; the convexity of the upper surface began to sink; and boggy matter flowed out at the edges. Not only did the substance of the bog move, but it carried with it the adjacent pasture-grounds, though separated by a large and deep ditch. The motion continued a considerable time, and the surface rose into undulations, but without bursting up or breaking. The pasture-land rose very high, and was urged on with the same motion, till it rested upon a neighbouring meadow, the whole surface of which it covered to a depth of sixteen feet. The site which the bog had occupied was left full of unsightly holes, containing foul water giving forth stinking vapours. It was pretty well ascertained that this catastrophe was occasioned by long-continued rain—not by softening the bog on which it fell, but by getting *under* it, and so causing it to slide away.

England, though it has abundance of fenny or marshy land in the counties lying west and south of the Wash, has very few such bogs as those which cover nearly three million acres of land in Ireland. There are some spots, however, such as Chat Moss in Lancashire, which belong to this character. Leland, who wrote in the time of Henry the Eighth, described, in his quaint way, an outflow of this moss: 'Chat Moss brast up within a mile of Mosley Haul, and destroied much grounde with mosse thereabout, and destroied much fresh-water fishche thereabout, first corrupting with stinkinge water Glasebrooke, and so Glasebrooke carried stinkinge water and mosse into Mersey water, and Mersey corrupted carried the roulling mosse, part to the shores of Wales, part to the isle of Man, and some unto Ireland. And in the very top of Chateley More, where the mosse was hyest and brake, is now a fair plaine valley as ever in tymes paste, and a rylle runnith int, and peaces of small trees be found in the bottom.' Let it be remembered that this is the same Chat Moss over which the daring but yet calculating genius of George Stephenson carried a railway. It is amusing now to look back at the evidence given, thirty-five years ago, before the Parliamentary Committee on the Liverpool and Manchester Railway. Engineers of some eminence vehemently denied the possibility of achieving the work. One of them said that no vehicle could stand on the Moss short of the bottom; that the whole must be scooped out, to the depth of thirty or forty feet, and an equivalent of hard earth filled in; and that even if a railway could be formed on the Moss, it would cost £200,000. Nevertheless Stephenson *did* it, and expended only £30,000; and there is the railway, sound to the present hour. The moss, over an area of nearly twelve square miles, is so soft as to yield to the foot; while some parts of it are a pulpy mass. Stephenson threw down thousands of cubic yards of firm earth, which gradually sank, and solidified sufficiently to form his railway upon; hurdles of heath and brushwood were laid upon the surface, and on these the wooden sleepers. There is still a gentle kind of undulation, as if the railway rested on a semi-fluid mass; nevertheless it is quite secure.

Scotland has many more bogs and peat-mosses than England. They are found chiefly in low districts, but sometimes even on the tops of the mountains. Mr Robert Chambers gives an account of an outburst which took place in 1629: 'In the fertile district between Falkirk and Stirling, there was a large moss with a little lake in the middle of it, occupying a piece of gradually-rising ground. A highly-cultivated district of wheat-land lay below. There had been a series of heavy rains, and the moss became overcharged with moisture. After some days, during which slight movements were visible on this quagmire, the whole mass began one night to leave its native situation, and slide gently down to the low grounds. The people who lived on these lands, receiving sufficient warning, fled and saved their lives; but in the morning light they beheld their little farms, sixteen in number, covered six feet deep with liquid moss, and hopelessly lost.' —*Domestic Annals of Scotland*, ii. 35.

Somewhat akin to this was the flowing moss described by Pennant. It was on the Scottish border, near the shore of the Solway. When he passed the spot during his First Journey to Scotland in 1768, he saw it a smiling valley; on his Second Journey, four years afterwards, it was a dismal waste. The Solway Moss was an expanse of semi-liquid bog covering 1600 acres, and lying somewhat higher than a valley of fertile land near Netherby. So long as the moderately hard crust near the edge was preserved, the moss did not flow over: but on one occasion some peat-diggers imprudently tampered with this crust; and the moss, moistened with very heavy rain, overcame further control. It was on the night of the 17th of November 1771, that a farmer who lived near the Moss was suddenly alarmed by an unusual noise. The crust had given way, and the black deluge was rolling towards his house while he was searching with a lantern for the cause of the noise. When he caught sight of a small dark stream, he thought it came from his own farm-yard dung hill, which by some strange cause had been set in motion. The truth soon flashed upon him, however. He gave notice to his neighbours with all expedition. 'Others,' said Pennant, 'received no other advice than what this Stygian tide gave them: some by its noise, many by its entrance into their houses; and I have been assured that some were surprised with it even in their beds. These passed a horrible night, remaining totally ignorant of their fate, and the cause of their calamity, till the morning, when their neighbours with difficulty got them out through the roof.' About 300 acres of bog flowed over 400 acres of land, utterly ruining and even burying the farms, overturning the buildings, filling some of the cottages up to the roof, and suffocating many cattle. The stuff flowed along like thick black paint, studded with lumps of more solid peat; and it filled every nook and crevice in its passage. 'The disaster of a cow was so singular as to deserve mention. She was the only one, out of eight in the same cow-house, that was saved, after having stood sixty hours up to the neck in mud and water. When she was relieved she did not refuse to eat, but would not touch water, nor would even look at it without manifest signs of horror.'

The same things are going on around us at the present day. During the heavy rains of August 1861, there was a displacement of Auchingray

Moss between Slamannan and Airdrie. A farmer, looking out one morning from his farm-door near the first-named town, saw, to his dismay, about twenty acres of the moss separate from its clay bottom, and float a distance of three quarters of a mile. The sight was wonderful, but the consequences were grievous; for a large surface of potato-ground and of arable land became covered with the offensive visitant.

JANUARY 4.

St Titus, disciple of St Paul. St Gregory, bishop, 541. St Rigobert, or Robert, about 750. St Rumon, bishop.

Born.—Archbishop Usher, 1580; Jacob Ludwig Karl Grimm, 1785.
Died.—The Maréchal Duc de Luxembourg, 1695; Charlotte Lennox, novelist, 1804; Rachel, *tragédienne*, 1858; Joseph John Gurney, philanthropist, 1847.

JACOB L. K. GRIMM.

Jacob Grimm (1785–1863) and his younger brother Wilhelm (1786–1859), natives of Hanau in the electorate of Hesse-Cassel, were distinguished as investigators of the early history and literature of Germany. They produced numerous works, including the fairy tales collected from various parts of Germany, and were finally engaged upon a large Dictionary of the German Language. 'All my labours,' says Jacob Grimm, 'have been either directly or indirectly devoted to researches into our ancient language, poetry, and laws. These studies may seem useless to many; but to me they have always appeared a serious and dignified task, firmly and distinctly connected with our common fatherland, and calculated to foster the love of it. I have esteemed nothing trifling in these inquiries, but have used the small for the elucidation of the great, popular traditions for the elucidation of written documents. Several of my books have been published in common with my brother William. We lived from our youth up in brotherly community of goods; money, books, and collectanea, belonged to us in common, and it was natural to combine our labours.' The publications of Jacob extended over fully half a century, the first having appeared in 1811.

MARÉCHAL DUC DE LUXEMBOURG, 1695.

Whatever glory or territory France gained by arms under Louis XIV. might be said to be owing to this singularly able general. It was remarked that each of his campaigns was marked by some brilliant victory, and as these were always blazoned on the walls of the principal church of Paris, he came to be called, by one of those epigrammatic flatteries for which the French are distinguished, *Le Tapissier de Notre Dame*. With his death the prosperities of Louis XIV. terminated.

MADEMOISELLE RACHEL.

The modern tragedy queen of France died at thirty-eight—that age which appears so fatal to genius; that is to say, the age at which an overworked nervous system comes naturally to a close. An exhausting professional tour in America, entered upon for needless money-making, is believed to have had much to do in bringing the great *tragédienne* to a premature grave. Rachel was the child of poor Hebrew parents, and her talents were first exercised in singing to a guitar on the streets of Paris. When at an early age she broke upon theatrical audiences in the characters of Roxane, Camille, and others of that class, she created a *furore* almost unexampled. Yet her style of acting was more calculated to excite terror than to melt with pity. She was in reality a woman without estimable qualities. The mean passion of avarice was her predominating one, and strange stories are told of the oblique courses she would resort to to gratify it. There was but one relieving consideration regarding it, that she employed its results liberally in behalf of the poor family from which she sprang. The feelings with which we heard in England in 1848 that Rachel had excited the greatest enthusiasm in the *Théâtre Français* by singing the Marseillaise hymn, and soon after that her lover M. Ledru Rollin, of the provisional government, had paid her song with a grant of public money, will not soon be forgotten.

INTRODUCTION OF THE SILK MANUFACTURES INTO EUROPE.

It was on the 4th of January 536, that two monks came from the Indies to Constantinople, bringing with them the means of teaching the manufacture of silk. Workmen instructed in the art carried it thence to Italy and other parts of Europe. In England, the manufacture was practised as early as the reign of Henry VI., in the middle of the fifteenth century.

ARREST OF THE FIVE MEMBERS.

The 4th of January 1641-2 is the date of one of the most memorable events in English history —the attempted arrest of the five members of the House of Commons—Pym, Hampden, Hollis, Haselrig, and Strode—by Charles I. The divisions between the unhappy king and his parliament were lowering towards the actual war which broke out eight months later. Charles, stung by the Grand Remonstrance, a paper in which all the errors of his past government were exposed, thought by one decisive act to strike terror into his outraged subjects, and restore his full authority. While London was on the borders of insurrection against his rule, there yet were not wanting considerable numbers of country gentlemen, soldiers of fortune, and others, who were eager to rally round him in any such attempt. His design of coming with an armed band to the House and arresting the five obnoxious members, was communicated by a lady of his court; so that, just as he approached the door of the House with his cavalier bands, the gentlemen he wished to seize were retiring to a boat on the river, by which they made their escape.

Mr John Forster has assembled, with great skill, all the facts of the scene which ensued. 'Within the House,' he says,* 'but a few minutes had elapsed since the Five Members had departed, and Mr Speaker had received instruction to sit still with the mace lying before him, when

* The Arrest of Five Members, by Charles I. A Chapter of English History re-written. By John Forster. 1860.

a loud knock threw open the door, a rush of armed men was heard, and above it (as we learn from Sir Ralph Verney) the voice of the King commanding "upon their lives not to come in." The moment after, followed only by his nephew, Charles, the Prince Elector Palatine, Rupert's eldest brother, he entered; but the door was not permitted to be closed behind him. Visible now at the threshold to all were the officers and desperadoes, of whom, D'Ewes proceeds: "some had left their cloaks in the hall, and most of them were armed with pistols and swords, and they forcibly kept the door of the House of Commons open, one Captain Hide standing next the door holding his sword upright in the scabbard." A picture which Sir Ralph Verney, also present that day, in his place, completes by adding that, "so the door was kept open, and the Earl of Roxburgh stood within the door, leaning upon it."'

The King walked uncovered along the hall, while the members stood uncovered and silent on each side. Taking a position on the step in front of the Speaker's chair, he looked round for the faces of Pym and his four associates, and not finding them, he thus spoke: 'Gentlemen, I am sorry for this occasion of coming among you. Yesterday I sent a serjeant-at-arms upon a very important occasion to apprehend some that by my command were accused of high treason; whereunto I did expect obedience, and not a message. And I must declare unto you here, that albeit no king that ever was in England, shall be more careful of your privileges, to maintain them to the uttermost of his power, than I shall be, yet you must know that in cases of treason no person hath a privilege. And therefore I am come to know if any of these persons that were accused are here.'

Still casting his eyes vainly around, he after a pause added, 'So long as those persons that I have accused (for no slight crime, but for treason) are here, I cannot expect that this House will be in the right way I do heartily wish it. Therefore I am come to tell you that I must have them, wherever I find them.'

After another pause, he called out, 'Is Mr Pym here?' No answer being returned, he asked if Mr Hollis was here. There being still no answer, he turned to the Speaker, and put these questions to him. The scene became painfully embarrassing to all, and it grew more so when Lenthal, kneeling before the King, entreated him to understand that he could neither see nor speak but at the pleasure of the House. Mr Forster has been enabled by D'Ewes to describe the remainder of the scene in vivid terms. After another long pause—a 'dreadful silence'—'Charles spoke again to the crowd of mute and sullen faces. The complete failure of his scheme was now accomplished, and all its possible consequences, all the suspicions and retaliations to which it had laid him open, appear to have rushed upon his mind. "Well, since I see all my birds are flown, I do expect from you that you will send them unto me as soon as they return hither. But, I assure you, on the word of a king, I never did intend any force, but shall proceed against them in a legal and fair way, for I never meant any other. And now, since I see that I cannot

do what I came for, I think this no unfit occasion to repeat what I have said formerly, that whatsoever I have done in favour, and to the good, of my subjects, I do mean to maintain it. I will trouble you no more, but tell you I do expect, as soon as they come to the House, you will send them to me; otherwise I must take my own course to find them." To that closing sentence, the note left by Sir Ralph Verney makes a not unimportant addition, which, however, appears nowhere in Rushworth's Report. "For their treason was foul, and such an one as they would all thank him to discover." If uttered, it was an angry assertion from amid forced and laboured apologies, and so far, would agree with what D'Ewes observed of his change of manner at the time. "After he had ended his speech, he went out of the House in a more discontented and angry passion than he came in, going out again between myself and the south end of the clerk's table, and the Prince Elector after him."

'But he did not leave as he had entered, in silence. Low mutterings of fierce discontent broke out as he passed along, and many members cried out aloud, so as he might hear them, *Privilege! Privilege!* With these words, ominous of ill, ringing in his ear, he repassed to his palace through the lane again formed of his armed adherents, and amid audible shouts of an evil augury from desperadoes disappointed of their prey.'

There was but an interval of six days between the King's entering the House of Commons, and his flight from Whitehall. Charles raised the issue, the Commons accepted it, and so began our Great Civil War.

LIFE-BOATS AND THEIR BOATMEN.

The northern coast of Wales, between the towns of Rhyl and Abergele, was thrown into excitement on the 4th of January 1847, by the loss of one gallant life-boat, and the success of another. A schooner, the *Temperance* of Belfast, got into distress in a raging sea. The Rhyl life-boat pushed off in a wild surf to aid the sufferers; whether the boat was injured or mismanaged, none survived to tell; for all the crew, thirteen in number, were overwhelmed by the sea, and found a watery grave. The *Temperance*, however, was not neglected; another life-boat set out from Point-of-Air, and braving all dangers, brought the crew of the schooner safe to land.

This event is a type of two important things in relation to the shipping of England—the enormous amount of wreck on our coasts, and the heroic and unselfish exertions made to save human life imperilled by those catastrophes. The wreck is indeed terrible. There is a 'Wreck Chart' of the British Islands now published annually, spotted with death all over; little black marks are engraved for every wreck, opposite the part of the coast where they occurred. More than one of these charts has had *a thousand* such spots, each denoting either a total wreck or a serious disaster, and involving the loss of a still larger number of lives. The collier ships which bring coal from the north to London are sadly exposed to these calamities during their ten or twelve thousand annual voyages. The eastern coast from the Tyne to the Humber, the coast opposite Yarmouth, the shoals off the mouth of the Thames, the Scilly Isles, the west coast of Wales, and Barnstaple Bay, are all dismal places for wrecks.

Little need is there to tell the story of ship-wreck: it is known full well. How the returning emigrant, with his belt full of gold, sinks to a briny grave when within sight of his native shore; how the outgoing emigrant meets with a similar death before his voyage has well commenced; how the soldier is overwhelmed when departing to fight on foreign shores; how friends are severed, valuable goods lost, merchants ruined—all this is known to every one who takes up a newspaper. Some may say, looking at the pro-digious activity of our shipping, that wreck is an inevitable accompaniment of such a system. When we consider that seven hundred over-sea voyages *per day* either begin or end at a port in the United Kingdom, we ought to expect disasters as one of the attendant consequences. True, *some* disasters: the question is, whether pruden-tial arrangements might not lessen the number.

About the end of last century, after a terrible storm on the Northumbrian coast, Mr Great-head, of South Shields, constructed what he called a *safety-boat* or *life-boat*, containing much cork in its composition, as a means of producing buoyancy. Other inventors followed and tried to improve the construction by the use of air-tight cases, india-rubber linings, and other light but impervious substances. Sometimes these boats were instrumental in saving life; sometimes a Grace Darling, daring all perils, would push forth to a distressed ship in a common open boat; but still the loss of life by shipwreck was every year distressingly great. It was under this state of things that the 'Insti-tution for the Preservation of Life from Ship-wreck' was founded in 1824, to establish life-boats and mortar-rockets at all the dangerous parts of our coasts; to induce the formation of local committees at the chief ports for a similar purpose; to maintain a correspondence with those committees; and to encourage the inven-tion of new or improved boats, buoys, belts, rocket apparatus, and other appliances for saving life. Right nobly has this work been done. Without fee or reward, without guarantee or 'subsidy,' the Institution, now called the 'Life-Boat Institution,' has been employed for nearly forty years in saving human life. Many an excit-ing narrative may be picked out of the pages of the *Life-Boat*, a journal in which the Institution occasionally records the story of shipwreck and of life-preserving.

The life-boat system is remarkable in all its points. In 1850 the Duke of Northumberland offered a prize for the best form of life-boat. The boat-builders set to work, and sent in nearly 300 plans; the winner was Mr Beeching, boat-builder at Yarmouth. Oddly enough, however, the examiners did not practically adopt any one of them, not even Mr Beeching's; they got a member of their own body (Mr Peake, master shipwright at Woolwich dockyard) to construct a life-boat that should comprise all the best points of all the best plans. This boat, slightly im-proved by later alterations, is the one now adopted by the Life-Boat Institution, and coming

into use in other countries besides our own. It is about thirty feet long, seven wide, and four deep; nearly alike at both ends, and ingeniously con-trived with air chambers, passages, and valves. It possesses in a high degree these qualities—great lateral stability; speed against a heavy sea; facility for landing and for taking the shore; im-mediate self-discharge of sea-water; facility of self-righting if upset; great strength of construction; and stowage room for a number of passengers. Gallantly the boatmen manage these life-boats. The Institution maintains life-boat stations all round the coast, each of which is a little *impe-rium* in itself—a life-boat, generally a boat-house to keep it in, a carriage on which to drag it out to the sea, and a complete service of all the articles necessary for the use of the men. There is a captain or coxswain to each boat, and he can command the services of a hardy crew, obtained partly by salaries and partly by reward when actually engaged in saving life. The Institution can point to over 24,000 lives saved between 1824 and 1876, either directly by the boats and boatmen, or by exertions encouraged and rewarded by the Institution.

Nor should the gallant life-boatmen be grudged their bit of honest pride at what they have done. They can tell of the affair of October 7th, 1854, when, in an easterly gale at Holm Sand on the Suffolk coast, the life-boat boldly struck out, and finding a Norwegian brig in distress, was baffled by the drunken state of the eight sea-men on board, but succeeded, on a second at-tempt next morning, in bringing all safely off, the men being by that time sobered and manage-able. They can tell of the affair of the 2nd of May, 1855, when the Ramsgate beachmen saw signal rockets at the light-vessels moored off the Good-win Sands, denoting that a ship was in danger. The life-boat gallantly started on her mission of mercy. Then was there seen a hapless ship, the *Queen of the Teign*, high and dry on the Goodwins, with a foaming sea on the edge of the sand. How to get near it? The boatmen waited till the morning tide supplied a sufficiency of water; they went in, ran on the sand among the breakers, and aided the poor exhausted crew of the ship to clamber on board the life-boat. All were saved; and by dexterous management the ship was saved also. There was the Whitby case of January the 4th, 1857, when one of the boatmen was clearly washed out of the life-boat, *over the heads of all his companions*, by a raging sea; and yet all were saved, ship's crew and boatmen alike. But most of all do the life-boatmen pleasurably reflect on the story of the *Northern Belle*, and what they achieved for the crew of that ship. It was a fine vessel, an American trader of 1100 tons. On the 5th of January 1857, she was off the North Foreland, struck by a terrible sea, and placed in imminent peril. The Broadstairs boatmen harnessed them-selves to their life-boat carriage, and dragged it with the boat a distance of no less than two miles, from Broadstairs to Kingsgate, over a heavy and hilly country. In the dead of a winter's night, amid hail, sleet, and rain, the men could not see where to launch their boat. They waited through the darkness. At day-break on the next morning, a distressing sight presented itself : twenty-three poor fellows were clinging to the rigging of the only remaining mast of the *Northern Belle*, to which they had held on during this appalling night. Off went the life-boat, the *Mary White*, manned by seven daring boatmen, who braved the raging sea which washed over them repeatedly. They went to the wreck, brought off seven men, and were obliged to leave the rest for fear of involving all in destruction. Meanwhile another life-boat, the *Culmer White*, was wheeled overland from Broadstairs, then launched, and succeeded in bringing away fourteen of the sufferers. There remained only two others, the captain and the pilot, who refused to leave the wreck so long as a spar was standing. The *Culmer White* dashed out a second time, rescued these two mariners, and left the hapless ship to its watery grave. How the poor American sailors were warmed and cared for at the little hostelry, the 'Captain Digby,' at Kingsgate ; how the life-boats returned in triumphant procession to Broadstairs; and how the quiet heroism of the life-boatmen was the admiration of all—the newspapers of the period fully told.

EVIDENCE ABOUT A CHIMNEY.

A claim having been made in the year 1826, at the Marlborough-street Police Office, for a reward on account of the detection of a brewery chimney on fire, it was resisted on the ground that the flue, which was above eighty feet high, was so constructed and managed that it *could not* take fire. A witness on this side, who gave the (unnecessary) information that he was a chimney-sweep, set forth his evidence in the following terms : 'This here man (pointing to the patrol) has told a false affidavit, your wortship. I knows that ere chimley from a hinfant, and she knows my foot as well as my own mother. The ways I goes up her is this—I goes in all round the boiler, then I twists in the chimley like the smoke, and then up I goes with the wind, for, your wortship, there's a wind in her that would blow you out like a feather, if you didn't know her as well as I do, and that makes me always go to the top myself, because there isn't a brick in her that doesn't know my foot. So that you see, your wortship, no soot or blacks is ever in her; the wind won't let 'em stop : and besides they knows that I go up her regular. So that she always keeps herself as clean as a new pin. I'll be bound the sides of her is as clean this minute as I am (not saying much for the chimney) ; therefore, your wortship, that ere man as saw two yards of fire coming out of her, did not see no such thing, I say ; and he has told your wortship, and these here gentlemen present, a false affidavit, I say. I was brought up in that chimley, your wortship, and I can't abear to hear such things said—lies of her ; and that's all as I knows at present, please your wortship.'

Handsel Monday.

The first Monday of the year* is a great holiday among the peasantry of Scotland, and

* The year 1864 being assumed as the basis of the *Book of Days*, the popular Scotch festival of *Handsel-Monday* comes to be treated under the 4th of January.

children generally, as being the day peculiarly devoted in that country to the giving and receiving of presents. It is on this account called *Handsel Monday*, handsel being in Scotland the equivalent of a Christmas box, but more specially inferring a gift at the commencement of a season or the induing of some new garment. The young people visit their seniors in expectation of *tips* (the *word*, but not the *action*, unknown in the north). Postmen, scavengers, and deliverers of newspapers look for their little annual guerdons. Among the rural population, *Auld Hansel Monday*. i. e. Handsel Monday old style, or the first Monday after the 12th of the month, is the day usually held. The farmers used to treat the whole of their servants on that morning to a liberal breakfast of roast and boiled, with ale, whiskey, and cake, to their utmost contentment ; after which the guests went about seeing their friends for the remainder of the day. It was also the day on which any disposed for change gave up their places, and when new servants were engaged. Even now, when most old fashions are much decayed, *Auld Handsel Monday* continues to be the holiday of the year to the class of farm-labourers in Scotland.

'It is worth mentioning that one William Hunter, a collier (residing in the parish of Tillicoultry, in Clackmannanshire), was cured in the year 1738 of an inveterate rheumatism or gout, by drinking freely of new ale, full of barm or yeast. The poor man had been confined to his bed for a year and a half, having almost entirely lost the use of his limbs. On the evening of Handsel Monday, as it is called, some of his neighbours came to make merry with him. Though he could not rise, yet he always took his share of the ale, as it passed round the company, and in the end he became much intoxicated. The consequence was that he had the use of his limbs next morning, and was able to walk about. He lived more than twenty years after this, and never had the smallest return of his old complaint.'—(Sinclair's) *Statistical Account of Scotland*, xv. 201, *note*.

The Man in the Moon.

This is a familiar expression, to which few persons attach any definite idea. Many would be found under a belief that it refers merely to that faint appearance of a face which the moon presents when full. Those who are better acquainted with natural objects, and with folk-lore, are aware that the Man in the Moon—the object referred to under that name—is a dusky resemblance to a human figure which appears on the western side of the luminary when eight days old, being somewhat like a man carrying a thorn-bush on his back, and at the same time engaged in climbing, while a detached object in front looks like his dog going on before him. It is a very old popular notion amongst various nations, that this figure is the man referred to in the book of Numbers (chap. xv. v. 32 *et seq*.), as having been detected by the children of Israel in the wilderness, in the act of gathering sticks on the Sabbath-day, and whom the Lord directed (in absence of a law on the subject) to be stoned to death without the camp. One would have thought this poor stick-gatherer sufficiently punished in the actual history: nevertheless, the popular mind has assigned him the additional pain of a perpetual pillorying in the moon. There he is with his burden of sticks upon his back, continually climbing up that shining height with his little dog before him, but never getting a step higher! And so it ever must be while the world endures!

Our poets make clear to us how old is this notion. When *Moonshine* is to be represented in the famous play of Pyramus and Thisbe (Shakspeare's *Midsummer Night's Dream*), Mr Quince, the carpenter, gives due directions, as follows: 'One must come in with a bush of thorns and a lantern, and say he comes in to disfigure, or to present, the person of moonshine.' And this order is realised. 'All I have to say,' concludes the performer of this strange part, 'is, to tell you, that the lantern is the moon; I the man in the moon; this thorn-bush my thorn-bush; and this dog my dog.' Chaucer adverts to the Man in the Moon, with a needless aggravation of his criminality:

'On her brest a chorle painted ful even,
  Bearing a bush of thorns on his backe,
  Which for his *theft* might clime so ne'r the heaven.'

Dante, too, the contemporary of Chaucer, makes reference, in his *Inferno*, to the Man in the Moon, but with a variation upon the popular English idea, in as far as he calls him Cain.

In Ritson's *Ancient Songs*, there is one extracted from a manuscript of the time of Edward II., on the Man in the Moon, but in language which can scarcely now be understood. The first verse, in modern orthography, will probably satisfy the reader:

'Man in the Moon stand and stit (?)
  On his bot fork his burden he beareth,
It is much wonder that he na down slit,
  For doubt lest he fall he shudd'reth
    and shi'ereth.
When the frost freezes must chill he byde,
  The thorns be keen his hattren * so
    teareth,
Nis no wight in the world there wot when
    he syt (?)
  Ne bote it by the hedge what weeds he
    weareth.'

JANUARY 5.

Twelfth-Day Eve.

St Simeon Stylites, 459; St Telesphorus, seventh bishop of Rome, 128; St Syncletica (4th century?), virgin.

ST SIMEON STYLITES,

so named from the Greek word *stylos*, a pillar, was the founder of an order of monks, or rather solitary devotees, called pillar-saints. Of all the forms of voluntary self-torture practised by the early Christians this was one of the most extraordinary. Originally a shepherd in Cilicia about the year 408, when only thirteen years of age,

* Attire.

Simeon left his flocks, and obtained admission into a monastery in Syria, but afterwards withdrew to a mountain about thirty or forty miles east from Antioch, where he at first confined himself within a circle of stones. Deeming this mode of penance not sufficiently severe, in the year 423 he fixed his residence on the top of a pillar, which was at first nine feet high, but was successively raised to the somewhat incredible height of sixty feet (forty cubits). The diameter of the top of the pillar was only three feet, but it was surrounded by a railing which secured him from falling off, and afforded him some relief by leaning against it. His clothing consisted of the skins of beasts, and he wore an iron collar round his neck. He exhorted the assembled people twice a day, and spent the rest of his time in assuming various postures of devotion. Sometimes he prayed kneeling, sometimes in an erect attitude with his arms stretched out in the form of a cross, but his most frequent exercise was that of bending his meagre body so as to make his head nearly touch his feet. A spectator once observed him make more than 1240 such reverential bendings without resting. In this manner he lived on his pillar more than thirty years, and there he died in the year 459. His remains were removed to Antioch with great solemnity. His predictions and the miracles ascribed to him are mentioned at large in Theodoretus, who gives an account of the lives of thirty celebrated hermits, ten of whom were his contemporaries, including St Simeon Stylites. The pillar-saints were never numerous, and the propagation of the order was almost exclusively in the warm climates of the East. Among the names recorded is that of another Simeon, styled the younger, who is said to have dwelt sixty years on his pillar.

Born.—Dr Benjamin Rush, 1745, *Philadelphia;* Thomas Pringle, traveller and poet, 1789.

Died.— Edward the Confessor, 1066, *Westminster;* Catharine 'de' Medici, Queen of France, 1589; James Merrick, 1769, *Reading;* John Howie, author of *The Scots Worthies*, 1793; Isaac Reed, commentator on Shakspeare, 1807; Marshal Radetsky, 1858.

EDWARD THE CONFESSOR.

Towards the close of 1065, this pious monarch completed the rebuilding of the Abbey at Westminster, and at Christmas he caused the newly-built church to be hallowed in the presence of the nobles assembled during that solemn festival.

The king's health continued to decline; and early in the new year, on the 5th of January, he felt that the hand of death was upon him. As he lay, tradition says, in the painted chamber of the palace at Westminster, a little while before he expired, Harold and his kinsman forced their way into the apartment, and exhorted the monarch to name a successor, by whom the realm might be ruled in peace and security. 'Ye know full well, my lords,' said Edward, 'that I have bequeathed my kingdom to the Duke of Normandy, and are there not those *here* whose oaths have been given to secure his succession?' Harold stepped nearer, and interrupting the king, he asked of Edward upon whom the crown should be bestowed. 'Harold! take it, if such be thy wish; but the gift will be thy ruin. Against the Duke and his baronage no power of thine can avail thee!' Harold replied that he did not fear the Norman or any other enemy. The dying king, wearied with importunity, turned himself upon his couch, and faintly intimated that the English nation might name a king, Harold, or whom they liked; and shortly afterwards he expired. In the picturesque language of Sir Francis Palgrave, 'On the festival of the Epiphany, the day after the king's decease, his obsequies were solemnised in the adjoining abbey, then connected with the royal

abode by walls and towers, the foundations whereof are still existing. Beneath the lofty windows of the southern transept of the Abbey, you may see the deep and blackened arches, fragments of the edifice raised by Edward, supporting the chaste and florid tracery of a more recent age. Westward stands the shrine, once rich in gems and gold, raised to the memory of the Confessor by the devotion of his successors, despoiled, indeed, of all its ornaments, neglected, and crumbling to ruin, but still surmounted by the massy iron-bound oaken coffin which contains the ashes of the last legitimate Anglo-Saxon king.'—*History of England: Anglo-Saxon Period.*

DEATH AND BURIAL OF THE CONFESSOR, FROM THE BAYEUX TAPESTRY.

We long possessed many interesting memorials of the Confessor in the coronation insignia which he gave to the Abbey Treasury—including the rich vestments, golden crown and sceptres, dalmatic, embroidered pall, and spurs—used at the coronations of our sovereigns, until the reign of Charles II. The death and funeral of the Confessor are worked in a compartment of the Bayeux Tapestry, believed to be of the age of the Conquest. The crucifix and gold chain and ring were seen in the reign of James II. The sculptures upon the frieze of the present shrine represent fourteen scenes in the life of the Confessor. He was the first of our sovereigns who touched for the king's-evil; he was canonized by Pope Alexander about a century after his death. The use of the Great Seal was first introduced in his reign: the original is in the British Museum. He was esteemed the patron-saint of England until superseded in the 13th century by St George; the translation of his relics from the old to his new shrine at Westminster, in 1263, still finds a

place, on the 13th of October, in the English Calendar: and more than twenty churches exist, dedicated either to him or to Edward the king and martyr.

JOHN HOWIE

was author of a book of great popularity in Scotland, entitled the *Scots Worthies,* being a homely but perspicuous and pathetic account of a select number of persons who suffered for 'the covenanted work of Reformation' during the reigns of the last Stuarts. Howie was a simple-minded Ayrshire moorland farmer, dwelling in a lonely cot amongst bogs, in the parish of Fenwick, a place which his ancestors had possessed ever since the persecuting time, and which continued at a recent period to be occupied by his descendants. His great-grandfather was one of the persecuted people, and many of the unfortunate brethren had received shelter in the house when they did not know where else to lay their head. One friend, Captain Paton, in Meadowhead, when executed at Edinburgh in 1684, handed down his bible from the scaffold to his wife, and it soon after came into the hands of the Howies, who still preserve it. The captain's sword, a flag for the parish of Fenwick, carried at Bothwell Bridge, a drum believed to have been used there, and a variety of manuscripts left by covenanting divines, were all preserved along with the captain's bible, and rendered the house a museum of Presbyterian antiquities. People of great eminence have pilgrimised to Lochgoin to see the home of John Howie and his collection of curiosities, and generally have come away acknowledging the singular interest attaching to both. The simple worth, primitive manners, and strenuous faith of the elderly sons and daughters of John Howie, by whom the little farm was managed, formed a curious study in themselves. Visitors also fondly lingered in the little room, constituting the only one besides the kitchen, which formed at once the parlour and study of the author of the Worthies; also over a bower in the little cabbage-garden, where John used to spend hours—nay, days—in religious exercises, and where, he tells us, he formally subscribed a covenant with God on the 10th of June 1785. A stone in the parish churchyard records the death of the great-grandfather in 1691, and of the grandfather in 1755, the latter being ninety years old, and among the last survivors of those who had gone through the fire of persecution. John Howie wrote a memoir of himself, which no doubt contains something one cannot but smile at, as does his other work also. Yet there is so much pure-hearted earnestness in the man's writings, that they cannot be read without a certain respect. The Howies of Lochgoin may be said to have formed a monument of the religious feelings and ways of a long by-past age, protracted into modern times. We see in them and their cot a specimen of the world of the century before the last. It is to be feared that in a few more years both the physical and the moral features of the place will be entirely changed.

ATTEMPTED ASSASSINATION OF LOUIS XV.

On the 5th of January 1757, an attempt was made upon the life of the worthless French king, Louis XV., by Robert Francis Damiens. 'Between five and six in the evening, the king was getting into his coach at Versailles to go to the Trianon. A man, who had lurked about the colonnades for two days, pushed up to the coach, jostled the dauphin, and stabbed the king under the right arm with a long knife ; but, the king having two thick coats, the blade did not penetrate deep. Louis was surprised, but thinking the man had only pushed against him, said, 'Le coquin m'a donné un furieux coup de poing,' but putting his hand to his side, and feeling blood, he said, ' Il m'a blessé ; qu'on le saisisse, et qu'on ne lui fasse point de mal.' The king being carried to bed, it was quickly ascertained that the wound was slight and not dangerous.

'Damiens, the criminal, appeared clearly to be mad. He had been footman to several persons, had fled for a robbery, had returned to Paris in

a dark and restless state of mind ; and by one of those wonderful contradictions of the human mind, a man aspired to renown that had descended to theft. Yet in this dreadful complication of guilt and frenzy, there was room for compassion. The unfortunate wretch was sensible of the predominance of his black temperament ; and the very morning of the assassination, asked for a surgeon to let him blood ; and to the last gasp of being, he persisted that he should not have committed this crime, if he had been blooded. What the miserable man suffered is not to be described. When first raised and carried into the guard-chamber, the Garde-desceaux and the Duc d'Ayen ordered the tongs to be heated, and pieces torn from his legs, to make him declare his accomplices. The industrious art used to preserve his life was not less than the refinement of torture by which they meant to take it away. The inventions to form the bed on which he lay (as the wounds on his leg prevented his standing), that his health might in no shape be affected, equalled what a reproving tyrant would have sought to indulge his own luxury.

'When carried to the dungeon, Damiens was wrapped up in mattresses, lest despair might tempt him to dash his brains out, but his madness was no longer precipitate. He even amused himself by indicating a variety of innocent persons as his accomplices ; and sometimes, more harmlessly, by playing the fool with his judges. In no instance he sank either under terror or anguish. The very morning on which he was to endure the question, when told of it, he said with the coolest intrepidity, " La journée sera rude "—after it, insisted on some wine with his water, saying, " Il faut ici de la force." And at the accomplishment of his tragedy, studied and prolonged on the precedent of Ravaillac's, he supported all with unrelaxed firmness ; and even unremitted torture of four hours, which succeeded to his being two hours and a-half under the question, forced from him but some momentary yells.' —*Memoirs of the Reign of King George the Second*, ii., 281.

That, in France, so lately as 1757, such a criminal should have been publicly torn to pieces by horses, that many persons of rank should have been present on the occasion, and that the sufferer allowed ' quelques plaisanteries ' to escape him during the process, altogether leave us in a strange state of feeling regarding the affair of Damiens.

Twelfth-Day Eve.

Twelfth-day Eve is a rustic festival in England. Persons engaged in rural employments are, or have heretofore been accustomed to celebrate it ; and the purpose appears to be to secure a blessing for the fruits of the earth.

'In Herefordshire, at the approach of the evening, the farmers with their friends and servants meet together, and about six o'clock walk out to a field where wheat is growing. In the highest part of the ground, twelve small fires, and one large one, are lighted up. The attendants, headed by the master of the family, pledge the company in old cider, which circulates freely on these occasions. A circle is formed round the large fire, when a general shout and hallooing takes place, which you hear answered from all the adjacent villages and fields. Sometimes fifty or sixty of these fires may be all seen at once. This being finished, the company return home, where the good housewife and her maids are preparing a good supper. A large cake is always provided, with a hole in the middle. After supper, the company all attend the bailiff (or head of the oxen) to the wain-house, where the following particulars are observed: The master, at the head of his friends, fills the cup (generally of strong ale), and stands opposite the first or finest of the oxen. He then pledges him in a curious toast: the company follow his example, with all the other oxen, and addressing each by his name. This being finished, the large cake is produced, and, with much ceremony, put on the horn of the first ox, through the hole above mentioned. The ox is then tickled, to make him toss his head: if he throw the cake behind, then it is the mistress's perquisite; if before (in what is termed the boosy), the bailiff himself claims the prize. The company then return to the house, the doors of which they find locked, nor will they be opened till some joyous songs are sung. On their gaining admittance, a scene of mirth and jollity ensues, which lasts the greatest part of the night.'—*Gentleman's Magazine, February*, 1791. The custom is called in Herefordshire *Wassailing*. The fires are designed to represent the Saviour and his apostles, and it was customary as to one of them, held as representing Judas Iscariot, to allow it to burn a while, and then put it out and kick it about the materials.

At Pauntley, in Gloucestershire, the custom has in view the prevention of the smut in wheat. 'All the servants of every farmer assemble in one of the fields that has been sown with wheat. At the end of twelve lands, they make twelve fires in a row with straw; around one of which, made larger than the rest, they drink a cheerful glass of cider to their master's health, and success to the future harvest; then returning home, they feast on cakes made with carraways, soaked in cider, which they claim as a reward for their past labour in sowing the grain.'*

'In the south hams [villages] of Devonshire, on the eve of the Epiphany, the farmer, attended by his workmen, with a large pitcher of cider, goes to the orchard, and there encircling one of the best bearing trees, they drink the following toast three several times:—

'Here's to thee, old apple-tree,
Whence thou mayst bud, and whence thou mayst blow!
And whence thou mayst bear apples enow!
Hats full! caps full!
Bushel—bushel—sacks full,
And my pockets full too! Huzza!'

This done, they return to the house, the doors of which they are sure to find bolted by the females, who, be the weather what it may, are inexorable to all entreaties to open them till some one has

* Rudge's Gloucester.

56

guessed at what is on the spit, which is generally some nice little thing, difficult to be hit on, and is the reward of him who first names it. The doors are then thrown open, and the lucky clodpole receives the tit-bit as his recompense. Some are so superstitious as to believe, that if they neglect this custom, the trees will bear no apples that year.'—*Gentleman's Magazine*, 1791, p. 403.

OLD ENGLISH PRONUNCIATIONS.

The history of the pronunciation of the English language has been little traced. It fully appears that many words have sustained a considerable change of pronunciation during the last four hundred years: it is more particularly marked in the vowel sounds. In the days of Elizabeth, high personages pronounced certain words in the same way as the common people now do in Scotland. For example, the wise Lord Treasurer Burleigh said *whan* instead of when, and *war* instead of were; witness a sentence of his own: 'At Enfield, fyndying a dozen in a plump, *whan* there was no rayne, I bethought myself that they *war* appointed as watchmen, for the apprehendyng of such as are missyng,' &c.—Letter to Sir Francis Walsingham, 1586. (Collier's *Papers to Shakspeare Society*.) Sir Thomas Gresham, writing to his patron in behalf of his wife, says: 'I humbly beseech your honour to be a *stey* and some comfort to her in this my absence.' Finding these men using such forms, we may allowably suppose that much also of their colloquial discourse was of the same homely character.

Lady More, widow of the Lord Chancellor Sir Thomas More, writing to the Secretary Cromwell in 1535, beseeched his 'especial *gude maistership*,' out of his 'abundant *gudeness*' to consider her case. 'So, bretherne, here is my *maister*,' occurs in Bishop Lacy's Exeter Pontifical about 1450. These pronunciations are the broad Scotch of the present day.

Tway for two, is another old English pronunciation. 'By whom came the inheritance of the lordship of Burleigh, and other lands, to the value of *twai* hundred pounds yearly,' says a contemporary life of the illustrious Lord Treasurer. *Tway* also occurs in Piers Ploughman's Creed in the latter part of the fourteenth century:

'——Thereon lay a litel chylde lapped in cloutes,
And tweyne of *tweie* yeres olde,' &c.

So also an old manuscript poem preserved at Cambridge:

' Dame, he seyde, how schalle we doo,
He fayleth *twaye* tethe also.'

This is the pronunciation of Tweeddale at the present day; while in most parts of Scotland they say *twa*. Tway is nearer to the German *zwei*.

A Scotsman, or a North of England man, speaking in his vernacular, never says 'all:' he says 'a'.' In the old English poem of *Havelok*, the same form is used:

' He shall haven in his hand
A Denemark and Engeland.'

The Scotsman uses *ony* for any :

> ' Aye keep something to yoursel'
> Ye scarcely tell to *ony*.'
> BURNS.

This is old English, as witness Caxton the printer in one of his publishing advertisements issued about 1490 : 'If it ples *ony* man, spirituel or temporel,' &c. An Englishman in those days would say *ane* for one, even in a prayer :

> ' Thus was Thou aye, and evere salle be,
> Thre yn *ane*, and *ane* yn thre.'

A couplet, by the way, which gives another Scotch form in *sal* for shall. He also used *amang* for among, *sang* for song, *faught* for fought,

> (' They faught with Heraud everilk ane.'
> *Guy of Warwick*.)

tald for told, *fand* for found, *gane* for gone, and *awn* for own. The last four occur in the curious verse inscriptions on the frescoes representing scenes in St Augustine's life in Carlisle Cathedral, and in many other places, as a reference to Halliwell's *Dictionary of Archaisms* will shew.

In a manuscript form of the making of an abbess, of probably the fifteenth century, *mainteyne* for maintain, *sete* for seat, and *quere* for quire, shew the prevalence at that time in England of pronunciations still retained in Scotland. (*Dugdale's Monasticon*, i. 437.) *Abstein* for abstain, persevered down to the time of Elizabeth : ' He that will doo this worke shall *absteine* from lecherousness and dronkennesse,' &c. *Scot's Discoverie of Witchcraft*, 1584, where *contein* also occurs. The form *sook* for suck, which still prevails in Scotland, occurs in Capgrave's metrical *Life of St Katherine*, about 1450.

> ' Ah ! Jesu Christ, crown of maidens all,
> A maid bare thee, a maid gave thee *sook*.'

Stree for straw—being very nearly the Scottish pronunciation—occurs in Sir John Mandeville's Travels, of the fourteenth century. Even that peculiarly vicious northern form of *shooter* for suitor would appear, from a punning passage in Shakspeare, to have formerly prevailed in the south also :

> *Boyet.*—Who is the suitor?
> *Rosaline.*—Well, then, I am the *shooter*.
> *Love's Labour Lost*.

It is to be observed of Shakspeare that he uses fewer old or northern words than some of his contemporaries ; yet the remark is often made by Scotsmen, that much of his language, which the commentators explain for English readers, is to them intelligible as their vernacular, so that they are in a condition more readily to appreciate the works of the bard of Avon than even his own countrymen.

The same remark may be made regarding Spenser, and especially with respect to his curious poem of the *Shepherd's Calendar*. When he there tells of a ewe, that ' She mought ne gang on the greene,' he uses almost exactly the language that would be employed by a Selkirkshire shepherd, on a like occasion, at the present day. So also when Thenot says : ' Tell me, good Hobbinol, what gars thee greete ?' he speaks pure Scotch. In this poem, Spenser also uses *tway* for two, *gait* for goat, *mickle* for much, *wark* for work, *wae* for woe, *ken* for know, *craig* for the neck, *warr* for worse, *hame* for home, and *teen* for sorrow, all of these being Scottish terms.

From that rich well of old English, Wycliffe's translation of the Bible, we learn that in the fourteenth century *aboon* stood for above (' Gird *abowen* with knychtis gyrdill,' 2 *Kings* iii. 21), *nowther* was neither, and *breed* was bread (' Give to us this day oure breed,' &c.), all of these being Scottish pronunciations of the present day.

Wycliffe also uses many words, now obsolete in England, but still used in Scotland, as *oker* for interest, *orison* for oration, *almery*, a press or cupboard, *sad* for firm or solid, *tolbooth*, a place to receive taxes (' He seith a man syttynge in a tolbothe, Matheu by name,' *Matt.* ix. 9) ; *toun* for a farm (' The first saide, Y have bought a toun, and Y have nede to go out and se it,' *Luke* xiv. 19), *scarry* for precipitous, *repe* for a handful of corn-straw (' Here's a *rip* to thy auld baggie.'—*Burns*. ' Whanne thou repest corn in the feeld, and forgetist and leeuest a repe, thou schalt not turn agen to take it,' *Deut.* xxiv. 19), *forleit* for left altogether. The last, a term which every boy in Scotland applies to the forsaking of a nest by the bird, was used on a remarkable public occasion to describe the act of James II. in leaving his country. ' Others,' says Sir George Mackenzie, ' were for declaring that the king had *forleited* the kingdom.'

The differences of pronunciation which now exist between the current English and cognate languages chiefly lie in the vowel sounds. The English have flattened down the broad A in a vast number of cases, and played a curious legerdemain with E and I, while other nations have in these particulars made no change. It seems to have been a process of refinement, or what was thought to be such, in accordance with the advancing conditions of domestic life in a country on the whole singularly fortunate in all the circumstances that favour civilization. Whether there is a real improvement in the case may be doubted ; that it is a deterioration would scarcely be asserted in any quarter. Even those, however, who take the most favourable view of it, must regret that the change should have extended to the pronunciation of Greek and Latin. To introduce the flat A for the broad one, and interchange the sounds of E and I, in these ancient languages, must be pronounced as an utterly unwarrantable interference with something not our own to deal with—it is like one author making alterations in the writings of another, an act which justice and good taste alike condemn.

Chalk.—Mrs Delany says : ' I have found remarkable benefit from having chalk in everything I drink ; a lump put into the jug of water, and the tea-water managed in the same way. It is a great sweetener of the blood.'

Price of Tea in 1728.—' The man at the Poultry has tea of all prices—Bohea from thirteen to twenty shillings, and green from twelve to thirty.'—*Mrs. Delany's Correspondence*.

JANUARY 6.

Epiphany, or Twelfth-Day.

(Old Christmas Day.)

St Melanius, bishop, 490. St Nilammon, hermit. St Peter, abbot of St Austin's, Canterbury, 608.

Born.—Richard II., King of England, 1366; Joan d'Arc, 1402; Peter Metastasio, poet, 1698; Benjamin Franklin, philosopher, *Boston, U.S.*, 1706; David Dale, philanthropist, 1739; George Thomas Doo, engraver, 1800.

Died.—Seth Ward, Bishop of Salisbury, mathematician, 1689; John Dennis, critic, 1734; Madame d'Arblay (Frances Burney), novelist, 1840; James Smith, comic poet, 1840; Fanny Wright, lady politician, 1853.

BENJAMIN FRANKLIN.*

Modern society has felt as if there were something wanting in the character of Franklin; yet what the man positively had of good about him was, beyond all doubt, extremely good. Self-denial, energy, love of knowledge, sagacity to discern and earnestness to pursue what was calculated to promote happiness amongst mankind, scientific ingenuity, courage in the protection of patriotic interests against misrule—all were his. How few men possess half so many high qualities!

It is an extremely characteristic circumstance that, landing at Falmouth from a dangerous voyage, and going to church with his son to return thanks to God for their deliverance, he felt it as an occasion when a Catholic would have vowed to build a chapel to some saint: 'not being a Catholic,' said the philosopher, 'if I were to vow at all, it would be to build a *lighthouse*' [the article found chiefly wanting towards the end of their voyage].

It is little known that it was mainly by the advice of Franklin that the English government resolved to conquer Canada, and for that purpose sent out Wolfe's expedition.

While in our island at that time (1759), as agent for the colony of Pennsylvania, he made an ex-

BENJAMIN FRANKLIN.

cursion to Scotland, accompanied by his son. His reputation as a man of science had made him well known there, and he was accordingly received with distinction by Hume, Robertson, Lord Kames, and other literary men of note, was made a doctor of St Andrew's University, and a burgess by the Town Council of Edinburgh. Franklin paid a long visit to Lord Kames at his seat of Kames in Berwickshire, and when he came away, his host and hostess gave him a convoy into the English border. Some months after, writing to his lordship from London, he said: 'How much more agreeable would our journey have been, if we could have enjoyed you as far as York! We could have beguiled the way by discoursing on a thousand things that now we may never have an opportunity of considering together; for conversation warms the mind, enlivens the imagination, and is continually starting fresh game that is immediately pursued and taken, and which would never have occurred in the duller intercourse of epistolary correspondence. So that whenever I reflect on the great pleasure and advantage I received from the free communication of sentiment in the conversation we had at Kames, and in the agreeable little rides to the Tweedside, I shall ever regret our premature parting.'

'Our conversation,' he added, 'until we came to York, was chiefly a recollection of what we had seen and heard, the pleasure we had enjoyed, and the kindnesses we had received in Scotland, and how far that country had exceeded our expectations. On the whole, I must say, I think the time we spent there was six weeks of the *densest* happiness I have ever met with in any part of my life; and the agreeable and instructive society we found there in such plenty, has left so pleasing an impression on my memory, that, did not strong connections draw me elsewhere, I believe Scotland would be the country I should choose to spend the remainder of my days in.'

Soon after, May 3rd, 1760, Franklin communicated to Lord Kames a plan he had formed to write a little book under the title of *The Art of Virtue.* 'Many people,' he said, 'lead bad lives that would gladly lead good ones, but do not know how to make the change. They have frequently resolved and endeavoured it; but in vain, because their endeavours have not been properly

---

* Franklin is sometimes said to have been born on the 17th of January. He was, in reality, born on what was held at the time of birth as the 6th, being *old style.* Considering that the day of the birth of remarkable men, *as expressed in their own time*, is that round which our associations arrange themselves, it is intended in this work to adhere to that date, in all cases where it is known.

conducted. To expect people to be good, to be just, to be temperate, &c., without shewing them how they should become so, seems like the ineffectual charity mentioned by the Apostle, which consisted in saying to the hungry, the cold, and the naked, "Be ye fed, be ye warmed, be ye clothed," without shewing them how they should get food, fire, or clothing.

'Most people have naturally some virtues, but none have naturally *all* the virtues.

'To inquire those that are wanting, and secure what we require as well as those we have naturally, is the subject of an art. It is properly an art, as painting, navigation, or architecture. If a man would become a painter, navigator, or architect, it is not enough that he is *advised* to be one, that he is *convinced* by the arguments of his adviser that it would be for his advantage to be one, and that he resolves to be one; but he must also be taught the principles of the art, be shewn all the methods of working, and how to acquire the habits of using properly all the instruments; and thus regularly and gradually he arrives, by practice, at some perfection in the art. If he does not proceed thus, he is apt to meet with difficulties that might discourage him, and make him drop the pursuit.

'My *Art of Virtue* has also its instruments, and teaches the manner of using them.

'Christians are directed to have faith in Christ, as the effectual means of obtaining the change they desire. It may, when sufficiently strong, be effectual with many; for a full opinion, that a teacher is infinitely wise, good, and powerful, and that he will certainly reward and punish the obedient and disobedient, must give great weight to his precepts, and make them much more attended to by his disciples. But many have this faith in so weak a degree, that it does not produce the effect. Our *Art of Virtue* may, therefore, be of great service to those whose faith is unhappily not so strong, and may come in aid of its weakness. Such as are naturally well-disposed, and have been so carefully educated as that good habits have been early established and bad ones prevented, have less need of this art; but all may be more or less benefited by it.'*

Between two men of such sentiments as Franklin and Lord Kames, thrown together for six weeks, the subject of religious toleration we may well suppose to have been frequently under discussion. Franklin communicated to his Scotch friend a small piece, of the nature of an apologue, designed to give a lesson of toleration, and which Kames afterwards published. It has often been reprinted as an original idea of the American philosopher; but, in reality, he never pretended to anything more than giving it its literary style, and the idea can be traced back through a devious channel to Saadi, the Persian poet, who, after all, relates it as coming from another person. It was as follows:—

'1. And it came to pass after these things, that Abraham sat in the door of his tent, about the going down of the sun.

'2. And behold a man, bowed with age, came from the way of the wilderness, leaning on a staff.

* Sparkes's *Life and Correspondence of Franklin.* 10 vols. 8vo. Philadelphia. Vol. ix.

'3. And Abraham arose and met him, and said unto him, "Turn in, I pray thee, and wash thy feet, and tarry all night, and thou shalt arise early on the morrow, and go on thy way."

'4. But the man said, "Nay, for I will abide under this tree."

'5. And Abraham pressed him greatly; so he turned, and they went into the tent, and Abraham baked unleavened bread, and they did eat.

'6. And when Abraham saw that the man blessed not God, he said unto him, "Wherefore dost thou not worship the most high God, Creator of heaven and earth?"

'7. And the man answered and said, "I do not worship the God thou speakest of, neither do I call upon his name; for I have made to myself a god which abideth alway in mine house, and provideth me with all things."

'8. And Abraham's zeal was kindled against the man, and he arose and fell upon him, and drove him forth with blows into the wilderness.

'9. And at midnight God called unto Abraham, saying, "Abraham, where is the stranger?"

'10. And Abraham answered and said, "Lord, he would not worship thee, neither would he call upon thy name; therefore have I driven him out from before my face into the wilderness."

'11. And God said, "Have I borne with him these hundred ninety and eight years, and nourished him, and clothed him, notwithstanding his rebellion against me; and couldst not thou, that art thyself a sinner, bear with him one night?"

'12. And Abraham said, "Let not the anger of the Lord wax hot against his servant; lo, I have sinned; forgive me, I pray thee."

'13. And Abraham arose, and went forth into the wilderness, and sought diligently for the man and found him, and returned with him to the tent: and when he had entreated him kindly, he sent him away on the morrow with gifts.'

That Franklin should have ascended from the condition of a journeyman compositor to be a

PRINTING PRESS WORKED AT BY FRANKLIN
IN LONDON.

great philosopher and legislator, and 'to stand before kings,' is certainly one of the most interesting biographical facts which the eighteenth century presents. Without that frugal use of means, the want of which so signally keeps our toiling millions poor, it never could have been.

Of ever memorable value is the anecdote he tells of his practice in a London printing-office. 'I drank only water,' says he; 'the other workmen, near fifty in number, were great drinkers of beer. On one occasion, I carried up and down stairs a large form of types in each hand, when others carried but one in both hands. They wondered to see that the *Water American*, as they called me, was stronger than themselves who drank *strong* beer. We had an alehouse boy, who always attended in the house to supply the workmen. My companion at the press drank every day a pint before breakfast, a pint at breakfast with his bread and cheese, a pint between breakfast and dinner, a pint at dinner, a pint in the afternoon about six o'clock, and another when he had done with his day's work. I thought it a detestable custom; but it was necessary, he supposed, to drink *strong* beer that he might be *strong* to labour. I endeavoured to convince him that the bodily strength afforded by beer could only be in proportion to the grain or flour of the barley dissolved in the water of which it was made; that there was more flour in a pennyworth of bread; and therefore, if he could eat that with a pint of water, it would give him more strength than a quart of beer. He drank on, however, and had four or five shillings to pay out of his wages every Saturday night for that vile liquor; an expense I was free from. And thus these poor devils kept themselves always under.'

THE RETREAT FROM CABUL, 1842.

The British power went into Afghanistan, in 1839, upon an unrighteous cause. The punishment which Providence, in the natural course of events, brings upon such errors, overtook it towards the close of 1841, and on the 6th of January it became a necessity that an army of about 4,500 men, with 12,000 camp followers, should commence a precipitate retreat from its Cabul cantonments, through a difficult country, under frost and snow, which it was ill fitted to endure, and harassed by hordes of implacable enemies. The *Noche Triste* of Cortez's troops on their retirement from Mexico, the terrible retreat of Napoleon's army from Moscow, even the fearful scenes which attended the destruction of Jerusalem, scarcely afford a more distressing narrative of human woe. The first day's march took them five miles through the snow, which was in many places dyed with their blood. They had to bivouack in it, without shelter, and with scarcely any food, and next morning they resumed their journey, or rather flight,—a long confused line of soldiery mixed with rabble, camels and other beasts of burden, and ladies with their children; while the native bands were continually attacking and plundering. The second evening saw them only ten miles advanced upon their fatal journey, and the night was again spent in the snow, which proved the winding-sheet of many before morning. It is believed that if they had started more promptly, and could have advanced more rapidly, the enemy, scarcely prepared to follow them, could not have proved so destructive. But the general—Elphinstone, — and other chief officers, were tempted to lose time in the hope of negotiating with the hostile chiefs, and particularly Akbar-Khan, for a purchased safety. Unfortunately, the native chiefs had little or no control over their followers. It was on this third day that they had to go through the celebrated Koord-Caubul Pass. The force, with its followers, in a long disorderly string, struggled on through the narrow defile, suffering under a constant and deadly fire from the fanatical Ghilzyes, or falling under their knives in close encounter. Thus, or by falling exhausted in the snow, 3,000 are said to have perished. Another night of exposure, hunger, and exhaustion followed. Next day, the sadly reduced files were stayed for a while, to try another negotiation for safety. The ladies and the married officers were taken under the protection of Akbar-Khan, and were thus saved. The remaining soldiery, and particularly the Indian troops, were now paralysed with the effects of the cold, and scarcely able to handle or carry their arms. Many were butchered this day. They continued the march at night, in the hope of reaching Jugdulluck, and next day they still went on, doing their best to repel the enemy as they went. Reduced to a mere handful, they still exhibited the devoted courage of British soldiers. While the wretched remnant halted here, the general and two other officers gave themselves up to Akbar-Khan, as pledges that Jellalabad would be delivered up for the purchase of safety to the troops. The arrangement only served to save the lives of those three officers. The subsequent day's march was still harassed by the natives, and at a barrier which had been erected in the Jugdulluck Pass, the whole of the remainder were butchered, excepting about twenty officers and forty-five soldiers. After some further collisions with the foe, there came to be only six officers alive at a place about sixteen miles from Jellalabad. On the 13th of January, the garrison of that fortress saw a single man approaching their walls, mounted on a wretched little pony, and hanging exhausted upon its neck. He proved to be Dr Bryden, the only one of the force which left Cabul a week before, who had escaped to tell the tale.

It is easy to shew how the policy of particular commanders had a fatal effect in bringing about this frightful disaster to the British power—how, with better management on their part, the results might have been, to some extent, otherwise; but still the great fact remains, that a British army was where it ought never to have been, and of course exposed to dangers beyond those of fair warfare. An ancient Greek dramatist, in bringing such a tragedy before the attention of his audience, would have made the Chorus proclaim loudly the wrath of the gods. Ignorant men, of our own day, make comments not much different. The remark which a just philosophy makes on the subject is, that God has arranged that justice among men should have one set of effects, and injustice another. Where nations violate the Divine rule to do to others as they would have others to do to them, they lay themselves open to all the calamitous consequences which naturally flow from the act, just as surely as do individuals when they act in the same manner.

Twelfth-Day.

This day, called Twelfth-Day, as being in that number after Christmas, and Epiphany from the Greek Ἐπιφάνεια, signifying *appearance*, is a festival of the Church, in commemoration of the *Manifestation of Christ to the Gentiles;* more expressly to the three Magi, or Wise Men of the East, who came, led by a star, to worship him immediately after his birth. (*Matt.* ii. 1-12.) The Epiphany appears to have been first 'observed as a *separate* feast in the year 813. Pope Julius I. is, however, reputed to have taught the Church to distinguish the Feasts of the Nativity and Epiphany, so early as about the middle of the fourth century. The primitive Christians celebrated the Feast of the Nativity for twelve days, observing the first and last with great solemnity; and both of these days were denominated Epiphany, the first the greater Epiphany, from our Lord having on that day become Incarnate, or made His appearance in "the flesh;" the latter, the lesser Epiphany, from the threefold manifestation of His Godhead—the first, by the appearance of the blazing star which conducted Melchior, Jasper, and Balthuzar, the three Magi, or wise men, commonly styled the three Kings of Cologne, out of the East, to worship the Messiah, and to offer him presents of "Gold, Frankincense, and Myrrh"—Melchior the *Gold,* in testimony of his royalty as the promised King of the Jews; Jasper the *Frankincense,* in token of his Divinity; and Balthuzar the *Myrrh,*

in allusion to the sorrows which, in the humiliating condition of a man, our Redeemer vouchsafed to take upon him: the second, of the descent of the Holy Ghost in the form of a Dove, at the Baptism: and the third, of the first miracle of our Lord turning water into wine at the marriage in Cana. All of which three manifestations of the Divine nature happened on the same day, though not in the same year.

'To render due honour to the memory of the ancient Magi, who are supposed to have been kings, the monarch of this country himself, either personally or through his chamberlain, offers annually at the altar on this day, Gold, Frankincense, and Myrrh; and the kings of Spain, where the Feast of Epiphany is likewise called the "Feast of the Kings," were accustomed to make the like offerings.'—*Brady.*

In the middle ages, the worship by the Magi was celebrated by a little drama, called the Feast of the Star. 'Three priests, clothed as kings, with their servants carrying offerings, met from different directions before the altar. The middle one, who came from the east, pointed with his staff to a star. A dialogue then ensued; and, after kissing each other, they began to sing, "Let us go and inquire;" after which the precentor began a responsory, "Let the Magi come." A procession then commenced; and as soon as it began to enter the nave, a crown, with a star resembling a cross, was lighted up, and pointed out to the Magi, with, "Behold the Star in the East." This being concluded, two priests standing at each side of the altar, answered meekly, "We are those whom you seek;" and, drawing a curtain, shewed them a child, whom, falling down, they worshipped. Then the servants made the offerings of gold, frankincense, and myrrh, which were divided among the priests. The Magi, meanwhile, continued praying till they dropped asleep; when a boy, clothed in an alb, like an angel, addressed them with, "All things which the prophets said are fulfilled." The festival concluded with chanting services, &c. At Soissons, a rope was let down from the roof of the church, to which was annexed an iron circle having seven tapers, intended to represent Lucifer, or the morning star; but this was not confined to the Feast of the Star.'—Fosbroke's *Antiquities*, ii. 700.

At Milan, in 1336, the *Festival of the Three Kings* was celebrated in a manner that brings forcibly before us the tendency of the middle ages to fix attention on the historical externals of Christianity. The affair was got up by the Preaching Friars. 'The three kings appeared, crowned, on three great horses richly habited, surrounded by pages, body guards, and an innumerable retinue. A golden star was exhibited in the sky, going before them. They proceeded to the pillars of St Lawrence, where King Herod was represented with his scribes and wise men. The three kings ask Herod where Christ should be born, and his wise men, having consulted their books, answer, at Bethlehem. On which the three kings, with their golden crowns, having in their hands golden cups filled with frankincense, myrrh, and gold, the star going before, marched to the church of St Eustorgius, with all their attendants, preceded by trumpets, horns, asses, baboons, and a great variety of animals. In the church, on one side of the high altar, there was a manger with an ox and ass, and in it the infant Christ in the arms of his mother. Here the three kings offer Him gifts. The concourse of the people, of knights, ladies, and ecclesiastics, was such as was never before beheld.'*

In its character as a popular festival, Twelfth-Day stands only inferior to Christmas. The leading object held in view is to do honour to the three wise men, or, as they are more generally denominated, the three kings. It is a Christian custom, ancient past memory, and probably suggested by a pagan custom, to indulge in a pleasantry called the *Election of Kings by Beans.*† In England, in later times, a large cake was formed, with a bean inserted, and this was called *Twelfth-Cake*. The family and friends being assembled, the cake was divided by lot, and whoever got the piece containing the bean was accepted as king for the day, and called King of the Bean. The importance of this ceremony in France, where the mock sovereign is named *Le Roi de la Fève*, is indicated by the proverbial

phrase for good luck, 'Il a trouvé la fève au gâteau,' He has found the bean in the cake. In Rome, they do not draw king and queen as in England, but indulge in a number of jocularities, very much for the amusement of children. Fruit-stalls and confectioners' shops are dressed up with great gaiety. A ridiculous figure, called Beffana, parades the streets, amidst a storm of popular wit and nonsense. The children, on going to bed, hang up a stocking, which the Beffana is found next morning to have filled with cakes and sweetmeats if they have been good, but with stones and dirt if they have been naughty.

In England, it appears there was always a queen as well as a king on Twelfth-Night. A writer, speaking of the celebration in the south of England in 1774, says: 'After tea, a cake is produced, with two bowls containing the fortunate chances for the different sexes. The host fills up the tickets, and the whole company, except the king and queen, are to be ministers of state, maids of honour, or ladies of the bed-chamber. Often the host and hostess, more by design than accident, become king and queen. According to Twelfth-Day law, each party is to support his character till midnight.

In the sixteenth century, it would appear that some peculiar ceremonies followed the election of the king and queen. Barnaby Goodge, in his paraphrase of the curious poem of Nageorgus, *The Popish Kingdom*, 1570, states that the king, on being elected, was raised up with great cries to the ceiling, where, with chalk, he inscribed crosses on the rafters to protect the house against evil spirits.

The sketch on the opposite page is copied from an old French print, executed by J. Mariatte, representing *Le Roi de la Fève* (the King of the Bean) at the moment of his election, and preparing to drink to the company. In France, this act on his part was marked by a loud shout of 'Le Roi boit!' (The king drinks,) from the party assembled.

A Twelfth-Day custom, connected with Paget's Bromley in Staffordshire, went out in the seventeenth century. A man came along the village with a mock horse fastened to him, with which he danced, at the same making a snapping noise with a bow and arrow. He was attended by half-a-dozen fellow-villagers, wearing mock deers' heads, and displaying the arms of the several chief landlords of the town. This party danced *the Hays*, and other country dances, to music, amidst the sympathy and applause of the multitude. There was also a huge pot of ale with cakes by general contribution of the village, out of the very surplus of which 'they not only repaired their church, but kept their poor too; which charges,' quoth Dr Plot, 'are not now, perhaps, so cheerfully borne.'*

On Twelfth-Night, 1606, Ben Jonson's masque of *Hymen* was performed before the Court; and in 1613, the gentlemen of Gray's Inn were permitted by Lord Bacon to perform a Twelfth-Day masque at Whitehall. In this masque the character of Baby Cake is attended by 'an

---

* Warton's *History of English Poetry*, quoting a Chronicle of Milan, by Gualvanei de la Flamma.

† 'Some maintain it to have been derived from the custom observed by the Roman children, who, at the end of their Saturnalia, drew lots with beans, to see who would be king.'—*Brady*

* *Natural History of Staffordshire*, 1680, p. 434.

THE KING OF THE BEAN.

usher bearing a great cake with a bean and a pease.'

On Twelfth-Day, 1563, Mary Queen of Scots celebrated the French pastime of the King of the Bean at Holyrood, but with a queen instead of a king, as more appropriate, in consideration of herself being a female sovereign. The lot fell to the real queen's attendant, Mary Fleming, and the mistress good-naturedly arrayed the servant in her own robes and jewels, that she might duly sustain the mimic dignity in the festivities of the night. The English resident, Randolph, who was in love with Mary Beton, another of the queen's maids of honour, wrote in excited terms about this festival to the Earl of Leicester. 'Happy was it,' says he, 'unto this realm, that her reign endured no longer. Two such sights, in one state, in so good accord, I believe was never seen, as to behold two worthy queens possess, without envy, one kingdom, both upon a day. I leave the rest to your lordship to be judged of. My pen staggereth, my hand faileth, further to write. . . . The queen of the bean was that day in a gown of cloth of silver; her head, her neck, her shoulders, the rest of her whole body, so beset with stones, that more in our whole jewel-house were not to be found. . . . The cheer was great. I never found myself so happy, nor so well treated, until that it came to the point that the old queen [Mary] herself, to show her mighty power, contrary unto the assurance granted me by the younger queen [Mary Fleming], drew me into the dance, which part of the play I could

with good will have spared unto your lordship, as much fitter for the purpose.' *

Charles I. had his masque on Twelfth-Day, and the Queen hers on the Shrovetide following, the expenses exceeding £2000; and on Twelfth-Night, 1633, the Queen feasted the King at Somerset House, and presented a pastoral, in which she took part.

Down to the time of the Civil Wars, the feast was observed with great splendour, not only at Court, but at the Inns of Court, and the Universities (where it was an old custom to choose the king by the bean in a cake), as well as in private mansions and smaller households.

Then, too, we read of the English nobility keeping Twelfth-Night otherwise than with cake and characters, by the diversion of blowing up pasteboard castles; letting claret flow like blood, out of a stag made of paste; the castle bombarded from a pasteboard ship, with cannon, in the midst of which the company pelted each other with egg-shells filled with rose-water; and large pies were made, filled with live frogs, which hopped and flew out, upon some curious person lifting up the lid.

Twelfth-Night grew to be a Court festival, in which gaming was a costly feature. Evelyn tells us that on Twelfth-Night, 1662, according to custom, his Majesty [Charles II.] opened the revels of that night by throwing the dice himself in the Privy Chamber, where was a table set on purpose, and lost his £100. [The year before

* Strickland's *Lives of the Queens of Scotland*, iv. 20.

63

ne won £1500.] The ladies also played very deep. Evelyn came away when the Duke of Ormond had won about £1000, and left them still at passage, cards, &c., at other tables.

The Rev. Henry Teonge, chaplain of one of Charles's ships-of-war, describes Twelfth-Night on board: 'Wee had a great kake made, in which was put a beane for the king, a pease for the queen, a cloave for the knave, &c. The kake was cut into several pieces in the great cabin, and all put into a napkin, out of which every one took his piece as out of a lottery; then each piece is broaken to see what was in it, which caused much laughter, and more to see us tumble one over the other in the cabin, by reason of the ruff weather.' The celebrated Lord Peterborough, then a youth, was one of the party on board this ship, as Lord Mordaunt.

The Lord Mayor and Aldermen and the guilds of London used to go to St Paul's on Twelfth-Day, to hear a sermon, which is mentioned as an old custom in the early part of Elizabeth's reign.

A century ago, the king, preceded by heralds, pursuivants, and the Knights of the Garter, Thistle, and Bath, in the collars of their respective orders, went to the Royal Chapel at St James's, and offered gold, myrrh, and frankincense, in imitation of the Eastern Magi offering to our Saviour. Since the illness of George III., the procession, and even the personal appearance of the monarch, have been discontinued. Two gentlemen from the Lord Chamberlain's office now appear instead, attended by a box ornamented at top with a spangled star, from which they take the gold, frankincense, and myrrh, and place them on an alms-dish held forth by the officiating priest.

In the last century, *Twelfth-Night Cards* represented ministers, maids of honour, and other attendants of a court, and the characters were to be supported throughout the night. John Britton, in his *Autobiography*, tells us he 'suggested and wrote a series of Twelfth-Night Characters, to be printed on cards, placed in a bag, and drawn out at parties on the memorable and merry evening of that ancient festival. They were sold in small packets to pastrycooks, and led the way to a custom which annually grew to an extensive trade. For the second year, my pen-and-ink characters were accompanied by prints of the different personages by Cruikshank (father of the inimitable George), all of a comic or ludicrous kind.' Such characters are still printed.

The celebration of Twelfth-Day with the costly and elegant Twelfth-cake has much declined within the last half-century. Formerly, in London, the confectioners' shops on this day were entirely filled with Twelfth-cakes, ranging in price from several guineas to a few shillings; the shops were tastefully illuminated, and decorated with artistic models, transparencies, &c. We remember to have seen a huge Twelfth-cake in the form of a fortress, with sentinels and flags; the cake being so large as to fill two ovens in baking.

One of the most celebrated and attractive displays was that of Birch, the confectioner,

No. 15, Cornhill, probably the oldest shop of its class in the metropolis. This business was established in the reign of King George I., by a Mr Horton, who was succeeded by Mr Lucas Birch, who, in his turn, was succeeded by his son, Mr Samuel Birch, born in 1757; he was many years a member of the Common Council, and was elected alderman of the ward of Candlewick. He was also colonel of the City Militia, and served as Lord Mayor in 1815, the year of the battle of Waterloo. In his mayoralty, he laid the first stone of the London Institution; and when Chantrey's marble statue of George III. was inaugurated in the Council Chamber, Guildhall, the inscription was written by Lord Mayor Birch. He possessed considerable literary taste, and wrote poems and musical dramas, of which the *Adopted Child* remained a stock piece to our time. The alderman used annually to send, as a present, a Twelfth-cake to the Mansion House. The upper

NO. 15, CORNHILL.

portion of the house in Cornhill has been rebuilt, but the ground-floor remains intact, a curious specimen of the decorated shop-front of the last century, and here are preserved two door-plates, inscribed, 'Birch, Successor to Mr Horton,' which are 140 years old. Alderman Birch died in 1840, having been succeeded in the business in Cornhill in 1836 by the present proprietors, Ring and Brymer. Dr Kitchiner extols the soups of Birch, and his skill has long been famed in civic banquets.

We have a Twelfth-Night celebration recorded in theatrical history. Baddeley, the comedian (who had been cook to Foote), left, by will, money to provide cake and wine for the performers, in the green-room at Drury-lane Theatre, on Twelfth-Night; but the bequest is not now observed in this manner.

The Carnival.

The period of Carnival—named as being *carnivale*, a farewell to flesh—is well known as a time of merry-making and pleasure, indulged in in Roman Catholic countries, in anticipation of the abstemious period of Lent: it begins at Epiphany, and ends on Ash Wednesday. Selden remarks: 'What the Church debars one day, she gives us leave to take out in another. First, we fast, then we feast; first, there is a Carnival, then a Lent.' In these long revels, we trace some of the licence of the Saturnalia of the Christian Romans, who could not forget their pagan festivals. Milan, Rome, and Naples were celebrated for their carnivals, but they were carried to their highest perfection at Venice. Bishop Hall, in his *Triumphs of Rome*, thus describes the *Jovial Carnival* of that city: 'Every man cries *Sciolta*, letting himself loose to the maddest of merriments, marching wildly up and down in all forms of disguises; each man striving to outgo others in strange pranks of humorous debauchedness, in which even those of the holy order are wont to be allowed their share; for, howsoever it was by some sullen authority forbidden to clerks and votaries of any kind to go masked and misguised in those seemingly abusive solemnities, yet more favourable construction hath offered to make them believe it was chiefly for their sakes, for the refreshment of their sadder and more restrained spirits, that this free and lawless festivity was taken up.'

In modern Rome, the masquerading in the streets and all the out-of-door amusements are limited to eight days, during which the grotesque maskers pelt each other with sugar-plums and bouquets. These are poured from baskets from the balconies down upon the maskers in carriages and afoot; and they, in their turn, pelt the company at the windows: the *confetti* are made of chalk or flour, and a hundredweight is ammunition for a carriage-full of roisterers.

The Races, however, are one of the most striking out-of-door scenes. The horses are without riders, but have spurs, sheets of tin, and all sorts of things hung about them to urge them onward; across the end of the Piazza del Popolo is stretched a rope, in a line with which the horses are brought up; in a second or two, the rope is let go, and away the horses fly at a fearful rate down the Corso, which is crowded with people, among whom the plunging and kicking of the steeds often produce serious damage.

Meanwhile, there is the Church's Carnival, or the *Carnivale Sanctificato*. There are the regular spiritual exercises, or retreats, which the Jesuits and Passionists give in their respective houses for those who are able to leave their homes and shut themselves up in a monastery during the whole ten days; the *Via Crucis* is practised in the Coliseum every afternoon of the Carnival, and this is followed by a sermon and benediction; and there are similar devotions in the churches. In the colleges are given plays, the scenery, drops, and acting being better than the average of public performances; and between the acts

are played solos, duets, and overtures, by the students or their friends.

The closing revel of the Carnival is the *Moccoletti*, when the sport consists in the crowd carrying lighted tapers, and trying to put out each other's taper with a handkerchief or towel, and shouting *Sens moccolo*. M. Dumas, in his *Count of Monte Christo*, thus vividly describes this strange scene:

'The *moccolo* or *moccoletti* are candles, which vary in size from the paschal taper to the rushlight, and cause the actors of the great scene which terminates the Carnival two different subjects of anxiety: 1st, how to preserve their *moccoletti* lighted; secondly, how to extinguish the *moccoletti* of others. The *moccolo* is kindled by approaching it to a light. But who can describe the thousand means of extinguishing the *moccoletti*? The gigantic bellows, the monstrous extinguishers, the superhuman fans? The night was rapidly approaching: and, already, at the shrill cry of *Moccoletti!* repeated by the shrill voices of a thousand vendors, two or three stars began to twinkle among the crowd. This was the signal. In about ten minutes, fifty thousand lights fluttered on every side, descending from the Palais de Venise to the Plaza del Popolo, and mounting from the Plaza del Popolo to the Palais de Venise. It seemed the *fête* of Jack-o'-Lanterns. It is impossible to form any idea of it without having seen it. Suppose all the stars descended from the sky, and mingled in a wild dance on the surface of the earth; the whole accompanied by cries such as are never heard in any other part of the world. The *facchino* follows the prince, the *transtavere* the citizen: every one blowing, extinguishing, re-lighting. Had old Æolus appeared at that moment, he would have been proclaimed king of the *moccoli*, and Aquilo the heir-presumptive to the throne. This flaming race continued for two hours: the Rue du Cour was light as day, and the features of the spectators on the third and fourth stories were plainly visible. Suddenly the bell sounded which gives the signal for the Carnival to close, and at the same instant all the *moccoletti* were extinguished as if by enchantment. It seemed as though one immense blast of wind had extinguished them all. No sound was audible, save that of the carriages which conveyed the masks home; nothing was visible save a few lights that gleamed behind the windows. The Carnival was over.'

In Paris, the Carnival is principally kept on the three days preceding Ash Wednesday; and upon the last day, the procession of the *Bœuf-gras*, or Government prize ox, passes through the streets; then all is quiet until the Thursday of Mid-Lent, or *Mi-carême*, on which day only the revelry breaks out wilder than ever.

RHYTHMICAL PUNS ON NAMES.

One of the best specimens of this kind of composition is the poem said to have been addressed by Shakspeare to the Warwickshire beauty, Ann Hathaway, whom he afterwards married. Though his biographers assert that not a fragment of the

Bard of Avon's poetry on this lady has been res-cued from oblivion, yet, that Shakspeare had an early disposition to write such verses, may be reasonably concluded from a passage in *Love's Labour Lost*, in which he says:

'Never durst poet teach a pen to write,
Until his ink were tempered with love's sighs.'

The lines, whether written by Shakspeare or not, exhibit a clever play upon words, and are inscribed:

'TO THE IDOL OF MY EYE, AND DELIGHT OF MY
HEART, ANN HATHAWAY.

Would ye be taught, ye feathered throng,
With love's sweet notes to grace your song,
To pierce the heart with thrilling lay,
Listen to mine Ann Hathaway!
She hath a way to sing so clear,
Phœbus might wondering stop to hear.
To melt the sad, make blithe the gay,
And Nature charm, Ann hath a way;
    She hath a way,
      Ann Hathaway;
To breathe delight, Ann hath a way.

When Envy's breath and rancorous tooth
Do soil and bite fair worth and truth,
And merit to distress betray,
To soothe the heart Ann hath a way.
She hath a way to chase despair,
To heal all grief, to cure all care,
Turn foulest night to fairest day.
Thou know'st, fond heart, Ann hath a way;
    She hath a way,
      Ann Hathaway;
To make grief bliss, Ann hath a way.

Talk not of gems, the orient list,
The diamond, topaze, amethyst,
The emerald mild, the ruby gay;
Talk of my gem, Ann Hathaway!
She hath a way, with her bright eye,
Their various lustre to defy,—
The jewels she, and the foil they,
So sweet to look Ann hath a way;
    She hath a way,
      Ann Hathaway;
To shame bright gems, Ann hath a way.

But were it to my fancy given
To rate her charms, I'd call them heaven;
For though a mortal made of clay,
Angels must love Ann Hathaway;
She hath a way so to control,
To rapture the imprisoned soul,
And sweetest heaven on earth display,
That to be heaven Ann hath a way;
    She hath a way,
      Ann Hathaway;
To be heaven's self, Ann hath a way!'

When James I. visited the house of Sir Thomas Pope in Oxfordshire, the knight's in-fant daughter was presented to the king, with a piece of paper in her hands, bearing these lines:

'See! this little mistress here
Did never sit in Peter's chair,
Neither a triple crown did wear;
    And yet she is a Pope!

No benefice she ever sold,
Nor did dispense with sin for gold;
She hardly is a fortnight old,
    And yet she is a Pope!

No king her feet did ever kiss,
Or had from her worse looks than this;
Nor did she ever hope
To saint one with a rope,
    And yet she is a Pope!

"A female Pope!" you'll say—"a second Joan!"
No, sure—she is Pope Innocent, or none.'

The following on a lady rejoicing in the name of Rain is not unworthy of a place here:

'Whilst shivering beaux at weather rail,
Of frost, and snow, and wind, and hail,
    And heat, and cold, complain,
My steadier mind is always bent
On one sole object of content—
    I ever wish for Rain!

Hymen, thy votary's prayer attend,
His anxious hope and suit befriend,
    Let him not ask in vain;
His thirsty soul, his parched estate,
His glowing breast commiserate—
    In pity give him Rain!'

Another amorous rhymester thus writes:

'ON A YOUNG LADY NAMED CARELESS.

Careless by name, and Careless by nature
Careless of shape, and Careless of feature.
Careless in dress, and Careless in air;
Careless of riding, in coach or in chair;
Careless of love, and Careless of hate;
Careless if crooked, and Careless if straight.
Careless at table, and Careless in bed.
Careless if maiden, not Careless if wed.
Careless at church, and Careless at play ·
Careless if company go, or they stay.
E'en Careless at tea, not minding chit-chat;
So Careless! she's Careless for this or for that.
Careless of all love or wit can propose;
She's Careless—so Careless, there's nobody knows.
Oh! how I could love thee, thou dear Careless thing!
(Oh, happy, thrice happy! I'd envy no king.)
Were you Careful for once to return me my love,
I'd care not how Careless to others you'd prove.
I then should be Careless how Careless you were;
And the more Careless you, still the less I should care.'

Thomas Longfellow, landlord of the 'Golden Lion' inn at Brecon, must have pulled a rather long face, when he observed the following lines, written on the mantelshelf of his coffee-room:

'Tom Longfellow's name is most justly his due:
Long his neck, long his bill, which is very long too;
Long the time ere your horse to the stable is led,
Long before he's rubbed down, and much longer till
    fed;
Long indeed may you sit in a comfortless room,
Till from kitchen long dirty your dinner shall come;
Long the often-told tale that your host will relate,
Long his face while complaining how long people eat;
Long may Longfellow long ere he see me again—
Long 'twill be ere I long for Tom Longfellow's inn.'

Nor has the House of Lords, or even the Church, escaped the pens of irreverent rhyming punsters. When Dr Goodenough preached before the Peers, a wag wrote:

''Tis well enough, that Goodenough
    Before the Lords should preach;
For, sure enough, they're bad enough
    He undertakes to teach.'

Again, when Archbishop Moore, dying, was succeeded by Dr Manners Sutton, the following lines were circulated:

'What say you? the Archbishop's dead?
 A loss indeed!—Oh, on his head
   May Heaven its blessings pour!
 But if with such a heart and mind,
 In Manners we his equal find,
   Why should we wish for M-ore?'

Our next example is of a rather livelier description:

'At a tavern one night,
 Messrs More, Strange, and Wright
Met to drink and their good thoughts exchange.
 Says More, "Of us three,
 The whole will agree,
There's only one knave, and that's Strange."

 "Yes," says Strange, rather sore,
 "I'm sure there's one More,
A most terrible knave, and a bite,
 Who cheated his mother,
 His sister, and brother."
"Oh yes," replied More, "that is Wright."'

Wright again comes in very appropriately in these lines written

'ON MEETING AN OLD GENTLEMAN NAMED WRIGHT.

What, Wright alive! I thought ere this
That he was in the realms of bliss!
Let us not say that Wright is wrong,
Merely for holding out so long;
But ah! 'tis clear, though we're bereft
Of many a friend that Wright has left,
Amazing, too, in such a case,
That Wright and left should thus change place!
Not that I'd go such lengths as quite
To think him left because he's Wright:
But left he is, we plainly see,
Or Wright, we know, he could not be:
For when he treads death's fatal shore,
We feel that Wright will be no more.
He's, therefore, Wright while left; but, gone,
Wright is not left: and so I've done.'

When Sir Thomas More was Chancellor, it is said that, by his unremitting attention to the duties of his high office, all the litigation in the Court of Chancery was brought to a conclusion in his lifetime; giving rise to the following epigram:

'When More some years had Chancellor been,
 No more suits did remain.
 The same shall never more be seen,
 Till More be there again.'

More has always been a favourite name with the punsters—they have even followed it to the tomb, as is shown in the following epitaph in St Benet's Churchyard, Paul's Wharf, London:

'Here lies one More, and no more than he.
One More and no more! how can that be?
Why, one More and no more may well lie here alone;
But here lies one More, and that's more than one.'

Punning epitaphs, however, are not altogether rarities. The following was inscribed in Peterborough Cathedral to the memory of Sir Richard Worme:

'Does worm eat Worme? Knight Worme this truth
   confirms;
For here, with worms, lies Worme, a dish for worms.
Does Worme eat worm? Sure Worme will this
   deny;
For worms with Worme, a dish for Worme don't lie.
'Tis so, and 'tis not so, for free from worms
'Tis certain Worme is blest without his worms.'

In the churchyard of Barro-upon-Soar, in Leicestershire, there is another punning epitaph on one Cave:

'Here, in this grave, there lies a Cave:
   We call a cave a grave.
 If cave be grave and grave be Cave,
   Then, reader, judge, I crave,
 Whether doth Cave lie here in grave,
   Or grave here lie in Cave:
 If grave in Cave here buried lie,
 Then, grave, where is thy victory?
 Go, reader, and report, here lies a Cave,
 Who conquers death, and buries his own grave.'

JANUARY 7.

St Lucian, of Antioch, priest and martyr, 312. St Cedd, bishop of London, 7th century. St Thillo, 702. St Kentigerna, widow, 728. St Aldric, bishop of Mans, 856. St Canut, 1171.

St Lucian, whose name occurs in the calendar of the Church of England on the 8th of January, being the first Roman priest who occurs and is retained there, was a learned Syrian who busied himself in revising the Holy Scriptures—was for a while disaffected to orthodox doctrine, but afterwards conformed to it, and finally died at Nicomedia, after a long imprisonment.

St Cedd was an Anglo-Saxon saint, who took a prominent part in Christianising his hitherto heathen countrymen in the midland districts of England. He long served God in the monastery of Lindisfarne, and afterwards was appointed bishop of the East Saxons. Amongst his noted acts was the building of a monastery at Tilbury, near the mouth of the Thames.

Born.—Robert Nicoll, poet, 1814.
Died.—Fenelon de la Mothe, 1715; Allan Ramsay, the Scottish poet, 1758; J. H. Frere, poet, 1846.

FENELON.

François de Salignac de la Mothe Fenelon was born at Perigord, in 1651. He preached a sermon at the early age of fifteen, before a select assembly at Paris; but his uncle, the Marquis de Fenelon, fearing that the praises of the world would make the boy vain, caused him to enter the seminary of St Sulpice, where he remained several years and took orders. He was sent by Louis XIV. to Poitou, to convert the Protestants, when he nobly refused the aid of dragoons, relying solely on his powers of persuasion. He was appointed tutor to the young Duke of Burgundy, and in five years Louis made him Archbishop of Cambray. Thence began his troubles: he was suspected of favouring the doctrines of the

67

Quietists, and upon his refusing to condemn them, Bossuet denounced him to the king as a heretic, and he was eventually banished from the court; he, however, signed a recantation, and would have been restored to royal favour, had not his celebrated romance of *Télémaque*, which he had written some years before, been published against his will, through the treachery of a servant. Louis suspected several passages in this work to be directed against himself; it was suppressed in France, but rapidly circulated in Holland; and perhaps there is no book in the French language which has been more read. It is, at this day, a class-book in almost every European school. His work on Female Education, published in 1688, proceeds upon the uniformly indulgent theory,—teaching without tears. He wrote his *Dialogues of the Dead* for the use of his pupil, the Duke of Burgundy: his noble zeal in not sparing the vices of kings shines throughout the work. His political opinions were liberal; and his acts of benevolence were munificent: in the year 1709 he fed the French army at his own expense.

St Distaff's Day.

As the first free day after the twelve by which Christmas was formerly celebrated, the 7th of January was a notable one among our ancestors. They jocularly called it *St Distaff's Day*, or *Rock Day*, because by women the rock or distaff was then resumed, or proposed to be so. The duty seems to have been considered a dubious one, and when it was complied with, the ploughmen, who on their part scarcely felt called upon on this day to resume work, made it their sport to set the flax a-burning; in requital of which prank, the maids soused the men from the water-pails. Herrick gives us the popular ritual of the day in some of his cheerful stanzas:

'ST DISTAFF'S DAY; OR, THE MORROW AFTER
             TWELFTH-DAY.

Partly work and partly play
You must on St Distaff's Day:
From the plough soon free your team;
Then come home and fother them:
If the maids a-spinning go,
Burn the flax and fire the tow.
Bring in pails of water then,
Let the maids bewash the men.
Give St Distaff all the right:
Then bid Christmas sport good night,
And next morrow every one
To his own vocation.'

This mirthful observance recalls a time when spinning was the occupation of almost all women who had not anything else to do, or during the intervals of other and more serious work—a cheering resource to the solitary female in all ranks of life, an enlivenment to every fireside scene. To *spin*—how essentially was the idea at one time associated with the female sex! even to that extent, that in England *spinster* was a recognised legal term for an unmarried woman—the *spear* side and the *distaff* side were legal terms to distinguish the inheritance of male from that of female children—and the *distaff* became a

68

synonym for woman herself: thus, the French proverb was: 'The crown of France never falls to the distaff.' Now, through the change wrought by the organised industries of Manchester and Glasgow, the princess of the fairy tale who was destined to die by a spindle piercing her hand, might wander from the Land's End to John o' Groat's House, and never encounter an article of the kind, unless in an archæological museum.

Mr John Yonge Akerman, in a paper read before the Society of Antiquaries, has carefully traced the memorials of the early use of the distaff and spindle on the monuments of Egypt, in ancient mythology and ancient literature, and everywhere shews these implements as the insignia of womanhood. We scarcely needed such proof for a fact of which we have assurance in the slightest reflection on human needs and means, and the natural place of woman in human society. The distaff and spindle must, of course, have been coeval with the first efforts of our race to frame textures for the covering of their persons, for they are the very simplest arrangement for the formation of thread: the distaff, whereon to hang the flax or tow—the spindle, a loaded pin or stick, whereby to effect the twisting; the one carried under the arm, the other dangling and turning in the fingers below, and forming an axis round which to wind parcels of the thread as soon as it was made. Not wonderful is it that Solomon should speak of woman as laying her hands to the distaff (Prov. xxxi. 19), that the implement is alluded to by Homer and Herodotus, and that one of the oldest of the mythological ideas of Greece represented the Three Fates as spinning the thread of human destiny. Not very surprising is it that our own Chaucer, five hundred years ago, classed this art among the natural endowments of the fair sex in his ungallant distich:

'Deceit, weeping, spinning, God hath given
   To women kindly, while they may live.'

It was admitted in those old days that a woman could not quite make a livelihood by spinning; but, says Anthony Fitzherbert, in his *Boke of Husbandrie*, 'it stoppeth a gap,' it saveth a woman from being idle, and the product was needful. No rank was above the use of the spindle. Homer's princesses only had them gilt. The lady carried her distaff in her gemmed girdle, and her spindle in her hand, when she went to spend half a day with a neighbouring friend. The farmer's wife had her maids about her in the evening, all spinning. So lately as Burns's time, when lads and lasses came together to spend an evening in social glee, each of the latter brought her spinning apparatus, or *rock*,* and the assemblage was called a *rocking*:

'On Fasten's eve we had a *rocking*.'

It was doubtless the same with Horace's *uxor Sabina, perusta solibus*, as with Burns's bonnie Jean.

The ordinary spindle, throughout all times, was a turned pin of a few inches in length, having a nick or hook at the small and upper end, by which to fasten the thread, and a load of

* From the German, *rocken*.

some sort at the lower end to make it hang rightly. In very early times, and in such rude nations as the Laps, till more recent times, the load was a small perforated stone, many examples of which (called *whorls*) are preserved in antiquarian museums. It would seem from the Egyptian monuments as if, among those people, the whorl had been carried on the top.

Some important improvements appear to have been made in the distaff and spindle. In Stow's *Chronicle*, it is stated: 'About the 20th year of Henry VIII., Anthony Bonvise, an Italian, came to this land, and taught English people to spin with a distaff, at which time began the making of Devonshire kersies and Coxall clothes.' Again, Aubrey, in his *Natural History of Wiltshire*, says: 'The art of spinning is so much improved within these last forty years, that one pound of wool makes twice as much cloath (as to extent) as it did before the Civill Warres.'

SPINNING WITH THE DISTAFF.

It is hard to say when the spinning-wheel superseded the simpler process of the distaff and spindle. The wheel is stated, in the *Dictionnaire des Origines*, to have been invented by a citizen of Brunswick in 1533; three years before was printed the *Dictionary of Palsgrave*, wherein we find the phrase, 'I spynne upon a rock,' rendered 'Je file au rouet.'

We have, however, evidence, in a manuscript in the British Museum, written early in the fourteenth century, of the use of a spinning-wheel at that date: herein are several representations of a woman spinning with a wheel: she stands at her work, and the wheel is moved with her right hand, while with her left she twirls the spindle: this is the wheel called a *torn*, the term for a spinning-wheel still used in some districts of England. The spinning-wheel said to have been invented in 1533 was, doubtless, that to which women *sat*, and which was worked with the feet.

Spinning with the wheel was common with the recluses in England: Aubrey tells us that Wiltshire was full of religious houses, and that old Jacques 'could see from his house the nuns of Saint Mary's (juxta Kington) come forth into the Nymph Hay with their rocks and wheels to spin, and with their sewing work.' And in his

MS. *Natural History of Wiltshire*, Aubrey says: 'In the old time they used to spin with rocks; in Staffordshire, they use them still.'

The change from the distaff and spindle to the spinning-wheel appears to have been almost coincident with an alteration in, or modification of, our legal phraseology, and to have abrogated the use of the word *spinster* when applied to single women of a certain rank. Coke says: '*Generosus* and *Generosa* are good additions: and, if a gentlewoman be named spinster in any original writ, etc., appeale, or indictment, she may abate and quash the same; for she hath as good right to that addition as Baronesse, Viscountesse, Marchionesse, or Dutchesse have to theirs.' Blount, in his *Law Dictionary*, says of spinster: 'It is the addition usually given to all unmarried women, from the Viscount's daughter downward.' In his *Glossographia*, he says of spinster: 'It is a term or addition in our law dialect, given in evidence and writings to a *femme sole*, as it were calling her *spinner*: and this is the only addition for all unmarried women, from the Viscount's daughter downward.'

'I am unable' (says Mr Akerman) 'to trace these distinctions to their source, but they are too remarkable, as indicating a great change of feeling among the upper classes in the sixteenth century, to be passed unnoticed. May we suppose that, among other causes, the art of printing had contributed to bring about this change, affording employment to women of condition, who now devoted themselves to reading instead of applying themselves to the primitive occupation of their grandmothers; and that the wheel and the distaff being left to humbler hands, the time-honoured name of *spinster* was at length considered too homely for a maiden above the common rank.

Before the science of the moderns banished the spinning-wheel, some extraordinary feats were accomplished with it. Thus, in the year 1745, a woman at East Dereham, in Norfolk, spun a single pound of wool into a thread of 84,000 yards in length, wanting only 80 yards of 48 miles, which, at the above period, was considered a circumstance of sufficient curiosity to merit a place in the Proceedings of the Royal Society. Since that time, a young lady of Norwich has spun a pound of combed wool into a thread of 168,000 yards; and she actually produced from the same weight of cotton a thread of 203,000 yards, equal to upwards of 115 miles: this last thread, if woven, would produce about 20 yards of yard-wide muslin.

The spinning-wheel has almost left us—with the lace-pillow, the hour-glass, and the hornbook; but not so on the Continent. 'The art of spinning, in one of its simplest and most primitive forms, is yet pursued in Italy, where the countrywomen of Caia still turn the spindle, unrestrained by that ancient rural law which forbade its use without doors. The distaff has outlived the consular fasces, and survived the conquests of the Goth and the Hun. But rustic hands alone now sway the sceptre of Tanaquil, and all but the peasant disdain a practice which once beguiled the leisure of high-born dames.'

Sermon to the Jews.

7th January 1645, Mr John Evelyn was present at a peculiar ceremony which seems to have been of annual occurrence at Rome. It was a sermon preached to a compulsory congregation of Jews, with a view to their conversion. Mr Evelyn says: 'They are constrained to sit till the hour is done, but it is with so much malice in their countenances, spitting, humming, coughing, and motion, that it is almost impossible they should hear a word from the preacher. A conversion is very rare.' *

Cattle in January.

Worthy Thomas Tusser, who, in Queen Mary's time, wrote a doggrel code of agriculture under the name of *Five Hundred Points of Good Husbandry*, † recommends the farmer, as soon as Christmas observances are past, to begin to attend carefully to his stock.

' Who both by his calf and his lamb will be known,
  May well kill a neat and a sheep of his own;
And he that can rear up a pig in his house,
  Hath cheaper his bacon and sweeter his souse.'

He urges the gathering up of dung, the mending of hedges, and the storing of fuel, as employments for this month. The scarcity in those days of fodder, especially when frost lasted long, he reveals to us by his direction that all trees should be pruned of their superfluous boughs, that the cattle might browse upon them. The myrtle and ivy were the wretched fare he pointed to for the sheep. The homely verses of this old poet give us a lively idea of the difficulties of carrying cattle over the winter, before the days of field turnips, and of the miserable expedients which were had recourse to, in order to save the poor creatures from absolute starvation:

' From Christmas till May be well entered in,
  Some cattle wax faint, and look poorly and thin;
And chiefly when prime grass at first doth appear,
  Then most is the danger of all the whole year.

Take verjuice and heat it, a pint for a cow,
Buy salt, a handful, to rub tongue ye wot how:
That done with the salt, let her drink off the rest;
This many times raiseth the feeble up beast.'

Connection of Distant Ages by the Lives of Individuals.

The shortness at once and speed of human life are brought strongly before our minds when we cast the simplest look back upon our own career, find ourselves grandfathers so long before what appears the proper time, and finally discover that we are about to leave the world with not half of our plans and wishes accomplished. The matter is also very pointedly illustrated by the great changes which every one finds in the *personnel* of his surrounding world every ten years or so;

the boys become men, the little girls now reckoning each their two or three babies, the matronly hostesses who used to sit at the heads of hospitable tables now retired into quiet dowagerhood, the vigorous mature men now becoming shaky and unfit for business, the old and venerable now to be found only in the churchyard! On the other hand, one sometimes get an exhilaration as to human life and his own individual prospects, by instances of lives at once remarkably protracted and attended by singular health and vigour. To find a Brougham at eighty-two heading a great social gathering like that which took place at Glasgow in September 1860, or a Lyndhurst at eighty-eight pouring out the words of experience and sagacity in the House of Lords for four hours at a time, is felt by all younger persons as a moral glass of champagne. The day looks brighter by our even hearing such a fact alluded to. And the reason obviously is that we get from such facts a conviction of pleasant possibilities for ourselves. We all feel that such *may*, in favouring circumstances, be our own case. It seems to imply that Time is, after all, not so deadly an enemy to us as he is generally represented: if we use him well, he will use us well. There is, moreover, a spirit in man which gives him the desire and the power to resist the influence of surrounding agencies. We delight to brave cold, hunger, fatigue, and danger. The unconquerable will joyfully hardens itself to throw off the common effects of life's many evils. It is a joy to this spirit to find that some valorous souls can and do live on, and on, and on, so long, seeming as if they had acquired some mastery over fate itself—that Power—' *nil miserantis Orci*,'—before which, alas, we must all fall sooner or later.

There is, we must admit, a limit to this satisfaction; for when life becomes in any instance protracted to a decidedly extraordinary extent, the individual necessarily feels himself amongst strangers—perhaps helplessly dependent on them —the voice of every youthful companion hushed —wife, perhaps even children, removed from his side—new things in which he has no part or vocation all around him. Then, indeed, it were better for him to follow those who have gone before. Yet, while the spectacle of such a superfluous relic of past ages gives us, of course, little pleasure in the contemplation, and can inspire us with no pleasant anticipations, it may become a matter of considerable interest to a mind which dwells upon time with a regard to either its historical or its sentimental relations.

For example, while no one could wish to imitate the recently deceased American, Ralph Farnham, in length of days—the fact being that he lived to 107—no one could see him, as the Prince of Wales did in November 1860, and reflect that here was still in the body one of the little civic band which defended Bunker Hill in 1775, without feelings of extreme interest. Such a man, thus so long surviving the multitude amongst whom he once acted, becomes to us as one returned from the dead. He ought to be a shadow and a recollection, and behold he is a reality! The whole story of the War of American Independence is now so far removed into the

---

* Evelyn's *Diary*, i. p. 136.
† Reprint by Lackington, Allen and Co., 1812.

region of history, that any living link between it and the present time is necessarily heard of with extreme surprise. Yet Lord Lyndhurst, who still (1862) takes a part in our public affairs, was born in Boston, a British subject, the State of Massachusetts being then and for some years later a British province.

The affair of the *Forty-five* precedes the struggle for American independence by thirty years; yet even that event is brought into apparent closeness to us by many surprising connections. There were still one or two Culloden men living when George IV. was king: one came to see him at Holyrood in 1822, and greeted him as 'the last of his enemies.' It is worth noting that an uncle of the present Lord Torphichen (1862) was an officer in the royal army in 1745, was present at the battle of Prestonpans, and is noted by Dr Carlyle in his *Autobiography* as the only wounded man on the king's side who was carried to Bankton House, all the other wounded people taken there being Highlanders. [Lord Torphichen, however, had another *uncle*, who, when a boy in 1720, was supposed to be bewitched, and thus was the cause of a fast being held in Calder parish, and of three or four poor persons being imprisoned under suspicion of sorcery!] That there should be now moving in society in Edinburgh, a lady whose father-in-law attended the Prince in his wanderings, does not call for particular remark. It becomes more startling to hear Mr Andrew Coventry, of Edinburgh, a gentleman in the vigour of life, speak of having dined with the *mother-in-law* of the gallant Charles Edward. He did so in 1823, at the house of Mr Bethmann in Frankfort. This lady was the Princess Stolberg, then ninety years of age. Her daughter, the Princess Louisa de Stolberg, had married the Prince about fifty years before. It appears from a note in Earl Stanhope's History of England, that his lordship also was introduced to the Princess at Frankfort. He states that she was 'still lively and agreeable,' and that she lived till 1826. 'It is singular,' his lordship very naturally adds, 'that a man born eighty-five years after the Chevalier, should have seen his mother-in-law.'

When George IV. acceded to the throne in 1820, he had occasion to remark a very curious circumstance connecting his reign with one which we are accustomed to consider as remote. The decorations of the Order of the Garter, which then returned to the king from his deceased father, had only been worn by two persons since the reign of Charles II.! By that monarch they had been conferred upon the Duke of Somerset—he who was commonly called the Proud Duke—and by him they had been retained till his death in 1748, when they were conferred upon the young Prince of Wales, subsequently George III. The entire time embraced by the two tenures of the honour was about a hundred and forty years. It was remarkable of the Duke of Somerset, that he figured in the pageants and politics of six reigns. 'At the funeral of Charles II., he was one of the supporters of the chief mourner, Prince George of Denmark. He carried the orb at the coronation of James II.; at the coronation of William and Mary, he bore the queen's crown.

At the funeral of King William, he was again one of the supporters of the chief mourner, Prince George; and at the coronations of Queen Anne, George I., and George II., he carried the orb.' Mr Jesse, in relating these circumstances a few years ago, makes the remark, that there might be individuals still living, who had conversed with the Duke of Somerset, who had conversed with Charles II.* .

Lord Campbell quotes, in his *Lives of the Chief Justices*, the statement of the Earl of Mansfield to Mr Murray of Henderland, about 1787, that 'he had conversed with a man who was present at the execution of the Blessed Martyr.' Mr Murray, who died a very few years ago, accompanies his report of this statement with the remark, 'How wonderful it seems that there should be only one person between me and him who saw Charles's head cut off!'† Perhaps this is scarcely so wonderful as that the mother of Sir Walter Scott, who survived 1820, had seen a person who had seen Cromwell make his entry into Edinburgh in 1650; on which occasion, by the way, the individual in question remarked nothing in the victor of Dunbar but the extraordinary magnitude of his nose! It was also quite as singular that Charles James Fox, who might have lived to attend the levees of Queen Victoria without being much older than Lord Lyndhurst now is, had an uncle in office as joint paymaster of the forces in 1679! This last person was a son of Sir Stephen Fox by his first marriage. All Sir Stephen's first family having predeceased him, he wedded in his old age, in Queen Anne's time, a healthy young woman, the daughter of a Lincolnshire clergyman, and by her left two sons, one of whom was the father of Charles James.

Dr Routh, who died December 22, 1854, President of Magdalen College, Oxford, in the hundredth year of his age, 'knew Dr Theophilus Leigh, Master of Baliol, the contemporary of Addison, who pointed out to him the situation of Addison's rooms: and he had been told by a lady of her aunt, who had seen Charles II. walking round the parks at Oxford (when the parliament was held there during the plague of London) with his dogs, and turning by the cross path to the other side when he saw the heads of horses coming.'—*Times*, Dec. 25, 1854.

One more such case may be noticed in reference to the reign of Charles II. Dr John Mackenzie, who had been Burns's medical attendant at Mauchline, and who died in Edinburgh in 1841 at no very advanced age, had attended

* It would appear that George IV. could not, with strict truth, say that his father succeeded in the order of the Garter to Charles Duke of Somerset. He in reality succeeded to John first Earl of Poulett, who died 28th May 1743. But, the Duke of Somerset dying 2nd December 1748, John Earl Granville was invested as his grace's successor on the same day with Prince George, along with four other knights.

† A Mr Evans, who died October 9, 1780, at the age of 139, in the full possession of his faculties, 'could well remember the execution of Charles I., being seven years old at the time.'—*Bailey's Records of Longevity*. If this be a true statement, Mr Evans was probably the last person in life who remembered the Blessed Martyr's death.

professionally a lady of rank who was born eight years before the death of the Merry Monarch. This was the Countess of Loudon, widow of the third Earl. She was born in 1677 and died in 1777, having attained the venerable age of a hundred.

Elizabeth, Countess Dowager of Hardwicke, who died May 26, 1858, was daughter of a person who had been a naval officer of Queen Anne and a rebel at the battle of Sheriffmuir, namely, James, fifth Earl of Balcarres. This venerable lady could have said that at her grandfather's first marriage King Charles gave away the bride; an event which took place nearly a hundred and ninety years before her own death.

This marriage, by the way, was a remarkable one. The young Colin Earl of Balcarres was obtaining for his bride, a young Dutch lady, Mauritia de Nassau, daughter of a natural son of Maurice Prince of Orange. 'The Prince of Orange, afterwards William III., presented his fair kinswoman on this joyful occasion with a pair of magnificent emerald ear-rings, as his wedding-gift. The day arrived, the noble party were assembled in the church, and the bride was at the altar; but, to the dismay of the company, no bridegroom appeared! The volatile Colin had forgotten the day of his marriage, and was discovered in his night-gown and slippers, quietly eating his breakfast! Thus far the tale is told with a smile on the lip, but many a tear was shed at the conclusion. Colin hurried to the church, but in his haste left the ring in his writing-case;—a friend in the company gave him one,—the ceremony went on, and, without looking at it, he placed it on the finger of his fair young bride :—it was a mourning ring, with the mort-head and cross-bones. On perceiving it at the close of the ceremony, she fainted away, and the evil omen had made such an impression on her mind, that, on recovering, she declared she should die within the year, and her presentiment was too truly fulfilled.' *

When Mr and Mrs S. C. Hall in 1840 made a tour in Ireland, in order to prepare the beautiful book regarding that country which they afterwards published, they were startled one day by finding themselves in the company of a gentleman of the county of Antrim,† who could tell them that his father had been at the battle of the Boyne, fought exactly a hundred and fifty years before. The latter was fifteen at the time of the battle. He lived a bachelor life till, on approaching old age, he overheard one day some young collateral relations talking rather too freely of what they would do with his property after his death; whereupon, in disgust, he took an early opportunity of marrying, and became the father of the gentleman in question. It is even more

* Lives of the Lindsays, ii. 120.　Rings bearing a death's head were in great favour in the grim religious times then not long past.　In a will dated 1648, occurs this clause : ' Also I do will and appoint ten rings of gold to be made of the value of twenty shillings a-piece sterling, with a death's head upon some of them.'—Halliwell's Shakspeare, v. 318.

† Sir Edmund Macnaghten, of Bush Mills ; he was father of Sir William Macnaghten, political agent at Cabul, and who fell in the massacre at that place.

remarkable that Maurice O'Connell of Derrynane, who died in 1825 at the age of 99, knew Daniel M'Carthy, who had been at the battle of Aughrim (July 12, 1691),—who was indeed the first man to run away from it,—but who, being 108 at his death in 1740, might have equally well remembered Cromwell's massacre at Drogheda in 1649. The gentleman who relates this fact in the *Notes and Queries*,* says : ' I remember being told in the county of Clare, about 1828, of an individual then lately deceased, who remembered the siege of Limerick by General Ginkle, and the news of the celebrated Treaty of Limerick (October 3, 1691).'

If we go back to any former period of British history, we shall find precisely similar linkings of remote ages by the lives of individuals. Lettice Countess of Leicester, who died in 1634, was born about 1539; consequently might have remembered Henry VIII., whose queen, Anne Boleyn, was her great aunt. To pursue the remarks of a contemporary writer,† ' during the reign of Edward VI., the young Lettice was still a girl; but Sir Francis Knollys, her father, was about the court, and Lettice no doubt saw and was acquainted with the youthful sovereign. The succession of Mary threw the family of Lettice into the shade. As a relative of the Boleyns, and the child of a Puritan, she could expect no favour from the daughter of Catherine of Arragon; but Mary and Philip were doubtless personally known to her. At Elizabeth's succession, Lettice was in her eighteenth year, and in all the beauty of opening womanhood. About 1566, at the age of twenty-six, she was married to the young Walter Devereux, Viscount Hereford, created Earl of Essex in 1572. He died in 1576, and in 1578 his beautiful Countess was secretly married to Robert Dudley, Earl of Leicester. The great favourite died in 1588, and within the year of her weeds Lettice was again married to an unthrifty knight of doubtful character, Sir Christopher Blount. In 1601, Lettice became a widow for the third time : her husband was a party to the treasonable madness of her son, and both suffered on the scaffold. Such accumulated troubles would have sufficed to kill an ordinary woman; but Lettice retired to Drayton Bassett, and lived on in spite of her sorrows. In James's time her connections were in favour. She came up to London to share the smiles of the new dynasty, and to contest for her position as Countess of Leicester against the base-born son of her predecessor in the Earl's affections. At James's death she had attained the age of eighty-five, with faculties unimpaired. We may imagine that she was introduced to the new sovereign. The grandmother of the Earls of Holland and Warwick, and the relation of half the court, would naturally attract the attention and share the courtesies of the lively Henrietta and the grave, stately, formal Charles. He was the sixth English sovereign (or the seventh if Philip be counted) whom she had seen. The last few years of her life were passed at Drayton :

* April 12, 1851.
† John Bruce, *Notes and Queries*, 2nd ser. iii. 13.

' " Where she spent her days so well,
    That to her the better sort
    Came as to an holy court,
    And the poor that lived near
      Dearth nor famine could not fear
        Whilst she lived."

' Until a year or two of her death, we are told that she " could yet walk a mile of a morning." She died on Christmas Day in 1634, at the age of ninety-four.

' Lettice was one of a long-lived race. Her father lived till 1596, and one of her brothers attained the age of eighty-six, and another that of ninety-nine.

' There is nothing incredible, nor even very extraordinary, in the age attained by the Countess Lettice ; but even her years will produce curious results if applied to the subject of possible transmission of knowledge through few links. I will give one example : Dr Johnson, who was born in 1709, might have known a person who had seen the Countess Lettice. If there are not now, there were, amongst us, within the last three or four years, persons who knew Dr Johnson. There might therefore be only two links between ourselves and the Countess Lettice who saw Henry VIII.'

Even these cases, remarkable as they are when viewed by themselves, sink into comparative unimportance before some others now to be adverted to.

The first gives us a connection between the time of Cromwell and that of Queen Victoria by only two lives. William Horrocks, born in 1657, one year before the death of the Protector, was married at the usual time of life, and had a family. His wife was employed as a nurse in the family of the Chethams at Castleton Hall, near Rochdale. In 1741, when eighty-four years of age, he married for a second wife a woman of twenty-six, who, as his housekeeper, had treated him with a remarkable degree of kindness. The circumstance attracted some share of public attention, and the Chetham family got portraits of the pair painted, to be retained in their mansion as a curiosity ; which portraits were not long ago, and probably still are, in existence. To William Horrocks in 1744 there was born a son, named James, who lived down to the year 1844, on a small farm at Harwood, about three miles from Bolton. This remarkable centenarian, who could say that he had a brother born in the reign of Charles II., and that his father first drew breath as a citizen of the Commonwealth, is described as having been wonderfully well-preserved down almost to the last. At ninety, he had one day walked twenty-one miles, returning from Newton, where he had been recording his vote at an election.*

The second case we have in store for the reader is a French one, and quite as remarkable as the preceding. It may first be stated in this form : a lady, who might be described as a niece of Mary Queen of Scots, died so lately as 1713. She was the widow of the Duc d'Angoulême, a natural son of Charles IX., king of France, who

* See a full account of Horrocks, quoted from the *Manchester Guardian*, in *Notes and Queries*, 2nd ser. iii. 475.

died in 1574, so that she survived her father-in-law a hundred and thirty-nine years.* At the time when she left the world, a sixth generation of the posterity of Mary (Prince Frederick, father of George III.) was a boy of five years.

A third case may be thus stated : A man residing in Aberdeenshire, within the recollection of people still living there, not only had witnessed some of the transactions of the Civil War, but he had seen a man who was connected with the battle of Flodden, fought in September 1513. The person in question was Peter Garden, who died at Auchterless in 1775, aged 131. When a youth, he had accompanied his master to London, and there saw Henry Jenkins, who died in 1670, at the extraordinary age of 169. Jenkins, as a boy, had carried a horse-load of arrows to Northallerton, to be employed by the English army in resisting the invasion of James IV. of Scotland, and which were in reality soon after used at the battle of Flodden. Here two lives embraced events extending over two hundred and sixty-two years !

JANUARY 8.

St Apollinaris, the apologist, bishop, 175 ; St Lucian, of Beauvais, martyr, 290 ; St Nathalan, bishop, confessor, 452 ; St Severinus, abbot, 482 ; St Gudula, virgin, 712 ; St Pega, virgin, about 719 ; St Vulsin, bishop, confessor, 973.

STE GUDULA

is regarded with veneration by Roman Catholics as the patroness-saint of the city of Brussels. She was of noble birth, her mother having been niece to the eldest of the Pepins, who was Maire of the Palace to Dagobert I. Her father was Count Witger. She was educated at Nivelle, under the care of her cousin Ste Gertrude, after whose death in 664, she returned to her father's castle, and dedicated her life to the service of religion. She spent her future years in prayer and abstinence. Her revenues were expended on the poor. It is related of her, that going early one morning to the church of St Morgelle, two miles from her father's mansion, with a female servant bearing a lantern, the wax taper having been accidentally extinguished, she lighted it again by the efficacy of her prayers. Hence she is usually represented in pictures with a lantern. She died January 8th, 712, and was buried at Ham, near Villevord. Her relics were transferred to Brussels in 978, and deposited in the church of St Gery, but in 1047 were removed to the collegiate church of Michael, since named after her the cathedral of Ste Gudula. This ancient Gothic structure, commenced in 1010, still continues to be one of the architectural ornaments of the city of Brussels. Her Life was written by Hubert of Brabant not long after the removal of her relics to the church of St Michael.

* Francis II., the elder brother of Charles IX., was first husband of Mary of Scotland ; consequently this unfortunate princess was by marriage aunt of the Duchess d'Angoulême

GALILEO GALILEI.

Such (though little known) was the real full name of the famous Italian professor, who first framed and used a telescope for the observation of the heavenly bodies, and who may be said to have first given stability and force to the theory which places the sun in the centre of the planetary system. In April or May 1609, Galileo heard at Venice of a little tubular instrument lately made by one Hans Lippershey of Middleburg, which made distant objects appear nearer, and he immediately applied himself to experimenting on the means by which such an instrument could be produced. Procuring a couple of spectacle glasses, each plane on one side, but one convex and the second concave on the other side, he put these at the different ends of a tube, and applying his eye to the concave glass, found that objects were magnified three times, and brought apparently nearer. Soon afterwards, having made one which could magnify thirty times, Galileo commenced observations on the surface of the moon, which he discovered to be irregular, like that of the earth, and on Jupiter, which, in January 1610, he ascertained to be attended by four stars, as he called them, which afterwards proved to be its satellites. To us, who calmly live in the knowledge of so much that the telescope has given us, it is inconceivable with what wonder and excitement the first discoveries of the rude tube of Galileo were received. The first effects to himself were such as left him nothing to desire; for, by the liberality of his patron, the Grand Duke of Tuscany, he was endowed with a high salary, independent of all his former professional duties.

The world has been made well aware of the opposition which Galileo experienced from the ecclesiastical authorities of his age; but it is remarkable that the first resistance he met with came from men who were philosophers like himself. As he went on with his brilliant discoveries—the crescent form of Venus, the spots on the sun, the peculiar form of Saturn—he was met with a storm of angry opposition from the adherents of the old Aristotelian views; one of whom, Martin Horky, said he would 'never grant that Italian his new stars, though he should die for it.' The objections made by these persons were clearly and triumphantly refuted by Galileo: he appealed to their own senses for a sufficient refutation of their arguments. It was all in vain. The fact is equally certain and important that, while he gained the admiration of many men of high rank, he was an object of hostility to a vast number of his own order.

It was not, after all, by anything like a general movement of the Church authorities that Galileo was brought to trouble for his doctrines. The Church had overlooked the innovations of Copernicus: many of its dignitaries were among the friends of Galileo. Perhaps, by a little discreet management, he might have escaped censure. He was, however, of an ardent disposition; and

being assailed by a preacher in the pulpit, he was tempted to bring out a pamphlet defending his views, and in reality adding to the offence he had already given. He was consequently brought before the Inquisition at Rome, February 1615, and obliged to disavow all his doctrines, and solemnly engage never again to teach them.

From this time, Galileo became manifestly less active in research, as if the humiliation had withered his faculties. Many years after, recovering some degree of confidence, he ventured to publish an account of his *System of the World*, under the form of a dialogue, in which it was simply discussed by three persons in conversation. He had thought thus to escape active opposition; but he was mistaken. He had again to appear before the Inquisition, April 1633, to answer for the offence of publishing what all educated men now know to be true; and a condemnation of course followed. Clothed in sackcloth, the venerable sage fell upon his knees before the assembled cardinals, and, with his hands on the Bible, abjured the heresies he had taught regarding the earth's motion, and promised to repeat the seven penitential psalms weekly for the rest of his life. He was then conveyed to the prisons of the Inquisition, but not to be detained. The Church was satisfied with having brought the philosopher to a condemnation of his own opinions, and allowed him his liberty after only four days. The remaining years of the great astronomer were spent in comparative peace and obscurity.

That the discoverer of truths so certain and so important should have been forced to abjure them to save his life, has ever since been a theme of lamentation for the friends of truth. It is held as a blot on the Romish Church that she persecuted 'the starry Galileo.' But the great difficulty as to all new and startling doctrines is to say whether they are entitled to respect. It certainly was not wonderful that the cardinals did not at once recognise the truth contained in the heliocentric theory, when so many so-called philosophers failed to recognise it. And it may be asked if, to this day, the promulgator of any new and startling doctrine is well treated, so long as it remains unsanctioned by general approbation, more especially if it appears in any degree or manner inconsistent with some point of religious doctrine. It is strongly to be suspected that many a man has spoken and written feelingly of the persecutors of Galileo, who daily acts in the same spirit towards other reformers of opinions, with perhaps less previous inquiry to justify him in what he is doing.

JOHN, FIRST EARL OF STAIR.

The Earl of Stair above cited was eldest son of James Dalrymple, Viscount Stair, the President of the Court of Session in Scotland, and the greatest lawyer whom that country has produced. This first earl, as Sir John Dalrymple, was one of three persons of importance chosen to offer the crown of Scotland to William and Mary at the Revolution. As Secretary of State for Scotland, he was the prime instrument in causing the Massacre of Glencoe, which covered his name with infamy, and did not leave that of his royal master untarnished. He was greatly instrumental in bringing about the union of Scotland with England, though he did not live to see it effected. His son, the second earl, as ambassador to France in the time of the regency of Orleans, was of immense service in defeating the intrigues of the Stuarts, and preserving the crown for the Hanover dynasty.

The remarkable talents and vigour of three generations of one family on the Whig side, not to speak of sundry offshoots of the tree in eminent official situations, rendered the Dalrymples a vexation of no small magnitude to the Tory party in Scotland. It appears to have been with reference to them, that the Nine of Diamonds got the name of the *Curse of Scotland;* this card bearing a resemblance to the nine lozenges, *or,* arranged saltire-wise on their armorial coat.*

Various other reasons have, indeed, been suggested for this expression—as that, the game of Comète being introduced by Mary of Lorraine (alternatively by James, Duke of York) into the court at Holyrood, the Nine of Diamonds, being the winning card, got this name in consequence of the number of courtiers ruined by it; that in the game of Pope Joan, the Nine of Diamonds is the Pope—a personage whom the Scotch Presbyterians considered as a curse; that diamonds imply royalty, and every ninth king of Scotland was a curse to his country: all of them most lame and unsatisfactory suggestions, in comparison with the simple and obvious idea of a witty reference to a set of detested but powerful statesmen, through the medium of their coat of arms. Another supposition, that the Duke of Cumberland wrote his inhuman orders at Culloden on the back of the Nine of Diamonds, is negatived by the fact, that a caricature of the earlier date of October 21, 1745. represents the young chevalier attempting to lead a herd of bulls, laden with papal curses, excommunications, &c., across the Tweed, with the Nine of Diamonds lying before them.

LIEUTENANT WAGHORN.

This name will be permanently remembered in connection with the great improvements which have been made of late years in the postal communications between the distant parts of the British Empire and the home country. Waghorn was a man of extraordinary energy and resolution, as well as intelligence; and it is sad to think that his life was cut short at about fifty, before he had reaped the rewards due to his public services.

In the old days of four-month passages round Cape Horn, a quick route for the Indian mail was generally felt as in the highest degree desirable. It came to be more so when the Australian colonies began to rise into importance. A pas-

* In the arms of the Earl of Stair, this bearing stands first and fourth, for Dalrymple. The bearings in the second and third quarters are derived from marriages.

sage by the Euphrates, and the 120 miles of desert between that river and the Mediterranean, was favourably thought of, was experimented upon, but soon abandoned. Waghorn then took up the plan of a passage by Egypt and the Red Sea, which, after many difficulties, was at length realized in 1838. Such was his energy at this time, that, in one of his early journeys, when charged with important dispatches, coming one winter's day to Suez, and being disappointed of the steamer which was to carry him to Bombay, he embarked in an open boat to sail along the six hundred miles of the Red Sea, without chart or compass, and in six days accomplished the feat. A magnificent steam fleet was in time established on this route by the Peninsular and Oriental Steam Navigation Company, and has, we need scarcely say, proved of infinite service in facilitating personal as well as postal communications with the East.

BI-CENTENARY OF NEWSPAPERS.

There are several newspapers in Europe which have lived two hundred years or more—papers that have appeared regularly, with few or no interruptions, amid wars, tumults, plagues, famines, commercial troubles, fires, disasters of innumerable kinds, national and private. It is a grand thing to be able to point to a complete series of such a newspaper; for in it is to be found a record, however humble and imperfect, of the history of the world for that long period. The proprietors may well make a holiday-festival of the day when such a bi-centenary is completed. A festival of this kind was held at Haarlem on the 8th of January, 1856, when the *Haarlem Courant* completed its 200th year of publication. The first number had appeared on the 8th of January, 1656, under the title of *De Weekelycke Courant van Europa;* and a fac-simile of this ancient number was produced, at some expense and trouble, for exhibition on the day of the festival. Lord Macaulay, when in Holland, made much use of the earlier numbers of this newspaper, for the purposes of his *History.* The first number contained simply two small folio pages of news.

The Continent is rather rich in old newspapers of this kind. On the 1st of January, 1860, the *Gazette of Rostock* celebrated its 150th anniversary, and the *Gazette of Leipsic* its 200th. The proprietors of the latter paper distributed to their subscribers, on this occasion, fac-similes of two old numbers, of Jan. 1, 1660, and Jan. 1, 1760, representing the old typographical appearance as nearly as they could. It has lately been said that Russian newspapers go back to the year 1703, when one was established which Peter the Great helped both to edit and to correct in proof. Some of the proof sheets are still extant, with Peter's own corrections in the margin. The Imperial Library at St Petersburg is said to contain the only two known copies of the first year complete. The *Hollandsche Mercurius* was issued more than two centuries ago, a small quarto exactly in size like our *Notes and Queries;* we can there see how the news of our civil war was from time to time received among the people of Holland, who were generally well affected to the royalist cause. At the assumption of power by

Cromwell in 1653, the paper hoisted a wood-cut title representing various English matters, including Cromwell seated in council; and this, as an historical curiosity, we have caused to be here reproduced. In the original; there is a copy of verses by some Dutch poet, describing the subjects of the various designs on this carved page. He tells us that the doors of Westminster were opened to Oliver; that both the council and the camp bowed to him; and that London, frantic

FRONTISPIECE OF A DUTCH NEWSPAPER, 1653.

with joy, solicited his good services in connection with peace and commerce. The *Hollandsche Mercurius* was, after all, a sort of Dutch 'Annual Register,' rather than a newspaper: there are many such in various countries, much more than 200 years old. Old newspapers have been met with, printed at Nürnberg in 1571, at Dillingen in 1569, at Ratisbon in 1528, and at Vienna even so early as 1524. There may be others earlier than this, for aught that is at present known.

Modern investigators of this subject, however, have found it previously necessary to agree upon an answer to the question, 'What is a newspaper?' Many small sheets were issued in old days, each containing an account of some one event, but having neither a preceding nor a following number under the same title. If it be agreed that the word 'newspaper' shall be applied only to a publication which has the following characteristics—a treatment of news from various parts of the world, a common title for every issue, a series of numbers applied to them all, a date to each number, and a regular period between the issues—then multitudes of old publications which have hitherto been called newspapers must be expelled from the list. It matters not what we call them, provided there be a general agreement as to the scope of the word used.

A very unkind blow was administered to our national vanity somewhat more than twenty years ago. We fancied we possessed in our great National Library at the British Museum, a real printed English newspaper, two centuries and a half old. Among the Sloane MSS. is a volume containing what purport to be three numbers of the *English Mercurie*, a newspaper published in 1588: they profess to be Nos. 50, 51, and 54 of a series: and they give numerous particulars of the Spanish Armada, a subject of absorbing interest in those days. Each number consists of four pages somewhat shorter and broader than that which the reader now holds in his hand. Where they had remained for two centuries nobody knew; but they began to be talked about at the close of the last century—first in Chalmers' *Life of Ruddiman*, then in the *Gentleman's Magazine*, then in Nichols' *Literary Anecdotes*, then in D'Israeli's *Curiosities of Literature*, then in the English edition of *Beckmann*, then in various English and Foreign Cyclopædias, and then, of course, in cheap popular periodicals. So the public faith remained firm that the *English Mercurie* was the earliest English newspaper. The fair edifice was, however, thrown down in 1839. Mr Thomas Watts, the able Assistant Librarian at the British Museum, on subjecting the sheets to a critical examination, found abundant evidence that the theory of their antiquity was not tenable. Manuscript copies of three numbers are bound up in the same volume; and from a scrutiny of the paper, the ink, the handwriting, the type (which he recognised as belonging to the Caslon foundry), the literary style, the spelling, the blunders in fact and in date, and the corrections, Mr Watts came to a conclusion that the so-called *English Mercurie* was printed in the latter half of the last century. The evidence in support of this opinion was collected in a letter addressed to Mr Panizzi, afterwards printed for private circulation. Eleven years later, in 1850, Mr Watts furnished to the *Gentleman's Magazine* the reasons which led him to think that the fraud had been perpetrated by Philip Yorke, second Earl of Hardwicke: in other words, that the Earl, for some purpose not now easy to surmise, had written certain paragraphs in a seemingly Elizabethan style, and caused them to be printed as if belonging to a newspaper of 1588. Be this as it may, concerning the identity of the writer, all who *now* look at the written and printed sheets agree that they are not what they profess to be; and thus a pretty bit of national complacency is set aside; for we have become ashamed of our *English Mercurie*.

Mr Knight Hunt, in his *Fourth Estate*, gives us credit, however, for a printed newspaper considerably more than two centuries old. He says: 'There is now no reason to doubt that the puny ancestor of the myriads of broad sheets of our time was published in 1622; and that the most prominent of the ingenious speculators who offered the novelty to the world was Nathaniel Butter. His companions in the work appear to have been Nicholas Bourne, Thomas Archer, Nathaniel Newberry, William Sheppard, Bartholomew Donner, and Edward Allde. All these different names appear in the imprint of the early numbers of the first newspaper, the *Weekly News*. What appears to be the earliest sheet bears the date 23d of May 1622.' About 1663, there was a newspaper called *Kingdom's Intelligencer*, more general and useful than any of its predecessors. Sir Roger L'Estrange was connected with it; but the publication ceased when the *London Gazette* (first called the *Oxford Gazette*) was commenced in 1665. A few years before this, during the stormy times of the Commonwealth, newspapers were amazingly numerous in England; the chief writers in them being Sir John Birkenhead and Marchmont Needham.

If it were any part of our purpose here to mention the names of newspapers which have existed for a longer period than one century and a half, we should have to make out a pretty large list. Claims have been put forward in this respect for the *Lincoln, Rutland, and Stamford Mercury*, the *Scotch Postman*, the *Scotch Mercury*, the *Dublin News-Letter*, the *Dublin Gazette*, *Pue's Occurrences*, *Faulkner's Journal*, and many others, some still existing, others extinct. The *Edinburgh Evening Courant* has, we believe, never ceased to appear thrice a week (latterly daily) since the 15th of December 1718; and its rival, the *Caledonian Mercury*, now incorporated with the *Weekly Scotsman*, was but by two years less venerable. *Saunders's News-Letter*, now stopped, had a vitality in Dublin of about one hundred and thirty years.

In connection with these old newspapers, it is curious to observe the original meaning of the terms *Gazette* and *News-Letter*. During the war between the Venetians and the Turks in 1563, the Venetian Government, being desirous of communicating news on public affairs to the people, caused sheets of military and commercial intelligence to be written: these sheets were read out publicly at certain places, and the fee paid for hearing them was a small coin called a *gazzetta*. By degrees, the name of the coin was transferred to the written sheet; and an official or government newspaper became known as a Gazzetta or Gazetta. For some time afterwards, the Venetian Government continued the practice, sending several written copies to several towns, where they were read to those who chose to listen to them. This rude system, however, was not calculated to be of long duration: the printing-press speedily superseded such written sheets. The name, however, survives; the official newspapers of several European countries being called *Gazettes.*

Concerning *News-Letters*, they were the precursors of newspapers generally. They were really letters, written on sheets of writing-paper. Long after the invention of printing, readers were too few in number to pay for the issue of a regular periodically-printed newspaper. How, then, could the wealthy obtain information of what was going on in the world? By *written* newspapers or news-letters, for which they paid a high price. There were two classes of news-writers in those days—such as wrote privately to some particular person or family, and such as wrote as many copies as they could dispose of. Whitaker, in his *History of Craven*, says that the Clifford family preserves a record or memorandum to the following effect: 'To Captain Robinson, by my Lord's commands, for writing letters of newes to his Lordship for half a year, five pounds.' In or about the year 1711, the town-council of Glasgow kept a news-writer for a weekly 'letter.' A collection of such letters was afterwards found in Glammis Castle. During the time of Ben Jonson, and down to a later period, there were many news-writers living in London, some of them unemployed military men, who sought about in every quarter for news. Some would visit the vicinity of the Court, some the Exchange, some Westminster Hall, some (old) St Paul's—the nave of which was, in those days, a famous resort for gossips. All that they could pick up was carried to certain offices, where they or other writers digested the news, and made it sufficient to fill a sheet of certain size. The number of copies of this sheet depended on the number of subscribers, most of whom were wealthy families residing in the country. Ben Jonson frequently satirizes these news-writers, on account of the unscrupulous way in which the news was often collected. Even in the days of Queen Anne, when mails and posts were more numerous, and when the printing-press had superseded the written news-letter, the caterers for the public were often suspected of manufacturing the news which they gave. Steele, in No. 42 of the *Tatler*, represents a news-writer as excusing himself and his craft in the following way: 'Hard shifts we intelligencers are forced to. Our readers ought to excuse us, if a westerly wind, blowing for a fortnight together, generally fills every paper with an order of battle; when we shew our mental skill in every line, and according to the space we have to fill, range our men in squadrons and battalions, or draw out company by company, and troop by troop: ever observing that no muster is to be made but when the wind is in a cross-point, which often happens at the end of a campaign, when half the men are deserted or killed. The *Courant* is sometimes ten deep, his ranks close; the *Postboy* is generally in files, for greater exactness; and the *Postman* comes down upon you rather after the Turkish way, sword in hand, pell-mell, without form or discipline; but sure to bring men enough into the field; and wherever they are raised, never to lose a battle for want of numbers.'

GETTING INTO A SCRAPE.

This phrase, involving the use of an English word in a sense quite different from the proper one, appears to be a mystery to English lexicographers. Todd, indeed, in his additions to Johnson, points to *skrap*, Swedish, and quotes from Lye, ' Draga en in i *scraeper*—to draw any one into difficulties.' But it may be asked, what is the derivation of the Swedish phrase? It is as likely that the Swedes have adopted our phrase as that we have adopted theirs. It may be suspected that the phrase is one of those which are puzzling in consequence of their having originated in special local circumstances, or from some remarkable occurrence.

There is a game called golf, almost peculiar to Scotland, though also frequently played upon Blackheath, involving the use of a small, hard, elastic ball, which is driven from point to point with a variety of wooden and iron clubs. In the north, it is played for the most part upon downs (or *links*) near the sea, where there is usually abundance of rabbits. One of the troubles of the golf-player is the little hole which the rabbit makes in the sward, in its first efforts at a burrow; this is commonly called a *rabbit's scrape*, or simply a *scrape*. When the ball gets into a scrape, it can scarcely be played. The rules of most golfing fraternities, accordingly, include one indicating what is allowable to the player *when he gets into a scrape.* Here, and here alone, as far as is known to the writer, has the phrase a direct and intelligible meaning. It seems, therefore, allowable to surmise that this phrase has originated amongst the golfing societies of the north, and in time spread to the rest of the public.

JANUARY 9.

SS. Julian and Basilissa, martyrs, 313. St Peter of Sebaste, bishop and confessor, about 387. St Marchiana, virgin and martyr, about 305. St Vaneng, confessor, about 688. St Fillan, abbot, 7th century. St Adrian, abbot at Canterbury, 710. St Brithwald, archbishop of Canterbury, 731.

ST FILLAN

is famous among the Scottish saints, from his piety and good works. He spent a considerable part of his holy life at a monastery which he built in Pittenweem, of which some remains of the later buildings yet exist in a habitable condition. It is stated that, while engaged here in transcribing the Scriptures, his left hand sent forth sufficient light to enable him, at night, to continue his work without a lamp. For the sake of seclusion, he finally retired to a wild and lonely vale, called from him Strathfillan, in Perthshire, where he died, and where his name is still attached to the ruins of a chapel, to a pool, and a bed of rock.

'At Strathfillan, there is a deep pool, called the Holy Pool, where, in olden times, they were wont to dip insane people. The ceremony was performed after sunset on the first day of the quarter, O.S., and before sunrise next morning. The dipped persons were instructed to take three stones from the bottom of the pool, and, walking three times round each of three cairns on the bank, throw a stone into each. They were next conveyed to the ruins of St Fillan's chapel; and in a corner called St Fillan's bed, they were laid on their back, and left tied all night. If next morning they were found loose, the cure was deemed perfect, and thanks returned to the saint. The pool is still (1843) visited, not by parishioners, for they have no faith in its virtue, but by people from other and distant places.'—*New Statistical Account of Scotland, parish of Killin*, 1843.

Strange as it may appear, the ancient bell of the chapel, believed to have been St Fillan's bell, of a very antique form, continued till the beginning of the nineteenth century to lie loose on a grave-stone in the churchyard, ready to be used, as it occasionally was, in the ceremonial for the cure of lunatics. The popular belief was, that it was needless to attempt to appropriate and carry it away, as it was sure, by some mysterious means, to return. A curious and covetous English traveller at length put the belief to the test, and the bell has been no more heard of. The head of St Fillan's crosier, called the *Quigrich*, of silver gilt, elegantly carved, and with a jewel in front, remained at Killin with the Dewar family, by the representative of which it was conveyed to Canada. The story is that this family obtained possession of the Quigrich from King Robert Bruce, after Bannockburn, on his becoming offended with the abbot of Inchaffray, its previous keeper; and there is certainly a document proving its having been in their possession in the year 1487. Partly by purchase, and partly by gift, this relic became the property of the Society of Antiquaries of Scotland.

QUIGRICH OF ST FILLAN, FROM WILSON'S 'PRE-HISTORIC ANNALS OF SCOTLAND.'

A relic of St Fillan figures in Hector Boece's account of the battle just alluded to. 'King Robert,' says he, 'took little rest the night before the battle, having great care in his mind for the surety of his army, one while revolving in his consideration this chance, and another while that: yea, and sometimes he fell to devout contemplation, making his prayer to God and St Fillan, whose arm, as it was set and enclosed in a silver case, he supposed had been the same time within his tent, trusting the better fortune to follow by the presence thereof. As he was thus making his prayers, the case suddenly opened and clapped to again. The king's chaplain being present, astonished therewith, went to the altar where the case stood, and finding the arm within it, he cried to the king and others that were present, how there was a great miracle wrought, confessing that he brought the empty case to the field, and left the arm at home, lest that relic should have been lost in the field, if anything chanced to the army otherwise than well. The king, very joyful of this miracle, passed the remnant of the night in prayer and thanksgiving.'

Born.—John Earl St Vincent (Admiral Jervis), 1734.
Died. — Bernard de Fontenelle, philosopher, 1757; Thomas Birch, biographical and historical writer, 1766, Elizabeth O. Benger, historian, 1822; Caroline Lucretia Herschel, astronomer, 1848.

LORD ST VINCENT.

In the history of this great naval commander, we have a remarkable instance of early difficulties overcome by native hardihood and determination. The son of a solicitor who was treasurer to Greenwich Hospital, he received a good education, and was designed for the law; but this was not to be his course. To pursue an interesting recital given by himself—'My father's favourite plan was frustrated by his own coachman, whose confidence I gained, always sitting by his side on the coach-box when we drove out. He often asked what profession I intended to choose. I told him I was to be a lawyer. "Oh, don't be a lawyer, Master Jackey," said the old man; "all lawyers are rogues." About this time young Strachan (father of the late Admiral Sir Richard Strachan, and a son of Dr Strachan, who lived at Greenwich) came to the same school, and we became great friends. He told me such stories of the happiness of a sea life, into which he had lately been initiated, that he easily persuaded me to quit the school and go with him. We set out accordingly, and concealed ourselves on board of a ship at Woolwich.' After three days' absence, young Jervis returned home, and persisted in not returning to school. 'This threw my mother into much perplexity, and, in the absence of her husband, she made known her grief, in a flood of tears, to Lady Archibald Hamilton, mother of the late Sir William Hamilton, and wife of the Governor of Greenwich Hospital. Her ladyship said she did not see the matter in the same light as my mother did, that she thought the sea a very honourable and a very good profession, and said she would undertake to procure me a situation in some ship-of-war. In the meantime my mother sent for her brother, Mr John Parker, who, on being made acquainted with my determination, expostulated with me, but to no purpose. I was resolved I would not be a lawyer, and that I would be a sailor. Shortly afterwards Lady

Archibald Hamilton introduced me to Lady Burlington, and she to Commodore Townshend, who was at that time going out in the *Gloucester*, as Commander-in-Chief, to Jamaica. She requested that he would take me on his quarter-deck, to which the commodore readily consented; and I was forthwith to be prepared for a sea life. My equipment was what would now be called rather grotesque. My coat was made for me to grow up to; it reached down to my heels, and was full large in the sleeves; I had a dirk, and a gold-laced hat; and in this costume my uncle caused me to be introduced to my patroness, Lady Burlington. Here I acquitted myself but badly. I lagged behind my uncle, and held by the skirt of his coat. Her ladyship, however, insisted on my coming forward, shook hands with me, and told me I had chosen a very honourable profession. She then gave Mr Parker a note to Commodore George Townshend, who lived in one of the small houses in Charles Street, Berkeley Square, desiring that we should call there early the next morning. This we did; and after waiting some time, the commodore made his appearance in his night-cap and slippers, and in a very rough and uncouth voice asked me how soon I would be ready to join my ship? I replied, "Directly." "Then you may go to-morrow morning," said he, "and I will give you a letter to the first lieutenant." My uncle, Mr Parker, however, replied that I could not be ready quite so soon, and we quitted the commodore. In a few days after this we set off, and my uncle took me to Mr Blanchard, the master-attendant or the boatswain of the dockyard—I forget which—and by him I was taken on board the hulk or receiving-ship the next morning, the *Gloucester* being in dock at the time. This was in the year 1748. As soon as the ship was ready for sea we proceeded to Jamaica, and as I was always fond of an active life, I volunteered to go into small vessels, and saw a good deal of what was going on. My father had a very large family, with limited means. He gave me twenty pounds at starting, and that was all he ever gave me. After I had been a considerable time at the station, I drew for twenty more, but the bill came back protested. I was mortified at this rebuke, and made a promise, which I have ever kept, that I would never draw another bill, without a certainty of its being paid. I immediately changed my mode of living, quitted my mess, lived alone, and took up the ship's allowance, which I found to be quite sufficient; washed and mended my own clothes, made a pair of trousers out of the ticking of my bed, and, having by these means saved as much money as would redeem my honour, I took up my bill; and from that time to this' (he said this with great energy) 'I have taken care to keep within my means.'

FONTENELLE.

Fontenelle stands out amongst writers for having reached the extraordinary age of a hundred years. He was probably to a great extent indebted for that length of days to a calmness of nature which forbade the machine to be subjected to any rough handling. It was believed of him that he had never either truly laughed or truly

cried in the whole course of his existence. His leading characteristic is conveyed in somebody's excellent *mot* on hearing him say that he flattered himself he had a good heart: 'Yes, my dear Fontenelle, as good a heart as can be made out of brains.' Better still in an anecdote which has got into currency: 'One day, a certain *bon-vivant* abbé came unexpectedly to dine with him. The abbé was fond of asparagus dressed with butter; for which Fontenelle also had a great *goût*, but preferred it dressed with oil. Fontenelle said for such a friend there was no sacrifice he would not make: the abbé should have half the dish of asparagus he had ordered for himself, and, moreover, it should be dressed with butter. While they were conversing thus together, the poor abbé fell down in a fit of apoplexy; upon which his friend Fontenelle instantly scampered down stairs, and eagerly called out to his cook: "The whole with oil! the whole with oil, as at first!"'

Fontenelle was born at Rouen, 11th February, 1657, and was, by his mother's side, nephew of the great Corneille. He was bred to the law, which he gave up for poetry, history, and philosophy. His poetical pieces have, however, fallen into neglect and oblivion. The *Dialogues des Morts*, published in 1683, first laid the foundation of his literary fame. He was the first individual who wrote a treatise expressly on the Plurality of Worlds. It was published in 1686, the year before the publication of Newton's *Principia*, and is entitled *Conversations on the Plurality of Worlds*. It consists of five chapters, with the following titles: 1. The Earth is a planet which turns round its own axis and also round the sun. 2. The Moon is a habitable world. 3. Particulars concerning the world in the Moon, and that the other planets are inhabited. 4. Particulars of the worlds of Venus, Mercury, Mars, Jupiter, and Saturn. 5. The Fixed Stars are so many suns, each of which illuminates a world. In another edition of the work published in 1719, Fontenelle added a sixth chapter, entitled, 6. New thoughts which confirm those in the preceding conversations—the latest discoveries which have been made in the heavens. This singular work, written by a man of great genius, and with a sufficient knowledge of astronomy, excited a high degree of interest, both from the nature of the subject, and the vivacity and humour with which it is treated. The conversations are carried on with the Marchioness of G——, with whom the author is supposed to be residing. The lady is distinguished by youth, beauty, and talent, and the share which she takes in the dialogue is not less interesting than the more scientific part assumed by the philosopher.

The *Plurality of Worlds* (says Sir David Brewster) was read with unexampled avidity through every part of Europe. It was translated into all the languages of the Continent, and was honoured by annotations from the pen of the celebrated astronomer Lalande; and of M. Gottsched, one of its German editors. No fewer than three English translations of it were published; and one of these, we believe the first, had run through *six* editions so early as the year 1737.

We have given this outline of Fontenelle's

celebrated work in consequence of the great attention which its subject, the Plurality of Worlds, has of late excited in scientific circles. One of the leading controversialists has been the author of an Essay on the *Plurality of Worlds*, who urges the theological, not less than the scientific, reasons for believing in the old tradition of a single world: 'I do not pretend,' says this writer, 'to disprove the plurality of worlds; but I ask in vain for any argument which makes the doctrine probable.' . . . 'It is too remote from knowledge to be either proved or disproved.' Sir David Brewster has replied in *More Worlds than One*, emphatically maintaining that analogy strongly countenances the idea of all the solar planets, if not all worlds in the universe, being peopled with creatures, not dissimilar in being and nature to that of the inhabitants of the earth.

CAROLINE LUCRETIA HERSCHEL

was one of those women who occasionally come forth before the world, as in protest against the commonly accepted ideas of men regarding the mental capacity of the gentler sex. Of all scientific studies one would suppose that of mathematics to be the most repulsive to the female mind; yet what instances there are of the contrary! Jeanne Dumée, the widow who sought solace for her desolate state in the study of the Copernican theory; Marie Caunitz, who assisted her husband in making up his *Mathematical Tables*; the Marquise de Châtelet, the friend of Voltaire, Maupertuis, and Bernouilli, who published in 1740 her *Institution de Physique*, an exposition of the philosophy of Leibnitz, and who likewise translated the *Principia* of Newton; Nicole de Lahière, who helped her husband Lefante with a Treatise on the Lengths of Pendulums; the Italian Agnosi, who wrote and debated on all learned subjects, a perfect Admirable Crichton in petticoats, and whose mathematical treatises yet command admiration: finally, an-

CAROLINE LUCRETIA HERSCHEL.

other fair Italian, Maria Catarina Bassi, who was equally conversant with classical and mathematical studies, and actually attained the honours of a professor's chair in the university of Bologna. Such examples are certainly enough to prove that, whatever may be the ordinary or average powers and tendencies of the female mind, there is nothing in its organization absolutely to forbid an occasional competency for the highest subjects of thought.

Isaac Herschel and his wife Ilse little thought, when he was plying his vocation as a musician at Hanover, what a world-wide reputation was in store for their family. He taught them all music—four sons and a daughter. The second son, William, came to England to seek his fortune in 1758; and when, after many difficulties, he became organist at Bath, his sister Caroline came over to live with him. In time, turning his attention to telescopes and astronomy, and gaining the favour of George III., he became the greatest practical astronomer of his age. For more than forty years did the brother pursue his investigations at Slough, near Windsor, Caroline assisting him. It is stated that when he became for ten or twelve hours at a time absorbed in study, Miss Herschel sometimes found it necessary to put food into his mouth, as otherwise he would have neglected even that simplest of nature's needs. The support of the pair was assured by a pension from the king, who did himself honour by conferring on William Herschel the honour of knighthood.

In 1798 Caroline Herschel published a *Catalogue of Stars*, at the expense of the Royal Society, which has ever since been highly valued by practical astronomers. After a noble career, Sir William died in 1822; and his sister then went to spend the rest of her days at Hanover. She afterwards prepared a *Catalogue of Nebulæ and Star-Clusters*, observed by her brother.

It was an event worth remembering, when, on the 8th of February 1828, the Astronomical Society's gold medal was awarded to Caroline

Herschel. Her nephew John, afterwards the eminent Sir J. F. W. Herschel, was President of the Society, and shrank from seeming to bestow honour on his own family; but the Council worthily took the matter in hand. Sir James South, in an address on the occasion, after adverting to the labours of Sir William Herschel, said: 'Who participated in his toils? Who braved with him the inclemency of the weather? Who shared his privations? A female! Who was she? His sister. Miss Herschel it was who, by night, acted as his amanuensis. She it was whose pen conveyed to paper his observations as they issued from his lips; she it was who noted the right ascensions and polar distances of the objects observed; she it was who, having passed the night near the instruments, took the rough manuscripts to her cottage at the dawn of day, and produced a fine copy of the night's work on the subsequent morning; she it was who planned the labour of each succeeding night; she it was who reduced every observation and made every calculation; she it was who arranged everything in systematic order; and she it was who helped him to obtain an imperishable name. But her claims to our gratitude end not here. As an original observer, she demands, and I am sure has, our most unfeigned thanks. Occasionally, her immediate attention during the observations could be dispensed with. Did she pass the night in repose? No such thing. Wherever her illustrious brother was, there you were sure to find her also.' As one remarkable fact in her career, she discovered seven comets, by means of a telescope which her brother made expressly for her use.

It was not until the extraordinary age of *ninety-seven* that this admirable woman closed her career. Her intellect was clear to the last; and princes and philosophers alike strove to do her honour. The foregoing portrait—in which, notwithstanding age and decay, we see the lineaments of intellect and force of character,—is from a sketch in the possession of Sir John Herschel.

Touching for the Evil.

On this day in the year 1683, King Charles II. in council at Whitehall, issued orders for the future regulation of the ceremony of Touching for the King's Evil. It was stated that 'his Majesty, in no less measure than his royal predecessors, having had good success therein, and in his most gracious and pious disposition being as ready as any king or queen of this realm ever was, in any thing to relieve the necessities and distresses of his good subjects,' it had become necessary to appoint fit times for the 'Publick Healings;' which therefore were fixed to be from All-Hallow-tide till a week before Christmas, and after Christmas until the first week of March, and then cease till Passion week; the winter being to be preferred for the avoidance of contagion. Each person was to come with a recommendation from the minister or churchwardens of his parish, and these individuals were enjoined to examine carefully into the cases before granting such certificates, and in particular to make sure

that the applicant had not been touched for the evil before.*

Scrofula, which is the scientific name of the disease popularly called the *King's evil*, has been described as 'indolent glandular tumours, frequently in the neck, suppurating slowly and imperfectly, and healing with difficulty.' (Good's *Study of Medicine.*) This is the kind of disease most likely to be acted upon by the mind in a state of excitement. The tumours may be stimulated, and the suppuration quickened and increased, which is the ordinary process of cure. Whether the result be produced through the agency of the nerves, or by an additional flow of blood to the part affected, or by both, has not perhaps been clearly ascertained: but that cures in such cases are effected by some such natural means, is generally admitted by medical practitioners; and it is quite credible that, out of the hundreds of persons said to have been cured of king's evil by the royal touch, many may have been restored to health by the mind under excitement operating on the body. In all such cases, however, the probability of cure may be considered as in proportion to the degree of credulity in the person operated upon, and as likely to be greatest where the feeling of reverence or veneration for the operator is strongest. As society becomes instructed in the causes and nature of diseases, and the methods of cure established by medical experience, the belief in amulets, charms, and the royal touch passes away from the human mind, together with all the other superstitions which were so abundant in ages of ignorance, and of which only a few remains still linger among the most uninstructed classes of society.

The practice of touching for the king's evil had its origin in England from Edward the Confessor, according to the testimony of William of Malmesbury, who lived about one hundred years after that monarch. Mr Giles's translation of this portion of the *Chronicle of the Kings of England* is as follows: 'But now to speak of his miracles. A young woman had married a husband of her own age, but having no issue by the union, the humours collecting abundantly about her neck, she had contracted a sore disorder, the glands swelling in a dreadful manner. Admonished in a dream to have the part affected washed by the king, she entered the palace, and the king himself fulfilled this labour of love by rubbing the woman's neck with his hands dipped in water. Joyous health followed his healing hand; the lurid skin opened, so that worms flowed out with the purulent matter, and the tumour subsided; but as the orifice of the ulcer was large and unsightly, he commanded her to be supported at the royal expense till she should be perfectly cured. However, before a week was expired, a fair new skin returned, and hid the ulcers so completely that nothing of the original wound could be discovered. . . . . Those who knew him more intimately affirm that he often cured this complaint in Normandy; whence appears how false is their notion who in our times assert that the cure of this disease does not proceed from personal sanctity, but from hereditary virtue in the royal line.'

Shakspeare describes the practice of the holy

---

* Broadside printed by John Bill, 1683.

king in his tragedy of *Macbeth*, ' the gracious Duncan ' having been contemporary with Edward the Confessor :

> ' *Macduff.*—What's the disease he means ?
> *Malcolm.*—   'Tis called the evil ;
> A most miraculous work in this good king;
> Which often, since my here-remain in England,
> I've seen him do. How he solicits heaven
> Himself best knows ; but strangely-visited people,
> All swoln and ulcerous, pitiful to the eye,
> The mere despair of surgery, he cures ;
> Hanging a golden stamp about their necks,
> Put on with holy prayers : and 'tis spoken,
> To the succeeding royalty he leaves
> The healing benediction. With this strange virtue
> He hath a heavenly gift of prophecy ;
> And sundry blessings hang about his throne,
> That speak him full of grace.'

Holinshed's Chronicle is Shakspeare's authority, but by referring to the passage it will be seen that the poet has mixed up in his description the practice of his own times. Referring to Edward the Confessor, Holinshed writes as follows :— ' As it has been thought, he was inspired with the gift of prophecy, and also to have the gift of healing infirmities and diseases. He used to help those that were vexed with the disease commonly called the king's evil, and left that virtue, as it were, a portion of inheritance to his successors, the kings of this realm.'

Laurentius, first physician to Henry IV. of France, in his work *De Mirabili Strumas Sanando*, Paris, 1609, derives the practice of touching for the king's evil from Clovis, A.D. 481, and says that Louis I., A.D. 814, also performed the ceremony with success. Philip de Commines says (Danett's transl., ed. 1614, p. 203), speaking of Louis XI. when he was ill at Forges, near Chinon, in 1480: ' He had not much to say, for he was shriven not long before, because the kings of Fraunce use alwaies to confesse themselves when they touch those that be sick of the king's evill, which he never failed to do once a weeke.'

There is no mention of the first four English kings of the Norman race having ever attempted to cure the king's evil by touching ; but that Henry II. performed cures is attested by Peter of Blois, who was his chaplain. John of Gaddesden, who was physician to Edward II., and flourished about 1320 as a distinguished writer on medicine, treats of scrofula, and, after describing the methods of treatment, recommends, in the event of failure, that the patient should repair to the court in order to be touched by the king. Bradwardine, Archbishop of Canterbury, who lived in the reigns of Edward III. and Richard II., testifies as to the antiquity of the practice, and its continuance in the time when he lived. Sir John Fortescue, Lord Chief Justice of the Court of King's Bench in the time of Henry IV., and afterwards Chancellor to Henry VI., in his *Defence of the Title of the House of Lancaster*, written just after Henry IV.'s accession to the crown, and now among the Cotton manuscripts in the British Museum, represents the practice as having belonged to the kings of England from time immemorial. Henry VII. was the first English sovereign who established a particular ceremony to be used on the occasion of touching, and introduced the practice of presenting a small piece of gold.

We have little trace of the custom under the eighth Harry ; but Cavendish, relating what took place at the court of Francis I. of France, when Cardinal Wolsey was there on an embassy in 1527, has the following passage : ' And at his [the king's] coming into the bishop's palace [at Amiens], where he intended to dine with the Lord Cardinal, there sat within a cloister about 200 persons diseased with the king's evil, upon their knees. And the king, or ever he went to dinner, provised every of them with rubbing and blessing them with his bare hands, being bareheaded all the while ; after whom followed his almoner, distributing of money unto the diseased. And that done, he said certain prayers over them, and then washed his hands, and came up into his chamber to dinner, where my lord dined with him.'—*Life of Wolsey*, ed. 1825, i. 124.

In the reign of Queen Elizabeth, William Tookes published a book on the subject of the cures effected by the royal touch—*Charisma ; sive Donum Sanationis*. He is a witness as to facts which occurred in his own time. He states that many persons from all parts of England, of all ranks and degrees, were, to his own knowledge, cured by the touch of the Queen; that he conversed with many of them both before and after their departure from the court ; observed an incredible ardour and confidence in them that the touch would cure them, and understood that they actually were cured. Some of them he met a considerable time afterwards, and upon inquiry found that they had been perfectly free from the disease from the time of their being touched, mentioning the names and places of abode of several of the persons cured. William Clowes, surgeon to Queen Elizabeth, denominates scrofula ' the King's or the Queen's Evil, a disease repugnant to nature ; which grievous malady is known to be miraculously cured and healed by the sacred hands of the Queen's most royal majesty, even by Divine inspiration and wonderful work and power of God, above man's will, art, and expectation.'

In the State Paper Office there are preserved no less than eleven proclamations issued in the reign of Charles I. respecting the touching for the king's evil. They relate mostly to the periods when the people might repair to the court to have the ceremony performed. In the troubled times of Charles's reign he had not always gold to bestow ; for which reason, observes Mr Wiseman, he substituted silver, and often touched without giving anything.

Mr Wiseman, who was principal surgeon to Charles II. after the Restoration, says : ' I myself have been a frequent eye-witness of many hundreds of cures performed by his Majesty's touch alone, without any assistance from chirurgery.' The number of cases seems to have increased greatly after the Restoration, as many as 600 at a time having been touched, the days appointed for it being sometimes thrice a week. The operation was often performed at Whitehall on Sundays. Indeed, the practice was at its height in the reign of Charles II. In the first four years after his restoration he touched nearly 24,000 persons. Pepys, in his *Diary*, under the date June 23, 1660, says : ' To my lord's lodgings, where Tom Guy came to me, and then staid to see the king touch for the king's evil. But he did not come at all, it rained so ; and the poor people were forced to stand all the morning in the rain in the garden. Afterwards he touched them in the Banquetting House.' And again, under the date of April 10, 1661, Pepys says : ' Met my lord the duke, and, after a little talk with him, I went to the Banquet House, and there saw the king heal,—the first time that ever I saw him do it,—which he did with great gravity ; and it seemed to me to be an ugly office and a simple one.'

One of Charles II.'s proclamations, dated January 9, 1683, has been given above. Evelyn, in his *Diary*, March 28, 1684, says : ' There was so great a concourse of people with their children to be touched for the evil, that six or seven were crushed to death by pressing at the chirurgeon's door for tickets.' The *London Gazette*, October 7, 1686, contains an advertisement stating that his Majesty would heal weekly on Fridays, and commanding the attendance of the king's physicians and surgeons at the Mews, on Thursdays in the afternoon, to examine cases and deliver tickets.

Gemelli, the traveller, states that Louis XIV. touched 1600 persons on Easter Sunday, 1686. The words he used were : ' Le Roy te touche, Dieu te guérisse ' (' The King touches thee ; may God cure thee '). Every Frenchman received fifteen sous, and every foreigner thirty. — Barrington's *Observations on the Statutes*, p. 107.

But Charles II. and Louis XIV. had for a few years a rival in the gift of curing the king's evil by touching. Mr Greatrakes, an Irish gentleman of the county of Waterford, began, about 1662, to have a strange persuasion in his mind that the faculty of curing the king's evil was bestowed upon him, and upon trial found his touching succeed. He next ventured upon agues, and in time attempted other diseases. In January 1666, the Earl of Orrery invited him to England to attempt the cure of Lady Conway of a headache ; he did not succeed ; but during his residence of three or four weeks at Ragley, Lord Conway's seat in Warwickshire, cured, as he states, many persons, while others received benefit. From Ragley he removed to Worcester, where his success was so great that he was invited to London, where he resided many months in Lincoln's Inn Fields, and performed many cures.—*A brief Account of Mr Valentine Greatrakes, and divers of the strange cures by him performed ; written by himself, in a Letter addressed to the Hon. Robert Boyle, Esq., whereunto are annexed the testimonials of several eminent and worthy persons of the chief matters of fact there related.* London, 1666.

The ceremony of touching was continued by James II. In the *Diary* of Bishop Cartwright, published by the Camden Society, at the date of August 27, 1687, we read : ' I was at his Majesty's levee ; from whence, at nine o'clock, I attended him into the closet, where he healed

350 persons.' James touched for the evil while at the French court. Voltaire alludes to it in his *Siècle de Louis XIV*. William III. never performed the ceremony.

Queen Anne seems to have been the last of the English sovereigns who actually performed the ceremony of touching. Dr Dicken, her Majesty's sergeant-surgeon, examined all the persons who were brought to her, and bore witness to the certainty of some of the cures. Dr Johnson, in Lent, 1712, was amongst the persons touched by the Queen.

For this purpose he was taken to London, by the advice of the celebrated Sir John Floyer, then a physician in Lichfield. Being asked if he remembered Queen Anne, Johnson said he had ' a confused, but somehow a sort of solemn recollection of a lady in diamonds, and a long black hood.' Johnson was but thirty months old when he was touched.

Carte, the historian, appears to have been not only a believer in the efficacy of the royal touch, but in its transmission in the hereditary royal line ; and to prove that the virtue of the touch was not owing to the consecrated oil used at the coronation, as some thought, he relates an instance within his own knowledge of a person who had been cured by the Pretender. (*History of England*, vol. i. p. 357, *note*.) ' A young man named Lovel, who resided at Bristol, was afflicted with scrofulous tumours on his neck and breast, and having received no benefit from the remedies applied, resolved to go to the Continent and be touched. He reached Paris at the end of August 1716, and went thence to the place where he was touched by the lineal descendant of a race of kings who had not at that time been anointed. He touched the man, and invested him with a narrow riband, to which a small piece of silver was pendant, according to the office appointed by the Church for that solemnity. The humours dispersed insensibly, the sores healed up, and he recovered strength daily till he arrived in perfect health at Bristol at the beginning of January following. There I saw him without any remains of his complaint.' It did not occur to the learned historian that these facts might all be true, as probably they were, and yet might form no proof that an unanointed but hereditarily rightful king had cured the evil. The note had a sad effect for him, in causing much patronage to be withdrawn from his book.

A form of prayer to be used at the ceremony of touching for the king's evil was originally printed on a separate sheet, but was introduced into the Book of Common Prayer as early as 1684. It appears in the editions of 1707 and 1709. It was altered in the folio edition printed at Oxford in 1715 by Baskett.

Previous to the time of Charles II., no particular coin appears to have been executed for the purpose of being given at the touching. In the reign of Queen Elizabeth, the small gold coin called an angel seems to have been used. The touch-pieces of Charles II. are not uncommon, and specimens belonging to his reign and of the reigns of James II. and of Queen Anne may be seen in the British Museum. They have figures of St Michael and the dragon on one side, and a ship on the other. A piece in the British Museum has on one side a hand descending from a cloud

TOUCH-PIECE (TIME OF CHARLES II.).

TOUCH-PIECE (TIME OF QUEEN ANNE).

towards four heads, with ' He touched them' round the margin, and on the other side a rose and thistle, with ' And they were healed.'

We have engraved a gold touch-piece of Charles II., obverse and reverse; and the identical touch-piece, obverse and reverse, given by Queen Anne to Dr Johnson, preserved in the British Museum.

THE 'DAVY' AND THE 'GEORDY.'

On this day, in the year 1816, Davy's safety lamp, for the first time, shed its beams in the dark recesses of a coal-pit. The Rev. John Hodgson, rector of Jarrow, near Newcastle,—a man of high accomplishment, subsequently known for his laborious *History of Northumberland*,—had on the previous day received from Sir Humphry Davy, two of the lamps which have ever since been known by the name of the great philosopher. Davy, although he felt well-grounded reliance in the scientific correctness of his new lamp, had never descended a coal-pit to make the trial: and Hodgson now determined to do this for him. Coal mines are wont to give forth streams of gas, which, when mixed in certain proportions with atmospheric air, ignite by contact with an open flame, producing explosion, and scattering death and destruction around. Till this time, miners were in the habit, when working in foul air, of lighting themselves by a *steel mill*—a disk of steel kept revolving in contact with a piece of flint: such an arrangement being safe, though certainly calculated to afford very little light. Davy found the means, by enclosing the flame in a kind of lantern of wire-gauze, of giving out light without inviting explosion. Armed with one of these lamps, Mr Hodgson descended Hebburn pit, walked about in a terrible atmosphere of *fire-damp*, or explosive gas, held his lamp high and low, and saw it become full of blazing gas without producing any explosion. He approached gradually a miner working

by the spark light of a steel mill ; a man who had not the slightest knowledge that such a wonder as the new lamp was in existence. No notice had been given to the man of what was about to take place. He was alone in an atmosphere of great danger, 'in the midst of life or death,' when he saw a light approaching, apparently a candle burning openly, the effect of which he knew would be instant destruction to him and its bearer. His command was instantly, '*Put out the light !*' The light came nearer and nearer. No regard was paid to his cries, which then became wild, mingled with imprecations against the comrade (for such he took Hodgson to be) who was tempting death in so rash and certain a way. Still, not one word was said in reply ; the light continued to approach, and then oaths were turned into prayers that his request might be granted; until there stood before him, silently exulting in his success, a grave and thoughtful man, a man whom he well knew and respected, holding up in his sight, with a gentle smile, the triumph of science, the future safeguard of the pitmen.* The clergyman afterwards acknowledged that he had done wrong in subjecting this poor fellow to so terrible a trial.

Great and frequent as had been the calamities arising from fire-damp, it was not till after an unusually destructive explosion in 1812, that any concentrated effort was made to obtain from science the means of neutralising it. In August 1815, Sir Humphry Davy was travelling through Northumberland. In consequence of his notable discoveries in chemistry, Dr Gray, rector of Bishopwearmouth, begged him to make a short sojourn in Newcastle, and see whether he could suggest anything to cure the great danger of the mines. Mr Hodgson and Mr Buddle, the latter an eminent colliery engineer, explained all the facts to Davy, and set his acute mind thinking. He came to London, and made a series of experiments. He found that flame will not pass through minute tubes; he considered that a sheet of wire-gauze may be regarded as a series of little tubes placed side by side ; and he formed a plan for encircling the flame of a lamp with a cylinder of such gauze. Inflammable air can get through the meshes to reach the flame, but it cannot emerge again *in the form of flame*, to ignite the rest of the air in the mine. He sent to Mr Hodgson for *a bottle of fire-damp :* and with this he justified the results to which his reasoning had led him. At length, at the end of October, Davy wrote to Hodgson, telling all that he had done and reasoned upon, and that he intended to have a rough ' safety lamp' made. This letter was made public at a meeting in Newcastle on the 3d of November ; and soon afterwards Davy read to the Royal Society, and published in the *Philosophical Transactions*, those researches in flames which have contributed so much to his reputation. There can be no question that his invention of the safety lamp was due to his love of science and his wish to do good. He made the best lamp he could, and sent it to Mr Hodgson, and read with intense interest that gentleman's account of the

* Raine's *Life of the Rev. John Hodgson.*

eventful experiences of the 9th of January. It is pleasant to know that that identical lamp is preserved in the Museum of Practical Geology in Jermyn Street. Mr Buddle advised Sir Humphry to take out a patent for his invention, which he was certain would realise £5000 to £10,000 a year. But Davy would have none of this; he did not want to be paid for saving miners' lives. 'It might,' he replied, 'undoubtedly enable me to put four horses to my carriage; but what could it avail me to have it said that Sir Humphry drives his carriage and four?'

While the illustrious philosopher was thus effecting his philanthropic design by a strictly scientific course, a person then of little note, but afterwards the equal of Davy in fame,—George Stephenson, engine-wright at Killingworth Colliery, near Newcastle,—was taxing his extraordinary genius to effect a similar object by means more strictly mechanical. In August 1815, he devised a safety lamp, which was tried with success on the subsequent 21st of October. Accompanied by his son Robert, then a boy, and Mr Nicholas Wood, a superintendent at Killingworth, Stephenson that evening descended into the mine. 'Advancing alone, with his yet untried lamp, in the depths of those underground workings—calmly venturing his own life in the determination to discover a mode by which the lives of many might be saved and death disarmed in these fatal caverns—he presented an example of intrepid nerve and manly courage, more noble even than that which, in the excitement of battle and the impetuosity of a charge, carries a man up to the cannon's mouth. Advancing to the place of danger, and entering within the fouled air, his lighted lamp in hand, Stephenson held it firmly out, in the full current of the blower, and within a few inches of its mouth. Thus exposed, the flame of the lamp at first increased, and then flickered and went out; but there was no explosion of gas. . . . Such was the result of the first experiment with the first practical miner's safety lamp; and such the daring resolution of its inventor in testing its valuable qualities!'[*]

Stephenson's first idea was that, if he could establish a current within his lamp, by a chimney at its top, the gas would not take fire at the top of the chimney; he was gradually led to connect with this idea, an arrangement by a number of small tubes for admitting the air below, and a third lamp, so constructed—being a very near approach to Davy's plan—was tried in the Killingworth pit on the 30th of November, where to this day lamps constructed on that principle—and named the 'Geordy'—are in regular use.

No one can *now* doubt that both Davy and Stephenson really invented the safety lamp, quite independently of each other: both adopted the same principle, but applied it differently. To this day some of the miners prefer the 'Geordy;' others give their vote for the 'Davy;' while others again approve of lamps of later construction, the result of a combination of improvements. In those days, however, the case was very different. A fierce lamp-war raged throughout 1816 and 1817. The friends of each party accused the other of stealing fame. Davy having the advantage

[*] Smiles's *Life of George Stephenson.*

86

of an established reputation, nearly all the men of science sided with him. They affected superb disdain for the new claimant, George Stephenson, whose name they had never before heard. Dr Paris, in his *Life of Davy,* says: 'It will hereafter be scarcely believed that an invention so eminently philosophic, and which could never have been derived but from the sterling treasury of science, should have been claimed on behalf of an engine-wright of Killingworth, of the name of Stephenson—a person not even professing a knowledge of the elements of chemistry.' There were others, chiefly men of the district, who defended the rights of the ingenious engine-wright, whose modesty, however, prevented him from ever taking up an offensive position towards his illustrious rival.

MARRIAGE OF MR ABERNETHY.

January 9, 1800, Mr Abernethy, the eccentric surgeon, was married to Miss Ann Threlfall. 'One circumstance on the occasion was very characteristic of him; namely, his not allowing it to interrupt, even for a day, his course of lectures at the hospital. Many years after this, I met him coming into the hospital one day, a little before two (the hour of lecture), and seeing him rather smartly dressed, with a white waistcoat, I said, "You are very gay to-day, sir?" "Ay," said he; "one of the girls was married this morning." "Indeed, sir," I said. "You should have given yourself a holiday on such an occasion, and not come down to the lecture." "Nay," returned he; "egad! I came down to lecture the day I was married myself!" On another occasion, I recollect his being sent for to a case just before lecture. The case was close in the neighbourhood, and it being a question of time, he hesitated a little; but being pressed to go, he started off. He had, however, hardly passed the gates of the hospital before the clock struck two, when, all at once, he said: "No, I'll be —— if I do!" and returned to the lecture-room.'—*Macilvain's Memoirs of Abernethy.*

JANUARY 10.

St Marcian, priest, fifth century. St Agatho, pope, 682. St William, archbishop of Bourges, confessor, 1209.

St William was deemed a model of monastic perfection. 'The universal mortification of his senses and passions laid in him the foundation of an admirable purity of heart and an extraordinary gift of prayer; in which he received great heavenly lights and tasted of the sweets which God has reserved for those to whom he is pleased to communicate himself. The sweetness and cheerfulness of his countenance testified the uninterrupted joy and peace that overflowed his soul, and made a virtue appear with the most engaging charms in the midst of austerities. . . . He always wore a hair shirt under his religious habit, and never added, nor diminished, anything in his clothes either winter or summer.'—*Butler.*

Born.—Dr George Birkbeck, 1776.

Died.— Archbishop Laud (beheaded), 1645; Edward Cave, 1754; Admiral Boscawen, 1761; Linnæus, naturalist, 1778; Mary Russell Mitford, authoress, 1855.

DR BIRKBECK.

In inquiring into the origin of that movement for popular instruction which has occupied so broad a space during this century, we are met by the name of George Birkbeck standing out in conspicuous characters. The son of a banker at Settle, in Yorkshire, and reared as a medical practitioner, he was induced at an early period of life to accept a professorship in what was called the Andersonian Institution of Glasgow, —a kind of popular university which had just then started into being, under circumstances which will be elsewhere adverted to. Here Birkbeck found great difficulty in getting apparatus made for a course of lectures on Natural and Experimental Philosophy; and this suggested to him the establishment of popular lectures to working men, with a view to the spread of knowledge in various matters relating to the application of science to the practical arts. This was the germ from which Mechanics' Institutions afterwards sprang. The trustees of the Andersonian Institution had not Birkbeck's enthusiasm; they deemed the scheme visionary, and refused at first to support it. In the autumn of 1800 he went to Yorkshire for a vacation, and there digested a plan for forming a class 'solely for persons engaged in the practical exercise of the mechanical arts, men whose education ·in early life had precluded even the possibility of acquiring the smallest portion of scientific knowledge.'

DR BIRKBECK.

This mechanics' class was to be held in one of the rooms of the Andersonian Institution. On his return to Glasgow he opened communications with the chief owners of manufacturing establishments, offering to the more intelligent workmen free admission to his class. The first lecture was attended by 75 artisans; it excited so much interest that 200 came to the second lecture, 300 to the third, and 500 to the fourth. His grateful pupils presented him with a silver cup at the close of the course, as a token of their appreciation of his disinterested kindness. He repeated these labours year after year till 1804, when he resigned his position at Glasgow to Dr Ure, who, like him, was at that time struggling into fame. Birkbeck married, came to London, and settled down as a physician.

Many years elapsed, during which Dr Birkbeck was wholly absorbed in his professional duties. He did not, however, forget his early schemes; and, as he advanced in life, he found or made opportunities for developing them. In 1820 he gave a gratuitous course of seventeen lectures at the London Institution. Gradually a wish spread in various quarters to put in operation the plan which had so long occupied the thoughts of Birkbeck—viz., to give instructions in science to working men. In 1821 a School of Arts was established at Edinburgh, chiefly through the instrumentality of Mr Leonard Horner. In 1823 a Mechanics' Institution was founded at Glasgow, and another in London, of which last Dr Birkbeck was very appropriately elected President, an office he filled till his death eighteen years afterwards. There has been considerable controversy as to whether Mr Robertson, the first editor of the *Mechanics' Magazine*, is not entitled to the honour of being the first proposer of Mechanics' Institutions; let it suffice for our purpose to associate the three names of Brougham, Birkbeck, and Robertson in this useful labour, and leave to others the due apportionment of praise.

ARCHBISHOP LAUD.

The name of Laud does not savour agreeably in the minds of Englishmen; yet it will be generally admitted that he was unjustly and vindictively treated. The career of the man from a humble origin to the primate's throne, which he attained in 1633, need not be detailed. Led by a love of the old ceremonies of the church—though, as he always alleged, with no affection for Rome—he became the principal minister of Charles I., in those unhappy movements for introducing episcopacy in Scotland and checking puritanism in England, which, in combination with arbitrary political rule, brought on the Great Civil War.

He was called to the council of Charles I., according to his own statement, against his will; yet he devised and executed many unwarrantable revenue schemes: he, doubtless, believed in the divine right of kings, and being opposed, an unhappy infirmity of temper induced him to concur in many cruel and arbitrary schemes, to crush opposition, and render his master independent of parliaments. These expedients succeeded for a while, but, at length failing, the king was compelled to call his last parliament, Nov. 3, 1640; and early next year the Archbishop was impeached of treason by the Commons, and sent to the Tower, where he remained exposed to many hardships until his death. In 1643, he was accused of designs of overthrowing parliaments, and bringing about union with Rome. Prynne, the barrister, who was Laud's personal enemy, collected evidence against him, seized his private papers, and even his prayer-book, and took his Diary by force out of his pocket. Prynne tampered with the evidence to suit the views of his party, but the proofs were so weak that the Peers were disinclined to convict him. He has left a full and, on the whole, faithful account of his trial, in which he defended himself with courage and ability. The Commons then changed the impeachment to an ordinance for Laud's execution, to which the Lords assented; he had procured a pardon from the king, which was disregarded, and Laud was brought to the block on Tower-hill, mainly, it is alleged, to gratify the extreme Presbyterians of Scotland, and induce them to go heartily on with the war, this party having been inspired with bitter feelings regarding the unhappy primate, whom they considered as the main author of the calamities they had been for several years enduring. The last words of Laud were a solemn denial of the charge of affection for Rome: his chaplain, Dr Sterne, attended him to the scaffold, where, after some minutes spent in prayer, his head was cut off at one blow, in the 72nd year of his age. His body was buried in the church of Allhallows, Barking, near the Tower, but in 1663 was removed to his college at Oxford. He had been for several years Chancellor of that University, to which he gave many valuable MSS., and where many other proofs of his munificent patronage of learning yet remain. He employed Inigo Jones to build the picturesque eastern wing of St John's; here, in 1636, he entertained at dinner, the King and Queen and Prince Rupert. He restored the painted windows in the chapel at Lambeth, it was alleged, 'by their like in the mass-book,' but this he utterly denied.

Whitelock says: 'Laud was too full of fire, though a just and good man; and his want of experience in state matters and too much zeal for church ceremonies, if he proceeded in the way he was then in, would set the nation on fire.' Even at the University he had the character of being 'at least very popishly inclined.' 'His bigotry and cruelty in the execution of his high office ought assuredly not to have gone unpunished; but the sentence against him was, perhaps, the most unjustifiable act of the zealots of the Long Parliament; and it appears strongly one of the disadvantages of government by a large assembly of men: for the odium of the death of Laud, being divided among so many, has neither brought with it individual infamy, nor was likely to produce individual remorse.'—*Westminster Review*, vol. xvii.

SIR HENRY YELVERTON.

On the 10th January 1609-10, Sir Henry

Yelverton, Recorder of Northampton, and a member of Parliament, wrote out an account of the measures he took for regaining the favour of the King and some of his state-officers, which he had forfeited in consequence of the misunderstanding of some parts of his conduct and certain expressions which he had publicly used. From this document we get near glimpses of the King and some of his ministers, and it must be confessed that they do not suffer by being seen so near; on the contrary, one becomes rather inclined to think that they possessed at least the Christian graces of courtesy, patience, and placableness in a creditable degree, and might be much more tolerable personages than they are usually represented to be by modern historians.

According to Mr Foss, Sir Henry Yelverton, being returned by Northampton to the first parliament of King James, 'took an independent, but not a factious part.'[*] An English parliament was then like the Reichsrath of Austria in our own time: it was expected to deliberate, but not to be very obstinate in thwarting the royal wishes. Yelverton thought rather more of the interest of the public than of the desires of the King. He did not fully and freely concur in granting the subsidy which was desired, but advocated its being graduated over a series of years, that its payment might be more easy. His language was plain and direct, and perhaps did include a few expressions that might have been better omitted. It was reported to James that Sir Henry Yelverton did not act as one of his friends in parliament. Moreover, he was said to have spoken on several occasions disrespectfully of the Scottish nation, and in particular of Sir George Dunbar, the Lord Treasurer of Scotland, and of the Earl of Dunfermline, its Chancellor. He soon learned that the King and these two ministers were deeply offended with him, and that the royal disfavour might prove a serious impediment to his advance in life.

If Sir Henry Yelverton had been meaning to act the part of a high-flying patriot, he would, we may hope, have disregarded these hints and wrapped himself in his virtue, as many did in the next reign. But he had no such·thing in view, nor was there then any great occasion at this time for a high patriotism. He was a good-natured though honest and sincere man, well-affected to the King, his officers, and nation; and he saw no reason for remaining on bad terms with them, if a few words of explanation could restore him to their good graces. He therefore resolved, if possible, to see the persons offended, and put himself right with them.

The first step he took was to consult with a Scotch gentleman, 'one Mr Drummond,' as to the means of approaching the persons offended. We suspect this to have been William Drummond, the poet, who was just at this time returning from his legal studies at Paris, and would probably be passing through London on his way homewards; but we only can speak by conjecture. By 'Mr Drummond' Yelverton was recommended to use any favour he had with the Lady Arabella Stuart, the King's cousin, in order to make an advance to the Lord Chancellor Dunfermline,

[*] Foss's *Judges of England*, 1857, vol. vi. p. 391.

who was then living in London. By Lady Arabella's kind intervention, an interview was arranged between Yelverton and the Chancellor, which accordingly took place at the Scottish Secretary of State's house in *Warwick Lane.* This Chancellor, it may be remarked, was a Seton, a man of magnificent tastes, and most dignified and astute character. He frankly told Yelverton that the King had, on being spoken to on the subject, shewn himself grievously displeased, but yet not unwilling to listen to any certain and authentic expression of his regret for the past, if such should be presented to him; and the Chancellor undertook to lay a petition from Yelverton before his Majesty.

The petition sets forth that he, Sir Henry Yelverton, had long been vexed with the grief of his Highness' displeasure, and that it added much to the petitioner's unhappiness that he could not see the way how to make known to his Highness his sorrow and the truth of his subjection; he adds : 'Pardon, most merciful Sovereign, him who, by misconstruction only, hath thus been wrapped and chained in your Highness' displeasure ; for if ever, either by way of comparison or otherwise, any word did ever slip me either in disgrace or diminution of the state of the Scottish nation, I neither wish mercy from God, nor grace from your Majesty ; yea, vouchsafe, most renowned and noble Sovereign, to credit me thus far, that I never so much as lisped out any word against the Union, which I as heartily seek as any subject can ; neither did ever in Parliament so much as whisper against the general naturalisation it seemed your Highness upon weighty reasons did desire.'

The arrangements for the interview being completed, Sir H. Yelverton thus narrates the details : 'After which, the 6th of January 1609, being sent for to court by his lordship, about five of the clock in the afternoon, he brought me into the King's presence, where his Majesty sat alone in his chair in his bedchamber ; but soon after my coming in, while I was on my knee, and his Majesty having entered into his speech, there came in, besides, my Lord of Dunbar (who was there at first), my Lord Chamberlain, and my Lord of Worcester, and stood all behind me.

'At my first coming in I made three low congees to his Majesty, and being somewhat far from him, stirring his hat, he beckoned his hand, and bade me come near ; so, coming on, the carpet was spread before his Majesty, and I kneeled on my right knee, and spake as followeth :

'"I humbly beseech your most excellent Majesty to vouchsafe your gracious pardon for all offences past, which I protest were not wilfully committed, but only out of the error of my judgment, which I ever was and ever will be ready to reform as I shall be taught from your Majesty."'

The King paused, and beckoning with his hand, thrice bade Sir Henry stand up, which he then did : stirring his hat again, 'with a mild countenance,' he addressed Sir Henry at considerable length, complaining of his proposing a Bill to naturalise my Lord Kinloss, 'because he was half English, making a hateful distinction between him that was all Scot, and him that was some part of this nation. If he were a mere Scot, away with him ; but if he came from hence of any late time, then dandle him, and welcome him as a home-born : which reason was the worse made by you, that knows much and can speak so sourly. For since my title to this crown hath fetched me out of Scotland, and that both nations are my subjects, and I their head, would you have the left side so strange from the right, as there should be no embracement nor intercourse between them ? Nay, you should rather have reasoned, We are now become brethren under one governor, and therefore what God hath joined let not us still keep in two.' The King then complained of Sir Henry's opposition to the subsidy, as well as to the union, to the general naturalisation of the Scots, to the commerce desirable between both nations, and to the abolition of the hostile laws.

'After his Majesty's speech, Sir Henry again knelt down, and, in whatsoever his Majesty should condemn him, would not labour to excuse himself ; but humbly desired to purge his offence by his lowliest submission and faithful promise of amendment hereafter.' Sir Henry then touched upon the several points of his Majesty's speech, and the King replied, and concluded with saying, 'I shut up all, and acquit you.' Sir Henry humbly thanked the King, who bade him stand up ; my Lord of Dunbar kneeling, desired that Sir Henry might kiss the king's hand, whereupon the king said, 'With all my heart,' and Sir Henry kissed the royal hand three times, bowed, and retired.

On the 10th of January, Sir Henry Yelverton went to the Lord Treasurer at Whitehall, and thanked his lordship for the furtherance of his peace and reconciliation with the King, to which the Lord Treasurer replied, concluding with the friendly assurance : ' " But now all is well, and persuade yourself you have lost nothing by this jar between the King and you, for as by this the world knows you to be honest and sufficient, so the judgment of the King is, that there is good matter in you ; for myself, I will desire your friendship as you do mine, and will promise to do you my best ; whereupon in pledge I give you my hand :" and so, shaking me by the hand, he bid me farewell.'

Soon after this reconciliation, viz. in 1613, Mr Yelverton was made Solicitor-General, and knighted ; and in 1616, Attorney-General. In 1625, he was made one of the Justices of the King's Bench, and afterwards of the Common Pleas : and had not the Duke of Buckingham been suddenly cut off, he would, in all probability, have been made Lord Keeper of the Great Seal.

THE PENNY POST.

The 10th of January 1840 will be a memorable day in the history of civilization, as that on which the idea of a Penny Postage was first exemplified. The practical benefits derived from this reform, are so well known that it is needless to dwell upon them. Let us rather turn attention for a few moments to the remarkable, yet most modest man, whom his species have to thank for this noble invention. Rowland Hill, born in 1795, was devoted through all his early years, even from boyhood, to the business of a teacher. At the age of forty, we find him engaged in conducting the colonization of South Australia upon the plan of Mr. Edward Gibbon Wakefield, for which his powers of organization gave him a great advantage, and in which his labours were attended with a high degree of success. It was about the year 1835, that he turned his attention to the postal system of the country, with the conviction that it was susceptible of reform. Under enormous difficulties, he contrived to collect information upon the subject, so as to satisfy himself, and enable him to satisfy others, that the public might be benefited by a cheaper postage, and yet the revenue remain ultimately undiminished.

The leading facts on which he based his conclusions have been detailed in an authoritative document. 'The cost of a letter to the Post-Office he saw was divisible into three branches. First, that of receiving the letter and preparing it for its journey, which, under the old régime, was troublesome enough, as the postage varied first in proportion to the distance it had to travel; and again, according as it was composed of one, two, or three sheets of paper, each item of charge being exorbitant. For instance, a letter from London to Edinburgh, if single, was rated at 1s. 1½d.; if double, at 2s. 3d.; and if treble, at 3s. 4½d.; any — the minutest — inclosure being treated as an additional sheet. The duty of taxing letters, or writing upon each of them its

SIR ROWLAND HILL.

postage, thus became a complicated transaction, occupying much time and employing the labour of many clerks. This, and other duties, which we will not stop to specify, comprised the first of the three branches of expense which each letter imposed on the office. The second was the cost of transit from post-office to post-office. And this expense, even for so great a distance as from London to Edinburgh, proved, upon careful examination, to be no more than the ninth part of a farthing! The third branch was that of delivering the letter and receiving the postage —letters being for the most part sent away unpaid. Rowland Hill saw that, although a considerable reduction of postage might and ought to be made, even if the change rested there, yet that, if he could cheapen the cost to the Post-

office, the reduction to the public could be carried very much further, without entailing on the revenue any ultimate loss of serious amount. He therefore addressed himself to the simplification of the various processes. If, instead of charging according to the number of sheets or scraps of paper, a weight should be fixed, below which a letter, whatever might be its contents, should only bear a single charge, much trouble to the office would be spared, while an unjust mode of taxation would be abolished. For, certainly, a double letter did not impose double cost, nor a treble letter three-fold cost upon the Post-office. But, if the alteration had rested there, a great source of labour to the office would have remained; because postage would still have been augmented upon each letter in proportion to the distance it had to travel. In the absence of knowledge as to the very minute cost of mere transit, such an arrangement would appear just; or, to place the question in another light, it would seem unjust to charge as much for delivering a letter at the distance of a mile from the office at which it was posted as for delivering a letter at Edinburgh transmitted from London. But when Rowland Hill had, by his investigation, ascertained that the difference between the cost of transit in the one instance and the other was an insignificant fraction of a farthing, it became obvious that it was a nearer approximation to perfect justice to pass over this petty inequality than to tax it even to the amount of the smallest coin of the realm. With regard to the third head, all that could be done for lessening the cost attendant on delivering the letters from house to house, was to devise some plan of pre-payment which should be acceptable to the public (so long accustomed to throw the cost of correspondence on the receiver of a letter instead of the sender), and which, at the same time, should not transfer the task of collection to the receiving-office, while it relieved the letter-carriers attached to the distributing office; otherwise comparatively little would have been gained by the change. This led to the proposal for pre-payment by stamped labels, whereby the Post-office is altogether relieved from the duty of collecting postage. Thus, one by one, were the impediments all removed to the accomplishment of a grand object—uniformity of postage throughout the British Isles.' *

It necessarily followed, from the economy thus proposed, that the universal rate might be a low one, which again might be expected to react favourably on the new system, in enabling a wider public to send and receive letters. A brother of Mr Hill had, a few years before, suggested the *Penny Magazine.* Perhaps this was the basis of Mr Rowland Hill's conception, that each letter of a certain moderate weight should be charged one penny. The idea was simple and intelligible, and, when announced in a pamphlet in 1837, it was at once heartily embraced by the public. Neither the government nor the opposition patronised it. The Post-office authorities discountenanced it as much as possible. Nevertheless, from the mere force of public sentiment, it was introduced into parliament and ratified in 1839.

The Whig ministry of the day were so far just to Mr Hill, that they gave him a Treasury appointment to enable him to work out his plan, and this he held till the Conservative party came into power in 1841. Having been by them bowed out of office, on the allegation that his part of the business was accomplished, he might have shared the fate of many other public benefactors, if the community had not already become profoundly impressed with a sense of the value of his scheme. They marked their feeling towards him by a subscription which amounted to fifteen thousand pounds. On the replacement of the Whigs in 1846, he was brought back into office as Secretary to the Postmaster-

* *Our Exemplars, Poor and Rich.* Edited by Matthew D. Hill. London, 1861, p. 317.

General; in which position, and as Secretary to the Post-Office from 1854 till 1864, he was active in effecting improvements. Of these one of the chief was the organisation of the Money-Order Office, by which upwards of twenty-five millions sterling are annually transmitted. Later developments of the system are the Post-Office Savings Banks and Post-Office Insurance; and the Post-Office now manages the telegraph system of the country. Forty years after the establishment of Penny Postage, the British Post-Office carried 1128 millions of letters, besides 115 millions of halfpenny post-cards and 345 millions of newspapers. Nor has England alone to thank Rowland Hill, for there is no civilised country which has not adopted his scheme. He well deserved his honours of K.C.B., D.C.L., and a parliamentary grant of £20,000. He died 27th August 1879; and an interesting biography, published by his nephew the year after, tells the story of his life and of the Penny Postage.

JANUARY 11.

St Hyginus, pope and martyr, 142. St Theodosius, the Cœnobiarch, 529. St Salvius or Sauve, bishop of Amiens, 7th century. St Egwin, bishop, confessor, 717.

ST THEODOSIUS, THE CŒNOBIARCH.

St Theodosius died in 529, at the age of 104. He was a native of Cappadocia, but when a young man removed to Jerusalem, in the vicinity of which city he resided during the remainder of his life. He is said to have lived for about thirty years as a hermit, in a cave, but having been joined by other saintly persons, he finally established a monastic community not far from Bethlehem. He was enabled to erect a suitable building, to which by degrees he added churches, infirmaries, and houses for the reception of strangers. The monks of Palestine at that period were called Cœnobites; and Sallustius, bishop of Jerusalem, having appointed Theodosius superintendent of the monasteries, he received the name of Cœnobiarch. He was banished by the Emperor Anastasius about the year 513, in consequence of his opposition to the Eutychian heresy, but was recalled by the Emperor Justinus.

'The first lesson which he taught his monks was, that the continual remembrance of death is the foundation of religious perfection; to imprint this more deeply in their minds, he caused a great grave or pit to be dug, which might serve for the common burial-place of the whole community, that by the presence of this memorial of death, and by continually meditating on that object, they might more perfectly learn to die daily. The burial-place being made, the abbot one day, when he had led his monks to it, said: "The grave is made; who will first perform the dedication?" Basil, a priest, who was one of the number, falling on his knees, said to St Theodosius: "I am the person; be pleased to give me your blessing." The abbot ordered the prayers of the Church for the dead to be offered up for him, and on the fortieth day, Basil wonderfully departed to our Lord in peace, without any apparent sickness.'— *Butler.*

It may not be superfluous, in all reverence, to remark that, while a remembrance of our mortality is an essential part of religion, it is not necessary to be continually thinking on that subject. Life has active duties calling for a different exercise of our thoughts from day to day and throughout the hours of the day, and which would necessarily be neglected if we were to be obedient to the mandate of the Cœnobiarch. Generally, our activity depends on the hopes of living, not on our expectation of dying; and perhaps it would not be very difficult to shew that the *fact* of our not being naturally disposed to dwell on the idea of an end to life, is one to be grateful for to the Author of the Universe, seeing that not merely our happiness, but in some degree our virtues, depend upon it.

Born.—Francesco Mazzuoli Parmigiano, painter, *Parma,* 1503 ; Henry Duke of Norfolk, 1654.
Died.—Sir Hans Sloane, M.D., 1753 ; François Roubiliac, sculptor, 1762 ; Dominic Cimarosa, musician, 1801; F. Schlegel, German critic, 1829.

HENRY DUKE OF NORFOLK.

Mr E. Browne (son of Sir Thomas Browne) tells us in his journal (*Sloane MSS.*) of the celebration of the birthday of Mr Henry Howard (afterwards Duke of Norfolk) at Norwich, January 11, 1664, when they kept up the dance till two o'clock in the morning. The festivities at Christmas, in the ducal palace there, are also described by Mr Browne, and we get an idea from them of the extravagant merry-makings which the national joy at the Restoration had made fashionable. 'They had dancing every night, and gave entertainments to all that would come ; he built up a room on purpose to dance in, very large, and hung with the bravest hangings I ever saw ; his candlesticks, snuffers, tongs, fireshovels, and andirons, were silver ; a banquet was given every night after dancing ; and three coaches were employed to fetch ladies every afternoon, the greatest of which would hold fourteen persons, and cost five hundred pound, without the harness, which cost six score more.

'January 5, Tuesday. I dined with Mr Howard, where we drank out of pure gold, and had the music all the while, with the like, answerable to the grandeur of [so] noble a person : this night I danc'd with him also.

'January 6. I din'd at my aunt Bendish's, and made an end of Christmas, at the duke's palace, with dancing at night, and a great banquet. His gates were open'd, and such a number of people flock'd in, that all the beer they could set out in the streets could not divert the stream of the multitudes, till very late at night.'

SIR HANS SLOANE.

Sir Hans Sloane, Bart., the eminent physician and naturalist, from whose collections originated the British Museum, born at Killeleagh, in the north of Ireland, April 16, 1660, but of Scotch extraction—his father having been the head of a colony of Scots settled in Ulster under

James I.—gives us something like the model of a life perfectly useful in proportion to powers and opportunities. Having studied medicine and natural history, he settled in London in 1684, and was soon after elected a Fellow of the Royal Society, to which he presented some curiosities. In 1687 he was chosen a Fellow of the College of Physicians, and in the same year sailed for Jamaica, and remained there sixteen months, when he returned with a collection of 800 species of plants, and commenced publishing a *Natural History of Jamaica,* the second volume of which did not appear until nearly twenty years subsequent to the first ; his collections in natural history, &c., then comprising 8,226 specimens in botany alone, besides 200 volumes of dried samples of plants. In 1716 George I. created Sloane a baronet—a title to which no English physician had before attained. In 1719 he was elected President of the College of Physicians, which office he held for sixteen years ; and in 1727 he was elected President of the Royal Society. He zealously exercised all his official duties until the age of fourscore. He then retired to an estate which he had purchased at Chelsea, where he continued to receive the visits of scientific men, of learned foreigners, and of the Royal Family ; and he never refused admittance or advice to rich or poor, though he was so infirm as but rarely to take a little air in his garden in a wheeled chair. He died after a short illness, bequeathing his museum to the public, on condition that £20,000 should be paid to his family ; which sum scarcely exceeded the intrinsic value of the gold and silver medals, and the ores and precious stones in his collection, which he declares, in his will, cost at least £50,000. His library, consisting of 3,556 manuscripts and 50,000 volumes, was included in the bequest. Parliament accepted the trust on the required conditions, and thus Sloane's collections formed the nucleus of the British Museum.

Sir Hans Sloane was a generous public benefactor. He devoted to charitable purposes every shilling of his thirty years' salary as physician to Christ's Hospital ; he greatly assisted to establish the Dispensary set on foot by the College of Physicians ; and he presented the Apothecaries' Company with the freehold of their Botanic Gardens at Chelsea. Sloane also aided in the formation of the Foundling Hospital. His remains rest in the churchyard of St Luke's, by the river-side, Chelsea, where his monument has an urn entwined with serpents. His life was protracted by extraordinary means : when a youth he was attacked by spitting of blood, which interrupted his education for three years ; but by abstinence from wine and other stimulants, and continuing, in some measure, this regimen ever afterwards, he was enabled to prolong his life to the age of ninety-three years ;[*] exemplifying the truth of his favourite maxim—that sobriety,

* Sir Edward Wilmot, the physician, was, when a youth, so far gone in consumption, that Dr. Radcliffe, whom he consulted, gave his friends no hopes of his recovery, yet he lived to the age of ninety-three ; and Dr Heberden notes : " This has been the case with some others, who had many symptoms of consumption in youth."

temperance, and moderation are the best preservatives that nature has granted to mankind.

Sir Hans Sloane was noted for his hospitality, but there were three things he never had at his table—salmon, champagne, and burgundy.

LOTTERIES.

The first lottery in England, as far as is ascertained, began to be drawn on the 11th of January, 1569, at the west door of St Paul's Cathedral, and continued day and night till the 6th of May. The scheme, which had been announced two years before, shews that the lottery consisted of forty thousand lots or shares, at ten shillings each, and that it comprehended 'a great number of good prizes, as well of ready money as of plate, and certain sorts of merchandize.' The object of any profit that might arise from the scheme was the reparation of harbours and other useful public works.

Lotteries did not take their origin in England; they were known in Italy at an earlier date; but from the year above named, in the reign of Queen Elizabeth, down to 1826, (excepting for a short time following upon an Act of Queen Anne,) they continued to be adopted by the English government, as a source of revenue. It seems strange that so glaringly immoral a project should have been kept up with such sanction so long. The younger people at the present day may be at a loss to believe that, in the days of their fathers, there were large and imposing offices in London, and pretentious agencies in the provinces, for the sale of lottery tickets; while flaming advertisements on walls, in new books, and in the public journals, proclaimed the preferableness of such and such 'lucky' offices—this one having sold two-sixteenths of the last twenty thousand pounds prize; that one a half of the same; another having sold an entire thirty thousand pound ticket the year before; and so on. It was found possible to persuade the public, or a portion of it, that where a blessing had once lighted it was the more likely to light again.

The State lottery was framed on the simple principle, that the State held forth a certain sum to be repaid by a larger. The transaction was usually managed thus. The government gave £10 in prizes for every share taken, on an average. A great many blanks, or of prizes under £10, left, of course, a surplus for the creation of a few magnificent prizes wherewith to attract the unwary public. Certain firms in the city, known as lottery-office-keepers, contracted for the lottery, each taking a certain number of shares; the sum paid by them was always *more* than £10 per share; and the excess constituted the government profit. It was customary, for many years, for the contractors to give about £16 to the government, and then to charge the public from £20 to £22. It was made lawful for the contractors to divide the shares into halves, quarters, eighths, and sixteenths; and the contractors always charged relatively more for these aliquot parts. A man with thirty shillings to spare could buy a sixteenth; and the contractors made a large portion of their profit out of such customers.

The government sometimes paid the prizes in terminable annuities instead of cash; and the loan system and the lottery system were occasionally combined in a very odd way. Thus, in 1780, every subscriber of £1000 towards a loan of £12,000,000, at four per cent., received a bonus of four lottery tickets, the value of each of which was £10, and any one of which might be the fortunate number for a twenty or thirty thousand pounds prize.

Amongst the lottery offices, the competition for business was intense. One firm, finding an old woman in the country named Goodluck, gave her fifty pounds a year on condition that she would join them as a nominal partner, for the sake of the attractive effect of her name. In their advertisements each was sedulous to tell how many of the grand prizes had in former years fallen to the lot of persons who had bought at *his* shop. Woodcuts and copies of verses were abundant, suited to attract the uneducated. Lotteries, by creating illusive hopes, and supplanting steady industry, wrought immense mischief. Shopmen robbed their masters, servant girls their mistresses, friends borrowed from each other under false pretences, and husbands stinted their wives and children of necessaries—all to raise the means for buying a portion or the whole of a lottery ticket. But, although the humble and ignorant were the chief purchasers, there were many others who ought to have known better. In the interval between the purchase of a ticket and the drawing of the lottery, the speculators were in a state of unhealthy excitement. On one occasion a fraudulent dealer managed to sell the same ticket to two persons; it came up a five hundred pound prize; and one of the two went raving mad when he found that the real ticket was, after all, not held by him. On one occasion circumstances excited the public to such a degree that extravagant biddings were made for the few remaining shares in the lottery of that year, until at length one hundred and twenty guineas were given for a ticket on the day before the drawing. One particular year was marked by a singular incident: a lottery ticket was given to *a child unborn*, and was drawn a prize of one thousand pounds on the day after his birth. In 1767 a lady residing in Holborn had a lottery ticket presented to her by her husband; and on the Sunday preceding the drawing her success was *prayed for* in the parish church, in this form: 'The prayers of this congregation are desired for the success of a person engaged in a new undertaking.' In the same year the prize (or a prize) of twenty thousand pounds fell to the lot of a tavern-keeper at Abingdon. We are told, in the journals of the time—'The broker who went from town to carry him the news he complimented with one hundred pounds. All the bells in the town were set a ringing. He called in his neighbours, and promised to assist this with a capital sum, that with another; gave away plenty of liquor, and vowed to lend a poor cobbler money to buy leather to stock his stall so full that he should not be able to get into it to work; and lastly, he promised to buy a new coach for the coachman who brought him down the ticket, and to give a set of as good horses as could be bought for money.'

The theory of 'lucky numbers' was in great

favour in the days of lotteries. At the drawing, papers were put into a hollow wheel, inscribed with as many different numbers as there were shares or tickets; one of these was drawn out (usually by a Blue-coat boy, who had a holiday and a present on such occasions), and the number audibly announced; another Blue-coat boy then drew out of another wheel a paper denoting either 'blank' or a 'prize' for a certain sum of money; and the purchaser of that particular number was awarded a blank or a prize accordingly. With a view to lucky numbers, one man would select his own age, or the age of his wife; another would select the date of the year; another a row of odd or of even numbers. Persons who went to rest with their thoughts full of lottery tickets were very likely to dream of some one or more numbers, and such dreams had a fearful influence on the wakers on the following morning. The readers of the *Spectator* will remember an amusing paper (No. 191, Oct. 9th, 1711), in which the subject of lucky numbers is treated in a manner pleasantly combining banter with useful caution. The man who selected 1711 because it was the year of our Lord; the other who sought for 134, because it constituted the minority on a celebrated bill in the House of Commons; the third who selected the 'mark of the Beast,' 666, on the ground that wicked beings are often lucky—these may or may not have been real instances quoted by the *Spectator*, but they serve well as types of classes. One lady, in 1790, bought No. 17090, because she thought it was the nearest *in sound* to 1790, which was already sold to some other applicant. On one occasion a tradesman bought four tickets, consecutive in numbers: he thought it foolish to have them so close together, and took one back to the office to be exchanged; the one thus taken back turned up a twenty thousand pounds prize!

The lottery mania brought other evils in its train. A species of gambling sprang up, resembling time-bargains on the Stock Exchange; in which two persons, A and B, lay a wager as to the price of Consols at some future day; neither intend to buy or to sell, although nominally they treat for £10,000 or £100,000 of stock. So in the lottery days; men who did not possess tickets nevertheless lost or won by the failure or success of particular numbers, through a species of insurance which was in effect gambling. The matter was reduced almost to a mathematical science, or to an application of the theory of probabilities. Treatises and Essays, Tables and Calculations, were published for the benefit of the speculators. One of them, *Painter's Guide to the Lottery*, published in 1787, had a very long title-page, of which the following is only a part:—'The whole business of Insuring Tickets in the State Lottery clearly explained; the several advantages taken by the office keepers pointed out; an easy method given, whereby any person may compute the Probability of his Success upon purchasing or insuring any particular number of tickets; with a Table of the prices of Insurance for every day's drawing in the ensuing Lottery; and another Table, containing the number of tickets a person ought to purchase to make it an equal chance to have any particular prize.'

94

Plough Monday.

This being in 1864 the first Monday after Twelfth Day, is for the year *Plough Monday.* Such was the name of a rustic festival, heretofore of great account in England, bearing in its first aspect, like St Distaff's Day, reference to the resumption of labour after the Christmas holidays. In Catholic times, the ploughmen kept lights burning before certain images in churches, to obtain a blessing on their work; and they were accustomed on this day to go about in procession, gathering money for the support of these *plough-lights*, as they were called. The Reformation put out the lights; but it could not extinguish the festival. The peasantry contrived to go about in procession, collecting money, though only to be spent in conviviality in the public-house. It was at no remote date a very gay and rather pleasant-looking affair. A plough was dressed up with ribbons and other decorations—the *Fool Plough.* Thirty or forty stalwart swains, with their shirts over their jackets, and their shoulders and hats flaming with ribbons, dragged it along from house to house, preceded by one in the dress of an old woman, but much bedizened, bearing the name of *Bessy*. There was also a Fool, in fantastic attire. In some parts of the country, morris-dancers attended the procession; occasionally, too, some reproduction of the ancient Scandinavian sword-dance added to the means of persuading money out of the pockets of the lieges.

A Correspondent, who has borne a part (cow-horn blowing) on many a Plough Monday in Lincolnshire, thus describes what happened on these occasions under his own observation:—'Rude though it was, the Plough procession threw a life into the dreary scenery of winter, as it came winding along the quiet rutted lanes, on its way from one village to another; for the ploughmen from many a surrounding thorpe, hamlet, and lonely farm-house united in the celebration of Plough Monday. It was nothing unusual for at least a score of the "sons of the soil" to yoke themselves with ropes to the plough, having put on clean smock-frocks in honour of the day. There was no limit to the number who joined in the morris-dance, and were partners with "Bessy," who carried the money-box; and all these had ribbons in their hats and pinned about them wherever there was room to display a bunch. Many a hardworking country Molly lent a helping hand in decorating out her Johnny for Plough Monday, and finished him with an admiring exclamation of—"Lawks, John! thou does look smart, surely." Some also wore small bunches of corn in their hats, from which the wheat was soon shaken out by the ungainly jumping which they called dancing. Occasionally, if the winter was severe, the procession was joined by threshers carrying their flails, reapers bearing their sickles, and carters with their long whips, which they were ever cracking to add to the noise, while even the smith and the miller were among the number, for the one sharpened the plough-shares and the other ground the corn; and Bessy rattled his box and danced so high that he shewed his worsted stockings and corduroy breeches; and very often, if there was a thaw, tucked up his gown skirts under his waistcoat, and shook the bonnet off his head, and disarranged the long ringlets that ought to have concealed his whiskers. For Betsy is to the procession of Plough Monday what the leading *figurante* is to an opera or ballet, and dances about as gracefully as the hippopotami described by Dr Livingstone. But these rough antics were the cause of much laughter, and rarely do we ever remember hearing any coarse

PROCESSION OF THE PLOUGH ON PLOUGH MONDAY.

jest that would call up the angry blush to a modest cheek.

'No doubt they were called "plough bullocks," through drawing the plough, as bullocks were formerly used, and are still yoked to the plough in some parts of the country. The rubbishy verses they recited are not worth preserving beyond the line which graces many a public-house sign of "God speed the plough." At the large farm-house, besides money they obtained refreshment, and through the quantity of ale they thus drank during the day, managed to get what they called "their load" by night. Even the poorest cottagers dropped a few pence into Bessy's box.

'But the great event of the day was when they came before some house which bore signs that the owner was well-to-do in the world, and nothing was given to them. Bessy rattled his box and the ploughmen danced, while the country lads blew their bullocks' horns, or shouted with all their might; but if there was still no sign, no coming forth of either bread-and-cheese or ale, then the word was given, the ploughshare driven into the ground before the door or window, the whole twenty men yoked pulling like one, and in a minute or two the ground before the house was as brown, barren, and ridgy as a newly-ploughed field. But this was rarely done, for everybody gave something, and were it but little the men never murmured, though they might talk about the stinginess of the giver afterwards amongst themselves, more especially if the party was what they called "well off in the world." We are not aware that the ploughmen were ever summoned to answer for such a breach of the law, for they believe, to use their own expressive language, "they can stand by it, and no law in the world can touch 'em, 'cause it's an old charter;" and we are sure it would spoil their "folly to be wise."

'One of the mummers generally wears a fox's skin in the form of a hood; but beyond the laughter the tail that hangs down his back awakens by its motion as he dances, we are at a loss to find a meaning. Bessy formerly wore a bullock's tail behind, under his gown, and which he held in his hand while dancing, but that appendage has not been worn of late.

'Some writers believe it is called White Plough Monday on account of the mummers having worn their shirts outside their other garments. This they may have done to set off the gaudy-coloured ribbons; though a clean white smock frock, such as they are accustomed to wear, would shew off their gay decorations quite as well. The shirts so worn we have never seen. Others have stated that Plough Monday has its origin from ploughing again commencing at this season. But this is rarely the case, as the ground is generally too hard, and the ploughing is either done in autumn, or is rarely begun until February, and very often not until the March sun has warmed and softened the ground. Some again argue that Plough Monday is a festival held in remembrance of "the plough having ceased from its labour." After weighing all these arguments, we have come to the conclusion that the true light in which to look at the origin of this ancient custom is that thrown upon the subject by the ploughman's candle, burnt in the church at the shrine of some saint, and that to maintain this light contributions were collected and sanctioned by the Church, and that the priests were the originators of Plough Monday.'

At Whitby, in Yorkshire, according to its historian, the Rev. G. Young, there was usually an extra band of six to dance the sword-dance. With one or more musicians to give them music on the violin or flute, they first arranged themselves in a ring with their swords raised in the air. Then they went through a series of evolutions, at first slow and simple, afterwards more rapid and complicated, but always graceful. 'Towards the close each one catches the point of his neighbour's sword, and various movements take place in consequence; one of which consists in joining or plaiting the swords into the form of an elegant *hexagon* or rose, in the centre of the ring, which rose is so firmly made that one of them holds it up above their heads without undoing it. The dance closes with taking it to pieces, each man laying hold of his own sword. During the dance, two or three of the company called *Toms* or *Clowns*, dressed up as harlequins, in most fantastic modes, having their faces painted or masked, are making antic gestures to amuse the spectators; while another set called *Madgies* or *Madgy Pegs*, clumsily dressed in women's clothes, and also masked or painted, go from door to door rattling old canisters, in which they receive money. Where they are well paid they raise a huzza; where they get nothing, they shout "hunger and starvation!"'

Domestic life in old times, however rude and comfortless compared with what it now is, or may be, was relieved by many little jocularities and traits of festive feeling. When the day came for the renewal of labour in earnest, there was a sort of competition between the maids and the men which should be most prompt in rising to work. If the ploughmen were up and dressed at the fireside, with some of their field implements in hand, before the maids could get the kettle on, the latter party had to furnish a cock for the men next Shrovetide. As an alternative upon this statute, if any of the ploughmen, returning at night, came to the kitchen hatch, and cried 'Cock in the pot,' before any maid could cry 'Cock on the dunghill!' she incurred the same forfeit.

DUTIES OF A DAY IN JANUARY FOR A PLOUGH-MAN IN THE SEVENTEENTH CENTURY.

Gervase Markham gives an account of these in his *Farewell to Husbandry*, 1653; and he starts with an allusion to the popular festival now under notice. 'We will,' says he, 'suppose it to be after Christmas, or about Plow Day, (which is the first setting out of the plow,) and at what time men either begin to fallow, or to break up pease-earth, which is to lie to bait, according to the custom of the country. At this time the Plowman shall rise before four o'clock in the morning, and after thanks given to God for his rest, and the success of his labours, he shall go into his stable or beast-house, and first he shall fodder his cattle, then clean the house, and make the booths

[stalls?] clean; rub down the cattle, and cleanse their skins from all filth. Then he shall curry his horses, rub them with cloths and wisps, and make both them and the stable as clean as may be. Then he shall water both his oxen and horses, and housing them again, give them more fodder and to his horse by all means provender, as chaff and dry pease or beans, or oat-hulls, or clean garbage (which is the hinder ends of any grain but rye), with the straw chopped small amongst it, according as the ability of the husbandman is.

'And while they are eating their meat, he shall make ready his collars, hames, treats, halters, mullers, and plow-gears, seeing everything fit and in its due place, and to these labours I will also allow two hours; that is, from four of the clock till six. Then he shall come in to breakfast, and to that I allow him half an hour, and then another half hour to the yoking and gearing of his cattle, so that at seven he may set forth to his labours; and then he shall plow from seven o'clock in the morning till betwixt two and three in the afternoon. Then he shall unyoke and bring home his cattle, and having rubbed them, dressed them, and cleansed them from all dirt and filth, he shall fodder them and give them meat. Then shall the servants go in to their dinner, which allowed half an hour, it will then be towards four of the clock; at what time he shall go to his cattle again, and rubbing them down and cleansing their stalls, give them more fodder; which done, he shall go into the barns, and provide and make ready fodder of all kinds for the next day. . . . .

'This being done, and carried into the stable, ox-house, or other convenient place, he shall then go water his cattle, and give them more meat, and to his horse provender; and by this time it will draw past six o'clock; at what time he shall come in to supper, and after supper he shall either sit by the fireside, mend shoes both for himself and their family, or beat and knock hemp or flax, or pick and stamp apples or crabs for cider or vinegar, or else grind malt on the querns, pick candle rushes, or do some husbandly

THE QUERN.

office till it be fully eight o'clock. Then shall he take his lanthorn and candle, and go see his cattle, and having cleansed his stalls and planks, litter them down, look that they are safely tied, and then fodder and give them meat for all night. Then, giving God thanks for benefits received that day, let him and the whole household go to their rest till the next morning.'

It is rather surprising to find the quern, the hand-mill of Scripture, continuing in use in England so late as the time of the Commonwealth, though only for the grinding of malt. It is now obsolete even in the Highlands, but is still used in the Faröe Islands. The stone mill of Bible times appears to have been driven by two women; but in Western Europe it was fashioned to be driven by one only, sometimes by a fixed handle, and sometimes by a movable stick inserted in a hole in the circumference.

JANUARY 12.

St Arcadius, martyr. St Benedict, commonly called Bennet, 690. St Tygrius, priest. St Ælred, 1166.

ST BENEDICT BISCOP.

Biscop was a Northumbrian monk, who paid several visits to Rome, collecting relics, pictures, and books, and finally was able to found the two monasteries of Wearmouth and Jarrow. Lambarde, who seems to have been no admirer of ornamental architecture or the fine arts, thus speaks of St Benedict Biscop: 'This man laboured to Rome five several tymes, for what other thinge I find not save only to procure pope-holye privileges, and curious ornaments for his monasteries, Jarrow and Weremouth; for first he gotte for theise houses, wherein he nourished 600 monks, great liberties; then brought he them home from Rome, painters, glasiers, free-masons, and singers, to th' end that his buildings might so shyne with workmanshipe, and his churches so sounde with melodye, that simple souls ravished therewithe should fantasie of theim nothinge but heavenly holynes. In this jolitie continued theise houses, and other by theire example embraced the like, till Hinguar and Hubba, the Danish pyrates, A.D. 870, were raised by God to abate their pride, who not only fyred and spoyled them, but also almost all the religious houses on the north-east coast of the island.'

Born.—George, fourth Earl of Clarendon, 1800.
Died.—The Emperor Maximilian I., 1519; the Duke of Alva, *Lisbon*, 1583; John C. Lavater, 1801, *Zurich*.

THE DUKE OF ALVA.

This great general of the Imperial army and Minister of State of Charles V., was educated both for the field and the cabinet, though he owed his promotion in the former service rather to the caprice than the perception of his sovereign, who promoted him to the first rank in the army more as a mark of favour than from any consideration of his military talents. He was undoubtedly the ablest general of his age. He was principally distinguished for his skill and prudence in choosing his positions, and for maintaining strict discipline in his troops. He often obtained, by patient stratagem, those advantages which would have been thrown away or dearly acquired by a precipitate encounter with the enemy. On the Emperor wishing to know his opinion about attacking the Turks, he advised

him rather to build them a golden bridge than offer them a decisive battle. Being at Cologne, and avoiding, as he always did, an engagement with the Dutch troops, the Archbishop urged him to fight. 'The object of a general,' answered the Duke, 'is not to fight, but to conquer: he fights enough who obtains the victory.' During a career of so many years, he never lost a battle.

While we admire the astute commander, we can never hear the name of Alva without horror for the cruelties of which he was guilty in his endeavours to preserve the Low Countries for Spain. During his government in Holland, he is reckoned to have put 18,000 of the citizens to death. Such were the extremities to which fanaticism could carry men generally not deficient in estimable qualities, during the great controversies which rose in Europe in the sixteenth and seventeenth centuries.

GREAT EATERS.

Under January 12, 1722-3, Thomas Hearne, the antiquary, enters in his Diary, what he had learned regarding a man who had been at Oxford not long before,—a man remarkable for a morbid appetite, leading him to devour large quantities of raw, half-putrid meat. The common story told regarding him was, that he had once attempted to imitate the Saviour in a forty days' Lent fast, broke down in it, and 'was taken with this unnatural way of eating.'

One of the most remarkable gluttons of modern times was Nicholas Wood, of Harrison, in Kent, of whom Taylor, the Water Poet, wrote an amusing account, in which the following feat is described: 'Two loynes of mutton and one loyne of veal were but as three sprats to him. Once, at Sir Warham St Leger's house, he shewed himself so violent of teeth and stomach, that he ate as much as would have served and sufficed thirty men, so that his belly was like to turn bankrupt and break, but that the servingman turned him to the fire, and anointed his paunch with grease and butter, to make it stretch and hold; and afterwards, being laid in bed, he slept eight hours, and fasted all the while; which, when the knight understood, he commanded him to be laid in the stocks, and there to endure as long as he had laine bedrid with eating.'

In a book published in 1823, under the title of *Points of Humour*, having illustrations by the unapproachable George Cruikshank, there is a droll anecdote regarding an inordinate eater: 'When Charles Gustavus, King of Sweden, was besieging Prague, a boor of a most extraordinary visage desired admittance to his tent; and being allowed to enter, he offered, by way of amusement, to devour a large hog in his presence. The old General Kœnigsmark, who stood by the King's side, hinted to his royal master that the peasant ought to be burnt as a sorcerer. "Sir," said the fellow, irritated at the remark, "if your Majesty will but make that old gentleman take off his sword and spurs, I will eat him before I begin the pig." General Kœnigsmark, who, at the head of a body of Swedes, performed wonders against the Austrians, could not stand this proposal, especially as it was accompanied by a most hideous expansion of the jaws and mouth. Without uttering a word, the veteran turned pale, and suddenly ran out of the tent; nor did he think himself safe till he arrived at his quarters.'

EARLY RISING IN WINTER.

Lord Chatham, writing to his nephew, January 12, 1754, says:—' *Vitanda est improba Syren, Desidia,* I desire may be affixed to the curtains of your bedchamber. If you do not rise early, you can never make any progress worth mentioning. If you do not set apart your hours of reading; if you suffer yourself or any one else to break in upon them, your days will slip through your hands unprofitably and frivolously, unpraised by all you wish to please, and really unenjoyed by yourself.'

It must, nevertheless, be owned that to rise early in cold weather, and in the gloomy dusk of a January morning, requires no small exertion of virtuous resolution, and is by no means the least of life's trials. Leigh Hunt has described the trying character of the crisis in his *Indicator*:

'On opening my eyes, the first thing that meets them is my own breath rolling forth, as if in the open air, like smoke out of a cottage-chimney. Think of this symptom. Then I turn my eyes sideways and see the window all frozen over. Think of that. Then the servant comes in. "It is very cold this morning, is it not?"—"Very cold, sir."—"Very cold indeed, isn't it?"—"Very cold indeed, sir."—"More than usually so, isn't it, even for this weather?" (Here the servant's wit and good nature are put to a considerable test, and the inquirer lies on thorns for the answer.) "Why, sir, ... I think it *is*." (Good creature! There is not a better or more truth-telling servant going.) "I must rise, however. Get me some warm water."—Here comes a fine interval between the departure of the servant and the arrival of the hot water; during which, of course, it is of "no use" to get up. The hot water comes. "Is it quite hot?"—"Yes, sir."—"Perhaps too hot for shaving: I must wait a little?"—"No, sir; it will just do." (There is an over-nice propriety sometimes, an officious zeal of virtue, a little troublesome.) "Oh—the shirt—you must air my clean shirt:—linen gets very damp this weather."—"Yes, sir." Here another delicious five minutes. A knock at the door. "Oh, the shirt—very well. My stockings —I think the stockings had better be aired too." —"Very well, sir."—Here another interval. At length everything is ready, except myself. I now cannot help thinking a good deal—who can?— upon the unnecessary and villanous custom of shaving; it is a thing so unmanly (here I nestle closer) — so effeminate, (here I recoil from an unlucky step into the colder part of the bed.)— No wonder, that the queen of France took part with the rebels against that degenerate king, her husband, who first affronted her smooth visage with a face like her own. The Emperor Julian never showed the luxuriancy of his genius to better advantage than in reviving the flowing beard. Look at Cardinal Bembo's picture—at Michael Angelo's—at Titian's—at Shakspeare's —at Fletcher's—at Spenser's—at Chaucer's— Alfred's—at Plato's. I could name a great man for every tick of my watch. Look at the Turks, a grave and otiose people—Think of Haroun Al Raschid and Bed-ridden Hassan—Think of Wortley Montague, the worthy son of his mother, a man above the prejudice of his time— Look at the Persian gentlemen, whom one is ashamed of meeting about the suburbs, their dress and appearance are so much finer than our own—Lastly, think of the razor itself — how totally opposed to every sensation of bed—how cold, how edgy, how hard! how utterly different from anything like the warm and circling amplitude which

> Sweetly recommends itself
> Unto our gentle senses.

Add to this, benumbed fingers, which may help you to cut yourself, a quivering body, a frozen towel, and an ewer full of ice; and he that says there is nothing to oppose in all this, only shews, at any rate, that he has no merit in opposing it.'

Running Footmen.

Down to the time of our grandfathers, while there was less conveniency in the world than now, there was much more *state*. The nobility lived in a very dignified way, and amongst the particulars of their grandeur was the custom of keeping running footmen. All great people deemed it a necessary part of their travelling equipage, that one or more men should run in front of the carriage, not for any useful purpose, unless it might be in some instances to assist in lifting the carriage out of ruts, or helping it through rivers, but principally and professedly as a mark of the consequence of the traveller. Roads being generally bad, coach travelling was not rapid in those days; seldom above five miles an hour. The strain required to keep up with his master's coach was accordingly not very severe on one of these officials; at least, it was not so till towards the end of the eighteenth century, when, as a consequence of the acceleration of travelling, the custom began to be given up.

Nevertheless, the running footman required to be a healthy and agile man, and both in his dress and his diet a regard was had to the long and comparatively rapid journeys which he had to perform. A light black cap, a jockey coat, white linen trousers, or a mere linen shirt coming to the knees, with a pole six or seven feet long, constituted his outfit. On the top of the pole was a hollow ball, in which he kept a hard-boiled egg, or a little white wine, to serve as a refreshment in his journey; and this ball-topped pole seems to be the original of the long silver-headed cane which is still borne by footmen at the backs of the carriages of the nobility. A clever runner in his best days would undertake to do as much as seven miles an hour, when necessary, and go three-score miles a day; but, of course, it was not possible for any man to last long who tasked himself in this manner.

The custom of keeping running footmen survived to such recent times that Sir Walter Scott remembered seeing the state-coach of John Earl of Hopetoun attended by one of the fraternity, 'clothed in white, and bearing a staff.' It is believed that the Duke of Queensberry who died in 1810, kept up the practice longer than any other of the London grandees: and Mr

Thoms tells an amusing anecdote of a man who came to be hired for the duty by that ancient but far from venerable peer. His grace was in the habit of trying their paces by seeing how they could run up and down Piccadilly, he watching and timing them from his balcony. They put on a livery before the trial. On one occasion, a candidate presented himself, dressed, and ran. At the conclusion of his performance he stood before the balcony. 'You will do very well for me,' said the duke. 'And your livery will do very well for me,' replied the man, and gave the duke a last proof of his ability as a runner by then running away with it.*

Running footmen were employed by the Austrian nobility down to the close of the last century. Mrs St George, describing her visit to Vienna at that time,† expresses her dislike of the custom, as cruel and unnecessary. 'These unhappy people,' she says, 'always precede the carriage of their masters in town, and sometimes even to the suburbs. They seldom live above three or four years, and generally die of consumption. Fatigue and disease are painted in their pallid and drawn features; but, like victims, they are crowned with flowers, and adorned with tinsel.'

The dress of the official abroad seems to have been of a very gaudy character. A contributor to the *Notes and Queries* describes in vivid terms the appearance of the three footmen who preceded the King of Saxony's carriage, on a road near Dresden, on a hot July day in 1845: 'First, in the centre of the dusty *chaussée*, about thirty yards ahead of the foremost horses' heads, came a tall, thin, white-haired old man; he looked six feet high, about seventy years of age, but as lithe as a deer; his legs and body were clothed in drawers or tights of white linen; his jacket was like a jockey's, the colours blue and yellow, with lace and fringes on the facings; on his head a sort of barret cap, slashed and ornamented with lace and embroidery, and decorated in front with two curling heron's plumes; round his waist a deep belt of leather with silk and lace fringes, tassels, and quaint embroidery, which seemed to serve as a sort of pouch to the wearer. In his right hand he held, grasped by

* Notes and Queries, 2nd ser., i. 9.

† Journal kept during a visit to Germany, in 1799, 1800. Privately printed. 1861.

the middle, a staff about two feet long, carved and pointed with a silver head, and something like bells or metal drops hung round it, that jingled as he ran. Behind him, one on each side of the road, dressed and accoutred in the same style, came his two sons, handsome, tall young fellows of from twenty to twenty-five years of age; and so the king passed on.'

In our country, the running footman was occasionally employed upon simple errands when unusual dispatch was required. In the neighbourhood of various great houses in Scotland, the country people still tell stories illustrative of the singular speed which these men attained. For example: the Earl of Home, residing at Hume Castle in Berwickshire, had occasion to send his footman to Edinburgh one evening on important business. Descending to the hall in the morning, he found the man asleep on a bench, and, thinking he had neglected his duty, prepared to chastise him, but found, to his surprise, that the man had been to Edinburgh (thirty-five miles) and back, with his business sped, since the past evening. As another instance: the Duke of Lauderdale, in the reign of Charles II., being to give a large dinner-party at his castle of Thirlstane, near Lauder, it was discovered, at the laying of the cloth, that some additional plate would be required from the Duke's other seat of Lethington, near Haddington, fully fifteen miles distant across the Lammermuir hills. The running footman instantly darted off, and was back with the required articles in time for dinner! The great boast of the running footman was that, on a long journey, he could beat a horse. 'A traditional anecdote is related of one of these fleet messengers (rather half-witted), who was sent from Glasgow to Edinburgh for two doctors to come to see his sick master. He was interrupted on the road with an inquiry how his master was now. "He's no dead yet," was the reply; "but he'll soon be, for I'm fast on the way for twa Edinburgh doctors to come and visit him." ' *

Langham, an Irishman, who served Henry Lord Berkeley as running footman in Elizabeth's time, on one occasion, this noble's wife being sick, 'carried a letter from Callowdon to old Dr Fryer, a physician dwelling in Little Britain in London, and returned with a glass bottle in his hand, compounded by the doctor, for the recovery of her health, a journey of 148 miles performed by him in less than forty-two hours, notwithstanding his stay of one night at the physician's and apothecary's houses, which no one horse could have so well and safely performed; for which the Lady shall after give him a new suit of clothes.'—*Berkeley Manuscripts*, 4to, 1821, p. 204.

The memory of this singular custom is kept alive in the ordinary name for a man-servant—a *footman*. In Charles Street, Berkeley Square, London, there is a particular memorial of it in the sign of a public-house, called *The Running Footman*, much used by the servants of the neighbouring gentry. Here is represented a tall, agile man in gay attire, and with a stick having a metal ball at top; he is engaged in running.

* Notes and Queries, 2nd ser., i. 121.

Underneath is inscribed, 'I am the only Running Footman.' Of this sign a transcript is presented on the preceding page.

JANUARY 13.

NEW-YEAR'S DAY, O. S.

St Kentigern (otherwise St Mungo), of Glasgow, 601; St Veronica of Milan, 1497.

The 13th of January is held as St Hilary's day by the Church of England. On this day, accordingly, begins the Hilary Term at Cambridge, though on the 14th at Oxford; concluding respectively on the Friday and Saturday next before Palm Sunday.

ST VERONICA.

St Veronica was originally a poor girl working in the fields near Milan. The pious instructions of her parents fell upon a heart naturally susceptible in a high degree of religious impressions, and she soon became an aspirant for conventual life. Entering the nunnery of St Martha in Milan, she in time became its superioress; in which position her conduct was most exemplary. Some years after her death, which took place in 1497, Pope Leo X. allowed her to be honoured in her convent in the same manner as if she had been beatified in the usual form.

Veronica appears as one whose mind had been wholly subdued to a religious life. She was evangelical perfection according to the ideas of her Church and her age. Even under extreme and lingering sickness, she persisted in taking her share of the duties of her convent, submitting to the greatest drudgeries, and desiring to live solely on bread and water. 'Her silence was a sign of her recollection and continual prayer; in which her gift of abundant and almost continual tears was most wonderful. She nourished them by constant meditation on her own miseries, on the love of God, the joys of heaven, and the sacred passion of Christ. She always spoke of her own sinful life, as she called it, though it was most innocent, with the most profound compunction. She was favoured by God with many extraordinary visits and comforts.'—*Butler*.

The name Veronica conducts the mind back to a very curious, and very ancient, though obscure legend of the Romish Church. It is stated that the Saviour, at his passion, had his face wiped with a handkerchief by a devout female attendant, and that the cloth became miraculously impressed with the image of his countenance. It became VERA ICONICA, or a true portrait of those blessed features. The handkerchief, being sent to Abgarus, king of Odessa, passed through a series of adventures, but ultimately settled at Rome, where it has been kept for many centuries in St Peter's Church, under the highest veneration. There seems even to be a votive mass, ' de Sancta Veronica seu vultu Domini,' the idea being thus personified, after a manner peculiar to the ancient Church. From the term *Vera Iconica* has come the name Veronica, the image being thus, as it were, personified in the character of a female saint, who, however, remains without biography and date. As a curiosity amongst ancient religious ideas, a picture of the revered handkerchief is here given.

From a series of papers contributed to the *Art Journal* for 1861, by Mr Thomas Heaphy, artist, London, entitled *An Examination of the Antiquity of the Likeness of our Blessed Lord*, it appears

that the legendary portrait of Christ can be traced with a respectable amount of evidence, much farther back than most persons are aware of. In the early days of the Christian Church at Rome, before it received the protection of the empire, the worshippers, rendered by their hopes of resurrection anxious to avoid burning the bodies of their friends, yet living amongst a people who burnt the dead and considered any other mode of disposing of them as a nuisance, were driven

to the necessity of making subterranean excavations for purposes of sepulture, generally in secluded grounds belonging to rich individuals. Hence the famous Catacombs of Rome, dark passages in the rock, sometimes three above each other, having tiers of recesses for bodies along their sides, and all wonderfully well preserved. In these recesses, not unfrequently, the remains of bodies exist; in many, there are tablets telling who was the deceased; in some, there are recesses containing lachrymatories, or tear-vials, and little glass vessels, the sacramental cups of the primitive church, on which may still be traced pictures of Christ and his principal disciples. A vast number, however, of these curious remains have been transferred to the Vatican, where they are guarded with the most jealous care.

Mr Heaphy met with extraordinary difficulties in his attempts to examine the Catacombs, and scarcely less in his endeavours to see the stores of reliques in the Vatican. He has nevertheless placed before us a very interesting series of the pictures found, generally wrought in gold, on the glass cups above adverted to. Excepting in one instance, where Christ is represented in the act of raising Lazarus from the dead (in which case the face is an ordinary one with a Brutus crop of hair), the portrait of Jesus is invariably repre-

sented as that peculiar oval one, with parted hair, with which we are so familiar; and the fact becomes only the more remarkable from the contrast it presents to other faces, as those of St Peter or St Paul, which occur in the same pictures, and all of which have their own characteristic forms and expressions. Now, Tertullian, who wrote about the year 160, speaks of these portraits on sacramental vessels as a practice of the *first Christians*, as if it were, even in his time, a thing of the past. And thus the probability of their being found very soon after the time of Christ, and when the tradition of his personal appearance was still fresh, is, in Mr Heaphy's opinion, established.

We are enabled here to give a specimen of these curious illustrations of early Christianity, being one on which Mr Heaphy makes the following remarks: 'An instance of what may be termed the transition of the type, being apparently executed at a time when some information respecting the more obvious traits in the true likeness had reached Rome, and the artist felt no longer at liberty to adopt the mere conventional type of a Roman youth, but aimed at giving such distinctive features to the portrait as he was able from the partial information which had reached him. We see in this instance that our Saviour,

who is represented as giving the crown of life to St Peter and St Paul, is delineated with the hair divided in the middle (distinctly contrary to the fashion of that day) and a beard, being so far an approximation to the true type. . . . . One thing to be specially noticed is, that the portraits of the two apostles were at that time already depicted under an easily recognised type of character, as will be seen by comparing this picture with two others which will appear hereafter, in all of which the short, curled, bald head and thick-set features of St Peter are at once discernible, and afford direct evidence of its being an exact portrait likeness, [while] the representation of St Paul is scarcely less characteristic.'

ST KENTIGERN.

Out of the obscurity which envelops the history of the northern part of our island in the fifth and sixth centuries, when all of it that was not provincial Roman was occupied by Keltic tribes under various denominations, there loom before us three holy figures, engaged in planting Christianity. The first of these was Ninian, who built a church of stone at Whithorn, on the promontory of Wigton; another was Serf, who some time after had a cell at Culross, on the north shore of the Firth of Forth; a third was Kentigern, pupil of the last, and more notable than either. He appears to have flourished throughout the sixth century, and to have died in 601. Through his mother, named Thenew, he was connected with the royal family of the Cumbrian Britons—a rude state stretching along the west side of the island between Wales and Argyle. After being educated by Serf at Culross, he returned among his own people, and planted a small religious establishment on the banks of a little stream which falls into the Clyde at what is now the city of Glasgow. Upon a tree beside the clearing in the forest, he hung his bell to summon the savage neighbours to worship; and the tree with the bell still figures in the arms of Glasgow. Thus was the commencement made of what in time became a seat of population in connexion with an episcopal see; by and by, an industrious town; ultimately, what we now see, a magnificent city with half a million of inhabitants. Kentigern, though his amiable character procured him the name of Mungo, or the Beloved, had great troubles from the then king of the Strathclyde Britons; and at one time he had to seek a refuge in Wales, where, however, he employed himself to some purpose, as he there founded, under the care of a follower, St Asaph, the religious establishment of that name, now the seat of an English bishopric.

Resuming his residence at Glasgow, he spent many years in the most pious exercises—for one thing reciting the whole psalter once every day. As generally happened with those who gave themselves up entirely to sanctitude, he acquired the reputation of being able to effect miracles. Contemporary with him, though a good deal his junior, was Columba, who had founded the celebrated monastery of I-colm-kill. It is recorded that Columba came to see St Kentigern at his little church beside the Clyde, and that they interchanged their respective pastoral staves, as a token of brotherly affection. For a time, these two places were the centres of Christian missionary exertion in the country now called Scotland. St Kentigern, at length dying at an advanced age, was buried on the spot where, five centuries afterwards, arose the beautiful cathedral which still bears his name.

Born.—Charles James Fox, statesman, 1748.
Died.—George Fox, founder of the sect of Quakers, 1690; Dr James Macknight, 1800; Earl of Eldon (formerly Lord Chancellor of England), 1838.

CHARLES JAMES FOX.

Of Charles James Fox, the character given by his friends is very attractive: 'He was,' says Sir James Mackintosh, 'gentle, modest, placable, kind, of simple manners, and so averse from parade and dogmatism, as to be not only unostentatious, but even somewhat inactive in conversation. His superiority was never felt, but in the instruction which he imparted, or in the attention which his generous preference usually directed to the more obscure members of the company. His conversation, when it was not repressed by modesty or indolence, was delightful. The pleasantry, perhaps, of no man of wit had so

unlaboured an appearance. It seemed rather to escape from his mind than to be produced by it. His literature was various and elegant. In classical erudition, which, by the custom of England, is more peculiarly called learning, he was inferior to few professed scholars. Like all

CHARLES JAMES FOX.

men of genius, he delighted to take refuge in poetry, from the vulgarity and irritation of business. His own verses were easy and pleasing, and might have claimed no low place among those which the French call *vers de société*. He disliked political conversation, and never willingly took any part in it. . . . . From these qualities of his private as well as from his public character, it probably arose that no English statesman ever preserved, during so long a period of adverse fortune, so many affectionate friends, and so many zealous adherents.'

The shades of Fox's history are to be found in his extravagance, his gambling habits (which reduced him to the degradation of having his debts paid by subscription), and his irregular domestic life; but how shall the historian rebuke one whose friends declared that they found his faults made him only the more lovable?

Viewing the unreasonableness of many party movements and doings, simply virtuous people sometimes feel inclined to regard *party* as wholly opposed in spirit to truth and justice. Hear, however, the defence put forward for it by the great Whig leader: 'The question,' says he, 'upon the solution of which, in my opinion, principally depends the utility of party, is, in what situations are men most or least likely to act corruptly—in a party, or insulated? and of this I think there can be no doubt. There is no man so pure who is not more or less influenced, in a doubtful case, by the interests of his fortune or his ambition. If, therefore, a man has to decide upon every new question, this influence will have so many frequent opportunities of exerting itself that it will in most cases ultimately prevail; whereas, if a man has once engaged in a party, the occasions for new decisions are more rare, and consequently these corrupt influences operate less. This reasoning is much strengthened when you consider that many men's minds are so framed that, in a question at all dubious, they are incapable of any decision; some, from narrowness of understanding, not seeing the point of the question at all; others, from refinement, seeing so much on both sides, that they do not know how to balance the account. Such persons will, in nine cases out of ten, be influenced by interest, even without their being conscious of their corruption. In short, it appears to me that a party spirit is the only substitute that has been found, or can be found, for public virtue and comprehensive understanding; neither of which can be reasonably expected to be found in a very great number of people. Over and above all this, it appears to me to be a constant incitement to everything that is right: for, if a party spirit prevails, all power, aye, and all rank too, in the liberal sense of the word, is in a great measure elective. To be at the head of a party, or even high in it, you must have the confidence of the party; and confidence is not to be procured by abilities alone. In an Epitaph upon Lord Rockingham, written I believe by Burke, it is said, " *his virtues were his means;*" and very truly; and so, more or less, it must be with every party man. Whatever teaches men to depend upon one another, and to feel the necessity of conciliating the good opinion of those with whom they live, is surely of the highest advantage to the morals and happiness of mankind; and what does this so much as party? Many of these which I have mentioned are only collateral advantages, as it were, belonging to this system; but the decisive argument upon this subject appears to me to be this: Is there any other mode or plan in this country by which a rational man can hope to stem the power and influence of the Crown? I am sure that neither experience nor any well-reasoned theory has ever shewn any other. Is there any other plan which is likely to make so great a number of persons resist the temptations of titles and emoluments? And if these things are so, ought we to abandon a system from which so much good has been derived, because some men have acted inconsistently, or because, from the circumstances of the moment, we are not likely to act with much effect?'

Mr Fox was the third son of Henry Fox, afterwards Lord Holland, and of Lady Georgina Caroline Fox, eldest daughter of Charles, second Duke of Richmond. As a child he was remarkable for the quickness of his parts, his engaging disposition, and early intelligence. 'There's a clever little boy for you!' exclaims his father to Lady Caroline Fox, in repeating a remark made *à propos* by his son Charles, when hardly more than two years and a half old. 'I dined at home to-day,' he says, in another letter to her, ' *tête-à-tête* with Charles, intending to do business, but he has found me pleasanter employment, and was very sorry to go away so soon.' He is, in another letter, described as 'very pert, and very argumentative, all life and spirits, motion, and good humour; stage-mad, but it makes him read a good deal.' That he was excessively indulged is certain: his father had promised that he should be present when a garden wall was to be flung down, and having forgotten it, the wall was built up again—it was said, that he might fulfil his promise.

DR MACKNIGHT.

Dr James Macknight, born in 1721, one of the

ministers of Edinburgh, wrote a laborious work on the Apostolical Epistles, which was published in 1795, in four volumes 4to. He had worked at it for eleven hours a day for a series of years, and, though well advanced in life, maintained tolerable health of body and mind through these uncommon labours; but no sooner was his mind relieved of its familiar task, than its powers, particularly in the department of memory, sensibly began to give way; and the brief remainder of his life was one of decline. Dibdin recommends the inviting quartos of Macknight, as containing 'learning without pedantry, and piety without enthusiasm.'

A SERMON BY THE POPE.

It is a circumstance not much known in Protestant countries, that the head of the Roman Catholic Church does not ascend the pulpit. Whether it is deemed a lowering of dignity for one who is a sovereign prince as well as a high priest to preach a sermon like other priests, or whether he has not time—certain it is that priests cease to be preachers when they become popes. One single exception in three hundred years tends to illustrate the rule. Pope Pius IX. supplied that exception. It was his lot to be, and to do, and to see many things that lie out of the usual path of pontiffs, and this among the number.

On the 2nd of June 1846, Pope Gregory XVI. died. Fifty-one cardinals assembled at the palace of the Quirinal at Rome, on Sunday the 14th, to elect one of their body as a successor to Gregory. The choice fell on Giovanni Maria Mastaï Ferretti, Cardinal-Archbishop of Imola; and he ascended the chair of St Peter as Pope Pius IX. He was a liberal man, who had won much popular esteem by his general kindness, especially to the poor and afflicted. While yet an archbishop, he occupied the pulpit one day in an unexpected manner; the officiating priest was taken ill during his sermon, and the cardinal, who was present, at once took his place, his text, and his line of argument. It was equally an unforeseen incident for him to preach as a pope. The matter is thus noticed in Count de Liancourt's *Pius the Ninth: the First Year of his Pontificate*, under the date January 13th, 1847: 'This circumstance has been noticed in the chronological tables of the year as an event which had not occurred before for three hundred years. But it is as well that it should be known that it was not a premeditated design on the part of his Holiness, but merely the result of accident. On the day in question, the Octave of the Epiphany, the celebrated preacher Padre Ventura, whose eloquence attracted crowds of eager listeners, had not arrived at the church (de Santa Andrea della Valle, at Rome); and the disappointed congregation, thinking indisposition was the cause of his absence, were on the point of retiring, when suddenly the bells rang, and announced the unexpected arrival of the Sovereign Pontiff. It is impossible to describe the feelings of the congregation, or the deep interest and excitement which were produced in their minds when they saw Pius IX. advance towards the pulpit, or the profound silence with which they listened to his discourse.' It was a simple, good, plain sermon, easily intelligible to all.

This was a day to be remembered, for Pius IX. was held almost in adoration at that time by the excitable Italians. He was a reforming pope, a liberal pope. He offended Austria and all the petty despots of Italy by his measures as an Italian prince, if not as the head of the Church. He liberated political prisoners; gave the first sign of encouragement to the construction of railways in the papal dominions; gave increased freedom to the press; encouraged scientific meetings and researches; announced his approval of popular education; surrounded himself with liberal ministers; and purified the papal household. It was hard work for him to contend against the opposition of Lambruschini and other cardinals; but he did so. Alas! it was all too good to be permanent. The year 1848 arrived, and with it those convulsions which agitated almost every country in Europe. Pope Pius became thoroughly frightened. He either really believed that nations are not fitted for so much liberty and liberalism as he had hitherto been willing to give them, or else the power brought to bear against him by emperors, kings, princes, grand-dukes, cardinals, and archbishops, was greater than he could withstand. He changed his manners and proceedings, and became like other popes. What followed all this, belongs to the history of Italy.

THE CHANGE OF THE STYLE IN BRITAIN.

The Act for the change of the style (24 Geo. II. cap. 23) provided that the legal year in England 1752 should commence, not on the 25th of March, but on the 1st of January, and that after the 3rd of September in that year, the next ensuing day should be held as the 14th, thus dropping out eleven days. The Act also included provisions regarding the days for fairs and markets, the periods of legal obligations, and the future arrangements of the calendar. A reformed plan of the calendar, with tables for the moveable feasts, &c. occupies many pages of the statute.

The change of the style by Pope Gregory in the sixteenth century was well received by the people of the Catholic world. Miracles which took place periodically on certain days of the year, as for example the melting of the blood of St Gennaro at Naples on the 19th of September, observed the new style in the most orthodox manner, and the common people hence concluded that it was all right. The Protestant populace of England, equally ignorant, but without any such quasi-religious principle to guide them, were, on the contrary, violently inflamed against the statesmen who had carried through the bill for the change of style; generally believing that they had been defrauded of eleven days (as if eleven days of their destined lives) by the transaction. Accordingly, it is told that for some time afterwards, a favourite opprobrious cry to unpopular statesmen, in the streets and on the hustings, was, ' Who stole the eleven days? Give us back the eleven days!'

Near Malwood Castle, in Hampshire, there was an oak tree which was believed to bud every Christmas, in honour of Him who was born on that day. The people of the neighbourhood said they would look to this venerable piece of timber as a test of the propriety of the change of style. They would go to it on the new Christmas Day, and see if it budded: if it did not, there could be no doubt that the new style was a monstrous mistake. Accordingly, on Christmas Day, new style, there was a great flocking to this old oak, to see how the question was to be determined. On its being found that no budding took place, the opponents of the new style triumphantly proclaimed that their view was approved by Divine wisdom—a point on which it is said they became still clearer, when, on the 5th January, being old Christmas Day, the oak was represented as having given forth a few shoots. These people were unaware that, even although there were historical grounds for believing that Jesus was born on the 25th of December, we had been carried away from the observance of the true day during the three centuries which elapsed between the event and the Council of Nice.

The change of style has indeed proved a sad discomfiture to all ideas connected with particular days and seasons. It was said, for instance, that March came in like a lion and went out like a lamb; but the end of the March of which this was said, is in reality the 12th of April. Still more absurd did it become to hold All Saints' Eve (October 31) as a time on which the powers of the mystic world were in particular vigour and activity, seeing that we had been observing it at a wrong time for centuries. We had been continually for many centuries gliding away from the right time, and yet had not perceived any difference—a pretty good proof that the assumedly sacred character of the night was all empty delusion.

Recovered Rings.

In the *Acta Sanctorum* a curious legend is related in connexion with the life of Kentigern, as to the finding of a lost ring. A queen, having formed an improper attachment to a handsome soldier, put upon his finger a precious ring which her own lord had conferred upon her. The king, made aware of the fact, but dissembling his anger, took an opportunity, in hunting, while the soldier lay asleep beside the Clyde, to snatch off the ring, and throw it into the river. Then returning home along with the soldier, he demanded of the queen the ring he had given her. She sent secretly to the soldier for the ring, which could not be restored. In great terror, she then dispatched a messenger to ask the assistance of the holy Kentigern. He, who knew of the affair before being informed of it, went to the river Clyde, and having caught a salmon, took from its stomach the missing ring, which he sent to the queen. She joyfully went with it to the king, who, thinking he had wronged her, swore he would be revenged upon her accusers; but she, affecting a forgiving temper, besought him to pardon them as she had done. At the same time, she confessed her error to Kentigern, and solemnly vowed to be more careful of her conduct in future.*

In the armorial bearings of the see of Glasgow, and now of the city, St Kentigern's tree with its bell forms the principal object, while its stem is crossed by the salmon of the legend, bearing in its mouth the ring so miraculously recovered.

GLASGOW ARMS.

Fabulous as this old church legend may appear, it does not stand quite alone in the annals of the past. In Brand's *History of Newcastle*, we find the particulars of a similar event which occurred at that city in or about the year 1559. A gentleman named Anderson—called in one account Sir Francis Anderson—fingering his ring as he was one day standing on the bridge, dropped the bauble into the Tyne, and of course gave it up as lost. After some time a servant of this gentleman bought a fish in Newcastle market, in the stomach of which the identical lost ring was found.†

An occurrence remarkably similar to the above is related by Herodotus as happening to Polycrates, after his great success in possessing himself of the island of Samos. Amasis, king of Egypt, sent Polycrates a friendly letter, expressing a fear for the continuance of his singular prosperity, for he had never known such an instance of felicity which did not come to calamity in the long run; therefore advising Polycrates to throw away some favourite gem in such a way that he might never see it again, as a kind of charm against misfortune. Polycrates consequently took a valuable signet-ring—an emerald set in gold—and sailing away from the shore in a boat, threw this gem, in the sight of all on board, into the deep. 'This done, he returned home and gave vent to his sorrow.

'Now it happened, five or six days afterwards, that a fisherman caught a fish so large and beautiful that he thought it well deserved to be made a present of to the king. So he took it with him to the gate of the palace, and said that he wanted to see Polycrates. Then Polycrates allowed him to come in, and the fisherman gave him the fish with these words following—"Sir king, when I took this prize, I thought I would not carry it to market, though I am a poor man who live by

my trade. I said to myself, it is worthy of Polycrates and his greatness; and so I brought it here to give it you." The speech pleased the king, who thus spoke in reply: "Thou didst well, friend, and I am doubly indebted, both for the gift and for the speech. Come now, and sup with me." So the fisherman went home, esteeming it a high honour that he had been asked to sup with the king. Meanwhile, the servants, on cutting open the fish, found the signet of their master in its belly. No sooner did they see it than they seized upon it, and hastening to Polycrates with great joy, restored it to him, and told him in what way it had been found. The king, who saw something providential in the matter, forthwith wrote a letter to Amasis, telling him all that had happened. . . . Amasis . . . perceived that it does not belong to man to save his fellowman from the fate which is in store for him; likewise he felt certain that Polycrates would end ill, as he prospered in everything, even finding what he had thrown away. So he sent a herald to Samos, and dissolved the contract of friendship. This he did, that when the great and heavy misfortune came, he might escape the grief which he would have felt if the sufferer had been his loved friend.'*

In Scottish family history there are at least two stories of recovered rings, tending to support the possible verity of the Kentigern legend. The widow of Viscount Dundee—the famous Claverhouse—was met and wooed at Colzium House, in Stirlingshire, by the Hon William Livingstone, who subsequently became Viscount Kilsyth. The gentleman gave the lady a pledge of affection in the form of a ring, having for its posy, 'YOURS ONLY AND EVER.' She unluckily lost it in the garden, and it could not again be found; which was regarded as an unlucky prognostic for the marriage that soon after took place. Nor was the prognostic falsified by the event, for not long after her second nuptials, while living in exile in Holland, she and her only child were killed by the fall of a house. Just a hundred years after, the lost ring was found in a clod in the garden; and it has since been preserved at Colzium House. The other story is less romantic, yet curious, and of assured verity. A large silver signet ring was lost by Mr Murray of Pennyland, in Caithness, as he was walking one day on a shingly beach bounding his estate. Fully a century afterwards, it was found in the shingle, in fair condition, and restored to Mr Murray's remote heir, the present Sir Peter Murray Threipland of Fingask, baronet.

Professor De Morgan, in *Notes and Queries* for December 21, 1861, relates an anecdote of a recovered ring nearly as wonderful as that connected with the life of Kentigern. He says he does not vouch for it; but it was circulated and canvassed, nearly fifty years ago, in the country town close to which the scene is placed, with all degrees of belief and unbelief. 'A servant boy was sent into the town with a valuable ring. He took it out of its box to admire it, and in passing over a plank bridge he let it fall on a muddy bank. Not being able to find it, he ran away, took to the sea, finally settled in a colony, made a large fortune, came back after many

* *Acta Sanctorum*, i. 820.   † Brand's *Newcastle*, i. 45.   * Rawlinson's *Translation of Herodotus*, ii. 438.

106

years, and bought the estate on which he had been servant. One day, while walking over his land with a friend, he came to the plank bridge, and there told his friend the story. "I could swear," said he, pushing his stick into the mud, "to the very spot on which the ring dropped." When the stick came back the ring was on the end of it.'

Wild Oats.—We are more familiar with wild oats in a moral than in a botanical sense; yet in the latter it is an article of no small curiosity. For one thing, it has a self-inherent power of moving from one place to another. Let a *head* of it be laid down in a moistened state upon a table, and left there for the night, and next morning it will be found to have walked off. The locomotive power resides in the peculiar hard *awn* or spike, which sets the grain a-tumbling over and over, sideways. A very large and coarse kind of wild oats, brought many years ago from Otaheite, was found to have the ambulatory character in uncommon perfection. When ordinary oats is allowed by neglect to degenerate, it acquires this among other characteristics of wild oats.

JANUARY 14.

Sts Isaias and Sabbas, 273. St Barbasceminus, 346. St Hilary, B. 368. St Felix.

ST HILARY.

St Hilarius lived in the fourth century, and the active and influential part of his life was passed under the Emperor Constantius in the East, though he is included among the Fathers of the Western or Latin Church. He belonged to a family of distinction resident at Poitiers, in Gaul, and was brought up in paganism, but became a convert to Christianity, and in the year 354 was elected bishop of Poitiers. The first general council, held at Nice (Nicæa) in Bithynia, in 325, under the Emperor Constantine, had condemned the doctrine of Arius, but had not suppressed it; and Hilarius, about thirty years afterwards, when he had made himself acquainted with the arguments, became an opponent of the Arians, who were then numerous, and were patronised by the Emperor Constantius. The council of Arles, held in 353, had condemned Athanasius and others, who were opponents of the Arian doctrine; and Hilarius, in the council of Beziers, held in 356, defended Athanasius, in opposition to Saturninus, bishop of Arles. He was in consequence deposed from his bishopric by the Arians, and banished by Constantius to Phrygia. There he remained about four years, occupied in composing his principal work, *On the Trinity*, in twelve books. Hilarius, besides his twelve books *On the Trinity*, wrote a work *On Synods* addressed to the bishops of Gaul and Britain, in which he gives an account of the various creeds adopted in the Eastern church subsequent to the council of Nice; and he addressed three books to the Emperor Constantius, of whose religious opinions he was always an energetic and fearless opponent. He continued, indeed, from the time when he became a bishop till the termination of his life in 368, to be zealously engaged in the Trinitarian controversy; and the final triumph of the Nicene creed over the Arian may be attributed in a great degree to his energetic exertions. After the death of Constantius, in 361, he was restored to his bishopric, and returned to Poitiers, where he died.

Born.—Prince Adam Czartoryski, 1770.
Died.—Edward Lord Bruce, 1610; Dr John Boyse, translator of the Bible, 1643; Madame de Sevigné, 1696; Edmund Halley, astronomer, 1742; Dr George Berkeley, Bishop of Cloyne, 1753.

DR JOHN BOYSE.

A minute and interesting memoir of this eminent scholar, in Peck's *Desiderata Curiosa*, makes us aware of his profound learning, his diligence in study, and his many excellences of character. Ultimately he was a prebendary of Ely; but when engaged in his task of translating the Bible, he was only rector of Boxworth. Boyse was one of a group of seven scholars at Cambridge to whom were committed the Apocryphal books; and when, after four years, this task was finished, he was one of two of that group sent to London to superintend the general revision. With other four learned men, Boyse was engaged for nine months at Stationers' Hall, in the business of revising the entire translation; and it is not unworthy of notice, as creditable to the trade of literature. that, while the task of translation passed unrewarded of the nation, that of revision was remunerated by the Company of Stationers sending each scholar *thirty shillings a week*. The idea of a guerdon for literary exertion was then a novelty—indeed a thing scarcely known in England.

Boyse was employed with Sir Henry Savile in that serious task of editing Chrysostom, which led to a celebrated witticism on the part of Sir Henry. Lady Savile, complaining one day to her husband of his being so abstracted from her society by his studies, expressed a wish that she were a book, as she might then receive some part of his attention. 'Then,' said Sir Henry, 'I should have you to be an almanack, that I might change you every year.' She threatened to burn Chrysostom, who seemed to be killing her husband; whereupon Dr Boyse quietly remarked, 'That were a great pity, madam.' 'Why, who was Chrysostom?' inquired she. 'One of the sweetest preachers since the Apostles' times,' he calmly answered. 'Then,' said she, corrected by his manner and words, 'I would not burn him for the world.'

Boyse lived to eighty-two, though generally engaged eight hours a day in study. He seems to have been wise before his time as to the management of his physical system under intellectual labour, and his practice may even yet be described with advantage. 'He made but two meals, dinner and supper;* betwixt which he never so much as drank, unless, upon trouble of flatulency, some small quantity of *aqua-vitæ* and sugar. After meat he was careful, almost to curiosity, in picking and rubbing his teeth;

* In the days of Elizabeth and the first James, few gentlemen took anything but a draught of ale by way of breakfast.

esteeming that a special preservative of health; by which means he carried to his grave almost a Hebrew alphabet of teeth [twenty-two]. When that was done, he used to sit or walk an hour or more, to digest his meat, before he would go to his study. . . . He would never study at all, in later years, between supper and bed; which time, two hours at least, he would spend with his friends in discourse, hearing and telling harmless, delightful stories, whereof he was exceedingly full. . . . The posture of his body in studying was always standing, except when for ease he went upon his knees.' No modern physiologist could give a better set of rules than these for a studious life, excepting as far as absence of all reference to active exercise is concerned.

MADAME DE SEVIGNÉ.

This celebrated woman, who has the glory of being fully as conspicuous in the graces of style as any writer of her age, died, after a few days' illness, at the town of Grignan. Her children were throughout life her chief object, and especially her daughter, to her affection for whom we owe the greater part of that admirable collection of Letters upon which the fame of Madame de Sevigné is raised. La Harpe describes them as 'the book of all hours, of the town, of the country, on travel. They are the conversations of a most agreeable woman, to which one need contribute nothing but one's own; which is a great charm to an idle person.'

Her Letters were not published till the eighteenth century, but they were written in the mid-day of the reign of Louis XIV. 'Their ease and freedom from affectation,' says Hallam, 'are more striking by contrast with the two epistolary styles which had been most admired in France—that of Balzac, which is laboriously tumid, and that of Voiture, which becomes insipid by dint of affectation. Everyone perceives that in the *Letters of a Mother to her Daughter*, the public, in a strict sense, is not thought of; and yet the habit of speaking and writing what men of wit and taste would desire to hear and read, gives a certain mannerism, I will not say air of effort, even to the letters of Madame de Sevigné. The abandonment of the heart to its casual impulses is not so genuine as in some that have since been published. It is at least clear that it is possible to become affected in copying her unaffected style; and some of Walpole's letters bear witness to this. Her wit and talent of painting by single touches are very eminent; scarcely any collection of letters, which contain so little that can interest a distant age, are read with such pleasure. If they have any general fault, it is a little monotony and excess of affection towards her daughter, which is reported to have wearied its object, and, in contrast with this, a little want of sensibility towards all beyond her immediate friends, and a readiness to find something ludicrous in the dangers and sufferings of others.' Thus, in one letter she mentions that a lady of her acquaintance, having been bitten by a mad dog, had gone to be dipped in the sea, and amuses herself by taking off the provincial accent with which she will express herself on the first plunge. She makes a jest of La Voisin's execution, and

108

thought that person was as little entitled to sympathy as any one; yet, when a woman is burned alive, it is not usual for another woman to turn it into drollery.—*Literature of Europe.*

Madame de Sevigné's taste has been arraigned for slighting Racine; and she has been charged with the unfortunate prediction: "*Il passera comme le café.*" But it has been denied that these words can be found, though few like to give up so diverting a miscalculation of futurity.

BISHOP BERKELEY AND TAR-WATER.

Berkeley was a poet, as well as a mathematician and philosopher; and his mind was not only well stored with professional and philosophical learning, but with information upon trade, agriculture, and the common arts of life. Having received benefit from the use of tar-water, when ill of the colic, he published a work on the Virtues of Tar-water, on which he said he had bestowed more pains than on any other of his productions. His last work, published but a few months before his death, was *Further Thoughts on Tar-water;* and it shews his enthusiastic character, that, when accused of fancying he had discovered a panacea in tar-water, he replied, that 'to speak out, he freely owns he suspects tar-water is a panacea.' Walpole has taken the trouble to preserve, from the newspapers of the day, the following epigram on Berkeley's tar-water:

'Who dare deride what pious Cloyne has done?
　The Church shall rise and vindicate her son;
　She tells us all her bishops shepherds are,
　And shepherds heal their rotten sheep with tar.'

In a letter written by Mr John Whishaw, solicitor, May 25, 1744, we find this account of Berkeley's panacea: 'The Bishop of Cloyne, in Ireland, has published a book, of two shillings price, vpon the excellencies of tar-water, which is to keep ye bloud in due order, and a great remedy in many cases. His way of making it is to put, I think, a gallon of water to a quart of tar, and after stirring it together, to let it stand forty-eight hours, and then pour off the clear and drink a glass of about half a pint in ye morn, and as much at five in ye afternoon. So it's become common to call for a glass of tar-water in a coffee-house, as a dish of tea or coffee.'

GREAT FROSTS.

On this day, in 1205, 'began a frost which continued till the two and twentieth day of March, so that the ground could not be tilled; whereof it came to pass that, in summer following, a quarter of wheat was sold for a mark of silver in many places of England, which for the more part in the days of King Henry the Second was sold for twelve pence; a quarter of beans or peas for half a mark; a quarter of oats for forty pence, that were wont to be sold for fourpence. Also the money was so sore clipped that there was no remedy but to have it renewed.'—*Stowe's Chronicle.*

It has become customary in England to look to St Hilary's Day as the *coldest in the year;* perhaps from its being a noted day about the middle of the notedly coldest month. It is, however, just possible that the commencement of the extraordinary and fatal frost of 1205, on this day, may have had something to do with the notion; and it may be remarked, that in 1820 the 14th of January *was* the coldest day of the year, one gentleman's thermometer falling to four degrees Fahrenheit below zero. On a review of the greatest frosts in the English chronicles, it can only be observed that they have for the most part occurred throughout January, and only, in general, diverge a little into December on the one hand, and February on the other. Yet one of the most remarkable of modern frosts began quite at the end of January.

It was at that time in 1814 that London last saw the Thames begin to be so firmly frozen as to support a multitude of human beings on its surface. For a month following the 27th of the previous December, there had been a strong frost in England. A thaw took place on the 26th January, and the ice of the Thames came down in a huge 'pack,' which was suddenly arrested between the bridges by the renewal of the frost. On the 31st the ice pack was so firmly frozen in one mass, that people began to pass over it, and next day the footing appeared so safe, that thousands of persons ventured to cross. Opposite to Queenhithe, where the mass appeared most solid, upwards of thirty booths were erected, for the sale of liquors and viands, and for the playing of skittles. A sheep was set to a fire in a tent upon the ice, and sold in shilling slices, under the

appellation of *Lapland mutton*. Musicians came, and dances were effected on the rough and slippery surface. What with the gay appearance of the booths, and the quantity of favourite popular amusements going on, the scene was singularly cheerful and exciting. On the ensuing day, faith in the ice having increased, there were vast multitudes upon it between the London and Blackfriars' Bridges; the tents for the sale of refreshments, and for games of hazard, had largely multiplied; swings and merry-go-rounds were added to skittles; in short, there were all the appearances of a Greenwich or Bartholomew Fair exhibited on this frail surface, and *Frost Fair* was a term in everybody's mouth. Amongst those who strove to make a trade of the occasion, none were more active than the humbler class of printers. Their power of producing an article capable of preservation, as a memorial of the affair, brought them in great numbers to the scene. Their principal business consisted, accordingly, in the throwing off of little broadsides referring to Frost Fair, and stating the singular circumstances under which they were produced, in rather poor verses—such as the following:

' Amidst the arts which on the Thames appear,
  To tell the wonders of this icy year,
  Printing claims prior place, which at one view
  Erects a monument of THAT and YOU.'

Another peculiarly active corps was the ancient fraternity of watermen, who, deserting their proper trade, contrived to render themselves ser-

FAIR ON THE THAMES, 1716.

viceable by making convenient accesses from the landings, for which they charged a moderate toll. It was reported that some of these men realized as much as ten pounds a day by this kind of business.

All who remember the scene describe it as having been singular and picturesque. It was not merely a white icy plain, covered with flag-bearing booths and lively crowds. The peculiar circumstances under which this part of the river

had finally been frozen, caused it to appear as a variegated ice country—hill and dale, and devious walk, all mixed together, with human beings thronging over every bit of accessible surface.

After Frost Fair had lasted with increasing activity for four days, a killing thaw came with the Saturday, and most of the traders who possessed any prudence struck their flags and departed. Many, reluctant to go while any customers remained, held on past the right time, and towards evening there was a strange medley of tents, and merry-go-rounds, and printing presses seen floating about on detached masses of ice, beyond recovery of their dismayed owners, who had themselves barely escaped with life. A large refreshment booth, belonging to one Lawrence, a publican of Queenhithe, which had been placed opposite Brook's Wharf, was floated off by the rising tide, at an early hour on Sunday morning, with nine men in the interior, and was borne with violence back towards Blackfriars' Br.dge, catching fire as it went. Before the conflagration had gone far, the whole mass was dashed to pieces on one of the piers of the bridge, and the men with difficulty got to land. A vast number of persons suffered immersion both on this and previous days, and three men were drowned. By Monday nothing was to be seen where Frost Fair had been, but a number of ice-boards swinging lazily backwards and forwards under the impulse of the tide.

There has been no recurrence of Frost Fair on the Thames since 1814; but it is a phenomenon which, as a rule, appears to recur several times each century. The next previous occasion was in the winter of 1788–9; the next again in January 1740, when people dwelt in tents on the Thames for weeks. In 1715–16, the river was thickly frozen for several miles, and became the scene of a popular *fête* resembling that just described, with the additional feature of an ox roasted whole for the regalement of the people. The next previous instance was in January 1684. There was then a constant frost of seven weeks, producing ice eighteen inches thick. A contemporary, John Evelyn, who was an eye-witness of the scene, thus describes it:

'The frost continuing, more and more severe, the Thames, before London, was still planted with booths in formal streets, all sorts of trades and shops, furnished and full of commodities, even to a *printing press*, where the people and ladies took a fancy to have their names printed, and the day and the year set down when produced on the Thames: this humour took so universally, that it was estimated the printer gained five pounds a day, for printing a line only, at sixpence a name, besides what he got by ballads, &c. Coaches plied from Westminster to the Temple and from other stairs, to and fro, as in the streets; sheds, sliding with skates, or bull-baiting, horse and coach races, puppet-shows and interludes, cooks, tippling and other lewd places; so that it seemed to be a bacchanalian triumph or carnival on the water: while it was a severe judgment on the land, the trees not only splitting as if lightning-struck, but men and cattle perishing in divers places, and the very seas so locked up with ice, that no vessels could stir out or come in; the fowls, fish, and birds, and all our exotic plants and greens, universally perishing. Many parks of deer were destroyed; and all sorts of fuel so dear, that there were great contributions to keep the poor alive. Nor was this severe weather much less intense in most parts of Europe, even as far as Spain in the most southern tracts.

'London, by reason of the excessive coldness of the air hindering the ascent of the smoke, was so filled with the fuliginous stream of the sea-coal, that hardly could any one see across the streets; and this filling of the lungs with the gross particles exceedingly obstructed the breath, so as one could scarcely breathe. There was no water to be had from the pipes or engines; nor could the brewers and divers other tradesmen work; and every moment was full of disastrous accidents.'

King Charles II. visited the diversions on the Thames, with other personages of the royal family; and the names of the party were printed upon a quarto piece of Dutch paper, within a type border, as follows:

> CHARLES, KING.
> JAMES, DUKE.
> KATHERINE, QUEEN.
> MARY, DUCHESS.
> ANNE, PRINCESS.
> GEORGE, PRINCE.
> HANS IN KILDER.
>
> London: Printed by G. Croome, on the Ice on the River of Thames, Jan. 31, 1684.

Hollinshed describes a severe frost as occurring at the close of December 1564: 'On New Year's even,' he says, 'people went over and along the Thames on the ice from London Bridge to Westminster. Some played at the foot-ball as boldly there as if it had been on dry land. Divers of the court, being daily at Westminster, shot daily at pricks set upon the Thames; and the people, both men and women, went daily on the Thames in greater number than in any street of the city of London. On the 3d day of January it began to thaw, and on the 5th day was no ice to be seen between London Bridge and Lambeth; which sudden thaw caused great floods and high waters, that bare down bridges and houses, and drowned many people, especially in Yorkshire.'

A protracted frost necessarily deranges the lower class of employments in such a city as London, and throws many poor persons into destitution. Just as sure as this is the fact, so sure is it that a vast horde of the class who systematically avoid regular work, preferring to live by their wits, simulate the characteristic appearances of distressed labourers, and try to excite the charity of the better class of citizens. Investing themselves in aprons, clutching an old spade, and hoisting as their signal of distress a turnip on the top of a pole or rake, they will wend their way through the west-end streets, proclaiming themselves in sepulchral tones as *Frozen-out Gardeners*, or simply calling, 'Hall frozen hout!' or chanting 'We've got no work to do!' The faces of the corps are duly dolorous; but one can nevertheless observe a sharp eye kept on the doors and windows they are passing, in order that if possible they may arrest some female gaze on which to practise their spell of pity. It is alleged on good grounds that the generality of these victims of the frost are impostors, and that their daily gatherings will often amount to double a skilled workman's wages. Nor do they usually discontinue the trade till long after the return of milder airs has liquidated even real claims upon the public sympathy.

FROZEN-OUT GARDENERS.

FROST PICTURES.

When, like a sullen exile driven forth,
Southward, December drags his icy chain,
He graves fair pictures of his native North
　　On the crisp window-pane.

So some pale captive blurs, with lips unshorn,
The latticed glass, and shapes rude outlines there,
With listless finger and a look forlorn,
　　Cheating his dull despair.

The fairy fragments of some Arctic scene
I see to-night; blank wastes of polar snow,
Ice-laden boughs, and feathery pines that lean
　　Over ravines below.

Black frozen lakes, and icy peaks blown bare,
Break the white surface of the crusted pane,
And spear-like leaves, long ferns, and blossoms fair
　　Linked in silvery chain.

Draw me, I pray thee, by this slender thread;
Fancy, thou sorceress, bending vision-wrought
O'er that dim well perpetually fed
　　By the clear springs of thought!

Northward I turn, and tread those dreary strands,—
Lakes where the wild fowl breed, the swan abides;
Shores where the white fox, burrowing in the sands,
　　Harks to the droning tides.

And seas, where, drifting on a raft of ice,
The she-bear rears her young; and cliffs so high,
The dark-winged birds that emulate their rise
　　Melt through the pale blue sky.

There, all night long, with far diverging rays,
And stalking shades, the red Auroras glow;
From the keen heaven, meek suns with pallid blaze
　　Light up the Arctic snow.

Guide me, I pray, along those waves remote,
That deep unstartled from its primal rest;
Some errant sail, the fisher's lone light boat
　　Borne waif-like on its breast!

Lead me, I pray, where never shallop's keel
Brake the dull ripples throbbing to their caves;
Where the mailed glacier with his armed heel
　　Spurs the resisting waves!

Paint me, I pray, the phantom hosts that hold
Celestial tourneys when the midnight calls;
On airy steeds, with lances bright and bold,
　　Storming her ancient halls.

Yet, while I look, the magic picture fades;
Melts the bright tracery from the frosted pane;
Trees, vales, and cliffs, in sparkling snows arrayed,
　　Dissolve in silvery rain.

Without, the day's pale glories sink and swell
Over the black rise of yon wooded height;
The moon's thin crescent, like a stranded shell,
　　Left on the shores of night.

Hark how the north wind, with a hasty hand,
Rattling my casement, frames his mystic rhyme.
House thee, rude minstrel, chanting through the land,
　　Runes of the olden times.*

* By Edith May, in Hale's *Selections from Female Writers.* 1853.

INFERNAL MACHINES.

The 14th of January 1858 was made memorable in France by an attempt at regicide, most diabolical in its character, and yet the project of a man who appears to have been by no means devoid of virtue and even benevolence. It was, however, the third time that what the French call an Infernal Machine was used in the streets of Paris, for regicidal purposes, within the present century.

The first was a Bourbonist contrivance directed against the life of the First Consul Bonaparte. 'This machine,' says Sir Walter Scott, in his *Life of Napoleon*, 'consisted of a barrel of gunpowder, placed on a cart, to which it was strongly secured, and charged with grape-shot, so disposed around the barrel as to be dispersed in every direction by the explosion. The fire was to be communicated by a slow match. It was the purpose of the conspirators, undeterred by the indiscriminate slaughter which such a discharge must occasion, to place the machine in the street, through which the First Consul must go to the opera; having contrived that it should explode exactly as his carriage should pass the spot.' Never, during all his eventful life, had Napoleon a narrower escape than on this occasion, on the 14th of December 1800. St Regent applied the match, and an awful explosion took place. Several houses were damaged, twenty persons were killed on the spot, and fifty-three wounded, including St Regent himself. Napoleon's carriage, however, had just got beyond the reach of harm. This atrocity led to the execution of St Regent, Carbon, and other conspirators.

Fieschi's attempt at regicide in 1835 was more elaborate and scientific; there was something of the artillery officer in his mode of proceeding, although he was in truth nothing but a scamp. Fieschi hired a front room of a house in Paris, in a street through which royal *cortéges* were sometimes in the habit of passing; he proceeded to construct a weapon to be fired off through the open window, on some occasion when the king was expected to pass that way. He made a strong frame, supported by four legs. He obtained twenty-five musket barrels, which he ranged with their butt ends raised a little higher than the muzzles, in order that he might fire *downwards*, from a first floor window into the street. The barrels were not ranged quite parallel, but were spread out slightly like a fan; the muzzles were also not all at the same height; so that by this combined plan he obtained a sweep of fire, both in height and breadth, more extensive than he would otherwise have obtained. Every year during Louis Philippe's reign there were certain days of rejoicing in July, in commemoration of the circumstances which placed him on the throne. On the 28th, the second day of the festival in 1835, a royal *cortége* was proceeding along this particular street, the Boulevard du Temple. Fieschi adjusted his machine, heavily loaded with ball (four to each barrel), and connected the touch-holes of all his twenty-five barrels with a train of gunpowder. He had a blind at his window, to screen his operations

from view. Just as the *cortége* arrived, he raised his blind and fired, when a terrific scene was presented. Marshal Mortier, General de Verigny, the aide-de-camp of Marshal Maison, a colonel, several grenadiers of the Guard, and several by-standers, were killed, while the wounded raised the number of sufferers to nearly forty. In this, as in many similar instances, the person aimed at escaped. One ball grazed the king's arm, and another lodged in his horse's neck: but he and his sons were in other respects unhurt. Fieschi was executed; and his name obtained for some years that kind of notoriety which Madame Tussaud could give it.

We now come to the attempt of Orsini and his companions. A Birmingham manufacturer was commissioned to make six missiles according to a particular model. The missile was of oval shape, and had twenty-five nipples near one end, with percussion caps to fit them. The greatest thickness and weight of metal were at the nipple end, to ensure that it should come foremost to the ground. The inside was to be filled with detonating composition, such as fulminate of mercury; a concussion would explode the caps on the nipples, and communicate the explosion to the fulminate, which would burst the iron shell into innumerable fragments. A Frenchman residing in London bought alcohol, mercury, and nitric acid; made a detonating compound from these materials, and filled the shells with it. Then ensued a very complicated series of manœuvres to get the conspirators and the shells to Paris, without exciting the suspicion of the authorities. On the evening of the 14th of January 1858, the Emperor and Empress were to go to the opera; and Orsini and his confederates prepared for the occasion. At night, while the imperial carriage was passing, three explosions were heard. Several soldiers were wounded; the Emperor's hat was perforated; General Roquet was slightly wounded in the neck; two footmen were wounded while standing behind the Emperor's carriage; one horse was killed; the carriage was severely shattered; and the explosion extinguished most of the gas-lights near at hand. The Emperor, cool in the midst of danger, proceeded to the opera as if nothing had happened. When the police had sought out the cause of this atrocity, it was ascertained that Orsini, Pierri, Rudio, and Gomez were all on the spot; three of the shell-grenades had been thrown by hand, and two more were found on Orsini and Pierri. The fragments of the three shells had inflicted the frightful number of more than five hundred wounds—Orsini himself had been struck by one of the pieces. Rudio and Gomez were condemned to the galleys; Orsini and Pierri were executed. Most readers will remember the exciting political events that followed this affair in England and France, nearly plunging the two countries into war.

The Feast of the Ass.

Formerly, the Feast of the Ass was celebrated on this day, in commemoration of the 'Flight into Egypt.' Theatrical representations of Scripture history were originally intended to impress religious truths upon the minds of an illiterate people, at a period when books were not, and few could read. But the advantages resulting from this mode of instruction were counterbalanced by the numerous ridiculous ceremonies which they originated. Of these probably none exceeded in grossness of absurdity the Festival of the Ass, as annually performed on the 14th of January. The escape of the Holy Family into Egypt was represented by a beautiful girl holding a child at her breast, and seated on an ass, splendidly decorated with trappings of gold-embroidered cloth. After having been led in solemn procession through the streets of the city in which the celebration was held, the ass, with its burden, was taken into the principal church, and placed near the high altar, while the various religious services were performed. In place, however, of the usual responses, the people on this occasion imitated the braying of an ass; and, at the conclusion of the service, the priest, instead of the usual benediction, brayed three times, and was answered by a general *hee-hawing* from the voices of the whole congregation. A hymn, as ridiculous as the ceremony, was sung by a double choir, the people joining in the chorus, and imitating the braying of an ass. Ducange has preserved this burlesque composition, a curious medley of French and mediæval Latin, which may be translated thus :

' From the country of the East,
Came this strong and handsome beast :
This able ass, beyond compare,
Heavy loads and packs to bear.
　Now, seignior ass, a *noble* bray,
　Thy beauteous mouth at large display ;
　Abundant food our hay-lofts yield,
　And oats abundant load the field.
　　Hee-haw ! He-haw ! He-haw !

' True it is, his pace is slow,
Till he feels the quickening blow ;
Till he feel the urging goad,
On his hinder part bestowed.
　Now, seignior ass, &c.

' He was born on Shechem's hill ;
In Reuben's vales he fed his fill ;
He drank of Jordan's sacred stream,
And gambolled in Bethlehem.
　Now, seignior ass, &c.

' See that broad majestic ear !
Born he is the yoke to wear :
All his fellows he surpasses ;
He 's the very lord of asses !
　Now, seignior ass, &c.

' In leaping he excels the fawn,
The deer, the colts upon the lawn ;
Less swift the dromedaries ran,
Boasted of in Midian.
　Now, seignior ass, &c.

' Gold from Araby the blest,
Seba myrrh, of myrrh the best,
To the church this ass did bring ;
We his sturdy labours sing.
　Now, seignior ass, &c.

' While he draws the loaded wain,
Or many a pack, he don't complain.
With his jaws, a noble pair,
He doth craunch his homely fare.
　Now, seignior ass, &c.

' The bearded barley and its stem,
And thistles, yield his fill of them :
He assists to separate,
When it 's threshed, the chaff from wheat.
　Now, seignior ass, &c.

' With your belly full of grain,
Bray, most honoured ass, Amen !
Bray out loudly, bray again,
Never mind the old Amen ;
Without ceasing, bray again,
Amen ! Amen ! Amen ! Amen !
　Hee-haw ! He-haw ! He-haw ! '

The ' Festival of the Ass,' and other religious burlesques of a similar description, derive their origin from Constantinople ; being instituted by the Patriarch Theophylact, with the design of weaning the people's minds from pagan ceremonies, particularly the Bacchanalian and calendary observances, by the substitution of Christian spectacles, partaking of a similar spirit of licentiousness,—a principle of accommodation to the manners and prejudices of an ignorant people, which led to a still further adoption of rites, more or less imitated from the pagans. According to the pagan mythology, an ass, by its braying, saved Vesta from brutal violence, and, in consequence, ' the coronation of the ass ' formed a part of the ceremonial feast of the chaste goddess.

An elaborate sculpture, representing a kneeling ass, in the church of St Anthony at Padua, is said to commemorate a miracle that once took place in that city. It appears that one morning, as St Anthony was carrying the sacrament to a dying person, some profane Jews refused to kneel as the sacred vessels were borne past them. But they were soon rebuked and put to contrition and shame, by seeing a pious ass kneel devoutly in honour of the host. The Jews, converted by this miracle, caused the sculpture to be erected in the church. It takes but little to make a miracle. The following anecdote, told by the Rev John Wesley, in his *Journal*, would, in other hands, have made a very good one. ' An odd circumstance,' says Mr Wesley, ' happened at Rotherham during the morning preaching. It was well only serious persons were present. An ass walked gravely in at the gate, came up to the door of the house, lifted up his head, and stood stock still, in a posture of deep attention. Might not the dumb beast reprove many, who have far less decency, and not much more understanding ? '

A somewhat similar asinine sensibility was differently displayed in the presence of King Henry IV. of France—the ass, on this occasion, not exhibiting itself as a dumb animal. When passing through a small town, just as the King was getting tired of a long stupid speech delivered by the mayor, an ass brayed out loudly ; and Henry, with the greatest gravity and politeness of tone, said : ' Pray, gentlemen, speak one at a time, if you please.'

Mallard Day.

The 14th of January is celebrated in All Souls College, Oxford, by a great merrymaking, in commemoration of the finding of an overgrown mallard in a drain, when they were digging a foundation for the college buildings, anno 1437.

The following extract from a contemporary chronicle gives an account of the incident: 'Whenas Henrye Chichele, the late renowned archbishope of Cantorberye, had minded to founden a collidge in Oxenforde, for the hele of his soule and the soules of all those who peryshed in the warres of Fraunce, fighteing valiantlye under our most gracious Henrye the fifthe, moche was he distraughten concerning the place he myghte choose for thilke purpose. Him thinkyth some whylest how he myghte place it withouten the eastern porte of the citie, both for the pleasauntnesse of the meadowes and the clere streamys therebye runninge. Agen him thinkyth odir whylest howe he mote builden it on the northe side for the heleful ayre there coming from the fieldes. Nowe while he doubteth thereon he dremt, and behold there appereth unto him one of righte godelye personage, sayinge and adviseing as howe he myghte placen his collidge in the highe strete of the citie, nere unto the chirche of our blessed ladie the Virgine, and in witnesse that it was sowthe, and no vain and deceitful phantasie, wolled him to laye the first stane of the foundation at the corner which turneth towards the Cattys Strete, where in delvinge he myghte of a suretye finde a schwoppinge mallarde imprisoned in the sinke or sewere, wele yfattened and almost ybosten. Sure token of the thrivaunce of his future college.

'Moche doubteth he when he awoke on the nature of this vision, whethyr he mote give hede thereto or not. Then advisyth he there with monie docters and learnyd clerkys, who all seyde howe he oughte to maken trial upon it. Then comyth he to Oxenforde, and on a daye fixed, after masse seyde, proceedeth he in solemnee wyse, with spades and pickaxes for the nonce provided, to the place afore spoken of. But long they had not digged ere they herde, as it myghte seme, within the wam of the erthe, horrid strugglinges and flutteringes, and anon violent quaakinges of the distressyd mallarde. Then Chichele lyfteth up his hondes and seyth Benedicite, &c. &c. Nowe when they broughte him forth, behold the size of his bodie was as that of a bustarde or an ostridge. And moch wonder was thereat; for the lycke had not been seene in this londe, ne in onie odir.'

We obtain no particulars of the merrymaking beyond a quaint song said to have been long sung on the occasion:

'THE MERRY OLD SONG OF THE ALL SOULS' MALLARD.

'Griffin, bustard, turkey, capon,
Let other hungry mortals gape on;
And on the bones their stomach fall hard,
But let All Souls' men have their MALLARD.
　　Oh! by the blood of King Edward,*
　　Oh! by the blood of King Edward,
　　It was a wopping, wopping MALLARD.

'The Romans once admired a gander
More than they did their chief commander;

---

* The allusion to King Edward is surely an anachronism, as King Henry VI. was reigning at the time of the foundation of this college.

114

Because he saved, if some don't fool us,
The place that's called th' head of Tolus.
　　Oh! by the blood, &c.

'The poets feign Jove turned a swan,
But let them prove it if they can;
As for our proof, 'tis not at all hard,
For it was a wopping, wopping MALLARD.
　　Oh! by the blood, &c.

'Therefore let us sing and dance a galliard,
To the remembrance of the MALLARD:
And as the MALLARD dives in pool,
Let us dabble, dive, and duck in bowl.
　　Oh! by the blood of King Edward,
　　Oh! by the blood of King Edward,
　　It was a wopping, wopping MALLARD.'

MISERRIMUS.

In the north aisle of the cloister of Worcester Cathedral is a sepulchral slab, which bears only the word MISERRIMUS, expressing that a most miserable but unknown man reposes below. The most heedless visitor is arrested by this sad voice speaking, as it were, from the ground; and it is no wonder that the imaginations of poets and romancists have been awakened by it:

'"Miserrimus!" and neither name nor date,
Prayer, text, or symbol, graven upon the stone;
Nought but that word assigned to the unknown,
That solitary word—to separate
From all, and cast a cloud around the fate
Of him who lies beneath. Most wretched one!
Who chose his epitaph?—Himself alone
Could thus have dared the grave to agitate,
And claim among the dead this awful crown;
Nor doubt that he marked also for his own,
Close to these cloistral steps, a burial-place,
That every foot might fall with heavier tread,
Trampling upon his vileness. Stranger, pass
Softly!—To save the contrite Jesus bled!'

There has of course been much speculation regarding the identity of Miserrimus: even a novel has been written upon the idea, containing striking events and situations, and replete with pathos. It is alleged, however, that the actual person was no hero of strikingly unhappy story, but only a 'Rev Thomas Morris, who, at the Revolution refusing to acknowledge the king's supremacy [more probably refusing to take the oaths to the new monarch], was deprived of his preferment, and depended for the remainder of his life on the benevolence of different Jacobites.' At his death, viewing merely, we suppose, the extreme indigence to which he was reduced, and the humiliating way in which he got his living, he ordered that the only inscription on his tomb should be—MISERRIMUS! *

Such freaks are not unexampled, and we cannot be always sure that there is a real correspondence between the inscription and the fact. For instance, a Mr Francis Cherry of Shottesbrooke, who died September 23, 1713, had his grave inscribed with no other words than HIC JACET PECCATORUM MAXIMUS (Here lies the Chief of Sinners), the truth being, if we are to believe his friend Hearne, that he was an upright and amiable man, of the most unexceptionable religious practice—in Hearne's own words, 'one

---

* Britton's Cathedral Antiquities, quoting Lees's Worcestershire Miscellany.

of the most learned, modest, humble, and virtuous persons that I ever had the honour to be acquainted with.'*

The writer can speak on good authority of a similar epitaph which a dying person of unhappy memory desired to be put upon his coffin. The person referred to was an Irish ecclesiastic who many years ago was obliged, in consequence of a dismal lapse, to become as one lost to the world. Fully twenty-five years after his wretched fall, an old and broken down man, living in an obscure lodging at Newington, a suburb of Edinburgh, sent for one of the Scottish Episcopal clergy, for the benefit of his ministrations as to a dying person. Mr F—— saw much in this aged man to interest him; he seemed borne down with sorrow and penitence. It was tolerably evident that he shunned society, and lived under a feigned name and character. Mr F—— became convinced that he had been a criminal, but was not able to penetrate the mystery. The miserable man at length had to give some directions about his funeral—an evidently approaching event; and he desired that the only inscription on his coffin should be 'A CONTRITE SINNER.' He was in due time deposited without any further memorial in Warriston Cemetery, near Edinburgh.

JANUARY 15.

St Paul, the First Hermit, 342. St Isidore, priest and hermit, c. 390. St Isidore, priest and hospitaller of Alexandria, 403. St John Calybite, recluse, 450. St Maurus, abbot, 584. St Main, abbot. St Ita or Mida, virgin abbess, 569. St Bonitus, bishop of Auvergne, 710.

Born.—Dr Samuel Parr, 1747, *Harrow;* Dr John Aikin, 1747, *Knibsworth;* Talma, French tragedian, 1763, *Paris;* Thomas Crofton Croker, 1798.
Died.—Father Paul Sarpi, 1623; Sir Philip Warwick, 1683.

DR PARR,

as a literary celebrity, occupied no narrow space in the eyes of our fathers. In our own age, he has shrunk down into his actual character of only a literary eccentricity. It seems almost incredible that, after his death in 1825, there should have been a republication of his WORKS—in eight volumes octavo. Successively an assistant at Harrow, and the proprietor of an academy at Stanmore, he was at the basis a schoolmaster, although he spent the better part of his life as perpetual curate of Hatton, and even attained the dignity of a prebendal stall in St. Paul's.

It is related of Parr, that, soon after setting up at Stanmore, he found himself in need of a wife. By some kind friends, a person thought to be a suitable partner was selected for him; but the union did not prove a happy one. It was remarked that he had wanted a housekeeper, and that the lady had wanted a house. She was of a good family in Yorkshire, an only child, who had been brought up by two maiden aunts, 'in rigidity and frigidity,' and she described her

* Reliquiæ Hearnianæ. i. 294.

husband as having been 'born in a whirlwind, and bred a tyrant.' She was a clever woman and a voluble talker, and took a pleasure in exposing his foibles and peculiarities before company. At Stanmore Dr Parr assumed the full-bottomed wig, which afterwards became a distinguishing part of his full dress. The Rev. Sydney Smith has given a humorous description of this ornament of his person: 'Whoever has had the good fortune to see Dr Parr's wig, must have observed, that while it trespasses a little on the orthodox magnitude of perukes in the anterior parts, it scorns even episcopal limits behind, and swells out into boundless convexity of frizz, the μέγα θαῦμα of barbers, and the terror of the literary world.' At Stanmore he abandoned himself to smoking, which became his habit through life. He would sometimes ride in prelatical pomp through the streets on a black saddle, bearing in his hand a long cane or wand, with an ivory head like a crosier. At other times he was seen stalking through the town in a dirty striped morning gown.

In 1787 Dr Parr published, in conjunction with his friend the Rev Henry Homer, a new edition of *Bellendenus De Statu.* William Bellenden was a learned Scotchman, who was a Professor in the University of Paris, and wrote in Latin a work in three books, entitled *De Statu Principis, De Statu Reipublicæ,* and *De Statu Prisci Orbis.* The three books of this republication were dedicated respectively to Mr Burke, Lord North, and Mr Fox; and Dr Parr prefixed a Latin Preface, exhibiting in high eulogistic relief the characters of those three statesmen, the 'Tria Lumina Anglorum.' The book was published anonymously, and excited the curiosity of the literary world. Parr anticipated the fame which his preface would confer upon him. His vanity was excessive, and so obvious as frequently to expose him to ridicule. If the different passages of his letters, in which he has praised himself, were collected together, they would make a book; but the one which he wrote to Mr Homer, when he had completed the Preface to *Bellendenus,* contains an outburst of self-conceit and self-laudation, which is probably without a parallel. As such it is worth transcribing:

'Dear Sir,—What will you say, or rather, what shall I say myself, of myself? It is now ten o'clock at night, and I am smoking a quiet pipe, after a most vehement, and, I think, a most splendid effort of composition—an effort it was indeed, a mighty and a glorious effort; for the object of it is, to lift up Burke to the pinnacle where he ought to have been placed before, and to drag down Lord Chatham from that eminence to which the cowardice of his hearers, and the credulity of the public, had most weakly and most undeservedly exalted the impostor and father of impostors. Read it, dear Harry; read it, I say, aloud; read it again and again; and when your tongue has turned its edge from me to the father of Mr Pitt, when your ears tingle and ring with my sonorous periods, when your heart glows and beats with the fond and triumphant remembrance of Edmund Burke—then, dear Homer, you will forgive me, you will love me, you will congratulate me, and readily will you take upon yourself the trouble of printing what in writing has cost me much greater though not longer trouble. Old boy, I tell you that no part of the Preface is better conceived, or better

DR PARR.

written; none will be read more eagerly, or felt by those whom you wish to feel it, more severely. Old boy, old boy, it is a stinger; and now to other business,' &c. — *Correspondence*, vol. ii., p. 196.

Soon after the death of Mr Fox, Dr Parr announced his intention of publishing a life of the statesman whom he so much admired. The expectations of the public were disappointed by the publication, in 1809, of *Characters of the late Charles James Fox, selected, and in part written, by Philopatris Varvicensis*, two vols. 8vo. Of the first volume one hundred and seventy-five pages are extracted *verbatim* from public journals, periodical publications, speeches, and other sources; and of these characters the best is by Sir James Mackintosh; next, a panegyric on Mr Fox by Dr Parr himself occupies one hundred and thirty-five pages. The second volume is entirely occupied by notes upon a variety of topics which the panegyric has suggested, such as the penal code, religious liberty, and others, plentifully inlaid with quotations from the learned languages.

Dr Parr's knowledge on ecclesiastical, political, and literary subjects, was extensive, and his conversation was copious and animated. He had a great reputation in his day as a table-talker, although his utterance was thick, and his manner overbearing, and often violent. Sydney Smith, several years after Dr Parr's death, remarked, that 'he would have been a more considerable man if he had been more knocked about among his equals. He lived with country gen-

116

tlemen and clergymen, who flattered and feared him.' When he met with Dr Johnson, who was more than his equal, at Mr Langton's, as recorded in Boswell (*Life*, edited by Croker, royal 8vo, p. 659), he was upon his good behaviour, and the Doctor praised him. 'Sir, I am much obliged to you for having asked me this evening. Parr is a fair man. I do not know when I have had an occasion of such free controversy. It is remarkable how much of a man's life may pass without meeting any instance of this kind of open discussion.'

In the performance of his clerical duties Dr Parr was assiduous; he was an advocate for more than the pomp and circumstance of the established forms of public worship. His wax candles were of unusual length and thickness, his communion-plate massive, and he decorated his church, at his own expense, with windows of painted glass. He had an extraordinary fondness for church-bells, and in order to furnish his belfry up to the height of his wishes he made many appeals to the liberality of his friends and correspondents. He himself writes, 'I have been importunate, and even impudent.' In one of his letters he intimates an intention of writing a work on Campanology; but even if he had done so, he would hardly have reached the height of enthusiasm of Joannes Barbricius, who, in his book, *De Cœlo et Cœlesti Statu*, Mentz, 1618, employs four hundred and twenty-five pages to prove that the principal employment of the blessed in heaven will be the ringing of bells.

His style, as a writer of English, is exceedingly artificial. Sydney Smith, in reviewing his Spital Sermon, preached in 1800, gives a description of it which is generally applicable to all his compositions. 'The Doctor is never simple and natural for a single moment. Everything smells of the rhetorician. He never appears to forget himself, or to be hurried by his subject into obvious language. . . . . Dr Parr seems to think that eloquence consists not in an exuberance of beautiful images, not in simple and sublime conceptions, not in the feelings of the passions, but in a studious arrangement of sonorous, exotic, and sesquipedal words.' He had a very high opinion of himself as a writer of Latin epitaphs, of which he composed about thirty. At a dinner, when Lord Erskine had delighted the company with his conversation, Dr Parr, in an ecstasy, called out to him, 'My Lord, I mean to write your epitaph.' Erskine, who was a younger man, replied, 'Dr Parr, it is a temptation to commit suicide.' The epitaph on Dr Johnson, inscribed on his monument in St Paul's Cathedral, was written by Dr Parr. At the end of the fourth volume of his works, is a long correspondence respecting this epitaph, between Parr, Sir Joshua Reynolds, Malone, and other friends of the deceased Doctor. The reader 'will be amused at the burlesque importance which Parr attaches to epitaph-writing.'—*Croker*.

Dr Parr's handwriting was very bad. Sir William Jones writes to him—'To speak plainly with you, your English and Latin characters are so badly formed, that I have infinite difficulty to read your letters, and have abandoned all hopes of deciphering many of them. Your Greek is wholly illegible; it is perfect algebra.'*

TALMA.

Though Talma displayed in early boyhood a remarkable tendency to theatricals, his first attempt on a public stage, in 1783, was such as to cause his friends to discommend his pursuing the histrionic profession. It was not till a second attempt at the Théâtre Français (four years later) that he fixed the public approbation. On the retirement of Lavire, he became principal tragedian at that establishment; and no sooner was he launched in his career than his superior intellect began to work towards various reformations of the stage, particularly in the department of costume. He is said to have been the first in his own country who performed the part of Titus in a Roman toga.

Talma was an early acquaintance of the first Napoleon, then Captain Buonaparte, to whom he was first introduced in the green-room of the Théâtre Français; and he used to relate that, about this time, Buonaparte, being in great pecuniary distress, had resolved to throw himself into the Seine, when he fortunately met with an old schoolfellow, who had just received a considerable sum of money, which he shared with the future emperor. 'If that warm-hearted comrade,' said he, 'had accidentally passed down another street, the history of the next twenty years would have been written without the names of Lodi, Marengo, Austerlitz, Jena, Friedland, Moscow, Leipzig, and Waterloo.'

When his friend Buonaparte was setting out on his expedition to Egypt, the great tragedian offered, in the warmth of his friendship, to accompany him; but Napoleon would not listen to the proposal. 'Talma,' said he, 'you must not commit such an act of folly. You have a brilliant course before you; leave fighting to those who are unable to do anything better.' When Napoleon rose to be First Consul, his reception of Talma was as cordial as ever. When he in time became Emperor, the actor conceived that the intimacy would be sure to cease; but he soon received a special invitation to the Tuileries.

Talma was a man of cultivated mind, unerring taste, and amiable qualities. 'His dignity and tragic powers on the stage,' says Lady Morgan, 'are curiously but charmingly contrasted with the simplicity, playfulness, and gaiety of his most unassuming, unpretending manners in private life.' He had long been married to a lady of fortune. He lived in affluence principally at his villa in the neighbourhood of Paris, whither, twice a week, he went to perform.

Talma, when near his sixtieth year, achieved one of his greatest triumphs in Jouy's tragedy of *Sylla*. Napoleon had then (December, 1821) been dead only a few months. The actor, in order to recal the living image of his friend and patron, dressed his hair exactly after the well-remembered style of the deceased emperor, and

*The Works of Samuel Parr, LL.D., Prebendary of St Paul's, Curate of Hatton, &c., with Memoirs of his Life and Writings, and a Selection from his Correspondence, by John Johnstone, M.D. 8 vols. 8vo, 1828.

his dictator's wreath was a fac-simile of the laurel crown in gold which was placed upon Napoleon's brow at Notre Dame. The intended identity was recognised at once with great excitement. The government thought of interdicting the play; but Talma was privately directed to curl his hair in future, and adopt a new arrangement of the head.

'Talma was taken ill at Paris, where he expired without pain, 19th October 1826. His majestic features have been preserved to us by David in marble. The body was borne to the cemetery of Père la Chaise, attended by at least 100,000 mourners; and his friend, comrade, and rival, Lafont, placed upon the coffin a wreath of *immortelles*, and pronounced an affectionate funeral oration.'—Cole's *Life of Charles Kean*.

Talma was no less honoured and esteemed by Louis XVIII. than by Napoleon. In 1825 he published some reflections on his favourite art; and, June 11, 1826, he appeared for the last time on the stage in the part of Charles VI. He is said altogether to have created seventy-one characters, the most popular of which were Orestes, Œdipus, Nero, Manlius, Cæsar, Cinna, Augustus, Coriolanus, Hector, Othello, Leicester, Sylla, Regulus, Leonidas, Charles VI., and Henry VIII. He spoke English perfectly; he was the friend and guest of John Kemble, and was present in Covent Garden Theatre, when that great actor took his leave of the stage.

THE BURLESQUE ENGAGEMENT.

'—— many to the steep of Highgate hie;
Ask, ye Bœotian shades! * the reason why?
'Tis to the worship of the solemn Horn,
Grasped in the holy hand of Mystery,
In whose dread name both men and maids are sworn,
And consecrate the oath with draught and dance till morn.'   BYRON.

The poet here alludes to a curious old custom which has been the means of giving a little gentle merriment to many generations of the citizens of London, but is now fallen entirely out of notice. It was localised at Highgate, a well-known village on the north road, about five miles from the centre of the metropolis, and usually the last place of stoppage for stage coaches on their way thither. Highgate has many villas of old date clustering about it, wealthy people having been attracted to the place on account of the fine air and beautiful views which it derives from its eminent site: Charles Mathews had his private box here; and Coleridge lived with Mr Gillman in one of the Highgate terraces. The village, however, was most remarkable about 1820, and at earlier dates, for the extraordinary number of its inns and taverns, haunts of recreation-seeking Londoners, and partly deriving support from the numerous travellers who paused there on their way to town.

When Mr William Hone was publishing his *Every Day Book* in 1826, he found there were no fewer than nineteen licensed houses of entertainment in this airy hamlet. The house of greatest

* Byron wrote this verse in Thebes, the capital of Bœotia.

dignity and largest accommodation was the *Gate House*, so called from the original building having been connected with a gate which here closed the road, and from which the name of the village is understood to have been derived. Another hostelry of old standing was 'The Bell.' There were also 'The Green Dragon,' 'The Bull,' 'The Angel,' 'The Crown,' 'The Flask,' &c. At every one of these public-houses there was kept a pair of horns, either ram's. bull's, or stag's, mounted on a stick, to serve in a burlesque ceremonial which time out of mind had been kept up at the taverns of Highgate, commonly called 'Swearing on the Horns.' It is believed that this custom took its rise at 'The Gatehouse,' and gradually spread to the other houses—perhaps was even to some extent a cause of other houses being set up, for it came in time to be an attraction for jovial parties from London. In some cases there was also a pair of mounted horns over the door of the house, as designed to give the chance passengers the assurance that the merry ceremonial was there practised.

And the ceremonial—in what did it consist? Simply in this, that when any person passed through Highgate for the first time on his way to London, he, being brought before the horns at one of the taverns, had a mock oath administered to him, to the effect that he would never drink small beer when he could get strong, unless he liked it better; that he would never, except on similar grounds of choice, eat brown bread when he could get white, or water-gruel when he could command turtle-soup; that he would never make love to the maid when he might to the mistress, unless he preferred the maid; and so on with a number of things, regarding which the preferableness is equally obvious. Such at least was the bare substance of the affair; but of course there was room for a luxuriance of comicality, according to the wit of the imposer of the oath, and the simplicity of the oath-taker; and, as might be expected, the ceremony was not a dry one. Scarcely ever did a stage-coach stop at a Highgate tavern in those days, without a few of the passengers being initiated amidst the laughter

SWEARING ON THE HORNS.

of the rest, the landlord usually acting as high-priest on the occasion, while a waiter or an ostler would perform the duty of clerk, and sing out 'Amen' at all the proper places.

Our artist has endeavoured to represent the ceremonial in the case of a simple countryman, according to the best traditionary lights that can now be had upon the subject.

It is acknowledged that there were great differences in the ceremonial at different houses, some landlords having much greater command of wit than others. One who possessed the qualifications more eminently than the rest, would give an address warning the neophyte to avoid the allurements of the metropolis, in terms which provoked shouts of laughter from the bystanders. He would tell him—if, on his next coming to Highgate, he should see three pigs lying in a ditch, it was his privilege to kick the middle one out and take her place; if he wanted a bottle of wine and had no money, he might drink one on credit if anybody felt inclined to trust him. He would also be told, at the end of the oath, to kiss the horns, *or* any pretty girl in the company who would allow him. Another part of the jocularity was to tell him to take notice of the first word of the oath—he must be sure to mind *that*. If he forgot *that*, he would be liable to have to take the oath over again. *That*, in short, was a word to him of infinite importance, a forgetting of which could not fail to be attended with troublesome consequences. The privileges of Highgate had always to be paid for in some liquor for the company, according to the means and inclination of the person sworn.

In those old unthinking days of merry England, societies and corporations and groups of work-people, who were admitting a new member or associate, would come out in a body to Highgate to have him duly sworn upon the Horns and enjoy an afternoon's merrymaking at his expense. If we can put faith in Byron, parties of young people of both sexes, under (it is to be hoped) proper superintendence, would dance away the night after an initiation at the Horns. Once a joke of that sort was established, it was wonderful what a great deal could be made of it, and how ill it was to wear out. For thirty years past, however, the Horns have disappeared from Highgate, and the taverns of that tidy village have now as grave an aspect as their neighbours.

With regard to the origin of the custom in connexion with Highgate, it seems impossible to obtain any light. Most probably the custom was long ago not an uncommon one at favourite inns, and only survived at Highgate when it had gone out elsewhere. The only historical fact which has been preserved regarding it, is that a song embodying the burlesque oath was introduced in a pantomime at the Haymarket Theatre in 1742.

BREAD, ITS MAKING AND SALE IN THE MIDDLE AGES.

In the chronicles and records of the Middle Ages that have survived to us, we find many items of curious information relative to the supply in those days of what was, from the absence of the potato and other articles of food, even more than now, the staff of human life. We cull a few of these particulars for the information—and, we trust, also the amusement—of those among our readers who care to know something about the usages of the olden time.

The bread that was in common use in England from five to six centuries ago, was of various degrees of fineness (or 'bolting,'* as it was called) and colour. The very finest and the whitest probably that was known, was *simnel-bread*, which (in the thirteenth and fourteenth centuries at least) was as commonly known under the name of *pain-demayn* (afterwards corrupted into *payman*); a word which has given considerable trouble

* From the bolter, bolting-sieve, or bolting clot (cloth), as it was indifferently named.

to Tyrrwhitt and other commentators upon Chaucer, but which means no more than 'bread of our Lord,' from the figure of our Saviour, or the Virgin Mary, impressed upon each round flat loaf, as is still the usage in Belgium with respect to certain rich cakes much admired there. This bread of course was only consumed by persons of the highest rank, and in the most affluent circumstances.

The next in quality to this was *wastel bread*, in common use among the more luxurious and more wealthy of the middle classes, and the name of which it seems not improbable is closely allied to the old French *gasteau*, 'a cake.' Nearly resembling this in price and quality, though at times somewhat cheaper, was *light bread*, or *puffe*, also known as 'French bread,' or 'cocket,' though why it was called by the latter appellation is matter of doubt. Bread of a still inferior quality was also sometimes known as 'cocket;' and it seems far from improbable that it was so called from the word *cocket*, as meaning a seal, it being a strict regulation in London and elsewhere that each loaf (at all events each loaf below a certain quality) should bear the impress of its baker's seal. The halfpenny loaf of simnel was at times of the same weight as the farthing loaf of wastel or puff; the relative proportions, however, varied considerably at different periods.

The next class of bread was *tourte*, made of unbolted meal, and the name of which has much puzzled the learned. It seems not improbable, however, that this kind of bread was originally so called from the loaves having a twisted form (*torti*), to distinguish them from those of a finer quality. Tourte was in common use with the humbler classes and the inmates of monasteries. *Trete bread*, or *bread of trete*, was again an inferior bread to *tourte*, being made of wheat meal once bolted, or from which the fine flour at one sifting had been removed. This was also known as '*bis*,' or *brown bread*, and probably owed its name to the fact of bran being so largely its constituent, that substance being still known in the North of England as '*trete*.' An inferior bread to this seems to have passed under the name of *all-sorts*, or some similar appellation, being also known as *black bread*. It was made of various kinds of grain inferior to wheat.

In the reign of Edward III. we find mention made of a light, or French, bread, made in London (and resembling simnel probably), and known by the name of '*wygge*,' an appellation still given in Scotland to a kind of small cake. Another kind of white bread is also spoken of in the reigns of Edward II. and III., under the still well-known name of '*bunne*' (or *boun*). *Horse-bread* also was extensively prepared by the bakers, in the form of loaves duly sealed, beans and peas being the principal ingredients employed.

The profits of the bakers from very remote times were strictly a matter for legislatorial enactment. A general regulation was in force, from the days of King John until the reign of Edward I., if not later, throughout England (the City of London perhaps excepted), that the profit of the baker on each quarter of wheat was to be, for his own labour, three pence and such bran as might be sifted from the meal; and that he was to add to the prime cost of the wheat, for fuel and wear of the oven, the price of two loaves; for the services of three men, he was to add to the price of the bread three halfpence; and for two boys one farthing; for the expenses attending the seal, one halfpenny; for yeast, one halfpenny; for candle, one halfpenny; for wood, threepence; and for wear and tear of the bolter, or bolting-sieve, one halfpenny.

In London, only farthing loaves and halfpenny loaves were allowed to be made, and it was a serious offence, attended by forfeiture and punishment, for a baker to be found selling loaves of any other size. Loaves of this description seem to have been sometimes smuggled into market beneath a towel, or beneath the folds of the garments, under the arms. For the better identification of the latter, in case of necessity, each loaf was sealed with the baker's seal; and this from time to time, and at the Wardmotes more especially, was shewn to the alderman of the Ward, who exacted a fee for registering it in his book. In London, from time to time, at least once in the month, each baker's bread (or, at all events, some sample loaves) was taken from the oven by the officers of the assayers, who seem to have had the appellation of 'hutch-reves,' and duly examined as to quality and weight; it being enacted, however, in favour of the baker, that the scrutiny should always be made while the bread was hot; the 'assay,' or sample loaves, which were given out to the bakers periodically for their guidance as to weight and quality, being delivered to them while hot.

In the City of London, if the baker sold his bread himself by retail, he was particularly forbidden —for reasons apparently not easy now to be appreciated or ascertained—to sell it in his house, or before his house, or before the oven where it was baked; in fact, he was only to sell it in the 'King's Market,' and such market as was assigned to him, and not elsewhere; by which term apparently, in the fourteenth century, the markets of Eastcheap, Cornhill, and Westcheap were meant. The *foreign* baker, however, or non-freeman, was allowed to store his bread for a single night. In the market, the loaves were exposed for sale in *panyers* (bread-baskets), or in boxes or chests, in those days known as 'hutches;' the latter being more especially employed in the sale of tourte bread. The principal days for the sale of bread in the London markets seem to have been Tuesday and Saturday, though sale there on Sundays is also mentioned: in the days of Henry III. and Edward I., the king's toll on each basket of bread was one halfpenny on week days, and three halfpence on Sundays. In other instances, we find bread delivered in London from house to house by *regratresses*, also called '*hucksters*,' or female retailers. These dealers, on purchasing their bread from the bakers, were privileged by law to receive thirteen articles for twelve, such being apparently the limit of their legitimate profits; though it seems to have been the usage in London, at least at one period, for the baker to give to each regratress who dealt with him sixpence every Monday morning, by way of *estrene*, or hansel-money, and threepence

as *curtesy* or good-bye money, on delivery upon Friday of the last batch of the week; a practice, however, which was forbidden by the authorities —the bakers being also ordered not to give credit to these regratresses when known to be in debt to others, and not to take bread back from them when once it had become cold. No regratress was allowed to cross London Bridge, or to go out of the City, to buy bread for the purpose of retailing it. The baker of tourte bread was also forbidden to sell to a regratress in his shop, but only from his hutch, in the King's market.

Though considerable favour was shewn to such bakers as were resident within the walls of the City, and though at times the introduction of *foreign* bread, as being 'adulterine' or spurious, was strictly prohibited; still, in general, a large proportion of the London supply was brought from a distance, Stratford le Bow, Stepney (Stevenhethe), Bromley (Bremble) in Essex, Paddington, and Saint Albans being among the places which we find mentioned; the carriage being by horse or in carts, the loaves being packed in the latter (at least sometimes, and as to the coarser kinds) without baskets. Bread seems to have been brought from the villages of Buckinghamshire and Oxfordshire, in barges known as '*scuts*,' or '*scows*.' We read that, occasionally, the country bakers contrived to undersell their London brethren by making the public gainers of two ounces in the penny-worth of bread. Against bread made in South-wark there appears to have been an extraordinary degree of prejudice, the reason on one occasion assigned being, 'because the bakers of Suthewerk are not amenable to the justice of the City.' A common piece of fraud with knavish bakers seems to have been the making of bread of pure quality on the outside and coarse within; a practice which was forbidden by enactment, it being equally forbidden to make loaves of bran, or purposely mixed with bran.

The baker of white bread was on no account to make tourte or brown bread, and similar restrictions were put upon the '*tourter*,' or baker of brown bread, as to the making of white. Tourte bread being made of unbolted meal, we find the tourte bakers of the City of London forbidden (in the reign of Richard II.) to have a bolting-sieve in their possession, as also to sell flour to a cook—the latter enactment being evidently intended to insure the comparative fineness of their bread, by preventing them from subtracting the flour from the meal. Bakers within the City were forbidden to heat their ovens with fern, stubble, or straw; and in the reign of King John (A.D. 1212), in consequence of the recent devastation of the City by fire, they were not allowed to bake at night. They were also at times reminded by the civic authorities that it was their duty to instruct their servants so many times in the year, how to bolt the flour and knead their dough; and for the latter purpose they were not to use fountain-water, as being probably too hard.

Hostelers and herbergeours (keepers of inns and lodging-houses) were not allowed to bake bread. Private individuals who had no ovens of their own, were in the habit of sending their flour to be kneaded by their own servants at the 'moulding-boards' belonging to the bakers, the loaves being then baked in the baker's oven. Persons of respectability also had the right to enter bake-houses to see the bread made. Bakers were allowed, in London, to keep swine in their houses at times when other persons were forbidden, with a view probably to the more speedy consumption of the refuse bran, and as an inducement to the baker not to make his bread of too coarse a quality. The swine, however, were to be kept out of the public streets and lanes. No baker was allowed in the city to withdraw the servant or journeyman of another, nor was he to admit such a person into his service without a licence from the master whom he had previously served.

JANUARY 16.

St Marcellus, pope, martyr, 310. St Macarius, the elder, of Egyyt, 390. St Honoratus, archbishop of Arles, 429. St Fursey, son of Fintan, king of part of Ireland, 650. Five Friars, minors, martyrs. St Henry, hermit, 1127.

Born.—Richard Savage, poet, 1697.
Died.—Edmund Spenser, poet, 1599 ; Edward Gibbon, historian, 1794 ; Sir John Moore, 1809 ; Edmund Lodge, herald, 1839.

EDWARD GIBBON.

The confessions or statements of an author regarding the composition of a great work are

EDWARD GIBBON.

generally interesting. Gibbon gives an account both of the formation of the design of writing his

Decline and Fall of the Roman Empire, and of the circumstances under which that magnificent book was finished. At about twenty-seven years of age he inspected the ruins of Rome under the care of a Scotchman 'of experience and taste,' named Byers ; and 'it was at Rome,' says he, 'on the 15th of October 1764, as I sat musing amidst the ruins of the Capitol, while the bare-footed friars were singing vespers in the Temple of Jupiter, that the idea of writing the decline and fall of the city first started to my mind.' It is to be observed that he thought only of the history of the city, not of the empire, to which his ideas finally expanded.

Gibbon commenced the writing of his history after settling in a house in London about 1772. The latter moiety of the work was composed in an elegant mansion at Lausanne, in Switzerland,

RESIDENCE OF GIBBON AT LAUSANNE.

to which he retreated on being disappointed in a political career in England. The whole work occupied about fifteen years. 'It was,' says he— and the passage can never be read without the deepest interest—'it was on the day, or rather night, of the 27th of June 1787, between the hours of eleven and twelve, that I wrote the last lines of the last page, in a summer-house in my garden. After laying down my pen, I took several turns in a *berceau*, or covered walk of acacias, which commands a prospect of the country, the lake, and the mountains. The air was temperate, the sky was serene, the silver orb of the moon was reflected from the waters, and all nature was silent. I will not dissemble the first emotions of joy on recovering my freedom, and, perhaps, the establishment of my fame. But my pride was soon humbled, and a sober melancholy was spread over my mind, by the idea that I had taken an everlasting leave of an old and agreeable companion, and that whatsoever might be the future fate of my History, the

121

life of the historian must be short and precarious.'

The historian was then fifty.

Gibbon, as is well known, spent his life in celibacy, and was thus the better fitted for undertaking and carrying through a great literary work. Partly in consequence of the sedentary life to which his task confined him, he became extremely obese. There is a story representing him as falling in love, while at Lausanne, with a young lady of great beauty and merit, and which goes on to describe him as one day throwing himself at her feet to declare his passion, when it was found impossible for him to rise again till he was extricated by the laughing damsel from his ludicrous position. George Coleman the Younger has painted the scene in verse of by no means great merit.

'—— the fair pursued
Her prattle, which on literature flowed;
Now changed her author, now her attitude,
And much more symmetry than learning showed.
Eudoxus watched her features, while they glowed,
Till passion burst his puffy bosom's bound;
And rescuing his cushion from its load,
Flounced on his knees, appearing like a round
Large fillet of hot veal just tumbled on the ground.

'Could such a lover be with scorn repulsed?
Oh no! disdain befitted not the case;
And Agnes at the sight was so convulsed
That tears of laughter trickled down her face.
Eudoxus felt his folly and disgrace,
Looked sheepish, nettled, or wished himself away;
And thrice he tried to quit his kneeling place;
But fat and corpulency seemed to say,
Here's a petitioner that must for ever pray!'

The falling in love with a young lady at Lausanne is undoubtedly true; but it happens that the incident took place in Gibbon's youth, when, so far from being fat or unwieldy, he was extremely slender—for, be it observed, the illustrious historian was in reality a small-boned man, and of more than usually slight figure in his young days. He was about twenty years of age, and was dwelling in Switzerland with a Protestant pastor by his father's orders, that he might recover himself (as he ultimately did) from a tendency to Romanism which had beset him at College, when Mademoiselle Susan Curchod, the daughter of the pastor of Crassy in Burgundy, came on a visit to some relations in Lausanne. The father of the young lady, in the solitude of his village situation, had bestowed upon her a liberal education. 'She surpassed,' says Gibbon, 'his hopes, by her proficiency in the sciences and languages; and in her short visits to some relations at Lausanne, the wit, the beauty, and erudition of Mademoiselle Curchod were the theme of universal applause. The report of such a prodigy awakened my curiosity; I saw and loved. I found her learned without pedantry, lively in conversation, pure in sentiment, and elegant in manners; and the first sudden emotion was fortified by the habits and knowledge of a more familiar acquaintance. She permitted me to make two or three visits at her father's house. I passed some happy days there in the mountains of Burgundy, and her parents honourably encouraged the connection. In a calm retirement,

the vanity of youth no longer fluttered in her bosom; she listened to the voice of truth and passion, and I might presume to hope that I had made some impression on a virtuous heart. At Crassy and Lausanne, I indulged my dream of felicity; but, on my return to England, I soon found that my father would not hear of this strange alliance, and that without his consent I was myself destitute and helpless. After a painful struggle I yielded to my fate: I sighed as a lover, I obeyed as a son. My wound was insensibly healed by time, absence, and the habits of a new life. My cure was accelerated by a faithful report of the tranquillity and cheerfulness of the lady herself, and my love subsided into friendship and esteem.'

The subsequent fate of Susan Curchod is worthy of being added. 'The minister of Crassy soon after died; his stipend died with him: his daughter retired to Geneva, where, by teaching young ladies, she earned a hard subsistence for herself and her mother; but in her lowest distress she maintained a spotless reputation and a dignified behaviour. A rich banker of Paris, a citizen of Geneva, had the good fortune and good sense to discover and possess this inestimable treasure; and in the capital of taste and luxury, she resisted the temptation of wealth, as she had sustained the hardships of indigence. The genius of her husband has exalted him to the most conspicuous situation in Europe. In every change of prosperity and disgrace, he has reclined on the bosom of a faithful friend; and Mademoiselle Curchod is now the wife of M. Necker, the Minister, and perhaps the Legislator, of the French monarchy.'

Gibbon wrote when the husband of his old love was trying to redeem France from destruction by financial reforms. Not long after, he and his family were obliged to fly from France, after which they spent several years in Switzerland. They were the parents of Madame de Stael Holstein.

SIR JOHN MOORE.

The battle of Corunna, January 16, 1809, was heard of with profound feeling by the British public. An army had failed in its mission: deceived by the Spanish junta and British minister (Mr Frere), it had made an advance on Madrid, and was forced to commence a retreat in the depth of winter. But the commander, Sir John Moore, more than redeemed himself from any censure to which he was liable, by the skill and patience with which he conducted the troops on their withdrawal to the coast. Our army was in great wretchedness, but the pursuing French were worse; and when the gallant Moore stood at bay at Corunna, he gave the pursuers a thorough repulse, though at the expense of his own life.

The handsome and regular features of Moore bear a melancholy expression, in harmony with his fate. He was in reality an admirable soldier. He had from boyhood devoted himself to his profession with extreme ardour, and his whole career was one in which duty was never lost sight of. He perished at the too early age of forty-seven, survived by his mother, at the mention of whose name, on his death-bed, he manifested the only symptom of emotion which escaped him in that trying hour.

While a boy of eleven years old, Moore had a great advantage, for his education in matters

MONUMENT OF SIR JOHN MOORE, AT CORUNNA.

of the world, by accompanying his father, Dr Moore, on a tour of Europe, in company with the minor Duke of Hamilton, to whom Dr Moore acted as governor or preceptor. The young soldier, constantly conversing with his highly enlightened parent, and introduced to many scenes calculated to awake curiosity, became a man in thoughts and manners while still a mere boy. At thirteen he danced, fenced, and rode with uncommon address. His character was a fine compound of intelligence, gentleness, and courage.

The connection with the Duke of Hamilton had very nearly cost Moore his life. The Duke, though only sixteen, was allowed to wear a sword. One day, 'in an idle humour, he drew it, and began to amuse himself by fencing at young Moore, and laughed as he forced him to skip from side to side to shun false thrusts. The Duke continued this sport till Moore unluckily started in the line of the sword, and received it in his flank.' The elder Moore was speedily on the spot, and found his son wounded on the outside of the ribs. The incident led to the formation of a lasting friendship between the penitent young noble and his almost victim.—*Life of Sir John Moore, by his brother, James Carrick Moore.*

THE BOTTLE HOAX.

On the 16th of January 1749, there took place in London a bubble or hoax, which has somehow become unusually well impressed upon the public mind. 'A person advertised that he would, this evening, at the Haymarket Theatre, play on a common walking cane the music of every instrument now used, to surprising perfection; that he would, on the stage, get into a tavern quart bottle, without equivocation, and while there, sing several songs, and suffer any spectator to handle the bottle; that if any spectator should come masked, he would, if requested, declare who they were; and that in a private room he would produce the representation of any person dead, with which the person requesting it should converse some minutes, as if alive.' The prices proposed for this show were—gallery, 2s.; pit, 3s.; boxes, 5s.; stage, 7s. 6d.

At the proper time, the house was crowded with curious people, many of them of the highest rank, including no less eminent a person than the Culloden Duke of Cumberland. They sat for a little while with tolerable patience, though uncheered with music; but by and by, the performer not appearing, signs of irritation were evinced. In answer to a sounding with sticks and catcalls, a person belonging to the theatre came forward and explained that, in the event of a failure of performance, the money should be returned. A wag then cried out, that, if the ladies and gentlemen would give double prices, the conjurer would go into a pint bottle, which proved too much for the philosophy of the audience. A young gentleman threw a lighted candle upon the stage, and a general charge upon that part of the house followed. According to a private letter, to which we have had access— (it was written by a Scotch Jacobite lady)— 'Cumberland was the first that flew in a rage, and called to pull down the house. . . . . He drew his sword, and was in such a rage, that somebody slipped in behind him and pulled the sword out of his hand, which was as much as to say, "Fools should not have chopping sticks." This sword of his has never been heard tell of, nor the person who took it. Thirty guineas of reward are offered for it. Monster of Nature, I am sure I wish he may never get it!

'The greater part of the audience made their way out of the theatre; some losing a cloak, others a hat, others a wig, and others, hat, wig, and swords also. One party, however, stayed in the house, in order to demolish the inside; when, the mob breaking in, they tore up the benches, broke to pieces the scenes, pulled down the boxes, in short dismantled the theatre entirely, carrying away the particulars above-mentioned into the street, where they made a mighty bonfire; the curtain being hoisted in the middle of it by way of flag.'

There is a want of explanation as to the intentions of this conjurer. The proprietor of the theatre afterwards stated that, in apprehension of failure, he had reserved all the money taken, in order to give it back, and he would have returned it to the audience if they would have stayed their hands from destroying his house. It therefore would appear that either money was not the object aimed at, or, if aimed at, was not attained, by the conjurer. Most probably he only meant to try an experiment on the credulity of the public.

The bottle hoax proved an excellent subject for the wits, particularly those of the Jacobite party. The following advertisement appeared in the paper called *Old England :*

'Found, entangled in a slit of a lady's demolished smock-petticoat, a gilt-handled sword of martial temper and length, not much the worse of wearing, with the Spey curiously engraven on one side, and the Scheld on the other ; supposed to be taken from the fat sides of a certain great general in his hasty retreat from the battle of Bottle-noddles in the Haymarket. Whoever has lost it may inquire for it at the sign of the Bird and Singing Lane in Potters' Row.' *

JANUARY 17.

St Anthony, patriarch of monks, 356. SS Speusippus, Eleusippus, Meleusippus, martyrs. St Nennius, abbot, 6th century. St Sulpicius the Pious, archbishop, 591. St Sulpicius the second, archbishop, 644. St Milgithe, virgin, 7th century.

ST ANTHONY.

Antonius, reputed as amongst the earliest of anchorets, and commonly called the Patriarch of Monks, was a native of Egypt, born about the year 251. After leading an ascetic life for some time in his native village, he withdrew from human society and took up his abode in a cave. His abstinence, his self-inflicted punishments, the temptations of the evil one, the assaults of dæmons, and the efficacy of his prayers, are all narrated by St Athanasius. His manner of life was imitated by a great number of persons, who occasionally resorted to him for advice and instruction. Antonius seems indeed to have been the founder of the solitary mode of living, which soon extended from Egypt into other countries. During the persecution under Maximinus, about the year 310, some of the solitaries were seized in the wilderness, and suffered martyrdom at Alexandria, whither Antonius accompanied them, but was not subjected to punishment. After his return, he retired farther into the desert, but went on one occasion to Alexandria in order to preach against the Arians.

The two monastic orders of St Anthony originated long after the time of the saint,—one in Dauphiné, in the eleventh century ; and the other, a military order, in Hainault, in the fourteenth century. In Dauphiné, the people were cured of the erysipelas, by the aid, as they thought, of St Anthony ; and the disease was afterwards called St Anthony's Fire.

It is scarcely necessary to remark that St Anthony is one of the most notable of all the saints in the Romish calendar. One cannot travel anywhere in Europe at the present day, and particularly in Italy, without finding, in churches and monasteries, and the habits and familiar ideas of the people, abundant memorials of this early Egyptian anchorite. Even in Scotland, at Leith, a street reveals by its name where a monastery of St Anthony once stood ; while,

* Gentleman's and Scots Magazines, 1749. Bishop Forbes's MSS.

124

on the hill of Arthur's Seat, overhanging Edinburgh, we still see a fragment of a small church that had been dedicated to him, and a fountain called St Anton's Well.

The Temptations of St Anthony have, through St Athanasius's memoir, become one of the most familiar of European ideas. Scores of artists, from Salvator Rosa downwards, have exerted their talents in depicting these mystic occurrences. Satan, we are informed, first tried, by bemudding his thoughts, to divert him from the design of becoming a monk. Then he appeared to him in the form successively of a handsome woman and a black boy, but without in the least disturbing him. Angry at the defeat, Satan and a multitude of attendant fiends fell upon him during the night, and he was found in his cell in the morning lying to all appearance dead. On another occasion, they expressed their rage by making such a dreadful noise that the walls of his cell shook. 'They transformed themselves into shapes of all sorts of beasts, lions, bears, leopards, bulls, serpents, asps, scorpions, and wolves ; every one of which moved and acted agreeably to the creatures which they represented : the lion roaring and seeming to make towards him ; the bull to butt ; the serpent to creep ; and the wolf to run at him, and so, in short, all the rest ; so that Anthony was tortured and mangled by them so grievously that his bodily pain was greater than before.' But, as it were laughingly, he taunted them, and the devils gnashed their teeth. This continued till the roof of his cell opened, a beam of light shot down, the devils became speechless, Anthony's pain ceased, and the roof closed again.

Bishop Latimer relates a 'pretty story' of St Anthony, 'who, being in the wilderness, had there a very hard and strait life, insomuch that none at that time did the like ; to whom came a voice from heaven, saying, "Anthony, thou art not so perfect as is a cobbler that dwelleth at Alexandria." Anthony, hearing this, rose up forthwith and took his staff and went till he came to Alexandria, where he found the cobbler. The cobbler was astonished to see so reverend a father come to his house ; when Anthony said unto him, "Come and tell me thy whole conversation, and how thou spendest thy time." "Sir," said the cobbler, "as for me, good works have I none, for my life is but simple and slender ; I am but a poor cobbler. In the morning when I rise, I pray for the whole city wherein I dwell, especially for all such neighbours and poor friends as I have : after I set me at my labour, where I spend the whole day in getting my living ; and I keep me from all falsehood, for I hate nothing so much as I do deceitfulness ; wherefore, when I make to any man a promise, I keep to it, and perform it truly. And thus I spend my time poorly with my wife and children, whom I teach and instruct, as far as my wit will serve me, to fear and dread God. And this is the sum of my simple life." In this story, you see how God loveth those who follow their vocation and live uprightly without any falsehood in their dealing. Anthony was a great holy man ; yet this cobbler was as much esteemed before God as he.'

Born.—B. de Montfaucon, antiquary, 1655 ; Archibald Bower, historical writer, 1686 ; George Lord Lyttelton, historian and poet, 1709 ; Victor Alfieri, poet, 1749 ; J. C. W. G. Mozart, musician, 1756.

Died.—John Ray, naturalist, 1705 ; Bishop Horne, 1792.

MONTFAUCON.

A model of well-spent literary life was that of Bernard de Montfaucon. Overlooking many minor works, it is enough to regard his great ones: *Antiquity explained by Figures*, in fifteen folios, containing twelve hundred plates (descriptive of all that has been preserved to us of ancient art); and the *Monuments of the French Monarchy*, in five volumes. 'He died at the Abbey of St Germain des Prés, in 1741, at the age of eighty-seven, having preserved his faculties so entire, that nearly to the termination of his long career he employed eight hours a day in study. A very regular and abstemious life had so fortified his constitution that, during fifty years, he never was indisposed; nor does it appear that his severe literary labours had any tendency to abridge his days.'

Several other literary Nestors could be cited to prove that the life of an author is not necessarily unhealthful or short. It is only when literary labour is carried to an extreme transcending natural power, or complicated with harassing cares and dissipation, that it proves destructive. When we see a man of letters sink at an early age, supposing there has been no original weakness of constitution, we may be sure that there has been some of these causes at work. When, as often happens, a laborious writer like the late Mr. Britton or Mr. John Nichols goes on, with the pen in his hand every day, till he has passed eighty, then we may be equally sure there has been prudence and temperance. But the case is general. Health and longevity are connected to a certain extent with habit. And there is some sense at bottom in what a quaint friend of ours often half jocularly declares; namely, that it would, as a rule, do invalids some good, if they were not so much sympathised with as they are, if they were allowed to know that they would be better (because more useful) members of society if they could contrive to avoid bad health; which most persons can to a certain extent do by a decent degree of self-denial, care, and due activity.

'Deep-thinking philosophers have at all times been distinguished by their great age, especially when their philosophy was occupied in the study of Nature, and afforded them the divine pleasure of discovering new and important truths. . . . The most ancient instances are to be found among the Stoics and the Pythagoreans, according to whose ideas, subduing the passions and sensibility, with the observation of strict regimen, were the most essential duties of a philosopher. We have already considered the example of a Plato and an Isocrates. Apollonius of Tyanæa, an accomplished man, endowed with extraordinary powers both of body and mind, who, by the Christians, was considered as a magician, and by the Greeks and Romans as a messenger of the gods, in his regimen a follower of Pythagoras, and a friend to travelling, was above 100 years of age. Xenophilus, a Pythagorean also, lived 106 years. The philosopher Demonax, a man of the most severe manners and uncommon stoical apathy, lived likewise 100 years.

'Even in modern times philosophers seem to have obtained this pre-eminence, and the deepest thinkers appear in that respect to have enjoyed, in a higher degree, the fruits of their mental tranquillity. Newton, who found all his happiness and pleasure in the higher spheres, attained to the age of eighty-four. Euler, a man of incredible industry, whose works on the most abstruse subjects amount to above three hundred, approached near to the same age: and Kant, the first philosopher now alive, still shews that philosophy not only can preserve life, but that it is the most faithful companion of the greatest age, and an inexhaustible source of happiness to one's self and others.'—*Hufeland's Art of Preserving Life.*

THE DISCONTINUED 'SERVICES.'

It is a curious proof of that tendency to *continuity* which marks all public institutions in England, that the services appointed for national thanksgiving on account of the Gunpowder Plot, for national humiliation regarding the execution of Charles I., and for thanksgiving with respect to the Restoration of Charles II., should have maintained their ground as holidays till after the middle of the nineteenth century. National good sense had long ceased to believe that the Deity had inspired James I. with 'a divine spirit to interpret some dark phrases of a letter,' in order to save the kingdom from the 'utter ruin' threatened by Guy Fawkes and his associates. National good feeling had equally ceased to justify the keeping up of the remembrance of the act of a set of infuriated men, to the offence of a large class of our fellow-Christians. We had most of us become very doubtful that the blood of Charles I. was 'innocent blood,' or that he was strictly a 'martyred sovereign,' though few would now-a-days be disposed to see him punished exactly as he was for his political shortcomings and errors. Still more doubt had fallen on the blessing supposed to be involved in the 'miraculous providence' by which Charles II. was restored to his kingdom. Indeed, to say the very least, the feeling, more or less partial from the first, under which the services on these holidays had been appointed, had for generations been dead in the national heart, and their being still maintained was a pure solecism and a farce.

It was under a sense of this being the case that, at the convocation of 1857, Dr Milman, Dean of St Paul's, expressed a doubt whether we ought to command the English nation to employ in a systematic way opprobrious epithets towards Roman Catholics, and to apply divine epithets to the two Charleses. He was supported by Dr Martin, Chancellor of the diocese of Exeter. Enough transpired to shew that Convocation did not attach much value to the retention of the services. In 1858, Earl Stanhope brought the matter formally before the House of Lords. He detailed the circumstances under which the services had originated; and then moved an address to the Crown, praying that the Queen would, by royal consent, abolish the services, as being derogatory to the present age. He pointed out that, although a nest of scoundrels planned a wicked thing early in the seventeenth century, it does not follow that the Queen should command her subjects to use offensive language towards Roman Catholics in the middle of the nineteenth. He also urged that we, in the present day, have a right to think as we please about the alleged divine perfections of the sovereigns of the Stuart family. From first to last there have been differences of opinion as to the propriety of these services; many clergymen positively refused to read them; and the Dean and Chapter of Canterbury Cathedral omitted them without waiting for royal authority. I was striking to observe how general was the support which Earl Stanhope's views obtained in the House of Lords. The Archbishop of Canterbury, the Bishops of London and Oxford, the Earl of Derby, besides those who generally ranked among liberal peers, supported the address, which was forthwith carried. A similar address was passed by the House of Commons. The Queen returned answers which plainly shewed what the advisers of the Crown thought on the matter. Accordingly, on the 17th of January 1859, a royal warrant was issued, abolishing the special services for the three days named. It was immediately seen, however, that if the Acts of Parliament still remained in the Statute-book, clergymen might occasionally be embarrassed in reference to them; and, accordingly, a new Act was passed in the same year, repealing the obnoxious statutes.

Thus was a small but wholesome work done once for all. The pith of the whole subject is contained in a sensible observation made by the Archbishop of Canterbury: 'I hold it to be impossible, even if it were desirable, that we, at a distance of two or three centuries, should entertain the feelings or sympathise with the expressions which are found in these services; and it is very inexpedient that the people should be invited to offer up prayers and thanksgivings in which their hearts take no concern.'

A remark may be offered in addition, at the hazard of appearing a little paradoxical—that it might be well if a great deal of history, instead of being remembered, could be forgotten. It would be a benefit to Ireland, far beyond the Encumbered Estates Act, if nearly the whole of her history could be obliterated. The oblivion of all that Sir Archibald Alison has chronicled would be a blessing to both France and England. Happy were it for England if her war for the subjugation of America could be buried in oblivion; and happy, thrice happy, would it be for America in future, if her warlike efforts of 1861 could be in like manner forgotten. Above all, it is surely most desirable that there should be no regular celebration by any nation, sect, or party, of any special transaction, the memory of which is necessarily painful to some neighbouring state, or some other section of the same population. Let us just reflect for a moment on what would be thought of a man who, in private society,

loved to taunt a neighbour with a law-suit he had lost fifty years ago, or some criminality which had been committed by his great-grand-uncle! What better is it to remind the people of Ireland of their defeat at the Boyne, or our Catholic fellow-Christians of the guilt of the infatuated Catesby and his companions?

St Anthony and the Pigs: Legal Prosecutions of the Lower Animals.

[See note on p. 778.]

St Anthony has been long recognised as the patron and protector of the lower animals, and particularly of pigs. Quaint old Fuller, in his *Worthies*, says: 'St Anthony is universally known for the patron of hogs, having a pig for his page in all pictures, though for what reason is unknown, except, because being a hermit, and having a cell or hole digged in the earth, and having his general repast on roots, he and hogs did in some sort enter-common both in their diet and lodging.' Stow, in his *Survey*, mentions a curious custom prevalent in his time in the London markets: 'The officers in this city,' he says, 'did divers times take from the market people, pigs starved or otherwise unwholesome for man's sustenance; these they did slit in the ear. One of the proctors of St Anthony's Hospital tied a bell about the neck, and let it feed upon the dunghills; no one would hurt or take it up; but if any one gave it bread or other feeding, such it would know, watch for, and daily follow, whining till it had somewhat given it; whereupon was raised a proverb, such a one will follow such a one, and whine as if it were an Anthony pig.' This custom was generally observed, and to it we are indebted for the still-used proverbial simile—Like a tantony pig.

At Rome, on St Anthony's day, the religious service termed the *Benediction of Beasts* is annually performed in the church dedicated to him, near Santa Maria Maggiore. It lasts for some days; for not only every Roman, from the pontiff to the peasant, who has a horse, mule, or ass, sends his cattle to be blessed at St Anthony's shrine; but all the English send their job-horses and favourite dogs, and for the small offering of a couple of *paoli* get them sprinkled, sanctified, and placed under the immediate protection of the saint. A similar custom is observed on the same day at Madrid and many other places.

On the Continent, down to a comparatively late period, the lower animals were in all respects considered amenable to the laws. Domestic animals were tried in the common criminal courts, and their punishment on conviction was death; wild animals fell under the jurisdiction of the ecclesiastical courts, and their punishment was banishment and death by exorcism and excommunication. Nor was the latter a light punishment. We all know how St Patrick exorcised the Irish reptiles into the sea; and St Bernard, one day, by peevishly saying, 'Be thou excommunicated' to a blue-bottle fly, that annoyed him by buzzing about his ears, unwittingly destroyed the flies of a whole district. The prerogative of trying the domestic animals was founded on the Jewish law, as laid down in Exodus xxi. 28, and other places in the Old Testament. In every instance advocates were assigned to defend the animals, and the whole proceedings, trial, sentence, and execution, were conducted with all the strictest formalities of justice. The researches of French antiquaries have brought to light the records of ninety-two processes against animals, tried in their courts from 1120 to 1740, when the last trial and execution, that of a cow, took place.

The trials of wild animals of a noxious description, as rats, locusts, caterpillars,. and such like, were, as has been already mentioned, conducted in the ecclesiastical courts. The proceedings were exceedingly complicated, and, not having the sanction of the Mosaical law, were founded on the following thesis: As God cursed the serpent, David the mountains of Gilboa, and our Saviour the barren fig-tree; so, in like manner, the church had full power and authority to exorcise, anathematise, and excommunicate all animate and inanimate things. But as the lower animals, being created before man, were the elder-born and first heirs of the earth, as God blessed them and gave them 'every green herb for meat,' as they were provided for in the ark, and entitled to the privileges of the sabbath, they must ever be treated with the greatest clemency, consistent with justice.

Some learned canonists, however, disputed those propositions, alleging that authority to try and punish offences, under the law, implied a contract, quasi-contract, pact, or stipulation, between the supreme power that made and administered the law, and those subjected to it. They contended, that, the lower animals being devoid of intelligence, no such pact ever had been or could be made; and that punishments for injuries committed unintentionally and in ignorance of the law, were unjust. They questioned, also, the authority of the Church to anathematise those whom she did not undertake to baptize, and adduced the example of the Archangel Michael, who, when contending with Satan for the body of Moses, did not make a railing accusation against the 'Old Serpent,' but left it to the Lord to rebuke him. Such discussions appear like the amusing inventions of Rabelais, or Swift; but they were no jesting matter to the simple agriculturists who engaged in those litigations.

The general course of a process was as follows: The inhabitants of the district being annoyed by certain animals, the court appointed experts to survey and report upon the damage committed. An advocate was then appointed to defend the animals, and shew cause why they should not be summoned. They were then cited three several times, and not appearing, judgment was given against them by default. The court next issued a *monitoire*, warning the animals to leave the district within a certain time, under penalty of adjuration; and if they did not disappear on or before the period appointed, the exorcism was with all solemnity pronounced. This looks straightforward enough, but the delays and uncertainties of the law—ecclesiastical law especially—have long been proverbial. The courts, by every available means of delay, evaded the last extremity of pronouncing the exorcism, probably lest the animals should neglect to pay attention to it. Indeed, it is actually recorded that, in some instances, the noxious animals, instead of 'withering off the face of the earth,' after being anathematised, became more abundant and destructive than before. This the doctors, learned in the law, attributed neither to the injustice of the sentence, nor want of power of the court, but to the malevolent antagonism of Satan, who, as in the case of Job, is at certain times permitted to tempt and annoy mankind.

A law-suit between the inhabitants of the commune of St Julien, and a coleopterous insect, now known to naturalists as the *Eynchitus aureus*, lasted for more than forty-two years. At length the inhabitants proposed to compromise the matter by giving up, in perpetuity, to the insects, a fertile part of the district for their sole use and benefit. Of course the advocate of the animals demurred to the proposition; but the court, overruling the demurrer, appointed assessors to survey the land, and, it proving to be well wooded and watered, and every way suitable for the insects, ordered the conveyance to be engrossed in due form and executed. The unfortunate people then thought they had got rid of a trouble imposed on them by their litigious fathers and grandfathers; but they were sadly mistaken. It was discovered that there had formerly been a mine or quarry of an ochreous earth, used as a pigment, in the land conveyed to the insects; and though the quarry had long since been worked out and exhausted, some one possessed an ancient right of way to it, which if exercised would be greatly to the annoyance of the new proprietors. Consequently the contract was vitiated, and the whole process commenced *de novo*. How or when it ended, the mutilation of the recording documents prevents us from knowing; but it is certain that the proceedings commenced in the year 1445, and that they had not concluded in 1487. So what with the insects, the lawyers, and the church, the poor inhabitants must have been pretty well fleeced. During the whole period of a process, religious processions and other expensive ceremonies that had to be well paid for, were strictly enjoined. Besides, no district could commence a process of this kind unless all its arrears of tithes were paid up; and this circumstance gave rise to the well-known French legal maxim—'The first step towards getting rid of locusts is the payment of tithes;' an adage that in all probability was susceptible of more meanings than one.

The summonses were served by an officer of the court, reading them at the places where the animals frequented. These citations were written out with all technical formality, and, that there might be no mistake, contained a description of the animals. Thus, in a process against rats in the diocese of Autun, the defendants were described as dirty animals in the form of rats, of a greyish colour, living in holes. This trial is famous in the annals of French law, for it was at it that Chassanee, the celebrated jurisconsult—the Coke of France—won his first laurels. The rats not appearing on the first citation, Chassanee, their counsel, argued that the summons was of a too local and individual character; that, as all the rats in the diocese were interested, all the rats should be summoned, in all parts of the diocese. This plea being admitted, the curate of every parish in the diocese was instructed to summon every rat for a future day. The day arriving, but no rats, Chassanee said that, as all his clients were summoned, including young and old, sick and healthy, great preparations had to be made, and certain arrangements carried into effect, and therefore he begged for an extension of time. This also being granted, another day was appointed, and no rats appearing, Chassanee objected to the legality of the summons, under certain circumstances. A summons from that court, he argued, implied full protection to the parties summoned, both on their way to it and on their return home; but his clients, the rats, though most anxious to appear in obedience to the court, did not dare to stir out of their holes on account of the number of evil-disposed cats kept by the plaintiffs. Let the latter, he continued, enter into bonds, under heavy pecuniary penalties, that their cats shall not molest my clients, and the summons will be at once obeyed. The court acknowledged the validity of this plea;

but, the plaintiffs declining to be bound over for the good behaviour of their cats, the period for the rats' attendance was adjourned *sine die;* and thus, Chassanee gaining his cause, laid the foundation of his future fame.

Though judgment was given by default, on the non-appearance of the animals summoned, yet it was considered necessary that some of them should be present when the *monitoire* was delivered. Thus, in a process against leeches, tried at Lausanne, in 1451, a number of leeches were brought into court to hear the *monitoire* read, which admonished them to leave the district in three days. The leeches, proving contumacious, did not leave, and consequently were exorcised. This exorcism differing slightly from the usual form, some canonists adversely criticised, while others defended it. The doctors of Heidelberg, then a famous seat of learning, not only gave it their entire and unanimous approbation, but imposed silence upon all impertinents that presumed to speak against it. And, though they admitted its slight deviation from the recognised formula made and provided for such purposes, yet they triumphantly appealed to its efficiency as proved by the result; the leeches.

TRIAL OF A SOW AND PIGS AT LAVEGNY.

immediately after its delivery, having died off, day by day, till they were utterly exterminated.

Among trials of individual animals for special acts of turpitude, one of the most amusing was that of a sow and her six young ones, at Lavegny, in 1457, on a charge of their having murdered and
128

partly eaten a child. Our artist has endeavoured to represent this scene; but we fear that his sense of the ludicrous has incapacitated him for giving it with the due solemnity. The sow was found guilty and condemned to death; but the pigs were acquitted on account of their youth, the bad example of their mother, and the absence of direct proof as to their having been concerned in the eating of the child.

These suits against animals not unfrequently led to more serious trials of human beings, on charges of sorcery. Simple country people, finding the regular process very tedious and expensive, purchased charms and exorcisms from empirical, unlicensed exorcists, at a much cheaper rate. But, if any of the parties to this contraband traffic were discovered, death by stake and fagot was their inevitable fate—infernal sorcerers were not to presume to compete with holy church. Still there was one animal, the serpent, which, as it had been cursed at a very early period in the world's history, might be exorcised and charmed (so that it could not leave the spot where it was first seen) by any one, lay or cleric, without the slightest imputation of sorcery. The formula was simply thus :—

'By Him who created thee, I adjure thee, that thou remain in the spot where thou art, whether it be thy will to do so or otherwise; and I curse thee with the curse with which the Lord hath cursed thee.'

But if a wretched shepherd was convicted of having uttered the following nonsense, termed 'the prayer of the wolf,' he was burned at the stake :

'Come, beast of wool, thou art the lamb of humility ! I will protect thee. Go to the right about, grim, grey, and greedy beasts ! Wolves, she-wolves, and young wolves, ye are not to touch the flesh, which is here. Get thee behind me, Satan !'

French shepherds suffered fearfully in the olden time, through being frequently charged with sorcery ; and, among the rustic population, they are still looked upon as persons who know and practise dark and forbidden arts.

Legal proceedings against animals were not confined to France. At Basle, in 1474, a cock was tried for having laid an egg. For the prosecution it was *proved* that cocks' eggs were of inestimable value for mixing in certain magical preparations; that a sorcerer would rather possess a cock's egg than be master of the philosopher's stone; and that, in pagan lands, Satan employed witches to hatch such eggs, from which proceeded animals most injurious to all of the Christian faith and race. The advocate for the defence admitted the facts of the case, but asked what evil animus had been proved against his client, what injury to man or beast had it effected? Besides, the laying of the egg was an involuntary act, and as such, not punishable by law. If the crime of sorcery were imputed, the cock was innocent; for there was no instance on record of Satan ever having made a compact with one of the brute creation. In reply, the public prosecutor alleged that, though the devil did not make compacts with brutes, he sometimes entered into them ; and though the swine possessed by devils, as mentioned in Scripture, were involuntary agents, yet they, nevertheless, were punished by being caused to run down a steep place into the sea, and so perished in the waters. The pleadings in this case, even as recorded by Hammerlein, are voluminous ; we only give the meagre outlines of the principal pleas; suffice it to say, the cock was condemned to death, not as a cock, but as a

sorcerer or devil in the form of a cock, and was with its egg burned at the stake, with all the due form and solemnity of a judicial punishment.

As the lower animals were anciently amenable to law in Switzerland, so, in peculiar circumstances, they could be received as witnesses. And we have been informed, by a distinguished Sardinian lawyer, that a similar law is still, or was to a very late period, recognised in Savoy. If a man's house was broken into between sunset and sunrise, and the owner of the house killed the intruder, the act was considered a justifiable homicide. But it was considered just possible that a man, who lived all alone by himself, might invite or entice a person, whom he wished to kill, to spend the evening with him, and after murdering his victim, assert that he did it in defence of his person and property, the slain man having been a burglar. So when a person was killed under such circumstances, the solitary householder was not held innocent, unless he produced a dog, a cat, or a cock that had been an inmate of the house, and witnessed the death of the person killed. The owner of the house was compelled to make his declaration of innocence on oath before one of those animals, and if it did not contradict him, he was considered guiltless ; the law taking for granted, that the Deity would cause a miraculous manifestation, by a dumb animal, rather than allow a murderer to escape from justice.

In Spain and Italy the lower animals were held subject to the laws, as in France. Azpilceuta of Navarre, a renowned Spanish canonist, asserts that rats when exorcised were ordered to depart for foreign countries, and that the obedient animals would, accordingly, march down in large bodies to the sea-coast, and thence set off by swimming in search of desert islands, where they could live and enjoy themselves, without annoyance to man. In Italy, also, processes against caterpillars and other 'small deer' were of frequent occurrence ; and certain large fishes called terons, that used to break the fishermen's nets, were annually anathematised from the lakes and headlands of the north-western shores of the Mediterranean. *Apropos* of fishes, Maffei, the learned Jesuit, in his *History of India*, tells a curious story. A Portuguese ship, sailing to Brazil, fell becalmed in dangerous proximity to a large whale. The mariners, terrified by the uncouth gambols of the monster, improvised a summary process, and duly exorcised the dreaded cetacean, which, to their great relief, immediately sank to the lowest depths of ocean.

THE SHREWSBURY TRIPLE FIGHT.

On the 17th January 1667-8, there took place a piece of private war which, in its prompting causes, as well as the circumstances under which it was fought out, forms as vivid an illustration of the character of the age as could well be desired. The parties were George Villiers, Duke of Buckingham, attended by Sir Robert Holmes and Captain William Jenkins, on one side ; and Francis Talbot, Earl of Shrewsbury, attended by Sir John Talbot, a gentleman of the King's

Privy Chamber, and Bernard Howard, a younger son of the Earl of Arundel, on the other.

Pepys, in reference to this 'duell,' as he terms it, says, it was all 'about my Lady Shrewsbury, at that time, and for a great while before, a mistress to the Duke of Buckingham; and so her husband challenged him, and they met; and my Lord Shrewsbury was run through the body, from the right breast through the shoulder; and Sir John Talbot all along up one of his arms; and Jenkins killed upon the place, and the rest all in a little measure wounded.' (Pepys's *Diary*, iv. 15.) A pardon under the great seal, dated on February the 5th following, was granted to all the persons concerned in this tragical affair; the result of which proved more disastrous than had at first been anticipated, for Lord Shrewsbury died in consequence of his wound, in the course of the same year.

It is reported that during the fight the Countess of Shrewsbury held her lover's horse, in the dress of a page. This lady was Anna Maria Brudenell, daughter of Robert Earl of Cardigan. She survived both her gallant and her first husband, and was married, secondly, to George Rodney Brydges, of Keynsham, in Somersetshire.

JANUARY 18.

St Peter's Chair at Rome. St Paul and Thirty-six Companions in Egypt. St Prisca, virgin and martyr, about 275. St Deicolus, abbot, 7th century. St Ulfrid, bishop and martyr, 1028.

The festival of St Peter's Chair, annually celebrated at Rome on this day, appears to be meant as an act of gratitude for the founding of the papacy. Butler tells us that it is well evidenced for a great antiquity, being adverted to in a martyrology copied in the time of St Willibrod, in 720. 'Christians,' he says, 'justly celebrate the founding of this mother church, the centre of Catholic communion, in thanksgiving to God for his mercies on his church, and to implore his future blessing.' The celebration takes place in St Peter's Church, under circumstances of the greatest solemnity and splendour. It is one of the very few *funzioni* (functions), as they are called, which are celebrated in that magnificent temple. The affair is thus described by Lady Morgan in her work, *Italy*:

'The splendidly dressed troops that line the nave of the cathedral, the variety and richness of vestments which clothe the various church and lay dignitaries, abbots, priests, canons, prelates, cardinals, doctors, dragoons, senators, and grenadiers, which march in procession, complete, as they proceed up the vast space of this wondrous temple, a spectacle nowhere to be equalled within the pale of European civilization. In the midst of swords and crosiers, of halberds and crucifixes, surrounded by banners, and bending under the glittering tiara of threefold power, appears the aged, feeble, and worn-out pope, borne aloft on men's shoulders, in a chair of crimson and gold, and environed by slaves, (for such they look,) who waft, from plumes of ostrich

feathers mounted on ivory wands, a cooling gale, to refresh his exhausted frame, too frail for the weight of such honours. All fall prostrate, as he passes up the church to a small choir and throne, temporarily erected beneath the chair of St Peter. A solemn service is then performed, hosannas arise, and royal votarists and diplomatic devotees parade the church, with guards of honour and running footmen, while English gentlemen and ladies mob and scramble, and crowd and bribe, and fight their way to the best places they can obtain.

'At the extremity of the great nave behind the altar, and mounted upon a tribune designed or ornamented by Michael Angelo, stands a sort of throne, composed of precious materials, and supported by four gigantic figures. A glory of seraphim, with groups of angels, sheds a brilliant light upon its splendours. This throne enshrines the real, plain, worm-eaten, wooden chair, on which St Peter, the prince of the apostles, is said to have pontificated; more precious than all the bronze, gold, and gems, with which it is hidden, not only from impious, but from holy eyes, and which once only, in the flight of ages, was profaned by mortal inspection.'

Her ladyship then narrates how the French, when in occupation of Rome in the days of the first Napoleon, made an examination of the chair, and found upon it the well-known confession of the Mahometan faith, '*There is but one God, and Mahomet is his prophet;*' whence it was inferred that the chair had been brought from the East in the middle ages, probably among the spoils of the Crusaders. But Lady Morgan here made a mistake, the chair with the Mahometan inscription being in reality one preserved in similar circumstances at Venice.

The saints referred to in the second article of the list for this day appear to have been a group of missionaries, who went at an early but unknown period into Egypt to propagate the faith, and there became martyrs. St Deicolus or St Deel was an Irish priest, who spent his best days in France, and whose memory is preserved in Franche-comté, where his name Deel is still frequently given in baptism.

Born.—Ch. Montesquieu, 1689; Dr. John Gillies, historian, 1747.

Died.—Archangelo Corelli, 1713; Sir Samuel Garth, 1719; J. Baskerville, 1775; Sir John Pringle, 1782.

DEATH OF CORELLI.

The melancholy end of Archangelo Corelli, founder of the Roman or ancient school of violinists, is thought to have been hastened by the unfeeling treatment which he experienced from the King of Naples, and the successes of inferior Neapolitan artists. Their fiery genius presented a curious contrast to the meek, timid, and gentle character of Corelli, so analogous to the style of his music. He had published his admirable concertos but six weeks, when he fell into a state of melancholy and chagrin, and died. He was buried in the church of Santa Maria della Rotondo, in the ancient Pantheon, where a monument with a marble bust is erected to his memory, near that of Raphael. For many years after the decease of Corelli, a solemn service, consisting of selections from his own works, was performed in the Pantheon, on the anniversary of his funeral; and this solemnity continued so long as any of his immediate scholars survived to conduct the performance. One great point of Corelli's excellence was, the nice management of his band, their bows moving exactly together, so that at rehearsals he would immediately stop the band if he saw an irregular bow. There was little or no melody in instrumental music before Corelli's time; and though his productions have yielded to the superior genius and talents of Haydn, Mozart, Beethoven, and Cherubini, the works of Corelli are still admired for their grace and eloquence; and they have continued longer in favour in England than in the great composer's own country, or, indeed, in any other part of Europe.

BASKERVILLE, THE PRINTER.

John Baskerville, a native of Worcestershire, having acquired considerable wealth by the japanning business at Birmingham, devoted himself to the perfection of the art of printing, more particularly in the shape of the letters. He is said to have spent six hundred pounds before he could obtain a single letter to please himself, and many thousands before he made a profit of his pursuit, which he prosecuted so ardently that he manufactured his own printing-ink, presses, moulds for casting, and all the apparatus for printing. His typography is extremely beautiful, uniting the elegance of Plantin with the clearness of the Elzevirs; in his Italic letters he stands unrivalled, such freedom and perfect symmetry being in vain to be looked for among the specimens of Aldus and Colinæus. He was a man of eccentric tastes; he had each panel of his carriage painted with a picture of his trades. He was buried in his garden; and in 1821, his remains being accidentally disturbed, the leaden coffin was opened, and the body was found in a singular state of preservation—the shroud was perfect and very white, and a branch of laurel on the breast of the corpse was, though faded, entire. He died Jan. 8, 1775.

THE PEASANT COUNTESS.

Died, on the 18th January 1797, Sarah Countess of Exeter, the heroine of a singular *mésalliance*. The story has been several times handled in both prose and verse. Tennyson tells it under the title of *The Lord of Burleigh*, relating how, under the guise of a poor landscape painter, Henry Cecil wooed a village maiden, and gained her hand; how he conducted her on a tour, seeing

'Parks with oak and chesnut shady,
    Parks and ordered gardens great;
Ancient homes of lord and lady,
    Built for pleasure or for state;'

until they came to a majestic mansion, where the domestics bowed before the young lover, whose wife then, for the first time, discovered his rank.

'All at once the colour flushes
    Her sweet face from brow to chin:
As it were with shame she blushes,
    And her spirit changed within.
Then her countenance all over
    Pale again as death did prove:
But he clasped her like a lover,
    And he cheered her soul with love.
So she strove against her weakness,
    Though at times her spirits sank:
Shaped her heart with woman's meekness,
    To all duties of her rank.
And a gentle consort made he,
    And her gentle mind was such,
That she grew a noble lady,
    And the people loved her much.
But a trouble weighed upon her,
    And perplexed her, night and morn,
With the burden of an honour
    Unto which she was not born.
Faint she grew and even fainter,
    As she murmured, "Oh that he
Were once more that landscape painter,
    Which did win my heart from me!"
So she drooped and drooped before him,
    Fading slowly from his side;
Three fair children first she bore him,
    Then before her time she died.'

The real details of this romantic story are not quite so poetical as Tennyson represents, but yet form a curious anecdote of aristocratic eccentricity. It appears that Mr Henry Cecil, while his uncle held the family titles, married a lady of respectable birth, from whom, after fifteen years of wedded life, he procured a divorce. Before that event, being troubled with heavy debts, he put on a disguise, and came to live as a poor and humble man, at Bolas Common, near Hodnet, an obscure village in Shropshire. No one came to inquire after him; he had vanished from the gaze and the knowledge of all his relatives. He was known to none, and having no ostensible means of living, there were many surmises as to who and what he was. The general belief at one moment was, that he gained his bread as a highwayman. In anticipation of the divorce he paid addresses to a young lady of considerable attractions, named Taylor, who, however, being engaged, declined his hand. He lodged with a cottage labourer named Hoggins, whose daughter Sarah, a plain but honest girl, next drew the attention of the noble refugee. He succeeded, notwithstanding the equivocal nature of his circumstances, in gaining her heart and hand. It has been set forth that Mr Cecil, disgusted with the character of his fashionable wife, resolved to seek some peasant mistress who should love him for his own sake alone; but the probability is that the young noble was simply eccentric, or that a craving for sympathy in his solitary life had disposed him to take up with the first respectable woman who should come in his way. Under the name of Mr John Jones, he purchased a piece of land near Hodnet, and built a house upon it, in which he lived for some years with his peasant bride, who never all that time knew who he really was. It has been stated that he did not appear fastidious about what he did. He on one occasion gratified his father-in-law by carrying a large pig to be given as a present to a neighbouring squire. He took his turn of service in the vestry, in which duty, having occasion to attend the Shrewsbury sessions, he was noticed by a brother magistrate, who had been his school-fellow; but it did not lead to a detection. He disappeared for a short time occasionally, in order, as is supposed, to obtain supplies of money. The marriage took place on the 3rd of October 1791, not long after the divorce of the first Mrs Henry Cecil was accomplished.

Two years after the marriage (December 27, 1793), Mr Cecil succeeded to the peerage and estates in consequence of the death of his uncle; and it became necessary that he should quit his obscurity at Hodnet. Probably the removal of the pair to Burleigh House, near Stamford, was effected under the circumstances described by the Laureate. It is also true that the peasant countess did not prove quite up to the part she had been unwittingly drawn into. Being, as it chanced, a ruddy-faced and rather robust woman,* she did not pine away in the manner described by Tennyson; but after having borne her husband three children (amongst whom was the peer who succeeded), she sickened and died, January 18, 1797. The earl was afterwards created a marquis, married a third wife, the Dowager Duchess of Hamilton, and died in 1804.†

DEATH AND FUNERAL OF A SQUAW IN LONDON.

Examples of the Red Men of North America—so absurdly called Indians—have at various times visited England. The readers of the *Spectator* will remember Addison's interesting account of four kings of the nations lying between New York and Canada, who came to London in 1710, and were introduced to Queen Anne. So lately as 1835, a party of the Michigan tribe, including the chief, Muk Coonee (the Little Boar), appeared amongst us, the object being a negotiation for the sale of certain lands. Arrangements were made for their being presented to King William on the 18th of January; but the chief found on that day a very different affair on his hands. His squaw, the *Diving Mouse*, of only twenty-six years, sickened and on that day died, at the lodging which the party occupied in the Waterloo Road.

When this lady of the wild felt a mortal sickness upon her, she refused all medicine, saying if the Great Spirit intended that she should then die, he would be angry at any attempt on her part to avert the doom. The only thing she would allow to be done for her was the administration of the rite of baptism, and this was only submitted to because she was told there might consequently be more ceremony at her funeral. Loud were the wailings of the chief and his friends round the couch of the dead squaw.

When preparations were necessary for the funeral, he took a pride in making them as handsome as he could. He placed her in a richly

* Such are the accounts usually given; but in a portrait of the noble pair, by Lawrence, kept in Burleigh House, the lady appears possessed of an oval countenance, of what we would call very considerable beauty, and the reverse of rustic in style.

† Tennyson's Poems, 10th ed., p. 355. Notes and Queries, 1st ser., xii. 280, 355; 2nd ser., i. 437; ii. 457. Collins's Peerage, by Brydges, ii. 609.

ornamented coffin, with a silver plate bearing an inscription. An elaborate shroud was laid over her Indian garments; laurel leaves and a bouquet were placed on her breast; her earrings were laden with ornaments; her cheeks were painted red; and a splendid Indian shawl was thrown over all. The funeral took place at St John's churchyard, in the Waterloo Road. The clergyman read the service in the usual English form. The coffin was lowered, a white rose thrown upon it, and then the dull cold earth. Shaw Whash ('Big Sword') pronounced an oration in his native language; and then the funeral *cortége* returned to the lodgings. The chief, with much dignity, addressed to the persons assembled a few words, which were translated by his French interpreter, M. Dunord. 'For three years prior to my visit to this country,' he said, 'I rested on the bosom of my wife in love and happiness. She was everything to me; and such was my fear that illness or accident might part us in England, that I wished her to remain behind in our settlements. This she would not consent to, saying, "That I was all the world to her, and in life or death she would remain with me!" We came, and I have lost her. She who was all my earthly happiness is now under the earth; but the Great Spirit has placed her there, and my bosom is calm. I am not, I never was, a man of tears; but her loss made me shed many.'

This was not the last sorrow of poor Muk Coonee. A few days after the burial of the squaw, another of his companions was taken from him. This was 'Thunder and Lightning,' a young Indian about the same age as the squaw. He, in like manner, was baptized, and was buried in the same churchyard. It was observed that the chief had been looking anxiously around at various times during the ceremony; and it now appeared that he entertained distrust as to whether the grave of his wife had been disturbed. He had in some way marked on or near her grave his *totam*, or symbol, something which would denote the tribe and rank of the deceased, and which was intended to secure inviolable respect for the sacred spot. Some of the appearances around led the poor fellow to suspect that the grave had been tampered with. Earnest were the endeavours made to assure him that his fears were groundless, and he at length was induced to believe that the grave of the 'Diving Mouse' had not been opened.

Prussic Acid.—The peach (we gather from Dr Daubeny's *Lectures on Roman Husbandry*) was brought from Persia, and Columella alludes to the fable of its poisonous qualities. 'Could this mistake arise,' asks Dr Daubeny, 'from a knowledge of the poisonous properties of the prussic acid existing in the kernels of the peach?' It may be observed that a notion prevailed in Egypt, probably referring to the secret of the Psylli, that a citron eaten early in the morning was an antidote against all kinds of poison. Its juice. injected into the veins, would have a similar effect. Blackberries, when perfectly ripe, were eaten by the Romans, and by the Greeks were considered a preventive of gout.

JANUARY 19.

Ss Maris, Martha, Audifax, and Abachum, martyrs, 270. St Lomer, 593. St Blaithmaic, abbot in Scotland, 793. St Knut (Canutus), king of Denmark, martyr, 1036. St Wulstan, bishop of Worcester, 1095. St Henry of England, martyr in Finland, 1151.

WULSTAN, BISHOP OF WORCESTER.

St Wulstan was the last saint of the Anglo-Saxon Church, the link between the old English Church and hierarchy and the Norman. He was a monk, indeed, and an ascetic; still, his vocation lay not in the school or cloister, but among the people of the market-place and the village, and he rather dwelt on the great broad truths of the Gospel than followed them into their results. Though a thane's son, a series of unexpected circumstances brought him into the religious profession, and he became prior of a monastery at Worcester. Born at Long Itchington, in Warwickshire, and educated at the monasteries of Evesham and Peterborough, the latter one of the richest houses and the most famous schools in England, he was thoughtful above his years, and voluntarily submitted to exercises and self-denials from which other children were excused. To Wulstan, the holy monk, the proud Earl Harold once went thirty miles out of his way, to make his confession to him, and beg his prayers. He was a man of kind yet blunt and homely speech, and delighted in his devotional duties; the common people looked upon him as their friend, and he used to sit at the church door listening to complaints, redressing wrongs, helping those who were in trouble, and giving advice, spiritual and temporal. Every Sunday and great festival he preached to the people: his words seemed to be the voice of thunder, and he drew together vast crowds, wherever he had to dedicate a church. As an example of his practical preaching, it is related that, in reproving the greediness which was a common fault of that day, Wulstan confessed that a savory roast goose which was preparing for his dinner, had once so taken up his thoughts, that he could not attend to the service he was performing, but that he had punished himself for it, and given up the use of meat in consequence.

At length, in 1062, two Roman cardinals came to Worcester, with Aldred the late bishop, now Archbishop of York; they spent the whole Lent at the Cathedral monastery, where Wulstan was prior, and they were so impressed with his austere and hard-working way of life, that partly by their recommendation, as well as the popular voice at Worcester, Wulstan was elected to the vacant bishopric. He heard of this with sorrow and vexation, declaring that he would rather lose his head than be made a bishop; but he yielded to the stern rebuke of an aged hermit, and received the pastoral staff from the hands of Edward the Confessor. The Normans, when they came, thought him, like his church, old-fashioned and homely; but they admired, though in an Englishman, his unworldly and active life, which was not that of study and thoughtful retirement, but of ministering to the common people, supplying the deficiencies of the parochial clergy, and preaching. He rode on horseback, with his retinue of clerks and monks, through his diocese, repeating the Psalter, the Litanies, and the office for the dead; his chamberlain always had a purse ready, and 'no one ever begged of Wulstan in vain.' In these progresses he came into personal contact with all his flock, high and low—with the rude crowds, beggars and serfs, craftsmen and labourers, as well as with priests and nobles. But everything gave way to his confirming children — from sunrise to sunset he would go without tasting food, blessing batch after batch of the little ones.

Wulstan was a great church builder: he took care that on each of his own manors there should be a church, and he urged other lords to follow his example. He rebuilt the cathedral of his see, and restored the old ruined church of Westbury. When his new cathedral was ready for use, the old one built by St Oswald was to be demolished; Wulstan stood in the churchyard looking on sadly and silently, but at last burst into tears at this destruction, as he said, of the work of saints, who knew not how to build fine churches, but knew how to sacrifice themselves to God, whatever roof might be over them.

Still, with a life of pastoral activity, Wulstan retained the devotional habits of the cloister. His first words on awaking were a psalm; and some homily or legend was read to him as he lay down to rest. He attended the same services as when in the monastery; and each of his manor houses had a little chapel, where he used to lock himself in to pray in spare hours.

It cannot be said of Wulstan that he was much of a respecter of persons. He had rebuked and warned the headstrong Harold, and he was not less bold before his more imperious successor. At a council in Winchester, he bluntly called upon William to restore to the see some lands which he had seized. He had to fight a stouter battle with Lanfranc, who, ambitious of deposing him for incapacity and ignorance, in a synod held before the king, called upon the bishop to deliver up his pastoral staff and ring; when, according to the legend, Wulstan drove the staff into the stone of the tomb of the Confessor, where it remained fast imbedded, notwithstanding the efforts of the Bishop of Rochester, Lanfranc, and the king himself, to remove it, which, however, Wulstan easily did, and thenceforth was reconciled to Lanfranc; and they subsequently co-operated in destroying a slave trade which had long been carried on by merchants of Bristol with Ireland.

Wulstan outlived William and Lanfranc. He passed his last Lent with more than usual solemnity, on his last Maundy washing the feet and clothes of the poor, bestowing alms and ministering the cup of 'charity;' then supplying them, as they sat at his table, with shoes and victuals; and finally reconciling penitents, and washing the feet of his brethren of the convent. On Easter-day, he again feasted with the poor.

At Whitsuntide following, being taken ill, he prepared for death, but he lingered till the first day of the new year, when he finally took to his bed. He was laid so as to have a view of the altar of a chapel, and thus he followed the psalms which were sung. On the 19th of January 1095, at midnight, he died in the eighty-seventh year of his age, and the thirty-third of his episcopate. Contrary to the usual custom, the body was laid out, arranged in the episcopal vestments and crosier, before the high altar, that the people of Worcester might look once more on their good bishop. His stone coffin is, to this day, shewn in the presbytery of the cathedral, the crypt and early Norman portions of which are the work of Wulstan.*

Born.—Nicholas Copernicus, 1472 ; James Watt, 1736.
Died.—Charles Earl of Dorset, 1706 ; William Congreve, poet, 1729 ; Thomas Ruddiman, grammarian, 1757 ; Isaac Disraeli, miscellaneous writer, 1848.

JAMES WATT.

James Watt was, as is well known, a native of the then small seaport of Greenock, on the Firth of Clyde. His grandfather was a teacher of mathematics. His father was a builder and contractor—also a merchant,—a man of superior sagacity, if not ability, prudent and benevolent. The mother of Watt was noted as a woman of fine aspect, and excellent judgment and conduct. When boatswains of ships came to the father's shop for stores, he was in the habit of throwing in an extra quantity of sail-needles and twine, with the remark, 'See, take that too ; I once lost a ship for want of such articles on board.'† The young mechanician received a good elementary education at the schools of his native town. It was by the overpowering bent of his own mind that he entered life as a mathematical-instrument-maker.

When he attempted to set up in that business at Glasgow, he met with an obstruction from the corporation of Hammermen, who looked upon him as an intruder upon their privileged ground. The world might have lost Watt and his inventions through this unworthy cause, if he had not had friends among the professors of the University,—Muirhead, a relation of his mother, and Anderson, the brother of one of his dearest school-friends,— by whose influence he was furnished with a workshop within the walls of the college, and invested with the title of its instrument-maker. Anderson, a man of an advanced and liberal mind, was Professor of Natural Philosophy, and had, amongst his class apparatus, a model of Newcomen's steam-engine. He required to have it repaired, and put it into Watt's hands for the purpose. Through this trivial accident it was that the young mechanician was led to make that improvement of the steam-engine which gave a new power to civilized man, and has revolutionised the world. The model of Newcomen has very

* The writer of this article acknowledges his obligations to the *Lives of English Saints*, 1844.
† Williamson's Memorials of James Watt. 4to, 1856. p. 155.

fortunately been preserved, and is now in the Hunterian Museum at Glasgow College.

MODEL OF NEWCOMEN'S STEAM-ENGINE.

Watt's career as a mechanician, in connection with Mr Boulton, at the Soho Works, near Birmingham, was a brilliant one, and ended in raising him and his family to fortune. Yet it cannot be heard without pain, that a sixth or seventh part of his time was diverted from his proper pursuits, and devoted to mere ligitation, rendered unavoidable by the incessant invasions of his patents.

He was often consulted about supposed inventions and discoveries, and his invariable rule was to recommend that a *model* should be formed and tried. This he considered as the only true test of the value of any novelty in mechanics.

CONGREVE AND VOLTAIRE.

Congreve died at his house in Surrey-street, Strand, from an internal injury received in being overturned in his chariot on a journey to Bath— after having been for several years afflicted with blindness and gout. Here he was visited by Voltaire, who had a great admiration of him as a writer. 'Congreve spoke of his works,' says Voltaire, 'as of trifles that were beneath him, and hinted to me, in our first conversation, that I should visit him on no other footing than upon that of a gentleman who led a life of plainness and simplicity. I answered, *that, had he been so unfortunate as to be a mere gentleman*, I should never have come to see him ; and I was very much disgusted at so unreasonable a piece of vanity.'

This is a fine rebuke.

Congreve's remains lay in state in the Jerusalem Chamber, and he was buried in Westminster Abbey, where a monument was erected to his memory by Henrietta, Duchess of Marlborough, to whom he bequeathed £10,000, the accumulation of attentive parsimony. The Duchess purchased with £7,000 of the legacy a diamond necklace. 'How much better,' says Dr Young, 'it would have been to have given the money to Mrs Bracegirdle, with whom Congreve was very intimate for years; yet still better would it have been to have left the money to his poor relations in want of it.'

ISAAC DISRAELI.

Few miscellanies have approached the popularity enjoyed by the *Curiosities of Literature,* the work by which Mr Disraeli is best known. This success may be traced to the circumstances of his life, as well as his natural abilities, favouring the production of exactly such a work. When a boy, he was sent to Amsterdam, and placed under a preceptor, who did not take the trouble to teach him anything, but turned him loose into a good library. Nothing could have been better suited to his taste, and before he was fifteen he had read the works of Voltaire and dipped into Bayle. When he was eighteen he returned to England, half mad with the sentimental philosophy of Rousseau. He declined to enter mercantile life, for which his father had intended him; he then went to Paris, and stayed there, chiefly living in the public libraries until a short time before the outbreak of the French Revolution. Shortly after his return to England he wrote a poem on the *Abuse of Satire,* levelled at Peter Pindar: it was successful, and made Disraeli's name known. In about two years, after the reading of Andrews's *Anecdotes,* Disraeli remarked that a very interesting miscellany might be drawn up by a well-read man from the library in which he lived. It was objected that such a work would be a mere compilation of dead matter, and uninteresting to the public. Disraeli thought otherwise, and set about preparing a volume from collections of the French Ana, the author adding as much as he was able from English literature. This volume he called *Curiosities of Literature.* Its great success induced him to publish a second volume; and after these volumes had reached a fifth edition, he added three more. He then suffered a long illness, but his literary habits were never laid aside, and as often as he was able he worked in the morning in the British Museum, and in his own library at night. He published works of great historical research, including the *Life and Reign of Charles I.* in five volumes, and the *Amenities of Literature* in three volumes; but the great aim of his life was to write a *History of English Literature,* of which the *Amenities* were to be the materials. His literary career was cut short in 1839 by a paralysis of the optic nerve. He died at the age of eighty-two, retaining to the last, his sweetness and serenity of temper and cheerfulness of mind. Shortly before, his son wrote, for a new edition of the *Curiosities of Literature,* a memoir of the author, in which he thus happily sketched the features of his father's character:

'He was himself a complete literary character, a man who really passed his life in his library. Even marriage produced no change in these habits; he rose to enter the chamber where he lived alone with his books, and at night his lamp was ever lit within the same walls. Nothing, indeed, was more remarkable than the isolation of this prolonged existence; and it could only be accounted for by the united influences of three causes: his birth, which brought him no relations or family acquaintance; the bent of his disposition; and the circumstance of his inheriting an independent fortune, which rendered unnecessary those exertions that would have broken up his self-reliance. He disliked business, and he never required relaxation; he was absorbed in his pursuits. In London his only amusement was to ramble among booksellers; if he entered a club, it was only to go into the library. In the country, he scarcely ever left his room but to saunter in abstraction upon a terrace; muse over a chapter, or coin a sentence. He had not a single passion or prejudice; all his convictions were the result of his own studies, and were often opposed to the impressions which he had early imbibed. He not only never entered into the politics of the day, but he could never understand them. He never was connected with any particular body or set of men; comrades of school or college, or confederates in that public life which, in England, is, perhaps, the only foundation of real friendship. In the consideration of a question, his mind was quite undisturbed by traditionary preconceptions; and it was this exemption from passion and prejudice which, although his intelligence was naturally somewhat too ingenious and fanciful for the conduct of close argument, enabled him, in investigation, often to shew many of the highest attributes of the judicial mind, and particularly to sum up evidence with singular happiness and ability.'

FAC-SIMILES OF INEDITED AUTOGRAPHS.
ISABEL, QUEEN OF DENMARK.

Died at Ghent, of a broken heart, January 19, 1525, Isabel of Austria, Queen of Denmark, a 'nursing mother' of the Reformation. Isabel was the second daughter of Philip the Fair of Austria, and Juana *la Loca,* the first Queen of Spain. She was born at Brussels in 1501, and married at Malines, August 12, 1515, to Christiern of Denmark, who proved little less than her murderer. When he, 'the Nero of the North,' was deposed by his infuriated subjects, she followed him into exile, soothed him and nursed him, for which her only reward was cruel neglect, and, some add, more cruel treatment, descending even to blows. The frail body which shrined the bright, loving spirit, was soon worn out; and Isabel died, as above stated, aged only twenty-four years.

It will be seen that the Queen spells her name Elizabeth, probably as more consonant with Danish ideas, for she was baptized after her grandmother, Isabel the Catholic. It is well known that our ancestors (mistakenly) considered Elizabeth and Isabel identical. The autograph here given is from the Cotton MSS. (Brit. Mus.) Vesp. F. III.

Scarborough Warning.—Toby Matthew, Bishop of Durham, in the postscript of a letter to the Archbishop of York, dated January 19, 1603, says : ' When I was in the midst of this discourse, I received a message from my Lord Chamberlain, that it was his Majesty's pleasure that I should preach before him on Sunday next; which *Scarborough Warning* did not only perplex me, &c.' 'Scarborough warning' is alluded to in a ballad by Heywood, as referring to a summary mode of dealing with suspected thieves at that place ; by Fuller, as taking its rise in a sudden surprise of Scarborough Castle by Thomas Stafford in 1557 ; and it is quoted in Harrington's old translation of Ariosto—

' They took them to a fort, with such small treasure,
　As in to Scarborow warning they had leasure.'

There is considerable likelihood that the whole of these writers are mistaken on the subject. In the parish of Anwoth, in the stewartry of Kirkcudbright, there is a rivulet called *Skyreburn*, which usually appears as gentle and innocent as a child, being just sufficient to drive a mill ; but from having its origin in a spacious bosom of the neighbouring hills, it is liable, on any ordinary fall of rain, to come down suddenly in prodigious volume and vehemence, carrying away hayricks, washings of clothes, or anything else that may be exposed on its banks. The abruptness of the danger has given rise to a proverbial expression, generally used throughout the south-west province of Scotland,—*Skyreburn warning*. It is easy to conceive that this local phrase, when heard south of the Tweed, would be mistaken for *Scarborough warning ;* in which case, it would be only too easy to imagine an origin for it connected with that Yorkshire watering-place.

Shakspeare's Geographical Knowledge.—The great dramatist's unfortunate slip in representing, in his *Winter's Tale,* a shipwrecked party landing in Bohemia, has been palliated by the discovery which some one has made, that Bohemia, in the thirteenth century, had dependencies extending to the sea-coast. But the only real palliation of which the case is susceptible, lies in the history of the origin of the play. Our great bard, in this case, took his story from a novel named *Pandosto*. In doing so, for some reason which probably seemed to him good, he transposed the respective circumstances said to have taken place in Sicily and Bohemia, and, simply through advertence, failed to observe that what was suitable for an island like Sicily was unsuitable for an inland country like Bohemia.

Shakspeare did not stand alone in his defective geographical knowledge. We learn from his contemporary, Lord Herbert of Cherbury, that Luines, the Prime Minister of France, when there was a question

136

made about some business in Bohemia, asked whether it was an inland country, or lay upon the sea.

We ought to remember that in the beginning of the seventeenth century, from the limited intercourse and interdependence of nations, there was much less occasion for geographical knowledge than there now is, and the means of obtaining it were also infinitely less.

JANUARY 20.

ST AGNES' EVE.

St Fabian, pope, 250. St Sebastian, 288. St Euthymius, 473. St Fechin, abbot in Ireland, 664. St Fabian is a saint of the English calendar.

Born.—Frederick, Prince of Wales, 1707, *Hanover ;* Jean Jacques Barthélemy, 1716, *Cassis.*

Died.—Cardinal Bembo, 1547 ; Rodolph II., emperor, 1612 ; Charles, first Duke of Manchester, 1722 ; Charles VII., emperor, 1745 ; Sir James Fergusson, 1759 ; Lord Chancellor Yorke, 1770 ; David Garrick, 1779 ; John Howard, 1790.

ANNE OF AUSTRIA.

This extraordinary woman, daughter of Philip II. of Spain and queen of Louis XIII., exercised great influence upon the fortunes of France, at a critical period of its history ; thus in part making good the witty saying,—that when queens reign, men govern ; and that when kings govern, women eventually decide the course of events. Soon after the marriage of Anne, the administration fell into the hands of Cardinal Richelieu, who took advantage of the coldness and gravity of the queen's demeanour to inspire Louis with dislike and jealousy. Induced by him to believe that the queen was at the head of a conspiracy to get rid of him, Louis compelled her to answer the charge at the council table, when her dignity of character came to her aid ; and she observed contemptuously, that 'too little was to be gained by the change to render such a design on her part probable.' Alienated from the king's affection and council, the queen remained without influence till death took away monarch and minister and left to Anne, as mother of the infant monarch (Louis XIV.), the undisputed reins of power. With great discernment, she chose for her minister, Mazarin, who was entirely dependent upon her, and whose abilities she made use of without being in danger from his ambition. But the minister became unpopular: a successful insurrection ensued, and Anne and the court were detained for a time prisoners in the Palais Royal, by the mob. The Spanish pride of the queen was compelled to submit, and the people had their will. But a civil war soon commenced between Anne, her ministers and their adherents, on one side; and the *noblesse*, the citizens and people of Paris, on the other. The former triumphed, and hostilities were suspended; but the war again broke out: the court had secured a defender in Turenne, who triumphed over the young *noblesse* headed by the great Condé! The nobles and middle classes were never afterwards able to raise their heads, or offer resistance to the royal power up to the period of the great Revolution; so that Anne of Austria may be said to have founded absolute monarchy in France, and not the subsequent imperiousness of Louis XIV. Anne's portrait in the Vienna gallery shews her to have been of pleasing exterior. Her Spanish haughtiness and love of ceremonial were impressed by education upon the mind of her son, Louis XIV., who bears the blame and the credit of much that was his mother's. She died at the age of sixty-four.

DEATH OF GARRICK.

Garrick, who 'never had his equal as an actor, and will never have a rival,' at Christmas 1778, while on a visit to Lord Spencer, at Althorpe, had a severe fit, from which he only recovered sufficiently to enable him to return to town, where he expired on the 20th of January 1779, in his own house, in the centre of the Adelphi Terrace,* in his sixty-third year. Dr Johnson said, 'his death eclipsed the gaiety of nations.' Walpole, in the opposite extreme: 'Garrick is dead; not a public loss; for he had quitted the stage.' Garrick's remains lay in state at his house previous to their interment in Westminster Abbey, with great pomp: there were not at Lord Chatham's funeral half the noble coaches that attended Garrick's, which is attributable to a political cause. Burke was one of the mourners, and came expressly from Portsmouth to follow the great actor's remains.

SIR JOHN SOANE.

This successful architect died at his house in Lincoln's Inn Fields, surrounded by the collection of antiquities and artistic treasures which he bequeathed to the British nation, as "the Soanean Museum." He was a man of exquisite taste, but of most irritable temperament, and the tardy settlement of the above bequest to the country was to him a matter of much annoyance. His remains rest in the burial-ground of St Giles's-in-the-Fields, St Pancras, where two tall cypresses overshadow his tomb. At his death, the trustees appointed by parliament took charge of the Museum, library, books, prints, manuscripts,

* The ceiling of the front drawing-room was painted by Antonio Zucchi, A.R.A.: the chimney-piece is said to have cost £300. Garrick died in the back drawing-room, and his widow in the same house and room in 1822.

drawings, maps, models, plans and works of art, and the house and offices; providing for the admission of amateurs and students in painting, sculpture, and architecture; and general visitors. The entire collection cost Soane upwards of £50,000.

THE FIRST PARLIAMENT.

It was a great date for England, that of the First Parliament. There had been a Council of the great landholders, secular and ecclesiastic, from Anglo-Saxon times; and it is believed by some that the Commons were at least occasionally and to some extent represented in it. But it was during a civil war, which took place in the middle of the thirteenth century, marvellously like that which marked the middle of the seventeenth, being for law against arbitrary royal power, that the first parliaments, properly so called, were assembled. Matthew of Paris, in his *Chronicle*, first uses the *word* in reference to a council of the barons in 1246. At length, in December 1264, when that extraordinary man, Simon de Montfort Earl of Leicester—a mediæval Cromwell—held the weak King Henry III. in his power, and was really the head of the state, a parliament was summoned, in which there should be two knights for each county, and two citizens for every borough; the first clear acknowledgment of the Commons' element in the state. This parliament met on the 20th of January 1265, in that magnificent hall at Westminster * which still survives, so interesting a monument of many of the most memorable events of English history. The representatives of the Commons sat in the same place with their noble associates, probably at the bottom of the hall, little disposed to assert a controlling voice, not joining indeed in any vote, for we hear of no such thing at first, and far of course from having any adequate sense of the important results that were to flow from their appearing there that day. There, however, they were—an admitted Power, entitled to be consulted in all great national movements, and, above all, to have a say in the matter of taxation. The summer months saw Leicester overpowered, and himself and nearly all his associates slaughtered; many changes afterwards took place in the constitutional system of the country; but the *Commons*, once allowed to play a part in these great councils, were never again left out. Strange that other European states of high civilization and intelligence should be scarcely yet arrived at a principle of popular representation, which England, in comparative barbarism, realised for herself six centuries ago!

THE COLDEST DAY IN THE CENTURY, JAN. 20, 1838.

Notwithstanding the dictum of M. Arago, that 'whatever may be the progress of the sciences, never will observers who are trustworthy and careful of their reputation, venture to foretell the state of the weather,'—this pretension received a singular support in the winter of 1838. This was the first year in which the noted Mr Murphy

* Fabyan's Chronicle, i. 356.

published his *Weather Almanac;* wherein his indication for the 20th day of January is ' Fair. Prob. lowest deg. of Winter temp.' By a happy chance for him, this proved to be a remarkably cold day. At sunrise, the thermometer stood at 4° below zero; at 9 a.m., +6°; at 12 (noon), +14°; at 2 p.m., 16½°; and then increased to 17°, the highest in the day; the wind veering from the east to the south.

The popular sensation of course reported that the lowest degree of temperature for the season appeared to have been reached. The supposition was proved by other signal circumstances, and particularly the effects seen in the vegetable kingdom. In all the nursery-grounds about London, the half-hardy, shrubby plants were more or less injured. Herbaceous plants alone seemed little affected, in consequence, perhaps, of the protection they received from the snowy covering of the ground.

Two things may be here remarked, as being almost unprecedented in the annals of meteorology in this country: first, the thermometer below zero for some hours; and secondly, a rapid change of nearly fifty-six degrees. — *Correspondent of the Philosophical Magazine,* 1838.

Still, there was nothing very remarkable in Murphy's indication, as the coldest day in the year is generally about this time (January 20). Nevertheless, it was a fortunate hit for the weather prophet, who is said to have cleared £3000 by that year's almanac!

It may amuse the reader to see what were the results of Murphy's predictions throughout the year 1838:

	Days.	Decidedly wrong days.
January, partly right on	23	8
February	8	20
March	11	20
April	15	15
May	12	19
June	18	12
July	10	20
August	15	15
September	15	15
October	11	20
November	14	16
December	15	16

[The cold of January 1838 was much exceeded by that of January 1881. The average for the former month was 28·2°; for the latter, 27·8°. On 17th January 1881, the thermometer fell to 9° in the air and 7° on the ground. On the 20th, it was 15°.]

SKATING.

This seems a fair opportunity of adverting to the winter amusement of skating, which is not only an animated and cheerful exercise, but susceptible of many demonstrations which may be called elegant. Holland, which with its extensive water surfaces affords such peculiar facilities for it, is usually looked to as the home and birthplace of skating; and we do not hear of it in England till the thirteenth century. In the former country, as has been remarked in an early page of this volume, the use of skates is in great favour; and it is even taken advantage of as a

means of travelling, market-women having been known, for a prize, to go in this manner thirty miles in two hours. Opportunities for the exercise are, in Britain, more limited. Nevertheless, wherever a piece of smooth water exists, the due freezing of its surface never fails to bring forth hordes of enterprising youth to enjoy this truly inviting sport.

Skating has had its bone age before its iron one. Fitzstephen, in his *History of London,* tells us that it was customary in the twelfth century for the young men to fasten the leg-bones of animals under their feet by means of thongs, and slide along the ice, pushing themselves by means of an iron-shod pole. Imitating the chivalric fashion of the tournament, they would start in a career against each other, meet, use their poles for a push or a blow, when one or other was pretty sure to be hurled down, and to slide a long way in a prostrate condition, probably with some considerable hurt to his person, which we may hope was generally borne with good humour. In Moorfields and about Finsbury, specimens of these primitive skates have from time to time been exhumed, recalling the time when these were marshy fields, which in winter were resorted to by the youth of London for the amusements which Fitzstephen describes. A pair preserved in the British Museum is here delineated.

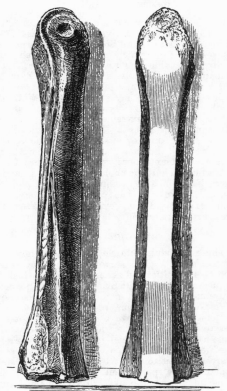

PRIMITIVE BONE SKATES.

The iron age of skating—whenever it might come—was an immense stride in advance. A pair of iron skates, made in the best modern fashion, fitted exactly to the length of the foot, and, well fastened on, must be admitted to be an instrument satisfactorily adapted for its purpose. With unskilled skaters, who constitute the great multitude, even that simple onward movement in which they indulge, using the *inner* edge of the skates, is something to be not lightly appreciated, seeing that few movements are more exhilarating. But this is but the *walk* of the art. What may be called the *dance* is a very different thing. The highly trained skater aims at performing a series of movements of a graceful kind, which may be looked upon with the same pleasure as we experience from seeing a fine picture. Throwing himself on the *outer* edge of his instrument, poising himself out of the perpendicular line in attitudes which set off a handsome person to uncommon advantage, he performs a series of curves within a certain limited space, cuts the figure 8,

SKATING SCENE.

the figure 3, or the circle, *worms and screws* backwards and forwards, or with a group of companions goes through what he calls waltzes and quadrilles. The calmness and serenity of these movements, the perfect self-possession evinced, the artistic grace of the whole exhibition, are sure to attract bystanders of taste, including examples of the fair,—

> ———'whose bright eyes
> Rain influence.'

Most such performers belong to skating clubs,— fraternities constituted for the cultivation of the art *as an art*, and to enforce proper regulations. In Edinburgh, there is one such society of old standing, whose favourite ground is Duddingston Loch, under the august shadow of Arthur's Seat. The writer recalls with pleasure skating exhibitions which he saw there in the hard winters early in the present century, when Henry Cockburn and the philanthropist James Simpson were conspicuous amongst the most accomplished of the club for their handsome figures and great skill in the art. The scene of that loch 'in full bearing,' on a clear winter day, with its busy stirring multitude of sliders, skaters, and curlers, the snowy hills around glistening in the sun, the ring of the ice, the shouts of the careering youth, the rattle of the curling stones and the shouts of the players, once seen and heard, could never be forgotten.

In London, the amusements of the ice are chiefly practised upon the artificial pieces of water in the parks. On Sunday the 6th of January 1861, during an uncommonly severe frost, it was calculated that of sliders and skaters, mostly of the humbler grades of the population, there were about 6000 in St James's Park, 4000 on the Round Pond in Kensington Gardens, 25,000 in the Regent's Park, and 30,000 on the Serpentine in

Hyde Park. There was, of course, the usual proportion of heavy falls, awkward collisions, and occasional immersions, but all borne good-humouredly, and none attended with fatal consequences. During the ensuing week the same pieces of ice were crowded, not only all the day, but by night also, torches being used to illuminate the scene, which was one of the greatest animation and gaiety. On three occasions there were refreshment tents on the ice, with gay flags, variegated lamps, and occasional fire-works; and it seemed as if half London had come to look on from the neighbouring walks and drives.

In these ice-festivals, as usually presented in London, there is not much elegant skating to be seen. The attraction of the scene consists mainly in the infinite appearances of mirth and enjoyment which meet the gaze of the observer.

The same frost period occasioned a very remarkable affair of skating in Lincolnshire. Three companies of one of the Rifle Volunteer regiments of that county assembled on the Witham, below the Stamp End Loch (December 29, 1860), and had what might be called a skating parade of several hours on the river, performing various evolutions and movements in an orderly manner, and on some occasions attaining a speed of fourteen miles an hour. In that province, pervaded as it is by waters, it was thought possible that, on some special occasion, a rendezvous of the local troops might be effected with unusual expedition in this novel way.

St. Agnes's Eve.

The feast of St Agnes was formerly held as in a special degree a holiday for women. It was thought possible for a girl, on the eve of St Agnes, to obtain, by divination, a knowledge of her future husband. She might take a row of pins, and plucking them out one after another, stick them in her sleeve, singing the whilst a paternoster; and thus insure that her dreams would that night present the person in question. Or, passing into a different country from that of her ordinary residence, and taking her right-leg stocking, she might knit the left garter round it, repeating:—

'I knit this knot, this knot I knit,
To know the thing I know not yet,
That I may see
The man that shall my husband be,
Not in his best or worst array,
But what he weareth every day;
That I to-morrow may him ken
From among all other men.'

Lying down on her back that night, with her hands under her head, the anxious maiden was led to expect that her future spouse would appear in a dream and salute her with a kiss.

On this superstition, John Keats founded his beautiful poem, *The Eve of St Agnes*, of which the essence here follows:—

'They told her how, upon St Agnes's Eve,
Young virgins might have visions of delight,
And soft adorings from their loves receive
Upon the honey'd middle of the night,
If ceremonies due they did aright;

140

As, supperless to bed they must retire,
And couch supine their beauties, lily white;
Nor look behind, nor sideways, but require
Of Heaven with upward eyes for all that they desire.

*   *   *   *   *   *   *

'Out went the taper as she hurried in;
Its little smoke, in pallid moonshine, died:
She closed the door, she panted, all akin
To spirits of the air, and visions wide.
No utter'd syllable, or, woe betide!
But to her heart, her heart was voluble,
Paining with eloquence her balmy side;
As though a tongueless nightingale should swell
Her throat in vain, and die, heart-stifled, in her dell.

'A casement high and triple arch'd there was,
All garlanded with carven imag'ries
Of fruits, and flowers, and bunches of knot grass,
And diamonded with panes of quaint device
Innumerable of stains and splendid dyes,
As are the tiger-moth's deep damask'd wings;
And in the midst, 'mong thousand heraldries,
And twilight saints, with dim emblazonings,
A shielded 'scutcheon blush'd with blood of queens and
    kings.

'Full on this casement shone the wintry moon,
And threw warm gules on Madeline's fair breast,
As down she knelt for Heaven's grace and boon;
Rose-bloom fell on her hands, together prest,
And on her silver cross soft amethyst,
And on her hair a glory, like a saint.

*   *   *   *   *   *   *

                         Her vespers done,
Of all its wreathed pearls her hair she frees;
Unclasps her warmed jewels one by one;
Loosens her fragrant bodice; by degrees
Her rich attire creeps rustling to her knees:
Half-hidden, like a mermaid in sea-weed,
Pensive awhile she dreams awake, and sees,
In fancy, fair St Agnes in her bed,
But dares not look behind, or all the charm is fled.

'Soon, trembling in her soft and chilly nest,
In sort of wakeful swoon, perplex'd she lay;
Until the poppied warmth of sleep oppress'd
Her soothed limbs, and soul fatigued away;
Flown, like a thought, until the morrow day,
Blissfully haven'd both from joy and pain;
Clasp'd like a missal where swart Paynims pray;
Blinded alike from sunshine and from rain,
As though a rose should shut, and be a bud again.

'Stol'n to this paradise, and so entranced,
Porphyro gazed upon her empty dress,
And listened to her breathing.

*   *   *   *   *   *   *

                    He took her hollow lute,—
Tumultuous,—and, in chords that tenderest be,
He played an ancient ditty, long since mute,
In Provence call'd "La belle dame sans mercy:"
Close to her ear touching the melody;—
Wherewith disturb'd, she utter'd a soft moan:
He ceased—she panted quick—and suddenly
Her blue affrayed eyes wide open shone:
Upon his knees he sank, pale as smooth-sculptured
    stone.

'Her eyes were open, but she still beheld,
Now wide awake, the vision of her sleep:
There was a painful change, that nigh expell'd
The blisses of her dream so pure and deep,
At which fair Madeline began to weep,
And moan forth witless words with many a sigh;
While still her gaze on Porphyro would keep;
Who knelt, with joined hands and piteous eye,
Fearing to move or speak, she look'd so dreamingly.

" Ah, Porphyro !" said she, "but even now
  Thy voice was at sweet tremble in mine ear,
  Made tuneable with every sweetest vow ;
  And those sad eyes were spiritual and clear :
  How changed thou art ! how pallid, chill, and
    drear !
Give me that voice again, my Porphyro,
  Those looks immortal, those complainings dear !
Oh, leave me not in this eternal woe,
For if thou diest, my love, I know not where to go."

 'Beyond a mortal man impassion'd far
  At these voluptuous accents, he arose,
  Ethereal, flush'd, and like a throbbing star,
  Seen 'mid the sapphire heaven's deep repose,
  Into her dream he melted, as the rose
  Blendeth its odour with the violet,—
  Solution sweet : meantime the frost-wind blows,
  Like Love's alarum pattering the sharp sleet
Against the window-panes.

     *   *   *   *   *   *   *

" Hark ! 'tis an elfin-storm from faëry land,
  Of haggard seeming, but a boon indeed.
Arise—arise ! the morning is at hand ;—
  Let us away, my love, with happy speed.—

     *   *   *   *   *   *   *

And they are gone : ay, ages long ago
These lovers fled away into the storm.'

JANUARY 21.

St Fructuosus, 259.   St Agnes, virgin-martyr, 304 or
305.   St Epiphanius, 497.   St Vimin, or Vivian (?),
615.   St Publius.

ST AGNES.

St Agnes—than whom there is no saint more
revered by the Romish church—is usually described as a young Roman girl, who suffered
savage persecution, and finally martyrdom, under
Diocletian. Upon the place of her supposed
death, a church was built, and may still be seen
without the walls of Rome ; another was dedicated
to her within the city. There is at Rome an
annual procession in her honour, when a lamb,
highly decorated, is led through the city. The
connection of her name with the Latin for a lamb
(*agnus*) has probably led to the association of this
animal with her memory.

Born.—Henry VII., King of England, *Pembroke Castle*,
1456 ; Thomas Lord Erskine, 1750 ; Admiral William
Smyth, 1788.

Died.—Miles Coverdale, translator of the Scriptures,
1568 ; Joseph Scaliger, 1609 ; James Quin, actor, *Bath*,
1766 ; J. H. Bernard de St Pierre, 1814 ; Dr Robert
Macnish, miscellaneous writer, 1837 ; Henry Hallam, historian, 1859.

ERRONEOUS ESTIMATES OF AGES.

Partly from the crafty and astute character of
the man, partly from the tedious bad health
of his latter years, partly perhaps from our hearing of him so much in the relation of a father, we
always think of Henry VII. as an elderly person.
Yet he died in the fifty-third year of his age.
There is something of the like illusion regarding
several other royal personages in English history.
For example, the deposed Henry VI. is usually
thought of as a man well up in years at the time

of his death; but he never got beyond his
forty-sixth. His ancestor John of Gaunt, whom
(following Shakspeare) we think of as 'time-
honoured Lancaster,' died at fifty-nine. At the
same period of life died James I., whom we always
represent to ourselves as an old man. The manner in which historical personages are spoken of,
in respect of age, by their contemporaries, has
helped us in some measure into this illusion.
Malone remarks as follows : ' Our ancestors, in
their estimate of old age, appear to have estimated
somewhat differently from us, and to have considered men as old whom we should now esteem
middle-aged. With them every man who had
passed fifty seems to have been accounted an old
man. King Henry is represented as old by
Daniel, in his poem of *Rosamond*. Henry was
born in 1133, and died in 1189, at the age of
fifty-six. Robert Earl of Leicester is called an
old man by Spenser in a letter to Gabriel Harvey
in 1582, at which time Leicester was not fifty
years old ; and the French Admiral Coligny is
represented by his biographer Lord Huntington,
as a very old man, though at the time of his death
he was but fifty-three.'

LORD ERSKINE.

It is well known that Lord Erskine had experienced what he considered as a ghostly visitation.
The circumstances, as related by himself, are given
in Lady Morgan's *Book of the Boudoir*.

 ' When I was a very young man, I had been for
some time absent from Scotland. On the morning
of my arrival in Edinburgh, as I was descending
the steps of a close, or coming out from a bookseller's shop, I met our old family butler. He
looked greatly changed, pale, wan, and shadowy
as a ghost. "Eh! old boy," I said, "what brings
you here ?" He replied, "To meet your honour,
and solicit your interference with my lord, to
recover a sum due to me, which the steward at
the last settlement did not pay." Struck by his
looks and manner, I bade him follow me to the
bookseller's, into whose shop I stepped back ; but
when I turned round to speak to him, he had
vanished.

 ' I remembered that his wife carried on some
little trade in the Old Town. I remembered even
the house and flat she occupied, which I had
often visited in my boyhood. Having made it
out, I found the old woman in widow's mourning.
Her husband had been dead for some months,
and had told her on his death-bed, that my
father's steward had wronged him of some
money, but that when Master Tom returned, he
would see her righted. This I promised to do,
and shortly after I fulfilled my promise. The
impression was indelible——.' *

An amusing circumstance regarding Lord
Erskine arose from his becoming possessed of a
Sussex estate, which grew nothing but stunted
birches, and was found totally irreclaimable.
That it might not be wholly a loss to him, he

  * Lord Erskine was born in 1750, and entered the navy
as a midshipman at the age of fourteen : at eighteen he
transferred his services to the army, and at twenty-seven
settled in the study of that profession in which he acquired
such celebrity. He died in 1823.

commenced getting the birches converted into brooms, which were sold throughout the country. One of the broom-sellers being taken before a magistrate for acting thus without a licence, Erskine went to defend him, and contended there was a clause to meet this very case. Being asked which it was, he answered, 'The *sweeping* clause, your worship, which is further fortified by a proviso, that "nothing herein contained shall prevent any proprietor of land from vending the produce thereof in any manner that to him shall seem fit."'

DEATH OF LOUIS XVI.

The 21st of January will long be a memorable day in the history of France, as that on which an agonised nation, driven frantic by the threats of external enemies, threw down the bloody head of their king as a gage of defiance to all gainsayers. Innocent and amiable, but fallen upon evil times, Louis XVI. warmly engages our interest, as a victim who suffered for the evil doings of those who went before him. The story of his imprisonment and death, including the final parting with his family, is one of the saddest ever put on record.

Early on a gloomy winter morning, Paris was astir with the movements of large bodies of troops, forming a guard along the line by which the unfortunate king was conducted from his prison to the scaffold. He had made all religious preparations for death; yet is believed to have still entertained some hope of a rescue, it being understood that five hundred devoted adherents had vowed to interfere in his behalf even at the scaffold. Hence his last moments did not exhibit that serenity and meek submission which would have best become an innocent sufferer. There may, however, be room for debate as to the exact degree in which an unsubmissive spirit manifested itself. Somewhat to the surprise of our generation, it is thus described in Louis Blanc's *Histoire de la Révolution Française*, tom. viii., published in 1856:—

'At ten minutes past ten, they reached the foot of the scaffold. It had been erected in front of the Palace of the Tuileries, in the square called after Louis the Fifteenth, and near the spot where stood the statue of the most corrupt of kings—a king who died tranquilly in his bed. The condemned was three minutes descending from the carriage. Upon quitting the Temple he had refused the redingote which Cléry had offered him, and now appeared in a brown coat, white waistcoat, grey breeches, and white stockings. His hair was not disordered, nor was any change perceptible in his countenance. The Abbé Firmont was dressed in black. A large open space had been kept round the scaffold,—with cannon ranged on every side,—while beyond, as far as the eye could reach, stood an unarmed multitude gazing. . . . Descending from his carriage, Louis fixed his eyes upon the soldiers who surrounded him, and with a menacing voice cried, "Silence!" The drums ceased to beat, but at a signal from their officer, the drummers again went on. "What treason is this?" he shouted; "I am lost! I am lost!" For it was evident that up to this moment he had been

clinging to hope. The executioners now approached to take off a part of his clothes; he repulsed them fiercely, and himself removed the collar from his neck. But all the blood in his frame seemed to be turned into fire when they sought to tie his hands. "Tie my hands!" he shrieked. A struggle was inevitable:—it came. It is indisputable, says Mercier, that Louis fought with his executioners. The Abbé Edgeworth stood by, perplexed, horrified, speechless. At last, as his master seemed to look inquiringly at him, he said, "Sir, in this additional outrage I only see a last trait of the resemblance between your Majesty and the God who will give you your reward." At these words the indignation of the man gave way to the humility of the Christian, and Louis said to the executioners, "I will drain the cup to the dregs." They tied his hands, they cut off his hair, and then, leaning on the arm of his confessor, he began, with a slow tread and sunken demeanour, to mount the steps, then very steep, of the guillotine. Upon the last step, however, he seemed suddenly to rouse, and walked rapidly across to the other side of the scaffold; when, by a sign commanding silence, he exclaimed, "I die innocent of the crimes imputed to me." His face was now very red, and, according to the narrative of his confessor, his voice was so loud that it could be heard as far as the Pont-Tournant. Some other expressions were distinctly heard, "I pardon the authors of my death, and I pray Heaven that the blood you are about to shed may never be visited upon France." He was about to continue, when his voice was drowned by the renewed rolling of the drums, at a signal which, it is affirmed, was given by the comedian Dugayon, in anticipation of the orders of Santerre. "Silence! be silent!" cried Louis the Sixteenth, losing all self-control, and stamping violently with his foot. Richard, one of the executioners, then seized a pistol, and took aim at the king. It was necessary to drag him along by force. With difficulty fastened to the fatal plank, he continued to utter terrible cries, only interrupted by the fall of the knife.'

THE FATE OF CAPTAIN ALLEN GARDINER.

It was a mournful spectacle that met the eyes of the crew of H.M.S. *Dido*, when, on the 21st of January, 1852, they found the remains of Captain Allen Gardiner and his hapless companions, on the dismal shore of Terra del Fuego, at the southern extremity of America. First came to light some direction, rudely written on a rock; then a boat lying on the beach at the mouth of a small river; then the unburied bodies of Gardiner and his friend Maidment; then a packet of papers and books; then the shattered remains of another boat, with part of her gear and stores, and various articles of clothing; then two more dead bodies; and lastly, the graves of the rest of the party.

Allen Gardiner was a remarkable man; one of those in whom the hardy seaman is combined with the deeply pious Christian: so strongly imbued, indeed, was he with piety, that the last years of his life were those of a missionary rather than of a sea-captain. He made many attempts at rescuing barbarous tribes from heathendom in various parts of the world. On returning from one of his voyages, in 1849, Gardiner formed a plan for sending out a missionary ship to Terra del Fuego, in the hope of Christianizing the rude Fuegians and Patagonians. During a year or more his efforts were unavailing. First the Moravian Brethren, then the Scottish National Church. declined to enter into his views. At last, a lady at Cheltenham provided him with £700; and this, with £300 from his own private purse, formed the resources on which he acted. Unable to afford a brigantine or schooner, as he had wished, he contented himself with four open boats, which he caused to be built at Liverpool. Two of these were launches of considerable size, named by him the *Pioneer* and the *Speedwell;* the other two were small dingies, used as tenders or luggage boats. He sought and found six companions willing to share his perilous enterprise— a surgeon, a missionary, and four hardy, God-fearing Cornish boatmen. In September 1850, the ship *Ocean Queen*, bound from Liverpool to California, took out Gardiner. his companions, his boats, and six months' provisions. They were landed on the inhospitable foreign shore on the 5th of December.

From the day when the *Ocean Queen* left them to pursue her voyage round Cape Horn, the eye of no civilized man ever saw these brave sailor-missionaries alive. All that is known of them has been gathered from the papers subsequently found. Their life must have been one of continual hardship, cheered by nothing but the consciousness of a good motive. Seven men, in four open boats, went to convert barbarians, whose language they did not understand, and in a country singularly bare of food. Such was the enterprise, noble in intent, but deficient in practical foresight. They soon found the boats to be much encumbered with stores, and the *Pioneer* somewhat leaky. In several short voyages from island to island, and from shore to shore, they encountered numberless mishaps. Sometimes the natives came down to the beach and drove them away; sometimes they appeared more friendly, but robbed those whose mission they could not of course understand. During a storm both dingies were lost, with their contents ; during another, the anchors and the spare timber were lost. Next, they found that all their gunpowder had been forgetfully left behind in the *Ocean Queen*, and that they had no means of shooting birds or other animals for food. Thus wore away the month of January, 1851. So far from their missionary labours having been begun, it was with them a struggle for the maintenance of their own lives. As time advanced, their dangers were increased. On the 1st of February their poor *Pioneer* was shattered during a storm; and now they had only the *Speedwell* to voyage in—a boat whose name almost mocked them in their misery. From this day their anxious eyes were turned, not to the rude Fuegians, but to the arrival of some ship from England with succour. Arrangements had been made for sending out further supplies to them; Gardiner and his companions did not know of the various mischances that retarded (till too late) the carrying out of these plans. Some of the men became ill with the scurvy ; some lived in a cavern, that the boats might become more comfortable as hospitals for the others. A few fish and fowl were caught ; but nothing that required shooting. So March and April passed : and then the Antarctic winter began, adding snow and ice to their other troubles. From the middle of May they were all put on short allowance, owing to the rapid disappearance of their six months' stores. At the end of June one of the brave Cornishmen, Badcock, died, worn out with scurvy. There is an entry in Gardiner's diary, about the end of June, enumerating the articles still left ; and among them were 'six mice,' concerning which he said : 'The mention of this last item in our list of provisions may startle some of our friends, should it ever reach their ears ; but circumstanced as we are, we partake of them with a relish, and have already eaten several of them ; they are very tender, and taste like rabbit.' A solitary penguin, a dead fox, a half-devoured fish thrown up on shore,—all were welcomed by the half-starved men.

When August arrived, the strength of all was nearly exhausted. A few garden seeds were made into a kind of gruel ; and mussel-broth was served to the invalids. Captain Gardiner himself lived on mussels for a fortnight, and was then compelled to give up this diet. He was about to lie down resignedly to die, when the discovery of a kind of rock-weed gave him a little further respite. On the 23rd, Erwin the boatman died, exhausted by hunger and disease; and on the 26th another boatman, Bryant, followed him. Pearce, the remaining boatman, went nearly mad at the loss of his companions. Mr Maidment, the missionary, had just strength sufficient to dig a grave and deposit the last remains of the two poor fellows in it. He then made a pair of crutches with two sticks, on which Captain Gardiner might lean while walking a little ; for these two, with their cavern and their shattered *Pioneer*, were at some little distance from the *Speedwell;* and Gardiner wished that he and the remnant of his little band, if God willed them to die on that dismal spot, should at least die in companionship. It was not to be, however; his strength failed him too soon, and he returned to the cavern. The heroic, unrepining Maidment died on the 2nd of September. Gardiner was helpless: there was no Maidment to find a bit of food for him, and he could not rise to search for it himself. Hunger on the 3rd and 4th, hunger on the 5th and 6th ; no food ; and only just strength enough to write a few lines on paper which he hoped might one day reach friendly hands. It is supposed that he sank into the arms of death on the evening of the 6th, but none was near to make the record; nor can we know whether the remaining two of the unfortunate band (Mr Williams the surgeon, and Pearce the boatman, who were in or near the *Speedwell*) died a little before or a little after their chief. The difference of date could not be much ; for health, strength, and food were alike wanting to all.

It matters little here to notice by what cross-purposes supplies of food and other necessaries failed to reach Patagonia till too late. When Captain Moorshead, in the *Dido,* touched at that spot, (which he was permitted by the Government to do, on the earnest solicitation of Gardiner's friends,) various writings guided him from place to place, till he came to the poor shattered *Pioneer*. 'Captain Gardiner's body was lying beside the boat, which apparently he had left, and being too weak to climb into it again, had died by the side of it. We were directed to the cavern by a hand painted on the rock, with Psalm lxii. 5—8, under it.' Mr Maidment's body was found in the cavern.

Here is the last scene of the tragedy. 'Their remains,' says Captain Moorshead, speaking of the seven deceased men, 'were collected together and buried close to the spot, and the funeral service read by Lieutenant Underwood. A short inscription was placed on the rock near his own text; the colours of the boats and ships were struck half mast; and three volleys of musketry were the only tribute of respect I could pay to this lofty-minded man and his devoted companions.'

JANUARY 22.

St Vincent, martyr at Valencia, 304. St Anastasius, martyr in Assyria, 628.

ST VINCENT.

Vincent was a Spanish saint, martyred under the proconsul Dacian in the fourth century. The recital of his pious serenity and cheerfulness under unheard-of tortures, is very striking. After having been cruelly broiled over a fire, he was put into a dungeon, bound in stocks, and left without provisions. 'But God,' says Butler, 'sent his angels to comfort him, with whom he sung the praises of his protector. The gaoler, observing through the chinks the prison filled with light, and the saint walking and praising God, was converted upon the spot to the Christian faith, and afterwards baptized.' The bones of the martyr were afterwards kept with the utmost veneration, and Butler speaks of some parts of the body as being still preserved in religious houses in France.

St Vincent's Day.

It is not surprising that a saint with such a history as that of St Vincent should have made a deep impression on the popular mind, and given rise to superstitious ideas. The ancient remark on his day was couched in somewhat obscure terms: 'Vincenti festo, si sol radiet, memor esto;' merely calling us to remember if the sun shone on that day. The matter was a mystery to modern investigators of folk lore, till a gentleman residing in Guernsey, looking through some family documents of the sixteenth century, found a scrap of verse expressed in old provincial French:

> ' Prens garde au jour St Vincent,
> Car, sy ce jour tu vois et sent
> Que le soleil soiet cler et biau,
> Nous érons du vin plus que l'eau.' *

* Notes and Queries, ix. 307.

Not, as might at first sight be supposed, an intimation to *bon-vivants*, that in that case there would be a greater proportion of wine than of water throughout the year, but a hint to the vine-culturing peasantry that the year would be a dry one, and favourable to the vintage. It will be found that St Vincent's is not the only day from whose weather that of the future season is prognosticated.

Born.—Francis Bacon, Lord Verulam, 1561 ; Sir Robert Cotton, 1570 ; P. Gassendi, 1592 ; Gotthold Lessing, 1729 ; George Lord Byron, *London*, 1788.

Died.—George Steevens, editor of Shakspeare, *Hampstead*, 1800 ; John F. Blumenbach, physiologist, 1840 ; Richard Westall, painter, 1850.

FRANCIS BACON.

Ours is a white-washing age, and, perhaps, to speak in all seriousness, justice and generosity alike do call for the reconsideration of some of the verdicts of the past. Bacon—whose intellectual greatness as the expositor of the inductive philosophy has always been admitted, but whose bribe-receiving as a judge has laid him open to the condemnation of Pope, as

'The wisest, greatest, meanest of mankind'—

has found a defender in these latter days in Mr Hepworth Dixon. The great fact which stares us in the face is, that Bacon, when about to be

MONUMENT TO LORD BACON.

prosecuted for bribe-receiving by the House of Lords, gave in a paper, in which he used the words : 'I confess that I am guilty of corruption, and do renounce all defence, and put myself upon the grace and mercy of your lordships.' One would think this fact, followed as it duly was by his degradation from the post of Lord Chancellor, enough to appal the most determined white-washer. Nevertheless, Mr Dixon has come valiantly to the rescue, and really made out a wonderfully good case for his client.

His explanations chiefly come to this : the wife of the king's favourite, the Duke of Buckingham, wished to get Bacon's place for a friend of her own ; and Coke, a rival and enemy of Bacon, made common cause with her grace. In the loose and bad practice of that age, when it was customary to give presents even to royalty every new-year's morning, and influence and patronage were sought in all directions by these means, it was not difficult to get up a charge against a chancellor so careless and indifferent to conceal-ment as Bacon. He, taken at a disadvantage under sickness, at first met the twenty-two cases of alleged bribery with an indignant declaration of his innocence of all beyond failing in some instances to inform himself whether the cause was fully at an end before receiving the alleged gift. And it really did, after all, appear that only in three instances was the case still before the court at the time when the gifts were made ; and in these there were circumstances fully shewing that no thought of bribery was entertained, nor any of its ordinary results experienced. Bacon, how-ever, was soon made to see that his ruin was determined on, and unavoidable ; while by yield-ing to the assault he might still have hopes from the king's grace. Thus was he brought to make the confession which admitted of a certain degree of guilt ; in consequence of which he was expelled the House of Peers, prohibited the court, fined forty thousand pounds, and cast into the Tower. The guilt which he admitted, however, was not that of taking bribes to pervert justice, but that of allowing fees to be paid into his court at irregular times.

Mr Dixon says : 'A series of public acts in which the King and Council concurred, attested the belief in his substantial innocence. By separate and solemn acts he was freed from the Tower ; his great fine was remitted ; he was allowed to reside in London ; he was summoned to take his seat in the House of Lords. Society reversed his sentence even more rapidly than the Crown. When the fight was over, and Lord St Albans was politically a fallen man, no con-temporary who had any knowledge of affairs ever dreamt of treating him as a convicted rogue. The wise and noble loved him, and courted him more in his adversity than they had done in his days of grandeur. No one assumed that he had lost his virtue because he had lost his place. The good George Herbert held him in his heart of hearts ; an affection which Bacon well repaid. John Selden professed for him unmeasurable veneration. Ben Jonson expressed, in speaking of him after he was dead, the opinion of all good scholars, and all honest men : "My conceit of his person," says Ben, "was never increased towards him by his place or honours ; but I have and do reverence him for the greatness that was proper only to himself, in that he seemed to me ever by his work one of the greatest of men, and most worthy of admiration that hath been in many ages. In his adversity, I ever prayed that God would give him strength, for greatness he

could not want. Neither could I condole in a word or syllable for him, as knowing no accident could do harm to virtue, but rather help to make it manifest." '

In the dedication of his *Essays* to the Duke of Buckingham, Bacon uses this expression : 'I do conceive that the Latin volume of them, being in the universal language, may last as long as books last.'

The present writer once, at a book-sale, lighted upon a copy of the *Essays*, which bore the name of Adam Smith as its original owner. It con-tained a note, in what he presumes to have been the writing of Mr Smith on this passage, as follows : 'In the preface, what may by some be thought vanity, is only that laudable and innate confidence which any good man and good writer possesses.'

SIR ROBERT BRUCE COTTON, AND THE COTTONIAN LIBRARY.

The life and labours of this distinguished man present a remarkable instance of the application of the study of antiquities to mat-ters of political importance and public benefit Descended from an ancient family, he was born at Denton, in Huntingdonshire, and educated at Trinity College, Cambridge. Having settled in London, he there formed a society of learned men attached to antiquarian pursuits, and soon became a diligent collector of records, charters, and other instruments relating to the history of his country ; a vast number of which had been dispersed among private hands at the dissolution of the monasteries. In the year 1600, we find Cotton assisting Camden in his *Britannia*; and in the same year he wrote an Abstract of the question of Precedency between England and Spain, in consequence of Queen Elizabeth having desired the thoughts of the Society already men-tioned upon that point. Cotton was knighted by James I., during whose reign he was much con-sulted by the privy councillors and ministers of state upon difficult points relating to the consti-tution. He was also employed by King James to vindicate Mary Queen of Scots from the supposed misrepresentations of Buchanan and Thuanus ; and he next, by order of the king, examined, with great learning, the question whether the Papists ought, by the laws of the land, to be put to death or to be imprisoned. From his intimacy with Carr, Earl of Somerset, he was suspected by the Court of having some knowledge of the circumstances of Sir Thomas Overbury's death ; and he was consequently detained in the custody of an alderman of London for five months, and interdicted the use of his library. He sat in the first parliament of King Charles I., for whose honour and safety he was always zealous. In the following year, a manuscript tract, entitled *How a Prince may make himself an absolute Tyrant*, being found in Cotton's library, though unknown to him, he was once more parted from his books by way of punishment. These harassing persecu-tions led to his death, at Cotton House, in West-minster, May 6, 1631. His library, much increased by his son and grandson, was sold to the Crown, with Cotton House (at the west end of Westminster Hall); but in 1712, the mansion falling into decay, the library was removed to Essex House, Strand; thence, in 1730, to Ashburnham House, Westminster, where, by a fire, upwards of 200 of the MSS. were lost, burnt, or defaced; the remainder of the library was removed into the new dormitory of the Westminster School, and, with Major Edwards's bequest of 2000 printed volumes, was transferred to the British Museum. The Cottonian collection originally contained 938 volumes of Charters, Royal Letters, Foreign State Correspondence, and Ancient Registers. It was kept in cases, upon which were the heads of the Twelve Cæsars; above the cases were portraits of the three Cottons, Spelman, Camden, Lambard, Speed, &c., which are now in the British Museum collection of portraits. Besides MSS. the Cottonian collection contained Saxon and English coins, and Roman and English antiquities, all now in the British Museum. Camden, Speed, Raleigh, Selden, and Bacon, all drew materials from the Cottonian library; and in our time the histories of England, by Sharon Turner and Lingard, and numerous other works, have proved its treasures unexhausted.

THE SOUTH SEA BUBBLE.

This day, in the year 1720, inaugurated the most monstrous commercial folly of modern times—the famous *South Sea Bubble*.

In the year 1711, Harley, Earl of Oxford, with the view of restoring public credit, and discharging ten millions of the floating debt, agreed with a company of merchants that they should take the debt upon themselves for a certain time, at the interest of six per cent., to provide for which, amounting to £600,000 per annum, the duties upon certain articles were rendered permanent. At the same time was granted the monopoly of trade to the South Seas, and the merchants were incorporated as the South Sea Company; and so proud was the minister of his scheme, that it was called, by his flatterers, 'the Earl of Oxford's masterpiece.' In 1717, the Company's stock of ten millions was authorised by Parliament to be increased to twelve millions, upon their advancing two millions to Government towards reducing the national debt. The name of the Company was thus kept continually before the public; and though their trade with the South American States was not profitable, they continued to flourish as a monetary corporation. Their stock was in high request; and the directors, determined to fly at high game, proposed to the Government a scheme for no less an object than the paying off the national debt; this proposition being made just on the explosion in Paris of its counterpart, the Mississippi scheme of the celebrated John Law. The first propounder of the South Sea project was Sir John Blount, who had been bred a scrivener, and was a bold and plausible speculator. The Company agreed to take upon themselves the debt, amounting to £30,981,712, at five per cent. per annum, secured until 1727, when the whole was to become redeemable at the pleasure of the Legislature, and the interest to be reduced to four per cent. Upon the 22nd of January 1720, the House of Commons,

in a committee, received the proposal with great favour; the Bank of England was, however, anxious to share in the scheme, but, after some delay, the proposal of the Company was accepted, and leave given to bring in the necessary Bill.

At this crisis an infatuation regarding the South Sea speculation began to take possession of the public mind. The Company's stock rose from 130 to 300, and continued to rise while the Bill was in progress. Mr Walpole was almost the only statesman in the House who denounced the absurdity of the measure, and warned the country of the evils that must ensue; but his admonition was entirely disregarded.

Meanwhile, the South Sea directors and their friends, and especially the chairman of the Company, Blount, employed every stratagem to raise the price of the stock. It was rumoured that Spain would, by treaty with England, grant a free trade to all her colonies, and that silver would thus be brought from Potosi, until it would be almost as plentiful as iron; also, that for our cotton and woollen goods the gold mines of Mexico were to be exhausted. The South Sea Company were to become the richest the world ever saw, and each hundred pound of their stock would produce hundreds per annum to the holder. By this means the stock was raised to near 400; it then fluctuated, and settled at 330, when the Bill was passed, though not without opposition.

Exchange Alley was the seat of the gambling fever; it was blocked up every day by crowds, as were Cornhill and Lombard-street with carriages. In the words of the ballads of the day:

'There is a gulf where thousands fell,
　There all the bold adventurers came;
A narrow sound, though deep as hell,
　'Change Alley is the dreadful name.'—*Swift.*

'Then stars and garters did appear
　Among the meaner rabble;
To buy and sell, to see and hear
　The Jews and Gentiles squabble.
The greatest ladies thither came,
　And plied in chariots daily,
Or pawned their jewels for a sum
　To venture in the Alley.'

On the day the Bill was passed, the shares were at 310; next day they fell to 290. Then it was rumoured that Spain, in exchange for Gibraltar and Port Mahon, would give up places on the coast of Peru; also that she would secure and enlarge the South Sea trade, so that the company might build and charter any number of ships, and pay no per-centage to any foreign power. Within five days after the Bill had become law, the directors opened their books for a subscription of a million, at the rate of £300 for every £100 capital; and this first subscription soon exceeded two millions of original stock. In a few days, the stock advanced to 340, and the subscriptions were sold for double the price of the first payment. Then the directors announced a midsummer dividend of ten per cent. upon all subscriptions. A second subscription of a million at 400 per cent. was then opened, and in a few hours a million and a half was subscribed for.

Meanwhile, innumerable bubble companies started up under the very highest patronage.

The Prince of Wales, becoming governor of one company, is said to have cleared £40,000 by his speculations. The Duke of Bridgewater and the Duke of Chandos were among the schemers. By these deceptive projects, which numbered nearly a hundred, one million and a half sterling was won and lost by crafty knaves and covetous fools. The absurdity of the schemes was palpable: the only policy of the projectors was to raise the shares in the market, and then to sell out, leaving the bubble to burst, perhaps, next morning. One of the schemes was 'A company for carrying on an undertaking of great advantage, but nobody to know what it is:' each subscriber, for £2 deposit, to be entitled to £100 per annum per share; of this precious scheme 1000 shares were taken in six hours, and the deposits paid.

In all these bubbles, persons of both sexes alike engaged ; the men meeting their brokers at taverns and coffee-houses, and the ladies at the shops of milliners and haberdashers ; and such was the crowd and confusion in Exchange Alley, that shares in the same bubble were sold, at the same instant, ten per cent. higher at one end of the Alley than at the other. All this time Walpole continued his gloomy warnings, and his fears were impressed upon the Government ; when the King, by proclamation, declared all unlawful projects to be public nuisances, and to be prosecuted accordingly, and any broker trafficking in them to be liable to a penalty of £5000. Next, the Lords Justices dismissed all petitions for patents and charters, and dissolved all the bubble companies. Notwithstanding this condemnation, other bubbles sprang up daily, and the infatuation still continued. Attempts were made to ridicule the public out of their folly by caricature and satire. Playing-cards bore caricatures of bubble companies, with warning verses, of which a specimen is annexed, copied from a print called *The Bubbler's Medley*.

In the face of such exposures, the fluctuations of the South Sea stock grew still more alarming. On the 28th of May it was quoted at 550, and in four days it rose to 890. Then came a tremendous rush of holders to sell out; and on June 3, so few buyers appeared in the Alley, that stock fell at once from 890 to 640. By various arts of the directors to keep up the price of stock, it finally rose to 1000 per cent. It then became known that Sir John Blount, the chairman, and others, had sold out; and the stock fell throughout the month of August, and on September 2 it was quoted at 700 only.

The alarm now greatly increased. The South Sea Company met in Merchant Taylors' Hall, and endeavoured to appease the unfortunate holders of stock, but in vain : in a few days the price fell to 400. Among the victims was Gay, the poet, who, having had some South Sea stock presented to him, supposed himself to be master of £20,000. At that crisis his friends importuned him to sell, but he rejected the counsel : the profit and principal were lost, and Gay sunk under the calamity, and his life became in danger.

The ministers grew more alarmed, the directors were insulted in the streets, and riots were ap-

prehended. Despatches were sent to the king at Hanover, praying his immediate return. Walpole was implored to exercise his influence with the Bank of England, to induce them to relieve the Company by circulating a number of South Sea bonds. To this the Bank reluctantly con-

sented, but the remedy failed : the South Sea stock fell rapidly : a run commenced upon the most eminent goldsmiths and bankers, some of whom, having lent large sums upon South Sea stock, were obliged to abscond. This occasioned a great run upon the Bank, but the intervention of a holiday gave them time, and they weathered the storm. The South Sea Company were, however, wrecked, and their stock fell ultimately to 150 ; when the Bank, finding its efforts unavailing to stem the tide of ruin, contrived to evade the loosely-made agreement into which it had partially entered.

Public meetings were now held all over England, praying the vengeance of the Legislature upon the South Sea directors, though the nation was as culpable as the Company. The king returned, and parliament met, when Lord Molesworth went so far as to recommend that the people, having no law to punish the directors, should treat them like Roman parricides—tie them in sacks, and throw them into the Thames. Mr Walpole was more temperate, and proposed inquiry, and a scheme for the restoration of public credit, by engrafting nine millions of South Sea stock into the Bank of England, and the same into the East India Company ; and this plan became law. At the same time a Bill was brought in to restrain the South Sea directors, governor, and other officers, from leaving the kingdom for a twelvemonth; and for discovering their estates and effects, and preventing them from transporting or alienating the same. A strange confusion ensued: Mr Secretary Craggs was accused by Mr Shippen, 'downright Shippen,' of collusion in the South Sea business, when he promised to explain his conduct, and a committee of inquiry was appointed. The Lords had been as active as the Commons. The Bishop of Rochester likened the scheme to a pestilence; and Lord Stanhope said that every farthing possessed by the criminals, directors or not, ought to be confiscated, to make good the public losses. The cry out-of-doors for justice was equally loud: Mr Aislabie, the Chancellor of the Exchequer, and Mr Craggs, were openly accused : five directors. including Mr Edward Gibbon, the grandfather of the celebrated historian, were ordered to the custody of the Black Rod, and the Chancellor absented himself from parliament until the charge against him had been inquired into. Meanwhile, Knight, the treasurer of the Company, taking with him the books and documents, and secrets of the directors, escaped disguised in a boat on the Thames, and was conveyed thence to Calais, in a vessel hired for the purpose. Two thousand pounds' reward was, by royal proclamation, offered for his apprehension. The doors of the House of Commons were locked, and the keys placed upon the table, and the inquiry proceeded. The South Sea directors and officers were secured; their papers were seized, and such as were Members of Parliament were expelled the House, and taken into custody. Sir John Blount was examined, but little could be drawn from him; and Lord Stanhope, in replying to a reflection made upon him by the Duke of Wharton, spoke with such vehemence that he fell into a fit, and on the next evening expired. Meanwhile, the treasurer of the Company was apprehended near Liège, and lodged in the citadel of Antwerp; but the States of Brabant refused to deliver him up to the British authorities, and ultimately he escaped from the citadel. There is an admirable caricature of this manœuvre, entitled 'The Brabant Skreen,' in which the Duchess of Kendal, from behind the screen, is supplying Knight with money, to enable him to effect his escape.

On the 10th of February, the Committee of Secrecy reported to Parliament the results of their inquiry, shewing how false and fictitious entries had been made in the books, erasures and alterations made, and leaves torn out; and some of the most important books. had been destroyed altogether. The properties of many thousands of persons, amounting to many millions of money, had been thus made away with. Fictitious stock had been distributed among members of the Government, by way of bribe. to facilitate the passing of the Bill: to the Earl of Sunderland was assigned £50,000; to the Duchess of Kendal, £10,000; to Mr Secretary Craggs, £30,000. Mr Charles Stanhope, one of the Secretaries to the Treasury, had received £250,000, as the difference in the price of some stock, and the account of the Chancellor of the Exchequer shewed £794,451. He had also advised the Company to make their second subscription a

million and a half, instead of a million, without any warrant. In the third subscription his name was down for £70,000; Mr Craggs, senior, for £659,000; the Earl of Sunderland for £160,000; and C. Stanhope for £47,000. Upon this report, the practices were declared to be corrupt, infamous, and dangerous, and a Bill was brought in for the relief of the unhappy sufferers. In the examination of the accused persons, Charles Stanhope was acquitted by a majority of three only, which caused the greatest discontent through the country. Mr Chancellor Aislabie was, however, the greatest criminal, and without a dissentient voice he was expelled the House, all his estate seized, and he was committed a close prisoner to the Tower of London. Next day Sir George Caswall, of a firm of jobbers who had been implicated in the business, was expelled the House, committed to the Tower, and ordered to refund £250,000. The Earl of Sunderland was acquitted, lest a verdict of guilty against him should bring a Tory ministry into power; but the country was convinced of his criminality. Mr Craggs the elder died the day before his examination was to have come on. He left a fortune of a million and a half, which was confiscated for the benefit of the sufferers by the delusion which he had mainly assisted in raising. Every director was mulcted, and two millions and fourteen thousand pounds were confiscated, each being allowed a small residue to begin the world anew. As the guilt of the directors could not be punished by any known laws of the land, a Bill of Pains and Penalties—a retro-active statute—was passed. The characters of the directors were marked with ignominy, and exorbitant securities were imposed for their appearance. To restore public credit was the object of the next measure. At the end of 1720, the South Sea capital stock amounted to £37,800,000, of which the allotted stock only amounted to £24,500,000. The remainder, £13,300,000, was the profit of the Company by the national delusion. Upwards of eight millions were divided among the proprietors and subscribers, making a dividend of about £33 6s. 8d. per cent. Upon eleven millions, lent by. the Company when prices were unnaturally raised, the borrowers were to pay 10 per cent., and then be free; but it was long before public credit was thoroughly restored.

There have been many bubble companies since the South Sea project, but none of such enormity as that national delusion. In 1825, over-speculation led to a general panic; in 1836, abortive schemes had nearly led to results as disastrous; and, in 1845, the grand invention of the railway led to a mania which ruined thousands of speculators. But none of these bubbles was countenanced by those to whom the government of the country was entrusted, which was the blackest enormity in the South Sea Bubble.

The powerful genius of Hogarth did not spare the South Sea scheme, as in the emblematic print here engraved, in which a group of persons riding on wooden horses, the devil cutting fortune into collops, and a man broken on the wheel, are the main incidents,—the scene being at the base of a monument of the folly of the age. Beneath are some rhymes, commencing with

'See here the causes why in London
So many men are made and undone.'

The scene in Exchange Alley has also been excellently painted in our time by Mr E. M. Ward, R.A., with the motley throng of beaux and ladies turned gamblers, and the accessory

THE SOUTH SEA BUBBLE.—CARICATURE BY HOGARTH.

pawnbroker's shop, in a truly Hogarthian spirit. The picture is in the Vernon collection, South Kensington.

ANCIENT WIDOWS.

January 22, 1753, died at Broomlands, near Kelso, Jean Countess of Roxburgh, aged 96. No way remarkable in herself, this lady was notable in some external circumstances. She had undergone one of the longest widowhoods of which any record exists—no less than seventy-one years; for her first and only husband, Robert third Earl of Roxburgh, had been lost in the *Gloucester* frigate. in coming down to Scotland with the Duke of York, on the 7th of May 1682. She must also have been one of the last surviving persons born under the Commonwealth. Her father, the first Marquis of Tweeddale, fought at Long Marston Moor in 1644.

Singular as a widowhood of seventy-one years must be esteemed, it is not unexampled, if we are to believe a sepulchral inscription in Camberwell Church, relating to Agnes Skuner, who died in 1499, at the age of 119, having survived her husband Richard Skuner *ninety-two years!*

These instances of long-enduring widowhoods lead us by association of ideas to a noble lady who, besides surviving her husband without second nuptials during a very long time, was further noted for reaching a much more extraordinary age. Allusion is here made to the celebrated Countess of Desmond, who is usually said to have died early in the seventeenth century, after seeing a hundred and forty years. There has latterly been a disposition to look with doubt on the alleged existence of this venerable person; and the doubt has been strengthened by the discovery that an alleged portrait of her, published by Pennant, proves to be in reality one of Rembrandt's mother. There is, however, very fair evidence that such a person did live, and to a very great age. Bacon, in his *Natural History*, alludes to her as a person recently in life. 'They tell a tale,' says he, 'of the old Countess of Desmond who lived till she was seven score years old, that she did *dentire* [produce teeth] twice or thrice; casting her old teeth, and others coming in their place.' Sir Walter Raleigh, moreover, in his *History of the World*, says: 'I myself *knew* the old Countess of Desmond, of Inchiquin, in Munster, who lived in the year 1589, and many years since, who was married in Edward the Fourth's time, and held her jointure from all the Earls of Desmond since then; and that this is true all the noblemen and gentlemen in Munster can witness.'[*] Raleigh was in Ireland in 1589, on his homeward voyage from Portugal, and might then form the personal acquaintance of this aged lady.

We have another early reference to the Countess from Sir William Temple, who, speaking of cases of longevity, writes as follows: 'The late Robert Earl of Leicester, who was a person of great learning and observation, as well as of truth, told me several stories very extraordinary upon this subject; one of a Countess of Desmond, married out of England in Edward IV.'s time, and who lived far in King James's reign, and was counted to have died some years above a hundred and forty; at which age she came from Bristol to London, to beg some relief at Court, having long been very poor by reason of the ruin of that Irish family into which she was married.'[†]

Several portraits alleged to represent the old Countess of Desmond are in existence: one at Knowle in Kent; another at Bedgebury, near Cranbrook, the seat of A. J. Beresford-Hope, Esq.:

[*] Hist. of World, book i. chap. 5. sec. 5.

[†] Sir W. Temple on Health and Long Life. Works (ed. 1814), iii. 283.

and a third in the house of Mr Herbert at Mucross Abbey, Killarney. On the back of the last is the following inscription : ' Catharine Countesse of Desmonde, as she appeared at ye court of our Sovraigne Lord King James, in this preasent A.D. 1614, and in ye 140th yeare of her age. Thither she came from Bristol to seek relief, ye house of Desmonde having been ruined by Attainder. She was married in the Reigne of King Edward IV., and in ye course of her long Pilgrimage renewed her teeth twice. Her principal residence is at Inchiquin in Munster, whither she undoubtedlye proposeth (her purpose accomplished) incontinentlie to return. LAUS DEO.' Another portrait considered to be that of the old

THE OLD COUNTESS OF DESMOND.

Countess of Desmond has long been in the possession of the Knight of Kerry. It was engraved by Grogan, and published in 1806, and a transcript of it appears on this page. The existence of so many pictures of old date, all alleged to represent Lady Desmond, though some doubt may rest on them all, forms at least a corroborative evidence of her existence. It may here be remarked that the inscription on the back of the Mucross portrait is most probably a production, not of her own day, as it pretends to be, but of some later time. On a review of probabilities, with which we need not tire the reader, it seems necessary to conclude that the old Countess died in 1604, and that she never performed the journey in question to London. Most probably, the Earl of Leicester mistook her in that particular for the widow of the forfeited Garrett Earl of Desmond, of whom we shall presently have to speak.

The question as to the existence of the so-called Old Countess of Desmond was fully discussed a few years ago by various writers in the *Notes and Queries*, and finally subjected to a thorough sifting in an article in the *Quarterly*

Review,[*] evidently the production of one well acquainted with Irish family history. The result was a satisfactory identification of the lady with Katherine Fitzgerald, of the Fitzgeralds of Dromana, in the county of Waterford, the second wife of Thomas twelfth earl of Desmond, who died at an advanced age in the year 1534. The family which her husband represented was one of immense possessions and influence—able to bring an array of five or six thousand men into the field ; but it went to ruin in consequence of the rebellion of Garrett the sixteenth Earl in 1579. Although Countess Katherine was not the means of carrying on the line of the family, she continued in her widowhood to draw her jointure from its wealth ; did so even after its forfeiture. Thus a state paper dated 1589 enumerates, among the forfeitures of the attainted Garrett, ' the castle and manor of Inchiquin, now in the hands of Katherine Fitz-John, late wife to Thomas, sometyme Earl of Desmond, for terme of lyef as for her dower.' It appears that Raleigh had good reason to know the aged lady, as he received a grant out of the forfeited Desmond property, with the obligation to plant it with English families ; and we find him excusing himself for the non-fulfilment of this engagement by saying, ' There remaynes unto me but an old castle and demayne, which are yet in occupation of the old Countess of Desmond for her jointure.'

After all, Raleigh did lease at least two portions of the lands, one to John Cleaver, another to Robert Reve, both in 1589, for rents which were to be of a certain amount ' after the decease of the Lady Cattelyn old Countess Dowager of Desmond, widow,' as the documents shew.[†]

Another important contemporary reference to the old Countess is that made by the traveller Fynes Morrison, who was in Ireland from 1599 to 1603, and was, indeed, shipwrecked on the very coast where the aged lady lived. He says in his *Itinerary* : ' In our time the Countess of Desmond lived to the age of about one hundred and forty years, being able to go on foot four or five miles to the market-town, and using weekly so to do in her last years ; and not many years before she died, she had all her teeth renewed.' After hearing on such good authority of her ladyship's walking powers, we may the less boggle at the tradition regarding the manner of her death, which has been preserved by the Earl of Leicester. According to him, the old lady might have drawn on the thread of life somewhat longer than she did, but for an ..ccident. ' She must needs,' says he, ' climb a nut-tree to gather nuts ; so, falling down, she hurt her thigh, which brought a fever, and that brought death.'

It is plain that, if the Countess was one hundred and forty in 1604, she must have been born in the reign of Edward IV. in 1464, and might be married in his reign, which did not terminate till 1483. It might also be that the tradition about the Countess was true, that she had danced at the English Court with the Duke of Gloucester (Richard III.), of whom it is said she used to affirm that ' he was the handsomest man in the room except his brother Edward, and was very well made.'

JANUARY 23.

St Emerantia, virgin, martyr, about 304. St Clement of Ancyra, martyr, 304. St Agathangelus, 304. St Eusebius, abbot in Assyria, 4th century. Ildefonsus, archbishop of Toledo, 667. St John the Almoner, patriarch of Alexandria, about 7th century. St Raymond of Pennafort, 1275.

ST EUSEBIUS.

St Eusebius 'took nourishment only once in four days, but would not allow any of his monks to pass above two days without eating.'—*Butler.* The intervals were rather long, but, on Eusebius's part, the proportions were generous.

ST RAYMOND.

Raymond of Pennafort was a Spanish saint, who derived his fame from having been one of the earliest and most devoted of the order of St Dominick. By wonderful exertions as a missionary preacher, he restored large portions of his country to Christianity, which had previously been wholly in possession of the Moors. Towards the end of his life, having been taken by James king of Arragon to the island of Majorca, he met there with the most brilliant success in converting the pagan inhabitants, but found all his happiness blighted by the personal immorality of the king. Failing to bring him to a better life, he desired to leave the island ; but this the king would not permit. He even threatened with death any one who should help the holy man to make his escape. What followed may be stated in the words of Butler. 'The saint, full of confidence in God, said to his companion, "A king of the earth endeavours to deprive us of the means of retiring ; but the King of heaven will supply them." He then walked boldly to the waters, spread his cloak upon them, tied up one corner of it to a staff for a sail, and having made the sign of the cross, stepped upon it without fear, whilst his timorous companion stood trembling and wondering on the shore. On this new kind of vessel the saint was wafted with such rapidity that in six hours he reached the harbour of Barcelona, sixty leagues distant from Majorca. Those who saw him arrive in this manner met him with acclamations. But he, gathering up his cloak dry, put it on, stole through the crowd, and entered his monastery. A chapel and a tower, built on the place where he landed, have transmitted the memory of this miracle to posterity. This relation,' says our author, with all desirable gravity, 'is taken from the bull of his canonization, and the earliest historians of his life. The king became a sincere convert, and governed his conscience, and even his kingdoms, by the advice of St Raymond, from that time till the death of the saint.'

Died.—James Earl of Moray, Regent of Scotland, 1570 ; William Pitt, statesman, 1806 ; Sir Francis Burdett, political character, 1844 ; Archdeacon Hare, 1855.

DEATH OF MR PITT.

The last months of the life of this great statesman were embittered by a succession of defeats and reverses, such as might break the proudest or the most stoical spirit that ever swayed the destinies of a great nation. The overthrow of the new coalition which he had succeeded in forming against the French ascendency in the latter part of 1805, is supposed to have combined with the vexation arising from the impeachment of his friend, Lord Melville, to destroy him. Nevertheless, the vigour of his intellectual faculties, and the intrepid haughtiness of his spirit, remained to appearance unaltered. But he could not conceal from the public eye the decay of his health, and the constant anxiety which gnawed at his heart. He had staked everything on a great venture. When the news came of Napoleon's defeat of the great Austrian army and the surrender of Ulm, the minister would give no credit to the rumour ; when it was confirmed, he tried to bear up, but death was in his face. The news of the victory of Trafalgar, which arrived in a few days, seemed to revive him ; and in two days more, when he dined on Lord Mayor's day in Guildhall, in returning thanks for his health being drunk, he said, " Let us hope that England, having saved herself by her energy, may save Europe by her example." These were the last words that he uttered in public. But Austerlitz soon completed what Ulm had begun ; and the peculiar look which Pitt wore after this calamitous event, was described by Wilberforce as the *Austerlitz look.*

Early in December, Pitt retired to Bath, hoping that he might there gather strength for the coming session of Parliament. While there the news reached him of a decisive battle that had been fought and lost in Moravia, and that the coalition was dissolved. He sank under the blow. He came up from Bath by slow journeys, and on the 11th of January, 1806, reached his villa at Putney. On the 20th was to be the parliamentary dinner at the house of the First Lord of the Treasury, in Downing-street ; and the cards were already issued. But the days of the great minister were numbered.

The villa is pleasantly situated upon Putney Heath, surrounded by a few acres of pleasure ground ; and the minister's only chance for life was, that he should spend some months in such repose as this rural retreat afforded. His colleagues in the ministry paid him short visits, and carefully avoided conversation on politics. But his spirit was not quenched even in this extremity. His friend, the Marquess Wellesley, had, a few days before Mr Pitt's return to Putney, arrived in England, after an absence of eight years in India. He wrote to Mr Pitt, who, on the 12th of January, replied from Putney Hill, acknowledging to have received, with inexpressible pleasure, the Marquess's 'most friendly and affectionate letter, requesting to see him at the first possible moment,' adding, 'I am recovering rather slowly from a series of stomach complaints, followed by severe attacks of gout ; but I believe I am now in the way of real amendment.'

This was one of the last letters Mr Pitt ever

wrote. He received the Marquess with his usual kindness and good humour; he talked cheerfully, and with an unclouded mind, and spoke in the warmest terms of commendation of the Marquess's brother, Arthur, saying, 'I never met with any military officer with whom it was so satisfactory to converse. He states every difficulty before he undertakes any service, but none after he has undertaken it.' But the Marquess saw that the hand of death was upon the minister, although the melancholy truth was not known nor believed by either his friends or his opponents.

The excitement of this interview was too much for the sick man; he fainted away, and Lord Wellesley left the house, convinced that the close was fast approaching.

Lord Wellesley having learned that an amendment hostile to Mr Pitt was to be proposed in the House of Commons, warned Lord Granville of the minister's approaching death; he received the fatal intelligence with a burst of tears, and on the first day there was no debate. It was rumoured that evening that Mr Pitt was better; but on the following morning his physicians pronounced that there were no hopes. 'The commanding faculties,' says Lord Macaulay, 'of which he had been too proud, were now beginning to fail. His old tutor and friend, the Bishop of Lincoln, informed him of his danger, and gave such religious advice and consolation as a confused and obscured mind could receive. Stories were told of devout sentiments fervently uttered by the dying man. But these stories found no credit with anybody who knew him. Wilberforce pronounced it impossible that they could be true. "Pitt," he added, "always said less than he thought on such topics." It was asserted in many after-dinner speeches, Grub-street elegies, and academic prize poems, and prize declamations, that the great minister died exclaiming, "Oh! my country!" This is a fable; but it is true that the last words which he uttered, while he knew what he said, were broken exclamations about the alarming state of public affairs. He ceased to breathe on the morning of the 23rd of January 1806, the twenty-fifth anniversary of the day on which he first took his seat in Parliament. He was in his forty-seventh year, and had been, during near nineteen years, excepting for a short interval, First Lord of the Treasury, and undisputed chief of the administration. Since parliamentary government was established in England, no English statesman had held supreme power so long. Walpole, it is true, was First Lord of the Treasury during more than twenty years; but it was not till Walpole had been some time First Lord of the Treasury that he could be properly called Prime Minister.'

With respect to the last moments of the great minister. it was told to a visitor to the house at Putney Hill, in 1817, by a person who was in the chamber a little before Mr Pitt's death, that 'it was heated to a very high and oppressive temperature; and that the deep voice of the dying minister, as he asked his valet a question, startled the visitor who had been unused to it. He died calmly, and apparently under none of those political perturbations which, at the period, were ascribed to his last moments.'

152

A public funeral and a monument were voted to Pitt by Parliament. The funeral took place on the 22nd of February: the corpse, having lain in state during two days in the Painted Chamber, was borne, with great pomp, to the northern transept of Westminster Abbey. A splendid train of princes, nobles, and privy councillors followed. The grave of Pitt had been made near to the spot where his great father, Lord Chatham, lay, and near also to the spot where his great rival (Fox) was soon to lie:

'The mighty chiefs sleep side by side;
Drop upon Fox's grave the tear,
'Twill trickle to his rival's bier.'—*Scott.*

Wilberforce, who carried the banner before Pitt's hearse, described the ceremony with deep feeling. As the coffin descended into the earth, he said, the eagle face of Chatham from above seemed to look down with consternation into the dark house which was receiving all that remained of so much power and glory.

OPENING OF THE FIRST ROYAL EXCHANGE.

In the sixteenth century, Antwerp had led the way in preparing a house specially for the daily assembling of merchants—what was then called a Byrsa or Burse, a term of mediæval Latin, implying expressly a purse, but more largely a place of treasure. The want of such a point of daily rendezvous was felt in London as early as the reign of Henry VIII.; but it was not till the days of his lion-hearted daughter that the idea was realised, through the exertions and liberality of the celebrated Sir Thomas Gresham, a London merchant, who had been royal agent at Antwerp, and ambassador at the minor Italian Court of Parma.

Sir Thomas met with innumerable difficulties in the preliminary arrangements for building his Burse. Some of the merchants preferred the old place of assembling in Lombard-street; others advocated a site between Lombard-street and Cornhill. At length we find the wardens of the twelve principal companies calling upon Gresham at his mansion in Bishopsgate-street, at eight o'clock in the morning, to make arrangements for the site. It was then settled that the houses to be removed for the site—including a 'little old house in Cornehill, inhabited by a widow, which the cytte was driven to buy' for 100 marks—should all be cleared away for the workmen 'to fall in hand with the foundation.' Thirty-eight houses—some of them cottages. a store-house, and two gardens—were demolished in order to make room for the Burse.

The simple manner in which the edifice was given to the citizens is not the least striking incident. On the 9th of February 1565-6, Sir Thomas Gresham, at the house of Alderman Rivers, in company with Sir William Garrard, Sir William Cheeton, Thomas Rowe, and other citizens, 'most frankly and lovingly promised' that within a month after the Burse should be fully finished, he would present it, in equal moieties, to the City and the Mercers' Company. In token of his sincerity, he thereupon gave his hand to Sir William Garrard, and, in the presence of his assembled friends, *drank a carouse* to his kinsman, Thomas Rowe. 'How rarely,' remarks

Mr Burgon, 'do ancient documents furnish us with such a picture of ancient manners!' The first stone of the building was laid by Gresham, June 7, 1566.

On the 23rd of January 1570-1, the building was opened by Queen Elizabeth. Stow relates that 'the Queen's Majesty, attended with her nobility, came from her house at the Strande, called Somerset House, and entred the citie by Temple-bar, through Fleete-streete, Cheap, and so by the north side of the Burse, to Sir Thomas Gresham's in Bishopsgate-streete, where she dined.

THE ROYAL EXCHANGE, LONDON, AS BUILT BY SIR THOMAS GRESHAM.

After dinner, her Majestie, returning through Cornhill, entered the Burse on the south side; and after that she had viewed every part thereof above the ground, especially the Pawn, which was richly furnished with all sorts of the finest wares in the city, she caused the same Burse by an herald and trumpet to be proclaimed the *Royal Exchange*, and so to be called from thenceforth, and not otherwise.'

Such is the brief account which has been transmitted to us of the event from which the Burse, as it was then called, dates its present name; by one who was probably an eye-witness of the scene he describes. The only other contemporary notice Mr Burgon has met with of this memorable passage in the annals of the metropolis occurs in the accounts of the churchwardens of St Margaret's, Westminster; where is recorded that the bell-ringers were paid 4d. 'for ringing when the Queen's Majesty went to the Bursse;' and 8d. 'for ringing when the Queen's Majesty went to Sir Thomas Gresham's and came back again.'

In the Bodleian Library is a Latin play, in five acts, entitled *Byrsa Basilica, &c.*, being a dramatic account of the building and opening of the Exchange, conceived in the most fantastic strain, according to the taste of the age. There is also extant a play, by Thomas Heywood, describing the building of the Burse, and referring in every page to Gresham. It is entitled, *If you know not me you know nobody: or, the Troubles of Queen Elizabeth.* 4to, 1606. In this play Heywood has followed Stow's narrative very faithfully till the queen comes to visit Gresham, and name the Burse: but here the poet can no longer restrain his invention. Gresham purchases a pearl which no one could afford to buy, and, in imitation of Cleopatra, drinks it, reduced to powder, in a cup of wine.

> ' Here fifteen hundred pound at one clap goes!
> Instead of sugar, Gresham drinks the pearl
> Unto his queen and mistress: pledge it, lords!'

That Gresham drank a *carouse* to the queen is not unlikely, but there is no reason for believing that the royal merchant was addicted to such royal draughts as Heywood describes. The incident was probably borrowed from the history of Sir William Capel, of whom a similar story is related by Fuller, in his *Worthies.—Burgon's Life and Times of Sir Thomas Gresham*, vol. ii. pp. 351—354.

AN ALE-TASTER IN OLD TIMES.

It is noted in Dr Langbaine's Collections, under January 23, 1617, that John Shurle had a patent from Arthur Lake, Bishop of Bath and Wells, and Vice-Chancellor of Oxford, 'for the office of ale-taster [to the University] and the making and assizing of bottles of hay. The office of ale-tasting requires that he go to every ale-brewer that day they brew, according to their courses, and taste their ale; for which his ancient fee is one gallon of strong ale and two gallons of small wort, worth a penny.' *

* Reliquiæ Hearnianæ, i. 38.

WONDERS IN THE AIR.

23rd January 1642 [1643], was published 'A great Wonder in Heaven, shewing, &c.,'—a thin *brochure* now exceedingly rare. Its statement was to the effect, that on a Saturday in the by-past Christmas time, there had occurred at Keniton, in Northamptonshire, the apparition and noise of a battle in the air, a ghostly repetition of the conflict which two months before had taken place on the adjacent fields at Edgehill between the forces of the King and the Parliament. It was between twelve and one in the morning that there was 'heard, by some shepherds and other countrymen and travellers, first the sound of drums afar off, and the noise of soldiers, as it were, giving out their last groans; at which they were much amazed, and amazed stood still, till it seemed by the nearness of the noise to approach them; at which, too much affrighted, they sought to withdraw as fast as possibly they could; but then on a sudden, while they were in these cogitations, appeared in the air the same incorporeal soldiers that made those clamours, and immediately, with ensigns displayed, drums beating, muskets going off, cannons discharged. horses neighing, which also to these men were visible. the alarum or entrance to this game of death was struck up; one army, which gave the first charge, having the King's colours, and the other the Parliament's, in their head or front of the battles, and so pell-mell to it they went; the battle that appeared to [be] the King's forces seeming at first to have the best, but afterwards to be put into apparent rout. But till two or three in the morning in equal scale continued this dreadful fight, the clattering of arms, noise of cannons, cries of soldiers, so amazing and terrifying the poor men, that they could not believe they were mortal, or give credit to their ears and eyes. Run away they durst not, for fear of being made a prey to these infernal soldiers; and so they, with much fear and affright, stayed to behold the success of the business. . . . After some three hours' fight, that army which carried the King's colours withdrew, or rather appeared to fly; the other remaining, as it were, masters of the field, stayed a good space triumphing, and expressing all the signs of joy and conquest, and then, with all their drums, trumpets, ordnance, and soldiers, vanished. The poor men, glad they were gone, made with all haste to Keniton; and there knocking up Mr Wood, a justice of the peace, who called up his neighbour, Mr Marshall, the minister, they gave them an account of the whole passage, and averred it upon their oaths to be true.'

What follows is most remarkable of all. The gentlemen thus apprised of what had taken place, 'suspending their judgments till the next night about the same hour, they, with the same men, and all the substantial men of that and the neighbouring parishes, drew thither; where, about half an hour after their arrival, on Sunday, being Christmas night, appeared, in the same tumultuous warlike manner, the same two adverse armies. fighting with as much spite and spleen as formerly. . . . The next night they appeared not, nor all that week. . . . But on

154

the ensuing Saturday night, in the same place, and at the same hour, they were again seen with far greater tumult, fighting in the manner above mentioned for four hours, or very near, and then vanished, appearing again on Sunday night, and performing the same actions of hostility and bloodshed. . . . Successively the next Saturday and Sunday the same tumults and prodigious sights and actions were put in the state and condition they were formerly. The rumour whereof coming to his Majesty at Oxford, he immediately dispatched thither Colonel Lewis Kirke, Captain Dudley, Captain Waithman, and three other gentlemen of credit, to take the full view and notice of the said business; who, first hearing the relation of Mr Marshall and others, stayed there till Saturday night following, wherein they saw and heard the fore-mentioned prodigies, and so on Sunday, distinctly knowing divers of the apparitions by their faces, as that of Sir Edmund Varney, and others that were there slain; of which, upon oath, they made testimony to his Majesty.'*

HON. CHARLES TOWNSHEND.

January 23, 1748, the Hon. Charles Townshend, writing to a friend, says, 'I cannot go to the Opera, because I have forsworn all expense which does not end in pleasing me.'† If this were a rule generally followed, and the reserved means bestowed in judicious efforts for the good of others, what an improved world it would be!

Charles Townshend is one of the minor celebrities of the last century: he died in 1767, at the age of forty-two. Burke, referring some years after to his services in parliament, said he could not even then speak of Charles Townshend without some degree of sensibility. 'He was the delight and ornament of this House, and the charm of every private society which he honoured with his presence. Perhaps there never arose in this country, nor in any country, a man of more pointed and finished wit, and (where his passions were not concerned) of a more refined, exquisite and penetrating judgment.

It was the good fortune of Charles to gain favour with a young and noble widow, the Countess of Dalkeith (daughter of John Duke of Argyll, and mother of Henry Duke of Buccleuch). Sir Walter Scott relates the following anecdote regarding this alliance: 'When he [Charles Townshend] came to Scotland [after the marriage], the tide of relations, friends, and vassals, who thronged to welcome the bride, were so negligent of her husband, as to leave him in the hall, while they hurried his lady forwards into the state apartments, until he checked their haste by exclaiming, "For Heaven's sake, gentlemen, consider I am at least Prince George of Denmark!"' ‡

This union introduced Mr Townshend to the society of the then brilliant circle of Scottish literati. But, if we may depend upon the judgment of the Rev. Alexander Carlyle, these gentlemen judged his talents to be more of a showy

---

* Copied (with modernised spelling) from a transcript of the original *brochure*, Appendix to Lord Nugent's Life of John Hampden, ii. 468.

† Jesse's Life of George Selwyn.

‡ Quarterly Review, xxxiv. 202.

than a solid character; and 'at the end of two months,' says this shrewd observer, 'he had stayed long enough here.' Carlyle gives the following sketch of an afternoon spent with the English stranger :

'I called on him one morning at Dalkeith, when he said I had come most *à-propos*, if not engaged, for that he was going to ride to Edinburgh to make some calls: and his wife being engaged to dine with the Duchess of Gordon, he would be very glad of a small party in a tavern, I agreed, and we rode to Edinburgh together. When we drew near that city, he begged me to ride on and bespeak a small dinner at a tavern, and get a friend or two if I could to join us, as he must turn to the left to call on some people who lived in that direction. I went to town directly, and luckily found Home and Ferguson in Kincaid[the bookseller]'s shop, and sent a cady* to Robertson, to ask him to meet us at the Cross Keys soon after two o'clock, who likewise came. During dinner, and for almost an hour after, Charles, who seemed to be fatigued by his morning visits, spoke not a single word, and we four went on with our kind of conversation without adverting to Mr Townshend's absence. After he had drunk a pint of claret, he seemed to awaken from his reverie, and then silenced us all with a torrent of colloquial eloquence, which was highly entertaining, for he gave us all our own ideas over again, embodied in the finest language, and delivered in the most impressive manner. When he parted from us, my friends remarked upon his excellence in this talent, in which Robertson agreed with them, without, perhaps, being conscious that he was the most able proficient in that art.'†

Charles Townshend fully appears to have been one of those persons with showy and superficial talents who make an impression on all around them, but produce no permanent good results. He could move and delight men, but not improve or guide them. In some peculiar circumstances, and at certain crises, his gift of the tongue might have proved serviceable; but, usually, such powers are only calculated to create or support delusions, by making the worse appear the better reason. Public men possessed of fascinating eloquence should in general be viewed with suspicion, and carefully guarded against, for they are apt to do great mischief. To make a pulpit orator a leader in a church, or raise a clever special pleader to a place in the cabinet council, are dangerous movements. In general, the powers which have made them famous are, at the best, useless in grave and important circumstances; often, the *prestige* which these powers have given, only enables them to interfere injuriously with the course pointed out by the wise. Perilous it is for a country to have a political system in which brilliant parliamentary oratory is allowed any but a moderate sway. It might be of some service to inquire how often mere oratory has been on the side of what was just, reasonable, and for the good of a state, and how often the reverse; and whether, on the whole, the affairs of

* A street message-carrier was so called in the northern capital.

† Autobiography of Alexander Carlyle, 1860, p. 391.

nations and of individuals would not have been in a better case at this moment, if there never had existed any man capable of standing up and sawing the air, and puffing and sweating, while pouring out an ocean of exaggerated phrases calculated to work on the feelings of a multitude.

DEATH OF SIR FRANCIS BURDETT.

This event took place on the 23rd of January 1844, when Sir Francis had attained his seventy-fourth year. The strain of political sentiment which made him the idol of the populace in the reign of George III., had long given place to strong conservatism, and he necessarily became a man of little political note in his latter years. When we remember the Gracchus-like position of Sir Francis in April 1810—ordered to the Tower for a libel on the House of Commons, and standing a siege of horse and foot in his house in Piccadilly for several days before the warrant could be executed—the story of his death reads strangely. It was the fortune of this fine old English gentleman to be united to a daughter of Mr Coutts the banker; and the pair had lived together with singular attachment and harmony for upwards of fifty years. Towards the close of 1843, Lady Burdett's state of health excited great alarm in her family. She died on the 10th of January 1844. Her death sounded her husband's knell. She who had so long been the partner and sharer of his joys and troubles, the mother of his children, the friend of his soul, being now removed, from that instant life became an insupportable burthen to him. Resolutely refusing food or nourishment of any kind, he died on the 23rd of the same month ; and man and wife were buried side by side in the same vaults, at the same hour, on the same day, in the church of Ramsbury, Wilts.

MR PITT AND HIS SERVANT.

Obviously a good end would be served if examples of a reasonable treatment of servants, followed by good results, were occasionally presented for the consideration of masters and mistresses. Mr Pitt, who was so able a servant of the state, was also a good master to his own domestics : that is, he did not fail to recognise good conduct in his servants, and to treat them with due consideration of their numerous duties. He was likewise very quick in the perception of qualities which recommend an individual for domestic service, of which the following is an interesting instance :

Mr Pitt once obtained a servant in a very odd way. Riding on the moors with a friend, they came up with a flock of geese, driven by a boy, with a bit of red rag at the end of a long stick. 'We must ride round,' said Mr Pitt, 'we shall never get through this immense flock.' 'Yes, but you may,' cried a sharp-looking boy, who had heard him, 'if you will only keep your horses quiet. Sh—sh—ee—ayi—ayi !' and the boy waved his stick here and there, and in a minute or two the flock opened, and, wheeling to the left and right in regular columns, made a passage through which they rode. 'That must be a clever lad,' observed Mr Pitt ; 'he manœuvres his little army in a wonderful manner—a general could not do it better;' and he ordered the groom to inquire to whom he belonged. A day or two afterwards, he was sent for, and put in the stables. Next he was made an under-groom ; then taken to town to wait on the upper servants, and afterwards made a footman. One day, Mr Pitt went down to Holwood, in Kent, with Mr Dundas and three or four friends, to talk over parliamentary business : some time before the dinner-hour, the cook was seized with apoplexy, which so affected the butler and occasional valet that he fell with a fit of gout. Mr Pitt grew anxious about the dinner, when the young man whom he had advanced from gooseherd to footman, said, 'Don't, sir, send off any express for a cook ; if you think proper, the maid shall cook the dinner. These are your intimate friends, and will take no notice : their servants as yet know nothing of the matter, for I thought they might be frightened to be where there is a dead man. Let me manage, and all will go well, without any alarm being spread.' He accordingly dressed Mr Pitt, saw to everything, and acquitted himself so well, that Mr Pitt soon after made him his valet ; but he did not live much longer, to have his services recompensed. He was an excellent servant. Mr Pitt would sometimes order him to precede him a day or two to a place he was about to visit. 'You will excuse me, sir,' the man would reply : 'but I mustn't go ; for if I do, who will attend you when you take your physic to-morrow ? You will be busy, and put it off ; and nobody knows how to give it but myself.' 'Well, well,' Mr Pitt would answer, 'do so, then ;' and would add, 'Ah ! he is very anxious about me—I must let him have his own way.'

JANUARY 24.

St Timothy, disciple of St Paul, martyr at Ephesus, 97. St Babylas, bishop of Antioch, about 250. St Macedonius of Syria, 5th century. St Cadocus or Cadoc, abbot of Wales, 6th century. St Suranus, abbot in Umbria, martyr, 7th century.

Born.—Charles Earl of Dorset, poet, 1637 ; Frederick the Great, 1712 ; Pierre A. Caron de Beaumarchais, musical composer, *Paris*, 1732.
Died.—Justice Henry Yelverton, 1650 ; James Ralph, political writer, 1762.

CHARLES EARL OF DORSET.

A wit among lords, a generous friend to literary men, himself a fair writer of verses, gay but not reckless, honest far above his time, so much a favourite that, do what he liked, the world never thought him in the wrong,—Dorset claims some respect even in a later and better age. His poems are merely a bunch of trifles ; yet there is some heart, and also some feeling of the deeper realities of life, under the rosy badinage of his well-known ballad, *To all you ladies now at land*, professedly indited at sea the night before an engagement with the Dutch fleet, but stated to have been in reality the work of about a week :*

'When any mournful tune you hear,
　　That dies in every note,
As if it sighed with each man's care,
　　For being so remote ;
Think how often love we've made
To you, when all those tunes were played.

'In justice you can not refuse
　　To think of our distress,
When we, for hopes of honour, lose
　　Our certain happiness ;
All those designs are but to prove
Ourselves more worthy of your love.'

* Life by A. Chalmers, Brit. Poets, viii. 339.

Frederick II., King of Prussia, son of Frederick William I. and of Sophia Dorothea, Princess of Hanover, and surnamed the Great for his talents and successes, was, in his boyhood, treated with extreme severity, through the antagonism of his parents. His youthful tuition was rigid, its sole object being military exercises ; but he received the rudiments of his education from a French lady. The taste he acquired through her means for polite literature, was strongly opposed to the system of his coarse father, who would say, ' My eldest son is a coxcomb, proud, and has a fine French spirit, that spoils all my plans.' The conduct of the old savage towards him was both harsh and cruel ; it was still more so to any one to whom he was attached, or who was in any way, agreeable to the prince. A young girl, who had played on the pianoforte while the prince accompanied her on the flute, was publicly flogged by the executioner in the streets of Potsdam. The queen could not endure this injustice towards her son, and arranged that he should seek refuge in England with his maternal uncle George II. This secret plan, which was confided only to the prince's sister, and two lieutenants, his friends, was discovered by the King, who, finding that his son had already quitted the palace, sent soldiers in search of him, and he was discovered just as he was getting into a chariot to carry him to Saxony. One of the lieutenants, his companions, escaped by the fleetness of his horse ; but the other was carried back to Potsdam with the prince ; both being handcuffed like malefactors, and thrown into separate dungeons ; and the princess, who implored the king to pardon her brother, was thrown from one of the palace windows.

The King had made up his mind that his son should die on the scaffold : 'He will always be a disobedient subject,' said he, 'and I have three other boys who are more than his equals.' His life was only saved by the intercession of the Emperor of Austria, Charles VI., through his ambassador, Count Seckendorf. Nor could the King bring his son to trial ; for neither the ministers nor generals would sit in judgment upon the heir to the crown of Prussia, which so enraged the King that he sent the prince to be confined for life in a fortress at Custrin. Previously to his being conveyed to prison, the lieutenant who had been taken with him, was, by the King's order, executed upon a lofty scaffold, opposite the windows of the apartment in which the prince was confined. At Custrin, he saw no one but the governor of the fortress ; books, pens, paper, and his flute, were all denied him. When he had been imprisoned a year, the resentment of his father abated ; he was ordered to Berlin ; and there, at a grand fête at the palace, Frederick, in a grey suit, the only one he had been permitted to wear since his disgrace, was placed behind the chair of his mother. He then grew in favour with his father, who, however, could not forgive his disinclination for military exercises, and his love of music and the fine arts ; but above all his preference of foreign fashions to the plain, inelegant Prussian uniform, which the King so liked. Yet this prince, having ascended the throne, established the military renown of Prussia, and became one of the most famous generals in history; leaving to his successor a kingdom enlarged from 2190 to 3515 German square miles, and an army of 200,000 men.

Notwithstanding his fame as a monarch, legislator, and man of letters, Frederick, according to his own account, spent the happiest years of his life, when he was a youth, in the chateau of Rheinsberg, not far from Berlin.

WEATHERCOCKS.

The invention of the vane, or weathercock, must have been of very early date. Vitruvius calls it *triton*, probably from its having in his time the form of a triton. The usual form on towers, castles, and secular buildings, was that of a banner; but on ecclesiastical edifices, it generally was a representation of the male of the barn-door fowl. According to Ducange, the cock was originally devised as an emblem of clerical vigilance, or what it ought to be. Apart from symbolism, the large tail of the cock was well adapted to turn with the wind.

Many churches have for a vane the emblem of the saints to whom they are dedicated: thus, St Peter's, Cornhill, London, is surmounted with a key, St Peter being said to keep the key of heaven. St Laurence has for a vane, a gridiron; and St Laurence, at Norwich, has the gridiron, with the holy martyr extended upon the bars. The vane upon St Mildred's Church, in the Poultry, is a gilt ship in full sail; and that of St Michael's, Queenhithe, is a ship, the hull of which will hold a bushel of grain, referring to the former traffic in corn at the hithe.

St Sepulchre's Church, Skinner-street, has four pinnacles, each with a vane, which led Howell to say: 'Unreasonable people are as hard to reconcile as the vanes of St Sepulchre's tower, which never looked all four upon one point of the heavens.'

The grasshopper of the Royal Exchange is the vane which surmounted the former Exchange. It is of copper-gilt, eleven feet long, and represents the crest of Sir Thomas Gresham, the founder of the first Exchange.

MOTHER SHIPTON.

Mother Shipton is one of those half-mythical persons about whom it is exceedingly difficult to discover the exact truth. During her lifetime she was the reputed author of many curious 'prophecies,' and was looked upon as a witch or prophetess. According to a common tradition she was born on the banks of the river Nidd, near Knaresborough, about 1488. Her maiden name was Agatha Sonthiel; she married an artisan named Toby Shipton, and settled near York, where she died about 1561. After an interval of about eighty years, her sayings appeared in the form of a pamphlet in 1641, entitled *The Prophesie of Mother Shipton in the Raigne of Henry the Eighth. Foretelling the death of Cardinal Wolsey, the Lord Percy, and others, as also what should happen in ensuing times.* Other editions followed, to which great additions were made by their respective editors or authors. One edition by Richard Head, with its pretended biography of Mother Shipton, is thought to be a pure fiction. Her prophecies were still familiar to many around her native district a hundred years ago. Amongst the editions of her productions are the following: *Two Strange Prophecies*, 1642; *Life and Death of Mother Shipton*, 1677; *Mother Shipton's Life and Curious Prophecies*, 1797; *Mother Shipton's Prophecies*, 1877.

JANUARY 25.

St Juventinus and Maximinus, martyrs at Antioch, 363. St Apollo, abbot in Thebais, about 393. St Publius, abbot in Syria, 4th century. St Projectus (or St Prix), bishop of Clermont, martyr, 674. St Poppo, abbot of Stavello, 1048.

St Paul's Day.

The festival of the Conversion of St Paul, instituted by the church in gratitude for so miraculous and so important an instance of the Divine power, 'a perfect model of a true conversion,' is mentioned in several calendars and missals of the eighth and ninth centuries. 'It was for some time kept a holiday of obligation in most churches of the West; and we read it mentioned as such in England in the council of Oxford, in 1222, in the reign of King Henry III.' —*Butler.* It is still a festival of the Anglican, as well as other churches.

The day has also a celebrity of another description, the origin of which has not yet been discovered. It has been an article of constant belief in Western Europe, during the middle ages, and even down to our own time, that the whole character of the coming year is prognosticated by the condition of the weather on this day; and this is the more singular, as the day itself was one of those to which the old prognosticators gave the character of a *dies Ægyptiacus*, or unlucky day. The special knowledge of the future, which it was believed might be derived from it, were arranged under four heads, in four monkish Latin verses, which are found very frequently in the manuscripts of the middle ages, and prevailed equally on the continent and in our own island. The following is the most correct copy of these verses that we have been able to obtain (in copies of a later date, attempts were made to improve the style of the Latin, which in some degree destroyed their quaintness):

'Clara dies Pauli bona tempora denotat anni;
Si nix vel pluvia, designat tempora cara;
Si fiant nebulæ, pereunt animalia quæque;
Si fiant venti, designat prælia genti.'

Fair weather on St Paul's day thus betided a prosperous year; snow or rain betokened a dear year, and therefore an unfruitful one; clouds foreboded great mortality among cattle; and winds were to be the forerunners of war. Several old translations of these lines into verse in French and English are met with; the following is one of the English versions:

'If St Paul's day be fair and clear,
It does betide a happy year;
But if it chance to snow or rain,
Then will be dear all kind of grain;
If clouds or mists do dark the skie,
Great store of birds and beasts shall die;
And if the winds do flie aloft,
Then war shall vexe the kingdome oft.'

Other days in the month of January enjoyed at different times, and in different places, a similar reputation among the old prognosticators, but none of them were anything like so generally held and believed in as the day of the Conversion of St Paul.

In the reign of Philip and Mary (1555), this day was observed in the metropolis with great processional state. In the *Chronicle of the Grey Friars of London*, we read that 'on St Paul's day there was a general procession with the children of all the schools in London, with all the clerks, curates, and parsons, and vicars, in copes, with their crosses ; also the choir of St Paul's ; and divers bishops in their habits, and the Bishop of London, with his pontificals and cope, bearing the sacrament under a canopy, and four prebends bearing it in their gray *amos ;* and so up into Leadenhall, with the mayor and aldermen in scarlet, with their cloaks, and all the crafts in their best array ; and so came down again on the other side, and so to St Paul's again. And then the king, with my lord cardinal, came to St Paul's, and heard masse, and went home again ; and at night great bonfires were made through all London, for the joy of the people that were converted likewise as St Paul was converted.'

Down to about this time there was observed, in connection with St Paul's Cathedral, a custom arising from an obligation incurred by Sir William Baud in 1375, when he was permitted to enclose twenty acres of the Dean's land, in consideration of presenting the clergy of the cathedral with a fat buck and doe yearly on the days of the Conversion and Commemoration of St Paul. 'On these days, the buck and the doe were brought by one or more servants at the hour of the procession, and through the midst thereof, and offered at the high altar of St Paul's Cathedral : after which the persons that brought the buck received of the Dean and Chapter, by the hands of their Chamberlain, twelve pence sterling for their entertainment ; but nothing when they brought the doe. The buck being brought to the steps of the altar, the Dean and Chapter, apparelled in copes and proper vestments, with garlands of roses on their heads, sent the body of the buck to be baked, and had the head and horns fixed on a pole before the cross, in their procession round about the church, till they issued at the west door, where the keeper that brought it blowed the death of the buck, and then the horns that were about the city answered him in like manner ; for which they had each, of the Dean and Chapter, three and fourpence in money, and their dinner ; and the keeper, during his stay, meat, drink, and lodging, and five shillings in money at his going away ; together with a loaf of bread, having in it the picture of St Paul.'[*]

Born.—Robert Boyle, 1627, *Lismore ;* Thomas Tanner, antiquary, 1674 ; Paul Whitehead, 1709 ; Robert Burns, 1759 ; Sir Francis Burdett, 1770 ; James Hogg (the Ettrick Shepherd), poet, 1772 ; Benjamin Robert Haydon, painter, 1786, *Plymouth ;* Daniel Maclise, artist, 1811, *Cork.*

Died.—William Shield, dramatic composer, 1829.

ROBERT BURNS.

Robert Burns, the Scottish poet, first saw the light on the 25th January 1759 in a small cottage by the wayside near the Bridge of Doon, two

miles from Ayr. A wonderful destiny was that of the peasant's babe born that day—a life of toil, imprudence, poverty, closed in early death, but to be followed by an afflatus of popular admiration and sympathy such as never before nor since attended a literary name in any country. The strains of Burns touch all hearts. He has put words together, as scarcely any writer ever did before him. His name has become a stenograph for a whole system of national feelings and predilections. Other poets, after death, have a tablet in Westminster Abbey, and occasional

ROBERT BURNS ; FROM A SILHOUETTE BY MIERS.

allusions in critical writings. But when the centenary of Burns's birth arrives, it is celebrated in every town in the country ; nay, wherever our language is spoken—alike in Canada, the United States, Australia, New Zealand, and Cape Colony—there is a pouring out of grateful sentiment in honour of Burns.

BIRTH OF BURNS.

BY THOMAS MILLER.

Upon a stormy winter night
Scotland's bright star first rose in sight ;
Beaming upon as wild a sky
As ever to prophetic eye
Proclaimed, that Nature had on hand
Some work to glorify the land.
Within a lonely cot of clay,
That night her great creation lay.

Coila—the nymph who round his brow
Twined the red-berried holly-bough—
Her swift-winged heralds sent abroad,
To summon to that bleak abode
All who on Genius still attend,
For good or evil to the end.

They came obedient to her call :—
The immortal infant knew them all.

Sorrow and Poverty—sad pair—
Came shivering through the wintry air :
Hope, with her calm eyes fixed on Time,
His crooked scythe hung with flakes of rime :
Fancy, who loves abroad to roam,
Flew gladly to that humble home :

Pity and Love, who, hand in hand,
Did by the sleeping infant stand :
Wit, with a harem-skarem grace,
Who smiled at Laughter's dimpled face :
Labour, who came with sturdy tread,

By high-souled Independence led .
Care, who sat noiseless on the floor ;
While Wealth stood up outside the door,
Looking with scorn on all who came,
Until he heard the voice of Fame,

COTTAGE AT ALLOWAY, THE BIRTH-PLACE OF BURNS.

And then he bowed down to the ground :—
Fame looked on Wealth with eyes profound,
Then passed in without sign or sound.

Then Coila raised her hollied brow,
And said, 'Who will this child endow ?'
Said Love, 'I'll teach him all my lore,
As it was never taught before ;
Its joys and doubts, its hopes and fears,
Smiles, kisses, sighs, delights, and tears.'
Said Pity, 'It shall be my part
To gift him with a gentle heart.'
Said Independence, 'Stout and strong
I'll make it to wage war with wrong.'
Said Wit, 'He shall have mirth and laughter,
Though all the ills of life come after.'
'Warbling her native wood-notes wild,'
Fancy but stooped and kissed the child ;
While through her fall of golden hair
Hope looked down with a smile on Care.

Said Labour, 'I will give him bread.'
'And I a stone when he is dead,'
Said Wealth, while Shame hung down her head.

'He'll need no monument,' said Fame ;
'I'll give him an immortal name ;
When obelisks in ruin fall,
Proud shall it stand above them all ;
The daisy on the mountain side
Shall ever spread it far and wide ;
Even the road-side thistle down
Shall blow abroad his high renown.'

Said Time, 'That name, while I remain,
Shall still increasing honour gain ;
Till the sun sinks to rise no more,
And my last sand falls on the shore
Of that still, dark, and unsailed sea,
Which opens on Eternity.'

Time ceased : no sound the silence stirr'd,
Save the soft notes as of a bird
Singing a low sweet plaintive song,
Which murmuring Doon seemed to prolong,
As if the mate it fain would find
Had gone and 'left a thorn' behind.

Upon the sleeping infant's face
Each changing note could Coila trace.

Then came a ditty, soft and slow,
Of Love, whose locks were white as snow.

The immortal infant heaved a sigh,
As if he knew such love must die.

That ceased : then shrieks and sounds of laughter,
That seemed to shake both roof and rafter,
Floated from where Kirk Alloway
Half buried in the darkness lay.

A mingled look of fun and fear
Did on the infant's face appear.

There was a hush : and then uprose
A strain, which had a holy close,
Such as with Cotter's psalm is blended
After the hard week's labour's ended,
And dawning brings the hallowed day.

In sleep the infant seemed to pray.

Then there was heard a martial tread,
As if some new-born Wallace led
Scotland's armed sons in Freedom's cause.

Stern looked the infant in repose.

The clang of warriors died away,
And then 'a star with lessening ray'
Above the clay-built cottage stood ;
While Ayr poured from its rolling flood
A sad heart-rending melody,
Such as Love chants to Memory,
When of departed joys he sings,
Of 'golden hours on angel wings'
Departed, to return no more.

Pity's soft tears fell on the floor,
While Hope spake low, and Love looked pale,
And Sorrow closer drew her veil.

Groans seemed to rend the infant's breast,
Till Coila whispered him to rest ;
And then, uprising, thus she spake :
'This child unto myself I take.

159

All hail! my own inspired Bard,
In me thy native Muse regard!' *
Around the sleeping infant's head
Bright trails of golden glory spread.
'A love of right, a scorn of wrong,'
She said, 'unto him shall belong;
A pitying eye for gentle woman,
Knowing "to step aside is human;"
While love in his great heart shall be
A living spring of poetry.
Failings he shall have, such as all
Were doomed to have at Adam's fall;
But there shall spring above each vice
Some golden flower of Paradise,
Which shall, with its immortal glow,
Half hide the weeds that spread below;
So much of good, so little guile,
As shall make angels weep and smile,
To think how like him they might be
If clothed in frail humanity;
His mirth so close allied to tears,
That when grief saddens or joy cheers,
Like shower and shine in April weather,
The tears and smiles shall meet together.
A child-like heart, a god-like mind,
Simplicity round Genius twined :
So much like other men appear,
That, when he's run his wild career,
The world shall look with wide amaze,
To see what lines of glory blaze
Over the chequered course he passed—
Glories that shall for ever last.

Of Highland hut and Lowland home,
His songs shall float across the foam,
Where Scotland's music ne'er before
Rang o'er the far-off ocean shore.
To shut of eve from early morn,
They shall be carolled mid the corn,
While maidens hang their heads aside,
Of Hope that lived, and Love that died;
And huntsmen on the mountains steep,
And herdsmen in the valleys deep,
And virgins spinning by the fire,
Shall catch some fragment of his lyre.
And the whole land shall all year long
Ring back the echoes of his song.
The world shall in its choice records
Store up his common acts and words,
To be through future ages spread;
And how he looked, and what he said,
Shall in wild wonderment be read,
When coming centuries are dead.'

' "And wear thou this,"' she solemn said,
' And bound the holly round' his 'head;
The polished leaves, and berries red,
            Did rustling play;
And, like a passing thought, she fled
            In light away.' †

It is amusing to learn that Burns, when just
emerging from obscurity, jocularly anticipated
that his birthday would come to be noted among
other remarkable events. In a letter to his early
patron, Gavin Hamilton, in 1786, he says: 'For
my own affairs, I am in a fair way of becoming
as eminent as Thomas à Kempis, or John Bun-
yan; and you may expect henceforth to see my
birthday inscribed among the wonderful events,
in the Poor Robin and Aberdeen Almanacks,
along with the Black Monday and the Battle of
Bothwell-bridge.'

* 'The Vision,' by Burns.   † Ibid., last verse.
160

It is an affecting circumstance that Burns,
dying in poverty, and unable to remunerate
his medical attendant in the usual manner,
asked the doctor's acceptance of his pair of
pistols as a memorial of their friendship. Dr
Maxwell, who proved a generous friend to
the poor bard's surviving widow and children, retained these weapons till his death in 1834, after
which they were preserved for some years by his
sister. On her death, they were presented
to the Society of Antiquaries of Scotland, in
whose museum in Edinburgh they are now kept
in an elegant coffer, but open to the inspection of
the public.*

EDWARD II. OF ENGLAND.

25th January 1327, is the date of the deposition of the silly king, Edward II., whose reign
of twenty years had been little else than one
continual wrangle regarding the worthless royal
favourites, Gaveston and Despencer. Edward is
remarkable in one respect, that, weak and pusil-
lanimous himself, he was the son of one and
father of another of the most vigorous of English
monarchs. Wisdom, dignity, and every manly
quality had fairly leaped over this hapless generation.

There is an authentic manuscript which gives
an account of the expenses of Edward II. during
a part of his reign; and it contains striking
evidence of his puerile character. There are
repeated entries of small sums, disbursed to
make good the losses which the king incurred in
playing at *cross and pile*, which is neither more
nor less than the pitch and toss of modern schoolboys. He played at this game with the usher of
his chamber, and he would borrow from his
barber the money wherewith to play. He did
not disdain to travel on the Thames, in a returned barge which had brought fagots to his
court. There is a sum entered, as paid by the
king's own hands, to James of St Albans, who
had danced before his highness upon a table, and
made him laugh heartily; and another was conferred on Morris Ken of the Kitchen, who, in a
hunt at Windsor, made the king laugh heartily
by frequently tumbling off his horse.† An
elaborate history of the reign could not make us
better appreciate the misfortune of the English
people in being for twenty years under such a
monarch.

MARRIAGE OF THE PRINCESS MARGARET OF
ENGLAND.

On St Paul's day, 1502-3, there took place a
marriage in the royal family of England, which
has been attended with most important consequences to the welfare of the entire island. The

* At a sale of Dr Maxwell's effects in Dumfries,
several pairs of pistols of an ordinary make were disposed
of—for the Doctor had been a weapon-fancier to some
extent—and two of these sets have since been severally
set forth as Burns's pistols. One of them, which had
been bought for the sum of fifteen and sixpence, fell into
the hands of a modern bard, and was enshrined by him
in an elegant case. See a curious paper on Burns's Pistols,
by the Right Rev. Bishop Gillis, of Edinburgh, 1859.
† Antiquarian Repertory, 4 vols. 4to, vol. ii. p. 406.

Princess Margaret, eldest daughter of Henry VII., was then united at the manor of Richmond to King James IV. of Scotland, as represented by his proxy, Patrick Earl of Bothwell. It was foreseen by the English king that this union might lead to that of the two kingdoms, which had so long been at enmity with each other; and when some of his council objected, that in this event England would become a province of Scotland, he shewed his deeper wisdom by remarking that it never could be so, as the smaller would ever follow the larger kingdom.

The young Queen of Scots was at this time only thirteen years and a quarter old; nevertheless, a learned Scotsman, Walter Ogilvy, who was present at the marriage, describes her as if she had already acquired all the graces, mental as well as bodily, of mature womanhood. She was 'decens, urbana, sagax.' Beauty and modesty were united in her. She was of tall stature, had lively eyes, smooth arms, beautiful hands, golden hair, and a tongue enriched with various languages. Her complexion united the beauty of both the roses of her father and mother. Whether she walked or lay, stood or sat, or spoke, a grace attended her.

GEORGE SELWYN.

January 25, 1791, died the celebrated wit, George Selwyn, in the seventy-second year of his age.

The Earl of Carlisle, writing to George Selwyn from Trentham, Sept. 20, 1774, tells him that a man is about to be tried at the assizes in Carlisle for murder. His lordship adds, 'If you should happen to be with us at the time of the assizes, I will take care to get you a good place at the execution; and though our Tyburn may not have all the charms which that has where you was brought up and educated, yet it may be better than no Tyburn.'

Lord Carlisle here alludes to the singular taste of George Selwyn for attending executions, in order to watch the conduct of the criminal under his extraordinary circumstances; a propensity the more remarkable in him, that he was a man of the greatest benevolence and tenderness of nature, and the undisputed prince of the men of wit and humour of his day. It was perhaps to gratify the very benevolence of his nature, by giving it a hearty sensation, that he was so fond of looking upon the sufferings of evil-doers.

His friend Horace Walpole, writing in 1750, speaks of him as one 'whose passion it was to see coffins, corpses, and executions.' Walpole having spoken of one Arthur More, recently deceased, George instantly remarked the curious fact that More had had his coffin chained to that of his mistress. 'How do you know?' inquired Walpole in some surprise. 'Why,' replied Selwyn, 'I saw them the other day in a vault at St Giles's.' 'He was walking this week,' says Walpole, 'in Westminster Abbey, with Lord Abergavenny, and met the man who shews the tombs. "Oh, your servant, Mr Selwyn; I expected to have seen you here the other day, when the old Duke of Richmond's body was taken up."' George had probably been out of town when the event happened.

The trial of the unfortunate rebel lords, in 1746, proved a rich treat for Selwyn. He attended most assiduously, and went fully into the spirit of the scene. Observing a Mrs. Bethel, who had what is called a *hatchet* face, he said, 'What a shame of her to turn her face to the prisoners before they are condemned!' Going to get a tooth extracted, he told the dentist he would drop his handkerchief for the signal. Some ladies rallied him about his want of feeling in having gone to see Lord Lovat's head cut off; 'Why,' said he, 'I made amends by going to the undertaker's to see it sewn on again.' And such was really the fact. He attended this last ceremony with an appearance of great solemnity, concluding the affair by calling out in the manner of the Lord Chancellor at the trial, 'My Lord Lovat, your lordship may rise!'

Henry, first Lord Holland, who, with all his faults as a statesman, possessed both wit and good nature, touched off the ruling passion of George Selwyn in the neatest manner when on his death-bed. Being informed that George had been inquiring for him, he said to his servant, The next time Mr Selwyn calls, show him up: if I am alive, I shall be delighted to see him; and if I am dead, he will be glad to see me.'

The story has been often told of George Selwyn, that he went to Paris, in 1756, on purpose to see the execution of Damien, for his attempt to assassinate Louis XV. 'On the day of the execution, he mingled with the crowd, in a plain undress and bob-wig; when a French nobleman, observing the deep interest he took in the scene, and imagining, from the plainness of his attire, that he must be a person in the humbler ranks of life, chose to imagine that he must infallibly be a hangman. "Eh, bien, monsieur," he said, "êtes-vous arrivé pour voir ce spectacle?"—"Oui, monsieur."—"Vous êtes bourreau?"—"Non, non, monsieur; je n'ai pas cette honneur; je ne suis qu'un amateur."'*

HONOUR TO MAGISTRATES.

On this day, in 1821, there were read before the Society of Antiquaries, some notes by Mr John Adey Repton, on the custom which prevailed in the seventeenth century of erecting two ornamental posts beside the gates of chief magistrates. Of the examples presented by Mr Repton, one may be here copied, being the posts erected beside the door of Thomas Pettys, Mayor of Norwich in 1592. This feature of old municipal usage is often alluded to by the contemporary dramatists. Thus, in *Lingua, or a Combat of the Tongue and the five Senses for Superiority: a Pleasant Comedie*, 1607, 4to, occurs the following passage:

'*Communis Sensus*.—Crave my counsel, tell me what manner of man is he? Can he entertain a man into his house? Can he hold his velvet cap in one hand, and vail his bonnet with the other? Knows he how to become a scarlet gown? Hath he *a pair of fresh posts at his door?*

'*Phantastes*.—He's about some hasty state matters; he talks of posts, methinks.

'*Com. S.*—Can he part a couple of dogs brawling in the street? Why, then, chuse him Mayor, &c.'

* Jesse's Memoirs of George Selwyn, i. 11.

In Beaumont and Fletcher's play of *The Widow*, is the following passage:

' I'll love your door the better while I know it.
' *Widow.*—A pair of such brothers were fitter for posts without door, indeed *to make a show at a new-chosen magistrate's gate*, than to be used in a woman's chamber.'

MAYORAL DOOR-POSTS, NORWICH, 1592.

Similar posts were erected at the sheriff's gate, and used for the display of proclamations. In Rowley's play of *A Woman Never Vexed*, 1632, a character says:

' If e'er I live to see thee sheriff of London,
I'll *gild thy posts*.'

A trace of this old custom is still to be found in Edinburgh, where it is a rule that a pair of gilded lamp-posts are always erected before the door of the Lord Provost.

THE AUTHORIZED VERSION OF THE BIBLE.

(*Ordered in January*, 1604.)

The month of January is memorable as that of the celebrated Hampton Court Conference, held at the beginning of the reign of James I. in England (1604), for the regulation of questions of religion, agitated by the violent opposition between the High Church party and the Puritans. Among other grievances brought forward on this occasion was the unsatisfactory state of the translations of the Bible then existing; and one of the most important and lasting results was the formation of the Authorized translation of the Scriptures which still remains in use in this country, and which was ordered by King James soon after the Conference separated. The

162

history of the English versions of the Bible is a subject of interest to everybody.

There was no principle or doctrine in the Roman Catholic religion opposed to the translation of the Holy Scriptures. In fact, the Latin text of the Bible used by the Catholics, and known as the Vulgate, was itself only a translation; and it was translated into the languages of various countries without reluctance or hesitation. Among the Anglo-Saxons, Aldhelm is said to have translated the Psalms as early as the seventh century; and an Anglo-Saxon translation of the Psalms, partly in prose and partly in verse, is still preserved in the Imperial Library in Paris, and was printed at Oxford in 1835, under the editorial care of Mr Benjamin Thorpe. The Anglo-Saxon translation of the Gospels, which has been ascribed to the ninth century, has also been printed; and a distinguished Anglo-Saxon ecclesiastic, Alfric, towards the close of the tenth century, translated into Anglo-Saxon a great part of the Old Testament, which is still preserved in manuscript. The whole of the Scriptures are supposed to have been translated into Anglo-Norman, but detached portions only are preserved. An English harmony of the Gospels was compiled in verse in the beginning of the thirteenth century, by a man named Orm, who gave to it the title of Ormulum, after his own name. Several versions of the Psalms were also written in early English, but the first translation of the entire Bible into English was that which was completed in the course of the latter half of the fourteenth century, and which is known as Wycliffe's Bible, as being the work either of that reformer himself, or at least of his followers There are two texts of this English version, differing considerably from each other—which are printed side by side in the edition in 3 vols. 4to edited by Forshall and Madden—and it must have been circulated very widely, from the great number of manuscript copies still in existence.

Though the mediæval churchmen did not object to the Scriptures being translated, they had a strong objection to the communication of them to the vulgar. In this respect the publication of translations of the Bible before and after the invention of printing, presented totally different questions. A manuscript book was very expensive, could be multiplied but slowly, and could only be possessed by the wealthy. The translations, therefore, to which we have alluded, were mostly, no doubt, made for ecclesiastics themselves, for abbesses and nuns, or for pious ladies of rank. But the Wycliffites openly professed that their object in translating the Scriptures was to communicate them to the people, and even to the lowest orders, by reading them, and causing them to be read, in the vernacular tongue. The whole mass of the Romish clergy who were opposed to reform took the alarm, horrified at the idea of imparting religious knowledge to the people, whom they wished to keep in a condition of blind subjection to themselves, with which such knowledge was quite incompatible. The first attempt to proscribe the Wycliffite translation was made in parliament in 1390, and was defeated by the influence of the Duke of

Lancaster, John of Gaunt. But in 1408, the clergy, under Archbishop Arundel, succeeded in their object : Wycliffe's and every other translation of the Scriptures into English were prohibited by an act of Convocation; and all who were known or suspected to read them were subjected to bitter persecution, which continued without intermission until the reign of Henry VIII.

The English Reformers were quick at taking advantage of the new art of printing, and they soon entered into communication with their brethren on the Continent, where only they could find a free press. In the year 1526, an English translation of the New Testament was printed, it is said, at Antwerp, and copies were surreptitiously passed into England. This translation, which is said to have been made direct from the Greek original, was the work of William Tyndal, a canon of the then new foundation of Christ Church, Oxford, who had been obliged to leave his native country on account of his religious opinions, assisted by John Fry, or Fryth, and William Roy, who were both put to death as heretics. It was the first *printed* translation of any part of the Scriptures in English. The chiefs of the Catholic party in England seem to have been much embarrassed with this book, and

they attempted to meet the difficulty by buying up all the copies and burning them; and thus created an artificial sale, which enabled Tyndal to bring out another and more correct edition. It was not till 1530, that Sir Thomas More, as Lord Chancellor, with the high ecclesiastics, issued a declaration against all English translations of the Scriptures; and that same year Tyndal printed his translation of the Pentateuch at Hamburg. He had now undertaken, with the assistance of another learned English Reformer, Miles Coverdale, a translation of the whole Bible; but in the middle of his labours he was suddenly arrested and thrown into prison by order of the Emperor, and his opinions were punished with death in 1536, the year of the first act for the dissolution of the English monasteries. In the previous year, the great work on which he had laboured with so much zeal had been completed. Miles Coverdale, who had been his assistant from the commencement, had continued the work alone after Tyndal's imprisonment; and this first English Bible was published in 1535, in a huge folio volume, believed from the character of the types to have been printed at Zurich, under the sole name of Coverdale. It was dedicated to King Henry VIII. of England.

By this time the Reformation had made such

HENRY VIII. DELIVERING THE BIBLE TO CRANMER AND CROMWELL.
(*Being a portion of the Engraved Title of ' Cranmer's Bible.'*)

advances in England, that the King himself was induced to allow the Bible to be circulated in the language of the people; and early in the year 1536 the English clergy were enjoined by royal authority to place a Latin Bible and an English Bible in the choir of every church, where it could be freely read by the people. The number of copies of Coverdale's Bible was insufficient to supply such a demand; and a new English Bible was now ordered to be printed under the direction of Cranmer, on which it is believed that Coverdale was the chief person employed. Leave was obtained from the King of France to print this Bible in Paris, where the typographic art

was then carried to the greatest perfection, and the care of the printing was entrusted to Richard Grafton and Edward Whitchurch; but they were interrupted by the interference of the French clergy, who seized and burnt nearly the whole impression, and Grafton and Whitchurch were obliged to withdraw to London, where the printing was completed in the spring of 1539. This book was sometimes called Cranmer's Bible, and sometimes spoken of as the 'Great Bible.' It was to it that reference was made in the royal proclamation of the following year, which enjoined the curates and parishioners of every parish to provide themselves with the

163

Bible of the largest size, under a penalty of forty shillings a month as long as they remained without it. At the latter end of Henry's reign, in consequence of a change in the religious policy of the Court, a check was again put on the free reading of the Scriptures, which was of course removed on the accession of Edward VI.

The persecutions of Queen Mary's reign drove the English Reformers into exile, when a number of the more zealous of them assembled at Geneva, and, while there, employed themselves upon a new translation of the Scriptures, with annotations, to which was given a strong Calvinistic colouring, and which contained political notions of a democratic character. The New Testament was first published, and was completed in 1557: the Old Testament followed in 1560. This is generally known as the Geneva Bible, and was in favour among the Puritan party and in Scotland. Elizabeth, at the beginning of her reign, determined to have an English translation of the Bible in accordance with her views in religious matters; and she entrusted the direction of it to Archbishop Parker, who distributed the work among a certain number of learned men.

It was published in 1568, and, from the circumstance that there was a considerable number of bishops among the translators, it is often spoken of as the Bishops' Bible.

Such was the state of things at the time of the Hampton Court Conference. There were at least four different English translations of the Bible, which had gone through numerous editions, differing very much from each other, not only verbally, but very often in the interpretation of Holy Writ, and not one of which had any absolute authority over the other. Moreover, most of these older translations, in the Old Testament at least, had been made in a great measure from the Latin vulgate, the old Romanist version. It cannot be denied that one authorized and correct version of the Bible was greatly wanted, and this seems to have been allowed by all parties. It appears, however, that the proposal originated with the Puritans, and that it was their speaker in the Conference, Dr. Reynolds, who brought the subject before the King. James had no partiality for any of the translations which then existed; he is understood to have disliked the Geneva Bible, partly on account of its rather

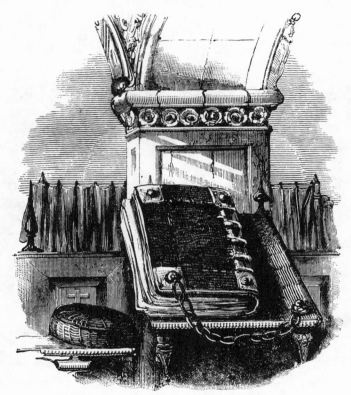

CHAINED BIBLE IN CUMNOR CHURCH, LEICESTERSHIRE.

low tone on his favourite 'kingcraft;' it was a flattering idea that his reign in England should be inaugurated by a translation of the Scriptures from the original Hebrew. He, accordingly, embraced the proposal with eagerness,

and drew up with his own pen the rules for translating. In the course of the year 1604, James appointed a Commission of learned men selected from the two Universities and from Westminster, consisting at first of fifty-four individuals, but reduced subsequently to forty-seven. To each of these a portion of the Scriptures was given to translate. They began their labours in the spring of 1607, and completed them in three years; and then a select committee was appointed, consisting of two from each University, and two from Westminster, who met at Stationers' Hall, in London, to correct the work of the rest. The Bishop of Winchester (Bilson) and Dr. Myles Smith finally revised the whole, and prefixed the arguments to the several books. It is supposed that Bancroft, Bishop of London, had the chief direction of the whole work.

Thus was formed the Authorized Version of the Scriptures, which was published in 1611, and has ever since been the only English translation acknowledged by the Anglican Church. For the time at which it was written, it is truly a very wonderful work; but still it is acknowledged by modern scholars to be far from perfect. During the two centuries and a half since the time of James I., Hebrew philology and the knowledge of biblical antiquities have made great advance; and there can be no doubt that the Authorized translation of the Bible contains many errors and many mistranslations, which it would be very desirable to see corrected. Many men of great learning have therefore, from time to time, asked for a new translation, or at least a revision of the present Authorised Version.

A copy of the Authorised Version was, as before, placed in each parish church, that it might be accessible to all; and, usually, after the fashion of the old libraries, it was chained to the place. A sketch of such a Bible, yet surviving in Cumnor Church, Leicestershire, is given in the preceding page.

[A committee of sixty Oriental and Biblical scholars was formed in 1870 for the revision of the Bible, one half of whom were engaged on the Old Testament, the remainder on the New Testament. After ten years' labour the New Testament was finished in 1880, and issued by the Oxford and Cambridge University Press authorities in 1881.]

JANUARY 26.

St Polycarp, bishop of Smyrna, 166. St Paula, widow, 404. St Conon, bishop of Man, about 648.

ST POLYCARP.

Polycarpus is the earliest of the Christian fathers. An unusual and peculiar interest attaches to him, as one who might have known, if he did not actually know, the evangelist John. At Smyrna, of which he was bishop, Polycarp suffered martyrdom by burning, in 167. Of his writings there remains but an epistle to the Philippians, exhorting them to maintain the purity of the faith.

ST CONON.

Conon is a Scotch saint of the seventh century. He was for some years Bishop of Man or of the Southern Isles, and his name continued to be remembered with veneration in the Highlands till the Reformation. 'Claw for claw,' as Conon said to Satan, 'and the devil take the shortest nails,' is a proverb of the Highlanders, apparently referring to some legend of an encounter between the holy man and the great spiritual enemy of our race.

Born.—Lord George Sackville, 1716; J. B. Bernadotte, king of Sweden, 1764, *Pau;* Thomas Noon Talfourd, 1795.

Died.—Henry Brigges, 1630, *Oxford;* Dr E. Jenner, 1823, *Berkeley;* Francis Jeffrey, 1850, *Edinburgh;* Adam Gottlob Ochlenschläger, Danish poet, 1850.

FRANCIS JEFFREY.

The first recognised editor of the *Edinburgh Review* was a man of small and slight figure, and of handsome countenance; of fine conversational powers, and, what will surprise those who think of him only as the uncompromising critic, great goodness of heart and domestic amiability. In his latter years, when past the psalmist-appointed term of life, he grew more than ever tender of heart and amiable, praised nursery songs, patronised mediocrities, and wrote letters of almost childish gentleness of expression. It seemed to be the natural strain of his character let loose from some stern responsibility, which had made him sharp and critical through all his former life.

His critical writings had a brilliant reputation in their day. He was too much a votary of the regular old rhetorical style of poetry to be capable of truly appreciating the Lake school, or almost any others of his own contemporaries. The greatest mistake he made was as to Wordsworth, whose *Excursion* he saluted (*Edinburgh Review,* November 1814) with an article beginning, 'This will never do;' a free and easy condemnation which, now contrasted with the reputation of Wordsworth, returns a fearful revenge upon the critic.

Jeffrey, however, is not without his companions in this kind of misfortune. Home, the author of *Douglas,* could not see the merit of Burns; and Ritson, while appreciating him as a poet generally, deemed his songs a failure. 'He does not,' says the savage Joseph, 'appear to his usual advantage in song: *non omnia possumus.'*

It would be a curious task, and something like a fair revenge upon the sanguinary brotherhood of Critics, to run over their works, and select the unhappy cases in which, from prejudice or want of natural penetration, they have passed judgments and made prophecies which now appear ludicrously inappropriate. Some unlucky pronouncements by unprofessional hands may meanwhile be noted.

It was Waller who wrote of *Paradise Lost* on its first appearance: 'The old blind schoolmaster. John Milton, hath published a tedious poem on the fall of man; if its length be not considered a merit, it has no other.'

Walpole, led by political prejudice, on several occasions wrote disparagingly of Smollett. *Humphry Clinker,* which has ever been a favourite with the British public, is passed over ignominiously by the lord of Strawberry Hill, as 'a party novel written by the profligate hireling Smollett.

We find a tolerably fair offset to the short-comings of Whig Review criticism, in the way in which the poetry of Hunt, Shelley, and Keats was treated in the early volumes of the *Quarterly*. In the noted article on the *Endymion* of Keats (April 1818), which Byron speaks of in his couplet—

> ' 'Tis strange the mind, that very fiery particle,
> Should let itself be snuffed out by an article'—

(which, however, was a mistake), the critic pro-fesses to have been utterly unable to read the poem, and adds : 'The author is a copyist of Mr Hunt . . . more unintelligible, almost as rugged, twice as diffuse, and ten times more tiresome and absurd than his prototype.'

BISHOP LOW.

Died on the 26th January 1855, the Right Rev. David Low, Bishop of Ross and Argyll, in the episcopal communion of Scotland. The prin-cipal reason for noticing this prelate is the fact that he was the last surviving clergyman in Scotland, who had, in his official character, acted upon scruples in behalf of the house of Stuart. At the time of the excellent bishop's entrance to the Church, in 1787—when he was ordained a deacon—the body to which he belonged omitted the prayer for the king and royal family from their service, being unostentatiously but firmly attached to the fortunes of the family which forfeited the British crown nearly a hundred years before ; and it was not till after the death of the unfortunate Charles Edward, in January 1788, that they at length (not without some diffi-culty) agreed to pray for King George.

An obituary notice of Bishop Low speaks of him as follows : ' His appearance was striking—tall, attenuated, but active—his eye sparkling with intelligence, his whole look that of a vene-rable French *abbé* of the old *régime*. His mind was eminently buoyant and youthful, and his memory was a fount of the most interesting historical information, especially in connection with the Cavalier or Jacobite party, to which he belonged by early association and strong religious and political predilection. Born in a district (at that time) devoted to the cause of the Stuarts, almost under the shadow of Edzell Castle, the ancient stronghold of the Lindsays in Forfarshire, and having lived much from time to time in his early years in the West Highlands, among the Stuarts of Ballachulish and Appin, he had enjoyed familiar intercourse with the veterans of 1715 and 1745, and he detailed the minutest events and adven-tures of those times with a freshness and a graphic force which afforded infinite delight to his younger auditors. His traditional knowledge extended even to the wars of Claverhouse and Montrose.'

Those who know of bishops and their style of living only from the examples afforded by the English Protestant Church, will hear with sur-prise and incredulity of what we have to tell regarding Bishop Low. This venerable man, who had never been married, dwelt in a room of the old priory of Pittenweem, on the coast of Fife, where he ministered to a congregation for which a good dining-room would have furnished

tolerably ample accommodation. He probably never had an income above a hundred a year in his life ; yet of even this he spent so little, that he was able at the last to bequeath about eight thousand pounds for purposes connected with his communion. A salt herring and three or four potatoes often formed the home dinner of the Bishop of Ross and Argyll.

Even in Scotland, chiefly from the introduc-tion of English clergymen of fortune into the episcopate, a bishop is beginning to be, typically, a tolerably well-off and comfortable-looking personage. It therefore becomes curious to re-call what he, typically, was not many years ago. The writer has a perfect recollection of a visit he paid, in the year 1826, to the venerable Dr Jolly, Bishop of Moray, who was esteemed as a man of learning, as well as a most devoted officer of his church. He found the amiable prelate living at the fishing town of Fraserburgh, at the north-east corner of Aberdeenshire, where he officiated to a small congregation. The bishop, having had a little time to prepare himself for a visitor, was, by the time the writer made his call, dressed in his best suit and his Sunday wig. In a plain two-story house, such as is common in Scotch towns, having a narrow wooden stair ascending to the upper floor, which was composed of two *coomceiled* apartments, *a but and a ben*, and in one of these rooms, the beautiful old man—for he *was* beautiful—sat, in his neat old-fashioned black suit, buckled shoes, and wig as white as snow, surrounded entirely by shelves full of books, most of them of an antique and theo-logical cast. Irenæus or Polycarp could not have lived in a style more simple. The look of the venerable prelate was full of gentleness, as if he had never had an enemy, or a difficulty, or anything else to contend with, in his life. His voice was low and sweet, and his conversation most genial and kindly, as towards the young and unimportant person whom he had admitted to his presence. The whole scene was a his-torical picture which the writer can never forget, or ever reflect on without pleasure. Bishop Jolly lived in a style nearly as primitive as Bishop Low ; but the savings which consequently arose from his scanty income were devoted in a different way. His passion apart from the church was for books, of which he had gathered a wonderful quantity, including many that were of considerable value for their rarity.

The series of non-jurant English bishops, which began with those who refused to acknowledge William and Mary, including Sancroft, Arch-bishop of Canterbury, came to an end with the Rev. Mr Gordon, who died on the 19th of No-vember 1779. There was, however, a succession of separatists, beginning with one bishop, and which did not terminate till 1805.[*]

SEVENTH SONS AND THEIR SEVENTH SONS.

There has been a strong favour for the number Seven, from a remote period in the world's his-tory. It is, of course, easy to see in what way the Mosaic narrative gave sanctity to this number in connection with the days of the week, and led

<hr>

[*] Notes and Queries, 2nd ser., xi. 273.

to usages which influence the social life of all the countries of Europe. But a sort of mystical goodness or power has attached itself to the number in many other ways. Seven wise men, seven champions of Christendom, seven sleepers, seven-league boots, seven churches, seven ages of man, seven hills, seven senses, seven planets, seven metals, seven sisters, seven stars, seven wonders of the world,—all have had their day of favour ; albeit that the number has been awkwardly interfered with by modern discoveries concerning metals, planets, stars, and wonders of the world.

Added to the above list is the group of *Seven Sons*, especially in relation to the youngest or seventh of the seven ; and more especially still if this person happen to be the seventh son of a seventh son. It is now, perhaps, impossible to discover in what country, or at what time, the notion originated ; but a notion there certainly is, chiefly in provincial districts, that a seventh son has something peculiar about him. For the most part, the imputed peculiarity is a healing power, a faculty of curing diseases by the touch, or by some other means.

The instances of this belief are numerous enough. There is a rare pamphlet called the *Quack Doctor's Speech*, published in the time of Charles II. The reckless Earl of Rochester delivered this speech on one occasion, when dressed in character, and mounted on a stage as a charlatan. The speech, amid much that suited that licentious age, but would be frowned down by modern society, contained an enumeration of the doctor's wonderful qualities, among which was that of being a ' seventh son of a seventh son,' and therefore clever as a curer of bodily ills. The matter is only mentioned as affording a sort of proof of the existence of a certain popular belief. In Cornwall, the peasants and the miners entertain this notion ; they believe that a seventh son can cure the king's evil by the touch. The mode of proceeding usually is to stroke the part affected thrice gently, to blow upon it thrice, to repeat a form of words, and to give a perforated coin or some other object to be worn as an amulet. At Bristol, about forty years ago, there was a man who was always called ' Doctor,' simply because he was the seventh son of a seventh son. The family of the Joneses of Muddfi, in Wales, is said to have presented seven sons to each of many successive generations, of whom the seventh son always became a doctor—apparently from a conviction that he had an inherited qualification to start with. In Ireland, the seventh son of a seventh son is believed to possess prophetical as well as healing power. A few years ago, a Dublin shopkeeper, finding his errand-boy to be generally very dilatory in his duties, inquired into the cause, and found that, the boy being a seventh son of a seventh son, his services were often in requisition among the poorer neighbours, in a way that brought in a good many pieces of silver. Early in the present century, there was a man in Hampshire, the seventh son of a seventh son, who was consulted by the villagers as a doctor, and who carried about with him a collection of crutches and sticks, purporting to have once belonged to persons whom he had cured of lame-

ness. Cases are not wanting, also, in which the seventh daughter is placed upon a similar pinnacle of greatness. In Scotland, the *spae wife*, or fortune-teller, frequently announces herself as the seventh daughter of a seventh daughter, to enhance her claims to prophetic power. Even so late as 1851, an inscription was seen on a window in Plymouth, denoting that a certain doctress was ' the third seventh daughter,'—which the world was probably intended to interpret as the seventh daughter of the seventh daughter of a seventh daughter.

Sometimes this belief is mixed up with curious family legends. The *Winchester Observer*, a few years ago, gave an account of the ' Tichborne Dole,' associated with one of the very oldest Hampshire families. The legend tells that, at some remote period, a Lady Mabella, on her death-bed, besought her lord, the Tichborne of those days, to supply her with the means for bequeathing a gift or *dole* of bread to any one who should apply for it annually on the Feast of the Annunciation of the Blessed Virgin. Sir Roger promised her the proceeds of as much land as she could go over while a brand or billet of a certain size was burning : she was nearly bedridden, and nearly dying ; and her avaricious lord believed that he had imposed conditions which would place within very narrow limits the area of land to be alienated. But he was mistaken. A miraculous degree of strength was given to her. She was carried by her attendants into a field, where she crawled round many goodly acres. A field of twenty-three acres, at Tichborne, to this day, bears the name of the *Crawl*. The lady, just before her death, solemnly warned her family against any departure from the terms of the dole ; she predicted that the family name would become extinct, and the fortunes impoverished, if the dole were ever withdrawn. The Tichborne dole, thus established, was regarded as the occasion of an annual festival during many generations. It was usual to bake fourteen hundred loaves for the dole, of twenty-six ounces each, and to give twopence to any applicant in excess of the number that could be then served. This custom was continued till about the middle of the last century ; when, under pretence of attending Tichborne Dole, vagabonds, gipsies, and idlers of every description, assembled from all quarters, pilfering throughout the neighbourhood ; and at last, in 1796, on account of the complaints of the magistrates and gentry, it was discontinued. This gave great offence to many who had been accustomed to receive the dole. And now arose a revival of old traditions. The good Lady Mabella, as the legend told, had predicted that, if the dole should be withheld, the mansion would crumble to ruins ; that the family name would become extinct through the failure of male heirs ; and that this failure would be occasioned by a generation of seven sons being followed by a generation of seven daughters. Singularly enough, the old house partially fell down in 1803 ; the baronet of that day had seven sons ; the eldest of these had seven daughters ; and the owner of the family estates became a Doughty instead of a Tichborne. If this story be correctly told, it is certainly a very tempting one for those who have a leaning towards the number seven.

France, as well as our own country, has a belief in the Seventh Son mystery. The *Journal de Loiret*, a French provincial newspaper, in 1854 stated that, in Orleans, if a family has seven sons and no daughter, the seventh is called a *Marcou*, is branded with a *fleur-de-lis*, and is believed to possess the power of curing the king's evil. The Marcou breathes on the part affected, or else the patient touches the Marcou's *fleur-de-lis*. In the year above-named, there was a famous Marcou in Orleans named Foulon; he was a cooper by trade, and was known as 'le beau Marcou.' Simple peasants used to come to visit him from many leagues in all directions, particularly in Passion week, when his ministrations were believed to be most efficacious. On the night of Good Friday, from midnight to sunrise, the chance of cure was supposed to be especially good, and on this account four or five hundred persons would assemble. Great disturbances hence arose; and as there was evidence, to all except the silly dupes themselves, that Foulon made use of their superstition to enrich himself, the police succeeded, but not without much opposition, in preventing these assemblages.

In some of the States of Germany there used formerly to be a custom for the reigning prince to stand sponsor to a seventh son (no daughter intervening) of any of his subjects. Whether still acted upon is doubtful; but there was an incident lately which bore on the old custom in a curious way. A West Hartlepool newspaper stated that Mr J. V. Curths, a German, residing in that busy colliery town, became, toward the close of 1857, the father of one of those prodigies —a seventh son. Probably he himself was a Saxe Gothan by birth; at any rate he wrote to the Prince Consort, reminding him of the old German custom, and soliciting the honour of his Royal Highness' sponsorship to the child. The Prince was doubtless a little puzzled by this appeal, as he often must have been by the strange applications made to him. Nevertheless, a reply was sent in the Prince's name, very complimentary to his countryman, and enclosing a substantial *souvenir* for the little child; but the newspaper paragraph is not sufficiently clear for us to be certain whether the sponsorship really was assented to, and, if so, how it was performed.

Three Wonderful Things.—Sir James Stewart, of Coltness, was accustomed to say, that after having lived fifty years, and gone through almost all the geographical and literary world, three things only had surmounted his most sanguine expectations—The Amphitheatre at Verona, the Church of St Peter's at Rome, and Mr Pitt in the House of Commons.

Smoking was formerly forbidden among schoolmasters. In the rules of the school at Chigwell, founded in 1629, it was declared that 'the master must be a man of sound religion, neither Papist nor Puritan, of a grave behaviour, and sober and honest conversation, no tippler or haunter of alehouses, and no *puffer of tobacco.*'

'*To the good.*'—We find this homely phrase in the speech of Charles I. to the House of Commons on 'The Arrest of the Five Members,' as follows: 'Whatsoever I have done in favour and *to the good*,' &c.

JANUARY 27.

St Julian, bishop, 3rd century. St John Chrysostom, archbishop, 407. St Marius, abbot, 555.

ST JOHN CHRYSOSTOM.

St John *Chrysostomus* is one of the most celebrated of the fathers of the Eastern or Greek church. He was born about the year 347, at Antioch. His father was commander of the Imperial army in Syria. He was educated for the bar, but became a convert to Christianity; and the solitary manner of living being then in great estimation, and very prevalent in Syria, he retired to a mountain not far from Antioch, where he lived some years in solitude, practising the usual austerities. He returned to the city in 381, and was ordained by Meletius, Bishop of Antioch, to the office of deacon, and to that of presbyter in 386. He became one of the most popular preachers of the age; his reputation extended throughout the Christian world; and in 398, on the death of Nectarius, he was elected Bishop of Constantinople. He was zealous and resolute in the reform of clerical abuses, and two years after his consecration, on his visitation in Asia Minor, he deposed no less than thirteen bishops of Lydia and Phrygia. His denunciations of the licentious manners of the court drew upon him the resentment of the Empress Eudoxia, who encouraged Theophilus, patriarch of Alexandria, to summon a synod at Chalcedon, in which a number of accusations were brought against Chrysostom. He was condemned, deposed, and banished to Cucusus, a place in the mountain-range of Taurus, whence, after the death of the Empress, it was determined to remove him to a desert place on the Euxine. He travelled on foot, and caught a fever, which occasioned his death at Comana, in Pontus, September 14, 407, at the age of sixty.

The works of Chrysostom are very numerous, consisting of 700 homilies and 242 epistles, as well as commentaries, orations, and treatises on points of doctrine. His life has been written by Socrates, Sozomen, Theodorèt, and other early writers, and by Neander in more recent times.

The name Chrysostomus, or golden-mouthed, on account of his eloquence, was not given to him till some years after his death. Socrates and the other early writers simply call him John, or John of Constantinople.

Born.—Dr Thomas Willis, 1622, *Bodmin;* J. C. W. Mozart, 1756.

Died.—Sir William Temple, 1699; Thomas Woolston, 1733, *King's Bench Prison;* Admiral Lord Hood, 1816; Dr C. Hutton, mathematician, 1823; Rev. Dr Andrew Bell, originator of the Madras System of Juvenile Education, 1832; John James Audubon, naturalist, 1851, *New York.*

DR ANDREW BELL.

Dr Andrew Bell, being a holder of rich livings, was able, by the aid of very frugal or rather penurious habits, to realise a large fortune, all of which he devoted at his death to exemplify and perpetuate that system of juvenile education, the introduction of which, first in Madras and afterwards in England, had given him celebrity, but of which, it need scarcely be remarked, the merits are now found to have been largely over-estimated. It is sad to reflect that, among the founders of useful institutions, several, if not many, or the greatest number, have been wretched egotists, or noted in life rather for the unfavourable aspect they bore towards their fellow-creatures, than for anything of a benevolent or genial cast. Thus Guy, the bookseller, whose money established the medical hospital bearing his name, is alleged to have made it chiefly by purchasing seamen's tickets, and a not very creditable success in the affair of the South Sea bubble. Of George Watson, founder of an hospital for the nurture of boys in Edinburgh, the papers preserved in his cabinet shew how penuriously he lived, and how rigorous beyond measure he was as a creditor. James Donaldson, who left a quarter of a million for a similar purpose, overlooked in his will all his old servants and retainers, and assigned but one or two poor annuities to those nearest him in blood. There are, of course, many instances in which benevolent intentions have solely or mainly ruled; but, certainly, many have been of the opposite complexion here indicated. Among such must be reckoned Andrew Bell, who left £120,000 Three per Cent. Consols. to found an extensive establishment for juvenile education in his native city of St Andrews. The egotism of this old gentleman, as indicated in his ordinary conversation, and in his leaving a considerable sum for the composition and publication of a memoir to glorify him, allow no room to doubt that, in the hoarding of money, and in the final disposal of what he acquired, he had purely an eye to himself.

Thomas De Quincey tells some things of a domestic nature regarding Dr Bell, which, in the case of any reasonably respectable man, one would not desire to see repeated, but which, regarding him, do not call for being put under any restriction. 'Most men,' says the Opium-eater, 'have their enemies and calumniators; Dr Bell had *his*, who happened rather indecorously to be his wife, from whom he was legally separated . . . divorced *à mensâ et thoro*. This legal separation did not prevent the lady from persecuting the unhappy doctor with everlasting letters, endorsed outside with records of her enmity and spite. Sometimes she addressed her epistles thus: "To that supreme of rogues, who looks the hang-dog that he is, Doctor (such a doctor!) Andrew Bell." Or again: "To the ape of apes, and the knave of knaves, who is recorded to have once paid a debt—but a small one, you may be sure, it was that he selected for this wonderful experiment—in fact, it was 4½d. Had it been on the other side of 6d., he must have died before he could have achieved so dreadful a sacrifice." Many others, most ingeniously varied in the style of abuse, I have heard rehearsed by Coleridge, Southey, Lloyd, &c.; and one, in particular, addressed to the doctor, when spending a summer at the cottage of Robert Newton, an old soldier, in Grasmere, presented on the back two separate adjurations, one specially addressed to Robert himself, pathetically urging him to look sharply after the rent of his lodgings; and the other more generally addressed to the unfortunate person as yet

undisclosed to the British public (and in this case turning out to be myself), who might be incautious enough to pay the postage at Ambleside. "Don't grant him an hour's credit," she urged upon the person unknown, "if I had any regard to my family." "*Cash down!*" she wrote twice over. Why the doctor submitted to these annoyances, nobody knew. Some said it was mere indolence; but others held it to be a cunning compromise with her inexorable malice. The letters were certainly open to the "public" eye; but meantime the "public" was a very narrow one: the clerks in the post-office had little time for digesting such amenities of conjugal affection; and the chance bearer of the letters to the doctor would naturally solve the mystery by supposing an *extra* portion of madness in the writer, rather than an *extra* portion of knavery in the reverend receiver.'

ROBERT BURTON.

On the 27th January 1639, there was interred in Christ Church Cathedral, Oxford, one of the most singular men of genius that England has at any time produced,—the famous Robert Burton, author of the *Anatomy of Melancholy*. Though occupying a clerical charge in his native county of Leicester, he lived chiefly in his rooms in Christ Church College, and thus became a subject of notice to Anthony Wood, who, in his *Athenæ Oxonienses*, thus speaks of him: 'He was an exact mathematician, a curious calculator of nativities, a general-read scholar, a thorough-paced philologist, and one that understood the surveying of lands well. As he was by many accounted a severe student, a devourer of authors, a melancholy and humorous person, so, by others who knew him well, a person of great honesty, plain-dealing, and charity. I have heard some of the ancients of Christ Church say, that his company was very merry, facete, and juvenile; and no man in his time did surpass him for his ready and dexterous interlarding his common discourse among them with verses from the poets, or sentences from classical authors, which, being then all the fashion in the University, made his company more acceptable.'

The Anatomy of Melancholy was the only work which Burton produced. After the 8th edition (1676), the book seems to have fallen into neglect, till Dr Johnson's remark, that it was the only book that ever took him out of bed two hours sooner than he wished to rise, again directed attention to it. Dr Ferrier has shewn that Sterne was largely indebted to it, and other authors have been poachers on the same preserve. The work contains a vast number of quotations, nearly all Latin, combined with his own reflections on the large mass of historical and other materials which he has collected. His humour is quaint and peculiar. His melancholy resembles that of Jacques in *As you Like it*. The fine stanzas prefixed to his book, beginning—

'When I goe musing all alone,'—

exhibit the meaning which Burton attaches to

the word, which seems to be, not depression of spirits, but rather a habit of rumination, during which the feelings are cheerful or sad according to the succession of thoughts which pass through the mind.

These lines are thought to have suggested to Milton many ideas in his *Il Penseroso:*

'When I goe musing all alone,
　Thinking of divers things fore-known,
When I would build castles in the air,
　Void of sorrow and void of fear,
Pleasing myself with phantasms sweet,
　Methinks the time runs very fleet :
　　All my joys to this are folly,
　　Nought so sweet as Melancholy.

'When I goe walking all alone,
　Recounting what I have ill done,
My thoughts on me then tyrannise,
　Fear and sorrow me surprise;
Whether I tarry still or go,
　Methinks the time moves very slow :
　　All my griefs to this are jolly,
　　Nought so sad as Melancholy.

'When to my selfe I act and smile,
　With pleasing thoughts the time beguile,
By a brookside or wood so green,
　Unheard, unsought for, or unseen,
A thousand pleasures doe me bless,
　And crown my soul with happiness.
　　All my joyes besides are folly,
　　None so sweet as Melancholy.

'When I lie, sit, or walk alone,
　I sigh, I grieve, making great mone,
In a dark grove, or irksome den,
　With discontents and furies then,
A thousand miseries at once
　Mine heavy heart and soul ensconce.
　　All my griefs to this are jolly,
　　None so sour as Melancholy.'

MONUMENT OF BURTON IN CHRISTCHURCH.

An edition of the work was published in 1849. in 8vo, with notes, in which the quotations are translated, explained, and referred to the respective works from which they have been derived.

Burton died at or very near the time which he had some years before foretold from the calculations of his own nativity, and which, says Wood, 'being exact, several of the students did not forbear to whisper among themselves, that rather than there should be a mistake in the calculation, he sent up his soul to heaven through a slip about his neck.' We have no other evidence of the truth of this than an obscure hint in the epitaph on his tomb, which was written by the author himself, a short time before his death.   Over his grave, against the upper pillar of the aisle, was raised a monument, with the bust of Burton, painted to the life; and on the right-hand, is the calculation of his nativity; and under the bust is the epitaph :

'Paucis notus, paucioribus ignotus,
　Hic jacet *Democritus* junior,
　　Cui vitam dedit et mortem
　　　Melancholia.
Ob. 8, Id. Jan.   A.C. MD.XXXIX.'

EARLY NOTICES OF COFFEE IN ENGLAND, FROM BROADSIDES IN THE LUTTREL COLLECTION.

A manuscript note, written by Oldys, the celebrated antiquary, states that 'The use of coffee in England was first known in 1657. Mr Edwards, a Turkey merchant, brought from Smyrna to London one Pasqua Rosee, a Ragusan youth, who prepared this drink for him every morning.   But the novelty thereof drawing too much company to him, he allowed his said servant, with another of his son-in-law, to sell it publicly, and they set up the first coffee-house in London, in St Michael's alley in Cornhill.   The sign was Pasqua Rosee's own head.'   Oldys is slightly in error here; Rosee commenced his coffee-house in 1652, and one Jacobs, a Jew, had established a similar undertaking at Oxford, a year or two earlier.   One of Rosee's original shop or hand-bills, the only mode of advertising in those days, is now before us; and considering it to be a remarkable record of a great social innovation, we here reprint it for the amusement of the reader :

THE VERTUE OF THE COFFEE DRINK,
First made and publickly sold in England by Pasqua Rosee.

The grain or berry called coffee, groweth upon little trees only in the deserts of Arabia. It is brought from thence, and drunk generally throughout all the Grand Seignour's dominions.   It is a simple, innocent thing, composed into a drink, by being dried in an oven, and ground to powder, and boiled up with spring water, and about half a pint of it to be drunk fasting an hour before, and not eating an hour after, and to be taken as hot as possibly can be endured; the which will never fetch the skin off the mouth, or raise any blisters by reason of that heat.

The Turks' drink at meals and other times is usually water, and their diet consists much of fruit; the crudities whereof are very much corrected by this drink.

The quality of this drink is cold and dry; and

though it be a drier, yet it neither heats, nor inflames more than hot posset. It so incloseth the orifice of the stomach, and fortifies the heat within, that it is very good to help digestion; and therefore of great use to be taken about three or four o'clock afternoon, as well as in the morning. It much quickens the spirits, and makes the heart lightsome; it is good against sore eyes, and the better if you hold your head over it and take in the steam that way. It suppresseth fumes exceedingly, and therefore is good against the head-ache, and will very much stop any defluxion of rheums, that distil from the head upon the stomach, and so prevent and help consumptions and the cough of the lungs.

It is excellent to prevent and cure the dropsy, gout, and scurvy. It is known by experience to be better than any other drying drink for people in years, or children that have any running humours upon them, as the king's evil, &c. It is a most excellent remedy against the spleen, hypochondriac winds, and the like. It will prevent drowsiness, and make one fit for business, if one have occasion to watch, and therefore you are not to drink of it after supper, unless you intend to be watchful, for it will hinder sleep for three or four hours.

It is observed that in Turkey, where this is generally drunk, that they are not troubled with the stone, gout, dropsy, or scurvy, and that their skins are exceeding clear and white. It is neither laxative nor restringent.

Made and sold in St Michael's-alley in Cornhill, by Pasqua Rosee, at the sign of his own head.

The new beverage, as may readily be supposed, had its opponents, as well as its advocates. The following extract from *A Broadside against Coffee*, published about the same period, informs us that Rosee's partner, the servant of Mr Edwards's son-in-law, was a coachman; while it controverts the statement that hot coffee will not burn the mouth, and ridicules the broken English of the Ragusan:

A BROADSIDE AGAINST COFFEE.

A coachman was the first (here) coffee made,
And ever since the rest drive on the trade:
'*Me no good Engalash!*' and sure enough,
He played the quack to salve his Stygian stuff;
'*Ver boon for de stomach, de cough, de phthisick,*'
And I believe him, for it looks like physic.
Coffee a crust is charred into a coal,
The smell and taste of the mock china bowl;
Where huff and puff, they labour out their lungs,
Lest, Dives-like, they should bewail their tongues.
And yet they tell ye that it will not burn,
Though on the jury blisters you return;
Whose furious heat does make the waters rise,
And still through the alembics of your eyes.
Dread and desire, you fall to 't snap by snap,
As hungry dogs do scalding porridge lap.
But to cure drunkards it has got great fame;
Posset or porridge, will 't not do the same?
Confusion hurries all into one scene,
Like Noah's ark, the clean and the unclean.
And now, alas! the drench has credit got,
And he's no gentleman that drinks it not;
That such a dwarf should rise to such a stature!
But custom is but a remove from Nature.
A little dish and a large coffee-house,
What is it but a mountain and a mouse?

But, in spite of opposition, coffee soon became a favourite drink, and the shops, where it was sold, places of general resort.

One of the most noted was at the Sultan Morat or Amurath's head in Exchange-alley; another was 'Ward's' in Bread-street, at the sign of the Sultan Solyman's head. Tokens, to serve as small money, were issued by both of these establishments, and are here represented. Another of

the earliest houses was the Rainbow, near Temple-bar, which still flourishes, but altogether in a new style. There can be little doubt that the coffee-house, as a substitute for the beerseller's fire-side, was a movement towards refinement, as well as temperance. There appears to have been a great anxiety that the coffee-house, while open to all ranks, should be conducted under such restraints as might prevent the better class of customers from being offended. Accordingly, the following regulations, printed on large sheets of paper, were hung up in conspicuous positions on the walls:

THE RULES AND ORDERS OF THE COFFEE-HOUSE.

Enter, sirs, freely, but first, if you please,
Peruse our civil orders, which are these.

First, gentry, tradesmen, all are welcome hither,
And may without affront sit down together:
Pre-eminence of place none here should mind,
But take the next fit seat that he can find:
Nor need any, if finer persons come,
Rise up for to assign to them his room;
To limit men's expense, we think not fair,
But let him forfeit twelve-pence that shall swear:
He that shall any quarrel here begin,
Shall give each man a dish t' atone the sin;
And so shall he, whose compliments extend
So far to drink in coffee to his friend;
Let noise of loud disputes be quite forborne,
Nor maudlin lovers here in corners mourn,
But all be brisk, and talk, but not too much;
On sacred things, let none presume to touch,
Nor profane Scripture, nor saucily wrong
Affairs of State with an irreverent tongue:
Let mirth be innocent, and each man see
That all his jests without reflection be;

To keep the house more quiet and from blame,
We banish hence cards, dice, and every game ;
Nor can allow of wagers, that exceed
Five shillings. which ofttimes do troubles breed ;
Let all that 's lost or forfeited be spent
In such good liquor as the house doth vent,
And customers endeavour, to their powers,
For to observe still, seasonable hours.
Lastly, let each man what he calls for pay,
And so you 're welcome to come every day.

The above rules are ornamented, with an engraved representation of a coffee-house. Five persons, one of them smoking, and, evidently, from their dresses of different ranks in life, are seated at a table, on which are small basins, without saucers, and tobacco pipes, while a waiter is engaged in serving coffee. Believing that the public will feel some interest in the seventeenth century coffee-house—the resort of Dryden, Wycherley, and the wits and poets generally— we have caused a transcript of this print to be here presented.

Immediately after their first establishment, the coffee-houses became the resort of *quidnuncs,* and the great marts for news of all kinds, true and false. A broadside song, published in 1667, thus describes the principal subjects of coffee-house conversation :

COFFEE-HOUSE. TEMP. CHARLES II.

NEWS FROM THE COFFEE-HOUSE, OR THE
NEWSMONGERS' HALL.

You that delight in wit and mirth,
　And long to hear such news
As come from all parts of the earth,
　Dutch, Danes, and Turks, and Jews,
I'll send you to a rendezvous,
　Where it is smoking new ;
Go hear it at a coffee-house,
　It cannot but be true.

There battles and sea-fights are fought,
　And bloody plots displayed ;
They know more things than ere was thought,
　Or ever was betrayed :
No money in the Minting-house
　Is half so bright and new ;
And, coming from the coffee-house.
　It cannot but be true.

Before the navies fall to work,
　They know who shall be winner ;
They there can tell you what the Turk
　Last Sunday had to dinner ;
Who last did cut De Ruyter's corns,
　Amongst his jovial crew ;
Or who first gave the devil horns,
　Which cannot but be true.

　　*　　*　　*　　*

Another swears by both his ears,
　Monsieur will cut our throats ;
The French king will a girdle bring,
　Made of flat-bottomed boats,
Shall compass England round about,
　Which must not be a few,
To give our Englishmen the rout ;
　This sounds as if 'twere true.

There 's nothing done in all the world,
　From monarch to the mouse,
But every day or night 'tis hurled
　Into the coffee-house.
What Lily, or what Booker can
　By art not bring about,
At coffee-house you'll find a man
　Can quickly find it out.

They'll tell you there what lady-ware
　Of late is grown too light ;
What wise man shall from favour fall,
　What fool shall be a knight ;
They'll tell you when our failing trade
　Shall rise again and flourish,
Or when Jack Adams shall be made
　Churchwarden of the parish.

　　*　　*　　*　　*

They know all that is good or hurt,
　To bless ye, or to save ye ;
There is the college, and the court,
　The country, camp, and navy ;
So great a university,
　I think there ne'er was any,
In which you may a scholar be
　For spending of a penny.

A merchant's prentice there shall show
　You all and everything
What hath been done, and is to do,
　'Twixt Holland and the King ;
What articles of peace will be
　He can precisely shew ;
What will be good for them or we
　He perfectly doth know.

　　*　　*　　*　　*

The drinking there of chocolate
Can make a fool a Sophy ;
'Tis thought the Turkish Mahomet
Was first inspired with coffee,
By which his powers did overflow
The land of Palestine ;
Then let us to the coffee-house go,
'Tis cheaper far than wine.

You shall know there what fashions are,
How periwigs are curled ;
And for a penny you shall hear
All novells in the world.
Both old and young, and great and small,
And rich and poor, you'll see ;
Therefore let 's to the coffee all,
Come all away with me.

In 1675 a proclamation was issued for shutting up and suppressing all coffee-houses. The government of the day, however, found that, in making this proclamation, they had gone a step too far. So early as this period, the coffee-house had become a power in the land—as Macaulay tells us—a most important political institution, when public meetings, harangues, resolutions, and the rest of the machinery of agitation, had not come into fashion, and nothing resembling a newspaper existed. In such circumstances, the coffee-houses were the chief organs through which the public opinion of the metropolis vented itself. Consequently, on a petition of the merchants and retailers of coffee, permission was granted to keep the coffee-houses open for six months, under an admonition that the masters of them should prevent all scandalous papers, books, and libels from being read in them; and hinder every person from declaring, uttering, or divulging all manner of false and scandalous reports against government, or the ministers thereof. The absurdity of constituting every maker of a cup of coffee a censor of the press, was too great for even those days; the proclamation was laughed at, and no more was heard of the suppression of coffee-houses. Their subsequent history does not fall within our present limits, but may be referred to at another opportunity.

THE ORIGIN OF SOME WELL-KNOWN LINES.

' His angle-rod made of a sturdy oak ;
His line a cable, which in storms ne'er broke ;
His hook he baited with a dragon's tail,
And sat upon a rock, and bobbed for whale.'

The origin of these somewhat famous lines seems not to be generally known. In our contemporary *Notes and Queries* (for November 30, 1861, p. 448) they are spoken of as 'Dr King's well-known quatrain upon *A Giant Angling.*' This is a mistake; at least, if Dr William King, the Oxford wit and poet, is the person meant; indeed, there seems every reason to suppose that they were composed before Dr King was born. With one or two trifling variations, they are to be found in the *Mock Romance*, a rhapsody attached to *The Loves of Hero and Leander*, a small 12mo published in London in the years 1653 and 1677 ; the following being the context :

' This day (a day as fair as heart could wish)
This giant stood on shore of sea to fish :
For angling-rod, he took a sturdy oak ;
For line a cable, that in storm ne'er broke ;
His hook was such as heads the end of pole,
To pluck down house ere fire consumes it whole :

His hook was baited with a dragon's tail,
And then on rock he stood to bob for whale :
Which straight he caught, and nimbly home did
    pack,
With ten cart-load of dinner on his back.'

Dr King, however, is not the only unsuccessful claimant of the above four lines. They are printed in the fifth volume of Dryden's *Miscellany*, and have been attributed to Daniel Kenrick, a quack physician, at Worcester. As, however, Kenrick was thirty-two years of age in 1685, it is as impossible that they can have been written by him as by Dr King. Their true origin we have given above ; their authorship is, and probably always will be, unknown.

JANUARY 28.

St Agnes, virgin and martyr. St Cyril, patriarch of Alexandria, 444. Sts Thyrsus, Leucius, and Callinicus, martyrs. St John of Reomay, abbot, 6th century. St Paulinus, patriarch of Aquileia, 804. B. Charlemagne, emperor, 814. St Glastian, of Scotland, 830. St Margaret, princess of Hungary, 1271.

ST CYRIL.

St Cyrillus was educated at Alexandria, where his uncle Theophilus was patriarch, through whose influence St John Chrysostom was deposed and banished from Constantinople. On the death of Theophilus in 412, St Cyrillus was elected as his successor in the patriarchate. He is generally described as a man of revengeful disposition, and a violent persecutor of those whom he considered heretics. The story of the murder of Hypatia, the daughter of the mathematician Theon of Alexandria, has been related by Socrates, Nicephorus, and other ecclesiastical historians. Hypatia was a lady of such extraordinary ability and learning as to have been chosen to preside over the school of Platonic philosophy in Alexandria, and her lectures were attended by a crowd of students from Greece and Asia Minor. She was also greatly esteemed and treated with much respect by Orestes, the governor of Alexandria, who was a decided opponent of the patriarch. Hence the malice of Cyril, who is related to have excited a mob of fanatical monks to assault her in the street, who dragged her into a church, and there murdered her, actually tearing her body to pieces.

Cyril had a long and violent dispute with Nestorius, bishop of Constantinople, concerning the divine nature of Christ, and whether Mary was entitled to the appellation of 'Mother of God,' and other mysterious matters. Nestorius was condemned and deposed by Pope Celestine, and Cyril was appointed to carry out the sentence, for which purpose he summoned a council of sixty bishops at Ephesus ; but John, patriarch of Antioch, summoned a counter-council of forty bishops, who supported Nestorius, and excommunicated Cyril. The rival patriarchs appealed to the Emperor Theodosius, who committed both Cyril and Nestorius to prison, where they remained some time under rigorous treatment. Cyril, by the influence of Pope Celestine, was liberated, and restored in 431 to his see of Alexandria, which he retained till his death in 444. His works are numerous, mostly on difficult points of doctrine, which are rendered more obscure by a perplexed style, and the barbarous Greek in which they are written. They have been published in seven vols. folio, Greek and Latin, Paris, 1638.

***

Born.—Captain Maclure, Arctic voyager, 1807.

Died.—Charlemagne, 814 ; King Henry VIII., 1547, *Windsor ;* Sir Francis Drake, 1596 ; Sir Thomas Bodley, founder of the Bodleian Library, Oxford, 1612 ; Peter the Great of Russia, 1725 ; Mrs Johnson (*Stella*), 1728, *Dublin ;* J. B. Danville, 1782, *Paris ;* Mademoiselle Clairon, actress, 1803 ; Sir William Beechey, painter, 1839 ; W. H. Prescott, historian, 1859.

PETER THE GREAT IN ENGLAND.

On the 28th of January 1725, died Peter I., Czar of Russia, deservedly named the Great ; one of the most extraordinary men that ever appeared on the great theatre of the world, in any age or country—a being full of contradictions, yet consistent in all he did ; a promoter of literature, arts, and sciences, yet without education himself. ' He gave a polish,' says Voltaire, ' to his people, and was himself a savage ; he taught them the art of war, of which he was himself ignorant ; from the sight of a small boat on the river Moskwa he erected a powerful fleet, made himself an expert and active shipwright, sailor, pilot, and commander ; he changed the manners, customs, and laws of the Russians : and lives in their memory as the father of his country.'

His taste for everything connected with ships and navigation amounted, in early life, to a passion. When he had resolved to visit the countries of Western Europe, to learn how to improve his own barbarous subjects, he went straight to Saardam, in Holland, and there, with his companions, worked in the dockyards as a common shipwright, by the name of Pieter Timmerman ; he rose early, boiled his own pot, and received wages for his labour. When well advanced in the manual art, he proceeded, in January 1698, to England, to study the theory of ship-building, and the method of making draughts and laying them off in the mould-lofts. Arriving in honourable state with his companions in three English ships, which had been dispatched for him, he was kindly received by King William, but without state ceremonial, his wish being to remain in England simply as a private gentleman ; accordingly, his name never once appears in the *London Gazette*, then, as now, the only official paper. A large house was hired for him and his suite, at the bottom of York-buildings, now Buckingham-street, in the Adelphi,—the last house on the east side, looking on the Thames. It contained spacious apartments, in which some of the decorations that existed at the time of the imperial visit may still be seen.* As the Czar came not in any public character, he was placed under the especial charge of the Marquis of Carmarthen, with whom he became very intimate. It is stated in a private letter, that they used to spend

* Pepys, the diarist, lived in the house opposite, the last on the west side of the street, but it has been since rebuilt.

174

their evenings frequently together in drinking hot pepper and brandy. Peter loved strong liquors ; and we learn from one of the papers of the day, that he took a particular fancy to the *nectar ambrosia*, a new cordial which the compounder presented to his Majesty, who sent for more of it.

The Czar sojourned in England four months. In the *Postboy* it is stated that, on the day after his arrival, he went to Kensington Palace, to dine with King William and the Court ; but he was all the while *incognito*. On the Saturday following, the Czar went to the opera ; and on the Friday night he was present at the last of the Temple revels. On the following Sunday, he went in a hackney-coach to Kensington Palace, and returned at night to his lodgings (in Norfolk-street), where he was attended by several of the King's servants. His movements, during the rest of the month, were a journey to Woolwich and Deptford, to see the dockyards ; then to the theatre, to see the *Rival Queens ; or Alexander the Great ;* to St James's, to be present at a fine ball ; to Redriff, where a ship was building for him ; and he was present at the launch of a man-of-war at Chatham.

The Czar was continually annoyed by the crowds in the streets of London, as he had been at Amsterdam, and he could not bear the jostling with becoming patience. As he was one day walking along the Strand with the Marquis of Carmarthen, a porter, with a load on his shoulder, rudely pushed against him, and drove him into the road. He was extremely indignant, and ready to knock the man down ; but the Marquis interfering, saved the offender, only telling him that the gentleman whom he had so rudely run against was ' the Czar.' The porter turning round, replied with a grin, ' Czar ! we are all Czars here.'

After a month's residence in London, the Czar and his suite removed to John Evelyn's house, Sayes-court, close to Deptford dockyard. It had been let by Evelyn to Admiral Benbow, whose term had just expired. A doorway was broken through the boundary-wall of the dockyard, to communicate with the dwelling-house. The grounds, which were beautifully laid out and planted, had been much damaged by the Admiral ; but the Czar proved a worse tenant. Evelyn's servant wrote to him : ' There is a house full of people *right nasty.* The Czar lies next your library, and dines in the parlour next your study. He dines at ten o'clock, and six at night ; is very often at home a whole day ; very often in the King's yard, or by water, dressed in several dresses. The King is expected there this day ; the best parlour is pretty clean for him to be entertained in. The King pays for all he has.' But this was not all : Evelyn had a favourite holly-hedge, which the Czar is said to have spoiled, by trundling a wheelbarrow through it every morning, for the sake of exercise. The Czar and his retinue remained here only three weeks ; but the damage done to the house and gardens was estimated at £150.

We have scarcely any evidence that the Czar ever worked in Deptford dockyard as a shipwright ; he seems to have been employed in collecting information connected with naval architecture, from the Commissioner and Surveyor of the Navy, Sir Anthony Deane. Peter might be seen almost daily on the Thames, in a sailing yacht, or rowing a boat ; and the King made him a present of

SAYES COURT, DEPTFORD, THE RESIDENCE OF PETER THE GREAT.

the *Royal Transport*, with orders to change her masts, rigging, sails, &c., in any such way as the Czar might think proper for improving her sailing qualities. But his great delight was to get into a small decked boat from the dockyard, and taking Menzikoff, and three or four of his suite, to work the vessel with them, he being the helmsman ; by which practice he said he should be able to teach them how to command ships when they got home. Having finished their day's work, they used to resort to a public-house in Great Tower-street, close to Tower-hill, to smoke their pipes, and drink beer and brandy. The landlord had the Czar of Muscovy's head painted and put up for a sign, which continued till the year 1808, when a person named Waxel took a fancy to the old sign, and offered the then landlord of the house to paint him a new one for it. A copy was accordingly made, which maintained its station until the house was rebuilt. when the sign was not replaced, and the name only remains.

The Czar, in passing up and down the river, was much struck with the magnificent building of Greenwich Hospital, which, until he had visited it, and seen the old pensioners, he thought to be a royal palace ; and one day, when King William asked him how he liked his hospital for decayed seamen, the Czar answered, 'If I were the adviser of your Majesty, I should counsel you to remove your court to Greenwich, and convert St James's into a hospital.'

It being term-time while the Czar was in London, he was taken into Westminster Hall ; he inquired who all those busy people in black gowns and flowing wigs were, and what they were about? Being answered 'They are lawyers, sir,' 'Lawyers!' said he, much astonished, 'why, I have but *two* in my whole dominions, and I believe I shall hang one of them the moment I get home.'

Two sham fights at sea were got up for the

Czar ; the ships were divided into two squadrons. and every ship took her opposite, and fired three broadsides *aloft and one alow*, without shot. On returning from Portsmouth, Peter and his party, twenty-one in all, stopped at the principal inn at Godalming, and, according to the landlord's bill. which is preserved in the Bodleian Library, there consumed, at breakfast, half a sheep, a quarter of lamb, ten pullets, twelve chickens. three quarts of brandy, six quarts of mulled wine, seven dozen of eggs, with salad in proportion : and at dinner, five ribs of beef, weighing three stone ; one sheep, 56 lbs. ; three-quarters of lamb, a shoulder and loin of veal boiled, eight pullets, eight rabbits, two dozen and a half of sack, and one dozen of claret. Peter was invariably a hard-drinker, for he is known to have drunk a pint of brandy and a bottle of sherry for his morning draught ; and after dinner eight bottles of sack, 'and so went to the playhouse.'

The Czar had an extraordinary aversion to a crowd : at a birthday-ball at St James's, instead of joining the company, he was put into a small room. whence he could see all that passed without being himself seen. When he went to see the King in Parliament, he was placed upon the roof of the house to peep in at the window, when King and people so laughed at him that he was obliged to retire. The Czar had a favourite monkey, which sat upon the back of his chair, and one day annoyed the King by jumping upon him, while he paid Peter a visit.

Bishop Burnet accompanied the Czar to shew him the different churches in the metropolis, and to give information upon ecclesiastical matters. While residing at Deptford, Peter frequently invited Dr. Halley from the Royal Observatory, in Greenwich Park, to dine with him, and give him his opinion and advice, especially upon his plan of building a fleet. He also visited several manufactories and workshops in London, and bought a famous geographical clock of its maker, Carte, at the sign of the Dial and Crown, near Essex-street, in the Strand. The Czar was very fond of mechanism, and it is said that before he left England he could take a watch to pieces, and put it together again. The King promised Peter that there should be no impediment to his engaging and taking with him to Russia, English artificers and scientific men ; and when he returned to Holland, there went with him captains of ships, pilots, surgeons, gunners, mast-makers, boat-builders, sail-makers, compass-makers, carvers, anchor-smiths, and copper-smiths ; in all, nearly 500 persons. At his departure, he presented to the King a ruby, valued at £10,000, which he brought in his waistcoat-pocket, and placed in William's hand, wrapped up in a piece of brown paper !

The memory of Peter, among his countrymen, is held in the highest veneration. The magnificent equestrian statue erected by Catherine II. ; the waxen figure of Peter in the museum of the Academy, founded by himself ; the dress, the sword, and the hat, which he wore at the battle of Pultowa, the last pierced with a ball ; the horse that he rode in that battle ; the trowsers, worsted stockings, shoes, and cap, which he wore at Saardam,—all in the same apartment; his two favourite dogs, his turning-lathe, and tools, with specimens of his workmanship; the iron bar which he forged with his own hand at Olonitz; the *Little Grandsire*, so carefully preserved as the first germ of the Russian navy; and the wooden hut in which he lived while superintending the first foundation of Petersburg:—these, and a thousand other tangible memorials, all preserved with the utmost care, speak in the most intelligible language the opinion which the Russians hold of the *Father of his Country*.

CLAIRON'S UNSEEN PERSECUTOR.

Mademoiselle Clairon, the theatrical idol of Paris in the middle of the last century, relates in her Memoirs, that in her early days she attracted the affections of a Breton gentleman, whom, as he was gloomy and despotic, she found it impossible to love. He died of chagrin on her account, without succeeding even in inducing her to come and see him in his last moments. The event was followed by a series of occurrences which, notwithstanding their mysterious nature, she relates with the appearance of perfect sincerity. First, there was every night, at eleven o'clock, a piercing cry heard in the street before her house. And, in several instances, on friends speaking of it incredulously, it took place on the instant, to the consternation of all who heard it. After an interval of some weeks, the annoyance was renewed in the form of a musket-shot, which seemed to be fired against her window, and was heard by all in her apartment, but never could be traced by the police to any living agent. Then another interval took place, after which an invisible clapping of hands followed: this was followed in its turn by a strain of fine music. Finally, after two years and a half, this strange persecution from the invisible ceased. Madame Clairon states that she afterwards received a visit from an old lady, who had attended her lover on his death-bed, and who informed her that with his latest breath he had inveighed against the object of his unfortunate passion, and threatened to pursue her as long after his death as she had pursued him during his life, being exactly two years and a half.

The Duchess d'Abrantes, in her Memoirs, relates how she had heard Clairon give a solemn recital of these occurrences, 'laying aside all affectation and everything that could be construed into speaking for effect.' The wonder is how, if such things happen, they should so entirely fail to obtain credence; how, if they do not happen, they should be so often related as if they did, and on what, in ordinary matters, would pass as sufficient evidence.

Clairon was a great favourite with Voltaire: it would be curious to learn what he thought of her story of the invisible persecutor. She appears to have had her full share of theatrical caprices and jealousies, under one of which she prematurely withdrew from the stage, though not without a considerable fortune. Garrick, asked what he thought of her as an actress, said she was 'too much an actress;' which gives a tolerable idea of her attitudinary style. It is said she was equally an actress off the stage, maintaining a

176

grand manner even before her domestics. She died at eighty-one, in full possession of her faculties.

W. H. PRESCOTT.

America has great honour in William Hickling Prescott, author of the histories of *Ferdinand and Isabella of Spain*, of *Cortez*, and of *Pizarro*, who died on the 28th of January 1859, at the age of 63. The historical writings of Prescott are among the few finished and classical productions of the kind in our age, which are worthy to rank with those of Gibbon, Hume, and others, in the last century. Fortunate in having the power of devoting himself to those studies in which it was his ambition to excel, this eminent American was just as unfortunate in the deficiency of certain requisites which one would have previously said were indispensable for such a career. He had from an early period of life lost in a great measure the use of his eyes. How he contrived by patience and the use of adroit arrangements to overcome this prodigious difficulty, is detailed by himself in a manner extremely interesting:

'Having settled,' he says, 'on a subject for a particular history, I lost no time in collecting the materials, for which I had peculiar advantages. But just before these materials arrived, my eye had experienced so severe a strain that I enjoyed no use of it again for reading for several years. It has, indeed, never since fully recovered its strength, nor have I ever ventured to use it again by candlelight. I well remember the blank despair which I felt when my literary treasures arrived from Spain, and I saw the mine of wealth lying around me which I was forbidden to explore. I determined to see what could be done with the eyes of another. I remembered that Johnson had said, in reference to Milton, that the great poet had abandoned his projected history of England, finding it scarcely possible for a man without eyes to pursue a historical work, requiring reference to various authorities. The remark piqued me to make an attempt.

'I obtained the services of a reader who knew no language but his own. I taught him to pronounce the Castilian in a manner suited, I suspect, much more to my ear than to that of a Spaniard; and we began our wearisome journey through Mariana's noble History. I cannot even now call to mind without a smile the tedious hours in which, seated under some old trees in my country residence, we pursued our slow and melancholy way over pages which afforded no glimmering of light to him, and from which the light came dimly struggling to me through a half-intelligible vocabulary. But in a few weeks the light became stronger, and I was cheered by the consciousness of my own improvement; and when we had toiled our way through seven quartos, I found I could understand the book when read about two-thirds as fast as ordinary English. My reader's office required the more patience; he had not even this result to cheer him in his labour.

'I now felt that the great difficulty could be overcome; and I obtained the services of a reader whose acquaintance with modern and ancient tongues supplied, so far as it could be supplied, the deficiency of eyesight on my part. But though in this way I could examine various authorities, it was not easy to arrange in my mind the results of my reading, drawn from different and often contradictory accounts. To do this I dictated copious notes as I went along; and when I had read enough for a chapter—from thirty to forty and sometimes fifty pages in length—I had a mass of memoranda in my own language, which would easily bring before me at one view the fruits of my researches. Those notes were carefully read to me; and while my recent studies were fresh in my recollection, I ran over the whole of my intended chapter in my mind. This process I repeated at least half-a-dozen times, so that when I finally put my pen to paper it ran off pretty glibly, for it was an effort of memory rather than creation. This method had the advantage of saving me from the perplexity of frequently referring to the scattered passages in the originals, and it enabled me to make the corrections in my own mind which are usually made in the manuscript, and which with my mode of writing—as I shall explain—would have much embarrassed me. Yet I must admit that this method of composition, when the chapter was very long, was somewhat too heavy a strain on the memory to be altogether recommended.

'Writing presented me a difficulty even greater than reading. Thierry, the famous blind historian of the Norman Conquest, advised me to cultivate dictation; but I have usually preferred a substitute that I found in a writing-case made for the blind, which I procured in London forty years since. It is a simple apparatus, often described by me for the benefit of persons whose vision is imperfect. It consists of a frame of the size of a piece of paper, traversed by brass wires as many as lines are wanted on the page, and with a sheet of carbonated paper, such as is used for getting duplicates, pasted on the reverse side. With an ivory or agate stylus the writer traces his characters between the wires on the carbonated sheet, making indelible marks, which he cannot see, on the white page below. This treadmill operation has its defects; and I have repeatedly supposed I had accomplished a good page, and was pro-

ceeding in all the glow of composition to go ahead when I found I had forgotten to insert a sheet of my writing-paper below, that my labour had been all thrown away, and that the leaf looked as blank as myself. Notwithstanding these and other whimsical distresses of the kind, I have found my writing-case my best friend in my lonely hours, and with it have written nearly all that I have sent into the world the last forty years.

'The manuscript thus written and deciphered—for it was in the nature of hieroglyphics—by my secretary was then read to me for correction, and copied off in a fair hand for the printer. All this, it may be thought, was rather a slow process, requiring the virtue of patience in all the parties concerned. But in time my eyes improved again. Before I had finished *Ferdinand and Isabella*, I could use them some hours every day. And thus they have continued till within a few years, though subject to occasional interruptions, sometimes of weeks and sometimes of months, when I could not look at a book. And this circumstance as well as habit, second nature, has led me to adhere still to my early method of composition. Of late years I have suffered not so much from inability of the eye as dimness of the vision, and the warning comes that the time is not far distant when I must rely exclusively on the eyes of another for the prosecution of my studies. Perhaps it should be received as a warning that it is time to close them altogether.'

LORD NORTH'S ADMINISTRATION.

On this day in 1770 commenced the long administration of Lord North, during which the American colonies were lost to the British crown. The fatal misjudgment and obstinacy which led to such a disastrous result can scarcely be thought of in our times with patience; and, when we think of the evils inflicted on America in the vain attempt to drag her back into subjection, a feeling of indignation at all persons in administration, and particularly the chief, is apt to take possession of the mind. Yet, strange to say, the head of the cabinet which carried on the wretched

MEDAL STRUCK IN HONOUR OF LORD NORTH.

contest, was undeniably one of the most amiable and pleasant-natured men in existence. His character is brought out in a charming manner by a daughter of the minister, who wrote in compliance with a request of Lord Brougham:

'His manners were those of a high-bred gentleman, particularly easy and natural; indeed, good

breeding was so marked a part of his character that it would have been affectation in him to have been otherwise than well-bred. With such good taste and good breeding, his raillery could not fail to be of the best sort—always amusing and never wounding. He was the least fastidious of men, possessing the happy art of extracting any good that there was to be extracted out of anybody. He never would let his children call people *bores;* and I remember the triumphant joy of his family, when, after a tedious visit from a very prosy and empty man, he exclaimed, " Well, that man *is* an insufferable bore ! " He used frequently to have large parties of foreigners and distinguished persons to dine with him at Bushy Park. He was himself the life and soul of these parties. To have seen him then, you would have said that he was there in his true element. Yet I think that he had really more enjoyment when he went into the country on a Saturday and Sunday, with only his own family, or one or two intimate friends : he then entered into all the jokes and fun of his children, was the companion and intimate friend of his elder sons and daughters, and the merry, entertaining playfellow of his little girl, who was five years younger than any of the others. To his servants he was a most kind and indulgent master : if provoked by stupidity or impertinence, a few hasty, impatient words might escape him ; but I never saw him *really out of humour.* He had a drunken, stupid groom, who used to provoke him ; and who from this circumstance was called by the children " the man that puts papa in a passion ; " and I think he continued all his life putting papa in a passion, and being forgiven, for I believe he died in his service.' *

Lord John Russell, in his *Life and Times of Charles James Fox* (1859), remarks that Lord North had borne his elevation with modesty, and shewed equanimity in his fall. 'A trifling circumstance evinced his good humour. On the evening when he announced his resignation in the House of Commons [March 20, 1782], snow was falling, and the weather was bitterly cold. Lord North kept his carriage. As he was passing through the great-coat room of the House of Commons, many members (chiefly his opponents) crowded the passage. When his carriage was announced, he put one or two of his friends into it, and then making a bow to his opponents, said, " Good night, gentlemen ; it is the first time I have known the advantage of being in the secret." '

COMMENCEMENT OF GAS-LIGHTING.

January 28, 1807, Pall Mall was lighted with gas,—the first street of any city so illuminated. The idea of using carburetted hydrogen gas for purposes of illumination first occurred to Mr William Murdoch, a native of Ayrshire, holding a position of trust at the mines of Redruth, in Cornwall. He made his first experiments in 1792, at Redruth. Removing in 1798 to the machine-making establishment of Messrs Watt and Boulton, at Birmingham, he there followed up his

MESSRS. WATT AND BOULTON'S ESTABLISHMENT, BIRMINGHAM.

experiments, and succeeded in lighting up the buildings with gas for the celebration of the Peace of Amiens. He also fitted up the works of Philips and Lee, at Manchester, with gas-lights in 1805, and there fully proved the economical value of the scheme. Murdoch was a man

* Letter by Lady Charlotte Lindsay, youngest daughter of Lord North, written in 1839 for Lord Brougham's *Statesmen of George III.*

of sagacious and accurate understanding, worthy to be associated with his countryman Watt. A portrait of him is preserved in the hall of the Royal Society of Edinburgh.

The merit of bringing gas-light into use in London belongs to a German named Winser, a man of an opposite type of intellect to Murdoch, yet having the virtue of perseverance. In the pamphlets issued by this person for the promotion of gas-lighting schemes and companies, there was such extravagance, quackery, and fanaticism, as tended to retard their success. Sir Walter Scott wrote from London that there was a *madman* proposing to light London with—what do you think?—why, with smoke! Even the liberal mind of Sir Humphry Davy failed to take in the idea that gas was applicable to purposes of street or house lighting. Yet, Winser having succeeded after all in obtaining some supporters, the long line between St James's Palace and Cockspur-street did blaze out in a burst of gas-lamps on the night in question, to the no small admiration of the public.

When we consider that gas-light has since been extended all over London, over nearly every town of above a thousand inhabitants in the empire, and pretty generally throughout the towns of both Europe and America, producing a marvellous saving in the expense of artificial light, it becomes curious to observe the great hesitation expressed in the scientific and popular literature of 1807-8-9 regarding the possibility of applying it economically to general use. The reader will readily find the expression of contemporary public opinion on the subject in a paper in the *Edinburgh Review* for January 1809, written by James Pillans, afterwards professor of Latin (1820—1863) in the University of Edinburgh.

In London, about 1810, before any company had been established, Mr Ackermann's shop, in the Strand, was regularly lighted with gas. It is said, that a lady calling there one evening, was so delighted with the beautiful white jets she saw on the counter, that she offered any money for permission to carry them home to light her drawing-room.

Gas-lighting had a ridiculous objection to contend with, worthy to be ranked with that which insisted for years, without experiment, that the wheels of steam locomotives would go on whirling without creating any forward movement. It was generally assumed that the pipes conveying gas would be hot, and apt to produce conflagrations. People used to touch them cautiously with their hands, under the belief that a careless touch would burn them. The lamp-lighters, to a man, were opposed to the new mode of lighting.

A company being formed in 1810 (the shareholders, of course, being pitied as idiots), the system was put in practice for the first time on Westminster Bridge in the last night of the year 1812. Some districts of London had gas introduced on the streets in 1814. It then gradually found its way into other cities, and finally into other countries. It is calculated that on the capital of about twenty millions laid out on gas manufactories in this country, there is an average return of $6\frac{1}{4}$ per cent.—a good commentary on the objections originally made to this mode of lighting.

COURT FOOLS AND JESTERS.

In connection with the name of Henry VIII., it may not be improper to advert to a custom of which he was a noted observer,—the custom, once universally prevalent, of keeping professional fools and jesters in palaces and other great houses. It was founded upon, or at least was in strict accordance with, a physiological principle, which may be expressed under this formula—the *Utility of Laughter*. Laughter is favourable to digestion, for by it the organs concerned in digestion get exercise, the exercise necessary for the process. And, accordingly, we usually find an ample meal more easily disposed of where merriment is going on, than a light one which has been taken in solitude, and under a sombre state of feeling.

According to the ideas of modern society, cheerful after-dinner conversation is sufficient stimulus for the digestive organs. Our forefathers, less refined, went at once to the point, and demanded a fixed and certain means of stirring up merriment; and perhaps it may be doubted if they were not nearer to a true philosophy of the matter than we are. Anyhow, the fact is, that all through the middle ages men of means and consequence did keep officers for the promotion of laughter in their households, and especially at meals. Such officers were of two kinds. One was an imperfect-witted man, or fool, whose follies were deemed to be amusing;

GROUP OF COURT FOOLS.

he wore a parti-coloured dress, including a cowl, which ended in a cock's head, and was winged with a couple of long ears; he, moreover, carried in his hand a stick called his bauble, terminating either in an inflated bladder, or some other ludicrous object, to be employed in slapping inadvertent neighbours. The other, called a jester, was a ready-witted, able, and perhaps well-educated man, possessed of those gifts of representing character, telling droll stories, and making pointed remarks, which we have seen giving distinction to a Charles Mathews, and occasionally find in a certain degree in private society. The fool was a very humble person, haunting kitchen and scullery, messing almost with the dogs, and liable, when malapert, to a whipping. The jester was comparatively a companion to the sovereign or noble who engaged his services. The importance of Berdic, 'joculator' to William the Conqueror, is shewn by the fact of three towns and five carucates in Gloucestershire having been conferred upon him.

And the names of Scogan, Will Somers, John Heywood, Pace, Tarleton, and Archie Armstrong, who were 'jesters' to a succession of Tudor and Stuart sovereigns of England, have all been sufficiently notable to be preserved. We

WILL SOMERS.

introduce a correct portraiture of Somers, jester to Henry VIII., as a very fair representative of his class. It will be admitted that he is a perfectly well-arranged and respectable-looking person. It is a curious illustration of the natural need that seems to exist in a certain state of society for the services of a fun-maker, that

Montezuma, Emperor of Mexico, was found by Cortez to have such an officer about his court.

A pleasant volume, by Dr. John Doran, entitled *The History of Court Fools*, was published in 1858, and seemed a tolerably exhaustive treatise on the subject. Nevertheless, the ingenious author has since found some additional details, which he is pleased to communicate through these pages.

A Supplementary Chapter to the ' History of Court Fools.'

When the author of the last *History of Court Fools* wrote ' Finis' to his volume, he had not fully satisfied himself on two points,—first, the date of the existence of the earliest jester; and, secondly, whether such an individual as an official fool, or fool by right of office, was still maintained in any public court or private household. On those two points he has since arrived at a more satisfactory conclusion; and the result of his researches, on those and other points referring to the same subject, he submits to the consideration of the readers of these pages.

It can scarcely be doubted that the female official fool had precedence of the male court and household jester. When Ceres went in search of Proserpine, the Queen of Eleusis sent with her one of the merriest of her maids, named Iambe. This maid, renowned at court for her wit, frolicsome humour, power of repartee, and skill in saying smart things generally, was expressly sent with the bereaved mother to divert her sorrow by her quips and cranks, her jokes, gambols, and her laughter-compelling stories. This commission was, to the very letter, that which especially belonged to the official jester; and there is no reason to hesitate in assigning to Iambe the distinction of having been the founder of a race which is not yet extinct, and the godmother, so to speak, of satires in sharp measure which bear the name of Iambic.

With regard to existing jesters officially appointed, there are several who presume so to describe themselves, but of the genuineness or authenticity of whose pretensions much might be said, particularly in an adverse sense. It has become the fashion of clowns to travelling circuses to style themselves ' Queen's Jesters;' and there is one of these, named Wallet, whose portrait has been engraved among those of the Eminent Men of the Age, and who writes himself down as Court Jester to Queen Victoria, by her Majesty's appointment! We can only say that we should feel grateful for a sight of the Lord Chamberlain's warrant confirming this authority.

The fool by right of office must be looked for beyond the seas. The jester who figured at the Eglintoun tournament, and his brother who jokes and tumbles in the procession of Lady Godiva, may be mountebanks by profession, but they are only jesters for the nonce. The descendants of the old jesters are to be traced, however, in England as well as on the Continent. The dramatic writer, Mr Fitzball, refers to his descent from an illegitimate son of the Conqueror, who was lord of an estate called Fitz-Follie. It has been suggested that this name may have been indicative of the calling exercised at court by the owner of the estate. It might, indeed, have reference to the King's folly; and if the original designation was Fitz-Folle, it would serve to point to the vocation of the lucky young gentleman's mother. However this may be, we have not to go far abroad for another illustration, to see how a pedigree may improve in the persons last enrolled.

It is scarcely to be supposed that Gonella, the renowned Italian jester, of several centuries back, ever thought that among the future possessors of his name would be found a Monsignore, exercising the office, not of court fool, but of papal nuncio, at Brussels.

From Italy, as from England, the professional Merry Andrew in households has passed away. There is a relic of some of them at Mantua,—the apartments assigned to the old, comic ducal dwarfs. These rooms, six in number, and little more than as many feet square, are mere white-washed cells, long since stripped of all furniture. At the end of one of them, said to have been their kitchen, there is a raised platform, on which the jocular little men used to dine.

It is a singular fact that as the female jester had precedence, in point of date of origin, of her brother in the vocation, so has she survived that brother, and still holds her own in the court of the Sultan and the households of his great pashas. When Mrs Edmund Hornby was ' In and about Stamboul,' in 1858, she, in company with other ladies, visited the hareem of Kiza Pasha. The visitors accepted an invitation to a banquet, at which warm rye bread, covered with seeds, pleasant soups, smoking *pilaufs*, and pancakes swimming in honey, were among the chief dishes. The native ladies gave loose and unseemly rein to their appetites, stimulated by official female buffoons who served the dishes with accompanying jokes, the utterance of which excited the most uproarious laughter, not only from the ladies their mistresses, but also from their less witty, yet wit-appreciating, slaves. Mrs Hornby describes the chief jester as ' a wild and most extraordinary-looking woman, with an immensity of broad humour and drollery in her face.' The quality of the fun seems to have been of the coarsest; and the English ladies congratulated themselves on their lack of apprehension of jokes at which the lovely Circassian, the second wife of the Pasha, ' between the intervals of licking her fingers and spoon, and popping tit-bits on our plates, laughed so complacently, which sometimes obliged the Arabs and eunuchs at the door to dive under the arras, to conceal their uncontrollable fits of mirth.' Whether the modern female Turkish jester be the descendant or not of a long line of predecessors, we are not informed. We *do* know, however, that when Lady Wortley Montagu paid a similar visit, at the beginning of the last century, she was only amused by indifferent dancing, and by another exhibition, of which she speaks in the free and easy style of the fine ladies of her day.

This female table-jester—and this again is a singular circumstance—was of old a personage common enough at inns on the Continent. The readers of Erasmus will remember among his *Colloquies* one entitled ' Diversorium.' In that graphic paper we are taken to an inn at Lyons. The guests are received by handsome women, young maidens, and younger girls, all of whom also wait at table and enliven the company, whose digestion they make easy by narrating joyous stories, bandying witticisms, playing give-and-take with the visitors, and shewing themselves as ready to meet a jest by a sharp reply, as to provoke a reply by a galliard jest. The youngest of these pretty and carefully trained fools was never unequal to the task of meeting the heaviest fire of broad wit from a whole room full of revellers. These they stimulated and provoked by showers of humorous epithets and a world of pretty ways. They followed the guests to their chamber doors, laughing, jesting, and sporting; nor did they take leave of them till they had performed offices which young princesses in the Odyssey render to the guests of their royal sires, carrying off the linen of the travellers, dropping their foolery, and then seriously addressing themselves to the office of laundresses.

In the East, beyond the Bosphorus, there is still to be found in one and the same individual, in some families, a mixture of the domestic and the buffoon. These, however, probably resemble rather the impudent French or Spanish, and even some English *valets* of the drama, than the official jester; men whose impudent wit was tolerated, rather than solicited or expected. The male fool, by right of office, is now to be met with only in Russia. 'In St Petersburg,' says an English lady, in her *Six Years' Travels in Russia*, 'they are by no means rare.' The old Russian joke of serving up dwarfs in a pie, still pleases imperial Grand Dukes. The professional Russian fools, this lady tells us, 'wear a ridiculous dress, but dwarfs usually appear in plain clothes.'

In the recently-published Life of Bishop Doyle, of Kildare and Leighlin, by Mr Fitzpatrick, the author fixes on that Roman Catholic prelate as being the last person within these realms who kept a fool in his household. Dr Doyle, however, who has been dead about a score of years, was, in the case cited, simply giving shelter to a village idiot, for sufferers of which class there was no public asylum in Ireland. The poor idiot did not fill, in Dr Doyle's household, such an office as was executed in that of the late Pope Gregory XVI., by Cardinal Soglia. In the gardens of the Vatican, the illustrious men there used to pass away the long summer evening hours, by playing at blindman's buff, Soglia being always hoodwinked, and armed with a stick. It was his object to strike at those whose aim was, of course, to evade him. On one of these occasions, the holy father stooped to remove a flower-vase which stood in peril of being shattered by the Cardinal's upraised stick, which, however, descended so rapidly as to put the papal skull in danger, but that some officials present unceremoniously pulled his holiness backward. Soglia, as concoctor of fun to the Roman court, was succeeded by Monsignore Aopi, who was also the Pope's confessor. It is, moreover, added, that Gregory took great delight in the jokes of certain Capuchins, particularly when they were tipsy. So, at least, says Della Galtina, according to whom the old court-foolery was sustained with great spirit at Rome to the very last.

It must be allowed, that the legendary saints themselves afforded the Popes good authority for this sort of buffoonery. St Kened, for instance, though a weak, decrepit, and sickly little fellow, was an inveterate joker. When

the Welsh St David succeeded, by his prayers, in getting him strong and straight, it was the other saint's most favourite joke, by dint of his own prayers, to get himself bent double again! And this course went on alternately, till St David, unable to see any fun in it, gave up his task, and left the wit to his double crookedness of mind and body. The act, however, was just one which might have entered into a fool's head. In a better sort of wit, remarkable for its boldness, the religious men who hung about courts enjoyed the admiration and impunity awarded to the jesters. For example: 'What is the difference between a Scot and a sot?' asked Charles of Burgundy of Duns Scotus, as the two sat opposite each other at or after dinner. 'There is only a table between them!' answered the holy clerk, whose reply was received with unbounded applause, either for its finely small wit, or its incontrovertible truth.

Some potentates have been satisfied with less than wit; of such was the Grand Duchess Catherine of Russia, who maintained a Finnish girl on her establishment, in whose incomparable mimicry of all the great people at court her highness experienced a never-failing delight. A similar pleasure is still enjoyed by the negro king of Dahomey, concerning whom Duncan, the Life-guardsman, who travelled in Africa in 1849, states a curious circumstance. In that uncivilized monarch's dominions, it is considered highly disgraceful for a man to be guilty of drunkenness. Immunity, in this respect, is the privilege of the king's mimics and jesters only. Of these the black sovereign possesses many, and in their degradation and jollity he finds occasion for much mirth and laughter.

In England, those merry serving-men whose success was sometimes rewarded by making them lords of landed estates, were occasionally employed rather for sedative than stimulating purposes. Strutt records that it was not unusual to engage them as story-tellers to kings and princes who required to be gently talked into sleep. This office has expired, but well-qualified candidates for it survive. In our own courts, however, it was the more rattling fool who enjoyed the greater share of admiration. He spoke so boldly, when there was need for it, that honest and merry men of note, desirous to serve their royal master, borrowed the liberty, as it were, and told valuable truth under the form of an idle joke. When Richard II. was pressed by all classes of his people for reform in a government under which they were sorely oppressed, his plumed and dainty flatterers advised him to place himself at the head of his army, and destroy nobles and commons alike, who were thus unreasonable. The King was perplexed; 'but,' says John Trussell, the historian, 'there was present old Sir John Linne, a good soldier, but a shuttlebrain, of whom the King in merriment demanded, in this case, what was, as he thought, the fittest to be done. Sir John swore, "Blood and wounds! let us charge home and kill every mother's son, and so we shall make quick despatch of the best friends you have in the kingdom." This giddy answer,' adds Trussell, 'more weighed with the King than if it had been spoken in grave and sober sort : and thus it often happens, that wise counsel is more sweetly followed when it is tempered with folly ; and earnest is the less offensive, if it be delivered in jest.'

Indeed, it may be said, that on such principle was founded the very institution of court fools. Even the grave Queen Elizabeth of York could thus listen to her Greenwich jester, William. It was otherwise with her husband, Henry VII., who neither kept fools himself, nor admired those maintained by the English nobility. This is little to be wondered at, if all the jesters of lords resembled him who was kept by Thomas Lord Derby. Henry VII. was the guest of the latter, soon after his Majesty had so ungratefully exe-cuted Sir William Stanley, Lord Derby's own brother ! Host and guest were standing on the leads of Latham House, viewing the country. Lord Derby was close against the parapet, the King immediately behind him. The house fool ob-served this propinquity, and chose to suspect the King of present, or was eager to remind him of past, treachery. Drawing near to his master, he exclaimed gruffly, ' Tom, remember Will !' This fool's bolt, so swiftly shot, reached the King's conscience, and his Majesty withdrew, in un-dignified hurry, into the house.

Henry's son, the eighth of the name, restored the banished official to court. Of his own Sir Merrymans, none is better known to us than Will Somers, whose effigy is at Hampton Court. This good fellow's memory was perpetuated by the establishment of the ' Will Somers Tavern,' in Old Fish-street. When tavern-tokens were allowed to be issued—a permission in existence as late as the reign of Charles II.—the landlord of the above hostelry issued one, with a figure of Will Somers on it, by way of distinction.

It is to be remembered, that a time ensued when a distinction was made between a jester and a fool. A dramatist like Heywood did not dis-dain to be the former, mingling with gentlemen and scholars ; but we see that the fool, in the days of Mary and Philip, was of a lower degree. When the illustrious two, just mentioned, visited Faversham, the Chamberlain kept a book, in which he entered moneys given to the members of the royal retinue. The entry of—' To the King's and Queen's jester—2s.,' indicates the position of the fool ; two shillings was the lowest sum awarded to the lowest menial in the royal train. The keeper of the bears seems to have been a more important personage than the baser fool at Queen Elizabeth's court, where her jester, Tarleton the actor, was held in some honour. When fool and bearward followed her Majesty to Canterbury, the corporation gave liberally to her retinue ; but while the bearward received an angel, or ten shillings, the fool, Walter, was put off with the odd money, which, added to the angel, just made an English mark. ' Three and fourpence' was the sum that fell to the fool.

Let it not be considered irreverent if the words ' Shakspeare' and ' jester' be com-bined. They naturally occur here. There are four years, 1585-89, during which nothing certain is known of Shakspeare's whereabouts. In a letter addressed by Sir Philip Sidney, from

Utrecht, 1586, to his father-in law, Walsingham, there is a passage to this effect : ' I wrote to you a letter, by Will, my Lord of Leicester's jesting player.' In the first volume of the Shaks-peare Society papers, Mr John Bruce asks, ' Who was this Will, my Lord of Leicester's jesting player ?' He may have been Will John-son, Will Sly, Will Kimpe, or, as some have thought, even the immortal William himself ! This knotty point cannot be unravelled here. The circumstance serves, however, to shew that ' jesting players' followed their patrons even to the tented field.

Under our first Stuart kings, the court fools revived in dignity. They were allowed serving-men to wait upon them, and some of these were pensioned for their good services. The author of *Letters from the Mountains* states that in some Scottish families of the olden time, down to the present century, was often to be found an individual who united in himself the offices of gamekeeper and warlock or wizard, and that in the latter capacity he in some degree resembled the court or household jester. There was a stranger combination than this in the person of the famous Archie Armstrong, official fool to James I. and his son Charles. Archie was a sort of gentleman groom of the chambers to the first King, preceding him when in progress, and look-ing after the royal quarters. In this capacity,

ARCHIE ARMSTRONG.

Armstrong was made a free citizen of Aberdeen, and held that freedom till his death. James must have loved him, at one period ; for despite his hatred of tobacco, he granted a patent to Archie for the manufacture of tobacco pipes. The fool, moreover, gained no trifling addition to his salary, in bribes administered to him for presenting petitions, even those of recusants ; at which last, however, James was not so well pleased as he was with Archie's jokes. The position of Armstrong, who was on most familiar terms with his second master, Charles, is significantly indicated by his demand, when appointed to accompany that Prince to Spain. He claimed to have the service of an attendant, the same as was awarded to the gentlemen of the royal suite. The claim caused a tumult among the gentlemen in question, and Archie was fain to go abroad in less state than he thought became him. In the gloomy days that succeeded, the fool raised laughter at court, but not such an honest laughter as used to shake the house of Charles's brother, Prince Henry, where 'sweetmeats and Coryat,' that prince of non-official jesters and coxcombs, used to finish and gladden every repast.

Although the jester was not to be found on the household list of Oliver Cromwell, there were occasions when buffoons, hired for sport, appeared at Whitehall. One of these was the marriage of the Protector's daughter, Frances, with Mr. Rich. At the festival which followed the ceremony, some of the buffoons attempted to blacken with a burnt cork the face of Sir Thomas Hillingsby, as he was dancing. The solemn old gentleman-usher to the Queen of Bohemia was so enraged at this liberty, that he drew his dagger and would have made short work with the jester's life, had not others present interfered. There was, however, very wide licence at this feast. It was there that Oliver descended to practical foolery, snatched off his son Richard's wig, and, pretending to fling it into the fire, contrived to slip it under him, and, sitting on it, affected to deplore its loss.

When Wharton, in the *True Briton*, compared two of the Chancellors of Charles II. (Nottingham and Shaftesbury), he reckoned among the superior characteristics of the former, the absence of buffoons from his household. The last man of the next reign whom one might expect to see with a fool in his suite, was the infamous Judge Jeffreys. His official jester, however, attended him on his bloody circuit. The judge loved and laughed at the fool's power of wit and mimicry; and at Taunton he tossed to the buffoon the 'pardon' of a convicted victim, leaving the victim's friends to purchase it of him, if such was desired, and lay within the compass of their means!

After this, the official jester disappeared, or his calling was modified. Thus, in the early part of the last century, there was a well-known Cheshire dancing-master, named Johnson, who was hired out at parties given by the northern nobility, at which he had licence to utter or enact anything that was likely to move the guests to laughter. Johnson was familiarly known as 'Lord Flame,' the name of a character played by him, in his own extravaganza, entitled *Hurlothrumbo*, a piece acted at the Haymarket in 1729. Johnson was among the last of the paid English jesters. The genuine *ultimus scurrarum* in this country is said to have been a retainer in the house of Mr. Bartlett, of Castlemorton, Worcestershire. The date of his death is not precisely known, but it would seem to have been in the last half of the last century. He is still spoken

of; and 'as big a fool as Jack Hafod,' at once preserves his name and indicates his quality. Since Hafod's days, we have only had fools for the nonce, in England. Such is he who struts in anniversary processions, or who is only reproduced as a memorial of the past, like the dramatic jester who figures in the gay doings at Sudeley Castle, where Mr and Mrs Dent, the occupiers of that old residence of Katherine Parr, preside at fancy balls, in the ancient mansion, in the gallant costume of Henry and his Queen.

There is not much to be added to the history of the Court Fools of France. Of one of the most renowned of these, Triboulet, the present writer saw a capital portrait, the property of Walter Savage Landor, sold at Christie's, in 1859. It is the work of Licinio, the great rival of Titian, and is worthy of either hand. Triboulet appears to have been a man of strongly-marked but 'jolly' features; just such a man, in short, as history, but not the dramatic historians, have made him.

The most extraordinary combination of two offices that ever occurred, existed at the court of Louis XVIII., in the person of Coulon, a medical man of great skill, who ultimately abandoned all practice except with respect to the King, to whom he was at once doctor and jester. When a medical student, Coulon was wont, by his powers of mimicry, to keep a whole hospital-ward in roars of laughter. On one occasion, when officiating as assistant to the great Alibert, as the latter was bandaging the swollen legs of the suffering sovereign, Coulon so exquisitely mimicked his master behind his back, that the delighted Louis retained him thenceforward near his person. For the amusement of his royal patron, Coulon gave daily imitations. If the King asked him whom he had met, the medical jester would at once assume the bearing, voice, and the features of the person he desired to represent. It mattered not at all what the sex or the quality might be, or whether the mimicked individuals were the King's friends or relations, or otherwise. In either case, the monarch was in an ecstasy of hilarity as he promptly recognised each personage thus presented to him.—'Coulon,' said the Duke of Orleans to him, one day, 'I happened to see and hear your imitation of me, yesterday. It was capital, but not quite perfect. You did not wear, as I do, a diamond pin in your cravat. Allow me to present you with mine; it will make the resemblance more striking.' 'Ah! your highness,' replied Coulon, fixing the pin in his own cravat, and putting on such a look of the prince that the latter might have thought he was standing before a mirror, 'as a poor imitator, I ought, properly, to wear only paste!'

His imitations, however, were so approximate to reality that he sat for portraits of Thiers and Molé; but Coulon's greatest triumph, in this way, was through a harder task. There was no efficient portrait extant of the deceased minister, Villèle. Gros was regretting this. 'Ay,' said Coulon, 'no likeness of him represents the profound subtlety of his character, and his evanescent expression.' As he said this, a living Villèle seemed to stand before the artist, who then and there took from this singular personage, the well-known portrait which so truthfully represents the once famous statesman of the old Bourbon times.

The only man who ever resembled Coulon at the court of France was Dufresnoy, the poet, playwright, actor, gardener, glass manufacturer, spendthrift, wit, and beggar. Louis XIV. valued him as Louis XVIII. valued Coulon, and many dramatists of his day used to 'book' his loose, brilliant sayings, and reproduce them as original. His royal protector appointed him his honorary fool; and it must be allowed that Dufresnoy had more of the old official about him than the refined and wealthy Coulon. The earlier jester, having got into debt with his washerwoman, settled the claim by making her his wife. It was a poor joke, and his wit seems to have suffered from it. He ventured, one day, to rally the Abbé Pelligrini on the soiled look of his linen. 'Sir,' said the piqued Abbé, 'it is not everyone who has the good luck to marry his laundress!' The joker was dumb; and he stood no bad illustration of that line in Churchill, which speaks of men

'O'errun with wit and destitute of sense.'

The combination of a serious with a jesting vocation was not at all uncommon at the court of Russia. In the household of the Czarina Elizabeth, Professor Stehlin, teacher of mathematics and history to the Grand Duke, afterwards Peter II., was also buffoon to his illustrious and imbecile pupil. This, indeed, was an office shared by all the young gentlemen of the Grand Duke's household, for they jumped to his humour, and danced to his fiddling, in his wife's bed-room, at all hours of the night, in all sorts of disguises, and to the accompaniment of most undignified figures of speech. The Czarina's own fool, Aksakoff, was a mere stolid brute, who used to place mice and hedgehogs in his mistress's way, for no better reason than that the sight of those animals terrified her to death. The selfishness of this fellow is in strong contrast with the disinterested folly of poor Bluet d'Arbères, another of the few men who have joined earnestness of life with a fool's calling. At the beginning of the seventeenth century, when the plague was devastating Paris, this heroic ex-fool to the Duke of Mantua conceived the heroically-foolish idea, that the pestilence would be stayed, if he made sacrifice of his own life by way of expiation. Under this impression, he starved himself to death.

It is certain that the Hanoverian family brought no official jesters with them to England. The reason may be found in the assertion of Palmblad, that the fashion of keeping fools was going out of German courts when Ernest Augustus was Elector of Hanover. Yet this father of our George I. retained a buffoon—Burkard Kaspar Adelsburn—for two reasons; as a remnant of good old German manners, and because the fashion was dying away in France, which country he just then detested. This jester exercised great influence over the Elector; not merely in a witty, but also in a ghostly sense, for Burkard would ever and anon lecture his libertine sovereign with all the freedom and earnestness of Whitefield when belabouring a reprobate collier.

That the fashion lingered on in Germany is clear, from a letter written by Lady Featherstonehaugh, in 1753, and quoted by Lady Chatterton in the recently-published *Memorials of Lord Gambier*. The former lady writes from Dresden, and alludes to the court-doings of Frederick Augustus. 'In the evening,' she says, 'we were at the apartments of the Royal Family, and were much surprised at seeing an ancient custom kept up here, and in no other court besides, except that of Prussia, of keeping buffoons. There are no less than three at this court.'

Nevertheless, when the official court fool ceased to be found in palace households, some princes began to be their own fools. This, however, is a portion of a subject which cannot here be entered upon. Sufficient for this article is the 'folly' thereof. J. D.

A surprise is felt that one of the Armstrongs— that border clan remarkable only for *stouthreif*— should have ever found his way to court, even in so equivocal a position as that of the King's Jester. The traditionary story on this point has been thus reported to us. A shepherd with the carcase of a sheep on his shoulders, was tracked by the officers of justice to a cottage in the moorlands, where, however, they found no one but a vacant-looking lad, who sat rocking a cradle, apparently altogether unconscious of their object. Searching somewhat narrowly, they at length found that, instead of a baby, the carcase of the missing sheep occupied the cradle. No longer doubting that the rocker of the cradle was the delinquent, they seized and brought him to Jedburgh, where King James VI. had just arrived to hold one of his *justice aires*.

Condemned to die for his crime, Archie Armstrong—for it was he—pleaded with the king that he was a poor ignorant man—he had heard of the Bible, and wished to read it through— would his Highness please respite him till this should have been, for his soul's weal, accomplished. The good-natured monarch granted the prayer, and Archie immediately rejoined with a sly look, 'Then deil tak me an I ever read a word o't, as lang as my een are open!' James saw from this that there was humour in the man, and had him brought to court.

WINTER EVENING.

Winter ——————
I love thee when the day is o'er,
Spite of the tempest's outward roar;
Queen of the tranquil joys that weave
The charm around the sudden eve ;
The thick'ning footsteps thro' the gloom,
Telling of those we love come home;
The candles lit, the cheerful board,
The dear domestic group restored ;
The fire that shows the looks of glee,
The infants standing at our knee ;
The busy news, the sportive tongue,
The laugh that makes us still feel young ;
The health to those we love, that now
Are far as ocean winds can blow ;
The health to those who with us grew,
And still stay with us tried and true ;
The wife that makes life glide away,
One long and lovely marriage day.
Then music comes till—round us creep
The infant list'ners half asleep ;
And busy tongues are loud no more,
And, Winter, thy sweet eve is o'er.— *Anonymous.*

JANUARY 29.

St Sulpicius Severus, about 407. St Gildas, the Albanian or Scot, 512. St. Gildas, the Wise, or Badonicus, abbot (570?). St Francis of Sales, 1622.

ST GILDAS.

This saint, according to his legend, was the son of Can, a king of the Britons of Alcluyd or Dumbarton, and was born some time in the latter part of the fifth century. He was one of twenty-four brothers, the rest of whom were warriors, and were, with their father, usually at war with King Arthur. But Gildas, having shewn a disposition for learning, was sent to the school of the Welsh saint Iltutus. He afterwards went to study in Gaul, whence he returned to Britain, and set up a school of his own in South Wales. Subsequently, at the invitation of St Bridget, he visited Ireland, where he remained a long time, and founded several monasteries. He returned to England, bringing with him a wonderful bell, which he was carrying to the Pope; and after having been reconciled with King Arthur, who had killed his eldest brother in battle, he proceeded on his journey to Rome. He went from Rome to Ravenna, and on his way home stopped at Ruys, in Brittany, which was so tempting a place for a hermit, that he determined to remain there, and he founded a monastery, of which he was himself the first abbot. The Bretons pretended that he died there, and that they possessed his relics; but, according to the Welsh legend, he returned to Wales, bringing back the wonderful bell, which was long preserved at Lancarvan, where he first took up his residence. He there became intimate with St Cadoc, and, having the same tastes, the two friends went to establish themselves as hermits in two desert islands, in the estuary of the Severn, and fixed upon those which are now known by the names of Steepholm and Flatholm, Gildas choosing the latter; and here they remained until they were driven away by the attacks of the Northern pirates. Gildas then settled at Glastonbury, where he died, and was buried in the church of St Mary.

Such is the outline of the story of St Gildas, which, in its details, is so full of inconsistencies and absurdities, that many writers have tried to solve the difficulty by supposing that there were two or several saints of the name of Gildas, whose histories have been mixed up together. They give to one the title of Gildas Badonicus, or the Historian, because, in the tracts attributed to him, he says that he was born in the year when King Arthur defeated the Saxons in the battle of Mount Badon, in Somersetshire; the other they call Gildas the Albanian or Scot, supposing that he was the one who was born at Alcluyd. The first has also been called Gildas the Wise. Gildas is known as the author, or supposed author, of a book entitled *De Excidio Britanniæ*, consisting of a short and barren historical sketch of the history of the struggle between the Britons and the Picts and Saxons, and of a declamatory epistle addressed to the British princes, reproaching them for their vices and misconduct, which are represented as the cause of the ruin of their country. Some

modern writers are of opinion that this book is itself a forgery, compiled in the latter half of the seventh century, amid the bitter disputes between the Anglo-Saxon and British churches; and that, in the great eagerness of the middle ages to find saints, the name was seized upon with avidity; and in different places where they wished to profit by possessing his relics, they composed legends of him, intended to justify their claim, which therefore agreed but partially with each other. Altogether, the legend of St Gildas is one of the most mysterious and controvertible in the whole Roman Calendar, and its only real interest arises from the circumstance of the existence of a book written in this island, and claiming so great an antiquity.

ST FRANCIS OF SALES.

If any one is at a loss to understand how so much of the influence which the Church of Rome lost in Europe at the Reformation was afterwards regained, let him read the Life of this remarkable man. Francis Count of Sales, near Annecy, threw rank and fortune behind his back, to devote himself to the interests of religion. His humility of spirit, his austerities, his fervid devotion, gave him distinction as a preacher at a comparatively early age. In his provostship at Geneva, his sermons were attended with extraordinary success. 'He delivered the word of God with a mixture of majesty and modesty; had a sweet voice and an animated manner; but what chiefly affected the hearts of his hearers, was the humility and unction with which he spoke from the abundance of his own heart.' He went about among the poor, treating them with a meekness and kindness which wonderfully gained upon them. To this, in a great degree, it was owing that he brought, as has been alleged, above seventy thousand of the Genevese Calvinists back to the Romish church.

Afterwards, in 1594, Francis and a cousin of his undertook a mission to Chablais, on the Lake of Geneva. On arriving at the frontiers, they sent back their horses, the more perfectly to imitate the apostles. The Catholic religion was here nearly extinct, and Francis found his task both difficult and dangerous. Nevertheless, in four years, his efforts began to have an effect, and soon after he had so gained over the people to his faith, that the Protestant forms were put down by the state. 'It is incredible,' says Butler, 'what fatigues and hardships he underwent in the course of this mission; with what devotion and tears he daily recommended the work of God; with what invincible courage he braved the greatest dangers; with what meekness and patience he bore all manner of affronts and calumnies." St Francis de Sales died in 1622, at the age of fifty-six.

Born.—Emmanuel de Swedenborg, 1688-9; Thomas Paine, political writer, 1737; William Sharp, line-engraver, 1749, *London*.
Died.—Emperor Aurelian, 275; Bishop Sanderson, 1663; John Theophilus Fichte, philosopher, 1814, *Berlin;* George III., 1820, *Windsor;* Agnes Berry, 1852; Mrs Gore, novelist, 1861.

SWEDENBORG.

The life-history of Swedenborg is very remarkable for its complete division into two parts, utterly alien from each other; the first fifty-five years devoted to pure science and to official business under the King of Sweden, the last twenty-eight to spiritual mysticism and the foundation of a new religion. His voluminous works on the latter class of subjects, are generally felt to be unreadable. There can, however, be no reasonable doubt (as we believe) that the author was as sincere in his descriptions of the spiritual world as he had ever been in regard to the most material of his original studies. Perhaps, after all, there is some psychological problem yet to be satisfactorily made out regarding such mystics as he, resolving all into some law at present unknown.

A letter written by the celebrated philosopher Kant, in 1764, and which is published in his Works, gives the following curious details regarding Swedenborg, of whose possession of an extraordinary gift he considers it an indubitable proof. 'In the year 1756,' says he [the true date, however, was 1759], 'when M. de Swedenborg, towards the end of February, on Saturday, at 4 o'clock p.m., arrived at Gottenburg from England, Mr William Costel invited him to his house, together with a party of fifteen persons. About 6 o'clock, M. de Swedenborg went out, and after a short interval returned to the company quite pale and alarmed. He said that a dangerous fire had broken out in Stockholm at the Suderhalm (Stockholm is about 300 miles from Gottenburg), and that it was spreading very fast. He was restless and went out often: he said that the house of one of his friends, whom he named, was already in ashes, and that his own was in danger. At 8 o'clock, after he had been out again, he joyfully exclaimed, "Thank God! the fire is extinguished the third door from my house." This news occasioned great commotion through the whole city, and particularly amongst the company in which he was. It was announced to the Governor the same evening. On the Sunday morning, Swedenborg was sent for by the Governor, who questioned him concerning the disaster. Swedenborg described the fire precisely, how it had begun, in what manner it had ceased, and how long it had continued. . . . On the Monday evening, a messenger arrived at Gottenburg, who was dispatched during the time of the fire. In the letters brought by him, the fire was described precisely in the manner stated by Swedenborg. On Tuesday morning, the royal courier arrived at the Governor's with the melancholy intelligence of the fire, of the loss it had occasioned, and of the houses it had damaged and ruined, not in the least differing from that which Swedenborg had given immediately after it had ceased, for the fire was extinguished at 8 o'clock.'

Kant adds: 'What can be brought forward against the authenticity of this occurrence? My friend, who wrote this to me, has not only examined the circumstances of this extraordinary case at Stockholm, but also about two months ago, at Gottenburg, where he is acquainted with the most respectable houses, and where he could obtain the most complete and authentic information.'

GEORGE III.

The death of George III. on this day in the year 1820, was an event of no political consequence, as for ten years he had been secluded under mental eclipse. But his people reflected with a feeling of not unkindly interest on his singularly long reign—so long it was that few remembered any other—on his venerable age—eighty-two—his irreproachable character as a family man—and the many remarkable things which had fallen out in his time. Amiable people of little reflection viewed him as 'the good old King,' the supporter of safe principles in church and state, the friend of religion and virtue. Others of keener intelligence pointed to the vast amount of disaster which had been brought upon the country, mainly through his wrong judgment and obstinacy—the American colonies lost, a fatal interference with the concerns of France in 1793, an endangerment of the peace of the country through a persistent rejection of the claim for Catholic emancipation. To these people the rule of George III. appeared to have been unhappy from the beginning. He had never ceased to struggle for an increase of the kingly authority. He could endure no minister who would not be subservient to him. Any officer who voted against his favourite ministers in parliament, he marked in a black-list which he kept, and either dismissed him at once or stopped his promotion. A particular cohort amounting to fifteen or twenty in the House of Commons, were recognised as 'the King's Friends,' from the readiness they shewed to do his bidding and act for his interest on all occasions; and this unconstitutional arrangement was calmly submitted to. A great deal of what was amiss in the king's system of government might be traced to mis-education under a bad mother, who continually dinned into his ear, 'George, be a king!' and preceptors who were disaffected to Revolution principles. Like other weak men, he could not understand a conscientious dissent from his own opinion. He argued thus:—'I think so and so, and I am conscientious in thinking so: ergo, any other opinion must be unconscientious.' It is perfectly certain, accordingly, that he looked upon Mr Fox, and the Whigs generally, as base and profligate men—his son included in the number; and adhered to the policy which cost him America under a perfect conviction that only worthless people could sympathise with the claims of the disaffected colonists. It is, on the other hand, remarkable of the king, that whenever resistance reached the point where it became clearly dangerous, he gave way. After he had conceded peace and independence to America, there was something heroic in his reception of Mr Adams, the first ambassador of the new republic, when he said that, though he had been the last man in England to resolve on the pacification, he should also be the last to seek to break it. The mistaken policy which inflicted such wretchedness on the patriots in America, is in some measure redeemed by his grateful generosity to the loyalists. It was found after his death, that he had, all through the war, kept a private register, in which he entered the name of any one who suffered for his loyalty to Great Britain, and full particulars regarding him, that he might, as far as possible, afford him compensation. One is struck by the *English* character of King George—English in his doggedness and his prejudices, but equally English in his conscientiousness and his frankness. It is strange to reflect on the evils incurred by the United Kingdom through the accident of her wrongheaded ruler being a virtuous man. Had that latter particular been reversed, such huge political aberrations would have been impossible.

Mr Thackeray, in his Lectures on the Four Georges, touches on the last days of the third with a pathos rarely reached in modern literature. The passage is a gem of exquisite beauty. 'I have,' says he, 'seen his picture as it was taken at this time, hanging in the apartment of his daughter, the Landgravine of Hesse Hombourg—amidst books and Windsor furniture, and a hundred fond reminiscences of her English home. The poor old father is represented in a purple gown, his snowy beard falling over his breast—the star of his famous Order still idly shining on it. He was not only sightless: he became utterly deaf. All light, all reason, all sound of human voices, all the pleasures of this world of God, were taken from him. Some slight lucid moments he had; in one of which, the queen, desiring to see him, found him singing a hymn, and accompanying himself on the harpsichord. When he had finished, he knelt down and prayed aloud for her, and then for his family, and then for the nation, concluding with a prayer for himself, that it might please God to avert his heavy calamity from him, but, if not, to give him resignation to submit. He then burst into tears, and his reason again fled.

'What preacher need moralise on this story; what words save the simplest are requisite to tell it? It is too terrible for tears. The thought of such a misery smites me down in submission before the Ruler of kings and men, the Monarch supreme over empires and republics, the inscrutable Dispenser of life, death, happiness, victory. "O brothers," I said to those who heard me first in America—"O brothers! speaking the same dear mother tongue—O comrades, enemies no more, let us take a mournful hand together as we stand by this royal corpse, and call a truce to battle! Low he lies to whom the proudest used to kneel once, and who was cast lower than the poorest: dead, whom millions prayed for in vain. Driven off his throne; buffeted by rude hands, with his children in revolt; the darling of his old age killed before him untimely; our Lear hangs over her breathless lips and cries, "Cordelia, Cordelia, stay a little!

"Vex not his ghost—oh! let him pass—he hates him,
That would upon the rack of this tough world
Stretch him out longer!"

Hush! Strife and Quarrel, over the solemn grave. Sound, trumpets, a mournful march! Fall, dark curtain, upon his pageant, his pride, his grief, his awful tragedy!'

188

JANUARY 30.

St Barsimæus, bishop and martyr, 2nd century. St Martina, virgin and martyr, 3rd century. St Aldegondes, virgin and abbess, 660. St Bathildes, queen of France, 680.

Born.—Charles Rollin, 1661, *Paris;* Walter Savage Landor, 1775; Charles Lord Metcalfe, 1785.
Died—William Chillingworth, 1644; King Charles I., 1649; Dr John Robison, mechanical philosopher, 1805.

LORD METCALFE.

Charles Metcalfe—raised at the close of a long official life to the dignity of a peer of the realm—was a notable example of that kind of Englishman, of whom Wellington was the type,—modest, steady, well-intending, faithful to his country and to his employers; in a word, the devotee of duty. A great part of his life was spent in India—some years were given to Jamaica—finally, he took the government of Canada. There, when enjoying at fifty-nine the announcement of his peerage, he was beset by a cruel disease. His biographer Mr Kaye tells us—'One correspondent recommended Mesmerism, which had cured Miss Martineau; another, Hydropathy, at the "pure springs of Malvern;" a third, an application of the common dock-leaf; a fourth, an infusion of couch grass; a fifth, the baths of Docherte, near Vienna; a sixth, the volcanic hot springs of Karlsbad; a seventh, a wonderful plaster, made of rose-leaves, olive oil, and turnip juice; an eighth, a plaster and powder in which some part of a young frog was a principal ingredient; a ninth, a mixture of copperas and vinegar; a tenth, an application of pure ox-gall; an eleventh, a mixture of Florence oil and red precipitate; whilst a twelfth was certain of the good effects of Homœopathy, which had cured the well-known "Charlotte Elizabeth." Besides these varied remedies, many men and women, with infallible recipes or certain modes of treatment, were recommended to him by themselves and others. Learned Italian professors, mysterious American women, erudite Germans, and obscure Irish quacks—all had cured cancers of twenty years' standing, and all were pressing, or pressed forward, to operate on Lord Metcalfe.'

The epitaph written upon Lord Metcalfe by Lord Macaulay gives his worthy career and something of his character in words that could not be surpassed:

'Near this stone is laid Charles Theophilus, first and last Lord Metcalfe, a statesman tried in many high posts and difficult conjunctures, and found equal to all. The three greatest dependencies of the British crown were successively entrusted to his care. In India his fortitude, his wisdom, his probity, and his moderation are held in honourable remembrance by men of many races, languages, and religions. In Jamaica, still convulsed by a social revolution, he calmed the evil passions which long-suffering had engendered in one class, and long domination in another. In Canada, not yet recovered from the calamities of civil war, he reconciled contending factions to each other and to the mother country. Public esteem was the just reward of his public virtue; but those only who enjoyed the privilege of his friendship could appreciate the whole worth of his gentle and noble nature. Costly monuments in Asiatic and American cities attest the gratitude of nations which he ruled; this tablet records the sorrow and the pride with which his memory is cherished by private affection. He was born the 30th day of January 1785. He died the 5th day of September 1846.'

EXECUTION OF CHARLES I.

Though the anniversary of the execution of Charles I. is very justly no longer celebrated with religious ceremonies in England, one can scarcely on any occasion allow the day to pass without a feeling of pathetic interest in the subject. The meek behaviour of the King in his latter days, his tender interviews with his little children when parting with them for ever, the insults he bore so well, his calmness at the last on the scaffold, combine to make us think leniently of his arbitrary rule, his high-handed proceedings with

Nonconformists, and even his falseness towards the various opposing parties he had to deal with. When we further take into account the piety of his meditations as exhibited in the *Eikon Basilike*, we can scarcely wonder that a very large proportion of the people of England, of his own generation, regarded him as a kind of martyr, and cherished his memory with the most affectionate regard. Of the highly inexpedient nature of the action, it is of no use to speak, as its consequences in causing retaliation and creating a reaction for arbitrary rule, are only too notorious.

Charles was put to death upon a scaffold raised in front of the Banqueting House, Whitehall. There is reason to believe that he was conducted to this sad stage through a window, from which the frame had been taken out, at the north extremity of the building near the gate. It was not so much elevated above the street, but that he could hear people weeping and praying for him below. A view of the dismal scene was taken at the time, engraved, and published in Holland, and of this a transcript is here presented.

EXECUTION OF CHARLES I.

The scaffold, as is well known, was graced that day by two executioners in masks; and as to the one who used the axe a question has arisen, who was he? The public seems to have been kept in ignorance on this point at the time; had it been otherwise, he could not have long escaped the daggers of the royalists. Immediately after the Restoration, the Government made an effort to discover the masked headsman; but we do not learn that they ever succeeded. William Lilly, the famous astrologer, having dropped a hint that he knew something on the subject, was examined before a parliamentary committee at that time, and gave the following information:

'The next Sunday but one after Charles the First was beheaded, Robert Spavin, Secretary unto Lieutenant-General Cromwell, invited himself to dine with me, and brought Anthony Peirson and several others along with him to dinner. Their principal discourse all dinner-time was only, who it was that beheaded the King. One said it was the common hangman; another, Hugh

Peters; others were nominated, but none concluded. Robert Spavin, so soon as dinner was done, took me to the south window. Saith he, "These are all mistaken; they have not named the man that did the fact: it was Lieutenant-Colonel Joyce. I was in the room when he fitted himself for the work—stood behind him when he did it—when done went in again with him. There's no man knows this but my master (viz. Cromwell), Commissary Ireton, and myself." "Doth not Mr Rushworth know it?" said I. "No, he doth not," saith Spavin. The same thing Spavin since had often related to me when we were alone. Mr Prynne did, with much civility, make a report hereof in the house.'*

Nevertheless, the probability is that the King's head was in reality cut off by the ordinary executioner, Richard Brandon. When, after the Restoration, an attempt was made to fix the guilt on one William Hulett, the following evidence was given

* Lilly's History of his Life and Times ed. 1715, p. 89.

in his defence, and there is much reason to believe that it states the truth. 'When my Lord Capell, Duke Hamilton, and the Earl of Holland, were beheaded in the Palace Yard, Westminster [soon after the King], my Lord Capell asked the common hangman, "Did you cut off my master's head?" "Yes," saith he. "Where is the instrument that did it?" He then brought the axe. "Is this the same axe? are you sure?" said my lord. "Yes, my lord," saith the hangman; "I am very sure it is the same." My Lord Capell took the axe and kissed it, and gave him five pieces of gold. *I heard him say,* "Sirrah, wert thou not afraid?" Saith the hangman, "They made me cut it off, and I had thirty pounds for my pains."'

We have engraved two of the relics associated with this solemn event in our history. First is the Bible believed to have been used by Charles, just previous to his death, and which the King is said to have presented to Bishop Juxon, though

KING CHARLES I.'S BIBLE.

this circumstance is not mentioned in any contemporaneous account of the execution. The only notice of such a volume, as a dying gift, appears to be that recorded by Sir Thomas Herbert, in his narrative, which forms a part of *The Memoirs of the last Two Years of the Reign of that unparalleled Prince, of ever-blessed memory, King Charles I.;* London, 1702, p. 129, in the following passage:—'The King thereupon gave him his hand to kiss, having the day before been graciously pleased, under his royal hand, to give him a certificate, that the said Mr Herbert was not imposed upon him, but by his Majesty made choice of to attend him in his bedchamber, and had served him with faithfulness and loyal affection. His Majesty also delivered him his Bible, in the margin whereof he had, with his own hand, written many annotations and quotations, and charged him to give it to the Prince so soon as he returned.' That this might be the book above represented is rendered extremely probable, on the assumption that the King would be naturally anxious that his son should possess that very copy of the Scriptures which had been provided for himself when he was Prince of Wales. It will be observed that the cover of the Bible is decorated with the badge of the Principality within the Garter, surmounted by a royal coronet (in silver gilt), enclosed by an embroidered border;

190

the initial P. being apparently altered to an R., and the badges of the Rose and Thistle upon a ground of blue velvet: the book was, therefore, bound between the death of Prince Henry in 1612, and the accession of Charles to the throne in 1625, when such a coronet would be no longer used by him. If the Bible here represented be that referred to by Herbert, the circumstance of Bishop Juxon becoming the possessor of it might be accounted for by supposing that it was placed in his hands to be transmitted to Charles II., with the George of the Order of the Garter belonging to the late King, well known to have been given to that prelate upon the scaffold. The Bible was, when Mr Roach Smith wrote the above details in his *Collectanea Antiqua,* in the possession of James Skene, Esq. of Rubislaw.*

Next is engraved the silver clock-watch, which had long been used by King Charles, and was given by him to Sir Thomas Herbert, on the morning of his execution. The face is beautifully engraved; and the back and rim is elaborately chased, and pierced with foliage and scrollwork. It has descended as an heir-loom to William Townley Mitford, Esq.; and from its undoubted

* Mr. Skene, the last survivor of the six friends to whom Sir Walter Scott dedicated the respective cantoes of *Marmion,* now (1862) resides in Oxford.

genuineness must be considered as one of the most interesting relics of the monarch.

The body of the unfortunate King was embalmed immediately after the execution, and taken to Windsor to be interred. A small group of his friends, including his relative the Duke of Richmond, was permitted by Parliament to conduct a funeral which should not cost above five hundred pounds. Disdaining an ordinary grave, which had been dug for the King in the

KING CHARLES I.'S WATCH.

floor of the chapel, they found a vault in the centre of the choir, containing two coffins, believed to be those of Henry VIII. and his queen Jane Seymour; and there his coffin was placed, with no ceremony beyond the tears of the mourners, the Funeral Service being then under prohibition. The words 'King Charles, 1648,' inscribed on the outside of the outer wooden coffin, alone marked the remains of the unfortunate monarch. These sad rites were paid at three in the afternoon of the 19th of February, three weeks after the execution.

The coffin of King Charles was seen in the reign of William III., on the vault being opened to receive one of the Princess Anne's children. It remained unobserved, forgotten, and a matter of doubt for upwards of a century thereafter, till, in 1813, the vault had once more to be opened for the funeral of the Duchess of Brunswick. On the 1st of April, the day after the interment of that princess, the Prince Regent, the Duke of Cumberland, the Dean of Windsor, Sir Harry Halford, and two other gentlemen assembled at the vault, while a search was made for the remains of King Charles. The leaden coffin, with the inscription, was soon found, and partially opened, when the body of the decapitated king was found tolerably entire and in good condition, amidst the gums and resins which had been employed in preserving it. 'At length the whole face was disengaged from its covering. The complexion of the skin of it was dark and discoloured. The forehead and temples had lost little or nothing of their muscular substance; the cartilage of the nose was gone; but the left eye, in the first moment of exposure, was open and full, though it vanished almost immediately: and the pointed beard, so characteristic of the reign of King Charles, was perfect. The shape of the face was a long oval; many of the teeth remained. . . . . When the head had been entirely disengaged from the attachments which confined it, it was found to be loose, and without any difficulty was taken up and held to view. . . . . . The back part of the scalp was perfect, and had a remarkably fresh appearance; the pores of the skin being more distinct, as they usually are when soaked in moisture; and the tendons and filaments of the neck were of considerable substance and firmness. The hair was thick at the back part of the head, and, in appearance, nearly black. . . . On holding up the head to examine the place of separation from the body, the muscles of the neck had evidently retracted themselves considerably; and the fourth cervical vertebra was found to be cut through its substance, transversely, leaving the surfaces of the divided portions perfectly smooth and even.'[*]

The first Lord Holland used to relate, with some pleasantry, a usage of his father, Sir Stephen Fox, which proves the superstitious veneration in which the Tories held the memory of Charles I. During the whole of the 30th of January, *the wainscot of the house used to be hung with black*, and no meal of any sort was allowed till after midnight. This attempt at rendering the day melancholy by fasting had a directly contrary effect on the children; for the housekeeper, apprehensive that they might suffer from so long an abstinence from food, used to give the little folks clandestinely as many comfits and sweetmeats as they could eat, and Sir Stephen's in-

[*] Sir Henry Halford's Account of what appeared on opening the coffin of King Charles I., &c. 1813.

tended fast was looked to by the younger part of the family as a holiday and diversion.—*Correspondence of C. J. Fox, edited by Earl Russell.*

There is a story told regarding a Miss Russell, great-grand-daughter of Oliver Cromwell, who was waiting-woman to the Princess Amelia, daughter of George II., to the effect that, while engaged in her duty one 30th of January, the Prince of Wales came into the room, and sportively said, 'For shame, Miss Russell! why have you not been at church, humbling yourself with weepings and wailings for the sins on this day committed by your ancestor?' To which Miss Russell answered, 'Sir, for a descendant of the great Oliver Cromwell, it is humiliation sufficient to be employed, as I am, in pinning up the tail of your sister!'—*Rede's Anecdotes, 1799.*

The Calves'-Head Club.

The *Gentleman's Magazine* for 1735, vol. v., p. 105, under the date of January 30, gives the following piece of intelligence:—'Some young noblemen and gentlemen met at a tavern in Suffolk Street [Charing Cross], called themselves the Calves'-Head Club, dressed up a calf's head in a napkin, and after some huzzas threw it into a bonfire, and dipt napkins in their red wine and waved them out at window. The mob had strong beer given them, and for a time hallooed as well as the best, but taking disgust at some healths proposed, grew so outrageous that they broke all the windows, and forced themselves into the house; but the guards being sent for, prevented further mischief.' The *Weekly Chronicle*, of February 1, 1735, states that the

THE CALVES'-HEAD CLUB.

damage was estimated at 'some hundred pounds,' and that 'the guards were posted all night in the street, for the security of the neigh-bourhood.' Horace Walpole says the mob destroyed part of the house. Sir William (called Hellfire) Stanhope was one of the members. This riotous occurrence was the occasion of some verses in *The Grub Street Journal*, of which the following lines may be quoted as throwing some additional light on the scene :

> ' Strange times ! when noble peers, secure from riot,
> Can't keep Noll's annual festival in quiet,
> Through sashes broke, dirt, stones, and brands
>   thrown at 'em,
> Which, if not scand- was brand- alum magnatum.
> Forced to run down to vaults for safer quarters,
> And in coal-holes their ribbons hide and garters.'

The manner in which Noll's (Oliver Cromwell's) ' annual festival ' is here alluded to, seems to shew that the bonfire, with the calf's-head and other accompaniments, had been exhibited in previous years. In confirmation of this fact, there exists a print entitled *The True Effigies of the Members of the Calves'-Head Club, held on the 30th of January* 1734, *in Suffolk Street, in the County of Middlesex ;* being the year before the riotous occurrence above related. This print, as will be observed in the copy above given, shews a bonfire in the centre of the foreground, with the mob ; in the background, a house with three windows, the central window exhibiting two men, one of whom is about to throw the calf's-head into the bonfire below. The window on the right shews three persons drinking healths, that on the left two other persons, one of whom wears a mask, and has an axe in his hand.

It is a singular fact that a political club of this revolutionary character should have been in existence at so late a period as the eighth year of the reign of George II. We find no mention of it for many years preceding this time, and after the riot it was probably broken up.

The first notice that we find of this strange club is in a small quarto tract of twenty-two pages, which has been reprinted in the *Harleian Miscellany*. It is entitled *The Secret History of the Calves-Head Club ; or, the Republican unmask'd. Wherein is fully shewn the Religion of the Calves-Head Heroes, in their Anniversary Thanksgiving Songs on the 30th of January, by them called Anthems, for the Years* 1693, 1694, 1695, 1696, 1697. *Now published to demonstrate the restless implacable Spirit of a certain Party still amongst us, who are never to be satisfied until the present Establishment in Church and State is subverted.* The Second Edition. London, 1703. The *Secret History*, which occupies less than half of the twenty-two pages, is vague and unsatisfactory, and the five songs or anthems are entirely devoid of literary or any other merit. As Queen Anne commenced her reign in March 1702, and the second edition of this tract is dated 1703, it may be presumed that the first edition was published at the beginning of the Queen's reign. The author states, that ' after the Restoration the eyes of the Government being upon the whole party, they were obliged to meet with a great deal of precaution, but now they meet almost in a public manner, and apprehend nothing.' Yet all the evidence which he produces concerning their meetings is hearsay. He had never himself been present at the club. He states, that ' happening in the late reign to be in company of a certain active Whig,' the said Whig

informed him that he knew most of the members of the club, and had been often invited to their meetings, but had never attended : ' that Milton and other creatures of the Commonwealth had instituted this club (as he was informed) in opposition to Bishop Juxon, Dr Sanderson, Dr Hammond, and other divines of the Church of England, who met privately every 30th of January, and though it was under the time of the usurpation had compiled a private form of service of the day, not much different from what we now find in the Liturgy.' From this statement it appears that the author's friend, though a Whig, had no personal knowledge of the club. The slanderous rumour about Milton may be passed over as unworthy of notice, this untrustworthy tract being the only authority for it.

But the author of the *Secret History* has more evidence to produce. ' By another gentleman, who, about eight years ago, went, out of mere curiosity, to their club, and has since furnished me with the following papers [the songs or anthems], I was informed that it was kept in no fixed house, but that they removed as they saw convenient ; that the place they met in when he was with them was in a blind alley about Moorfields ; that the company wholly consisted of Independents and Anabaptists (I am glad, for the honour of the Presbyterians, to set down this remark) ; that the famous Jerry White, formerly chaplain to Oliver Cromwell (who, no doubt of it, came to sanctify with his pious exhortations the ribaldry of the day), said grace ; that, after the cloth was removed, the anniversary anthem, as they impiously called it, was sung, and a calf's skull filled with wine, or other liquor, and then a brimmer, went round to the pious memory of those worthy patriots who had killed the tyrant, and delivered the country from his arbitrary sway.' Such is the story told in the edition of 1703 ; but in the edition of 1713, after the word Moorfields, the narrative is continued as follows : —' where an axe was hung up in the club-room, and was reverenced as a principal symbol in this diabolical sacrament. Their bill of fare was a large dish of calves'-heads, dressed several ways, by which they represented the king, and his friends who had suffered in his cause ; a large pike with a small one in his mouth, as an emblem of tyranny ; a large cod's head, by which they pretended to represent the person of the king singly ; a boar's head, with an apple in its mouth, to represent the king. . . . After the repast was over, one of their elders presented an *Ikon Basilike*, which was with great solemnity burned upon the table, whilst the anthems were singing. After this, another produced Milton's *Defensio Populi Anglicani*, upon which all laid their hands, and made a protestation, in form of an oath, for ever to stand by and maintain the same. The company wholly consisted of Anabaptists,' &c.

As a specimen of the verses, the following stanzas may be quoted from the anthem for 1696, in reference to Charles I. :—

> ' This monarch wore a peaked beard,
>   And seemed a doughty hero,
> A Diocletian innocent,
>   And merciful as Nero.

' The Church's darling implement,
    And scourge of all the people,
He swore he'd make each mother's son
    Adore their idol steeple ;

' But they, perceiving his designs,
    Grew plaguy shy and jealous,
And timely chopt his calf's head off,
    And sent him to his fellows.'

This tract appears to have excited the curiosity of the public in no small degree ; for it passed, with many augmentations as valueless as the original trash, through no less than nine editions. The fifth edition, published in 1705, contains three additional songs, and is further augmented by ' Reflections ' on each of the eight songs, and by ' A Vindication of the Royal Martyr Charles the First, wherein are laid open the Republicans' Mysteries of Rebellion, written in the time of the Usurpation by the celebrated Mr Butler, author of *Hudibras ;* with a Character of a Presbyterian, by Sir John Denham, Knight.' To a certainty the author of *Hudibras* never wrote anything so stupid as this ' Vindication,' nor the author of *Cooper's Hill* the dull verses here ascribed to him.

The sixth edition is a reprint of the fifth, but has an engraving representing the members of the club seated at a table furnished with dishes such as are described in the extract above quoted, and with the axe hung up against the wainscot. A man in a priest's dress is saying grace, and four other persons are seated near him, two on each side ; two others seem by their dress to be men of rank. A black personage, with horns on his head, is looking in at the door from behind ; and a female figure, with snakes among her hair, probably representing Rebellion, is looking out from under the table.

The eighth edition, published in 1713, contains seven engravings, including the one just described, and the text is augmented to 224 pages. The additional matter consists of the following articles :—' An Appendix to the Secret History of the Calf's Head Club ;' ' Remarkable Accidents and Transactions at the Calf's Head Club, by way of Continuation of the Secret History thereof,'— these ' Accidents ' extend over the years 1708-12, and consist of narratives apparently got up for the purpose of exciting the public and selling the book ; ' Select Observations of the Whigs ;' ' Policy and Conduct in and out of Power.' Lowndes mentions another edition published in 1716.

Hearne tells us that on the 30th January 1706-7, some young men in All Souls' College, Oxford, dined together at twelve o'clock, and amused themselves with cutting off the heads of a number of woodcocks, ' in contempt of the memory of the blessed martyr.' They had tried to get calves'-heads, but the cook refused to dress them.*

MEMORIALS OF CHARLES I.

It is pleasanter to contemplate the feelings of tenderness and veneration than those of contempt and anger. We experience a relief in turning from the coarse doings of the Calves'-Head Club,

* Reliquiæ Hearnianæ, i. 121.

194

to look on the affectionate grief of those who, on however fallacious grounds, mourned for the royal martyr. It is understood that there were seven mourning rings distributed among the more intimate friends of the unfortunate king, and one of them was latterly in the possession of Horace Walpole at Strawberry Hill, being a gift to him from Lady Murray Elliott. The stone presents the profile of the king in miniature. On the obverse of this, within, is a death's head, surmounting a crown, with a crown of glory above ; flanked by the words, GLORIA—VANITAS ; while round the interior runs the legend, *Gloria Ang. Emigravit, Ja. the* 30, 1648.

There are also extant several examples of a small silver case or locket, in the form of a heart, which may be presumed each to have been suspended near the heart of some devoted and tearful loyalist. In the example here presented, there is an engraved profile head of the king within, opposite to which, on the inside of the lid, is inscribed, ' *Prepared be to follow me,* C.R.' On one of the exterior sides is a heart stuck through with arrows, and the legend, ' *I liue and dy in*

loyaltye.' On the other exterior side is an eye dropping tears, surmounted by ' Quis temperet a lacrymis, January 30, 1648.' Other examples of this mourning locket have slight variations in the ornaments and legends.

CONVIVIAL CLUBS IN LANCASHIRE.

What is a club ? A voluntary association of persons for a common object, and contributing equally to a common purse. The etymology of the word is a puzzle. Some derive it from the Anglo-Saxon *cleofan,* to cleave, *q. d.* the members ' stick together ;' but this seems a little far-fetched. Others consider it as from the Welsh verb *clapiaw*, to form into a lump; or to join together for a common end. Whencesoever our name for it, the institution is ancient; it was known among the ancient Greeks, every member contributing his share of the expenses. They had even their benefit-clubs, with a common chest, and monthly payments for the benefit of members in distress. Our Anglo-Saxon forefathers had like confederations, only they called them *gylds* or *guilds*, from *gyldan*, to pay, to contribute a share. Religious guilds were succeeded by trade guilds and benevolent guilds, which were a sort of sick and burial clubs, some of which still survive. The club convivial, in essence if not in name, has always been a cherished institution amongst us. We need only name the Mermaid, of the time of Shakspeare, Ben Jonson, and their fellows. It would be an interesting inquiry to trace the succession of such clubs, in the metropolis alone, from' the days of Elizabeth to those of Anne; the clubs of the latter period being so delightfully pictured to us by Addison, Steele, and others of their members. From the coffee-house clubs of the time of Charles II., including the King's Head or Green Ribbon Club of the Shaftesbury clique, —it would be curious to trace the gradual development of the London clubs, into their present palatial homes at the West-end. But our task is a much more limited one. We wish to perpetuate a few of the fast-fading features of some of these institutions in a northern shire,—clubs in which what Carlyle terms the 'nexus' was a love of what was called 'good eating and drinking, and good fellowship.'

What its inhabitants designate 'the good old town' of Liverpool might naturally be expected, as the great seaport of Lancashire, to stand pre-eminent in its convivial clubs. But we must confess we have been unable to find any very distinct vestiges, or even indications, of such institutions having once enjoyed there 'a local habitation and a name.' To deny to the inhabitants of Liverpool, the social character and convivial habits out of which such clubs naturally spring, would be to do them a great injustice. But the only peep we get into their habits in the latter half of the 18th century, is that afforded by some published *Letters to the Earl of Cork*, written by Samuel Derrick, Esq., then Master of the Ceremonies at Bath, after a visit to Liverpool in 1767. After describing the fortnightly assemblies, 'to dance and play cards;' the performances at the one theatre which then sufficed; the good and cheap entertainment provided for at Liverpool's three inns, where 'for tenpence a man dines elegantly at an ordinary consisting of a dozen dishes,'—Mr Derrick lauds the private hospitality which he enjoyed, and the good fellowship he saw: 'If by accident one man's stock of ale runs short, he has only to send his pitcher to his neighbour to have it filled.' He celebrates the good ale of Mr Thomas Mears, of Paradise-street, a merchant in the Portuguese trade, 'whose malt was bought at Derby, his hops in Kent, and his water brought by express order from Lisbon.' 'It was, indeed,' says Derrick, 'an excellent liquor.' He speaks of the tables of the merchants as being plenteously furnished with viands well served up, and adds that, 'of their excellent rum they consumed large quantities in punch, when the West India fleet came in mostly with limes,' which he praises as being 'very cooling, and affording a delicious flavour.'* Still, these are the tipplings around the private 'mahogany,' if such a material were then used for the festive board; and Mr Derrick nowhere narrates a visit to a club. Indeed, the only relic of such an assemblage is to be found in a confederation which existed in Liverpool for some time about the middle of the 18th century.

Its title was 'The Society of Bucks.' It seems to have been principally convivial, though to some slight extent of a political complexion. On Monday, 4th June 1759, they advertise a celebration of the birthday of George Prince of Wales, (afterwards George III.) On Wednesday, July 25, their anniversary meeting is held 'by the command of the grand,'—(a phrase borrowed from the Freemasons)—dinner on the table at two o'clock. On August 3, they command a play at the theatre; and on the 8th February 1760, the Society is recorded as 'having generously subscribed £70 towards clothing our brave troops abroad, and the relief of the widows and orphans of those who fell nobly in their country's and liberty's cause. This is the second laudable subscription made by them, as they had some time since remitted 50 guineas to the Marine Society.'

From an early period in the 18th century, the amusements of the inhabitants of Manchester consisted of cards, balls, theatrical performances, and concerts. About 1720 a wealthy lady named Madam Drake, who kept one of the three or four private carriages then existing in the town, refused to conform to the new-fashioned beverages of tea and coffee; so that, whenever she made an afternoon's visit, her friends presented her with that to which she had been accustomed,—a tankard of ale and a pipe of tobacco! The usual entertainment at gentlemen's houses at that period included wet and dry sweetmeats, different sorts of cake and gingerbread, apples, or other fruits of the season, and a variety of home-made wines, the manufacture of which was a great point with all good housewives. They made an essential part of all feasts, and were brought forth when the London or Bristol dealers came down to settle their accounts with the Manchester manufacturers, and to give orders. A young manufacturer about this time, having a valuable customer to sup with him, sent to the tavern for a pint of foreign wine, which next morning furnished a subject for the sarcastic remarks of all his neighbours. About this period there was an evening club of the most opulent manufacturers, at which the expenses of each person were fixed at 4½d.; viz., 4d. for ale, and a halfpenny for tobacco. At a much later period, however, sixpennyworth of punch, and a pipe or two, were esteemed fully sufficient for the evening's tavern amusement of the principal inhabitants. After describing a common public-house in which a

* Derrick's Letters from Chester, Liverpool, &c.

large number of respectable Manchester trades-men met every day after dinner,—the rule being to call for six-pennyworth of punch, the amuse-ment to drink and smoke and discuss the news of the town, it being high 'change at six o'clock and the evening's sitting peremptorily terminated at 8 p.m.,—the writer we are quoting adds, 'To a stranger it is very extraordinary, that merchants of the first fortunes quit the elegant drawing-room, to sit in a small, dark dungeon, for this house cannot with propriety be called by a better name—but such is the force of long-established custom!'*

The club which originated at the house just de-scribed has some features sufficiently curious to be noted as a picture of the time. A man named John Shaw, who had served in the army as a dragoon, having lost his wife and four or five children, solaced himself by opening a public-house in the Old Shambles, Manchester; in conducting which he was ably supported by a sturdy woman servant of middle age, whose only known name was 'Molly.' John Shaw, having been much abroad, had acquired a knack of brewing punch, then a favourite beverage; and from this attraction, his house soon began to be frequented by the prin-cipal merchants and manufacturers of the town, and to be known as 'John Shaw's Punch-house.' Sign it had none. As Dr Aikin says in 1795 that Shaw had then kept the house more than fifty years, we have here an institution dating prior to the memorable '45. Having made a comfortable competence, John Shaw, who was a lover of early hours, and, probably from his military training, a martinet in discipline, insti-tuted the singular rule of closing his house to customers at eight o'clock in the evening. As soon as the clock struck the hour, John walked into the one public room of the house, and in a loud voice and imperative tone, proclaimed 'Eight o'clock, gentlemen; eight o'clock.' After this no entreaties for more liquor, however urgent or suppliant, could prevail over the inexorable land-lord. If the announcement of the hour did not at once produce the desired effect, John had two modes of summary ejectment. He would call to Molly to bring his horsewhip, and crack it in the ears and near the persons of his guests; and should this fail, Molly was ordered to bring her pail, with which she speedily flooded the floor, and drove the guests out wet-shod. On one occasion of a county election, when Colonel Stanley was returned, the gentleman took some friends to John Shaw's to give them a treat. At eight o'clock John came into the room and loudly announced the hour as usual. Colonel Stanley said he hoped Mr Shaw would not press the matter on that occasion, as it was a special one, but would allow him and his friends to take another bowl of punch. John's characteristic reply was:—'Colonel Stanley, you are a law-maker, and should not be a law-breaker; and if you and your friends do not leave the room in five minutes, you will find your shoes full of water.' Within that time the old servant, Molly, came in with mop and bucket, and the repre-sentative for Lancashire and his friends retired

* Dr Aikin's Description of the Country from thirty to forty miles round Manchester.

in dismay before this prototype of Dame Parting-ton. After this eight o'clock law was established. John Shaw's was more than ever resorted to. Some of the elderly gentlemen, of regular habits, and perhaps of more leisure than their juniors, used to meet there at four o'clock in the after-noon, which they called 'watering time,' to spend each his sixpence, and then go home to tea with their wives and families about five o'clock. But from seven to eight o'clock in the evening was the hour of high 'change at John Shaw's; for then all the frequenters of the house had had tea, had finished the labours of the day, closed their mills, warehouses, places of business, and were free to enjoy a social hour. Tradition says that the punch brewed by John Shaw was some-thing very delicious. In mixing it, he used a long-shanked silver table-spoon, like a modern gravy-spoon; which, for convenience, he carried in a side pocket, like that in which a carpenter carries his two-foot rule. Punch was usually served in small bowls (that is, less than the 'crown bowls' of later days) of two sizes and prices; a shilling bowl being termed 'a P of punch,'—'a Q of punch' denoting a sixpenny bowl. The origin of these slang names is un-known. Can it have any reference to the old saying—'Mind your P's and Q's.?' If a gentle-man came alone and found none to join him, he called for 'a Q.' If two or more joined, they called for 'a P;' but seldom more was spent than about 6d. per head. Though eccentric and austere, John won the respect and esteem of his customers, by his strict integrity and stedfast adherence to his rules.

For his excellent regulation as to the hour of closing, he is said to have frequently received the thanks of the ladies of Manchester, whose male friends were thus induced to return home early and sober. At length this nightly meeting of friends and acquaintances at John Shaw's grew into an organised club, of a convivial character, bearing his name. Its objects were not political; yet, John and his guests being all of the same political party, there was sufficient unanimity among them to preserve harmony and concord. John's roof sheltered none but stout, thorough-going Tories of the old school, genuine 'Church and King' men; nay, even 'rank Jacobites.' If perchance, from ignorance of the character of the house, any unhappy Whig, any unfortunate par-tisan of the house of Hanover, any known mem-ber of a dissenting conventicle, strayed into John Shaw's, he found himself in a worse posi-tion than that of a solitary wasp in a beehive. If he had the temerity to utter a political opinion, he speedily found 'the house too hot to hold him,' and was forthwith put forth into the street. When the club was duly formed, a President was elected; and there being some contest about a Vice-President, John Shaw summarily abolished that office, and the club had perforce to exist without its 'Vice.' The war played the mischief with John's inimitable brew; limes became scarce; lemons were substituted: at length of these too, and of the old pine-apple rum of Jamaica, the supplies were so frequently cut off by French privateers, that a few years before John Shaw's death, the innovation of 'grog' in place of punch struck a heavy blow at the old man's heart. Even autocrats must die, and at length, on the 26th January 1796, John Shaw was gathered to his fathers, at the ripe old age of eighty-three, having ruled his house upwards of fifty-eight years; namely, from the year 1738. But though John Shaw ceased to rule, the club still lived and flourished. His successor in the house carried on the same 'early closing movement,' with the aid of the same old servant Molly. At length the house was pulled down, and the club was very migratory for some years. It finally settled down in 1852, in the Spread Eagle Hotel, Corporation Street, where it continued to prosper and flourish. From the records of the club, which commenced in 1822 and extend to a recent date, it appears that its government consisted of a President, a Vice-President, a Recorder [i.e. Secretary], a Doctor [generally some medical resident of 'the right sort'], and a Poet Laureate: these are termed 'the staff;' its number of members fluctuated between thirty and fifty; these gentlemen were in the habit of closing their sittings, as of old, at curfew. Its presidents have included several octogenarians; but we do not venture to say whether such longevity is due to its punch or its early hours. One of its presidents, Edmund Buckley, was formerly (1841–47) M.P. for Newcastle-under-Lyne; he continued to be a member of the club for upwards of forty years, although approaching the patriarchal age of some of his predecessors. In 1834, John Shaw's absorbed into its venerable bosom another club of similar character, entitled 'The Sociable Club.' The club possessed amongst its relics oil paintings of John Shaw and his maid Molly, and of several presidents of past years. Many years ago, a singular old China punch-bowl, which had been the property of John Shaw himself, was restored to the club as its rightful property, by the descendant of a trustee. It is a barrel-shaped vessel, suspended as on a stillage, with a metal tap at one end, whence to draw the liquor; which it received through a large opening or bung-hole. Besides assembling every evening, winter and summer, between five and eight o'clock, a few of the members dined together every Saturday at 2 P.M.; and they had an annual dinner, when old friends and members drank old wine, toasted old toasts, told old stories, or 'fought their battles o'er again.' Such was John Shaw's famous Manchester club—in its more prosperous days, in the year of grace 1862.

From a punch-drinking club we turn to a dining club. About the year 1806 a few Manchester gentlemen were in the habit of dining together, as at an ordinary, at what was called 'Old Froggatt's,' the Unicorn Inn, Church Street, High Street. They chiefly consisted of young Manchester merchants and tradesmen, just commencing business and keen in its pursuit, with some of their country customers. They rushed into the house, about one o'clock, ate a fourpenny pie, drank a glass of ale, and rushed off again to 'change and to business. At length it began to be thought that they might just as well dine off a joint; and this was arranged with host and hostess, each diner paying a penny for cooking and twopence for catering and providing. The meal, however, continued to be performed with wonderful dispatch, and one of the traditionary stories of the society is that, a member one day, coming five minutes behind the hour, and casting a hasty glance through the window as he approached, said disappointedly to a friend, 'I need not go in—all their necks are up!' As soon as dinner was over, Old Froggatt was accustomed to bring in the dinner bill, in somewhat primitive fashion. Instead of the elegant, engraved form of more modern times, setting forth how many 'ports,' 'sherries,' 'brandies,' 'gins,' and 'cigars,' had been swallowed or consumed,—Froggatt's record was in humble chalk, marked upon the loose, unhinged lid of that useful ark in old cookery, the salt-box. A practical joke perpetrated one day on this cretaceous account, and more fitted for ears of a generation ago than those now existing, led to a practice of giving as the first toast after every Tuesday's dinner at the club, 'The Salt-box lid,'—a cabala which usually causes great perplexity to the uninitiated guest. About Christmas 1810, these gentlemen agreed to form themselves into a regular club. Having to dine in a hurry and hastily to return to business, the whole thing had much the character of every one scrambling for what he could get; and the late Mr Jonathan Peel, a cousin of the first Sir Robert, and one of its earliest members, gave it in joke the name of the 'Scramble Club.' which was felt to be so appropriate, that it was at once adopted for the club's title, and it has borne the name ever since. The chief rule of the club was, that every member should spend sixpence in drink for the good of the house; and the law was specially levelled against those 'sober-sides' who would otherwise have sneaked off with a good dinner, washed down with no stronger potations than could be supplied by the pump of the Unicorn. The club had its staff of officers, its records and its register; but alack! incautiously left within the reach of servants, the first volume of the archives of the ancient and loyal Scramblers served the ignoble purpose of lighting the fires of an inn. We are at once reminded of the great Alexandrian library, whose MS. treasures fed the baths of the city with fuel for more than eight months! The club grew till the Unicorn could no longer accommodate its members; and after various 'flittings' from house to house, it finally folded its wings and alighted under the hospitable roof of the Clarence Hotel, Spring-gardens; where it still, 'nobly daring, dines,' and where the dinners are too good to be scrambled over. Amongst the regalia of the club are some portraits of its founder and early presidents, a very elaborately carved snuff-box, &c. The members dine together yearly in grand anniversary. Amongst the laws and customs of the club, was a system of forfeit, or fines. Thus if any member removed to another house, or married, or became a father, or won a prize at a horse-race, he was mulcted in one, two, or more bottles of wine, for the benefit of the club. Again, there were odd rules (with fines for infraction) as to not taking the chair, or leaving it to ring a bell, or asking a stranger to ring it, or allowing a stranger to pay anything. These delinquencies were formally brought before the club, as charges, and if proved, a fine of a bottle or more followed ; if not proved, the membe bringing the charge forfeited a bottle of wine There were various other regulations, all tending to the practical joking called 'trotting,' and of course resulting in fines of wine.

Leaving the Scramble Club to go on dining, as it has done for more than half a century, we come next to a convivial club in another of the ancient towns of Lancashire—'Proud Preston.' It seems that from the year 1771 down to 1841, a period of seventy years, that town boasted its 'Oyster and Parched Pea Club.'* In its early stages the number of its members was limited to a dozen of the leading inhabitants ; but. like John Shaw's Club, they were all of the same political party, and they are said to have now and then honoured a Jacobite toast with a bumper. It possesses records for the year 1773, from which we learn that its president was styled 'the Speaker.' Amongst its staff of officers was one named 'Oystericus,' whose duty it was to order and look after the oysters, which then came 'by fleet' from London ; a Secretary, an Auditor, a Deputy Auditor, and a Poet Laureate, or 'Rhymesmith,' as he was generally termed. Among other officers of later creation, were the 'Cellarius,' who had to provide 'port of first quality,' the Chaplain, the Surgeon-general, the Master of the *Rolls* (to look to the provision of bread and butter), the 'Swig-Master,' whose title expresses his duty, Clerk of the *Peas*, a Minstrel, a Master of the Jewels, a Physician-in-Ordinary, &c. Among the Rules and Articles of the club, were 'That a barrel of oysters be provided every Monday night during the winter season, at the equal expense of the members ; to be opened exactly at half-past seven o'clock.' The bill was to be called for each night at ten o'clock, each member present to pay an equal share. 'Every member, on having a son born, shall pay a gallon—for a daughter half a gallon—of port, to his brethren of the club, within a month of the birth of such child, at any public-house he shall choose.' Amongst the archives of the club is the following curious entry, which is *not* in a lady's hand :—

'The ladies of the Toughey [? Toffy] Club were rather disappointed at not receiving, by the hands of the respectable messenger, despatched by the still more respectable members, of the Oyster Club, a few oysters. They are just sitting down, after the fatigues of the evening, and take the liberty of reminding the worthy members of the Oyster Club, that oysters were *not made for man alone.* The ladies have sent to the venerable president a small quantity of sweets [? pieces of Everton toffy] to be distributed, as he in his wisdom shall think fit.

'Monday Evening.'

It does not appear what was the result of this pathetic appeal and sweet gift to the venerable president of the masculine society. In 1795 the club was threatened with a difficulty, owing, as stated by 'Mr Oystericus,' to the day of the wagon—laden with oysters—leaving London

* We derive our information as to this club from the *Preston Chronicle.*

198

having been changed. Sometimes, owing to a long frost, or other accident, no oysters arrived. and then the club must have solaced itself with 'parched peas' and 'particular port.' Amongst the regalia of the club was a silver snuff-box, in the lid of which was set a piece of oak, part of the quarter-deck of Nelson's ship *Victory.* On one occasion the master of the jewel-office, having neglected to replenish this box with snuff, was fined a bottle of wine. At another time (November 1816), the Clerk of the *Peas* was reprimanded for neglect of duty, there being no peas supplied to the club. The Rhymesmith's poetical effusions must provoke a laugh by local allusion ; but they are scarcely good enough to record here, at least at length. A few of the best lines may be given, as a sample of the barrel :—

' A something monastic appears amongst oysters,
  For gregarious they live, yet they sleep in their
    cloisters ;
'Tis observed too, that oysters, when placed in their
    barrel,
Will never presume with their stations to quarrel.

*   *   *   *

' From this let us learn what an oyster can tell us,
And we all shall be better and happier fellows.
Acquiesce in your stations, whenever you've got
    'em ;
Be not proud at the top, nor repine at the bottom,
But happiest they in the middle who live,
And have something to lend, and to spend, and to
    give.'

        ———

' The Bard would fain exchange, alack !
  For precious gold, his crown of laurel ;
His sackbut for a butt of sack,
  His vocal shell for oyster barrel.'

Three lines for an ode in 1806 :—

' Nelson has made the seas our own,
  Then gulp your well-fed oysters down,
    And give the French the *shell.*'

Such were and are some of the Convivial Clubs of Lancashire in the last or present century. Doubtless, similar institutions have existed, and may still exist, in other counties of England. If so, let some of their Secretaries, Recorders, or Rhymesmiths tell in turn their tale.   J. H.

        ———

Old Lady's Pharmacopœia a Hundred Years Ago. —Mrs Delany writes in January 1758 : ' Does Mary cough in the night? Two or three snails boiled in her barley-water or tea-water, or whatever she drinks, might be of great service to her ; taken in time, they have done *wonderful cures. She* must know nothing of it. They give no manner of taste. It would be best nobody should know it but yourself, and I should imagine *six or eight* boiled in a quart of water and strained off and put into a bottle, would be a good way, adding a spoonful or two of that to *every liquid* she takes. They must be fresh done every two or three days, otherwise they grow too thick.'

The Laconic.—In 1773, Mr Fox, when a Lord of the Treasury, voted against his chief, Lord North ; accordingly, on the next evening, while seated on the ministerial bench in the House of Commons, Fox received from the hands of one of the doorkeepers the following laconic note : 'Sir,—His Majesty has thought proper to order a new Commission of the Treasury, in which I do not perceive the name of Charles James Fox.—NORTH.'

JANUARY 31.

St Marcella, widow, 410. St Maidoc, called also Aidan, bishop of Ferus in Ireland, 632. St Serapion, martyr, 1240. St Cyrus and St John, martyrs. St Peter Nolasco, 1258.

Born.—Ben Jonson, 1574, *Westminster.*
Died.—Prince Charles Edward Stuart, 1788; Clara Clairon, 1803, *Paris.*

CHARLES EDWARD STUART.

This unfortunate prince, so noted for his romantic effort to recover a forfeited crown in 1745, and the last person of the Stuart family who maintained any pretensions to it, expired at his house in Florence, at the age of sixty-eight. (It is alleged that, in reality, he died on the 30th of January, but that his friends disguised a fact which would have been thought additionally ominous for the house of Stuart.) The course of

Charles Edward for many years after the *Forty-five* was eccentric; latterly it became discreditable, in consequence of sottishness, which not only made his friends and attached servants desert him, but caused even his wife to quit his house, to which she would never return. All that can be said in extenuation is, that he had been a greatly disappointed man : *magnis incidit ausis.* There is, however, a more specific and effective excuse for his bad habits ; they had been acquired in the course of his extraordinary adventures while skulking for five months in the Highlands. The use of whisky and brandy in that country was in those days unremitting, when the element could be had; and Charles's physical sufferings from hunger, exposure, and fatigue, made him but too eager to take the cup when it was offered to him. Of this fact there are several unmistakeable illustrations in a work quoted below—such as this, for example : Charles, arriving at a hovel belonging to Lochiel, ' took,' says the eye-witness, narrator of the incident, ' a hearty dram, *which he pretty often called for there-*

CHARLES EDWARD STUART.

after, to drink his friends' healths.' ' I have learned,' he said on another occasion, ' to take a hearty dram, while in the Highlands.' *

We often hear of the long perseverance of a certain cast of features, or of some special features in families ; and of the truth of the remark there is no lack of illustrations. The portraits of our own royal family furnish in themselves a very clear example of resemblance continued through a series of generations. The most observable

* Fourth edition of R. Chambers's *History of the Rebellion of* 1745-6. 1845.

peculiarity may be said to consist of a fulness in the lower part of the cheek. It can be traced back not only to the first monarch of the family of Brunswick Lunenburg, but to his mother, the Electress Sophia of Hanover; which shews that it did not come from the paternal line of the family, but more probably from the house of Stuart, of which the Electress was an immediate descendant, being grand-daughter to King James I. No attempt, as far as the writer is aware, has ever been made to trace this physiognomy farther back than the Electress Sophia; and certainly in her mother Elizabeth, the Electress Palatine of Rhine, and in Elizabeth's father, King James, we do not find any such peculiarity prominently brought out.

There is, nevertheless, reason to believe that common points of physiognomy in the Stuart and Hanover families can be traced to a generation prior to the sovereign last-mentioned, who is the common ancestor. The writer, at least, must own that he has been very much struck by the resemblance borne by the recent portraits of our present amiable sovereign to one representing Prince Charles Edward in his later years. Our means of representing the two countenances are limited; yet even in the above wood engraving the parity is too clear not to be generally acknowledged. The fulness of cheek is palpable in both portraits; the form of the mouth is the same in both; and the general aspect, when some allowances are made for difference of age and sex, is identical. It is four generations back from the Prince, and eight from the Queen, to King James—two centuries and a half have elapsed since the births of the two children from whom the subjects of the two portraits are respectively descended: yet there is a likeness exceeding what is found in half the cases of brother and sister. The peculiarity, however, is apparent also in a portrait of Mary of Scotland, taken in her latter years; and it may further be remarked that between the youthful portraits of Prince Charles Edward and those of Albert Edward, Prince of Wales, in his early manhood, a very striking resemblance exists. Thus the perseverance of physiognomy may be said to extend over *three centuries* and *eleven generations*. Most of her Majesty's loyal and affectionate subjects will probably feel that the matter is not without some interest, as reminding them of the connection between the present royal family and that ancient one which it superseded, and as telling us emphatically that Possessor and Pretender are now happily ONE.

THE LIGHTING OF THE BEACONS.

During the threats of invasion from France in 1803-4, the spirit of the people for national defence was wound up to a high pitch of enthusiasm. On the evening of the 31st of January 1804, a beacon at Hume Castle in Berwickshire was lighted in consequence of a mistake, and, other beacons following the example, the volunteers throughout nearly all the southern counties of Scotland were in arms before next morning, and pouring fast to their respective places of rendezvous. It was held to be a most creditable example of earnest and devoted patriotism, and undoubtedly served to create a general feeling of confidence in the self-defensive powers of the island.

Some particulars of this affair have been set down by Sir Walter Scott, who had opportunities of observing what happened on the occasion. 'The men of Liddesdale,' says he, 'the most remote point to the westward which the alarm reached, were so much afraid of being late in the field, that they put in requisition all the horses they could find; and when they had thus made a forced march out of their own county, they turned their borrowed steeds loose to find their

way back through the hills, and they all got back safe to their own stables. Another remarkable circumstance was, the general cry of the inhabitants of the smaller towns for arms, that they might go along with their companions. The Selkirkshire yeomanry made a remarkable march; for although some of the individuals lived at twenty and thirty miles' distance from the place where they mustered, they were nevertheless embodied and in order in so short a period, that they were at Dalkeith, which was their alarm-post, about one o'clock on the day succeeding the first signal, with men and horses in good order, though the roads were in a bad state, and many of the troopers must have ridden forty or fifty miles without drawing bridle.

'The account of the ready patriotism displayed by the country on this occasion, warmed the hearts of Scottishmen in every corner of the world. It reached [in India] the ears of the well-known Dr Leyden, whose enthusiastic love of Scotland, and of his own district of Teviotdale, formed a distinguished part of his character. The account, which was read to him when on a sick-bed, stated (very truly) that the different corps, on arriving at their alarm-posts, announced themselves by their music playing the tunes peculiar to their own districts, many of which have been gathering-signals for centuries. It was particularly remembered, that the Liddesdale men, before mentioned, entered Kelso playing the lively tune—

O wha dare meddle wi' me!
And wha dare meddle wi' me!
My name it is little Jock Elliot,
And wha dare meddle wi' me!

The patient was so delighted with this display of ancient Border spirit, that he sprung up in his bed, and began to sing the old song with such vehemence of action and voice, that his attendants, ignorant of the cause of excitement, concluded that the fever had taken possession of his brain; and it was only the entry of another Borderer, Sir John Malcolm, and the explanation which he was well qualified to give, that prevented them from resorting to means of medical coercion.'

A local newspaper of February 3, 1860, chronicled a festive meeting which had taken place four days before at the village of St Boswells in Roxburghshire, and gave the following curious details *à-propos*: 'On the memorable night in 1804, when the blazing beacons on the Scottish hills told the false tale of a French invasion, a party of volunteers were enjoying themselves in a licensed toll-house at Ancrum Bridge, Roxburghshire. They rushed out on hearing that the beacon was lit on the Eildons, and, in their hurry to march to the appointed rendezvous, forgot to settle the reckoning with their host of the toll-house. When the alarm had subsided, and the volunteers had returned to their homes, they remembered the bill was still to pay, but the difficulty of assembling the whole party retarded the settlement till the anniversary of the day of the false alarm, the 31st January, drew near. They considered this a proper occasion to meet and clear off the old score, and it was then determined to hold an annual meeting by way of commemorating the lighting of the beacons. The toll-keeper removed first to New-town, and then to St Boswells, but the party followed him, and the festival is still held in the Buccleuch Arms' Inn, St Boswells, though none of the members of the original party of 1804 remain to take part in it.'

PERSEVERING PHYSIOGNOMIES.

The remarkable case of resemblance of distant relatives given under the title 'Charles Edward Stuart' could be supported by many others.

Dr Fosbroke, in his valuable historical work entitled *The Berkeley Manuscripts*, gives some interesting anecdotes of Dr Jenner, and, amongst others, makes the following statement: 'A lady whom Dr Jenner met at John Julius Angerstein's, remarked how strongly Dr Jenner's physiognomy re-sembled that of her own ancestor, Judge Jenner, of a family of the name seated in Essex. It is presumed that a branch of this line migrated from Essex into Gloucestershire, where, in the parish of Standish, they have been found for two centuries.'*

The thick under-lip of the imperial family of Austria is often alluded to. It is alleged to have been derived through a female from the princely Polish family of Jagellon. However this may be, we have at least good evidence that the remark is of old date; for Burton, in his *Anatomy of Melancholy*, says, ' The Austrian lip, and those Indians' flat noses, are propagated.'

In the *Notes and Queries* of March 13, 1852, a writer signing VOKAROS presented the following state-ment: 'To trace a family likeness for a century is not at all uncommon. Any one who knows the face of the present Duke of Manchester, will see a strong family likeness to his great ancestor through six generations, the Earl of Manchester of the Com-monwealth, as engraved in Lodge's Portraits. The following instance is more remarkable. Elizabeth Harvey was Abbess of Elstow in 1501. From her brother Thomas is descended, in a direct line, the pre-sent Marquis of Bristol. If any one will lay the portrait of Lord Bristol, in Mr Gage Rokewode's *Thingoe Hundred*, by the side of the sepulchral brass of the Abbess of Elstow, figured in Fisher's *Bedford-shire Antiquities*, he cannot but be struck by the strong likeness between the two faces. This is valuable evi-dence on the disputed point whether portraits were attempted in sepulchral brasses.' A writer in a sub-sequent number, signing 'H. H.,' considered this 'a strong demand on credulity,' and alleged that the Abbess's brass gives the same features as are generally found on brasses of the period, implying that likeness was not then attempted on sepulchral monuments. Yet, on the specific alleged fact of the resemblance between the abbess and the marquis, 'H. H.' gave no contradiction; and the fact, if truly stated by Vo-karos, is certainly not unworthy of attention.

The writer is tempted to add an anecdote which he has related elsewhere. In the summer of 1826, as he was walking with a friend in the neighbourhood of the town of Kirkcudbright, a carriage passed, con-taining a middle-aged gentleman, in whose burly figure and vigorous physiognomy he thought he observed a resemblance to the ordinary portraits of Sir William Wallace. The friend to whom he instantly remarked the circumstance, said, 'It is curious that you should have thought so, for that gentleman is General Dunlop, whose mother [Burns's correspondent] was a Wallace of Craigie, a family claiming to be descended from a brother of the Scottish hero!' As the circumstance makes a rather 'strong demand upon credulity,' the writer, besides averring

* Berkeley Manuscripts, &c., 4to. 1821. P. 220.

that he states no more than truth, may remark that possibly the ordinary portrait of Wallace has been derived from some intermediate member of the Craigie-Wallace family, though probably one not later than the beginning of the seventeenth century. Of the improbability of any portrait of Wallace having ever been painted, and of the anachronisms of the dress and armour, he is, of course, well aware.

In regard to the question of hereditary physiognomy, it might be supposed that, unless where a family keeps within its own bounds, as that of Jacob has done, we are not to expect a perseverance of features through more than a very few generations, seeing that the ancestry of every human being increases enormously in number at each step in the retrogression, so as to leave a man but little chance of deriving any feature from (say) any particular great-great-great-great-grandfather. On the other hand, it is to be considered that there *is* a chance, however small, and it may be only in those few instances that the transmission of likeness is remarked. It is in favour of this view that we so often find a family feature or trait of coun-tenance re-emerging after one or two generations, or coming out unexpectedly in some lateral offshoot. The writer could point to an instance where the beauty of a married woman has passed over her own children to reappear with characteristic form and complexion in her grandchildren. He knows very intimately a young lady who, in countenance, in port, and in a peculiar form of the feet, is precisely a revival of a *great-grandmother*, whom he also knew intimately. He could also point to an instance where a woman of deep olive complexion and elegant oriental figure, the inheritress, perhaps, of the style of some remote an-cestress, has given birth to children of the same brown, sanguineous type as her own brothers and sisters; the whole constitutional system being thus shewn as liable to sinkings and re-emergences. In the case of Queen Victoria and Prince Charles, it is probably re-emergence of type that is chiefly concerned; and the parity may accordingly be considered as in a great degree accidental.

There are some curious circumstances regarding family likenesses, not much, if at all, hitherto noticed, but which have a value in connection with this ques-tion. One is, that a family characteristic, or a resem-blance to a brother, uncle, grandfather, or other rela-tive, may not have appeared throughout life, but will emerge into view after death. The same result is occasionally observed when a person is labouring under the effects of a severe illness. We may presume that the mask which has hitherto concealed or smo-thered up the resemblance, is removed either by emaciation or by the subsidence of some hitherto predominant expression. Another fact equally or even more remarkable, is, that an artist painting A.'s por-trait will fail to give a true likeness, but produce a face strikingly like B.'s,—a brother or cousin,—a person whom he never saw. The writer was once shewn a small half-length portrait, and asked if he could say who was the person represented. He instantly mentioned Mr Gilbert Burns, the poet's brother, whom he had slightly known a few years before. He was then told that the picture had been painted from the poet's own countenance by an artist named Taylor, who never obtained any reputation. This artist had certainly never seen Gilbert Burns. Gilbert and Robert were, moreover, well known to have been of different types, the one taking from the mother, the other from the father. The curious con-sideration arising from this class of facts is, that the same *variation* or *transition*, which nature makes in producing a second child of one set of parents, appears to be made in the mysterious recesses of the plastic mind of the artist.

FEBRUARY

—— Then came old February, sitting
In an old wagon, for he could not ride,
Drawn of two fishes for the season fitting,
Which through the flood before did softly slide
And swim away; yet had he by his side
His plough and harness fit to till the ground,
And tools to prune the trees, before the pride
Of hasting prime did make them bourgeon wide.

SPENSER.

(DESCRIPTIVE.)

FEBRUARY comes in like a sturdy country maiden, with a tinge of the red, hard winter apple on her healthy cheek, and as she strives against the wind, wraps her russet-coloured cloak well about her, while with bent head, she keeps throwing back the long hair that blows about her face, and though at times half blinded by the sleet and snow, still continues her course courageously. Sometimes she seems to shrink. and while we watch her progress, half afraid that she will be blown back again into the dreary waste of Winter. we see that her course is still forward, that she never takes a backward step, but keeps journeying along slowly, and drawing nearer, at every stride, to the Land of Flowers. Between the uplifted curtaining of clouds, that lets in a broad burst of golden sunlight, the skylark hovers like a dark speck, and cheers her with his brief sweet song. while the mellow-voiced blackbird and the speckle-breasted thrush make music

202

among the opening blossoms of the blackthorn, to gladden her way; and she sees faint flushings of early buds here and there, which tell her the long miles of hedgerows will soon be green.

Now there is a stir of life in the long silent fields, a jingling of horse-gear, and the low wave-like murmur of the plough-share, as it cuts through the yielding earth, from the furrows of which there comes a refreshing smell, while those dusky foragers, the rooks, follow close upon the ploughman's heels. Towards the end of the month the tall elm-trees resound with their loud 'cawing' in the early morning, and the nests they are busy building shew darker every day through the leafless branches, until Spring comes and hides them beneath a covering of foliage. Even in smoky cities, in the dawn of the length-ening days, the noisy sparrows come out from under the blackened eaves, and, as they shake the soot from off their wings, give utterance to the delight they feel in notes that sound like the grating jar of a knife-grinder's dry wheel. Now and then the pretty goldfinch breaks out with its short song, then goes peeping about as if wonder-ing why the young green groundsel is so long before putting forth its dull golden flowers. The early warbling of the yellow-hammer is half drowned by the clamorous jackdaws that now congregate about the grey church steeples. Then Winter, who seems to have been asleep, shews his cloudy form once more above the bare hill-tops, from whence he scatters his snow-flakes; while the timid birds cease their song, and again shelter in the still naked hedgerows, seeming to marvel to themselves why he has returned again, after the little daisy buds had begun to thrust their round green heads above the earth, announcing his departure. But his long delay prevents not the willow from shooting out its silvery catkins, nor the graceful hazel from unfurling its pen-dulous tassels; while the elder, as if bidding defiance to Winter, covers its stems with broad buds of green.

The long-tailed field-mouse begins to blink at intervals, and nibble at the stores he hoarded up in autumn; then peeping out and seeing the snow lie among the young violet leaves, at the foot of the oak amid whose roots he has made his nest, he coils himself up again after his repast, and enjoys a little more sleep. Amid the wide-spreading branches over his head, the raven has begun to build; and as he returns with the lock of wool he has rent from the back of some sickly sheep to line his nest, he disturbs the little slumberer below by his harsh, loud croaking. That ominous sound sends the affrighted lambs off with a scamper to their full-uddered dams, while the raven looks down upon them with hungry eye, as if hoping that some one will soon cease its pitiful bleating, and fall a sacrifice to his horny beak. But the silver-frilled daisies will soon star the ground where the lambs now race against each other, and the great band of summer-birds will come from over the sunny sea, and their sweet piping be heard in place of the ominous croaking of the raven.

The mild days of February cause the beauti-fully-formed squirrel to wake out of his short winter sleep, and feed on his hoarded nuts; and he may now be seen balanced by his hind legs and bushy tail, washing his face, on some bare bough near his dray or nest, though at the first sound of the voices of the boys who come to hunt him, he is off, and springs from tree to tree with the agility of a bird. It is only when the trees are naked that the squirrel can be hunted, for it is difficult to catch a glimpse of him when 'the leaves are green and long;' and it is an old country saying, when anything unlikely to be found is lost, that 'you might as well hunt a squirrel when the leaves are out.' Country boys may still be seen hiding at the corner of some out-building, or behind some low wall or fence, with a string in their hands attached to the stic' that supports the sieve, under which they have scattered a few crumbs, or a little corn, to tempt the birds, which become more shy every day, as insect-food is now more plentiful. With what eager eyes the boys watch, and what a joyous shout they raise, as the sieve falls over some feathered prisoner! But there is still ten chances to one in favour of the bird escaping when they place their hands under the half-lifted sieve in the hope of laying hold of it. The long dark nights are still cold to the poor shepherds, who are compelled to be out on the windy hills and downs. attending to the ewes and lambs, for thousands would be lost at this season were it not for their watchful care. In some of the large farmhouses, the lambs that are ailing, or have lost their dams, may be seen lying before the fire in severe weather; and a strange expression—as it seemed to us—beamed from their gentle eyes, as they looked around, bleating for something they had lost; and as they licked our hands, we felt that we should make but poor butchers. And there they lie sheltered, while out-of-doors the wind still roars, and the bare trees toss about their naked arms like maniacs, shaking down the last few withered leaves in which some of the insects have folded up their eggs. Strange power! which we feel, but see not; which drives the fallen leaves before it, like routed armies; and ships, whose thunder shakes cities, it tosses about the deep like floating sea-weeds, and is guided by Him 'who gathereth the winds in His fists.'

'February fill-dyke' was the name given to this wet slushy month by our forefathers, for when the snow melted, the rivers overflowed, the dykes brimmed over, and long leagues of land were under water, which have been drained within the last century; though miles of marshes are still flooded almost every winter, the deep silt left, enriching future harvests. It has a strange appearance to look over a wide stretch of country, where only the tops of the hedgerows or a tree or two are here and there visible. All the old familiar roads that led along pleasant streams to far-away thorpe or grange in summer, are buried beneath the far-spreading waters. And in those hedges water-rats, weasels, field-mice, and many another seldom-seen animal, find harbourage until the waters subside: we have there found the little harvest-mouse, that when full grown is no bigger than a large bee, shivering in the bleak hedgerow.

And in those reedy fens and lonesome marshes

203

where the bittern now booms, and the heron stands alone for hours watching the water, while the tufted plover wails above its head, the wild-fowl shooter glides along noiseless as a ghost in his punt, pulling it on by clutching the over-hanging reeds, for the sound of a paddle would startle the whole flock, and he would never come within shot but for this guarded silence. He bears the beating rain and the hard blowing winds of February without a murmur, for he knows the full-fed mallard—feathered like the richest green velvet—and the luscious teal will be his reward, if he perseveres and is patient. In the midnight moonlight, and the grey dawn of morning, he is out on those silent waters, when the weather almost freezes his very blood, and he can scarcely feel the trigger that he draws; while the edges of frosted water-flags which he clutches, to pull his punt along, seem to cut like swords. To us there has seemed to be at such times 'a Spirit brooding on the waters,' a Presence felt more in those solitudes than ever falls upon the heart amid the busy hum of crowded cities, which has caused us to exclaim unawares, 'God is here!'

Butterflies that have found a hiding-place some-where during winter again appear, and begin to lay their eggs on the opening buds, which when in full leaf will supply food for the future cater-pillars. Amongst these may now be found the new-laid eggs of the peacock and painted-lady butterflies, on the small buds of young nettles, though the plants are only just above ground. Everybody who has a garden now begins to make some little stir in it, when the weather is fine, for the sweet air that now blows abroad mellows and sweetens the newly-dug earth, and gives to it quite a refreshing smell. And all who have had experience, know that to let the ground lie fallow a few weeks after it is trenched, is equal to giving it an extra coating of manure, such virtue is there in the air to which it lies exposed. Hard clods that were difficult to break with the spade when first dug up, will, after lying exposed to the sun and frost, crumble at a touch like a ball of sand. It is pleasant, too, to see the little children pottering about the gardens, unconscious that, while they think they are help-ing, they are in the way of the workmen; to see them poking about with their tiny spades or pointed sticks, and hear their joyous shouts, when they see the first crocus in flower, or find beneath the decaying weeds the upright leaves of the hyacinth. Even the very smallest child, that has but been able to walk a few weeks, can sit down beside a puddle and help to make 'dirt-pies,' while its little frock slips off its white shoulders, and as some helping sister tries to pull it on again, she leaves the marks of her dirty fin-gers on the little one's neck. But a fire kindled to burn the great heap of weeds which Winter has withered and dried, is their chief delight. What little bare sturdy legs come toddling up, the cold red arms bearing another tiny load which they throw upon the fire, and what a clapping of hands there is, as the devouring flame leaps up and licks in the additional fuel which cracks again as the February wind blows the sparks about in starry showers! Pleasant is it also to watch them beside the village brook, after the icy chains of Winter

are unloosened, floating their sticks and bits of wood which they call boats—all our island chil-dren are fond of water—while their watchful mothers are sewing and gossiping at the open cot-tage doors, round which the twined honeysuckles are now beginning to make a show of leaves. All along beside the stream the elder-trees are shew-ing their emerald buds, while a silvery light falls on the downy catkins of the willows, which the country children call palm; while lower down we see the dark green of the great marsh-marigolds, which ere long will be in flower, and make a golden light in the clear brook, in which the leaves are now mirrored. Happy children! they feel the increasing warmth, and find enjoy-ment in the lengthening of the days, for they can now play out-of-doors an hour or more longer than they could a month or two ago, when they were bundled off to bed soon after dark, 'to keep them,' as their mothers say, 'out of mischief.' Sometimes, while digging in February, the gar-dener will turn up a ball of earth as large as a moderate-sized apple; this when broken open will be found to contain the grub of the large stag-beetle in a torpid state. When uncoiled, it is found to be four inches in length. About July it comes out a perfect insect—the largest we have in Britain. Some naturalists assert that it re-mains underground in a larva state for five or six years, but this has not been proved satisfactorily. Many a meal do the birds now gather from the winter greens that remain in the gardens, and unless the first crop of early peas is protected, all the shoots will sometimes be picked off in a morn-ing or two, as soon as they have grown a couple of inches above ground. The wild wood-pigeons are great gatherers of turnip-tops, and it is nothing unusual in the country to empty their maws, after the birds are shot, and wash and dress the tender green shoots found therein. No finer dish of greens can be placed on the table, for the birds swallow none but the young eye-shoots. Larks will at this season sometimes unroof a portion of a corn-stack, to get at the well-filled sheaves. No wonder farmers shoot them; for where they have pulled the thatch off the stack, the wet gets in, finds its way down to the very foundation, and rots every sheaf it falls through. We can never know wholly, what birds find to feed upon at this season of the year; when the earth is sometimes frozen so hard, that it rings under the spade like iron, or when the snow lies knee-deep on the ground. We startle them from under the sheltering hedges; they spring up from the lowly moss, which remains green all through the winter; we see them pecking about the bark, and de-cayed hollow of trees; we make our way through the gorse bushes, and they are there: amid withered grass, and weeds, and fallen leaves, where lie millions of seeds, which the autumn winds scattered, we find them busy foraging; yet what they find to feed upon in many of these places, is still to us a mystery. We know that at this season they pass the greater portion of their time in sleep,—another proof of the great Creator's providence,—so do not require so much food as when busy building, and breed-ing, in spring and summer. They burrow in the snow through little openings hardly visible to human eyes, beneath hedges and bushes, and there they find warmth and food. From the corn-house, stable, or cart-shed, the blackbird comes rushing out with a sound that startles us, as we enter; for there he finds something to feed upon: while the little robin will even peck at the window frame if you have been in the habit of feeding him. On the plum-tree, before the window at which we are now writing, a robin has taken his stand every day throughout the winter, eyeing us at our desk, as he waited for his accustomed crumbs. When the door was opened and all still, he would hop into the kitchen, and there we have found him perched on the dresser, nor did we ever attempt to capture him. If strangers came down the garden-walk, he never flew further away than the privet-hedge, until he was fed. Generally, as the day drew to a close, he mounted his favourite plum-tree, as if to sing us a parting song. We generally threw his food under a thorny, low-growing japonica, which no cat could penetrate, although we have often seen our own Browney girring and swearing and switching his tail, while the bird was safely feeding within a yard of him.

Primroses are now abundant, no matter how severe the Winter may have been. Amid the din and jar of the busy streets of London, the pleasant cry of ' Come buy my pretty primroses' falls cheerfully on the ear, at the close of February. It may be on account of its early appearance, that we fancy there is no yellow flower so delightful to look upon as the delicately-coloured primrose; for the deep golden hue of the celandine and buttercup is glaring when compared with it. There is a beauty, too, in the form of its heart-shaped petals, also in the foliage. Examined by an imaginative eye, the leaves when laid down look like a pleasant green land, full of little hills and hollows, such as we fancy insects—invisible to the naked glance—must delight in wandering over. Such a world Bloomfield pictured as he watched an insect climb up a plantain leaf, and fancied what an immense plain the foot or two of short grass it overlooked must appear in the eye of a little traveller, who had climbed a summit of six inches. In the country they speak of things happening at 'primrose-time:' he died or she was married 'about primrose-time;' for so do they mark the season that lies between the white ridge of Winter, and the pale green border of Spring. Then it is a flower as old and common as our English daisies, and long before the time of Alfred must have gladdened the eyes of Saxon children by its early appearance, as it does the children of the present day. The common coltsfoot has been in flower several weeks, and its leaves are now beginning to appear, for the foliage rarely shews itself on this singular plant until the bloom begins to fade. The black hellebore is also in bloom, and, on account of its resemblance to the queen of summer, is called the Christmas-rose, as it often flowers at that season. It is a pretty ornament on the brow of Winter, whether its deep cup is white or pale pink, and in sheltered situations remains a long time in flower.

Every way there are now signs that the reign of Winter is nearly over: even when he dozes he can no longer enjoy his long sleep, for the snow melts from under him almost as fast as it falls, and he feels the rounded buds breaking out beneath him. The flush of golden light thrown from the primroses, as they catch the sunshine, causes him to rub his dazed eyes, and the singing of the unloosened meadow-runnels falls with a strange sound on his cold, deadened ear. He knows that Spring is hiding somewhere near at hand, and that all Nature is waiting to break out into flower and song, when he has taken his departure.

A great change has taken place almost unseen. We cannot recall the day when the buds first caught our eye—tiny green dots which are now opening into leaves that are covering the lilac-trees. We are amazed to see the hawthorn hedge, which a week or two ago we passed unnoticed, now bursting out into the pale green flush of Spring—the most beautiful of all green hues. We feel the increasing power of the sun; and windows which have been closed, and rendered air-tight to keep out the cold, are now thrown open to let in the refreshing breeze, which is shaking out the sweet buds, and the blessed sunshine—the gold of heaven — which God in His goodness showers alike upon the good and the evil.

(HISTORICAL.)

February was one of the two months (January being the other) introduced into the Roman Calendar by Numa Pompilius, when he extended the year to twelve of these periods. Its name arose from the practice of religious expiation and purification which took place among the Romans at the beginning of this month (*Februare*, to expiate, to purify). It has been on the whole an ill-used month, perhaps in consequence of its noted want (in the northern hemisphere) of what is pleasant and agreeable to the human senses. Numa let fall upon it the doom which was unavoidable for some one of the months, of having, three out of four times, a day less than even those which were to consist of thirty days. That is to say, he arranged that it should have only twenty-nine days, excepting in leap years; when, by the intercalation of a day between the 23rd and 24th, it was to have thirty. No great occasion here for complaint. But when Augustus chose to add a thirty-first day to August, that the month named from him might not lack in the dignity enjoyed by six other months of the year, he took it from February, which could least spare it, thus reducing it to twenty-eight in all ordinary years. In our own parliamentary arrangement for the reformation of the calendar, it being necessary to drop a day out of each century excepting those of which the ordinal number could be divided by four, it again fell to the lot of February to be the sufferer. It was deprived of its 29th day for all such years, and so it befell in the year 1800, and will in 1900, 2100, 2200, &c.

Verstegan informs us that, among our Saxon ancestors, the month got the name of *Sprout-kale*, from the fact, rather conspicuous in gardening, of the sprouting of cabbage at this ungenial season. The name of Sol-monatt was afterwards conferred upon it, in consequence of the return of the luminary of day from the low course in the heavens which for some time he had been running. ' The common emblematical representation of February is, a man in a sky-coloured dress, bearing in his hand the astronomical sign Pisces.'—*Brady.*

CHARACTERISTICS OF FEBRUARY.

The average temperature of January, which is the lowest of the year, is but slightly advanced in February ; say from 40° to 41° Fahrenheit. Nevertheless, while frosts often take place during the month, February is certainly more characterised by rain than by snow, and our unpleasant sensations during its progress do not so much arise from a strictly low temperature, as from the harsh damp feeling which its airs impart. Usually, indeed, the cold is intermitted by soft vernal periods of three or four days, during which the snow-drop and crocus are enabled to present themselves above ground. Gloomy, chilly, rainy days are a prominent feature of the month, tending, as has been observed, to a flooding of the country ; and we all feel how appropriate it is that the two signs of the zodiac connected with the month— Aquarius and Pisces—should be of such watery associations. Here, again, however, we are liable to a fallacy, in imagining that February is the most rainy of the months. Its average depth of fall, 4·21 inches, is, in reality, equalled by three other months, January, August, and September, and exceeded by October, November, and December, as shewn by a rain-gauge kept for thirty years in the Isle of Bute.

At London, the sun is above the horizon on the 1st of February from 7h. 42m. to 4h. 47m., in all 9h. 5m. At the last day of the month, the sun is above the horizon 10h. 45m.

PROVERBS REGARDING FEBRUARY.

The tendency of this month to wet and its uncertain temperature, as hovering between Winter and Spring, are expressed proverbially :

' February fill the dyke [ditch]
Either with the black or white :'

i. e. either with rain or snow. Popular wisdom, however, recognises an advantage in its adhering to the wintry character, the above rhyme having occasionally added to it,

' If it be white, it 's the better to like ;'

while other rhymes support the same view. Thus, in Ray's collection of English proverbs, we have :

' The Welshman would rather see his dam on her bier,
Than see a fair Februeer ; '

and from the Scotch collections :

' A' the months o' the year
Curse a fair Februeer.'

The Norman peasant pronounces virtually to the same purpose :

' Février qui donne neige,
Bel été nous pleige.'

Connected evidently with this general idea about February, is the observation regarding Candlemas Day, to be adverted to in its place.

First of February.

ST IGNATIUS.

Ignatius occupies an important place in the history of Christianity, as an immediate disciple and successor of the apostles. As bishop of Antioch, in which position he acted for forty years, he is admitted to have been a perfect model of virtue and pious zeal. Under the Emperor Trajan, this holy man was sent to Rome to be devoured by wild beasts —a martyrdom to which he submitted with the usual resignation and joy. What was left of the feeble old man was carefully brought back to Antioch, and preserved for the veneration of the faithful. There are, however, more important relics of the martyr in four epistles, a translation of which was published by Archbishop Wake, in 1693.

ST BRIDGET, OR ST BRIDE.

St Bridget was a native of Ireland, and has the honour to share with St Patrick the distinction of exercising the spiritual patronage of that island. She was a daughter of one of the princes of Ulster, and was born at Fochart, in that province, soon after the first conversion of Ireland to the Christian faith. As she grew up she became remarkable for her piety, and having taken the monastic vow, she was the first nun in Ireland, and has ever since been reverenced by the Irish Romanists as the mother of nunneries in that country. She built her first cell under a large oak, which had perhaps been the site of pagan worship in earlier times, and from whence it was named Kil-dara, or the cell of the oak. Round this first Irish nunnery eventually arose the city of Kildare. After having astonished the Catholic world by a number of extraordinary miracles, which are duly chronicled in her legends, she died on the 1st of February 523, and was buried at Kildare. A tradition was current among the Irish, that she was buried in the church at Downpatrick, which boasted also of possessing the bodies of St Patrick and St Columba. Giraldus Cambrensis has recorded how, in 1185, soon after the conquest of Ulster by John de Courci, the bodies of the three saints were found, lying side by side, in a triple vault, St Patrick occupying the place in the middle, and how they were all three translated into the cathedral. This event appears to have created a great sensation at the time, and was commemorated in the following Latin distich, which is frequently quoted in the old monastic chronicles:

' In burgo Duno tumulo tumulantur in uno
Brigida, Patricius, atque Columba pius.''

For some cause or other Bridget was a popular saint in England and Scotland, where she was better known by the corrupted or abbreviated name of St Bride, and under this name a number of churches were dedicated to her. We need only mention St Bride's Church in Fleet-street, London.

Adjoining to St Bride's Churchyard, Fleet-street, is an ancient well dedicated to the saint, and commonly called Bride's Well. A palace erected near by took the name of Bridewell. This being given by Edward VI. to the city of London as a workhouse for the poor and a house of correction, the name became associated in the popular mind with houses having the same purpose in view. Hence it has arisen that the pure and innocent Bridget—the first of Irish nuns—is now inextricably connected in our ordinary national parlance with a class of beings of the most opposite description.

Born.—Tiberius Hemsterhuys, 1685. *Groningen;* Edward Coke, Lord Chief Justice, 1551-2, *Mileham ;* John Philip Kemble, actor, 1757, *Prescot.*

Died.—Pope Alexander VIII., 1691; Charles Duke of Shrewsbury, 1717 : Sir Hew Dalrymple, President of the Court of Session, 1737 ; William Aiton, botanist, 1793, *Kew ;* Dr John Lemprière (*Classical Dictionary*), 1824 ; Edward Donovan, naturalist, 1837 ; Mary Wollstonecraft Shelley (*née* Godwin), novelist, 1851.

THE DUKE OF SHREWSBURY.

The fortunes of this distinguished nobleman present a remarkable instance of the attainment of the highest honours of rank and state, but limited to his own individual enjoyment of such distinctions. He was the elder son of the eleventh Earl of Shrewsbury, who died of a wound received in his duel with George Villiers, second Duke of Buckingham, at Barnes, as described at page 129. He was born in the year of the Restoration, and had Charles the Second for his godfather. In 1694, he was created Marquis of Alton and Duke of Shrewsbury, and installed a Knight of the Garter. His grace was a prominent statesman in the reigns of William and Mary, Queen Anne, and George I., and filled some of the highest official situations. He had quitted the Church of Rome and become a Protestant in 1679, and by his steady adherence to the Protestant cause had incurred the displeasure of

James II. He was one of the seven who, in June 1688, joined the celebrated association, inviting over the Prince of Orange. At the demise of Queen Anne (who delivered to him the Treasurer's staff on her death-bed), the Duke of Shrewsbury was, at the same time, Lord Lieutenant of Ireland, Lord High Treasurer of Great Britain, and Lord Chamberlain,—a circumstance, says Sir Bernard Burke, (*Peerage and Baronetage,* edit. 1862,) previously unparalleled in our history. His grace, on that occasion, secured the Hanoverian accession, by at once signing the order for proclaiming George I. The Duke married the daughter of the Marquis of Palliotti, but died without issue, when the dukedom and marquisate expired, and the earldom, &c., reverted to his cousin.

THE TWO PRINCES OF ANAMABOE.

In the London season of 1749, two black princes of Anamaboe were in fashion at all the assemblies. Their story is very much like that of Oroonoko, and is briefly this : A Moorish king, who had entertained, with great hospitality, a British captain trafficking on the coast of Africa, reposed such confidence in him as to intrust him with his son, about eighteen years of age, and another sprightly youth, to be brought to England and educated in the European manners. The captain received them, and basely sold them for slaves. He shortly after died ; the ship coming to England, the officers related the whole affair ; upon which the Government sent to pay their ransom, and they were brought to England, and put under the care of the Earl of Halifax, then at the head of the Board of Trade, who had them clothed and educated. They were afterwards received in the higher circles, and introduced to the King (George II.) on the 1st of February. In this year they appeared at Covent Garden Theatre, to see the tragedy of *Oroonoko,* where they were received with a loud clap of applause, which they returned with ' a genteel bow.' The tender interview between Imoinda and Oroonoko so affected the Prince, that he was obliged to retire at the end of the fourth act. His companion remained, but wept all the time so bitterly, that it affected the audience more than the play.

WILLIAM AITON AND THE 'HORTUS KEWENSIS.'

In the neatly kept churchyard of Kew, in Surrey, rest the remains of William Aiton, ' late gardener to his Majesty at Kew,' a reputation which he largely extended by the publication of the famed Catalogue of Plants in the royal gardens, entitled the *Hortus Kewensis.* He had been superintendent of the gardens from their first establishment ; and in honour of his professional abilities and private worth, at his funeral the pall was supported by Sir Joseph Banks, the Rev D. Goodenough, Dr Pitcairne, Mr Dundas (of Richmond), and Zoffany, the painter.

THE BELL ROCK LIGHTHOUSE.

For more than half a century has this noble structure braved the storms of the German Ocean without any of its masonry being displaced. It was first lighted on the 1st of February 1811.

The Inch Cape Rock, Scape Rock, as it is termed in the oldest charts,* or Bell Rock, lies on

THE BELL ROCK LIGHTHOUSE.

the coast about twenty-four miles east of Dundee harbour, in the track of all vessels making for the estuaries of the Friths of Forth and Tay, from a foreign voyage. It was, from a very remote period, the scene of numerous shipwrecks. The top of the rock being visible at low water, one of the abbots of Aberbrothock attached to it a framework and a bell, which, being rung by the waves, warned mariners to avoid the fatal reef. A tradition respecting this bell has been embodied by Southey in his ballad of 'Ralph the Rover.' A notorious pirate of this name is said to have cut the bell from the framework, 'to plague the Abbot of Aberbrothock,' and some time after he is said to have received the just punishment of his wickedness, by being shipwrecked on the spot.

The necessity of erecting a lighthouse upon this rock was painfully shewn in the year 1799, when about seventy vessels were wrecked on the coast of Scotland in a terrific storm. This calamity drew the attention of the Commissioners of the Northern Lighthouses to the Inch Scape, and Mr Robert Stevenson, the scientific engineer of the Lighthouse Board, erected the present edifice from his own designs, between the years 1807 and 1811. The rock being bare only during short daily intervals, the work necessarily became very troublesome, as well as in some degree critical. All the stones were shaped and prepared at

* Inch Scaup appears to be the true old name of the rock, implying something at once an island and a bed of shell-fish.

208

Arbroath; and the several courses having been dove-tailed, and cemented together by joggles of stone and oaken trenails, the whole building, when erected upon the rock and properly fixed and cramped, was constituted into one solid mass, which seems likely to defy the elements for centuries. The light-room is of cast-iron, and the entire height of the pillar is 115 feet. The cost was £60,000. In the arrangements, the primitive contrivance of the bell has not been forgotten: during stormy and foggy weather, the machinery which causes the reflectors to revolve, is made to ring two large bells, each weighing about 12 cwt., in order to warn the seaman of his danger when too nearly approaching the rock.

When Sir Walter Scott visited this lighthouse in 1815, he wrote in the album kept there the following lines:

PHAROS LOQUITUR.

'Far on the bosom of the deep,
    O'er these wild shelves my watch I keep:
A ruddy gem of changeful light,
    Bound on the dusky brow of Night;
The seaman bids my lustre hail,
    And scorns to strike his tim'rous sail.'

A work precisely similar to the erection of the Bell Rock Lighthouse—the formation of a lighthouse on the rock called Skerryvore, in the Hebrides—was executed between 1835 and 1844, by Alan Stevenson, son of Robert, under circumstances of even greater difficulty and peril: such are among the works which give great engineers a kind of parallel place in our pacific age to that of the mythic heroes of a primitive one. Of each work, an elaborate detail has been published by their respective chiefs.

A curious circumstance connected with the building of the Inch Scape Lighthouse is mentioned in a late work: 'One horse, the property of James Craw, a labourer in Arbroath, is believed to have drawn the entire materials of the building. This animal latterly became a *pensioner* of the Lighthouse Commissioners, and was sent by them to graze on the island of Inchkeith, where it died of old age in 1813. Dr John Barclay, the celebrated anatomist, had its bones collected and arranged in his museum, which he bequeathed at his death to the Royal College of Surgeons [Edinburgh], and in their museum the skeleton of the *Bell Rock horse* may yet be seen.'*

The way Shrews were Tamed long ago.

'Madam,' said Dr Johnson, in a conversation with Mrs Knowles, 'we have different modes of restraining evil: stocks for the men, a *ducking-stool for women*, and a pound for beasts.' On other occasions, the great lexicographer speaks very complacently of the famous remedy for curing shrews, so much approved by our forefathers, but, fortunately, already a little out of fashion in the worthy Doctor's time. One of the last instances on record in which the ducking-stool is mentioned as an instrument of justice, is in the *London Evening Post* of April 27, 1745. 'Last week,' says the journal, 'a woman that

* Jervise's Memorials of Angus and the Mearns. 4to 1861, p. 175.

keeps the Queen's Head ale-house at Kingston, in Surrey, was ordered by the court to be ducked for scolding, and was accordingly placed in the chair, and ducked in the river Thames, under Kingston bridge, in the presence of 2,000 or 3,000 people.'

According to verbal tradition, the punishment of the ducking-stool was inflicted at Kingston and other places up to the beginning of the present century. However, the 'stool' was but rarely used at this period; though it was very extensively employed in the sixteenth and seventeenth centuries.

M. Misson, an intelligent Frenchman, who travelled in England about the year 1700, gives the following interesting description of the ducking-stool. 'This method,' he says, 'of punishing scolding women is funny enough. They fasten an arm-chair to the end of two strong beams, twelve or fifteen feet long, and parallel to each other. The chair hangs upon a sort of axle, on which it plays freely, so as always to remain in the horizontal position. The scold being well fastened in her chair, the two beams are then placed, as near to the centre as possible, across a post on the water-side; and being lifted up behind, the chair, of course, drops into the cold element.

The ducking is repeated according to the degree of shrewishness possessed by the patient, and

DUCKING STOOL, AS PRACTISED AT BROADWATER, NEAR LEOMINSTER.

generally has the effect of cooling her immoderate heat, at least for a time.' An illustration exactly answering to this description is given as the frontispiece of an old chap-book, entitled *Strange and Wonderful Relation of the Old Woman who was drowned at Ratcliff Highway, a fortnight ago.*

DUCKING-CHAIR AT A VILLAGE WELL.

Apparently, in the case of this aged person, the administrators of the punishment had given a dip too much; and, of course, in such rough proceedings, a safe measure must have been difficult to

hit. A second illustration, which has been furnished by a gentleman well acquainted with English village life, represents the apparatus as erected close to a watering trough, into which the patient, of course, was let down by the cross-tree, from which the seat depended. Presuming this to be the place whither the females of the village resorted for supplies of water for domestic purposes, we must see that the site was appropriate; for, somehow, places where water is obtained, are often the scene of very fiery displays. To make the fountain of the evil the means of the punishment was in accordance with the fitness of things. It is but natural to suppose that before any scold was dipped, the community must have suffered a good deal at her hands. When at length the hour of retribution arrived, we can imagine the people to have been in a state of no small excitement. Labour would be deserted. All the world would be out of doors. The administrators would appear in young eyes to have something of a heroic bearing. Men would shout; women would look timidly from doors; dogs would yelp. The recalcitrations of the peccant dame, her *crescendo* screamings and invectives, the final smotherment of her cries in the cold but not cooling element, must have furnished a scene for a Hogarth or a Wilkie. Failing such illustrations, the reader will accept one from Clarke's *History of Ipswich*, in which a good deal of what is characteristic of such scenes is displayed. It is impossible to view

the picture with perfect gravity; and yet modern humanity, it must be admitted, cannot quite sanction the idea of employing such means of correction for one of the weaker, if not always the gentler sex.

Mr Cole, the antiquary, writing about 1780, says: 'In my time, when I was a boy and lived with my grandfather in the great corner house at the bridge-foot, next to Magdalen College, Cambridge, and rebuilt since by my uncle, Joseph Cock, I remember to have seen a woman ducked for scolding. The chair hung by a pulley fastened to a beam about the middle of the bridge; and the woman having been fastened in the chair, she was let under water three times successively, and then taken out. The bridge was then of timber,

before the present stone bridge of one arch was built. The ducking-stool was constantly hanging in its place, and on the back panel of it was an engraving representing devils laying hold of scolds. Some time after, a new chair was erected in the place of the old one, having the same device carved on it, and well painted and ornamented.' That the cold water cure had a wholesome effect upon the tongues of not a few of the fair sex is agreed on by all old writers who mention the subject, poets as well as prosaists. John Gay, in his *Pastorals*, expresses himself very decisively on this point:

'I'll speed me to the pond, where the high stool
  On the long plank hangs o'er the muddy pool:
  That stool, *the dread of every scolding quean.*'

210

The term *Cucking-stool* is sometimes used interchangeably for ducking-stool, the resemblance of the names having apparently led to an idea that they meant the same thing. In reality, the cucking-stool was a seat of a kind which delicacy forbids us particularly to describe, used for the exposure of flagitious females at their own doors or in some other public place, as a means of putting upon them the last degree of ignominy. In Scotland. an ale-wife who exhibited bad drink to the public was put upon the *Cock stule*, and the ale, like such relics of John Girder's feast as were totally uneatable (see *Bride of Lammermoor*), was given to 'the pure folk.' In Leicester, in 1457, a scold was put upon the cuck-stool before her own door, and then carried to the four gates of the town. The practice seems a strange example of the taste of our ancestors; yet in connection with the fact, it is worthy of being kept in mind, that among the ceremonies formerly attending the installation of the Pope, was the public placing of him in a similar chair, called the *Sedes Stercoraria*, with a view to remind him that he was after all but a mortal man.

In Lysons's *Environs of London*, there is an account for the making of a cucking-stool for Kingston-upon-Thames; it is dated 1572, and is as follows:

	£	s.	d.
The making of the cucking-stool .	0	8	0
Iron-work for the same . . .	0	3	0
Timber for the same	0	7	6
Three brasses for the same, and three wheels	0	4	10
	£1	3	4

This rather expensive cucking-stool must have been in very frequent use in the good town of Kingston ; for in the old account books there are numerous entries of money paid for its repairs. In fact, Kingston seems to have enjoyed quite a pre-eminence in the matter of shrews, to judge by the amount of money laid out in their taming. Shrewsbury itself lags far behind in the cold-water cure ; for, as stated in the *History of Shropshire*, it was only in the year 1669 that an order was issued by the corporation of the town, that 'a ducking-stool be erected for the punishment of scolds.'

The ducking-stool, the oldest known remedy for evil tongues—so old, indeed, that it is mentioned in the Doomsday Survey, in the account of the city of Chester—was superseded to a certain extent, in the seventeenth century and later, by another piece of machinery, called the *Branks*. The branks was homœopathic rather than hydropathic ; and connoisseurs were enthusiastic in asserting that it possessed great advantages over the ducking-stool. Old Dr Plot, in his *History of Staffordshire*, informs his readers that 'they have an artifice at Newcastle-under-Lyne and Walsall, for correcting of scolds, which it does so effectually, that I look upon it as much to be preferred to the cucking-stool, which not only endangers the health of the party, but also gives the tongue liberty 'twixt every dip, to neither of which this is at all liable : it being such a bridle for the tongue as not only quite deprives them of speech, but brings shame for the trans-

gression and humility thereupon, before 'tis taken off: which being put upon the offender by order of the magistrate, and fastened with a padlock behind, she is led round the town by an officer, to her shame, nor is it taken off till after the party begins to shew all external signes imaginable of humiliation and amendment.' The warm-hearted Doctor gives a representation of a pair of branks, as seen in various cities of Staffordshire about the year 1680. The instruments look formidable

SCOLD'S BRIDLE OR BRANK.

enough, consisting of hoops of metal passed round the neck and head, opening by means of hinges at the sides, and closed by a staple with a padlock at the back ; a plate within the hoop projecting inwards pressed upon the tongue, and formed an effectual gag. We must take it upon the assurance of so learned a man as Dr Plot, who was keeper of the Ashmolean Museum, and Professor of Chemistry at Oxford, and who dedicated his work to King James II., that the brank was a very harmless instrument, and 'much to be preferred to the cucking-stool.'

That the brank, or 'scold's bridle,' is of much more modern origin than the ducking-stool, there seems little doubt. The latter was certainly in use among our Saxon forefathers, whereas no example of the brank has been noticed of greater antiquity than that preserved in the church of Walton-on-Thames, Surrey, which bears the date 1633, with the distich :

'Chester presents Walton with a bridle,
　To curb women's tongues that talk so idle.'

Tradition alleges that the instrument was given for the use of the parish by a neighbouring gentleman, of the name of Chester, who lost an estate through the indiscreet babbling of a mischievous woman to an uncle, from whom he had considerable expectations. This Walton bridle—which may still be seen in the vestry of the parish church—is a far less terrible-looking engine than Dr Plot's. It is made of thin iron, and so contrived as to pass over and round the head, where the whole clasps together, and is fastened at the back of the neck by a small padlock. The bridle-bit, as it is called, is a flat piece of iron. about two inches long and one inch broad, which goes into the mouth, and keeps down the tongue by its pressure, while an aperture in front admits the nose.

There are still numerous specimens of branks preserved in different private and public antiquarian collections throughout England. There was, until lately, a brank in the old Chesterfield poor-house, Derbyshire ; and there is still one at the Guildhall, Lichfield ; one at Hamstall-Ridware, Staffordshire ; one at Walsall, near Wolverhampton ; and one at Holme, Lancashire. There was one in the town-hall at Leicester, now in private hands in that town. A brank which is recorded in 1623 as existing at Macclesfield. and is still seen in the town-hall, has been actually used, as stated by a writer in the *Archæological Journal* of September 1856, within the memory of an aged official of the municipal authorities in that town. In Scotland, likewise, there are sundry specimens of gossips' bridles still extant; and it seems, from various notices, that its use was quite as frequent formerly in the northern kingdom as south of the Tweed. Pennant, in his *Tour in Scotland*, in 1772, records its use at Langholm, in Dumfriesshire, where the local magistrates had, it appears, their little piece of machinery in constant readiness for any emergency. Dr Wilson, in his *Prehistoric Annals of Scotland*, mentions the brank as a Scottish instrument of ecclesiastical punishment, for the coercion of scolds and slanderous gossips. The use of the apparatus occurs in the Burgh Records of Glasgow as early as 1574, when two quarrelsome females were bound to keep the peace, or, on further offending, 'to be brankit.' In the records of the Kirk Session at Stirling, for 1600, 'the brankes' are mentioned as the punishment for a shrew. In St Mary's church, at St Andrew's, a memorable specimen still exists, known as the 'Bishop's brank,' sketched and noticed in the Abbotsford edition of *The Monastery*.

Ducking-stools and branks, however, with all their terrors, seem to have been insufficient to frighten the shrews of former days out of their bad propensities. In addition to them the terrors of the Ecclesiastical Courts were held over their heads, as seen, among others, in the records of the diocese of London, which contain numerous entries of punishments awarded to scolds. The same in the provinces. In 1614, dame Margaret, wife of John Bache, of Chaddesley, was prosecuted at the sessions as a 'comon skould, and a sower of strife amongste her neyghbours, and hath bynn presented for a skoulde at the leetc houlden for the manour of Chadsley, and for misbehavying her tonge towards her mother-in-law, at a visytacon at Bromsgrove, and was *excommunicated* therefore.' The excommunication appears to have had little effect in these and other cases ; for only a few years after the date above recorded, the magistrates of the town of Kidderminster, not far from Chadsley, voted the purchase of 'a bridle for scolds.' Whether the 'bridle' was ever more popular than the 'stoole' is an open question; but, at any rate, both carried it, in the majority of instances, over the thunder of the Church. The thing called excommunication somehow never did thrive in England—not even for the taming of shrews.*

WILL OF A SMALL FARMER OF THE THIRTEENTH CENTURY.

From an inventory of the effects of Reginald Labbe, a small farmer, who died in 1293, we obtain a curious view of the circumstances of an individual of the agricultural class, at that early period.

* Notices regarding the Ducking-Stool and Branks are scattered throughout *Notes and Queries*. There are also some papers on the subject in the *Archæologia* and *Gentleman's Magazine*. The most exhaustive treatment of it is to be found in a paper by Mr Llewellynn Jewitt, in his very pleasing antiquarian miscellany entitled *The Reliquary*.

Reginald Labbe died worth chattels of the value of thirty-three shillings and eight pence, leaving no ready money. His goods comprised a cow and calf, two sheep and three lambs, three hens, a bushel and a half of wheat, a seam of barley, a seam and a half of fodder, a seam of 'dragge' or mixed grain, and one halfpenny worth of salt. His wardrobe consisted of a tabard, tunic, and hood ; and his 'household stuffe' seems to have been limited to a bolster, a rug, two sheets, a brass dish, and a tripod or trivet, the ordinary cooking apparatus of those times. Possessing no ready money, his bequests were made in kind. A sheep worth ten pence is left to the high altar of 'Neweton,' perhaps Newton-Valence, near Alton, Hants ; and another of the same value to the altar and fabric fund of 'Eakewode,' possibly Oakwood, near Dorking, Surrey. His widow Ida received a moiety of the testator's cow, which was valued at five shillings, and Thomas Fitz-Norreys was a co-partner in its calf, to the extent of a fourth. It is worthy of note, that the expenditure of the executors upon the funeral, the 'month's-mind,' and in proving the will of Reginald Labbe, consumed something more than a third of all he left behind him, being in the proportion of 11s. 9d. to 33s. 8d. Some of the items are singular. One penny was paid for digging his grave, twopence for tolling the bell, sixpence for making his will, and eightpence for proving it, 'with the counsel of clerks ;' in other words, under legal advice. We may safely multiply these sums by fifteen, perhaps by twenty, to arrive at the value of money in the thirteenth as compared with the nineteenth century ; and by this process we shall find that the lawyer or clerk who prepared the will received a fee not greatly disproportioned to the modern charge for such professional assistance. The mourners bidden to the funeral, some of whom, probably, bore Reginald's body to its resting-place, were refreshed with bread and cheese and beer to the amount of six shillings: the same homely fare at the 'month's-mind' cost the estate two shillings and eightpence. The scribe who prepared this account for the executors was remunerated with threepence, a large sum having regard to the amount of labour.

The document is in Latin, from which Mr Hudson Turner prepared the preceding abstract.

FEBRUARY 2.

The Purification of the Virgin, commonly called Candlemas Day.

St. Lawrence, Archbishop of Canterbury, 619.

Born.—Bishop W. Thomas, 1613, *Bristol ;* William Borlase, D.D., 1696, *Cornwall ;* John Nichols, 1744, *Islington.*

Died.—Sir Owen Tudor, 1461 ; Baldassarre Castiglione, 1529 ; Giovanni di Palestrina, 1594 ; Archbishop John Sharp, 1714 ; Pope Clement XIII., 1769 ; Francis Hayman, painter, 1776 ; James Stuart, 1788 ; Dr Olinthus G. Gregory, mathematician, 1841.

DR BORLASE, THE CORNISH ANTIQUARY.

This accomplished gentleman was born at Pendeen, in the parish of St Just, in Cornwall, where his family had been settled from the reign of King William Rufus. He was vicar of St Just, and rector of Ludgvan ; and by collecting mineral fossils in the rich copper-works of the latter parish.

he was encouraged to investigate the natural history of his native county. Its numerous monuments of remote antiquity, which had till then been nearly neglected, next led him to study the religion and customs of the ancient Britons. He wrote a *Natural History of Cornwall*, as well as illustrated its Antiquities, historical and monumental, and he contributed many curiosities to the Ashmolean Museum. He was equally attentive to his pastoral duties; he greatly improved the high roads of St Just, which were more numerous than in any parish in Cornwall. He was the friend of Pope, whom he furnished with the greater part of his materials for forming his grotto at Twickenham. Pope acknowledged the gift, in a letter to Dr Borlase, in which he says, 'I am much obliged to you for your valuable collection of Cornish diamonds. I have placed them where they may best represent yourself, *in a shade, but shining.*'

Over one of the arches of the entries to Pope's grotto—which in reality was a passage to his garden under the adjacent public road — is fixed, among other notable objects, a large ammonite; over a corresponding arch, balancing this object, is the cast of the fossil. One feels it to be a curious circumstance that the great poet should have thus become familiar with an example of the huge cephalopoda of the primitive world, long before any one knew that singular history which geology now assigns them. It must be matter of conjecture whether Pope got his ammonite and its cast from Dr Borlase or some other naturalist.

Candlemas.

From a very early, indeed unknown date in the Christian history, the 2nd of February has been held as the festival of the Purification of the Virgin, and it is still a holiday of the Church of England. From the coincidence of the time with that of the *Februation* or purification of the people in pagan Rome, some consider this as a Christian festival engrafted upon a heathen one, in order to take advantage of the established habits of the people; but the idea is at least open to a good deal of doubt. The popular name Candlemas is derived from the ceremony which the Church of Rome dictates to be observed on this day; namely, a blessing of candles by the clergy, and a distribution of them amongst the people, by whom they are afterwards carried lighted in solemn procession. The more important observances were of course given up in England at the Reformation; but it was still, about the close of the eighteenth century, customary in some places to light up churches with candles on this day.

At Rome, the Pope every year officiates at this festival in the beautiful chapel of the Quirinal. When he has blessed the candles, he distributes them with his own hand amongst those in the church, each of whom, going singly up to him, kneels to receive it. The cardinals go first; then follow the bishops, canons, priors, abbots, priests, &c., down to the sacristans and meanest officers of the church. According to Lady Morgan, who witnessed the ceremony in 1820—'When the last of these has gotten his candle, the poor *conser-*

vatori, the representatives of the Roman senate and people, receive theirs. This ceremony over, the candles are lighted, the Pope is mounted in his chair and carried in procession, with hymns chanting, round the ante-chapel; the throne is stripped of its splendid hangings; the Pope and cardinals take off their gold and crimson dresses, put on their usual robes, and the usual mass of the morning is sung.' Lady Morgan mentions that similar ceremonies take place in all the parish churches of Rome on this day.

It appears that in England, in Catholic times, a meaning was attached to the size of the candles, and the manner in which they burned during the procession; that, moreover, the reserved parts of the candles were deemed to possess a strong supernatural virtue:

'This done, each man his candle lights,
　　Where chiefest seemeth he,
Whose taper greatest may be seen;
　　And fortunate to be,
Whose candle burneth clear and bright:
　　A wondrous force and might
Doth in these candles lie, which if
　　At any time they light,
They sure believe that neither storm
　　Nor tempest doth abide,
Nor thunder in the skies be heard,
　　Nor any devil's spide,
Nor fearful sprites that walk by night,
　　Nor hurts of frost or hail,' &c. *

The festival, at whatever date it took its rise, has been designed to commemorate the churching or purification of Mary; and the candle-bearing is understood to refer to what Simeon said when he took the infant Jesus in his arms, and declared that he was a *light to lighten the Gentiles*. Thus literally to adopt and build upon metaphorical expressions, was a characteristic procedure of the middle ages. Apparently, in consequence of the celebration of Mary's purification by candle-bearing, it became customary for women to carry candles with them, when, after recovery from child-birth, they went to be, as it was called, *churched*. A remarkable allusion to this custom occurs in English history. William the Conqueror, become, in his elder days, fat and unwieldy, was confined a considerable time by a sickness. 'Methinks,' said his enemy the King of France, 'the King of England lies long in childbed.' This being reported to William, he said, 'When I am churched, there shall be a thousand lights in France!' And he was as good as his word; for, as soon as he recovered, he made an inroad into the French territory, which he wasted wherever he went with fire and sword.

At the Reformation, the ceremonials of Candlemas day were not reduced all at once. Henry VIII. proclaimed in 1539: 'On Candlemas day it shall be declared, that the bearing of candles is done in memory of Christ, the spiritual light, whom Simeon did prophesy, as it is read in the church that day.' It is curious to find it noticed as a custom down to the time of Charles II., that when lights were brought in at nightfall, people would say—'God send us the light of

* Barnaby Googe's Translation of Naogeorgus, in the *Popish Kingdom*. Ellis's Edition of Brand's *Popular Antiquities*.

heaven!' The amiable Herbert, who notices the custom, defends it as not superstitious. Somewhat before this time, we find Herrick alluding to the customs of Candlemas eve: it appears that the plants put up in houses at Christmas were now removed.

> 'Down with the rosemary and bays,
>   Down with the mistletoe:
> Instead of holly now upraise
>   The greener box for show.
>
> The holly hitherto did sway,
>   Let box now domineer,
> Until the dancing Easter day
>   Or Easter's eve appear.
>
> The youthful box, which now hath grace
>   Your houses to renew,
> Grown old, surrender must his place
>   Unto the crisped yew.
>
> When yew is out, then birch comes in,
>   And many flowers beside,
> Both of a fresh and fragrant kin',
>   To honour Whitsuntide.
>
> Green rushes then, and sweetest bents,
>   With cooler oaken boughs,
> Come in for comely ornaments,
>   To re-adorn the house.
> Thus times do shift; each thing in turn does hold;
> New things succeed, as former things grow old.'

The same poet elsewhere recommends very particular care in the thorough removal of the Christmas garnishings on this eve:

> ' That so the superstitious find
> No one least branch left there behind;
> For look, how many leaves there be
> Neglected there, maids, trust to me,
> So many goblins you shall see.'

He also alludes to the reservation of part of the candles or torches, as calculated to have the effect of protecting from mischief:

> ' Kindle the Christmas brand, and then
>   Till sunset let it burn,
> Which quenched, then lay it up again,
>   Till Christmas next return.
>
> Part must be kept, wherewith to tend
>   The Christmas log next year;
> And where 'tis safely kept, the fiend
>   Can do no mischief there.'

There is a curious custom of old standing in Scotland, in connection with Candlemas day. On that day it is, or lately was, an universal practice in that part of the island, for the children attending school to make small presents of money to their teachers. The master sits at his desk or table, exchanging for the moment his usual authoritative look for one of bland civility, and each child goes up in turn and lays his offering down before him, the sum being generally proportioned to the abilities of the parents. Sixpence and a shilling are the most common sums in most schools; but some give half and whole crowns, and even more. The boy and girl who give most are respectively styled King and Queen. The children, being then dismissed for a holiday, proceed along the streets in a confused procession, carrying the King and Queen in state,

214

exalted upon that seat formed of crossed hands which, probably from this circumstance, is called the *King's Chair*. In some schools, it used to be customary for the teacher, on the conclusion of the offerings, to make a bowl of punch and regale each urchin with a glass to drink the King and Queen's health, and a biscuit. The latter part of the day was usually devoted to what was called the *Candlemas bleeze*, or blaze, namely, the conflagration of any piece of furze which might exist in their neighbourhood, or, were that wanting, of an artificial bonfire.

Another old popular custom in Scotland on Candlemas day was to hold a football match, the east end of a town against the west, the unmarried men against the married, or one parish against another. The Candlemas Ba', as it was called, brought the whole community out in a state of high excitement. On one occasion, some years ago, when the sport took place in Jedburgh, the contending parties, after a struggle of two hours in the streets, transferred the contention to the bed of the river Jed, and there fought it out amidst a scene of fearful splash and dabblement, to the infinite amusement of a multitude looking on from the bridge.

Considering the importance attached to Candlemas day for so many ages, it is scarcely surprising that there is a universal superstition throughout Christendom, that good weather on this day indicates a long continuance of winter and a bad crop, and that its being foul is, on the contrary, a good omen. Sir Thomas Browne, in his *Vulgar Errors*, quotes a Latin distich expressive of this idea:

> ' Si sol splendescat Maria purificante,
>   Major erit glacies post festum quam fuit ante;'

which may be considered as well translated in the popular Scottish rhyme:

> ' If Candlemas day be dry and fair,
>   The half o' winter 's to come and mair;
> If Candlemas day be wet and foul,
>   The half o' winter 's gane at Yule.'

In Germany there are two proverbial expressions on this subject: 1. The shepherd would rather see the wolf enter his stable on Candlemas day than the sun; 2. The badger peeps out of his hole on Candlemas day, and when he finds snow, walks abroad; but if he sees the sun shining, he draws back into his hole. It is not improbable that these notions, like the festival of Candlemas itself, are derived from pagan times, and have existed since the very infancy of our race. So at least we may conjecture, from a curious passage in Martin's *Description of the Western Islands*. On Candlemas day, according to this author, the Hebrideans observe the following curious custom: —' The mistress and servants of each family take a sheaf of oats and dress it up in women's apparel, put it in a large basket, and lay a wooden club by it, and this they call Brüd's Bed: and then the mistress and servants cry three times, " Brüd is come; Brüd is welcome!" This they do just before going to bed, and when they rise in the morning they look among the ashes, expecting to see the impression of Brüd's club there; which, if they do, they reckon it a *true presage of a good crop and prosperous year*, and the contrary they take as an ill omen.'

THE PURIFICATION FLOWER.

Our ancestors connected certain plants with certain saints, on account of their coming into blossom about the time of the occurrence of those saints' days. Thus the snowdrop was called the *Purification Flower* (also the Fair Maid of February), from its blossoming about Candlemas; the crocus was dedicated to St Valentine; the daisy to St Margaret (hence called by the French *La belle Marguerite*); the Crown Imperial to St Edward, king of the West Saxons, whose day is the 18th of March; the Cardamine, or Lady's Smock, to the Virgin, its white flowers appearing about Lady-day. The St John's Wort was connected, as its name expresses, with the blessed St John. The roses of summer were said to fade about St Mary Magdalen's Day.* There were also the Lent Lily or Daffodil, the Pasque-flower or Anemone, Herb Trinity, Herb Christopher, St Barnaby's Thistle, Canterbury Bell (in honour of St Augustine of England), Herb St Robert, and Mary Wort.

COINS CUT INTO HALVES AND QUARTERS.

The discovery of Silver Pennies cut into halves and quarters, though not uncommon in England, is apt to be overlooked by numismatists. In the great find of coins which took place at Cuerdede, in Lancashire, in 1840, were several pennies of Alfred and Edward the Elder so divided. The same was the case with coins of Edward the Confessor, found at Thwaite, in Suffolk; and with those of William the Conqueror, discovered at Benworth, in Hampshire, in 1833. On the latter discovery, Mr Hawkins has remarked that the halves and quarters were probably issued from the mints in that form, as the whole collection had evidently been in circulation. The great find of silver pennies (mostly of Henry II.) at Worcester, in 1854, comprised a half coin of Eustace, Count of Boulogne, and about thirteen halves and as many quarters of Henry's pennies. The collections in the British Museum contain specimens of divided coins of nearly every monarch from Alfred to Henry III., with whose reign they cease. The practice of dividing the coins no doubt arose from the scarcity of small change, which was in part remedied under the reign of Edward I. by the coinage of halfpence and farthings. —*A. W. Franks; Archæologia,* vol. xxxviii. part 1.

FEBRUARY 3.

St Blaize, bishop of Sebaste, 316. St Auscharius, archbishop of Hamburg and Bremen, 865. St Wereburge, patroness of Chester, 699. St Margaret of England, 12th century.

ST WEREBURGE.

Wereburge was one of the earlier and more celebrated of the Anglo-Saxon saints, and was not only contemporary with the beginning of Christianity in Mercia, but was closely mixed up with the first movement for the establishment of nunneries in England. Her father, Wulfhere, king of the Mercians, though nominally a Christian, was not a zealous professor, but, under the influence of his queen, all his children were

* 2nd Notes and Queries, vii. 312.

earnest and devout believers. These children were three princes, — Wulfhad, Rufinus, and Keured,—and one daughter, Wereburge. The princess displayed an extraordinary sanctity from her earliest years, and, though her great beauty drew round her many suitors, she declared her resolution to live a virgin consecrated to Christ. Among those who thus sought her in marriage was the son of the king of the West Saxons; but she incurred greater danger from a noble named Werbode, a favourite in her father's court, who was influenced, probably, by ambition as much as by love. At this time there are said to have been already five bishops' sees in Mercia,—Chester, Lichfield, Worcester, Lincoln, and Dorchester; and to that of Lichfield, which was nearest to the favourite residence of King Wulfhere, near Stone, in Staffordshire, St Chad (Ceadda) had recently been appointed. It appears that Chad had an oratory in the solitude of the forest, where he spent much of his time; and that Wulfhere's two sons Wulfhad and Rufinus, while following their favourite diversion, discovered him there. The legend, which is not quite consistent, represents them as having been pagans down to that time, and as being converted by Chad's conversation.

Werbode, also, is said to have been a perverse pagan, and, according to the legend, his influence had led Wulfhere to apostatise from Christianity. The king approved of Werbode as a husband for Wereburge, but he was stoutly opposed by the queen and the two young princes; and the royal favourite, believing that the two latter were the main obstacles to his success, and having obtained information of their private visits to St Chad, maligned them to their father, and obtained an order from King Wulfhere for putting them to death. This barbarous act was no sooner accomplished, than Werbode was poisoned by an evil spirit, and died raving mad; while King Wulfhere, overcome with deep repentance, returned to Christianity, and became renowned for his piety.

Wereburge now, with her father's consent, became a nun, and entered the monastery of Ely, which had been but recently founded, and which was then governed by her cousin Etheldrida. As a nun of Ely, Wereburge soon became celebrated for her piety, and, according to the legend, her sanctity was made manifest by numerous miracles. Ethelred, Wulfhere's brother, succeeded him on the throne of the Mercians in 675; and one of his first cares was to call his niece Wereburge from Ely, and entrust to her care the establishment of nunneries in Mercia. Within a very short time, assisted by his munificence, she founded religious houses for nuns at Trentham and Hanbury (near Tutbury), in Staffordshire, and at Wedon in Northamptonshire, of all which she was superior at the same time. She died at Trentham, on the 3rd of February, 699, having declared her will that her body should be buried at Hanbury; when the people of Trentham attempted to detain it by force, those of Hanbury were aided by a miracle in obtaining possession of it, and carried it for interment to their church. Years afterwards, when the Danes ravaged this part of the

215

island, the body of St Wereburge was carried for safety from Hanbury to Chester, and deposited in the abbey church there (now the cathedral), of which she henceforth became the patroness.

Such is the history of St Wereburge as we gather it partly from tolerably authentic history, but more largely from the legend. The latter was set forth in English verse early in the sixteenth century, by a monk of Chester named Henry Bradshaw, whose book was printed in a black-letter volume, now very rare, by Pynson, in 1521.* Bradshaw's verses are too dull to be worth quotation as specimens of old English poetry, and the posthumous miracles he relates are certainly not worth repeating. There is one, however, which gives us such a curious picture of the proceedings of the citizens when a mediæval town was on fire, and bears also such curious points of resemblance to the description of the confusion in London at the great fire of 1666, that, as shewing how little progress had been made during the period between the time of Henry Bradshaw and the reign of Charles II., we are tempted to give some verses from it. Some houses had accidentally taken fire while the inhabitants were at their devotions in the churches:

' This fearefull fire encreased more and more,
Piteously wastyng hous, chambre, and hall.
The citizens were redy their cité to succour,
Shewed all their diligence and labour continuall;
Some cried for water, and some for hookes dyd call;
Some used other engins by crafte and policy;
Some pulled downe howses afore the fire truly.

' Other that were impotent mekely gan praye
Our blessed Lorde on them to have pité.
Women and children cried, "Out and waile away!"
Beholdyng the daunger and perill of the cité.
Prestes made hast divine service to supplé [complete],
Redy for to succour their neyghbours in distres
(As charité required), and helpe their hevynes.

' The fire contynued without any cessynge,
Fervently flamyng ever contynuall,
From place to place mervaylously rennyng [running],
As it were tynder consumyng toure and wall.
The citezens sadly laboured in vayne all;
By the policie of man was founde no remedy
To cesse [stop] the fire so fervent and myghty.

*   *   *   *   *   *

' Many riall [royal] places fell adowne that day,
Riche marchauntes houses brought to distruction;
Churches and chapels went to great decay.
That tyme was brent [burnt] the more [greater] part of the towne;
And to this present day is a famous opinion
Howe a mighty churche, a mynstre of saynt Michaell,
That season was brent and to ruyne fell.'

The citizens, finding themselves powerless to put out the fire, addressed their prayers to St Wereburge, and the monks then brought out her shrine, and carried it in procession through the flaming streets. This, it was believed, stopped the progress of the conflagration.

* It may be well to state that this curious poem has been reprinted by the Chetham Society.

216

Born.—Henry Cromwell (N. S.), 1627.
Died.—Sweyn (of Denmark), 1014; John of Gaunt, 1399; Charles X. of Sweden, 1660; Sir Thomas Lombe, 1738; Richard Nash (Bath), 1761; John Beckmann, 1811, Göttingen; Admiral Strachan, 1828.

JOHN OF GAUNT.

Edward the Third's fourth son, John, born at Ghent, or, as it was then spelt, Gaunt, during his father's expedition to Flanders, in February 1340, and called from that circumstance, John of Gaunt, has obtained a greater name amongst celebrated princes than his own merits would perhaps justify, probably in some measure from his inheriting the popularity of his elder and greater brother, the Black Prince. John, when two years old, was created Earl of Richmond. After the death of the great warrior, Henry Duke of Lancaster, in 1360, John of Gaunt, who had married his daughter the princess Blanche, was raised by his father, King Edward, to that dukedom. In the adventurous expedition which the Black Prince made into Spain in 1367, his brother John accompanied him. Two years later, accompanying the Black Prince on a march which he made through France to the English possessions in the south, John took the command of the army, on his brother being obliged by the state of his health to return to England. Immediately afterwards John of Gaunt married the Spanish princess Constance, eldest daughter of Don Pedro, whom he had first seen at Bordeaux in 1367; and, as her father had been murdered by his rival, the usurper Don Erique, the Duke of Lancaster assumed in his wife's right the title of King of Castile and Leon. In the continuous wars with France which followed, John of Gaunt was a brave but not a successful commander, and they were put an end to by the truce of 1374.

The Black Prince died on the 8th of June 1376, two years after this peace. Since his return to England, he had espoused the popular cause against his father's government, and thus became a greater favourite than ever with the nation. His brother of Lancaster, on the contrary, was unpopular, and supported the abuses of the court. After his death, John of Gaunt became all powerful in the parliament, and high in favour with his father the king; but in his hostility to the opposition which had been supported by the Black Prince, he quarrelled violently with the Church, and especially with William of Wickham, Bishop of Winchester, whom he persecuted with inveterate hatred. It is believed that the Duke's hostility to the bishops was the main cause of the support he gave to John Wycliffe, the great Church reformer, by which he certainly did good service to the English Reformation in its first beginning, and gained popularity among the Lollards. But even here he proceeded with the intemperance which especially marked his character. The prelates, provoked by the encouragement thus openly given to innovators in Church doctrines and government, cited Wycliffe to appear in St Paul's Church, before Courtenay, Bishop of London, to answer for his opinions. He came there on the 19th of February 1377, supported by the Duke of Lancaster and the Lord Henry Percy, Marshal of England, in person, with a formidable array of knights. The bishop was highly offended by this bold advocacy of men who came there to be tried as heretics, and high words passed between him and the Duke, who is said to have threatened ' to pull down the pride of him, and of all the bishops of England,' and to have talked of dragging him out of the church by the hair of his head. A great crowd of citizens, who were present, shewed an inclination to take part with the bishop, and, further irritated by some proceedings in parliament which threatened their municipal rights, they rose tumultuously next morning, and rushing first to the house of the Marshal, broke into it, and committed various acts of violence. Not, however, finding Lord Henry Percy there, they hastened to the Savoy, the palace of the Duke of Lancaster, where ' a priest chancing to meete them, asked of some, what that busines meant. Whereunto he was answered, that they went to take the Duke and the Lord Percy, that they might be compelled to deliver to them Sir Peter de la More, whome they unjustly kept in prison. The priest sayde that Peter de la More was a traytour to the king, and was worthie to be hanged. With which words they all cryed, " This is Percy ! this is the traytour of England ! his speech bewrayeth him, though hee bee disguised in apparel." Then ranne they all upon him, striving who should give him his deaths wound, and after they had wounded him, they caryed him to prison, where he dyed.' The Bishop of London now arrived and appeased the rioters, but not till the great courtiers against whom their wrath had been excited were in great terror. The Duke and the Lord Henry Percy happened to be dining with a Flemish merchant named John of Yprès ; ' but the Londoners knew it not, for they thought that he and the duke had beene at the Savoy, and therefore with all hast posted thither. But one of the dukes knights seeing these things, in great haste came to the place where the duke was, and, after that he had knocked and could not get in, hee sayd to Haverland the porter, " If thou love my lord and thy life, open the gate ! " with which wordes hee got entrey, and with great feare hee telles the duke that without the gate were infinite numbers of armed men, and, unlesse hee tooke great heede, that day should bee his last. With which words, when the duke heard them, he leapt so hastily from his oysters, that he hurt both his legges against the fourme. Wine was offered to his oysters, but hee would not drinke for haste. Hee fledde with his fellow Syr Henry Percy, no manne following them, and, entring the Thamis, never stinted rowing untill they came to a house neere the manor of Kenington (besides Lambeth), where at that tyme the princesse was, with the young prince, before whom he made his complaint.' The Londoners were summoned before the King, who effected a reconciliation between them and the Duke ; but, old Stow adds in his quaint manner, ' in the meane space some men ceased not to make rymes in reproch of the duke, and to fasten them in divers places of the city, whereby the greater fury of the people might be kindled, the

dukes fame blotted, and his name had in detestation.'

This was one of the last public audiences given by King Edward III.. who died on the 21st of June following. At the beginning of the following reign, the hostile feeling between the Londoners and John of Gaunt continued. but his power had greatly declined, and for a while he took little part in public business. In Wat Tyler's rebellion, when the insurgents had obtained possession of London, they proclaimed the Duke of Lancaster as one of the arch-traitors, and burnt his palace of the Savoy to the ground. John of Gaunt was at this time in Scotland, employed in a diplomatic mission. He had not long returned from a hostile expedition to France, the ill success of which had increased his unpopularity. From this time forward the Duke was involved in frequent quarrels with his nephew the young king. and they became more and more difficult to reconcile, until at last Richard was glad to get rid of him by allowing him to carry an army of ten thousand men to Spain in order to recover by force the kingdom of Castile. He landed at Corunna in the month of July 1385, and marched through Galicia into Portugal, where the King of Portugal not only joined him with an army, but married Philippa, John of Gaunt's eldest daughter by his first wife. He was at first successful against the Spaniards, but eventually having lost the greater part of his troops by famine and disease, he was obliged to make his retreat into Guienne, and was glad to conclude a treaty with the *de facto* King of Castile, by which John of Gaunt abandoned all his claim to the throne of Castile and Leon, in consideration of a large sum of money, and of the marriage of Henry Prince of the Asturias, the heir of Castile, with his daughter by his second wife. On the return of the Duke of Lancaster from the Continent, he appears to have become suddenly popular, perhaps on account of his hostility to his nephew's favourites. He had been always accused of aiming at the English crown, and of a design to supplant the young King Richard; and it is said that he incurred Richard's final displeasure, by pressing the king too urgently to acknowledge his son Henry of Bolingbroke, heir to the throne. From this time John of Gaunt lived retired from court until his death, which occurred at Ely House, in Holborn, on the 3rd of February 1399. It is hardly necessary to add, that within a few weeks afterwards his son became King of England, as Henry IV.

BEAU NASH.

This extraordinary man, to whose amenities the city of Bath owes so much, was born at Swansea, in 1673 ; educated at Carmarthen School, and thence sent to Jesus College, Oxford, where his college life was mostly marked by his assiduity in intrigue. He next purchased for himself a pair of colours in the army, which, however, he soon quitted. He then entered himself at the Temple, to study for the law, but led so gay a town life without any visible means of supporting it, that his companions suspected him of being a highwayman.

Disgusted at these suspicions, Nash retired to Bath, then one of the poorest and meanest cities in England. It had its public amusements for the company who flocked there to drink the Bath waters, consisting chiefly of a band of musicians, who played under some fine old trees, called the Grove. In 1704, Nash was appointed 'master of the ceremonies,' and immediately removed the music to the Pump-room. His laws were so strictly enforced that he was styled 'King of Bath:' no rank would protect the offender, nor dignity of station condone a breach of the laws. Nash desired the Duchess of Queensberry, who appeared at a dress ball in an apron of point-lace, said to be worth 500 guineas, to take it off, which she did, at the same time desiring his acceptance of it; and when the Princess Amelia requested to have one dance more after 11 o'clock, Nash replied that the laws of Bath, like those of Lycurgus, were unalterable. Gaming ran high at Bath, and frequently led to disputes and resort to the sword, then generally worn by well-dressed men. Swords were, therefore, prohibited by Nash in the public rooms; still, they were worn in the streets, when Nash, in consequence of a duel fought by torchlight, by two notorious gamesters, made the law absolute, 'That no swords should, on any account, be worn in Bath.' He also wrote certain 'Rules, by general consent determined,' to be observed at all public places of amusement: these he concluded as follows:—

'N.B.—Several men of no character, old women, and young ones of questionable reputation, are great authors of lies in this place, being of the sect of levellers.'

Nash was a sleeping partner in one of the principal gambling-houses in Bath; consequently, his life was chequered with vicissitudes. In 1732, he possessed six fine black coach-horses, which were so well matched and paced so well in full trot, that it appeared as if one horse drew the carriage. He kept a coachman, postilion, two footmen in livery, a gentleman out of livery, and a running footman. Many instances of Nash's benevolence are recorded. He gave away his money freely. A broken gamester, observing him one day win two hundred guineas at picquet, and put the money into his pocket with indifference, exclaimed, 'How happy that money would make me!' Nash, overhearing this, placed the money in his hand, saying, 'Go, then, and be happy!'

Of Nash's gambling life some expiatory anecdotes are related. The Earl of T——, when a young man, being fond of play, was desirous to have 'the King of Bath' for his opponent, for whom, however, he was no match. Nash, after winning from him several trifling stakes, resolved to attempt his cure. Accordingly, he engaged his lordship one evening to a serious amount; and having first won all his ready money, then the title-deeds of his estates, and finally the very watch in his pocket and the rings on his fingers, Nash read him a lecture on the flagrant impropriety of attempting to make money by gambling, when poverty could only be pleaded in justification of such conduct. He then returned him all his winnings, at the same time exacting from him a promise that he would never play again. Not less generously did Nash behave to an Oxford student, who had come to spend the long vacation at Bath. This greenhorn, who also affected to be a gamester, was lucky enough to win a large sum of money from Nash, and after the game was ended was invited by him to supper. 'Perhaps,' said Nash, 'you think I have asked you for the purpose of securing my revenge; but I can assure you that my sole motive in requesting your company is to set you on your guard, and to entreat you to be warned by my experience, and to shun play as you would the devil. This is strange advice for one like me to give; but I feel for your youth and inexperience, and am convinced that if you do not stop where you now are, you will infallibly be ruined.' Nash was right. A few nights afterwards, having lost his entire fortune at the gaming table, the young man blew his brains out!

The Corporation of Bath so highly respected Nash, that the Chamber voted a marble statue of him, which was erected in the Pump-room, between the busts of Newton and Pope; this gave rise to a stinging epigram by Lord Chesterfield, concluding with these lines:

'The *statue* placed these busts between
Gives satire all its strength;
Wisdom and *Wit* are little seen,
But *Folly* at full length.'

Except a few months annually passed in superintending the amusements at Tunbridge, Nash lived at Bath until his health was worn out; and after one of Nature's serious warnings, he expired at his house in St John's-place, on the 3rd of February, 1761, aged eighty-seven years. He was buried in the Abbey Church with great ceremony: a solemn hymn was sung by the charity-school children, three clergymen preceded the coffin, the pall was supported by aldermen, and the Masters of the Assembly Rooms followed as chief mourners; while the streets were filled and the housetops covered with spectators, anxious to witness the respect paid to the venerable founder of the prosperity of the city of Bath.

SURRENDER OF HUME CASTLE.

Under the date February 3, 1651, we have, in Whitlocke's *Memorials*, intelligence of the siege of Hume Castle in Berwickshire, by Colonel Fenwick, an officer of Cromwell's army. This seat of a once powerful family occupied a commanding position at the western extremity of the great plain of the Merse. On its being summoned by Colonel Fenwick to surrender to Cromwell (who had recently beaten the Scots at Dunbar and overrun nearly the whole of Scotland south of the Forth), the governor answered, 'That he knew not Cromwell, and for his castle it was built upon a rock.' Four days later, there was intelligence in London, that Colonel Fenwick was playing with his guns upon Hume Castle, and that the governor sent this letter to him:

'I William of the Wastle
Am now in my castle,
And awe the dogs in the town
Shand garre me gang down.'

218

So Whitlocke prints or misprints the governor's brave answer, which in reality was only a somewhat confused version of a rhyme used by boys in one of their games. This sport, as practised to the present day in Scotland, is as follows. One of the party takes his station upon a large stone, heap of sand, rubbish, or any other materials, with a handkerchief in his hand, and cries out, as a defiance to his companions:

> I Willie Wastle
> Stand in my castle,
> And a' the dogs in the town
> 'll no ding Willie Wastle down.

They assail him, trying to drive him from his position, while he endeavours to repel them with the handkerchief. Any one who succeeds in driving him off, takes the vacated position, and seeks to maintain it in the same manner; and so on. The quaint act of the governor in adopting this defiance against the Cromwellian officer, has been the means of certifying to us that the antiquity of the boy's game is not less than two centuries.

The governor—whose name we learn from another source to have been Thomas Cockburn—appears to have made a resistance in conformity with his answer to the English commander; and it is not till three days after, that Whitlocke records the great execution which the mortar pieces had done against Hume Castle. The shot had made great breaches and spoilt many rich goods, and Fenwick was preparing for a storm, when the governor beat a parley. 'Fenwick refused to treat unless they would presently surrender upon quarter for life; which they did; and Fenwick appointed some officers to look to the equal sharing of the goods among his soldiers; only the governor's lady had liberty to carry out some of her goods and bedding.'[*]

The rhyme of Willie Wastle was used later in the century with reference to another public event. Mr William Veitch, a zealous Presbyterian clergyman who had been persecuted under the Stuarts, but after the Revolution became a prominent minister under the new establishment, is stated to have preached one day at Linton in Roxburghshire, when it pleased him to make allusion to the late episcopal frame of church government. 'Our bishops,' he said, 'had for a long time thought themselves very secure, like

> Willie, Willie Wastle,
> I am in my castle;
> A' the dogs in the town
> Dare not ding me down.

Yea, out there is a doggie in heaven that has dung them all down.'[†]

St Blaize's Day.

St. Blasius is generally represented as bishop of Sebaste in Armenia, and as having suffered martyrdom in the persecution of Licinius in 316. The fact of iron *combs* having been used in tear-ing the flesh of the martyr appears the sole reason for his having been adopted by the woolcombers as their patron saint. The large flourishing communities engaged in this business in Bradford and other English towns, are accustomed to hold a septennial jubilee on the 3rd of February, in honour of Jason of the Golden Fleece and St Blaize; and, not many years ago, this fête was conducted with considerable state and ceremony. First went the masters on horseback, each bearing a white sliver; then the masters' sons on horseback; then their colours; after which came the apprentices, on horseback, in their uniforms. Persons representing the king and queen, the royal family, and their guards and attendants, followed. Jason, with his golden fleece and proper attendants, next appeared. Then came BISHOP BLAIZE in full canonicals, followed by shepherds and shepherdesses, woolcombers, dyers, and other appropriate figures. some wearing *wool wigs*. At the celebration in 1825, before the procession started, it was addressed by Richard Fawcett, Esq., in the following lines suitable to the occasion:

> 'Hail to the day, whose kind auspicious rays
> Deigned first to smile on famous Bishop Blaize!
> To the great author of our combing trade,
> This day's devoted, and due honour's paid;
> To him whose fame through Britain's isle resounds.
> To him whose goodness to the poor abounds;
> Long shall his name in British annals shine,
> And grateful ages offer at his shrine!
> By this our trade are thousands daily fed,
> By it supplied with means to earn their bread.
> In various forms our trade its work imparts,
> In different methods and by different arts;
> Preserves from starving, indigents distressed,
> As combers, spinners, weavers, and the rest.
> We boast no gems, or costly garments vain,
> Borrowed from India, or the coast of Spain;
> Our native soil with wool our trade supplies,
> While foreign countries envy us the prize.
> No foreign broil our common good annoys,
> Our country's product all our art employs;
> Our fleecy flocks abound in every vale,
> Our bleating lambs proclaim the joyful tale.
> So let not Spain with us attempt to vie,
> Nor India's wealth pretend to soar so high;
> Nor Jason pride him in his Colchian spoil,
> By hardships gained and enterprising toil,
> Since Britons all with ease attain the prize,
> And every hill resounds with golden cries.
> To celebrate our founder's great renown,
> Our shepherd and our shepherdess we crown;
> For England's commerce, and for George's sway
> Each loyal subject give a loud HUZZA.
> HUZZA!'[*]

A significant remark is dropped by the local historian of these fine doings, that they were most apt to be entered upon when trade was flourishing.

There was also a general popular observance of St Blaize's day in England. Apparently for no better reason than the sound of the venerated prelate's name, it was customary to light fires on this day, or evening, on hill-tops or other conspicuous places. Perhaps the Scotch custom of the *Candlemas Bleeze*, already adverted to, was only St Blaize's fire transferred back to his eve. So determinedly anxious were the country

* Whitlocke's Memorials, p. 463.
† Scots Presbyterian Eloquence Displayed.

* *Leeds Mercury*, Feb. 5, 1825.

people for the celebration by a blaze, that they would sacrifice articles of some importance to make one. Country women went about during the day in an idle merry humour, making good cheer: and if they found a neighbour spinning, they thought themselves justified in making a conflagration of the distaff.

In the simple days when England was Catholic, it was believed that, by a charm in name of St Blaize, a thorn could be extracted from the flesh, or a bone from the throat. It was only necessary to hold the patient, and say, 'Blaize, the martyr and servant of Jesus Christ, commands thee [in the case of a bone in the throat] to pass up or down; [in the case of a thorn] to come forth;' and the command was instantly effectual.

The Wedding Ring.

Mystic significance has, from the earliest period, been associated with the ring. In its circular continuity it was accepted as a type of eternity, and hence of the stability of affection. The Greek and Roman rings are often inscribed with sentences typical of this feeling. *May you live long* is engraved on one published by Caylus; *I bring good fortune to the wearer*, was another usual inscription; sometimes a stone was inserted in the ring, upon which was engraved an intaglio, representing a hand pulling the lobe of an ear, with the one word *Remember* above it. Others have the wish *Live happy*, or *I give this love pledge*. They were lavishly displayed by the early nations; but, except as an indication of gentility or wealth, they appear to have been little valued until Greek sentimentalism gave them a deeper significance. As a gift of love, or a sign of betrothal, they came into ancient use. The Jews make the ring a most important feature of the betrothal in the marriage ceremony. They were sometimes of large size, and much elaboration of

workmanship, as in the specimen here engraved, selected from the curious collection of rings formed by the late Lord Londesborough. It is beautifully wrought of gold filigree, and richly enamelled. Upon it are the words *Joy be with you*, in Hebrew characters. According to the Jewish law, it is necessary that this ring be of a certain value; it is therefore examined and certified by the officiating Rabbi and chief officers of the synagogue, when it is received from the bridegroom; whose absolute property it must be, and not obtained on credit or by gift. When this is properly certified, the ring is returned to him, and he places it on the bride's finger, calling attention to the fact that she is, by means of this ring, consecrated to him; and so completely binding is this action that, should the marriage not be further consecrated, no other could be contracted by either party without a legal divorce.

In the middle ages, solemn betrothal by means of the ring often preceded matrimony, and was sometimes adopted between lovers who were about to separate for long periods. Chaucer, in his *Troilus and Cresseide*, describes the heroine as giving her lover a ring, upon which a love-motto was engraved, and receiving one from him in return. Shakespeare has more than one allusion to the custom, which is absolutely enacted in his *Two Gentlemen of Verona*, when Julia gives Proteus a ring, saying, 'Keep you this remembrance for thy Julia's sake;' and he replies, 'Why, then, we'll make exchange; here, take you this.' The invention of the *gimmal* or linked ring gave still greater force and significance to the custom. Made with a double and sometimes a triple link, which turned upon a pivot, it could shut up into one solid ring. This will be better understood by our second cut, which represents one of these rings. It is shewn first as it appears when closed; to the sides of

each outer hoop a small hand is attached, each fitting into the other, as the hoops are brought together, and enclosing a heart affixed to the central notched ring. It was customary to break these rings asunder at the betrothal, which was ratified in a solemn manner over the Holy Bible, and sometimes in the presence of a witness, when the man and the woman broke away the upper and lower rings from the central one, which the witness retained; when the marriage contract was fulfilled at the altar, the three portions of the ring were again united, and the ring used in the ceremony.

The fourth finger of the left hand has from long usage been consecrated to the wedding ring, from an ancient belief that from this finger a nerve went direct to the heart. So completely was this fanciful piece of physiology confided in by the Greeks and Romans, that their physicians term this the medical or healing finger, and used it to stir their mixtures, from a notion that nothing noxious could communicate with it, without its giving immediate warning by a palpitation of the heart. This superstition is retained in full force in some country places in England, particularly in Somersetshire, where all the fingers of the hand are thought to be injurious except the ring-finger, which is thought to have the power of curing any sore or wound which is stroked by it. That a sanatory power is imparted to the wedding ring, is believed by the peasantry, both in England and Ireland, who fancy any growth like a wart, on the skin, may be removed by rubbing a wedding ring upon them.

The clasped hands adopted on the gimmal rings became a frequent emblem on the solid wedding ring. The Londesborough collection furnishes us with a peculiarly curious example of the Shakspearian era; throwing a side light upon a passage in the great dramatist's *Twelfth Night*, where Malvolio, breaking open the letter purporting to be in his mistress's handwriting, says: 'By your leave, wax. Soft!—and the impressure her Lucrece, with which she uses to seal.' The bust of Lucretia, with her hand directing the fatal dagger, appears on the face of this ring; at the back are two clasped hands; the whole being enriched by niello engraving.

This fashion of ring is still in use in that curious local community of fishermen inhabiting the Claddagh at Galway, on the Irish western coast. They number with their families between five and six thousand, and are particularly exclusive in their tastes and habits, rarely intermarrying with other than their own people. The wedding ring is an heir-loom in the family; it is regularly transferred from the mother to the daughter who

is first married, and so passes to her descendants. Many of them still worn there are very old, and show traces of still older design, like that in our cut, whose prototype may have been made in the Elizabethan era. The hands in this instance support a crowned heart, typical of the married state.

Within the hoop of the ring, it was customary, from the middle of the sixteenth to the close of the seventeenth century, to inscribe a motto or 'posy,' consisting frequently of a very simple sentiment in commonplace rhyme. The following are specimens:

'Our contract
Was Heaven's act.'

'In thee, my choice,
I do rejoyce.'

'God above
Encrease our love.'

The engraving exhibits one of these 'posyrings,' of the simplest form, such as would be in ordinary use in the early part of the seventeenth century. The posy was always on the flat inner side of the ring. Shakspeare has alluded more than once in contemptuous terms to these rhyming effusions. In the *Merchant of Venice*, Act v., sc. 1, when Portia asks Gratiano the reason of his quarrel with Nerissa, he answers:

'About a hoop of gold, a paltry ring
That she did give me; whose *posy* was,
For all the world, like Cutler's poetry
Upon a knife, *Love me, and leave me not.*'

Hamlet asks at the conclusion of the triple lines of rhyme uttered by the players at the commencement of their tragedy—'Is this a prologue, or the posy of a ring?' Yet the composition of such posies exercised the wits of superior men occasionally, and they were sometimes terse and epigrammatic. In 1624, a small collection of them was printed with the quaint title, *Love's Garland, or posies for Rings, Handkerchiefs, and Gloves; and such pretty tokens, that lovers send their loves.* It is curious that the second of the posies given above, and which was copied from a ring of the time of the publication of this volume, is given with a very slight variation in the series. The custom of placing the heart on the ring is also alluded to in the following posy :

'My heart and I,
Until I dye.'

The joined hands is also notified in another :

'Not two, but one
Till life be gone.'

One of the most complete jingles is the following :

'Desire,
Like fire,
Doth still aspire.'

Of a more meritorious kind, are the following specimens from a manuscript of the same period :

'Constancy and heaven are round,
And in this the Emblem's found.'

'Weare me out, Love shall not waste,
Love beyond Tyme still is plac'd.'

'Weare this text, and when you looke
Uppon your finger, sweare by th' booke.'

Lilly, in his address to the ladies, prefixed to the second part of his *Euphues*, 1597, hopes they will be favourable to his work, 'writing their judgments as you do the Posies in your rings, which are always next to the finger, not to be seene of him that holdeth you by the hand, and yet knowne by you that weare them on your hands.'

The Rev. Giles Moore notes in his Journal, 1673-4 (Sussex Archæological Collections, vol. i.), 'I bought for Ann Brett a gold ring, this being the posy: "When this you see, remember me."'

One of the most whimsical of these inscriptions was used by Dr John Thomas, Bishop of Lincoln in 1753, who had been married three times; on his fourth marriage he placed as a motto on the wedding ring :

'If I survive,
I'll make them five !'

'My Lady Rochford,' writes Horace Walpole, 'desired me t'other day to give her a motto for a ruby ring,' proving the late continuance of the custom. The most modern form of sentimental or significant ring was ingeniously constructed by French jewellers in the early part of the present century, and afterwards adopted by English ones, in which a motto was formed by the arrangement of stones around the hoop ; the initial letter of the name of each stone forming amatory words, when combined; as in the following examples :

R uby.	L apis Lazuli.
E merald.	O pal.
G arnet.	V erde antique.
A methyst.	E merald.
R uby.	M alachite.
D iamond.	E merald.

AN ODD FUNERAL IN THE TIME OF THE COMMONWEALTH.

Dugdale has preserved for us an account of the funeral of the wife of a gentleman, of good means, but cynical temper, during the Commonwealth. The gentleman was Mr Fisher Dilke, Registrar of Shustoke ; his wife was sister of Sir Peter Wentworth, one of the regicide judges. 'She was a frequenter of conventicles ; and dying before her husband, he first stripped his barn-wall to make her a coffin ; then bargained with the clerk for a groat to make a grave in the churchyard, to save eightpence by one in the church. This done, he speaketh about eight of his neighbours to meet at his house, for bearers ; for whom he provided three twopenny cakes and a bottle of claret [this treat would cost 2s. at the utmost]. And some being come, he read a chapter in Job to them till all were then ready ; when, having distributed the cake and wine among them, they took up the corpse, he following them to the grave. Then, putting himself in the parson's place, (none being there,) the corpse being laid in the grave, and a spade of mould cast thereon, he said, "Ashes to ashes, dust to dust ;" adding, "Lord, now lettest thou thy servant depart in peace, for mine eyes have seen thy salvation ;" and so returned home.'*

FEBRUARY 4.

St Phileas and Philoromus, martyrs in Egypt, *circ.* 309. St Isidore of Pelusium, 449. St Modan, abbot in Scotland, 7th century. St Rembert, archbishop of Bremen, 888. St Gilbert, abbot in England, 1190. St Andrew Corsini, bishop, 1373. St Jane (or Joan), queen of France, 1505. St Joseph of Leonissa, 1612.

Born.—George Lillo, dramatist, 1693, *Moorgate.*
Died.—Lucius Septimius Severus, 211, *York ;* Egbert (*of England*), 836 ; John Rogers, burnt at *Smithfield*, 1555 ; Giambatista Porta, natural philosopher, inventor of the camera obscura, 1615, *Naples ;* George Abbot, archbishop of Canterbury, 1648 ; Rev. Robert Blair, poet, 1746 ; Louis, Duke of Orleans, 1752 ; Charles de la Condamine, astronomer, 1774 ; John Hamilton Mortimer, historical painter, 1779, *Aylesbury.*

THE EMPEROR SEVERUS.

Several of the Roman emperors had visited Britain, but Severus was the only one who came to die in this distant island. Britain had then been a Roman province full a hundred years, and as such had become peaceable and prosperous, for even the Caledonians in the North had ceased to

* Life of Sir William Dugdale, 4to, p. 106.

222

be troublesome, and Roman roads, with accompanying towns, had been carried up to the borders of the wild highlands. A still greater proof of the prosperous state of this province is found in the circumstance that its governors could interfere actively in the affairs of the Continent, raise formidable rebellions, and even contend for the empire. Such was the case when, in A.D. 193, the imperial throne became an object of dispute between three competitors,—Severus, Pescennius Niger, and Albinus ; the last being governor of Britain. Albinus marched with the legions of Britain, and soon made himself master of Gaul ; but Severus, to equal courage and great military skill, joined an amount of craft and treachery which soon gave him the superiority over both his rivals. Having defeated and slain Niger, he reached Rome with his troops in 196, and hastening to Gaul, fought the great battle of Lyons on the 19th of February 197, in which Albinus also perished. Severus, thus left master of the empire, had his attention soon called to the state of Britain.

It appears that during these events the Caledonians had again become formidable, partly through some great ethnological change which was going on in the North, partly it is conjectured through an immigration on a large scale of foreign tribes, perhaps from the North of Europe. Virius Lupus, the new propraetor or governor of Britain appointed by Severus, found himself unable effectually to repress their turbulency ; and he was obliged, in the year 208, to write to the Emperor for assistance. Severus displayed in this last act of his life all the qualities which had raised him to power. He determined to assist his propraetor in person ; and although it was already late in the year, he collected his army, took with him his two sons, Caracalla and Geta, and, arriving in Britain in an incredibly short space of time, fixed his court at the city then called Eburacum, but now York, which was the station of the sixth legion. The Northern tribes, astonished at the rapidity of his movements, sent envoys to ask for peace, but in vain ; and the vigorous old soldier, who was in his sixty-third year and crippled with painful disease, placed himself at the head of his army, marched directly into the wilds of the North, in spite of obstacles in overcoming which no less than fifty thousand of his men are said to have perished, and never stopped till he reached the extreme northern coast of Scotland, where he is said to have observed the parallax of the sun, and the comparative length of the days and nights. During this arduous campaign, the Emperor was often carried in a litter, which he was unable to leave for several successive days, but everything yielded before his stern and inflexible will. To add to his sufferings, his son Caracalla, who accompanied him while Geta remained in the south, grieved him by his unfilial conduct, and not only entered into culpable intrigues against him, but actually on one occasion attempted his life.

After having thus reduced the Caledonians and Maeatae, as the two great tribes who then shared North Britain were called, Severus returned in triumph to Eburacum, or York,—it is supposed towards the end of the year 209 ; but he had not been there long before news arrived that the Caledonians and Mæatæ, false to their oaths, had risen again and invaded the Roman province. Without delay he gave orders for reassembling the army, and, declaring in a quotation from Homer that he would this time entirely extirpate the faithless barbarians, prepared to place himself again at its head. He was at this moment in such a state of exhaustion that he was unable even to walk, and during his absence from the troops Caracalla recommenced his intrigues, and persuaded them to choose him for their emperor. When Severus was informed of this act of rebellion, all his energies were roused, and, mounting the tribunal, caused all who had taken part in it to appear before him, and addressing them fiercely said, ' Soldiers, it is not the feet, but the head which discharges the duties of a general.' At the same moment he gave the order to march against the enemy ; but the effort was too much for him, and they had not proceeded far before his disease assumed so dangerous a character, that they were obliged to carry him back to Eburacum, where he died on the 4th of February 211. His body was consumed in a funeral pile in the city where he died, and it has been said that the great tumulus still remaining at York was raised over the spot as a monument. His ashes were gathered into an urn of alabaster, and carried to Rome.

FATE OF LA CONDAMINE.

The leading incidents of the life of this eminent philosopher entitle him to be considered as a *martyr of science.* A native of Paris, upon leaving college he entered the army, and shewed great intrepidity in the siege of Rosas. Upon his return to Paris, he entered the Academy of Sciences, as assistant chemist. When the Academy were arranging for a voyage to the equator, for measuring an arc of the meridian, with a view more accurately to determine the dimensions and figure of the earth, La Condamine was fascinated by the project. ' The very desire,' says Condorcet, ' of being connected with so perilous an undertaking, made him an astronomer.' His proposals having been accepted by the Academy, in 1735, in company of MM. Bouguer and Godin, he proceeded to Peru; on reaching which the natives suspected the philosophers of being either heretics or sorcerers, come in search of new gold mines : the surgeon to the expedition was assassinated ; the people were excited against them ; and the country was difficult and dangerous. Bouguer and La Condamine and the Spanish Commissioners quarrelled, and conducted their operations separately ; but the results did not differ from their average by a five-thousandth part of the whole, in the length of a degree of the meridian. They encountered great fatigues and hardships, until their return in 1743 ; when La Condamine published an account of his voyage up the Amazon, and his travels in South America. His determination of the figure of the earth, conjointly with Bouguer, appeared later. Among his other scientific labours was his proposition to adopt the length of the seconds pendulum as an invariable unit of measure. On the 4th of February 1774, he died while voluntarily undergoing an experimental operation for the

removal of a malady contracted in Peru. Always occupied, he appears to have needed time to feel his misfortunes ; and, notwithstanding his sufferings, he appears never to have been unhappy ; his wit and amiability of temper made him many friends, and his humour was generally successful in blunting the attacks of enmity.

A ROYAL SPEECH BY CANDLELIGHT.

The opening-day of the Session of Parliament in 1836 (February 4), was unusually gloomy, which, added to an imperfection in the sight of King William IV., and the darkness of the House, rendered it impossible for his Majesty to read the royal speech with facility. Most patiently and good-naturedly did he struggle with the task, often hesitating, sometimes mistaking, and at others correcting himself. On one occasion, he stuck altogether, and after two or three ineffectual efforts to make out the word, he was obliged to give it up ; when, turning to Lord Melbourne, who stood on his right hand, and looking him most significantly in the face, he said in a tone sufficiently loud to be audible in all parts of the House, ' Eh! what is it ?' Lord Melbourne having whispered the obstructing word, the King proceeded to toil through the speech ; but by the time he got to about the middle, the librarian brought him two wax-lights, on which he suddenly paused ; then raising his head, and looking at the Lords and Commons, he addressed them, on the spur of the moment, in a perfectly distinct voice, and without the least embarrassment or the mistake of a single word, in these terms :

' My Lords and Gentlemen,—

' I have hitherto not been able, from want of light, to read this speech in the way its importance deserves ; but as lights are now brought me, I will read it again from the commencement, and in a way which, I trust, will command your attention.'

The King then again, though evidently fatigued by the difficulty of reading in the first instance, began at the beginning, and read through the speech in a manner which would have done credit to any professor of elocution.

Early Lending Library.— In the reign of Henry IV. was built a library in Durham College (now Trinity College), Oxford, for the large collection of books of Richard of Bury, said to consist of more volumes than all the bishops of England had then in their possession. Richard had bestowed certain portions of his valuable library upon a company of scholars residing in a Hall at Oxford ; and he drew up ' A provident arrangement by which books may be lent to strangers,' meaning students of Oxford not belonging to that Hall. The custody of the books was deputed to five of the scholars, of which three, and in no case fewer, could lend any books for inspection and use only ; but for copying and transcribing, they did not allow any book to pass without the walls of the house. And when any scholar, whether secular or religious, was qualified for the favour, and demanded the loan of a book, the keepers, provided they had a duplicate of the book, might lend it to him, taking a security exceeding in value the book lent. The reader may smile at the caution ; but we have known some possessors of books in our own day to adopt similar rules.

FEBRUARY 5.

St Agatha, virgin martyr, patroness of Malta, 251. The martyrs of Pontus, 304. St Abraamius, bishop of Arbela, martyr, 348. St Avitus, archbishop of Vienne, 525. St Alice (or Adelaide), abbess at Cologne, 1015. The twenty-six martyrs of Japan, 1697.

Born.—Bishop Thomas Tanner, 1674 (N. S.), *Market Lavington ;* Rev. Dr John Lingard, historian, 1771, *Winchester ;* Sir Robert Peel, Bart., statesman, 1788, *Bury, Lancashire ;* Dr John Lindley, botanist, 1799, *Catton.*

Died.—Marcus Cato, B.C. 46, *Utica ;* James Meyer, Flemish scholar, 1552 ; Adrian Reland, Orientalist and scholar, 1718, *Utrecht ;* James, Earl Stanhope, political character, 1721, *Chevening ;* Dr William Cullen, 1790, *Kirknewton ;* Lewis Galvani, discoverer of galvanism, 1799, *Bologna ;* Thomas Banks, sculptor, 1805 ; General Paoli, Corsican patriot, 1807.

DEATH OF THE FIRST EARL STANHOPE.

This eminent person carried arms under King William in Flanders ; and his Majesty was so struck with his spirit and talent that he gave him a captain's commission in the Foot Guards, with the rank of lieutenant-colonel, he being then in his 21st year. He also served under the Duke of Schomberg and the Earl of Peterborough ; and subsequently distinguished himself as Commander-in-chief of the British forces in Spain. At the close of his military career, he became an active Whig leader in Parliament ; took office under Sunderland, and was soon after raised to the peerage. His death was very sudden. He was of constitutionally warm and sensitive temper, with the impetuous bearing of the camp, which he had never altogether shaken off. In the course of the discussion on the South Sea Company's affairs, which so unhappily involved some of the leading members of the Government, the Duke of Wharton (Feb. 4, 1721) made some severe remarks in the House of Lords, comparing the conduct of ministers to that of Sejanus, who had made the reign of Tiberius hateful to the old Romans. Stanhope, in rising to reply, spoke with such vehemence in vindication of himself and his colleagues, that he burst a blood-vessel, and died the next day. 'May it be eternally remembered,' says the *British Merchant,* 'to the honour of Earl Stanhope, that he died poorer in the King's service than he came into it. Walsingham, the great Walsingham, died poor ; but the great Stanhope lived in the time of South Sea temptations.'

GENERAL PAOLI AND DR JOHNSON.

When, in 1769, this patriotic General, the Garibaldi of his age, was overpowered in defending Corsica against the French, he sought refuge in England, where he obtained a pension of £1200 a year, and resided until 1789. Boswell, who had travelled in Corsica, anticipated introducing him to Johnson ; 'for what an idea,' says he, in his account of the island, 'may we not form of an interview between such a scholar and philosopher as Mr Johnson, and such a legislator and general as Paoli !' Accordingly, upon his arrival in England, he was presented to Johnson by Boswell, who tells us, they met with a manly ease,

mutually conscious of their own abilities, and the abilities of each other. 'The General spoke Italian, and Dr Johnson English, and understood one another very well, with a little interpretation from me, in which I compared myself to an isthmus, which joins two great continents.' Johnson said, 'General Paoli had the loftiest port of any man he had ever seen.'

Paoli lived in good style, and with him, Johnson says, in one of his letters to Mrs Thrale, 'I love to dine.' Six months before his death, June 25, 1784, the great Samuel was entertained by Paoli at his house in Upper Seymour-street, Portman-square. 'There was a variety of dishes much to his (Johnson's) taste, of all of which he seemed to me to eat so much, that I was afraid he might be hurt by it ; and I whispered to the General my fear, and begged he might not press him. "Alas !" said the General, " see how very ill he looks ; he can live but a very short time. Would you refuse any slight gratifications to a man under sentence of death? There is a humane custom in Italy, by which persons in that melancholy situation are indulged with having whatever they like to eat and drink, even with expensive delicacies."

On the breaking out of the French Revolution, it was thought that Paoli, by the influence of his name with his countrymen, might assist in preserving their loyalty against the machinations of the liberals. Repairing to Paris, he was graciously received by Louis XVI., and appointed Lieutenant-General of the island. The Revolutionists were at first too much for him ; but, on the war breaking out between England and France, he, with the aid of the English, drove the French garrisons out of the island. On departing soon after, he strongly recommended his countrymen to persist in allegiance to the British crown. He then returned to England, where he died February 5, 1807. A monument, with his bust by Flaxman, was raised to his memory in Westminster Abbey.

THE BELL-SAVAGE INN—BANKS'S HORSE.

On the 5th February, in the 31st year of Henry VI., John French gave to his mother for her life 'all that tenement or inn, with its appurtenances, called *Savage's Inn,* otherwise called the *Bell on the Hoop,* in the parish of St Bridget, in Fleet-street, London, to have and to hold, ... without impeachment of waste.'* From this piece of authentic history we become assured of the fallacy of a great number of conjectures that have been indulged in regarding the origin of the name ' Bell and Savage,' or ' Bell-Savage,' which was for ages familiarly applied to a well-known, but now extinct inn, on Ludgate-hill. The inn had belonged to a person named Savage. Its pristine sign was a bell, perched, as was customary, upon a hoop. ' Bell Savage Inn' was evidently a mass made up in the public mind, in the course of time, out of these two distinct elements.

Moth, in *Love's Labour Lost,* wishing to prove how simple is a certain problem in arithmetic, says, ' The dancing horse will tell you.' This is believed to be an allusion to a horse called

* Archæologia, xviii. 198.

Morocco, or Marocco, which had been trained to do certain extraordinary tricks, and was publicly exhibited in Shakspeare's time by its master, a Scotchman named Banks. The animal made his appearance before the citizens of London, in the yard of the Belle Savage Inn, the audience as usual occupying the galleries which surrounded the court in the centre of the building, as is partially delineated in the annexed copy of a contemporary wood-print, which illus-

THE WONDERFUL HORSE OF AN. 1595.

trates a brochure published in 1595, under the name of 'Maroccus Exstaticus: or Bankes Bay Horse in a Traunce; a Discourse set downe in a merry dialogue between Bankes and his Beast . . . . . intituled to Mine Host of the Belsauage and all his honest guests.' Morocco was then a young nag of a chestnut or bay colour, of moderate size. The tricks which the animal performed do not seem to us now-a-days very wonderful; but such matters were then comparatively rare, and hence they were regarded with infinite astonishment. The creature was trained to erect itself and leap about on its hind legs. We are gravely told that it could dance *the Canaries.* A glove being thrown down, its master would command it to take it to some particular person: for example, to the gentleman in the large ruff, or the lady with the green mantle; and this order it would correctly execute. Some coins being put into the glove, it would tell how many they were by raps with its foot. It could, in like manner, tell the numbers on the upper face of a pair of dice. As an example of comic performances, it would be desired to single out the gentleman who was the greatest slave of the fair sex; and this it was sure to do satisfactorily enough. In reality, as is now well known, these feats depend upon a simple training to obey a certain signal, as the call of the word *Up.* Almost any young horse of tolerable intelligence could be trained to do such feats in little more than a month.

Morocco was taken by its master to be exhibited in Scotland in 1596, and there it was thought to be animated by a spirit. In 1600, its master astonished London by making it override the vane of St Paul's Cathedral. We find in the Jest-books of the time, that, while this performance was going on in presence of an enormous crowd, a serving-man came to his master walking about in the middle aisle, and entreated him to come out and see the spectacle. 'Away, you fool!' answered the gentleman; 'what need I go so far to see a horse on the top, when I can see so many asses at the bottom!' Banks also exhibited his horse in France, and there, by way of stimulating popular curiosity, professed to believe that the animal really was a spirit in equine form. This, however, had very nearly led to unpleasant consequences, in raising an alarm that there was something diabolic in the case. Banks very dexterously saved himself for this once by causing the horse to select a man from a crowd with a cross on his hat, and pay homage to the sacred emblem, calling on all to observe that nothing satanic could have been induced to perform such an act of reverence. Owing, perhaps, to this incident, a rumour afterwards prevailed that Banks and his curtal [nag] were burned as subjects of the Black Power of the World at Rome, by order of the Pope. But more authentic notices shew Banks as surviving in King Charles's time, in the capacity of a jolly vintner in Cheapside.*

It may at the same time be remarked that there would have been nothing decidedly extraordinary in the horse being committed with its master to a fiery purgation. 'In a little book entitled *Le Diable Bossu*, Nancy, 1708, 18mo, there is an obscure allusion to an English horse whose master had taught him to know the cards, and which was burned alive at Lisbon in 1707; and Mr Granger, in his *Biographical History of England* (vol. iii., p. 164, edit. 1779), has informed us that, within his remembrance, a horse which had been taught to perform several tricks was, with his owner, put into the Inquisition.' —*Douce's Illustrations of Shakspeare*, i. 214.

THE BATTLE OF PLASSEY.

On February 4, 1757, Robert Clive had attacked the forces of Surajah Dowlah with success, and driven them from the neighbourhood of Calcutta. Surajah Dowlah, the youthful Viceroy or Nabob of Bengal, had overpowered the British factory at Calcutta, and committed the monstrous cruelty of shutting up a hundred and forty-six English in the famous Black Hole, where, before morning, all but twenty-three had perished miserably. Against him came from Madras the 'heaven-born soldier' Robert Clive, with about three thousand troops, of which only a third were English, together with a fleet under Admiral Watson. Aided by a conspiracy in the Nabob's camp in favour of Meer Jaffier, and using many artifices and tricks which seemed to him justified by the practices of the enemy, Clive at length found himself at Cossimbuzar, a few miles from Plassey, where lay Surajah Dowlah with sixty thousand men. He had to consider that, if he crossed the intermediate river and failed in his attack, himself and his troops would be utterly lost. A council of war advised him against advancing. Yet, inspired by his wonderful genius, he determined on the bolder course. The Bengalese army advanced upon him with an appearance of power which would have appalled most men; but the first cannonade from the English threw it into confusion. It fled; Surajah descended into obscurity; and the English found India open to them. This memorable battle took place on 23d June 1757. One hardly knows whether to be most astonished at the courage of Clive, or at the perfidious arts to which he at the same time descended in order to out-manœuvre a too powerful enemy. The conduct of the English general is defended by his biographer Sir John Malcolm, but condemned by Lord Macaulay, who remarks that the maxim 'Honesty is the best policy' is even more true of states than of individuals, in as far as states

* See Halliwell's *Shakspeare*, notes to *Love's Labour Lost*, for a great assemblage of curious notices regarding Banks and Morocco; also Chambers's *Domestic Annals of Scotland*, under April 1596.

are longer-lived, and adds, 'It is possible to mention men who have owed great worldly prosperity to breaches of private faith; but we doubt whether it is possible to mention a state which has on the whole been a gainer by a breach of public faith.'

Insignificant as was the English force employed on this occasion, we must consider the encounter as, from its consequences, one of the great battles of the world.

FEBRUARY 6.

St Dorothy, virgin martyr, 304. St Mel, bishop of Ardagh, 488. St Vedast, bishop of Arras, 539. St Barsanuphius, of Palestine, 6th century. St Amandus, 675.

Born.—Antoine Arnauld, French theologian, 1612, *Paris;* Anne, Queen of England, 1665, *St James's;* Augustine Calmet, 1672.

Died.—Jacques Amyot, Great Almoner of France, 1593; Charles II., King of England, 1685, *Whitehall;* Pope Clement XII., 1740; Dr Joseph Priestley, chemist and electrician, 1804, *Pennsylvania*.

DEATH OF CHARLES THE SECOND.

The winter of 1684-5 had been spent by the Court at Whitehall, amid the gaieties common to the season. Evelyn could never forget 'the inexpressible luxury and profaneness, gaming, and all dissoluteness, and, as it were, a total forgetfulness of God (it being Sunday evening)' which he was witness of; 'the King sitting and toying with his concubines, Portsmouth, Cleveland, Mazarine, &c., a French boy singing love-songs in that glorious gallery, whilst about twenty of the great courtiers and other dissolute persons were at basset, round a large table, a bank of at least £2000 in gold before them; upon which two gentlemen who were with me made strange reflections. Six days after, all was in the dust.' Burnet tells us that the King 'ate little all that day, and came to Lady Portsmouth, his favourite mistress, at night, and called for a porringer of spoon meat. Being made too strong for his stomach, he ate little, and had a restless night.' Another account states that the revels extended over Sunday night until the next morning, when at eight o'clock the King swooned away in his chair, and was seized with a fit of apoplexy; and, according to Evelyn, had not Dr King, who was accidentally present, and had a lancet in his pocket, bled his Majesty, 'he would certainly have died that moment, which might have been of direful consequence, there being nobody else present with the King, save his doctor and one more. It was a mark of extraordinary dexterity, resolution, and presence of mind in the doctor, to let him blood in the very paroxysm, without staying the coming of other physicians, which regularly should have been done, and for want of which he must have a regular pardon, as they tell me.' The Privy Council, however, approved of what he had done, and ordered him £1000, but which was never paid him. This saved the King for the instant; but next morning he had another fit, and the physicians told the Duke of York that his majesty was not likely to live through the day.

Then took place a scene, revealing the hypocrisy of a lifetime; that is, shewing that Charles, while professing Protestantism, had all along been, as far as he was any thing, a Catholic. 'The Duke,' says Burnet, 'ordered Huddleston, the priest, who had mainly contributed to the saving of Charles at Worcester, to be brought to the lodgings under the bedchamber. When Huddleston was told what was to be done, he was in great confusion, for he had not brought the host. He went, however, to another priest, who lived in the court, who gave him the pix, with an host in it. Everything being prepared, the Duke whispered the King in the ear; upon that the King ordered that all who were in the bedchamber should withdraw, except the Earls of Bath and Feversham; and the door was double-locked. The company was kept out half an hour; only Lord Feversham opened the door once, and called for a glass of water. Cardinal Howard told Bishop Burnet that, in the absence of the company, Huddleston, according to the account he sent to Rome, made the King go through some acts of contrition, and, after obtaining such a confession as he was then able to give, he gave him absolution. The consecrated wafer stuck in the King's throat, and that was the reason of calling for a glass of water. Charles told Huddleston that he had saved his life twice, first his body, then his soul.

'When the company were admitted, they found the King had undergone a marvellous alteration. Bishop Ken then vigorously applied himself to the awaking of the King's conscience, and pronounced many short ejaculations and prayers, of which, however, the King seemed to take no notice, and returned no answer. He pressed the King six or seven times to receive the sacrament; but the King always declined, saying he was very weak. But Ken pronounced over him absolution of his sins. * * * The King suffered much inwardly, and said he was burnt up within. He said once that he hoped he should climb up to heaven's gates, which was the only word savouring of religion that he used.'

During the night Charles earnestly recommended the Duchess of Portsmouth and her boy to the care of James; 'and do not,' he good-naturedly added, 'let poor Nelly starve.' The Queen sent excuses for her absence, saying she was too much disordered to resume her post by the couch, and implored pardon. 'She ask my pardon, poor woman!' cried Charles; 'I ask hers, with all my heart.'

'The morning light began to peep through the windows of Whitehall, and Charles desired the attendants to pull aside the curtains, that he might once more look at the day. He remembered that it was time to wind up a clock which stood near his bed. These little circumstances were long remembered, because they proved beyond dispute that, when he declared himself a Roman Catholic, he was in full possession of his faculties. He apologised to those who stood round him all night for the trouble which he had caused. He had been, he said, a most unconscionable time dying, but he hoped they would excuse it.

This was the last glimpse of that exquisite urbanity so often found potent to charm away the resentment of a justly incensed nation. Soon after dawn the speech of the dying man failed. Before ten his senses were gone. Great numbers had repaired to the churches at the hour of morning service. When the prayer for the King was read, loud groans and sobs shewed how deeply his people felt for him. At noon, on Friday, the 6th of February, he passed away without a struggle.'*

It was the belief of many at the time that Charles II. was poisoned. It was common then and in the preceding age to attribute the sudden death of any great man to poison; but, in Charles's case, the suspicions are not without authority. Sheffield, Duke of Buckingham, says: 'The most knowing and the most deserving of all his physicians did not only believe him poisoned, but thought himself so too, not long after, for having declared his opinion a little too boldly.'† Bishop Patrick strengthens the supposition from the testimony of Sir Thomas Mellington, who sat with the King for three days, and never went to bed for three nights.‡ Lord Chesterfield, the grandson of the Earl of Chesterfield who was with Charles at his death, states positively that the King was poisoned.§ The Duchess of Portsmouth, when in England in 1699, is said to have told Lord Chancellor Cowper that Charles II. was poisoned at her house by one of her footmen in a dish of chocolate; and Fox had heard a somewhat similar report from the family of his mother, who was grand-daughter to the Duchess.

This historical evidence is, however, invalidated by more recent investigation. On examining King Charles's head, a copious effusion of lymph was found in the ventricles and at the base of the cranium; from which Sir Henry Halford was disposed to think that the King might have been still further bled with advantage. It is quite evident from Sir Henry's account, that Charles II. died of apoplexy—the only too probable consequence of his excesses—and consequently that his indifference to the solicitations of those about him, on religious matters, can only, with charity, be attributed to the effects of his disease.||

A WONDERFUL CHILD.

The annals of precocity present no more remarkable instance than the brief career of Christian Heinecker, born at Lubeck, February 6, 1721. At the age of ten months he could speak and repeat every word which was said to him: when twelve months old, he knew by heart the principal events narrated in the Pentateuch: in his second year he learned the greater part of the history of the Bible, both of the Old and New Testaments: in his third year he could reply to most questions on universal history and geography, and in the same year he learned to speak Latin and French: in his fourth year he employed himself in the study of religion and the

* Macaulay's History of England, vol. i.
† Buckingham's Works, vol. ii.
‡ Bishop Patrick's Autobiography.
§ Letters to his Son.
|| Paper read to the College of Physicians, by Sir Henry Halford, in 1835.

history of the church, and he was able not only to repeat what he had read, but also to reason upon it, and express his own judgment. The King of Denmark wishing to see this wonderful child, he was taken to Copenhagen, there examined before the court, and proclaimed to be a wonder. On his return home, he learned to write, but, his constitution being weak, he shortly after fell ill; he died on the 27th of June 1725, without, it is said, shewing much uneasiness at the approach of death. This account of him by his teacher is confirmed by many respectable contemporary authorities. Martini published a dissertation at Lubeck, in which he attempted to account for the circumstances of the child's early development of intellect.

It cannot be too generally known that extreme precocity like this is of the nature of disease and a subject for the gravest care. In a precocious child, the exercise of the intellect, whether in lessons or otherwise, should be discouraged and controlled, not, as it too often is, stimulated, if there be any sincere desire that the child should live.

THE TWO UNKNOWN SISTERS—A CORNISH LEGEND.

I.

It is from Nectan's sainted steep
The foamy waters flash and leap:
It is where shrinking wild flowers grow,
They lave the nymph that dwells below!

II.

But wherefore, in this far off dell,
The reliques of a human cell?
Where the sad stream, and lonely wind,
Bring man no tidings of his kind!

III.

Long years agone, the old man said,
'Twas told him by his grandsire dead,
One day two ancient sisters came,
None there could tell their race or name!

IV.

Their speech was not in Cornish phrase,
Their garb had marks of loftier days;
Slight food they took from hands of men,
They wither'd slowly in that glen!

V.

One died!—the other's shrunken eye
Gush'd, till the fount of tears was dry;
A wild and wasting thought had she,
'I shall have none to weep for me!'

VI.

They found her, silent, at the last,
Bent, in the shape wherein she pass'd;
Where her lone seat long used to stand,
Her head upon her shrivell'd hand!

VII.

Did fancy give this legend birth,
The grandame's tale for winter hearth?
Or some dead bard by Nectan's stream,
People these banks with such a dream?

VIII.

We know not: but it suits the scene,
To think such wild things here have been,
What spot more meet could grief or sin
Choose at the last to wither in!

R. S. HAWKER.

FEBRUARY 7.

St Theodorus (Stratilates), martyred at Heraclea, 319. St Augulus, bishop of London, martyr, 4th century. St Tresain, of Ireland, 6th century. St Richard, king of the West Saxons, *circ.* 722. St Romualdo, founder of the order of Camaldoli, 1027.

ST ROMUALDO.

Romualdo was impelled to a religious life by seeing his father in a fit of passion commit manslaughter. Assuming the order of St Benedict, he was soon scandalised by the licentious lives generally led by his brethren, and to their reformation he zealously devoted himself. The result was his forming a sub-order, styled from the place of its first settlement, the *Camaldolesi*, who, in their asceticism and habits of solemn and silent contemplation, remind us of the early Egyptian anchorets. St Romualdo, who died at an advanced age in 1027, was consequently held in great veneration, and Dante has placed him in his *Paradiso*, 'among the spirits of men contemplative.'

Born.—Rev. Sir Henry Moncrieff, D.D., 1750; Charles Dickens, novelist, 1812.

Died.—James Earl of Moray (the Bonny), murdered 1592; Dr Bedell, bishop of Kilmore, 1642; Anne Radcliffe, novelist, 1823, *Pimlico;* Henry Neele, poet, 1828, *London;* M. Bourrienne, formerly Secretary to Napoleon Bonaparte, died in a madhouse at *Caen. Normandy*, 1834.

MRS RADCLIFFE'S ROMANCES.

This admirable writer had, in her youth, the benefit of the society of Mr Bentley, the well-known man of letters and taste in the arts, and of Mr Wedgwood, the able chemist; and she became thus early introduced to Mrs Montague, Mrs Piozzi, and the Athenian Stuart. Her maiden name was Ward, and she acquired that which made her so famous by marrying Mr William Radcliffe, a graduate at Oxford and a student at law, afterwards proprietor and editor of the *English Chronicle.* Her first work was a romance styled *The Castles of Athlin and Dunbayne;* her second, which appeared in 1790, *The Sicilian Romance,* of which Sir Walter Scott, then a novel reader of no ordinary appetite, says: 'The scenes were inartificially connected, and the characters hastily sketched, without any attempt at individual distinction; being cast in the mould of ardent lovers, tyrannical parents, with domestic ruffians, guards, and others, who had wept or stormed through the chapters of romance, without much alteration in their family habits or features, for a quarter of a century before Mrs Radcliffe's time.' Nevertheless, 'the praise may, be claimed for Mrs Radcliffe, of having been the first to introduce into her prose fictions a beautiful and fanciful tone of natural description and impressive narrative, which had hitherto been exclusively applied to poetry.'

The Romance of the Forest, which appeared in 1791, placed the author at once in that rank and pre-eminence in her own particular style of composition, which she ever after maintained. Next year, after visiting the scenery of the

Rhine, Mrs Radcliffe is supposed to have written her *Mysteries of Udolpho*, or, at least, corrected it, after the journey. For the *Mysteries*, Mrs Radcliffe received the then unprecedented sum of £500; for her next production, the *Italian*, £800. This was the last work published in her lifetime. This silence was unexplained : it was said that, in consequence of brooding over the terrors which she had depicted, her reason had been overturned, and that the author of the *Mysteries of Udolpho* only existed as the melancholy inmate of a private madhouse ; but there was not the slightest foundation for this unpleasing rumour.

Of the author of the *Mysteries of Udolpho*, the unknown author of the *Pursuits of Literature* spoke as 'a mighty magician, bred and surrounded by the Florentine muses in their secret solitary caverns, amid the paler shrines of Gothic superstition, and in all the dreariness of enchantment.' Dr Joseph Warton, the head master of Winchester School, then at a very advanced period of life, told Robinson, the publisher, that, happening to take up the *Mysteries of Udolpho*, he was so fascinated that he could not go to bed until he had finished it, and that he actually sat up a great part of the night for that purpose. Mr Sheridan and Mr Fox also spoke of the *Mysteries* with high praise.

The great notoriety attained by Mrs Radcliffe's romances in her lifetime, made her the subject of continually recurring rumours of the most absurd and groundless character. One was to the effect that, having visited the fine old Gothic mansion of Haddon Hall, she insisted on remaining a night there, in the course of which she was inspired with all that enthusiasm for hidden passages and mouldering walls which marks her writings. The truth is, that the lady never saw Haddon Hall.

Mrs Radcliffe died in Stafford-row, Pimlico, February 7, 1823, in her fifty-ninth year; and was buried in the vault of the chapel, in the Bayswater-road, belonging to the parish of St George, Hanover-square.

THE GREAT BED OF WARE.

When Sir Toby Belch (*Twelfth Night*, Act iii., scene 2) wickedly urges Aguecheek to pen a challenge to his supposed rival, he tells him to put as many lies in a sheet as will lie in it, 'although the sheet were big enough for the bed of Ware in England.' The enormous bed here

THE GREAT BED OF WARE.

alluded to was a wonder of the age of Shakspeare, and it still exists in Ware. It is a square of 10 feet 9 inches, 7 feet 6 inches in height, very elegantly carved, and altogether a fine piece of antique furniture. It is believed to be not older than Elizabeth's reign. It has for ages been an inn wonder, visited by multitudes, and described by many travellers. There are strange stories of people engaging it to lie in, twelve at a time, by way of putting its enormous capacity for accommodation to the proof. It was long ago customary for a company, on seeing it, to drink from a can of beer a toast appropriate to it. In the same room, there hung a pair of horns, upon which all new-comers were sworn, as at Highgate.

THE PORTLAND VASE.

In one of the small rooms of the old British Museum (Montague House), there had been exhibited, for many years, that celebrated production of ceramic art—the Portland Vase; when, on the 7th of February 1845, this beautiful work was wantonly dashed to pieces by one of the visitors to the Museum, named William Lloyd.

The Portland Vase was found about the year 1560, in a sarcophagus in a sepulchre under the Monte del Grano, two miles and a half from Rome. It was deposited in the palace of the Barberini family until 1770, when it was purchased by Byres, the antiquary, who subsequently sold it to Sir William Hamilton. From Sir William it was bought for 1800 guineas, by the Duchess of Portland; and at the sale of her Grace's property, after her decease, the Vase was *bought in* by the Portland family for £1029. The Vase is 9¾ inches high, and 7¼ inches in diameter, and has two handles. Four authors of note considered it to be stone, but all differing as to the *kind* of stone: Breval regarded it as chalcedony; Bartoli, sardonyx; Count Tetzi, amethyst; and De la Chausse, agate. In reality it is composed of glass, ornamented with white opaque figures, upon a dark-blue semi-transparent ground; the whole having been originally covered with white enamel, out of which the figures have been cut after the manner of a cameo. The glass foot is thought to have been cemented on, after bones or ashes had been placed in the vase. This mode of its manufacture was discovered by examination of the fractured pieces, after the breaking of the vase in 1845; a drawing of the pieces is preserved in the British Museum.

The subject of the figures is involved in mystery; for as much difference of opinion exists respecting it as formerly did regarding the materials of the vase. The seven figures, each five inches high, are said by some to illustrate the fable of Thaddeus and Theseus; Bartoli supposed the group to represent Proserpine and Pluto; Count Tetzi, that it had reference to the birth of Alexander Severus, whose cinerary urn it is thought to be; whilst the late Mr Thomas Windus, F.S.A., considered the design as representing a lady of quality consulting Galen, who at length discovered her sickness to be love for a celebrated rope-dancer.

The vase was engraved by Cipriani and Bartolozzi, in 1786. Copies of it were executed by Wedgwood at fifty guineas each; the model having cost 500 guineas. Sir Joseph Banks and Sir Joshua Reynolds bore testimony to the excellent execution of these copies, which were chased by a steel rifle, after the bas-relief had been wholly or partially fired. One of these copies may be seen in the British Museum.

The person who so wantonly broke the original vase was sentenced to pay a fine, or to undergo imprisonment; and the sum was paid by a gentleman, anonymously. The pieces, being gathered up, were afterwards put together by Mr Doubleday, so perfectly, that a blemish can scarcely be detected; and the restored Vase is now kept in the Medal-room of the Museum.

FEBRUARY 8.

St Paul, bishop of Verdun, 631. St Cuthman of England, 8th century. St Stephen of Grandmont, 1124. St John of Matha, founder of the Order of Trinitarians, 1213.

Born.—St Proclus, patriarch of Constantinople, 412; Mary I., Queen of England, 1516, *Greenwich;* William Earl of Pembroke, 1580; Samuel Butler, author of *Hudibras*, 1612, *Strensham;* Peter Daniel Huet, bishop of Avranches, 1630; Charles Henault, *littérateur*, 1685. *Caen;* John Andrew de Luc, Genevese philosopher, 1727.

Died.—Mary, Queen of Scotland, beheaded at Fotheringay, 1586-7; Richard Penderel, who aided in the escape of Charles II., 1671, *St. Giles's, London;* Dr George Sewel, historian of the Quakers, 1727, *Hampstead;* Aaron Hill, poet, 1750, *Strand.*

EXECUTION OF MARY QUEEN OF SCOTS.

The judicial murder of Mary Queen of Scots —whose life, according to the Earl of Kent, would have been the death of our religion, and whose death was calculated to be its preservation —was performed at Fotheringay Castle, on the 8th of February 1586-7. The minute accounts of the scene, which are too familiar to be here repeated, exhibit a religious dignity, resignation, and apparent serenity of conscience, that tend greatly to counteract the popular impressions regarding the guilt of the Scottish queen. One is at a loss to believe that one who had not lived well could die so well.

Heretofore, the strange conduct of Elizabeth regarding her unfortunate cousin, has not tended to exculpate her from the guilt of authorising the Fotheringay tragedy. But it now begins to appear that she really did not give the final order for the act, but that the whole affair was managed without her consent by Burleigh, Walsingham, and Davison, the signature to the warrant being forged at Walsingham's command by his secretary Thomas Harrison;[*] so that the queen's conduct to these men afterwards was not hypocritical, as hitherto believed. The act was so far of an occult and skulking nature, that a fortnight and a day elapsed before King James, while hunting at Calder, was certified of it. It put him into 'a very great displeasure and grief,' as it well might, and he 'much lamented and mourned for her many days.'[†]

AARON HILL.

This extraordinary person—a small poet and great projector—died on the 8th of February 1750, '*in the very minute of the earthquake,*' says

* See Strickland's *Lives of the Queens of Scotland*, vii. 465.

+ Patrick Anderson's *History of Scotland*, MS.

Davies, 'the shock of which, though speechless, he appeared to feel.' Aaron Hill was of good family, fortune, and connexions, born February 10, 1685, in a house upon the site of Beaufort-buildings, in the Strand. He was for a short time at Westminster School: when fifteen years of age, he made a voyage to Constantinople, purposely to pay a visit to his relative Lord Paget, ambassador there, and who sent him, with a clerical tutor, to travel through Egypt and Palestine, and great part of the East; he subsequently travelled in Europe, with Sir William Wentworth, for two or three years. In 1709 he published his first poem, *Camillus*, in honour of the Earl of Peterborough, who made him his secretary. He next wrote eight books of an epic poem, *Gideon*, but did not complete it. He then produced for Drury-lane Theatre his first tragedy of *Elfrida*, and was next appointed manager of the Italian Opera-house in the Haymarket, and wrote *Rinaldo*, being the libretto of the first opera that Handel composed after he came to England. For a poem in praise of the Czar Peter, he was rewarded with a gold medal. He appears to have been such a person as Swift loved to ridicule—a projector, trying various schemes, and succeeding in none. We now find him patenting an oil as sweet as that of olives, from beech-masts; next organising a company for raising plantations in Georgia; afterwards clearing the woods in the Highlands of Scotland, to furnish timber for the navy, and making potash to rival that brought from Russia. These several schemes failed. All this time he was writing turgid, declamatory tragedies, or translating plays from the French theatre: his greatest success was a translation of Voltaire's *Zara*, in which Mrs T. Cibber, the excellent tragic actress, made her first appearance on the stage. He was intimate with Bolingbroke and Pope. The latter, falling into a misunderstanding with Hill, classed him with the flying fishes, 'who now

and then rise upon their fins, and fly out of the profound; but their wings are soon dry, and they drop down to the bottom.' Hill rejoined by an epigram, and Pope marked him out for a place in the *Dunciad*; a violent controversy ensued, in which Hill appeared to no advantage; he threatened Pope with vengeance, which led the little bard of Twickenham for some time to carry loaded pistols, and to be accompanied by his big, faithful Danish dog, Bounce.

Hill lost all his property by his schemes; but he for literary fame confidently appealed to posterity:

'Yet while from life my setting prospects fly,
Fain would my mind's weak offspring shun to die;
Fain would their hope some light through time explore,
The name's kind passport when the man's no more.'

It is, however, a fact worthy of the consideration of the literary class, that Aaron Hill worked much for fame, and in his lifetime enjoyed a share of it; yet, of all the writings which he issued and which had their day, there is but one little piece—an epigram—which can be said to have survived to our time:

'Tender-handed stroke a nettle,
　And it stings you for your pains;
Grasp it like a man of mettle,
　And it soft as silk remains.

' 'Tis the same with common natures,
　Use them kindly, they rebel;
But be rough as nutmeg-graters,
　And the rogues obey you well.'

SEDANS.

Evelyn, writing at Naples on the 8th February 1645, describes the gay appearance of the city and its inhabitants, adding, 'The streets are full of gallants on horseback, in coaches and sedans,' which last articles, he tells us, were 'from hence brought first into England by Sir Sanders Duncomb.' It would appear that Sir Sanders introduced this convenience into England in 1634,

LADY CARRIED IN A SEDAN, TEMP. GEO. II.

and, obtaining a patent for it from the king, prepared forty or fifty examples for public use.

It is thus, in regard to its starting in England, very nearly contemporaneous with the hackney-coach, which dates from 1625. Not inconsistent, however, with this statement of the general use of sedans, may be another given on good authority, that *one* such convenience had previously been used by the favourite Buckingham, much to the disgust of the people, who exclaimed that he was employing his fellow-creatures to do the service of beasts.

In any community where elegant life was cultivated, the SEDAN was sure of favour, being a very handy and pleasant means of getting carried from one's home either to a private or a public entertainment. In the first three quarters of the eighteenth century, when the style of dress was highly refined, and the least derangement to the hair of either lady or gentleman was fatal, the sedan was at its zenith of usefulness. Then was the gentleman, with his silk clothes and nicely arranged toupee and curls, as fain to take advantage of this careful casing as he went from house to house, as any of the softer sex. The nobility, and other wealthy persons, used to keep their own sedans, and have them very handsomely decorated. They stood in the lobby of the town-mansion, ready to be used when required. It must have been a fine sight to see several gilt sedans passing along, with a set of ladies and gentlemen of one family, through the west-end streets of London, attended by link-boys, and being one by one ushered into some luxurious mansion, where company was received for the evening. When the whole party had been duly delivered, the link-boys thrust their flambeaux into the trumpet-like extinguishers which flourished at each aristocratic door-cheek in the metropolis, and withdrew till the appointed time when their services were required for returning home.

In Edinburgh, in the middle of the eighteenth century, there were far more sedans in use than coaches. The sedan was better suited for the steep streets and narrow lanes of the Scottish capital, besides being better fitted in all circumstances for transporting a finely dressed lady or gentleman in a cleanly and composed condition. The public sedans of that city were for the most part in the hands of Highlanders, whose uncouth jargon and irritability amidst the confusions of a dissolving party, or a dismissed theatre, used to be highly amusing. Now, there is no such thing in Edinburgh, any more than in London, as a private sedan; and within the last few years the use of public ones has nearly, if not entirely ceased.

EARTHQUAKES IN ENGLAND.

The last earthquake of any considerable violence in England occurred on the 8th of February 1750. Such commotions are not so infrequent in our island as many suppose; but it must be admitted that they are generally innocuous or nearly so. Even in that notoriously mobile district about Comrie in Perthshire,—where during the winter of 1839-40 they had a hundred and forty earthquakes, being at the rate of about a shock a day at an average,—they seldom do much harm. Still, seeing that movements capable of throwing down buildings do at rare intervals take place, it might be well to avoid the raising of public structures.

as church towers and obelisks, beyond a moderate elevation. Perhaps it will yet be found that the Victoria Tower at Westminster is liable to some danger from this cause.

According to Mrs Somerville (*Physical Geography*, ed. 1858), there have been 255 earthquakes put on record in England, most of them slight and only felt in certain districts. The notices of such events given by our chronicles are generally meagre, little to purpose, of no scientific value, and more calculated to raise curiosity than to gratify it. Still, they are better than nothing.

In 1101 all England was terrified 'with a horrid spectacle, for all the buildings were lifted up and then again settled as before.'[*] In 1133 many houses were overthrown, and flames issued from rifts in the earth, which defied all attempts to quench them. On the Monday in the week before Easter in 1185, 'chanced a sore earthquake through all the parts of this land, such a one as the like had not been heard of in England, since the beginning of the world; for stones that lay couched fast in the earth were removed out of their places, houses were overthrown, and the great church of Lincoln rent from the top downwards.' (Holinshed.) The next earthquake of any moment occurred on St Valentine's Eve in 1247, and did considerable damage in the metropolis: this was preceded by a curious phenomenon —for three months prior to the shock the sea ceased to ebb and flow on the English coast, or the flow at least was not perceptible; the earthquake was followed by a season of such foul weather that the spring was a second winter. On the 12th of September 1275, St Michael's Church, Glastonbury, was destroyed by an earthquake. John Harding, in his metrical chronicle for 1361. records

> 'On St Mary's Day
> The great wind and earthquake marvellous,
> That greatly gan the people all affraye,
> So dreadful was it then, and perilous.'

Twenty years afterwards another was experienced, of which Fabyan, while omitting all particulars, says, 'The like thereof was never seen in England before that day nor since;' but the very next year (1382) Harding writes:

> 'The earthquake was, that time I saw,
> That castles, walls, towers, and steeples fyll,
> Houses, and trees, and crags from the hill.'

This happened on the 21st of May, and was followed three days afterwards by a 'watershake,' when the ships in the harbours were driven against each other with great violence.

About six o'clock on the evening of the 17th of February 1571, the earth near Kinaston, Herefordshire, began to open; 'and a hill, called Marclay Hill, with a rock under it, made at first a mighty bellowing noise, which was heard afar off, and then lifted up itself a great height and began to travel, carrying along with it the trees that grew upon it, the sheepfolds and flocks of sheep abiding thereon at the same time. In the place from whence it removed, it left a gaping distance 40 feet wide, and 80 ells long,—the whole field was almost 20 acres. Passing along, it overthrew

[*] William of Malmesbury.

a chapel standing in the way, removed a yew-tree growing in the churchyard from the west to the east ; with the like violence it thrust before it highways, houses and trees, made tilled ground pasture, and again turned pasture into tillage.' (Burton's *General History of Earthquakes*.) Three years later, in the same month, York, Worcester, Gloucester, Bristol, Hereford, and some less important towns, felt the shock of an earthquake, which so alarmed the good people of Norton, who were at evening prayer, that they fled from the chapel, fearing the dead were about to rise from their graves ; but this was nothing to the excitement created in London by a similar event which took place on the evening of Easter Wednesday (April 6), 1580. The great clock bell at Westminster struck at the shock, and the bells of the various churches were set jangling ; the people rushed out of the theatres in consternation, and the gentlemen of the Temple, leaving their supper, ran out of the hall with their knives in their hands. Part of the Temple Church was cast down, some stones fell from St Paul's, and two apprentices were killed at Christ Church by the fall of a stone during sermon-time. This earthquake was felt pretty generally throughout the kingdom, and was the cause of much damage in Kent, where many castles and other buildings were injured ; and at Dover, a portion of a cliff fell, carrying with it part of the castle wall. So alarmed were all classes, that Queen Elizabeth thought it advisable to cause a form of prayer to be used by all householders with their whole family, every evening before going to bed. About a century after, according to the compilers of chronologies, Lyme Regis was nearly destroyed by an earthquake ; but the historian of Dorsetshire makes no allusion to such an event. On the 8th of September 1692, the merchants were driven from Change and the people from their houses by a shock, and the streets of London were thronged with a panic-stricken crowd, some swooning, some aghast with wonder and amazement. This earthquake was felt in most of the home counties. Evelyn, writing from Sayes Court to Bishop Tenison, says, 'As to our late earthquake here, I do not find it has left any considerable marks, but at Mins, it is said, it has made some demolitions. I happened to be at my brother's at Wotton, in Surrey, when the shaking was, and at dinner with much company ; yet none of us at table were sensible of any motion. But the maid who was then making my bed, and another servant in a garret above her, felt it plainly ; and so did my wife's laundrymaid here at Deptford, and generally, wherever they were above in the upper floors, they felt the trembling most sensibly. In London, and particularly in Dover-street, they were greatly affrighted.' Although the earthquake did little damage, it sufficed to set afloat sundry speculations as to the approaching end of the world, and frightened the authorities into ordering a strict enforcement of the laws against swearing, drunkenness, and debauchery.

The year 1750 is, however, the year *par excellence* of English earthquakes. It opened with most unseasonable weather. the heat being, according to Walpole, 'beyond what was ever known in any other country ;' and on the 8th of February a pretty smart shock was experienced, followed exactly a month afterwards by a second and severer one, when the bells of the church clocks struck against the chiming-hammers, dogs howled, and fish jumped high out of the water. The lord of Strawberry Hill, in a letter to Sir Horace Mann, draws a lively picture of the effect created by the event, and we cannot do better than borrow his narration :

' "Portents and prodigies are grown so frequent,
That they have lost their name."

'My text is not literally true ; but as far as earthquakes go towards lowering the price of wonderful commodities, to be sure we are overstocked. We have had a second, much more violent than the first ; and you must not be surprised if, by next post, you hear of a burning mountain springing up in Smithfield. In the night between Wednesday and Thursday last, the earth had a shivering fit between one and two ; but so slight that, if no more had followed. I don't believe it would have been noticed. I had been awake, and had scarce dozed again,—on a sudden I felt my bolster lift my head. I thought somebody was getting from under my bed, but soon found it was a strong earthquake that lasted nearly half a minute, with a violent vibration and great roaring. I got up and found people running into the streets, but saw no mischief done. There has been some ; two old houses flung down, several chimnies, and much earthenware. The bells rang in several houses. Admiral Knowles, who has lived long in Jamaica, and felt seven there, says this was more violent than any of them. The wise say, that if we have not rain soon we shall certainly have more. Several people are going out of town, for it has nowhere reached above ten miles from London : they say they are not frightened, but that it is such fine weather, "Lord, one can't help going into the country !" The only visible effect it has had was in the Ridotto, at which, being the following morning, there were but 400 people. A parson who came into White's the morning after earthquake the first, and heard bets laid on whether it was an earthquake or the blowing up of powder mills, went away exceedingly scandalised, and said, "I protest they are such an impious set of people, that I believe, if the last trumpet was to sound, they would bet puppet-show against judgment !" The excitement grew intense: following the example of Bishops Secker and Sherlock, the clergy showered down sermons and exhortations, and a country quack sold pills "as good against an earthquake." A crazy Life-guardsman predicted a third and more fatal earthquake at the end of four weeks after the second, and a frantic terror prevailed among all classes as the time drew near. On the evening preceding the 5th of April, the roads out of London were crowded with vehicles, spite of an advertisement in the papers threatening the publication "of an exact list of all the nobility and gentry who have left or shall leave this place through fear of another earthquake." "Earthquake gowns"—warm gowns to wear while sitting out of doors all night—were in great request with women. Many people sat in coaches all night in Hyde Park, passing away the time with the aid of cards and candles:' and Walpole asks his correspondent, 'What will you think of Lady Catherine Pelham, Lady Frances Arundel, and Lord and Lady Galway, who go this evening to an inn ten miles out of town, where they are to play brag till four o'clock in the morning, and then come back, I suppose, to look for the bones of their husbands and families under the rubbish?' However, the soldier proved a false prophet, and expiated his folly in the madhouse. On the 18th of March in this year an earthquake was felt at Portsmouth, Southampton, and the Isle of Wight. In April, Cheshire, Flintshire, and Yorkshire were startled in like manner: this was followed by an earthquake in Dorsetshire in May, by another in Somersetshire in July, and in Lincolnshire in August, the catalogue being completed on the 30th of September by an earthquake extending through the counties of Suffolk, Leicester, and Northampton.

The great earthquake which destroyed Lisbon in 1755, agitated the waters of the three kingdoms, and even affected the fish-pond of Peerless Pool, in the City-road, London; but it produced no damage. Since then several shocks have been experienced here from time to time, but unattended with any circumstances calling for notice; the last one recorded being a slight earthquake felt in the north-western counties of England on the 9th of November 1852.

FEBRUARY 9.

St Apollonia, virgin martyr at Alexandria, 249. St Nicephorus, martyr at Antioch, 260. St Attracta, virgin in Ireland, 5th century. St Theliau, bishop of Llandaff, *circ.* 580. St Ansbert, archbishop of Rouen, 695. St Erhard, of Scotland, 8th century.

Born.—Daniel Bernouilli, a celebrated Swiss mathematician, 1700, *Gröningen;* C. F. Volney, French philosopher, 1757.

Died.—Agnes Sorel, 1450, *Memel;* Bishop Hooper, burnt at *Gloucester,* 1555; Dr Rowland Taylor, burnt at *Hadleigh,* 1555; Henry Lord Darnley, consort of Mary Queen of Scots, murdered, 1567; Dr John Gregory, author of *A Father's Legacy to his Daughters,* 1773, *Edinburgh;* Dr William Boyce, 1779; Benjamin Martin, philosophical writer, 1782; Nevil Maskelyne, astronomer-royal, 1811, *Flamsteed House.*

DANIEL BERNOUILLI, THE EMINENT
MATHEMATICIAN.

This eminent man, one of a family which is known in the history of mathematics by the services of eight of its members, was the second son of John Bernouilli, and was born at Gröningen, February 9, 1700. His father, though highly famous as a mathematician, was jealous of his own son: it is related that, one day, he proposed to Daniel, then a youth, a little problem to try his strength; the boy took it with him, solved it, and came back, expecting some praise from his father. '*You ought to have done it on the spot,*' was all the observation made, and with a tone and gesture which his son remembered to the

latest day of his life. That Daniel in mature life was not deficient in ready power is proved by the following anecdote. Koenig, another great mathematician, dining with him one day, mentioned a difficult problem which had long baffled him; but he added with some pride, 'I accomplished it at last.' Bernouilli said little at the moment, but went on attending to his guests, and before they rose from table he had solved the problem in his mind.

The elder Bernouilli, John, was succeeded in the Academy of Sciences by Daniel, at whose death, in 1782, his brother John succeeded him. Thus for ninety years the Academy never wanted a Bernouilli in its list of members. Daniel spent a great part of his life in Basle, where he was held in such esteem that it was part of the education of every child to learn to take off the hat to him. The fact of so peculiar a talent passing from father to son, and spreading into so many branches, is very noteworthy; and it will be found that the subject is followed out in a paper a page onward.

THE EXPERIMENT AT SCHIEHALLION.

Dr Maskelyne, the astronomer-royal, amongst many investigations in astronomy and general physics, distinguished himself in a special manner by one which had for its object directly to ascertain the attraction of mountains, and remotely the mean density of the earth. The scene of this great labour was the mountain Schiehallion, in Perthshire. Arriving there in the latter part of June 1774, the philosopher and his assistant, Mr Burrow, had a station prepared for themselves half way up the south side of the hill; afterwards another on the north side. It is a long bare mountain of 3,500 feet in elevation, in the midst of a country purely Alpine, and subject to the dreariest climatal influences. Three weeks elapsed before the learned investigator got a clear day for the ascertainment of a meridian line wherein to place his astronomical quadrant. Amidst the greatest difficulties—for the season was the worst seen for several years —he was just enabled, before November, to fix approximately the declination which the plumb-line made from the perpendicular on the respective sides of the mountain, being 5″ 8; whence it was afterwards deduced by Dr Charles Hutton, that, if the rock of the hill be taken as that of free-stone, or 2·5 of water, the earth's density will be 4·5 of the same measure (subsequently corrected by Professor Playfair into 4·867).

The writer of this notice has often amused himself by reflecting on what would be the feelings of the English philosopher, fresh from the Greenwich Observatory, and Crane-court, Fleet-street, on finding himself in a wilderness, whence, but thirty years before, there had poured down a host of half-naked barbarians upon the plains of his native country, and where there had recently died an old Highland chief and bard (Robertson, of Struan) who had been out with both Dundee and Mar. What, also, would be the conception of his enterprise, his instruments, his measurements and surveyings, adopted by the Clan Donnochie, of the Moor of Rannoch? What would they think when they were told that a man had come to Schiehallion to weigh it,—nay, to weigh the earth? Maskelyne tells us, however, in his paper in the *Philosophical Transactions*, that Sir Robert Menzies, the chief gentleman near Schiehallion, paid him many hospitable attentions, and that he received visits from Wilson, Reid, and Anderson, professors in Glasgow, and from various other men of science, throughout the autumn—' so great a noise had the attempt of this uncommon experiment made in the country, and so many friends did it meet with interested in the success of it.'

The mountain Schiehallion was adopted for the experiment, because it was a lofty and narrow one, whereof the longer axis lay nearly east and west, thus giving a small difference of latitude between the two stations in proportion to the bulk of the mass lying between. Maskelyne himself, and even his geological friend and visitor Playfair, might have felt some additional interest in the affair, if they had known that the mountain had been shaped for their purpose by the great ice-flow of the glacial period, the marks of whose passage can be clearly traced along its sides and ridge, up to nearly the summit.

MURDER OF DAVID RIZZIO—PERMANENCY OF BLOOD-STAINS.

On the night of the 9th February 1567, Lord Darnley was murdered, the house in which he slept beside the Kirk of the Field having been blown up by gunpowder. And just about a year before, on the 9th March 1565–6, David Rizzio, the Italian secretary of Mary of Scotland, was murdered in Holyrood Palace, by certain Protestant leaders of her court, with the assistance of her husband, Lord Darnley. The poor foreigner was torn from her side as she sat at supper, and dragged through her apartments to the outer door, where he was left on the floor for the night, dead with fifty-six wounds, each conspirator having been forced to give a stab, in order that all might be equally involved in guilt and consequent danger. The queen, who was then pregnant of her son (James I. of England), deeply resented the outrage. This murder was the first of the series of tragic events in which the queen was involved.

The floor at the outer door of the queen's apartments presents a large irregular dark mark, which the exhibitor of the palace states to be the blood of the unfortunate Rizzio. Most strangers hear with a smile of a blood-stain lasting three centuries, and Sir Walter Scott himself has made it the subject of a jocular passage in one of his tales,* representing a Cockney traveller as trying to efface it with the patent scouring drops which it was his mission to introduce into use in Scotland. The scene between him and the old lady guardian of the palace is very amusing; but it may be remarked of Scott, that he entertained some beliefs in his secret bosom which his worldly wisdom and sense of the ludicrous led him occasionally to treat comically or with an appearance of scepticism. In another of his novels—the *Abbot*—he alludes with a feeling of awe and horror to the Rizzio blood-stain; and in

* Introduction to *Chronicles of the Canongate.*

his *Tales of a Grandfather*, he deliberately states that the floor at the head of the stair still bears visible marks of the blood of the unhappy victim. Joking apart, there is no *necessity* for disbelieving in the Holyrood blood-mark. There is even some probability in its favour. In the first place, the floor is very ancient, manifestly much more so than the late floor of the neighbouring gallery, which dated from the reign of Charles II. It is in all likelihood the very floor which Mary and her courtiers trod. In the second place, we know that the stain has been shewn there since a time long antecedent to that extreme modern curiosity regarding historical matters which might have induced an imposture; for it is alluded to by the son of Evelyn as being shewn in 1722. Finally, it is matter of experiment, and fully established, that wood not of the hardest kind (and it may be added, stone of a porous nature) takes on a permanent stain from blood, the oxide of iron contained in it sinking deep into the fibre, and proving indelible to all ordinary means of washing. Of course, if the wearing of a blood-stained floor by the tread of feet were to be carried beyond the depth to which the blood had sunk, the stain would be obliterated. But it happens in the case of the Holyrood mark, that the two blotches of which it consisted are out of the line over which feet would chiefly pass in coming into or leaving the room. Indeed, that line appears to pass through and divide the stain,—a circumstance in no small degree favourable to its genuineness.

Alleged examples of blood-stains of old standing both upon wood and stone are reported from many places. We give a few extracted from the *Notes and Queries*. Amidst the horrors of the French Revolution, eighty priests were massacred in the chapel of the convent of the Carmelites at Paris. The stains of blood are still to be seen on the walls and floor. 'At Cothele, a mansion on the banks of the Tamar, the marks are still visible of the blood spilt by the lord of the manor, when, for supposed treachery, he slew the warder of the drawbridge.' 'About fifty years ago, there was a dance at Kirton-in-Lindsey: during the evening a young girl broke a blood-vessel and expired in the room. I have been told that the marks of her blood are still to be seen. At the same town, about twenty years ago, an old man and his sister were murdered in an extremely brutal manner, and their cottage floor was deluged with blood, the stains of which are believed yet to remain.'

TALENTS—FROM WHICH PARENT USUALLY DERIVED?

There is a prevalent, but nowhere well-argued idea, that talents are usually, if not always, derived from the mother. One could wish that a notion so complimentary to the amiable sex were true; but it scarcely is so.

There are, certainly, some striking instances of mother-derived abilities; none more so than that presented by the man perhaps the most distinguished for general abilities in our age—Henry Lord Brougham, whose mother, a niece of Principal Robertson, was a woman of the finest intellectual properties, while the father was of but ordinary gifts. Of like notableness is the case of Sir Walter Scott; the mother sagacious in an extraordinary measure, the father a plain good man, and no more. But look, on the other hand, at two other able men of the last and present epochs, Lord Macaulay and Robert Burns. In their cases, the phenomenon was precisely the converse : that is, clever father, ordinary mother.

It is only too easy to point to instances of father and son standing as noted for talent, while we hear nothing of the mother. Binities like Bernardo and Torquato Tasso, John and Daniel Bernouilli, William and John Herschel. James and John Stuart Mill, Chatham and William Pitt. George and Robert Stephenson, Carlo and Horace Vernet, abound in our biographical dictionaries. Another fact, connected less pointedly with the subject, but in itself of some value, is also pretty clearly shewn in these compilations ; namely, how often a man of eminence in the world of thought and taste is the son of a man who was engaged in some humble capacity connected with the departments in which his son excelled :—Mozart, for instance, the son of a capell-meister; James Watt, the son of a teacher of mathematics.

There are, however, instances of the descent of superior mental qualities through a greater number of generations than two, with a presumable transmission from the father to the son, while mothers are unheard of. The amiable Patrick Fraser Tytler, who wrote the best history of Scotland extant, was son to the accomplished Alexander Fraser Tytler (commonly styled Lord Woodhouselee), who wrote several books of good repute, and was, in turn, the son of William Tytler, author of the *Enquiry into the Evidence against Mary Queen of Scots*. The late Professor William Gregory, a man of the highest scientific accomplishments, was the son of Dr James Gregory, a professor of distinguished ability, author of the well-known *Conspectus Medicinœ*, who was the son of Dr John Gregory, author of the *Father's Legacy to his Daughters*, and other works; whose father, an eminent Aberdeen professor, was the son of James Gregory, right eminent as a mathematician, and the inventor of the reflecting telescope. It is, however, to be remarked that the talents of this last gentleman, and of his scarcely less distinguished brother David, are supposed to have been inherited from their mother, who was the daughter of an ingenious, busy-brained man of some local celebrity.

Not less remarkable is the series of the Sheridans. It seems to have started as a line of able men with Dr Thomas Sheridan, of Dublin, the friend of Swift; who was the son of another Dr Thomas Sheridan, and the nephew of a Bishop of Kilmore. Next came Mr Thomas Sheridan, of elocution-teaching memory, a man of lively talents; next the famed Richard Brinsley; next Thomas Sheridan, in whom there were brilliant abilities, though through unfortunate circumstances they never came to any effective demonstration. Among the children of this last, we find Lady Dufferin and the Hon Mrs Norton, both brilliant women ; and from Lady Dufferin, again, comes a son, Lord Dufferin,

whose Arctic yacht voyage has given his name the stamp of talent at a very early age. Of the five Sheridans, who stand here in succession, we hear of but one (Richard) whose mother has left any fame for abilities.

With these facts before us, and it would be easy to multiply them, it must plainly appear that the inheritance of talent from a mother is not a rule. At the utmost, it is a fact only possible, or which has an equal chance of occurring with its opposite. Most probably, people are led to make a rule of it by the propensity to paradox, or by reason of their remarking mother-descended talent as something unexpected, while they overlook the instances of the contrary phenomenon.

Let us speculate as we may, there are mysteries about the rise of uncommon abilities that we shall probably never penetrate. Whence should have come the singular genius of a Lawrence—son to a simple inn-keeping pair on the Bath-road ? Whence the not less wonderful gifts of a Wilkie—child of a plain Scotch minister and his wife—the mother so commonplace that, hearing how David was so much admired, she expressed surprise at their never saying anything of George—a respectable young grocer, who, being of goodly looks, had more pleased a mother's eye ? Whence should the marvellous thought-power of Shakspeare have been derived —his parents being, to all appearance, undistinguished from thousands of other Stratfordians who never had sons or daughters different from the multitude ?

Shrove Tuesday.

Shrove Tuesday derives its name from the ancient practice, in the Church of Rome, of confessing sins, and being *shrived* or *shrove*, *i. e.* obtaining absolution, on this day. Being the day prior to the beginning of Lent, it may occur on any one between the 2nd of February and the 8th of March. In Scotland, it is called Fasten's E'en, but is little regarded in that Presbyterian country. The character of the day as a popular festival is mirthful: it is a season of carnival-like jollity and drollery—' Welcome, merry Shrovetide ! ' truly sings Master Silence.

The merriment began, strictly speaking, the day before, being what was called *Collop Monday*, from the practice of eating collops of salted meat and eggs on that day. Then did the boys begin their Shrovetide perambulations in quest of little treats which their senior neighbours used to have in store for them—singing :

> ' Shrovetide is nigh at hand,
> And I be come a shroving ;
> Pray, dame, something,
> An apple or a dumpling.'

When Shrove Tuesday dawned, the bells were set a ringing, and everybody abandoned himself to amusement and good humour. All through the day, there was a preparing and devouring of pancakes, as if some profoundly important religious principle were involved in it. The pancake and Shrove Tuesday are inextricably associated in the popular mind and in old literature. Before being eaten, there was always a great deal of contention among the eaters, to see which could most adroitly toss them in the pan.

Shakspeare makes his clown in *All's Well that Ends Well* speak of something being ' as fit as a pancake for Shrove Tuesday.' It will be recollected that the parishioners of the Vicar of Wakefield ' religiously ate pancakes at Shrovetide.' Hear also our quaint old friend, the Water Poet—' Shrove Tuesday, at whose entrance in the morning all the whole kingdom is in quiet, but by that time the clock strikes eleven, which (by the help of a knavish sexton) is commonly before nine, there is a bell rung called Pancake Bell, the sound whereof makes thousands of people distracted, and forgetful either of manners or humanity. Then there is a thing called wheaten flour, which the cooks do mingle with water, eggs, spice, and other tragical, magical enchantments, and then they put it by little and little into a frying-pan of boiling suet, where it makes a confused dismal hissing (like the Lernian snakes in the reeds of Acheron), until at last, by the skill of the cook, it is transformed into the form of a flip-jack, called a pancake, *which ominous incantation the ignorant people do devour very greedily.*'

It was customary to present the first pancake to the greatest slut or lie-a-bed of the party. ' which commonly falls to the dog's share at last for no one will own it their due.' Some allusion is probably made to the latter custom in a couplet placed opposite Shrove Tuesday in *Poor Robin's Almanack* for 1677 :

' Pancakes are eat by greedy gut,
  And Hob and Madge *run for the slut.*'

In the time of Elizabeth, it was a practice at Eton for the cook to fasten a pancake to a crow (the ancient equivalent of the knocker) upon the school door.

At Westminster School, the following custom is observed to this day :—At 11 o'clock a.m. a verger of the Abbey, in his gown, bearing a silver bâton, emerges from the college kitchen, followed by the cook of the school, in his white apron, jacket, and cap, and carrying a pancake. On arriving at the school-room door, he announces himself, ' The cook,' and having entered the school-room, he advances to the bar which separates the upper school from the lower one, twirls the pancake in the pan, and then tosses it over the bar into the upper school, among a crowd of boys, who scramble for the pancake ; and he who gets it unbroken, and

THROWING THE PANCAKE ON SHROVE TUESDAY IN WESTMINSTER SCHOOL.

carries it to the deanery, demands the honorarium of a guinea (sometimes two guineas), from the Abbey funds, though the custom is not mentioned in the Abbey statutes : the cook also receives two guineas for his performance.

Among the revels which marked the day, football seems in most places to have been conspicuous. The London apprentices enjoyed it in Finsbury Fields. At Teddington, it was conducted with such animation that careful householders had to protect their windows with hurdles and bushes. There is perhaps no part of the United Kingdom where this Shrovetide sport is kept up with so much energy as at the village of Scone, near Perth, in Scotland. The men of the parish assemble at the cross, the married on one side and the bachelors on the other; a ball is thrown up, and they play from two o'clock till sunset. A person who witnessed the sport in the latter part of the last century, thus describes it : 'The game was this : he who at any time got the ball into his hands, ran with it till overtaken by one of the opposite party ; and then, if he could shake himself loose from those on the opposite side who seized him, he ran on ; if not, he threw the ball from him, unless it was wrested from him by the other party, but no party was allowed to kick it. The object of the married men was to *hang* it, that is, to put it three times into a small hole on the moor, which was the *dool*, or limit, on the one hand : that of the bachelors was to *drown* it, or dip it three times in a deep place in the river, the limit on the other : the party who could effect either of these objects won the game ; if neither one, the ball was cut into equal parts at sunset. In the course of the play, there was usually some violence between the parties ; but it is a proverb in this part of the country, that " A' is fair at the ba' o' Scone." '

Taylor, the Water Poet, alludes to the custom of a fellow carrying about ' an ensign made of a piece of a baker's mawkin fixed upon a broomstaff,' and making orations of nonsense to the people. Perhaps this custom may have been of a similar nature and design to one practised in France on Ash Wednesday. The people there ' carry an effigy, similar to our Guy Fawkes, round the adjacent villages, and collect money for his funeral, as this day, according to their creed, is the burial of good living. After sundry absurd mummeries, the corpse is deposited in the earth.'* In the latter part of the last century, a curious custom of a similar nature still survived in Kent. A group of girls engaged themselves at one part of a village in burning an uncouth image, which they called a *holly boy*, and which they had stolen from the boys ; while the boys were to be found in another part of the village burning a like effigy, which they called the *ivy girl*, and which they had stolen from the girls ; the ceremony being in both cases accompanied by loud huzzas.† These are fashions, we humbly opine, smacking of a very early and probably pagan origin. At Bromfield, in Cumberland, there used to be a still more remarkable custom. The scholars of the free school of that parish assumed a right, from old use and wont, *to bar out the master*, and keep him out for three days. During the period of this expulsion, the doors were strongly barricaded within ; and the boys, who defended it like a besieged city, were armed in general with guns made of the hollow

twigs of the elder, or bore-tree. The master, meanwhile, made various efforts, by force and stratagem, to regain his lost authority. If he succeeded, heavy tasks were imposed, and the business of the school was resumed and submitted to ; but it more commonly happened that all his efforts were unavailing. In this case, after three days' siege, terms of capitulation were proposed by the master and accepted by the boys. The terms always included permission to enjoy a full allowance of Shrovetide sports.*

In days not very long gone by, the inhumane sport of *throwing at cocks* was practised at Shrovetide, and nowhere was it more certain to be seen than at the grammar-schools. The poor animal was tied to a stake by a short cord, and the unthinking men and boys who were to throw at it, took their station at the distance of about twenty yards. Where the cock belonged to some one disposed to make it a matter of business, twopence was paid for three *shies* at it, the missile used being a broomstick. The sport was continued till the poor creature was killed outright by the blows. Such tumult and outrage attended this inhuman sport a century ago, that, according to a writer in the *Gentleman's Magazine*, it was sometimes dangerous to be near the place where it was practised. Hens were also the subjects of popular amusement at this festival. It was customary in Cornwall to take any one which had not laid eggs before Shrove-Tuesday, and lay it on a barn-floor to be thrashed to death. A man hit at her with a flail ; and if he succeeded in killing her therewith, he got her for his pains. It was customary for a fellow to get a hen tied to his back, with some horse-bells hung beside it. A number of other fellows, blindfolded, with boughs in their hands, followed him by the sound of the bells, endeavouring to get a stroke at the bird. This gave occasion to much merriment, for sometimes the man was hit instead of the hen, and sometimes the assailants hit each other instead of either. At the conclusion, the hen was boiled with bacon, and added to the usual pancake feast. Cock-fights were also common on this day. Strange to say, they were in many instances the sanctioned sport of public schools, the master receiving on the occasion a small tax from the boys under the name of a *cock-penny*. Perhaps this last practice took its rise in the circumstance of the master supplying the cocks, which seems to have been the custom in some places in a remote age. Such cock-fights regularly took place on Fasten's E'en in many parts of Scotland till the middle of the eighteenth century, the master presiding at the battle, and enjoying the perquisite of all the runaway cocks, which were technically called *fugies*. Nay, so late as 1790, the minister of Applecross, in Ross-shire, in the account of his parish, states the schoolmaster's income as composed of two hundred merks, with 1s. 6d. and 2s. 6d. per quarter from each scholar, and *the cock-fight dues*, which are equal to one quarter's payment for each scholar.†

The other Shrovetide observances were chiefly

* *Morning Chronicle*, March 10, 1791.
† *Gentleman's Magazine*, 1779.

* Hutchinson's History of Cumberland.
† Cock-fighting is now legally a misdemeanour, and punishable by penalty.

of a local nature. The old plays make us aware of a licence which the London prentices took on this occasion to assail houses of dubious repute, and cart the unfortunate inmates through the city. This seems to have been done partly under favour of a privilege which the common people assumed at this time of breaking down doors for sport, and of which we have perhaps some remains, in a practice which still exists in some remote districts, of throwing broken crockery and other rubbish at doors. In Dorsetshire and Wiltshire, if not in other counties, the latter practice is called *Lent Crocking.* The boys go round in small parties, headed by a leader, 'who goes up and knocks at the door, leaving his followers behind him, armed with a good stock of potsherds—the collected relics of the washing-pans, jugs, dishes, and plates, that have become the victims of concussion in the hands of unlucky or careless housewives for the past year. When the door is opened, the hero,—who is perhaps a farmer's boy, with a pair of black eyes sparkling under the tattered brim of his brown milking-hat,—hangs down his head, and, with one corner of his mouth turned up into an irrepressible smile, pronounces the following lines :

> A-shrovin, a-shrovin,
> I be come a-shrovin ;
> A piece of bread, a piece of cheese,
> A bit of your fat bacon,
> Or a dish of dough-nuts,
> All of your own makin !
>
> A-shrovin, a-shrovin,
> I be come a-shrovin,
> Nice meat in a pie,
> My mouth is very dry !
> I wish a wuz zoo well-a-wet
> I'de zing the louder for a nut !
>
> *Chorus*—A-shrovin, a-shrovin,
>   We be come a-shrovin !

Sometimes he gets a bit of bread and cheese, and at some houses he is told to be gone ; in which latter case, he calls up his followers to send their missiles in a rattling broadside against the door. It is rather remarkable that, in Prussia, and perhaps other parts of central Europe, the throwing of broken crockery at doors is a regular practice at marriages. Lord Malmesbury, who in 1791 married a princess of that country as proxy for the Duke of York, tells us, that the morning after the ceremonial, a great heap of such rubbish was found at her royal highness's door.

OLD GRAMMAR-SCHOOL CUSTOMS.

Mr R. W. Blencowe, in editing certain extracts from the journal of Walter Gale, schoolmaster at Mayfield, in the *Sussex Archæological Collections*, tells us that the salary of the Mayfield schoolmaster was only £16 a-year, which was subsequently increased by the bequest of a house and garden, which let for £18 a-year. There were none of those perquisites so common in old grammar-schools, by which the scanty fortunes of the masters were increased, and the boys instructed in the humanities, as in the Middle School at Manchester, where the master provided the cocks, for which he was liberally paid, and which were to be buried up to their necks

to be shied at by the boys on Shrove Tuesday, and at the feast of St Nicholas, as at Wyke, near Ashford. No Mr Graham had bequeathed a silver bell to Mayfield, as he had done to the school at Wreay in 1661, to be fought for annually, when two of the boys, who had been chosen as captains, and who were followed by their partisans, distinguished by blue and red ribbons, marched in procession to the village-green, where each produced his cocks ; and when the fight was won, the bell was suspended to the hat of the victor, to be transmitted from one successful captain to another. There were no potation pence, when there were deep drinkings, sometimes for the benefit of the clerk of the parish, when it was called clerk's ale, and more often for the schoolmaster, and in the words of some old statutes, 'for the solace of the neighbourhood :' potations which Agnes Mellers, avowess, the widow of a wealthy bellfounder of Nottingham, endeavoured, in some degree, to restrain when she founded the grammar-school in that town in 1513, by declaring that the schoolmaster and usher of her school should not make use of any potations, cock-fightings, or drinkings, with his or their wives, hostess, or hostesses, *more than twice a year.* There were no 'delectations' for the scholars, such as the barring out of the schoolmaster, which Sir John Deane, who founded the grammar-school at Wilton, near Northbeach, to prevent all quarrels between the teacher and the taught, determined should take place only twice a year, a week before Christmas and Easter, 'as the custom was in other great schools.' No unhappy ram was provided by the butcher, as used to be the case at Eton in days long gone by, to be pursued and knocked on the head by the boys, till on one occasion, the poor animal, being sorely pressed, swam across the Thames, and, reeling into the market-place at Windsor, followed by its persecutors, did such mischief, that this sport was stopped, and instead thereof it was hamstrung, after the speech on Election Saturday, and clubbed to death. None of these humanising influences were at work at Mayfield : there was not even the customary charge of 5s. to each boy for rods.

No such rules as those in force at the free grammar-school at Cuckfield prevailed at Mayfield. They were not taught 'on every working day one of the eight pearls of reason, with the word according to the same, that is to say, *Nomen* with *Amo, Pronomen* with *Amor,* to be said by heart ; nor as being a modern and a thoroughly Protestant school, were they called upon before breakfast each Friday to listen to a little piece of the Pater Noster, or Ave Maria, the Credo, or the verses of the Mariners, or the Ten Commandments, or the Five Evils, or some other proper saying in Latin meet for babies.' Still less, as in the case of the grammar-school at Stockport, did any founder will 'that some cunning priest, with all his scholars, should, on Wednesday and Friday of every week, come to the church to the grave where the bodies of his father and mother lay buried, and there say the psalm of *De Profundis,* after the Salisbury use, and pray especially for his soul, and for the souls of his father and mother, and for all Christian souls.' Neither did the trustees, that they might sow the seeds of ambition in the minds of the scholars, ordain, as was done at Tunbridge and at Lewisham, 'that the best scholars and the best writers should wear some pretty garland on their heads, with silver pens well fastened thereunto, and thus walk to church and back again for at least a month.' A ceremony which in these days would infallibly secure for them all sorts of scoffings, and probably a broken head. *

* The above mention of *silver pens* would seem to carry the use of metal pens back to a period long antecedent to the date generally attributed.

It is deemed appropriate to append hereunto a memorial of one of the ancient grammar-school customs, more honoured in the breach than the observance, but which nevertheless still retains a certain hold. It is the stool or altar of punishment which was formerly in use at the Free School of Lichfield—the school at which Addison, Ashmole, Garrick, Johnson, and Wollaston received their education. When our artist visited this venerable temple of learning a few

years ago, there was a head-master receiving a good salary, *but no scholars.* The flogging-horse, here delineated, stood in the lower room, covered with dust.

FEBRUARY 10.

St Soteris, virgin-martyr, 4th century. St Scholastica, virgin, 543. St Erlulph, of Scotland, bishop, martyr at Verdun, 830. St William of Maleval, 1157.

Lent—Ash Wednesday.

It is an ancient custom of the Christian church to hold as a period of fasting and solemnity the forty days preceding Easter, in commemoration of the miraculous abstinence of Jesus when under temptation. From *lengten-tide,* a Saxon term for spring (as being the time of the lengthening of the day), came the familiar word for this period—LENT. Originally, the period began on what is now the first Sunday in Lent; but, it being found that, when Sundays, as improper for fasting, were omitted, there remained only thirty-six days, the period was made by Pope Gregory to commence four days earlier; namely, on what has since been called Ash Wednesday. This name was derived from the notable ceremony of

the day in the Romish church. It being thought proper to remind the faithful, at commencement of the great penitential season, that they were but dust and ashes, the priests took a quantity of ashes, blessed them, and sprinkled them with holy water. The worshipper then approaching in sackcloth, the priest took up some of the ashes on the end of his fingers, and made with them the mark of the cross on the worshipper's forehead, saying, ' *Memento, homo, quia cinis es, et in pulverem reverteris* ' (Remember, man, that you are of ashes, and into dust will return). The ashes used were commonly made of the palms consecrated on the Palm Sunday of the previous year. In England, soon after the Reformation, the use of ashes was discontinued, as 'a vain show,' and Ash Wednesday thence became only a day of marked solemnity, with a memorial of its original character in a reading of the curses denounced against impenitent sinners.

The popular observances on Ash Wednesday are not of much account. The cocks being now dispatched, a thin scare-crow-like figure or puppet was set up, and shied at with sticks, in imitation of one of the sports of the preceding day. The figure was called a *Jack-a-lent,* a term which is often met with in old literature, as expressive of a small and insignificant person. Beaumont and Fletcher, in one of their plays, make a character say—

> 'If I forfeit,
> Make me a Jack o' Lent and break my shins
> For untagged points and counters.'

Boys used to go about *clacking* at doors, to get eggs or bits of bacon wherewith to make up a feast among themselves; and when refused, would stop the keyhole with dirt, and depart with a rhymed denunciation. In some parts of Germany, the young men gathered the girls into a cart, and drove them into a river or pool, and there ' washed them favouredly,'—a process which shews that abstinence from merriment was not there held as one of the proprieties of the day.

' Among the ancient customs of this country which have sunk into disuse, was a singularly absurd one, continued even to so late a period as the reign of George I. During the Lenten season, an officer denominated, the *King's Cock Crower* crowed the hour each night, within the precincts of the Palace, instead of proclaiming it in the ordinary manner of watchmen.* On the first *Ash Wednesday* after the accession of the House of Hanover, as the Prince of Wales, afterwards George II., sat down to supper, this officer abruptly entered the apartment, and according to accustomed usage, proclaimed in a sound resembling the shrill pipe of a cock, that it was " past ten o'clock." Taken by surprise, and imperfectly acquainted with the English language, the astonished prince naturally mistook the tremulation of the assumed crow, as some mockery intended to insult him, and instantly rose to resent the affront: nor was it without difficulty that the interpreter explained the nature of the custom, and satisfied him, that a

* In Debrett's *Imperial Calendar* for the year 1822, in the list of persons holding appointments in the Lord Steward's department of the Royal Household, occurs the ' Cock and Cryer at Scotland-yard.'

compliment was designed, according to the court etiquette of the time. From that period we find no further account of the exertion of the imitative powers of this important officer; but the court has been left to the voice of reason and conscience, to remind them of their errors, and not to that of the cock, whose clarion called back Peter to repentance, which this fantastical and silly ceremony was meant to typify.'—*Brady.*

Born.—William Congreve, poet and dramatist (baptized), 1670, *Bardsey;* Aaron Hill, poet, 1685, *Strand;* Dr Benjamin Hoadly, 1706, *Broad-street, London;* James Smith, comic poet, 1775, *London;* Rev. Dr Henry H. Milman, historian, 1791, *London.*

Died.—Sir William Dugdale, historian and antiquary, 1686, *Shustoke;* Isaac Vossius, scholar, of Leyden, 1689, *Windsor;* Thomas Chubb, Wiltshire divine, 1747, *Salisbury;* Montesquieu, French jurist, 1755, *Paris;* Dr James Nares, musical composer, 1783, *Westminster;* Samuel Prout, painter in water-colours, 1852.

ISAAC VOSSIUS: A STRANGE CANON.

This eccentric Dutch scholar, a son of Gerard Vossius, a still more learned man, died on the 10th of February, 1688-9, in Windsor Castle, where Charles II. had assigned him apartments fifteen years previously, when he came to England from Holland, and the king made him a canon of Windsor. Never did a man undertake the clerical office who was more unfit for it. Although a canon of Windsor, he did not believe in the divine origin of the Christian religion, and he treated religious matters with contempt, although in all other things he was exceedingly credulous. Charles, on one occasion, said, 'This learned divine is a strange man; he will believe anything except the Bible.' When he attended divine service in the chapel at Windsor, it is said that he used to read Ovid's *Ars Amandi* instead of the prayer-book. He knew all the European languages, without being able to speak one of them correctly. He was familiar with the manners and customs of the ancients, but profoundly ignorant of the world and the affairs of ordinary life. On his death-bed he refused the sacrament, and was only prevailed upon to take it by the remark of one of his colleagues, that if he would not do it for the love of God, he ought to do it for the honour of the chapter to which he belonged.

Vossius took an odd delight in having his hair combed in a measured or rhythmical manner. He would have it done by barbers or other persons skilled in the rules of prosody. A Latin treatise on rhythm, published by him at Oxford in 1673, contains this curious passage: 'Many people take delight in the rubbing of their limbs, and the combing of their hair; but these exercises would delight much more, if the servants at the baths, and of the barbers, were so skilful in this art, that they could express any measure with their fingers. I remember that more than once I have fallen into the hands of men of this sort, who could imitate any measure of songs in combing the hair; so as sometimes to express very intelligibly iambics, trochees, dactyles, &c., from whence there arose to me no small delight.'

16

RIOT AT OXFORD ON ST SCHOLASTICA'S DAY.

On the 10th of February 1354, in the reign of Edward III., a dire conflict took place between the students of the University of Oxford and the citizens. The contest continued three days. On the second evening, the townsmen called into their assistance the country people; and thus reinforced, completely overpowered the scholars, of whom numbers were killed and wounded. The citizens were, consequently, debarred the rites and consolations of the church; their privileges were greatly narrowed; they were heavily fined; and an annual penance for ever was enjoined that on each anniversary of St Scholastica, the mayor and sixty-two citizens attend at St Mary's Church, where the Litany should be read at the altar, and an oblation of one penny made by each man.

HISTORY OF THE UMBRELLA.

The designation of this useful contrivance (from *umbra,* shade) indicates the earliest of its twofold uses. Johnson describes it as 'a screen used in hot countries to keep off the sun, and in others to bear off the rain;' and Kersey, many years before (1708), had described it as 'a kind of broad fan or screen, commonly used by *women to shelter them from rain;* also, a wooden frame, covered with cloth, to keep off the sun from a window.' Phillips, in his *New World of Words,* edit. 1720, describes the umbrella as 'now commonly used by women to shelter them from rain.'

As a shade from the sun, the umbrella is of great antiquity. We see it in the sculptures and paintings of Egypt, and Sir Gardner Wilkinson has engraved a delineation of an Ethiopian princess, travelling in her chariot through Upper Egypt to Thebes, wherein the car is furnished with a kind of umbrella fixed to a tall staff rising from the centre, and in its arrangement closely resembling the chaise umbrella of the present time. The recent discoveries at Nineveh shew that the umbrella (or parasol) 'was generally carried over the king in time of peace, and even in war. In shape,' says Layard, 'it resembled very closely those now in common use, but it is always seen open in the sculptures. It was edged with tassels, and was usually adorned at the top by a flower or some other ornament. On the later bas-reliefs, a long piece of linen or silk, falling from one side, like a curtain, appears to screen the king completely from the sun. The parasol was reserved exclusively for the monarch, and is never represented as borne over any other person. On several bas-reliefs from Persepolis, the king is represented under an umbrella, which a female slave holds over his head.'

From the very limited use of the parasol in Asia and Africa, it seems to have passed, both as a distinction and a luxury, into Greece and Rome. The *Skiadeion,* or day-shade of the Greeks, was carried over the head of the effigy of Bacchus; and the daughters of the aliens at Athens were required to bear parasols over the heads of the maidens of the city at the great festival of the Panathenea. We see also the parasol figured in the hands of a princess on the Hamilton vases in

241

the British Museum. At Rome, when the veil could not be spread over the roof of the theatre, it was the custom for females and effeminate men to defend themselves from the sun with the *umbrella* or *umbraculum* of the period; and this covering appears to have been formed of skin or leather, capable of being raised or lowered, as circumstances might require.

Although the use of the umbrella was thus early introduced into Italy, and had probably been continued there as a vestige of ancient Roman manners, yet so late as 1608, Thomas Coryat notices the invention in such terms as to indicate that it was not commonly known in his own country. After describing the fans of the Italians, he adds: 'Many of them do carry other fine things, of a far greater price, that will cost at least a ducat (5s. 6d.), which they commonly call, in the Italian tongue, *umbrellaes*; that is, things that minister shadow unto them, for shelter against the scorching heat of the sun. These are made of leather, something answerable to the form of a little canopy, and hooped in the inside with divers little wooden hoopes, that extend the *umbrella* into a pretty large compasse. They are used especially by *horsemen*, who carry them in their hands when they ride, fastening the end of the handle upon one of their thighs; and they impart so long a shadow unto them, that it keepeth the heate of the sun from the upper part of their bodies.' It is probable that a similar contrivance existed, at the same period, in Spain and Portugal, whence it was taken to the New World. Defoe, it will be remembered, makes Robinson Crusoe describe that he had seen umbrellas employed in the Brazils, and that he had constructed his own umbrella in imitation of them. 'I covered it with skins,' he adds, 'the hair outwards, so that it cast off the rain like a penthouse, and kept off the sun so effectually, that I could walk out in the hottest of the weather with greater advantage than I could before in the coolest.' In commemoration of this ingenious production, one species of the old heavy umbrellas was called 'The Robinson.'

The umbrella was used in England as a luxurious sun-shade early in the seventeenth century. Ben Jonson mentions it by name in a comedy produced in 1616; and it occurs in Beaumont and Fletcher's *Rule a Wife and Have a Wife*, where Altea says:

'Are you at ease? Now is your heart at rest?
Now you have got a shadow, an umbrella,
To keep the scorching world's opinion
From your fair credit.'

In those days, as we may infer from a passage in Drayton, the umbrella was composed exteriorly of feathers, in imitation of the plumage of water-birds. Afterwards, oiled silk was the ordinary material. In the reign of Queen Anne, the umbrella appears to have been in common use in London as a screen from rain, but only for the weaker sex. Swift, in the *Tatler*, October 17, 1710, says, in 'The City Shower:'

'The tuck'd up seamstress walks with hasty strides,
While streams run down her oiled umbrella's sides.'

Gay speaks of it in his *Trivia; or, the Art of Walking the Streets of London:*

242

'Good housewives all the winter's rage despise,
Defended by the riding-hood's disguise:
Or underneath th' umbrella's oily shed,
Safe through the wet on clinking pattens tread.
Let Persian dames th' umbrella's ribs display,
To guard their beauties from the sunny ray;
Or sweating slaves support the shady load,
When Eastern monarchs shew their state abroad:
Britain in winter only knows its aid,
To guard from chilly showers the walking maid.'

This passage, which points to the use of the umbrella exclusively by women, is confirmed by another passage in the *Trivia*, wherein the surtout is recommended for men to keep out 'the drenching shower:'

'By various names, in various countries known,
Yet held in all the true surtout alone,
Be thine of kersey firm, though small the cost;
Then brave unwet the rain, unchill'd the frost.'

At Woburn Abbey is a full-length portrait of the beautiful Duchess of Bedford, painted about 1730, representing the lady as attended by a black servant, who holds an open umbrella to shade her. Of about the same period is the sketch engraved on the next page, being the vignette to a song of Aaron Hill's, entitled *The Generous Repulse*, and set to a tolerable air by Carey:

'Thy vain pursuit, fond youth, give o'er.
What more, alas! can Flavia do?
Thy worth I own, thy fate deplore,
All are not happy that are true.

* * * * * *

'But if revenge can ease thy pain,
I'll soothe the ills I cannot cure,
Tell thee I drag a hopeless chain,
And all that I inflict endure.'

Flavia, as will be observed, administers this poorish consolation, seated on a flowery bank, and keeping off the sunshine with a long-stalked umbrella, or what we should now call a parasol, while the 'fond youth' reclines bare-headed by her side.

The eighteenth century was half elapsed before the umbrella had even begun to be used in England by both sexes, as we now see it used. In 1752, Lieutenant-Colonel (afterwards General) Wolfe, writing from Paris, says: 'The people here use umbrellas in hot weather to defend them from the sun, and *something of the same kind to save them from the snow and rain*. I wonder a practice so useful is not introduced in England.' Just about that time, a gentleman did exercise the moral courage to use an umbrella in the streets of London. He was the noted Jonas Hanway, newly returned from Persia, and in delicate health, by which, of course, his using such a convenience was justified both to himself and the considerate part of the public. 'A parapluie,' we are told, 'defended Mr Hanway's face and wig.' For a time, no others than the dainty beings then called Macaronies ventured to carry an umbrella. Any one doing so was sure to be hailed by the mob as 'a mincing Frenchman.' One John Macdonald, a footman, who has favoured the public with his memoirs, found as late as 1770, that, on appearing with a fine silk umbrella which he had brought from Spain, he was saluted with the cry of 'Frenchman, why don't you get a coach?' It appears, however, as if there had previously been a kind of transition period, during which an umbrella was kept at a coffee-house, liable to be used by gentlemen on special occasions by night, though still regarded as the resource of effeminacy. In the *Female Tatler* of December 12, 1709, there occurs the following announcement: 'The young gentleman belonging to the Custom House, who, in the fear of rain, borrowed the umbrella at Will's coffee-house, in Cornhill, of the mistress, is hereby advertised that to be dry from head to foot on the like occasion, he shall be welcome to the maid's pattens.' It is a rather early fact in the history of the general use of umbrellas, that in 1758, when Dr Shebbeare was placed in the pillory, a servant stood beside him with an umbrella to protect him from the weather, physical and moral, which was raging around him.

'THE GENEROUS REPULSE.'

Much of the clamour which was raised against the general use of the umbrella originated with the chairmen and hackney-coachmen, who, of course, regarded rainy weather as a thing especially designed for their advantage, and from which the public were entitled to no other protection than what their vehicles could afford.

In all the large towns of the empire, a memory is preserved of the courageous citizen who first carried an umbrella. In Edinburgh, it was a popular physician named Spens. In the *Statistical Account of Glasgow*, by Dr Cleland, it is related that, about the year 1781, or 1782, the late Mr John Jameson, surgeon, brought with him an umbrella, on his return from Paris, which was the first seen in the city, and attracted universal attention. This umbrella was made of heavy wax-cloth, with cane ribs, and was a ponderous article. Cowper mentions the umbrella twice in his *Task*, published in 1784.

The early specimens of the English umbrella made of oiled silk, were, when wet, exceed-ingly difficult to open or to close; the stick and furniture were heavy and inconvenient, and the article generally very expensive; though an umbrella manufacturer in Cheapside, in 1787, advertised pocket and portable umbrellas superior to any kind ever *imported* or manufactured in this kingdom; and 'all kinds of common umbrellas prepared in a particular way, that will never stick together.' The substitution of silk and gingham for the oiled silk, however, remedied the above objection.

The umbrella was originally formed and carried in a fashion the reverse of what now obtains. It had a ring at top, by which it was usually carried on the finger when furled (and by which also it could be hung up within doors), the wooden handle terminating in a rounded point to rest on the ground. The writer remembers umbrellas of this kind being in use among old ladies so lately as 1810. About thirty years ago, there was living in Taunton, a lady who recollected when there were but two umbrellas in that town ; one belonged to a clergyman, who, on proceeding to his duties on Sunday, hung up the umbrella in the church porch, where it attracted the gaze and admiration of the townspeople coming to church.

ANECDOTE PRESERVED BY DUGDALE.

The laboriously industrious antiquary, Sir William Dugdale, to whom we owe a large proportion of what has been preserved of the ecclesiastical antiquities of England, died at the ripe age of eighty-six. His son, Sir John Dugdale, preserved from his conversation some brief anecdotes, and among the rest a merry tale regarding the Scotch covenanting minister, Patrick Gillespie. This esteemed leader having fallen into a grievous sin, the whole of his party felt extremely scandalised, and ' nothing less would serve them than to hold a solemn convention, for seeking the Lord (as their term was) to know of him wherefore he allowed this holy brother to fall under the power of Satan. That a speedy solution might be given them, each of them by turn vigorously wrestled with God, till (as they pretended) he had solved their question ; viz.: that this fall of their preacher was not for any fault of his own, but for the sins of his parish laid upon him. Whereupon the convention gave judgment that the parish should be fined for public satisfaction, as was accordingly done.'—*Life of Dugdale*, 4to, 1827, p. 60, *note*.

FEBRUARY 11.

Saints Saturninus, Dativus, and others, martyrs of Africa, 304. St Severinus, 507. St Theodora, empress, 867. (In the Anglo-Romish calendar) Cædmon, about 680.

CÆDMON.

Cædmon is the most ancient English poet whose name is known. He lived in Northumbria, near the monastery which was then called Streanes-halch, but which has since been known by the name of Whitby. The name of its abbess, Hilda, is known to every one acquainted with Northern legend and poetry.

It was a favourite custom of the Anglo-Saxons to meet together at drinking-parties, and there, in the midst of their mirth, the harp was passed round, and each in his turn was expected to sing or chant some poem to the instrument—and these, as we may gather from the story, were often the composition of the singer, for the art of composing poetry seems to have been very extensively cultivated among our Saxon forefathers. Now the education of Cædmon, who was apparently the son of a small landholder, had been so much neglected that he had been unable either to compose, or to repeat or sing ; and when on these occasions he saw the harp approach him, he felt so overwhelmed with shame that he rose from his seat and went home. An important part of the wealth of an Anglo-Saxon landholder at this time—the events of which we are speaking occurred in the latter half of the seventh century—consisted in cattle, and it was the duty of the sons or retainers of the family to guard them at night ; for this could not be done by the agricultural serfs, as none but a freeman was allowed to bear arms. Now it happened on one of the occasions when Cædmon thus slunk from the fes-

tive beer-party (*gebeorscipe*) in disgrace, that it was his turn to guard the cattle, and proceeding from the hall to his post, he laid himself down there with a feeling of vexation and despondency, and immediately fell asleep. In his slumber a stranger appeared to him, and, addressing him by his name, said, ' Cædmon, sing me something.' Cædmon answered, ' I know nothing to sing, or I should not have left the hall to come here so soon.' ' Nay,' said the stranger, ' but thou hast something to sing ! ' ' What must I sing ? ' said Cædmon. ' Sing the Creation,' was the reply. Cædmon immediately began to sing verses ' which he had never heard before,' and which are given in Anglo-Saxon in some of the old manuscripts. When he awoke, he was not only able to repeat the lines which he had composed in his dream, but he went on at will in the most excellent poetry. In the morning he presented himself before the reeve, or bailiff, of Whitby, and informed him of his miraculous gift of poetry, and the reeve took him to the abbess Hilda. Hilda and a number of high and pious ecclesiastics listened to his story, and witnessed his performance, after which they read to him a short portion of the Scripture in Anglo-Saxon, and he went home, and on his return next morning he repeated it in Anglo-Saxon verse, excelling in beauty everything they had heard before. Such a heaven-born poet was a prize not to be thrown away, and Cædmon yielded to Hilda's earnest solicitations, and became a monk of her house— for the early Anglo-Saxon nunneries contained monks and nuns in the same establishment. He was here employed by the pious abbess in translating into Anglo-Saxon verse the whole of the sacred history. Bede gives an affecting account of Cædmon's death, which took place about the year 680. He was regarded as a saint by the Anglo-Saxon Church, and his death is placed in the Anglo-Romish Calendar on the 11th of February, but there is no known authority for fixing it on that day.

Cædmon is, indeed, only known even by name through his story, as told by the historian Bede, who was almost his contemporary, or at least lived only a generation later, and it would have been perhaps no more thought of than other legends, but for a rather curious circumstance. The celebrated Archbishop Usher became possessed of an early manuscript of Anglo-Saxon poetry, which he afterwards gave to Junius, a distinguished Anglo-Saxon scholar, and it proved to be a paraphrase in Anglo-Saxon verse of some parts of the Scripture history, bearing so many points of resemblance to the works of Cædmon, as described by Bede, that Junius did not hesitate to print it under Cædmon's name (at Amsterdam, in 1655). One excellent edition, with an English translation, has since been printed by Mr Benjamin Thorpe. The original MS. is now among Junius's manuscripts in the Bodleian library, at Oxford. The earlier part of this poetry, containing the history of the Creation and of the fall of man, is much more poetical than the rest, and may very probably be the same which, in Anglo-Saxon times, was ascribed to Cædmon, though it bears no name in the manuscript. The story of the temptation and fall is told with great dramatic effect, and in some circumstances bears such close resemblance to Milton's *Paradise Lost*, that it has been supposed that the latter poet must have been acquainted with the poetry of Cædmon, though the latter was printed by Junius in a very unreadable form, and without any translation.

Born. — The Princess Elizabeth (of York), 1466 ; Bernard de Bovier de Fontenelle, *littérateur*, 1657, *Rouen.*

Died.—The Emperor Heraclius, 641 ; Elizabeth Plantagenet *of York*, 1502 ; René Descartes, French philosopher, 1650, *Stockholm ;* William Shenstone, poet, 1763, *Hales Owen ;* Macvey Napier, editor of the *Encyclopædia Britannica*, 1847.

PREMATURE DEATH OF DESCARTES.

The death of this eminent philosopher was indirectly brought about by the means which he had taken to escape from the persecution of his enemies. After completing his travels, he determined to devote his attention exclusively to philosophical and mathematical inquiries, with the ambition of renovating the whole circle of the sciences. At the age of thirty-three he sold a portion of his patrimony, and retired into Holland, where he remained eight years so completely aloof from the distractions of the world, that his very place of residence was unknown, though he preserved an intercourse of letters with many friends in France. Meanwhile with the increase of his fame arose a spirit of controversy against his writings. Shrinking from the hostility of the church, he gladly accepted an invitation of Christina, Queen of Sweden, by whom he was treated with the greatest distinction, and was relieved from the observance of any of the humiliating usages so generally exacted by sovereigns of those times from all whom they admitted into their presence. The queen, however, probably from the love of differing from every one else, chose to pursue her studies with Descartes at five o'clock in the morning ; and as his health was peculiarly delicate, the rigour of the climate, and the unseasonable hour, brought on a pulmonary disease, of which he very soon died, being then only in the fifty-fourth year of his age. The queen wished to inter him with great honour in Sweden; but the French ambassador interposed, and his remains were conveyed for sepulture amongst his countrymen in Paris. Thus fell one of the greatest men of his age, a victim to the absurd caprice of the royal patron who had afforded him shelter from the persecutions of the church.

Probably, no man has given a greater impulse to mathematical and philosophical inquiry than Descartes. He was the first who successfully applied algebra to geometry ; he pointed out the important law of the sines ; in an age in which optical instruments were extremely imperfect, he discovered the changes to which light is subjected in the eye by the crystalline lens; and he directed attention to the consequences resulting from the weight of the atmosphere. He was not only the greatest geometrician of the age, but by the clearness and admirable precision of his style, he became one of the founders of French prose. In his laborious experiments upon the animal frame,

he recognised Harvey's researches on the circulation of the blood, and made it the basis of the physiological part of his work on Man. He is the author of what is emphatically called Modern Philosophy ; his name has revived in some measure of late years, chiefly owing, among ourselves, to Dugald Stewart, and in France to the disposition of the philosophers to cast away their idols of the eighteenth century.

SHENSTONE'S QUATRAIN.

Shenstone has furnished an inn-window quatrain which is oftener heard from the lips of our generation than any of his dulcet pastoral verses.

' Whoe'er has travelled life's dull round,
　Where'er his stages may have been,
Must sigh to think he still has found
　His warmest welcome at an inn.'

Dr Percy, who more than once visited ' the wailing poet of the *Leasowes*,' told Miss Hawkins that he always thought Shenstone and found him a man unhappy in his temper. In his taste for rural pleasures he was finical to a ludicrous degree of excess. In the purchase of a cow, he regarded nothing but the spots on her hide ; if they were beautiful, all other requisites were disregarded. His man-servant, whose office it was to shew his grounds, had made a grotto, which Shenstone approved. This was always made the test of the visitor's judgment : if he admired William's grotto, his master thought him worth accompanying round the place, and, on a signal from the man, appeared ; but if it was passed with little notice, he kept out of the way.

PERUQUIERS' PETITION.

On the 11th of February, 1765, a petition was presented to King George III., by the master peruke-makers of the metropolis, setting forth the distresses of themselves and an incredible number of others dependent on them, from the almost universal decline of their trade, in consequence of gentlemen so generally beginning to wear their own hair. What business remained to their profession was, they said, nearly altogether taken from them by French artists. They had a further ground of complaint in their being obliged to work on Sunday, which they would much rather have spent in their religious duties, ' learning to fear God and honour the king [a bit of flattery].' Under these circumstances, the distressed peruke-makers prayed his majesty for means of relief. The king—though he must have scarcely been able to maintain his gravity—returned a gracious answer. But the public, albeit but little converted from the old views regarding the need of protection to industry, had the sense to see the ludicrous side of the petition, and some one quickly regaled them by publishing a petition from the *Body Carpenters*, imploring his majesty to wear a wooden leg, and to enjoin all his servants to appear in the royal presence with the same graceful decoration.*

POLITICAL WINDOW-BREAKING.

The foolish excesses in which the politicians of the last century occasionally indulged, were

* *Gentleman's Magazine*, 1765, p. 95.

strangely exemplified upon the acquittal of Admiral Keppel, February 11, 1779, after a trial of thirty days, on charges of misconduct and incapacity exhibited against him by Sir Hugh Palliser. In the evening, a courier brought to London the news of Keppel's acquittal, couched in the most honourable terms for him, and most ignominious to his antagonist. Public feeling was much excited in favour of Keppel. Palliser himself was fain to make his escape out of Portsmouth (where the trial took place), at five in the morning, in a hired post-chaise, to avoid insults and outrage from the mob, and sheltered himself in the Admiralty. The news spread rapidly through London, and by eleven at night most houses were illuminated, both in London and Westminster. Guns were discharged by the servants of some of the great lords in the Opposition, and squibs and crackers thrown plentifully by the populace. The ministers, and some of the Scots, were sullen, and would not exhibit lights ; yet the mob was far more temperate than usual, the Opposition having taken no pains to inflame them, nor even to furnish them with any *cri de guerre.* Late at night, as the people grew drunk, an empty house in Pall Mall, recently inhabited by Sir Hugh Palliser, and still supposed to belong to him, was attacked; the windows were broken, and at last, though some guards had been sent for, the mob forced their way into it, and demolished whatever remained. The windows of Lord Mulgrave and Captain Hood were likewise broken, and some others accidentally that were not illuminated. It happened at three in the morning that Charles Fox, Lord Derby, and his brother, Major Stanley, and two or three other young men of quality, having been drinking at Almack's till that late hour, suddenly thought of making the tour of the streets, and were joined by the Duke of Ancaster, who was very drunk, and, what shewed that it was no premeditated scheme, the latter was a courtier, and had actually been breaking windows. Finding the mob before Palliser's house, some of the young lords said, 'Why don't you break Lord George Germaine's windows ?' The populace had been so little tutored, that they asked who he was, and receiving some further encouragement, they quickly proceeded to break Lord George's windows. The mischief pleasing the juvenile leaders, they marched to the Admiralty, forced the gates, and demolished Palliser's and Lord Lilburne's windows. Lord Sandwich, exceedingly terrified, escaped through the garden with his mistress, Miss Reay, to the Horse Guards, and there betrayed a most manifest panic. The rioters then proceeded to Lord North's, who got out on to the top of his house ; but the alarm being now given, the Guards arrived, and prevented any further mischief.—*Walpole's Last Journals,* vol. ii., pp. 342—344.

SUSSEX SMUGGLERS.

The coast of Sussex appears to have been greatly frequented by smugglers in the middle of the last century, and their affrays with Custom-house officers were at that time very desperate. In the year 1749, there was sent to Chichester a special commission, with Sir Michael Forster as president, to try seven smugglers for the murder of two Custom-house officers ; an act

perpetrated under circumstances of atrocity too horrible to be related. They were convicted, and, with the exception of one who died the night before the execution, they were all executed and hanged in chains, in different parts of Sussex. The state of public feeling regarding these culprits made it necessary that a company of foot-guards and a troop of horse should attend to prevent all chances of rescue. Seven more were tried and convicted at the following assizes at East Grinstead, for highway robbery and for the barbarous murder of a poor fellow named Hawkins, who was suspected of giving information against them, and who was literally flogged to death. Six of them were executed. Most of them belonged to a celebrated set called the Hawkhurst gang, who were the terror of the counties of Kent and Sussex. Three more were tried at the Old Bailey, also with sixty others, who had broken open the Custom-house at Poole, and taken away a quantity of tobacco, which had been seized and deposited there. They were executed at Tyburn. A place called Whitesmith was celebrated as a nest of smugglers long after this time ; and about 1817, one of the outstanding debts in the overseers' books was due to a well-known smuggler of Whitesmith, for 'two gallons of gin to be drunk in the vestry.'

There were places of deposit for the smuggled goods, most ingeniously contrived, in various parts of Sussex. Among others, it is said, was the manorial pond at Fulmer, under which there was dug a cavern, which could hold 100 tubs of spirits : it was covered with planks, carefully strewed over with mould, and this remained undiscovered for many years.

In the churchyard at Patcham is an inscription on a monument, now nearly illegible, to this effect :

> 'Sacred to the memory of
> DANIEL SCALES,
> who was unfortunately shot, on Tuesday evening, Nov. 7, 1796.
>
> 'Alas ! swift flew the fatal lead,
> Which pierced through the young man's head.
> He instant fell, resigned his breath,
> And closed his languid eyes in death.
> And you who to this stone draw near,
> Oh! pray let fall the pitying tear.
> From this sad instance may we all
> Prepare to meet Jehovah's call.'

The real story of his death is this : Daniel Scales was a desperate smuggler, and one night he, with many more, was coming from Brighton, heavily laden, when the Excise officers and soldiers fell in with them. The smugglers fled in all directions ; a riding officer, as such persons were called, met this man, and called upon him to surrender his booty, which he refused to do. The officer knew that 'he was too good a man for him, for they had tried it out before; so he shot Daniel through the head.'

A COWED AMBASSADOR.

In a grave work by Archbishop Parker, entitled *The Defence of Priestes Marriages,* 4to, there occurs unexpectedly an amusing anecdote.* 'It chanced that there came a French ambassador to the king's highness, King Henry the Eighth, with letters, I trow, from the French king, not long before that sent to him from the holy father of Rome. This ambassador, sitting at the council-table, began to set up a stout countenance with a weak brain, and carped English exceedingly fast ; which he thought should have been his only sufficient commendation of them all that were at the table, that he could speak so readily.

* In the present extract a modern orthography is assumed.

The matter of his talk was universal; but the substance was much noting the *gluttony of Englishmen*, which devoured so much victual in the land; partly magnifying the great utility of the French tongue, which he noted to be almost throughout the world frequented. And in his conference he marvelled of divers noblemen that were present, for that they could not keep him talk, or yet so much as understand him to perceive his great wit.

'Among the number of the lords, there sat the old honourable Captain, the Lord Earl of Shrewsbury, looking at his meat, and gave neither ear nor countenance to this *folie* man, but gave others leave to talk, and sat as he might, shaking his head and hands in his palsy, which was testimony enough whether he were not in his days a warrior lying abroad in the field, to take air of the ground. This French ambassador was offended with him, and said, "What an honour it were for yonder nobleman, if he could speak the French tongue! Surely it is a great lack to his nobility." One of the lords that kept him talk, asking leave of this *mounsire* to report part of the communication to the Lord Shrewsbury, made report thereof, yet in his most courteous manner, with [as] easy and favourable rehearsal as might touch a truth.

'When he heard it, where before his head, by the great age, was almost grovelling on the table, he roused himself up in such wise, that he appeared in length of body as much as he was thought ever in all his life before. And, knitting his brows, he laid his hand on his dagger, and set his countenance in such sort, that the French *hardie* ambassador turned colour wonderfully. "Saith the French [fellow] so?" saith he; "marry, tell the French dog again, by sweet St Cuthbert, If I knew that I had but one pestilent French word in all my body, I would take my dagger and dig it out, before I rose from the table. And tell that tawny [varlet] again, howsoever he hath been hunger-starved himself at home in France, that if we should not eat our beasts, and make victual of them as fast as we do, they would so increase beyond measure, that they would make victual of us, and eat us up!"

'When these words were reported again to the French guest, he spoiled no more victual at the dinner after that, but drank wondrous oft . . . . his eyes were never off him [the Earl of Shrewsbury] all that dinner while after.'

FEBRUARY 12.

St Eulalia, virgin of Barcelona, martyr, about 305. St Meletius, patriarch of Antioch, 381. St Benedict, of Anian, abbot, 821. St Anthony Cauleas, patriarch of Constantinople, 896.

Born.—Gabriel Naudé, *littérateur*, 1600, *Paris;* Bishop (John) Pearson, 1613, *Snoring;* Dr Cotton Mather (writer on Witchcraft), 1663, *Boston, N. A.;* Elias de Crebillon, French romancist, 1707, *Paris;* Edward Forbes, naturalist, 1815, *Douglas, Isle of Man.*

Died.—Bishop David ap Owen, 1512; Lady Jane Grey, beheaded, 1555, *Tower;* Sir Nicholas Throckmorton, chief butler of England, *temp.* Elizabeth, 1571; George Heriot, founder of 'Heriot's Hospital,' 1624; Gabriel Brotier, editor of *Tacitus*, 1789, *Paris;* Lazaro Spallanzani, naturalist, 1799, *Paris;* Immanuel Kant, philosopher, 1804; Sir Astley Cooper, surgeon, 1841.

SIR NICHOLAS THROCKMORTON.

Sir Nicholas Throckmorton, the head of the ancient Warwickshire family, after which our well-known London street is named, filled several offices of state, but led a troubled life. He was sewer to Henry VIII., in which capacity it was his duty to attend the

> 'marshall'd feast,
> Serv'd up in hall with sewer and seneschal.'

He also headed a troop in the armament against France which Henry VIII. commanded in person. After the king's death, he attached himself to the Queen-dowager Katherine Parr, and to the Princess Elizabeth. He next distinguished himself in Scotland, under the Protector Somerset, by whom he was sent to London with the news of the victory of Pinkie. Afterwards created a knight, and appointed to a place in the Privy Chamber, he was admitted to great intimacy by Edward VI. Having witnessed the death of the boy king at Greenwich, in 1553, he came immediately to London, and dispatched Mary's goldsmith to announce to her the king's demise. On the 2nd of February 1554, Sir Nicholas was arrested and committed to the Tower, on the well-founded charge of being concerned in the rebellion of Sir Thomas Wyatt. He was tried at Guildhall, and his case was thought to be hopeless; but having undertaken to conduct his own defence, he did it with such adroitness, promptness of reply, and coolness of argument, intermixed with retorts, spirited, fearless, and reiterated, in answer to the partial remarks of the Lord Chief Justice, and followed up by an impassioned appeal to the jury, that, in defiance of the threats of the Chief Justice and the Attorney-General,—in defiance too of the proverb on the subject,—he obtained a verdict of acquittal. He was directed to be discharged, but was remanded, and kept in prison till January 18, 1555. Nearly all the jury were fined and imprisoned for their independent verdict.

Sir Nicholas afterwards served in Queen Mary's army, under the Earl of Pembroke; but he devoted himself chiefly to the Princess Elizabeth, whom he privately visited at Hatfield. When Queen Mary died, he was admitted to see her corpse, and, as Elizabeth had requested, took from her finger the wedding-ring which had been given to her by Philip, and delivered it to Elizabeth. By this Protestant queen he was appointed to high offices, and sent on a special embassy to Edinburgh to remonstrate with Mary Queen of Scots, against her intended marriage with Darnley. When Mary was imprisoned at Lochleven, Throckmorton was commissioned by Elizabeth to negotiate with the rebel lords for her release.

A few years later we find Throckmorton sent to the Tower on a well-founded charge of intriguing for a marriage between the Scottish queen and the Duke of Norfolk. He was not kept long in confinement, but never regained the confidence of Elizabeth; and his distress of mind is thought to have hastened his death, which took place, February 12, 1571, at the house of the Earl of Leicester,—not, it is also said, without suspicion of poison. There is a monument to his memory, a recumbent figure in the church of St Catherine Cree, in Leadenhall-street.

Sir Francis Walsingham, in a letter to the Earl of Leicester, on Throckmorton's death, says of him, that 'for counsel in peace and for conduct in war, he hath not left of like sufficiency, that I know.' Camden says, he was 'a man of large experience, piercing judgment, and singular prudence; but he died very luckily for himself and his family, his life and estate being in great danger by reason of his turbulent spirit.' He was the court favourite of three sovereigns, but fell by his love of intrigue.

The late Sir Henry Halford used to relate that he had seen a prescription in which *a portion of the human skull* was ordered, in powder, for Sir Nicholas Throckmorton. It was dug out of the ruins of a house in Duke-street, Westminster, which had belonged to Oliver Cromwell's apothecary.

ASSASSINATION OF MR THYNNE IN PALL MALL.

As the visitor to Westminster Abbey passes through the south aisle of the choir, he can scarcely fail to notice sculptured upon one of the most prominent monuments a frightful scene of assassination, which was perpetrated in one of

SCULPTURE ON THYNNE'S MONUMENT IN WESTMINSTER ABBEY.

the most public streets of the metropolis, late in the reign of Charles the Second. The victim of this atrocity was Thomas Thynne, Esq., who had a short time before succeeded in carrying off the youthful widow of Lord Ogle. The handsome Count Köningsmark, who had been rejected by the lady, was tempted by disappointed passion to plot, if not to perpetrate, this barbarous revenge upon his rival.

Thomas Thynne, of Longleat, in Wiltshire, was descended from an ancient family, and from his large income was called 'Tom of Ten Thousand.' He had been a friend of the Duke of York, afterwards James II.; but having quarrelled with his royal highness, Thynne had latterly attached himself with great zeal to the Whig or Opposition party, and had become an intimate associate of their head, the Duke of Monmouth. At Longleat, where he lived in a style of magnificence, Thynne was often visited by Monmouth; and he is the Issachar of Dryden's glowing description of the Duke's progresses, in the *Absalom and Achitophel*:

248

'From east to west his glories he displays,
And, like the sun, the Promised Land surveys.
Fame runs before him, as the morning star,
And shouts of joy salute him from afar;
Each house receives him as a guardian god,
And consecrates the place of his abode.
But hospitable treats did most commend
Wise Issachar, his wealthy western friend.'

It was on the night of Sunday, the 12th of February 1681-2, that the west end of London was startled by the news that Thynne had been shot while passing in his coach along Pall Mall. King Charles, sitting at Whitehall, might almost have heard the report of the assassin's musketoon; and so might Dryden, sitting in his favourite front room, on the ground-floor of his house on the south side of Gerrard-street, also hardly more than a couple of furlongs distant. The murderers escaped. Thynne survived his mortal wound only a few hours, during which the Duke of Monmouth sat by the bedside of his dying friend.

An active search, conducted by Sir John Reresby and the Duke of Monmouth, resulted in the speedy apprehension of the three inferior instruments in this murder, including one Boroski, a Pole, who had fired the fatal shot. The instigator of the murder, Count Köningsmark, was apprehended a week after the commission of the murder. A few days later, the four men were brought to the bar at the Old Bailey, to be arraigned and tried—Boroski, Vratz, and Stern, as principals in the murder, and Count Köningsmark as accessory before the fact. At the trial, the evidence, and indeed their own confession, clearly proved the fact of Boroski shooting Thynne, and Vratz and Stern being present assisting him. With respect to Köningsmark, besides the testimony of his accomplices, the other evidence shewed him living concealed in a humble lodging, and holding communication with the murderers, before and almost at the time of the fact. He had also fled immediately after the offence was committed. To this it was answered by Köningsmark, that the men accused were his followers and servants, and that of necessity he frequently communicated with them, but never about this murder; that when he arrived in London, he was seized with a distemper, which obliged him to live privately till he was cured; and finally, that he never saw, or had any quarrel with, Mr Thynne. This defence, though morally a weak one, was strengthened by the absence of any legal proof to connect the Count with the assassination, and by the favourable summing-up of Chief Justice Pemberton, who seemed determined to save him. The three principals were found guilty, and Köningsmark was acquitted.

Reresby, in his *Memoirs*, tells us how a Mr Foubert, who kept an academy in London, where he had for a pupil a younger Count Köningsmark —apparently brother to the murderer—came and offered him a large bribe to interfere in the course of justice; which bribe he instantly rejected, because he did not believe that any one was the better for money acquired in such a way.

The convicted prisoners were hanged at the

place of the murder, in Pall Mall, on the 10th of March following; and Boroski was afterwards suspended in chains, a little beyond Mile-end Town. Evelyn records in his *Diary*, under the 10th March : 'This day was executed Colonel Vratz and some of his accomplices, for the execrable murder of Mr Thynne, set on by the principal Köningsmark ; he went to execution like an undaunted hero, as one that had done a friendly office for that base coward,—Count Köningsmark, who had hopes to marry his [Mr Thynne's] widow, the rich Lady Ogle, and was acquitted by a corrupt jury, and so got away. Vratz told a friend of mine, who accompanied him to the gallows, and gave him some advice, that he did not value dying a rush, and hoped and believed God would deal with him like a gentleman.'

Count Köningsmark, after he had paid his fees, and got out of the hands of the officers of justice at the Old Bailey, made a quick retreat from England. According to the *Amsterdam Historical Dictionary*, he went to Germany to visit his estates, in 1683 ; was wounded at the siege of Cambray, which happened that same year ; he afterwards went with his regiment to Spain, where he distinguished himself on several occasions ; and finally, in 1686, he accompanied his uncle, Otto William, to the Morea, where he was present at the battle of Argas, and so overheated himself, that he was seized with a pleurisy, which carried him off. Such, at the early age of twenty-seven, was the end of Köningsmark, within little more than four years after the tragedy of his supposed victim Thynne, and his own narrow escape from the gibbet, to which he had been the cause of consigning his three associates or instruments.

SIR ASTLEY PASTON COOPER, BART., SERJEANT-SURGEON TO THE QUEEN.

This eminent practitioner and excellent man was the fourth son of the rector of Great Yarmouth, in Norfolk ; and was born at Brooke, in that county, August 23, 1768. His mother sprung from the ancient family of the Pastons, and was the authoress of a novel, entitled *The Exemplary Mother.* He was chiefly educated by his father, a sound scholar. An accidental circumstance is said to have influenced his future career : when a boy, he saw a lad fall from a cart, and tear his thigh in such a manner as to wound the femoral artery. Young Cooper immediately took his handkerchief, and applied it round the thigh so tightly, as to control the bleeding until further assistance could be procured. At the age of fifteen, he was placed with a surgeon and apothecary at Yarmouth ; he next came to London, and was apprenticed to his uncle, one of the surgeons of Guy's Hospital ; but, in a few months, was transferred, by his own desire, to Mr Cline, the eminent surgeon of St Thomas's Hospital. Here his zeal and application were incessant ; and he laid the foundation of his fame and fortune by giving a course of lectures on the principles and practice of surgery, which had previously only formed part of the anatomical course. His class of students rose to 400, by far

the largest number ever known in London. He made no attempt at oratory, but was plain and practical in his details, and very successful in his illustrations ; while he carefully avoided the introduction of controversial subjects connected with physiological science. In 1792, he visited Paris, and made himself master of the theory and practice of French surgery. In the same year, he commenced practice in London : when at its zenith, his annual receipt of fees far exceeded that of any other member of the profession : in one year he received £21,000 ; and for many years after, his annual receipt was £15,000 and upwards. His success in practice, it is supposed, consisted chiefly in his knowing how and when to operate ; yet, on an important occasion, his courage had nearly forsaken him. In 1821, George the Fourth having a small tumour in the scalp, an operation for its removal was resolved upon, and Cooper was selected to perform it. On the day appointed, he waited upon his majesty. Lord Liverpool and other cabinet ministers occupied a room adjoining that in which the king was. A short time before the operation was commenced, Cooper was observed to be pale and nervous, when Lord Liverpool, taking hold of his hand, said, 'You ought to recollect that this operation either makes or ruins you. Courage, Cooper!'—and he was so impressed with this timely rebuke that every appearance of anxiety vanished from his countenance, and he performed the operation with his wonted coolness and dexterity. In the course of a few months after this, he received from the king a baronetcy, with remainder, in default of male issue, to his nephew Astley Paston Cooper, who in due time succeeded to the title.

Sir Astley Cooper had long retired from practice, when he died, February 12. 1841, in his seventy-third year, bequeathing a large fortune. His extensive practice had small beginnings : in the first year, his income was but £5 5s. ; the second, £26 ; the third, £64 ; the fourth, £96 ; the fifth, £100 ; the sixth, £200 ; the seventh, £400 ; the eighth, £610. He received some very large fees, among which was that of a thousand guineas thrown at him in his nightcap by a patient whom he had cut for the stone ; an anecdote which he told with no small degree of animation, on retiring from a patient upon whom he had just performed the same operation, and who had likewise, in his agony, flung his cap at the surgeon, but *without* the cheque which gave so much force to the original incident. Probably, no surgeon of ancient or modern times enjoyed a greater share of reputation during his life than fell to the lot of Sir Astley. The old and new world alike rung with his fame. On one occasion, his signature was received as a passport among the mountains of Biscay by the wild followers of Don Carlos. A young English surgeon, seeking for employment, was carried as a prisoner before Zumalacarregui, who demanded what testimonials he had of his calling or his qualifications. Our countryman presented his diploma of the College of Surgeons ; and the name of Astley Cooper, which was attached to it, no sooner struck the eye of the Carlist leader, than he at once received his prisoner with friendship, and appointed him as a surgeon in his army.

Sir Astley Cooper, by his unwearied assiduity in the dissecting-room, produced some of the most important contributions to modern surgery, which he published without regard to profit. His influence on the surgery of the day was great: 'He gave operations a scientific character, and divested them in a great degree of their terrors, by performing them unostentatiously, simply, confidently, and cheerfully, and thereby inspiring the patient with hope of relief, where previously resignation under misfortune had too often been all that could be expected from the sufferer.'—*Sir John Forbes.*

THE DINTON HERMIT.

A letter of Hearne, the antiquary, dated February 12, 1712-13,* gives an account of an extraordinary object preserved in the Ashmolean Museum under the name of the *Buckinghamshire Shoe*. The corresponding shoe for the other foot is preserved at Dinton Hall, near Aylesbury. Each of these shoes is not merely composed of patches, like a beggar's cloak, but it presents a load of such patches, layer above layer, to the amount, it is believed, of many hundreds of individual pieces. The shoes were made and worn by an eccentric man named John Bigg, not without parts or education, who was for some time clerk to the regicide Judge Mayne; but, after the ruin of his master's cause at the Restoration, grew morbid, retired from the world, and lived like a hermit in a hut or cave, near his former master's house of Dinton, only adjourning in summer to the woods near Kimble. Bigg was little over thirty at the time of his retirement, and he lived to 1696, when he must have been sixty-seven. A portrait engraved in Lipscomb's *Buckinghamshire†* presents us a handsome, composed-looking man, dressed in clothes and shoes all alike composed of small patches, the head being covered by a sort of stiff hood, terminating in two divergent peaks, and composed in like manner with the rest of the dress, while two (leather?) bottles hang at the girdle, and a third is carried in the left hand. Bigg lived upon charity, but never asked anything excepting leather; and when he got any of that article, his amusement was to patch it upon his already overladen shoes. People, knowing his tastes, brought him food, likewise ale and milk. The last article he carried in one of his bottles; in the other two he carried strong and small ale. The man was perfectly inoffensive, and conduct so extraordinary is only to be accounted for in his case by supposing a slight aberration of the intellect, the consequence perhaps of disappointed hopes.

COMPLETION OF THE REVOLUTION OF 1688.

The 12th of February is the memorable anniversary of the perfecting of the Revolution of 1688. James II. having, with his family, withdrawn in terror to France, a convention called by the Prince of Orange met on the 22nd of

* Reliquiæ Hearnianæ, i. 281.

† The portrait of Bigg is also engraved in Kirby's *Wonderful Museum*, vol. v.

January 1688-9, and proceeded under his protection to deliberate on the settlement of the kingdom. To find that James had abdicated was an easy matter; how to dispose of the vacant throne was not so easy. There was a large party for a regency; others were disposed to accept the Princess of Orange, the eldest daughter of the ex-king, as their sovereign. It was not till after much debating, and a threat of the Prince to go back to Holland and leave them to settle their own affairs, that the convention at length, on the 12th of February, adopted the resolution, 'That William and Mary, Prince and Princess of Orange, be declared King and Queen of England, France, and Ireland, and the dominions thereunto belonging.' The crown was next day formally offered to them in the Banqueting Room, at Whitehall, and accepted; and the Revolution was complete.

Mary had arrived in London so recently as the 11th, by which time it was tolerably certain that she and her husband were to be nominated to a joint sovereignty. However glad she might naturally be at her husband's successful expedition, however excited by the prospect of being a regnant queen of England, the crisis was calculated to awaken sober feelings. She was displacing a father; her husband was extruding an uncle. 'It was believed,' says the contemporary Evelyn, 'that both, especially the Princess, would have shewed some seeming reluctance of assuming her father's crown, and made some apology, testifying by her regret that he should by his mismanagement necessitate the nation to so extraordinary a proceeding; which would have shewn very handsomely to the world. . . . Nothing of all this appeared. She came into Whitehall, laughing and jolly, as to a wedding, so as to seem quite transported. She rose early the next morning, and in her undress, as was reported, before her women were up, went about from room to room to see the convenience of Whitehall; lay in the same bed where the late queen lay; and, within a night or two, sat down to play at basset, as the queen her predecessor used to do. She smiled upon and talked to everybody. . . . This carriage was censured by many.' It outraged even Dr Burnet, the new queen's chaplain.

It now appears that Mary acted under orders from her husband, who wished to give a check to those who desired to see his wife made sole monarch and deemed her ill-used, because he was associated with her. Lord Macaulay even makes it out to be a fine case of self-devotion on the part of the queen. To betray levity regarding an unfortunate father in order to please a triumphant husband, was a strange piece of self-devotion. For a husband to ask his wife to do so was not very wise, as fully appeared from the disgust which it excited. There cannot truly be said to have been either taste, judgment, or good feeling, on either side in the case. As the one drawback to the felicity of this great event was a consideration of the relationship of the new sovereigns to the old, it would have been much better policy for them to make a feeling for King James prominent in their conduct, even though it bore no place in their hearts.

THE RESURRECTIONISTS.

The name of Sir Astley Cooper recals a traffic in the recent existence of which amongst us young men of our time might hesitate to believe. It is indeed a startling chapter in the history of civilization which is supplied by the methods formerly resorted to by anatomical teachers, for the purpose of obtaining subjects for dissection. From the year 1800 until the alteration of the law in 1832, the Resurrectionists, or 'Body-snatchers,' were almost the only sources of this supply : they were persons generally of the worst character, if we except the watchmen of that time, who were set to guard the burial-grounds, all of whom received a regular percentage on the sum obtained by the Resurrectionists. The public were for many years aware of church-yards being robbed; it was known to be effected with wonderful rapidity and dexterity; but the *modus* was never fathomed by the public, and, curiously enough, no accidental circumstance occurred to furnish the explanation ; even the members of the medical profession, with very few exceptions, were kept in ignorance of it, so careful were the Resurrectionists to remove all traces of their mode of working after the completion of their task. It was generally supposed that the body-snatcher, in exhuming a body, first proceeded, as a novice would have done, to remove all the earth with which the grave had been recently filled ; and having at length arrived at the coffin, that he then, with proper implements, forced off the lid, and so removed the body. This would have occupied considerable time, and rendered the body-snatchers proportionately more liable to detection. To avoid this, they only cleared away the earth above the head of the coffin, taking care to leave that which covered the other end as far as possible undisturbed. As soon as about one-third of the coffin was thus exposed, they forced a very strong crowbar, made of a peculiar form for the purpose, between the end of the coffin and the lid, which latter, by using the lever as one of the first order, they generally pressed up, without much difficulty. It usually happened, at this stage of the proceedings, that the superincumbent weight of the earth on the other portion of the coffin-lid caused it to be snapped across at a distance of about one-third of its length from the end. As soon as this had been effected, the body was drawn out, the death-gear removed from it, and replaced in the coffin, and finally the body was tied up and placed in its receptacle, to be conveyed to its destination. By this means, in the case of a shallow grave of loose earth, free from stones, the Resurrectionist would remove a body in a quarter of an hour. Silence was essential for the safety of the Resurrectionists ; and in gravelly soils they had a peculiar mode of flinging out the earth, in order to prevent the rattling of the stones against the iron spade.

As soon as the body was raised, it was generally placed in a sack, and then carried to a hackney-coach or spring-cart, usually the latter. When bodies were sent from the country to the metropolis, they were generally packed in hat-crates, or in the casks in which hardwares are sent. Sometimes the subject, instead of being deposited in a sack, was laid on a large square green baize cloth, the four corners of which were tied together, so as to inclose the body. It was not directly conveyed to any dissecting-room, but was generally deposited in some half-built house, or other convenient building, until the following day. The body-snatcher would then, dressed as a porter, swing the load over his shoulders, and often, even in broad daylight, carry it to its place of destination through the most crowded streets of the metropolis. At other times, the students would receive the bodies at their own houses, and convey them in a hackney-coach to the dissecting-rooms, the coachman being well paid for his job. Sometimes the driver was exorbitant in his demands, and was somewhat ingenious in enforcing them : a pupil who was conveying a body by coach to his hospital was astonished by finding himself in front of the Bow-street police-office, when the coachman, tapping at the front window, said to the affrighted youth, 'Sir, my fare to so-and-so is a guinea, unless you wish to be put down here.' The reply, without any hesitation, was, 'Quite right, my man ; drive on.'

At the commencement of a new session at the hospitals, the leading Resurrectionists might be seen looking out for lecturers ; and 'fifty pounds down, and nine guineas a body,' was often acceded to ; the former being the opening fee from each school promised an exclusive supply. The competition for subjects, which the exhumators pretended to get up between the different schools, sometimes raised the prices so exorbitantly as to leave scarcely any remuneration for the lecturers. In some cases twenty pounds have been given for a single subject, in healthy seasons.

The competition occasionally led to revolting scenes of riot. Mr Bransby Cooper, in his *Life of Sir Astley Cooper*, relates that two Resurrectionists, having gained access to a private burial-ground near Holywell Mount by bribing the gravedigger, sometimes brought away six bodies in one night. Two other exhumators, hearing of this prosperity, threatened to expose the gravedigger if he did not admit them to share his plunder; but he was beforehand with them, and pointed them out to a public-house full of labourers, as body-snatchers come to bribe him to let them steal from his ground, when the whole crowd rushed after the Resurrectionists, who narrowly escaped their vengeance. They ran to a police-office, and, in a loud voice, told the sitting magistrate if he sent officers to Holywell Mount burial-ground they would find every grave robbed of its dead ; the grave-digger having sold them to the body-snatchers. The indignant people rushed to the burial-ground, broke open the gates, dug up the graves, and finding in them empty coffins, seized the gravedigger, threw him into one of the deepest excavations, began shovelling the earth over him, and would have buried him alive, but for the activity of the constables. The mob then went to his house, broke every article of his furniture, seized his wife and children, and dragged them through a stagnant pool in the neighbourhood.

Such outrages as these, and the general indignation which arose from them, having interrupted the supply of bodies, other stratagems were resorted to. The Resurrectionists, by associating with the lower class of undertakers, obtained possession of the bodies of the poor which were taken to their establishments several days before interment, and often a clergyman read the funeral service over a coffin filled with brick-bats, or other substitute for the stolen body.

The bodies of suicides were sometimes stolen from the charge of persons appointed to sit up with them ; or they were obtained from poor-houses and infirmaries by the Resurrectionists pretending relationship with the deceased, and claiming the bodies for burial. By this means, one Patrick got a number of subjects, chiefly from St Giles's workhouse, his wife being employed, under various disguises, to own the bodies. At other times, the body-snatchers would destroy the tombs, vaults, and expensive coffins of the wealthy, to obtain their prey ; and their exactions, villany, and insolence grew intolerable. The sale of a drunken man in a sack, as a subject, to Mr Brookes the ana-tomist, is a well-known incident.

Nevertheless, so useful were the services of the regular Resurrectionists, that when they got into trouble, the surgeons made great exertions in their favour, and advanced large sums of money to keep them out of gaol, or support them during imprisonment. Sir Astley Cooper expended hundreds of pounds for this purpose : a single liberation has been known to cost £160 ; and an anatomical teacher has paid £5 as a weekly allowance, continued for two years, to a Resurrectionist confined in prison.

A leading Resurrectionist once received £144 for twelve subjects in one evening, out of which he had to pay his underlings £5 each. These high prices not unfrequently led persons, while alive, to offer to sell their bodies for dissection after death ; but very rarely did any surgeon accede to such a proposal, since the law did not recognise any right of property in a dead body. Among the papers left by Sir Astley Cooper was found the following : 'Sir, I have been informed you are in the habit of purchasing bodys, and allowing the person a sum weekly. Knowing a poor woman that is desirous of doing so, I have taken the liberty of calling to know the truth. I remain, your humble servant, * * *.' Sir Astley Cooper's answer (copied on the back of the application) was brief : 'The *truth* is, that you deserve to be hanged for making such an unfeeling offer.—A. C.'

The graves were not always disturbed to obtain possession of the entire body, for the *teeth* alone, at one time, offered tempting remuneration. Mr Cooper relates an instance of a Resurrectionist feigning to look out a burial-place for his poor wife, and thus obtaining access to the vault of a meeting-house, the trap-door of which he unbolted, so that at night he let himself down into the vault, and secured the front teeth of the whole congregation, by which he cleared £60.

For nearly thirty years had this nefarious traffic flourished, when a Select Committee of the House of Commons was appointed to investigate the matter. In reply to the following question : 'Does the state of the law actually prevent the teachers of anatomy from obtaining the body of any person, which, in consequence of some peculiarity of structure, they may be particularly desirous of procuring ?' Sir Astley Cooper stated : 'The law does not prevent our obtaining the body of an individual if we think proper ; for there is no person, let his situation in life be what it may, whom, if I were disposed to dissect, I could not obtain.' In reply to another question, Sir Astley Cooper said, 'The law only enhances the price, and does not prevent the exhumation : nobody is secured by the law, it only adds to the price of the subject.'

The profession had for many years been anxious to devise some plan to prevent the exhumation of bodies ; but it was thought too hazardous to attempt the enactment of laws on the subject, in consequence of the necessary publicity of the discussions upon them. The horrible murders committed at Edinburgh, under the system of *Burking*, and exposed in the year 1828, at last rendered it peremptorily necessary for the Government to establish some means of legalizing dissection, under restrictions regulated by the ministers of the Crown. An inspector was appointed, to whom the certificate of the death of the individual, and the circumstances under which he died, were to be submitted before the body could be dissected, and then only in the schools in which anatomizing was licensed by the Government ; and this new system has much raised the characters of those who are teaching anatomy, as well as the science itself, in the estimation of the public.

The Resurrectionists mostly came to bad ends. There were but few *regulars ;* the others being composed of Spitalfields weavers, or thieves, who found

252

the disguise of this occupation convenient for carrying on their own peculiar avocations. One was tried, and received sentence of death, for robbing the Edinburgh mail, but was pardoned upon the intercession of the Archdukes John and Lewis, who were much interested by finding the criminal at work in his cell, articulating the bones of a horse ; he left the country, and was never after heard of. Another Resurrectionist, after a long and active career, withdrew from it in 1817, and occupied himself principally in obtaining and disposing of teeth. As a licensed sutler, in the Peninsula and France, he had drawn the teeth of those who had fallen in battle, and had plundered the slain : with the produce of these adventures, he built a large hotel at Margate, but his previous occupation being disclosed, his house was avoided, and disposed of at a very heavy loss : he was subsequently tried, and imprisoned for obtaining money under false pretences, and was ultimately found dead in a public-house near Tower-hill. It is credibly reported of one body-snatcher, that, at his death, he left nearly £6000 to his family. One, being captured, was tried and found guilty of stealing the clothes in which the bodies were buried, and was transported for seven years. A man who was long superintendent to the dissecting-room at St Thomas's Hospital, was dismissed for receiving and paying for bodies sent to his employer, and re-selling them at an advanced price, in Edinburgh ; he then turned Resurrectionist, was detected and imprisoned, and died in a state of raving madness.

FEBRUARY 13.

St Polyeuctus, martyr at Melitine, 250. St Martinianus, hermit, of Athens, *circ.* 4th century. St Medomnoc (or Dominic), bishop of Ossory, 6th century. St Stephen, abbot in Italy, 6th century. St Licinius, bishop of Angers, 618. St Gregory II. (Pope), 631. Roger, abbot of Elan in Champagne, *circ.* 1175. St Catherine de Ricci, virgin, 1589.

Born.—Alexander Wedderburn, Earl of Rosslyn, 1733, *Chesterhall ;* David Allan, Scottish painter, 1744, *Alloa ;* Charles Maurice de Talleyrand-Perigord, diplomatist, 1754.

Died.—Catherine Howard, beheaded, 1543, *Tower ;* Benvenuto Cellini, Florentine sculptor, 1576 ; Elizabeth (of Bohemia), 1662, *Leicester House ;* Dr Cotton Mather, 1728, *Boston, N. A. ;* Dr Samuel Croxall, fabulist, 1752 ; Charles Count de Vergennes, French diplomatist, 1787, *Versailles ;* the Duke de Berri, assassinated, 1820, *Paris ;* Henry Hunt, political character, 1835 ; Sharon Turner, historian, 1847.

St Valentine's Eve.

At Norwich, St Valentine's eve appears to be still kept as a time for a general giving and receiving of gifts. It is a lively and stirring scene. 'The streets swarm with carriers, and baskets laden with treasures ; bang, bang, bang go the knockers, and away rushes the banger, depositing first upon the door-step some packages from the basket of stores—again and again at intervals, at every door to which a missive is addressed, is the same repeated, till the baskets are empty. Anonymously, St Valentine presents his gifts, labelled only with "St Valentine's love," and "Good morrow, Valentine." Then within the houses of destination, the screams, the shouts, the rushings to catch the bang-bangs,—the flushed faces, sparkling eyes, rushing feet to pick up the fairy-gifts—inscriptions to be interpreted, mysteries to be unravelled, hoaxes to be found out —great hampers, heavy and ticketed "With care, this side upwards," to be unpacked, out of which jump live little boys with St Valentine's love to the little ladies fair,—the sham bang-bangs, that bring nothing but noise and fun—the mock parcels that vanish from the door-step by invisible strings when the door opens—monster parcels that dwindle to thread papers denuded of their multiplied envelopes, with fitting mottoes, all tending to the final consummation of good counsel. " Happy is he who expects nothing, and he will not be disappointed." It is a glorious night ; marvel not that we would perpetuate so joyous a festivity.'—*Madders's Rambles in an Old City* (*Norwich*).

FEBRUARY 14.

St Valentine, priest and martyr, *circ.* 270. St Abraames, bishop of Carres, 422. St Maro, abbot in Syria, 433. St Auxentius, hermit, of Bithynia, *circ.* 470. St Conran, bishop of Orkney, 7th century.

Born.—Camille, Duke de Tallard, 1652, *Dauphiné ;* Archdeacon Waterland, eminent theologian, 1683, *Wasely.*
Died.—Pope Innocent I., 417 ; Richard II., King of England, murdered, 1400 ; Lord Chancellor Talbot, 1737 ; Captain James Cook, killed at *Owhyhee,* 1779 ; Sir William Blackstone, author of the *Commentaries on the Laws of England,* 1780, *Wallingford.*

CAPTAIN COOK.

The career of James Cook—son of a farm-servant[*]—originally a cabin-boy and common sailor, rising to command and to be the successful conductor of three great naval expeditions for discovery in seas heretofore untraversed, presents an example of conduct rarely matched ; and it is not wonderful that scarcely the name of any Englishman is held in greater respect.

It was on a second visit to the Sandwich Islands in the Pacific Ocean, that Cook's life was abruptly ended by an unfortunate collision with the natives, February 14, 1779, when he had just turned his fiftieth year.

The squabble which led to this sad event arose from a miserable cause, the theft of a pair of tongs and a chisel by a native on board one of the ships. One now-a-days hears with surprise that the sailors, pursuing this man towards the shore, fired at him. All might have been ended amicably if an English officer had not attempted to seize the boat of another native, by way of

[*] The father of Captain Cook, named likewise James, was a native of Ednam parish in Berwickshire, and the father of James Cook (grandfather of the navigator) was an elder of that parish in 1692, when Thomas Thomson, father of the poet of the *Seasons,* was its minister. These particulars are given with documentary evidence in Johnston's *Botany of the Eastern Borders,* 1853 (p. 177).

guarantee that the thief would be given up. These high-handed proceedings naturally created a hostile feeling, and during the night an English boat was taken away. Cook went ashore at seven o'clock on a Sunday morning, to secure the person of the king, as a means of obtaining justice, and before eight he was a dead man on the beach, with the natives over his body cutting it to pieces.

Cook was a man of extraordinary natural sagacity, fortitude, and integrity. He was extremely kind-hearted ; yet, as often happens with such persons, somewhat hasty and irritable. He was very modest and unassuming ; not forward in discourse, yet always affable. In personal respects, he was chiefly remarkable for a tall and vigorous frame of body ; his head is described as small, but in his portraits the forehead seems a large expanse, and what the phrenologists call the ' knowing organs ' are well advanced. He had one peculiarity of great consequence to him : in the most critical circumstances, when he had given all proper directions, he could take sleep with perfect calmness. His death through the paltry squabble just described, was the more remarkable, as his benevolence of disposition led him in general to look mildly on the depredations of the natives.

Cook's widow, *née* Elizabeth Batts, who had been married to him in 1762, survived him fifty-six years, dying in 1835.

LADY SARAH LENNOX.

Lady Sarah Lennox — born 14th February 1745—is an interesting figure of a subordinate class in modern English history. Her father, the second Duke of Richmond of his creation (grandson of King Charles II.), had made, in early life, not exactly a romantic marriage, but a marriage which was followed by romantic circumstances. The bride was Lady Sarah Cadogan, daughter of Marlborough's favourite general.

' Their union was a bargain to cancel a gambling debt between the parents, and the young Lord March was brought from college, the lady from the nursery, for the ceremony. The bride was amazed and silent, but the bridegroom exclaimed—" Surely you are not going to marry me to that dowdy ?" Married he was, however, and his tutor instantly carried him off to the Continent . . . . . Three years afterwards, Lord March returned from his travels an accomplished gentleman, but having such a disagreeable recollection of his wife that he avoided home, and repaired on the first night of his arrival to the theatre. There he saw a lady of so fine an appearance that he asked who she was. " The reigning toast, the beautiful Lady March." He hastened to claim her, and they lived together so affectionately, that, one year after his decease in 1750, she died of grief.'[*]

Lady Sarah, one of the numerous children of this loving pair, grew up an extraordinary beauty. Of this we get some testimony from the great domestic chronicler of the last century,

[*] Life of Sir Charles James Napier, by Sir W. Napier, i. 2.

Horace Walpole, who had occasion, in January 1761, to write to his friend George Montagu, regarding some private theatricals which he had witnessed at Holland House. By what appears to us a strange taste, the play selected to be performed by children and very young ladies was *Jane Shore*; Lady Sarah Lennox enacting the heroine, while the boy, afterwards eminent as Charles James Fox, was Hastings. Walpole praises the acting of the performers, but particularly that of Lady Sarah, which he admits to have been full of nature and simplicity. 'Lady Sarah,' he says, 'was more beautiful than you can conceive . . . . in white, with her hair about her ears, and on the ground, no Magdalen by Correggio was half so lovely and expressive.'[*]

The charms of this lovely creature had already made an impression on the heart of George III., then newly come to the throne at two and twenty. There seems no reason to doubt that the young monarch formed the design of raising his lovely cousin (for such she was) to the throne. The idea was of course eagerly embraced by her ladyship's relations, and particularly by her eldest sister's husband, Mr Fox, who held the office of Paymaster of the Forces, and was anxious to strengthen the party to which he belonged. Any such project was, on the other hand, calculated extremely to offend the King's mother, the Princess of Wales, who, for the support of her power over her son, was desirous that his future wife should be beholden to herself for her brilliant position. Early in the winter 1760-1, the King took an opportunity of speaking to Lady Sarah's cousin, Lady Susan Strangeways, expressing a hope at the drawing-room, that her ladyship was not soon to leave town. She said she should. 'But,' said the King, 'you will return in summer for the coronation.' Lady Susan answered that she did not know—she hoped so. 'But,' said the King again, 'they talk of a wedding. There have been many proposals; but I think an English match would do better than a foreign one. Pray tell Lady Sarah Lennox I say so.' Here was a sufficiently broad hint to inflame the hopes of a family, and to raise the head of a blooming girl of sixteen to the fifth heavens.

It happened, however, that Lady Sarah had already allowed her heart to be pre-occupied, having formed a girlish attachment for the young Lord Newbottle, grandson of the Marquis of Lothian. She did not therefore enter into the views of her family with all the alacrity which they desired. According to a narrative of Mr Grenville, 'She went the next drawing-room to St James's, and stated to the King, in as few words as she could, the inconveniences and difficulties in which such a step would involve him. He said, that was his business: he would stand them all: his part was taken, he wished to hear hers was likewise.

'In this state it continued, whilst she, by advice of her friends, broke off with Lord Newbottle,[†] very reluctantly on her part. She went

into the country for a few days, and by a fall from her horse broke her leg. The absence which this occasioned gave time and opportunities for her enemies to work; they instilled jealousy into the King's mind upon the subject of Lord Newbottle, telling him that Lady Sarah still continued her intercourse with him, and immediately the marriage with the Princess of Strelitz was set on foot; and, at Lady Sarah's return from the country, she found herself deprived of her crown and her lover Lord Newbottle, who complained as much of her as she did of the King. While this was in agitation, Lady Sarah used to meet the King in his rides early in the morning, driving a little chaise with Lady Susan Strangeways; and once it is said that, wanting to speak to him, she went dressed like a servant-maid, and stood amongst the crowd in the Guard-room, to say a few words to him as he passed by.'[*] Walpole also relates that Lady Sarah would sometimes appear as a haymaker in the park at Holland House, in order to attract the attention of the King as he rode past;[†] but the opportunity was lost. The habit of obedience to his mother's will carried the day, and he allowed an emissary to go on a mission to obtain a bride for him in the Protestant courts of Germany.

It is believed that Lady Sarah was allowed to have hopes till the very day when the young sovereign announced to his council that he had resolved on wedding the Princess Charlotte of Mecklenburg Strelitz. She felt ill-used, and her friends were all greatly displeased. With the King she remained an object of virtuous admiration,—perhaps also of pity. He wished to soften the disappointment by endeavouring to get her established in a high position near his wife; but the impropriety of such a course was obvious, and it was not persisted in.

Lady Sarah, however, was asked by the King to take a place among the ten unmarried daughters of dukes and earls who held up the train of his queen at the coronation; and this office, which we cannot help thinking in the circumstances derogatory, she consented to perform. It is said that, in the sober, duty-compelled mind of the sovereign, there always was a softness towards the object of his youthful attachment. Walpole relates that he blushed at his wedding service, when allusion was made to Abraham and *Sarah*.

Lady Sarah Lennox in 1764 made a marriage which proved that ambition was not a ruling principle in her nature, her husband being 'a clergyman's son,' Sir Thomas Charles Bunbury, Bart. Her subsequent life was in some respects infelicitous, her marriage being dissolved by Act of Parliament in 1776. By a subsequent marriage to the Hon. Major-General George Napier, she became the mother of a set of remarkable men, including the late Sir Charles James Napier, the conqueror of Scinde, and Lieut.-General Sir William Napier, the historian of the Peninsular War. Her ladyship died at the age of eighty-two, in 1826, believed to be the last surviving great grand-daughter of Charles II.

---

[*] Walpole's Letters.

[†] He must have been William John, who became fifth Marquis of Lothian, and died in 1815, at the age of eighty.

[*] Grenville's Diary, Grenville Papers, 1853, iv. 209.

[†] Walpole's Memoirs of the Reign of George III., 1845, vol. i. p. 64.

St Valentine's Day.

ALENTINE'S DAY is now almost everywhere a much degenerated festival, the only observance of any note consisting merely of the sending of jocular anonymous letters to parties whom one wishes to *quiz,* and this confined very much to the humbler classes. The approach of the day is now heralded by the appearance in the print-sellers' shop windows of vast numbers of missives calculated for use on this occasion, each generally consisting of a single sheet of post paper, on the first page of which is seen some ridiculous coloured caricature of the male or female figure, with a few burlesque verses below. More rarely, the print is of a sentimental kind, such as a view of Hymen's altar, with a pair undergoing initiation into wedded happiness before it, while Cupid flutters above, and hearts transfixed with his darts decorate the corners. Maid-servants and young fellows interchange such epistles with each other on the 14th of February, no doubt conceiving that the joke is amazingly good; and, generally, the newspapers do not fail to record that the London postmen delivered so many hundred thousand more letters on that day than they do in general. Such is nearly the whole extent of the observances now peculiar to St Valentine's Day.

At no remote period it was very different. Ridiculous letters were unknown; and, if letters of any kind were sent, they contained only a courteous profession of attachment from some young man to some young maiden, honeyed with a few compliments to her various perfections, and expressive of a hope that his love might meet with return. But the true proper ceremony of St Valentine's Day was the drawing of a kind of lottery, followed by ceremonies not much unlike what is generally called the game of forfeits. Misson, a learned traveller, of the early part of the last century, gives apparently a correct account of the principal ceremonial of the day. 'On the eve of St Valentine's Day,' he says, 'the young folks in England and Scotland, by a very ancient custom, celebrate a little festival. An equal number of maids and bachelors get together; each writes their true or some feigned name upon separate billets, which they roll up, and draw by way of lots, the maids taking the men's billets, and the men the maids'; so that each of the young men lights upon a girl that he calls his *valentine,* and each of the girls upon a young man whom she calls hers. By this means each has two valentines; but the man sticks faster to the valentine that has fallen to him than to the valentine to whom he is fallen. Fortune having thus divided the company into so many couples, the valentines give balls and treats to their mistresses, wear their billets several days upon their bosoms or sleeves, and this little sport often ends in love.'

In that curious record of domestic life in England in the reign of Charles II., *Pepys's Diary,* we find some notable illustrations of this old custom. It appears that married and single were then alike liable to be chosen as a valen-

ST VALENTINE'S LETTER-SHOWER.

tine, and that a present was invariably and necessarily given to the choosing party. Mr Pepys enters in his diary, on Valentine's Day, 1667: 'This morning came up to my wife's bedside (I being up dressing myself) little Will Mercer to be her valentine, and brought her name written upon blue paper in gold letters, done by himself, very pretty; and we were both well pleased with it.

But I am also this year my wife's valentine, and it will cost me £5; but that I must have laid out if we had not been valentines.' Two days after, he adds: 'I find that Mrs Pierce's little girl is my valentine, she having drawn me: which I was not sorry for, it easing me of something more that I must have given to others. But here I do first observe the fashion of drawing mottoes as well as names, so that Pierce, who drew my wife, did draw also a motto, and this girl drew another for me. What mine was, I forget; but my wife's was "Most courteous and most fair," which, as it may be used, or an anagram upon each name, might be very pretty.' Noticing, soon afterwards, the jewels of the celebrated Miss Stuart, who became Duchess of Richmond, he says: 'The Duke of York, being once her valentine, did give her a jewel of about £800; and my Lord Mandeville, her valentine this year, a ring of about £300.' These presents were undoubtedly given in order to *relieve* the obligation under which the being drawn as valentines had placed the donors. In February 1668, Pepys notes as follows—' This evening my wife did with great pleasure shew me her stock of jewels, increased by the ring she hath made lately, as my valentine's gift this year, a Turkey-stone set with diamonds. With this, and what she had, she reckons that she hath above one hundred and fifty pounds' worth of jewels of one kind or other; and I am glad of it, for it is fit the wretch should have something to content herself with.' The reader will understand wretch to be used as a term of endearment.

Notwithstanding the practice of *relieving*, there seems to have been a disposition to believe that the person drawn as a valentine had some considerable likelihood of becoming the associate of the party in wedlock. At least, we may suppose that this idea would be gladly and easily arrived at, where the party so drawn was at all eligible from other considerations. There was, it appears, a prevalent notion amongst the common people, that this was the day on which the birds selected their mates. They seem to have imagined that an influence was inherent in the day, which rendered in some degree binding the lot or chance by which any youth or maid was now led to fix his attention on a person of the opposite sex. It was supposed, for instance, that the first unmarried person of the other sex whom one met on St Valentine's morning in walking abroad, was a destined wife or a destined husband. Thus Gay makes a rural dame remark—

'Last Valentine, the day when birds of kind
Their paramours with mutual chirpings find,
I early rose just at the break of day,
Before the sun had chased the stars away:
A-field I went, amid the morning dew,
To milk my kine (for so should housewives do).
Thee first I spied—and the first swain we see,
In spite of Fortune shall our true love be.'

A forward Miss in the *Connoisseur*, a series of essays published in 1754-6, thus adverts to other notions with respect to the day: 'Last Friday was Valentine's Day, and the night before, I got five bay-leaves, and pinned four of them to the four corners of my pillow, and the fifth to the middle; and then, if I dreamt of my sweetheart, Betty said we should be married before the year

256

was out. But to make it more sure, I boiled an egg hard, and took out the yolk, and filled it with salt; and when I went to bed, ate it, shell and all, without speaking or drinking after it. We also wrote our lovers' names upon bits of paper, and rolled them up in clay, and put them into water; and the first that rose up was to be our valentine. Would you think it?—Mr Blossom was my man. I lay a-bed and shut my eyes all the morning, till he came to our house; for I would not have seen another man before him for all the world.'

St Valentine's Day is alluded to by Shakspeare and by Chaucer, and also by the poet Lydgate (who died in 1440). One of the earliest known writers of valentines, or poetical amorous addresses for this day, was Charles Duke of Orleans, who was taken at the battle of Agincourt. Drayton, a poet of Shakspeare's time, full of great but almost unknown beauties, wrote thus charmingly

TO HIS VALENTINE.

'Muse, bid the morn awake,
   Sad winter now declines,
Each bird doth choose a mate,
   This day's St Valentine's:
For that good bishop's sake
   Get up, and let us see,
   What beauty it shall be
   That fortune us assigns.

But lo! in happy hour,
   The place wherein she lies,
In yonder climbing tower
   Gilt by the glittering rise;
Oh, Jove! that in a shower,
   As once that thunderer did,
   When he in drops lay hid,
   That I could her surprise!

Her canopy I'll draw,
   With spangled plumes bedight,
No mortal ever saw
   So ravishing a sight;
That it the gods might awe,
   And powerfully transpierce
   The globy universe,
   Out-shooting every light.

My lips I'll softly lay
   Upon her heavenly cheek,
Dyed like the dawning day,
   As polish'd ivory sleek:
And in her ear I'll say,
   "Oh thou bright morning-star!
   'Tis I that come so far,
   My valentine to seek."

Each little bird, this tide,
   Doth choose her loved peer,
Which constantly abide
   In wedlock all the year,
As nature is their guide:
   So may we two be true
   This year, nor change for new,
   As turtles coupled were.

Let's laugh at them that choose
   Their valentines by lot;
To wear their names that use,
   Whom idly they have got.
Such poor choice we refuse,
   Saint Valentine befriend;
   We thus this morn may spend,
   Else, Muse, awake her not.'

Donne, another poet of the same age, remarkable for rich though scattered beauties, writes an epithalamium on the marriage of the Princess Elizabeth to Frederick Count Palatine of the Rhine—the marriage which gave the present royal family to the throne—and which took place on St Valentine's Day, 1614. The opening is fine—

  ' Hail, Bishop Valentine ! whose day this is ;
    All the air is thy diocese,
    And all the chirping choristers
    And other birds are thy parishioners :
    Thou marryest every year
    The lyric lark and the grave whispering dove ;
    The sparrow that neglects his life for love,
    The household bird with the red stomacher ;
    Thou mak'st the blackbird speed as soon
    As doth the goldfinch or the halcyon—
    This day more cheerfully than ever shine,
    This day which might inflame thyself, old Valentine !'

The origin of these peculiar observances of St Valentine's Day is a subject of some obscurity. The saint himself, who was a priest of Rome, martyred in the third century,* seems to have had nothing to do with the matter, beyond the accident of his day being used for the purpose. Mr Douce, in his *Illustrations of Shakspeare*, says : ' It was the practice in ancient Rome, during a great part of the month of February, to celebrate the Lupercalia, which were feasts in honour of Pan and Juno, whence the latter deity was named Februata, Februalis, and Februlla. On this occasion, amidst a variety of ceremonies, the names of young women were put into a box, from which they were drawn by the men as chance directed. The pastors of the early Christian church, who, by every possible means, endeavoured to eradicate the vestiges of pagan superstitions, and chiefly by some commutations of their forms, substituted, in the present instance, the names of particular saints instead of those of the women ; and as the festival of the Lupercalia had commenced about the middle of February, they appear to have chosen St Valentine's Day for celebrating the new feast, because it occurred nearly at the same time. This is, in part, the opinion of a learned and rational compiler of the *Lives of the Saints*, the Rev. Alban Butler. It should seem, however, that it was utterly impossible to extirpate altogether any ceremony to which the common people had been much accustomed—a fact which it were easy to prove in tracing the origin of various other popular superstitions. And, accordingly, the outline of the ancient ceremonies was preserved, but modified by some adaptation to the Christian system. It is reasonable to suppose, that the above practice of choosing mates would gradually become reciprocal in the sexes, and that all persons so chosen would be called Valentines, from the day on which the ceremony took place.'

  * Valentine met a sad death, being first beaten with clubs and then beheaded. The greater part of his remains are preserved in the church of St Praxedes at Rome, where a gate (now the Porta del Popolo) was formerly named from him *Porta Valentini*.

FEBRUARY 15.

Saints Faustinus and Jovita, martyrs at Brescia, about 121. St Sigefride of York, apostle in Sweden, 1002.

Born.—Galileo Galilei, astronomer, 1564, *Pisa ;* Louis XV. (of *France*), 1710.
Died.—Oswy (of *Northumbria*), 670 ; John Philips, poet, 1708, *Hereford ;* Anthony Earl of Shaftesbury, author of *Characteristics*, 1713, *Naples ;* Bishop Atterbury, 1732 ; John Hadley, inventor of the sextant, 1744; Charles Andrew Vanloo, historical painter, 1765.

PHILIPS, THE CIDER POET.

John Philips, the artificial poet who parodied the style of Milton in the *Splendid Shilling*, is better known by his poem upon *Cider*, 'which continued long to be read as an imitation of Virgil's Georgics, which needed not shun the presence of the original.' Johnson was told by Miller, the eminent gardener and botanist, that there were many books written on cider in prose which do not contain so much truth as Philips's poem. 'The precepts which it contains,' adds Johnson, 'are exact and just; and it is, therefore, at once a book of entertainment and science.' It is in blank verse, and an echo of the numbers of *Paradise Lost*. 'In the disposition of his matter, so as to intersperse precepts relating to the culture of trees, with sentiments more generally alluring, and in easy and graceful transitions from one subject to another, he has very diligently imitated his master ; but he unhappily pleased himself with blank verse, and supposed that the numbers of Milton, which impress the mind with veneration, combined as they are with subjects of inconceivable grandeur, could be sustained by images which at most can only rise to eloquence. Contending angels may shake the regions of heaven in blank verse ; but the flow of equal measures, and the embellishment of rhyme, must recommend to our attention the art of engrafting, and decide the merit of the " redstreak " and " pearmain." '—*Johnson.*

Philips was cut off by consumption, when he had just completed his thirty-second year. He was buried in the cathedral of Hereford; and Sir Simon Harcourt, afterwards Lord Chancellor, gave him a monument in Westminster Abbey, which bears a long inscription, in flowing Latinity, said by Johnson to be the composition of Bishop Atterbury, though commonly attributed to Dr Freind.

EXTRAORDINARY MARRIAGES.

Among the many remarkable marriages on record, none are more curious than those in which the bridegroom has proved to be of the same sex as the bride. Last century there lived a woman who dressed in male attire, and was constantly going about captivating her sisters, and marrying them ! On the 5th of July 1777, she was tried at a criminal court in London for thus disguising herself, and it was proved that at various times she had been married to three women, and 'defrauded them of their money and their clothes.' The fair deceiver was required by the justices to give the daughters of the citizens an opportunity of making themselves acquainted with her features by standing in the pillory at Cheapside : and after going through this ordeal, she was imprisoned for six months. In 1773 a woman went courting a woman, dressed as a man, and was very favourably received. The lady to whom these not very delicate attentions were paid was much older than the lover, but she was possessed of about a hundred pounds, and this was the attraction to her adventurous friend. But the intended treachery was discovered; and, as the original chronicler of the story says, 'the old lady proved too knowing.' A more extraordinary case than either of these was that of two women who lived together by mutual consent as man and wife for six-and-thirty years. They kept a public-house at Poplar, and the 'wife,' when on her death-bed, for the first time told her relatives the fact concerning her marriage. The writer in the *Gentleman's Magazine* (1776) who records the circumstances, states that 'both had been crossed in love when young, and had chosen this method to avoid further importunities.' It seems, however, that the truth was suspected, for the 'husband' subsequently charged a man with extorting money from her under the threat of disclosing the secret, and for this offence he was sentenced to stand three times in the pillory, and to undergo four years' imprisonment.

It is usually considered a noteworthy circumstance for a man or woman to have been married three times, but of old this number would have been thought little of. St Jerome mentions a widow that married her twenty-second husband, who in his turn had been married to twenty wives—surely an experienced couple ! A woman named Elizabeth Masi, who died at Florence in 1768, had been married to seven husbands, all of whom she outlived. She married the last of the seven at the age of 70. When on her death-bed she recalled the good and bad points in each of her husbands, and having impartially weighed them in the balance, she singled out her fifth spouse as the favourite, and desired that her remains might be interred near his. The death of a soldier is recorded in 1784 who had had five wives; and his widow, aged 90, wept over the grave of her fourth husband. The writer who mentioned these facts naïvely added : 'The said soldier was much attached to the marriage state.' There is an account of a gentleman who had been married to four wives, and who lived to be 115 years old. When he died he left twenty-three 'children' alive and well, some of the said children being from three to four score. A gentleman died at Bordeaux in 1772, who had been married sixteen times.

In July 1768 a couple were living in Essex who had been married eighty-one years, the husband being 107, and the wife 103 years of age. At the church of St Clement Danes, in 1772, a woman of 85 was married to her sixth husband.

Instances are by no means rare of affectionate attachment existing between man and wife over a period longer than is ordinarily allotted to human life. In the middle of the last century a farmer of Nottingham died in his 107th year. Three days afterwards his wife died also, aged 97. They had lived happily together upwards of eighty years. About the same time a yeoman of

Coal-pit Heath, Gloucestershire, died in his 104th year. The day after his funeral his wife expired at the age of 115 ; they had been married eighty-one years.

The announcements of marriages published in the *Gentleman's Magazine* during the greater part of last century included a very precise statement of the portions brought by the brides. Here are a few of such notices :

'Mr N. Tillotson, an eminent preacher among the people called Quakers, and a relative of Archbishop Tillotson, to Miss ——, with £7000.'

'Mr P. Bowen to Miss Nicholls, of Queenhithe, with £10,000.'

'Sir George C. to the widow Jones, with £1000 a-year, besides ready money.'

The following announcement follows the notice of a marriage in the *Gentleman's Magazine* for November 1774 :—'They at the same time ordered the sexton to make a grave for the interment of the lady's father, then dead.' This was unusual ; but a stranger scene took place at St Dunstan's church on one occasion, during the performance of the marriage ceremony. The bridegroom was a carpenter, and he followed the service devoutly enough until the words occurred, 'With this ring I thee wed.' He repeated these, and then shaking his fist at the bride added, 'And with this fist I'll break thy head.' The clergyman refused to proceed, but, says the account, 'the fellow declared he meant no harm,' and the confiding bride 'believed he did but jest,' whereupon the service was completed. A still more unpleasant affair for the lady once happened. A young couple went to get married, but found on their arrival at church that they had not money to pay the customary fees. The clergyman not being inclined to give credit, the bridegroom went out to get the required sum, while the lady waited in the vestry. During his walk the lover changed his mind, and never returned to the church. The young girl waited two hours for him, and then departed, —'Scot free,' dryly remarks one narrator. A bridegroom was once arrested at the church door on the charge of having left a wife and family chargeable to another parish, 'to the great grief and shame of the intended bride.'

In Scotland, in the year 1749, there was married the 'noted bachelor, W. Hamilton.' He was so deformed that he was utterly unable to walk. The chronicler draws a startling portrait of the man : 'His legs were drawn up to his ears, his arms were twisted backwards, and almost every member was out of joint.' Added to these peculiarities, he was eighty years of age, and was obliged to be carried to church on men's shoulders. Nevertheless, his bride was fair, and only twenty years of age ! A wedding once took place in Berkshire under remarkable circumstances : the bridegroom was of the mature age of eighty-five, the bride eighty-three, and the bridesmaids each upwards of seventy — neither of these damsels having been married. Six grand-daughters of the bridegroom strewed flowers before the 'happy couple,' and four grandsons of the bride sung an epithalamium composed by the parish clerk on the occasion. On the 5th February, in the eighteenth year of Elizabeth (corresponding to 1576), Thomas Filsby, a deaf man, was married in St Martin's parish, Leicester. Seeing that, on account of his natural infirmity, he could not, for his part, observe the order of the form of marriage, some peculiarities were introduced into the ceremony, with the approbation of the Bishop of Lincoln, the commissary Dr Chippendale, and the Mayor of Leicester. 'The said Thomas, for expressing of his mind, instead of words, of his own accord used these signs : first he embraced her [the bride, Ursula Russet] with his arms ; took her by the hand and put a ring on her finger ; and laid his hand upon his heart, and held up his hands towards heaven ; and, to shew his continuance to dwell with her to his life's end, he did it by closing his eyes with his hands, and digging the earth with his feet, and pulling as though he would ring a bell, with other signs approved.'* At the more recent marriage of a deaf and dumb young man at Greenock, the only singularity was in the company. The bridegroom, his three sisters, and two young men with them were all deaf and dumb. There is a case mentioned in Dodsley's *Annual Register* of an ostler at a tavern in Spilsby who walked with his intended wife all the way to Gretna Green to get married—240 miles.

Some of the most remarkable marriages that have ever taken place are those in which the brides came to the altar partly, or in many cases entirely, divested of clothing. It was formerly a common notion that if a man married a woman *en chemisette* he was not liable for her debts ; and in *Notes and Queries* there is an account by a clergyman of the celebration of such a marriage some few years ago. He tells us that, as nothing was said in the rubric about the woman's dress, he did not think it right to refuse to perform the marriage service. At Whitehaven a wedding was celebrated under the same circumstances, and there are several other instances on record.

A curious example of compulsory marriage once took place in Clerkenwell. A blind woman, forty years of age, conceived a strong affection for a young man who worked in a house near to her own, and whose 'hammering' she could hear early and late. Having formed an acquaintance with him, she gave him a silver watch and other presents, and lent him £10 to assist him in his business. The recipient of these favours waited on the lady to thank her, and intimated that he was about to leave London. This was by no means what the blind woman wanted, and as she was determined not to lose the person whose industrial habits had so charmed her, she had him arrested for the debt of £10 and thrown into prison. While in confinement she visited him, and offered to forgive him the debt, on condition that he married her. Placed in this strait, the young man chose what he deemed the least of the two evils, and married his 'benefactress,' as the writer in the *Gentleman's Magazine* calls her. The men who arrested him gave the bride away at the altar. In 1767 a young blacksmith of Bedford was paying his addresses to a maiden, and upon calling to see her one evening

* From the parish register, quoted in *Notes and Queries*, 2nd ser., iv. 489.

was asked by her mother, what was the use of marrying a girl without money ? Would it not be better for him to take a wife who could bring £500 ? The blacksmith thought it would, and said he should be 'eternally obliged' to his adviser if she could introduce him to such a prize. 'I am the person, then,' said the mother of his betrothed, and we are told that 'the bargain was struck immediately.' Upon the return of the girl, she found her lover and parent on exceedingly good terms with each other, and they were subsequently married. The bride was sixty-four years of age, and the bridegroom eighteen. This disparity of years is comparatively trifling. A doctor of eighty was married to a young woman of twenty-eight ; a blacksmith of ninety (at Worcester, 1768) to a girl of fifteen ; a gentleman of Berkshire, aged seventy-six, to a girl whom his *third* wife had brought up. The husband had children living 'thrice the age' of his fourth wife. At Hill farm, in Berkshire, a blind woman of ninety years was married to her ploughman, aged twenty ; a gentleman of Worcester, upwards of eighty-five, to a girl of eighteen ; a soldier of ninety-five, 'who had served in King William's wars, and had a ball in his nose,' to a girl of fifteen. In 1769 a woman of Rotherhithe, aged seventy, was married to a young man aged twenty-three—just half a century difference between their ages. A girl of sixteen married a gentleman of ninety-four—but he had £50,000.

TIME-CANDLES.

In the Life of Alfred the Great, by Asserius, we read that, before the invention of clocks, Alfred caused six tapers to be made for his daily use ; each taper, containing twelve pennyweights of wax, was twelve inches long, and of proportionate breadth. The whole length was divided into twelve parts, or inches, of which three would burn for one hour, so that each taper would be consumed in four hours ; and the six tapers, being lighted one after the other, lasted for twenty-four hours. But the wind blowing through the windows and doors, and chinks of the walls of the chapel, or through the cloth of his tent, in which they were burning, wasted these tapers, and, consequently, they burnt with no regularity : he therefore designed a lantern made of ox or cow horn, cut into thin plates, in which he inclosed the tapers ; and thus protecting them from the wind, the period of their burning became a matter of certainty.

This is an amusing and oft-quoted story, but, like many other old stories, it lacks authenticity. The work of Asser, there is reason to believe, is not genuine. See the arguments in Wright's *Biog. Brit. Lit.* vol. i. pp. 408—412. It moreover appears that some of the institutions popularly ascribed to Alfred, existed before his time.—*Kemble's Saxons in England.*

Still, there is nothing very questionable in this mode of Alfred's to measure time ; and, possibly, it may have suggested an 'improvement,' which was patented so recently as 1859, and which consists in making marks on the side or around the sides of candles either by indentation or colouring at intervals, and equal distances apart, according to the size of the candle, to indicate the time by the burning of the candle. The marks are to consist of hours, half-hours, and if necessary quarter-hours, the distance to be determined by the kind of candle used ; the mark or other announcement may be made either in the process of manufacture or after.

THE GREAT TUN OF HEIDELBERG.

In a large under room, in the castle or palace of the Princes Palatine of the Rhine at Heidelberg, the eccentric traveller Thomas Coryat found this vast vessel, in its original form, of which he has given a picture representing himself as perched on its top,

THE GREAT TUN OF HEIDELBERG.

with a glass of its contents in his hands. To him it appeared the greatest wonder he had seen in his travels, fully entitled to rank with those seven wonders of the world of which ancient authors inform us.

Its construction was begun in the year 1589 and finished in 1591, one Michael Warner being the principal fabricator. It was composed of beams twenty-seven feet long, and had a diameter of eighteen feet. The iron hooping was eleven thousand pounds in weight. The cost was eleven score and eighteen pounds sterling. It could hold a hundred and thirty-two fuders of wine, a fuder being equal to four English hogsheads, and the value of the Rhenish contained in it when Coryat visited Heidelberg (1608) was close upon two thousand pounds.

'When the cellarer,' says Coryat, 'draweth wine out of the vessel, he ascendeth two several degrees of wooden stairs made in the form of a ladder, and so goeth up to the top ; about the middle whereof there is a bung-hole or venting orifice, into the which he conveyeth a pretty instrument of some foot and a half long, made in the form of a spout, wherewith he draweth up the wine and so poureth it after a pretty manner into a glass.' The traveller advises visitors to beware lest they be inveigled to drink more than is good for them. *

Murray's *Handbook of the Rhine* represents the present tun as made in 1751, as thirty-six feet long and twenty-four in height, and as capable of containing 800 hogsheads, or 283,200 bottles. It has been disused since 1769.

FEBRUARY 16.

St Onesimus, disciple of St Paul, martyr, 95. Saints Elias, Jeremy, Isaias, Samuel, and Daniel, Egyptian martyrs, 309. St Juliana, virgin martyr at Nicomedia, about 309. St Tanco (or Tatto), of Scotland, bishop, martyr at Verdun, about 815. St Gregory X. (Pope), 1276.

Born.—Philip Melanchthon, reformer, 1497, *Bretten ;* Gaspard de Coligny. Admiral of France, and Protestant leader, 1516, *Chatillon ;* Archbishop (John) Sharp, 1644, *Bradford ;* Baron Trenck, 1726.

Died.—Alphonso III. (of *Portugal*), 1279 ; Archbishop Henry Deane, 1502, *Canterbury ;* John Stoffler, German astronomer, 1531 ; Dr Richard Mead, virtuoso, 1754, *St Pancras ;* Peter Macquer, French chemist, 1784, *Paris ;* Giovan Batista Casti, Italian poet, 1803, *Paris ;* Lindley Murray, grammarian, 1826 ; Dr Kane, American Arctic explorer, 1857, *Havana.*

BARON TRENCK.

The career of this extraordinary man presents several remarkable instances of the fatal influence of vanity and ungovernable passion upon a life which, at the outset, was brilliant with good fortune.

Born February 16, 1726, of parents belonging to the most ancient and wealthy houses in East Prussia, the young Baron distinguished himself in his thirteenth year, at his University ; one year later he wounded and disarmed in a duel one of the most celebrated swordsmen of Königsberg ; and in his sixteenth year, Frederick (after-

wards the Great) appointed him a cadet, and soon afterwards the King gave him a cornetcy in his body-guard, then the most splendid and gallant regiment in Europe. Trenck was a great favourite at court ; but about two years afterwards an imprudent attachment was formed between him and the Princess Amelie, which had a fatal influence upon his fortunes. During the war between Prussia and Austria, Trenck, being detected in a correspondence with the enemy, was sent prisoner to the fortification of Glatz. It was at the same time ascertained that large sums of money had been remitted to him by the princess. From that time must be dated Frederick's intense and obdurate hatred of Trenck. Making his escape by bribery, he went to Russia, where he was appointed captain of a troop of hussars : he was in high favour with the empress, and acquired considerable wealth through the legacy of a Russian princess ; but the Prussian ambassador left nothing undone to injure him, in accordance, as he pretended, with instructions from the King, his master. In 1748, Trenck returned to Prussia, to visit his family, and at Dantzic he was arrested by a party of hussars, and taken prisoner to Berlin : he was at first treated well, but his intemperate conduct led to his being sent to Magdeburg, and confined in a cell underground, and almost without light : his sufferings may be read in his own memoirs. After two soldiers had suffered death for conniving at his attempts to escape, and other plots

* Coryat's *Crudities*, ed. 1776, ii. 351.

260

were discovered, a prison was built on purpose for him, in which he was chained to the walls with fetters of fifty-six pounds weight. Here he remained eight years, when Frederick consented to his release upon condition of his leaving the kingdom. He went first to Vienna, where he was again arrested on account of his violent language against Frederick; but he was soon set free, and advised to retire. He settled at Aix-la-Chapelle, married, and commenced business as a wine-merchant, but did not prosper, and became bankrupt. He next wrote articles of a democratic tendency for several periodical publications; and in 1787, after the death of Frederick the Great, he published his memoirs, for the copyright of which he received a very large sum. The work was translated into almost all the European languages; the ladies at Paris, Berlin, and Vienna, wore rings, necklaces, bonnets, and dresses à la Trenck, and he was made the hero of seven pieces on the French stage. He subsequently commenced a weekly journal at Aix-la-Chapelle, under the title of L'Ami des Hommes, in which he advocated the new French doctrines. In 1792, he went to Paris, joined a Jacobin club, and was afterwards a zealous adherent of the Mountain party, which, nevertheless, betrayed and accused him, and he was thrown into prison. He would, however, have escaped by the fall of Robespierre, had it not been for his restlessness. 'He was,' said Du Roure, 'the greatest liar I ever knew. To that, his favourite propensity, he owed his fate. Our hope of escape in the prison was to remain unnoticed by the gaoler, and wait events. Upon the least complaint, the order from the authorities was à la mort, sometimes without the ceremony of a trial. The prisoners were numerous, and for some days a rumour had been circulated among them, and continually kept up, as if with fresh information, that the Prussians were marching upon Paris, carrying all before them. We knew of nothing certain that went on outside the prison walls, and were not without hopes that this intelligence was correct. Still, we were puzzled to discover how such information could be promulgated amongst us, as it thus was, early every morning, with some new addition. This prevalent topic of conversation, it seems, had, with its daily additions, reached the ears of the gaoler, who caused the gates of the prison to be closed to ingress or egress until the day was far advanced, in order to try whether any fresh news thus circulated came from without, or was concocted within the walls. Trenck that morning circulated some additional particulars about the Prussians' vicinity to Paris, which were traced to him through those to whom he had communicated them, with the addition, that his information was certain, for he had just received it, which was impossible. He was thus caught in circulating false rumours, complained of by the gaoler, and lost his head by the guillotine, near the Barrière du Trône, on the 26th of July 1794. On the scaffold, and in his sixty-ninth year, he gave proof of his ungovernable passions. He harangued the crowd, and when his head was on the block, his vehemence was such, that the executioner had to hold him by his silver locks to meet the fatal stroke. He was buried, with the other victims of that sanguinary period, in a spot of ground not more than thirty feet square, in the corner of the garden of the canonesses of St Augustine, near the ancient village of Picpus, now inclosed in the Faubourg Antoine.'

Baron Trenck was a man of considerable literary talents, and was fully as familiar with English as with French literature. In person he was stout and thick-set, his countenance by no means prepossessing, from a disease which had disfigured it; and he was slovenly in his dress.

DR MEAD AND HIS MUSEUM.

Foremost among the medical men of the last century, for his professional skill, his amiable manners, and princely munificence, ranks Dr Richard Mead, who was consulted beside the death-bed of Queen Anne, and became physician to George II. He was born at Stepney, near London, in 1675; and after studying in continental schools, and taking the degree of Doctor of Medicine at Padua, he settled at his native village, and there established his reputation. Among his early services were his researches in experimental physiology, for which no small degree of courage was necessary. He handled vipers, provoked them, and encouraged them to seize hold of hard bodies, on which he imagined that he could collect their venom in all its force. Having obtained the matter, he conveyed it into the veins of living animals, mixed it with human blood, and even ventured to taste it, in order to establish the utility of sucking the wounds inflicted by serpents.

Mead was instrumental in promoting inoculation for the small-pox: the Prince of Wales desired him, in 1721, to superintend the inoculation of some condemned criminals, intending afterwards to encourage the practice by employing it in his own family; the experiment amply succeeded, and the individuals on whom it was made recovered their liberty. When the terrible plague ravaged Marseilles, and its contagious origin was discredited, Dr Mead, after a careful examination of the subject, declared the plague to be a contagious distemper, and a quarantine was enjoined; and he proposed a system of Medical Police, in a tract of which seven editions were sold in one year. Through Dr Mead's influence, Sutton's invention for expelling the foul and corrupted air from ships was tried, and its simplicity and efficacy proved; a model of Sutton's machine made in copper was deposited in the museum of the Royal Society, and the ships of his Majesty's navy were provided with it. The fact that, in each of these cases, Mead's results have been superseded by more recent discoveries, does not in the least detract from his merit. What he effected was, for his time, wonderful.

Mead was fast approaching the summit of his fortune, when his great protector, Radcliffe, died, and Mead moved into his house in Bloomsbury-square. After the most brilliant career of professional and literary reputation, of personal honour, of wealth, and of notoriety, which ever fell in combination to the lot of any medical man in any age or country, Mead took to the bed from which he was to rise no more, on the 11th of February, and expired on the 16th of the same month, 1754. His death was unaccompanied by any visible signs of pain.

In practice, Dr Mead was without a rival; his receipts averaging, for several years, between six and seven thousand pounds, an enormous sum in relation to the value of money at that period. He daily sat in Batson's coffee-house, in Cornhill, and at Tom's, in Russell-street, Coventgarden, to inspect written, or receive oral, statements from the apothecaries, prescribing without seeing the patient, for a half-guinea fee. He gave advice gratuitously, not merely to the indigent, but also to the clergy, and all men of learning.

Dr Mead had removed into Great Ormondstreet, Queen-square, several years before his death: the house is No. 49, corner of Powisplace; behind his house was a good garden, in which he built a gallery and museum. There Mead gave *conversazioni*, which were the first meetings of the kind. He possessed a rare taste for collecting; but his books, his statues, his medals, were not to amuse only his own leisure: the humble student, the unrecommended foreigner, the poor inquirer, derived almost as much enjoyment from these treasures as their owner; and he constantly kept in his pay several scholars and artists, who laboured, at his expense, for the benefit of the public. His correspondence extended to all the principal literati of Europe, who consulted him, and sent him many curious presents. At his table might be seen the most eminent men of the age. Pope was a ready guest, and the delicate poet was always sure to be regaled with his favourite dish of *sweetbreads*. Politics formed no bar of separation: the celebrated physicians, Garth, Arbuthnot, and Freind, were not the less his intimate associates because they were Tories. When Freind was sent to the Tower for some supposed political offence, Mead frequently visited him, and attended his patients in his absence; from Sir Robert Walpole he procured his liberation, and then presented him with a large sum, being the fees which he had received from his brother practitioner's clients. He also persuaded the wealthy citizen, Guy, to bequeath his fortune towards the noble hospital which bears his name.

Although Mead's receipts were so considerable, and two large fortunes were bequeathed to him, his benevolence, public spirit, and splendid mode of living, prevented him from leaving great wealth to his family. He whose mansion was a sort of open house for men of genius and talent, who kept a second table for his humbler dependents, and who was driven to his country house, near Windsor, by six horses, was not likely to amass wealth; but he did better: he acted according to his own conviction, that what he had gained from the public could not be more worthily bestowed than in the advancement of the public mind; and he truly fulfilled the inscription which he had chosen for his motto: 'Non sibi, sed toti.'*

After Dr Mead's death, the sale of his library and museum realized between fifteen and sixteen

* Pettigrew's *Lives of British Physicians.*

262

thousand pounds, his pictures alone producing £3400. The printed catalogue of the library contains 6592 separate numbers; Oriental, Greek, and Latin manuscripts forming no inconsiderable part: the greater portion of the library he bequeathed to the College of Physicians. The collection included prints and drawings, coins and medals, marble statues of Greek philosophers and Roman emperors; bronzes, gems, intaglios, Etruscan and other vases; marble busts of Shakspeare, Milton, and Pope, by Scheemakers; statues of Hygeia and Antinöus; a celebrated bronze head of Homer; and an iron cabinet (once Queen Elizabeth's), full of coins, among which was a medal, with Oliver Cromwell's head in profile; legend 'The Lord of Hosts,' the word at Dunbar, 1650; on the reverse, the Parliament sitting.

Of so worthy a man as Dr Mead memorials are interesting: in the College of Physicians is a fine bust of him, by Roubiliac; and here is his portrait, and the gold-headed cane which he received from Radcliffe, and which was afterwards carried by Askew, Pitcairn, and Matthew Baillie. Among the pictures at the Foundling Hospital is Dr Mead's portrait, by Allan Ramsay; and in the nave of Westminster Abbey is a monument to our worthy physician.

Dr Mead was a clever person, but Dr Woodward had the better of him in wit: when they fought a duel under the gate of Gresham College, Woodward's foot slipped, and he fell. 'Take your life!' exclaimed Mead. 'Anything but *your physic*,' replied Woodward. The quarrel arose from a difference of opinion on medical subjects.

LINDLEY MURRAY.

As many spoke of Robin Hood who never shot with his bow, so many hear of Lindley Murray who know nothing of him but that he composed a book of English grammar. He was an American — native of Pennsylvania — and realized a competency at New York, partly as a barrister and partly as a merchant. The necessities of health obliged him to remove to England, where he spent the last forty years of his protracted life at Holdgate, near York, a feeble invalid, but resigned and happy. Besides his well-known *Grammar*, he wrote a book on *The Power of Religion on the Mind*. He was a man of mild and temperate nature, entirely beloved by all connected with him. In a series of autobiographical letters, he gives a statement as to the moderation of his desires, well worthy of being brought under general notice.

' My views and wishes with regard to property were, in every period of my life, contained within a very moderate compass. I was early persuaded that, though "a competence is vital to content," I ought not to annex to that term the idea of much property. I determined that when I should acquire enough to enable me to maintain and provide for my family in a respectable and moderate manner, and this according to real and rational, not imaginary and fantastic wants, and a little to share for the necessities of others, I would decline the pursuits of property, and devote a great part of my time, in some way or other, to the benefit of my fellow-creatures, within the sphere of my abilities to serve them. I perceived that the desire of great possessions generally expands with the gradual acquisition and full attainment of them; and I imagined that charity and a generous application do not sufficiently correspond with the increase of property. I thought, too, that procuring great wealth has a tendency to produce an elated independence of mind, little connected with that humility which is the ground of all our virtues; that a busy and anxious pursuit of it often excludes views and reflections of infinite importance, and leaves but little time to acquire that treasure which would make us rich indeed . . . I was persuaded that a truly sincere mind could be at no loss to discern the just limits between a safe and competent portion and a dangerous profusion of the good things of life. These views of the subject I reduced to practice; and terminated my mercantile concerns when I had acquired a moderate competency.'

DR KANE.

There are not many American names that have made a more purely satisfactory impression on European minds than that of Elisha Kent Kane. Born in 1822, and educated as a surgeon, he spent all his youthful years in adventurous explorations, first in the Philippine Islands, afterwards in India, then in Africa: he next took a bold and prominent part in the war which his countrymen waged against Mexico; finally, he accompanied the expedition which American generosity (chiefly represented by Mr Grinnell) sent in search of Sir John Franklin. All this was over, and Kane had become the historian of the expedition, before he had passed thirty. Another Arctic exploration being determined on, Kane was appointed as its commander, and started on his voyage in May 1853. With indefatigable perseverance he carried his vessel, the *Advance*, into Smith's Sound, to a point at latitude 78° 43′ N., where the thermometer in February was so low as 70° *minus* Fahrenheit. Further progress in the vessel being impossible, Kane took to a boat, and made further explorations of a most remarkable kind, finally discovering an iceless sea north of 80° N. The sufferings of the whole party in these movements were extreme; but they became insignificant in comparison with those of a return which was necessitated in open boats to the most northerly Danish Greenland settlement, and which occupied eighty-four days. Immense credit was due to Kane for the skill and energy which enabled him to bring back his people with scarcely diminished numbers through such unheard-of difficulties and perils. The able and highly illustrated book, in which he subsequently detailed this heroic enterprise, and described the new regions he had explored, must remain an enduring monument to his memory. It is alleged that, after all he had suffered, his constitution was not seriously injured. Yet the melancholy fact is that this extraordinary man sunk into the grave the year after his book was published.

CASTI AND THE GIULI TRE.

February 16, 1803, died, at above eighty years of age, the Italian poet, Giovan Batista Casti, known chiefly by his clever comic poem the *Animali Parlanti*, which our Mr Stewart Rose has partially translated under the name of the *Court of Beasts*. He was in early life a priest at Montefiascone, in the States of the Church, but afterwards became the *protégé* in succession of the Grand Duke of Tuscany and the Emperor of Germany (Joseph II.), and was only recognised as a gay and free-thoughted court poet. He spent his latter years in ease at Paris. He was generally known as the *Abate* Casti, owing to his early connexion with the Church, though towards the close of his life he dropped the title, and was desirous that it should be forgotten.

Casti displayed the remarkable ingenuity and resources of his mind in a poetical work which stands quite unique in point of subject in the literature of all nations. It appeared in 1762 (being his first work, though published when he was upwards of forty) under the title of the *Tre Giuli*, and consisted of two hundred sonnets descriptive of the troubles which the author was pleased to represent himself as having incurred in consequence of borrowing three giuli which he was never able to repay. A giulio (Julius), worth about a groat English, is a small silver coin first struck by Julius II. and called after him.

Captain Montagu Montagu published a translation of this remarkable book in 1826, and a second edition in 1841. Mr Leigh Hunt, in the *Liberal*, published in 1822, had drawn the attention of English readers to the poem, and given an English version of several of the sonnets. It could hardly be that Mr Hunt should fail to be struck with the humour and grace of Casti, and indeed the *Tre Giuli* seems to have made upon him an extraordinary impression.

'The fertility of fancy and learned allusion,' he writes, 'with which the author has written his 200 sonnets on a man's coming to him every day and asking him for Tre Giuli is inferior only to what Butler or Marvell might have made of it. The very recurrence of the words becomes a good joke. Let statesmen say what they will of "the principle of reiteration," the principles of imagination and continuation are the intense things in this our mortal state: as the perpetual accompaniment and exaggeration of one image is the worst thing in sorrow, so it is the merriest thing in a piece of wit.' 'The Giuli Tre are henceforth among our standing jokes—among our lares and penates of pleasantry.' 'Nobody that we have met with in Italy could resist the mention of them. The priest did not pretend it. The ladies were glad they could find something to approve in a poet of so erroneous a reputation. The man of the world laughed as merrily as he could. The patriot was happy to relax his mustachios. Even the bookseller of whom we bought them laughed with a real laugh, evidently not the mercenary and meretricious grin with which he laughs at the customer instead of the book, when he has the luck to get rid of some heavy facetiosity by a chance sale—not "the bought smile—

——Loveless, joyless, unendeared,
    Casual fruition."'

It should be mentioned, however, that one great source of drollery in the original is lost in the translation. It has been elegantly said that work of this kind is like pouring a perfume from one vessel into another, which, if it be ever so carefully done, must result in a certain loss of fragrance by evaporation in the transfusion. But, in addition to this, the *Tre Giuli* is written in a style which is without an English equivalent; its *versi tronchi*, or truncated verses, have the final word in every line accented on the last syllable, which has an effect extremely ludicrous in Italian. The style of verse is only employed in burlesque or humorous subjects; it is mock-heroic, and possesses, to Italian ears, a drollery in sound quite apart from, and in addition to, the humour of the sense of the verse.

The *Tre Giuli* is a kind of small-debts epic. It is in poetry what Paganini's fantasia on one string was in music. It is a literary *tour de force*. The 'pay me' of the creditor Chrysophilus comes beating through the verse in all sorts of places, just as the injunction 'Forward' tolls incessantly throughout the story of the *Wandering Jew*. A poem essentially of one idea is yet made to possess the most infinite variety; the story is without beginning, or middle, or end, and yet is full of interest. We know what is coming, and are constantly expecting it, and yet we are somehow surprised when it does come. The insatiable dun never appears at quite the time or place at which we had been looking for him. Just as the legerdemainist twists a sheet of paper into all manner of forms, or makes a piece of money shew itself to us in all sorts of places, so does the idea of this poem change and twist, and appear and disappear. The Tre Giuli are now a lump of metal in our hands. Now they are hammered out into a tissue sheet that seems to cover the whole globe.

And as in all the superior kinds of burlesque there is a touch of seriousness and real feeling—for truth and nature enhance even travestie—so in the *Tre Giuli*, in spite of the triviality and humorousness of the subject, our interest and sympathies are excited in an extraordinary degree by the earnestness and persistence, almost the pathos of the narrator. His agony seems now and then so real, that we are tempted to forget how ridiculous is the cause of it. He so impresses us with his want of three groats, that we feel for him quite as much as though he were crying for three kingdoms. His need for so small a matter is so urgent, that both become endowed with colossal proportions, and the farcical subject by its serious treatment becomes lifted up to tragic importance. As in a kaleidoscope the slightest turn of the tube gives the same pieces of glass quite a different character, owing to their new combination, so does this one want of *Tre Giuli* shift itself in the poet's hands into an endless variety of presentments. Now he defies his creditor, now he cajoles him, now point blank he refuses to pay him, now he puts him off with promises, he sues to him, he abuses him, expostulates, insults, entreats, flatters, runs from him. The debt is now near, now far; it will be settled immediately, to-morrow, the day after—now never— not till doomsday—not even then; it is now large, now small, now laughably trivial, now of a fearful importance. The poet steeps his three coins in verse, and they come out endowed with the attributes of fairy money, and we can conceive their being capable of anything, and its being possible to do anything with them.

Let others, says Casti in an early sonnet, celebrate the deeds and wars of Enëas, the feats of kings, battles, love, beauty. 'This,' (to quote Captain Montagu's translation) :

'This is the subject matter of my lay :
  Chrysophilus, one time, three groats me lent,
And for them asked me a hundred times a day.
He kept on asking, and I would not pay,
  And this importunate dun 'tis my intent
Herein in various fashion to display.'

And so on, reiterating in the third sonnet :

'Hence, dreams or fables, hence! whoever quotes:
  Meanwhile the Muse relates in artless tone
The genuine story of the triple groats.'

Or to take Mr Leigh Hunt's rendering of the lines:

'Ye dreams and fables keep aloof, I pray :
  While thus my Muse keeps spinning as she goes
The genuine history of the *Giuli Tre*.'

The poet states that, just as the beating of a steel upon a flint produces a stream of sparks, so the repeated entreaties of his creditor, beating upon his breast, have awoke the dormant seeds of song, and compelled him to make the three groats the theme of his lyre, while he hopes that at least the charm of novelty may attach to his efforts. His dun, he vows, has no right to wonder that to all his applications for the amount of the loan he receives the same unvarying answer ; for, he argues ingeniously :

'As one, who constantly shall sound A flat
  Upon the hautboy or the organ, may
Expect the instrument to utter what
  Will be the note that answers to flat A :
Thus every time my creditor this way
  One similar question makes me undergo,
He hears one similar tone in answering notes ;
  Yet still I don't repay him his three groats ;
And should he ask me a hundred times a day,
  He'd hear a hundred times the selfsame "No."'

He next proceeds rather to insult and defy his creditor, deprecates all charity from him, vows he may go hang himself, but still he won't get back his money! Yet, after this burst of courage and confidence, he sinks into a very complaining mood.

'Those triple groats still haunt my mind, and balk
  My heart continually of joy and rest.
His hateful likeness, who has ever been
  The troubler of my peace and evil star,
Is always in my eyes.'

The shadow of the relentless dun haunts him worse than Asmodeus. Any one in search of Chrysophilus is bid to look for his debtor; it is simply impossible that the creditor can be far from him. Now he contemplates travelling to the moon, and covets 'a residence aloft.'

'Yet should I fear that travelling through the air
  Thou'dst come one day to find me out up there ! '

'—— I nothing doubt
That, should he chance to learn my hiding-place,
  In Calicut or China tho' I were,
He'd straight post horses take and find me out ! '

More calmly, then, he reflects that Chrysophilus must be drawn to him by the power of gravitation, 'or by centripetal cohesion's laws,' or a natural affinity, or by attraction. Next he asks why he may not, like Orestes, be at last in a measure forgiven by the Fates. Suddenly, as he is about to quit the town secretly, his creditor appears behind him, offering to accompany him upon his journey. Chrysophilus himself is one day seen booted, spurred, and horsed,—he is going a journey. The poet does not wish him harm ; but oh ! if he should be taken prisoner by the Turks, or made Grand Vizier or Mufti, and never come back ! Never ! Let him have a prosperous voyage, and, that completed, may there be a perpetual hurricane to prevent him ever returning. His creditor gone, he experienced all the feelings of a city long invested, and the siege raised at last. His joy is boundless, but there comes a letter by the post. Chrysophilus, the relentless, writes :

'Get me the three groats ready,—do not miss,—
  As soon as possible, for I shall be
By Sunday or Monday at latest, unremiss,
  On horse or foot—dead or alive—with thee ! '

He finds the letter like one of those papers impregnated with arsenic—

'Whoever reads, or even opens, dies.'

He compares himself to a truant schoolboy suddenly caught by his preceptor ; to king Priam finding the Greek horse open, and the enemy in Troy. He becomes a moral teacher. 'Ah ! never run in debt,' he says ; then prudently qualifies his precept :

'But to your sorrow,
If so compelled, take care that first ye see
What natured man he is from whom ye borrow.'

He complains that, whereas he was wont to be stoically indifferent to all misfortune, he is now made miserable by this contemptible debt—just as a lion that has conquered panthers and tigers finds it agony to endure the sting of a gadfly. His debt is an evil, but his creditor is a greater one ; he condemns the latter, not the former so much. The application and the refusal have now got to be matters of rote, performed without volition. The creditor comes with a parrot-cry for his money. The debtor answers with a parrot-cry that he has not got it, and derides the creditor for being, after all, merely a 'dunning automaton.'

'The whispering breeze, that speaks in softest breath,
The verdant hill, the cool, umbrageous vale,
The bird that spreads his pinions to the gale,
The brook that jets with bounding leap beneath,
And makes sweet music in its noisy fall,—
The dance and song of laughter-loving youth
At times, oh Dun ! with calm delights these soothe
My mind, till *thou* comest back to chase them all.'

Leigh Hunt has happily rendered the 35th sonnet—

'No : none are happy in this best of spheres.
Lo ! when a child we tremble at a look ;
Our freshest age is withered o'er a book ;
The fine arts bite us, and great characters.

Then we go boiling with our youthful peers,
In love and hate ; in riot and rebuke ;
By hook misfortune has us, or by crook,
And griefs and gouts come thickening with our years.

In fine, we've *debts ;* and, when we've debts, no ray
Of hope remains to warm us to repose.
Thus has my own life passed from day to day ;
And now, by way of climax, though not close,
The fatal debit of the Giuli Tre
Fills up the solemn measure of my woes.'

Heartily the poet wishes he were a child again,—to know nothing of duns and debts ; or a bird, that he might fly off, out of the reach of his creditor ; or that, like Gyges, he had a ring that could render him invisible at pleasure. He next congratulates himself that he is unmarried and childless, dreading that if he had children they would be of little comfort to him, for they would certainly grow up to resemble his creditor, and would dun accordingly. Then he entreats the dun not to forget that, after all, dunning is of little use ; it cannot fill the creditor's purse. He expresses his regret that there is not, as amongst the Jews, a custom of periodically extinguishing debt, which he denounces as a

——— 'heartache of the keenest kind,
To which no other pain can be compared ;
An inward rack that night and day doth grind.'

All pleasures now pall upon him ; his liability haunts his imagination everywhere ; he is dunned by the echo of his own voice ; compares his debt to perpetual motion ; implores oblivion to set his cares at rest ; condemns sleep because it augments his ills, by giving him dreams—for he dreams of his debt, just as a sailor dreams of storms ; sighs for a keg of Lethe ; laments the good times, when duns, and writs, and bailiffs were not ; contemplates the agony the thought of his debt will be to him in his old age, and believes

that his dun gets wind of him a mile off or more ! Next he reflects that his debt is not really much in itself, but is made to appear considerable by the insufferable importunity of his dun, just as a slight pimple, from being scratched and irritated, becomes a serious sore. He begins to suspect that the climate in which he lives in some way produces hard creditors, just as 'diversities of clime' resulted in the luxuriousness of the Persian and the Assyrian, the savageness of the Thracian, the mendacity of the Greeks, the courage of the Romans. He buys a ticket in a lottery, as a means of paying his debt, but he draws a blank. He suspects the Evil One of informing the dun as to the whereabouts of the debtor. Now he is declaring that the dun must be ubiquitous ; now that he is as frightful to him as the hangman to the condemned felon ; he can cure himself, he says, of all disease but that of debt ; thinks that money and blood have some extraordinary affinity, and that, as there are times when, according to Galen and Hippocrates, patients should not be bled, so on certain days debtors should not be asked for money. In allusion to the story of words frozen at the pole, the poet holds that if he were there with his creditor, and a thaw were to occur, the only words they would hear would be a cry for the Three Groats.

'The devious comet that on high careers
With sanguine splendour girt, athwart the night,
Ne'er gave the bigot crowd so much affright,
From dread of war—plague—famine—when it nears,
As oft it makes me palpitate with fears ;
When unexpectedly upon my sight
The Dun, whose presence is to me the plight
And harbinger of future ill, appears.'

For the return of the comets may be calculated, but none can be sure of the advent of the creditor. Now and then Chrysophilus is very pleasant in manner ; puts questions upon, and discusses, all sorts of indifferent topics—then suddenly asks for his money.

'Thus sometimes playing with a mouse, ere nip,
The cat will on her helpless victim smile,
Until, at length, she gives the fatal grip.'

The poet now arrives at the conclusion that Platonic love must be about as difficult a thing as the payment of his debt. Next he wishes he had found the philosopher's stone, so as to be able to pay his debt.

'To get the triple groats' true ore,
I'd study chymic properties—which found,
I'd break the pot, nor think about them more.'

He imagines there were no duns in Mahomet's time, as he has left no instruction in the Koran as to the cursing of duns. He declares that his language should be called the Tongue of NO. Wishes his creditor had king Midas's gold-transmuting attribute, and then he might perhaps give up his claim for the three groats. The quadrature of the circle may be discovered, he says, but never any money in his pockets. He sighs for Cicero's eloquence, who paid his creditors with words, not money. Accompanying a lover of the antique to explore the statues of the Campidoglio, he recognises in one of the figures a resemblance to his dun—

'Which with an inward terror did me strike ;
Then like a thief, that flies the sheriff's men,
Down stairs I ran as quick as I could tread it,
And while I live I'll ne'er go there again.'

Further on we gather particulars of the loan—

'This is the fatal spot, sir ! where one day
Chrysophilus lent three groats—'twas there
He drew his purse, and opening it with care,
Told out the money, warning to repay.

It wa'n't a step beyond the place or ere
  He 'gan already asking me to pay,
  And from that time tormenting me this way,
The stingy dun has followed everywhere.

The spot is baleful, sir, and we must purge
  With logs of wood hewn by the moon's cold rays,
Now make a magic fire, and round its verge
  Keep turning barefoot—twice and thrice then cry,
(With lustral water sprinkling o'er the blaze,)
  " Get out of this ; hence, evil spirit, fly ! "'

He laments the primeval age when *mine* and *thine*
were synonymous ; when a community of goods prevailed, and money was undiscovered. His debt has
jaundiced his whole life. Wont to find pleasure in
contemplating ' the golden hair, neat foot, and lovely
face,' of his Nisa, the charm is lost to him now. He
gazes into her beauteous countenance, but by the
strangest metamorphosis he finds it suddenly change—
his Nisa becomes his Chrysophilus. In the 200th
sonnet we find Apollo rebuking the poet for wasting
his time on such a trivial subject. The poet ceases,
in obedience to his divine protector, not because he
has nothing more to say about his debt—not because
he has paid it. He bids good night for ever to his
dun and the three groats. The curtain that rose
discovering the poet a debtor, appears to descend
leaving him in the same plight. Certainly, Chrysophilus never got his money.

It may further be noted, as of interest in the history
of Casti, that among his dramatic compositions for
the court opera at Vienna, was *Il Re Teodoro in
Venezia*, which, owing chiefly perhaps to the music
of Paisello, had a great success on the Continent at
the time of its production. Another work, *La Grotto
di Trofonio*, was produced, with alterations, at Drury
Lane, in 1791. It was Casti, too, who versified the
Figaro of Beaumarchais, for the music of Mozart, in
1786.

FEBRUARY 17.

Saints Theodulus and Julian, martyrs in Palestine,
309. St Flavian, archbishop of Constantinople, martyr
in Lydia, 449. St Loman, or Luman, first bishop of
Trim, 5th century. St Fintan, abbot in Leinster, 6th
century. St Silvin, of Auchy, bishop, 718.

Born.—Francis Duke of Guise, French warrior, 1519 ;
Horace Benedict de Saussure, Genevese traveller, 1740 ;
John Pinkerton, historian and antiquary, 1758, *Edinburgh.*
Died.—Michael Angelo Buonarotti, painter, sculptor,
architect, and engineer, 1563-4 ; Giordano Bruno, Neapo-
litan philosopher, burnt at *Rome*, 1600 ; Jean Baptiste
Poquelin Molière, 1673. *Paris ;* Antoine Galland, trans-
lator of the *Arabian Nights' Entertainments*, 1715 ; John
Martin, historical painter, 1854 ; John Braham, singer
and composer, 1856, *London.*

MOLIÈRE.

France, having Molière for one of her sons,
may .be said to have given birth to the greatest
purely comic writer of modern times. Born the
son of a humble valet-de-chambre and *tapissier* in
Paris, in 1620, this singular genius pressed through
all the trammels and difficulties of his situation, to
education and the exercise of that dramatic art
in which he was to attain such excellence. The
theatre was new in the French capital, and he at
once raised it to glory. His *Etourdi*, his *Pre-*

cieuses Ridicules, his *Menteur*, his *Tartuffe*,[*] his
Femmes Savantes, what a brilliant series they constitute ! The list is closed by the *Malade Imagi-
naire*, which came before the world when the
poor author was sick in earnest ; dying indeed
of a chest complaint, accompanied by spitting of
blood. On the third night of the representation,
he was advised not to play ; but he resolved to
make the effort, and it cost him his life. He
was carried home dying to his house in the Rue
Richelieu, and there soon breathed his last,
choked with a gush of blood, in the arms of two
stranger priests who happened to lodge in the
same house.

It was maliciously reported by prejudiced
people that Molière had expired when in the act
of counterfeiting death in his *rôle* on the stage,
and this made it the more difficult to obtain for
him the Christian burial usually denied to
players. His widow flew to the king, exclaiming against the priesthood, but was glad to make
very humble representations to the Archbishop
of Paris, and to stretch a point regarding
Molière's wish for religious consolations, in
order to have the remains of her husband treated
decently. On its being shewn that he had
received the sacrament at the preceding Easter,
the archbishop was pleased to permit that this
glory of France should be inhumed without any
pomp, with two priests only, and with no church
solemnities. The Revolutionists, more just,
transferred the remains of the great comedian
from the little chapel where they were first
deposited to the Museum of French Monuments.

M. GALLAND.

The English people, who for generations have
enjoyed that most attractive book, the *Arabian
Nights' Entertainments*, know in general very
little of its origin. The western world received
it from the hands of a French savant of the
seventeenth century, who obtained it in its
original form during a residence in the East.

---

[*] ' The history of *Tartuffe* is a curious example of the
impediments so frequently thrown in the way of genius.
The whole of the play was not publicly performed until
after a severe struggle with the bigots of Paris, the first
three acts only having been produced at Versailles on the
12th of May 1664, but not the complete play until 1669.
It took five years to convince the religiously-affected that
an attack on the immoral pretender to religious fervour
was not an attack on religion. It may easily be supposed
that a character so symbolical of cant and duplicity,
under whatever creed it might choose to cloak itself,
would soon be transferred to other countries, and consequently we find it transplanted to our own theatre as early
as 1670, by a comedian of the name of Medbourne, a
Roman Catholic, who in his adaptation chose to make
the *Tartuffe* a French Huguenot, thereby gratifying his
own religious prejudices, and more closely satirizing the
English puritan of the time. Ozell, a dramatic writer,
known only to literary antiquaries and the readers of the
Dunciad, also translated it, with the rest of Molière's dramatic works; but the chief introducer and adapter of this
celebrated play to the English stage was Colley Cibber,
who, in 1718, under the name of the *Non-Juror*, produced and wrote the principal part of what is now known
as *The Hypocrite*, Isaac Bickerstaffe doing little more
than adding the coarse character of *Mawworm* for Weston,
the chief low comedian of his time.'—*Anonymous.*

Antoine Galland, born of poor parents in 1646, shewed such talents in early life that he not only obtained a finished education, but received an appointment as *attaché* to the French embassy at Constantinople while still a young man. He devoted himself to Oriental travel, the collection of Oriental literature, and the study of Eastern authors. His learning was as prodigious in amount as its subjects were for that age extraordinary; but of all his laborious works little memory survives, while his light task of translating the *Mille et Une Nuits* has ensured him a kind of immortality.

In the first editions of this work, the translator preserved the whole of the repetitions respecting Schecherezade and her vigilant sister; which the quick-witted French found insufferably tedious. It was resolved by some young men that they would try to make Galland feel how stupid were these endless wakenings. Coming in the middle of a cold January night to his house in the Faubourg St Jacques, they began to cry vehemently for M. Galland. He speedily appeared upon the balcony, dressed only in his *robe de chambre* and night-cap, and in great anger at this inopportune disturbance. 'Have I the honour,' said one of the youths, 'to speak to Monsieur Galland—the celebrated Monsieur Galland—the learned translator of the *Mille et Une Nuits?*' 'I am he, at your service, gentlemen,' cried the savant, shivering from top to toe. 'Ah then, Monsieur Galland, if you are not asleep, I pray you, while the day is about to break, that you will tell us one of those pleasant stories which you so well know.' The hint was taken, and the tiresome formula of the wakening of the sultaness was suppressed in all but the first few *nuits*.

DE SAUSSURE'S ASCENT OF MONT BLANC.

M. de Saussure was a Geneva professor, who distinguished himself in the latter part of the eighteenth century by his researches in the natural history of the Alps. His investigations were embodied in a laborious work, entitled *Voyage dans les Alpes*, which yet bears an honoured place in European libraries. Previous to De Saussure's time, there had been scarcely any such bold idea entertained as that the summit of Mont Blanc could be reached by human foot. Under his prompting, a few guides made the attempt on three several occasions, but without success. The great difficulty lay in the necessity of undergoing the whole exertion required within the time between two indulgences in repose, for there was no place where, in ascending or descending, the shelter necessary for sleep could be obtained. The case might well appear the more hopeless, when the extraordinary courage and powers of exertion and endurance that belong to the Alpine guides were considered: if they generally regarded the enterprise as impossible, who might attempt it?

Nevertheless, a new and favourable route

DE SAUSSURE ASCENDING MONT BLANC.

having been discovered, and a hut for shelter during an intermediate night having been prepared, M. de Saussure attempted an ascent in September 1785. Having spent a night at the hut, the party set out next morning with great confidence to ascend the remaining thousand toises along the ridge called the Aiguille du Goûté; and they had advanced a considerable way when the depth of the fresh-fallen snow proved an insurmountable barrier.

A second attempt was made by De Saussure in June 1786; and, though it failed, it led to the discovery, by a guide named Jacques Balmat, of a preferable route, which proved to be the only one at all practicable. Unfortunately, De Saussure, who, from his persevering efforts, deserved to be the Conqueror of Mont Blanc, was anticipated in the honour by a gentleman named Paccard, to whom Balmat imparted his secret, and who, under Balmat's guidance, gained the summit of the mountain in August of the last-named year.

It was not till August 1787, and after a second successful attempt by Balmat, in company with two other guides, that De Saussure finally accomplished his object. On this occasion, he had a tent carried, in which he might take a night's rest at whatever place should prove suitable; and all his other preparations were of the most careful kind. The accompanying illustration, which is from his own work, exhibits the persevering philosopher calmly ascending along the icy track, with his *cortège* of guides, and certain men carrying his tent, his scientific instruments, and other articles. It will be observed that the modern expedient of tying the members of the party together had not then been adopted; but some of them held by each other's alpenstocks, as is still the fashion. De Saussure spent the first night on the top of a comparatively small mountain called the Côte, near Chamouni; the second was passed in an excavation in the snow on what was called the second plateau, with the tent for a covering. On the third day, the party set out at an early hour, undauntedly climbing a snow or ice slope at an angle of thirty-nine degrees, and at eleven o'clock gained the summit, after suffering incredible inconvenience from the heat and the rarity of the air. To give an idea of the latter difficulty, it is only necessary to mention that De Saussure, by his barometer, found the column of the atmosphere above him represented by *sixteen inches and one line.*

'My first looks,' says he, 'were directed on Chamouni, where I knew my wife and her two sisters were, their eyes fixed to a telescope, following all our steps with an uneasiness too great, without doubt, but not less distressing to them. I felt a very pleasing and consoling sentiment when I saw the flag which they had promised to hoist the moment they observed me at the summit, when their apprehensions would be at least suspended.'

All Europe rang with the news of De Saussure's ascent of Mont Blanc and his observations on the mountain; and it was long before he found many followers. Now scarcely a season passes but some enterprising Englishman performs this once almost fabulous feat.

JOHN BRAHAM.

It is hardly conceivable that this famous vocalist died so recently as 1856, for one occasionally meets with his figure in favourite characters as the frontispiece of plays dating in the eighteenth century. There is scarcely anybody so old as to remember when Braham was a new figure on the stage. In reality, he did appear there so long ago as 1785, when, however, he was only eleven years of age. He was of Hebrew parentage, was a worthy and respected man, and joined to the wonderful powers of his voice a very fair gift of musical composition. The large gains he made in his own proper walk he lost, as so many have done, by going out of it into another—that of a theatre-proprietor. But his latter days were passed in comfort, under the fostering care of his daughter, the Countess Waldegrave.

MYSTIC MEMORY.

In February 1828, Sir Walter Scott was breaking himself down by over-hard literary work, and had really fallen to some extent out of health. On the 17th he enters in his Diary, that, on the preceding day at dinner, although in company with two or three beloved old friends, he was strangely haunted by what he would call 'the sense of pre-existence;' namely, a confused idea that nothing that passed was said for the first time—that the same topics had been discussed, and the same persons had stated the same opinions on them. The sensation, he adds, 'was so strong as to resemble what is called a *mirage* in the desert, or a calenture on board of ship, when lakes are seen in the desert, and sylvan landscapes in the sea. . . . There was a vile sense of want of reality in all that I did and said.'

This experience of Scott is one which has often been felt, and often commented on by authors, by Scott himself amongst others. In his novel of *Guy Mannering,* he represents his hero Bertram as returning to what was, unknown to him, his native castle, after an absence from childhood, and thus musing on his sensations: 'Why is it that some scenes awaken thoughts which belong, as it were, to dreams of early and shadowy recollection, such as my old Brahmin Moonshie would have ascribed to a state of previous existence? How often do we find ourselves in society which we have never before met, and yet feel impressed with a mysterious and ill-defined consciousness that neither the scene, the speakers, nor the subject are entirely new; nay, feel as if we could anticipate that part of the conversation which has not yet taken place.' Warren and Bulwer Lytton make similar remarks in their novels, and Tennyson adverts to the sensation in a beautiful sonnet:

'As when with downcast eyes we muse and brood,
　　And ebb into a former life, or seem
　　To lapse far back in a confused dream
To states of mystical similitude;
If one but speaks, or hems, or stirs his chair,
　　Ever the wonder waxeth more and more,
　　So that we say, All this hath been before.
All this *hath* been, I know not when or where;
　　So, friend, when first I looked upon your face,
　　Our thoughts gave answer each to each, so true

Opposed mirrors each reflecting each—
  Although I knew not in what time or place,
Methought that I had often met with you,
And each had lived in the other's mind and speech.'

Theological writers have taken up this strange state of feeling as an evidence that our mental part has actually had an existence before our present bodily life, souls being, so to speak, created from the beginning, and attached to bodies at the moment of mortal birth. Glanvil and Henry More wrote to this effect in the seventeenth century; and in 1762, the Rev Capel Berrow published a work entitled *A Pre-existent Lapse of Human Souls demonstrated*. More recently, we find Southey declaring: 'I have a strong and lively faith in a state of continued consciousness from this stage of existence, and that we shall recover *the consciousness of some lower stages through which we may previously have passed* seems to me not improbable.' Wordsworth, too, founds on this notion in that fine poem where he says—

  ' Our birth is but a sleep and a forgetting;
    The soul that rises in us, our life's star,
  Has had elsewhere its setting,
    And cometh from afar.'

With all respect for the doctrine of a previous existence, it appears to us that the sensation in question is no sort of proof of it; for it is clearly absurd to suppose that four or five people who had once lived before, and been acquainted with each other, had by chance got together again, and in precisely the same circumstances as on the former occasion. The notion, indeed, cannot for a moment be seriously maintained.' We must leave it aside, as a mere poetical whimsy.

In a curious book, published in 1844 by Dr Wigan, under the title of *The Duality of the Mind*, an attempt is made to account for the phenomenon in a different way. Dr Wigan was of opinion that the two hemispheres of the brain had each its distinct power and action, and that each often acts singly. Before adverting to this theory of the illusion in question, let us hear a remarkably well described case which he brings forward as part of his own experience:

' The strongest example of this delusion I ever recollect in my own person was on the occasion of the funeral of the Princess Charlotte. The circumstances connected with that event formed in every respect a most extraordinary psychological curiosity, and afforded an instructive view of the moral feelings pervading a whole nation, and shewing themselves without restraint or disguise. There is, perhaps, no example in history of so intense and so universal a sympathy, for almost every conceivable misfortune to one party is a source of joy, satisfaction, or advantage to another. . . . One mighty all-absorbing grief possessed the nation, aggravated in each individual by the sympathy of his neighbour, till the whole people became infected with an amiable insanity, and incapable of estimating the real extent of their loss. No one under five-and-thirty or forty years of age can form a conception of the universal paroxysm of grief which then superseded every other feeling.

' I had obtained permission to be present on the occasion of the funeral, as one of the lord chamberlain's staff. Several disturbed nights previous to that ceremony, and the almost total privation of rest on the night immediately preceding it, had put my mind into a state of hysterical irritability, which was still further increased by grief and by exhaustion from want of food; for between breakfast and the hour of interment at midnight, such was the confusion in the town of Windsor, that no expenditure of money could procure refreshment.

' I had been standing four hours, and on taking my place by the side of the coffin, in St George's chapel, was only prevented from fainting by the interest of the scene. All that our truncated ceremonies could bestow of pomp was there, and the exquisite music produced a sort of hallucination. Suddenly after the pathetic Miserere of Mozart, the music ceased, and there was an absolute silence. The coffin, placed on a kind of altar covered with black cloth (united to the black cloth which covered the pavement), sank down so slowly through the floor, that it was only in measuring its progress by some brilliant object beyond it that any motion could be perceived. I had fallen into a sort of torpid reverie, when I was recalled to consciousness by a paroxysm of violent grief on the part of the bereaved husband, as his eye suddenly caught the coffin sinking into its black grave, formed by the inverted covering of the altar. In an instant I felt not merely an *impression*, but a *conviction* that I had seen the whole scene before on some former occasion, and had heard even the very words addressed to myself by Sir George Naylor.'

Dr Wigan thinks he finds a sufficient explanation of this state of mind in the theory of a double brain. ' The persuasion of the same being a repetition,' says he, ' comes on when the attention has been roused by some accidental circumstance, and we become, as the phrase is, wide awake. I believe the explanation to be this : only · one brain has been used in the immediately preceding part of the scene : the other brain has been asleep, or in an analogous state nearly approaching it. When the attention of both brains is roused to the topic, there is the same vague consciousness that the ideas have passed through the mind before, which takes place on re-perusing the page we had read while thinking on some other subject. The ideas *have* passed through the brain before : and as there was not sufficient consciousness to fix them in the memory without a renewal, we have no means of knowing the length of time that had elapsed between the *faint* impression received by the single brain, and the *distinct* impression received by the double brain. It may seem to have been many years.' It is a plausible idea ; but we have no proof that a single hemisphere of the brain has this distinct action ; the analogy of the eyes is against it, for there we never find one eye conscious or active, and the other not. Moreover, this theory does not, as will be seen, explain all the facts ; and hence, if for no other reason, it must be set aside.

The latest theory on the subject is one started by a person giving the signature ' F' in the *Notes and Queries* (February 14, 1857). This person thinks that the cases on record are not to be explained otherwise than as cases of fore-knowledge. 'That under certain conditions,' says he, 'the human mind is capable of foreseeing the future, more or less distinctly, is hardly to be questioned. May we not suppose that, in dreams or waking reveries, we sometimes anticipate what will befall us, and that this impression, forgotten in the interval, is revived by the actual occurrence of the event foreseen?' He goes on to remark that in the *Confessions* of Rousseau there is a remarkable passage which appears to support this theory. This singular man, in his youth, taking a solitary walk, fell into a reverie, in which he clearly foresaw 'the happiest day of his life,' which occurred seven or eight years afterwards. 'I saw myself,' says Jean Jacques, 'as in an ecstasy, transported into that happy time and occasion, where my heart, possessing all the happiness possible, enjoyed it with inexpressible raptures, without thinking of anything sensual. I do not remember being ever thrown into the future with more force, or of an illusion so complete as I then experienced; and that which has struck me most in the recollection of that reverie, now that it has been realized, is to have found objects so exactly as I had imagined them. If ever a dream of man awake had the air of a prophetic vision, that was assuredly such.' Rousseau tells how his reverie was realized at a *fête champêtre*, in the company of Madame de Warens, at a place which he had not previously seen. 'The condition of mind in which I found myself, all that we said and did that day, all the objects which struck me, recalled to me a kind of dream which I had at Annecy seven or eight years before, and of which I have given an account in its place. The relations were so striking, that in thinking of them I could not refrain from tears.' 'F' remarks that 'if Rousseau, on the second of these occasions, had forgotten the previous one, save a faint remembrance of the ideas which he then conceived, it is evident that this would have been a case of the kind under consideration.'

Mr Elihu Rich, another correspondent of the useful little periodical above quoted, and who has more than once or twice experienced 'the mysterious sense of having been surrounded at some previous time by precisely the same circumstances, and taken a share in the same conversation,' favours this theory of explanation, and presents us with a curious illustration. 'A gentleman,' says he, 'of high intellectual attainments, now deceased, told me that he had dreamed of being in a strange city, so vividly that he remembered the streets, houses, and public buildings as distinctly as those of any place he ever visited. A few weeks afterwards he was startled by seeing the city of which he had dreamed. The likeness was perfect, except that one additional church appeared in the picture. He was so struck by the circumstance that he spoke to the exhibitor, assuming for the purpose the air of a traveller acquainted with the place. He was informed that the church was a recent erection.'

To the same purport is an experience of a remarkable nature which Mr John Pavin Phillips, of Haverfordwest, relates as having occurred to

himself, in which a second reverie appears to have presented a renewal of a former one. 'About four years ago,' says he, 'I suffered severely from derangement of the stomach, and upon one occasion, after passing a restless and disturbed night, I came down to breakfast in the morning, experiencing a sense of general discomfort and uneasiness. I was seated at the breakfast-table with some members of my family, when suddenly the room and objects around me vanished away, and I found myself, without surprise, in the street of a foreign city. Never having been abroad, I imagined it to have been a foreign city from the peculiar character of the architecture. The street was very wide, and on either side of the roadway there was a foot pavement elevated above the street to a considerable height. The houses had pointed gables and casemented windows overhanging the street. The roadway presented a gentle acclivity; and at the end of the street there was a road crossing it at right angles, backed by a green slope, which rose to the eminence of a hill, and was crowned by more houses, over which soared a lofty tower, either of a church or some other ecclesiastical building. As I gazed on the scene before me I was impressed with an overwhelming conviction that I had looked upon it before, and that its features were perfectly familiar to me; I even seemed *almost* to remember the name of the place, and whilst I was making an effort to do so a crowd of people appeared to be advancing in an orderly manner up the street. As it came nearer it resolved itself into a quaint procession of persons in what we should call fancy dresses, or perhaps more like one of the guild festivals which we read of as being held in some of the old continental cities. As the procession came abreast of the spot where I was standing I mounted on the pavement to let it go by, and as it filed past me, with its banners and gay paraphernalia flashing in the sunlight, the irresistible conviction again came over me that I had seen this same procession before, and in the very street through which it was now passing. Again I *almost* recollected the name of the concourse and its occasion; but whilst endeavouring to stimulate my memory to perform its function, the effort dispelled the vision, and I found myself, as before, seated at my breakfast-table, cup in hand. My exclamation of astonishment attracted the notice of one of the members of my family, who inquired "what I had been staring at?" Upon my relating what I have imperfectly described, some surprise was manifested, as the vision, which appeared to me to embrace a period of considerable duration, must have been almost instantaneous. The city, with its landscape, is indelibly fixed in my memory, but the sense of previous familiarity with it has never again been renewed. The "spirit of man within him" is indeed a mystery; and those who have witnessed the progress of a case of catalepsy cannot but have been impressed with the conviction that there are dormant faculties belonging to the human mind, which, like the rudimentary wings said to be contained within the skin of the caterpillar, are only to be developed in a higher sphere of being.' *

In the same work the Rev. Mr W. L. Nichols,

* *Notes and Queries*, 2nd ser., iii. 132.

of Bath, adduces a still more remarkable case from a memoir of Mr William Hone, who, as is well-known, was during the greater part of his life a disbeliever of all but physical facts. He had been worn down to a low condition of vitality by a course of exertion of much the same character as that which gave Scott an experience of the mystic memory. Being called, in the course of business, to a particular part of London, with which he was unacquainted, he had noticed to himself, as he walked along, that he had never been there before. ' I was shewn,' he says, ' into a room to wait. On look-ing round, everything appeared perfectly fami-liar to me; I seemed to *recognise* every object. I said to myself, " What is this? I was never here before, and yet I have seen all this; and, if so, there is a very peculiar knot in the shut-ter."' He opened the shutter, and found the knot! ' Now then,' thought he, ' here is some-thing I cannot explain on my principles; there must be some power beyond matter.' This con-sideration led Mr Hone to reflect further on the wonderful relations of man to the Unseen, and the ultimate result was his becoming an earnestly religious man.

Mr Nichols endeavours to shew the case might be explained by Dr Wigan's theory of a double brain; but it is manifestly beyond that theory to account for the preconception of the knot in the shutter, or the extraneous church in the visioned city. These explanations failing, we are in a manner compelled to think of clair-voyance or the prophetic faculty, because no other explanation is left. On this assumption, an experience of mystic memory might be sup-posed to arise from a previous dream, or it may be a day reverie, perhaps one of only an instant's duration and very recent occurrence, in which the assemblage of objects and transactions was *foreseen* :—it appears as the recollection of a more or less forgotten vision.

FEBRUARY 18.

St Simeon, or Simon, bishop of Jerusalem, martyr, 116. Saints Leo and Paragorius, martyrs, 3rd century.

Born.—Mary I., Queen of England, 1517, *Greenwich;* Isaac Casaubon, scholar, 1559, *Geneva;* James Cassini, astronomer, 1677, *Paris;* Alexander Volta, discoverer of *Voltaism,* 1745, *Como;* David Bogue, eminent Indepen-dent divine, 1750, *Dowlaw, near Eyemouth, Berwickshire;* Charles Lamb, essayist, 1775, *London.*

Died.—Pope Gregory V., 999; George Duke of Clarence, murdered, 1478; Martin Luther, Protestant Reformer, *Wittenberg,* 1546; Sir Richard Baker, chroni-cler, 1645, *Fleet Prison;* John Louis de Balzac, *littéra-teur,* 1654, *Angoulême;* Dr Thomas Hyde, Orientalist, 1702, *Hamburg;* John Ernest Count Bernstorf, Hanove-rian minister, 1772, *Hamburg;* Sir Jeffry Wyatville, architect (Windsor Castle restoration), 1840, *Windsor;* Baron von Biela, astronomer, 1856.

GEORGE DUKE OF CLARENCE—WAS HE DROWNED IN MALMSEY?

Among the old historic traditions of the Tower of London is the story that George Duke of Clarence, brother of Edward the Fourth, who met his death on February 18, 1478, was, by order of his other brother, Richard Duke of Glou-cester, drowned in a butt of Malmsey wine in the above prison. It is said that, being con-demned to die, the Duke's partiality for Malm-sey led him to select this strange mode of quitting life. There is considerable confusion in the narra-tives: first, Sir Thomas More insinuates that Gloucester's efforts to save Clarence were feeble; next, Lord Bacon accuses him of contriving his brother's death; and Shakspeare characterizes him as the associate of the murderers; while Sandford makes him the actual murderer. It is conjectured that Clarence was sentenced to be poisoned, and that the fatal drug may have been conveyed to him in 'malvoisie,' or Malmsey, then a favourite wine. The scene of the murder is disputed: by some it is said to have been a room in the Bowyer Tower; but Mrs Hutchinson, the daughter of Sir Allan Apsley, Lieutenant of the Tower, and herself born in it, and therefore well acquainted with the traditions of the building, states that the drowning took place in a chamber in the Bloody Tower.

The only contemporary, or nearly contempo-rary authorities for the story, are Fabyan and Comines: now, Fabyan was an Englishman, and a Londoner, and had no doubt about it whatever. ' The Duke of Clarence,' he says, ' was secretly put to death, and drowned in a butt of malmsey within the Tower;' and Comines considered the authority good, otherwise he would scarcely have mentioned it in the way he has done.

FUNERAL GARLANDS.

Among the many customs which have been handed down to us from early times, but which have now, unfortunately, become obsolete, one of the most beautiful, simple, and most poetically symbolic, was that of carrying garlands before the corpses of unmarried females on their way to the grave, and then hanging up the garland in the church as a memento of the departed one. This sweetly pretty custom was in former ages observed in most parts of the kingdom, but in Derbyshire—that land of wild and beautiful scenery, where remnants of old customs, of popu-lar beliefs and superstitions, and of the sports and habits of past generations linger in plenty about its mountains and its dales, its farms, its old halls, and its humbler homesteads—its obser-vance has, perhaps, been continued to a much later period than in any other district. Indeed, in some of the Peak villages the garland has been carried even within memory of their more aged inhabitants.

Flowers have ever been an emblem of purity, and even in the primitive Christian church it was usual to place them, formed into wreaths or crowns, at the heads of deceased virgins. In every age, indeed, true virginity has been honoured in its purity by flowers pure as itself, and fresh from the hands of their Maker.

The same feeling which tempts the bride to adorn her beautiful tresses with a wreath of orange blossoms for her nuptials—which gives rise to the offering of a bouquet of flowers, and to the custom of strewing the pathway she is to tread on her way to the altar—has been the origin of the custom of adorning the corpse, the coffin, and the grave of the virgin with the same frail but lovely and appropriate emblems. The same feeling which calls virginity itself 'a flower,' is that which places flowers in the hair of the bride, in the hands or around the face of the corpse, and in the garlands at the grave.

In early ages, doubtless, the funeral garlands were composed of real flowers, but this gradually gave way to those composed of hoops and paper intermixed with ribands, which were much more durable, and had a better appearance when suspended in the churches. The custom has been referred to by many of the old writers, and Shakspeare himself alludes to it when he says, (*Hamlet*, Act v. scene 1,) 'Yet here she is allowed her virgin *crants*'—'crants' signifying garlands.'

Old John Marston, in 1605, wrote in his *Dutch Courtezan*, 'I was afraid, i' faith, that I should ha' seene *a garland on this beautie's hearse ;* ' and a ballad of a later date runs thus :

' But since I'm resolved to die for my dear,
   I'll chuse six young virgins my coffin to bear ;
   And all those young virgins I now do chuse,
   Instead of green ribbands, green ribbands, green
      ribbands,
   Instead of green ribbands, a *garland* shall wear ;
   And when in the church in my grave I lie deep,
   Let all those fine garlands, fine garlands, fine gar-
      lands,
   Let all those fine *garlands hang over my feet.*
   And when any of my sex behold the sight,
   They may see I've been constant, been constant,
   They may see I've been constant to my heart's
      delight.'

William Sampson, in 1636, thus alludes to this charming custom, in his lines on the death of Miss E. Tevery :—

' Why did the *Lilly, Paunce,* and *Violet* weepe,
  The *Marigold* ere sun-set in did creepe ?
  At whose reflexion she us'd for to rise
  And at his way-gate to close up her eies.
  Why were the beaten waies with flowers strowne,
  And set with needy *Lazar's,* hanging downe
  Their mournful heades ? why did the Pulpit mourne,
  As if prepared for some Funerall urne ?
  And yet *the Temple was with garlands hung,*
  Of sweet-smelling Flowers, which might belong
  Unto some bridall ! Noe ! heaven knows the cause,
  'Twas otherwise decreed in Nature's Lawes ;
  Those smelling sweetes with which our sense was
     fed,
  Were for *the buriall of a maiden,* dead ;
  Which made an *Autumne* just in the mid-spring,
  And all things contrary their births to bring ;
  Herbs, Plants, and *Flowers* contrariously grew,
  Because they now received not Nature's dew ;
  The needy beggars hung their heads for thee,
  Thou matchlesse map of maiden modesty,
  From whose faire handes they had an almner's pay,
  As often as they met thee every day.
  The sacred Temple, where thy holy fires
  Of incense was pow'red on, in chast desires
  Was thus prepar'd, and deck'd on every side
  To welcome thee, as her sole soveraigne Bride ;
  Whose goodness was inimitable, whose vertues
     shone,
  *l*ike to the sun in his bright *Horizon :*

The Maiden Vestalls, that with wat'ry eies,
  Bore thee to th' Church for *Vesta's* sacrifize,
  Were all in white ! carracts of innocence
  Prefiguring thy greater eminence.
  So great their losse, that with watery eine,
  They offer teares still to thy virgin shrine ;
  And if that teares, sighes, or praires could save
     thee,
  What would not they expresse now to have thee ?
  Sacred divinity allows of no such wish,
  Therefore, emparadic'd soule, rest thou in blisse.'

Gay, in his poems, has more than allusion to the custom. He says :—

' To her sweet memory flow'ry garlands strung
  On her now empty seat aloft were hung.'

Of the garlands themselves but few examples remain, but they may still be seen in some of the churches of Derbyshire. It is curious that, although allusions to the custom are not unfrequent, no representation of a garland had ever been engraved until within the last few months, when some examples were given in *The Reliquary* quarterly journal.* Two of these engravings we are now enabled to reproduce.

The first engraving shows five garlands as they at present exist in the north aisle of Ashford-in-the-Water Church, and the second exhibits on a larger scale a particular garland, one of eight which formerly existed in Matlock Church, but are now preserved in a local museum. They are thus described in *The Reliquary :*—

' The garlands are each composed of two hoops of wood, with bands crossing each other at right angles, and attached to the hoops ; thus forming a kind of open arched crown. The hoops and bands are all of wood, wrapped round with white paper, and at the top is a loop for suspension. The hoops and bands of the smaller one, as shewn in the accompanying woodcut, are decorated with paper flowers and rosettes, and at the top is a flower formed of hearts, and having somewhat the appearance of that of the *Clarkia pulchella.* From between the rosettes of the upper hoop, a paper riband, gimped on the edges, and ornamented by diamonds cut out with scissors, hangs down to below the lower band, to which they are not attached.

' In another example, the hoops and bands are decorated with paper flowers, or rosettes, intermixed with bunches of narrow slips, or shreds of paper ; and at the top is a bunch of the same, over paper folded like a fan. Originally, the flowers have been formed, some of plain, and others of folded or crimped paper ; and others again of both ; and in some parts the paper has been afterwards coloured red or blue, thus producing a somewhat gay appearance. From the centre of the top are suspended a pair of gloves, cut out of white paper, and a kerchief or collar, also of paper, gimped on the edges and carefully folded. In most instances the name of the female in whose honour these garlands were prepared was written on the collar, gloves, or handkerchief. On this under notice no name occurs, but its date is probably of the latter part of last century. Through age the colours on the paper have nearly disappeared.

* Edited by Llewellynn Jewitt, F.S.A. London : John Russell Smith. Vol. i. p. 7.

'The garlands at Ashford-in-the-Water, although in general character resembling the others we have described, differ from them in detail. They are not so profusely ornamented with rosettes, bear no bunches of shreds of paper, and have no "pinked" or cut ribands. Each garland contains a single glove, and a kerchief or collar. On the collar or kerchief of each has been written a verse of poetry, and the name, age, and date of death of the virgin in whose

FUNERAL GARLANDS, ASHFORD-IN-THE-WATER CHURCH.

honour they were prepared. Owing to age, the decay of the paper, and the fading of the ink, the writing on most of them is obliterated. On one, however, the date of April 12th, 1747, occurs;

FUNERAL GARLAND, MATLOCK CHURCH.

there has also on this one been six lines of poetry, now perfectly illegible, and the name of the female appears to have been Ann Howard, who died at the age of twenty-one. On another of a later date, we succeeded with considerable difficulty in deciphering the following lines :—

> " Be always ready, no time delay,
> I in my youth was called away,
> Great grief to those that's left behind,
> But I hope I'm great joy to find.
> Ann Swindel,
> Aged 22 years,
> Dec. 9th, 1798." '

The form of garland of course varied in different localities, but the same general design prevailed wherever the custom was observed. In some of the metropolitan churches the garland, instead of being composed of real flowers, or of paper ones, was frequently composed of wire formed into filagree work resembling flowers and leaves, ornaments of gum, wax, and of dyed horn, and other materials, and sometimes had a gay, instead of a simple and pure appearance. A garland of this time has thus been described in the *Antiquarian Repertory* :

'These garlands at the funerals of the deceased were carried solemnly before the corpse by two maids, and afterwards hung up in some conspicuous place within the church, and they were made in the following manner, viz. :—the lower rim or circlet was a broad hoop of wood, whereunto was fixed at the sides thereof two other hoops, crossing each other at the top at right angles, which formed the upper part, being about one-third longer than the width. These hoops were wholly covered with artificial flowers of paper, dyed horn, and silk, and more or less beautiful, according to the skill or ingenuity of the performer. In the vacancy inside, from the top, hung white paper cut in form of gloves, whereon was written deceased's name, age, &c., together with long slips of various coloured paper, or ribands; these were many times intermixed with gilded or painted shells of blown eggs, as farther ornaments, or it may be as emblems of bubbles, or the bitterness of this life; while other garlands had only a solitary hourglass hanging therein, as a more significant symbol of mortality.'

Of garlands, and the funeral rites generally of a virgin, a most interesting account is to be found in a very scarce little book entitled *The Virgin's Pattern*, which describes the funeral of a lady at Hackney, named Perwich: 'The hearse, covered with velvet, was carried by six servant maidens of the family, all in white. The sheet was held up by six of those gentlewomen in the school that had most acquaintance with her, in mourning habit, with white scarfs and gloves. A rich costly garland of gum-work adorned with banners and 'scutcheons, was borne immediately before the hearse, by two proper young ladies that entirely loved her. Her father and mother, with other near relations and their children, followed next the hearse in due order, all in mourning: the kindred next to them; after whom came the whole school of gentlewomen, and then persons of chief rank from the neighbourhood and from the city of London, all in white gloves; both men, women, children, and servants having been first served with wine. The hearse having been set down, with the garland upon it, the Rev. Dr Spurstow preached her funeral sermon. This done, the coffin, anointed with rich odours, was put down into the grave, in the middle alley of the said (Hackney) church.'

In a singular old book entitled the *Comical Pilgrim's Pilgrimage*, the author says: 'When a virgin dies, a garland made of all sorts of flowers and sweet herbs, is carried by a young woman on her head, before the coffin, from which hang down two black ribands, signifying our mortal state, and two white, as an emblem of purity and innocence. The ends thereof are held by four young maids, before whom a basket full of herbs and flowers is supported by two other maids, who strew them along the streets to the place of burial; then, after the deceased, follow all her relations and acquaintance.'

In some districts the garlands were only allowed to remain suspended in the church for a twelvemonth after the burial of the young woman. In others the garland was buried in the same grave with her. In Derbyshire, however, they appear to have remained hung up on the arches or on the beams of the roof, until they have either decayed away or been removed by order of some one whose love of change was greater than his veneration for these simple memorials of the dead.

274

In 1662, an inquiry in the diocese of Ely was made as follows: 'Are any garlands and other ordinary funeral ensigns suffered to hang where they hinder the prospect, or until they grow foul and dusty, withered and rotten?' At Heanor, not many years ago, a number of these interesting relics, which had hung there for years, were removed at a general church-cleaning which took place on the coming in of a new incumbent, and at many other places they have been as ruthlessly destroyed. At Llandovery the garlands and gloves hang a year in the church, and are then taken down, and on each anniversary of the death of the virgin the grave is by some friend decorated with flowers, and a pair of white gloves is laid upon it. These gloves are taken away by the nearest relative who visits the grave that day.

Beautifully and touchingly has Anna Seward sung:

' Now the low beams with paper garlands hung,
　　In memory of some village youth or maid,
Draw the soft tear, from thrill'd remembrance sprung;
　　How oft my childhood marked that tribute paid!
The gloves suspended by the garland's side,
White as its snowy flowers with ribands tied.
Dear village! long these wreaths funereal spread,
Simple memorial of the early dead!'

and it is much to be hoped that wherever any of these 'simple memorials of the early dead' exist, they may long escape the hand of the spoliator, and be allowed to remain where the loving hands and the sorrowing hearts of the mourners, generations past, had placed them.

FUNERAL FEAST OF SIR JOHN PASTON.

In 1466 died in London, Sir John Paston, the head of the wealthy family whose correspondence, known as the *Paston Letters*, presents so many pictures of the life of the English gentry of that age. The body of Sir John was conveyed, for interment, to the Priory of Bromholm, in the parish of Barton, a little village on the north-east coast, and within sight of the sea. A curious roll of accounts of the expenses of the funeral is preserved, from which we gather that for the feast, during three continuous days, one man was occupied in flaying beasts; and provision was made of thirteen barrels of beer, twenty-seven barrels of ale, one barrel of beer of the greatest assize, and a runlet of red wine of fifteen gallons. All these, however, copious as they seem, proved inadequate to the demand; for the account goes on to state that five coombs of malt at one time, and ten at another, were brewed up expressly for the occasion. Meat, too, was in proportion to the liquor; the country round about must have been swept of geese, chickens, capons, and such small gear, all which, with thirteen hundred eggs, thirty gallons of milk, and eight of cream, forty-one pigs, forty calves, and ten 'nete,' slain and devoured, give a fearful picture of the scene of festivity within the priory walls. Amongst such provisions, the article of bread bears nearly the same proportion as in Falstaff's bill of fare. On the other hand, the torches, the many pounds weight of wax to burn over the grave, and the separate candle of enormous stature and girth, form prodigious items. No less than £20 was changed from gold into smaller coin that it might be showered amongst the attendant throng; and twenty-six marks in copper had been used for the same object in London, before the procession began to move. A barber was occupied five days in smartening up the monks for the ceremony; and 'the reke of the torches at the dirge' was so great that the glazier had to remove two panes to permit the fumes to escape.

FEBRUARY 19.

St Barbatus, bishop of Benevento, 684.

Born.—Nicolaus Copernicus, astronomer, 1473, *Thorn, in Prussia* ; Henry Frederick Prince of Wales, 1594, *Stirling Castle ;* Admiral Lord Rodney, 1718, *Walton-on-Thames ;* Richard Cumberland, dramatist. 1732, *Cambridge ;* Sir Roderick I. Murchison, geologist. 1792. *Tarradale. Ross-shire.*

Died.—Dec. Albinus (Emperor), killed, 198, *Rhone River ;* Erasmus Reinhold, astronomer, 1553, *Thuringen ;* Lucilio Vanini, 1619, burnt as an atheist, at *Toulouse ;* Sir Henry Savile, mathematician, 1622, *Eton College ;* Francis de Sauvages, nosologist, 1767, *Montpelier ;* Elizabeth Carter, classical scholar, 1806, *London ;* Bernard Barton, poet, 1849 ; Sir William Napier, military historian, 1860.

HENRY PRINCE OF WALES.

It is blessed to die in promise, rather than after all the blots and mischances of performance. We naturally credit the young dead with much which might never have been realized. Nevertheless, in the early death of Henry Prince of Wales there is no room to doubt that the national bewailment was just. All accounts concur in representing him as a youth of bright talents, most generous dispositions, and the noblest aspirations. At sixteen, he had the figure, the proportions, and the sentiments of a full-grown man. With the love of study which belonged to his father, he possessed what his father entirely

wanted, a love of manly military exercises. In riding, in archery. in the use of arms, he was

without a superior. He studied ship-building and the whole art of war with as much zeal as if he had had no taste for elegant learning. When, at Christmas 1609, the romantic spectacle called his *Barriers* was presented in the Banqueting House at Whitehall,—when he and six other youths met each in succession eight others, at pike and sword play,—all clad in the beautiful armour of the period,—Henry was remarked, to the surprise of all, to have given and received thirty-two pushes of pike and about three hundred and sixty strokes of sword, in one evening.

It was in the midst of active study and exercise, and while the nation was becoming fully aware of the promise he gave as their future ruler, that this accomplished prince was seized with a fever, the consequence, apparently, of the too violent fatigues to which he occasionally subjected himself. What immediately affected him to a fatal illness, seems to have been his playing at tennis one evening without his coat. In the simple act of stripping off and laying aside that coat, was involved an incalculable change of the current of English history; for, had Henry survived and reigned, the country would probably have escaped a civil war—and who can say, in that event, how much our national destinies might have been changed, for good or evil? During the twelve days of the prince's illness, the public mind was wrought up to a pitch of intense anxiety regarding him; and when, on one occasion, he was thought to have yielded up the ghost, the cry of grief went out from St James's Palace into the street, and was there repeated and spread by the sympathising multitude. All that the medical skill of that age could do was done to save so valuable a life, including some applications that sound strangely in our ears : for example, pigeons applied to the head, and a split cock to the feet. Sir Walter Raleigh sent from his prison in the Tower a 'quintescence' which he believed to be of wonderful power ; and it did give the prince the only approach to a restoring perspiration which he had had. But all was in vain. Henry died on the 6th of November 1612, when three months less than nineteen years of age. As a historical event, his death ranks with a very small class in which deceased royalty has been mourned by the nation's *heart;* the deaths of the Princess Charlotte and of the Prince Consort Albert being almost the only other instances.

The national admiration of this young prince is shewn in some quaint lines, hitherto inedited. in the Burleigh MSS. :

' Loe ! where he shineth yonder,
　A fixed star in heaven ;
Whose motion heere came under
　None of your planets seaven.
If that the moone should tender
　The sunne her love, and marry,
They both would not engender
　Soe great a star as Harry.'—1617.

SIR WILLIAM NAPIER.

The public was for some years startled from time to time by the publication of letters signed William Napier, speaking passionately and unmeasuredly on some subject, generally military : it came to be recognised as a *Napierian* style of writing. The writer of these fiery missives was one of the worthiest and ablest of men, the younger brother of the eminent commander Sir Charles James Napier, and *par excellence* the historian of the Peninsular War. William Napier, born in 1785, commanded a regiment (the 43rd) all through that war, and was well fitted to be its annalist. His work, begun in 1828, and finished in six volumes, is a masterpiece of detailed history. Passages of it are said to have been recounted round the watch-fires and told in the trenches before Sebastopol, and never without warming the soldier's heart, firing his mind, and nerving his arm. Sir William also wrote *The Conquest of Scinde*, and a Life of his brother Charles, both of them valuable books. He is not the least memorable of the extraordinary brood of sons which Sarah Lennox, after some other singular passages of life, was fated to bring into the world. He died February 12, 1860.

THE DREAM OF THE GOOD KING GONTRAN.

The late Hugh Miller, in his interesting work, *My Schools and Schoolmasters*, when speaking of a cousin named George, says :—

'Some of his Highland stories were very curious. He communicated to me, for example, beside the broken tower, a tradition illustrative of the Celtic theory of dreaming, of which I have since often thought. Two young men had been spending the early portion of a warm summer day in exactly such a scene as that in which he communicated the anecdote. There was an ancient ruin beside them, separated, however, from the mossy bank on which they sat by a slender runnel, across which there lay, immediately over a miniature cascade, a few withered grass-stalks. Overcome by the heat of the day, one of the young men fell asleep ; his companion watched drowsily beside him, when all at once the watcher was aroused to attention by seeing a little, indistinct form, scarce larger than a humble-bee, issue from the mouth of the sleeping man, and, leaping upon the moss, move downwards to the runnel, which it crossed along the withered grass-stalks, and then disappeared amid the interstices of the ruin. Alarmed by what he saw, the watcher hastily shook his companion by the shoulder, and awoke him ; though, with all his haste, the little, cloud-like creature, still more rapid in its movements, issued from the interstice into which it had gone, and, flying across the runnel, instead of creeping along the grass-stalks and over the sward, as before, it re-entered the mouth of the sleeper, just as he was in the act of awakening. "What is the matter with you?" said the watcher, greatly alarmed ; "what ails you?" "Nothing ails me," replied the other, "but you have robbed me of a most delightful dream. I dreamed I was walking through a fine rich country, and came at length to the shores of a noble river ; and, just where the clear water went thundering down a precipice, there was a bridge all of silver, which I crossed ; and then, entering a noble palace on the opposite side, I saw great heaps of gold and jewels ; and I was

276

just going to load myself with treasure, when you rudely awoke me, and I lost all." '

The above story is by no means uncommon in the Highlands, and the writer has frequently heard it related by an old native of Ross-shire—who firmly believed it—as an indisputable evidence of the immortality of the soul, the 'little indistinct form' being assumedly the soul of the man, in full life, sense, and motion, while his body was wrapped in the death-like torpor of sleep. And he further stated that in the Highlands, under peculiar circumstances, the little form has been seen leaving the mouths of certain persons at the last gasp of life.

It is a curious fact that a similar legend, having, however, a much more practical conclusion, is related of Gontran the Good, king of Burgundy, who lived, reigned, and died so far back as the sixth century. One day, Gontran, wearied with the chase, and attended but by one faithful squire, laid himself down to rest near a small rivulet, and soon fell asleep. The squire, while carefully guarding his royal master, with great astonishment perceived a small beast (*bestion*) emerge from the king's mouth, and proceed to the bank of the rivulet, where it ran up and down for some time, seemingly wishing to cross the water, but unable to do so. Thereupon the squire, determined to see the end of the adventure, drew his sword, and laid it over the stream from bank to bank. The little animal seeing this improvised bridge, ran over it, and speedily disappeared in a small hole, at the foot of a hill on the opposite side. After remaining there for a very short period, it returned along the sword, and into the king's mouth. Soon after, Gontran, awakening, said that he had just had a most extraordinary dream, in which he thought that he had crossed a foaming torrent on a bridge of polished steel, and entered a subterranean palace full of gold and jewels. The squire then relating what he had seen, the king, on his return to his palace, summoned all the learned men in Burgundy, and having stated the whole occurrence, demanded of them the immediate interpretation thereof. For once in the world's history, the opinion of the savans was unanimous ; they declared there could be no reasonable doubt on the matter. A large treasure was concealed under the hill, and, its existence being by a special miracle disclosed to the king, he alone was destined to be its possessor. Gontran immediately set a great number of men to work, the hill was undermined, and the treasure discovered. Receiving this treasure as an especial gift of Providence, Gontran devoted the principal part of it to purposes of charity and religion. He founded hospitals for the poor, and ecclesiastical edifices for the clergy ; he made extensive roads through his kingdom, that the poor might be the better enabled to perform pilgrimages ; and covered the shrine of St Marcel, at Châlons-sur-Saone, with a thick layer of beaten gold. Still further to commemorate the wonderful event, the King ordered that the hill should ever after be termed Mont-Trésor, the name which it bears at the present day.

Claud Paradin, in his *Symbola Heroica*, has

recorded the wonderful dream of Gontran, by the accompanying engraving and the motto:

'SIC SOPOR IRRUPIT.'

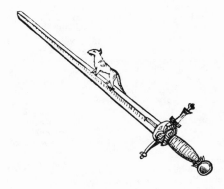

'SO SLEEP CAME UPON HIM.'

FEBRUARY 20.

Saints Tyrannio, Zenobius, and others, martyrs in Phœnicia, about 310   St Sadoth, bishop of Seleucia and Ctesiphon, with 128 companions, martyrs, 342.   St Eleutherius, bishop of Tournay, martyr, 522.   St Mildred, virgin abbess in Thanet, 7th century.   St Eucherius, bishop of Orleans, 743.   St Ulrick, of England, 1154.

Born.—François-Marie Arouet de Voltaire, poet, dramatist, historical and philosophical writer, 1694, *Chatenay ;* David Garrick, actor and dramatist, 1716, *Hereford ;* Rev. James Dallaway, antiquary, 1763, *Bristol.*

Died.—Archbishop Arundel, 1413-14, *Canterbury ;* Sir Nicholas Bacon, Lord Keeper, 1579, *York House, Strand ;* Dorothy Sidney, Countess of Sunderland, 1684, *Brington ;* Mrs Elizabeth Rowe, philanthropic-religious writer, 1737; Charles III. (of *Savoy*), 1773; Joseph II. (Emperor), 1790; Dr John Moore, novelist, 1802, *Richmond ;* Richard Gough, antiquary, 1809, *Wormley ;* Andreas Hofer, Tyrolese patriot, shot by the French, 1810 ; Joseph Hume, statesman, 1855.

JOSEPH HUME.

The name of Joseph Hume has become so inseparably associated with his long-continued exertions to check extravagance in the use of public money, that most persons will hear with a feeling of surprise that he was in reality disposed to a liberal use of the state funds wherever a good object was to be served, and especially if that object involved the advancement of knowledge among the people. The Earl of Ellesmere, in his address to the Geographical Society, in 1855, bore strong testimony to the help which Mr Hume had given in promoting the claim of that body for assistance towards giving it a better place of meeting, and enabling it to throw open to the public the use of its 'instruments' of research and instruction.' The present writer can add a grateful testimony, in regard to the Scottish Society of Antiquaries. That body, being a few years ago hardly rich enough to keep a person to shew its valuable

museum, a proposal was made that it should hand its collection over to the state, who might then keep it open for the instruction and gratification of the public at its own expense.   Mr Hume became satisfied that the proposal was an honest one, calculated to prove serviceable to the public ; and the Society had no such friend and advocate as he in getting the transaction with the Treasury effected.   The result has been such as fully to justify the zeal he shewed on the occasion.

Mr Hume was a native of Montrose, made his way through poverty to the education of a physician, and, realizing some wealth in India, devoted himself from about the age of forty to political life.   As a member of Parliament, it was the sole study of this remarkable man to protect and advance the interests of the public ; he specially applied himself, in the earlier part of his career, to the advocacy of an economical use of the public purse.   He met with torrents of abuse and ridicule from those interested in opposite objects, and he encountered many disappointments ; but nothing ever daunted or disheartened him. Within an hour of a parliamentary defeat, he would be engaged in merry play with his children, having entirely cast away all sense of mortification.   The perfect single-heartedness and honesty of Joseph Hume in time gained upon his greatest enemies, and he died in the enjoyment of the respect of all classes of politicians.

TWO POET FELONS.

On the 20th of February 1749, the vulgar death of felons was suffered at Tyburn by two men different in some respects from ordinary criminals, Usher Gahagan and Terence Conner, both of them natives of Ireland.   They were young men of respectable connexions and excellent education ; they had even shewn what might be called promising talents.   Gahagan, on coming to London, offered to translate Pope's *Essay on Man* into Latin for the booksellers, and, from anything that appears, he would have performed the task in a manner above mediocrity. There was, however, a moral deficiency in both of these young men.   Falling into vicious courses, and failing to supply themselves with money by honest means, they were drawn by a fellow-countryman named Coffey into a practice of filing the coin of the realm, a crime then considered as high treason.   For a time, the business prospered, but the usual detection came.   It came in a rather singular manner.   A teller in the Bank of England, who had observed them frequently drawing coin from the bank, became suspicious of them, and communicated his suspicions to the governors.   Under direction from these gentlemen, he, on the next occasion, asked the guilty trio to drink wine with him in the evening at the Crown Tavern, near Cripplegate.   As had been calculated upon, the wine and familiar discourse opened the hearts of the men, and Gahagan imparted to the teller the secret of their life, and concluded by pressing him to become a confederate in their plans.   Their apprehension followed, and, on Coffey's evidence, the two others were found guilty and condemned to death.

Just at that time, the young Prince George

(afterwards George III.) and his younger brother Edward had appeared in the characters of Cato and Juba, in a boy-acted play at court. Poor Gahagan sent a poetical address to the young prince, hoping for some intercession in his behalf. It was as well expressed and as well rhymed as most poetry of that age. After some of the usual compliments, he proceeded thus:

'	Roused with the thought and impotently vain,
	I now would launch into a nobler strain;
	But see! the captive muse forbids the lays,
	Unfit to stretch the merit I would praise.
	Such at whose heels no galling shackles ring,
	May raise the voice, and boldly touch the string;
	Cramped hand and foot while I in gaol must stay,
	Dreading each hour the execution day;
	Pent up in den, opprobrious alms to crave,
	No Delphic cell, ye gods, nor sybil's cave;
	Nor will my Pegasus obey the rod,
	With massy iron barbarously shod,' &c.

Conner in like verse claimed the intercession of the Duchess of Queensberry, describing in piteous terms the hard usage and meagre fare now meted out to him, and entreating that she, who had been the protectress of Gay, would not calmly see another poet hanged. All was in vain.

WARWICK LANE.

Few of the thoroughfares of old London have undergone such mutations of fortune as may be traced in Warwick-lane, once the site of the house of the famed Beauchamps, Earls of Warwick, afterwards distinguished by including in its precincts the College of Physicians, now solely remarkable for an abundance of those private shambles which are still permitted to disgrace the English metropolis.

In the coroners' rolls of five centuries ago, we read of mortal accidents which befel youths in attempting to steal apples in the neighbouring orchards of Paternoster-row and Ivy-lane, then periodically redolent of fruit-blossoms.

Warwick Inn, as the ancient house was called, was, in the 28th of Henry VI. (about 1450) possessed by Cecily, Duchess of Warwick. Eight years later, when the greater estates of the realm were called up to London, Richard Neville, Earl of Warwick, the *King-maker*, 'came with 600 men, all in red jackets, embroidered with ragged staves before and behind, and was lodged in Warwick-lane; in whose house there was oftentimes six oxen eaten at a breakfast, and every tavern was full of his meat; for he that had any acquaintance in that house, might have there so much of sodden and roast meat as he could prick and carry on a long dagger.'

The Great Fire swept away the Warwick-lane of Stow's time; and when it was rebuilt, there was placed upon the house at its north-west end, a bas-relief of Guy, Earl of Warwick, in memory of the princely owners of the inn, with the date '1668' upon it. This memorial-stone, which was renewed in 1817, by J. Deykes, architect, is a counterpart of the figure in the chapel of St Mary Magdalen, in Guy's Cliff, near Warwick.

The College of Physicians, built by Wren to replace a previous fabric burnt down in the Great Fire, may still be seen on the west side of the lane, but sunk into the condition of a butcher's shop. Though in a confined situation, it seems to have formerly been considered an impressive structure, the exterior being thus described in Garth's witty satire of the *Dispensary*:

'	Not far from that most celebrated place, *
	Where angry Justice shews her awful face,
	Where little villains must submit to fate,
	That great ones may enjoy the world in state.
	There stands a dome majestic to the sight,
	And sumptuous arches bear its awful height;
	A golden globe, placed high with artful skill.
	Seems to the distant sight a gilded pill.'

This simile is a happy one; though Mr Elmes, Wren's biographer, ingeniously suggests that the gilt globe was perhaps intended to intimate the universality of the healing art. Here the physicians met until the year 1825, when they removed to their newly-built College in Pall Mall East. The interior of the edifice in Warwick-lane was convenient and sumptuous; and one of the minute accounts tells us that in the garrets were dried the herbs for the use of the Dispensary. The College buildings were next let to the Equitable Loan (or Pawnbroking) Company; next to Messrs. Tylor, braziers, and as a meat-market: oddly enough, on the left of the entrance portico, beneath a bell-handle there remains the inscription 'Mr Lawrence, Surgeon,' along with the words 'Night Bell,' recalling the days when the house belonged to a learned institution.

We must, however, take a glance at the statues of Charles II. and Sir John Cutler, within the court; especially as the latter assists to expose an act of public meanness. It appears by the College books

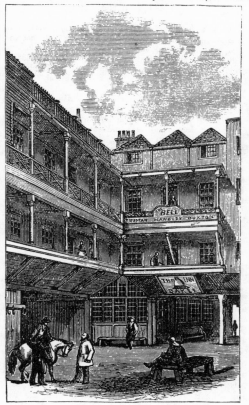

BELL INN, WARWICK LANE.

that, in 1674, Sir John Cutler promised to bear the expense of a specified part of the new building: the

* Newgate.

committee thanked him, and in 1680, statues of the King and Sir John were voted by the members : nine years afterwards, when the College was completed, it was resolved to borrow money of Sir John, to discharge the College debt ; what the sum was is not specified ; it appears, however, that in 1699, Sir John's executors made a demand on the College for £7,000, supposed to include money actually lent, money pretended to be given, and interest on both. The executors accepted £2,000, and dropped their claim for the other five. The statue was allowed to stand ; but the inscription, 'Omnis Cutleri cedat Labor Amphitheatro,' was very properly obliterated.

In the Lane are two old galleried inns, which carry us back to the broad-wheeled travelling wagons of our forefathers. About midway, on the east side, is the Bell Inn, where the pious Archbishop Leighton ended his earthly pilgrimage, according to his wish, which Bishop Burnet states him to have thus expressed in the same peaceful and moderate spirit, as that by which, in the troublous times of the Commonwealth, Leighton won the affections of even the most rigid Presbyterians. 'He used often to say, that, if he were to choose a place to die in, it should be an inn ; it looking like a pilgrim's going home, to whom this world was all as an inn, and who was weary of the noise and confusion in it. He added that the officious tenderness and care of friends was an entanglement to a dying man ; and that the unconcerned attendance of those that could be procured in such a place would give less disturbance. And he obtained what he desired ; for he died [1684] at the Bell Inn, in Warwick-lane.' — *Burnet's Own Times.*

Dr Fall, who was well acquainted with Leighton, after a glowing eulogy on his holy life and 'heavenly converse,' proceeds : 'Such a life, we may easily persuade ourselves, must make the thought of death not only tolerable, but desirable. Accordingly, it had this noble effect upon him. In a paper left under his own hand, (since lost,) he bespeaks that day in a most glorious and triumphant manner ; his expressions seem rapturous and ecstatic, as though his wishes and desires had anticipated the real and solemn celebration of his nuptials with the Lamb of God. . . . He sometimes expressed his desire of not being troublesome to his friends at his death ; and God gratified to the full his modest humble choice ; he dying at an inn in his sleep.'

Somewhat lower in the Lane is the street leading to Newgate-market, which Gay has thus signalized :

' Shall the large mutton smoke upon your boards ?
  Such Newgate's copious market best affords.'
                              Trivia, book ii.

Before the Great Fire, this market was kept in Newgate-street, where there was a market-house formed, and a middle row of sheds, which afterwards were converted into houses, and inhabited by butchers, tripe-sellers, &c. The stalls in the open street grew dangerous, and were accordingly removed into the open space between Newgate-street and Paternoster-row, formerly the orchards already mentioned ; and here were the houses of the Prebends of St Paul's, overgrown with ivy ; whence Ivy-lane takes its name, although amidst the turmoil of the market, with the massive dome of St Paul's on one side, and that of

OXFORD ARMS INN, WARWICK LANE.

the old College of Physicians on the other, it is hard to associate the place with the domain of a nymph so lovely as Pomona.

The other galleried inn of Warwick-lane is the Oxford Arms, within a recess on the west side, and nearly adjoining to the residentiary houses of St Paul's in Amen-corner. It is one of the best specimens of the old London inns remaining in the metropolis. As you advance you observe a red brick pedimented façade of the time of Charles II., beneath which you enter the inn-yard, which has, on three of its sides, two stories of balustraded wooden galleries, with exterior staircases leading to the chambers on each floor ; the fourth side being occupied by stabling, built against part of old London wall. The house was an inn with the sign of the Oxford Arms before the Great Fire, as appears by the following advertisement in the *London Gazette* for March, 1672-3, No. 762 :—'These are to give notice, that Edward Bartlett, Oxford carrier, hath removed his inn, in London, from the *Swan*, at Holborn-bridge, to the *Oxford Arms*, in Warwick-lane, where he did inn before the Fire ; his coaches and wagons going forth on their usual days,—Mondays, Wednesdays, and Fridays. He hath also a hearse, with all things convenient, to carry a corpse to any part of England.' The *Oxford Arms* was not part of the Earl of Warwick's property, but belonged to the Dean and Chapter of St Paul's, who hold it to this day. From the inn premises is a door opening into one of the back yards of the residentiary houses, and it is stated that, during the riots of 1780, this passage facilitated the escape of certain Roman Catholics, who then frequented the Oxford Arms, on their being attacked by the mob ; for which reason, as is said, by a clause inserted in the Oxford Arms lease, that door is forbidden to be closed up. This inn appears to have been longer frequented by carriers, wagoners, and stage-coaches, than the Bell Inn, on the east side of the Lane ; for in the list in Delaune's *Present State of London*, 1690, the Oxford Arms occurs frequently, but mention is not made of the *Bell* Inn.

'At the Oxford Arms, in Warwick-lane,' lived John Roberts, the bookseller, from whose shop issued the majority of the squibs and libels on Pope.

In Warwick-square, about midway on the west side of the Lane, was the early office of the *Public Ledger* newspaper, in which Goldsmith wrote his *Citizen of the World*, at two guineas per week ; and here succeeded to a share in the property John Crowder, who, by diligent habits, rose to be alderman of the ward (Farringdon Within), and Lord Mayor in 1829-30. The *London Packet* (evening paper) was also Crowder's property. The *Independent Whig* was likewise localized in the square ; and at the south-west corner was the printing-office of the inflexible John Wheble, who befriended John Britton, when cellarman to a wine-merchant, and set him to write the *Beauties of Wiltshire*. Wheble was, in 1771, apprehended for abusing the House of Commons, in his *Middlesex Journal*, but was discharged by Wilkes ; of a better complexion was his *County Chronicle*, and the *Sporting Magazine*, which he commenced with John Harris, the bookseller. In this dull square, also, was the office of Mr Wilde, solicitor, the father of Lord Chancellor Truro, who here mounted the office-stool *en route* to the Woolsack.

Happy Accidents.—In 1684, a poor boy, apprenticed to a weaver at his native village of Wickwar, in Gloucestershire, in carrying, according to custom on a certain day in the year, a dish called 'whitepot' to the baker's, let it fall and broke it, and fearing to face his mistress, ran away to London, where he prospered, and, remembering his native village, founded the schools there which bear his name. At Monmouth, tradition relates that one William Jones left that place to become a shopboy to a London merchant, in the time of James I., and, by his good conduct, rose first to the counting-house, and then to a partnership in the concern ; and having realized a large fortune, came back in the disguise of a pauper, first to his native place, Newland, in Gloucestershire, from whence, having been ill received there, he betook himself to Monmouth, and meeting with kindness among his old friends, he bestowed £9,000 in founding a free grammar-school.

FEBRUARY 21.

Saints Daniel, priest, and Verda, virgin, martyrs, 344. St Severianus, bishop of Scythopolis, martyr, about 452. Blessed Pepin of Landen, mayor of the palace, 640. Saints German, abbot, and Randaut, martyrs, about 666.

Born.—Pierre du Bosc, 1623, *Bayeux ;* Mrs Anne Grant, author of *Letters from the Mountains*, 1755, *Glasgow.*

Died.—Caius Cæsar Agrippa, A.D. 4 ; James I. (of Scotland), murdered, 1437, *Perth ;* Pope Julius II., 1513 ; Henry Grey, Duke of Suffolk, beheaded, 1555 ; Robert Southwell, poet, executed at *Tyburn*, 1595 ; Secretary John Thurloe, 1668, *Lincoln's-inn ;* Benedict de Spinoza, philosopher, 1677 ; Pope Benedict XIII., 1730 ; Eugène de Beauharnais, Duke of Leuchtenberg, 1824, *Munich ;* Rev. Robert Hall, Baptist preacher, 1831, *Bristol ;* Charles Rossi, R.A., sculptor, 1839.

POPE JULIUS II.

Julius de la Rovere, who ascended the papal throne in 1503, under the title of Julius II., is one of the most famous of all the Popes. He was the founder of the church of St Peter at Rome ; but his most remarkable acts were of a warlike character. During his papacy of ten years, he was continually engaged in war, first, against the Venetians, to recover the Romagna, in which affair he was assisted by the French and Germans ; afterwards with the Germans against the French, in order to get these dangerous friends driven out of Italy. It was not till he had formed what he called ' a holy league,' in which he united to himself Spain, England, Venice, and the Swiss, that he succeeded in his object. In this war, he assumed all the characters and duties of a military commander, and few have exceeded him in spirit and resolution. As examples of the far-reaching policy of the man, he sent a splendid sword of state to the King of Scotland (James IV.) ; it still exists among the Scottish regalia, exhibiting the armorial bearings of Pope Julius. In the great chest at Reikiavik cathedral in Iceland, are robes which he sent to the bishop of that remote island.

Julius struck a medal to commemorate the great events of his reign ; it represented him in pontificals, with the tiara on his head, and a whip in his hand, chasing the French, and trampling the shield of France under his feet. When Michael Angelo was making a statue of the pope, he said to him, ' Holy Father, shall I place a book in your hand ?' ' No,' answered his Holiness, ' a sword rather—I know better how to handle it.' He was indeed much more of a soldier than an ecclesiastic, in any recognised sense of the term. He was the first pope who allowed his beard to grow, in order to inspire the greater respect among the faithful ; a fashion in which he was followed by Charles V. and other kings, and which spread through the courtiers to the people.

THE CAMERONIANS—EPIGRAM BY BURNS.

In the churchyard of the parish of Balmaghie, in the stewartry of Kirkcudbright, are the grave-stones of three persons who fell victims to the boot-and-saddle mission sent into Scotland under the last Stuarts. One of these rude monuments bears the following inscription :

'Here lyes David Halliday, portioner of Maifield, who was shot upon the 21st of February 1685, and David Halliday, once in Glengape, who was likewise shot upon the 11th of July 1685, for their adherence to the principles of Scotland's Covenanted Reformation

' Beneath This Stone Two David Hallidays
  Do Lie, Whose Souls Now Sing Their Master's praise.
To know If Curious Passengers desire,
For What, By Whom, And How They Did Expire ;
They Did Oppose This Nation's Perjury,
Nor Could They Join With Lordly Prelacy.
Indulging Favours From Christ's Enemies
Quenched Not Their Zeal. This Monument Then cries,
These Were The Causes, Not To Be Forgot,
Why They By Lag So Wickedly Were Shot ;
One Name, One Cause, One Grave, One Heaven, Do Tie
Their Souls To That One God Eternally.'

The reverend gentleman who first printed this epitaph in his parochial contribution to the Statistical Account of Scotland (1794), made upon it the unlucky remark—'The author of which no doubt supposed himself to have been writing poetry'— unlucky when we consider the respect due to the earnestness of these men in a frame of religious opinion which they thought right, and for which they had surrendered life. Burns, who got the Statistical Account out of the subscription library of Dumfries, experienced the just feeling of the occasion, and rebuked the writer for his levity in a quatrain, which he inscribed on the margin, where it is still clearly to be traced :

' The Solemn League and Covenant
  Now brings a smile—now brings a tear—
But sacred Freedom too was theirs ;
  If thou'rt a slave, indulge thy sneer.'

It will perhaps be learned with some surprise that a remnant of those Cameronians who felt unsatisfied with the Presbyterian settlement at the Revolution, still exists in Scotland. Numbering about seven hundred persons, scattered chiefly throughout the south-west provinces of Scotland, they continue to decline taking the oath of allegiance to the reigning monarch, or to accept of any public office, holding that monarch and people have broken their pledge or covenant, by which they were bound in 1644 to extirpate popery, prelacy, and other errors. Holding out their testimony on this subject, they abstain from even exercising the elective franchise, alleging that to do so would be to sanction the aforesaid breach of covenant, to which they trace all the evils that befall the land. In May 1861, when this Reformed Presbytery met in Edinburgh, a trying question came before them ; there were young men in their body who felt anxious to join in the volunteer movement ; some had even done it. There were also some members who had exercised the elective franchise. To pursue a contemporary record : 'A lengthened discussion took place as to what should be done, and numerous reverend members urged the modification of the

testimony, as regards the assumed identity of the representative and the voter, and as regards the interpretation of the oath of allegiance. Highly patriotic and almost loyal views were expressed on the Volunteer question, and warm expressions of admiration and love for Her Majesty were uttered, and of willingness to defend her person and protect the soil from invasion, so far as their service could be given apart from rendering fealty to the constitution. Another party in the Synod denounced the proposal to modify the testimony, as a backsliding and defection from the testimony. It was ultimately resolved, by 30 to 11, to appoint a committee to inquire into the soundness of the views contained in the testimony on the points mooted, and to relieve kirk sessions from the obligation to expel members who entertained doubts and difficulties on these matters, but meantime to recommend members of the Church to abstain from voting at elections. No similar recommendation having been made as to holding aloof from the Volunteer movement. it may be presumed that that point has been conceded.'

THE FOLK-LORE OF PLAYING CARDS.

The long disputed questions respecting the period of the invention of playing-cards, and whether they were first used for purposes of divination or gambling, do not fall within the prescribed limits of this paper. Its object is simply to disclose—probably for the first time in print—the method or system of divination by playing-cards, constantly employed and implicitly depended upon, by many thousands of our fellow-countrymen and women at the present day. The smallest village in England contains at least one 'card-cutter,' a person who pretends to presage future events by studying the accidental combinations of a pack of cards. In London, the name of these fortune-tellers is legion, some of greater, some of lesser repute and pretensions : some willing to draw the curtains of destiny for a sixpence, others unapproachable except by a previously paid fee of from one to three guineas. And it must not be supposed that all of those persons are deliberate cheats ; the majority of them ' believe in the cards ' as firmly as the silly simpletons who employ and pay them. Moreover, besides those who make their livelihood by ' card-cutting,' there are numbers of others, who, possessing a smattering of the art, daily refer to the pasteboard oracles, to learn their fate and guide their conduct. And when a ticklish point arises, one of those crones will consult another, and then, if the two cannot pierce the mysterious combination, they will call in a professed mistress of the art, to throw a gleam of light on the darkness of the future. In short, there are very few individuals among the lower classes in England who do not know something respecting the cards in their divinatory aspect, even if it be no more than to distinguish the lucky from the unlucky ones ; and it is quite common to hear a person's complexion described as being of a heart, or club colour. For these reasons, the writer—for the first time as he believes—has applied the well-known term folk-lore to this system of divination by playing cards, so extensively known and so continually practised in the British dominions.

The art of cartomancy, or divination by playing-cards, dates from an early period of their obscure history. In the museum of Nantes there is a painting, said to be by Van Eyck, representing Philippe le Bon, Archduke of Austria, and subsequently King of Spain, consulting a fortune-teller by cards. This picture, of which a transcript is here given, cannot be of a later date than the fifteenth century. When the art was introduced into England is unknown; probably, however, the earliest printed notice of it in this country is the following curious story, extracted from Rowland's *Judicial Astrology*

Condemned : 'Cuffe, an excellent Grecian, and secretary to the Earl of Essex, was told, twenty years before his death, that he should come to an untimely end, at which Cuffe laughed, and in a scornful manner intreated the soothsayer to shew him in what manner he should come to his end, who condescended to him, and calling for cards, intreated Cuffe to draw out of the pack any three which pleased him. He did so, and drew three knaves, and laid them on the table by the wizard's direction, who then told him, if he desired to see the sum of his bad fortune, to take up those cards. Cuffe, as he was prescribed, took up the first card, and looking on it, he saw the portraiture of himself *cap-à-pie*, having men encompassing him with bills and halberds. Then he took up the second, and there he saw the judge

THE ARCHDUKE OF AUSTRIA CONSULTING A FORTUNE-TELLER.

that sat upon him; and taking up the last card, he saw Tyburn, the place of his execution, and the hangman, at which he laughed heartily. But many years after, being condemned, he remembered and declared this prediction.'

The earliest work on cartomancy was written or compiled by one Francesco Marcolini, and printed at Venice in 1540. There are many modern French, Italian, and German works on the subject; but, as far as the writer's knowledge extends, there is not an English one. The system of cartomancy, as laid down in those works, is very different from that used in England, both as regards the individual interpretations of the cards, and the general method of reading or deciphering their combinations. The English system, however, is used in all British settlements over the globe, and has no doubt been carried thither by soldiers' wives, who, as is well known to the initiated, have ever been considered peculiarly skilful practitioners of the art. In-

deed, it is to a soldier's wife that this present exposition of the art is to be attributed. Many years ago the exigencies of a military life, and the ravages of a pestilential epidemic, caused the writer, then a puny but not very young child, to be left for many months in charge of a private soldier's wife, at an out-station in a distant land. The poor woman, though childless herself, proved worthy of the confidence that was placed in her. She was too ignorant to teach her charge to read, yet she taught him the only accomplishment she possessed,—the art of 'cutting cards,' as she termed it; the word cartomancy, in all probability, she had never heard. And though it has not fallen to the writer's lot to practise the art professionally, yet he has not forgotten it, as the following interpretations of the cards will testify.

DIAMONDS.

King. A man of very fair complexion; quick to anger, but soon appeased.

Queen. A very fair woman, fond of gaiety, and a coquette.
Knave. A selfish and deceitful relative ; fair and false.
Ten. Money. Success in honourable business.
Nine. A roving disposition, combined with honourable and successful adventure in foreign lands.
Eight. A happy prudent marriage, though rather late in life.
Seven. Satire. Scandal. Unpleasant business matters.
Six. Marriage early in life, succeeded by widowhood.
Five. Unexpected news, generally of a good kind.
Four. An unfaithful friend. A secret betrayed.
Trey. Domestic troubles, quarrels and unhappiness.
Deuce. A clandestine engagement. A card of caution.
Ace. A wedding ring. An offer of marriage.

HEARTS.

King. A fair, but not very fair, complexioned man ; good natured, but rather obstinate, and, when angered, not easily appeased.
Queen. A woman of the same complexion as the king; faithful, prudent, and affectionate.
Knave. An unselfish relative. A sincere friend.
Ten. Health and happiness, with many children.
Nine. Wealth. High position in society. The wish-card.
Eight. Fine clothes. Pleasure. Mixing in good society. Going to balls, theatres, &c.
Seven. Many good friends.
Six. Honourable courtship.
Five. A present.
Four. Domestic troubles caused by jealousy.
Trey. Poverty, shame and sorrow, caused by imprudence. A card of caution.
Deuce. Success in life, position in society, and a happy marriage, attained by virtuous discretion.
Ace. The house of the person consulting the decrees of fate.

SPADES.

King. A man of very dark complexion, ambitious and unscrupulous.
Queen. A very dark complexioned woman, of malicious disposition. A widow.
Knave. A lawyer. A person to be shunned.
Ten. Disgrace ; crime ; imprisonment. Death on the scaffold. A card of caution.
Nine. Grief ; ruin ; sickness ; death.
Eight. Great danger from imprudence. A card of caution.
Seven. Unexpected poverty caused by the death of a relative. A lean sorrow.
Six. A child. To the unmarried a card of caution.
Five. Great danger from giving way to bad temper. A card of caution.
Four. Sickness.
Trey. A journey by land. Tears.
Deuce. A removal.
Ace. Death ; malice ; a duel ; a general misfortune.

CLUBS.

King. A dark complexioned man, though not so dark as the king of spades ; upright, true, and affectionate.
Queen. A woman of the same complexion, agreeable, genteel, and witty.
Knave. A sincere, but rather hasty-tempered friend.
Ten. Unexpected wealth, through the death of a relative. A fat sorrow.

Nine. Danger caused by drunkenness. A card of caution.
Eight. Danger from covetousness. A card of caution.
Seven. A prison. Danger arising from the opposite sex. A card of caution.
Six. Competence by hard-working industry.
Five. A happy, though not wealthy marriage.
Four. Danger of misfortunes caused by inconstancy, or capricious temper. A card of caution.
Trey. Quarrels. Or in reference to time may signify three years, three months, three weeks, or three days. It also denotes that a person will be married more than once.
Deuce. Vexation, disappointment.
Ace. A letter.

The foregoing is merely the alphabet of the art ; the letters, as it were, of the sentences formed by the various combinations of the cards. A general idea only can be given here of the manner in which those prophetic sentences are formed. The person who desires to explore the hidden mysteries of fate is represented, if a male by the king, if a female by the queen, of the suit which accords with his or her complexion. If a married woman consults the cards, the king of her own suit, or complexion, represents her husband ; but with single women, the lover, either in *esse* or *posse*, is represented by his own colour ; and all cards, when representing persons, lose their own normal significations. There are exceptions, however, to these general rules. A man, no matter what his complexion, if he wear uniform, even if he be the negro cymbal-player in a regimental band, can be represented by the king of diamonds :—note, the dress of policemen and volunteers is not considered as uniform. On the other hand, a widow, even if she be an albiness, can be represented only by the queen of spades.

The ace of hearts always denoting the house of the person consulting the decrees of fate, some general rules are applicable to it. Thus the ace of clubs signifying a letter, its position, either before or after the ace of hearts, shews whether the letter is to be sent to or from the house. The ace of diamonds, when close to the ace of hearts, foretells a wedding in the house ; but the ace of spades betokens sickness and death.

The knaves represent the thoughts of their respective kings and queens, and consequently the thoughts of the persons whom those kings and queens represent, in accordance with their complexions. For instance, a young lady of a rather but not decidedly dark complexion, represented by the queen of clubs, when consulting the cards, may be shocked to find her fair lover (the king of diamonds) flirting with a wealthy widow (the queen of spades, attended by the ten of diamonds), but will be reassured by finding his thoughts (the knave of diamonds) in combination with a letter (ace of clubs), a wedding ring (ace of diamonds), and her house (the ace of hearts) ; clearly signifying that, though he is actually flirting with the rich widow, he is, nevertheless, thinking of sending a letter, with an offer of marriage, to the young lady herself. And look, where are her own thoughts, represented by the knave of clubs ; they are far away with the old lover, that dark man (king of spades) who, as is plainly shewn by his being attended by the nine of diamonds, is prospering at the Australian diggings or elsewhere. Let us shuffle the cards once more, and see if the dark man, at the distant diggings, ever thinks of his old flame, the club-complexioned young lady in England. No! he does not. Here are his thoughts (the knave of spades) directed to this fair, but rather gay and coquettish woman (the queen of diamonds); they are separated but by a few hearts, one of them, the sixth (honourable courtship), shewing the excellent understanding that exists between them. Count, now, from the six of hearts to the ninth card from it, and lo! it is a wedding ring (the ace of diamonds); they will be married before the expiration of a twelvemonth.

The general mode of manipulating the cards, when fortune-telling, is very simple. The person, who is desirous to know the future, after shuffling the cards *ad libitum*, cuts the pack into three parts. The seer, then, taking up these parts, lays the cards out, one by one, face upwards, upon the table, sometimes in a circular form, but oftener in rows consisting of nine cards in each row. Nine is the mystical number. Every nine consecutive cards form a separate combination, complete in itself; yet, like a word in a sentence, no more than a fractional part of the grand scroll of fate. Again, every card, something like the octaves in music, is *en rapport* with the ninth card from it; and these ninth cards form other complete combinations of nines, yet parts of the general whole. The nine of hearts is termed the 'wish-card.' After the general fortune has been told, a separate and different manipulation is performed, to learn if the pryer into futurity will obtain a particular wish; and, from the position of the wish-card in the pack, the required answer is deduced.

In conclusion, a few words must be said on the professional fortune-tellers. That they are, generally speaking, wilful impostors is perhaps true. Yet, paradoxical though it may appear, the writer feels bound to assert that those 'card-cutters' whose practice lies among the lowest classes of society, really do a great deal of good. Few know what the lowest classes in our large towns suffer when assailed by mental affliction. They are, in most instances, utterly destitute of the consolations of religion, and incapable of sustained thought. Accustomed to live from hand to mouth, their whole existence is bound up in the present, and they have no idea of the healing effects of time. Their ill-regulated passions brook no self-denial, and a predominant element of self rules their confused minds. They know of no future, they think no other human being ever suffered as they do. As they term it themselves, 'they are upset.' They perceive no resource, no other remedy than a leap from the nearest bridge, or a dose of arsenic from the first chemist's shop. Haply some friend or neighbour, one who has already suffered and been relieved, takes the wretched creature to a fortune-teller. The seeress at once perceives that her client is in distress, and, shrewdly guessing the cause, pretends that she sees it all in the cards. Having thus asserted her superior intelli-

284

gence, she affords her sympathy and consolation, and points to hope and a happy future; blessed hope! though in the form of a greasy playing card. The sufferer, if not cured, is relieved. The lacerated wounds, if not healed, are at least dressed; and, in all probability, a suicide or a murder is prevented. Scenes of this character occur every day in the meaner parts of London.

Unlike the witches of the olden time, the fortune-tellers are generally esteemed and respected in the districts in which they live and practise. And, besides that which has already been stated, it will not be difficult to discover sufficient reasons for this respect and esteem. The most ignorant and depraved have ever a lurking respect for morality and virtue; and the fortune-tellers are shrewd enough to know and act upon this feeling. They always take care to point out what they term 'the cards of caution,' and impressively warn their clients from falling into the dangers those cards foreshadow, but do not positively foretell, for the dangers may be avoided by prudence and circumspection. By referring to the preceding significations of the cards, it will be seen that there are cards of caution against dangers arising from drunkenness, covetousness, inconstancy, caprice, evil temper, illicit love, clandestine engagements, &c. Consequently the fortune-tellers are the moralists, as well as the consolers of the lower classes. They supply a want that society either cannot or will not do. If the great gulf which exists between rich and poor cannot be filled up, it would be well to try if, by any process of moral engineering, it could be bridged over.

FEBRUARY 22.

Saints Thalasius and Limneus, 5th century. St Baradat, 5th century. St Margaret, of Cortona, 1297.

Born.—Dr Richard Price, statist, 1723, *Tynton;* George Washington, President of the United States, 1731, *Bridge's Creek, Virginia;* Charles Duke of Richmond, 1735; Rev. Gilbert Wakefield, classical scholar, 1756, *Nottingham.*

Died.—David II. (of Scotland), 1371, *Edinburgh Castle;* Frederick I. (of Tuscany), 1609; Frederick Ruysch, anatomist, 1639, *The Hague;* James Barry, painter, 1806, *Marylebone;* Smithson Tennant, chemist, 1815, *Boulogne;* Dr Adam Ferguson, historian, 1816, *St Andrews;* Rev. Sydney Smith, wit and *littérateur*, 1845, *St George's, Hanover-square.*

GEORGE WASHINGTON.

'George Washington, without the genius of Julius Cæsar or Napoleon Bonaparte, has a far purer fame, as his ambition was of a higher and holier nature. Instead of seeking to raise his own name, or seize supreme power, he devoted his whole talents, military and civil, to the establishment of the independence and the perpetuity of the liberties of his own country. In modern history no man has done such great things without the soil of selfishness or the stain of a grovelling ambition. Cæsar, Cromwell, Napoleon attained a higher elevation, but the love of dominion was the spur that drove them on. John Hampden, William Russell, Algernon Sydney, may have had motives as pure, and an ambition as sustained; but they fell. To George Washington alone in modern times has it been given to accomplish a wonderful revolution, and yet to remain to all future times the theme of a people's gratitude, and an example of virtuous and beneficent power.'—*Earl Russell: Life and Times of Charles James Fox.*

The pre-eminence here accorded to Washington will meet with universal approval. He clearly and unchallengeably stands out as the purest great man in universal history. While America feels a just pride in having given him birth, it is something for England to know that his ancestors lived for generations upon her soil. His great-grandfather emigrated about 1657, having previously lived in Northamptonshire. The Washingtons were a family of some account. Their history has been traced by the Rev. J. N. Simpkinson, rector of Brington, near Northampton, with tolerable clearness, in a volume

entitled *The Washingtons*, published in 1860, but more concisely in a speech which he delivered at a meeting of American citizens in London, on Washington's birthday, two years later:

'The Washingtons,' he says, 'were a Northern family, who lived some time in Durham, and also in Lancashire. It was from Lancashire that they came to Northamptonshire. It is a pleasure to me to be able to point out what induced them to come to Northamptonshire. The uncle of the first Lawrence Washington was Sir Thomas Kitson, one of the great merchants who, in the time of Henry VII. and Henry VIII., developed the wool trade of the country. That wool trade depended mainly on the growth of wool, and the creation of sheep farms in the midland counties. I have no doubt, therefore, that the reason why Lawrence Washington settled in Northamptonshire, leaving his own profession, which was that of a barrister, was that he might superintend his uncle's transactions with the sheep-proprietors in that county. Lawrence Washington soon became Mayor of

GEORGE WASHINGTON.

Northampton, and at the time of the dissolution of the monasteries, being identified with the cause of civil and religious liberty, he gained a grant of some monastic lands. Sulgrave was granted to him. It will be interesting to point out the connexion which existed between him and my parish of Brington. In that parish is situated Althorp, the seat of the Spencers. The Lady Spencer of that day was herself a Kitson, daughter of Washington's uncle, and the Spencers

were great promoters of the sheep-farming movement. Thus, then, there was a very plain connexion between the Washingtons and the Spencers. The rector of the parish at that time was Dr Layton, who was Lord Cromwell's prime commissioner for the dissolution of monasteries. Therefore we see another cause why the lands of Sulgrave were granted to Lawrence Washington. For three generations they remained at Sulgrave, taking rank among the nobility and gentry of the county. At the end of three generations their fortunes failed. They were obliged to sell Sulgrave, and they then retired to our parish of Brington, being, as it were, under the wing of the Spencer family. . . . From this depression the Washingtons recovered by a singular marriage. The eldest son of the family had married the half-sister of George Villiers, Duke of Buckingham, which at this time was not an alliance above the pretensions of the Washingtons. They rose again into great prosperity. . . . . . About the emigrant I am not able to discover much : except that he, above all others of the family, continued to be on intimate terms with the Spencers down to the very eve of the civil war ; that he was knighted by James I. in 1623 ; and that we possess in our county not only the tomb of his father, but that of the wife of his youth, who lies buried at Islip-on-the-Nen. When the civil war broke out, the Washingtons took the side of the King. . . . . You all know the name of Sir Henry Washington, who led the storming party at Bristol, and defended Worcester. We have it, on the contemporary authority of Lloyd, that this Colonel Washington was so well known for his bravery, that it became a proverb in the army when a difficulty arose : " Away with it, quoth Washington." The emigrant who left England in 1657, I leave to be traced by historians on the other side of the Atlantic.'

In Brington Church are two sepulchral stones, one dated 1616 over the grave of the father of the emigrant, in which his arms appear impaled with those of his wife ; the other covering the remains of the uncle of the same person, and presenting on a brass the simple family shield, with the extraneous crescent appropriate to a younger brother. Of the latter a transcript is here given, that the reader may be enabled to ex-

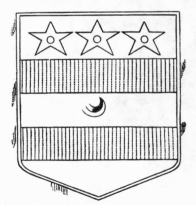

ercise a judgment in the question which has been raised as to the origin of the American flag. It is supposed that the stars and stripes which figure in that national blazon were taken from the shield of the illustrious general, as a compliment no more than due to him. In favour of this idea it is to be remarked that the stripes of the Washingtons are alternate gules and white, as are those of the national flag ; the stars in

286

chief, moreover, have the parallel peculiarity of being five-pointed, six points being more common.

The scene at the parting of Washington with his officers at the conclusion of the war of Independence, is feelingly described by Mr Irving : ' In the course of a few days Washington prepared to depart for Annapolis, where Congress was assembling, with the intention of asking leave to resign his command. A barge was in waiting about noon on the 4th of December at Whitehall ferry, to convey him across the Hudson to Paulus Hook. The principal officers of the army assembled at Fraunces' tavern in the neighbourhood of the ferry, to take a final leave of him. On entering the room, and finding himself surrounded by his old companions in arms, who had shared with him so many scenes of hardship, difficulty, and danger, his agitated feelings overcame his usual self-command. Filling a glass of wine, and turning upon them his benignant but saddened countenance, " With a heart full of love and gratitude," said he, " I now take leave of you, most devoutly wishing that your latter days may be as prosperous and happy as your former ones have been glorious and honourable." Having drunk this farewell benediction, he added with emotion, " I cannot come to each of you to take my leave, but I shall be obliged if each of you will come and take me by the hand." General Knox, who was the nearest, was the first to advance. Washington, affected even to tears, grasped his hand and gave him a brother's embrace. In the same affectionate manner he took leave severally of the rest. Not a word was spoken. The deep feeling and manly tenderness of these veterans in the parting moment could not find utterance in words. Silent and solemn they followed their loved commander as he left the room, passed through a corps of light infantry, and proceeded on foot to Whitehall ferry. Having entered the barge, he turned to them, took off his hat, and waved a silent adieu. They replied in the same manner, and having watched the barge until the intervening point of the battery shut it from sight, returned still solemn and silent to the place where they had assembled.'

THE REV. SYDNEY SMITH.

The witty canon of St Paul's (he did not like to be so termed) expired on the 22nd of February 1845, in his seventy-fourth year, at his house, No. 56, Green-street, Grosvenor-square. He died of water on the chest, consequent upon disease of the heart. He bore his sufferings with calmness and resignation. The last person he saw was his brother Bobus, who survived him but a few days,—literally fulfilling the petition in a letter written by Sydney two-and-thirty years before, ' to take care of himself, and wait for him.' He adds : ' We shall both be a brown infragrant powder in thirty or forty years. Let us contrive to last out for the same time, or nearly the same time.' His daughter, Lady Holland, thus touchingly relates an incident of his last days :

' My father died in peace with himself and with all the world ; anxious to the last to promote the comfort and happiness of others. He sent messages of kindness and forgiveness to the few he thought had injured him. Almost his last act was bestowing a small living of £120 per annum on a poor, worthy, and friendless clergyman, who had lived a long life of struggle with poverty on £40 per annum. Full of happi-

REV. SYDNEY SMITH.

ness and gratitude, he entreated he might be allowed to see my father; but the latter so dreaded any agitation, that he most unwillingly consented, saying, "Then he must not thank me; I am too weak to bear it." He entered—my father gave him a few words of advice—the clergyman silently pressed his hand, and blessed his death-bed. Surely, such blessings are not given in vain.'

Of all the estimates which have been written of the genius and character of the Rev. Sydney Smith, none exceeds in truthful illustration that which Earl Russell has given in the *Memoirs, &c., of Thomas Moore:* 'His (Sydney Smith's) great delight was to produce a succession of ludicrous images : these followed each other with a rapidity that scarcely left time to laugh ; he himself laughing louder, and with more enjoyment than any one. This electric contact of mirth came and went with the occasion ; it cannot be repeated or reproduced. Anything would give occasion to it. For instance, having seen in the newspapers that Sir Æneas Mackintosh was come to town, he drew such a ludicrous caricature of Sir Æneas and Lady Dido, for the amusement of their namesake, that Sir James Mackintosh rolled on the floor in fits of laughter, and Sydney Smith, striding across him, exclaimed "Ruat Justitia." His powers of fun were, at the same time, united with the strongest and most practical common sense. So that, while he laughed away seriousness at one minute, he destroyed in the next some rooted prejudice which had braved for a thousand years the battle of reason and the breeze of ridicule. The *Letters of Peter Plymley* bear the greatest likeness to his conversation ;

the description of Mr Isaac Hawkins Brown dancing at the court of Naples, in a volcano coat, with lava buttons, and the comparison of Mr Canning to a large blue-bottle fly, with its parasites, most resemble the pictures he raised up in social conversation. It may be averred for certain, that in this style he has never been equalled, and I do not suppose he will ever be surpassed.'

'Sydney,' says Moore, 'is, in his way, inimitable ; and as a conversational wit, beats all the men I have ever met. Curran's fancy went much higher, but also much *lower*. Sydney, in his gayest flights, though boisterous, is never vulgar.'

It was for the first time learned, from his daughter's book, in what poverty Sydney Smith spent many years of his life, first in London, afterwards at a Yorkshire parsonage. It was not, however, that painful kind of poverty which struggles to keep up appearances. He wholly repudiated appearances, confessed poverty, and only strove, by self-denial, frugality, and every active and economic device, to secure as much comfort for his family as could be legitimately theirs. In perfect conformity with this conduct, was that most amusing anecdote of his preparations to receive a great lady—paper lanterns on the evergreens, and a couple of jack-asses with antlers tied on to represent deer in the adjacent paddock. He delighted thus to mock aristocratic pretensions. The writer has heard (he believes) an inedited anecdote of him, with regard to an over-flourishing family *annonce* in a newspaper, which would have made him out to be a man of high grade in society. 'We are not great people at all,' said he, 'we are common honest people—people that pay our bills.' In the like spirit was his answer to a proposing county historian, who inquired for the Smythe arms—'The Smythes never had any arms, but have always sealed their letters with their thumbs.' Even when a little gleam of prosperity enabled him at last to think that his family wanted a carriage, observe the philosophy of his procedure: 'After diligent search, I discovered in the back settlements of a York coachmaker an ancient green chariot, supposed to have been the earliest invention of the kind. I brought it home in triumph to my admiring family. Being somewhat dilapidated, the village tailor lined it, the village blacksmith repaired it ; nay, (but for Mrs. Sydney's earnest entreaties,) we believe the village painter would have exercised his genius upon the exterior ; it escaped this danger, however, and the result was wonderful. Each year added to its charms, it grew younger and younger ; a new wheel, a new spring ; I christened it the "Immortal ;" it was known all over the neighbourhood ; the village boys cheered it, and the village dogs barked at it ; but "*Faber meæ fortunæ*" was my motto, and we had no false shame.'

FRENCH DESCENT IN WALES.

This day is memorable as being that on which, in the year 1797, the last invasion by an enemy was made on the shores of the island of Great Britain. At ten o'clock in the morning, three ships of war and a lugger were seen to pass 'the

Bishops '—a group of rocks off St David's Head in Pembrokeshire. The ships sailed under English colours; but the gentleman by whom they were discovered had been a sailor in his youth, and readily recognised them as French men-of-war with troops on board. He at once despatched one of his domestics to alarm the inhabitants of St David's, while he himself watched the enemy's motions along the coast towards Fishguard. At this latter town the fort was about to fire a salute to the British flag, when the English colours were struck on board the fleet, and the French ensign hoisted instead. Then the true character of the ships was known, and the utmost alarm prevailed. Messengers were despatched in all directions to give notice of a hostile invasion; the numbers of the enemy were fearfully exaggerated; vehicles of all kinds were employed in transporting articles of value into the interior. The inhabitants of St David's mustered in considerable numbers; the lead of the cathedral roof was distributed to six blacksmiths and cast into bullets; all the powder to be obtained was divided amongst those who possessed fire-arms; and then the whole body marched to meet the enemy. On the 23rd, several thousand persons, armed with muskets, swords, pistols, straightened scythes on poles, and almost every description of offensive weapon that could be obtained, had assembled. The enemy, meanwhile, whose force consisted of 600 regular troops and 800 convicts and sweepings of the French prisons, had effected a landing unopposed at Pencaer, near Fishguard. About noon on the following day the ships that had brought them sailed unexpectedly, and thus the troops were cut off from all means of retreat. Towards evening all the British forces that could be collected, consisting of the Castlemartin yeomanry cavalry, the Cardiganshire militia, two companies of fencible infantry, and some seamen and artillery, under the command of Lord Cawdor, arrived on the scene, and formed in battle array on the road near Fishguard. Shortly afterwards, however, two officers were sent by the French commander (Tate) with an offer to surrender, on the condition that they should be sent back to Brest by the British Government. The British commander replied that an immediate and unconditional surrender was the only terms he should allow, and that unless the enemy capitulated by two o'clock, and delivered up their arms, he would attack them with 10,000 men. The 10,000 men existed, for available purposes, only in the speech of the worthy commander; but the French general did not seem disposed to be very inquisitive, and the capitulation was then signed. On the morning of the 25th the enemy accordingly laid down their arms, and were marched under escort to various prisons at Pembroke, Haverfordwest, Milford, and Carmarthen. Five hundred were confined in one jail at Pembroke; of these one hundred succeeded in making their escape through a subterranean passage, 180 feet long, which they had dug in the earth at a depth of three feet below the surface.

Many wonderful stories are told in reference to this invasion. What follows is related in *Tales and Traditions of Tenby:* 'A tall, stout, masculine-looking female, named Jemima Nicholas, took a pitchfork, and boldly marched towards Pencaer to meet the foe; as she approached, she saw twelve Frenchmen in a field; she at once advanced towards them, and either by dint of her courage, or rhetoric, she had the good fortune to conduct them to, and confine them in, the guardhouse at Fishguard.' . . . . 'It is asserted that Merddin the prophet foretold that, when the French should land here, they would drink of the waters of Finon Crib, and would cut down a hazel or nut tree that grew on the side of Finon Well, along with a white-thorn. The French drank of that water, and cut down the trees as prophesied. We must also give our readers an account of Enoch Lake's dream and vision. About thirty years before the French invasion, this man lived near the spot where they landed. One night, he dreamed that the French were landing on Carreg Gwasted Point; he told his wife, and the impression was so strong, that he arose, and went to see what was going on, when he distinctly saw the French troops land, and heard their brass drums. This he told his wife and many others, who would not believe him till it had really happened.'

FAMILIAR NAMES.

In the hearty familiarity of old English manners, it was customary to call all intimates and friends by the popular abbreviations of their Christian names. It may be, therefore, considered as a proof at once of the popularity of poets and the love of poetry, that every one who gained any celebrity was almost invariably called Tom, Dick, Harry, &c. Heywood in his curious work, the *Hierarchie of Blessed Angels,* complains of this as an indignity to the worshippers of the Muse.

' Our modern poets to that end are driven,
  Those names are curtailed which they first had given,
  And, as we wished to have their memories drowned,
  We scarcely can afford them half their sound.
  Greene, who had in both academies ta'en
  Degree of Master, yet could never gain
  To be called more than Robin; who, had he
  Profest aught but the muse, served and been free
  After a seven years' 'prenticeship, might have,
  With credit too, gone Robert to his grave.
  Marlowe, renowned for his rare art and wit,
  Could ne'er attain beyond the name of Kit;
  Although his *Hero and Leander* did
  Merit addition rather. Famous Kid
  Was called but Tom. Tom Watson, though he wrote
  Able to make Apollo's self to dote
  Upon his muse, for all that he could strive,
  Yet never could to his full name arrive.
  Tom Nash, in his time of no small esteem,
  Could not a second syllable redeem;
  Excellent Beaumont, in the foremost rank
  Of th' rarest wits, was never more than Frank.
  Mellifluous Shakespeare, whose enchanting quill
  Commanded mirth or passion, was but Will.
  And famous Jonson, though his learned pen
  Be dipt in Castaly, is still but Ben.
  Fletcher, and Webster, of that learned pack
  None of the mean'st, yet neither was but Jack.
  Decker's but Tom, nor May, nor Middleton,
  And here's now but Jack Ford that once was John.

Soon after, however, he takes the proper view of the subject, and attributes the custom to its right cause.

> 'I, for my part,
> Think others what they please, accept that heart
> That courts my love in most familiar phrase ;
> And that it takes not from my pains or praise,
> If any one to me so bluntly come ;
> I hold he loves me best that calls me Tom.'

FEBRUARY 23.

St Serenus, a gardener, martyr, 307. St Boisil, prior of Melrose, 664. St Milburge, virgin, abbess in Shropshire, 7th century. Dositheus, monk of Palestine. Peter Damian, cardinal, 1072.

Born.—Samuel Pepys, diarist, Secretary to the Admiralty, 1632, *Brampton* (or *London*) ; George Frederick Handel, musical composer, 1685, *Halle* (see page 292) ; William Mason, poet, 1725, *Hull ;* Prince Henry Benedict Stuart, Cardinal York, 1725.

Died.—Pope Eugenius IV., 1447 ; Sir Thomas Wyatt, beheaded, 1555, *Tower ;* Stanislaus I. (of Poland), 1766 ; Sir Joshua Reynolds, painter, 1792, *Leicester-square ;* Dr Joseph Warton, Professor of Poetry, Oxon, 1800, *Wickham, Hants ;* John Keats, poet, 1821, *Rome ;* Joanna Baillie, poet and dramatist, 1851, *Hampstead.*

DEATH OF SIR JOSHUA REYNOLDS.

For some time previous to his decease this great painter felt that his end was approaching. The failure of his powers is touchingly recorded. In July 1789, when Sir Joshua had nearly finished the portrait of Lady Beauchamp (the last female portrait he ever painted), his eyesight was so affected that he found it difficult to proceed. He laid down his pencil, and sat a while in mute consideration. In his pocket-book is this note of the calamity : 'Monday, the 13th of July,—prevented by my eye beginning to be obscured.' He soon totally lost it, and then violently apprehended that the other was going too. This was not the case ; but the dread of what might happen if he used it much, entirely deterred him from either painting, writing, or reading : he amused himself by sometimes cleaning or mending a picture, for his ruling passion still continued in force, and he enjoyed his pictures as much as ever. His health was perfect, and his spirits were good ; he enjoyed company in a quiet way, and loved a game at cards as well as ever.

Sir Joshua's niece, Miss Palmer, speaks, in March 1790, of his still painting ; another authority dates his entire cessation from work in November 1791 : 'His last male portrait was that of Charles James Fox ; and when the final touches were given to this picture, the hand of Reynolds fell to rise no more.'

Sir Joshua now became much depressed in spirits ; a tumour and inflammation above the eye that had perished could not be dispersed, and he dreaded that the other eye might be affected. He grew melancholy and sorrowfully silent. A concealed malady was sapping his life and spirits. Mr Burke tells us that the great painter's 'illness was long, but borne with a mild and cheerful fortitude, without the least mixture of anything irritable or querulous, agreeable to the placid and even tenor of his whole life. He

had, from the beginning of his malady, a distinct view of his dissolution, which he contemplated with an entire composure, that nothing but the innocence, integrity, and usefulness of his life, and an unaffected submission to the will of Providence, could bestow.'

'I have been fortunate,' said Reynolds, ' in long good health and constant success, and I ought not to complain. I know that all things on earth must have an end.' With these simple words of resignation, Sir Joshua expired, without any visible symptoms of pain, at his house in Leicester-square, on the night of February 23, 1792, in the sixty-ninth year of his age.

Next day his body was opened by Mr Hunter, the eminent surgeon, when his liver was found to have become preternaturally enlarged, from about five pounds to nearly eleven pounds. It was also somewhat scirrhous. The optic nerve of the left eye was quite shrunk, and more flimsy than it ought to have been ; the other,

STAIRCASE IN SIR JOSHUA REYNOLDS'S HOUSE, LEICESTER-SQUARE.

which Sir Joshua was so apprehensive of losing, was not affected. In his brain was found more water than is usual with men of his age. Malone tells us that Reynolds had long enjoyed such constant health, looked so young, and was so active, that he thought, though sixty-nine years old, he was as likely to live eight or ten years longer as any of his younger friends.

The remains of the illustrious painter, after lying in state in the great room of the Royal Academy at Somerset House, were interred, with much ceremony, in St Paul's Cathedral, in a grave in the south aisle of the crypt ; in the nave above is a marble portrait-statue of England's finest painter, Reynolds, by her best sculptor, Flaxman. At the close of the funeral,

Mr Burke, who was one of Sir Joshua's executors, attempted to thank the members of the Royal Academy for the respect shewn to the remains of their late President; but the orator's feelings could only find vent in tears—he could not utter a word. A memorial print, engraved by Bartolozzi, was presented to each of the gentlemen attending the funeral.

'Sir Joshua Reynolds,' says Burke, 'was on very many accounts one of the most memorable men of his time. He was the first Englishman who added the praise of the elegant arts to the other glories of his country. In taste, in grace, in facility, in happy invention, in the richness and harmony of colouring, he was equal to the greatest inventors of the renowned ages. . . . . He had too much merit not to excite some jealousy, too much innocence to provoke any enmity. The loss of no man of his time can be felt with more sincere, general, and unmixed sorrow.'

CATO-STREET CONSPIRACY.

The popular discontents following the close of the great war—after efflorescing in radicalism, Manchester meetings, street oratory, Cobbett's *Registers*, &c.—came to a sort of head in the early part of 1820. A combination of mean men was then formed, with a view to the effecting a revolution by means of sanguinary violence. The chief man concerned was one named Arthur Thistlewood, who had been a soldier, who had been involved in a trial for sedition, but acquitted, and who had afterwards suffered a year's imprisonment for sending a challenge to the minister, Lord Sidmouth. He was a desperate man, animated by a spirit of revenge which overpowered reason. It seemed to him not impossible, by some such stroke as that contemplated in the Gunpowder Treason, to create a national confusion out of which a better government might be evoked; and he found a number of extreme radicals, of like fortunes with himself, to join in his enterprise. In all such movements of the common sort of people, there are always some whose virtue does not enable them to resist bribery. The Government never remained unacquainted with the conspiracies formed against it.

Months before the development of the plot, it was fully known to the ministers, who, according to the wretched policy which necessity suggested to them, employed spies named Oliver and Edwards to stimulate its authors, so as to make them clearly amenable to the law. Thistlewood and a group of associates went on meeting in some den in Gray's Inn-lane, arranging their plans, unconscious of the traitors in their midst. Their main design was to assassinate the ministers, each in his own house; but, at length learning that there was to be a cabinet dinner at the house of Earl Harrowby, President of the Council, in Grosvenor-square, on the 23rd of February, they resolved to wait for it, Thistlewood remarking with savage glee, 'It will be a rare haul to murder them all together.'

It was arranged that some of the conspirators should watch Lord Harrowby's house; one was to call and deliver a dispatch-box at the door;

the others were then to rush in, and having secured the servants, they were to assassinate the ministers as they sat at dinner; bringing away as special trophies, the heads of Lord Sidmouth and Lord Castlereagh, in two bags provided for the purpose! They were then to set fire to the cavalry barracks; and the Bank of England and the Tower of London were to be taken by the people, who, it was hoped, would rise upon the spread of the news. It can scarcely be believed that such a scheme should have been seriously planned in the metropolis at so late a date; yet such was the fact.

With a view to the attack in Grosvenor-square, their place of meeting was a loft over a stable in Cato-street, near the Edgware-road. Here the conspirators having mustered to the number of twenty-four, took the precaution of placing one as a sentinel below, whilst they prepared for their dreadful work. Meanwhile, the ministers, fully apprised of what was going on, did not arrive at Lord Harrowby's: the Archbishop of York, who lived next door, happened to give a dinner-party at the same hour as that appointed at Lord Harrowby's, and the arrival of carriages at the Archbishop's deceived those of the conspirators who were on the watch in the square, and they did not discover their mistake until it was too late to give warning to their comrades assembled in Cato-street. Here, while the traitors were arming themselves by the light of one or two candles, a party of Bow-street officers, mounting by a ladder, forcibly entered the loft: the foremost of them, in attempting to seize Thistlewood, was run by him through the body, and instantly fell; the lights were extinguished, a few shots were exchanged, and Thistlewood and some of his companions escaped through a window at the back of the premises: nine were taken that evening, with their arms and ammunition; and the intelligence was conveyed to the ministers, who had met at Lord Liverpool's, at Westminster, to await the result. A reward of £1,000 was immediately offered for the apprehension of Thistlewood, and he was captured next morning, while in bed, at the house of a friend in Little Moorfields.

The conspirators were sent to the Tower, the last persons imprisoned in that fortress. On the 20th of April, Thistlewood was condemned to death after three days' trial; and on May 1, he and his four principal accomplices,—Ings, Brunt, Tidd, and Davidson, who had been severally tried and convicted,—were hanged at the Old Bailey. The remaining six pleaded guilty; one received a pardon, and five were transported for life. To efface recollection of the conspiracy, Cato-street has been re-named Homerstreet.

SCENT-BALLS AND POMANDERS.

Among the minor objects of personal use which appear, from an inventory, to have belonged to Margaret de Bohun, daughter of Humphrey de Bohun, Earl of Hereford and Essex, slain at the battle of Boroughbridge, March 16, 1321, is a 'poume de aumbre,' or scent-ball, in the composition of which ambergris probably formed a principal ingredient. We here learn also that a nutmeg was occasionally used for the like purpose; it was set in silver, decorated with stones and pearls, and was evidently an object rare and highly prized. Amongst the valuable effects of Henry V., according to the inventory taken A.D. 1423, are enumerated a musk-ball of gold, weighing eleven ounces, and another of silver gilt. At a later period, the pomander was very commonly worn as the pendant of a lady's girdle. A receipt for compounding it may be found in the *Treasury of Commodious Conceits*, 1586.

The orange appears to have been used as a pomander soon after its introduction into England. Cavendish describes Cardinal Wolsey entering a crowded chamber 'holding in his hand a very fair orange, whereof the meat or substance within was taken out, and filled up again with the part of a sponge, wherein was vinegar and other confections against the pestilent airs; the which he most commonly smelt unto, passing among the press, or else he was pestered with many suitors.'

Sir Thomas Gresham, in his celebrated portrait by Sir Antonio Möre, holds in his left hand a small object resembling an orange, but which is a *pomander*. This sometimes consisted of a dried Seville orange, stuffed with cloves and other spices; and being esteemed a fashionable preservative against infection, it frequently occurs in old portraits, either suspended to the girdle or held in the hand. In the eighteenth century, the signification of this object had become so far forgotten, that, instead of pomanders, *bonâ fide* oranges were introduced into portraits, a practice which Goldsmith has happily satirized in his *Vicar of Wakefield*, where seven of the Flamboroughs are drawn with seven oranges, &c.

When the pomander was made of silver, it was

A SILVER POMANDER.

perforated with holes, to let out the scent. Hence the origin of the *vinaigrette* of our day.

The earliest mention of *coral* is that which occurs in the inventory of Alianore de Bohun, namely, the paternoster of coral, with gilded *gaudeer* (the larger beads), which belonged to Margaret de Bohun, and the three branches of coral which Alianore possessed. The above use of coral explains its being worn, in later times, as an amulet, or defence against infection.

MR FOX; AN OLD ENGLISH NURSERY STORY.

In Shakspeare's *Much Ado About Nothing*, Benedict (Act I., Sc. 1) alludes to 'the old tale—it is not so, nor 'twas not so, but indeed God forbid it should be so.' It is believed by his laborious commentator, Mr Halliwell, that Shakspeare here had in his recollection a simple English nursery story which he had probably heard in his infancy at Stratford, and of which some memory still survives. The story is given by the

learned commentator as follows: 'Once upon a time there was a young lady, called Lady Mary, who had two brothers. One summer they all went to a country seat of theirs, which they had not before visited. Among the other gentry in the neighbourhood who came to see them, was a Mr Fox, a bachelor, with whom they, particularly the young lady, were much pleased. He used often to dine with them, and frequently invited Lady Mary to come and see his house. One day that her brothers were absent elsewhere, and she had nothing better to do, she determined to go thither; and accordingly set out unattended. When she arrived at the house, and knocked at the door, no one answered. At length she opened it and went in; over the portal of the hall was written, "Be bold, be bold—but not too bold, lest that your heart's blood should run cold." She opened it; it was full of skeletons and tubs full of blood. She retreated in haste, and coming down stairs she saw Mr Fox advancing towards the house with a drawn sword in one hand, while with the other he dragged along a young lady by her hair. Lady Mary had just time to slip down, and hide herself under the stairs, before Mr Fox and his victim arrived at the foot of them. As he pulled the young lady upstairs, she caught hold of one of the banisters with her hand, on which was a rich bracelet. Mr Fox cut it off with his sword: the hand and bracelet fell into Lady Mary's lap, who then contrived to escape unobserved, and got home safe to her brothers' house. After a few days, Mr Fox came to dine with them as usual. After dinner, when the guests began to amuse each other with extraordinary anecdotes, Lady Mary at length said she would relate to them a remarkable dream she had lately had. "I dreamt," said she, "that as you, Mr Fox, had often invited me to go to your house, I would go there one morning. When I came to the house I knocked, but no one answered. When I opened the door, over the hall was written, 'Be bold, be bold—but not too bold.' But," said she, turning to Mr Fox, and smiling, "it is not so, nor it was not so." Then she pursued the rest of the story, concluding at every turn with "It is not so, nor it was not so," till she came to the room full of dead bodies, when Mr Fox took up the burden of the tale, and said, "It is not so, nor it was not so; and God forbid it should be so," which he continues to repeat at every subsequent turn of the dreadful story, till she came to the circumstance of the cutting off the young lady's hand, when, upon his saying as usual, "It is not so, nor it was not so; and God forbid it should be so," Lady Mary retorts, "But it is so, and it was so, and here's the hand I have to show;" at the same time producing the bracelet from her lap; whereupon the guests drew their swords, and cut Mr Fox into a thousand pieces.'

It is worthy of notice that the mysterious inscription seen by the lady in Mr Fox's house is identical with that represented by Spenser (*Faerie Queen*, III. xi. 54), as beheld by Britomart in

'———— the house of Busyrane,
Where Love's spoyles are exprest.'

It occurs in the following stanza:

'And as she lookt about she did behold
How over that same dore was likewise writ,
Be bold, be bold, and everywhere *Be bold*;
That much she mus'd, yet could not construe it
By any ridling skill or commune wit.
At last she spyde at that rowme's upper end
Another yron dore, on which was writ,
Be not too bold; whereto. though she did bend
Her earnest mind, yet wist not what it might intend.

It cannot be said that there is much in the story of Mr Fox; but it is curious to find it a matter of familiar knowledge to two writers like Shakspeare and Spenser; and we learn from their allusions that, rude and simple as it is, it has existed for about three centuries, if not more.

FEBRUARY 24.

St Matthias, the Apostle, *Colchis.* Saints Montanus, Lucius, Flavian, Julian, Victoricus, Primulus, Rhenus, and Donatian, martyrs at Carthage, 259. St Pretextatus, archbishop of Rouen, martyr, about 585. St Lethard, bishop of Senlis, 596, *Canterbury.* St Ethelbert, first Christian king of England, 616. Robert of Arbrissel, 111.

Born.—John Picus, Count of Mirandola, 1463; Charles V. (of Spain), 1500, *Ghent;* James Quin, actor, 1693, *Covent-garden;* Robert Lord Clive, conqueror of Bengal, 1726; Charles Lamb, humorous essayist, 1775, *London;* Robert Lord Gifford, Master of the Rolls, 1779.

Died.—Richard de la Pole, Francis Duke of Lorraine, and General de la Tremouille, killed at *Pavia,* 1525; Francis Duke of Guise, assassinated, 1563; James Earl of Derwentwater, beheaded, 1716; Joseph (of Portugal), 1777; Charles Buonaparte, 1785; Hon. Henry Cavendish, amateur chemist, 1810; Thomas Coutts, banker, 1822; John VI. (of Portugal), 1826.

MEMORIALS OF HANDEL.

George Frederick Handel, although a native of Germany (born at Halle, in Saxony, on the 23d of February 1685), from having passed nearly the whole of his life in England, and produced in it all his great works, is almost claimed by us as an Englishman. When a child, he sacrificed his play-hours, and sometimes even his meals, to his passion for music, which was so successfully cultivated, that, when only ten years of age, he composed a set of sonatas, not without their value as pieces of music.

At the outset of his professional life in 1703, he had nearly been lost to the world. It was at Hamburg that he got embroiled with Mattheson, an able musician, who violently assaulted him. A duel ensued, and nothing but a *score,* buttoned under Handel's coat, on which his antagonist's weapon broke, saved a life that was to prove of inestimable value. Handel was never married: the charms of his music impressed many beauties and singers in his favour; but he shewed no disposition to avail himself of their partialities. His thoughts were nearly all absorbed by his art, and a high sense of moral propriety distinctly marked his conduct through life.

Handel, as a composer, was great in every style. In sacred music, especially of the choral kind, he throws at an immeasurable distance all who preceded and followed him.

Handel first arrived in London in 1710, and was soon honoured by the notice of Queen Anne. Aaron Hill was then manager of the opera, and his *Rinaldo* was set to music by Handel, and produced in March, 1711. At the peace of Utrecht, he composed for that event a *Te Deum* and *Jubilate;* and a pension of £200 was the reward of this service. In 1714, when the Elector of Hanover was placed on the British

throne, Handel, not having kept his promise to return to Hanover, durst not present himself at court: but he got over the difficulty by a pleasant stratagem: his friend, Baron Kilmansegge, contrived that he should meet the King, during a royal excursion on the Thames, with a band of wind instruments, playing the charming *Water Music,* written for the occasion; the composer was received again into favour, his pension was doubled; and many years after, when appointed to teach the Princesses, Queen Caroline, consort of George II., added another £200, making altogether £600 per annum, no small income a century ago.

Next he became chapel-master to the Duke of Chandos, at Canons, and there he produced most of his concertos, sonatas, lessons, and organ fugues; besides his *Acis and Galatea,* for which Gay wrote the poetry. Then he carried out the conversion of the Italian Theatre into an Academy of Music; he was engaged as manager, and produced fifteen new operas; but the Italians virulently opposed 'the German intruder;' the cabal became insupportable, and the great composer and able manager retired with a loss of £10,000 and broken health. He next attempted operas at Covent Garden Theatre, but this speculation proved equally unfortunate. He next gave Lent oratorios, but with no better success; even his sublimest work, *The Messiah,* was ill attended and received in the metropolis, when first produced in 1741. These failures were caused by the hostility of the nobility, notwithstanding the patronage of the Royal family. He then took refuge in Ireland, where he began by performing *The Messiah* for the benefit of the city prison. He returned to London in 1742, renewed his oratorios at Covent Garden Theatre, and henceforth was uniformly successful; and he continued his oratorios with great profit nearly to the last day of his life.

Handel died on a Good Friday (according to his own wish), April 13, 1759, and was buried in Westminster Abbey. Late in life he was afflicted with blindness; but he continued to perform and even composed pieces, and assisted at one of his oratorios only a week before his death.

Handel will long be remembered for his munificent aid to the Foundling Hospital in London. In 1749, he gave a performance of his own compositions, by which the charity realized five hundred guineas, and every subsequent year he superintended the performance of *The Messiah* in the Foundling Hospital Chapel, which netted altogether £7,000; he also presented an organ, and bequeathed to the charity a fair copy of the score and parts of the oratorio of *The Messiah.*

The memory of Handel has been preserved by a series of performances of his works under the roof which covers his dust. At a century from his birth, in 1784, was given the first *Commemoration,* zealously patronised by George III., who was so fond of music that he was accustomed to write out the programmes of his own concerts. Handel's 'Abbey Commemoration' was repeated annually till 1791; these performances benefiting different metropolitan charities to the amount of £50,000. In 1834, took place another Commemoration in the Abbey. Festivals of Handel's music have since been given by the Sacred Harmonic Society, and in the Crystal Palace at Sydenham, upon a very grand scale.

We possess in England many memorials of the genius and character of this excellent man. Roubiliac's first and last works in this country were his statue of Handel, for Vauxhall Gardens, and his monumental statue of the great composer in Poet's Corner, Westminster Abbey. His autographs are highly treasured: in the Queen's library are the original MSS. of nearly all Handel's works, filling eighty-two folio volumes; and his MS. scores and letters are preserved in the board-room of the Foundling Hospital. Portraits of Handel are numerous: he was painted by Thornhill, Kyte, Denner, Wolfand, Hudson, and Grafoni. The portrait by Denner was in Handel's own possession, and is most trustworthy, though Walpole describes Hudson's portrait as 'honest similitude;' it is at Gopsal, the seat of Earl Howe. The statue of Handel from Vauxhall is now in the possession of the Sacred Harmonic Society; and a cast of Handel's features, taken after death by Roubiliac for the Abbey statue, is carefully preserved, as are a few impressions from the mould. A harpsichord and book-case, which once belonged to the great composer, are also treasured as relics. He lived many years in the house No. 57, on the south side of Brook-street, four doors from Bond-street, and here he gave rehearsals of his oratorios.

Handel was fond of society, enjoyed his pipe over a cup of coffee, and was a lively wit in conversation. He was very fond of Mrs Cibber, at whose house, on Sunday evenings, he often met Quin, the comedian. One evening Handel, having delighted the company by playing on the harpsichord, took his leave. After he was gone, Quin was asked by Mrs Cibber whether he did not think Mr Handel had a charming hand. 'A *hand*, madam! you mistake, it is a *foot*.' 'Poh! poh!' said she, 'has he not a fine finger?' 'Toes, madam!' In fact, his hand was so fat, that the knuckles, which usually appear convex, were, like those of a child, dinted or dimpled in; however, his touch was so smooth, that his fingers seemed to grow to the keys. They were so curved and compact when he played, that no motion, and scarcely the fingers themselves, could be perceived. In performing on the organ, his command of the instrument was amazing, as was the fulness of his harmony, and the grandeur and dignity of his style. He wore an enormous white wig, and when things went well at the oratorios, it had a certain nod or vibration, which denoted his pleasure and satisfaction. Without this signal, nice observers were certain that he was out of humour. At the close of an air, the voice with which he used to cry out 'Chorus!' was formidable indeed. Handel died possessed of £20,000, which, with the exception of £10,000 to the fund for decayed musicians, he chiefly bequeathed to his relations on the Continent.

MRS MIDNIGHT'S ANIMAL COMEDIANS.

'The town,' as Beau Tibbs would say, was regaled, in 1753, with a new pleasure, under the

BALLET OF DOGS AND MONKEYS:
On the left, below, a monkey cavalier on dog-back.

293

A MONKEY TOWN BESIEGED BY DOGS.

appellation of Mrs Midnight's Animal Comedians. With incredible labour and patience, a number of dogs and monkeys had been trained to go through certain scenic representations, which were generally acknowledged to be a marvellously good imitation of the doings of human actors. The performance took place in a small theatre, which was fitted up with appropriate scenery, decorations, &c., and was, we believe, well attended. A representation of the stage as it appeared from the pit, is reproduced on the preceding page from a contemporary print, in which, however, there are compartments exhibiting other performances by the animal comedians.

Taking these compartments as evidence on the subject, we find that there was a *Monkeys' Entertainment*, two of these animals being seated in full dress at a table with wine and cake, while another of the same species attended with a plate under his arm. Two dogs, accoutred like soldiers, shewed their agility by jumping over a succession of bundles of sticks. Three personated Harlequin, Pero (?), and Columbine, the last attired in a prodigious hoop. Two monkeys, in cloaks and cocked hats, were exercised upon the backs of a couple of dogs. Another monkey, mounted on dog-back, went through a series of quasi-equestrian performances, mounting and dismounting with the greatest propriety. There was also a grand *Ballet Dance* of dogs and monkeys in the formal dresses of the period, powdered hair, &c., and of this we have caused a copy to be prepared (p. 293). In the original a 'lady' has just been brought in in a sedan. Certainly, however, the principal performance was a *Siege*, of which also a copy here appears. The stage in this instance presented the exterior of a fortified town. Monkeys manned the walls, and fired at a multitude of canine besiegers. The army of dogs, under their brave commanders, came forward with unflinching courage, and, a couple of ladders being planted, they mounted the ramparts with the greatest agility, and entered the city sword in hand, disregarding such casualties as the fall of two or three of the storming party into the ditch.

The simial defenders, as we may suppose, gave a determined resistance; but all was in vain against canine courage, and soon the flag of the assailants waved upon the battlements. When the smoke cleared away, the besieged and besiegers were observed in friendly union on the top of the fore-wall, taking off their hats to the tune of *God save the King*, and humbly saluting the audience. Tradition intimates to us that Mrs Midnight's Animal Comedians were for a season in great favour in London; yet, strange to say, there is no notice of them in the *Gentleman's Magazine*, or any other chronicle of the time which we have been able to consult.

FISH AND FISH PIES IN LENT.

The strictness with which our ancestors observed Lent and fast-days led to a prodigious consumption of fish by all classes; and great quantities are entered in ancient household accounts as having been bought for family use. In the 31st year of the reign of Edward III., the following sums were paid from the Exchequer for fish supplied to the royal household:

Fifty marks for five lasts (9,000) red herrings, twelve pounds for two lasts of white herrings, six pounds for two barrels of sturgeon, twenty-one pounds five shillings for 1300 stock-fish, thirteen shillings and ninepence for eighty-nine congers, and twenty marks for 320 mulwells.

The cooks had many ways of preparing the fish. Herring-pies were considered as delicacies even by royalty. The town of Yarmouth, by ancient charter, was bound to send a hundred herrings, baked in twenty-four pies or pasties, annually to the king; and Eustace de Corson, Thomas de Berkedich, and Robert de Withen, in the reign of Edward I., held thirty acres by tenure of supplying twenty-four pasties of fresh herrings, for the king's use, on their first coming into season.

'Lampreys were the favourite dish of the mediæval epicures; they were always considered a great delicacy. So great was the demand for this fish in the reign of King John, as to have induced that monarch to issue a royal licence to one Sampson, to go to Nantes to purchase lampreys for the use of the Countess of Blois. The same king issued a mandate to the sheriffs of Gloucester (that city being famous for producing lampreys), forbidding them, on their first coming in, to be sold for more than two shillings a piece. In the reign of Edward III., they were sometimes sold for eightpence or tenpence a piece, and they often produced a much higher price. In 1341, Walter Dastyn, sheriff of Gloucester, received the sum of £12, 5s. 8d. for forty-four lampreys supplied for the king's use.'* The corporation of Gloucester presented to the sovereign every Christmas, as a token of their loyalty, a lamprey-pie, which was sometimes a costly gift, as lampreys at that season could scarcely be procured at a guinea a piece. (See *Fish, how to choose, how to dress*. Printed at Launceston.) The Severn is noted for its lampreys, and Gloucester noted for its peculiar mode of stewing them; indeed, a Gloucester lamprey will almost excuse the royal excess of Henry I., who died at Rouen, of an illness brought on by eating too freely of this choice fish, after a day spent in hunting.

In addition to these favourite dishes, the choice 'vianders' of the fourteenth century paid epicurean prices for delicious morsels of the whale, the porpoise, the grampus, and the sea-wolf. These animals, being then considered as fish, were held as allowable food in Lent: it is lamentable to think how much sin they thus occasioned among our forefathers, before they were discovered to be mammalian. The flesh of the porpoise was cooked in various ways: a manuscript in the British Museum contains a receipt for making 'puddynge of porpoise' (Harl. MSS., No. 279); and we find it served at table as late as the time of Henry VIII., and in the north to a later period.

Use of Militia Drilling and Tactics.—Gibbon, who at one part of his life was a captain in the Hampshire regiment of militia, remained ever after sensible of a benefit from it. He says, 'It made me an Englishman and a soldier. In this peaceful service I imbibed the rudiments of the language and science of tactics, which opened a new field of study and observation. The discipline and evolutions of a modern battalion gave me a clearer notion of the phalanx and the legion; and the captain of the Hampshire grenadiers (the reader may smile) has not been useless to the historian of the Roman empire.'—*Miscellaneous Works*, vol. i., p. 136.

* Parker's Domestic Architecture in England, 14th cent., p. 131.

FEBRUARY 25.

St Victorinus, and six companions, martyrs, 284. St Cæsarius, physician of Constantinople, 369. St Walburge, virgin, of England, 779. St Tarasius, patriarch of Constantinople, 806.

Born.—Germain de Saint Foix, 1703, *Rennes*.

Died.—William Lily, master of St Paul's School, London, 1523; Robert Earl of Essex, beheaded, 1600; Count Wallenstein, commander, assassinated, 1634, *Eger;* Frederick I. (of Prussia), 1713; Sir Christopher Wren, architect, 1723, *St James's;* Dr William Buchan, 1805, *St Pancras;* George Don, naturalist, 1856.

WILLIAM LILY, THE GRAMMARIAN.

This famous schoolmaster, the friend of Erasmus and Sir Thomas More, was born at Odiham, Hants, about 1468; he was educated at Oxford University, and then travelled to the East, to acquire a knowledge of the Greek language. On his return to England he set up a private grammar-school, and was the first teacher of Greek in the metropolis. In 1512, Dean Colet, who had just founded St Paul's School, appointed Lily the first master. In the following year he produced his *Grammar*, which has probably passed through more editions than any work of its kind, and is used to this day in St Paul's School; the English rudiments were written by Colet, and the preface to the first edition by Cardinal Wolsey; the Latin syntax chiefly by Erasmus; and the remainder by Lily; the book being thus the joint production of four of the greatest scholars of the age. Lily held the mastership of St Paul's School for nearly twelve years; he died of the plague in London, and was buried in the north churchyard of St Paul's, within bow-shot of the school to whose early celebrity he had so essentially contributed.

COUNT WALLENSTEIN.

There is scarcely a personage in history of more awe-striking character than Count Wallenstein, the commander of the Emperor's armies in that struggle with Protestantism, the Thirty Years' War.

Born of high rank in 1583, Wallenstein found himself at forty chief of the imperial armies, and the possessor of immense wealth. Concentrating a powerful mind on one object, the gratification of his ambition, he attained it to a remarkable degree, and was for some time beyond doubt the greatest subject in Europe. In managing troops by a merciless discipline, in making rapid marches, in the fiery energy of his attacks upon the enemy, he was unrivalled. In but one battle, that of Lutzen, where he met the Protestant army under Gustavus of Sweden, was he unsuccessful.

The personality and habits of the man have been strikingly described by Michiels in his *History of the Austrian Government*. 'Wallenstein's immense riches, his profound reserve, and theatrical manners, were the principal means he employed to exalt the imagination of the masses. He always appeared in public surrounded by extraordinary pomp, and allowed all those attached to his house to share in his luxury. His officers

lived sumptuously at his table, where never less than one hundred dishes were served. As he rewarded with excessive liberality, not only the multitude but the greatest personages were dazzled by this Asiatic splendour. Six gates gave entrance to his palace at Prague, to make room for which he had pulled down one hundred houses. Similar châteaux were erected by his orders on all his numerous estates. Twenty-four chamberlains, sprung from the most noble families, disputed the honour of serving him, and some sent back the golden key, emblem of their grade, to the Emperor, in order that they might wait on Wallenstein. He educated sixty pages, dressed in blue velvet and gold, to whom he gave the first masters; fifty trabants guarded his antechamber night and day; six barons and the same number of chevaliers were constantly within call to bear his orders. His *maître-d'hôtel* was a person of distinction. A thousand persons usually formed his household, and about one thousand horses filled his stables, where they fed from marble mangers. When he set out on his travels, a hundred carriages, drawn by four or six horses, conveyed his servants and baggage; sixty carriages and fifty led horses carried the people of his suite; ten trumpeters with silver bugles preceded the procession. The richness of his liveries, the pomp of his equipages, and the decoration of his apartments, were in harmony with all the rest. In a hall of his palace at Prague he had himself painted in a triumphal car, with a wreath of laurels round his head, and a star above him.

'Wallenstein's appearance was enough in itself to inspire fear and respect. His tall thin figure, his haughty attitude, the stern expression of his pale face, his wide forehead, that seemed formed to command, his black hair, close-shorn and harsh, his little dark eyes, in which the flame of authority shone, his haughty and suspicious look, his thick moustaches and tufted beard, produced, at the first glance, a startling sensation. His usual dress consisted of a justaucorps of elk skin, covered by a white doublet and cloak; round his neck he wore a Spanish ruff; in his hat fluttered a large red plume, while scarlet pantaloons and boots of Cordova leather, carefully padded on account of the gout, completed his ordinary attire. While his army devoted itself to pleasure, the deepest silence reigned around the general. He could not endure the rumbling of carts, loud conversations, or even simple sounds. One of his chamberlains was hanged for waking him without orders, and an officer secretly put to death because his spurs had clanked when he came to the general. His servants glided about the rooms like phantoms, and a dozen patrols incessantly moved round his tent or palace to maintain perpetual tranquillity. Chains were also stretched across the streets, in order to guard him against any sound. Wallenstein was ever absorbed in himself, ever engaged with his plans and designs. He was never seen to smile, and his pride rendered him inaccessible to sensual pleasures. His only fanaticism was ambition. This strange chief meditated and acted incessantly, only taking counsel of himself, and disdaining strange advice and inspirations. When he gave any orders or explanations, he could not bear to be looked at curiously; when he crossed the camp, the soldiers were obliged to pretend that they did not see him. Yet they experienced an involuntary shudder when they saw him pass like a supernatural being. There was something about him mysterious, solemn, and awe-inspiring. He walked alone, surrounded by this magic influence, like a saddening halo.'

The end of Wallenstein was such as might have been anticipated. Becoming too formidable for a subject, he was denounced to the Emperor by Piccolomini, who obtained a commission to take the great general dead or alive. On the 25th of February 1634, he was assailed in the Castle of Eger by a band, in which were included one Gordon, a Scotsman, and one Butler, an Irishman, and fell under a single stroke of a partizan, dying in proud silence, as he had lived.

DEATH OF SIR CHRISTOPHER WREN.

Wren's long and useful life, although protracted by activity and temperance much beyond the usual term of man's existence, was brought to a close by an accident. After his dismissal from the office of Surveyor-General, he occupied a town residence in St James's-street, Piccadilly, and continued to superintend the repairs of Westminster Abbey. He also rented from the Crown a house at Hampton Court, where he often retired, and there he passed the greater part of the last five years of his life in study and contemplation. On his last journey from Hampton Court to London, he contracted a cold, which accelerated his death. The good old man had, in his latter days, accustomed himself to sleep a short time after his dinner, and on the 25th of February 1723, his servant, thinking his master had slept longer than usual, went into his room, and found him dead in his chair. He was in his ninety-first year.

The funeral of Wren was attended by an assemblage of honourable and distinguished personages, from his house in St James's-street to St Paul's Cathedral, where his remains were deposited in the crypt, adjoining to others of his family, in the recess of the south-eastern window, under the choir. His grave is covered with a black marble slab, with a short inscription in English; and on the western jamb of the window recess is a handsome tablet, with a Latin inscription written by the architect's son, Christopher, in which are the words, ' Lector, si monumentum quæris, circumspice,' which instruction, to ' look around,' has led to the conclusion that the tablet was intended for the body of the cathedral, where the public might read it. It is understood that the malice of the commissioners for rebuilding St Paul's pursued Wren beyond the grave, and condemned the explanatory epitaph to the crypt, where it could be read but by comparatively few persons. Many years afterwards, Mr Robert Mylne, architect, had a copy of the inscription placed over the marble screen to the choir, which has since been removed.

Wren adorned London with no fewer than forty public buildings, but was the worst paid architect of whom we have any record: his annual salary as architect of St Paul's was £200; and his pay for rebuilding the churches in the city was only £100 a year.

DR BUCHAN AND HIS ' DOMESTIC MEDICINE.'

Who has not heard of Buchan's *Domestic Medicine*, the medical Mentor, 'the guide, philosopher, and friend' of past generations, and scarcely yet superseded by Graham and Macaulay? This book, bearing on its title-page the epigraph, ' The knowledge of a disease is half its cure,' a sort of temptation to the reading of medical books in general, first appeared in 1769: it speedily obtained popularity by the plain and familiar style in which it is written; and no less than nineteen editions of the book, amounting to 80,000 copies, were sold during the author's life-time.

Dr Buchan, who was born in Roxburghshire, in 1729, long enjoyed a good London practice as a physician. He lived many years at the house of his son, Dr Alexander Buchan, No. 6, Percy-street, Bedford-square; and there he died, at the age of seventy-six: he was buried in the west cloister of Westminster Abbey church.

It was Buchan's practice to see patients at the Chapter Coffee-house, in Paternoster-row, where he usually might be found in ' the *Wittenagemot*,' a box in the north-east corner of the coffee-room. Though he was a high Tory, he heard the political discussions of the place with good humour, and commonly acted as a moderator, an office for which his fine physiognomy, and his venerable white hairs, highly qualified him. His son belonged to the same club or set, and though somewhat dogmatical, added to the variety and intelligence of the discussions, which, from the mixture of the company, were as various as the contents of a newspaper.

Of this same *Wittenagemot* Dr George Fordyce and Dr Gower were also members; and it was very amusing to hear them in familiar chat with Dr Buchan. On subjects of medicine they seldom agreed, and when such were started, they generally laughed at one another's opinions. They liberally patronised Chapter punch, which always bore a high reputation in London. If any one complained of being indisposed, Buchan would exclaim, ' Now, let me prescribe for you. Here, John or Isaac, bring a glass of punch for Mr ——, unless he likes brandy-and-water better. Take that, sir, and I'll warrant you'll soon be well—you're a peg too low, you want stimulus; and if one glass won't do, call for a second.'

The *Domestic Medicine* was written in Sheffield; and James Montgomery, in his *Memoirs*, relates the following particulars of the author: ' I remember seeing the old gentleman when I first went to London. He was of venerable aspect, neat in his dress, his hair tied behind with a large black ribbon, and a gold-headed cane in his hand, quite realizing my idea of an Esculapian dignitary.' Montgomery acknowledges that he never spoke to the Doctor, as he was quite out of his reach; but he looked upon him with respect, as a man who had published *a book.* In one of the Scottish editions of Buchan, there was an astounding misprint, in which a prescription containing *one hundred ounces of laudanum*, instead of that number of drops, is recommended.

In no other science does Pope's maxim that ' a little learning is a dangerous thing' hold so strongly as in medicine; for those who read medical works, professing to be popular, are almost certain to suppose themselves affected with every disease about which they read. They forthwith take alarm at the probable consequences, and having some lurking suspicion that they may have mistaken the symptoms, they follow the prescriptions laid down in their book in secret, lest they should bring themselves into open ridicule. Goethe shrewdly remarks: ' He who studies his body too much becomes diseased —his mind, becomes mad;' and there is an old Italian epitaph which, with a little amendment, would run thus: 'I was well—I wished to be better—*read medical books*—took medicine—and died.'

INVASION PANIC.

Towards the close of February 1744, the threatened invasion of England by the French, accompanied by the young Pretender, caused a general alarm throughout the kingdom, and all Roman Catholics were prohibited from appearing within ten miles of London. We had then three ships in the Downs; but the landing was expected to be in Essex or Suffolk. Walpole writes from the House of Commons, February 16th: ' We have come nearer to a crisis than I expected! After the various reports about the Brest squadron, it has proved that they are sixteen ships of the line off Torbay; in all probability to draw our fleet from Dunkirk, where they have two men-of-war, and sixteen large Indiamen to transport eight thousand foot and two thousand horse which are there in the town. There has been some difficulty to persuade the people of the imminence of our danger; but yesterday the King sent a message to both Houses to acquaint us that he has certain information of the young Pretender being in France, and of the designed invasion from thence, in concert with the disaffected here.' Immediately addresses were moved to assure the King of standing by him with lives and fortunes. All the troops were sent for, in the greatest haste, to London; and an express to Holland to demand six thousand men. On the 23rd, Walpole writes: 'There is no doubt of the invasion: the young Pretender is at Calais, and the Count de Saxe is to command the embarkation. Sir John Norris was to sail yesterday to Dunkirk, to try to burn their transports; we are in the utmost expectation of the news. The Brest squadron was yesterday on the coast of Sussex.' On the 25th of February, the English Channel fleet under Sir John Norris came within a league of the Brest squadron. Walpole says the coasts were covered with people to see the engagement; but at seven in the evening the wind changed, and the French fleet escaped. A violent storm shattered and wrecked the transports, and the expedition was glad to put back to Dunkirk. The dread of the invasion was then at an end.

With regard to ' the disaffected' mentioned

298

in the King's message, Mr. P. Yorke notes in his *Parliamentary Journal:* ' 1744, February 13. Talking upon this subject with Horace Walpole, he told me confidently that Admiral Matthews intercepted last summer a felucca in her passage from Toulon to Genoa, on board of which were found several papers of great consequence, relating to a French invasion in concert with the Jacobites; one of them particularly was in the style of an invitation from several of the nobility and gentry of England to the Pretender. These papers, he thought, had not been sufficiently looked into, and were not laid before the cabinet council until the night before the message was sent to both Houses.' The invasion designed for 1744 did not take place, but in the next year the young Pretender, as is well known, came with only seven men, and nearly overturned the government.

TIME—DAY—AND NIGHT.
By Geoffrey Whitney, 1589.

Two horses free, a third doth swiftly chase,
The one is white, the other black of hue;
None bridles have for to restrain their pace,
And thus they both the other still pursue;
　　And never cease continual course to make,
　　Until at length the first they overtake.

The foremost horse that runs so fast away,
It is our time, while here our race we run;
The black and white presenteth night and day,
Who after haste, until the goal be won;
　　And leave us not, but follow from our birth,
　　Until we yield, and turn again to earth.

FEBRUARY 26.

St Alexander, patriarch of Alexandria, 326. St Parphyrius, bishop of Gaza, 420. St Victor, of Champagne, 7th century.

Born.—Anthony Cooper, Earl of Shaftesbury, 1671, *Exeter House;* Rev. James Hervey, author of *Meditations*, 1714, *Hardingstone;* François J. D. Arago, natural philosopher, 1786; Victor Hugo, fictitious writer, 1802.

Died.—Manfred (of Tarento), killed, 1266; Robert Fabian, chronicler, 1513, *Cornhill;* Sir Nicholas Crispe, Guinea trader, 1665, *Hammersmith;* Thomas D'Urfey, wit and poet, 1723, *St James's;* Maximilian (of Bavaria), 1726, *Munich;* Joseph Tartiné, musical composer, 1770, *Padua;* Dr Alexander Geddes, theologian, 1802, *Paddington;* John Philip Kemble, actor, 1823, *Lausanne;* Dr William Kitchiner, *littérateur*, 1827, *St Pancras;* Sir William Allan, R.A., painter, 1850; Thomas Moore, lyric poet, 1852; Thomas Tooke, author of the *History of Prices*, &c., 1858, *London.*

ECCENTRICITIES OF DR KITCHINER.

Eccentricity in cookery-books is by no means peculiar to our time. We have all read of the oddities of Mrs Glasse's instructions; and most olden cookery-books savour of such humour, not to mention as oddities the receipts for doing out-of-the-way things, such as 'How to Roast a Pound of Butter,' which we find in the *Art of Cookery*, by a lady, 1748. To the humour of Dr Kitchiner in this way we doubtless owe a very good book —his *Cook's Oracle*, in which the instructions are given with so much come-and-read-me pleasantry and gossiping anecdote as to win the dullest reader. But Kitchiner was not a mere book-making cook: he practised what he taught, and he had ample means for the purpose. From his father, a coal-merchant in an extensive way of business in the Strand, he had inherited a fortune of £60,000 or £70,000, which was more than sufficient to enable him to work out his ideal of life.* His heart overflowed with benevolence and good humour, and no man better understood the art of making his friends happy. He shewed equal tact in his books: his *Cook's Oracle* is full of common-sense practice; and lest his reader should stray into excess, he wrote *The Art of Invigorating and Prolonging Life*, and a more useful book in times when railways were not—*The Traveller's Oracle, and Horse and Carriage Keeper's Guide*. With his ample fortune, Kitchiner was still an economist, and wrote a *Housekeeper's Ledger*, and a coaxing volume entitled *The Pleasures of Making a Will*. He also wrote on astronomy, telescopes, and spectacles. In music he was a proficient; and in 1820, at the coronation of George IV., he published a collection of the *National Songs of Great Britain*, a folio volume, with a splendid dedication plate to His Majesty. Next he edited *The Sea Songs of Charles Dibdin*. But, merrily and wisely as Kitchiner professed to live, he had scarcely reached his fiftieth year when he was taken from the circle of friends. At this time he resided at No. 43, Warren-street, Fitzroy-square. On the 26th of February he joined a large dinner-party given by Mr Braham, the celebrated singer: he had been in high spirits, and had enjoyed the company to a later hour than his usually early habits allowed. Mathews was present, and rehearsed a portion of a new comic entertainment, which induced Kitchiner to amuse the party with some of his whimsical reasons for inventing odd things, and giving them odd names. He returned home, was suddenly taken ill, and in an hour he was no more!

Though always an epicure, and fond of experiments in cookery, and exceedingly particular in the choice of his viands, and in their mode of preparation for the table, Kitchiner was regular, and even abstemious, in his general habits. His dinners were cooked according to his own method; he dined at five; supper was

* The Doctor's father was a Roman Catholic, and in the riots of 1780, Beaufort-buildings, in the Strand, were filled with soldiers to protect Kitchiner's coal-wharf in the rear of the buildings by the river-side.

served at half-past nine; and at eleven he retired. Every Tuesday evening he gave a *conversazione* at which he delighted to bring together professors and amateurs of the sciences and the polite arts. For the regulation of the party the Doctor had a placard over his drawing-room chimney-piece, inscribed 'Come at seven, go at eleven.' It is said that George Colman the younger, being introduced to Kitchiner on one of his evenings, and reading this admonition, found an opportunity to insert in the placard after 'go' the pronoun 'it,' which, it must be admitted, materially

WILLIAM KITCHINER, M.D.

altered the reading. In these social meetings, when the Doctor's servant gave the signal for supper, those who objected to take other than tea or coffee departed; and those who remained descended to the dining-room, to partake of his friendly fare. A cold joint, a lobster salad, and some little *entremets*, usually formed the summer repast; in winter some nicely-cooked hot dishes were set upon the board, with wine, *liqueurs*, and ales from a well-stocked cellar. Such were the orderly habits at these evening parties, that, 'on the stroke of eleven,' hats, umbrellas, &c., were brought in, and the Doctor attended his guests to the street-door, where, first looking at the stars, he would give them a cordial shake of the hand, and a hearty 'good night,' as they severally departed.

Kitchiner's public dinners, as they may be termed, were things of more pomp, ceremony, and etiquette: they were announced by notes of invitation, as follows:—

'Dear Sir,—The honour of your company is requested, to dine with the Committee of Taste, on Wednesday next, the 10th instant.

'The specimens will be placed on the table at five o'clock precisely, when the business of the day will immediately commence.

'I have the honour to be
'Your most obedient Servant,
'W. KITCHINER, Sec.

August, 1825,
'43, Warren-street, Fitzroy-square.

'At the last general meeting, it was unanimously resolved—that

'1st. An invitation to ETA BETA PI must be answered in writing, as soon as possible after it is received—within twenty-four hours at latest, —reckoning from that at which it was dated; otherwise the secretary will have the profound regret to feel that the invitation has been definitely declined.

'2nd. The secretary having represented that the perfection of the several preparations is so exquisitely evanescent that the delay of *one minute*, after the arrival at the meridian of concoction, will render them no longer worthy of men of taste:

'Therefore, to ensure the punctual attendance of those illustrious gastrophilists who, on this occasion, are invited to join this high tribunal of taste—for their own pleasure, and the benefit of their country—it is irrevocably resolved—"That the janitor be ordered not to admit any visitor, of whatever eminence of appetite, after the hour at which the secretary shall have announced that the specimens are ready."

'By Order of the Committee,
'W. KITCHINER, Sec.'

At the last party given by the Doctor on the 20th February, as the first three that were bidden entered his drawing-room, he received them seated at his grand pianoforte, with 'See the Conquering Hero comes!' accompanying the air by placing his feet on the pedals, with a peal on the kettle-drums beneath the instrument. Alas, the conquering hero was not far off!

The accompanying whole-length portrait of Dr Kitchiner has been engraved from a well-executed mezzotint—a private plate—'painted and engraved by C. Turner, engraver in ordinary to His Majesty.' The skin of the stuffed tiger on the floor of the room was brought from Africa by Major Denham, and presented by him to his friend Kitchiner.

SUSPENSION OF CASH PAYMENTS IN 1797.

In the great war which England commenced against France in 1793, the first four years saw

two hundred millions added to the national debt, without any material advantage being gained: on the contrary, France had become more formidable than at first, had made great acquisitions, and was now less disposed to peace than ever. So much coin had left the country for the payment of troops abroad, and as subsidies to allies, that the Bank during 1796 began to feel a difficulty in satisfying the demands made upon it. At the close of the year, the people began to hoard coin, and to make a run upon the country banks. These applied to the Bank of England for help, and the consequence was, that a run upon it commenced in the latter part of February 1797. This great establishment could only keep itself afloat by paying in sixpences. Notwithstanding the sound state of its ultimate resources, its immediate insolvency was expected,—an event the consequences of which must have been dreadful. In that exigency, the Government stepped in with an order in council (February 26), authorizing the notes of the bank as a legal tender, until such time as proper remedies could be provided.

This suspension of cash payments by the Bank of England—a virtual insolvency—was attended by the usual effect of raising the nominal prices of all articles; and, of course, it deranged reckonings between creditors and debtors. It was believed, however, to be an absolutely indispensable step, and the Conservative party always regarded it as the salvation of the country. A return to cash payments was from the first promised and expected to take place in a few months; but, as is well known, King Paper reigned for twenty-two years. During most of that time, a guinea bought twenty-seven shillings worth of articles. It was just one of the dire features of the case that even a return to what should never have been departed from, could not be effected without a new evil; for of course, whereas creditors were in the first instance put to a disadvantage, debtors were so now. The public debt was considered as enhanced a third by the act of Sir Robert Peel for the resumption of cash payments, and all private obligations rose in the same proportion.

On a review of English history during the last few years of the eighteenth century, one gets an idea that there was little sound judgment and much recklessness in the conduct of public affairs; but the spirit of the people was unconquerable, and to that a very poor set of administrators were indebted for eventual successes which they did not deserve.

NELSON AND THE SPANISH ADMIRAL'S SWORD.

In the council-chamber of the Guildhall, Norwich, is a glass case containing a sword, along with a letter shewing how the weapon came there. When, in the midst of unexampled national distress, and an almost general mutiny of the sailors, the English fleet under Sir John Jervis engaged and beat the much superior fleet of Spain off Cape St Vincent, February 14, 1797, Captain Nelson, in his ship the *Captain*, seventy-four, disabled several vessels, and received the surrender of one, the *San Josef*, from its commander, after having boarded it. [This unfortunate officer soon after died of his wounds.] It would appear that, a few days after the action, Nelson bethought him of a proper place to which to assign the keeping of the sword of the Spanish commander, and he determined on sending it to the chief town of his native county. This symbol of victory accordingly came to the Mayor of Norwich, accompanied by a letter which is here exactly transcribed :

Irresistible, off Lisbon, Feb. 26th, 1797.

Sir,

Having the good fortune on the most glorious 14th February to become possessed of the sword of the Spanish Rear Admiral Don Xavier Francesco Wintheysen in the way sett forth in the paper transmitted herewith

And being Born in the County of Norfolk, I beg leave to present the sword to the City of Norwich in order to its being preserved as a memento of this event. and of my affection for my native County.

I have the honor to Be, Sir, your most Obedient servant, HORATIO NELSON.

To the Mayor of Norwich.

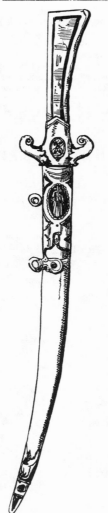

SPANISH COMMANDER'S SWORD, PRESENTED BY NELSON TO NORWICH.

CHURCH BELLS.

Large bells in England are mentioned by Bede as early as A.D. 670. A complete peal, however, does not occur till nearly 200 years later, when Turketul, abbot of Croyland, in Lincolnshire, presented his abbey with a great bell, which was called Guthlac, and afterwards added six others, named Pega, Bega, Bettelin, Bartholomew, Tatwin, and Turketul. At this early period, and for some centuries later, bell-founding, like other scientific crafts, was carried on by the monks. Dunstan, who was a skilful artificer, is recorded by Ingulph as having presented bells to the western churches. When in after times bell-founding became a regular trade, some founders were itinerant, travelling from place to place, and stopping where they found business ; but the majority had settled works in large towns. Among other places London, Gloucester, Salis-

bury, Bury St Edmunds, Norwich, and Colchester have been the seats of eminent foundries.

Bells were anciently consecrated, before they were raised to their places, each being dedicated to some divine personage, saint, or martyr. The ringing of such bells was considered efficacious in dispersing storms, and evil spirits were supposed to be unable to endure their sound. Hence the custom of ringing the 'passing bell' when any one was *in articulo mortis*, in order to scare away fiends who might otherwise molest the departing spirit, and also to secure the prayers of such pious folk as might chance to be within hearing. An old woman once related to the writer, how, after the death of a wicked squire, his spirit came and *sat upon the bell*, so that all the ringers together could not toll it. The bell-cots, so common on the gable-ends of our old churches, in former times contained each a 'Sancte' bell, so called from its being rung at the elevation of the host ; one may be seen, still hanging in its place, at Over, Cambridgeshire.

It is scarcely probable that any bells now remain in this country of date prior to the 14th or at most the 13th century, and of the most ancient of these the age can only be ascertained approximately, the custom of inserting the date in the inscription (which each bell almost invariably bears) not having obtained until late in the 16th century.

The very old bells expand more gradually from crown to rim than the modern ones, which splay out somewhat abruptly towards the mouth. It may be added that the former are almost invariably of excellent tone, and as a rule far superior to those cast now-a-days. There is a popular idea that this is in consequence of the older founders adding silver to their bell-metal ; but recent experiments have shewn that the presence of silver spoils instead of improving the tone, in direct proportion to the quantity employed.

A cockney is usually defined as a person born within hearing of Bow bells ; Stow, however, who died early in 1605, nowhere mentions this notion, so that it is probably of more recent origin. The Bow bell used to be rung regularly at nine o'clock at night ; and by will dated 1472, one John Donne, Mercer, left two tenements with appurtenances, to the maintenance of Bow bell. 'This bell being usually rung somewhat late, as seemed to the young men 'prentices and other in Cheape, they made and set up a rhyme against the clerk, as followeth :

' Clarke of the Bow bell with the yellow locks,
  For thy late ringing thy head shall have knocks.'

Whereunto the clerk replying, wrote—

' Children of Cheape, hold you all still,
  For you shall have the Bow bell rung at your will.'*

One of the finest bits of word-painting in Shakspeare occurs in the mention of a bell, where King John, addressing Hubert, says

     ' If the midnight bell
Did with his iron tongue and brazen mouth
Sound one unto the drowsy race of night.'

Here ' brazen' implies not merely that particular mixture of copper and calamine, called brass,

    * Stow's *Survey of London.*

but in a broader sense, any metal which is compounded with copper. This acceptation of the term is noticed by Johnson, and in confirmation occurs the fact that the name of *Brasyer* was borne of old by an eminent family of east-country bell-founders; being, like Bowyer, Miller, Webber, &c. &c., a trade-name, *i.e.* derived from the occupation of the bearer.

The inscriptions on the oldest bells are in the Lombardic and black-letter characters, the former probably the more ancient; the black-letter was superseded by the ordinary Roman capitals, towards the close of the sixteenth century. Even later, however, than this, some founders employed a sort of imitation of the old Lombardic. The following are genuine Lombardic inscriptions:

SALVET NVNC ADAM QVI CVNC ACREAVIT ET ADAM ∗

NAC CAMPANELLA COLITUR RATERINA PUELLA

SANCT ANDREU IS MI NAME

The next ten are transcripts of black-letter inscriptions.

'Sum Rosa Pulsata Mundi Katerina Vocata.'
'Est Michi Collatum, Ihē istud nomen amatum.'
'Plebs ōis plaudit ut me tam sepius audit.'
'Stella Maria Maris Succurre Piissime Nobis.'
'Virginis Egregie Vocor Campana Marie.'
'Xpō Perpetue Det Nobis Gaudia Vite.'

　∗ Salvet nunc Adam qui cuncta creavit et Adam.

'Me Melior bere, non est Campana sub ere.'
'In Multis annis resonat Campana Johannis.'
'Fac Margareta Nobis Hæc Munera Leta.'
'Laudem Resono Michael.'

The commonest black-letter inscription is a simple invocation, as 'Ave Maria,' or 'Sancte ———, ora pro nobis.' After the Reformation these invocations of course disappeared, and founders then more frequently placed their names on the bells, with usually some rhyme or senti-

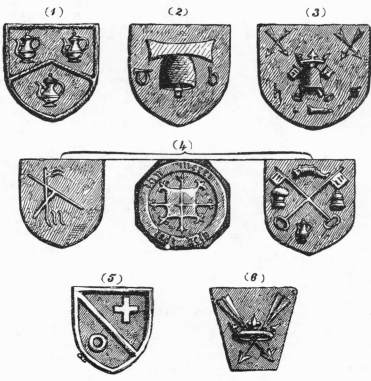

(1)　　　(2)　　　(3)

(4)

(5)　　　(6)

ANCIENT BELL FOUNDRY STAMPS.

ment, which, as some of the following specimens will prove, is often sad doggrel :—

'This bell was broake and cast againe. as plainly doth appeare,
John Draper made me in 1618, wich tyme chvrch-wardens were
Edward Dixson for the one, whoe stode close to his tacklin,
And he that was his partner there was Alexander Jacklin.'

'Of all the bells in Benet I am the best,
And yet for my casting the parish paid lest.'

'Repent, I say, be not too late,
Thyself al times redy make.'

'I value not who doth me see,
For Thomas Bilbie casted me ;
All tho my voice it is but small
I will be heard among you all.'

'My sound is good, which that you hear,
Young Bilbie * made me sound so clear.'

'My treble voice your hearts rejoice.'

'Let us all sound out,
Ile keep my place no doubt.'

'Hethatwilpvrchashonorsgaynemvstancient lathers [sic] stillmayntayne.'

Four bells at Graveley, Cambridgeshire, are thus inscribed :—

'*Treble.* God of his marce heareth us all,
2.   Whenvpon that we do call.
3.   O priese the Lord thearefore I say,
Tenor. I sound vnto the living when the sovle doth part way.'

The older founders, as we have seen, seldom placed their names on their bells ; yet the black-letter and later Lombardic inscriptions are often accompanied by their *Foundry-stamps*, or trade marks, some specimens of which are engraved above: (1) Occurs on two bells at Brent-Tor, Devon, and elsewhere ; the three vessels so like coffee-pots are founders' lave-pots. (2) Is supposed to be the stamp of a London foundry ; it may be seen on four bells at St Bartholomew's, Smith-field. (3) Is the stamp of a Bury St Edmund's foundry ; the gun and bullet indicate that H. S. was also a gun-founder. (6) Is the mark of Stephen Tonni, who founded at Bury about 1570. The crown and arrows are typical of the martyr-dom of St Edmund.

During the Civil War, many church bells were melted down and cast into cannon. Not quite so honourable was the end of four large bells which once, hung in a clockier or clock-tower in St Paul's Cathedral, which tower was pulled down by Sir Miles Partridge in the reign of Henry VIII., and the common speech then was that 'he did set a hundred pounds upon a cast of dice against it, and so won the said clockier and bells of the King, and then causing the bells to be broken as they hung, the rest was pulled down.'†

* These Bilbies were great west-country founders. One of them is said to have committed suicide because he could not get Cullompton bells in tune.
† Stow's *Survey of London.*

THE SILENT TOWER OF BOTTREAUX.*

The church at Boscastle, in Cornwall, has no bells, while the neighbouring tower of Tintagel contains a fine peal of six ; it is said that a peal of bells for Boscastle was once cast at a foundry on the Continent, and that the vessel which was bringing them went down within sight of the church tower. The Cornish folk have a legend on this subject, which has been embodied in the following stanzas by Mr Hawker:

Tintagel bells ring o'er the tide,
The boy leans on his vessel's side,
He hears that sound, and dreams of home
Soothe the wild orphan of the foam
  ' Come to thy God in time,'
    Thus saith their pealing chime ;
  ' Youth, manhood, old age past,
    Come to thy God at last.'

But why are Bottreaux's echoes still ?
Her tower stands proudly on the hill,
Yet the strange chough that home hath found,
The lamb lies sleeping on the ground.
  ' Come to thy God in time,'
    Should be her answering chime ;
  ' Come to thy God at last,'
    Should echo on the blast.

The ship rode down with courses free,
The daughter of a distant sea,
Her sheet was loose, her anchor stored,
The merry Bottreaux bells on board.
  ' Come to thy God in time,'
    Rung out Tintagel chime ;
  ' Youth, manhood, old age past,
    Come to thy God at last.'

The pilot heard his native bells
Hang on the breeze in fitful spells.
' Thank God,' with reverent brow, he cried,
' We make the shore with evening's tide.'
  ' Come to thy God in time,'
    It was his marriage chime ;
  ' Youth, manhood, old age past,
    Come to thy God at last.'

' Thank God, thou whining knave, on land,
But thank at sea the steersman's hand,'
The captain's voice above the gale,
' Thank the good ship and ready sail.'
  ' Come to thy God in time,'
    Sad grew the boding chime ;
  ' Come to thy God at last,'
    Boomed heavy on the blast.

Up rose that sea, as if it heard
The Mighty Master's signal word.
What thrills the captain's whitening lip?
The death-groans of his sinking ship.
  ' Come to thy God in time,'
    Swung deep the funeral chime,
  ' Grace, mercy, kindness, past—
    Come to thy God at last.'

Long did the rescued pilot tell,
When grey hairs o'er his forehead fell,
While those around would hear and weep,
That fearful judgment of the deep.
  ' Come to thy God in time,'
    He read his native chime ;
  ' Youth, manhood, old age past,
    Come to thy God at last.'

* Bottreaux is the old name for Boscastle.

Still, when the storm of Bottreaux's waves
Is waking in his weedy caves,
Those bells, that sullen surges hide,
Peal their deep tones beneath the tide.
' Come to thy God in time,'
Thus saith the ocean chime ;
' Storm, whirlwind, billow past,
Come to thy God at last.'

THE ROOKS AND NEW STYLE.

The 26th of February, N.S., corresponds to the day which used to be assigned for the rooks beginning to search for materials for their nests, namely, the twelfth day after Candlemas, O.S.

The Rev. Dr Waugh used to relate that, on his return from the first year's session at the University of Edinburgh, his father's gardener undertook to give him a few lessons in natural history. Among other things, he told him that the 'craws' (rooks) always began building twelve days after Candlemas. Wishful to shew off his learning, young Waugh asked the old man if the craws counted by the old or by the new style, just then introduced by Act of Parliament. Turning upon the young student a look of contempt, the old gardener said—'Young man, craws care naething for acts of parliament.'

FEBRUARY 27.

St Nestor, bishop in Pamphylia, martyr, 250. Saints Julian, Chronion, and Besas, martyrs, 3rd century. St Thalilæus, 5th century. St Leander, bishop of Seville, 596. St Galmier, of Lyons, about 650. St Alnoth, of England, martyr, about 7th century.

Born.—George Morley, bishop of Winchester, 1597, *Cheapside ;* John David Michaelis, Orientalist, 1717, *Halle ;* James Robinson Planché, *littérateur*, 1796, *London ;* Lord William George Frederick Bentinck, 1802 ; Henry W. Longfellow, poet, 1807.

Died.—The Emperor Geta, murdered, 212 ; Philip Nye, Nonconformist, 1673, *London ;* John Evelyn, diarist, 1706, *Wotton ;* Dr John Arbuthnot, 1735, *Cork-street, London ;* Sir John B. Warren, G.C.B., 1822 ; William Woolnoth, engraver, 1837.

JOHN EVELYN, THE DIARIST.

This excellent man,—the perfect model of an English gentleman of the seventeenth century, and known as ' Sylva Evelyn,' from his work with that title, on Forest Trees—was born of an ancient and honourable family, at Wotton House, in Surrey, on the 31st of October 1620. At four years old, he was taught to read by one Frier, in the church porch, at Wotton. He next learnt Latin in a school at Lewes, in Sussex ; his father proposed sending him to Eton, but was deterred from doing so by the report of the severe discipline in that school. He completed his education at Balliol College, Oxford ; and in 1640 was entered at the Middle Temple, London, but soon relinquished what he calls ' the unpolished study ' of the law. Having stored his mind with travel and study, he entered on a long career of active, useful, and honourable employment. He was not, however, without some share in the intrigues connected with the Restoration of Charles the Second, after which he was often at court. On the foundation of the Royal Society,

in 1662, he was appointed one of the fellows, and a member of the council. Among the various official duties to which he was appointed, was the commissionership for building Greenwich Hospital, the first stone of which edifice he laid on the 30th of June 1696.

But the delight of Evelyn was in the pursuits of rural economy. He was the great improver of English gardening, and first laid out his gardens at Sayes Court, Deptford, which he let to the Czar Peter the Great, who damaged them to the extent of £150 in three weeks. Evelyn then retired to his paternal home at Wotton, ' sweetly environed with delicious streams and venerable woods,' the latter valued at £100,000. His love of planting, and the want of timber for the navy, led him to write his *Sylva ; a Discourse on Forest Trees*, the first book printed by order of the Royal Society ; it led to the planting of many millions of forest trees, and is one of the very few books in the world which completely effect what they were designed to do. Another valuable work by Evelyn is his *Diary, or Kalendarium*, a most interesting picture of the time in which he lived, and the manuscript of which was accidentally saved from being used as waste paper. Evelyn's *Diary* is, however, an after compilation : unlike Pepys's *Diary*, which is an unstudied record from day to day.

John Evelyn died in his 86th year, at his town house, called *The Head*, in Dover-street, Piccadilly, on the 27th of February 1705-6 : his remains rest in a raised coffin-shaped tomb in Wotton Church, where also is interred his estimable wife, the daughter of Sir Richard Browne.

THE FIRST RUSSIAN EMBASSY TO ENGLAND.

February 27, 1557-8, the first Russian embassy arrived in the neighbourhood of London. It came in rather remarkable circumstances. The Russian Emperor, Ivan Vasilivich, thought the time had now arrived when his country ought to enter upon formal commercial relations with England. He therefore charged a noble named Osep Napea to proceed thither with a goodly company, and bearing suitable presents for ' the famous and excellent princes, Philip and Mary, King and Queen of England.' It appears that among the gifts were a number of the skins of the sable, with the teeth, ears, and claws of the animal preserved, four living sables, with chains and collars, ' thirty luzarnes rich and beautiful,' six great skins such as the emperor himself wore, and a great jer-falcon, with a silver drum used for a lure to it in hawking.

The expedition sailed in several English vessels from the port of St Nicolas, in Russia, but was very unfortunate in the voyage. Several vessels being thrown away, or forced to seek shelter on the coast of Norway, one called the *Edward Bonaventure*, containing the ambassador, arrived with difficulty, after a four months' voyage, on the east coast of Aberdeenshire, in Scotland, along with a smaller vessel, called her pink. There they were driven ashore by a violent storm, near Kinnaird Head, when a boat containing the grand pilot, with the ambassador and seven other Russian gentlemen, making for land in the dark, was overwhelmed and beaten on the rocks : thus the pilot and several of the Russians and mariners were drowned, and only the ambassador himself and two or three others were saved. The ship became a total wreck, and such of her valuable goods as came on shore, including the gifts to the English monarchs, were pillaged by the rude people of the coast ; but the ambassador and his small company were speedily received under care of the gentry of the district, and treated with the greatest kindness.

Stow relates in his *Chronicle*—'As soon as it was known to the company in London of the loss of their pilot, men, goods, and ships, the merchants obtained the Queen's letters to the Lady Dowager of Scotland [Mary of Lorraine, widow of James V., and Regent of the kingdom], for the gentle entertainment of the said ambassador with his train, and restitution of his goods, and also addressed two gentlemen, Mr Laurence Hassey, Doctor of the Civil Law, and George Gilpin, with money and other requisites, into Scotland, to comfort him and his there, and also to conduct him into England.'

We learn from a contemporary Scottish writer, Bishop Lesley, that the ambassador and his friends were brought to Edinburgh, and there entertained handsomely by the Queen Regent for some time ; after which they set out for Berwick, attended by Lord Hume on the part of the Queen, and accompanied by the two English gentlemen who had come for their succour, besides 500 gentlemen of Scotland on horseback. Arriving within twelve miles of London on the 27th February 1557-8, the Russian ambassador was there received in formal style by eighty merchants, in goodly apparel, and with chains of gold, all mounted on horseback, by whom he was conducted to a merchant's house, four miles from the city, and there honourably lodged. ' Next day,' says Stow, ' he was, by the merchant adventurers for Russia, to the number of 140 persons, and so many or more servants in one livery, conducted towards the city of London, where by the way he had not only the hunting of the fox, &c., but also, by the Queen's Majesty's commandment was received by the Viscount Montague ; he, being accompanied by divers lusty knights, esquires, gentlemen, and yeomen, to the number of 300 horses, led him to the north parts of the city of London, where, by four merchants richly apparelled, was presented to him a fair, richly-trapped horse, together with a footcloth of crimson velvet, enriched with gold laces ; whereupon the ambassador mounted, riding toward Smithfield bars, the Lord Mayor, accompanied with the aldermen in scarlet, did receive him, and so riding through the city of London, between the Lord Mayor and Viscount Montague, a great number of merchants and notable persons riding before, was conducted to his lodgings in Fenchurch-street, &c. &c.

' At his first entrance into his chamber, there was presented unto him on the Queen's behalf, for a gift and present, one rich piece of cloth of tissue, a piece of cloth of gold, another piece of cloth of gold raised with crimson velvet, a piece

of crimson velvet in grain, a piece of purple velvet, a piece of damask purpled, a piece of crimson damask ; which he thankfully accepted.'

It was not till the 25th of March, exactly a twelvemonth after his taking leave of his master, that he came before the English court. Being conducted by water to Westminster, he was there honourably received by six lords, who conducted him into a chamber, where he was saluted by the Lord Chancellor, the Treasurer, Privy Seal, the Admiral, the Bishop of Ely, and other counsellors. Then he was brought into the presence of the King and Queen, ' sitting under a stately cloth of honour,' and permitted to make his oration, and deliver his letters. Two days after, the Bishop of Ely and Sir William Peter, chief secretary, came to his lodging and concluded the commercial treaty which was desired by his master.

On the 3rd of May, having received sundry rich gifts for the Muscovian Emperor, including the singular one of a pair of lions, male and female, Osep Napea departed from the Thames in four goodly ships full of English merchandise. ' It is to be remarked,' says Stow, ' that during the whole abode of the said ambassador in England, the company of merchants did frankly give to him and his all manner of costs and charges in victuals, riding from Scotland to London, during his abode there, and until setting of sail aboard of ship.'

FEBRUARY 28.

Martyrs who died of the great pestilence in Alexandria, 261-3. St Romanus, about 460, and St Lupicinus, abbots, 479. St Proterius, patriarch of Alexandria, martyr, 557.

Born.—Michael de Montaigne, essayist, 1533, *Perigord ;* Henry Stubbe, ' the most noted Latinist and Grecian of his age,' 1631, *Partney ;* Dr Daniel Solander, naturalist, 1736, *Nordland, Sweden.*

Died.—Humphrey, Duke of Gloucester, murdered, 1447, *St Albans ;* George Buchanan, historian, 1582, *Edinburgh ;* Christian IV. (of *Denmark*), 1646 ; Edward Moore, dramatist, 1757 ; Dr Richard Grey, 1771.

MRS SUSAN CROMWELL.

On the 28th of February 1834, died, at the age of ninety, Mrs Susan Cromwell, youngest daughter of Thomas Cromwell, Esq., the great-grandson of the Protector. She was the last of the Protector's descendants who bore his name. The father of this lady, whose grandfather, Henry Cromwell, had been Lord Lieutenant of Ireland, spent his life in the modest business of a grocer on Snow-hill ; he was, however, a man of exemplary worth, fit to have adorned a higher station. His father, who was a major in King William's army, had been born in Dublin Castle during his father's lieutenancy.

It may be remarked that the family of the Lord Protector Oliver Cromwell was one of good account, his uncle and godfather, Sir Oliver Cromwell, possessing estates in Huntingdonshire alone which were afterwards worth £30,000 a-year. The Protector's mother, by an odd chance, was named Stewart; but it is altogether imaginary that she bore any traceable relationship to the royal family. The race was originally Welsh, and bore the name of Williams; but the great-grandfather of the Protector changed it to Cromwell, in compliance with a wish of Henry VIII., taking that particular name in honour of his relation, Thomas Cromwell, Earl of Essex.

INSTITUTION OF THE ORDER OF ST PATRICK.

On the 28th of February 1783, George III. signed at St James's the statutes constituting the Order of St Patrick. The forming of this order of knighthood was prompted by the recent appearances of a national Irish spirit which would no longer sit patiently under neglect and misgovernment. It was thought by the new cabinet of Lord Shelburne a good policy to seek to conciliate the principal peers of Ireland by conferring marks of distinction upon them. The whole arrangements were after the model of those of the Order of the Garter. Besides the King as 'Sovereign,' there were a Grand Master, and fifteen Companions (since extended to twenty-two), besides a Chancellor, a Registrar, a Secretary, a Genealogist, an Usher, and a King-at-Arms, a Prelate being afterwards added. The first companions elected were the Prince Edward (afterwards Duke of Kent, father of Queen Victoria), the Duke of Leinster, and thirteen Earls of Ireland, amongst whom was the Earl of Mornington, afterwards Marquis Wellesley, eldest brother of the Duke of Wellington. Proper dresses and insignia were ordered for the knights and officers, and the hall of Dublin Castle, under the new name of ST PATRICK'S HALL, was assigned as their place of meeting. It was designed, of course, as a concession to the national feelings, that the order was named from St Patrick, the tutelar saint of Ireland, and that the cross of St Patrick (a red saltire), and a golden harp, the ancient Irish ensign, together with the national badge, the shamrock or trefoil, to which the saint had given celebrity, were made its principal symbols.

It will surprise no one, not even amongst the people of the sister island itself, and probably it will amuse many, that a few anomalous circumstances attended the formation of the order of St Patrick. First, the saint's 'day' was not chosen for the institution of the order, and is not celebrated by them. Second, the Grand Master, though entitled to preside in absence of the sovereign, is not necessarily a member of the order. Further, the secretary has no duties (though he draws fees); the letters patent of foundation are not known to exist (no one can tell if they ever passed the great seal either of England or Ireland); and there are no arrangements for degradation or expulsion.*

ODDITIES OF FAMILY HISTORY.

Human life and its relations have certain tolerably well-marked bounds, which, however, are sometimes overpassed in a surprising manner.

One of the most ancient observations regarding

* Nicholas's *History of the Orders of Knighthood of the British Empire*, iv. 3-92.

human life, and one yet found acceptable to our sense of truth, is that a life passed healthily, and unexposed to disastrous accident, will probably extend to seventy years. Another is that there are usually just about three generations in a century. And hence it arises that one generation is usually approaching the grave when the third onward is coming into existence:—in other words, a man is usually well through his life when his son's children are entering it, or a man's son is usually near the tomb about a hundred years after his own birth,—a century rounding the mortal span of two generations and seeing a third arrived at the connubial period.

It is well known, nevertheless, that some men live much beyond seventy years, and that more than three generations are occasionally seen in life at one time.

Dr Plot, in his *Natural History of Staffordshire*, 1686, gives many instances of centenarians of his time, and of persons who got to a few years beyond the hundred,—how far well authenticated we cannot tell. He goes on to state the case of 'old Mary Cooper of King's Bromley in this county, not long since dead, who lived to be a *beldam*, that is, to see the sixth generation, and could say the same I have,' says he, 'heard reported of another, viz. " *Rise up, daughter, and go to thy daughter, for thy daughter's daughter hath a daughter;*" whose eldest daughter Elizabeth, now living, is like to do the same, there being a female of the fifth generation near marriageable when I was there. Which is much the same that Zuingerus reports of a noble matron of the family of Dolburges, in the archbishopric of Mentz, who could thus speak to her daughter:

" (1) Mater ait (2) natæ, Dic (3) natæ, Filia, (4) natam
Ut moveat, (5) natæ flangere (6) filiolam."

That is, the mother said to her daughter, daughter bid thy daughter tell her daughter, that her daughter's daughter cries.'

He adduces, as a proof how far this case is from being difficult of belief, that a Lady Child of Shropshire, being married at twelve, had her first baby before she was complete thirteen, and this being repeated in the second generation, Lady Child found herself a grandmother at twenty-seven! At the same rate, she might have been a *beldam* at sixty-six; and had she reached 120, as has been done by others, it was possible that *nine* generations might have existed together!

Not much less surprising than these cases is one which Horace Walpole states in a letter dated 1785 to his friend Horace Mann: 'There is a circumstance,' he says, 'which makes me think myself an antediluvian. I have literally seen seven descents in one family. . . . I was schoolfellow of the two last Earls of Waldegrave, and used to go to play with them in the holidays, when I was about twelve years old. They lived with their grandmother, natural daughter of James II. One evening when I was there, came in her mother Mrs Godfrey, that king's mistress, ancient in truth, and so superannuated, that she scarce seemed to know where she was. I saw her another time in her chair in St James's Park, and have a perfect idea of her face, which was pale, round, and sleek. Begin with her; then count her daughter, Lady Waldegrave; then the latter's son the ambassador; his daughter Lady Harriet Beard, her daughter, the present Countess Dowager of Powis, and her daughter Lady Clive; there are six, and the seventh now lies in of a son, and might have done so six or seven years ago, had she married at fourteen. When one has beheld such a pedigree, one may say, "And yet I am not sixty-seven!"'

While two generations, moreover, are usually disposed of in one hundred years, there are many instances of their extending over a much longer space of time. In our late article on the connection of distant ages by the lives of individuals, the case of James Horrox was cited, in which the father was born in 1657, and the son died in 1844, being eighty-seven years beyond the century. Benjamin Franklin, who died in 1790, was the grandson of a man who had been born in the sixteenth century, during the reign of Elizabeth, three generations thus extending over nearly two centuries. The connubial period of most men is eminently between twenty-eight and forty; but if men delay marriage to seventy, or undertake second or third nuptials at that age with young women—both of them events which sometimes happen—it must arise, as a matter of course, that not a century, but a century and a half, or even more, will become the bounds of two generations. The following instance speaks for itself. 'Wednesday last,' says the *Edinburgh Courant* of May 3, 1766, 'the lady of Sir William Nicolson, of Glenbervy, was safely delivered of a daughter. What is very singular, Sir William is at present ninety-two years of age, and has a daughter alive of his first marriage, aged sixty-six. He married his present lady when he was eighty-two, by whom he has now had six children.' If the infant here mentioned had survived to ninety-two also, she might have said at her death, in 1858, 'My father was born a hundred and eighty-four years ago, in the reign of Charles II.'

There are also average bounds to the number of descendants which a man or a woman may reckon before the close of life. To see three, four, or five children, and three or four times the number of grandchildren, are normal experiences. Some pairs, however, as is well known, go much beyond three, four, or five. Some marry a second, or even a third time, and thus considerably extend the number of the immediate progeny. In these cases, of course, the number of grandchildren is likely to be greatly extended. Particular examples are on record, that are certainly calculated to excite a good deal of surprise. Thus we learn from a French scientific work that the wife of a baker at Paris produced one-and-twenty children—at only seven births, moreover, and in the space of seven years! Boyle tells of a French advocate of the sixteenth century who had forty-five children. He is, by-the-bye, spoken of as a great water-drinker—'aquæ Tiraquellus amator.' We learn regarding Catherine Leighton, a lady of the time of Queen Elizabeth, that she married in succession husbands named Wygmore, Lymmer, Collard, and Dodge, and had children by all four; but we do not learn how many.

Thomas Urquhart of Cromarty and his wife Helen Abernethy—the grandparents of that singular genius Sir Thomas Urquhart, the translator of *Rabelais*—are stated to have had thirty-six children, twenty-five of them sons, and they lived to see the whole of this numerous progeny well provided for. 'The sons were men of great reputation, partly on account of their father's, and partly for their own personal merits. The daughters were married in families not only equal to their quality, but of large, plentiful estates, and they were all of them (as their mother had been) very fruitful in their issue.' Thomas Urquhart, who lived in the early part of the sixteenth century, built for himself a lofty, many-turreted castle, with sundry picturesque and elegant features, which Hugh Miller has well described in his account of Cromarty, but which was unfortunately taken down in 1772. It was also remembered of this many-childed laird, that he used to keep fifty servants. The entire population of Cromarty Castle must therefore have been considerable. Notwithstanding the great expense thus incurred, the worthy laird died free of debt, and transmitted the family property unimpaired to his posterity.

As to number of descendants, two cases in the annals of English domestic life come out very strongly. First, there was Mrs Honeywood of

MARY HONEYWOOD, AGED NINETY-THREE.

Charing, in Kent, who died on the 10th of May 1620, aged ninety-three, having had sixteen children, a hundred and fourteen grandchildren, two hundred and twenty-eight great-grandchildren, and nine great-great-grandchildren. Dr Michael Honeywood, dean of Lincoln, who died in 1681, at the age of eighty-five, was one of the grandchildren.* The second instance was even more wonderful. It represents Lady Temple of Stow, as dying in 1656, having given birth to four sons and nine daughters, and lived to see *seven hundred descendants.*

In as far as life itself goes in some instances considerably beyond an average or a rule, so does it happen that men occasionally hold office or practise a profession for an abnormally long time. Hearne takes notice of a clergyman, named Blower, who died in 1643, vicar of White-Waltham, which office he had held for sixty-seven years, though it was not his first cure. 'It was said he never preached but one sermon in his life, which was before Queen Elizabeth. Going after this discourse to pay his reverence to her Majesty, he first called her My Royal Queen, and afterwards My Noble Queen; upon which Elizabeth smartly said, "What! am I ten groats worse than I was?" Blower was so mortified by this good-natured joke, that he vowed to stick to the homilies for the future.'†

The late Earl of Aberdeen had enjoyed the honours of his family for the extraordinary period of sixty years,—a fact not unexampled, however, in the Scottish peerage, as Alexander, ninth Earl of Caithness, who died in 1765, had been peer for an equal time, and Alexander, fourth Duke of Gordon, was duke for seventy-five years, namely from 1752 to 1827. It is perhaps even more remarkable that for the Gordon dukedom, granted in 1684, there were but four possessors in a hundred and forty-three years, and for the Aberdeen earldom, granted in 1682, there were but four possessors in a hundred and seventy-eight years! In connection with these particulars, we may advert to the long reign of Louis XIV. of France—seventy-two years.

Odd matrimonial connections are not infrequent. For example, a man will marry the niece of his son's wife. Even to marry a grandmother, though both ridiculous and illegal, is not unexampled (the female, however, being not a blood relation).

'Dr Bowles, doctor of divinity, married the daughter of Dr Samford, doctor of physic, and, *vice versâ*, Dr Samford the daughter of Dr

* In the *Topographer and Genealogist*, edited by John Gough Nichols (1846), vol. i., is given an enumeration of the progeny of Mary Honeywood, shewing how eleven of her children had each a considerable family, three as many as eleven, one twelve, and two thirteen, children; the eldest grandchild having twenty, &c. The Dean of Lincoln, one of the grandsons, used to relate that he was present at a dinner given by the old lady to a family party of two hundred of her descendants. She died in 1620, aged ninety-three, having outlived her marriage seventy-seven years.

† Hearne found, in the register of White-Waltham, the figure of the key of the west door of the church, which Blower had there delineated, in accordance with a custom which had in view to prevent any alteration being made in the key. Formerly, the bishop of the diocese used to deliver the keys of a church in a formal manner to the ostiarii, or doorkeepers, the deacons at the same time delivering the doors; latterly the minister performed these formalities, always taking a sketch of the keys in the parish registers, so that, in case of their being lost or unwarrantably altered, they might have them restored.— *Leland's Itinerary,* v. 153

Bowles; whereupon the two women might say, These are our fathers, our sons, and our husbands.'—*Arch. Usher's MSS. Collections, quoted in Reliquiæ Hearnianæ,* i. 124.

The rule in matrimonial life where no quarrel has taken place is to continue living together. Yet we know that in this respect there are strange eccentricities. From the biography of our almost divine Shakspeare, it has been inferred that, on going to push his fortune in London, he left his Anne Hathaway (who was eight years his senior) at Stratford, where she remained during the sixteen or seventeen years which he spent as a player and play-writer in the metropolis; and it also appears that, by and by returning there as a man of gentlemanly means, he resumed living with Mrs Shakspeare, as if no sort of alienation had ever taken place between them. There is even a more curious, and, as it happens, a more clear case, than this, in the biography of the celebrated painter, George Romney. He, it will be remembered, was of peasant birth in Lancashire. In 1762, after being wedded for eight years to a virtuous young woman, he quitted his home in the north to try his fortune as an artist in London, leaving his wife behind him. There was no quarrel—he supplied her with ample means of support for herself and her two children out of the large income he realized by his profession; but it was not till *thirty-seven years had passed,* namely, in 1799, when he was sixty-five, and broken in health, that the truant husband returned home to resume living with his spouse. It is creditable to the lady, that she was as kind to her husband as if he had never left her; and Romney, for the three or four years of the remainder of his life, was as happy in her society as ill health would permit. It is a mystery which none of the great painter's biographers, though one of them was his son, have been able to clear up.

LINES ON THE GRAVE OF JACKSON THE PUGILIST,

In the West London and Westminster Cemetery.

'Stay, Traveller,' the Roman record said,
  To mark the classic dust beneath it laid;
'Stay, Traveller,' this brief memorial cries,
  And read the moral with attentive eyes:
Hast thou a lion's heart, a giant's strength,
Exult not, for these gifts must yield at length;
Do health and symmetry adorn thy frame,
The mouldering bones below possessed the same;
Does love, does friendship, every step attend,
This man ne'er made a foe, nor lost a friend;
But death full soon dissolves all human ties,
And, his last combat o'er, here Jackson lies.

THE RACE-HORSE ECLIPSE.

On the 28th of February 1789, died at Canons, in Middlesex, the celebrated horse Eclipse, at the advanced age of twenty-five. The animal had received his name from being born during an eclipse, and it became curiously significant and appropriate when, in mature life, he was found to surpass all contemporary horses in speed. He was bred by the Duke of Cumberland, younger brother of George III., and afterwards became the property of Dennis O'Kelly, Esq., a gentleman of large fortune, who died in December

1787, bequeathing this favourite horse and another, along with all his brood mares, to his brother Philip, in whose possession the subject of this memoir came to his end. For many years, Eclipse lived in retirement from the turf, but in another way a source of large income to his master, at Clay Hill, near Epsom, whither many curious strangers resorted to see him. They used to learn with surprise,—for the practice was not common then, as it is now,—that the life of Eclipse was insured for some thousands of pounds. When, after the death of Dennis O'Kelly, it became necessary to remove Eclipse to Canons, the poor beast was so worn out that a carriage had to be constructed to carry him. The secret of his immense success in racing was revealed after death in the unusual size of his heart, which weighed thirteen pounds.

FEBRUARY 29.

St Oswald, bishop of Worcester, and archbishop of York, 992.

ST OSWALD.

Oswald was an Anglo-Saxon prelate who was rewarded with the honour of canonization for the zeal with which he had assisted Dunstan and Odo in revolutionizing the Anglo-Saxon church, and substituting the strict monachism of the Benedictines for the old genial married clergy; or, in other words, reducing the Church of England to a complete subjection to Rome. Oswald was Odo's nephew, and was, like him, descended from Danish parents, and having at an early age distinguished himself by his progress in learning, was called to Canterbury by his uncle, Archbishop Odo, who made him a canon of the Old Minster there. He had already, however, begun to display his passion for monachism, and became so dissatisfied with the manners of the married clergy of Canterbury, that he left England to enter the abbey of Fleury in France, which was then celebrated for the severity of its discipline; yet even there Oswald became celebrated for the strictness of his life. Archbishop Odo died in 961, and, as he felt his health declining, he sent for his nephew, who arrived only in time to hear of his death. He returned to Fleury, but was finally persuaded to come back to England with his kinsman Oskitel, Archbishop of York, who was on his way from Rome with his pallium. On their arrival in England they found Dunstan just elected to the see of Canterbury; and that celebrated prelate, fearful that the see of Worcester, which he had previously held, should fall into the hands of a bishop not sufficiently devoted to the cause of monachism, persuaded Oswald to accept it. The new bishop, in fact, found plenty to do at Worcester, for Dunstan himself had not been able to dislodge the married canons from the church, and they offered an equally resolute resistance to his successor. Having struggled for some time in vain, Oswald gave up the contest, left the church and the canons, and built a new church and monastery near it, within the same churchyard, which he dedicated to the Virgin Mary; he also established there a colony of monks from Fleury. The people, we are told, attended sometimes one church and some-

times the other at will, until, gained over by the superior holiness which Oswald's clergy appeared to display, they gradually deserted the old church, and the married canons found themselves obliged to yield.

In 972, Oswald was, through Dunstan's interest, raised to the archbishopric of York, and Dunstan, fearing for the interests of monachism in Mercia, where Oswald had still made no great progress, insisted on his retaining the bishopric of Worcester along with the archiepiscopacy. The triumph of Dunstan's craftiness as well as talents in the conference at Calne, in 978, finally turned the scale against the old Anglo-Saxon clergy; and soon after that event Oswald succeeded in turning the clergy (who, according to the phraseology of the old writers of his party, 'preferred their wives to the church') from most of the principal churches in the diocese of Worcester, and substituting monks in their places. In 986, Oswald founded the important abbey of Ramsey, on land which he had obtained from the gift of Earl Aylwin; and he here established a school, which became one of the most celebrated seats of learning in England during the latter part of the tenth century, under the direction of the learned Abbo, one of the foreign monks whom Oswald had brought hither from Fleury. Oswald's favourite residence appears to have been at Worcester, where his humility and charity were celebrated. It was only towards the close of his life that he finally triumphed over the secular clergy of the old church of St Peter, and from that time his new church of St Mary superseded it and became the cathedral of the diocese. He was present to consecrate the church of Ramsey on the 8th of November 991, and, after some stay there, returned to Worcester, where, in the middle of his duties, he was seized with a disease which carried him off very suddenly, and he was buried in his church of St Mary. Oswald died on the day before the kalends of March, that is, on the last day of the previous month; and he is the only saint who takes his place in the calendar for that day.

Born.—Edward Cave, printer, 1692, *Newton, Warwick;* Gioacchino Rossini, 1792, *Pesaro.*

Died.—St Barbas, bishop of Benevento, 684; Archbishop John Whitgift, 1603-4, *Croydon;* John Landseer, engraver, 1852.

ARCHBISHOP WHITGIFT.—HIS HOSPITAL AT CROYDON.

Whitgift, 'one of the worthiest men that ever the English hierarchy did enjoy,' was the third primate of the Protestant Church of England after the Reformation, in the reign of Queen Elizabeth, upon whose death the Archbishop was afraid lest King James should make alterations in the government and Liturgy of the church; and his death was accelerated by this anxiety. He took a prominent part in explaining and defending before the King the doctrines and practices of the church, and was at the head of the Commission appointed for printing a uniform translation of the Bible, but he did not live to assist in its execution. He caught cold while sailing to Fulham in his barge; and on the following Sunday, after a long interview with the King, was seized with a fit, which ended in an attack of palsy and loss of speech. The King visited him at Lambeth, and told him that he 'would pray for his life; and if he could obtain it, he should think it one of the greatest temporal blessings that could be given him in this kingdom.' He died on the 29th of February, in the seventy-third year of his age, and was buried in the parish church of Croydon, on the second day after his death; his funeral was solemnized on the 27th of March, in a manner suitable to the splendour in which he had lived.

The Archbishop always took a lively interest in the management of public charities, and he left several instances of his munificence. He built and endowed, entirely from his own revenues, a hospital, free-school, and chapel, at Croydon, which he completed during his own lifetime. He commenced building the hospital on the 14th of February 1596, and finished it within three years. It is a brick edifice, in the Elizabethan style, at the entrance of the town from London: over the entrance are the armorial bearings of the see of Canterbury, and this inscription: 'QVI DAT PAVPERI NON INDIGEBIT.' The original yearly revenue was only £185, 4s. 2d.; but, by improved rents and sundry benefactions, it now exceeds £2000 per annum. Each poor brother and sister is to receive £5 per annum, besides wood, corn, and other provisions. Amongst the crimes to be punished by expulsion, are 'obstinate heresye, sorcerye, any kind of charmynge, or witchcrafte.' In the chapel is a portrait of the Archbishop, painted on board; and an outline delineation of Death, as a skeleton and gravedigger. Among the documents are the patent granted to the founder, with a drawing of Queen Elizabeth, on vellum; and on the Archbishop's deed of foundation is a drawing of himself, very beautifully executed. In the hall, where the brothren dine together three times yearly, is a folio Bible, in black letter, with wooden covers, mounted with brass; it has Cranmer's prefaces, and was printed in 1596. Here also, formerly, were three ancient wooden goblets, one of which was inscribed:

'What, sirrah! hold thy pease!
Thirst satisfied, cease.'

END OF 'LA BELLE JENNINGS.'

29th February, 1730, in a small private nunnery of Poor Clares, in King-street, Dublin, an aged lady was found in the morning, fallen out of bed, stiff with cold, and beyond recovery. The person who died in this obscure and miserable manner had once been the very prime lady of the land, the mistress of Dublin Castle, where she had received a monarch as her guest. At an early period of her life, she had been one of the loveliest figures in the gay and luxurious court of Charles II. She was, in short, the person celebrated as *La Belle Jennings,* and latterly the wife of that Duke of Tyrconnel who nearly recovered Ireland for King James II. She entered life soon after the Restoration, as maid of honour to the Duchess of York, and in that position had conducted herself with a pro-

priety all the more commendable that it was in her time and place almost unique. As wife of the Duke of Tyrconnel, during his rule in Dublin in 1689-90, her conduct appears to have been as dignified, as it had formerly been pure. It is presented in a striking light in Mrs Jameson's account of what happened after the battle of the Boyne—'where fifteen Talbots of Tyrconnel's family were slain, and he himself fought like a hero of romance.' 'After that memorable defeat,' says our authoress, 'King James and Tyrconnel reached Dublin on the evening of the same day. The Duchess, who had been left in the Castle, had passed four-and-twenty hours in all the agonies of suspense; but when the worst was known, she showed that the spirit and strength of mind which distinguished her in her early days was not all extinguished. When the King and her husband arrived as fugitives from the lost battle, on which her fortunes and her hopes had depended, harassed, faint, and so covered with mud, that their persons could scarcely be distinguished, she, hearing of their plight, assembled all her household in state, dressed herself richly, and received the fugitive King and his dispirited friends with all the splendour of court etiquette. Advancing to the head of the grand staircase with all her attendants, she kneeled on one knee, congratulated him on his safety, and invited him to a banquet, respectfully inquiring what refreshment he would be pleased to take at the moment. James answered sadly that he had but little stomach for supper, considering the sorry breakfast he had made that morning. She, however, led the way to a banquet already prepared; and did the honours with as much self-possession and dignity as Lady Macbeth, though racked at the moment with equal terror and anxiety.'*

JOHN DUNS SCOTUS.

It is a pity that such obscurity rests on the personal history of this light of the middle ages. He was an innovator upon the stereotyped ideas of his age, and got accordingly a dubious reputation among formalists. If he had been solely the author of the following sentence—'Authority springs from reason, not reason from authority—true reason needs not be confirmed by any authority'—it would have been worth while for Scotland to contend for the honour of having given him birth.

School Exercise.—In several old grammar-schools there was a liberal rule that the boys should have an hour from three till four for their drinkings. Sometimes the schoolmaster, for want of occupation, employed himself oddly enough. One day a visitor to the school of —— observing some deep-coloured stains upon the oaken floor, inquired the cause. He was told that they were occasioned by the leakage of a butt of Madeira, which the master of the grammar school, who had grown lusty, not having had for some time any scholar who might afford him the opportunity of taking exercise, employed himself upon a rainy day in rolling up and down the schoolroom for the purpose of ripening the wine, and keeping himself in good condition.

* *Memoirs of the Beauties of the Court of Charles II.,* vol. ii. p. 223

MARCH

—— Sturdy March, with brows full sternly bent,
And armed strongly, rode upon a ram,
The same which over Hellespontus swam,
Yet in his hand a spade he also bent
And in a bag all sorts of weeds, y same
Which on the earth he strewed as he went,
And filled her womb with fruitful hope of nourishment.

SPENSER.

(DESCRIPTIVE.)

MARCH is the first month of Spring. He is Nature's Old Forester, going through the woods and dotting the trees with green, to mark out the spots where the future leaves are to be hung. The sun throws a golden glory over the eastern hills, as the village-clock from the ivy-covered tower tolls six, gilding the hands and the figures that were scarcely visible two hours later a few weeks ago.

The streams now hurry along with a rapid motion, as if they had no time to dally with, and play round the impeding pebbles, but were eager to rush along the green meadow-lands, to tell the flowers it is time to awaken. We hear the cottagers greeting each other with kind 'Good morning,' across the paled garden-fences in the sunrise, and talking about the healthy look of the up-coming peas, and the promise in a few days of a dish of early spinach. Under the old oak, surrounded with rustic seats, they congregate on the village-green, in the mild March evenings,

311

and talk about the forward spring, and how they have battled through the long hard winter, and, looking towards the green churchyard, speak in low voices of those who have been borne thither to sleep out their long sleep since 'last primrose-time,' and they thank God that they are still alive and well, and are grateful for the fine weather 'it has pleased Him to send them at last.'

Now rustic figures move across the landscape, and give a picturesque life to the scenery. You see the ploughboy returning from his labour, seated sideways on one of his horses, humming a line or two of some love-lorn ditty, and when his memory fails to supply the words, whistling the remainder of the tune. The butcher-boy rattles merrily by in his blue-coat, throwing a saucy word to every one he passes; and if he thinks at all of the pretty lambs that are bleating in his cart, it is only about how much they will weigh when they are killed. The old woman moves slowly along in her red cloak, with basket on arm, on her way to supply her customers with new-laid eggs. So the figures move over the brown winding roads between the budding hedges in red, blue, and grey, such as a painter loves to seize upon to give light, and colour, to his landscape. A few weeks ago those roads seemed uninhabited.

The early-yeaned lambs have now become strong, and may be seen playing with one another, their chief amusement being that of racing, as if they knew what heavy weights their little legs will have to bear when their feeders begin to lay as much mutton on their backs as they can well walk under—so enjoy the lightness of their young lean days. There is no cry so childlike as that of a lamb that has lost its dam, and how eagerly it sets off at the first bleat the ewe gives: in an instant it recognises that sound from all the rest, while to our ears that of the whole flock sounds alike. Dumb animals we may call them, but all of them have a language which they understand; they give utterance to their feelings of joy, love, and pain, and when in distress call for help, and, as we have witnessed, hurry to the aid of one another. The osier-peelers are now busy at work in the osier-holts; it is almost the first out-of-door employment the poor people find in spring, and very pleasant it is to see the white-peeled willows lying about to dry on the young grass, though it is cold work by a windy river side for the poor women and children on a bleak March day. As soon as the sap rises, the bark-peelers commence stripping the trees in the woods, and we know but few country smells that equal the aroma of the piled-up bark. But the trees have a strange ghastly look after they are stripped—unless they are at once removed—standing like bleached skeletons when the foliage hangs on the surrounding branches. The rumbling wagon is a pretty sight moving through the wood, between openings of the trees, piled high with bark, where wheel never passes, excepting on such occasions, or when the timber is removed. The great ground-bee, that seems to have no hive, goes blundering by, then alights on some green patch of grass in the underwood, though what he finds there to feed upon is a puzzle to you, even

if you kneel down beside him, as we have done, and watch ever so narrowly.

How beautiful the cloud and sunshine seem chasing each other over the tender grass! You see the patch of daisies shadowed for a few moments, then the sunshine sweeps over them, and all their silver frills seem suddenly touched with gold, which the wind sets in motion. Our forefathers well named this month 'March many-weathers,' and said that 'it came in like a lion, and went out like a lamb,' for it is made up of sunshine and cloud, shower and storm, often causing the horn-fisted ploughman to beat his hands across his chest in the morning to warm them, and before noon compelling him to throw off his smock-frock and sleeved waistcoat, and wipe the perspiration from his forehead with his shirt sleeve, as he stands between the plough-stilts at the end of the newly-made furrow. Still we can now plant our 'foot upon nine daisies,' and not until that can be done do the old-fashioned country people believe that spring is really come. We have seen a grey-haired grandsire do this, and smile as he called to his old dame to count the daisies, and see that his foot fairly covered the proper number.

Ants now begin to run across our paths, and sometimes during a walk in the country you may chance to stumble upon the nest of the wood-ant. At a first glance it looks like a large heap of litter, where dead leaves and short withered grass have been thrown lightly down upon the earth; perhaps at the moment there is no sign of life about it, beyond a straggler or two at the base of the mound. Thrust in the point of your stick, and all the ground will be alive in a moment; nothing but a mass of moving ants will be seen where you have probed. Nor will it do to stay too long, for they will be under your trousers and up your boots, and you will soon feel as if scores of red-hot needles were run into you, for they wound sharply. If you want the clean skeleton of a mouse, bird, or any other small animal, throw it on the nest of the wood-ant, and on the following day you will find every bone as bare and clean as if it had been scraped. Snakes may now be seen basking in some sunny spot, generally near a water-course, for they are beautiful swimmers and fond of water. They have slept away the winter under the dead leaves, or among the roots, and in the holes of trees, or wherever they could find shelter. In ponds and ditches may also be seen thousands of round-headed long-tailed tadpoles, which, if not devoured, will soon become nimble young frogs, when they have a little better chance of escaping the jaws of fishes and wildfowl, for no end of birds, fishes, reptiles, and quadrupeds feed on them. Only a few weeks ago the frogs were in a torpid state, and sunk like stones beneath the mud. Since then they left those black spots, which may be seen floating in a jellied mass on the water, and soon from this spawn the myriads of lively tadpoles we now see sprang into life. Experienced gardeners never drive frogs out of their grounds, as they are great destroyers of slugs, which seem to be their favourite food. Amongst the tadpoles the water-rat may now be seen swimming about and nibbling at some leaf, or overhanging blade of grass, his tail acting as a rudder, by which he can steer himself into any little nook, wheresoever he may take a fancy to go. If you are near enough, you will see his rich silky hair covered with bright silver-like bubbles as they sink into the water, and he is a most graceful swimmer. The entrance to his nest is generally under the water ; throw a stone and he will dive down in a moment, and when he has passed the watery basement, he at once ascends his warm dry nest, in which, on one occasion, a gallon of potatoes was found, that he had hoarded up to last him through the winter. Pleasant is it on a fine March day to stand on some rustic bridge—it may be only a plank thrown across the stream—and watch the fishes as they glide by, or pause and turn in the water, or to see the great pike basking near the surface, as if asleep in the sunshine. Occasionally a bird will dart out from the sedge, or leave off tugging at the head of the tall bulrush, and hasten away between the willows, that seem to give a silvery shiver, every time the breeze turns up the underpart of their leaves to the light. In solitary places, by deep watercourses, the solemn plunge of the otter may sometimes be heard, as he darts in after his prey, or you may start him from the bank where he is feeding on the fish he has captured.

Violets, which Shakspeare says are 'sweeter than the lids of Juno's eyes,' impregnate the March winds with their fragrance, and it is amazing what a distance the perfume is borne on the air from the spot where they grow ; and, but for thus betraying themselves, the places where they nestle together would not always be found. Though called the wood-violet, it is oftener found on sunny embankments, under the shelter of a hedge, than in the woods ; a woodside bank that faces the south may often be seen diapered with both violets and primroses. Though it is commonly called the 'blue violet,' it approaches nearer to purple in colour. The scentless autumn violets are blue. No lady selecting a violet-coloured dress would choose a blue. The 'dark-velvet' is a name given to it by our old poets, who also call it 'wine-coloured;' others call the hue 'watchet,' which is blue. But let it be compared with the blue-bell, beside which it is often found, and it will appear purple in contrast. Through the frequent mention made of it by Shakspeare, it must have been one of his favourite flowers; and as it still grows abundantly in the neighbourhood of Stratford-on-Avon, it may perhaps yet be found scenting the March air, and standing in the very same spots by which he paused to look at it. Like the rose, it retains its fragrance long after the flower is dead. The perfume of violets and the song of the blackcap are delights which may often be enjoyed together while walking out at this season of the year, for the blackcap, whose song is only equalled by that of the nightingale, is one of the earliest birds that arrives. Though he is a droll-looking little fellow in his black wig, which seems too big for his head, yet, listen to him! and if you have never heard him before, you will hear such music as you would hardly think such an organ as a bird's throat could make. There is one silvery shake which no other bird can compass : it sinks down to the very lowest sound music is capable of making, and yet is as distinct as the low ring of a silver bell. The nightingale has no such note : for there is an unapproachable depth in its low sweetness. While singing, its throat is wonderfully distended, and the whole of its little body shivers with delight. Later in the season, it often builds its compact nest amid the sheltering leaves of the ivy, in which it lays four or five eggs, which are fancifully dashed with darker spots of a similar hue.

Daisies, one of the earliest known of our old English flowers that still retains its Saxon name, are now in bloom. It was called the day's-eye, and the eye-of-day, as far back as we have any records of our history. 'It is such a wanderer,' says a quaint old writer, 'that it must have been one of the first flowers that strayed and grew outside the garden of Eden.' Poets have delighted to call them 'stars of the earth,' and Chaucer describes a green valley 'with daisies powdered over,' and great was his love for this beautiful flower. He tells us how he rose early in the morning, and went out again in the evening, to see the day's-eye open and shut, and that he often lay down on his side to watch it unfold. But beautiful as its silver rim looks, streaked sometimes with red, 'as if grown in the blood of our old battle-fields,' says the above-quoted writer, still it is a perfect compound flower, as one of those little yellow florets which form its 'golden boss' or crown will show, when carefully examined. Whatever may be said of Linnæus, Chaucer was the first who discovered that the daisy slept, for he tells us how he went out,

'To see this flower, how it *will go to rest*,
For fear of night, so hateth it the darkness.'

He also calls the opening of the daisy 'its resurrection,' so that nearly five centuries ago the sleep of plants was familiar to the Father of English Poetry. Now the nests of the blackbird and thrush may be seen in the hedges, before the leaves are fully out, for they are our earliest builders, as well as the first to awaken Winter with their songs. As if to prepare better for the cold, to which their young are exposed, through being hatched so soon as they are, they both plaster their nests inside with mud, until they are as smooth as a basin. They begin singing at the first break of dawn, and may be heard again as the day closes. We have frequently heard them before three in the morning in summer. The blackbird is called 'golden bill' by country people, and the 'ouzel cock' of our old ballad poetry. It is not easy to tell males from females during the first year, but in the second year the male has the 'golden bill.' If undisturbed, the blackbird will build for many seasons in the same spot, often only repairing its old nest. No young birds are more easily reared, as they will eat almost anything. Both the nests and eggs of the thrush and blackbird are much alike.

Sometimes, while peeping about to discover these rounded nests, we catch sight of the germander-speedwell, one of the most beautiful of our March flowers, bearing such a blue as is only at times seen on the changing sky; we know no blue flower that can be compared with it. The ivy-leaved veronica may also now be found, though it is a very small flower, and must be sought for very near the ground. Now and then, but not always, we have found the graceful wood-anemone in flower in March, and very pleasant it is to come unaware upon a bed of these pretty plants in bloom, they shew such a play of shifting colours when stirred by the wind, now turning their reddish-purple outside to the light, then waving back again, and showing the rich white-grey inside the petals, as if white and purple lilacs were mixed, and blowing together. The leaves, too, are very beautifully cut; and as the flower has no proper calyx, the pendulous cup droops gracefully, 'hanging its head aside,' like Shakspeare's beautiful Barbara. If—through the slightest breeze setting its drooping bells in motion—the old Greeks called it the wind flower, it was happily named, for we see it stirring when there is scarce more life in the air than

'———— On a summer's day
Robs not one light seed from the feathered grass.'

The wheat-ear, of which country children say, 'some bird blackened its eye for going away,' now makes its appearance, and is readily known by the black mark which runs from the ear to the base of the bill. Its notes are very low and sweet, for it seems too fat to strain itself, and we have no doubt could sing much louder if it pleased. It is considered so delicious a morsel, that epicures have named it the British ortolan, and is so fat it can scarcely fly when wheat is ripe. Along with it comes the pretty willow-wren, which is easily known by being yellow underneath, and through the light colour of its legs. It lives entirely on insects, never touching either bloom or fruit like the bullfinch, and is of great value in our gardens, when at this season such numbers of insects attack the blossoms. But one of the most curious of our early comers is the little wryneck, so called because he is always twisting his neck about. When boys, we only knew it by the name of the willow-bite, as it always lays its eggs in a hole in a tree, without ever troubling itself to make a nest. When we put our hand in to feel for the eggs, if the bird was there it hissed like a snake, and many a boy have we seen whip his fingers out when he heard that alarming sound, quicker than ever he put them in, believing that a snake was concealed in the hole. It is a famous destroyer of ants, which it takes up so rapidly on its glutinous tongue, that no human eye can follow the motion, for the ants seem impelled forward by some secret power, as one writer observes: 'as if drawn by a magnet.' This bird can both hop and walk, though it does not step out so soldier-like as the beautiful wagtail. Sometimes, while listening to the singing birds in spring, you will find all their voices hushed in a moment, and unless you are familiar with country objects, will be at a loss to divine the cause. Though you may not have heard it, some bird has raised a sudden cry of alarm, which causes them all to rush into the hedges and bushes for safety. That bird had

seen the hovering hawk, and knew that, in another moment or so, he would drop down sudden as a thunderbolt on the first victim that he fixed his far-seeing eyes upon; and his rush is like the speed of thought. But he always remains nearly motionless in the air before he strikes, and this the birds seem to know, and their sight must be keen to see him so high up as he generally is before he strikes. In the hedges they are safe, as there is no room there for the spread of his wings; and if he misses his quarry, he never makes a second dart at it. Sometimes the hawk catches a Tartar, as one did that pounced upon and carried off a weasel, which, when high in the air, ate into the hawk's side, causing him to come down dead as a stone, when the weasel, who retained his hold of the hawk, ran off, not appearing to be the least injured after his unexpected elevation.

What a change have the March winds produced in the roads; they are now as hard as they were during the winter frost. But there was no cloud of dry dust then as there is now. When our forefathers repeated the old proverb which says, 'A peck of March dust is worth a king's ransom,' did they mean, we wonder, that its value lay in loosening and drying the earth, and making it fitter to till? In the old gardening books a dry day in March is always recommended for putting seed into the ground.

To one who does not mind a noise there is great amusement to be found now in living near a rookery, for there is always something or another going on in that great airy city overhead, if it only be, as Washington Irving says, 'quarrelling for a corner of the blanket' while in their nests. They are nearly all thieves, and think nothing of stealing the foundation from one another's houses during the building season. When some incorrigible blackguard cannot be beaten into order, they all unite and drive him away; neck and crop do they bundle him out. Let him only shew so much as his beak in the rookery again after his ejectment, and the whole police force are out and at him in a moment. No peace will he ever have there any more during that season, though perhaps he may make it up again with them during the next winter in the woods. We like to hear them cawing from the windy high elm-trees, which have been a rookery for centuries, and which overhang some old hall grey with the moss and lichen of forgotten years. The sound they make seems to give a quiet dreamy air to the whole landscape, and we look upon such a spot as an ancient English home, standing in a land of peace.

———

(HISTORICAL.)

We derive the present name of this month from the Romans, among whom it was at an early period the first month of the year, as it continued to be in several countries to a comparatively late period, the legal year beginning even in England on the 25th of March, till the change of the style in 1752. For commencing the year with this month there seems a sufficient reason in the fact of its being the first season, after the *dead* of the year, in which decided symptoms of a renewal of growth take place. And for the Romans to dedicate their first month to Mars, and call it *Martius*, seems equally natural, considering the importance they attached to war, and the use they made of it.

Among our Saxon forefathers, the month bore the name of *Lenet-monat*,—that is, length-month, —in reference to the lengthening of the day at this season,—the origin also of the term Lent.

' The month,' says Brady, ' is portrayed as a man of a tawny colour and fierce aspect, with a helmet on his head—so far typical of Mars— while, appropriate to the season, he is represented leaning on a spade, holding almond blossoms and scions in his left hand, with a basket of seeds on his arm, and in his right hand the sign Aries, or the Ram, which the sun enters on the 20th of this month, thereby denoting the augmented power of the sun's rays, which in ancient hiero- glyphics were expressed by the horns of animals.

CHARACTERISTICS OF MARCH.

March is noted as a dry month. Its dust is looked for, and becomes a subject of congratu- lation, on account of the importance of dry weather at this time for sowing and planting. The idea has been embodied in proverbs, as ' A peck of March dust is worth a king's ransom,' and ' A dry March never begs its bread.' Blus- tering winds usually prevail more or less through- out a considerable part of the month, but mostly in the earlier portion. Hence, the month appears to change its character as it goes on ; the re- mark is, ' It comes in like a lion, and goes out like a lamb.' The mean temperature of the month for London is stated at 43·9° ; for Perth, in Scotland, at 43° ; but, occasionally, winter reappears in all its fierceness. At London the sun rises on the first day at 6.46 ; on the last at 5.38, being an extension of upwards of an hour.

First of March.

St David, archbishop of Caerleon, patron of Wales, 544. St Albinus, of Angers, 549. St Swidbert, or Swibert, of Northumberland, bishop, 713. St Monan, of Scotland, martyr, 374.

St David.

David, popularly termed the titular saint of Wales, is said to have been the son of a prince of Cardiganshire of the ancient regal line of Cunedda Wledig ; some, also, state that he was the son of Xanthus, son of Ceredig, lord of Cere- digion, and Non, daughter of Gynyr of Caergawh, Pembrokeshire. St David has been invested by his legendary biographers with extravagant de- coration. According to their accounts, he had not merely the power of working miracles from the moment of his birth, but the same preter- natural faculty is ascribed to him while he was yet unborn ! An angel is said to have been his constant attendant on his first appearance on earth, to minister to his wants, and contribute to his edification and *relaxation ;* the Bath waters became warm and salubrious through his agency ; he healed complaints and re-animated the dead ; whenever he preached, a snow-white dove sat upon his shoulder ! Among other things,—as pulpits were not in fashion in those times,—the earth on which he preached was raised from its level, and became a hill ; from whence his voice was heard to the best advantage. Among these popular legends, the pretended life of St David, in Welsh, in the Cotton MSS. (D. xxii.), is the most remarkable for its spurious embellishments. His pedigree is here deduced from the Virgin Mary, of whom it makes him the lineal eigh- teenth descendant ! But leaving the region of fiction, there is no doubt that the valuable services of St David to the British church entitle him to a very distinguished position in its early annals. He is numbered in the *Triads* with Teilo and Catwg as one of the 'three canonized saints of Britain.' Giraldus terms him 'a mirror and pattern to all, instructing both by word and example, excellent in his preaching, but still more so in his works. He was a doctrine to all, a guide to the religious, a life to the poor, a support to orphans, a protection to widows, a father to the fatherless, a rule to monks, and a model to teachers; becoming all to all, that so he might gain all to God.'

To this, his moral character, St David added a high character for theological learning; and two productions, a *Book of Homilies*, and a *Treatise against the Pelagians*, have been ascribed to him. St David received his early education at Menevia, (derived from Main-aw, 'a narrow water,' frith or strait), named afterwards Ty Ddewi, 'David's House,' answering to the present St David's, which was a seminary of learning and nursery of saints. At this place, some years after, he founded a convent in the Vale of Rhos. The discipline which St David enjoined in this monastic retreat is represented as of the most rigorous nature. After the Synod at Brevy, in 519, Dubricius, or Dyvrig, Archbishop of Caerleon, and consequently Primate of Wales, resigned his see to St David, who removed the archiepiscopal residence to Menevia, the present St David's, where he died about the year 544, after having attained a very advanced age. The saint was buried in the cathedral, and a monument raised to his memory. It is of simple construction, the ornaments consisting of one row of four quatrefoil openings upon a plain tomb.

St David appears to have had more superstitious honours paid to him in England than in his native country. Thus, before the Reformation, the following collect was read in the old church of Sarum on the 1st of March :—'Oh God, who by thy angel didst foretel thy blessed Confessor St David, thirty years before he was born, grant unto us, we beseech thee, that celebrating his memory, we may, by his intercession, attain to joys everlasting.'

Inscription for a monument in the Vale of Ewias.

'Here was it, stranger, that the *Patron Saint*
Of *Cambria* passed his age of penitence,
A solitary man ; and here he made
His hermitage, the roots his food, his drink
Of Hodney's mountain stream.　Perchance thy youth
Has read, with eager wonder, how the knight
Of Wales, in Ormandine's enchanted bower,
Slept the long sleep : and if that in thy veins
Flow the pure blood of Britain, sure that blood
Hath flowed with quicker impulse at the tale
Of DAVID's deeds, when thro' the press of war
His gallant comrades followed his *green crest*
To conquest.　　Stranger ! Hatterill's mountain heights
And this fair vale of Ewias, and the stream
Of Hodney, to thine after-thoughts will rise
More grateful, thus associate with the name
Of David, and the deeds of other days.'—SOUTHEY.

Born.—Dr John Pell, mathematician, 1610, *Southwick ;* Caroline, of England, 1683 ; Dr David Bogue, Scottish missionary, 1750, *Halidown ;* Sir Samuel Romilly, lawyer and politician, 1757, *Marylebone.*

Died.—Francis Rabelais, French romancist, 1553 : Anne, Queen of England, 1619, *Hampton Court ;* Matthias, Emperor of Germany, 1619 ; Sir Thomas Herbert, 1682, *York ;* Leopold II., Emperor of Germany, 1792, *Prague ;* Manuel Johnson, astronomer, 1859, *Oxford.*

RABELAIS.

Francis Rabelais, the son of an apothecary, was born at Chinon, a town of Touraine, in 1483. Brimming over with sport and humour, by a strange perversity it was decided to make the boy a monk, and Rabelais entered the order of Franciscans. His gaiety proved more than they could endure, and he was transferred to the easier fraternity of the Benedictines; but his high spirits were too much for these likewise, and he escaped to Montpelier, where he studied medicine, took a doctor's degree, and practised with such success, that he was invited to the court at Paris. In the train of an ambassador he went to Rome in 1536, and received absolution from the Pope for his violation of monastic vows. On his return to France he was appointed curé of Meudon, and died in 1553, aged 70.

Wit was the distinction of Rabelais. He was learned, and he had seen much of the world ; and for the pedantry of scholars, the cant of priests, and the folly of kings, he had a quick eye and a light-hearted contempt. It was an age of deadly intolerance : to dissent from the church was to burn at the stake, and to criticise governors was mutilation or death on the scaffold. Rabelais had not earnestness for a martyr, but the contempt and fun that stirred within him demanded utterance, and donning the fool's cap and bells, he published the romance of Gargantua and Pantagruel. Gargantua was a giant who lived several centuries and begot a son, Pantagruel, as big and wonderful as himself. Beneath his tongue an army took shelter from the rain, and in his mouth and throat were populous cities. Under the mask of their adventures Rabelais contrived to speak his mind concerning kings, priests, and scholars, just as Swift, following his example, did in *Gulliver's Travels.* He was accused of heresy and irreligion, but Francis I. read and enjoyed the story of Gargantua and Pantagruel, and said he could see no harm in it. Calvin at one time thought he had found in Rabelais a Protestant, and was prepared to number him among his disciples, but gravely censuring him for his profane jesting, Rabelais, in revenge, made Panurge, one of the characters in his romance, discourse in Calvinistic phrases. The obscenity which is inwrought in almost every page of Rabelais prevents his enjoyment by modern readers, although his coarseness gave no offence to the generation for which he wrote. Coleridge, whose opinion is worth having, says : 'Beyond a doubt Rabelais was among the deepest, as well as boldest, thinkers of his age. His buffoonery was not merely Brutus's rough stick, which contained a rod of gold : it was necessary as an amulet against the monks and legates.

Never was there a more plausible, and seldom, I am persuaded, a less appropriate line, than the thousand times quoted

" Rabelais laughing in his easy chair,"

of Mr Pope. The caricature of his filth and zanyism show how fully he both knew and felt the danger in which he stood. . . . I class Rabelais with the great creative minds of the world, Shakspeare, Dante, Cervantes, &c.'

LABORIOUS ASTRONOMICAL OBSERVATIONS.

Mr Manuel Johnson was for many years ' the Radcliffe observer' at the noble observatory at Oxford, built by the munificence of Dr Radcliffe. Mr Johnson was a devoted and disinterested worker, and allowed nothing to interfere with the regular duties of the observatory. Night after night, with not more than a rare periodical break of a week or two, he was at the same task, steadily travelling through the region of the circumpolar heavens which he had marked out for his observation, to which latterly were added the important labours connected with the heliometer. Taking the Groombridge Catalogue as his foundation, he re-observed all the stars—more than 4000—included in that catalogue, and added 1500 other stars not found in Groombridge. The meridian instruments of the Radcliffe observatory were, for several years, almost wholly employed for this work, and volumes 40—53 of the *Radcliffe Observatory* are filled with observations and special catalogues, all designed for ultimate collection into a large catalogue of circumpolar stars, of which some sheets had already passed through the press at the time of Mr Johnson's death.

There is surely something affecting in the contemplation of a life devoted with such unslackening zeal to a task of such a nature as this—calculated to prove serviceable, but under such circumstances that the individual worker could never derive any benefit from it.

WILLIAM CAXTON.

On the 1st of March 1468-69, William Caxton began, at the city of Bruges, to translate the *Recueil of the Histories of Troy* from the French, at the command of Margaret, Duchess of Burgundy, sister of the English King Edward IV. The work was finished on the 19th of September 1471, and formally presented to the Duchess. It was a noted literary undertaking, and by a very notable person. Caxton, a native of the Weald of Kent, supposed to have been born about 1422, and brought up as a mercer in London, had for several years occupied the eminent position of *Governor of the English in Bruges*, there being at that time many of our countrymen following merchandize in the capital of the Duchy of Burgundy, insomuch, that they required a governor of their own for the maintenance of order among them, for the preservation of their privileges, and for various diplomatic purposes. (It seems to have been a position like that of Conservator of the Scots Privileges at Campvere, which was kept in force down to the last century.) Caxton was a well-educated man,

wealthy, and of great application. It could only be the impulse of his own tastes which led him to take up the pen of an author, and translate the *Recueil of Histories*. The step, however, once taken, seems to have led to a complete change in the current of his life.

The book being finished was multiplied in the way then customary, by manuscript, and sold at a good price. Books, dear as they necessarily were in the fifteenth century, were in good and increasing demand, for the intellect of Europe was getting into an activity it had never known before. The *Recueil* was a remarkable and popular book, and we can imagine an author of such a practical turn of mind as the Governor of the English in Bruges feeling a little impatience at the slow means of producing copies which the pen of the copyist supplied. Well, there was an art beginning at that time to be practised for the multiplication of books by printing from blocks and

CAXTON'S HOUSE.

moveable types. It had been obscurely attempted by one Coster at Haarlem before the year 1440; afterwards it was brought to a tolerable efficiency at Mentz, in Germany, by three men named Faust, Gutenberg, and Schœffer; these men had even produced an edition of the Latin Bible, which scarcely could be distinguished from the finest manuscript. Just about this time, one Colard Mansion was beginning or professing to introduce this somewhat mysterious art into Bruges. It could scarcely fail to catch the attention of so enterprising a man as Caxton, even if he had not a book of his own to be printed.

An arrangement was made between Caxton and Mansion, whereby the former furnished money, and the latter set up a printing office.

of which the first or at least a very early emanation was an impression of *The Recuyell of the Historyes of Troye.* This was a most remarkable tome, for it was the first English book that ever was printed :—the first of so many !

The second was a translation by Caxton from a French moral treatise, entitled *The Game and Playe of the Chesse,* which was finished on the last day of March 1474. and printed under his care, most probably at Bruges, though some consider it as the first issue of his press after he had removed to England. To convey some idea of the style of typography in these early days of the art, we present a fac-simile of a passage of the *Game and Playe of the Chesse,* being the dedication to the unfortunate Duke of Clarence.

To the right noble/right excellent & vertuous prince George duc of Clarence Erle of warwyk and of salisburye/grete chamberlayn of Englond & leutenant of Irelond oldest broder of kynge Edward by the grace of god kynge of England and of fraunce / your most humble seruant william Caxton amonge other of pour seruantes sendes vnto yow pees . helthe . Joye and victorye vpon your Enempes /

How it came about we do not know, although it is not difficult to surmise. Caxton is soon after found to have returned to his own country, and commenced business as a printer and publisher, being for certain the first who practised the typographic art in this island. He was wealthy; he had been in a high employment; it looks to us as a descent, that such a man, past fifty years of age. should have gone into such a business, for certainly it was no more dignified then than it is now. We can only suppose that Caxton had all along had strong literary tastes—had prudentially kept them in check while realising an independence, and now felt at liberty to indulge his natural bent, while yet pleasing himself with the idea that he was usefully and not unprofitably occupied. Whatever his motives might be, there we find him practising typography, and also selling books, in a house called the Almonry (*i.e.* alms-distributing house), near the western door of Westminster Abbey,* and this from about 1476 till 1491, when he died, about seventy years of age. His publications were for their time meritorious, and in some instances he was author as well as printer. They include *Dictes and Sayings,* 1477; *Chronicles of England,* 1480; *Mirror of the World,* 1481; [Gower's] *Confessio Amantis,*

1483; *Æsop,* 1484; *King Arthur,* 1485, &c. An advertisement of one of his productions is extremely quaint and simple : 'If it ples ony man spirituel or temporel to bye ony pyes [piece] of two and three comemoraciõs of salisburi vse enpryntid after the forme of this presēt lettre whiche ben wel and truly correct, late hym come to westmonester in to the almonesrye at the reed pale, and he shall have them good chepe.' *

COMMENCEMENT OF THE 'SPECTATOR.'

On the 1st of March 1711, appeared the first number of the *Spectator,* the most popular work that England had up to that time produced,— alike the recreation of the learned, the busy, and the idle. This work was printed daily in the same form, and at the same price, as the *Tatler,* and supported by the same able contributors, but was, altogether, a work of far more elevated pretensions than its predecessor. The *Tatler* and the *Spectator* were the first attempts made in England, or any other country, to instruct and amuse unlearned readers by short papers, appearing at stated intervals, and sold at a cheap rate. The object of the writers was 'to bring philosophy out of closets and libraries, schools and colleges, to dwell in clubs, and assemblies, at tea-tables and at coffee-houses.'

The *Spectator* was planned by Addison in concert with Sir Richard Steele, and its success was chiefly owing to the matchless pen of the former. Addison's papers are designated by the letters C.L.I.O., which some have supposed he adopted as composing the name of the muse Clio; but Mr Nichols thinks, rather as being the initials of the places where the papers were written, Chelsea, London, Islington, and the Office. This supposition is strengthened by transposing the letters (for there is no absolute

The house in which Caxton is said to have lived stood on the north side of the Almonry, with its back against that of a house on the south side of Tothill-street. Bagford describes this house as of brick, with the sign of the King's Head'; it fell down in November 1845, before the removal of the other dwellings in the Almonry, to form the new Victoria-street. A beam of wood was sawed from the materials of this house, and from it were made a chess board and two sets of chessmen, as appropriate memorials of Caxton's *Game and Playe of the Chesse.* Caxton's House was a three-storied house, with a bold gable, and a gallery running along the upper story. It is said that wooden types were found on clearing away the materials of the house ; its precise site was immediately adjoining the spot now occupied by the principal entrance to the Westminster Palace Hotel.

* *Life and Typography of William Caxton,* compiled from original sources, by William Blades. 4to, vol. i. 1861.

rule by which their order should be fixed) into the Latin word *loci*, or 'at the place' where he might have resided. The publication of the *Spectator* continued regularly to the close of the seventh volume; after an interval of about eighteen months, the eighth volume commenced and terminated December 20, 1714.

The notion of a club in which the *Spectator* is formed, not only gave the work a dramatic air, but a sort of unity to the conduct of it; as it tied together the several papers into what may be called one work, by the reference they all have to the same common design.

The origin of some of the numbers of the *Spectator* is not a little curious, and shews with what talent the contributors of the essays converted the most trifling subjects into articles of interest. No. 71, which contains 'the epistle of an enamoured footman in the country to his mistress,' and signed 'James,' originated in the following circumstance. In the year 1711, James Hirst lived as servant with the Hon. Edward Wortley. It happened one day, that in delivering a letter to his master, he, by mistake, gave him one which he had written to his sweetheart, and kept back Mr Wortley's. He soon discovered his error, and immediately hurried to his master in order to retrieve it, but it happened to be the first that presented itself, and before his return, Mr Wortley had perused the enamoured footman's love story. James entreated to have it returned. 'No,' said Mr Wortley, 'No, James; you shall be a great man; this letter shall appear in the *Spectator*.' It was accordingly communicated to Sir Richard Steele, and published in James's own words, 'Dear Betty,' &c.

THE VICTORIA CROSS.

The 1st of March 1857, is one among many days associated with the bestowal of the Victoria Cross upon heroic soldiers and sailors. The affair is in itself a trifle; yet it involves a principle of some importance. England cannot be said to be altogether happy in her modes of rewarding merit. The friendless and the unobtrusive are apt to be pushed aside, and to be supplanted by those who can call boldness and influence to their aid. Such at any rate has been the case in the army and navy; the humble soldiers and sailors have always received their full share of hard knocks, while the officers have carried off the honours and rewards. The nation has often felt and said that this was wrong; and the authorities of the War Office have judiciously yielded to the public sentiment in this among many other matters. It was in the middle of the Crimean war that the War Office undertook to 'consider' the subject; but a period of many months passed before the 'consideration' led to any results. At length on the 8th of February 1856, the *London Gazette* announced that Her Majesty had under her Royal Sign Manual been pleased to institute a new naval and military decoration entitled the 'Victoria Cross.' Unlike any other decoration recognised in our army and navy, this order is to be conferred *for valour only*—irrespective of rank or station; and the recipient becomes also entitled

to a pension of £10 a year for life. The Victoria Cross is a simple affair as a work of art. It consists of a bronze Maltese cross with the royal crest in the centre, and underneath it a scroll bearing the words 'FOR VALOUR;' it is suspended by a red ribbon if worn on the breast of a soldier, and by a blue ribbon if worn by a sailor. Trifling as it is, however, the men highly prize it, for hitherto it has been honestly bestowed. The reader will call to mind that remarkable ceremony in the summer of 1857, when the Queen bestowed the Victoria Cross, with her own hand, on sixty-one noble fellows in Hyde-park. Of those thus honoured, twenty-five were commissioned officers, fifteen were warrant and non-commissioned officers, and the remaining twenty-one were private soldiers and common seamen. In every instance there was a distinct recognition in the *Official Gazette* of the specific act of valour for which the cross was bestowed—whether arising out of the Crimean, the Chinese, or the Indian wars—in order to afford proof that merit, not favour, won the reward. Here we are told that Joseph Trewvas, seaman, 'cut the hawsers of the floating-bridge in the Straits of Genitchi under a heavy fire of musketry;' on which occasion he was wounded. 'The late gallant Captain Sir William Peel,' we are told, 'took up a live shell that fell among some powder cases; the fuse was still burning, and the shell burst as he threw it over the parapet.' Here is an incident which warms one's blood while we read it: 'In the charge of the Light Cavalry Brigade at Balaklava, Trumpet-Major Crawford's horse fell and dismounted him, and he lost his sword; he was attacked by two Cossacks, when private Samuel Parkes (whose horse had been shot) saved his life by placing himself between them and the Trumpet-Major, and drove them away by his sword. In the attempt to follow the Light Cavalry Brigade in the retreat, they were attacked by six Russians, whom Parkes kept at bay, and retired slowly fighting, and defending the Trumpet-Major for some time.' In spite of the wretched official English of this description (in which 'he' and 'his,' 'they' and 'whose' are hopelessly wandering to find their proper verbs), we cannot fail to take a liking for the gallant trooper Parkes. Then there was Serjeant-Major Henry, of the Artillery, who at the terrible battle of Inkermann, 'defended the guns of his battery until he had received twelve bayonet wounds.' During the siege of Sebastopol, a rifle-pit was occupied by two Russians, who annoyed our troops by their fire, whereupon 'Private M'Gregor, of the Rifles, crossed the open space under fire, and taking cover under a rock, dislodged them, and occupied the pit.' In India some of the Victoria Crosses were given to the gallant fellows by their commanding officers, in the Queen's name; and when those officers were men of tact and good feeling, they contrived to enhance the value of the reward by a few well-chosen remarks. Thus, Brigadier Stidste, in giving Crosses to two men of the 52nd Foot, pointed out to them the difference between the Order of the Bath and the Order of Valour, adding, in reference to the latter, 'I only wish I had it myself.'

The Emblem of Wales.

Various reasons are assigned by the Welsh for wearing the leek on St David's Day. Some affirm it to be in memory of a great victory obtained over the Saxons. It is said that, during the conflict, the Welshmen, by order of St David, put leeks into their hats to distinguish themselves from their enemies. To quote the *Cambria* of Rolt, 1759:

———'Tradition's tale
Recounting tells how famed Menevia's priest
Marshalled his Britons, and the Saxon host
Discomfited ; how the green leek his bands
Distinguished, since by Britons annual worn,
Commemorates their tutelary saint.'

In the *Diverting Post*, 1705, we have the following lines :

' Why, on St David's Day, do Welshmen seek
To beautify their hat with verdant leek
Of nauseous smell ? For *honour* 'tis, hur say,
" *Dulce et decorum est pro patria* "—
Right, Sir, to die or fight it is, I think,
But how is't *Dulce*, when you for it stink ?'

Shakspeare makes the wearing of the leek to have originated at the battle of Cressy. In the play of *Henry V*. Fluellin, addressing the monarch, says :

' Your grandfather, of famous memory, an't please your Majesty, and your great uncle, Edward the Black Prince of Wales, as I have read in the chronicles, fought a most prave pattle here in France.
' *King.* They did, Fluellin !
' *Fluellin.* Your Majesty says very true ; if your Majesty is remembered of it, the Welshman did goot service in a garden where leeks did grow ; wearing leeks in their Monmouth caps, which your Majesty knows to this hour is an honourable padge of the service ; and I do believe your Majesty takes no scorn to wear leek upon St Tavy's Day.'

The observance of St David's Day was long countenanced by royalty. Even sparing Henry VII. could disburse two pounds among Welshmen on their saint's anniversary ; and among the Household Expenses of the princess Mary for 1544. is an entry of a gift of fifteen shillings to the Yeomen of the King's Guard for bringing a leek to Her Grace on St David's Day. Misson, alluding to the custom of wearing the leek, records that His Majesty William III. was complaisant enough to bear his Welsh subjects company, and two years later we find the following paragraph in *The Flying Post* (1699) : ' Yesterday, being St David's Day, the King, according to custom, wore a leek in honour of the Ancient Britons, the same being presented to him by the sergeant-porter, whose place it is, and for which he claims the clothes His Majesty wore that day ; the courtiers in imitation of His Majesty wore leeks also.'

We cannot say now as Hierome Porter said in 1632, ' that it is sufficient theme for a jealous Welshman to ground a quarrel against him that doth not honour his cap' with the leek on St David's Day ; our modern head-dress is too ill-adapted for such verdant decorations to allow of their being worn, even if the national sentiment was as vigorous as ever ; but gilt leeks are still carried in procession by the Welsh branches of

320

Friendly Societies, and the national badge may be seen decorating the mantelpiece in Welsh houses on the anniversary of the patron saint of the principality.

Whatever may be the conflicting opinions on the origin of wearing the leek in Wales, it is certain that this vegetable appears to have been a favourite dish with Welshmen as far back as we can trace their history. In Caxton's *Description of Wales*, speaking of the Maners and Rytes of the Welshmen, he says :

' They have gruell to potage,
And *Leekes* kynde to companage.'

As also :

' Atte meete, and after eke,
Her solace is salt and *Leeke*.'

Worlidge mentions the love of the Welsh for this alliaceous food. ' I have seen the greater part of a garden there stored with leeks, and part of the remainder with onions and garlic.' Owen in his *Cambrian Biography*, 1803, observes that the symbol of the leek, attributed to St David, probably originated from the custom of Cymhortha, when the farmers, assisting each other in ploughing, brought their leeks to aid the common repast.

Perhaps the English, if not the Welsh reader will pardon us for expressing our inclination to believe that the custom had no romantic origin whatever, but merely sprung up in allusion to the prominence of the leek in the *cuisine* of the Welsh people.

MARCH 2.

St Simplicius, Pope, buried 483. Martyrs under the Lombards, 6th century. St Joavan, or Joevin, bishop in Armorica, 6th century. St Marnan, of Scotland, 620. St Ceadda, or Chad, bishop of Lichfield, 673. St Charles the Good, Earl of Flanders, martyr, 1124.

ST CEADDA, OR CHAD.

St Chad is regarded as the missionary who introduced Christianity among the East Saxons. He was educated at the monastery of Lindisfarne, or Holy Island, of which he became the bishop. He exercised at the same time the like jurisdiction over the extensive diocese of Mercia, first fixing that see at Lichfield, so called from the great number of martyrs slain and buried there, under Maximinanus Herudeus ; the name signifying the field of carcases.* Bede assures us that St Chad zealously devoted himself to all the laborious functions of his charge, visiting his diocese on foot, preaching the gospel, and seeking out the poorest and most abandoned persons in the meanest cottages and in the fields, that he might instruct them. When old age compelled him to retire, he settled with seven or eight monks near Lichfield. Tradition described him as greatly affected by storms ; he

* Such is the tradition ; but according to Dr. Harwood, the name refers to the marshy nature of the surrounding country, the Saxon word *lych* signifying a marsh.

called thunder 'the voice of God,' regarding it as designed to call men to repentance, and lower their self-sufficiency. On these occasions, he would go into the church, and continue in prayer until the storm had abated; it is related that seven days before his death, a monk named Arvinus, who was outside the building in which he lay, heard a sound as of heavenly music attendant upon a company of angels, who visited the saint to forewarn him of his end.

Upon his canonization, St Chad became the patron saint of medicinal springs. His bones were removed from Stow, where he died, to the site of Lichfield cathedral, about the year 700, and were inclosed in a rich shrine, which, being resorted to by multitudes of pilgrims, caused the gradual rise of the city of Lichfield from a small village. The whole place is rich with memorials of the good St Chad; there is a small church dedicated to him, being erected on the site of St Mary's church, which he built, and hard by which he was buried. It is related that the saint's tomb here had a hole in it, through which the pilgrims used to take out portions of the dust, which, mixed with holy water, they gave to men and animals to drink.

The history of the cathedral has this romantic episode: In 1643, the Royalists, under the Earl of Chesterfield, fortified the close. They were attacked by the Parliamentary troops under Lord Brooke, of whom it is told that, on approaching the city, he prayed, if his cause was unjust, he might presently be cut off: whereupon he was killed by a brace of bullets from a musket, or wall piece, discharged by a deaf and dumb gentleman named Dyott, from the middle tower of the church, and fell at a spot now marked by an inscription:

'　'Twas levelled when fanatic Brooke
　　The fair cathedral stormed and took;
　　But thanks to heaven and good St Chad,
　　A guerdon meet the spoiler had!'—
　　　　　　　　　　　　Marmion, vi. 36.

This occurring on the 2nd of March, the anniversary of St Chad, was looked upon by the Royalists as a signal interference of Providence.

On the east side of the town is St Chad's Well, which Leland describes as 'a spring of pure water, with a stone in the bottom of it, on which, some say, St Chad was wont, naked, to stand in the water and pray; at this stone St Chad had his oratory in the time of Wulfere, King of the Mercians.' Sir John Floyer, the celebrated physician, of Lichfield,* who, in 1702, published a curious essay *To Prove Cold Bathing both Safe and Useful*, describes St Chad as 'one of the first converters of our nation, who used immersion in the baptism of the Saxons. And the well near Stow, which may bear his name, was probably his baptistery, it being deep enough for immersion, and conveniently seated near the church; and that has the reputation of curing sore eyes, &c., as most holy wells in England do, which got that name from the baptizing the first Christians in them, and to the memory of the holy bishops

* It was by the advice of Sir John Floyer that Dr Johnson was taken to London, to be touched for the King's evil by Queen Anne.

21

who baptized in them they were commonly dedicated, and called by their name.' Sir John gives a table of diseases for which St Chad's bath is efficacious, ' with some directions to the common people;' and he finds diseases for nearly every letter in the alphabet. A small temple-like edifice has been erected over the well, in memory of St Chad. Sir John Floyer, it should be added, set up a sort of rival bath, the water of which he shews to be the coldest in the neighbourhood, the success of which he foretells when he has 'prevailed over the prejudices of the common people, who usually despise all cheap and common remedies, which have ordinarily the greatest effects.'

In London we possessed a *St Chad's Well*, on the east side of the Gray's Inn-road, near King's Cross, in Fifteen-foot lane. Here a tenement was, about a century ago, called St Chad's Well-house, from the medicinal spring there, which was strongly recommended by the medical faculty of the day. It long remained one of the favourite spas of the metropolis, with Bagnigge Wells, and the spring which gave name to Spa-fields. Two of these spas have almost gone out of recollection; but St Chad's remained to our time, with its neat garden, and economical medicine at a half-penny per glass. Old Joseph Munden, the comedian, when he resided at Kentish Town, was for many years in the habit of visiting St Chad's three times a-week, and drinking its waters; as did the judge, Sir Allan Chambre, when he lived at Prospect-house, Highgate. Mr Alexander Mensall, who, for fifty years, kept the Gordon House Academy at Kentish Town, used to walk, with his pupils, once a week, to St Chad's, to drink its waters, as a means of 'keeping the doctor out of the house.' In 1825, Mr Hone wrote, 'The miraculous water is aperient, and was some years ago quaffed by the bilious, and other invalids, who flocked thither in crowds. . . . . A few years, and it will be with its water, as with the water of St Pancras Well, which is inclosed in the garden of a private house, near old St Pancras churchyard.'

London is, however, still more extensively associated with St Chad, through its excellent citizen Sir Hugh Myddelton; for the New River takes its rise from Chad's Well springs, situated in the meadows, about midway between Hertford and Ware; and when this water reached the north of London, it there gave name to Chad-well-street.

Born.—D. Junius Juvenal, Latin poet, A.D. *circ.* 40, *Aquinum;* Sir Thomas Bodley (Bodleian Library), 1544, *Exeter;* William Murray, Earl of Mansfield, Lord Chief Justice, 1705, *Perth;* Suchet, Duke of Albuera, 1772, *Lyons;* Hugh Edward Strickland, naturalist, 1811, *Righton, York.*

Died.—Pope Pelagius I., 560; Lothaire III., of France, 986, poisoned, *Compiègne;* Robert Abbot, Bishop of Salisbury, 1618; Cardinal Bouillon, 1715, *Rome;* Francesco Bianchini, mathematician, 1729, *Rome;* Solomon Gessner, painter and poet, 1788, *Zurich:* John Wesley, founder of Methodism, 1791, *London;* Horace Walpole, Earl of Orford, 1797, *Berkeley-square;* Francis, fifth Duke of Bedford, 1802, *Woburn Abbey;* Francis II., Emperor of Austria, 1835; W. H. M. Olbers, astronomer, 1840; Giambattista Rubini, singer. 1854.

SIR THOMAS BODLEY.

Among the great men who adorn the reign of the virgin queen, not one of the least dignified figures is that of Sir Thomas Bodley, founder of the public library at Oxford.

Bodley, in consequence of his father being unable to live in England during the reign of Mary, commenced his education at Geneva, and on returning home at fourteen was already a good scholar. Entering afterwards at Magdalen College, Oxford, he became in succession a fellow of Merton, and the orator of the University. At a mature age, he travelled on the Continent, chiefly that he might acquire the modern languages; then, returning to his college, he devoted himself to the study of history and politics. In 1583, he was made gentleman usher to Queen Elizabeth; and in 1585 he married a rich widow of Bristol. From soon after this date until 1597, Bodley was employed by Queen Elizabeth in several embassies and commissions, and he resided nearly five years in Holland. It need scarcely be remarked how largely this continental education, travel, and experience must have qualified Bodley for the noble task which he had set himself—the restoration of the public library of the University of Oxford.

Bodley, having succeeded in all his negotiations for his royal mistress, obtained his final recall in 1597, when, finding his advancement at court obstructed by the jealousies and intrigues of great men, he retired from it, and all public business. In the same year he set about founding anew the public library, by offering to restore the buildings in which had been deposited the books and manuscripts left by Humphrey, the good Duke of Gloucester, all of which had been destroyed or dispersed before the year 1555, the room continuing empty until restored by Sir Thomas Bodley. His offer being gladly accepted, he settled a fund for the purchase of books, and the maintenance of proper officers, and commenced his undertaking by presenting a large collection of books purchased on the Continent, and valued at £10,000. Other collections and contributions followed, to such an amount that the old building was no longer sufficient to contain them, when Sir Thomas Bodley proposed to enlarge the edifice; and, his liberal example being followed, the University was enabled to add three other sides, forming the quadrangle and rooms for the schools, &c. He did not, however, live to see the whole completed. This illustrious person died in 1612.

The Bodleian Library was first opened to the public on the 8th of November 1602. Sir Thomas, then lately knighted, was declared the founder; and in 1605, Lord Buckhurst, Earl of Dorset, and Chancellor of the University, placed his bust in the library. An annual speech in praise of Sir Thomas Bodley was founded in 1681, and is delivered on the visitation-day of the library, November the 8th.

Casaubon visited the Bodleian Library very shortly after the completion of the first building, in 1606. 'None of the colleges,' he writes, ' attracted me so much as the Bodleian Library, a work rather for a king than a private man. It

is certain that Bodley, living or dead, must have expended 200,000 livres on that building. The ground-plot is the figure of the letter T. The part which represents the perpendicular stem was formerly built by some prince, and is very handsome; the rest was added by Bodley with no less magnificence. . . . . The upper story is the library itself, very well built, and fitted with an immense quantity of books. Do not imagine that such plenty of manuscripts can be found here as in the Royal Library (of Paris); there are not a few manuscripts in England, but nothing to what the King possesses. But the number of books is wonderful, and increasing every year; for Bodley has bequeathed a considerable revenue for that purpose. As long as I remained at Oxford I passed whole days in the Library; for books cannot be taken out, but the library is open to all scholars for seven or eight hours every day. You might always see, therefore, many of these greedily enjoying the banquet prepared for them, which gave me no small pleasure.'

As you enter the library you are struck by an excellent portrait of the founder, by Cornelius Jansen; and by its side and opposite, those of the first principal librarians. There are also other portraits of much interest, particularly that of Junius, the famous Teutonic scholar, by Vandyck; of Selden, an exquisite painting by Mytens; and of Humphrey Wanley, some time under-librarian here. The ceiling is painted with the arms of the University, and those of Bodley. The books in this part of the library retain still their ancient classified arrangement, according to Bodley's will.

It would require a volume to enumerate the many important additions in books and manuscripts, made to this library by its numerous benefactors. The famous library of more than 200 Greek manuscripts, formed by Giacomo Baroccio, a Venetian nobleman, was added in 1627, by will of Herbert, Earl of Pembroke, then Chancellor of the University. In 1633, nearly the same number of manuscripts, chiefly Latin and English, were given by Sir Kenelm Digby. Both these collections are supposed to have been presented at the instigation of Archbishop Laud, who succeeded the Earl as Chancellor, and who himself enriched the library with more than 1300 manuscripts in the Oriental and European tongues. The Selden Library, of more than 8000 volumes of printed books and manuscripts, was next deposited here by Selden's executors. In the two succeeding centuries we find among the benefactors Junius, Marshall, Hyde, Lord Crewe, Tanner, Bishop of St Asaph, Rawlinson, Browne Willis, Thomas Hearne, and Godwin. Among the subsequent additions were the collections of early plays and English poetry, by Malone; and of topography by Gough. To these, prompted by a similar feeling of princely munificence, the late Mr Francis Douce added his tastefully collected library of printed books and manuscripts, coins and medals, prints and drawings, the result of years of patient and untiring research.

The funds of the library are kept up by small fees paid by members of the University at their matriculation, and by a trifling annual contribution from all as soon as they shall have taken their B.A. degree. This, with legacies bequeathed to it, independent of the University chest, has enabled the library, from time to time, to increase its treasures. The collections of manuscripts of D'Orville ; Clarke, the celebrated traveller ; the Abbate Canonici of Venice ; the printed books and manuscripts of the Oppenheimer family, comprising the finest library of Rabbinical literature ever got together, have, by these means, been purchased. A large addition of books is also made annually by new publications sent to the library, under the Act of Parliament for securing copyright.

HORACE WALPOLE.

A person to whom the second stratum of modern history is so much indebted as Horace Walpole, could not well be overlooked in the present work. Born just within the verge of aristocratic rank—third son of the great minister Sir Robert Walpole, who was ennobled as Earl of Orford—and living through a century of unimportant events and little men—the subject of this notice devoted talents of no mean order to comparatively trifling pursuits, and yet with the

effect of conferring an obligation on the world. His works on royal and noble authors and on artists are valuable books ; his letters, in which he has chronicled all the curious and memorable affairs, both public and private, during sixty years, are of inestimable value as a general picture of the time, though perhaps we are disposed to rest too securely on them for details of fact. It is vain to hanker on the essential effeminacy and frivolity of Horace Walpole, or even to express our fears that he did not possess much heart. Take him for what he is, and what he did for us, and does any one not feel that we could well have spared a better man ?

Horace had twenty-eight years of parliamentary life, without acquiring any distinction as a politician. He professed strenuous Whig opinions, but in his heart was without popular sympathies. His historical works shew that he was capable of considerable literary efforts. Being, however, a well-endowed sinecurist, and a member of the highest aristocratic circles, he had no motive for any great exertion of his faculties. It literally became the leading business of this extraordinary man to make up a house of curiosities. His great 'work' was *Strawberry Hill*. He had purchased this little mansion as a mere cottage in 1747, and

STRAWBERRY HILL, GRAND GALLERY.

for the remaining fifty years of his life he was constantly adding to it, decorating it, and increasing the number of the pictures, old china, and other objects of *virtu* which he had assembled in it. The pride of his life—old bachelor as he was—was to see pretty duchesses and countesses wandering through its corridors and basking on its little terrace. There is one redeeming trait in the fantastic aristocrat. When he succeeded in old age to the family titles, he could hardly be induced to act the peer's part, and still signed with his ordinary name, or as 'Uncle of the late Earl of Orford.' The love of books and articles of taste was at least sufficient to overpower in his mind the glitter of the star.

The glories of Strawberry Hill came to an end in 1842, when the whole of the pictures and curiosities which it contained were dispersed by a twenty-four days' sale, through the agency of the renowned auctioneer, George Robins. On that occasion, a vast multitude of people flocked to the house to see it, and for the chance of picking up some of its multifarious contents. The general style of the mansion was too unsubstantial and trashy to give much satisfaction. Yet it was found to contain a Great Staircase, highly decorated, an Armoury, a room called the Star-chamber, a Gallery, and some other apartments. All were as full as they could hold of pictures, armour, articles of bijouterie, china, and other curiosities. One room was devoted to portraits by Holbein. In another was the hat of Cardinal Wolsey, together with a clock which had been presented by King Henry VIII. as a morning gift to Anne Bullen. The dagger of King Henry VIII. and a mourning ring for Charles I., vied with the armour of Francis I. in attracting attention. One article of great elegance was a silver bell, which had been formed

PAPAL CURSING BELL FOR ANIMALS.

by Benvenuto Cellini, for Pope Clement VII., with a rich display of carvings on the exterior, representing serpents, flies, grasshoppers, and other insects, the purpose of the bell having been to serve in a papal cursing of these animals, when they on one occasion became so troublesome as to demand that mode of castigation. Another curious article, suggestive of the beliefs of a past age, was the *shew-stone* of Dr Dee, a piece of polished cannel coal, which had been

used by that celebrated mystic as a mirror in which to see spirits. The general style of Strawberry Hill was what passed in Walpole's days as Gothic. However really deficient it might be in correctness, or inferior in taste, the effect of the interior of the Great Gallery was interesting. Conspicuous in this room was a portrait of Lady Falkland in white by Van Somer, which suggested to Walpole the incident of the figure walking out of its picture frame in his tale of the *Castle of Otranto*.

Strawberry Hill, if in its nature capable of being preserved, would have been the best memorial of Horace Walpole. This failing, we find his next best monument in the collective edition of his letters, as arranged and illustrated by Mr Peter Cunningham. Allowing for the distortions of whim and caprice, and perhaps some perversions of truth through prejudice and spleen, this work is an inestimable record of the era it represents. Its prominent characteristic is garrulity. In the language of the *Edinburgh Review* (Dec. 1818): 'Walpole was, indeed, a garrulous *old* man nearly all his days; and, luckily for his gossiping propensities, he was on familiar terms with the gay world, and set down as a man of genius by the Princess Amelia, George Selwyn, Mr Chute, and all persons of the like talents and importance. His descriptions of court dresses, court revels, and court beauties, are in the highest style of perfection,—sprightly, fantastic, and elegant: and the zeal with which he hunts after an old portrait or a piece of broken glass, is ten times more entertaining than if it were lavished on a worthier object. He is indeed the very prince of gossips,—and it is impossible to question his supremacy, when he floats us along in a stream of bright talk, or shoots with us the rapids of polite conversation. He delights in the small squabbles of great politicians and the puns of George Selwyn,—enjoys to madness the strife of loo with half a dozen bitter old women of quality,—revels in a world of chests, cabinets, commodes, tables, boxes, turrets, stands, old printing, and old china,—and indeed lets us loose at once amongst all the frippery and folly of the last two centuries with an ease and a courtesy equally amazing and delightful. His mind, as well as his house, was piled up with Dresden china, and illuminated through painted glass; and we look upon his heart to have been little better than a case full of enamels, painted eggs, ambers, lapis-lazuli, cameos, vases, and rock crystals. This may in some degree account for his odd and quaint manner of thinking, and his utter poverty of feeling. He could not get a plain thought out of that cabinet of curiosities, his mind;—and he had no room for feeling,—no place to plant it in, or leisure to cultivate it. He was at all times the slave of elegant trifles; and could no more screw himself up into a decided and solid personage, than he could divest himself of petty jealousies and miniature animosities. In one word, everything about him was in little; and the smaller the object, and the less its importance, the higher did his estimation and his praises of it ascend. He piled up trifles to a colossal height—and made a pyramid of nothings "most marvellous to see."'

THE FIFTH DUKE OF BEDFORD AND BLOOMS-BURY HOUSE.

On the 2nd of March 1802, died Francis, fifth Duke of Bedford, unmarried, at the age of thirty-seven, deeply lamented on account of his amiable character and the enlightened liberality with which he had dispensed the princely fortunes of his family. In his tenure of the honours and estates of the house of Bedford, we find but one incident with which we are disposed to find fault, or at which we might express regret, the taking down of that family mansion in Bloomsbury-square which had been the residence of the patriot lord, and toward which he had thrown a look of sorrow on passing to the scaffold in Lincoln's Inn Fields. That house should have been kept up by the race of Russell as long as two bricks of it would hold together.

This mansion, which was taken down in 1800, had been built in the reign of Charles II. for Thomas Wriothesley, Earl of Southampton, and it came into the Bedford family by the marriage of the patriot Lord Russell to the admirable daughter of the Earl, Lady Rachel. It occupied the whole north side of the square, with gardens extending behind towards what is now the City-road, the site of Russell-square, and of many handsome streets besides. There was something not easily to be accounted for in the manner in which the house and its contents were disposed of. The whole were set up to auction (May 7, 1800). A casual dropper-in bought the whole of the furniture and pictures, including Thornhill's copies of the cartoons (now in the Royal Academy), for the sum of £6,000. In *Dodsley's Annual Register*, 1800, the gallery is described as the only room of consequence in the mansion. This was fitted up by the fourth Duke of Bedford, who placed in it the copies of the cartoons by Thornhill, at the sale of whose collection they had been bought by the Duke for £200. The prices fetched by some of the pictures at the Bloomsbury House sale, by Mr Christie, appear very small: as, St John preaching in the Wilderness, by Raphael, 95 guineas; an Italian Villa, by Gainsborough, 90 guineas; four paintings of a Battle, by Cassinovi, which cost the Duke £1,000, were sold for 60 guineas; a fine Landscape, by Cuyp, 200 guineas; two beautiful bronze figures, Venus and Antinous, 20 guineas, and Venus couchant, from the antique, 20 guineas. Among the pictures was the Duel between Lord Mohun and the Duke of Hamilton, in Hyde Park. The celebrated statue of Apollo, which stood in the hall of Bedford House, was removed to Woburn: it originally cost 1000 guineas.

The week after, there were sold the double rows of lime-trees in the garden, and the ancient stem of the light and graceful acacia which stood in the court before the house, and which Walpole commends in his *Essay on Landscape Gardening*. The house was immediately pulled down; and, says the *Annual Register*, 'the site of a new square, of nearly the same dimensions as Lincoln's Inn Fields, and to be called Russell-square, has been laid out.'

The Bedford property in Bloomsbury has realized enormous sums: for example, New Oxford-street, occupying the site of the *Rookery* of St Giles, was made at a cost of £290,227 4s. 10d., of which £113,963 was paid to the Duke of Bedford alone, for freehold purchases.

HORACE WALPOLE ON BALLOONS.

On March 2, 1784, Blanchard, the aëronaut, made his first ascent from Paris, in a hydrogen balloon, to which he added wings and a rudder, proved on trial to be useless.

This was a busy year in ballooning; and among those who took interest in the novelty was Horace Walpole, who, in a letter of Jan. 13, thus speculates upon the chances of turning aërostation to account: 'You see the Airgonauts have passed the Rubicon. By their own account they were exactly birds; they flew through the air; perched on the top of a tree, some passengers climbed up, and took them in their nest. The smugglers, I suppose, will be the first that will improve upon the plan. However, if the project be ever brought to perfection, (though I apprehend it will be addled, like the ship that was to live under water and never came up again,) it will have a different fate from other discoveries, whose inventors are not known. In this age all that is done (as well as what is never done) is so faithfully recorded, that every improvement will be registered chronologically. Mr Blanchard's *Trip to Calais* puts me in mind of Dryden's *Indian Emperor*:

'"What divine monsters, O ye gods, are these,
    That float in air, and fly upon the seas?"

Dryden little thought that he was prophetically describing something more exactly than ships as conceived by Mexicans. If there is no air-sickness, and I were to go to Paris again, I would prefer a balloon to the packet-boat, and had as lief roost in an oak as sleep in a French inn, though I were to caw for my breakfast like the young ravens.'

In the autumn of the same year, Walpole is writing a letter at Strawberry Hill, when his servants call him away to see a balloon; he supposes Blanchard's, that was to be let off at Chelsea in the morning. He is writing to a friend, Mr Conway, and thus continues: 'I saw the balloon from the common field before the window of my round tower. It appeared about a third of the size of the moon, or less, when setting, something above the tops of the trees on the level horizon. It was then descending; and after rising and declining a little, it sunk slowly behind the trees, I should think about or beyond Sunbury, at five minutes after one.' This ascent leads Walpole to say, 't'other night I diverted myself with a sort of meditation on future *airgonation*, supposing it will not only be perfected, but will depose navigation. I did not finish it, because I am not skilled, like the gentleman that used to write political ship-news, in that style which I wanted to perfect my essay; but in the prelude I observed how ignorant the ancients were in supposing Icarus melted the wax of his wings by too near access to the sun, whereas he would have been frozen to death before he made the first port on that road. Next I discovered an alliance between

Bishop Wilkins's art of flying and his plan of universal language; the latter of which he, no doubt, calculated to prevent the want of an interpreter when he should arrive at the moon.

'But I chiefly amused myself with ideas of the change that would be made in the world by the substitution of balloons for ships. I supposed our seaports to become *deserted villages;* and Salisbury Plain, Newmarket Heath, (another canvass for alteration of ideas,) and all downs (but *the* Downs), arising into dockyards for aërial vessels. Such a field would be ample in furnishing new speculations. But to come to my ship-news:

'The good balloon, Dædalus, Captain Wingate, will fly in a few days for China; he will stop at the Monument to take in passengers.

' Arrived on Brand-sands, the Vulture, Captain Nabob; the Tortoise snow, from Lapland; the Pet-en-l'air, from Versailles; the Dreadnought, from Mount Etna, Sir W. Hamilton commander; the Tympany, Montgolfier. Foundered in a hurricane, the Bird of Paradise, from Mount Ararat; the Bubble, Sheldon, took fire, and was burnt to her gallery; and the Phœnix is to be cut down to a second-rate.'

' In these days Old Sarum will again be a town, and have houses in it. There will be fights in the air with wind-guns, and bows and arrows; and there will be prodigious increase of land for tillage, especially in France, by breaking up all public roads as useless.'

In December he writes: 'This enormous capital (London), that must have some occupation, is most innocently amused with those philosophic playthings, air-balloons. But, as half-a-million of people that impassion themselves for any object are always more childish than children, the good souls of London are much fonder of the *airgonauts* than of the toys themselves. Lunardi, the Neapolitan secretary, is said to have bought three or four thousand pounds in the stocks, by exhibiting his person, his balloon, and his dog and cat, at the " Pantheon," for a shilling each visitor. Blanchard, a Frenchman, is his rival, and I expect that they will soon have an air-fight in the clouds, like a stork and a kite.'

Since Walpole's time there have been changes in the value of public roads and the serviceableness of sea-ports, but from causes apart from aërial navigation—in which art comparatively little progress has been made since the year 1784.

ESCAPE OF LOUIS PHILIPPE TO ENGLAND, 1848.

It was on the 2nd of March 1848, that Louis Philippe, King of the French, after a career of vicissitude, perhaps unexampled in modern times, finally left France, and sought a sheltering place in England. The particulars of the King's escape form an episode of singular interest in the life of the dethroned monarch, and are related in the *Quarterly Review* for March 1850, being further confirmed to the Editor of the BOOK OF DAYS by one of the principal agents engaged in the transaction.

Our engraving represents the summer-house on the Côte de Grâce at Honfleur, in which King

Louis Philippe and Queen Marie-Amélie were concealed previous to their departure for England.

'Every one who has sailed in front of Honfleur, must have remarked a little chapel situated on the top of the wooded hill that overhangs the town. It was dedicated by the piety of the sailors of ancient days to Notre Dame de Grâce, as was a similar one on the opposite shore. From it, Mr de Perthuis' cottage is commonly called La Grâce; and we can easily imagine the satisfaction of the Royal guests at finding themselves under the shelter of a friendly roof with a name of such good omen.

'On Thursday, the 2nd of March (1848), just at daybreak, the inmates of La Grâce were startled by the arrival of a stranger, who, however, turned out to be Mr Jones, the English Vice-Consul at Hâvre, with a message from the Consul, Mr Featherstonhaugh, announcing that the *Express* steam-packet had returned, and was placed entirely at the King's disposal, and that Mr Jones would concert with his Majesty the means of embarkation. He also brought news, if possible, more welcome—a letter from Mr Besson, announcing that the Duke de Nemours, his little daughter, the Princess Marguerite, and the Princess Clementine, with her husband and children, were safe in England. This double good news reanimated the whole party, who were just before very much exhausted both in body and mind. But the main difficulty still remained; how they were to get to the *Express?*

' Escape became urgent; for not only had the Procureur de la République of the district hastened to Trouville with his gendarmes to seize the stranger (who, luckily, had left it some hours), but, having ascertained that the stranger was the King, and that Mr de Perthuis was in his company, that functionary concluded that his Majesty was at La Grâce, and a domiciliary visit to the Pavilion was subsequently made.

' The evening packet (from Hâvre to Honfleur) brought back Mr Besson and Mr Jones, with the result of the council held on the other side of the water, which was, that the whole party should instantly quit La Grâce, and, taking advantage of the dusk of the evening, embark in the same packet by which these gentlemen had arrived, for a passage to Hâvre, where there were but a few steps to be walked between leaving the Honfleur boat and getting on board the *Express*. The Queen was still to be Madame Lebrun; but the King, with an English passport, had become Mr William Smith. Not a moment was to be lost. The King, disguised as before, with the addition of a coarse great-coat, passed, with MM. de Rumigny and Thuret, through one line of streets; Madame Le Brun, leaning on her *nephew's* arm, by another. There was a great crowd on the quay of Honfleur, and several gendarmes; but Mr Smith soon recognised Mr Jones, the Vice-Consul, and, after a pretty loud salutation in English (which few Mr Smiths speak better), took his arm, and stepped on board the packet, where he sat down immediately on board one of the passengers' benches. Madame Le Brun took a seat on the other side. The vessel, the *Courier*, happened to be one that the King had employed the summer before at Tréport. M. Lamartine, who mistakes even the place, and all the circumstances of this embarkation, embroiders it with a statement that the King was recognised by the crew, who, with the honour and generosity inherent in all Frenchmen, would not betray him. We are satisfied that there are very few seamen who would have betrayed him; but the fact is, that he was not recognised; and, when the steward went about to collect the fares and some gratuity for the band, Mr Smith shook his head, as if understanding no French, and his friend Mr Jones paid for both. On landing at the quay of Hâvre, amidst a crowd of people and the *crieurs* of the several hotels was Mr Featherstonhaugh, who, addressing Mr Smith as his *uncle*, whom he was delighted to see, conducted him a few paces further on, into the *Express*, lying at the quay, with her steam up; Madame Le Brun following.'

MARCH 3.

St Marinus and Asterius, martyrs in Palestine, about 272. Saints Emeterius and Chelidonius, martyrs in Spain. St Winwaloe, abbot in Armorica, about 529. St Lamalisse, of Scotland, 7th century. St Cunegundes, empress, 1040.

Born.—Gisbert Voet, Leyden theologian, 1589; Edmund Waller, poet, 1605, *Coleshill*; Sir William Davenant, poet laureate, 1606, bapt. *Oxford*; Thomas Otway, dramatic poet, 1651. *Trotten, Sussex*; William Godwin, novelist, 1756, *Wisbeach*; W. C. Macready, tragedian, 1793. *London*.

Died.—Sir Nicholas Carew, beheaded, 1539, *Aldgate*; John Frederick, the Magnanimous, of Saxony, 1554; John Sturm, Lutheran teacher, 1589; George Herbert, poet, rector of *Bemerton*, 1633; Robert Hooke, philosopher, 1703; Camillo, Duke de Tullard, French Marshal, 1728; Rev. Dr William Stukeley, antiquary, 1765, *East Ham*; Dr William Hunter, 1783. *London*; Robert Adam, architect, 1792; Copley Fielding, landscape painter, 1855.

WALLER, DAVENANT, AND OTWAY.

This day is the anniversary of the birth of three English poets: Edmund Waller, in 1605; Sir William Davenant, in 1606; and Thomas Otway, in 1651.

Waller was the descendant of an ancient and honourable family in Buckinghamshire, and his mother was the sister of the patriot, John Hampden. He was educated at Eton, subsequently took his degree at King's College, Cambridge, and was sent to Parliament at the age of seventeen, as representative of the family borough of Agmondesham, having even then obtained considerable reputation as a poet. He was twice married, between the death of the first, and his union with the second, the more valuable productions of his muse were given to the world. He had become the suitor of the Lady Dorothea Sydney, daughter of the Earl of Leicester, whom he immortalized as *Sacharissa*, a name, 'formed,' as he used to say, 'pleasantly,' from sacharum, sugar. Yet he describes her as haughty and scornful. Sacharissa and her lover met long after the spring of life had passed, and on her asking him, 'When he would write such fine verses upon her again?' the poet ungallantly replied, 'Madam, when you are as young again.' As a politician, he was fickle and unsteady. The affair called his Plot, which terminated in his securing his own safety by appearing against his associates, has condemned his name to infamy. During the Commonwealth, he panegyrised Cromwell, but from no sincere conviction. The act, however, is almost redeemed by the wit of his reply to Charles II., with reference to the verses, that poets usually succeed best in fiction. He died in London in the autumn of 1688. Waller is described as possessing rare personal advantages, exceedingly eloquent, and as one of the most witty and gallant men of his time; so much so, that, according to Clarendon, 'his company was acceptable where his spirit was odious.' The first edition of his poems was printed in 1645. Prefixed to it was a whimsical address, purporting to be 'from the Printer to the Reader,' assigning as a reason for their publication, that surreptitious copies had found their way into the world, ill set forth under his name—so ill that he might justly disown them.

As a specimen of Waller's 'smoothness,' (which was the admiration of Pope), we give one of his lyrical poems, well known, but which can never be met with anywhere without giving pleasure:

' Go, lovely Rose,
Tell her that wastes her time and me.
　　That now she knows,
When I resemble her to thee,
How sweet and fair she seems to be.

Tell her that's young,
And shuns to have her graces spied,
　　That hadst thou sprung
In deserts, where no men abide,
Thou must have uncommended died.

Small is the worth
Of beauty from the light retired:
　　Bid her come forth,
Suffer herself to be desired,
And not blush so to be admired.

Then die, that she
The common fate of all things rare
　　May read in thee:
How small a part of time they share,
That are so wondrous sweet and fair.

In the churchyard of Beaconsfield, near the place of his birth, Waller lies buried beneath a handsome monument of white marble.

Davenant, aptly designated by Leigh Hunt, ' as the restorer of the stage in his time, and the last of the deep-working poetical intellects of the age that followed that of Elizabeth,' was the son of an innkeeper at Oxford. His mother was ' a very beautiful woman, of a good wit and conversation,' and as Shakspeare had frequented ' The Crown ' in his journeys from Warwickshire to London, scandal assigned other motives than those of friendship to the interest he early manifested to the youth, his namesake and godson. Davenant succeeded to the laureateship on the death of Ben Jonson. He was a great favourite with the Earl of Newcastle, who appointed him lieutenant-general of his ordnance.

In the civil war he obtained credit as a soldier, and was knighted by Charles I. at the siege of Gloucester. On the decline of the king's affairs, his life was saved, it is said, chiefly by the interference of Milton ; and it is believed that the intercession of Davenant afterwards mainly contributed to preserve Milton from the scaffold when matters changed· in England. After the Restoration, Davenant obtained a patent for the representation of dramatic pieces at the Duke's Theatre, in Lincoln's Inn Fields, and the house was opened with a new play of his own, entitled the *Siege of Rhodes*, in which he introduced a variety of beautiful scenery and machinery.

He wrote, in all, about twenty-five dramatic pieces. He died in 1668, and was interred in Westminster Abbey.

The only poem by Davenant, if we except his dramas, and a few minor addresses, is *Gondibert*, which he unfortunately left unfinished. Opinions differ greatly on the merits of this production ; but it is generally acknowledged to be ' without the charm of reality, and cold and abstracted ; yet full of chivalrous grandeur, noble thoughts, harmonious diction, and displays an accurate knowledge of human nature, and a deep spirit of philosophy.'

As a sample of Sir William Davenant's muse, we give the following song :

' The lark now leaves his wat'ry nest,
　And climbing, shakes his dewy wings ;
He takes this window for the east ;
　And to implore your light, he sings,
Awake, awake, the morn will never rise,
Till she can dress her beauty at your eyes.

' The merchant bows unto the seaman's star,
　The ploughman from the sun his season takes ;
But still the lover wonders what they are,
　Who look for day before his mistress wakes.
Awake, awake, break through your veils of lawn,
Then draw your curtains, and begin the dawn.'

Otway was not more remarkable for moving the tender passions, than for the variety of fortune to which he himself was subjected. Born the son of a clergyman, he was educated for the church, but on quitting Oxford, and coming to London, he became an actor, but performed with indifferent success. Otway was more valued for the sprightliness of his conversation and wit, which procured him the friendship of the Earl of Plymouth, who obtained for him a

328

cornet's commission in the troops which then served in Flanders. Otway was always in necessitous circumstances, and particularly so on his return from abroad. He had recourse to writing for the stage, and this was the only employment that nature seems to have fitted him for. Leigh Hunt terms Otway ' the poet of sensual pathos ; for, affecting as he sometimes is, he knows no way to the heart but through the senses.' In comedy, he has been considered too licentious, which, however, was no great objection to those who lived in the profligate days of Charles II. ; but in tragedy ' where he does not intend to be sublime, but confines himself to his own element, the pathetic, no writer can produce more powerful effects than his.'

But although Otway possessed, in so eminent a degree, the rare talent of writing to the heart, he was not favourably regarded by some of his contemporary poets, nor was he always successful in his dramatic compositions. After experiencing many reverses of fortune in regard to his circumstances, but generally changing for the worse, he died April 13, 1685, at a public-house on Tower-hill, whither he had retired to avoid the pressure of his creditors. The horrible story of his having been choked by attempting too eagerly to swallow a piece of bread, of which he had been some time in want, has been successfully controverted.

Besides ten plays, Otway composed some miscellaneous poems, and wrote several translations. The beauty and delicacy of Otway's imagery will be seen in the following example :

' You took her up a little tender flower,
　Just sprouted on a bank, which the next frost
Had nipt, and with a careful, loving hand,
Transplanted her into your own fair garden,
Where the sun always shines. There long she
　flourished ;
Grew sweet to sense, and lovely to the eye ;
Till at the last a cruel spoiler came,
Cropped this fair rose, and rifled all its sweetness,
Then threw it like a loathsome weed away.'

―――

GEORGE HERBERT.

Through Izaak Walton the personal memory of George Herbert has been preserved. He was born on the 3rd of April 1593, in Montgomery Castle, Wales, being the fifth brother of Lord Herbert of Cherbury. He was educated at Trinity College, Cambridge, and in 1619 was chosen orator for the University. In those days King James used to go hunting about Newmarket and Royston, and was frequently invited to Cambridge, where Herbert, as orator, had to receive him. The King was so charmed by Herbert's fine speeches that he gave him a sinecure of £120 a-year, with hopes of yet better things. Lord Bacon, whom Walton happily designates ' the great secretary of Nature,' made Herbert's acquaintance at Cambridge, and so estimated his powers, that he submitted some writings to his criticism and revision. With the death of King James, in 1625, ended all Herbert's cherished hopes of promotion at court. After some severe struggles with his ambition, he resolved to take sacred orders, and in 1626 he was appointed prebend of Layton Ecclesia, a village in Hunts. Plagued with ague, he removed in 1630 to the healthier parsonage of Bemerton, a mile from Salisbury, where he died in 1632, at the early age of thirty-nine.

Herbert's fame rests on a posthumous publication. When dying, he handed a manuscript to a friend, saying, ' Sir, I pray deliver this little book to my dear brother Farrer, and tell him he shall find in it a picture of the many spiritual conflicts that have passed betwixt God and my soul. Desire him to read it, and then, if he can think it may turn to the advantage of any poor dejected soul, let it be made public ; if not, let him burn it.' The little book was *The Temple, or Sacred Poems and Private Ejaculations*. Mr Farrer had it printed at Cambridge in 1633, and it at once rose into high popularity. Walton, writing in 1670, says that 20,000 copies had been sold, a large number for the seventeenth century. Herbert's imagination found its joy and exercise in the services and rites of the Church of England; what Nature was to Wordsworth, the Prayer-book was to him ; and until Keble wrote, he was *par spécialité* the ecclesiastical poet. Our enjoyment of his verses is greatly marred through his free use of quaint conceits and fantastic imagery, by which his pious and often profound thoughts are obscured rather than illustrated. Herbert had a passion for music, and composed many of his hymns, that he might sing them to his lute and viol.

DR STUKELEY, THE ANTIQUARY, AND HIS SPECULATIONS.

This writer on Roman and British antiquities, the next distinguished investigator after Strype, died at the rectory-house of St George the Martyr, Queen-square, London.

He was born at Holbeach, in Lincolnshire, in 1687, and completed his education at Benet College, Cambridge. Here, natural science was his favourite pursuit, and with his friend and fellow-collegian, Stephen Hales, he used to ramble over Gogmagog Hills and the bogs of Cherry Hunt Moor, gathering simples ; they also studied together anatomy and chemistry, and performed many curious dissections and experiments. After practising for a time as a physician, first at Boston, then in London, finally at Grantham, Stukeley relinquished medicine, and took orders. At first he obtained good preferments in Lincolnshire, but in 1747, being presented to the rectory of St George the Martyr, in Queen-square, he once more settled in the metropolis, where, and at Kentish-town, he spent the rest of his life. Stukeley obtained this living from the Duke of Montague, with whom he had become acquainted some years before, when they were associated as founders of the Egyptian Society. It is curious to us now-a-days to hear Stukeley thus describing his first lodging, at one Mrs Machin's, Ormond-street. 'On one side of my lodgings we have a *beau* street, and those sorts of entertainments it affords, and in my study backwards I have a fine view to Hampstead, and the rural scene of haymakers, &c. Next door I have the beautiful sight of Lord

Powis's house, the most regular piece of architecture of any house in London, and a sharp fresh air, so that I enjoy a perfect *rus in urbe.*' He next lived in Queen-square, the north side of which ' was left open,' it is said, for the sake of the beautiful landscape view.

Stukeley's first antiquarian work was an account of the celebrated *Arthur's Oven*, in Scotland ; next, his *Itinerarium Curiosum*, of which the second volume, or *Centuria*, is of all Stukeley's works the most sought after. He next published two works on Abury and Stonehenge, and he was the first to investigate the tumuli of that neighbourhood. He carefully studied the form and arrangement of Abury, and his engravings and restorations of Stonehenge are valuable ; he regarded this work as a temple of the British Druids ; but, in both cases, his essays are full of fanciful and irrelevant speculation, which, John Britton tells us, for many years so harassed and distressed him, that he was ' often tempted to relinquish the pursuit [of antiquities], in despair of ever arriving at anything like proof, or rational evidence.'

In 1757, Stukeley printed his account of the work of Richard of Cirencester, *De Situ Britanniæ*,' from the MS. sent to him as having been recently discovered at Copenhagen, by Charles Julius Bertram. The *Itinerary* contains eighteen journeys, which Richard says he compiled from certain fragments by a Roman general, from Ptolemy, and other authors ; he mentions 176 stations (while Antoninus has only 113), some of them considerably north of the wall of Severus. The credit and fidelity of Richard have been doubted, but wherever the subject has admitted of local investigation, the result has been favourable to his authenticity. Gibbon says of him, that ' he shews a genuine knowledge of antiquity very extraordinary for a monk of the fourteenth century.'

In 1758, Stukeley published his *Account of the Medallic History of Marcus Aurelius Valerius Carausius, Emperor of Britain*, of which work Gibbon somewhat ungratefully says, ' I have used his materials, and rejected most of his fanciful conjectures.' It was this lively and licentious fancy which brought the ingenuity and learning which he really possessed into discredit. He undoubtedly described much that was curious and valuable, and which would probably have been lost but for his record of it. But his theories were his bane. Among his Stonehenge speculations, he laments the loss of a tablet of tin found there in the time of Henry VIII., inscribed with strange characters, which Sammes thought to be Punic, but Stukeley himself Irish. He adds : ' No doubt but what it was a memorial of the founders, wrote by the Druids, and had it been preserved till now, would have been an invaluable curiosity.'

Horace Walpole, adverting to the earthquake speculations of 1750, tells us : ' One Stukeley, a parson, has accounted for it, and I think prettily, by electricity—but that is the fashionable cause, and everything is resolved into electrical appearances, as formerly everything was accounted for by Des Cartes's vortices and Sir Isaac's gravitation.'

Regarding Stukeley's Lincolnshire life there is some pleasant gossip in Thompson's *History of Boston*, gleaned from letters and diaries, and affording some glimpses of the social life of that period.

In London, as he tells us, he frequented no levees, but 'took a vast deal of solitude,' and, instead of running from the Royal Society to the Antiquaries, retreated every night at six o'clock to his contemplative pipe. 'I love solitude in London,' he writes, 'and the beauty of living there is, that we can mix in company and solitude in just proportion; whilst in the country we have nothing else but solitude?'

Dr Stukeley was buried at East Ham, in Essex, where, by his own particular desire, there is no monument to denote his resting-place. He appears to have been a single-hearted, good man, who, after some experience of public life, found that 'home was most agreeable.'

In the library of the Gentlemen's Society at Spalding are preserved several of Stukeley's letters, in one of which he strenuously maintains the opinion that Britain was originally settled by Brute or Brito, the descendant of Æneas and Lavinia. 'In confidence of the truth of this descent from Æneas,' says Stukeley, 'I have endeavoured to unravel his pedigree through all the labyrinths of Grecian fable up to Noah, wherein one way or other is comprehended some part at least of all the famous men and kingdoms of Greece, Italy, and Egypt, where there is any mutual relation by marriage or descent; and this will be particularly useful to me in reading the classics.'

The only geological opinion to be found in these letters is the following : 'At Edmondthorp, in Leicestershire, I saw some huge and perfect scallop-shells, antediluvian, in the stone. You know Leicestershire consists of a red stone, brimful of the petrified shells of the old world, especially all round the bottom of the great cliff, which generally bounds Lincolnshire and that county. 'Tis easy to conceive that when the whole face of the county was an ocean, this cliff of ours, which begins at Hambledon, in Rutlandshire, and ends at Lincoln, stopped these shells from rolling down with the declining waters of the cataclysm into the sea, and so left them incrusted in the stone. I know this is the case all along the bottom of the cliff.'

THE MERRY UNDERTAKERS.

One of the favourite bequests of our ancestors in the time preceding the Reformation, was for the purpose of keeping up an annual visit to the tomb of the testator, attended by a feast. This 'commemoration guttle,' as Dr Fosbroke calls it,[*] probably took its rise in the Pagan institution of anniversaries, but it was less spiritual and elegant. Mr Douce tells us that one of the meetings taking place at an inn, where the sign was the arms of a nobleman, one having asked a clergyman present to translate the motto, '*Virtus post funera vivit*,' he made answer, '*Virtus*, a parish clerk, *vivit*, lives well, *post funera*, at funeral feasts.'

    * History of Gloucester, 4to, 1819, p. 350.

THE MERRY UNDERTAKERS.

The joyous private behaviour of those whose business it is to take part in funeral pageantry has supplied material of humorous description to authors, from Richard Steele down to Charles Dickens. These officials necessarily put on looks of grave concern with their mourning habiliments; and, after all, having a part to act, is it not well that they act it? How should we regard them if, instead of an outward solemnity, they presented faces of merriment, or even of indifference? Still, in an official assumption of woe, there is something which we cannot view in other than a ludicrous light.

In the last quarter of the eighteenth century, there flourished, at the corner of the lane leading from the Wandsworth-road to Battersea-bridge, a tavern, yclept the Falcon, kept by one Robert Death, a man whose figure is said to have ill comported with his name, seeing that it displayed the highest appearances of jollity and good condition. A merry-hearted artist, named John Nixon, passing this house one day, found an undertaker's company regaling themselves at *Death's Door*. Having just discharged their duty to a rich nabob in a neighbouring cemetery, they had, the first time for three or four hours, found an opportunity of refreshing exhausted nature; and well did they ply the joyful work before them. The artist, tickled at a festivity among such characters in such a place, sketched them on the spot, and his sketch was soon after published, accompanied with a cantata from another hand, of no great merit, in which Sable, the foreman of the company, is represented as singing as follows, to the tune of 'I've kissed and I've prattled with fifty fair maids:'

Dukes, lords, have I buried, and squires of fame,
　　And people of every degree;
But of all the fine jobs that came in my way,
　　A fun'ral like this for me.
　　　　This is the job
　　　　That fills the fob,
　　O! the burying a nabob for me!

Unfeather the hearse, put the pall in the bag,
　　Give the horses some oats and some hay;
Drink our next merry meeting and quackery's increase,
　　With three times three and huzza, &c.'

Death has now submitted to his mighty namesake, and the very place where the merry undertakers regaled themselves can scarce be distinguished among the spreading streets which now occupy this part of the environs of the metropolis.

St Dunstan.—Walter Gale, the Sussex schoolmaster, records that in 1749, 'there was at Mayfield a pair of tongs, which the inhabitants affirmed, and many believed, to be that with which St Dunstan, Archbishop of Canterbury, who had his residence at a fine ancient dome in this town, pinched the devil by the nose when, in the form of a handsome maid, he tempted him.' What made it more terrible to this sightly tempter was, that the tongs happened to be red-hot, the pair being one that St Dunstan made use of at his forge, for it seems that the Archbishop was a blacksmith as well as a saint.

Lord Bute.—Some idea of the unpopularity of this minister may be gathered from his brother, Mr Stuart Mackenzie, being described as a very amiable man, to whom no objection was ever raised beyond his relationship to Lord Bute.

MARCH 4.

St Lucius, pope and martyr, 253. St Adrian, bishop of St Andrews, martyr in Scotland 874. St Casimir, Prince of Poland, 1482.

Born.—Don Pedro, of Portugal, 1394; James Earl Waldegrave, 1715; Lord Chancellor Somers, 1652, *Worcester.*

Died.—Saladin, 1193, *Damascus;* Bernard Gilpin, rector of *Houghton-le-Spring,* 1583; Matthias Hoe, 1645, *Dresden;* J. Vanderlinden, 1664, *Leyden;* John Anstis, Garter King-at-Arms, 1744; the Rev. Thomas Seward, 1790, *Lichfield;* Thomas Rickman, architect, 1841, *Birmingham;* Charles Leopold von Buch, German geologist, 1853.

SALADIN.

The famous sultan of Egypt and Syria, who overthrew the short-lived Latin kingdom of Jerusalem, and successfully bore the brunt of the third crusade, was very much a soldier of fortune after the type of the modern Mehemet Ali. It was in the course of a career of conquest, beginning with Egypt and going on to Syria, that he fought Guy de Lusignan, King of Jerusalem, at Tiberias, in 1187, and obtained possession of that city. Then did Philip Augustus of France and Richard I. of England deem themselves called upon by Christian duty to fly to the rescue of the holy sepulchre. The energies of this third crusade were concentrated on a two years' siege of Acre, which they took, notwithstanding the efforts of Saladin for its rescue; but they vainly endeavoured to force a way to Jerusalem, and were finally obliged to rest satisfied with leaving the Christians in possession of a strip of the coast between Tyre and Jaffa.

In this contest between Europeans and Asiatics, there was a wonderful display of valour on both sides; but the struggle is mainly interesting to us through the magnanimity of Saladin. The lion-hearted King of England, being one day on the point of being taken prisoner, was saved from that fate by the generosity of a Norman gentleman, Guillaume de Préau, who called out, 'I am the king,' in a voice expressive of a wish to secure good treatment. Guillaume was instantly surrounded and taken, and he was quickly brought before Saladin, who at once knew that he was not Richard. On the stratagem being explained, the Sultan could only praise him for the self-devotion he had displayed.

On entering Jerusalem, after a successful battle, the people surrounded him, clamouring for their fathers, brothers, and sons whom he had taken prisoners. He could not resist this sad spectacle, but at once ordered the prisoners to be released.

Having established good laws in his territories, he was determined that they should be executed without respect of persons. His own nephew being cited in judgment, he compelled him to appear. Nay, a merchant venturing to accuse Saladin himself of some wrong, and the cadi having come to the sultan to ask what should be done, 'That which is just,' answered he. He went to the court, pleaded his own cause, and so far from punishing the plaintiff, thanked and rewarded him for shewing so much confidence in his integrity.

Though Saladin was a usurper, with the stain of ingratitude to his early masters, there must have been splendid qualities in a man who, born a Khoord in a moderate rank of life, raised himself to be the ruler of Egypt, Arabia, Syria, Mesopotamia, and the finest tracts of Asia Minor, all in the course of a life of fifty-seven years.

He left his vast territories amongst his seventeen sons ; but their rule was everywhere of short duration.

BERNARD GILPIN, HIS HOSPITALITY AND PREACHING.

This good man, born in Westmoreland in 1517, and by his mother related to Cuthbert Tunstall, the enlightened Bishop of Durham, through that prelate was appointed to the valuable rectory of Houghton-le-Spring. This was in the reign of Mary, a dangerous time for one of such Protestant tendencies as he. Entering at once upon his duties, he did not hesitate to preach the doctrines of the Reformation, and was accordingly very soon accused to Bishop Bonner. Gilpin obeyed the summons of the unpitying prelate, and, fully expecting to suffer at the stake, before setting out he said to his house-steward, ' Give me a long garment, that I may die with decency.' As he journeyed with the ministers of the bishop, he is said to have broken his leg, which, delaying his journey, saved his life, Mary dying in the interval. Gilpin then returned in joy and peace to his parishioners at Houghton. Queen Elizabeth offered him the bishopric of Carlisle, which he declined; and he continued to his death the rector of Houghton. He visited the ruder parts of Northumberland, where the people subsisted mostly on plunder, fearlessly holding forth to them the commands and sanctions of Christianity, and thus did much to change the character of the county. From these useful services he was often called the *Northern Apostle*.

Houghton, being then, as now, a rich benefice, yielded Gilpin an ample income. His hospitality resembled that of the primitive bishops : every fortnight, forty bushels of corn, twenty bushels of malt, and a whole ox, besides other provisions, were consumed in the rectory-house, which was open to all travellers. With equal zeal and assiduity, he settled differences among his parishioners, provided instruction for the young, and prayed by the bedsides of the sick and poor.

THOMAS RICKMAN.

To Thomas Rickman belongs the merit of discriminating and classifying the styles resulting from progressive changes in the Gothic architecture of the middle ages, as clearly as to William Smith belongs the honour of first classifying strata by their respective shells. It must ever be felt as a curious and anomalous circumstance, that the genius who did us this service, and who ultimately gained celebrity by the vast number of Gothic churches which he built in

England, was by birth and up-bringing a member of the Society of Friends, whose principle it is to attach no consequence whatever to the forms of ' steeple-houses.'

'DEMANDS JOYOUS.'

How our ancestors managed to pass the long winter evenings in the olden time, has never been satisfactorily explained. They had no new books, indeed few books of any kind, to read or talk about. Newspapers were unknown; a wandering beggar, minstrel, or pedler circulated the very small amount of news that was to be told. The innumerable subjects of interest that form our ordinary topics of conversation were then utterly unknown. So we can only conclude that our ancestors, like some semi-savage tribes at the present day, passed their spare hours in relating often-told stories, and exercised their wits in asking each other puzzling questions or riddles. Many copies of what we would now term riddle-books, are found in both the French and English collections of old manuscripts, and some were printed at an early period. One of these, entitled *Demands Joyous*, which may be rendered *Amusing Questions*, was printed in English by Wynkyn de Worde, in 1511. From this work, of which one copy only is said to be extant, we cull a few ' demands,' with their responses, for the amusement of the reader ; the greater part of them being too strongly impregnated with indecency and profanity to be presentable here :

Dem. What bare the best burden that ever was borne ?

Res. The ass that carried our Lady, when she fled with our Lord into Egypt.

Dem. What became of that ass ?

Res. Adam's mother ate her.

Dem. Who was Adam's mother ?

Res. The earth.

Dem. How many calves' tails would it take to reach from the earth to the sky ?

Res. No more than one, if it be long enough.

Dem. What is the distance from the surface of the sea to the deepest part thereof ?

Res. Only a stone's throw.

Dem. When Antichrist appears in the world, what will be the hardest thing for him to understand ?

Res. A hand-barrow, for of that he shall not know which end ought to go foremost.

Dem. What is it that never was and never will be ?

Res. A mouse's nest in a cat's ear.

Dem. Why do men make an oven in a town ?

Res. Because they cannot make a town in an oven.

Dem. How may a man discern a cow in a flock of sheep ?

Res. By his eyesight.

Dem. Why doth a cow lie down ?

Res. Because it cannot sit.

Dem. What is it that never freezeth ?

Res. Boiling water.

Dem. Which was first, the hen or the egg ?

Res. The hen, at the creation.

Dem. How many straws go to a goose's nest ?

Res. Not one, for straws not having feet cannot go anywhere.

Dem. Who killed the fourth part of all the people in the world ?

Res. Cain when he killed Abel.

Dem. What is it that is a builder, and yet not a

man, doeth what no man can do, and yet serveth both God and man ?

Res. A bee.

Dem. What man getteth his living backwards?

Res. A ropemaker.

Dem. How would you say two paternosters, when you know God made but one paternoster ?

Res. Say one twice over.

Dem. Which are the most profitable saints of the church ?

Res. Those painted on the glass windows, for they keep the wind from wasting the candles.

Dem. Who were the persons that made all, and sold all, that bought all and lost all ?

Res. A smith made an awl and sold it to a shoe-maker, who lost it.

Dem. Why doth a dog turn round three times before he lieth down ?

Res. Because he knoweth not his bed's head from the foot thereof.

Dem. What is the worst bestowed charity that one can give ?

Res. Alms to a blind man ; for he would be glad to see the person hanged that gave it to him.

Dem. What is the age of a field-mouse ?

Res. A year. And the age of a hedgehog is three times that of a mouse, and the life of a dog is three times that of a hedge-hog, and the life of a horse is three times that of a dog, and the life of a man is three times that of a horse, and the life of a goose is three times that of a man, and the life of a swan is three times that of a goose, and the life of a swallow three times that of a swan, and the life of an eagle three times that of a swallow, and the life of a ser-pent three times that of an eagle, and the life of a raven is three times that of a serpent, and the life of a hart is three times that of a raven, and an oak groweth five hundred years, and fadeth five hundred years.

MARCH 5.

Saints Adrian and Eubulus, of Palestine, martyrs, 309. St Kiaran, of Ireland, bishop, 4th century. St Roger, a Franciscan, 1236.

Born.—John Collins, F.R.S., accountant, 1624, *Wood-eaton ;* Dr George Stanhope, Dean of Canterbury, 1660, *Hartshorne.*

Died.—Odoacer, King of Italy, A.D. 493 ; Alphonso II. (of Portugal), 1223, *Alcobaça ;* Antonio Allegri Cor-reggio, painter, 1534, *Correggio ;* Henri I., Prince of Condé, 1588; Pope Clement VIII., 1605; James Duke of Hamilton, 1649, beheaded, *Old Palace Yard ;* Arthur, Lord Capell, beheaded, 1649; Henry Earl of Holland, beheaded, 1649; Bishop Beveridge, 1708; the Rev. Dr Philip Francis, 1773, *Bath ;* Dr Thomas Arne, musical composer, 1778; the Marquis de la Place, philosopher, 1827; Alexander Volta (*Voltaism*), 1827, *Como ;* Dr Lant Carpenter, miscellaneous writer, 1840; M. J. B. Orfila, physician and chemist, 1853.

DR ARNE, THE MUSICAL COMPOSER.

Dr Thomas Augustine Arne, with whose lank features we are familiar through the character-istic portrait of him by Bartolozzi, was the son of an upholsterer, in King-street, Covent-garden, at whose house were lodged the Indian kings, mentioned in the *Spectator* as visiting England in the reign of Queen Anne. Young Arne was educated at Eton, and intended for the profession

of the law ; but progress in that or any other such pursuit was impossible. Every energy of the young man's mind was absorbed in music. The father having positively forbidden him this study, he secreted a spinet in his room, and, muffling the strings, practised in the night, while the rest of the family were asleep. It is also related that the youth would steal in the disguise of a livery into the servants' gallery of the opera-house. Nevertheless, he served a three years' clerkship to the law. In the meantime, he took lessons on the violin of Festing, under whom he made rapid progress, of which his father had no suspicion, till going to a concert one evening, he was asto-nished to see his son playing the first fiddle most skilfully. The elder Arne now gave up resist-ance, and consented to his son teaching his sister, Mrs Cibber, to sing ; and for her he set Addi-son's opera of *Rosamond.* In 1738, the young musician established his reputation by his *Comus,* which he composed in the back parlour of a house in Craven-buildings, Wych-street. The melody of Arne at this time, and of his Vaux-hall-gardens songs afterwards, forms an era in English music, and was long the standard of per-fection at our theatres and public gardens. But the work which has most contributed to his fame is his *Artaxerxes,* translated from Metas-tasio's *Artacerses,* which with the talents of Tenducci, Peretti, and Arne's pupil, Miss Brent, had very great success: he sold the copyright for sixty guineas, then considered a large sum for such a property. Its general melody has been analysed as neither Italian nor English, but an agreeable mixture of Italian, English, and Scots. His music for the dramatic songs of Shakspeare attained great popularity, which it still enjoys. Of his song of ' Rule, Britannia,' it may be said that it would have preserved and endeared his name with the English nation throughout all time, though he had never com-posed another. Altogether, he arranged for the stage upwards of thirty musical pieces. He died March 5, 1778, and was buried in the church of St Paul, Covent-garden. He was a singular instance of that predestinate taste, which is to be accounted for only by peculiar organization, the existence of which, among other less splendid instances, has been since confirmed by Crotch, Himmel, and Mozart. Arne's was, indeed, the pure and unbought love of the art, generated by the pleasurable perception of sweet sounds.

THE FIRST LOCOMOTIVE IN THE BRITANNIA TUBE.

It must have been an anxious day for the late Robert Stephenson when he first sent a locomo-tive engine through the wonderful Britannia tubular bridge over the Menai Straits,—an anxious day, but probably not a distrustful one ; for he, like all our great engineers, knew his own strength, and relied on the soundness of the principles which had guided him.

Assuredly it was no small difficulty which he had been called upon to overcome. While the Chester and Holyhead Railway was being con-structed, Stephenson pondered how it should cross the Menai. Telford's beautiful suspension bridge being deemed too slight for the purpose, he planned a tube or hollow girder, through which a train might pass as through a tunnel. To make such a tunnel of sheet iron, stiff enough to resist any tendency to bending, was a formidable task. The Menai Strait, at the point selected for the crossing, is about eleven hundred feet wide at high water; in the middle is a rock called the Britannia rock, rising a few feet above high water level. Stephenson resolved to erect a pier of masonry on the rock, so as to break the span of the strait into two portions. To ensure manageable dimensions, it was determined that there should be two tubes, one for the up and one for the down trains. A masonry tower was to support the Caernarvon end of the tubes, and another to support the Anglesea end. There would thus therefore be four separate tubes, forming two when joined end to end.

Mighty were the engineering agencies brought to bear upon the work, and long was the period during which the operations continued. Should the tube be of cast iron or wrought? Should the cross section be square, circular, or oval? Before these questions could be properly answered, the skill of Stephenson, Fairbairn, Hodgkinson, and other eminent engineers was taxed to the utmost, and the company spent a large sum of money in preliminary experiments. Years rolled on; and it was not until 1850, that the trains could cross the bridge that was commenced in 1845. There was the Britannia Tower to build, a large mass of masonry higher than the Monument near London-bridge, and containing twenty thousand tons of stone. There were the Caernarvon and Anglesea Towers to construct, on nearly as massive a scale. There were the vast abutments further inland; for which Mr Thomas, whose carvings in stone at the new Houses of Parliament display so much skill, was employed to sculpture four lions _couchant_ twenty-five feet long, majestic in their colossal repose. But the tubes were the most important achievement; each tube is a hollow trunk varying from twenty-five to thirty feet in height, and about fifteen feet wide. The top and bottom are cellular, to insure increased strength. All parts alike, sides and cells, are formed of very thick sheet or plate iron, strengthened with angle-irons, and riveted. Never, perhaps, was there such another job of riveting as this; more than _two million_ rivets were driven red hot into holes punched in the plates! Four gigantic tubes were thus built up piece by piece, on platforms ranged along the Caernarvon shore.

Probably the greatest _lift_, in a mechanical sense, ever effected, was the lifting of these tubes —each of which weighed nearly two thousand tons, and had to be raised a clear height of one hundred feet. Each tube was removed from its platform to eight floating pontoons, and was towed upon them to its place between the towers. Then, by a most extraordinary combination of chains, pulleys, hydraulic-machines, and steam-power, each tube was steadily raised inch by inch, until at length it reached its proper elevation, where suitable supports for its ends were provided. The Menai Strait had never before known such a holiday as that which marked the day selected for

raising the first of the tubes. Engineers of eminence came from all parts of the United Kingdom, and from foreign countries, to mark critically Stephenson's great achievements; directors and shareholders came to witness a work on which so many hundred thousand pounds of their capital had been expended; while curiosity-seekers, congregating from the neighbouring counties, swelled the number of those who lined both sides of the strait. Amid the busy hum of preparations, and movements which could be understood only by those versed in engineering science, one figure was above or apart from all others—it was Robert Stephenson, directing and controlling the work of vast bodies of mechanics and labourers. It was a long day, a day of eighteen hours' continuous work, to raise each tube to its height of a hundred feet. Many may guess, but none can know, the feelings that agitated the mind of the great engineer on this day. Perhaps 'agitate' is not the proper word, he was too self-possessed to be agitated; but the ordeal must nevertheless have been a terrible one —seeing that a mishap might bring the whole enterprise to ruin.

And when, many months afterwards, the tubes were properly adjusted end to end, and a continuous tunnel made, the passage of the first locomotive through it was another great event to be recorded in the history of the mighty Britannia-bridge. Each portion of tube had shewn itself firm and stiff enough to bear bravely the lifting process; but would the tubes, as a continuous tunnel, bear the rush and pressure, the rattle and vibration, of a ponderous locomotive? The 5th of March 1850, was the day selected for practically solving this problem; and the solution bore out in every way the calculations of the engineer. Three locomotives, of the heaviest character known to the narrow gauge, were chained end to end. They were decked with the flags of all nations. Robert Stephenson acted as driver of the leading locomotive, and other men of science stood or sat wherever it was most convenient. This weight of ninety tons was driven to the centre of one of the tubes, where it was allowed to remain stationary, with its full dead weight, for a few minutes; and the same took place on the return trip. Then a coal-train of three hundred tons was driven through, and then another train of two hundred tons was allowed to rest with all its weight, for two hours, in the centre of the tube. The plates and rivets bore the test triumphantly; and thus was completed a modern wonder of the world.*

* We are not aware whether Mr Stephenson, before his death, rectified his views concerning the relative claims of himself and Mr W. Fairbairn, concerning the tubular principle for bridges. In the elaborate researches carried on in 1845, Mr Fairbairn was the principal experimentalist; but when the reports came to be made public, it appeared that Mr Stephenson spoke of himself as the originator of the main idea, realized under his own eye by the aid of Messrs Fairbairn and Hodgkinson; whereas Mr Fairbairn has always contended and supported his argument in full in his engineering works, that _he_ was the veritable inventor of the most important feature in the bridge.

MARCH 6.

St Fridolin, abbot, 538. St Baldred, of Scotland, about 608. Saints Kyneburge, Kyneswide, and Tibba, 7th century. St Chrodegang, bishop of Metz, 766. St Cadroe, about 975. Colette, virgin and abbess, 1447.

Born.—Michael Angelo Buonarotti, painter, sculptor, and architect, 1474, *Chiusi;* Francesco Guicciardini, diplomatist, 1482, *Florence;* Bishop Francis Atterbury, 1662, *Milton;* Vice-Admiral Sir Charles Napier, 1786, *Merchistoun.*

Died.—Roger Lord Grey de Ruthyn, 1352; Sir John Hawkwood, first English general, 1393, *Florence,* Zachary Ursinus, German divine, 1583, *Neustadt;* Philip, third Earl of Leicester, 1693; Lord Chief Justice Sir John Holt, 1710, *Redgrave;* Philip. first Earl of Hardwicke, Lord Chancellor, 1764, *Wimpole;* G. T. F. Raynal, philosophical historian, 1796, *Passey;* the Rev. Dr Samuel Parr, 1825. *Hatton;* George Mickle Kemp, architect (Scott Monument), 1844, *Edinburgh;* Professor Heeren, history and antiquities, 1842; Benjamin Travers, surgeon, 1858.

BISHOP ATTERBURY.

In Atterbury we find one of the numerous shipwrecks of history. Learned, able, eloquent, the Bishop of Rochester lost all through hasty, incorrect thinking, and an impetuous and arrogant temper. He had convinced himself that the exiled Stuart princes might be restored to the throne by the simple process of bringing up the next heir as a Protestant, failing to see that the contingency on which he rested was unattainable. One, after all, admires the courage which prompted the fiery prelate, at the death of Queen Anne, to offer to go out in his lawn sleeves and proclaim the son of James II., which would have been a directly treasonable act; we must also admit that, though he doubtless was guilty of treason in favour of the Stuarts, the bill by which he lost his position and was condemned to exile (1723), proceeded on imperfect evidence, and was a dangerous kind of measure. To consider Atterbury as afterwards attached to the service of the so-called Pretender,—wasting bright faculties on the petty intrigues of a mock court, and gradually undergoing the stern correction of Fact and Truth for the illusory political visions to which he had sacrificed so much,—is a reflection not without its pathos, or its lesson. Atterbury ultimately felt the full weight of the desolation which he had brought upon himself. He died at Paris, on the 15th of February 1732.

A specimen of the dexterous wit of Atterbury in debate is related in connection with the history of the Occasional Conformity and Schism Bills, December 1718. On that occasion, Lord Coningsby rebuked the Bishop for having, the day before, assumed the character of a prophet. 'In Scripture,' said this simple peer, 'I find a prophet very like him, namely Balaam, who, like the right reverend lord, drove so very furiously, that the ass he rode upon was constrained to open his mouth and reprove him.'

The luckless lord having sat down, the bishop rose with a demure and humble look, and having thanked his lordship for taking so much notice of him, went on to say that 'the application of Balaam to him, though severe, was certainly very happy, the terms prophet and priest being often promiscuously used. There wanted, however, the application of the ass; and it seemed as if his lordship, being the only person who had reproved him, must needs take that character upon himself.' From that day, Lord Coningsby was commonly recognised by the appellation of 'Atterbury's Pad.'

G. M. KEMP.

The beauty of the monument to Sir Walter Scott at Edinburgh becomes the more impressive when we reflect that its designer was a man but recently emerged at the time from the position of a working carpenter. It is a Gothic structure, about 185 feet high, with exquisite details, mostly taken from Melrose Abbey. Kemp's was one of a number of competing plans, given in with the names of the designers in sealed envelopes; so that nothing could be more genuine than the testimony thus paid to his extraordinary genius. In his earlier days as a working carpenter, Kemp adopted the plan of travelling from one great continental dom-kirk or cathedral to another, supporting himself by his handicraft while studying the architecture of the building. It was wonderful how much knowledge he thus acquired, as it were at his own hand, in the course of a few years. He never obtained any more regular education for his eventual profession. Kemp was a man of modest, almost timid demeanour, very unlike one designed to push his way in the world. After becoming a person of note, as entrusted with the construction of Scotland's monument to the most gifted of her sons, he used to relate, as a curious circumstance, the only connexion he had ever had with Scott in life. Travelling toilsomely one hot day between Peebles and Selkirk, with his tools over his back, he was overtaken by a carriage containing a grey-haired gentleman, whom he did not know. The gentleman, observing him, stopped the carriage, and desired the coachman to invite the wayfaring lad to a seat on the box. He thus became the subject of a characteristic piece of benevolence to the illustrious man with whose name he was afterwards to meet on so different a level.

Most sad to relate, while the monument was in the progress of construction, the life of the architect was cut short by accident, he having fallen into a canal one dark evening, in the course of his homeward walk.

MIDLENT, OR MOTHERING SUNDAY.

In the year 1864, the 6th of March is the fourth Sunday in Lent, commonly called Midlent Sunday. Another popular name for the day is Mothering Sunday, from an ancient observance connected with it.

The harshness and general painfulness of life in old times must have been much relieved by certain simple and affectionate customs which modern people have learned to dispense with. Amongst these was a practice of going to see parents, and especially the female one, on the mid Sunday of Lent, taking for them some little present, such as a cake or a trinket. A youth engaged in this amiable act of duty was said to go *a-mothering*, and thence the day itself came to be called Mothering Sunday. One can readily imagine how, after a stripling or maiden had gone to service, or launched in independent housekeeping, the old bonds of filial love would be brightened by this pleasant annual visit, signalised, as custom demanded it should be, by the excitement attending some novel and perhaps surprising gift. There was also a cheering and peculiar festivity appropriate to the day, the prominent dish being *furmety*—which we have to interpret as wheat grains boiled in sweet milk, sugared and spiced. In the northern parts of England, and in Scotland, there seems to have been a greater leaning to steeped pease fried in butter, with pepper and salt. Pancakes so composed passed by the name of *carlings*; and so conspicuous was this article, that from it Carling Sunday became a local name for the day.

> 'Tid, Mid, and Misera,
> *Carling*, Palm, Pase-egg day,'

remains in the north of England as an enumeration of the Sundays of Lent, the first three terms probably taken from words in obsolete services for the respective days, and the fourth being the name of Midlent Sunday from the cakes by which it was distinguished.

Herrick, in a canzonet addressed to Dianeme, says—

> 'I'll to thee a *simnel* bring,
> 'Gainst thou go a-mothering;
> So that, when she blesses thee,
> Half that blessing thou'lt give me.'

He here obviously alludes to the sweet cake which the young person brought to the female parent as a gift; but it would appear that the term 'simnel' was in reality applicable to cakes which were in use all through the time of Lent. We are favoured by an antiquarian friend with the following general account of

Simnel Cakes.

It is an old custom in Shropshire and Herefordshire, and especially at Shrewsbury, to make during Lent and Easter, and also at Christmas, a sort of rich and expensive cakes, which are called *Simnel Cakes*. They are raised cakes, the crust of which is made of fine flour and water, with sufficient saffron to give it a deep yellow colour, and the interior is filled with the materials of a very rich plum-cake, with plenty of candied lemon peel, and other good things. They are made up very stiff, tied up in a cloth, and boiled for several hours, after which they are brushed over with egg, and then baked. When ready for sale the crust is as hard as if made of wood, a circumstance which has given rise to various stories of the manner in which they have at times been treated by persons to whom they were sent as presents, and who had never seen one before, one ordering his simnel to be boiled to soften it, and a lady taking hers for a footstool. They are made of different sizes, and, as may be supposed from the ingredients, are rather expensive, some large ones selling for as much as half-a-guinea, or even, we believe, a guinea, while smaller ones may be had for half-a-crown. Their form, which as well as the ornamentation is nearly uniform, will be best understood by the accompanying engraving, representing large and small cakes as now on sale in Shrewsbury.

The usage of these cakes is evidently one of great antiquity. It appears from one of the epigrams of the poet Herrick, that at the beginning of the seventeenth century it was the custom at Gloucester for young people to carry simnels as presents to their mothers on Midlent Sunday (or Mothering Sunday).

It appears also from some other writers of this age, that these simnels, like the modern ones, were boiled as well as baked. The name is found in early English and also in very old French, and it appears in mediæval Latin under the form *simanellus* or *siminellus*. It is considered to be derived from the Latin *simila*, fine flour, and is usually interpreted as meaning the finest quality of white bread made in the middle ages. It is evidently used, however, by the mediæval writers in the sense of a cake, which they called in Latin of that time *artocopus*, which is constantly explained by *simnel* in the Latin-English vocabularies. In three of these, printed in Mr Wright's *Volume of Vocabularies*, all belonging to the fifteenth century, we have 'Hic *artocopus, anglice symnelle*,' 'Hic *artocopus, a symnylle*,' and 'Hic *artocopus, anglice a symnella*;' and in the latter place it is further explained by a contemporary pen-and-ink drawing in the margin, representing the simnel as seen from above and sideways, of which we give below a fac-simile. It is quite evident that it is a rude representation of a cake exactly like those still made in Shropshire. The ornamental border, which is clearly identical with that of the modern cake, is, perhaps, what the authorities quoted by Ducange v. *simila*, mean when they spoke of the cake as being *foliata*. In the *Dictionarius* of John de Garlande, compiled at Paris in the thirteenth century, the word *simineus* or *simnels*, is used as the equivalent to the Latin *placentæ*, which are described as cakes exposed in the windows of the hucksters to sell to the scholars of the University and others. We learn from Ducange that it was usual in early times to

SIMNEL CAKES.

mark the simnels with a figure of Christ or of the Virgin Mary, which would seem to shew that they had a religious signification. We know that the Anglo-Saxon, and indeed the German race in general, were in the habit of eating consecrated cakes at their religious festivals. Our hot cross buns at Easter are only the cakes which the pagan Saxons ate in honour of their goddess Eastre, and from which the Christian clergy, who were unable to prevent people from eating, sought to expel the paganism by marking them with the cross.

It is curious that the use of these cakes should have been preserved so long in this locality, and still more curious are the tales which have arisen to explain the meaning of the name, which had been long forgotten. Some pretend that the father of Lambert Simnel, the well-known pretender in the reign of Henry VII., was a baker, and the first maker of simnels, and that in consequence of the celebrity he gained by the acts of his son, his cakes have retained his name. There is another story current in Shropshire, which is much more picturesque, and which we tell as nearly as possible in the words in which it was related to us. Long ago there lived an honest old couple, boasting the names of Simon and Nelly, but their surnames are not known. It was their custom at Easter to gather their children about them, and thus meet together once a year under the old homestead. The fasting season of Lent was just ending, but they had still left some of the unleavened dough which had been from time to time converted into bread during the forty days. Nelly was a careful woman, and it grieved her to waste anything, so she suggested that they should use the remains of the Lenten dough for the basis of a cake to regale the assembled family. Simon readily agreed to the proposal, and further reminded his partner that there were still some remains of their Christmas plum pudding hoarded up in the cupboard, and that this might form the interior, and be an agreeable surprise to the young people when they had made their way through the less tasty crust. So far, all things went on harmoniously ; but when the cake was made, a subject of violent discord arose, Sim insisting that it should be boiled, while Nell no less obstinately contended that it should be baked. The dispute ran from words to blows, for Nell, not choosing to let her province in the household be thus interfered with, jumped up, and threw the stool she was sitting on at Sim, who on his part seized a besom, and applied it with right good will to the head and shoulders of his spouse. She now seized the broom, and the battle became so warm, that it might have had a very serious result, had not Nell proposed as a compromise that the cake should be boiled first, and afterwards baked. This Sim acceded to, for he had no wish for further acquaintance with the heavy end of the broom. Accordingly, the big pot was set on the fire, and the stool broken up and thrown on to boil it, whilst the besom and broom furnished fuel for the oven. Some eggs, which had been broken in the scuffle, were used to coat the outside of the pudding when boiled, which gave it the shining gloss it possesses as a cake. This new and remarkable production

in the art of confectionery became known by the name of the cake of Simon and Nelly, but soon only the first half of each name was alone preserved and joined together, and it has ever since been known as the cake of Sim-Nel, or Simnel !

TRADITION AND TRUTH.

The value of popular tradition as evidence in antiquarian inquiries cannot be disputed, though in every instance it should be received with the greatest caution. A few instances of traditions, existing from a very remote period and verified in our own days, are worthy of notice.

On the northern coast of the Firth of Forth, near to the town of Largo, in Fifeshire, there has existed from time immemorial an eminence known by the name of Norie's Law. And the popular tradition respecting this spot, has ever been that a great warrior, the leader of a mighty army, was buried there, clad in the silver armour he wore during his lifetime. Norie's Law is evidently artificial, and there can be no wonder that the neighbouring country people should suppose that a great chief had been buried underneath it, for the interment of warrior chieftains under artificial mounds, near the sea, is as ancient as Homer. Hector, speaking of one whom he intended to slay in single combat, says :

> ' The long-haired Greeks
> To him, upon the shores of Hellespont,
> A mound shall heap ; that those in after times,
> Who sail along the darksome sea, shall say,
> This is the monument of one long since
> Borne to his grave, by mighty Hector slain.'

Our Anglo-Saxon ancestors buried their warrior leaders in the same manner. The foregoing quotation seems almost parodied in the dying words of the Saxon Beowulf :

> ' Command the famous in war
> To make a mound,
> Bright after the funeral fire,
> Upon the nose of the promontory ;
> Which shall, for a memorial
> To my people, rise high aloft,
> On Heonesness ;
> That the sea-sailors
> May afterwards call it
> Beowulf's Barrow,
> When the Brentings,
> Over the darkness of the flood,
> Shall sail afar.'

So it was only natural for the rustic population to say that a chief was buried under Norie's Law. Agricultural progress has, in late years, thrown over hundreds of burial barrows, exposing mortuary remains, and there are few labourers in England or Scotland who would not say, on being pointed out a barrow, that a great man, at some distant period, had been interred beneath it. But silver armour, with one single exception, has never been found in barrows ; and as Norie's Law is actually the barrow in which silver accoutrements were found, the tradition of the people was fully verified. For only by tradition, and that from a very distant period, could they have known that the person interred at Norie's Law was buried with silver armour.

It appears that, about the year 1819, a man in

humble life and very moderate circumstances, residing near Largo, was—greatly to the surprise of his neighbours—observed to have suddenly become passing rich for one of his position and opportunities. A silversmith, in the adjacent town of Cupar, had about the same time been offered a considerable quantity of curious antique silver for sale; part of which he purchased, but a larger part was taken to Edinburgh, and disposed of there. Contemporary with these events, a modern excavation was discovered in Norie's Law, so it did not require a witch to surmise that a case of treasure-trove had recently occurred. The late General Durham, then owner of the estate, was thus led to make inquiries, and soon discovered that the individual alluded to, induced by the ancient tradition, had made an excavation in the Law, and found a considerable quantity of silver, which he had disposed of as previously noticed. But influenced, as some say, by a feeling of a conscientious, others of a superstitious character, he did not take all the silver he discovered, but left a large quantity in the Law. Besides, as this ingenious individual conducted his explorations at night, it was supposed that he might have overlooked part of the original deposit. Acting in accordance with this intelligence, General Durham caused the Law to be carefully explored, and found in it several lozenge-shaped plates of silver, that undoubtedly had been the scales of a coat of mail, besides a silver shield and sword ornaments, and the mounting of a helmet in the same metal. Many of these are still preserved at Largo House, affording indisputable evidence of the very long perseverance and consistency which may characterise popular tradition.

Our next illustration is from Ireland, and it happened about the commencement of the last century. At Ballyshannon, says Bishop Gibson, in his edition of Camden's *Britannia*, were two pieces of gold discovered by a method very remarkable. The Bishop of Derry being at dinner, there came in an old Irish harper, and sang an ancient song to his harp. His lordship, not understanding Irish, was at a loss to know the meaning of the song; but upon inquiry, he found the substance of it to be this, that in such a place, naming the very spot, a man of gigantic stature lay buried; and that over his breast and back were plates of pure gold, and on his fingers rings of gold so large that an ordinary man might creep through them. The place was so exactly described, that two persons there present were tempted to go in quest of the golden prize which the harper's song had pointed out to them. After they had dug for some time, they found two thin pieces of gold, circular, and more than two inches in diameter. This discovery encouraged them to seek next morning for the remainder, but they could find nothing more. In all probability they were not the first inquisitive persons whom the harper's song had sent to the same spot.

Since the ancient poetry of Ireland has become an object of learned research, the very song of the harper has been identified and printed, though it was simply traditional when sung before the Bishop. It is called *Moira Borb*; and

the verse, which more particularly suggested the remarkable discovery, has been translated thus :—

' In earth, beside the loud cascade,
    The son of Sora's king we laid;
And on each finger placed a ring
    Of gold, by mandate of our King.'

The 'loud cascade' was the well-known waterfall at Ballyshannon, now known as 'the Salmon-leap.'

Another instance of a similar description occurred in Wales. Near Mold, in Flintshire, there had existed from time immemorial a burial mound or barrow, named by the Welsh peasantry *Bryn-yr-ellylon*, the Hill of the Fairies. In 1827, a woman returning late from market, one night, was extremely frightened by seeing, as she solemnly averred, a spectral skeleton standing on this mound and clothed in a vestment of gold, which shone like the noon-day sun. Six years afterwards, the barrow, being cleared away for agricultural purposes, was found to contain urns and burnt bones, the usual contents of such places. But besides these, there was a most unusual object found, namely, a complete skeleton, round the breast of which was a corslet of pure gold, embossed with ornaments representing nail heads and lines. This unique relic of antiquity is now in the British Museum; and, if we are to confine ourselves to a natural explanation, it seems but reasonable to surmise that the vision was the consequence of a lingering remembrance of a tradition, which the woman had heard in early life, of golden ornaments buried in the goblin hill.

CANTERBURY PILGRIM-SIGNS.

The Thames, like the Tiber, has been the conservator of many minor objects of antiquity, very useful in aiding us to obtain a more correct knowledge of the habits and manners of those who in former times dwelt upon its banks. Whenever digging or dredging disturbs the bed of the river, some antique is sure to be exhumed. The largest amount of discovery took place when old London-bridge was removed, but other causes have led to the finding of much that is curious. Among these varied objects not the least interesting are a variety of small figures cast in lead, which prove to be the 'signs' worn by the pilgrims returned from visiting the shrine of St Thomas-à-Becket at Canterbury, and who wore them in their hats, or as brooches upon some portion of their dress, in token of their successful journey.

The custom of wearing these brooches is noted by Giraldus Cambrensis as early as the twelfth century. That ecclesiastic returned from a continental journey by way of Canterbury, and stayed some days to visit Becket's shrine; on his arrival in London he had an interview with the Bishop of Winchester, and he tells us that the Bishop, seeing him and his companions with signs of St Thomas hanging about their necks, remarked that he perceived they had just come from Canterbury. Erasmus, in his colloquy on pilgrimages, notes that pilgrims are 'covered on every side with images of tin and lead. The cruel and superstitious Louis XI. of France, customarily wore such signs stuck around his hat. The anonymous author of the Supplement to Chaucer's *Canterbury Tales*, described that famed party of pilgrims upon their arrival at the archiepiscopal city, and says:

' Then, as manner and custom is, *signs* there they bought,
     For men or contré should know whom they had sought.
Each man set his silver in such thing as he liked,
And in the meanwhile, the matter had y-piked
His bosom full of Canterbury brooches.'

The rest of the party, we are afterwards told,

' Set their *signs* upon their heads, and some upon their cap.'

They were a considerable source of revenue to the clergy who officiated at celebrated shrines, and have been found abroad in great numbers, bearing the figures of saints to whom it was customary to do honour by pilgrimages in the middle ages. The shells worn by the older pilgrims to Compostella, may have originated  the practice ; which still survives in Catholic countries, under the form of the medalets, sold on saints' days, which have touched sacred relics, or been consecrated by ecclesiastics.

The first specimen of these Canterbury brooches we engrave, and which appears to be a work of the fourteenth century, has a full length of St Thomas in pontificals in the act of giving the pastoral benediction. The pin which was used to attach it to the person, will be perceived behind the figure ; it seems best fitted to be secured to, and stand upright upon, the hat or cap of the pilgrim. Our second specimen takes the ordinary form of a brooch, and has in the centre the head only of Becket ; upon the rim are inscribed the words *Caput Thome*. The skull of the saint was made a separate exhibition in the reign of Edward III., and so continued until the days of Henry VIII. The monks of Canterbury thus made the most of their saint, by exhibiting his shrine at one part of the cathedral, his skull at another, and the point of the sword of Richard Brito, which fractured it, in a third place. The wealth of the church naturally became great, and no richer prize fell into the rapacious hands of the Royal suppressor of monasteries than Canterbury.

These signs were worn, not only as indications of pilgrimage performed, but as charms or protections against accidents in the journey ; and it would appear that the horses of the pilgrims were supplied with small bells inscribed with the words *Campana Thome*, and of which also we give a specimen. All these curious little articles have been found at various times in the Thames,

and are valuable illustrative records, not only of the most popular of the English pilgrimages, but of the immortal poem of Geoffrey Chaucer, who has done so much toward giving it an undying celebrity.

MARCH 7.

Saints Perpetua and Felicitas, martyrs at Carthage, 203. St Paul the Simple, anchoret, about 330. St Thomas of Aquino, Doctor of the Church and Confessor, 1274.

Born.—Sir John Fortescue Aland, 1670 ; Antonio Sanchez, 1699.
Died.—Antoninus Pius, Roman Emperor, 162, *Lorium ;* William Longsword, first Earl of Salisbury, 1226 ; Pope Innocent XIII., 1724 ; Bishop Thomas Wilson, 1755, *Isle of Man ;* Blanchard, aëronaut, 1809 ; Admiral Lord Collingwood, 1810.

BISHOP WILSON.

The benign and saintly Thomas Wilson was born at Burton, in Cheshire, on the 20th of December 1663. He was educated at Trinity College, Dublin, whither most of the young gentlemen of Lancashire and Cheshire were at that time sent. In 1692, the Earl of Derby chose him for his domestic chaplain, and tutor to his son, Lord Strange, and in 1697 appointed him to the bishopric of Sodor and Man, then in the gift of the Derby family. The episcopal revenue was only £300 a-year, and he found his palace in ruins, the house having been uninhabited for eight years. The people of the island were ignorant and very poor ; but the bishop at once took measures to improve their condition. He taught them to work, to plant, dig, and drain, and make roads ; he opened schools, chapels, and libraries ; he had studied medicine, and was able to cure the sick. Nearly all that Oberlin did in the Ban-de-la-Roche, Wilson anticipated in the Isle of Man. His whole income, after providing for the modest needs of his household, he expended in alms and improvements. It was said that ' he kept beggars from every door in Man but his own.' He published several devotional works and sermons, which are to this day widely read and admired. Queen Anne offered him an English bishopric, which he declined ; George I.

repeated the offer, with the same result. Queen Caroline was very anxious to keep him in London, and one day, when she had several prelates with her, she said, pointing to Wilson, 'See, here, my lords, is a bishop who does not come for translation.' 'No, indeed, and please your Majesty,' said Wilson, 'I will not leave my wife in my old age because she is poor.' Cardinal Fleury wanted much to see him, and invited him to France, saying he believed that they were the two oldest and poorest bishops in Europe, and he obtained an order from the government that no French privateer should ravage the Isle of Man. Wilson's goodness, like Oberlin's, overcame all differences of creed. Catholics and Dissenters came to hear him preach, and Quakers visited at his palace. He died at the age of ninety-three, and in the fifty-eighth year of his tenure of the office of bishop.

LORD COLLINGWOOD.

The personal history of this great naval commander furnishes a remarkable example of everything sacrificed to duty. He might be said to have lived and died at sea. The case becomes the more remarkable, when we know that Collingwood, beneath the panoply of the hero, cherished the finest domestic and social feelings. Born at Newcastle-on-Tyne in 1750, he was sent to sea as a midshipman at the age of eleven. After twenty-five years' uninterrupted service, he returned to Northumberland, making, as he says, acquaintance with his own family, to whom he had hitherto been, as it were, a stranger. In 1793, the war with the French Republic called him away from a young wife and two infant daughters, whom he most tenderly loved, though he was never permitted to have much of their society. He bore a conspicuous part in Lord Howe's victory, June 1, 1794, and in Jervis's victory off Cape St Vincent in 1797. In 1799, he was raised to the rank of Rear-Admiral. The peace of Amiens, for which he had long prayed, restored him to his wife and children for a few months in 1802, but the renewed war called him to sea in the spring of 1803, and he never more returned to his happy home. This constant service made him frequently lament that he was hardly known to his own children; and the anxieties and wear and tear incidental to it, shortened his valuable life. Passing over many less brilliant, but still very important services, Collingwood was second in command in the battle of Trafalgar. His ship, the *Royal Sovereign*, was the first to attack and break the enemy's line; and upon Nelson's death, Collingwood finished the victory, and continued in command of the fleet. He was now raised to the peerage. After a long and wearying blockade, during which, for nearly three years, he hardly ever set foot on shore, he sailed up the Mediterranean, where his position involved him in difficult political transactions; at length, completely worn out in body, but with a spirit intent on his duties to the last, Collingwood died at sea, on board the *Ville de Paris*, near Port Mahon, on the 7th of March 1810.

Nelson had a greater affection for Lord Collingwood than for any other officer in the service. In command he was firm, but mild, most considerate of the comfort and health of his men : the sailors called him father. He was a scientific seaman and naval tactician ; of strong enlightened mind, considering the circumstances of his life; the official letters and dispatches of this sailor, who had been at sea from his childhood, are admirable, even in point of style ; and his letters to his wife on the education of his daughters are full of good sense and feeling. The people of Newcastle, reasonably proud of so excellent a fellow-townsman as Lord Collingwood, have erected, by public subscription, a portrait statue of him in their town, and one of its leading streets bears his honoured name.

MOLLY MOGG.

On the 7th March 1766, died Mrs Mary Mogg, of the Rose Tavern, Wokingham, who had been, forty years before, the subject of a droll ballad by Gay, in association (as is believed) with Pope and Swift. This ballad almost immediately found its way into print, through the medium of *Mist's Journal* of August 27, 1726, prefaced with a notice stating that 'it was writ by two or three men of wit (who have diverted the public both in prose and verse), upon the occasion of their lying at a certain inn at Wokingham where the daughter of that house was remarkably pretty, and whose name is Molly Mogg.'

MOLLY MOGG.

The schoolboy delights in a play-day,
　　The schoolmaster's joy is to flog ;
The milkmaid's delight is in May-day,
　　But mine is in sweet Molly Mogg.

Will-a-wisp leads the traveller a-gadding,
　　Through ditch and through quagmire and bog ;
No light can e'er set me a-padding,
　　But the eyes of my sweet Molly Mogg.

For guineas in other men's breeches
　　Your gamesters will palm and will cog ;
But I envy them none of their riches,
　　So I palm my sweet Molly Mogg.

The hart that's half-wounded is ranging,
　　It here and there leaps like a frog ;
But my heart can never be changing,
　　It's so fixed on my sweet Molly Mogg.

I know that by wits 'tis recited,
　　That women at best are a clog ;
But I'm not so easily frighted
　　From loving my sweet Molly Mogg.

A letter when I am inditing,
　　Comes Cupid and gives me a jog ;
And I fill all my paper with writing,
　　Of nothing but sweet Molly Mogg.

I feel I'm in love to distraction,
　　My senses are lost in a fog ;
And in nothing can find satisfaction,
　　But in thoughts of my sweet Molly Mogg.

If I would not give up the three Graces,
　　I wish I were hanged like a dog,
And at court all the drawing-room faces,
　　For a glance at my sweet Molly Mogg.

For those faces want nature and spirit,
　　And seem as cut out of a log ;
Juno, Venus, and Pallas's merit
　　Unite in my sweet Molly Mogg.

Were Virgil alive with his Phillis,
And writing another Eclogue,
Both his Phillis and fair Amaryllis
He'd give for my sweet Molly Mogg.

When she smiles on each guest like her liquor,
Then jealousy sets me a-gog :
To be sure, she's a bit for the Vicar,
And so I shall lose Molly Mogg.

It appears that the ballad—perhaps to the surprise of its authors—attained instant popularity. Molly and the Rose at Wokingham became matter of public interest, and literary historians have not since disdained to inquire into the origin of the verses. We learn that Swift was at this time on a visit to Pope at Twickenham, while preparing for the publication of his *Travels of Lemuel Gulliver ;* that Gay joined his two brother bards, and that the tuneful trio were occasionally at the Rose in the course of their excursions that summer. The landlord, John Mogg, had two fair daughters, Molly and Sally, of whom Sally was in reality the cruel beauty referred to in the ballad ; but ' the wits were too far gone to distinguish, and so the honour, if honour it be, has clung to Molly, who, after all, died a spinster at the age of sixty-six.' The inn had in these latter days its *Pope's Room,* and its chair called *Pope's Chair,* and there was an inscription on a pane of glass said to have been written by Pope. The house, however, is now transformed into a mercer's shop.*

UNDER THE SNOW.

It is a well-ascertained fact that snow affords a comparatively warm garment in intensely cold weather. This is difficult for non-scientific persons to understand ; but it is based on the circumstance that snow, on account of its loose flocculent nature, conducts heat slowly. Accordingly, under this covering, exactly as under a thick woollen garment, the natural heat of the body is not dissipated rapidly, but retained.

Instances are abundant to shew that snow really protects substances from cold of great intensity. Farmers and gardeners well know this ; and, knowing it, they duly value a good honest fall of snow on their fields and gardens in winter. There are not the same tests to apply in reference to the human body ; nevertheless, the fact is equally undeniable. The newspapers every winter record examples. Thus the Yorkshire papers contained an account, in 1858, of a snow storm at or near Market Weighton, in which a woman had a remarkable experience of the value of a snow garment. On the 7th of March she was overtaken by the storm on the neighbouring moors, and was gradually snowed up, being unable to move either forward or backward. Thus she remained forty-three hours. Cold as she of course was, the snow nevertheless prevented the cold from assuming a benumbing tendency ; and she was able to the last to keep a breathing place about her head. On the second day after, a man crossing the moor saw a woman's bonnet on the snow ; he soon found that there was a living woman beneath the bonnet ; and a course of judicious treatment restored her to health.

* See *Notes and Queries,* 2nd ser. viii. 84, 129 172.

The remarkable case of Elizabeth Woodcock is still more striking. In the winter of 1799 she was returning on horseback from Cambridge to her home in a neighbouring village ; and having dismounted for a few minutes, the horse ran away from her. At seven o'clock on a winter evening she sat down under a thicket, cold, tired, and disheartened. Snow came on ; she was too weak to rise, and the consequence was that by the morning the snow had heaped up around her to a height of two feet above her head as she sat. She had strength enough to thrust a twig, with her handkerchief at the top of it, through the snow, to serve as a signal, and to admit a little daylight. Torpor supervened ; and she knew little ·more of what passed around her. Night succeeded day, and day again broke, but there she remained, motionless and foodless. Not senseless, however, for she could hear church bells and village sounds—nay, even the voice and conversation of some of her neighbours. Four whole days she thus remained—one single pinch of snuff being her only substitute for food during the time, and this, she found to her sorrow, had lost its pungency. On the fifth day a thaw commenced, and then she suffered greatly, but still without being able to extricate herself. It was not until the eighth day that the handkerchief was espied by a villager, who, with many others, had long been seeking for her. Stooping down he said, ' Are you there, Elizabeth Woodcock ? ' She had strength enough to reply faintly, ' Dear John Stittle, I know your voice. For God's sake, help me out ! ' She died half a year afterwards, through mismanagement of frost-bitten toes ; but it was fully admitted that no one, unless cased in snow, could have lived out those eight days and nights in such a place without food.

Similar in principle was the incident narrated by Hearne, the antiquary, in the last century, in a letter addressed to Mr Charry, of Shottesbrooke. In the severe winter of 1708-9, a poor woman, near Yeovil, in Somersetshire, having been to Chard, to sell some of her home-spun yarn, was returning home, when, falling ill by the wayside, she requested to be allowed to sit by the fire in a cottage. This being unfeelingly refused, she lay down under a hedge in the open air, being too weak to proceed farther. Snow soon came on. A neighbour passed by, and helped for a few minutes to guide her steps ; but her strength soon failed her, and *he,* in like manner, left her to her fate. Once more laid prostrate, she became gradually covered with the snow. Day after day passed, for a whole week, during which time her friends made search and inquiry for her in every direction. The only person who could give information was the man who had abandoned her, after her failure in the attempt to walk ; and he remained silent, lest his conduct should bring reproaches on him. There then occurred one of those strange sleep-revelations which, explain them how we may, are continually reported as playing a part in the economy of human life. A poor woman dreamed that the missing person lay under a hedge in a particular spot denoted. The neighbours, roused by the narration she gave, sallied forth with sticks, which they thrust through the snow in various places. One of them thought he heard a groan ; he thrust again in a particular spot, when a feeble voice cried out, ' Oh, for God's sake, don't kill me !' The poor, imprisoned wayfarer was taken out, to the astonishment of all. ' She was found,' says the writer of the letter, ' to have taken great part of her upper garment for sustenance ; but how she could have digested a textile fabric of wool or flax is not easy to understand. She surprised her neighbours by the assertion that she had lain very warm, and had slept most part of the time. One of her legs lay just under a bush, and was not quite covered with snow ; this became in consequence frost-bitten, but not too far for recovery. Her spirits revived, and she was able shortly to resume her ordinary duties.'

In these two last-named instances the person was a full week under the snow blanket ; and the covering evidently prevented the natural warmth of the body from being abstracted to so great a degree as to be fatal.

MARCH 8.

Saints Apollonius, Philemon, and others, martyrs of Egypt, about 311. St Senan, Bishop in Ireland, about 544. St Psalmoid, or Saumay, of Ireland, about 589. St Felix, Bishop of Dunwich, 646. St Julian, Archbishop of Toledo, 690. St Rosa, virgin of Viterbo, buried 1252. St Duthak, Bishop of Ross, 1253. St John of God, founder of the Order of Charity, 1550.

Born.—St John of God, 1495; Dr John Campbell, historical writer, 1708, *Edinburgh;* Dr John Fothergill (Quaker), 1712, *Carr-end;* William Roscoe, miscellaneous writer, 1753, *Liverpool ;* Austin H. Layard, M.P., explorer of the antiquities of Nineveh, 1817, *Paris.*

Died.—King William III., of England, 1702, *Kensington;* Bishop John Hough, 1743 ; Thomas Blackwell, LL.D., classical scholar, 1757, *Edinburgh;* Sir William Chambers, R.A., architect, 1796 ; Francis Duke of Bridgewater (canal navigation), 1803, *St James's ;* W. Sawrey Gilpin, landscape painter, 1807, *Brompton ;* Joseph Jekyll, F.R.S., noted wit, 1837, *London ;* Karl Johann (Bernadotte), King of Sweden, 1844.

SIR WILLIAM CHAMBERS.

In our day, which is distinguished by an unprecedentedly high culture of architecture, the attainments of Sir William Chambers, the great English architect of the eighteenth century, are apt to be set down as mediocre. There must, nevertheless, have been some considerable gifts in possession of the man who could design such a noble pile as Somerset House.

Chambers was born at Stockholm (1726), the son of a Scotchman who had gone there to prosecute some claims of debt for warlike stores which he had furnished to Charles XII. Educated in England, he started in life as supercargo in a mercantile ship trading with China. In that country he busied himself in taking sketches of the peculiar buildings of the country, and thus laid the foundations of a taste which clung to him in his subsequent professional career. He was afterwards able to study architecture both in Italy and France. His command

of the pencil seems to have been the main means of his advancement. It recommended him to the Earl of Bute as a teacher of architectural drawing to the young Prince George, afterwards George III. Having thus secured an opening into important fields of professional exertion, his energetic character and assiduity did all the rest ; and Chambers reigned for thirty years the acknowledged architectural chief of his day, received a Swedish order of knighthood, and retired from business with a handsome fortune.

It was in 1775, that Sir William, as Comptroller of his Majesty's works, proceeded to the great work of his life, the reconstruction of Somerset House. He is admitted to have shewn in the internal arrangements of this great quadrangle all desirable taste and skill, while the exterior is the perfection of masonry. Many of the ornamental details were copied from models executed at Rome, under Chambers's direction : the sculptors employed were Carlini, Wilton, Geracci, Nollekens, and Bacon. Telford, the engineer, when he came to London, in 1782, was employed on the quadrangle. Chambers received £2,000 a-year during the erection of Somerset House ; it cost more than half a million of money ; but it is one of the noblest structures in the metropolis, and, in some respects, superior to any ; the street-front and vestibule have always been much admired. After Somerset House, Chambers's most successful designs are the Marquis of Abercorn's mansion at Duddingstone near Edinburgh ; and Milton Abbey, in Dorsetshire, which he built in the Gothic style for Lord Dorchester.

Sir William Chambers also designed the royal state coach, which has now been used by our sovereigns for a century. Walpole describes it as a beautiful object, though crowded with improprieties ; its palm-trees denote the architect's predilection for oriental objects. The bill was £8,000, but being taxed, was reduced nearly £500.

JOSEPH JEKYLL.

The wit of Mr Jekyll has given him a traditionary fame superior to, and which will probably be more lasting than, that which some worthy men derive from solid works. He was, however, the author of several books, one of them of an antiquarian nature (on the monuments in the Temple Church), and he had attained, some time before his death, the senior position both among the King's Counsel and the Benchers. He reached the age of eighty-five. His *bon mots* were for a long course of years the delight of the bar of London, and of the brilliant society to which his powers of conversation gave him access. An obituary notice states that they would fill volumes. It is nevertheless probable that now, at the distance of a quarter of a century, it would be difficult to gather as many pleasantries of Mr Jekyll as would fill a page of the present work.

A general remark with regard to *bon mots* may here be properly appended—namely, that they are extremely apt to be reproduced. It is not necessarily that jokers are plagiarists, but that the relations of things out of which *bon mots* spring are of limited number and liable to recur. It is therefore not without good cause that the determined joker utters his well-known malediction—'Perish those who have said all our good things before us!'

There is an old French collection of *bon mots*, called the *Nain Jaune* (Yellow Dwarf), in which some of the most noted of English jokes will be found anticipated. For example, the recommendation of Dr Johnson to the lady author who sent him a manuscript poem, and told him she had other irons in the fire—'I advise you to put the poem with the irons.' Of this the prototype appears as follows : 'M. N——, que la ciel a donné du malheureux talent d'écrire, sans penser, tous les mois, un volume, consultait le très franc et le très malin P., sur un ouvrage nouveau dont il menace le public—"Parlez-moi franchement," lui disait-il, "car si cela ne vaut rien, *j'ai d'autres fers au feu."*—"Dans ce cas," lui respondit P., "je vous conseille *de mettre votre manuscrit où vous avez mis vos fers."*

As another example, though rather in the class of comic occurrences than criticisms—Mrs Piozzi, in her *Autobiography*, relates that her mother Mrs Salusbury used to narrate the following circumstance in connection with the name of Lord Harry Pawlett. A lady, to whom that nobleman had paid attentions, and whom Mrs Salusbury knew, requested of his lordship that he would procure for her a couple of monkeys of a particular kind, from the East Indies. 'Lord Harry, happy to oblige her, wrote immediately, depending on the best services of a distant friend, whom he had essentially served. Writing a bad hand, however, and spelling what he wrote with more haste than correctness, he charged the gentleman to send him over two monkeys; but the word being written *too*, and all the characters of one height (100), what was Lord Harry Pawlett's dismay, when a letter came to hand with the news, that he would receive fifty monkeys by such a ship, and fifty more by the next conveyance, making up the hundred, according to his lordship's commands!'

We rather think there is a counterpart to this story, in which a Virginia planter is represented as writing to his factor in England to send him over *two* virtuous young women; in consequence of which, through a misapprehension of the characters forming the word two, the factor sent him fifty examples of the sex, with a promise of fifty more as soon as the number of volunteers for Virginia could be made up.

Whether this be the case or not, it appears that the joke about the monkeys is a hundred years older than the time of Mrs Salusbury and Lord Harry Pawlett. In a letter dated the 19th of January 1635-6, Sir Edward Verney, Knight Marshal to Charles I., wrote to his son, Ralph Verney, from London, as follows : * 'To requite your news of your fish, I will tell you as good a tale from hence, and as true. A merchant of London that writ to a factor of his beyond sea, desired him by the next ship to send him 2 or 3 apes. He forgot the *r*, and then it was 203 apes. His factor sent him four score, and says he shall have

* Communicated by John Bruce to *Notes and Queries*, April 26, 1862.

the rest by the next ship, conceiving the merchant had sent for two hundred and three apes. If yourself or friends will buy any to breed on, you could never have had such choice as now.'

THE BOWYER BIBLE.

About ninety years ago, a poor youth was walking through Newgate-street listlessly looking into the shops, and lamenting his own poverty. His fancy was taken by a portrait in one of the windows; and something within him said that *he* too, perchance, might be able to paint portraits, and to earn a living thereby. He went home, procured paints, brushes, and a bit of broken looking-glass, and painted a small portrait of himself. It was a success in his eyes, and apparently in the eyes of others; for he gradually got employment as a miniature painter, and numbered among his sitters such great personages as George III. and Queen Charlotte. One Sunday, when the poor King was too far gone in his mental malady to sit to portrait-painters, the artist drew *on his thumb nail* a portrait of the King, which he afterwards transferred on the same scale to ivory; the Prince Regent liked the miniature so well, that he at once purchased it at the price named by the artist—a hundred guineas.

The person here treated of was William Bowyer, whose name is now little known or thought of as that of a regular artist. Perhaps he found that he was really deficient in the higher powers of art, and that it would be wise for him to turn his attention to other fields of labour. Be this as it may, he became a printer, and gradually realized a competency in that trade. The Stationers' Company, to this day, have the management of a small endowment which he established for the benefit of poor working printers. The most remarkable work printed by him was an Edition of *Hume's History of England*, so costly that only a few copies could be disposed of.

William Bowyer is now chiefly remembered in connexion with one particular copy of the Bible. Macklin ventured on the most costly edition of the Bible ever issued from the press; and Bowyer, possessing one copy of this work, devoted the leisure of nearly thirty years to illustrating it. He procured from every part of Europe engravings, etchings, and original drawings, relating to biblical subjects; and these, to the number of *seven thousand*, he interleaved with his Bible. From Michael Angelo and Raffaelle to Reynolds and West, every artist whose Scripture subjects had been engraved was brought into requisition. Bowyer having only his own taste to please, gave a very wide scope to the meaning of the words 'scriptural' and 'biblical;' insomuch that he included plates of natural history that *might* possibly illustrate the cosmogony of the Bible. The collection included the best Scripture atlases. Its most original features were two hundred drawings by Lautherbourg. Thus he went on, step by step, until his Bible expanded to forty-five folio volumes, including examples from nearly 600 different engravers.

This extraordinary work seems to have occupied Mr Bowyer from about 1798 to 1824. The work, with costly binding, and an oak cabinet to contain all the forty-five volumes, is said to have cost him *four thousand guineas*. He insured it in the Albion Fire Office for £3,000. After his death, a lottery was got up for the benefit of his daughter, Mrs Parkes, with this Bible as the sole prize. One Mr Saxon, a Somersetshire farmer, won the prize. It is just possible that, as in the famous case of the family picture of the Vicar of Wakefield, the dimensions were not found compatible with domestic convenience; for the work has changed hands several times. At Messrs Puttick and Simpson's a few years ago, it became the property of Mr Moreland of Manchester; after which it passed into the hands of Mr Albinson of Bolton. In the early part of March 1856, there was a seven days' sale of the extensive library of the last-named gentleman; and among the lots the chief was the celebrated Bowyer Bible. The biddings began at £400, and the lot was ultimately knocked down at £550 to Mr Robert Heywood of Bolton. Ponderous as such a work must be for any private library, it would nevertheless be a pity that so unique a collection should ever be broken up and scattered.

LIFE-SAVING DOGS.

We owe to two principles which have been ably illustrated by modern naturalists—namely, the educability of animals, and the transmission of the acquired gifts to new generations—that the young pointer, without ever having seen a field of game, is no sooner introduced to one than it *points*, as its father and mother did before it. To this also we owe the even more interesting speciality of certain varieties of the canine species, that they unpromptedly engage in the business of saving human life in situations of danger. We have all heard of the dogs of St Bernard, which for ages have been devoted to the special duty of rescuing travellers who may be lost in Alpine snows. Early in the present century, one of these noble creatures was decorated with a medal, in reward for having saved the lives of no less than twenty-two snow-bound travellers. Sad to say, it lost its own life in the winter of 1816. A Piedmontese courier, after resting for a while at the Hospice during a terrible snow storm, was earnestly desirous of proceeding that same night to the village of St Pierre, on the Italian side of the mountain. The monks, after endeavouring in vain to dissuade him, lent him the aid of two guides and two dogs, including the one bearing the medal. The courier's family knowing of his intended return, and anxious for his safety, ascended part of the way to meet him; and thus it happened that the whole were nearly together when an avalanche broke away from the mountain pinnacle, and buried human beings and dogs together. So keen is the sense of smell possessed by these dogs, that though a perishing man lie beneath a snow drift to a depth of several feet, they will detect the spot, scrape away the snow with their feet, make a howling that can be heard at a great distance, and exert themselves to the utmost in his behalf. An anecdote is told of one of the dogs that found a child whose mother had just been destroyed by an avalanche; the child, alive

344

and unhurt, was in some way induced to get upon the dog's back, and was safely conveyed to the Hospice.

Of the aptitude of the Newfoundland dog to take to the water, and courageously help drowning or endangered persons, the instances are abundant. We will cite only two. A Mr William Phillips, while bathing at Portsmouth, ventured out too far, and was in imminent peril. Two boatmen, instead of starting off to assist him, selfishly strove to make a hard bargain with some of the bystanders, who urged them. While the parley was going on, a Newfoundland dog, seeing the danger, plunged into the water, and saved the struggling swimmer. It is pleasantly told that Mr Phillips, in gratitude for his deliverance, bought the dog from his owner, a butcher, and thereafter gave an annual festival, at which the dog was assigned the place of honour, with a good ration of beefsteaks. He had a picture of the dog painted by Morland, and engraved by Bartolozzi; and on all his table-linen he had this picture worked in the tissue, with the motto, 'Virum extuli mari.'

The other anecdote is of more recent date. On the 8th of March 1834, two little boys were playing on the banks of the Grosvenor Canal at Pimlico (now filled up to make the Victoria and Crystal Palace Railway). The younger of the two, in his gambols, fell into the water; the elder, about nine years of age, plunged in with the hope of saving him. Both sank, and their lives were greatly imperilled. It happened that at that critical moment Mr Ryan, an actor at Astley's Amphitheatre, was passing, with a fine Newfoundland dog, which, under the name of *Hero*, was wont to take part in some of the performances. A bystander threw a pebble into the water, to shew the spot where the two poor boys were immersed. The dog plunged in and brought up the elder one; the clothes were rent, and the boy sank again; but the dog, making a second attempt, succeeded in bringing him to the shore, and afterwards his brother. Mr Horncroft, the father of the children, gave a dinner that evening, at which Hero was a specially invited guest; and his gambols with the two boys whom he had saved, shewed how he appreciated the joyousness of the meeting.

Some years ago, it was resolved at Paris to take advantage of the gifts of the Newfoundland dog, for a general purpose resembling the practice at St Bernard. Ten select dogs were brought to the French capital, and appointed as savers of human life in the river Seine. They were first exercised in drawing stuffed figures of men and children from the water, and in time they acquired such skill and facility in their business, as to prove eminently serviceable.

Bequests of Worsted Beds.—Bequests of beds with worsted hangings frequently occur in the middle ages. The Countess of Northampton, in 1356, bequeathed to her daughter the Countess of Arundel 'a bed of red worsted embroidered. Lady Despencer, in 1409, gave her daughter Philippa 'a bed of red worsted, with all the furniture appertaining thereto.' Lady Elizabeth Andrews, in 1474, gave to William Wyndsore 'a red bed of worsted, with all the hangings.'—*Testamenta Vetusta.*

MARCH 9.

St Pacian, Bishop of Barcelona, 4th century. St Gregory, of Nyssa, bishop, 400. St Frances, widow, of Rome, foundress of the Collatines, 1440. St Catherine, of Bologna, virgin, 1463.

Born.—Lewis Gonzaga (*St Aloysius*), 1568; Dr Joseph Franz Gall, founder of phrenology, 1757, *Tiefenbrunn, Suabia;* William Cobbett, political writer, 1762, *Farnham.*

Died.—Sultan Bajazet I., *Antioch;* David Rizzio, 1566, murdered, *Holyrood;* William Warner, poet, 1609, *Amwell;* Francis Beaumont, dramatist, 1616; Cardinal Jules Mazarine, 1661, *Vincennes;* Bishop Joseph Wilcocks, 1756; John Calas, broken on the wheel, 1762, *Toulouse;* William Guthrie, historical and geographical writer, 1771, *London;* Dr Samuel Jebb, 1772. *Derbyshire;* Dr Edward Daniel Clarke, traveller, 1822, *Pall Mall;* Anna Letitia Barbauld, writer of books for the young, 1825, *Stoke Newington;* Miss Linwood, artist in needlework, 1845; Professor Oersted, Danish natural philosopher, 1851.

WILLIAM COBBETT.

Were we asked to name the Englishman who most nearly answers to the typical John Bull which Leech delights to draw in *Punch*, we should pause between William Hogarth and William Cobbett, and likely say—Cobbett. His bluff speech, his hearty and unreasonable likes and dislikes, his hatred of craft and injustice, his tenderness, his roughness, his swift anger and gruff pity, his pugnacity, his pride, his broad assurance that his ways are the only right ways, his contempt for abstractions, his exaltation of the solidities over the elegancies of life, these and a score of other characteristics identify William Cobbett with John Bull.

Cobbett was, in his origin, purely an English peasant. He was born in a cottage-like dwelling on the south side of the village of Farnham, in Surrey. Since the Cobbetts left it, about 1780, it has been used as a public-house under the name of the 'Jolly Farmer,'—noted, as we understand, for its home-brewed ale and beer, the produce of the Farnham hops. Behind it is a little garden and steep sand-rock, to which Cobbett makes allusion in his writings. 'From my infancy,' says he,—'from the age of six years, when I climbed up the side of a steep sand-rock, and there scooped me out a plot of four feet square to make me a garden, and the soil for which I carried up in the bosom of my little blue

WILLIAM COBBETT.

smock frock (a hunting shirt), I have never lost one particle of my passion for these healthy and rational, and heart-charming pursuits.'

Cobbett, having a hard-working, frugal man for his father, was allowed no leisure and little education in his boyhood. 'I do not remember,' he says, 'the time when I did not earn my own living. My first occupation was driving the small birds from the turnip-seed, and the rooks from the pease. When I first trudged a-field, with my wooden bottle and my satchel slung over my shoulders, I was hardly able to climb the gates and stiles; and at the close of the day, to reach home was a task of infinite difficulty. My next employment was weeding wheat, and leading a single horse at harrowing barley. Hoeing pease followed; and hence I arrived at the honour of joining the reapers in harvest, driving the team, and holding the plough. We were all of us strong and laborious; and my father used to boast, that he had four boys, the eldest of whom was but fifteen years old, who did as much work as any three men in the parish of Farnham. Honest pride and happy days!

The father, nevertheless, contrived, by his own exertions in the evening, to teach his sons to read and write. The subject of this memoir in time advanced to a place in the garden of Waverley Abbey, afterwards to one in Kew Garden, where George III. took some notice of him, and where he would lie reading Swift's *Tale of a Tub* in the evening light. In 1780, he went to Chatham and enlisted as a foot-soldier, and immediately after his regiment was shipped off to Nova Scotia, and thence moved to New Brunswick. He was not long in the army ere he was promoted over the heads of thirty sergeants to the rank of sergeant-major, and without exciting any envy. His steadiness and his usefulness were so marked, that all the men recognised it as a mere matter of course that Cobbett should be set over them. He helped to keep the accounts of the regiment, for which he got extra pay. He rose at four every morning, and was a marvel of order and industry. 'Never,' he writes, 'did any man or thing wait one moment for me. If I had to mount guard at ten, I was ready at nine.' His leisure he diligently applied to study. He learnt grammar when his pay was sixpence a-day. 'The edge of my berth, or that of my guard-bed,' he tells us, 'was my seat to study in; my knapsack was my bookcase; a bit of board lying on my lap was my writing table. I had no money to buy candle or oil; in winter time it was rarely I could get any light but that of the fire, and only my turn even of that. To buy a pen, or a sheet of paper, I was compelled to forego some portion of food, though in a state of half starvation. I had no moment to call my own, and I had to read and write amidst the talking, laughing, singing, whistling, and brawling of at least half a score of the most thoughtless men.' That was at the outset, for he soon rose above these miseries, and began to save money. While in New Brunswick he met the girl who became his wife. He first saw her in company for about an hour one evening. Shortly afterwards, in the dead of winter, when the snow lay several feet thick on the ground, he chanced in his walk at break of day to pass the house of her parents. It was hardly light, but there was she out in the cold, scrubbing a washing tub. That action made her mistress of Cobbett's heart for ever. No sooner was he out of hearing, than he exclaimed, 'That's the girl for me!' She was the daughter of a sergeant of artillery, and then only thirteen. To his intense chagrin, the artillery was ordered to England, and she had to go with her father. Cobbett by this time had managed to save 150 guineas, the produce of extra work. Considering that Woolwich, to which his sweetheart was bound, was a gay place, and that she there might find many suitors, who, moved by her beauty, might tempt her by their wealth, and, unwilling that she should hurt herself with hard work, he sent her all his precious guineas, and prayed that

she would use them freely, for he could get plenty more; to buy good clothes, and live in pleasant lodgings, and be as happy as she could until he was able to join her. Four long years elapsed before they met. Cobbett, when he reached England, found her a maid-of-all-work, at £5 a-year. On their meeting, without saying a word about it, she placed in his hands his parcel of 150 guineas unbroken. He obtained his discharge from the army, and married the brave and thrifty woman. She made him an admirable wife; never was he tired of speaking her praises, and whatever comfort and success he afterwards enjoyed, it was his delight to ascribe to her care and to her inspiration. At this time he brought a charge of peculation against four officers of the regiment to which he had belonged. A court-martial was assembled, witnesses were summoned, but Cobbett was not forthcoming. He had fled to France, and for his conduct no fair explanation was ever given. From France he sailed to New York in 1792, and settled in Philadelphia. Shunned and persecuted in England, Dr Priestley sought a home in Pennsylvania in 1794. Cobbett attacked him in ' *Observations on the Emigration of a Martyr to the Cause of Liberty,* by Peter Porcupine.' The pamphlet took amazingly, and Cobbett followed it up with a long series of others discussing public affairs in a violent anti-democratic strain. He drew upon himself several prosecutions for libel, and to escape the penalties he returned to England in 1800, and tried to establish *The Porcupine,* a daily Tory newspaper, in London. It failed after running a few months, and then he started his famous *Weekly Register,* which he continued without interruption for upwards of thirty-three years. The *Register* at first advocated Toryism, but it soon veered round to that Radicalism with which its name became synonymous. The unbridled invective in which Cobbett indulged kept actions for libel continually buzzing about his ears. The most serious of these occurred in 1810, and resulted in his imprisonment for two years and a fine of £1,000 to the King. In 1817, he revisited America, posting copy regularly for his *Register ;* and he returned in 1819, bearing with him the bones of Thomas Paine. Again he tried a daily newspaper in London, but he was only able to keep it going for two months. He wished to get into Parliament, and unsuccessfully contested Coventry in 1820, and Preston in 1826; but in 1832 he was returned for Oldham. His parliamentary career was comparatively a failure. He was too precipitate and dogmatic for that arena. The late hours sapped his health, and he died after a short illness, on the 18th of June 1835, aged seventy-three. The *Weekly Register,* whilst it alone might stand for the sole business of an ordinary life, represented merely a fraction of Cobbett's activity. He farmed, he travelled, he saw much society, and wrote books and pamphlets innumerable. His *Register* was denounced as 'two-penny trash.' He thereon issued a series of political papers entitled *Two-penny Trash,* which sold by the hundred thousand. His industry, early rising, and methodical habits enabled him to get through an amount of work incredible to ordinary men. He wrote easily but spared no pains to write well; his terse, fluent, and forcible style has won the praise of the best critics. He had no abstruse thoughts to communicate; he knew what he wanted to say, and had the art of saying it in words which anybody who could read might comprehend. Few could match him at hard hitting in plain words, or in the manufacture of graphic nick-names. Dearly did he enjoy fighting, and a plague, a terror, and a horror he was to many of his adversaries. Jeremy Bentham said of him: 'He is a man filled with *odium humani generis*. His malevolence and lying are beyond anything.' Many others spoke of him with equal bitterness, but years have toned off these animo-sities, and the perusal of his fiercest sayings now only excites amusement. Cobbett's character is at last understood as it could scarcely be in the midst of the passions which his wild words pro-voked. It is clearly seen that his understanding was wholly subordinate to his feelings; that his feelings were of enormous strength; and that his understanding, though of great capacity, had a very limited range. His feelings were kindly, and they were firmly interwoven with the poor and hard-working people of England. Whatever men or measures Cobbett thought likely to give Englishmen plenty of meat and drink, good rai-ment and lodging, he praised; and whatever did not directly offer these blessings he denounced as impostures. Doctrine more than this he had not, and would hear of none. Thus it was that he came to ridicule all arts and studies which did not bear on their face the promise of physical comfort. Shakspeare, Milton, the British Mu-seum, Antiquaries, Philanthropists, and Political Economists, all served in turn as butts for the arrows of his contempt. Of the craft of the demagogue he had little; he made enemies in the most wanton and impolitic manner; and thoughts of self-interest seldom barred for an instant the outflow of his feelings. Fickle and inconsistent as were those feelings, intellectually considered, in them Cobbett wrote himself out at large. From his multitudinous and diffuse writings a most entertaining volume of readings might be selected. His love of rural life and rural scenes is expressed in many bits of compo-sition which a poet might envy; and his tren-chant criticisms of public men and affairs, and his grotesque opinions, whilst they would prove what power can live in simple English words, would give the truest picture of him who holds high rank among the great forces which agitated England in the years anterior to the Reform Bill.

DEATH OF CARDINAL MAZARIN.

Mazarin, an Italian by birth, and a pupil of Richelieu, but inferior to his master, was the minister of the Regency during the minority of Louis XIV. He was more successful at the close of his career in his treaties of peace than he had been in his wars and former negotiations. In February 1661, he had concluded at Vincennes a third and last treaty with Charles, duke of Lorraine, by which Strasburg, Phalsburg, Stenai, and other places were given up to France. A fatal malady had seized on the Cardinal whilst engaged in the conferences of the treaty, and, worn by mental agony, he brought it home with him to the Louvre. He consulted Grenaud, the great physician, who told him that he had two months to live. This sad assurance troubled the Cardinal greatly; his pecuniary wealth, his valuables and pictures, were immense. He was fond of hoarding, and his love of pictures was as strong as his love of power—perhaps even stronger. Soon after his physician had told him how short a time he had to live, Brienne per-ceived the Cardinal in night-cap and dressing-gown tottering along his gallery, pointing to his pictures, and exclaiming, 'Must I quit all these?' He saw Brienne, and seized him: 'Look!' he exclaimed, 'look at that Correggio! this Venus of Titian! that incomparable Deluge of Caracci! Ah! my friend, I must quit all these! Farewell, dear pictures, that I loved so dearly, and that cost me so much!' His friend surprised him slumbering in his chair at another time, mur-muring, 'Grenaud has said it! Grenaud has said it!' A few days before his death, he caused himself to be dressed, shaved, rouged, and painted, 'so that he never looked so fresh and vermilion' in his life. In this state he was carried in his chair to the promenade, where his envious courtiers cruelly rallied him with ironical compliments on his appearance. Cards were the amusement of his death-bed, his hand being held by others; and they were only interrupted by the visit of the Papal Nuncio, who came to give the Cardinal that plenary indulgence to which the prelates of the Sacred College are officially entitled.

MRS BARBAULD.

Anna Letitia Aiken, by marriage Mrs Bar-bauld, spent most of her long life of eighty-two years in the business of teaching and in writing for the young. Of dissenting parentage and connexions, and liberal tendencies of mind, she was qualified to confer honour on any denomina-tion or sect she might belong to by her consum-mate worth, amiableness, and judgment. She was at all times an active writer, and her writings both in prose and verse display many admirable qualities; nevertheless, the public now knows little about them, her name being chiefly kept in re-membrance by her contributions to the well-known children's book, mainly of her brother's composition, the *Evenings at Home*.

Amongst Mrs Barbauld's miscellaneous pieces, there is an essay *Against Inconsistency in our Expectations*, which has had the singular honour of being reprinted for private distribution by more than one person, on account of its remark-able lessons of wisdom which it is calculated to convey. She starts with the idea that 'most of the unhappiness of the world arises rather from disappointed desires than from positive evil.' It becomes consequently of the first importance to know the laws of nature, both in matter and in mind, that we may reach to equity and modera-tion in our claims upon Providence. 'Men of merit and integrity,' she remarks, 'often censure the dispositions of Providence for suffering characters they despise to run away with advantages which, they yet know, are purchased by such means as a high and noble spirit could never submit to. If you refuse to pay the price, why expect the purchase?' This may be called the key-note of the whole piece.

Say that a man has set his heart on being rich. Well, by patient toil, and unflagging attention to the minutest articles of expense and profit, he may attain riches. It is done every day. But let not this person also expect to enjoy 'the pleasures of leisure, of a vacant mind, of a free, unsuspicious temper.' He must learn to do hard things, to have at the utmost a homespun sort of honesty, to be in a great measure a drudge. 'I cannot submit to all this.' Very good, be above it; only do not repine that you are not rich.

How strange to see an illiterate fellow attaining to wealth and social importance, while a profound scholar remains poor and of little account! If, however, you have chosen the riches of knowledge, be content with them. The other person has paid health, conscience, liberty for *his* wealth. Will you envy him his bargain? 'You are a modest man—you love quiet and independence, and have a delicacy and reserve in your temper, which renders it impossible for you to elbow your way in the world and be the hero of your own merits. Be content then with a modest retirement, with the esteem of your intimate friends, with the praises of a blameless heart, and a delicate, ingenuous spirit; but resign the splendid distinctions of the world to those who can better scramble for them.'

The essayist remarks that men of genius are of all others most inclined to make unreasonable claims. 'As their relish for enjoyment,' says she, ' is strong, their views large and comprehensive, and they feel themselves lifted above the common bulk of mankind, they are apt to slight that natural reward of praise and admiration which is ever largely paid to distinguished abilities; and to expect to be called forth to public notice and favour: without considering that their talents are commonly unfit for active life; that their eccentricity and turn for speculation disqualifies them for the business of the world, which is best carried on by men of moderate genius; and that society is not obliged to reward any one who is not useful to it. The poets have been a very unreasonable race, and have often complained loudly of the neglect of genius and the ingratitude of the age. The tender and pensive Cowley, and the elegant Shenstone, had their minds tinctured by this discontent; and even the sublime melancholy of Young was too much owing to the stings of disappointed ambition.'

MISS LINWOOD'S EXHIBITION OF NEEDLEWORK.

For nearly half a century, in old Savile House, on the north side of Leicester-square, was exhibited the gallery of pictures in needlework which Miss Mary Linwood, of Leicester, executed through her long life. She worked her first picture when thirteen years old, and the last piece when seventy-eight; beyond which her life was extended twelve years. Genius, virtue, and

unparalleled industry had, for nearly three-quarters of a century, rendered her residence an honour to Leicester. As mistress of a boarding-school, her activity continued to her last year. In 1844, during her annual visit to her Exhibition in London, she was taken ill, and conveyed in an invalid carriage to Leicester, where her health rallied for a time, but a severe attack of influenza terminated her life in her ninetieth year. By her death, many poor families missed the hand of succour, her benevolent disposition and ample means having led her to minister greatly to the necessities of the poor and destitute in her neighbourhood.

No needlework, either of ancient or modern times, (says Mr Lambert,) has ever surpassed the productions of Miss Linwood. So early as 1785, these pictures had acquired such celebrity as to attract the attention of the Royal Family, to whom they were shewn at Windsor Castle. Thence they were taken to the metropolis, and shewn privately to the nobility at the Pantheon, Oxford-street; in 1798, they were first exhibited publicly at the Hanover-square Rooms; whence they were removed to Leicester-square.

The pictures were executed with fine crewels, dyed under Miss Linwood's own superintendence, and worked on a thick tammy woven expressly for her use: they were entirely drawn and embroidered by herself, no background or other important parts being put in by a less skilful hand—the only assistance she received, if such it may be called, was in the threading of her needles.

The pictures appear to have been cleverly *set* for picturesque effect. The principal room, a fine gallery, was hung with scarlet cloth, trimmed with gold; and at the end was a throne and canopy of satin and silver. A long dark passage led to a prison cell, in which was Northcote's *Lady Jane Grey Visited by the Abbot and Keeper of the Tower at Night;* the scenic illusion being complete. Next was a cottage, with casement and hatch-door, and within it Gainsborough's cottage children, standing by the fire, with chimney-piece and furniture complete. Near to this was a den, with lionesses; and further on, through a cavern aperture was a brilliant sea-view and picturesque shore. The large picture by Carlo Dolci had appropriated to it an entire room. The large saloons of Savile House were well adapted for these exhibition purposes, by insuring distance and effect.

The collection ultimately consisted of sixty-four pictures, most of them of large or gallery size, and copied from paintings by great masters. The gem of the collection, *Salvator Mundi,* after Carlo Dolci, for which 3,000 guineas had been refused, was bequeathed by Miss Linwood to her Majesty Queen Victoria.

In the year after Miss Linwood's death, the pictures were sold by auction, by Christie and Manson; and the prices they fetched denoted a strange fall in the money-value of these curious works. *The Judgment on Cain,* which had occupied ten years working, brought but £64 1s.; *Jephtha's Rash Vow,* after Opie, sixteen guineas; two pictures from Gainsborough, *The Shepherd Boy,* £17 6s. 6d., and *The Ass and Children,* £23 2s. *The*

Farmer's Stable, after Morland, brought £32 11s. A portrait of Miss Linwood, after a crayon picture by Russell, R.A.. brought eighteen guineas; and *A Woodman in a Storm*, by Gainsborough. £33 1s. 6d. Barker's *Woodman* brought £29 8s. *The Girl and Kitten*, by Sir Joshua Reynolds,

MISS LINWOOD'S EXHIBITION OF NEEDLEWORK.

£10 15s.; and *Lady Jane Grey*, by Northcote, £24 13s. In the Scripture-room, *The Nativity*, by Carlo Maratti, was sold for £21; *Dead Christ*, L. Caracci, fourteen guineas; but *The Madonna della Sedia*, after Raffaelle, was bought in at £38 17s. A few other pictures were reserved; and those sold did not realize more than £1,000.

OLD LONDON SHOPS.

Business in the olden time was conducted in a far more open way than among ourselves. Advertising in print was an art undiscovered. A dealer advertised by word of mouth from an open shop, proclaiming the qualities of his wares, and inviting passengers to come and buy them. The principal street of a large town thus became a scene of noisy confusion. The little we know of the ancient state of the chief London thoroughfares, shews this to have been their peculiarity. In the south of Europe we may still see something of the aspect which the business streets of old London must have presented in the middle ages; but the eastern towns, such as Constantinople or Cairo, more completely retain these leading characteristics, in ill-paved streets, crowded markets, open shops disconnected with dwelling-houses, and localities sacred to particular trades. The back streets of Naples still possess similar arrangements, which must have existed there unchanged for centuries. The shops are vaulted cells in the lower story of the houses, and are closed at night by heavy doors secured by iron bars and massive padlocks. In the drawings preserved in mediæval manuscripts we see such shops delineated. Our first cut, copied from one of the best of these pictures, executed about 1490, represents the side of a street apparently devoted to a confraternity of mercers, who exhibit hats, shoes, stockings, scarfs, and other articles in front of their respective places of business; each taking their position at the counter which projects on the pathway, and from whence they addressed wayfarers when they wanted a customer. Lydgate, the monk of Bury, in his curious poem called *London Lack-penny*, has described the London shops as he saw them at the close of the fourteenth century:

'Where Flemyngs to me began to cry,
　"Master, what will you cheapen or buy?
　Fine felt hats, or spectacles to read;
　Lay down your silver and here you may speed."'

He afterwards describes the streets crowded with

peripatetic traders. 'Hot peascods' one began to cry, and others strawberries and cherries, while 'one bade me come near and buy some spice;' but he passes on to Cheapside, then the grand centre of trade, and named from the great market or *cheap* established there from very early time :

'Then to the Cheap my steps were drawn,
　Where much people I there saw stand ;
　One offered me velvet, silk, and lawn,
　　"Here is Paris thread, the finest in the land !"'

Tempting as all offers were, his lack of money brought him safely through the throng :

'Then went I forth by London stone,
　Throughout all Canwyke-street ;
　Drapers much cloth me offered anon,
　　Then comes me one, cried, "Hot sheepes feet !"'

Among the crowd another cried 'Mackerell!' and he was again hailed by a shopkeeper, and invited to buy a hood. The *Liber Albus*, a century before Lydgate, describes these shops, which consisted of open rooms closed at night by shutters, the tenants being enjoined to keep the space before their shops free of dirt, nor were they to sweep it before those of other people. At that time paving was unknown, open channels drained the streets in the centre, and a few rough stones might be placed in some favoured spots ; but mud and mire, or dust and ruts, were the most usual condition of the streets. On state occasions, such as the entry of a sovereign, or the passage to Westminster of a coronation procession from the Tower, the streets were levelled, ruts and gulleys filled in, and the road new gravelled ; but these attentions were seldom bestowed, and the streets,

350

of course, soon lapsed into their normal condition of filthy neglect.

The old dramatists, whose works often preserve unique and valuable records of ancient usages, incidentally allude to these old shops ; thus in Middleton's comedy, *The Roaring Girl*, 1611, Moll Cutpurse, from whom the play is named, refuses to stay with some jovial companions : 'I cannot stay now, 'faith : I am going to buy a shag-ruff : the shop will be shut in presently.' One of the scenes of this play occurs before a series of these open shops of city traders, and is thus described : 'The three shops open in a rank [like those in our cut]: the first an apothecary's shop; the next a feather shop; the third a sempster's shop ;' from the last the passengers are saluted with 'Gentlemen, what is't you lack ? what is't you buy ? see fine bands and ruffs, fine lawns, fine cambricks : what is't you lack, gentlemen ? what is't you buy ? ' This cry for custom is often contemptuously alluded to as a characteristic of a city trader ; and in the capital old comedy *Eastward Hoe*, the rakish apprentice Quick-silver asks his sober fellow-apprentice, 'What ! wilt thou cry, what is't ye lack ? stand with a bare pate, and a dropping nose, under a wooden penthouse.' This dialogue takes place in the shop of their master, 'Touchstone, a honest goldsmith in the city ;' its uncomfortable character, and the exposure of the shopkeeper to all weathers, is fully confirmed by the glimpses of street scenery we obtain in old topographic prints. Faithorne's view of Fish-street and the Monument represents a goldsmith's open shop with its wooden pent-

house ; it appears little better than a shed, with a few shelves to hold the stock ; and a counter, behind which the master is ensconced. It shews that no change for the better as regarded the comfort of shopkeepers was made by the Great Fire of London.

With the Revolution came a government well-defined in the Bill of Rights, and a consequent additional security to trade and commerce. Traders increased, and London enlarged itself ; yet local government continued lax and bad ; streets were unpaved, ill-lighted, and dangerous at night. Shops were still rude in construction, open to wind and weather, and most uncomfortable to both salesman and buyer. A candle stuck in a lantern swung in the night breezes, and gave a dim glare over the goods. The wooden penthouse, which imperfectly protected the wares from drifts of rain, was succeeded by a curved projection of lath and plaster. Our third cut, from a print dated 1736, will clearly exhibit this, as well as the painted sign (a greyhound) over the door ; the shop front is furnished with an open railing, which encloses the articles exposed for

sale ; in this instance, fruit is the vendible commodity, and oranges in baskets appear piled under the window. The lantern ready for lighting hangs on one side.

The custom of noting inns by signs, was succeeded by similarly distinguishing the houses of traders ; consequently in the seventeenth century sign-painting flourished, and the practice of the 'art' of a sign-painter was the most profitable branch of the fine arts left open to Englishmen. The houses in London not being numbered, a tradesman could only be known by such means ; hence every house in great leading thoroughfares displayed its sign ; and the ingenuity of traders was taxed for new and characteristic devices by which their shops might be distinguished. The sign was often engraved as a 'heading' to the shop-bill ; and many whimsical and curious combinations occurred from the custom of an apprentice or partner in a well-known house adopting its sign in addition to a new device of his own. These signs were sometimes stuck on posts, as we see them in country inns, between the foot and carriage way. In narrow streets they were slung across the road. More generally they projected over the footpath, supported by ironwork which was wrought in an elaborate, ornamental style. A young tradesman made his first and chiefest outlay in a new sign, which was conspicuously painted and gilt, surrounded by a heavy, richly carved, and painted frame, and then suspended from massive decorative ironwork. Cheapside was still the coveted locality for business, and the old views of that favoured locality are generally curious from the delineation of the line of shops, and crowd of signs, that are presented on both sides the way. From a view of Bow Church and neighbourhood published by Bowles in 1751, we select the two examples of shops engraved below. The two modes of suspending the signs are those generally in vogue. In one instance the shop is enclosed by glazed windows ; in the other it is open. The latter is a pastrycook's ; a cake on a stand occu-

pies the centre of the bracketed counter, which is protected by a double row of glazing above. Still the whole is far from weatherproof, and a

heavy drifting rain must have been a serious inconvenience when it happened, not to speak of the absolute damage it must have done. The mercers, hatters, and shoemakers made their places of business distinguished by throwing out poles, such as we see at the shops of country barbers, at an angle from the shop-front over the foot-path, hanging rows of stockings, or lines of hats, &c., upon them. When a shower came, these could at once be hauled in, and saved from damage ; but the signs swung and grated in the breeze, or collected water in the storm, which descended on the unlucky pedestrian, for whom no umbrella had, as yet, been invented. The spouts from the houses, too, were ingeniously contrived to condense and pour forth a volume of water which wavered in the wind, and made the place of its fall totally uncertain ; a few rough semi-globular stones formed a rude pavement in places ; but it was often in bad condition, for each householder was allowed to do what he pleased in this way, and sometimes he solved the difficulty of doubting what was best by doing nothing at all. The pedestrian was protected from carriages by a line of posts, as seen in our cut ; but he was constantly liable to be thrust in the gutter, or driven into a doorway or shop, by the sedan-chairs that crowded the streets, and which were thoroughly hated by all but the wealthy who used them, and those who profited by their use. 'The art of walking the streets of London' was therefore an art, necessary of acquirement by study, and Gay's poem, which bears the title, is an amusing picture of all the difficulties which beset pedestrianism when the wits of Queen Anne's reign rambled from tavern to tavern, to gather news or enjoy social converse.

These ponderous signs, with their massive iron frameworks, as they grew old, grew dangerous ; they would rot and fall, and when this did not occur, they 'made night hideous' by the shrieks and groans of the rusty hinges on which they swung. They impeded sight and ventilation in narrow streets, and sometimes hung inconveniently low for vehicles. At last they were doomed by Act of Parliament, and in 1762 ordered to be removed, or, if used, to be placed flat against the fronts of the houses. They had increased so enormously that every tradesman had one, each trying to hide and outvie his neighbour by the size or colour of his own, until it became a tedious task to discover the shop wanted. Gay, in his 'Trivia,' notes how—

> ——'Oft the peasant, with inquiring face,
> Bewildered, trudges on from place to place ;
> He dwells on every sign with stupid gaze,
> Enters the narrow alley's doubtful maze,
> Tries every winding court and street in vain,
> And doubles o'er his weary steps again.'

In addition to swinging painted sign-boards, it was sometimes the habit with the rich and ambitious trader to engage the services of the wood-carver to decorate his house with figures or emblems, the figures being those of some animal or thing adopted for his sign, as the stag seen over one of the doors in the cut of the Cheapside shops ; or else representations, modelled and coloured 'after life,' of pounds of candles, rolls of tobacco, cheeses, &c. &c.

There existed in St Martin's-lane, a number of years ago, a fine example of a better-class Lon-

don shop, of which we here give a wood-cut. It had survived through many changes in all its essential features. The richly carved private door-case told of the well-to-do trader who had erected it. The shop was an Italian warehouse ; and the window was curiously constructed, carrying out the traditional form of the old open shop with its projecting stall on brackets, and its slight window above, but effecting a compromise for security and comfort by enclosing the whole in a sort of glass box ; above which the trade of the occupant was shewn more distinctly in the small oil-barrels placed upon it, as well as by the models of candles which hung in bunches from the canopy above. The whole of this framework was of timber richly carved throughout with

foliated ornament, and was unique as a surviving example of the better class shops of the last century.

It was in the early part of the reign of George I. that shops began to be closed in with sash-windows, allowing them to be open in fine weather, but giving the chance of closing them in winter and during rain. Addison alludes to it in the *Tatler*, as if it was a somewhat absurd luxury. 'Private shops,' says he, 'stand upon Corinthian pillars, and whole rows of tin pots show themselves, in order to their sale, through a sash window.' A great improvement of the most economic and simple kind succeeded the old and expensive signs. This was numbering houses in a street. The first street so numbered was New Burlington-street, in June 1764. The fashion spread eastward, and the houses in Lincoln's-inn-fields were the next series thus distinguished. The old traders who stuck pertinaciously to their signs, affixed them flat to their walls, and a few thus preserved rot in obscurity in some of our lonely old streets ; one of the earliest and most curious is 'The Doublet,' in Thames-street, which seems to have originated in the days of Elizabeth, and to have been painted and repainted from time to time, till it is now scarcely distinguishable. The once-famed inn, used by Shakspeare, 'The Bell,' in Great Carter-lane, is no longer an inn ; but its sign, a bell, boldly sculptured in high relief, and rich in decoration, is still on its front. Other sculptured signs remain on city houses, but units now represent the hundreds that once existed. At the corner of Union-street, Southwark, where it opens on the Blackfriars-road, is a well-executed old sign ; a gilt model, life-size, representing a dog licking an overturned cooking-pot. It is curious that this very sign is mentioned in that strange old poem, 'Cock Lorell's Boat' (published by Wynkyn de Worde, in the early part of the reign of Henry VIII.) : one of the passengers is described as dwelling

> 'at the Sygne of the dogges hed in the pot.'

In Holywell-street, Strand, is the last remain-

ing shop sign *in situ*, being a boldly-sculptured half-moon, gilt, and exhibiting the old conventional face in the centre. About the year 1840 it was a mercer's shop, and the bills made out for customers were 'adorned with a picture' of this sign. It was afterwards occupied by a print-seller and dealer in old china, and the shop windows, instead of being open as represented in the woodcut, are now glazed. The corner-post, next door, which was decorated with a boldly-carved lion's head and paws, disappeared when the adjoining house was rebuilt. This street altogether is a good, and now an almost unique specimen of those which once were the usual style of London business localities, crowded, tortuous, and ill-ventilated, having shops closely and inconveniently packed, but which custom had made familiar and inoffensive to all; while the old traders, who delighted in 'old styles,' looked on improvements with absolute horror, as ' a new-fashioned way ' to bankruptcy.

A FORTUNE-TELLER OF THE LAST CENTURY.

Early in the year 1789, died in the Charter-house, Isaac Tarrat, a man of some literary merit, who had actually practised the arts of a fortune-teller. Originally a linendraper in the city, and a thriving one, he had from various causes proved ultimately unsuccessful, and at seventy knew not how to obtain his bread. One who had contributed, as he had done, to the *Ladies' Diary* and the *Gentleman's Magazine*, would have now been at no loss to live by the press; it was different in those days, and Tarrat was reduced to become a fortune-teller. In a mean street near the Middlesex Hospital, there was an obscure shop kept by an elderly woman, who had long made a livelihood by means of an oracle maintained on the premises. It became the office of Mr. Tarrat to sit in an upper room, in a fur cap, a white beard, and a flowing worsted damask night-gown, and tell the fortunes of all who might apply. The woman sat in the front shop, receiving the company, and taking their money. ' The Doctor ' was engaged in this duty at a shilling a day and his food. He admitted that his mistress treated him kindly, always giving him a small bowl of punch after supper; there was no great discomfort in his situation, beyond the constant distress of mind he suffered from reflecting on the infamous character of his occupation. He had occasion to remark with surprise that many of his customers were of less mean and illiterate appearance than might be expected. At length, having scraped together a small amount of cash, Tarrat gave up his place—and he did so just in time, as his successor had not been a month in office when he was taken up as an impostor. Poor Tarrat afterwards found a retreat in the Charter-house, and there contrived to make the thread of life spin out to eighty-eight.

The Profession of a Conjurer, a hundred years ago, was by no means uncommon, nor does it seem to have been thought a discreditable one. A person named Hassell was in full practice as a cunning man in the neighbourhood of Tunbridge Wells, very recently. One of the best known of his craft (in Sussex), was a man of the name of Sanders, of Heathfield, who died about 1807. He was a respectable man, and at one time in easy circumstances, but he neglected all earthly concerns for astrological pursuits, and, it is said, died in a workhouse.

MARCH 10.

The Forty Martyrs of St Sebaste, 320. St Mackessog (or Kessog), Bishop in Scotland, 560. St Droctovæus, Abbot, about 580.

Born.—Bishop Duppa, 1598-9, *Lewisham ;* Marcellus Malpighi, microscopic anatomist, 1628, *Bologna ;* Professor Playfair (Natural Philosophy), *Benvie,* 1748 ; William Etty, R.A., painter, 1787, *York ;* E. H. Baily, R.A., sculptor, 1788, *Bristol.*

Died.—Heliogabalus (Emperor), beheaded, A.D. 222 ; Pope Benedict III., 858 ; Ladislaus III. of Poland, 1333 ; Thomas Lord Seymour, of Sudley, beheaded, 1549 ; William Paulet, first Marquis of Winchester, 1572, *Basing ;* Sir Hugh Myddleton, engineer (*New River*), 1636 ; Sir John Denham, poet, 1668 ; John, Earl of Bute, (prime minister, 1762-3,) *South Audley-street, London,* 1792 ; Benjamin West, painter, P.R.A., 1820 ; John VI., King of Portugal, 1826.

GOOD BISHOP DUPPA.

As you ascend Richmond Hill, by the roadside, near the Terrace, you see an old pile of red brick which testifies the benevolence of a good Bishop, who lived in troublous times, but ended his days in peace, one of his latest works being the erection and endowment of the above edifice. The following inscription is on a stone tablet, over the outer entrance :—' *Votiva Tabula,* I will pay my vows which I made to God in my trouble.' It was founded by Dr Brian Duppa, towards the close of his life. He had been chaplain to Charles I., and tutor to his children, the Prince of Wales and Duke of York. After the decapitation of his royal master, he retired to Richmond, where he led a solitary life until the Restoration ; soon after which he was made Bishop of Winchester, and Lord-almoner. He died at Richmond, in 1662 ; having been visited, when on his death-bed, by Charles II., a few hours only before he expired. In the previous year the good bishop had founded the above almshouse, endowing it for ten poor women, unmarried, and of the age of fifty years and upwards ; for whose support he settled the rentals of certain properties in the county. The almswomen are elected by the minister and vestry of Richmond ; and are each allowed £1 monthly, and a further £1 at Midsummer and Christmas ; together with a gown of substantial cloth, called *Bishop's blue,* every other year. They have each, also, a Christmas dinner of a barn-door fowl and a pound of bacon, secured to them by the lease of a farm at Shepperton.

REVERSES OF THE PAULETS.

The first Marquis of Winchester was one of those members of the peerage who stand out as prominent persons in the national history, giving direction to public affairs, exercising vast influence, acquiring great accumulations of honours and wealth, and leaving families to dwindle behind them in splendid insignificance. Born about 1475, the son of a small Somersetshire gentleman, William Paulet or Powlett (for the name is spelt both ways) devoted himself to court life, and in time prospered so well that he became successively Comptroller and Treasurer of the Household to King Henry VIII. Under the boy king who succeeded, he rose to be Lord Treasurer, the highest office in the state, being then over seventy years of age. Under the same reign he was ennobled, and finally made Marquis of Winchester. It has never been said that he possessed masterly abilities; he is only presented to us as a man of great policy and sagacity. When the death of the young king raised a dynastic difficulty, old Powlett saw that the popular sentiment would not ratify the pretensions of Lady Jane Grey, and, throwing himself into the opposite scale, he was the chief instrument in preserving the crown for Mary. Through that bloody reign, he continued to be Lord Treasurer. When Elizabeth and Protestantism succeeded, he still contrived to keep his place. In fact, this astute old man maintained uninterrupted prosperity down to his death in 1571-2, when he was ninety-seven, enormously wealthy, and had upwards of a hundred descendants. It might well excite surprise that a statesman should have kept high place from Edward's reign, *through Mary's*, into Elizabeth's; and the question was one day put to him, how it was that he did so. He answered that 'he was born of the willow, not of the oak.' He seems to have been remarkable for pithy sayings. One is recorded—'That there was always the best justice when the court was absent from London.'

The old Marquis amused himself in his latter years by building a superb house at Basing, in Hants; it is said to have been more like a palace than a nobleman's mansion. But we hear no more of the cautious wisdom which founded the greatness of the family. We hear of the third marquis writing poetry and giving away large estates among four illegitimate sons; of the fourth impoverishing himself by a magnificent entertainment to Queen Elizabeth; and of the fifth taking the losing side in the Civil War. After all, the conduct of this last lord was not the least creditable part of the family history. On the breaking out of that great national strife, Lord Winchester fortified Basing House for the king, enclosing about fourteen acres within the exterior ramparts. A large garrison, well provisioned, enabled him not merely to defy a powerful besieging force, but to make upon it many deadly sallies. He wrote on every window of the house the words, *Aimez loyauté*, which have since continued to be the motto of the family crest. He swore to maintain his position so long as a single stone of his mansion remained. It was not till after a siege of two years (October 1645), that the investing army succeeded in their object. The house, in which the captors found valuables amounting to £300,000, was burnt to the ground. The Marquis survived to 1674, and his loyal faith and courage were acknowledged in an epitaph by Dryden.

A curious particular in the subsequent history of the family is the marriage, by its representative Charles Duke of Bolton, of Lavinia Fenton, the actress, remarkable for having first performed *Polly Peachum* in the Beggar's Opera. To this subject we shall have occasion to make reference on a future occasion (*see April* 11).

HONEYCOMBS IN TIMBER.

Among the many interesting facts concerning bees which attract the attention not only of naturalists, but of other persons acquainted with country life, is the existence of honeycombs in timber. The little workers select their dwellings in accordance with instincts which are yet but little understood; penetrating through or into solid substances by means apparently very inadequate to the work to be done. M. Réaumur proposed the name of *carpenter-bees* to denote those which work in wood, to distinguish them from the *mason-bees* that work in stone, and the *mining-bees* that work underground. Mr Rennie (*Insect Architecture*) says, 'We have frequently witnessed the operations of these ingenious little workers, who are particularly partial to posts, palings, and the wood-work of houses which has become soft by beginning to decay. Wood actually decayed, or affected by dry rot, they seem to reject as unfit for their purpose; but they make no objections to any hole previously drilled, provided it be not too large.' It is always, so far as is known, a female bee that thus engages in carpentry. Mr Rennie describes one which he saw actually at work. She chiselled a place in a piece of wood, for the nest, with her jaws; she gnawed the wood, little bits at a time, and flew away to deposit each separate fragment at a distance. When the hole was thus made, she set out on repeated journeys to bring pollen and clay; she visited every flower near at hand fitted to yield pollen, and brought home a load of it on her thighs; and alternated these journeys with others which resulted in bringing back little pellets of clay. After several days' labour, she had brought in pollen enough to serve as food for the future generation, and clay enough to close up the door of her dwelling. Several days afterwards, Mr Rennie cut open the wooden post in which these operations had been going on. He found a nest of six cells; the wood formed the lateral walls, but the cells were separated one from another by clay partitions no thicker than cardboard. The wood was worked as smooth as if it had been chiselled by a joiner.

Such instances are of repeated occurrence, more or less varied in detail. Thus, on the 10th of March 1858, some workmen employed by Mr Brumfitt, of Preston, while sawing up a large solid log of baywood, twenty feet long by two feet square, discovered a cavity in it about eight feet long, containing a full-formed honeycomb. Many carpenter-bees dig perpendicular galleries of great depth in upright posts and palings. Réaumur describes a particular kind, called by him the violet carpenter-bee (on account of the beautiful colour of the wings), which usually selects an upright piece of wood, into which she bores obliquely for about an inch, and then, changing the direction, works perpendicularly for twelve or fifteen inches, and half an inch in breadth. She sometimes scoops out three or four such channels in one piece of wood. Each channel is then partitioned into cells about an inch in depth; the partitions being made in a singular way from the sawdust or rather gnawings of the wood. The depositing of the eggs, the storing of them with pollen, and the building up of the partitions, proceed in regular order, thus. The bee first deposits an egg at the bottom of the excavation; then covers it with a thick layer of paste made of pollen and honey; and then makes over or upon this a wooden cover, by arranging concentric rings of little chips or gnawings, till she has formed a hard flooring about as thick as a crown-piece, exhibiting (from its mode of construction) concentric rings like those of a tree, and cemented by glue of her own making. She deposits an egg on this flooring or partition, then another layer of soft food for another of her children, and then builds another partition—and so on, for a series of perhaps ten or twelve in height. Few things are more wonderful in their way than this; for the little worker has no tools but two sharp teeth to help her; she bores a tunnel ten or twelve times her own length quite smooth at the side; and makes ten or twelve floors to her house by a beautiful kind of joinery. This labour occupies several weeks. The egg first deposited develops into a grub, a pupa, and a perfect bee earlier than the others; and the mother makes a side door out of the bottom cell for the elder children to work their way out when old enough; they can penetrate the partitions between the cells, but not the hard wood of a piece of timber.

THE BROWNIE BEE.

(A Cornish Croon.)

I.

Behold those wingèd images !
   Bound for their evening bowers ;
They are the nation of the bees,
   Born from the breath of flowers !
Strange people they ! A mystic race,
In life and food and dwelling-place !

II.

They first were seen on earth, 'tis said,
   When the rose breathes in spring :
Men thought her blushing bosom shed
   These children of the wing :
But lo ! their hosts went down the wind,
Filled with the thoughts of God's own mind !

III.

They built them houses made with hands,
   And there, alone, they dwell ;
No man to this day understands
   The mystery of their cell :
Your cunning sages cannot see
The deep foundations of the bee !

IV.

Low in the violet's breast of blue
   For treasured food they sink ;
They know the flowers that hold the dew
   For their small race to drink :
They glide—King Solomon might gaze
With wonder on their awful ways !

V.

And once—it is a grandame's tale,
   Yet filled with secret lore—
There dwelt within a woodland vale,
   Fast by old Cornwall's shore,
An ancient woman, worn and bent,
Fallen Nature's mournful monument.

VI.

A home had they—the clustering race,
   Beside her garden-wall ;
All blossoms breathed around the place,
   And sunbeams fain would fall ;
The lily loved that combe the best,
Of all the valleys of the west !

VII.

But so it was that on a day,
   When summer built her bowers,
The waxen wanderers ceased to play
   Around the cottage flowers :
No hum was heard ; no wing would roam ;
They dwelt within their cloistered home !

VIII.

This lasted long—no tongue could tell
   Their pastime or their toil !

What binds the soldier to his cell,
   Who should divide the spoil ?
It lasted long—it fain would last,
Till Autumn rustled on the blast !

IX.

Then sternly went that woman old,
   She sought the chancel floor :
And there, with purpose bad and bold,
   Knelt down amid the poor :
She took, she hid, the blessed bread,
Which is, what Jesu master said !

X.

She bare it to her distant home,
   She laid it by the hive,—
To lure the wanderers forth to roam,
   That so her store might thrive :
'Twas a wild wish, a thought unblest,
Some cruel legend of the west !

XI.

But lo ! at morning-tide, a sign !
   For wondering eyes to trace ;
They found, above that bread, a shrine
   Reared by the harmless race :
They brought their walls from bud and flower,
They built bright roof and beamy tower !

XII.

Was it a dream ? or did they hear
   Float from those golden cells,
A sound, as of some psaltery near,
   Or soft and silvery bells ?
A low, sweet psalm, that grieved within,
In mournful memory of the sin !

XIII.

Was it a dream ? 'tis sweet no less,
   Set not the vision free ;—
Long let the lingering legend bless,
   The nation of the bee !
So shall they bear upon their wings,
A parable of sacred things !

XIV.

So shall they teach, when men blaspheme,
   Or sacrament or shrine,
That humbler things may fondly dream
   Of mysteries divine :
And holier hearts than his may beat,
Beneath the bold blasphemer's feet !

                  R. S. H.

Open air Preaching is sometimes heard from a great distance. It must of course depend much on the character of the speaker's voice, but also to a considerable extent on conditions of the surface and on the hygrometric state of the atmosphere. Mrs Oliphant, in her Life of the Rev. Edward Irving, states that he had been on some occasions clearly heard at the distance of half a mile. It has been alleged, however, that Black John Russell of Kilmarnock, celebrated by Burns in no gracious terms, was heard, though not perhaps intelligibly, at the distance of a full mile. It would appear that even this is not the utmost stretch of the phenomenon. A correspondent of *Jameson's Journal*, in 1828, states that, being at the west end of Dumferline, he overheard part of a sermon then delivering at a tent at Cairneyhill by Dr Black : he did not miss a word, 'though the distance must be something about two miles :' the preacher has, perhaps, seldom been surpassed for distinct speaking and a clear voice : 'and the wind, which was steady and moderate, came in the direction of the sound.'

MARCH 11.

St Constantine, of Scotland, martyr, 6th century. St Sophronius, Patriarch of Jerusalem, 639. St Ængus, the Culdee, bishop in Ireland, 824. St Eulogius, of Cordova, 859.

Born.—Torquato Tasso, Italian poet, 1544, *Sorrento ;* John Peter Niceron, French biographer, 1685, *Paris ;* William Huskisson, statesman, 1770, *Birch Moreton Court, Worcestershire.*

Died.—John Toland, miscellaneous writer, 1722, *Putney ;* Hannah Cowley, dramatic writer, 1809, *Tiverton.*

THE WITCHES OF BELVOIR.

On the 11th of March 1618-19, two women named Margaret and Philippa Flower, were burnt at Lincoln for the alleged crime of witchcraft. With their mother, Joan Flower, they had been confidential servants of the Earl and Countess of Rutland, at Belvoir Castle. Dissatisfaction with their employers seems to have gradually seduced these three women into the practice of hidden arts in order to obtain revenge. According to their own confession, they had entered into communion with familiar spirits, by which they were assisted in their wicked designs. Joan Flower, the mother, had hers in the bodily form of a cat, which she called *Rutterkin.* They used to get the hair of a member of the family and burn it; they would steal one of his gloves and plunge it in boiling water, or rub it on the back of Rutterkin, in order to effect bodily harm to its owner. They would also use frightful imprecations of wrath and malice towards the objects of their hatred. In these ways they were believed to have accomplished the death of Lord

Ross, the Earl of Rutland's son, besides inflicting frightful sicknesses upon other members of the family.

It was long before the earl and countess, who were an amiable couple, suspected any harm in these servants, although we are told that for some years there was a manifest change in the countenance of the mother, a diabolic expression being assumed. At length, at Christmas, 1618, the noble pair became convinced that they were the victims of a hellish plot, and the three women were apprehended, taken to Lincoln jail, and examined. The mother loudly protested innocence, and, calling for bread and butter, wished it might choke her if she were guilty of the offences laid to her charge. Immediately, taking a piece into her mouth, she fell down dead, probably, as we may allowably conjecture, overpowered by consciousness of the contrariety between these protestations and the guilty design which she had entertained in her mind.

Margaret Flower, on being examined, acknowledged that she had stolen the glove of the young heir of the family, and given it to her mother, who stroked Rutterkin with it, dipped it in hot water, and pricked it; whereupon Lord Ross fell ill and suffered extremely. In order to prevent Lord and Lady Rutland from having any more children, they had taken some feathers from their bed, and a pair of gloves, which they boiled in water, mingled with a little blood. In all these particulars, Philippa corroborated her sister. Both women admitted that they had familiar spirits, which came and sucked them at various parts of their bodies; and they also described visions of devils in various forms which they had had from time to time.

Associated with the Flowers in their horrible

THE THREE WITCHES OF BELVOIR.

practices were three other women, of the like grade in life,—Anne Baker, of Bottesford; Joan Willimot, of Goodby; and Ellen Greene, of Stathorne, all in the county of Leicester, whose confessions were to much the same purpose. Each had her own familiar spirits to assist in working out her malignant designs against her neighbours. That of Joan Willimot was called *Pretty*. It had been blown into her mouth by her master, William Berry, in the form of a fairy, and immediately after came forth again and stood on the floor in the shape of a woman, to whom she forthwith promised that her soul should be enlisted in the infernal service. On one occasion, at Joan Flower's house, she saw two spirits, one like an owl, the other like a rat, one of which sucked her under the ear. This woman, however, protested that, for her part, she only employed her spirit in inquiring after the health of persons whom she had undertaken to cure.

Greene confessed to having had a meeting with Willimot in the woods, when the latter called two spirits into their company, one like a kitten, the other like a mole, which, on her being left alone, mounted on her shoulders and sucked her under the ears. She had then sent them to bewitch a man and woman who had reviled her, and who, accordingly, died within a fortnight. Anne Baker seems to have been more of a visionary than any of the rest. She once saw a hand, and heard a voice from the air; she had been visited with a flash of fire; all of them ordinary occurrences in the annals of hallucination. She also had a spirit, but, as she alleged, a beneficent one, in the form of a white dog. From the frontispiece of a contemporary pamphlet giving an account of this group of witches, we transfer a homely picture of Baker, Willimot, and Greene, attended each by her familiar spirit. The entire publication is reprinted in Nichols's *Leicestershire*.

The examinations of these wretched women were taken by magistrates of rank and credit, and when the judges came to Lincoln the two surviving Flowers were duly tried, and on their own confessions condemned to death by the Chief Justice of the Common Pleas, Sir Henry Hobbert.

THE FIRST DAILY PAPER.

The British journal entitled to this description was *The Daily Courant*, commenced on the 11th of March 1702, by 'E. Mallet, against the Ditch at Fleet Bridge,' a site, we presume, very near that of the present *Times'* office. It was a single page of two columns, and professed solely to give foreign news, the editor or publisher further assuring his readers that he would not take upon himself to give any comments of his own, 'supposing other people to have sense enough to make reflections for themselves.' The *Daily Courant* very soon passed into the hands of Samuel Buckley, 'at the sign of the Dolphin in Little Britain,'—a publisher of some literary attainments, who afterwards became the printer of the *Spectator*, and pursued on the whole a useful and respectable career. As a curious

trait of the practices of the government of George I., we have Buckley entered in a list of persons laid before a Secretary of State (1724), as ' Buckley, Amen-corner, the worthy printer of the *Gazette*—well-affected;' *i.e.* well-affected to the Hanover succession, a point of immense consequence at that epoch.

The *Daily Courant* was in 1735 absorbed in the *Daily Gazetteer.* *

THE LUDDITES.

' Who makes the quartern-loaf and Luddites rise?'
JAMES SMITH.

March 11th, 1811, is a black-letter day in the annals of Nottinghamshire. It witnessed the commencement of a series of riots which, extending over a period of five years, have, perhaps, no parallel in the history of a civilized country for the skill and secrecy with which they were managed, and the amount of wanton mischief they inflicted. The hosiery trade, which employed a large part of the population, had been for some time previously in a very depressed state. This naturally brought with it a reduction in the price of labour. During the month of February 1811, numerous bands of distressed frameworkknitters were employed to sweep the streets for a paltry sum, to keep the men employed, and to prevent mischief. But by the 11th of March their patience was exhausted; and flocking to the market-place from town and country, they resolved to take vengeance on those employers who had reduced their wages. The timely appearance of the military prevented any violence in the town, but at night no fewer than sixtythree frames were broken at Arnold, a village four miles north of Nottingham. During the succeeding three weeks 200 other stocking frames were smashed by midnight bands of distressed and deluded workmen, who were so bound together by illegal oaths, and so completely disguised, that very few of them could be brought to justice. These depredators assumed the name of *Luddites;* said to have been derived from a youth named *Ludlam*, who, when his father, a framework-knitter in Leicestershire, ordered him to 'square his needles,' took his hammer and beat them into a heap. Their plan of operation was to assemble in parties of from six to sixty, as circumstances required, under a leader styled *General* or *Ned Ludd*, all disguised, and armed, some with swords, pistols, or firelocks, others with hammers and axes. They then proceeded to the scene of destruction. Those with swords and firearms were placed as a guard outside, while the others broke into the house and demolished the frames, after which they reassembled at a short distance. The leader then called over his men, who answered not to names, but to certain numbers; if all were there, and their work for the night finished, a pistol was fired, and they then departed to their homes, removing the black handkerchiefs which had covered their faces. In consequence of the continuance of these daring outrages, a large military force was brought into the neighbourhood, and two of the London police magistrates, with several other officers, came down

* Andrews's *History of British Journalism*. 2 vols. 1859.

to Nottingham, to assist the civil power in attempting to discover the ringleaders; a *secret committee* was also formed, and supplied with a large sum of money for the purpose of obtaining private information; but in spite of this vigilance, and in contempt of a Royal Proclamation, the offenders continued their devastations with redoubled violence, as the following instances will shew. On Sunday night, November 10th, a party of Luddites proceeded to the village of Bulwell, to destroy the frames of Mr Hollingworth, who, in anticipation of their visit, had procured the assistance of three or four friends, who with fire-arms resolved to protect the property. Many shots were fired, and one of the assailants, John Westley, of Arnold, was mortally wounded, which so enraged the mob that they soon forced an entrance: the little garrison fled, and the rioters not only destroyed the frames, but every article of furniture in the house. On the succeeding day they seized and broke a waggon-load of frames near Arnold; and on the Wednesday following proceeded to Sutton-in-Ashfield, where they destroyed thirty-seven frames; after which they were dispersed by the military, who took a number of prisoners, four of whom were fully committed for trial. During the following week only one frame was destroyed, but several *stacks were burned*, most probably, as was supposed, by the Luddites, in revenge against the owners, who, as members of the yeoman cavalry, were active in suppressing the riots. On Sunday night, the 24th of November, thirty-four frames were demolished at Basford, and eleven more the following day. On December the 6th, the magistrates published an edict, which ordered all persons in the disturbed districts to remain in their houses after ten o'clock at night, and all public-houses to be closed at the same hour. Notwithstanding this proclamation, and a great civil and military force, thirty-six frames were broken in the villages around Nottingham within the six following days. A Royal Proclamation was then issued, offering £50 reward for the apprehension of any of the offenders; but this only excited the men to further deeds of daring. They now began to plunder the farmhouses both of money and provisions, declaring that they 'would not starve whilst there was plenty in the land.' In the month of January 1812, the frame-breaking continued with unabated violence. On the 30th of this month, in the three parishes of Nottingham, no fewer than 4,348 families, numbering 15,350 individuals, or nearly half the population, were relieved out of the poor rates. A large subscription was now raised to offer more liberal rewards against the perpetrators of these daring outrages; and at the March assize seven of them were sentenced to transportation. In this month, also, an Act of Parliament was passed, making it *death to break a stocking or a lace frame*. In April, a Mr Trentham, a considerable manufacturer, was shot by two ruffians while standing at his own door. Happily the wound did not prove mortal; but the offenders were never brought to justice, though a reward of £600 was offered for their apprehension. This evil and destructive spirit continued to manifest itself from time to time till

October 1816, when it finally ceased. Upwards of a thousand stocking frames and a number of lace machines were destroyed by it in the county of Nottingham alone, and at times it spread into the neighbouring counties of Leicester, Derby, and York, and even as far as Lancaster. Its votaries discovered at last that they were injuring themselves as much or more than their employers, as the mischief they perpetrated had to be made good out of the county rate.

BITING THE THUMB.

In *Romeo and Juliet* the servants of Capulet and Montague commence a quarrel by one biting his thumb, apparently as an insult to the others. And the commentators, considering the act of biting the thumb as an insulting gesture, quote the following passage from Decker's *Dead Term* in support of that opinion:—'What swearing is there' (says Decker, describing the groups that daily frequented the walks of St Paul's Church), 'what shouldering, what jostling, what jeering, what biting of thumbs to beget quarrels!' Sir Walter Scott, referring to this subject in a note to the *Lay of the Last Minstrel*, says:—'To bite the thumb or the glove seems not to have been considered, upon the Border, as a gesture of contempt, though so used by Shakspeare, but as a pledge of mortal revenge. It is yet remembered that a young gentleman of Teviotdale, on the morning after a hard drinking bout, observed that he had bitten his glove. He instantly demanded of his companions with whom he had quarrelled? and learning that he had had words with one of the party, insisted on instant satisfaction, asserting that, though he remembered nothing of the dispute, yet he never would have bitten his glove without he had received some unpardonable insult. He fell in the duel, which was fought near Selkirk in 1721 [1707].'

It is very probable that the commentators are mistaken, and the act of biting the thumb was not so much a gesture of insulting contempt as a threat—a solemn promise that, at a time and place more convenient, the sword should act as the arbitrator of the quarrel; and, consequently, a direct challenge, which, by the code of honour of the period, the other party was bound to accept. The whole history of a quarrel seems to be detailed in the graphic quotation from Decker. We almost see the ruffling swashbucklers strutting up and down St Paul's-walk, full of braggadocio, and 'new-turned oaths.' At first they shoulder, as if by accident; at the next turn they jostle; fiery expostulation is answered by jeering, and then, but not till then, the thumb is bitten, expressive of dire revenge at a convenient opportunity, for fight they dare not within the precincts of the cathedral church. A curious illustration of this subject will be found in the following extract from evidence given at a court-martial held on a sergeant of Sir James Montgomery's regiment, in 1642. It may be necessary to state that, though the regiment was nominally raised in Ireland, all the officers and men were Scotch by birth, or the immediate descendants of Scottish settlers in Ulster. Sergeant Kyle was accused of killing Lieutenant

Baird, and one of the witnesses deposed as follows :—

The witness and James McCullogh going to drink together a little after nightfall on the twenty-second of February, the said lieutenant and sergeant ran into the room where they were drinking, and the sergeant being first there, offered the chair he sat on to the lieutenant, but the lieutenant refused it, and sat upon the end of a chest. Afterwards, the lieutenant and sergeant fell a-jeering one another, upon which the sergeant told the lieutenant that if he would try him, he would find him a man, if he had aught to say to him. Also, Sergeant Kyle threw down his glove, saying there is my glove, lieutenant, unto which the lieutenant said nothing. Afterwards, many ill words were (exchanged) between them, and the lieutenant threatening him (the said sergeant), the sergeant told him that he would defend himself, and take no disgrace at his hands, but that he was not his equal, he being a lieutenant and the said Kyle a sergeant. Afterwards the sergeant threw down his glove a second time, and the lieutenant not having a glove, demanded James McCullogh his glove to throw to the sergeant, who would not give him his glove ; upon that, the lieutenant *held up his thumb licking on it with his tongue, and saying,* 'There is my parole for *it.'* Afterwards, Sergeant Kyle went to the lieutenant's ear, and asked him, 'When ?' The lieutenant answered, 'Presently.' Upon that Sergeant Kyle went out, and the lieutenant followed with his sword drawn under his arm, and being a space distant from the house said, ' Where is the villain now ?' 'Here I am for you,' said Kyle, and so they struck fiercely one at another.

Licking of the thumb—and why not biting ?— is a most ancient form of giving a solemn pledge or promise, and has remained to a late period in Scotland as a legalized form of undertaking, or bargain. Erskine, in his *Institutes*, says it was ' a symbol anciently used in proof that a sale was perfected; which continues to this day in bargains of lesser importance among the lower ranks of the people—the parties licking and joining of thumbs; and decrees are yet extant, sustaining sales upon " *summonses of thumblicking*," upon this, " That the parties had licked thumbs at finishing the bargain."'

Proverbs and snatches of Scottish song may be cited as illustrative of this ancient custom ; and in the parts of Ulster where the inhabitants are of Scottish descent, it is still a common saying, when two persons have a community of opinion on any subject, 'We may lick thooms upo' that.'

Jamieson, in his *Scottish Dictionary*, remarks

—'This custom, though now apparently credulous and childish, bears indubitable **marks of**

THE INTERIOR OF OLD ST PAUL'S.

great antiquity. Tacitus, in his *Annals*, states that it existed among the Iberians; and Ihre alludes to it as a custom among the Goths. I am well assured by a gentleman, who has long resided in India, that the Moors, when concluding a bargain, do it, in the very same manner as the vulgar in Scotland, by licking their thumbs.'

According to Ducange, in the mediæval period the thumb pressed on the wax was recognised as a seal to the most important documents, and secretaries detected in forging or falsifying documents were condemned to have their thumbs cut off. The same author gives an account of a northern princess who had entered a convent and became a nun. Subsequently, circumstances occurred which rendered it an important point of high policy that she should be married, and a dispensation was obtained from Rome, abrogating her conventual vow, for that purpose. The lady, however, obstinately refused to leave her convent, and marry the husband which state policy had provided for her, so arrangements were made for marrying her by force. But the nun, placing her right thumb on the blade of a sword, swore that she would never marry, and as an oath of this solemn character could not be broken, she was allowed to remain in her convent. Hence it appears that a vow made with the thumb on a sword blade was considered more binding than that on taking the veil; and that, though the Pope could grant a dispensation for the latter, he could not or would not give one for the former.

Something of the same kind prevailed among the Romans; and the Latin word *polliceri*—to promise, to engage—has by many been considered to be derived from *pollex—pollicis*, the thumb.

THE BUTCHERS' SERENADE.

Hogarth, in his delineation of the Marriage of the Industrious Apprentice to his master's daughter, takes occasion to introduce a set of butchers coming forward with marrowbones and cleavers, and roughly pushing aside those who doubtless considered themselves as the legitimate musicians. We are thus favoured with a memorial of what might be called one of the old institutions of the London vulgar—one just about to expire, and which has, in reality, become obsolete in the greater part of the metropolis. The custom in question was one essentially connected with marriage. The performers were the butchers' men,—'the bonny boys that wear the sleeves of blue.' A set of these lads, having duly accomplished themselves for the purpose, made a point of attending in front of a house containing a marriage party, with their cleavers, and each provided with a marrowbone, wherewith to perform a sort of rude serenade, of course with the expectation of a fee in requital of their music. Sometimes, the group would consist of four, the cleaver of each ground to the production of a certain note; but a full band—one entitled to the highest grade of reward—would be not less than eight, producing a complete octave; and, where there was a fair skill, this series of notes would have all the fine effect of a peal of bells. When this serenade happened in the evening, the men would be dressed neatly in clean blue aprons, each with a portentous wedding favour of white paper in his breast or hat. It was wonderful with what quickness and certainty, under the

THE BUTCHERS' SERENADE.

enticing presentiment of beer, the serenaders got wind of a coming marriage, and with what tenacity of purpose they would go on with their performance until the expected crown or half-crown was forthcoming. The men of Clare Market were reputed to be the best performers, and their *guerdon* was always on the highest scale accordingly. A merry rough affair it was; troublesome somewhat to the police, and not always relished by the party for whose honour it was designed; and sometimes, when a musical band came upon the ground at the same time, or a set of boys would please to interfere with pebbles rattling in tin canisters, thus throwing a sort of burlesque on the performance, a few blows would be interchanged. Yet the Marrowbone-and-Cleaver epithalamium seldom failed to diffuse a good humour throughout the neighbourhood; and one cannot but regret that it is rapidly passing among the things that were.

MARCH 12.

St Maximilian of Numidia, martyr, **296**. St Paul of Cornwall, bishop of Leon, about **573**. St Gregory the Great, Pope, **604**.

ST GREGORY THE GREAT.

There have been Popes of every shade of human character. Gregory the Great is one distinguished by modesty, disinterestedness, and sincere religious zeal, tempered by a toleration which could only spring from pure benevolence. The son of a Roman senator, with high mental gifts, and all the accomplishments of his age, he was drawn forward into prominent positions, but always against his will. He would have fain continued to be an obscure monk or a missionary, but his qualities were such that at length even the popedom was thrust upon him (on the death of Pelagius II. in 590). On this occasion he wrote to the sister of the Emperor, 'Appearing to be outwardly exalted, I am really fallen. My endeavours were to banish corporeal objects from my mind, that I might spiritually behold heavenly joys. . . . . I am come into the depths of the sea, and the tempest hath drowned me.'

The writings of Pope Gregory, which fill four folio volumes, are said to be very admirable. The English King Alfred showed his appreciation of one treatise by translating it. In exercising the functions of his high station, Gregory exhibited great mildness and forbearance. He eagerly sought to convert the heathen, and to bring heretics back to the faith; but he never would sanction the adoption of any harsh measures for these purposes. One day—before he attained the papal chair—walking through the market in Rome, he was struck by the beauty of a group of young persons exposed to be sold as slaves. In answer to his inquiry of who they were, and whence they came, he was told they were *Angli*, from the heathen island of Britain. 'Verily, *Angeli*,' he said, punning on the name; 'how lamentable that the prince of darkness should be the master of a country containing such a beautiful people! How sad that, with so fair an outside, there should be nothing of God's grace within!' His wish was immediately to set out as a missionary to England, and it was with difficulty he was prevented. The incident, however, led to a mission being ere long sent to our then benighted country, which thus owed its first reception of Christian light to Gregory.

Almsgiving, in such Protestant countries as England, is denounced as not so much a lessening of human suffering as a means of engendering and extending pauperism. Gregory had no such fears to stay his bountiful hand. With him to relieve the poor was the first of Christian graces. He devoted a large proportion of his revenue and a vast amount of personal care to this object. He in a manner took the entire charge of the poor upon his own hands. 'He relieved their necessities with so much sweetness and affability, as to spare them the confusion of receiving alms; the old men among them he, out of deference, called his fathers. He often entertained several of them at his own table. He kept by him an exact catalogue of the poor, called by the ancients *matriculæ*; and he liberally provided for the necessities of each. In the beginning of every month he distributed to all the poor corn, wine, pulse, cheese, fish, flesh, and oil; he appointed officers for every street, to send every day necessaries to all the needy sick; before he ate, he always sent off meats from his own table to some poor persons.' There may be some bad moral results from this wholesale system of relief for poverty, but certainly the motives which prompted it must be acknowledged to have been highly amiable.

Gregory was a weakly man, often suffering from bad health, and he did not get beyond the age of sixty-four. We owe to him a phrase which has become a sort of formula for the popes—'Servant of the servants of God.' His name, which is the same as *Vigilantius* or *Watchman*, became, from veneration for him, a favourite one; we find it borne, amongst others, by a Scottish prince of the eighth century, the reputed progenitor of the clan M'Gregor. It is curious to think of this formidable band of Highland outlaws of the seventeenth century as thus connected by a chain of historical circumstances with the gentle and saintly Gregory, who first caused the lamp of Christianity to be planted in England.

Born.—Godfrey Bidloo, anatomist, 1649, *Amsterdam;* John Thomas Desaguliers, philosophical writer, 1683, *Rochelle;* Bishop G. Berkeley, philosopher, 1684, *Kilcrin, Kilkenny;* John Frederick Daniell, chemist and meteorologist, 1790, *Essex-street, Strand.*

Died.—Cæsar Borgia, killed, 1508, *Castle of Viana;* Alexander Piccolomini, Italian miscellaneous writer, 1578, *Siena;* Ludovick Muggleton, sectarian (Muggletonians), 1697; the Rev. Dr George Gregory, editor of the *New Annual Register*, 1808, *West Ham;* Rev. R. Polwhele, topographer and poet, 1838.

BISHOP BERKELEY.

Dr George Berkeley, better known as Bishop Berkeley, the mathematician and ideal philosopher, graduated at Trinity College, Dublin, which he entered as a pensioner at the early age of fifteen. Very different opinions prevailed about him at College; those who knew little of him took him for a fool, while those who were most intimate with him considered him a prodigy of learning. His most intimate friends were the best judges in this case, for before he reached his twenty-third year he competed for and obtained a fellowship. Within the next three years he published his *Theory of Vision*, a work of remarkable sagacity, and the first of its kind. Its object may be roughly stated to be an attempt, and a successful one, to trace the boundary line between our ideas of sight and touch. He supposed that if a man born blind could be enabled to see, it would be impossible for him to recognise any object by sight which he had previously known by touch, and that such a person would have no idea of the relative distance of objects. This supposition was confirmed in a very surprising manner in the year 1728, eighteen years after the publication of Mr Berkeley's book, by a young man who was born blind and couched by Mr Cheseldon. He said that all objects seemed to touch his eyes ; he was unable to distinguish the *dog* from the *cat* by sight, and was so sorely puzzled between his newly-acquired sense and that of touch that he asked which was the *lying* sense. In the next year Berkeley published his *Principles of Human Knowledge*, in which he set forth his celebrated system of *immaterialism*, attempting to prove that the common notion of the existence of matter is false, and that such things as bricks and mortar, chairs and tables, are nonentities, except as ideas in the mind. A further defence of this system, in *Three Dialogues between Hylas and Philonous*, established his reputation as a writer, and his company was sought even where his opinions were rejected. Through Dean Swift he was introduced to the celebrated Earl of Peterborough, whom he accompanied to Italy in the capacity of chaplain.

His first piece of preferment was the deanery of Derry. And no sooner was he settled in this than he conceived and carried out to the utmost of his power a project which entitles him to the admiration of posterity. It was nothing less than a scheme for the conversion of the savage Americans to Christianity. He proposed to erect a college in Bermuda as a missionary school, to resign his deanery, worth £1,100 a year, and to go out himself as its first president, on the stipend of £100 a year. His plan was approved by parliament, and he set out, taking with him three other noble and kindred spirits. For seven years Sir R. Walpole delayed him with various excuses, and at last gave him to understand that the promised grant would not be paid till it suited ' public convenience,' thus rendering the whole scheme abortive.

In 1733, he was appointed to the bishopric of Cloyne. The rest of his life was devoted to the earnest discharge of his episcopal duties and the further prosecution of his studies. His custom was to rise between three and four o'clock, summon his family to a music lesson, and spend the rest of the morning in study. In this part of his life, he published *The Analyst*, which was followed by several other works, among which was a letter to the Roman Catholics of his diocese, entitled *A Word to the Wise*, for which in the *Dublin Journal* of November 18, 1749, they returned ' their sincere and hearty thanks to the worthy author, assuring him that they are determined to comply with every particular recommended in his address to the utmost of their power.'

Suffering a good deal from a nervous colic towards the end of his life, and finding relief from tar-water, he wrote a treatise on its virtues, which, with its sequel, *Further Thoughts on Tar-water*, was his last work for the press.* He died at Oxford, suddenly, in the midst of his family, on Sunday evening, January 14, 1753, while listening to a sermon of Dr Sherlock's which Mrs Berkeley was reading to him. He was interred in Christ Church, Oxford.

* For a fuller account of the work on tar-water, see under January 14.

362

LUDOVICK MUGGLETON.

A time of extraordinary religious fervour is sure to produce its monsters, even as the hot mud of the Nile was fabled to do by Lucretius. Several arose amidst the dreadful sectarian contendings of the period of the civil war, and scarcely any more preposterous than Ludovick Muggleton, who is said to have been a working tailor, wholly devoid of education. About 1651, when this man was between forty and fifty years of age, he and a brother in trade, named Reeves, announced themselves as the two last witnesses of God that would ever be appointed on earth ; professed a prophetic gift, and pretended to have been invested with an exclusive power over the gates of heaven and hell. When Reeves died, Muggleton continued to set himself forth in this character, affecting to bless those who respectfully listened to him, and cursing all who scoffed at him, assuming, in short, to have the final destiny of man, woman, and child entirely in his own hand. By ravings in speech and print, he acquired a considerable number of followers, chiefly women, and became at length such a nuisance, that the public authorities resolved, if possible, to put him down. His trial at the Old Bailey, January 17, 1677, ended in his being sentenced to stand in the pillory on three days in three several parts of London, and to pay a fine of £500, or be kept in jail in failure of payment. His books were at the same time ordered to be publicly burnt. All this severity Muggleton outlived twenty years, dying at length at the age of ninety, and leaving a sect behind him, called from him Muggletonians.

It would serve to little good purpose to go farther into the history of this wretched fanatic. One anecdote, however, may be related of him. It happened on a day, when Muggleton was in his cursing mood, that he very energetically devoted to the infernal deities a gentleman who had given him some cause of offence. The gentleman immediately drew his sword, and placing its point at the cursing prophet's breast, demanded that the anathemas just pronounced should be reversed upon pain of instant death. Muggleton, who had no relish for a martyrdom of this kind, assumed his blessing capacity, and gave the fiery gentleman the fullest satisfaction.

There is no mention of Muggletonians in the official report of the census of 1851, though it included about a dozen small sects, under various uncouth denominations. As late as 1846, some of Muggleton's incomprehensible rhapsodies were reprinted and published, it is sincerely to be hoped for the last time.

THE TRAFFIC OF WOMEN'S HAIR.

As a rule, the women of England do not sell their hair. There is, however, in England, a large and regular demand for this article, to make those supposititious adornments which one sees in every hair-dresser's window. It is stated that a hundred thousand pounds' weight of human hair is required to supply the demand of the English market. It is mainly brought from the continent, where women of the humbler rank may be said to cherish their hair with a view to selling it for money. Light hair comes mostly from Belgium and Germany, dark from France and Italy. There is a Dutch company, the agents of which make annual visits to the towns and villages of Germany, buying the tresses of poor women. In France the trade is mostly in the hands of agents, sent out by large firms at Paris. These agents, going chiefly to the Breton villages, take with them a supply of silks, laces, ribbons, haberdashery, and cheap jewellery, which they barter with the peasant women and girls for their tresses. Mr Trollope, while travelling in Brittany, saw much of this singular hair-cropping going on; as the women in that province all wear close-fitting caps, the difference between the cropped and the uncropped was not so perceptible as it otherwise would have been. The general price is said to vary from about one franc to five francs for a head of hair half a pound to a pound in weight; but choice specimens occasionally command more than their weight in silver, owing to the eager competition of buyers to obtain them.

In England, something of this kind is going on in country villages, but not (it is supposed) to any great extent. A feeling of womanly pride rebels against it. Occasionally, however, evidence peeps out to show that poor Englishwomen know that there is a market for such a commodity. One instance of a ludicrous kind occurred at a metropolitan police-court some years ago. On March 12th, 1825, the court was thronged by a number of poor women, who seemed excited and uncomfortable, and who whispered among themselves as to who should be the spokeswoman to tell the tale which all evidently desired should be told. At length one of them, with a manner half ashamed, told the magistrate that one Thomas Rushton, a barber, called at her poor abode one day, and asked politely to look at her hair. Whether she guessed his errand, is not clear; but she took off her cap at his bidding. He professed to be in raptures with the beauty of her hair, and offered her a guinea for it. Being in straitened circumstances she accepted the offer. The rogue at once took out his scissors, and cut off the whole of her hair. 'See, your worship,' said she, 'what he has done.' His worship *did* see, and found that there were only little stumps of hair left like pig's bristles. The fellow put her hair in his hat, put the hat on his head, and ran off without giving her a single coin. All the other women in the court had been defrauded of their tresses in a similar way, and probably all on the same day—for the rogue could not afford to wait until the exploit got wind. The poor women declared that they had been rendered quite miserable when they came to show their husbands their cropped heads—which may well be imagined.

It may be added that, about a hundred years ago, when false hair was perhaps more in use than it is now, a woman residing in a Scotch burgh used to get a guinea from time to time for her tresses, which were of a bright golden hue.

MARCH 13.

St Euphrasia, virgin, 410. St Mochoemoc, abbot in Ireland, 655. St Gerald, bishop in Ireland, 732. St Theophanes, abbot, 818. St Nicephorus, patriarch of Constantinople, 828. St Kennocha, virgin in Scotland, 1007.

Born.—Esther Johnson (Swift's *Stella*), 1681, *Sheen, Surrey;* Dr Joseph Priestley, philosophical writer, 1733, *Field-head;* Joseph II. (of Germany), 1741; Charles, Earl Grey, statesman, 1764, *Howick.*

Died.—Belisarius, general, 565, *Constantinople;* Cardinal d'Ossat, 1604, *Rome;* Bartholo, Legate, burned, 1614; Richard Cowley, actor, 1618, *Shoreditch;* John Gregory, scholar, 1646; Jean de la Fontaine, French poet, 1695; Peter Mignard, French painter, 1695; Nicolas Boileau, French poet, 1711; Archbishop Herring, 1757, *Croydon;* Sophia Lee, novelist, 1824; J. F. Daniell, chemist and meteorologist, 1845; Regina Maria Roche, novelist, (*Children of the Abbey.*) 1845; Sir T. N. Talfourd, dramatist and lawyer, 1854; Richard, Lord Braybrooke, editor of Pepys's *Diary,* 1858.

BELISARIUS.

Belisarius is one of those historical names which, from accidental circumstances, are more impressed on our memories than some of greater importance. As not unfrequently happens, the circumstance which has most enlisted our sympathies with it proves on investigation to be a mere fiction. The picture of the aged hero, deprived of his eyes, and reduced to beggary by the ingratitude of his imperial master, and seeking individual charity in the memorable words, *Date obolum Belisario,* is familiar to every schoolboy as a touching example of the inconstancy of fortune. Yet it is a story inconsistent with the facts of history, invented apparently several centuries after the period at which it was supposed to have occurred, and first mentioned by John Tzetzes, a Greek writer of no authority, who lived in the twelfth century.

The origin of Belisarius is doubtful, but he has been conjectured to have been a Teuton, and to have been at least bred in his youth among the Goths. We find him first serving as a barbarian recruit among the private guards of Justinian, before he ascended the imperial throne, and, after that event, which took place in A.D. 527, he was raised to a military command, and soon displayed qualities as a warrior and a man which give him a rank among the most celebrated names of antiquity. His great services to the Empire commenced with the arduous campaign in 529, in which he protected it against the invasions of the Persians. He returned to Constantinople to save the Emperor from the consequences of a great and dangerous insurrection in the capital. In 533, he received the command of an expedition against the Vandals, who had made themselves masters of Carthage and Africa, and by his marvellous skill and constancy, as well as by his moderation and policy, he restored that province to the Empire. In the command of his army he had to contend with troops who, as well as their officers, were demoralized and turbulent, and in reducing them to discipline and obedience he performed a more difficult task than even that of conquering the enemy. The consequence was that the officers who served under Belisarius indulged their jealousy and personal hostility by writing to Constantinople, disparaging his exploits, and privately accusing him of a design to usurp the kingdom of Africa. Justinian himself was jealous of his benefactor, and indirectly recalled him to the Court, where, however, his presence silenced envy, if it did not overcome it, and he obtained the honours of a triumph, the first which had yet been given in the city of Constantinople. It was adorned by the presence of Gelimer, the captive king of the Vandals of Africa; and immediately afterwards Belisarius was declared consul for the following year.

Belisarius was soon called upon to march at the head of the Roman armies against the Goths of Italy, where new victories and new conquests attended him, and Italy also was restored to the Imperial crown. During this war, Rome was besieged by the Goths, and only saved from them by the conduct of the great imperial commander. The glory of Belisarius was now at its height, and, though the praise of the court was faint and hollow, he was beloved by the soldiers, and almost adored by the people, whose prosperity he had secured. After another brief expedition against the Persians, Belisarius fell under the displeasure of the empress, the infamous Theodora, and was disgraced, and even in danger of his life. He only escaped by submission, and again left Constantinople to take the command of an Italian war. The Gothic king Totilas had again invaded that province, and was threatening Rome. Unsupported and unsupplied with troops and the necessaries of war, Belisarius was obliged to remain an idle spectator of the progress of the Goths, until, in A.D. 546, they laid siege to Rome, and proceeded to reduce it by famine. Before any succour could arrive, the imperial city was surrendered to the barbarians, and the king of the Goths became its master. It was, however, preserved from entire destruction by the remonstrances of Belisarius, who recovered possession of it in the following year, and repaired its walls and defences. But treachery at home continued to counteract the efforts of the general in the provinces, and, after struggling gloriously against innumerable and insurmountable difficulties, Belisarius was finally recalled to Constantinople in the year 548. After his departure, the Goths again became victorious, and the following year Rome was again taken by Totilas.

The last exploit of Belisarius saved Constantinople from the fury of the Bulgarians, who had invaded Macedonia and Thrace, and appeared within sight of the capital. Now an aged veteran, he attacked them with a small number of troops hastily collected, and inflicted on them a signal defeat; but Justinian was guided by treacherous councils, and prevented his general from following up the success. On his return, he was welcomed with acclamations by the inhabitants of Constantinople; but even this appears to have been imputed to him as a crime, and the emperor received him coldly, and treated him with neglect. This, which occurred in 559,

364

was his last victory; two years afterwards, an occasion was taken to accuse Belisarius of complicity in a conspiracy against the life of the emperor. He presented himself before the imperial council with a conscious innocence which could not be gainsayed; but Justinian had prejudged his guilt; his life was spared as a favour, but his wealth was seized, and he was confined a prisoner in his own palace. After he had been thus confined a few months, his entire innocence was acknowledged, and he was restored to his liberty and fortune; but he only survived about eight months, and died on the 13th of March, 565. The emperor immediately confiscated his treasures, restoring only a small portion to his wife Antonina.

JOHN GREGORY.

'This miracle of his age for critical and curious learning,' as Anthony Wood describes him, was born at Amersham, in Buckinghamshire, on the 10th November, 1607, and baptized at the parish church on the 15th of the same month. He was the son of John and Winifred Gregory, who were, says Fuller, 'honest though mean (poor), yet rich enough to derive unto him the hereditary infirmity of the gout.' Having been found a boy of talent, he was probably educated and sent to Oxford at the expense of some member of the Drake family, for in 1624 we find him at Christ Church in the capacity of servitor to Sir William Drake, where 'he and his master,' says Wood, 'were placed under the tuition of the learned Mr George Morley, afterwards Bishop of Winchester.' Young Gregory was an indefatigable student, devoting no less than 'sixteen out of every four-and-twenty hours' to the pursuit of learning. This almost incredible application he continued for years; and when, in 1631, he took the degree of Master of Arts, he astonished his examiners with the amount of his learning. Dr Duppa, the Dean of Christ's Church, struck with Gregory's erudition, took him under his especial patronage, and gave him a minor canonry in his cathedral; subsequently, on becoming Bishop of Chichester, he appointed Gregory his domestic chaplain, and conferred on him a prebend in his cathedral; and, on being translated to the see of Salisbury, he also gave him a stall in that cathedral. Wood's account of Gregory's acquirements is too curious to be given in any but his own words. 'He attained,' says this biographer, 'to a learned elegance in English, Latin, and Greek, and to an exact skill in Hebrew, Syriac, Chaldee, Arabic, Ethiopic, &c. He was also well versed in philosophy, had a curious faculty in astronomy, geometry, and arithmetic, and a familiar acquaintance with the Jewish Rabbins, Ancient Fathers, modern critics, commentators, and what not.' His works, which are still extant,* though scarce, corroborate

* His works were—1. *Notes on the View of the Civil and Ecclesiastical Law by Sir Thomas Ridley, Knt.*
These notes, which evinced great learning, indefatigable investigation, and critical acumen, were published when he was only twenty-six, and passed through several editions.

2. *Notes and Observations on some passages of Scriptures.* This work also passed through several editions.

the above account; yet while he necessarily brings forth his learning in discussing abstruse questions, he makes no display of it, and Fuller, after stating that he was 'an exquisite linguist and general scholar,' adds, 'his modesty setting the greater lustre on his learning.' Nor does he appear to have taken any active part in the contentions of his day. His works are confined to learned and scientific subjects, and scarcely manifest a bias to any party. Yet neither his modesty, nor humble birth, nor his profound learning, nor his quiet inoffensive habits could save him from the animosity that was then rampant in the two contending parties. He was deprived of all his preferments, and reduced to destitution—without a home, and without the means of procuring one. His case was but a common one in those days of national strife and bloodshed.

At length he found a place of refuge—a miserable one it was, at 'an obscure ale-house standing on the green at Kidlington, near Oxford, and kept by a man named Sutton.' Gregory, in the days of his prosperity, had taken Sutton's son into his service ; had treated him with kindness and benevolence ; had improved his education, and endeavoured to advance his condition in life. What became of the boy is not known, but Gregory's kindness to him had reached the father's heart, and now Sutton, with meritorious gratitude, offered Gregory an asylum and a home. Here the learned prebendary lingered out the last years of his life, tormented with gout, and in all his afflictions subject to the noise and discomfort of a village alehouse. He died on the 13th of March, 1646, and his friends, who during his life were either unwilling or

afraid to alleviate his sufferings, contributed towards his funeral expenses, and gave him honourable burial in the choir of Christ Church cathedral. Many and extravagantly eulogistic were the elegies which now appeared in praise of his erudition, his humility, and his piety.

DANIELL AND METEOROLOGY.

Professor Daniell died in a moment, in the Council-room of the Royal Society, immediately after concluding some remarks on a scientific subject, the day after he had completed his fifty-fifth year. He was one of the most accomplished men of science of his day, distinguished as a professor of chemistry, and as a writer of treatises on chemistry and electricity, but is perhaps most notable to us as one of the first in our country to attempt philosophical authorship on meteorological subjects. This science is now cultivated assiduously, under favour of the British Association and the Board of Trade, and has observers contributing to its results in all parts of the world ; but in 1823, when Mr Daniell published his *Meteorological Essays*, it was in a most rudimentary state.

Mr Daniell owned in this volume his obligations to the works of preceding workers—the foundation-stones, as he called them, of the science,—but in an especial manner to Mr (afterwards Dr) Dalton, who had recently explained the constitution of the mixed gases. He had been enabled to arrive at the conclusion that there are, as it were, two distinct atmospheres surrounding the earth— the air, and the suspended vapour — whose relations to heat are different, and whose conditions of equilibrium are incompatible with each other. Owing to the antagonisms of these two fluids, a continual movement is kept up, tending to the most important results. After tracing the phenomena, the philosopher, in a devout strain, which was characteristic of him, proceeded to say : ' In tracing the harmonious results of such discordant operations, it is im-

3. *Eight learned Tracts*, published after his death under the title of *Gregorii Posthuma*, with a short account of the Author's Life set before them, written by his dearest friend John Gurgany (Son of Hugh Gurgany, Priest), sometimes a Servitor of Christ Church, afterwards Chaplain of Merton College ; dedicated to Edward Bysshe, Clar. King of Arms, a Patron not only to the Author, but to Gurgany in the time of their afflictions.

possible not to pause to offer up a humble tribute of admiration of the designs of a beneficent Providence, thus imperfectly developed in a department of creation where they have been supposed to be most obscure. By an invisible, but ever-active agency, the waters of the deep are raised into the air, whence their distribution follows, as it were, by measure and weight, in proportion to the beneficial effects which they are calculated to produce. By gradual, but almost insensible expansions, the equipoised currents of the atmosphere are disturbed, the stormy winds arise, and the waves of the sea are lifted up; and that stagnation of air and water is prevented which would be fatal to animal existence. But the force which operates is calculated and proportioned; the very agent which causes the disturbance bears with it its own check; and the storm, as it vents its force, is itself setting the bounds of its own fury.'

When we consider the activity now shown in the prosecution of meteorology, it will appear scarcely credible that, so lately as the date of Mr Daniell's book, there were no authorized instruments for observation in this department but those at the Royal Society's apartments in London, which had long been in such a state that no dependence whatever could be placed upon them. The barometer had been filled without any care to remove the moisture from the glass, and in taking the observations no correction was ever applied for the alteration of level in the mercury of the cistern, or for the change of density in the metal from variations of temperature. With respect to the thermometers, no care had been taken to secure correct graduation. The Society had never possessed a vane; it learned the course of the winds from a neighbouring weathercock. The rain-gauge, the elevation of which was stated with ostentatious precision, was placed immediately below a chimney, in the centre of one of the smokiest parts of London, and it was part of the duty of the Society's clerk ever and anon to pass a wire up the funnel to clear it of soot. To complain, after this, that the water was left to collect for weeks and months before it was measured, ' would,' says Mr Daniell, be comparatively insignificant criticism.'

DISCOVERY OF THE PLANET URANUS.

The astronomical labours of the self-taught genius William Herschel at Slough, under shadow of the patronage of George III., and his addition of a first-class planet to the short list which had remained unextended from the earliest ages, were amongst the matters of familiar interest which formed conversation in the days of our fathers.

It was on the evening of the 13th of March, 1781, that the patient German, while examining some small stars in the constellation Gemini, marked one that was new to him; he applied different telescopes to it in turn, and found the results different from those observable with fixed stars. Was it a comet? He watched it night after night, with a view of solving this question; and he soon found that the body was moving among the stars. He continued his observations

till the 19th of April, when he communicated to the Royal Society an account of all he had yet ascertained concerning the strange visitor. The attention of astronomers both at home and abroad was excited; and calculations were made to determine the orbit of the supposed comet. None of these calculations, however, accorded with the observed motion; and there arose a further question, ' Is it a planet?' This question set the computers again at work; and they soon agreed that a new planet really had been discovered in the heavens. It was at first supposed that the orbit was circular; but Laplace, in 1783, demonstrated that, as in the case of all the other planets, it is elliptical. It then became duly recognised as the outermost of the members of the solar system, and so remained until the recent days when the planet Neptune was discovered. The discoverer, wishing to pay a compliment to the monarch who so liberally supported him, gave the name of the *Georgium Sidus*, or Georgian Star, to the new planet; other English astronomers, wishing to compliment the discoverer himself, suggested the name of *Herschel;* but Continental astronomers proposed that the old mythological system should be followed; and this plan was adopted, the name *Uranus*, suggested by Bode, being now accepted by all the scientific world as a designation for the seventh planet.

WEATHER NOTIONS.

Amongst weather notions one of the most prevalent is that which represents the moon as exercising a great influence. It is supposed that upon the time of day at which the moon changes depends the character of the weather during the whole of the ensuing month; and we usually hear the venerable name of Sir William Herschel adduced as authorising this notion. Foster, in his *Perennial Calendar*, transfers from the *European Magazine* what he calls an excellent table of the prospective weather, founded on ' a philosophical consideration of the attraction of the sun and moon in their several positions respecting the earth.' Modern science in reality rejects all these ideas as vain delusions; witness the following letter written by the late ingenious professor of astronomy in the university of Glasgow, in answer to a gentleman who wrote to him, making inquiries upon this subject.

' Observatory, July 5, 1856.—Dear Sir, I am in receipt of your letter regarding the supposed influence of the moon on the weather. You are altogether correct. *No relation exists between these classes of phenomena.* The question has been tested and decided over and over again by the discussion of long and reliable meteorological tables; nor do I know any other positive way of testing any such point. I confess I cannot account for the origin of the prevalent belief. J. P. NICHOL.'

Admiral Fitzroy, through the publications authorized by the Board of Trade, has stated such of the observations of common weather wisdom as may be depended upon.

The old remark about a ruddy evening and a grey morning (alluded to in the gospel of Matthew) as indicating good weather, meets full approval; as also that a red sky in the morning foretells bad weather, or much rain, if not wind. The Admiral adds, that a high dawn denotes wind, and a low dawn fair weather. When clouds have a soft and delicate appearance, fair weather may be looked for; when they are hard and ragged, wind is to be expected.

'Misty clouds forming or hanging on heights show wind and rain coming, if they remain or descend. If they rise or disperse, the weather will improve, or become fine.

'When sea-birds fly out early and far to seaward, moderate wind and fair weather may be expected. When they hang about the land or over it, sometimes flying inland, expect a strong wind, with stormy weather. When birds of long flight, such as swallows, hang about home, and fly low, rain or wind may be expected; also when pigs carry straw to their sties, and when smoke from chimneys does not ascend readily.

'Dew is an indication of fine weather; so is fog. Remarkable clearness of atmosphere near the horizon, distant objects, such as hills unusually visible or raised by refraction; what is called a *good hearing day;* may be mentioned among signs of wet, if not wind, to be expected.'

SIGNS OF FOUL WEATHER.
By Dr Jenner.

The *hollow winds* begin to blow;
The *clouds look black*, the *glass is low;*
The *soot falls down*, the *spaniels sleep;*
And *spiders* from their *cobwebs peep.*
Last night the *sun* went *pale to bed;*
The *moon* in *halos* hid her head.
The boding shepherd heaves a sigh,
For, see, a *rainbow* spans the sky.
The *walls are damp*, the *ditches smell*,
Clos'd is the pink-ey'd *pimpernel.*
Hark! how the *chairs* and *tables crack*,
Old Betty's joints are on the rack:
Her *corns* with *shooting pains* torment her,
And to her bed untimely sent her.
Loud *quack the ducks*, the *sea fowl cry*,
The *distant hills* are *looking nigh.*
How restless are the *snorting swine!*
The *busy flies* disturb the *kine.*
Low o'er the *grass* the *swallow wings*,
The *cricket*, too, how *sharp he sings!*
Puss on the hearth, with *velvet paws*,
Sits *wiping* o'er her *whisker'd jaws.*
The *smoke* from *chimneys right ascends*,
Then spreading, *back to earth it bends.*
The *wind* unsteady *veers around*,
Or settling in the *South is found.*
Through the clear stream the *fishes rise*,
And *nimbly catch* the incautious *flies.*
The *glow-worms* num'rous, clear and bright,
Illum'd the *dewy hill* last night.
At dusk the squalid *toad* was seen,
Like *quadruped*, stalk o'er the green.
The *whirling wind* the dust obeys,
And in the *rapid eddy* plays.
The *frog* has chang'd his *yellow vest*,
And in a *russet coat* is drest.
The *sky is green*, the air is still,
The *mellow* blackbird's voice is shrill.
The *dog*, so alter'd in his taste,
Quits mutton-bones, on *grass* to feast.
Behold the *rooks*, how odd their flight,
They imitate the *gliding kite*,
And seem *precipitate to fall*,
As if they felt the piercing ball.
The *tender colts on back do lie*,
Nor heed the traveller passing by.
In *fiery red* the *sun* doth *rise*,
Then *wades through clouds* to mount the skies.
'Twill *surely rain*, we see't with sorrow,
No *working in the fields to-morrow.*

MARCH 14.

St Acepsimas, bishop in Assyria, Joseph, and Aithilahas, martyrs, 380. St Boniface, bishop of Ross, in Scotland, 630. St Maud, Queen of Germany, 968.

Died.—John, Earl of Bedford, 1555; Simon Morin, burned, 1663; Marshal-General Wade, 1751; Admiral John Byng, shot at *Portsmouth*, 1757; William Melmoth, accomplished scholar, 1799, *Bath;* Daines Barrington, antiquary, lawyer, and naturalist, 1800, *Temple;* Frederick Theophilus Klopstock, German poet, 1803, *Ottensen;* George Papworth, architect and engineer, 1855.

JOHN RUSSELL, FIRST EARL OF BEDFORD.

The importance of the noble house of Bedford during the last three centuries may be traced to the admirable personal qualities of a mere private gentleman—'a Mr Russell'—in connection with a happy fortuitous occurrence. The gentleman here referred to was the eldest, or only son of James Russell of Berwick, a manor-place in the county of Dorset, about a mile from the seacoast. He was, however, born at Kingston-Russell in the same county, where the elder branch of the family had resided from the time of the Conquest. At an early age he was sent abroad to travel, and to acquire a knowledge of the continental languages. He returned in 1506 an accomplished gentleman, and a good linguist, and took up his residence with his father at Berwick. Shortly after his arrival a violent tempest arose, and on the next morning, 11th January, 1506, three foreign vessels appeared on the Dorset coast making their way for the port of Weymouth. Information being given to the Governor, Sir Thomas Trenchard, he repaired to the coast with a body of men prepared to meet the vessels whether belonging to friends or foes. On reaching the harbour they were found to be part of a convoy under the command of Philip, Archduke of Austria, and only son of Maximilian I., Emperor of Germany.

This young prince had just married Johanna, daughter of Ferdinand and Isabella, King and Queen of Castile and Aragon, and was on his way to Spain when overtaken by the storm which had separated the vessel in which he was sailing and two others from the rest of the convoy, and had forced them to take shelter in Weymouth Harbour.

Sir Thomas Trenchard immediately conducted the Archduke to his own castle, and sent messengers to apprize the King, Henry the Seventh, of his arrival. While waiting for the King's reply, Sir Thomas invited his cousin and neighbour, young Mr Russell of Berwick, to act as interpreter and converse with the Archduke on topics connected with his own country, through which Mr Russell had lately travelled. '"It is an ill wind," says Fuller, referring to this incident, "that blows nobody profit:" so this accident (of the storm) proved the foundation of Mr Russell's preferment.' For the Archduke was so delighted with his varied knowledge and courteous bearing, that, on deciding to proceed at once to Windsor, he requested Mr Russell to accompany him, and when they arrived there, he recommended him so highly to the King's notice, that he granted him an immediate interview. Henry was extremely struck with Mr Russell's conversation and appearance: 'for,' says Lloyd, 'he had a moving beauty that waited on his whole body, a comportment unaffected, and such a comeliness in his mien, as exacted a liking, if not a love, from all that saw him; the whole set off with a person of a middle stature, neither tall to a formidableness, nor short to a contempt, straight and proportioned, vigorous and active, with pure blood and spirits flowing in his youthful veins.' Mr Russell was forthwith appointed a gentleman of the Privy Chamber.

Three years afterwards, Henry VIII. ascended the throne, and was not slow to perceive Mr Russell's great and varied talents. He employed him in important posts of trust and difficulty, and found him an able and faithful diplomatist on every occasion. Consequently he rewarded him with immense grants of lands,—chiefly from the dissolved monasteries,—and loaded him with honours. He was knighted; was installed into the Order of the Garter, and was raised to the peerage as Baron Russell of Chenies. He was made Marshal of Marshalsea; Controller of the King's Household; a Privy Councillor; Lord Warden of the Stannaries in the counties of Devon and Cornwall; President of these counties and of those of Dorset and Somerset; Lord Privy-Seal; Lord Admiral of England and Ireland; and Captain-General of the Vanguard in the Army. Lastly, the King, on his death-bed, appointed Lord Russell, who was then his Lord Privy-Seal, to be one of the counsellors to his son, Prince Edward. On Edward VI. ascending the throne, Lord Russell still retained his position and influence at Court. On the day of the coronation he was Lord High Steward of England for the occasion, and soon afterwards employed by the young Protestant king to promote the objects of the Reformation, which he did so effectually that, as a reward, he was created Earl of Bedford, and endowed with the rich abbey of Woburn, which soon afterwards became, as it still continues to be, the principal seat of the family.

On the accession of the Catholic Mary, though Lord Russell had so zealously promoted the Reformation, and shared so largely in the property of the suppressed monasteries, yet he was almost immediately received into the royal favour, and re-appointed Lord Privy-Seal. Within the same year he was one of the noblemen commissioned to escort Philip from Spain to become the Queen's husband, and to give away her Majesty at the celebration of her marriage. This was his last public act. And it is remarkable that as Philip, the Archduke of Austria, first introduced him to Court, so that Duke's grandson, Philip of Spain, was the cause of his last attendance there. It was more remarkable that he was able to pursue a steady upward course through those great national convulsions which shook alike the altar and the throne; and to give satisfaction to four successive sovereigns, each differing widely from the other in age, in disposition, and in policy. From the wary

368

Henry VII., and his capricious and arbitrary son; from the Protestant Edward and the Romanist Mary, he equally received unmistakeable evidences of favour and approbation. But the most remarkable, and the most gratifying fact of all is, that he appears to have preserved an integrity of character through the whole of his extraordinary and perilous career.

There is nothing in his correspondence, or in any early notice of him that betrays the character of a time-serving courtier. The true cause of his continuing in favour doubtless lay in his natural urbanity, his fidelity, and, perhaps, especially in that skill and experience in diplomacy which made his services so valuable, if not essential, to the reigning sovereign.

He died, 'full of years as of honours,' on the 14th of March, 1555, and was buried at Chenies, in Bucks, the manor of which he had acquired by his marriage. The countess, who survived him only three years, built for his remains a large vault and sepulchral chapel adjoining the parish church; and a magnificent altar tomb, bearing their effigies in life-size, was erected to commemorate them by their eldest son, Francis, second Earl of Bedford. The chapel, which has ever since been the family burial-place, now contains a fine series of monuments, all of a costly description, ranging from the date of the Earl's death to the present century; and the vault below contains between fifty and sixty members of the Russell family or their alliances. The last deposited in it was the eighth Duke of Bedford, who died in May 1872.*

The Earl of Bedford, when simply Sir John Russell, was frequently sent abroad both on friendly and hostile expeditions, and had many narrow escapes of life. On one occasion, after riding by night and day through rough and circuitous roads to avoid detachments of the enemy, he came to a small town, and rested at an obscure inn, where he thought he might with safety refresh himself and his horse. But before he could begin the repast which had been prepared for him, he was informed that a body of the enemy, who were in pursuit of him, were approaching the town. He sprang on his horse, and without tasting food, rode off at full speed, and only just succeeded in leaving the town at one end while his pursuers entered it at the other.

On another occasion the hotel in which he was staying was suddenly surrounded by a body of men who were commissioned to take him alive and send him a captive to France. From this danger he was rescued by Thomas Cromwell, who passed himself off to the authorities as a Neapolitan acquaintance of Russell's, and promised that if they would give him access to him, he would induce him to yield himself up to them without resistance. This adventure was introduced into a tragedy entitled *The Life and Death of Thomas, Lord Cromwell*, which is supposed to have been written by Heywood, in the reign of Elizabeth; and from which the following is a brief extract:

* See Wiffen's *Memoirs of the House of Russell*, vol. i.; Dugdale's *Baronetage*, vol. ii.; Hutchin's *History of Dorset*, vol. ii.; Collins' *Peerage*, vol. i.

'*Bonoma. A Room in an Hotel divided by a curtain. Enter Sir John Russell and the Host.*

Russell. Am I betrayed ? Was Russell born to die
By such base slaves, in such a place as this ?
Have I escaped so many times in France,
So many battles have I overpassed,
And made the French scour when they heard my
    name,
And am I now betrayed unto my death ?
Some of their hearts' blood first shall pay for it.
    Host. They do desire, my lord, to speak with you.
    Russell. The traitors do desire to have my blood ;
But by my birth, my honour, and my name,
By all my hopes, my life shall cost them dear !
Open the door ! I'll venture out upon them ;
And if I must die, then I'll die with honour.
    Host. Alas, my lord, that is a despert course ; —
They have begirt you round about the house :
Their meaning is, to take you prisoner,
And to send your body unto France.
    Russell. First shall the ocean be as dry as sand,
Before alive they send me unto France.
I'll have my body first bored like a sieve,
And die as Hector 'gainst the Myrmidons,
Ere France shall boast Russell's their prisoner !
Perfidious France ! that 'gainst the law of arms
Hast thus betrayed thine enemy to death :
But, be assured, my blood shall be revenged
Upon the best lives that remain in France.'

Cromwell, under the guise of a Neapolitan, enters with his servant, dismisses the Host, reveals himself to Russell as the son of his Farrier at Putney; says he is come to rescue him, and persuades him to exchange garments with his servant. The exchange effected, Russell says :

'How dost thou like us, Cromwell ? Is it well ?
    Cromwell. O excellent ! Hodge, how dost thou feel
        thyself ?
    Hodge. How do I feel myself ? Why, as a nobleman should do. O, how I feel honour come creeping on ! My nobility is wonderful melancholy. Is it not most gentlemanlike to be melancholy ?
    Russell. Ay, Hodge. Now go sit down in my study, and take state upon thee.
    Hodge. I warrant you, my lord ; let me alone to take state upon me.'

Cromwell and Sir John Russell pass through the soldiers unmolested, and reach Mantua in safety, from whence Sir John proceeded to England without further interruption. He recommended Cromwell to Wolsey, and thus was the cause of his subsequent greatness.

MARSHAL WADE.

Field-Marshal George Wade died at the age of eighty, possessed of above £100,000. In the course of a military life of fifty-eight years, his most remarkable, though not his highest service was the command of the forces in Scotland in 1724, and subsequent years, during which he superintended the construction of those roads which led to the gradual civilization of the Highlands.

'Had you seen those roads before they were made,
    You'd have lifted up your hands and blessed General
        Wade,'

sung an Irish ensign in quarters at Fort William, referring in reality to the tracks which had previously existed on the same lines, and

which are roads in all respects but that of being *made*, i. e. regularly constructed ; and, doubtless, it was a work for which the general deserved infinite benedictions. Wade had also much to do in counteracting and doing away with the Jacobite predilections of the Highland clans ; in which kind of business it is admitted that he acted a humane and liberal part. He did not so much force, as reason the people out of their prejudices.

The general commenced his Highland roads in 1726, employing five hundred soldiers in the work, at sixpence a-day of extra pay, and it was well advanced in the three ensuing years. He himself employed, in his surveys, an English coach, which was everywhere, even at Inverness, the first vehicle of the kind ever seen ; and great was the wonder which it excited among the people, who invariably took off their bonnets to the driver, as supposing him the greatest personage connected with it. When the men had any extra hard work, the general slaughtered an ox and gave them a feast, with something liquid wherewith to drink the king's health. On completing the great line by Drumuachter, in September 1729, he held high festival with his *highwaymen*, as he called them, at a spot near Dalnaspidal, opposite the opening of Loch Garry, along with a number of officers and gentlemen, six oxen and four ankers of brandy being consumed on the occasion.*

Walpole relates that General Wade was at a low gaming house, and had a very fine snuff-box, which on a sudden he missed. Everybody denied having taken it, and he insisted on searching the company. He did ; there remained only one man who stood behind him, and refused to be searched unless the general would go into another room alone with him. There the man told him that he was born a gentleman, was reduced, and lived by what little bets he could pick up there, and by fragments which the waiters sometimes gave him. 'At this moment I have half a fowl in my pocket. I was afraid of being exposed. Here it is ! Now, sir, you may search me.' Wade was so affected, that he gave the man a hundred pounds ; and 'immediately the genius of generosity, whose province is almost a sinecure, was very glad of the opportunity of making him find his own snuff-box, or another very like it, in his own pocket again.'

DEATH OF ADMIRAL BYNG.

The execution of Admiral Byng for not doing the utmost with his fleet for the relief of Port Mahon, in May 1756, was one of the events of the last century which made the greatest impression on the popular mind. The account of his death in Voltaire's *Candide*, is an exquisite bit of French epigrammatic writing :

'Talking thus, we approached Portsmouth. A multitude of people covered the shore, looking attentively at a stout gentleman who was on his knees with his eyes bandaged, on the quarter-deck of one of the vessels of the fleet. Four soldiers, placed in front of him, put each three balls in his head, in the most peaceable manner,

* *Domestic Annals of Scotland*, by R. Chambers, iii. 526, 561.

24

and all the assembly then dispersed quite satisfied. "What is all this?" quoth *Candide*, "and what devil reigns here?" He asked who was the stout gentleman who came to die in this ceremonious manner. "It is an Admiral," they answered. "And why kill the Admiral?" "It is because he has not killed enough of other people. He had to give battle to a French Admiral, and they find that he did not go near enough to him." "But," said *Candide*, "the French Admiral was as far from him as he was from the French Admiral." "That is very true," replied they; "but in this country it is useful to kill an Admiral now and then, just to encourage the rest [*pour encourager les autres*].'"

THE REFORM ACT OF 1831-2: OLD SARUM.

The 14th of March 1831 is a remarkable day in English history, as that on which the celebrated bill for parliamentary reform was read for the first time in the House of Commons. The changes proposed in this bill were sweeping beyond the .expectations of the most sanguine, and caused many advocates of reform to hesitate. So eagerly, however, did the great body of the people lay hold of the plan—demanding, according to a phrase of Mr Rintoul of the *Spectator* newspaper, the 'Bill, the whole Bill, and nothing but the Bill,'—that it was found impossible for all the conservative influences of the country, including latterly that of royalty itself, to stay, or greatly alter the measure. It took fourteen months of incessant struggle to get the bill

passed; but no sooner was the contest at an end than a conservative reaction set in, falsifying alike many of the hopes and fears with which the measure had been regarded. The nation calmly resumed its ordinary *aplomb*, and moderate thinkers saw only occasion for congratulation that so many perilous anomalies had been removed from our system of representation.

Amongst these anomalies there was none which the conservative party felt it more difficult to defend, than the fact that at least two of the boroughs possessing the right of returning two members, were devoid of inhabitants, namely Gatton and Old Sarum. 'Gatton and Old Sarum' were of course a sort of *tour de force* in the hands of the reforming party, and the very names became indelibly fixed in the minds of that generation. With many Old Sarum thus acquired a ridiculous association of ideas, who little knew that, in reality, the attributes of the place were calculated to raise sentiments of a beautiful and affecting kind.

Old Sarum, situated a mile and a half north of Salisbury—now a mere assemblage of green mounds and trenches—is generally regarded as the Sorbiodunum of the Romans. Its name, derived from the Celtic words, *sorbio*, dry, and *dun*, a fortress, leads to the conclusion that it was a British post: it was, perhaps, one of the towns taken by Vespasian, when he was engaged in the subjugation of this part of the island under the Emperor Claudius. A number of Roman roads meet at Old Sarum, and it is mentioned in

OLD SARUM.

the *Antonine Itinerary*, thus shewing the place to have been occupied by the Romans, though, it must be admitted, the remains present little resemblance to the usual form of their posts. In the Saxon times, Sarum is frequently noticed by

historians; and under the Anglo-Saxon and Anglo-Norman princes, councils, ecclesiastical and civil, were held here, and the town became the seat of a bishopric. There was a castle or fortress, which is mentioned as early as the time of Alfred, and which may be regarded as the citadel. The city was defended by a wall, within the enclosure of which the cathedral stood. Early in the thirteenth century, the cathedral was removed to its present site; many or most of the citizens also removed, and the rise of New Sarum, or Salisbury, led to the decay of the older place; so that, in the time of Leland (sixteenth century), there was not one inhabited house in it. The earthworks of the ancient city are very conspicuous, and traces of the foundation of the cathedral were observed about thirty years ago. Mr Constable, R.A., was so struck with the desolation of the site, and its lonely grandeur, that he painted a beautiful picture of the scene, which was ably engraved by Lucas.

The plate was accompanied with letter-press, of which the following are passages: 'This subject, which seems to embody the words of the poet, "Paint me a desolation," is one with which the grander phenomena of nature best accord. Sudden and abrupt appearances of light—thunder-clouds—wild autumnal evenings—solemn and shadowy twilights, "flinging half an image on the straining sight"—with variously tinted clouds, dark, cold, and grey, or ruddy bright—even conflicts of the elements heighten, if possible, the sentiment which belongs to it.

'The present appearance of Old Sarum, wild, desolate, and dreary, contrasts strongly with its former splendour. This celebrated city, which once gave laws to the whole kingdom, and where the earliest parliaments on record were convened, can only now be traced by vast embankments and ditches, tracked only by sheep-walks. "The plough has passed over it." In this city, the wily Conqueror, in 1086, confirmed that great political event, the establishment of the feudal system, and enjoined the allegiance of the nobles. Several succeeding monarchs held their courts here; and it too often screened them after their depredations on the people. In the days of chivalry, it poured forth its Longspear and other valiant knights over Palestine. It was the seat of the ecclesiastical government, when the pious Osmond and the succeeding bishops diffused the blessings of religion over the western kingdom: thus it became the chief resort of ecclesiastics and warriors, till their feuds and mutual animosities, caused by the insults of the soldiery, at length occasioned the separation of the clergy, and the removal of the Cathedral from within its walls, which took place in 1227. Many of the most pious and peaceable of the inhabitants followed it, and in less than half a century after the completion of the new church, the building of the bridge over the river Harnham diverted the great western road, and turned it through the new city. This last step was the cause of the desertion and gradual decay of Old Sarum.'

SMITHFIELD MARTYRS' ASHES.

Fanaticism sent many Protestants to the stake at Smithfield in the time of Queen Mary. The place of their suffering is supposed to have been on the south-east side of the open area, for old engravings still extant represent some of the buildings known to have existed on that side, as backing the scene of the burnings. Ashes

and bones have more than once been found, during excavations in that spot; and it has long been surmised that those were part of the remains of the poor martyrs. A discovery of this kind occurred on the 14th March 1849. Excavations were in progress on that day, connected with the construction of a new sewer, near St Bartholomew's church. At a depth of about three feet beneath the surface, the workmen came upon a heap of unhewn stones, blackened as if by fire, and covered with ashes and human bones, charred and partially consumed. One of the city antiquaries collected some of the bones, and carried them away as a memorial of a time which has happily passed. If there had only been a few bones present, their position might possibly be explained in some other way; and so might a heap of fire-blackened stones; but the juxtaposition of the two certainly gives the received hypothesis a fair share of probability.

THE GREYBEARD, OR BELLARMINE.

The manufacture of a coarse strong pottery, known as 'stoneware,' from its power of withstanding fracture and endurance of heat, originated in the Low Countries in the early part of the sixteenth century. The people of Holland particularly excelled in the trade, and the productions of the town of Delft were known all over Christendom. During the religious feuds which raged so horribly in Holland, the Protestant party originated a design for a drinking jug, in ridicule of their great opponent, the famed Cardinal Bellarmine, who had been sent into the Low Countries to oppose in person, and by his pen, the progress of the Reformed religion. He is described as 'short and hard-featured,' and thus he was typified in the corpulent beer-jug

here delineated. To make the resemblance greater, the Cardinal's face, with the great square-cut beard then peculiar to ecclesiastics, and termed 'the cathedral beard,' was placed in front of the jug, which was as often called 'a grey-beard' as it was 'a Bellarmine.' It was so popular as to be manufactured by thousands, in all sizes and qualities of cheapness; sometimes the face was delineated in the rudest and fiercest style. It met with a large sale in England, and many fragments of these jugs of the reign of Elizabeth and James I. have been exhumed in London. The writers of that era very frequently allude to it. Bulwer, in his *Artificial Changeling*, 1653, says of a formal doctor, that 'the fashion of his beard was just, for all the world, like those upon Flemish jugs, bearing in gross the form of a broom, narrow above and broad beneath.' Ben Jonson, in *Bartholomew Fair*, says of a drunkard, '*The man with the beard* has almost struck up his heels.' But the best description is the following in Cartwright's play, *The Ordinary*, 1651:

'—— Thou thing!
Thy belly looks like to some strutting hill,
O'ershadowed with thy rough beard like a wood;
Or like a larger jug, that some men call
A *Bellarmine*, but we a conscience,
Whereon the tender hand of pagan workman
Over the proud ambitious head hath carved
An idol large, with beard episcopal,
Making the vessel look like tyrant Eglon!'

The term *Greybeard* is still applied in Scotland to this kind of stoneware jug, though the face of Bellarmine no longer adorns it. A story connected with Greybeards was taken down a few years ago from the conversation of a venerable prelate of the Scottish Episcopal church; and though it has appeared before in a popular publication, we yield to the temptation of bringing it before the readers of the BOOK OF DAYS:

About 1770, there flourished a Mrs Balfour of Denbog, in the county of Fife. The nearest neighbour of Denbog was a Mr David Paterson, who had the character of being a good deal of a humorist. One day when Paterson called, he found Mrs Balfour engaged in one of her half-yearly brewings, it being the custom in those days each March and October to make as much ale as would serve for the ensuing six months. She was in a great pother about bottles, her stock of which fell far short of the number required, and she asked Mr Paterson if he could lend her any.

'No,' said Paterson, 'but I think I could bring you a few Greybeards that would hold a good deal; perhaps that would do.' The lady assented, and appointed a day when he should come again, and bring his Greybeards with him. On the proper day, Mr Paterson made his appearance in Mrs Balfour's little parlour.

'Well, Mr Paterson, have you brought your Greybeards?'

'Oh yes. They're down stairs waiting for you.'

'How many?'

'Nae less than ten.'

'Well, I hope they're pretty large, for really I find I have a good deal more ale than I have bottles for.'

'I'se warrant ye, mem, ilk ane o' them will hold twa gallons.'

'Oh, that will do extremely well.'

Down goes the lady.

372

'I left them in the dining-room,' said Paterson. When the lady went in, she found ten of the most bibulous old lairds of the north of Fife. She at once perceived the joke, and entered into it. After a hearty laugh had gone round, she said she thought it would be as well to have dinner before filling the greybeards; and it was accordingly arranged that the gentlemen should take a ramble, and come in to dinner at two o'clock.

The extra ale is understood to have been duly disposed of.

———

MARCH 15.

St Abraham, hermit of Mesopotamia, and his niece, St Mary, 4th century. St Zachary, Pope, 752. St Leocritia, of Cordova, virgin, martyr, 859.

LONGINUS THE KNIGHT.

One would suppose that the mediæval legendaries were very hard-set for saints, if we judge by the strange names which are sometimes introduced in their lists. A very slight ground was sufficient for building a legend, as may be instanced by a saint who, in the old calendars, especially the English and German calendars, was commemorated on this day. The Evangelists St Matthew and St Mark, describing the crucifixion, tell us that a centurion who was on guard saw the signs which attended the death of the Saviour, and became converted, and exclaimed, 'Truly this man was the Son of God;' and St John adds how, while Christ still remained on the cross, 'one of the soldiers with a spear pierced his side, and forthwith came thereout blood and water.' The mediæval ecclesiastics made one individual of these two persons, and gave him the name of Longinus, more usually written in mediæval French, Longinas or Longis, and in old English Longeus, under which he was one of the most popular personages of mediæval legend. He was said to have been blind (how a blind man came to be made a centurion is not quite clear); when ordered by Pontius Pilate to pierce our Saviour's side with his spear, the blood, according to the story, ran down into his eyes, and restored him miraculously to sight, which was partly the cause of his conversion to Christianity. He now associated with the Apostles, becoming an active 'soldier of the faith,' and distinguishing himself by the fervency of his zeal. He was thus, in the twenty-eighth year of his age, living at Cæsarea of Cappadocia, when information of his behaviour was carried to the prefect or governor, Octavius, who immediately summoned him to his presence. When questioned, Longinus told the prefect his name, said that he was a Roman soldier, of the province of Isauria, and acknowledged that he was a zealous follower of Christ. After some discussion on the relative merits of Christianity and paganism, Longinus was commanded to worship the idols, and eat of the sacrifice offered to them, but he refused; whereupon the tormentors or executioners (*quæstionarii*) were ordered to cut off his tongue and knock out his teeth. He long bears this and other outrages with great fortitude; but at length he proposes a curious sort of compromise, to which Octavius consents. It had been shewn, said Longinus, how little all the torments of the pagans affected him, but now, if he might have leave, he would undertake to break all their idols and overcome their gods, it being made a condition that, if he were successful, the pagans should desert their idols, and believe in the true God; but if their gods were able to do him any injury, he would become a pagan. Longinus immediately 'broke to pieces the idol, overthrew his altars and all his marble statues, and spilt all the offerings,' and the devils who dwelt in them fled, but they were arrested by Longinus, who chose to obtain some information from them. The demons acknowledged that his was the greatest God. He asked them further how they came to dwell in the idols, and they said that they came to seek comfortable places of refuge, and, finding beautiful images of stone, on which the name of Christ had not been invoked, nor the sign of the cross made, they immediately took possession of them, as well as of the people of the neighbourhood, who were equally unprotected; and now that he had driven them out, they supplicated him to let them go where they would, and begged not to be 'precipitated into the abyss.' This is a very curious illustration of the mediæval notion of the nature of the heathen idols. When the citizens heard this revelation, they set up a great shout of joy, and, as soon as the devils were driven out of them, they all embraced the Christian faith. This, however, did not save the saint from martyrdom; for Octavius, terrified lest the emperor should punish him and the city for its apostasy from the imperial faith, caused the head of Longinus to be cut off, and then repented, and became a Christian himself. 'These things,' says the legend, 'were acted in the city of Cæsarea of Cappadocia, on the Ides of March, under Octavius the prefect.' The legend is found in mediæval manuscripts in Latin and in other languages.

Born.—Theophilus Bonet, eminent Genevese physician, 1620; Jean Barbeyrac, eminent jurist, 1674, *Beziers;* General Andrew Jackson, 1767.

Died.—Julius Cæsar, assassinated, B.C. 44, *Rome;* Thomas Lord Chancellor Egerton, 1617, *Dodleston, Cheshire;* Sir Theodore Mayerne, physician to James I. and Charles I., 1655, *Chelsea;* John Earl of Loudon, Chancellor of Scotland, 1663; the Rev. Dr Thomas Franklin, eminent Greek scholar, 1784, *London;* Admiral John Jervis, Earl St Vincent, 1823, *Stone;* John Liston, comic actor, 1846; Otto Kotzebue, navigator, 1846; Cardinal Mezzofanti, extraordinary linguist, 1849; Captain Sir Samuel Brown, civil engineer, 1852.

JEAN BARBEYRAC.

The circumstances under which the ideas were developed, that led to the production of noted works in literature or art, would, if it were possible to collect them, form a remarkable history, affording strange illustrations of the multifarious phases presented by the human mind. Fancy, for instance, a learned professor and doctor of jurisprudence, compelled by fate to reside with a gambling mother-in-law, and to sit for hours listening to the wearisome conversation of a party of old women playing at cards; and yet improving the occasion, by mentally laying the foundation of the most elaborate work on gaming that ever has been written. These were exactly the circumstances which gave origin to Barbeyrac's celebrated *Traité de Jeu.*

Barbeyrac was a native of France; but, being a Calvinist, was compelled by the revocation of the edict of Nantes to take refuge in Switzerland. He became professor of law at Lausanne, and subsequently at Gröningen; and published many works on jurisprudence, besides a translation of Tillotson's *Sermons.* But the work on which his reputation is founded, and by which he is known at the present day, is his treatise on gaming, dedicated to Ann Princess of Orange, eldest daughter of George II., the text-book for all who wish to study the subject.

The *Traité de Jeu* abounds in the most recondite learning. The first of its four books contains arguments to prove that gaming is not inconsistent with natural laws, morality, or religion. In the second book the author applies these arguments specifically to the various kinds of games that have been played at different periods in the history of the world. The third book states the limitations under which the previous arguments are to be considered; and the fourth enumerates the various abuses of gaming. Finally, he comes to the rather startling conclusion that gambling is not in itself immoral or illegal, and that it is nowhere, directly or indirectly, forbidden in the Holy Scriptures.

Barbeyrac starts with the undeniable proposition that man is essentially a worker, his whole existence depending upon labour; consequently God had designed that man should be employed in works of usefulness for himself and others. But, as man cannot work without rest, food, and relaxation, the Deity had expressly sanctioned all those requirements, by the mere act of creating man a working animal—the evil consisting in the abuse, not in the use of those indispensable requisites.

'There are persons, however,' says Barbeyrac, 'who unreasonably suppose that use and abuse cannot be separated; and who, forming to themselves strange mystical notions of virtue and piety, would persuade us that every kind of diversion and amusement, being neither more nor less than the consequences of man's fallen nature, is unworthy of rational creatures. Such persons may be above the common limits of human nature, in a sphere of perfection unattainable by the great mass of mankind. Still, they ought to allow those, who cannot arrive at such a high degree of perfection, to follow in low humility the path which nature and providence have pointed out to them, to enjoy their opinions in peace, and their consciences devoid of scruple.'

'I maintain,' he continues, 'as an irrefragable principle, that, for the sake of relaxation, man may indulge in such amusements as are free from vice. This being admitted, if a person takes pleasure in playing at cards or dice, there is no reason why he may not amuse himself in that manner, quite as innocently as in painting, dancing, music, hunting, or any other similar diversions. The question then arises, whether the game be played for nothing, or for a stake of value. In the first case, it is a mere relaxation, bearing not the slightest semblance of criminality; with regard to the second, there can be no evil in it, looking at the matter generally, without taking into consideration peculiar circumstances. For, if I am at liberty to promise and give my property, absolutely and unconditionally, to whomsoever I please, why may I not promise and give a certain sum, in the event of a person proving more fortunate or more skilful than I, with respect to the result of certain contingencies, movements, or combinations, on which we had previously agreed? And why may not this person honestly avail himself of the result, either of his skill, or of a favourable concurrence of fortuitous circumstances, on the issue of which I had voluntarily contracted an obligation? And though but one of the parties gains an advantage, yet there is nothing contrary to strict equity in the transaction, the terms having been previously agreed on by both. Every person, being at liberty to determine the conditions on which he will concede a right to another, may make it dependent on the most chance circumstances. *A fortiori*, then, a person may fairly and honestly avail himself of these winnings, when he has risked on the event as much as he was likely to gain. In fact, gaming is a contract, and in every contract the mutual consent of the parties is the supreme law; this is an incontestable maxim of natural equity.'

Many of Barbeyrac's arguments and quotations are taken from our old Puritan writers, who admitted that a kind of gambling, under the designation of lots, was sanctioned by the Scriptures; though only to be used to decide matters connected with religion and the church. The able authoress of *Silas Marner* has shewn us something of the working of this lot system, though it certainly is more a kind of divination than gambling.

To conclude, Barbeyrac's arguments must be considered as a series of clever paradoxes, written by a learned philosopher unacquainted with the world and the manifold wickednesses of its ways. Though we may certainly employ our time better, there can be no great harm in a friendly game of whist or backgammon; but the undeniable vice and folly of gambling has received and ever will receive the direct condemnation of all good men able to form an opinion on the matter.

SIR THEODORE MAYERNE.

Collectors of heads, for such is the ghastly phrase used by the *cognoscenti* to indicate engraved portraits, fancy themselves fortunate when they can obtain a folio engraving, representing a jolly-looking, well-kept individual, apparently of not more than sixty summers, holding a skull in the left hand, and bearing the following inscription:

'Theodore Turquet de Mayerne, knight, aged eighty-two years, by birth a Frenchman, by religion a Protestant; in his profession a second

Hippocrates; and what has seldom happened to any but himself, first physician to three kings; in erudition unequalled, in experience second to none, and as the result of all these advantages, celebrated far and near.'

If the inscription stated that Mayerne had been physician to four kings, it would be nearer the mark, for he really served in that capacity Henry IV. of France, James I., Charles I., and Charles II., of England. He was born at Geneva, in 1573, and named Theodore after his godfather, the celebrated reformer Beza. He studied at Montpelier, and soon after taking his degrees, received the appointment of physician to Henry IV.; but, his profession of Protestant principles being a bar to his advancement in France, he came to England, and was warmly received by James the First. His position in the history of medical science is well defined, by his being among the earliest practitioners who applied chemistry to the preparing and compounding of medicines. His skill and celebrity enabled him to acquire a large fortune, and to live unmolested and respected during the terrible convulsions of the civil war. Though a noted *bon vivant*, he attained the advanced age of eighty-two years, dying in 1655, at his own house in Chelsea, a favourite place of residence among the physicians of the olden time. The immediate cause of his death he attributed to drinking bad wine with a convivial party, at a tavern in the Strand. 'Good wine,' he used to say, 'is slow poison: I have drunk it all my lifetime, and it has not killed me yet; but bad wine is sudden death.'

In hours of relaxation, Mayerne applied his chemical knowledge to the improvement of the arts of painting and cookery, in both of which he was no mean proficient, as an amateur. The famous artist Petitot owed the perfection of his colouring in enamel to Mayerne's experiments, and the best cookery book of the period was written by the learned physician himself. Indeed it is not generally known how much cookery is indebted to medicine. Mayerne, in the seventeenth, Hunter and Hill in the eighteenth, and Kitchiner in the nineteenth century, have given to the world the best cookery books of their respective eras. Indeed, in ancient times, cookery was specifically considered as an important branch of the healing art; the word *curare*, among the Romans, signifying to dress a dinner, as well as to cure a disease. Mayerne's cookery-book bears the high sounding title of *Archimagirus Anglo-Gallicus*, and the following specimen of its contents will testify that it well merited its appellation. The jolly physician often participated in the hospitalities of my Lord Mayor, and the great commercial guilds and companies; so, as a fitting token of his gratitude, he named his *chef-d'œuvre*, the first and principal recipe in his book,

A City of London Pie.

'Take eight marrow bones, eighteen sparrows, one pound of potatoes, a quarter of a pound of eringoes, two ounces of lettuce stalks, forty chesnuts, half a pound of dates, a peck of oysters, a quarter of a pound of preserved citron, three artichokes, twelve eggs, two sliced lemons, a handful of pickled barberries, a quarter of an ounce of whole pepper, half an ounce of sliced nutmeg, half an ounce of whole cinnamon, a quarter of an ounce of whole cloves, half an ounce of mace, and a quarter of a pound of currants. Liquor when it is baked, with white wine, butter, and sugar.'

Some years ago, with very slight alterations —only adopted after deep consultation, to suit the palates of the present day—a pie was made from the above recipe, which gave complete satisfaction to the party of connoisseurs in culinary matters, who heartily and merrily partook of it.

MEZZOFANTI'S WONDERFUL MEMORY.

This celebrated linguist, born at Bologna, in 1774, was the son of a carpenter, and was intended for the same occupation, had not a priest observed the remarkable intelligence of the boy, and had him educated for the priesthood, when he acquired, before the completion of his university career, the Latin, Greek, Hebrew, Arabic, Spanish, French, German, and Swedish languages. At the early age of twenty-two, he was appointed professor of Arabic in the university, and next of Oriental languages; but through political changes, he lost both these appointments, and was for some years reduced to great distress. Meanwhile, Mezzofanti made his all-engrossing pursuit the study of languages. One of his modes of study was calling upon strangers at the hotels of Bologna, interrogating them, making notes of their communications, and taking lessons in the pronunciation of their several languages. 'Nor did all this cost me much trouble,' says Mezzofanti; 'for, in addition to an excellent memory, God had gifted me with remarkable flexibility of the organs of speech.' He was now reinstated in his appointments; and his attainments grew prodigious. Mr Stewart Rose, in 1817, reported him as reading twenty languages, and speaking eighteen. Baron Tach, in 1820, stated the number at thirty-two. Lord Byron, about the same time, described him as 'a walking polyglot, a monster of languages, and a Briareus of parts of speech.' In 1831, he settled in Rome, accepted a prebend in the church of St Mary Major, which he exchanged for a canonry in St Peter's; he was next appointed keeper of the Vatican library, and in 1838 was elevated to the Cardinalate.

Mezzofanti's residence at Rome gave a new impulse to his linguistic studies. Herr Guido Görres, the eminent German scholar, writes of him, in 1841, ' He is familiar with all the European languages; and by this I understand not only the ancient classical tongues, and the modern ones of the first class, such as the Greek and Latin, or the Italian, French, German, Spanish, Portuguese, and English; his knowledge extends also to languages of the second class, viz., the Dutch, Danish, and Swedish, to the whole Sclavonic family, Russian, Polish, Bohemian, or Czechish, to the Servian, the Hungarian, the Turkish, and even to those of the third and fourth classes, the Irish, the Welsh, the Wallachian, the Albanian, the Bulgarian, and the Illyrian. Even the Romani of the Alps, and the Lettish, are not unknown to him; nay, he has made himself acquainted with Lappish. He is master of the languages which fall within the Indo-Germanic family, the Sanscrit and Persian, the Koordish, the Georgian, the Armenian; he is familiar with all the members of the Semitic family, the Hebrew, the Arabic, the Syriac, the Samaritan, the Chaldee, the Sabaic, nay, even with the Chinese, which he not only reads, but speaks. Among the Hamitic languages,

he knows Coptic, Ethiopic, Abyssinian, Amharic, and Angolese.' He is described as invariably speaking in each language with the precision, and in most cases with the fluency of a native. His pronunciation, his idiom, his vocabulary, were alike unexceptionable; even the familiar words of every-day life, and the delicate turns of conversational speech, were at his command. He was equally at home in the pure Parisian of the Faubourg St Germain and in the Provençal of Toulouse. He could accommodate himself to the rude jargon of the Black Forest, or to the classic vocabulary of Dresden.

Cardinal Wiseman, the friend of Mezzofanti, has thus spoken of his extraordinary power of acquiring and remembering a number of languages—that is, knowing them thoroughly, grammatically, and familiarly,—so as to speak each with its own accentuation, read it with facility and point, express himself technically through its medium, and, above all, write a familiar note in it. Of this power, says Wiseman, no one, perhaps, ever attained such pre-eminence in philology, and no one could have made a more noble use of the wonderful gift entrusted to him to improve. His labours were in the prisons, in which he found confined natives of every habitable country—Croats, Bulgarians, Wallachians, Bohemians, Hungarians, Poles, Lithuanians. As may be supposed, in a provincial city in Italy there was but small chance that any of these should meet with priests of their own nation. Cardinal Mezzofanti was moved with a burning desire to converse with them and offer them the consolations of religion. He set himself to work, and in a few days was able to speak with them readily and fluently. Cases have been known of persons coming to this extraordinary man for confession, but speaking only some out-of-the-way language which debarred them from intercommunication with all priests within their reach. On such occasions Cardinal Mezzofanti would request a delay of three weeks, during which time he would so completely master the language, however difficult, that he could apprehend the most minute particulars communicated to him. At the age of fifty he was thoroughly versed in fifty languages, and before his death the number he knew must have amounted to seventy or eighty. Of these, it must be added, he was acquainted with all the varieties of dialect, provincialisms, and patois. He would detect the particular county in England from which a person came, or the province in France, and was conversant not only with the grammar, but with the literature of all those nations. By a Portuguese he was once, to his (Cardinal Wiseman's) own knowledge, taken for a countryman; and on another occasion he was similarly mistaken for an Englishman. He could write a note or an apology (perhaps, after all, the greatest test) without an error in form, language, style, or title of address of his correspondent, and would turn his sentences without ever losing sight of the little niceties, idioms, and peculiarities which form the distinctive characteristics of a language. His method of studying a language was to take the grammar and read it through, after which he was its master. He used to say he had never forgotten anything he had ever read or heard. Cardinal Wiseman states that he one day met Mezzofanti hurrying away, as he said, to a Propaganda—'What are you going to do there?' 'To teach the Californians their language.' 'How did you learn Californian?' 'They taught me, but they had no grammar; I have made a grammar, and now I am going to teach them to read and write it.'—(*Lectures on the Phenomena of Memory*, 1857.)

Mezzofanti died on the 15th of March 1849; and was buried in the church of St Onofrio, beside the grave of Torquato Tasso.

CAPTAIN SIR SAMUEL BROWN.

Many nations in past times sought to find how a bridge might so be constructed that the weight of the roadway, instead of resting upon arches of masonry, or on a rigid iron or wooden framework, might be supported by the tension of ropes or chains. Kircher described a bridge of chains which the Chinese constructed many centuries ago in their country. Turner, in his *Account of Bootan or Bhotan in India*, describes several very ingenious bridges devised by the natives for crossing the ravines which intersect that mountainous country. One is a bridge consisting of a number of iron chains supporting a matted platform ; another is formed of two parallel chains, around which creepers are loosely twisted, with planks for a roadway suspended ; while a third is formed of two rattan or osier ropes, encircled by a hoop of the same material : the passenger propelling himself by sitting in the hoop, holding a rope in each hand, and making the hoop slide along. Some of the rude bridges constructed by the natives in South America, such as that at Taribita, consist each of a single rush rope, on which a kind of carriage is swung, and drawn along by another rope held by a person on the bank. At Apurima the natives have constructed a bridge nearly 400 feet long, by 6 feet wide, by placing two bark ropes parallel, and interweaving cross-pieces of wood from one to the other.

Of an actual iron suspension bridge, the first made in Europe seems to have been one over the Tees near Middleton, constructed rather more than a century ago. Two chains were stretched in a nearly straight line, steadied by inclined ties from the banks below ; and the roadway (only a narrow path for foot-passengers) was supported immediately by the chains. In 1816, a little bridge was constructed over Gala Water in Scotland, made chiefly of wire, at the orders of a manufacturer named Richard Lees ; and another of similar kind was soon afterwards constructed across the Tweed at King's Meadows, near Peebles, with a platform four feet wide resting on the wires. It was about that date, or a little earlier, that Captain Brown made an important advance in the construction of chain bridges, by changing altogether the form of the links. Instead of making them short and circular or oval, he made them several feet long, with eyes drilled at each end, and connecting them with short links and bolt-pieces. Every main link, in fact, consisted of a series of flat bars, pivoted at the ends to each other and to the adjacent links. He also devised an ingenious mode of removing a defective link without disturbing the continuity of the chain. These two capital inventions laid the basis for the plans of most of the great suspension bridges since constructed, including Brown's Bridge over the Tweed at Berwick, Brown's Trinity Pier at Newhaven near Leith, Telford's beautiful Menai and Conway bridges, Brown's Chain-pier at Brighton, Tierney Clark's bridge at Hammersmith, Brown's bridge at Montrose, and the grandest suspension bridge, perhaps, ever constructed—that built by

Mr Tierney Clark over the Danube at Pesth. It was no small merit in an engineer to render such works possible.

JULIUS CÆSAR.

' It is possible,' says a living author, ' to be a very great man, and to be still very inferior to Julius Cæsar, the most complete character, so Lord Bacon thought, of all antiquity. Nature seems incapable of such extraordinary combinations as composed his versatile capacity, which was the wonder even of the Romans themselves. The first general—the only triumphant politician—inferior to none in eloquence —comparable to any in the attainments of wisdom, in an age made up of the greatest commanders, statesmen, orators, and philosophers that ever appeared in the world—an author who composed a perfect specimen of military annals in his travelling carriage—at one time in a controversy with Cato, at another writing a treatise on punning, and collecting a set of good sayings—fighting and making love at the same moment, and willing to abandon both his empire and his mistress for a sight of the Fountains of the Nile. Such did Cæsar appear to his contemporaries.' [*]

The assassination of Cæsar on the Ides of March, B.C. 44, was immediately preceded by certain prodigies, which it has greatly exercised the ingenuity of historians and others to attempt to explain.

First, on the night preceding the assassination, Cæsar dreamt, at intervals, that he was soaring above the clouds on wings, and that he placed his hand within the right hand of Jove. It would seem that perhaps some obscure and half-formed image floated in Cæsar's mind of the eagle, as the king of birds,—secondarily, as the tutelary emblem under which his conquering legions had so often obeyed his voice ; and thirdly, as the bird of Jove. To this triple relation of the bird, the dream covertly appears to point. And a singular coincidence is traced between the dream and a circumstance reported to us, as having actually occurred in Rome, about twenty-four hours before Cæsar's death. A little bird, which by some is represented as a very small kind of sparrow, but which, both to the Greeks and Romans, was known by a name implying a regal station (probably from the audacity which at times prompted it to attack the eagle), was observed to direct its flight towards the senate-house, consecrated by Pompey, whilst a crowd of other birds were seen to hang upon its flight in close pursuit, towards Pompey's Hall. Flight and pursuit were there alike arrested ; the little bird-king was overtaken by his enemies, who fell upon him as so many conspirators, and tore him limb from limb. [†]

The other prodigies were—2. A dream of Cæsar's wife, Calpurnia, that their house had fallen in, that he had been wounded by assassins, and had taken refuge in her bosom. 3. The arms of Mars, deposited in Cæsar's house, rattled at night. 4. The doors of the room wherein he slept flew open spontaneously. 5. The victims and birds were inauspicious. 6. Solitary birds appeared in the Forum. 7. There were lights in the sky, and nocturnal noises. 8. Fiery figures of men were seen ; a flame issued from the hand of a soldier's slave without hurting him. 9. After the murder of Cæsar, it was remembered that the attendant removed his gilded chair from the senate-room, thinking that he would not attend the meeting.

The last words of Cæsar, as he fell before the blows of his assassins, have become proverbial, being generally given as ' Et tu, Brute !' (And thou too,

[*] Lord Broughton (John Cam Hobhouse) in notes to *Childe Harold*, Canto IV.

[†] See a paper by De Quincey, in *Blackwood's Edinburgh Magazine*, 1832.

Brutus !)—certainly a most natural expression on seeing a youthful and beloved friend among those prepared to shed his blood. There is, however, a doubt as to the words used by Cæsar. They have been given as composed of the Greek language, ' Καὶ σὺ τέκνον !' (What, thou, too !) Some even express a doubt if he was heard to utter any expression at all after the stabbing began, or did anything more than adjust his mantle, in order that, when fallen, the lower part of his person might be covered.

LAST WORDS OF REMARKABLE PERSONS.

It may amuse the reader, in connection with the preceding matter, to glance over a small collection of the final expressions of remarkable persons, as these are communicated by biographers and historians. In most instances, the authorities are given, along with such explanations as may be presumed to be necessary.

SOCRATES. (To a friend, when about to drink the cup of poison :) ' Krito, we owe a cock to Æsculapius ; discharge the debt and by no means omit it.'—*Grote.*

' I consider the sacrifice of the cock as a more certain evidence of the tranquillity of Socrates, than his discourse on Immortality.'—*Dr Cullen.*

MAHOMET. ' Oh Allah ! be it so—among the glorious associates in Paradise !'—*Irving's Life of Mahomet.*

SIR HUGH PERCY. ' I have saved the bird in my bosom.'

Sir Hugh, fighting unsuccessfully for Henry VI. at Hedgely Moor, April 1464, used this expression on feeling himself mortally wounded, in reference to the faith he had pledged to his unfortunate sovereign, while so many deserted him.

COLUMBUS. ' In manus tuas, Domine, commendo spiritum meum.'

PIZARRO. ' Jesu !'

' At that moment he received a wound in the throat, and, reeling, sank on the floor, while the swords of Rada and several of the conspirators were plunged into his body. "Jesu !" exclaimed the dying man, and, tracing a cross with his finger on the bloody floor, he bent down his head to kiss it, &c.'—*Prescott.*

KING JAMES V. OF SCOTLAND. ' It came with a lass, and it will go with one !'

Alluding to the intelligence brought to him, that his wife was delivered of a daughter, the heiress of the crown, and to the fact of the crown having come into his family by the daughter of King Robert Bruce.

CARDINAL BEATON (assassinated 1546). ' Fy, fy, all is gone !'

' And so he (James Melvin) stroke him twyse or thrise trowght him with a stog sweard ; and so he fell ; never word heard out of his mouth, but "I am a preast, I am a preast : fy, fy, all is gone !"'—*Knox's Hist. Reformation in Scot.,* edit. 1846, i. 177.

TASSO. ' Into thy hands, O Lord !'—*Wiffen's Life of Tasso.*

CHARLES V. ' Ay, Jesus !'—*Stirling's Cloister Life of Charles V.*

FERRAR, BISHOP OF ST DAVID'S. March 30, 1555. (On being chained to the stake at Carmarthen Cross :) ' If I stir through the pains of my burning, believe not the doctrine I have taught.'

JOHN KNOX. ' Now it is come.'—*M'Crie's Life of John Knox.*

DR DONNE. ' Thy will be done.'

' He lay fifteen days earnestly expecting his hourly

change, and in the last hour of his last day, as his body melted away, and vapoured into spirit, his soul having, I verily believe, some revelation of the beatific vision, he said, "I were miserable if I might not die ;" and after those words, closed many periods of his faint breath by saying often, "Thy kingdom come, thy will be done !"'—*Walton's Life of Dr Donne.*

GEORGE HERBERT. ' And now, Lord—Lord, now receive my soul !'

RALEIGH. (To the executioner, who was pausing :) ' Why dost thou not strike ? Strike, man !'

GROTIUS. ' Be serious.'

ROBERT CECIL, FIRST EARL OF SALISBURY, *Minister to James I.* ' Ease and pleasure quake to hear of death ; but my life, full of cares and miseries, desireth to be dissolved.'

It may be remarked that Lord Salisbury died when, to all appearance, at the summit of earthly glory.

DUKE OF BUCKINGHAM. ' Traitor, thou hast killed me !' [To the assassin Felton.]

CHARLES I. ' Remember !'

To Bishop Juxon, on the scaffold ; supposed to refer to a message to his son, commanding him to forgive his enemies and murderers.

CROMWELL. ' It is not my design to drink or sleep, but my design is to make what haste I can to be gone.' Followed by a few pious ejaculations.—*Carlyle's Cromwell.*

CHARLES II. ' Don't let poor Nelly starve.' [Referring to his mistress, Nell Gwynne.]

WILLIAM III. ' Can this last long ?' [To his physician.]

This is not an uncommon death-bed expression. A lady, a victim by burning to a preposterous fashion of dress once in vogue, and who survived the accident a few hours, was heard to breathe, ' Shall I be long in dying ?'

LOCKE. ' Cease now.' [To Lady Marsham, who had been reading the Psalms to him.]

POPE. ' There is nothing that is meritorious but virtue and friendship, and, indeed, friendship itself is but a part of virtue.'

GENERAL WOLFE. ' What, do they run already ? then I die happy.'

Alluding to the intelligence given him as he lay wounded on the field, that the French were beaten.

WILLIAM, DUKE OF CUMBERLAND. ' It is all over.'

' On the 30th of October [1766], his Royal Highness was playing at picquet with General Hodgson. He grew confused and mistook the cards. The next day he recovered enough to appear at Court, but after dinner was seized with a suffocation, and ordered the window to be opened. One of his *valets de chambre,* who was accustomed to bleed him, was called, and prepared to tie up his arm ; but the Duke said, "It is too late !—it is all over !" and expired.'—*Walpole's Mem. of Reign of George III.*

HAYDN. ' God preserve the Emperor.'

HALLER. ' The artery ceases to beat.'

MADAME DE POMPADOUR, 1764. (To the curé of the Madeleine, who had called to see her, and was taking his leave, as she seemed just about to expire :) ' Un moment, Monsieur le Curé, nous nous en irons ensemble.'

EARL OF CHESTERFIELD. ' Give Dayrolles a chair.'

' Upon the morning of his decease, and about half an hour before it happened, Mr Dayrolles [a friend] called upon him to make his usual visit. When he had entered the room, the *valet de chambre* opening the curtains of the bed, announced Mr Dayrolles to his lordship. The earl just found strength in a faint voice to say, *Give Dayrolles a chair.* These were the last words he was heard to speak. They were characteristic, and were remarked by the very able and attentive physician then in the room [Dr Warren]. "His good breeding," said that gentleman, "only quits him with life."'—*Maty's Memoirs of Philip Earl of Chesterfield*, 1779.

DR FRANKLIN. 'A dying man can do nothing easy.'

To his daughter, who had advised him to change his position in bed, that he might breathe more easily. These are the last words recorded in his biography; but they were pronounced a few days before his decease.

DR WILLIAM HUNTER. 'If I had strength enough to hold a pen, I would write how easy and pleasant a thing it is to die.'

GOLDSMITH.

'It then occurred to Dr Turton to put a very pregnant question to his patient. "Your pulse," he said, "is in greater disorder than it should be, from the degree of fever you have. *Is your mind at ease?*" "*No, it is not,*" was Goldsmith's melancholy answer. They are the last words we are to hear him utter in this world.'—*Forster's Life and Times of Oliver Goldsmith.*

FONTENELLE. 'Je ne souffre pas, mes amis, mais je sens une certaine difficulté d'être.' (I do not suffer, my friends; but I feel a certain difficulty of existing.)

THURLOW. 'I'm shot if I don't believe I'm dying.'

JOHNSON. 'God bless you, my dear.'

To Miss Morris, a friend's daughter, who came to him at the last to ask his blessing.

GIBBON. 'Mon Dieu, mon Dieu!'

MARAT. 'A moi, ma chère!' (Help, my dear!)

To his waiting maid, on feeling himself stabbed in his bath by Charlotte Corday.

MADAME ROLAND. 'Oh, Liberty, how many crimes are committed in thy name!'

Addressed to the statue of Liberty, at her execution.

MIRABEAU. 'Let me die to the sounds of delicious music.'

GAINSBOROUGH. 'We are all going to heaven, and Vandyke is of the company.'—*A. Cunningham's Lives of Painters.*

BURNS. 'That scoundrel, Matthew Penn!'

The solicitor who had written to him about a debt, and inspired the poor poet with fears of a jail.

WASHINGTON. 'It is well.'

NELSON. 'I thank God I have done my duty.'

WILLIAM PITT. 'Oh my country! how I leave my country!'

There was long a doubt as to the last words of Mr Pitt. The Earl of Stanhope, in his Life of the great minister (1862), gave them from a manuscript left by his lordship's uncle, the Hon. James H. Stanhope, as, 'Oh my country! how I love my country!' But his lordship afterwards stated in a letter in the *Times*, April 26, 1862, that, on re-examination of the manuscript,—a somewhat obscure one,—no doubt was left on his mind that the word 'love' was a mistake for 'leave.' The expression, as now in this manner finally authenticated, is in a perfect and most sad conformity with the state of the national affairs at the time when Mr Pitt was approaching his end. A new coalition, which England had with great difficulty and at vast expense formed against Napoleon, had been dashed to pieces by the prostration of Austria; and Pitt must have had the idea in his mind that

hardly now a stay against that prodigious power remained. It was indeed generally believed that the overthrow of the coalition was what brought him to his end.

SIR JOHN MOORE. 'Stanhope, remember me to your sister.'

Addressed to one of his aides-de-camp, the Hon. Captain Stanhope, son of the Earl of Stanhope. The person referred to was the celebrated Lady Hester Stanhope.—*Life of Sir John Moore, by his brother, James Carrick Moore.*

DR ADAM, *Rector of the High School of Edinburgh*, 1809. 'It grows dark, boys; you may go.'

The venerable teacher thought he was exercising his class in Buchanan's Psalms, his usual practice on a Monday. The delirium ended with these words.

DE STAEL. 'I have loved God, my father, and liberty.'

NAPOLEON. 'Mon Dieu—La Nation Française—Tête d'armée.'—*Alison.*

'He expired at length without pain and in silence, during a convulsion of the elements, on the night of the 5th of May 1821. The last words he stammered out were *Army* and *France*, but it could not be ascertained whether it was a dream, delirium, or adieu.'—*Lamartine.*

JOHN ADAMS, SECOND PRESIDENT OF THE UNITED STATES. 'Thomas Jefferson still survives.'

Adams died on the 4th July 1826, the fiftieth anniversary of the declaration of Independence. As he found his end approaching at so interesting a crisis, he reflected that there would yet remain the writer of that famous document, his associate in so many trying scenes. He was in reality mistaken in the point of fact, for Jefferson at a distant part of the country had died that morning.

THOMAS JEFFERSON. 'I resign my soul to God, my daughter to my country.'

BYRON. 'I must sleep now.'

TALMA. 'The worst of all is that I cannot see.'

GEORGE IV. 'Watty, what is this? It is death, my boy—they have deceived me.'

To his page, Sir Wathen Waller, who was assisting him on a seat when the last qualm came.

SIR WALTER SCOTT. 'God bless you all!'

To his family, surrounding his death-bed.

SIR JAMES MACKINTOSH. 'Happy.'

'Upon our inquiring how he felt, he said he was "happy."'—*Life by his Son.*

GOETHE. 'More light!'

'His speech was becoming less and less distinct. The last words audible were, *More light!* The final darkness grew apace, and he whose eternal longings had been for more light, gave a parting cry for it, as he was passing under the shadow of death.'—*G. H. Lewes's Life of Goethe.*

EDWARD IRVING. 'If I die, I die unto the Lord. Amen!'—*Oliphant's Life of Edward Irving.*

CHARLES MATHEWS. 'I am ready.'

'I approached him,' says his widow biographer, 'and, kissing his head, said, "I want you to go to bed now." He closed the Bible which he had been reading; and, looking up at me, replied meekly, "I am ready." . . . "*I am ready!*" memorable words! —they were his last, and they recurred to me as I was taken from him in a *twofold sense*, and ought in some degree to have tempered the anguish of the time.'

EARL OF ELDON. 'It matters not to me, where I am going, whether the weather be cold or hot.'

To Mr Pennington, who had made the remark that it was a cold day.—*Campbell's Lives of the Chancellors.*

PRINCESS CHARLOTTE. 'You make me drunk. Pray leave me quiet. I find it affects my head.' To her medical attendants, who had been administering brandy, hot wine, and sal volatile.—*Raikes's Correspondence with the Duke of Wellington.*

PROFESSOR EDWARD FORBES. 'My own wife.' To Mrs Forbes, who inquired as he was dying if he still knew her.—*Memoir of Edward Forbes by George Wilson, &c.*

It is remarkable how few of these last words of noted persons express what may be called the ruling passion of the life—contrary to Pope's idea:

' And you, brave Cobham, to the latest breath,
Shall feel your ruling passion strong in death ;
Such in those moments as in all the past,
"Oh, save my country, Heaven!" shall be your last.'

In many instances the matter referred to is trivial, in some surprisingly so. In others, there is only an allusion to what was passing at the moment. In few is there any great thought. Some express only the enfeebled mind. Perhaps the most striking is that of Dr Adam of the Edinburgh High School, for it reveals in fact what dying is—a darkening and fading away of the faculties. There is, however, this general lesson to be derived from the expressions of the dying, that there is usually a calmness and absence of strong sensation of any kind at the last moment. On this point, we quote a short passage from the *Quarterly Review.*

' The pain of dying must be distinguished from the pain of the previous disease ; for when life ebbs, sensibility declines. As death is the final extinction of corporeal feelings, so numbness increases as death comes on. The prostration of disease, like healthful fatigue, engenders a growing stupor—a sensation of subsiding softly into a coveted repose. The transition resembles what might be seen in those lofty mountains, whose sides exhibiting every climate in regular gradation, vegetation luxuriates at their base, and dwindles in the approach to the regions of snow, till its feeblest manifestation is repressed by the cold. The so-called agony can never be more formidable than when the brain is the last to go, and the mind preserves to the end a rational cognizance of the state of the body. Yet persons thus situated commonly attest that there are few things in life less painful than the close. "If I had strength enough to hold a pen," said William Hunter, "I would write how easy and delightful it is to die." "If this be dying," said the niece of Newton, of Olney, " it is a pleasant thing to die;" " the very expression," adds her uncle, " which another friend of mine made use of on her death-bed a few years ago." The same words have so often been uttered under similar circumstances, that we could fill pages with instances which are only varied by the name of the speaker. "If this be dying," said Lady Glenorchy, " it is the easiest thing imaginable." " I thought that dying had been more difficult," said Louis XIV. "I did not suppose it was so sweet to die," said Francis Saurez, the Spanish theologian. An agreeable surprise was the prevailing sentiment with them all. They expected the stream to terminate in the dash of the torrent, and they found it was losing itself in the

gentlest current. The whole of the faculties seem sometimes concentrated on the placid enjoyment. The day Arthur Murphy died, he kept repeating from Pope :

" Taught half by reason, half by mere decay,
To welcome death, and calmly pass away."

'Nor does the calm partake of the sensitiveness of sickness. There was a swell in the sea the day Collingwood breathed his last upon the element which had been the scene of his glory. Captain Thomas expressed a fear that he was disturbed by the tossing of the ship. " No, Thomas," he replied, " I am now in a state in which nothing in this world can disturb me more. I am dying ; and am sure it must be consolatory to you, and all who love me, to see how comfortably I am coming to my end." '

MARRIAGE FORTUNES.

Under the 15th March 1735, the *Gentleman's Magazine* records—'John Parry, Esq., of Carmarthenshire, (married) to a daughter of Walter Lloyd, Esq., member for that county ; a fortune of £8,000.' It seems to us indecorous thus to trumpet forth a little domestic particular, of no importance to any but the persons concerned ; but it was a regular custom in the reign of George II., and even considerably later. There is scarcely a single number of the magazine here quoted which does not include several such announcements, sometimes accompanied by other curious particulars. For example, in 1731, we have—' Married, the Rev. Mr Roger Waina, of York, about twenty-six years of age, to a Lincolnshire lady, upwards of eighty, with whom he is to have £8,000 in money, £300 per annum, and a coach-and-four during life only.' What would now be matter of gossip in the locality of the marriage was then deemed proper information for the whole community. Thus, in March 1735, the *Gentleman's Magazine* gives this *annonce*—' The Earl of Antrim, of Ireland, to Miss Betty Pennefeather, a celebrated beauty and toast of that kingdom.' It is to be feared that Miss Betty Pennefeather was without fortune ; otherwise it would have been sure to be stated, or at least alluded to.

Towards the end of the century, such announcements were given with less glaring precision. Thus in the *Gazette* of January 5, 1789, we find—' Sunday se'nnight, at St Aulkman's Church, Shrewsbury, A. Holbeche, Esq., of Slowley Hill, near Coleshill, in this county, to Miss Ashby, of Shrewsbury, a very agreeable lady, *with a good fortune.*' On the 2nd of January 1792—' Yesterday, at St Martin's Church, William Lucas, Esq., of Holywell, in Northamptonshire, to Miss Legge, only daughter of the late Mr Francis Legge, builder, of this town ; an agreeable young lady, *with a handsome fortune.*' And on the 29th of October 1798—' A few days ago, at St Martin's Church, in this town, Mr William Barnsley, of the Soho, to Miss Sarah Jorden, of Birmingham Heath ; an agreeable young lady, *with a genteel fortune.*' In other cases, where possibly the bride was penniless, her personal qualifications alone were mentioned ; as this, in April 1783—[' MARRIED] on Saturday last, Mr George Donisthorpe, to the *agreeable* Mrs Mary Bowker, both of this town.'

One of the latest notices of the kind occurs in *Aris's Birmingham Gazette,* of July 14, 1800, being that of the Right Hon. Mr Canning, Under Secretary of State, to Miss Scott, sister to the Marchioness of Titchfield, ' *with £100,000 fortune.*'

MARCH 16.

St Julian, of Cilicia, martyr, about 303. St Finian, surnamed Lohbar (or the Leper), of Ireland, 8th century.

Born.—René de Bossu, classical scholar, 1631, *Paris ;* Jacques Boileau, French theologian, 1635 ; Caroline Lucretia Herschel, astronomer, 1750, *Hanover ;* Madame Campan, historical writer, 1752.

Died.—Tiberius Claudius Nero, A.D. 37, *Misenum ;* the Emperor Valentinian III., assassinated 455 ; Alexander III. of Scotland, 1286 ; Lord Berners, translator of Froissart, 1532, *Calais ;* Richard Burbage, original performer in Shakspeare's plays, 1618-19, *Shoreditch ;* Johann Severin Vater, German linguist and theologian, 1826, *Halle ;* Gottfried Nees von Esenbach, botanist, 1858 ; M. Camille Jullien, musician, 1860.

RICHARD BURBAGE.

Everything connected with Shakspeare and his works possesses a powerful interest to cultivated Englishmen. So little, indeed, is known of our great dramatist, that we are in some instances, perhaps, too ready to make the most of the simplest trifles pertaining to his meagre history. But Richard Burbage, the actor, who first personated Shakspeare's leading characters, and whose eminence in his art may have suggested many of the noble mind creations which now delight us, merits a niche in the temple of Shakspearean history, second only in rank to that of the great master of nature himself. Burbage, the son of a player, was born about 1564. His name stands next to that of Shakspeare in the licences for acting, granted to the company at the Globe Theatre, by James I., in 1603. Little more can be learned regarding his career, than what is stated in the many funeral elegies written on his death. One of these, of which an incorrect copy was first printed in the *Gentleman's Magazine,* 1825, thus enumerates the principal characters he performed :

' He's gone, and with him what a world are dead,
  Friends, every one, and what a blank instead !
Take him for all in all, he was a man
Not to be matched, and no age ever can.
No more young Hamlet, though but scant of breath,
Shall cry, "Revenge !" for his dear father's death.
Poor Romeo never more shall tears beget
For Juliet's love and cruel Capulet :
Harry shall not be seen as king or prince,
They died with thee, dear Dick (and not long
    since),
Not to revive again, Jeronimo
Shall cease to mourn his son Horatio :
They cannot call thee from thy naked bed
By horrid outcry ; and Antonio's dead.
Edward shall lack a representative ;
And Crookback, as befits, shall cease to live.
Tyrant Macbeth, with unwashed bloody hand,
We vainly now may hope to understand.
Brutus and Marcius henceforth must be dumb,
For ne'er thy like upon the stage shall come,
To charm the faculties of ears and eyes,
Unless we could command the dead to rise.
Vindex is gone, and what a loss was he !
Frankford, Brachiano, and Malvole.
Heart-broken Philaster, and Amintas too,
Are lost for ever ; with the red-haired Jew,
380

Which sought the bankrupt merchant's pound of
    flesh,
By woman-lawyer caught in his own mesh.
What a wide world was in that little space,
Thyself a world—the Globe thy fittest place !
Thy stature small, but every thought and mood
Might throughly from thy face be understood ;
And his whole action he could change with ease
From ancient Lear to youthful Pericles.
But let me not forget one chiefest part,
Wherein, beyond the rest, he moved the heart ;
The grieved Moor, made jealous by a slave,
Who sent his wife to fill a timeless grave,
He slew himself upon the bloody bed.
All these, and many more, are with him dead.'

It must be cited as no mean evidence of Burbage's merit as an actor, that the fame of his abilities held a prominent place in theatrical tradition, down to the days of Charles the Second, when Flecknoe wrote a poem in his praise, inscribed to Charles Hart, the great performer after the Restoration.

Burbage was performing at the Globe Theatre on the 29th of June 1613, when that classic edifice was burned down, very shortly after Shakspeare had given up the stage, and retired to his native town. And it is, in all probability, owing to this irremediable disaster,

THE GLOBE THEATRE.

that not one line of a drama by Shakspeare, in the handwriting of the period, has been preserved to us. The play in performance, when the fire broke out, was called *All This is True*—supposed, with good reason, to be a revival of *King Henry the Eighth,* under a new name. This we learn from a contemporary ballad, *On the Pitiful Burning of the Globe Play-house,* in which Burbage is thus mentioned :

' Out ran the knights, out ran the lords,
    And there was great ado,
Some lost their hats, some lost their swords,
    Then out ran Burbage too ;
The reprobates, though drunk on Monday,
Prayed for the fool, and Henry Condy.
Oh ! sorrow, pitiful sorrow, and yet
    All This is True.'

Elegiac effusions poured forth like a torrent on the death of Burbage. The poets had been under heavy obligations to the great actor, and felt his loss severely. By one of those written by Middleton, the dramatist, the tradition which represents Burbage to have been a successful painter in oil, as well as an actor, is corroborated:

ON THE DEATH OF THAT GREAT MASTER IN HIS ART AND QUALITY, PAINTING AND PLAYING, R. BURBAGE.

'Astronomers and star-gazers this year,
　Write but of four eclipses—five appear:
Death interposing Burbage, and their staying,
Hath made a visible eclipse of playing.'

The lines remind one of Dr Johnson's saying, that the death of Garrick had eclipsed the gaiety of nations. The word 'staying,' at the end of the third line, refers to the players being then inhibited from acting, on account of the death of Anne of Denmark, Queen of James the First; who died at Hampton Court, just a fortnight before Burbage.

The abilities and industry of Burbage earned their due reward. He left landed estate at his death producing £300 per annum; equivalent to about four times the amount at the present day.

He was buried in the church of St Leonard's, Shoreditch, and the only inscription put over his grave were the simple and expressive words,

'EXIT BURBAGE.'

M. JULLIEN.

M. Jullien is likely to be under-estimated by those who remember only his peculiarities. His name is so closely associated with Promenade Concerts, that the one is almost certain to suggest the other; and his appearance at those concerts was so remarkable, so unusually conspicuous, that many persons remember his vanity rather than his ability. In dress and manner he always seemed to say, 'I am the great Jullien;' and it is not surprising that he should, as a consequence, earn a little of that contempt which is awarded to vain persons. But the estimate ought not to stop here. Jullien had really a feeling for good music. Although not the first to introduce high-class orchestral music to the English public at a cheap price, he certainly was the first who succeeded in making such a course profitable night after night for two or three months together. His promenade concerts were repeated for many successive years, and so well were they attended, that the locomotion implied by the word 'promenade' became almost an impossibility. Of the quadrilles and mazurkas, the waltzes and polkas, played on those occasions, high-class musicians thought nothing; but when Jullien, with a band of very admirable performers, played some of the finest instrumental works due to the genius of Beethoven, Mozart, Mendelssohn, and Haydn, such as the 'Choral' and 'Pastoral Symphonies,' the 'Symphony Eroica,' the 'Jupiter Symphony,' the 'Italian' and 'Scotch Symphonies,' and the like, persons of taste crowded eagerly to hear them. He knew his players well, and they knew him; each could trust the other, and the consequence was that the symphonies, concertos, and overtures were always admirably performed. He found the means of making his shilling concerts pay, even when hiring the services of an entire opera or philharmonic band; and by his tact in doing this, he was enabled year after year to present some of the highest kind of music to his hearers. The rapt attention with which the masterpieces were listened to was always remarkable; the noisy quadrilles were noisily applauded, but Jullien shewed that he could appreciate music of a higher class, and so did his auditors. His life was a remarkable one, humble at the beginning, showy in the meridian, melancholy at the close. Born in 1810, he was in early life a sailor-boy, and served as such at the battle of Navarino. About 1835 his musical taste lifted him to the position of manager of one of the public gardens of Paris. His success in this post induced him to visit London, where his Promenade Concerts were equally well received. In 1851 his troubles began, owing to unsuccessful speculations at the Surrey Gardens and Covent Garden Theatre. Barely had he recovered from these when his mind became affected, and his death, in 1860, took place in a lunatic asylum at Paris.

PRINCE HOHENLOHE'S MIRACULOUS CURES.

On the 16th of March 1823, Prince Hohenlohe wrote a letter which, connected with subsequent events, produced a great sensation among that class of religious persons who believe that the power of working miracles still exists. Three or four years before that date, Miss O'Connor, a nun in the convent of New Hall, near Chelmsford, began to be affected with swellings in one hand and arm. They became gradually worse, and the case assumed an aggravated form. A surgeon of Chelmsford, after an unsuccessful application of the usual modes of cure, proposed to send for Dr Carpue, an eminent London practitioner. He also failed; and so did Dr Badeley, the physician of the convent. At length, after more than three years of suffering, the poor nun tried spiritual means. The Superioress or Lady Abbess, having heard of certain extraordinary powers alleged to be possessed by Prince Hohenlohe, wrote to him, soliciting his prayers and advice in reference to Miss O'Connor. In his reply, dated as above, the Prince directed that on the 3d of May (a high festival in the Roman Catholic Church), at eight o'clock in the morning, the sufferer should make confession, partake of the Sacrament, and offer up fervent prayers; and stating that, on the same day and hour, he also would pray for her. At the appointed time, Miss O'Connor did as had been directed; and, according to the account given, her pains immediately left her, and she gradually recovered. The facts were attested by Dr Badeley; and the authorities of the convent mentioned that he was a Protestant, as if to disarm suspicion concerning the honesty of his testimony.

This Prince Hohenlohe was a young religious enthusiast. There is no just ground to believe that he was an impostor. Like Joanna Southcote, he sincerely credited his own possession of some kind of miraculous power. He belonged to a branch of an ancient sovereign family in Bavaria. Having become an ecclesiastic, he was very fervent in his devotions. In 1821, when about twenty-nine years of age, his fame as a miraculous curer of diseases began to spread abroad. The police were ordered to watch the matter; for there were hundreds of believers in him at Bamberg; and even princesses came to solicit his prayers for their restoration to health and beauty. The police required that his proceedings should be open and public, to shew that there was no collusion; this he resisted, as being contrary to the sacred character of such devotional exercises. They therefore forbade him to continue the practice; and he at once retired into Austria, where the Government was likely to be more indulgent.

His fame spread to England, and on the 3d of January 1822, there appeared an advertisement so remarkable that we will give it in full: —'To Germans, Foreign Merchants, and Others. —Prince Alexander of Hohenlohe.—Whereas several public journals, both foreign and domestic, have announced most extraordinary cures to have been performed by Prince Alexander of Hohenlohe: This is to entreat that any one who can give unerring information concerning him, where he now is, or of his intended route, will immediately do so; and they will thereby confer on a female, labouring under what is considered an incurable malady, an obligation which no words can describe. Should a gentleman give the information, his own feelings would sufficiently recompense him; but if a person in indigent circumstances, ten guineas will with pleasure be given, provided the correctness of his information can be ascertained.—Address to A. B., at Mrs Hedge's, Laundress, 9, Mount Row, Davies Street, Berkeley Square.' There is a touching earnestness about this, which tells of one yearning to fly to any available succour as a relief from suffering: whether it was obtained, we do not know.

In France, twelve witnesses deposed to a fact which was alleged to have occurred in the Convent of St Benoit, at Toulouse. One of the nuns, named Adelaide Veysre, through an injury in the leg, had her foot twisted nearly round; and for six months she endured great suffering. During a visit which the Cardinal Bishop of Toulouse paid to her, to administer spiritual consolation, she begged him to apply to Prince Hohenlohe. He did so, and penned a letter dated May 22, 1822. The Prince, in reply, directed that on the 25th of July, the feast of St James (patron of monks), solemn prayer should be offered up for her recovery. The Bishop performed mass in the invalid's chamber on the appointed day; and, it is asserted, that when the Holy Wafer was raised, the foot resumed its proper position, the first stage in a complete recovery.

In 1823, Dr Murray, Roman Catholic Archbishop of Dublin, avowed his belief in the following narrative:—Miss Mary Stuart, a nun in the Ranelagh Convent at Dublin, who had been afflicted with a nervous malady for four years, having heard that the 1st of August was a day on which Prince Hohenlohe advised all sufferers to pray solemnly for relief, begged that everything should be done to give effect to the ceremony. Two priests and four nuns joined her in mass, and before the day was ended, her reco-

382

very had commenced. The facts were sworn to before a Dublin magistrate. The Rev. Robert Daly afterwards wrote to Dr Cheyne, an eminent physician who had previously attended Miss Stuart, asking whether in his opinion there was any miraculous interposition, or whether he could account for the cure by natural causes. The physician, in a courteous but cautious reply, simply stated that he found it quite easy to explain the phenomenon according to principles known in every-day practice. Dr Cheyne seems to have considered the ailments of such persons as in a great measure dependent on nervous exhaustion and depression of mind, and the convalescence as arising chiefly from mental elevation and excitement.

There is no necessity for suspecting wilful distortion of truth in these recitals. All, or nearly all the Prince's patients were young females of great nervous susceptibility; and they as well as he were doubtless sincere in believing that the cures were miraculous. Modern medical science regards such facts as real, but to be accounted for on simply natural principles.

MARCH 17.

St Joseph of Arimathæa, the patron of Glastonbury. Many martyrs of Alexandria, about 392. St Patrick, apostle of Ireland, 464 or 493. St Gertrude, virgin, abbess in Brabant, 659.

Legendary History of St Patrick.

Almost as many countries arrogate the honour of having been the natal soil of St Patrick, as made a similar claim with respect to Homer. Scotland, England, France, and Wales, each furnish their respective pretensions; but, whatever doubts may obscure his birthplace, all agree in stating that, as his name implies, he was of a patrician family. He was born about the year 372, and when only sixteen years of age, was carried off by pirates, who sold him into slavery in Ireland; where his master employed him as a swineherd on the well-known mountain of Sleamish, in the county of Antrim. Here he passed seven years, during which time he acquired a knowledge of the Irish language, and made himself acquainted with the manners, habits, and customs of the people. Escaping from captivity, and, after many adventures, reaching the Continent, he was successively ordained deacon, priest, and bishop; and then once more, with the authority of Pope Celestine, he returned to Ireland to preach the Gospel to its then heathen inhabitants.

The principal enemies that St Patrick found to the introduction of Christianity into Ireland, were the Druidical priests of the more ancient faith, who, as might naturally be supposed, were exceedingly adverse to any innovation. These Druids, being great magicians, would have been formidable antagonists to any one of less miraculous and saintly powers than Patrick. Their obstinate antagonism was so great, that, in spite of his benevolent disposition, he was compelled to curse their fertile lands, so that they became dreary bogs; to curse their rivers, so that they produced no fish; to curse their very kettles, so that with no amount of fire and patience could they ever be made to boil; and, as a last resort, to curse the Druids themselves, so that the earth opened and swallowed them up.

A popular legend relates that the saint and his followers found themselves, one cold morning, on a mountain, without a fire to cook their breakfast, or warm their frozen limbs. Unheeding their complaints, Patrick desired them to collect a pile of ice and snow-balls; which having been done, he breathed upon it, and it instantaneously became a pleasant fire—a fire that long after served to point a poet's conceit in these lines:

> ' Saint Patrick, as in legends told,
> The morning being very cold,
> In order to assuage the weather,
> Collected bits of ice together;
> Then gently breathed upon the pyre,
> When every fragment blazed on fire.
> Oh! if the saint had been so kind,
> As to have left the gift behind
> To such a lovelorn wretch as me,
> Who daily struggles to be free;
> I'd be content—content with part,
> I'd only ask to thaw the heart,
> The frozen heart, of Polly Roe.'

The greatest of St Patrick's miracles was that of driving the venomous reptiles out of Ireland, and rendering the Irish soil, for ever after, so obnoxious to the serpent race, that they instantaneously die on touching it. Colgan seriously relates that St Patrick accomplished this feat by beating a drum, which he struck with such fervour that he knocked a hole in it, thereby endangering the success of the miracle. But an angel appearing mended the drum; and the patched instrument was long exhibited as a holy relic. In 1831, Mr James Cleland, an Irish gentleman, being curious to ascertain whether the climate or soil of Ireland was naturally destructive to the serpent tribe, purchased half-a-dozen of the common harmless English snake (*natrix torquata*), in Covent Garden market in London. Bringing them to Ireland, he turned them out in his garden at Rath-gael, in the county of Down; and in a week afterwards, one of them was killed at Milecross, about three miles distant. The persons into whose hands this strange monster fell, had not the slightest suspicion that it was a snake, but, considering it a curious kind of eel, they took it to Dr J. L. Drummond, a celebrated Irish naturalist, who at once pronounced the animal to be a reptile and not a fish. The idea of a 'rale living sarpint' having been killed within a short distance of the very burial-place of St Patrick, caused an extraordinary sensation of alarm among the country people. The most absurd rumours were freely circulated, and credited. One far-seeing clergyman preached a sermon, in which he cited this unfortunate snake as a token of the immediate commencement of the millennium; while another saw in it a type of the approach of the cholera morbus. Old prophecies were raked up, and all parties and sects, for once, united in believing that the snake foreshadowed 'the beginning of the end,' though they very widely differed as to what that end was to

be. Some more practically minded persons, however, subscribed a considerable sum of money, which they offered in rewards for the destruction of any other snakes that might be found in the district. And three more of the snakes were not long afterwards killed, within a few miles of the garden where they were liberated. The remaining two snakes were never very clearly accounted for; but no doubt they also fell victims to the reward. The writer, who resided in that part of the country at the time, well remembers the wild rumours, among the more illiterate classes, on the appearance of those snakes; and the bitter feelings of angry indignation expressed by educated persons against the—very fortunately then unknown—person who had dared to bring them to Ireland.

A more natural story than the extirpation of the serpents, has afforded material for the pencil of the painter, as well as the pen of the poet. When baptizing an Irish chieftain, the venerable saint leaned heavily on his crozier, the steel-spiked point of which he had unwittingly placed on the great toe of the converted heathen. The pious chief, in his ignorance of Christian rites, believing this to be an essential part of the ceremony, bore the pain without flinching or murmur; though the blood flowed so freely from the wound, that the Irish named the place *Struth-fhuil* (stream of blood), now pronounced Struill, the name of a well-known place near Downpatrick. And here we are reminded of a very remarkable fact in connection with geographical appellations, that the footsteps of St Patrick can be traced, almost from his cradle to his grave, by the names of places called after him. Thus, assuming his Scottish origin, he was born at Kilpatrick (the cell or church of Patrick), in Dumbartonshire. He resided for some time at Dalpatrick (the district or division of Patrick), in Lanarkshire; and visited Crag-phadrig (the rock of Patrick), near Inverness. He founded two churches, Kirkpatrick at Irongray, in Kircudbright; and Kirkpatrick at Fleming, in Dumfries; and ultimately sailed from Portpatrick, leaving behind him such an odour of sanctity, that among the most distinguished families of the Scottish aristocracy, Patrick has been a favourite name down to the present day. Arriving in England, he preached in Patterdale (Patrick's dale), in Westmoreland; and founded the church of Kirkpatrick, in Durham. Visiting Wales, he walked over Sarn-badrig (Patrick's causeway), which, now covered by the sea, forms a dangerous shoal in Carnarvon Bay; and departing for the Continent, sailed from Llan-badrig (the church of Patrick), in the island of Anglesea. Undertaking his mission to convert the Irish, he first landed at Innis-patrick (the island of Patrick), and next at Holmpatrick, on the opposite shore of the mainland, in the county of Dublin. Sailing northwards, he touched at the Isle of Man, sometimes since, also, called Innis-patrick, where he founded another church of Kirkpatrick, near the town of Peel. Again landing on the coast of Ireland, in the county of Down, he converted and baptized the chieftain Dichu, on his own threshing-floor. The name of the parish of Saul, derived from Sabbal-patrick (the barn of Patrick), perpetuates the event. He then proceeded to Temple-patrick, in Antrim, and from thence to a lofty mountain in Mayo, ever since called Croagh-patrick.

He founded an abbey in East Meath, called Domnach-Padraig (the house of Patrick), and built a church in Dublin on the spot where St Patrick's Cathedral now stands. In an island of Lough Derg, in the county of Donegal, there is St Patrick's Purgatory; in Leinster, St Patrick's Wood; at Cashel, St Patrick's Rock; the St Patrick's Wells, at which the holy man is said to have quenched his thirst, may be counted by dozens. He is commonly stated to have died at Saul on the 17th of March 493, in the one hundred and twenty-first year of his age.

Poteen, a favourite beverage in Ireland, is also said to have derived its name from St Patrick; he, according to legend, being the first who instructed the Irish in the art of distillation. This, however, is, to say the least, doubtful; the most authentic historians representing the saint as a very strict promoter of temperance, if not exactly a teetotaller. We read that in 445 he commanded his disciples to abstain from drink in the day-time, until the bell rang for vespers in the evening. One Colman, though busily engaged in the severe labours of the field, exhausted with heat, fatigue, and intolerable thirst, obeyed so literally the injunction of his revered preceptor, that he refrained from indulging himself with one drop of water during a long sultry harvest day. But human endurance has its limits: when the vesper bell at last rang for evensong, Colman dropped down dead—a martyr to thirst. Irishmen can well appreciate such a martyrdom; and the name of Colman, to this day, is frequently cited, with the added epithet of *Stadhach*—the Thirsty.

As the birthplace of St Patrick has been disputed, so has that of his burial. But the general evidence indicates that he was buried at Downpatrick, and that the remains of St Columb and St Bridget were laid beside him; according to the old monkish Leonine distich:

' In Burgo Duno, tumulo tumulantur in uno,
    Brigida, Patricius, atque Columba pius.'

Which may be thus rendered:—

' On the hill of Down, buried in one tomb,
    Were Bridget and Patricius, with Columba the pious.'

One of the strangest recollections of a strange childhood is the writer having been taken, by a servant, unknown to his parents, to see a silver case, containing, as was said, the jaw-bone of St Patrick. The writer was very young at the time, but remembers seeing one much younger, a baby, on the same occasion, and has an indistinct idea that the jaw-bone was considered to have had a very salutary effect on the baby's safe introduction into the world. This jaw-bone, and the silver shrine enclosing it, has been, for many years, in the possession of a family in humble life near Belfast. In the memory of persons living, it contained five teeth, but now retains only one—three having been given to members of the family, when emigrating to America; and the fourth was deposited under the altar of the Roman Catholic Chapel of Derriaghy, when re-

384

built some years ago. The curiously embossed case has a very antique appearance, and is said to be of an immense age; but it is, though certainly old, not so very old as reported, for it carries the ' Hall-mark ' plainly impressed upon it. This remarkable relic has long been used for a kind of extra-judicial trial, similar to the Saxon *corsnet*, a test of guilt or innocence of very great antiquity; accused or suspected persons freeing themselves from the suspicion of crime, by placing the right hand on the reliquary, and declaring their innocence, in a certain form of words, supposed to be an asseveration of the greatest solemnity, and liable to instantaneous, supernatural, and frightful punishment, if falsely spoken, even by *suppressio veri*, or *suggestio falsi*. It was also supposed to assist women in labour, relieve epileptic fits, counteract the diabolical machinations of witches and fairies, and avert the baleful influence of the evil eye. We have been informed, however, that of late years it has rarely been applied to such uses, though it is still considered a most welcome visitor to a household, where an immediate addition to the family is expected.

The shamrock, the well-known trefoil plant, and Irish national emblem, is almost universally worn in the hat over all Ireland, on St Patrick's day. The popular notion is, that when St Patrick was preaching the doctrine of the Trinity to the pagan Irish, he used this plant, bearing three leaves upon one stem, as a symbol or illustration of the great mystery. To suppose, as some absurdly hold, that he used it as an argument, would be derogatory to the saint's high reputation for orthodoxy and good sense; but it is certainly a curious coincidence, if nothing more, that the trefoil in Arabic is called *shamrakh*, and was held sacred in Iran as emblematical of the Persian Triads. Pliny, too, in his *Natural History*, says that serpents are never seen upon trefoil, and it prevails against the stings of snakes and scorpions. This, considering St Patrick's connexion with snakes, is really remarkable, and we may reasonably imagine that, previous to his arrival, the Irish had ascribed mystical virtues to the trefoil or shamrock, and on hearing of the Trinity for the first time, they fancied some peculiar fitness in their already sacred plant to shadow forth the newly revealed and mysterious doctrine. And we may conclude, in the words of the poet, long may the shamrock,

' The plant that blooms for ever,
    With the rose combined,
    And the thistle twined,
Defy the strength of foes to sever.
    Firm be the triple league they form,
    Despite all change of weather ;
In sunshine, darkness, calm, or storm,
    Still may they fondly grow together.'

W. P.

In the Galtee or Gaultie Mountains, situated between the counties of Cork and Tipperary, there are seven lakes, in one of which, called Lough Dilveen, it is said Saint Patrick, when banishing the snakes and toads from Ireland, chained a monster serpent, telling him to remain there till Monday.

The serpent every Monday morning calls out in Irish, 'It is a long Monday, Patrick.'

That St Patrick chained the serpent in Lough Dilveen, and that the serpent calls out to him every Monday morning, is firmly believed by the lower orders who live in the neighbourhood of the Lough.

Noah and his Wife.

The early English calendars pretend that on the 17th of March Noah entered the ark (*introitus Noæ in arcam*), and they add, under the 29th of April, *egressus Noæ de arca*, Here Noah went out of the ark. It would not be easy to determine why this particular day was chosen as that of Noah's entrance into the ark; but the poetic and romantic spirit of the middle ages habitually seized upon certain persons and facts in biblical history, and gave them a character and clothed them in incidents which are very different from those they present in the Scriptures. In this respect mediæval legend took greater liberties with Noah's wife than with Noah himself. This lady was, for some reason or other, adopted as the type of the mediæval shrew; and in the religious plays, or mysteries, the quarrels between Noah and his helpmate were the subject of much mirth to the spectators. In the play of Noah in the Towneley mysteries (one of the earliest of these collections), when Noah carries to his dame the news of the imminence of the flood which had just been announced to him by the Creator, she is introduced abusing him for his credulity, sneering at him as an habitual bearer of bad news, and complaining of the ill life she leads with him. He tells her to 'hold her tongue,' but she only becomes more abusive, till he is provoked to strike her; she returns the blow, and they fall a-fighting, until Noah has had enough, and runs away to his work. When the ark is finished another quarrel arises, for Noah's wife laughs at his ark, and declares that she will not go into it. In reply to the first invitation, she says scornfully (we modernize the orthography):

'I was never barred ere, as ever might I the [*prosper*],
    In such an oyster as this!
In faith, I cannot find
Which is before, which is behind;
But shall we here be pinned,
    Noah, as have thou bliss?'

The water is now rising, and she is pressed still more urgently to go into the ark, on which she returns for answer:

'Sir, for Jack nor for Gill will I turn my face,
Till I have on this hill spun a space
    On my rock;
Well were he might get me!
Now will I down set me;
Yet rede [*counsel*] I no man let [*hinder*] me
    For dread of a knock.'

The danger becomes now so imminent, that Noah's wife jumps into the ark of her own will, where she immediately picks up another quarrel with her husband, and they fight again, but this time Noah is conqueror, and his partner complains of being beaten 'blue,' while their three sons lament over the family discords.

25

In the similar play in the Chester mysteries, the wife assists in tolerably good temper during the building of the ark, but when it is finished she refuses to go into it, and behaves in a manner which leads Noah to exclaim:

'Lorde, that wemen be crabbed aye!
    And non are meke, I dare well saye.'

Noah's wife becomes so far reconciled that she assists in carrying into the ark the various couples of beasts and birds; but when this labour is achieved, she refuses to go in herself unless she be allowed to take her gossips with her, telling Noah, that unless he agree to her terms, he may row whither he likes, and look out for another wife. Then follows a scene at the tavern, where the good dame and her gossips join in the following chant:

'The good gossippes songe.
The flude comes flittinge in full faste,
On everye syde that spreades full farre;
For feare of drowninge I am agaste;
Good gossippes, lett us drawe nere,
And lett us drinke or [*ere*] we departe,
For ofte tymes we have done soe.
For att a draughte thou drinkes a quarte,
And soe will I doe or I goe.
Heare is a pottill full of malmsine, good and
    stronge;
Itt will rejoice bouth hearte and tonge;
Though Noye thinke us never so longe,
Heare we will drinke alike.'

At this moment, her three sons arrive and drag her away to the ark, which she has no sooner entered than she falls a-beating her husband.

These will serve as curious examples of the corrupt and not very reverent form in which the events of Scripture history were during the middle ages communicated to the vulgar. The quarrels of Noah and his wife formed so popular a story that they became proverbial. The readers of Chaucer will remember how, in the Canterbury Tales, Nicholas, when examining the carpenter on his knowledge of Noah's flood, asks him—

'"Hast thou not herd," quod Nicholas, "also
The sorwe of Noe, with his felawship,
Or that he mighte get his wif to ship?
Him had be lever, I dare wel undertake,
At thilke time, than all his wethers blake,
That she had had a ship hireself alone."'

Born.—Francesco Albano, painter, 1578, *Bologna*; David Ancillon, learned French Protestant clergyman, 1617, *Metz*; Samuel Patterson, first book auctioneer, 1728, *London*; Carsten Niebuhr, celebrated traveller, 1733, *West Ludingworth*; the Rev. Dr Thomas Chalmers, 1780, *Anstruther*; Ebenezer Elliott, 'Corn Law Rhymer,' 1781, *Masborough, York.*

Died.—Cneius Pompeius, Labienus, and Attius Varus, B.C. 45, killed, *Munda*; Marcus Aurelius Antoninus, A.D. 180, *Sirmium*; William Earl of Pembroke, 1570, *London*; Thomas Randolph, poet, 1634, *Blatherwick*; Philip Massinger, dramatic poet, 1640; Bishop Gilbert Burnet, historian, 1715, *Clerkenwell*; Jean Baptiste Rousseau, eminent French lyric poet, 1741, *Brussels*; George Earl of Macclesfield, astronomer, P.R.S., 1764; Daniel Bernouilli, mathematician, 1782, *Basle*; David Dale, philanthropist, 1806; Sir J. E. Smith, first president of the Linnean Society, 1828, *Norwich*; J. J Grandier, the eminent designer of book illustrations, 1847; Mrs Anna Jameson, writer on art. 1860.

DAVID DALE.

Died, on the 17th March 1806, David Dale, one of the fathers of the cotton manufacture in Scotland. He was the model of a self-raised, upright, successful man of business. Sprung from humble parents at Stewarton in Ayrshire, he early entered on a commercial career at Glasgow, and soon began to grapple with great undertakings. In company with Sir Richard Arkwright, he commenced the celebrated New Lanark Cotton Mills in 1783, and in the course of a few years he had become a rich man. Mr Dale in this career had great difficulties to overcome, particularly in the prejudices and narrow-sightedness of the surrounding country gentlefolk. He overcame them all. He took his full share of public duty as a magistrate. The poor recognised him as the most princely of philanthropists. He was an active lay preacher in a little body of Independents to which he belonged, and whose small, poor, and scattered congregations he half supported. Though unostentatious to a remarkable degree, it was impossible to conceal that David Dale was one of those rare mortals who hold all wealth as a trust for a general working of good in the world, and who cannot truly enjoy anything in which others are not participators. Keeping in view certain prejudices entertained regarding the moral effects of the factory system, it is curious to learn what were the motives of the philanthropic Dale in promoting cotton mills. His great object was to furnish a profitable employment for the poor, and train to habits of industry those whom he saw ruined by a semi-idleness. He aimed at correcting evils already existing, evils broad and palpable; and it never occurred to him to imagine that good, well-paid work would sooner or later harm any body.

By a curious chance, Robert Owen married the eldest daughter of Mr Dale, and became his successor in the management of the New Lanark Mills. Both were zealous in promoting education among their people; but there was an infinite difference between the views of the two men as to education. Dale was content with little more than impressing the old evangelical faith of western Scotland upon the youth under his charge. Owen contemplated modes of moralising the people such as no Scotchman had ever dreamt of. The father-in-law was often put upon the defensive by the son-in-law, regarding his simple unmistrusting faith, and was obliged to admit that there was force in what Owen said, assuming the truth of his view of human nature. But he would generally end the discussion by remarking with his affectionate smile, 'Thou needest to be very right, for thou art very positive.'

David Dale was a remarkably obese man, insomuch it was said he had not for years seen his shoe-buckles as he walked. He one day spoke of having fallen all his length on the ice; to which his friend replied that he had much reason to be thankful that it was not all his breadth. The name of the worthy philanthropist has been commemorated in the names of two of his grandchildren—Robert Dale Owen (died in 1877), ambassador for the United States to the King-

dom of the Two Sicilies, and David Dale Owen, author of a laborious work on the *Geology of Wisconsin, Iowa, and Minnesota* (1852).

MARCH 18.

St Alexander, Bishop of Jerusalem, martyr, 251. St Cyril, Archbishop of Jerusalem, 336. St Fridian, Bishop of Lucca, 578. St Edward, King of England, and martyr, 978. St Anselm, Bishop of Lucca, 1086.

EDWARD THE KING AND MARTYR.

The great King Edgar had two wives, first Elfleda, and, after her death, Elfrida, an ambitious woman, who had become queen through the murder of her first husband, and who survived her second; and Edgar left a son by each, Edward by Elfleda, and Ethelred by Elfrida. At the time of their father's death, Edward was thirteen, and Ethelred seven years of age; and they were placed by the ambition of Elfrida, and by political events, in a position of rivalry. Edgar's reign had been one continued struggle to establish monarchism, and with it the supremacy of the Church of Rome, in Anglo-Saxon England; and the violence with which this design had been carried out, with the persecution to which the national clergy were subjected, now caused a reaction, so that at Edgar's death the country was divided into two powerful parties, of which the party opposed to the monks was numerically the strongest. The queen joined this party, in the hope of raising her son to the throne, and of ruling England in his name; and the feeling against the Romish usurpation was so great, that, although Edgar had declared his wish that his eldest son should succeed him, and his claim was no doubt just, the crown was only secured to him by the energetic interference of Dunstan. Edward thus became King of England in the year 975.

Edward appears, as far as we can learn, to have been an amiable youth, and to have possessed some of the better qualities of his father; but his reign and life were destined to be cut short before he reached an age to display them. He had sought to conciliate the love of his stepmother by lavishing his favour upon her, and he made her a grant of Dorsetshire, but in vain; and she lived, apparently in a sort of sullen state, away from court, with her son Ethelred, at Corfe in that county, plotting, according to some authorities, with what may be called the national party, against Dunstan and the government. The Anglo-Saxons were all passionately attached to the pleasures of the chase, and one day—it was the 18th of March 978—King Edward was hunting in the forest of Dorset, and, knowing that he was in the neighbourhood of Corfe, and either suffering from thirst or led by the desire to see his half-brother Ethelred, for whom he cherished a boyish attachment, he left his followers and rode alone to pay a visit to his mother. Elfrida received him with the warmest demonstrations of affection, and, as he was unwilling to dismount from his horse, she offered him the cup with her own hand. While he was in the act of drinking, one of the queen's attendants, by her command, stabbed him with a dagger. The prince hastily turned his horse, and rode toward the wood, but he soon became faint and fell from his horse, and his foot becoming entangled in the stirrup, he was dragged along till the horse was stopped, and the corpse was carried into the solitary cottage of a poor woman, where it was found next morning, and, according to what appears to be the most trustworthy account, thrown by Elfrida's directions into an adjoining marsh. The young king was, however, subsequently buried at Wareham, and removed in the following year to be interred with royal honours at Shaftesbury. The monastic party, whose interests were identified with Edward's government, and who considered that he had been sacrificed to the hostility of their opponents, looked upon him as a martyr, and made him a saint. The writer of this part of the Anglo-Saxon chronicle, who was probably a contemporary, expresses his feelings in the simple and pathetic words, 'No worse deed than this was done to the Anglo race, since they first came to Britain.'

The story of the assassination of King Edward is sometimes quoted in illustration of a practice which existed among the Anglo-Saxons. Our forefathers were great drinkers, and it was customary with them, in drinking parties, to pass round a large cup, from which each in turn drunk to some of the company. He who thus drank, stood up, and as he lifted the cup with both hands, his body was exposed without any defence to a blow, and the occasion was often seized by an enemy to murder him. To prevent this, the following plan was adopted. When one of the company stood up to drink, he required the companion who sat next to him, or some one of the party, to be his *pledge*, that is, to be responsible for protecting him against anybody who should attempt to take advantage of his defenceless position; and this companion, if he consented, stood up also, and raised his drawn sword in his hand to defend him while drinking. This practice, in an altered form, continued long after the condition of society had ceased to require it, and was the origin of the modern practice of pledging in drinking. At great festivals, in some of our college halls and city companies, the custom is preserved almost in its primitive form in passing round the ceremonial cup—the loving cup, as it is sometimes called. As each person rises and takes the cup in his hand to drink, the man seated next to him rises also, and when the latter takes the cup in his turn, the individual next to him does the same.

Born.—Philip de Lahire, French geometrician, 1640, *Paris*; John Caldwell Calhoun, American statesman, 1782, *South Carolina.*

Died.—Edward, King and Martyr, 978; Pope Honorius III., 1227; Bishop Patrick Forbes, 1635, *Aberdeen*; Dr George Stanhope, eminent divine, 1728, *Lewisham*; Sir Robert Walpole, (Earl of Orford,) prime minister to George I. and II., 1745, *Houghton*; the Rev. Lawrence Sterne, author of *Tristram Shandy*, 1768, *Bond-street*;

John Horne Tooke, political writer, 1812, *Ealing*; Sebastian Pether, painter of moonlight scenery, 1844, *Battersea*; Sir Henry Pottinger, G.C.B., military commander in India, 1856; W. H. Playfair, architect, 1857, *Edinburgh.*

LAWRENCE STERNE.

The world is now fully aware of the moral deficiencies of the author of *Tristram Shandy.* Let us press lightly upon them for the sake of the bright things scattered through his writings —though these, as a whole, are no longer read. The greatest misfortune in the case is that Sterne was a clergyman. Here, however, we may charitably recall that he was one of the many who have been drawn into that profession, rather by connection than their own inclination. If Sterne had not been the great-grandson of an Archbishop of York, with an influential pluralist uncle, who could give him preferment, we should probably have been spared the additional pain of considering his improprieties as made the darker by the complexion of his coat. He spent the best part of his life as a life-enjoying, thoughtless, but not particularly objectionable country pastor, at Sutton in Yorkshire, and he had attained the mature age of forty-seven when the first volumes of his singular novel all at once brought him into the blaze of a London reputation. It was mainly during the remaining eight years of his life that he incurred the blame which now rests with his name. These years were made painful to him by wretched health. His constitution seems to have been utterly worn out. A month after the publication of his *Sentimental Journey*, while it was reaping the first fruits of its rich lease of fame, the poor author expired in solitary and melancholy circumstances, at his lodgings in Old Bond-street. There is something peculiarly sad in the death of a merry man. One thinks of Yorick—'Where be your gibes now? your gambols? your songs? your flashes of merriment, that were wont to set the table in a roar?' We may well apply to Sterne—since he applied them to himself—the mournful words, 'Alas, poor Yorick!' Dr Dibdin found, in the possession of Mr James Atkinson, an eminent medical practitioner at York, a very curious picture, done rather coarsely in oil, representing two figures in the characters of quack doctor and mountebank on a stage, with an indication of populace looking on. An inscription, to which Mr Atkinson appears to have given entire credence, represented the doctor as Mr T. Brydges, and the mountebank as Lawrence Sterne; and the tradition was that each had painted the other. It seems hardly conceivable that a parish priest of Yorkshire in the middle of the eighteenth century should have consented to be enduringly presented under the guise and character of a stage mountebank; but we must remember how much he was at all times the creature and the victim of whim and drollery, and how little control his profession and calling ever exercised over him. Mr Atkinson, an octogenarian, told Dibdin that his father had been acquainted with Sterne, and he had thus acquired many anecdotes of the whims and crotchets of the far-famed sentimental traveller. Amongst other things which Dibdin learned here was the fact that Sterne possessed the talent of an amateur draughtsman, and was | fond of exercising his pencil. In our copy of the picture in question, albeit it is necessarily given

BRYDGES AND STERNE.

on a greatly reduced scale, it will readily be observed that the face of Sterne wears the characteristic comicality which might be expected.

BURNING OF TWO HERETICS.

On Wednesday, the 18th of March 1611-12, one Bartholomew Legat was burnt at Smithfield, for maintaining thirteen heretical (Arian) opinions concerning the divinity of Christ. It was at the instance of the king, himself a keen controversialist, that the bishops, in consistory assembled, tried, and condemned this man. The lawyers doubted if there were any law for burning heretics, remarking that the executions for religion under Elizabeth were 'done *de facto* and not *de jure*.' Chamberlain, however, thought the King would 'adventure to burn Legat with a good conscience.' And adventure he did, as we see, taking self-sufficiency of opinion for conscience, as has been so often done before and since. Nor did he stop there, for on the 11th of April following, 'another miscreant heretic,' named William Wightman, was burnt at Lichfield. We learn that Legat declared his contempt for all ecclesiastical government, and refused all favour. He 'said little, but died obstinately.'

King James had no mean powers as a polemic. He could argue down heretics and papists to the admiration (not wholly insincere) of his courtiers.

It was scarcely fair that he should have had so powerful an ally as the executioner to close the argument. It is startling to observe the frequency of bloodshed in this reign for matters of opinion. As an example—on the Whitsun-eve of the year 1612, four Roman Catholic priests, who had previously been 'twice banished, but would take no warning' (such is the cool phrase of Chamberlain), were hanged at Tyburn. It is remarked, as a fault of some of the officials, that, being very confident at the gallows, they were allowed to 'talk their full' to the assembled crowd, amongst whom were several of the nobility, and others, both ladies and gentlemen, in coaches.

THE OMNIBUS TWO HUNDRED YEARS AGO.

It may appear strange, but the omnibus was known in France two centuries ago. Carriages on hire had already been long established in Paris: coaches, by the hour or by the day, were let out at the sign of St Fiacre; but the hire was too expensive for the middle classes. In 1662, a royal decree of Louis XIV. authorized the establishment of a line of twopence-halfpenny omnibuses, or *carosses à cinq sous*, by a company, with the Duke de Roanès and two marquises at its head, and the gentle Pascal among the shareholders. The decree expressly stated that these coaches, of which there were originally seven, each containing eight places, should run at fixed hours, full or empty, to and from certain extreme quarters of Paris, 'for the benefit of a great number of persons ill provided for, as persons engaged in lawsuits, infirm people, and others, who have not the means to ride in chaise or carriage, which cannot be hired under a pistole, or a couple of crowns a day.'

The public inauguration of the new conveyances took place on the 18th of March 1662, at seven o'clock in the morning, and was a grand and gay affair. Three of the coaches started from the Porte St Antoine, and four from the Luxembourg. Previous to their setting out, two commissaries of the Chatelet, in legal robes, four guards of the grand provost, half a score of city archers, and as many cavalry, drew up in front of the people. The commissaries delivered an address upon the advantages of the twopence-halfpenny carriages, exhorted the riders to observe good order, and then, turning to the coachmen, covered the body of each with a long blue frock, with the arms of the King and the city showily embroidered on the front. With this badge off drove the coachmen; but throughout the day, a provost-guard rode in each carriage, and infantry and cavalry, here and there, proceeded along the requisite lines, to keep them clear.

There are two accounts of the reception of the novelty. Sanval, in his *Antiquities of Paris*, states the carriages to have been pursued with the stones and hisses of the populace, but the truth of this report is doubted; and the account given by Madame Perrier, the sister of the great Pascal, describing the public joy which she witnessed on the appearance of these low-priced conveyances, in a letter written three days after, is better entitled to credit; unless the two accounts may relate to the reception by the people in different parts of the line. For a while all Paris strove to ride in these omnibuses, and some stood impatiently to gaze at those who had succeeded better than themselves. The twopence-halfpenny coach was the event of the day; even the *Grand Monarque* tried a trip in one at St Germains, and the actors of the Marais played the *Intrigue des Carosses à Cinq Sous*, in their joyous theatre. The wealthier classes seem to have taken possession of them for a considerable time; and it is singular that when they ceased to be fashionable, the poorer classes would have nothing to do with them, and so the speculation failed.

The system reappeared in Paris in 1827, with this inscription placed upon the sides of the vehicles: *Enterprise générale des Omnibus*. In the *Monthly Magazine* for 1829, we read: 'The *Omnibus* is a long coach, carrying fifteen or eighteen people, all inside. Of these carriages, there were about half a dozen some months ago, and they have been augmented since; their profits are said to have repaid the outlay within the first year; the proprietors, among whom is Lafitte, the banker, are making a large revenue out of the Parisian sous, and speculation is still alive.'

The next item in the history of the omnibus is of a different cast. In the struggle of the Three Days of July 1830, the accidental upset of an omnibus suggested the employment of the whole class of vehicles for the forming of a barricade. The help thus given was important, and so it came to pass that this new kind of coach had something to do in the banishing of an old dynasty.

The omnibus was readily transplanted to London. Mr Shillibeer, in his evidence before the Board of Health, stated that, on July 4, 1829, he started the first pair of omnibuses in the metropolis, from the Bank of England to the Yorkshire Stingo, New Road. Each of Shillibeer's vehicles carried twenty two passengers inside, but only the driver outside; each omnibus was drawn by three horses abreast, the fare was one shilling for the whole journey, and sixpence for half the distance, and for some time the passengers were provided with periodicals to read on the way. The first *conductors* were two sons of British naval officers, who were succeeded by young men in velveteen liveries. The first omnibuses were called 'Shillibeers,' and the name is common to this day in New York.

The omnibus was adopted in Amsterdam in 1839; and it has since been extended to all parts of the civilized world.

INTRODUCTION OF INOCULATION.

March 18th 1718, Lady Mary Wortley Montagu, at Belgrade, caused her infant son to be inoculated with the virus of small-pox, as a means of warding off the ordinary attack of that disease. As a preliminary to the introduction of the practice into England, the fact was one of importance; and great credit will always be due to this lady for the heroism which guided her on the occasion.

LADY MARY WORTLEY MONTAGU.

At the time when Dr Sydenham published the improved edition of his work on fevers, in 1675, small-pox appears to have been the most widely diffused and the most fatal of all the pestilential diseases, and was also the most frequently epidemic. The heating and sweating plan of treatment prevailed universally. Instead of a free current of air and cooling diet, the patient was kept in a room with closed windows and in a bed with closed curtains. Cordials and other stimulants were given, and the disease assumed a character of malignity which increased the mortality to a frightful extent. The regimen which Dr Sydenham recommended was directly the reverse, and was gradually assented to and adopted by most of the intelligent practitioners.

Inoculation of the small-pox is traditionally reported to have been practised in some mode in China and Hindustan; and Dr Russell, who resided for some years at Aleppo, states, as the result of his inquiries, that it had been in use among the Arabians from ancient times; but he remarks, that no mention is made of it by any of the Arabian medical writers known in Europe. (*Phil. Trans.* lviii. 142.) None of the travellers in Turkey have noticed the practice previous to the eighteenth century. The first accounts are by Pylarini and Timoni, two Italian physicians, who, in the early part of the eighteenth century, sent information of the practice to the English medical professors, by whom, however, no notice was taken of it.*

It was in the course of her residence in Turkey, with her husband Mr Edward Wortley Montagu, the British ambassador there, that Lady Mary made her famous experiment in inoculation. Her own experience of small-pox had led her, as she acknowledged, to observe the Turkish practice of inoculation with peculiar interest. Her only brother, Lord Kingston, when under age, but already a husband and a father, had been carried off by small-pox; and she herself had suffered severely from the disease, which, though it had not left any marks on her face, had destroyed her fine eyelashes, and had given a fierceness of expression to her eyes which impaired their beauty. The hope of obviating much suffering and saving many lives induced her to form the resolution of introducing the practice of inoculation into her native country.

In one of her letters, dated Adrianople, April 1st, 1717, she gives the following account of the observations which she had made on the proceedings of the Turkish female practitioners.

'The small-pox, so general and so fatal amongst us, is entirely harmless by the invention of *ingrafting*, which is the term they give it. There is a set of old women who make it their business to perform the operation every autumn, in the month of September, when the great heat is abated. People send to one another to know if any one has a mind to have the small-pox. They make parties for this purpose, and when they are met (commonly fifteen or sixteen together), the old woman comes with a nut-shell full of the matter of the best sort of small-pox, and asks you what vein you please to have opened. She immediately rips open that you offer to her with a large needle (which gives you no more pain than a common scratch), and puts into the vein as much

* The communications of the two Italian physicians are recorded in the abridged edition of the *Philosophical Transactions*, vol. v. p. 370.

matter as can lie upon the head of her needle, and after that binds up the little wound with a hollow bit of shell, and in this manner opens four or five veins. . . . . . The children or young patients play together all the rest of the day, and are in perfect health till the eighth. Then the fever begins to seize them, and they keep their beds two days, very seldom three. They have very rarely above twenty or thirty on their faces, which never mark, and in eight days' time they are as well as they were before their illness. Where they are wounded there remain running sores during the distemper, which, I don't doubt, is a great relief to it. Every year thousands undergo the operation; and the French ambassador says pleasantly that they take the small-pox here by way of diversion, as they take the waters in other countries. There is no example of any one that has died of it; and you may believe me that I am well satisfied of the safety of this experiment, since I intend to try it upon my dear little son. I am patriot enough to try to bring this useful invention into fashion in England.'

While her husband, for the convenience of attending to his diplomatic duties, resided at Pera, Lady Mary occupied a house at Belgrade, a beautiful village surrounded by woods, about fourteen miles from Constantinople, and there she carried out her intention of having her son inoculated. On Sunday, the 23rd of March 1718, a note addressed to her husband at Pera contained the following passage : 'The boy was ingrafted on Tuesday, and is at this time singing and playing, very impatient for his supper. I pray God my next may give you as good an account of him. I cannot ingraft the girl: her nurse has not had the small-pox.'

Lady Mary Wortley Montagu, after her return from the East, effectively, though gradually and slowly, accomplished her benevolent intention of rendering the malignant disease as comparatively harmless in her own country as she had found it to be in Turkey. It was an arduous, a difficult, and, for some years, a thankless undertaking. She had to encounter the pertinacious opposition of the medical professors, who rose against her almost to a man, predicting the most disastrous consequences; but, supported firmly by the Princess of Wales (afterwards Queen Caroline) she gained many supporters among the nobility and the middle classes. In 1721 she had her own daughter inoculated. Four chief physicians were deputed by the government to watch the performance of the operation, which was quite successful; but the doctors were apparently so desirous that it should not succeed, that she never allowed the child to be alone with them for a single instant, lest it should in some way suffer from their malignant interference. Afterwards four condemned criminals were inoculated, and this test having proved successful, the Princess of Wales had two of her own daughters subjected to the operation with perfect safety. While the young princesses were recovering, a pamphlet was published which denounced the new practice as unlawful, as an audacious act of presumption, and as forbidden in Scripture by the express command : 'Thou shalt not tempt the Lord thy God.' Some of the nobility followed the example of the Princess, and the practice gradually extended among the middle classes. The fees at first were so expensive as to preclude the lower classes from the benefit of the new discovery.

Besides the opposition of the medical professors, the clergy denounced the innovation from their pulpits as an impious attempt to take the issues of life and death out of the hands of Providence. For instance, on the 8th of July 1722, a sermon was preached at St Andrew's, Holborn, in London, by the Rev. Edward Massey, Lecturer of St Alban's, Wood-street, 'against the dangerous and sinful practice of inoculation.' The sermon was published, and the text is Job ii. 7 : ' So went Satan forth from the presence of the Lord, and smote Job with sore boils from the sole of his foot unto his crown.' The preacher says : ' Remembering our text, I shall not scruple to call that a diabolical operation which usurps an authority founded neither in the laws of nature or religion ; which tends, in this case, to anticipate and banish Providence out of the world, and promote the increase of vice and immorality.' The preacher further observes that ' the good of mankind, the seeking whereof is one of the fundamental laws of nature, is, I know, pleaded in defence of the practice ; but I am at a loss to find or understand how that has been or can be promoted hereby ; for if by *good* be meant the preservation of life, it is, in the first place, a consideration whether *life* be a *good or not.*' In addition to denunciations such as these from high places, the common people were taught to regard Lady Mary with abhorrence, and to hoot at her, as an unnatural mother who had risked the lives of her own children.

So annoying was the opposition and the obloquy which Lady Mary had to endure, that she confessed that, during the four or five years which immediately succeeded her return to England, she often felt a disposition to regret having engaged in the patriotic undertaking, and declared that if she had foreseen the vexation and persecution which it brought upon her she would never have attempted it. In fact, these annoyances seem at one time to have produced a depression of spirits little short of morbid ; for in 1725 she wrote to her sister Lady Mar, ' I have such a complication of things both in my head and my heart, that I do not very well know what I do ; and if I cannot settle my brains, your next news of me will be that I am locked up by my relations. In the meantime I lock myself up, and keep my distraction as private as possible.'

It is remarkable that Voltaire should have been the first writer in France to recommend the adoption of inoculation to the inhabitants of that country. In 1727 he directed the attention of the public to the subject. He pointed out to the ladies especially the value of the practice, by informing them that the females of Circassia and Georgia had by this means preserved the beauty for which they have for centuries been distinguished. He stated that they inoculated their children at as early an age as six months ; and observed that most of the 20,000 inhabitants of Paris who died of small-pox in 1720 would probably have been saved if inoculation had been then in use.

Dr Gregory has observed, that the first ten years of the progress of inoculation in England were singularly unfortunate. It fell into bad hands, was tried on the most unsuitable subjects, and was practised in the most injudicious manner. By degrees the regular practitioners began to patronise and adopt it, the opposition of the clergy ceased, and the public became convinced of the fact that the disease in the new form was scarcely ever fatal, while they were aware from experience that when it occurred naturally, one person died out of about every four.

A new era in the progress of inoculation commenced when the Small-pox Hospital was founded by voluntary subscription in 1746, for the extension of the practice among the poor of London. Dr Mead, who had been present when the four criminals were inoculated, wrote a treatise in favour of it in 1748, and the College of Physicians published a strong recommendation of it in 1754. Mr Sutton and his two sons, from about 1763, became exceedingly popular as inoculators ; in 1775 a dispensary was opened in London for gratuitous inoculation of the poor, and Mr Dimsdale at the same time practised with extraordinary success. The Small-pox Hospital having adopted the plan of promiscuous inoculation of out-patients, carried it on to an immense extent between 1790 and 1800. In 1796, Dr Jenner announced his discovery of vaccination, and inoculation of the small-pox was gradually superseded by inoculation of the cow-pox.

On the 23d of July 1840, the practice of inoculation of the small-pox was prohibited by an act of the British Parliament, 3 and 4 Vict. c. 29. This statute, entitled ' An Act to Extend the Practice of Vaccination,' enacted that any person who shall produce or attempt to produce by inoculation of variolous matter the disease of small-pox, shall be liable on conviction to be imprisoned in the common gaol or house of correction for any term not exceeding one month.'

MARCH 19.

St Joseph, husband of the Virgin Mary, 1st century. St Alemund, of England, martyr, about 819.

Born.—John Astruc, eminent French physician, 1684, *Sauve* ; the Rev. Edward Bickersteth, writer on religious subjects, 1786, *Kirkby-Lonsdale.*
Died.—Alexander Severus, murdered, A.D: 235; Spencer Compton, Earl of Northampton, 1643, killed at *Hopton Heath ;* Bishop Thomas Ken, 1711, *Frome ;* Pope Clement II., 1721 ; Nicholas Hawksmoor, architect, pupil of Wren, 1736 ; Admiral Sir Hugh Palliser, 1786, *Greenwich Hospital ;* Stephen Storace, musical composer, 1796, *London ;* John Duke of Roxburghe, bibliophilist, 1804; Sir Joseph Banks, naturalist, forty-two years P.R.S., 1820, *Spring-grove, Middlesex ;* Thomas William Daniell, R.A., painter of Oriental scenery, 1840.

JOHN DUKE OF ROXBURGHE.

John Duke of Roxburghe, remarkable for the magnificent collection of books which wealth and taste enabled him to form, and to whom a venerative reference is made in the name of the Rox-burghe Club, died at the age of sixty-four. His Grace's library in St James's Square comprised upwards of ten thousand distinct articles, the richest department being early English literature. It cost its noble collector forty years, but pro-bably a moderate sum of money, in comparison with what was realized by it when, after his death, it was brought to the hammer. On that occasion, a single book—Boccaccio's *Decamerone*, printed at Venice in 1471—was sold at £2,260, the highest price known to have ever been given for a book. Dr Dibdin's account of the sale, or as he chooses to call it, *the fight*, which took place in May 1812, is in an exaggerative style, and extremely amusing.

'It would seem,' says the reverend biblio-maniac, 'as if the year of our Lord 1811 was destined, in the annals of the book auctions, to be calm and quiescent, as a prelude and contrast to the tremendous explosion or contest which, in the succeeding year, was to rend asunder the bibliomaniacal elements. It is well known that Mr George Nichol had long prepared the cata-logue of that extraordinary collection; and a sort of avant-courier or picquet guard preceded the march of the whole army, in the shape of a *preface*, privately circulated among the friends of the author. The publication of a certain work, ycleped the *Bibliomania*, had also probably stirred up the mettle and hardened the sinews of the contending book-knights. At length the hour of battle arrived. . . . For *two-and-forty* succes-sive days—with the exception only of Sundays—was the voice and hammer of Mr Evans heard, with equal efficacy, in the dining-room of the late duke, which had been appropriated to the vendition of the books; and within that same space (some thirty-five feet by twenty) were such deeds of valour performed, and such feats of book-heroism achieved, as had never been pre-viously beheld, and of which the like will pro-bably never be seen again. The shouts of the victors and the groans of the vanquished stunned and appalled you as you entered. The throng and press, both of idle spectators and deter-mined bidders, was unprecedented. A sprink-ling of Caxtons and De Wordes marked the first day; and these were obtained at high, but, com-paratively with the subsequent sums given, moderate prices. *Theology, jurisprudence, philo-sophy*, and *philology*, chiefly marked the earlier days of this tremendous contest; and occasion-ally, during these days, there was much stirring up of courage, and many hard and heavy blows were interchanged; and the combatants may be said to have completely wallowed themselves in the conflict! At length came *poetry*, Latin, Italian, and French; a steady fight yet continued to be fought: victory seemed to hang in doubt-ful scales—sometimes on the one, sometimes on the other side of Mr Evans—who preserved throughout (as it was his bounden duty to pre-serve) a uniform, impartial, and steady course; and who may be said, on that occasion, if not to have "rode the whirlwind," at least to have "directed the storm." At length came ENGLISH POETRY!! and with that came the tug and trial of war: Greek met Greek; in other words,

grandee was opposed to grandee; and the indo-mitable Atticus was compelled to retire, stunned by the repeated blows upon his helmet. The lance dropped from his hand, and a swimming darkness occasionally skimmed his view; for on that day, the *Waterloo* among book-battles, many a knight came far and wide from his retirement, and many an unfledged combatant left his father's castle to partake of the glory of such a contest. Among these knights from a "far countree" no one shot his arrows with a more deadly effect than Astiachus! But it was re-served for Romulus to reap the greatest victories in that poetic contest! He fought with a choice body-guard: and the combatants seemed amazed at the perseverance and energy with which that body-guard dealt their death-blows around them!

'*Dramatic Poetry* followed; what might be styled rare and early pieces connected with our ancient poetry; but the combat now took a more tranquil turn: as after "a smart brush" for an *early Shakspeare* or two, Atticus and Coriolanus, with a few well-known dramatic aspirants, ob-tained almost unmolested possession of the field.

'At this period, to keep up our important metaphor, the great *Roxburghe day* of battle had been somewhere half gone through, or decided. There was no disposition, however, on either side to relax from former efforts; when (prepare for something terrific!) the *Romances* made their appearance; and just at this crisis it was that more blood was spilt, and more ferocity exhibited, than had ever been previously wit-nessed.'

At length came the *Valdarfer Boccaccio*, of which it may be remarked that it had been acquired by the Duke's father for a hundred guineas. It was supposed to be the only fault-less copy of the edition in existence.

'I have a perfect recollection,' says Dibdin, 'of this notorious volume, while in the library of the late Duke. It had a faded yellow morocco bind-ing, and was a sound rather than a fine copy. The expectations formed of the probable price for which it would be sold were excessive; yet not so excessive as the price itself turned out to be. The marked champions were pretty well known beforehand to be the Earl Spencer, the Marquis of Blandford (now Duke of Marl-borough), and the Duke of Devonshire. Such a rencontre, such a "shock of fight," naturally begot uncommon curiosity. My friends, Sir Egerton Brydges, Mr Lang, and Mr G. H. Free-ling, did me the kindness to breakfast with me on the morning of the sale—and upon the con-clusion of the repast, Sir Egerton's carriage con-veyed us from Kensington to St James's Square.

———The morning lowered,
And heavily with clouds came on the day—
Big with the fate of . . . and of . . . .

In fact the rain fell in torrents, as we lighted from the carriage and rushed with a sort of im-petuosity to gain seats to view the contest. The room was crowded to excess; and a sudden darkness which came across gave rather an addi-tional interest to the scene. At length the moment of sale arrived. Evans prefaced the putting up of the article by an appropriate oration, in which he expatiated upon its excessive rarity, and concluded by informing the company of the regret and even " anguish of heart " expressed by Mr Van Praet [librarian to the Emperor Napoleon] that such a treasure was not to be found in the imperial collection at Paris. Silence followed the address of Mr Evans. On his right hand, leaning against the wall, stood Earl Spencer: a little lower down, and standing at right angles with his lordship, appeared the Marquis of Blandford. Lord Althorp stood a little backward to the right of his father, Earl Spencer. Such was " the ground taken up " by the adverse hosts. The honour of firing the first shot was due to a gentleman of Shropshire, unused to this species of warfare, and who seemed to recoil from the reverberation of the report himself had made !—" One hundred guineas," he exclaimed. Again a pause ensued ; but anon the biddings rose rapidly to 500 guineas. Hitherto, however, it was evident that the firing was but masked and desultory. At length all random shots ceased ; and the champions before named stood gallantly up to each other, resolving not to flinch from a trial of their respective strengths. " *A thousand guineas* " were bid by Earl Spencer —to which the marquis added " *ten.*" You might have heard a pin drop. All eyes were turned— all breathing well-nigh stopped—every sword was put home within its scabbard—and not a piece of steel was seen to move or to glitter, except that which each of these champions brandished in his valorous hand. See, see !—they parry, they lunge, they bet: yet their strength is undiminished, and no thought of yielding is entertained by either. *Two thousand pounds* are offered by the marquis. Then it was that Earl Spencer, as a prudent general, began to think of a useless effusion of blood and expenditure of ammunition—seeing that his adversary was as resolute and " fresh " as at the onset. For a quarter of a minute he paused : when my Lord Althorp advanced one step forward, as if to supply his father with another spear for the purpose of renewing the contest. His countenance was marked by a fixed determination to gain the prize—if prudence, in its most commanding form, and with a frown of unusual intensity of expression, had not made him desist. The father and son for a few seconds converse apart ; and the biddings are resumed. " *Two thousand two hundred and fifty pounds,*" said Lord Spencer. The spectators were now absolutely electrified. The marquis quietly adds his usual " *ten,*" . . . and there is an *end of the contest.* Mr Evans, ere his hammer fell, made a due pause—and indeed, as if by something preternatural, the ebony instrument itself seemed to be charmed or suspended " in the mid air." However, at length down dropped the hammer. . . . . The spectators,' continues Mr Dibdin in his text, ' stood aghast ! and the sound of Mr Evans's prostrate sceptre of dominion reached, and resounded from, the utmost shores of Italy. The echo of that fallen hammer was heard in the libraries of Rome, of Milan, and St Mark. Boccaccio himself started from his slumber of some five hundred years ; and Mr

Van Praet rushed, but rushed in vain, amidst the royal book-treasures at Paris, to see if a copy of the said *Valdarfer Boccaccio* could there be found ! The price electrified the bystanders, and astounded the public ! The marquis's triumph was marked by a plaudit of hands, and presently after he offered his hand to Lord Spencer, saying, " We are good friends still ! " His lordship replied, " Perfectly, indeed I am obliged to you." " So am I to you," said the marquis, " so the obligation is mutual." He declared that it was his intention to have gone as far as £5,000. The noble marquis had previously possessed a copy of the same edition, wanting five leaves ; " for which five leaves," Lord S. remarked, " he might be said to have given £2,600."

' What boots it to recount minutely the various achievements which marked the conclusion of the *Roxburghe contest*, or to describe, in the manner of Sterne, the melancholy devastations which followed that deathless day ? The battle languished towards its termination (rather, we suspect, from a failure of ammunition than of valour or spirit on the part of the combatants) ; but notwithstanding, there was oftentimes a disposition manifested to resume the glories of the earlier part of the day, and to show that the spirit of bibliomania was not made of poor and perishable stuff. Illustrious be the names of the book-heroes, who both conquered and fell during the tremendous conflict just described ! And let it be said, that John Duke of Roxburghe both deserved well of his country and the book-cause.'

Dibdin had afterwards occasion (*Reminiscences of a Literary Life*) to make the following addition to the history of this precious volume : ' Of all EXTRAORDINARY RESULTS, what could exceed that of the Boccaccio of 1471, coming eventually into the possession of the *former* nobleman (Earl Spencer), at a price less than ONE-HALF of that for which he had originally contended with the latter, who had become its first purchaser at the above sale ? Such, however, is the FACT. At the sale of the Marquis of Blandford's library in 1819, this volume was purchased by the house of Longman and Co. for £918, it having cost the Marquis £2,260.' It came from them to Lord Spencer at that price, and is now in the beautiful library at Althorpe, Northamptonshire.

PERSONAL DEFECTS OVERCOME.

March 19, 1638, John Rous enters in his diary: ' Some years since I saw in Holborn, London, near the bridge, an Italian, who with his mouth did lay certain sheets of paper together, one upon another lengthwise, between the right hand and the left ; and then he took a needle and pricked it through the one end, and so then the other, so that the paper lay sure. Then he took a short-text pen, and dipped it in a standish or ink-horn of lead, and therewith wrote *Laus Deo semper*, in a very fair text hand (not written with his hand, but his mouth) ; then with another pen he flourished daintily about these letters in divers forms. He did with his mouth also take up a needle and thread, pricking the needle right down, out of which he pulled the thread, and took another by (fitter), and put it into the needle.

Then therewith he took three stitches in a cloth with a linen wheel (prepared with a turner's device for the foot). He did spin with his mouth. He wrote fair with his left foot. He used a pencil and painted with his mouth. He took a pretty piece or gun with his toes, and poured in a paper of powder, pulled out the scouring stick very nimbly, rammed in the powder, put up the stick, pulled up the cock with his toes, then another short piece charged (that had a Swedish firelock) being put in his mouth by another man, he held it forth and discharged it, and forthwith, with his toes, he discharged the other. He gathered up four or five small dice with his foot, and threw them out featly. His hands were both shrimped and lame.'*

MURDER OF MURDOCH GRANT.

The wild and sequestered district of Assynt, in Sutherlandshire, was, in the spring of 1830, the scene of a murder, remarkable on account of the allegation of one of the witnesses at the subsequent trial, that he had been prompted to a knowledge of some of the circumstances in a dream.

Murdoch Grant, an itinerant pedler, had attended a rustic wedding and merry-making at the hamlet of Assynt on the 19th of March in the above year, and for some time after he was not heard of. When four weeks had elapsed, a farm servant passing a lonely mountain lake, called Loch-tor-na-eigin, observed a dead body in the water, and, on this being dragged ashore, the features of the missing pedler were recognised. From the marks of violence about the head, and the fact of the pockets being empty and turned inside out, no doubt was entertained that the unfortunate man had met his death by foul means. But for some time all the efforts of the authorities to discover the perpetrator of the deed proved vain. The sheriff, Mr Lumsden, was much assisted in his investigations by a young man named Hugh Macleod, who had recently attempted to set up a school, but was now living idly with his parents.

One day, Mr Lumsden calling at the post-office of the district, it chanced to be mentioned by the postmaster, that, soon after the murder, he had changed a ten-pound note for a man whom he did not expect to find so rich, namely Hugh Macleod. Mr Lumsden afterwards asked Macleod how he came to have so large a note, and finding the latter deny the fact, his suspicions were so much excited that he deemed it justifiable to have the young man arrested. On his house being searched, none of the pedler's property was found in it, and, after a while, there seemed so little probability in the suspicion, that the young man was on the point of being liberated. At that juncture, however, a remarkable event took place.

A tailor named Kenneth Fraser came voluntarily forward with an averment that he had had a dream in which some particulars of the murder were revealed. In his sleep the image of the Macleods' cottage was presented to him, and a voice said to him in Gaelic, 'The merchant's pack is lying in a cairn of stones, in a hole near

* Diary of John Rous (Camden Society), p. 84.

394

their house.' The authorities went with him to the house in question, and there, certainly, under a pile of stones, lay some articles which had belonged to Grant. When accident afterwards discovered that Macleod was in possession of a pair of stockings which had belonged to the unfortunate pedler, there was no longer any hesitation felt in bringing him before a Court of Justice. He was tried by Lord Moncreiff, at the Circuit Court in Inverness, September 27th, when Kenneth Fraser gave the evidence regarding his dream with the greatest firmness and consistency. Macleod was found guilty, condemned, and executed, ultimately confessing that he had been the murderer of the pedler.*

It has not been stated to what extent Fraser's evidence weighed with the jury in the making up of their verdict. In so sceptical an age as ours, one would suppose that his tale of the dream would tend to invalidate the force of his evidence; but we must remember that the trial took place at Inverness. The supposition indulged in by ordinary people was, that Fraser, in the course of his carousings with Macleod, had got a glimpse of the terrible secret, and only affected to put it in the form of a dream, though how he should have thought such a falsehood advantageous when so many were sure to treat it with derision, is difficult to see. The case being so peculiar, we deem it worth while to reprint the report of Fraser's depositions from the *Inverness Courier* (Sept. 28, 1830).

'Kenneth Fraser, "the dreamer," was in the employ of John Macleod, tailor in Clachtoll, in the spring of 1830. Had some drink with the prisoner on the 5th April, and saw him have £1 11s. 0d. in money, and a red pocket-book; prisoner said he got the money from Lochbroom, where he was a schoolmaster, but told witness to say nothing about it. They went about drinking together for a day or two, prisoner paying all. Witness was at the Loch searching for the pack this year. It was in April when a messenger came for him to search for it. It had been said that witness had seen in a dream where the pack was lying. He said so himself at Hugh Graham's in Lynnmore, and it was true. "I was at home when I had the dream in the month of February.† It was said to me in my sleep, by a voice like a man's, that the pack was lying in such a place. I got a sight of the place just as if I had been awake; I never saw the place before. The voice said in Gaelic, 'The pack of the merchant is lying in a cairn of stones in a hole near their house.' The voice did not name the Macleods, but he got a sight of the ground fronting the south with the sun shining on it, and a burn running beneath Macleods house. I took the officer to the place I had got a sight of. It was on the south-west side of Loch-tor-na-eigin. We found nothing there. We went to search on the south side of the burn. I had not seen this place in my dream. It was not far

* Newspapers of the day. *Fraser's Magazine*, December 1856. For a striking account of the conduct of Macleod under sentence, see *Quarterly Review*, September 1851.

† There is obviously an anachronism here. February is, probably, a mistake for April.

from the place seen in my dream that the things were found. There were five silk handkerchiefs lying in a hole." The witness, having recounted this marvellous occurrence, said he saw the prisoner in about a fortnight after the 6th April, at church. Did not go with prisoner, who went home. Never heard Macleod's voice after that time. Witness was at Dornoch when Macleod was in jail, but no message was sent to him from the prisoner. Witness saw Murdoch Grant at the wedding of Betty Fraser. Never was told the articles were put in the hole, and knew nothing of them but from the dream.'

A judicial case resembling the above happened in London in the reign of William III. One Stockden, a victualler in Grub-street, was murdered on the 23d of December, 1695, by some person or persons unknown. Justice appeared to be baffled in its attempts to discover the guilty, when a Mrs Greenwood came voluntarily forward with the declaration that Stockden had appeared to her in a dream, and shewn her a house in Thames-street, where he alleged one of the murderers lived. Afterwards he appeared a second time, and shewed her the likeness of one Maynard, as that of the guilty person in question. Maynard was consequently put in Newgate prison, where he confessed the fact, and impeached three accomplices. It is stated that in a third dream Stockden displayed to Mrs Greenwood the portrait of one of these wretched men, and that she, from her recollection of the likeness, identified him in prison. Three of the criminals suffered on the scaffold. A sober account of this case was published by the Rev. William Smithies, curate of St Giles, Cripplegate, the parish in which the murdered man had lived.

Many will have a recollection of the case of Corder, who was tried at Bury St Edmunds, in August 1828, for the murder of Maria Marten, at Polsted, in Suffolk, about sixteen months before. Corder, after murdering his victim, a young woman whom he had seduced, concealed her body in a solitary building called the Red Barn. The stepmother of the deceased, a witness on the trial, gave testimony that she had received in a dream that knowledge of the situation of the body which led to the detection of the murder.

MARCH 20.

St Cuthbert, Bishop of Lindisfarne, 687. St Wulfran, Archbishop of Sens, and apostolic missionary in Friesand, 720.

ST CUTHBERT.

In the seventh century, when the northern part of Britain was a rude woody country occupied by a few tribes of half-savage inhabitants, and Christianity was planted in only a few establishments of holy anchorets, a high promontory, round which swept the waters of the Tweed, was the seat of a small monastery, bearing the descriptive name of *Muilros*.* A shepherd boy of the neighbouring

* The name and establishment were afterwards shifted a few miles up the Tweed, leaving 'Old Melrose' in decay. Only the faintest traces of it now exist.

vale of the Leader had seen this primitive abode of religious zeal and self-denial, and he became impelled by various causes to attach himself to it. Soon distinguished by his ardent, but mild piety, and zeal for the conversion of the heathen, he in time rose to be superior or prior of Muilros ; and was afterwards transferred to be prior of a similar establishment on Lindisfarne, an island on the Northumbrian coast. The holy Cuthbert excelled all his brethren in devotion ; he gave himself so truly to the spirit of prayer and heavenly contemplation, that he appeared to others more like an angel than a man. To attain to still greater heights in devotion, he raised a solitary cell for his own habitation in the smaller island of Farne, where at length he died on the 20th of March 687.

His brother monks, raising the body of Cuthbert eleven years afterwards, that it might be placed in a conspicuous situation, found it uncorrupted and perfect ; which they accepted as a miraculous proof of his saintly character. It was put into a fresh coffin, and placed on the ground, where very soon it proved the means of working miraculous cures. A hundred and seventy-four years afterwards, on the Danes invading Northumberland, the monks carried away the body of Cuthbert, and for many years wandered with it from place to place throughout Northumbria and southern Scotland, everywhere willingly supported by the devout ; until at length, early in the eleventh century, it was settled at the spot where afterwards, in consequence, arose the beautiful cathedral of Durham. There, for five centuries, the shrine over the incorrupt body of Cuthbert was enriched by the offerings of the faithful : it became a blaze of gold and jewellery, dazzling to look upon. The body was inspected in 1104, and found still fresh. In 1540, when commissioners came to reduce Durham to a conformity with the new ecclesiastical system, the body of Cuthbert was again inspected, and found fresh ; after which it was buried, and so remained for nearly three centuries more. In May 1827, eleven hundred and thirty-nine years after the death of the holy man on Farne island, the coffin was exhumed, and the body once more and perhaps finally examined, but this time more rigorously than before, for it was found a mere skeleton swaddled up so as to appear entire, with plaster balls in the eye-sockets to plump out that part of the visage. It thus appeared that a deception had been practised ; but we are not necessarily to suppose that more than one or two persons were concerned in the trick. Most probably, at the various inspections, the examiners were so awed as only to look at the exterior of the swaddlings, the appearance of which would satisfy them that the body was still perfect within. The case is, however, a very curious one, as exhibiting a human being more important dead than alive, and as having what might be called a posthumous biography infinitely exceeding in interest that of his actual life.

Palm Sunday.

The brief popularity which Jesus experienced on his last entry into Jerusalem, when the people 'took branches of palm trees, and went forth to meet Him, crying Hosanna, &c.,' has been commemorated from an early period in the history of the Church on the Sunday preceding Easter, which day was consequently called PALM SUNDAY. Throughout the greater part of Europe, in defect of the palm tree, branches of some other tree, as box, yew, or willow, were blessed by the priests after mass, and distributed among the people, who forthwith carried them in a joyous procession, in memory of the Saviour's triumphant entry into the holy city; after which they were usually burnt, and the ashes laid aside, to be sprinkled on the heads of the congregation on the ensuing Ash Wednesday, with the priest's blessing.

Before the change of religion, the Palm Sunday customs of England were of the usual elaborate character. The flowers and branches designed to be used by the clergy were laid upon the high altar; those to be used by the laity upon the south step of the altar. The priest,

PROCESSION OF THE ASS.

arrayed in a red cope, proceeded to consecrate them by a prayer, beginning, 'I conjure thee, thou creature of flowers and branches, in the name of God the Father,' &c. This was to displace the devil or his influences, if he or they should chance to be lurking in or about the branches. He then prayed—'We humbly beseech thee that thy truth may [here a sign of

the cross] sanctify this creature of flowers and branches, and slips of palms, or boughs of trees, which we offer,' &c. The flowers and branches were then fumed with frankincense from censers, after which there were prayers and sprinklings with holy water. The flowers and branches being then distributed, the procession commenced, in which the most conspicuous figures were two priests bearing a crucifix. When the procession had moved through the town, it returned to church, where mass was performed, the communion taken by the priests, and the branches and flowers offered at the altar.

In the extreme desire manifested under the ancient religion to realize all the particulars of Christ's passion, it was customary in some places to introduce into the procession a wooden figure of an ass, mounted on wheels, with a wooden human figure riding upon it, to represent the Saviour. Previous to starting, a priest declared before the people who was here represented, and what he had done for them; also, how he had come into Jerusalem thus mounted, and how the people had strewn the ground as he went with palm branches. Then it set out, and the multitude threw their willow branches before it as it passed, till it was sometimes a difficulty for it to move; two priests singing psalms before it, and all the people shouting in great excitement. Not less eager were the strewers of the willow branches to gather them up again after the ass had passed over them, for these twigs were deemed an infallible protection against storms and lightning during the ensuing year.

Another custom of the day was to cast cakes from the steeple of the parish church, the boys scrambling for them below, to the great amusement of the bystanders. Latterly, an angel appears to have been introduced as a figure in the procession: in the accounts of St Andrew Hubbard's parish in London, under 1520, there is an item of eightpence for the hire of an angel to serve on this occasion. Angels, however, could fall in more ways than one, for, in 1537, the hire was only fourpence. Crosses of palm were made and blessed by the priests, and sold to the people as safeguards against disease. In Cornwall, the peasantry carried these crosses to 'our lady of Nantswell,' where, after a gift to the priest, they were allowed to throw the crosses into the well, when, if they floated, it was argued that the thrower would outlive the year; if they sunk, that he would not. It was a saying that he who had not a palm in his hand on Palm Sunday, would have his hand cut off.

After the Reformation, 1536, Henry VIII. declared the carrying of palms on this day to be one of those ceremonies not to be contemned or dropped. The custom was kept up by the clergy till the reign of Edward VI., when it was left to the voluntary observance of the people. Fuller, who wrote in the ensuing age, speaks of it respectfully, as 'in memory of the receiving of Christ into Hierusalem a little before his death, and that we may have the same desire to receive him into our hearts.' It has continued down to a recent period, if not to the present day, to be customary in many parts of England to go *a-palming* on the Saturday before Palm Sunday; that is, young persons go to the woods for slips of willow, which seems to be the tree chiefly employed in England as a substitute for the palm, on which account it often receives the latter name. They return with slips in their hats or button-holes, or a sprig in their mouths, bearing the branches in their hands. Not many years ago, one stall-woman in Covent-garden market supplied the article to a few customers, many of whom, perhaps, scarcely knew what it meant. Slips of the willow, with its velvety buds, are still stuck up on this day in some rural parish churches in England.

The ceremonies of Easter at Rome—of what is there called *Holy Week*—commence on Palm Sunday.* To witness these rites, there are seldom fewer than ten thousand foreigners assembled in the city, a large proportion of them English and American, and of course Protestant. During Holy Week, the shops are kept open, and concerts and other amusements are given; but theatrical performances are forbidden. The chief external differences are in the churches, where altars, crucifixes, and pictures are generally put in mourning.

About nine on Palm Sunday morning, St Peter's having received a great crowd of people, all in their best attire, one of the papal regiments enters, and forms a clear passage up the central aisle. Shortly afterwards the 'noble guard,' as it is called, of the Pope—a superior body of men —takes its place, and the corps diplomatique and distinguished ecclesiastics arrive, all taking their respective seats in rows in the space behind the high altar, which is draped and fitted up with carpets for the occasion. The Pope's chief sacristan now brings in an armful of so-called palms, and places them on the altar. These are stalks about three feet long, resembling a walking-cane dressed up in scraps of yellow straw; they are sticks with bleached palm leaves tied on them in a tasteful but quite artificial way. The preparation of these substitutes for the palm is a matter of heritage, with which a story is connected. When Sextus V. (1585—90) undertook to erect in the open space in front of St Peter's, the tall Egyptian obelisk which formerly adorned Nero's circus, he forbade any one to speak on pain of death, lest the attention of the workmen should be diverted from their arduous task. A naval officer of St Remo, who happened to be present, foreseeing that the ropes would take fire, cried out to 'apply water.' He was immediately arrested, and conducted before the pontiff. As the cry had saved the ropes, Sextus could not enforce the decree, and to shew his munificence he offered the transgressor

* The Holy Week of 1862 is described in this work by a gentleman who witnessed the ceremonies.

his choice of a reward. Those who have observed the great abundance of palms which grow in the neighbourhood of St Remo, between Nice and Genoa, will not be surprised to hear that the wish of the officer was to enjoy the privilege of supplying the pontifical ceremonies with palms. The Pope granted him the exclusive right, and it is still enjoyed by one of his family.

At 9.30 a burst of music is heard from the choir, the soldiers present arms, all are on the tiptoe of expectation, and a procession enters from a side chapel near the doorway. All eyes are turned in this direction, and the Pope is seen borne up the centre of the magnificent basilica in his *sedia gestatoria*. This chair of state is fixed on two long poles covered with red velvet, and the bearers are twelve officials, six before and six behind. They bear the ends of the poles on their shoulders, and walk so steadily as not to cause any uneasy motion. On this occasion, and always keeping in mind that the church is in mourning, the Pope is plainly attired, and his mitre is white and without ornament. There are also wanting the *flabelli*, or large fans of feathers, which are carried on Easter Sunday. Thus slowly advancing, and by the movement of his hand giving his benediction to the bowing multitude, the Pope is carried to the front of his throne at the further end of the church. Descending from his *sedia gestatoria*, his Holiness, after some intermediate ceremonies and singing, proceeds to bless the palms, which are brought to him from the altar. This blessing is effected by his reading certain prayers, and incensing the palms three times. An embroidered apron is now placed over the Pope's knees, and the cardinals in turn receive a palm from him, kissing the palm, his right hand, and knee. The bishops kiss the palm which they receive and his right knee; and the mitred abbots and others kiss the palm and his foot. Palms are now more freely distributed by sacristans, till at length they reach those among the lay nobility who desire to have one. The ceremony concludes by reading additional prayers, and more particularly by chanting and singing. The *Benedictus qui venit* is very finely executed. In conclusion, low mass is performed by one of the bishops present, and the Pope, getting into his *sedia gestatoria*, is carried with the same gravity back to the chapel whence he issued, and which communicates with his residence in the Vatican. The entire ceremonial lasts about three hours, but many, to see it, endure the fatigue of standing five to six hours. Among the strangers present, ladies alone are favoured with seats, but they must be in dark dresses, and with black veils on their heads instead of bonnets.

Until lately, there existed at Caistor, in Lincolnshire, a Palm Sunday custom of a very quaint nature, and which could not have been kept up if it had not been connected with a tenure of property. It has been thus described: 'A person representing the proprietor of the estate of Broughton comes into the porch of Caistor Church while the first lesson is reading, and three times cracks a gadwhip, which he then folds neatly up. Retiring for the moment to a seat in the church, he must come during the second lesson to the minister, with the whip held upright, and at its upper end a purse with thirty pieces of silver contained in it; then he must kneel before the clergyman, wave the whip thrice round his head, and so remain till the end of the lesson, after which he retires.

The precise origin of this custom has not been ascertained. We can see in the purse and its thirty pieces of silver a reference to the misdeeds of Judas Iscariot; but why the use of a whip? Of this the only explanation which conjecture has hitherto been able to supply, refers us back to the ancient custom of the Procession of the Ass, before described. Of that procession it is supposed that the gadwhip of Caistor is a sole-surviving relic. The term *gadwhip* has been a puzzle to English antiquaries; but a gad [goad] for driving horses, was in use in Scotland so lately as the days of Burns, who alludes to it. A portraiture of the gad-whip employed on a recent occasion, with the purse at its upper end, is here presented. The land which was held by the singular tenure now described, having been sold in 1845, the custom ceased.

THE GAD-WHIP.

Born.—Publius Ovidius Naso, B.C. 43; Bishop Thomas Morton, 1564; Napoleon, Duke of Reichstadt, 1811.

Died.—The Emperor Publius Gallienus, A.D. 268, assassinated at *Milan;* Henry IV. King of England, 1413, *Westminster;* Ernest, Duke of Luneburg, 1611; Bishop Samuel Parker, 1687, *Oxford;* Sir Isaac Newton, philosopher, 1727, *Kensington;* Frederick, Prince of Wales, 1751, *Leicester House;* Gilbert West, classical scholar, 1756, *Chelsea;* Firmin Abauzit, Genevese theological writer, 1767; Lord Chief Justice, Earl of Mansfield, 1793; H. D. Inglis (*Derwent Conway*), traveller, 1835; Mademoiselle Mars, celebrated French comic actress, 1847.

THE DEATH OF HENRY THE FOURTH.
AMBIGUOUS PROPHECIES.

Robert Fabian, alderman and sheriff of London, a man of learning, a poet, and historian, in his *Concordance of Stories* (a history commencing with the fabulous Brute, and ending in the reign of Henry VII.), was the first to relate the since often-quoted account of the circumstances attending the death of the fourth Henry.

'In this year' [1412], says the worthy citizen, 'and twentieth day of the month of November, was a great council holden at the Whitefriars of London, by the which it was, among other things, concluded, that for the King's great journey he intended to take in visiting the Holy Sepulchre of our Lord, certain galleys of war should be made, and other purveyance concerning the same journey.

'Whereupon, all hasty and possible speed was made, but after the feast of Christmas, while he was making his prayers at St Edward's shrine, to take there his leave, and so to speed him on his journey, he became so sick, that such as were about him feared that he would have died right there; wherefore they, for his comfort, bare him into the Abbot's place, and lodged him in a chamber; and there, upon a pallet, laid him before the fire, where he lay in great agony a certain of time.

'At length, when he was come to himself, not knowing where he was, freyned [inquired] of such as then were about him, what place that was; the which shewed to him, that it belonged unto the Abbot of Westminster; and for he felt himself so sick, he commanded to ask if that chamber had any special name. Whereunto it was answered, that it was named Jerusalem. Then said the king—"Loving be to the Father of Heaven, for now I know I shall die in this chamber, according to the prophecy of me before said that I should die in Jerusalem;" and so after, he made himself ready, and died shortly after, upon the day of St Cuthbert, or the twentieth day of March 1413.'

This story has been frequently told with variations of places and persons; among the rest, of Gerbert, Pope Sylvester II., who died in 1003. Gerbert was a native of France, but, being imbued with a strong thirst for knowledge, he pursued his studies at Seville, then the great seat of learning among the Moors of Spain. Becoming an eminent mathematician and astronomer, he introduced the use of the Arabic numerals to the Christian nations of Europe; and, in consequence, acquired the name and fame of a most potent necromancer. So, as the tale is told, Gerbert, being very anxious to inquire into the future, but at the same time determined not to be cheated, by what Macbeth terms the juggling fiends, long considered how he could effect his purpose.

At last he hit upon a plan, which he put into execution by making, under certain favourable planetary conjunctions, a brazen head, and endowing it with speech. But still dreading diabolical deception, he gave the head power to utter only two words—plain 'yes' and 'no.' Now, there were two all-important questions, to which Gerbert anxiously desired responses. The first, prompted by ambition, regarded his advancement to the papal chair; the second referred to the length of his life,—for Gerbert, in his pursuit of magical knowledge, had entered into certain engagements with a certain party who shall be nameless; which rendered it very desirable that his life should reach to the longest possible span, the reversion, so to speak, being a very uncomfortable prospect. Accordingly Gerbert asked the head, 'Shall I become Pope?' The head replied, 'Yes!' The next question was, 'Shall I die before I chant mass in Jerusalem?' The answer was, 'No!' Of course, Gerbert had previously determined, that if the answer should be in the negative, he would take good care never to go to Jerusalem. But the certain party, previously hinted at, is not so easily cheated. Gerbert became Pope Sylvester, and one day while chanting mass in a church at Rome, found himself suddenly very ill. On making inquiry, he learned that the church he was then in was named Jerusalem. At once, knowing his fate, he made preparations for his approaching end, which took place in a very short time.

Malispini relates in his Florentine history that the Emperor Frederick II. had been warned, by a soothsayer, that he would die a violent death in Firenze (Florence). So Frederick avoided Firenze, and, that there might be no mistake about the matter, he shunned the town of Faenza also. But he thought there was no danger in visiting Firenzuolo, in the Appenines. There he was treacherously murdered in 1250, by his illegitimate son Manfred. Thus, says Malispini, he was unable to prevent the fulfilment of the prophecy.

The old English chroniclers tell a somewhat similar story of an Earl of Pembroke, who, being informed that he would be slain at Warwick, solicited and obtained the governorship of Berwick-upon-Tweed; to the end that he might not have an opportunity of even approaching the fatal district of Warwickshire. But a short time afterwards, the Earl being killed in repelling an invasion of the Scots, it was discovered that Barwick, as it was then pronounced, was the place meant by the quibbling prophet.

The period of the death of Henry IV. was one of great political excitement, and consequently highly favourable to the propagation of prophecies of all kinds. The deposition of Richard and usurpation of Henry were said to have been foretold, many centuries previous, by the enchanter Merlin; and both parties, during the desolating civil wars that ensued, invented prophecies whenever it suited their purpose. Two prophecies of the ambiguous kind, 'equivocations of the fiend that lies like truth,' are recorded by the historians of the wars of the roses, and noticed by Shakspeare.

William de la Pole, first Duke of Suffolk, had been warned by a wizard, to beware of water and avoid the tower. So when his fall came, and he was ordered to leave England in three days, he made all haste from London, on his way to France, naturally supposing that the Tower of London, to which traitors were conveyed by water, was the place of danger indicated. On his passage across the Channel, however, he was captured by a ship named Nicholas of the Tower, commanded by a man surnamed Walter. Suffolk, asking this captain to be held to ransom, says—

'Look on my George, I am a gentleman;
Rate me at what thou wilt, thou shalt be paid.'
Captain. 'And so am I; my name is Walter Whitmore—
How now? why start'st thou? What, doth death affright?'
Suffolk. 'Thy name affrights me, in whose sound is death;
A cunning man did calculate my birth,
And told me that by water I should die;
Yet let not this make thee be bloody-minded,
Thy name is Gaultier being rightly sounded.'

Of course, the prophecy was fulfilled by Whitmore beheading the Duke.

The other instance refers to Edmund Beaufort, Duke of Somerset, who is said to have consulted Margery Jourdemayne, the celebrated witch of Eye, with respect to his conduct and fate during the impending conflicts. She told him that he would be defeated and slain at a castle; but as long as he arrayed his forces and fought in the open field, he would be victorious and safe from harm. Shakspeare represents her familiar spirit saying—

'Let him shun castles.
Safer shall he be on the sandy plain
Than where castles mounted stand.'

After the first battle of St Albans, when the trembling monks crept from their cells to succour the wounded and inter the slain, they found the dead body of Somerset lying at the threshold of a mean alehouse, the sign of which was a castle. And thus,

'Underneath an alehouse' paltry sign,
The Castle, in St Albans, Somerset
Hath made the wizard famous in his death.'

Cardinal Wolsey, it is said, had been warned to beware of Kingston. And supposing that the town of Kingston was indicated by the person who gave the warning, the cardinal took care never to pass through that town; preferring to go many miles about, though it lay in the direct road between his palaces of Esher and Hampton Court. But after his fall, when arrested by Sir William Kingston, and taken to the Abbey of Leicester, he said, 'Father Abbot, I am come to leave my bones among you,' for he knew that his end was at hand.

SIR ISAAC NEWTON.

It was an equally just and generous thing of Pope to say of Newton, that his life and manners would make as great a discovery of virtue and goodness and rectitude of heart, as his works have done of penetration and the utmost stretch of human knowledge. Assuredly, Sir Isaac was the perfection of philosophic simplicity. His plays in childhood were mechanical experiments. His relaxations in mature life from hard thinking and investigation, were dabblings in ancient chronology and the mysteries of the Apocalypse. The passions of other men, for love, for money, for power, were in him non-existent; all his energies were devoted to pure study. Sir David Brewster, in his able *Life of Newton*, has successfully defended his character from imputations brought upon it by Flamsteed. He has also, however, printed a letter attributed to Sir Isaac —a love-letter—a love-letter written when he was sixty, proposing marriage to the widow of his friend Sir William Norris. It is quite impossible for us to believe that the author of the *Principia* ever wrote such a letter, until more decisive proof of the fact can be adduced, and scarcely even then.

The subjoined autograph of Sir Isaac is furnished to us from an inedited letter. It precisely resembles one which we possess, extracted from the books of the Mint, of which Sir Isaac was master.

LORD CHIEF JUSTICE, EARL OF MANSFIELD.

Lord Campbell, in his *Lives of the Chief Justices*, has traced the career of William Murray, Earl of Mansfield, with great precision and a good deal of fresh light. He shews us how he came of a very poor Scotch peer's family, the eleventh of a brood of fourteen children, reared on oatmeal porridge in the old mansion of Scoon, near Perth, which our learned author persists in calling a *castle*, while it was nominally a palace, but in reality a plain old-fashioned house. One particular of some importance in the Chief Justice's history does not seem to have been known to his biographer—that, while the father (David, fifth Viscount Stormont) was a good-for-little man of fashion, the mother, Marjory Scott, was a woman of ability, who was supposed to have brought into the Stormont family any talent—and it is not little—which it has since exhibited, including that of the illustrious Chief Justice. She came of the Scots (so they spelt their name) of Scotstarvit, in Fife, a race which produced an eminent patron of literature in Sir John Scot, Director of the Chancery in the time of Charles I., and author of a bitingly clever tract, entitled *The Staggering State of Scots Statesmen*, which was devoted to the amiable purpose of shewing all the public and domestic troubles that had fallen upon official persons in Scotland from the days of Mary downward. Marjory, Viscountess of Stormont, was the great-granddaughter of Sir John, whose wife again was of a family of talent, Drummond of Hawthornden. In the history of the lineage of intellect we could scarcely find a clearer pretension to ability than what lay at the door of the youth William Murray.

It is not our business to trace, as Lord Campbell has done, the steps by which this youth rose at the English bar, attained office, prosecuted Scotch peers, his cousins, for treason against King George, became a great parliamentary orator, and the highest criminal judge in the kingdom, and, without political office, was the director of several successive cabinets.

We may remark, however, what has hitherto been comparatively slurred, that the Jacobitism of Murray's family was unquestionable. His father was fully expected to join in the insurrection of 1715, and he was thought to avoid doing so in a way not very creditable to him. An elder brother of William was in the service of 'the Pretender' abroad. When Charles Edward, in 1745, came to Perth, he lodged in the house of Lord Stormont, and one of the ladies of the family (sister to the Chief Justice) made his Royal Highness's bed with her own fair hands. After this, the remark of Lovat at his trial to the Solicitor-General, that his mother had been very kind to the Frasers as they marched through Perth, may well be accepted as a simple reference to a matter of fact.

The most important point in the life of the Lord Chief Justice, all things considered, is his transplantation to England. His natural destiny was, as Lord Campbell remarks, to have lived the life of an idle younger brother, fishing in the Tay, and hunting deer in Atholl. How comes it that he found a footing in the south? On this subject, Murray himself must have studied to preserve an obscurity. It was given out that he had been brought to London at three years of age, and hence the remark of Johnson to Boswell, that much might be made of a Scotsman 'if caught young.' To Lord Campbell belongs the credit of ascertaining that young Murray in reality received his juvenile education at the Grammar-school of Perth, and did not move to England till the age of fourteen, by which time he had shown great capacity, being, for one thing, able to converse in Latin. The Jacobite elder brother was the means of bringing 'Willie' southward. As a Scotch member during the Harley and Bolingbroke administration, he had gained the friendship of Atterbury, then Dean of Westminster. In the Stuart service himself, and anxious to bring Willie into the same career, he recommended that he should be removed to Westminster school, and brought up under the eye of the dean; professing to believe that he was sure of a scholarship at Christchurch, and of all desirable advancement that his talent fitted him for. Willie was accordingly sent on horseback by a tedious journey to London, in the spring of 1718, and never saw his country or his parents again. In a year he had obtained a king's scholarship, and it is suspected that the interest of Atterbury was the means of his getting it.

Lord Campbell duly tells us of the elegant elocution to which Murray attained. He succeeded, it seems, in getting rid of his Scotch accent; and yet 'there were some *shibboleth* words which he could never pronounce properly to his dying day: for example, he converted *regiment* into *reg'ment*; at dinner he asked not for *bread*, but *brid*; and in calling over the bar, he did not say, 'Mr *Solicitor*,' but 'Mr *Soleester*, will you move anything?'

MARCH 21.

St Serapion (called the Sindonite), about 388. St Serapion (the scholastic), Bishop in Egypt, 4th century. St Serapion, abbot. St Benedict (or Bennet), abbot of Mount Casino, patriarch of the Western monks, 543. St Enna, abbot in Ireland, 6th century.

ST BENEDICT.

The history of St Benedict is chiefly interesting to us from the circumstance that he was in a manner the father of Western monachism, and especially of that portion of it which exercised so great and durable an influence on the social history of this part of Europe. He was born about the year 480, and was a native of Norcia, in Umbria, from whence he was sent to study at Rome, but he had imbibed a strong taste for asceticism, and when about fourteen or fifteen, he fled to the wild mountains of Subiaco, disgusted, as it is said, by the vices practised in

Rome. He took up his residence alone in a cavern which is now called the Holy Grotto, and his hiding-place was known only to a monk of a neighbouring monastery, named Romanus, who supplied him scantily with food. After three years passed in this manner, Benedict became endowed with sanctity, and his reputation began soon to spread over the country, so that he was at length elected Abbot of Vicovara, between Subiaco and Tivoli; but he disagreed with the monks, and returned to his old place of retirement. His fame drew so many monks to the desert, that he established twelve monasteries; placing in each twelve monks, and a superior. Here he received a continual accession of monks, and is said to have performed many miracles; but at length becoming an object of persecution to some of his flock, he left Subiaco, and went to Monte Cassino, a lofty mountain in the kingdom of Naples. On the brow of the mountain stood an ancient temple of Apollo, surrounded by a grove, where some of the inhabitants of this district appear to have remained still addicted to their old idolatrous worship. Benedict converted these by his preaching, and by the miracles which accompanied it, broke the idol, and overthrew the altar; and having demolished the temple and cut down the grove, built on the spot two small oratories, which were the first beginning of the celebrated abbey of Monte Cassino. When he founded this abbey in the year 529, Benedict was forty-eight years of age. While Abbot of Monte Cassino, Benedict founded several other similar establishments, and he drew up the rule for their governance, which became subsequently that of the whole Benedictine order. The great principle of this rule was absolute obedience, the other main duties being charity and voluntary poverty. The monks were to employ seven hours of the day in manual labour, and two in pious reading. They were to abstain entirely from animal food, and were allowed only a fixed quantity of food daily. They were to possess everything in common, and this article was at first enforced so strictly, that in some of the monasteries in France a monk was considered to have merited punishment when he said, ‘my cloak,’ or ‘my hat,’ as no individual was allowed to possess anything of his own. In course of time, however, this injunction was generally evaded, and the Benedictine monasteries became celebrated for their immense possessions, which they excused on the ground that the wealth of the monasteries belonged to the monks not individually but collectively—that they were so many pauper members of a rich foundation. Benedict ruled the abbey of Monte Cassino about fourteen years, and died on Saturday the 21st of March, it is believed in the year 543, and was buried in the church of his monastery. In England the name of this saint is usually known by its popular form of Benet or Bennet.

After his death the rule of St Benedict was adopted by nearly all the monks of the West. In England the rule of the earlier Anglo-Saxon monks was very loose, and their monasteries partook more of the character of secular than of religious establishments. In the tenth century,

St Dunstan, with the aid of some other ecclesiastics of his time, and after an obstinate struggle, forced the Benedictine order upon the Anglo-Saxons, and it was still more completely established in this island by the Normans. But the more onerous parts of the rule were no longer observed, and the monks and nuns had become celebrated for their luxurious living, and for the secular character of their lives. Frequent attempts were made to restore the order to somewhat of its religious purity, and these various reformations produced numerous branch orders, among which the most powerful and celebrated were the monks of Cluny, and the Cistercians.

Born.—Robert Bruce, King of Scotland, 1274; Humphrey Wanley, antiquary, 1672, *Coventry;* John Sebastian Bach, musical composer, 1685, *Eisenach;* J. B. J. Fourier, mathematician, 1768; Henry Kirke White, poet, 1785, *Nottingham.*

Died.—Edmond of Woodstock, Earl of Kent, beheaded, 1330; Archbishop Cranmer, burnt at *Oxford,* 1556; Peter Ernest, Count de Mansfeld, 1604, *Luxembourg;* Tomasso Campanella, Dominican metaphysician and politician, 1639, *Paris;* Archbishop Usher, 1656, *Reigate, Surrey;* Charlotte Tremouille, Countess of Derby, heroic defender of Latham House, and of the Isle of Man, 1663, *Ormskirk,* Richard Dawes, eminent Greek scholar, 1766, *Haworth;* Duc d'Enghien, shot at Vincennes, 1804; Michael Bryan, biographer of painters and engravers, 1821; Baron La Motte-Fouqué, poet and novelist, 1843; Robert Southey, LL.D., poet laureate, 1843, *Keswick;* Rev. W. Scoresby, Arctic voyager, 1857.

CRANMER.

It is startling to note in how many instances the future destiny of a great man seems at one time or other to have hung on a thread. One little chance, one event, in itself most trivial, substituted for another at some critical point, and the great man's name might have been omitted in Fame's scroll. Had Thomas Cranmer not met with Henry VIII. accidentally, we might never have heard of him; for he was not a man to push his way to distinction. He was in no way a very extraordinary man. Henry found him a fellow of his college, a widower, a private tutor, learned in divinity, and a staunch believer in the King's supremacy. Whatever may be said of Henry, he had undoubtedly a shrewd insight into character. He saw at once that Cranmer was an acquisition. He at once employed him. He sent him on an embassy to the Pope, as well as to Germany, and made him archbishop in four years, against his will. He stood by him to the last.

Cranmer must have been the most useful man of the Reformation. His cautious prudence enabled him to steer safely where bolder guides would have endangered the vessel, and to keep in harbour when others would have risked the storm. He pushed on the cause indefatigably, but never agitated. During Henry's reign he supported the King's supremacy, laboured at the English Bible, and began a revised Liturgy. Edward VI., reigning from nine years old to fifteen, afforded him a golden opportunity for cautiously, but surely, advancing the great cause. Cranmer was the chief compiler of the new Liturgies, Articles, Homilies, &c., and the chief allayer of disputes which began to harass the unity of the Reformers. In Mary's reign the old man was duped into recantations, and burnt at Oxford.

Cranmer is by some described as a weak man, and by others elaborately defended. It is easier to detract from or extol a character, than to analyse it. As a man he was vacillating, as a Christian strong, as both prudent. A man naturally weak may be often courageous, and an upright conscience is easily confused in a weak mind. Prudence was Cranmer's chief character- istic, and prudence begets compromise, compro- mise vacillation. When he took contradictory oaths on his instalment, he was content with a protest: he said, 'What could I have done more?' And the key to his whole course is given in his own words : ' It pertains not to private subjects to reform things, but quietly to suffer what they cannot amend '—a difficult rule in those days as a guide to consistent conduct. No doubt it was by aid of this principle that his enemies at the last undermined his consistency.

Yet he was a most pure Christian. When he saw his duty clearly, he never turned from it. He strongly opposed Henry's Six Articles, and almost seditiously circulated his disapproval of Mary. Worldly we are sure he was not, though Dr Hook would have it so, building an imaginary charge on an obscure transaction. Ever would he plead for those condemned. He uniformly forgave his enemies, and confided in his friends with a childish simplicity. 'Do my lord of Canterbury an ill turn, and he is your friend for ever,' was the world's testimony of him. 'When he was informed of their treachery and ingrati- tude, he led aside Thornden and Barber into his garden, told them that some whom he trusted had disclosed his secrets and accused him of heresy, and asked how they thought such persons ought to be treated. They were loud in express- ing their indignation, and declared that such traitors deserved to die. "Know ye these letters, my masters?" said the primate, and shewed them the proof of their own falsehood. The two offenders fell upon their knees to implore for- giveness ; for it was evident that their lives were in his power, but all the revenge he took was to bid them ask God's forgiveness.'

'Kind, gentle, good, and weak.'

Shakspeare puts it very well :

' Look, the good man weeps ! He's honest, on mine honour. God's bless'd mother ! I swear he is true-hearted; and a soul None better in my kingdom.'

HENRY KIRKE WHITE.

White was remarkable at the schools he attended in Nottingham for extraordinary appli- cation. Such was his early passion for reading, that, when seated in his little chair with a large book on his knee, his mother would have to say more than once, 'Henry, my love, come to dinner,' ere she could rouse him from his reverie. At the age of seven he used to steal into the kitchen to teach the servant to read and write. But so little sympathy did his father, who was a butcher, show with his tastes and predilections,

that he not only kept him from school one whole day a week to carry out meat, but actually, for a time, occupied nearly all his leisure hours besides in this ungenial task.

At the age of fourteen he was sent to work at the stocking-loom, with a view to future promo- tion to the hosier's warehouse. It would be impossible to imagine a more disagreeable occu- pation for poor Henry ; and while he drudged at

HOUSE AT NOTTINGHAM IN WHICH HENRY KIRKE WHITE WAS BORN.

it most unwillingly for a twelvemonth, his thoughts were roaming along the banks of the silvery Trent, or resting in the welcome shade of Clifton Grove. At fifteen, his mother succeeded in pro- curing his admission into a lawyer's office, where, as no premium could be paid with him, he had to serve two years before he could be articled—a form which took place in 1802. He now began to learn Latin and Greek. Such, we are told, was his assiduity, that he used to decline Greek nouns and verbs as he went to and from the office, gave up supping with the family, and ate his meal in his own little room, in order to pursue his studies more uninterruptedly,—studies which often extended far into the night, and became almost encyclopædic in their range. He com- menced as author by sending contributions to the *Monthly Preceptor* and *Monthly Mirror*. From the former he received a pair of 12-inch globes as a prize for the best imaginary tour from London to Edinburgh, which he wrote one even- ing after tea, and read to the family at supper. He was then only sixteen. Through the latter he attracted the notice of Mr Hill and Capel Loft, who persuaded him to prepare a volume of poems, which appeared in 1803, dedicated to the Duchess of Devonshire—a lady more interested in elections than books of poetry, and who con- sequently took no further notice of the volume or its author. Henry's great desire now was to enter the Church. He disliked the drudgery of an attorney's office; a deafness, too, which was gaining upon him, threatened to make him useless as a lawyer, and his mind was deeply imbued with religious feelings. He hoped that the publication of his poems might in some way or other further this object. For a time, however, he was doomed to disappointment. At length, through the influence of Mr Simeon, the author of the well-known *Skeleton Sermons*, his fondest hopes were realized. In October 1805, he went to Cambridge, where, by unexampled industry, he speedily attained distinction, was first at every examination, and was looked upon as a future Senior Wrangler. But he had long overtaxed his strength. At the end of one short year from his entering the College, exhausted nature sank beneath incessant toil and anxiety. He died October 19, 1806.

Byron, in his *English Bards and Scotch Reviewers*, has finely said of him:

' Science' self destroy'd her favourite son !

*　　*　　*　　*　　*

'Twas thine own genius gave the final blow,
And help'd to plant the wound that laid thee low :
So the struck eagle, stretch'd upon the plain,
No more through rolling clouds to soar again,
View'd his own feather on the fatal dart,
And wing'd the shaft that quiver'd in his heart :
Keen were his pangs, but keener far to feel,
He nursed the pinion which impell'd the steel,
While the same plumage that had warm'd his nest
Drank the last life-drop of his bleeding breast.'

MARCH 22.

St Paul, Bishop of Narbonne, 3d century. St Basil, of Ancyra, martyr, 362. St Lea, widow, of Rome, 384. St Deogratias, Bishop of Carthage, 457. St Catharine, of Sweden, Abbess, 1381.

Born.—Henry de Beauchamp, Earl and last Duke of Warwick, 1424, *Hanley Castle;* Sir Anthony Vandyck, painter, 1599, *Antwerp;* Edward Moore, dramatic writer, 1712, *Abingdon;* Rosa Bonheur, artist, 1822.

Died.—Thomas Earl of Lancaster, beheaded at *Pontefract,* 1322; Thomas Duke of Clarence, slain in *Anjou,* 1421; Anne Clifford, Countess of Pembroke, 1676, *Brougham;* Jean Baptiste Lully, Father of French dramatic music, 1687, *Paris;* Jonathan Edwards, Calvinistic minister, 1758, *New Jersey;* John Canton, electrician, 1772; J. W. von Goethe, German poet and prose writer, 1832, *Weimar;* Rev. David Williams, warden of New College, 1860.

GOETHE.

When the spirit of Goethe passed away, all Europe took note of the event, and pondered on those last words, ' Let the light enter.' He was venerable with age and honours, a wise many-sided mind, and the greatest poet of Germany. ' In virtue of a genius such as modern times have only seen equalled once or twice,' says Mr Lewes, ' Goethe deserves the epithet of great; unless we believe a great genius can belong to a small mind. Nor is it in virtue of genius alone that he deserves the name. Merck said of him that what he lived was more beautiful than what he

wrote; and his life, amid all its weaknesses and all its errors, presents a picture of a certain grandeur of soul, which cannot be contemplated unmoved.'

Johann Wolfgang Goethe was born in 1749, in the busy old-fashioned town of Frankfort-on-the-Maine; a child so precocious that we find it recorded that he could write German, French, Italian, Latin, and Greek, before he was eight. His age fulfilled the promise of youth: he grew up a genuine man, remarkable for endless activity of body and mind, a sage minister, a noble friend, and a voluminous writer.

He commenced his collegiate course at Leipsic in 1765, but gave himself little to prescribed studies. Jurisprudence suited him as little at Strasburg, whither he went in 1770; yet in the following year he duly became Dr Goethe. He gave himself chiefly to literature and society. At length, in 1775, at the request of Karl August, he went to Weimar, ' where his long residence was to confer on an insignificant duchy the immortal renown of a German Athens.' He remained the Duke's counsellor, prime minister, and personal friend for more than fifty years; busying himself in acts of public utility and private benevolence, and studying and writing upon everything which came in his way.

When Napoleon and the Emperor of Russia met at Erfurt, near Weimar, in 1808, the former patronised Goethe by summoning him to a private audience. It lasted nearly an hour, and seems to have given mutual satisfaction. On Nov. 7, 1825, Goethe was honoured with a Jubilee, on the fiftieth anniversary of his residence at Weimar. His own play *Iphigenia* was performed in the Theatre, and the whole town was illuminated. An anecdote will illustrate his exalted position. ' Karl August came into his study accompanied by the King of Bavaria, who brought with him the Order of the Grand Cross as a homage. In strict etiquette a subject was not allowed to accept such an order without his sovereign granting permission; and Goethe, ever punctilious, turned to the Grand Duke, saying: " If my gracious sovereign permits;" upon which the Duke called out: "Du alter Kerl! mache doch kein dummes Zeug!" " Come, old fellow, no nonsense!" He received another noteworthy honour. A handsome seal, with a motto, " Without haste, without rest," taken from his poems, reached him from England. The accompanying letter expressed its desires "to shew reverence where reverence is due," and was signed by fifteen English admirers of the " spiritual teacher," among whom were Carlyle, Dr Carlyle, Sir Walter Scott, Lockhart, Wordsworth, Southey, and Professor Wilson.' He died in his eighty-fourth year, at least in mind still young.

His juvenile production, *The Sorrows of Werther,* seized upon the sentimental spirit of the time, and rendered him famous. Though a genuine and characteristic work, he outgrew its philosophy and lived to regret it. *Faust* is his great work, but can never be popular, as its wisdom does not lie on the surface. *Hermann and Dorothea* is immortal as the *Vicar of Wakefield.* His minor poems have widely influenced modern verse. He wrote an *Autobiography* and many prose works, and was by no means insignificant as a pioneer to the noble host of modern veterans in science.

His friendship and co-operation with Schiller is one of the most lovable parts of Goethe's life. Those two great minds were essentially diverse. Yet we find them, to their eternal honour, 'brought into brotherly union only by what was highest in their natures and their aims.' When Schiller's death was concealed from him, Goethe discovered it by the shyness of his domestics. He saw Schiller must be ill, and at night was heard to weep. 'In the morning he said to a friend, "Is it not true that Schiller was very ill yesterday?" The friend (it was a woman) sobbed. "He is dead?" said Goethe faintly. "You have said it," was the answer. "He is dead," repeated Goethe, and covered his face with his hands.' Then he wrote with truth, doubtless, 'The half of my existence is gone from me.'

There is something in Goethe's greatness not always pleasing. He feared to marry, lest he should cripple his freedom. Not that he professed such a motive, but this is the only explanation of the fact that so many loves stopped short of marriage. The names of women in his works mostly belong to real characters. Continually in his biography we are coming upon 'traces of a love-affair;' and besides obscure cases, we have Gretchen, Käthchen, Frederica, Lotte, Lili, Bettina, Frau von Stein, &c. &c. Frederica he treated badly in his youthful days, unless the reader can excuse Hamlet's conduct to Ophelia. Bettina he only petted, and seemingly did not ill-treat. Frau von Stein he was faithful to during many years, and she was a married woman. With Christine Vulpius he lived sixteen years, in defiance of public opinion; and then, in defiance again of the same public opinion, when she was fat, ugly, and intemperate, he honourably married her. Yes, and when she died, let us thoughtfully take note, he wrote thus to Zelter : 'When I tell thee, thou rough and sorely-tried son of earth, that my dear little wife has left me, thou wilt know what that means.'

Genius is often whimsical. Poet Goethe wasted as much precious time in trying to be an artist, as artist Turner wasted in vainly labouring to express himself in verse.

SUPPRESSION OF THE ORDER OF THE KNIGHTS TEMPLARS, MARCH 22, 1312.

The origin of the celebrated order of Templars is due to the piety of nine French knights, who in 1118 had followed Godfrey de Bouillon to the Crusades, and there dedicated themselves to insure the safety of the roads against the attacks of the infidels who maltreated the pilgrims to the Holy City. Their numbers rapidly increased; men of every nation, rank, and riches joined themselves to the generous militia who gained such glory on the battle-field. The council of Troyes approved them, encouragements and recompenses were awarded to their devotion, and a rule was granted them. St Bernard thus describes them in their early days : 'They lived without anything they could call their own, not even their will : they are generally simply dressed, and covered with dust, their faces em-

404

browned with the burning sun, and a fixed severe expression. On the eve of a battle, they arm themselves with faith within, and steel without; these are their only decoration, and they use them with valour, in the greatest perils fearing neither the number nor the strength of the barbarians. Their whole confidence is placed in the God of armies, and fighting for His cause they seek a certain victory, or a holy and honourable death. O happy way of life, in which they can await death without fear, desire it with joy, and receive it with assurance!'

The statutes of the order had for their basis all military and Christian virtues. The formula of the oath they took on their entrance was found in the archives of the Abbey of Alcobaza, in Aragon; it is as follows :

'I swear to consecrate my words, my arms, my strength, and my life to the defence of the mysteries of the faith, and that of the unity of God. I also promise to be submissive and obedient

GRAND MASTER OF THE TEMPLARS.

to the Grand Master of the Order. Whenever it is needful, I will cross the seas to fight, I will give help against all infidel kings and princes; and in the presence of three enemies I will not fly but fight, if they are infidels.'

At their head they carried their celebrated standard, called the Beaucéant, which bore the motto : 'Non nobis, Domine, non nobis, sed nomini tuo, da gloriam;' and after this they marched to battle, reciting prayers, having first received the holy sacrament. It was in 1237 that the knight who carried the Beaucéant in an action where the Mussulmans had the advantage, held it raised above his head until his conquerors, with redoubled blows, had pierced his whole body and cut off both his hands : such was their determined courage, while many authentic witnesses prove that, faithful to their oath, they respected the laws of religion and honour.

It is not fair for an impartial seeker after truth to judge the conduct of the Templars from works written after their misfortunes ; seldom indeed do the proscribed find courageous apologists : we must rather look to contemporary historians, the witnesses of their virtues and exploits ; and to the honourable testimony of popes, kings, and princes, who shortly after became their oppressors. They are never denounced by the troubadours, and it is well known that these bold poets were the severest censors of their age, and attacked without pity the popes, clergy, and great men : nor was the favourite proverb, ' to drink like a Templar,' ever imagined until after their abolition : whilst our own king, Edward II., who afterwards so weakly gave in to the prevailing cry, wrote at the first to the kings of Portugal, Castile, Sicily, and Aragon, praying them not to give credence to the calumnies which were spread against them.

It was in France that the storm burst out with all violence : the unscrupulous king, Philip le Bel, with his minister Marigny, had cast a covetous eye upon the wealth acquired by the knights, and determinedly used every means to obtain it. The first accusations were made by two men, the Prior of Montfaucon and Naffodei, a Florentine, who had been banished from his country, and whom none believed to have ever been one of the order. The prior had been condemned to perpetual imprisonment by the Grand Master, for heresy and infamous conduct, so that revenge was evidently his motive.

The first act was to recal the Grand Master from Cyprus upon another pretext, and on the 13th of October 1307, he, with one hundred and thirty-nine knights, were arrested in their own Palace of the Temple at Paris, their possessions were confiscated, and the king himself took up his abode at the Temple on that day, and seized their treasures. All the knights throughout France were at the same time thrown into prison. Their accusation was that new statutes had been established in place of the old ones, by which the knight on his admittance was required to deny his faith in Christ, to spit upon the cross, and to suffer other scandalous liberties : they were spoken of as 'ravening wolves, a perfidious idolatrous society, whose works and words alone are sufficient to pollute the earth and infect the air.' The inhabitants of Paris were convoked in the king's garden, the heads of the parishes and communities assembled, whilst the commissioners and monks preached against the condemned.

They were put into irons, and the Inquisitor, Guillaume de Paris, questioned them, not permitting them to employ any counsel. Warriors, who by their privileges and riches had walked beside princes, were left without the necessaries of life. The comforts of religion were even refused, under the pretext that they were heretics, and unworthy to participate in them. Life, liberty, and rewards were offered to those knights who would confess the crimes of which their order was accused ; twenty-six grandees of the court declared themselves their accusers ; and from all quarters archbishops, bishops, abbés, chapters,

and corporate bodies of the cities and villages, sent in their adhesion. After the barbarous fashion of the age, the Inquisitor commanded the trial to begin by torture ; one hundred and forty were thus tried in order to wring from them a confession, and it appears that only three resisted all entreaties ; the remainder attested the pretended crimes imputed to them, but throughout there is so much improbability, absurdity, and contradiction in the evidence, that it is easy to see under what constraint it was given. The Pope, Clement the Fifth, who claimed the right of being their sole judge, called the fathers of the church to a council at Vienne. Numbers of proscribed Templars were wandering among the mountains near Lyons, and with praiseworthy resolution they chose nine knights to go and plead their cause, in spite of the instruments of torture and the still smoking fagots by which thirty-six had died in Paris alone. They presented themselves as the representatives of from fifteen hundred to two thousand knights, under the safe-conduct of the public faith ; but Clement immediately arrested and put them in chains, augmenting his guard to save himself from the despair the others might be driven to. The Council were scandalised at such a proceeding, and refused their sentence until they had an opportunity of hearing the accused ; but this suited neither the Pope nor Philip, and after trying in vain to bend the just decision of the fathers, the former pronounced, in a secret consistory, the suppression of the order.

Jacques de Molay, a brave and virtuous knight, was at this time the Grand Master. Of a noble family of Burgundy, he had been received into the order in 1265, and gained himself an honourable place at the French court, so much so as to stand at the baptismal font for Robert, the fourth son of the king. During his absence in the East he was unanimously elected to his high office, and when the calumnies which began to be whispered reached his ear, he returned to the Pope and demanded an immediate examination into the conduct of the order. His own character would stand the highest test for probity and morality, his prosecutors even never imputing to him the shameful and dissolute crimes of which they so readily accused his associates ; but this was no protection, for he too was loaded with chains, and severe tortures applied. His sufferings, the menaces of the Inquisitor, the assurance that the knights would be condemned to death, and the order destroyed, if they did not yield to the king's projects, the pardonable desire of sparing their blood, and the hope of appeasing the King and Pope, induced him to condescend to an acknowledgment that he had against his own will denied his Saviour. But this he retracted very speedily, and kept stedfast to it through many sufferings and privations ; the cardinals, however, refused credence to the withdrawal, and in May 1310, they read the sentence in the church of Notre Dame, condemning him to perpetual imprisonment. To the great astonishment of those present, the Grand Master and one of his companions proclaimed the retractation of their confession, accusing themselves only of the crime of having ever made it. The cardinals, taken by surprise, entrusted these two prisoners to the care of the Provost, but when the king heard of it, he called his council together, among whom there was not a single ecclesiastic, and it was decided that De Molay and the knights should be immediately burnt.

An immense pile of wood was prepared for them, when, as a last effort on the part of the king, he sent the public crier to offer pardon and liberty to any one who would avow his participation in these pretended crimes. Neither the sight of horrible preparations for death, nor the tears of their relatives, nor the entreaties of their friends, could shake any of these inflexible souls; the offers of the king were reiterated, but cunning, prayers, and menaces, all were useless.

They had already submitted to the shame of an untrue confession, and now a noble repentance, with the feelings of virtue and truth, made them prefer death on the scaffold to a life redeemed by ignominy and untruth. The Grand Master was the first to ascend the steps, and the heroic old man addressed the multitude thus : 'None of us have betrayed either our God or our country ; we die innocent ; the decree which condemns us is an unjust one, but there is in heaven an august tribunal where the oppressed never implore in vain : to that tribunal I cite thee, O Roman Pontiff ; within forty days thou shalt be there : and thee, O Philip, my master and my king ; in vain do I pardon thee, thy life is condemned ; within the year I await thee before God's throne.'

Such citations were not uncommon in the middle ages, but perhaps the deaths of the pope and king, who survived De Molay but a short time, were the occasion of the popular tradition which has been retained by historians—Justus Lipsius, for instance. This at least is certain, that the Templars died without a groan, shewing an admirable firmness of courage, invoking the name of God, blessing Him, and calling Him to witness to their innocence.

Time has rendered them justice. The great Arnaud did not hesitate to believe them guiltless. 'There is scarcely any one,' he says, ' who now believes there was any justice in accusing the Templars of committing impiety, idolatry, and impurity.' The whole charge belonged to the spirit of the age, which, shortly after the death of Philip le Bel, degraded his minister Marigny, and gained over his wife and sister to swear that he had employed a magician to attempt the king's life, by moulding wax images of him and running them through with pins, using at the same time magical incantations. The magician was imprisoned, whereupon he hung himself in despair ; his wife was burnt as an accomplice, and Marigny himself was hung.

Philip had done all he could to induce the other European sovereigns to follow his example in the suppression of the Templars ; the greater part were only too ready to seize upon their vast treasures. In England sealed orders were sent to all the sheriffs, which when opened were to be executed suddenly. The Templars were imprisoned, but torture does not seem to have been used ; they were finally dispersed among various monasteries to live on a miserable pittance granted

by the king out of their own enormous revenues. The final decree against them was issued on the 22nd March 1312.

PETER CUMMIN AND OTHER CENTENARIANS.

March 22, 1724, was buried in Alnwick churchyard, Peter Cummin, a day-labourer reputed as upwards of a hundred and twenty years old. His name could not be found in the parish register of baptisms, because all previous to 1645 were lost. In his latter years this venerable person used to live from house to house amongst the gentry of the district. It is related of him that, coming to the house of Mr Brown, of Shawdon, near Alnwick, he looked round him, and expressed wonder at the great changes that had taken place since he was there last. He was asked how long that was ago, when, on a comparison of circumstances, the family found it was just a hundred years.[*]

It may be added that, at Newcastleton in Roxburghshire, they point to a field in the neighbourhood, where one day about 1770, amongst those engaged in reaping, was a woman of great age, but still in possession of a fair share of strength. Chatting with some of her neighbours, she told them she had once reaped in that field before, when she was a girl ; and after some discussion, this proved to have been exactly a hundred years before.

As an additional pendant to the case of Peter Cummin, the reader may take that of a noted vagrant, named James Stuart, who died at Tweedmouth, April 11, 1844, aged 116, having been born in South Carolina on 25th December 1728. A few charitable persons having combined to make the last days of this veteran comfortable, he naïvely remarked to an inquiring friend one day, that ' he had na been see weel off this hunder year.'

One of the most curious, though not the most extreme instances of longevity, was described in a letter by Thomas Atkins, dated Windsor, September 28, 1657, addressed to Fuller, and printed by him in his *Worthies*. The subject of the recital was the Rev. Patrick M'Ilvain, minister of Lesbury, near Alnwick. He was a hundred and ten years of age, having been born at Whithorn, in Wigtonshire, in 1546. Atkins heard this ancient pastor perform the service and preach, as was his custom, using neither spectacles for reading, nor notes for his sermon. 'His text was, " Seek you the kingdom of God, and all things shall be added unto you." In my poor judgment he made an excellent good sermon, and went cleverly through, without the help of any notes.' It appeared that, many years before, he had exhibited the usual symptoms of decay ; but latterly his eyesight had been restored, he had got a fresh crop of thin flaxen hair, and three new teeth appeared in his gums. He had always been a spare man, and very abstemious in his habits. Having married when above eighty, he had four youthful daughters living with him, besides his wife, who was only about fifty. It does not appear how long the veteran survived 1657.

[*] Antiquarian Repertory, iii. 435.

MARCH 23.

St Victorian, proconsul of Carthage, and others, martyrs, **484**. St Edelwald, of England, 699. St Alphonsus Turibius, Archbishop of Lima, 1606.

Wednesday in Holy Week in Rome.

On this occasion the only ceremony that attracts attention is the singing of the first *Miserere* in the Sistine Chapel. This commences at half-past four in the afternoon. The crowding is usually very great. The service, which is sometimes called Tenebræ, from the darkness of the night in which it was at one time celebrated, is repeated on the two following days in the Sistine Chapel, and singing not greatly different takes place also in St Peter's. The whole office of Tenebræ is a highly-finished musical composition, performed by the organ and the voices of one of the finest choirs in the world. Some parts are of exquisite beauty and tenderness. We give the following account of the composition from a work quoted below. 'In no other place has this celebrated music ever succeeded. Baini, the director of the pontifical choir, in a note to his Life of Palestrina, observes that on Holy Wednesday, 1519 (pontificate of Leo X.), the singers chanted the *Miserere* in a new and unaccustomed manner, alternately singing the verses in symphony. This seems to be the origin of the far-famed *Miserere*. Various authors, whom Baini enumerates, afterwards composed *Miserere;* but the celebrated composition of Gregorio Allegri, a Roman, who entered the papal college of singers in 1629, was the most successful, and was for some time sung on all the days of Tenebræ. Ultimately, the various compositions were eclipsed by the *Miserere* composed by Bai; but since 1821 the compositions of Baini, Bai, and Allegri are sung on the three successive days, the two latter sometimes blended together. The first verse is sung in harmony, the second in plain chant, and so successively till the last verse.'*

At the office of the *Miserere*, a ceremony takes place that may be described from the same authority: 'A triangular candlestick, upon which are fifteen candles, corresponding to the number of psalms recited, is placed at the epistle side of the altar. After each psalm one of the candles is extinguished by a master of the ceremonies, and after the Benedictus the candle on the top is alone not extinguished, but it is removed and concealed behind the altar, and brought out at

* The Ceremonies of Holy Week at Rome, by Right Rev. Monsignor Baggs. (Rome, Piale, 1854.)

the end of the service; while that canticle is sung the six candles on the altar also are extinguished, as well as those above the rails. The custom of concealing the last and most elevated candle, and of bringing it forward burning at the end of the service, is in allusion to the death and resurrection of Christ, whose light is represented by burning tapers. In the same manner, the other candles extinguished one after another, may represent the prophets successively put to death before their divine Lord.'

Born.—Pierre Simon Laplace, French savant, author of *Mécanique Céleste*, 1749, *Beaumont-en-Ange;* William Smith, 'The Father of English Geology,' 1769.

Died.—Peter the Cruel, king of Castile, 1369; Pope Julius III., 1556; Justus Lipsius, eminent historical writer, 1606, *Louvain;* Paul, Emperor of Russia, assassinated, 1801, *St Petersburg;* Thomas Holcroft, miscellaneous writer, 1809; Duchess of Brunswick, sister of George III., 1813; Augustus Frederick Kotzebue, German dramatist, 1819, assassinated at *Mannheim;* Carl Maria von Weber, German musical composer, 1829, *London;* Archdeacon Nares, philologist, 1829.

FACSIMILES OF INEDITED AUTOGRAPHS.
PEDRO THE CRUEL.

The following facsimile presents the autograph of Pedro I., King of Castile, styled the Cruel. The original is the signature to a treaty, and is copied from Cott. MS. Vesp. C. xii. The ink is thick, and of a brown colour, and it will be seen that Pedro, for a king in the fourteenth century, wrote a very good hand. He has been stigmatised as unnatural, cruel, an infidel, and a fratricide; but Pedro's fratricide consisted in executing an illegitimate brother who was about to assassinate him, and his infidelity appears chiefly to have been hatred of the monks. The latter, in their turn, hated him, and as their pens were more lasting than his sceptre, Pedro's name has descended to posterity blackened by the accusation of almost every crime which man could commit.

Don Pedro was born in 1334, and died by the dagger of his illegitimate brother Enrique (who usurped his throne) at Montièl, on the 23d of March 1369, aged thirty-five. His two surviving daughters became the wives of John of Gaunt and Edmund of Langley, sons of Edward III. of England.

This Prince is one of the first modern kings who possessed the accomplishment of writing. Our Henry I. ('Beauclerc') could not write, and signed with a mark, as any one may see who will take the trouble to consult Cott. MS. Vesp. F. iii. (British Museum).

'YO EL REY'—'I THE KING.'

ENGLAND LAID UNDER INTERDICT.

On the 23d of March 1208, England underwent the full vengeance of the papal wrath. King John had occupied the throne during nearly nine years, and had contrived to lose his continental territories, and to incur the hatred of his subjects ; and he now quarrelled with the Church —then a very formidable power. The ground of dispute was the appointment of an Archbishop of Canterbury ; and as the ecclesiastics of Canterbury espoused the papal choice, John treated them with a degree of brutality which could not fail to provoke the utmost indignation of the Court of Rome. Innocent III., who at this time occupied the papal chair, expostulated with the king of England, and demanded redress following up these demands with threats of laying an interdict upon the kingdom, and excommunicating the king. When these threats were announced to John, ' the king,' to use the words of the contemporary historian, Roger de Wendover, ' became nearly mad with rage, and broke forth in words of blasphemy against the Pope and his cardinals, swearing by God's teeth that, if they or any other priests soever presumptuously dared to lay his dominions under an interdict, he would banish all the English clergy, and confiscate all the property of the church ;' adding that, if he found any of the Pope's clerks in England, he would send them home to Rome with their eyes torn out and their noses split, 'that they might be known there from other people.' Accordingly, on Easter Monday, 1208, which that year fell on the 23d of March, the three bishops of London, Ely, and Winchester, as the Pope's legates, laid a general interdict on the whole of England, by which all the churches were closed, and all religious service was discontinued, with the exception of confession, the administration of the viaticum on the point of death, and the baptism of children. Marriages could no longer be celebrated, and the bodies of the dead 'were carried out of cities and towns, and buried in roads and ditches, without prayers or the attendance of priests.' The king retaliated by carrying out his threat of confiscation; he seized all the church property, giving the ecclesiastical proprietors only a scanty allowance of food and clothing. 'The corn of the clergy was everywhere locked up,' says the contemporary writer, ' and distrained for the benefit of the revenue ; the concubines of the priests and clerks were taken by the king's servants, and compelled to ransom themselves at a great expense; monks and other persons ordained, of any kind, when found travelling on the roads, were dragged from their horses, robbed, and basely ill-treated by the king's satellites, and no one would do them justice. About that time the sergeants of a certain sheriff on the borders of Wales came to the king, bringing in their custody, with his hands tied behind him, a robber who had robbed and murdered a priest on the high road; and on their asking the king what it was his pleasure should be done to a robber in such a case, the king immediately replied, " He has only slain one of my enemies ; release him, and let him go." ' In such a state of things, it is not to be won-

dered at if the higher ecclesiastics fled to the Continent, and as many of the others as could make their escape followed their example. This gloomy period, which lasted until the taking off the interdict in 1214, upwards of six years, was long remembered in the traditions of the peasantry.

We have heard a rather curious legend, on tradition, connected with this event. Many of our readers will have noticed the frequent occurrence, on old common lands, and even on the sides of wild mountains and moorlands, of the traces of furrows, from the process of ploughing the land at some very remote period. To explain these, it is pretended that King John's subjects found an ingenious method of evading one part of the interdict, by which all the cultivated land in the kingdom was put under a curse. People were so superstitious that they believed that the land which lay under this curse would be incapable of producing crops, but they considered that the terms of the interdict applied only to land in cultivation at the time when it was proclaimed, and not to any which began to be cultivated afterwards ; and to evade its effect, they left uncultivated the land which had been previously cultivated, and ploughed the commons and other uncultivated lands : and that the furrows we have alluded to are the remains of this temporary cultivation. It is probable that this interpretation is a very erroneous one ; and it is now the belief of antiquaries that most of these very ancient furrow-traces, which have been remarked especially over the Northumbrian hills, are the remains of the agriculture of the Romans, who obtained immense quantities of corn from Britain, and appear to have cultivated great extents of land which were left entirely waste during the middle ages.

Our mediæval forefathers frequently shewed great ingenuity in evading the ecclesiastical laws and censures. We have read in an old record, the reference to which we have mislaid, of a wealthy knight, who, for his offences, was struck with the excommunication of the Church, and, as he was obstinate in his contumacy, died under the sentence. According to the universal belief, a man dying under such circumstances had no other prospect but everlasting damnation. But our knight had remarked that the terms of the sentence were that he would be damned whether buried within the church or without the church, and he gave orders to make a hole in the exterior wall of the building, and to bury his body there, believing that, as it was thus neither within the church nor without the church, he would escape the effects of the excommunication. Curiously enough, one or two examples have been met with of sepulchral interments within church walls, but it may perhaps be doubted if they admit of this explanation.

CAMPDEN HOUSE, KENSINGTON.

On the morning of Sunday, March 23, 1862, at about four o'clock, the mansion known as Campden House, built upon the high ground of Kensington just two centuries and a half before, was almost entirely destroyed by fire. It was one of the few old mansions in the environs of the metropolis which time has spared to our day; it belonged to a more picturesque age of architecture than the present; and though yielding in extent and beauty to its more noble neighbour, Holland House, built within five years of the same date, and which in general style it resembled, was still a very interesting fabric. It was built for Sir Baptist Hicks, about the year 1612; and his arms, with that date, and those of his son-in-law, Edward Lord Noel, and Sir Charles Morison, were emblazoned upon a large bay-window of the house. In the same year (1612), he built the Sessions House in the broad part of St John Street, Clerkenwell; it was named after him, Hicks's Hall, a name more familiar than Campden House, from the former being inscribed upon scores of milestones in the suburbs of London, the distances being measured 'from Hicks's Hall.' This Hall lasted about a century and a half, when it fell into a ruinous condition, and a new Hall was built on Clerkenwell Green, and thither was removed a handsomely carved wood mantelpiece from the old Hall, together with a portrait of Sir Baptist Hicks, painter unknown, and stated by Sir Bernard Burke to have never been engraved: it hung in the dining-room at the Sessions House.

Baptist Hicks was the youngest son of a wealthy silk-mercer, at the sign of the White Bear, at Soper Lane end, in Cheapside. He was brought up to his father's business, in which he amassed a considerable fortune. In 1603, he was knighted by James I., which occasioned a contest between him and the alderman, respecting precedence; and in 1611, being elected alderman of Bread Street ward, he was discharged, on paying a fine of £500, at the express desire of the King. Strype tells us that Sir Baptist was one of the first citizens that, after knighthood, kept their shops; but being charged with it by some of the aldermen, he gave this answer: 'That his servants kept the shop, though he had a regard to the special credit thereof; and that he did not live altogether upon interest, as most of the alderman knights did, laying aside their trade after knighthood; and that, had two of his servants kept their promise and articles concluded between them and him, he had been free of his shop two years past; and did then but seek a fit opportunity to leave the same.' This was in the year 1607. Sir Baptist was created a baronet 1st July 1620; and was further advanced to the peerage as Baron Hicks, of Ilmington, in the county of Warwick; and Viscount Campden, in Gloucestershire, 5th May 1628. He died at his house in the Old Jewry, 18th October 1629, and was buried at Campden. He was a distinguished member of the Mercers' Company, to which his widow made a liberal bequest, one object of which was to assist young freemen beginning business as shopkeepers, with the gratuitous loan of £1000. Lady Campden was also a benefactress to the parish of Kensington.

The Campden House estate was purchased by Sir Baptist Hicks from Sir Walter Cope, or, according to a tradition in the parish, was won of him at some game of chance. Bowack, in his *Antiquities of Middlesex*, describes it as 'a very

noble pile, and finished with all the art the architects of that time were masters of; the situation being upon a hill, makes it extreme healthful and pleasant.' Sir Baptist Hicks had two daughters, coheiresses, who are reputed to have had £100,000 each for their fortune: the eldest, Juliana, married Lord Noel, to whom the title devolved at the first Viscount Campden's decease; Mary, the youngest daughter, married Sir Charles Morison, of Cashiobury, Herts. Baptist, the third Lord Campden, who was a zealous royalist, lost much property during the Civil Wars, but was permitted to keep his estates on paying the sum of £9000 as a composition, and making a settlement of £150 per annum on the Commonwealth Ministry. He resided chiefly at Campden House during the Protectorate: the Committee for Sequestrations held their meetings here.

At the Restoration, the King honoured Lord Campden with particular notice; and we read in the *Mercurius Politicus*, that on June 8, 1666, 'His Majesty was pleased to sup with Lord Campden at Kensington.' In 1662, an Act was passed for settling Campden House upon this nobleman and his heirs for ever; and in 1667, his son-in-law, Montague Bertie, Earl of Lindsey, who so nobly distinguished himself by his filial piety at the battle of Edge Hill, and who was wounded at Naseby, died in this house.

In 1691, Anne, Princess of Denmark, hired Campden House from the Noel family, and resided there for about five years with her son, William Duke of Gloucester, then heir-presumptive to the throne. The adjoining house is said to have been built at this time for the accommodation of her Royal Highness's household: it was named Little Campden House, and was for some time the residence of William Pitt; it had an outer arcaded gallery, and was subsequently called The Elms, and tenanted by Mr Egg, the painter: it was greatly injured by the fire.

At Campden House, the young Duke's amusements were chiefly of a military cast; and at a very early age he formed a regiment of boys, chiefly from Kensington, who were on constant duty here. He was placed under the care of the Earl of Marlborough and of Bishop Burnet. When King William gave him into the hands of the former, 'Teach him to be what you are,' said the King, 'and my nephew cannot want accomplishments.' Bishop Burnet, who had superintended his education for ten years, describes him as an amiable and accomplished prince, and in describing his education, says, 'The last thing I explained to him was the Gothic constitution, and the beneficiary and feudal laws: I talked of these things, at different times, near three hours a day. The King ordered five of his chief ministers to come once a quarter, and examine the progress he had made.' They were astonished at his proficiency. He was, however, of weak constitution; 'but,' says the Bishop, 'we hoped the dangerous time was over. His birthday was on the 24th of July 1700, and he was then eleven years old: he complained the next day, but we imputed that to the fatigue of a birthday, so that he was too much neglected; the day after, he grew much worse, and it proved to be a malignant fever. He died (at Windsor) on the fourth day of his illness : he was the only remaining child of seventeen that the Princess had borne.' Burnet adds, ' His death gave great alarm to the whole nation. The Jacobites grew insolent upon it, and said, now the chief difficulty was removed out of the way of the Prince of Wales's succession.' Mr Shippen, who then resided at Holland House, wrote the following lines upon the young Prince's death :

'So, by the course of the revolving spheres,
 Whene'er a new discovered star appears,
 Astronomers, with pleasure and amaze,
 Upon the infant luminary gaze.
 They find their heaven's enlarged, and wait
   from thence
 Some blest, some more than common influence ;
 But suddenly, alas ! the fleeting light,
 Retiring, leaves their hopes involved in endless
   night.'

In 1704, Campden House was in the occupation of the Dowager Countess of Burlington, and of her son the architect Earl, then in his ninth year. In the latter part of Queen Anne's reign, Campden House was sold to Nicholas Lechmere, an eminent lawyer, who became Chancellor of the Duchy of Lancaster, and Attorney-General. In 1721, he was created a peer, and Swift's ballad of *Duke upon Duke*, in which the following lines occur, had its origin in a quarrel between his lordship, who then occupied this mansion, and Sir John Guise :

'Back in the dark, by Brompton Park,
   He turned up through the Gore,
 So slunk to Campden House so high,
   All in his coach and four.
 The Duke in wrath call'd for his steeds,
   And fiercely drove them on ;
 Lord ! Lord ! how rattled then thy stones,
   O kingly Kensington !
 Meanwhile, Duke Guise did fret and fume,
   A sight it was to see,
 Benumbed beneath the evening dew,
   Under the greenwood tree.'

The original approach to Campden House from the town of Kensington was through an avenue of elms, which extended nearly to the High-street and great western road, through the grounds subsequently the cemetery. About the year 1798, the land in front of the house was planted with trees, which nearly cut off the view from the town ; and at the same time a new road was made to the east, and planted with a shrubbery. About this time, Lyons describes a caper-tree, which had flourished in the garden of Campden House for more than a century. Miller speaks of it in the first edition of his *Gardener's Dictionary*; it was sheltered from the north, having a south-east aspect, and though not within the reach of any artificial heat, it produced fruit every year.

The olden celebrity of Campden House may be said to have ceased a century since ; for Faulkner, in his *History and Antiquities of Kensington*, 1820, states it to have then been occupied more than sixty years as a boarding-school for ladies. He describes the piers of the old gateway as then surmounted by two finely sculptured dogs, the supporters of the Campden arms, which were

placed there when the southern avenue was removed in the year 1798. The mansion was built of brick, with stone finishings ; and a print of the year 1793 shews the principal or southern

CAMPDEN HOUSE.

front, of three stories, to have then consisted of three bays, flanked by two square turrets, surmounted with cupolas ; the central bay having an enriched Jacobean entrance porch, with the Campden arms sculptured above the first-floor bay-windows ; a pierced parapet above ; and dormer windows in the roof. As usual with old mansions, as the decorated portions decay, they are not replaced ; and Faulkner's view of this front, in 1820, shews the turrets without the cupola roofs ; the main roof appears flat, and the ornamental porch has given way to a pair of plain columns supporting the central bay-window. He describes this front as having lost most of its original ornaments, and being then covered with stucco. His view also shews the eastern end, with its bays and gables, its stacks of chimneys in the form of square towers, and the brickwork panelled according to the original design. The north or garden front was, at the same period, more undermined than the south front ; and westward the mansion adjoined Little Campden House.

Faulkner described—so lately as 1820, be it remembered—the entrance-hall lined with oak panelling, and having an archway leading to the grand staircase ; on the right was a large parlour, modernised ; and on the west were the domestic offices. The great dining-room, in which Charles II. supped with Lord Campden, was richly carved in oak ; and the ceiling was stuccoed, and ornamented with the arms of the Campden family. But the glory of this room was the tabernacle oak mantelpiece, consisting of six Corinthian columns, supporting a pediment ; the intercolumniations being filled with grotesque devices, and the whole supported by two caryatidal figures, finely carved. The *state apartments* on the first floor consisted of three large rooms facing the south ; that on the east, 'Queen Anne's bed-chamber,' had an enriched plaster ceiling, with pendants, and the walls were hung with red damask tapestry, in imitation of foliage. The central apartment originally had its large bay-window filled with painted glass.

shewing the arms of Sir Baptist Hicks, Lord Noel, and Sir Charles Morison; and the date of the erection of the mansion, 1612. The eastern wing, on the first floor, contained 'the globe-room,' which Faulkner thought to have been originally a chapel; but we rather think it had been the theatre for puppets, fitted up for the amusement of the young Duke of Gloucester; it communicated with a terrace in the garden by a flight of steps, made, it is said, for the accommodation of the Princess Anne. The apartment adjoining that last named had its plaster ceiling enriched with arms, and a mantelpiece of various marbles. Such was the Campden House of last century. A few years before the fire, large sums had been expended upon the restoration and embellishment of the interior: a spacious theatre had been fitted up for amateur performances, and the furniture and enrichments were in sumptuous taste, if not in style accordant with the period of the mansion; but, whatever may have been their merits, the whole of the interior, its fittings and furniture, were destroyed in the conflagration of March 23; and before the Londoners had risen from their beds that Sunday morning, all that remained of Campden House, or 'Queen Anne's Palace,' as it was called by the people of Kensington, were its blackened and windowless walls. As the abode of the ennobled merchant of the reign of James I.; where Charles II. feasted with his loyal chamberlain; and as the residence of the Princess, afterwards Queen Anne, and the nursing home of the heir to the British throne, Campden House is entitled to special record, and its disappearance to a passing note.

SWALLOWING A PADLOCK.

Medical men see more strange things, perhaps, than any other persons. They are repeatedly called upon to grapple with difficulties, concerning which there is no definite line of treatment generally recognised; or to treat exceptional cases, in which the usual course of proceeding cannot with safety be adopted. If it were required to name the articles which a woman would *not* be likely to swallow, a *brass padlock* might certainly claim a place in the list; and we can well imagine that a surgeon would find his ingenuity taxed to grapple with such a case. An instance of this kind took place at Edinburgh in 1837; as recorded in the local journals, the particulars were as follows: On the 23d of March, the surgeons at the Royal Infirmary were called upon to attend to a critical case. About the middle of February, a woman, while engaged in some pleasantry, put into her mouth a small brass padlock, about an inch and two-thirds in length, and rather more than an inch in breadth. To her consternation, it slipped down her throat. Fear of distressing her friends led her to conceal the fact. She took an emetic, but without effect; and for twenty-four hours she was in great pain, with a sensation of suffocation in the throat. She then got better, and for more than a month suffered but little pain. Renewed symptoms of inconvenience led her to apply to the Infirmary. One of the professors believed the story she told; others deemed it incredible; and nothing immediately was done. When, however, pain, vomiting, and a sense of suffocation returned, Dr James Johnson, hospital-assistant to Professor Lizars, was called upon suddenly to attend to her. He saw that either the padlock must be extracted, or the

woman would die. An instrument was devised for the purpose by Mr Macleod, a surgical instrument maker; and, partly by the skill of the operator, partly by the ingenious formation of the instrument, the strange mouthful was extracted from the throat. The woman recovered.

MARCH 24.

St Irenæus, Bishop of Sirmium, martyr, 304. St William, martyr at Norwich (aged eleven years), 1137. St Simon (an infant), martyr at Trent, 1472.

Maundy Thursday.

The day before Good Friday has been marked from an early age of the church by acts of humility, in imitation of that of Christ in washing the feet of his disciples on the eve of his passion. Ecclesiastics small and great, laymen of eminence, not excepting sovereign princes, have thought it fitting, in the spirit of their religion, to lay by personal dignity on this occasion, and condescend to the menial act of washing the feet of paupers. It is in consequence of an associated act of charity, the distribution of food in baskets, or *maunds*, that the day has come to be distinguished in England as Maundy Thursday. In Rome, however, and throughout Catholic Europe generally, the day is known as Holy Thursday. Another popular old name of the day in England is *Shere* Thursday, from the custom of shearing the hair which the priesthood used to observe.*

The observance of Maundy Thursday among the religious of old is duly described by Neogeorgus in his *Popish Kingdom*, as thus translated by Googe:

'And here the monks their maundies make with sundry solemn rites,
And signs of great humility, and wondrous pleasant sights.
Each one the other's feet doth wash, and wipe them clean and dry,
With hateful mind and secret fraud, that in their hearts doth lie;
As if that Christ with his examples did these things require,
And not to help our brethren here with zeal and free desire;
Each one supplying other's want, in all things that they may,
As he himself a servant made, to serve us every way.
Then straight the loaves do walk, and pots in every place they skink,
Wherewith the holy fathers oft to pleasant damsels drink.'

Cardinal Wolsey, at Peterborough Abbey, in

* By a natural inversion, maund and maundy have come to signify articles given in charity or from kindness. In an old jest-book, there is a story of a rich merchant dictating a testament to a scrivener, while a poor nephew stood by, hoping to hear of something to his advantage. While the testator was still enumerating the debts due to him, the nephew cried, 'Ha, ha! what saith my uncle now?—does he now make his *maundies*?' 'No,' answered the cool man of business, 'he is yet in his *demands*.' This is a good example of the secondary meaning.

1530, 'made his maund in our lady's chapel, having fifty-nine poor men whose feet he washed and kissed; and after he had wiped them, he gave every of the said poor men twelve pence in money, three ells of good canvas to make them shirts, a pair of new shoes, a cast of red herrings, and three white herrings; and one of these had two shillings'—the number of the poor men being probably in correspondence with the years of his age. About the same period, the Earl of Northumberland, on Maundy Thursday, gave to each of as many poor men as he was years old, and one over, a gown with a hood, a linen shirt, a platter with meat, an ashen cup filled with wine, and a leathern purse containing as many pennies as he was years old, and one over; besides miscellaneous gifts to be distributed in like manner in name of his lady and his sons.

The king of England was formerly accustomed on Maundy Thursday to have brought before him as many poor men as he was years old, whose feet he washed with his own hands, after which his majesty's maunds, consisting of meat, clothes, and money, were distributed amongst them. Queen Elizabeth, when in her thirty-ninth year, performed this ceremony at her palace of Greenwich, on which occasion she was attended by thirty-nine ladies and gentlewomen. Thirty-nine poor persons being assembled, their feet were first washed by the yeomen of the laundry with warm water and sweet herbs, afterwards by the sub-almoner, and finally by the queen herself, kneeling; these various persons, the yeomen, the sub-almoner, and the queen, after washing each foot, marked it with the sign of the cross above the toes, and then kissed it. Clothes, victuals, and money were then distributed. This strange ceremonial, in which the highest was for a moment brought beneath the lowest, was last performed in its full extent by James II.

King William left the washing to his almoner; and such was the arrangement for many years afterwards. 'Thursday, April 15 [1731], being Maundy Thursday, there was distributed at the Banqueting House, Whitehall, to forty-eight poor men and forty-eight poor women (the king [George II.]'s age being forty-eight), boiled beef and shoulders of mutton, and small bowls of ale, which is called dinner; after that large wooden platters of fish and loaves, viz. undressed, one large old ling, and one large dried cod; twelve red herrings and twelve white herrings, and four half-quarter loaves. Each person had one platter of this provision; after which were distributed to them shoes, stockings, linen and woollen cloth, and leather bags, with one penny, two-penny threepenny, and fourpenny pieces of silver and shillings; to each about four pounds in value. His Grace the Lord Archbishop of York, Lord High Almoner, performed the annual ceremony of washing the feet of a certain number of poor in the Royal Chapel, Whitehall, which was formerly done by the kings themselves, in imitation of our Saviour's pattern of humility.' For a considerable number of years, the washing of the feet has been entirely given up; and since the beginning of the reign of Queen Victoria, an additional sum of money has been given in lieu

of provisions. Some examples of the *Maundy money* recently used by English royalty are here represented.

In Austria, the old rite of the *Fusswaschung* is still kept up by the Emperor, under circumstances of great ceremony.

The ceremonies of Holy Thursday at Rome call for being described in detail.

1. *Blessing the Oils.*—This ceremony takes place in St Peter's during mass, the cardinal arch-priest, or a bishop in his stead, officiating. There are three varieties of the oil to be blessed. The first is the oil of catechumens, used in blessing baptism, in consecrating churches and altars, in ordaining priests, and in blessing and crowning sovereigns. The second is the oil used in administering extreme unction to the apparently dying. Third, the sacred chrism, composed of oil and balm of Gilead or of the West Indies, and which is used in confirmation, the consecration of bishops, patens, and chalices, and in the blessing of bells. The Roman Pontifical prescribes, that besides the bishop and the usual ministers, there should be present twelve priests, seven deacons, and seven sub-deacons, all habited in white vestments. The bishop sits down before a table facing the altar, and exorcises and blesses the oil for the sick, which is brought in by a sub-deacon. He then proceeds with the mass, during which the balsam is brought in, and also the oil for the chrism and that for the catechumens, by two deacons. The bishop blesses the balsam and mixes it with some oil; he then breathes three times in the form of a cross over the vessel of the chrism, as do the twelve priests also. Next follows the blessing, and then the salutation of the chrism; the latter is made three times, by the bishop and each of the twelve priests in succession saying, 'Hail, holy chrism,' after which they kiss the vessel which contains it. The oil of catechumens is blessed and saluted in like manner; and with the remaining part of the mass the rite terminates. Roman Catholic writers adduce various authorities and traditions sanctioning these ceremonies.

2. *Silencing the Bells.*—In the Sistine chapel, at the performance of mass, after the Gloria in Excelsis is sung, no bells are allowed to be rung in Rome, except at the Papal benediction, until the same canticle is sung in the Papal chapel on the following Saturday morning. In other words, all the bells in Rome are mute from about half-past eleven on Thursday morning till

the same time on Saturday. During this period of two days, such is the force of the custom, that hand-bells, usually employed in hotels to be rung for dinner, are silent. So likewise bells rung for school remain mute. As a substitute for bells, it is the practice to use a kind of wooden clappers, or *troccola*. These are in the form of wooden boxes, with some interior mechanism turned by a handle, so as to make a disagreeable clattering noise. This species of troccole is said to have been used anciently by the Greeks. The silencing of the bells—a signal comfort to the ears in some parts of Rome—being prescribed in ancient rituals, is thus enforced as one of the old customs of the church.

3. *Feet Washing at St Peter's.*—The Pope, who officiates at this and other ceremonies, is this day dressed very plainly, in white, with a red cope, and a small white skull-cap; and instead of being carried he walks, for the object of the usages in which he is concerned is to typify the humility of Christ on the night of the Last Supper. After mass at the Sistine chapel, his Holiness, about one o'clock, proceeds to the balcony over the central door of St Peter's, and there pronounces his general benediction. As this is repeated in grander style on Easter Sunday, there is usually no great concourse of spectators. Descending to the church, the Pope proceeds to the northern transept, which is fitted up for the occasion. On the north is his chair of state; on the west and ranged along the draped wall, embellished with a tapestry picture of the Last Supper, is a bench or seat elevated on a platform so as to be conspicuous. The other parts of the transept are fitted with seats for distinguished persons, also for ladies who are suitably dressed and provided with tickets. Just as the Pope is about to take his seat, there enter from a side door thirteen bishops dressed in high white caps and white garments. Twelve of these represent the apostles, whose feet were washed by Christ, and the thirteenth represents an angel, who, according to the legend, appeared to Gregory the Great (590—604), while he was performing an act of charity to poor persons. These thirteen bishops, who are all habited alike, take their seats gravely on the bench along the wall, and are the objects of general attention; for it is their feet which the Pope is about to wash. After some singing and reading of passages of Scripture, the Pope's cope is taken off, an embroidered apron is put on, and a towel is fastened to his waist by the assisting cardinal deacons; and then he washes and kisses the right foot of each of the thirteen priests. It is to be understood that the washing is of the slightest possible kind. Little time is occupied. The ceremony terminates by each receiving from the Pope a towel and a nosegay, besides a gold and silver medal which are presented by the treasurer. The Pope now washes his hands, is re-invested in his red cope, and proceeds immediately to the next act of humiliation.

4. *The Pope Serving at Supper.*—Conducted in procession from the northern transept, the Pope walks across the nave of St Peter's to a stair which leads to a large apartment above the portico. Here a table is laid, as for a regular meal, the recipients of which are the thirteen priests who have just been honoured by having their feet washed. He gives them water to wash their hands, helps them to soup and other dishes, and pours out wine and water for them to drink. The plates are handed to him by prelates. During the ceremony, one of his chaplains reads prayers. He then blesses them, washes his hands, and departs. The priests who are the objects of these attentions are selected from different countries by the favour of diplomatic agents. Some of them, however, are Italians, selected by officials on the spot, the captain of the Pope's Swiss guard having the privilege of appointing one.

5. *The Grand Penitentiary.*—Among the remarkable things in St Peter's, are the number of confessionals, in which are seated clergymen ready to hear the confessions of those who apply to them, and who seem so many religious sentinels at their posts. Still more to accommodate applicants, the confessionals, as is seen by inscriptions on them, are for the French, German, Spanish, Portuguese, English, and Greek, as well as Italian languages. Besides this usual arrangement, the Grand Cardinal Penitentiary sits in a confessional in the afternoon of Holy Thursday to give absolution for mortal sins which are beyond the sphere of ordinary confession, and which cannot otherwise be absolved. This day, the altars of St Peter's are all stripped, the hundred lamps that usually burn round the tomb of St Peter are extinguished, and with the chanting of the *Miserere* a general gloom prevails.

6. *Washing the Feet of Pilgrims.*—The ceremonies connected with the so-called pilgrims, take place at the *Trinità de' Pellegrini*, an establishment adapted for accommodating pilgrims and situated in one of the populous parts of Rome. Poor persons are admitted to the benefit of the charity, who have come to visit the holy places from a greater distance than sixty miles, and who bring certificates from their bishop. The ceremonies on the evening of Holy Thursday consist in washing the feet of pilgrims of both sexes, the men in one place, and the women in another. To the female department ladies only are admitted as spectators. After the feet-washing, each class is entertained at supper. The following account of the affair is by an eye-witness in the year 1862:—'I went to the feet-washing of the male pilgrims about eight o'clock. On entering a passage, I saw a tremendous crush at the further end, where there was a door opening on a lower floor, in which the ceremony takes place. With some little squeezing, I got through the doorway, down a few steps, and found myself in a hot and close apartment, crowded nearly to suffocation. Along one end and side was a bench to be used as a seat, with a foot-board raised off the floor. A paling and guards kept back the crowd. In half an hour, a troop of poor-looking people, very much resembling the ragged beggars whom one sees in the streets of Rome, entered by a side door, and ranging themselves along the bench, proceeded to take off their shoes and stockings. Several priests now appear, and one of them having read some prayers, they join the body of operators. These are gentlemen and persons in

business in Rome, who form a confraternity devoted to this and other acts of charity. They are habited in a red jacket, a little cravat, and apron, and sit chatting and laughing till the tubs with warm water are brought in, and set, one before each poor person. They now begin the operation of washing, the general remark of the on-lookers being that to all appearance the feet had previously been cleaned, so that the act of voluntary humiliation does not seem particularly nauseous, nor does it last long. The priests get their hands washed by having hot water poured on them, along with a squeeze of lemon, and another prayer ends the ceremony, which, to say the least of it, is not pleasing. The pilgrims afterwards adjourn to a hall, where, at long tables, the same operators wait upon them at supper. To my mind, the whole thing had a got-up look, and one wonders how it should be perpetuated. Similar ceremonies take place in the female department, where the operators are ladies of distinction. These ceremonies are repeated on Friday and Saturday evenings. The pilgrims are lodged and otherwise entertained during this period, and are dismissed with small money presents.'

At Rome, on the evening of this day, the shops of sausage-makers, candle-makers, and pork-dealers are decorated and illuminated in a fantastic way. The most prominent object in each is a picture of the Virgin and Child, enshrined amidst flowers and candles, as on a sort of altar. Festoons of flowers and evergreens are otherwise stuck about, and there is a profusion of patches of divers colours on the pork, candles, and other articles on the shelves. These grotesque illuminations draw crowds of strangers and others to witness them; the shops so lighted up doing apparently a little more business than usual.

Born.—Mahomet II., 1430, *Adrianople;* Henry Benedict, Cardinal York, 1725, *Rome.*

Died.—Haroun-al-Raschid, twenty-fifth Caliph, 809 ; Pope Nicholas V., 1455 ; Elizabeth, Queen of England, 1603, *Sheen (Richmond)* ; Dr Daniel Whitby, celebrated divine, 1726, *Salisbury ;* Philip, Earl of Chesterfield, author of the celebrated *Letters,* 1773, *Chesterfield House, May Fair ;* John Harrison, maker of 'The Longitude Watch,' 1776, *Red Lion-square, London ;* Mrs Mary Tighe, classic poetess, 1810, *Woodstock, Ireland ;* Bertel Thorvaldsen, Danish sculptor, 1844 ; Rev. Thomas Gisborne, miscellaneous writer, 1846.

FACSIMILES OF INEDITED AUTOGRAPHS.
QUEEN ELIZABETH.

Elizabeth was born at Greenwich, September 7, 1533, and died March 24, 1602-3, in her seventieth year. This is one of her earliest autographs, being the signature of a letter (Cott. MSS. Vesp. F. III.) written in 1558, the year of her accession to the throne. Her hand changed much for
414

the worse in her latter years. The present autograph is, however, slightly injured, in consequence of the edges of the letter having been burnt away.

DEATH OF QUEEN ELIZABETH.

A variety of relations and reports of the circumstances of the death of this great queen are current ; but that which appears deserving of most credit has been least noticed. It is found in the manuscript diary of a contemporary, a barrister named Maningham, which is preserved among the Harleian manuscripts in the British Museum ¡No. 5353). Maningham was acquainted with men at court well situated to give him correct information, especially with the queen's chaplain, Dr Parry, and, anxious to ascertain the real condition of the queen, he went to Richmond, where the court was then established, on the 23d of March 1603. He has entered in considerable detail the facts of this visit. 'March 23. I was at the court at Richmond to heare Dr Parry, one of her majesties chaplens, preache, and be assured whether the queane were living or dead. I heard him, and was assured shee was then living.' After the service, he dined with the preacher, and gathered from him the following interesting information :

'I dyned with Dr Parry in the privy chamber, and understood by him, the Bishop of Chichester, the Deane of Canterbury, the Deane of Windsore, &c., that her majestie hath bin by fits troubled with melancholy some three or four moneths ; but for this fortnight extreame oppressed with it, in soe much that she refused to eate anything, to receive any phisicke, or admit any rest in bedd, till within these two or three dayes. Shee hath bin in a manner speachlesse for two dayes ; very pensive and silent since Shrovetides, sitting sometymes with her eye fixed upon one object many houres togither ; yet she alwayes had her perfect senses and memory, and yesterday signified by the lifting up of her hand and eyes to heven, a signe which Dr Parry entreated of hir, that shee beleeved that fayth which she had caused to be professed, and looked faythfully to be saved by Christ's merits and mercy onely, and no other meanes. She tooke great delight in hearing prayers, would often at the name of Jesus lift up hir hands and eyes to heaven. She would not heare the archbishop speake of hope of hir longer lyfe, but when he prayed, or spake of heaven and those joyes, she would hug his hand, &c. It seems she might have lived yf she would have used meanes, but shee would not be persuaded, and princes must not be forced. Hir physicians sayd she had a body of a firme and perfect constitution, likely to have lived many yeares. A royal majesty is not privilege against death.'

Next day, Maningham was again at Richmond, probably he had remained all night.

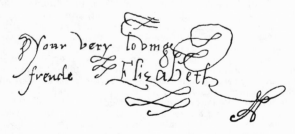

and he added the following entry in his diary :
—'March 24. This morning about three at
clocke, her majestie departed this lyfe, mildly
like a lambe, easely like a ripe apple from the
tree ; *cum levi quâdam febre, absque gemitu.* Dr
Parry told me that he was present, and sent his
prayers before hir soule ; and I doubt not but
shee is amongst the royall saints in heaven in
eternall joyes.'

It will be seen that our diarist makes no allusions to the manner in which Elizabeth was
rumoured to have signified her wish that James
of Scotland should be her successor on the
English throne ; but a few days later we find the
following curious entry :

'April 4. Dr Parry told me the Countess
Kildare assured him that the queane caused the
ring wherewith shee was wedded to the crowne to
be cutt from hir finger some six weekes before hir
death ; but wore a ring which the Earl of Essex
gave hir unto the day of hir death.'

THE OLD MANOR-HOUSE AT STOKE POGIS,
BUCKINGHAMSHIRE.

This venerable mansion was built, or begun
to be built by George Hastings, first Earl of
Huntingdon, who died on the 24th of March
1544, and was buried in Stoke church. Like
many other manor-houses of the same, or of an

MANOR-HOUSE OF STOKE POGIS.

earlier period, that of Stoke was invested with
considerable interest from its association with
persons who were remarkable in their generation, if not of historic fame. This interest in
Stoke manor-house has been preserved and
enhanced by Gray, who, in his amusing poem of
' A Long Story,' has thus described it :

  ' In Britain's isle, no matter where,
    An ancient pile of building stands,
  The Huntingdons and Hattons there
    Employed the power of fairy hands
  To raise the building's fretted height,
    Each panel in achievement clothing,

  Rich windows that exclude the light,
    And passages that lead to nothing.
  Full oft within the spacious walls,
    When he had fifty winters o'er him,
  My grave Lord Keeper led the brawls ;
    The seal and maces danced before him.
  His bushy beard, and shoe-strings green,
    His high-crowned hat, and satin doublet,
  Moved the stout heart of England's Queen,
    Though Pope and Spaniard could not trouble it.

This ' grave Lord Keeper ' was Sir Christopher Hatton, who, it must be remarked, was
never the owner or occupier of this old mansion,
although generally supposed to have been so by
topographers, and by commentators on Gray's
Poems. The old manor-house, indeed, was not
completely finished till it came into the possession of Henry, the third Earl of Huntingdon,
who, although it might have been burdened by a
mortgage, certainly retained possession of it till
his death.

One of his letters now in existence is dated at
Stoke, on 13th December 1592,[*] and among the
payments after his funeral, occurs this item—
'Charges about the vendition of my Lord's goods
in the county of Bucks, £8.'[†] This most probably refers to the sale of his property at Stoke.
Now Sir Christopher Hatton died in November
1591, a year before the date of the Earl's letter
from Stoke, and four years before his death,
which occurred in 1595. But we have more
conclusive evidence to the same effect. Sir
Christopher has left numerous letters from which
his proceedings during the latter years of his
life—the only time in which he could have been
at Stoke—may be traced from month to month,
almost from day to day, and not one of these
letters affords the slightest indication of his
connexion with Stoke.[‡] Nor is such connexion
noticed in any parish record at Stoke. The idea
rests solely on tradition, and can easily be
accounted for.

On the death of the third Earl of Huntingdon,
Sir Edward Coke, the great lawyer, purchased
the manor and resided at Stoke ; and soon after,
in 1598, married for his second wife, Lady
Hatton, widow of Sir William Hatton, nephew
and heir of the ' Lord Keeper.' This lady was
sufficiently conspicuous to stamp the name of
Hatton on the traditions of Stoke. She was a
daughter of Lord Burleigh, and while priding
herself on her ' gentle blood,' was imperious,
officious, and vindictive. From her first husband
she received a rich jointure, and retained his
three places of residence in her own hands.
She also retained his name after her marriage
with Sir Edward Coke, who was old enough to
have been her father, and towards whom she
always affected great contempt. She stipulated
that her marriage should be secretly performed
in a private house, late in the evening, and
without banns or licence. For this irregular
marriage the ' great oracle of the law,' his bride,
her father Lord Burleigh, and the officiating
minister, were cited into the ecclesiastical court.

[*] History of Stoke Pogis.
[†] Bell's *Huntingdon Peerage*, p. 80.
[‡] See *Life of Sir Christopher Hatton*, by Sir Harris
Nicolas. 1847.

Thus commenced 'the honeymoon of the happy pair.'* Lady Hatton next forbade her spouse to enter her house in Holborn except by a back door. For many years the stern lawyer submitted to be hen-pecked in silence. At length he was driven to have recourse to law; for while he was professionally engaged in London, his faithful wife was at Stoke dismantling his house. She collected all his plate, and other valuable moveables, and carried them off to one of her own houses.

She is also supposed to have influenced Lord Bacon and others to prejudice the King against him, by casting discredit on his official proceedings. Certain it is that about this time he lost the King's favour; was deprived of his office as Lord Chief Justice, and advised to 'live privately at home, and take into consideration and review his book of Reports, wherein, as his Majesty is informed, be many extravagant and exorbitant opinions set down and published for positive and good law.' Poor Sir Edward!—'to live privately at home,' in a dismantled house, with a sullied reputation, and his wife entertaining his enemies with his property, and at the expense of his character. This was too much to bear. The lion was roused; and he who was such a stickler for the law set the law at defiance, and, forcibly entering Lady Hatton's houses in search of his property, not only carried off his own, but some of hers also. This led to legal proceedings against each other. Sir Edward accused his lady of having 'embezzled all his gilt and silver plate and vessell, and instead thereof foisted in alkumy of the same sorte, fashion, and use, with the illusion to have cheated him of the other.' Lady Hatton, on her part, alleged that 'Sir Edward broke into Hatton House, seased upon my coach and coach horses, nay, my apparel, which he detains; thrast all my servants out of doors without wages, sent down his men to Corfe Castle [another of her ladyship's residences] to inventory, seize, ship, and carry away all the goods, which being refused him by the castle-keeper, he threats to bring your lordship's warrant for the performance thereof. Stop, then, his high tyrannical courses; for I have suffered beyond the measure of any wife, mother, nay, of any ordinary woman in this kingdom, without respect to my father, my birth, my fortunes, with which I have so highly raised him.' Judgment was given in favour of Lady Hatton; and a reconciliation took place, for Sir Edward 'flattered himself she would still prove a very good wife.'

In the following year these domestic broils took another course. Sir Edward Coke and Lady Hatton had one child, a daughter, and when she was about fourteen years old, her father negotiated for her marriage with Sir John Villiers, brother of Buckingham, the King's favourite, hoping through this alliance to regain the King's favour. The proposal was graciously received, and Sir Edward was delighted with the prospect of success. It is true that his wife and daughter, who were then residing with him at Stoke, did not relish his scheme; but this did

* Disraeli's *Curiosities of Literature*, and *The Story of Corfe Castle*, by Bankes.

416

not much trouble him, as he considered that his daughter, in such a case, was bound to obey her father's mandate. Highly gratified with this prospect, he retired to rest, and enjoyed a quiet, undisturbed slumber. But the first intelligence of the morning was that Lady Hatton and her daughter had left Stoke at midnight, and no one knew where they were gone. Here was a blow to his promising scheme. Day after day passed, and yet he could learn no tidings of the fugitives. At last he ascertained that they were concealed at Oatlands, a house then rented by a cousin of Lady Hatton. Without waiting for a warrant, Sir Edward, accompanied by a dozen sturdy men, all well armed, hastened to Oatlands, and, after two hours' resistance, took the house by assault and battery. This curious piece of family warfare is admirably described by Lady Hatton herself as 'Sir Edward Cook's most notorious riot, committed at my Lord of Arguyl's house, when, without constable or warrant, associated with a dozen fellows well weaponed, without out cause being beforehand offered, to have what he would, he took down the doors of the gatehouse and of the house itself, and tore the daughter in that barbarous manner from the mother, and would not suffer the mother to come near her.'

Having thus gained possession of his daughter, he carried her off to Stoke, locked her up in an upper chamber, and kept the key of the door in his pocket. Lady Hatton made an attempt to recover her daughter by forcible means; but to her astonishment, for this attempt, and her other proceedings, her husband, now fortified by the King's favour, succeeded in throwing her into prison. Thus with his wife incarcerated in a public prison, and his daughter safely locked up in his own house, the great lawyer, to use his own expression, 'had got upon his wings again,' and forced both his wife and daughter to promise a legal consent to the marriage. Lady Hatton was even induced by the severities of prison to write to the king and promise to settle her lands on her daughter and Sir John Villiers. Thus Sir Edward Coke effected his object. His daughter and Sir John Villiers were married in 1617, at Hampton Court, in the presence of the King and Queen and all the chief nobility of England. The bridal banquet was most splendid, and a masque was performed in the evening; but Lady Hatton was still in confinement. Shortly afterwards she was liberated, and gave a magnificent entertainment at Hatton House, which was honoured by the presence of the King and Queen, but Sir Edward Coke and all his servants were peremptorily excluded. Two years afterwards Sir John Villiers was raised to the peerage, as Viscount Purbeck and Baron Villiers of Stoke Pogis. But the sequel of these family broils was melancholy. Lady Purbeck deserted her husband, and lived with Sir Robert Howard, which rapidly brought on her degradation, imprisonment, and an early death. Lady Hatton pursued her husband with rancorous hatred, and openly avowed her impatience for his death. A report of his death having one day reached her, she immediately left London for Stoke to take possession of his mansion, but on reaching Colnbrook, she met one of his physicians, who informed her of his amendment. On hearing this she returned to London in evident disappointment.

Sir Edward, in his solitary old age, must have viewed the fruits of his own scheme with bitter compunction. When eighty years of age, we are told, he 'felt himself alone on the earth, was suspected by his king, deserted by his friends, and detested by his wife.' His only domestic solace, during the last two years of his life, was the company of his daughter, Lady Purbeck, who, much to her credit, left her paramour to watch over the last hours of her aged father.

Three days before his death, being suspected of possessing seditious writings, his peace was disturbed by Sir Francis Windebank, who came with an order of Council to search his papers, and who carried off more than fifty manuscripts, including his will, which were not returned to the family till 1641. Sir Edward Coke died on the 3rd of September 1634, in his eighty-fourth year. Lady Purbeck then left Stoke, and soon after was imprisoned in the Gatehouse at Lambeth.*

Lady Hatton now took possession of the old manor-house, and occasionally resided in it till her death in 1644. From her, who must have long been the subject of local gossip, the name of Hatton might well be mixed up with the traditions of Stoke; and Gray, by poetic licence, or from want of better information, applied it to the Lord Keeper, who certainly never possessed the old manor-house, nor 'led the brawls' in it. It was, however, honoured by the presence of his royal mistress. Queen Elizabeth, in 1601, paid a visit at Stoke to Sir Edward Coke, who entertained her very sumptuously, and presented her on the occasion with jewels worth from ten to twelve hundred pounds.† In 1647, the old manor-house was for some days the residence of Charles I., when a prisoner in the custody of the parliamentary army.‡ It would have been visited by another of our monarchs had not its then owner refused to admit him. This was Sir Robert Gayer, who, by the bequest of his brother, came into possession of the manor in 1657. At the coronation of Charles II. this eccentric gentleman was made a knight of the Bath, which so strengthened his previous attachment to the House of Stuart that he never would be reconciled to any other dynasty. Soon after William III. had ascended the throne, he visited Stoke, and signified his desire to see the old manor-house. But the irascible old knight burst into a violent rage, vehemently declaring that the king should never come under his roof. ' He has already,' said he, ' got possession of another man's house—he is an usurper—tell him to go back again !' Lady Gayer expostulated; she entreated; she even fell on her knees, and besought her husband to admit the king, who was then actually waiting at the gate. All her efforts were useless. The obstinate knight only became more furious, vociferating—' An Englishman's house is his castle. I shall open and close my door to whom I please. The king,

I say, shall not come within these walls !' So his majesty returned as he came,—a stranger to the inside of the mansion, and the old knight gloried in his triumph.*

Thus the old manor-house at Stoke was possessed by some very remarkable characters; it entertained one sovereign in all the state and magnificence of royalty ; it received another as a prisoner in the custody of his own subjects ; it closed its doors against a third, and dismissed him as though he had been an insignificant intruder, and after having thus witnessed the strange and changing scenes of two centuries and a half, it was itself pulled down, with the exception of one wing, in 1789, by its then owner, Granville Penn, Esq., a descendant of the celebrated William Penn, the founder of Pennsylvania. The existing wing of the old house, though only a portion of an inferior part of the mansion, affords a specimen of Tudor architecture, and conveys some idea of the internal arrangement of the aristocratic residences of that period.   W. H. K.

MARCH 25.

THE ANNUNCIATION OF THE BLESSED VIRGIN MARY (Lady Day). St Cammin, of Ireland, abbot.

The Annunciation.

This day is held in the Roman Catholic Church as a great festival, in the Anglican Reformed Church as a feast, in commemoration of the message of the angel Gabriel to the Virgin Mary, informing her that the Word of God was become flesh. In England it is commonly called *Lady Day; in France, Notre Dame de Mars*. It is a very ancient institution in the Latin Church. Among the sermons of St Augustine, who died in 430, are two regarding the festival of the Annunciation.

' In representations of the Annunciation, the Virgin Mary is shewn kneeling, or seated at a table reading. The lily (her emblem) is usually placed between her and the angel Gabriel, who holds in one hand a sceptre surmounted by a fleur-de-lis, on a lily stalk; generally a scroll is proceeding from his mouth with the words *Ave Maria gratiâ plenâ;* and sometimes the Holy Spirit, represented as a dove, is seen descending towards the Virgin.'—*Calendar of the Anglican Church.*†

In the work here quoted, we find a statement affording strong proof of the high veneration in which the Virgin was formerly held in England, as she still is in Catholic countries; namely, that no fewer than two thousand one hundred and twenty churches were named in her sole honour, besides a hundred and two in which her name was associated with that of some other saint.

Born.—Archbishop John Williams, 1582, *Aberconway ;* Bishop George Bull, 1634, *Wells ;* Sir Richard Cox, Lord Chancellor of Ireland, 1650, *Bandon ;* Joachim Murat, King of Naples, 1771, *Bastide Frontonière.*

---

* Disraeli's *Curiosities of Literature.* vol. v. p. 1—18. Bankes' *Story of Corfe Castle*, pp. 36—57.
† Lysons' *Magna Britannia.*
‡ Idem.

* Lipscomb's *Bucks*, vol. iv. *in loco.*
† J. H. Parker, Oxford and London, 1851.

Died.—Sir Thomas Elyot. eminent English writer *temp.* Henry VIII., 1546; Bishop Aldrich, 1556, *Horncastle;* Archbishop John Williams, 1650, *Llandegay;* Henry Cromwell, fourth son of the Protector, 1674, *Soham, Cambridgeshire;* Nehemiah Grew, celebrated for his work on the Anatomy of Vegetables, 1711; Anna Seward, miscellaneous writer, 1809, *Lichfield.*

Good Friday.

The day of the Passion has been held as a festival by the Church from the earliest times. In England, the day is one of two (Christmas being the other) on which all business is suspended. In the churches, which are generally well attended, the service is marked by an unusual solemnity.

Before the change of religion, Good Friday was of course celebrated in England with the same religious ceremonies as in other Catholic countries. A dressed figure of Christ being mounted on a crucifix, two priests bore it round the altar, with doleful chants; then, laying it on the ground with great tenderness, they fell beside it, kissed its hands and feet with piteous sighs and tears, the other priests doing the like in succession. Afterwards came the people to worship the assumedly dead Saviour, each bringing some little gift, such as corn and eggs. There was finally a most ceremonious burial of the image, along with the 'singing bread,' amidst the light of torches and the burning of incense, and with flowers to strew over the grave.

The king went through the ceremony of blessing certain rings, to be distributed among the people, who accepted them as infallible cures for cramp. Coming in state into his chapel, he found a crucifix laid upon a cushion, and a carpet spread on the ground before it. The monarch crept along the carpet to the crucifix, as a token of his humility, and there blessed the rings in a silver basin, kneeling all the time, with his almoner likewise kneeling by his side. After this was done, the queen and her ladies came in, and likewise crept to the cross. The blessing of cramp-rings is believed to have taken its rise in the efficacy for that disease supposed to reside in a ring of Edward the Confessor, which used to be kept in Westminster Abbey. There can be no doubt that a belief in the medical power of the cramp-ring was once as faithfully held as any medical maxim whatever. Lord Berners, the accomplished translator of Froissart, while ambassador in Spain, wrote to Cardinal Wolsey June 21, 1518, entreating him to reserve a few cramp-rings for him, adding that he hoped, with God's grace, to bestow them well.

A superstition regarding bread baked on Good Friday appears to have existed from an early period. Bread so baked was kept by a family all through the ensuing year, under a belief that a few gratings of it in water would prove a specific for any ailment, but particularly for diarrhœa. We see a memorial of this ancient superstition in the use of what are called hot cross-buns, which may now be said to be the most prominent popular observance connected with the day. In London, and all over England (not, however, in Scotland), the morning of Good Friday

is ushered in with a universal cry of *Hot Cross-Buns!* A parcel of them appears on every breakfast table. It is a rather small bun, more than usually spiced, and having its brown sugary surface marked with a cross. Thousands of poor children and old frail people take up for this day the business of disseminating these quasi-religious cakes, only intermitting the duty during church hours; and if the eagerness with which young and old eat them could be held as expressive of an appropriate sentiment within their hearts, the English might be deemed a pious people. The ear of every person who has ever dwelt in England is familiar with the cry of the street bun-vendors:

> One a penny, buns,
> Two a penny, buns,
> One a penny, two a penny,
> Hot cross-buns!

Whether it be from failing appetite, the chilling effects of age, or any other fault in ourselves, we cannot say; but it strikes us that neither in the bakers' shops, nor from the baskets of the street-vendors, can one now get hot cross-buns comparable to those of past times. They want the spice, the crispness, the everything they once had. Older people than we speak also with mournful affection of the two noted bun-houses of Chelsea. Nay, they were *Royal* bun-houses, if their signs could be believed, the popular legend always insinuating that the King himself had stopped there, bought, and eaten of the buns. Early in the present century, families of the middle classes walked a considerable way to taste the delicacies of the Chelsea bun-houses, on the seats beneath the shed which screened the pavement in front. An insane rivalry, of course, existed between the two houses, one pretending to be *The* Chelsea Bun-house, and the other the Real Old Original Chelsea Bun-house. Heaven knows where the truth lay, but one thing was certain and assured to the innocent public, that the buns of both were so very good that it was utterly impossible to give an exclusive verdict in favour of either.

A writer, signing himself H. C. B., gives in the *Athenæum* for April 4, 1857, an account of an ancient sculpture in the Museo Borbonico at Rome, representing the miracle of the five barley loaves. The loaves are marked each with a cross on the surface, and the circumstance is the more remarkable, as the *hot cross-bun* is not a part of the observance of the day on the Continent. H. C. B. quotes the late Rev. G. S. Faber for a train of speculation, having for its conclusion that our eating of the hot cross-buns is to be traced back to a pagan custom of worshipping the Queen of Heaven with cakes— a custom to be found alike in China and in ancient Mexico, as well as many other countries. In Egypt, the cakes were horned to resemble the sacred heifer, and thence called *bous*, which in one of its oblique cases is *boun*—in short, *bun!* So people eating these hot cross-buns little know what, in reality, they are about.

WASHING MOLLY GRIME.

In the church of Glentham, Lincolnshire, there is a tomb with a figure, popularly called

Molly Grime; and this figure was regularly washed every Good Friday by seven old maids of Glentham, with water brought from Newell Well, each receiving a shilling for her trouble, in consequence of an old bequest connected with some property in that district. About 1832, the property being sold without any reservation of the rent-charge of this bequest, the custom was discontinued.*

GOOD FRIDAY IN ROME.

At Rome, the services in the churches on Good Friday are of the same solemn character as on the preceding day. At the Sistine Chapel, the yellow colour of the candles and torches, and the nakedness of the Pope's throne and of the other seats, denote the desolation of the church. The cardinals do not wear their rings; their dress is of purple, which is their wearing colour; in like manner, the bishops do not wear rings, and their stockings are black. The mace, as well as the soldiers' arms, are reversed. The Pope is habited in a red cope; and he neither wears his ring nor gives his blessing. A sermon is preached by a conventual friar. Among other ceremonies, which we have not space to describe, the crucifix is partially unveiled, and kissed by the Pope, whose shoes are taken off on approaching, to do it homage. A procession takes place (across a vestibule) to the Paolina Chapel, where mass is celebrated by the Grand Penitentiary. In the afternoon, the last *Miserere* is chanted in the Sistine Chapel, on which occasion the crowding is very great. After the *Miserere,* the Pope, cardinals, and other clergy, proceed through a covered passage to St Peter's, in order to venerate the relics of the *True Cross,* the *Lance,* and the *Volto Santo,* which are shewn by the canons from the balcony above the statue of St Veronica. Notwithstanding the peculiar solemnity of the religious services of the day, the shops, public offices, and places of business, also the palazzos where galleries of pictures are shewn, are open as usual—the only external indications of the religious character of the day being the muteness of the bells. This disregard of Good Friday at Rome contrasts strangely with the fact, that Roman Catholics shut their shops and abstain from business on that day in Scotland and other countries where it is in no respect a legal *non dies.*

THE MYSTERY PLAY OF GOOD FRIDAY AT MONACO.

The principality of Monaco is one of the smallest, yet one of the prettiest, possessions in the world. Three short streets, an ancient château well fortified, good barracks, a tolerably large square or place, a church, and fine public gardens, placed on a rock which descends perpendicularly into the Mediterranean five hundred feet deep, and you have there the whole of this Lilliputian principality. High mountains rise behind the town, and shelter it from the north wind, whilst the mildness of the climate is attested by the vigorous growth of the palm trees and cactus, which stretches its knotty arms, set with thorns, over the rocks, reminding the passer-by of beggars

* Edwards's *Remarkable Charities,* 100.

who hold out their malformations or solicit attention by their contortions. The mountain tops dazzle you with their snowy mantle, whilst the gardens are filled with the sweet perfume of Bengal roses, orange blossom, geraniums, and Barbary figs, which seem to have found here their natal soil. This little spot was given in the tenth century to the Grimaldi family, of Genoa, by a special favour of the Emperor, but it was a source of continual jealousy; the Republic of Genoa attacking it on the one side, and Charles of Anjou on the other.

In 1300 it was restored to the Grimaldi, but shortly after fell into the hands of the Spinolas, an equally illustrious Genoese family, when it became one of the centres for the Ghibellin faction. Yet in 1329 it was restored to its rightful owners, and remained in their hands by the female side up to the last prince. The château is an interesting edifice of the middle ages, with its two towers and double gallery of arcades. The court is large, and adorned with fine frescoes by Horace de Ferrari; whilst the staircase is as magnificent as that at Fontainebleau, and entirely of white marble.

We will enter this little city with the crowd of strangers which the procession of Good Friday annually collects. When the services of the evening are over, about nine o'clock preparations are made for a display which is allegorical, symbolical, and historical; the intention is to depict the different scenes of Christ's passion, and his path to the cross. The members of a brotherhood act the different parts, and a special house preserves the costumes, decorations, lay figures, and other articles necessary for the representation. Torches are lighted, and the drums of the national guard supply the place of bells, which are wanting. There are numbers of stations on the way to Calvary, and a different scene enacted at each; the same person who represents Christ does not do so throughout, but there is one who drinks the vinegar, another who is scourged, another bears the cross. Each is represented by an old man with white hair and beard, clothed in scarlet robes, a crown of thorns, and the breast painted with vermilion to imitate drops of blood. The four doctors of the law wear black robes and an advocate's cap; from time to time they draw a large book from their pocket, and appearing to consult together, shew by significant gestures that the text of the law is decisive, and they can do no other than condemn Jesus. Pontius Pilate is near to them, escorted by a servant, who carries a large white parasol over his head; whilst the Roman prefect wears the dress of the judge of an assize court, short breeches and a black toga. Behind this majestic personage walks a slave in a large white satin mantle, carrying a silver ewer, which he presents to the Governor when he pronounces the words 'I wash my hands of it.' King Herod is not forgotten in the group; he will be recognised by his long scarlet mantle, his wig with three rows of curls, his grand waistcoat, and gilt paper crown placed on his grey hair. Then comes the *Colonel of Pontius Pilate's Army* (so described in the list), distinguished by his great height and extreme leanness: his white trousers were fastened round his legs after the fashion of the Gauls, he had a Roman cuirass, the epaulettes of a general, a long rapier, white silk stockings, a gigantic helmet, over which towered a still higher plume of feathers. This military figure was mounted on a horse of the small Sardinian breed, so that the legs of the rider touched the ground. St Peter with the cock, Thomas the incredulous, the Pharisees and Scribes, were all there; none were forgotten. As for Judas, his occupation consisted in throwing himself every moment into his master's arms, and kissing him in a touching manner. Adam and Eve must not be forgotten, under the form of a young boy and girl, in costumes of Louis Quinze, with powdered wigs, and eating apples off the bough of an orange tree!

The procession advances; the Jewish nation, represented by young persons dressed in blue blouses with firemen's helmets, form in rank to insult the martyred God as he passes. Here it is a tall rustic who gives him a blow with his fist; there a woman offers vinegar and gall; still further, the Roman soldiers, at a signal from the beadle, throw themselves forward, lance in hand, and make a feint of piercing him with sanguinary fury, drawing back only to repeat the same formidable movement. The Jews brandish menacing axes, whilst the three Maries, dressed in black, their faces covered with lugubrious veils, weep and lament bitterly.

Finally, there is Christ on the cross, and Christ laid in the tomb; but this part of the scene is managed by puppets suitably arranged.

If we place all these scenes in the narrow old streets of Monaco, passing through antique arcades, and throw over the curious spectacle the trembling light of a hundred torches and a thousand wax lights, the stars shining in the dark blue sky, the distant chanting of the monks, the charm of mystery and poetry, and the scent of orange blossoms and geraniums, we shall feel that we have retrograded many centuries, and can fancy ourselves transported into the dark middle ages, to the time when the mystery plays, of which this is a relic, replaced the Greek tragedy.

The Holy Coat of Treves.

The ancient archiepiscopal city of Treves, on the Moselle, is remarkable for possessing among its cathedral treasures, the coat reputed to be that worn by the Saviour at his execution, and for which the soldiers cast lots. Its history is curious, and a certain antiquity is connected with it, as with many other 'relics' exhibited in the Roman Catholic Church, and which gives them an interest irrespective of their presumed sacred character. This coat was the gift of the famed Empress Helena, the mother of Constantine the Great, and the 'discoverer' of so large a number of memorials of the founders of Christianity. In her day, Treves was the capital of Belgic Gaul, and the residence of the later Roman Emperors; it is recorded that she converted her palace into the Cathedral, and endowed it with this treasure —the seamless coat of the Saviour. That it was a treasure to the Cathedral and city is apparent from the records of great pilgrimages performed at intervals during the middle ages, when this coat was exhibited; each pilgrim offered money

to the shrine, and the town was enriched by their general expenditure. Unlike other famed relics, this coat was always exhibited sparingly. The Church generally displays its relics at intervals of a few years, but the Holy Coat was only seen once in a century; it was then put away by the chief authorities of the Cathedral in some secret place known only to a few. In Murray's *Handbook for Travellers*, 1841, it is said, 'The existence of this relic, at present, is rather doubtful—at least, it is not visible; the attendants of the church say it is walled up.' All doubts were soon after removed, for in 1844 the Archbishop Arnoldi announced a centenary jubilee, at which the Holy Coat was to be exhibited. It produced a great effect, and Treves exhibited such scenes as would appear rather to belong to the fourteenth than the nineteenth century. Pilgrims came from all quarters, many in large bands preceded by banners, and marshalled by their village priests. It was impossible to lodge the great mass of these foot-sore travellers, and they slept on inn-stairs, in outhouses, or even in the streets, with their wallets for their pillows. By the first dawn they took up their post by the Cathedral doors; and long before these were opened, a line of many hundreds was added: sometimes the line was more than a mile in length, and few persons could reach the high altar where the coat was placed in less time than three hours. The heat, dust, and fatigue were too much for many, who fainted by the way; yet hour after hour, a dense throng passed round the interior of the Cathedral, made their oblation, and retired. The coat is a loose garment with wide sleeves, very simple in form, of coarse material, dark brown in colour, probably the result of its age, and entirely without seam or decoration. Our cut is copied from the best of the prints published

THE HOLY COAT OF TREVES.

at Treves during the jubilee, and will convey a clear impression of a celebrated relic which few are destined to examine. The dimensions given on this engraving state that the coat measures from the extremity of each sleeve, 5 feet 5 inches; the length from collar to the lowermost edge being 5 feet 2 inches. In parts it is tender, or threadbare; and some few stains upon it are reputed to be those of the Redeemer's blood. It is reputed to have worked many miracles in the way of cures, and its efficacy has never been doubted in Treves.

The *éclat* which might have attended the exhibition of 1844, was destined to an opposition from the priestly ranks of the Roman Catholic Church itself. Johann Ronge, who already had become conspicuous as a foremost man among the reforming clergy of Germany, addressed an eloquent epistle to the Archbishop of Treves, indignantly denouncing a resuscitation of the superstitious observances of the middle ages. This letter produced much effect, and so far excited the wrath of Rome, that Ronge was excommunicated; but he was far from weakened thereby. Before the January of the following year he was at the head of an organized body of Catholics prepared to deny the supremacy of Rome; but the German governments, alarmed at the spread of freedom of opinion, suppressed the body thus called into vitality, and Ronge was ultimately obliged to leave his native land. In 1850 he came to England, and it is somewhat curious to reflect that the bold priest who alarmed Rome, lived for a time the quiet life of a teacher in the midst of busy London, very few of whose inhabitants were conversant with the fact of his residence among them.

PENITENT WITH CROWN OF THORNS.

In the Lent processions of Penitents which take place in the Southern Italian states, the persons who form them are so completely enveloped in a peculiar dress that nothing but the

ITALIAN PENITENT IN LENT PROCESSIONS.

eyes and hands are visible. A long white gown covers the body, and a high pointed hood envelops the head, spreading like a heavy tippet over the shoulders; holes are cut to allow of sight, but there are none for breathing. The sketch here engraved was made at Palermo, in Sicily, on the Good Friday of 1861, and displays these peculiarities, with the addition of others, seldom seen even at Rome. Each penitent in the procession wore upon the hood a crown of thorns twisted round the brow and over the head. A thick rope was passed round the neck, and looped in front of the breast, in which the uplifted hands of the penitent rested in the attitude of prayer. Thus, deprived of the use of hands and almost of sight, the slow movement of these lines of penitents through the streets was regulated by the clerical officials who walked beside and marshalled them.

MARCH 26.

St Braulio, Bishop of Saragossa, 646.　St Ludger, Bishop of Munster, Apostle of Saxony, 809.

HOLY SATURDAY IN ROME.

On the reading of a particular passage in the service of the Sistine Chapel, which takes place about half-past eleven o'clock, the bells of St Peter's are rung, the guns of St Angelo are fired, and all the bells in the city immediately break forth, as if rejoicing in their renewed liberty of ringing. This day, at St Peter's, the only ceremony that need be noticed is the blessing of the fire and the paschal candle. For this purpose, *new fire*, as it is called, is employed. At the beginning of mass, a light, from which the candles and the charcoal for the incense is enkindled, is struck from a flint in the sacristy, where the chief sacristan privately blesses the water, the fire, and the five grains of incense which are to be fixed in the paschal candle. Formerly, all the fires in Rome were lighted anew from this holy fire, but this is no longer the case. After the service, the cardinal vicar proceeds to the baptistry of St Peter's; there having blessed and exorcised the water for baptism, and dipped into the paschal candle, concludes by sprinkling some of the water on the people. Catechumens are afterwards baptized, and deacons and priests are ordained, and the tonsure is given.

Born.—Conrad Gesner, eminent scholar and naturalist, 1516, *Zurich ;* William Wollaston, author of *The Religion of Nature Delineated,* 1659, *Coton Clanford, Staffordshire ;* George Joseph Bell, writer on law and jurisprudence, 1770, *Fountainbridge, Edinburgh.*

Died.—Bishop Brian Duppa, 1662, *Richmond ;* William Courten, traveller and virtuoso, 1702, *Kensington ;* Sir John Vanbrugh, architect and dramatist, 1726, *Whitehall ;* C. P. Duclos, French romance writer, 1772, *Paris ;* John Mitchell Kemble, Anglo-Saxon scholar and historian, 1857; John Seaward, engineer, 1858.

DEATH OF SIR JOHN VANBRUGH.

In a diminutive house, which he had built for himself at Whitehall with the ruins of the old palace, died Sir John Vanbrugh, 'a man of wit and man of honour,' leaving a widow many years younger than himself, but no children, his only son having been killed at the battle of Tournay.

Vanbrugh was of Dutch descent, and the son of a sugar-baker at Chester, where he was born in 1666. We have no account of his being educated for the profession of an architect : he is believed to have been sent to France at the age of nineteen, and there studied architecture; and being detected in making drawings of some fortifications, he was imprisoned in the Bastile. He became a dramatic writer and a herald ; in the first he excelled, but his wit and vivacity were of a loose kind: hence Pope says, 'Van wants grace,' &c. Still he borrowed little, and when he translated, he enriched his author. He built, as a speculation of his own, a theatre in the Haymarket, which afterwards became the original Opera-house, on the site of the present building. In this scheme he had Congreve for his dramatic coadjutor, and Betterton for manager, by whom the house was opened in 1706 ; and here Vanbrugh's admirable comedy of *The Confederacy* was first brought out.

Many years before this, Vanbrugh had acquired some reputation for architectural skill ; for in 1695 he was appointed one of the commissioners for completing the palace at Greenwich, when it was about to be converted into an hospital. In 1702, he produced the palace of Castle Howard for his patron, the Earl of Carlisle, who being then Earl Marshal of England, bestowed upon Vanbrugh the not unprofitable appointment of Clarencieux, King-at-Arms. His work of Castle Howard recommended him as architect to many noble and wealthy employers, and to the appointment to build a palace to be named after the victory at Blenheim. This brought the architect vexation as well as fame ; for Duchess Sarah, 'that wicked woman of Marlborough,' as Vanbrugh calls her, discharged him from his post of architect, and refused to pay what was due to him as salary. Sir Joshua Reynolds declared Vanbrugh to have been defrauded of the due reward of his merit, by the wits of the time, who knew not the rules of architecture. 'Vanbrugh's fate was that of the great Perault : both were objects of the petulant sarcasms of factious men of letters ; and both have left some of the fairest monuments which, to this day, decorate their several countries,—the façades of the Louvre, Blenheim, and Castle Howard.' Reynolds was among the first to express his approbation of Vanbrugh's style, and to bear his testimony as an artist to the picturesque magnificence of Blenheim.'

The wits were very severe on Vanbrugh. Swift, speaking of his diminutive house at Whitehall, and the stupendous pile at Blenheim, says of the former :

'At length they in the corner spy
A thing resembling a goose pye.'

Of the palace at Blenheim :

'That, if his Grace were no more skill'd in
The art of battering walls than building,
We might expect to see next year
A mousetrap man chief engineer.'

This ridicule pursued Vanbrugh to his epitaph,

422

for after his remains had been deposited in Wren's beautiful church of St Stephen's, Walbrook, Dr Evans, alluding to Vanbrugh's massive style, wrote :

' Lie heavy on him, earth, for he
Laid many a heavy load on thee

A ZEALOUS FRIEND OF ST PAUL'S CATHEDRAL.

On the 26th of March 1620, being Midlent Sunday, a remarkable assemblage took place around St Paul's Cross, London.

St Paul's Cathedral had lain in a dilapidated state for above fifty years, having never quite recovered the effects of a fire which took place in 1561. At length, about 1612, an odd busy being, called Henry Farley—one of those people who are always going about poking the rear of the public to get them to do something—took up the piteous call of the fine old church, resolved never to rest till he had procured its thorough restoration. He issued a variety of printed appeals on the subject, beset state officers to get bills introduced into Parliament, and in 1616 had three pictures painted on panel; one representing a procession of grand personages, another the said personages seated at a sermon at St Paul's Cross, both being incidents which he wished to see take place as a commencement to the desired work. The cut on next page is a reduction of the latter extraordinary picture, which Farley lived to see realized on the day cited at the head of this little article.

The picture represents that curious antique structure, the Preaching Cross, which for centuries existed in the vacant space at the northeast corner of St Paul's churchyard, till it was demolished by a Puritan lord mayor at the beginning of the Civil War. A gallery placed against the choir of the church contains, in several compartments, the King, Queen, and Prince of Wales, the Lord Mayor, &c., while a goodly corps of citizens sit in the area in front of the Cross. Most probably, when the King came in state with his family and court, to hear the sermon which was actually preached here on Midlent Sunday, 1620, the scene was very nearly what is here presented.

One of Farley's last efforts for the promotion of the good work he had taken in hand, was the publication of a tract in twenty-one pages, in the year 1621. After some other matters, it gives a petition to the King, written in the name of the church, which introduces Farley to notice as 'the poore man who hath been my voluntary servant these eight years, by books, petitions, and other devises, even to his owne dilapidations.' It also contains a petition which Farley had prepared to be given to the King two days before the Midlent sermon, but which the Master of Bequests had taken away before the King could read it, 'as many had been so taken before, to the great hindrance and grief of the poore author.' In this address, the church thus speaks :—' Whereas, to the exceeding great joy of all my deare friends, there is certaine intelligence that your Highnesse will visit me on Sunday next, and the rather I believe it, for that I have had more sweeping, brushing, and cleansing than I have had in forty years before.' Then the author adds a recital of the various efforts he had made to attract the royal attention to St Paul's. He had assailed him with 'carols' on various occasions. He had published a ' Dream,' prefiguring what he wished to see effected. Towards the last, he tells the church, ' I grew much dismayed . . . . Many rubs I ran through; many scoffes and scornes I did undergo; forsaken by butterflie friends; laughed at and derided by your enemies; pursued after by wolves of Wood Street and foxes of the Poultrey, ... sometimes at the point of death and despaire. Instead of serving my Prince (which I humbly desired, though but as a doorkeeper in you), I was presst for the service of King Lud [put into Lud-gate prison], when all the comfort I had was that I could see you, salute you, and condole with your mise-ries [the prison being in a tower crossing the street of Ludgate Hill; consequently commanding a view of the west front of the church]. My poore clothes and ragges I could not compare to any-thing better than to your west end, and my service to you nothing lesse than bond-age.' In the midst of his troubles, when thinking of quitting all and going to Virginia, he heard of the King's intended visit, and was comforted. The tract ends with St Paul's giving Mr Farley a promise that, for his long and faithful services, he should have a final resting-place within her walls.

MARCH 27.

St John, of Egypt, hermit, **394**.   St Rupert, or Robert, Bishop of Saltzburg, **718**.

Easter.

Easter, the anniversary of our Lord's resurrec-tion from the dead, is one of the three great festivals of the Christian year,—the other two being Christmas and Whitsuntide. From the earliest period of Christianity down to the pre-sent day, it has always been celebrated by believers with the greatest joy, and accounted the Queen of Festivals. In primitive times it was usual for Christians to salute each other on the morning of this day by exclaiming, ' Christ is risen;' to which the person saluted replied, ' Christ is risen indeed,' or else, ' And hath appeared unto Simon;'—a custom still retained in the Greek Church.

THE PREACHING CROSS, ST PAUL'S.

The common name of this festival in the East was the *Paschal Feast*, because kept at the same time as the *Pascha*, or Jewish passover, and in some measure succeeding to it. In the sixth of the Ancyran Canons it is called the *Great Day*. Our own name *Easter* is derived, as some suppose, from *Eostre*, the name of a Saxon deity, whose feast was celebrated every year in the spring, about the same time as the Christian festival— the name being retained when the character of the feast was changed; or, as others suppose, from *Oster*, which signifies rising. If the latter supposition be correct, Easter is in name, as well as reality, the feast of the resurrection.

Though there has never been any difference of opinion in the Christian church as to *why* Easter is kept, there has been a good deal as to *when* it ought to be kept. It is one of the moveable feasts; that is, it is not fixed to one particular day—like Christmas Day, *e. g.*, which is always kept on the 25th of December—but moves back-wards or forwards according as the full moon next after the vernal equinox falls nearer or further from the equinox. The rule given at the beginning of the Prayer-book to find Easter is this: ' Easter-day is always the first *Sunday* after the full moon which happens upon or next after the twenty-first day of *March*; and if the full moon happens upon a *Sunday*, Easter-day is the *Sunday* after.'

423

The paschal controversy, which for a time divided Christendom, grew out of a diversity of custom. The churches of Asia Minor, among whom were many Judaizing Christians, kept their paschal feast on the same day as the Jews kept their passover; *i. e.* on the 14th of Nisan, the Jewish month corresponding to our March or April. But the churches of the West, remembering that our Lord's resurrection took place on the Sunday, kept their festival on the Sunday following the 14th of Nisan. By this means they hoped not only to commemorate the resurrection on the day on which it actually occurred, but also to distinguish themselves more effectually from the Jews. For a time this difference was borne with mutual forbearance and charity. And when disputes began to arise, we find that Polycarp, the venerable bishop of Smyrna, when on a visit to Rome, took the opportunity of conferring with Anicetas, bishop of that city, upon the question. Polycarp pleaded the practice of St Philip and St John, with the latter of whom he had lived, conversed, and joined in its celebration; while Anicetas adduced the practice of St Peter and St Paul. Concession came from neither side, and so the matter dropped; but the two bishops continued in Christian friendship and concord. This was about A.D. 158.

Towards the end of the century, however, Victor, bishop of Rome, resolved on compelling the Eastern churches to conform to the Western practice, and wrote an imperious letter to the prelates of Asia, commanding them to keep the festival of Easter at the time observed by the Western churches. They very naturally resented such an interference, and declared their resolution to keep Easter at the time they had been accustomed to do. The dispute henceforward gathered strength, and was the source of much bitterness during the next century. The East was divided from the West, and all who, after the example of the Asiatics, kept Easter-day on the 14th, whether that day were Sunday or not, were styled *Quartodecimans* by those who adopted the Roman custom.

One cause of this strife was the imperfection of the Jewish calendar. The ordinary year of the Jews consisted of 12 lunar months of 29½ days each, or of 29 and 30 days alternately; that is, of 354 days. To make up the 11 days' deficiency, they intercalated a thirteenth month of 30 days every third year. But even then they would be in advance of the true time without other intercalations; so that they often kept their passover before the vernal equinox. But the Western Christians considered the vernal equinox the commencement of the natural year, and objected to a mode of reckoning which might sometimes cause them to hold their paschal feast twice in one year and omit it altogether the next. To obviate this, the fifth of the apostolic canons decreed that, 'If any bishop, priest, or deacon, celebrated the Holy Feast of Easter before the vernal equinox, as the Jews do, let him be deposed.'

At the beginning of the fourth century, matters had gone to such a length, that the Emperor Constantine thought it his duty to take steps to allay the controversy, and to insure uniformity

of practice for the future. For this purpose, he got a canon passed in the great Œcumenical Council of Nice (A.D. 325), 'That everywhere the great feast of Easter should be observed upon one and the same day; and that not the day of the Jewish passover, but, as had been generally observed, upon the Sunday afterwards.' And to prevent all future disputes as to the time, the following rules were also laid down:

1. 'That the twenty-first day of March shall be accounted the vernal equinox.'
2. 'That the full moon happening upon or next after the twenty-first of March, shall be taken for the full moon of Nisan.'
3. 'That the Lord's-day next following that full moon be Easter-day.'
4. 'But if the full moon happen upon a Sunday, Easter-day shall be the Sunday after.'

As the Egyptians at that time excelled in astronomy, the Bishop of Alexandria was appointed to give notice of Easter-day to the Pope and other patriarchs. But it was evident that this arrangement could not last long; it was too inconvenient and liable to interruptions. The fathers of the next age began, therefore, to adopt the golden numbers of the Metonic cycle, and to place them in the calendar against those days in each month on which the new moons should fall during that year of the cycle. The Metonic cycle was a period of nineteen years. It had been observed by Meton, an Athenian philosopher, that the moon returns to have her changes on the same month and day of the month in the solar year after a lapse of nineteen years, and so, as it were, to run in a circle. He published his discovery at the Olympic Games, B.C. 433, and the cycle has ever since borne his name. The fathers hoped by this cycle to be able always to know the moon's age; and as the vernal equinox was now fixed to the 21st of March, to find Easter for ever. But though the new moon really happened on the same day of the year after a space of nineteen years as it did before, it fell an hour earlier on that day, which, in the course of time, created a serious error in their calculations.

A cycle was then framed at Rome for 84 years, and generally received by the Western church, for it was then thought that in this space of time the moon's changes would return not only to the same day of the month, but of the week also. Wheatley tells us that, 'During the time that Easter was kept according to this cycle, Britain was separated from the Roman empire, and the British churches for some time after that separation continued to keep Easter according to this table of 84 years. But soon after that separation, the Church of Rome and several others discovered great deficiencies in this account, and therefore left it for another which was more perfect.'— *Book on the Common Prayer*, p. 40. This was the Victorian period of 532 years. But he is clearly in error here. The Victorian period was only drawn up about the year 457, and was not adopted by the Church till the fourth Council of Orleans, A.D. 541. Now from the time the Romans finally left Britain (A.D. 426), when he supposes both churches to be using the cycle of 84 years, till the arrival of St Augustine (A.D. 596). the error can hardly have amounted to a difference worth disputing about. And yet the time the Britons kept Easter must have varied considerably from that of the Roman missionaries to have given rise to the statement that they were Quartodecimans, which they certainly were not; for it is a well-known fact that British bishops were at the Council of Nice, and doubtless adopted and brought home with them the rule laid down by that assembly. Dr Hooke's account is far more probable, that the British and Irish churches adhered to the Alexandrian rule, according to which the Easter festival could not begin before the 8th of March; while according to the rule adopted at Rome and generally in the West, it began as early as the fifth. 'They (the Celts) were manifestly in error,' he says; 'but owing to the haughtiness with which the Italians had demanded an alteration in their calendar, they doggedly determined not to change.'—*Lives of the Archbishops of Canterbury*, vol. i. p. 14. After a good deal of disputation had taken place, with more in prospect, Oswy, King of Northumbria, determined to take the matter in hand. He summoned the leaders of the contending parties to a conference at Whitby, A.D. 664, at which he himself presided. Colman, bishop of Lindisfarne, represented the British church. The Romish party were headed by Agilbert, bishop of Dorchester, and Wilfrid, a young Saxon. Wilfrid was spokesman. The arguments were characteristic of the age; but the manner in which the king decided irresistibly provokes a smile, and makes one doubt whether he were in jest or earnest. Colman spoke first, and urged that the custom of the Celtic church ought not to be changed, because it had been inherited from their forefathers, men beloved of God, &c. Wilfrid followed: 'The Easter which we observe I saw celebrated by all at Rome: there, where the blessed apostles, Peter and Paul, lived, taught, suffered, and were buried.' And concluded a really powerful speech with these words: 'And if, after all, that Columba of yours were, which I will not deny, a holy man, gifted with the power of working miracles, is he, I ask, to be preferred before the most blessed Prince of the Apostles, to whom our Lord said, "Thou art Peter, and upon this rock will I build my church, and the gates of hell shall not prevail against it; and to thee will I give the keys of the kingdom of heaven"?'

The King, turning to Colman, asked him, 'Is it true or not, Colman, that these words were spoken to Peter by our Lord?' Colman, who seems to have been completely cowed, could not deny it. 'It is true, O King.' 'Then,' said the King, 'can you shew me any such power given to your Columba?' Colman answered, 'No.' 'You are both, then, agreed,' continued the King, 'are you not, that these words were addressed principally to Peter, and that to him were given the keys of heaven by our Lord?' Both assented. 'Then,' said the King, 'I tell you plainly, I shall not stand opposed to the door-keeper of the kingdom of heaven; I desire, as far as in me lies, to adhere to his precepts and obey his commands, lest by offending him who keepeth

the keys, I should, when I present myself at the gate, find no one to open to me.'

This settled the controversy, though poor honest Colman resigned his see rather than submit to such a decision.

On Easter-day depend all the moveable feasts and fasts throughout the year. The nine Sundays before, and the eight following after, are all dependent upon it, and form, as it were, a body-guard to this Queen of Festivals. The nine preceding are the six Sundays in Lent, Quinquagesima, Sexagesima, and Septuagesima; the eight following are the five Sundays after Easter, the Sunday after Ascension Day, Whit Sunday, and Trinity Sunday.

Easter Customs.

The old Easter customs which still linger among us vary considerably in form in different parts of the kingdom. The custom of distributing the 'pace' or 'pasche ege,' which was once almost universal among Christians, is still observed by children, and by the peasantry in Lancashire. Even in Scotland, where the great festivals have for centuries been suppressed, the young people still get their hard-boiled dyed eggs, which they roll about, or throw, and finally eat. In Lancashire, and in Cheshire, Staffordshire, and Warwickshire, and perhaps in other counties, the ridiculous custom of 'lifting' or 'heaving' is practised. On Easter Monday the men lift the women, and on Easter Tuesday the women lift or heave the men. The process is performed by two lusty men or women joining their hands across each other's wrists; then, making the person to be heaved sit down on their arms, they lift him up aloft two or three times, and often carry him several yards along a street. A grave clergyman who happened to be passing through a town in Lancashire on an Easter Tuesday, and having to stay an hour or two at an inn, was astonished by three or four lusty women rushing into his room, exclaiming they had come 'to lift him.' 'To lift me!' repeated the amazed divine; 'what can you mean?' 'Why, your reverence, we're come to lift you, cause it's Easter Tuesday.' 'Lift me because it's Easter Tuesday? I don't understand. Is there any such custom here?' 'Yes, to be sure; why, don't you know? all us women was lifted yesterday; and us lifts the men to-day in turn. And in course it's our reights and duties to lift 'em.' After a little further parley, the reverend traveller compromised with his fair visitors for half-a-crown, and thus escaped the dreaded compliment. In Durham, on Easter Monday, the men claim the privilege to take off the women's shoes, and the next day the women retaliate. Anciently, both ecclesiastics and laics used to play at ball in the churches for tansy-cakes on Eastertide; and, though the profane part of this custom is happily everywhere discontinued, tansy-cakes and tansy-puddings are still favourite dishes at Easter in many parts. In some parishes in the counties of Dorset and Devon, the clerk carries round to every house a few white cakes as an Easter offering; these cakes, which are about the eighth of an inch thick, and of two sizes,—the larger being seven or eight inches, the smaller about five in diameter,

—have a mingled bitter and sweet taste. In return for these cakes, which are always distributed after Divine service on Good Friday, the clerk receives a gratuity according to the circumstances or generosity of the householder.

W. H. K.

Easter Sunday in Rome.

At Rome, as might be expected, Easter Sunday is celebrated with elaborate ceremonials, for which preparations have been making all the previous week.* The day is ushered in by the firing of cannons from the castle of St Angelo, and about 7 o'clock, carriages with ladies and gentlemen are beginning to pour towards St Peter's. That magnificent basilica is found to be richly decorated for the occasion, the altars are freshly ornamented, and the lights around the tomb and figure of St Peter are now blazing after their temporary extinction. According to

THE POPE CARRIED IN ST PETER'S CHURCH ON EASTER DAY.

usage, the Pope officiates this day at mass in St Peter's, and he does so with every imposing accessory that can be devised. From a hall in the adjoining palace of the Vatican, he is borne into the church, under circumstances of the utmost splendour. Seated in his *Sedia Gestatoria*, his vestments blaze with gold; on his head he wears the Tiara, a tall round gilded cap representing a

* The description which follows is prepared by a gentleman who witnessed the ceremonials in 1862.

triple crown, and which is understood to signify spiritual power, temporal power, and a union of both. Beside him are borne the *flabelli*, or large fans, composed of ostrich feathers, in which are set the eye-like parts of peacocks' feathers, to signify the eyes or vigilance of the church. Over him is borne a silk canopy richly fringed. After officiating at mass at the high altar, the Pope is, with the same ceremony, and to the sound of music, borne back through the crowded church, and then ascends to the balcony over the central doorway. There rising from his chair of state, and environed by his principal officers, he pronounces a benediction, with indulgences and absolution. This is the most imposing of all the ceremonies at Rome at this season, and the concourse of people in the area in front of St Peter's is immense. On the occasion in 1862, there were, in addition, at least 10,000 French troops. The crowd is most dense almost immediately below the balcony at which the Pope appears ; for there papers are thrown down containing a copy of the prayers that have been uttered, and ordinarily there is a scramble to catch them. The prayers, it need hardly be said, are in Latin.* On the evening of Easter Sunday, the dome and other exterior parts of St Peter's are beautifully illuminated with lamps.

THE BIDDENDEN CAKES.

Hasted, in his *History of Kent* (1790), states that, in the parish of Biddenden, there is an endowment of old, but unknown date, for making a distribution of cakes among the poor every Easter Sunday in the afternoon. The source of the benefaction consists in twenty acres of land, in five parcels, commonly called the *Bread and Cheese Lands.* Practically, in Mr Hasted's time, six hundred cakes were thus disposed of, being given to persons who attended service, while 270 loaves of three and a half pounds weight each, with a pound and a half of cheese, were given in addition to such as were parishioners.

The cakes distributed on this occasion were impressed with the figures of two females side by side and close together. Amongst the country people it was believed that these figures represented two maidens named Preston, who had left the endowments ; and they further alleged that these ladies were twins, who were born in bodily union—that is, joined side to side, as represented on the cakes ; who lived nearly thirty years in this connection, when at length one of them died, necessarily causing the death of the other in a few hours. It is thought by the Biddenden people that the figures on the cakes are meant as a memorial of this natural prodigy, as well as of the charitable disposition of the two ladies. Mr Hasted, however, ascertained that the cakes had only been printed in this manner within the preceding fifty years, and concluded more rationally that the figures were meant to represent two widows, ' as the general objects of a charitable benefaction.'

If Mr Hasted's account of the Biddenden cakes be the true one, the story of the conjoined twins

* A translation, along with a number of details we have not space to notice, will be found in Murray's *Handbook to Rome.*

—though not inferring a thing impossible or unexampled—must be set down as one of those cases, of which we find so many in the legends of the common people, where a tale is invented to account for certain appearances, after the real meaning of the appearances was lost. It is a process most natural and simple. First, apparently, some one suggests how the circumstance *might be* accounted for ; next, some one blunderingly states that the circumstance *is* so accounted for, the only change being one from the subjunctive to the indicative mood. In this way, a vast number of old monuments, and a still greater number of the names of places, come to have grandam tales of the most absurd kind connected with them, as histories of their origin.

There is, for example, in the Greyfriars' churchyard, Edinburgh, a mausoleum composed of a recumbent female figure with a pillar-supported canopy over her, on which stand four female figures at the several corners. The popular story is, that the recumbent lady was poisoned by her four daughters, whose statues were afterwards placed over her in eternal remembrance of their wickedness ; the fact being, that the four figures were those of Faith, Charity, Justice, &c., favourite emblematical characters in the age when the monument was erected, and the object in placing them there was merely ornamental.

About Easter 1333, a curious occurrence took place at Durham. ' The Queen of Edward III. having followed the king to that city, was conducted by him through the gate of the abbey to the prior's lodgings, where, having supped and gone to bed with her royal lord, she was soon disturbed by one of the monks, who readily intimated to the king that St Cuthbert by no means loved the company of her sex. The queen, upon this, got out of bed, and having hastily dressed herself, went to the castle for the remaining part of the night, asking pardon for the crime she had inadvertently been guilty of against the patron saint of their church.'—Brand's *History of Newcastle*, ii. 408.

Born.—James Keill, mathematician, 1671, *Edinburgh.*
Died.—Ptolemy XIII. of Egypt, B.C. 47, drowned in the Nile ; Pope Clement III., A.D. 1191 ; Alphonso II. (of Castile), 1350, *Gibraltar ;* Pope Gregory XI., 1378 ; James I., King of England, 1625, *Theobalds ;* Bishop Edward Stillingfleet, polemical writer, 1699, *Westminster ;* Leopold, Duke of Lorraine, 1729, *Luneville ;* R. C. Carpenter, architect, 1855.

JEMMY CAMBER, ONE OF KING JAMES'S FOOLS.

During his reign in Scotland, King James had a fool or court jester, named Jemmy Camber, who lodged with a laundress in Edinburgh, and was making love to her daughter, when death cut him off in an unexpected and singular manner, as related by Robert Armin in his *Nest of Ninnies*, published in 1608.

' The chamberlaine was sent to see him there (at the laundress's), who, when he came, found him fast asleepe under the bed stark naked, bathing in nettles, whose skinne when we wakened him was all blistred grievously. The king's chamberlaine bid him arise and come to the king. "I will not," quoth he, " I will go make my grave." See how things chanced ; he spake truer than he was aware. For the chamberlaine, going home without him, tolde the king his answere. Jemmy rose, made him ready, takes his horse, and rides to the churchyard in the high towne, where he found the sexton (as the custom is there) making nine graves—three for men, three for women, and three for children; and whoso dyes next, first comes, first served. "Lend mee thy spade," says Jemmy, and with that digs a hole, which hole hee bids him make for his grave; and doth give him a French crowne; the man, willing to please him (more for his gold than his pleasure), did so; and the foole gets upon his horse, rides to a gentleman of the towne, and on the sodaine within two houres after dyed; of whom the sexton telling, he was buried there indeed. Thus you see, fooles have a guesse at wit sometime, and the wisest could have done no more, nor so much. But thus this fat foole fills a leane grave with his carkasse; upon which grave the king caused a stone of marble to bee put, on which poets writ these lines in remembrance of him:

"He that gaed all men till jeare,
    Jemy a Camber he ligges here;
Pray for his saule, for he is geane,
    And here a ligges beneath this steane." '

MARCH 28.

Saints Priscus, Malchus, and Alexander, of Cæsarea, in Palestine, martyrs, 280. St Sixtus III., Pope, 440. St Gontran, King of Burgundy, 593.

EASTER FESTIVITIES IN CHESTER.

Most people are aware how much of a mediæval character still pertains to the city of Chester, —how its gable-fronted houses, its 'Rows' (covered walks over the ground-floors), and its castellated town walls, combine to give it an antique character wholly unique in England. It is also well known how, in the age succeeding the Conquest, this city was the seat of the despotic military government of Hugh d'Avranches, commonly called, from his savage character, *Hugo Lupus*, whose sword is still preserved in the British Museum.

Chester was endowed by Hugo with two yearly fairs, at Midsummer and Michaelmas, on which occasions criminals had free shelter in it for a month, as indicated by a glove hung out at St Peter's Church,—for gloves were a manufacture at Chester. It was on these occasions that the celebrated Chester mysteries, or scriptural plays, were performed.

As the tourist walks from the Watergate along the ancient walls towards the Cathedral, he cannot fail to notice the beautiful meadow lying between him and the river; it is the Rood-eye, or as formerly written, the Roodee; the scene of the sports for which Chester was so long famous, eye being a term used for a waterside meadow; and the legend of the rood or cross was the following:—A cross was erected at Hawarden, by which a man was unfortunately killed; and in accordance with the superstition of those days, the cross was made to bear the blame of the accident, and was thrown into the river; for which sacrilegious act the men received the name of Ha'rden Jews. Floated down the stream, it was taken up at the Rood-eye, and became very

celebrated for the number of miracles it wrought. Sad to relate, after the Reformation it again became the subject of scorn and contempt; for

HIGH CROSS OF CHESTER.

the master of the grammar-school converted it into a block on which to chastise his refractory pupils, and it was finally burnt, perhaps by the very scholars who had suffered on it.

We need not wonder that in so ancient and thriving a city old customs and games were well kept up; and to begin with those of the great festival of Easter. Then might be seen the mayor and corporation, with the twenty guilds established in Chester, with their wardens at their heads, setting forth in all their pageantry to the Rood-eye to play at football. The mayor, with his mace, sword, and cap of maintenance, stood before the cross, whilst the guild of Shoemakers, to whom the right had belonged from time immemorial, presented him with the ball of the value of 'three and four pence or above,' and all set to work right merrily. But, as too often falls out in this game, 'greate strife did arise among the younge persons of the same cittie,' and hence, in the time of Henry the Eighth, this piece of homage to the mayor was converted into a present from the shoemakers to the drapers of six gleaves or hand-darts of silver, to be given for the best foot-race; whilst the saddlers, who went in procession on horseback, attired in all their bravery, each carrying a spear with a wooden ball, decorated with flowers and arms, exchanged their offering for a silver bell, which should be a 'rewarde for that horse which with speedy runninge should run before all others.'

It would appear that the women were not banished from a share in the sports, but had their own football match in a quiet sort of way; for as the mayor's daughter was engaged with other maidens in the Pepper-gate at this game, her lover, knowing well that the father was too busy on the Rood-eye with the important part he had to play at these festivities, entered by the gate and carried off the fair girl,—nothing loth, we may suppose. The angry father, when he discovered the loss, ordered the Pepper-gate to be for ever closed, giving rise to the Chester proverb—'When the daughter is stolen, shut the Pepper-gate;' equivalent to our saying, 'When the steed is stolen, shut the stable door.'

The good and healthful practice of archery was not forgotten at these Shrove Tuesday and Easter Monday meetings; the reward for the best shot was provided, not by the guilds, but by the bride-grooms. All those happy men who had not closed their first year of matrimonial bliss, if they had been married in the said city, were bound to deliver to the guild of drapers there before the mayor, an arrow of silver, instead of the ball of silk and velvet which had been the earlier offering, to be given as a prize for the exercise of the long-bow. In this the sheriffs had to take their part, for there was a custom, 'the memory of man now living not knowinge the original,' that on Black Monday (a term used for Easter Monday, owing, it is supposed, to the remarkably dark and in-clement weather which happened when Edward the Third lay with his army before Paris) the two sheriffs should shoot for a breakfast of calves' head and bacon. The drum sounded the procla-mation through the city, and from the stalwart yeomen on the Rood-eye, the sheriffs each chose one, until they had got the number of twelve-score; the shooting began on one side and then on the other, until the winners were declared; they then walked first, holding their arrows in their hands, whilst the losers followed with their bows only, and marching to the Town Hall took their breakfast together in much loving jollity, 'it being a commendable exercise, a good recrea-tion, and a lovinge assembly;' a remark of the old writer with which our readers will not disagree. But time, which changes all things, led the sheriffs in 1640 to offer a piece of plate to be run for instead of the calves' head breakfast; we may be sure there were some Puritans at work here, but with the Englishman's natural love of good fare, this resolution was rescinded in 1674, and it was decided that the breakfast was established by ancient usage, and could not be changed at the pleasure of the sheriffs; yet these great men were not easily persuaded, for we find that two years after they were fined ten pounds for not keeping the calves' head feast. When the last of these festivities came off, we know not: it is now kept as an annual dinner, but not on any fixed day. The shooting has, alas! disappeared; the care with which they trained their children in this vigorous exercise may be traced from a curious order we find in the common council book, that, 'For the avoiding of idleness, all children of six years old and upwards, shall, on week days, be set to school, or some virtuous labour, where-by they may hereafter get an honest living; and on Sundays and holy days they shall resort to their parish churches and there abide during the time of divine service, and in the afternoon all the said male children shall be exercised in shooting with bows and arrows, for pins and points only; and that their parents furnish them

with bows and arrows, pins and points, for that purpose, according to the statute lately made for maintenance of shooting in long-bows and artillery, being the ancient defence of the kingdom.'

If we walk through the streets of the city on this festive Easter Monday, we shall probably see a crowd of young and gay gallants carrying about a chair, lined with rich white silk, from which garlands of flowers and streamers of ribbon depend; as they meet each fair damsel, she is requested to seat herself in the chair, no oppo-sition being allowed, nor may we suppose, in those times of free and easy manners, that any would be offered. The chair is then lifted as high as the young men can poise it in the air, and on its descent a kiss is demanded by each, and a fee must be also paid. It would seem that this custom called 'lifting' still prevails in the counties of Cheshire, Lancashire, Shropshire, and War-wickshire, but is confined to the streets; formerly they entered the houses, and made every inmate undergo the lifting. The late Mr Lysons, keeper of the records of the Tower of London, gave an extract from one of the rolls in his custody to the Society of Antiquaries, which mentioned a payment to certain ladies and maids of honour for taking King Edward the First in his bed, and lifting him; so it appears that no rank was exempt. The sum the King paid was no trifle, being equal to about £400 in the present day. The women take their revenge on Easter Tuesday, and go about in the same manner three times must the luckless wight be elevated his escape is in vain, if seen and pursued. Strange to say, the custom is one in memory of the Re-surrection, a vulgar and childish absurdity into which so many of the Romish ceremonies de-generated.

We may be sure that the Pace, Pask, or Easter eggs were not forgotten by the Chester children. Eggs were in such demand at that season that they always rose considerably in price; they were boiled very hard in water coloured with red, blue, or violet dyes, with inscriptions or landscapes traced upon them; these were offered as presents among the 'valentines' of the year, but more frequently played with by the boys as balls, for ball-playing on Easter Monday was universal in every rank. Even the clergy could not forego its delights, and made this game a part of their service. Bishops and deans took the ball into the church, and at the commencement of the anti-phone began to dance, throwing the ball to the choristers, who handed it to each other during the time of the dancing and antiphone. All then retired for refreshment: a gammon of bacon eaten in abhorrence of the Jews was a standard dish; with a tansy pudding, symbolical of the bitter herbs commanded at the paschal feast. An old verse commemorates these customs:

'At stool-ball, Lucia, let us play,
　For sugar, cakes, or wine;
Or for a tansy let us pay,
　The loss be thine or mine.
If thou, my dear, a winner be
　At trundling of the ball,
The wager thou shalt have, and me,
　And my misfortunes all.'

The churches were adorned at this season like

theatres, and crowds poured in to see the sepulchres which were erected, representing the whole scene of our Saviour's entombment. A general belief prevailed in those days that our Lord's second coming would be on Easter Eve; hence the sepulchres were watched through the night, until three in the morning, when two of the oldest monks would enter and take out a beautiful image of the Resurrection, which was elevated before the adoring worshippers during the singing of the anthem, 'Christus resurgens.' It was then carried to the high altar, and a procession being formed, a canopy of velvet was borne over it by ancient gentlemen: they proceeded round the exterior of the church by the light of torches, all singing, rejoicing, and praying, until coming again to the high altar it was there placed to remain until Ascension-day. In many places the monks personated all the characters connected with the event they celebrated, and thus rendered the scene still more theatrical.

Another peculiar ceremony belonging to Chester refers to the minstrels being obliged to appear yearly before the Lord of Dutton. In those days when the monasteries, convents, and castles were but dull abodes, the insecurity of the country and the badness of the roads making locomotion next to impossible, the minstrels were most acceptable company 'to drive dull care away,' and were equally welcomed by burgher and noble. They generally travelled in bands, sometimes as Saxon gleemen, sometimes having instrumentalists joined to the party, as a tabourer, a bagpiper, dancers, and jugglers. At every fair, feast, or wedding, the minstrels were sure to be; arrayed in the fanciful dress prevailing during the reigns of the early Norman kings—mantles and tunics, the latter having tight sleeves to the wrist, but terminating in a long depending streamer which hung as low as the knees; a hood or flat sort of Scotch cap was the general head-dress, and the legs were enveloped in tight bandages, called *chausses*, with the most absurd peak-toed boots and shoes, some being intended to imitate a ram's horn or a scorpion's tail. In all the old books of household expenses, we meet with the largesses which were given to the minstrels, varying, of course, according to the riches and liberality of the donor: thus when the Queen of Edward I. was confined of the first Prince of Wales in Carnarvon Castle, the sum of £10 was given to the minstrels (Welsh harpers, we may suppose them to have been) on the day of her churching. In another old record of the brotherhood feasts at Abingdon, we find them much more richly rewarded than the priests themselves; for whilst twelve of the latter got fourpence each for singing a dirge, twelve minstrels had two-and-threepence each, food for themselves and their horses, to make the guests merry: wise people were they, and knew the value of a good laugh during the process of digestion.

430

It was customary for the minstrels of certain districts to be under the protection of some noble lord, from whom they received a licence at the holding of an annual court; thus the Earls of Lancaster had one at Tutbury, on the 16th of August, when a king of the minstrels and four stewards were chosen: any offenders against the rules of the society were tried, and all complaints brought before a regular jury. This jurisdiction belonged in Chester to the very ancient family of the Duttons, who took their name from a small township near Frodshaw, which was purchased for a coat of mail and a charger, a palfrey and a sparrowhawk, by Hugh the grandson of Odard, son of Ivron, Viscount of Constantine, one of William the Conqueror's Norman knights. Nor did the Duttons soon lose the warlike character of their race, for we find them long after joining in any rebellion or foray that the licentious character of the times permitted. Harry Hotspur inveigled Peter, the eleventh knight, to join him in his ill-fated expedition; happily, however, the king pardoned him. Much more unfortunate were they at Bloreheath; at that battle Sir Peter's grandson, Sir Thomas, was killed, with his brother and eldest son. The way in which they gained the jurisdiction over the Cheshire minstrels was characteristic. We have previously mentioned the extraordinary privilege granted of exemption from punishment during the Chester fairs, a privilege which could not fail in those days to draw together a large concourse of lawless and ruffianly people. During one of these fairs, Ranulph de Blundeville, Earl of Chester, was besieged in his Castle of Rhuddlan, by the yet unsubdued Welsh; when the news of this reached the ears of John Lacy, constable of Chester, he called together the minstrels who were present at the fair, and with their assistance collected a large number of disorderly people, armed but indifferently with whatever might be at hand, and sent them off under the command of Hugh Dutton, in the hope of effecting some relief for the Earl. When they arrived in sight of the castle their numbers had a highly imposing appearance; and the Welsh, taking them for the regular

TRUMPETER AND HERALD IN THE CHESTER FESTIVITIES.

army, and not waiting to try their discipline, or discover their lack of arms, immediately raised the siege, and marched back to their own fastnesses, leaving the Earl full of gratitude to his deliverers; as a token of which, he gave to their captain jurisdiction over the minstrels for ever.

This, then, was the origin of the grand procession which took place yearly on St John the Baptist's day, and was continued for centuries, being only laid aside in the year 1756. In the fine old Eastgate Street, the minstrels assembled, the lord of Dutton or his heir giving them the meeting. His banner or pennon waved from the window of the hostelry where he took up his abode, and where the court was to be held; a drummer being sent round the town to collect the people, and inform them at what time he would meet them. At eleven o'clock a procession was formed: a chosen number of their instrumentalists formed themselves into a band and walked first; two trumpeters in their gorgeous attire followed, blowing their martial strains; the remainder of the minstrels succeeded, white napkins hung across their shoulders, and the principal man carried their banner. After these came the higher ranks, the Lord of Dutton's steward bearing his token of office, a white wand; the tabarder, or herald, his short gown, from which he derived his name, being emblazoned with the Dutton arms; then the Lord of Dutton himself, the object of all this homage, accompanied by many of the gentry of the city and neighbourhood—and Cheshire can number more ancient families than any other county in England; of whom old Fuller tells us, 'They are remarkable on a fourfold account: their numerousness, not to be paralleled in England in the like extent of ground; their antiquity, many of their ancestors being fixed here before the Norman conquest; their loyalty; and their hospitality.' Thus they moved forward to the church of St John the Baptist, the which having entered, the musicians fell upon their knees, and played several pieces of sacred music in this reverent attitude; the canons and vicars choral then performed divine service, and a proclamation was made, 'God save the King, the Queen, the Prince, and all the Royal family; and the honourable Sir Peter Dutton, long may he live and support the honour of the minstrel court.' The procession returned as it came, and then entered upon the important business of satisfying the appetite with the fine rounds of beef, haunches of venison, and more delicate dishes of peacock, swan, and fowls; followed by those wondrous sweet compounds called 'subtleties,' with stout, ale, hippocras, and wine, to make every heart cheerful. The minstrels did not forget to make their present of four flagons of wine, and a lance, as a token of fealty to their lord, with the sum of fourpence-halfpenny for the licence which he granted them, and in which they were commanded 'to behave themselves lively as a licensed minstrel of the court ought to do.' The jury were empanelled during the afternoon, to inquire if they knew of any treason against the King or the Earl of Chester, or if any minstrel were guilty of using his instrument without licence, or had in any way misdemeaned himself; the verdicts were pronounced, the oaths administered, and all separated, looking forward to their next merry meeting.

EASTER SINGERS IN THE VORARLBERG.

If there be any country which has hitherto escaped the invasion of civilization and a revolution in manners, it is assuredly the Vorarlberg in the Tyrol. This primitive region begins where the ordinary traveller stops, wearied with the beauties of Switzerland and hesitating whether he should abandon the high roads to rough it in the difficult passes of these mountains. At Rochach the steamer leaves Switzerland and five times changes its flag on Lake Constance before reaching Bregentz, where the two-headed eagle announces to the traveller that he has set foot in Austrian territory. There he disembarks, and after passing through the formalities of the custom-house and passport office, he can go about, act, and talk with the greatest freedom, delivered from the fear of any espionage even on the part of the gens-d'armes of his Apostolic Majesty, the Emperor Francis Joseph. It is only in more recent years that the inhabitants have had to submit to a police, who are looked upon with an evil eye by these free mountaineers; they say that it is not required by reason of the tranquillity of the country, no robbery or assassination having ever been committed.

About a league from Lake Constance the mountains assume a wild and savage character; a narrow defile leads to a high hill which must be crossed to reach the valley of Schwartzenberg. I gained the summit of the peak at sunset; the rosy vapour which surrounded it hid the line of the horizon, and gave to the lake the appearance of a sea; the Rhine flowed through the bottom of the valley and emptied itself into the lake, to recommence its course twelve leagues farther on. On one side were the Swiss mountains; opposite was Landau, built on an island; on the other side the dark forests of Wurtemberg, and over the side of the hill the chain of the Vorarlberg mountains. The last rays of the setting sun gilded the crests of the glaciers, whilst the valleys were already bathed in the soft moonlight. From this high point the sounds of the bells ringing in the numerous villages scattered over the mountains were distinctly heard, the flocks were being brought home to be housed for the night, and everywhere were sounds of rejoicing.

'It is the evening of Holy Saturday,' said our guide; 'the Tyrolese keep the festival of Easter with every ceremony.' And so it was; civilization has passed that land by and not left a trace of its unbelieving touch; the resurrection of Christ is still for them the tangible proof of revelation, and they honour the season accordingly. Bands of musicians, for which the Tyrolese have always been noted, traverse every valley, singing the beautiful Easter hymns to their guitars; calling out the people to their doors, who join them in the choruses and together rejoice on this glad anniversary. Their wide-brimmed Spanish hats are decorated with bouquets of flowers; crowds of children accompany them, and when the darkness of night comes on, bear lighted

431

torches of the pine wood, which throw grotesque shadows over the spectators and picturesque wooden huts. The Pasch or Paschal eggs, which have formed a necessary part of all Easter offer-

EASTER SINGERS IN THE TYROL.

ings for centuries past, are not forgotten : some are dyed in the brightest colours and boiled hard ; others have suitable mottoes written on the shells, and made ineffaceable by a rustic process of chemistry. The good wife has these ready prepared, and when the children bring their baskets they are freely given : at the higher class of farmers' houses wine is brought out as well as eggs, and the singers are refreshed and regaled in return for their Easter carols.

Born.—Sir Thomas Smith, author of *The English Commonwealth*, 1514-15, *Saffron Walden* ; Dr Andrew Kippis, Nonconformist divine, editor of *Biographia Britannica*, 1725, *Nottingham*.

Died.—Pope Martin IV., 1285 ; Lord Fitzwalter, and Lord John de Clifford, killed at *Ferrybridge*, 1461 ; Sanzio Raffaelle, painter, 1520, *Rome* ; Jacques Callot, eminent engraver, 1636, *Nanci* ; Wentzel Hollar, celebrated engraver, 1677, *Westminster* ; Margaret Woffington, celebrated actress, 1760 ; Dr James Tunstall, vicar of *Rochdale*, 1772 ; Marquis de Condorcet, philosophical writer, 1794 ; General Sir Ralph Abercrombie, battle of Alexandria, 1801 ; Henry Hase, Bank of England, 1829 ; Rev. Dr Valpy, classical scholar, *Reading*, 1836 ; Thomas Morton, dramatist, 1838.

WENTZEL HOLLAR.

Wentzel Hollar, an eminent engraver, and scion of an ancient Bohemian family, was born at Prague in 1607. His parents destined him for the profession of the law, but his family being ruined and driven into exile by the siege and capture of Prague, he was compelled to support himself by a taste and ability, which he had very early exhibited, in the use of the pen and pencil. In 1636, Thomas Earl of Arundel, an accomplished connoisseur, when passing through Frankfort, on his way to Vienna, as Ambassador to the Emperor Frederick II., met Hollar, and was so pleased with the unassuming manner and talent of the young engraver, that he attached him to the suit of the embassy. On his return to England, the earl introduced Hollar to Charles the First, and procured him the appointment of drawing-master to the young prince, subsequently Charles the Second. For a short period all went well with Hollar, for he now enjoyed the one fitful gleam of sunshine which illumined his toil-worn life. He resided in apartments in Arundel House, and was constantly employed by his noble patron, in engraving those treasures of ancient art still known as the Arundelian marbles. But soon the great civil war broke forth; Lord Arundel was compelled to seek a refuge on the Continent, while Hollar, with two other artists, Peake and Faithorne, accepted commissions in the King's service. All three, under the command of the heroic Marquis of Winchester, sustained the memorable protracted siege in Basing House, and though most of the survivors were put to the sword by the parliamentary party, yet, through some means now unknown, the lives of the artists were spared.

When he regained his liberty, Hollar followed his patron to Antwerp, and resumed his usual employment; but the early death of Lord Arundel compelled him to return to England, and earn a precarious subsistence by working for print-dealers. His patient industry anticipated a certain reward at the Restoration; but when that event occurred, he found himself as much neglected as the generality of the expectant Royalists were. A fallacious prospect of advantage was opened to him in 1669. He was appointed by the Court to proceed to Tangier, and make plans and drawings of the fortifications and principal buildings there. On his return, the vessel in which he sailed was attacked by seven Algerine pirates, and after a most desperate conflict, the English ship succeeded in gaining the protection of the port of Cadiz, with a loss of eleven killed and seventeen wounded. Hollar, during the engagement, coolly employed himself in sketching the exciting scene, an engraving of which he afterwards published. For a year's hard work, under an African sun, poor Hollar received no more than one hundred pounds and the barren title of the King's Iconographer.

His life now became a mere struggle for bread. The price he received for his work was so utterly inadequate to the extraordinary care and labour he bestowed upon it, that he could scarcely earn a bare subsistence. He worked for fourpence an hour, with an hour-glass always before him, and was so scrupulously exact with respect to his employer's time, that at the least interruption, he used to turn the glass on its side to prevent the sand from running. Hollar was not what may be termed a great artist. His works, though characterised by a truthful air of exactness, are deficient in picturesque effect; but he is the engraver whose memory is ever faithfully cherished by all persons of antiquarian predilections. Hundreds of ancient monuments, buildings, costumes, ceremonies, are preserved in his works, that, had they not been engraved by his skilful hand, would have been irretrievably lost in oblivion.

He died as poor as he had lived. An execution was put into his house as he lay dying. With characteristic meekness, he begged the bailiff's forbearance, praying that his bed might be left for him to die on; and that he might not be removed to any other prison than the grave. And thus died Hollar, a man possessed of a singular ability, which he exercised with an industry that permitted neither interval nor repose for more than fifty years. He is said to have engraved no

less than 24,000 plates. Of a strictly moral character, unblemished by the failings of many men of genius, and of unceasing industry, he passed a long life in adversity, and ended it in destitution of common comfort. Yet of no engraver of his age is the fame now greater, or the value of his works enhanced to so high a degree.

TRIAL OF FATHER GARNET.

On the 28th of March 1606, took place the trial of Father Garnet, chief of the Jesuits in England, for his alleged concern in the Gunpowder Treason. He was a man of distinguished ability and zeal for the interests of the Romish Church, and had been consulted by the conspirators Greenway and Catesby regarding the plot, on an evident understanding that he was favourable to it. Being found guilty, he was condemned to be hanged, which sentence was put in execution on the ensuing 3rd of May, in St Paul's-churchyard. There has ever since raged a controversy about his criminality; but an impartial person of our day can scarcely but admit that Garnet was all but actively engaged in forwarding the conspiracy. He himself acknowledged that he was consulted by two of the plotters, and that he ought to have revealed what he knew. At the same time, one must acknowledge that the severities then practised towards the professors of the Catholic faith were calculated in no small measure to confound the sense of right and wrong in matters between them and their Protestant brethren.

PRIESTS' HIDING CHAMBERS.

During a hundred and fifty years following the Reformation, Catholicism, as is well known, was generally treated by the law with great severity, insomuch that a trafficking priest found in England was liable to capital punishment for merely performing the rites of his religion. Nevertheless, even in the most rigorous times, there was always a number of priests concealed in the houses of the Catholic nobility and gentry, daring everything for the sake of what they thought their duty. The country-houses of the wealthy Catholics were in many instances provided with secret chambers, in which the priests lived concealed probably from all but the lord and lady of the mansion, and at the utmost one or two confidential domestics. It is to be presumed that a priest was rarely a permanent tenant of the Patmos provided for him, because usually these concealed apartments were so straitened and inconvenient that not even religious enthusiasm could reconcile any one long to occupy them. Yet we are made aware of an instance of a priest named Father Blackhall residing for a long series of years in the reign of Charles I. concealed in the house of the Viscountess Melgum, in the valley of the Dee, in Scotland.[*]

As an example of the style of accommodation, two small chambers in the *roof* formed the priest's retreat in the old half-timber house of Harborough Hall, midway between Hegley and

* See his Memoirs, published by the Spalding Society.

Kidderminster.* At Watcomb, in Berks, there is an old manor-house, in which the priest's chamber is accessible by lifting a board on the staircase.

A similar arrangement existed at Dinton Hall, near Aylesbury, the seat of Judge Mayne, one of the Regicides, to whom it gave temporary shelter at the crisis of the Restoration. It was at the top of the mansion, under the beams of the roof, and was reached by a narrow passage lined with cloth. Not till three of the steps of an ordinary stair were lifted up, could one discover the entrance to this passage, along which Mayne could crawl or pull himself in order to reach his den.†

Captain Duthy, in his *Sketches of Hampshire*, notices an example which existed in that part of England. In the old mansion of Woodcote, he says, 'behind a stack of chimneys, accessible only by removing the floor boards, was an apart-ment which contained a concealed closet . . . a *priest's hole.*'

The arrangements thus indicated give a striking idea of the dangers which beset the ministers of the Romish faith in times when England lived in continual apprehension of changes which they might bring about, and when they were accordingly treated with all the seve-rity due to public enemies.

One of the houses most remarkable for its means of concealing proscribed priests was Hend-lip Hall, a spacious mansion situated about four miles from Worcester, supposed to have been built late in Elizabeth's reign by John Abingdon, the queen's cofferer, a zealous partisan of Mary Queen of Scots. It is believed that Thomas Abingdon, the son of the builder of the mansion, was the person who took the chief trouble in so fitting it up. The result of his labours was that there was scarcely an apartment which had not

HENDLIP HOUSE.

secret ways of going in and out. Some had back staircases concealed in the walls; others had places of retreat in their chimneys; some had trap-doors, descending into hidden recesses. 'All,' in the language of a writer who ex-amined the house, 'presented a picture of gloom, insecurity, and suspicion.'‡ Standing, moreover, on elevated ground, the house afforded the means of keeping a watchful look-out for the approach of the emissaries of the law, or of persons by whom it might have been dangerous for any skulking priest to be seen, supposing his reverence to have gone forth for an hour to take the air.

Father Garnet, who suffered for his guilty knowledge of the Gunpowder Treason, was con-cealed in Hendlip, under care of Mr and Mrs Abingdon, for several weeks, in the winter of 1605-6. Suspicion did not light upon his name at first, but the confession of Catesby's servant, Bates, at length made the government aware of his guilt. He was by this time living at Hendlip, along with a lady named Anne Vaux, who devoted herself to him through a purely religious feeling, and another Jesuit, named Hall. Just as we have surmised regarding the general life of the skulking priesthood, these persons spent most of their hours in the apartments occupied by the family, only resorting to places of strict conceal-ment when strangers visited the house. When Father Garnet came to be inquired after, the government, suspecting Hendlip to be his place of retreat, sent Sir Henry Bromley thither, with

* *Notes and Queries*, 2nd ser. ii. 337.
† Lipscomb's *Buckinghamshire*, ii. 156.
‡ Beauties of England, xv. part i. p. 184.

instructions which reveal to us much of the character of the arrangements for the concealment of priests in England. 'In the search,' says this document, 'first observe the parlour where they use to dine and sup; in the east part of that parlour it is conceived there is some vault, which to discover you must take care to draw down the wainscot, whereby the entry into the vault may be discovered. The lower parts of the house must be tried with a broach, by putting the same into the ground some foot or two, to try whether there may be perceived some timber, which, if there be, there must be some vault underneath it. For the upper rooms, you must observe whether they be more in breadth than the lower rooms, and look in which places the rooms be enlarged; by pulling up some boards, you may discover some vaults. Also, if it appear that there be some corners to the chimneys, and the same boarded, if the boards be taken away there will appear some. If the walls seem to be thick, and covered with wainscot, being tried with a gimlet, if it strike not the wall, but go through, some suspicion is to be had thereof. If there be any double loft, some two or three feet, one above another, in such places any may be harboured privately. Also, if there be a loft towards the roof of the house, in which there appears no entrance out of any other place or lodging, it must of necessity be opened and looked into, for these be ordinary places of hovering [hiding].'

Sir Henry invested the house, and searched it from garret to cellar, without discovering anything suspicious but some books, such as scholarly men might have been supposed to use. Mrs. Abingdon—who, by the way, is thought to have been the person who wrote the letter to Lord Monteagle, warning him of the plot—denied all knowledge of the person searched for. So did her husband when he came home. 'I did never hear so impudent liars as I find here,' says Sir Henry in his report to the Earl of Salisbury, forgetting how the power and the habit of mendacity was acquired by this persecuted body of Christians. After four days of search, two men came forth half dead with hunger, and proved to be servants. Sir Henry occupied the house for several days more, almost in despair of further discoveries, when the confession of a conspirator condemned at Worcester put him on the scent for Father Hall, as for certain lying at Hendlip. It was only after a search protracted to ten days in all, that he was gratified by the voluntary surrender of both Hall and Garnet. They came forth from their concealment, pressed by the need for air rather than food, for marmalade and other sweetmeats were found in their den, and they had had warm and nutritive drinks passed to them by a reed 'through a little hole in a chimney that backed another chimney, into a gentlewoman's chamber.' They had suffered extremely by the smallness of their place of concealment, being scarcely able to enjoy in it any movement for their limbs, which accordingly became much swollen. Garnet expressed his belief that, if they could have had relief from the blockade for but half a day, so as to allow of their sending away books and furniture by which

the place was hampered, they might have baffled inquiry for a quarter of a year.*

MARCH 29.

Saints Jonas, Barachisius, and their companions, martyrs, 327. St Mark, Bishop of Arethusa, in Syria, 4th century. Saints Armogastes, Archinimus, and Satur, martyrs, 457. St Gundleus, a Welsh King, 5th century. St Eustasius (or Eustachius), abbot of Luxeu, 625.

Born.—Sanzio Raffaelle, painter, 1483, *Urbino*; † Dr John Lightfoot, Scripture commentator, 1602, *Stoke-upon-Trent*, Joseph Ignace Guillotin, physician, originator of the guillotine in France, 1738, *Xaintes*; Marshal Jean de Dieu Soult, Duke of Dalmatia, 1769, *St Amand-du-Tarn*; Sir Edward Geoffrey Stanley, fourteenth Earl of Derby, statesman, 1799.

Died.—Pope Stephen X., 1058, *Florence*; Raymond Lully, 'the enlightened doctor,' 1315, *Majorca*; Henry Percy, third Earl of Northumberland, killed at the battle of Towton, 1461; Archbishop Tobias Matthew, 1629, *York*; Theophilus Bonet, eminent Genevese physician, 1689; Captain Thomas Coram, originator of the Foundling Hospital in London, 1751; Emanuel Swedenborg, 1772, *Coldbath Fields, London*; Gustavus III. of Sweden, 1792, *Stockholm*; Charles Dignum, singer, 1827; Sir William Drummond, learned historian, 1828; Thomas Harrison, of Chester, architect, 1829; Lieutenant Stratford, R.N., editor of the *Nautical Almanac*, 1853.

SIR THOMAS PARKYNS—CORNISH WRESTLING.

Sir Thomas Parkyns, Bart., of Bunny Park, Nottinghamshire, who died on the 29th of March 1741, was the author of a curious work, entitled *The Inn Play, or Cornish Hugg Wrestler.* Nor was he a mere writer on wrestling; he was an able and skilful athlete himself, as well as a ripe scholar, subtle disputant, and energetic country magistrate. Slightly eccentric, he was equally at home in the wrestling ring or on the magisterial bench; and it was said that he could throw an antagonist, combat a paradox, quote the classics, and lay down the law at quarter sessions, with any man in all England. It was when a boy, under the famous Dr Busby, at Westminster School, that the attention of Sir Thomas was first attracted to wrestling, by his having to construe the well-known epigram of Martial, commencing with the line:

'Rure morans, quid agam? respondi pauca, rogatus,'

which has been thus translated:

‘ When to my farm retired, how do I live?
　If any ask, this short account I give;
　The gods, at the first light, I do adore,
　And place this care all other cares before.
　My grounds I visit then, and servants call,
　And their just tasks I do impose on all.

* Jardine's *Narrative of the Gunpowder Plot*, p. 189. 1857.

† Sometimes the 28th of March is given as the date of the birth of the illustrious Raphael. The original statement on the subject is that Raphael was born on Good Friday (he died also on Good Friday). A French work, entitled *Ephémérides*, 1812, affirms that Good Friday of 1483 was the 29th of March, and this authority we follow.

I study next, rouse my poetic vein ;
My body then anoint, and gently strain
With some meet exercise ; exult in mind
At every turn, myself both free to find
From crimes and debts ; last, I bathe, sup, laugh,
    drink,
Jest, sing, rest, and, on all that passes, think.
A little lamp the while sends forth a ray,
Which to my nightly studies makes a day.'

From Westminster, Sir Thomas went to Cambridge, where his principal study was mathematics and mechanics, in their applications to feats of strength and dexterity. We next find him a student at Gray's-inn, relieving the dry study of the law by instructions in wrestling, boxing, and fencing, from the best masters that the metropolis could produce. Succeeding to the title early in life, he settled down on his ancestral estate at Bunny, and established an annual wrestling match in his park, open to all comers. The prize was a gold-laced hat, value twenty-two shillings, and three shillings for the second best. The amount was small, but the glory was great. Sir Thomas was no idle patron of the contests; he never objected to go in for a fall with the best man on the ground, and often won and wore the gold-laced hat himself. His servants were all upright, muscular, young fellows, and good wrestlers. Indeed, his favourite coachman and footman had defeated the baronet himself in the wrestling ring, throwing him on his back in such consummate style, that his heart warmed to them at once, and, like Robin Hood of yore, he immediately took them into his service. There was a policy in this, for he well knew that a good and powerful wrestler could be no other than a sober man. 'Whoever would be a complete wrestler,' says Sir Thomas, 'must avoid being overtaken in drink, which very much enervates, or, being in a passion at the sight of his adversary, or having received a fall, in such cases he is bereaved of his senses, not being master of himself is less of his art, but sheweth too much play, or none at all, or rather pulleth, kicketh, and ventureth beyond all reason and his judgment when himself.

    That man's a fool, that hopes for good
    From flowing bowls and feverish blood.'

He also further informs us, that the greatest of wrestling masters is one Bacchus, who has many assistants, among others : 'Brandy a Frenchman, Usquebaugh an Irishman, Rum a Molossonian— these masters teach mostly the trip, which I assure you is no safe and sound play. You may know them by their walkings and gestures, they stagger and reel, and cross legs, which I advise my scholars to avoid, and receive many a foul fall in the sink or kennel: and were your constitutions of porphyry, marble, or steel, they will make you yield to your last and only fair fall.'

Speaking of the antiquity of wrestling, he says :—'Though at the beginning of the preface I take notice that wrestling was in vogue, great credit, reputation, and estimation in Martial the poet's days, wrestling without all doubt is of greater antiquity, as appears by Genesis, Jacob wrestled with an angel. Whether it was real

and corporeal, or mystical and spiritual in its signification, I leave the divines to determine. But I advise all my scholars to avoid wrestling with angels; for, though they may maintain the struggle till break of day, and seem to lay their adversaries supine and on their backs, yet they will have the fall and be out of joint with Jacob's thigh.'

A good specimen of what may be termed the wrestling style of Sir Thomas is found in the following directions for giving an opponent the throw called by adepts

'THE FLYING HORSE.

'Take him by the right hand with your left, your palm being upwards as if you designed only to shake him by the hand in a friendly manner in the beginning, and twist it outwards, and lift it upwards to make way for your head, and put your head under his right arm-pit, and hold his hand down to your left side, hold your head stiff backwards, to hold him out of his strength, then put your right arm up to the shoulder between his grainings, and let your hand appear behind past his breech, but if you suspect they will cavil at that arm, as a breeching, lay your arm along his belly, and lift him up as high as your head and in either hold, when so high, lean backward, and throw him over your head.'

There is a good-humoured quaintness in the description of this encounter. How placidly it commences with taking the opponent's hand 'in a friendly manner,' reminding us of Izaak Walton's words, 'use him as though you loved him,' when directing how to impale a wretched frog on a fishing-hook. Anon, the plot thickens, until, at last, the astonished novice finds himself performing the flying-horse—the spread eagle the Americans more analogically term it—over his friend's head !

One of the wrestling baronet's whims was to form a collection of stone coffins ; and a rare and probably unexampled collection he did form, and keep with great nicety, in the churchyard at Bunny. It was not from any antiquarian tastes, however, that he made this collection ; neither was it for the mere empty desire of possessing a few score stone coffins. He was one who loved to read a moral in all around him ; to find tongues in trees, books in the running brooks, and good in everything. The coffins ranged before him were emblems of mortality, teaching the athletic champion of the wrestling ring that the great wrestler Death would inevitably overcome him in the end. And to carry this impression of humility even into the house of prayer, he caused his own monument—the marble effigies of Sir Thomas Parkyns, as he termed it—to be placed opposite his pew in the chancel—his own chancel —of Bunny Church, that he might look on it every Lord's day, and say—What is life ! This monument was carved out of a 'fair piece of marble,' in his own great barn, by his own domestic chaplain ; and from what remains of it now, we may hope that the chaplain was a much better clergyman than sculptor. On this monument Sir Thomas is depicted in the centre, standing in his wrestling dress, potent and postured, ready for either flying-horse or

Cornish-hug. His attitude is the first position of wrestling, as well as a moralising posture, and emblematises 'the divine and human struggle for the glorious mastery.' On one side is a well-

EFFIGY OF SIR THOMAS PARKYNS.

limbed figure lying *above* the scythe of time, the sun rising gloriously over it, showing that the strong man and wrestler is in the prime of youth. On the other side we see the same figure stretched in a coffin, with Time, scythe in hand, standing triumphantly over *it ;* the sun gone down, marking the darkness of the tomb, the fate of all, strong or feeble. There are some Latin verses on the monument, that have been translated as follows :—

'At length, by conquering Time subdued,
  Lo ! here Britannia's wrestler lies ;
Till now he still unshaken stood,
  Whene'er he strove, and gain'd the prize.

Long was the doubtful strife—beset
  With years, he long eludes the fall ;
Nor yet inglorious his defeat,
  O'ermatch'd by Him who conquers all.

To life restored, the day will come,
  When he, though now he faint and fail,
Shall rise victorious from the tomb,
  And over Time himself prevail.'

Thus did Sir Thomas Parkyns moralise in marble, and decorate with solemn emblems the church at Bunny.

Though no training will enable a man to wrestle successfully against a century, still temperance, wholesome toil, and manly exercise, will carry him bravely over several scores of years. Sir Thomas Parkyns never knew a day's illness until his seventy-eighth year, when death at last gave him the backfall, and he died universally beloved and lamented. The wrestling matches he instituted were annually kept up for many years after his death, and were not finally done away with till about the year 1810. His monument, though considerably dilapidated, is still to be seen in the chancel of Bunny Church ; we had almost forgotten to say that, having selected one of his stone coffins for his own use, he left the remainder to such parishioners of Bunny as might choose to be interred in them.

CORAM AND THE FOUNDLING HOSPITAL.

Captain Thomas Coram was born at Lyme Regis, in Dorsetshire, in 1668. He emigrated to Massachusetts, where, after working a while as a shipwright, he became master of a trading vessel, made some money, and at last settled in London. In 1720, when living at Rotherhithe, and walking to and from the city early in the morning and late at night, his feelings were often keenly tried in coming across infants exposed and deserted in the streets. His tender heart at once set his head devising some remedy. There were hospitals for foundlings in France and Holland, and why not in England? Coram was an honest mariner, without much learning or art of address; but he had energy and patience, and for seventeen years he spent the most of his time in writing letters and visiting in advocacy of a home for foundlings. After long striking, a spark caught

CAPTAIN CORAM, BY HOGARTH.

the tinder of the fashionable world; such an institution was voted a necessity of the age; and in 1739, the Foundling Hospital was established by Royal Charter. Subscriptions poured freely in, and in 1741 the Lamb's Conduit estate of 56 acres was bought as a site and grounds for £5,500. It was a fortunate investment. London rapidly girdled the Hospital, which now lies at its very centre, and from the leases of superfluous outskirts the Hospital draws an annual income equal to the original purchase-money. Hogarth was a great friend of the Hospital, and was one of its earliest Governors. For its walls he painted Coram's portrait, 'one of the first,' he writes, 'that I did the size of life, and with a particular desire to excel.' He and other painters displayed

their works in the rooms of the Foundling, and out of the practice grew the first Exhibition of the Royal Academy in the Adelphi, in 1760. The show of pictures drew 'the town' to the Hospital, and its grounds became the morning lounge of the belles and beaux of London in the last years of George II. Handel also served the Foundling nobly. To its chapel he presented an organ, and for eleven years, from 1749 to his death in 1759, he conducted an oratorio for its benefit, from which sums varying from £300 to £900 were annually realized. The original score of his 'Messiah' is preserved among the curiosities of the Hospital.

The Governors commenced work in a house in Hatton Garden on 25th March 1741, having exhibited a notice the previous day, that 'To-morrow at 8 o'clock in the evening this house will be opened for the reception of 20 children.' Any person bringing a child rang the bell at the inner door, and waited to hear if there were no objections to its reception on account of disease. No questions were asked as to whom the infant belonged to, or why it was brought. When the full number of babes had been received, a board was hung out over the door, 'The House is full.' Sometimes a hundred children were brought when only twenty could be admitted, and in the crush for precedence riots ensued; in consequence, a ballot was instituted, and the women drew out of a bag, white, red, and black balls. Those who drew black had to go away, those who drew white were accepted, and those who drew red remained in case the child of any woman who had drawn white should be found ineligible from infectious disease. The fame of the charity spread far and wide, and the country began to consign foundlings to its care. A tinker was tried at Monmouth for drowning a child he had received to carry to London. Seven out of eight infants a waggoner undertook to bring to town were found dead at the end of the journey. One man with five in a basket got drunk on his way, fell asleep on a common, and when he awoke three of his charge were suffocated. A horseman from Yorkshire was asked on Highgate Hill what he carried in his panniers, and he shewed two infants, saying that he got eight guineas for the trip, but that others were offering to do it cheaper.

In 1754, the governors moved into the present Hospital, erected from the designs of architect Jacobson, with 600 children, whom they were supporting at an expense of five times the amount of their income! In their distress they applied to Parliament for aid, which voted them £10,000, but plunged them into new difficulties by ordering the reception of all infants that might be brought to them, and opening country branches. At one of these, Ackworth, near Pontefract, cloth was made, in suits of which some of the patrons of the Hospital appeared at the annual festivals. At another, Aylesbury, John Wilkes, M.P., was treasurer, and when he left the kingdom in 1764, it was found that he was in possession of some of the funds.

In compliance with the Act of Parliament a basket was hung at the gate of the Hospital, in which the foundling was deposited, and a bell rung to give notice to the officers in attendance.

From 1741 to 1756 the Governors had accepted the charge of 1384 children, but under the new parliamentary arrangement the traffic developed amazingly. On the 2d of June 1756, the first day of the basket, 117 infants were put into it. In 1757, bills were posted through the streets, apprising the public of their privilege. The workhouses got rid of all their infantile encumbrances in the convenient basket. Women stood at the gate, stripped their babies naked, popped them into the basket, and rang the bell. In the first year, 3,296 were put in; in the second, 4,025; in the third, 4,229; and in ten months of the fourth, 3,324. Out of the total of 14,874, it is scarcely surprising, however horrible, to learn that only 4,000 lived to be apprenticed, a mortality of 70 per cent. ! The expense of the charity thus far was nearly £500,000. Of course results like these alarmed the most Quixotic, and in 1760 Parliament revoked the order for indiscriminate admission, and agreed to bear the charge of the children who had flooded the charity at their invitation. Warned by this terrible experience, the Governors were content to work with much humbler aims. They still accepted any infant that might be brought, if a purse of £100 was given with it, but even this privilege they felt it wise to abolish in 1801.

The annual revenue of the Hospital at this day from its estate and funded property is nearly £11,000, and with this sum 460 boys and girls are maintained and educated, from infancy until their fifteenth year. The Queen is a donor of fifty guineas annually, following the precedent set by George II. The conditions of admission now are 'that the child be illegitimate, except that the father be a soldier or sailor killed in the service of his country, and that the mother shall have borne a good character previous to her misfortune, and that she be poor and have no relations able or willing to maintain her child.' The object of the Governors is to hide the shame of the mother, as well as to preserve the life of her child, and dismiss her with the charge, ' Sin no more.' The average admissions are thirty-seven annually. No infant is received older than twelve months. The treasurer gives each babe a name, and when christened it is sent into the country to nurse, and on the attainment of its third year is brought to the Hospital in London. There all receive a plain education in reading, writing, and arithmetic. The girls, taught sewing and household work, are put out to domestic service in respectable families. There is a constant demand, much in excess of the supply, for servants bred at the Foundling. The boys are apprenticed to various trades, and about fifty of them are instructed in music, and draughted into the bands of the army and navy. The children on the whole turn out well in the world, and generally bear the home of their youth in kindly remembrance.

From Handel the Foundling has inherited a high musical reputation. Several blind children, received during the years of indiscriminate admission, were trained as a choir, and their sweet voices were a great attraction to the chapel. Mr. Grenville, the organist, Mr.

Printer, Jenny Freer, and Miss Thetford, noted singers, were all blind foundlings. On Sundays the chapel is usually filled in every corner by crowds who come to hear the excellent music, which is led by professionals, and supported by the voices of 500 children. The pew rents, and collections at the door, average from £600 to £900 a year, after paying all expenses. The altar-piece, ' Christ presenting a Child,' is by West, who retouched the picture in 1816. From the pulpit Sterne and Sidney Smith, not to run over other names, have pleaded for the charity.

The collection of pictures at the Foundling is worth seeing. They are nearly all gifts, and illustrate very fairly the state of British art in the third quarter of last century. There is Hogarth's portrait of Coram, of which he said that ' it had stood the test of twenty years' competition, notwithstanding the first painters in the kingdom exerting all their talents to vie with it;' also his March to Finchley, and his Moses brought to Pharaoh's Daughter. There is a portrait of Lord Dartmouth, by Sir Joshua Reynolds; of George II., by Shackleton; of Handel, by Kneller; of Dr Mead, by Allan Ramsay; views of various London hospitals, by Gainsborough, Richard Wilson, Haytley, and Wale; three sacred subjects by Hayman, Highmore, and Wills; a bas-relief by Rysbrack, and a bust of Handel by Roubiliac.

Captain Coram's fortune appears never to have been large, and his credit in the institution of the Foundling lay, not in any pecuniary endowment, but in the undaunted pertinacity with which he fought down public apathy, and at last induced wealth and power to work out his philanthropic design. Two years before his death it was discovered that he had lost all his means. His friends thereon bestirred themselves to raise him to independence by subscription; and in order that the good old man might not be offended, Dr Brocklesby broke to him the project. His answer was, ' I have not wasted the little money I once had in self-indulgence or vanity, and am not ashamed to confess that in my old age I am poor.' In 1749 they secured him an annuity of £170. He happily did not live to see the charity he had founded, in the years of its frightful efflorescence. He died on the 29th of March 1751, aged eighty-four, when the Hospital which preserves his memory was in course of erection; and in the new stone catacombs of the chapel his body was the first to be laid. There, also, Lord Tenterden was buried in 1832 —the Canterbury barber's boy, who rose to be Lord Chief Justice of England. An excellent statue of Coram, by Calder Marshall, was set up at the gates of the Hospital in 1856; but the stone out of which it is cut has already proved so friable, that it has had to be painted over to save it from destruction.

THE BERKSHIRE LADY'S GARLAND.

'March 29, 1679,' is the date of a baronetcy conferred on a Berkshire gentleman, William Kenrick, of Whitley, which, however, expired with the second generation about the close of the century. The second baronet left his property to an only daughter, who is understood to have soon after disposed herself in marriage in a very extraordinary way. Tradition and a contemporary *broadside* ballad concur in representing this young gentlewoman as paid court to by many, but refusing all, and keeping her affections disengaged, until, attending a wedding at Reading, she met a young and handsome but poor attorney, named Benjamin Child, with whom she fell violently in love on the spot. For some days she reasoned with herself on the subject, trying to shake herself free of this sudden passion, but all in vain. Then, feeling that something must be done, but unable from confusion of mind to devise a proper course, she took the extraordinary step of sending the young man a letter, demanding satisfaction for injuries she alleged he had inflicted on her, and appointing time and place for a hostile meeting. Mr. Child was much surprised, and quite at a loss to conceive who the challenger could be. By the advice of a friend, however, he resolved to attend. The meeting may be described in the words of the ballad:

' Early on a summer's morning,
When bright Phœbus was adorning
Every bower with his beams,
The fair lady came, it seems.

At the bottom of a mountain,
Near a pleasant crystal fountain,
There she left her gilded coach,
While the grove she did approach.

Covered with her mask, and walking,
There she met her lover, talking
With a friend that he had brought,
So she asked him whom he sought.

"I am challenged by a gallant
Who resolves to try my talent ;
Who he is I cannot say,
But I hope to shew him play."

" It is I that did invite you ;
You shall wed me, or I'll fight you
Underneath those spreading trees ;
Therefore choose from which you please.

"You shall find I do not vapour,
I have sought my trusty rapier ;
Therefore take your choice," said she :
"Either fight or marry me ! "

Said he, "Madam, pray what mean you ?
In my life I've never seen you ;
Pray unmask, your visage shew
Then I'll tell you ay or no."

" I will not my face uncover
Till the marriage ties are over ;
Therefore choose you which you will,
Wed me, sir, or try your skill.

"Step within that pleasant bower
With your friend one single hour ;
Strive your thoughts to reconcile,
And I'll wander here the while."

While this beauteous lady waited,
The young bachelors debated
What was best for to be done.
Quoth his friend, " The hazard run ;

" If my judgment can be trusted,
Wed her first, you can't be worsted ;
If she's rich you'll rise to fame,
If she's poor, why, you're the same."

He consented to be married ;
All three in a coach were carried
To a church without delay,
Where he weds the lady gay.

Though sweet pretty Cupids hover'd
Round her eyes, her face was cover'd
With a mask,—he took her thus,
Just for better or for worse.'

The ballad goes on to state that the pair went in her coach to the lady's elegant mansion, where, leaving him in a parlour, she proceeded to dress herself in her finest attire, and by and by broke upon his vision as a young and handsome woman and his devoted wife:

' Now he's clothed in rich attire,
Not inferior to a squire ;
Beauty, honour, riches' store,
What can man desire more ?'

It appears that Mr Child took a position in society suitable to the fortune thus conferred upon him, and was high sheriff of the county in 1714.*

MRS FITZHERBERT.

29th March 1837, died at Brighton, Mrs Fitzherbert, at the age of eighty-one. Born Mary Anne Smythe (daughter of Walter Smythe, Esq., of Brambridge, in the county of Hants), she was first married to Edward Weld, Esq., of Lulworth Castle, Dorsetshire ; secondly to Thomas Fitzherbert, Esq., of Swinnerton, Staffordshire. She was a second time a widow, living on a handsome jointure, and greatly admired in society on account of her beauty and accomplishments, when, in 1785, being twenty-nine years of age, she became acquainted with the Prince of Wales, who was six years younger. He fell distractedly in love with her, and was eager to become her third husband ; but she, well aware that the royal marriage-act made the possibility of anything more than an appearance of decent nuptials in this case extremely doubtful, resisted all his importunities. It has been stated, on good authority, that, to overcome her scruples, he caused himself one day to be bled, put on the appearance of having made a desperate attempt on his own life, and sent some friends to bring her to see him. She was thus induced to allow him to engage her with a ring in the presence of witnesses ; but she afterwards broke off, went abroad, and for a long time resisted all the efforts he made to induce her to return. It is told, as a curious fact in this strange love history, that one of the chief instruments in bringing about the union of the ill-assorted pair, was the notorious Duke of Orleans (Philip Egalité.)

Towards the close of 1785, it became known that the heir-apparent of the British crown was about to marry a Catholic widow lady named Mrs Fitzherbert. Charles Fox, to whose party the prince had attached himself, wrote to his royal highness on the 10th of December, a long letter, pointing out the dangerous nature of the course he was following. 'Consider,' said he, 'the circumstances in which you stand ; the King not feeling for you as a father ought ; the Duke of York

* See the entire ballad, with notes, in *Ancient Ballads and Songs of the Peasantry*, edited by Robert Bell, 1857.

professedly his favourite, and likely to be married to the King's wishes; the nation full of its old prejudices against Catholics, and justly dreading all disputes about succession.' Then the marriage could not be a real one. 'I need not,' said he, 'point out to your good sense what a source of uneasiness it must be to you, to her, and above all, to the nation, to have it a matter of dispute and discussion whether the Prince of Wales is or is not married.' The whole letter, written in a tone of sincere regard for the prince, was highly creditable to the wisdom of the writer.

The prince answered on the instant, thanking Mr Fox for his advices and warnings, but assuring them they were needless. 'Make yourself easy, my dear friend; believe me, the world will now soon be convinced that there not only is [not], but never was, any ground for those reports which have of late been so malevolently circulated.'

Ten days after the date of this letter, namely, on the 21st of December, the Prince and Mrs Fitzherbert were married by an English clergyman, before two witnesses. Mr Fox, misled by the Prince, took it upon him to deny the fact of the marriage in the House of Commons; but society was never blinded on the subject. Mrs Fitzherbert lived for several years with great openness, as the wife of the Prince of Wales, and in the enjoyment of the entire respect of society, more especially of her husband's brothers. A separation only took place about 1795, when the prince was about to marry (for the payment of his debts) the unfortunate Caroline of Brunswick. Mrs Fitzherbert survived this event forty-two years, and never during the whole time ceased to be 'visited.' The case is a very peculiar one, from its standing in so dubious a position both with respect to law and morality.

MARCH 30.

St John Climacus, the Scholastic, abbot of Mount Sinai, 605. St Zozimus, Bishop of Syracuse, 660. St Regulus (or Rieul), Bishop of Senlis.

Born.—Sir Henry Wotton, Provost of Eton College, and poetical and prose writer, 1568, *Boughton Hall, Kent;* Archbishop Somner, antiquary, 1606, *Canterbury;* Francis Pilatre de Rozier, aëronaut, 1756, *Metz;* Field-Marshal Henry Viscount Hardinge (Peninsular war and Sutlej campaign), 1785, *Wrotham, Kent.*

Died.—Phocion, Athenian general and statesman, B.C. 317; Cardinal Bourchier, early promoter of printing in England, 1486, *Knowle, Kent;* Sir Ralph Sadler, diplomatist (Sadler Papers), 1587, *Standon, Herts;* Dr John King, Bishop of London, 1621; Archbishop Somner, 1669, *Canterbury;* Sebastian de Vauban, military engineer (fortification), 1707, *Paris;* Dr William Hunter, 1783, *Windmill-street, St James's;* James Morier, traveller and novelist, 1849.

SIR HENRY WOTTON.

Boughton Hall, in Kent, situated, as Izaak Walton tells us, 'on the brow of such a hill as gives the advantage of a large prospect, and of equal pleasure to all beholders,' was the birthplace of Sir Henry Wotton. After going through

the preliminary course at Winchester School, he proceeded to Oxford, where he studied until his twenty-second year; and then, laying aside his books, he betook himself to the useful library of travel. He passed one year in France, three in Germany, and five in Italy. Wherever he stayed, to quote Walton again, 'he became acquainted with the most eminent men for learning and all manner of arts, as picture, sculpture, chemistry, and architecture; of all which he was a most dear lover, and a most excellent judge. He returned out of Italy into England about the thirtieth year of his age, being noted by many, both for his person and comportment; for indeed he was of a choice shape, tall of stature, and of a most persuasive behaviour, which was so mixed with sweet discourse and civilities as gained him much love from all persons with whom he entered into an acquaintance.'

One of his acquaintances was Robert Devereux, Earl of Essex, and there can be little doubt that Wotton was, some way or another, implicated in the rash plot of that unfortunate nobleman. For when Essex was sent to the Tower, as a step so far on his way to the scaffold, Wotton thought it prudent, 'very quickly and as privately, to glide through Kent unto Dover,' and, with the aid of a fishing-boat, to place himself on the shores of France. He soon after reached Florence, where he was taken notice of by Ferdinand de Medici, Grand Duke of Tuscany, who sent him, under the feigned name of Octavio Baldi, on a secret mission to James VI. of Scotland. The object of this mission had reference to James's succession to the English throne, and a plot to poison him, said to be entered into by some Jesuits. After remaining three months in Scotland, Wotton returned to Italy, but soon after, hearing of the death of Elizabeth, he waited on the King at London. 'Ha,' said James, when he observed him at Court, 'there is my old friend Signor Octavio Baldi.' The assembled courtiers, among whom was Wotton's brother, stared in confusion, none of them being aware of his mission to Scotland. 'Come forward and kneel, Signor Octavio Baldi,' said the king; who, on Wotton obeying, gave him the accolade, saying, 'Arise, Sir Henry Wotton.' James, as from his character may readily be supposed, highly enjoyed the state of mystification the courtiers were thrown into by the unexpected scene. Immediately after, Wotton received the appointment of ambassador to the city of Venice.

It was on this journey to Venice, that Sir Henry, when passing through Augsburg, wrote in the album of his friend Flecamore, the punning and often quoted definition of an ambassador—an honest man sent to lie abroad for the good of his country. Certainly ambassadors had no good repute for veracity in those days, yet in all probability Wotton's diplomatic tactics were of a different description. On an occasion, his advice on this rather delicate question being asked, by a person setting out for a foreign embassy, he said, 'Ever speak the truth; for if you do so, you shall never be believed, and 'twill put your adversaries (who will still hunt counter) to a loss in all their disquisitions and undertakings.'

For twenty years Sir Henry represented the

English court at Venice, and during that time successfully sustained the Doge in his resistance to the aggression of the Papal power. And finally returning to his native country, he received what Thomas Fuller styles, 'one of the genteelest and entirest preferments in England,' the Provostship of Eton College.

To Wotton's many accomplishments was added a rich poetical taste, which he often exercised in compositions of a descriptive and elegiac character. He also delighted in angling, finding it, 'after tedious study, a cheerer of his spirits, a diverter of sadness, a calmer of unquiet thoughts, a moderator of passions, a procurer of contentedness; and that it begat habits of peace and patience in those who professed and practised it.' So when settled down in life as Provost of Eton, he built himself a neat fishing-lodge on the banks of the Thames, where he was often visited by his friend and subsequent biographer, Walton. The site is still occupied by a fishing-lodge, though not the one that Wotton erected. It is on an island, a green lawn sloping gently down to the pleasant river. On one side, the turrets of Windsor Castle are seen, through a vista of grand old elm trees; on the other the spires and antique architecture of Eton Chapel and College. The property still belongs to the College, and it is said that it never has been untenanted by a worthy and expert brother of the angle since the time of Wotton. And there it was, 'with peace and patience cohabiting in his heart,' as Walton tells us, that Sir Henry, when beyond seventy years of age, 'made this description of a part of the present pleasure that possessed him, as he sat quietly, on a summer's evening, on a bank a-fishing. It is a description of the Spring; which, because it glided as softly and sweetly from his pen as that river does at this time, by which it was then made, I shall repeat it unto you:

" This day dame Nature seemed in love;
  The lusty sap began to move;
Fresh juice did stir th' embracing vines,
And birds had drawn their valentines.
The jealous trout, that low did lie,
Rose at a well-dissembled fly;
There stood my friend, with patient skill
Attending on his trembling quill.
Already were the eaves possest
With the swift pilgrim's daubed nest;
The groves already did rejoice
In Philomel's triumphant voice;
The showers were short, the weather mild,
The morning fresh, the evening smiled.
Joan takes her neat-rubbed pail, and now
She trips to milk the sand-red cow,
Where, for some sturdy foot-ball swain,
Joan strokes a syllabub or twain.
The fields and gardens were beset
With tulips, crocus, violet:
And now, though late, the modest rose
Did more than half a blush disclose.
Thus all looks gay, and full of cheer,
To welcome the new-liveried year." '

As Sir Henry, in the quiet shades of Eton, found himself drawing towards the end of life, he felt no terror; he was only inspired with hope for the future and kindly remembrances of the past. Among these last, was the wish to revisit the school where he had played and

studied when a boy; so for this purpose he travelled to Winchester, and here is his commentary:—'How useful was that advice of a holy monk, who persuaded his friend to perform his customary devotions in a constant place, because in that place we usually meet with those very thoughts which possessed us at our last being there. And I find it thus far experimentally true; that, at my now being in that school, and seeing that very place, where I sat when I was a boy, occasioned me to remember those very thoughts of my youth which then possessed me; sweet thoughts indeed, that promised my growing years numerous pleasures, without mixtures of cares; and those to be enjoyed when time (which I then thought slow-paced) had changed my youth into manhood. But age and experience have taught me that those were but empty hopes. For I have always found it true, as my Saviour did foretell, " sufficient for the day is the evil thereof."' Returning to Eton from this last visit to Winchester, he died in 1639, and was buried in the College chapel, according to his own direction, with no other inscription on his tomb than—

> ' HERE LIES THE AUTHOR OF THIS SENTENCE :
> THE ITCH OF DISPUTATION IS THE SCAB OF THE
>   CHURCH.'

We translate the inscription, for, strange to say, the original Latin words were incorrectly written, and, as gossiping Pepys tells us, so basely altered that they disgrace the stone.

THE SICILIAN VESPERS.

On this day, five hundred and eighty years ago, the people of Sicily rescued themselves from the tyranny of a foreign dynasty by an insurrection which has become a celebrated event in history, and which presents some points of resemblance to the revolution in the same island which we have so recently witnessed. In our time the Neapolitan tyrant was a Prince of the French house of Bourbon; at the most distant period he was of the French house of Anjou. The secret prompter of it was in the both cases an Italian patriot,—Garibaldi in 1860, and in 1282 John of Procida. It is difficult to say in which the tyranny had been most galling, but in the earlier period the revolt was directed with less skill, and was carried on with greater ferocity.

Sicily and Naples were at that time ruled by a conqueror and usurper, to whom they had been handed over by the will of a pope, and they were occupied by a French soldiery, of whose unbounded greediness and brutal licentiousness, the properties and persons of the inhabitants of all ranks were the prey. In Sicily, more even than in the continental provinces of Naples, the Italians were subjected, without any chance of redress, to the oppressions of their French rulers; and almost incredible anecdotes are told by the old chroniclers of the manner in which they were treated. They were attacked especially in that point on which all people feel sensitive, the honours of their wives and daughters. A French baron named Ludolph, who was governor of Menone, is said to have taken by force a young girl every week to satisfy his passions; and a knight of Artois named Faramond, who commanded in Noto, made a regular practice of causing all the handsomest women of his government to be brought to his palace, where they were sacrificed to his violence. John of Procida, who had been himself robbed of his lands by the French, was indefatigable in his efforts to rouse the spirits of the Sicilians, secretly visited and encouraged their chiefs, and secured the aid of the King of Arragon, Don Pedro, who was tempted by the prospect of obtaining for himself the crown of Sicily, to which he made out a claim through his wife. Yet, though John of Procida had made the Sicilians eager for revolt, we have no reason for supposing that there was any organised plan of insurrection, when it burst out suddenly and by accident; and we must probably ascribe in a great measure to this circumstance the sanguinary character which it assumed.

The 30th of March in the year 1282 was Easter Monday, and, as was customary on such festive occasions, the people of Palermo determined to go in procession to hear vespers at a church a short distance out of the town. The French looked upon all such gatherings with suspicion, and caused the people thus assembled to be searched for arms, which appears to have been made a pretext by the French soldiery for insulting the Sicilian females. Such was the case on the present occasion. As a young lady of great beauty, and the daughter of a gentleman of condition, was proceeding to the church, a French soldier laid hands upon her, and, under pretence of ascertaining if she had weapons concealed under her dress, offered her publicly a brutal insult. Her screams threw the multitude into a furious excitement, and, led by her father and husband and their friends, they seized whatever weapons came to hand, and massacred the whole of the French in Palermo, sparing neither sex nor age. To such a degree had the hatred of the population been excited, that even the monks issued from their monasteries to encourage and assist in the slaughter. Saint Remi, the governor of Palermo, attempted to make his escape in disguise, but was taken and killed, and the father of the young lady whose insult had been the signal for the rising, was chosen governor of the city for the Sicilians.

This signal, once given, was quickly acted upon in other parts of the island. The same day similar massacres took place in Monte Reale. Conigio, Carini, Termini, and other neighbouring towns; on the morrow, the example spread to Cefaladi, Mazaro, and Marsala; and on the 1st of April at Gergenti and Liceta. Burdac, the governor of Marsala, had just issued an order to the inhabitants of his government, to bring in all their gold and silver to the royal treasury, when the insurgents came to put him to death; and Louis de Montpellier, governor of San Giovanni, was poignarded by an injured husband, and his corpse hung out ignominiously at the castle window. Another unprovoked insult led to the revolt of Catania on the 4th of April. A young Frenchman named Jean Viglemada, notorious for his libertinism, attempted to take liberties with a lady named Julia Villamelli, when he was prevented by the unexpected en-

trance of her husband, whom he slew. The lady rushed through the street screaming for vengeance; and the people assembled, and, falling furiously on the Frenchmen, made a horrible carnage of them. Eight thousand are said to have perished in the massacre; all who escaped sought refuge in a strong fortress, where some perished with hunger and the rest were killed in attempting to leave it in disguise. The people of Palermo had meanwhile raised troops, and with these they laid siege to Taormina, took the place by assault, and slaughtered the whole of its French garrison. Messina alone remained in the possession of the French, and this was soon lost by their own imprudence. A citizen named Collura, supposed to have been employed by conspirators, made his appearance armed in the most public place of the town. As the Sicilians had been forbidden under the most severe penalties to carry or even possess arms, this was an act of defiance to the French authority, and four archers came to take the offender to prison. He offered a vigorous resistance, and some friends came to his assistance. The municipal authorities, believing that the citizens were not strong enough to overcome the French garrison, assisted in arresting the rioters, who, after an obstinate struggle, were all secured and committed to prison. The affair would probably have ended here, but the viceroy, not satisfied with imprisoning the men who had resisted his officers, sent to seize their wives also; and the citizens, provoked at this act of injustice, flew to arms, and, taking the French unprepared, massacred about three thousand of them. The rest retired into the fortresses, which were taken by assault, and their defenders put to the sword. The fate of the viceroy is a matter of doubt.

Such are the circumstances, as far as known, of this celebrated insurrection, which, from the circumstance of its having begun on the occasion of a public procession of the people of Palermo to attend vespers, received the name of the *Sicilian Vespers*. It is stated by some of the old writers that the numbers of the French who perished in the massacres throughout the island were not less than from twenty-four to twenty-eight thousand; but this number is supposed by historical writers to be greatly exaggerated. The King of Naples, Charles of Anjou, was at Monte-Fiascone, treating with the Pope, when the news of these events was brought to him, and he was so overcome with rage and indignation that it was some time before he could speak, but he gnawed a cane which he used to carry in his hand, and rolled his eyes furiously from side to side. When at length he opened his mouth, it was to give vent to frightful threats against the 'traitorous' Sicilians. But from that time nothing prospered with him. While the Pope laboured to overwhelm the insurgents with his excommunications, the King assembled an immense force, and laid siege to Messina, the inhabitants of which were reduced to propose terms of capitulation; but the conditions he insisted on imposing were so harsh that they resolved on continuing their defence, which they did until they were relieved by the King of Arragon, who had now thrown off the mask, and arrived with a numerous fleet. Charles was obliged to raise the siege of Messina, and nearly the whole naval armament was taken or destroyed by the Arragonese. Don Pedro had already been crowned King of Sicily at Palermo. In the war which followed, Charles had to submit to defeats and disappointments until he died in 1285, not only deprived of Sicily, but threatened by revolt in Naples.

MARRIAGE OF ELIZA SPENCER.

Sir John Spencer, Lord Mayor of London in 1594, was a citizen of extraordinary wealth. At his death, March 30, 1609, he was said to have left £800,000, a sum which must have appeared utterly fabulous in those days. His funeral was attended by a prodigious multitude, including three hundred and twenty poor men, who each had a large dole of eatable, drinkable, and wearable articles given him.

Ten years before his death, 'Rich Spencer,' as he was called, had his soul crossed by a daughter, who insisted upon giving her hand to a slenderly endowed young nobleman, the Lord Compton. It seems to have been a rather perilous thing for a citizen in those times to thwart the matrimonial designs of a nobleman, even towards a member of his own family. On the 15th March 1598-9, John Chamberlain, the Horace Walpole of his day, as far as the writing of gossipy letters is concerned, adverted in one of his epistles to the troubles connected with the love affairs of Eliza Spencer. 'Our Sir John Spencer,' says he, 'was the last week committed to the Fleet for a contempt, and hiding away his daughter, who, they say, is contracted to the Lord Compton; but now he is out again, and by all means seeks to hinder the match, alleging a pre-contract to Sir Arthur Henningham's son. But upon his beating and misusing her, she was sequestered to one Barker's, a proctor, and from thence to Sir Henry Billingsley's, where she yet remains till the matter be tried. If the obstinate and self-willed fellow should persist in his doggedness (as he protests he will), and give her nothing, the poor lord should have a warm catch.'*

Sir John having persisted in his self-willed course of desiring to have something to say in the disposition of his daughter in marriage, the young couple became united against his will, and for some time he steadily refused to take Lady Compton back into his good graces. At length a reconciliation was effected by a pleasant stratagem of Queen Elizabeth. When Lady Compton had her first child, the queen requested that Sir John would join her in standing as sponsors for the first offspring of a young couple happy in their love, but discarded by their father; the knight readily complied, and her Majesty dictated her own surname for the Christian name of the child. The ceremony being performed, Sir John assured the Queen that, having discarded his own daughter, he should adopt this boy as his son. The parents of the child being introduced, the knight, to his great surprise, discovered that he had adopted his own grandson; who, in

* Letters of John Chamberlain during the Reign of Queen Elizabeth, edited from the originals by Sarah Williams. Camden Society, 1861, p. 50.

reality, became the ultimate inheritor of his wealth.

There is extant a curious characteristic letter of Lady Compton to her husband, apparently written on the paternal wealth coming into their hands:

'My sweete Life,

'Now I have declared to you my mind for the settling of your state, I supposed that it were best for me to bethink, or consider with myself, what allowance were meetest for me. For, considering what care I ever had of your estate, and how respectfully I dealt with those, which, by the laws of God, of nature, and civil polity, wit, religion, government, and honesty, you, my dear, are bound to, I pray and beseech you to grant to me, your most kind and loving wife, the sum of £1600 per annum, quarterly to be paid.

'Also, I would (besides the allowance for my apparel) have £600 added yearly (quarterly to be paid) for the performance of charitable works, and those things I would not, neither will, be accountable for.

'Also, I will have three horses for my own saddle, that none shall dare to lend or borrow; none lend but I; none borrow but you.

'Also, I would have two gentlewomen, lest one should be sick, or have some other lett. Also, believe that it is an indecent thing for a gentlewoman to stand mumping alone, when God hath blessed their lord and lady with a great estate.

'Also, when I ride a-hunting, or hawking, or travel from one house to another, I will have them attending; so, for either of these said women, I must and will have for either of them a horse.

'Also, I will have six or eight gentlemen; and I will have my two coaches, —one lined with velvet, to myself, with four very fair horses, and a coach for my women, lined with cloth; one laced with gold, the other with scarlet, and laced with watch-lace and silver, with four good horses.

'Also, I will have two coachmen; one for my own coach, the other for my women's.

'Also, at any time when I travel, I will be allowed, not only carriages and spare horses for me and my women, but I will have such carriages as shall be fitting for all, or duly; not pestering my things with my women's, nor theirs with chambermaids', or theirs with washmaids'.

'Also, for laundresses, when I travel, I will have them sent away with the carriages, to see all safe; and the chambermaids I will have go before with the grooms, that the chambers may be ready, sweet, and clean.

'Also, for that it is indecent to crowd up myself with my gentleman usher in my coach, I will have him to have a convenient horse to attend me either in city or country; and I must have two footmen; and my desire is, that you defray all the charges for me.

'And, for myself (besides my yearly allowance), I would have twenty gowns of apparel; six of them excellent good ones, eight of them for the country, and six others of them very excellent good ones.

'Also, I would have put into my purse £2000 and £200, and so you to pay my debts.

'Also, I would have £6,000 to buy me jewels, and £4,000 to buy me a pearl chain.

'Now, seeing I have been and am so reasonable unto you, I pray you do find my children apparel, and their schooling; and all my servants, men and women, their wages.

'Also, I will have all my houses furnished, and all my lodging-chambers to be suited with all such furniture as is fit; as beds, stools, chairs, suitable cushions, carpets, silver warming-pans, cupboards of plate, fair hangings, and such like. So, for my drawing-chamber, in all houses, I will have them delicately furnished, both with hangings, couch, canopy, glass, chairs, cushions, and all things thereunto belonging.

'Also, my desire is, that you would pay your debts, build Ashby-house, and purchase lands, and lend no money (as you love God) to the Lord Chamberlain,* which would have all, perhaps your life, from you. Remember his son, my Lord Waldon, what entertainment he gave me when you were at Tilt-yard. If you were dead, he said, he would marry me. I protest I grieve to see the poor man have so little wit and honesty, to use his friends so vilely. Also, he fed me with untruths concerning the Charter-house; but that is the least: he wished me much harm; you know him. God keep you and me from him, and such as he is.

'So, now that I have declared to you what I would have, and what that is I would not have, I pray, when you be an earl, to allow me £1,000 more than now desired, and double attendance.

'Your loving wife,
'ELIZA COMPTON.'

The Passover of the Modern Jews.

Jewish life, which is every day losing its originality in towns, has still preserved in some village communities on the Continent its strong traditional impress. It is among the Vosges mountains and on the banks of the Rhine that we must look for the superstitious, singular customs, and patriarchal simplicity of ancient Judea.

Having an invitation to witness the festival of Paeçach at the house of a fine old Jew, at Bolwiller, near Basle, I set off on the fourteenth of their month Nisan, corresponding to our 29th of March, to be ready for the ceremony which was to celebrate the flight of Israel from Egypt with their kneading troughs upon their shoulders. Hence its name of the 'Feast of Azymes,' or unleavened bread. As I was passing down the street, I marked the first sign; children were running in all directions with baskets of bottles, the presents of the rich tradespeople to the rabbi, schoolmaster, beadle, &c., of wine of the best quality, that the poor as well as the rich may make merry.

My host received me on the threshold with the classical salutation, 'Alechem Salem,' 'Peace be with you,' and I was soon in the midst of his numerous family, who had just concluded the week's preparations. These consist of the most extensive washings and cleanings; every cup to be used must be boiled in water, the floors are washed and sprinkled with red and yellow sand; the *matsès*, or Passover cakes, are kneaded by robust girls, on immense tables near the flaming stove; others take it from the bright copper bowls, roll it out into the round cakes, prick and bake it. Enormous chaplets of onions are hung round the kitchen, and shining tin plates are ranged by dozens on the shelves, to be used only at the Passover. White curtains adorn every window; the seven-branched lamp is brought out; the *misrach*, a piece of paper on which this word, meaning *east*, is written, is reframed and hung on the side of the room towards Jerusalem,

* Thomas Howard, Earl of Suffolk, made Lord Treasurer in 1613.

in which direction they turn at prayer; the raised sofa on which the master of the house passes the first two nights is fitted with cushions.

Our conversation was interrupted by the three knocks of the *Schuleklopfer*, who comes to each house to call the faithful to prayer; we followed him immediately, and found the synagogue splendidly illuminated, and when the service was over, each family returned home to hold the *seder*, the most characteristic ceremony of the festival. The table in the dining-room was covered with a cloth, the lamp lighted, plates were set, but no dishes; on each plate a small book was laid, called the *Haggada*, in Hebrew, consisting of the chants and prayers to be used, and illustrated with engravings of the departure of the Israelites from Egypt. My host took the sofa at the head of the table, his wife and daughters were on one side, his sons on the other, all dressed in new clothes, and their heads covered. At the end of the table I noticed an angular-faced man in far-worn clothes. I found he was a sort of beggar who always partook of Herr Salomon's festivals. In the middle of the table, on a silver dish, were laid three Passover-cakes, separated by a napkin; above these, on smaller dishes, was a medley of lettuce, marmalade flavoured with cinnamon, apples, and almonds, a bottle of vinegar, some chervil, a hard-boiled egg, horse-radish, and at one side a bone with a little flesh on it. All these were emblems: the marmalade signified the clay, chalk, and bricks in which the Hebrew slaves worked under Pharaoh; the vinegar and herbs, the bitterness and misery they then endured; and the bone the paschal lamb. Each guest had a silver cup; the master's was of gold; on a side-table were several bottles of Rhenish Falernian; the red recalling the cruelty of Pharaoh, who, tradition says, bathed in the blood of the Hebrew children.

The master of the house opened the ceremony with the prayer of blessing; the cups having first been filled to the brim, then the eldest son rose, took a ewer from another table, and poured water over his father's hands, all present rising and stretching out their hand to the centre dish, repeating these words from the *Haggada*: 'Behold the bread of sorrow our fathers ate in Egypt! Whoever is hungry let him come and eat with us. Whoever is poor let him take his Passover with us.' The youngest son asks his father in Hebrew, 'What is the meaning of this ceremony?' and his father replies, 'We were slaves in Egypt, and the Lord our God has brought us out with a mighty hand and a stretched out arm.' All then repeated the story of the departure from Egypt in Bible words, and tasted the various symbolical articles arranged in the dish. By the side of the master's cup stood one of much larger dimensions, which was now filled with the best wine; it is set apart for the prophet Elijah, the good genius of Israel, an invisible guest it is true, but always and everywhere present at high festivals.

Thus ends the first part of the *seder*: the evening meal is set on the table, good cheer and cheerful conversation follow. At a certain time every one resumes his former position, and the table is arranged as at the first. Herr Salomon returns to his cushions, and half a Passover-cake covered with a napkin is laid before him, which division typifies the passage of the Red Sea; he gave a piece of it to each. A prayer followed, and he then desired his eldest son to open the door. The young man left his place, opened the door into the corridor very wide, and stood back as if to let some one pass. The deepest silence prevailed; in a few minutes the door was closed, the prophet had assuredly entered, he had tasted the wine which was exclusively set apart for him, and sanctified the house by his presence as God's delegate. The cups of wine are now emptied for the fourth time; the 115th, 116th, 118th, and 150th Psalms are sung with their traditional inflexions; and each rivals his neighbour in spirit and voice; the women even are permitted to join on this evening, though prohibited at all other times.

Thus ends the religious part of the festival, but the singing continues, the libations become more and more copious; at nine the women retire, and leave the men, until the influence of the Rhenish wine reminds them it is time to separate. The usual evening prayer is never offered on this night and the following one; they are special occasions, when God watches, as formerly in Egypt, over all the houses of the Jews. The ceremonies we have described are repeated on the following day, which is a great festival. All the people go early to the synagogue in their new clothes. Dinner is prepared at noon, and the afternoon is devoted to calling on friends; the dessert remains on the table, and a plate and glass of wine are presented to each guest with the hospitable salutation, 'Baruch-haba,' 'Blessed be he who cometh.'

The feast lasts a week, but four days are only half feasts, during which the men attend to necessary business, and the women pay visits, and make the arrangements for marriages, which are scarcely ever concluded without the intervention of a marriage agent, who receives so much from the dowry at the completion of the affair.

On bidding adieu to my host at the conclusion of the feast, he begged me to be careful during my journey, as we were in the time of *omer*. This is the interval between the Passover and Pentecost, the seven weeks elapsing from the departure from Egypt and the giving of the law, marked in former days by the offering of an omer of barley daily at the temple. Now there is no offering, but all the villagers after the evening prayer count the days, and look forward to its close with a sort of impatience; it is considered a fearful time, during which a thousand extraordinary events take place, and when every Jew is particularly exposed to the influence of evil spirits. There is something dangerous and fatal in the air; every one should be on the watch, and not tempt the *schédim* (demons) in any way; the smallest and most insignificant things require attention. These are some of the recommendations given by Jewish mothers to their children : 'Do not whistle during the time of omer, or your mouth will be deformed; if you go out in your shirt sleeves, you will certainly come in with a lame arm; if you throw stones in the air, they will fall back upon you.' Let not

men of any age ride on horseback, or in a carriage, or sail in a boat; the first will run away with you, the wheels of the second will break, the last will take in water. Have a strict eye upon your cattle, for the sorcerers will get into your stables, mount your cows and goats, bring diseases upon them, and turn their milk sour. In the latter case, try to lay your hand upon the suspected person, shut her up in a room with a basin of the sour milk, and beat the milk with a hazel wand, pronouncing God's name three times. Whilst you are doing this, the sorceress will make great lamentation, for the blows are falling upon her. Only stop when you see blue flames dancing on the surface of the milk, for then the charm is broken. If at nightfall a beggar comes to ask for a little charcoal to light his fire, be very careful not to give it, and do not let him go without drawing him three times by his coat tail, and without losing time, throw some large handfuls of salt on the fire. This beggar is, probably, a sorcerer, for they seize upon every pretext, and take all disguises to enter into your houses. Such are the dangers of omer.

PRETENDED MURDERS OF CHRISTIAN CHILDREN BY THE JEWS.

The Christians of the middle ages, especially in the west of Europe, regarded the Jews with bitter hatred, and assailed them with horrible calumnies, which served as the excuses for persecution and plunder. One of the most frequent of these calumnies was the charge of stealing Christian children, whom, on Good Friday, or on Easter day, they tormented and crucified in the same way that Christ was crucified, in despite of the Saviour and of all true believers. Rumours of such barbarous atrocities were most frequent during the twelfth and thirteenth centuries. The Anglo-Saxon Chronicle informs us, under the year 1137, how, 'in his (King Stephen's) time, the Jews of Norwich bought a Christian child before Easter, and tortured him with all the same torture with which our Lord was tortured; and on Long Friday (the name among the Anglo-Saxons and Scandinavians for Good Friday) hanged him on a rood for hatred of our Lord, and afterwards buried him. They imagined it would be concealed, but our Lord shewed that he was a holy martyr. And the monks took him and buried him honourably in the monastery; and through our Lord he makes wonderful and manifold miracles, and he is called St William.' The writer of this was contemporary with the event, and, although his testimony is no proof that the child was murdered by the Jews, it leaves no doubt of the fact of their being accused of it, or of the advantage which the English clergy took of it. The later chroniclers, John of Bromton, and Matthew of Westminster, repeat the story, and represent it as occurring in the year 1145. The Roman Catholic Church made a saint of Hugh, who, they say, was twelve years of age, and had been apprenticed to a tanner, and his martyrdom is commemorated in the calendar on the 24th of March. The words of the Anglo-Saxon Chronicle would seem to shew that the old practice of selling children for slaves con-

446

tinued to exist at Norwich in the time of Stephen. St William's shrine at Norwich was long an object of pilgrimage; and the people of that city built and dedicated a chapel to him in Thorp-Wood, near Norwich, where his body is said to have been found.

A child is said to have been put to death in the same manner by the Jews of Gloucester, in the year 1160; and again, in the year 1181, the Jews of Bury St Edmunds are accused of having crucified a child named Robert, on Easter day, at whose shrine in the church there numerous miracles were believed to be performed. Two years afterwards, Philippe Auguste, King of France, banished the Jews from his kingdom on a similar charge, which was again brought against the Jews of Norwich in 1235 and 1240, on which charge several Jews were punished. Matthew of Westminster states that the Jews of Lincoln circumcised and crucified a Christian child in 1250, at whose tomb miracles were performed; but this is perhaps only a mistake of date for the more celebrated child martyr, whose story we will now relate.

As the story is related by Matthew Paris,—who also, it must be remarked, lived at the time of the event,—the Jews of Lincoln, about the feast of Peter and Paul (June 29), stole a Christian child eight years of age, whose name was Hugh, and kept him secretly till they had given information to all the Jews throughout England, who sent deputies to be present at the ceremony of crucifying him. This was alleged to have been done with all the particularities which attended the passion of our Saviour. The mother of the child, meanwhile, was in great distress, went about the city inquiring for it, and, informed that it had been last seen playing with some Jewish children and entering a certain Jew's house there, she suddenly entered the Jew's house, and discovered the body of her child thrown into a well. The alarm was given to the citizens, who forced the house, and carried away the body of the murdered child. In the middle of this tumult, King Henry's Justiciary, John de Lexington, was in Lincoln, and he caused the Jew who lived in this house, and was called Copin, to be seized and strictly examined. Copin, on a pardon for his life and limbs, made a confession of all the circumstances of the murder, and declared that it was the custom of the Jews thus to sacrifice Christian children every year. The canons of Lincoln obtained the body of the child, and buried it under a shrine in their cathedral, and for ages, according to the belief of the Catholic Church, miracles continued to be performed at the tomb of St Hugh. That the public circumstances of this story took place,—namely, that the Jews of Lincoln were accused of murdering a child under these circumstances, that many of them were imprisoned and brought to punishment on this charge, and that the body of the child was buried honourably in Lincoln Cathedral,—there is no room for doubt. In the Chronicle of London, known as the *Liber de Antiquis Legibus*, it is stated that on St Cecilia's day (Nov. 22), then a Monday, ninety-two Jews were brought from Lincoln to Westminster, accused of having slain a male Christian child, and were all committed to the Tower of London. There is a peculiar interest attached to this event, from the circumstance that it appears to be the first instance we know in which the right of a foreigner to be tried by a mixed jury was insisted upon, in this case unsuccessfully. The London Chronicle, by a contemporary writer, adds, 'of which number eighteen, who refused to submit to the verdict of Christians without Jews, when the king was at Lincoln, and when they were indicted for that murder before the king, were the same day drawn, and after dinner in the evening hanged. The rest were sent back to the Tower.' Official documents relating to these Jews in the Tower are also printed in Rymer's *Fœdera*. A ballad in Anglo-Norman has been preserved in the National Library in a contemporary manuscript, and has been printed by M. Francisque Michel in a little volume entitled *Hugues de Lincoln*, which gives an account of the pretended martyrdom of the child 'St Hugh,' resembling generally the narrative of Matthew Paris, except that it gives considerably more details of the manner in which the child was treated. But the most remarkable proof of the firm hold which this story had taken upon men's minds in the middle ages is the existence of a ballad, more romantic in its details, which has been preserved orally down to our own time, and is still recited from time to time in Scotland and the north of England. Several copies of it have been printed from oral recitation, among our principal collections of old ballads, of which perhaps the best is that given by Jamieson.

HUGH OF LINCOLN.

Four and twenty bonny boys
　Were playing at the ba';
And by it came him, sweet sir Hugh,
　And he play'd o'er them a'.

He kick'd the ba' with his right foot,
　And catch'd it wi' his knee;
And throuch-and-thro' the Jew's window,
　He gar'd the bonny ba' flee.

He's done him to the Jew's castell,
　And walk'd it round about;
And there he saw the Jew's daughter
　At the window looking out.

'Throw down the ba', ye Jew's daughter,
　Throw down the ba' to me!'
'Never a bit,' says the Jew's daughter,
　'Till up to me come ye.'

'How will I come up? How can I come up?
　How can I come to thee?
For as ye did to my auld father,
　The same ye'll do to me.'

She's gane till her father's garden,
　And pu'd an apple, red and green;
'Twas a' to wyle him, sweet sir Hugh,
　And to entice him in.

She's led him in through ae dark door,
　And sae has she thro' nine;
She's laid him on a dressing table,
　And stickit him like a swine.

And first came out the thick thick blood,
　And syne came out the thin;
And syne came out the bonny heart's blood;
　There was nae mair within.

447

She's row'd him in a cake o' lead,
    Bade him lie still and sleep;
She's thrown him in Our Lady's draw-well,
    Was fifty fathom deep.

When bells were rung, and mass was sung,
    And a' the bairns came hame,
When every lady gat hame her son,
    The Lady Maisry gat nane.

She's ta'en her mantle her about,
    Her coffer by the hand;
And she's gane out to seek her son,
    And wander'd o'er the land.

She's done her to the Jew's castell,
    Where a' were fast asleep;
'Gin ye be there, my sweet sir Hugh,
    I pray you to me speak.'

She's done her to the Jew's garden,
    Thought he had been gathering fruit;
'Gin ye be there, my sweet sir Hugh,
    I pray you to me speak.'

She near'd Our Lady's deep draw-well,
    Was fifty fathom deep;
'Where'er ye be, my sweet sir Hugh,
    I pray you to me speak.'

'Gae hame, gae hame, my mither dear;
    Prepare my winding sheet;
And, at the back o' merry Lincoln,
    The morn I will you meet.'

Now lady Maisry is gane hame;
    Made him a winding sheet;
And, at the back o' merry Lincoln,
    The dead corpse did her meet.

And a' the bells o' merry Lincoln,
    Without men's hands, were rung;
And a' the books o' merry Lincoln,
    Were read without man's tongue;
And ne'er was such a burial
    Sin Adam's days begun.

THE BORROWED DAYS.

It was on the 30th of March 1639, that the Scottish covenanting army, under the Marquis of Montrose, marched into Aberdeen, in order to put down a reactionary movement for the king and episcopacy which had been raised in that city. The day proved a fine one, and therefore favourable for the march of the troops, a fact which occasioned a thankful surprise in the friends of the Covenant, since it was one of the *Borrowed Days*, which usually are ill. One of their clergy alluded to this in the pulpit, as a miraculous dispensation of Providence in favour of the good cause.

The Borrowed Days are the three last of March. The popular notion is, that they were borrowed by March from April, with a view to the destruction of a parcel of unoffending young sheep—a purpose, however, in which March was not successful. The whole affair is conveyed in a rhyme thus given at the firesides of the Scottish peasantry :—

' March said to Aperill,
    I see three hoggs * upon a hill,
And if you'll lend me dayes three,
    I'll find a way to make them dee.
The first o' them was wind and weet,
The second o' them was snaw and sleet,

* Hogg, a sheep in its second year.

The third o' them was sic a freeze,
It froze the birds' nebs to the trees :
When the three days were past and gane,
The three silly hoggs came hirpling * hame.'

Sir Thomas Browne, in his *Vulgar Errors*, alludes to this popular fiction, remarking, 'It is usual to ascribe unto March certain *Borrowed Daies from April*.' But it is of much greater antiquity than the time of Browne. In the curious book entitled the *Complaynt of Scotland*, printed in 1548, occurs the following passage :— 'There eftir i entrit in ane grene forest, to contempill the tender yong frutes of grene treis, becaus the borial blastis of the *thre borouing dais of Marche* hed chaissit fragrant flureise of evyrie frut-tree far athourt the fieldis.' Nor is this all, for there is an ancient calendar of the church of Rome often quoted by Brand,† in which allusion is made to 'the rustic fable concerning the nature of the month [March]; the rustic names of six days which shall follow in *April, or may be last in March.*'

No one has yet pretended fully to explain the origin or meaning of this fable. Most probably, in our opinion, it has taken its rise in the observation of a certain character of weather prevailing about the close of March, somewhat different from what the season justifies; one of those many wintry relapses which belong to the nature of a British spring. This idea we deem to be supported by Mrs. Grant's account of a similar superstition in the Highlands :—' The *Faoilteach*, or those first days of February, serve many poetical purposes in the Highlands. They are said to have been borrowed for some purpose by February from January, who was bribed by February with three young sheep. These three days, by Highland reckoning, occur between the 11th and 15th of February; and it is accounted a most favourable prognostic for the ensuing year that they should be as stormy as possible. If these days should be fair, then there is no more good weather to be expected through the spring. Hence the Faoilteach is used to signify the very ultimatum of bad weather.'—*Superstitions of the Highlanders*, ii. 217.

FANTOCCINI.

In the simulative theatricals of the streets, the Fantoccini, when they existed, might be considered as the legitimate drama; Punch as sensational melodrama. The Punch puppets, as is well known—but what a pity it should be known!—are managed by an unseen performer below the stage, who has his fingers thrust up within their dresses, so as to move the head and arms only. In the case of the Fantoccini, all the figures have moveable joints, governed by a string, and managed by a man who stands behind the scene, passing his arms above the stage, and so regulating the action of his *dramatis personæ*. The Fantoccini were in considerable vogue in the bye streets of London in the reign of George IV., on the limited scale represented by our artist. Turks, sailors, clowns, &c., dangled and danced through the scene with great propriety

* Limping.
+ Popular Antiquities, edit. 1854, ii. 41.

448

of demeanour, much to the delight of the young, and the gaping wonderment of strangers.

Few persons who gazed upon the grotesque movements of these figures imagined the profound age of their invention. The Fantoccini, introduced as a novelty within our own remembrance, in reality had its chief features developed in the days of the Pharaohs; for in the tombs of ancient Egypt, figures have been found whose limbs were made moveable for the delight of children before Moses was born. In the tombs of Etruria similar toys have been discovered; they were disseminated in the East; and in China and India are now made to act dramas, either as moveable figures, or as shadows behind a curtain. As 'ombres Chinoises' these figures made a novelty for London sightseers at the end of the last century; and may still be seen on winter nights in London performing a brief, grotesque, and not over-delicate drama, originally produced at Astley's Amphitheatre, and there known as 'The Broken Bridge.'

It requires considerable dexterity to 'work'

FANTOCCINI IN LONDON.

these figures well; and when several are grouped together, the labour is very great, requiring a quick hand and steady eye. The exhibition does not 'pay' now so well as Punch; because it is too purely mechanical, and lacks the bustle and fun, the rough practical joking and comicality of that great original creation. The proprietors of these shows complain of this degenerate taste; but it is as possible for the manager of a street show to be in advance of the taste of his audience, as for the manager of a Theatre Royal; and the 'sensation dramas' now demanded by the theatregoers, are to better plays what Punch is to the Fantoccini.

29

MARCH 31.

St Acacius (or Achates), Bishop of Antioch, 3rd century. St Benjamin, Deacon, martyr, 424. St Guy (or Witen), Abbot at Ferrara, 1046.

Born.—Prince Arthur, Duke of Brittany, 1187; Henry II. of France, 1518, *St Germain*; René Descartes, French philosopher, 1596, *La Haye*; Pope Benedict XIV., *Bologna*; Frederick V. of Denmark, 1732; Francis Joseph Haydn, musical composer, 1732, *Rohrau*; Dr Joseph Towers, 1737, *Southwark*; General Richard D. Guyon, commander in the Hungarian patriotic army, 1813, *Walcot, Somerset*.

Died.—Francis I. of France, 1547, *Rambouillet*; Philip III. of Spain, 1621, *Madrid*; Dr John Donne, poet, 1631; Peter Burman, law-writer and Leyden professor, 1741; George, Earl Macartney, Ambassador to China, 1806, *Chiswick*; Ludwig Beethoven, musical composer, 1827, *Vienna*; John Constable, R.A., landscape painter, 1837; John C. Calhoun, American statesman, 1850; Edward Riddle, mathematician, 1854; Charlotte Brontë (Mrs Nicol), novelist, 1855; Lady Charlotte Bury, novelist, 1861, *Sloane-street*.

GEORGE, EARL MACARTNEY.

George Macartney, a descendant of the Macartneys of Auchenleck, near Kirkcudbright, was born at his father's seat, Lissanoure, in the county of Antrim, Ireland, on the 14th of May 1737. So quick was he to learn, and so well instructed by a private tutor named Dennis, that, at the early age of thirteen, he was admitted a fellow commoner of Trinity College, Dublin. His choice of profession inclined towards medicine, until accidentally reading 'certain curious old tracts on chronology' (the Book of Days of the period), his circle of ideas became enlarged, and an honourable spirit of ambition changed his first design. And long after, when he had it in his power to reward his tutor's care with two rich benefices, he emphatically acknowledged that 'the events, dates, and other facts' gleaned up, when a boy, from those old chronological works, not only pointed out the way, but were of the greatest service to him as he travelled the arduous path which eventually led to wealth and distinction. Having obtained the degree of M.A., he spent some time in travel, during which he fortunately made the acquaintance of Stephen, son of Lord Holland, and elder brother of the renowned orator and statesman, Charles James Fox. Here was the tide that led to fortune, nor was the ambitious youth, whose head was stored with 'facts, dates, and other events,' slow to take advantage of the flood. The abilities and personal advantages of the young Irishman were soon recognised at Holland House; and, after a short course of political training, he was brought into Parliament for the borough of Midhurst, then at the command of his influential patron. He did not disappoint the expectations of his friends. Just at that period, statesmen of all parties were puzzled by the attitude of Russia. Scarcely permitted, by the public opinion of Europe, to hold a place among civilized states, the empire of the Czars had, at one bound, stepped into the first class, under the clever guidance of an ambitious woman, whom romantically unexpected events had placed upon the throne. Macartney was the first to see the position and accept it, in the following oracular words,—'Russia,' he said, 'is no longer to be gazed at as a distant glimmering star, but as a great planet, that has obtruded itself into our system, whose place is yet undetermined, but whose motions must powerfully affect those of every other orb.'

It was necessary, for many important reasons, that England should stand well with the newly-born, semi-savage giant of the North. Yet three ambassadors from the Court of St James's had failed in persuading the Empress Elizabeth to renew the treaty which expired in 1734. To all three she flatly refused to continue the close connection that had long existed between the two countries, on the simple and unanswerable grounds, that Russia would not enter into exclusive relations with any particular European power. In this emergency, Macartney was appointed Envoy Extraordinary to the Empress; and having received the honour of knighthood, departed on his delicate mission. He was eminently successful. His consummate tact enabled him to obviate the difficulty of access to the Empress, which had utterly discomfited the previous envoys; while his penetration and discretion enabled him to triumph over other obstacles. At his first public audience with the Czarina, he completely gained her consideration by a piece of flattery. After assuring her of his master, George the Third's inviolable attachment to her person, he added:—'And forgive me, Madam, if here I express my own particular satisfaction in having been chosen for so pleasing, so important an employment. By this means, I shall have the happiness of more nearly contemplating those extraordinary accomplishments, those heroic virtues, which make you the delight of that half of the globe over which you reign, and which render you the admiration of the other.' He succeeded in persuading the Court of St Petersburg to agree to a treaty as nearly as possible in accordance with his instructions; and many distinguished testimonials were conferred upon him, for this important service. From being a simple envoy, he was elevated to the position of ambassador and plenipotentiary; the Empress gave him a magnificent gold snuff-box, inlaid with diamonds; and the king of Poland sent him the insignia of the White Eagle.

On his return, he was appointed Chief Secretary for Ireland, and soon after made a Knight Companion of the Bath. For several stormy sessions, he sat in the Irish House of Commons, and on one occasion, being taunted with his red ribbon and White Eagle, he gave a reply which effectually prevented any other attacks of that kind; observing in conclusion—'Thus, Sir, I was employed at a very early age, whilst some of my opponents were engaged in the weighing of syllables, the measurement of words, and the construction of new phrases. If, in my embassies, I have received testimonies never before granted but to my superiors; if my person is adorned with extraordinary proofs of distinction, let me tell these

gentlemen that they are badges of honour, not of shame and disgrace. Let me tell them that, if, from my public situation, my name should ever pass to posterity, it will be transmitted as a testimony of my services and integrity, not as a record of infamy and crimes.'

We next find Sir George in the British parliament, representing the burghs of Ayr, Irvine, Rothesay, &c., most probably by the influence of Lord Bute, whose daughter, Lady Jane Stewart, he had lately married. In 1775 he was appointed Governor of Grenada, and in the following year advanced to the Irish peerage, under the title of Lord Macartney, Baron of Lissanoure.

A more important field for his public services soon after presented itself in the governorship of the Madras Presidency. He entered upon this office with all the zeal and discretion by which he was so eminently distinguished. His arrival in India was hailed with joy as an event presaging some hopes of relief from the difficulties and degradations into which the Presidency had sunk. There was disunion in the council, and danger without. The country was overrun by Hyder Ali; while famine relentlessly swept away the wretched natives; but, worse than all, there existed a shameless system of gross and complicated corruption, in every branch of the Company's service. In reforming these abuses, the Governor was subjected to the grossest calumnies, and actual personal danger. Yet, in the short space of four years, by indomitable, unceasing effort, he introduced better arrangements. His wisdom was as beneficial to his country, as his unsullied integrity was honourable to himself. Nor were his services unrecognised. In approbation of his conduct, he was appointed to the high office of Governor-General, which after due consideration he declined. The Company, however, in acknowledgment of his eminent services, bestowed on him an unsolicited life-pension of £1500 per annum.

For six years after his return from Madras, Lord Macartney lived on his paternal estate at Lissanoure; finding full scope for his active mind in building houses for his tenantry, draining bogs, and planting trees. But the services he could render his country were much too valuable to be absorbed in the simple affairs of private life. In 1792, he was appointed ambassador to China. A detailed account of this embassy, prepared by Sir George Staunton from Lord Macartney's own papers, was, till a very late period, the standard authority on all matters relating to the Chinese empire. On his return, he was sent on a peculiar mission to Italy, the precise objects of which have never transpired; but the service was evidently conducted to the entire satisfaction of the Government, as we find him about this time created a British peer, under the title of Baron Macartney of Parkhurst. He was subsequently appointed Governor of the Cape Colony, an office he was compelled by ill health to resign shortly afterwards. On leaving the Cape, he deemed it right to place on record a declaration, similar to one he previously had made when resigning the governorship of Madras. This declaration consisted simply of a solemn form of oath, to the effect that he had lived exclusively on his salary, never received bribes, nor engaged in trafficking speculations for his own benefit. In speaking of this public act, he says,—' I trust that it will not be imputed to me as proceeding from any motive of vanity, ostentation, or parade, but from a sense of that propriety and consistency, which I wish to preserve through the whole course of my political life, now drawing near to its conclusion. If it be a gratification to my private feelings, it is equally the discharge of a debt, which the public has a right to demand from every public man.' After his return from the Cape, Lord Macartney engaged no more in public affairs. During the latter part of his life, he resided at Chiswick, enjoying the society of the leading literary and scientific men of the day.

JOHN C. CALHOUN.

Amongst the statesmen of powerful intellect who arose in America in the age succeeding Independence, a prominent place is due to Mr Calhoun, who occupied the position of Secretary of War during the whole presidency of Mr Monroe (1817-25), and was himself Vice-President of the States during the ensuing six years. The name (identical with Colquhoun) indicates a Scottish extraction; but the father of Mr. Calhoun was an Irishman, who emigrated to Pennsylvania. At New Haven College, at the bar in South Carolina, as representative of that State in Congress, and in all his administrative capacities, the massive talents of Mr Calhoun were conspicuous, nor was the grandeur of his moral nature held in less esteem.

It was in 1831, during Jackson's presidency, and while Mr Calhoun was senator for South Carolina, that that state and others threatened to secede from the Union, on account of the system of protection adopted in the interest of the manufacturers of the Northern States. Mr Calhoun was the earnest and powerful advocate of Free Trade and of State Rights and State Sovereignty. South Carolina actually passed an Act of Nullification, or a refusal to pay the duties of a highly protective tariff, and the dissolution of the Union and war were imminent, when a compromise, proposed by Mr Clay, was agreed to, a lower tariff adopted, and the danger for the time averted. A speech pronounced by Mr Calhoun at this period, contained the following passage :—' We are told that the Union must be preserved. And how is it proposed to preserve the Union ? By force ! Does any man in his senses believe that this beautiful structure, —this harmonious aggregate of States, produced by the joint consent of all,—can be preserved by force ? Its very introduction will be certain destruction to the Federal Union. No, no ! You cannot keep the States united in their constitutional and federal bonds by force. Force may, indeed, hold the parts together ; but such union would be the bond between the master and slave—a union of exaction on one side, and of unqualified *obedience* on the other. It is madness to suppose that the Union can be preserved by force. Disguise it as you may, the contest is one between power and liberty.' In 1843, Mr Calhoun became Secretary of State under the admi-

nistration of Mr Tyler, who, by the death of General Harrison, had become President. In 1845 he returned to the Senate, of which he remained a member until his death.

Mr Calhoun is considered by many as the greatest of American statesmen. Loved, admired, trusted, and almost idolized in South Carolina and throughout the Southern States, he was necessarily less popular in the north. His free-trade principles were opposed to northern interests ; his defence of State rights, and the right of nullification and secession, were opposed to the territorial passion of the north ; while his opinions on the necessity, and even philanthropy of negro slavery, were such as only local feelings have ever been able to sanction. But while Mr Calhoun's political opinions found little favour, except in his own section, his commanding talents, and the purity of his public and private character, made him everywhere respected. His influence in his native state was unbounded, and he, more than any other man, moulded the public opinion of the Southern States, and prepared them for the steps which they took at the election of Mr Lincoln.

FRANCIS I.

The era of Francis I. in France was that of revived learning and skill in the arts. Up to his time, notwithstanding that the use of the vernacular language had been introduced in the legal proceedings of Germany, England, and other countries, they continued in France to employ a barbarous Latin, to the great bewilderment of all sorts of people. Francis ordered a change in this respect, in order that those who had the unhappiness to go to law might at least have the satisfaction of reading their ruin in their own tongue. He likewise introduced the fashion of long hair and short beards, after Pope Julius II. As soon as it was observed that the courtiers allowed their beards to grow, it became an object with magistrates and grave elderly men generally to get themselves well-shaven. The courtiers and petit-maîtres by and by grew disgusted with their long beards, and took once more to close shaving. Then the grave men, determined to be unlike those people, immediately began to allow their beards to grow.

Francis was cut off at fifty-three in consequence of his immoralities. The bishop of Mâcon, preaching his funeral sermon, had the *hardiesse* to assure his auditors that the king's soul had gone straight to paradise, without passing through purgatory. To the credit, however, of the Sorbonne, it rebuked the bishop for this piece of courtliness, and forbade his sermon to be printed.

BEETHOVEN.

This eminent composer was the son of a tenor-singer, who in his turn was the son of a bass-singer, both being of course obscure men. It is remarkable how often the genealogy of brilliant musical power is of this nature. Bach came of a tribe of humble musicians, commencing, it is said, with a miller. Haydn's father was an amateur harpist in humble life. Mozart was the son of an ordinary kapell-meister and teacher of the violin. The father of Rossini was a horn-blower in the orchestra of a strolling company. It seems as if, for the production of the musical genius, the antecedence of musical temperament and a moderate ability were necessary ; or as if the family musical gift, in that case, only became somewhat intensified—screwed up an octave higher, as it were.

APRIL

Next came fresh April, full of lustyhed,
And wanton as a kid whose horne new buds;
Upon a bull he rode, the same which led
Europa floating through th' Argolick fluds:
His horns were gilden all with golden studs,
And garnished with garlands goodly dight,
Of all the fairest flowers and freshest buds,
Which th' earth brings forth; and wet he seemed in sight
With waves through which he waded for his love's delight.

SPENSER.

(DESCRIPTIVE.)

APRIL presents no prettier picture than that of green fields, with rustic stiles between the openings of the hedges, where old footpaths go in and out, winding along, until lost in the distance; with children scattered here and there, singly or in groups, just as the daisies are, all playing or gathering flowers.

With what glee they rush about! chasing one another in zigzag lines like butterflies, tumbling here, and running there; one lying on its back, laughing and shouting in the sunshine; another, prone on the grass, is pretending to cry, in order to be picked up. A third, a quiet little thing, with her silky hair hanging all about her sweet face, sits patiently sticking daisy-buds on the thorns of a leafless branch, that she may carry home a tree of flowers. Some fill their pinafores, others sit decorating their caps and bonnets, while one, whose fair brow has been garlanded, dances as she holds up the skirt of her little frock daintily

452

with her fingers. Their graceful attitudes can only be seen for a few moments; for if they catch a strange eye directed towards them, they at once cease their play, and start off like alarmed birds. We have often wished for a photograph of such a scene as we have here described and witnessed while sheltered behind some hedge or tree.

Dear to us all are those old footpaths that, time out of mind, have gone winding through the pleasant fields, beside hedges and along watercourses, leading to peaceful villages and far-away farms, which the hum and jar of noisy cities never reach; where we seem at every stride to be drawing nearer the Creator, as we turn our backs upon the perishable labours of man.

Only watch some old man, bent with the weight of years, walking out into the fields when April greens the ground—

'Making it all one emerald.'

With what entire enjoyment he moves along, pausing every here and there to look at the opening flowers! Yes, they are the very same he gazed upon in boyhood, springing from the same roots, and growing in the very spots where he gathered them fifty long years ago. What a many changes he has seen since those days, while they appear unaltered! He thinks how happy life then passed away, with no more care than that felt by the flowers that wave in the breeze and sunshine, which shake the rain from their heads, as he did when a boy, darting in and out bareheaded, when he ran to play amid the April showers. Tears were then dried and forgotten almost as soon as shed. He recalls the companions of his early manhood, who stood full-leaved beside him, in the pride of their summer strength and beauty, shewing no sign of decay, but exulting as if their whole life would be one unchanged summerhood. Where are they now? Some fell with all their leafy honours thick upon them. A few reached the season of the 'sere and yellow leaf' before they fell, and were drifted far away from the spot where they flourished, and which now 'knoweth them no more for ever.' A few stood up amid the silence of the winter of their age, though they saw but little of one another in those days of darkness. And now he recalls the withered and ghastly faces, which were long since laid beneath the snow. He alone is spared to look through the green gates of April down those old familiar footpaths, which they many a time traversed together. 'Cuckoo! cuckoo!' Ah, well he knows that note! It brings again the backward years—the sound he tried to imitate when a boy—home, with its little garden—the very face of the old clock, whose ticking told him it was near schooltime. And he looks for the messenger of spring now as he did then, as it flies from tree to tree; but all he can discover is the green foliage, for his eyes are dim and dazed, and he cannot see it now. He hears the song of some bird, which was once as familiar to him as his mother's voice, and tries to remember its name, but cannot; and as he tries, he thinks of those who were with him when he heard it; and so he goes on unconsciously unwinding link by link the golden chain which reaches from the grave to heaven. And when he returns home, he carries with him a quiet heart, for his thoughts scarcely seem allied to earth, and lie 'too deep for tears.' He seems to have looked behind that gray misty summit, where the forgotten years have rolled down, and lie buried, and to have seen that dim mustering-ground beyond the grave, where those who have gone before are waiting to receive him.

Many of the trees now begin to make 'some little show of green.' Among these is the elm, which has a beautiful look with the blue April sky seen through its half-developed foliage. The ash also begins to shew its young leaves, though the last year's 'keys,' with the blackened seed, still hang among the branches, and rattle again in every wind that blows. The oak puts out its red buds and bright metallic-looking leaves slowly, as if to shew that its hardy limbs require as little clothing as the ancient Britons did, when hoary oaks covered long leagues of our forest-studded island. The chesnut begins to shoot forth its long, finger-shaped foliage, which breaks through the rounded and gummy buds that have so firmly enclosed it. On the limes we see a tender and delicate green, which the sun shines through as if they were formed of the clearest glass. The beech throws from its graceful sprays leaves which glitter like emeralds when they are steeped in sunshine; and no other tree has such a smooth and beautiful bark, as rustic lovers well know when they carve the names of their beloved ones on it. The silver birch throws down its flowers in waves of gold, while the leaves drop over them in the most graceful forms, and the stem is dashed with a variety of colours like a bird. The laburnums stand up like ancient foresters, clothed in green and gold. But, beautiful above all, are the fruit-trees, now in blossom. The peaches seem to make the very walls to which they are trailed burn again with their bloom, while the cherry-tree looks as if a shower of daisies had rained on it, and adhered to the branches. The plum is one mass of unbroken blossom, without shewing a single green leaf, while, in the distance, the almond-tree looks like some gigantic flower, whose head is one tuft of bloom, so thickly are the branches embowered with buds. Then come the apple-blossoms, the loveliest of all, looking like a bevy of virgins peeping out of their white drapery, covered with blushes; while all the air around is perfumed with the fragrance of the bloom, as if the winds had been out gathering flowers, and scattered the perfume everywhere as they passed. All day long the bees are busy among the bloom, making an unceasing murmur, for April is beautiful to look upon; and if she hides her sweet face for a few hours behind the rain-clouds, it is only that she may appear again peeping out through the next burst of sunshine in a veil of fresher green, through which we see the red and white of her bloom.

Numbers of birds, whose names and songs are familiar to us, have, by the end of this month, returned to build and sing once more in the bowery hollows of our old woods, among the bushes that dot our heaths, moors, and commons, and in the hawthorn-hedges which stretch for weary miles over green Old England, and will soon be covered with May-buds. We find the 'time of their coming' mentioned in the pages of the Bible, shewing that they migrated, as they do now, and were noticed by the patriarchs of old, as they led their flocks to the fresh spring-pastures. The sand-martin—one of the earliest swallows that arrives—sets to work like a miner, making a pick-axe of his beak, and hewing his way into the sandbank, until he hollows out for himself a comfortable house to dwell in, with a long passage to it, that goes sloping upward to keep out the wet, and in which he is caverned as dry and snug as ever were our painted forefathers. The window-swallow is busy building in the early morning,—we see his shadow darting across the sunny window-blind while we are in bed; and if we arise, and look cautiously through one corner of the blind, we see it at work, close to us, smoothing the clay with its throat and the under part of the neck, while it moves its little head to and fro, holding on to the wall or window-frame all the time by its claws, and the flattening pressure of the tail. It will soon get accustomed to our face, and go on with its work, as if totally unconscious of our presence, if we never wilfully frighten it. Other birds, like hatters, felt their nests so closely and solidly together, that they are as hard to cut through as a well-made mill-board. Some fit the materials carefully together, bending one piece and breaking another, and making them fit in everywhere like joiners and carpenters, though they have neither square, nor rule, nor tool, only their tiny beaks, with which they do all. Some weave the materials in and out, like basket-makers; and by some unknown process—defying all human ingenuity—they will work in, and bend to suit their purpose, sticks and other things so brittle and rotten that were we only to touch them ever so gently, they would drop to pieces. Nothing seems to come amiss to them in the shape of building materials, for we find their nests formed of what might have been relics of mouldering scarecrows, bits of old hats, carpets, wool-stockings, cloth, hair, moss, cotton in rags and hanks, dried grass, withered leaves, feathers, lichen, decayed wood, bark, and we know not what beside; all put neatly together by these skilful and cunning workmen. They are the oldest miners and masons, carpenters and builders, felters, weavers, and basket-makers; and the pyramids are but as the erections of yesterday compared with the time when these ancient architects first began to build. As for their nests—

> 'What nice hand,
> With every implement and means of art,
> And twenty years' apprenticeship to boot,
> Could make us such another?'
> HURDIS.

Amongst the arrivals in April is the redstart, which is fond of building in old walls and ruins. Where the wild wallflower waves from some crumbling castle, or fallen monastery, there it is pretty sure to be seen, perched perhaps on the top of a broken arch, constant at its song from early morn, and shaking its tail all the time with a tremulous motion. We also recognise the pleasant song of the titlark, or tree-pipit, as it is often called; and peeping about, we see the bird perched on

some topmost branch, from which it rises, singing, into the air a little way up, then descends again, and perches on the same branch it soared from, never seeming at rest. We also see the pretty whitethroat, as it rises up and down, alighting a score times or more on the same spray, and singing all the time, seeming as if it could neither remain still nor be silent for a single minute on any account. Sometimes it fairly startles you, as it darts past, its white breast flashing on the eye like a sudden stream of light. Country children, when they see it, call out,

> 'Pretty Peggy Whitethroat,
> Come stop and give us a note.'

The woodlark is another handsome-looking bird, that sings while on the wing as well as when perched on some budding bough, though its song is not so sweet as that of Shakspeare's lark, which

> 'At heaven's gate sings.'

Then there are the linnets, that never leave us, but only shift their quarters from one part of the country to another, loving most to congregate about the neighbourhood of gorse-bushes, where they build and sing, and live at peace among the thousands of bees that are ever coming to look for honey in the golden baskets which hang there in myriads. We hear also the pretty goldfinch, that is marked with black and white, and golden brown; and pleasant it is to watch a couple of them, tugging and tearing at the same head of groundsel. But all the land is now musical: the woods are like great cathedrals, pillared with oaks and roofed with the sky, from which the birds sing, like hidden nuns, in the green twilight of the leafy cloisters.

Now the angler hunts up his fishing-tackle, for the breath of April is warm and gentle; a golden light plays upon the streams and rivers, and when the rain comes down, it seems to tread with muffled feet on the young leaves, and hardly to press down the flowers. But to hear the sweet birds sing, to feel the refreshing air blowing gently on all around, and see Nature arraying herself in all her spring beauty, has ever seemed to us a much greater pleasure than that of fishing. Few care about reading the chapters in delightful old Izaak Walton, that treat upon fishes alone: it is when he quits his rod and line, and begins to gossip about the beauty of the season; when he sits upon that primrose bank, and tells us that the meadows 'are too pleasant to be looked at but only on holidays;' making, while so seated, 'a brave breakfast with a piece of powdered beef, and a radish or two he has in his bag,'—that we love most to listen to him. Still, angling is of itself a pleasant out-of-door sport; for, if tired, there is the bank ready to sit down upon; the clear river to gaze over; the willows to watch as they ever wave wildly to and fro; or the circle in the water—made by some fish as it rises at a fly—to trace, as it rounds and widens, and breaks among the pebbles on the shore, or is lost amid the tangles of the overhanging and ever-moving sedge. Then comes the arrowy flight of the swallows, as they dart after each other through the arch of the bridge, or dimple the water every here and there as they sweep over it. Ever shifting our position, we can 'dander' along, where little curves and indentations form tiny bays and secluded pools, which, excepting where they open out riverward, are shut in by their own overhanging trees and waving sedges. Or, walking along below the embankment, we come to the great sluice-gates, that are now open, and where we can see through them the stream that runs between far-away meadows where all is green, and shadows are thrown at noonday over the haunts of the water-hen and water-rat. Saving the lapping of the water, all is silent. There a contemplative man may sit and hold communion with Nature, seeing something new every time he shifts his glance, for many a flower has now made its appearance which remained hidden while March blew his windy trumpet, and in these green moist shady places the blue bell of spring may now be found. It is amongst the earliest flowers—such as the cowslips and daisies—that country children love to place the bluebell, to ornament many an open cottage-window in April; it bears no resemblance to the blue harebell of summer, as the latter flowers grow singly, while those of the wild hyacinth nearly cover the stem with their closely-packed bells, sometimes to a foot in height. The bells which are folded are of a deeper blue than those that have opened; and very gracefully do those hang down that are in full bloom, shewing the tops of their fairy cups turning backward. The dark upright leaves are of a beautiful green, and attract the eye pleasantly long before the flowers appear. Beside them, the delicate lily-of-the-valley may also now be found, one of the most graceful of all our wildflowers. How elegantly its white ivory-looking bells rise, tier above tier, to the very summit of the flower-stalk, while the two broad leaves which protect it seem placed there for its support, as if a thing of such frail beauty required something to lean upon! Those who have inhaled the perfume from a whole bed of these lilies in some open forest-glade, can fancy what odours were wafted through Eden in the golden mornings of the early world. At the end of the month, cowslips are sprinkled plentifully over the old deep-turfed pastures in which they delight to grow, for long grass is unfavourable to their flowering, and in it they run all to stalk. What a close observer of flowers Shakspeare must have been, to note even the 'crimson drops i' th' bottom' of the cowslip, which he also calls 'cinque-spotted!' The separate flowers or petals are called 'peeps' in the country, and these are picked out to make cowslip wine. We have counted as many as twenty-seven flowers on one stalk, which formed a truss of bloom larger than that of a verbena. A pile of cowslip 'peeps,' in a clean basket, with a pretty country child, who has gathered them and brought them for sale, is no uncommon sight at this season in the market-place of some old-fashioned country town. The gaudy dandelion and great marsh-marigold are now in flower, one lighting up our wayside wastes almost everywhere, and the other looking like a burning lamp as its reflection seems blazing in the water. It is pleasant to see a great bed of tall dandelions on a windy April day shaking all their golden heads together; and common as it may appear,

it is a beautiful compound flower. And who has not, in the days of childhood, blown off the downy seed, to tell the hours of the day by the number of puffs it took to disperse the feathered messengers? How beautifully, too, the leaves are cut! and when bleached, who does not know that it is the most wholesome herb that ever gave flavour to a salad? Shakspeare's

'Lady-smock all silver white,'

is also now abundant in moist places, still retaining its old name of 'cuckoo-flower,' though we know that several similar flowers are so called in the country through coming into bloom while the cuckoo sings. The curious arum or cuckoo-pint, which children call 'lords and ladies,' in the midland counties, is now found under the hedges. Strip off the spathe or hood, and inside you will find the 'parson-in-his-pulpit,' for that is another of its strange country names. Few know that this changing plant, with its spotted leaves, forms those bright coral-berries which give such a rich colouring to the scenery of autumn. It must have furnished matter of mirth to our easily pleased forefathers, judging from the many merry names they gave to it, and which are still to be found in our old herbals.

Leaves, also, are beautiful to look upon without regarding the exquisite forms and colours of the flowers; and strange are the names our botanists have been compelled to adopt to describe their different shapes. Awl, arrow, finger, hand, heart, and kidney-shaped are a few of the names in common use for this purpose. Then the margin or edges of leaves are saw-toothed, crimped, smooth, slashed, notched, torn out, and look even as if some of them have been bitten by every variety of mouth; as if hundreds of insects had been at work, and each had eaten out its own fanciful pattern. Others, again, are armed, and have a 'touch-me-not' look about them, like those of the holly and thistles; while some are covered underneath with star-shaped prickles, hair-like particles, or soft down, making them, to the touch, rough, smooth, sticky, or soft as the down of velvet. To really see the form of a leaf, it must be examined when all the green is gone and only the skeleton left, which shews all the ribs and veins that were before covered. A glass is required to see this exquisite workmanship. The most beautiful lace is poor in comparison with the patterns which Nature weaves in her mysterious loom; and skilful lace-makers say that no machine could be made to equal the beautiful patterns of the skeleton leaves, or form shapes so diversified. Spring prepares the drapery which she hangs up in her green halls for the birds to shelter and build and sing among; and soon the hawthorn will light up these hanging curtains with its silver lamps, and perfume the leafy bowers with May.

In a work entitled *The Twelve Moneths*, published in 1661, April is described with a glow of language that recalls the Shaksperian era:
'The youth of the country make ready for the morris-dance, and the merry milkmaid supplies them with ribbons her true love had given her. The little fishes lie nibbling at the bait, and the porpoise plays in the pride of the tide. The

shepherds entertain the princes of Arcadia with pleasant roundelays. The aged feel a kind of youth, and youth hath a spirit full of life and activity; the aged hairs refreshen, and the youthful cheeks are as red as a cherry. The lark and the lamb look up at the sun, and the labourer is abroad by the dawning of the day. The sheep's eye in the lamb's head tells kind-hearted maids strange tales, and faith and troth make the true-lover's knot. It were a world to set down the worth of this month; for it is Heaven's blessing and the earth's comfort. It is the messenger of many pleasures, the courtier's progress, and the farmer's profit; the labourer's harvest, and the beggar's pilgrimage. In sum, there is much to be spoken of it; but, to avoid tediousness, I hold it, in all that I can see in it, the jewel of time and the joy of nature.

'Hail April, true Medea of the year,
  That makest all things young and fresh appear,
  What praise, what thanks, what commendations due,
  For all thy pearly drops of morning dew?
  When we despair, thy seasonable showers
  Comfort the corn, and cheer the drooping flowers;
  As if thy charity could not but impart
  A shower of tears to see us out of heart.
  Sweet, I have penned thy praise, and here I bring it,
  In confidence the birds themselves will sing it.'

(HISTORICAL.)

In the ancient Alban calendar, in which the year was represented as consisting of ten months of irregular length, April stood first, with thirty-six days to its credit. In the calendar of Romulus, it had the second place, and was composed of thirty days. Numa's twelve-month calendar assigned it the fourth place, with twenty-nine days; and so it remained till the reformation of the year by Julius Cæsar, when it recovered its former thirty days, which it has since retained.

It is commonly supposed that the name was derived from the Latin *aperio*, I open, as marking the time when the buds of the trees and flowers open. If this were the case, it would make April singular amongst the months, for the names of none of the rest, as designated in Latin, have any reference to natural conditions or circumstances. There is not the least probability in the idea. April was considered amongst the Romans as Venus's month, obviously because of the reproductive powers of nature now set agoing in several of her departments. The first day was specially set aside as *Festum Veneris et Fortunæ Virilis*. The probability, therefore, is, that *Aprilis* was *Aphrilis*, founded on the Greek name of Venus (*Aphrodite*).

Our Anglo-Saxon forefathers called the month

456

Oster-monath; and for this appellation the most plausible origin assigned is—that it was the month during which east winds prevailed. The term Easter may have come from the same origin.

CHARACTERISTICS OF APRIL.

It is eminently a spring month, and in England some of the finest weather of the year occasionally takes place in April. Generally, however, it is a month composed of shower and sunshine rapidly chasing each other; and often a chill is communicated by the east winds. The sun enters Taurus on the 20th of the month, and thus commences the second month past the equinox. At the beginning of April, in London, the sun rises at 5.33 A.M., and sets at 6.27 P.M.; at the end, the times of rising and setting are 4.38 and 7.22. The mean temperature of the air is 49° 9'.

Proverbial wisdom takes, on the whole, a kindly view of this flower-producing month. It even asserts that—

A cold April
The barn will fill.

The rain is welcomed:

An April flood
Carries away the frog and his brood.

And

April showers
Make May flowers.

Nor is there any harm in wind:

When April blows his horn,
It's good for both hay and corn.

AN APRIL DAY.

This day Dame Nature seemed in love;
The lusty sap began to move;
Fresh juice did stir th' embracing vines,
And birds had drawn their valentines.
The jealous trout that low did lie,
Rose at a well-dissembled fly;
Already were the eaves possess'd
With the swift pilgrim's daubed nest:
The groves already did rejoice,
In Philomel's triumphant voice:
The showers were short, the weather mild,
The morning fresh, the evening smiled.
Joan takes her neat-rubbed pail, and now
She trips to milk the sand-red cow.
The fields and gardens were beset
With tulips, crocus, violet;
And now, though late, the modest rose
Did more than half a blush disclose.
Thus all looks gay and full of cheer,
To welcome the new-liveried year.
                                    SIR H. WOTTON.

First of April.

St Melito, Bishop of Sardis, in Lydia, 2d century. St Hugh, Bishop of Grenoble, 1132. St Gilbert, Bishop of Caithness, in Scotland, 1240.

Born.—William Harvey, discoverer of the circulation of the blood, 1578, *Folkestone;* Charles de St Evremond, 1613, *St Denis le Gât;* Solomon Gesner, painter and poet, author of 'The Death of Abel,' 1730, *Zurich ;* Robert Surtees, historical antiquary, 1779, *Durham ;* Sir Thomas F. Buxton, Bart., philanthropist, 1786, *Essex.*

Died.—Sultan Timur (Tamerlane), conqueror of Persia, &c., 1405 (the date otherwise given as 19th of February) ; Robert III., King of Scots, 1406, *Paisley ;* Sigismund I., King of Poland, 1548 ; Jean Baptiste Thiers, miscellaneous writer, 1702 ; Dr John Langhorne, poet, translator of Plutarch, 1779, *Blagdon ;* Dr Isaac Milner, Dean of Carlisle, theological writer, 1820, *Kensington Gore ;* Reginald Heber, Bishop of Calcutta, 1826, *Trichinopoly.*

ROBERT SURTEES.

It was very appropriate that Mr Surtees should be born on the 1st of April, as he was the perpetrator of one of the most dexterous literary impostures of modern times. Be it observed, in the first place, that he was a true and zealous historical antiquary, and the author of a book of high merit in its class, the *History and Antiquities of the County Palatine of Durham.* Born to a fair landed estate, educated at Oxford, possessed of an active and capacious mind, marked by a cheerful, social temper, the external destiny of Surtees was such as to leave little to be desired. Residing constantly on his paternal acres at Mainsforth, near Durham, in the practice of a genial hospitality, he fulfilled most of the duties of his station in a satisfactory manner, and was really a very popular person.

It was not till after the death of Surtees in 1835, that any discovery was made of the literary imposture above referred to. Sir Walter Scott, upon whom it was practised, had died three years earlier, without becoming aware of the deception. Scott had published three editions of his *Border Minstrelsy,* when, in 1806, he received a letter from Mr Surtees (a stranger to him), containing remarks upon some of the ballads composing that work. Scott sent a cordial answer, and by and by there came from Mr Surtees, a professedly old ballad 'on a feud between the Ridleys and the Featherstones,' which he professed to have taken down from the recitation of an old woman on Alston Moor. It is, to the apprehension of the writer of this article, a production as coarse as it is wild and incoherent; but it was accompanied by historical notes calculated to authenticate it as a narrative of actual events, and Scott, who was then full of excitement about ballads in general, did not pause to criticise it rigorously. He at once accepted it as a genuine

relic of antiquity—introduced a passage of it in *Marmion,* and inserted it entire in the next edition of his *Minstrelsy.*

Supposing a person generally truthful to have been for once tempted to practise a deception like this, one would have expected him, on finding it successful, to be filled with a concern he had never anticipated, wishful to repair the error, and, above all, determined to commit no more such mistakes. Contrary to all this, we find Mr Surtees in the very next year passing off another ballad of his own making upon the unsuspicious friend whose confidence he had gained. In a letter, dated the 28th of February in that year, he proceeds to say :

'I add a ballad of *Lord Ewrie,* apparently a song of gratulation on his elevation to the peerage, which I took by recitation from a very aged person, Rose Smith, of Bishop Middleham, æt. 91, whose husband's father and two brothers were killed in the Rebellion of 1715. I was interrogating her for Jacobite songs, and instead acquired *Lord Ewrie.* The person intended is William Lord Eure,' &c. In this, as in the former case, he added a number of historical notes to support the deception, and Scott did not hesitate in putting *Lord Ewrie* in a false character before the world in the next edition of his *Border Minstrelsy.* This, however, was not all. Tempted, apparently, by the very faith which Scott had in his veracity, he played off yet a third imposture.

There is, in the later editions of the *Minstrelsy,* a ballad of very vigorous diction, entitled *Barthram's Dirge,* beginning :

'They shot him dead on the Nine-stone Rig,
  Beside the Headless Cross ;
And they left him lying in his blood,
  Upon the moor and moss.'

The editor states that it was obtained from the recitation of an old woman by his 'obliging friend' Mr Surtees, who communicated it to him, with only a few missing lines replaced by himself, as indicated by brackets. In reality, this ballad was also by Mr Surtees. The missing lines, supplied within brackets, were merely designed as a piece of apparent candour, the better to blind the editor to the general falsehood of the story. When we turn to the letter, in which Surtees sent the ballad to Scott, we obtain a good notion of the plausible way in which these tricks were framed : 'The following romantic fragment,' says Surtees, '(which I have no further meddled with than to fill up a hemistich, and complete rhyme and metre), I have from the imperfect recitation of Ann Douglas, a withered crone who weeded in my garden :

"They shot him dead on the Nine-stone Rig," &c.

I have no local reference to the above. The

name of Bartram bids fair for a Northumbrian hero; but the style is, I think, superior to our Northumbrian ditties, and more like the Scotch. There is a place called Headless Cross, I think, in old maps, near Elsdon, in Northumberland; but this is too vague to found any idea upon.'—*Letter of November 9, 1809.*

Thus, we see the deceptions of the learned historian of Durham were carefully planned, and very coolly carried out. There was always the simple crone to recite the ballad. Quotations from old wills and genealogies established the existence of the persons figuring in the recital. And, when necessary, an affectation was made of supplying missing links in modern language. A friendship was established with the greatest literary man of his age on the strength of these pretended services. Scott was not only misled himself, but he was induced to mislead others. The impostor looked coolly on, as, from day to day, his too trusting friend was allowed to introduce into his book fictitious representations, calculated, when detected, to take away its credit. It is difficult to understand how the person so acting should be, in the ordinary affairs of life, honourable and upright. But it was so. We are left no room to doubt that Mr Robert Surtees was faithful in his own historical narrations, and wholly above mendacity for a sordid or cowardly purpose. It was simply this —that men of honourable principles have heretofore had but imperfect ideas of the obligation to speak the truth in the affairs of ancient traditionary literature—we might almost say, of literature generally.

If they judged aright, they would see that the natural consequence of deceptions regarding professedly old ballads is to create and justify doubts regarding all articles of the kind. Seeing that one so well skilled in such matters as Scott was deceived in at least three instances, how shall we put trust in a single other case where he states that a ballad was taken down for him from popular recitation? A whole series of his legends were professedly obtained from a Mrs Brown of Falkland; another series from a Mrs Arnot of Arbroath: what guarantee have we that these were not female Surteeses? How rapidly would belief extend in cases where it was justified, if there were no liars and impostors! Every instance of deception sensibly dashes faith; and not even the slightest departure from truth can be practised without consequences of indefinite mischief.

THE REV. RICHARD NAPIER, ASTROLOGER AND PHYSICIAN, DIED APRIL 1, 1634.

Astrology was so much in vogue in the seventeenth century, that neither learning, nor rank, nor piety secured persons from becoming its dupes. James I. was notorious for his credulity about such delusions. Sir Kenelm Digby, though one of the most learned and scientific men of his day, as well as an able statesman, was scarcely less credulous. Charles I., and his supplanter Cromwell, are alike said to have consulted astrologers. Even the clergy, who ought to have denounced such delusions, not

only sanctioned, but in some instances practised, astrology. Thus the Rev. Richard Napier, though remarkable for piety, was no less remarkable for his supposed skill in astrology. He was a son of Sir Robert Napier, of Luton-Hoo, in Bedfordshire, and became rector of Great Linford, in the adjoining county of Buckingham, in 1589. He was instructed in astrology and physic by the celebrated Dr Forman, who, as Lilly informs us, 'used to say, on his first becoming his pupil, that he would be a dunce, yet, in continuance of time, he proved a singular astrologer and physician.' Dr Forman eventually thought so highly of his pupil, that he bequeathed him ' all his rarities and secret manuscripts of what sort soever.'

Napier was an M.A., and was usually styled Dr; 'but,' says Aubrey, 'whether doctorated by degree or courtesy, because of his profession, I know not. He was a person of great abstinence, innocence, and piety, and spent two hours every day in family prayer.' When a patient or 'querent' came to consult him, he immediately retired to his closet for prayer, and was heard as holding conversations with angels and spirits. He asked them questions respecting his patients, and by the answers, which he fancied they returned, he was guided more than by his professed skill in medicine or astrology. In fact, he privately acknowledged that he practised astrology chiefly as the ostensible means of information, while he really depended on his (supposed) communications from spiritual beings. 'He did,' says Aubrey, ' converse with the angel Raphael.' 'The angel told him if the patient were curable or incurable.' The angel Raphael 'did resolve him, that Mr Booth of Cheshire should have a son that should inherit three years hence. This was in 1619, and we are informed that in 1622 his son George was born, who eventually became Lord Delamere.' 'At some times,' continues Aubrey, 'upon great occasions, he had conference with Michael, but very rarely. He outwent Forman in physick and holiness of life; cured the falling-sickness perfectly by constellated rings; some diseases by annulets, &c.' Lilly, in his Autobiography, says: 'I was with him (Napier) in 1632 or 1633, upon occasion; he had me up into his library, being excellently furnished with very choice books; there he prayed almost one hour. He invocated several angels in his prayer —viz., Michael, Gabriel, Uriel, &c.'

One or two examples may suffice to illustrate the nature of his practice. When 'E. W——, Esq.,' was about eight years old, he was troubled with worms, and was taken by his grandfather, 'Sir Francis ——,' to Dr Napier. The doctor retired to his closet, and E. W—— peeped in, and saw him on his knees at prayer. The doctor, duly instructed by his angelic adviser, returned to Sir Francis, and ordered his grandson to take a draught of muscadine every morning, and predicted he would be free from the disorder when fourteen years old!

A woman afflicted with ague applied to the doctor, who gave her a spell to cure it; but 'a minister' seeing it, sharply reproved her for using such a diabolical aid, and ordered her to burn it. She burned it; but the ague returned so severely, that she again applied to the doctor for the spell, and was greatly benefited by its use. But the minister, on discovering what she was doing, so alarmed her with its consequences, that she again burned the spell. 'Whereupon she fell extremely ill, and would have had the spell the third time; but the doctor refused, saying, that she had contemned and slighted the power and goodness of the blessed spirits, and so she died.'

In 1634, the Earl of Sunderland placed himself for some months under the care of Dr Napier; the Earl of Bolingbroke and Lord Wentworth also patronised him, and protected him from the interference of magistrates, extending their protection even to his friends and fellow-practitioners of the unlawful art. For the doctor, we are told, 'instructed many other ministers in astrology,' 'lent them whole cloak-bags full of books,' and protected them from harm and violence, especially one William Marsh of Dunstable, a recusant, who, 'by astrology, resolved thievish questions, and many times was in trouble, but by Dr Napier's interest was still enabled to continue his practice, no justice of the peace being permitted to vex him.' 'This man had only two books, Guido and Haly, bound together. He had so numbled and thumbled the leaves of both, that half one side of every leaf was torn even to the middle. He did seriously confess to a friend of mine that astrology was but the countenance, and that he did his business by the help of the blessed spirits, with whom only men of great piety, humility, and charity could be acquainted.'

Dr Napier does not appear to have been assisted by Raphael in his clerical ministrations; for 'miscarrying one day in the pulpit, he never after used it, but all his lifetime kept in his house some excellent scholar or other to officiate for him!' ''Tis certain,' says Aubrey, 'he told his own death to a day and hour, and died praying upon his knees, being of a very great age, on April 1st, 1634. His knees were horny with frequent praying.' His burial is thus entered in the parish register: 'April 15, 1634. Buried, Mr. Richard Napier, rector, the most renowned physician both of body and soul.'

His manuscripts, which contained a diary of his practice for fifty years, fell into the hands of Elias Ashmole, who had them bound in several folio volumes, and deposited with his own in the library at Oxford which bears his name, and where they still remain, together with a portrait of Dr Napier. Many of the medical recipes in these manuscripts are marked by Dr Napier, as having been given him by the angel Raphael.

W. H. K.

ORIGIN OF HACKNEY-COACH STANDS.

On the 1st of April 1639, Mr Garrard, writing in London to Wentworth, Earl of Strafford, then Lord-lieutenant of Ireland, says:

'I cannot omit to mention any new thing that comes up amongst us, though never so trivial. Here is one Captain Baily; he hath been a sea-captain, but now lives on the land, about this city, where he tries experiments. He hath erected, according to his ability, some four hackney-coaches, put his men in a livery, and appointed them to stand at the Maypole in the Strand, giving them instructions at what rate to carry men into several parts of the town, where all day they may be had. Other hackneymen seeing this way, they flocked to the same place, and performed their journeys at the same rate; so that sometimes there is twenty of them together, which disperse up and down, that they and others are to be had everywhere, as watermen are to be had by the water-side. Everybody is much pleased with it; for, whereas before coaches could not be had but at great rates, now a man may have one much cheaper.'

'Gossip Garrard,' as he has been termed, was scarcely correct in saying that everybody was pleased with the new and convenient system of metropolitan conveyances introduced by the retired sea-captain. The citizen shopkeepers bitterly complained that they were ruined by the coaches. 'Formerly,' they said, 'when ladies and gentlemen walked in the streets, there was a chance of obtaining customers to inspect and purchase our commodities; but now they whisk past in the coaches before our apprentices have time to cry out "What d'ye lack!"' Another complaint was, that in former times the tradesmen in the principal streets earned as much as paid their rents by letting out their upper apartments to members of parliament, and country gentlemen visiting London on pleasure or business, until the noise made by the coaches drove the profitable lodgers to less frequented thoroughfares.

Taylor, the water-poet, being a waterman, one of the class whose business was most injured by the coaches, felt exceedingly bitter against the new system, and wrote an invective, entitled *The World Runs upon Wheels*, in which he adduces all the inconveniences of coaches, enumerating, in his peculiar style, all the disadvantages caused by them. 'We poor watermen,' he says, 'have not the least cause to complain against this infernal swarm of trade-spoilers, who, like grasshoppers or caterpillars of Egypt, have so overrun the land, that we can get no living on the water; for I dare truly affirm, that every day, especially if the court be at Whitehall, they do rob us of our livings, and carry five hundred and sixty fares daily from us.'

In another publication, entitled *The Thief*, Taylor says:

'Carroches, coaches, jades, and Flanders mares,
Do rob us of our shares, our wares, our fares:
Against the ground, we stand and knock our heels,
Whilst all our profit runs away on wheels;
And, whosoever but observes and notes
The great increase of coaches and of boats,
Shall find their number more than e'er they were,
By half and more, within this thirty year.
The watermen at sea had service still,
And those that staid at home had work at will:
Then upstart helcart-coaches were to seek,
A man could scarce see twenty in a week;
But now, I think, a man may daily see
More than the wherrys on the Thames can be.'

The stillness of London streets in the olden time is unexpectedly exemplified by the serious complaints made regarding the noise of coaches. We might wonder what an ancient citizen would say if he could possibly hear the incessant roar of the cabs, omnibuses, vans, &c., of the present day! Taylor, when there were only some dozen hackney-coaches, and a very few private carriages, thus entreats his readers:

'I pray you but note the streets, and the chambers or lodgings in Fleet Street or the Strand, how they are pestered with coaches, especially after a masque or play at the court, where even the very earth shakes and trembles, the casements shatter, tatter, and clatter, and such a confused noise is made, as if all the devils were at barley-break,* so that a man can neither sleep, speak, hear, write, or eat his dinner or supper quiet for them; besides, their tumbling din (like a counterfeit thunder) doth sour wine, beer, and ale most abominably, to the impairing of their healths that drink it, and the making of many a victualler trade-fallen.'

'A coach,' he continues, 'like a heathen, a pagan, an infidel, or an atheist, observes neither Sabbath nor holiday, time nor season, robustiously breaking through the toil or net of divine and human law, order, and authority, and, as it were, condemning all Christian conformity, like a dog

that lies on a heap of hay, who will eat none of it himself, nor suffer any other beast to eat any. Even so, the coach is not capable of hearing what

* The game now called ' Thread-the-Needle.'

a preacher saith, nor will it suffer men or women to hear that would hear, for it makes such a hideous rumbling in the streets by many church doors, that people's ears are stopped with the noise, whereby they are debarred of their edifying, which makes faith so fruitless, good works so barren, and charity as cold at midsummer as if it were a great frost, and by this means souls are robbed and starved of their heavenly manna, and the kingdom of darkness replenished. To avoid which they have set up a cross-post in Cheapside on Sundays, near Wood Street end, which makes the coaches rattle and jumble on the other side of the way, further from the church, and from hindering of their hearing.'

Public convenience, however much it may be opposed at first, invariably triumphs in the end over private interests. The four hackney-coaches started by Captain Baily in 1634, increased so rapidly, that their number in 1637 was confined by law to 50; in 1652, to 200; in 1659, to 300; in 1662, to 400; in 1694, to 700; in 1710, to 800; in 1771, to 1000. It is not our purpose to continue their history further.

At first the hackney coach-driver sat in a kind of chair, in front of the vehicle, as may be seen by a rude wood-cut in a ballad of the period, preserved in the Roxburghe collection, written by Taylor, and entitled *The Coache's Overthrow.* Subsequently, in the reign of Charles II., the driver sat on one of the horses, in manner of a modern postilion. This is clearly evident, by the short whip and spurs of the man in the preceding illustration, taken from a contemporary engraving, representing a hackney-coachman of that reign. In the early part of the last century the custom had changed, the driver sitting in front on a box, in which was kept food for the horses, and a piece of rope, nails, and hammer to repair the vehicle in case of accident. Subsequently, this rude box was, for neatness' sake, covered with a cloth, and thus we now have the terms box-seat and hammer-cloth.

It is said that the sum of £1500, arising from the duty on hackney-coaches, was applied in part payment of the cost of rebuilding Temple Bar.

April Fools.

The 1st of April, of all days in the year, enjoys a character of its own, in as far as it, and it alone, is consecrated to practical joking. On this day it becomes the business of a vast number of people, especially the younger sort, to practise innocent impostures upon their unsuspicious neighbours, by way of making them what in France are called *poissons d'Avril,* and with us April fools. Thus a knowing boy will despatch a younger brother to see a public statue descend from its pedestal at a particular appointed hour. A crew of giggling servant-maids will get hold of some simple swain, and send him to a bookseller's shop for the *History of Eve's Grandmother,* or to a chemist's for a pennyworth of *pigeon's milk,* or to a cobbler's for a little *strap oil,* in which last case the messenger secures a hearty application of the strap to his shoulders, and is sent home in a state of bewilderment as to what the affair means. The urchins in the kennel make a sport of calling to some passing beau to look to his coat-skirts; when he either finds them with a piece of paper pinned to them or not; in either of which cases he is saluted as an April fool. A waggish young lady, aware that her dearest friend Eliza Louisa has a rather empty-headed youth dangling after her with little encouragement, will send him a billet, appointing him to call upon Eliza Louisa at a particular hour. when instead of a welcome, he finds himself treated as an intruder, and by and by discovers that he has not advanced his reputation for sagacity or the general prospects of his suit. The great object is to catch some person off his guard, to pass

off upon him, as a simple fact, something barely possible, and which has no truth in it; to impose upon him, so as to induce him to go into positions of absurdity, in the eye of a laughing circle of bystanders. Of course, for successful April fooling, it is necessary to have some considerable degree of coolness and face; as also some tact whereby to know in what direction the victim is most ready to be imposed upon by his own tendencies of belief. It may be remarked, that a large proportion of the business is effected before and about the time of breakfast, while as yet few have had occasion to remember what day of the year it is, and before a single victimisation has warned people of their danger.

What compound is to simple addition, so is Scotch to English April fooling. In the northern part of the island, they are not content to make a neighbour believe some single piece of absurdity. There, the object being, we shall say, to befool simple Andrew Thomson, Wag No. 1 sends him away with a letter to a friend two miles off, professedly asking for some useful information, or requesting a loan of some article, but in reality containing only the words:

' This is the first day of April,
    Hunt the gowk another mile.'

Wag No. 2, catching up the idea of his correspondent, tells Andrew with a grave face that it is not in his power, &c.; but if he will go with another note to such a person, he will get what is wanted. Off Andrew trudges with this second note to Wag No. 3, who treats him in the same manner; and so on he goes, till some one of the series, taking pity on him, hints the trick that has been practised upon him. A successful affair of this kind will keep rustic society in merriment for a week, during which honest Andrew Thomson hardly can shew his face. The Scotch employ the term gowk (which is properly a cuckoo) to express a fool in general, but more especially an April fool, and among them the practice above described is called *hunting the gowk.*

Sometimes the opportunity is taken by ultra-jocular persons to carry out some extensive hoax upon society. For example, in March 1860, a vast multitude of people received through the post a card having the following inscription, with a seal marked by an inverted sixpence at one of the angles, thus having to superficial observation an official appearance : ' Tower of London.— Admit the Bearer and Friend to view the Annual Ceremony of Washing the White Lions, on *Sunday, April 1st,* 1860. Admitted only at the White Gate. It is particularly requested that no gratuities be given to the Wardens or their Assistants.' The trick is said to have been highly successful. Cabs were rattling about Tower Hill all that Sunday morning, vainly endeavouring to discover the White Gate.

It is the more remarkable that any such trick should have succeeded, when we reflect how identified the 1st of April has become with the idea of imposture and unreality. So much is this the case, that if one were about to be married, or to launch some new and speculative proposition or enterprise, one would hesitate to select April 1st for the purpose. On the other hand, if one had to issue a mock document of any kind with the desire of its being accepted in its proper character, he could not better insure the joke being seen than by dating it the 1st of April.

The literature of the last century, from the *Spectator* downwards, has many allusions to April fooling ; no references to it in our earlier literature have as yet been pointed out. English antiquaries appear unable to trace the origin of the custom, or to say how long it has existed among us. In the Catholic Church, there was the Feast of the Ass on Twelfth Day, and various mummings about Christmas ; but April fooling stands apart from these dates. There is but one plausible-looking suggestion from Mr Pegge, to the effect that, the 25th of March being, in one respect, New Year's Day, the 1st of April was its *octave*, and the termination of its celebrations ; but this idea is not very satisfactory. There is much more importance in the fact, that the Hindoos have, in their *Huli*, which terminates with the 31st of March, a precisely similar festival, during which the great aim is to send persons away with messages to ideal individuals, or individuals sure to be from home, and enjoy a laugh at their disappointment. To find the practice so widely prevalent over the earth, and with so near a coincidence of day, seems to indicate that it has had a very early origin amongst mankind.

Swift, in his Journal to Stella, enters under March 31, 1713, that he, Dr Arbuthnot, and Lady Masham had been amusing themselves that evening by contriving ' a lie for to-morrow.' A person named Noble had been hanged a few days before. The lie which these three laid their heads together to concoct, was, that Noble had come to life again in the hands of his friends, but was once more laid hold of by the sheriff, and now lay at the Black Swan in Holborn, in the custody of a messenger. ' We are all,' says Swift, ' to send to our friends, to know whether they have heard anything of it, and so we hope it will spread.' Next day, the learned Dean duly sent his servant to several houses to inquire among the footmen, not letting his own man into the secret. But nothing could be heard of the resuscitation of Mr Noble ; whence he concluded that ' his colleagues did not contribute ' as they ought to have done.

April fooling is a very noted practice in France,

and we get traces of its prevalence there at an earlier period than is the case in England. For instance, it is related that Francis, Duke of Lorraine, and his wife, being in captivity at Nantes, effected their escape in consequence of the attempt being made on the 1st of April. ' Disguised as peasants, the one bearing a hod on his shoulder, the other carrying a basket of rubbish at her back, they both at an early hour of the day passed through the gates of the city. A woman, having a knowledge of their persons, ran to the guard to give notice to the sentry. "April fool!" cried the soldier ; and all the guard, to a man, shouted out, "April fool!" beginning with the sergeant in charge of the post. The governor, to whom the story was told as a jest, conceived some suspicion, and ordered the fact to be proved ; but it was too late, for in the meantime the duke and his wife were well on their way. The 1st of April saved them.'

It is told that a French lady having stolen a watch from a friend's house on the 1st of April, endeavoured, after detection, to pass off the affair as *un poisson d'Avril*, an April joke. On denying that the watch was in her possession, a messenger was sent to her apartments, where it was found upon a chimney-piece. ' Yes,' said the adroit thief, ' I think I have made the messenger a fine *poisson d'Avril !*' Then the magistrate said she must be imprisoned till the 1st of April in the ensuing year, *comme un poisson d'Avril.*

THE WISE FOOLS OF GOTHAM.

On an eminence about a mile south of Gotham, a village in Nottinghamshire, stands a bush known as the ' Cuckoo Bush,' and with which the following strange legend is connected. The present bush is planted on the site of the original one, and serves as a memorial of the disloyal event which has given the village its notoriety.

King John, as the story goes, was marching towards Nottingham, and intended to pass through Gotham meadow. The villagers believed that the ground over which a king passed became for ever afterwards a public road ; and not being minded to part with their meadow so cheaply, by some means or other they prevented the king from passing that way. Incensed at their proceedings, he sent soon after to inquire the reason of their rudeness and incivility, doubtless intending to punish them by fine or otherwise. When they heard of the approach of the messengers, they were as anxious to escape the consequences of the monarch's displeasure as they had been to save their meadow. What time they had for deliberation, or what counsels they took we are not told, but when the king's servants arrived they found some of the inhabitants endeavouring to drown an eel in a pond ; some dragging their carts and wagons to the top of a barn to shade a wood from the sun's rays ; some tumbling cheeses down a hill in the expectation that they would find their way to Nottingham Market, and some employed in hedging in a cuckoo, which had perched upon an old bush ! In short they were all employed in such a manner as convinced the king's officers that they were a village of *fools*, and consequently unworthy of his majesty's notice. They, of course, having outwitted the king, imagined that they were *wise*. Hence arose the saying 'The wise fools of Gotham.' Fuller says, alluding to this story, and some others to which this gave rise, such as 'The Merry Tales of the Mad Men of Gotham,' published in the time of Henry VIII, 'Gotham doth breed as *wise* people as any which causelessly laugh at their simplicity.'

But they have other defenders besides Fuller. Some sceptical poet, whose production has not immortalised his name, writes:

'Tell me no more of Gotham fools,
Or of their eels, in little pools,
    Which they, we're told, were drowning;
Nor of their carts drawn up on high
When King John's men were standing by,
    To keep a wood from browning.

Nor of their cheese shov'd down the hill,
Nor of the cuckoo sitting still,
    While it they hedged round:
Such tales of them have long been told,
By prating boobies young and old,
    In drunken circles crowned.

The fools are those who thither go,
To see the cuckoo bush, I trow,
    'The wood, the barn, and pools;
For such are seen both here and there,
And passed by without a sneer,
    By all but errant fools.'

APRIL 2.

St Apian, of Lycia, martyr, 306. St Theodosia, of Cæsarea, martyr, 308. St Nicetius, archbishop of Lyons, 577. St Ebba, or Abba, abbess, martyr, 874. B. Constantine, King of Scotland, 874. St Bronacha, of Ireland. St Francis of Paula, founder of the order of Minims, 1508.

Born.—C. N. Oudinot, Marshal of France, Duke of Reggio, 1767, *Bar-sur-Ornain* (sometimes the 25th is given as the date).

Died.—Arthur, Prince of Wales, 1502, *Ludlow;* Jean Barth, French naval commander, 1702; Thomas Carte, historian, 1754, *Yattendon;* Comte de Mirabeau, 1791, *Paris;* Dr James Gregory, professor of medicine, author of 'Conspectus Medicinæ,' 1821, *Edinburgh;* John Le Keux, architectural engraver, 1846.

ARTHUR, PRINCE OF WALES.

King Henry VII., the first of our Tudor monarchs, had three sons, Arthur, Henry, and Edmond, the last of whom died in his childhood. Arthur was born on the 20th of September 1486, at Winchester. His birth was the subject of universal joy throughout the kingdom, as in him were united the claims of the rival houses of York and Lancaster, and the general satisfaction was soon increased by the early display of precocious talents, and of a gentle and amiable disposition. In 1489, Arthur was created Prince of Wales. This title, as given to the king's eldest son, had been created originally as a measure of conciliation towards the Welsh, and it would be still more gratifying to that people when the House of Tudor came to the throne. The House of York had also, before its attainment of royalty, had close relations with Wales;

and Edward IV., as a stroke of wise policy, had sent his eldest son to reside in his great castle of Ludlow, on the border, and had established there a court of government for Wales and the Marches, which had now become permanent. Henry VII., in continuation of this policy, sent his son, Prince Arthur, to Ludlow, to reside there under the governance of a distant relative of the Tudor family, named Sir Rhys ap Thomas, and Ludlow Castle became Arthur's home. Little is said of the actions of the youthful prince, except that his good qualities became more and more developed, until the year 1501, when, in the month of November, Arthur, who had just completed his fifteenth year, was married with great ceremony to Catherine of Aragon, a Spanish princess, then in her eighteenth year. The young prince and his bride repaired to Ludlow immediately after the marriage, which he survived but a short time, dying in Ludlow Castle, on the 2nd of April 1502. His corpse was conveyed in solemn procession to Worcester, and was there buried in the cathedral, and a rich shrine, which still remains, raised over the tomb. The untimely death of this amiable prince was the subject of sincere and universal grief, but indirectly it led to that great revolution which gave to England her present religious and ecclesiastical forms. Henry VII., for political reasons, and on the plea that the marriage had never been consummated, married the widow of Arthur to his younger brother Henry, who became afterwards King Henry VIII. Henry, who subsequently declared that the marriage was forced upon him, divorced his wife, and the dispute, as every one knows, was, under the direction of Providence, the cause of the separation of the English church from Rome. In a somewhat similar manner the untimely death of Henry, Prince of Wales, the son of James I., led perhaps indirectly to that great convulsion in the middle of the following century, to which we owe the establishment of the freedom of the English political constitution.

A GROUP OF OLD LADIES.

Died at Edinburgh, on the 2nd of April 1856, Miss Elizabeth Gray, at the age of 108, having been born in May 1748. That cases of extraordinary longevity are seldom supported by clear documentary evidence has been very justly alleged; it has indeed been set forth that we scarcely have complete evidence for a single example of the centenarian. In this case, however, there was certainly no room for doubt. Miss Gray had been known all her life as a member of the upper circle of society in the Scottish metropolis, and her identity with the individual Elizabeth Gray, the daughter of William Gray, of Newholm, writer in Edinburgh, whose birth is chronicled in the register of her father's parish of Dolphington, in Lanarkshire, as having occurred in May 1748, is beyond dispute in the society to which the venerable lady belonged. It may be remarked that she was a very cheerful person, and kept up her old love of whist till past the five score. Her mother attained ninety-six, and two of her sisters died at ninety-four and ninety-six respectively. She had, however, survived her father upwards of a hundred years, for he died in 1755; nay, a more remarkable thing than even this was to be told of Betty Gray—a brother of hers (strictly a half-brother) had died so long ago as 1728. A faded marble slab in the wall of Dolphington Kirk, which records the decease of this child—for such he was—must have been viewed with strange feelings, when, a hundred and twenty-eight years later, the age-worn sister was laid in the same spot.

Little more than two years after the death of Miss Gray, there died in Scotland another centenarian lady, about whose age there could be no ground for doubt, as she had lived in the eye of intelligent society all her days. This person was the Hon. Mrs Hay Mackenzie, of Cromartie. She died in October 1858, at the age of 103; she was grandmother to the Duchess of Sutherland; her father was the sixth Lord Elibank, brother and successor of Lord Patrick, who entertained Johnson in Edinburgh; her maternal grandfather was that unfortunate Earl of Cromartie who so narrowly escaped accompanying Kilmarnock and Balmerino to the scaffold in 1746. She was a most benevolent woman—a large giver—and enjoyed universal esteem. Her conversation made the events of the first half of the eighteenth century pass as vividly before the mind as those of the present day. It was remarked as a curious circumstance, that of Dunrobin Castle, the place where her grandfather was taken prisoner as a rebel, her granddaughter became mistress.

It is well known that female life is considerably more enduring than male; so that, although boys are born in the proportion of 105 to 100 of girls —a fact that holds good all over Europe—there are always more women in existence than men. It really is surprising how enduring women sometimes become, and how healthily enduring too, after passing the more trying crises of female existence. Mrs Piozzi, who herself thought it a person's own fault if they got old, gives us in one of her letters a remarkable case of vigorous old-ladyism.

'I must tell you,' says she, 'a story of a Cornish gentlewoman hard by here [Penzance], Zenobia Stevens, who held a lease under the Duke of Bolton by her own life only ninety-nine years—and going at the term's end ten miles to give it up, she obtained permission to continue in the house as long as she lived, and was asked of course to drink a glass of wine. She did take one, but declined the second, saying she had to ride home in the twilight upon a young colt, and was afraid to make herself giddy-headed.'*

The well known Countess Dowager of Cork, who died in May 1840, had not reached a hundred —she had but just completed her ninety-fourth year—but she realized the typical character of a veteran lady who, to appearance, was little affected by age. Till within a few days of her death she was healthy and cheerful as in those youthful days when she charmed Johnson and Boswell, the latter of whom was only six years her senior. She was in the custom to the last of dining out every day when she had not company

* Mrs Piozzi's *Remains, sub anno* 1821.

at home. As to death, she always said she was ready for him, come when he might; but she did not like to see him coming. Lady Cork was daughter of the first Lord Galway, and she lived to see the *sixth*, her great grand-nephew.

Mr Francis Brokesby, who writes a letter on antiquities and natural curiosities from Shottesbrooke in 1711 (published by Hearne in connection with *Leland's Itinerary*, vi. 104), mentions several instances of extremely protracted female life. He tells of a woman then living near the Tower in London, aged about 130, and who remembered Queen Elizabeth. Hearne himself subsequently states that this woman was Jane Scrimshaw, who had lived for four score years in the Merchant Tailors' alms-houses, near Little Tower-hill. She was, he says, born in the parish of Mary-le-Bow, London, on the 3rd of April 1584, so that she was then in the 127th year of her age, 'and likely to live much longer.' She, however, died on the 26th of December 1711. It is stated that even at the last there was scarcely a grey hair on her head, and she never lost memory or judgment. Mr Brokesby reported another venerable person as having died about sixty years before—that is, about 1650— who attained the age of a hundred and forty. She had been the wife of a labouring man named Humphry Broadhurst, who resided at Hedgerow, in Cheshire, on the property of the Leighs of Lyme. The familiar name she bore, *The Cricket in the hedge*, bore witness to her cheerful character; a peculiarity to which, along with great temperance and plainness of living, her great age was chiefly to be attributed. A hardly credible circumstance was alleged of this woman, that she had borne her youngest child at four score. Latterly, having been reduced by gradual decay to great bodily weakness, she used to be carried in the arms of this daughter, who was herself sixty. She was buried in the parish church of Prestbury. It was said of this woman that she remembered Bosworth Field; but here there must be some error, for to do so in 1650 she would have needed to be considerably more than 140 years old, the battle being fought in 1485. It is not unlikely, however, that her death took place earlier than 1650, as the time was only stated from memory.

THE GAME OF PALL MALL.

April 2, 1661, Pepys enters in his Diary, 'To St James's Park, where I saw the Duke of York playing at Pelemele, the first time that I ever saw the sport.'

The Duke's brother, King Charles II., had recently formed what is called the Mall in St James's-park for the playing of this game, which, however, was not new in England, as there had previously existed a walk for the purpose (lined with trees) on the ground now occupied by the street called Pall Mall. It was introduced from France, probably about the beginning of the seventeenth century; but the derivation of the name appears to be from the Italian, *Palamaglio*, i. e., *palla*, a ball, and *maglio*, a mallet; though we derived the term directly from the French *Palemaille*. The game answers to this name, the object being by a mallet to drive a ball along a straight alley and through an elevated ring at the end: victory being to him who effects this object at the smallest number of strokes. Thus

THE GAME OF PALL MALL.

pall-mall may be said in some degree to resemble golf, being, however, less rustic, and more suitable for the man of courts.* King Charles II. would appear to have been a good player. In Waller's poem on St James's Park, there is a well-known passage descriptive of the Merry Monarch engaged in the sport:

' Here a well-polished mall gives us the joy,
To see our Prince his matchless force employ;
His manly posture and his graceful mien,
Vigour and youth in all his motions seen;
No sooner has he touched the flying ball,
But 'tis already more than half the mall.
And such a fury from his arm has got,
As from a smoking culverin 'twere shot.'

MALLET AND BALL FORMERLY USED IN THE GAME OF PALL MALL.

(*Length of Mall 3 ft. 8 in., diameter of the Ball 2¼ in.*)

The phrase 'well polished' leads to the remark that the alley for pall-mall was hardened and strewn with pounded shells, so as to present a perfectly smooth surface. The sides of the alley appear to have been boarded, to prevent the ball from going off the straight line. We do not learn anywhere whether, as in golf, mallets of different shapes and weights were used for a variety of strokes,—a light and short one, for instance, for the final effort to ring the ball. There is, however, an example of a mallet and

ball preserved in London from the days when they were employed in Pall Mall; and they are here represented.*

The game was one of a commendable kind, as it provoked to exercise in the open air, and was of a social nature. It is rather surprising that it should have so entirely gone out, there being no trace of it after the Revolution. The original alley or avenue for the game in London began, even in the time of the Commonwealth, to be converted into a street—called, from the game, Pall Mall—where, if the reader will pardon a

* See an interesting paper on the Game of Pall Mall, by Mr Albert Way, in the *Archæological Journal*, volume xi. p. 253.

* These curious relics of an extinct game were long in the possession of the late Mr Benjamin L. Vulliamy.

very gentle pun, clubs now take the place of mallets.

THE FLEET PRISON OF OLD.

April 2, 1844, the Fleet Prison in London was abolished, after existing as a place of incarceration for debtors more than two centuries; all that time doing little credit to our boasted civilization.

In the spring of the year 1727 a Committee of the House of Commons, appointed to inquire into the management of Debtors' prisons, brought to light a series of extortions and cruelties practised by the jailers towards the unfortunate debtors in their charge, which now appear scarcely credible, but which were not only true, but had been practised continually for more than a century by these monsters, who had gone on unchecked from bad to worse, until this commission disclosed atrocities which induced the House of Commons to address the King, desiring he would prosecute the wardens and jailers for cruelty and extortion, and they were committed prisoners to Newgate.

Hogarth has chosen for the subject of one of

THE OLD FLEET PRISON.

his most striking pictures the examination of the acting warden of the Fleet—Thomas Bambridge —before a Committee of the House of Commons. In the foreground of the picture a wretched prisoner explains the mode by which his hands and neck were fastened together by metal clamps. Some of the Committee are examining other instruments of torture, in which the heads and necks of prisoners were screwed, and which seem rather to belong to the dungeons of the Inquisition than to a debtors' prison in the heart of London. Bambridge and his satellites had used these tortures to extort fees or bribes from the unfortunate debtors; at the same time allowing full impunity to the dishonest, whose cash he shared. At the conclusion of the investigation, the House unanimously came to the conclusion that he had wilfully permitted several debtors to escape; had been guilty of the most notorious breaches of trust, great extortions, and the highest crimes and misdemeanours in the execution of his office; that he had arbitrarily and unlawfully loaded with irons, put into dungeons, and destroyed, prisoners for debt under his charge, treating them in the most barbarous and cruel manner, in high violation and contempt of the laws of the kingdom. Yet this wretch, probably by means of the cash he had accumulated in his cruel extortions, managed to escape justice, dying a few years afterwards, not as he might and ought to have done, at Tyburn, but by his own hands.

When the Commissioners paid their first and unexpected visit to the Fleet prison, they found an unfortunate baronet, Sir William Rich, confined in a loathsome dungeon, and loaded with irons, because he had given some slight offence to Bambridge. Such was the fear this man's cruelty excited, that a poor Portuguese, who had been manacled and shackled in a filthy dungeon for months, on being examined before the Commissioners, and surmising wrongly, from something said, that Bambridge might return to his post, 'fainted, and the blood started out of his mouth and nose.'

Thirty-six years before this Committee gave the death-blow to the cruel persecution which awaited an unfortunate debtor, the state of this and other prisons was fully exposed in a little volume, 'illustrated with copper plates,' and termed *The Cries of the Oppressed.* The frontispiece gives the curious view of the interior of the Prison, here produced on a larger scale. It is a unique view in old London, and gives the general aspect of the place, its denizens and its visitors, in 1691, when the plate was engraved. In the foreground, some persons of the better class, who may have come to visit friends, are walking; and one male exquisite, in a wig of fashionable proportions, carries some flowers, and perhaps a few scented herbs, to prevent 'noisome smells' (which we learn were very prevalent in the jail) from injuring his health. A charitable gentleman places in the begging-box some cash for the benefit of the destitute prisoners, who are seen at grated windows clamouring for charity. In the archway which connects the forecourt with the prisoners' yard, are seated some visitors waiting their turn; a female is about to leave the jail, and walks towards the jailer, seated on the opposite bench, who bears the key of the gate in his hand; the gate is provided with a grated opening, through which to examine and question applicants for admission; the wall is surmounted by a formidable row of spikes; and over these (by aid of a violent use of perspective) we see the hats of those who walk Farringdon Street, or Fleet Market, as it

was then called, the view being bounded by the old brick houses opposite the prison.

Moses Pitt, who published this now rare little volume, was at one time an opulent man. He rented from Dr Fell, Bishop of Oxford, 'the printing house called the Theatre' in the time of Charles the Second, where he commenced an Atlas in 12 vols. folio, and, as he says, 'did in the latter end of King Charles's time print great quantities of Bibles, Testaments, Commonprayers, &c., whereby I brought down the price of Bibles more than half, which did great good at that time, popery being then likely to overflow us.' His troubles began in building speculations at Westminster, in King Street, Duke Street, and elsewhere. He tells that he 'also took care to fill up all low grounds in that part of St James's Park between the bird-cages and that range of buildings in Duke Street, whose back front is toward the said park.'*

He erected a great house in Duke Street, which he let to the famed Lord Chancellor Jeffreys; but the Revolution prevented him from getting a clear title to all the ground, though Sir Christopher Wren, the King's Architect, had begun to negotiate the matter. Then creditors came on Pitt, and a succession of borrowings, and lawsuits consequent thereto, led rapidly to his incarceration in the Fleet Prison for debt.

Pitt's book is the result of communications addressed to 65 debtors' prisons in England. It is, as he says, 'a small book as full of tragedies as pages; they are not acted in foreign nations among Turks and Infidels, Papists and Idolaters, but in this our own country, by our own countrymen and relations to each other,—not acted time out of mind, by men many thousand or hundred years agone; but now at this very day by men now living in prosperity, wealth, and grandeur; they are such tragedies as no age or country can parallel.' He, among many others, narrates the case of Mr Morgan, a surgeon of Liverpool, who, being put in prison there, was ultimately reduced so low by poverty, neglect, and hunger, as to catch by a cat mice for his sustenance. On his complaining of the barbarity of his jailer, instead of redress, he was beaten and put into irons. In the Castle of Lincoln, one unfortunate, because he had asked for a purse the jailers had taken from him, he being destitute thereby, was treated to 'a ride in the jailer's coach,' as they termed it; that is, he was placed in a hurdle,

* These bird-cages gave the name still retained of 'Bird-cage walk' to the southern avenue in the park, and there Charles the Second kept his feathered favourites. The park seems to have been left in a comparatively neglected state, for Pitt says, he 'filled the low ground near Storey's Gate with garden mould, and sowed it with hay seed, where the water in moist weather stagnated, and was the cause of fogs and mists, so that thereby that part of the park is clear from fogs, and healthy. I also, at my own cost, cleansed a great part of the common shoars, not only about the said park, but Westminster also, and laid out about £12,000 in buildings, whereby I have made Westminster as healthy a place as any other part about London, and as commodious for gentry to live in, which has brought a considerable trade to that part of the town.'

with his head on the stones, and so dragged about the prison yard, ' by which ill-usage he so became not altogether so well in his intellects as formerly.' From Appleby, in Westmoreland, an unfortunate debtor writes, 'Certainly no prisoners' abuses are like ours. Our jail is but eight yards long, and four and a half in breadth, without any chimney, or place of ease; several poor prisoners have been starved and poisoned in it; for whole years they cannot have the benefit of the air, or fires, or refreshment.' It was the custom of the jailers to charge high fees for bed or lodging; to force prisoners to purchase from them all they wanted for refreshment at extortionate charges, to continually demand gratuities, and to ill-treat and torture all who would not or could not gratify their rapacity. One wretched man at St Edmundbury jail, for daring to send out of the prison for victuals, had thumbscrews put upon him, and was chained on tip-toe by the neck to the wall.

All these cruelties resulted from the easy possibility of making money. The office of prime warden was let at a large price, and the money made by forced fees. The debtor was first taken to a sponging-house, charged enormously there; if too poor to pay, removed to the prison, but subjected to high charges for the commonest necessaries. Even if he lived 'within the rules,' as the privileged houses of the neighbourhood were termed, he was always subjected to visits from jailers, who would declare his right to that little liberty forfeit unless their memory was refreshed by a fee. The Commission already alluded to remedied much of this, but still gross injustice remained in many minor instances.

The state of the prison in 1749 may be gathered from a poem, entitled ' The Humours of the Fleet,' written by a debtor, the son of Dance, the architect of old Buckingham House and of Guy's Hospital. It is 'adorned' with a frontispiece shewing the prison yard and its denizens. A new-comer is treating the jailer, cook, and others to drink; others play at rackets against the high brick-wall, which is furnished with a formidable row of spikes at right angles with it, and above that a high wooden hoarding. A pump and a tree in one corner do not obliterate the unpleasant effect of the ravens who are feeding on garbage thrown about.

The author describes the dwellers in this ' poor, but merry place,' the joviality consisting in ill-regulated, noisy companionship. Some, we are told, play at rackets, or wrestle; others stay indoors at billiards, backgammon, or whist.

' Some, of low taste, ring hand-bells, direful noise !
　And interrupt their fellows' harmless joys ;
　Disputes more noisy now a quarrel breeds,
　And fools on both sides fall to loggerheads :
　Till wearied with persuasive thumps and blows,
　They drink to friends, as if they ne'er were foes.'

The prisoners had a mode of performing rough justice among themselves on disturbers of the general peace, by taking the offending parties to the common yard, and well drenching them beneath the pump !

' Such the amusement of this merry jail,
　Which you'll not reach, if friends or money fail :

' For ere its three-fold gates it will unfold,
The destined captive must produce some gold ;
Four guineas at the least for different fees
Completes your *Habeas*, and commands the keys ;
Which done and safely in, no more you're bled.
If you have cash, you'll find a friend and bed ;
But that deficient, you'll but ill betide,
Lie in the hall, perhaps, or common side.'

' The chamberlain' succeeded the jailers, and he expected a ' tip,' or gratuity, to shew proper lodgings ; a ' master's fee,' consisting of the sum of £1 2s. 8d., had then to be paid for the privilege of choosing a decent room. This, however, secured nothing, as the wily chamberlain,

' When paid, puts on a most important face,
　And shows *Mount-scoundrel* as a charming place.'

This term was applied to wretched quarters on the common side at the top of the building, where no one stayed if he could avoid it ; hence ' this place is first empty, and the chamberlain commonly shews this to raise his price upon you for a better.' A fee of another half-guinea induces him to shew better rooms, for which half-a-crown a-week rent has to be paid ; unless ' a chum' or companion be taken who shares the charge, and sponges on the freshman ; for generally ' the chum' was an old denizen, who made the most of new-comers. The one our author describes seems to have startled him by his appearance ; but the chamberlain comforts him with the assurance :

' The man is now in dishabille and dirt,
　He shaves to-morrow though, and turns his shirt.'

The first night is spent over a heavy supper and drinking bout, ordered lavishly by the old stager and jailers, and paid for by the new-comer.

One custom may be noted in the words of this author as a ' wind-up to a day in prison.' He tells us that ' Watchmen repeat *Who goes out ?* from half an hour after nine, till St Paul's clock strikes ten, to give visitors notice to depart ; when the last stroke is given, they cry *All told ;* at which time the gates are locked, and nobody suffered to go out upon any account.'

The cruelties which had been repeatedly complained of from 1586 by the poor prisoners, who charged the wardens with murder and other misdemeanours, continued unchecked in the midst of London until 1727. The simpler, but still unwarrantable extortions, which we have described from Dance's poem, as existing in 1749, continued with very little modification until the suppression of the jail in 1844. The same may be said of other debtors' jails in the kingdom. All good rules were abandoned or made of no avail by winking at their breakage. Thus, spirituous liquors were not permitted to be brought in by visitors for prisoners' use, yet dram-shops were established in the prison itself, under the name of ' tape shops,' where liquor at an advanced charge might be bought, under the name of *white* or *red tape*, as gin, rum, or brandy was demanded. In the same way game, not allowed to be sold outside, was publicly sold inside the prison's walls. Any luxuries or extravagances might be obtained by a dishonest or rich prisoner. The rules for living outside were equally lax, and though the person who availed himself of the privilege was supposed to never go beyond their precincts, country trips were often taken, *if paid for :* one of the denizens of the rules of the King's Bench, a sporting character of the name of Hetherington, drove the coach from London to Birmingham for more than a month consecutively, during the illness of his friend the coachman, for whom he often ' handled the ribbons.' On festival occasions, such as Easter Monday, the prisoners invited their friends, who came in shoals ; and 'the mirth and fun grew fast and furious' during the day ; hopping in sacks, footraces, and other games were indulged in, and on one occasion a mock election was got up within the walls, which has been immortalized on canvas by the artist, B. R. Haydon, then in the King's Bench for debt. It was considered one of his best works, was purchased for £500 by King George the Fourth, and is now at Windsor Castle.

DR GREGORY AND THE MODERATE MAN.

Dr James Gregory, Professor of the Practice of Physic in the University of Edinburgh, was a man of vigorous talents and great professional eminence. He was what is called a *starving doctor*, and, not long after his death, the following anecdote was put in print, equally illustrative of this part of the learned professor's character, and of the habits of life formerly attributed to a wealthy western city :

Scene—*Doctor's Study.*　Enter *a grave-looking Glasgow Merchant.*

Patient.—Good morning, doctor ; I'm just come to Edinburgh about some law business, and I thought, when I was here at any rate, I might just as weel tak your advice, sir, anent my trouble.

Doctor.—And pray what may your trouble be, my good sir ?

P.—'Deed, doctor, I'm no very sure ; but I'm thinking it's a kind of weakness that makes me dizzy at times, and a kind of pinkling about my stomach—I'm just no right.

Dr.—You're from the west country, I should suppose, sir ?

P.—Yes, sir, from Glasgow.

Dr.—Ay. Pray, sir, are you a gourmand—a glutton ?

P.—God forbid, sir ! I'm one of the plainest men living in all the west country.

Dr.—Then, perhaps, you're a drunkard ?

P.—No, doctor ; thank God, no one can accuse me of that : I'm of the Dissenting persuasion, doctor, and an elder ; so ye may suppose I'm nae drunkard.

Dr.—(*Aside*—I'll suppose no such thing, till you tell me your mode of life.) I'm so much puzzled with your symptoms, sir, that I should wish to hear in detail what you eat and drink. When do you breakfast, and what do you take to it ?

P.—I breakfast at nine o'clock. I tak a cup of coffee, and one or two cups of tea ; a couple of eggs, and a bit of ham or kipper'd salmon, or may be both, if they're good, and two or three rolls and butter.

Dr.—Do you eat no honey, or jelly, or jam, to breakfast ?

P.—O yes, sir ; but I don't count that as anything.

Dr.—Come, this is a very moderate breakfast. What kind of dinner do you make ?

P.—Oh, sir, I eat a very plain dinner indeed. Some soup, and some fish, and a little plain roast or boiled ; for I dinna care for made dishes ; I think, some way, they never satisfy the appetite.

Dr.—You take a little pudding, then, and afterwards some cheese ?

P.—Oh yes ; though I don't care much about them.

Dr.—You take a glass of ale or porter with your cheese ?

P.—Yes, one or the other, but seldom both.

Dr.—You west country people generally take a glass of Highland whisky after dinner ?

P.—Yes, we do ; it's good for digestion.

Dr.—Do you take any wine during dinner ?

P.—Yes, a glass or two of sherry ; but I'm indifferent as to wine during dinner. I drink a good deal of beer.

Dr.—What quantity of port do you drink ?

P.—Oh, very little ; not above half a dozen glasses or so.

Dr.—In the west country, it is impossible, I hear, to dine without punch ?

P.—Yes, sir ; indeed 'tis punch we drink chiefly ; but, for myself, unless I happen to have a friend with me, I never tak more than a couple of tumblers or so, —and that's moderate.

Dr.—Oh, exceedingly moderate, indeed ! You then, after this slight repast, take some tea, and bread and butter ?

P.—Yes, before I go to the counting-house to read the evening letters.

Dr.—And, on your return, you take supper, I suppose ?

P.—No, sir, I canna be said to tak supper ; just something before going to bed : a rizzer'd haddock, or a bit of toasted cheese, or half a hundred oysters, or the like o' that ; and, may be, two-thirds of a bottle of ale ; but I tak no regular supper.

Dr.—But you take a little more punch after that ?

P.—No, sir ; punch does not agree with me at bedtime. I tak a tumbler of warm whisky toddy at night ; it's lighter to sleep on.

Dr.—So it must be, no doubt. This, you say, is your every-day life ; but, upon great occasions, you perhaps exceed a little ?

P.—No, sir, except when a friend or two dine with me, or I dine out, which, as I am a sober family man, does not often happen.

Dr.—Not above twice a-week ?

P.—No ; not oftener.

Dr.—Of course you sleep well, and have a good appetite ?

P.—Yes, sir, thank God, I have ; indeed, any wee harl o' health that I hae is about mealtime.

Dr.—(Assuming a severe look, knitting his brows, and lowering his eyebrows.) Now, sir, you are a very pretty fellow, indeed ; you come here and tell me that you are a moderate man, and I might have believed you, did I not know the nature of the people in your part of the country ; but, upon examination, I find, by your own shewing, that you are a most voracious glutton : you breakfast in the morning in a style that would serve a moderate man for dinner ; and, from five o'clock in the afternoon, you undergo one almost uninterrupted loading of your stomach till you go to bed. This is your moderation ! You told me, too, another falsehood—you said you were a sober man ; yet, by your own shewing, you are a beer swiller, a dram-drinker, a wine-bibber, and a guzzler of Glasgow punch,—a liquor, the name of which is associated, in my mind, only with the ideas of low company and beastly intoxication. You *tell* me you eat indigestible suppers, and swill toddy to force sleep —I *see* that you chew tobacco. Now, sir, what human stomach can stand this ? Go home, sir, and leave off your present course of riotous living—take some dry toast and tea to your breakfast—some plain meat and soup for dinner, without adding to it anything to spur on your flagging appetite ; you may take a cup of tea in the evening, but never let me hear of haddocks and toasted cheese, and oysters, with their accompaniments of ale and toddy at night; give up chewing that vile narcotic, nauseous abomination, and there are some hopes that your stomach may recover its tone, and you be in good health like your neighbours.

P.—I'm sure, doctor, I'm very much obliged to you —(taking out a bunch of bank-notes)—I shall endeavour to——

Dr.—Sir, you are not obliged to me—put up your money, sir. Do you think I'll take a fee from you for telling you what you knew as well as myself? Though you are no physician, sir, you are not altogether a fool. You have read your Bible, and must know that drunkenness and gluttony are both sinful and dangerous; and, whatever you may think, you have this day confessed to me that you are a notorious glutton and drunkard. Go home, sir, and reform, or, take my word for it, your life is not worth half a year's purchase.

[*Exit Patient, dumbfounded, and looking blue.*
Dr.—(*Solus.*) Sober and temperate! Dr Watt tried to live in Glasgow, and make his patients live moderately, and purged and bled them when they were sick; but it would not do. Let the Glasgow doctors prescribe beefsteaks and rum punch, and their fortune is made.

APRIL 3.

Sts Agape, Chionia, and Irene, martyrs, 304 St Ulpian, of Tyre, martyr. St Nicetias, abbot, 824. St Richard, 1253, *Dover.*

Born.—Richard II., King of England, 1366, *Bordeaux ;* Rev. George Herbert (religious poetry), 1593, *Montgomery Castle ;* Roger Rabutin, Count de Bussy, 1618, *Epiry ;* Washington Irving, American miscellaneous writer, 1783, *New York ;* Rev. Dionysius Lardner, scientific and miscellaneous writer, 1793, *Dublin.*

Died.—Prince Arthur, Duke of Brittany, English prince, murdered, 1203, *Rouen ;* John Napier of Merchiston, inventor of logarithms, 1617, *Merchiston ;* Edward, Marquis of Worcester, 1667, *Raglan ;* Jacques Ozanam, French mathematical writer, 1717, *Paris ;* Dr John Berkenhout (medical and scientific writings), 1791.

PRINCE ARTHUR.

A peculiar interest seems to attach itself to the fate of most of the princes known in history by the name of Arthur, and none of them has attracted more general sympathy than the youthful nephew of Richard Cœur de Lion, the manner of whose death is itself a subject of mysterious doubt. This sympathy is probably in some measure owing to the touching scene in which he has been introduced by Shakspeare.

In the order of succession of the five sons of King Henry II., Geoffrey Duke of Brittany intervened between Richard and John. Geoffrey was accidentally slain in a tournament, leaving his wife Constance advanced in pregnancy, and she subsequently, in 1187, gave birth to Prince Arthur, who was acknowledged as the successor to his father as Duke of Brittany. On the death of King Richard, in 1199, Arthur, then twelve years of age, was no doubt his rightful heir, but John, as is well known, seized at once upon the crown of England, and people in general seem to

have preferred, according to principles which were strictly constitutional, the prince who could govern to the one who was for the time incapacitated by his age. But the barons of Anjou, Touraine, and Maine espoused the cause of Arthur, and took the oath of allegiance to him and to his mother Constance as his guardian. Cœur de Lion, at the time of his death, had just signed a truce with the King of France, Philippe Auguste, and it was to this monarch that Constance carried her young son when the territories of the barons who supported him were invaded and barbarously ravaged by King John and his mercenary troops. Philippe, who was waiting eagerly for the opportunity of depriving the King of England of his continental possessions, embraced the cause of Arthur with the utmost zeal, and not only sent troops to assist the barons of Anjou and Brittany, but invaded Normandy. It was soon, however, evident that Philippe was fighting for himself and not for Arthur, and the barons of Arthur's party became so certain of his designs, that their leader, Guillaume des Roches, seneschal of Anjou, effected a reconciliation with King John, and succeeded in carrying the young prince away from the court of France. This was hardly done, when the seneschal learnt from secret information that John was acting treacherously, and only sought to gain possession of his nephew in order to poison him; and he carried Arthur by night to Angers, and placed himself again under the protection of Philippe. The latter made peace with the king of England at the beginning of the year 1200, when Arthur was induced by the French king to remain contented with the Duchy of Brittany, and renounce all claims to the crown of England, as well as to the continental provinces of Normandy, Maine, Anjou, Touraine, and Poitou.

Affairs remained in this position until the beginning of the year 1202, when Philippe Auguste resumed his hostile designs against Normandy, and again put forward the claims of Arthur, who was now fifteen years old. As the continental barons were nearly all ready to rise against King John, Philippe immediately invested Arthur with the counties of Poitou, Anjou, Maine, and Touraine, and sent him with an escort into Poitou to head the insurrection there; but, unfortunately, the young prince was persuaded to make an attempt upon Mirabeau, and he was there surprised by King John, on the 1st of August 1202, and captured with all the barons who accompanied him. Arthur was carried a prisoner to Falaise, from whence he was subsequently transferred to Rouen, and nothing further is satisfactorily known of him, although there is no doubt that he was murdered.

Many accounts of the circumstances of the murder, probably all more or less apocryphal, were afterwards current, and some of them have been preserved by the old chroniclers. According to that given by Ralph of Coggeshall, John, at the suggestion of some of his evil councillors, resolved on putting out Arthur's eyes, and sent some of his creatures to Falaise, to execute this barbarous design in his prison; but it was prevented by Hubert de Burgh, then governor of

Falaise, who took time to communicate personally with the king. In consequence of Hubert's humanity, Arthur was removed from Falaise to Rouen, where, on the 3rd of April 1203, he was taken from the tower in which he was confined, placed in a boat where King John with his esquire, Peter de Maulac, waited for him, and there murdered by the latter at the king's command. According to another version, Maulac shrunk from the deed, and John murdered his nephew with his own hand. This account is evidently the foundation of part of the story adapted by Shakspeare, who, however, strangely lays the scene at Northampton. Roger de Wendover, who is quite as good authority as the abbot of Coggeshall, gives an entirely different explanation of the cause of the prisoner's removal from Falaise to Rouen. He says that 'after some lapse of time, King John came to the castle of Falaise, and ordered his nephew Arthur to be brought into his presence. When he appeared, the King addressed him kindly, and promised him many honours, requiring him to separate himself from the French king, and to adhere to the party of himself, as his lord and uncle. But Arthur illadvisedly replied with indignation and threats, and demanded of the King that he should give up to him the kingdom of England, with all the territories which King Richard possessed at the time of his death; and, inasmuch as all those possessions belonged to him by hereditary right, he affirmed with an oath that unless King John immediately restored the territories aforesaid to him, he should never enjoy peace for any length of time. The King was much troubled at hearing these words, and gave orders that Arthur should be sent to Rouen, to be imprisoned in the new tower there, and placed under close guard; but shortly afterwards the said Arthur suddenly disappeared.' Popular tradition was from a rather early period almost unanimous in representing the murder as having been perpetrated by the king's own hand; but this perhaps arose more out of hatred to John's memory than from any accurate knowledge of the truth. Arthur was sixteen years of age at the time of his death.

___

LORD WORCESTER AND HIS 'CENTURY OF INVENTIONS.'

In respect of his pursuits and tastes, Edward, Marquis of Worcester, stands much isolated in the British peerage, being a speculative mechanical inventor. His little book, called *A Century of Inventions*, is one of the most curious in English literature. It appears to have been written in 1655, and strictly consists of descriptions of a hundred projects, as its title imports; none of them, however, so explicit as to enable a modern adventurer to carry them out in practice. The objects in view were very multifarious. Secret writing, by cipher, or by peculiar inks; telegraphs or semaphores; explosive projectiles that would sink any ship; ships that would resist any explosive projectiles; floating gardens for English rivers; automaton figures; machines for dredging harbours; an engine to raise ships for repair; an instrument for teaching perspective; a method of fixing shifting sands on the seashore; a cross-

bow that will discharge two arrows at once; an endless watch, that never wants winding up; a key that will fasten all the drawers of a cabinet by one locking; a large cannon that could be shot six times in a minute; flying machines; a brass mould to cast candles; hollow-handled pocket-combs, knives, forks, and spoons, for carrying secret papers; calculating machines for addition and subtraction; a pistol to discharge a dozen times with once loading; an apparatus for lighting its own fire and candle at any predetermined hour of the night; a complete portable ladder, which, taken out of the pocket, may be fastened to a point a hundred feet high; a way to make a boat work against wind and tide; nothing came amiss to the mechanical Marquis. Knowing to how extraordinary a degree many of those projects foreshadow inventions which have brought renown to other men in later days, it is tantalizing to be unable to discover how far he had really proceeded in any one of them. It is a generally accepted fact, however, that he had worked out in his mind a clear conception of a steam-engine (as we should now call it); indeed he is believed to have set a model of a steam-engine at work shortly before his death. He employed, too, a German artizan, Casper Kaltoff, for many years in constructing models and new machines of various kinds.

A brave, loyal, and worthy man was the Marquis of Worcester. Like many other noble cavaliers, he impoverished himself in befriending Charles the First; and, like them again, he failed in obtaining any recompense from Charles the Second. He was the owner and occupier of Raglan Castle during the troubles of the Civil War; and it is to him that the incident relates (carefully told ever since to visitors to the Castle), concerning the practical aid given by his ingenuity to his loyalty. He had constructed some hydraulic engines and wheels for conveying water from the moat to the top of the great tower. Some of the Roundheads approaching, the Marquis resolved to startle them by a display of his engineering powers. He gave private orders to set the water works in play. 'There was such a roaring,' he afterwards wrote, 'that the poor silly men stood so amazed as if they had been half dead; and yet they saw nothing. At last, as the plot was laid, up comes a man staring and running, crying out before he came to them, "Look to yourselves, my masters, for the lions are got loose." Whereupon the searchers gave us such a loose, that they tumbled so over one another down the stairs, that it was thought one half of them had broke their necks: never looking behind them till they were sure they had got out of the Castle.'

___

THE POET LAUREATESHIP.

On April 3rd, 1843, we find Sir Robert Peel writing to Wordsworth, kindly urging him to overcome his reluctance, and become poet-laureate. The bard of Rydal Mount being seventy-four, feared he might be unfit to undertake the tasks expected of him; but on being assured it would be a sinecure as far as he chose, he accepted the office. We are most of us aware that this office was, in no remote times, one of real duty, an ode being expected on the king's birthday and other occasions. According to modern conceptions, a genuine poet conferred as much honour on the office, as the office upon him. Originally, the title inferred a great public honour to some special bard. placing him high above his fellows. Among the ancients, as late as the Emperor Theodosius, the ceremony of crowning with the laurel wreath was actually performed; even in modern times, from so far back as the thirteenth century, Abbé Resnel conjectures the custom was revived and retained in Italy and Germany. In England and France it does not seem to have been at any time regularly established.

Petrarch, in Italy, wore his laurel with true dignity. The curious formula used at his coronation has been preserved. 'We, count and senator, for us and our college, declare Francis Petrarch great poet and historian; and for a special mark of his quality of poet, we have placed with our hands on his head a *crown of laurel*, granting to him by the tenor of these presents, and by the authority of King Robert, of the senate, and the people of Rome, in the poetic as well as in the historic art, and generally in whatsoever relates to the said arts, as well in this holy city as elsewhere, our free and entire power of reading, disputing, and interpreting all ancient books, to make new ones, *and compose poems, which God assisting, shall endure from age to age.*'

It was not all Francis Petrarch's successors who composed such poems. Mad Querno, 'Antichrist of wit,' laureate of Leo X., wrote twenty thousand verses, but no god assisted, save Bacchus, and the wits twisted slily among the laurels vine-leaf and cabbage-leaf.

Chaucer is often called poet-laureate. He held sundry appointments under Edward III., Richard II., and Henry IV., and several curious grants were made to him, among which was a pipe of wine. Edward III. made him comptroller of the custom of wool, but not in the way of sinecure: on the contrary, we find it enjoined 'that the said Geffrey write with his own hand his rolls touching the said office, and continually reside there, and do and execute all things pertaining to the said office in his own proper person, and not by his substitute.'

The Reverend 'Master Skelton, poet laureate,' as he terms himself, figured in Henry VIII.'s time as a most hearty reviler of bad customs and worse clergy. To wit:—

'Salt-fish, stock-fish, nor herring,
It is not for your wearing,
Nor in holy Lenten season
Ye will neither beanes ne peason,
But ye looke to be let loose
To a pygge or to a goose,
Your george not endewed,
Without a capon stewed.'

And much more, equally scurrilous, till at last Wolsey punished him for alluding to his (Wolsey's) 'greasy genealogy.'

The office of laureate should never be more than an honour; or, at least, it should never

472

impose taskwork. Only so far as the laureate feels, let him speak. If the true poet endeavour to offer such a sacrifice on the altar of public taste, as to sing of unheroic or unpoetic events, the spirit of inspiration will go up from him in the smoke, like the angel at Manoah's offering. Let any one read through Warton's Birthday Odes, for June 4, in regular succession, and he will discover the difficulties of this jobbing. Of many national effusions, practically imposed or prompted by his office, Tennyson cannot shew one,—nor even the ode to the Duke,—worthy to stand by the side of his other noble poems.

APRIL 4.

St Isidore, bishop of Seville, 606.   St Plato, abbot, 813.

Born.—John Jackson, learned English divine, 1686, *Thirsk, Yorkshire.*

Died.—St Ambrose, 397, *Milan;* Pope Nicolas IV., 1292; Sir Robert Naunton, 1634; Simon Episcopius (Bisschop), Dutch theological writer, 1643, *Amsterdam;* Robert Ainsworth (Latin Dictionary), 1743, *Poplar;* Oliver Goldsmith, poet and miscellaneous writer, 1774, *Temple, London;* Lloyd Kenyon, Lord Chief Justice of England, Lord Kenyon, 1802, *Bath;* Lalande, French mathematician, 1807; Andrea Massena, Duke of Rivoli, Marshal of France, 1817, *Ruel;* Rev. John Campbell, missionary to South Africa, 1840.

SAINT AMBROSE AND THE EMPEROR.

The election of Ambrose to the bishopric of Milan is perhaps unequalled in the singularity of all its circumstances. He was carefully educated when young for the civil service, became an advocate, and practised with such success that, at the age of thirty-one, he was appointed governor of Liguria. In this capacity he had resided five years at Milan, and was renowned for his prudence and justice, when Auxentius the bishop died, A.D. 374.

The city was at that time divided between Arians and Orthodox. Party disputes ran high respecting the election of a new bishop, and a tumult appeared imminent, when Ambrose, hearing of these things, hastened to the church where the people had assembled, and exhorted them to peace and submission to the laws. His speech was no sooner ended than an infant's voice was heard in the crowd, 'Ambrose is Bishop.' The hint was taken at once, and the whole assembly cried out, 'Ambrose shall be the man!' The contending factions agreed, and a layman whose pursuits seemed to exclude him altogether from the notice of either party, was suddenly elected by universal consent. It was in vain he refused, affected an immoral course of life, and twice fled from the city: the emperor seconded the choice of the people, and Ambrose was at length compelled to yield. Valentinian gave thanks to God that it had pleased Him to make choice of the very person to take care of men's souls whom he had himself before appointed to preside over their temporal concerns. And Ambrose, having given all his property to the church and the poor, reserving only an annual income for his sister Marcellina, set about his new duties with a determination to honestly discharge them.

The most striking instance of the manner in which he executed this resolve is found in his treatment of the Emperor Theodosius. This august person was naturally hot tempered. And it so happened that, in a popular tumult in Thessalonica, A.D. 390, Botheric, the imperial officer, was slain. This was too much for the emperor's forbearance, and he ordered the sword to be let loose upon them. Seven thousand were massacred in three hours, without distinction and without trial. Ambrose wrote him a faithful letter, reminding him of the charge in the prophecy, that, if the priest does not warn the wicked, he shall be answerable for it. 'I love you,' he says, 'I cherish you, I pray for you, but blame not me if I give the preference to God.' On these principles he refused to admit Theodosius into the church at Milan. The emperor pleaded that David had been guilty of murder and adultery. 'Imitate him then,' said the zealous bishop, 'in his repentance as well as his sin.' He submitted, and kept from the church eight months. Ruffinus, the master of the offices, now undertook to persuade the bishop to admit him. He was at once reminded of the impropriety of his interference, inasmuch as he, by his evil counsels, had been in some measure the author of the massacre. 'The emperor,' he said, 'is coming.' 'I will hinder him,' said Ambrose, 'from entering the vestibule: yet if he will play the king, I shall offer him my throat.' Ruffinus returned and informed the emperor. 'I will go,' he exclaimed, 'and receive the refusal which I desire:' and as he approached the bishop, he added, 'I come to offer myself to submit to what you prescribe.' Ambrose enjoined him to do public penance, and to suspend the execution of all capital warrants for thirty days in future, that the ill effects of intemperate anger might be prevented.

The writings of St Ambrose, many of which breathe a touching eloquence, were collected in two volumes, folio, 1691.

OLIVER GOLDSMITH.

That exhibition of serio-comic sprightliness and naïve simplicity which gives a peculiar character to Goldsmith's works, shewed itself equally in his life. In his writings it amuses us. But when we think of the poverty, and hardship, and drudgery which fell to his lot, we cannot smile at the man with the same hearty goodwill. Still the ludicrous element remains. Even in his outward appearance his biographer, Mr Forster, has to admit it, and make the best of it. 'Though his complexion was pale, his face round and pitted with the small-pox, and a somewhat remarkable projection of his forehead and his upper lip suggested excellent sport for the caricaturists, the expression of intelligence, benevolence, and good humour predominated over every disadvantage, and made the face extremely pleasing.'

At school and at college he shewed all the symptoms of a dunce, and many of those of a fool. Then, after idling some time, he succeeded

in failing utterly in a very fair number of attempts to set up in life, as much out of sheer negligence and simplicity, as incapacity; and when his friends had pretty well given him up, he set out, with a flute in his hand, and nothing in his pocket, to see the world. He passed through many countries, and much privation; and finally returned, bringing with him a degree in medicine, some medical knowledge, and that wide experience of manners which ever fed his genius more than reading or books. Now he became usher in a school, apothecary's journeyman, poor physician, press-corrector, and other things, alternately or simultaneously starving and suffering: thought of going to Mount Sinai to interpret the inscriptions; but at length became reviewer. He made one attempt more to escape from bondage; got an appointment as medical officer at Coromandel; lost it; and then finally settled down to the profession of author. Fame soon came to the side of Sorrow, and Pleasure often joined them; till death, fifteen years later, took him away by disease arising from sedentary habits. He was buried in the Temple burial-ground, and Johnson wrote the Latin epitaph in Westminster Abbey.

Undoubtedly, Goldsmith's greatest works are those which were labours of love. *The Traveller* and *The Deserted Village* stand first, with their graceful simplicity, without humour. Then, *The Vicar of Wakefield*, which joins shrewd humour to simplicity. His comedies proved most remunerative. In all his works, self-chosen, or dictated by necessity, his style remains attractive.

He preserved his independence and honesty through much drudgery and many vexations, which tried him even in his best days. Yet, after all the laments about the sufferings of authors, many of his might by common sense and prudence have been avoided. He failed in these. He was all innocence, humour, good-nature, and sensibility. To be a simpleton is not a necessary qualification of an author. Goldsmith has accurately sketched himself: 'Fond of enjoying the present, careless of the future, his sentiments those of a man of sense, his actions those of a fool; of fortitude able to stand unmoved at the bursting of an earthquake, yet of sensibility *to be affected by the breaking of a tea-cup.*' Prosperity added to his difficulties as well as to his enjoyments: the more money he had, the more thoughtlessly he expended, wasted, or gave it away.

Yet his heart was right, and right generous. He squandered his money quite as often in reckless benevolence as in personal indulgence. When at College, and in poverty, he would write ballads, and sell them for a few shillings; then give the money to some beggar on his way home. This habit continued through his life. He would borrow a guinea, to give it away; he would give the clothes off his own bed. In private life, or at the famous *Literary Club*, where he figured both in great and little, in wisdom, wit, and blue silk, his friends, who laughed at him, loved and valued him. Edmund Burke, the gentle Reynolds, Johnson, Hogarth,—all but jealous Bozzy,—delighted in him. When he died, it was 'Poor Goldy!' Burke wept. Reynolds laid his work aside. Johnson was touched to the quick : ' Let not his failings be remembered : he was a very great man.'

His failings have been dragged to light more than need have been. He spoke out every thought, and so occasionally foolish ones. There-fore Garrick (though but in joke) must write this :

'Here lies Nolly Goldsmith, for shortness called Noll,
Who wrote like an angel, but talked like poor Poll.'

He liked to appear to advantage on great occa-sions, and had a child's eye for colour ; so his tailor's bills have been hunted up and paraded, revealing glimpses of ' Tyrian bloom, satin-grain, and garter-blue silk breeches ' (£8, 2s. 7d.) ; or when Bozzy gives a dinner, ' a half dress suit of ratteen, lined with satin, a pair of silk stocking breeches, and a pair of bloom-coloured ditto,' costing £16. Yet a man less unsophisticated could easily have concealed such weaknesses as Goldsmith indulged.

One thing is strange. Not a trace of love or love-making in forty-six years, save one obscure tale of his being with difficulty dissuaded from 'carrying off and marrying' a respectable needle-woman, probably as a kindness ; and a guess that he might have had that sort of fancy for a young lady friend, at whose house he often visited, and who, when he was dead, begged, with her sister, a lock of his brown hair.

LADY BURLEIGH AND HER THREE LEARNED SISTERS.

In the reign of Elizabeth, and even from an earlier period, it was customary for ladies to receive a classical education. The ' maiden Queen' herself was a good Greek scholar, and could speak Latin with fluency. But amongst the learned ladies of that day, the four daughters of Sir Anthony Cooke, the preceptor of Edward VI., were pre-eminent. Mildred, his eldest daughter, married William Cecil, afterwards Lord Burleigh. She was equally remarkable for learning, piety, and benevolence. She could read with critical accuracy Hebrew, Greek, and Latin. She presented a Hebrew Bible to the University of Cambridge, and accompanied it with a letter written by herself in Greek. She had not only read most of the Greek and Latin classics, but the chief works in those languages by early Christian writers, from some of which she made very able English translations. She was a general patroness of literature ; she supported two poor students at St John's College, Cambridge ; made large presents of books to both universities, and provided various facilities for the encouragement of learning. Amongst her acts of benevolence, she provided the Haberdashers' Company with the means of lending to six poor tradesmen twenty pounds each, every two years : and a similar charity for the poor people of Waltham and Cheshunt in Hertfordshire ; four times every year she relieved all the poor prisoners in London ; and expended large sums in other acts of bene-volence and charity, far too numerous to specify. She lived forty-three years with her husband, who speaks of her death, which occurred 4th

April 1589, as the severest blow he had ever experienced, but says, ' I ought to comfort myself with the remembrance of hir manny vertuouss and godly actions wherein she contynued all her liff.'

Anna, the second daughter of Sir Anthony Cooke, was also a good Latin and Greek scholar, and well acquainted with some of the continental languages. At an early age she translated twenty-five sermons from the Italian of Barnar-dine Ochine, which were published in an octavo volume. From the Latin she translated Bishop Jewel's *Apology for the Church of England*, which was so faithfully and skilfully executed, that the bishop, on revising the manuscript, did not find it necessary to alter a single word. On sending her translation of the *Apology* to the bishop, she wrote him a letter in Greek, which he answered in the same language. She married Sir Nicholas Bacon, and was the mother of the famous Sir Anthony Bacon, and the still more famous Francis Bacon, created Lord Verulam.

Elizabeth, the third daughter of Sir Anthony Cooke, was equally remarkable for her learning. She wrote epitaphs and elegies on her friends and relations in Greek, in Latin, and in English verse ; and published an English translation from a French work. She married, first, Sir Thomas Hobby, of Bisham, Berks, and accom-panied him to France, when he went thither as ambassador from Queen Elizabeth, and where he died in 1566. She brought his body back to Bisham, and, building there a sepulchral chapel, buried him and his brother Sir Philip therein, and wrote epitaphs on them in Greek, Latin, and English. She next married John, Lord Russell, and surviving him, wrote epitaphs on him in the same languages, for his tomb in Westminster Abbey.

Katherine, fourth daughter of Sir Anthony Cooke, was famous for her scholarship in Hebrew, Greek, and Latin ; and for considerable talent in poetry. She married Sir Henry Killegrew, and was buried in the Church of St Thomas the Apostle, in Vintry Yard, London, where a hand-some monument was erected to her memory, in-scribed with the following epitaph, written by herself :—

' Dormio nunc Domino, Domini virtute resurgam ;
Et σωτῆρα meum carne videbo mea.
Mortua ne dicar, fruitur pars altera Christo :
Et surgam Capiti, Tempore, tota mea.'

' To God I sleep, but I in God shall rise,
And, in the flesh, my Lord and Saviour see.
Call me not dead, my soul to Christ is fled,
And soon both soul and body joined shall be.'

There is a curious ghost story about Lady Russell. She was buried at Bisham by the remains of her first husband, Sir Thomas Hobby, and in the adjoining mansion still hangs her portrait, representing her in widow's weeds, and with a very pale face. Her ghost, resembling this portrait, is still supposed to haunt a certain chamber ; which is thus accounted for by local tradition. Lady Russell had by her first husband a son, who, so unlike herself, had a natural antipathy to every kind of learning, and such was his obstinate repugnance to learning to write, that he would wilfully blot over his copy-books in the most slovenly manner. This conduct so irritated his refined and intellectual mother, that to cure him of the propensity, she beat him again and again severely, till at last she beat him to death. As a punishment for her cruelty, she is now doomed to haunt the room where the fatal catastrophe happened, and as her apparition glides through the room it is always seen with a river passing close before her, in which she is ever trying, but in vain, to wash off the blood-stains of her son from her hands. It is remark-able that about twenty years ago, in altering a window-shutter, a quantity of antique copy-books were discovered pushed into the rubble between the joists of the floor, and one of these books was so covered with blots, that it fully answered the description in the story.

There is generally some ground for an old tradition. And certain it is that Lady Russell had no comfort in her sons by her first husband. Her youngest son, a posthumous child, especially caused her much trouble, and she wrote to her brother-in-law, Lord Burleigh, for advice how to treat him. This may have been the naughty boy who was flogged to death by his mamma, though he seems to have lived to near man's estate.   W. H. K.

HAYDON THE PAINTER AND TOM THUMB.

It is scarcely an exaggeration to say that poor Haydon, the historical painter, was killed by Tom Thumb. The lucky dwarf was 'the feather that broke the back' of the unhappy artist. Of that small individual it is not necessary here to say much. He was certainly, from his smallness, a great natural curiosity; nor could it be denied that, with a happy audacity, surprising in one so young, he exhibited some cleverness, and a few rather extraordinary attainments.

Haydon had from boyhood entertained a noble estimate of the province of art, and strove to rise to eminence in the highest form of painting, instead of descending to mere portraiture. The world, however, never gave him credit for such an amount of genius or ability as he believed himself to possess, although he was everywhere recognised as a remarkable and deserving artist. He was one of those men who make enemies for themselves. Conceited, obstinate, and irritable, he was always quarrelling—now with the Royal Academy, now with individuals, and gradually relapsed into the conviction that he was an ill-understood and ill-used man. In 1820 he pro-duced a large picture, 'Christ entering Jeru-salem,' and he gained a considerable sum of money by exhibiting it to shilling visitors, in London and throughout the provinces. After this, however, his troubles began; his historical pictures were too large for private mansions, and failed to meet with purchasers.

Few diaries are more sad than that which Haydon kept, and which accumulated at length to twenty six large MS. volumes. Despondency marked nearly every page. At one time he mourned over the absence of customers for his pictures; at another, of some real or fancied slight he had received from other painters, while his entries made repeated reference to debts, creditors, insolvencies, applications to friends for loans, and appeals to ministers for Government supply. One great and honourable ambition he had cherished—to illustrate the walls of the new Houses of Parliament with historical pictures; but this professional eminence was denied to him, as he believed, through unworthy favouritism.

Such was the mental condition of the unhappy painter in the early part of the year 1846, when the so-called General Tom Thumb came to Eng-land. Haydon had then just finished a large picture on which he had long been engaged, 'The Banishment of Aristides.' He hoped to redeem his fallen fortunes, and to relieve him-self of some of his debts, by exhibiting the pic-ture. He engaged a room at the Egyptian Hall in Piccadilly, under the roof where the dwarf was attracting his crowds, and sent hundreds of invitations to distinguished persons and critics to attend a private view. An entry in his diary on April 4th was 'the beginning of the end,' shewing how acutely the poor man felt his com-parative want of success:—' Opened; rain hard; only Jerrold, Baring, Fox Maule, and Hobhouse came. Rain would not have kept them away twenty-six years ago. Comparison—

1st day of "Christ entering Jerusalem,"
1820   .   .   .   .   .   £19 16 0
1st day of "Banishment of Aristides,"
1846   .   .   .   .   .   .   1 1 6

I trust in God, Amen!' Soon afterwards he wrote, 'They rush by thousands to see Tom Thumb. They push, they fight, they scream, they faint, they cry "Help!" and "Murder!" They see my bills and caravan, but do not read them; their eyes are on them, but their sense is gone. It is an insanity, a *rabies furor*, a dream, of which I would not have believed England could have been guilty.' He had exhibited his 'Aristides' as an appeal to the public against the Commis-sioners for the Houses of Parliament, who had reported slightingly of his cartoons for a series of large pictures; and now the public gave hardly any response whatever to his appeal. About a fortnight after the opening of his exhi-bition he recorded in his diary, with few but bitter words, the fact that in one week 12,000 persons had paid to see Tom Thumb, while only 133½ (the fraction being doubtless a child at half-price) paid to see the 'Aristides.' After five weeks' struggle he closed the Exhibition, with a positive loss of more than a hundred pounds; and thus, in the midst of poverty and misery, relieved only by a kind of pious tenderness which distinguished him in his domestic relations, he renewed work upon the fondly cherished series of pictures intended by him for the House of Lords. One piteous entry in his diary was to the effect—'Oh, God! let it not be presumptuous in me to call for thy bless-ing on my six works!' The end was not long delayed. One morning in June, the hapless man was found in his painting-room, prostrate in front of his picture of 'Alfred the Great and the First British Jury.' His diary, a small portrait of his wife, his prayer-book, his watch, and letters to his wife and children, were all orderly arranged; but, for the rest—a pistol and a razor had ended his earthly troubles.

MARRIAGE ARRANGEMENTS IN OLD TIMES.

Such of our ancestors as possessed rank and wealth had a very arbitrary mode of arranging the alliances of their children. So late as the reign of James I., the disposal of a young orphan heiress lay with the monarch on the throne, by whom it was generally deputed to some favourite possessed of sons to whom the marriage might be important. The union of the ward to a son of that person, or some other person chosen by him, was then inevitable. No one, hardly even the young persons themselves, appear even to have entertained a doubt that this arrangement was all in the natural and legitimate course of things. The subordination of the young in all respects to their seniors was, indeed, one of the most remarkable peculiarities of social life two or three centuries ago.

There is preserved the agreement entered into on the 4th April 1528, between Sir William Sturton, son and heir apparent of Edward Lord Sturton, on the one part, and Walter Hungerford, squire of the body to the king, on the other, for the disposal of Charles, the eldest son of the former, in marriage to one of the three daughters of the latter, Elinor, Mary, or Anne, whichever *Sir William* might choose. It was at the same time agreed that Andrew, the second son of Sir William Sturton, should marry another of the young ladies. The terms under which the covenant was made give a striking idea of the absolute rigour with which it would be carried out. Hungerford was to have the *custody of the body* of Charles Sturton, or, in case of his death, of Andrew Sturton, in order to make sure of at least one marriage being effected. On the other hand, the father of the three girls undertook to pay Sir William eight hundred pounds, two hundred 'within twelve days of the deliverance of the said Charles,' and the remainder at other specified times.

The covenant included an arrangement for the return of the money in case the young gentleman should refuse the marriage, or if by the previous decease of Sir William the wardship of his sons should fall to the crown.[*]

JOE HAINES.

Funny Joe Haines, a celebrated comedian, who flourished in the latter part of the seventeenth century, was the first to introduce the absurd, but mirth-provoking performance of delivering a speech from the back of an ass on the stage. Shuter, Liston, Wilkinson, and a host of minor celebrities have since adopted the same method of raising the laughter of an audience. When a boy, at a school in St Martin's Lane, the abilities and ready wit of Haines induced some gentlemen to send him to pursue his studies at Oxford, where he became acquainted with Sir Joseph Wilkinson; who, when appointed Secretary of State, made Joe his Latin secretary. But the wit, being incapable of keeping state secrets, soon lost this honourable situation, finding a more congenial position as one of the king's company of actors at Drury Lane. Here he was in his true element, the excellence of his acting and brilliancy of wit having the effect, in that dissolute era, of causing his society to be eagerly sought for by both men and women of high rank. The manners of the period are well indicated by the fact that a noble Duke, when going as an ambassador to France, took Haines with him as an agreeable companion. In Paris, the actor assumed a new character. Dubbing himself Count Haines, he commenced the career of sharper and swindler, which afterwards gave him a high position in the extraordinary work of Theophilus Lucas entitled *The Lives of the Gamesters*.

When he could no longer remain in France, Haines made his escape to London, and returned to the stage. Subsequently he went to Rome, in the suite of Lord Castlemaine, when that nobleman was sent by James II. on an embassy to the Pope. Here Haines professed to be a Roman Catholic, but, on his return to England, after the Revolution, he made a public recantation — sufficiently public, it must be admitted, since it was read on the stage. Nor did the indecorum of this exhibition prevent it from being one of the most popular performances of the day.

Haines was the author of but one play, entitled *The Fatal Mistake*, but he wrote many witty prologues and epilogues, and a *Satire against Brandy* has been ascribed to him. Numberless anecdotes are related of his practical jokes,

JOE HAINES ADDRESSING A THEATRICAL AUDIENCE FROM THE BACK OF AN ASS.

[*] Antiquarian Repertory, by Grose and Astle, 1809, vol. iv., p. 669.

swindling tricks, and comical adventures, but the only one fit to appear here is the following adventure with two bailiffs and a bishop.

One day Joe was arrested by two bailiffs for a debt of twenty pounds, just as the Bishop of Ely was riding by in his carriage. Quoth Joe to the bailiffs, 'Gentlemen, here is my cousin the Bishop of Ely; let me but speak a word to him, and he will pay the debt and costs.' The bishop ordered his carriage to stop, whilst Joe close to his ear whispered: 'My lord, here are a couple of poor waverers, who have such terrible scruples of conscience that I fear they will hang themselves!' 'Very well,' replied the bishop. So, calling to the bailiffs, he said—'You two men, come to me to-morrow, and I will satisfy you.' The bailiffs bowed, and went their way. Joe (tickled in the midriff, and hugging himself with his device) went his way too. In the morning the bailiffs repaired to the bishop's house. 'Well, my good men,' said his reverence, 'what are your scruples of conscience?'—'Scruples!' replied the bailiffs, 'we have no scruples; we are bailiffs, my lord, who yesterday arrested your cousin, Joe Haines, for twenty pounds. Your lordship promised to *satisfy* us to-day, and we hope you will be as good as your word.' The bishop, to prevent any further scandal to his name, immediately paid the debt and costs.

Haines's choice companion was a brother actor, named Mat Coppinger, a man of considerable abilities. Coppinger wrote a volume of *Poems, Songs, and Love Verses,* which he dedicated to the Duchess of Portsmouth, and all that can be said of them is, that they are exactly what might have been written by such a man to such a woman. Coppinger one night, after personating a mock judge in the theatre, took the road in the character of a real highwayman. The consequence was that, a few days afterwards, the unfortunate Mat found himself before a real judge, receiving the terrible sentence of death. The town was filled with indignation and dismay; for a paltry 'watch, and seven pounds in money,' the amusing Coppinger was to lose his precious life! Petitions poured in from every quarter; expressing much the same sentiments as those of ancient Pistol:

'Let gallows gape for dog, let man go free,
　And let not hemp his windpipe suffocate.'

But in vain: a stave of an old song tells us that

'Mat didn't go dead, like a sluggard in bed,
　But boldly in his shoes, died of a noose
　That he found under Tyburn Tree.'

Haines died in 1701, at the age of fifty-three. As with all the notorieties of the time, his decease was commemorated by poetical honours, as is thus testified by—

An Elegy on the Death of Mr. Joseph Haines, the late Famous Actor, in the King's Play-house.

'Lament, ye beaus and players, every one,
　The only champion of your cause is gone;
　The stars are surly, and the fates unkind,
　Joe Haines is dead, and left his ass behind.
　Ah! cruel fate, our patience thus to try,
　Must Haines depart, while asses multiply?

If nothing but a player down should go,
　There's choice enough, without great Haines the beau!
In potent glasses, when the wine was clear,
　His very looks declared his mind was there.
Awful majestic on the stage at night,
　To play, not work, was all his chief delight;
Instead of danger, and of hateful bullets,
　He liked roast beef and goose, and harmless pullets!
Here lies the famous Actor, Joseph Haines,
　Who while alive in playing took great pains,
　Performing all his acts with curious art,
　Till Death appeared, and smote him with his dart.'

LORD KENYON ON FORESTALLERS.

Considering how completely the British public is now emancipated from the illusion that there is any harm to them from what was called forestalling and regrating, it sounds strange that a judge so recent as Chief Justice Kenyon presided at various trials where punishment was inflicted for this imaginary offence. In charging a jury in the case of one Rusby, who was indicted for purchasing a quantity of oats and selling them at a profit on the same day, his lordship adverted with scorn to the doctrines of Adam Smith. 'I wish,' said he, 'Dr Smith had lived to hear the evidence of to-day. If he had been told that cattle and corn were brought to market, and there bought by a man whose purse happened to be longer than his neighbour's, so that the poor man who walks the streets and earns his daily bread by his daily labour could get none but through his hands, and at the price he chooses to demand; that it had been raised 3d., 6d., 9d., 1s., 2s., and more a quarter on the same day, would he have said there is no danger from such an offence?' On a verdict of guilty being pronounced, the judge added: 'Gentlemen, you have done your duty, and conferred a lasting obligation on your country.' Sydney Smith remarks that 'this absurdity of attributing the high price of corn to combinations of farmers and the dealings of middlemen was the common nonsense talked in the days of my youth. I remember when ten judges out of twelve laid down this doctrine in their charges to the various grand juries on their circuits.'

ONLY ONE.

Mr W. S. Gilpin, a nephew of the well-known author of various works on the picturesque, practised the business of a landscape gardener at Painesfield, East Sheen, till his death at an advanced age on the 4th April, 1843. 'When, in the course of a conversation upon the crowded state of all professions, it was casually remarked to Mr Gilpin that *his* profession at least was not numerous, he quietly remarked, "No, there is but *one.*" He afterwards admitted that there was one Pontet, a *gardener,* in Derbyshire.'—*Gentleman's Magazine,* August 1843.

James Hogg, the Ettrick Shepherd, used to relate with much humorous relish a similar anecdote of the author of *The Excursion.* At a meeting in the house of Professor Wilson, on Windermere, in the autumn of 1817, where Wordsworth, Hogg, and several other poets were present, the evening became distinguished by a remarkably brilliant bow of the nature of the aurora borealis across the heavens. The party came out to see it, and looked on for some time in admiration. Hogg remarked, 'It is a triumphal arch got up to celebrate this meeting of the poets.' He afterwards heard the future poet-laureate whispering unconsciously to himself—'Poets—poets! what does the fellow mean? Where are they?' In his conception there was but one poet present. *

* The writer oftener than once heard James Hogg relate this story.

APRIL 5.

St Tigernach, of Ireland, 550. St Becan, of Ireland, abbot, 6th century. St Gerald, abbot of Seauve, near Bordeaux, 1095. St Vincent Ferrer, of Spain, confessor, 1419.

Born.—Thomas Hobbes, philosophical writer, 1588, *Malmesbury ;* Dr Edmund Calamy, 1671, *Aldermanbury ;* Catharine I. of Russia, 1689, *Ringen.*

Died.—John Stow (history and antiquities of London), 1605, *London ;* William Lord Brounker, mathematician, P.R.S., 1684, *St Catherine's ;* Rev. William Derham, D.D., scientific writer, 1735, *Upminster ;* Sir Thomas Hanmer, Speaker of the House of Commons in the reign of Queen Anne, editor of Shakspeare, 1746 ; Danton, guillotined, 1794 ; Rev. William Gilpin, writer on scenery, 1804, *Boldre, Hampshire ;* Robert Raikes, first institutor of Sunday-schools, 1811, *Gloucester.*

JOHN STOW.

One of the most remarkable and precious preservations of the past,—a photograph, as it were, of old London,—is the well-known *Survey* of the venerable John Stow. From it we acquire a knowledge not of the topography alone, but also of the manners, habits, and customs of London and its inhabitants in the palmy days when the Lord Mayor was little less than a monarch, and Shakspeare was holding horses at the Globe Theatre on Bankside. In fact, we possess from Stow's indefatigable labours a more intimate knowledge of Queen Elizabeth's capital than we do of the same city at any other period, or, indeed, of any other city at any age of the world. Nor is the *Survey* the mere dry bones of antiquarian research. A distinguished critic has designated it as the most picturesque of narratives. The very minuteness that gave an air of ridicule to the work, causing Fuller to describe Stow as 'such a smell-feast that he cannot pass by Guildhall but his pen must taste of the good cheer therein,' renders the *Survey* all the more valuable to us now. For instance, after giving a complete account of the abbey of St Clair, he says :—

'Near adjoining to this abbey, on the south side thereof, was some time a farm belonging to the said nunnery, at which farm I myself, in my youth, have fetched many a halfpennyworth of milk, and never had less than three ale pints for a halfpenny in the summer, nor less than one ale quart for a halfpenny in the winter, always hot from the kine, as the same was milked and strained. One Trolop, and afterwards Goodman, were farmers there, and had thirty or forty kine to the pail. Goodman's son, being heir to his father's purchase, let out the ground first for the grazing of horses, and then for garden plots, and lived like a gentleman thereby.'

Here we have a part of his own autobiography, an account of the price and quality of the milk then sold in London, and the source from which the now crowded district of Goodman's Fields derived its name.

Stow was born in the parish of St. Michael's, Cornhill, and brought up to his father's business of a tailor. It is rather a singular circumstance

that Speed and Stow, the two most distinguished historians of the sixteenth century, were both tailors, which led Sir Henry Spelman to say, 'We are beholden to Mr Speed and Mr Stow for *stitching* up for us our English history.'

To unceasing industry, Stow added an unquenchable love of truth. In his earliest writings, he announced his views of historical composition. No amount of fine phrases or elegant composition, he considered, could atone for the slightest deviation from fact. 'In history,' he said, 'the chief thing that is to be desired is truth ;' and adds this rhythmical caution to the 'phrasemakers :'

'Of smooth and flattering speech,
  Remember to take heed,
For truth in plain words may be told,
  But craft a lie doth need.'

A life devoted to the study of history affords the biographer but few incidents. Stow was ever engaged in travelling on foot from place to place, in search of materials ; or employed in transcribing, translating, abstracting, and compiling the materials so collected. Nor was the painful, patient labourer allowed to live in peace. The vulgar scoffed at him, as the 'lazy pricklouse,' who would not work at his honest trade ; and the higher powers, fearing that his researches in antiquity might injure the Reformed religion, threw him into prison, and ransacked his humble dwelling. From the report of those enforcers of the law, we have a pleasant peep at his library, which consisted of 'great collections of his own for his English Chronicles, also a great sort of old books printed ; some fabulous, as *Sir Gregory Triamour*, &c., and a great parcel of old manuscript chronicles in parchment and paper ; besides miscellaneous tracts touching physic, surgery, herbs, and medical receipts ; and also fantastical popish books printed in old time, and others written in Old English on parchment.'

Such a man could never be expected to become wealthy ; accordingly we find Stow in his old age struggling with poverty. Yet his good-humour never forsook him. Being troubled with pains in his feet, he observed that his afflictions lay in the parts he had formerly made so much use of. And this elucidates a passage in the Hawthornden MSS. Ben Jonson, conversing with Drummond respecting Stow, said, 'He and I walking alone, he asked two cripples what they would have to take them to their order.'

At last, when eighty years of age, Stow received a state acknowledgment of his public services. He petitioned James I. for a licence to beg, as he himself expresses in the petition—

'A recompense for his (the petitioner's) labour and travel of forty-five years, in setting forth the *Chronicles of England*, and eight years taken up in the *Survey* of the cities of London and Westminster, towards his relief in his old age : having left his former means of living, and only employing himself for the service and good of his country.'

The prayer was granted by Letters Patent under the Great Seal, reciting that—

'Whereas our loving subject, John Stow (a very aged and worthy member of our city of

London), this five-and-forty years hath to his great charge, and with neglect of his ordinary means of maintenance (for the general good, as well of posterity as of the present age), compiled and published divers necessary books and chronicles; and therefore we, in recompense of these his painful labours, and for the encouragement to the like, have, in our Royal inclination, been pleased to grant our Letters Patent, under our great Seal of England, thereby authorizing him, the said John Stow, to collect among our loving subjects their voluntary contributions and kind gratuities.'

These Letters were granted for one year, but produced so little, that they were extended for another twelve months, one entire parish in the city of London giving the munificent sum of seven-and-sixpence. Such was the public remuneration of the man who had been useful to his country but not to himself—the reward of the incessant labours of a well-spent life—of, as Stow himself said, many a weary day's travel, and cold winter night's study.

His person and character are thus described by his literary executor, Edmond Howes:—

'He was tall of stature, lean of body and face, his eyes small and crystalline, of a pleasant and cheerful countenance; his sight and memory very good; very sober, mild, and courteous to any that required his instructions; and retained the true use of all his senses unto the day of his death, being of an excellent memory. He always protested never to have written anything either for malice, fear, or favour, nor to seek his own

STOW'S MONUMENT.

particular gain or vainglory; and that his only pains and care was to write the truth. He could never ride, but travelled on foot unto divers

cathedral churches, and other chief places of the land to search records. He was very careless of scoffers, backbiters, and detractors. He lived peacefully and died at fourscore years of age, and was buried in his parish church of St Andrew's Undershaft; whose mural monument near to his grave was there set up at the charges of Elizabeth, his wife.'

It is a curious circumstance—one which, in some countries, would be termed a miracle—that the Great Fire in 1666 spared the monument of Stow: the man from whose records alone we know what London was previous to the devouring conflagration. Independent of its interest, it is a remarkable curiosity, from its being made of terra cotta, coloured to resemble life; very few sepulchral memorials of that kind being now in existence. It represents the venerable antiquary in a sitting posture, poring over one of the three hundred and thirty-nine manuscripts from which he extracted and condensed his imperishable *Annals*.

WILTSHIRE SHEPHERDS.

John Aubrey was a native of Wiltshire, and therefore proud of its downs, which, in his odd, quaint way, he tells us, 'are the most spacious plaines in Europe, and the greatest remaines that I can hear of the smooth primitive world when it lay all under water. The turfe is of a short sweet grasse, good for the sheep. About Wilton and Chalke, the downes are intermixt with boscages, that nothing can be more pleasant, and in the summer time doe excell Arcadia in verdant and rich turfe.' Then, pursuing the image, he says, 'The innocent lives of the shepherds here doe give us a resemblance of the Golden Age. Jacob and Esau were shepherds; and Amos, one of the royall family, asserts the same of himself, for he was among the shepherds of Tecua (Tekoa) following that employment. The like, by God's own appointment, prepared Moses for a scepter, as Philo intimates in his life, when he tells us that a shepherd's art is a suitable preparation to a kingdom. The same he mentions in his Life of Joseph, affirming that the care a shepherd has over his cattle very much resembles that which a king hath over his subjects. The same St Basil, in his Homily de St Mamene, Martyre, has, concerning David, who was taken from following the ewes great with young ones to feed Israel. The Romans, the worthiest and greatest nation in the world, sprang from shepherds. The augury of the twelve vultures placed a sceptre in Romulus's hand, which held a crook before; and as Ovid says,

"His own small flock each senator did keep."

Lucretius mentions an extraordinary happinesse, and as it were divinity, in a shepherd's life:—

"Thro' shepherds' care, and their divine retreats."

And to speake from the very bottome of my heart, not to mention the integrity and innocence of shepherds, upon which so many have insisted and copiously declaimed, methinks he is much more happy in a wood that at ease contemplates the universe as his own, and in it the sunn and starrs, the pleasing meadows, shades, groves, green banks, stately trees, flowing springs, and the wanton windings of a river, fit objects for quiet innocence, than he that with fire and sword disturbs the world, and measures his possessions by the waste that lies about him.'

Then the old Wiltshire man tells us how the plains abound with hares, fallow deer, partridges, and bustards ; the fallow deer and bustards have disappeared. In this delightful part of the country is the Arcadia about Wilton which ' did no doubt conduce to the heightening of Sir Philip Sydney's phansie. He lived much in these parts, and the most masterly touches of his pastoralls he wrote here upon the spott where they were conceived. 'Twas about these purlieus that the Muses were wont to appeare to Sir Philip Sydney, and where he wrote down their dictates in his table-book, though on horseback,' and some old relations of Aubrey's remembered to have seen Sir Philip do this.

Aubrey then proceeds to trace many of the shepherds' customs of his district to the Romans, from whom the Britons received their knowledge of agriculture. The festivals at sheep-shearings he derives from the Parilia. In Aubrey's time, the Wiltshire sheepmasters gave no wages to their shepherds, but they had the keeping of so many sheep *pro ratâ*, ' soe that the shepherd's lambs doe never miscarry ;' and Plautus gives a hint of this custom amongst the Romans in his time. In Scotland, it is still the custom to pay shepherds partly in this manner. The Wiltshire antiquary goes so far as to say that the habit of his time was that of the Roman, or Arcadian shepherds, as delineated by Drayton, in his *Polyolbion*, i.e., a long white cloak with a very deep cape, which comes half way down their backs, made of the locks of the sheep. There was a sheep-crook, as we read of in Virgil and Theocritus ; a sling, a scrip, their tar box, a pipe or flute, and their dog. But since 1671 (when Aubrey wrote) they are grown so luxurious as to neglect their ancient warm and useful fashion, and go *à la mode*. T. Randolph, in an Eclogue on the Cotswold Hill games, says :

' What clod pates, Thenot, are our British swaines,
How lubber-like they loll upon the plaines !'

And, as additional evidence of their luxurious taste, Aubrey remembered that before the Civil War many of them made straw hats, which was then left off ; ' and the shepherdesses of late yeares (1680) doe begin to worke point, whereas before they did only knitt coarse stockings.' Evelyn notes that, instead of the slings, the shepherds had, in his time, a hollow iron, or piece of horn not unlike a shoeing horne, fastened to the other end of the crosier, by which they took up stones, and kept their flocks in order.

It is curious to find that the shepherds and other villagers, in Aubrey's time, took part in welcoming any distinguished visitors to their country by rustic music and pastoral singing. We read of the minister of Bishop's Cannings, an ingenious man and excellent musician, making several of his parishioners good musicians, both vocal and instrumental ; and they sung psalms in concert with the organ in the parish church. When King James I. visited Sir Edward Bayn-

ton, at Bromham, the minister entertained his Majesty, at the Bush, in Cotefield, with bucolics of his own making and composing, of four parts ; which were sung by his parishioners, who wore frocks and whips like carters. Whilst his Majesty was thus diverted, the eight bells rang merrily, and the organ was played. The minister afterwards entertained the king with a football match of his own parishioners ; who, Aubrey tells us, ' would, in those days, have challenged all England for musique, football, and ringing.' For the above loyal reception King James made the minister of Bishop's Cannings one of his chaplains in ordinary.

When Anne, Queen of James I., returned from Bath, the worthy minister received her at Shepherd-shard, with a pastoral performed by himself and his parishioners in shepherds' weeds. A copy of this song was printed, with an emblematic frontispiece of goats, pipes, sheep-hooks, cornucopias, &c. The song was set for four voices, and so pleased the queen, that she liberally rewarded the singers.

APRIL 6.

St Sixtus, pope, martyr, 2nd century. Hundred and twenty martyrs of Hadiab in Persia, 345. St Celestine, pope, 432. St Prudentius, bishop of Troyes, 861. St Celsus, archbishop of Armagh, 1129. St William, abbot of Eskille, confessor, 1203.

Born.—Jean Baptiste Rousseau, French poet, 1669, *Paris ;* James Mill, historian and political economist, 1773.

Died.—Richard I. (*Cœur-de-Lion*), King of England, 1199, *Fontevrault ;* Laura de Noves, the subject of Petrarch's amatory poetry, 1348, *Avignon ;* Sanzio Raffaelle, painter, 1520 ; Albert Dürer, artist, 1528, *Nuremberg ;* Sir Francis Walsingham, statesman, 1590, *London ;* David Blondel, French historical writer, 1655, *Amsterdam ;* Dr Richard Busby, teacher, 1695, *Westminster ;* William Melmoth, the elder, author of *The Great Importance of a Religious Life*, 1743, *Lincoln's Inn, London ;* Sir William Hamilton, British ambassador at Naples (work on Vesuvius), 1803.

RICHARD CŒUR-DE-LION.

The outlines of the history of Richard I. are tolerably well known to all readers. After a very turbulent youth during the reign of his father, Henry II., Richard succeeded to the throne of England on the 6th of July 1189, though he was only crowned on Sunday, the 3rd of September following, when his reign is considered as beginning. On the 11th of December he started for the Holy Land, and spent nearly two years on the way, engaged in a variety of adventures in the Mediterranean. At length he joined the King of France in Syria, and they took the city of Acre on the 12th of July 1192 ; but the two kings soon quarrelled, and Philip returned home, while Richard remained, performing marvellous exploits against the Saracens, until the latter end of September, when the King of England made a truce with Saladin, and embarked on his return to his own dominions. He was wrecked near Aquileia, and fell into the hands of his enemy, the Duke of Austria, who sent him prisoner to the Emperor; and the latter, as we all know, kept him in close confinement until the beginning of February 1194, when Richard's subjects paid an immense ransom for his release. The remainder of his reign was occupied chiefly in profitless wars with France; and at last, on the 6th of April 1199, this brilliant hero perished in a paltry squabble with a continental feudatory, who, having found a treasure in his own lands, refused to give more than half of it to his suzerain, who claimed the whole.

Richard Cœur-de-Lion had spent no more than a few months in his own kingdom, and he had never been anything but a burthen to his subjects; yet, for some cause or other, perhaps partly from comparison with his still more worthless brother John, the strange brilliance of his exploits, and particularly his efforts to wrest the Holy Land from the infidels, his tyranny and vices have been thrown into oblivion, and he takes the place of an imaginary hero rather than of an ordinary king. He furnishes us with the example of a king whose whole history actually became a romance within half a century after his death. The romance of Richard Cœur-de-Lion is supposed to have been composed in French, or Anglo-Norman, towards the middle of the thirteenth century, and a version of it in English verse was composed about the end of the same century, or at the beginning of the fourteenth. From this time we frequently find, even in the sober chroniclers, the incidents of the romance confounded with those of history.

This romance furnishes us with a curious instance of the ease with which history becomes perverted in popular tradition. Richard is here a mythic personage, even supernatural by his mother's side; for his father, King Henry, is represented as marrying a sort of elf-woman, daughter of the King of Antioch (of course an infidel prince), by whom he has three children, named Richard, John, and Topias, the latter a daughter. As was usual with such beings, the lady was unable to remain at the performance of Christian worship; and one day, when she was obliged to be present at the sacrament, she fled away through the roof of the church, taking with her her youngest son and her daughter, but John was dropped, and broke his thigh by the fall. Richard, the eldest son, was no sooner crowned, than he proclaimed a tournament, where he jousted with his knights in three disguises, in order to discover who was the most worthy, and he selected two, named Sir Thomas Multon and Sir Fulk Doyly, as his companions, and engaged them to go with him in the guise of palmers to see the Holy Land, preparatory to his intended crusade. After wandering through the principal countries of the East, they returned overland, still in their disguise, and one day, on their way, they put up at a tavern, and cooked themselves a goose for their dinner. When they had dined, and 'had well drunken,' which appears to have been their habit, a minstrel presented himself, and offered them minstrelsy. Richard, as we know, was himself a poet and loved minstrelsy; but on this occasion, perhaps through the effect of the drinking, the king treated the minstrel with

rudeness, and turned him away. The latter was an Englishman, and knew King Richard and his two knights, and, in revenge, he went to the King of Almayn (Germany), who is here named Modard, and informed him who the three strangers were. Modard immediately seized them, and threw them into a loathsome prison. The son of the King of Almayn, who was an insolent fellow, and thought himself the strongest man in the world, insulted the King of England, and challenged him to fight with fists, and Richard struck him down dead with the first blow. The king, enraged at the loss of his son and the heir to his kingdom, condemned his prisoner to be put to death, but Richard was saved by the king's daughter, the Princess Margery, with whom he formed an illicit intercourse. King Modard discovered by accident the disgrace done to him in the person of his daughter, and was more firm than ever in his resolution to put the King of England to death; and a powerful and ferocious lion which the king possessed was chosen as the executioner, was kept three days and nights without food to render him more savage, and was then turned into the chamber where Richard was confined. Richard fearlessly encountered the lion, thrust his arm down his throat, tore out his heart, and killed him on the spot. Not content with this exploit, he took the lion's heart into the hall where King Modard and his courtiers were seated at table, and dipping it in salt, ate it raw, 'without bread!' Modard, in astonishment, gave him the nickname of Richard Cœur-de-Lion, or Richard Lion's-heart:

> 'I wis, as I undyrstande can,
> This is a devyl, and no man,
> That has my stronge lyoun slawe,
> The harte out of hys body drawe,
> And has it eeten with good wylle!
> He may be callyd, be ryght skylle,
> King icrystenyd off most renoun,
> Stronge Rychard Coer-de-Lyoun.'

Modard now voluntarily allows Richard to be ransomed, and the latter returns to England, where he immediately prepares for the crusade, which occupies the greater part of the romance, in the course of which Richard not only kills innumerable Saracens with his own hand, but he cooks, eats, and relishes them.

Such is a very brief outline of the earlier part of the romantic history of Richard Cœur-de-Lion, which was extremely popular through the middle ages of England, and exercised a wide influence on the popular notions of history. We know well that Richard's nickname, if we may so call it, of Cœur-de-Lion, was intended merely to express his characteristic bravery, and that it meant simply the Lion-hearted; but the old legendary explanation continued to be received even as late as the time of Shakspeare, and still more recently. In the second act of *King John*, the dauphin Louis speaks of—

> 'Richard, that robb'd the lion of his heart;'

and the bastard Faulconbridge describes King Richard as one—

> 'Against whose fury and unmatched force
> The aweless lion could not wage the fight,
> Nor keep his princely heart from Richard's hand.

He that perforce robs lions of their hearts
May easily win a woman's.

King John, Act i. Sc. 1.

But perhaps of all the romantic incidents of Richard's life, the one which has remained most strongly impressed upon people's minds, is that of the discovery of his place of confinement by his favourite minstrel Blondel. The story has been very differently told, and has been altogether discredited by some, while other historians have looked upon it as authentic. We are enabled to give, from a manuscript of the thirteenth century, in the British Museum (MSS. Addit. No. 7103), the earliest version of this story which has yet been published. We translate from the old French:

'We will now,' this narrative proceeds, 'go on to tell you more of King Richard, whom the Duke of Austria held in his prison; and nobody knew what had become of him, except the duke and his counsellors. Now it happened that the king had bred up from his childhood a minstrel, who was named Blondel; and it came into his mind that he would seek his lord through all lands until he obtained intelligence of him. Accordingly, he went on his way, and wandered so long through strange countries that he had employed full a year and a half, and still could obtain no satisfactory news of the king. And he continued his search so long that, as chance would have it, he entered Austria, and went straight to the castle where the king was in prison, and he took his lodgings at the house of a widow woman. And he asked her whose castle that was, which was so strong and fair, and well-placed. His hostess replied that it belonged to the Duke of Austria. "Ah! fair hostess," said Blondel, "tell me now, for love, is there no prisoner within this castle?" "Truly," said the good dame, "yes, there has been one this four years, but we cannot by any means know who he is. And I can tell you for truth that they keep him close and watchfully; and we firmly believe that he is of gentle blood and a great lord." And when the good Blondel heard these words, he was marvellously glad; and it seemed to him in his heart that he had found what he sought; but he was careful not to let his hostess perceive his joy. That night he was much at his ease, and slept till day; and when he heard the watch proclaim the day with his horn, he rose and went straight to the church to pray God to help him. And then he returned to the castle, and addressed himself to the castellan within, and told him that he was a minstrel, and would very gladly stay with him if he would. The castellan was a young and joyous knight, and said that he would retain him willingly. Then was Blondel very joyful, and went and fetched his viol and his instruments, and served the castellan so long that he was a great favourite with him, and was much in favour in the castle and household. Thus he remained at the castle all the winter, but without getting to know who the prisoner was. And it happened that he went one day at Easter all alone in the garden which was near the tower, and looked about, and thought if by any accident he might see the prison. And while he was in this thought, the king looked

through a loophole, and saw Blondel, who had been his minstrel, and considered how he should make himself known to him. And he bethought himself of a song which they had made between them two, and which nobody in that country knew except them, and he began to sing the first verse loud and clear, for he sang right well. And when Blondel heard it, he then knew for certain that it was his lord; and he had in his heart the greatest joy that ever he had in his life. And immediately he left the garden, and went to his chamber where he lay, and took his viol and began to play a note; and in playing he rejoiced for his lord whom he had found. Thus Blondel remained from that time till Pentecost, and kept his secret so well that nobody suspected him. And then came Blondel to the castellan and said to him: "For God's sake! dear sir, if it pleased you, I would willingly return to my country, for it is a long time since I have had any intelligence thence." "Blondel, dear brother, that you will not do, if you will believe me; but, continue to dwell here, and I will do you much good." "In faith," said Blondel, "I will remain on no terms." When the castellan saw that he could not retain him, he gave him leave with great reluctance. So Blondel went his way, and journeyed till he came to England, and told King Richard's friends and barons that he had found his lord the king, and told them where he was.'

Richard was slain by a *quarrel* from a crossbow, shot by Bertram de Gordon from the castle of Chalun, in Aquitaine, which the king was besieging in order to put down a rebellion. He 'was buried at Fontevrault, at his father's feet, whom he confessed he had betrayed. His heart was buried in Rouen, in testimony of the love he had ever borne unto that city, for the stedfast love he always found in the citizens thereof, and his bowels at the foresaid Chalun.'—*Stow*.

The visitor of the cathedral of Rouen sees a recumbent full-length statue of the lion-hearted King. An English gentleman informs us, in the work quoted below, that, on his visiting the Museum of Antiquities at Rouen, in 1857, he 'observed a small portion of dust, having a label attached, marking it to be the dust of the heart of Richard Cœur-de-Lion from the cathedral.'[*]

That lion heart now transformed into 'a little dust,' exposed in a paper with a label, in a Museum, for the gratification of the curious!

The case, however, is not unexampled. In the last century, a stone coffin was dug up in front of the mansion-house of Eccles, in Berwickshire. 'As it had been buried above two hundred years, every part of the body was reduced to ashes. As the inside of the stone was pretty smooth, and the whole portrait of the person visible (though in ashes), Sir John Paterson had the curiosity to collect the whole, and (wonderful to tell!) it did not exceed in weight one ounce and a-half.'[†]

LAURA DE NOVES.

This far-famed woman was long held to be nothing more than an imaginary personage, until

[*] Notes and Queries, March 30, 1861.
[†] Statistical Account of Scotland, 1794, vol. xi., p. 239.

satisfactory information established the facts of her actual history. The angel upon earth, clothed in ideal grace, and only fit to live in the seventh heaven, of whom we catch such bright glimpses in Petrarch's poems, was imaginary enough; but there was a Laura of real flesh and blood.

When Petrarch first saw her he was twenty-two, and she not yet twenty, though already married; and from that minute to her death, upwards of twenty years after, he bestowed on her a poet's devotion, making her the theme of that wonderful series of sonnets which constitutes the bulk of his poetical writings; raving of her beauty, her gentleness, her many admirable qualities, and yet so controlled by her prudence that the history of Laura de Noves is as pure as it is interesting.

It fully appears that her life could not have been one of the happiest. Though it must have bred a proud delight to be the subject of such verse and the talk of all Italy, the relation was one full to her of embarrassment, and most probably even sorrow. The sonnets of Petrarch added jealousy to her lord's natural moroseness; and even without any such pretext, there is little ground for thinking that he cared much for her. For when, after a life entirely faithful to her marriage vow, as there is every reason to believe, after putting up with his unkindness more than twenty years, and bearing him ten children, she died of the plague, this husband married again within seven months of her death.

In his manuscript copy of Virgil—a valuable relic, afterwards removed from Italy by the French —Petrarch is discovered to have made the following marginal note: 'The sainted Laura, illustrious for her virtues, and for a long time celebrated in my verses, was first seen of me in my early youth on the 6th of April 1327, in the church of St. Clara, at Avignon, at the first hour of the day; and in the same city, in the same month of April, on the same sixth day, and at the same hour, in the year 1348, this light disappeared from our day, when I was then by chance at Verona, ignorant, alas! of my calamity. The sad news reached me at Parma, by letter from my friend Ludovico, on the morning of the 19th of May. This most chaste and beautiful lady was buried on the same day of her death, after vespers, in the church of the Cordeliers. Her soul, as Seneca says of Africanus, returned, I feel most assured, to heaven, whence it came. These words, in bitter remembrance of the event, it seemed good to me to write, with a sort of melancholy pleasure, in this place' (that is, in the Virgil) 'especially, which often comes under my eyes, that nothing hereafter in this life may seem to me desirable, and that I may be warned by continual sight of these words and remembrance of so swiftly-fleeting life,—by this strongest cord broken,—that it is time to flee from Babylon, which, God's grace preventing, will be easy to me, when I think boldly and manfully of the fruitless cares of the past, the vain hopes, and unexpected events.'

Petrarch contrived to survive the loss of Laura twenty-six years; yet his was a strange passion. It is hard to decide how much he really feels, or does not feel, in his enamoured laments. A poet will write according to the habit of his time; and the fact that Petrarch has clothed his sorrows in a fanciful garb of cold conceit and whimsical expression, does not disprove the existence of real feeling underlying them. Although it may have been kept alive by artificial means; though there may have been pleasure mixed with the bitterness—the pleasure of making verses, of winning fame—there must have been a solid substratum of real passion for this one theme to have engrossed a long life. We may quote a fragment of Petrarch's correspondence as an interesting comment on these remarks: 'You are befooling us all,' writes the bishop of Lombes from Rome to Avignon, where Laura resided, and from whence, now nine years after his first meeting with her, the poet still continued to pour forth his sonnets, 'and it is wonderful that at so tender age' (his age was thirty-one) 'you can deceive the world with so much art and success. . . . . Your Laura is a phantom created by your imagination for the exercise of your poetry. Your verse, your love, your sighs, are all a fiction; or, if there is anything real in your passion, it is not for the lady Laura, but for the *laurel*, that is, the crown of poets.' To which Petrarch answers: 'As to Laura, would to heaven she were only an imaginary personage, and my passion for her only a pastime! Alas! it is a madness, which it would be difficult and painful to feign for any length of time, and what an extravagance it would be to affect such a passion! . . . . How often have you yourself been witness of *my paleness and sufferings*. I know very well that you speak only in irony. . . .'

The reader must believe this passion real, however reluctantly. Perhaps he would like a specimen of the poems themselves.

First, a piece of absurd conceit, written when Laura was in danger of death, a specimen of the worst:

How Laura, if she dies, will certainly enjoy an exalted position in Heaven.

'This lovely spirit, if ordained to leave
Its mortal tenement before its time,
Heaven's fairest habitation shall receive,
And welcome her to breathe its sweetest clime.
If she establish her abode between
Mars and the planet-star of beauty's queen,
The sun will be obscured, so dense a cloud
Of spirits from adjacent stars will crowd
To gaze upon her beauty infinite.
Say that she fixes on a lower sphere,
Beneath the glorious sun, her beauty soon
Will dim the splendour of inferior stars—
Of Mars, of Venus, Mercury, and the Moon.
She'll choose not Mars, but higher place than Mars;
She will eclipse all planetary light,
And Jupiter himself will seem less bright.'

Now a specimen extremely beautiful, of the best:

Depicts the heavenly beauty of his lady, and vows to love her always.

'Time was, her tresses, by the breathing air,
Were wreathed to many a ringlet golden bright.
Time was, her eyes diffused unmeasured light,
Tho' now their lovely beams are waxing rare;

483

Her face methought that in its beauty showed
Compassion, her angelic shape and walk,
Her voice that seemed with heaven's own speech to
    talk.
At these, what wonder that my bosom glowed !
A living sun she seemed,—a spirit of heaven !
Those charms decline ; but does my passion ? no !
I love not less—the slackening of the bow
Assuages not the wound its shaft has given.'

The above are Thomas Campbell's translations.

ADVENTURES OF THE KOH-I-NOOR.

Large diamonds, like first-class pictures, have a European reputation, because they are few in number, are not susceptible of reproduction, are everywhere prized, and can only be bought by the wealthy. Only a few *very* large diamonds (called *paragons*) are known in the world. The standard here in view is a minimum weight of one hundred carats (a carat being about 3⅕th Troy grains, or 100 carats equal to ⅔rds of a Troy ounce). The 'Koh-i-noor,' in its present perfected state, weighs 102 carats ; the 'Star of the South,' 125 ; the Regent, or Pitt diamond, 137 ; the great Austrian diamond, 139 ; the Orloff, or great Russian diamond, 193 ; one in possession of the Rajah of Maltan, in Borneo, weighs 367 carats, in the uncut state. The Porter Rhodes diamond, found at Kimberley, South Africa, weighed 150 carats uncut, and £60,000 was refused for it.

A romantic history is attached to every one of these jewels. The Rajah of Maltan, it is said, was once offered by the Governor of Batavia a hundred and fifty thousand dollars, two large war-brigs, and a complete store of guns and ammunition, for his diamond ; but he refused the offer. A portion of this eagerness is attributable to a belief on the part of Orientals in certain mystical and medical properties in the diamond.

The Koh-i-noor, which left India on the 6th of April 1850, to pass into the hands of Queen Victoria, has had an especially notable history. It was found in the mines of Golconda. How many ages this was ago no one can tell ; but the Hindoos, who are fond of high numbers, say that it belonged to Kama, King of Anga, three thousand years ago. Viewed within more modest limits, the diamond is said to have been stolen from one of the Kings of Golconda by a treacherous general named Mininzola, and by him presented to the Great Mogul, Shah Jehan, father of Aurungzebe, about the year 1640. It was then in a rough uncut state, very much larger than at present. Shah Jehan employed a Venetian diamond-worker, Hortensio Borgis, to cut it, in order to develop its brilliancy : this was done so badly that more than half of the gem was cut away, and the rest very imperfectly treated. The Mogul, in a rage, fined the jeweller ten thousand ducats, instead of paying him for his misdirected labours. When Tavernier, the French traveller, was in India, about two hundred years ago, he saw the Koh-i-noor, and told of the intense wonderment and admiration with which it was regarded in that country. After his time, the treasure changed hands frequently among the princes of India, generally by means either of fraud or violence ; but it is not worth while to trace the particulars. Early in the present

century the possessor was the Khan of Cabul. From him it was obtained in an audacious way by the famous chief of Lahore, Runjeet Singh. ' Having heard that the Khan of Cabul possessed a diamond that had belonged to the Great Mogul, the largest and purest known, he invited the unfortunate owner to his court, and there, having him in his power, demanded the diamond. The guest, however, had provided himself against such a contingency, with a perfect imitation of the coveted jewel. After some show of resistance, he reluctantly acceded to the wishes of his powerful host. The delight of Runjeet was extreme, but of short duration : the lapidary to whom he gave orders to mount his new acquisition pronouncing it to be merely a bit of crystal. The mortification and rage of the despot were unbounded. He immediately ordered the palace of the Khan to be invested, and ransacked from top to bottom. For a long while, all search was vain. At last a slave betrayed the secret ; the diamond was found concealed beneath a heap of ashes. Runjeet Singh had it set in an armlet, between two diamonds, each the size of a sparrow's egg.'* When the Hon. W. G. Osborne was at Lahore some years afterwards, and visited the great Sikh potentate, 'the whole space behind the throne was crowded with Runjeet's chiefs, mingled with natives from Candahar, Cabul, and Afghanistan, blazing with gold and jewels, and dressed and armed with every conceivable variety of colour and fashion. Cross-legged in a golden chair sat Runjeet Singh, dressed in simple white, wearing no ornaments but a single string of enormous pearls round the waist, and the celebrated Koh-i-noor, or "Mountain of Light," upon his arm.' Sometimes, in a fit of Oriental display, Runjeet decked his horse with the Koh-i-noor, among other jewels. After his death, the precious gem passed into the hands of his successors on the throne of Lahore ; and when the Punjaub was conquered by the English in 1850, the Koh-i-noor was included among the spoil. Colonel Mackesan and Captain Ramsay brought it to England in the *Medea*, as a present from the East India Company to the Queen.

The Koh-i-noor, when examined by European diamond merchants, was pronounced to be badly cut ; and the Court jeweller employed Messrs. Coster, of Amsterdam, to re-cut it—a work that occupied the labours of thirty-eight days, of twelve hours each. This is not really cutting, it is grinding ; the gem being applied to the surface of a flat iron plate, moistened with oil and diamond powder, and rotating with great velocity, in such a way as to produce new reflecting facets. The late Duke of Wellington gave the first touch to this work, as a sort of honorary amateur diamond-cutter. The world-renowned gem has since been regarded as far more dazzling and beautiful than at any former time in its history.

Voltaire having paid some high compliments to the celebrated Haller, was told that Haller was not in the habit of speaking so favourably of him. 'Ah !' said Voltaire, with an air of philosophic indulgence, 'I dare say, we are both of us very much mistaken.' —*Lord Jeffrey : Ed. Review.*

* Barrera on *Gems and Jewels.*

APRIL 7.

St Hegesippus, a primitive father, 2nd century. St Aphraates, anchoret, 4th century. St Finan, of Ireland. St Aibert, recluse, 1140. St Herman Joseph, confessor, 1226.

———

Born.—St Francis Xavier, Christian missionary, 1506, *Xavier Castle, Pyrenees ;* Dr Hugh Blair, author of *Lectures on Rhetoric,* &c., 1718, *Edinburgh ;* William Wordsworth, poet, 1770, *Cockermouth ;* François M. C. Fourier, French socialist, 1772 ; R. W. Elliston, actor, 1774, *London ;* Sir Francis Chantrey, sculptor, 1782 ; Giambattista Rubini, ' the greatest of tenor singers,' 1795 ; Sir J. E. Tennent, author of works on Belgium, Ceylon, &c., 1804, *Belfast.*

Died.—Charles VIII. of France, 1498, *Amboise ;* Jerome Bignon, French historical writer, 1656; Sir William Davenant, poet, 1668 ; Charles Colardean, French dramatic writer, 1776, *Paris ;* Peter Camper, Dutch anatomist, 1789, *Leyden ;* Rev. William Mason, poet, 1797 ; William Godwin, novelist and miscellaneous writer, 1836, *London ;* Sir James Scarlett, Lord Abinger, Chief Baron of the Court of Exchequer, 1844, *Bury St Edmunds ;* William L. Bowles, poet, 1850, *Salisbury.*

FOURIER.

Among the dreamers and contrivers of new social worlds, Fourier is unquestionably the prince ; no one ever brought to the task a more imperial intellect, or evolved a grander, more complex, and more detailed Utopia. His works are voluminous, and to master the laws and ordinances of his ideal kingdom would be a labour more than equivalent to the comprehension of Blackstone and the Code Napoleon.

Fourier, the son of a linendraper, was born at Besançon. His father dying in narrow circumstances, he commenced life behind a haberdasher's counter in Rouen, from whence he moved to Lyons, in which city, as a clerk and as a merchant, he spent a large part of his life. The Revolution had filled the air with daring social speculations, and Fourier quickly arrived at the conviction that the existing constitution of society was radically rotten. In 1796 he was draughted into the army as a private soldier, but after two years of service he was discharged as an invalid, and bearing with him a notable stock of ideas derived from his experience of military discipline and organization. Whilst a clerk at Marseilles, in 1799, he was ordered to superintend the sinking of a quantity of corn in the sea at midnight, which had become spoiled by hoarding when the people were dying of famine. This, and sundry encounters with commercial knavery, inspired him with an increasing aversion to trade. He gave all his spare hours to study, and among his acquaintances had a repute for universal knowledge, and for some unfathomable notions on the reconstruction of society. Excited by their curiosity, he was induced to publish, in 1808, a book as a prospectus of his scheme, to be developed in eight volumes ; but the poor book did not find above a dozen purchasers. Six years elapsed, when by chance a copy of the neglected work fell into the hands of M. Just Muiron, a gentleman of Besançon, who read it with delight, entered into correspondence with Fourier, and avowed himself his disciple. He urged Fourier to fulfil his programme, and offered to bear a great part of the cost of publication. The result was, that Fourier gave up business, and retired into the country, and between the years 1816 and 1821 produced the bulk of his writings. He printed two large volumes at Besançon, and at the end of 1822 carried them to market in Paris ; but no one would buy or even read them. The reviewers dismissed them as voluminous and abstruse. To meet this objection he produced an abridgment, but it fared no better. Worn out with waiting, and unable to bear the expense of a Parisian residence, he was compelled to return to Lyons in 1825, and take a situation as cashier at £50 a year. Meanwhile his work found receptive readers here and there throughout France, who encouraged him to go on writing. Madame Clarissa Vigoureux became a most effective ally, devoting her fortune and a skilful pen to the propagation of his views. In 1829, he made his abode permanently in Paris. The Revolution of 1830 brought the St Simonian sect of socialists into notoriety, and Fourier sent copies of his books to its leaders, but they paid them no attention. He tried the Owenites of England in the same way, and met with the same neglect. Irritated by their indifference, he attacked them in a sarcastic pamphlet, *The Fallacy and Charlatanry of the St Simonians and the Owenites,* which created a great sensation, and put an end to his weary years of obscurity. Several of the cleverest St Simonians became his adherents, and in June 1832 they started a weekly paper, *The Phalanstery,* which Fourier edited. Some disciples, anxious to realize the paradisiacal life of *The Phalanstery,* set up a joint-stock society, with a nominal capital of £20,000, at Rambouillet, but it turned out an utter failure. Fourier protested against the experiment, as entered into with wild haste, and without the completion of the conditions essential to success. Whilst waiting in the confident expectation that some great capitalist would knock at his door, and give him power to transform into fact the dream of his life, Fourier died on the 10th of October 1837, in his sixty-sixth year. He was never married.

Fourier was a thin, nervous man, of about five feet seven inches. His head, which was not large, was high in front, depressed behind (what phrenologists call the bankrupt form of head, as indicating an over-generous and too little selfish nature), and very full on each side. His hair was light brown, his eyes blue, his nose aquiline, his chin large, and his lips thin and closely compressed. In manner he was dignified, yet simple and earnest ; and in his later years there was a sphere of sadness, if not bitterness, around him from long travail and hope deferred. His income was scarcely ever more than £60 a year, but his wants were few ; he was a good economist, and at his death £40 was found in his cash-box. Music and flowers were his perpetual delights.

Fourier's writings extend over eight thick volumes, and about an equal quantity remains in manuscript. They deal with a wide variety of subjects, and a well-read Fourierite is seldom at a loss for a quotation from his master on any

485

matter under discussion. In many points there is a close resemblance between Fourier and Swedenborg: both were equally ready to evolve the unknown from their internal consciousness, and to deliver it with all the assurance of certainty. Fourier's grand aim was to assort mankind according to their characters, powers, and propensities; to band them together in such a way, that friendship, work, and pleasure should coincide. He was never tired of asserting that the Newtonian law of attraction was equally applicable to the world of mind as the world of matter; and that all the disorder and misery of society springs from the infraction and resistance of its benign operation. His socialism had thus a spiritual side; and many who would have been repelled from the dead level of a material communion, were fascinated with his glorious pictures of harmonious hierarchies of workers, where each man should do what he loved to do, and could do best, in fellowship with those whose tastes and feelings were kindred to his own. Fourier's language is graphic and striking, but seldom elegant, and often incorrect. His wealth of imagination and his logical power, as remarkable in construction as in destruction, amaze, while they excite regret that such genius should have been squandered so fruitlessly. Had he tried to govern a single village or workshop, he might have discovered the vanity of drawing out schemes of society on paper, the folly of legislating for men as though they were bricks and mortar, and the hopelessness of doing them good in any way save through the consent of their erratic, perverse, and incalculable wills.

Fourierism found many adherents in France and the United States, and various abortive attempts were made to institute associations after his model. The Revolution of 1848 brought a flush of promise to the Parisian Fourierites, but the reaction which followed blighted all. Fourier's doctrines are far too complicated to enter into popular politics, and the day is probably not distant when they will altogether lapse out of any faith into the condition of literary and psychological curiosities.

LOVE AND MADNESS.

On the evening of the 7th of April 1779, a handsome, well-dressed lady was stepping out of Covent Garden Theatre, to take her coach, when a young man in the dress of a clergyman moved abruptly towards her, and firing a pistol into her head, killed her in a moment. Immediately he fired another at himself, but without fatal effect, and then began to beat his head with its butt, as if eager in any way to deprive himself of life. He was, however, secured, and carried, all bespattered with his own blood and that of his victim, to a magistrate. The dead body was taken to a neighbouring tavern to await a coroner's inquest.

No more romantic story broke the dull tenor of English aristocratic life in the eighteenth century. The lady was Miss Reay, well known as the mistress of the Earl of Sandwich, an elderly statesman of great ability, who conducted the whole of the naval affairs of England during the war with the American colonies. Miss Reay was of humble origin, but possessed beauty, intelligence, and an amiable character. She had borne four children to the Earl, who treated her with the greatest tenderness and affection. Rather more than three years before the above date, a young military officer named Hackman, in quarters at Huntingdon, was, in the course of an ordinary hospitality, invited by Lord Sandwich to Hitchinbroke, his lordship's country residence. Though the time is so near our own, it was different in some of the essentials of good taste, if not of morals; and we learn with some little surprise that this distinguished statesman had Miss Reay established as the mistress of his house, for the reception of such society as visited him. The young man, who was of an enthusiastic temperament, fell violently in love with Miss Reay, and sought to win her affections with a view to matrimony. The poor girl, who had the grace to wish she were not what she was, opened her heart to his addresses. They corresponded, they met; the young man was permitted to believe that the most cherished hope of his heart would be realized. To fit himself the better to maintain her as his wife, he studied for the church, took orders, and actually entered upon a curacy (Wiverton, in Norfolk). Miss Reay's situation became always more and more embarrassing, as the number of her children increased. Well disposed to Hackman, she was yet bound by strong ties of gratitude to Lord Sandwich. In short, she could not summon sufficient moral courage to break through her bondage. She seems to have striven to temper the violent transports of her lover; but his was not a constitution to bear with such a disappointment. His letters, afterwards published, fully shew how his love for this unfortunate woman gradually fixed itself as a morbid idea in his mind. For some weeks before the fatal day, he dwells in his letters on suicides, and cases of madmen who murdered the objects of their affections. The story of Chatterton seems to have had a fascination for him. He tells a friend on the 20th of March, that he did not believe he could exist without Miss Reay. He then, and for some time further, appears to have only contemplated his own death, as the inevitable consequence of his blighted passion. On the morning of the 7th of April he was employed in reading Blair's *Sermons;* but afterwards having traced Miss Reay to the theatre, he went back to his lodgings for a brace of pistols, which he employed in the manner which has been described.

The wretchedness of the unhappy man during the few days left to him on earth was extreme. He woke to a just view of his atrocious act, but only to condemn himself, and the more eagerly to long for death. After his condemnation, the following note reached him:

'17 April, '79.

'To Mr Hackman, in Newgate.

'If the murderer of Miss Reay wishes to live, the man he has most injured will use all his interest to procure his life.'

His answer was:

' Condemned cell, Newgate,
'17 April, 1779.

' The murderer of her whom he preferred, far preferred, to life, suspects the hand from which he has just received such an offer as he neither desires nor deserves. His wishes are for death, not for life. One wish he has : could he be pardoned in this world by the man he has most injured? Oh, my lord, when I meet her in another world, enable me to tell her (if departed spirits are not ignorant of earthly things) that you forgive us both, that you will be a father to her dear infants! 'J. H.'

Two days after this date, Hackman expiated his offence at Tyburn.*

The surviving children of Miss Reay were well educated by their father; and the fourth, under the name of Basil Montagu, attained the rank of Queen's Counsel, and distinguished himself by a Life of Bacon and other works.

SALE OF A WIFE.

The *Annual Register* for 1832 gave an account of a singular wife-sale which took place on the 7th of April in that year. Joseph Thomson, a farmer, had been married for three years without finding his happiness advanced, and he and his wife at length agreed to separate. It is a prevalent notion amongst the rude and ignorant in England that a man, by setting his wife up to public auction, and so parting with her, legally dissolves the marriage tie, and escapes from all its obligations. Thomson, under this belief, came into Carlisle with his wife, and by the bellman announced that he was about to sell her. At twelve o'clock at noon the sale commenced, in the presence of a large number of persons. Thomson placed his wife on a large oak chair, with a rope or halter of straw round her neck. He then spoke as follows :—' Gentlemen, I have to offer to your notice my wife, Mary Anne Thomson, otherwise Williams, whom I mean to sell to the highest and fairest bidder. Gentlemen, it is her wish as well as mine to part for ever. She has been to me only a born serpent. I took her for my comfort, and the good of my home; but she became my tormentor, a domestic curse, a night invasion, and a daily devil. Gentlemen, I speak truth from my heart when I say—may God deliver us from troublesome wives and frolicsome women! Avoid them as you would a mad dog, a roaring lion, a loaded pistol, cholera morbus, Mount Etna, or any other pestilential thing in nature. Now I have shewn you the dark side of my wife, and told you her faults and failings, I will introduce the bright and sunny side of her, and explain her qualifications and goodness. She can read novels and milk cows; she can laugh and weep with the same ease that you could take a glass of ale when thirsty. Indeed, gentlemen, she

reminds me of what the poet says of women in general :

" Heaven gave to women the peculiar grace,
    To laugh, to weep, to cheat the human race."

She can make butter and scold the maid; she can sing Moore's melodies, and plait her frills and caps; she cannot make rum, gin, or whisky, but she is a good judge of the quality from long experience in tasting them. I therefore offer her with all her perfections and imperfections, for the sum of fifty shillings.' If this speech is correctly reported, the man must have been a humorist in addition to his other qualities. The account concludes with the statement that, after waiting about an hour, Thomson knocked down the lot to one Henry Mears, for twenty shillings and a Newfoundland dog; they then parted in perfect good temper—Mears and the woman going one way, Thomson and the dog another.

Of course an affair of this kind is simply an outrage upon decency, and has no legal effect whatever. It can only be considered as a proof of the besotted ignorance and brutal feelings of a portion of our rural population. Rather unfortunately, the occasional instances of wife-sale, while remarked by ourselves with little beyond a passing smile, have made a deep impression on our continental neighbours, who seriously believe that it is a habit of all classes of our people, and constantly cite it as an evidence of our low civilization. It would never occur to us as a proof of any such thing, for we recognise it as only an eccentricity; yet it may be well for us to know that it really does take place now and then,—more frequently, indeed, than almost any are aware of,—and is a social feature by no means unworthy of the grave consideration of educationists.

In 1815, a man held a regular auction in the market-place at Pontefract, offering his wife at a minimum bidding of one shilling, and 'knocking her down' for eleven shillings. In 1820, a man named Brouchet led his wife, a decent-looking woman, into the cattle-market at Canterbury, from the neighbouring village of Broughton; he asked a salesman to sell her for him; the salesman replied that his dealings were with cattle, not with women, and he refused. The man thereupon hired a pen or stall, for which he paid the usual tollage of sixpence, and led his wife into it by a halter; and soon afterwards he sold her to a young man at Canterbury for five shillings. In 1834, a man led his wife by a halter, in precisely a similar way, into the cattle-market at Birmingham; but the local journals did not report the sum at which the unfortunate 'lot' was knocked down. A case occurred in 1835, in which a woman was sold by her husband for fifteen pounds; she at once went home with the buyer; she survived both buyer and seller, and then married again. Some property came to her in the course of years from her first husband; for, notwithstanding claims put forth by other relations, she was able to maintain in a court of law that the sale did not and could not vitiate her rights as his widow. A good deal of surprise was felt in many villages of ignorant peasantry, in 1837, at

---

* The correspondence of Hackman with Miss Reay was published by Mr. Herbert Croft, under the appropriate title which has been assumed as a heading for this article. The book has become extremely rare; but the bulk of the letters are reprinted in a Collection of Criminal Trials, 6 vols. Knight and Lacy, 1825.

the result of a trial at the West Riding Sessions in Yorkshire, where a man was committed to a month's imprisonment and hard labour for selling, or attempting to sell, his wife: the right to do this being believed in more extensively than we are apt to imagine. In 1858, in a beer-shop at Little Horton, near Bradford, a man named Hartley Thompson put up his wife, described by the local journals as a pretty young woman, for sale; he even announced the sale beforehand by means of a crier or bellman; he brought her in with a ribbon round her neck, by way of halter. These two persons had lived unhappily together, and both entertained a belief that by such a process as this they might legally separate for life. It is difficult, indeed, to credit how such things can be, unless the wife be more or less a consenting party; this supposition once made, however, so cheap a substitute for the Divorce Court becomes intelligible. Doubtless, in some cases the husband acts wholly for himself in the matter; as happened in 1859 at Dudley, where a man sold his wife for sixpence, under the full belief that by so doing she would have no further legal claim on him for support.

There are not wanting instances of a belief that the marital tie may be legally dissolved by a document partaking of the character of a lease. In the feudal days there was the famous case of Sir John de Camoys, who regularly leased his wife to Sir William de Paynel; the lady was, however, not a consenting party to the transaction; and on appealing to the law, the lease was declared null and void. In recent times one particular instance presented a curious variation from this course of proceeding. The Birmingham Police Court, in 1853, had to adjudicate on an assault case; and in the evidence the strange fact came out that a husband had leased, not his wife, but *himself*. He had deserted his wife, and had paid a lawyer thirty-five shillings to draw up a regular contract between him and another woman. In proper form the man was described as a 'carpenter,' and the woman as a 'spinster.' Omitting the names, the opening sentences ran thus:—'Wherein the said —— and —— have mutually agreed with each other to live and reside together, and to mutually assist in supporting and maintaining each other during the remainder of their lives, and also to sign the agreement hereinafter contained to that effect: now, therefore, it is hereby mutually agreed by and between the said —— and ——, that they shall live and reside together during the remainder of their lives, and that they shall mutually exert themselves by work and labour, and by following all their business pursuits, to the best of their abilities, skill, and understanding, and by aiding and assisting each other, for their mutual benefit and advantage, and also to provide for themselves and each other the best support and comforts in life which their means and income can afford, &c. &c.' The man had allowed himself, or had been allowed, to believe that the existence of this document would be a bar to any claim on the part of his poor wife. It is no wonder that the magistrate administered a severe reproof to the lawyer who lent himself to such a scandal.

APRIL 8.

St Dionysius, of Corinth, 2nd century. St Ædesius, martyr, 306. St Perpetuus, bishop of Tours, 491. St Walter, abbot of St Martin's, near Pontoise, 1099. B. Albert, patriarch of Jerusalem, 1214.

Born.—John C. Loudon, writer on botany, &c., 1783, *Cambuslang, Lanarkshire.*

Died.—Caracalla, Roman emperor, assassinated, 217, *Edessa;* Pope Benedict III., 858; John the Good, King of France, 1364, *Savoy Palace, London;* Lorenzo de Medici, 'the Magnificent,' 1492, *Florence;* Dr Thomas Gale, learned divine and editor, 1702, *York.*

THE CAPTIVITY OF JOHN, KING OF FRANCE,
AT SOMERTON CASTLE.

John I. (surnamed 'Le Bon') mounted the throne of France in 1350, at the age of thirty. He began his reign most inauspiciously by beheading the Count d'Eu, an act which alienated the affections of all his greater nobles from him, and which he in vain endeavoured to repair by instituting the order of the 'Star,' in imitation of that of the 'Garter,' founded by the sovereign of England. Next he was much perplexed by the continued enmity of Charles d'Evereux, King of Navarre. Finally, the Black Prince, invading his realm, ravaged Limousin, Auvergne, Berri, and Poitou. Incensed by the temerity of his English assailants, John hastily raised an army of 60,000 men, swearing that he would give battle to the prince immediately. The two armies met at Maupertuis, near Poitiers, September 19, 1356, when the Black Prince, with only 8,000 men under his command, succeeded in routing the French army most completely, and taking the king and his fourth son, Philip, a brave youth of fifteen, prisoners. The royal captives were first taken to Bordeaux, and thence brought to England, where they landed, May 4, 1357. During the first year of his captivity, John resided at the palace of the Savoy in London, where he was well entertained, enjoying full liberty, and often receiving visits from King Edward and Queen Philippa. Towards the close of the year 1358, a series of restrictions began to be imposed upon the captives, accompanied by reductions of their suite; but this change was the result of political caution, not of any unnecessary severity, and ended in their transfer to Somerton Castle, near Navenby, in Lincolnshire, August 4, 1359. William Baron d'Eyncourt, a noble in whom the king could place the utmost confidence, was appointed custodian of the royal prisoners.

Previous to this coming into Lincolnshire, in accordance with an edict of Edward III., John had been forced to dismiss forty-two of his attendants; he still, however, retained about the same number around his person. Among these were two chaplains, a secretary, a clerk of the chapel, a physician, a maître d'hôtel, three pages, four valets, three wardrobe men, three furriers, six grooms, two cooks, a fruiterer, a spiceman, a barber, and a washer, besides some higher officers, and a person bearing the exalted name of 'le roy de menestereulx,' who appears to have been a maker of musical instruments and clocks as well as a minstrel; and last, but not least, 'Maître Jean le fol.' The Somerton Castle furniture being utterly insufficient for such a vast increase of inmates, the captive king added a number of tables, chairs, forms, and trestles, besides fittings for the stables, and stores of firewood and turf. He also fitted up his own chamber, that of the Prince Philip, and of M. Jean le fol, besides the chapel, with hangings, curtains, cushions, ornamented coffers, sconces, &c., the furniture of each of these filling a separate waggon when the king left Somerton.

Large consignments of good Bordeaux wines were transmitted from France to the port of Boston for the captive king's use, as much as a hundred and forty tuns being sent at one time as a present, intended partly for his own use and partly as a means of raising money to keep up his royal state. One of the costly items in the king's expenditure was sugar, together with spices bought in London, Lincoln, and Boston, immense quantities of which we may infer were used in the form of confectionery; for in the household books we meet constantly with such items as eggs to clarify sugar, roses to flavour it with, and cochineal to colour it. These bon-bons appear to have cost about three shillings the pound; at least such is the price of what is termed 'sucre roset vermeil,' and especial mention is made of a large silver gilt box made for the king as a 'bonbonière,' or receptacle for such sweets.

In the article of dress John was most prodigal. In less than five months he ordered eight complete suits, besides one received as a present from the Countess of Boulogne, and many separate articles. One ordered for Easter was of Brussels manufacture, a marbled violet velvet, trimmed with miniver; another for Whitsuntide, of rosy scarlet, lined with blue taffeta. The fur and trimmings of these robes formed a most costly additional item, there having been paid to William, a furrier of Lincoln, £17, 3s. 9d. for 800 miniver skins, and 850 ditto of 'gris;' also £8, 10s. to Thornsten, a furrier of London, for 600 additional miniver skins, and 300 of 'gris,' all for one set of robes. Thus 2,550 skins, at a cost of £25,13s. 9d., were used in this suit, and the charge for making it up was £6, 8s. Indeed, so large were the requirements of the captive king and his household in this particular, that a regular tailoring establishment was set up in Lincoln by his order, over which one M. Tassin presided.

The pastimes he indulged in were novel-reading, music, chess, and backgammon. He paid for writing materials in Lincolnshire three shillings to three shillings and sixpence for one dozen parchments, sixpence to ninepence for a quire of paper, one shilling for an envelope with its silk binder, and fourpence for a bottle of ink. The youthful tastes of the valorous Prince Philip appear to have been of what we should consider a more debased order than his royal father's. He had dogs, probably greyhounds, for coursing on the heath adjoining Somerton, and falcons, and, I am sorry to add, game cocks, too; a charge appearing in the royal household accounts for

the purchase of one of these birds, termed, in language characteristic of the period, 'un coc à faire jouster.'

One very marked trait in King John's character was his love of almsgiving. His charitable gifts, great and small, public and private, flowed in a ceaseless stream when a captive in adversity, no less than when on the throne in prosperity. Wherever he was he made a small daily offering to the curate of the parish, besides presenting larger sums on the festivals of the church. For instance, he gave to the humble Curé of Boby (Boothby) a sum equal to twelve shillings, for masses offered by him at Christmas; eight shillings at the Epiphany; and four shillings and fourpence at Candlemas. The religious orders also received large sums at his hands; on each of the four mendicant societies of Lincoln he bestowed fifteen escuz, or ten pounds. On his way from London to Somerton, he offered at Grantham five nobles (£1, 13s. 4d.); gave five more nobles to the preaching friars of Stamford, and the same sum to the shrine of St Albans. In fact, wherever he went, churches, convents, shrines, recluses, and the poor and unfortunate, were constant recipients of his bounty.

On the 21st of March 1360, King John was removed from Somerton, and lodged in the Tower of London, the journey occupying seven days. Two months after (May 19), he was released on signing an agreement to pay to England 3,000,000 of gold crowns (or £1,500,000) for his ransom, of which 600,000 were to be paid within four months of his arrival in France, and 400,000 a year, till the whole was liquidated, and also that his son, the Duc d'Anjou, and other noble personages of France, should be sent over as hostages for the same. The last act of this unfortunate monarch shews his deep-seated love of truth and honour. On the 6th of December 1363, the Duc d'Anjou and the other hostages broke their parole, and returned to Paris. Mortified beyond measure at this breach of trust, and turning a deaf ear to the remonstrances of his council, John felt himself bound in honour to return to the English coast, and accordingly four days afterwards he crossed the sea once more, and placed himself at the disposal of Edward. The palace of the Savoy was appointed as his residence, where he died after a short illness in the spring of 1364.

THE TURNSPIT.

Many years ago the writer happened to be at an auction of what are technically termed fixtures; in this instance, the last moveable furnishings of an ancient country-house about to be pulled down to make room for a railway station. Amongst the many lots arranged for sale, was a large wooden wheel enclosed in a kind of circular box, which gave rise to many speculations respecting the use it had been put to. At last, an old man, the blacksmith of the neighbouring village, made his appearance, and solved the puzzle, by stating that it was a 'dog-wheel,'—a machine used to turn a spit by the labour of a dog; a very common practice down to a not distant period, though now scarcely within the memory of living men. Besides the blacksmith, the writer has met with only one other person who can remember seeing a turnspit dog employed in its peculiar vocation ; but no better authority can be cited than that of Mr Jesse, the well-known writer on rural subjects, who thus relates his experiences :—

'How well do I recollect in the days of my youth watching the operations of a turnspit at the house of a worthy old Welsh clergyman in Worcestershire, who taught me to read ! He was a good man, wore a bushy wig, black worsted stockings, and large plated buckles in his shoes. As he had several boarders as well as day scholars, his two turnspits had plenty to do. They were long-bodied, crook-legged, and ugly dogs, with a suspicious, unhappy look about them, as if they were weary of the task they had to do, and expected every moment to be seized upon to perform it. Cooks in those days, as they are said to be at present, were very cross ; and if the poor animal, wearied with having a larger joint than usual to turn, stopped for a moment, the voice of the cook might be heard rating him in no very gentle terms. When we consider that a large solid piece of beef would take at least three hours before it was properly roasted, we

may form some idea of the task a dog had to perform in turning a wheel during that time. A pointer has pleasure in finding game, the terrier worries rats with eagerness and delight, and the bull-dog even attacks bulls with the greatest energy, while the poor turnspit performs his task with compulsion, like a culprit on a tread-wheel, subject to scolding or beating if he stops a moment to rest his weary limbs, and is then kicked about the kitchen when the task is over.'

The services of the turnspit date from an early period. Doctor Caius, founder of the college at Cambridge which bears his name, and the first English writer on dogs, says,—'There is comprehended under the curs of the coarsest kind a certain dog in kitchen service excellent. For when any meat is to be roasted, they go into a wheel, which they turning about with the weight of their bodies, so diligently look to their business, that no drudge nor scullion can do the feat more cunningly, whom the popular sort hereupon term turnspits.'

The annexed illustration, taken from *Remarks on a Tour to North and South Wales*, published in 1800, clearly exhibits how the dog was enabled to perform his curious and uncongenial task. The letterpress in reference to it says :—'New-

A TURNSPIT AT WORK.

castle, near Carmarthen, is a pleasant village ; at a decent inn here a dog is employed as turnspit ; great care is taken that this animal does not observe the cook approach the larder ; if he does, he immediately hides himself for the remainder of the day, and the guest must be contented with more humble fare than intended.'

One dog being insufficient to do all the roasting

for a large establishment, two or more were kept, working alternately ; and each animal well knowing and noting its regular turn of duty, great difficulty was experienced in compelling it to work out of the recognised system of rotation. Buffon relates that two turnspits were employed in the kitchen of the Duc de Lianfort at Paris, taking their turns every other day to go into the wheel. One of them, in a fit of laziness, hid itself on a day that it should have worked, so the other was forced to go into the wheel instead. When the meat was roasted, the one that had been compelled to work out of its turn began to bark and wag its tail till it induced the scullions to follow it; then leading them to a garret, and dislodging the skulker from beneath a bed, it attacked and killed its too lazy fellow-worker.

A somewhat similar circumstance occurred at the Jesuits' College of La Flèche. One day, the cook, having prepared the meat for roasting, looked for the dog whose turn it was to work the wheel for that day; but not being able to find it, he attempted to employ the one whose turn it was to be off duty. The dog resisted, bit the cook, and ran away. The man, with whom the dog was a particular favourite, was much astonished at its ferocity; and the wound being severe and bleeding profusely, he went to the surgeon of the College to have it dressed. In the meantime the dog ran into the garden, found the one whose turn it was to work the spit for that day, and drove it into the kitchen; where the deserter, seeing no opportunity of shirking its day's labour, went into the wheel of its own accord, and began to work.

Turnspits frequently figure in the old collections of anecdotes. For instance, it is said that the captain of a ship of war, stationed in the port of Bristol for its protection in the last century, found that, on account of some political bias, the inhabitants did not receive him with their accustomed hospitality. So, to punish them, he sent his men ashore one night, with orders to steal all the turnspit dogs they could lay their hands upon. The dogs being conveyed on board the ship, and snugly stowed away in the hold, consternation reigned in the kitchens and dining-rooms of the Bristol merchants; and roast meat rose to a premium during the few days the dogs were confined in their floating prison. The release of the turnspits was duly celebrated by many dinners to the captain and his officers.

In an exceeding rare collection of poems, entitled *Norfolk Drollery*, there are the following lines:—

Upon a dog called Fuddle, turnspit at the Popinjay, in Norwich.

'Fuddle, why so? Some fuddle-cap sure came
Into the room, and gave him his own name;
How should he catch a fox?* he'll turn his back
Upon tobacco, beer, French wine, or sack.
A bone his jewel is; and he does scorn,
With Æsop's cock, to wish a barley-corn.
There's not a soberer dog, I know, in Norwich,
What . . . . . would ye have him drunk with porridge?
This I confess, he goes around, around,
A hundred times, and never touches ground;
And in the middle circle of the air
He draws a circle like a conjuror.
With eagerness he still does forward tend,
Like Sisyphus, whose journey has no end.
He is the soul (if wood has such a thing?)
And living posy of a wooden ring.
He is advanced above his fellows, yet
He does not for it the least envy get.

* An old slang term for becoming fuddled.

He does above the Isle of Dogs commence,
And wheels the inferior spit by influence.
This, though, befalls his more laborious lot,
He is the Dog-star, and his days are hot.
Yet with this comfort there's no fear of burning,
'Cause all the while the industrious wretch is turning.
Then no more Fuddle say; give him no spurns,
But wreak your spleen on one that never turns,
And call him, if a proper name he lack,
A four-foot hustler, or a living Jack.'

The poets not unfrequently used the poor turnspit as an illustration or simile. Thus Pitt, in his *Art of Preaching*, alluding to an orator who speaks much, but little to the purpose, says:—

'His arguments in silly circles run,
Still round and round, and end where they begun.
So the poor turnspit, as the wheel runs round,
The more he gains, the more he loses ground.'

A curious political satire, published in 1705, and entitled *The Dog in the Wheel*, shews, under the figure of a turnspit dog, how a noisy demagogue can become a very quiet placeman. The poem commences thus:—

'Once in a certain family,
Where idleness was dis-esteemed;
For ancient hospitality,
Great plenty and frugality,
'Bove others famous deemed.
No useless thing was kept for show,
Unless a paroquet or so;
Some poor relation in an age,
The chaplain, or my lady's page:
All creatures else about the house
Were put to some convenient use.
Nay, ev'n the cook had learned the knack
With cur to save the charge of jack;
So trained 'em to her purpose fit,
And made them earn each bit they ate.
Her ready servants knew the wheel,
Or stood in awe of whip and bell;
Each had its task, and did it well.'

The poem as it proceeds describes the dogs in office lying by the kitchen fire, and discussing some savoury bones, the well-earned rewards of the day's exertions. The demagogic cur, entering, calls them mean, paltry wretches, to submit to such shameful servitude; unpatriotic vermin to chew the bitter bones of tyranny. For his part, he would rather starve a thousand times over than do so. Woe be to the tyrannic hand that would attempt to make him a slave, while he had teeth to defend his lawful liberty—and so forth. At this instant, however, the cook happens to enter—

'And seeing him (the demagogue) among the rest,
She called him very gently to her,
And stroked the smooth, submissive cur:
Who soon was hushed, forgot to rail,
He licked his lips, and wagged his tail,
Was overjoyed he should prevail
　　Such favour to obtain.
Among the rest he went to play,
Was put into the wheel next day,
He *turned* and ate as well as they,
　　And never *speeched* again.'

APRIL 9.

Roman captives, martyrs in Persia, 362. St Mary of Egypt, 5th century. Massylitan martyrs in Africa. St Eupsychius, martyr. St Dotto, abbot in Orkney, 6th century. St Waltrude, 686. St Gautier, abbot in Limousin, 1130.

Born.—Fisher Ames, American statesman, President of Harvard College, 1758, *Dedham, Massachusetts;* George Peacock, Dean of Ely, mathematician, 1791, *Denton.*

Died.—Constantine II., Roman emperor, assassinated, 340 ; Zenon, Emperor of the East, 491 ; Pope Constantine, 715; Edward IV., King of England, 1483 ; Gabrielle d'Estrées ('La Belle Gabrielle'), 1599; Francis Bacon, 1626, *St Albans ;* William, Earl of Craven, 1697; Simon, Lord Lovat, beheaded, 1747 ; Christian Wolf, philosophical writer, 1754, *Halle ;* Jacques Necker, French financial minister (1788), 1804, *Geneva ;* John Opie, painter, 1807 ; Dr William Prout, scientific writer, 1850, *London.*

EDWARD IV.

On this day, in the year 1483, died Edward IV., a king who makes a figure in history rather through the circumstances of the period in which he lived, than from the personal influence he exercised over them. He was the instrument of a revolution rather than the hero of it. That revolution was virtually the overthrow of feudalism, which had, through its own inherent defects and its increasing incongruity with the advance in the political and social condition of the world, been long tending to its fall. The disastrous government of a weak monarch on the throne, Henry VI., and the violent animosities of the feudal nobles, fomented by the intrigues of the Duke of York, the representative of a rival dynasty which had been displaced by a former revolution, brought on the long and furious civil wars known as the Wars of the Roses, in which the feudal nobles and great families were occupied much more in the indulgence of personal hatred and in mutual destruction than in carrying out any important political principles. When the power of the aristocracy had exhausted itself, the fortunes, perhaps we may say the accidents of war had left the party of the house of York the stronger of the two divisions into which the country had fallen ; and to this circumstance, without any remarkable merits of his own, Edward owed the throne. His claim on the score of descent was no doubt according to strict law better than that of the dynasty he displaced, inasmuch as he was descended from Lionel, Duke of Clarence, the second son of Edward III., while the branch of Lancaster was descended only from that monarch's third son. In the savage war of feudal rivalry in which the old aristocracy had almost worn itself out, Edward's father, Richard, Duke of York, perished at the moment when the crown of England was within his grasp, in consequence chiefly of his own want of caution and foresight in the battle of Wakefield, fought on the 31st of December 1460. Edward, who now succeeded his father in his claim to the crown, was a brave and able soldier, with more perseverance and less hesitation in pursuing his object. After having

inflicted a severe defeat on the Lancastrians at Mortimer's Cross, on the northern borders of Herefordshire, he advanced upon London, to which place Queen Margaret had also directed her retreat after the defeat and death of the Duke of York. She had gained a victory over the Yorkists near St Albans and delivered her husband from imprisonment, when consciousness of the superiority of Edward's forces obliged her to retrace her steps northward. Edward, who was then only in the nineteenth year of his age, was proclaimed King of England on the 2nd of March 1461.

Edward possessed many of the qualities which then in a prince conciliated the attachment of the multitude. He was bold and active, princely in bearing, one of the handsomest men of his time, and popular in his manners. Even his more apparent vices were such as were easily pardoned by popular opinion ; but under a brilliant exterior he was selfish and unscrupulous, eager of pleasure, and at the same time treacherous and cruel. The precarious character of the tenure by which he held the throne was shewn within the first few years of his reign. He had hardly ascended the throne, before he was obliged to hurry to the north to meet his opponents, who had already brought together a very powerful army under Queen Margaret and the Duke of Somerset. On Palm Sunday, the 29th of the same month of March 1461, Edward defeated the Lancastrians with frightful slaughter, at Towton, in Yorkshire ; and Queen Margaret, with her husband, Henry VI., and their son, the young prince Edward, were obliged to seek safety in Scotland. Queen Margaret subsequently entered England, and renewed the struggle, but the only result was the capture of the deposed king, who was imprisoned in the Tower.

King Edward was at this time popular among his subjects, but he seems to have given himself up entirely to his pleasures, and to have neglected the great feudal chiefs to whom he owed his throne. Perhaps they, on the other side, were unreasonable in their wishes to monopolise favour and power. The great Earl of Warwick had formed a design for the marriage of his daughter with the Duke of Clarence, to which Edward refused his consent; and Warwick is said to have been further offended by the neglect which the king shewed to him in the circumstances of his marriage with Lady Elizabeth Wydville. The powerful nobleman now quitted Edward, and became reconciled to Queen Margaret, and the civil war having recommenced, King Edward was taken prisoner, but he succeeded in making his escape, and fled to Holland. During his absence, Henry VI. was restored to the throne, and Edward was deposed, and proclaimed a traitor. But within a short time Edward returned with the assistance of the Duke of Burgundy, landed in Yorkshire in March 1471, and directing his march south, entered London and recovered the throne almost without resistance. On Easter Sunday, the 14th of April, Edward gained a great victory over the Lancastrians at Barnet, in which the Earl of Warwick was slain ; and on the 14th of May he defeated Queen Margaret's army in the battle of Tewkesbury. King Henry had again become a prisoner at Barnet ; and Queen Margaret and her son Edward, Prince of Wales, were captured at Tewkesbury, and the young prince was barbarously murdered in King Edward's presence. King Henry himself was murdered in the Tower, on the 21st of May, so that Edward could now enjoy the crown without a competitor. Queen Margaret was some time afterwards set at liberty on the payment of a considerable ransom by her brother the King of France.

Edward, thus relieved from further uneasiness, now gave himself up to his pleasures, in which he is said to have indulged indiscriminately, and not always with dignity. He died of the results of a surfeit, on the 9th of April 1483, in the forty-second year of his age. He exercised little influence on the political or social condition of his country, although the parliament took the opportunity of his weakness or inattention to obtain some concessions which were important for the strengthening of the national liberty. It was under Edward IV. that the art of printing was introduced into England, and it received encouragement from him personally, and from his ministers. Otherwise King Edward's reign seems best known, in popular remembrance, as the age of Jane Shore, his favourite mistress. The dynasty which Edward had founded was short-lived, and was soon driven out to give place to the house of Tudor, which destroyed the feudal power, only weakened by the successor of the Yorkists.

WILLIAM, EARL OF CRAVEN.

In the latter half of the sixteenth century, a poor lad, named Craven, trudged his weary way from Yorkshire to London, with the laudable design of seeking his fortune. Assisting to drive a long string of pack-horses, he found protection and companionship on the road ; and when the carrier was delivering a pack of Yorkshire cloth to a draper in Watling Street, he recommended the boy to the service of the citizen. The youth was soon advanced to be an apprentice ; steady industry claiming its due reward, he in course of time set up for himself in Leadenhall ; and ultimately becoming Lord Mayor, received the honour of knighthood from King James. The accession of wealth and honour did not cause him to forget his native Wharfdale. He beautified and repaired the church of Burnsall, in which he had sat when a poor boy ; founded and endowed alms-houses and other charitable institutions for indigent Yorkshiremen, and when death called him, full of years, he left an immense fortune to his only son William.

At that period, wealth alone, without the addition of a long pedigree, had not the position which it now enjoys; though military renown was considered a sufficient cover for any deficiency of birth. Probably for this reason, William Craven, the wealthy grandson of a Yorkshire peasant, at an early age took service in the army of Henry, Prince of Orange, and acquitted himself with honour and distinction. Afterwards, being one of the English volunteers who joined Gustavus Adolphus. he led the

forlorn hope at the storming of Creutznach. Though the first assault was repulsed, Craven, with determined bravery, led on a second, which proved gloriously successful. Though smarting under a severe wound, our hero generously granted quarter to the vanquished enemy, and Gustavus coming up knighted him as he lay wounded on the ground.

One of the avowed objects of Gustavus was the reinstatement of the Count-Palatine Frederick in the palatinate. The character of Frederick was not of a description to excite the respect or admiration of bold and politic men ; but his wife, the Princess Elizabeth, daughter of James I., was endowed with all the romantic qualities of a true heroine, as certainly as she was the heroine of a sad but true romance. The days of chivalry had not then quite passed away. Harte tells us that the courage and presence of mind of the princess were so conspicuous, and her figure and manners so attractive—though not to be termed a consummate beauty—that half the army of Gustavus was in love with her. The ferocious Christian, Duke of Brunswick, was her most tractable slave ; so was young Thurm, and so was Sir William Craven. But the death of Gustavus destroyed the last hope of recovering the palatinate, and Sir William Craven entered the service of the States of Holland, and continued in their army till the Restoration.

Though Sir William took no part in the civil war of England, yet from his great wealth, combined with his exceedingly simple, soldier-like habits of life, he was enabled to afford the exiled royal family very considerable pecuniary supplies. As a single instance of his liberality in this respect, he gave Charles II. no less than fifty thousand pounds in one sum and at one time. On this account the Parliament confiscated his estates, and though the States-General interfered through their ambassador, no effect ensued from the mediation. At the Restoration he regained his estates, and Charles conferred upon him the title of Earl.

On returning to England, Craven's first care was to purchase a grand old edifice called Drury House, from its having belonged to the knightly family of that name, and from which also the street called Drury-lane derives its appellation. This building, part of which was in existence within the memory of persons now living, stood on the site of the Olympic Theatre and the adjoining tavern called the "Craven Arms." After he had fitted up this house in a style of regal magnificence, the Princess Elizabeth, then twelve years a widow, came to reside in it with Lord Craven. Whether any stronger tie than pure friendship existed between them, it is not our place to inquire. When she came to live in Drury House, Craven was fifty-three years of age, and the Princess was sixty-five. It has been said, however, that they had previously been privately married on the Continent, and that the fifty thousand pounds given to Charles II. was the price of his consent to the marriage of his unfortunate aunt.

When the Princess arrived in England, Earl Craven began to build a magnificent palace for her, on his estate of Hampstead Marshall, in

Berkshire; but Elizabeth scarcely lived a year after her return from the Continent, and this house, intended to rival the castle of Heidelberg, was burned to the ground ere its completion. During the great plague of 1665, Lord Craven remained in London to succour the wretched, encourage the timid, and preserve order. On the death of Monk, he received the colonelcy of the Coldstream Guards, and during the latter part of the seventeenth century, the stout old Earl was one of the most conspicuous characters in London. Whenever a fire took place, he was sure to be present, to render assistance and preserve order; so it became a common saying that his horse could smell a fire ere it happened. His city birth, warlike fame, and romantic connexion with a queen—for Elizabeth was always styled in England by her fatal title of Queen of Bohemia—rendered him the most popular man in London, and his quiet remonstrances would disperse a riotous mob more effectively than a regiment of soldiers. He died in 1696, at the advanced age of eighty-eight years.

Across the end of Craven Buildings in Drury-lane, there will be observed a wall, on which is inscribed, at the present day, the name and business of a neighbouring tradesman. There was formerly a fresco painting on this wall, representing Lord Craven on a white charger, with a marshal's bâton in his hand. This portrait was frequently repainted in oil, and down to the present century was considered one of the sights of London; but it is now completely obliterated.

LA BELLE GABRIELLE.

The gallant, chivalrous, favourite French monarch, Henri Quatre, when starting on one of his warlike exploits in 1590, sojourned for a night at the Château de Cauvers, belonging to an artillery officer whom he had much befriended, the Chevalier D'Estrées. The daughter of the house, Gabrielle, a gentle, beautiful creature, about nineteen, had long honoured the king secretly, as belonging to the type of heroes whom women love. Her enthusiasm gave a warmth to the grace that naturally belonged to her; and she fairly captured the heart of Henri, without, so far as appears, any predetermined design of so doing. The king could not then delay his military proceedings; but he carried away with him recollections that were not likely to die. He found opportunities to see her again, and to work both upon her love and her gratitude. The state of court morals in those days in France, as in many other countries, points to what followed—how that she was married to Damerval de Liancourt, as a means of appeasing or blinding her father; how that the king procured a divorce for her on some pretext, well or ill founded; and how that she then lived with Henri during the remainder of her brief life, ennobled as a duchess, in order to give her station at court. Abating the one fact that she was his mistress and not his wife, all other parts of her career have met with the general encomiums of French writers. She was exceedingly beautiful, and was known everywhere as 'La Belle Gabrielle.' She spent her life royally, almost as a queen; yet she

494

was without haughtiness or arrogance. She never abused the favour she received, and withal was so affable, gentle, and benevolent, that she won the good-will of courtiers and people alike. The king loved her deeply; once, when engaged in a military enterprise of which the issue was doubtful, he wrote to her: 'If I am defeated, you know me well enough to be certain I shall not flee; my last thought will be of God—my last but one, of thee.' Her only quarrels were with the great minister, Sully, who disapproved of some of the persons promoted or rewarded through her means. The king well knew what an inestimable servant or friend he had in his unyielding minister; and once, when Gabrielle appealed to him, he told her honestly that he would rather lose her than Sully, if one must be lost. Her good sense came to the aid of her other qualities, and she no longer opposed Sully's views. Gabrielle's end was a sad one. On the 9th of April 1599, a fit of apoplexy carried her off, accompanied by such frightful contortions as to induce a suspicion that she had been poisoned; but no proof of such a crime ever came to light. The king mourned for her as he would for a princess of the blood royal, and felt her loss deeply. French song and poem, drama and opera, have had much to say concerning Henri Quatre and La Belle Gabrielle.

THE PONY EXPRESS.

The Pacific States, as they are called, of America, being separated from the rest by the wide sierra of the Rocky Mountains,—canal, railway, or even good roads not yet being practicable in that region,—communication necessarily becomes a difficulty. Even to convey letters over two thousand miles of prairie, mountain, and forest, was a task of a sufficiently formidable character. This difficulty was, however, overcome in 1860, by the enterprise of a private firm. Messrs. Russell, Major, and Waddell, who had been engaged as contractors for the conveyance of government stores, determined to establish a kind of express mail, by which letters should be conveyed in about a week between the two extreme points; depending partly on the commercial public and partly on the government for an adequate return. The contractors first built stations along the line of route, at convenient intervals, stocking them plentifully; then purchased six hundred ponies, or strong serviceable horses; then engaged a corps of fearless and trustworthy riders; and finally provided an equipment of riding-dress, letter-bags, revolvers, and rifles for the men. On the 9th of April 1860, the service commenced. Two pony-couriers started on the same day; one from St Francisco, to come east; the other from St Joseph on the Missouri, to go west. When a pony had done his stage, at twelve miles an hour, he was replaced by another; and when a courier had done as many stages as he could accomplish without rest, another took his place. Thus the mail-bags were travelling incessantly at the rate of twelve miles an hour. Each mail accomplished the nineteen hundred miles of distance in about seven days and a half. The system very soon became comparatively consolidated. The men suffered from fatigue, hunger, cold, heat, and especially from the attacks of Indians, but they persevered undauntedly ; and the Pony Express served its purpose until the opening of the Pacific Railway in 1869 superseded other means of communication.

APRIL 10.

St Bademus, abbot, martyr. 376. B. Mechtildes, virgin and abbess, 14th century.

Born.—Hugo Grotius, historical and theological writer, 1583, *Delft ;* Sir John Pringle, P.R.S., medical writer, 1707, *Stitchel, Roxburghshire ;* William Hazlitt, miscellaneous writer, 1778, *Maidstone.*

Died.—Louis II., King of France, 'Le Bèque,' 879 ; William, Earl of Pembroke, 1630 ; Jean Lebeuf, French antiquarian writer, 1760 ; Prince Eugène of Savoy, 1736, *Vienna ;* William Cheselden, anatomist, 1752 ; Admiral John Byron, 1786 ; Erasmus Darwin, poet, 1802 ; Lagrange, French mathematician, 1813, *Paris ;* Paul Courier, French novelist, 1825 ; Cardinal Weld, 1837, *Rome ;* Alexander Nasmyth, painter, 1840, *Edinburgh.*

INTRODUCTION OF THE ORGAN INTO A CHURCH AT COMPIÈGNE.

The only incident of religious history connected with the 10th of April that is noticed in a French work resembling the present, is the introduction by King Pepin, of France, of an organ into the Church of St Corneille at Compiègne, in the year 787—rather a minute fact to be so signalised ; suggesting, however, the very considerable antiquity of the instrument in association with devotion. It may be remarked that the bagpipe is believed by the historians of music to be the basis of the organ : the organ is, in its primitive form, a bagpipe put into a more mechanical form, and furnished with a key-board. And this, again, suggests how odd it is that Scotland, which still preserves the bagpipe as a national instrument, should have all along, in her religious history, treated its descendant, the organ, with such contumely.

'When the Scots invaded the northern parts in 1640, a sergeant-major was billeted in one Mr Calvert's house, who was musically disposed, and had a portative organ for his pleasure in one of his chambers. The Scotchman, being of the preciser strain, and seeing the instrument open, "Art thou a kirkman ?" says he. "No, sir," says he (Mr Calvert). "Then, what the de'il, man," returns the Scot, " dost thou with this same great box o' whistles here ? " '—*Thoms's Anecdotes and Traditions.*

THE 'TENTH OF APRIL.'

The name of this day is almost the only one applied in England, in the manner of our French neighbours, as a denomination for an event. And yet the event was, after all, one of slight ultimate importance. It was an apparent danger to the peace of the country, and one which was easily turned aside and neutralised.

The Parisian Revolution of February, 1848, had, as usual, stirred up and brought into violent action all the discontents of Europe. Even in happy England there was a discontent,

one involving certain sections of the working classes, and referring rather to certain speculative political claims than to any practical grievance. The Chartists, as they were called, deemed this a good opportunity for pressing their claims, and they resolved to do so with a demonstration of their numbers, thus hinting at the physical force which they possessed, but probably without any serious designs against the peace of their fellow-citizens. It was arranged that a monster petition should be presented to parliament on the 10th of April, after being paraded through London by a procession. The Government, fearing that an outbreak of violence might take place, as had happened already at Manchester, Glasgow, and other large towns, assembled large bodies of troops, planted cannon in the neighbourhood of Westminster Bridge, and garrisoned the public offices ; at the same time a vast number of the citizens were sworn in as special constables to patrol the streets. The Chartists met on Kennington Common, under the presidency of Mr Feargus O'Connor, M.P., but their sense of the preparations made for the preservation of the peace, and a hint that they would not be allowed to cross the bridges in force, took away all hope of their intended demonstration. Their petition was quietly taken ' in three cabs ' along Vauxhall Bridge, and presented to the House of Commons ; the multitude dispersed; by four o'clock in the afternoon London had resumed its ordinary appearances, and the *Tenth of April* remained only a memory of an apprehended danger judiciously met and averted.

HOARDED TREASURES AND TREASURE TROVE.

The custom of hoarding or burying money belongs either to a rude or a disturbed state of society. Where matters are more systematic and peaceful, spare cash can always be made to yield interest. Sometimes, in past years, the hiding of treasure arose from a sort of diseased activity of the money-loving propensity. A singular case of this kind occurred in 1843. On the 10th of April, eight labourers were employed in grubbing up trees at Tufnell Park, near Highgate, and during their labours they lighted upon two jars containing nearly four hundred sovereigns in gold. They divided the money, and one of them spent his share ; but soon afterwards Mr Tufnell, lord of the manor, claimed the whole of it as *treasure-trove.* There is a complex law, partly statute and partly civil, relating to the recovery of treasure for which the original owner does not apply ; and according to the circumstances of the finding, the property belongs to the Crown, to the lord of the manor, or to the finder, or to two out of these three. While the eight labourers were anxiously puzzling over Mr Tufnell's claim, the real owner stepped forward, and told a singular tale. He was a brass-founder living in Clerkenwell ; and being about nine months before under a temporary mental delusion, he one night took out two jars of sovereigns with him, and buried them in the field at Tufnell Park. Being able to prove these facts, his claim to the money was admitted. In other cases, the burying of treasure results not from any delusion, but from the ignorance of the owner as to any better mode of securing it. In 1820, some labouring men, on clearing out a ditch at Bristol, found a number of guineas and half-guineas, and a silver snuff-box. Some time afterwards a sailor was seen to be disconsolately grubbing at that spot; and on inquiry, it appeared that, before starting on his last voyage, he had hidden behind the ditch his few worldly treasures, and had cut a notch in a tree to denote the spot.

Times of trouble, as we have said, led to frequent buryings of treasure. In 1820, the foundations of some old houses were being removed at Exeter, and during the operations the workmen came upon a large collection of silver coins. They made merry and got drunk on the occasion, which attracted the attention of their employer; he caused more careful examination to be made, which resulted in the discovery of a second heap of coins, in a hole covered with a flat stone. The coins were of all dates, from Henry the Eighth to Charles the First or the Commonwealth; and it is not improbable that the disturbed state of affairs in the middle of the seventeenth century led to this mode of securing treasure. The French Revolution was fruitful in such proceedings, some of which came to light in our own country. In January 1836, at Great Stanmore, the rector's coachman and gardener found in a field on the side of a ditch, a heap of more than three hundred and sixty foreign gold coins, comprising louis d'ors, Napoleons, doubloons, and other kinds, worth on an average more than a guinea a-piece. The wife of one of the men told the rector's wife; and then came an inquiry—to whom did or should the treasure belong? As soon as the news became noised abroad, excited villagers rushed to the spot, and found stores far more rich than that which had set the place in commotion, amounting to nearly four thousand pounds in value. The finders naturally claimed it; then the rector claimed it, because it had been found on glebe-land; and then the Crown appointed a regular coroner's inquest (in accordance with an ancient usage) to investigate the whole matter. During the inquiry, some singular evidence came out. About twenty years earlier, when the downfall of Napoleon had led to the resuscitation of the Bourbons, a foreigner came to reside at Stanmore; he used to walk about the fields in an abstracted manner, and was naturally regarded by the villagers as a singular character. He suddenly left the place, and never re-appeared. Two years after the stranger's departure, another person came, searched about the fields, and made minute inquiries concerning some hidden wealth. He stated that the foreigner who had formerly lived at Stanmore was dead; that on his death-bed he had revealed the fact of having hidden considerable treasure; and that he had sketched a ground-plan of the field where the hoard lay. On comparing notes it appeared that, during the long intervening period, two ash-trees had been removed from the side of the ditch; that this change had prevented the foreigner's agent or heir from identifying the spot; and that a change in the watercourse had gradually washed away the earth and left the coins exposed. As a question of probability, we may conjecture that the

496

troubled state of France had something to do with this burying of the foreigner's treasure; as a question of law, the amount reverted to the Crown as *treasure-trove*.

BELLMAN'S VERSES.

In London, and probably other English cities, in the seventeenth century, the Bellman was the recognised term for what we would now call a night watchman, being derived from the hand-bell which the man carried in order to give alarm in case of fire. In the Luttrell Collection of Broadsides (Brit. Mus.) is one dated 1683-4, entitled ' A Copy of Verses presented by Isaac Ragg, Bellman, to his Masters and Mistresses of Holbourn Division, in the parish of St Giles's-in-the-Fields.' It is headed by a wood-cut representing Isaac in professional accoutrements, a pointed pole in the left hand, and in the right

THE BELLMAN OF HOLBORN.

a bell, while his lantern hangs from his jacket in front. Below is a series of verses, on St Andrew's Day, King Charles the First's Birthday, St Thomas's Day, Christmas Day, St John's Day, Childermas Day, New Year's Day, on the thirtieth of January, &c., all of them very proper and very insufferable; the 'prologue' is, indeed, the only specimen worth giving here, being the expression of Mr Ragg's official duty; it is as follows:

' Time, Master, calls your bellman to his task,
   To see your doors and windows are all fast,
   And that no villany or foul crime be done
   To you or yours in absence of the sun.
   If any base lurker I do meet,
   In private alley or in open street,
   You shall have warning by my timely call,
   And so God bless you and give rest to all.'

In a similar, but unadorned broadside, dated

1666, Thomas Law, bellman, greets his masters of 'St Giles, Cripplegate, within the Freedom,' in twenty-three dull stanzas, of which the last may be subjoined :

' No sooner hath St Andrew crowned November,
But Boreas from the North brings cold December,
And I have often heard a many say,
He brings the winter month Newcastle way ;
For comfort here of poor distressed souls,
Would he had with him brought a fleet of coals !'

It seems to have been customary for the bellman to go about at a certain season of the year, probably Christmas, amongst the householders of his district, giving each a copy of his broadside—firing a broadside at each, as it were—and expecting from each in return some small gratuity, as an addition to his ordinary salary. The execrable character of his poetry is indicated by the contempt with which the wits speak of ' bellman's verses.'

Robert Herrick has a little poem giving his friends a blessing in the form of the nightly addresses of

THE BELLMAN.

From noise of scare fires rest ye free,
From murders benedicitie ;
From all mischances that may fright
Your pleasing slumbers in the night ;
Mercie secure ye all, and keep
The goblin from ye, while ye sleep.
Past one o'clock, and almost two,
My masters all, ' good day to you.'

APRIL 11.

St Leo the Great, Pope, 461. St Antipas, martyr. St Maccai, abbot, 5th century (?). St Aid, abbot in Ireland. St Guthlac, hermit, patron of the abbey of Croyland, 716.

ST GUTHLAC.

Of St Guthlac, one of the most interesting of the old Saxon anchorets, we have a good biography by a nearly contemporary monk named Felix. From this it appears that the saint was at first devoted to warlike enterprises, but after a time was moved to devote himself wholly to a contemplative religious life in Croyland Isle in the fen countries. Here he performed, as usual, many miracles, was tortured by devils, and had many blessed experiences ; at length, on the 11th of April 716, he was favoured with a quiet and easy passage to a higher state of existence, at the age of forty-one.

There is much that is admirable in this biography, and the character it ascribes to St Guthlac. The account contains no trace of those monstrous asceticisms which so often disgust us. He wore skins instead of linen, and had one daily meal only, of barley-bread and water; but no self-inflictions are recorded, only abstemious habits and incessant devotion. 'The blessed man Guthlac was a chosen man in divine deeds, and a treasure of all wisdom ; and he was stedfast in his duties, as also he was earnestly intent on Christ's service, so that never was aught else in his mouth but Christ's praise, nor

in his heart but virtue, nor in his mind but peace and love and pity ; nor did any man ever see him angry nor slothful to Christ's service : but one might ever perceive in his countenance love and peace ; and evermore sweetness was in his temper, and wisdom in his breast, and there was so much cheerfulness in him, that he always appeared alike to acquaintances and to strangers.' We must confess,—not a revolting character.

Monk Felix describes the fen wilderness : 'There are immense marshes, now a black pool of water, now foul-running streams, and also many islands, and reeds, and hillocks, and thickets.' Doubtless, a true description. The villages were mostly built on beds of gravel, which afforded comparative security.

Ethelbald founded an abbey in Croyland Isle, St Guthlac's retreat, which was destroyed by the Danes when they sacked Ely and Peterborough. It was rebuilt, and destroyed by fire ; and again rebuilt. The monks in after time got to be somewhat ill-famed for drunkenness, revellings, and such like.

Croyland Isle, like the Isle of Ely, is now no more. Of the four streams which enclosed it, the drainage has removed all trace of three, changing them to quiet pastures and rich farming land ; and the Welland itself now runs wide of the village, in a new channel. The curious old triangular bridge stands high and dry in the centre of the village square, lorn of its three streams ; and on it sits a robed figure in stone, with a great stone in its hand, supposed to be, amongst other things, a loaf. The modern church is built out of part of the old abbey, and a beautiful portion of ruin remains, though the restorers, alas ! are at it. We ourselves can testify to the beautiful peace of those Croyland fens, even at this day ; and they must have been much more beautiful in the saint's time.

Born.—Christopher Smart, poet, 1722, *Shepburne in Kent ;* David Hamilton, architect, 1768, *Glasgow ;* Marshal Lannes, Duke of Montebello, 1769, *Lectoure ;* George Canning, statesman, 1770, *London.*

Died.—Cardinal Beaufort, 1447, *Winchester ;* Gaston de Foix, French warrior, 1512, *Ravenna ;* Pope Gregory XIII., 1585 ; Stanislaus Poniatowski, last king of Poland, 1798, *St Petersburg ;* John Galt, novelist and miscellaneous writer, 1839.

CARDINAL BEAUFORT.

Henry of Beaufort, who was a very good example of the political prelates of our papal middle ages, and is well known in the annals of England during the fifteenth century, was the second son of John of Gaunt, by that prince's third wife, the Lady Catherine Swynford, and he was therefore half-brother of King Henry IV. He took his name from the castle of Beaufort, in France, where he was born. His birth occurred before the marriage of his parents, but he was legitimatized in the 20th of Richard II., along with his brothers, the eldest of whom was Marquis of Dorset and Lord High Admiral of England, and the other became distinguished as a warrior, and was created Duke of Exeter by Henry V. From the former the present ducal house of Beaufort claims descent. Henry of Beaufort was thus allied by blood both with the crown and with the most powerful men of the day. He studied at Aix-la-Chapelle and at Oxford, and appears to have been well versed in the civil and canon laws. In 1397, and therefore immediately after his legitimization, he was intruded by Pope Boniface IX. into the bishopric of Lincoln, and the new prelate appears to have been in favour with Richard II., for he accompanied that prince in his last expedition into Ireland, and was with him on his return when he met Beaufort's half-brother, Henry of Lancaster, and became his prisoner.

No doubt Bishop Beaufort stood high in the favour of his brother when the latter ascended the throne. On the death of William of Wickham, in 1405, he was translated from the see of Lincoln to that of Winchester, which he continued to hold during the rest of his life. It is recorded of him, that when Henry V., obliged to obtain large sums for his wars, meditated a heavy taxation of the ecclesiastical body, the Bishop of Winchester did not oppose his nephew's demand, but he bought off the danger by lending the king, out of his own great wealth, the sum of twenty thousand pounds. That his power in England was great, and that he was not unpopular, was proved by the circumstance that on the death of Henry V. he was chosen by the Parliament to be, with the Earl of Warwick, guardian of the infant prince, who had now become Henry VI. He seems to have taken an active part in the government from the first, but he differed in many of his views from the Duke of Gloucester, and the disagreement rose to such a height that the bishop wrote to the Duke of Bedford to call him from France to interfere, and his presence alone effected a reconciliation. Nor was this reconciliation easy, for though the regent Bedford arrived in London on the 10th of January, private negotiations produced so little effect that, after several months' discussion, it was found necessary to submit the matter to a parliament, the members of which were forbidden to appear in arms, lest it might end in a fight. 'The twentie-one of February,' says Stow, 'began a great councell at St Albans, which was afterwarde rejorned to Northampton, but, for that no due conclusion might be made, on the 15 of March was called a parliament at Leicester, the which endured till the 25 day of June. This was called the parliament of battes, because men being forbidden to bring swords or other weapons, brought great battes and staves on their neckes, and when those weapons were inhibited them, they took stones and plomets of lead. During this parliament, the variance betwixt the two lords was debated, insomuch that the Duke of Gloucester put a bill of complaint against the byshop, containing sixe articles, all which articles were by the bishop sufficiently answered; and finally, by the counsel of the lord regent, all the matters of variance betweene the sayde two lords were put to the examination and judgement of certain lords of the parliament.' The bishop, however, seems not to have been fully satisfied, for soon afterwards he resigned his office of Lord Chancellor.

Immediately after this reconciliation, on the 23rd of June 1426, Bishop Beaufort's ambition

498

was gratified by his election at Rome to the dignity of a cardinal (of St Eusebius), and on the Duke of Bedford's return to France in the February of the following year he accompanied him to Calais to receive there the cardinal's hat. In the autumn of 1429, Cardinal Beaufort was appointed by the Pope the papal legate in the army which he was sending against the Bohemian heretics, who at the same time enjoined him to bring with him out of England a body of soldiers to assist in the expedition, for the raising of which he authorised him to levy a tax of one-tenth on the incomes of the spirituality in England. Cardinal Beaufort raised the money, collected upwards of four thousand English soldiers, and was on his way to the Continent, when he received a message from the Regent Bedford, earnestly requesting him to carry him whatever troops he could to reinforce him in Paris. The cardinal's patriotism overcame his devotion to the Pope, and he proceeded with his soldiers to Paris, where he was gladly received, but, after remaining no long while there, the cardinal continued his journey to Bohemia. He soon, however, returned thence to England, having, as far as is known, performed no act worth recording.

Cardinal Beaufort continued to take an active part in political affairs, and he appears to have been generally considered as a friend to reforms. He was popular, because he seems to have steadily supported the French policy of Henry V., and to have been opposed to all concessions to the enemy. The remarkable political poem entitled the *Libel of English Policy*, written in the year 1436, was dedicated to him. Yet he acted in concert with the Duke of Suffolk in concluding the truce of 1444, and in bringing about the marriage of the young King of England with Margaret of Anjou, which was the fertile source of so many troubles in England. From this time the cardinal's political party became identified with Suffolk's party, that is, with the party of the queen. Beaufort was himself perhaps falling into dotage, for he was now an octogenarian, and he did not long survive this event, for he died in his episcopal palace of Walvesey, on the 11th of April 1447. He had ruled the see of Winchester during the long period of nearly forty-three years. Cardinal Beaufort was usually considered to be a selfish, hard, and unfeeling man, yet it must be remembered to his credit that, when Joan d'Arc was brought into the market-place of Rouen for execution, Beaufort, who sat on a scaffold with the prelates of France, rose from his seat in tears, and set the example to the other bishops of leaving the place. He was certainly ambitious, for at the advanced age of eighty he still cherished the hope of securing his election to the papacy.

HOCK-TIDE.

A fortnight after Easter our forefathers celebrated a popular anniversary, the origin and meaning of which has been the subject of some dispute. It was called Hoke-tide, or Hock-tide, and occupied two days, the Monday and Tuesday following the second Sunday after Easter, though the Tuesday was considered the principal day. On this day it was the custom for the women to go out into the streets and roads with cords, and stop and bind all those of the other sex they met, holding them till they purchased their release by a small contribution of money. On the Monday, the men had proceeded in the same way towards the women. The meaning of the word *hoke,* or *hock,* seems to be totally unknown, and none of the derivations yet proposed seem to be deserving of our consideration. The custom may be traced, by its name at least, as far back as the thirteenth century, and appears to have prevailed in all parts of England, but it became obsolete early in the last century. At Coventry, which was a great place for pageantry, there was a play or pageant attached to the ceremony, which, under the title of 'The old Coventry play of Hock Tuesday,' was performed before Queen Elizabeth during her visit to Kenilworth, in July 1575. It represented a series of combats between the English and Danish forces, in which twice the Danes had the better, but at last, by the arrival of the Saxon women to assist their countrymen, the Danes were overcome, and many of them were led captive in triumph by the women. Queen Elizabeth 'laughed well' at this play, and is said to have been so much pleased with it, that she gave the actors two bucks and five marks in money. The usual performance of this play had been suppressed in Coventry soon after the Reformation, on account of the scenes of riot which it occasioned.

It will be seen that this Coventry play was founded on the statement which had found a place in some of our chroniclers as far back as the fourteenth century, that these games of Hock-tide were intended to commemorate the massacre of the Danes on St Brice's day, 1002 ; while others, alleging the fact that St Brice's day is the 13th of November, suppose it to commemorate the rejoicings which followed the death of Hardicanute, and the accession of Edward the Confessor, when the country was delivered from Danish tyranny. Others, however, and probably with more reason, think that these are both erroneous explanations ; and this opinion is strongly supported by the fact that Hock Tuesday is not a fixed day, but a moveable festival, and dependent on the great Anglo-Saxon pagan festival of Easter, like the similar ceremony of heaving, still practised on the borders of Wales on Easter Monday and Tuesday. Such old pagan ceremonies were preserved among the Anglo-Saxons long after they became Christians, but their real meaning was gradually forgotten, and stories and legends, like this of the Danes, afterwards invented to explain them. It may also be regarded as a confirmation of the belief, that this festival is the representation of some feast connected with the pagan superstitions of our Saxon forefathers, that the money which was collected was given to the church, and was usually applied to the reparation of the church buildings. We can hardly understand why a collection of money should be thus made in commemoration of the overthrow of the Danish influence, but we can easily imagine how, when the festival was continued

by the Saxons as Christians, what had been an offering to some one of the pagan gods might be turned into an offering to the church. The entries on this subject in the old churchwardens' registers of many of our parishes, not only shew how generally the custom prevailed, but to what an extent the middle classes of society took part in it. In Reading these entries go back to a rather remote date, and mention collections by men as well as women while they seem to shew that there the women, 'hocked,' as the phrase was, on the Monday, and the men on the Tuesday. In the registers of the parish of St Laurence, under the year 1499, we have—

'Item, received of Hock money gaderyd of women, xxs.
    Item, received of Hok money gaderyd of men, iiijs.'

And, in the parish of St Giles, under the date 1535—

'Hoc money gatheryd by the wyves (*women*), xiijs. ixd.'

And, in St Mary's parish, under the year 1559—

'Hoctyde money, the mens gatheryng, iiijs. The womens, xijs.'

Out of this money, it would appear that the 'wyves,' who always gained most, were in Reading treated with a supper, for we find in the churchwardens' accounts of St Giles's parish, under the year 1526, this entry—

'Paid for the wyves supper at Hoctyde, xxiiijd.'

In the year 1450, a bishop of Worcester inhibited these 'Hoctyde' practices, on the ground that they led to all sorts of dissipation and licentiousness. It may be added that it appears, from the entries in the churchwardens' registers of various parishes, that in the fifteenth and sixteenth centuries Hock-tide was called in London Hob-tide.

APRIL 12.

St Victor, of Braga, martyr. St Julius, Pope, 352. St Sabas, the Goth, martyr, 372. St Zeno, bishop of Verona, 380.

Born.—Edward Bird, eminent 'genre' painter, 1772, *Wolverhampton ;* Henry Clay, American statesman, 1777 ; John George, Earl of Durham, statesman, 1792, *Durham.*

Died.—Seneca, Roman philosopher, ordered to death by Nero, 65, *Rome ;* Jacques-Benique Bossuet, Bishop of Cordan, orator, philosopher, and historian, 1704, *Meaux ;* Dr George Cheyne, eminent physician, 1742, *Bath ;* William Kent, painter, sculptor, and architect, 1748, *Burlington House, Chiswick ;* Pietro Metastasio, Italian poet, 1782, *Vienna ;* Dr Edward Young, poet, 1765, *Welwyn.*

LUCIUS ANNÆUS SENECA.

Lucius Annæus Seneca, the Roman philosopher, was born B.C. 6. His life may be considered as an ineffectual protest against the corruption of his time. At length the tyranny and excesses of the emperors were indulged in unchecked, where only a few opposed what the majority were not sorry to reap the fruits of.

Seneca was educated in all that was to be

learned, and became a pleader at the bar. This vocation he had to abandon through the jealousy of Caligula, who deemed himself an able orator. Nevertheless, the emperor took occasion to banish him to Corsica ; where he remained, till recalled by Agrippina to educate her son Nero. After being Nero's tutor, he became his minister, and endeavoured to restrain his excesses. Suspecting danger, he asked to be allowed to surrender to his master all his wealth, and to go into studious retirement But the tyrant refused this request ; and taking hold of the first pretext, ordered him to put an end to himself. This he did like a philosopher, before his wife and friends. First his veins were opened. Then he took a draught of poison. But still dying slowly, he was put into a warm bath ; and at last, it is said, suffocated in a stove.

His manner of life was abstemious and noble. His philosophy was somewhat eclectic — a fusion of all the existing systems, though the stoical predominated. His style was somewhat florid and ostentatious, yet both the style and the philosophy are frequently admirable, and often filled with such a spirit as we are apt to think Christianity alone has inculcated.

We subjoin, in illustration, an extract from his essay *On Anger*, which is a fair specimen of this spirit :—' Verily, what reason is there for hating those who fall into the hands of the law ? or into sins of any kind ? It is not the mark of a wise man to hate those that err : indeed, if he does, he himself should hate himself. Let him think how much of what he does is base, how many of his actions call for pardon. Will he hate himself then ? Yet a just judge does not give one decision in his own case, another in a stranger's. No one is found who can absolve himself. Whoever says he is innocent, looks at the proof rather than his conscience. How much more human is it to shew a mild, kind spirit to those who do wrong ; not to drive them headlong, but to draw them back ! If a man wander out of his path through ignorance of the country, it is better to set him right again, than to urge him on further.' (*Seneca, De Ira*, i. 14.)

DR GEORGE CHEYNE.

Dr George Cheyne, a physician of considerable eminence in his day, was born in Aberdeenshire, and educated at Edinburgh under the celebrated Doctor Pitcairne. After a youth passed in severe study and prudent abstinence, Cheyne came to London, with the determination of entering on practice. On his first arrival, being a stranger, and having to make friends, he was compelled to conform to the general style of life, which was to be described as free. The consequence of the sudden change from abstemiousness to epicurean indulgence, was, that Cheyne increased daily in bulk, swelling to such an enormous size, that he weighed no less than thirty-two stones ; and was compelled to have the whole side of his carriage made open to receive him. With this increase of size came its natural concomitants, shortness of breath, habitual lethargy, and a crowd of nervous and scorbutic symptoms. In this deplorable condition, having vainly exhausted the powers of medicine, he determined to try a milk

and vegetable diet, the good effects of which speedily appeared. His size was reduced almost to a third ; and he recovered his strength, activity, and cheerfulness, with the perfect use of all his faculties. And by a regular adherence to a milk and vegetable regimen, he lived to a good age, dying at Bath in his seventy-second year. He wrote several works that were well received by the medical and scientific world, two of which— *An Essay on Health and Long Life,* and *The English Malady, or a Treatise of Nervous Diseases,* —contained the results of his own experience, and, as may be supposed, met with considerable ridicule from the free-living doctors and critics of the day. On the publication of the first work, Winter, a well-known physician of the period, addressed the following epigram to Cheyne :

' Tell me from whom, fat-headed Scot,
   Thou didst thy system learn ;
From Hippocrate thou hadst it not,
   Nor Celsus, nor Pitcairne.

Suppose we own that milk is good,
   And say the same of grass ;
The one for babes is only food,
   The other for an ass.

Doctor ! one new prescription try,
   (A friend's advice forgive ;)
Eat grass, reduce thyself, and die,
   Thy patients then may live.'

To which Cheyne made the following reply :

' My system, doctor, is my own,
   No tutor I pretend ;
My blunders hurt myself alone,
   But yours your dearest friend.

Were you to milk and straw confined,
   Thrice happy might you be ;
Perhaps you might regain your mind,
   And from your wit get free.

I can't your kind prescription try,
   But heartily forgive ;
'Tis natural you should wish me die,
   That you yourself may live.'

KENT AND HIS ST CLEMENT'S ALTAR-PIECE.

William Kent was a distinguished mediocrity in a mediocre time. The favour of the Earl of Burlington and some other men of rank, enabled him, without genius or acquired skill, to realize good returns, first for pictures, afterwards as an architect. It is fully admitted that he was deficient in all the qualities of the artist, that his portraits were without likeness, his ceilings and staircases coarse caricatures of Olympus—that he was, in short, wholly a bad artist. And yet, in a worldly point of view, Kent, to the discredit of the age, was anything but a failure.

Amongst a few pictures which Kent had interest to get bought and introduced into London churches, was one which the vestry of St Clement's in the Strand—Johnson's church— had unhappily placed above their communiontable. It was such a muddle, in point of both design and execution, that nobody could pretend to say what was the meaning of it. The wags, at length getting scent of it, began to lay bets as to what it was all about ; some professing to believe one thing and some another. The Bishop of London became so scandalised at what was going on, that—probably feeling as much bewildered as anybody—he ordered the picture to be taken down.

Then came in Wag-in-chief, William Hogarth, professing to clear up the mystery, or at least to solve several dubious points in it, by an engraving representing the picture; which engraving being placed under the piece, might, he said, enable the vestry to restore it to its place, and so save 'the sixty pounds which they wisely gave for it.' On this engraving he had letters with references below for explanation. Thus, said he, 'No. 1 is not the Pretender's wife and children, as our weak brethren imagine. No. 2 is not St

KENT'S DUBIOUS ALTAR-PIECE.

Cecilia, as the connoisseurs think, but a choir of angels playing in concert.' The other explanations betray the fine secretive humour of Hogarth: 'A, an organ; B, an angel playing on it. C, the shortest joint of the arm; D, the longest joint. E, an angel tuning a harp; F, the inside of his leg, *but whether right or left is not yet discovered.* G, a hand playing on a lute; H, the other leg, judiciously omitted to make room for the harp. J and K, smaller angels, *as appears from their wings.*'

Kent must have writhed under this play upon

his precious work; but the sixty pounds secured in his pocket would doubtless be a sort of consolation.

YOUNG'S NARCISSA.

The 'Third Night' of Young's *Complaint* is entitled 'Narcissa,' from its being dedicated to the sad history of the early death of a beautiful lady, thus poetically designated by the author. Whatever doubts may exist with respect to the reality or personal identity of the other characters noticed in the *Night Thoughts*, there can be none whatever as regards Narcissa. She was the daughter of Young's wife by her first husband, Colonel Lee. When scarcely seventeen years of age, she was married to Mr Henry Temple, son of the then Lord Palmerston.* Soon afterwards being attacked by consumption, she was taken by Young to the south of France in hopes of a change for the better; but she died there about a year after her marriage, and Dr Johnson, in his *Lives of the Poets*, tells us that 'her funeral was attended with the difficulties painted in such animated colours in *Night the Third*.' Young's words in relation to the burial of Narcissa, eliminating, for brevity's sake, some extraneous and redundant lines, are as follows:

> 'While nature melted, superstition raved;
> That mourned the dead; and this denied a grave.
> For oh! the curst ungodliness of zeal!
> While sinful flesh relented, spirit nursed
> In blind infallibility's embrace,
> Denied the charity of dust to spread
> O'er dust! a charity their dogs enjoy.
> What could I do? What succour? What resource?
> With pious sacrilege a grave I stole;
> With impious piety that grave I wronged;
> Short in my duty; coward in my grief!
> More like her murderer than friend, I crept
> With soft suspended step, and muffled deep
> In midnight darkness, whispered my last sigh.
> I whispered what should echo through their realms,
> Nor writ her name, whose tomb should pierce the skies.'

All Young's biographers have told the same story, from Johnson down to the edition of the *Night Thoughts* edited by George Gilfillan, who, speaking of Narcissa, says, 'her remains were brutally denied sepulture as the dust of a Protestant.'

Le Tourneur translated the *Night Thoughts* into French about 1770, and, strange to say, the work soon became exceedingly popular in France, more so probably than ever it has been in England. Naturally enough, then, curiosity became excited with respect to where the unfortunate Narcissa was buried, and it was soon discovered that she had been interred in the Botanic Garden of Montpellier. An old gate-keeper of the garden, named Mercier, confessed that many years previously he had assisted to bury an English lady in a hollow, waste spot of the garden. As he told the story, an English clergyman came to him and begged that he would bury a lady; but he refused, until the Englishman, with tears in his eyes, said that she was his only

* By a second wife, grandfather of Lord Palmerston (1784—1865), the well-known English politician.

502

daughter; on hearing this, he (the gate-keeper), being a father himself, consented. Accordingly, the Englishman brought the dead body on his shoulders, his eyes 'raining' tears, to the garden at midnight, and he there and then buried the corpse. The dismal scene has been painted by a French artist of celebrity; and there cannot be many persons who have not seen the engravings from that picture, which are sold as *souvenirs* of Montpellier. About the time this confession was made, Professor Gouan, an eminent botanist, was writing a work on the plants in the garden, into which he introduced the above story, thus giving it a sort of scientific authority; and consequently the grave of Narcissa became one of the treasures of the garden, and one of the leading lions of Montpellier. A writer in the *Evangelical Magazine* of 1797 gives an account of a visit to the garden, and a conversation with one Bannal, who had succeeded Mercier in his office, and who had often heard the sad story of the burial of Narcissa from Mercier's lips. Subsequently, Talma, the tragedian, was so profoundly impressed with the story, that he commenced a subscription to erect a magnificent tomb to the memory of the unfortunate Narcissa; but as the days of bigotry in matters of sepulture had nearly passed away, it was thought better to erect a simple monument, inscribed, as we learn from Murray's *Handbook*, with the words:

'PLACANDIS NARCISSÆ MANIBUS.'

The *Handbook* adding, 'She was buried here at a time when the atrocious laws which accompanied the Revocation of Nantes, backed by the superstition of a fanatic populace, denied Christian burial to Protestants.'

Strange to say, this striking story is almost wholly devoid of truth. Narcissa never was at Montpellier; she died and was buried at Lyons. That she died at Lyons, we know from Mr Herbert Crofts's account of Young, published by Dr Johnson; that she was buried there, we know by her burial registry and her tombstone, both of which are yet in existence. And by these we also learn that Young's 'animated' account of her funeral in the *Night Thoughts* is simply untrue. She was not denied a grave:

> 'Denied the charity of dust to spread
> O'er dust;'

nor did he steal a grave, as he asserts, but bought and paid for it. Her name was not left unwrit, as her tombstone still testifies.

The central square of the Hôtel de Dieu at Lyons was long used as a burial-place for Protestants; but the alteration in the laws at the time of the great Revolution doing away with the necessity of having separate burial-places for different religions, the central square was converted into a medical garden for the use of the hospital. The Protestants of Lyons being of the poorer class, there were few memorials to remove when the ancient burying-ground was made into a garden. The principal one, however, consisting of a large slab of black marble, was set up against a wall, close by an old Spanish mulberry-tree. About twenty years ago, the increasing growth of this tree necessitated the removal of the marble slab, when it was found that the side that had been placed against the wall contained a Latin inscription to the memory of Narcissa. The inscription, which is too long to be quoted here, leaves no doubt upon the matter. It mentions the names of her father and mother, her connexion with the noble family of Lichfield, her descent from Charles II., and the name of her husband, and concludes by stating that she died on the 8th of October 1736, aged eighteen years.

On discovering this inscription, M. Ozanam, the director of the Hôtel de Dieu, searched the registry of Protestant burial, still preserved in the Hôtel de Ville of Lyons, and found an entry, of which the following is a correct translation:

'Madam Elizabeth Lee, daughter of Colonel Lee, aged about eighteen years, wife of Henry Temple, English by birth, was buried at the Hôtel de Dieu at Lyons, in the cemetery of persons of the Reformed religion of the Swiss nation, the 12th of October 1736, at eleven o'clock at night, by order of the Prévôt of the merchants. Received 729 livres, 12 sols.

'Signed, PARA, Priest and Treasurer.'

From this document, the authenticity of which is indisputable, we learn the utter untruthfulness of Young's recital. True, Narcissa was buried at night, and most probably without any religious service, and a considerable sum charged for the privilege of interment, but she was not denied the 'charity their dogs enjoy.' Calculating according to the average rate of exchange at the period, 729 livres would amount to thirty-five pounds sterling. Was it this sum that excited a poetical indignation so strong as to overstep the bounds of veracity? We could grant the excuse of poetical licence, had not Young declared in his preface that the poem 'was real, not fictitious.' The subject is not a pleasing one, and we need not carry it any further; but may conclude in the words of Mr Cecil, who, alluding to Young's renunciation of the world in his writings, when he was eagerly hunting for church preferment, says: 'Young is, of all other men, one of the most striking examples of the sad disunion of piety from truth.'

RODNEY'S NAVAL VICTORY.

The victory achieved by Admiral Rodney over the French fleet in the West Indies, on the 12th of April 1782, was brilliant in itself, but chiefly remarkable for the service which it rendered to Britain at a critical time. The English military force had been baffled in America; France, Spain, and Holland were assailing her in the weakness to which her contest with the colonies had reduced her; the very coasts of Britain were insulted by the cruisers of her many enemies. There was at the best before her a humiliating peace. Rodney's victory came to hold up her drooping head, and enable her to come respectably out of the war.

The French fleet, consisting of thirty vessels, under Count de Grasse, was placed at Martinique. It designed to make a junction with the Spanish fleet, that the two might fall with full force upon Jamaica. It became of the first importance for the British fleet under Sir George Rodney to prevent this junction. With a somewhat greater number of vessels, but less aggregate weight of metal, he followed the French for three or four days, fighting a partial and inconclusive action on the 9th of April; finally bringing it to a general action on the morning of the 12th, in a basin of water bounded by the islands of Guadaloupe, Dominique, Saintes, and Marigalante.

The battle began at seven in the morning, and consisted throughout the day of a close hand-to-hand fight, in which the English ships poured destruction upon the largely manned vessels of the enemy. A little after noon, the English admiral made a movement of a novel character; with four vessels he broke through the enemy's line near the centre, and doubled back upon it, thus assailing it on both sides, and throwing all into confusion. The French admiral's vessel, the *Ville de Paris*, was a superb one of 110 guns, a present from the French capital to Louis XV. at the close of the preceding war. An English 74, the *Canada*, grappled with it, and in a two-hours' combat reduced it nearly to a wreck. It finally surrendered to Sir Samuel Hood, commander of the English van, when only two men besides the admiral were left unhurt. The whole affair was a series of hand-to-hand conflicts, in which the English displayed all their characteristic audacity and perseverance. When evening came with the abruptness peculiar to the tropical regions, the French obtained some advantage from it, as it permitted some of their vessels to escape. Seven, however, remained in the hands of the victors. The killed and wounded on that side reached the astounding amount of nine thousand, while that of the English was under one thousand. Rodney also had the glory of carrying the French commander as his prisoner to London.

The British nation, on receiving intelligence of this great victory, broke out in a tumult of joy which had scarcely had a precedent since the acquittal of the seven bishops. Rodney, who previously had been in rather depressed personal circumstances, was made a peer, and pensioned.

APRIL 13.

St Hermengild, martyr, 586. St Guinoch, of Scotland, 9th century. St Caradoc, priest and martyr, 1124.

Born.—Thomas Wentworth, Earl of Strafford, statesman, 1593, *Chancery-lane, London;* Jean Pierre Crousaz, Swiss divine, philosopher, and mathematician, 1663 *Lausanne;* Frederick North, Earl of Guildford, statesman, 1732; Philip Louis, Duke of Orleans, 1747, *St Cloud;* Dr Thomas Beddoes, writer on medicine and natural history, 1760.

Died.—Henry, Duke of Rohan, French military commander, 1638, *Switzerland;* Charles Leslie, controversialist, 1722, *Glaslough;* Christopher Pitt, translator of Virgil, 1748, *Blandford;* George Frederick Handel, musical composer, 1759; Dr Charles Burney, musician, and author of *History of Music*, 1814, *Chelsea;* Captain Hugh Clapperton, traveller, 1827; Sir Henry de la Beche, geologist, 1855; Sydney Lady Morgan, miscellaneous writer, 1859, *London.*

SIR HENRY DE LA BECHE.

The chief of the Geological Survey of England and Wales, who died at the too early age of fifty-nine, was one of those men who, using moderate faculties with diligence, and under the guidance of sound common sense, prove more serviceable as examples than the most brilliant geniuses. His natural destiny was the half-idle, self-indulgent life of a man of fortune; but his active mind being early attracted to the rising science of geology, he was saved for a better fate. With ceaseless assiduity he explored the surface of the south-western province of England, completing its survey in a great measure at his own expense. He employed intervals in composing works expository of the science, all marked by wonderful clearness and a strong practical bearing. Finally, when in office as chief of the survey, he was the means of founding a mineralogical museum and school in London, which has proved of the greatest service in promoting a knowledge of the science, and which forms the most suitable monument to his memory.

THE EDICT OF NANTES.

With a view to the conclusion of a series of troubles which had harassed his kingdom for several years, Henry IV. of France came to an agreement with the Protestant section of his subjects, which was embodied in an edict, signed by him at Nantes, April 13, 1598. By it, Protestant lords *de fief haut-justicier* were entitled to have the full exercise of their religion in their houses; lords *sans haute-justice* could have thirty persons present at their devotions. The exercise of the Reformed religion was permitted in all places which were under the jurisdiction of a parliament. The Calvinists could, without any petition to superiors, print their books in all places where their religion was permitted [some parts of the kingdom were, in deference to particular treaties, exempted from the edict]. What was most important, Protestants were made competent for any office or dignity in the state. Considering the prejudices of the bulk of the French people, it is wonderful that the Protestants obtained so much on this occasion. After all, Henry was not able to get the edict registered till next year, when the Pope's legate had quitted the kingdom.

KING CHARLES'S STATUE AT CHARING-CROSS.

The bronze statue at Charing-cross has been the subject of more vicissitudes, and has attracted a larger amount of public attention, than is usual among our statues. In 1810, the newspapers announced that 'On Friday night (April 13th), the sword, buckler, and straps fell from the equestrian statue of King Charles the First at Charing-cross. The appendages, similar to the statue, are of copper [bronze?]. The sword, &c., were picked up by a man of the name of Moxon, a porter, belonging to the Golden Cross Hotel, who deposited them in the care of Mr Eyre, trunk-maker, in whose possession they remain till that gentleman receives instructions from the Board of Green Cloth at St James's Palace relative to their reinstatement.'

Something stranger than this happened to the statue in earlier times. It may be here stated that this statue is regarded as one of the finest

in London. It was the work of Hubert le Sœur, a pupil of the celebrated John of Bologna. Invited to this country by King Charles, he modelled and cast the statue for the Earl of Arundel, the enlightened collector of the Arundelian marbles. The statue seems to have been placed at Charing-cross at once; for immediately after the death of the king, the Parliament ordered it to be taken down, broken to pieces, and sold. It was bought by a brazier in Holborn, named John River. The brazier having an eye for taste, or, possibly, an eye for his own future profit, contrived to evade one of the conditions of the bargain; the statue, instead of being broken up, was quietly buried uninjured in his garden, while some broken pieces of metal were produced as a blind to the Parliament. River was, unquestionably, a fellow alive to the tricks of trade; for he made a great number of bronze handles for knives and forks, and sold them as having been made from the fragments of the statue; they were bought by the loyalists as a mark of affection to the deceased king, and by the republicans as a memorial of their triumph. When Charles the Second returned, the statue was brought from its hiding-place, repurchased, and set up again at Charing-cross, where it was for a long time regarded as a kind of party memorial. While the scaffolding was up for its re-erection, Andrew Marvell wrote some sarcastic stanzas, of which the following was one:

' To comfort the heart of the poor Cavalier,
 The late King on horseback is here to be shewn.
What ado with your kings and your statues is
 here!
Have we not had enough, pray, already of one?'

About the year 1670, Sir Robert Vyner, merchant and Lord Mayor, set up an equestrian statue of Charles the Second at Stocks Market, the site of the present Mansion House; and as there was some reason to believe that Vyner had venal reasons for flattering the existing monarch, Andrew Marvell took advantage of the opportunity to make an onslaught on both the monarchs at once. He produced a rhymed dialogue for the two bronze horses: the Charing-cross horse reviled the profligacy of Charles the Second; while the Stocks Market horse retaliated by abusing Charles the First for his despotism. Among the bitter things said by the Charing-cross horse, was:

' That he should be styled Defender of the Faith,
 Who believes not a word what the Word of God
  saith!'
and

' Though he changed his religion, I hope he's so
 civil,
Not to think his own father is gone to the devil!'

And when the Stocks Market horse launched out at Charles the First for having fought desperately for ' the surplice, lawn sleeves, the cross, and the mitre,' the Charing-cross horse retorted with a sneer—

' Thy king will ne'er fight unless for his queans.'

In much more recent days, the Charing-cross statue became an object of archæological solicitude on other grounds. In *Notes and Queries* for 1850 (p. 18), Mr Planché asked, 'When did the *real* sword of Charles the First's time, which but a few years back hung at the side of that monarch's equestrian figure at Charing-cross, disappear; and what has become of it? This question was put, at my suggestion, to the official authorities by the Secretary of the British Archæological Association; but no information could be obtained on the subject. That the sword *was* a real one of that period, I state upon the authority of my learned friend, the late Sir Samuel Meyrick, who had ascertained the fact, and pointed out to me its loss.' To this query Mr Street shortly afterwards replied, 'The sword disappeared about the time of the coronation of her present majesty, when some scaffolding was erected about the statue, which afforded great facilities for removing the rapier (for such it was); and I always understood that it found its way, by some means or other, to the Museum (so called) of the notorious Captain D.; where, in company with the wand of the Great Wizard of the North, and other well-known articles, it was carefully labelled and numbered, and a little account appended of the circumstance of its acquisition and removal.' The editor of *Notes and Queries* pointedly added, 'The age of chivalry is certainly past; otherwise the idea of *disarming a statue* would never have entered the head of any man of arms even in his most frolicsome of moods.' We may conclude, then, that the *present* sword of this remarkable statue is a modern substitute.

RUSHES AND RUSH-BEARING.

In ages long before the luxury of carpets was known in England, the floors of houses were covered with a much more homely material.

When William the Conqueror invested his favourites with some of the Aylesbury lands, it was under the tenure of providing 'straw for his bed-chamber; three eels for his use in winter, and in summer straw, *rushes*, and two green geese thrice every year.'

It is true that in the romance of *Ywaine and Gawin*, we read:

> 'When he unto chamber yede,
> The chamber flore, and als ye bede,
> With klathes of gold were al over spred;'

but even in the palaces of royalty the floors were generally strewed with rushes and straw, sometimes mixed with sweet herbs. In the household roll of Edward II. we find an entry of money paid to John de Carleford, for going from York to Newcastle to procure straw for the king's chamber. Froissart, relating the death of Gaston, Count de Foix, says,—that the count went to his chamber, which he found ready strewed with rushes and green leaves, and the walls were hung with boughs newly cut for perfume and coolness, as the weather was marvellously hot. Adam Davie, Marshal of Stratford-le-bow, who wrote about the year 1312, in his poem of the *Life of Alexander*, describing the marriage of Cleopatra, says—

> 'There was many a blithe grome;
> Of olive, and of ruge floures,
> Weren y strewed halls and bowres;
> With samytes and bandekyns
> Weren curtayned the gardyns.'

This custom of strewing the 'halle and bowres' was continued to a much later period. Hentzner, in his *Itinerary*, says of Queen Elizabeth's presence chamber at Greenwich, 'The floor, after the English fashion, was strewed with *hay*,' meaning rushes. If, however, we may trust to an epistle, wherein Erasmus gives an account of this practice to his friend Dr Francis, physician to Cardinal Wolsey, it would appear that, the rushes being seldom thoroughly changed, and the habits of those days not very cleanly, the smell soon became anything but pleasant. He speaks of the lowest layer of rushes (the top only being renewed) as remaining unchanged sometimes for twenty years; a receptacle for beer, grease, fragments of victuals, and other organic matters. To this filthiness he ascribes the frequent pestilences with which the people were afflicted, and Erasmus recommends the entire banishment of rushes, and a better ventilation, the sanitary importance of which was thus, we see, perceived more than two centuries since.

When Henry III., King of France, demanded of Monsieur Dandelot what especial things he had noted in England during the time of his negotiation there, 'he answered that he had seen but three things remarkable; which were, that the people did drinke in bootes, eate rawe fish, and strewed all their best roomes with *hay;* meaning blacke jacks, oysters, and rushes.'—(*Wits, Fits, and Fancies*, 4to. 1614.)

The English stage was strewed with rushes in Shakspeare's time; and the Globe Theatre was roofed with rushes, or as Taylor, the water-poet, describes it, the old theatre 'had a thatched hide,' and it was through the rushes in the roof taking fire that the first Globe Theatre was burnt down. Killigrew told Pepys how he had improved the stage from a time when there was 'nothing but rushes upon the ground, and everything else mean.' To the rushes succeeded matting; then for tragedy black hangings, after which came the green cloth still used—the cloth, as Goldsmith humorously observes, spread for bloody work.

The strewing of rushes in the way where processions were to pass, is attributed by our poets to all times and countries. Thus, at the coronation of Henry V., when the procession is coming, the grooms cry:

> 'More rushes, more rushes!'
> *Henry IV.* Act v. Sc. 5.

Thus also at a wedding:

> ' Full many maids, clad in their best array,
> In honour of the bride, come with their flaskets
> Fill'd full with flowers: others in wicker baskets
> Bring from the marish rushes, to o'erspread
> The ground, whereon to church the lovers tread.'
> Browne's *Brit. Past.*, i. 2.

They were used green:

> ' Where is this stranger? Rushes, ladies, rushes,
> Rushes as green as summer for this stranger.'
> —Beaumont and Fletcher's *Valentinian*, ii. 4.

Not worth a rush became a common comparison for anything worthless; the rush being of so little value as to be trodden under foot. Gower has:

> ' For til I se the daie springe,
> I sette slepe nought at a rushe.'

We find the rush used in Devonshire in a charm for the thrush, as follows: 'Take three rushes from any running stream, and pass them separately through the mouth of the infant, then plunge the rushes again into the stream, and as the current bears them away, so will the thrush depart from the child.'—*Notes and Queries*, No. 203.

In the *Herball to the Bible*, 1587, mention is made of 'sedge and rushes, the whiche manie in the countrie doe use in sommer-time to strewe their parlors or churches, as well for coolness as for pleasant smell.' The species preferred was the *Calamus aromaticus*, which, when bruised, gives forth an odour resembling that of the myrtle;

in the absence of this, inferior kinds were used. Provision was made for strewing the earthen or paved floors of churches with straw or rushes, according to the season of the year. We find several entries in parish accounts for this purpose.

Brand quotes from the churchwardens' accounts of St Mary-at-hill, London, of which parish he was rector: '1504. Paid for 2 Berden Rysshes for the strewing the newe pewes, 3d.' '1493. For 3 Burdens of rushes for ye new pews, 3d.'

We find also in the parish account-book of Hailsham, in Sussex, charges for strewing the church floor with straw or rushes, according to the season of the year; and in the books of the city of Norwich, entries for pea-straw used for such strewing.

The Rev. G. Miles Cooper, in his paper on the Abbey of Bayham, in the *Sussex Archæological Collections*, vol. ix. 1857, observes:

'Though few are ignorant of this ancient custom, it may not perhaps be so generally known, that the strewing of churches grew into a religious festival, dressed up in all that picturesque circumstance wherewith the old church well knew how to array its ritual. Remains of it linger to this day in remote parts of England. In Westmoreland, Lancashire, and districts of Yorkshire, there is still celebrated between haymaking and harvest a village fête called the Rushbearing. Young women dressed in white, and carrying garlands of flowers and rushes, walk in procession to the parish church, accompanied by a crowd of

RUSH-BEARING.

rustics, with flags flying and music playing. There they suspend their floral chaplets on the chancel rails, and the day is concluded with a simple feast. The neighbourhood of Ambleside was, until lately, and may be still, one of the chief strongholds of this popular practice; respecting which I will only add, as a curious fact, that up to the passing of the recent Municipal Reform Act, the town clerk of Norwich was accustomed to pay to the subsacrist of the cathedral an annual guinea for strewing the floor of the cathedral with rushes on the Mayor's Day, from the western door to the entrance into the choir; this is the most recent instance of the ancient usage which has come to my knowledge.'

The annual rush-bearing wake, as formerly observed in Cheshire, has been thus described: A large quantity of rushes—sometimes a cart-load—

is collected, and being bound on the cart, are cut evenly at each end, and on Saturday evening a number of men sit on the top of the rushes, holding garlands of artificial flowers, tinsel, &c. The cart is drawn round the parish by three or four spirited horses, decked with ribbons, the collars being surrounded with small bells. It is attended by morris-dancers fantastically dressed; there are men in women's clothes, one of whom, with his face blackened, has a belt with a large bell attached, round his waist, and carries a ladle to collect money from the spectators. The party stop and dance at the public-house in their way to the parish church, where the rushes are deposited, and the garlands are hung up, to remain till the next year. *

* Communication to *Notes and Queries*, i. 358.

The uses of the rush in domestic economy are worth notice. Rush-lights, or candles with rush wicks, are of the greatest antiquity; for we learn from Pliny that the Romans applied different kinds of rushes to a similar purpose, as making them into flambeaux and wax-candles for use at funerals. The earliest Irish candles were rushes dipped in grease and placed in lamps of oil; and they have been similarly used in many districts of England. Aubrey, writing about 1673, says that at Ockley, in Surrey, 'the people draw peeled rushes through melted grease, which yields a sufficient light for ordinary use, is very cheap and useful, and burnes long.' This economical practice was common till towards the close of the last century. There was a regular utensil for holding the rush in burning; of which an example is here presented.

THE RUSH-HOLDER.

The Rev. Gilbert White has devoted one letter to 'this simple piece of domestic economy,' in his *Natural History of Selborne*. He tells us:

'The proper species is the common soft rush, found in most pastures by the sides of streams, and under hedges. Decayed labourers, women, and children, gather these rushes late in summer; as soon as they are cut, they must be flung into water, and kept there, otherwise they will dry and shrink, and the peel will not run. When peeled they must lie on the grass to be bleached, and take the dew for some nights, after which they are dried in the sun. Some address is required in dipping these rushes into the scalding fat or grease. The careful wife of an industrious Hampshire labourer obtains all her fat for nothing: for she saves the scummings of her bacon pot for this use; and if the grease abound with salt she causes the salt to precipitate to the bottom, by setting the scummings in a warm oven. Where hogs are not much in use, and especially by the sea-side, the coarse animal oils will come very cheap. A pound of common grease may be procured for fourpence; and about six pounds of grease will dip a pound of rushes, which cost one shilling, so that a pound of rushes ready for burning will cost three shillings. If men that keep bees will mix a little wax with the grease, it will give it a consistency, render it more cleanly, and make the rushes burn longer: mutton suet will have the same effect.'

A pound avoirdupois contains 1600 rushes; and supposing each to burn on an average but half-an-hour, then a poor man will purchase 1800 hours of light, a time exceeding thirty-three entire days, for three shillings. According to this account, each rush, before dipping, costs one thirty-third of a farthing, and one-eleventh afterwards. Thus a poor family will enjoy five and a-half hours of comfortable light for a farthing. An experienced old housekeeper assured Mr White that one pound and a half of rushes completely supplied her family the year round, since working-people burn no candle in the long days, because they rise and go to bed by daylight.

Little farmers use rushes in the short days both morning and evening, in the dairy and kitchen; but the very poor, who are always the worst economists, and therefore must continue very poor, buy a halfpenny candle every evening, which in their blowing, open rooms, does not burn much longer than two hours. Thus, they have only two hours' light for their money, instead of eleven.

APRIL 14.

Saints Tiburtius, Valerian, and Maximus, martyrs in Rome, 229. Saint Carpus of Thyatira, and others, 251. St Benezet, patron of Avignon, 1184. Saints Antony, John, and Eustachius, martyrs, about 1342. B. Lidwina, of Schiedam, 1433.

Born.—William Henry, Duke of Portland, statesman, 1738; Dr George Gregory, miscellaneous writer, 1754, *Dublin.*

Died.—Richard **Neville**, Earl of Warwick (the King-maker), killed, 1471, *Barnet;* Earl of Bothwell, husband of Mary Queen of Scots, 1577; Thomas Otway, poet, 1685, *London;* Madame de Sévigné (Letters), 1696, *Grignan;* Madame Pompadour, mistress of Louis XV., 1764; John Gilbert Cooper, poet, 1769; Rev. James Granger (*Biographical History of England*), 1776, *Shiplake;* William Whitehead, 1785, *London.*

WARWICK, THE KING-MAKER.

Richard Neville, Earl of Warwick, may be looked upon as the hero of the wars of the Roses. He was the eldest son of the Richard Neville who had obtained through his marriage with the heiress of the Montacutes the earldom of Salisbury, and who stood high in court favour in the earlier part of the reign of Henry VI. The other sons of the Earl of Salisbury were Thomas John, afterwards created Marquis of Montagu, and George, who became Archbishop of York. The eldest brother, Richard, who had married the heiress of the Beauchamps, Earl of Warwick, inherited their estates, and was created Earl of Warwick in 1449. Both earls, Salisbury and Warwick, espoused warmly the cause of the house of York, and were bitter opponents of the Queen's favourite, the Duke of Suffolk, and of the Duke of Somerset, who succeeded him. At the beginning of the year 1452, the Duke of York, alarmed by the intrigues at court, withdrew to his castle of Ludlow, in Shropshire, where he assembled his forces, and may be said to have commenced the civil war. He no doubt reckoned on the support of Salisbury and Warwick, who, however, were not with him on this occasion; but, when he was again obliged to assemble his friends at Ludlow in the beginning of 1455, they joined him there with their forces, as well as the Duke of Norfolk and other great feudal barons. Marching thence direct to London, they came upon the king's army at St Albans by surprise, and the first victory of the Yorkists was gained there on the 22nd March, in a great measure by the military talents of the Earl of Warwick. The Duke of York was again made protector of the kingdom, and he immediately made Salisbury Lord Chancellor, and gave the important post of Captain-General of Calais to the Earl of Warwick. The Duke of Somerset and other Lancastrian lords had been slain in the battle; but the courage and activity of the queen soon restored the court party to its strength. The battle of St Albans had excited personal animosities among the feudal barons which left little hopes of peace, though both parties hesitated long in commencing the war. At length, at a council held at Coventry at the end of the month of February 1456, an outward reconciliation was effected, which was concluded at a general meeting of the great lords in London, about a fortnight afterwards. Some of the terms of this reconciliation shew how much of the personal feelings of the chiefs were mixed up in the old feudal wars. The Yorkist chiefs were to pacify the families of the lords slain in the battle of St Albans by expenditure of blood-money, of which the Duke of York was to pay to Somerset's widow and children five thousand marks, the Earl of Warwick to Lord Clifford a thousand marks, and Salisbury to Lord Egremont a similar consideration, while all three were to build at their own expense a chapel for the souls of the slain lords. In the solemn procession which took place on the 25th of March, to confirm this reconciliation, the Duke of York walked hand in hand with the queen, the Earl of Salisbury with the Duke of Somerset, and the Earl of Warwick with the Duke of Exeter, and all hostile feelings appeared to be laid aside. It was soon, however, seen how hollow are all such reconciliations.

The Earl of Warwick was now looked upon as the real head of the Yorkist party, and he furnished the occasion of the first outward breach of the late reconciliation. He had repaired to his government at Calais, where his power and popularity were unlimited, and which he had now made his head-quarters. In the month of May, he considered himself justified in attacking a large fleet of ships which was proceeding from the Hanse Towns to Spain, which he defeated, sinking some and capturing others. The Hanseatic League complained, and Warwick was called upon for explanations. The earl did not hesitate in presenting himself at court to answer the charges brought against him; but his reception seems to have been such as to give him suspicion of personal danger. On the 9th of November 1455, when Warwick was attending the court at Westminster, he was attacked by some of the queen's household, and escaped with difficulty to his barge on the Thames, in which he immediately dropped down the river and made the best of his way to Calais.

It was soon after so evident to the Yorkist lords that the queen was concerting measures for their destruction, that they determined on providing for their own defence. We find them in the autumn of 1459 mustering in the north and west of England, fighting, dispersing tempo-

rarily, finally re-assembling in great force in the summer of 1460. Warwick was then able to enter London, and soon after (July 10) to overthrow the royal forces at Northampton. The imbecile Henry being here taken prisoner, and his queen and their son driven to seek refuge in Scotland, York first definitely advanced his claim to the crown. Soon after, fortune deserted him at the battle of Wakefield (Dec. 31, 1460), when he and the Earl of Salisbury's second son, Sir Thomas Neville, were slain, and the Earl of Salisbury himself taken prisoner and beheaded. Warwick was defeated in a second battle of St Albans, fought on the 17th February 1461; but the success of the young Duke of York at Mortimer's Cross had turned the tide again in favour of that house; the queen again retired to the north; young Edward, joined by Warwick, marched to London, and was proclaimed king, under the title of Edward IV. (March 4, 1461); and three weeks after, by the bloody defeat of Towton, the hopes of the house of Lancaster appeared extinguished.

There could be no doubt that to the Earl of Warwick Edward owed his throne, and for a while he appeared to reign only under the earl's protection. Rewards, honours, places of emolument were monopolised by the family and friends of Warwick. At this time he was perhaps the most potent noble that had ever lived in feudal England. He dwelt in his palace in London, known as Warwick House, occupying the site of what is now called Warwick-lane, in a style of princely magnificence, and with profuse hospitality, which we can now hardly understand. 'When hee came to London,' the old chronicler tells us, 'hee helde such an house, that sixe oxen were eaten at a breakfast, and everie taverne was full of his meate, for who that had any acquaintance in that house, he should have as much sodden and rost as he might carry upon a long dagger.' The earl became thus extremely popular among the commonalty, but the young king grew gradually weary of the sort of tutelage in which he was held, and gathered round him friends who were not likely to encourage him to bear it. While Edward sought to escape from the thrall of the great earl, and began to distribute his favours among his new friends, Warwick appears to have become personally more ambitious, and perhaps more imperious. He had two daughters, Isabel and Anne, and he evidently aimed at approaching nearer to the crown by marrying the eldest to the Duke of Clarence, the king's brother, who was then heir presumptive to his throne, and over whom he had gained great influence. Edward, however, refused his consent to this match, and Warwick is said to have taken further offence at the king's marriage with Elizabeth Wydville, in 1464, and with the influence gained by her relatives. Still, though greatly dissatisfied, Warwick continued in appearance the friend of the king of his own making, and who had loaded him with honours and wealth, for he was at the same time Prime Minister, Commander-in-Chief, and Admiral of England, besides a multitude of other lucrative offices. The first subject of open disagreement arose out of a foreign marriage, the heir of the Duke of Burgundy having solicited the hand of Edward's sister Margaret, while Louis XI. of France also demanded her for one of his sons. Warwick advocated the latter, and went as negotiator with great pomp to France, and had many familiar and secret interviews with Louis, at which were said to have been discussed less the terms of the marriage than the means of a reconciliation between Warwick and the Lancastrian party. During his absence, Edward yielded to other influence, and concluded the match with the heir of Burgundy. Warwick, on his return, complained bitterly of the way in which he had been treated, and retired to his castle of Middleham, in Yorkshire. A reconciliation was effected through the intercession of the Archbishop of York, and the great earl returned to court; but the time he spent there was occupied chiefly by intrigues on both sides, with which we are very imperfectly acquainted. In spite of the king's opposition, the Duke of Clarence was married to the Lady Isabel Neville, at Calais, in July 1469, the Archbishop of Canterbury performing the ceremony; and there can be little doubt that at this time Warwick contemplated the design of dethroning Edward and placing the crown on the head of his son-in-law Clarence. During their absence serious insurrections broke out in England, and the king was reduced to such distress that he called them urgently to his assistance. Warwick and Clarence had, however, no sooner arrived, than the king found himself placed under restraint, and was carried as a virtual prisoner to the castle of Middleham. Both kings were now prisoners at the same time, for Henry VI. was confined in the Tower of London. Towards the end of 1469, after Warwick and his friends had exacted various grants and conditions, Edward was set at liberty, and another hollow reconciliation took place. In the month of February 1470, an entertainment was given by Warwick's brother, the archbishop, at the Moor, in Hertfordshire, to the king, the earl, and the Duke of Clarence; when, as Edward was washing his hands before supper, an attendant whispered some words of suspicion into his ear, which caused him to slip out of the room, take horse, and fly in haste to the castle of Windsor. The king and the earl were reconciled again, by the intermediation of Edward's mother, the Duchess of York, but this reconciliation was shorter even than the former. Popular insurrections broke out, which Edward believed to be secretly promoted by Warwick and his friends, and his suspicions were further excited by the slowness with which they proceeded against the rebels. Edward hastily raised a considerable army, defeated the rebels, and then marched against his minister and brother, and Warwick and Clarence were now compelled to seek safety in flight. They succeeded in getting to France, where they were well received by Louis XI. This crafty monarch seized upon the occasion to carry into effect a new plan of his own contriving. Warwick was introduced secretly to Queen Margaret, and these two bitter enemies became reconciled, Warwick undertaking to dethrone Edward, and restore Henry VI., under

certain conditions, one of which was the marriage of his second daughter, Anne, to the youthful Prince of Wales. He thus secured, in any event, a fair prospect of one of his daughters becoming Queen of England; and he had sufficient influence over the Duke of Clarence to induce him to join in this arrangement.

King Edward's fears appear to have been lulled by the treacherous professions of Warwick's two brothers, the Marquis of Montagu and the Archbishop of York, and he made no preparations against the impending danger. Warwick, with assistance from the King of France, set sail, and landed on the coast of Devon on the 13th of September 1470, while Edward was in the north, drawn thither by reports of an insurrection of the Nevilles. The earl had thus time to carry out his plans in the south. He was speedily joined by his friends, took possession of the capital, and directed his march northwards with a powerful army to meet his opponent. Edward, on the other hand, was deserted by many of the chief men in attendance upon him, who were kinsmen or friends of Warwick, and in despair he took ship and fled to Holland, to seek a temporary refuge at the court of Burgundy. So rapid was the succession of events, that, on the 6th of October, Warwick returned to London in triumph, and, taking King Henry from the Tower, replaced him on the throne. On this occasion, he did not forget to reserve to himself all the offices and quite as much power as he had held under the reign of his Yorkist sovereign.

The triumph, however, was a short one. Edward, aided by the Duke of Burgundy, landed at Ravenspur, in Yorkshire, on the 15th of March 1471. Warwick advanced to meet him as far as Coventry; but there he experienced the uncertainty of such alliances as he had been making. No sooner did the rival armies come into each other's presence at Coventry, than the Duke of Clarence, who is believed to have been secretly tampered with, led away his troops from Warwick's army, and joined his brother, King Edward. The earl was now obliged to retire, and Edward succeeded in placing himself between him and the capital. The decisive battle was fought on Easter Sunday, the 14th of April, and the result is well known. The Lancastrians were defeated with great slaughter, and the Earl of Warwick, and his brother, the Marquis of Montagu, were both among the slain. The French historian of these events, Comines, tells us that it was the custom of the Earl of Warwick never to fight on foot, but that his manner was, when he had dismounted to lead his men to the charge, to remount again immediately, so that if the fortune of the day was against him, he could ride away in time. The historian adds, that on this occasion the Earl had been persuaded by his brother, the Marquis of Montagu, to send away his horse, so that when he left the field he was soon overtaken and slain. His death left King Edward far more firmly established on the throne than when he had held it under the protection of the *King-maker*.

BLACK MONDAY.

'It is to be noted that the 14 day of April, and the morrow after Easter Day (1360), King Edward [III.] with his host lay before the city of Paris; which day was full dark of mist and hail, and so bitter cold, that many men died on their horsebacks with the cold; wherefore unto this day it hath been called the *Black Monday.*'—*Stow's Chronicle.*

ACCESSION OF A BOURBON PRINCE TO THE SPANISH THRONE.

Philip, the grandson of Louis XIV., being called to the throne of Spain by the will of the preceding monarch, Charles II., made his entry into Madrid on the 14th of April 1701. To receive him with the more magnificence, they had prepared a splendid auto-da-fé for his arrival, at which several Jews were ready to be burnt; but the new sovereign declared firmly that he had no wish to behold any such ceremony, and signalised his accession to the throne by an act of clemency which must have seemed very extraordinary to his subjects.

On the same day ten years after, died Monseigneur, the father of this young sovereign. It is told of him that when he heard of the brilliant destiny opening for his second son, he remarked that he had never wished to be able to say more than *the king my father, and the king my son;* fine words, if they had not been prompted by indolence more than by moderation. Nothing was more common for many years before his death than to hear people saying of him, '*Fils de roi, père de roi, jamais roi.*' The event seemed to favour the credulity of those who have faith in such predictions; but the saying was founded on the obvious fact that his father, King Louis, from superior constitution and health, was likely to outlive him.

MOUNTEBANKS.

The *Gazette* of April 14, 1684, contains an order suppressing all mountebanks, rope-dancers, and ballad-singers, who had not taken a licence from the Master of the Revels, and particularly Samuel Rutherford, —— Irish, Willian Bevel, and Richard Olsworth. The Master of the Revels was at this time the celebrated player Killigrew, who was thus allowed, by favour of the king, to tax all makers of fun but those of his own order, and whose function seems to have been of an oppressive character, strangely at issue with its festive appellation.

The mountebank and the merry-andrew played their fantastic tricks in country towns within memory; but scarcely with such state as a hundred and forty years since, when they were thus sketched in *A Tour through England* (1723): 'I cannot leave Winchester without telling you of a pleasant incident that happened there. As I was sitting at the George Inn, I saw a coach with six bay horses, a calash and four, a chaise and four, enter the inn, in a yellow livery turned up with red; four gentlemen on horseback, in blue, trimmed with silver; and as yellow is the colour given by the dukes in England, I went out to see

510

what duke it was; but there was no coronet on the coach, only a plain coat-of-arms on each, with this motto:

"ARGENTO LABORAT FABER."

Upon inquiry, I found this great equipage belonged to a mountebank, and that his name being Smith, the motto was a pun upon his name. The footmen in yellow were his tumblers and trumpeters, and those in blue his merry-andrew, his apothecary, and spokesman. He was dressed in black velvet, and had in his coach a woman that danced on the ropes. He cures all diseases, and sells his packets for sixpence a-piece. He erected stages in all the market towns twenty miles round; and it is a prodigy how so wise a people as the English are gulled by such pickpockets. But his amusements on the stage are worth the sixpence, without the pills. In the morning he is dressed up in a fine brocade nightgown, for his chamber practice, when he gives advice, and gets large fees.'

Cowper, in describing the newspaper of his day, adverts to one of this class of vagabonds in a well-remembered couplet:

'And Katerfelto, with his hair on end
　At his own wonders, wondering for his bread.'
　　　　　　Task: the Winter Evening.

Cowper probably wrote this passage in 1782; the *Task* was published complete in 1785. But, who was Katerfelto?

In a pamphlet on quackery, published at Kingston-upon-Hull, in 1805, it is stated that Dr Katerfelto practised on the people of London in the influenza of 1782; that he added to his nostrums the fascinations of hocus-pocus; and that with the services of some extraordinary *black cats* he astonished the vulgar. In 1790 or 1791, he visited the city of Durham, accompanied by his wife and daughter. His travelling equipage consisted of an old rumbling coach, drawn by a pair of sorry hacks; and his two black servants wore green liveries with red collars. They were sent round the town, blowing trumpets, and delivering bills of their master's performances. These were—in the day-time, a microscope; in the evening, electrical experiments, in which the black cats—'the Doctor's devils'—played their parts in yielding electric sparks; tricks of legerdemain concluded the entertainments.

He was a tall, thin man, dressed in a black gown and square cap; he is said to have been originally a soldier in the Prussian service. In one of his advertisements he states that he was a Colonel in the 'Death's Head' regiment of Hussars, a terrific prognostic of his ultimate profession. He had many mishaps in his conjuring career: once he sent up a fire-balloon, which, falling upon a haystack, set it on fire, and it was consumed, when Katerfelto was sued for its value, and was sent to prison in default of payment. And, not long before his death, he was committed by the Mayor of Shrewsbury to the House of Correction in that city as a vagrant and impostor.

Katerfelto mixed up with his quackery some real science, and by aid of the solar microscope astonished the world with insect wonders. In one of his advertisements in the *Morning Post,* of July 1782, he says that by its aid the insects on the hedges will be seen larger than ever, and those insects which caused the late influenza will be seen as large as a bird; and in a drop of water the size of a pin's head there will be seen above 50,000 insects; the same in beer, milk, vinegar, blood, flour, cheese, &c., and there will be seen many surprising insects in different vegetables, and above 200 other dead objects.' He obtained good prices for his show:—'The admittance to see these wonderful works of Providence is only—front seats, three shillings; second seats, two shillings; and back seats, one shilling only, from eight o'clock in the morning till six in the afternoon, at No. 22, Piccadilly.' He fully understood the advantages of puffing, and one of his advertisements commences with a story of 'a gentleman of the faculty belonging to Oxford University, who, finding it likely to prove a fine day, set out for London purposely to see those great wonders which are advertised so much by that famous philosopher, Mr Katerfelto;' that the said gentleman declared 'if he had come 300 miles on purpose, the knowledge he had then received would amply reward him; and that he should not wonder that some of the nobility should come from the remotest part of Scotland to hear Mr Katerfelto, as the people of that country in particular are always searching after knowledge.' He elsewhere declares himself 'the greatest philosopher in this kingdom since Sir Isaac Newton.' 'And Mr Katerfelto, as a divine and moral philosopher, begs leave to say that all persons on earth live in darkness, if they are able to see, but will not see his wonderful exhibition.'

A still more famous quack flourished in London at the same time. This was Dr Graham, who opened what he called a Temple of Health, in the Adelphi, in which he expatiated on the advantages of electricity and magnetism. He says in one of his advertisements that he will explain 'the whole art of enjoying health and vigour of body and mind, and of preserving and exalting personal beauty and loveliness; or in other words, of living with health, honour, and happiness in this world, for at least a hundred years.'

One of the means for ensuring this was the frequent use of mud-baths; and that the doctor might be observed to practise what he preached, he was to be seen, on stated occasions, immersed in mud to the chin; accompanied by a lady to whom he gave the name of Vestina, Goddess of Health, and who afterwards became celebrated as the wife of Sir William Hamilton, and the great counsellor and friend of Lord Nelson. At this time she had only recently ceased to be a nurse-maid; but her beauty attracted general attention in London. It is to be remarked that while she remained in the mud-bath, she had her hair elaborately dressed in the prevailing fashion, with powder, flowers, feathers, and ropes of pearl; the doctor appearing in an equally elaborate wig.

From the Adelphi Graham removed to Schomberg House, Pall Mall, which he christened the Temple of Health and Hymen, and fitted up with much magnificence. The admittance was five shillings, yet the place was crowded by a silly audience, brought together by his audacious puffs and impudent lectures on subjects now impossible to be alluded to. One of them may be a sufficient sample of the whole:

'If there be one human being, rich or poor, male or female, in or near this great metropolis of the world, who has not had the good fortune and the happiness of hearing the celebrated lecture, and of seeing the grand celestial state bed, the magnificent electrical apparatus, and the supremely brilliant and unique decorations of this magical edifice, of this enchanting Elysian palace! where wit and mirth, love and beauty— all that can delight the soul, and all that can ravish the senses, will hold their court, this, and every evening this week in chaste and joyous assemblage! let them now come forth, or for ever afterwards let them blame themselves, and bewail their irremediable misfortune.'

Graham engaged the services of two gigantic porters, whom he stationed at the door in the showiest liveries covered with gold lace. His rooms at night were superbly lighted by wax, and nothing spared to attract visitors. The doctor alternated his lectures with those of the lady just alluded to, and thus he advertised her performances: 'Vestina, the rosy Goddess of Health, presides at the evening lecture, assisting at the display of the celestial meteors, and of that sacred vital fire over which she watches, and whose application in the cure of diseases she daily has the honour of directing. The descriptive exhibition of the apparatus in the daytime is conducted by the officiating junior priest.' This latter office was performed by a young medical man, who afterwards became Dr Mitford, and was father to the famed authoress. Graham's expenses, always large, continued when his popularity waned, and he died poor in the neighbourhood of Glasgow. He may fairly be considered as the last of the unblushing quack-doctors.

We get a very good and clear account of mountebanks, as existing in Venice in the beginning of the seventeenth century, from that extraordinary compound of sense and oddity, Tom Coryat, who then travelled over Europe and into India, and published an account of his adventures under the modest, yet not very inappropriate name of *Coryat's Crudities*. He first tells us that mountebanks are common throughout Italy, but more especially abundant in Venice, the name being of the language of that country, *Monta in banco*, from their mounting on a bench, ' because these fellows do act their part upon a stage, which is compacted of benches of forms. . . . . The principal place where they act is the first part of St Mark's street that reacheth betwixt the west front of St Mark's church and the opposite front of St Germinian's church. Twice a day, that is in the morning and in the afternoon, you may see five or six several stages erected for them. . . . . These mountebanks at one end of their stage place their trunk, which is replenished with a world of new-fangled trumperies. After the whole rabble of them is gotten up to the stage,—whereof some wear vizards like fools in a play, some that are women are attired with habits according to that person that they sustain,—the music begins; sometimes vocal, sometimes instrumental, sometimes both.

'While the music plays, the principal mountebank opens his trunk and sets abroad his wares. [Then] he maketh an oration to the audience of half an hour long, wherein he doth most hyperbolically extol the virtue of his drugs and confections—though many of them are very counterfeit and false. I often wondered at these natural orators; for they would tell their tales with such admirable volubility and plausible grace, *extempore*, and seasoned with that singular variety of elegant jests and witty conceits, that they did often strike great admiration into strangers . . . . . [He then] delivereth his commodities by little and little, the jester still playing his part, and the musicians singing and playing upon their instruments. The principal things that they sell are oils, sovereign waters, amorous songs printed, apothecary drugs, and a commonweal of other trifles. The head mountebank, every time he delivereth out anything, maketh an extemporal speech, which he doth eftsoons intermingle with such savoury jests (but spiced now and then with singular scurrility), that they minister passing mirth and laughter to the whole company, which may perhaps consist of a thousand people.'

Coryat saw a mountebank one day play with a viper; another he saw cut and gash his arm till the blood streamed, and heal it all up in a few minutes. There was one who had been born and still continued blind, who was noted for his extemporal songs, 'and for a pretty kind of music which he made with two bones betwixt his fingers.' The scene would last a couple of hours, when, having cloyed the audience with their jests, and sold as many of their wares as they could, they would 'remove their trinkets and stage till the next meeting.'

Ben Jonson in his comedy of *Volpone; or,* *the Fox*, has given in full the scene of a mountebank's stage at Venice, and the speech of the quack, who vends his medicines in a style singularly like that adopted by 'Cheap Jack' at country fairs in the present day. Thus he says: 'You all know, honourable gentlemen, I never valued this ampulla, or vial, at less than eight crowns; but for this time I am content to be deprived of it for six: six crowns is the price, and less in courtesy I know you cannot offer me. Take it or leave it, however both it, and I, am at your service! Well! I am in a humour at this time to make a present of the small quantity my coffer contains: to the rich in courtesy, and to the poor for God's sake. Wherefore, now mark: I asked you six crowns, and six crowns at other times you have paid me; you shall not give me six crowns, nor five, nor four, nor three, nor two, nor one, nor half a ducat. Sixpence it will cost you, (or six hundred pounds); expect no lower price, for I will not bate.' The latter part of this speech might pass for a short-hand report of a modern speech at a fair, the words with which bargains are still sold being identical with those Ben Jonson puts into the mouth of his *Volpone*.

The Earl of Rochester whose vices and eccentricities made him famous in the days of Charles the Second, on one occasion personated a mountebank doctor, and delivered a speech which obtained some celebrity. His example was followed by the legitimate comedians. Thus Leveridge and Penkethman appeared at fairs as '*Doctor Leverigo, and his Jack-Pudding Pinkanello,*' and the still more famous actor Joe Haines as '*Watho Van Claturbank, High German Doctor.*' His burlesque speech was published as a broadside, with an engraving representing his temporary stage, which we here copy.

The scene is Tower-hill, then a rendezvous of

MOUNTEBANK DISTRIBUTING HIS WARES ON THE STAGE.

mountebanks : Joe is represented delivering his speech, medicine in hand ; beside him is a harlequin ; behind, his 'Jack-Pudding' sounds lustily on the trumpet to call attention to his work. A gouty patient is seated in the operating chair ; behind are boxes of medicines and phials for 'retail trade.' Patients on sticks hobble towards the stage ; an itinerant vendor of 'strong waters,' in days when no excise interfered with extreme indulgence in cheap liquors, keeps up the courage of one waiting his turn on the stage for cure. A mass of all kinds of people are in front, among them a juvenile pickpocket. It is a perfect transcript of the genuine mountebank's stage of the days of Queen Anne ; his speech burlesques their high-flown pretensions and inflated verbosity. He calls himself 'High German Doctor, Chymist, and Dentifricator, native of Arabia Deserta, citizen and burgomaster of the City of Brandipolis, seventh son of a seventh son, unborn doctor of above sixty years' experience. Having studied over Galen, Hypocrates, Albumazar, and Paracelsus, I am now become the Esculapius of the age ; having been educated at twelve universities, and travelled through fifty-two kingdoms, and been counsellor to the counsellors of several monarchs.

'By the earnest prayers and entreaties of several lords, earls, dukes, and honourable personages, I have been at last prevailed upon to oblige the world with this notice. That all persons, young and old, blind or lame, deaf or dumb, curable or incurable, may know where to repair for cure, in all cephalalgias, paralytic paroxysms, palpitations of the pericardium, empyemas, syncopes, and nasieties ; arising either from a plethory or a cachochymy, vertiginous vapours, hydrocephalous dysenteries, odontalgic, or podagrical inflammations, and the entire legion of lethiferous distempers.

'This is Nature's palladium, health's magazine ; it works seven manner of ways, as Nature requires, for it scorns to be confined to any particular mode of operation ; so that it effecteth the cure either hypnotically, hydrotically, cathartically, poppismatically, pneumatically, or synedochically ; it mundifies the hypogastrium, extinguishes all supernatural fermentations and ebullitions, and, in fine, annihilates all nosotrophical morbific ideas of the whole corporeal compages. A drachm of it is worth a bushel of March dust ; for, if a man chance to have his brains beat out, or his head dropped off, two drops—I say two drops ! gentlemen, seasonably applied, will recall the fleeting spirits, re-enthrone the deposed archeus, cement the discontinuity of the parts, and in six minutes restore the lifeless trunk to all its pristine functions, vital, natural, and animal ; so that this, believe me, gentlemen, is the only sovereign remedy in the world.

'*Venienti occurite morbo.*—Down with your dust.

'*Principiis obsta.*—No cure, no money.

'*Quærenda pecunia primum.*—Be not sick too late.'

One of the last, if not the very last, of the genuine foreign mountebank doctors, was a German, known as Doctor Bossy ; who had considerable reputation, and ended as a practitioner

in a good house with a fair competence. He used to mount his stage in the early part of the present century, on alternate days at Tower-hill or Covent Garden Market, that the East and West of London might alike avail themselves of his services. There is a story of Colonel Kelly's famous parrot once disconcerting the doctor ; when he had induced an old woman to mount his stage in the market, and narrate the wonderful cures he had effected with her. The parrot had learnt much coarse language in that locality, which was sometimes applied as if intentionally. The old lady having concluded her narrative, ' Lying old —— !' exclaimed the bird. The doctor, for the moment discomfited by the roar of laughter from his audience, soon gravely stepped forth with his hand on his heart, and said with due solemnity : 'It is no lie, you wicked bird !—it is all true as is de Gospel !'

Very few of these practitioners now remain. Where they do exist it is in very humble form, and they sell little else than corn-plasters and cheap cough medicines. The author of this paper saw one at York three years ago, who aspired somewhat higher, and sold medicines on a stage in the old style, but without the merry-andrew or the music ; he presented himself in shabby black clothes, with a dirty white neckcloth. The genuine mountebank doctor, with his roomy phaeton, his band of music behind, and his jester on the box, is only to be met with in the country towns of the south of France, or in Italy. The writer remembers one at Marseilles, who shared his duties with his wife ; the lady occasionally drawing the teeth of persons who mounted the phaeton, and whose cries were drowned by the brass band seated in the rear. The best idea of an Italian travelling doctor of this sort was afforded to opera-goers by the late Signor Lablache, in his whimsically humorous personation of Doctor Dulcamara in the popular opera of *L'Elisor d'Amore.* His gorgeous equipage, with its musical and other attendants ; his vast size, and still vaster pomposity ; the exuberance of his dress, and the greater exuberance of his style when descanting on his nostrums, left nothing to desire in perfecting the picture of a full-blown quack and mountebank.

AN ECCENTRIC.

Lysons, in his *Environs of London,* gives a singular account of one Russell, a native of Streatham, who, as appears by the register, was buried on the 14th of April 1772, the following passage being annexed to the entry :—'This person was always known under the guise or habit of a woman, and answered to the name of *Elizabeth,* as registered in this parish, Nov. 21st 1669, but on death proved to be a man.' John Russell, his father, had three daughters, and two sons, William and John, who were baptized respectively in 1668 and 1672. 'There is little doubt, therefore, that the person here recorded was one of the two,' and must consequently have been either 100 or 104 years of age at the time of his death ; but he himself used to aver that he was 108 years old. Early in life he associated with gipsies, and he accompanied the celebrated Bampfylde Moore Carew in many of his rambles. He also visited most parts of the Continent as a stroller and vagabond ; and having acquired a knowledge of astrology and quackery, he returned to

England, and practised both arts with much profit. This was after his assumption of the female garb, and Lysons remarks that 'his long experience gained him the character of a most infallible *doctress ;'* he was likewise ' an excellent sempstress, and celebrated for making a good shirt.' In 1770, he applied for a certificate of his baptism, under the name of his sister Elizabeth, who had been christened in November 1669. About the same time he became a resident of his native place, where his extraordinary age obtained him the charitable notice of many respectable families, and among others that of Mr Thrale, at whose house ' Dr Johnson, who found him a shrewd sensible person, with a good memory, was very fond of conversing with him.' He died suddenly, and his true sex was then discovered, to the extreme surprise of all the neighbourhood.

APRIL 15.

Saints Basilissa and Anastasia, martyrs, 1st century. Saint Paternus, Bishop of Avranches, 563. St Ruadhan, abbot, 584. St Munde, abbot, 962. St Peter Gonzales, 1246.

Born.—William Augustus, Duke of Cumberland, 1721, *London ;* Sir James Clark Ross, navigator, 1800.

Died.— George Calvert, Lord Baltimore, 1632; Dominico Zampieri (Domenichino), Italian painter, 1641, *Naples ;* Madame de Maintenon, 1719, *St Cyr ;* William Oldys, antiquary, 1761, *London ;* Madame de Pompadour, mistress of Louis XV., 1764, *Paris ;* Dr Alexander Murray, philologist, 1813 ; John Bell, eminent surgeon, 1820, *Rome ;* Thomas Drummond, eminent in physical science, 1840, *Dublin.*

WILLIAM OLDYS.

Quaint and simple-minded William Oldys gave himself up, heart and soul, to the pleasant task of searching among old literary stores. The period in which he lived and laboured was not one to appreciate the value of such an enthusiast. Booksellers and men of letters found it worth while to make use of him, but it was little in their power to benefit him in return. So he rummaged old book-stalls undisturbed, made his honest notes, collected materials for mighty works contemplated, jotted down gentle indignation at unworthy treatment in endless diaries, and left all these invaluable treasures at his death to be scattered and lost and destroyed.

Little is known of his life, and that little, not always of a pleasing nature. ' His parents ' relates Grose—antiquary himself, after another fashion—' dying when he was very young, he soon squandered away his small patrimony, when he became, at first attendant in Lord Oxford's library, and afterwards librarian.' Possibly, the patrimony was very small; possibly, it went in books ; be that as it may, it is pleasing to find him in a post so congenial to his tastes. But Lord Oxford died, and Oldys became dependent on the booksellers. How this served his ends, we may judge by an anecdote communicated by the son of a friend of his. It was made known to the Duke of Norfolk one day at dinner, that Oldys had been passing ' *many years in quiet obscurity in the Fleet Prison.*' The Duke, to his honour, set him free, and got him appointed Norroy King-at-arms

Oldys wrote many valuable articles on various subjects ; but his chief remains were manuscript materials laboriously collected for works to come. ' His discoveries and curiosities,' says D'Israeli, ' were dispersed on many a fly-leaf, in occasional memorandum-books ; in ample marginal notes on his authors. They were sometimes thrown into what he calls his *Parchment Budgets,* or *Bags of Biography—Of Botany—Of Obituary—*of *Books Relative to London,* and other titles and bags, which he was every day filling.' His annotated edition of *Langbaine's Dramatic Poets,* preserved in the British Museum, is ' not interleaved, but overflowing with notes, written in a very small hand about the margins, and inserted between the lines ; nor may the transcriber pass negligently over its corners,' stored with date and reference. He also kept *diaries,* in which he jotted down work to be done, researches to be made, his feelings, his sorrows, with an infinitude of items, whose loss is to be regretted. In one volume, which has been preserved, he grows melancholy about his work, and sets down a pious misgiving, —' he heapeth up riches, and cannot tell who shall gather them.' In sadder mood still, he includes the contents in a quaint couplet :

' Fond treasurer of these stores, behold thy fate
    In Psalm the thirty-ninth, 6, 7, and 8.'

He sighs over books he has lent, which have not returned. He tells how he wrote some valuable article, of nearly two sheets, and how the booksellers ' for sordid gain, and to save a little expense in print and paper, got Mr John Campbell to cross it and cramp it, and play the devil with it, till they squeezed it into less compass than a sheet.' Or again, he growls humorously at ' old counsellor Fane, of Colchester, who, *in formâ pauperis,* deceived me of a good sum of money which he owed me, and not long after set up his chariot,' and who ' gave me a parcel of manuscripts, and promised me others, which he never gave me, nor anything else, besides a barrel of oysters.'

Probably ' old counsellor Fane ' knew his man, not only in the bribe of manuscript, but that of oysters. We know, at least, that when his throat was dry with the dust of folios, Oldys was wont to moisten it. Here is a song ' *made extempore by a gentleman, occasioned by a fly drinking out of his cup of ale,*' which D'Israeli traces to Oldys :

' Busy, curious, thirsty fly !
    Drink with me, and drink as I !
    Freely welcome to my cup,
    Couldst thou sip and sip it up ;
    Make the most of life you may :
    Life is short and wears away.

' Both alike are mine and thine,
    Hastening quick to their decline !
    Thine's a summer, mine no more,
    Though repeated to threescore !
    Threescore summers, when they're gone,
    Will appear as short as one !'

THE NIGHTINGALE AND ITS SONG.

The nightingale is pre-eminently the bird of April. Arriving in England about the middle of the month, it at once breaks forth into full song, which gradually decreases in compass and volume, as the more serious labours of life, nest-building, incubating, and rearing the young, have to be performed. The peculiar mode of migration, in reference to the limited range of this bird, has long been a puzzling problem for naturalists. In some districts they are to be heard filling the air with their sweet melody in every hedge-row ; while in other places, to all appearance quite as well suited to their habits, not one has ever been observed. And, stranger still, this marked difference, between abundance and total absence of nightingales, exists between places only a few miles apart. It might be supposed that the warmer districts of the kingdom would be most congenial to their habits, yet they are not found in Cornwall, nor in the south of Devonshire, where, in favourable seasons, the orange ripens in the open air. On the other hand, they are seldom heard to the northward of York, while they are plentiful in Denmark.

The migration of the nightingale to and in England seems to be conducted in an almost due north and south direction ; its eastern limits being bounded by the sea, and its western by the third degree of west longitude, which latter a very few stragglers only ever cross. This line completely cuts off Devonshire and Cornwall, nearly all Wales, and of course Ireland. Its northern limit, on the eastern side, is York ; but on the west it has been heard as far north as the neighbourhood of Carlisle.

The patriotic Sir John Sinclair, acting on the general rule that migratory song-birds almost always return to their native haunts, endeavoured to establish the nightingale in Scotland, but unfortunately without success. The attempt was conducted on a scale large enough to exhibit very palpable results, in case that the desired end had been practicable. Sir John commissioned a London dealer to purchase as many nightingales' eggs as he could get at the liberal price of one shilling each ; these were well packed in wool, and sent down to Scotland by mail. A number of trustworthy men had previously been engaged to find and take especial care of all robin-redbreasts' nests, in places where the eggs could be hatched in perfect safety. As regularly as the parcels of eggs arrived from London, the robins' eggs were removed from their nests and replaced by those of the nightingale ; which in due course were sat upon, hatched, and the young reared by their Scottish fosterers. The young nightingales, when full fledged, flew about, and were observed for some time afterwards apparently quite at home, near the places where they first saw the light, and in September, the usual period of migration, they departed. They never returned.

The poets have applied more epithets to this bird than, probably, to any other object in creation. The gentleman so favourably known to the public under the pseudonym of Cuthbert Bede, collected and published in *Notes and Queries* no less than one hundred and thirteen simple adjectives epithetically bestowed upon the nightingale by British poets ; and the present writer, in the same periodical, added sixty-five more to the number. The great difference, however, among the poets, is with reference to the character of its song. Milton speaks of it as the—

'Sweet bird, that shuns the noise of folly,
　Most musical, most melancholy.'

To this, Coleridge almost indignantly replies :—

'"Most musical, most melancholy bird !"
A melancholy bird ? O idle thought,
In nature there is nothing melancholy ;
But some night wandering man, whose heart was pierced
With the remembrance of a grievous wrong,
Or slow distemper, or neglected love,
And so, poor wretch, filled all things with himself,
And made all gentle sounds tell back the tale
Of his own sorrows—he, and such as he,
First named thy notes a melancholy strain.
＊　＊　＊　＊　'Tis the merry nightingale,
That crowds, and hurries, and precipitates,
With fast thick warble, his delicious notes,
As he were fearful that an April night
Would be too short for him to utter forth
His love chant, and disburden his full soul
Of all its music.'

The classical fable of the unhappy Philomela may have given an ideal tinge of melancholy to the Daulian minstrel's midnight strain ; as well as an origin to the once, and even now not altogether forgotten popular error, that the bird sings with its breast impaled upon a thorn. In an exquisite sonnet by Sir Philip Sidney, set to music by Bateson in 1604, we read :—

'The nightingale, as soon as April bringeth
　Unto her rested sense a perfect waking,
While late bare earth, proud of her clothing springeth,
　Sings out her woes, a thorn her song-book making ;
And mournfully bewailing,
　Her throat in tunes expresseth,
　While grief her heart oppresseth,
For Tereus o'er her chaste will prevailing.'

The earliest notice of this myth by an English poet is, probably, that in the *Passionate Pilgrim* of Shakspeare :

'Everything did banish moan,
　Save the nightingale alone ;
She, poor bird, as all forlorn,
　Leaned her breast up till a thorn,
And there sung the dolefull'st ditty,
　That to hear it was great pity.'

Hartley Coleridge, alluding to the controversy respecting the song of the nightingale, says :— 'No doubt the sensations of the bird while singing are pleasurable ; but the question is, what is the feeling which its song, considered as a succession of sounds produced by an instrument, is calculated to convey to a human listener ? When we speak of a pathetic strain of music, we do not mean that either the fiddle or the fiddler is unhappy, but that the tones or intervals of the air are such as the mind associates with tearful sympathies. At the same time, I utterly deny that the voice of Philomel expresses present pain. I could never have imagined that the pretty creature sets its breast against a thorn, and could not have perpetrated the abominable story of Tereus.' And to still further illustrate his opinion, he compares the songs of the nightingale and lark in the following lively poem, extracted from a little known limp volume published at Leeds :—

' 'Tis sweet to hear the merry lark,
  That bids a blithe good morrow;
But sweeter to hark, in the twinkling dark,
  To the soothing song of sorrow.
Oh, nightingale! what doth she ail?
  And is she sad or jolly?
For ne'er on earth was sound of mirth
  So like to melancholy.
The merry lark, he soars on high,
  No worldly thought o'ertakes him;
He sings aloud to the clear blue sky,
  And the daylight that awakes him.
As sweet a lay, as loud as gay,
  The nightingale is trilling;
With feeling bliss, no less than his,
  Her little heart is thrilling.
Yet ever and anon a sigh
  Peers through her lavish mirth;
For the lark's bold song is of the sky,
  And hers is of the earth.
By night and day she tunes her lay,
  To drive away all sorrow;
For bliss, alas! to night must pass,
  And woe may come to-morrow.'

Tennyson, in his *In Memoriam*, fully recognises the characteristics of both joy and grief in the nightingale's song:

' Wild bird! whose warble liquid, sweet,
  Rings echo through the budded quicks,
Oh, tell me where the senses mix,
Oh, tell me where the passions meet,
  Whence radiate? Fierce extremes employ
    Thy spirit in the lurking leaf,
    And in the midmost heart of grief
  Thy passion clasps a secret joy.'

Again, he expresses a similar idea in *The Gardener's Daughter*:

' Yet might I tell of weepings, of farewells,—
Of that which came between more sweet than each,
In whispers, like the whispers of the leaves,
That tremble round a nightingale—in sighs
Which perfect joy, perplexed for utterance,
Stole from her sister sorrow.'

Faber, in *The Cherwell Water Lily*, gives an angelic character to the strains of Philomel:

' I heard the raptured nightingale
Tell from yon elmy grove his tale
  Of jealousy and love,
In thronging notes that seem'd to fall,
As faultless and as musical
  As angels' strains above.
So sweet, they cast on all things round
A spell of melody profound;
They charmed the river in its flowing,
They stayed the night wind in its blowing,
They lulled the lily to her rest,
Upon the Cherwell's heaving breast.'

It seems very probable that Faber had read the following lines by Drummond, of Hawthornden :—

' Sweet artless songster, thou my mind doth raise
To airs of spheres, yes, and to angels' lays.'

The beautiful prose passage on the nightingale in Walton's *Angler* has been frequently quoted, amongst others by Sir Walter Scott, Sir Humphry Davy, and Bishop Horne; Dr Drake, too, in his *Literary Hours*, asserts that this description surpasses all that poets have written on the

subject. ' The nightingale,' says Walton, 'breathes such sweet, loud music out of her little instrumental throat, that it might make mankind to think miracles are not ceased. He that at midnight, when the very labourer sleeps securely, should hear, as I have very often, the clear airs, the sweet descants, the natural rising and falling, the doubling and redoubling of her voice, might well be lifted above earth, and say, Lord, what music hast thou provided for the saints in heaven, when thou affordest bad men such music on earth?'

More than two hundred years ago, a learned Jesuit, named Marco Bettini, attempted to reduce the nightingale's song to letters and words; and his attempt has been considered eminently successful. Towards the close of the last century, one Bechstein, a German, neither a scientific naturalist nor a scholar, simply a sportsman and observer of nature, but whose name must ever be connected with singing-birds, improved Bettini's attempt into the following form; which, however uncouth it may look, must be acknowledged by all acquainted with the song a very remarkable imitation, as far as the usual signs of spoken language can represent the different notes and modulations of the voice of the nightingale :—

Tiouou, tiouou, tiouou, tiouou,
    Shpe tiou tokoua;.
    Tio, tio, tio, tio,
Kououtio, kououtiou, kouotiou, koutioutio,
  Tokuo, tskouo, tskouo, tskouo,
Tsii, tsii, tsii, tsii, tsii, tsii, tsii, tsii, tsii, tsii, tsii,
  Kouorror, tiou, tksoua, pipitksouis,
Tso, tso, tso, tso, tso, tso, tso, tso, tso, tso, tso, tso,
    tsirrhading,
Tsi, tsi, si, tosi, si, si, si, si, si, si, si, si,
  Tsorre, tsorre, tsorre, tsorreki;
Tsatu, tsatu, tsatu, tsatu, tsatu, tsatu, tsatu, tsi,
Dlo, dlo, dlo, dla, dlo, dlo, dlo, dlo, dlo,
    Kouiou, trrrrrrrritzt,
Lu, lu, lu, ly, ly, ly, li, li, li, li.

Chalons, a celebrated Belgian composer, has set this to music, and Nodier asserts that there is nothing equal to it in the language of imitation. Yet, in the writer's own opinion, it is surpassed in expression, compass of voice, emphasis on the notes, and trill of terminating cadence, by the following rather ungallant imitation, sung by the French peasantry :—

Le bon Dieu m'a don-né une femme, Que j'ai
tant, tant, tant, tant, bat-tue, Que
s'il m'en donne une autre, Je ne la bat-ter-ais plus,
plus, plus, plus, Qu'un petit, qu'un pet-it, qu'un pet-it!

A ROYAL OPINION ON THE INCOMES OF THE CLERGY.

'The Duke of Cumberland heard a Mr Mudge, one of our angelic order [a clergyman], and who had a most seraphic finger for the harpsichord, play him a tune at some friendly knight or squire's house, where he was ambushed for him on his way to or from Scotland, and very honestly expresssed great satisfaction at the performance. "And would your highness think," says his friend, "that with such a wonderful talent, this worthy clergyman has not above a hundred a-year?" "And do you not think, sir," replied his highness, "that when a priest has more, it generally spoils him?"'—*Rev. Dr Warner, in Jesse's 'George Selwyn and his Contemporaries,'* iii. 336.

APRIL 16.

Eighteen martyrs of Saragossa, 304. St Turibius, Bishop of Astorga, about 420. St Fructuosus, Archbishop of Braga, 665. St Magnus, of Orkney, martyr, 1104. St Druon, recluse, patron of shepherds, 1186. St Joachim of Sienna, 1305.

Born.—Sir Hans Sloane, naturalist, 1660, *Killileagh;* Charles Montagu, Earl of Halifax, 1661, *Horton;* John Law, speculative financier, 1671, *Edinburgh.*

Died.—Aphra Behn, poetess 1689; George Louis, Comte de Buffon, naturalist, 1788, *Montbard;* Muzio Clementi, celebrated pianist, 1832; Henry Fuseli, artist, 1825, *Putney Hill;* F. Reynolds, dramatist, 1841; Pietro Dragonetti, eminent musician, 1846, *London;* Madame Tussaud, artist and exhibitor of wax figures, 1850, *London.*

APHRA BEHN.

Aphra Behn, celebrated as a writer and a wit, was born in the city of Canterbury, in the reign of Charles I. Her father, whose name was Johnson, being of a good family and well connected, obtained, through the interest of his relative, Lord Willoughby, the appointment of Lieutenant-General of Surinam, and set out with his wife and children to the West Indies. Mr Johnson died on the voyage, but his family reached Surinam, and settled there for some years. While here, Aphra became acquainted with the American Prince Oroonoka, and his beloved wife Imoinda, and the adventures of this pair became the materials of her first novel. On returning to London, she became the wife of Mr Behn, a Dutch merchant resident in that city. How long Mr Behn lived after his marriage is not known, but, probably, not long; for when we next hear of Mrs Behn, her wit and abilities had brought her into high repute at the Court of Charles II.; so much so, that Charles thought her a fit and proper person to be entrusted with the transaction of some affairs of importance abroad during the Dutch war. Our respect for official English is by no means increased when we learn that these high-sounding terms merely mean that she was to be sent over to Antwerp as a *spy!* However, by her skill and intrigues, but more by the influence she possessed over Vander Albert, she succeeded so well as to obtain information of the design of the Dutch to sail up the

Thames and burn the English ships in their harbours, and at once communicated her information to the English Court. Although subsequent events proved her intelligence to be well founded, it was only laughed at at the time, which probably determined her to drop all further thoughts of political affairs, and during the remainder of her stay at Antwerp to give herself up to the gallantries and gaieties of the place. On her voyage back to England, she was very near being lost. The vessel foundered in a storm, but fortunately in sight of land, so that the passengers were saved by boats from the shore. The rest of her life was devoted to pleasure and the muses.

Her writings, which are numerous, are nearly forgotten now, and from the opinion of several writers, it is well they should be. The following are the principal: three vols. of *Miscellany Poems;* seventeen *Plays;* two volumes of *History and Novels;* and a translation of M. Fontenelle's *History of Oracles* and *Plurality of Worlds.*

A plain black marble slab covers her grave in the cloisters of Westminster Abbey, bearing the following inscription:

' MRS APHARRA BEHN DIED APRILL THE 16TH, 1689.

    ' Here lies a proof that wit can never be
      Defence enough against mortality.
      Great poetess, O thy stupendous lays
      The world admires, and the Muses praise.'

MADAME TUSSAUD.

The curious collection of wax-work figures exhibited in Baker-street, London, under the name of Madame Tussaud, is well known in England. Many who are no longer in their first youth must also have a recollection of the neat little figure of Madame Tussaud·herself, seated in the stair of approach, and hard to be distinguished in its calm primness from the counterfeits of humanity which it was the business of her life to fabricate. Few, however, are aware of the singularities which marked the life of Madame Tussaud, or of the very high moral merits which belonged to her.

She had actually lived among the celebrated men of the French Revolution, and framed their portraits from direct observation. It was her business one day to model the horrible countenance of the assassinated Marat, whom she detested, and on another to imitate the features of his beautiful assassin, Charlotte Corday, whom she admired and loved. Now, she had a Princess Lamballe in her hands; anon, it was the atrocious Robespierre. At one time she was herself in prison, in danger of the all-devouring guillotine, having there for her associates Madame Beauharnais and her child, the grandmother and mother of the Emperor Napoleon III. Escaping from France, she led for many years a life of struggle and difficulty, supporting herself and her family by the exercise of her art. Once she lost her whole stock by shipwreck on a voyage to Ireland. Meeting adversity with a stout heart, always industrious, frugal, and considerate, the ingenious little woman at length was enabled to set up her models in London, where she had forty years of constant prosperity, and where she died at the age of ninety, in the midst of an attached

and grateful family, extending to several generations. Let ingenuity be the more honoured when
it is connected, as in her case, with many virtues.

THE SWEATING SICKNESS.

April 16, 1551, the sweating sickness broke
out at Shrewsbury. This was the last appearance of one of the most remarkable diseases
recorded in history. Its first appearance was
in August 1485, among the followers of Henry
VII. who fought and gained the memorable battle
of Bosworth Field. The battle was contested on
the 22nd of August, and on the 28th the king
entered London, bringing in his train the fatal and
previously unknown pestilence. The 'Swetynge
Sykenesse,' as it is termed by the old chroniclers,
immediately spread its ravages among the
crowded, unhealthy dwellings of the citizens of
London. Two lord mayors and six aldermen,
having scarcely laid aside the state robes in which
they had received the Tudor king, died in the first
week of the terrible visitation. The national joy
and public festivities, consequent on the conclusion
of the long struggle between the rival houses of
York and Lancaster, were at once changed to
general terror and lamentation. The coronation
of Henry, an urgent measure, as it was expected
to extinguish the last scruples that some might
entertain regarding his right to the throne, was
of necessity postponed. The disease spread over
all England with fearful rapidity. It seems to
have been a violent inflammatory fever, which,
after a short rigor, prostrated the vital powers
as with a blow; and, amidst a painful oppression
at the stomach, head-ache, and lethargic stupor,
suffused the whole body with a copious and dis-
gustingly foetid perspiration. All this took place
in a few hours, the crisis being always over
within the space of a day and night; and scarcely
one in a hundred recovered of those who were
attacked by it. Hollinshed says :—'Suddenly,
a deadly burning sweat so assailed their bodies
and distempered their blood with a most ardent
heat, that scarce one among an hundred that
sickened did escape with life, for all in manner,
as soon as the sweat took them, or a short time
after, yielded the ghost. Kaye, the founder of
Caius College, Cambridge, and the most eminent
physician of his day, who carefully observed the
disease at its last visitation, relates that its
'sudden sharpness and unwont cruelness passed
the pestilence (the plague). For this (the plague)
commonly giveth three or four, often seven,
sometimes nine, sometimes eleven, and sometimes
fourteen days respect to whom it vexeth. But
that (the sweating sickness) immediately killed.
Some in opening their windows, some in playing
with their children at their street doors, some in
one hour, many in two, it destroyed, and, at the
longest, to them that merrily dined it gave a
sorrowful supper. As it found them, so it took
them, some in sleep, some in wake, some in
mirth, some in care, some fasting, and some full,
some busy, and some idle, and in one house,
sometimes three, sometimes four, sometimes
seven, sometimes eight, sometimes more, sometimes all.'

Though the sweating sickness of 1485 desolated the English shores of the Irish Channel,
and the northern border counties of England.
yet it did not penetrate into either Ireland or
Scotland. It disappeared about the end of the
year; a violent tempest that occurred on the
1st of January 1486, was supposed to have swept
it away for ever.

The slight medical knowledge of the period
found itself utterly unable to cope with the new
disease. No resource was therefore left to the
terrified people, but their own good sense, which
fortunately led them to adopt the only efficient
means that could be pursued. Violent medicines
were avoided. The patient was kept moderately
warm, a small quantity of mild drink was given,
but total abstinence from food was enjoined
until the crisis of the malady had passed.
Those who were attacked in the day, in order
to avoid a chill, went immediately to bed without taking off their clothes, and those who
sickened at night did not rise, carefully avoiding
the slightest exposure to the air of either hand
or foot. Thus they carefully guarded against
heat or cold, so as not to encourage the perspiration by the former, nor check it by the latter;
bitter experience having taught that either was
certain death.

In 1506, the sweating sickness broke out in
London for the second time, but the disease exhibited a much milder character than it did during
its first visitation; numbers who were attacked
by it recovered, and the physicians of the day
rejoiced triumphantly, attributing the cures to
their own skill, instead of to the milder form of
the epidemic. It was not long till they discovered
their error. In 1517, the disease broke out in
England for the third time, with all its pristine
virulence. It ravaged England for six months,
and as before did not penetrate into Ireland or
Scotland. It reached Calais, however, then an
English possession, but did not spread farther
into France.

As eleven years elapsed between the second
and third visitation of this fell destroyer, so the
very same period intervened between its third
and fourth appearance, the latter taking place in
1528. The previous winter had been so wet,
that the seed corn had rotted in the ground.
Some fine weather in spring gave hopes to the
husbandman, but scarcely had the fields been
sown when a continual series of heavy rains
destroyed the grain. Famine soon stalked over
the land, and with it came the fatal sweating
sickness. This, as far as can be collected, was
its most terrible visitation, the old writers describing it as *The Great Mortality*. All public
business was suspended. The Houses of Parliament and courts of law were closed. The
king, Henry VIII., left London, and endeavoured
to avoid the epidemic by continually travelling
from place to place, till, becoming tired of so
unsettled a life, he determined to await his
destiny at Tittenhanger. There, with his first
wife, Catherine of Aragon, and a few favourites,
he lived in total seclusion from the outer world.
the house being surrounded with large fires,
which night and day were kept constantly burning, as a means of purifying the atmosphere.
There are no accurate data by which the number
of persons destroyed by this epidemic can be

estimated, but they must have been many, very many. The visitation lasted much longer than the previous ones. Though the greater number of deaths occurred in 1528, the disease was still prevalent in the following summer. As before, the epidemic did not extend to Scotland or Ireland. It was even affirmed and believed that natives of those countries were never attacked by it, though dwelling in England; that in Calais it spared the French, the men of English birth alone becoming its victims; that, in short, it was a disease known only in England, and fatal only to Englishmen; consequently, the learned gave it the name of *Sudor Anglicus*—the English sweat. And the learned writers of the period all cordially agreed in ascribing the English pestilence to the sins of Englishmen, though they differed in opinion as to the particular sins which called down so terrible a manifestation of Divine displeasure. Not one of them conjectured the real causes of the epidemic, namely, the indescribable filthiness of English towns and houses, and the scarcity and disgusting unwholesomeness of the people's food.

The disease soon gave the lie to the expression *Sudor Anglicus* by spreading into Germany, and there committing frightful ravages. On its last visit to England, in April 1551, it made its first appearance at Shrewsbury. It was found to have undergone no change. It attacked its hapless victims at table, on journeys, during sleep, at devotion or amusement, at all times of the day or night. Nor had it lost any of its malignity, killing its victims sometimes in less than an hour, while in all cases the space of twenty-four hours decided the fearful issue of life or death.

Contemporary historians say that the country was depopulated. Women ran about negligently clothed, as if they had lost their senses, and filled the air with dismal outcries and lamentations. All business came to a stand. No one thought of his daily avocations. The funeral bells tolled night and day, reminding the living of their near and inevitable end. Breaking out at Shrewsbury, it spread westward into Wales, and through Cheshire to the north-western counties; while on the other side, it extended to the southern counties, and easterly to London, where it arrived in the beginning of July. It ravaged the capital for a month, then passed along the east coast of England towards the north, and finally ceased about the end of September. Thus, in the autumn of 1551, the sweating sickness vanished from the earth; it has never reappeared, and in all human probability never will, for the conditions under which a disease of its nature and malignity could occur and extend itself do not now exist. Modern medical science avers that the *Sudor Anglicus* was a rheumatic fever of extraordinary virulence; still of a virulence not to be wondered at, when we take into consideration the deficiency of the commonest necessaries of life, that prevailed at the period in which it occurred.

BATTLE OF CULLODEN.—PRINCE CHARLES'S
KNIFE-CASE.

On the 16th of April 1746, was fought the battle of Culloden, insignificant in comparison with many other battles, from there being only about eight thousand troops engaged on each side, but important as finally setting at rest the claims of the expatriated line of the house of Stuart to the British throne. The Duke of Cumberland, who commanded the army of the government, used his victory with notable harshness and cruelty; not only causing a needless slaughter among the fugitives, but ordering large numbers of the wounded to be fusilladed on the field: a fact often doubted, but which has been fully proved. He probably acted under an impression that Scotland required a severe lesson to be read to her, the reigning idea in England being that the northern kingdom was in rebellion, whereas the insurgents represented but a small party of the Scottish people, to whom in general the descent of a parcel of the Highland clans with Charles Edward Stuart was as much a surprise as it was to the court of St James's. The cause of the Stuarts had, indeed, extremely declined in Scotland by the middle of the eighteenth century, and the nation was turning its whole thoughts to improved industry, in peaceful submission to the Brunswick dynasty, when the romantic enterprise of Prince Charles, at the head of a few hundred Camerons and Macdonalds, came upon it very much like a thunder-cloud in a summer sky. The whole affair of the Forty-five was eminently *an affair out of time*, an affair which took its character from a small number of persons, mainly Charles himself and a few West Highland chieftains, who had pledged themselves to him, and after all went out with great reluctance.

The wretched wanderings of the Prince for five months, in continual danger of being taken and instantly put to death, form an interesting pendant to the romantic history of the enterprise itself. Thirty thousand pounds was the fee offered for his capture; but, though many scores of persons had it in their power to betray him, no one was found so base as to do it. A curious circumstance connected with his wanderings has only of late been revealed, that, during nearly the whole time, he himself had a large command of money, a sum of about twenty-seven thousand pounds in gold having come for him too late to be of any use in the war, and been concealed in the bed of a *burn* in the Cameron's country, whence, from time to time, portions of it were drawn for his use and that of his friends.

When George IV. paid his visit to Scotland in 1822, Sir Walter Scott was charged by a lady in Edinburgh, with the duty of presenting to him the pocket knife, fork, and spoon which Charles Edward was believed to have used in the course of his marches and wanderings in 1745-6. The lady was, by Sir Walter Scott's acknowledgment,* Mary Lady Clerk, of Penicuik. This relic of Charles, having subsequently passed to the Marquis of Conyngham, and from him to his son Albert, first Lord Londesborough, is now preserved with great care amidst the valuable collection of ancient plate and *bijouterie* at Grimston Park, Yorkshire. The case is a small one covered with black shagreen; for portability, the knife,

* Note to Croker's *Boswell*, 8vo. ed. p. 329.

fork, and spoon are made to screw upon handles, so that the three articles form six pieces, allowing

of close packing, as shewn in our first cut. The second cut exhibits the articles themselves, on a scale of half their original size; one of the handles being placed below, while the rose pattern on the knob of each is shewn at *a*. They are all engraved with an ornament of thistle leaves, and the spoon and fork marked with the initials

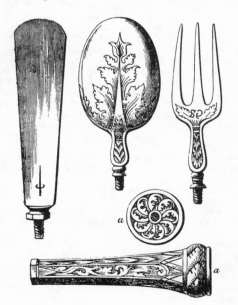

C. S., as will be better seen on reversing the engraving. The articles being impressed with a Dutch plate stamp, we may presume that they were manufactured in Holland.

On reverting to the chronicles of the day,[*] we find that the king, in contemplation of his visit to Scotland, expressed a wish to possess some relic of the 'unfortunate Chevalier,' as he called him; and it was in the knowledge of this fact, that Lady Clerk commissioned Sir Walter Scott to present to his Majesty the articles here described. On the king arriving in Leith Road, Sir Walter went out in a boat to present him with a silver cross badge from 'the ladies of Scotland,' and he took that opportunity of handing him the gift of Lady Clerk, which the king received with marked gratification. At a ball a few days afterwards, he gave the lady his thanks in person, in terms which shewed his sense of the value of the gift. He was probably by that time aware of an interesting circumstance in her own history connected with the Forty-five. Born Mary Dacres, the daughter of a Cumberland gentleman, she had entered the world at the time when the Prince's forces were in possession of Carlisle. While her mother was still confined to bed, a Highland party came to the house; but the officer in command, on learning the circumstances, not only restrained his men from giving any molestation, but pinned his own white rosette or cockade upon the infant's breast, that it might protect the household from any trouble from others. This rosette the lady kept to her dying day, which was not till several years subsequent to the king's visit. Her ladyship retained till past eighty an erect and alert carriage, which, together with some peculiarities of dressing, made her one of the most noted street figures of her time. With Sir Walter she was on the most intimate terms. The writer is enabled to recall a walk he had one day with this distinguished man, ending at Mr Constable's warehouse in Princes-street, where Lady Clerk was purchasing some books at a side counter. Sir Walter, passing through to the stairs by which Mr Constable's room was reached, did not recognise her ladyship, who, catching a sight of him as he was about to ascend, called out, 'Oh, Sir Walter, are you really going to pass me?' He immediately turned to make his usual cordial greetings, and apologised with demurely waggish reference to her odd dress, 'I'm sure, my lady, by this time I might know your back as well as your face.'

It is understood in the Conyngham family, that the knife-case came to Lady Clerk 'through the Primrose family,' probably referring to the widow of Hugh third Lord Primrose, in whose house in London Miss Flora Macdonald was sheltered after her liberation from a confinement she underwent for her concern in promoting the Prince's escape. We are led to infer that Lady Primrose had obtained the relic from some person to whom the Chevalier had given it as a *souvenir* at the end of his wanderings.[†]

* *Edinburgh Observer*, quoted in *Gentleman's Magazine*, September 1822.

† We learn from Boswell that the Prince gave a similar knife-case to Dr Macleod, brother of 'Rasay,' who had promoted his escape; and it appears that this relic was lately in the possession of Dr Macleod's great grandson, Mr Shaw, sheriff-substitute, Lochmaddy.

APRIL 17.

St Anicetus, Pope and martyr, 173. St Simeon, Bishop of Ctesiphon, 341. St Stephen, abbot of Citeaux, 1134.

Born.—John Ford, dramatist (baptized), 1586, *Islington ;* Bishop Edward Stillingfleet, 1635, *Cranbourn, Dorset.*

Died.—Marino Falieri, doge of Venice, executed, 1355 ; Joachim Camerarius, German Protestant scholar, 1574, *Leipzig ;* George Villiers, second duke of Buckingham, 1688, *Kirkby-Moorside ;* Bishop Benjamin Hoadley ; 1761, *Winchester ;* Dr Benjamin Franklin, 1790, *Philadelphia ;* James Thom, 'The Ayrshire sculptor,' 1850, *New York.*

GEORGE VILLIERS, SECOND DUKE OF BUCKINGHAM.

This nobleman, whose miserable end is described by Pope, was about six or seven years old when, on his father's murder, he succeeded to his titles and estates. During his long minority, which he passed chiefly on the Continent, his property so greatly accumulated as to have become, it is said, fifty thousand a year, equal to at least four times that sum at the present day.

At the battle of Worcester, he was General of the king's horse, and, after the loss of that contest, he escaped with much difficulty. Travelling on foot through bye lanes, obtaining refreshment at cottages, and changing his dress with a woodman, he was enabled to elude the vigilance of his pursuers. At the restoration of Charles II., he was appointed to several offices of trust and honour ; but such were his restless disposition and dissolute habits, that he soon lost the confidence of the king, and made a wreck of his property. ' He gave himself up,' says Burnet, ' to a monstrous course of studied immoralities.' His natural abilities, however, were considerable, and his wit and humour made him the life and admiration of the court of Charles. ' He was,' says Granger, ' the alchymist and the philosopher ; the fiddler and the poet ; the mimic and the statesman.'

His capricious spirit and licentious habits unfitted him for the permanent leadership of any political party, nor did he generally take much interest in politics, but occasionally he devoted himself to some special measure, and would then become its principal advocate ; though even on such occasions his captious, ungoverned temper often led him to give personal offence, and to infringe the rules of the House, for which he was more than once committed to the Tower. Lord Clarendon relates an amusing anecdote of him on one of these occasions, which is also a curious illustration of the manner of conducting public business at that period. ' It happened,' says the Chancellor, ' that upon the debate of the same affair, the Irish Bill, there was a conference appointed with the House of Commons, in which the Duke of Buckingham was a manager, and as they were sitting down in the Painted Chamber, which is seldom done in good order, it chanced that the Marquis of Dorchester sate next the Duke of Buckingham, between whom there was no good correspondence. The one changing his posture for his own ease, which made the station

of the other more uneasy, they first endeavoured by justling to recover what they had dispossessed each other of, and afterwards fell to direct blows. In the scuffle, the Marquis, who was the lower of the two in stature, and was less active in his limbs, was deprived of his periwig, and received some rudeness, which nobody imputed to his want of courage. Indeed, he was considered as beforehand with the Duke, for he had plucked off much of his hair to compensate for the loss of his own periwig.' For this misdemeanour they were both sent to the Tower, but were liberated in a few days.

The Duke of Buckingham began to build a magnificent mansion at Cliefden, in Buckinghamshire, on a lofty eminence commanding a lovely view on the banks of the Thames, where he is said to have carried on his gallantries with the notorious Countess of Shrewsbury, whose husband he killed in a duel, an account of which has already been given in this volume (page 129).

Large as was his income, his profligate habits reduced him to poverty, and he died in wretchedness at Kirkby-Moorside, in Yorkshire, in 1688. The circumstances of his death have thus been, somewhat satirically, described by Pope in his third Epistle to Lord Bathurst :

' Behold ! what blessings wealth to life can lend,
And see, what comfort it affords our end !
In the worst inn's worst room, with mat half-hung,
The floors of plaster, and the walls of dung,
On once a flock-bed, but repaired with straw,
With tape-tied curtains, never meant to draw,
The George and Garter dangling from that bed
Where tawdry yellow strove with dirty red,
Great Villiers lies—alas ! how changed from him,
That life of pleasure, and that soul of whim,
Gallant and gay, in Cliefden's proud alcove,
The bower of wanton Shrewsbury and Love ;
Or just as gay at council, in a ring
Of mimick'd statesmen and their merry king.
No wit to flatter, reft of all his store !
No fool to laugh at, which he valued more.
There, victor of his health, of fortune, friends,
And fame, this lord of useless thousands ends.'

The house in which the Duke died is still in existence. There is no tradition of its ever having been an inn, and it is far from being a mean habitation. It is built in the Elizabethan style, with two projecting wings ; and at the time of the Duke's decease, must have been, with but one exception, the best house in the town. The room in which he expired is the best sleeping room in the house, and had then, as now, a good boarded floor. His Yorkshire place of residence was Helmsley Castle, which is about six miles from Kirkby-Moorside, and now a mere ruin. While hunting in the neighbourhood of Kirkby, the manor of which belonged to him, he was seized with hernia and inflammation, which caused his detention and death at the above-mentioned house, then occupied, probably, by one of his tenants.

So little did the house in which the Duke died really resemble Pope's description. Nor was his death-bed altogether without proper attendants. It so happened that just about the time of his seizure, the Earl of Arran, his kinsman, was passing through York, and hearing of the Duke's illness he hastened to him, and, on finding the condition he was in, immediately sent for a physician from York, who, with other medical men, attended on the Duke till his death. Lord Arran also sent for a Mr Gibson, a neighbour and acquaintance of the Duke's, and apprized his family and connexions of the circumstances of his case; so that Lord Fairfax, Mr Brian Fairfax, Mr Gibson, and Colonel Liston, were speedily in attendance. Lord Arran also informed the Duke of his immediate danger, and, supposing him to be a Roman Catholic, proposed to send for a priest of that persuasion, but the Duke declared himself to be a member of the Church of England, and after some hesitation agreed to receive the clergyman of the parish, who offered up prayers for him, 'in which he freely joined;' and afterwards administered to him the Holy Communion.

Shortly after this he became speechless, and died at eleven o'clock on the night of the 16th of April.* Lord Arran ordered the body to be carried to Helmsley Castle, and, after being disbowelled and embalmed, to remain there till orders were received from the Duchess. It was subsequently taken to London, and interred in Westminster Abbey. This circumstantial account of the Duke's death is given, because Pope's has been received as historical, instead of a poetic exaggeration of the real facts of the case.

Of the Duke's dissolute habits, of his unprincipled character, of his self-sacrificed health, and his ruined fortune, it is scarcely possible to speak too strongly. His possession of Helmsley Castle at his death was only nominal. In reference to his funeral, Lord Arran says: 'There is not so much as one farthing towards defraying the least expense.' Soon after his death all his property, which had long been deeply mortgaged, was sold, and did not realize sufficient to pay his debts; and dying issueless, his titles, which had been undeservedly conferred on his father and only disgraced by himself, became extinct. Indeed all the titles, nine in number, conferred by James on his favourite George Villiers and his brothers, became extinct in the next generation. Strange to say, this profligate Duke married Mary, daughter and heir of the puritan Lord Fairfax, the Parliamentary General, whom he deserted while living and left without a memento at his death.

Many years after the Duke's decease, a steel seal, with his crest on it, was found in a crevice in the room wherein he died, and is still possessed by the present owner of the house; and an old parish register at Kirkby contains the following curious entry:

'Burials; 1687, April 17th, Georges Viluas Lord dooke of bookingham.'†

W. H. K.

GREYSTEIL.

The books of the Lord Treasurer of Scotland indicate that, when James IV. was at Stirling on

* Lord Arran's letter to the Bishop of Rochester, from which this account is taken, is dated 'Kerby-moor-Syde, April 17, 1687.' He probably died on the 16th, although generally said to have died on the 17th. [The discrepancy as to the year of his death may be accounted for by a different method of reckoning the beginning of the year.]

† For this extract, the writer is indebted to the Rev. C. R. Hay, late vicar of Kirkby-Moorside.

the 17th April 1497, there was a payment 'to twa fithalaris [fiddlers] that sang Greysteil to the king, ixs.' Greysteil is the title of a metrical tale which originated at a very early period in Scotland, being a detail of the adventures of a chivalrous knight of that name. It was a favourite little book in the north throughout the sixteenth and seventeenth centuries, sold commonly at sixpence; yet, though there was an edition so late as 1711, so entirely had it lost favour during the eighteenth century, that Mr David Laing, of Edinburgh, could find but one copy, from which to reprint the poem for the gratification of modern curiosity. We find a proof of its early popularity, not merely in its being sung to King James IV., but in another entry in the Lord Treasurer's books, as follows:— Jan. 22, 1508, to Gray Steill, lutar, vs.; '* from which it can only be inferred that one of the royal lute-players, of whom there appear to have been four or five, bore the nickname of Greysteil, in consequence of his proficiency in singing this old minstrel poem. It appears to have been deemed, in the sixteenth and seventeenth centuries, as high a compliment as could well be paid to a gallant warrior, to call him Greysteil. For example, James V. in boyhood bestowed this pet name upon Archibald Douglas, of Kilspindie; and even when the Douglas was under banishment, and approaching the king in a kind of disguise for forgiveness, 'Yonder is surely my Greysteil,' exclaimed the monarch, pleased to recall the association of his early days. Another personage on whom the appellation was bestowed was Alexander, sixth Earl of Eglintoun, direct ancestor of the present Earl. A break in the succession (for Earl Alexander was, paternally, a Seton, not a Montgomery) had introduced a difficulty about the descent of both the titles and estates of the family, and the lordship of Kilwinning was actually given away to another by Act of Parliament, in 1612. In a family memoir we are told, 'Alexander was not a man tamely to submit to such injustice, and the mode which he adopted to procure redress was characteristic. He had repeatedly remonstrated, but in vain. Irritated by the delay on the part of the crown to recognise his right to the earldom, and feeling further aggrieved by the more material interference with his barony of Kilwinning, he waited personally on the Earl of Somerset, the King's favourite, with whom he supposed the matter mainly rested. He gave the favourite to understand that, as a peer of the realm, he was entitled to have his claims heard and justice done him, and that though but little skilled in the subtleties of law and the niceties of court etiquette, he knew the use of his sword. From his conduct in this affair, and his general readiness with his sword, the Earl acquired the sobriquet of Greysteil, by which he is still known in family tradition.'†

It will probably be a surprise to most of our readers that the tune of old called Greysteil, and probably the same which was sung to James

* Dauney's Ancient Scottish Melodies, 4to, Edinburgh, 1838, p. 358.

† Memorials of the Earls of Eglintoun, by William Fraser. 2 vols. 4to. Edinburgh [privately printed], 1859.

IV. of Scotland in 1497, still exists, and can now be forthcoming. The piece of music we refer to is included, under the name *Greysteil*, in 'Ane Playing Booke for the Lute, noted and collected at Aberdeen by Robert Gordon in 1627,' a manuscript which some years ago was in the possession of George Chalmers, the historian. The airs in this book being in tablature, a form of notation long out of use, it was not till about 1840 that the tune of Greysteil was with some difficulty read off from it, and put into modern notation, and so communicated to the writer of this notice by his valued friend Mr William Dauney, advocate, editor of the ancient Scottish melodies just quoted. Mr Dauney, in sending it, said, ' I have no doubt that it is in substance the air referred to in the Lord Treasurer's accounts. . . . . . The ballad or poem to which it had been chanted, was most probably the popular romance of that name, which you will find in Mr Laing's *Early Metrical Tales,* and of which he says in the preface that, "along with the poems of Sir David Lyndsey, and the histories of Robert Bruce and of Sir William Wallace, it formed the standard production of the vernacular literature of the country." . . . . The tune,' Mr Dauney goes on to say, ' is not Scottish in its structure or character; but it bears a resemblance to the somewhat monotonous species of chant to which some of the old Spanish and even English historical ballads were sung. In this respect it is suitable to the subject of the old romance, which is not Scottish.' There is a serviceable piece of evidence for the presumed antiquity of the air, in the fact that a satirical Scotch poem on the unfortunate Earl of Argyle, dated 1686, bears on it, ' appointed to be sung to the tune of old Greysteil.' We must, however, acknowledge that, but for this proof of poetry being actually sung to 'Old Greysteil,' we should have been disposed to think that the tune here printed was only presented by the luters as a sort of prelude or refrain to their chanting of the metrical romance in question. The abruptness of the end is very remarkable.

The tune of *Greysteil,* for certain as old as 1627, and presumed to be traditional from at least 1497, is as follows :

When on the subject of so early a piece of Scotch music, it may not be inappropriate to advert to another specimen, which we can set forth as originally printed in 1588, being the oldest piece in print as far as we know. It is only a simple little *lilt*, designed for a homely dance, but still, from its comparative *certain antiquity*, is well worthy of preservation. Mr Douce has transferred it into his *Illustrations of Shakspeare*, from the book in which it originally appeared, a volume styled *Orchesographie*, professedly by Thionot Arbeau (in reality by a monk named Jean Tabouret), printed at Lengres in the year above mentioned. He calls it a *branle* or *brawl*, 'which was performed by several persons uniting hands in a circle and giving each other continual shakes, the steps changing with the tune. It usually consisted of three *pas* and a *pied-joint* to the time of four strokes of the bow; which being repeated, was termed a *double brawl*. With this dance balls were usually opened.'

The copy given in the original work being in notation scarcely intelligible to a modern musician, we have had it read off and harmonised as follows:

BRING THEM IN AND KEEP THEM AWAKE.

On the 17th April 1725, John Rudge bequeathed to the parish of Trysull, in Staffordshire, twenty shillings a year, that a poor man might be employed to go about the church during sermon and keep the people awake; also to keep dogs out of church. A bequest by Richard Dovey, of Farmcote, dated in 1659, had in view the payment of eight shillings annually to a poor man, for the performance of the same duties in the church of Claverley, Shropshire. In the parishes of Chislet, Kent, and Peterchurch, Herefordshire, there are similar provisions for the exclusion of dogs from church, and at Wolverhampton there is one of five shillings for keeping boys quiet in time of service.*

We do not find any very early regulations made to secure the observance of festivals among Christians. A solicitude on the subject becomes apparent in the middle ages. Early in the thirteenth century, we meet with a document of a curious nature, the principal object of which is to awaken a reverence for the Lord's day. It professes to be 'a mandate which fell from heaven, and was found on the altar of

* Edwards's *Remarkable Charities*, 220.

St Simon, on Mount Golgotha, in Jerusalem,' and humbly taken by the patriarch, and the Archbishop Akarias, 'after that for three days and three nights the people, with their pastors, had lain prostrate on the ground, imploring the mercy of God.' A copy of it was brought to England by Eustachius, abbot of Hay; who, on his return from the Holy Land, preached from city to city against the custom of buying and selling on the Sunday. 'If you do not obey this command,' says this celestial message, 'verily, I say unto you, that I will not send you any other commands by another letter, but I will open the heavens, and instead of rain I will pour down upon you stones and wood, and hot water by night; so that ye shall not be able to guard against it, but I will destroy all the wicked men. This I say unto you; ye shall die the death, on account of the holy day of the Lord; and of the other festivals of my saints which ye do not keep, I will send upon you wild beasts to devour you,' &c.

Yet the sacredness of the day had been attested by extraordinary interpositions of divine power. At Beverley, a carpenter who was making a peg, and a weaver who continued to work at his web after three o'clock on the

Saturday, were severally struck with palsy. In Nasurta, a village which belonged to one Roger Arundel, a man who had baked a cake in the ashes after the same hour, found it bleed when he tried to eat it on Sunday, and a miller who continued to work his mill was arrested by the blood which flowed from between the stones, in such quantity as to prevent their working; while in some places, not named, in Lincolnshire, bread put by a woman into a hot oven after the forbidden hour, remained unbaked on the Monday; when another piece, which by the advice of her husband she put away in a cloth, because the ninth hour was past, she found baked on the morrow.—(Notes to *Feasts and Fasts*, by E. V. Neale.)

Leland presents evidence of the same kind of feeling in a story told of Richard de Clare, Earl of Gloucester, by annalists, to this effect. In the year 1260, a Jew of Tewkesbury fell into a sink on the Sabbath, and out of reverence for the day, would not suffer himself to be drawn out; the earl, out of reverence for the Sunday, would not permit him to be drawn out the next day, and between the two he died.

By the 5th and 6th Edward VI., and by 1st Elizabeth, it was provided, that every inhabitant of the realm or dominion shall diligently and faithfully, having no lawful or reasonable excuse to be absent, endeavour themselves to their parish church or chapel accustomed; or, upon reasonable let, to some usual place where common prayer shall be used,—on Sundays and holidays,—upon penalty of forfeiting for every non-attendance twelve pence, to be levied by the churchwardens to the use of the poor. But the application of these provisions to the attendance upon other holidays than Sundays, seems to have been soon dropped. The statute of James I., re-enacting the penalty of one shilling for default in attendance at church, is limited to Sundays; and the latter day alone is mentioned in the Acts of William and Mary, and George III., by which exceptions in favour of dissenters from the Church of England were introduced.

As the statute of James applied solely to Sundays, there was no civil punishment left for this neglect; though it remained punishable, under the 5th and 6th of Edward VI., by ecclesiastical censures. Mr Vansittart Neale, in his *Feasts and Fasts*, however, cites several cases which appear to settle that the ecclesiastical courts had not the power to compel any person to attend his parish church, because they have no right to decide the bounds of parishes.

There were, however, from time to time, suits commenced against individuals for this neglect of attendance at church; these actions being generally instigated by personal motives rather than with religious feeling. Professor Amos, in his Treatise on Sir Matthew Hale's *History of the Pleas of the Crown*, states the following cases : 'In the year 1817, at the Spring Assizes for Bedford, Sir Montague Burgoyne was prosecuted for having been absent from his parish church for several months; when the action was defeated by proof of the defendant having been indisposed. And in the Report of Prison Inspectors to the House of Lords, in 1841, it appeared, that in 1830, ten persons were in prison for recusancy in not attending their parish churches. A mother was prosecuted by her own son.' These enactments remained in our Statute-book, until, in common with many other penal and disabling laws in regard to religious opinions, they were swept away by the statute 9th and 10th Vict., c. 59.

It also appears that in old times many individuals considered it their duty to set aside part of their worldly wealth for keeping the congregation awake. Some curious provisions were made for this purpose. At Acton church in Cheshire, about five and twenty years ago, one of the churchwardens or the apparitor used to go round the church during service, with a long wand in his hand; and if any of the congregation were asleep, they were instantly awoke by a tap on the head. At Dunchurch, a similar custom existed : a person bearing a stout wand, shaped liked a hay fork at the end, stepped stealthily up and down the nave and aisle, and, whenever he saw an individual asleep, he touched him so effectually that the spell was broken; this being sometimes done by fitting the fork to the nape of the neck.

We read of the beadle in another church, going round the edifice during service, carrying a long staff, at one end of which was a fox's brush, and at the other a knob; with the former he gently tickled the faces of the female sleepers, while on the heads of their male compeers he bestowed with the knob a sensible rap.

In some parishes, persons were regularly appointed to whip dogs out of church; and 'dog-whipping' is a charge in some sexton's accounts to the present day.

APRIL 18.

St Apollonius, the Apologist, martyr, 186. St Laserian, Bishop of Leighlin, Ireland, 638. St Galdin, Archbishop of Milan, 1176.

Born.—Sir Francis Baring, baronet, eminent merchant, 1740 ; George H. Lewes, miscellaneous writer, 1817, *London.*

Died.—John Leland, eminent English antiquary, 1552, *London ;* John Fox, author of *The Acts and Monuments of the Church*, 1587, *London ;* Robert Parsons, Jesuit controversialist, 1610, *Rome ;* Sir Symonds D'Ewes, collector of English historical records, 1650 ; George Lord Jeffreys, Chancellor of England, 1689, *Tower of London ;* Alexandre Lainez, French poet, 1710 ; Charles Pratt, Earl Camden, Chancellor of England 1766-1770, statesman, 1794 ; Dr Erasmus Darwin, poet, 1802, *Breadsall ;* John Abernethy, eminent surgeon, 1831.

LORD CHANCELLOR JEFFREYS.

As even Nero had some one to strew flowers over his grave, so was there a bard who found the notorious Jeffreys worthy of a gratulatory ode on his acceding to the Chief Justiceship. It appears in a broadside, dated October 23, 1683, and is wholly composed of panegyric. The circumstance becomes the more remarkable as the effusion is in Latin verse, arguing that the author was a man of good education. It ends with—

'I, secli presentis amor, longumque futuri
Exemplar, qui sic titulos virtutibus ornas,
Virtutem celsis titulis! Antiqua Britannum
Gesta sepultorum per te rediviva resurgant,
Angliacumque novis cumulant annalibus orbem.'*

ERASMUS DARWIN.

Erasmus Darwin, poet and physician, was
born at Elton, near Newark, in Nottinghamshire.
From his early youth, he was inclined to the
easily enjoyed pleasures of the imagination,
rather than to the hard-earned rewards of scientific studies. The following anecdote shews how
open to vivid impressions his mind was in youth.
Journeying from Newark, to enter upon his collegiate education at Cambridge, he rested for the
night at the house of two old bachelor brothers.
They were delighted with the vivacity of the
young student, and were rendered by it so painfully sensible that they were childless and solitary, that he heard one say regretfully to the
other, 'Why did not one of us marry!' The
tone and the circumstances never allowed that
sentence to fade from Darwin's memory, and it
was the origin of that strong condemnation of an
unmarried life, which for ever afterwards he
was so ready to utter. In due course, Darwin
graduated in medicine at Cambridge; but even
there he distinguished himself more by poetic
exercises than proficiency in science. Indeed, he
never attained to any particular eminence as a
physician, and would now be completely forgotten
were it not for his principal poem, *The Loves of
the Plants*. This work formed part only of a
poem entitled *The Botanic Garden*, in which
the physiology and classification of the vegetable
world is related in high-sounding, but not unmelodious verse, and illustrated with many
notes amusing, though not profound. The di-
gressions are many, and the flights of imagination
widely discursive. These flights are not always
characterised by scientific accuracy, but reach
the extreme limits of poetic frenzy. One, however, as a prognostication of steam-vessels and
locomotive engines, has become among the most
hackneyed quotations in our language—

'Soon shall thy arm, unconquered steam! afar
Drag the slow barge, or drive the rapid car.'

The *Loves of the Plants* had a great popularity
in its day, but was at last snuffed out by the
able but severe burlesque, *The Loves of the Tri-
angles*. [A life of Erasmus Darwin has been
issued in Germany by Ernst Krause. The English
translation of this book is graced by a preliminary notice by his distinguished grandson, Charles
Darwin. Krause has shewn that the vein of intellectual thought and speculation in the works of
the latter was more or less anticipated in those
of Erasmus Darwin.]

FOLK LORE OF NAIL-CUTTING.

A man had better ne'er been born
Than have his nails on a Sunday shorn.
Cut them on Monday, cut them for health;
Cut them on Tuesday, cut them for wealth;
Cut them on Wednesday, cut them for news;
Cut them on Thursday, for a pair of new shoes;

* Luttrel Collection of Broadsides, Brit. Mus.

Cut them on Friday, cut them for sorrow;
Cut them on Saturday, see your sweetheart to-
morrow.'

Sir Thomas Browne remarks: 'To cut nails upon a
Friday or a Sunday is accounted lucky amongst the
common people in many places. The set and statu-
tory times of paring nails and cutting hair is thought
by many a point of consideration, which is perhaps
but the continuation of an ancient superstition. To
the Romans it was piacular to pare their nails upon
the nundinæ, observed every ninth day,' &c.

APRIL 19.

St Ursmar, bishop and abbot, 713. St Elphege, Archbishop of Canterbury, martyr, 1012. St Leo IX., Pope,
1054.

THE MARTYRDOM OF ST ELPHEGE.

The Danes, emboldened by success, had determined at no distant time to conquer England;
and, as a measure of precaution, to anticipate
any league that might be formed against them,
they resolved on the murder of the king and
Witan. Their plan was disclosed, and Ethelred
and his nobles, panic-struck and frenzied, took
refuge in the last resource of cowards, assassination. Orders were secretly sent over the country
to exterminate the Danes, who were billeted on
the different Anglo-Saxon families, on the next
St Brice's Day, Nov. 13, 1002. A massacre
ensued which only finds a parallel in the Sicilian
Vespers, the atrocities of St Bartholomew's Day,
and the barbarism of the French Revolution.
The Danes vowed revenge, and for years after
kept their vow with desolating rigour.

Under these circumstances, Elphege became
Archbishop of Canterbury, A.D. 1006. He was
an enthusiastic Benedictine monk. It is told of
him that, in winter, he would rise at midnight,
and, issuing unseen from his house, kneel, exposed to the night air while praying, barefoot,
and without his great coat. Flesh he never
touched, except on extraordinary occasions; his
body was so attenuated, that, it is said, when he
held up his hand,

'It was so wan, and transparent of hue,
You might have seen the moon shine through.'

In 1011, the marauding Danes appeared, for
the second time, before Canterbury, and prepared
for an assault. The nobles fled; but the good
old archbishop buckled on his spiritual armour,
and shewed a vigour of mind but little expected
in one who had hitherto displayed only the virtues
of the recluse. He exhorted the citizens; and
they, encouraged by his example, for twenty
days successfully repelled the assaults of the
enemy. How the contest would have ended it
is impossible to say, had not the city been
betrayed by one Ælmær. While the plunder
was going on with every circumstance of cruelty,
the archbishop, trusting that his person would
be respected, resolved to address the Danes, in
the hope of moderating their excesses. He
arrived at a spot where the carnage and cruelty
were beyond all description. Women were exposed to worse than death, because they could

not reveal the hiding-place of treasures which did not exist; and their children were tossed from spear-point to spear-point before their eyes, amid the laughter of incarnate fiends, or crushed beneath the waggon-wheels which bore away the plunder. Eloquent from very anguish of heart, Elphege called upon them not to make war upon infants, and offered himself for death if they would but respect the women and spare the children. Instead of yielding to his entreaties, the Danes seized him, bound him, and by a refinement of cruelty dragged him to witness the destruction of his cathedral by fire. He knew that the church was filled with defenceless clergy, monks, and women. As the falling timbers and streams of melted lead drove them from the sanctuary, they were butchered amid shouts and merriment. Then to vary the sport, every tenth person was spared to become a slave. The archbishop himself was spared, his ransom being considered more profitable than his death. For seven months he was carried about with the army wherever they went, kept a close prisoner, and often in chains. On the day before Easter, he received notice that unless his ransom were paid within eight days—and it was fixed at 3,000 pieces of silver—his life would be forfeited. Paid it was not, and the anger of the Danes became excessive. At one of their feasts, when the men had gorged themselves, as was their fashion, and drunk themselves half mad with south-country wine, the archbishop was sent for to make them sport. 'Money, bishop, money!' was the cry which greeted him on all sides, as he was hurried into the hall. Breathless from fatigue, he sat down for a short time in silence. 'Money, money!' was still the cry. 'Your ransom, bishop, your ransom!' Having recovered his breath, the archbishop rose with dignity, and all were silent to hear if he would promise money for his ransom. 'Silver and gold,' he said, 'have I none; what is mine to give I freely offer, the knowledge of the one true God.' Here some one snatched up one of the ox-bones with which the floor was plentifully strewed, and threw it at the defenceless old man. Amid shouts of laughter, the cowardly example was followed, till he sank, severely bruised, but not dead. Some one standing near—it is said in pity for the sufferings of Elphege—raised his battle-axe, and with one blow ended his mortal agony. From a feeling of remorse, the body was given up to his friends, without ransom, for burial, and was first interred in London with great pomp; and then, only ten years after, conveyed in the barge of a Danish king, and attended by a Danish guard of honour, to Canterbury, and deposited by the side of the illustrious Dunstan.

——

Born.—Edward Pellew, Viscount Exmouth, naval commander, 1757.

Died.—King Robert II. of Scotland, 1390, *Dundonald Castle, Ayrshire;* Philip Melanchthon, German Protestant scholar, 1560, *Wittenberg;* Thomas Sackville, Earl of Dorset, poet, Lord Treasurer of England, 1608; Queen Christina, of Sweden, 1689, *Rome;* Jean Gallois, French scholar and critic, 1707; Nicholas Saunderson, blind scholar and mathematician, 1739, *Boxworth;* Dr Richard Price, calculator, 1791, *Hackney;* George, Lord Byron,

poet, 1824, *Missolonghi, Greece;* John Carne, miscellaneous writer, 1844, *Penzance;* Professor Robert Jameson, naturalist, 1854, *Edinburgh.*

QUEEN CHRISTINA OF SWEDEN.

Gustavus Adolphus, the heroic king of Sweden, was succeeded at his death in 1632 by his daughter Christina. This princess, having reigned as gloriously as her father had fought, having presided at the treaty of Westphalia, which gave peace to Germany, astonished Europe by abdicating at the age of twenty-seven. It was certainly a strange event, yet one that might not have been discreditable to her, if she had not had the weakness to repent of it.

The design of Queen Christina in quitting the Swedish throne was that she might have freedom to gratify her taste for the fine arts. She knew eight languages; she had been the disciple of Descartes, who died in her palace at Stockholm. She had cultivated all the arts in a climate where they were then unknown. She wished to live amongst them in Italy. With this view, she resolved also to accommodate her religion to her new country, and became a Roman Catholic.

Self-denying and self-repudiating acts do not always leave the character the sweeter. It is fully admitted that Christina was not improved by descending into private life. There remains one terrible stain upon her memory, the murder of her equerry, Monaldeschi, which she caused to be perpetrated in a barbarous manner in her own presence, during her second journey in France. During the thirty-five years of her ex-queenship, her conduct was marked by many eccentricities, the result of an almost insane vanity.

LORD BYRON.

George Gordon, Lord Byron, born in London, January 22nd, 1788, the chief of the English poets of his day—endowed with rank, fortune, brilliant intellect, fed full of literary fame, an object of intense interest to the mass of enlightened society,—what more seemed necessary to make an enviable fate? and yet, as we all know, no man seemed in his time more unhappy —perhaps really was so. An explanation of all this is only to be found in some elements of his own nature. He was, we must remember, the son of a man of almost insane profligacy, by a woman whose violent temper often appeared to approach frenzy. The genius of Byron was as much distemper as ability.

He was unlucky in a congenital malformation of the limbs, which he could only conceal by careful padding; it was such a defect as a man of well-balanced mind would have been little affected by. With him, we may fear, it was a source of misanthropical bitterness, poisoning all the springs of happiness. Early extravagances led him into a marriage, which proved another source of misery, not from any demerit in his partner, for she was in reality an excellent woman, but from the want of congeniality between the pair. Twelve months after the union, one only after the birth of a daughter, Lady Byron formed the resolution of separating from him, his conduct being such that only on the supposition of his insanity (which her lawyers negatived), could she have excused it. Byron then, in the very zenith of literary fame, and only six-and-twenty, became an exile from his native country.

He spent the remainder of his life at Venice, at Ravenna, at Pisa, finally at Genoa, never ceasing to write actively, till passing to Greece, for the purpose of throwing himself into the service of its patriots, he was struck down by fever at Missolonghi, and died when little over six-and-thirty.

The freakish, mysterious life of Byron, his egotistical misanthropical poetry, so expressive of an unsatisfied and unhappy mind, latterly his giving himself to the composition of works trenching on the indecent and immoral, caused him to be the subject of intense curiosity and infinite discussion in his own day and for some years after. The melancholy tone of his poetry infected all young persons of a susceptible nature, and more particularly those who attempted verse. He set a fashion of feeling, which only died out with its generation. We can now estimate his productions more coolly, and assign them their true place, as not poetry of the highest order; and we can now better judge of the faults of the man. If Lady Byron's lawyers had been more enlightened in psychology, they would have saved their client from throwing off her unfortunate husband. A lawyer only inquires if there appear in the general actions a knowledge of right and wrong; he knows nothing of the infinite shades of unsoundness which often mingle with the strains of a character able to pass muster in this respect. In Byron there was an eccentricity of feeling which can only be interpreted as a result of unhealthiness of brain, obviously derived from his parents. The common sense of the multitude understands these matters in a rough sort of way, and is never at a loss to judge of those who, apparently fit to conduct their own affairs, have yet an undeclared *queerness*, which is apt to shew itself in certain circumstances.

There is something extremely touching in the references which Byron made in certain of his poems to the infant daughter whom he never saw after she was a month old. The third book of *Childe Harold*, written in 1816, begins with a kind of dedication to Ada:

' Is thy face like thy mother's, my fair child?
Ada! sole daughter of my house and heart!
When last I saw thy young blue eyes they smiled,
And then we parted, not as now we part,
But with a hope.'

And with Ada it ends:

' My daughter! with thy name this song began—
My daughter! with thy name thus much shall end—
I see thee not,—I hear thee not,—but none
Can be so wrapt in thee; thou art the friend
To whom the shadows of far years extend;
Albeit my brow thou never shouldst behold,
My voice shall with thy future visions blend,
And reach into thy heart, when mine is cold,—
A token and a tone, even from thy father's mould.

' To aid thy mind's development,—to watch
Thy dawn of little joys,—to sit and see
Almost thy very growth,—to view thee catch
Knowledge of objects,—wonders yet to thee!

528

To hold thee lightly on a gentle knee,
And print on thy soft cheek a parent's kiss,—
This, it would seem, was not reserved for me;
Yet this was in thy nature:—as it is,
I know not what is there, yet something like to this.'

She was but eight years old at the time of her father's lamented and premature death. At the age of nineteen, in 1835, she was married to Lord King, who subsequently became Earl of Lovelace, and to whom she bore three children. It is said that she did not resemble her father in features—still less did she in the tendencies of her mind, which were wholly to scientific and mathematical studies. She had a presentiment that she would die at the same age as her father, and it was fulfilled, her decease taking place in November 1852, when she was several months less than thirty-seven.

APRIL 20.

St Serf or Servanus, of Scotland, 5th century. St Agnes of Monte Pulciano, 1317. St James of Sclavonia, 1485.

Died.—Eliza Barton, 'the Maid of Kent,' executed, 1534, *Tyburn;* Prince Eugène of Savoy, military commander, 1736, *Vienna;* John Lewis Petit, 'in his time the most renowned surgeon in Europe,' 1760, *Paris;* Robert Mudie, miscellaneous writer, 1842, *London.*

CROMWELL'S DISSOLUTION OF THE RUMP PARLIAMENT.

The 20th of April 1653, is the date of this memorable event. The Parliament by which Charles I. had been met and overcome, was dwindled down by various purgations to about fifty-three members, who aimed at becoming a sort of mild oligarchy for the administration of the affairs of the commonwealth. They were deliberating on a bill for the future representation, in which they should have a permanent place, when Cromwell resolved to make an end of them. It was the last incident in the natural series of a revolution, placing military power above all other.

Cromwell, having ordered a company of musketeers to follow him, entered the House ' in plain black clothes and grey worsted stockings,' and, sitting down, listened for a while to their proceedings. Hearing at length the question put, that the bill do pass, he rose, put off his hat, and began to speak. In the course of his address, he told them of their self-seeking and delays of justice, till at length Sir Peter Wentworth interrupted him with a remonstrance against such language. Then blazing up, he said, ' We have had enough of this—I will put an end to your prating.' Stepping into the floor of the House, and clapping on his hat, he commenced a violent harangue, which he occasionally emphasized by stamping with his feet, and which came mainly to this, ' It is not fit you should sit here any longer—you have sat too long for any good you have been doing lately. You shall now give place to better men.' ' Call them in!' he exclaimed; and his officer Harrison and a file of soldiers entered the House. Then proceeding,

'You are no parliament! Some of you are drunkards'—bending a stern eye upon Mr Chaloner; 'some of you are ——,' a word expressive of a worse immorality, and he looked here at Henry Marten and Sir Peter Wentworth—'living in open contempt of God's commandments. Some of you are corrupt, unjust persons—how can you be a parliament for God's people? Depart, I say, and let us have done with you. Go!'

He litted the mace from the table, and gave it to a musketeer to be taken away. He caused Harrison to give his hand to Speaker Lenthal, and lead him down from the chair. The members, cowed by his violence, and the sight of the armed men, moved gloomily out of the House. 'It is the Lord that hath caused me to do this,' he said. 'I have sought that He would rather slay me than put me upon doing this work.' Sir Harry Vane venturing a remonstrance, 'Oh, Sir Harry Vane!' exclaimed the Lord-General; 'the Lord deliver me from Sir Harry Vane!' When all had gone out, he came out too, and locked the door. From that time he was master of the three kingdoms for about five and a half years.

JAMES WOOD, BANKER, GLOUCESTER.

This wealthy and most extraordinary individual died on the 20th of April 1836, having attained the age of eighty years. 'Jemmy Wood' —for by such name he was usually recognised— was the sole proprietor of the old Gloucester Bank, which had been established by his grandfather in the year 1716, being one of those primitive banking concerns which took their rise in

JEMMY WOOD'S HOUSE, GLOUCESTER.

a shop business, and of which, perhaps, hardly one example now survives. Wood's bank was conducted to the last by the proprietor and two or three clerks, at the end of a common chandlery shop, which they also attended to. Wood was latterly considered as the richest commoner in the kingdom. His habits were those of a thrifty old bachelor. In the bank or shop his whole time was passed: he went to no one's house, and never invited any person to his. It was his habit on Sundays to go to church regularly, eat his dinner on his return, and then take a short walk into the country. He left several wills of a conflicting character, and, as a matter of course, these documents caused litigation, and gave employment to lawyers and attorneys for years.

Many anecdotes illustrating his penuriousness are told; amongst others the following: One Sunday before leaving his house to proceed to church, he gave to a little boy, who acted as his servant, a chicken, which he intended to be roasted for dinner. The cooking process commenced; and as the bird was turned and basted, the savoury steam which it gave forth sharpened the boy's appetite, and he ventured to rub his finger on the breast, which was being gradually browned, and apply his finger to his mouth. The taste was delicious! He became bolder, and picked away a morsel of the breast of the bird; then another; other bits followed, until none of the breast remained. Hunger was gnawing at the boy's heart, and he could not resist temptation; so the whole chicken speedily disappeared. His hunger now appeased, he saw his fault, and, trembling at the prospect of meeting his thrifty master, like most little boys after doing wrong, he thought of hiding. On entering a closet adjoining the room, his eye fell on a small bottle, having on it a label with the awful word 'poison' in legible characters. He feared death much, but his master still more, and in a minute he resolved to end his days; accordingly, he drained the bottle, and was, as he thought, safe from his master's rage. In a short time, the old banker appeared on the scene, resolved to enjoy his chicken and glass of brandy-and-water. Great was his astonishment to see the spit empty, and find the boy away. On making a search he found the latter lying on the pantry floor with the empty bottle, which quickly brought before his mind a solution of the mystery. The boy was drunk, for the bottle contained old Wood's brandy, which was marked 'poison,' to guard it from the possibility of being touched by the servants. What the old gentleman did with the lad is not recorded.

The Cuckoo.

The 20th of April is the fair-day of Tenbury, in Worcestershire, and there is a belief in that county that you never hear the cuckoo till Tenbury fair-day, or after Pershore fair-day, which is the 26th of June.*

The following is a very common rhyme in England, regarding the period of the cuckoo:—

In April
The cuckoo shows his bill;
In May
He is singing all day;
In June
He changes his tune;

* Notes and Queries, 2nd ser. i. 429.

In July
He prepares to fly;
In August
Fly he must.

It is a popular belief in Norfolk that whatever you are doing the first time you hear the cuckoo, that you will do most frequently all the year. Another is that an unmarried person will remain single as many years as the cuckoo, when first heard, utters its call.*

Mr Marryat found a curious legend among the Danes regarding the cuckoo. 'When in early spring-time the voice of the cuckoo is first heard in the woods, every village girl kisses her hand, and asks the most question, "Cuckoo! cuckoo! when shall I be married?" and the old folks, borne down with age and rheumatism, inquire, "Cuckoo! cuckoo! when shall I be released from this world's cares?" The bird, in answer, continues singing "Cuckoo!" as many times as years will elapse before the object of their desires will come to pass. But as some old people live to an advanced age, and many girls die old maids, the poor bird has so much to do in answering the questions put to her, that the building season goes by; she has no time to make her nest, but lays her eggs in that of the hedge-sparrow.'

Several of our English birds were objects of superstition in the Middle Ages, and none more so than the cuckoo. Our forefathers looked upon it as the harbinger of spring, and as the merriest songster of summer, and it is the subject of the oldest of English popular songs now remaining. This song, which is preserved in MSS. Harl. No. 978, must be of the earlier half of the thirteenth century, and is remarkable for being accompanied with musical notes, and as being the oldest sample of English secular music. The words are as follows:

'Sumer is icumen in,
  Lhude sing Cuccu;
Groweth sed, and bloweth med,
  And springth the wde nu.
    Sing Cuccu.
Awe bleteth after lomb,
  Lhouth after calve cu;
Bulluc sterteth, bucke verteth;
  Murie sing Cuccu,
    Cuccu, Cuccu.
Wel singes thu, Cuccu;
Ne swik thu naver nu.'

Which may be thus interpreted in modern English:

'Summer is come in,
  Loud sing Cuckoo;
Grows the seed, and blooms the mead,
  And sprouts the wood now.
    Sing Cuckoo.
The ewe bleats after the lamb,
  The cow lows after the calf,
The bullock leaps, the buck verts (goes to
    the fern);
  Merrily sing Cuckoo,
    Cuckoo, Cuckoo.
Well singest thou, Cuckoo;
Cease thou never to sing, Cuckoo.'

The reader will remember the somewhat similar song of spring in Shakspeare's Love's Labour's Lost, where spring is 'maintained by the cuckoo.'

* Notes and Queries, 2nd ser. i. 523.

It was the spring, indeed, and not the summer, that the cuckoo was considered to represent in the Middle Ages. There is an early Latin poem on the cuckoo in connexion with spring, which is ascribed, no doubt incorrectly, to Bede, in which the cuckoo is called upon to awake, because the spring had arrived:

'Tempus adest veris, cuculus, modo rumpe soporem.'

It is the popular belief in some parts of the country that the cuckoo always makes its first appearance on the 21st of April.

The cuckoo was often celebrated in the mediæval poetry of all ages and all languages, and was looked upon as possessing some share of supernatural knowledge. In some parts it seems to have been an article of belief that it was one of the gods who took the form of the bird, and it was considered a crime to kill it. Its most singular quality, in this superstitious lore, was the power of telling how long people would live, the faith in which is still preserved among the peasantry of many parts of Germany and the north of Europe. It was believed that if, when you first heard a cuckoo in the morning, you put the question in a respectful manner, it would immediately repeat its note just as many times as you had years to live. This superstition is the foundation of many stories in the mediæval Latin writers, of which the following, told by Cæsarius of Heisterbach, belongs to the year 1221. A 'converse' in a certain monastery—that is, a layman who had become a monk—was walking out one day, when, hearing a cuckoo and counting the number of times its note was repeated, he found it to be twenty-two. 'Ah!' said he, 'if I am yet to live twenty-two years more, why should I mortify myself all this long time in a monastery? I will return to the world, and give myself up to the enjoyment of its pleasures for twenty years, and then I shall have two years to repent in.' So he returned to the world, and lived joyously two years, and then died, losing twenty out of his reckoning.

In another given in Wright's Selection of Latin Stories, a woman is described as lying on her death-bed, when her daughter urged her to send for a priest, that she might confess her sins. To whom her mother replied, 'Why? if I am ill to-day, to-morrow or next day I shall be well.' But the daughter, seeing she became worse, brought in several of her neighbours, who urged the same thing. To whom she said, 'What do you talk about? or, what do you fear? I shall not die these twelve years; I have heard the cuckoo, who told me so.' At length she became speechless, and was at the point of death. Then her daughter sent for the priest, who came, bringing what was necessary [to perform the last duties], and approaching her he asked if she had anything to confess. All she said was 'kuckuc' [cuckoo]. Again the priest offered her the sacrament, and asked her if she believed the Lord was her Saviour, and she replied 'kuckuc,' so the priest went away, and shortly afterwards she died.

In one of the branches of the celebrated romance of Renart (Reynard the Fox), written in French verse in the thirteenth century, and published by Meon (vol. iv., p. 9), Renart and his wife, dame Ermengart, are introduced reposing together in the early morning, and discoursing of ambitious prospects, when Renart suddenly hears the note of the cuckoo:

> ' A cest mot Renart le cucu
> Entent, si jeta un faus ris ;
> "Jou te conjur," fait il, "de cris,
> Cucus, que me dise le voir,
> Quans ans j'ai à vivre ; savoir
> Le veil, cucu."'

> ' At this word Renart the cuckoo
> Hears, and broke into a false laugh ;
> "I conjure you," said he, "earnestly,
> Cuckoo, that you tell me the truth,
> How many years I have to live ; to know
> It I wish, Cuckoo."'

The cuckoo responded at once, and repeated his note thirteen times,—

> ' Atant se taist, que plus ne fu
> Li oisiaus illuec, ains s'envolle.
> Et Renars maintenant acole
> Dame Ermengart ; "Avés oi ?"
> "Sire," dist-ell, "des cuer joi ;
> Vos semons que me baisies."
> "Dame," dist-il, "j'en suis tos lies.
> *   *   *   *   *   *   *
> M'a li cucus treize ans d'aé
> A vivre encore ci après."'

> Then he ceased, for no longer was
> The bird there, but flew away.
> And Renart now embraced
> Dame Ermengart ; "Have you heard ?"
> "Sir," said she, "I have heard it gladly ;
> I demand that you kiss me."
> "Dame," said he, "I am quite rejoiced.
> *   *   *   *   *   *   *
> To me has the cuckoo thirteen years of life
> To live yet here taught."'

The notion which couples the name of the cuckoo with the character of the man whose wife is unfaithful to him, appears to have been derived from the Romans, and is first found in the Middle Ages in France, and in the countries of which the modern language is derived from the Latin. We are not aware that it existed originally among the Teutonic race, and we have doubtless received it through the Normans. The opinion that the cuckoo made no nest of its own, but laid its eggs in that of another bird which brought up the young cuckoo to the detriment of its own offspring, was well known to the ancients, and is mentioned by Aristotle and Pliny. But they more correctly gave the name of the bird not to the husband of the faithless wife, but to her paramour, who might justly be supposed to be acting the part of the cuckoo. They gave the name of the bird in whose nest the cuckoo's eggs were usually deposited, *curruca*, to the husband. It is not quite clear how, in the passage from classic to mediæval, the application of the term was transferred to the husband.

There are, or have been not long ago, in different parts of England, remnants of other old customs, marking the position which the cuckoo held in the superstitions of the Middle Ages. In Shropshire, till very recently, when the first cuckoo was heard, the labourers were in the habit of leaving their work, making

holiday of the rest of the day, and carousing in what they called the cuckoo ale. Among the peasantry in some parts of the kingdom, it is considered to be very unlucky to have no money in your pocket when you hear the cuckoo's note for the first time in the season. It was also a common article of belief, that if a maiden ran into the fields early in the morning, to hear the first note of the cuckoo, and when she heard it took off her left shoe and looked into it, she would there find a man's hair of the same colour as that of her future husband.

APRIL 21.

St Eingan, or Enean, King of Scots, about 590. St Anastasius, surnamed the Younger, patriarch of Antioch, 610. St Anastasius, the Sinaite, anchoret, after 678. St Beuno, abbot of Clynnog, in Carnarvonshire, 7th century. St Malrubius, martyr, of Ireland, 721. St Anselm, Archbishop of Canterbury, 1109.

Born.—Prince George of Denmark, consort of Anne, Queen of England, 1653 ; James Harris, Earl of Malmesbury, statesman, 1746, *Salisbury ;* Samuel Hibbert Ware, M.D., scientific writer, 1782, *Manchester ;* Reginald Heber, poet, Bishop of Calcutta, 1783, *Malpas, Cheshire ;* Thomas Wright, historical and antiquarian writer, 1810.

Died.—Alexander the Great, B.C. 323, *bur. Alexandria ;* Diogenes the cynic, B.C. 323, *Corinth ;* Anselm, Archbishop of Canterbury, 1109, *Canterbury ;* Peter Abelard, eminent French scholar, 1142 ; Jean Racine. French dramatic poet, 1699 ; David Mallet, poet, 1765, *Drury Lane, London.*

ARCHBISHOP ANSELM.

Few English prelates have exercised so great an influence on the politics and on the literature and learning of their age, as Anselm, Archbishop of Canterbury. He was born at Aosta, in Piedmont, about the year 1033, and exhibited from a very early age a strongly marked love for learning and a monastic life. As these tastes were sternly opposed by his father, young Anselm secretly left his home, and after wandering in Burgundy and France full three years, he at length reached Bec, in Normandy, and entered himself in the school which had just then been rendered famous by the teaching of Lanfranc. Here he soon distinguished himself by the rapidity with which he acquired learning, but, when pressed to become a teacher himself, he preferred the monastic state, and became a monk in the abbey of Bec in the year 1060 ; six years afterwards he was chosen prior of that abbey, and in 1078 he was still further advanced to the high office of abbot. During this period he wrote most of his important works, nearly all of a theological character, which soon spread his fame through Western Europe. His piety and numerous virtues were at the same time so remarkable, that his brethren in the abbey of Bec believed him to be capable of working miracles. His friend Lanfranc had been made Archbishop of Canterbury, and soon after Anselm became abbot of Bec he paid a visit to England, and passed some time at Canterbury. He again visited England in 1092, at the invitation of Hugh, Earl of Chester, who chose to establish monks from Bec in his newly-founded monastery at Chester.

At this time the see of Canterbury had been vacant about four years, King William Rufus having refused to fill it up, in order that he might retain the revenues in his own hands, and it appears that the English clergy had been already looking to Anselm as a suitable successor to Lanfranc. It is probable that he had already become known as a staunch champion of the temporal power of the Church. During Anselm's second visit to England, the urgent expostulations of the prelates had overcome William's selfishness; and early in 1093, while Anselm was still in England, the King announced his election to the archbishopric of Canterbury. Anselm at first refused the proffered honour, but his reluctance was overcome by the persuasions of his clerical brethren, and he was finally consecrated on the 4th of December. The archbishop and the king quarrelled at Christmas, not much more than a fortnight after his consecration. The subject of dispute was the heriot then usually paid to the king on the decease of the archbishop, Anselm refusing to give so large a sum as the king demanded. A second quarrel soon followed, occasioned by Anselm's attempt to restrain the king from trespassing on the rights of the Church. On the return of the king from Normandy, in November 1094, a third dispute arose, on a subject of still greater moment in regard to the papal supremacy in England. Urban II. had been elected Pope on the 12th of March 1088, but he had not yet been officially acknowledged by the English monarch, for the papal election had been disputed. Anselm had recently written a learned book, his treatise *De Incarnatione Verbi*, which he had dedicated to Pope Urban, and he now demanded the king's permission to go to Rome to receive the pallium from the pope's hands. The king not only refused, but burst into a violent passion, declaring that no one was acknowledged pope in England without the king's consent. Anselm refused to yield this point, and a grand council of prelates and nobles was held, in which nearly all the English prelates took part on this question with the king against the Archbishop of Canterbury. Soon afterwards the king acknowledged Pope Urban, and Anselm received the pallium, and was outwardly reconciled with the king; but other quarrels soon occurred, and in 1097 Anselm obtained with difficulty the king's permission to proceed to Rome. He remained in Italy some time, and in the spring of 1099 he went to Lyons to wait there the effect of the pope's expostulations with William Rufus, but Urban died (July 1099) before this could be known, and the king himself was killed in August 1100, while Anselm was still at Lyons. Anselm was recalled by Henry I., and taken into favour, but he had now become the unflinching champion of the temporal power of the Church of Rome, and we can hardly excuse him for being himself the cause of many of his quarrels with the crown, since, in spite of all that King Henry was willing to do to conciliate the Church, Anselm remained on no better terms with him than with his predecessor. On Anselm's return to England began the great dispute on

532

the question of the investiture. The prelates of the Church had been accustomed to receive from the hands of the sovereign the investiture of the ring and crozier, by which the temporalities of the see were understood to be conveyed. The pope had been long seeking to deprive the king of this right, the question it involved being simply whether the clergy in England should hold their estates, and be the subjects of the king or the pope. The council of Rome in 1099, at which Anselm was present, declared against the secular power, and decided that any layman presuming to grant such investiture, or any priest accepting it, should thereby incur sentence of excommunication. On Anselm's return to England, it would have been his duty to receive the investiture from the new monarch, but, when required to do so, he absolutely refused, referring the king to the acts of the council. Henry was equally firm in withstanding this new encroachment of the court of Rome, and the question was finally referred to the new pope, and Anselm again repaired to Rome, where he had been preceded by an envoy from the king. Pascacius II. decided against the king, but Anselm, on his way back, was met by a message from King Henry intimating that he would not be allowed to enter England, and he again sought an asylum at Lyons. The dispute between the king and the pope was at last settled by mutual concession, the secular sovereign being allowed the right of exacting homage, but not of investing, and Anselm returned to England in the autumn of 1106. He spent the remainder of his days in reforming abuses in the Church and in writing books, and died, 'laid in sackcloth and ashes,' on the 21st of April 1109, in the seventy-sixth year of his age. With the exception of his violent and unyielding advocacy of the temporal power of the Church, Anselm's character was no less exemplary as a prelate than as a man. He was a person of great intellectual powers, and it is to him really that we owe the introduction of metaphysical reasoning into theology, and therefore a new school for the latter science. His works have always held a very high rank in the Catholic church.

PAPER-MARKS.

The water-marks adopted by the old papermakers to distinguish their own manufactures, have engaged the attention of antiquaries, particularly bibliographers; as by their aid a proximate date to books or documents may be obtained. In courts of law such evidence has been of use, and especially so when brought to bear on cases of forgery, where the paper could be proved of a much more modern date than the document purported to be.

One of the earliest papermarks consists of a circle surmounted by a cross, resembling those borne in the hands of sovereign princes on coronations or state occasions, and typical of the Christian faith — the cross planted on earth. This very interesting mark is met on documents as early as 1301.

The papers manufactured in the Low Countries, for the use of the first printers, have a great variety of marks, and shew that the new art soon gave impetus to the trade of the paper-makers. Many of them were the marks or badges of noble families, whose tenants fabricated the paper. Thus the letter P and the letter Y, sometimes separate and sometimes conjoined, are the initials of Philip the Good, Duke of Burgundy (who reigned from 1419 to 1467), and his wife Isabella, daughter of John, King of Portugal (married 1429), and whose name was, in accordance with the custom of the age, spelt Ysabella. The letter P had been used alone as a paper-mark from the time of the Duke Philip de Rouvere (1349), so that for 116 years it had been a national water-mark. Other symbols of the house of Burgundy also appear; particularly the single fleur-de-lys, which was the peculiar cognizance of this important family, and is borne on the shield of arms of the famous Jean-sans-peur. The Unicorn, the Anchor, and the Bull's head, were also badges of the family. The

Unicorn was the supporter of the armorial bearings of the Dukes; it was typical of power and purity, and Monstrelet relates the fondness of Duke Philip for displaying it on all occasions.

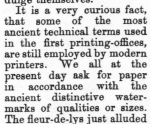

The Bull as typical of power, and the Anchor of stability and hope, were part of the fanciful imaginings with which the great of the Middle Ages delighted to indulge themselves.

It is a very curious fact, that some of the most ancient technical terms used in the first printing-offices, are still employed by modern printers. We all at the present day ask for paper in accordance with the ancient distinctive water-marks of qualities or sizes. The fleur-de-lys just alluded to has long been the distinctive mark of *demy* paper; but a still more curious instance occurs in the *foolscap* paper, originally marked with a fool's head, wearing the cap and bells, such as the privileged jesters of the old nobility and gentry appear to have worn, from the thirteenth to the seventeenth century. This curious mark distinguished the paper until the middle of the seventeenth century, when the English paper-makers adopted the figure of Britannia, and the continental makers other devices.

Equal in general interest is the post-horn; from which *post* paper takes its name. This mark was in use as early as 1370. It sometimes

appears on a shield, and in the seventeenth century is surmounted by a ducal coronet, in which form it still appears on our ordinary writing paper.

An open hand sometimes surmounted by a star or cross; with the fingers occasionally disposed as if in the act of giving the pastoral benediction of a Churchman, is one of the oldest paper-marks. It was in use at the commencement of the fifteenth century and probably earlier. It occurs on letters preserved in the Record Office of that early date, and constantly appears on books which issued from the presses of Germany and the Netherlands, in the very infancy of the art of printing; continuing to a comparatively recent date, and giving the name to what is still called *hand* paper.

Most of our readers will no doubt be familiar with the small square quartoes, known as pot-quartoes which were extremely popular in the sixteenth and seventeenth centuries, for printing editions of plays and pamphlets; and which will be more familiar to modern readers as the size chosen for the publications of the Camden Society. This paper takes its name from the pot or tankard in common use at the time of its original manufacture. It was particularly characteristic of Dutch paper, and is found in the account books of Matilda, Duchess of Holland, still preserved at the Hague. It continued to be used on paper of different forms and sizes, made in the Low Countries, and is found on the paper of books printed at Gouda, Louvain, Delft, and other places in the Netherlands, during the fifteenth century.

The excellence of Dutch paper, its purity and durability, have never been excelled. Dr Dibdin, that genuine bibliomaniac, speaks of the music of the rustle of leaves when turned over in a good old book. The modern papers, though whiter and more beautiful to the eye, obtain their qualities by chemical agencies that carry the elements of decay in them; and equal in name only the coarser looking but stronger papers of a past era.

THUNDER AND THE DAYS OF THE WEEK.

'Some write (their ground I see not) that Sunday's thunder should bring the death of learned men, judges, and others; Monday's thunder the death of women; Tuesday's thunder plenty of grain; Wednesday's thunder the death of harlots; Thursday's thunder plenty of sheep and corn; Friday's thunder, the slaughter of a great man, and other horrible murders; Saturday's thunder a general plague and great dearth.' —LEONARD DIGGES's *Prognostication Everlasting of right good Effect*, Lond. 1556.

APRIL 22.

Saints Epipodius and Alexander, martyrs at Lyons, 2nd century. Saints Soter and Caius, Popes, martyrs, 2nd and 3rd centuries. St Leonides, father of Origen, 202. Saints Azades, Tharba, and others, martyrs in Persia, 341. St Rufus, or Rufin, anchoret at Glendalough, near Dublin. St Theodorus of Siceon, Bishop and Confessor, 613. St Opportuna, Abbess of Montreuil, 770.

Born.—Henry Fielding, dramatist and novelist, 1707; Immanuel Kant, German philosopher, 1724, *Königsberg ;* James Grahame, poet, 1765, *Glasgow.*

Died.—King Henry VII. of England, 1509, *Richmond ;* Antoine de Jussieu, eminent French botanist, 1758; Chrétien Gillaume de Malsherbes, advocate, beheaded, 1794, *Paris ;* Thomas Haynes Bailey, lyrical poet, 1839, *Cheltenham.*

THE WANDERING JEW.

The story of the Jew who had witnessed the Crucifixion, and had been condemned to live and wander over the earth until the time of Christ's second coming, while it is one of the most curious of the mediæval legends, has a peculiar interest for us, because, so far as we can distinctly trace its history, it is first heard of with any circumstantial details in our island. The chronicler of the abbey of St Albans, whose book was copied and continued by Matthew Paris, has recorded how, in the year 1228, 'a certain archbishop of Armenia Major came on a pilgrimage to England to see the relics of the saints, and visit the sacred places in this kingdom, as he had done in others ; he also produced letters of recommendation from his Holiness the Pope to the religious men and prelates of the churches, in which they were enjoined to receive and entertain him with due reverence and honour. On his arrival, he came to St Albans, where he was received with all respect by the abbot and monks ; and at this place, being fatigued with his journey, he remained some days to rest himself and his followers, and a conversation took place between him and the inhabitants of the convent, by means of their interpreters, during which he made many inquiries relating to the religion and religious observances of this country, and told many strange things concerning the countries of the East. In the course of conversation he was asked whether he had ever seen or heard anything of Joseph, a man of whom there was much talk in the world, who, when our Lord suffered, was present and spoke to him, and who is still alive, in evidence of the Christian faith ; in reply to which a knight in his retinue, who was his interpreter, replied, speaking in French, " My Lord well knows that man, and a little before he took his way to the western countries, the said Joseph ate at the table of my lord the archbishop in Armenia, and he has often seen and held converse with him." He was then asked about what had passed between Christ and the said Joseph, to which he replied, " At the time of the suffering of Jesus Christ, he was seized by the Jews and led into the hall of judgment before Pilate, the governor, that he might be judged by him on the accusation of the Jews ; and Pilate finding no cause for adjudging him to death, said to them, ' Take him and judge

him according to your law ;' the shouts of the Jews, however, increasing, he, at their request, released unto them Barabbas, and delivered Jesus to them to be crucified. When therefore the Jews were dragging Jesus forth, and had reached the door, Cartaphilus, a porter of the hall, in Pilate's service, as Jesus was going out of the door, impiously struck him on the back with his hand, and said in mockery, ' Go quicker, Jesus, go quicker ; why do you loiter ?' and Jesus, looking back on him with a severe countenance, said to him, ' I am going, and you will wait till I return.' And, according as our Lord said, this Cartaphilus is still awaiting his return. At the time of our Lord's suffering he was thirty years old, and, when he attains the age of a hundred years, he always returns to the same age as he was when our Lord suffered. After Christ's death, when the Catholic faith gained ground, this Cartaphilus was baptized by Ananias (who also baptized the apostle Paul), and was called Joseph. He dwells in one or other division of Armenia, and in divers Eastern countries, passing his time amongst the bishops and other prelates of the church ; he is a man of holy conversation, and religious ; a man of few words, and circumspect in his behaviour, for he does not speak at all unless when questioned by the bishops and religious men, and then he tells of the events of old times, and of those which occurred at the suffering and resurrection of our Lord, and of the witnesses of the resurrection, namely, those who rose with Christ, and went into the holy city, and appeared unto men. He also tells of the creed of the apostles, and of their separation and preaching. And all this he relates without smiling or levity of conversation, as one who is well practised in sorrow and the fear of God, always looking forward with fear to the coming of Jesus Christ, lest at the last judgment he should find him in anger, whom, when on his way to death, he had provoked to just vengeance. Numbers come to him from different parts of the world, enjoying his society and conversation ; and to them, if they are men of authority, he explains all doubts on the matters on which he is questioned. He refuses all gifts that are offered to him, being content with slight food and clothing.'''

Such is the account of the Wandering Jew left us by a chronicler who was contemporary with what he relates, and we cannot doubt that there was such a person as the Armenian in question, and that some impostor had assumed the character of the Jew who was supposed to be still wandering about the world, until in the middle of the sixteenth century he made his appearance in Germany. He had now changed his name to Ahasuerus, and somewhat modified his story. It was again a bishop who had seen him, when he attended a sermon at Hamburg, where a stranger appeared in the winter of 1542, who made himself remarkable by the great devotion with which he listened. When questioned, he said that he was by nation a Jew, that his original occupation had been that of a shoemaker, that he had been present at the passion of Jesus Christ, and that since that time he had wandered through many countries. He said that he was one of the Jews who dragged Christ before Pilate and were clamorous for his death, and on the way to the place of crucifixion, when Jesus stopped to rest, he pushed him forward, and told him rudely to go on. The Saviour looked at him, and said, 'I shall stop and repose, but thou shalt go on ;' upon which the Jew was seized with an irresistible desire to wander, and had left his wife and children, whom he had never seen since, and had continued to travel from one country to another, until he now came to Germany. The bishop described him as a tall man, apparently of about fifty years of age, with long hair, which hung down to his shoulders, who went barefooted, and wore a strange costume, consisting of sailor's trousers which reached to the feet, a petticoat which descended to the knees, and a mantle which also reached to the feet. He was always taciturn, was never seen to laugh, ate and drank little, and, if anybody offered him money, he never took more than two or three pence, which he afterwards gave away in charity, declaring that God contributed to all his wants. He related various events which he had seen in different countries and at different times, to people's great astonishment. All these details, and many more, are told in a letter, dated the 29th of June 1564, which was printed in German and in French. On this occasion the Jew spoke good German, in the dialect of Saxony ; but when he, or another person under the same character, appeared in the Netherlands in 1575, he spoke Spanish. A few years later the Wandering Jew arrived in Strasburg, and, presenting himself before the magistrates, informed them that he had visited their city just two hundred years before, 'which was proved to be true by a reference to the registers of the town.'

The Wandering Jew proceeded next to the West Indies, and returned thence to France, where he made his appearance in 1604, and appears to have caused a very considerable sensation. As during the time he was there the country was visited by destructive hurricanes, it was believed that these visitations accompanied the Jew in his wanderings, and this belief became so general that at the present day, in Brittany and Picardy, when a violent hurricane comes on, the peasantry are in the habit of making the sign of the cross, and exclaiming, 'C'est le Juif-errant qui passe !' Various accounts of the appearance of the Wandering Jew in differents parts of France at this time were printed, and he became the subject of more than one popular ballad, one of which is well known as still popular in France, and is sold commonly by the hawkers of books, the first lines of which are,—

> 'Est-il rien sur la terre
> 　　Qui soit plus surprenant
> Que la grande misère
> 　　Du pauvre Juif-errant ?
> Que son sort malheureux
> 　　Paraît triste et fâcheux !'

There is a well-known English ballad on the Wandering Jew, which is perhaps as old as the time of Elizabeth, and has been reprinted in *Percy's Reliques*, and in most English collections of old ballads. It relates to the Jew's appearance in Germany and Flanders in the sixteenth

century. The first stanza of the English ballad is,—

> 'When as in fair Jerusalem
> 　　Our Saviour Christ did live,
> And for the sins of all the world
> 　　His own dear life did give ;
> The wicked Jews with scoffs and scorn
> 　　Did dailye him molest,
> That never till he left his life
> 　　Our Saviour could not rest.'

On the 22nd of April 1774, the Wandering Jew, or some individual who had personated him, appeared in Brussels, where he told his story to the *bourgeois*, but he had changed his name, and now called himself Isaac Laquedem. The wanderer has not since been heard of, but is supposed to be travelling in some of the unknown parts of the globe. The *Histoire admirable du Juif-errant*, still printed and circulated in France, forms one of the class of books which our antiquaries call chap-books, and is full of fabulous stories which the Jew is made to tell with his own mouth.

THE TRIUMPH TAVERN.—LONDON INNS,
THEIR SIGNS AND TOKENS.

April 22, 1661, Charles II. made a formal procession from the Tower to Westminster, as a preliminary to his coronation, which was effected next day. The arches raised on this occasion were allowed to remain for a year, and the whole affair was commemorated by a new tavern at Charing-cross, taking to itself the name of the Pageant Tavern—alternately the Triumph Tavern—and on whose token money a specimen of the arches was given, as appears from the accompanying representation of one of the pieces. Pepys

notes a visit he made to the Triumph Tavern in May 1662, in company with Captain Ferrars, to have a sly peep at the Portuguese maids of honour who had accompanied the queen, Catherine of Braganza, to England, and who do not seem to have pleased the worthy diarist, as he styles them 'sufficiently unagreeable.'

These trivial particulars may serve as a fit starting-point for a few notes regarding London taverns and hostelries of past ages, and the token money which they issued. The tavern life of old London opens a large field for the study of national manners, for they were not only places of convenient sojourn, or pleasant sociality, but the rendezvous of politicians and traders. In days when newspapers were scarce, and business was conducted more privately than at present, the nearest tavern took the place with the ordinary shopkeeper that the Royal Exchange occupied with the merchant. They lined the main thoroughfares of London, particularly the great leading one from High-street, Southwark, to the northern extremity of Bishopsgate; and that still more important 'main artery' which followed the course of the river from London-bridge by way of Cheapside, Fleet-street, and the Strand, to Westminster.

We will follow this latter roadway, noting the chief hostelries on our way, as they are among the most celebrated which London possessed, and are enough to indicate the associations of the whole class.

On the Southwark side of London-bridge stood a tavern known as 'The Bear at the Bridge-foot,' which retained a celebrity for some centuries. It was the house to which travellers resorted who wished to pass by water to Gravesend in the 'tilt-boats' which, in about two days, conveyed them to that—then—far-off locality. Of such convenience was this house to voyagers, that in 1633, when others were closed, this was exempted, 'for the convenience of passengers to Greenwich.' Pepys in his *Diary* more than once mentions this tavern; and, among other things, notes that the Duke of Richmond arranged that the king's cousin, the fair Frances Stewart, should leave the court privily, and join him 'at The Beare at the Bridge-foot,' where a coach was ready, and they are stole away into Kent, without the king's leave.' The antiquity of the house is noted in a poem of 1691, entitled 'The Last Search after Claret in Southwark:'

'We came to the Bear, which we soon understood,
 Was the first house in Southwark built after the flood.'

It took its sign, doubtless, from the popular sport of bear-baiting, which was indulged in by the Londoners in the Southwark bear gardens, and the 'token' issued by one of the owners of this hostelry exhibits a chained and muzzled bear, as may be seen in our cut issued from the original in the British Museum. Cornelius Cook,

who issued this coin, was connected with the parish of St Olave's as early as 1630; he was a captain in the civic trainband, and afterwards a colonel in Cromwell's army; but at the Restoration he subsided into private life as mine host of the Bear, and took to the mintage of his own coin, like other innkeepers and traders.

We must now say a few words of this generally usurped privilege of coinage so universal in the middle of the seventeenth century. The want of an authorized money as small change had been felt long, and complained of. Farthings, half-pence, and pence, were all struck by the Government in silver, the farthings necessarily so small and thin as to be losses rather than gain to the trader: hence an authorized currency was established, and larger copper coins, known as 'Abbey-pieces,' and 'Nuremberg counters,' were issued by the great monastic establishments, and

by traders, who exchanged each other's 'tokens,' they being, in fact, small accommodation bills payable at sight. The Abbey-pieces were large, about the size of a florin, and generally had a religious inscription in Latin around them; the 'Nuremberg counters' have sometimes a counting-table on one side and an emblematic device on the other. They originated at Nuremberg, and were imported in large quantities; the name of one maker, 'Hans Krauwinkel,' is of most frequent occurrence.

An attempt was made during the reign of Elizabeth to supersede this *pseudo moneta* by a legitimate copper currency; but her majesty had a magnificent contempt for any other than the precious metal to bear her authorized effigy, and never favoured the scheme. James the First granted a monopoly to Lord Harrington for the exclusive manufacture of copper tokens, but the whole affair was so discreditable to both parties, and dishonourable toward the public, that those issued privately by tradesmen were preferred, and rapidly increased during the reign of Charles I.; and throughout the Commonwealth nearly every innkeeper and tradesman struck his own 'for necessarie chainge,' as they sometimes inscribed upon them. Soon after the Restoration, the Government took the matter into their serious consideration; and in 1665, pattern farthings were struck in copper, having, for the first time, a figure of Britannia on the reverse; but it was not until 1671 that half-pence and farthings were generally issued, and it was not until 1674 that the traders' tokens were effectually prohibited by royal proclamation.

One of the most interesting of the tavern tokens is that issued by the host at the Boar's

Head, in Eastcheap—the house immortalized by Shakspeare as the scene of Falstaff's jollities, and the resort of the bard and his dramatic brethren. It was destroyed in the Fire of London, afterwards rebuilt, and a stone-carved boar's head (as upon the token) placed over the door, with the date 1668 upon it, which 'sign' was removed to the Guildhall Library when the house was demolished to form the approaches to London-bridge.

Arrived at the Poultry (so called, says Stowe, because 'poulterers in the olden time dwelt and sold poultry at their stalls in the High-street'), the Rose Tavern first invites attention, as a house of ancient repute for good wines; here were also the 'Three Cranes,' and 'The Exchange Tavern,' all issuing tokens, the latter with a curious view of the building after which it was named.

Of the Cheapside taverns, the most renowned from its associations was the Mermaid, the resort of Ben Jonson and his literary friends, members of a club established by Sir Walter Raleigh in

1603, and numbering among them Shakspeare.

Beaumont, Fletcher, Donne, Selden, and the noblest names in English authorship. Truly might Beaumont, in his poetical epistle to Jonson, exclaim :

'What things have seen
Done at the Mermaid ; heard words that have been
So nimble, and so full of subtle flame,
As if that every one from whom they came
Had mean'd to put his whole wit in a jest!'

This celebrated tavern stood behind the houses between Bread-street and Friday-street. The Mitre was close beside it, a house celebrated for its good cheer, and popularity with the *bon-vivants* of the days of Elizabeth and James the First. At the corner of Friday-street, nearly opposite, stood the famed 'Nag's Head,' a tavern the pretended scene of the consecration of the first Protestant archbishop—Parker of Canterbury—in the reign of Elizabeth (1559). His confirmation really took place at the church of St Mary-le-Bow ; but the party prejudices of the papistical writers induced them to transfer the locality to the Nag's Head tavern, where they frequently asserted the meeting and ordination took place; a fable fully refuted in Strype's *Life of Parker*.

At the north-west angle of St Paul's there still remains one of the most whimsical of the old London signs—'The Goose and Gridiron.' This tavern was in existence long before the Great Fire, up to which time it bore the graver designation of 'The Mitre.' It had become known through the concerts given here by the Society of Musicians, and their arms displaying the lyre of Apollo, surmounted by the crest of the swan, when the house was rebuilt, these figures, being adopted for the sign, were soon jocularly converted into the Goose and Gridiron ; and now we have a veritable representation of the latter absurdity over the door. In the same way we have a giant's mouth with a bull in it to indicate the Bull and Mouth in Aldersgate-street, the sign originally being the mouth or harbour of Boulogne ; and the 'Swan with Three Necks,' in Lad-lane, a bird represented with three heads on one body, though originally meant to indicate the three nicks or marks of ownership made on its bill. Well might Ben Jonson exclaim :

'——— It even puts Apollo
To all his strength of art to follow
The flights, and to divine
What's meant by every sign.'

Thus the Bell Savage on Ludgate-hill, when emblazoned with a painting of a savage man standing beside a bell, destroyed the reminiscences of its origin, which lay in the name of the innkeeper, Savage, attached to his hostelry 'The Bell.' We shall look long at 'The Pig and Tinder-box' ere we find its prototype in 'The Elephant and Castle,' but that it undoubtedly is. The 'Devil and Bag o' nails' is a vulgar corruption of the Satyr and Bacchanals which some art-loving landlord placed over his door. The faithful governor of Calais—'Caton Fidèle'—is transformed into 'The Cat and Fiddle ;' Sir Cloudesley Shovel, Queen Anne's brave admiral, into 'The Ship and Shovel;' and Mercury, the messenger of the gods, into 'The Goat in Boots.' A writer in the *British Apollo*, 1707, says :

'I'm amused at the signs
As I pass through the town,
To see the odd mixture—
A Magpie and Crown,
The Whale and the Crow,
The Razor and Hen,
The Leg and Seven Stars,
The Scissors and Pen,
The Axe and the Bottle,
The Tun and the Lute,
The Eagle and Child,
The Shovel and Boot.'

Such strange combinations are, however, easily comprehensible when we remember that it was the custom to combine a new sign with an old one, that apprentices placed their masters' with their own, and that others, like 'The Eagle and Child,' are the badges of old families. From the latter come our red lions, blue boars, antelopes, griffins, swans, and dragons. To have a large showy sign, brilliantly painted and gilt, was the chief desire of a tavern in the old time, and there were many artists who lived well by sign-painting. Chief among them was Isaac Fuller, whom Vertue notes as 'much employed to paint the great taverns in London,' the chief rooms being often adorned on walls and ceiling after the fashion of noble mansions. When the first exhibition of pictures by living English artists was opened in 1760, the sneerers at native talent announced by advertisements in the daily papers that preparations were making for a rival 'exhibition of curious signs by brokers and sign-painters.'

Fleet-street has been long celebrated for its taverns. Many of old foundation and with quaint signs still remain ; others have passed away, leaving an undying celebrity. 'The Bolt-in-Tun' was the punning heraldic badge of Prior Bolton, the last of the ancient clerical rulers of St. Bartholomew's prior to the Reformation. Peele's coffee-house, at the corner of Fetter-lane, now rebuilt, was noted for its useful files of newspapers. 'The Hole-in-the-Wall,' near it, is a characteristic house, behind the main line of building, approached by a passage or hole in the wall of the front house; this is the case with most of the old inns here, which had originally ground in front of them, afterwards encroached on by building. 'The Rainbow' was celebrated as the first coffee-house opened in London. 'The Mitre' was established here after the Great Fire had destroyed the original tavern in Cheapside. 'The King's Head' stood at the corner of Chancery-lane, and was as old as the time of Edward VI. It was a picturesque pile, and is more familiar to modern men than any of the famed hostelries of the past, as it was the residence of Isaac Walton, and appears in all illustrated editions of his 'Angler,' which he advertises to be 'sold at his shopp in Fleet-street, under the King's Head tavern,' the public rooms of the tavern being on the first floor. Nearly opposite, and again behind the houses, is 'Dick's Tavern,' which stands on the site of the printing office of Richard Tottel, law-stationer in the reign of Henry VIII. Facing this is another famed tavern, 'The Cock,' also approached by an alley; it was a favourite retreat of lawyers and law-students in the last century, and is renowned in modern lyrics by Alfred Tennyson in 'Will Waterproof's Monologue.' Its proprietor during the Great Plague closed it entirely, and advertised the fact 'to all persons who have any accompts with the master, or farthings belonging to the said house,' that they might be paid or exchanged for the proper currency. We engrave one of this honest man's farthings.

None of the Fleet-street taverns are surrounded with an interest equal to that known as 'The Devil,' which stood within two doors of Temple Bar, on the south side of the street, where Child's bank is now situated. It was a favourite haunt of the wits and lawyers, and the latter placarded their chamber doors with the announcement 'gone to the Devil,' when they needed refreshment. The sign represented St Dunstan seizing the devil by the nose when he came to tempt him during his labour at the goldsmith's forge, according to the old legend. As this tale was depicted on the sign, it is shewn in the 'token' of its landlord, here engraved, which was issued

in the early part of the reign of Charles the Second. The fame of the saint was completely submerged in that of his sable opponent, and the tavern only known by the name of the latter from the days of Ben Jonson, who has given it endless fame. It was then kept by Simon Wadloe, and appears to have been in the hands of his descendants when this token was issued. Aubrey tells us that 'Ben Jonson, to be near the Devil Tavern, lived without Temple Bar, at a combmaker's shop.' Here he removed the wits from the Mermaid at Cheapside, and founded the renowned Apollo club, writing his admirable 'sociable rules' for its guidance, in his favourite Latin, which has been translated into English verse by Brome, one of his poetic 'sons,' for thus he termed the men

admitted. Near the door was placed a gilded bust of Apollo, and a 'Welcome' in flowing hearty rhymes, by the great poet. When the famed old tavern gave place to other buildings, this bust and inscribed board found a resting-place in Child's bank, where they may still be seen; they have been re-gilt and re-painted from time to time, but the original lettering of Ben's era may be still detected under the more modern paint.

Palsgrave-place, a little beyond Temple Bar, marks the spot where once stood the 'Palsgrave's Head Tavern,' a sign adopted in the reign of James the First, in honour of Frederick, Palsgrave of the Rhine, who married the king's daughter, the Princess Elizabeth. Ship-yard, opposite, denotes the sign of the Ship, a house established in honour of Sir Francis Drake, and taking for its sign the bark in which he circumnavigated the world.

Such are a few of the interesting associations connected with London taverns and their money tokens. The subject of London tokens generally has been treated in an octavo volume by Mr Akerman, the late Secretary of the Society of Antiquaries; also by Mr J. H. Burn, whose excellent volume was published at the expense of the Corporation of London; since these were printed, a more extensive quarto volume, with an abundance of illustration, has been published by Mr Boyne, and devoted to the description of all issued throughout the kingdom.

FAMOUS LONDON TAVERN KEEPERS.

One of the most noted tavern keepers of the last century was Le Beck, whose portrait was painted by Sir Godfrey Kneller, wearing a linen cap, and holding a glass. Le Beck distinguished himself by providing the best food, exquisitely cooked, and the most admirable wines; nor did he yield to any of his compeers in the extravagance of his charges. Perhaps Le Beck's temple was the best provided in London for the devotees of the Epicurean sect; and their high priest seems to have been a huge, powerful-looking man, fit for the ancient office of killing the largest victims offered at their altars. His mighty head became the sign of a noted tavern in the reign after Le Beck himself had disappeared.

Le Beck was not, however, without his rivals. In the *Hind and Panther Transversed* is mentioned, with Epicurean honour, Pontack's, a celebrated French eating-house, in Abchurch-lane, in the City, where the annual dinners of the Royal Society were held until 1746:

'What wretch would nibble on a hanging shelf,
 When at Pontack's he may regale himself?
 *   *   *   *   *   *   *
 Drawers must be trusted, through whose hands conveyed
 You take the liquor, or you spoil the trade;
 For sure those honest fellows have no knack
 Of putting off stum'd claret* for Pontack.'

Evelyn describes Pontack as son to the famous and wise prime President of Bordeaux, whose head was painted for the tavern sign. Defoe, in 1722, describes the best French claret as named after him: 'here you may bespeak a dinner from four or five shillings a head to a guinea, or what sum you please;' and Swift

* Stumed wine was wine strengthened by extraneous infusions.

describes the wine at seven shillings a flask, adding, 'Are not these pretty rates?'

Among its extravagances, in the bill of fare of 'a guinea ordinary figure,' we read 'a ragout of fatted snails,' and 'chickens not two hours out of the shell.'

The Castle, near Covent Garden, was memorable for its celebrated cook, Tom Pierce. Here a most gallant act was performed by some men of gaiety, who, taking off one of the shoes from a noted belle, filled it with wine, and drank her health, and then consigned it to Pierce to dress for them; when Tom produced it exquisitely ragooed for their supper. The wits of that day wrote against its luxuries, though they did not refuse to partake of them. Garth sings the happiness of the contented rural rector, who has good plain food nicely dressed; for, with him,

'No cook with art increased physicians' fees,
Nor served up death in soups and fricassees.'

APRIL 23.

St George, martyr, about **303**. St Ibar, or Ivor, Bishop in Ireland, about 500. St Gerard, Bishop of Toul, confessor, **994**. St Adalbert, Bishop of Prague, martyr, 997.

St George.

If Gibbon's sketch of St George's career be correct, that martial hero owes his position in the Christian calendar to no merit of his own. Born

in a fuller's shop in Epiphania, Cilicia, he contrived to ingratiate himself with those above him by servilely flattering them, and so gradually rose from his original obscurity. A lucrative contract for supplying the army with bacon, proved, under his unscrupulous management, a mine of wealth; but as soon as he had made his fortune, he was compelled to fly the country, to escape the consequences of the discovery of his dishonest practices. He afterwards became a zealous convert to Arianism, and made himself so conspicuous in his new vocation, that he was

sent by Constantius to supersede Athanasius in the archbishopric of Alexandria. To satisfy his avarice, the pagan temples were plundered, and the pagan and Christian inhabitants taxed, till the oppression became unendurable. The people rose and expelled the ex-contractor, but he was quickly reinstated by the army of Constantius. The accession of Julian was the signal for retribution. George and two of his most obnoxious adherents were dragged to prison by the exultant Alexandrians, where they lay for twenty-four days, when the impatience of the people refused to wait longer for revenge. The prison doors were broken open, the archbishop and his friends murdered, and their bodies, after being carried through the city in triumph, thrown into the sea. This death at the hands of the pagans made the tyrant a martyr in the eyes of the Arians, and canonization followed as a matter of course. When the Arians re-entered the church, they brought back their saint with them; and although he was at first received with distrust, the sixth century saw him firmly established as one of the first order. The Crusades added to his renown. He was said to have fought for Godfrey of Bouillon at the battle of Antioch, and appeared to Cœur-de-Lion before Acre as the precursor of victory, and from that time the Cappadocian adventurer became the chosen patron of arms and chivalry. Romance cast its halo around him, transforming the symbolical dragon into a real monster slain in Libya to save a beautiful maiden from a dreadful death.

Butler, the historian of the Romish calendar, repudiates George of Cappadocia, and will have it that the famous saint was born of noble Christian parents, that he entered the army, and rose to a high grade in its ranks, until the persecution of his co-religionists by Diocletian compelled him to throw up his commission, and upbraid the emperor for his cruelty, by which bold conduct he lost his head and won his saintship. Whatever the real character of St George might have been, he was held in great honour in England from a very early period. While in the calendars of the Greek and Latin churches he shared the twenty-third of April with other saints, a Saxon Martyrology declares the day dedicated to him alone; and after the Conquest his festival was celebrated after the approved fashion of Englishmen. In 1344, this feast was made memorable by the creation of the noble Order of St George, or the Blue Garter, the institution being inaugurated by a grand joust, in which forty of England's best and bravest knights held the lists against the foreign chivalry attracted by the proclamation of the challenge through France, Burgundy, Hainault, Brabant, Flanders, and Germany. In the first year of the reign of Henry V., a council held at London decreed, at the instance of the king himself, that henceforth the feast of St George should be observed by a double service; and for many years the festival was kept with great splendour at Windsor and other towns.* Shakspeare, in *Henry VI.*, makes the Regent Bedford say, on receiving the news of disasters in France:

* Betts's *Memorials of the Order of the Garter.*

' Bonfires in France I am forthwith to make
To keep our great St George's feast withal !'

Edward VI. promulgated certain statutes severing the connexion between the 'noble order' and the saint; but on his death, Mary at once abrogated them as 'impertinent, and tending to novelty.' The festival continued to be observed until 1567, when, the ceremonies being thought incompatible with the reformed religion, Elizabeth ordered its discontinuance. James I., however, kept the 23rd of April to some extent, and the revival of the feast in all its glories was only prevented by the Civil War. So late as 1614, it was the custom for fashionable gentlemen to wear blue coats on St George's day, probably in imitation of the blue mantle worn by the Knights of the Garter.

In olden times, the standard of St George was borne before our English kings in battle, and his name was the rallying cry of English warriors. According to Shakspeare, Henry V. led the attack on Harfleur to the battle-cry of 'God for Harry! England! and St George!' and 'God and St George' was Talbot's slogan on the fatal field of Patay. Edward of Wales exhorts his peace-loving parents to

' Cheer these noble lords,
And hearten those that fight in your defence ;
Unsheath your sword, good father, cry St George !'

The fiery Richard invokes the same saint, and his rival can think of no better name to excite the ardour of his adherents :

' Advance our standards, set upon our foes,
Our ancient word of courage, fair St George,
Inspire us with the spleen of fiery dragons.'

England was not the only nation that fought under the banner of St George, nor was the Order of the Garter the only chivalric institution in his honour. Sicily, Arragon, Valencia, Genoa, Malta, Barcelona, looked up to him as their guardian saint ; and as to knightly orders bearing his name, a Venetian Order of St George was created in 1200, a Spanish in 1317, an Austrian in 1470, a Genoese in 1472, and a Roman in 1492, to say nothing of the more modern ones of Bavaria (1729), Russia (1767), and Hanover (1839).

DRAGON LEGENDS.

In all the wide domain of the mythical and marvellous, no legends occur so frequently, or in so many various forms, as those which describe a monstrous winged serpent, or dragon, devouring men, women, and children, till arrested by the miraculous valour or saintly piety of some hero. In nearly all of these legends, a maiden, as the special victim of the monster, and a well, cave, or river, as its dwelling-place, are mixed up with the accessory objects of the main story. The Grecian mythology abounds with such narrations, apparently emblematical of the victory gained by spring over winter, of light over darkness, of good over evil. Nor was this pagan myth antagonistic to the language or spirit of Christianity. Consequently we find a dragon—as the emblem of sin in general, and paganism in particular—vanquished by a saint, a perpetually recurring myth running through all the ancient

Christian legends. At first the monster was used in its figurative sense alone ; but in the darker ages, the idea being understood literally, the symbol was translated into an acknowledged fact.

In many instances the ravages caused by inundations have been emblematized as the malevolent deeds of dragons. In the seventh century, St Romanus is said to have delivered the city of Rouen from one of those monsters. The feat was accomplished in this very simple manner. On Ascension day, Romanus, taking a condemned criminal out of prison, ordered him to go and fetch the dragon. The criminal obeyed, and the dragon following him into the city, walked into a blazing fire that had previously been prepared, and was burned to death. To commemorate the event, King Dagobert gave the clergy of Rouen the annual privilege of pardoning a condemned criminal on Ascension day ; a right exercised with many ceremonies, till the period of the first Revolution. This dragon, named Gargouille (a water-spout), lived in the river Seine ; and as Romanus is said to have constructed embankments to defend Rouen from the overflowing of that river, the story seems to explain itself. The legends of Tarasque, the dragon of the Rhone, destroyed by St Martha, and the dragon of the Garonne, killed by St Martial at Bordeaux, admit of a similar explanation. The winding rivers resembling the convolutions of a serpent, are frequently found to take the name of that animal in common language, as well as in poetical metaphor. The river Draco, in Bithynia, is so called from its numerous windings, and in Italy and Germany there are rivers deriving their names from the same cause. In Switzerland the word *drach* has been frequently given to impetuous mountain torrents, which, suddenly breaking out, descend like avalanches on the lower country. Thus we can easily account for such local names as *Drachenlok*, the dragon's hole ; *Drachenreid*, the dragon's march ; and the legends of Struth, of Winkelreid, and other Swiss dragon-slayers.

But the inundation theory will not explain all dragon legends. Indeed, it would be as easy for a supernaturally endowed power to arrest the overflowing of a river as to destroy a dragon, admitting there were animals of that description. But such a comparison cannot be applied to the limited power of an ordinary man, and we find not only saints, but sinners of all kinds, knights, convicts, deserters, and outlaws, figuring as dragon-killers. And this may readily be accounted for. In almost every strange object the ignorant man fancies he discovers corroboration of the myths learned in his childhood ; and, as different periods and places exhibit different phenomena, legends in course of time are varied by being mixed up with other myths and facts originally unconnected with them. The mediæval naturalists, too, by recognising the dragon as a genuine existing animal known to science and travellers, laid a foundation for innumerable varieties of the legend. Thus, at Aix, the fossilized head of an extinct Saurian reptile is shewn as the veritable head of the dragon slain by St Martha.

In churches at Marseilles, Lyons, Ragusa, and Cimiers, skins of stuffed alligators are exhibited as the remains of dragons. The best authenticated of all the dragon stories is that of the one said to have been killed by Dieudonne, of Gozo, a knight of Rhodes, and afterwards Grand Master of the Order, in the fourteenth century. The head of this dragon was carefully preserved as a trophy at Rhodes, till the knights were driven out of the island. The Turks, respecting bravery even in a Christian enemy, preserved the head with equal care, so that it was seen by Thevenot as late as the middle of the seventeenth century; and from his account it appears to have been no other than the head of a hippopotamus.

Real persons have, in some instances, been made the heroes of legends as wild as that of Perseus. The ignorant, unable to appreciate or even to comprehend the mere idea of literary fame, have ever given a mythical reputation to men of letters. In Italy, Virgil is still spoken of as a potent necromancer; and a sculptured representation of St George and the dragon on the portal of a church at Avignon has conferred on Petrarch the renown of a dragon-killer. According to the tale, as Petrarch and Laura were one day hunting, they chanced to pass the den of a dragon. The hideous monster, less ravenous than amorous, attacked Laura; but the poet rushing to her assistance, killed the beast with his dagger. If the story be doubted, the narrator triumphantly points to the sculpture as a proof of its correctness; just as the painted representation of a dragon, on the wall of Mordiford church, in Herefordshire, has been innumerable times pointed out as the exact resemblance and memorial of a reptile killed by a condemned criminal in the neighbouring river Lug. To vulgar minds such evidence appears incontrovertible. As a local poet sings—

' Who has not heard, of Herefordian birth,
    Who has not heard, as winter evenings lag on,
  That tale of awe to some—to some of mirth—
    Of Mordiford's most famous huge green dragon?
  Who has not seen the figure on its church,
    At western end outspread to all beholders,
  Where leaned the beggar pilgrim on his crutch
    And asked its meaning—body, head, and shoulders?
  There still we see the place, and hear the tale,
    Where man and monster fought for life and glory;
  No one can righteously the facts assail,
    For even the church itself puts it before ye.'

A fertile source of mythical narrations is found in the ancient names of places; legends being invented to account for the names, and then we are gravely informed that the names were derived from the alleged facts of the legends. Near Dundee, in Forfarshire, there is a well called The Nine Maidens' Well, and adjoining are places named respectively Pittempton, Baldragon, Strathmartin, and Martinstane. From these simple circumstances we have a dragon story, which may be thus abridged. A dragon devoured nine maidens at the well near Pittempton. Martin, the lover of one of the maidens, finding life a burden, determined to kill the reptile, or perish in the attempt. Accord-

ingly, he attacked it with a club, striking the first blow at Strath—pronounced by the country people Strike—martin. The venomous beast was scotched, not killed, by this blow; but as it dragged — Scottice, *draiglet* —'its slow length along' through a morass, the hero of the adventure followed up the attack, and finally killed the monster at Martinstane. The dragon, like other great criminals of the olden time, made a 'last speech, confession, and dying declaration,' in the following words:

' I was tempit (tempted) at Pittempton,
    Draiglit (draggled) at Baldragon,
  Stricken at Strikemartin,
    And killed at Martinstane.'

The festival of the Rogations, anciently held on the three days preceding Ascension Day, were the prime source of dragon legends. During these days the clergy, accompanied by the church officers and people, walked round the boundaries of their respective parishes; and at certain prescribed spots offered up prayers, beseeching blessings on the fruits of the earth, and protection from the malevolent spirit of all evil. To a certain extent, the custom is still observed in many English parishes. In the ancient processions, there was always carried the image of a dragon, the emblem of the infernal spirit, whose overthrow was solicited from heaven, and whose final defeat was attributed to the saint more particularly revered by the people of the diocese or parish. On the third day of the processions, the dragon was stoned, kicked, buffeted, and treated in a very ignominious, if not indecent manner. Thus every parish had its dragon as well as its saint, with a number of dragon localities—the dragon's rock, the dragon's well, &c., so named from being the spots where the dragon was deposited, when the processions stopped for refreshment or prayer.

The processional dragon has descended down even to our own day. Previous to the Municipal Corporations Act of 1835, Snap, the famous Norwich dragon, annually went in procession with the mayor and corporation on the Tuesday preceding the eve of St John the Baptist. Snap was a magnificent reptile, all glittering in green and gold. He was witty, too, bandying jokes on men and things in general, with his admiring friends in the crowd. Guarded by four *whifflers*, armed with drawn swords, Snap seemed to be quite at home among the bands and banners of the procession. But, true to his ancient traditionary instincts, though on that important anniversary the cathedral was strewn with rushes to receive the civic dignitaries in the olden manner, Snap never presumed to enter the sacred edifice, but sat upon a stone—the dragon's stone—till the service was concluded, and the procession resumed its onward march. But the act previously referred to has ruthlessly swept away Snap, with all the grand corporate doings and feastings for which the East Anglian city was once so famous. Yet the rabble, affectionately clinging to their time-honoured friend the dragon, have more than once attempted to get up a mock Snap, to be speedily put to flight by the 'Move on there!' of a blue-coated policeman. Such are the inevitable changes of time.

Born.—King Louis IX. of France, 1215; Julius Cæsar Scaliger, eminent scholar, 1484; George, Lord Anson, navigator, 1697, *Shuckborough*; Sir Gilbert Elliot, first Earl of Minto, statesman, 1751.

Died.—Pierre Danès, eminent French scholar, 1577; William Shakspeare, 1616, *Stratford-on-Avon*; Maurice de Nassau, Prince of Orange, 1625; Jean Barbeyrac, eminent jurist, 1744; Andrew Baxter, philosophical writer, 1750; Joseph Nollekins, sculptor, 1823, *London*; Aaron Arrowsmith, geographer, 1823, *London*; William Wordsworth, poet, 1850; Count de Volney, French philosophical writer, 1820.

SHAKSPEARE.

'He was a man of universal genius, and from a period soon after his own era he has been universally idolized. It is difficult to compare

him to any other individual. The only one to whom I can at all compare him is the wonderful Arabian dervise who dived into the body of each [person], and in that way became familiar with the thoughts and secrets of their hearts. He was a man of obscure origin, and, as a player, limited in his acquirements; but he was born evidently with a universal genius. His eye glanced at the various aspects of life, and his fancy portrayed with equal felicity the king on the throne and the clown who cracked his chestnuts at a Christmas fire. Whatever note he took, he struck it just and true, and awakened a corresponding chord in our bosoms.'—*Sir Walter Scott's speech on proposing the Memory of Shakspeare at the Edin. Theat. Fund Dinner, February 23, 1827.*

As is well known, a house in Henley Street, Stratford, is traditionally famous as that in which Shakspeare was born, though the fact has been the subject of considerable doubt. It is but the beginning of the obscurities which rest on the biography of the Bard of Avon. The facts established regarding him by documentary evidence form but a handful: that he was baptized on the 26th of April 1564; that his father was a man

542

of substance, at one time high bailiff of the burgh, but subsequently fell into difficulties; that he himself, at eighteen, married Anne Hathaway, who was twenty-seven, and who brought him a

THE BIRTHPLACE OF SHAKSPEARE.

daughter six months after, and subsequently a daughter and a son together; that, in 1589, he is found as a shareholder in the Blackfriars Theatre in London, afterwards a shareholder in that called the Globe; that, as a writer of plays for these houses, he realized large gains, and in 1597 began to buy houses and land at his native town, to which he latterly retired to spend the evening of his days in comfort and dignity; and that, on the 23rd of April 1616, he died at Stratford, and was buried in the chancel of the parish church, where there is a monument, presenting a portrait bust to his memory. Such is nearly all we know for certain; it is from the uncertain voice of tradition alone that we hear of his having been apprenticed to a butcher, of his having got into trouble by a deer-stealing adventure, and of his first occupation in London having been that of holding gentlemen's horses at the theatre door. One or two faint allusions to his writings in those of his contemporaries complete the effective materials of what may be by courtesy called the Life of Shakspeare. Let us not forget, however, one other particular to which we should cling with great and affectionate interest, that he was characterised by these contemporaries as the *Gentle Shakspeare*. It conveys the idea of a union of amiability and modest dignity, especially pleasing.

Driven to deductions and surmises regarding Shakspeare, we hope that the following remarks may appear allowable. First, we would say that the shade of family misfortune and difficulty which fell upon him in early manhood is sufficient to account for his leaving his native borough. We conceive that, his father being impoverished, and himself feeling anxious for the future of his own little family, he bethought him, as so many young men in similar circumstances still do, of attempting to advance his fortunes in London. An acquaintance with the London players, who we know occasionally visited Stratford, and the impulse of his own genius, probably determined him to the stage. There, in adapting plays which had been written by other persons, he fully discovered his wonderful powers, and was gradually drawn on to write original plays, deriving his subjects from history and from collections of prose tales. Fortune following on these exertions, his mind took only the firmer hold of Stratford and his loved relatives there. It became the dream of his life to restore his family to the comfort and respectability from which they had fallen—to become, if possible, a man of some consequence there. In this he might be said to resemble Scott, who, comparatively indifferent to literary *éclat*, concentrated his highest aspirations on founding a laird's family in the county of his race—Roxburghshire. As in Scott's case there was a basis for the idea in the gentle blood of which he was descended, so was there in Shakspeare's. Through at least the mother, Mary Arden, of Wilmcote, if not also through the father, there was a trace of connexion with land and birth. It is a highly significant circumstance that, in 1596, when Shakspeare was getting his head above water in London, his father is found applying to the Heralds' College for a coat-of-arms, on the basis of family service to King Henry VII., of official dignity, of the possession of property, and the fact of having married a daughter of Arden of Wilmcote; an application which was extended three years later, to one for the privilege of impaling the Shakspeare arms with those of Arden. There can of course be no doubt that William the poet prompted these ambitious applications, and designed them for the benefit of himself and his descendants. They take their place with the investments at Stratford as part of the ultimate plan of life which the great poet had in view. Let it be observed that with this conception of his idea of life all the other known and even the negative circumstances are in conformity. He thought not of taking a high place in London—he rather kept retired, and saved money. To this voluntary obscurity it may be attributed that he has passed so notelessly amongst his fellows in the metropolis, and been left so wholly without a biography amongst them. In about ten years from his coming to London—namely in 1597—he was beginning to make his purchases of property in Stratford, and in a few years more he had wholly withdrawn to live like a private gentleman in the handsome house of the New Place—probably the best house in the town—where he lived till the end of his days. Let it be observed — strange that it should not have been observed before!—that this whole course of procedure is peculiar,—stands quite singular among the literary, and still more the theatrical lives of that day, arguing a character in Shakspeare as original and self-dependent as

his talents were exalted. It seems to us to speak strongly for a just and rational view of the ends of life on his part; it shews him as a man whose original healthy tastes had never become spoilt by town life, as one who never allowed himself to be carried away by love of excitement and applause: the smoke of the stage lamps had never smirched him; the homage of the Pembrokes and the Northamptons had never misled him. He desired simply to be a gentleman, living on his own acres, *procul à negotiis*. It was an idea of life both modest and dignified. We hear not of his seeking any external honours beyond the coat-of-arms. We hear of no ovations at his retirement from the stage; most probably he was too proud a man to undergo a testimonial, even had such things been then fashionable. He had come to town for a purpose, and when that was accomplished, he quietly resumed the calm existence he loved by the banks of that beautiful river of his youth, ever pressing along its green and umbrageous meadows. Could anything be more worthy of 'a gentleman of Nature's making' or of a man of genius?

One of the few certainties about Shakspeare is the date of his baptism, for it is inserted in the baptismal register of his native town of Stratford in the following clear, though ungrammatical fashion: '1564, April 26, Gulielmus, filius Joannes Shakspere.' We know, then, that he was baptized on the 26th of April 1564. When was he born? A fond prepossession in favour of St George's day has led to an assumption that the 23rd of April might be his natal morn, thus allowing him to be three days old at the time of his baptism; and accordingly it has long been customary to hold festivals in his honour on that day.

The question that first arises here is, Did three days form a customary interval in that age between the birth and baptism of a child? We must answer that there are examples of its doing so.[*] But there are also many instances of a longer interval. Milton, who was born in Shakspeare's lifetime, was baptized when eleven days old. In the case of the family of Thomas Godfrey, the eldest of whom was born in 1609, not one of the fifteen was christened in less than six days from birth, the entire series giving us the following intervals: 13, 6, 8, 15, 11, 12, 14, 21, 13, 10, 14, 10, 18, 15, and 11 days.[†]

There is, however, something like positive, though hitherto almost unnoticed evidence, that the Bard of Avon sang his first song some time before the 23rd of April. It is to be found on his tomb-stone in the legend—'OBIIT ANO. DOI. 1616. ÆTATIS 53. DIE 23, AP.'[‡] As this was

---

[*] Arthur Dee was born on the 13th of July 1579, and christened on the 16th ; and Katherine Dee was born on the 7th of June, and christened on the 10th. On the other hand, Theodore Dee was born on the 28th of February, and christened on the 1st of March ; and Margaret Dee was not christened till a fortnight after her birth. These instances are selected from Dr Dee's *Diary*, and tend to shew that there was no great regularity observed in such matters.'—*Halliwell.*

[†] J. G. Nichols's *Topographer and Genealogist*, ii 450.

[‡] Notes and Queries, 2nd ser. vii. 337.

inscribed under the care of relatives and contemporaries, it could scarcely but be correct;

SHAKSPEARE'S BURIAL-PLACE AND MONUMENT, STRATFORD-UPON-AVON CHURCH.
From an Original Drawing.

and, if so, we must accept it as an intimation that, on the 23rd of April 1616, Shakspeare had passed the fifty-two years which would have been exactly his age if he had been born on the 23rd of April 1564, and gone some way into his fifty-third year. In other words, being in his fifty-third year on the 23rd of April 1616, he must have been born some time before the same day in 1564.

The date of the baptism, nevertheless, gives us tolerable assurance that the birthday was one *very short while prior to the 23rd;* and there is a likelihood that it was the 22nd. 'One only argument,' says Mr de Quincey,* 'has sometimes struck us, for supposing that the 22nd might be the day, and not the 23rd; which is, that Shakspeare's sole grand-daughter, Lady Barnard, was married on the 22nd of April 1626, ten years exactly from the poet's death; and the reason for choosing this day might have had a reference to her illustrious grandfather's birthday, which, there is good reason for thinking, would be celebrated as a festival in the family for generations.'

The 23rd of April being usually given as the date of the death of Cervantes, a supposition has arisen, and become the subject of some rather puerile remark, that Shakspeare and the illustrious author of *Don Quixote* died on the same

* Encyclopædia Britannica, 8th ed. art. SHAKSPEARE.

day. It has not heretofore been pointed out that, if Shakspeare died on the day reckoned the 23rd of April in England, and Cervantes on that reckoned the 23rd of April in Spain, these two great, and in some measure kindred geniuses, necessarily did not die on the same day. Spain had adopted the Gregorian calendar on its first promulgation in 1582, and consequently the 23rd day of April in Spain corresponded with the 13th in England; there being at that time ten days' difference between the new and old style. It is to be hoped, then, that we shall have no more carefully-laboured, semi-mystical disquisitions on the now [we believe for the first time] exploded fallacy of Shakspeare and Cervantes having died on the same day.

AN IDEA AND A RHYME.

On the title-page of the first folio edition of Shakspeare's plays, there is an engraved portrait of the immortal bard, from the burin of Martin Droeshout, accompanied by some verses written by Ben Jonson, and commencing thus,

'The figure that thou here see'st put,
It was for gentle Shakspeare cut;
Wherein the graver had a strife
With nature, to outdo the life.'

When Betterton, the English Roscius, possessed the painting, now termed the Chandos portrait of Shakspeare, he allowed Dryden to have a copy taken from it by the pencil of Kneller. The poet paid the painter for his trouble, in flattery, a medium most convenient for Dryden, and, next to coin, the most acceptable to Kneller. In Dryden's poetic epistle to Kneller, on this occasion, we find the following lines :

'Such are thy pieces, imitating life
So near, they almost conquer in the strife.'

On the publication of the above, the coffee-house critics of the day, uproariously bellowing plagiarism, reviled Dryden for so servilely appropriating the idea and rhyme of Jonson, overlooking the actual fact that Jonson himself had appropriated both from Shakspeare's *Venus and Adonis*, where we may read :

'Look, where a painter would surpass the life,
His art's with nature's workmanship at strife.'

The rhyme thus repeated was not suffered to lie idle even, though the original idea was lost sight of. Thus, in an epilogue to the play of the *Brothers*, written by Cumberland, we find the following allusion to Reynolds's celebrated picture of Garrick, between Tragedy and Comedy—

'Who but hath seen the celebrated strife,
Where Reynolds calls the canvas into life,
And 'twixt the tragic and the comic muse,
Courted of both, and dubious which to chose.
Th' immortal actor stands?'

And in reference to the very same subject, we find in a *Critical Epistle to Sir Joshua Reynolds*—

> ' Your pencil summoned into life,
> For Garrick's choice, the ardent strife.'

Both the rhyme and the original idea might be hunted much further, and found in many unexpected places, were the result of sufficient interest to merit further attention here.

HENRY CLIFFORD ' THE SHEPHERD LORD.'

The life of Henry Clifford, commonly called the Shepherd Lord, is a striking illustration of the casualties which attended the long and disastrous contest between the Houses of York and Lancaster. The De Cliffords were zealous and powerful adherents of the Lancastrian interest. In this cause Henry's grandfather had fallen at the battle of St Alban's; and his father at the battle of Towton, that bloody engagement at which nearly 40,000 Englishmen perished by the hands of their fellow-countrymen. But scarcely had the Yorkists gained this victory, which placed their leader on the throne as Edward the Fourth, than search was made for the sons of the fallen Lord Clifford. These were two boys, of whom Henry, the eldest, was only seven years old. But the very name of Clifford was so hated and dreaded by the Yorkists, that Edward, though acknowledged king, could be satisfied with nothing less than the lives of these two boys. The young Cliffords were immediately searched for, but their mother's anxiety had been too prompt even for the eagerness of revenge; they could nowhere be found. Their mother was closely and peremptorily examined about them. She said, ' She had given direction to convey them beyond sea, to be bred up there; and that being thither sent, she was ignorant whether they were living or not.' This was all that could be elicited from their cautious mother. Certain it is that Richard, her younger son, was taken to the Netherlands, where he shortly afterwards died. But Henry, the elder, and heir to his father's titles and estates, was either never taken out of England; or, if he were, he speedily returned, and was placed by his mother at Lonsborow, in Yorkshire, with a trustworthy shepherd, the husband of a young woman who had been under-nurse to the boy whom she was now to adopt as her foster-son. Here, in the lowly hut of this humble shepherd, was the young heir of the lordly Cliffords doomed to dwell—to be clothed, fed, and employed as the shepherd's own son. In this condition he lived month after month, and year after year, in such perfect disguise, that it was not till he had attained the fifteenth year of his age that a rumour reached the court of his being still alive and in England. Happily the Lady Clifford had a friend at court, who forewarned her that the king had received an intimation of her son's place of concealment. With the assistance of her then husband, Sir Lancelot Threlkeld, Lady Clifford instantly removed ' the honest shepherd with his wife and family into Cumberland,' where he took a farm near the Scottish Borders. Here, though his mother occasionally held private communications

with him, the young Lord Clifford passed fifteen years more, disguised and occupied as a common shepherd; and had the mortification of seeing his Castle and Barony of Shipton in the hands of his adversary, Sir William Stanley; and his Barony of Westmoreland possessed by the Duke of Gloucester, the king's brother.

On the restoration of the Lancastrian line by the accession of Henry the Seventh, Henry Clifford, now thirty-one years old, was summoned to the House of Lords, and restored to his father's titles and estates. But such had been his humble training, that he could neither write nor read. The only book open to him during his shepherd's life was the book of nature; and this, either by his foster-father's instruction, or by his own innate intelligence, he had studied with diligence and effect. He had gained a practical knowledge of the heavenly bodies, and a deep-rooted love for Nature's grand and beautiful scenery.

> ' Among the shepherd-grooms, no mate
> Had he—a child of strength and state !
>   *   *   *   *
> Among the heavens his eye could see
> Face of thing that is to be;
> And, if man report him right,
> He could whisper words of might.'
>   *Wordsworth.*

Having regained his property and position, he immediately began to repair his castles and improve his education. He quickly learnt to write his own name; and, to facilitate his studies, built Barden Tower, near Bolton Priory, that he might place himself under the tuition of some learned monks there, and apply himself to astronomy, and other favourite sciences of the period.

Thus this strong-minded man, who, up to the age of thirty, had received no education, became by his own determination far more learned than noblemen of his day usually were, and appears to have left behind him scientific works of his own composition.

His training as a warrior had been equally defective. Instead of being practised from boyhood to the use of arms and the feats of chivalry, as was common with the youth of his own station, he had been trained to handle the shepherd's crook, and tend, and fold, and shear his sheep. Yet scarcely had he emerged from his obscurity and quiet pastoral life, when we find him become a brave and skilful soldier,—an able and victorious commander. At the battle of Flodden he was one of the principal leaders, and brought to the field a numerous retinue. He died the 23rd of April 1523, being then about seventy years old.

A CELEBRATED JOCKEY.

It was said of Tregonwell Frampton, Royal Stud Keeper at Newmarket, and ' Father of the Turf,' that he was ' a thorough good groom, yet would have made a good minister of state, if he had been trained for it.' Frampton was supposed to be better acquainted with the genealogy of the most celebrated horses than any man of his time, for he could reckon up the sires, grandsires, great grandsires, and great-great-grandsires, which he had himself seen. As few genealogists can trace the pedigrees of the most noted running horses for more than ten or twelve descents, it has been regretted that a kind of Heralds' Office was never created for horses, by which Childers in the last, and some of the great racers in the present age, might prove their descent from Bucephalus.

Frampton could choose the best racers equally well, from the thorough English black to the best-bred bay; and 'not a splint, or sprain, or bad eye, or old broken knee, or pinched foot, or low heel, escaped in the choice of a horse.' But the longest heat will come to an end; and even Frampton finished his course, in 1727, aged 86.

APRIL 24.

St Mellitus, third Archbishop of Canterbury, 624. Saints Beuve and Doda, of Rheims, 7th century. St Robert, of Chase-dieu, Auvergne, 1067. St Fidelis, martyr, 1622.

Born.—Edmund Cartwright, inventor of the power loom, 1743, *Marnham, Notts.*

Died.—James Beaton, archbishop of Glasgow, 1603, *Paris*; Daniel Defoe, author of *Robinson Crusoe*, &c., 1731, *London*; William Seward, miscellaneous writer, 1799.

BEAUMARCHAIS.

Pierre Augustine Caron de Beaumarchais, the son of an eminent Parisian watchmaker, served an apprenticeship to his father's business, and gained a prize from the French Academy of Sciences, for an improvement in watchmaking, when only twenty-one years of age. His knowledge of musical instruments, and skill in music, obtained him the high post of music-master to the daughters of Louis the Fifteenth. Possessed of an attractive figure, great talents, and an unbounded assurance, he was early employed in political intrigues by the leading statesmen of France, yet still found time to distinguish himself as an author and dramatist, as well as to realize a large fortune by financial and mercantile speculations. Two of the most popular and best known dramatic pieces in the world, the *Barber of Seville* and *Marriage of Figaro*, are from his witty and prolific pen. His many accomplishments, however, were obscured by an inordinate self-conceit, which he never cared to suppress; and it has been wittily remarked, that if he had been condemned to be hanged, he would have petitioned for a gallows as high as Haman's, to render his end the more conspicuous. But, with all his egotism, he had the good sense never to blush at the lowness of his birth. One day, a number of noblemen of high rank having been kept waiting for a considerable time in an ante-room while Beaumarchais was closeted with a minister in high office, it was determined to insult the *ci-devant* watchmaker, when he came out from the audience chamber. On Beaumarchais appearing, one of them said aloud:—'Pray, Monsieur de Beaumarchais, have the goodness to examine my watch, and inform me what is the matter with it; it very often stops, and I am sure from your youthful experience you will be able to tell me the cause.' 'Certainly, my lord,' replied Beaumarchais, with a profound bow, 'I served my apprenticeship to the watchmaking

trade under my respected father.' So, taking the proffered watch from the nobleman's hand, Beaumarchais opened and examined it with profound interest, a number of courtiers crowding round to witness the curious scene. All at once, as if by an awkward inadvertence, he let the valuable watch fall heavily on the floor, and, amidst the uproarious laughter of the by-standers, walked away, begging ten thousand pardons of the enraged nobleman for the unlucky *accident.*

SWINTON MAY-SONGS.

A correspondent sends us the following account of a custom in South Lancashire, which, he says, is new to him, and of which he can find no notice in Brand, or Strutt, or Hone, or in *Notes and Queries*, and which has therefore the recommendation of novelty, though old:

While reading one evening towards the close of April, 1861, I was on a sudden aware of a party of waits or carollers who had taken their stand on the lawn in my garden,[*] and were serenading the family with a song. There were four singers, accompanied by a flute and a clarinet; and together they discoursed most simple and rustic music. I was at a loss to divine the occasion of this local custom, seeing the time was not within any of our great festivals—Easter, May-day, or Whitsuntide. Inquiry resulted in my obtaining from an old 'Mayer' the words of two songs, called by the singers themselves 'May Songs,' though the rule and custom are that they *must* be sung before the first day of May. My chief informant, an elderly man named Job Knight, tells me that he 'went out' a May-singing for about fourteen years, but has now left it off. He says that the Mayers usually commence their singing rounds about the middle of April, though some parties start as early as the beginning of that month. The singing invariably ceases on the evening of the 30th April. Job says he can remember the custom for about thirty years, and he never heard any other than the two songs which follow. These are usually sung, he says, by five or six men, with a fiddle or flute and clarinet accompaniment. The songs are verbally as recited by Job Knight, and when I ventured to hint that one line (the third in the third verse of the New May Song), was too long, he sang the verse, to show that all the words were deftly brought into the strain. The first song bears marks of some antiquity, both in construction and phraseology. There is its double refrain—the second and fourth lines in every stanza—which, both musically and poetically, are far superior to the others. Its quaint picture of manners, the worshipful master of the house in his chain of gold, the mistress with gold along her breast, &c; the phrases, 'house and harbour,' 'riches and store,'—all seem to point to earlier times. The last line of this song appears to convey its object and to indicate a simple superstition, that these songs were charms to draw or drive ' these cold winters away.' There are several lines in both songs, in which the

[*] In the hamlet of Swinton, township of Worsley, parish of Eccles.

sense, no less than the rhythm, seems to have been marred, from the songs having been handed down by oral tradition alone; but I have not ventured on any alteration. In the second, and more modern song, the refrain in the fourth line of each stanza is again the most poetical and musical of the whole. But I detain your readers too long from the ballads themselves.

OLD MAY SONG.

All in this pleasant evening, together comers
　　[? come are] we,
　For the Summer springs so fresh, green, and gay;
We'll tell you of a blossom and buds on every tree,
　　Drawing near to the merry month of May.

Rise up, the master of this house, put on your chain
　　of gold,
　For the Summer springs so fresh, green, and gay;
We hope you're not offended, [with] your house we
　　make so bold,
　　Drawing near to the merry month of May.

Rise up, the mistress of this house, with gold along
　　your breast,
　For the Summer springs so fresh, green, and gay;
And if your body be asleep, we hope your soul's at
　　rest,
　　Drawing near to the merry month of May.

Rise up, the children of this house, all in your rich
　　attire,
　For the Summer springs so fresh, green, and gay;
For every hair upon your head[s] shines like the
　　silver wire,
　　Drawing near to the merry month of May.

God bless this house and harbour, your riches and
　　your store,
　For the Summer springs so fresh, green, and gay;
We hope the Lord will prosper you, both now and
　　evermore,
　　Drawing near to the merry month of May.

So now we're going to leave you, in peace and
　　plenty here,
　For the Summer springs so fresh, green, and gay;

We shall not sing you May again until another
　　year,
　For to draw you these cold winters away.

NEW MAY SONG.

Come listen awhile unto what we shall say,
Concerning the season, the month we call May;
For the flowers they are springing, and the birds
　　they do sing,
And the baziers* are sweet in the morning of May.

When the trees are in bloom, and the meadows are
　　green,
The sweet-smelling cowslips are plain to be seen;
The sweet ties of nature, which we plainly do see,
For the baziers are sweet in the morning of May.

All creatures are deem'd, in their station below,
Such comforts of love on each other bestow;
Our flocks they're all folded, and young lambs
　　sweetly do play,
And the baziers are sweet in the morning of May.

So now to conclude, with much freedom and love,
The sweetest of blessings proceeds from above;
Let us join in our song that right happy may we be,
For we'll bless with contentment in the morning of
　　May.†

From Job Knight I obtained the airs of both songs, which have been arranged or harmonised for me by a musical friend. They are as follows:—

* The *bazier* is the name given in this part of Lancashire to the auricula, which is usually in full bloom in April. This name for it is not to be found in Gerard's *History of Plants*, or Culpepper's *British Herbal*, or in the Glossaries of Halliwell, Nares, &c. The auricula was introduced into this country from Switzerland about the year 1567. Can its Lancashire name, say *base-ear* (*i.e.*, low ear) have any relation to the name *auricula*? (q. d. little ear).

† This last line would read better thus:
'For we're blest with content in the morning of May.'

OLD MAY SONG. I.

'All in this pleasant Evening.'

NEW MAY SONG. II.

'Come listen awhile.'

THE PASSING BELL.

There are many practices and ceremonies in use amongst us at the present day for the existence of which we are at a loss to account. The change which takes place in circumstances, as well as in the opinions of men, as time rolls on, causes us no longer to see the origin of numberless institutions which we still possess, and which we retain with respect and affection, although we no longer know their cause or their meaning, and in which we often unconsciously celebrate that of which we might not approve. Of such is the ceremony of tolling the bell at the time of death, formerly called the passing-bell, or the soul-bell, which seems to be as ancient as the first introduction of bells themselves, about the seventh century. Venerable Bede is the first who makes mention of bells, where he tells us that, at the death of St Thilda, one of the sisters of a distant monastery, as she was sleeping, thought she heard the bell which called to prayers when any of them departed this life. The custom was therefore as ancient as his days, and the reason for the institution was not, as some imagine, for no other end than to acquaint the neighbourhood that such a person was dead, but

chiefly that whoever heard the bell should put up their prayers for the soul that was departing, or *passing.*

In Bourne's *Antiquitates Vulgares* there is this passage on the subject, which goes to show that at times the custom had been disapproved :—' In a vestry-book belonging to the chapel of All Saints, in Newcastle-upon-Tyne, it is observable that the tolling of the bell is not mentioned in the parish accounts from the year 1643 till 1655, when we find it ordered to be tolled again at a vestry holden January 21st, 1655. The order stands thus :— "Whereas for some years past the collecting of the duty for bell and tolling hath been foreborne and laid aside, which hath much lessened the revenue of the church, by which, and such like means, it is brought into dilapidation, and having now taken the same into serious consideration, and fully debated the objections made by some against the same, and having had the judgment of our ministers concerning any superstition that might be in it, which being made clear, it is this day ordered, that from henceforth the church-officer appointed thereunto do collect the same, and bring the money unto the church wardens, and that those who desire to have the use of the bells may freely have them as formerly, paying the accustomed fees!" It is certain they laid it aside because they thought it superstitious, and it is probable, if they had not wanted money, they had not seen the contrary.'

There are also some regulations belonging to the parish of Wolchurch for the fines of the ringing and tolling of bells, amongst which one item is : ' The clerke to have for tollynge of the passynge belle, for manne, womanne, or childes, if it be in the day, four-pence ; if it be in the night, eight-pence for the same.'*

Of the reason for calling it the soul-bell, Bishop Hall says : ' We call them soul-bells because they signify the departure of the soul, not because they help the passage of the soul.' Whatever its origin and meaning, as it remains to us at present, it is a ceremony which accords well with our feelings upon the loss of a friend, and when we hear the tolling of the bell, whether at the hour of death or at the hour of burial, the sound is to us like the solemn expression of our grief.

APRIL 25.

St Mark, evangelist [68 ?]. St Anianus, second bishop of Alexandria [86 ?]. St Kebius of Cornwall, 4th century. St Phæbadius, bishop of Agen, after 392. St Maughold or Macallius, of Isle of Man, 6th century. St Ivo, 7th century.

St Mark's Eve.

' 'Tis now, replied the village belle,
    St Mark's mysterious eve,
And all that old traditions tell
    I tremblingly believe ;
How, when the midnight signal tolls,
    Along the churchyard green,
A mournful train of sentenced souls
    In winding-sheets are seen.
The ghosts of all whom death shall doom
    Within the coming year,
In pale procession walk the gloom,
    Amid the silence drear.'
                                        MONTGOMERY.

In the northern parts of England, it is still believed that if a person, on the eve of St Mark's day, watch in the church porch from eleven at night till one in the morning, he will see the apparitions of all those who are to be buried in the churchyard during the ensuing year. The following illustration of this superstition is found among the Hollis manuscripts, in the Lansdowne Collection. The writer, Gervase Hollis, of Great Grimsby, in Lincolnshire, was a colonel in the service of Charles the First, and by no means one who could be termed a superstitious man, even in his own day. He professes to have received the tale from Mr Liveman Rampaine, minister of God's word at Great Grimsby, in Lincolnshire, who was household chaplain to Sir Thomas Munson, of Burton, in Lincoln, at the time of the incident.

' In the year 1634, two men (inhabitants of Burton) agreed betwixt themselves upon St Mark's eve at night to watch in the churchyard at Burton, to try whether or no (according to the ordinary belief amongst the common people) they should see the Spectra, or Phantasma of those

* Strutt's *Manners and Customs.*

persons which should die in that parish the year following. To this intent, having first performed the usual ceremonies and superstitions, late in the night, the moon shining then very bright, they repaired to the church porch, and there seated themselves, continuing there till near twelve of the clock. About which time (growing weary with expectation and partly with fear) they resolved to depart, but were held fast by a kind of insensible violence, not being able to move a foot. About midnight, upon a sudden (as if the moon had been eclipsed), they were environed with a black darkness ; immediately after, a kind of light, as if it had been a resultancy from torches. Then appears, coming towards the church porch, the minister of the place, with a book in his hand, and after him one in a winding-sheet, whom they both knew to resemble one of their neighbours. The church doors immediately fly open, and through pass the apparitions, and then the doors clap to again. Then they seem to hear a muttering, as if it were the burial service, with a rattling of bones and noise of earth, as in the filling up of a grave. Suddenly a still silence, and immediately after the apparition of the curate again, with another of their neighbours following in a winding-sheet, and so a third, fourth, and fifth, every one attended with the same circumstances as the first. These all having passed away, there ensued a serenity of the sky, the moon shining bright, as at the first ; they themselves being restored to their former liberty to walk away, which they did sufficiently affrighted. The next day they kept within doors, and met not together, being both of them exceedingly ill, by reason of the affrightment which had terrified them the night before. Then they conferred their notes, and both of them could very well remember the circumstances of every passage. Three of the apparitions they well knew to resemble three of their neighbours; but the fourth (which seemed an infant), and the fifth (like an old man), they could not conceive any resemblance of. After this they confidently reported to every one what they had done and seen ; and in order designed to death those three of their neighbours, which came to pass accordingly. Shortly after their deaths, a woman in the town was delivered of a child, which died likewise. So that now there wanted but one (the old man), to accomplish their predictions, which likewise came to pass after this manner. In that winter, about mid-January, began a sharp and long frost, during the continuance of which some of Sir John Munson's friends in Cheshire, having some occasion of intercourse with him, despatched away a foot messenger (an ancient man), with letters to him. This man, travelling this bitter weather over the mountains in Derbyshire, was nearly perished with cold, yet at last he arrived at Burton with his letters, where within a day or two he died. And these men, as soon as ever they see him, said peremptorily that he was the man whose apparition they see, and that doubtless he would die before he returned, which accordingly he did.'

It may readily be presumed that this would prove a very pernicious superstition, as a malignant person, bearing an ill-will to any neighbour, had only to say or insinuate that he had seen him forming part of the visionary procession of St Mark's Eve, in order to visit him with a serious affliction, if not with mortal disease. Of a similar tendency was a custom indulged in among cottage families on St Mark's Eve, of riddling out all the ashes on the hearth-stone over night, in the expectation of seeing impressed upon them, in the morning, the footstep of any one of the party who was to die during the ensuing year. In circles much given to superstition, great misery was sometimes created by a malicious or wanton person coming slily into the kitchen during the night, and marking the ashes with the shoe of one of the party.

St Mark's Eve appears to have enjoyed among our simple ancestors a large share of the privileges which they assigned to All Saints' Eve (the Scottish Halloween.) In Poor Robin's Almanack for 1770, occurs this stanza:

> 'On St Mark's eve, at twelve o'clock,
> The fair maid will watch her smock,
> To find her husband in the dark,
> By praying unto good St Mark.'

We presume that the practice was to hang up the smock at the fire before going to bed; the rest of the family having retired, the anxious damsel would plant herself to wait till the resemblance of him who was to be her husband should come in and turn the garment. The divination by nuts was also in vogue. A row being planted amongst the hot embers on the hearth, one from each maiden, and the name of the loved one being breathed, it was expected that if the love was in any case to be successful, the nut would jump away; if otherwise, it would go on composedly burning till all was consumed:

> ' If you love me, pop and fly,
> If not, lie there silently.'

Until lately, St Mark's Day was marked at Alnwick by a ridiculous custom, in connection with the admission of *freemen of the common*, and described as follows: 'The persons who are to receive this privilege march on horseback, in great ceremony, dressed in white, with their swords by their sides, to the common, headed by the Duke of Northumberland's chamberlains and bailiff. Arrived at the *Freemen's Well*, a large dirty pool on the border of the common, they all deliberately walk into and through it, coming out on the other side begrimed with mud, and dripping all over.

Then hastily changing their clothes, and having comforted themselves with a dram, they make a round of the common, return into the town, where a ceremonial reception by fantastically dressed women awaits them, and end by calling at each other's houses, and imbibing more liquor. It is alleged that this singular procedure has reference to a visit which King John paid to Alnwick. Having been "laired" in this pool, he punished the inhabitants for their bad roads by imposing upon them, in the charter of their common, an obligation each to subject himself, on his entry, to the same filthy ablution.' Alnwick common lands being now enclosed, this absurd custom is abolished. The last time the freemen passed through the well was April 25, 1854.

———

Born.—King Edward II., of England, 1284, *Carnarvon ;* Oliver Cromwell, Protector of England, 1599, *Huntingdon ;* Sir Mark Isambard Brunel, engineer of the Thames Tunnel, 1769.

Died.—Torquato Tasso, Italian poet, 1595, *Rome ;* James Hay, Earl of Carlisle, statesman, 1636 ; Dr Henry Hammond, theologian, 1660 ; Dr John Woodward, naturalist, 1728 ; Samuel Wesley, the elder, 1735, *Epworth ;* William Cowper, poet, 1800, *East Dereham ;* Dr Patrick Colquhoun, writer on police and social improvements, 1820.

THE BIRTH OF EDWARD OF CARNARVON,

The first Prince of Wales, A.D. 1284.

Weep, noble lady, weep no more,
　The woman's joy is won ;
Fear not, thy time of dread is o'er,
　And thou hast borne a son !

Then ceased the Queen from pain and cry,
　And as she proudly smiled,
The tear stood still within her eye—
　A mother saw her child !

' Now bear him to the Castle-gate !'
　Thus did the King command,
There, stern and stately all, they wait,
　The warriors of the land.

They met ! another lord to claim,
　And loud their voices rung,
' We will not brook a stranger's name,
　Nor serve the Saxon tongue !

' Our King shall breathe a British birth,
　And speak with native voice :—
He shall be lord of Cymryan earth,
　The Chieftain of our choice !'

Then might you hear the drawbridge fall,
　And echoing footsteps nigh :—
And hearken ! by yon haughty wall
　A low and infant cry !

' God save your Prince !' King Edward said,
　' Your wayward wish is won,
Behold him ! from his mother's bed,
　My child ! my firstborn son !

' Here in his own, his native place,
　His future feet shall stand,
And rule the children of your race,
　In language of the land !'

'Twas strange to see ! so sternly smiled
　The warriors gray and grim :—
How little thought King Edward's child
　Who thus would welcome him !

Nor knew they then how proud the tone
　They taught their native vales :—
The shout, whole nations lived to own,
　God *bless* the Prince of Wales !

　　　　　　　　　　R. S. H

CROMWELL'S BAPTISMAL REGISTER.

The Protector, as is well known, was born at Huntingdon, April 25, 1599, the son of Robert Cromwell, a gentleman well connected in that county. Through the favour of an obliging correspondent, there is here presented a fac-simile of the entry of his birth and baptism in the parish register.

Thus extended and translated:—'Anno Domini

1599 Oliverus filius Roberti Cromwell generosi, et Elizabethæ uxoris ejus, natus vicesimo-quinto die Aprilis, et baptizatus vicesimo nono ejusdem mensis.' In the year of our Lord 1599, Oliver, son of Robert Cromwell, gentleman, and Elizabeth his wife, born on the 25th of April, baptized the 29th of the same month.

It will further be observed that some zealous cavalier has inserted, under the year of our Lord, the words ' *England's Plague for five years,*' which have subsequently been erased.

DR HAMMOND.—NAT. CROUCH.

Dr Henry Hammond must be held as a somewhat notable figure in the history of English literature, if it be true, as is alleged of him by Hearne, that he was ' the first man in England that had copy-money, *i.e.,* a price for the copyright of a literary work. ' He was paid such a sum of money (I know not how much) by Mr Royston, the king's printer, for his *Annotations on the New Testament.*'

One naturally feels some curiosity about a man who was the first of the long list who have written for booksellers' pay. He was one of the most noted of the many divines who lost their benefices (his was that of Penshurst, in Kent) under the Cromwellian rule. He was devoted to the monarchy, and bewailed the martyred Charles with bitter tears. His activity was thereafter given to the investigation of the literature and antiquities of the Bible, in which he had in his own age no rival. There could not be a more perfect ideal of a student. He ate little more than one meal a-day; five hours of his bed sufficed; he read in walking, and had books read to him while dressing. Finally, he could compose faster than any amanuensis could transcribe—a most serviceable quality at first sight for one who looked to be paid by the sheet. Five sheets a-day were within his range of power. It is related of him that, on two several occasions, he sat down at eleven at night, and composed a pamphlet for the press before going to rest. Dr Fell, however, who wrote his life, seems to have found that easy writing made rather hard reading, for he speaks of Hammond's compositions as incumbered with parentheses. It is also to be observed that the learned doctor did not thrive upon his assiduity in study, for he died of the stone at fifty-five.

In connexion with this article, it may be mentioned that *the first book published in England by subscription* was a polyglot Bible, prepared under the care of Dr Brian Walton, and published in six volumes in 1657. The learned editor became, at the Restoration, Bishop of Chester, but enjoyed the honour a very short time, dying November 29, 1661.

It may also be worth while to introduce to notice the first person who made any efforts in that business of *popularising literature* which now occupies so broad a space. It was unquestionably Nathaniel Crouch, a bookseller at the sign of the Bell, in the Poultry, London. He flourished in the reigns of William III. and Queen Anne, but very little of his personal history is known. With probably little education, but something of a natural gift for writing in his native language, Crouch had the sagacity to see that the works of the learned, from their form and price, were kept within a narrow circle of readers, while there was a vast multitude outside who were able and willing to read, provided that a literature suited to their means and capacities were supplied to them. He accordingly set himself to the task of transfusing the matter of large and pompous books into a series of small, cheap volumes, modestly concealing his authorship under the *nom de plume* of Robert Burton, or the initials R. B. Thus he produced a *Life of Cromwell*, a *History of Wales*, and many other treatises,* all printed on very plain paper, and sold at an

* Amongst the publications of Mr Crouch were: *Historical Rarities in London and Westminster*, 1681. *Wars in England, Scotland, and Ireland*, 1681. *Surprising Miracles of Nature and Art. Life of Sir F. Drake*, 1687. *Unfortunate Court Favourites of England*, 1706. *General History of Earthquakes*, 1736. This is the last date known, shewing that Mr Crouch's publications extended over a period of fifty-five years.

exceedingly reasonable rate. His enterprise and diligence were rewarded by large sales and considerable wealth. He must have appeared as something of a phenomenon in an age when authors were either dignified men in the church and the law, or vile Grub-streeters, whose lives were a scandal to the decent portion of society. John Dunton, a contemporary bookseller, who was pleased to write and publish an account of his own life, speaks of Crouch in such terms as betray a kind of involuntary respect. He says, 'He [Crouch] prints nothing but what is very useful and very entertaining. . . . . . . His talent lies at *collection*. He has melted down the best of our English histories into twelve-penny books, which are filled with wonders, rarities, and curiosities. . . . . . Nat. Crouch is a very ingenious person, and can talk fine things on any subject. He is . . . the only man who gets an estate by writing books. He is, or ought to be, an honest man; and I believe the former, for all he gets will wear well. . . . . His whole life is one continued lecture, wherein all his friends, but especially his two sons, may legibly read their duty.'

FASTERS.

Among the wonderful things believed in by our ancestors were instances of long-protracted fasts. In Rymer's *Fœdera* (vol. vi., p. 13), there is a rescript of King Edward III., having reference to a woman named Cecilia, the wife of John de Rygeway, who had been put up in Nottingham gaol for the murder of her husband, and there had remained mute and abstinent from meat and drink for forty days, as had been represented to the king on fully trustworthy testimony; for which reason, moved by piety, and for the glory of God and the Blessed Virgin, to whom the miracle was owing, his grace was pleased to grant the woman a pardon. The order bears date the 25th of April, in the 31st year of the king's reign, equivalent to A.D. 1357.

About the year 1531, one John Scott, a Teviotdale man, attracted attention in Scotland by his apparent possession of the ability to fast for many days at a time. Archbishop Spottiswood gives an account of him. 'This man,' says the historian, 'having succumbed in a plea at law, and knowing himself unable to pay that wherein he was adjudged, took sanctuary in the abbey of Holyrood-house, where, out of a deep displeasure, he abstained from all meat and drink the space of thirty or forty days together. Public rumour bringing this about, the king would have it put to trial, and to that effect, shutting him up in a private room within the Castle of Edinburgh, whereunto no man had access, he caused a little bread and water to be set by him, which he was found not to have tasted in the space of thirty-two days. This proof given of his abstinence, he was dimitted, and coming forth into the street half naked, made a speech to the people that flocked about him, wherein he professed to do all this by the help of the Blessed Virgin, and that he could fast as long as he pleased. Many did take it for a miracle, esteeming him a person of singular holiness; others thought him to be frantic and mad; so as in a short time he came to be neglected, and thereupon leaving the country, went to Rome, where he gave the like proof to Pope Clement the Seventh.

'From Rome he came to Venice, apparelled with holy vestures, such as the priests use when they say mass, and carrying in his hand a testimonial of his abstinence under the Pope's seal. He gave there the like proof, and was allowed some fifty ducats to make his expense towards the Holy Sepulchre, which he pretended to visit. This voyage he performed, and then returned home, bringing with him some palm-tree leaves and a scriptul of stones, which he said were a part of the pillar to which our Saviour was tied when he was scourged ; and coming by London, went up into the pulpit in Paul's churchyard, where he cast forth many speeches against the divorce of King Henry from Katherine his queen, inveighing bitterly against him for his defection from the Roman see, and thereupon was thrust into prison, in which he continued fifty days fasting.'

John Scott, the faster, is alluded to by his relative Scott of Satchells, an old soldier of the German wars, who, about 1688, drew up a strange rhyming chronicle of the genealogies of the Scotts and other Border families, which he published, and of which a new edition appeared at Hawick in 1784. The author plainly tells that he was

> '———ane that can write nane
> But just the letters of his name,'

and accordingly his verses are far from being either elegant in form or clear in meaning. Yet we can gather from him that the faster was John Scott of Borthwick, son of Walter Scott, of the family of Buccleuch, since ennobled.

Hearne states (*Leland's Itinerary*, vi., preface) that the story of John Scott, the fasting-man, was investigated with great care by Signor Albergati, of Bononia, and set down by him in a paper which is preserved, and of which he prints a copy. The learned signor affirms that he himself took strict means of testing the verity of Scott's fasting power during a space of eleven days in his own house, and no fallacy was detected. He put the man into clothes of his own, locked him up, kept the key himself, and did not allow meat or drink to come near him. He ends the document, which is dated the 1st of September 1532, with a solemn protestation of its truthfulness.

The industrious Dr Robert Plot quotes these two fasting cases in his *Natural History of Staffordshire*, and adds a third, of a somewhat different nature. Mary Waughton, of Wigginton, in Staffordshire, had been accustomed, he tells us, from her cradle to live upon an amount of food and liquor so much below what is customary, that she had become a local wonder. She does not eat in a day, he says, 'a piece above the size of half-a-crown in bread and butter ; or, if meat, not above the quantity of a pigeon's egg at most. She drinks neither wine, ale, or beer, but only water or milk, or both mixed, and of either of these scarce a spoonful in a day. And yet she is a maiden of a fresh complexion, and healthy enough, very piously disposed, *of the Church of England*, and therefore the less likely to put a trick upon the world; besides, 'tis very well known to many worthy persons with whom she has lived, that any greater quantities, or different liquors, have always made her sick.'[*]

In 1751, a young French girl, Christina Michelot, was attacked with a fever, which was followed by many distressing consequences, one of which was an inability or disinclination to take food. Water was her constant beverage, unaccompanied by any solid food whatever. From November in the year above named, until July 1755, this state of things continued. She was about eleven years old when the attack commenced ; and M. Lardillon, a physician who attended her three years afterwards, expressed a belief that she would yet surmount her strange malady, and eat again. This opinion was borne out by the result. Her case attracted much attention among the medical men of France, who tested its credibility by various observations. In 1762, Ann Walsh, of Harrowgate, a girl of twelve years old, suddenly lost her appetite. For eighteen months her daily sustenance consisted solely of one-third of a pint of wine and water. Her good looks and general state of health suffered little ; and she gradually recovered her normal condition. About the same time a boy was living at Chateauroux, in France, who was not known to have taken any kind of food for a whole year ; he had strength enough to assist his father's labourers in field work, but he became very thin and cadaverous. The accounts recorded lead to the conclusion that his inclination for food returned when the malady was removed which had brought on the abstinence. The journals of 1766 noticed with wonder the case of a gentleman at Clapham, who for twenty-five years had tasted no butcher's meat, and no beverage but water ; but the professed vegetarians can doubtless adduce many instances analogous to this. In 1771, a man at Stamford, for a wager of ten pounds, kept himself for fifty-one days without any kind of solid food or milk ; he won his wager, but probably inflicted more than ten pounds worth of damage upon his constitution. In 1772, occurred the case which has become known as Pennant's fasting woman of Ross-shire, Pennant having described it in his *Tour*. Katherine M'Leod, aged thirty-five, was attacked with fever, which occasioned partial blindness, and almost total inability to take food. Her parents sometimes put a little into her mouth ; but for a year and three-quarters they had no evidence that either food or drink passed down her throat. Once, now and then, by a forcible opening of the mouth and depression of the tongue, they sought to compel the passage of food ; but a suffocating constriction led them to desist from their course. When Pennant saw her, she was in a miserable state of body and mind. In 1774, attention was drawn to the case of Monica Mutcheteria, a Swabian woman, about thirty-seven years of age, who had been attacked by fever and nervous maladies several years before. For two years she could take no other sustenance than a little curds and whey and water ; for another year, she took (according to

[*] Plot's *Staffordshire*, p. 287.

the narrative) not a single atom of food or drop of liquid, and she did not sleep during the three years. The difficulty in all such narratives is not to believe the main story, but to believe that the truth goes so far as the story asserts. Monica, it is said, swallowed a bit of the consecrated wafer once a month, when the Eucharist was administered to her; if this were so, other small efforts at swallowing might have been practicable. In 1786, Dr Willan, an eminent physician whose labours have been noticed by Dr Marshall Hall, was called in to attend a monomaniac who had been sixty-one days without food. The physician adopted a course which threw a little sustenence into the system, and kept the man alive for seventeen days longer; but there seems to have been no doubt entertained that he really fasted for the space of time named.

One of the most curious cases of the kind was the exploit of Ann Moore, the 'Fasting woman of Tutbury,' who, in and about the year 1809, astonished the public by her assertion, or the assertion made by others concerning her, of a power to remain without food. The exposure, while it showed the possibility of really wonderful things in this way, equally showed how possible is deception in such matters. Several gentlemen in the neighbourhood, suspecting that Ann Moore's performances were not quite genuine, formed a plan by which they should become cognizant of any attempt to give this woman food or drink. She held on resolutely till the *ninth* day; when, worn out with debility and emaciation, she yielded, partook of food like other persons, and signed the following confession—' I, Ann Moore, of Tutbury, humbly asking pardon of all persons whom I have attempted to deceive and impose upon, and, above all, with the most unfeigned sorrow and contrition imploring the Divine mercy and forgiveness of that God whom I have so greatly offended, do most solemnly declare that I have occasionally taken sustenance during the last six years.' Of course, the detection of one imposture does not condemn other cases, for simulation of truth is a course open to every one. It gives us, however, to suspect that if equal care had been taken in other cases, similar detections might have followed. The question of the possibility must remain unresolved. We know that the need of nutrition depends on the fact of waste. If, in certain abnormal circumstances, waste be interrupted, the need of nutrition must be interrupted also, and a fasting woman like Cecilia Ridgway, or a fasting man like John Scott, will become a possibility of nature.

THINGS BY THEIR RIGHT NAMES.

The sportsmen of the middle ages invented a peculiar kind of language, with which it was necessary to be acquainted when speaking of things belonging to the chase. Different kinds of beasts, when going together in companies, were distinguished each by their own particular epithet, which was in some way descriptive of the nature or habits of the animal to which it was applied; and to have made a wrong use of one of these would have subjected him who made the mistake to undisguised ridicule; indeed, such is still the case, and to use that word *dog*, when sporting language would have that animal called a *hound*,

554

would be an offence which the ears of a sportsman would not tolerate, and of which it would be no palliation to argue that, though every dog is not a hound, still, every hound is a *dog*.

Of the epithets applied to companies of beasts in past times several are in use at the present day, though the greater part have passed away from us; or if they have not entirely done so, they are not all universally employed, though perhaps every one of them might still be found in existence if sought in the different counties of England. Of those which we daily apply we are at a loss to account for the origin in many cases, though no doubt when first employed the application seemed natural and descriptive enough; but as words are continually undergoing change in their spelling, or are subject to become obsolete or repudiated because *old-fashioned*, we come, in time, no longer to recognise their source.

The following list * will show what were those invented in the middle ages and what we retain. There was said to be a *pride* of lions; a *lepe* of leopards; a *herde* of harts, of bucks, and of all sorts of deer; a *bevy* of roes; a *sloth* of bears; a *singular* of boars; a *sounder* of wild swine; a *doylt* of tame swine; a *route* of wolves; a *harras* of horses; a *rag* of colts; a *stud* of mares; a *pace* of asses; a *baren* of mules; a *team* of oxen; a *drove* of kine; a *flock* of sheep; a *tribe* of goats; a *skulk* of foxes; a *cete* of badgers; a *richesse* of martins; a *fesynes* of ferrets; a *huske*, or *down* of hares; a *nest* of rabbits; a *clowder* of cats, and a *kindle* of young cats; a *shrewdness* of apes, and a *labour* of moles. Also, of animals when they retired to rest, a hart was said to be *harbored*, a buck *lodged*, a roebuck *bedded*, a hare *formed*, a rabbit *set*. Two greyhounds were called a *brace*, and three a *leash*, but two harriers or spaniels were called a *couple*. We have also a *mute* of hounds for a number, a *kennel* of raches, a *litter* of whelps, and a *cowardice* of curs.

This kind of descriptive phraseology was not confined to birds and beasts and other of the brute creation, but extended to the human species and their various natures, propensities, and callings, as shown in the list below, in which the meaning of the epithets is more obvious than in many of the foregoing.

Here we have: a *state* of princes; a *skulk* of friars; a *skulk* of thieves; an *observance* of hermits; a *subtiltie* of sergeants; a *safeguard* of porters; a *stalk* of foresters; a *blast* of hunters; a *draught* of butlers; a *temperance* of cooks; a *melody* of harpers; a *poverty* of pipers; a *drunkenship* of cobblers; a *disguising* of tailors; a *wandering* of tinkers; a *fighting* of beggars; a *ragful* (a netful) of knaves; a *blush* of boys; a *bevy* of ladies; a *nonpatience* of wives; a *gagle* of women and a *gagle* of geese. As applied to inanimate things, there was a *cluster* of grapes, a *cluster* of nuts, a *caste* of bread, &c.

The cluster of grapes and of nuts we are well acquainted with, but the *caste* of bread is quite gone, probably because bread is no longer baked in the same way as formerly, for by the word *caste* is meant that whole quantity of bread which was baked in a tin with divisions in it, or in a set of moulds all run together, and in that way the word is used as of something cast in a mould, as we say of metal. No doubt there was as much reason in all the terms when they were invented, and, as to the use of them, we are as rigorous as ever where we have them at all. Who would dare to call two horses anything but a *pair* when they are harnessed to a carriage, though they may be *two* in any other situation, and although four horses are *four*, let them be where they will. Then, two pheasants are a *brace*, two fowls are a *pair*, and two ducks are a *couple*, and so we might go on with an endless number.

* Strutt's *Sports and Pastimes.*

APRIL 26.

Saints Cletius and Marcellinus, popes and martyrs, 1st and 3rd centuries. St Riquier, or Ricardus, French anchoret, about 645. St Paschasius Radbert, abbot of Corwei, in Saxony, about 865.

Born.—Thomas Reid (moral philosophy), 1710, *Strachan, Kincardineshire*; David Hume, philosopher and historian, 1711, *Edinburgh*; Johann Ludwig Uhland, German poet, 1787.

Died.—Ferdinand Magellan, Portuguese navigator, killed, 1521, *Isle of Matan*; John, Lord Somers, Lord High Chancellor of England, 1697-1700, statesman, 1716, *North Mims*; Jeremy Collier, writer against the stage, 1726, *London*; Sir Eyre Coote, military commander, 1783, *Madras*; Carsten Niebuhr, traveller, 1815, *Meldorf in Holstein*; Henry Cockburn, author of 'Memorials of Edinburgh,' &c., 1854.

DAVID HUME, HIS NATIVITY AND EARLY CIRCUMSTANCES.

The exact or parochial nativity of David Hume has never been stated. It was the Tron church parish in Edinburgh, as appears from a memorandum in his father's handwriting among the family papers. The father was a small laird on the Whitadder, in Berwickshire, within sight of English ground, and the family mansion, where David must have spent many of his early years, was a plain small house, as here represented, taking its name of Ninewells from a remarkable spring, which breaks out in the steep bank, descending from the front of the house to the river.

The sketch of Ninewells House here given—the more curious, as the house has long since been superseded by a neat modern mansion—is from *Drummond's History of Noble British Families*. The eccentric author of the work says, underneath: 'It is a favourable specimen of the best Scotch lairds' houses, by the possession of which they think themselves entitled to modify their family coats, and establish coats of their own.'

A remarkable circumstance in the early history of the philosopher has been little regarded. Though of good descent, and the nephew of a Scotch peer, he was compelled, by the narrow circumstances of the family, to attempt a mercantile career at Bristol when a little over twenty years of age. We know nothing of what he did, with whom he was placed, or how he chiefly spent his time while aiming at a mercantile life in the city of the west; but we are made aware by himself that the scene was an alien one. He seems to have looked back with some degree of bitterness to his sojourn in Bristol, if we may judge from a little quiet sarcasm at the place which he utters in his *History of England*. He is there describing James Naylor, the Quaker's, entry into the city at the time of the civil war, in imitation of that of Christ into Jerusalem. 'He was mounted,' says Hume, 'on a horse;' then adds, 'I suppose from the difficulty in that place *of finding an ass.*'

NINEWELLS HOUSE.

Doubtless, David believed there could have been no difficulty in finding an ass in Bristol.

It is a curious fact, sometimes adverted to in Edinburgh, but which we cannot authenticate, that in the room in which David Hume died, the Bible Society of Edinburgh was many years afterwards constituted, and held its first meeting.

SUNDAY SPORTS AUTHORIZED BY QUEEN ELIZABETH.

The antiquary Hearne, as an illustration of the views of the early reformed church of England regarding amusements for the people on Sundays, brings forward the following license issued by Elizabeth on the 26th of April, in the eleventh year of her reign (1569).* 'To all mayors, sheriffs, constables, and other head officers within the county of Middlesex. After our hearty commendations, whereas we are informed that one John Seconton, poulter, dwelling within the parish of St Clement's Danes, being a poor man, having four small children, and fallen into decay, is licensed to have and use some plays and games at or upon several Sundays, for his better relief, comfort, and sustentation, within the county of Middlesex, to commence and begin at and from the 22nd of May next coming, after the date hereof, and not to remain in one place not above three several Sundays ; and we considering that great resort of people is like to come thereunto, we will and require of you, as well for good order as also for the preservation of the Queen's Majesty's peace, that you take with you four or five of the discreet and substantial men within your office or liberties where the games shall be put in practice, then and there to foresee and do your endeavour to your best in that behalf, during the continuance of the games or plays, which games are hereafter severally mentioned ; that is to say, the shooting with the standard, the shooting with the broad arrow, the shooting at twelve score prick, the shooting at the Turk, the leaping for men, the running for men, the wrestling, the throwing of the sledge, and the pitching of the bar, with all such other games as have at any time heretofore or now be licensed, used, or played. Given the 26th day of April, in the eleventh year of the Queen's Majesty's reign.'†

In connexion with the above, it may be worth while to advert to the fact that, on the 27th September, 1631, being Sunday, the play of the *Midsummer Night's Dream* was privately performed in the Bishop of Lincoln's house in London. The Puritans had influence to get this affair inquired into and visited with punishment, and there is something rather humorous in what was decreed to the performer of Bottom the weaver : 'We do order that Mr. Wilson, as he was a special plotter and contriver of this business, and did in such a brutish manner act the same with an ass's head, shall upon Tuesday next, from six o'clock in the morning till six o'clock at night, sit in the porter's lodge at my lord bishop's house, with his feet in the stocks,

* The spelling in our transcript is modernized.
† Hearne's edition of Camden, i. xxviii.

556

and attired with an ass's head, and a bottle of hay before him, and this subscription on his breast :

> 'Good people, I have played the beast,
> And brought ill things to pass ;
> I was a man, but thus have made,
> Myself a silly ass.' *

APRIL 27.

St Anthimus, bishop, and other martyrs at Nicomedia, 303. St Anastasius, pope and confessor, 401. St Zita, virgin, of Lucca, 1272.

Born.—Edward Gibbon, historian, 1737, *Putney;* Mary Wolstonecraft (Mrs Godwin), 1759 ; Maria Christina, consort of Ferdinand VII., of Spain, 1806, *Naples.*

Died.—Philip the Bold, Duke of Burgundy, 1404, *Hall in Hainault ;* John James Ankerström, regicide, executed 1792, *Stockholm ;* Sir William Jones, poet and scholar, 1794, *Calcutta ;* James Bruce, traveller in Africa, 1794, *Kinnaird, Stirlingshire ;* Thomas Stothard, R.A., 1834, *London.*

BRUCE THE TRAVELLER.

Amongst the noted men of the eighteenth century, Bruce stands out very clearly distinguished to us by his dignified energy and perseverance as a traveller in barbarous lands. Of imposing person (six feet four), of gentlemanly birth and position, accomplished in mind, possessed of indomitable courage, self-reliance, and sagacity, powerful, calm, taciturn, he was quite the kind of man to press his way through the deserts of Abyssinia, Nubia, and Ethiopia, and bring back accounts of them. On 14th November 1770, he reached the source of the Abawi, then considered the main stream of the Nile ; the accomplishment of the chief object of his journey filling him with the greatest exultation. He was altogether twelve years absent from his country, engaged in these remarkable travels.

When at length, after great labour and care, he published his travels in five quartos, with an additional volume of illustrations, a torrent of sceptical derision in a great measure drowned the voice of judicious praise which was their due. We must say the public appears to us to have shown remarkable narrow-mindedness and ignorance on this occasion. How foolish, for instance, to object to the story of the people under an obligation to live on lion's flesh for the purpose of keeping down the breed of that race, that the converse case, the devouring of man by the lion, had alone been heretofore known. There was nothing physically impossible in man's eating lion's flesh. If it were practicable to save the country from a dangerous animal by putting a premium upon its destruction, why should not the plan have been resorted to ? Equally absurd was it to deny that there could be a people so barbarous as to cut steaks from the living animal. Why, in the northern parts of Mr Bruce's own country, it was at that very time customary for the people to bleed their cattle, for the sake of a little sustenance to themselves, in times of dearth. It was creditable to

* Halliwell's *Shakspeare,* v. 12.

George III., that he always stood up for the veracity of Bruce, while men who thought themselves better judges, denounced him as a fabulist. The end of Bruce was striking. While enjoying the evening of his laborious life in his mansion of Kinnaird, on the Carse of Falkirk, he had occasion one night to hand a lady to her carriage. His foot slipped on the stair, and he fell on his head. Taken up speechless, he expired that night, at the age of sixty-four.

A PERSEVERING SLEEPER.

April 27th 1546, 'being Tuesday in Easter week, William Foxley, pot-maker for the Mint in the Tower of London, fell asleep, and so continued sleeping, and could not be wakened with pinching, cramping, or otherwise burning whatsoever, till the first day of term, which was fourteen days and fifteen nights. The cause of his thus sleeping could not be known, although the same were diligently searched after by the king's physicians and other learned men: yea, and the king himself examined the said William Foxley, who was in all points found at his waking to be as if he had slept but one night; and he lived more than forty years after in the Tower.'—*Stow.*

Instances of abnormal sleepiness are not uncommon. In the middle of the last century a woman of twenty-seven years of age, residing near Toulouse, had fits of sleep, each lasting from three to thirteen days, throughout a space of half a year. About the same time a girl of nineteen years, residing at Newcastle, slept fourteen weeks without waking, notwithstanding many cruel tests to which she was subjected. Her awaking was a process which lasted three days, after which she seemed in good health, but complained of faintness. Of cases of this nature on record, an over proportion refer to females.

APRIL 28.

St Vitalis, martyr, about 62. Saints Didymus and Theodore, martyrs, 304. St Pollio and others, martyrs in Pannonia, 304. St Patricius, bishop of Pruse, in Bithynia, martyr. St Cronan, abbot of Roscrea, Ireland, about 640.

Born.—Charles Cotton, poet, 1630, *Ovingden;* Anthony, seventh Earl of Shaftesbury, philanthropist, statesman, 1801.

Died.—Thomas Betterton, actor, 1710, *London;* Count Struensee, executed, 1772, *Copenhagen;* Baron Denon, artist, learned traveller, 1825, *Paris;* Sir Charles Bell, anatomist and surgeon, 1842, *Hallow Park, near Worcester;* Sir Edward Codrington, naval commander, 1851, *London;* Gilbert A. à Becket, comic prose writer, 1856.

CHARLES COTTON.

High on the roll of England's minor poets must be placed the well-known name of ' Charles Cotton, of Beresford in the Peak, Esquire.' He was descended from an honourable Hampshire family; his father, also named Charles, was a man of parts and accomplishments, and in his youth a friend and fellow-student of Mr Hyde, subsequently Lord Chancellor Clarendon. The elder Cotton, marrying an heiress of the Beresford family in Derbyshire, settled on an estate of that name near the Peak, and on the romantic banks of the river Dove. The younger, Charles,

studied at Cambridge, from whence he returned to his father's house, and, seemingly not being intended for any profession, passed the early part of his life in poetical studies, and the society of the principal literary men of the day. In 1656, being then in his twenty-sixth year, he married a distant relative of his own, the daughter of Sir Thomas Hutchinson; and this marriage appears from the husband's verses to have been a very happy one. He soon after succeeded to the paternal acres, but found them almost inundated with debt; mainly the consequence, it appears, of the imprudent living in which his father had long indulged. The poet was often a fugitive from his creditors: a cave is shown in Dovedale which proved a Patmos to him in some of his direst extremities.

It was not till after the Restoration that he began to publish the productions of his muse. There is a class of his writings very coarse and profane, which were extremely popular in their day, but from which we gladly avert our eyes, in order to feast on his serious and sentimental effusions, and contemplate him as a votary of the most gentle of sports, that of the angle. Coleridge says, ' There are not a few of his poems replete with every excellence of thought, image, and passion, which we expect or desire in the poetry of the minor muse.' The long friendship and unfeigned esteem of such a man as Izaak Walton is a strong evidence of Cotton's moral worth.

An ardent angler from youth, being brought up on the banks of one of the finest trout streams in England, we need not be surprised to find Cotton intimately acquainted with his contemporary brother-angler, author, and poet, Izaak Walton. How the acquaintance commenced is easier to be imagined than discovered now; but it is certain that they were united in the strictest ties of friendship, and that Walton frequently visited Beresford Hall, where Cotton had erected a fishing house, on a stone in the front of which was inscribed their incorporated initials, with the motto, *Sacrum Piscatoribus.*

A pleasant primitive practice then prevailed of adepts in various arts adopting their most promising disciples as *sons* in their special pursuits. Thus Ben Jonson had a round dozen of poetical sons; Elias Ashmole was the alchemical son of one Backhouse, thereby inheriting his adopted father's most recondite secrets; and Cotton became the angling son of his friend Walton. But though Walton was master of his art in the slow-running, soil-coloured, weed-fringed rivers of the south, there was much that Cotton could teach his angling parent with respect to fly-fishing in the rapid sparkling streams of the north country. So, when the venerable Walton was preparing the fifth edition of his *Compleat Angler,* he solicited his son Cotton to write a second part, containing *Instructions how to Angle for a Trout or Grayling in a Clear Stream;* and this second part, published in 1676, has ever since formed one book with the first. As is well known, Cotton's addition is written, like the first part, in the form of a dialogue, and though it may, in some respects, be inferior to its forerunner, yet in others it probably possesses more interest, from its description of wild romantic scenery, and its representation of Cotton himself, as a well-bred country gentleman of his day : courteous, urbane, and hospitable, a scholar without a shadow of pedantry ; in short, a cavalier of the old school, as superior to the fox-hunting squire of the eighteenth century as can readily be conceived. As there are now no traces of Walton on his favourite fishing-river, the Lea, Dovedale has become the Mecca of the angler, as well as a place of pilgrimage for all lovers of pure English literature, honest simplicity of mind, unaffected piety, and the beautiful in nature.

It is more than thirty years ago since the writer made his first visit to Dovedale, and easily identified every point in the scenery as described by Cotton. Beresford Hall was then a farm-house ; the semi-sacred Walton chamber

WALTON CHAMBER.

a store-room for the produce of the soil ; and the world-renowned fishing-house in a sorrowful state of dilapidation. The estate has since then been purchased by Viscount Beresford, who, by a very slight expenditure of money, with exercise of good taste, has restored everything as nearly as possible to the same state as when Cotton lived. Mr Anderdon, the most enthusiastic of Walton's admirers, who seems to have caught the good old angler's best style of composition, thus describes the Walton chamber as it now is. The scene is Beresford Hall, the time during Cotton's life, who is supposed to be from home. The Angler and Painter are travellers, guided by the host of the inn at the neighbouring village of Alstonefields. The servant is showing the Hall.

'Servant.—We have a chamber that my master calls Mr Walton's own chamber.

'Angler.—Indeed ! I must tell you I profess myself to be a scholar of his, and we call him the father of anglers ; may we therefore have permission to see that apartment ?

'Servant.—With pleasure, sir.—Sir, here is the chamber I told you of.

'Painter.—I declare, a goodly apartment, and his bed with handsome coverlid and hangings ; and I observe three angels' heads stamped on the ceiling in relief.

'Angler.—A fit emblem of the peaceful slumbers of the innocent ; and so, I am sure, are Mr Walton's. And whose picture is that over the mantel ?

'Servant.—That is my master, sir. It was painted at court, and brought last summer from London.

'Painter.—This portraiture is so delicately limned, and the colours so admirable, it could only be of a master's hand.

'Angler.—Beseech you, brother, may not this chamber deserve to be highly esteemed of all anglers ! Think—here it was Viator had his lodgings when Mr Cotton brought him to his house.

'Host.—There is the very bed where he was promised " sheets laid up in lavender ; " and you may be sure he had them.

'Painter.—And see the panels of oak wood, in figured patterns, over the chimney.

'Angler.—It is a rich work, and falls in with the rest of the chamber ; look at this fine cabinet chiselled in oak, and inlaid with painting.

'Host.—And here, again, the latticed windows, set with the arms of Beresford and Cotton.'*

Cotton's attached wife died about 1670, and he some time after married the Countess Dowager of Ardglass, who had a jointure of fifteen hundred pounds per annum. This second marriage relieved his more pressing necessities ; but at his death, which took place in 1687, the administration of his estate was granted to his creditors, his wife and children renouncing their claims.

IMPIOUS CLUBS.

An order in council appeared, April 28, 1721, denouncing certain scandalous societies which were believed to hold meetings for the purpose of ridiculing religion. A bill was soon after brought forward in the House of Peers for the suppression of blasphemy, which, however, was not allowed to pass, some of the lords professing to dread it as an introduction to persecution. It appears that this was a time of extraordinary profligacy, very much in consequence of the large windfalls which some had acquired in stock-jobbing and extravagant speculation. Men had waxed fat, and were come to be unmindful of their position on earth, as the creatures of a superior power. They were unbounded in indulgence, and an outrageous disposition to mock at all solemn things followed.

Hence arose at this time fraternities of free-living gentlemen, popularly recognised then, and remembered since, as Hell-fire clubs. Centring in London, they had affiliated branches at Edinburgh and at Dublin, among which the metropolitan secretary and other functionaries would occasionally perambulate, in order to impart to them, as far as wanting, the proper spirit. Grisly nicknames, as Pluto, the Old Dragon, the King of Tartarus, Lady Envy, Lady Gomorrah (for there were female members too), prevailed among them. Their toasts were blasphemous beyond modern belief. It seemed an ambition with these misguided persons how they should most express their contempt for everything which ordinary men held sacred. Sulphurous flames and fumes were raised at their meetings to give them a literal resemblance to the infernal regions.

* *The River Dove : with some Quiet Thoughts on the happy Practice of Angling, near the Seat of Mr Charles Cotton, at Beresford Hall, in Staffordshire.* We make no apology for so long an extract from this exquisite work, which being originally printed for private circulation, is very little known, even to those most competent to appreciate its numerous beauties.

Quiet, sober-living people heard of the proceedings of the Hell-fire clubs with the utmost horror, and it is not wonderful that strange stories came into circulation regarding them. It was said that now and then a distinguished member would die immediately after drinking an unusually horrible toast. Such an occurrence might well take place, not necessarily from any supernatural intervention, but from the moral strain required for the act, and possibly the sudden revulsion of spirits under the pain of remorse.

In Ireland, before the days of Father Mathew, there used to be a favourite beverage termed *scaltheen*, made by brewing whisky and butter together. Few could concoct it properly, for if the whisky and butter were burned too much or too little, the compound had a harsh or burnt taste, very disagreeable, and totally different from the soft, creamy flavour required. Such being the case, a good scaltheen-maker was a man of considerable repute and request in the district he inhabited. Early in the present century there lived in a northern Irish town a very respectable tradesman, noted for his abilities in making scaltheen. He had learned the art in his youth, he used to say, from an old man, who had learned it in his youth from another old man, who had been scaltheen-maker in ordinary to what we may here term, for propriety's sake, the H. F. club in Dublin. With the art thus handed down, there came many traditional stories of the H. F.'s, which the writer has heard from the noted scaltheen-maker's lips. How, for instance, they drank burning scaltheen, standing in impious bravado before blazing fires, till, the marrow melting in their wicked bones, they fell down dead upon the floor. How there was an unaccountable, but unmistakeable smell of brimstone at their wakes; and how the very horses evinced a reluctance to draw the hearses containing their wretched bodies to the grave. Strange stories, too, are related of a certain large black cat belonging to the club. It was always served first at dinner, and a word lightly spoken of it was considered a deadly insult, only to be washed out by the blood of the offender. This cat, however, as the story goes, led to the ultimate dissolution of the club, in a rather singular manner. As a rule, from their gross personal insults to clergymen, no member of the sacred profession would enter the club-room. But a country curate, happening to be in Dublin, boldly declared that if the H. F.'s asked him to dinner, he would consider it his duty to go. Being taken at his word, he was invited, and went accordingly. In spite of a torrent of execrations, he said grace, and on seeing the cat served first, asked the president the reason of such an unusual proceeding. The carver drily replied that he had been taught to respect age, and he believed the cat to be the oldest individual in company. The curate said he believed so, too, for it was not a cat but an imp of darkness. For this insult, the club determined to put the clergyman to instant death, but, by earnest entreaty, allowed him five minutes to read one prayer, apparently to the great disgust of the cat, who expressed his indignation by yelling and growling in a terrific

manner. Instead of a prayer, however, the wily curate read an exorcism, which caused the cat to assume its proper form of a fiend, and fly off, carying the roof of the club-house with it. The terrified members then, listening to the clergyman's exhortations, dissolved the club, and the king, hearing of the affair, rewarded the curate with a bishopric.

Other stories equally absurd, but not quite so fit for publication, are still circulated in Ireland. It is said that in the H. F. clubs blasphemous burlesques of the most sacred events were frequently performed; and there is a very general tradition, that a person was accidentally killed by a lance during a mocking representation of the crucifixion. A distinguished Irish antiquary has very ingeniously attempted to account for these stories, by supposing that traditionary accounts of the ancient mysteries, miracle plays, and ecclesiastical shows, once popular in Ireland, have been mixed up with traditions of the H. F. clubs; the religious character of the former having been forgotten, and their traditions merged into the alleged profane orgies of the latter. But, more probably, the recitals in question are merely imaginations arising from the extreme sensation which the H. F. system excited in the popular mind.

CAPTAIN MOLLOY.

On the 28th of April 1795, a naval court-martial, which had created considerable excitement, and lasted for sixteen days, came to a conclusion. The officer tried was Captain Anthony James Pye Molloy, of His Majesty's ship *Cæsar;* and the charge brought against him was, that he did not bring his ship into action, and exert himself to the utmost of his power, in the memorable battle of the 1st of June 1794. The charge in effect was the disgraceful one of cowardice; yet Molloy had frequently proved himself to be a brave sailor. The court decided that the charge had been made good; but, 'having found that on many previous occasions Captain Molloy's courage had been unimpeachable,' he was simply sentenced to be dismissed his ship, instead of the severe penalty of death.

A very curious story is told to account for this example of the 'fears of the brave.' It is said that Molloy had behaved dishonourably to a young lady to whom he was betrothed. The friends of the lady wished to bring an action of breach of promise against the inconstant captain, but she declined doing so, saying that God would punish him. Some time afterwards, they accidentally met in a public room at Bath. She steadily confronted him, while he, drawing back, mumbled some incoherent apology. The lady said, 'Captain Molloy, you are a bad man. I wish you the greatest curse that can befall a British officer. When the day of battle comes, may your false heart fail you!' His subsequent conduct and irremediable disgrace formed the fulfilment of her wish.

A TRAVELLED GOAT.

On the 28th April 1772, there died at Mile End a goat that had twice circumnavigated the globe; first, in the discovery ship *Dolphin*, under Captain

Wallis; and secondly, in the renowned *Endeavour*, under Captain Cook. The lords of the Admiralty had, just previous to her death, signed a warrant, admitting her to the privileges of an in-pensioner of Greenwich Hospital, a boon she did not live to enjoy. On her neck she had for some time worn a silver collar, on which was engraved the following distich, composed by Dr Johnson.

'Perpetui ambita bis terra præmia lactis,
  Hac habet, altrici capra secunda Jovis.'

APRIL 29.

St Fiachna of Ireland, 7th century. St Hugh, abbot of Cluni, 1109; St Robert, abbot of Molesme, 1110. St Peter, martyr, 1252.

Born.—King Edward IV. of England, 1441 (?) *Rouen;* Nicolas Vansittart, Lord Bexley, English statesman, 1766.
Died.—John Cleveland, poet, 1659, *St Michael's, College Hill;* Michael Ruyter, Dutch admiral, 1676, *Syracuse;* Abbé Charles de St Pierre, philanthropist, 1743, *Paris.*

A BRACE OF CAVALIER POETS.

John Cleveland, the noted loyalist poet during the reign of Charles the First and the Commonwealth, was a tutor and fellow of St John's College, Cambridge. His first appearance in political strife was the determined opposition he organized and maintained against the return of Oliver Cromwell, then a comparatively obscure candidate in the Puritan interest, as member of Parliament for Cambridge. Cromwell's stronger genius prevailing, he gained the election by one vote; upon which Cleveland, with the combined foresight of poet and prophet, exclaimed that a single vote had ruined the church and government of England. On the breaking out of the civil war, Cleveland joined the king at Oxford, and greatly contributed to raise the spirits of the cavaliers by his satires on the opposite party. After the ruin of the royal cause, he led a precarious fugitive life for several years, till, in 1655, he was arrested, as 'one of great abilities, averse, and dangerous to the Commonwealth.' Cleveland then wrote a petition to the Protector, in which, though he adroitly employed the most effective arguments to obtain his release, he did not abate one jot of his principles as a royalist. He appeals to Cromwell's magnanimity as a conquerer, saying:—'Methinks, I hear your former achievements interceding with you not to sully your glories with trampling on the prostrate, nor clog the wheel of your chariot with so degenerous a triumph. The most renowned heroes have ever with such tenderness cherished their captives, that their swords did but cut out work for their courtesies.'* He thus continues: —'I cannot conceit that my fidelity to my prince should taint me in your opinion; I should rather expect it would recommend me to your favour.

* This idea was paraphrased in *Hudibras,*—
  'The ancient heroes were illustr'ous
    For being benign, and not blust'rous
  Against a vanquished foe: their swords
  Were sharp and trenchant, not their words,
  And did in fight but cut work out
  T' employ their courtesies about.'

My Lord, you see my crimes; as to my defence, you bear it about you. I shall plead nothing in my justification but your Highness' clemency, which, as it is the constant inmate of a valiant breast, if you be graciously pleased to extend it to your suppliant, in taking me out of withering durance, your Highness will find that mercy will establish you more than power, though all the days of your life were as pregnant with victories as your twice auspicious third of September.'

The transaction was highly honourable to both parties. Cromwell at once granted full liberty to the spirited petitioner; though, personally, he had much to forgive, as is clearly evinced by Cleveland's

DEFINITION OF A PROTECTOR.

'What's a Protector? He's a stately thing,
  That apes it in the nonage of a king;
A tragic actor—Cæsar in a clown,
He's a brass farthing stamped with a crown;
A bladder blown, with other breaths puffed full;
Not the Perillus, but Perillus' bull:
Æsop's proud ass veiled in the lion's skin;
An outward saint lined with a devil within:
An echo whence the royal sound doth come,
But just as barrel-head sounds like a drum;
Fantastic image of the royal head,
The brewer's with the king's arms quartered;
He is a counterfeited piece that shows
Charles his *effigies* with a copper nose;
In fine, he's one we must Protector call—
From whom, the King of kings protect us all.'

After his release, Cleveland went to London, where he found a generous patron, and ended his days in peace; though he did not live to be rejoiced (or disappointed) by the Restoration.

Cleveland's poetry, at one time highly extolled, now completely sunk in oblivion, has shared the common fate of all works composed to support and flatter temporary opinions and prejudices. Contemporary with Milton, Cleveland was considered immeasurably superior to the author of *Paradise Lost.* Even Philips, Milton's nephew, asserts that Cleveland was esteemed the best of English poets. Milton's sublime work could scarcely struggle into print, while edition after edition of Cleveland's coarse satires were passing through the press; now, when Cleveland is forgotten, we need say nothing of the estimation in which Milton is held.

In connexion with the life of Cleveland, it may be well to notice a brother cavalier poet, Richard Lovelace, who in April 1642, was imprisoned by the parliament in the Gatehouse, for presenting a petition from the county of Kent, requesting them to restore the king to his rights. It was looked upon as an act of *malignancy*, or anti-patriotic loyalism, as we might now explain it. There is something fascinating in the gay, cavalier, self-devoted, poet nature, and tragic end of Lovelace. It was while in prison that he wrote his beautiful lyric, so heroic as to his sufferings, so charmingly sweet to his love, so delightful above all for its assertion of the independence of the moral on the physical and external conditions:

'When love with unconfined wings
  Hovers within my gates,
  And my divine Althea brings
  To whisper at my grates;

When I lye tangled in her haire,
  And fettered with her eye,
The birds that wanton in the aire
  Know no such libertie.

When flowing cups ran swiftly round
  With no allaying Thames,
Our caresse heads with roses crowned,
  Our hearts with loyal flames ;
When thirsty griefe in wine we steepe,
  When healths and draughts goe free,
Fishes, that tipple in the deepe,
  Know no such libertie.

When, linnet-like, confined I
  With shriller note shall sing
The mercye, sweetness, majestye,
  And glories of my king ;
When I shall voyce aloud how good
  He is, how great should be,
Th' enlarged winds, that curl the flood,
  Know no such libertie.

Stone walls do not a prison make,
  Nor iron barres a cage,
Mindes innocent and quiet take
  That for an hermitage :
If I have freedom in my love,
  And in my soule am free,
Angels alone, that soare above,
  Enjoy such libertie.'

Lovelace, according to Anthony Wood, was 'the most amiable and beautiful person that eye ever beheld.' He had a gentleman's fortune, which he spent in the royal cause, and in succouring royalists more unfortunate than himself.

Perhaps there was a dash of thoughtlessness and extravagance about him also—for we must remember he was a poet. The end was, that Lovelace, the high-spirited cavalier, poet, and lover, died in obscurity and poverty in a lodging in Shoe Lane, Fleet Street—memorable in the history of another poet, Chatterton—and was buried notelessly at the end of Bride's Church.

RUYTER.

From the condition of a common sailor arose the singular man who, in the seventeenth century, made the little half-ruined country of Holland the greatest maritime power in Europe. In 1672, while Louis XIV. overran that state, it triumphed over him by Ruyter's means at sea, just as Nelson checked the Emperor Napoleon in the midst of his most glorious campaigns. In the ensuing year, he met the combined fleets of France and England in three terrible battles, and won from D'Estrees, the French commander, the generous declaration that for such glory as Ruyter acquired he would gladly give his life. In a minor expedition against the French in Sicily, the noble Dutch commander was struck by a cannon-ball, which deprived him of life, at the age of sixty-nine.

COWPER THORNHILL'S RIDE.

April 29, 1745, Mr Cowper Thornhill, keeper of the Bell Inn at Stilton, in Huntingdonshire, performed a ride which was considered the

COWPER THORNHILL'S RIDE.

greatest ever done in a day up to that time. A contemporary print, here copied, presents the following statement on the subject: 'He set out from his house at Stilton at four in the morning, came to the Queen's Arms against Shoreditch Church in three hours and fifty-two minutes; returned to Stilton again in four hours and twelve minutes; came back to London again in four hours and thirteen minutes, for a wager of five hundred guineas. He was allowed fifteen hours to perform it in, which is 213 miles, and he did it in twelve hours and seventeen minutes. It is reckoned the greatest performance of the kind ever yet known. Several thousand pounds were laid upon the affair, and the roads for many miles were lined with people to see him pass and repass.'

Mr Cowper Thornhill is spoken of in the *Memoirs of a Banking-house*, by Sir William Forbes (Edin. 1860), as a man carrying on a large business as a corn-factor, and as 'much respected for his gentlemanly manners, and generally brought to table by his guests.'

Stow records a remarkable feat in riding as performed on the 17th July 1621, by Bernard Calvert of Andover. Leaving Shoreditch in London that morning at three o'clock, he rode to Dover, visited Calais in a barge, returned to Dover and thence back to St George's church in Shoreditch, which he reached at eight in the evening of the same day. Dover being seventy-one miles from London, the riding part of this journey was, of course, 142 miles.

A ride remarkable for what it accomplished in the daylight of three days, was that of Robert Cary, from London to Edinburgh, to inform King James of the death of Queen Elizabeth. Cary, after a sleepless night, set out on horseback from Whitehall between nine and ten o'clock of Thursday forenoon. That night he reached Doncaster, 155 miles. Next day he got to his own house at Witherington, where he attended to various matters of business. On the Saturday, setting out early, he would have reached Edinburgh by mid-day, had he not been thrown and kicked by his horse. As it was, he knelt by King James's bed-side at Holyrood, and saluted him King of England, soon after the King had retired to rest; being a ride of fully 400 miles in three days.

The first rise of Wolsey from an humble station was effected by a quick ride. Being chaplain to Henry VII. (about 1507), he was recommended by the Bishop of Winchester to go about a piece of business to the Emperor Maximilian, then at a town in the Low Countries. Wolsey left London at four one afternoon by a boat for Gravesend, there took post-horses, and arrived at Dover next morning. The boat for Calais was ready to sail. He entered it, reached Calais in three hours; took horses again, and was with the Emperor that night. Next morning, the business being dispatched, he rode back without delay to Calais, where he found the boat once more on the eve of starting. He reached Dover at ten next day. and rode to Richmond, which he reached in the evening, having been little more than two days on the journey.—*Cavendish's Life of Wolsey.*

APRIL 30.

St Maximus, martyr, 251. Saints James, Marian, and others, martyrs in Numidia, 259. St Sophia, virgin, martyr, 3rd century. St Erkonwald, bishop of London, about 686. St Adjutre, recluse, Vernon in Normandy, 1131. St Catherine of Sienna, virgin, 1380.

Born.—Queen Mary II. of England, 1662.
Died.—Marcus Annæus Lucanus, Roman poet, 65, *Rome;* Chevalier Bayard, killed, 1524 ; John, Count de Tilly, military commander, 1632, *Ingoldstadt ;* Dr Robert Plot, naturalist, topographer, 1696, *Borden ;* G. Farquhar, dramatist, 1707, *London ;* Jean Jacques Barthelemi, 1795, *Paris ;* Thomas Duncan, Scottish artist, 1845, *Edinburgh ;* Samuel Maunder, author of books of information, 1849, *London ;* Sir Henry Bishop, musical composer, 1855 ; James Montgomery, poet, 1854, *Sheffield.*

BAYARD.

The compatibility of high warlike qualities with the gentlest nature is strikingly shown in the case of Bayard, who at once gave the hardest strokes in the battle and the tournament, and was in society the most amiable of men. Simple, modest, kindly, the delicate lover, the sincere friend, the frank cavalier, pious, humane, and liberal, nothing seems wanting to complete the character of the *Chevalier sans peur et sans reproche.* He ought to be the worship of all soldiers, for no one has done more to exalt the character of the profession.

The exploits of Bayard fill the chronicles of his age, which embraces the whole reign of Louis XII., and the first nine years of that of Francis I. His end was characteristic. Engaged in the unfortunate campaign of Bonnivet, in Northern Italy, where the imperial army under the traitor De Bourbon pressed hard upon the retreating French troops, he was entreated to take the command and save the army if possible. 'It is too late,' he said ; 'but my soul is God's, and my life is my country's.' Then putting himself at the head of a body of men-at-arms, he stayed the pressure of the enemy till struck in the reins by a ball, which brought him off his horse. He refused to retire, saying he never had shown his back to an enemy. He was placed against a tree, with his face to the advancing host. In the want of a cross, he kissed his sword ; in the absence of a priest, he confessed to his maître-d'hôtel. He uttered consolations to his friends and servants. When De Bourbon came up, and expressed regret to see him in such a condition, he said, 'Weep for yourself, sir. For me, I have nothing to complain ; I die in the course of my duty to my country. You triumph in betraying yours ; but your successes are horrible, and the end will be sad.' The enemy honoured the remains of Bayard as much as his own countrymen could have done.

FARQUHAR THE DRAMATIST AT LICHFIELD.

This admirable comic writer appears, in other respects, to have been wedded to misfortune throughout his brief life. He was born at Londonderry in 1678, and educated in the University of Dublin. He appeared early at the Dublin theatre, made no great figure as an actor, and accidentally wounding a brother-comedian with a real sword, which he mistook for a foil, he forsook the stage, being then only seventeen years old. He accompanied the actor Wilks to London, and there attracted the notice of the Earl of Orrery, who gave him a commission in his own regiment. Wilks persuaded him to try his powers as a dramatist, and his first comedy, *Love and a Bottle*, produced in 1698, was very successful. In 1703, he adapted Beaumont and Fletcher's *Wildgoose Chase*, under the title of *The Inconstant*, which became popular. Young Mirabel in this play was one of Charles Kemble's most finished performances.

Farquhar was married to a lady who deceived him as to her fortune; he fell into great difficulties, and was obliged to sell his commission; he sunk a victim to consumption and over-exertion, and died, in his thirtieth year, leaving two helpless girls; one married 'a low tradesman,' the other became a servant, and the mother died in poverty.

Our dramatist has laid the scene of two of his best comedies at Lichfield. He has drawn from his experience as a soldier the incidents of his *Recruiting Officer*, produced in 1706, and of his *Beaux' Stratagem*, written during his last illness. One of his recruiting scenes is a street at Lichfield, where Kite places one of his raw recruits to watch the motion of St Mary's clock, and another the motion of St Chad's. We all remember in the *Beaux' Stratagem* the eloquent jollity of Boniface upon his Lichfield 'Anno Domini 1706 ale.' 'The Dean's Walk' is the avenue described by Farquhar as leading to the house of Lady Bountiful, and in which Aimwell pretends to faint.

The following amusing anecdote is also told of Farquhar at Lichfield. It was at the top of Market-street, that hastily entering a barber's shop, he desired to be shaved, which operation was immediately performed by a little deformed man, the supposed master of the shop. Dining the same day at the table of Sir Theophilus Biddulph, Farquhar was observed to look with particular earnestness at a gentleman who sat opposite to him; and taking an opportunity of following Sir Theophilus out of the room, he demanded an explanation of his conduct, as he deemed it an insult to be seated with such inferior company. Sir Theophilus, amazed at the charge, assured the captain the company were every one gentlemen, and his own particular friends. This, however, would not satisfy Farquhar; he was, he said, certain that the little humpbacked man who sat opposite to him at dinner was a barber, and had that very morning shaved him. Unable to convince the captain of the contrary, the baronet returned to the company, and stating the strange assertion of Farquhar, the mystery was elucidated, and the gentleman owned having, *for joke's sake*, as no other person was in the shop, performed the office of terror to the captain.

SIR HENRY R. BISHOP.

' In every house where music, more especially vocal music, is welcome, the name of Bishop has long been, and must long remain, a household word. Who has not been soothed by the sweet melody of " Blow, gentle gales ;" charmed by the measures of " Lo! here the gentle lark ;" enlivened by the animated strains of " Foresters, sound the cheerful horn ;" touched by the sadder music of " The winds whistle cold." Who has not been haunted by the insinuating tones of " Tell me, my heart ;" " Under the greenwood tree ;" or, " Where the wind blows," which Rossini, the minstrel of the south, loved so well? Who has not felt sympathy with

　　" As it fell upon a day,
　　　In the merry month of May ;"

admired that masterpiece of glee and chorus, " The chough and crow ;" or been moved to jollity at some convivial feast by " Mynheer Van Dunck," the most original and genial of comic glees?'—*Contemporary Obituary Notice.*

THE QUARTER-STAFF.

Contentions with the quarter-staff take their place among the old amusements of the people of England : rather rough for the taste of the present day, yet innocent in comparison with other sports of our forefathers. The weapon, if

QUARTER-STAFF, SHERWOOD FOREST.

it be worthy of such a term—perhaps we should content ourselves with calling it implement—was a tough piece of wood, of about eight feet long, not of great weight, which the practitioner grasped in the middle with one hand, while with the other he kept a loose hold midway between the middle and one end. An adept in the use of the staff might be, to one less skilled, a formidable opponent.

Dryden speaks of the use of the quarter-staff in a manner which would imply that in his time, when not in use, the weapon was hung upon the back, for he says

' His quarter-staff, which he could ne'er forsake,
    Hung half before and half behind his back.'

Bacon speaks of the use of cudgels by the captains of the Roman armies; but it is very questionable whether these cudgels partook of the character of the quarter-staff. Most persons will remember how often bouts at quarter-staff occur in the ballads descriptive of the adventures of Robin Hood and·Little John. Thus, in the encounter of Robin with the tanner, Arthur-a-Bland:

' Then Robin he unbuckled his belt,
    And laid down his bow so long;
He took up a staff of another oak graff,
    That was both stiff and strong.

 *   *   *   *   *

" But let me measure," said jolly Robin,
    " Before we begin our fray;
For I'll not have mine to be longer than thine,
    For that will be counted foul play."

" I pass not for length," bold Arthur replied,
    " My staff is of oak so free;
Eight foot and a half it will knock down a calf,
    And I hope it will knock down thee."

Then Robin could no longer forbear,
    He gave him such a knock,
Quickly and soon the blood came down,
    Before it was ten o'clock.

 *   *   *   *   *

About and about and about they went,
    Like two wild boars in a chase,
Striving to aim each other to maim,
    Leg, arm, or any other place.

And knock for knock they hastily dealt,
    Which held for two hours and more;
That all the wood rang at every bang,
    They plied their work so sore.'

In the last century games or matches at cudgels were of frequent occurrence, and public subscriptions were entered into for the purpose of finding the necessary funds to provide prizes. We have in our possession the original subscription list for one of these cudgel matches, which was played for on the 30th of April 1748, at Shrivenham, in the county of Berks, the patrons on that occasion being Lord Barrington, the Hons. Daniel and Samuel Barrington, Witherington Morris, Esq., &c. The amount to be distributed in prizes was a little over five pounds. We find now-a-days pugilists engage in a much more brutal and less scientific display for a far less sum. The game appears to have almost gone out of use in England, although we occasionally hear of its introduction into some of our public schools.

WONDERS OF THE GLASTONBURY WATERS.

Under the 30th April 1751, Richard Gough enters in his diary—' At Glastonbury, Somerset, a man thirty years afflicted with an asthma, dreamed that a person told him, if he drank of such particular waters, near the Chain-gate, seven Sunday mornings, he should be cured, which he

accordingly did and was well, and attested it on oath. This being rumoured abroad, it brought numbers of people from all parts of the kingdom to drink of these *miraculous waters* for various distempers, and many were healed, and great numbers received benefit.'

Five days after, Mr Gough added: ' 'Twas computed 10,000 people were now at Glastonbury, from different parts of the kingdom, to drink the waters there for various distempers.'

Of course, a therapeutical system of this kind could not last long. Southey preserves to us in his *Common-place Book* a curious example of the cases. A young man, witnessing the performance of *Hamlet* at the Drury Lane Theatre, was so frightened at sight of the ghost, that a humour broke out upon him, which settled in the king's evil. After all medicines had failed, he came to these waters, and they effected a thorough cure. Faith healed the ailment which fear had produced.

The last of April may be said to have in it a tint of the coming May. The boys, wisely provident of what was to be required to-morrow, went out on this day to seek for trees from which they might obtain their proper supplies of the May blossom. Dryden remarks the vigil or eve of May day:

' Waked, as her custom was, before the day,
    To do th' observance due to sprightly May,
For sprightly May commands our youth to keep
    The vigils of her night, and breaks their rugged
        sleep.' *

EARLY HISTORY OF SILK STOCKINGS.

April 30th 1560. Sir Thomas Gresham writes from Antwerp to Sir William Cecil, Elizabeth's great minister, ' I have written into Spain for silk hose both for you and my lady, your wife; to whom it may please you I may be remembered.' These silk hose, of black colour, were accordingly soon after sent by Gresham to Cecil.†

Hose were, up to the time of Henry VIII., made out of ordinary cloth: the king's own were formed of yard-wide taffata. It was only by chance that he might obtain a pair of silk hose from Spain. His son Edward VI. received as a present from Sir Thomas Gresham—Stow speaks of it as a great matter— ' a pair of long Spanish silk stockings.' For some years longer, silk stockings continued to be a great rarity. ' In the second year of Queen Elizabeth,' says Stow, ' her silk woman, Mistress Montague, presented her Majesty with a pair of black knit silk stockings for a new-year's gift; the which, after a few days wearing, pleased her Highness so well that she sent for Mistress Montague, and asked her where she had them, and if she could help her to any more; who answered, saying, " I made them very carefully, of purpose only for your Majesty, and seeing these please you so well, I will presently set more in hand." " Do so," quoth the Queen, " for indeed I like silk stockings so well, because they are pleasant, fine, and delicate, that henceforth I will wear no more cloth stockings." And from that time to her death the Queen never wore cloth hose, but only silk stockings.' ‡

* *Palamon and Arcite, B.L.*
† Burgon's *Life of Sir Thomas Gresham*, 2 vols., 1839, vol i., p. 110, 302.
‡ Stow's *Chronicle*, edit. 1631, p. 887.

MAY

Then came fair MAY, the fayrest mayd on ground,
  Deckt all with dainties of her season's pryde,
And throwing flowres out of her lap around :
Upon two brethren's shoulders she did ride,
The twinnes of Leda ; which on either side
  Supported her, like to their soveraine queene.
Lord ! how all creatures laught, when her they spide,
  And leapt and daunc't as they had ravisht beene !
And Cupid selfe about her fluttered all in greene.

SPENSER.

(DESCRIPTIVE.)

MAY brings with her the beauty and fragrance of hawthorn blossoms and the song of the nightingale. Our old poets delighted in describing her as a beautiful maiden, clothed in sunshine, and scattering flowers on the earth, while she danced to the music of birds and brooks. She has given a rich greenness to the young corn, and the grass is now tall enough for the flowers to play at hide-and-seek among, as they are chased by the wind. The grass also gives a softness to the dazzling white of the daisies and the glittering gold of the buttercups, which, but for this soft bordering of green, would almost be too lustrous to look upon. We hear the song of the milkmaid in the early morning, and catch glimpses of the white milkpail she balances on her head between the openings in the hedgerows, or watch her as she paces through the fields, with her gown drawn through the pockethole of her quilted petticoat, to prevent it draggling in the dew. We see the dim figure of the angler, clad in grey, moving through the white mist that still lingers beside the river. The early school-boy, who has a long way to go, loiters, and lays down his books to peep under almost every hedge and bush he passes, in quest of birds' nests. The village girl, sent on some morning errand, with the curtain of her cotton-covered bonnet hanging down her neck, ' buttons up' her little eyes to look at us, as she faces the sun, or shades her forehead with her hand, as she watches the skylark soaring and singing on its way to the great silver pavilion of clouds that stands amid the blue plains of heaven. We see the progress spring has made in the cottage gardens which we pass, for the broad-leaved rhubarb has now grown tall; the radishes are rough-leaved; the young onions show like strong grass; the rows of spinach are ready to cut, peas and young potatoes are hoed up, and the gooseberries and currants show like green beads on the bushes, while the cabbages, to the great joy of the cottagers, are beginning to 'heart.' The fields and woods now ring with incessant sounds all day long; from out the sky comes the loud cawing of the rook as it passes overhead, sometimes startling us by its sudden cry, when flying so low we can trace its moving shadow over the grass. We hear the cooing of ringdoves, and when they cease for a few moments, the pause is filled up by the singing of so many birds, that only a practised ear is enabled to distinguish one from the other; then comes the clear, bell-like note of the cuckoo, high above all, followed by the shriek of the beautifully marked jay, until it is drowned in the louder cry of the woodpecker, which some naturalists have com-pared to a laugh, as if the bird were a cynic, making a mockery of the whole of this grand, wild concert. In the rich green pastures there are sounds of pleasant life: the bleating of sheep, and the musical jingling of their bells, as they move along to some fresh patch of tempting herbage; the lowing of full-uddered cows, that morning and night brim the milkpails, and make much extra labour in the dairy, where the rosy-cheeked maidens sing merrily over their pleasant work. We see the great farm-house in the centre of the rich milk-yielding meadows, and think of cooling curds and whey, luscious cheesecakes and custards, cream that you might cut, and straw-berries growing in rows before the beehives in the garden, and we go along licking our lips at the fancied taste, and thinking how these pleasant dainties lose all their fine country flavour when brought into our smoky cities, while here they seem as if—

'Cool'd a long age in the deep-delved earth,
Tasting of Flora and the country green.'
KEATS.

Every way bees are now flying across our path, after making 'war among the velvet buds,' out of which they come covered with pollen, as if they had been plundering some golden treasury, and were returning home with their spoils. They, with their luminous eyes—which can see in the dark—are familiar with all the little in-habitants of the flowers they plunder, and which are only visible to us through glasses that magnify

largely. What a commotion a bee must make among those tiny dwellers in the golden courts of stamens and pistils, as its great eyes come peeping down into the very bottom of the calyx—the foundation of their flowery tower. Then, as we walk along, we remember that in those undated histories called the Welsh triads—which were oral traditions ages before the Romans landed on our shores—England was called the Island of Honey by its first discoverers, and that there was a pleasant murmur of bees in our primeval forests long before a human sound had disturbed their silence. But, beyond all other objects that please the eye with their beauty, and delight the sense with their fragrance, stand the May-buds, only seen in perfection at the end of this pleasant month, or a few brief days beyond. All our old poets have done reverence to the milk-white scented blossoms of the haw-thorn—the May of poetry—which throws an undying fragrance over their pages; nor does any country in the world present so beautiful a sight as our long leagues of English hedgerows sheeted with May blossoms. We see it in the cottage windows, the fireless grates of clean country parlours are ornamented with it, and rarely does anyone return home without bringing back a branch of May, for there is an old household aroma in its bloom which has been familiar to them from childhood, and which they love to inhale better than any other that floats around their breezy homesteads. The re-freshing smell of May-buds after a shower is a delight never to be forgotten; and, for aught we know to the contrary, birds may, like us, enjoy this delicious perfume, and we have fancied that this is why they prefer building their nests and rearing their young among the May blossoms. The red May, which is a common ornament of pleasure-grounds, derives its ruddy hue from having grown in a deep red clayey soil, and is not, we fancy, so fragrant as the white hawthorn, nor so beautiful as the pale pink May, which is coloured like the maiden blush rose. It is in the dew they shake from the pink May that our simple country maidens love to bathe their faces, believing that it will give them the complexion of the warm pearly May blossoms, which they call the Lady May. What a refreshing shower-bath, when well shaken, a large hawthorn, heavy with dew, and covered with bloom, would make!

The nightingale comes with its sweet music to usher in this month of flowers, and it is now generally believed that the male is the first that makes its appearance in England, and that his song increases in sweetness as the expected arrival of the female draws nearer. Nor will he shift his place, but continues to sing about the spot where he is first heard, and where she is sure to find him when she comes. We have no doubt these birds understand one another, and that the female finds her mate by his song, which was familiar to her before her arrival, and that she can distinguish his voice from all others. Could the nightingales which are said to be seen together in the countries to which they migrate be caught and marked before they return to England, this might be proved.

One bird will answer another, taking up the

song where the first ceases, when they are far beyond our power of hearing, as has been proved by persons placed midway, and close to the rival songsters, who have timed the intervals between, and found that, to a second, one bird began the instant the other was silent; though the distance between was too far apart for human ears to catch a note of the bird farthest from the listener, the hands which marked the seconds on the watches showed that one bird had never begun to sing until the other had ended. You may throw a stone among the foliage where the nightingale is singing, and it will only cease for a few moments, and move away a few feet, then resume its song. At the end of this month, or early in June, its nest, which is generally formed of old oak leaves, may be found, lined only with grass—a poor home for so sweet a singer, and not unlike that in which many of our sweetest poets were first cradled. As soon as the young are hatched the male ceases to sing, losing his voice, and making only a disagreeable croaking noise when danger is near, instead of giving utterance to the same sweet song

'That found a path
Through the sad heart of Ruth, when, sick for home,
She stood in tears amid the alien corn.'

KEATS.

How enraptured must good old Izaak Walton have been with the song of the nightingale, when he exclaimed, 'Lord, what music hast Thou provided for the saints in heaven, when Thou affordest bad men such music on earth.'

Butterflies are now darting about in every direction, here seeming to play with one another —a dozen together in places—there resting with folded wings on some flower, then setting off in that zig-zag flight which enables them to escape their pursuers, as few birds can turn sudden enough, when on the wing, to capture them. What is that liquid nourishment, we often wonder, which they suck up through their tiny proboscis; is it dew, or the honey of flowers? Examine the exquisite scales of their wings through a glass, and then you will say that, poetical as many of the names are by which they are known, they are not equal to the beauty they attempt to designate. Rose-shaded, damask-dyed, garden-carpet, violet-spotted, green-veined, and many another name beside, conveys no notion of the jewels of gold and silver, and richly-coloured precious stones, set in the forms of the most beautiful flowers, which adorn their wings, heads, and the under part of their bodies, some portions of which appear like plumes of the gaudiest feathers. Our old poet Spenser calls the butterfly 'Lord of all the works of Nature,' who reigns over the air and earth, and feeds on flowers, taking

'Whatever thing doth please the eye.'

What a poor name is Red Admiral for that beautiful and well-known butterfly which may be driven out of almost any bed of nettles, and is richly banded with black, scarlet, and blue! Very few of these short-lived beauties survive the winter; such as do, come out with a sad, tattered appearance on the following spring,

and with all their rich colours faded. By the end of this month most of the trees will have donned their new attire, nor will they ever appear more beautiful than now, for the foliage of summer is darker; the delicate spring-green is gone by the end of June, and the leaves then no longer look fresh and new. Nor is the foliage as yet dense enough to hide the traces of the branches, which, like graceful maidens, still show their shapes through their slender attire—a beauty that will be lost when they attain the full-bourgeoned matronliness of summer. But trees are rarely to be seen to perfection in woods or forests, unless it be here and there one or two standing in some open space, for in these places they are generally too crowded together. When near, if not over close, they show best in some noble avenue, especially if each tree has plenty of room to stretch out its arms, without too closely elbowing its neighbour; then a good many together can be taken in by the eye at once, from the root to the highest spray, and grand do they look as the aisle of some noble cathedral. In clumps they are 'beautiful exceedingly,' scattered as it were at random, when no separate branch is seen, but all the foliage is massed together like one immense tree, resting on its background of sky. Even on level ground a clump of trees has a pleasing appearance, for the lower branches blend harmoniously with the grass, while the blue air seems to float about the upper portions like a transparent veil. Here, too, we see such colours as only a few of our first-rate artists succeed in imitating; the sunshine that falls golden here, and deepens into amber there, touched with bronze, then the dark green, almost black in the shade, with dashes of purple and emerald—green as the first sward of showery April. We have often fancied, when standing on some eminence that overlooked a wide stretch of woodland, we have seen such terraces along the sweeps of foliage as were too beautiful for anything excepting angels to walk upon. While thus walking and musing through the fields and woods at this pleasant season of the year, a contented and imaginative man can readily fancy that all these quiet paths and delightful prospects were made for him, or that he is a principal shareholder in Nature's great freehold. He stops in winter to see the hedger and ditcher at work, or to look at the men repairing the road, and it gives him as much pleasure to see the unsightly gap filled up with young 'quicksets,' the ditch embankment repaired, and the hole in the high road made sound, as it does the wealthy owner of the estate, who has to pay the men thus employed for their labour. And when he passes that way again, he stops to see how much the quicksets have grown, or whether the patch on the embankment is covered with grass and wild flowers, or if the repaired hollow in the road is sound, and has stood the drying winds of March, the heavy rains of April, and is glad to find it standing level and hard in the sunshine of May. If it is a large enclosed park, and the proprietor has put up warnings that within there are steel traps, spring guns, and 'most biting laws' for trespassers, still the contented wanderer is sure to find some gentle eminence that over-

567

looks at least a portion of it. From this he will catch glimpses of glen and glade, and see the deer trooping through the long avenues, standing under some broad-branched oak, or, with their high antlers only visible, couching among the cool fan-leaved fern. They cannot prosecute him for looking through the great iron gates, which are aptly mounted with grim stone griffins, who ever stand rampant on the tall pillars, and seem to threaten with their dead eyes every intruder, nor prevent him from admiring the long high avenue of ancient elms, through which the sunshine streams and quivers on the broad carriage way as if it were canopied with a waving network of gold. He sees the great lake glimmering far down, and making a light behind the perspective of dark branches, and knows that those moving specks of silver which are ever crossing his vision are the stately swans sailing to and fro; the cawing of rooks falls with a pleasant sound upon his ear, as they hover around the old ancestral trees, which have been a rookery for centuries. Once there were pleasant footpaths between those aged oaks, and beside those old hawthorns—still covered with May-buds—that led to neighbouring villages, which can only now be reached by circuitous roads, that lie without the park: alas, that no 'village Hampden' rose up to do battle for the preservation of the old rights of way! Here and there an old stile, which forms a picturesque object between the heavy trunks to which it was clamped, is allowed to remain, and that is almost all there is left to point out the pleasant places through which those obliterated footpaths went winding along.

We have now a great increase of flowers, and amongst them the graceful wood-sorrel—the true Irish shamrock—the trefoil leaves of which are heart-shaped, of a bright green, and a true weather-glass, as they always shut up at the approach of rain. The petals, which are beautifully streaked with lilac, soon fade when the flower is gathered, while the leaves yield the purest oxalic acid, and are much sourer than the common sorrel. Buttercups are now abundant, and make the fields one blaze of gold, for they grow higher than the generality of our grasses, and so overtop the green that surrounds them. Children may now be seen in country lanes and suburban roads carrying them home by armfuls, heads and tails mixed together, and trailing on the ground. This common flower belongs to that large family of plants which come under the ranunculus genus, and not a better flower can be found to illustrate botany, as it is easily taken to pieces, and readily explained; the number five being that of the sepals of calyx, petals, and nectar-cup, which a child can remember. Sweet woodruff now displays its small white flowers, and those who delight in perfuming their wardrobes will not fail to gather it, for it has the smell of new hay, and retains its scent a length of time, and is by many greatly preferred before lavender. This delightful fragrance is hardly perceptible when the plant is first gathered, unless the leaves are bruised or rubbed between the fingers; then the powerful odour is inhaled. The sweet woodruff is rather a scarce plant, and must be sought for in woods, about the trunks of oaks—oak-leaf mould being the soil it most delights in; though small, the white flowers are as beautiful as those of the star-shaped jessamine. Plentiful as red and white campions are, it is very rare to find them both together, though there is hardly a hedge in a sunny spot under which they are not now in bloom. Like the ragged robin, they are in many places still called cuckoo-flowers, and what the 'cuckoo buds of yellow hue' are, mentioned by Shakspere, has never been satisfactorily explained. We have little doubt, when the names of flowers two or three centuries ago were known to but few, that many which bloomed about the time the cuckoo appeared, were called cuckoo-flowers; we can find at least a score bearing that name in our old herbals. Few, when looking at the greater stitchwort, now in flower, would fancy that that large-shaped bloom was one of the family of chickweeds; as for the lesser stitchwort, it is rarely found excepting in wild wastes, where gorse and heather abound; and we almost wonder why so white and delicate a flower should choose the wilderness to flourish in, and never be found in perfection but in lonely places. Several of the beautiful wild geraniums, commonly called crane's-bill, dove's-bill, and other names, are now in flower, and some of them bear foliage as soft and downy as those that are cultivated. Some have rich rose-coloured flowers, others are dashed with deep purple, like the heart's-ease, while the one known as herb Robert is as beautiful as any of our garden flowers. But it would make a long catalogue only to give the names of all these beautiful wild geraniums which are found in flower in May. But the most curious of all plants now in bloom are the orchises, some of which look like bees, flies, spiders, and butterflies; for when in bloom you might, at a distance, fancy that each plant was covered with the insects after which it is named. An orchis has only once to be seen, and the eye is for ever familiar with the whole variety, for it resembles no other flower, displaying nothing that would seem capable of forming a seed vessel, as both stamen and style are concealed. Like the violet, it has a spur, and the bloom rises from a twisted stalk. The commonest, which is hawked about the streets of London in April, is the Early Purple, remarkable for the dark purple spots on the leaves, but it seldom lives long. Kent is the county for orchises, where several varieties may now be found in flower.

(HISTORICAL.)

'May was the second month in the old Alban calendar, the third in that of Romulus, and the fifth in the one instituted by Numa Pompilius— a station it has held from that distant date to the present period. It consisted of twenty-two days in the Alban, and of thirty-one in Romulus's calendar; Numa deprived it of the odd day, which Julius Cæsar restored, since which it has remained undisturbed.'—*Brady.* The most receivable account of the origin of the name of the month is that which represents it as being assigned in honour of the *Majores,* or *Maiores,* the senate in the original constitution of Rome, June being in like manner a compliment to the

Juniores, or inferior branch of the Roman legislature. The notion that it was in honour of Maia, the mother by Jupiter of the god Hermes, or Mercury, seems entirely gratuitous, and merely surmised in consequence of the resemblance of the word. Amongst our Saxon forefathers the month was called *Tri-Milchi,* with an understood reference to the improved condition of the cattle under benefit of the spring herbage, the cow being now able to give milk thrice a-day.

It is an idea as ancient as early Roman times, stated by Ovid in his *Fasti,* and still prevalent in Europe, that May is an unlucky month in which to be married.

CHARACTERISTICS OF MAY.

While there is a natural eagerness to hail May as a summer month—and from its position in the year it ought to be one—it is after all very much a spring month. The mean temperature of the month in the British Islands is about 54°. The cold winds of spring still more or less prevail; the east wind has generally a great hold; and sometimes there are even falls of snow within the first ten or fifteen days. On this account proverbial wisdom warns us against being too eager to regard it as a time for light clothing :

> ' Change not a clout
> Till May be out.'

At London, the sun rises on the 1st of the month at 4.33; on the 31st at 3.51; the middle day of the month being 15h. 43m. long. The sun usually enters Gemini early in the morning of the 21st.

Other proverbs regarding May are as follow : —

> ' Be it weal or be it woe,
> Beans blow before May doth go.'

> ' Come it early or come it late,
> In May comes the cow-quake.'

> ' A swarm of bees in May
> Is worth a load of hay.'

> ' The haddocks are good,
> When dipped in May flood.'

> ' Mist in May, and heat in June,
> Make the harvest right soon.'

In Scotland, in parts peculiarly exposed, the east wind of May is generally felt as a very severe affliction. On this subject, however, a gentleman was once rebuked in somewhat striking terms by one *abnormis sapiens.* It was the late accomplished Lord Rutherfurd of the Edinburgh bench, who, rambling one day on the Pentland Hills, with his friend Lord Cockburn, encountered a shepherd who was remarkable in his district for a habit of sententious talking, in which he put everything in a triple form. Lord Rutherfurd, conversing with the man, expressed himself in strong terms regarding the east wind, which was then blowing very keenly. ' And what ails ye at the east wind?' said the shepherd. ' It is so bitterly disagreeable,' replied the judge. ' I wonder at you finding so much fault with it.' ' And pray, did you ever find any good in it ?' ' Oh, yes.' ' And what can you say of good for it? ' inquired Lord Rutherfurd. ' Weel,' replied the triadist, ' it dries the yird (soil), it slockens (refreshes) the ewes, and it's God's wull.' The learned judges were silent.

First of May.

St Philip and St James the Less, apostles. St Andeolus, martyr, 208. Saints Acius and Acheolus, martyrs, of Amiens, about 290. St Amator, Bishop of Auxerre, 418. St Briocus, of Wales, about 502. St Sigismund, King of Burgundy, about 517. St Marcon, abbot of Nanteu, in Normandy, 558. St Asaph, abbot and bishop at Llanelwy, in North Wales, about 590.

May 1st is a festival of the Anglican church, in honour of St Philip and St James the Less, apostles.

ST ASAPH.

Asaph is one of those saints who belong to the fabulous period, and whose history is probably but a legend altogether. According to the story, there was, in the sixth century, a bishop of Glasgow called Kentigern, called also by the Scots St Mungo, who was driven from his bishopric in 543, and took refuge in Wales with

St David. Kentigern also was a saint; so the two saints wandered about Wales for some time seeking unsuccessfully for a convenient spot to build a church for the fugitive, and had almost given up the search in despair, when the place was miraculously pointed out to them through the agency of a wild boar. It was a piece of rising ground on the banks of the little river Elwy, a tributary of the Clwyd, and Kentigern built upon it a small church of wood, which, from the name of the river, was called Llanelwy, and afterwards established a monastery there, which soon became remarkable for its numerous monks. Among these was a young Welshman, named Asaph, who, by his learning and conduct, became so great a favourite with Kentigern, that when the latter established an episcopal see at Llanelwy, and assumed the dignity of a bishop, he deputed to Asaph the government of the monastery. More than this, when at length St Kentigern's enemies in Scotland were appeased or silenced, and he was recalled to his native country, he resigned his Welsh bishopric to Asaph, who thus became bishop of Llanelwy, though what he did in his episcopacy, or how long he lived, is equally unknown, except that he is said, on very questionable authority, to have compiled the ordinances of his church, and to have written a life of his master, St Kentigern, as well as some other books. We can only say that nobody is known to have ever seen any such works. After his death, no bishops of Llanelwy have been recorded for a very long period of years—that is, till the middle of the twelfth century. The church and see still retained the name of Llanelwy, which, the supposed second bishop having been canonized, was changed at a later period to St Asaph, by which name it is still known.

Rogation Sunday. (1864.)

Rogation Sunday—the fifth after Easter— is one of the moveable festivals of the Anglican Church. It derived its name from the Gospel for the day, teaching us how we may *ask* of God so as to obtain. In former times there was a perambulation, in the course of which, at certain spots, thanksgiving psalms were sung. (See larger account under title ROGATION DAYS, May 2.)

Born.—William Lilly, astrologer, 1602, *Diseworth ;* Joseph Addison, miscellaneous writer, 1672, *Milston,* near *Amesbury, Wilts ;* Sebastian de Vauban, 1633, *Nivernois ;* Arthur, Duke of Wellington, 1769 ; Dr John Woodward, naturalist, 1665, *Derbyshire.*

Died.—Arcadius, emperor of the East, 408 ; Maud, Queen of England, 1118; Pope Pius V., 1572; John Dryden, poet, 1700, *London ;* François de Paris, 1727, *Paris ;* Miss Richmal Mangnall, author of *Miscellaneous Questions,* &c., 1820.

FRANÇOIS DE PARIS.

In the history of the great Jansenist schism which troubled the church in France for a hundred years, the name of the Deacon François de Paris bears a conspicuous place, not on account of anything he did or said in his life, but what happened regarding him after his death. Dying at thirty-seven, with a great reputation for sanctity and an infinite number of charitable works among the poor, his tomb in the cemetery of St Medard came to be regarded with much veneration among such of the Parisian populace as had contracted any sympathies for Jansenism. Within about four years of his interment, this tomb was the daily resort of multitudes, who considered it a good place for their extra devotions. It then began to be rumoured that, among such of these individuals as were diseased, miraculous cures took place at the tomb of Paris. The French capital chanced to be then in want of a new sensation. The strange tales of the doings in the cemetery of St Medard came very opportunely. It became a fashionable amusement to go there and witness the revivals of health which took place at the Deacon Paris's tomb. Scores of people afflicted with deep-seated rheumatism, sciatica, and contractions of

the limbs, or with epilepsy and neuralgia, went away professing to have been suddenly and entirely cured in consequence of their devotions at the shrine of this quasi-Protestant saint. The Jesuits were of course scornfully incredulous of miracles wrought at an opposite shop. But nevertheless the cures went on, and all Paris was excited.

In the autumn of 1731, the phenomena began to put on an even more striking shape. The votaries, when laid on the deacon's tomb, which was one slightly raised above the ground, began to experience strange convulsive movements, accompanied by dreadful pains, but always ending in cure. Some of them would be suddenly shot up several feet into the air, as by some explosive force applied below. Demonstrations of eloquence beyond the natural acquirements of the individual, knowledge of things beyond the natural scope of the faculties, powers of physical endurance above what seem to belong to human nature—in short, many of the phenomena alleged to happen in our own time under the influence of mesmerism—began to be exhibited by the *convulsionaires*. The scenes then daily presented in the St Medard churchyard became a scandal too great to be endured by the opponents of the Jansenists, and a royal decree was issued, shutting up the place except for its ordinary business of receiving the bodies of the dead. As the Parisian epigram went—for on what subject will not the gay ones of such a city make jokes ?—

' De par le roi, defense à Dieu
  De faire miracle en ce lieu.'

This prohibition, however, was only attended with the effect of shifting the scenes of the alleged miracles. The *convulsionaires* continued to meet in private, and it was found that a few particles of earth from the grave of Paris sufficed to produce all the usual phenomena. For years there continued to be assemblages of people who, under the professed influence of the deacon's miraculous power, could sustain enormous weights on their bellies, and undergo other tortures, such as human beings usually shrink from with terror. The Jesuits, unable to deny the facts, or account for them on natural grounds, could only attribute them to the devil and other evil spirits.

A gentleman of the name of Montgeron, originally sceptical, afterwards made a believer, employed himself for many years in collecting fully certified proofs of the St Medard cures and other phenomena. He published three large volumes of these evidences, forming one of the most curious books in existence ; bearing with patience several imprisonments in the Bastile as the punishment of his interference. There is no doubt of the sincerity of Montgeron. It cannot be disputed that few of the events of history are nearly so well evidenced as the convulsionaire phenomena. All that science can now say upon the subject is that the alleged facts are impossible, and therefore the evidence goes for nothing

May Day.

The outbreak into beauty which Nature makes at the end of April and beginning of May excites so joyful and admiring a feeling in the human breast, that there is no wonder the event should have at all times been celebrated in some way. The first emotion is a desire to seize some part of that profusion of flower and blossom which spreads around us, to set it up in decorative fashion, pay it a sort of homage, and let the pleasure it excites find expression in dance and song. A mad happiness goes abroad over the earth, that Nature, long dead and cold, lives and smiles again. Doubtless there is mingled with this, too, in bosoms of any reflection, a grateful sense of the Divine goodness, which makes the promise of seasons so stable and so sure.

Amongst the Romans, the feeling of the time found vent in their Floralia, or Floral Games, which began on the 28th of April, and lasted a few days. Nations taking more or less their origin from Rome have settled upon the 1st of May as the special time for fêtes of the same kind. With ancients and moderns alike it was one instinctive rush to the fields, to revel in the bloom which was newly presented on the meadows and the trees; the more city-pent the population, the more eager apparently the desire to get among the flowers, and bring away samples of them; the more sordidly drudging the life, the more hearty the relish for this one day of communion with things pure and beautiful. Among the barbarous Celtic populations of Europe, there was a heathen festival on the same day, but it does not seem to have been connected with flowers. It was called Beltein, and found expression in the kindling of fires on hill-tops by night. Amongst the peasantry of Ireland, of the Isle of Man, and of the Scottish Highlands, such doings were kept up till within the recollection of living people. We can see no identity of character in the two festivals; but the subject is an obscure one, and we must not speak on this point with too much confidence.

In England we have to go back several generations to find the observances of May-day in their fullest development. In the sixteenth century it was still customary for the middle and humbler classes to go forth at an early hour of the morning, in order to gather flowers and hawthorn branches, which they brought home about sunrise, with accompaniments of horn and tabor, and all possible signs of joy and merriment. With these spoils they would decorate every door and window in the village. By a natural transition of ideas, they gave to the hawthorn bloom the name of the May; they called this ceremony 'the bringing home the May;' they spoke of the expedition to the woods as 'going a-Maying.' The fairest maid of the village was crowned with flowers, as the 'Queen of the May;' the lads and lasses met, danced and sang together, with a freedom which we would fain think of as bespeaking comparative innocence as well as simplicity. In a somewhat earlier age, ladies and gentlemen were accustomed to join in the Maying festivities. Even the king and queen condescended to mingle on this occasion with their subjects. In Chaucer's *Court of Love*, we read that early on May-day 'Forth goeth all the court, both most and least, to fetch the flowers fresh.' And we know, as one illustrative fact, that, in the

reign of Henry VIII. the heads of the corporation of London went out into the high grounds of Kent to gather the May, the king and his queen, Catherine of Aragon, coming from their palace of Greenwich, and meeting these respected dignitaries on Shooter's Hill. Such festal doings we cannot look back upon without a regret that they are no more. They give us the notion that our ancestors, while wanting many advantages which an advanced civilization has given to us, were freer from monotonous drudgeries, and more open to pleasurable impressions from outward nature. They seem somehow to have been more ready than we to allow themselves to be happy, and to have often been merrier upon little than we can be upon much.

The contemporary poets are full of joyous references to the May festivities. How fresh and sparkling is Spenser's description of the going out for the May :

'Siker this morrow, no longer ago,
I saw a shole of shepherds outgo
With singing, and shouting, and jolly cheer;
Before them yode a lusty Tabrere,
That to the many a horn-pipe play'd,
Whereto they dancen each one with his maid.
To see these folks make such jouissance,
Made my heart after the pipe to dance.
Then to the greenwood they speeden them all,
To fetchen home May with their musical :
And home they bring him in a royal throne
Crowned as king; and his queen attone
Was Lady Flora, on whom did attend
A fair flock of fairies, and a fresh bend
Of lovely nymphs—O that I were there
To helpen the ladies their May-bush to bear!
         Shepherd's Calendar, Eclogue 5.

Herrick, of course, could never have overlooked a custom so full of a living poetry. 'Come, my Corinna,' says he,

'——— Come, and coming mark
How each field turns a street, and each street a
    park,
Made green and trimmed with trees : see how
Devotion gives each house a bough
Or branch; each porch, each door, ere this
An ark, a tabernacle is
Made up of white-thorn neatly interwove.

'A deal of youth ere this is come
Back, and with white-thorn laden home.
Some have dispatched their cakes and cream,
Before that we have left to dream.'

Not content with a garlanding of their brows, of their doors and windows, these merry people of the old days had in every town, or considerable district of a town, and in every village, a fixed pole, as high as the mast of a vessel of a hundred tons, on which each May morning they suspended wreaths of flowers, and round which they danced in rings pretty nearly the whole day. The May-pole, as it was called, had its place equally with the parish church or the parish stocks; or, if anywhere one was wanting, the people selected a suitable tree, fashioned it, brought it in triumphantly, and erected it in the proper place, there from year to year to remain. The Puritans—those most respectable people, always so unpleasantly shown as the enemies of mirth and good humour—caused May-poles to be uprooted, and a stop put to all their jollities ; but after the Restoration they were everywhere re-erected, and the appropriate rites re-commenced. Now, alas ! in the course of the mere gradual change of manners, the May-pole

RAISING OF THE MAY-POLE.

has again vanished. They must now be pretty old people who remember ever seeing one. Washington Irving, who visited England early in this century, records in his *Bracebridge Hall*, that he had seen *one*. ' I shall never,' he says, ' forget the delight I felt on first seeing a May-pole. It was on the banks of the Dee, close by the picturesque old bridge that stretches across the river from the quaint little city of Chester. I had already been carried back into former days by the anti-quities of that venerable place, the examination of which is equal to turning over the pages of a black-letter volume, or gazing on the pictures in Froissart. The May-pole on the margin of that poetic stream completed the illusion. My fancy adorned it with wreaths of flowers, and peopled the green bank with all the dancing revelry of May-day. The mere sight of this May-pole gave a glow to my feelings, and spread a charm over the country for the rest of the day ; and as I traversed a part of the fair plains of Cheshire, and the beautiful borders of Wales, and looked from among swelling hills down a long green valley, through which " the Deva wound its wizard stream," my imagination turned all into a perfect Arcadia. I value every custom that tends to infuse poetical feeling into the common people, and to sweeten and soften the rudeness of rustic manners, without destroying their simplicity.

Indeed, it is to the decline of this happy sim-plicity that the decline of this custom may be traced ; and the rural dance on the green, and the homely May-day pageant, have gradually disappeared, in proportion as the peasantry have become expensive and artificial in their pleasures, and too knowing for simple enjoyment. Some attempts, indeed, have been made of late years by men of both taste and learning to rally back the popular feeling to these standards of primi-tive simplicity ; but the time has gone by—the feeling has become chilled by habits of gain and traffic — the country apes the manners and amusements of the town, and little is heard of May-day at present, except from the lamentations of authors, who sigh after it from among the brick walls of the city.'

The custom of having a Queen of the May, or May Queen, looks like a relic of the heathen celebration of the day : this flower-crowned maid appears as a living representative of the goddess Flora, whom the Romans worshipped on this day. Be it observed, the May Queen did not join in the revelries of her subjects. She was placed in a sort of bower or arbour, near the May-pole, there to sit in pretty state, an object of admiration to the whole village. She herself was half covered with flowers, and her shrine was wholly composed of them. It must have

572

been rather a dull office, but doubtless to the female heart had its compensations. In our country, the enthronization of the May Queen has been longer obsolete than even the May-pole; but it will be found that the custom still survives in France. The only relic of the custom now surviving is to be found among the children of a few out-lying places, who, on May-day, go about with a finely-dressed doll, which they call *the Lady of the May*, and with a few small semblances of May-poles, modestly pre-senting these objects to the gentlefolks they

CHILDREN'S MAY-DAY CUSTOMS.

meet, as a claim for halfpence, to be employed in purchasing sweetmeats. Our artist has given a very pretty picture of this infantine represen-tation of the ancient festival.

In London there are, and have long been, a few forms of May-day festivity in a great measure peculiar. The day is still marked by a celebration, well known to every resident in the metropolis, in which the chimney-sweeps play the sole part. What we usually see is a small band, composed of two or three men in fantastic dresses, one smartly dressed female glittering with spangles, and a strange figure called Jack-in-the-green, being a man concealed within a tall frame of herbs and flowers, decorated with a flag at top. All of these figures or persons stop here and there in the course of their rounds, and dance to the music of a drum and fife, expecting of course to be remunerated by halfpence from the onlookers. It is now generally a rather poor show, and does not attract much regard; but many persons who have a love for old sports and day-observances, can never see the little troop without a feeling of interest, or allow it to pass without a silver remembrance. How this black profession should have been the last sus-tainers of the old rites of May-day in the metropolis does not appear.

At no very remote time—certainly within the present century—there was a somewhat similar demonstration from the milk-maids. In the course of the morning the eyes of the house-holders would be greeted with the sight of a milch-cow, all garlanded with flowers, led along by a small group of dairy-women, who, in light and fantastic dresses, and with heads wreathed in flowers, would dance around the animal to the sound of a violin or clarinet. At an earlier time, there was a curious addition to this choral troop, in the form of a man bearing a frame which covered the whole upper half of his person, on which were hung a cluster of silver flagons and dishes, each set in a bed of flowers. With this extraordinary burden, the legs, which alone were seen, would join in the dance,—rather clumsily, as might be expected, but much to the mirth of the spectators,—while the strange pile above floated and flaunted about with an air of heavy decorum, that added not a little to the general amusement. We are introduced to the prose of this old custom, when we are informed that the silver articles were regularly lent out for the purpose at so much an hour by pawn-brokers, and that one set would serve for a succession of groups of milk-maids during the day. In Vauxhall, there used to be a picture representing the May-day dance of the London milk-maids: from an engraving of it the accompanying cut is taken. It will be observed that the scene includes one or two chimney-sweeps as side figures.

In Scotland there are few relics of the old

MILK-MAIDS' DANCE ON MAY-DAY.

May-day observances—we might rather say none. beyond a lingering propensity in the young of the female sex to go out at an early hour, and wash their faces with dew. At Edinburgh this custom is kept up with considerable vigour, the favourite scene of the lavation being Arthur's Seat. On a fine May morning, the appearance of so many gay groups perambulating the hill sides and the intermediate valleys, searching for dew, and rousing the echoes with their harmless mirth, has an indescribably cheerful effect.

The fond imaginings which we entertain regarding the 1st of May—alas! so often disappointed—are beautifully embodied in a short Latin lyric of George Buchanan, which the late Archdeacon Wrangham thus rendered in English:

THE FIRST OF MAY.

' Hail! sacred thou to sacred joy,
    To mirth and wine, sweet first of May!
To sports, which no grave cares alloy,
    The sprightly dance, the festive play!

Hail! thou of ever circling time,
    That gracest still the ceaseless flow !
Bright blossom of the season's prime
    Age, hastening on to winter's snow!

When first young Spring his angel face
    On earth unveiled, and years of gold
Gilt with pure ray man's guileless race,
    By law's stern terrors uncontrolled :

Such was the soft and genial breeze,
    Mild Zephyr breathed on all around ;
With grateful glee, to airs like these
    Yielded its wealth th' unlaboured ground.

So fresh, so fragrant is the gale,
    Which o'er the islands of the blest
Sweeps ; where nor aches the limbs assail,
    Nor age's peevish pains infest.

Where thy hushed groves, Elysium, sleep,
    Such winds with whispered murmurs blow ;
So where dull Lethe's waters creep,
    They heave, scarce heave the cypress-bough.

And such when heaven, with penal flame,
    Shall purge the globe, that golden day
Restoring, o'er man's brightened frame
    Haply such gale again shall play.

Hail, thou, the fleet year's pride and prime!
    Hail ! day which Fame should bid to bloom !
Hail ! image of primeval time!
    Hail ! sample of a world to come !

May-poles—English and foreign.

One of the London parishes takes its distinctive name from the May-pole which in olden times overtopped its steeple. The parish is that of St Andrew *Undershaft*, and its May-pole is celebrated by the father of English poetry, Geoffry Chaucer, who speaks of an empty braggart :—

' Right well aloft, and high ye beare your head,
    As ye would beare the great shaft of Cornhill.'

Stow, who is buried in this church, tells us that in his time the shaft was set up ' every year, on May-day in the morning,' by the exulting Londoners, ' in the midst of the street before the south door of the said church; which shaft, when it was set on end, and fixed in the ground, was higher than the church steeple.' During the rest of the year this pole was hung upon iron hooks above the doors of the neighbouring houses, and immediately beneath the projecting penthouses which kept the rain from their doors. It was destroyed in a fit of Puritanism in the third year of Edward VI., after a sermon preached at St Paul's Cross against May games, when the inhabitants of these houses 'sawed it in pieces, everie man taking for his share as much as had layne over his doore and stall, the length of his house, and they of the alley divided amongst them so much as had lain over their alley gate.'

The earliest representation of an English May-pole is that published in the *variorum* Shak-speare, and depicted on a window at Betley, in Staffordshire, then the property of Mr Tollett,

and which he was disposed to think as old as the time of Henry VIII. The pole is planted in a mound of earth, and has affixed to it St George's red-cross banner, and a white pennon or streamer with a forked end. The shaft of the pole is painted in a diagonal line of black colour, upon a yellow ground, a characteristic decoration of all these ancient May-poles, as alluded to by Shak-speare in his *Midsummer Night's Dream*, where it gives point to Hermia's allusion to her rival Helena as a 'painted May-pole.' The fifth volume of Halliwell's folio edition of Shakspeare has a curious coloured frontispiece of a May-pole, painted in continuous vertical stripes of white, red, and blue, which stands in the centre of the village of Welford, in Gloucestershire, about five miles from Stratford-on-Avon. It may be an exact copy and legitimate successor of one standing there in the days when the bard himself visited the village. It is of great height, and is planted in the centre of a raised mound, to which there is an ascent by three stone steps: on this mound

probably the dancers performed their gyrations. Stubbes, in his *Anatomie of Abuses*, 1584, speaks of May-poles 'covered all over with flowers and hearbes, bounde rounde aboute with stringes, from the top to the bottom, and some tyme painted with variable colours.' The London citizen, Machyn, in his Diary, 1552, tells of one brought at that time into the parish of Fenchurch; 'a goodly May-pole as you have seene; it was painted whyte and green.'

In the illuminations which decorate the manu-script 'Hours' once used by Anne of Brittany and now preserved in the Bibliothèque Royale at Paris, and which are believed to have been painted about 1499, the month of May is illus-trated by figures bearing flower-garlands, and behind them the curious May-pole here copied,

which is also decorated by colours on the shaft, and ornamented by garlands arranged on hoops, from which hang small gilded pendents. The pole is planted on a triple grass-covered mound, em-banked and strengthened by timber-work.

That this custom of painting and decorating the May-pole was very general until a com-paratively recent period, is easy of proof. A Dutch picture, bearing date 1625, furnishes our third specimen (*see next page*); here the pole is surmounted by a flower-pot containing a tree, stuck all round with gaily-coloured flags; three hoops with garlands are suspended below it, from which hang gilded balls, after the fashion of the pendent decorations of the older French example. The shaft of the pole is painted white and blue.

London boasted several May-poles before the days of Puritanism. Many parishes vied with each other in the height and adornment of their own. One famed pole stood in Basing-lane, near St Paul's Cathedral, and was in the time of Stow kept in the hostelry called Gerard's Hall. 'In the high-roofed hall of this house,' says he, 'sometime stood a large fir pole, which reached

to the roof thereof,—a pole of forty feet long, and fifteen inches about, fabled to be the justing staff of Gerard the Giant.' A carved wooden figure of this giant, pole in hand, stood over the gate of this old inn, until March 1852, when the whole building was demolished for city improvements.

The most renowned London May-pole, and the latest in existence, was that erected in the Strand, immediately after the Restoration. Its history is altogether curious. The Parliament of 1644 had ordained that 'all and singular May-poles that are or shall be erected, shall be taken down,' and had enforced their decree by penalties that effectually carried out their gloomy desires. When the populace gave again vent to their May-day jollity in 1661, they determined on planting the tallest of these poles in the most conspicuous part of the Strand, bringing it in triumph, with drums beating, flags flying, and music playing, from Scotland Yard to the opening of Little Drury Lane, opposite Somerset House, where it was erected, and which lane was after termed 'May-pole Alley' in consequence. 'That stately cedar erected in the Strand, 134 feet high,' as it is glowingly termed by a contemporary author, was considered as a type of 'golden days' about to return with the Stuarts. It was raised by seamen, expressly sent for the purpose by the Duke of York, and decorated with three gilt crowns and other enrichments. It is frequently alluded to by authors. Pope wrote—

'Where the tall May-pole once o'erlooked the Strand.'

Our cut, exhibiting its features a short while before its demolition, is a portion of a long print by Vertue representing the procession of the members of both Houses of Parliament to St Paul's Cathedral to render thanks for the Peace of Utrecht, July 7th, 1713. On this occasion the London charity children were ranged on scaffolds, erected on the north side of

the Strand, and the cut represents a portion of one of these scaffolds, terminating at the opening

to Little Drury Lane, and including the pole, which is surmounted by a globe, and has a long streamer floating beneath it. Four years afterwards, this famed pole, having grown old and decayed, was taken down. Sir Isaac Newton arranged for its purchase with the parish, and it

was carried to Wanstead, in Essex, and used as a support to the great telescope (124 feet in length), which had been presented to the Royal Society by the French astronomer, M. Hugon. Its celebrity rendered its memory to be popularly preserved longer than falls to the lot of such relics of old London, and an anonymous author, in the year 1800, humorously asks :—

> 'What's not destroy'd by Time's relentless hand?
> Where's Troy?—and where's the May-pole in the
>   Strand?'

Scattered in some of the more remote English villages are a few of the old May-poles. One still does duty as the supporter of a weathercock in the churchyard at Pendleton, Manchester; others might be cited, serving more ignoble uses than they were originally intended for. The custom of dressing them with May garlands, and dancing around them, has departed from utilitarian England, and the jollity of old country customs given way to the ceaseless labouring monotony of commercial town life. The same thing occurs abroad as at home, except in lonely districts as yet unbroken by railways, and our concluding illustration is derived from such a locality. Between Munich and Salzburg are many quiet villages, each rejoicing in its May-pole; that we have selected for engraving is in the middle of the little village of St Egydien, near Salzburg. It is encircled by garlands, and crowned with a May-bush and flags. Beneath the garlands are figures dressed in the ordinary peasant costume, as if ascending the pole; they are large wooden dolls, dressed in linen and cloth clothing, and nailed by hands and knees to the pole. It is the custom here to place such figures, as well as birds, stags, &c., up the poles. In one instance a stag-hunt is so represented. The pole thus decorated remains to adorn the village green, until a renovation of these decorations takes place on the yearly May festival.

MAY, AS CELEBRATED IN OLD ENGLISH POETRY.

Our mediæval forefathers seem to have cherished a deep admiration for nature in all her forms; they loved the beauty of her flowers, and the song of her birds, and, whenever they could, they made their dwellings among her most picturesque and pleasant scenery. May was their favourite month in the year, not only because it was the time at which all nature seemed to spring into new life, but because a host of superstitions, dating from remote antiquity, were attached to it, and had given rise to many popular festivals and observances. The poets especially loved to dwell on the charms of the month of May. 'In the season of April and May,' says the minstrel who sang the history of the Fitz-Warines, 'when fields and plants become green again, and everything living recovers virtue, beauty, and force, hills and vales resound with the sweet songs of birds, and the hearts of all people, for the beauty of the weather and the season, rise up and gladden themselves.' The month of May is celebrated in the earliest attempts at English lyric poetry (*Wright's Specimens of Lyric Poetry of the Reign of Edward I.,* p. 45), as the season when 'it is pleasant at daybreak,'—

> 'In May hit murgeth when hit dawes;'

and

> 'Blosmes bredeth on the bowes.'
37

The 'Romance of Kyng Alisaunder,' as old, apparently, as the beginning of the fourteenth century, similarly speaks of the pleasantness of May (for it must be kept in mind that the old meaning of the word *merry* was pleasant)—

> 'Mery time it is in May;
> The foules syngeth her lay;
> The knighttes loveth the tornay;
> Maydens so daunceh and thay play.'—(l. 5,210, in
>   Weber.)

And the same poet alludes in another place (l. 2,547) to the melody of the birds—

> 'In tyme of May, the nyghtyngale
> In wode makith miry gale (*pleasant melody*);
> So doth the foules grete and smale,
> Som on hulle, som on dale.'

Much in the same tone is the 'merry' month celebrated in the celebrated 'Romance of the Rose,' which we will quote in the translation made by our own poet Chaucer. After alluding to the pleasure and joy which seemed to pervade all nature, after its recovery from the rigours of winter, now that May had brought in the summer season, the poet goes on to say that—

> '—than bycometh the ground so proude,
> That it wole have a newe shroude,
> And makith so quaynt his robe and faire,
> That it had hewes an hundred payre
> Of gras and flouris, ynde (*blue*) and pers (*grey*),
> And many hewes ful dyvers:
> That is the robe I mene, iwis (*truly*),
> Through which the ground to preisen is.
>   The briddes, that haven lefte her song,
> While thei han suffrid cold so strong
> In wedres gryl and derk to sight,
> Ben in May for the sonne bright
> So glade, that they shewe in syngyng
> That in her hertis is such lykyng (*pleasure*),
> That they mote syngen and be light.
> Than doth the nyghtyngale hir myght
> To make noyse and syngen blythe,
> Than is blisful many sithe (*times*)
> The chelaundre (*goldfinch*) and the papyngay
> Than young folk entenden ay
> For to ben gay and amorous;
> The tyme is than so saverous.
>   Hard is his hart that loveth nought
> In May, whan al this mirth is wrought;
> Whan he may on these braunches here
> The smale briddes syngen clere.'

The whole spirit of the poetry of mediæval England is embodied in the writings of Chaucer, and it is no wonder if we often find him singing the praises of May. The daisy, in Chaucer's estimate, was the prettiest flower in that engaging month—

> 'How have I thanne suche a condicion,
> That of al the floures in the mede
> Thanne love I most these floures white and rede,
> Suche as men callen daysyes in our toune.
> To hem have I so grete affeccioun,
> As I seyde erst, whanne comen is the May,
> That in my bed ther daweth (*dawns*) me no day
> That I nam (*am not*) uppe and walkyng in the mede,
> To seen this floure ayein (*against*) the sunne sprede
> Whan it up-ryseth erly by the morwe;
> That blisful sight softeneth al my sorwe.'
>   *Prologue to Legend of Goode Women.*

Chaucer more than once introduces the feathered minstrels welcoming and worshipping the month of May; as, for an instance, in his 'Court of Love,' where robin redbreast is introduced at the 'lectorn,' chaunting his devotions—

'"Hail now," quoth he, "o fresh sason of May,
Our moneth glad that singeu on the spray!
Hail to the floures, red, and white, and blewe,
Which by their vertue maketh our lust newe!"'

And so again in 'The Cuckow and the Nightingale,' when the poet sought the fields and groves on a May morning—

'There sat I downe among the faire floures,
And sawe the birdes trippe out of hir boures,
There as they rested hem alle the night;
They were so joyful of the dayes light,
They gan of May for to done honoures.'

It is the season which puts in motion people's hearts and spirits, and makes them active with life. 'For,' as we are told in the same poem—

'—every true gentle herte free,
That with him is, or thinketh for to be,
Againe May now shal have some stering (stirring)
Or to joye, or elles to some mourning,
In no season so muche, as thinketh me.
For whan they may here the birdes singe,
And see the floures and the leaves springe,
That bringeth into hertes remembraunce
A manner ease, medled (mixed) with grevaunce,
And lustie thoughtes full of grete longinge.'

May, in fact, was the season which was to last for ever in heaven, according to the idea expressed in the inscription on the gate of Chaucer's happy 'park'—

'Through me men gon into the blisful place
Of hertes, hele and dedly, woundes cure;
Through me men gon into the welle of grace,
There grene and lusty May shal ever endure.'
                    Chaucer's Assembly of Foules.

In the 'Court of Love,' when the birds have concluded their devotional service in honour of the month, they separate to gather flowers and branches, and weave them into garlands—

'Thus sange they alle the service of the feste,
And that was done right early, to my dome (as I
judged);
And forth goeth al the court, both moste and leste,
To feche the floures freshe, and braunche, and
blome;
And namely (especially) hawthorn brought both
page and grome,
With freshe garlandes party blew and white;
And than rejoysen in their grete delight,
Eek eche at other threw the floures bright,
The primerose, the violete, and the gold' (the mari-
gold).

The practice of going into the woods to gather flowers and green boughs, and make them into garlands on May morning, is hardly yet quite obsolete, and it is often mentioned by the other old poets, as well as by Chaucer. At the period when we learn more of the domestic manners of our kings and queens, in the sixteenth and seventeenth centuries, we find even royalty following the same custom, and rambling in the fields and woods at daybreak to fetch home 'the May.' So in Chaucer's 'Knightes Tale,' it was on a May morning that—

'Arcite, that is in the court ryal
With Theseus, his squyer principal,
578

Is risen, and loketh on the mery day.
And for to doon his observance to May,
Remembryng of the poynt of his desire,
He on his courser, stertyng as the fire,
Is riden into feeldes him to pleye,
Out of the court, were it a mile or tweye.
And to the grove, of which that I yow tolde,
By aventure his wey he gan to holde,
To make him a garland of the greves,
Were it of woodewynde or hawthorn leves;
And lowde he song agens the sonne scheene.'

MAY-DAY CAROL.

Some years ago we obtained the following song or carol from the mouths of several parties of little girls in the parish of Debden, in Essex, who on May morning go about from house to house, carrying garlands of different sizes, some large, with a doll dressed in white in the middle, which no doubt represents what was once the Virgin Mary. All who sing it, do so with various readings, or rather with corruptions, and it was only by comparing a certain number of these different versions, that we could make it out as intelligible as it appears in this text:

'I, been a rambling all this night,
And sometime of this day;
And now returning back again,
I brought you a garland gay.

A garland gay I brought you here,
And at your door I stand;
'Tis nothing but a sprout, but 'tis well budded out,
The works of our Lord's hand.

So dear, so dear as Christ lov'd us,
And for our sins was slain,
Christ bids us turn from wickedness,
And turn to the Lord again.'

Sometimes a sort of refrain is sung after each verse, in the following words:

'Why don't you do as we have done,
The very first day of May;
And from my parents I have come,
And would no longer stay.'

This is evidently a very old ballad, dating probably from as far back as the time of Elizabeth, when, according to the puritanical moralists, it was the custom for the youths of both sexes to go into the fields and woods on May eve, and remain out all night, returning early in the morning with green branches and garlands of flowers. The doll representing the Virgin Mary perhaps refers us back to a still older period. The puritans have evidently left their mark upon it, and their influence is still more visible in a longer version of it, preserved in a neighbouring parish, that of Hitchin, in Hertfordshire, which was communicated to Hone's *Every Day Book*, as sung in 1823 by the men in that parish. This also was, we believe, the case a few years ago in Debenham parish, where the girls have only taken it up at a comparatively recent period. The following is the Hitchin version:

'Remember us poor Mayers all,
And thus we do begin
To lead our lives in righteousness,
Or else we die in sin.

We have been rambling all this night,
 And almost all this day,
And now returned back again,
 We have brought you a branch of May.

A branch of May we have brought you,
 And at your door it stands ;
It is but a sprout, but it's well budded out
 By the work of our Lord's hands.

The hedges and trees they are so green,
 As green as any leek,
Our Heavenly Father he watered them
 With heavenly dew so sweet.

The heavenly gates are open wide,
 Our paths are beaten plain,
And, if a man be not too far gone,
 He may return again.

The life of man is but a span,
 It flourishes like a flower ;
We are here to-day, and gone to-morrow,
 And we are dead in one hour.

The moon shines bright, and the stars give a light,
 A little before it is day ;
So God bless you all, both great and small,
 And send you a joyful May !'

The same song is sung in some other parishes in the neighbourhood of Debenham, with further variations, which show us, in a curious and interesting manner, the changes which such popular records undergo in passing from one generation to another. At Thaxted, the girls wave branches before the doors of the inhabitants, but they seem to have forgotten the song altogether.

May-day Festivities in France.

In some parts of France, before the Revolution, it was customary to celebrate the arrival of May-day by exhibitions, in which the successors of William of Guienne and Abelard contended for the golden violet. The origin of these miniature Olympics is traced back to the year 1323, when seven persons of rank invited all the troubadours of Provence to assemble at Toulouse the first of May of the year following. Verses were then recited ; and amidst much glee, excitement, and enthusiasm, Arnauld Vidal de Castelraudari, cotemporary with Deguileville and Jean de Meung, bore off the first prize.

Every succeeding year was accompanied by similar competitions, and so profitable did the large concourse of people from the neighbouring countries become to the good burgesses of Toulouse, that at a later period, the ' Jeux Floraux,' as they were called, were conducted at their expense, and the prizes provided by the coffers of the city.

In 1540, Clémence Isaure, a lady of rank, and a patroness of the belles lettres, bequeathed the great bulk of her fortune for the purpose of perpetuating this custom, by providing golden and silver flowers of different design and value as rewards for the successful. It may be imagined with what enthusiasm the French people attended these lively meetings, where the gay sons of the South repeated their glowing praises of love, beauty, and knightly worth, in the soft numbers of the *langue d'oc.*

It may not be uninteresting that, in 1694, 'les Jeux Floraux' were continued by order of the Grand Monarque, when forty members (being the same number as that of the Académie Française) were elected into an academy for the purpose of having the fêtes conducted with more splendour and regularity. The academicians' office was to preside at the feasts, decide who were the victors, and distribute the rewards.

When I was quite a child, I went with my mother to visit her relatives at a small town in the South of France. We arrived about the end of April, when the spring had fully burst forth, with its deep blue sky, its balmy air, its grassy meadows, its flowering hedges and trees already green. One morning I went out with my mother to call upon a friend : when we had taken a few steps, she said :

'To-day is the first of May ; if the customs of my childhood are still preserved here, we shall see some " Mays " on our road.'

' Mays,' I said, repeating a word I heard for the first time, ' what are they ?'

My mother replied by pointing to the opposite side of the place we were crossing :

' Stop, look there,' she said ; ' that is a May.'

Under the gothic arch of an old church porch a narrow step was raised covered with palms. A living being, or a statue—I could not discern at the distance—dressed in a white robe, crowned with flowers, was seated upon it ; in her right hand she held a leafy branch ; a canopy above her head was formed of garlands of box, and ample draperies which fell on each side encircled her in their snowy folds. No doubt the novelty of the sight caused my childish imagination much surprise, my eyes were captivated, and I scarcely listened to my mother, who gave me her ideas on this local custom , ideas, the simple and sweet poetry of which I prefer to accept instead of discussing their original value.

' Because the month of May is the month of spring,' said she, ' the month of flowers, the month consecrated to the Virgin, the young girls of each *quartier* unite to celebrate its return. They choose a pretty child, and dress her as you see ; they seat her on a throne of foliage, they crown her and make her a sort of goddess ; she is May, the Virgin of May, the Virgin of lovely days, flowers, and green branches. See, they beg of the passers-by, saying, " For the May." People give, and their offerings will be used some of these days for a joyous festival.'

When we came near, I recognised in the May a lovely little girl I had played with on the previous day. At a distance I thought she was a statue. Even close at hand the illusion was still possible ; she seemed to me like a goddess on her pedestal, who neither distinguished nor recognised the profane crowd passing beneath her feet. Her only care was to wear a serene aspect under her crown of periwinkle and narcissus, laying her hand on her olive sceptre. She had, it is true, a gracious smile on her lips, a sweet expression in her eyes ; but these, though charming all, did not seem to seek or speak to any in particular ; they served as an adornment to her motionless physiognomy, lending life to the statue, but neither voice nor affections. Was it coquetry in so young a child thus studying to gain admiration? I know not, but to this day I can only think of the enchantment I felt in

contemplating her. An older sister of hers came forward as a collector, saying, 'For the

MAY-QUEEN IN THE SOUTH OF FRANCE.

May.' My mother stopped, and drawing some money from her purse, laid it on the china saucer that was presented; as for myself, I took a handful of sous, all that I could find in my pocket, and gave them with transport; I was too young to appreciate the value of my gift, but I felt the exquisite pleasure of giving.

In passing through the town we met with several other 'Mays,' pretty little girls, perhaps, but not understanding their part; always restless, arranging their veils, touching their crowns, talking, eating sweetmeats, or weary, stiff, half asleep, with an awkward, unpleasing attitude. None was the May, the representative of the joyous season of sweet and lovely flowers, but my first little friend.

[That there was a ceremony resembling this in England long ago has already been mentioned. It is thus adverted to by Browne, in *Britannia's Pastorals*—

'As I have seene the Lady of the May
  Set in an harbour — — —
  Built by the May-pole, where the jocund swains
  Dance with the maidens to the bagpipe's straines,

When envious night commands them to be gone,
Call for the merry yongsters one by one,
And for their well performance some disposes,
To this a garland interwove with roses ;
To that a carved hooke, or well wrought scrip ;
Gracing another with her cherry lip :
To one her garter, to another then
A handkerchiefe cast o're and o're again ;
And none returneth empty, that hath spent
His paynes to fill their rurall merriment.']

Robin Hood Games.

Mingling with the festivities of May-day, there was a distinct set of sports, in great vogue in the fifteenth and sixteenth centuries, meant to represent the adventures of the legendary Robin Hood. They have been described with (it is believed) historical fidelity in Mr Strutt's novel of *Queen Hoo Hall*, where the author has occasion to introduce them as performed by the dependents and servants of an English baron. (We abridge a little in the matter of costume.)

'In the front of the pavilion, a large square was staked out, and fenced with ropes, to prevent the crowd from pressing upon the performers, and interrupting the diversion; there were also two bars at the bottom of the enclosure, through which the actors might pass and repass, as occasion required. Six young men first entered the square, clothed in jerkins of leather, with axes upon their shoulders like woodmen, and their heads bound with large garlands of ivy leaves, intertwined with sprigs of hawthorn. Then followed six young maidens of the village, dressed in blue kirtles, with garlands of primroses on their heads, leading a fine sleek cow decorated with ribbons of various colours interspersed with flowers; and the horns of the animal were tipped with gold. These were succeeded by six foresters equipped in green tunics, with hoods and hosen of the same colour; each of them carried a bugle-horn attached to a baldrick of silk, which he sounded as he passed the barrier. After them came Peter Lanaret, the baron's chief falconer, who personified *Robin Hood;* he was attired in a bright grass-green tunic, fringed with gold; his hood and his hosen were parti-coloured, blue and white; he had a large garland of rosebuds on his head, a bow bent in his hand, a sheaf of arrows at his girdle, and a bugle-horn depending from a baldrick of light blue tarantine, embroidered with silver; he had also a sword and a dagger, the hilts of both being richly embossed with gold. Fabian, a page, as *Little John*, walked at his right hand; and Cecil Cellerman, the butler, as *Will Stukely*, at his left. These, with ten others of the jolly outlaw's attendants who followed, were habited in green garments, bearing their bows bent in their hands, and their arrows in their girdles. Then came two maidens, in orange-coloured kirtles with white courtpies, strewing flowers, followed immediately by the *Maid Marian*, elegantly habited in a watchet-coloured tunic reaching to the ground. She was supported by two bridemaidens, in sky-coloured rochets girt with crimson girdles. After them came four other females in green courtpies, and garlands of violets and cowslips. Then Sampson, the smith, as *Friar Tuck*, carrying a huge quarter-staff on his shoulder; and Morris, the mole-taker, who represented *Much*, the miller's son, having a long pole with an inflated bladder attached to one end. And after them the *May-pole*, drawn by eight fine oxen, decorated with scarfs, ribbons, and flowers of divers colours, and the tips of their horns were embellished with gold. The rear was closed by the hobby-horse and the dragon. When the May-pole was drawn into the square, the foresters sounded their horns, and the populace expressed their pleasure by shouting incessantly until it reached the place assigned for its elevation. During the time the ground was preparing for its reception, the barriers of the bottom of the enclosure were opened for the villagers to approach and adorn it with ribbons, garlands, and flowers, as their inclination prompted them. The pole being sufficiently onerated with finery, the square was cleared from such as had no part to perform in the pageant, and then it was elevated amidst the reiterated acclamations of the spectators. The *woodmen* and the *milkmaidens* danced around it according to the rustic fashion; the measure was played by Peretto

Cheveritte, the baron's chief minstrel, on the *bagpipes*, accompanied with the pipe and tabor, performed by one of his associates. When the dance was finished, Gregory the jester, who undertook to play the *hobby-horse*, came forward with his appropriate equipment, and frisking up and down the square without restriction, imitated the galloping, curvetting, ambling, trotting, and other paces of a horse, to the infinite satisfaction of the lower classes of the spectators. He was followed by Peter Parker, the baron's ranger, who personated a *dragon*, hissing, yelling, and shaking his wings with wonderful ingenuity; and to complete the mirth, Morris, in the character of *Much*, having small bells attached to his knees and elbows, capered here and there between the two monsters in the form of a dance; and as often as he came near to the sides of the enclosure, he cast slyly a handful of meal into the faces of the gaping rustics, or rapped them about their heads with the bladder tied at the end of his pole. In the meantime, Sampson, representing Friar Tuck, walked with much gravity around the square, and occasionally let fall his heavy staff upon the toes of such of the crowd as he thought were approaching more forward than they ought to do; and if the sufferers cried out from the sense of pain, he addressed them in a solemn tone of voice, advising them to count their beads, say a paternoster or two, and to beware of purgatory. These vagaries were highly palatable to the populace, who announced their delight by repeated plaudits and loud bursts of laughter; for this reason they were continued for a considerable length of time: but Gregory, beginning at last to falter in his paces, ordered the dragon to fall back. The well-nurtured beast, being out of breath, readily obeyed, and their two companions followed their example, which concluded this part of the pastime. Then the *archers* set up a target at the lower part of the green, and made trial of their skill in a regular succession. Robin Hood and Will Stukely excelled their comrades, and both of them lodged an arrow in the centre circle of gold, so near to each other that the difference could not readily be decided, which occasioned them to shoot again, when Robin struck the gold a second time, and Stukely's arrow was affixed upon the edge of it. Robin was therefore adjudged the conqueror; and the prize of honour, a garland of laurel embellished with variegated ribbons, was put upon his head; and to Stukely was given a garland of ivy, because he was the second best performer in that contest. The pageant was finished with the archery, and the procession began to move away to make room for the villagers, who afterwards assembled in the square, and amused themselves by dancing round the May-pole in promiscuous companies, according to the ancient custom.'

In Scotland, the Robin Hood games were enacted with great vivacity at various places, but particularly at Edinburgh; and in connection with them were the sports of the *Abbot of Inobedience*, or *Unreason*, a strange half serious burlesque on some of the ecclesiastical arrangements then prevalent, and also a representation called the *Queen of May*. A well-known historical work* thus describes what took place at these whimsical merry-makings: 'At the approach of May, they (the people) assembled and chose some respectable individuals of their number—very grave and reverend citizens, perhaps—to act the parts of Robin Hood and Little John, of the Lord of Inobedience or the Abbot of Unreason, and "make sports and jocosities" for them. If the chosen actors felt it inconsistent with their tastes, gravity, or engagements, to don a fantastic dress, caper and dance, and incite their neighbours to do the like, they could only be excused on paying a fine. On the appointed day, always a Sunday or holiday, the people assembled in their best attire and in military array, and marched in blithe procession to some neighbouring field, where the fitting preparations had been made for their amusement. Robin Hood and Little John robbed bishops, fought with pinners, and contended in archery among themselves, as they had done in reality two centuries before. The Abbot of Unreason kicked up his heels and played antics, like a modern pantaloon.' Maid Marian also appeared upon the scene, in flower-sprent kirtle, and with bow and arrows in hand, and doubtless slew *hearts* as she had formerly done *harts*. Mingling with the mad scene were the morris-dancers, with their fantastic dresses and jingling bells. So it was until the Reformation, when a sudden stop was put to the whole affair by severe penalties imposed by Act of Parliament.

MAY 2.

St Athanasius, 373.

ST ATHANASIUS.

The life of this holy man presents a long detail of troubles which he underwent as Patriarch of Alexandria, in consequence of his strenuous opposition to the heresies introduced by Arius, and through the injustice of several of the degenerate successors of the Emperor Constantine. It is not necessary in this place to cite the particulars of the story; suffice it, that Athanasius was six times driven from his see, had to take refuge in deserts from the wrath of his enemies, was often placed on trial under false charges, seldom knew any peace during nearly forty years, yet never swerved for a moment from the primitive orthodoxy, and finally died in his charge at Alexandria, with the esteem of all who truly knew him, and has ever since been one of the most venerated fathers of the church. There must have been a vast amount of quiet energy in St Athanasius. He always bore himself meekly; but he never yielded. The creed which bears his name, embodies his view of the mystery of the Trinity, but is believed to have been compiled in the fifth century.

Rogation Days.

The Rogation Days are the Monday, Tuesday, and Wednesday before Holy Thursday, or Ascension Day. It is said that Claudius Mamercus, Bishop of Vienna, about the year 452,

* *Domestic Annals of Scotland*, i. 7.

582

ordered these days to be observed as public fasts, with solemn processions and supplications, on the occasion of some great public calamity. The arrangement, meeting with approbation, was imitated and repeated, till at length it became a law in the Latin Church that they should be observed annually, with processions and supplications, to secure a blessing on the fruits of the earth, and the temporal interests of men. These three days are called *Rogation Days*, the week *Rogation Week*, and the Sunday preceding, *Rogation Sunday*, from the *Rogations* or *Litanies* chanted in the processions. The Church of England, at the Reformation, discontinued the public processions, but ordered these days to be observed as private fasts. There is no special office, or order of prayer, or even a single collect appointed in the prayer-book for the Rogation Days; but in the book of Homilies we find a Homily, divided into three parts, specially designed for the improvement of these three days.

Gange Days.

The Gange Days are the same as the three Rogation Days, and were so called from the ancient custom of perambulating the boundaries of the parish on those days, the name being derived from the Saxon word *gangen*, to go. In Roman Catholic times, this perambulation was a matter of great ceremony, attended with feastings and various superstitious practices. Banners, which the parish was bound to provide, hand-bells, and lights enlivened the procession. At one place the perambulators would stop to feast; and at another assemble round a cross to be edified with some godly admonition, or the legend of some saint or martyr, and so complete the circuit of the parish. When processions were forbidden, the useful part of these perambulations was retained. By the injunctions of Queen Elizabeth it was required that, in order to retain the perambulation of the circuits of parishes, the people should once in the year, at the time accustomed, with the curate and substantial men of the parish, walk about the parishes, as they were accustomed, and at their return to the church make their common prayers. And the curate in these perambulations was at certain convenient places to admonish the people to give thanks to God, as they beheld his benefits, and for the increase and abundance of the fruits upon the face of the earth. The 104th Psalm was appointed to be said on these occasions, and the minister was to inculcate such sentence as, ' *Cursed be he which translateth the bounds and doles of his neighbour.*'

The writer recollects one of these perambulations in his earlier days. The vicar of the parish was there; so were the 'substantial men,' and a goodly number of juveniles too; but the admonitions, the psalm, and the sentences, were certainly not. It was a merry two days' ramble through all sorts of odd places. At one time we entered a house by the door, and left it by a window on the opposite side; at another, men threw off their clothes to cross a canal at a certain point; then we climbed high walls, dived through the thickest part of a wood, and left everywhere in our track the conspicuous capitals, R. P. Buns and beer were served out to those who were lucky enough, or strong enough, to get them. And at one spot a large flat stone was pointed out, which had a hole in the middle; and the oracles of the day assured us that the parson used to have his head thrust into that hole, with his heels uppermost, for refusing to bury a corpse found there.

PAROCHIAL PERAMBULATIONS.

The ancient custom of perambulating parishes in Rogation week had a two-fold object. It was designed to supplicate the Divine blessing on the fruits of the earth; and to preserve in all classes of the community a correct knowledge of, and due respect for, the bounds of parochial and individual property. It appears to have been derived from a still older custom among the ancient Romans, called Terminalia, and Ambarvalia, which were festivals in honour of the god Terminus and the goddess Ceres. On becoming a Christian custom the heathen rites and ceremonies were of course discarded, and those of Christianity substituted. It was appointed to be observed on one of the Rogation days which were the three days next before Ascension Day. These days were so called from having been appropriated in the fifth century by Mamercus, Bishop of Vienna, to special prayer and fasting on account of the frequent earthquakes which had destroyed, or greatly injured vegetation. Before the Reformation parochial perambulations were conducted with great ceremony. The lord of the manor, with a large banner, priests in surplices and with crosses, and other persons with hand-bells, banners and staves, followed by most of the parishioners, walked in procession round the parish, stopping at crosses, forming crosses on the ground, 'saying or singing gospels to the corn,' and allowing 'drinkings and good cheer;'* which was remarkable, as the Rogation days were appointed fasts. From the different practices observed on the occasion the custom received the various names of *processioning, rogationing, perambulating,* and *ganging the boundaries;* and the week in which it was observed was called *Rogation week; Cross week,* because crosses were borne in the processions; and *Grass week,* because the Rogation days being fasts, vegetables formed the chief portion of diet.

At the Reformation, the ceremonies and practices deemed objectionable were abolished, and only 'the useful and harmless part of the custom retained.' Yet its observance was considered so desirable, that a homily was prepared for the occasion; and injunctions were issued requiring that for 'the perambulation of the circuits of parishes, the people should once in the year, at the time accustomed, with the rector, vicar, or curate, and the substantial men of the parish, walk about the parishes, as they were accustomed, and at their return to the church make their common prayer. And the curate, in their said common perambulations, was at certain convenient places to admonish the people to give thanks to God (while beholding of his benefits), and for

the increase and abundance of his fruits upon the face of the earth, with the saying of the 103rd Psalm. At which time also the said minister was required to inculcate these, or such like sentences, Cursed be he which translateth the bounds and doles of his neighbour; or such other order of prayers as should be lawfully appointed.'* In strict accordance with these directions, we find that 'the judicious Richard Hooker,' who is allowed by all parties to be a faithful exemplar of a true English Churchman, duly observed the custom of perambulation. 'He would by no means,' says his biographer, 'omit the customary time of procession, persuading all, both rich and poor, if they desired the preservation of love, and their parish rights and liberties, to accompany him in his perambulation, and most did so; in which perambulation he would usually express more pleasant discourse than at other times, and would then always drop some loving and facetious observations to be remembered against the next year, especially by the boys and young people; still inclining them and all his present parishioners to meekness, and mutual kindnesses, and love; because *love thinks not evil, but covers a multitude of infirmities.*'†

Those engaged in the processions usually had refreshments provided for them at certain parts of the parish, which, from the extent of the circuit of some parishes, was necessary; yet the cost of such refreshment was not to be defrayed by the parish, nor could such refreshment be claimed as a custom from any particular house or family. But small annuities were often bequeathed to provide such refreshments. In the parish of Edgcott, Buckinghamshire, there was about an acre of land, let at £3 a year, called 'Gang Monday Land,' which was left to the parish officers to provide cakes and beer for those who took part in the annual perambulation of the parish. At Clifton Reynes, in the same county, a bequest of land for a similar purpose directs that 'one small loaf, a piece of cheese, and a pint of ale, should be given to every married person, and half a pint of ale to every unmarried person, resident in Clifton, when they walked the parish boundaries in Rogation week.' A certain estate in Husborne Crawley, Bedfordshire, has to pay £4 on Rogation Day, once in seven years, to defray the expense of perambulating, and keeping up the boundaries of the parish.

Although perambulations were not to be at the cost of parishes, yet they were justified in maintaining the ancient circuit, though opposed by the owners of property over which they proceeded. Burns cites an instance in which this case was tried against the parishioners of Rudham, who, in their perambulation, had broken down two gates and a fence; and the court decided in favour of the parishioners, stating: 'parishioners may well justify the going over any man's land in the perambulation, according to their usage, and abate all nuisances in their way.'

This necessity or determination to perambulate along the old track often occasioned curious

* Grindal's *Remains*, pp. 141, 241, and *Note.* Whitgift's Works, iii. 266-7. Tindal's Works, iii. 62, 234 Parker Society's Edition.

* Burn's *Ecclesiastical Law*, vol. iii. 61. Grindal's *Remains*, p. 168.
† *Life of Hooker*, by Izaak Walton. Wordsworth's *Ecclesiastical Biography*, vol. iv. 276.

incidents. If a canal had been cut through the boundary of a parish, it was deemed necessary that some of the parishioners should pass through the water. Where a river formed part of the boundary line, the procession either passed along it in boats, or some of the party stripped and swam along it, or boys were thrown into it at customary places. If a house had been erected on the boundary line, the procession claimed the right to pass through it. A house in Buckinghamshire, still existing, has an oven only passing over the boundary line. It was customary in the perambulations to put a boy into this recess to preserve the integrity of the boundary line.

BEATING THE BOUNDS IN LONDON.

It was considered a good joke by the village lads, who, therefore, became ambitious of the honour, and, as they approached the house, generally settled by lot who should be the hero for the year. On one occasion, as the procession entered the house, they found the mistress just about to bake, and the oven full of blazing fagots. The boys, on seeing the flame issuing from the oven-mouth, exclaimed—'Tom Smith is the boy to go into the oven!' Poor Tom, expecting to be baked alive, uttered a fearful scream, and ran off home as fast as his legs could carry him. Another boy was made to scramble over the roof of the oven, and the boundary right was thus deemed sufficiently maintained. A more ludicrous scene occurred in London about the beginning of the present century. As the procession of churchwardens, parish officers, &c., followed by a concourse of cads, were perambulating the parish of St George's, Hanover-square, they came to the part of a street where a nobleman's coach was standing just across the boundary line. The carriage was empty, waiting for the owner, who was in the opposite house.

The principal churchwarden, therefore, himself a nobleman, desired the coachman to drive out of their way. 'I won't!' said the sturdy coachman; 'my lord told me to wait here, and here I'll wait, till his lordship tells me to move!' The churchwarden coolly opened the carriage door, entered it, passed out through the opposite door, and was followed by the whole procession, cads, sweeps, and scavengers. The last perambulation I witnessed was in 1818, at a small village in Derbyshire. It was of rather a degenerate character. There was no clergyman present, nor anything of a religious nature in the proceedings. The very name *processioning* had been transmuted (and not inaptly) into *possessioning*. The constable, with a few labourers, and a crowd of boys, constituted the procession, if such an irregular company could be so called. An axe, a mattock, and an iron crow, were carried by the labourers, for the purpose of demolishing any building or fence which had been raised without permission on the 'waste ground,' or for which the 'acknowledgment' to the lord of the manor had not been paid. At a small hamlet, rejoicing in the name of 'Wicked Nook,' some unfortunate rustic had unduly built a pig-sty. Poor grunty was turned adrift, and his luckless shed levelled to the ground. A new cottage, or mud hut, not much better than the pig's shed, was allowed to remain, on the cottager's wife proffering the 'acknowledgment.' At various parts of the parish boundaries, two or three of the village boys were 'bumped'—that is, a certain part of the person was swung against a stone wall, a tree, a post, or any other hard object which happened to be near the parish boundary. This, it will scarcely be doubted, was an effectual method of recording the boundaries in the memory of these *battering-rams*, and of those who witnessed this curious mode of registration.

The custom of perambulating parishes continued in some parts of the kingdom to a late period, but the religious portion of it was generally, if not universally, omitted. The custom has, however, of late years been revived in its integrity in many parishes, and certainly such a perambulation among the bounties of creation affords a Christian minister a most favourable opportunity for awakening in his parishioners a due sense of gratitude towards Him who maketh the 'sun to shine, and the rains to descend upon the earth, so that it may bring forth its fruit in due season.'

The Bezant.

On Monday in Rogation week was held, in the town of Shaftesbury or Shaston, in Dorsetshire, a festival called the Bezant, a festival so ancient, that no authentic record of its origin exists.

The Borough of Shaftesbury stands upon the brow of a lofty hill, having an extensive view over the vale of Blackmore. Until lately, from its situation, it was so deficient in water, that its inhabitants were indebted for a supply of this necessary article of life to the little hamlet of Enmore Green, which lies in the valley below. From two or three wells or tanks, situate in the village, the water with which the town was provided was carried up the then precipitous road, on the backs of horses and donkeys, and sold from door to door.

The Bezant was an acknowledgment on the part of the Mayor, Aldermen and Burgesses of the Borough, to the Lord of the Manor of Mitcombe, of which Enmore Green forms a part, for the permission to use this privilege; no charter, or deed, however, exists among their archives, as to the commencement of the custom, neither are there any records of interest connected with its observance, beyond the details of the expenses incurred from year to year.

On the morning of Rogation Monday, the Mayor and Aldermen accompanied by a lord and lady, appointed for the occasion, and by their mace-bearers carrying the Bezant, went in procession to Enmore Green. The lord and lady performed at intervals, as they passed along, a traditional kind of dance, to the sound of violins. The steward of the manor meeting them at the green, the mayor offered for his acceptance, as the representative of his lord, the Bezant, a calf's head uncooked, a gallon of ale, and two penny

loaves, with a pair of gloves edged with gold lace, and gave permission to use the wells, as of old, for another year. The steward, having accepted the gifts, retaining all for his own use, except the Bezant, which he graciously gave back, accorded the privilege, and the ceremony ended. The procession returned as it came, and the day, which was one of universal enjoyment to all classes of the population, was brought to a conclusion, according to the hospitable fashion of our country, in a dinner given by the Corporation to their friends.

The Bezant, which gave its name to the festival, is somewhat difficult to describe. It consisted of a sort of trophy, constructed of ribbons, flowers, and peacock's feathers, fastened to a frame, about four feet high, round which were hung jewels, coins, medals, and other matters of more or less value, lent for the purpose by persons interested in the matter, and many traditions prevailed of the exceeding value to which, in earlier times, it sometimes reached, and of the active part which persons of the highest rank in the neighbourhood took in its annual celebration.*

Latterly, however, the festival sadly degenerated, and in the year 1830, the Town and the Manor passing into the hands of the same proprietor, it ceased altogether, and is now one of those many ancient observances, not without their interest to the antiquary, which are numbered with the past. If this had not happened, however, the necessity for it no longer exists. The ancient Borough is no longer indebted to the lord of the manor for its water, for, through the liberality of the Marquis of Westminster, its present owner, the town is bountifully supplied with the purest water, from an artesian well sunk at his expense.

Born.—William Camden, English historical antiquary, 1551, *London*; William, Earl of Shelburne, first Marquis of Lansdowne, statesman, 1737; Rev. Robert Hall, Baptist preacher, 1764, *Arnsby*; John Galt, novelist, 1779, *Irvine, Ayrshire*; Sir John Malcolm, author of *History of Persia*, &c., 1769.

Died.—Leonardo da Vinci, painter, 1520, *Fontainebleau*; Sir Horace Vere, Lord Tilbury, military commander, 1635, *London*; James Sharpe, Archbishop of St Andrews, assassinated, 1679; Sir George Mackenzie, at one time King's Advocate for Scotland, miscellaneous writer, 1691, *Oxford*; Antoine Yves Goguet, author of a work on the Origin of Laws, 1758; William, Earl of Shelburne, first Marquis of Lansdowne, statesman, 1805; Hester Lynch Salusbury, Madame Piozzi, 1821, *Clifton*; William Beckford, author of *Vathek*, 1844, *Bath*.

WILLIAM BECKFORD.

Mr Beckford succeeded at an early period of life to immense wealth. He possessed great talents, and had cultivated and refined his mind to a singular degree. While still a mere youth, he surprised the world with his striking eastern tale of *Vathek*. The recluse nature of his life, in the indulgence of tastes equally magnificent and capricious, made him the subject of much remark and discussion. It seemed nothing to him

* Bezant being the recognised name of an ancient gold coin, we may presume that the ceremony took its name from such a piece of money being originally rendered to the lord of the manor.—*Ed.*

to take down a palace with which he was dissatisfied, and to build up a new one. The dash of whim which foreigners attribute to the English character, appeared in him to reach the highest point compatible with sanity.

The memoirs of Mr Beckford, published after his death, convey an anecdote, representing his whimsical character as not unsusceptible of having a certain 'method in it,' and that to a very fair purpose.

'I once,' said he, 'shut myself up at Fonthill to be out of the way of a lady—an ungallant thing to any lady on earth but her with whom it occurred. You must well remember the late Duchess of Gordon, as she was the continual talk of the town for her curious mercenary ways, and mode of entrapping men with her brood of daughters. I could have served no other lady so, I hope—I never enjoyed a joke so much. At that time everybody talked of Mr Beckford's enormous wealth—everything about me was exaggerated proportionately. I was in consequence a capital bait for the Duchess—so she thought; I thought very differently. She had been told that even a dog kennel at Fonthill was a palace—my house a Potosi. What more upon earth could be desired by a managing mother for a daughter? I might have been aged and imbecile — no matter, such is fashion's philosophy. I got a hint from town of her intention to surprise me with her hard face at Fonthill —a sight I could gladly dispense with. I resolved to give her a useful lesson. Fonthill was put in order for her reception, with everything I could devise to receive her magnificently—not only to receive her, but to turn the tables upon her for the presumption she had that I was to become the plaything of her purposes. The splendour of her reception must have stimulated her in her object. I designed it should operate in that manner. I knew her aim—she little thought so. My arrangements being made, I ordered my *major-domo* to say, on the Duchess's arrival, that it was unfortunate—everything being arranged for her Grace's reception, Mr Beckford had shut himself up on a sudden, a way he had at times, and that it was more than his place was worth to disturb him, as his master only appeared when he pleased; forbidding interruption, even if the King came to Fonthill. I had just received a large lot of books—nothing could be more opportune. I had them removed to the rooms of which I had taken possession. The Duchess conducted herself with wonderful equanimity, and seemed much surprised and gratified at what she saw, and the mode of her reception—just as I desired she should be, quite on tiptoe to have me for a son-in-law. When she got up in the morning, her first question was, "Do you think Mr Beckford will be visible to-day?"

'"I cannot inform your Grace—Mr Beckford's movements are so very uncertain—it is possible. Would your Grace take an airing in the park—a walk in the gardens?"

'Everything which Fonthill could supply was made the most of, whetting her appetite to her purpose still more. My master of the ceremonies to the Duchess did not know what to make of his master, the Duchess, or his own position. "Perhaps Mr Beckford will be visible to-morrow?" was the Duchess's daily consolation. To-morrow, and to-morrow, and to-morrow, came and went— no Mr Beckford. I read on, determined not to see her. Was it not serving a woman of such a coarse nature quite right?

'She remained seven or eight days, magnificently entertained, and then went away without seeing him. She was very angry, and said of him in her rage things too scandalous to have escaped any woman's lips but her own. Think of such a woman's vengeance—such a woman as the Duchess was, who never suffered anything to stand in the way of her objects!'

MAY 3.

Invention (or discovery) of the Holy Cross.

INVENTION OF THE CROSS.

On this day is commemorated the discovery — through the zeal of the Empress Helena, the mother of Constantine the Great—of the cross on which the Saviour was crucified. The statement usually given is that Helena went to Jerusalem, and there compelled the Jews to bring from their concealment and give up to her this and other crosses, and that its identity was established by a miracle: the body of a dead man was placed on each of the crosses, and when it touched the true one, the dead man immediately came to life. The cross was entrusted to the charge of the bishop of Jerusalem, and soon became an object of pilgrimage, and a source of profit, for small pieces were cut from it and given to the pilgrims, who made liberal offerings. In this manner the whole cross would naturally have been soon used up; but such a result was averted: it was found that the wood of the cross possessed the power of reproducing itself, and that, how much soever was cut off, the substance was not diminished. On the capture of Jerusalem, in 614, the true cross is said to have been carried into Persia, where it remained a few years, until it was recovered by the conquests of Heraclius, who carried it into Jerusalem on his back, in solemn procession: an event which is commemorated in the Roman Catholic church by the festival of the exaltation of the cross on the 14th of September, commonly called Holyrood-day. When the Empress Helena discovered the cross, she also obtained possession of the four nails with which Christ's body was attached to it, the spear which pierced his side, and other articles. Of the four nails, two were placed in the imperial crown, one was at a later period brought by Charlemagne to France, and a fourth was thrown into the Adriatic to calm the waters of that stormy sea.

The history of these and of the other numerous relics worshipped by the Roman Catholics, forms a curious picture of mediæval belief. The reformer Calvin published a book on the subject at a time when relic worship was at its height, which was translated into English by Stephen Wythers, in a quaint little black-letter volume, entitled 'A very profitable Treatise, made by M

Jhon Calvyne, declarynge what great profit might come to al Christendome, yf there were a regester made of all Sainctes' Bodies, and other Reliques,' printed in 1561. Calvin declares that so great a quantity of fragments of the true cross were scattered among the Christian churches in his time, that they would load a large ship; and that, whereas the original cross could be carried by one man, it would take three hundred men to support the weight of the existing fragments of it. The largest pieces of it were then preserved in the Sainte Chapelle, at Paris; at Poictiers; and at Rome. Calvin gives a list of the numerous relics connected with Christ's personal history which were preserved in his time, of which the following are a few examples:—The manger in which he was laid was preserved in the church of Sancta Maria Maggiore, at Rome; the cloth in which he was wrapped when born, in the church of St Paul, at Rome, and at San Salvador, in Spain; his cradle (!) and the shirt made for him by his mother, at Rome.

Following the events of the Saviour's life on earth, we find the jugs which held the water he turned into wine at the marriage at Cana, in considerable numbers, at Pisa, at Ravenna, Cluny, Angers, San Salvador, &c., and some of the wine into which the water was turned was preserved at Orleans; the table on which the last supper was served was shown in the church of St John Lateran; some of the bread he ate on that occasion, at San Salvador; the knife with which the paschal lamb was cut, at Treves; the cup in which he administered the wine, in a church near Lyons, as well as in an Augustine abbey in the district of the Albigeois; the platter on which the paschal lamb was placed, in three places; the towel with which he wiped the apostles' feet, at Rome, and at Aix; the palmbranch which he held in his hand when he entered Jerusalem, at San Salvador; a portion of the earth on which he stood when he raised Lazarus, in another church; and, in another, a portion of a fish which St. Peter caught, broiled, and offered to Jesus. In relation to the passion, the fragments of the cross, as already observed, were innumerable; and the nails were very numerous—one is still shown at Cologne; the spear with which his side was pierced had been greatly multiplied, for it is known to have been preserved in seven different places, among which were Rome, and the Sainte Chapelle, in Paris; in the latter locality was preserved the largest portion of the crown of thorns, fragments of which, however, were largely scattered, and many abbeys and churches were glad to boast of a single thorn; the seamless garment was shown at Treves, at Argenteuil, and at other places; and the dice with which the soldiers played for it, at Treves, and at San Salvador. Some of Christ's blood was shown in several places; and the celebrated French printer and reformer, Henry Stephens, mentions as shown in his time (the middle of the sixteenth century), in one church in France, a phial of glass containing some of Christ's tears, and in another church one full of his breath! His shoes were preserved at Rome. Hardly less numerous were the relics connected with the Virgin Mary. The slippers

of her husband, St Joseph, were preserved at Treves; one of Mary's shifts was shown at Aixla-Chapelle; many of her clothes were shown in different places; one of her combs was exhibited at Rome, and another at Besançon; and they showed her wedding ring (!) at Perugia; but the most popular relic of the Virgin Mary was her milk, portions of which were shown in almost as many places as fragments of the true cross. There were not a few samples of it in England. We might fill many pages with the often ridiculous relics of the innumerable saints of the Romish calendar. Some of the stones with which St Stephen was stoned were shown at Florence, at Arles, and at Vigaud, in Languedoc. The Augustine monks at Poitiers worshipped one of the arrows with which St Sebastian was slain, or at least made other people worship it; and there was another at Lambesc, in Provence. St Sebastian had become multiplied in a very extraordinary manner, for his body was found in four places, and his head in two others, quite independent of his body; while the grey friars at Angers exhibited his brains, which, when the case was broken up in the religious wars, were found to have been turned into a stone. St Philip appears to have had three feet—at least, a foot of St Philip's was found in three several places. Materialism in religion was carried to such a point, that the celebrated monastery of Mont St Michael, in Normandy, exhibited the sword and buckler with which the archangel Michael combated the spirit of evil, and we believe they were preserved there till the period of the great French Revolution; and one of the relic-mongers of earlier times is said to have exhibited a feather of the Holy Ghost—supposing, no doubt, from the pictorial representations, that the sacred spirit was a real pigeon.

The multiplicity of the same object seems sometimes to have embarrassed the exhibitors of relics. There is an old story of a rather sceptical visitor of sacred places in France, in the earlier part of the sixteenth century, to whom in a certain monastery the skull of John the Baptist was shown, on which he remarked, with some surprise, 'Ah! the monks of such a monastery showed me the skull of John the Baptist yesterday.' 'True,' said the monastic exhibitor, not disconcerted, 'but those monks only possess the skull of the saint when he was a young man, and ours was his skull when he was advanced in years and wisdom.' All the clergy, however, did not possess this peculiar style of ingenuity; but some labour was bestowed in sustaining the earlier doctrine, much enlarged in its application, that *all* holy relics possessed the miraculous power of multiplying themselves.

Born.—Nicolas Machiavelli, statesman and political writer, 1469, *Florence*; Dean Humphry Prideaux, theological writer, 1648, *Padstow*; William Windham, English statesman, 1750, *London*; Augustus Frederick Kotzebue, German poet, 1761, *Weimar.*

Died.—Dr Isaac Dorislaus, assassinated, 1649; Pope Benedict XIV., 1758; George Psalmanazar, miscellaneous writer, 1763; James Morison, hygeist, 1840; Thomas Hood, poet, 1845, *London.*

MACHIAVELLI.

What an unenviable immortality is that of Nicolas Machiavelli! Out of his surname has been coined a synonyme for treacherous craft; and some antiquaries hold with Butler, in *Hudibras*, that—' Nick Machiavel . . . gave his name to our Old Nick.' But like many other high coloured, popular beliefs, that of Machiavelli's unmitigated diabolism does not endure critical scrutiny.

Machiavelli was born in Florence, in 1469, of an ancient, but not wealthy family. He received a liberal education, and in his 29th year he was appointed secretary to the Ten, or committee of foreign affairs for the Florentine Republic. His abilities and penetration they quickly discerned, and despatched him from time to time on various and arduous diplomatic missions to the courts and camps of doubtful allies and often enemies. The Florentines were rich and weak, and the envy of the poor and strong; and to save themselves from sack and ruin, they had to trim adroitly between France, Spain, Germany, and neighbouring Italian powers. Machiavelli proved an admirable instrument in such difficult business; and his despatches to Florence, describing his own tactics and those of his opponents, are often as fascinating as a romance, while furnishing authentic pictures of the remorseless cruelty and deceit of the statesmen of his age.

In 1512 the brothers Giuliano and Giovanni de' Medici, with the help of Spanish soldiers, re-entered Florence, from which their family had been expelled in 1494, overthrew the government, and seized the reins of power. Machiavelli lost his place, and was shortly after thrown into prison, and tortured, on the charge of conspiring against the new *régime*. In the meanwhile Giovanni was elected Pope by the name of Leo X.; and knowing the Medicean love of literature, Machiavelli addressed a sonnet from his dungeon to Giuliano, half sad, half humorous, relating his sufferings, his torture, his annoyance in hearing the screams of the other prisoners, and the threats he had of being hanged. In the end a pardon was sent from Rome by Leo X., to all concerned in the plot, but not until two of Machiavelli's comrades had been executed.

Machiavelli now retired for several years to his country-house at San Casciano, about eight miles from Florence, and spent his days in literary pursuits. His exile from public life was not willing, and he longed to be useful to the Medici. Writing to his friend Vettori at Rome, 10th December, 1513, he says, ' I wish that these Signori Medici would employ me, were it only in rolling a stone. They ought not to doubt my fidelity. My poverty is a testimony to it.' In order to prove to them ' that he had not spent the fifteen years in which he had studied the art of government in sleeping or playing,' he commenced writing *The Prince*, the book which has clothed his name with obloquy. It was not written for publication, but for the private study of the Medici, to commend himself to them by proving how thoroughly he was master of the art and craft of Italian statesmanship.

About 1519 the Medici received him into favour, and drew him out of his obscurity. Leo X. employed him to draw up a new constitution for Florence, and his eminent diplomatic skill was brought into play in a variety of missions. Returning to Florence, after having acted as spy on the Emperor Charles Fifth's movements during his descent upon Italy, he took ill, and doctoring himself, grew worse, and died on the 22nd of June, 1527, aged fifty-eight. He left five children, with little or no fortune. He was buried in the church of Santa Croce, where, in 1787, Earl Cowper erected a monument to his memory.

The Prince was not published until 1532, five years after Machiavelli's death, when it was printed at Rome with the sanction of Pope Clement VII.; but some years later the Council of Trent pronounced it ' an accursed book.' *The Prince* is a code of policy for one who rules in a State where he has many enemies; the case, for instance, of the Medici in Florence. In its elaboration, Machiavelli makes no account of morality, probably unconscious of the principles and scruples we designate by that name, and displays a deep and subtle acquaintance with human nature. He advises a sovereign to make himself feared, but not hated; and in cases of treason to punish with death rather than confiscation, ' for men will sooner forget the execution of their father than the loss of their patrimony.' There are two ways of ruling, one by the laws and the other by force: ' the first is for men, the second for beasts;' but as the first is not always sufficient, one must resort at times to the other, ' and adopt the ways of the lion and the fox.' The chapter in which he discusses, ' in what manner ought a prince to keep faith?' has been most severely condemned. He begins by observing, that everybody knows how praiseworthy it is for a prince to keep his faith, and practise no deceit; but yet, he adds, we have seen in our own day how princes have prospered who have broken their faith, and artfully deceived their rivals. If all men were good, faith need never be broken; but as they are bad, and will cheat you, there is nothing left but to cheat them when necessary. He then cites the example of Pope Alexander VI. as one who took in everybody by his promises, and broke them without hesitation when he thought they interfered with his ends.

It can hardly excite wonder, that a manual of statesmanship written in such a strain should have excited horror and indignation throughout Europe. Different theories have been put forth concerning *The Prince* by writers to whom the open profession of such deceitful tactics has seemed incredible. Some have imagined, that Machiavelli must have been writing in irony, or with the purpose of rendering the Medici hateful, or of luring them to destruction. The simpler view is the true one: namely, that he wrote *The Prince* to prove to the Medici what a capable man was resting idly at their service. In holding this opinion, we must not think of Machiavelli as a sinner above others. He did no more than transcribe the practice of the ablest statesmen of his time into luminous and forcible language. Our feelings of repugnance at his teaching would have been incomprehensible, idiotic, or laughable to them. If they saw any fault in Machiavelli's book, it would be in its free exposure of the secrets of statecraft. Unquestionably, much of the odium which gathered round the name of Machiavelli arose from that cause. His posthumous treatise was conveniently denounced for its immorality by men whose true aversion to it sprang from its exposure of their arts. The Italians, refined and defenceless in the midst of barbarian covetousness and power, had many plausible excuses for Machiavellian policy; but every reader of history knows, that Spanish, German, French, and English statesmen never hesitated to act out the maxims of *The Prince* when occasion seemed expedient. If Machiavelli differed from his contemporaries, it was for the better. Throughout *The Prince* there flows a hearty and enlightened zeal for civilization, and a patriotic interest in the welfare of Italy. He was clearly a man of benevolent and honourable aims, but without any adequate idea of the wrongfulness of compassing the best ends by evil means. The great truth, which our own age is only beginning to incorporate into statesmanship, that there is no policy, in the long run, like honesty, was far beyond the range of vision of the rulers and diplomatists of the 15th and 16th centuries.

Machiavelli was a writer of singularly nervous and concise Italian. As a dramatist he takes high rank. His comedy of *Mandragola* is spoken of by Lord Macaulay as superior to the best of Goldoni, and inferior only to the best of Molière. It was performed at Florence with great success; and Leo X. admired it so much, that he had it played before him at Rome. He also wrote a *History of Florence*, which is a lively and graphic narrative, and an *Art of War*, which won the praise of so competent a judge as Frederick the Great of Prussia. These and other of his works form eight and ten volumes octavo in the collected editions.

AUGUSTUS FREDERICK KOTZEBUE.

Kotzebue, as a dramatic author, stands in some such relation to Schiller, the first master of the tragic art in his own country, as that in which our own Beaumont and Fletcher stand to Shakspeare. He had great fertility of invention, and the number of plays, on all subjects, which he favoured the world with, was in itself a marvel. He possessed considerable skill in producing tragic effects; but these were rather the results of exaggeration and sickly sentimentalism, of exhibiting things and events extraordinary and revolting, than of genuine human catastrophes, replete with fine passion, with high-souled interests, and happy exhibition of character. Hence that opposition between Kotzebue on the one hand, and Schiller and Goethe on the other, during the short time when all three together were doing their utmost at Weimar.

Nothing can convey a better idea of the sort of exaggeration which is chargeable upon Kotzebue, than an extract from an *autobiography* of the first fifty years of his life, which he published at Vienna in 1811; 'Come forth, ye magic images of my happy childhood. The recollection of you is scarcely connected with my present self. Come forth, ye lovely shadows, and delude my fancy; ascend like a thin vapour from the ocean of the past, and let those sweet hours float once again before my eyes. I stand as on the brink of the stream of time, watching the current as it bears away my flowers; I see them already yonder on the summit of a wave, about to be ingulfed and to disappear for ever. Let me catch that last glimmer. Do you see that boy who hangs with fixed eyes upon his mother's lips, while on a winter's evening she is reading some good book to him and to his sister? Such wast thou! See him again, making a table of his stool, and a seat of his foot-stool, while he is devouring a beloved romance, and leaves his ball and hobby-horse neglected in a corner. Such wast thou!'

Yes, so it seems, such was Kotzebue, even at fifty years old. But his life, if we can read it aright through such a haze, was eventful and full of interest.

He was born at Weimar, May 3, 1761. He proved a precocious child—precocious alike for sensibility and the gifts of an author. Unfortunately for him, and perhaps for the world, he had only a mother to direct him. He studied *Don Quixote* and *Robinson Crusoe*, and at the age of seven proposed to his future aunt in a letter. He stood three hours with a friend, in the snow and cold, outside the house of a sick girl, watching the window-blind, and burst into tears to see the shadow of a spoon administering physic. At this time, also, he wrote a comedy of one page in length—subject, *The Milkmaid and the Two Huntsmen*, which, the reader will surmise, was never printed. He describes himself as stealing under the stage of the theatre at Weimar, and hiding behind the drum, when he could not obtain admittance in the regular way; and he made himself a little wooden theatre, and pushed his figures hither and thither with wires, blowing *semen lycopodii* through a quill into a candle to produce lightning.

And so the child was father of the man. This taste for dramatic writing, and for setting up little theatres wherever he went, grew upon him; and when he was a student of the Jena Academy, in 1779, his first tragedy was acted in the private theatre. 'I succeeded,' he relates, 'in persuading our company to perform my drama, and Wolf, the deceased chapel-master, was so obliging as to compose a very fine *adagio* for it. This was played while the hero of the piece was at his prayers, and was by far the best thing in the whole performance. I myself personated the prince; but, alas! when at last I ought to have been shot, the pistol missed fire. Against this emergency, however, my murderer was prepared, as he had armed himself also with a dagger; but I was so eager to die, *that I fell at sight of the pistol*, before I had time to perceive the disaster. The hero, however, threw himself upon my prematurely dead body, and, equally resolved to kill as I was to die, gave me several desperate stabs with the dagger. The curtain dropped, *and the audience was very sparing of their applause.*'

When about nineteen, Kotzebue returned to

Weimar, and was admitted an advocate, but digressed continually to more congenial pursuits than those of the law. At length, in 1781, unforeseen good fortune placed him high in the world. Frederick William Von Bawr, who, after leading an active military life for some years, had entered the service of Catharine of Russia, in 1769, and risen to eminence, gave Kotzebue his unbounded patronage; and though the general died two years after the poet's arrival at St Petersburg, he contrived in that time to procure him in marriage a woman of condition, and have him appointed president of the government-magistracy for the province of Esthland. On a visit to Weimar, in 1790, Kotzebue lost his wife, and, to heal his grief, made a stay in Paris; after which he returned, and married another Russian lady. Then he came, for some reason or other, to reside in Weimar, and accepted the direction of the Imperial Theatre at Vienna. He was often in trouble on account of his writings; and soon after this, possibly on account of something he had written,—for he himself professes to be ignorant of the true cause,—he was entrapped into Russia, and banished to Siberia. He must have had influential friends about court, for he did not long remain in exile, being soon completely restored to the Emperor Paul's favour, and 'he slept in the imperial palace of Michailoff on the night of the 11th March, 1801, which transferred to Alexander the imperial dignity,' without, he maintains, any suspicion of what was to happen. He was further honoured in the new reign. Then, for some private reasons, after travelling in Italy some time, he finally settled in Mannheim, where his advocacy of Russian interests raised such a cry against him, as a traitor to his country and base spy, that conspiracies were formed to remove him; and on that same 11th day of March, in 1819. a young student, of excellent character previously, called on him in private, and stabbed him with a dagger. He may have been honestly advocating his own principles and opinions, influenced more or less by gratitude to the country which had done so much for him; yet, it must be confessed, much of his connection with Russia, and his own accounts of it, seem involved in obscurity.

Of Kotzebue's works, perhaps the best comedy is *False Shame*, and his principal tragic performance is *Gustavus Vasa*. *Misanthropy and Repentance*, a somewhat strange medley, is familiar to the English stage under the title of *The Stranger;* so have other pieces of his been introduced in England, with other titles and in various disguises. His interest is by no means confined to a limited range of subjects. We have scenes laid among the negroes, scenes laid in Russia, Spanish scenes, English scenes, comedies, tragedies, farces, in profuse abundance from Kotzebue's too prolific brain.

MORISON, THE 'HYGEIST.'

Died at Paris, May 3, 1840, James Morison, who styled himself 'Hygeist,' and was for many years notorious for his extensively advertised 'vegetable medicines.' It will be a surprise to many to know that Morison was a man of good family (in Aberdeenshire), and that he had

attained a competence by honourable merchandise in the West Indies before he came before the world in the capacity by which he has acquired fame. His own story, which there is no particular reason to discredit, always was that his own sufferings from bad health, and the cure he at length effected upon himself by vegetable pills, were what made him a disseminator of the latter article. He had found the pills to be the 'only rational purifiers of the blood.' By their use he had at fifty renewed his youth. His pains were gone; his limbs had become supple. He enjoyed sound sleep and high spirits. He feared neither heat nor cold, dryness nor humidity. Sensible that all this had come of the simple use of two or three pills at bed-time and a glass of lemonade in the morning, how should he be excused if he did not do his endeavour to diffuse the same blessing among his fellow-creatures? People may smile at this statement; but we can quite believe in its entire sincerity.

The pills were splendidly successful, giving a revenue of £60,000 to Government during the first ten years. Mr Morison had attained the age of seventy at his death. He had established a central institution called the British College of Health, in the New-road, London, which was carried on after his death.

THOMAS HOOD.

The births and deaths of many very notable men have to be left in this chronicle uncommented on; but the too early departure of Thomas Hood is associated with such feelings, that it cannot be passed over. Hood came of a family in humble life at Dundee, in Scotland, whence his father migrated to London. The young genius tried bookselling, which was his father's profession—also engraving—but was thrown out of all regular occupation by weak health. While little more than a stripling, he contributed prose and poetical pieces to periodical works, and soon attracted attention by his singular gift of humour. Of his *Comic Annual* and other subsequent publications, it is unnecessary to give a list. They have made for themselves a place in higher records than this. All have relished the exquisite drollery of Hood's writings; but it requires to be insisted on that they have qualities in addition, distinguishing them from nearly all such productions. There is a wonderful play of fancy over all that Hood wrote, and few writers surprise us so often with fine touches of humane feeling. It is most sad to relate that the life of this gifted man was clouded by misfortunes, mainly arising from his infirm health, and that he sunk into the grave, in poverty, at the age of forty-seven. In personal character he was extremely amiable; but his external demeanour was that of a grave and rather melancholy man.

SHAKSPEAREAN RELICS.

On the 3rd of May 1769, the freedom of Stratford-upon-Avon was presented to Mr Garrick, by the Mayor, Aldermen, and Burgesses, enclosed in the far-famed cassolette or casket, made from the veritable mulberry tree planted by Shakspeare. This precious relic is beautifully carved with the following devices :—In the front, Fame is represented holding the bust of Shakspeare, while the three Graces crown it with laurel. On the back, Garrick is delineated as King Lear, in the storm scene. On the sides are emblematical figures representing Tragedy and Comedy ; and the corners are ornamented with devices of Shakspeare's works. The feet are silver griffins with garnet eyes. The carving was executed by Davis, a celebrated artist of Birmingham, at the expense of fifty-five pounds.

It was purchased by the late Mr Mathews, the eminent comedian, at Mrs Garrick's sale. In 1835, it was again brought to the hammer, when Mr Mathews's library and curiosities were sold. Amidst a cloud of bidders, anxious to secure so matchless a relic, it was knocked down to Mr George Daniel, of Islington, at forty-seven guineas.

In September 1769, the Mayor and Corporation of Stratford-upon-Avon presented to Garrick a cup, about eleven inches in height, carved from the same far-famed mulberry tree. Garrick held this cup in his hand at the Jubilee, when he sang the beautiful song composed by himself for that occasion, commencing—

'Behold this fair goblet, 'twas carved from the tree,
Which, O my sweet Shakspeare, was planted by
    thee ;
As a relic, I kiss it, and bow at the shrine ;
What comes from thy hand must be ever divine !
    All shall yield to the mulberry tree ;
        Bend to thee,
        Blest mulberry ;
        Matchless was he
        Who planted thee ;
And thou, like him, immortal shall be.'

After the death of Mrs Garrick, the cup was sold, under a decree of Chancery, at Christie's auction-rooms, and purchased by a Mr Johnson, who afterwards offered it for sale at the price of two hundred guineas.

MAY 4.

St Mo ca, widow, 387.   St Godard, bishop, 1038.

Born.—Dr Francis Peck, English historical antiquary, 1692, *Stamford, Lincolnshire ;* John James Audubon, ornithologist, 1782, *Louisiana.*

Died.—Edward, Prince of Wales, son of Henry VI., 1471, *Tewkesbury ;* Ulysses Aldovrandi, naturalist, 1605; Louis XIII., King of France, 1643 ; Dr Isaac Barrow, eminent English divine, 1677; Sir James Thornhill, painter, 1734 ; Eustace Budgel, contributor to the *Spectator,* drowned in the Thames, 1737 ; Tippoo Sahib, Sultan of Mysore, killed at the siege of Seringapatam, 1799 ; Sir Robert Ker Porter, traveller, artist, 1842, *St Petersburg ;* Horace Twiss, miscellaneous writer, 1849.

AUDUBON.

One of those enthusiasts who devote themselves to one prodigious task, of a respectable, but not remunerative nature, and persevere in it till it, or their life, is finished. He was born of French parents, in the then French colony of Louisiana, in North America, and received a good education at Paris. Settled afterwards by his father on a farm near Philadelphia, he married, engaged in trade, and occasionally cultivated a taste for drawing. Gradually, a love of natural history, and an intense relish for the enjoyment of forest life, led him away from commercial pursuits ; and before he was thirty, we find him in Florida, with his rifle and drawing materials, thinking of nothing but how he might capture and sketch the numerous beautiful birds of his native country. At that time, there was a similar enthusiast in the same field, the quondam Scotch pedlar and poet, Alexander Wilson. They met, compared drawings, and felt a mutual respect. Wilson, however, saw in young Audubon's efforts the promise of a success beyond his own.

Years of this kind of life passed over. The stock of drawings increased, notwithstanding the loss at one time of two hundred, containing a thousand subjects, and in time the resolution of publishing was formed. He estimated that the task would occupy him fifteen more years, and he had not one subscriber ; but, notwithstanding the painful remonstrances of friends, he persevered. In the course of his preparations, about 1828, he visited London, Edinburgh, and Paris. We remember him at the second of these cities, a hale man of forty-six, nimble as a deer, and with an aquiline style of visage and eye that reminded one of a class of his subjects ; a frank, noble, natural man. Professor Wilson took to him wonderfully, and wrote of him, ' The hearts of all are warmed toward Audubon. The man himself is just what you would expect from his productions, full of fine enthusiasm and intelligence, most interesting in his looks and manners, a perfect gentleman, and esteemed by all who know him, for the simplicity and frankness of his nature.'

In 1830, he published his first volume, with ninety-nine birds, and one hundred plates. His birds were life-size and colour. The kings of England and France placed their names at the head of his subscription list. He was made a fellow of the Royal Society of London, and member of the Natural History Society of Paris.

In 1834, the second volume of the birds of America was published, and then Audubon went to explore the State of Maine, the shores of the Bay of Fundy, the Gulf of St Lawrence, and the Bay of Labrador. In the autumn of 1834, the second volume of *Ornithological Biography* was published in Edinburgh. People subscribed for the birds of America, with a view to posterity, as men plant trees. Audubon mentions a nobleman in London, who remarked, when subscribing, ' I may not live to see the work finished, but my children will.' The naturalist, though a man of faith, hope, and endurance, seems to have been afflicted by this remark. ' I thought—what if I should not live to finish my work ?' But he comforted himself by his reliance on Providence. After the publication of his third volume, the United States government gave him the use of an exploring vessel, and he went to the coast of Florida and Texas. Three years after this, the fourth volume of his engravings, and the fifth of his descriptions, were published. He had now

435 plates, and 1,165 figures, from the eagle to the humming-bird, with many land and sea views.

Audubon never cultivated the graces of style. He wrote to be understood. His descriptions are clear and simple. He describes the mocking-bird with the heart of a poet, and the eye of a naturalist. His description of a hurricane proves that he never ceased to be a careful and accurate observer in the most agitating circumstances.

Audubon died at his home, near New York, on the 27th January, 1851.

SIR JAMES THORNHILL.

This artist was an example of those who are paid for their services, not according to the amount of genius shown, but according to the area covered. His paintings were literally estimated by the *square yard*, like the work of the bricklayer or plasterer. He generally painted the ceilings and walls of large halls, staircases, and corridors, and was very liberal in his supply of gods and goddesses. Among his works were —the eight pictures illustrating the history of St Paul, painted in chiaroscuro on the interior of the cupola of St Paul's Cathedral; the princess's chamber at Hampton Court; the staircase, a gallery, and several ceilings at Kensington Palace; a hall at Blenheim; the chapel at Wimpole, in Cambridgeshire; and the ceiling of the great hall at Greenwich Hospital. For the pictures at St Paul's he was paid at the rate of forty shillings per square yard. Walpole, in his 'Anecdotes of Painters,' makes the following observations on the petty spirit in which the payments to Thornhill were made :—'High as his reputation was, and laborious as his work, he was far from being generously rewarded for some of them; and for others he found it difficult to obtain the stipulated prices. His demands were contested at Greenwich; and though La Fosse received £2,000 for his work at Montague House, and was allowed £500 for his diet besides, Sir James could obtain but forty shillings a square yard for the cupola of St Paul's, and, I think, no more for Greenwich. When the affairs of the South Sea Company were made up, Thornhill, who had painted their staircase and a little hall, by order of Mr Knight, their cashier, demanded £1,500; but the directors, hearing that he had been paid only twenty-five shillings a yard for the hall at Blenheim, would allow no more. He had a longer contest with Mr Styles, who had agreed to give him £3,500 (for painting the saloon at Moor Park); but not being satisfied with the execution, a law-suit was commenced; and Dahl, Richardson, and others, were appointed to inspect the work. They appeared in court bearing testimony to the merit of the performance; Mr Styles was condemned to pay the money.' Notwithstanding this mode of paying for works of art by the square, Sir James, who was an industrious man, gradually acquired a handsome competency. Artists in our day, who seldom have to work upon ceilings, conduct their labours under easier bodily conditions than Thornhill. It is said that he was so long lying on his back while painting the great hall at

Greenwich Hospital, that he could never afterwards sit upright with comfort.

TAKING OF SERINGAPATAM.

On the 4th of May 1799, Seringapatam was taken, and the empire of Hyder Ali extinguished by the death of his son, the Sultan Tippoo Sahib. The storming of this great fortress by the British troops took place in broad day, and was on that account unexpected by the enemy. The commander, General Sir David Baird, led one of the storming parties in person, with characteristic gallantry, and was the first man after the forlorn hope to reach the top of the breach. So far, well; but when there, he discovered to his surprise a second ditch within, full of water. For a moment he thought it would be impossible to get over this difficulty. He had fortunately, however, observed some workmen's scaffolding in coming along, and taking this up hastily, was able by its means to cross the ditch; after which all that remained was simply a little hard fighting. Tippoo came forward with apparent gallantry to resist the assailants, and was afterwards taken from under a heap of slain. It is supposed he made this attempt in desperation, having just ordered the murder of twelve British soldiers, which he might well suppose would give him little chance of quarter, if his enemy were aware of the fact.

It was remarkable that, fifteen years before, Baird had undergone a long and cruel captivity in this very fort, under Tippoo's father, Hyder Ali. The hardships he underwent on that occasion were extreme; yet, amidst all his sufferings, he never for a moment lost heart, or ceased to hope for a release. He was truly a noble soldier. As with Wellington, his governing principle was a sense of *duty*. In every matter, he seemed to be solely anxious to discover *what was right to be done, that he might do it*. He was a Scotchman, a younger son of Mr Baird, of Newbyth, in East Lothian (born in 1757, died in 1829). His person was tall and handsome, and his look commanding. In all the relations of his life he was a most worthy man, his kindness of heart winning him the love of all who came in contact with him.

An anecdote of Sir David Baird's boyhood forms the key to his character. When a student at Mr Locie's Military Academy at Chelsea, where all the routine of garrison duty was kept up, he was one night acting as sentinel. A companion, older than himself, came and desired leave to pass out, that he might fulfil an engagement in London. Baird steadily refused—' No,' said he, ' *that* I cannot do; but, if you please, you may knock me down, and walk out over my body.'[*]

The taking of Seringapatam gave occasion for a remarkable exercise of juvenile talent in a youth of nineteen, who was studying art in the Royal Academy, and whose name appears in the obituary list at the head of this day. He was then simply Robert Ker Porter, but afterwards, as Sir Robert, became respectfully known for his *Travels in Persia*; while his two sisters Jane and Anna

[*] Theodore Hook's *Life of Sir David Baird*.

Maria, attained a reputation as prolific writers of prose fiction. There had been such a thing before as a *panorama*, or picture giving details of a scene too extensive to be comprehended from one point of view; but it was not a work entitled to much admiration. With marvellous enthusiasm this boy artist began to cover a canvas of two hundred feet long with the scenes attending the capture of the great Indian fort; and, strange to say, he had finished it in six weeks. Sir Benjamin West, President of the Royal Academy, got an early view of the picture, and pronounced it a miracle of precocious talent. When it was arranged for exhibition, vast multitudes both of the learned and the unlearned flocked to see it. 'I can never forget,' says Dr Dibdin, 'its first impression upon my own mind. It was as a thing dropped from the clouds,—all fire, energy, intelligence, and animation. You looked a second time, the figures moved, and were commingled in hot and bloody fight. You saw the flash of the cannon, the glitter of the bayonet, and the gleam of the falchion. You longed to be leaping from crag to crag with Sir David Baird, who is hallooing his men on to victory! Then again you seemed to be listening to the groans of the wounded and the dying—and more than one female was carried out swooning. The oriental dress, the jewelled turban, the curved and ponderous scimitar—these were among the prime favourites of Sir Robert's pencil, and he treated them with literal truth. The colouring was sound throughout; the accessories strikingly characteristic. . . . . The public poured in thousands for even a transient gaze.'*

THE BEGGARS' OPERA.

In the spring and early summer of 1728, the *Beggars' Opera* of Gay had its unprecedented run of sixty-two nights in the theatre of Lincoln's-Inn Fields. No theatrical success of Dryden or Congreve had ever approached this; probably the best of Shakspeare's fell far short of it. We learn from Spence, that the idea of a play, with malefactors amongst its characters, took its rise in a remark of Swift to Gay, 'What an odd, pretty sort of thing a Newgate pastoral might make.' And, Gay proceeding to work out the idea in the form of a comedy, Swift gave him his advice, and now and then a correction, but believed the piece would not succeed. Congreve was not so sure—he said it would either take greatly or be condemned extremely. The poet, who was in his fortieth year, and had hitherto been but moderately successful in his attempts to please the public, offered the play to Colley Cibber for the Drury Lane Theatre, and only on its being rejected there took it to Mr Rich, of the playhouse just mentioned, where it was presented for the first time on the 29th of January, 1727-8. Strange to say, the success of the piece was considered doubtful for the greater part of the first act, and was not quite determined till Polly sang her pathetic appeal to her parents,—

'Oh, ponder well, be not severe,
To save a wretched wife,
For on the rope that hangs my dear
Depends poor Polly's life.'

* *Reminiscences of a Literary Life*, i. 145.

Then the audience, completely captivated, broke out into an applause which established the success of the play. It has ever since been a stock piece of the British stage, notwithstanding questionable morality, and moderate literary merit both in the dialogue and the songs; the fifty beautiful airs introduced into it being what apparently has chiefly given it its hold upon the public. It is to be remarked, that in the same season the play was presented for at least twenty nights in succession at Dublin; and even into Scotland, which had not then one regular theatre, it found its way very soon after.

The author, according to usage, got the entire receipts of the third, sixth, ninth, and fifteenth nights, amounting in the aggregate to £693,13s. 6d. In a letter to Swift, he takes credit for having 'pushed through this precarious affair without servility or flattery;' and when the play was published, Pope complimented him on not prefacing it with a dedication, thus deliberately foregoing twenty guineas (the established price of such things in those days). So early as the 20th of March, when the piece had only been acted thirty-six times, Mr Rich had profited to the extent of near four thousand pounds. So it might well be said that this play had made Rich *gay*, and Gay *rich*. Amongst other consequences of the *furore* for the play was a sad decline in the receipts at the Italian opera, which Gay had all along meant to rival. The wags had it that *that* should be called the Beggars' Opera.

The king, queen, and princesses came to see the *Beggars' Opera* on the twenty-first night of its performance. What was more remarkable, it was honoured on another night with the presence of the prime minister, Sir Robert Walpole, whose corrupt practices in the management of a majority in the House of Commons were understood to be glanced at in the dialogues of *Peachum* and *Lockit*. Sir Robert, whose good humour was seldom at fault, is said to have laughed heartily at *Lockit's* song:

'When you censure the age,
Be cautious and sage,
Lest the courtiers offended should be;
If you mention vice or bribe,
'Tis so fit to all the tribe,
Each cries—That was levelled at me;'

and so he disarmed the audience.

We do not hear much of any of the first actors of the *Beggars' Opera*, excepting Lavinia Fenton, who personated *Polly*. She was a young lady of elegant figure, but not striking beauty, a good singer, and of very agreeable conversation and manners. The performance of this part stood out conspicuous in its success, and brought her much notice. Her portrait was published in mezzotint; there was also a memoir of her hitherto obscure life. Her songs were printed on ladies' fans. The fictitious name became so identified with her, that her benefit was announced as *Polly's* night. One benefit having been given her on the 29th of April, when the *Beaux Stratagem* was performed, the public were so dissatisfied, that the *Beggars' Opera* had to be played for a second benefit to her on the 4th of May. The Duke of Bolton, a nobleman then in the prime of life, living apart from his wife, became inflamed with a violent passion for Miss Fenton, and came frequently to see the play. There is a large print by Hogarth, representing the performance at that scene in Newgate, towards the end of the second act, where *Polly* kneels to *Peachum,* to intercede for her husband. There we see two groups of fashionable figures in boxes raised at the sides of the stage; the Duke of Bolton is the nearest on the right hand side, dressed in wig, riband, and star, and with his eyes fixed on the kneeling *Polly.* At the end of the first season, his grace succeeded in inducing Miss Fenton to leave the stage and live with him, and when the opportunity arrived he married

THE BEGGARS' OPERA.

her. She was the first of a series of English actresses who have been raised to a connexion with the peerage. Warton tells us that he knew her, and could testify to her wit, good manners, taste, and intelligence. 'Her conversation,' says he, 'was admired by the first characters of the age, particularly the old Lord Bathurst and Lord Granville.'

Charles, third Duke of Bolton, who married Lavinia Fenton, died in 1754, without legitimate issue, though Miss Fenton had brought him before marriage several children, one of whom, a

Performers.—1. *Macheath,* Mr Walker; 2. *Lockit,* Mr Hall; 3. *Peachum,* Mr Hippesley; 4. *Lucy,* Mrs Egleton; 5. *Polly,* Miss Fenton.
 Audience.—6. Duke of Bolton; 7. Major Pounceford; 8. Sir Robert Fagg; 9. Mr Rich; 10. Mr Cook, the Auctioneer; 11. Mr Gay; 12. Lady Jane Cook; 13. Anthony Henley, Esq.; 14. Sir Conyers D'Arcy; 15. Lord Gage; 16. Sir Thos. Robinson.

clergyman, was living in 1809, when Banks mentioned the circumstance in his *Extinct Peerage of England*. The Bolton peerage fell into this condition in 1794, on the death of Harry, the fifth duke, and thus ended the main line of the Pauletts, so noted as statesmen and public characters in the days of Elizabeth and the first Stuarts.

MAY 5.

St Hilary, Archbishop of Arles, 449. St Mauront, abbot, 706. St Avertin, confessor, about 1189. St Angelus, Carmelite friar, martyr, 1225. St Pius V., pope, 1572.

Ascension Day (1864).

Ascension Day, or Holy Thursday, is a festival observed by the Church of England in commemoration of the glorious ascension of the Messiah into heaven, ' triumphing over the devil, and leading captivity captive;' ' opening the kingdom of heaven to all believers.' It occurs forty days after Easter Sunday, such being the number of days which the Saviour passed on earth after his resurrection. The observance is thought to be one of the very earliest in the church—so early, it has been said, as the year 68.

WELL-DRESSING AT TISSINGTON.

' Still, Dovedale, yield thy flowers to deck the fountains
    Of Tissington upon its holyday ;
The customs long preserved among the mountains
    Should not be lightly left to pass away.
They have their moral ; and we often may
    Learn from them how our wise forefathers wrought,
When they upon the public mind would lay
    Some weighty principle, some maxim brought
Home to their hearts, the healthful product of deep
    thought.'
Edwards.

Such was our feeling when our kind landlady at Matlock reminded us that on the following day, being Holy Thursday, or Ascension Day, there would take place the very ancient and well kept-up custom of dressing the wells of Tissington with flowers. She recommended us on no account to miss the opportunity, ' for the festivity draws together the rich and poor for many miles round,' said she ; ' and the village looks so pretty you cannot but admire it.' It was one of those lovely May mornings when we started on our twelve miles drive which give you the anticipation of enjoyment ; the bright sun was shining on the hills surrounding the romantically situated village of Matlock, the trees were already decked with the delicate spring tints of pale browns, olives, and greens, which form even a more pleasing variety to the artist's eye than the gorgeous colours of the dying autumn ; whilst the air had the crispness of a sharp frost, which had hardened the ground during the night, making our horses step merrily along.

We were soon at Willersley, with its woods and walks overhanging the Derwent, and connected in its historical associations with two remarkable but very different characters, having

been formerly a possession of the Earl of Shrewsbury, the husband of that ' sharpe and bitter

THE HALL WELL, TISSINGTON, AS DRESSED FOR ASCENSION DAY.

shrewe,' as the Bishop of Lichfield calls her, who figured so prominently in the reigns of Mary and Elizabeth. Married no less than four times, she was the ancestress of some of the most noble families in England. At the early age of fourteen she became the wife of Robert Barley, Esq., the union not lasting much more than a year. Sir William Cavendish then aspired to her hand, by which the fine old seat and lands of Hardwicke Hall, of which she was the heiress, came into the Devonshire family. Sir William was a man of eminent talent, and the zeal he displayed in the cause of the Reformation recommended him highly to his sovereign. He was better fitted to cope with his wife's masculine understanding and violent temper than her last husband, the Earl of Shrewsbury, who gives vent to some very undignified remonstrances in a letter to the Earl of Leicester, dated 1585. The queen had, it seems, taken the part of her own sex, and ordered the earl an allowance of five hundred a-year, leaving all the lands in the power of his wife : ' Sith that her majestie hathe sett downe this hard sentence againste me, to my perpetual infamy and dishonour, to be ruled and oberaune by my wief, so bad and wicked a woman; yet her majestie shall see that I obey her commandemente, thoughe no curse or plage in the erthe cold be more grievous to me. It is to much to make me my wiefe's pencyoner, and sett me downe the demeanes of Chatsworth, without the house and other landes leased.' From this time the pair lived separate; whilst the restless mind of the countess still pursued the political intrigues which had been the terror of her husband, and the aggrandizement of her family. She bought and sold estates, lent money, farmed, and dealt in lead, coals, and timber, patronized the wits of the day, who in return flattered but never deceived her, and died at the advanced age of eighty-seven, immensely rich, leaving the character behind her of being 'a proud, furious, selfish, and unfeeling woman.' She and the earl were for some time the custodians of the unfortunate Mary Queen of Scots, who passed a part of her imprisonment at Chatsworth, and at the old Hall at Hardwicke, which is now in ruins.

Very different from this has been the career of the present proprietor of beautiful Willersley, whose ancestor, Richard Arkwright, springing from a very humble origin, created his own fortune, and provided employment for thousands of his fellow-creatures by his improvements in cotton spinning. A history so well known needs no farther comment here, and we drive on through the Via Gellia, with its picturesque rocks and springing vegetation, gay with

> ' The primrose drop, the spring's own spouse,
> Bright daisies, and the lips-of-cows,
> The garden star, the queen of May,
> The rose, to crown the holyday.'   *Jonson.*

We cannot wonder that the Romans dedicated this lovely season to Flora, whom they depicted as strewing the earth with flowers, attended by her spouse, Zephyr; and in honour of whom they wove garlands of flowers, and carried branches of the newly-budded trees. From the entire disappearance of old customs, May comes upon us unwelcomed and unnoticed. In the writer's childhood a May-pole carried about in the hand was common even in towns; but now no children understand the pleasures of collecting the wayside and garden flowers, and weaving them into the magic circle. Still less applicable are L. E. L.'s beautiful lines:

> ' Here the Maypole rears its crest,
> With the rose and hawthorn drest;
> In the midst, like the young queen
> Flower-crowned, of the rural green,
> Is a bright-cheeked girl, her eye
> Blue, like April's morning sky.
> Farewell, cities! who could bear
> All their smoke and all their care,
> All their pomp, when wooed away
> By the azure hours of May?
> Give me woodbine-scented bowers,
> Blue wreaths of the violet flowers,
> Clear sky, fresh air, sweet birds, and trees,
> Sights and sounds, and scenes like these.'

We could not but notice, in passing through the meadows near Brassington, those singular limestone formations which crop out of the ground in the most fantastic forms, resembling arrows and spires, and which the people designate by various names, such as Peter's Pike, Reynard's Tor. Then came the village of Bradbourne, and the pretty foot-bridge, close by the mill, crossing Bentley Brook, a little stream mentioned by Walton as 'full of good trout and grayling.' This bridge is the direct foot-road to

Tissington, at which 'village of the holy wells' we soon arrived, and found it decked out in all its bravery. It has in itself many points of attraction independent of the ornaments of the day; the little stream that runs through the centre, the rural-looking cottages and comfortable farmhouses, the old church, which retains the traces of Saxon architecture, and, lastly, the Hall, a fine old edifice, belonging to the ancient family of the Fitzherberts, who reside there, the back of which comes to the village, the front looking into an extensive, well-wooded park.

When we drove into the village, though it was only ten o'clock, we found it already full of people from many miles round, who had assembled to celebrate the feast: for such indeed it was, all the characteristics of a village wake being there in the shape of booths, nuts, gingerbread, and toys to delight the young. We went immediately to the church, foreseeing the difficulty there would be in getting a seat, nor were we mistaken; for, though we were accommodated, numbers were obliged to remain outside, and wait for the service peculiar to the wells. The interior of the church is ornamented with many monuments of the Fitzherbert family, and the service was performed in rural style by a band of violinists, who did their best to make melody. As soon as the sermon was ended, the clergyman left the pulpit, and marched at the head of the procession which was formed into the village; after him came the band; then the family from the hall, and their visitors, the rest of the congregation following; and a halt was made at the first of the wells, which are five in number, and which we will now attempt to describe.

The name of 'well' scarcely gives a proper idea of these beautiful structures: they are rather fountains, or cascades, the water descending from above, and not rising, as in a well. Their height varies from ten to twelve feet; and the original stone frontage is on this day hidden by a wooden erection in the form of an arch, or some other elegant design: over these planks a layer of plaster of Paris is spread, and whilst it is wet, flowers without leaves are stuck in it, forming a most beautiful mosaic pattern. On one, the large yellow field ranunculus was arranged in letters, and so a verse of scripture or of a hymn was recalled to the spectator's mind; on another, a white dove was sculptured in the plaster, and set in a groundwork of the humble violet; the daisy, which our poet Chaucer would gaze upon for hours together, formed a diaper work of red and white; the pale yellow primrose was set off by the rich red of the ribes; nor were the coral berries of the holly, mountain ash, and yew forgotten; these are carefully gathered and stored in the winter, to be ready for the May-day *fête*. It is scarcely possible to describe the vivid colouring and beautiful effect of these favourites of nature, arranged in wreaths, and garlands, and devices of every hue; and then the pure, sparkling water, which pours down from the midst of them unto the rustic moss-grown stones beneath, completes the enchantment, and makes this feast of the well-flowering one of the most beautiful of all the old customs that are left in 'merrie England.'

The groups of visitors and country people, dressed in their holiday clothes, stood reverently round, whilst the clergyman read the first of the three psalms appointed for the day, and then gave out one of Bishop Heber's beautiful hymns, in which all joined with heart and voice. When this was over, all moved forwards to the next well, where the next psalm was read and another hymn sung; the epistle and gospel being read at the last two wells. The service was now over, and the people dispersed to wander through the village or park, which is thrown open; the cottagers vie with each other in showing hospitality to the strangers, and many kettles are boiled at their fires for those who have brought the materials for a pic-nic on the green. It is welcomed as a season of mirth and good fellowship, many old friends meeting then to separate for another year, should they be spared to see the well-dressing again; whilst the young people enjoy their games and country pastimes with their usual vivacity.

The origin of this custom of dressing the wells is by some persons supposed to be owing to a fearful drought which visited Derbyshire in 1615, and which is thus recorded in the parish registers of Youlgrave: 'There was no rayne fell upon the earth from the 25th day of March till the 2nd day of May, and then there was but one shower; two more fell betweene then and the 4th day of August, so that the greatest part of this land were burnt upp, bothe corn and hay. An ordinary load of hay was at £2, and little or none to be gotte for money.' The wells of Tissington were flowing during all this time, and the people for ten miles round drove their cattle to drink at them; and a thanksgiving service was appointed yearly for Ascension Day. But we must refer the origin much further back, to the ages of superstition, when the pastimes of the people were all out-of-doors, and when the wakes and daytime dances were on the village green instead of in the close ball-room; it is certainly a 'popish relic,'—perhaps a relic of pagan Rome. Fountains and wells were ever the objects of their adoration. 'Where a spring rises or a river flows,' says Seneca, 'there should we build altars and offer sacrifices;' they held yearly festivals in their honour, and peopled them with the elegant forms of the nymphs and presiding goddesses. In later times holy wells were held in the highest estimation: Edgar and Canute were obliged to issue edicts prohibiting their worship. Nor is this surprising, their very appearance being symbolic of loveliness and purity. The weary and thirsty traveller gratefully hails the 'diamond of the desert,' whether it be in the arid plains of the East, or in the cooler shades of an English landscape. May was always considered the favourable month for visiting the wells which possessed a charm for curing sick people; but a strict silence was to be preserved both in going and coming back, and the vessel in which the water was carried was not to touch the ground. After the Reformation these customs were strictly forbidden, as superstiticus and idolatrous, the cures which were wrought being doubtless owing to the fresh air, and what in these days we should call hydropathic remedies.

In consequence of this questionable origin, whether Pagan or Popish, we have heard some good but straitlaced people in Derbyshire condemn the well-dressing greatly, and express their astonishment that so many should give it their countenance, by assembling at Tissington; but, considering that no superstition is now connected with it, and that the meeting gives unusual pleasure to many, we must decline to agree with them, and hope that the taste of the well-dressers may long meet with the reward of an admiring company.

Born.—Emperor Justinian, 483, *Tauresium*, in *Bulgaria.*

Died.—Paulus Æmilius, 1529, *Paris;* Samuel Cooper, 1672; Stephen Morin, 1700, *Amsterdam;* John Pichon, 1751; Thomas Davies (dramatic biography), 1785, *London;* Pierre J. G. Cabanis, French materialist philosopher, 1808; Robert Mylne, architect, 1811; Napoleon Bonaparte, ex-Emperor of the French, 1821, *St Helena;* Rev. Dr Lant Carpenter, theologian, 1840; Sir Robert Harry Inglis, Bart., political character, 1855; Charles Robert Leslie, American artist, 1859, *London.*

ROBERT MYLNE.

Mr Mylne, the architect of Blackfriars Bridge in London, had aimed at perfecting himself in his profession by travel, by study, and a careful experience. His temper is said to have been rather peculiar, but his integrity and high sense of duty were universally acknowledged. He was born in Edinburgh in 1733, the son of one respectable architect, and nephew of another, who constructed the North Bridge in that city. The father and grandfather of his father were of the same profession; the latter (also named Robert) being the builder of Holyrood Palace in its present form, and of most of the fine, tall, ashlar-fronted houses which still give such a grandeur to the High-street. Considering that the son and grandson of the architect of Blackfriars Bridge have also been devoted to this profession, we may be said to have here a remarkable example of the perseverance of certain artistic faculties in one family; yet the whole case in this respect has not been stated. In the Greyfriars churchyard, in Edinburgh, there is a handsome monument, which the palace builder reared over his uncle, John Mylne, who died in 1667, in the highest reputation as an architect, and who was described in the epitaph as the last of *six generations*, who had all been 'master-masons' to the kings of Scotland. It cannot be shown that this statement is true, though it may be so; but it can be pretty clearly proved that there were at least three generations of architects before the one we have called the palace builder; exhibiting, even on this restricted ground, an example of persistent special talents in hereditary descent such as is probably unexampled in any age or country.

OPENING OF THE STATES-GENERAL OF FRANCE, 1789.

This event, so momentous in its consequences as to make it an era in the history of the world, took place at Versailles on the 5th of May, 1789. The first sitting was opened in the Salle de Menus. Nothing could be more imposing than the spectacle that presented itself. The deputies were introduced according to the order and etiquette established in 1614. The clergy, in cassocks, large cloaks, and square caps, or in violet robes and lawn sleeves, were placed on the right of the throne; the nobles, covered with cloth of gold and lace, were conducted to the left; whilst the commons, or *tiers état*, were ranged in front, at the end of the hall. The galleries were filled with spectators, who marked with applause those of the deputies who were known to have been favourable to the convention. When the deputies and ministers had taken their places, Louis XVI. arrived, followed by the queen, the princes, and a brilliant suite, and was greeted with loud applause. His speech from the throne was listened to with profound attention, and closed, with these words: 'All that can be expected from the dearest interest in the public welfare, all that can be required of a sovereign the first friend of his people, you may and ought to hope from my sentiments. That a happy spirit of union may pervade this assembly, and that this may be an ever-memorable epoch for the happiness and prosperity of the kingdom, is the wish of my heart, the most ardent of my desires; it is, in a word, the reward which I expect for the uprightness of my intentions, and my love of my subjects.' He was followed by Barentin, keeper of the seals, and then by Necker; but neither the king nor his ministers understood the importance of the crisis. A thousand pens have told how their anticipations of a happy issue were frustrated.

WHIPPING VAGRANTS.

Three centuries ago, the flagellation of vagrants and similar characters for slight offences was carried to a cruel extent. Owing to the dissolution of the monasteries, where the poor had chiefly found relief, a vast number of infirm and unemployed persons were suddenly thrown on the country without any legitimate means of support. These destitute persons were naturally led to wander from place to place, seeking a subsistence from the casual alms of any benevolent persons they might chance to meet. Their roving and precarious life soon produced its natural fruits, and these again produced severe measures of repression. By an act passed in 22 Henry VIII., vagrants were to be 'carried to some market town or other place, and there tied to the end of a cart naked, and beaten with whips throughout such market town or other place, till the body should be bloody by reason of such whipping.' The punishment was afterwards slightly mitigated; for by a statute passed in the 39th of Elizabeth's reign, vagrants were only 'to be stripped naked from the middle upwards, and whipped till the body should be bloody.'* Still vagrancy not only continued, but increased, so that several benches of magistrates issued special orders for the apprehension and punishment of vagrants found in their respective districts. Thus, in the quarter-sessions at Wycombe,

* *Burn's Justice*, vol. v. 501.

in Bucks, held on the 5th of May, 1698, an order was passed directing all constables and other parish officers to search for vagrants, &c.; 'and all such persons which they shall apprehend in any such search, or shall take begging, wandering, or misconducting themselves, the said constables, headboroughs, or tything-men, being assisted with some of the other parishioners, shall cause to be whipped naked from the middle upwards, and be openly whipped till the bodies shall be bloody.' This order appears to have been carried into immediate execution, not only within the magisterial jurisdiction of Wycombe, but throughout the county of Buckingham; and lists of the persons whipped were kept in the several parishes, either in the church registers, or in some other parish book. In the book kept in the parish of Lavenden, the record is sufficiently explicit. For example, 'Eliz. Roberts, lately the wife of John Roberts, a tallow-chandler in ye Strand, in Hungerford Market, in ye County of Middlesex, of a middle stature, brown-haired, and black-eyed, aged about — years, was whipped and sent to St Martin's-in-the-Field, in London, where she was born.' At Burnham, in the same county, there is in the church register a long list of persons who have been whipped, from which the following specimens are taken—'Benjamin Smat, and his wife and three children, vagrant beggars; he of middle stature, but one eye, was this 28th day of September 1699, with his wife and children, openly whipped at Boveney, in the parish of Burnham, in the county of Buck., according to ye laws. And they are assigned to pass forthwith from parish to parish by ye officers thereof the next direct way to the parish of St [Se]pulchers Lond., where they say they last inhabited three years. And they are limitted to be at St [Se]pulch. within ten days next ensuing. Given under our hands and seals. Will. Glover, Vicar of Burnham, and John Hunt, Constable of Boveney.' The majority of those in this list were females—as 'Eliz. Collins, a mayd pretty tall of stature;' 'Anne Smith, a vagrant beggar about fifteen years old;' 'Mary Web, a child about thirteen years of age, a wandering beggar;' 'Isabel Harris, a widd. about sixty years of age, and her daughter, Eliz. Harris, with one child.' Thus it appears that this degrading punishment was publicly inflicted on females without regard to their tender or advanced age. It is, however, only fair to mention, as a redeeming point in the parish officers of Burnham, that they sometimes recommended the poor women whom they had whipped to the tender mercies of the authorities of other parishes through which the poor sufferers had to pass.

The nature of these recommendations may be seen from copies of those still remaining in the register, one of which, after the common preamble, 'To all constables, headboroughs, and tything-men, to whom these presents shall come,' desires them 'to be as charitable as the law in such cases allows, to the bearer and her two children.' Cruelty in the first instance, and a recommendation of benevolence to others in the second, looks like an improved reading of Sidney Smith's celebrated formula—'A. never sees B.

in distress but he wishes C. to go and relieve him.'

The law of whipping vagrants was enforced in other counties much in the same manner as in Buckinghamshire.

The following curious items are from the constable's accounts at Great Staughton, Huntingdonshire:

169? Pd. in charges, taking up a distracted woman, watching her, and whipping her next day 0 8 6

171? Spent on nurse London for searching the woman to see if she was with child before she was whipped, 3 of them . 0 2 0

Pd. Tho. Hawkins for whipping 2 people yt had the small-pox 0 0 8

171¾ Paid for watching, victuals and drink, for Ma. Mitchell . . . 00 02 06

Pd. for whipping her . . . 00 00 04

171⅞ Pd. for whipping Goody Barry* . 00 00 04

'Men and women were whipped promiscuously at Worcester till the close of the last century, as may be seen by the corporation records. Male and female rogues were whipped at a charge of 4d. each for the whip's-man. In 1680 there is a charge of 4d. "for whipping a wench." In 1742, 1s. "for whipping John Williams, and exposing Joyce Powell." In 1759, "for whipping Elizabeth Bradbury, 2s. 6d." probably including the cost of the hire of the cart, which was usually charged 1s. 6d. separately.'†

Whipping, however, was not always executed at the 'cart's tail.' It was, indeed, so ordered in the statute of Henry VIII.; but by that passed in the 39th of Elizabeth it was not required, and about this time (1596), whipping-posts came into use. When the writings of John Taylor, 'the water-poet,' were published (1630), they appear to have been plentiful, for he says—

' In London, and within a mile I ween,
There are of jails or prisons full eighteen ;
And *sixty whipping-posts*, and stocks and cages.'

And in *Hudibras* we read of—

' An old dull sot, who toll'd the clock
For many years at Bridewell-dock ;
*　　*　　*　　*　　*
Engaged the constable to seize
All those that would not break the peace ;
Let out the stocks, and *whipping-post*,
And cage, to those that gave him most.'

On May 5th, 1713, the corporation of Doncaster ordered ' a whipping-post to be set up at the stocks at Butcher Cross, for punishing vagrants and sturdy beggars.'† The stocks were often so constructed as to serve both for stocks and whipping-post. The posts which supported the stocks being made sufficiently high, were furnished near the top with iron clasps to fasten round the wrists of the offender, and hold him securely during the infliction of the punishment. Sometimes a single post was made to serve both purposes; clasps being provided near the top for the wrists, when used as a whipping-post, and similar clasps below for the ankles when used as stocks, in which

* *Notes and Queries*, vol. xvii., 327.
† *Idem*, 425.
‡ *Idem*, 568.

case the culprit sat on a bench behind the post, so that his legs when fastened to the post were in a horizontal position. Stocks and whipping-

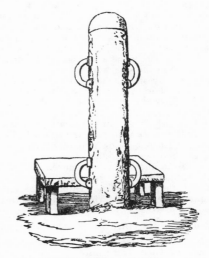

WHIPPING-POST AND STOOL.

posts of this description still exist in many places, and persons are still living who have been subjected to both kinds of punishment for which they were designed. Latterly, under the in-

PARISH STOCKS.

fluence, we may suppose, of growing humanity, the whipping part of the apparatus was dispensed with, and the stocks left alone. The weary knife-grinder of Canning, we may remember, only talks of being put in the stocks for a vagrant. The stocks was a simple arrangement for exposing a culprit on a bench, confined by having his ankles laid fast in holes under a movable board. Each parish had one, usually close to the churchyard, but sometimes in more solitary places. There is an amusing story told of Lord Camden, when a barrister, having been fastened up in the stocks on the top of a hill, in order to gratify an idle curiosity on the subject. Being left there by the absent-minded friend who had locked him in, he found it impossible to procure his liberation for the greater part of a day. On his entreating a chance traveller to release him, the man shook his head, and passed on, remarking that of course he was not put there for nothing. Now-a-days, the stocks are in most places removed as an unpopular object; or we see little more than a stump of them left. The whipping of female vagrants was expressly forbidden by a statute of 1791.

OATMEAL—ITS FORMER USE IN ENGLAND.

Edward Richardson, owner of an estate in the township of Ince, Lancashire, directed, in 1784, that for fifty years after his death there should be, on Ascension Day, a distribution of oatmeal amongst the poor in his neighbourhood, three loads to Ince, one to Abram, and another to Hindley.*

The sarcastic definition of oats by Johnson, in his *Dictionary*—'A grain which in England is generally given to horses, but in Scotland supports the people,' has been the subject of much remark. It is, however, worthy of notice that, when the great lexicographer launched this sneer at Caledonia, England herself was not a century advanced from a very popular use of oatmeal. Markham, in his *English Housewife*, 1653, speaks of oatmeal as a viand in regular family use in England. After giving directions how it should be prepared, he says the uses and virtues of the several kinds are beyond all reckoning. There is, first, the small ground meal, used in thickening pottage of meat or of milk, as well as both thick and thin gruel, 'of whose goodness it is needless to speak, in that it is frequent with every experience.' Then there are oat-cakes, thick and thin, 'very pleasant in taste, and much esteemed.' And the same meal may be mixed with blood, and the liver of sheep, calf, or pig; thus making 'that pudding which is called haggas, or haggus, of whose goodness it is in vain to boast, because there is hardly to be found a man that does not affect them.'

It is certainly somewhat surprising thus to find that the haggis of Scotland, which is understood now-a-days to be barely compatible with an Englishman remaining at table, was a dish which nearly every man in England *affected* in the time of the Commonwealth. More than this, Markham goes on to describe a food called *wash-brew*, made of the very small oatmeal by frequent steeping of it, and then boiling it into a jelly, to be eaten with honey, wine, milk, or ale, according

* Edwards's *Remarkable Charities*, 36.

to taste. 'I have,' says he, 'seen them of sickly and dainty stomachs which have eaten great quantities thereof, beyond the proportion of ordinary meats.' The Scotsman can be at no loss to recognise, in this description, the *sowens* of his native land, a dish formerly prevalent among the peasantry. but now comparatively little known. To illustrate Markham's remark as to the quantity of this mess which could be eaten, the writer may adduce a fact related to him by his grandmother, who was the wife of an extensive store-farmer in Peeblesshire, from 1768 to 1780. A new ploughman had been hired for the farm. On the first evening, coming home just after the sowens had been prepared, but when no person was present in the kitchen, he began with one of the cogs or bowls, went on to another, and in a little time had despatched the very last of the series; after which he coolly remarked to the maid, at that moment entering the house, 'Lass, I wish you would to-morrow night make my sowens all in one dish, and not in drippocks and drappocks that way!'

LESLIE, CHANTREY, AND SANCHO PANZA.

Leslie, the graceful and genial painter, whose death created a void in many a social circle, is chiefly associated in the minds of the public with two charming pictures—'Uncle Toby and the Widow,' and 'Sancho Panza and the Duchess;' pictures which he copied over and over again, with slight alterations—so many were the persons desirous of possessing them. A curious anecdote is told concerning the latter of the two pictures. When Leslie was planning the treatment of his subject, Chantrey, the sculptor, happened to come in. Chantrey had a hearty, jovial countenance, and a disposition to match. While in lively conversation, he put his finger to his nose in a comical sort of way, and Leslie directly cried out, 'That is just the thing for Sancho Panza,' or something to that effect. He begged Chantrey to maintain the attitude while he fixed it upon his canvas; the sculptor was a man of too much sterling sense to be fidgeted at such an idea; he complied, and the Sancho Panza of Leslie's admirable picture is indebted for much of its striking effect to Chantrey's portraiture. There has, perhaps, never been a story more pleasantly told by a modern artist than this—the half-shrewd, half-obtuse expression of the immortal Sancho; the sweet half-smile, tempered by high-bred courtesy, of the duchess; the sour and stern duenna, Doña Rodriguez; and the mirthful whispering of the ladies in waiting—all form a scene which Cervantes himself might have admired. Leslie painted the original for the Petworth collection; then a copy for Mr Rogers; then another for Mr Vernon; and then a fourth for an American collection. But these were none of them mere copies; Leslie threw original dashes of genius and humour into each of them, retaining only the main characteristics of the original picture.

A POETICAL WILL.

The will of John Hedges, expressed in the following quaint style, was proved on the 5th of July, 1737:—

> 'This fifth day of May,
> Being airy and gay,
> To hip not inclined,
> But of vigorous mind,
> And my body in health,
> I'll dispose of my wealth;
> And of all I'm to have
> On this side of the grave

To some one or other,
I think to my brother.
But because I foresaw
That my brothers-in-law,
If I did not take care,
Would come in for a share,
Which I noways intended,
Till their manners were mended—
And of that there's no sign—
I do therefore enjoin,
And strictly command,
As witness my hand,
That naught I have got
Be brought to hotch-pot ;
And I give and devise,
Much as in me lies,
To the son of my mother,
My own dear brother,
To have and to hold
All my silver and gold,
As th' affectionate pledges
Of his brother,

JOHN HEDGES.

MAY 6.

St John before the Latin Gate, 95.　St Eadbert, Bishop of Lindisfarne, confessor, about 698.　St John Damascen, 780.

Born.—Andrea Massena, French general, 1758, *Nice.*
Died.—Charles, Duc de Bourbon, killed at Rome, 1527 ; Sir Robert Bruce Cotton, English historical antiquary, 1631, *Conington ;* Cornelius Jansen (Jansenius), Bishop of Ypres, theologian, 1638 ; Samuel Bochart, French Protestant divine and orientalist, 1667, *Caen ;* Emperor Leopold I., 1705 ; Andrew Michael Ramsay, author of *Travels of Cyrus,* 1743, *St Germain-en-Laye.*

THE CONSTABLE DE BOURBON.

During the middle ages nothing inspired greater horror than false oaths and perjury. It was not enough to give up the guilty persons to the authorities who administered justice, but it was generally believed that God did not wait for the last judgment. The hand of the exterminating angel was always stretched out, menacing and implacable, over those who escaped the action of the law, or who placed themselves superior to it. Numbers of popular legends were current which related the awful divine judgments by which the anger of heaven was manifested against the impious. Such was the death of the Constable de Bourbon.

Born in the year 1489, he early displayed, under the careful training of his mother, a superiority to most men in mental and bodily accomplishments. His beauty and strength excited wonder and admiration ; whilst his correct understanding made friends of all around him. His first campaign was made in Italy, with Louis the Twelfth, during which the gallant Bayard became his most intimate friend ; and being raised by Francis the First to be a Constable of France, he accompanied him also to Italy, and to his talent was due the victory at Marignano. A coldness ensued between the king and his general, owing, it was supposed, to a pique of the queenmother, who had made advances to Bourbon, which were repulsed. She induced the king to refuse repayment of the money which Bourbon had borrowed to save the Milanese ; and afterwards various processes of law were commenced, which, by depriving him of his estates, would have left him penniless.

Provoked by his king's ingratitude, he entered into a secret correspondence with Charles the Fifth, Francis's great rival, and with some difficulty escaped from France, and was immediately appointed lieutenant-general to the emperor, in Italy.

When he had brought back victory under the flag of his new master, relieved Italy from the French rule, and given up the King of France, who was taken prisoner at the disastrous battle of Pavia, to his rival, he did not receive the price he expected for his treason. The emperor refused to give the hand of his sister Eleanor to a traitor, who covered himself in vain with military glory.

The indignant Bourbon returned into the midst of that army of which he was the soul, to hide his shame and rancour. Charles, in the meantime, forgetting the old Spanish bands to whom he owed the conquest of the Milanese, failed to send their pay, and the troops were many months in arrears. At first they supported the privations which their chief shared ; but soon murmurs broke out, and menaces of desertion to the enemy were heard. The constable, after having endeavoured to soften their complaints, no longer offered any opposition to the exactions of every kind that they levied on the duchy of Milan. The magistrates and inhabitants entreated him to put an end to this deplorable state of things, and to remove his army, who, according to the expression of the times, 'lived on the poor man.' He appeared to be touched with the unheard-of evils which the army had caused, and solemnly promised that they should cease, provided the city of Milan furnished him with thirty thousand ducats to pay his bands of mercenaries ; after which he would lead them out of the territory. Thus ran the oath, the breaking of which was fully believed to be the cause of his death by the superstitious : ' In case the least extortion,' said he, calling heaven to witness his promise, ' should be made on the poorest villager or citizen, I pray that, at the next battle or assault in which I shall be engaged, the first cannon-ball which is fired may be at me, and carry away my head.'

The money was paid, but the army remained ; robbery, burning, and murder marked the passage of madmen who cared nothing for their captain's oath ; the desolation of the country was so great, that some of the inhabitants, ruined, ill-used, and dishonoured, killed themselves with their own hands, praying heaven to avenge them. At length, the constable, who doubtless did not possess sufficient authority to keep his word, marched his army out of a country which could no longer maintain it, to Rome, which he intended to besiege and give up to the soldiers, who demanded money or pillage. A thousand sinister voices repeated in his ear the fatal oath he had so imprudently made.

The presentiment of his death seems to have oppressed him when he encamped on the 5th of May, 1527, before the walls of the Eternal City, where the rumour of his approach had spread the greatest alarm. His soldiers, even, who loved him as a father, and believed themselves invincible under his guidance—wild adventurers, who feared nothing either in this world or the next —shook their heads, and fixed their tearful eyes on the general's tent, where he had shut himself up, ordering that all should be ready for the attack on the following morning. During the night, he neither slept nor lay down, remaining in arms, with his brow resting on his hands.

At daybreak the trumpet sounded the assault : the constable, without saying a word, seized a ladder, and rushing before the boldest, himself planted it against the wall. At the same moment, an artillery-man (some say the famous sculptor, Benvenuto Cellini), who had recognised him from the battlements of the Castle of Saint-Angelo, directed his piece so skilfully that the ball carried away the head of Bourbon, who was just crying, 'The city is taken.' Rome was indeed taken, and given up to all the horrors of pillage, but at least the perjurer had received his punishment.

CORNELIUS JANSEN.

The world knows more about the Jansenists than about Jansen, for greater have been the disciples than the master. Cornelius Jansen was born, in 1585, at Akhoi, near Leerdam, in Holland. He was educated for the priesthood, and whilst acting as Professor of the Holy Scriptures at Louvain, he published a treatise, entitled *Mars Gallicus*, denouncing France for heresy on account of the alliances she was forming with Protestant states for the purpose of breaking the power of Spain. In acknowledgment of this service he was made Bishop of Ypres in 1635, but enjoyed his dignity for only three years, being cut off by the plague on the 6th of May, 1638, at the age of 53. If matters had rested here, Jansen would have been forgotten, wrapt in the odour of sanctity ; but for twenty years he had been engaged on a great theological work, in the preparation of which he had read over ten times the whole writings of St Augustine, collating them with the Fathers, and had studied thirty times every passage in which Augustine had referred to the Pelagian controversy. Two years after his death, his executors published the results of his persevering labours as *Augustinus Cornelii Jansenii*, and great was the amazement and horror of orthodox readers. Whilst holding firmly and faithfully to the ecclesiastical order of Rome, it turned out that Jansen had been doctrinally neither more nor less than a Calvinist. Louvain was thrown into a ferment, and attempts were made to suppress the work. The agitation spread to Paris. The inmates of the convent of Port Royal valiantly defended Jansen's positions, which the Jesuits as vigorously attacked. An abstract of Jansen's opinions was drawn up and laid before the pope, who, on 31st of May, 1653, pronounced them heretical. The Jansenists, who now numbered in their ranks men like Pascal and Nicole, admitted the justice of the papal decision, but evaded its force by saying the pope had rightly condemned the doctrines

602

included in the abstract, but that these doctrines were not to be found in Jansen. Again the Jesuits appealed to Rome, and the pope gratified them in asserting that the opinions condemned in the abstract were to be found in Jansen. Thereupon Louis XIV. expelled the Jansenists from Port Royal as heretics, and the Jesuits were triumphant. The controversy did not end here, but lingered on for years, absorbing other questions in its course. So late as 1713, Clement XI. issued his famous bull 'Unigenitus,' in which he condemned 101 propositions of a book by Father Quesnel, for its revival of the heresy of Jansen.

THE LAST OF THE ALCHEMISTS.

On the 6th of May 1782, a remarkable series of experiments was commenced, in his private laboratory at Guildford, by James Price, a distinguished amateur chemist, and Fellow of the Royal Society. Mr Price, during the preceding year, imagined he had succeeded in compounding a powder, capable, under certain circumstances, of converting mercury and other inferior metals into gold and silver. He hesitated before making public this extraordinary discovery ; but having communicated it to a few friends, and the matter becoming a subject of doubtful discussion among chemists, he determined to put it beyond cavil, by conducting a series of experiments in presence of a select assemblage of men of rank, science, and public character. The experiments, seven in number, commenced, as already observed, on the 6th of May, and ended on the twenty-fifth of the same month. They were witnessed by peers, baronets, clergymen, lawyers, and chemists, and in all of them gold and silver, in greater or less quantities, were apparently produced from mercury : to use the language of the alchemists, mercury was transmuted into gold and silver. Some of the gold thus produced was presented to the reigning monarch, George III., who received it with gracious condescension. The University of Oxford, where Price had been a fellow-commoner of Oriel College, bestowed on him the degree of M.D.; and his work, containing an account of the experiments, ran through two editions in the course of a few months.

The more sanguine and less scientific of the community saw in this work the approach of an era of prosperity for England such as the world had never previously witnessed. Who could doubt it? Had not the king honoured, and Oxford rewarded, the fortunate discoverer? Some, on the other hand, asserted that Price was merely a clever juggler; while others attempted to show in what manner he had deceived himself. On some points, however, there could be no difference of opinion. Unlike many professors of alchemy, Price was not a needy, nameless adventurer, but a man of wealth, family, and corresponding position in society. As a scientific man, he had already distinguished himself in chemistry, the study of which he pursued from a pure love of science ; and in private life his amiability of character had insured many worthy and influential friends.

In the fierce paper conflict that ensued on the

publication of the experiments, the Royal Society felt bound to interfere; and, accordingly, called upon Price, as a fellow of the society, to prove, to the satisfaction of his brother fellows, the truth of his alleged transmutations, by repeating his experiments in their presence. From this point Price seems to have lost confidence, and decided symptoms of equivocation and evasion appear in his conduct. He declined to repeat his experiments, on the grounds that the process of preparing the powder of projection was difficult, tedious, and injurious to health. Moreover, that the result of the experiments, though most valuable as a scientific fact, was not of the profitable character he at first believed and the public still supposed; the cost of making gold in this manner being equal to, in some instances more than, the value of the gold obtained; so much so, indeed, that, by one experiment, it cost about seventeen pounds sterling to make only one ounce of gold, which, in itself, was not of the value of four pounds. These excuses were taken for what they were worth; Sir Joseph Banks, the president of the society, reminding Price that not only his own honour, but the honour of the first scientific body in the world, was implicated in the affair. Price replied that the experiments had already been conducted in the presence of honourable and competent witnesses, and no advantage whatever could be gained by repeating them—'for, as the spectators of a fact must always be less numerous than those who hear it related, so the majority must at last believe, if they believe at all, on the credit of attestation.' Further, he adduced his case as an example of the evil treatment that has ever been the reward of great discoverers; and concluded by asserting that his wealth, position in society, and reputation as a scientific chemist, ought, in unenvious and unprejudiced minds, to free him from the slightest suspicion of deceit. To Price's friends this line of conduct was painfully distressing. Yielding at last to their urgent entreaties, he consented to make some more powder of projection, and satisfy the Royal Society. For this purpose, as he stated, he left London, in January 1783, for his laboratory at Guildford, faithfully promising to return in a month, and confound, as well as convince, all his opponents.

Arriving at Guildford, Price shut himself up in his laboratory, where he made it his first employment to distil a quantity of laurel-water, the quickest and deadliest poison then known. He next wrote his will, commencing thus—'Believing that I am on the point of departing from this world.' After these ominous preliminaries, he commenced the preparation of his promised powder of projection. One, two, three—six months passed, but nothing being heard of Price, even his most attached friends reluctantly confessed he had deceived them, when, to the surprise of every one, he reappeared in London, and formally invited as many members of the Royal Society as could make it convenient to attend, to meet him in his laboratory at Guildford on the 3rd of August. Although, scarcely a year previous, the first men in England were contending for the honour of witnessing the great chemist's marvellous experiments, such was

the change in public estimation caused by his equivocal conduct, that, on the appointed day, three members only of the Royal Society arrived at the laboratory, in acceptance of his invitation. Price received them with cordiality, though he seemed to feel acutely the want of confidence implied by their being so few. Stepping to one side for a moment, he hastily swallowed the contents of a flask of laurel-water. The visitors seeing a sudden change in his appearance, though then ignorant of the cause, called for medical assistance; but in a few moments the unfortunate man was dead. Many and various were the speculations hazarded on this strange affair. It is most probable that Price had in the first instance deceived himself, and then, by a natural sequence, attempted either wilfully or in ignorance to deceive others, and, subsequently discovering his error, had not the moral courage to confess openly and boldly that he had been mistaken.

Thus it was that alchemy, among scientific men at least, in England, came to an end with the last act of a tragedy; while in Germany, contrary to what might have been expected, it disappeared amidst the hilarious laughter of a comedy. Contemporary with Price, there lived at the University of Halle, a grave and learned professor of theology named Semler. In his youth, the professor had frequently heard a friend of his father, a crack-witted enthusiast, rejoicing in the appellation of Taubenschus, recount the dazzling marvels of the philosopher's stone. These youthful impressions were never completely obliterated from the mind of the theologian, who used to relieve his severer labours by performing a few chemical experiments in a small private laboratory. But an astute Jew coming to Halle, and informing Semler that he had picked up some wonderful alchemical secrets in Barbary, so completely cheated the simple professor, that he abandoned chemistry, as he then thought, for ever. But, long after, when Semler was well advanced in years, a Baron Hirschen discovered one of those universal medicines, which, like the tar-water, brandy-and-salt, and other nostrums of our own country, occasionally appear, create a furor, and then sink into oblivion. Semler tried some of this Salt of Life, as it was termed; and fancying it benefited his health, German professor-like, sat down and wrote three ponderous treatises on its astonishing virtues, greatly to the disgust of Hirschen, who felt that the theologian was rather ploughing with his heifer, as one might say; but in time he had his revenge.

While studying and developing the virtues of the Salt of Life, Semler could not fail to remember the ancient notion of the alchemists, that the philosopher's stone, when discovered, would also be a panacea. Here, thought he, is a universal medicine, powerful enough to change all diseases into pure and perfect health; why then, he continued, may it not be able to change an imperfect metal into pure and perfect gold? So he determined to fit up his laboratory once more, merely to try a few experiments; and in the meantime he placed an earthen jar, containing a solution of the Salt of Life in pure water, near a stove, to see how it would be affected by a moderate heat. On examining this jar a few days afterwards, to Semler's surprise he found it contained some thin scales of a yellowish metal, which, being tested, unmistakably proved to be pure gold. Here was a discovery!—gold, real, glittering gold, made without trouble or transmutation, furnace or crucible! proving that the dreams of the alchemists regarding transmutation were as absurd as they were proved fallacious; that gold, in accordance with Hermes Trismegistus, could be generated, but not transmuted. Semler's former experience, however, rendered him cautious: he repeated the experiment several times with the same success, till he became perfectly convinced. As conscientious as cautious, the professor considered that the benefits of this great discovery did not belong to him; Hirschen was the discoverer of the Salt of Life, and to him rightfully belonged all the advantages that might accrue from it. So Semler wrote to Hirschen a very minute account of his wonderful discovery; but such is the ingratitude of mankind, that the latter sent back a very contemptuous letter in reply, advising Semler to attend to his chair of theology, and not meddle with matters that he could not comprehend.

Thus repulsed, Semler thought it his duty to publish the matter to the world, which he accordingly did. All Germany was astounded. Salt of Life came into universal demand, and there were few houses in which a jar of it might not be seen near the stove; but fewer still were the houses in which it produced gold—only one, in fact, and that we need not say was Semler's.

The professor, in a lengthy memoir, attempted to explain how it was that his mixture produced gold, while that of others did not. It was owing, he considered, to a perfect regularity of temperature, which was necessary, by fecundating the salt, to produce the gold. But Klaproth, the most eminent chemist of the day, having analyzed the Salt of Life, found it to be a mixture of Glauber's salts and sulphate of magnesia, and utterly incapable of producing gold under any circumstances whatever. Semler then sent Klaproth some of his Salt of Life in powder, as well as in solution, and in both of these the chemist found gold, but not in combination with the other ingredients, as it could be removed from them by the mere process of washing. There could be only one conclusion on the matter; but Semler's known probity, and the absurdity of even the most ignorant person attempting a deception so easily discovered, rendered it very mysterious. As Semler was a theologian, and Klaproth a man of science, suspected of being imbued with the French philosophy, the common-sense view of the question was ignored, and the bitter controversy that ensued turned principally on the veracity of the respective leaders, whether the theologian was more worthy of belief than the chemist, or the contrary. And so hard did theology press upon science, that Klaproth condescended to analyze some of Semler's solution, in presence of the ministers of the king, and other distinguished persons, in Berlin. The result was more surprising than before.

In this public analysis Klaproth found a metal not gold, but a kind of brass called tombac; the substance we term 'Dutch metal.' This new discovery created shouts of laughter; but the government interfering, instituted a legal inquiry, and the police soon solved the mystery. Semler had a faithfully-attached old servant, who, for the simple purpose of gratifying his beloved master, used to slily slip small pieces of gold leaf into the professor's chemical mixtures. Having once commenced this course, the servant had to keep it up, as he well knew the disappointment at not finding gold would be much greater than in the first instance. But the old servant, being a pensioner, had to muster at head-quarters once a year. So, when the time came for him to depart, he entrusted the secret to his wife, giving her money to purchase the gold leaf as it might be required. But this woman, having a partiality for brandy, thought it a sin to waste so much money in gold leaf, and so bought Dutch metal instead, expending the balance on her favourite beverage. Semler fairly enough confessed his error when the laughable discovery was made, and no pretensions of that kind were ever again listened to in the German States.

THE TRIBUTE OF ROSES, A MAY-DAY CUSTOM.

In the times of the early kings of France, the parliament, placed between royalty and the church, formed one of the three great powers of the state. The kings felt a real esteem and respect for this judiciary body, and regularly attended its sittings; besides, it was not always stationary in Paris, but made an annual tour, when the princes and princesses of royal blood were accustomed to follow it in its laborious peregrinations, and thus added to the brilliancy and pomp of its meetings.

It was in 1227, during one of these judicial pilgrimages, that the custom called 'The Tribute of Roses' was founded; one of the most charming of which the parliamentary annals speak. The ceremony was created by a woman and for a woman; by a powerful and illustrious queen, for the wise and lovely daughter of the first president of the parliament of Paris, and possesses at the same time the majesty of all that comes from a throne, and the grace of all that comes from a woman. These, then, were the circumstances, according to ancient chronicles, under which the ceremony was instituted.

The parliament was convoked at Poitiers to judge of an important matter. The Vidame (or judge of a bishop's temporal jurisdiction) de Bergerac, who had been married three times, had left seven children of each union; and it was necessary to decide if those of the first marriage should take their share of the property in the same proportion as the junior branches, the written law and the customs of the provinces of Guyenne and Poitou not being agreed upon the point, and the parliament must settle the difference. The young Count Philibert de la Marche had been appointed judge to report the case; but as he was known to be much fonder of pleasure than work, the family counted little upon him; in addition to which the young man, one of the first peers of the court, had formed a warm attachment, and it is well known that love leaves little time for the serious duties of jurisprudence. They were, however, deceived.

On the 6th of May, Queen Blanche de Castille, widow of Louis VIII., and regent of the kingdom, made her entrance into Poitiers, followed by the principal lords of her court, the president and members of parliament. The streets were strewed with flowers, the houses hung with gay flags and cloth of gold, the cries of 'Vive le Roi,' 'Vive la Regente,' 'Noël, Noël,' mingled with the ringing of bells and the merry chimes of the Hotel de Ville. Mounted on a superb palfrey, the regent had at her right hand her son, twelve years of age, to whom she thus taught the respect which kings owe to justice; precious lessons, which made Louis the Ninth the most just and wise of kings, and gained for him a renown which will never perish. At her left was Thibault, Count of Champagne; then came the Lords of Crecy, of Zaintrailles, of Bourville, and Fécamp; the Earls of Ponthieu, of Toulouse, of Narbonne; the Vidames of Chartres and Abbeville; and a crowd of other gentlemen of renown, covered with their glittering armour. After these chosen warriors, the support and defence of the crown, came the members of parliament, mounted on their more peaceful mules.

At the head of the grave magistrates, every one must have noticed Pierre Dubuisson, the first of a long line of presidents, who, in spite of his eighty years, was fulfilling the serious duties of his appointment. At his side were the Nestors of the French magistracy, Philippe de Moirol, Clément Toutemain, Ange de Saint-Préval, Jacques Saint-Burge, and others who, if younger, were already celebrated for their ripened judgment. This brilliant procession went first to the cathedral, where a solemn mass was sung with due ceremony, in which the prayer was uttered that the Holy Spirit might descend on their proceedings; after which each received the holy communion from the hands of Claude de Blaisemont, Bishop of Poitiers. When this ceremony was ended, the procession again set forth to the house of Maturin de Surlauve, lord high treasurer to the crown.

The queen was anxious that the members, who usually brought their wives and families with them, should find lodgings in her immediate neighbourhood, and had fixed upon the field of roses—which were then in flower, and surrounded the magnificent and luxurious abode prepared for her—as the place for the court of justice to be held in; the first sitting was to take place the following day. The president, Pierre Dubuisson, had then apartments very near to the Regent. A widower for many years past, he had brought with him his daughter Marie, upon whom he lavished all his affections; she was endowed with remarkable beauty, as modest as wise, her wit equalling her elegance, and beloved and respected by the whole court. It was for her that the Count de la Marche felt such a violent passion; in his office as judge and peer of France, he had recourse to the learning of Dubuisson, and thus had often the opportunity of seeing Marie. His sentiments had been long avowed,

his title and coronet laid at her feet; but the modest young girl had always replied to these brilliant offers:—'Monseigneur, yours is an ancient race; your ancestors have left you a dozen turreted castles which adorn and defend France; you ought to have a wife worthy of your greatness, and I am only the daughter of a man of science and virtue. Permit me, then, to refuse your homage.'

This noble refusal, as often happens, had redoubled the ardour of the young count; hence he learnt with delight the determination of the Regent to accompany the parliament in its journey to Poitiers, and be present at its sittings; hoping that during the journey, while his functions obliged him to remain constantly near the princess, he should see Marie more frequently, as Blanche de Castille was much attached to her, and kept her at her side all the day; but the constraint of the royal presence did not permit him to express all he felt. It, however, made him imprudent; and when night came he ventured into the rose garden under Marie's windows, and to attract her attention, he sung one of Count Thibault de Champagne's romances. At the end of the second verse, Marie's window opened, and she addressed him in these words:—

'Are you not ashamed, Monseigneur, to employ the hours of work in vain gallantry? You will be called upon to-morrow to defend before a parliamentary assembly the honour and possessions of orphans, and you are wasting the hours of work in worthless pleasures. Look around you, and see the lights in the windows of the members who are preparing themselves for the important duties which you are called to fill; go and imitate them!'

Feeling the justice of this reproach, the young count felt that the only way of obtaining Marie's hand was to make himself worthy of it; and returning home, he began earnestly to study the cause which he was to plead.

On the morrow's sitting the succession of the Vidame de Bergerac's was the first case called for. The president, certain that the Count de la Marche was not prepared, proposed to pass on to another; but the Regent, who had heard all the previous evening, commanded that the cause should be tried. The count made his deferential bow to her majesty, and proceeded with a clear and luminous statement of the case. He offered conclusions based upon strict legal rules with an eloquence which astonished the wisest magistrates; and, carried away by the talent of the young nobleman, they received and adopted his opinion unanimously.

'Count,' said the Regent, after the sitting, 'you have just given us a marvellous proof of your erudition and eloquence; we thank you for it. But be candid, and tell us who has inspired you so well.'

'The voice of an angel descended from heaven to recall me to my duty,' replied the count.

'I knew it,' said the Regent; 'and I wish to recompense you for having followed the good advice that this angel gave you. Messire Pierre Dubuisson, you are created Chancellor of France; and you, my sweet Marie, shall after to-morrow be saluted by the name of Countess de la Marche.

And to perpetuate the remembrance of this day, to remind the young peers of France how they ought, like the Count de la Marche, to turn the most tender feelings to the advantage of justice, I shall expect them each year to give a tribute to my parliament.'

'And what shall the tribute be?' asked the Count de Champagne.

'A tribute of roses,' replied the Regent. 'Count de la Marche, you are the first to offer it to the parliament.'

In a moment the rose garden was despoiled of its most beautiful flowers, which the count presented in baskets to the grave members. Since then, every year on the first of May the youngest peer of France offered this tribute, which they called *la baillée aux roses*. In 1541 it gave rise to a dispute for precedence between the young Duke of Bourbon-Montpensier and the Duke de Nevers, one of whom was a prince of the blood. The claims of the two pretenders being submitted to the parliament, were argued by the two most celebrated lawyers of the period, François Marillac and Pierre Séguier. After both sides had been heard, the parliament gave its decree on Friday, the 17th of June 1541: 'that having regard to the rank of prince of the blood joined to his peerage, the court orders that the Duke de Montpensier shall offer the tribute of roses.'

This contest, which had excited in the highest degree both the court and the city, proves the value which the highest noblemen attached to the opportunity of paying respect, by this curious and graceful tribute, to the administrators of justice. But in 1589 the League, no longer considering the parliament as a court of peers, abolished the *baillée aux roses*, and since then the custom has been forgotten.

Bussy-Rabutin relates, that under the reign of Louis XIV. the President de Samoiguan proposed its re-establishment; but the Duke de Vivonne, to whom he spoke, replied—

'Monsieur le President, the peers of France, who support above all things the prerogatives of the crown, are not always on a good understanding with the parliament; believe me, it is better that we should both keep within our limits; let us not exhume old customs, which might perhaps become real subjects of dissension.'

These words induced the president to resign his intention; and this charming custom, so graceful in its origin, was for ever abolished.

MAY 7.

St Benedict II., Pope, confessor, 686. St John of Beverley, 721. St Stanislaus, Bishop of Cracow, martyr, 1079.

JOHN OF BEVERLEY.

Most of the early Anglo-Saxon saints were men and women of princely, or at least of noble birth; and such was the case with John of Beverley, who is commemorated on this day. He was born at Harpham, near Driffield, which latter place was apparently a favourite residence of the Northumbrian kings; and he was there-

fore a Yorkshireman. As was not very common among the Anglo-Saxons, he received a scriptural instead of an Anglo-Saxon name; and he was evidently intended for the church from his infancy, for we are told that when a boy his education was entrusted to the Abbess Hilda, and he afterwards went to Canterbury, and pursued his studies under Theodore the Great, who may be looked upon as the father of the Anglo-Saxon schools. On leaving Theodore, John set up as a teacher himself, and opened a school in his native district, in which his learning drew together a number of scholars, among whom was the historian Bede. About the year 685, John was made bishop of Hexham, one of the sees into which the then large diocese of York had been divided during the exile of Wilfred; but on Wilfred's return the see of York was restored to its former condition, and John resigned his bishopric, and retired into comparatively private life. Not long afterwards Hexham was again formed into a separate bishopric, and restored to John, who was removed thence to be made Archbishop of York, in the year 705.

From the account of this prelate given by his disciple Bede, it is evident that he was a man of learning, and of great piety, and that he exercised considerable influence over the Northumbrian church in his time; yet he was evidently not ambitious of public life, but preferred solitude and contemplation. Hence, both as bishop and archbishop, he selected places of retirement, where he could enjoy temporary seclusion from the world. With this view, he built a small monastic cell in an open place in the heart of the forest of the Deiri, which was so far removed from the haunts of men that its little stream was the resort of beavers, from which circumstance it was called in Anglo-Saxon Beofor-leag, or the lea of beavers, which, in the change of language, has been smoothed down into Beverley. From this circumstance, the Archbishop of York became known by the name of John of Beverley, which has distinguished him ever since. In 718, when he felt old age creeping upon him, John resigned his archbishopric, and retired to the solitude of Beverley, where he spent the remainder of his days. He died on the 7th of May 721. It is hardly necessary to add, that John's cell in the forest soon became a celebrated monastery, and that the flourishing town of Beverley gradually arose adjacent to it. Hither, during Roman Catholic times, numerous pilgrims resorted to the shrine of the saint, where great miracles and wonderful cures of diseases were believed to be performed; and his memory was held in such reverence, and his power as a saint supposed to be so great, that 'St John' became the usual war cry of the English of the North in their wars with the Scots.

Born.—Gerard Van Swieten, physician, 1700, *Leyden.*

Died.—Otho the Great, emperor, 973, *Magdeburg;* Jacques Auguste de Thou (Thuanus), French historian, 1617; John Gwillim, herald, 1621; Patrick Delany, D.D., miscellaneous writer, 1768, *Bath;* William, Marquis of Lansdowne, 1805; Richard Cumberland, English dramatist, 1811; H. W. Bunbury, amateur artist, 1811; Thomas Barnes, editor of the *Times,* 1841, *London.*

DE THOU.

The great work of the Sieur De Thou, the History of his own Time, is of a character to which no English writer has presented an exact parallel. According to one of his countrymen : 'That love of order, that courageous hatred of vice, that horror of tyranny and rebellion, that attachment to the rights of the crown and the ancient maxims of the monarchy, that force in the descriptions, that fidelity in the portraits,—all those characters of truth, of courage, and impartiality which shine in all parts of his work, have given it the distinction of being the purest source of the history of the sixteenth century.'

It must ever reflect credit on De Thou, while affording a noble incentive to others, that this truly great work was composed in the midst of the most laborious state employments.

THOMAS BARNES.

A future generation may perhaps enjoy the memoirs of some of the great editors who in the course of the present century have raised the political press to a power in the state. Common and natural is the curiosity to penetrate the mystery of the thunder of *The Times*, but discreetly and thoroughly has that mystery been preserved. We know the names of Walter, Stoddart, Barnes, Sterling, and Delane ; but of their mode of working and associates, little certainly.

Thomas Barnes, under whose editorship *The Times* became the greatest of newspapers, was born in 1785, and was educated as a Blue-coat boy. From Christ's Hospital he went to Cambridge ; after which, returning to London, he entered as a student for the bar at the Temple. The monotony of the law he relieved by light literary pursuits. He commenced writing a series of critical essays on English poets and novelists for a paper called *The Champion*, in which he manifested an eminent degree of power and taste. *The Champion* became sought after for the sake of Barnes's essays, which its conductors accordingly were anxious to see continued. There was, however, great difficulty in Barnes's irregular habits. Moved by their importunity, he had a table with books, paper, and ink, placed at his bedside, and ordered that he should be regularly called at four in the morning. Rising then, and wrapping round him a dressing-gown, he would dash off the coveted articles. Afterwards, having more ambitious views, he addressed a number of letters to *The Times*, on the men and events of the day, and was gratified by seeing them accepted. Mr Walter, struck with their merit, called on Barnes, and employed him, first as reporter, and then as editor. It is said Barnes wrote very few leaders, but spent his skill in appointing subjects to able writers, and in trimming and amplifying their productions. His life of incessant labour was unhappily closed by a premature death. After long suffering from stone, he was operated upon by Liston ; but his system, sapped by dissipation, and worn down by mental toil and bodily pain, gave way, and he died on the 7th of May 1841, at the age of fifty-six.

DON SALTERO.

In an entry of 'several presentments of Court Leet, relative to the repairs of walls on the banks of the Thames,' dated May 7th, 1685, there appears the name of James Salter, as one of the tenants who was fined the sum of five pounds, for suffering the river wall opposite his dwelling-house to become ruinous. The earliest notice, however, that we have of this person as the proprietor of a museum, is contained in a paper by Sir Richard Steele, published in *The Tatler*, in 1709, in which he is recognised by his nickname of Don Saltero, and several of his curiosities are incidentally mentioned. Salter had been valet to Sir Hans Sloane. On leaving service, he returned to his original trade of a barber,—combined, as it then was, with the arts of bleeding and tooth-drawing. In 1693, he set up a coffee-house, his late master giving him a few curiosities to place in the public room, as an attraction to customers. Salter being himself an oddity, his house soon became frequented by retired naval officers, and other residents of Chelsea, who contributed to his collection, and gave him the title of Don Saltero, from a fancied resemblance he bore to the celebrated knight of the woful countenance. Steele describes him as a sage of a thin and meagre countenance, enough to make one doubt whether reading or fretting had made it so philosophic. His first advertisement appears in *The Weekly Journal* of June 22nd, 1723, in the following words :—

'SIR,
Fifty years since, to Chelsea great,
  From Rodnam, on the Irish main,
I stroll'd, with maggots in my pate,—
  Where, much improv'd they still remain.
Through various employs I've past :
  A scraper, vertuos', projector,
Tooth-drawer, trimmer, and at last
  I'm now a grimcrack whim-collector.
Monsters of all sorts here are seen,
  Strange things in nature as they grew so ;
Some relicks of the Sheba queen,
  And fragments of the fam'd Bob Cruso.
Knick-knacks to dangle round the wall,
  Some in glass cases, some on shelf ;
But, what's the rarest sight of all,
  Your humble servant shows himself.
On this my chiefest hope depends,
  Now, if you will the cause espouse,
In journals pray direct your friends
  To my museum coffee-house ;
And, in requital for the timely favour,
I'll gratis bleed, draw teeth, and be your shaver ;
Nay, that your pate may with my noddle tally,
And you shine bright as I do—marry shall ye
Freely consult my revelation Molly ;
Nor shall one jealous thought create a huff,
For she has taught me manners long enough.
                                        DON SALTERO.
Chelsea Knackatory.'

Salter made no charge for seeing his museum, but visitors were expected to take refreshments ; and catalogues were sold for twopence each, headed with the words.

'O RARE !'

containing a list of the collection, and names of

607

the persons who had contributed to it. This catalogue went through forty-five editions, and the business was no doubt a profitable one. The time of Salter's death is not very certain, but his daughter, a Mrs Hall, kept the house in 1760.

Pennant, when a boy, saw in Don Saltero's collection 'a lignified hog,' that had been presented by his great uncle; it was simply the root of a tree, somewhat resembling the form of a pig. From one of the catalogues, now before us, we extract the following items, as a sample of the whole :—' A piece of Solomon's temple. Job's tears that grow on a tree. A curious piece of metal found in the ruins of Troy. A set of beads made of the bones of St Anthony of Padua. A curious flea-trap. A piece of Queen Catherine's skin. Pontius Pilate's wife's great-grandmother's hat. Manna from Canaan. A cockatrice serpent. The Pope's infallible candle. The lance of Captain How Tow Sham, King of the Darien Indians, with which he killed six Spaniards, and took a tooth out of each head, and put it in his lance as a trophy. Oliver's broadsword.' This last article had, in all probability, been presented by one of the earliest frequenters of the coffee-house, 'a little and very neat old man, with a most placid countenance,' named Richard Cromwell, the ex-protector of England. Sir John Cope and his sons, who lived in the neighbourhood, are included among the contributors to the museum; but there is no Highland broadsword mentioned in the catalogue. There is one remarkable item in it, which forms a curious link with the present day. It is described as 'a coffin of state for a friar's bones.' In Nichols's edition of The Tatler, we learn that this elaborately carved and gilt coffin, with its contents, was a present from the Emperor of Japan to the King of Portugal, that had been captured by an English privateer, whose captain gave it to Saltero. There can be little doubt that the bones it contained were the remains of one of 'the Japanese martyrs!'

One can hardly realize the fact, that in the last century, strangers in London made a point of visiting Don Saltero's, just as they now-a-days visit the British Museum. Franklin, in his 'Life,' says : 'We one day made a party to go by water to Chelsea, in order to see the college and Don Saltero's curiosities.' It was on the return from this party that the then journeyman printer, by displaying his skill in swimming, was induced to consider whether he would not try his fortunes in England as a teacher of swimming.

Everything has its day. So in 1799, after being an institution for more than a hundred years, Saltero's house and curiosities fell under the all-conquering and inevitable hammer of the auctioneer. In the advertisement which announces the sale, the house is described as 'a substantial and well-erected dwelling-house, delightfully situated facing the River Thames, commanding a beautiful view of the Surrey hills and adjacent country. Also, the valuable collection of curiosities.' The last fetched no more than £50. The highest price given for a lot was thirty-six shillings, which was paid for 'a very curious model of our blessed Saviour's sepulchre at Jerusalem, very neatly inlaid with mother-o'-pearl.'

608

MONKS OF ST FRANCIS.

May 7, 1772, died Sir William Stanhope, K.B., a younger brother of the celebrated Philip, Earl of Chesterfield. He resided at Eyethorpe in a handsome and hospitable manner, and exercised an attraction in society through his wit and literary talents. Sir William was a member of a convivial fraternity very characteristic of an age which, having material prosperity, and nothing to be fearful or anxious about, showed men of fortune generally in the light of pleasure-seekers rather than of duty-doers. The association bore the name of the Monks of St Francis, partly in allusion to the place of meeting, the house of Medmenham, in Bucks, which had been originally a Cistercian monastery. It comprised John Wilkes and Charles Churchill; the less-known poets, Lloyd and Paul Whitehead; also Francis Lord le Despencer, Sir John Dashwood King, Bubb Doddington, and Dr Benjamin Bates. The spirit of the society was shown by their putting up over the door of their place of meeting, the motto of the actual order of St Francis, 'Fais ce que tu voudras;' and it is understood that they took full advantage of the permission. Their orgies will not bear description. One can only express a regret that men possessed generally of some share of talents, and perhaps of impulses not wholly discreditable to their hearts, should have so far mistaken their way in the world.[*]

When Dr Lipscomb published his elaborate work on Buckinghamshire in 1847, he could hear of but one surviving member of the order of St Francis, and he in extreme old age, together with a gentleman who had been admitted to a few meetings while yet too young to be made a member.

While the orgies of the Medmenham monks must needs be buried in oblivion, it may be remarked that such societies were not uncommon in that full-fed, unthinking age. There was one called the Harry-the-Fifth Club, or The Gang, designed to exemplify in a more or less metaphorical manner the habits attributed to the hero of Agincourt. Of this fraternity, the then heir of British royalty, Frederick Prince of Wales, was a member; and there exists, or lately existed, at Windsor, a picture representing a sitting of the Gang, in which the Prince appears as president, with Sir Hugh Smithson, Lord Inchiquin, and other members. An example of the badge supposed to have belonged to this club represents the exploits of the tavern on one side, and those of the highway on the other, the latter containing, moreover, a view of a distant town, with stocks and a gibbet, with the motto, 'JACK GANG WARILY.'[†] Although the two latter words are an injunction to proceed with caution, it cannot be doubted that an extreme licence in all kinds of sensual enjoyments was assumed as the privilege of the Harry-the-Fifth Club.

* Lipscomb's Buckinghamshire, i. 481; iii. 615.
† Gentleman's Magazine, Sept. 1854. 'Gang Warily,' is the motto of the Drummonds, Earls of Perth, meaning simply, walk cautiously. The jingle of sound and sense between the name and motto might not be above the contemplation of this self-enjoying society.

MAY 8.

Apparition of St Michael. St Victor, martyr, 303. St Odrian, of Waterford (era unknown). St Wiro, o. Ireland, 7th century. St Gybrian, of Ireland, 8th century. St Peter, Archbishop of Tarentaise, in Savoy, 1174.

Born.—Alain René le Sage, French novelist, 1668, *Sargeau, in Brittany;* Dr Beilby Porteus, Bishop of London, 1731, *York;* Rev. William Jay, Congregationalist divine, 1769. *Tisbury. Wilts.*

Died.—Dr Peter Heylin, author of the *Life of Archbishop Laud,* &c., 1662 ; Marc René de Voyer de Paulmi, Marquis d'Argenson, French minister, 1721; Archbishop William King, 1729. *Donnybrook;* Bishop Hough, of *Worcester,* 1743 ; Pope Benedict XIV., 1758 ; Dr Samuel Chandler, 1766, *London;* Sebastian, Marquis de Pombal, Portuguese statesman, 1782, *Pombal;* Duc de Choiseul, French minister, 1785 ; Antoine L. Lavoisier, chemist, guillotined at Paris, 1794; W. C. Townsend, Q.C., author of *Lives of Eminent Judges.* 1850, *Wandsworth Common, near London;* Captain Barclay Allardice, noted athlete and pedestrian, 1854.

ARGENSON

Is worthy of a passing note as the first institutor of the modern system of police. He was a man of high family and no small personal merit, and when he took the position of lieutenant of the Parisian police, in 1697, he was considered as somewhat degrading himself. He contrived, however, to raise the office to his own level, by the improvements which he introduced, resulting in that system of easy and noiseless movement which not only checks ordinary breaches of the law, but assists so notably in preserving the government from its enemies. Argenson was a native of Venice, and received his first honours in that republic ; it was probably from the old secret practices of the Venetian state that he derived his idea of an improved police for Paris, that form of police which has since been extended to Austria, Prussia, and other governments. He finally became the French minister of finance, and died a member of the Academy.

BISHOP HOUGH'S MUNIFICENCE.

This memorable prelate, who had been elected to the presidentship of Magdalen College, Oxford, in opposition to the Roman Catholic recommended to the Fellows of the College by James II., attained the great age of ninety-three. Of his boundless munificence the following instance is related :—'He always kept a thousand pounds in the house for unexpected occurrences, perhaps to pay his funeral expenses, or legacies. One day, one of the excellent societies of his country came to him to apply for his contributions. The bishop told his steward to give them £500. The steward made signs to his master, intimating that he did not know where to find so large a sum. He replied, "You are right, Harrison ; I have not given enough. Give the gentleman the thousand pounds ; and you will find it in such a place;" with which the old steward was unwillingly, was forced to comply.' The good bishop was buried in his cathedral (Worcester), where is a fine monument to his memory, by Roubiliac ;

the scene of the above anecdote of his munificence being sculptured in bas-relief upon the memorial. The bishop, though he had acted a prominent part in public affairs, lived without an enemy. Pope says of him :

'Such as on Hough's unsullied mitre shine.'

Lord Lyttelton and Hawkins Browne also speak highly of Bishop Hough ; and Sir Thomas Bernard has introduced him as the principal speaker in his excellent colloquy—*The Comforts of Old Age.*

'CAPTAIN BARCLAY.'

By this name, without the affix of Allardice, was recognised, in the early part of the present century, a man whose pride and pleasure it was to exhibit the physical potentialities of human nature in their highest stretch. Rather oddly, he represented genealogically a man of wholly different associations, the celebrated Robert Barclay, who, in the reign of Charles II., wrote the *Apology for the Quakers.* It appears, however, that both the father and son of Robert were remarkable for their bodily strength. A powerful athletic figure was in fact hereditary in the family.

One of Captain Barclay's first notable feats— done, indeed, in his fifteenth year—was to walk, 'fair toe and heel,' six miles in an hour. In June 1801, when two and twenty, he walked from his family seat of Ury, in Kincardineshire, to Boroughbridge, in Yorkshire, a distance of 300 miles, in five oppressively hot days. It was on the 10th of November in the same year, that he completed the performance of one of his most notable feats, walking ninety miles in twenty-one and a half successive hours, on a bet of 5000 guineas. This he accomplished in an hour and eight minutes within time, without being greatly fatigued. Some years later, the task of walking 1000 miles in 1000 successive hours, a mile within each hour, in which many had before failed and none succeeded, was undertaken by Barclay, and about £100,000 was staked on the issue. He began his course at Newmarket, at midnight, on the 1st of June, and duly finished it at 3 p.m. on the 12th of July, amidst a vast concourse of spectators. Here, of course, the shortness of the periods of repose was what constituted the real difficulty. The pain undergone by the gallant captain is understood to have been excessive ; he had often to be lifted after resting, yet his limbs never swelled, nor did his appetite fail ; and, five days after, he was off upon duty in the luckless Walcheren expedition.

The great amateur athlete of the nineteenth century was a frank, honourable man, in universal esteem among his neighbours, and distinguished himself not a little as a promoter of agricultural improvements.

MASTER JOHN SHORNE.

The 8th of May 1308 is the date of the will of Master John Shorne, rector of North Marston, in Bucks, a very remarkable person, since he attained all the honours of a saint without ever being strictly pronounced one. There must have been something uncommon in the character of this country pastor to have so much impressed his contemporaries, and cast such an odour round his tomb for centuries after he was inurned. For one thing, he was thought to have a gift for curing the ague. He had greater powers than this, however, for it was reported of him that he once conjured the devil into a boot. Venerated profoundly, he was no sooner dead than his body was enclosed in a shrine, which immediately became an object of pilgrimage to vast numbers of people, and so continued till the Reformation. The allusions to the multitudes running to Master John Shorne, scattered about our mediæval literature, are endless. The votaries came mainly for cure of ague, which it was supposed the holy man could still effect; and so liberal were their oblations, that the rectory was enriched by them to the extent of £300 a year—a very large sum in those days. At one time the monks of Windsor contrived, by an adroit bargain with those of Osney, to get the body of Master Shorne removed to their church; but, though they advertised well—and this language is literally applicable—the saint did not 'take' in that quarter, and the body was afterwards returned to North Marston. At the same time, there was a well, near North Marston church, which passed by the name of Master John Shorne's Well, and whose waters were believed to be of great virtue for the cure of various diseases. It still exists, a neat square building, about eight feet by six, with an internal descent by steps; but its reputation is wholly gone.

MASTER JOHN SHORNE.
(*From the Rood Screen in Gately Church.*)

What is known of Master John Shorne gives

us a curious glimpse of the habits and ideas of our ancestors. To expect a miraculous cure by visiting the shrine of the saint, or drinking of the waters of his well, was a conviction from which no class was exempt. Equally undoubting were they as to the celebrated boot exorcism. On the ancient screen still existing in the church of Gately, in Norfolk, is a panel containing a tall figure, labelled underneath *Magister Johes Schorn*, exhibiting the saint with the boot in his left hand, and the devil peeping out of it; of which panel a representation appears in the cut. The same objects are painted on a screen at Cawston, in the same county. It would appear as if the saint were understood to keep the fiend in the boot and let it emerge occasionally, like a 'Jack in the box,' to impress the vulgar.

Fox in his *Martyrology* shews us that a pilgrimage to Master John Shorne was sometimes imposed as a penance. Of certain penitent heretics, he tells us, 'some were compelled to bear fagots; some were burned in their cheeks with hot irons; some condemned to perpetual prison; some compelled to make pilgrimages . . . some to the Rood at Wendover, some to Sir John Schorn, &c.' A Protestant ballad says—

'To Maister John Schorn, that blessed man born,
　For the ague to him we apply,
Which jugeleth with a bote, I beshrew his herte-rote,
　That will trust him, and it be I.'

EXHORTATION TO THE CONDEMNED AT NEWGATE.

Near to Newgate prison, in London, is a parish church bearing the grisly name of St Sepulchre's. On the 8th of May 1705, Robert Dowe gave fifty pounds to the vicar and churchwardens thereof, to the end that, through all futurity, they should cause a bell to be tolled, and a serious exhortation to be made to condemned prisoners in Newgate, during the night preceding their execution. For many years this custom was kept up in its full integrity, according to the will of the donor. At midnight, the sexton of St Sepulchre's came with a hand-bell to the window of the *condemned cell*—rang his bell—and delivered this address:

'All you that in the condemned hold do lie,
Prepare you, for to-morrow you shall die:
Watch all and pray, the hour is drawing near
That you before the Almighty must appear:
Examine well yourselves, in time repent,
That you may not to eternal flames be sent:
And when St Sepulchre's bell to-morrow tolls,
The Lord above have mercy on your souls!'

On the ensuing day, when the dismal procession, setting out for Tyburn, passed the gate of St Sepulchre's church, it paused for a brief space, while the clergyman addressed a prayer in behalf of the prisoner or prisoners, the great bell tolling all the time. There is something striking and impressive in the whole arrangement. By and by came a time when the executions took place in front of Newgate, and the clergyman's address was necessarily given up. Some years ago, it was stated that the sexton was still accustomed to come and offer his midnight address, that the terms of Mr Dowe's bequest might be fulfilled; but the offer was always declined, on the ground that all needful services of the kind were performed by the chaplain of the prison.

MAY 9.

St Hermas, 1st century.　St Gregory Nazianzen, 389. St Brynoth I., Bishop of Scara, in Sweden, 1317.　St Nicholas, Bishop of Lincopen, in Sweden, 1391.

Born.—Giovanni Paisiello, Italian musical composer, 1741, *Tarento.*

Died.—Cardinal de Bourbon, 1590; Francis, fourth Earl of Bedford, 1641; Count Zinzendorf, founder of the sect of Moravian Brethren, 1760, *Herrnhut ;* Comte de Lally, executed at Paris, 1766; Bonnel Thornton, miscellaneous writer, 1768 ; Frederick Schiller, illustrious German poet, 1805, *Weimar ;* Nicolas Francis Gay-Lussac, chemist, 1850, *Paris.*

SCHILLER.

' I will make Schiller as large as life,—that is, colossal.' ' Such,' says Emil Palleske, Schiller's latest German biographer, speaking of the sculptor Dannecker, ' were Dannecker's words, on hearing of the death of his friend. Sorrowful, but steadfast, he commenced his labour of love, and the work became what he aimed at—an apotheosis. No complicated details, no stamp of commonplace reality, dim the pure ether of these features : the traces of a sublime struggle on the lofty forehead, the knit brows, and the hollow cheeks, alone proclaim that this mighty spirit once wandered upon earth ; but the impress of past disquietude only serves to heighten the perfect repose which now designates the divinity. The earnest self-won harmony on the noble countenance irresistibly demands our reverence ; while its lofty resignation imperceptibly reminds us of many anxious cares which beat within our own restless hearts.'

This passage conveys a better idea than our words could give, of the reverential worship paid to Schiller in his own country. He was an intellectual giant, and a grateful people have placed him among their deities. Full of the spirit of his time, of powerful genius, of inexhaustible mental energy, devoted with passionate devotion to his own grand ideal of the beautiful and true, he mastered a wretched constitution, and revelled in the domains of mind. Poetry was to him no idle amusement, but conscience, religion, politics, and philosophy.

Johann Christoph Friedrich Schiller was born on the 10th of November 1759, at Marbach. His mother was a pious, worthy woman, of the true German mould, and his father an energetic, intelligent military man, in the service of Karl Eugen, Duke of Würtemberg. As a boy, he was chiefly remarkable for industry and strong feeling. He was intended for the church; but Karl Eugen had founded a military academy, and took care to press into it all the promising youth : so Schiller's views of life changed. As a student of the academy, he was devoted to his duke, and exercised his growing talent for verse in praise of the duchess, equally out of admiration and necessity. He became a regimental surgeon, and practised in Stuttgart. But with this post he was dissatisfied, and justly ; and when his *Robbers* appeared, and made him popular, he became still more restless. The duke looked with

suspicious eye on this mad youth, who spoke his mind so freely ; and fresh writings giving fresh offence, he prohibited the poet from writing again. At length he was put under arrest for fourteen days, and reprimanded, for stealing, without leave of absence, to Mannheim, to see his play acted. Then he fled in the night with a friend, and became an exile. After enduring much privation in many wanderings, he became theatre poet at Mannheim. Here he produced *Fiesco* and *Don Carlos,* toiled incessantly, indulged in numerous elective affinities, and got further into debt.

Debt—or rather uncertainty of income—was Schiller's bane. He trusted entirely to his pen and Providence for subsistence. In Mannheim, a friend, who had been bound for his Stuttgart debts, was arrested, and only set free at the expense of a poorer man, on whom the loss fell. Such are awkward incidents in the history of genius !

The Duke of Weimar, having encouraged Schiller in 1785, he set off to that diminutive Athens, where Jupiter Goethe reigned supreme, and staying at Leipsic on his way, commenced that remarkable friendship with Körner, which lasted through life, and which gave us a long series of noble letters. At last he came to Weimar, but Goethe kept aloof, finding how diametrically opposed their minds were. Years passed over before the restraint was removed. Here Schiller made many friends, as also at Jena, where he accepted a Professorship of History, with no salary. He laboured hard in his duties, and during this period wrote his *History of the Thirty Years' War,* a delight to youth and to age, sketched his great drama of *Wallenstein ;* loved, courted, and married Lotte von Lengefeld, a woman who proved worthy of him ; and enjoyed the friendship of Fichte and Wilhelm von Humboldt. He had a severe illness soon after his marriage, from the effects of which he never recovered. At last, in 1795, the bond of brotherhood was sealed, which reflects such honour on Schiller and Goethe, and which has caused the brother poets to be named the *Dioscuri.* After this, we have mutual plans and productions,— among them the *Xenien,* a series of fine satirical hits at all their numerous enemies, a book which set Germany on fire; mutual direction of the Weimar theatre; struggles with failing health; fresh cares, joys, hopes ; *Wallenstein ; Mary Stuart ; The Maid of Orleans ; The Bride of Messina ;* and lastly, *Wilhelm Tell ;* and so we draw near to the inevitable day.

Schiller's drama of *Wilhelm Tell* took possession of the hearts of the people more than any of its predecessors ; and yet, at the performance of an earlier work, very badly performed in Leipsic, we read that, ' after the first act, loud cries burst forth, from the whole of the crowded house, of " Long live Friedrich Schiller !" accompanied by a grand flourish of trumpets. At the end of the performance all the audience rushed out of the house to see their beloved poet more closely. When his tall form, bent by suffering, appeared, the crowd respectfully made way for him, all heads were quickly uncovered, and the poet was received in profound silence, as he passed through the long rows of people ; all hearts, all eyes, followed his steps; fathers and mothers holding their children aloft to see him, whispering, "That is he! that is he!"'

Schiller had a heart as fine and noble as his forehead. He deserved and won the love and esteem of all. Princes and people delighted to honour him. And posterity has not tarnished, but brightened, the lustre of the honours bestowed on him while he lived.

GAY-LUSSAC.

To Nicolas Francis Gay-Lussac unquestionably belongs the honour of first applying aërostation to scientific purposes on a great scale. True, ascents had been made by other philosophers, at Hamburg in 1803, and at St Petersburg in 1804, to determine in some degree the effect of altitude on magnetic action; but the scale of operations was in each case very limited. The Academy of Sciences, with the aid of the minister of the interior (Chaptal), organized an ascent in August 1804, which was to be managed by Gay-Lussac and Biot, with the aid of Conté, who had been the chief aëronaut with Bonaparte in Egypt. The ascent took place on the 23rd, from the garden of the Conservatoire des Arts et Metiers. The philosopher soon found that the rotatory motion of a balloon, as it ascends, ought to be taken into account in all delicate observations made while in the car; a precaution which had been neglected by the preceding observers. Gay-Lussac determined to make another ascent alone, to reach a still greater altitude. This was done on the 16th of September. He attained the unprecedented elevation of 7016 metres (about 23,000 English feet, upwards of four miles). A magnetic needle, a dipping needle, a centigrade thermometer, two hygrometers, two barometers, two little glass balloons, and one of copper; such were the instruments which the intrepid man took up with him, and which he undertook to observe, besides managing his balloon and car. His chief observations were recorded when he was at the heights of 3,032, 3,863, 4,511, 6,107, and 6,977 metres; and they were very valuable in reference ,o magnetism, pressure, temperature, and moisture. Biot and Gay-Lussac had lowered a pigeon out of their car when at the height of 10,000 feet, to notice its flight; Gay-Lussac made observations on his own respiration at high altitudes; he brought down specimens of rarefied air in his three little balloons; he determined the heights of the clouds he passed through; and he achieved other scientific results which have been brought largely into use by later savans.

The experiments of Mr Gay-Lussac may be said to have remained unrivalled till 1862, when the ardour of meteorological research led to others of a very remarkable character being made by Mr James Glaisher. After a number of preliminary ascents, Mr Glaisher made one at Wolverhampton, in company with Mr Coxwell, on the 6th of September in that year, when the balloon attained the height indicated by 9¾ inches of the barometer, reckoned as equal to 5¼ miles. This was certainly the highest point ever attained by a human being in any circumstances. When thus elevated, the rarity

of the air and extremely low temperature (for the thermometer stood a good way below zero) caused the adventurous aëronaut to fall into a state of insensibility, which was so far partaken of by Mr Coxwell, that the latter had to use his teeth in pulling the valve of the balloon, in order to cause a descent. 'On descending when the temperature rose to 17°, it was remarked as warm, and at 24° it was noted as very warm.' According to the narrative of Mr Glaisher, 'Six pigeons were taken up. One was thrown out at the height of three miles; it extended its wings, and dropped as a piece of paper. A second, at four miles, flew vigorously round and round, apparently taking a great dip each time. A third was thrown out between four and five miles, and it fell downwards. A fourth was thrown out at four miles when we were descending; it flew in a circle, and shortly after alighted on the top of the balloon. The two remaining pigeons were brought down to the ground; one was found to be dead.'

BLOOD'S ATTEMPT ON THE CROWN JEWELS.

This day, in the year 1671, witnessed one of the most extraordinary attempts at robbery recorded in the annals of crime. The designer was an Irishman, named Thomas Blood, whose father had gained property, according to the most probable account, as an iron-master, in the reign of Charles I. When the civil wars broke out, the son espoused the cause of the parliament, entered the army, and rose to the rank of colonel; at least, in subsequent times,

COLONEL BLOOD.

he is always spoken of as Colonel Blood. As, at the Restoration, we find him reduced to poverty, we may conclude that he had either squandered away his money, or that his property had been confiscated, perhaps in part both, for he seems to have laboured under the impression of having been injured by the Duke of Ormond, who had been appointed lord lieutenant of Ireland, and against whom he nourished the bitterest hatred. In 1663, he formed a plot for surprising Dublin Castle, and seizing upon the lord lieutenant, which, however, was discovered before it could be carried into execution. Blood then became a wandering adventurer, roaming from one country to another, until he established himself in London, in the disguise of a physician, under the name of Ayliffe. Such was his position in 1670, when he made another attempt on the life of his enemy, the Duke of Ormond. On the evening of the 6th of December in that year, as the duke was returning home from a dinner given to the young Prince of Orange, in St James's Street, he was stopped by six men on horseback, who dragged him from his coach, and having fastened him with a belt behind one of them, were carrying him off towards Tyburn, with the intention of hanging him there. But, by desperate struggling, he succeeded in slipping out of the strap which bound him, and made his escape, under favour of the darkness, but not without considerable hurt from the brutal treatment he had undergone. A reward of a thousand pounds was offered for the discovery of the ruffians concerned, but in vain.

It was not many months after this event, that Colonel Blood formed the extraordinary design of stealing the crown of England, and he contrived his plot with great artfulness. The regalia were at this time in the care of an aged but most trustworthy keeper, named Talbot Edwards, and Blood's first aim was to make his acquaintance. Accordingly, he one day in April went to the Tower, in the disguise of a parson, with a woman whom he represented as his wife, for the purpose of visiting the regalia. After they had seen them, the lady pretended to be taken ill, upon which they were conducted into the keeper's lodgings, where Mr Edwards gave her a cordial, and treated her otherwise with kindness. They parted with professions of thankfulness, and a few days afterwards the pretended parson returned with half-a-dozen pairs of gloves, as a present to Mrs Edwards, in acknowledgment of her courtesy. An intimacy thus gradually arose between Blood and the Edwardses, who appear to have formed a sincere esteem for him; and at length he proposed a match between their daughter and a supposed nephew of his, whom he represented as possessed of two or three hundred a-year in land. It was accordingly agreed, at Blood's suggestion, that he should bring his nephew to be introduced to the young lady at seven o'clock in the morning on the 9th of May (people began the day much earlier then than now); and he further asked leave to bring with him two friends, who, he said, wished to see the regalia, and it would be a convenience to them to be admitted at that early hour, as they were going to leave town in the forenoon.

Accordingly, as we are told by Strype, who received his narrative from the lips of the younger Edwards, 'at the appointed time, the old man had

got up ready to receive his guest, and the daughter had put herself into her best dress to entertain her gallant, when, behold! parson Blood, with three more, came to the jewel house, all armed with rapier blades in their canes, and every one a dagger and a pair of pocket pistols. Two of his companions entered in with him, and a third stayed at the door, it seems, for a watch.' At Blood's wish, they first went to see the regalia, that his friends might be at liberty to return; but as soon as the door was shut upon them, as was the usual practice, they seized the old man, and bound and gagged him, threatening to take his life if he made the smallest noise. Yet Edwards persisted in attempting to make all the noise he could, upon which they knocked him down by a blow on the head with a wooden mallet, and, as he still remained obstinate, they beat him on the head with the mallet until he became insensible; but recovering a little, and hearing them say they believed him to be dead, he thought it most prudent to remain quiet. The three men now went deliberately to work; Blood placing the crown for concealment under his cloak, while one of his companions, named Parrot, put the orb in his breeches, and the other proceeding to file the sceptre in two, for the convenience of putting it in a bag.

The three ruffians would probably thus have succeeding in executing their design, but for the opportune arrival of a son of Mr Edwards from Flanders, accompanied by his brother-in-law, a Captain Beckman, who, having exchanged a word with the man who watched at the door, proceeded upstairs to the apartments occupied by the Edwardses. Blood and his companions thus interrupted, immediately decamped with the crown and orb, leaving the sceptre, which they had not time to file. Old Edwards, as soon as they had left the room, began to shout out, 'Treason! Murder!' with all his might; and his daughter, rushing out into the court, gave the alarm, and cried out that the crown was stolen. The robbers reached the drawbridge without hindrance, but there the warder attempted to stop them, on which Blood discharged a pistol at him. As he fell down, though unhurt, they succeeded in clearing the other gates, reached the wharf, and were making for St Katherine's-gate, where horses were ready for them, when they were overtaken by Captain Beckman. Blood discharged his second pistol at the captain's head, but he escaped hurt by stooping, and immediately seized upon Blood, who struggled fiercely; but finding escape impossible, when he saw the crown wrested from his grasp, he is said to have exclaimed, in a tone of disappointment, 'It was a gallant attempt, however unsuccessful; for it was for a crown!' A few of the jewels fell from the crown in the struggle, but all that were of any value were recovered and restored to their places. Blood and Parrot (who had the orb and the most valuable jewel of the sceptre in his pocket) were secured and lodged in the White Tower, and three others of the party were subsequently captured.

The king, when informed of this extraordinary outrage, ordered Blood and Parrot to be brought to Whitehall to be examined in his presence.

There Blood behaved with insolent effrontery He avowed that he was the leader in the attempt upon the life of the Duke of Ormond, in the preceding year, and that it was his intention to hang him at Tyburn; and he further stated that he, with others, had on another occasion concealed themselves in the reeds by the side of the Thames, above Battersea, to shoot the king as he passed in his barge; and that he, Blood, had taken aim at him with his carbine, but that 'his heart was checked by an awe of majesty,' and that he had not only relented himself, but had prevented his companions from proceeding in their design. This story was probably false, but it seems to have had its designed effect on the king, which was no doubt strengthened by Blood's further declaration that there were hundreds of his friends yet undiscovered (he pretended to have acted for one of the discontented parties in the state), who were all bound by oath to revenge each other's death, which 'would expose his majesty and all his ministers to the daily fear and expectation of a massacre. But, on the other side, if his majesty would spare the lives of a few, he might oblige the hearts of many; who, as they had been seen to do daring mischief, would be as bold, if received into pardon and favour, to perform eminent services for the crown.' The singularity of the crime, the grand impudence of the offender, united perhaps with a fear of the threatened consequences, induced the king to save Blood from the vengeance of the law. He not only pardoned the villain, but gave him a grant of land in Ireland, by which he might subsist, and even took him into some degree of favour. It is alleged that Blood occasionally obtained court favours for others, of course for 'a consideration.' Charles received a rather cutting rebuke for his conduct from the Duke of Ormond, who had still the right of prosecuting Blood for the attempt on his life. When the king resolved to take the ruffian into his favour, he sent Lord Arlington to inform the duke that it was his pleasure that he should not prosecute Blood, for reasons which he was to give him; Arlington was interrupted by Ormond, who said, with formal politeness, that 'his majesty's command was the only reason that could be given; and therefore he might spare the rest.' Edwards and his son, who had been the means of saving the regalia—one by his brave resistance, and the other by his timely arrival—were treated with neglect; the only rewards they received being grants on the exchequer, of two hundred pounds to the old man, and one to his son, which they were obliged to sell for half their value, through difficulty in obtaining payment.

After he had thus gained favour at court, Blood took up his residence in Westminster; and he is said by tradition to have inhabited an old mansion forming the corner of Peter and Tufton streets. Evelyn, not long after the date of the attempt on the crown, speaks of meeting Blood in good society, but remarks his 'villanous, unmerciful look; a false countenance, but very well spoken, and dangerously insinuating.' He died on the 24th of August, 1680.

In the Luttrell Collection of Broadsides (*Brit.*

Mus.) is one styled 'An Elegie on Colonel Blood, notorious for stealing the Crown.'

'Thanks, ye kind fates, for your last favour shown,—
For stealing Blood, who lately stole the crown.'

The elegist is no flatterer. He boldly accuses Blood of having spent his whole life in villany. The first considerable affair he was engaged in

'Was rescuing from justice Captain Mason,
Whom all the world doth know to have been a base one;
The next ill thing he boldly undertook,
Was barbarously seizing of a duke,' &c.

The conclusion comes well off :—

'At last our famous hero, Colonel Blood,—
Seeing his projects all will do no good,
And that success was still to him denied,—
Fell sick with grief, broke his great heart, and died.'

The imperial crown now used by the British monarch on state occasions is different from that so nearly purloined by Colonel Blood. It was constructed in 1838, with jewels taken from old crowns, and others furnished by command of Her Majesty Queen Victoria. Professor Tennant, of King's College, laid the following account of it before the London and Middlesex Archæological Association, at Islington, July 7th, 1858 :—

'It consists of diamonds, pearls, rubies, sapphires, and emeralds, set in silver and gold; it has a crimson velvet cap, with ermine border, and is lined with white silk. Its gross weight is 39 oz. 5 dwts. Troy. The lower part of the band,

above the ermine border, consists of a row of 129 pearls, and the upper part of the band of a row of 112 pearls, between which, in front of the crown, is a large sapphire (partly drilled), purchased for the crown by King George the Fourth. At the back are a sapphire of smaller size and 6 other sapphires (three on each side), between which are 8 emeralds.

'Above and below the seven sapphires are 14 diamonds, and around the eight emeralds 128 diamonds. Between the emeralds and sapphires are sixteen trefoil ornaments, containing 160 diamonds. Above the band are 8 sapphires, surmounted by 8 diamonds, between which are eight festoons, consisting of 148 diamonds.

'In the front of the crown, and in the centre of a diamond Maltese cross, is the famous ruby said to have been given to Edward Prince of Wales, son of Edward the Third, called the Black Prince, by Don Pedro, King of Castile, after the battle of Najera, near Vittoria, A.D. 1367. This ruby was worn in the helmet of Henry the Fifth at the battle of Agincourt, A.D. 1415. It is pierced quite through, after the Eastern custom, the upper part of the piercing being filled up by a small ruby. Around this ruby, to form the cross, are 75 brilliant diamonds. Three other Maltese crosses, forming the two sides and back of the crown, have emerald centres, and contain, respectively, 132, 124, and 130 brilliant diamonds.

'Between the four Maltese crosses are four ornaments in the form of the French *fleur-de-lis*, with 4 rubies in the centre, and surrounded by rose diamonds, containing, respectively, 85, 86, 86, and 87 rose diamonds.

'From the Maltese crosses issue four imperial arches, composed of oak leaves and acorns; the leaves containing 728 rose, table, and brilliant diamonds; 32 pearls forming the acorns, set in cups containing 54 rose diamonds and 1 table diamond. The total number of diamonds in the arches and acorns is 108 brilliant, 116 table, and 559 rose diamonds.

'From the upper part of the arches are suspended 4 large pendant pear-shaped pearls, with rose diamond caps, containing 12 rose diamonds, and stems containing 24 very small rose diamonds. Above the arch stands the mound containing in the lower hemisphere 304 brilliants, and in the upper 244 brilliants; the zone and arc being composed of 33 rose diamonds. The cross on the summit has a rose-cut sapphire in the centre, surrounded by 4 large brilliants, and 108 smaller brilliants.'

Summary of Jewels comprised in the Crown.— large ruby irregularly polished; 1 large broad-spread sapphire; 16 sapphires; 11 emeralds; 4 rubies; 1363 brilliant diamonds; 1273 rose diamonds; 147 table diamonds; 4 drop-shaped pearls; 273 pearls.

PLATED CANDLESTICKS.

Candlesticks plated with silver were first made about a century since. Horace Walpole, in a letter to Mr Montagu, writes, Sept. 1, 1760: 'As I went to Lord Strafford's, I passed through Sheffield, which is one of the foulest towns in England, in the most charming situation; there are two-and-twenty thousand inhabitants making knives and scissors; they remit eleven thousand pounds a week to London. One man there has discovered *the art of plating copper with silver*; I bought a pair of candlesticks for two guineas that are quite pretty.'

MAY 10.

Saints Gordian and Epimachus, martyrs, 3rd and 4th centuries. St Comgall, abbot, 601. St Cataldus, Bishop of Tarentum, 7th century. St Isidore of Madrid, labourer, patron of Madrid, 1170. St Antoninus, Archbishop of Florence, 1459.

Born.—A. R. J. Turgot, illustrious finance minister of France, 1727, *Paris.*

Died.—Mareschal de Marillac, beheaded at Paris, 1632; La Bruyère, author of *Caractères*, 1696; Barton Booth, comedian, 1733, *Cowley, in Middlesex*; Louis XV., King of France, 1774; Caroline Matilda, Queen of Denmark, 1775, *Zelle*; General De Dampierre, killed at Tamars, 1793.

LOUIS XV.

Louis XV., though his private life was immoral, and his public conduct deficient in firmness and energy, was not without some of those merits which are always so much appreciated when they occur in high places. He has the credit of having been a liberal encourager of the useful arts. In connexion with this feature of his character a strange story is told.

A native of Dauphiné, named Dupré, who had passed his life in making experiments in chemistry, professed to have invented a kind of fire, so rapid and so devouring, that it could neither be evaded nor quenched, water only giving it fresh activity. On the canal of Versailles, in presence of the king, in the court of the arsenal of Paris, and in other places, Dupré made experiments, the results of which astonished the beholders. When it fully appeared that a man possessing this secret could burn a fleet or destroy a town in spite of all resistance, Louis forbade that the invention should be made public. Though he was then embarrassed with a war with the English, whose fleet it was most important that he should destroy, he declined to avail himself of an invention, the suppression of which he deemed to be required in the general interests of humanity. Dupré died some time after, carrying the secret with him to his grave. One naturally listens to all such stories with a certain degree of incredulity; yet it does not seem to be beyond the hopes of science to invent a fire which would, by the very tremendousness of its effects, make war an absurdity, and so force on the great expected day when a general police of nations will prevent any one from entering on hostilities afflicting to itself and others.

PUBLIC PLEASURE-GARDENS OF THE COMMONWEALTH.

Evelyn enters in his Diary, under May 10, 1654: 'My lady Gerrard treated us at Mulberry Garden, now the only place of refreshment about the town for persons of the best quality to be exceedingly cheated at;* Cromwell and his partizans having shut up and seized on Spring Garden, which till now had been the usual rendezvous for the ladies and gallants at this season.'

* Buckingham Palace now occupies the site of Mulberry Gardens.

Evelyn presently after adds: ' I now observed how women began to paint themselves, formerly a most ignominious thing, and used only by prostitutes.'

'SOMETHING TO YOUR ADVANTAGE.'

On the 10th of May 1830, there came before a London police magistrate a case involving a peculiar kind of fraud which for many years baffled the law, and consequently acquired a considerable degree of notoriety. Joseph Ady may be said to have been one of the newspaper celebrities of England during fully twenty years of the first half of the nineteenth century. Every now and then we were regaled with paragraphs headed, ' Joseph Ady again,' giving accounts of some one having been despoiled by him, and who had vainly sought for redress. Strange to say, a true and thorough notoriety ought to have been sufficient to guard the public against his practices; and yet, notorious as he appeared to most people, there must have been vast multitudes who had never heard of him, and who consequently were liable to become his victims. Ady was a decent-looking elderly man, a Quaker, with the external respectability attached to the condition of a householder, and to all appearance considered himself as pursuing a perfectly legitimate course of life. His *métier* consisted in this. He was accustomed to examine, so far as the means were afforded him, lists of unclaimed dividends, estates or bequests waiting for the proper owners, and unclaimed property generally. Noting the names, he sent letters to individuals bearing the same appellatives, stating that, on their remitting to him his fee of a guinea, they would be informed of ' something to their advantage.' When any one complied, he duly sent a second letter, acquainting him that in such a list was a sum or an estate due to a person of his name, and on which he might have claims worthy of being investigated. It was undeniable that the information *might* prove to the advantage of Ady's correspondent. Between this *might be* and the unconditional promise of something to the advantage of the correspondent, lay the debatable ground on which it might be argued that Ady was practising a dishonest business. It was rather too narrow a margin for legal purposes; and so Joseph went on from year to year, reaping the guineas of the unwary—seldom three months out of a police-court and its reports—till his name became a by-word; and still, out of the multitudes whom he addressed, finding a sufficient number of persons ignorant of his craft, and ready to be imposed upon— and these, still more strange to say, often belonging to the well-educated part of society.

In the case brought under notice on the 10th of May, 1830, Mr Blamire, a London solicitor, acting for a Mr Salkeld, had given in charge one Benjamin Ridgeway for defrauding him of a sovereign. Mr Salkeld, a solicitor in Cumberland, had received one of Ady's letters, had requested Mr Blamire to inquire into the matter; and a sovereign having consequently been given to Ridgeway, who was Ady's servant, a notice had been returned, stating that the name of Salkeld was in a list of persons having unclaimed money in the funds. Mr Blamire being of belief that there could be no connexion between the two Salkelds, demanded back the sovereign; and, on failing to obtain it, gave Ady's messenger, Ridgeway, into custody. The chief Bow-street police magistrate at that time was Sir Richard Birnie, who often indulged in rather undignified colloquies with the persons brought before him. Joseph Ady came forward to protect or assist his messenger, and then the following conversation occurred:—

Sir R. Birnie. Oh! you are the Mr Ady to whom so many persons, myself amongst the number, have been indebted for such valuable information; are you not?

Ady. I have come forward on behalf of my servant; but, if you have any charge against me, here I am.

Sir R. Birnie. You are charged, in conjunction with your servant, with having swindled Mr Blamire out of a sovereign, under pretence of furnishing a Mr Salkeld with information which turns out to be false.

Ady. I have lived for upwards of twenty-five years in Houndsditch, and, if I were a swindler, I could not have preserved my character so long.

Sir R. Birnie. Then you admit having empowered your agent to receive the money in your name?

Ady. I do. I have carried on transactions of a similar description for years; and although I have met with persons who were ungrateful enough to demand back the fee which I require for my trouble, I have always maintained my point, and I mean still to maintain it. If this gentleman has any demand against me, he knows my address, and the law is open to him. I insist that this is not the right place to try the question.

Sir R. Birnie. We will see that presently. Let the police constable who took this fellow's servant into custody stand forward, and produce the money he found upon him.

The constable accordingly produced two sovereigns and some halfpence; and, by direction of the magistrate, he handed one of the sovereigns to Mr Blamire. Ady said that he had not the least objection to his servant stating where and from whom he got the other. Ridgeway, looking significantly at his master, said he had forgotten the name of the gentleman who paid him the sovereign, but that he lived in Suffolk Place. An officer was sent to the address named, with directions that the gentleman should come forward and state the pretence under which Ridgeway had obtained the money. While the officer was gone, the magistrates conferred as to what should be done.

Sir R. Birnie. There is no doubt whatever that a gross system of fraud and imposition has been carried on for years by the defendant Ady. Upwards of fifty letters have been addressed to me upon the subject by persons who have been swindled out of their money.

Ady. I wonder, then, that you, as a magistrate, have not taken earlier notice of me. I am always to be found, and everybody knows there is law enough in England to reach every species of offence. If I had done wrong, I should have been punished long ago.

Sir R. Birnie. You are a clever fellow, and manage to keep within the law; but take care, Mr Ady, for I am determined to have my eye upon you.

Ady. So you may; you cannot say that you ever lost a sovereign by me yet.

Sir R. Birnie. No; but you tried hard for it, by sending me one of your swindling letters.

Ady. If I did, I dare say I could have told you something worth your notice.

Sir R. Birnie. Not you, indeed. And I'll tell you candidly, I never had a relation so rich as I am myself; therefore it would be quite useless to throw away your information upon me.

Ady. If that's the case, Sir Richard, your name shall be scratched from my books whenever I have your permission to go home.

The officer, on his return, whispered the result of his inquiry to Sir Richard, who exclaimed aloud— ' What! Mr Doherty, Solicitor-General for Ireland! Why, you pitch your game high indeed! So you have obtained the other sovereign from the Irish Solicitor-General!'

Ady. I did ; and that I think is a sufficient proof that my transactions are fair and above board. I should indeed be a hardy swindler to attempt to impose upon a Solicitor-General.

Sir R. Birnie. I have the honour to be acquainted with Mr Doherty ; and I dare say he will be good enough to tell me upon what pretence he parted with his money. He certainly could have known nothing of your character.

Ady. Perhaps not, Sir Richard.

The conversation ended here. The marked superiority of the cool, calm sense, and self-possession of Ady, over the inconsequential blustering of the magistrate, will enable the reader to understand how this singular man lived so many years upon the simplicity of the public.

CROMWELL'S COURTESY TO SIR WILLIAM SMYTH.

Sir William Smith, or Smyth, who on the 10th of May 1661, was created a baronet by Charles II. for his services during the civil war, was born at Buckingham about 1616. He was a member of the Middle Temple, and was in 1640 elected a burgess for Winchelsea. For some time he joined the side of the Parliament, but on perceiving its destructive tendencies, he deserted it, and entered the royal army, in which he soon became a colonel. He was governor, or commander of the king's garrison at Hillesden House, near Newport Paguell, when it was besieged and taken by Cromwell, in 1643. The garrison, however, had capitulated to march out with their arms, baggage, &c., unmolested. But as soon as they were out of the gate, one of Cromwell's soldiers snatched off Sir William Smyth's hat. He immediately complained to Cromwell of the man's insolence, and breach of the capitulation. 'Sir,' said Cromwell, 'if you can point out the man, or I can discover him, I promise you he shall not go unpunished. In the meantime (taking off a new beaver which he had on his own head) be pleased to accept of this hat instead of your own.' *

MAY 11.

St Mammertus, Archbishop of Vienna, 477. St Maieul, abbot of Cluni, 994.

Born.—Cardinal Pole, 1500, *Stoverton Castle ;* Peter Camper, anatomist, 1722, *Leyden.*

Died.—David I., King of Scots, 1153, *Carlisle ;* Jacques de Molay, Grand Master of the Templars, burnt at Paris, 1310 ; Jules-Hardouin Mansard, architect of Versailles, 1708 ; Catherine Cockburn, poetess, 1749 ; William Pitt, Earl of Chatham, 1778, *Hayes ;* Spencer Perceval, English minister, assassinated, 1812, *London ;* Madame Récamier, 1849.

ASSASSINATION OF MR SPENCER PERCEVAL.

A weak ministry, under a premier of moderate abilities, Mr Spencer Perceval, was broken up, May 11, 1812, by the assassination of its chief. On the evening of that day, Mr Perceval had just entered the lobby of the House of Commons, on his way into the house, when a man concealed behind the door shot him with a pistol. He staggered forward with a slight exclamation, and fell expiring. The incident was so sudden, that the assassin was at first disregarded by the

* Dr. King's *Anecdotes of his Own Times.*

bystanders. He was at length seized, and examined, when another loaded pistol was found upon him. He remained quite passive in the hands of his captors, but extremely agitated by his feelings, and when some one said, ' Villain, how could you destroy so good a man, and make a family of twelve children orphans ?' he only murmured in a mournful tone, 'I am sorry for it.' It was quickly ascertained that he was named John Bellingham, and that a morbid sense of some wrongs of his own alone led to the dreadful deed. His position was that of an English merchant in Russia : for some mercantile injuries there sustained he had sought redress from the British government ; but his memorials had been neglected. Exasperated beyond the feeble self-control which his mind possessed, he had at length deliberately formed the resolution of shooting the premier, not from any animosity to him, against which he loudly protested, but ' for the purpose,' as he said, ' of ascertaining, through a criminal court, whether his Majesty's ministers have the power to refuse justice to [for] a well-authenticated and irrefutable act of oppression committed by their consul and ambassador abroad.' His conduct on his trial was marked by great calmness, and he gave a long and perfectly rational address on the wrongs he had suffered, and his views regarding them. There was no trace of excitable mania in his demeanour, and he refused to plead insanity. The unhappy man, who was about forty-two years of age, met his fate a week after the murder with the same tranquillity. He probably felt death to be a kind relief from past distresses, for it was his own remark on his trial, ' Sooner than suffer what I have suffered for the last eight years, I should consider five hundred deaths, if it were possible for human nature to endure them, far more to be preferred.' He had left a wife of twenty years, with a babe at her breast, in St Petersburg, waiting to be called to England when his affairs should be settled. A more affecting image of human misery can scarcely be conceived.

It has often been stated that Mr John Williams of Scorrier House, near Redruth, in Cornwall—a man noted through a long life for his vigorous practical talents as a miner and mining speculator—had a dream representing the assassination of Mr Perceval on the night after its occurrence, when the fact could not be known to him by any ordinary means, and mentioned the fact to many persons during the interval between the dream and his receiving notice of its fulfilment. In a book of old world matters, it may be allowable to give such particulars of this alleged affair as can be gathered, more particularly as it is seldom that such occurrences can be stated on evidence so difficult to be dealt with by incredulity. It may be remarked that, unlike many persons who are supposed or alleged to have had such revelations, Mr Williams never made any secret of his story, but freely related every particular, even to individuals who meant to advert to it in print. Thus a minute account of it found its way into the *Times* of 28th August 1828, and another was furnished to Dr Aber-

617

crombie, and inserted by him in his *Inquiries Concerning the Intellectual Powers;* being directly drawn, he tells us, by an eminent medical friend of his own, 'from the gentleman to whom the dream occurred.' This latter account has been republished in a work by Dr Clement Carlyon,* formerly a Fellow of Pembroke College, who states that he had more than once heard the particulars from Mr Williams's own lips. Finally, Mr Hill, a barrister, and grandson of Mr Williams, communicated to Dr Carlyon a narrative which he drew up from the words of his grandfather, agreeing in all essential respects with the other recitals.

According to Dr Abercrombie's account, which Dr Carlyon mainly follows—'Mr Williams dreamt that he was in the lobby of the House of Commons, and saw a small man enter, dressed in a blue coat, and white waistcoat. Immediately after, he saw a man dressed in a brown coat with yellow basket buttons draw a pistol from under his coat and discharge it at the former, who instantly fell, the blood issuing from a wound a little below the left breast.' According to Mr Hill's account, 'he heard the report of the pistol, saw the blood fly out and stain the waistcoat, and saw the colour of the face change.' Dr Abercrombie's recital goes on to say, 'he saw the murderer seized by some gentlemen who were present, and observed his countenance, and on asking who the gentleman was who had been shot, he was told it was the Chancellor. (Mr Perceval was at the time Chancellor of the Exchequer.) He then awoke, and mentioned the dream to his wife, who made light of it.'† We now pursue the more detailed narrative of the *Times.* 'Mrs Williams very naturally told him it was only a dream, and recommended him to be composed, and go to sleep as soon as he could. He did so, and shortly after, again awoke her, and said that he had the second time had the same dream; whereupon she observed he had been so much agitated by his former dream, that she supposed it had dwelt on his mind, and begged of him to try to compose himself and go to sleep, which he did. A third time the vision was repeated; on which, notwithstanding her entreaties that he would be quiet, and endeavour to forget it, he arose, it being then between one and two o'clock, and dressed himself. At breakfast, the dreams were the sole subject of conversation: and in the forenoon Mr Williams went to Falmouth, where he related the particulars of them to all of his acquaintance that he met. On the following day, Mr Tucker, of Tremanton Castle, accompanied by his wife, a daughter of Mr Williams, went to Scorrier House about dusk. 'Immediately after the first salutations, on their entering the parlour, where were Mr, Mrs, and Miss Williams, Mr Williams began to relate to Mr Tucker the circumstances of his dream: and Mrs Williams observed to her daughter, Mrs Tucker, laughingly, that her father could not even suffer Mr Tucker to be seated before he told him of his nocturnal visitation: on the statement of

* *Early Years and Late Reflections.* By Clement Carlyon, M.D. 2 vols. Vol. i., p. 219.

† Dr Abercrombie's *Inquiries Concerning the Intellectual Powers.* Fifth ed. p. 301.

which, Mr Tucker observed that it would do very well for a dream to have the Chancellor in the lobby of the House of Commons, but he could not be found there in reality; and Mr Tucker then asked what sort of a man he appeared to be, when Mr Williams minutely described him; to which Mr Tucker replied, "Your description is not that of the Chancellor, but it is certainly that of Mr Perceval, the Chancellor of the Exchequer; and although he has been to me the greatest enemy I ever met with through life, for a supposed cause which had no foundation in truth (or words to that effect), I should be exceedingly sorry, indeed, to hear of his being assassinated, or of injury of the kind happening to him." Mr Tucker then inquired of Mr Williams if he had ever seen Mr Perceval, and was told that he had never seen him; nor had ever even written to him, either on public or private business; in short, that he never had anything to do with him, nor had he ever been in the lobby of the House of Commons in his life. Whilst Mr Williams and Mr Tucker were still standing, they heard a horse gallop to the door of the house, and immediately after Mr Michael Williams, of Treviner, (son of Mr Williams, of Scorrier), entered the room, and said that he had galloped out from Truro (from which Scorrier is distant seven miles), having seen a gentleman there who had come by that evening's mail from London, who said that he had been in the lobby of the House of Commons on the evening of the 11th, when a man called Bellingham had shot Mr Perceval; and that, as it might occasion some great ministerial changes, and might affect Mr Tucker's political friends, he had come as fast as he could to make him acquainted with it, having heard at Truro that he had passed through that place on his way to Scorrier. After the astonishment which this intelligence created had a little subsided, Mr Williams described most particularly the appearance and dress of the man that he saw in his dream fire the pistol, as he had before done of Mr Perceval.

'About six weeks after, Mr Williams, having business in town, went, accompanied by a friend, to the House of Commons, where, as has been already observed, he had never before been. Immediately that he came to the steps at the entrance of the lobby, he said, "This place is as distinctly within my recollection in my dream as any in my house," and he made the same observation when he entered the lobby. He then pointed out the exact spot where Bellingham stood when he fired, and which Mr Perceval had reached when he was struck by the ball, and when and how he fell. The dress both of Mr Perceval and Bellingham agreed with the description given by Mr Williams, even to the most minute particulars.'

It is worthy of remark that Mr Williams died in April 1841, after the publication of the two accounts of his dream which are here quoted, and no contradiction of the narrative, or of any particular of it, ever appeared. He is described in the obituary of the *Gentleman's Magazine,* as a man in the highest degree estimable. 'His integrity,' says this record, 'was proof against all temptation and above all reproach.'

MADAME RÉCAMIER.

Jeanne Françoise Julia Adelaide Bernard. Madame Récamier, was born on the 4th of December 1777. French memoirs record the histories of many remarkable women who have exercised no unimportant influence on the times in which they lived; and among these, Madame Récamier, not by any means one of the least remarkable, appears to have been in some respects almost unique. It is difficult to explain the source of her influence, which was so universal, which was exercised alike over princes and people, which drew politicians and generals, artists and savans, willingly captive to the feet of a woman during fully half a century. Madame Roland was a woman of indomitable spirit; Madame de Staël was a writer; many French beauties have reigned by a very bad kind of influence; but Madame Récamier had none of these recommendations. She never professed any political opinions decidedly; she was not a writer, nor remarkably witty, nor even high-born, nor yet licentious. But she was beautiful; and to this beauty she united a certain mysterious charm of placid and kind demeanour, a sweet natural manner, a dignified obsequiousness, which made all love her, because she seemed to love them. It was this artful simplicity which made her beauty all-powerful; it was this which made the populace follow after her in the streets of Lyons, where she was born; and this which drew unhappy Marie Antoinette to take notice of a child in a crowd.

A writer in *Fraser's Magazine* draws up a rough list of Madame Récamier's most distinguished admirers. 'There are crowned heads without number; first and foremost, he who was to be Napoleon I.; then Bernadotte, the future King of Sweden; the prince, afterwards King, of Würtemberg; the Hereditary Grand-Duke of Mecklenburg-Strelitz; the Prince of Bavaria; our Prince of Wales; the Dukes of Beaujolais and Montpensier, brothers of Louis Philippe; and last, not least, Prince Augustus of Prussia. . . . . Next we find more than crowned heads: Wellington, Metternich, Duke Mathieu de Montmorency, Benjamin Constant, Canova, Ballanche, and Chateaubriand:'—truly, conquests enough for one woman, and she but a notary's daughter!

Madame Récamier's influence over Napoleon is interesting. The first time he saw her was on a singular occasion. He was delivering his brief and pithy rejoinder to an address presented to him on his return from Italy in 1797, when he observed all eyes suddenly turned from him to another—Madame Récamier had stood up to gain a better sight of the general, and her beauty at once drew all eyes upon her; but so severe, she relates, was the look he directed towards her, that she resumed her seat in confusion. The only other occasion on which Napoleon personally encountered her was at his brother Lucien's house. It was then that Fouché whispered in her ear, 'The First Consul thinks you charming.' Napoleon endeavoured to be placed next to her at dinner; but, failing in this, he called out to Cambacérès, the second consul, who had proved on this occasion more fortunate than his comrade, 'Ah! ah!

citizen consul, close to the prettiest, eh!' A speech which affords a fair specimen of Napoleon's delicacy. After dinner, he endeavoured to open a conversation with her by saying, 'So you like music, madame,' but was interrupted by Lucien. The great man saw her no more. In after years she declined to figure at his court, and fell a victim to his jealousy, and, amongst other indignities, received an order of exile.

It is natural to pass from Napoleon to our own Duke. Wellington is said rather to have been enchanted than favourably received, and Madame Récamier's biographer, Madame Lenormant, charges him with want of good taste on one occasion. The latter statement remains altogether unsubstantiated; and for the former, it is quite plain that the fair dame tried her arts on the honest soldier. A specimen of his letters to her will be interesting for its novel French, as well as for being much more like a despatch than a love-letter.

'Paris, le 20 Octobre, 1814.

'J'étais tout hier à la chasse, madame, et je n'ai reçu votre billet et les livres qu'à la nuit, quand c'était trop tard pour vous répondre. J'esperais que mon jugement serait guide par le votre dans ma lecture des lettres de Mademoiselle Espinasse, et je desespère de pouvoir le former moi-même. Je vous suis bien obligé pour la pamphlète de Madame de Staël.

'Votre très obeissant et fidel serviteur,
'WELLINGTON.'

But, however much Madame Récamier coveted, and did her best to retain, the admiration of all admirers, she undoubtedly bestowed her best affections on Chateaubriand. She became, when they were both growing old, his champion, his priestess, and his nurse. Attachment to him was, latterly, the only merit which won her favour. He was devoted to her, in spite of all his selfishness, in spite of all his morbid sentimentality, with genuine and enduring, if somewhat romantic affection; and when his wife died, he offered her his hand, though she was almost blind, and he on the brink of the grave. This was in 1847; the old man died in 1848, and Madame Récamier in 1849. She had the good sense to refuse a proposal so absurd, but nursed him to the last, with great kindness and self-denial; and when we remember that this Platonic attachment was of thirty years' standing, we cannot refuse to be moved by the last melancholy scenes.

It may sound strange to say that Madame Récamier's life was praiseworthy for its purity and devotion, when we remember that she was a married woman: but, whether or not we approve, we have to bear in mind the difference between French and English customs in respect of marriage. She was married to M. Récamier, who was a wealthy banker, when he was forty-two and she sixteen; and though he always remained a father to her, he was in no sense her husband, except in the legal sense. Here was the error: it was too much to expect a beautiful girl to refuse the world's admiration, or not to have her head turned by the devotion of princes. Indeed, such self-command seems never to have been contemplated. When Lucien Bonaparte, who, by the way, is not set down in the list, paid his passionate addresses to her, M. Récamier recommended her to seem to encourage him, lest she should give some dangerous offence. At another time she even wrote to her husband to ask him to consent to a divorce, in order that she might marry Prince Augustus of Prussia, who had proposed to her; and he did not absolutely refuse, though he expostulated. It is curious, but certainly consistent, to find that the husband's failure in business, and loss of fortune, was afterwards considered sufficient reason for a separation. But there was not the least disagreement; he continued to dine with her daily, till he died in 1830.

Of all her admirers, Canova, whom she intruded herself upon in 1813, pleases us most. He behaved like a sensible man and an artist. He was devoted in a good practical way, lending her his pleasant villa. He shewed his admiration of her beauty not unbecomingly, and with no affectation. He did not talk such silly nonsense as Chateaubriand, who was always in such a vein as this : ' I fear I shall not be able to see you at half-past five, and yet I have but this happiness in the whole world ;' or, ' Je ne vis que quand je crois que je ne vous quitterai de ma vie ; ' but he quietly carved out of the marble an exquisite bust of the beauty ; and when she had the bad taste not to be pleased with it, put it as quietly aside, only, when she was gone, to wreath the brow with bays, and expose it as ' Beatrice.' Surely it was the beauty he loved, and not the woman. So can beauty rule the great and the mean, the artist and the clown. It is this same beauty that has spread the praise of Madame Récamier through the length and breadth of the world ; it is this same beauty which has buried in oblivion many an error such a woman must have been guilty of ; which blinds the eyes of biographers. ' Fleeting, transient, evanescent,' pleads the writer before quoted—' such are the terms invariably applied to beauty by the poet ; a fatal gift, more sadly still says the moralist ; and the wisdom of nations embodied in a popular adage vainly strives to persuade each succeeding generation that those alone are handsome who act handsomely ; yet who dare deny the lasting influence of beauty ? Even athwart the silent gulf which separates the living from the dead its pleadings are heard. Prove but that a woman was beautiful, and scarcely a historian remains impartial. Surely the charm which was sufficient to throw a halo round a Cleopatra, and better than her royal robes to hide the blood-stains on the life of a Mary Stuart, may procure forgiveness for the venial weaknesses which, in this country, will prevent the apotheosis of a Récamier.'

AN EARLY NORTHERN EXPEDITION.

The discoveries and conquests of the Spaniards and Portuguese in South America and India had greatly narrowed the limits of English maritime enterprise, when the discovery of North America by Sebastian Cabot suggested another and shorter route to the *El Dorado* of the East. ' Why,' it was naturally asked, ' should there not be a passage leading to the westward in the northern part of the great American continent, like that of Magellan in the southern ?' The

subject having been canvassed for some years, at last took a practical shape, and a company was formed under the name of *The Mystery, Company, and Fellowship of the Merchant Adventurers, for the Discovery of Unknown Lands*. Two hundred and forty shares of £25 each were rapidly subscribed, and the first three ships fitted out by the Merchant Adventurers weighed anchor at Deptford on the 11th of May 1553, and dropped down the Thames, their destination being to discover a way to China by a north-east passage. Great things being expected from the expedition, the day was made one of general rejoicing. As the ships passed Greenwich, where the court was then held, the courtiers came running out on the terraces of the palace, while the common people stood thick upon the shores below. The privy councillors, as became their dignity, merely looked out of the windows; but those of lesser degree crowded the battlements and towers. ' The ships discharged their ordnance, shooting off their great pieces after the manner of war, and of the sea, so that the tops of the hills sounded, and the valleys gave an echo, while the mariners shouted in such sort that the sky rang again.' It was a very triumph in all respects. ' But,' as the describer of the scene, the tutor of the royal pages, writes, ' alas ! the good King Edward, by reason of his sickness, was absent from this show; and, not long after the departure of these ships, the lamentable and most sorrowful accident of his death followed.'

Cabot drew out the instructions for the conduct of this expedition, being too far advanced in years to take command of it in person. Many bold adventurers offered their services for this important post ; ' but the Company of Merchants made greatest account of one Sir Hugh Willoughby, both by reason of his goodly personage, as also for his singular skill in war, so that they made choice of him for general of the voyage.' Willoughby, about three years previous, had acquired considerable fame by his long-sustained defence of Lauder Castle, in Berwickshire, against the French and Scots. Though suffering the greatest privations, he and a handful of brave men held the castle till peace was proclaimed ; and this circumstance most probably pointed him out to the Company as one whose courage, foresight, and fertility in resources, under the most trying circumstances, peculiarly fitted him for the command of their expedition. Richard Chancellor, the second in command, was recommended to the Company by Sir Henry Sidney, as a man whom he knew most intimately from daily intercourse, and one in the highest degree fitted for carrying out their purpose.

Cabot's instructions did not relate to the scientific part of the voyage alone, but took cognizance of the minutest details of discipline. Thus one clause directs :—' That no blaspheming of God, or detestable swearing, be used in any ship, nor communication of ribaldry, filthy tales, or ungodly talk be suffered in the company of any ship : neither dicing, tabling, carding, nor other devilish games to be frequented, whereby ensueth not only poverty to the players, but also strife, variance, brawling, fighting, and oftentimes murder, to the destruction of the parties and provoking of God's wrath and sword of vengeance.' Prayers, too, were to be said in each ship night and morning, but the explorers were not to attempt to force their religion upon any strange people they might discover; and they were to bear with any religious rites such people might have. The instructions conclude by assuring the explorers of their great likelihood of succeeding in the enterprise, adducing the examples of the Spaniards and Portuguese, who had, to the great wealth of their nations, discovered lands in places previously considered uninhabitable 'for extremities of heats and colds, and yet, when tried, found most rich, well-peopled, temperate, and so commodious that all Europe hath not the like.'

The three ships were respectively named the *Edward Bonadventure*, the *Bona Esperanza*, and the *Bona Confidentia*. Soon after sailing, at a consultation among the captains, Wardhuus in Norway was appointed as their place of rendezvous. A gale in the North Sea occasioned the separation thus foreseen and provided for; but they never met again. Willoughby, with the *Bona Esperanza* and *Bona Confidentia*, steering northwards, discovered Nova Zembla, and from thence was buffeted by opposing winds to the coast of Lapland. Here he anchored in a bay near the mouth of a river now called by the Russians the Varsina, merely intending to wait for a favourable wind to pursue his voyage; but extremely cold weather setting in, he resolved to winter there. This we learn from the last entry in his journal, written about the beginning of October, in the following words :—

'Thus remaining in this haven the space of a week, and seeing the year far spent, and also very evil weather—as frost, snow, hail, as though it had been the deep of winter—we thought best to winter there. Wherefore, we sent out three men south-south-west, to search if they could find people, who went three days' journey, but could find none; after that we sent other three westward, four days' journey, which also returned without finding people. Then sent we three men south-east, three days' journey, who in like sort returned without finding of people, or any similitude of habitation.'

The English at that time had no idea of the severity of a northern winter; and, consequently, the discovery ships were unprovided with the means of guarding against it. The crews of the two ships, six merchants, two surgeons, and Sir Hugh Willoughby, in all about seventy men, were frozen to death, about the same time as Sir Hugh's grand-niece, Lady Jane Grey, and many others of his relations, died on the scaffold. By a signature of Willoughby, attached to his will, it is known that he and some others were alive in January 1554, and may have been rejoiced by a glimpse of the sun at mid-day; but what a scene of horror it shone upon! Such as the poet only can depict :—

'Miserable they !
Who here entangled in the gathering ice,
Take their last look of the descending sun ;
While, full of death, and fierce with ten-fold frost,
The long, long night, incumbent o'er their heads,
Falls horrible ! Such was the Briton's fate,

As with first prow (what have not Britons dared !)
He for the passage sought, attempted since
So much in vain, and seeming to be shut
By jealous Nature with eternal bar.
In these fell regions, in Arzina caught,
And to the stony deep his idle ship
Immediate seal'd, he with his hapless crew,
Each full exerted at his several task,
Froze into statues; to the cordage glued
The sailor, and the pilot to the helm.'

When the gale by which Chancellor, in the *Edward Bonadventure*, was separated from the other ships, had moderated, he made the best of his way to the rendezvous at Wardhuus, where he waited some time for Willoughby; but the latter not arriving, and the season being far advanced, he determined to push on by himself. From this course he was earnestly dissuaded by some 'friendly Scottish men,' whom, to his great surprise, he found at this distant and inhospitable place. But we are not surprised to find Scotchmen there at that time, for the marriage of James III. with the daughter of Christian of Denmark opened up an early communication between Scotland and the extreme north of Europe. And among the Russian archives there is a notice of one David Coken (probably Cochran), a Scotch herald in the service of John, King of Denmark, who visited Russia, by way of the White Sea, three different times previous to 1502, half a century before it was known in England, by the result of Chancellor's voyage, that Russia could be reached in that direction. Chancellor, however, did not listen to the 'friendly Scottishmen,' 'being steadfastly and immutably determined to bring that to pass which he had undertaken to do, or die the death.' 'So,' to use the words of his chronicler, 'he sailed so far that he came at last to the place where he found no night at all, but a continual light and brightness of the sun shining on the mighty sea; and having the benefit of this perpetual light for certain days, at length it pleased God to bring him into a certain great bay, which was one hundred miles or thereabouts over.' This was the White Sea. Soon after he met with some fishermen, from whom he learned that the adjacent country was called Moscovy, and that 'one Juan Vasiliwich ruled far and wide in those places.'

Wintering his ship near the mouth of the Dwina, Chancellor proceeded to Moscow, where he was well received by the Czar; and in the following summer he returned to England as a great discoverer, equal to Columbus or Vasco da Gama. 'Will it not,' says old Hakluyt, 'be in all posterity as great a renown to our English nation to have been the first discoverers of a sea beyond the North Cape, and a convenient passage into the great empire of Russia, as for the Portuguese to have found a sea beyond the Cape of Good Hope, and consequently a passage to the East Indies; or for the Italians and Spaniards to have discovered unknown lands many hundred leagues westward of the Pillars of Hercules?'

In the spring of 1555, some Laplanders found Willoughby's ships uninjured, with their crews still frozen. The news being conveyed to the Czar, he ordered them to be brought to the

Dwina, and their cargoes preserved under seal for the benefit of their English owners. On Chancellor's second voyage to Russia, which immediately succeeded the first, he learned the recovery of these ships; and on his third voyage he brought out men to man and bring them to England. Sailors believe that there are what they term unlucky ships, and the fate of these would almost warrant the idea. In 1556, the three ships of the original expedition sailed from Russia, bound to England. Chancellor, in the *Edward Bonadventure*, returning from his third voyage, bringing with him a Russian ambassador and suite, and the *Bona Esperanza* and *Bona Confidentia*, rescued from the ice to be the agents of another disaster. Not one of the three reached England. The *Edward Bonadventure* was lost on the coast of Aberdeenshire; Chancellor, his son, and most of his crew perished, but the ambassador was miraculously saved.* The *Bona Confidentia* was lost, with all her crew, on the coast of Norway; and the *Esperanza* was swallowed up by the ocean, time and place unknown.

JOHN GILPIN.

Mr Beyer, an eminent linendraper at the end of Paternoster Row, where it adjoins to Cheapside—who died on the 11th of May 1791, at the ripe age of ninety-eight—is reported upon tolerable authority to have undergone in his earlier days the adventure which Cowper has depicted in his ballad of 'John Gilpin.' It appears from Southey's life of the poet, that, among the efforts which Lady Austen from time to time made to dispel the melancholy of Cowper, was her recital of a story told to her in her childhood of an attempted but unlucky pleasure-party of a London linendraper ending in his being carried past his point both in going and returning, and finally brought home by his contrarious beast without ever having come in contact with his longing family at Edmonton. Cowper is said to have been extremely amused by the story, and kept awake by it a great part of the ensuing night, during which he probably laid the foundations of his ballad embodying the incidents. This was in October 1782.

Southey's account of the origin of the ballad may be consistent with truth; but any one who candidly reads the marriage adventure of Commodore Trunnion, in *Peregrine Pickle*, will be forced to own that what is effective in the narration previously existed *there*.

MAY 12.

Saints Nereus and Achilleus, martyrs, 2nd century. St Flavia Domitilla, 2nd century. St Pancras, martyr, 304.

St Pancras, after whom many churches are called, in Italy, France, and Spain, and whose name designates a parish in London having a population equal to many large cities, was a Roman youth of only fourteen at the time of his martyrdom under Diocletion.

Born.—John Bell, eminent anatomist, 1763, *Edinburgh*; Hon. General Sir George Cathcart, 1784; John Russell Hind, astronomer, 1823, *Nottingham*.

* Of this ambassador's adventures and reception in England, an account is given in the present work, under 27th February.

Died.—Thomas Earl of Strafford, English minister, executed 1641, *Tower-hill, London*; John Rushworth, (historical collections), 1690, *Southwark*; Christopher Smart, poet, 1771, *London*; Francis Grose, antiquary, 1791.

THOMAS EARL OF STRAFFORD.

He deserted the popular cause, to become one of the most noted instruments of Charles I. in establishing an arbitrary government in England; he ruled Ireland with a rod of iron, and sowed the seeds of the great massacre in that kingdom. He was undoubtedly a great political culprit; yet the iniquitous nature of his trial and condemnation is equally undoubted; and every generous heart must sympathize with him when he found that the master he had served only too well yielded to sign his death-warrant. Political crime, too, is always so mixed up with sincere, though it may be blind opinion, that it seems hard to visit it with the punishment which we award to downright turpitude. The people made bonfires, and danced round them at his execution; but we, in a cooler time, may sigh over the idea of such a grand man being brought low on Tower-hill.

When Strafford lay in the Tower, he wrote several letters to members of his family, marking the existence in that proud bosom of all the natural affections. To his wife he thus wrote, on receiving the charge preferred by his enemies·

'Sweet Harte,—It is long since I writt unto you, for I am here in such a trouble as gives me little or noe respite. The chardge is now cum inn, and I am now able, I prayse God, to tell you that I conceave ther is nothing capitall; and for the rest, I knowe at the worste his Majestie will pardon all without hurting my fortune, and then we shall be happy by God's grace. Therefore comfort yourself, for I trust the clouds will pass away, and that we shall have fine weather afterwards. Farewell!—Your loving husbande,

'Tower of London,   'STRAFFORD.
4 Febr., 164$\frac{0}{1}$.'

The clouds did *not* pass away. The summer of 1641 was to be no summer for him. Less than a month before his death, when the bill for his attainder was passing to the House of Lords, he wrote in less confident, but still hopeful terms, to his little daughter—*

'My dearest Nan,—The time, I trust, draws on when I may hope to see you, which will be one of the best sightes I can look upon in this world. Your father, as you desired, has been hearde speake for himself, now thes three weekes together, and within a few days we shall see the conclusion. Ther is, I think, little fear of my life; soe I hope for a meanes to be left me to let you see how deare and much esteemed you are and ever shall be to me.

'Look that you learne to play the good housewife, for now, perchance, there may be need of it; yet, however fortune befall me, I shall ever willingly give you the first good of it, and content myself with the second.

'My dear hearte,—Plie your book and other learnings, which will be of use unto you hereafter, and you will see how we will live happily and contentedly, and live to see all these stormes blowen

* This interesting letter appeared in the Earl of Albemarle's work, *Memoirs of the Marquis of Rockingham*. 2 vols. 1852.

over; that so, at leisure, and in fairer weather, I may tell that which I am, and must infallibly be, in all the conditions of life,—Your loving father,

'Tower, this 19th April, 1641.   'STRAFFORD.'

FRANCIS GROSE.

Francis Grose, the son of a rich Swiss jeweller settled in London—at one time an officer in the Surrey militia, whence it was he derived his epithet of 'Captain,'—noted personally for his Falstaff-like figure, wit, and good-fellowship, was suddenly cut off by apoplexy at about the age of sixty. His voluminous works, depicting the ancient buildings of the three kingdoms, his treatises on military antiquities and on ancient arms and armour, may now be considered as superseded by better books; yet they were meritorious for their day. A huge, hearty, laughing figure he makes, through some twenty years of the last century; finally canonized in the verses of Burns, who was captivated by his good-humour, and wrote for him the wondrous tale of *Tam o' Shanter*. There were also some minor works by Grose, including one which embodied the slang and many of the curious local proverbs of England. In one of these lesser books he gives, apparently from his own observation in early life, a sketch of the small squire of England, as he existed before the days of modern improvement; it has something of the merit of Addison, and may be not inappropriately transferred to these pages:—

THE COUNTRY SQUIRE.

Another character, now worn out and gone, was the little independent gentleman, of £300 per annum, who commonly appeared in a plain drab or plush coat, large silver buttons, a jockey cap, and rarely without boots. His travels never exceeded the distance of the county town, and that only at assize and session time, or to attend an election. Once a week he commonly dined at the next market town with the attorneys and justices. This man went to church regularly, read the weekly journal, settled the parochial disputes between the parish officers at the vestry, and afterwards adjourned to the neighbouring ale-house, where he usually got drunk for the good of his country. He never played at cards but at Christmas, when a family pack was produced from the mantel-piece. He was commonly followed by a couple of greyhounds and a pointer, and announced his arrival by smacking his whip, or giving the view-halloo. His drink was generally ale, except at Christmas, the 5th of November, or some other gala days, when he would make a bowl of strong brandy punch, garnished with a toast and nutmeg. A journey to London was, by one of these men, reckoned as great an undertaking as is at present a voyage to the East Indies, and undertaken with scarcely less precaution and preparation.

The mansion of one of these squires was of plaster striped with timber, not unaptly called calamanco work, or of red brick, large casemented bow windows, a porch with seats in it, and over it a study; the eaves of the house well inhabited by swallows, and the court set round with holly-hocks. Near the gate a horse-block for the convenience of mounting. The hall was furnished with flitches of bacon, and the mantel-piece with guns and fishing-rods of various dimensions, accompanied by the broad-sword, partisan, and dagger, borne by his ancestors in the civil wars. The vacant spaces were occupied by stags' horns. Against the wall were posted King Charles's *Golden Rules*, Vincent Wing's *Almanack*, and a portrait of the Duke of Marlborough; in his window lay *Baker's Chronicle*, Foxe's *Book of Martyrs*, *Glanvil on Apparitions*, *Quincey's Dispensatory*, *The Complete Justice*, and a Book of Farriery.

In the corner, by the fire-side, stood a large wooden two-armed chair, with a cushion; and within the chimney corner were a couple of seats. Here, at Christmas, he entertained his tenants assembled round a glowing fire made of the roots of trees, and other great logs, and told and heard the traditionary tales of the village respecting ghosts and witches, till fear made them afraid to move. In the meantime the jorum of ale was in continual circulation.

The best parlour, which was never opened but on particular occasions, was furnished with Turk-worked chain, and hung round with portraits of his ancestors; the men in the character of shepherds, with their crooks, dressed in full suits and huge full-bottomed perukes; others in complete armour or buff coats, playing on the bass viol or lute. The females likewise as shepherdesses, with the lamb and crook, all habited in high heads and flowing robes.

Alas! these men and these houses are no more; the luxury of the times has obliged them to quit the country, and become the humble dependants on great men, to solicit a place or commission to live in London, to rack their tenants, and draw their rents before due. The venerable mansion, in the mean time, is suffered to tumble down, or is partly upheld as a farm-house; till, after a few years, the estate is conveyed to the steward of the neighbouring lord, or else to some nabob, contractor, or limb of the law.

THE 'PRENTICE'S PILLAR.

The beautiful collegiate church, commonly called *chapel*, of Roslin, near Edinburgh, which Britton allows to combine the solidity of the Norman with the finest tracery and ornamentation of the Tudor period, a gem of architectural

ANNIE WILSON OF ROSLIN.

beauty, and so entire that it has lately been refitted as a place of worship for an episcopalian congregation,* used to be shewn, in the earlier years of this century, by a venerable crone named Annie Wilson, of whom a counterfeit presentment is here given, borrowed from the sober pages of the *Gentleman's Magazine* (September 1817). You obtained from Annie a sort of cottage version of the legends of the place: how the barons of Roslin were always buried in mail—how when any evil or death was about to befall one of them, ' the *chaipel* aye appeared on fire the nicht afore '—how Sir William Sinclair's dog saved his master's life by bringing down a stag ' afore it crossed the March-burn,' and all the puffy accounts of the former dignity of the Sinclairs of Roslin, which their relative, Father Hay, has put on record. Mrs Wilson also gave her numerous visitors an account, not quite in the manner of Pugin or Willis, of the details of the architecture—the site of the high altar—the ' star in the east ' hanging from a drop in the groining over it—the seven acts of mercy and the seven deadly sins, carved on two lintels

THE 'PRENTICE'S PILLAR.

in the aisle—the legend on a stone, ' Strong is wine, stronger is the king, stronger are women, but above all truth conquers'—the mural tablet

* Roslin Chapel was desecrated by a mob at the Revolution, and remained for upwards of a century and a half windowless and mouldy, with great hazard of entire, though slow, destruction of its fine internal work. From this fate it has been rescued by the proprietor, the Earl of Rosslyn, to whom the further praise must be given of having effected a complete cleaning of the walls without the slightest injury to the carved work. The church was re-opened for worship on Easter Tuesday 1862, under the auspices of the Bishop of Edinburgh, the Bishop of Brechin, and other clergy of the Scottish episcopal communion.

and epitaph of the Earl of Caithness, of the Latin of which she made sad havoc ; all this in a monotonous voice, and without pauses, somewhat to the discomfiture of the hearers, who, however, never interrupted Annie with a question but they had reason to regret it, for she then recommenced her sing-song recital, and gave it all over again, it being impossible for her to resume the broken thread of her discourse.

Mrs Wilson's strong point was the *Apprentice's Pillar*. ' There ye see it, gentlemen, with the lace bands winding sae beautifully roond aboot it. The maister had gane awa to Rome to get a plan for it, and while he was awa his 'prentice made a plan himself and finished it. And when the maister cam back and fand the pillar finished, he was sae enraged that he took a hammer and killed the 'prentice. There you see the 'prentice's

face—up there in ae corner, wi' a red gash in the brow, and his mother greeting for him in the

corner opposite. And there, in another corner, is the maister, as he lookit just before he was hanged; it's him wi' a kind o' ruff roond his

face,' with a great deal more of the like twaddle, which Annie had told for fifty years without ever hearing a word of it doubted, and never once doubting it herself.

The 'Prentice's Pillar of Roslin is really a most beautiful specimen of Gothic tracery—a thing standing out conspicuously where all is beautiful. Viewing its exquisite workmanship, we need not wonder that such a story as that of the incensed master and his murder of the apprentice should be told regarding it. We have to fear, however, that, notwithstanding the faces of the master, the apprentice, and the apprentice's mother, exhibited on the walls, there is no real foundation for the tale. What chiefly gives cause for this apprehension is, that similar stories are told regarding particular pieces of work in other Gothic churches. In Lincoln cathedral, for example, there is a specially fine circular transept window, concerning which the verger tells you that an apprentice was the fabricator of it in the absence of his master, who, mortified at being so outdone, put an end to his own (not the apprentice's) existence in consequence. So also, in the cathedral of Rouen, there are two rose windows in the respective transepts, both fine, but one decidedly finer than the other. The guide's story is, that the master architect and his pupil strove which should plan the finest window. The pupil produced the north window, which proved 'plus belle que celle du midi,' and the humiliated master revenged himself by killing the pupil. We do not hear that in any of these cases there is any tangible memorial of the event, as at Roslin. How, it may be asked, should there be memorials of the event in that case, if the event be a fiction? We do not see that there is much force in this query. The faces, which are mere masks at the points in the architecture where such objects are commonly given, and not solitary objects (for there are two or three others without any story), may have been modified with a reference to the tale at a date subsequent to that of the building, or the apprentice's pillar and the faces together might all have been formed at the first, in playful or satirical allusion to similar stories told of previous Gothic churches.

All who have ever visited the noble minster of Lincoln must remember the tomb of Bishop Fleming, whereon he is represented twice above in full pontificals, and below in the form of an emaciated figure encompassed in a winding-sheet. All, too, must remember the verger's tale regarding this worthy bishop of Wickliffite memory, to the effect that he died while making an attempt to imitate the Saviour in his miraculous fast of forty days. Every Lincolnshire clown has heard of the 'mon that doyed foasting,' and of whose final condition a memorial is presented on his tomb. Now the truth is that similar figures are to be seen in many churches—as, for example, on the tomb of Canon Parkhouse in Exeter cathedral,—on that of Bishop Tully, of St David's, at Tenby, —on the tomb of John Baret, in the abbey church of Bury,—or that of Fox, bishop of Winchester, who died in 1528,—and always with the same story. Amongst well-informed persons no doubt is entertained that the story is a mere fiction of the plebeian mind, excogitated as a means of accounting for the extraordinary object presented to view. Such acts of asceticism are quite inappropriate regarding ecclesiastics of the fifteenth and sixteenth centuries. What was really aimed at was to give human pride a check, by showing what a great man was reduced to by wasting disease and the natural decay of extreme age. It was a sermon in stone.

Another romantic story, 'representing how a young bride on her marriage-day sportively hid herself in an old oak chest, which closed down upon her with a spring-lock, and how she was not discovered for many years after, by which time her husband had ended his life in melancholy fatuity,'—that tale which Mr Rogers narrated so well in his poem *Italy*, and which a popular ballad has made still more familiar to the English public,—is, in like manner told in several places besides Modena. For example, there is a large old oaken chest in the possession of the Rev. J. Haygarth, rector of Upham, which is said to have formerly been in the neighbouring mansion of Marwell Old Hall, between Winchester and Bishop's Waltham,—where it proved a living tomb to a young lady, precisely in the like circumstances described by Mr Rogers. Bramshall, Hampshire, has a similar chest and tale. The multiplicity of instances reveals the real character of the story, as one engendered by the popular mind in accordance with appearances. The chest is big enough to be a tomb for a human being: therefore it was so. The youth and bridal condition of the victim follow, as necessary to make the case the more telling.

MAY 13.

St Servatius, Bishop of Tongres, **384.** St John the Silent, Armenian anchoret, 559. St Peter Regalati, confessor, 1456.

Born.—Empress Maria Theresa, 1717; Charles, Marquis of Rockingham, statesman, 1730.
Died.—Johan Van Olden Barneveldt, Dutch statesman, beheaded, 1619, *Hague;* Louis Bourdaloue, French divine, 1704, *Paris;* James Basire, 1802; Cardinal Fesch, uncle of Napoleon Bonaparte, 1839.

BARNEVELDT.

This name is usually associated with ideas of national ingratitude. Another is evoked by it, that there is no party or body of men safe by their professions of liberal principles, or even their professed support of liberal forms of government, from the occasional perpetration of acts of the vilest tyranny and oppression. After William of Orange, the Netherlands owed their emancipation from the Spanish yoke to the advocate, Johan Van Olden Barneveldt. He it mainly was who obtained for his country a footing among the powers of Europe. As its chief civil officer, or advocate-general, he gained for it peace and prosperity, freed it from debt, restored its integrity by gaining back the towns which had been surrendered to England as caution for a loan, and extorted from Spain the recognition of its independence. It owed nearly everything to him. Nor could it be shewn that he ever was otherwise than an upright and disinterested administrator. He had, however, to oppose another and a dangerous benefactor of Holland in Prince Maurice of Orange. A struggle between the civil and the military powers took place. There was at the same time a struggle between the Calvinists and the Arminians. In British history, the former religious body has been associated with the cause of civil liberty

The history of the Netherlands is enough to shew that this was from no inherent or necessary affinity between liberty and the Genevan church. Barneveldt, who had embraced the tenets of Armin, contended that there should be no predominant sect in Holland; he desired toleration for all, even for the Catholics. The Calvinists, to secure their ascendency, united themselves with Prince Maurice, who, after all, was not of their belief. By these combined influences, the sage and patriotic Barneveldt was overwhelmed. After a trial, which was a mockery of justice, he was condemned to death; and this punishment was actually inflicted by decapitation, at the Hague, on the 13th of May 1619, when Barneveldt was seventy-two years of age.

MAY 14.

St Pontius, martyr, about 258. St Boniface, martyr, about 307. St Pachomius, abbot, 348. St Carthagh, Bishop of Lismore, about 637.

Born.—John Dunton, 1659, *Graffham*; Gabriel Daniel Fahrenheit, 1686, *Dantzig*; Robert Owen, philanthropic social reformer, 1771.

Died.—Henry IV. of France, assassinated at Paris, 1610; Louis XIII. of France, 1643, *St Germain-en-Laye*; Duc de Maine, 1736; Professor David Runkenius, 1798, *Leyden*; Sir William Congreve, Bart., inventor of warlike missiles, 1828, *Toulouse.*

JOHN DUNTON.

One of the most curious of autobiographies is the *Life and Errors of John Dunton*, a very erratic and versatile genius, who, combining the avocations of author and bookseller, wrote upwards of sixty works, and published more than six hundred. Dunton's mind has, not inaptly, been compared to 'a table, where the victuals were ill-sorted and worse dressed.' He was born at Graffham, in Huntingdonshire, and, at an early age, sent to school, where he passed through the general series of boyish adventures and mishaps — robbing orchards, swallowing bullets, falling into rivers, in short, improving in everything but learning, and not scrupling to tell lies when he could gain any advantage by concealing the truth. His family had been connected with the ministry for three generations; and though he felt prouder of this descent from the house of Levi, than if he had been a duke's son, yet being of too volatile a disposition to follow in the footsteps of his reverend ancestors, he was apprenticed to Thomas Parkhurst, a noted Presbyterian bookseller of the day, at the sign of the Bible and Three Crowns, Cheapside, London. Dunton and his master seem to have agreed very well together; a young lady, however, coming to visit Mr Parkhurst's family, the apprentice made love to her, and they met occasionally in Grocers' Hall Garden; but the master making a 'timely discovery,' sent Miss Susanna back to her friends in the country. Another slight difference occurred between master and apprentice. Parkhurst was a strict Presbyterian, and, according to the established custom of the period, Dunton was bound to attend the same place of worship as his master; but the rambling nature of the apprentice led him 'to break the order and harmony of the family,' by attending the ministrations of a Mr Doolittle, a famous Nonconformist. This course did not escape its merited punishment. One Sunday, as Dunton's eyes were wandering round Mr Doolittle's congregation, a certain beautiful Sarah Seaton gave him 'a mortal wound.' A courtship soon followed, with much letter-writing, to the loss of his master's time, and, worse still, clandestine visits to a dancing-school. How the affair ended we are not informed; in this instance love seems to have given place to politics; for the great struggle which led to the Revolution was in progress; the whole nation was divided into Whigs and Tories, and, of course, the bold 'prentices of London could not be neutral. So Dunton, joining the Whig apprentices, was chosen their treasurer, and one of a deputation that presented a petition bearing 30,000 signatures to the Lord Mayor. His lordship promised that he would acquaint the king with its contents, and then told them to return to their respective homes, and diligently attend to their masters' business.

At the expiration of his term of apprenticeship, Dunton gave his friends a feast to celebrate its 'funeral,' according to the usual custom. 'Such entertainments,' he truly observes, 'are vanity, and expensive;' and undoubtedly he had good reason to say so, for no less than one hundred apprentices were at the feast.

Soon afterwards, commencing trade on his own account, the cares of the world and business set him perfectly at ease from all inclinations to love or courtship. He was a bookseller now, but his great ambition was to be a publisher also. 'Printing,' he says, 'was uppermost in my thoughts, and authors began to ply me with specimens as earnestly, and with as much passion and concern, as the watermen do passengers with oars and sculls.' But Dunton had acquired a knowledge of the venal tribe of Grub-street when serving his time, and knew them to be 'paste and scissors hacks, and most inveterate liars also; for they will pretend to have studied six or seven years in the Bodleian library, and to have turned over all the Fathers, though you shall find that they can scarce tell whether they flourished before the Christian era or afterwards.' So avoiding those hack writers, Dunton's first publishing ventures were three religious works of sound doctrine, which did him good service. Moreover, discovering that politics, though very well for an apprentice, were not so suitable for a master tradesman, he avoided the pillory, in which more than one author and publisher of the time was uncomfortably exhibited; a notable instance being Benjamin Harris, bookseller, of Gracechurch-street, whose brave wife stood on the scaffold beside him, to protect her husband from the missiles of the brutal mob. And it is pleasing to know that this faithful couple, emigrating to America, prospered in New England; and after the Revolution, returned to their old shop in Gracechurch-street, where they lived honoured and respected.

Dunton, becoming 'a rising tradesman,' now turned his attention to matrimony, cautiously consulting his friends respecting his choice of a partner for life. After careful consideration, three ladies were selected, as the most eligible. First, there was Sarah Day, extremely pretty, well-bred, of considerable fortune, and the best natured creature in the world. But then Sarah Doolittle would make a better wife by ten degrees, for her father was a popular author as well as preacher; one of his works had reached the twentieth edition, and his son-in-law might naturally expect a few copyrights for nothing. There was even a third Sarah, a Miss Briscoe, of Uxbridge, handsome, rich, and religious. During his embarrassment as to which of the three Sarahs he should select, Dunton chanced, in his desultory way, to step into Dr Annesley's meeting-house one Sunday, where he saw a young lady, who almost charmed him dead, but on inquiry he found that she was pre-engaged. However, his friends advised him 'to make an experiment on her elder sister, they both being the daughters of Dr Annesley.' The experiment proving successful, the languishing Philaret, as Dunton styles himself, gives a history of the courtship, a sketch of his own and the lady's personal appearance, a recital of the love letters, an abstract of the wedding sermon preached by the father of the lovely Iris, an account of the wedding dinner, and a description of the wedding ring, the device being two hearts united, with the motto—

God saw thee
Most fit for me.

Dunton now removed to a large house, the sign of the Black Raven, near the Royal Exchange. The lovely Iris, whose real prose name was Elizabeth, becoming his bookseller and cash-keeper, managed all his affairs, leaving him entirely to his own rambling and scribbling humours. These were his 'golden days.' Among other works at this period, he published *Maggots; or Poems on several Subjects*, written, at the age of nineteen, by Samuel Wesley, his brother-in-law, and father of the celebrated founder of Methodism.

It is quite probable that his wife's business habits left Dunton too much to his own devices. When the Duke of Monmouth's rebellion was trampled down, Dunton, suddenly remembering that his debtors in New England owed him five hundred pounds, started off across the Atlantic. It is not unlikely that John, like many other citizens of London, was implicated in Monmouth's melancholy affair, and thought it best to get out of the way for a short time.

Dunton gives an amusing and interesting description of New England, as he observed it. In Boston, he saw a woman, who had been condemned to wear for life, on her right arm, the figure of an Indian cut out of red cloth; the mode of punishment so powerfully represented in Hawthorne's *Scarlet Letter*. The books he took over sold well, though the people of Boston were, even at that early period, 'smart' customers and slow paymasters. After a pleasant sojourn of some months, he returned to London, and found

that his wife had admirably managed business during his absence.

His next excursion was to Holland; and then, seeing a prospect of better times, he returned to England, removed to a new shop in the Poultry, and opened it on the same day the Prince of Orange entered London. The better times had arrived; Dunton set himself steadily to business, and soon became a leading and prosperous publisher. He says—'The world now smiled with me; I sailed with the wind and tide, and had humble servants enough among the booksellers, stationers, printers, and binders; but especially my own relations on every side were all upon the very height of love and tenderness.' His most fortunate speculation as a publisher, and of which he seems to have been proudest, was the *Athenian Mercury*, a weekly periodical. This work professed to answer all inquiries on matters of history, divinity, philosophy, love, or marriage. It had a great success, many men of mark were contributors, and it flourished for six years; till the great increase of similar publications of a lighter character caused Dunton to give it up. The complete series forms twenty folio volumes, and there have at various times been several selections of questions and answers reprinted from it. Dunton says, 'Mr Swift, a country gentleman, sent an ode, which, being an ingenious poem, was prefixed to the fifth supplement of the *Athenian Mercury*.' This country gentleman was subsequently the witty Dean of St Patrick's; and the ode has since been incorporated in his collected works. There is an anecdote respecting this poem worth noticing. On reading it Dryden said to Swift, 'Cousin, you will never be a poet;' and this denunciation is supposed to have been the cause of Swift's perpetual hostility to Dryden.

Prosperity still attended Dunton. Succeeding to some property by the death of a relative, he took up the livery of the Stationers' Company, and with the master, wardens, and a select few of the liverymen, dined with the Lord Mayor. The dinner was sumptuous, and his lordship presented each one of the guests with 'a noble spoon' to take home to his wife.

Evil days, however, were at hand. The lovely Iris sickened and breathed her last. John provided mourning for twenty of her relations, buried her handsomely in Bunhill Fields, and procured Mr Rogers, a learned divine, to preach her funeral sermon in her late father's meeting-house. Dunton published this sermon, and also erected a grave-stone to her memory, with a long inscription in verse of his own composition.

The extravagance of Dunton's grief for the loss of his wife clearly indicated that it would not last long. In about six months, he was married again to Sarah, daughter of Madame Jane Nicholas, of St Albans. Of this lady, whom he terms Valeria, he says, 'She seemed to be his first wife in a new edition, corrected and enlarged, or rather, in a new binding,' for he had only 'changed the person, not the virtues.' The marriage did not tend either to his comfort or happiness. His mother-in-law possessed some property, which Dunton wished her to sell, and invest the proceeds in his business, a course she very wisely refused to adopt. The disputes on this subject led to a separation ; and there being no one to look after business, the Black Raven was closed, Dunton setting off to Dublin with a venture of books. There he became involved in a ridiculous dispute with a rival bookseller, of which he published an account in a pamphlet termed *The Dublin Scuffle*. His wayward and unsettled disposition was now fast leading to its inevitable result. In 1705 we find him in terror of a gaol, hiding from his creditors, while writing his *Life and Errors*. As a bookseller he is no more known, though he long existed as a political pamphleteer, having written no less than forty tracts in favour of the Hanoverian succession. Swift says that one of Dunton's pamphlets, entitled *Neck or Nothing*, was one of the best ever published. In 1723, he petitioned George I. for a pension, comparing his unrequited services to those of Mordecai, but his application was unsuccessful. Surviving his second wife, he died in 1735, at the age of seventy-six ; and the last literary notice of him is in *The Dunciad*, where he is not unjustly termed a broken bookseller and abusive scribbler.

VACCINATION, AND ITS OPPONENTS.

On the 14th of May 1796, the immortal Edward Jenner conclusively established the important principles of vaccination ; proving that it was possible to propagate the vaccine affection by artificial inoculation from one human being to another, and thereby at will communicate security to all who were liable to small-pox. In a letter to his friend Gardner, the great discoverer thus modestly expresses himself on this memorable experiment : ' A boy of the name of Phipps was inoculated in the arm, from a pustule on the hand of a young woman,* who was infected by her master's cows. Having never seen the disease but in its casual way before, that is, when communicated from the cow to the hand of the milker, I was astonished at the close resemblance of the pustules, in some of their stages, to the variolous pustules. But now listen to the most delightful part of my story. The boy has since been inoculated for the small-pox, which, as I ventured to predict, produced no effect.'

Never was there a discovery so beneficial to the human race, and never did a discovery meet with so violent, so virulent an opposition. The lowest scribblers, excited by political animosity or personal rivalry, never vented such coarse, illiberal absurdities, as the learned physicians who opposed vaccination. Charges of murder and falsehood were freely made by them; nor was the war waged in the medical schools alone; it polluted the sanctity of the pulpit, and malignantly invaded the social harmonies of private life. Dr Mosely, one of the first of the anti-vaccinists, sagely asks :—' Can any person say what may be the consequences of introducing a bestial humour into the human frame, after a long lapse of years ? Who knows, besides, what ideas may rise in course of time from a brutal fever having excited its incongruous impressions on the brain ? Who knows but that the human

* Her name should be recorded—it was Sarah Nelmes.

character may undergo strange mutations from quadrupedan sympathy ? '

After vaccination had been for some time doing its benign work, a Dr Rowley adduced no less than five hundred cases ' of beastly new diseases ' produced by vaccination, in a pamphlet adorned by two coloured engravings, representing the ox-faced boy and the cow-manged girl. Nor does he confine himself to the medical part of the subject ; he asserts that small-pox is a visitation of God, while cow-pox is produced by impious and wicked men. The former being ordained by Heaven, the latter became neither more nor less than a daring impiety—' an attempt to wrest out of the hands of the Almighty the divine dispensations of Providence.'

Mosely described a boy whose face and part of his body, after vaccination, became covered with cow's hair ; and a Dr Smyth says :—' Among the numerous shocking cases of cow-pox which I have heard of, I know not if the most horrible of all has yet been published, viz., of a child at Peckham, who, after being inoculated with the cow-pox, had his former natural disposition absolutely changed to the brutal ; so that *it* ran upon all fours, bellowing like a cow, and butting with *its* head like a bull.'

Well, indeed, might a satirical poet of the day thus sing—

' O Mosely ! thy books mighty phantasies rousing,
    Full oft make me quake for my heart's dearest treasures :
For fancy, in dreams, oft presents them all browsing
    On commons, just like little Nebuchadnezzars.
There, nibbling at thistles, stand Jem, Joe, and Mary ;
    On their foreheads, oh, horrible ! crumpled horns bud :
Here Tom with a tail, and poor William all hairy,
    Reclined in a corner, are chewing the cud.'

The wildest opponent of vaccination was a certain Ferdinand Smyth Stuart, who described himself as 'physician, barrack-master, and great-grandson to Charles the Second.' The frontispiece to Smyth's work represents Dr Jenner, with a tail and hoofs, feeding a hideous monster with infants, out of baskets. Of course this monster is the pictorial representative of vaccination, and is thus described : ' A mighty and horrible monster, with the horns of a bull, the hind hoofs of a horse, the jaws of the kraken, the teeth and claws of a tiger, the tail of a cow, —all the evils of Pandora's box in his belly,— plague, pestilence, leprosy, purple blotches, fetid ulcers, and filthy sores, covering his body, —and an atmosphere of accumulated disease, pain, and death around him, has made his appearance in the world, and devours mankind, —especially poor, helpless infants ; not by scores only, or hundreds, or thousands, but by hundreds of thousands.' The spirit and wisdom of this member of a royal house will be sufficiently exemplified by one more quotation. Rising with his subject, he exclaims :—' The omnipotent God of nature, the inconceivable Creator of all existence, has permitted Evil, Buonaparte, and Vaccination to exist, to prosper, and even to triumph for a short space of time, perhaps as the scourge and punishment of mankind for their sins, and for reasons no doubt the best, far beyond the powers of our circumscribed and limited portion of penetration and knowledge to discover. But are we to worship, to applaud, or even to submit to Evil, to Buonaparte, or to Vaccination, because they have for some time been prosperous? No! Never let us degrade our honour, our virtue, or our conscience by such servility; let us contend against them with all our exertions and might, not doubting we shall ultimately triumph in a cause supported by truth, humanity, and virtue, and which therefore we well know Heaven itself will approve.'

MAY 15.

Saints Peter, Andrew, and companions, martyrs, 250. St Dympna, virgin, martyr, 7th century. St Genebrard, martyr, 7th century.

𝔚hit 𝔖unday. (1864.)

Whit Sunday is a festival of the Church of England, in commemoration of the descent of the Holy Ghost on the Apostles, when 'they were all with one accord in one place,' after the ascension of our Lord; on which occasion they received the gift of tongues, that they might impart the gospel to foreign nations. This event having occurred on the day of Pentecost, Whit Sunday is of course intimately associated with that great Jewish festival.

Born.—Cardinal Alberoni, Spanish minister, 1664, *Placentia, Italy ;* Constantine, Marquis of Normanby, 1797.

Died.—St Isidore, 1170, *Madrid ;* Mademoiselle Champmêle, celebrated French actress, 1698 ; Alexander Cunningham, historian, 1737, *London ;* Ephraim Chambers (*Cyclopœdia*), 1740, *London ;* Alban Butler, author of *Lives of the Saints,* 1773, *St Omer ;* Dr John Wall Callcott, musician, 1821 ; John Bonnycastle, 1821, *Woolwich ;* Edmund Kean, tragedian, 1833 ; Daniel O'Connell, 1847.

ALBAN BUTLER.

Supposing any one desired to take a course of reading in what is called hagiology, he might choose between the *Acta Sanctorum* and Alban Butler's *Lives of the Saints.* The first would be decidedly an alarming undertaking, for the *Acts of the Saints* occupy more than sixty folios. The great work was commenced more than two hundred years ago by Heribert Rosweyd, a Belgian Jesuit. His design was to collect, under each day of the year, the saints' histories associated therewith. After Rosweyd's death in 1629, the Jesuits commissioned J. Bolland to continue the work. He got through January and February in five folios, when he died in 1665. Under the auspices of his successor, Daniel Papebroch, March appeared in 1668, and April in 1675, each in three volumes. Other editors followed, bearing the unmelodious names of Peter Bosch, John Stilting, Constantine Suyskhen, Urban Sticken, Cornelius Bye, James Bue, and Ignacius Hubens ; and in 1762, one hundred and forty years after the appearance of

January, the month of September was completed in eight volumes, making forty-seven in all. In 1794, it had extended to fifty-three volumes, but owing to the invasion of Holland by the French, the work was not resumed till 1837 ; a new edition in 61 volumes appeared in Paris, 1863-67 ; and since that time it has now (1887) advanced to the sixty-third volume. Although abounding in stores of strange, recondite, and interesting information, the *Acta Sanctorum* do not find many readers outside the walls of convents ; and the secular inquirer into saintly history will, with better advantage, resort to Alban Butler's copious yet manageable narratives.

The Rev. Alban Butler, the son of a Northamptonshire gentleman of reduced fortune, was born in 1710, and in his eighth year was sent to the English college at Douay. There he became noted for his studious habits. He did nothing but read ; except when sleeping and dressing, a book was never out of his hand. Of those he deemed worthy he drew up abstracts, and filled bulky volumes with choice passages. With a passion for sacred biography, he early began to direct his reading to the collection of materials for his *Lives of the Saints.* He became Professor of Philosophy, and then of Divinity, at Douay, and in 1745 accompanied the Earl of Shrewsbury and his brothers, the Talbots, on a tour through France and Italy. On his return he was sent to serve as a priest in England, and set his heart on living in London, for the sake of its libraries. To his chagrin he was ordered into Staffordshire. He pleaded that he might be quartered in London for the sake of his work, but was refused, and quietly submitted. Afterwards he was appointed chaplain to the Duke of Norfolk. His *Lives of the Saints* he published in five quarto volumes, after working on them for thirty years. The manuscript he submitted to Challoner, the vicar apostolic of the London district, who recommended the omission of all the notes, on which Butler had expended years of research and pains. Like a good Catholic he yielded to the advice, but in the second edition he was allowed to restore them. He was ultimately chosen President of the English college of St Omer, where he died in 1773.

Of Alban Butler there is nothing more to tell, save that he was a man of a gentle and tolerant temper, and left kindly memories in the hearts of all who knew him. His *Lives* are written in a simple and readable style ; and Gibbon, in his *Decline and Fall,* perhaps gives the correct Protestant verdict when he says, 'It is a work of merit ; the sense and the learning belong to the author—his prejudices are those of his profession.'

𝔚hitsuntide.

The Pentecost was a Jewish festival, held, as the name denotes, fifty days after the feast of unleavened bread ; and its only interest in the history of Christianity arises from the circumstance that it was the day on which the Holy Ghost descended upon the apostles and imparted to them the gift of tongues. It is remarkable that this feast appears to have had no name peculiar to the early languages of Western Europe, for in all these languages its only name, like the German *Pfingst*, is merely derived from the Greek word, with the exception of our English Whit Sunday, which appears to be of comparatively modern origin, and is said to be derived from some characteristic of the Romish ceremonial on this day. We might suppose, therefore, that the peoples of Western Europe, before their conversion, had no popular religious festival answering to this day. Yet in mediæval Western Europe, Pentecost was a period of great festivity, and was considered a day of more importance than can be easily explained by the incidents connected with it, recorded in the gospel, or by any later Christian legends attached to it. It was one of the great festivals of the kings and great chieftains in the mediæval romances. It was that especially on which King Arthur is represented as holding his most splendid court. The sixth chapter of the *Mort d'Arthur* of Sir Thomas Malory, tells us how, 'Then King Arthur removed into Wales, and let crie a great feast that it should be holden at Pentecost, after the coronation of him at the citie of Carlion.' And chapter one hundred and eighteen adds, ' So King Arthur had ever a custome, that at the high feast of Pentecost especially, afore al other high feasts in the yeare, he would not goe that day to meat until he had heard or seene some great adventure or mervaile. And for that custom all manner of strange adventures came before King Arthur at that feast afore all other feasts.' It was in Arthur's grand *cour plenière* at the feast of Pentecost, that the fatal mantle was brought which threw disgrace on so many of the fair ladies of his court. More substantial monarchs than Arthur held Pentecost as one of the grand festivals of the year; and it was always looked upon as the special season of chivalrous adventure of tilt and tournament. In the romance of *Bevis of Hampton*, Pentecost, or, as it is there termed, Whitsuntide, appears again as the season of festivities—

' In somer at Whitsontyde,
  Whan knightes most on horsebacke ride,
  A cours let they make on a daye,
  Steedes and palfraye for to assaye,
  Whiche horse that best may ren.'

We seem justified from these circumstances in supposing that the Christian Pentecost had been identified with one of the great summer festivals of the pagan inhabitants of Western Europe. And this is rendered more probable by the circumstance, that our Whitsuntide still is, and always has been, one of the most popularly festive periods of the year. It was commonly celebrated in all parts of the country by what was termed the Whitsun-ale, and it was the great time for the morris-dancers. In Douce's time, that is, sixty or seventy years ago, a Whitsun-ale was conducted in the following manner : ' Two persons are chosen, previously to the meeting, to be lord and lady of the ale, who dress as suitably as they can to the characters they assume. A large empty barn, or some such building, is provided for the lord's hall, and fitted up with seats to accommodate the company. Here they assemble to dance and

regale in the best manner their circumstances and the place will afford ; and each young fellow treats his girl with a riband or favour. The lord and lady honour the hall with their presence, attended by the steward, sword-bearer, purse-bearer, and mace-bearer, with their several badges or ensigns of office. They have likewise a train-bearer or page, and a fool or jester, drest in a party-coloured jacket, whose ribaldry and gesticulation contribute not a little to the entertainment of some part of the company. The lord's music, consisting of a pipe and tabor, is employed to conduct the dance.' These festivities were carried on in a much more splendid manner in former times, and they were considered of so much importance, that the expenses were defrayed by the parish, and charged in the churchwardens' accounts. Those of St Mary's, at Reading, as quoted in Coates's History of that town, contain various entries on this subject, among which we have, in 1557 : ' Item payed to the morrys daunsers and the mynstrelles, mete and drink at Whytsontide, iij*s*. iiij*d*.' The churchwardens' accounts at Brentford, in the county of Middlesex, also contain many curious entries relating to the annual Whitsun-ales in the seventeenth century ; and we learn from them, as quoted by Lysons, that in 1621 there was ' Paid to her that was lady at Whitsontide, by consent, 5*s*.' Various games were indulged in on these occasions, some of them peculiar to the season, and archery especially was much practised. The money gained from these games seems to have been considered as belonging properly to the parish, and it is usually accounted for in the churchwardens' books, among the receipts, as so much profit for the advantage of the parish, and of the poor.

THE MORRIS-DANCE.

Antiquaries seem agreed that the old English morris-dance, so great a favourite in this country in the sixteenth century, was derived through Spain from the Moors, and that its name, in Spanish *Morisco*, a Moor, was taken from this circumstance. It has been supposed to be originally identified with the fandango. It was certainly popular in France as early as the fifteenth century, under the name of *Morisque*, which is an intermediate step between the Spanish *Morisco* and the English *Morris*. We are not aware of any mention of this dance in English writers or records before the sixteenth century ; but then, and especially in writers of the Shakspearian age, the allusions to it become very numerous. It was probably introduced into this country by dancers both from Spain and France, for in the earlier allusions to it in English it is sometimes called the *Morisco*, and sometimes the *Morisce* or *Morisk*. Here, however, it seems to have been very soon united with an older pageant dance, performed at certain periods in honour of Robin Hood and his outlaws, and thus a morris-dance consisted of a certain number of characters, limited at one time to five, but varying considerably at different periods. The earliest allusions to the morris-dance and its characters were found by Mr Lysons in the churchwardens' and chamberlains' books at Kingston-upon-Thames, and range through the last two years of the reign of Henry VII. and the greater part of that of his successor, Henry VIII. We learn there that the two principal characters in the dance represented Robin Hood and Maid Marian; and the various expenses connected with their different articles of dress, show that they were decked out very gaily. There was also a *frere*, or friar; a musician, who is sometimes called a minstrel, sometimes a piper, and at others a taborer,—in fact he was a performer on the pipe and tabor, and a 'dysard'

or fool. The churchwardens accounts of St Mary's, Reading, for 1557, add to these characters that of the hobby-horse. 'Item, payed to the mynstrels and the hobby-horse uppon May-day, 3*s*.' Payments to the morris-dancers are again recorded on the Sunday after May-day, and at Whitsuntide. The dancers, perhaps, at first represented Moors—prototypes of the Ethiopian minstrels of the present day, or at least there was one Moor among them; and small bells, usually attached to their legs, were indispensable to them. In the Kingston accounts of the 29th of Henry VIII. (1537-8), the wardrobe of the

THE MORRIS-DANCERS.

morris-dancers, then in the custody of the church-wardens, is thus enumerated :—'A fryers cote of russet, and a kyrtele weltyd with red cloth, a Mowrens (Moor's) cote of buckram, and four morres daunsars cotes of white fustian spangelid, and too gryne saten cotes, and disarddes cote of cotton, and six payre of garters with belles.'

There was preserved in an ancient mansion at Betley, in Staffordshire, some years ago, and we suppose that it exists there still, a painted glass window of apparently the reign of Henry VIII., representing in its different compartments the several characters of the morris-dance. George Tollett, Esq., who possessed the mansion at the beginning of this century, and who was a friend of the Shakspearian critic, Malone, gave a rather lengthy dissertation on this window, with an engraving, in the variorum edition of the works of Shakspeare. Maid Marian, the queen of May, is there dressed in a rich costume of the period referred to, with a golden crown on her head, and a red pink, supposed to be intended as the emblem of summer, in her left hand. This queen of May is supposed to represent the goddess Flora of the Roman festival ; Robin Hood appears as the lover of Maid Marian. An ecclesiastic also appears among the characters in the window, 'in the full clerical tonsure, with a chaplet of white and red beads in his right hand, his corded girdle and his russet habit denoting him to be of the Franciscan order, or one of the Grey Friars ; his stockings are red ; his red girdle is ornamented with a golden twist, and with a golden tassel.' This is supposed to be Friar Tuck, a well-known character of the *Robin Hood Ballads.* The fool, with his cock's comb and bauble, also takes his place in the figures in the window ; nor are the tabourer, with his tabor and pipe, or the hobby-horse wanting. The illustration on the preceding page throws these various characters into a group representing, it is conceived, a general morris-dance, for which, however, fewer performers might ordinarily serve. The morris-dance of the individual, with an occasional Maid Marian, seems latterly to have been more common. One of the most remarkable of these was performed by William Kemp, a celebrated comic actor of the reign of Elizabeth, being a sort of dancing journey from London to Norwich. This feat created so great a sensation, that he was induced to print an account of it, which was dedicated to one of Elizabeth's maids of honour. The pamphlet is entitled, '*Kemp's Nine Daies' Wonder*, performed in a daunce from London to Norwich. Containing the pleasure, paines, and kinde entertainment of William Kemp betweene London and that Citty, in his late *Morrice.*' It was printed in 1600 ; and the title-page is adorned with a woodcut, representing Kemp dancing, and his attendant, Tom the Piper, playing on the pipe and tabor. The exploit took place in 1599, but it was a subject of popular allusion for many years afterwards.

Kemp started from London at seven in the morning, on the first Monday in Lent, and, after various adventures, reached Romford that night, where he rested during Tuesday and Wednesday. He started again on Thursday morning, and made an unfortunate beginning by straining his

hip ; but he continued his progress, attended by a great number of spectators, and on Saturday morning reached Chelmsford, where the crowd assembled to receive him was so great, that it took him an hour to make his way through them to his lodgings. At this town, where Kemp remained till Monday, an incident occurred which curiously illustrates the popular taste for the morris-dance.

'At Chelmsford, a mayde not passing foureteene years of age, dwelling with one Sudley, my kinde friend, made request to her master and dame, that she might daunce the Morrice with me in a great large roome. They being intreated, I was soone wonne to fit her with bels ; besides, she would have the olde fashion, with napking on her armes ; and to our jumps we fell. A whole houre she held out ; but then being ready to lye downe, I left her off ; but thus much in her praise, I would have challenged the strongest man in Chelmsford, and amongst many I thinke few would have done so much.'

Other challenges of this kind, equally unsuccess-ful, took place on Monday's progress ; and on the Wednesday of the second week, which was Kemp's fifth day of labour,—in which he danced from Braintree, through Sudbury, to Melford,—he relates the following incidents.

'In this towne of Sudbury there came a lusty, tall fellow, a butcher by his profession, that would in a Morrice keepe me company to Bury. I being glad of his friendly offer, gave him thankes, and forward wee did set ; but ere ever wee had measur'd halfe a mile of our way, he gave me over in the plain field, protesting, that if he might get a 100 pound, he would not hold out with me ; for, indeed, my pace in dancing is not ordinary. As he and I were parting, a lusty country lasse being among the people, cal'd him faint-hearted lout, saying, "If I had begun to daunce, I would have held out one myle, though it had cost my life." At which words many laughed. "Nay," saith she, "if the dauncer will lend me a leash of his belles, I'le venter to treade one myle with him myselfe." I lookt upon her, saw mirth in her eies, heard boldness in her words, and beheld her ready to tucke up her russat petticoate ; I fitted her with bels, which she merrily taking, garnisht her thicke short legs, and with a smooth brow bad the tabrer begin. The drum strucke ; forward marcht I with my merry Mayde Marian, who shooke her fat sides, and footed it merrily to Melford, being a long myle. There parting with her (besides her skinfull of drinke), and English crowne to buy more drinke ; for, good wench, she was in a pittious heate ; my kindness she requited with dropping some dozen of short courtsies, and bidding God blesse the dauncer. I bade her adieu ; and, to give her her due, she had a good eare, daunst truly, and wee parted friends.'

Having been the guest of 'Master Colts,' of Melford, from Wednesday night to Saturday morning, Kemp made on this day another day's progress. Many gentlemen of the place ac-companied him the first mile, 'Which myle,' says he, 'Master Colts his foole would needs daunce with me, and had his desire, where leaving me, two fooles parted faire in a foule way ; I keeping on my course to Clare, where I a while rested, and then cheerfully set forward to Bury.' He reached Bury that evening, and was shut up there by an unexpected accident, so heavy a fall of snow, that he was unable to continue his progress until the Friday following. This Friday of the third week since he left London was only his seventh day's dancing; and he had so well reposed that he performed the ten miles from Bury to Thetford in three hours, arriving at the latter town a little after ten in the forenoon. 'But, indeed, considering how I had been booted the other journeys before, and that all this way, or the most of it, was over a heath, it was no great wonder; for I far'd like one that had escaped the stockes, and tride the use of his legs to out-run the constable; so light was my heeles, that I counted the ten myle as a leape.' At Thetford, he was hospitably entertained by Sir Edwin Rich, from Friday evening to Monday morning; and this worthy knight, 'to conclude liberally as hee had begun and continued, at my departure on Monday, his worship gave me five pounds,' a considerable sum at that time. On Monday, Kemp danced to Hingham, through very bad roads, and frequently interrupted by the hospitality or importunity of the people on the road On Wednesday of the fourth week Kemp reached Norwich, but the crowd which came out of the city to receive him was so great, that, tired as he was, he resolved not to dance into it that day; and he rode on horseback into the city, where he was received in a very flattering manner by the mayor, Master Roger Weld. It was not till Saturday that Kemp's dance into Norwich took place, his journey from London having thus taken exactly four weeks, of which period nine days were occupied in dancing the Morris.

The morris-dance was so popular in the time of James I., that when a Dutch painter of that period, Vinckenboom, executed a painting of Richmond palace, he introduced a morris-dance in the foreground of the picture. In Horace Walpole's time, this painting belonged to Lord Fitzwilliam; and Douce, in his dissertation on the morris-dance, appended to the 'Illustrations of Shakspeare,' has engraved some of the figures. At this time the favourite season of the morris-dance was Whitsuntide. In the well-known passage of the play of *Henry V.*, the Dauphin of France is made to twit the English with their love of these performances. When urging to make preparations against the English, he says—

'And let us do it with no show of fear;
No! with no more than if we heard that England
Were busied with a Whitsun morris-dance.'

In another play (*All's Well that Ends Well*, act ii., sc. 2), Shakspeare speaks of the fitness of 'a morris for May-day;' and it formed a not unimportant part of the observances on that occasion. A tract of the time of Charles I., entitled *Mythomistes*, speaks of 'the best taught country morris-dancer, with all his bells and napkins,' as being sometimes employed at Christmas; so that the performance appears not to have been absolutely limited to any period of the year, though it seems to have been considered as most appropriate to Whitsuntide and the month of May.

The natives of Herefordshire were celebrated for their morris-dancers, and it was also a county remarkable for longevity. A pamphlet, printed in the reign of James I., commemorates a party of Herefordshire morris-dancers, ten in number. whose ages together amounted to twelve hundred years. This was probably somewhat exaggerated; but, at a later period, the names of a party of eight morris-dancers of that county are given. the youngest of whom was seventy-nine years old, while the age of the others ranged from ninety-five to a hundred and nine, making together just eight hundred years. Morris-dancing was not uncommon in Herefordshire in the earlier part of the present century. It has been practised during the same period in Gloucestershire and Somerset, in Wiltshire, and in most of the counties round the metropolis. Hone saw a troop of Hertfordshire morris-dancers performing in Goswell-street Road, London, in 1826. Mrs Baker, in her *Glossary of Northamptonshire Words*, published in 1854, speaks of them as still met with in that county. And Halliwell, in his *Dictionary of Archaic and Provincial Words*, also speaks of the morris-dance as still commonly practised in Oxfordshire, though the old costume had been forgotten, and the performers were only dressed with a few ribbons.

THE WHITSUN MYSTERIES AT CHESTER.

The mystery or miracle plays, of which we read so much in old chronicles, possess an interest in the present day, not only as affording details of the life and amusements of the people in the middle ages—of which we have no very clear record but in them and the illuminated MSS.—but also in helping us to trace the progress of the drama from a very early period to the time when it reached its meridian glory in our immortal Shakspeare. It is said that the first of these plays, one on the passion of our Lord, was written by Gregory of Nazianzen, and a German nun of the name of Roswitha, who lived in the tenth century, and wrote six Latin dramas on the stories of saints and martyrs. When they became more common, about the eleventh or twelfth century, we find that the monks were generally not only the authors, but the actors. In the dark ages, when the Bible was an interdicted book, these amusements were devised to instruct the people in the Old and New Testament narratives, and the lives of the saints; the former bearing the title of mysteries, the latter of miracle plays. Their value was a much disputed point among churchmen: some of the older councils forbade them as a profane treatment of sacred subjects; Wickliffe and his followers were loud in condemnation; yet Luther gave them his sanction, saying, 'Such spectacles often do more good, and produce more impression, than sermons.' In Sweden and Denmark, the Lutheran ecclesiastics followed the example of their forefathers, and wrote and encouraged them to the end of the seventeenth century; it was about the middle of that century when they ceased in England. Relics of them may still be traced in the Cornish acting of 'St George and the Dragon,' and 'Beelzebub.'

They were usually performed in churches, but frequently in the open air, in cemeteries, market-places, and squares, being got up at a cost much exceeding the spectacles of the modern stage. We read of one at Palermo which cost 12,000 ducats for each performance, and comprised the entire story of the Bible, from the Creation to the Incarnation; another, of the Crucifixion, at the pretty little town of Aci Reale, attracted such crowds that all Sicily was said to congregate there. The stage was a lofty and large platform before the cathedral, whilst the senate-house served as a side scene, from which issued the various processions. The mixture of sacred and profane persons is really shocking: the Creator with His angels occupied the highest stage, of which there were three; the saints the next; the actors the lowest; on one side of this was the mouth of hell, a dark cavern, out of which came fire and smoke, and the cries of the lost; the buffoonery and coarse jests of the devils who issued from it formed the chief attraction to the crowd, and were considered the best part of the entertainment. Sometimes it was productive of real danger, setting fire to the whole stage, and producing the most tragic con-

sequences; as at Florence, where numbers lost their lives. Some of the accounts of these stage properties, in Mr Sharp's extracts, are amusing to read: 'Item, payd for mendyng hell mought, 2d.'—'Item, payd for kepyng of fyer at hell mothe, 4d.'—'Payd for settyng the world of fyer, 5d.'

We seem to have borrowed our plays chiefly from the French; there is indeed a great similarity between them and the Chester plays; but the play of wit is greater in the former than the latter, each partaking of the character of the nation. At first they were written in Latin, when of course the acting was all that the people understood:—that, however, was sufficient to excite them to great hilarity; afterwards they seem to have been composed for the neighbour-hood in which they were performed.

We have no very authentic account of the year when the mysteries were first played at Chester; some fix it about 1268, which is perhaps too early. In a note to one of the proclamations, we are told that they were written by a monk of Chester Abbey, Randall Higgenett, and played in 1327, on Monday, Tuesday, and Wednesday in Whitsun week. They were always acted in

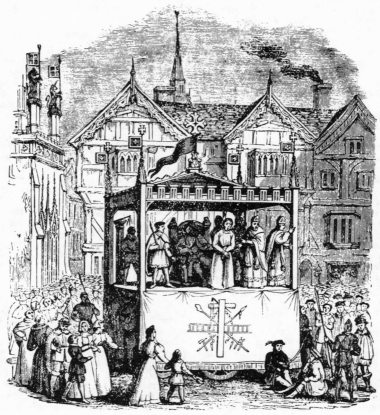

CHESTER MYSTERY PLAYS.

the open air, and consisted of twenty-four parts, each part or pageant being taken by one of the

guilds of the city; the tanners beginning with 'The Fall of Lucifer;' the drapers took the

'Creation;' the water-carriers of the Dee suitably enough acted 'The Flood,' and so on; the first nine being performed on Monday, the nine following on Tuesday, and the remaining seven on Wednesday. Twenty-four large scaffolds or stages were made, consisting of two tiers, or 'rowmes' as they are called, and fixed upon four wheels: in the lower one the actors dressed and undressed; the upper one, which was open on all sides for the spectators to see distinctly, was used for acting. By an excellent arrangement, to prevent crowding, each play was performed in every principal street; the first began before the old abbey gates, and when finished it was wheeled on to the market-cross, which was the mayor's position in all shows; by the time it was ended, the second pageant was ready to take its place, and it moved forward to Water-gate, and then to Bridge Street, so that all the pageants were going on at different places at the same time. Great order was preserved, in spite of the immense concourse of people who came from all quarters to enjoy the spectacle; and scaffolds were put up in all the streets, on which they might sit, for which privilege it is supposed that payment was received. It was wisely ordered that no man should wear any weapon within the precincts of the city during the time of the plays, as a further inducement, were any wanting, to make the people congregate to hear the 'holsome doctrine and devotion' taught by them. Pope Clement granted to each person attending a thousand days' pardon, and the Bishop of Chester forty days of the same grace.

They were introduced by 'banes', or proclamation, a word which is still retained in our marriage bans; three heralds made it with the sound of trumpets, and set forth in a lengthy prologue the various parts which were to be shown. 'The Fall of Lucifer' was a very popular legend from the earliest ages of Christianity, and its influence is felt to the present day, having been the original groundwork upon which Milton wrote some of his finest passages in *Paradise Lost*, which, as is well known, was intended to be a sacred drama commencing with Satan's address to the sun. Pride is represented as the cause of his fall; he declares, 'that all heaven shines through his brightness, for God hymselfe shines not so cleare;' and, on attempting to seat himself on the throne of God, he is cast down with Lightborn, and part of the nine orders of angels, among whom there follows a scene of bitter repentance and recrimination that they ever listened to the tempter. The stage directions for these scenes are curious enough; a great tempest is to spout forth fire, and a secret way underneath is to hide the evil angels from the spectators' sight.

It is unnecessary to describe each of these plays, as for the most part they follow the Bible narrative very closely; but, in passing, we will notice a few of the legends and peculiarities mixed up with them. Thus a very popular part was that of Noah's wife, who preferred staying with her gossips to entering the ark; and, with the characteristic perverseness of woman, had to be dragged into it by her son Shem, when she gives her husband a box on the ear. The play of the

'Shepherds of Bethlehem' gives some curious particulars of country life. The three shepherds meet and converse about their flocks, and then propose that each should bring out the food he has with him, and make a pic-nic of the whole. A wrestling match follows, and then the angels appear, and they go to Bethlehem; their gifts are curious, the first says—

'Heale kinge! borne in a mayden's bower,
Proffites did tell thou shouldest be our succore.
Loe, I bring thee a bell;
I praie thee save me from hell,
So that I maye with thee dwell,
And serve thee for aye.'

The next—

'Heale thee, blessed full barne (child),
Loe, sonne, I bring thee a flaggette,
Theirby heinges a spoune,
To eate thy pottage with all at noune.'

The last—

'Loe, sonne, I bring thee a cape,
For I have nothinge elles.'

Their boys follow with offerings: one 'a payre of ould hose;' another, 'a fayre bottill;' 'a pipe to make the woode ringe;' and lastly, 'a nutthooke to pull down aples, peares, and plumes, that oulde Joseph nede not hurte his thombes.' In the 'Passion,' the 'Tourmentoures' are very prominent, with their coarse rough jokes and rude buffetings. 'The Harrowing of Hell,' is a very singular part. Christ is represented as descending there, and choosing out Adam, Seth, Isaiah, and many other saints to go to Paradise, where they are met by Enoch and Elijah, who until this period had been its solitary inmates. There is in this piece a strong satire against a woman who is left behind; she says—

'Wo be to the tyme when I came heare.
Some tyme I was a taverner,
A gentill gossipe and a tapstere,
Of wyne and ale a trustie brewer,
Which wo hath me wroughte:
Of cannes I kept no trewe measuer,
My cuppes I soulde at my pleasure,
Deceavinge manye a creature.
With hoppes I made my ale stronge,
Ashes and erbes I blend amonge,
And marred so good maulte;
Therefore I may my handes wringe,
Shake my cannes, and cuppes ringe;
Sorrowful may I siche and singe
That ever I so dealt.'

These allusions to the taverners are so frequent in this description of writing, that we may feel sure they were guilty of much evil doing.

The play of 'Ezekiel' contains a summary of various prophecies, and especially the fifteen signs which were to precede the end of the world, a subject which then much engrossed the thoughts of mankind. The signs, as fixed by St Jerome, were as follow :—The first day the sea was to rise as a wall higher than the hills; the second, to disappear entirely; on the third, great fishes were to rise from it, and 'rore hideously;' the fourth, the sea and all waters were to be on fire; the fifth, a bloody dew was to fall on all trees and herbs; on the sixth, churches, cities, and houses were to be thrown down; the seventh, the rocks were to be rent;

the eighth, an earthquake; on the ninth, the hills and valleys were to be made plain; on the tenth, men who had hidden themselves in the caves were to come out mad; the eleventh, the dead should arise; the twelfth, the stars were to fall; the thirteenth, all men should die and rise again; on the fourteenth, earth and heaven should perish by fire; and the fifteenth would see the birth of the new heaven and new earth.

'Antichrist' the subject of the next play, was also a much expected character in the middle ages. He performs the miracle of self-resurrection, to deceive the kings who ask for proofs of his power; and brings all men to worship and sacrifice to him. Enoch and Elijah come from Paradise to expose their sin, and, after a long disputation, are martyred, Michael the archangel coming at the same moment and killing Antichrist, who is carried off by two demons; the martyrs rising and ascending with Michael. 'Doomsday' forms the last of the series, in which a pope, emperor, king, and queen are judged and saved; while a similar series confess their various sins, and are turned into hell. The queen says—

> 'Fie on pearls! fie on pride!
> Fye on gowne! fye on hyde! (skin)
> Fye on hewe! fye on guyde! (gold)
> Thes harrowe me to hell.'

Jesus descends with his angels, and complains of the injuries men have done to him: how his members bled afresh at every oath they swore, and that he had suffered more from them than from his Jewish persecutors.

There can be no doubt that the people of the most 'ancient, renowned citie of Caerleon, now named Chester,' were passionately fond of these 'Shewes;' and when the progress of enlightenment and refinement which the Reformation brought about banished the mystery plays, as bordering on profanity and licentiousness, as well as having a strong flavour of popery about them, they set about with alacrity to substitute in their place the pageants which became so general in the reigns of the Tudors and Stuarts, and are connected in history with the journeys or progresses of these monarchs. These pageants or triumphs have, like their predecessors, the mysteries, their relation to the English drama; not only were they composed for the purpose of flattering and complimenting their princes, but a moral end was constantly kept in view: virtue was applauded, while vice was set forth in its most revolting and unpleasing colours; and the altercations between these two leading personages often afforded the populace the highest amusement. The opportunity was also seized upon of presenting to royal ears some of the political abuses of the day; as in one offered by the Inns of Court to Charles the First, where ridicule was thrown upon the vexatious law of patents: a fellow appearing with a bunch of carrots on his head, and a capon on his fist, and asking for a patent of monopoly as the first inventor of the art of feeding capons with carrots, and that none but himself should have privilege of the said invention for fourteen years; whilst another came mounted on a little horse with an immense bit in his mouth, and the

request that none should be allowed to ride unless they purchased his bits.

Considerable sums of money were spent on these pageants; the expense falling sometimes on the guilds, who each took their separate part in the performance, or the mayor of the city would frequently give one at his own cost; whilst the various theatrical properties would seem to have been kept in order from the city funds, as we often read such entries as these in their books: 'For the annual painting of the city's four giants, one unicorn, one dromedarye, one luce, one asse, one dragon, six hobby-horses, and sixteen naked boys.' 'For painting the beasts and hobby-horses, forty-three shillings. For making new the dragon, five shillings; and for six naked boys to beat at it, six shillings.' The first of these pageants of which we have any record as performed at Chester, was in 1529; the title was 'Kynge Robart of Cicyle.' 'The History of Æneas and Queen Dido' was played on the Rood-eye in 1563, on the Sunday after Midsummer-day, during the time of the yearly fair, which attracted buyers and sellers in great numbers from Wales and the neighbouring counties. Earl Derby, Lord Strange, and other noblemen honoured these representations with their presence.

The pageant which we are about to describe, and which is the only one preserved to the present day, was given by Mr Robert Amory, sheriff of Chester in 1608, a liberal and public-spirited man, who benefited his city in many ways. It was got up in honour of Henry Frederic, the eldest son of James the First, on his creation as Prince of Wales; and perhaps no prince who ever lived was more worthy of the festival.

The author addresses his readers with a certain amount of self-approbation; he says, 'To be brief, what was done was so done, as being by the approbation of many said to bee well done; then, I doubt not, but it may merit the mercifull construction of some few who may chance to sweare 'twas most excellently ill done. Zeale procured it, loue deuis'd (devised) it, boyes performed it, men beheld it, and none but fooles dispraised it. As for the further discription of the businesse I referre to further relation; onely thus: The chiefest part of this people-pleasing spectacle consisted in three Bees, viz., Boyes, Beasts, and Bels: Bels of a strange amplitude and extraordinarie proportion; Beasts of an excellent shape and most admirable swiftnesse; and Boyes of a rare spirit and exquisite performance.'

These wonderful beasts consisted of two personages who took a leading part in all pageants, and were the 'greene or salvage men;' they were sometimes clothed completely in skins, but on this occasion ivy leaves were sewed on to an embroidered dress, and garlands of the same leaves round their heads; a 'huge blacke shaggie hayre' hung over their shoulders, whilst the 'herculean clubbes' in their hands made them fit and proper to precede and clear the way for the procession that followed. With them came the highly popular and important artificial dragon, 'very lively to behold: pursuing the savages, entring their denne, casting fire from his mouth; which afterwards was slaine, to the great pleasure of the spectators, bleeding, fainting, and staggering as though he endured a feelinge paine even at the last gaspe and farewell.'

The various persons who were to take part in the procession met at the old ' Highe Crosse,' which stood at the intersection of the four principal streets in Chester, and the proceedings were opened by a man in a grotesque dress climbing to the top of it, and fixing upon a bar of iron an 'Ancient,' or flag of the colours of St George; at the same time he called the attention of all present by beating a drum, firing off a gun, and brandishing a sword, after which warlike demonstrations he closed his exhibition by standing on his head with his feet in the air, on the bar of iron, 'very dangerously and wonderfully, to the view of the beholders, and casting fireworks very delightfull.' Envy was there on horseback, with a wreath of snakes about her head and one in her hand; Plenty came garlanded with wheat ears round her body, strewing wheat among the multitude as she rode along; St George, in full armour, attended by his squires and drummers, made a glorious show; Fame (with her trumpet), Peace, Joy, and Rumour were in their several places, spouting their orations; whilst Mercury, descending from heaven in a cloud, artificially winged, 'a wheele of fire burning very cunningly, with other fireworks,' mounted the Cross by the assistance of ropes, in the midst of heavenly melody. Other horsemen represented the City of Chester, the King, and the Prince of Wales, carrying the suitable colours, shields and escutcheons emblazoned on their dresses and horses' foreheads. The three silver gilt bells, which were to be run for, supported by lions rampant, were carried with many trumpets sounding before; and, when all were marshalled, eight voices sang the opening strain :—

'Come downe, thou mighty messenger of blisse,
    Come, we implore thee ;
Let not thy glory be obscured from us,
    Who most adore thee.
Then come, oh come, great Spirit,
    That we may joyful sing,
Welcome, oh welcome to earth,
    Joy's dearest darling.

Lighten the eyes, thou great Mercurian Prince,
    Of all that view thee,
That by the lustre of their optick sense
    They may pursue thee :
Whilst with their voyces
    Thy praise they shall sing,
Come away,
    Joy's dearest darling.

Mercury replies to this invocation, and then follow a series of most tedious speeches from each allegorical person, in praise of Britain in general, and Prince Henry in particular, with which we should be sorry to weary our readers. Envy comes in at the end, to sneer at the whole and spoil the sport; and in no measured terms explains the joy she feels,

'To see a city burnt, or barnes on fire,
    To see a sonne the butcher of his sire ;

To see two swaggerers eagerly to strive
Which of them both shall make the hangman
    thrive ;
To see a good man poore, or wise man bare,
To see Dame Virtue overwhelmed with care ;
To see a ruined church, a preacher dumbe,' &c.

But Joy puts her to flight, saying,—

'Envy, avaunt ! thou art no fit compeere
T' associate with these our sweet consociats here ;
Joy doth exclude thee,' &c.

Thus ends the pageant of 'Chester's Triumph in Honour of her Prince :' what followed cannot be better described than in the words of the author, one Richard Davies, a poet unknown to fame. 'Whereupon all departed for a while to a place upon the river, called the Roode, garded with one hundred and twentie halberders and a hundred and twentie shotte, bravely furnished. The Mayor, Sheriffs, and Aldermen of Chester, arrayed in their scarlet, having seen the said shewes, to grace the same, accompanied, and followed the actors unto the said Roode, where the ships, barques, and pinises, with other vessels harbouring within the river, displaying the armes of St George upon their maine toppes, with several pendents hanging thereunto, discharged many voleyes of shotte in honour of the day. The bels, dedicated, being presented to the Mayor. Proclamation being generally made to bring in horses to runne for the said bels, there was runne a double race, to the greate pleasure and delight of the spectators. Men of greate worthe running also at the ring for the saide cuppe, dedicated to St George, and those that wonne the prizes had the same, with the honour thereto belonging. The said several prizes, being with speeches and several wreathes set on their heads, delivered in ceremonious and triumphant manner, after the order of the Olympian sportes, whereof these were an imitation.'

THE WHITSUN-ALE.

Ale was so prevalent a drink amongst us in old times, as to become a part of the name of various festal meetings, as Leet-ale, Lamb-ale, Bride-ale [bridal], and, as we see, Whitsun-ale. It was the custom of our simple ancestors to have parochial meetings every Whitsuntide, under the auspices of the churchwardens, usually in some barn near the church, all agreeing to be good friends for once in the year, and spend the day in a sober joy. The squire and lady came with their piper and taborer; the young danced or played at bowls; the old looked on, sipping their ale from time to time. It was a kind of pic-nic, for each parishioner brought what victuals he could spare. The ale, which had been brewed pretty strong for the occasion, was sold by the churchwardens, and from its profits a fund arose for the repair of the church. In latter days, the festival degenerated, as has been the case with most of such old observances; but in the old times there was a reverence about it which kept it pure. Shakspeare gives us some idea of this when he adverts to the song in *Pericles*—

'It hath been sung at festivals,
    On ember eves, and *holy ales*.'

WHIT SUNDAY FÊTE AT NAPLES.

Among the religious festivals of the Neapolitans none is more joyously kept than that of the *Festa di Monte Vergine*, which takes place on Whit Sunday, but usually lasts three days. The centre of attraction is a church situated on a mountain near Avelino, and as this is a day's journey from Naples, carriages are in requisition. The re-markable feature of the festival is the gaiety of the crowds who attend from a wide district around. In returning home, the vehicles of all sorts which have been pressed into the service are decorated in a fantastic manner with flowers and boughs of trees; the animals which draw the carriages, consisting sometimes of a bullock and ass, as represented in the subjoined cut, are ornamented with ribbons; and numbers of the merry-makers, bearing sticks, with flowers and pictures of the Madonna, dance untiringly alongside. These festivities of the Neapolitans are traced to certain usages of their Greek ancestry, having possibly some relation to ancient Bacchanalian proces-sions.

WHIT SUNDAY FÊTE AT NAPLES.

FIRST SUNDAY MORNING OF MAY (OLD STYLE) AT CRAIGIE WELL, BLACKISLE OF ROSS.

Among the many relics of superstition still extant in the Highlands of Scotland, one of the most remarkable is the veneration paid to certain wells, which are supposed to possess eminent virtues as charms against disease, witchcraft, fairies, and the like, when visited at stated times, and under what are considered favourable auspices.

Craigie Well is situated in a nook of the parish of Avoch, which juts out to the south, and runs along the north shore of the Munlochy bay. The well is situated within a few yards of high-water mark. It springs out between two crags or boulders of trap rock, and immediately behind it the ground, thickly covered with furze, rises very abruptly to the height of about sixty feet. Probably the name of the well is suggested by the numerous masses of the same loose rock which are seen to protrude in so many places here and there through the gorse and broom which grow round about. There is a large briar bush growing quite near the two masses of rock mentioned, which is literally covered with small threads and patches of cloth, intended as offerings to the well. None, indeed, will dare go there on the day prescribed without bringing an offering, for such would be considered an insult to the 'healing waters!'

For more than a week before the morning ap-pointed for going upon this strange pilgrimage, there is scarcely a word heard among farm servants within five miles of the spot, but, among the English speaking people, 'Art thee no ganging to Craigack wall, to get thour health secured another year?' and, among the Gaelic speaking population, 'Dol gu topar Chreckack?'

Instigated more by curiosity than anything

else, I determined to pay this well a visit, to see how the pilgrims passed the Sunday morning there. I arrived about an hour before sunrise; but long before crowds of lads and lasses from all quarters were fast pouring in. Some, indeed, were there at daybreak, who had journeyed more than seven miles! Before the sun made his appearance, the whole scene looked more like a fair than anything else. Acquaintances shook hands in true highland style; brother met brother, and sister sister; while laughter and all manner of country news and gossip were so freely indulged in, that a person could hardly hear what he himself said. Some of them spoke tolerable English, others spoke Gaelic, while a third party spoke Scotch, very quaint in the phraseology and broad in the pronunciation.

Meantime crowds were eagerly pressing forward to get a tasting of the well before the sun should come in sight; for, once he made his appearance, there was no good to be derived from drinking of it. Some drank out of dishes, while others preferred stooping on their knees and hands to convey the water directly to their mouths. Those who adopted this latter mode of drinking had sometimes to submit to the inconvenience of being plunged in over head and ears by their companions. This practice was tried, however, once or twice by strangers, and gave rise to a quarrel, which did not end till some blows had been freely exchanged.

The sun was now shooting up his first rays, when all eyes were directed to the top of the brae, attracted by a man coming in great haste, whom all recognised as Jock Forsyth, a very honest and pious, but eccentric individual. Scores of voices shouted, 'You are too late, Jock: the sun is rising. Surely you have slept in this morning.' The new-comer, a middle-aged man, with a droll squint, perspiring profusely, and out of breath, pressed nevertheless through the crowd, and stopped not till he reached the well. Then, muttering a few inaudible words, he stooped on his knees, bent down, and took a large draught. He then rose up and said: 'O Lord! thou knowest that weel would it be for me this day an' I had stooped my knees and my heart before thee in spirit and in truth as often as I have stoopet them afore this well. But we maun keep the customs of our fathers.' So he stepped aside among the rest, and dedicated his offering to the briar-bush, which by this time could hardly be seen through the number of shreds which covered it.

Thus ended the singular scene. Year after year the crowds going to Craigach are perceptibly lessening in numbers.   J. S.

MAY 16.

St Brendan the Elder, 578. St Abdjesus, bishop, martyr. St Abdas, Bishop of Cascar, martyr. St Ubaldus, Bishop of Gubio, 1160. St Simon Stock, confessor, of Kent, 1265. St John Nepomuc, 1383.

THE LEGEND OF ST BRENDAN.

Mankind have ever had a peculiar predilection for stories of maritime adventure and discovery, of the mysterious wonders and frightful perils of the mighty ocean; and almost every nation can boast of its one great real or mythical navigator. The Greeks had their Ulysses, the Carthaginians their Hanno. The name of the adventurous Tyrian who first brought back a cargo of gold and peacocks from the distant land of Ophir may be unknown; but every school-boy has read with delight the voyages of the Arabian Sindbad. To come nearer home, as Denmark had its Gorm, and Wales its Madoc, so Ireland had its Brendan. Of all the saintly legends, this of Brendan seems to have been the most popular and widely diffused. It is found in manuscript in all the languages of Western Europe, as well as in the mediæval Latin of the monkish chroniclers, and several editions of it were printed in the earlier period of typography.

Historically speaking, Brendan, an Irishman of royal lineage, was the founder and first abbot of the monastery of Clonfert, in the county of Galway; several treatises on religion and church government, still extant, are attributed to him; and the year 578 is assigned as the date of his death.

According to the legend, Brendan, incited by a report he had heard from another abbot, named Berint, determined to make a voyage of discovery, in search of an island supposed to contain the identical paradise of Adam and Eve. So, having procured a good ship, and victualled it for seven years, he was about to start with twelve monks, his selected companions, when two more earnestly entreated that they might be allowed to accompany him. Brendan replied, 'Ye may sail with me, but one of you shall go to perdition ere ye return.' In spite, however, of this warning, the two monks entered the ship.

And, forthwith sailing, they were on the morrow out of sight of any land, and, after forty days and forty nights, they saw an island and sailed thitherward, and saw a great rock of stone appear above the water; and three days they sailed about it, ere they could get into the place. But at last they found a little haven, and there they went on land. And then suddenly came a fair hound, and fell down at the feet of St Brendan, and made him welcome in its manner. Then he told the brethren, 'Be of good cheer, for our Lord hath sent to us this messenger to lead us into some good place.' And the hound brought them to a fair hall, where they found tables spread with good meat and drink. St Brendan said grace, and he and his brethren sat down, and ate and drank of such as they found. And there were beds ready for them, wherein they took their rest.

On the morrow they returned to their ship, and sailed a long time ere they could find any land, till at length they saw a fair island, full of green pasture, wherein were the whitest and greatest sheep ever they saw, for every sheep was as big as an ox. And soon after there came to them a goodly old man, who welcomed them, and said, 'This is the Island of Sheep, and here is never cold weather, but ever summer; and that causes the sheep to be so big and so white.' Then this old man took his leave, and bade them sail forth right east, and, within

639

a short time, they should come into a place, the Paradise of Birds, where they should keep their Easter-tide

And they sailed forth, and came soon after to land, but because of little depth in some places, and in some places great rocks, they went upon an island, weening themselves to be safe, and made thereon a fire to dress their dinner; but St Brendan abode still in the ship. And when the fire was right hot, and the meat nigh sodden, then this island began to move, whereof the monks were afraid, and fled anon to the ship, and left their fire and meat behind them, and marvelled sore of the moving. And St Brendan comforted them, and said that it was a great fish named Jascon, which laboured night and day to put its tail in its mouth, but for greatness it could not.

The reader will recollect the similar story in the voyages of Sindbad; but Jascon, or Jasconius, as it is styled in the Latin version, turned out to be a much more useful fish than its Eastern counterpart, as will be seen hereafter.

After three days' sailing, they saw a fair land full of flowers, herbs, and trees; whereof they thanked God of His good grace, and anon they went on land. And when they had gone some distance they found a well, and thereby stood a tree, full of boughs, and on every bough sat a bird; and they sat so thick on the tree, that not a leaf could be seen, the number of them was so great; and they sang so merrily, that it was a heavenly noise to hear. And then, anon, one of the birds flew from the tree to St Brendan, and, with flickering of its wings, made a full merry noise like a fiddle, a joyful melody. And then St Brendan commanded the bird to tell him why they sat so thick on the tree, and sang so merrily. And then the bird said, 'Sometime we were angels in heaven; but when our master Lucifer fell for his high pride, we fell for our offences, some hither and some lower, after the nature of their trespass; and because our trespass is but little, therefore our Lord hath set us here, out of all pain, to serve Him on this tree in the best manner that we can.'

The bird, moreover, said to the saint: 'It is twelve months past that ye departed from your abbey, and in the seventh year hereafter ye shall see the place that ye desire to come to; and all these seven years ye shall keep your Easter here with us every year, and at the end of the seventh year ye shall come to the land of behest!' And this was on Easter-day that the bird said these words to St Brendan. And then all the birds began to sing even-song so merrily, that it was a heavenly noise to hear; and after supper St Brendan and his fellows went to bed and slept well, and on the morrow rose betimes, and then these birds began matins, prime, and hours, and all such service as Christian men use to sing.

Brendan remained with the birds till Trinity Sunday, and then returning to Sheep Island, he took in a supply of provisions, and sailed again into the wide ocean. After many perils, he discovered an island, on which was a monastery of twenty-four monks; with them Brendan spent Christmas, and on Twelfth-day again made sail.

On Palm Sunday they reached Sheep Island, and were received by the old man, who brought them to a fair hall, and served them. And on Holy Thursday, after supper, he washed their feet and kissed them, like as our Lord did to His disciples; and there they abode till Easter Saturday evening, and then departed and sailed to the place where the great fish lay; and anon they saw their caldron upon the fish's back, which they had left there twelve months before; and there they kept the service of the Resurrection on the fish's back; and after sailed the same morning to the island where was the tree of birds, and there they dwelt from Easter till Trinity Sunday, as they did the year before, in full great joy and mirth.

Thus they sailed, from island to island, for seven years; spending Christmas at the monastery, Palm Sunday at the Sheep Island, Easter-Sunday on the fish's back, and Easter Monday with the birds. There were several episodes, however, in this routine of sailings, of which space can be afforded for one of the strangest only.

After having been driven for many days to the northward by a powerful south wind, they saw an island, very dark, and full of stench and smoke; and there they heard great blowing and blasting of bellows, and heard great thunderings, wherefore they were sore afraid, and blessed themselves often. And soon after there came one, all burning in fire, and stared full ghastly on them, of whom the monks were aghast; and at his departure he made the horriblest cry that might be heard. And soon there came a great number of fiends, and assailed them with red hot iron hooks and hammers, in such wise that the sea seemed to be all on fire; but by the will of God, they had no power to hurt them nor the ship. And then they saw a hill all on fire, and a foul smoke and stench coming from thence; and the fire stood on each side of the hill, like a wall all burning. Then one of the monks began to cry and weep full sore, and say that his end was come, and that he might abide no longer in the ship; and anon he leapt into the sea, and then he cried and roared full piteously, cursing the time he was born; 'For now,' said he, 'I must go to perpetual torment.' And then the saying of St Brendan was verified, what he said to that monk ere he entered the ship. Therefore, it is good a man do penance and forsake sin, for the hour of death is uncertain.

According to the Latin version of the legend, the other monk, who voluntarily joined the expedition in defiance of the saint's solemn warning, came to an evil end also. On the first island where they landed, and were so hospitably entertained in 'a fair hall,' the wretched monk, overcome by temptation, stole a silver-mounted bridle and hid it in his vest; and in consequence of the theft died, and was buried on the island.

Their last visit to Jascon was marked by a more wonderful occurrence than on any of the previous occasions.

So they came to the great fish, where they used to say matins and mass on Easter Sunday. And when the mass was done, the fish began to move, and swam fast in the sea, whereof the monks were sore aghast. But the fish set the monks on land, in the Paradise of Birds, all whole and sound, and then returned to the place it came from. Then St Brendan kept Eastertide till Trinity Sunday, like as he had done before.

The prescribed wandering for seven years having been fulfilled, they were allowed to visit the promised land. After sailing for many days in darkness—

'The mist passed away, and they saw the fairest country that a man might see—clear and bright, a heavenly sight to behold. All the trees were loaded with fruit, and the herbage with flowers. It was always day, and temperate, neither hot nor cold; and they saw a river which they durst not cross. Then came a man who welcomed them, saying, "Be ye now joyful, for this is the land ye have sought. So lade your ship with fruit, and depart hastily, for ye may no longer abide here. Ye shall return to your own country, and soon after die. And this river that you see here parteth the world asunder, for on that side of the water may no man come that is in this life." Then St Brendan and his monks took of the fruit, and also plenty of precious stones, and sailed home into Ireland, where their brethren received them with great joy, giving thanks to God, who had kept them all those seven years from many perils, and at last brought them home in safety. To whom be glory and honour, world without end. Amen.'

This legend, absurd as it may appear, exercised considerable influence on geographical science down to a comparatively late period, and formed one of the several collateral causes which led to the discoveries of Columbus. The Spanish government sent out many vessels in search of the Island of St Brendan, the last in 1721. In the treaty of Evord, by which the Portuguese ceded the Canary Islands to the Castillians, the Island of St Brendan is mentioned as the island which cannot be found. The lower class of Spaniards still relate how Roderick, last of the Goths, made his escape thither; while the Portuguese assert that it served for a retreat to Don Sebastian, after the battle of Alcazar. On many old English charts it is to be found under its Irish name of I'Brazil. So common were voyages from Ireland in search of this island during the seventeenth century, that Ludlow, the regicide, when implicated in a conspiracy to seize Dublin Castle, made his escape to the Continent, by chartering a vessel at Limerick under the pretence of seeking for I'Brazil. Leslie of Glasslough, a man of judgment and enterprise, purchased a patent grant of this imaginary island from Charles I., and expended a fortune in seeking for—

> ' That Eden, where th' immortal brave
> 　Dwell in a land serene,—
> Whose towers beyond the shining wave,
> 　At sunset oft are seen.
> Ah ! dream too full of saddening truth !
> 　Those mansions o'er the main
> Are like the hopes I built in youth,
> 　As sunny, and as vain !'

ST JOHN NEPOMUC.

The fine and venerable old city of Prague, seated on the hill overlooking the new town, is decked out in all its bravery on this day. It is the *fête* of its favourite saint, the patron saint of Bohemia, St John Nepomuc. Hundreds, nay thousands, of people flock from the distant hills of the Tyrol, from Hungary, and from all parts of Bohemia, to the celebration. The old bridge dedicated to his memory, and on which his chapel stands, is so crowded that carriages are forbidden to cross it during the twenty-four hours. Service is going forward constantly, and as one party leaves, another fills the edifice. These poor people have walked all the distance, carrying their food, which often consists of cucumber, curds, and bread, in a bundle ; they join together in parties, and come singing along the road, so many miles each day. The town presents a most picturesque aspect ; the variety of costume worn in Hungary is well known ;* besides these, we find the loose green shooting-jackets of the Tyrol, the high-pointed hat, and tightly-fitting boots and stockings. The Bohemians, with their blue and red waistcoats, and large hats, remind you of the days of Luther ; whilst the women are gay with ribbons tied in their hair, and smartly embroidered aprons.

The legend of the saint is, that he lived in the days of a pagan king, whose queen he converted to the true faith, and who privately confessed to St John. Her husband, hearing of this, demanded to know her confession from the holy man, which he twice refused to reveal, on the plea of duty, though he was under threat of death. The consequence was that the king ordered him to be thrown over the old bridge into the Moldau, first barbarously cutting out his tongue. Tradition generally adds the marvellous to the true, and tells us that five stars shone in a crescent over his head. As a representation of this, a boat always sails between the arches of the bridge towards dusk on the *fête* day, with five lights, to remind the people of the stars which hung over the dying saint's head.

Born.—Sir William Petty, political economist, 1623, *Romsey, Hampshire ;* Sir Dudley North, merchant, traveller, author of *An Account of Turkey,* 1641.
Died.—Pope John XXI., killed at Viterbo, 1277 ; Samuel Bochard (history and languages), 1667, *Caen, Normandy ;* Paul Rapin de Thoyras, historian, 1725 ; Dr Daniel Solander, naturalist, 1782 ; Jean Baptiste Joseph, Baron Fourier, mathematician, 1830 ; George Clint, artist, 1854, *Kensington ;* Professor Henslow, botanist, 1861.

RAPIN AND HIS HISTORY.

The huge, voluminous history of England, by Rapin, kept a certain hold on the public favour, even down to a time which the present writer can remember. It was thought to be more impartial than other histories of England, the supposed fact being attributed to the country of the author.

* The photographs in the Austrian Court of the Exhibition of 1862 will be remembered by all who have seen them as striking examples of rich colouring, and taste in dress, even among the lower ranks.

But, in reality, Rapin had his twists like other people. A refugee from France under the revocation of the Edict of Nantes, he bore away a sense of wrongs extending back through many Protestant generations of his family, and this feeling expressed itself in a very odd way. In regard to the famous quarrel between Edward III. and Philip of Valois, he actually advocates the right of the former, which no Englishman of his own or any later time would have done.

Rapin came to England in the expedition of the Prince of Orange, served the new king in Ireland, and afterwards became governor to the son of William's favourite, the Duke of Portland.

DR SOLANDER.

The name of Solander, the Swedish botanist, the pupil of Linnæus, and the friend of Sir Joseph Banks, was honourably distinguished in the progress of natural science in the last century. He was born in Nordland, in Sweden, on the 28th of February, 1736; he studied at Upsala, under Linnæus, by whose recommendation he came to England in the autumn of 1760, and was employed at the British Museum, to which institution he was attached during the remainder of his life; he died, under-librarian of the Museum, in the year 1782.

It was, however, in voyages of discovery that Solander's chief distinction lay, especially in his contributions to botanical knowledge. In 1768, he accompanied Captain Cook in his first voyage round the world; the trustees of the British Museum having promised a continuance of his salary in his absence. During this voyage, Dr Solander probably saved a large party from destruction in ascending the mountains of Terra del Fuego; and very striking and curious is the story of this adventure in illustrating the effect of drowsiness from cold. It appears that Solander and Sir Joseph Banks had walked a considerable way through swamps, when the weather became suddenly gloomy and cold, fierce blasts of wind driving the snow before it. Finding it impossible to reach the ships before night, they resolved to push on through another swamp into the shelter of a wood, where they might kindle a fire. Dr Solander, well experienced in the effects of cold, addressed the men, and conjured them not to give way to sleepiness, but, at all costs, to keep in motion. 'Whoever sits down,' said he, 'will sleep; and whoever sleeps, will wake no more.' Thus admonished and alarmed, they set forth once again; but in a little time the cold became so intense as to produce the most oppressive drowsiness. Dr Solander himself was the first who felt the inclination to sleep too irresistible for him, and he insisted on being suffered to lie down. In vain Banks entreated and remonstrated; down he lay upon the snow, and it was with much difficulty that his friends kept him from sleeping. One of the black servants began to linger in the same manner. When told that if he did not go on, he would inevitably be frozen to death, he answered that he desired nothing more than to lie down and die. Solander declared himself willing to go on, but declared that he must first take some sleep.

It was impossible to carry these men; they were therefore both suffered to lie down, and in a few minutes were in a profound sleep. Soon after, some of those men who had been sent forward to kindle a fire, returned with the welcome news that a fire awaited them a quarter of a mile off. Banks then happily succeeded in awaking Solander, who, although he had not been asleep five minutes, had almost lost the use of his limbs, and his flesh was so shrunk that the shoes fell from his feet. He consented to go forward with such assistance as could be given; but no attempts to rouse the black servant were successful, and he, with another black, died there.

Dr Solander returned from this voyage in 1771, laden with treasures, which are still in the collection at the British Museum. He did not receive any remuneration for his perilous services beyond that extended by Sir Joseph Banks.

It will be recollected that the spot whereon Captain Cook first landed in Australia was named Botany Bay, from the profusion of plants which the circumnavigators found there, and the actual point of land was named, after one of the naturalists of the expedition, *Cape Solander;* the discovery has also been commemorated by a brass tablet, with an inscription, inserted in the face of the cliff, by Sir Thomas Brisbane, G.C.B., Governor of New South Wales.

PROFESSOR HENSLOW.

As Dr Buckland at Oxford, so Mr Henslow at Cambridge, did laudable service in leading off the attention of the university from the exclusive study of dead languages and mathematics to the more fruitful and pleasant fields of natural science.

John Stevens Henslow was born at Rochester, in 1796, and from a child displayed those tastes which distinguished his whole life. Stories are told of how he made the model of a caterpillar; dragged home a fungus, *Lycoperdon giganteum*, almost as big as himself; and how, having received as a prize *Travels in Africa*, his head was almost turned with a desire to become an explorer of that mysterious continent, and make acquaintance with its terrible beasts and reptiles. He went to Cambridge in 1814, where he took high mathematical honours, and in 1825 was appointed Professor of Botany. As Buckland bewitched Oxford with the charms of geology, Henslow did Cambridge with those of botany. All who came within the magic of his enthusiasm caught his spirit, and in his herborizing excursions round Cambridge he drew troops of students in his train. He was an admirable teacher; no one who listened to him could fail to follow and understand. At his lectures he used to provide baskets of the more common plants, such as primroses, and other species easily obtained in their flowering season; and as the pupils entered, each was expected to select a few specimens and bear them to his seat on a wooden plate, so that he might dissect for himself, and accompany the professor in his demonstration. He was also an excellent draughtsman, and by a free use of diagrams he was enabled to remove the last shade of obscurity from his expositions. At his house he held a *soirée* once a week, to which all were welcomed who had an interest in science. These evenings at the professor's became popular beyond measure, and to this day are held in affectionate remembrance by those who were his guests. In this useful activity, varied by other interests, theological and political, were Henslow's years passed at Cambridge, when in 1837, Lord Melbourne—who had almost given him the bishopric of Norwich—promoted him to the well-endowed rectory of Hitcham, in Norfolk. The people of his parish he found sunk almost to the lowest depth of moral and physical debasement, but Henslow bravely resolved to take them in hand, and spend his strength without reserve in their regeneration. His mode was entirely original. He got up a cricket-club, and encouraged ploughing matches, and all sorts of manly games. He gave every year an exhibition of fireworks on the rectory lawn, and tried to interest the more intelligent of his parishioners in his museum of curiosities. Then he took them annual excursions, sometimes to Ipswich, sometimes to Cambridge, Norwich, the sea-side, Kew, and London, leading through these places from one to two hundred rustics at his heels. Then he got up horticultural shows, to which the villagers sent their choice plants; and amid feasting and games he delivered at short intervals what he called 'lecturets' on various matters of morals and economy, brimming over with good sense and good-humour. Of course he paid special attention to his parish school, and from the first he made botany a leading branch of instruction. There were three botanical classes, and admission to the very lowest was denied to any child who could not spell, among other words, the terms Angiospermons, Glumaceons, and Monocotyledons. Under Henslow's enthusiasm and unequalled power of teaching, the hard and difficult vocabulary grew easy to the childhood of Hitcham, and ploughboys and dairymaids learned to discourse in phrases which would perplex a London drawing-room. Whilst looking after the labourers, he did not forget their employers, the farmers; and by lectures to the Hadleigh Farmers' Club he strove to 'convert,' as he expressed it, 'the *art* of husbandry into the *science* of agriculture.' In these secular labours Henslow believed that he laid the only durable basis for any spiritual culture that was worth the name. Under his ceaseless energy his parish gradually and surely changed its character from sloth and depravity to industry and virtue; and we scarcely know a more encouraging example of the good a clergyman may effect in the worst environment than that afforded by the story of Henslow's life at Hitcham. The last public appearance of the professor was as president of the natural history section of the British Association at Oxford in June, 1860. In 1861 a complication of disorders, arising, it was thought, from his long habit of overtasking mind and body, brought him to his death-bed. There, in his last hours, was seen the scientific instinct active as ever. In his sufferings he set himself to watch the signs of approaching dissolution, and discussed them with his medical attendants as though they were natural phenomena occurring outside himself.

GREENWICH FAIR.

In former times, the conception of Whit Monday in the mind of the great mass of Londoners had one central spot of intense brightness in—Greenwich Fair. For some years past, this has been a bygone glory, for magistrates found that the enjoyments of the festival involved much disorder and impropriety; and so its chief attractions were sternly forbidden. Strict justice owns that such an assemblage could not take place without some share of evil consequences; and yet one must sigh to think that so much pleasure, to all appearance purely innocent, has been subtracted from the lot of the industrious classes, and it may even be insinuated that the gain to morality is not entire gain.

If Whit Monday dawned brightly, every street in London showed, from an early hour, streams of lads and lasses pouring towards those outlets from the city by which Greenwich (five miles off) was then approached, the Kent Road and the river being the chief. No railway then—no steamers on the river—their place was supplied to some extent by stage-coaches and wherries. When the holiday-maker and his partner had, by whatever means, made their way to Greenwich, they found the principal street filled from end to end with shows, theatrical booths, and stalls for the sale of an infinite variety of merchandise. Usually, however, the first object was to get into the park; a terrible struggle it was, through accesses so much narrower than the multitude required. In this beautiful piece of ground, made venerable by the old oaks of Henry and Elizabeth, and dear to science by the towery Observatory, the youth and maidenhood of London carried on a series of sports during the whole forenoon. At one place there was kiss-in-the-ring; at another you might, for a penny, enjoy the chance of knocking down half-a-dozen pieces of gingerbread by throwing a stick; but the favourite amusement above all was to run your partner down the well-known slope between the high and low levels of the park. Generally, a row was drawn up at the top, and at a signal off they all set; some bold and successful in getting to the bottom on their feet, others, timid and awkward, tumbling headlong before they were half-way down. The strange disorders of this scene furnished, of course, food for no small merriment; the rule was to take every discomposure and spoiling of dress good-humouredly. Meanwhile there were other regalements. One of the old pensioners of the Hospital would be drawing halfpence for the use of his telescope, whereby you could see St Paul's Cathedral, Barking Church, Epping Forest, or the pirates hanging in chains along the river (the last a favourite spectacle). At another place, a sailor, or one assuming the character, would exemplify the nautical hornpipe to the sounds of a cracked violin. The game of 'thread-my-needle,' played by about a dozen lasses, also had its attractions.

After the charms of the park were exhausted, a saunter among the shows and players' booths occupied a few hours satisfactorily. Even the pictures on the exterior, and the musical bands and spangled dancers on the front platform, were no small amusement to minds vacant alike of care and criticism; but to plunge madly in, and see a savage baron get his deserts for a long train of cruelties, all executed in a quarter of an hour,—there lay the grand treat of this department. Here, however, there was nothing locally peculiar—nothing but what was to be seen at Bartholomew Fair, or any other fair of importance throughout the country.

Towards evening, the dancing booths began to drain off the multitudes from the street. Some of these were boarded structures of two and even three hundred feet long, each, of course, provided with its little band of violinists, each also presenting a bar for refreshments, with rows of seats for spectators. Sixpence was the ordinary price of admission, and for that sum the giddy youth might dance till he was tired, each time with a new partner, selected from the crowd. Here lay the most reprehensible part of the enjoyments of Greenwich Fair, and that which conduced most to bring the festival into disrepute, and cause its suppression. The names adopted for these temples of Terpsichore were often of a whimsical character, as 'The Lads of the Village,' 'The Moonrakers,' 'The Black Boy and Cat,' and so forth. The second of these names probably indicated an Essex origin, with reference to the celebrated fable of the Essex farmers trying to rake Luna out of a pool in which they saw her fair form reflected.

When the limbs were wearied with walking and dancing, the heart satiated with fun, or what passed as such, and perhaps the stomach a little disordered with unwonted meats and drinks, the holiday-makers would address themselves for home. Then did the stage-coaches and the hackneys make rich harvest, seldom taking a passenger to London under four shillings, a tax which but few could pay. The consequence was that vast multitudes set out on foot, and, getting absorbed in public-houses by the way, seldom reached their respective places of abode till an advanced hour of the night.

Fairs were originally markets—a sort of commercial rendezvous rendered necessary by the sparseness of population and the paucity of business; and merry-makings and shows were only incidental accompaniments. Now that population is dense, and commercial communications of all kinds are active and easy, the country fair is no longer a necessity, and consequently they have nearly everywhere fallen much off. At one time, the use being obvious and respectable, and the merriments not beyond what the general taste and morality could approve of, the gentlefolk of the manor-house thought it not beneath them to come down into the crowded streets and give their countenance to the festivities. Arm-in-arm would the squire and his dame, and other members of the family, move dignifiedly through the fair, receiving universal homage as a reward for the sympathy they thus showed

with the needs and the enjoyments of their inferiors. At the fair of Charlton, in Kent, not much beyond the recollection of living persons, the wife of Sir Thomas Wilson was accustomed to make her appearance with her proper attendants, walking forth from the family mansion into the crowded streets, where she was sure to be hailed with a musical band, got up gratefully in her especial honour. It surely is not in the giving up of such kindly customs that the progress of our age is to be marked. Does it not rather indicate something like a retrogression?

This fair of Charlton, which was held on St Luke's Day (18th of October), had some curious peculiarities. The idea of horns was somehow connected with it in an especial manner. From Deptford and Greenwich came a vast flock of holiday-makers, many of them bearing a pair of horns upon their heads. Every booth in the fair had its horns conspicuous in the front. Ram's horns were an article abundantly presented for sale. Even the gingerbread was marked by a gilt pair of horns. It seemed an inexplicable mystery how horns and Charlton fair had become associated in this manner, till an antiquary at length threw a light upon it by pointing out that a horned ox is the recognised mediæval symbol of St Luke, the patron of the fair, fragmentary examples of it being still to be seen in the painted windows of Charlton Church. This fair was one where an unusual license was practised. It was customary for men to come to it in women's clothes—a favourite mode of masquerading two or three hundred years ago—against which the puritan clergy launched many a fulmination. The men also amused themselves, in their way across Blackheath, in lashing the women with furze, it being proverbial that ' all was fair at horn fair.'*

All over the south of Scotland and north of England there are fairs devoted to the hiring of servants—more particularly farmers' servants —both male and female. In some districts, the servants open to an engagement stand in a row at a certain part of the street, ready to treat with proposing employers; sometimes exhibiting a straw in their mouths, the better to indicate their unengaged condition. It is a position which gives occasion for some coquetry and badinage, and an air of good-humour generally prevails throughout. When the business of the day is pretty well over, the amusement begins. The public houses, and even some of the better sort of hotels, have laid out their largest rooms with long tables and forms, for the entertainment of the multitude. It becomes the recognised duty of the lads to bring in the lasses from the streets, and give them refreshments at these tables. Great heartiness and mirth prevail. Some gallant youths, having done their duty to one damsel, will plunge down into the street, seize another with little ceremony, and bring her in also. A dance in another apartment concludes the day's enjoyments. The writer, in boyhood, has often looked upon these scenes with great amusement; he must now acknowledge that they involve too great an element of coarseness, if not

* Charlton fair, which long retained many of its old peculiarities, is now discontinued.

something worse; and he cannot but rejoice to hear that there is now a movement for conducting the periodical business of hiring upon temperance principles. It is one of the misfortunes of the lowly that, bound down to monotonous toil the greater part of their lives, they can scarcely enjoy an occasional day of relaxation or amusement without falling into excesses. Let us hope that in time there will be more frequent and more liberal intervals of relaxation, and consequently less tendency to go beyond reasonable bounds in merry-making.

MAY 17.

St Possidius, 5th century. St Maden, of Brittany. St Maw. St Cathan, 7th century. St Silave, 1100. St Paschal Baylon, 1592.

Born.—Dr Edward Jenner, discoverer of vaccination, 1749, *Berkeley;* Henry William, Marquis of Anglesey, statesman, 1768.

Died.—Heloise, 1163, *Paraclete Abbey;* Matthew Parker, Archbishop of Canterbury, 1575, *Lambeth;* Catharine I. of Russia, widow of Peter the Great, 1727; Dr Samuel Clarke, 1729, *London;* William Louth (biblical scholarship), 1732, *Buriton;* Samuel Boyse, poet, 1749, *London;* Alexis Claude Clairhaut, mathematician, 1756; Dr William Heberden, medical writer, 1801, *Windsor;* Prince Talleyrand, 1838, *Paris.*

HELOISE.

The story of Heloise and Abelard is one of the saddest on record. It is a true story of man's selfishness and woman's devotion and self-abnegation. If we wished for an allegory which should be useful to exhibit the bitter strife which has to be waged between the earthly and the heavenly, between passion and principle, in the noblest minds, we should find it provided for us in this painful history. We know all the particulars, for Abelard has written his own confessions, without screening himself or concealing his guilt; and several letters which passed between the lovers after they were separated, and devoted to the exclusive service of religion, have come down to posterity.

Not alone the tragic fate of the offenders, but also their exalted worth and distinguished position, helped to make notorious the tale of their fall. Heloise was an orphan girl, eighteen years old, residing with a canon of Nôtre Dame, at Paris, who was her uncle and guardian. This uncle took great pains to educate her, and obtained for her the advantage of Abelard's instruction, who directed her studies at first by letters. Her devotion to study rendered her remarkable among the ladies of Paris, even more than her beauty. ' In face,' Abelard himself informs us, ' she was not insignificant; in her abundance of learning she was unparalleled; and because this gift is rare in women, so much the more did it make this girl illustrious through the whole kingdom.' Abelard, though twice the age of Heloise, was a man of great personal attraction, as well as the most famous man of his time, as a rising teacher, philosopher, and divine. His fame was then at its highest. Pupils came to him by thousands. He was lifted up to that dangerous height of intellectual arrogance, from which the scholar has often to be hurled with violence by a hard but kind fate, that he may not let slip the true humility of wisdom. 'Where was found,' Heloise writes, 'the king or the philosopher that had emulated your reputation? Was there a village, a city, a kingdom, that did not ardently wish to see you? When you appeared in public, who did not run to behold you? And when you withdrew, every neck was stretched, every eye sprang forward to follow you. The women, married and unmarried, when Abelard was away, longed for his return!' And, becoming more explicit, she continues: 'You possessed, indeed, two qualifications—a tone of voice, and a grace in singing—which gave you the control over every female heart. These powers were peculiarly yours, for I do not know that they ever fell to the share of any other philosopher. To soften by playful instruments the stern labours of philosophy, you composed several sonnets on love, and on similar subjects. These you were often heard to sing, when the harmony of your voice gave new charms to the expression. In all circles nothing was talked of but Abelard; even the most ignorant, who could not judge of harmony, were enchanted by the melody of your voice. Female hearts were unable to resist the impression.' So the girl's fancies come back to the woman, and it must have caused a pang in the fallen scholar to see how much his guilt had been greater than hers.

It was a very thoughtless thing for Fulbert to throw together a woman so enthusiastic and a man so dangerously attractive. In his eagerness that his niece's studies should advance as rapidly as possible, he forgot the tendency of human instinct to assert its power over minds the most cultivated, and took Abelard into his house. A passionate attachment grew up between teacher and pupil: reverence for the teacher on the one hand, interest in the pupil on the other, changed into warmer emotions. Evil followed. What to lower natures would have seemed of little moment, brought to them a life of suffering and repentance. In his penitent confessions, no doubt conscientiously enough, Abelard represents his own conduct as a deliberate scheme of a depraved will to accomplish a wicked design; and such a terrible phase of an intellectual mind is real, but the circumstances in which the lovers were placed are enough to account for the unhappy issue. The world, however, it appears, was pleased to put the worst construction upon what it heard, and even Heloise herself expresses a painful doubt, long afterwards, for a moment, at a time when Abelard seemed to have forgotten her. 'Account,' she says, 'for this conduct, if you can, or must I tell you my suspicions, which are also the general suspicions of the world? It was passion, Abelard, and not friendship, that drew you to me; it was not love, but a baser feeling.'

The attachment of the lovers had long been publicly known, and made famous by the songs which Abelard himself penned, to the utter neglect of his lectures and his pupils, when the utmost extent of the mischief became clear at last to the unsuspicious Fulbert. Abelard contrived to convey Heloise to the nunnery of Argenteuil. The uncle demanded that a marriage should immediately take place; and to this Abelard agreed, though he knew that his prospects of advancement would be ruined, if the marriage was made public. Heloise, on this very account, opposed the marriage; and, even after it had taken place, would not confess the truth. Fulbert at once divulged the whole, and Abelard's worldly prospects were for ever blasted. Not satisfied with this, Fulbert took a most cruel and unnatural revenge upon Abelard, the shame of which decided the wretched man to bury himself as a monk in the Abbey of St Dennis. Out of jealousy and distrust, he requested Heloise to take the veil; and having no wish except to please her husband, she immediately complied, in spite of the opposition of her friends.

Thus, to atone for the error of the past, both devoted themselves wholly to a religious life, and succeeded in adorning it with their piety and many virtues. Abelard underwent many sufferings and persecutions. Heloise first became prioress of Argenteuil; afterwards, she removed with her nuns to the Paraclete, an asylum which Abelard had built and then abandoned. But she never subdued her woman's devotion for Abelard. While abbess of the Paraclete, Heloise revealed the undercurrent of earthly passion which flowed beneath the even piety of the bride of heaven, in a letter which she wrote to Abelard, on the occasion of an account of his sufferings, written by himself to a friend, falling into her hands. In a series of letters which passed between them at this time, she exhibits a pious and Christian endeavour to perform her duties as an abbess, but persists in retaining the devoted attachment of a wife for her husband. Abelard, somewhat coldly, endeavours to direct her mind entirely to heaven; rather affects to treat her as a daughter than a wife; and seems anxious to check those feelings towards himself which he judged it better for the abbess of the Paraclete to discourage than to foster. Heloise survived Abelard twenty-one years.

We have endeavoured to state the bare facts of this tragic history, and feel bound, in conclusion, to warn the reader that Pope's far-famed epistle of *Heloise to Abelard* conveys a totally erroneous notion of a woman who died a model of piety and universally beloved. She ever looked up to her husband with veneration, appreciating him as a great scholar and philosopher. She gave up everything on his account; and though once, when a mere girl, she was weak when she should have been strong, there is none of that sensuality traceable in her passionate devotion which is Pope's pet idea, and which he pursues with such assiduity. Perhaps the best passage in Pope's poem is one in which he represents Heloise as describing the melancholy of her convent's seclusion. We subjoin it as a specimen of the poem, without being very vain of it.

'The darksome pines, that o'er yon rocks reclined,
Wave high, and murmur to the hollow wind;
The wandering streams that shine between the hills,
The grots that echo to the tinkling rills;

The dying gales that pant upon the trees,
The lakes that quiver to the curling breeze ;—
No more these scenes my meditation aid,
Or lull to rest the visionary maid.
But o'er the twilight groves and dusky caves,
Long sounding isles, and intermingling graves,
Black Melancholy sits, and round her throws
A death-like silence and a dread repose :
Her gloomy presence saddens all the scene,
Shades every flower, and darkens every green ;
Deepens the murmur of the falling floods,
And wreathes a browner horror on the woods.'

TALLEYRAND.

At his death in 1838, Talleyrand had reached the age of eighty-four. He had figured as a bishop before the Revolution, made a narrow escape in that crisis of the national history, was Napoleon's minister for foreign affairs under both the Consulate and Empire, was the leading Frenchman in arranging the Restoration, and did not forsake public life under either the restored Bourbons or Louis Philippe. The character of the age in which he had lived was strongly brought before our thoughts when, on taking the oath to the new system of things in 1830, he said—'This is the thirteenth—I hope it will be the last.' He is generally reputed as the very type of the statesman of expediency and the slippery *diplomat ;* and yet there is reason to believe that Talleyrand, all through, acted for the best in behalf of his country. It is true, he had an extraordinary amount of that sagacity which, in the midst of general enthusiasm, can coolly calculate chances ; which is, accordingly, never *carried away ;* which plays with the passions and sentiments of men. But he was not necessarily on this account a wicked politician. He was even honest in certain great crises—for example, when he counselled Napoleon to moderation after obtaining the purple, and lost his favour by discommending the invasion of Spain, which he truly prophesied would be found ' the beginning of the end.' Being out of the immediate service of the Emperor, he was perfectly at liberty to move for the change of dynasty in 1814, and he continued faithful to the new one in the trying crisis of the ensuing year.

The reputation of Talleyrand has arisen more from his words than his actions. He could justly appreciate the ardour of other people, and make cool, witty remarks upon them. Hence it was thought that he had no heart, no generous feeling. He could point out the evil consequences of openness and zeal; hence it was thought that he had no probity or faithfulness. But he was in reality a kind-hearted man, and generally acted correctly. All we can truly say is just this, that in the various difficult matters he was concerned in, he could see the inevitable consequences of being the simpleton or the enthusiast; and that, being a wit, he loved to put his reflections on these things into epigrammatic form, thus unavoidably giving them an air of heartlessness. The generality of men, repining at the useful self-command they saw he could exercise, took their revenge by representing him as a monster of cold-heartedness and treachery—which was far from being his actual character. Their injustice was supported by a *sang-froid* which was constitutional with Talleyrand, but which was merely external.

The *bon mots* of Talleyrand had a great celebrity. There was something cynical about them, but they were also playful. When told that the Duke of Bassano was come back with Napoleon from Russia, he remarked, with an expression of doubt on his countenance, ' Those bulletins are always lying—they told us all the baggage had been left behind.' Such a fling at a stupid statesman many might have made. But what are we to say of the depth of such of his sayings as that the execution of the Duc D'Enghien was ' worse than a crime—it was a blunder'? There we see the comprehensive and penetrating intellect, as well as the epigrammatist. After all, as often happens with men's good things, some are traced to earlier wits. For instance, his saying that language was given to man ' not to express his thoughts, but to conceal them,' is traced back to South, the English divine. So also his reply to the question ' What had passed in the council ?' ' *Trois heures,*' had a prototype in a saying which Bacon records of Mr Popham, the Speaker of the House of Commons, who, being asked by Queen Elizabeth what had passed in the lower house, answered, ' Please your majesty, seven weeks.' It is not easy even for a Talleyrand to be original.

Some of his acts were practical witticisms, as when, at the death of Charles X., he appeared in a white hat in the republican quarters of Paris, and in the quartier St Germain put on a crape ; or, when asked by a lady for his signature in her album, he inscribed it at the very top of a page, so that there might be no order for ten thousand francs written over it.

Not long before the death of Talleyrand, an able English writer, speaking of his brilliant apothegms, said, ' What are they all to the practical skill with which this extraordinary man has contrived to baffle all the calamities of thirty years, full of the ruin of all power, ability, courage, and fortune ? Here is the survivor of the age of the Bastile, the age of the guillotine, the age of the prison-ship, the age of the sword. And after baffling the Republic, the Democracy, the Despotism, and the Restoration, he figures in his eightieth year as the Ambassador to England, the Minister of France, and retires from both offices only to be chief counsellor, almost the coadjutor of the king. That where the ferocity of Robespierre fell, where the sagacity of Napoleon fell, where the experience of the Bourbons fell, this one old man, a priest in a land of daring spirits—where conspiracy first, and soldiership after, were the great means of power—should survive all, succeed in everything, and retain his rank and influence through all change, is unquestionably among the most extraordinary instances of conduct exhibited in the world.'

SITTING BELOW THE SALT.

One of the customs of great houses, in former times, was to place a large ornamental *salt-vat* (commonly but erroneously called salt-foot) upon the table, about the centre, to mark the part below which it was proper for tenants and dependents to sit. The accompanying illustration represents a remarkably handsome article of this kind which belonged to Archbishop Parker, and

ARCHBISHOP PARKER'S SALT-VAT.

has since been preserved in Corpus Christi College, Cambridge, along with other plate presented to that institution by the venerable prelate, who was at one time its *Master*. The Corpus Christi salt-vat is an elegant fabric of silver and gold, beautifully carved externally, and twice the size of our illustration.

The salt-cellar of Bishop Fox, 1517, which is preserved in Corpus Christi College, Oxford, is a beautiful specimen of the goldsmiths' work of the period. It is silver-gilt, covered with ornaments elaborately chased, one of the chief figures being the pelican, which was the bishop's emblem.

This practice of old days, so invidiously distinguishing one part of a company from another, appears to have been in use throughout both England and Scotland, and to have extended at least to France. It would be an error to suppose that the distinction was little regarded on either hand, or was always taken good-humouredly on the part of the inferior persons. There is full evidence in old plays, and other early productions of the press, that both parties were fully sensible of what sitting below the salt inferred. Thus, in *Cynthia's Revels*, by Ben Jonson, we hear of a character who takes no notice of any ill-dressed person, and never drinks to anybody below the salt. One writing in 1613 about the miseries of a poor scholar in the houses of

648

the great,* says, 'he must sit under the salt—that is an axiom in such places.' Even, strange to say, the clerical preceptor of the children had to content himself with this inferior position, if we are to trust to a passage in Bishop Hall's satires—

'A gentle squire would gladly entertain
  Into his house some trencher-chapelaine,
Some willing man that might instruct his sons,
And that could stand to good conditions :
First, that he lie upon the truckle bed
Whiles his young maister lieth o'er his head ;
Second, that he do, on no default,
Ever presume to sit above the salt ;
Third, that he never change his trencher twice,' &c.

So also we find in an old English ballad the following sufficiently pointed allusion—

'Thou art a carle of mean degree,
  The salt it doth stand between me and thee ;
But, an' thou hadst been of a gentle strain,
  I would have bitten my gant† again.'

A Scotch noble, again, writing in 1680 about his family and its old neighbours, introduces a derogatory allusion to the self-raised son of one of those against whom he had a spite, as coming of a family who, in, visiting his (the noble's) relatives, 'never came to sit above the salt-foot.' ‡

THE BURIAL OF HELOISE.

The connexion of Heloise with Abelard, their separation, their subsequent lives, spent in penitence and religious exercises, not unmingled with human regrets, have employed a hundred pens. Heloise, surviving Abelard twenty-one years, was deposited in the same grave within Paraclete's white walls. The *Chronique de Tours* reports that, at the moment when the tomb of Abelard was opened for the body of Heloise, Abelard held out his hand to receive her. The author of a modern life of Abelard tells this tale, and, the better to support it, gives instances of similar miracles ; as, for example, that of a senator of Dijon, who, having been interred twenty-eight years, opened his arms to embrace his wife when she descended into the same tomb. These, being French husbands, may be supposed to have been unusually polite ; but that posthumous conjugal civilities are not necessarily confined to that nation, is shown by an anecdote told of the sainted Queen Margaret of Scotland. When, many years after her death, this royal lady was canonized, it was necessary to remove her body from a place in Dunfermline Abbey, where it lay beside her husband, King Malcolm, to a place more convenient for a shrine. It was found that the body was so preternaturally heavy that there was no lifting it. The monks were nonplused. At length, one suggested that the queen refused to be moved without her husband. Malcolm was then raised, and immediately the queen's body resumed its ordinary weight, and the removal was effected.

The bodies of Abelard and Heloise, after several migrations, were finally removed in 1800 to the cemetery of Père la Chaise, near Paris.

---

* *Strange Foot Post, with a Pocket full of Strange Petitions.* London, 1613. 4to.

† Glove, alluding to a challenge.

‡ *Memorie of the Somervilles.* Edinburgh. 2 vols. 1816. In an early volume of *Blackwood's Magazine* there is a keen controversy on this subject, in which Mr Riddell, the genealogical antiquary, bore a part.

MAY 18.

St Venantius, martyr, 250. St Theodotus, vintner, and seven virgins, martyrs, 303. St Potamon, martyr, 341. St Eric, King of Sweden, martyr, 1151.

Died.—Bishop Nicolas Longespee, 1297; Bishop Herbert Croft, 1691; Elias Ashmole, antiquary, 1692, *Great Lambeth;* Charles Perrault, miscellaneous writer, 1703; Ephraim Chambers, encyclopædist, 1740; Bishop John Douglas, 1807.

PERRAULT.

This name calls for a brief passing notice, as one associated with pleasures which we have all enjoyed in childhood. It is but little and even dubiously known, that the universally diffused *Tales of Mother Goose,* to wit, *Blue Beard, Tom Thumb, Cinderella,* &c., were a production of this celebrated French writer. After having spent a long life in more or less profound studies, and produced several learned dissertations, it pleased him to compose these fairy tales, probably to amuse a little son who had been born to him in his advanced age. It was in 1697 that these matchless stories were given to the world at Paris; not, however, as the production of Charles Perrault, the accomplished and esteemed scholar and critic, but as the work of Perrault d'Armancourt, his son, who was as yet a mere child. They have since been translated into nearly every language. Perrault died in the seventy-sixth year of his age.

A ROMANCE OF MILITARY HISTORY.

Early in the last century, the government raised six companies of highland soldiers, as a local force to preserve the peace and prevent robberies in the northern parts of Scotland. These companies, the famous Black Watch of Scottish song and story, were formed into a regiment in 1739, and four years after were marched to London, on their way to join the British army, then actively serving in Germany. Many of the men composing this regiment, believing that their terms of enlistment did not include foreign service, felt great dissatisfaction on leaving Scotland; but it being represented to them that they were merely going to London to be reviewed by the king in person, no actual disobedience to orders occurred. About the time, however, that the regiment reached London, the king departed for the Continent, and this the simple and high-minded Highlanders considered as a slight thrown upon either their courage or fidelity. Several disaffected persons, among the crowds that went to see the regiment in their quarters at Highgate, carefully fanned the flame of discontent; but the men, concealing any open expression of ill-feeling, sedulously prepared for a review announced to take place on the king's birthday, the 14th of May 1743. On that day Lord Sempill's Highland regiment, as it was then termed, was reviewed by General Wade, on Finchley Common. A paper of the day, says : ' The Highlanders made a very handsome appearance, and went through their exercise and firing with the utmost exactness. The novelty of the sight drew together the greatest concourse of people ever seen on such an occasion.'

The review having taken place, the dissatisfied portion of the regiment, considering that the duty for which they were brought to London had been performed, came to the wild resolution of forcing their way back to Scotland. So immediately after midnight, on the morning of the 18th of May, about one hundred and fifty of them, with their arms and fourteen rounds of ball-cartridge each, commenced their march northwards. On the men being missed, the greatest consternation ensued, and the most frightful apprehensions were entertained regarding the crimes likely to be perpetrated by the (supposed) savage mountaineers, on the peaceful inhabitants of English country-houses. Despatches were sent off to the officers commanding in the northern districts, and proclamations of various kinds were issued; among others, one offering a reward of forty shillings for every captured deserter. The little intercourse between different parts of the country, and the slow transmission of intelligence at the period, is remarkably exemplified by the fact that the first authentic news of the deserters did not reach London till the evening of the seventh day after their flight.

The retreat was conducted by a corporal, Samuel Macpherson, who exhibited considerable military skill and strategy. Marching generally by night, and keeping the line of country between the two great northern roads, they pushed forward with surprising celerity, carefully selecting strong natural positions for their resting-places. When marching by day, they directed their course from one wood or defensive position to another, rather than in a direct northern line—thus perplexing the authorities, who never knew where to look for the deserters, as scarcely two persons agreed when describing their line of march.

General Blakeney, who then commanded the north-eastern district, specially appointed Captain Ball, with a large body of cavalry, to intercept the Highlanders. On the evening of the 21st, Ball received intelligence that about three o'clock on the same day the fugitives had crossed the river Nen, near Wellingborough, in Northamptonshire. Conjecturing that they were making for Rutlandshire, he placed himself in an advantageous position at Uppingham, on the border of that county; Blakeney, with a strong force, being already posted at Stamford, on the border of Lincolnshire. But the Highlanders encamped for the night in a strong position on a hill surrounded by a dense wood, about four miles from Oundle, in Northamptonshire.

Early on the following morning, a country magistrate named Creed, hearing of the Highlanders' arrival in his neighbourhood, went to their camp, and endeavoured to persuade them to surrender. This they refused to do without a grant of pardon, which Creed could not give. After considerable discussion, both parties agreed to the following terms. Creed was to write to the Duke of Montague, Master-General of the Ordnance, stating that the deserters were willing to return to their duty on promise of a free pardon; they engaging to remain in the place they then occupied till a reply arrived from the duke; Creed also was to write to the military officer commanding in the district, desiring him not to molest the Highlanders until the duke's wishes were known. At five o'clock in the morning the letters were written by Creed, in the presence of the Highlanders, and immediately after despatched, by special messengers, to their respective destinations. In that to the military officer, Creed says, 'These Highlanders are a brave, bold sort of people, and are resolved not to submit till pardon comes down.'

In the meantime, a gamekeeper of Lord Gainsborough, having reported the position of the Highlanders to Captain Ball, that officer, arriving on the ground on the forenoon of the same day, demanded their immediate surrender. They replied that they were already in treaty with the civil authorities, and referred Captain Ball to Mr Creed. At the same time they wrote the following letter to Mr Creed, then attending church at Oundle :—

'Honoured Sir,—Just now came here a captain belonging to General Blakeney's regiment, and proposed to us to surrender to him, without regard to your honour's letter to the Duke of Montague, which we refused to do; wherefore he is gone for his squadron, and is immediately to fall on us. So that, if you think they can be kept off till the return of your letter, you'll be pleased to consider without loss of time.'

With this letter they also sent a verbal message, stating that they were strongly posted, and resolved to die to a man, rather than surrender on any other terms than those they had already proposed. Creed replied, advising them to surrender, and offering his good offices in soliciting their pardon. Ball, finding the position of the deserters unassailable by cavalry, rested till the evening, when General Blakeney's forces arrived. The Highlanders then sent out a request for another interview with Ball, which was granted. He told them he could grant no other terms than an unconditional surrender. They replied that they preferred dying with arms in their hands. They took him into the wood, and showed him the great strength of their position, which, from Ball's military description, seems to have been one of those ancient British or Roman earthworks which still puzzle our antiquaries. They said they were soldiers, and would defend it to the last. Ball replied that he too was a soldier, and would kill the last, if it came to the arbitrament of arms. They then parted, a guard of the Highlanders leading Ball out of the wood. On their way, Ball, by offering an absolute pardon to the two by whom he was accompanied, succeeded in inducing them to return to their duty. One went with him to the general; the other, returning to the wood, prevailed upon a number of his comrades to submit also; these persuaded others, so that in the course of the night the whole number surrendered to General Blakeney.

As the Highlanders in their retreat conducted themselves in the most unexceptionable manner, none of the fearful anticipations respecting them were realized. So, on their surrender, the public fright resolved itself into the opposite extreme of public admiration. The flight of the deserters was compared to the retreat of the Ten Thousand; and Corporal Macpherson was regarded as a

CORPORAL MACPHERSON.

second Xenophon. But the stern exigencies of military discipline had to be satisfied. By sentence of a court-martial, two corporals, Macpherson and his brother, and one private named Shaw, were condemned to be shot. The execution took place on the 12th of July, a newspaper of the day tells that—'The rest of the Highlanders were drawn out to see the execution, and joined in prayer with great earnestness. The unfortunate men behaved with perfect resolution and propriety. Their bodies were put into three coffins by three of their clansmen and namesakes and buried in one grave near the place of execution.'

General Stewart, in his *Sketches of the Highlanders,* says, 'There must have been something more than common in the case or character of these unfortunate men, as Lord John Murray, who was afterwards colonel of the regiment, had portraits of them hung up in his dining-room. I have not at present the means of ascertaining whether this proceeded from an impression on his lordship's mind that they had been victims to the designs of others, and ignorantly misled rather than wilfully culpable, or merely from a desire of preserving the resemblances of men who were remarkable for their size and handsome figure.'

Whatever stain may have been cast on the character of a brave and loyal regiment by this ill-judged affair, was soon after effectually washed away by their desperate courage on the sanguinary field of Fontenoy. One of Sempill's Highlanders, named Campbell, killed nine Frenchmen with his broadsword, and, while aiming a blow at a tenth, had his arm carried away by a cannon-ball. The Duke of Cumberland nominated him to a lieutenancy on the field; his portrait was engraved; and there was scarcely a village throughout England but had the walls of its cottages decorated with the representation of this warlike Celt. Sempill's regiment, losing its distinctive appellation about the middle of the last century, became the 42nd Highlanders, and as such can boast of laurels gained in every part of the globe where British valour and determination have stemmed and turned the headlong tide of battle.

THE MISCHIANZA.

On the 18th May 1778, a remarkable *fête*, known by the name of the Mischianza (Italian for a medley), took place in the city of Philadelphia. A British army, under General Sir William Howe had occupied the city as winter quarters for some months, while Washington lay with his shoeless army in a hutted camp a few miles off. The British troops had found the possession of Philadelphia barren of results, although they had friends in a portion of the population. Howe, disappointed, was about to retire from the command and go home. The army itself contemplated withdrawal, and did a month afterwards withdraw. It was, nevertheless, resolved to put a good face upon matters, and hold a festival, professedly in honour of the retiring general.

The affair took a character of romance and elegant gaiety from the genius of a young officer, named André. There was first a regatta on the river Delaware; then the main personages landed, and made a splendid procession for about a quarter of a mile to a piece of ground designed for the land *fête*. There a tournament took place between six knights of the *Blended Rose* on one side, and as many of the *Burning Mountain* on the other; all in fantastic silk dresses, with ribbons, devices, and mottoes, lances, shields, and pistols, each attended by his squire, and each professing to serve some particular lady of his love. Lord Cathcart, who acted as chief of the knights (and whom the writer remembers seeing thirty years afterwards in much soberer circumstances), rode at the head, with a squire on each hand; the device of his shield, a Cupid mounted on a lion, and professing to appear 'in honour of Miss Auchmuty.' One of the knights of the Blended Rose was the young Captain

THE MISCHIANZA TICKET.

Andrė, already alluded to, who stood forth for Miss P. Chew, with the device of two game cocks, and the motto, 'No Rival.' The first set of knights caused their herald to proclaim their intention to maintain by force of arms the supremacy of their ladies, in wit, beauty, and virtue; the herald of the other set responded with defiance, and they closed in mock fight, shivering lances, discharging pistols, and finally taking to their swords, until the Marshal of the Field, at the request of the ladies, ordered them to desist.

Then the gay party adjourned to a large and handsome house near by, where, in finely decorated rooms, they entered upon a series of dances. Afterwards, a pair of hitherto concealed doors being thrown open, they moved into a large pavilion laid out with an elegant supper. Fireworks completed this fantastic entertainment, the like of which had never before been seen on the west side of the Atlantic. A few days afterwards, General Howe withdrew to England, and three or four weeks later the English troops vacated Philadelphia.

The tragic fate which three years after befell the sprightly and ingenious André, the moving spirit of this show, gives it a sad interest. The writer, being not long ago in Philadelphia, sought out the scene of the *fête*, and with some difficulty found it, involved amidst the meaner details of that largely increased city. The house in which the ball and banquet took place appears as one which originally belonged to some opulent merchant, but is now sadly fallen from its once high estate, and used as a charity school. The spacious halls of the Mischianza we found rudely partitioned into smaller apartments for a variety of school classes. The walls, which were fantastically coloured for the ball, are now in a state of neglect. It was melancholy to tread the floors, and think of them as they were in May 1778, freighted with the festivity of gay, hopeful men and women, not one of whom is now in the land of the living.

DISRUPTION OF THE SCOTCH CHURCH, MAY 18, 1843.

This was an event of very great moment in Scotland, and perhaps of more importance to the rest of the United Kingdom than the rest of the United Kingdom was aware of. It took its origin in a movement of zeal in the Presbyterian Church of Scotland, mainly promoted by Dr Chalmers, and to which a stimulus was given by a movement in the Scotch dissenting bodies for putting an end to the connexion of church and state. Eager to show itself worthy of the status it enjoyed, and to obtain popular support, the church in 1834 passed a law of its own, ordaining that thenceforth no presentee to a parish church should be admitted or 'settled' (a duty of the presbytery of the district), if he was objected to by a majority of the male communicants of the congregation. This of course struck at the face of the system of patronage, long established—a system involving important civil rights. A presentee objected to next year claimed the protection of the civil courts, and had his claim allowed. The Veto law, as it was called, became a dead letter. It was after several years of vain struggling against the civil powers on points like this, that a large portion of the national clergy formed the resolu-

tion of withdrawing from an Establishment in which, as they held, ' Christ's sole and supreme authority as king in his church,' was dishonoured.

When the annual convocation or assembly of the church was approaching in May 1843, it was generally understood that this schism was about to take place; but nearly all cool on-lookers fully assured themselves that a mere handful of clergymen, chiefly those specially committed as leaders, would give up their comfortable stipends and manses, and all the other obvious advantages of their position. The result was such as to show that to judge of a probable course of action by a consideration of the grosser class of human motives only, is not invariably safe—on the contrary, may be widely wrong. The day of the meeting arrived. The assembly met in St Andrew's Church, in Edinburgh, under its Moderator or President, Dr Welsh, and with the usual sanctioning presence of the royal commissioner — an anomalous interference with the very principle concerned, which had been quietly submitted to by the church ever since the Revolution. There was a brilliant assemblage of spectators within, and a vast crowd without, most of them prepared to see the miserable show of eight or ten men voluntarily sacrificing themselves to what was thought a fantastic principle. When the time came for making up the roll of the members, Dr Welsh rose, and said that he must protest against further procedure, in consequence of proceedings affecting the rights of the church which had been sanctioned by her Majesty's government and by the legislature of the country. After reading a formal protest, he left his place and walked out of the church, followed first by Dr Chalmers, then by other prominent men, afterwards by others, till the number amounted to four hundred; who then walked along the streets to another place of meeting, and constituted themselves into the Free Church of Scotland — free, as distinguished from one fettered by the state connexion. There was of course general astonishment, mingled with some degree of consternation, at the magnitude of the separating body, indicating, as it did, something like the break-up of a venerable institution. But the full numbers of the seceding clergy were not yet ascertained; they reached four hundred and seventy, or not much less than a half of the entire body. It was a remarkable instance of the energy of religious (though, in the estimation of many, mistaken) principles, in an age of material things. When Lord Jeffrey was told, an hour after, what had taken place, he started up, exclaiming, 'Thank God for my country; there is not another upon earth where such a deed could have been done !'

Within four years the new church numbered 720 clergy, for whose subsistence a very fair provision was made by the contributions of their adherents; thus, by the way, proving the energy of that voluntary principle, to check which this movement had partly been made, and to which this sect still professed to be opposed. The real importance of the event lay in its taking away the support of a majority of the people from the Establishment, in one more of the three divisions of the empire.

MAY 19.

St Prudentiana, virgin, 1st century.   St Dunstan, Archbishop of Canterbury, 988. St Peter Celestine, Pope, 1296.

ST DUNSTAN.

St Dunstan was one of those men who stamp their own character on the age they live in. He was in every way a remarkable man. And, like most remarkable men, he has been unduly extolled on one hand, and vilified on the other. Monkish writers have embellished his life with a multitude of ridiculous, or worse than ridiculous miracles; and their opponents have represented him as ambitious, bigoted, and utterly unscrupulous as to means, so that he only gained his end.

In the following sketch we hope to keep clear of both these extremes, and present a truthful outline of the man.

Dunstan was born in the isle of Glastonbury, about the year 924 A.D. He was of noble, even royal descent. His father's name was Herstan, his mother's Cynedryda. Those who seek for the formation of character in first impressions derived from external objects, find them in this case in the scenery and local associations of his birthplace. Glastonbury was always esteemed a sacred spot. King Arthur, of imperishable memory, was buried there; and it was also believed that the remains of Joseph of Arimathea, and of St Patrick, the apostle of Ireland, rested within its hallowed precincts. On account of the clearness of the waters by which it was surrounded, the ancient British named it Ynyswytryn, or the 'Glassy Island;' the Romans knew it as Avalonia; and the Saxons called it Glæstingabyrig. Whatever its natural charms may have been, they can surely never have equalled those with which the poet laureate has invested it, when he describes it as

'The island valley of Avilion,
Where falls not hail, nor rain, nor any snow,
Nor ever wind blows loudly; but it lies
Deep-meadowed, happy, fair, with orchard lawns,
And bowery hollows, crowned with summer sea.'

Amid the scenery and associations of this favoured spot young Dunstan grew up, delicate in bodily health, but of prodigious mental powers. Ardent, and full of imagination, he aimed at everything, and easily accomplished nearly all he attempted. Besides Holy Scripture, the great divines of the church, poetry and history, he paid considerable attention to arithmetic, geometry, astronomy, and music. He excelled in drawing and sculpture. He spent much of his time in writing and illuminating books; and he also worked in gold and silver, copper and iron. Instead of moderating his too eager pursuit of knowledge, his parents and tutors made the grand mistake of inciting him to still greater efforts. The result was a brain fever. At the crisis of the disease, when his friends gave him up for dead, there was an access of delirium, and eluding the vigilance of his nurse, he rushed out of the room and went to the church. It was night, and the doors were closed; but he madly mounted some scaffolding, and by a perilous descent made his way into the building, where he was found the next morning, uninjured, and in a placid sleep. This was, of course, ascribed to a miracle—a belief which was confirmed both in his own mind and in that of others when he related, what was evidently a delirious dream, that he had been pursued by demons in the shape of wild dogs.

When the fever left him, change of scene was recommended, and his high connexions procured his admission into the court of Athelstan. Here he soon became a favourite, especially with the ladies, who frequently consulted him about their embroidery, &c. But the favourite at court is sure to have enemies there too. Whispers were spread abroad that he had learned to practise heathen charms and magic. Instead of allaying these reports, he freely indulged his wonder-loving propensities, till he proceeded a step too far. On one occasion he was in the bower of the noble Lady Ethelwyne, tracing some patterns for her embroidery, when the tune and words of a well-known anthem were heard proceeding from his harp, which hung against the wall, no hand being near it. The matron and her maidens rushed out of the apartment, declaring that Dunstan was wiser than he ought to be. Their statement confirmed the suspicions already excited; and he was banished from the court. The cold water ordeal was one specially provided for witches and wizards; and certain youngsters at court saw no reason why Dunstan should escape it. It would, at least, satisfy some old grudges to see whether he would sink or float, and perhaps it might do something towards clearing his character. So after him they went, as he was riding mournfully away, overtook him, dragged him from his horse, threw him into a pond, and, when he had succeeded in crawling to the bank, set their dogs to chase him. This cruel treatment disordered his imagination, and he again fancied that the demons of hell were let loose upon him.

Mortified by these indignities, and nearly heartbroken at being driven away from his lady-love—for he had become deeply enamoured of a young lady while at court—he betook himself to his uncle, Elphege the Bald, then bishop of Winchester. Elphege was a fanatic, and a fanatic in those days was sure to be an enemy to the married state. He was aware of the genius and talents of Dunstan, and he determined to enlist them on the monastic side, and, if possible, to make a monk of him. A return of fever aided the otherwise inconclusive arguments of the prelate, and Dunstan, on his recovery, was ordained priest, and went to Fleury to learn the rule of St Benedict, and conform to monastic discipline. He returned to Glastonbury an enthusiastic monk; for whatever he did, he did with all his might. He built himself a cell five feet long by two and a half feet wide, and not more than breast-high above ground, which served him for study, dormitory, and workshop, and in which he lived as an anchorite. As he entered manhood, his natural passions gained strength, and a hard conflict with himself ensued. To escape from his thoughts, he almost destroyed

653

himself with fasting and labouring at his forge. Osbern relates a story of this period of his life which has become one of the best known of monkish legends. The devil used to annoy the young saint by paying him nocturnal visits in the form of a bear, a serpent, or other noxious animal; but one night, as he was hammering away at his forge, Satan came in a human form as a woman, and looking in at his window, began to tempt him with improper conversation. Dunstan bore it till he had heated his pincers sufficiently, and then, with the red-hot instrument, seized his visitor by the nose. So, at least, he is reported to have told his neighbours in the morning, when they inquired what those horrible cries were which startled them from their sleep.

On the death of Athelstan, the new king, Edmund, recalled Dunstan to the court, made him abbot of the royal monastery of Glastonbury, and one of his counsellors. Having about this time inherited an ample fortune, he rebuilt and endowed the church, surrounded it with conventual buildings, introduced the Benedictine rule, and raised his favourite monastery to the rank of the first great public school in England during the rest of the Anglo-Saxon period. One great object of Dunstan's after life was to establish the Benedictine rule in all other monasteries in this country; and he succeeded so far as to be considered the father of the English Benedictines. His rule became the rule of the country.

Under Edred his power and influence were greatly increased. He was the personal friend of the king as well as his minister. And during the long illness with which he was afflicted, Dunstan not only conversed and prayed with him, but managed to convert his palace into a school of virtue. In fact, during this reign all real power was in the hands of Dunstan. Both the king and the Archbishop of Canterbury were governed by his superior mind. There could, therefore, be no temptation for him to leave the court; and when offered the bishopric of Winchester, and pressed by the king's mother to accept it, he could reply in all sincerity, 'Most assuredly the episcopal mitre shall never cover my brows while thy son liveth.' A change of fortune came with the accession of Edwy. The young king, though only sixteen years old, was married to the beautiful Elgiva. On his coronation day he rose from the table after dinner, leaving his guests over their cups, and went into an inner apartment to his wife and her mother. This gave offence to the nobles, and Odo desired that some persons would go and bring the king back. Dunstan and one of his kinsmen undertook this rude commission; and instead of persuading, they actually dragged the king back into the Mead-hall by force. Edwy, justly offended, called the minister to account for the public money committed to his care during the previous reign; and as this was not done to his satisfaction, he deprived him of his honours, confiscated his property, and banished him from the kingdom. This was such a triumph for the devil, that he was heard laughing and exulting over the saint's departure; but Dunstan told him

to moderate his joy, for his discomfiture would be as great at his return!—at least, so we read.

Edgar was shortly afterwards proclaimed king, and Dunstan returned in triumph. He was now made bishop of both Worcester and London, and still retained the abbey of Glastonbury. Shortly after he became Archbishop of Canterbury. In this position he was neither more nor less than an ecclesiastical statesman. He was the minister of Edgar, and though the king reigned, it was Dunstan who ruled. Clerical and monastic discipline were reformed by him. He encouraged the king to make royal progresses through the land, which brought him and his people together, and facilitated the administration of justice.

A splendid navy was also established and maintained in a state of efficiency through his instrumentality, and several public works were executed. Edgar was a most licentious wretch, and there can be little doubt that the archbishop connived at many of his disgraceful acts. At last, however, he went so far as to violate the sanctity of a convent. This raised an outcry. Dunstan was obliged to inflict a penance; and the king became more guarded in his amours for the future. Dr Hook sums up the result of Dunstan's administration as follows:—'Northumbria was divided into earldoms instead of kingdoms; the Danes were either subdued or conciliated; the sovereignty of the Anglo-Saxon king over the Scots was established; the navy was placed in such a state of efficiency that no enemy ventured to attack the coast; English pirates, who had infested our ports, were restrained and punished; while at home, trade was encouraged, family feuds were suppressed, and men were compelled, instead of taking the law into their own hands, to submit the decision of their quarrels to the magistrates. Regular circuits were established for the administration of justice, forming a court of appeal from the inferior judges. Standard measures were made and deposited at Winchester. Steps were taken to annihilate the wolves which still abounded in the country. Even to trivial matters could the mind of Dunstan descend; finding that quarrels very frequently arose in taverns, from disputes among the topers about their share of the liquor when they drank out of the same cup, he advised Edgar to order gold or silver pegs to be fastened in the pots, that whilst every man knew his just measure, shame should compel each to confine himself to his proper share.' Hence the expression, 'a peg too low.'

A reaction on behalf of the married clergy now commenced, and gathered strength; and although Dunstan remained minister of the crown under Edgar, his power was effectually shaken. Two circumstances took place about this time, which brought considerable disgrace on his name. At a council held at Winchester, the advocates of the regular clergy were getting the best of the argument, and beginning to demand the restitution of their benefices which had been taken from them, when a voice was heard as if proceeding from a crucifix on the wall, saying, 'Let it not be! let it not be! you have done well, and would do ill to change it.' The regulars, however, suspected trickery, and were not to be silenced so easily. A second meeting was held without effecting anything. A third was then called at Calne, in Wiltshire (A.D. 978), which was held, not in the open air, as was usual with the Anglo-Saxons, but in the upper room of a house. Another suspicious circumstance was, that the king, who had been present at both the previous councils, was kept away from this. When it came to Dunstan's turn to reply to the arguments of his adversaries, instead of doing so, he professed to commit his cause to Christ as judge, and immediately the floor of the room gave way, and all except the archbishop and his friends were precipitated to the floor beneath. Some were killed and some escaped. The populace sided with the Dunstanites, and it was supposed that the question was now settled by a miracle. This 'arch miracle-monger,' as Southey styles him, lived ten years after these exploits, to enjoy his victory and to establish his reforms. His death, like his life, was a scene of miracles. He expired in all the odour of monastic sanctity, on the 19th of May, in the year 988, and was buried in Canterbury cathedral.

Born.—John Theophilus Fichte, German philosophical writer, 1762, *Rammenau ;* Professor John Wilson, poet and miscellaneous writer, 1785, *Paisley.*

Died.—Flaccus Alcuinus, learned theologian, 804, *Tours ;* Anne Boleyn, queen of England, beheaded, 1536; John Hales, 'the ever memorable' scholar and critic, *Eton ;* Adam Billaut, French poet, 1662 ; Thomas Gent, printer, of York, 1778 ; James Boswell, author of *Life of Dr Johnson,* 1795; Charles James Apperley, writer on field sports, 1483.

ALCUIN.

Alcuin was one of the most remarkable Anglo-Saxons of the eighth century. He was born of noble and wealthy parents, at York, about the year 735, and was from his infancy dedicated to the church. York was at this period the great seat of learning among the Anglo-Saxons, and in the school of the celebrated Archbishop Egbert, Alcuin made such progress that he was subsequently appointed to the mastership, and became hardly less celebrated than his predecessor ; and was on more than one occasion sent on important ecclesiastical missions to Rome, which made him early acquainted with the continent. It was on the second of these visits, in the year 781, that he met Charlemagne, who was then meditating great intellectual reforms in his kingdom, and who soon formed for the Anglo-Saxon ecclesiastic a warm attachment. In 782, at Charlemagne's earnest desire, having obtained the consent of his spiritual and temporal superiors, Eanbald, Archbishop of York, and Alfwold, King of Northumbria, Alcuin left England to settle in France. He was received in the Frankish court as Charlemagne's friend and counsellor, as the companion of his private hours, and the instructor of his children ; and the revenues of the two monasteries of Ferrieres and St Lupus, at Troyes, were assigned to him for his income. About the year 790, he obtained the Emperor's reluctant consent to visit his native land, and that only on the condition that he

should return to France without delay. He had now, indeed, become an almost necessary minister of the great monarch, for he was a chief adviser in the plans of national instruction which had so great an influence on the civilization of Europe during the middle ages. He came in the character of ambassador from Charlemagne to King Offa, the great monarch of the Mercians, and remained till 792, when he left his native country for the last time, accompanied by a number of the Anglo-Saxon ecclesiastics.

Charlemagne had collected round him at this time an intellectual circle, which, by its refined learning and its philosophical spirit, reminds us almost of the intercourse of the philosophers and scholars of ancient Greece and Rome. Those who were admitted into this society assumed literary names and surnames in their intercourse and correspondence. Thus Charlemagne himself was called David ; Alcuin assumed the name of Flaccus Albinus ; Angilbert, another of the most distinguished men of this circle, took that of Homarus ; and Riculf, Archbishop of Mentz, was named Damotas. Under these names, when assembled together, they no doubt laid aside all the pomp of worldly dignity, and conversed together on an equality of intellectual enjoyment, enlivened by wit as well as learning ; and this spirit is reflected in many of the letters preserved among Alcuin's correspondence. Such a club appears as a bright light in the midst of the darkness of these remote ages.

When he was probably rather more than sixty years of age, Alcuin again formed the design of returning to his native country ; but his departure was prevented by the news of great troubles and revolutions in the kingdom of Northumbria, and he gave up all intention of quitting France. He died at Tours, in the abbey of St Martin, of which he was abbot, on the 19th of May 804. Alcuin left many works, which were highly esteemed in the middle ages, and most of them have been printed. The most interesting to modern readers are his epistles, which furnish us with many details of his life and thoughts, and throw no little light on the history and condition of his time.

ANNE BOLEYN.

The unhappy fate of Anne Boleyn has been celebrated in the popular histories of England, as that of an innocent woman sacrificed by her husband for the sake of a new affection. And to the acceptance of this view of her character and history, it can scarcely be doubted that her connection with the advance of the Protestant cause has largely conduced : it had become, as it were, a point of faith among the friends of the reformed religion, to suppose only what was favourable of the lovely woman from whose bright eyes the light of truth had first shone. We may attribute even more importance to the influence exercised by the popular veneration in which the unfortunate queen's daughter, Elizabeth, was held, and the necessity felt for upholding the idea of her legitimacy against the views of the Roman Catholics. During the reign of the Virgin Queen, when Protestantism had such a struggle with its antagonists, it became a political point of the greatest consequence to assert the innocence of Anne Boleyn, because on that, to some degree, depended the soundness of the queen's pretentions to the throne.

In our age, there is no consideration of any kind to interfere with a true verdict regarding Anne Boleyn. A modern historian may discuss the question, if he pleases, in an impartial spirit, without fear of blame from any quarter. We find that Mr Froude, in his *History of England under the Reign of Henry VIII.*, makes what he believes to be an effort to this effect, but perhaps not quite with success.

During seven years, while Henry was endeavouring to get quit of his first queen, Catherine of Aragon, on the shewing that his union with her was illegal, as she had previously been the wife of his brother, Anne Boleyn allowed herself to be entertained as a queen-elect in the royal household. There is presumably no guilt connected with her position there; but it argued a want of delicacy and just feeling on her part. At length the king wedded her in a private manner, and her coronation was soon after celebrated with extraordinary magnificence, as if to make up for any flaw that might be thought to derogate from her state as queen-consort. In due time Anne gave birth to a daughter, afterwards the famous Queen Elizabeth, and for two years and a half more she and her husband appeared to live in harmony. At length in April 1536, Henry professed to be troubled in mind by various rumours which had reached him regarding his wife. By his orders, four gentlemen of the court were arrested as having been guilty of adultery with the queen. Afterwards the queen's brother, Lord Rochfort, was put in custody on the same charge, to which, of course, his relationship gave a deeper hue. From the first, one of the four gentlemen, Smeton, a musician, confessed the truth of the charge.

Mr Froude shews, very conclusively, that the trials of the alleged participants in criminality, and of the queen, were conducted with even an unusual degree of solemnity and care. The special commission which first acted in that business was composed of the most respectable men connected with the administration, and it included the queen's father and uncle. The indictment found by the grand jury of Middlesex made no vague charges, but indicated certain days on which the offences were alleged to have been committed. The queen and her brother Rochfort were tried before twenty-seven of the peers of highest character in the realm. Unfortunately, the proceedings on the trials have not been preserved, but Mr Froude sees no reason to doubt that they were perfectly fair. Smeton, the musician, as before, admitted his guilt; the three commoners, his companions, were found guilty by the jury; and all were condemned to die the death of traitors. Anne and her brother were, in succession, found guilty by the House of Peers, and adjudged to die. 'We can form no estimate of the evidence,' says Mr Froude, 'for we do not know what it was. . . . But the fact remains to us, that these twenty-seven peers, who were not ignorant, as we are, but were fully acquainted with the grounds of the prosecution, did deliberately, after hearing the queen's defence, pronounce against her a unanimous verdict. . . . Men of all parties united in the sentence.' Including the grand jury, the petty jury, and the twenty-seven peers, 'we

have,' says Mr Froude, 'the judicial verdict of more than seventy noblemen and gentlemen, no one of whom had any interest in the deaths of the accused, and some of whom had interests the most tender in their acquittal; we have the assent of the judges who sat on the commission, and who passed sentence after full opportunities of examination, with all the evidence before their eyes.' Our author also states, that none of the male convicts denied, while several acknowledged their guilt on the scaffold. The queen, indeed, denied her guilt; and Mr Froude admits its 'antecedent improbability.' On the other hand, 'we have also the improbability, which is great, that the king, now forty-four years old, who in his earlier years had been distinguished for the absence of those vices in which contemporary princes indulged themselves, in wanton weariness of a woman for whom he had revolutionised the kingdom, and quarrelled with half Christendom, suddenly resolved to murder her.' Mr Froude further remarks the full approval given to the sentence on Anne and her paramours by parliament, the month after the execution, a fact to which he attaches great importance.

After all, however, the question of the criminality of the queen must be held as matter of doubt. It looks ill for the theory of Henry's belief in Anne's guilt, that, the very day after her death in the Tower green, he married Jane Seymour. We must also remember, that to get rid of one wife in order to obtain another, does not stand solitary in the history of King Henry. On the whole, it seems most probable that the poor queen had been simply imprudent in speaking with levity to those young courtiers, and that their confessions referred merely to gay and licentious talk, in which they had indulged in compliance with the lady's humours. The complaisance of ministers, courtiers, parliaments, and even judges to the imperious Tudor sovereigns, scarcely needs to be pointed out by us.

JAMES BOSWELL.

Boswell gets but hard measure from the world. We owe to him the best, because the most complete, account of a human being—in short, the best piece of *biography*—that the world possesses; and yet he is seldom respectfully spoken of. Even the completeness of the life of Johnson, proceeding as it does from his extreme veneration for the man, stands as a fact rather against than for him. True, Boswell did not exhibit in life many solid qualities; he failed in his profession as a counsel, both in his own country and in London; and he clouded his latter days and cut them short by dissipation. Surely many estimable men have done no better. True, also, he was vain, fickle, frivolous, to some extent; but have not many been so without forfeiting the regard of those who knew them? Perhaps the best defence that can be made for Boswell is to cite the regard in which he was held by his contemporaries—Johnson, above all. Invariable tradition represents him as the most pleasant of all pleasant companions. His high spirits, his drollery, his pure self-revealing simplicity, made him the delight of his friends. Surely, if a man had these good qualities, was at the same time honourable in his social and domestic relations, and possessed of the literary power and industry required for such a book as the *Life of Johnson*, he could not be quite a despicable being.

It is little known that Boswell occasionally wooed the Muses. The following is a song which he composed to an Irish air, in celebration of one of his many youthful love-affairs, and which can scarcely be said to have been published.*

' Oh, Larghan Clanbrassil, how sweet is thy sound,
To my tender remembrance, as Love's sacred ground :
For there Marg'ret Caroline first charmed my sight,
And filled my young heart with a fluttering delight.

When I thought her my own, ah ! too short seemed the day
For a jaunt to Downpatrick, or a trip on the sea ;
To express what I felt then, all language were vain—
'Twas in truth what the poets have studied to feign.

But too late I found even she could deceive,
And nothing was left but to weep and to rave ;
Distracted I fled from my dear native shore,
Resolved to see Larghan Clanbrassil no more.

Yet still, in some moments enchanted, I find
A ray of her softness beam soft on my mind ;
While thus in blest fancy my angel I see,
All the world is a Larghan Clanbrassil to me.'

OPENING OF THE CANAL OF LANGUEDOC.

In the reign of Louis XIV., long before any canal had been even projected in England, a noble one was executed in France, the famous canal of Languedoc, connecting the Mediterranean and the Atlantic. The obvious utility of such a communication had caused it to be projected so long ago as the reign of Francis I.; but it was reserved for that of Louis XIV. to see it effected. The difficulties overcome were prodigious. The meritorious engineer, Riquetti, unfortunately did not live to see his work completed ; but his place was supplied by his two sons, and the opening—a great day for France—took place on the 19th of May 1681. The effect of this canal in promoting agriculture, commerce, and the arts, in the south of France, has been very marked, and as universally admitted.

DELUSIONS OF JOHN MASON.

May 19, 1694, died John Mason, rector of Water Stratford, in Buckinghamshire ; a strange offshoot of the religious fervours of the seventeenth century. He is allowed to have shown in his earlier days both learning and abilities, and the simplicity of his character was never doubted. Through some cause, however, which has not been clearly stated, Mason fell into that condition, so apt to beset persons who allow their religious practice to press upon their bodily health, in which the patient (as he may well be called) is visited with apparent messages and addresses from a higher world. All that we learn on this subject is that he had given himself up to ' Calvinistic and millenary notions ; ' but this alone would scarcely account for the results. It became Mason's conviction that he was the Elias appointed to proclaim the second advent. Equally assured was he that the Saviour, at his re-descension upon earth, would commence his

* It is transcribed from a volume of songs which his son, Sir Alexander Boswell, gave anonymously to the world in 1803.

reign at Water Stratford. He promulgated his beliefs, probably in a style calculated to impress the vulgar, and in a short time his own delusion spread to others. Crowds of people, forsaking their homes, came to reside near him ; many sold their estates, or what else they had, in order to take up their quarters at Water Stratford. Every house and every out-house in that parish was filled to overflowing with these misled people, among whom community of goods prevailed, even to a point outraging decency. Browne Willis, the antiquary, anxious to have a correct notice of this delusion in his *History of Buckinghamshire*, wrote to a friend living near Mason's parish for full particulars. In reply, his friend, from his own and his mother's knowledge, gave him a minute account, from which the following is an extract.

' They went out most evenings into the fields and sung their hymns. My grandfather and mother went out to see them. The first object they met with was a countryman who lay on his face in Water Stratford churchyard, who was quite tired with singing, and when turned on his back was speechless, but came to himself. Then they went into the parsonage-house, and there was a congregation walking round the hall in a ring, making a most prodigious noise, and all of them crying out, "Glory ! Glory ! Glory !" and all in a sweat, and looking as if they were mad. My mother told them she thought theirs was an odd way of serving God, and wished they were not mad. At which they all stood still, with their mouths open, and stared fiercely on her, but said nothing ; and she verily believes, if my grandfather and another gentleman had not been with her, with their swords by their side, they would have served her as they did Mrs Lisle, of Imley, whose head-clothes they pulled off, and cried, "Avoid Satan !" Then my mother said, "Poor deluded people ! I am sorry for you. I wish I could speak with Mr Mason." Then one of their women went upstairs, and brought down word that Mr Mason was not to be seen or spoke with. Some time after this came the then Duke of Richmond, and a great many more noble persons, who, though denied access to him, forced their way up to him, and talked to him a good deal. And amongst other things he told them he had seen our Lord Christ in the room where they were then, with his fleshly eyes, and spoke to Him with his fleshly tongue ; and that our Lord Christ told him *He would come and appear in the air over Water Stratford, and judge the world on Whit Sunday following*.

' After this he looked out of his chamber window, and said the same things to the multitude that stood underneath.

' After this he was struck speechless, which was occasioned (as is supposed) by over talking himself ; on which Dr Paxton (a very eminent physician) was sent for from Buckingham, who came from visiting Mr Mason to our house, and told my father and mother that Mr Mason's ail was a squinacy, and that he would not recover ; and he accordingly died of it. He (Mr Mason) told his auditory when he was alive, that he should rise the third day after his decease, and with his body ascend into heaven. He was buried before the third day; and several of his people averring that they had seen him and spoke to him after his resurrection, on a piece of ground close behind the parsonage-house, which they called Holy Ground, his successor, Mr Rushworth, thought proper to take his body up, and had the coffin opened, and showed them the corpse. But this did not satisfy them. Still they would meet on Holy Ground, as they called it, and did so for sundry years; and when Mr Rushworth discharged them from coming there, they assembled in a house at Water Stratford. In the year 1710 (sixteen years after Mason's death), one Sunday my mother and a neighbouring lady went and saw them there, and they sung the same hymns, and made the same noise, and went round in a ring as they used to do.'

'Never was there,' says Granger, 'a scene of more frantic joy, expressed by singing, fiddling, dancing, and all the wildness of enthusiastic gestures and rapturous vociferations, than was seen at Stratford. Every vagabond and village fiddler that could be procured bore a part in the rude concert at this tumultuous jubilee.'

MARSHAL SOULT'S PICTURES.

On the 19th May 1852, began at Paris a sale of the pictures which had belonged to the deceased Marshal Soult. The prices realized for some of the articles were of unprecedented liberality. On the first day, three pieces by Murillo were disposed of, the 'Jesus and Child,' at 63,000 francs (£2,520); 'St Peter in Bonds,' at 151,000 francs (£6,040); and the 'Conception of the Virgin,' at the astounding price of 586,000 francs, which is equivalent to £23,440 sterling. The sums obtained for various articles on the ensuing days were on the same prodigious scale. It is understood that all Soult's valuable pictures were the plunder of Spanish convents, ruined during his occupation of the country. It was a brave show and enviable possession, but it was not without some accompanying qualms. When the Republic was established in the spring of 1848, the wary old soldier became nervous about these interesting pictures, lest, in some democratic freak, they should be reclaimed. He accordingly had them all quietly removed to Brussels, where they found an obscure, though temporary resting-place, in a gentleman's stable. At that crisis, many of them were offered in England at sums comparatively moderate, but not purchased; the 'Conception of the Virgin,' for instance, which brought £23,440 in 1852, might then have been had at £6,000.

MAY 20.

St Ethelbert, king of the East Angles, 793.   B. Yvo, Bishop of Chartres, 1115.   St Bernardine of Sienna.

Born.—Albert Durer, artist, 1471, *Nuremberg;* Elijah Fenton, poet, 1683, *Shelton, Staffordshire.*

Died.—Christopher Columbus, 1506, *Valladolid;* Bishop Thomas Sprat, 1713, *Bromley, Kent;* Nicholas Brady, D.D., joint translator of the Psalms into English, 1726, *Clapham;* Thomas Boston, popular Scotch writer in divinity, 1732, *Ettrick;* Charles Bonnet, naturalist, 1793, *Geneva;* Rev. Blanco White, miscellaneous writer, 1841.

BLANCO WHITE.

There is, perhaps, no more remarkable and affecting story of the conflict and suffering en-

dured by an earnest and honest mind in search for religious truth, than that afforded by the life of the Rev. Joseph Blanco White.

He was born at Seville, in 1775. His father belonged to an Irish family, and his mother was a Spaniard, connected with the old Andalusian nobility. His father was engaged in trade, and Blanco was placed in the counting-house, that he might at once learn writing and arithmetic, and become fitted for business. The drudgery he abhorred; his mother sympathized with him, and as a way of escape it was resolved that he should announce the church as his vocation. His father unwillingly assented. He was sent to college, became a priest, and attained sundry preferments. From an early age he had been afflicted with doubts. In reading Fenelon's *Telemaque*, before he was full eight years old, his delight in the story and sympathy with the courage and virtue of the characters, suggested the question, 'Why should we feel so perfectly sure that those who worshipped in that manner were wrong?' As a priest, graver doubts thickened in his mind, until at last he found himself 'worked to the madness of utter atheism.' He found other priests in the same case, but they were satisfied to perform their offices as matters of business or routine. This was impossible for White, and he longed to escape to some land where he should be free to speak openly all that he thought inwardly. In the excitement of the French invasion he sailed for England, and arrived in London in 1810. There he was fortunate enough to project and edit a monthly magazine, *El Español*, for circulation in Spain. It met the favour of the English government, and when discontinued in 1814, with the expulsion of the French from the Peninsula, White was rewarded with a pension of £250 a-year. The five years of hard work he passed through in the preparation of *El Español* ruined his health to such a degree, that his life was never afterwards free from suffering.

After his arrival in England he reviewed his opinions free from the antagonism and irritation he had endured in Spain, and which, he writes, 'had for ten years rendered the very name of religion so odious to me, that no language was strong enough to express my dislike.' After two years of serious consideration, in which he discovered 'that, with the exception of points essentially Popish, there is the most perfect agreement in the theological systems of Rome and England,' he became a member of the Church of England, and then a clergyman, by signing the twenty-four Articles, being all that is required to transform a Roman into an Anglican priest. His life henceforward for many years was spent in literary pursuits; he wrote some very popular works illustrative of his experience and opinions of Catholicism; and enjoyed the friendship of Lord Holland, Southey, Coleridge, Campbell, Mrs Hemans, and, above all, of Archbishop Whately. The peace he had at first enjoyed in the Church of England began to ebb away, and in 1818 difficulties about the Trinity were haunting him continually.

After a long and weary time of internal strife, the crisis arrived in December 1834, when residing at the archbishop's palace in Dublin. To

Dr Whately he wrote, ' My views in regard to the Scripture doctrine respecting our Saviour have gradually become Unitarian. The struggles which my mind has gone through on this point are indescribable.' The pain which this confession excited among his friends in the Church was intense. The Rev. J. H. Newman wrote him a letter from Oxford, which he describes as ' one long moan.' Many turned away from him, but Archbishop Whately, while regretting the change, preserved his friendship unaltered. To enjoy the worship and fellowship of the Unitarians, he settled in Liverpool, and there spent the remaining six years of his life. His health was wretched, but his days of pain were soothed by intercourse with congenial society, and correspondence with Dr Channing and other notable men in the Unitarian body. Worn with suffering, he obtained release in death, on the 20th of May 1841. On the morning of that day he woke, and said, ' Now I die ; ' and after sitting for about two hours in the attitude of expectation, it came to pass as he had said.

Blanco White was the author of a sonnet on ' Night,' which has been thought by many the best composition of the kind in our language ; as it is not much known, it is here inserted.

' Mysterious night ! when our first parent knew
  Thee from report Divine, and heard thy name,
  Did he not tremble for this lovely frame,
This glorious canopy of light and blue ?
Yet 'neath a curtain of translucent dew,
  Bathed in the rays of the great setting flame,
  Hesperus with the host of heaven came,
And lo ! Creation widened in man's view.
Who could have thought such darkness lay concealed
  Within thy beams, O Sun ! or who could find,
Whilst fly, and leaf, and insect stood revealed,
  That to such countless orbs thou madest us blind !
Why do we then shun death with anxious strife ?
If Light can thus deceive, wherefore not Life ? '

THE GARRAT ELECTIONS.

A comparatively obscure act of local injustice originated during the last century a political burlesque, which was so highly relished by the British public, that sometimes upwards of 80,000 persons assembled to take part in or enjoy the fun. The inhabitants of the hamlet of Garrat, situated between Wandsworth and Tooting, in Surrey, had certain rights in a small common, which had been encroached upon ; they therefore met in conclave, elected a president, resisted, and obtained their rights. As this happened at the time of a general election, it was determined that their president, or mayor, should hold office during parliament, and be re-elected with a new one. It was impossible that the ridiculous pomposity of the whole affair should not be felt and joked upon. When, therefore, party-spirit ran high, its effervescence was parodied by ' the storm in a tea-pot ' of a Garrat election. The public soon began to enjoy the joke, and the innkeepers and publicans of Wandsworth and the neighbourhood reaped so rich a harvest, that they ultimately made up a purse to pay necessary expenses ; the queerest and most facetious of candidates were brought from all quarters ; and all the paraphernalia of a serious election were parodied in this mock one. The culminating point of its popularity was reached in 1761, when Foote attended, and soon afterwards produced his farce, *The Mayor of Garrat*, at the Haymarket Theatre, where it had a great and deserved success, and immortalized elections that else would have been long since forgotten.

We possess no information as to who were the candidates for this important borough before 1747, when Squire Blowmedown and Squire Gubbins contested the honour. These were, as usual, assumed titles—the first being borne by John Willis, a waterman of Wandsworth ; the second by James Simmonds, keeper of a public-house known as the ' Gubbins' Head,' in Blackman Street, Borough. ' The Clerk and Recorder ' issued from an imaginary town-hall, at the order of the mayor, a due notification of the day of election ; and each candidate gave out handbills, in which he asserted his own merits, and abused his opponent in the style of the genuine elections. An ' Oath of Qualification ' was administered to electors, which was couched throughout in a strain of *double entendre*, and nothing was left undone that was usually done to insure success to the candidates.

From a somewhat large and curious collection of handbills and broadsides, printed during these elections, we may be enabled to give an idea of the wit of the day.* In 1747 the pretensions of Squire Blowmedown were enforced in ' a letter sent from an elector of the borough of Garrat to another,' and dated from St James's Market, in which we are assured that ' the greatest stranger must look upon himself as void of reason, entirely barren of wisdom, extinct of humanity, and unworthy the esteem of men of sense and veracity, should he neglect any opportunity to testify how ardent his wishes are that *this Phœnix* may be unanimously chosen.' For, ' as our worthy candidate judiciously observes, if drinking largely, heading a mob majestically, huzzaing eloquently, and feeding voraciously, be merits in any degree worthy the esteem of the good people of this land, *a Garrat*, I must ingeniously confess, is too mean an apartment for such a worthy · for Envy herself must confess, if the above qualifications are of any efficacy, the universal voice of the whole realm of Great Britain would not be equivalent to his wondrous deserts.'

In 1754, the same candidates came forward again, and, in imitation of their betters, bespattered each other in handbills. Thus Gubbins, while declaring himself ' zealously affected to his present Majesty King George, the Church and State,' asks—' where was Esquire Blowmedown when the Jew Bill, Matrimony Bill, and Wheel Bill passed ? ' Worse still, Blowmedown ' washes his boat every Sabbath-day, that he may not be induced to rise on Monday morning before high-water ! ' Of course, this meets with an indignant reply from the friends of the party attacked, ' a large majority of the most substantial and wealthy freeholders, electors of the ancient

* They have been obligingly communicated by T. Blackmore, Esq., of Wandsworth, who is also proprietor of Green's drawings, here copied.

659

borough of Garrat,' who state themselves to be 'not ashamed, much less afraid, to publicly declare that Blowmedown is the pride and glory of our minds, and that we will support him to the last.' The bill ends with an important— 'N.B. The Esquire entertains his friends at all the houses in Wandsworth on the day of election, which will be elegant and generous, without any other expense than that of every one paying for what they call for.'

The election of May 20, 1761, was alike remarkable for the number of candidates and for the efficient aid of their friends. Nine candidates came forward, and it is said that Foote, Garrick, and Wilkes wrote some of their addresses. Foote attended the election, and paid nine guineas for a room opposite Wandsworth church, for himself and friends to see the proceedings. The character of Snuffle, the sexton, in Foote's play, was derived from John Gardiner, a cobbler of Wandsworth and the parish gravedigger, who was one of the candidates under the name of Lord Twankum. That of Crispin Heeltap was copied from another candidate, a shoemaker, who came forward as Lord Lapstone. The other five were Kit Noisy, Esq. (one Christopher Beacham, a waterman), Lords Wedge and Paxford, Sir John Crambo and Beau Silvester. The claims of the latter were strongly enforced in an address to the electors of 'the antient, loyal, and renowned Boroughwick,' the principal point of the appeal being the resistance he is reputed to have made to an extra tax on beer, which at that time excited much popular ire. A lengthy and high-flown address was also issued by the Beau, in which he declares, 'I have given necessary orders for opening great plenty of public-houses in every hamlet throughout the electorate, for the reception of my friends and their acquaintance, desiring at the same time that they will be punctual in paying for what they call for; and not to overgorge, as it may endanger their health, and prejudice my election.' He then alludes to his fellow-candidates, giving his highest praise to Lord Lapstone, whose powers of drinking, he thinks, will produce 'a vast revenue' to his country, if he be 'spared for a long life!' We reprint entire another of his harangues, as it is one of the best specimens of the Garrat literature.

'*To the worthy Electors of the Antient and Opulent Borough of Garrat.*

'I return my unfeigned and hearty thanks to the numberless and worthy electors that have exerted themselves in my interest, in support of my election; and should I be so happy (as by almost a general voice I am already declared) to be your representative, the honour so conferred will lay on me such high obligations, as my best endeavours can never discharge; but my service shall be always at your command, and my study ever for your welfare. Without flattery I promise, and without delay I perform; and, worthy gentlemen, I doubt not your peculiar penetration, unbiased integrity, and renowned prudence in the choice of another, * worthy of such high honour and important trust. In your choice thereof, with submission I entreat you neither to choose one of fancied high blood, and certain low fortune, for by him your privileges will be at stake, either to maintain or

* Two members were returned for Garrat.

advance his honour; nor one either mean in descent or fortune, as the integrity of such will be always doubtful; nor yet proud, as your highest esteem of his merit will serve only for a footstool to his ambition; nor covetous, for he will be enamoured with your verdant lawns, and never rest till he has enclosed your extensive plains in his parchment noose, and confined your wide-spread space within the secure bounds of his coffers; nor impudent, because ignorance will be his only guide and your sure destruction. If one too venerable, he will require more respect from you than ever you will have service from him; and your remarkable temperance and sobriety demonstrates your abhorrence of a beastly glutton and a stupid sot; and common prudence will direct you to beware of one prompted by a complication of iniquities, for to his will the antique charter of your borough, your public treasure, your private properties, without remorse will he grasp, and without mercy snatch away your lives to feed his insatiable cruelty; against either of these may fate protect your borough and me from such connexions, but in them the devil will get his due. As for your humble servant, if my religion is not the most profound, 'tis the most universally applauded (20s. to the pound); and I fear not but by my pious example to increase the practice thereof. In honour I am upright, and downright in justice; immovably attached to my king and country, with an unbiased hatred to their enemies; my manners are untainted with gaudy politeness or fawning complaisance. My abilities will procure you the knowledge of your wants, if not the gratification of your desires; and those that dare advance the present price of the darling essence of Sir John Barley will highly incur my displeasure, if not feel the weight of my resentment. Through my purer and universal connexion, your liberty and commerce shall be spread to the Antipodes, and I will order yet undiscovered regions to be alarmed with your fame; in your borough I will erect a non-existent edifice for the transaction of your timber business, and in your suburbs plant an imaginary grove for your private affairs. My unknown fortune shall be ever ready for your assistance, my useless sword drawn in your defence; and my waste blood I'll freely spill in your protection. And, with permission,

   'I will, for ever and a day,
     'Subscribe myself, gentlemen,
       'Your most obedient servant,
'Bull Hall, May 4th 1761.   'BEAU SILVESTER.'

'N.B.—The Election will be the 20th instant. The Angel at Bull Stairs will be opened every day for the reception of all friends that please to honour me with their company.'

It is impossible to read this address without being forcibly reminded of Matthew Mug, the principal candidate in Foote's drama. He is a specious promiser of all good things to Garrat and its inhabitants, and, like Beau Silvester, particularly dilates on improving their trade. 'Should I succeed, you gentlemen may depend on my using my utmost endeavours to promote the good of the borough; to which purpose the encouragement of your trade and manufactories will most principally tend. Garrat, it must be owned, is an inland town, and has not, like Wandsworth, and Fulham, and Putney, the glorious advantage of a port; but what nature has denied, industry may supply. Cabbages, carrots, and cauliflowers may be deemed at present your staple commodities; but why should not your commerce be extended? Were I, gentlemen, worthy to advise, I should recommend the opening a new branch of trade ; sparrowgrass, gentlemen, the manufacturing of sparrowgrass ! Battersea, I own, gentlemen, bears at present the bell ; but where lies the fault ? In ourselves, gentlemen ; let us, gentlemen, but exert our natural strength, and I will take upon me to say, that a hundred of grass from the corporation of Garrat will, in a short time, at the London market, be held at least as an equivalent to a Battersea bundle !' There can be little doubt that Beau Silvester is 'the great original' of Matthew Mug.

Kitt Noisy's pretensions are summed up in a grandiloquent placard, which ends by confidently prognosticating his success : ' For I am well assured you know a Demosthenes from a madman, a Lycurgus from a libertine, and a Mark Anthony from a mountebank.' All this is sneered down by Sir Humphry Gubbins, who desires Noisy ' not to make so free with those capital ancients, Demosthenes, Lycurgus, &c. ; as they are gentlemen as little acquainted with the majority of his readers as with himself.' His abuse of his fellow-candidates is dismissed with the remark, that ' the regions of his ignorance and scurrility are so extensive, that was the ocean converted into ink, the sky into paper, and the stars into pens, it would not be adequate to the task ' of exposing it. He ends with—' A word or two by way of conclusion. It was the common saying of an old philosopher to his son, " I know what you have been doing, by knowing what company you have been in." As Moorfields, St Giles's, and Hockley-in-the-Hole are such recent and familiar phrases in the mouth of Mr Noisy's advocate, it requires no great skill in philosophy to learn at what academies he received his education. *Probatum est.*'

In 1763, we have again Lord Twankum, Kit Noisy, and the new candidate, Sir John Crambo, who declares, ' I will not only use my best endeavours to get repealed the late act on cyder and perry, but also my strongest efforts that you shall have strong beer again for threepence a quart.'

Seven candidates came forward for the next election in 1768. These were Sir Christopher Dashem, Lord Twankum, Sir George Comefirst, Sir William Airey, Sir William Bellows, one who signs himself ' Batt from the Workhouse,' and Sir John Harper. The latter was one James Anderson, a breeches-maker of Wandsworth, who became one of the most popular candidates during several elections.

This year's election was formally commenced by the following announcement :

' Whereas divers persons have thought proper to nominate themselves as candidates for this most antient and loyal borough without conforming to the several previous modes, forms, and methods to be observed and taken before such putting-up :
' This is therefore to give notice, that by antient records of the borough, each and every candidate who enters the list of fame must subscribe his name (either real or fictitious), his place of residence (if he has one), and occupation (if any), in the Doomsday-book of this borough, kept at the Mansion House, lest any disqualified person should dare to infringe, but

the least atom, on the privileges and immunities of this antient and most loyal borough.

'CROSS { Mayor and keeper of
the Archives.
' 9th of April, 1768.'

In another broadside the same mayor complains, ' That it hath been a custom of late for several people, strangers and foreigners, to erect booths for vending of beer and other liquors on this occasion, who have neither right, title, nor pretension to that privilege ; and that this custom is highly injurious to all the publicans of Garrat, to whom solely that privilege belongs by right of inheritance from time immemorial.' He therefore earnestly adjures the public not to patronize them, and ends his harangue thus :—' Now I must exhort you all to order and good breeding ; let the spirit of love reign amongst you—yea, and the spirit of Englishmen. Then, and in that case, will the greatest decorum and brightest example shine throughout your conduct ; which shall be the fervent prayer of him who will certainly suffer by the contrary, viz.,
'CROSS, *Mayor.* (His own fist !)'
On this occasion Lady Twankum played a conspicuous part with her lord. His bills announce that ' Lady Twankum desires those ladies who intend to honour her with their company to send their servants for tickets.' In a second announcement, ' Lady Twankum desires those ladies who are in the interest of her lord to come *full dressed,* and clean about the *heels.*' She also hopes they will honour her so far as to drink chocolate, tea, coffee, *or any other liquor* they please to order, on the morning of election ;' and adds, ' The lane and the whole borough will be grandly illuminated, according to custom, during the ball.'

Lord Twankum concludes his address by informing his constituents, ' The election will be on the 7th of June ensuing ; when I have given strict orders that every house on the road between Greenwich and Farnham shall be open from five o'clock in the morning to nine, and from nine all day long ; where you may please, drink, amuse, and regale yourselves at the moderate price of paying for what you use. Also by water, boats, barges, lighters, and wherries ; and by land, proper vehicles, viz., sand-carts, dust-carts, dung-carts, carrion-carts, trucks, and truckadoes, will be ready at the most convenient places for you all—if you will only take the trouble to seek them, and *pay the hire.*'

The election of 1775 is announced by ' Richard Penn, Mayor, Deputy Ranger of Wandsworth Common, and Superintendant of all the Gravel-pits thereto belonging ;' who recommends Sir William Blaize and Sir Christopher Dashem, and announces that two places of subscription are opened in Wandsworth and four in London, at various public houses, ' that the candidates shall not put themselves to a shilling expense.' He deprecates bribery, and notes a report ' as a caution to the worthy electors, that Sir John Harper has engaged a certain *famous dancing Punch,* who will exhibit during the whole election.' Sir William Blaize announces himself as ' Nephew to the late Lord Twankum,' and that he 'went as a volunteer from the artillery in the City of London to St James's, with 11,000 men to serve his majesty in the rebellion in the year '45, under the command of Sir William Bellows and Sir Joseph Hankey; [he] has been fourteen years since in the Surrey Militia, and exerted his abilities in such a manner [as] has gained him the applause of his country in general.'

The election of 1781 was as remarkable as those of 1761 and 1768 for the number of candidates; no less than nine contested the borough. Among them were our old friends Sir John Harper, Sir Christopher Dashwood, and Sir William Blaize; the new candidates being a Sir John Gnawpost, Sir William Swallowtail (one William Cook, a basketmaker, of Brentford), Sir Thomas Nameless, Sir Thomas Tubbs (a waterman), Sir Buggy Bates (one Robert Bates, a waterman and chimney-sweep), and Sir Jeffrey Dunstan, an itinerant dealer in old wigs, who turned out to be one of the most popular of the candidates that ever appeared on the Garrat hustings, and was retained member for three successive parliaments. He came forward in his own name with merely the prefix of a title, was much of a humorist, and possessed a fund of vulgar wit, and an extremely grotesque personal appearance. He had been long known about London, from his whimsical mode of crying his trade; and it was his pride to appear hatless, and regardless of personal grace, by wearing his shirt and waistcoat open to the waist, his breeches unbuttoned at the knees, and his stockings ungartered. He, however, assumed much mock dignity, spite of his dwarfish size, disproportioned head, and knock-knees; spoke of his daughters as 'Miss Dinah' and 'beautiful Miss Nancy,' the latter being elevated into 'Lady Ann' after she married 'Lord Thompson,' a dustman of Bethnal Green, where Sir Jeffrey resided until his death, by excess of drink, about 1797. He was in the habit of rehearsing his election speeches, and giving his imitations of popular London cries, on stated occasions, at the Whitechapel public-houses, in company with 'Ray the Tinker,' and 'Sir Charles Hartis,' a deformed fiddler and an unsuccessful candidate for Garrat. His quaint figure appears on some of the London tradesmen's tokens, and was used as a sign to public-houses.

Sir John Harper, in his address, speaks of 'having had the honour of serving Garrat in the last two parliaments *out-of-doors;*' calls himself 'principal rectifier of all mistakes and blunders;' promises 'to promote the trade and commerce of this land in general, and of every freeman in particular of this ancient and loyal borough of Garrat; to establish a firm, lasting, and universal peace with America; chastise the insolence and ingratitude of France, Spain, and Holland; and restore this nation to its ancient glory.' He also promises to call public servants to account in high places, to lighten taxes, shorten parliaments, and bring forward a scheme for the liquidation of the National Debt. He at the same time solemnly declares that he 'will never accept from government either place, pension, title, contract, or emolument whatsoever.' Sir John Harper and Sir Jeffrey Dunstan were unanimously returned, though an imputation was cast on the latter, to the effect that his daughter was to marry the son of the Premier, Lord North. Other candidates had wicked allegations levelled at them: Sir John Swallowtail was declared to have a contract to supply government with baskets; and Sir Buggy Bates another 'for a supply of soot, for the powder to destroy vermin in biscuit.'

There are preserved three very curious draw-

ings by Valentine Green,* delineating the chief features of this great electioneering farce. The most curious of the series represents Lady Blaize in her state barge passing through Wandsworth;

the principal inns, 'The Spread Eagle' and 'The Ram,' are indicated, with the entrance to Garrat Lane. Her ladyship carries in her boat a 'dancing Punch,' similar to that noted in 1775. She has

also two pages, one to shield her beauties under a huge umbrella, the other to ply an enormous

* They were copied in Hone's *Every-Day Book*, vol. ii., but with alterations and omissions, to compress them into two small cuts. We have re-engraved them strictly in accordance with the originals. Green is best known as a very good mezzotint engraver; he was born in Warwickshire, 1739, came to London in 1765, was appointed keeper of the British Institution upon its first foundation, a post he filled with zeal and integrity. He died 1813.

fan. She was graphically described to Hone by an old lady of Wandsworth. 'I remember her very well,' said she, ' and so I ought, for I had a good hand in the dressing of her. I helped to put together many a good pound of wool to make her hair up; I suppose it was more than three feet high, at least; and as for her stays, I also helped to make them, down in Anderson's barn. They were neither more nor less than a washing-tub without the bottom, well covered, and bedizened outside to look like a stomacher; as she sat in the boat she was one of the drollest creatures for size and dress ever seen!'

The boats were mounted on wheels and drawn by horses, though in one instance we see them dragged by men. The racket and semi-masquerading of the populace is a notable feature; many are habited in quaint wigs and hats, one drummer is in female costume; women join the rowers, quarrels and fights abound, and the scaffolding in front of the 'Spread Eagle' falls with its occupants. There is one remarkable spectator in the right-hand corner of this scene—a coatless, loosely-dressed, bald-headed man, with a porter-pot in his left hand; this is the publican, Sam House, celebrated at all Westminster elections for his zeal in the cause of Fox. He was never seen to wear either hat or coat, and has been spiritedly depicted by the famed caricaturist Gillray.

Sir John Harper addresses his constituents from a phaeton drawn by six horses, with mounted postilions, and preceded by horsemen carrying mops and brooms. Upon his carriage is inscribed, ' Harper for ever! No Whigs!' an allusion, possibly, to Sir Jeffrey Dunstan. He is speaking opposite the inn known as ' The Leathern Bottle,' which still stands unchanged in Garrat Lane, nearly opposite the common, which was the glory of the place. Sir William Swallowtail came to the poll in a wicker-chariot made by himself, and was preceded by hand-bell players. Sir Christopher Dashwood was drawn in a boat, with drums and fifes, and a Merry-Andrew mounted beside him. The road was kept by ' the Garrat Cavalry,' consisting of forty boys of all ages and sizes, so arranged that the smallest boys rode the largest horses, and *vice versâ;* who were commanded by a ' Master of the Horse,' in caricature regimentals, with a sword seven feet long, boots reaching to the hips, provided with enormous spurs, and mounted on the largest dray-horse that could be procured.

At the next election, in 1785, the death of Sir John Harper left Sir Jeffrey Dunstan without a rival; but in that for 1796 he was ousted by a new candidate, Sir Harry Dimsdale, a muffin-seller and dealer in tin-ware, almost as deformed as himself, but by no means so great a humorist. The most was made of his appearance, by dressing him in an ill-proportioned tawdry court suit, with an enormous cocked hat. He enjoyed his honour but a short time, dying before the next general election; he was ' the last' of the grotesque mayors, for no candidates started after his death, the publicans did not as before subscribe toward the expenses of the day, and the great saturnalia died a natural death.

'None but those who have seen a London mob on any great holiday,' says Sir Richard Philips, ' can form a just idea of these elections. On several occasions a hundred thousand persons, half of them in carts, in hackney coaches, and on horse and ass-back, covered the various roads from London, and choked up all the approaches to the place of election. At the two last elections, I was told that the road within a mile of Wandsworth was so blocked up by vehicles, that none could move backward or forward during many hours; and that the candidates, dressed like chimney-sweepers on May-day, or in the mock fashion of the period, were brought up to the hustings in the carriages of peers, drawn by six horses, the owners themselves condescending to become their drivers.'

After a lapse of thirty-four years, when the whim and vulgarity of a Garrat election was only remembered by a few, and recorded by Foote's drama, the general election of 1826 seems to have induced a desire to resuscitate the custom. A placard was prepared to forward the interests of a certain ' Sir John Paul Pry,' who was to come forward with Sir Hugh Allsides (one Callendar, beadle of All Saints' Church, Wandsworth), and Sir Robert Needall (Robert Young, surveyor of roads), described as a 'friend to the ladies who attend Wandsworth Fair.' The placard, which may be read in Hone's *Every-Day Book,* displays ' a plentiful lack of wit.' The project of revival failed; and Garrat has had no parliamentary representative ' out-of-doors' since the worthy muffin-seller was gathered to his fathers at the close of the last century.

CLIEFDEN HOUSE.

On the night of the 20th of May 1795, shortly after the family at Cliefden House had retired to rest, a maid-servant of the establishment, as

CLIEFDEN HOUSE AS BEFORE 1795.

she lay in bed, was reading a novel. Absorbed

in the story, she was perhaps supremely happy. But she was suddenly roused from her enjoyment by perceiving that her bed-curtains were in flames. Too terrified to alarm the family, she sank down on her bed and fainted. While she lay helpless and unconscious, the flames gathered strength, and spread to other parts of the building. Happily, many of the family were still awake, and in a few minutes the whole household was in motion. Such, according to tradition, was the origin of the conflagration. Certain it is, that however it originated, the fire occurred at the date mentioned, and calamitous were its effects. Every life indeed was saved, but the whole mansion, with the exception of its two end wings and the terrace, perished in the flames, and nearly all its rich furniture, its valuable paintings, and beautiful tapestry, shared the same fate. This house, which had been originally designed by Archer for the profligate George Villiers, second Duke of Buckingham, was built of red brick, with stone dressings. At each end was a square wing, connected with the main building by a colonnade, and a magnificent terrace about 440 feet long. The Duke of Buckingham, who purchased Cliefden from the family of Manfeld, its ancient proprietors, expended large sums, and evinced much taste in its arrangement and decoration. Regardless of expense, he procured the choicest productions of our own and other countries, and enriched this naturally lovely spot with a variety of trees, shrubs, and flowers, scarcely to be met with, at that period, in any other grounds of the same extent. He also adorned it, according to the fashion of the day, with alcoves and similar buildings.

Cliefden was his favourite place of residence; and here he carried on his amours with the infamous Countess of Shrewsbury, whose husband he killed in a duel.

> 'Gallant and gay, in Cliefden's proud alcove,
> The bower of wanton Shrewsbury and love.'

His gallantries, however, were often rudely curtailed by the want of money, and, from the same cause, he was unable to complete the mansion here; for, although the inheritor of immense property, his lavish expenditure had involved him deeply in debt, and he died in middle life, self-ruined in health, in fortune, and in reputation.

After the death of the Duke of Buckingham, Cliefden was purchased by Lord George Hamilton (fifth son of the Duke of Hamilton), who for his military services was created Earl of Orkney. At considerable cost he completed the house, and added new beauties to the ground. He died in 1737, and leaving no surviving male issue, his eldest daughter, Anne, became Countess of Orkney, and succeeded to the Cliefden estate. While in her possession, it was rented by his Royal Highness Frederick Prince of Wales, who for many years made it his summer residence. This amiable prince, unlike his father, who never appreciated the character of his British subjects, or sought their true interest, exerted his best energies to acquire a knowledge of the British laws and constitution, and to assimilate his own tastes and feelings to those of the people

he expected to be called on to govern. In his general behaviour he was courteous and considerate to all. He was a zealous promoter of every measure that he considered likely to forward the public good, and a special patron of the arts, sciences, and literature. Cliefden, as his residence, became the resort of the *literati* of the day, among whom Thomson and Mallet are still memorable in connexion with it. Mallet first received the prince's patronage, and was made his under-secretary, with a salary of two hundred pounds a year. Thomson's introduction to the prince, as described by Johnson, is amusing. The author of the *Castle of Indolence* appears to have been by no means diligent himself. His muse was a lazy jade, except under the sharp spur of necessity; and Thomson, having received a comfortable appointment under Government, indulged his love of ease and good living, paying little or no attention to his poetical mistress. But a change of ministry threw him out of his lucrative post; his finances were soon exhausted, and he lapsed into his former indigence. While in this condition he was introduced to the prince, and 'being gaily interrogated,' says Johnson, 'about the state of his affairs, he replied, they were in a more poetical posture than formerly.' He was then allowed a pension of one hundred pounds a year; but this being inadequate to his now luxurious habits, he began again to court his muse, and several dramatic productions were the result. One of them was a masque entitled *Alfred*, which he and Mallet in conjunction composed for the Prince of Wales, before whom it was performed for the first time, in 1740, at Cliefden. One of the songs in that masque was *Rule Britannia*. The masque is forgotten; the author of the song, and they who first heard its thrilling burst from the orchestra, are mouldering in their tombs; the halls through which the strain resounded have long since perished; but the enthusiasm then awakened still vibrates in the British heart to the sound of those words,

> 'Rule Britannia, Britannia rule the waves,
> For Britons never, never shall be slaves!'

Cliefden House, after the fire in 1795, remained nearly as the flames left it till 1830, when it was rebuilt by Sir George Warrender, who had purchased the estate. After the death of Sir George Warrender, Cliefden was purchased from his trustees by the Duke of Sutherland; and within a few months after his purchase was again burnt down, on the 15th of November, 1849, being the day of thanksgiving for the cessation of the cholera.

In the summer of 1850, the mansion was rebuilt by the Duke of Sutherland in a still more magnificent style, from designs by Barry. The centre portion, which is a revival of the design for old Somerset House, now extends to the wings, which, together with the terrace, are made to harmonize with the new building. It is indeed a magnificent and imposing structure, though by those who prefer the more picturesque appearance of the Tudor style, it may be considered heavy. It is now one of the seats of the Duke of Westminster.

But the grounds of Cliefden, which are about a hundred and thirty-six acres in extent, are its chief attraction. They have often been celebrated both in prose and verse. 'It is to Cliefden,' says a modern writer, ' that the river here owes its chief loveliness ; and whether we view the valley of the Thames from it, or float leisurely along the stream, and regard it as the principal object, we shall alike find enough to delight the eye and kindle the imagination. Cliefden runs along the summit of a lofty ridge which overhangs the river. The outline of this ridge is broken in the most agreeable way, the steep bank is clothed with luxuriant foliage, forming a hanging wood of great beauty, or in parts bare, so as to increase the gracefulness of the foliage by the contrast ; and the whole bank has run into easy flowing curves at the bidding of the noble stream which washes its base. A few islands deck this part of the river, and occasionally little tongues of land run out into it, or a tree overhangs it, helping to give vigour to the foreground of the rich landscape. In the early morning, when the sun has risen just high enough to illumine the summit of the ridge and highest trees, and all the lower part rests a heavy mass of shadow on the sleeping river, the scene is one of extraordinary grandeur.'*

THE SALTPETRE MAN.

It will perhaps surprise some readers to learn that chemical science was so far advanced in this country two hundred and forty years ago, that a patent was granted (dated 1625) to Sir John Brook and Thomas Russel, for obtaining saltpetre, for the manufacture of gunpowder, from animal exuviæ, from the soil of slaughter-houses and stables, and even from the floors of dwelling-houses. But it appears that the patent did not immediately produce a supply equal to the demand ; for in the year 1627, the third of the reign of Charles I., a proclamation was issued to remedy the inconvenience arising to the service from the want of a full and proper supply of *nitre* for the gunpowder manufactures. It first set forth that the saltpetre makers were never able to furnish the realm with a third part of the saltpetre required, more especially in time of war ; and then proceeded to state that, since a patent had been granted to Sir John Brook and Thomas Russel, for the making of saltpetre by a new invention, they were authorized to collect the animal fluids (which were ordered by this same proclamation to be preserved by families for this purpose) once in twenty-four hours, from house to house, in summer, and once in forty-eight hours in winter. It will not require a very fertile imagination to conceive that this proclamation was offensive and highly inconvenient to the people, and that the frequent visits of the *Saltpetre Man* and his agents would be anything but welcome. This, however, was not the worst. All soils throughout the kingdom which were impregnated with animal matter were claimed by the Crown for this peculiar purpose. And the same proclamation empowered the saltpetre makers to dig up the floors of all dove-houses, stables, cellars, slaughter-houses,

&c., for the purpose of carrying away the earth ; and prohibited the proprietors from relaying such floors with anything but ' mellow earth,' to afford greater facilities to the diggers. An obvious consequence was, that individuals anxious to preserve their premises from injury by this ruinous digging, resorted to bribery, and bought off the visits of the *Saltpetre Man*. He, on the other hand, conscious of the power his privileges gave him, became extortionate, and made his favours more ruinous than his duties. These vexatious and mischievous visits were put a stop to in 1656, by the passing of an act forbidding saltpetre makers from digging in houses or enclosed lands without leave of the owners. It also appears, from the extensive powers of the act under which the above-named patent was granted, that the corporate bodies of certain, or perhaps all, municipal towns were compelled at their own charge to maintain works for the manufacture of saltpetre from the refuse of their respective localities—a supposition which is confirmed by the fact that, in the year 1633, an order was made by the corporation of Nottingham, to the effect that no person, without leave from the mayor and common council, should remove any soil except to places appointed for the reception of such matter ; nor should any such material be sold to any foreigner (stranger) without their license. Four years later (1637) the hall book of the same corporation contains the following entry :—' William Burrows agreed to be made burgess on condition of freeing the town from all charges relating to the saltpetre works.' Doubtless the corporation were glad enough to rid themselves of the obnoxious character of the *Saltpetre Man*, with all its disagreeable contingencies, when relief could be had on such easy terms.

Troubles with the *Saltpetre Man* can be traced to a still earlier date than any we have mentioned, as the following curious memorial will show.

' To the Righte Honorable oure verie goode Lorde, the Lorde Burghley, Lorde Highe Threasiror of Englande.

' Righte Honorable, oure humble dewties to your good lordshippe premised, maye it please the same to be advertised, that at the Quarter Sessions holden at Newarke, within this countie of Nottingham, there was a general complaynte made unto us by the whole countrie, that one John Ffoxe, saltpetre maker, had charged the whole countrie by his precepts for the caryinge of cole from Selsona, in the countie of Nottingham, to the towne of Newarke, within the same countie, being sixteen miles distant, for the making of saltpetre, some townes with five cariages, and some with lesse, or else to give him four shillings for evrie loade, whereof he hath received a greate parte. Uppon which complaynte we called the same John Ffoxe before some of us at Newarke, at the sessions there, to answere the premises, and also to make us a proposition what lodes of coles would serve to make a thousand weight of saltpetre, to the end we might have sette some order for the preparing of the same ; but the saide Ffoxe will not sette down anie rate what would serve for the making of a thousand. Therefore, we have thoughte

* *Rambles by Rivers.*

good to advise youre good lordshippe of the premises, and have appoynted the clark of the peace of this countie of Nottingham to attend your lordshippe, to know your lordshippe's pleasure about the same, who can further inform your good lordshippe of the particularities thereof, if it shall please your lordshippe to give him hearinge : and so most humblie take our leaves. —Newark, the 8th of October, 1589.

> Ro. Markham.   William Sutton.
> Rauf Barton.   Nihs. Roos.
> Brian Lassels.   John Thornhagh.'

After the discovery and importation of rough nitre from the East Indies, the practice of obtaining it by such processes as those described in the patent of Brook and Russel fell into gradual disuse, and thus the country was relieved from one of the greatest annoyances to which it had ever been subject.

MAY 21.

St Hospitius, recluse in Provence, 881. St Godrick, hermit, of Finkley, near Durham, 1170. St Felix of Cantalicio, 1587.

Born.—Philip II. of Spain, 1527, *Valladolid ;* Francis Egerton, Duke of Bridgewater, promoter of canal navigation in England, 1736; Bryan Edwards, historian of the West Indies, 1743, *Westbury ;* John, Lord Lyndhurst, Chancellor of England, 1772, *Boston, U.S.*

Died.—James Graham, Marquis of Montrose, 1650, *Edinburgh ;* Cornelius Tromp, Dutch admiral, 1691, *Amsterdam ;* Jacques Maboul, French preacher, 1723, *Aeth ;* Robert Harley, Earl of Oxford, prime minister of Queen Anne, 1724; Sir John Hawkins, author of *A History of Music,* &c., 1789; Dr Thomas Warton, poet, Professor of Poetry, Oxford, 1790, *Trinity College, Oxford;* Maria Edgeworth, novelist, 1849.

THOMAS WARTON.

Thomas Warton was but a sorry singer himself, little better than an elegant 'gatherer and disposer of other men's stuff,' but he did good service to English literature, chiefly by the impulse he gave to a better appreciation of our early poets.

Warton was an Oxford Fellow, of an easy temperament, polished manners, and romantic taste. When only twenty-one—in 1749—he rendered himself notorious and popular by his early poem, *The Triumph of Isis,* a defence of Oxford against certain strictures of Mason. His *Observations on the Faerie Queen of Spenser* appeared in 1754, and showed where his greatest strength lay. Three years later he was made Professor of Poetry, which office he filled very efficiently for ten years, indulging in many excursions into general literature, and working chiefly at a handsome and elaborate translation of *Theocritus,* which he published in 1770. But his greatest and most elaborate work was a *History of English Poetry,* which he brought down to the end of the Elizabethan age. The completion of this useful and laborious task has often been projected, and not seldom commenced, but never fully accomplished, but will at some future day, it is to be hoped, find some one who will do it

justice, and supply a need, and merit the gratitude of a nation not—in this branch of literature —inferior to any.

Warton's *Notes on Milton,* though somewhat diffuse, possess great merit, and bear witness to extensive reading. This work, begun in 1785, the same year in which he was made Camden Professor of History and poet laureate, was not more fortunate than the *History of Poetry,* in that it was not completed when the author died.

Warton was a lounger in the pleasant fields of literature, and would have accomplished more had he undertaken less. He edited the works of poets, wrote biographies, histories of localities, comic scraps, papers in the *Idler,* and other periodicals, a history of Gothic architecture, of which the manuscript was lost, and produced a variety of heterogeneous matter; or at other times spent his life leisurely wandering in old cathedrals and by pleasant streams, or figuring at Johnson's literary club, or musing in his favourite haunts in his brother's garden at Winchester.

His *Sonnets* are the best of his poems, and that *To the River Lodon* the most natural of these.

To the River Lodon.

'Ah! what a weary race my feet have run
Since first I trod thy banks with alders crowned,
And thought my way was all thro' fairy ground,
Beneath thy azure sky and golden sun ;
Where first my muse to lisp her notes begun !
While pensive Memory traces back the round,
Which fills the varied interval between ;
Much pleasure, more of sorrow, marks the scene.
Sweet native stream ! those skies and suns so pure
No more return, to cheer my evening road !
Yet still one joy remains, that, not obscure,
Nor useless, all my vacant days have flowed,
From youth's gay dawn to manhood's prime mature ;
Nor with the muse's laurel unbestowed.'

AN EARTHQUAKE.

May 21, 1382, 'There was a great earthquake in England, at nine of the clock, fearing the hearts of many ; but in Kent it was most vehement, where it sunk some churches and threw them down to the earth.'—*Stow's Chronicles.*

A song written at the time upon this earthquake has been preserved,[*] and must be considered as something of a curiosity. It treats the matter as a great warning to an over-careless people.

'And also when this earth quoke,[†]
    Was none so proud he n'as aghast,
And all his jollity forsook,
    And thought on God while that it last ;
And as soon as it was over-past,
    Men wox as evil as they dead are ;
Each man in his heart may cast,
    This was a warning to beware.

Forsooth, this was a lord to dread,
    So suddenly made men aghast,
Of gold and silver they took none heed,
    But out of their houses full soon they passed ;

[*] *Political Poems and Songs relating to English History.* Published under direction of the Master of the Rolls. 1859. Vol. I.

[†] The original language is here given in modern spelling.

Chambers, chimneys, all to-brest [burst],
   Churches and castles foul 'gan fare ;
Pinnacles, steeples to ground it cast,
   And all for warning to beware.

*   *   *   *   *

Sickerly I dare well say,
   In such a plight this world is in,
Mony for winning would betray
   Father and mother and all his kin.
Now [it] were high time to begin
   To amend our lives and well to fare ;
Our bag hangeth on a slipper pin,
   But we of this warning beware.'

The effect of an earthquake in producing
serious feelings must of course depend on the
strength of the shock. We may presume that
the particular course which reformation is to
take will depend in great measure on the kinds
of profligacy and folly which happen to be
reigning at the time. A New England newspaper of 1727 announces* that 'a considerable
town in this province has been so *awakened* by
the awful providence in the earthquake, that the
women have generally laid aside their hoop-pet-
ticoats.' Many amongst us would probably
be glad to stand a shock of not immoderate violence, if any such reformation could be expected
from it.

THE MARINER'S COMPASS.

The history of the mariner's compass in Western Europe furnishes a curious illustration of
the danger of forming conclusions upon negative
evidence—that is, of supposing a thing did not
exist at any time, merely because no known
contemporary writer mentions its existence. It
had been long believed that this instrument, so
important an agent in the progress of man's
civilization, had been invented in Italy about
the year 1302, by one Flavio Gioïa. When the
celebrated orientalist, Jules Klaproth, discovered
that it had been known to the Chinese from a
very early period; that there were reasons for
believing that an implement made on the same
principles, and for the same object, had been in
use among that people at a date prior to the
Christian era; but that they certainly had the
mariner's compass, in a rather rude form, it is
true, before the end of the eleventh century of
our chronology ; it was immediately concluded
that the people of Europe had derived the
knowledge of this invention direct from the
Chinese. Subsequent to this discovery, other
orientalists have found evidence in a contemporary
Arab writer, that this instrument was in use
among the Mahometan sailors in the Mediterranean so early as the year 1242 ; and it was
therefore concluded that the Christians of the
West derived the mariner's compass from the
Chinese, not directly, but indirectly through the
Arabs. The more extensive researches into the
literature of Western Europe have, however,
shown that neither of these suppositions is
correct, but that the principles of the mariner's
compass were known among our forefathers at a
date considerably earlier than the one last
mentioned.

* As we learn from the *St James's Evening Post.*
Jan. 16, 1728.

668

A French poet, named Guyot de Provins, wrote
a satire on the vices of his time, which is known
by the title of *La Bible de Guyot de Provins,* and
which is supposed to have been completed in the
year 1205. In speaking of the pope, he uses
words which are literally translated as follows :
' I wish he resembled the star which never moves.
The mariners who take it for their guide, observe
it very carefully, and go and come directing their
way by it ; they call it the polar star. It is
fixed and motionless ; all the others move, and
change, and vary their position ; but this star
moves not. They have a contrivance which
never deceives them, through the qualities of
the magnet. They have an ugly brown stone,
which attracts iron ; they mark the exact quarter to
which the needle points, which they have rubbed
on this stone and afterwards stuck into a straw.
They merely put it in water, in which the straw
causes it to swim : then the point turns directly
towards the star, with such certainty that it will
never fail, and no mariner will have any doubt
of it. When the sea is dark and foggy, that
neither star nor moon can be seen, they place a
lighted candle beside the needle, and have then
no fear of losing their way ; the needle points
direct to the star, and the mariners know the
right way to take. This is a contrivance which
cannot fail. The star is very fair, and very
bright ; and so I wish our holy father (the pope)
were.' Another French poet, supposed to have
been contemporary with Guyot de Provins, has
left us a short amatory poem on his mistress,
whom he compares to the polar star, which, he
says, when they can see it, serves them as a
safe guide ; and he adds : ' Its position is still
known for their route, when the weather is quite
dark, to all those who employ the following
process : they insert a needle of iron, so that it is
almost all exposed to view, into a bit of cork,
and rub it on the brown stone of the magnet
(the loadstone). If this be placed in a vessel
full of water, so that nobody thrusts it out, as
soon as the water becomes motionless, to whatever side the point turns, there without any doubt
is the polar star.'

The use of this rude kind of mariner's compass must have been generally known, to
allow of its being referred to in this manner by
the popular poets ; and the *Bible* of Guyot de
Provins, at least, was so well known, that
Dante's preceptor, Brunetto Latine, when he tells
in one of his letters how, during a visit to
England, he had seen one of these instruments,
borrows the words of the poet to describe it.
One or two other Latin writers of the same
age also allude to it, though rather obscurely.

But a still more curious account has been
recently brought to light by the researches of
Mr T. Wright, who has found descriptions of
the mariner's compass in two different works by
Alexander Neckam, one of the most learned
English scholars of the latter half of the twelfth
century. He is said to have died in 1217, but
one, at least, of the works alluded to was probably
compiled when he was young ; both of these
passages had remained concealed in the obscurity
of mediæval manuscripts until they were published by Mr Wright. They reveal the fact

that already, in the twelfth century, the English navigators used a compass, which was so far an improvement upon that described above by writers of the thirteenth century, that the needle was placed on a pivot as at present, instead of being thrust into a straw or a bit of cork, and made to swim in a basin of water. Neckam speaks of this needle as one of the necessary parts of a ship's furniture.

It is thus quite evident that the mariner's compass, instead of being invented by an Italian at the beginning of the fourteenth century, was well known to English sailors as far back as the twelfth; and, in fact, that we find them using it earlier than any other people in Europe. M. D'Avezac, the eminent geographer, who pointed out the exact meaning and importance of these passages from Alexander Neckam, in several communications to the Society of Geography of Paris, suggests, and we think with great appearance of truth, that the real invention of Flavio Gioïa was that of placing the needle permanently in a box, instead of putting it in water, or placing it on a pivot raised permanently for the occasion; and he conjectures that its modern Italian and French name, *bussola, boussole*, is derived from the box in which it was thus placed, and which was probably made of box-wood.

It appears, therefore, to be established beyond doubt, that the invention of the mariner's compass, instead of being borrowed from the Chinese or Arabs, was one which developed itself gradually and independently in Western Europe. M. D'Avezac has further shown that the card of the compass (called in French the *rose des vents*, and in the mediæval Latin *stella maris*) was in use at the close of the thirteenth century; and that, so early as the year 1268, a French writer, Pierre de Maricourt, describes the variation of the compass, and that allowance was made for it, though this is commonly supposed not to have been observed before the end of the fifteenth century.

It is worthy of note that in England the French and Italian name was never adopted; but we have preserved our original word, 'needle,' which as we have seen, appears at first to have been the only permanent part of the instrument, the other parts being, when it had to be used, made or taken for the occasion.

MAY 22.

Saints Castus and Æmilius, martyrs, 250 (?). St Basiliscus, Bishop of Comana, in Pontius, martyr, 312. St Conall, abbot. St Bobo, confessor, 985. St Yvo, confessor, 1353.

Trinity Sunday (1864).

The mystery of the Holy Trinity has been from an early date commemorated by a festival, the observance of which is said to have been established in England by Thomas à Becket near the close of the twelfth century. In the fact of three hundred and ten churches in England being dedicated to the holy and un-divided Trinity, we read the reverence paid to the mystery in mediæval times; but even this is exceeded in our age, when one-fifth of all new churches are so dedicated. Architects and other artists in early times racked their brains for devices expressive of the Three in One, and many very curious ones are preserved.

Born.—Alexander Pope, 1688, *Lombard Street, London;* Jonathan Pereira, pharmacologist. 1804, *London.*

Died.—Emperor Constantine the Great, 337; Henry VI. of England, murdered in the Tower of London, 1471; Robert, Lord Molesworth, 1725; Rev. John Entick, author of *Naval History*, &c., 1773, *Stepney;* Jean Baptiste Beccaria, author of a work on crimes and punishments, 1781, *Turin;* General Duroc, killed at *Wurtschen,* 1813; Robert Vernon, bequeather of a gallery of pictures to the British nation, 1849, *London.*

RELICS OF HENRY VI.

After the battle of Hexham (15th May 1464), by which the fortunes of the House of Lancaster were for the time overthrown, the imbecile King Henry VI. fled from the field, and for some time was entirely lost to public observation; nor has English history been heretofore very clear as to what for a time became of him. It appears that, in reality, the unfortunate monarch was conducted by some faithful adherents into Yorkshire, and there, in the wild and unfrequented district of Craven, found a temporary and hospitable shelter in Bolton-hall, with Sir Ralph Pudsey, the son-in-law of a gentleman named Tunstall, who was one of the esquires of his body. It was an old and primitive mansion, of the kind long in use among the English squirearchy, having a hall and a few other apartments, forming three irregular sides of a square, which was completed by a screen wall. Remoteness of situation, and not any capacity of defence, must have been what recommended the house as the shelter of a fugitive king. Such as it was, Henry was entertained in it for a considerable time, till at length, tiring of the solitude, and fearful that his enemies would soon be upon him, he chose

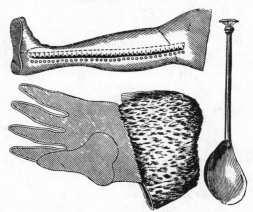

BOOT. GLOVE, AND SPOON OF HENRY VI.

to leave it, and was soon after seized and carried to the Tower.[*]

[*] *Antiquarian Repertory*, iii. 298.

The family of Pudsey was a hospitable and not over-prudent one. The spacious chimney-breast bore a characteristic legend, 'There ne'er was a Pudsey that increased his estate.' Nevertheless, and though for a number of years out of their old estate and house, the family is still in the enjoyment of both, although not in the person of a male representative.* They have for ages preserved certain articles which are confidently understood to have been left by King Henry when he departed from their house. These are, a boot, a glove, and a spoon, all of them having the appearances of great age. Engravings of these objects are here presented, taken from sketches made so long ago as 1777. The boot, it will be observed, has a row of buttons down the side. The glove is of tanned leather, with a lining of hairy deer's skin, turned over. The only remark which the articles suggest is, that King Henry appears to have been a man of effeminate proportions, as we know he was of poor spirit.

THE FOUNDER OF THE VERNON GALLERY.

The splendid collection of pictures preserved under this name in the South Kensington Museum was collected by a man whose profession suggests very different associations. Robert Vernon had risen from poverty to wealth as a dealer in horses. While practising this trade in a prudent and honourable manner, his natural taste led him to give much thought, as well as money (about £150,000, it was said), to the collection of a gallery of pictures. His pictures were selected by himself alone—with what sound discretion, consummate judgment, and exquisite taste, the Vernon collection still testifies. No greater contrast could possibly be than that between Mr Vernon and the connoisseur of the last century, represented by the satirist as saying—

'In curious matters I'm exceeding nice,
And know their several beauties by their price ;
Auctions and sales I constantly attend,
But choose my pictures by a skilful friend ;
Originals and copies much the same,
The picture's value is the painter's name.'

As a patron of art, no man has stood so high as Mr Vernon. He made it an invariable rule never to buy from a picture-dealer, but from the painter himself; thus securing to the latter the full value of his work, and stimulating him, by a higher and more direct motive, to greater exertions. Treating artists as men of genius and high feeling, he never cheapened their productions ; though, to a rising young painter, the honour of having a picture admitted into Mr Vernon's gallery was considered a far greater boon—as a test of merit and promise for the future—than any mere pecuniary consideration could bestow. And Mr Vernon did not confine his generous spirit to the public patronage of art and artists ; it was his pride and pleasure to seek out merit and foster it. Numerous were the instances in which his benevolent mind and princely fortune enabled him to smooth the path of struggling talent, and encourage fainting, toil-worn genius, in its dark hours of depression.

* *Gentleman's Magazine*, May 1841.

In forming his collection, Mr Vernon's leading idea was to exhibit to future times the best British Art of his period. So it was necessary, as any painter advanced in the practice of his profession, to secure his better productions ; consequently from time to time, at a great expenditure of money, Mr Vernon, as it is termed, weeded his collection ; never parting, however, with a picture without commissioning the artist to paint another and more important subject in his improved style.

It is not the mere money's worth of Mr Vernon's munificent gift to the nation that constitutes its real value, but the very peculiar nature of the collection ; it being in itself a select illustration of the state and progress of painting in this country from the commencement of the present century. Besides, it is an important nucleus for the formation of a gallery of British Art, both as regards its comprehensiveness and the general excellence of its examples, which are among the masterpieces of their respective painters. And we may conclude in the words of the *Times* newspaper, by stating that, 'there is nothing in the Vernon collection without its value as a representative of a class of art, and the classes are such that every eminent artist is included.'

FIRST CREATION OF BARONETS—MYTHS.

The 22nd May 1611 is memorable for the first creation of baronets. It is believed to have been done through the advice of the Earl of Salisbury to his master King James I., as a means of raising money for his majesty's service, the plan being to create two hundred on a payment of £1,000 each. On the king expressing a fear that such a step might offend the great body of the gentry, Salisbury is said to have replied, 'Tush, sire ; you want the money : it will do you good ; the honour will do the gentry very little harm.' At the same time care was professedly taken that they should all be men of at least a thousand a-year ; and the object held out was to raise a band for the amelioration of the province of Ulster—to build towns and churches in that Irish province, and be ready to hazard life in preventing rebellion in its native chiefs, each maintaining thirty soldiers for that purpose.

One curious little particular about the first batch of eighteen now created was, that to one—Sir Thomas Gerard, of Bryn, Lancashire—the fee of £1,000 was returned, in consideration of his father's great sufferings in the cause of the king's unfortunate mother.*

From the connexion of the first baronets with Ulster, they were allowed to place in their armorial coat the open red hand heretofore borne by the forfeited O'Neils, the noted *Lamh derg Eirin,* or red hand of Ulster. This heraldic device, seen in its proper colours on the escutcheons and hatchments of baronets, has in many instances given rise to stories in which it was accounted for in ways not so creditable to family pride as the possession of land to the extent of £1,000 per annum in the reign of King James.

For example, in a painted window of Aston

* Nichols's *Progresses of James I.* Vol. ii., 428.

Church, near Birmingham, is a coat-armorial of the Holts, baronets of Aston, containing the red hand, which is accounted for thus. Sir Thomas Holt, two hundred years ago, murdered his cook in a cellar, by running him through with a spit; and he, though forgiven, and his descendants, were consequently obliged to assume the red hand in the family coat. The picture represents the hand minus a finger, and this is also accounted for. It was believed that the successive generations of the Holts got leave each to take away one finger from the hand, as a step towards the total abolition of the symbol of punishment from the family escutcheon.

In like manner, the bloody hand upon a monument in the church of Stoke d'Abernon, Surrey, has a legend connected with it, to the effect that a gentleman, being out shooting all day with a friend, and meeting no success, vowed he would shoot at the first live thing he met; and meeting a miller, he fired and brought him down dead. The red hand in a hatchment at Wateringbury Church, Kent, and on a table on the hall of Church-Gresly, in Derbyshire, has found similar explanations. Indeed, there is scarcely a baronet's family in the country respecting which this red hand of Ulster has not been the means of raising some grandam's tale, of which murder and punishment are the leading features.

In the case of the armorial bearings of Nelthorpe of Gray's Inn, co. Middlesex, which is subjoined, the reader will probably acknowledge

that, seeing a sword erect in the shield, a second sword held upright in the crest, and a red hand held up in the angle of the shield, nothing could well be more natural, in the absence of better information, than to suppose that some bloody business was hinted at.

The fables thus suggested by the red hand of Ulster on the baronets' coats form a good example of a class which we have already done something to illustrate,—those, namely, called myths, which are now generally regarded as springing from a disposition of the human mind to account for actual appearances by some imagined history which the appearances suggest. It may be remarked that, from the disregard of the untutored intellect to the limits of the natural,

myths as often transcend their proper bounds as keep within them. Thus, wherever we have a deep, dark, solitary lake, we are sure to find a legend as to a city which it submerges. The city was a sink of wickedness, and the measure of its iniquities was at last completed by its inhospitality to some saint who came and desired a night's lodging in it; whereupon the saint invoked destruction upon it, and the valley presently became the bed of a lake. Fishermen, sailing over the surface in calm, clear weather, sometimes catch the forms of the towers and spires far down in the blue waters, &c. Also, wherever there is an ancient castle ill-placed in low ground, with fine airy sites in the immediate neighbourhood, there do we hear a story how the lord of the domain originally chose a proper situation for his mansion on high ground; but, strange to say, what the earthly workmen reared during each day was sure to be taken down again by visionary hands in the night-time, till at length a voice was heard commanding him to build in the low ground—a command which he duly obeyed. A three-topped hill is sure to have been split by diabolical power. A solitary rocky isle is a stone dropped from her apron by some migrating witch. Nay, we find that, a wear having been thrown across the Tweed at an early period for the driving of mills, the common people, when its origin was forgotten, came to view it as one of certain pieces of taskwork which Michael Scott the wizard imposed upon his attendant imps, to keep them from employing their powers of torment upon himself.

Flat rock surfaces and solitary slabs of stone very often present hollows, oblong or round, resembling the impressions which would be made upon a soft surface by the feet of men and animals. The real origin of such hollows we now know to be the former presence of concretions of various kinds which have in time been worn out. But in every part of the earth we find that these apparent footprints have given rise to legends, generally involving supernatural incidents. Thus a print about two feet long, on the top of the lofty hill called Adam's Peak, in Ceylon, is believed by the people of that island to be the stamp of Buddha's foot as he ascended to heaven; and, accordingly, it is amongst them an object of worship.

Even simpler objects of a natural kind have become the bases of myths. Scott tells us, in *Marmion*, how, in popular conception,

' St Cuthbert sits and toils to frame
  The sea-born beads that bear his name ; '

said beads being in fact sections of the stalks of encrinites, stone-skeletoned animals allied to the star-fish, which flourished in the early ages of the world. Their abundance on the shore of Holy Island, where St Cuthbert spent his holy life in the seventh century, is the reason why his name was connected with their supposed manufacture.

The so-called fairy-rings in old pastures—little circles of a brighter green, within which, it is supposed, the fairies dance by night—are now known to result from the outspreading propagation of a particular agaric, or mushroom, by which the ground is manured for a richer following vegetation.

At St Catherine's, near Edinburgh, is a spring containing *petroleum*, an oil exuding from the coal-beds below, but little understood before our own age. For many centuries this mineral oil was in repute as a remedy for cutaneous diseases, and the spring bore the pretty name of the Balm Well. It was unavoidable that anything so mysterious and so beneficial should become the subject of a myth. Boece accordingly relates with all gravity how St Catherine was commissioned by Margaret, the consort of Malcolm Canmore, to bring her a quantity of holy oil from Mount Sinai. In passing over Lothian, by some accident she happened to lose a few drops of the oil; and, on her earnest supplication, a well appeared at the spot, bearing a constant supply of the precious unguent.

Sound science interferes sadly with these fanciful old legends, but not always without leaving some doubtful explanation of her own. The presence of water-laid sand and gravel in many parts of the earth very naturally suggests tales of disastrous inundations. The geologist himself has heretofore been accustomed to account for such facts by the little more rational surmise of a discharged lake, although there might be not the slightest trace of any dam by which it was formerly held in. The highland fable which described the parallel roads of Glenroy as having been formed for the use of the hero Fingal, in hunting, was condemned by the geologist: but the lacustrine theory of Macculloch, Lauder, and other early speculators, regarding these extraordinary natural objects, is but a degree less absurd in the eyes of those who are now permitted to speculate on upheavals of the frame of the land out of the sea—a theory, however, which very probably will sustain great modifications as we become better acquainted with the laws of nature, and attain more clear insight into their workings in the old world before us.

QUARANTINE.

If a hundred persons were asked the meaning of the word quarantine, it is highly probable that ninety-nine would answer, 'Oh! it is something connected with shipping—the plague and yellow-fever.' Few are aware that it simply signifies *a period of forty days*; the word, though common enough at one time, being now only known to us through the acts for preventing the introduction of foreign diseases, directing that persons coming from infected places must remain forty days on shipboard before they be permitted to land. The old military and monastic writers frequently used the word to denote this space of time. In a truce between Henry the First of England and Robert Earl of Flanders, one of the articles is to the following effect:—'If Earl Robert should depart from the treaty, and the parties could not be reconciled to the king in three *quarantines*, each of the hostages should pay the sum of 100 marks.'

From a very early period, the founders of our legal polity in England, when they had occasion to limit a short period of time for any particular purpose, evinced a marked predilection for the quarantine. Thus, by the laws of Ethelbert, who died in 616, the limitation for the payment of the fine for slaying a man at an open grave was fixed to forty nights, the Saxons

reckoning by nights instead of days. The privilege of sanctuary was also confined within the same number of days. The eighth chapter of Magna Charta declares that 'A widow shall remain in her husband's capital messuage for forty days after his death, within which time her dower shall be assigned.' The tenant of a knight's fee, by military service, was bound to attend the king for forty days, properly equipped for war. According to Blackstone, no man was in the olden time allowed to abide in England more than forty days, unless he were enrolled in some tithing or decennary. And the same authority asserts that, by privilege of Parliament, members of the House of Commons are protected from arrest for forty days after every prorogation, and forty days before the next appointed meeting. By the ancient *Costumale* of Preston, about the reign of Henry II., a condition was imposed on every new-made burgess, that if he neglected to build a house within forty days, he should forfeit forty pence.

In ancient prognostications of weather, the period of forty days plays a considerable part. An old Scotch proverb states:

'Saint Swithin's day, gin ye do rain,
For forty days it will remain;
Saint Swithin's day, an ye be fair,
For forty days 'twill rain nae mair.'

There can be no reasonable doubt that this precise term is deduced from the period of Lent, which is in itself a commemoration of the forty days' fast of Christ in the wilderness. The period of forty days is, we need scarcely say, of frequent occurrence in Scripture. Moses was forty days on the mount; the diluvial rain fell upon the earth for forty days; and the same period elapsed from the time the tops of the mountains were seen till Noah opened the window of the ark.

Even the pagans observed the same space of time in the mysteries of Ceres and Proserpine, in which the wooden image of a virgin was lamented over during forty days; and Tertullian relates as a fact, well known to the heathens, that for forty days an entire city remained suspended in the air over Jerusalem, as a certain presage of the Millennium. The process of embalming used by the ancient Egyptians lasted forty days; the ancient physicians ascribed many strange changes to the same period; so, also, did the vain seekers after the philosopher's stone and the elixir of life.

MAY 23.

St Julia, martyr, 5th century. St Desiderius, Bishop of Langres, martyr, 411 (?). St Desiderius, bishop of Vienne, martyr, 612.

Born.—Elias Ashmole, antiquary, 1617, *Litchfield*; Dr William Hunter, 1718, *Kilbride, Lanarkshire*; Empress Catharine of Russia, 1729, *Zerbst Castle, Germany*; James Boaden, theatrical writer, biographer, 1762.

Died.—Emperor Henry V., 1125, *Utrecht*; Jerome Savonarola, religious and political reformer and orator, burnt at *Florence*, 1498; Francis Algarotti (physical science), 1764, *Pisa*; William Woollet, engraver, 1785; Richard Lalor Sheil, poet, politician, 1851, *Florence*.

SAVONAROLA.

The excessive corruption at which the church had arrived in the fifteenth century brought out an earlier and Italian Luther in the person of Gioralamo Savonarola, a Dominican preacher of

Florence, a man of great natural force of character, well fitted to be a reformer, but who was also one of those extreme pietists who derive their main energies from what they accept as divine promptings and commands whispered to them in their moments of rapture. Of Savonarola it was alleged that he had frequent conversations with God, and it was said the devils who infested his convent trembled at his sight, and in vexation never mentioned his name without dropping some of its syllables. His stern and daring eloquence caused his name to ring through Florence, and from Florence through Italy. He denounced the luxury and vices of the Florentines with a terrible thoroughness, and so effectually, that he quickly gathered around him a party of citizens as self-denying and earnest as himself. He openly resisted the despotism of the Medici, and sided with the democracy, prophesying judgment and woe for his adversaries. The lives led by the clergy and the papal court he pronounced infernal, and sure to sweep the church to perdition if repentance and amendment were not early sought and found. Pope Alexander VI. excommunicated and forbade him to preach; but he forbore only a while, and when he resumed preaching it was with greater vehemence and popular applause than before. The pope and the Medici then resolved to fight him with his own weapons. The Dominicans, glorified in their illustrious brother, were envied by the Franciscans. Savonarola had posted a thesis as a subject for disputation, and it was not difficult to prompt a Franciscan to prove it heretical. The strife between the two orders grew very hot. One of the Dominicans, in his zeal for the orthodoxy and sanctity of Savonarola, offered to prove them by walking through a fire unhurt. A Franciscan, not to be beaten, offered to do the same. The magistrates made arrangements for the trial. In the great square the city assembled to witness the spectacle. A pile of faggots was laid, but when set a-blaze, and everything was ready, Savonarola proposed that his champion should bear the consecrated host as his protection through his fiery walk. The magistrates would not listen to the proposal; its impiety, they said, was horrible. Savonarola was inflexible; he would not allow the ordeal to go forward except on that condition; and in the dispute the faggots consumed uselessly away. This business was his ruin with the Florentines. His enemies seized the advantage, broke into his convent of San Marco, and dragged him, his champion, and another monk to prison. The pope appointed a commission of clergy and laymen to try them, and the end was, that all three were strangled, and then burned, on the 23rd May 1498.

THE IRON CROWN OF ITALY.

On the 23rd of May 1805, when the Emperor Napoleon the First was crowned King of Italy at Milan, he, with his own hands, placed the ancient iron crown of Lombardy on his head, saying, 'God has given it to me, let him beware who would touch it;' thus assuming, as Sir Walter Scott observes, the haughty motto

attached to the antique diadem by its early possessors.

This celebrated crown is composed of a broad circle of gold, set with large rubies, emeralds,

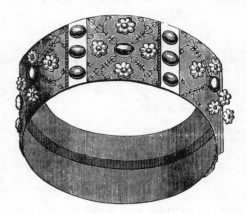

THE IRON CROWN OF ITALY.

and sapphires, on a ground of blue and gold enamel. The jewels and embossed gold exhibit a very close resemblance to the workmanship of an enamelled gold ornament, inscribed with the name of King Alfred the Great, which was found in the isle of Athelney, in Somersetshire, about the close of the seventeenth century, and is now carefully preserved in the Ashmolean museum at Oxford. But the most important part of the iron crown, from which, indeed, it derives its name, is a narrow band of iron, about three-eighths of an inch broad, and one-tenth of an inch in thickness, attached to the inner circumference of the circlet. This inner band of sacred iron—perfectly visible in the above engraving —is said to have been made out of one of the nails used at the crucifixion, given by the Empress Helena, the alleged discoverer of the cross, to her son Constantine, as a miraculous protection from the dangers of the battle-field. The ecclesiastics who exhibit the crown point out as a 'permanent miracle,' that there is not a single speck of rust upon the iron, though it has now been exposed more than fifteen hundred years. The earliest quasi-historical notice of the iron crown is, that it was used at the coronation of Agilulfus, King of Normandy, in the year 591.

Bonaparte, after his coronation at Milan, instituted a new order of knighthood for Italy, entitled the Iron Crown, on the same principles as that of the Legion of Honour for France.

MINISTERIAL FISH DINNER.

A ministerial fish dinner, in which whitebait forms a prominent feature, always signalizes the close of the parliamentary session—hilarious, we believe, as the break-out of boys from school on an unexpected holiday, whether the recent votes should have indicated approaching removal from the Treasury benches, or their continued and permanent occupation. Under this day, for reasons which will appear, we give an account (which was furnished to the *Times* in 1861) of the origin of the festival.

'Some of your readers have no doubt heard of Dagenham Reach, in Essex, a lake formed by the sudden irruption of the waters of the Thames over its banks nearly a century ago, covering the adjacent lands, from which they have never retired. On the banks of Dagenham Lake once stood, and, for aught I know, may still stand, a cottage occupied by a princely merchant named Preston, a baronet, of Scotland and Nova Scotia, and some time M.P. for Dover. He called it his "fishing cottage," and often in the spring went thither with a friend or two to escape the toils of parliamentary and mercantile duties. His most frequent guest was, as he was familiarly styled, Old George Rose, Secretary of the Treasury, and an Elder Brother of the Trinity House. Sir Robert also was an active member of that fraternity. Many a joyous day did these two worthies pass at Dagenham Reach, undisturbed by the storms that raged in the political atmosphere of Whitehall and St Stephen's Chapel. Mr Rose once intimated to Sir Robert that Mr Pitt, of whose friendship they were both justly proud, would, no doubt, much delight in the comfort of such a retreat. A day was named, and the Premier was accordingly invited, and received with great cordiality at the "fishing cottage." He was so well pleased with his visit and the hospitality of the baronet—they were all considered two, if not three-bottle men—that on taking leave Mr Pitt readily accepted an invitation for the following year, Sir Robert engaging to remind him at the proper time. For a few years Mr Pitt was an annual visitor at Dagenham Reach, and he was always accompanied by Old George Rose. But the distance was great, railways had not yet started into existence, and the going and coming were somewhat inconvenient for the First Minister of the Crown. Sir Robert, however, had his remedy, as have all such jovial souls, and he proposed that they should in future dine nearer London. Greenwich was suggested as a convenient *salle à manger* for the three ancients of the Trinity House — for Pitt was also a distinguished member of that august fraternity. The party was now changed from a trio to a quartet, Mr Pitt having requested to be permitted to bring Lord Camden. Soon after this migration a fifth guest was invited, Mr Long, afterwards Lord Farnborough. All still were the guests of Sir Robert Preston; but, one by one, other notables were invited (all of the Tory school), and at last Lord Camden considerately remarked that, as they were all dining at a tavern, it was only fair that Sir Robert Preston should be released from the expense. It was then arranged that the dinner should be given as usual by Sir Robert Preston, that is to say, at his invitation, and he insisted on still contributing a buck and champagne; but the rest of the charges of mine host were thenceforward defrayed by the several guests, and on this plan the meetings continued to take place annually till the death of Mr Pitt. Sir Robert was requested in the following year to summon the several guests, the list of whom by this time included most of the Cabinet Ministers. The time for meeting was usually after Trinity Monday, a short period before the end of the Session. By degrees a meeting, which was originally purely gastronomic, appears to have assumed, in consequence of the long reign of the Tories, a political or semi-political character. In the year 18— Sir Robert Preston died, but the affairs had become so consolidated by long custom, that the "fish dinner," as it was now called, survived; and Mr Long (I believe he was then Lord Farnborough) undertook to summon the several guests to the "Ministerial fish dinner," the private secretary of the late Sir Robert Preston furnishing to the private secretary of Lord Farnborough the names of the noblemen and gentlemen who had

been usually invited. Up to the decease of the baronet the invitations had been sent privately. I have heard that they now go in Cabinet boxes, and the party was certainly limited to the members of the Cabinet for some time. No doubt, eating and drinking are good for digestion, and a good digestion makes men calm and clear-headed, and calmness and a clear head promote logical reasoning, and logical reasoning aids the counsels of the nation, and *reipublicæ consilio* the nation goes on to glory. So I suppose, in one way or another, the "Ministerial Whitebait Dinner" conduces to the grandeur and prosperity of our beloved country.'

A HEREFORDSHIRE LADY IN THE TIME OF THE CIVIL WAR.

Amidst the leisure in the social life of two centuries since, time was found for recording a number of curious particulars bearing upon events, persons, circumstances, and manners, which are not to be found in the more pretentious histories of the period. Such information must be sought in the old family diaries, of which many specimens have been brought to light of late years, largely gratifying the fondness for archæological illustration by which the present age is distinguished from its predecessor.

A very interesting memorial of this sort is in the possession of Sir Thomas Edward Winnington, Bart., of Stanford Court, in the county of Worcester. It is the autograph account-book of Mrs Joyce Jefferies, a lady resident in Herefordshire and Worcestershire during the civil war, and who was half-sister and sole executrix of Humphrey Conyngesby, Esq., who travelled on the Continent between 1594 and 1610, in which latter year he left London for Venice, 'and was never after seen by any of his acquaintance on this side of the sea or beyond, nor any certainty known of his death, where, when, or how.' The book is kept in a clear hand, and comprises the receipt and expenditure of nine years; and besides containing many curious particulars of the manners of the age, sets forth her own very extraordinary self—the general representative of a class that is now exhibited only in the family pictures of the country ladies of the time. *

Mrs Jefferies lived in Widemarsh Street, Hereford, and her income amounted, on an average, to £500 per annum; she lived far beyond her means, not by over-indulgence in costly luxuries, for her own record is a tissue of benevolence from beginning to end, and three-fourths of the entries consist of sums bestowed in presents, excused in loans, or laid out in articles to give away. By being over free to her god-children,—by building her house in Widemarsh Street, which cost £800, and which was ordered to be pulled down in the time of the rebellion under Charles I., and the materials sold for £50—by other calamities of war—but worse, by knavish servants—she had so far consumed her means, that, had not her nephew received her in Holme Castle, she must have come to want in her old age.

Her personal appearance and style of dress may be gathered from her book. In 1638, in her palmy days, she wore a tawny camlet and kirtle, which, with trimmings and making, cost £10 17s. 5d. She had at the same time a black silk calimanco loose gown,

* The paper in *Archæologia*, vol. xxxvii., whence these details have been selected and condensed, is accompanied with *Historical Observations and Notes*, by John Webb, M.A., F.S.A., and was read to the Society of Antiquaries on April 17, and May 1, 1856. The first portion relates to points of character and domestic matters; and its sequel to the civil strife which at this period distracted the homes of our forefathers, and in which our benevolent lady had her share.

petticoat, and bodice, which, with the making, came to £18 1s. 8d. ; and a Polonia coat and kirtle cost in all £5 1s. 4d. Tailors were the male dressmakers of the time; and Mrs Jefferies employed them in Hereford, Worcester, and London. Sir Philip Warwick, describing the appearance of Cromwell in the House of Commons, remarks that his 'clothes were made by an ill country tailor.' But the country tailor was not the only artist who was unskilful in the trade; for the above tawny coat and silk calimanco dresses were so badly made in London, that they had to be altered by a country tailor. She had about the same period a head-dress of black tiffany; wore ruff-stocks, and a beaver hat with a black silk band, and adopted worsted hose of different colours, sometimes blue, sometimes grass-green. Among the articles of her toilet may be observed false curls and curling-irons; she had Cordovan gloves, sweet gloves, and embroidered gloves. She wore diamond and cornelian rings, used spectacles, and carried a whistle for a little dog, suspended at her girdle. A cipress (Cyprus?) cat, given to her by a Herefordshire friend, the Lady Dansey, of Brinsop, was no doubt a favourite; and she kept a throstle in a twiggen cage. The young lady above mentioned, who resided with her, was dressed at her expense, in a manner more suitable to her earlier time of life : for instance, she had in August 1638, a green silk gown, with a blue taffeta petticoat. At Easter following, she went to a christening, arrayed in a double cobweb lawn, and had a muff. In April 1639, she was dressed in a woollen gown, 'spun by the cook's wife, Whooper,' liver-coloured, and made up splendidly with a stomacher laced with twisted silver cord. Another article of this young lady's wardrobe was a gown of musk-coloured cloth; and when she rode out she was decked in a bastard scarlet safeguard coat and hood, laced with red, blue, and yellow; but none of her dresses were made by female hands.*

The household establishment of Mrs Jefferies is by no means, for a single person, on a contracted scale. Many female servants are mentioned; two having wages from £3 to £3 4s. per annum, with gowns of dark stuff at Midsummer. Her coachman, receiving 40s. per annum, had at Whitsuntide, 1639, a new cloth suit and cloak; and, when he was dressed in his best, exhibited fine blue silk ribbon at the knees of his hose. The liveries of this and another man-servant were, in 1641, of fine Spanish cloth, made up in her own house, and cost upwards of nine pounds. Her man of business, or steward, had a salary of £5 16s. A horse was kept for him, and he rode about to collect her rents and dues, and to see to her agricultural concerns. She appeared abroad in a coach drawn by two mares; a nag or two were in her stable; one that a widow lady in Hereford purchased of her, she particularly designated as 'a rare ambler.' She had a host of country cousins, and was evidently an object of great interest and competition among such as sought for sponsors to their children. She seems to have delighted in the office of gossip, and the number of her god-children became a serious tax upon her purse. A considerable list of her christening gifts includes, in 1638, a silver tankard to give her

* The spelling of this book is one of its curious features ; it is a transcript of speech as well as an exposition of thought ; for it corresponds closely with the mode of expression and pronunciation prevailing among the common people of Herefordshire, Worcestershire, and Salop, at the present day. Thus, in January 1642, we have a striking example in the dress of Miss Acton. ' A *yeard* and a half of scarlet baize was bought *to make her a waistcoate to dress her in*, and four yeards of red galoon to bind *him, i.e.*, the *waistcoate*.

god-daughter, little Joyce Walsh, £5 5s. 6d. ; 'at Heriford faier, for blue silk riband and taffetary lace for skarfs,' for a god-son and god-daughter, 8s. ; and 1642, 'paid Mr Side, gouldsmith in Heriford, for a silver bowle to give Mrs Lawrence daughter, which I found, too, called Joyse Lawrence, at 5s. 8d. an oz., 48s. 10d.' But to Miss Eliza Acton she was more than maternally generous, and was continually giving proofs of her fondness in all sorts of indulgence, supplying her lavishly with costly clothes and sums of money—money for gloves, for fairings, for cards against Christmas, and money repeatedly to put in her purse.

Of her system of housekeeping we get a glimpse. In summer, she frequently had her own sheep killed ; and at autumn a fat heifer, and at Christmas a beef or brawn were sometimes slaughtered, and chiefly spent in her house. She is very observant of the festivals and ordinances of the Church, while they continue unchanged; duly pays her tithes and offerings, and, after the old seignorial and even princely custom, contributes for her dependents as well as herself, in the offertory at the communion at Easter; has her pew in the church of All Saints at Hereford dressed, of course, with flowers at that season by the wife of the clerk ; gives to the poor's-box at the minster, and occasionally sends doles to the prisoners at Byster's Gate. Attached to ancient rules in town and country, she patronizes the fiddlers at sheep-shearing, gives to the wassail and the hinds at Twelfth Eve, when they light their twelve fires, and make the fields resound with toasting their master's health, as is done in many places to this day; and frequently in February is careful to take pecuniary notice of the first of the other sex, among those she knew, whom she met on Valentine's Day, and enters it with all the grave simplicity imaginable : 'Gave Tom Aston, for being my valentine, 2s. Gave Mr Dick Gravell, cam to be my valentine, 1s. I gave Timothy Pickering of Clifton, that was my valentine at Horncastle, 4d.' Sends Mr Mayor a present of 10s. on his ' law-day ;' and on a certain occasion dines with him, when the waits, to whom she gives money, are in attendance at the feast; and contributes to these at New Year and Christmas tide, and to other musical performers at entertainments or fairs ; seems fond of music, and strange sights, and 'rarer monsters.' She was liberal to Cherilickcome ' and his Jack-an-apes,' some vagrant that gained his living by exhibiting a monkey; and at Hereford Midsummer fair, in 1640, 'to a man that had the dawncing horse.' To every one who gratified her by a visit, or brought her a present, she was liberal; as well as to her own servants, and attendants at friends' houses. She provided medicine and advice for those who were sick and could not afford to call in medical aid ; and she took compassion upon those who were in the chamber of death and house of mourning, as may be seen in this entry : '1648, Oct. 29. For a pound of shugger to send Mrs Eaton when her son Fitz Wm. lay on his death-bed, 20d.'

In many instances, the feeling is worth more than the gift bestowed. She makes a little boy happy by threepence to put into his purse ; and to a poor fellow that was stationed to keep watch and ward at one of the city gates near her house, she contributed ' at several times,' 9d.

Not a single direct expression of ill-will can be detected in any of her comments. Mr Garnons, an occasional suitor for relief, she styles 'an unthrifty gentleman ;' amuses herself in setting down a small bad debt, and after recording the name of the borrower, and the trifling sum lent, adds, in a note, by way of anticipation, 'which he will never pay.' In another case, that of a legal transaction, in which a person had agreed to surrender certain premises to her use, and she had herself paid for drawing the instrument upon which he was to have acted, she observes, 'But he never did, and I lost my money.' In all matters she exhibits a gentle and a generous mind.

But it may be repeated that her greatest triumph, and one that her relations and acquaintance took care she should frequently enjoy, was at a *christening*. Here she was perfectly happy, if we may judge from what she herself tells us : 'Childe borne called Joyce. Memorand. that my cosin Mrs Jane Jeffrys, of Horncastle, was delivered of a daughter about a q'rter of an howre before 9 o'clock at night on Thursday night, being Christmas-eve's eve, and ye 23rd day of December 1647 ; and hitt was baptised on ye Munday following, being St John's-day, 27 day, 1647, and named Joyce. Ould Mrs Barckley and myself Joyse Jeffreys were gossips. God blesse hitt : Amen. Hitt went home with nurce Nott to the Smeeths in greate Chelsey's parish, ye same Munday after diner, to nurce.'

'December 27. Gave the midwyfe, good wyfe Hewes, of Upper Tedston, the christening day, 10s.' 'Munday. Gave nurce Nott ye same day, 10s.'

But what at this season gave the strong spur to her emotions was the circumstance of the infant having been called by her own Christian name. The exact period of her decease is unknown ; the codicil of her will carries her to 1650 ; and it is shown that she was buried in the chancel of the parish church of Clifton-upon-Tyne, on the border of Worcestershire.

MAY 24.

Saints Donatian and Rogatian, martyrs, about 287. St Vincent of Lerins, 450. St John de Prado, priest, martyr.

Born.—Bishop Jewel, 1522 ; Charles Von Linné (Linnæus), illustrious naturalist, 1707 ; Sir Robert Adair, ambassador, 1763 ; Albert Smith, comic writer, 1816, *Chertsey ;* John Henry Foley, artist, 1818, *Dublin ;* Her Majesty Queen Victoria, 1819, *Kensington.*

Died.—Pope Gregory VII., 1085 ; Nicolas Copernicus, astronomer, 1543, *Thorn, Prussia ;* Robert Cecil, Earl of Salisbury, minister to James I., 1612 : George Brydges, Lord Rodney, naval commander, 1792 ; Miss Jane Porter, novelist, 1850, *Bristol.*

LINNÆUS.

Carl Linné (usually Latinized to Linnæus) was born at Rashalt, a hamlet in the south of Sweden, on the 24th of May (N.S.) 1707. His father was a clergyman, whose house was situated in a delightful spot on the banks of a fine lake, surrounded by hills and valleys, woods and cultivated grounds. As Linné was wont to say, he walked out of his cradle into a garden. His father and an uncle had both a passion for horticulture, and they early inspired the child with their own spirit. Carl, however, was reckoned a dull boy. He was destined for the church ; but for theological studies he had a positive aversion, and, as a consequence, he made no progress in them. He was not disinclined to study, but his study was botany, and out of botany neither money nor advancement was to be had. It was finally resolved to make him a physician, and at the age of twenty he was sent to the University of Lund, where he was 'less

known for his knowledge of natural history than for his ignorance of everything else.' By good fortune he became a lodger in the house of the Professor of Medicine, Dr Stobœus, who discerning genius where others saw stupidity, gave Linné the free range of his library and museum, and treated him with all the kindness of a father. In this genial atmosphere he came to the determination to spend his life as a student of Nature, a resolve from which neither poverty nor misery ever moved him. To the regret of Stobœus he left Lund for Upsala, thinking that it was a better university. His father could allow him no more than eight pounds a year. Often he felt the pangs of hunger, and holes in his shoes he stuffed with paper ; but he read and attended lectures with an energy which let nothing slip, and was sure in the end to meet with reward.

LINNÆUS, AS HE TRAVELLED IN LAPLAND.

Celsius, the Professor of Divinity, himself a botanist, discovered Linné one day in the academical garden intently examining a plant, and, entering into conversation with the poor student, surprise followed surprise as the extent of his knowledge revealed itself. He led Linné to Rudbeck, the Professor of Botany, who took him into his house as tutor to his children, and allowed him to lecture as his deputy. In the quiet of Rudbeck's library Linné first conceived those schemes of classification by which he was to revolutionize botanical science. On the 12th of May 1732, he set forth on his celebrated journey to Lapland. Alone, sometimes on horseback and sometimes on foot, he skirted the borders of Norway, and returned by the eastern coast of the Gulf of Bothnia to Upsala on the 12th of October, having travelled 4,000 miles, and brought back upwards of one hundred plants before unknown or undescribed. The university rewarded him with £10, his travelling expenses. With £15 he had scraped together, he went to Holland in 1735, to seek a university where at a cheap rate he might obtain a diploma, to enable him to practise physic for a livelihood. At Hardervyck he succeeded in this object, defending on the occasion the hypothesis 'that intermittent fevers are owing to fine particles of clay, taken in with the food, lodging in the terminations of the arterial system.' In Holland, by the advice of Boerhaave, he tarried for three years, making many delightful acquaintances in that country of flowers. Cliffort, a rich Dutch banker, who had a fine garden and museum, committed them to his care to put in order. He paid liberally, but worked Linné very hard, especially in editing a grand folio, *Hortus Cliffartianus*, adorned with plates, and full of learned botanical lingo, for which Linné had nothing but contempt. In the same years he managed to get printed several works of his own, his *Flora Lapponica, Fundamenta Botanica, Genera Plantarum*, and *Critica Botanica*, by which he quickly became famous. From Holland he made an excursion to England, but was disappointed alike in his reception by English botanists, and in the state of their collections as compared with the Dutch. There is a tradition, that when he first saw the golden bloom of the furze on Putney Heath, he fell on his knees enraptured with the sight. He vainly endeavoured to preserve some specimens of the plant through the Swedish winter. On leaving Holland he had an interview with Boerhaave on his death-bed. His parting words were, ' I have lived out my time, and done what I could. May God preserve thee, from whom the world expects much more ! Farewell, my dear Linnæus !'

On his return to Sweden he married, and commenced business in Stockholm as a physician ; but in 1740 he was called to Upsala as Professor of Medicine, and shortly afterwards was transferred to the chair of Botany. In Upsala, as professor and physician, he spent the remaining eight-and-thirty years of his life. Honours from all nations, and wealth, flowed freely unto him. The king raised him to nobility, and he took the title of Von Linné. Ease, however, induced no cessation of his old habits of industry. To the end he laboured incessantly. He cared for nothing but science, and he knew no delight but to be busy in its service. Towards the close of his life he suffered from a complication of diseases, but from his bed he kept dictating to an amanuensis on his favourite subjects. He died on the 10th of January 1778, aged seventy years, seven months, and seven days ; closing in a blaze of honour and renown a life which had commenced in obscurity and poverty.

The labours of Linné were not confined to botany, but ranged over all branches of natural history ; but with botany his fame is indissolubly associated. The classification and nomenclature of plants he found in utter confusion—a confusion all the worse, inasmuch as it was formal, and the product of a pedantry jealous of innovation and proud of its jargon. The changes introduced by Linné were, however, such obvious improvements, that they attained general acceptance with surprising facility. It is true that Linné's classification of the vegetable kingdom was itself artificial, and that it has almost everywhere given place to the natural system of Jussieu, but none the less is the world his debtor. It is the glory of science that it is progressive, and that the high achievement of to-day makes way for a higher to-morrow. It is rarely the lot of the *savant* to set forth any system or hypothesis which is more than provisional, or which sooner or later does not suggest and yield place to a more comprehensive. But without the first it is not likely we should have the second ; without Linné, we should scarcely have enjoyed Jussieu.

A QUACK OCULIST.

Sir William Read, originally a tailor or a cobbler, became progressively a mountebank and a quack doctor, and gained, in his case, the equivocal honour of knighthood from Queen Anne. He is said to have practised by 'the light of nature' ; and though he could not read, he could ride in his own chariot, and treat his company with good punch out of a golden bowl. He had an uncommon share of impudence ; a few scraps of Latin in his bills made the ignorant suppose him to be wonderfully learned. He did not seek his reputation in small places, but practised at that high seat of learning, Oxford ; and in one of his addresses he called upon the Vice-Chancellor, University, and the City, to vouch for his cures—as, indeed, he did upon the people of the three kingdoms. Blindness vanished before him, and he even deigned to practise in other distempers ; but he defied all competition as an oculist.

Queen Anne and George I. honoured Read with the care of their eyes ; from which one would have thought the rulers, like the ruled, as dark intellectually as Taylor's (his brother quack) coach-horses were corporeally, of which it was said five were blind in consequence of their master having exercised his skill upon them.

Dr Radcliffe mentions this worthy as ' Read the mountebank, who has assurance enough to come to our table upstairs at Garraway's, swears he'll stake his coach and six horses, his two blacks, and as many silver trumpets, against a dinner at Pontack's.'

Read died at Rochester, May 24, 1715. After Queen Anne had knighted him and Dr Hannes, there appeared the following lines :—

'The Queen, like Heav'n, shines equally on all,
Her favours now without distinction fall :
Great Read and slender Hannes, both knighted, show
That none their honours shall to merit owe.
That Popish doctrine is exploded quite,
Or Ralph * had been no duke, and Read no knight.

* Ralph, first Duke of Montague.

That none may *virtue* or their *learning* plead,
This has no *grace*, and that can hardly *read*.'

There is a curious portrait of Read, engraved in a sheet, with thirteen vignettes of persons whose extraordinary cases he cured.

SUPERSTITIONS ABOUT ANIMALS.

The robin is very fortunate in the superstitions which attach to it. The legend which attributes its red breast to his having attended our Lord upon the cross, when some of His blood was sprinkled on it, may have died out of the memory of country-folk; but still—

'There's a divinity doth hedge—a robin,'

which keeps it from innumerable harms.

His nest is safe from the most ruthless bird-nesting boy. 'You must not take robin's eggs; if you do, you will get your legs broken,' is the saying in Suffolk. And, accordingly, you will never find their eggs on the long strings of which boys are so proud.

Their lives, too, are generally respected. 'It is unlucky to kill a robin.' 'How badly you write,' I said one day to a boy in our parish school; 'your hand shakes so that you can't hold the pen steady. Have you been running hard, or anything of that sort?' 'No,' replied the lad, 'it always shakes; I once had a robin die in my hand; and they say that if a robin dies in your hand, it will always shake.'

The cross on the donkey's back is still connected in the rustic mind with our Lord's having ridden upon one into Jerusalem on Palm Sunday; and I wish that it procured him better treatment than he usually meets with.

[A good many years ago a writer in *Blackwood's Magazine*, adverting to the fact that the ass must have borne this mark before the time of Christ, suggested that it might be a premonition of the honour which was afterwards to befall the species. But the naturalist comes rather roughly across this pleasant fancy, when he tells that the cross stripe is, as it were, the evanishment in this species of the multitude of stripes which we see in the allied species, the zebra.— *Swainson's Zoology.*]

It is lucky for you that martins should build against your house, for they will never come to one where there is strife. Soon after setting up housekeeping for myself, I was congratulated on a martin having built its nest in the porch over my front door.

It is unlucky to count lambs before a certain time; if you do, they will be sure not to thrive. With this may be compared the popular notion of the character of David's sin in numbering the people of Israel and Judah, related in the last chapter of the Second Book of Samuel—a narrative which makes some people look with suspicion and dislike upon our own decennial census.

It is unlucky to kill a *harvest man, i. e.*, one of those long-legged spiders which one sees scrambling about, perfectly independent of cobwebs: if you do kill one, there will be a bad harvest.

If there are superstitions about animals, it is satisfactory to find them leaning to the side of humanity; but the poor hedgehog finds to his cost that the absurd notion of his sucking the teats of cows serves as a pretext for the most cruel treatment.

It is currently believed that if you put horsehairs into a spring they will turn to eels. A few months ago, a labouring man told a friend of mine that 'he knew it was so, for he had proved it.' He had put a number of horsehairs into a spring near his house, and in a short time it was full of young eels.

Mermaids are supposed to abound in the ponds and ditches in this neighbourhood. Careful mothers use them as bugbears to prevent little children from going too near the water. I once asked a child what mermaids were, and he was ready with his answer at once, 'Them nasty things what crome you (*i. e.*, hook you) into the water!' Another child has told me, 'I see one wunst, that was a grit big thing loike a feesh.' Very probably it may have been a pike, basking in the shallow water. Uncaught fish are very likely to have their weight and size exaggerated. Everybody knows what enormous fish those are which anglers lose. A man has told me of carp, that he could 'compare them to nothing but great fat hogs,' which I have afterwards caught in a drag-net, and found to be not more than four pounds weight. No wonder, then, that a little child, with its mind prepared to believe in mermaids, should have seen something big enough for one in a pike.

The saying about magpies is well known—

'One, sorrow;
Two, mirth;
Three, a wedding;
Four, death.'

And it is a curious thing that, as the man said about the horsehairs being turned into eels,—'I have proved it;' for, as I was on my way to be married, travelling upon a coach-top to claim my bride the next day, three magpies—neither more nor less—flew across the road.

Suffolk.   C. W J.

MAY 25.

St Urban, pope and martyr, 230 (?). Saints Maximus (vulgarly Meuxe) and Venerand, martyrs in Normandy (5th century?). St Adhelm, first bishop of Sherburn (since Salisbury), 709. St Dumhade, abbot of Iona, 717, St Gregory VII., pope (Hildebrand), 1085. St Mary Magdalen of Pazzi, 1607.

Born.—John Mason Good, medical writer, 1764, *Epping*; John Pye Smith, D.D., learned theologian, 1774, *Sheffield;* Francis Edward Todleben (military engineering), 1818, *Mitau, Courland.*

Died.—Cardinal D'Amboise, minister of Louis XII., 1510; Dr George Fordyce, medical writer and teacher, 1802, *London;* Dr William Paley, author of *Natural Theology, Evidences of Christianity,* &c., 1805 · Edmund Malone, critical writer, 1812.

THE PLAGUE AT MARSEILLES, 1720.

The arrival of a ship from Sidon on this day, in 1720, at Marseilles, brought the plague into that city, and caused the death of an immense number of persons. It was the last time that this formidable disease appeared in Western Europe in any force. Only by the most active and rigorous arrangements was the evil prevented from extending into the rest of France. Severe as the affliction was, it brought out some gratifying results, in showing of how much abandonment of self human nature is capable. A monument was erected in 1802, to commemorate the courage shown on the occasion by the principal public functionaries of the city, and by upwards of 150 priests, and a great number of doctors and surgeons, who died in the course of their zealous efforts to relieve and console the afflicted. Amongst other matters adverted to on this interesting monument is 'Hommage au Dey Tunisien, qui respecta ce don qu'un pape (Clement XI.) faisoit au malheur.'

FLITTING-DAY IN SCOTLAND.

The 25th * of May, as the Whitsunday term (old style), is a great day in Scotland, being that on which, for the most part, people change their residences. For some unexplained reason the Scotch 'remove' oftener than their southern neighbours. They very generally lease their houses by the year, and are thus at every twelvemonth's end able to shift their place of abode. Whether the restless disposition has arisen from the short leases, or the short leases have been a result of the restless disposition, is immaterial. That the restlessness is a fact, is what we have mainly to deal with.

It haps, accordingly, that at every Candlemas a Scotch family gets an opportunity of considering whether it will, in the language of the country, sit or flit. The landlord or his agent calls to learn the decision on this point; and if 'flit' is the resolution, he takes measures by advertising to obtain a new tenant. The two or three days following upon the Purification, therefore, become distinguished by a feathering of the streets with boards projected from the windows, intimating 'A House to Let.' Then comes on a most lively excitement for individuals proposing to remove; you see them going about for weeks, inspecting the numerous houses offered to them. Considerations of position, accommodation, and rent, afford scope for endless speculation. The gentleman deliberates about the rent—whether it will suit his means. The lady has her own anxious thoughts about new furniture that may be required, and how far old carpets can be made to suit the new premises. Both have their reflections as to what the Thomsons and the Jacksons will say on hearing that they are going into a house so much handsomer, more ambitiously situated, and dearer than their last. At length the pleasing dream is over—they have taken the house, and the only thing that remains to be done is to 'flit.'

Intensely longed for, the 25th of May comes at last. The departing tenant knows he must vacate his house before twelve o'clock; consequently, he has to arrange for a quick transportation of his household gods that forenoon. What he is to the new tenant, the tenant of the house he is going to occupy is to him. He dreads—hates—to be pushed; but on the other hand he must push, lest his penates be left shelterless on the street. There is accordingly all that morning a packing up, a sending off, a pushing in—upholstery meeting upholstery in deadly contention; streets encumbered with card-tables and arm-chairs in the most awkward irrelation to their proper circumstances; articles even more sacredly domestic exposed to every idle passerby—a straw-and-ropiness everywhere. In the humbler class of streets, the show of poor old furniture is piteous to look upon, more especially if (as sometimes happens) Jove has chosen to make it a dropping morning. Each leaves his house dishevelled and dirty—marks of torn down brackets and departed pictures on the walls, floors loaded with unaccountable rubbish. But there

* By an Act of 1881, the Whitsunday term was fixed for 28th May, and the Martinmas term for 28th November.

is no time for cleaning, and in each must plunge. with all his goods and all his family, settle as they may. There is only a rude bivouac for the first twenty-four hours, with meals more confused and savage than the roughest pic-nic. And yet, such is the charm of novelty, that a 'flitting' is seldom spoken of as a time or occasion of serious discomfort. Nor are the drawbacks of the new dwelling much insisted on, however obvious. On the contrary, the tendency is to apologize for every less agreeable feature—to view hopefully the effect of a little cleaning here, a coat of size there; to trust that something will make that thorough draft in the lobby tolerable, and compensate for the absence of a sink in the back-kitchen. Jack does not think much of the lowness of the ceiling of the bedroom assigned to him, and Charlotte Louisa has the best hopes of the suitableness of the drawing-room (when the back-bedroom is added to it) for a dancing-party.

A few months generally serve to dispel much of this illusion, and show all the disadvantages of the new mansion in a sufficiently strong light. So when Candlemas next comes round, our tenant has probably become dissatisfied, and anxious for another change. If considerations of prudence stand in the way, the family must be content to stay where they are for another year or two. If able to encounter another change, they will undertake it, only perhaps to find new, though different discomforts, and long for other changes.

MAY 26.

St Quadratus, Bishop of Athens, 2nd century. St Eleutherius, pope, martyr, 192. St Augustine, apostle of the English (605?). St Oduvald, abbot of Melrose, 698. St Philip Neri, 1595.

ST AUGUSTINE.

Close upon thirteen hundred years ago, a monk named Gregory belonged to the great convent of St Andrew, situated on the Cœlian Mount, which, rising immediately behind the Colosseum, is so well known to all travellers at Rome. Whatever may have been the good or evil of this remarkable man's character is not a fit subject for discussion here. Let it suffice to say, both his panegyrists and detractors agree in stating that he was distinguished among his contemporaries for Christian charity, and a deep interest in the bodily and spiritual welfare of children. One day, as Gregory happened to pass through the slave market at Rome, his attention was attracted by an unusual spectacle. Among the crowd of slaves brought from many parts to be sold in the great mart of Italy, there were the ebony-coloured, simple-looking negroes of Africa, the dark, cunning-eyed Greeks, the tawny Syrians and Egyptians—these were the usual sights of the place. But on this eventful occasion Gregory perceived three boys, whose fair, red and white complexions, blue eyes, and flaxen hair, contrasted favourably with the dusky races by whom they were surrounded. Attracted by feelings of benevolent curiosity, the monk asked the slave-dealer from whence had those beautiful but strange-looking children been brought. 'From Britain, where all the people are of a similar complexion,' was the reply. To his next question, respecting their religion, he was told that they were pagans. 'Alas!' rejoined Gregory, with a profound sigh, 'more is the pity that faces so full of light and brightness should be in the hands of the Prince of Darkness; that such grace of outward appearance should accompany minds without the grace of God within.' Asking what was the name of their nation, he was told that they were called Angles, or English. 'Well said,' replied the monk; 'rightly are they called Angles, for they have the faces of angels, and they ought to be fellow-heirs of heaven.' Pursuing his inquiries, he was informed that they were 'Deirans,' from the land of Deira (the land of wild deer), the name then given to the tract of country lying between the rivers Tyne and Humber. 'Well said again,' answered Gregory; 'rightly are they called Deirans, plucked as they are from God's ire (*de ira Dei*), and called to the mercy of heaven.' Once more he asked, 'What is the name of the king of that country?' The reply was, 'Ella.' Then said Gregory, 'Allelujah! the praise of God their Creator shall be sung in those parts.'

Thus ended the memorable conversation, strangely exhibiting to us the character of Gregory and his age. The mixture of the playful and the serious, the curious distortions of words, which seem to us little more than childish punning, was to him and his contemporaries the most emphatic mode of expressing their own feelings, and instructing others. Nor was it a mere passing interest that the three English slaves had awakened in the mind of the monk; he went at once from the market-place to the Pope, and obtained permission to preach the Gospel to the English people. So, soon after, Gregory, with a small but chosen band of followers, set out from Rome for the far-distant shores of Britain. But on the third day of their journey, as they rested during the noontide heat, a locust leaped upon the book that Gregory was reading; and he then commenced to draw a moral from the act and name of the insect. 'Rightly is it called locusta,' he said, 'because it seems to say to us *loco sta*—stay in your place. I see that we shall not be able to finish our journey.' And as he spoke couriers arrived, commanding his instant return to Rome, a furious popular tumult having broken out on account of his absence.

Years passed away. Gregory became Pope; still affairs of state and politics did not cause him to forget the pagan Angles. At length, learning that one of the Saxon kings had married a Christian princess, he saw that the favourable moment had arrived to put his long-cherished project into execution. Remembering his old convent on the Cœlian Mount, he selected Augustine, its prior, and forty of the monks, as missionaries to England. The convent of St Andrew still exists, and in one of its chapels there is yet shown an ancient painting representing the departure of Augustine and his followers.

Let us now turn our attention to England

The Saxon Ethelbert, one of the dynasty of the Ashings, or sons of the Ash-tree, was then king of Kent, and had also acquired a kind of imperial sway over the other Saxon kings, as far north as the banks of the Humber. To consolidate his power, he had married Bertha, daughter of Caribert, King of Paris. Like all his race, Ethelbert was a heathen; while Bertha, as a descendant of Clovis, was a Christian; and one of the clauses in their marriage contract stipulated that she should enjoy the free exercise of her religion. Accordingly, she brought with her to England one Luidhard, a French bishop, as her chaplain; and she, and a few of her attendants, worshipped in a small building outside of Canterbury, on the site of which now stands the venerable church dedicated to St Martin. Of all the great saints of the period, the most famous was St Martin of Tours; and, in every probability, the name, as applied to this church, or the one which preceded it on the same site, was a memorial of the recollections the French princess cherished of her native country and religion while in a land of heathen strangers.

Augustine and his companions landed at a place called Ebbe's Fleet, in the island of Thanet. The exact date of this important event is unknown, but the old monkish chroniclers delight in recording that it took place on the very day the great impostor, Mahomet, was born. The actual spot of their landing is still traditionally pointed out, and a farm-house near it still bears the name of Ebbe's Fleet. It must be remembered that Thanet was at that period really an island, being divided from the mainland by an arm of the sea. Augustine selected this spot, thinking he would be safer there than in a closer contiguity to the savage Saxons; and Ethelbert, on his part, wished the Christians to remain for some time in Thanet, lest they might practise magical arts upon him.

At length a day was appointed for an interview between the missionary and king. The meeting took place under an ancient oak, that grew on the high land in the centre of Thanet. On one side sat the Saxon son of the Ash-tree, surrounded by his fierce pagan warriors; on the other the Italian prior, attended by his peaceful Christian monks and white-robed choristers. Neither understood the language of the other, but Augustine had provided interpreters in France, who spoke both Latin and Saxon, and thus the conversation was carried on. Augustine spoke first; the king listened with attention, and then replied to the following effect:—'Your words and promises are fair; but as they are new and doubtful, I cannot give my assent to them, and leave the customs I have so long observed with all my race. But as you have come hither strangers from a long distance, and as I seem to myself to have seen clearly that what you yourselves believed to be good you wish to impart to us, we do not wish to molest you; nay, rather we are anxious to receive you hospitably, and to give you all that is needed for your support; nor do we hinder you from joining all whom you can to the faith of your religion.'

Augustine and his followers, being then allowed

to reside in Canterbury, walked thither in solemn procession, headed by a large silver cross, and a banner on which was painted—rudely enough, no doubt — a representation of the Saviour. And as they marched the choristers sang one of the still famous Gregorian chants, a litany which Gregory had composed when Rome was threatened by the plague, commencing thus :—'We beseech thee, O Lord, in all thy mercy, that thy wrath and thine anger may be removed from this city, and from thy holy house, Allelujah!' And thus Gregory's grand wish was fulfilled; the Allelujah was heard in the wild country of Ella, among the pagan people of the Angles, who (as Gregory said, in his punning style) are situated in the extreme angle of the world.*

On the following Whit Sunday, June 2nd, A.D. 597, Ethelbert was baptized—with the exception of that of Clovis, the most important baptism the world had seen since the conversion of Constantine. The lesser chiefs and common people soon followed the example of their king, and it is said, on the authority of Gregory, that on the following Christmas ten thousand Saxons were baptized in the waters of the Swale, near Sheerness.

When Gregory sent Augustine to the conversion of England, the politic pope gave certain directions for the missionary's guidance. One referred to the delicate question of how the pagan customs which already existed among the Anglo-Saxons should be dealt with. Were they to be entirely abrogated, or were they to be tolerated as far as was not absolutely incompatible with the religion of the Gospel? Gregory said that he had thought much on this important subject, and finally had come to the conclusion that the heathen temples were not to be destroyed, but turned into Christian churches; that the oxen, which used to be killed in sacrifice, should still be killed with rejoicing, but their bodies given to the poor; and that the refreshment booths round the heathen temples should be allowed to remain as places of jollity and amusement for the people on Christian festivals. 'For,' he says, 'it is impossible to cut away abruptly from hard and rough minds all their old habits and customs. He who wishes to reach the highest place must rise by steps, and not by jumps.' And it would be inexcusable not to mention in *The Book of Days*, that it is through this judicious policy of Gregory that we still term the days of the week by their ancient Saxon appellations, derived in every instance from heathen deities. Christianity succeeded to Paganism, Norman followed Saxon, Rome has had to give way to Canterbury; yet the names of Odin, Thor, Tuisco, Saeter, and Friga are indelibly impressed upon our calendar.

Colonists in distant climes delight to give the familiar names of places in their loved native land to newly-established settlements in the wilderness. Something of this very natural feeling may be seen in Augustine. The first heathen temple he consecrated for Christian worship in England he dedicated to St Pancras. According to the legend, Pancras was a noble Roman youth, who, being martyred under Diocletian at the early age of fourteen years,

* *Gens Anglorum in mundi angulo posita.*

was subsequently regarded as the patron saint of children. There was a certain fitness, then, in dedicating the first church to him, in a country that owed its conversion to three children. But there was another and closer link connecting the first church founded in England by Augustine with St Pancras. The much-loved monastery of St Andrew, on the Cœlian Mount, which Gregory had founded, and of which Augustine was prior, had been erected on the very estate that had anciently belonged to the family of Pancras. Nor was the monastery without its own more particular memorial. When Augustine founded a cathedral on the banks of the Medway, he dedicated it to St Andrew, to perpetuate in barbarian Britain the old name so dear in civilized Italy; and subsequently St Paul's in London, and St Peter's in Westminster, represented on the banks of the Thames the great churches erected over the tombs of the two apostles of Rome beside the banks of the yellow Tiber.

Little is known of Augustine's subsequent career in England; he is said to have visited the Welsh, and journeyed into Yorkshire. He died on the 26th of May, but the year is uncertain.

Born.—Charles Duke of Orleans, 1391; Dr Michael Ettmuller, eminent German physician, 1644, *Leipzig;* John Gale, 1680, *London;* Shute Barrington, Bishop of Durham, 1734.

Died.—The Venerable Bede, historian, 735, *Jarrow, Durham;* Samuel Pepys, 1703, *Clapham;* Thomas Southern, dramatist, 1746; James Burnet, Lord Monboddo, 1799, *Edinburgh;* Francis Joseph Haydn, musical composer, 1809, *Grumpendorff, Vienna;* Capel Lofft, miscellaneous writer, 1824, *Moncallier, near Turin;* Admiral Sir Sidney Smith, G.C.B., 1840; Jacques Lafitte, eminent French banker and political character, 1844. *Paris.*

FAC-SIMILES OF INEDITED AUTOGRAPHS.
CHARLES DUKE OF ORLEANS.

The following is the signature of a remarkable and ill-fated man—the poet Duke of Orleans, father of Louis XII. of France. He was the son of the elegant, gentlemanly, and most unprincipled Duke Louis, murdered in the streets of Paris in 1407. His mother, Valentina of Milan, 'that gracious rose of Milan's thorny stem,' died of a broken heart for the loss of her much-loved and unloving lord. Charles, the eldest of their four children, was born May 26, 1391. He was married in 1409, to his cousin, Princess Isabelle, the little widow of Richard II. of England. She died in the following year, leaving one daughter. Charles exerted himself earnestly to procure the banishment of the Duke of Burgundy, suspected of inciting the murder of his father; but he was after some time most reluctantly persuaded to make peace with him. In 1415 he was taken prisoner at Agincourt, and confined in various English castles for the long term of twenty-five years. During his captivity he cultivated his poetical talent. In 1440 he was ransomed, and returned to France. His second wife, Bonne of Armagnac, having died without issue, Charles married, thirdly, Marie of Cleve, a lady with a fair face and fickle heart, by whom he had three children, Louis XII., and two daughters. He died on the 4th of June, 1465.

One of his poems has been translated by Longfellow, and the English version of another, an elegy on his first wife, will be found in her memoir, in the *Lives of the Queens of England*.

The autograph is the signature to a letter, in Cott. MSS. Vesp. F. III.

PEPYS AND HIS DIARY.

The publication of the *Diary* of Samuel Pepys, in 1825, has given us an interest in the man which no consideration of his place in society, his services to the state, or any other of his acts, could ever have excited. It is little to us that Pepys was clerk to the Admiralty through a great part of the reign of Charles II., sat in several parliaments, and died in honour and wealth at a good age. What we appreciate him for is, that he left us a chronicle of his daily life, written in a strain of such frank unreserve as to appear like thinking aloud; and which preserves for us a vast number of traits of the era of the Restoration which in no other way could we have obtained.

Mr Pepys's *Diary* was written in short-hand, and though it was left amongst his other papers at his death, it may be doubted if he ever entertained the least expectation that it would be perused by a single human being besides himself. Commencing in 1659, and closing in 1669, it comprises the important public affairs connected with the Restoration, the first Dutch war, the plague and fire of London. It exhibits the author as a zealous and faithful officer, a moderate loyalist, a churchman of Presbyterian leanings—on the whole, a respectably conducted man; yet also a great gossip, a gadder after amusements, fond of a pretty female face besides that of his wife, vain and showy in his clothing, and greatly studious of appearances before the world. The charm of his *Diary*, however, lies mainly in its deliberate registration of so many of those little thoughts and reflections on matters of self which pass through every one's mind at nearly all times and seasons, but which hardly any one would think proper to acknowledge, much less to put into a historical form.

The diarist's official duties necessarily brought him into contact with the court and the principal persons entrusted with the administration of affairs. Day by day he commits to paper his most secret thoughts on the condition of the state, on the management of affairs, on the silliness of the king, the incompetency of the king's advisers, and the shamelessness of the king's mistresses. He tells us of a child 'being dropped at a ball at court, and that the king had it in his closet a week after, and did dissect it;' of a dinner given to the king by the Dutch ambassador, where, 'among the rest of the king's company there was that worthy fellow my Lord of Rochester, and Tom Killigrew, whose mirth and raillery offended the former so much that he did give Tom Killigrew a box on the ear in the king's presence;' and of a score more such scandalous events. He also gives us an insight into church matters at the time of the Restoration, and into the difficulties attending a reimposition of Episcopacy. Under date 4th November 1660, for instance, he observes :—'In the morn to our own church, where Mr Mills did begin *to nibble at the Common Prayer*, by saying, "Glory be to the Father, &c.," but the people had been so little used to it, that *they could not tell what to answer*.' Pepys was an admirer and a good judge of painting, music, and architecture, and frequent allusions to these arts and their professors occur throughout the work; with respect to theatrical affairs he is very explicit. We are furnished with the names of the plays he witnessed, the names of their authors, the manner in which they were acted, and the favour with which they were received. His opinion of some well-known plays does not coincide with the judgment of more modern critics. For instance, of *Midsummer Night's Dream* he says :—' It is the most insipid, ridiculous play that ever I saw in my life;' and, again, of another of Shakspeare's he thus writes : 'To Deptford by water, reading *Othello, Moor of Venice*, which I ever heretofore esteemed a mighty good play; but having so lately read the *Adventures of Five Houres*, it seems a mean thing.' His notices of literary works are frequently interesting; of Butler's *Hudibras* he thought little—' It is so silly an abuse of the Presbyter Knight going to the warrs, that I am ashamed of it;' of Hobbes's *Leviathan*, he tells us that 30s. was the price of it, although it was heretofore sold for 8s., 'it being a book the bishops will not let be printed again.'

From 1684, Pepys occupied a handsome mansion at the bottom of Buckingham Street, Strand, the last on the west side, looking upon the Thames. Here, while president of the Royal Society, in 1684, he used to entertain the members. Another handsome house on the opposite side of the street, where Peter, the Czar of Russia, afterwards lived for some time, combines with Pepys's house, and the water-work tower of the York Buildings Company, to make this a rather striking piece of city scenery; and a picture of it, as it was early in the last century, is presented on next page. Pepys's house no longer exists.

How Mr Pepys spent his Sundays.

Pepys, as has been remarked, was a churchman inclined to favour the Presbyterians; he was no zealot, but he never failed to have prayers daily in his house, and he rarely missed a Sunday at church. We learn from his *Diary* how an average Christian comported himself with respect to religion in that giddy time.

Usually, before setting out for church, Pepys paid a due regard to the decoration of his person.

'The barber having done with me,' he says, 'I went to church.' We may presume that the

operation was tedious. In November 1663, he began to wear a peruke, which was then a new fashion, and he seems to have been nervous about appearing in it at public worship. 'To church, where I found that my coming in a periwig did not prove so strange as I was afraid it would, for I thought that all the church would presently cast their eyes upon me, but I found no such thing.' A day or two before, he had been equally anxious on presenting himself in this guise before his patron and principal, the Earl of Sandwich. The earl 'wondered to see me in my perukuque, and I am glad it is over.'

Pepys had a church to which he considered himself as attached; but he often—indeed, for the most part—went to others. One day, after attending his own church in the forenoon, and dining, he tells us, 'I went and ranged and ranged about to many churches, among the rest to the Temple, where I heard Dr Wilkins a *little.*' It was something like a man of fashion looking in at a succession of parties in an evening of the London season.

Very generally, Pepys makes no attempt to conceal how far secular feelings intruded both on his motives for going to church, and his thoughts while there. On the 11th August 1661, ' To our own church in the forenoon, and in the afternoon to Clerkenwell Church, *only to see the two fair Botelers.*' He got into a pew from which ' I had my full view of them both ; but I am out of conceit now with them.'

His general conduct at church was not good. In the first place, he allows his eyes to wander. He takes note of a variety of things :—' By coach to Greenwich Church, where a good sermon, a fine church, and a great company of handsome women.' On another occasion, attending a strange church, we are told, ' There was also my pretty black girl.'

Then, if anything ludicrous occurs, he has not a proper command of his countenance : ' Before sermon, I laughed at the reader, who, in his prayer, desired of God that he would imprint his Word on the thumbs of our right hands and on the right great toes of our right feet.' He even talks in church somewhat shamelessly, without excuse, or attempt at making excuse : ' In the pew both Sir Williams and I had *much talk* about the death of Sir Robert.'

Again, there was one more sad trick he had— he occasionally went to sleep : ' After dinner, to church again, my wife and I, where we had a dull sermon of a stranger, which made me sleep.' Here he satisfies his conscience with excuses. But sometimes he is without excuse, and then is sorry : ' Sermon again, at which I slept ; God forgive me ! '

At church he has a habit of criticizing alike service and parson ; and undeniably strange specimens of both seem to have come under his notice. First, the prayers. He goes to White Hall Chapel, ' with my lord,' but ' the ceremonies,' he says ' did not please me, *they do so overdo them.*' In fact, the singing takes his fancy much more. He is not without some skill himself : ' To the Abbey, and there meeting with Mr Hooper, he took me in among the quire, and there I sang with them their service.' It was very well for him he had this taste ; for on one occasion, he tells us, a psalm was set which lasted an hour, while some collection or other was being made. He criticizes the congregation also, instead of bestowing his whole attention on what is going on. He observes, ' The three sisters of the Thornburys, *very fine,* and the most zealous people that ever I saw in my life, even to admiration, *if it were true zeal.*' He has his personal observations to make of the parson, with little show of reverence sometimes : ' Went to the red-faced parson's church.' There, however, ' I heard a good sermon of him, better than I looked for.'

The sermon itself never escapes from his criticism. It is ' an excellent sermon,' or ' a dull sermon,' or ' a very good sermon,' or ' a lazy, poor sermon,' or ' a good, honest, and painful sermon.' He evidently expects the parson to take pains and be judicious : on one occasion ' an Oxford man gave us a most impertinent sermon,' and on another, ' a stranger preached like a fool.' But he does not seem to have minded these gentlemen availing themselves of the services of each other, or repeating their own discourses ; he seems to have been quite used to it : ' I heard a good sermon of Dr Bucks, *one I never heard before.*'

He goes home to dinner ; and, although he makes a point of remembering the text, he can seldom retain the exact words. It is generally after this fashion he has to enter it in the *Diary :* ' Heard a good sermon upon " teach us the right way," *or something like it.*' But, as a proof that he listened, he often favours us with a little abstract of how the subject was treated.

Pepys's Sunday dinner is generally a good one —he is particular about it : ' My wife and I alone to a leg of mutton, the sauce of which being made sweet, I was angry at it, and ate none :' not that he went without dinner,—he ' dined on the marrow-bone, that we had beside.' Fasting did not suit him. He began, one first day of Lent, and says, ' I do intend to try whether I can keep it or no ;' but presently we read, ' Notwithstanding my resolution, yet, for want of other victuals, *I did eat flesh this Lent.*' Now, how long would the reader fancy from that passage that he stood it ?—alas ! the register is made on the second day only !

Then, after dinner, what does Mr Pepys do ? To put it simply, he enjoys himself. Often, indeed, he goes out to dinner (his wife going also), or has guests (with their wives) at his own house ; but always, by some means or other, he contrives to get through a large amount of drinking before evening. ' At dinner and supper I drank, I know not how, *of my own accord,* so much wine, that I was even almost foxed, and my head aked all night.' Yet let us, in fairness, quote the rest : ' So home, and to bed, without prayers, *which I never did yet,* since I came to the house, of a Sunday night : I being now so out of order, that I durst not read prayers, for fear of being perceived by my servants in what case I was.'

But this is not Mr Pepys's only Sabbath amusement. He is musical : ' Mr Childe and I spent some time at the lute.' Or he takes a very sober walk, to which the strictest will not object. ' In the evening (July), my father and I walked round past home, and viewed all the fields, which was pleasant.' Sometimes he treats himself to a more doubtful indulgence : ' Mr Edward and I into Greye's Inn walks, and saw many beauties.' Nor was this an exceptional instance, or at a friend's instigation : ' I to Greye's Inn walk *all alone,* and *with great pleasure,* seeing the fine ladies walk there.'

On some part of the day, unless he was in very bad condition,—as, for instance, that night when there were no prayers,—Mr Pepys *cast up his accounts.* We read, ' Casting up my accounts, I do find myself to be worth £40 more, which I did not think.' Or, ' Stayed at home *the whole afternoon,* looking over my accounts.' And sometimes he so far hurts his conscience by this proceeding as to be fain to make excuses and apologies : ' *All the morning* at home, making up my accounts (God forgive me!) to give up to my lord this afternoon.'

SHUTE BARRINGTON.

The venerable Shute Barrington, Bishop of Durham, died on the 25th of March 1826, at the great age of ninety-two, having exercised episcopal functions for fifty-seven years. It was remarkable that there should have been living to so late a period one whose father had been the friend of Locke, and the confidential agent of Lord Somers in bringing about the union between Scotland and England. While the revenues of his see were large, so also were his charities; one gentleman stated that fully a hundred thousand pounds of the bishop's money had come through his hands alone for the relief of cases of distress and woe. A military friend of Mrs Barrington, being in want of an income, applied to the bishop, with a view to becoming a clergyman, thinking that his lordship might be enabled to provide for him. The worthy prelate asked how much income he required; to which the gentleman replied, that 'five hundred a year would make him a happy man.' 'You shall have it,' said the bishop; 'but not out of the patrimony of the church. I will not deprive a worthy and regular divine to provide for a necessitous relation. You shall have the sum you mention yearly out of my own pocket.' A curious circumstance connected with money occurred at the bishop's death. This event happening after 12 o'clock of the morning of the 25th, being quarter-day, gave his representatives the emoluments of a half-year, which would not have fallen to them had the event occurred before that hour. *

DUEL BETWEEN THE DUKE OF YORK AND COLONEL LENOX.

The political excitement caused by the mental alienation of George the Third, and the desire of the Prince of Wales, aided by the Whig party, to be appointed Regent, was increased rather than allayed by the unexpected recovery of the king, early in 1789, and the consequent public rejoicings thereon. At that time the Duke of York was colonel of the Coldstream Guards, and Charles Lenox, nephew and heir to the Duke of Richmond, was lieutenant-colonel of the same regiment. Colonel Lenox being of Tory predilections, and having proposed the health of Mr Pitt at a dinner-party, the Duke of York, who agreed with his brother in politics, determined to express his resentment against his lieutenant, which he did in the following manner:—At a masquerade given by the Duchess of Ancaster, a gentleman was walking with the Duchess of Gordon, whom the duke, suspecting him to be Colonel Lenox, went up to and addressed, saying that Colonel Lenox had heard words spoken to him at D'Aubigny's club to which no gentleman ought to have submitted. The person thus addressed was not Colonel Lenox, as the duke supposed, but Lord Paget, who informed the former of the circumstance, adding that, from the voice and manner, he was certain the speaker was no other than the Duke of York. At a field day which happened soon after, the duke was present at the parade of his regiment, when Colonel Lenox took the opportunity of publicly asking him what were the words he (Lenox) had submitted to hear, and by whom were they

* Nichols's *Illustrations of Literature.*

spoken. The duke replied by ordering the colonel to his post. After parade, the conversation was renewed in the orderly room. The duke declined to give his authority for the alleged words at D'Aubigny's, but expressed his readiness to answer for what he had said, observing that he wished to derive no protection from his rank; when not on duty he wore a brown coat, and hoped that Colonel Lenox would consider him merely as an officer of the regiment. To which the colonel replied that he could not consider his royal highness as any other than the son of his king.

Colonel Lenox then wrote a circular to every member of D'Aubigny's club, requesting to know whether such words had been used to him, begging an answer within the space of seven days; and adding that no reply would be considered equivalent to a declaration that no such words could be recollected. The seven days having expired, and no member of the club recollecting to have heard such words, Colonel Lenox felt justified in concluding that they had never been spoken; so he formally called upon the duke, through the Earl of Winchelsea, either to give up the name of his false informant, or afford the satisfaction usual among gentlemen. Accordingly, the duke, attended by Lord Rawdon, and Colonel Lenox, accompanied by the Earl of Winchelsea, met at Wimbledon Common (May 26th 1789). The ground was measured at twelve paces; and both parties were to fire at a signal agreed upon. The signal being given, Lenox fired, and the ball grazed his royal highness's side curl: the Duke of York did not fire. Lord Rawdon then interfered, and said he thought enough had been done. Lenox observed that his royal highness had not fired. Lord Rawdon said it was not the duke's intention to fire; his royal highness had come out, upon Colonel Lenox's desire, to give him satisfaction, and had no animosity against him. Lenox pressed that the duke should fire, which was declined, with a repetition of the reason. Lord Winchelsea then went up to the Duke of York, and expressed his hope that his royal highness could have no objection to say he considered Colonel Lenox a man of honour and courage. His royal highness replied, that he should say nothing: he had come out to give Colonel Lenox satisfaction, and did not mean to fire at him; if Colonel Lenox was not satisfied, he might fire again. Lenox said he could not possibly fire again at the duke, as his royal highness did not mean to fire at him. On this, both parties left the ground.

Three days afterwards, a meeting of the officers of the Coldstream Guards took place on the requisition of Colonel Lenox, to deliberate on a question which he submitted; namely, whether he had behaved in the late dispute as became an officer and a gentleman. After considerable discussion and an adjournment, the officers came to the following resolution: 'It is the opinion of the Coldstream regiment, that subsequent to the 15th of May, the day of the meeting at the orderly room, Lieut.-Col. Lenox has behaved with courage, but, from the peculiar difficulty of his case, not with judgment.'

The 4th of June being the king's birthday, a

grand ball was held at St James's Palace, which came to an abrupt conclusion, as thus described in a magazine of the period : ' There was but one dance, occasioned, it is said, by the following circumstance. Colonel Lenox, who had not danced a minuet, stood up with Lady Catherine Barnard. The Prince of Wales did not see this until he and his partner, the princess royal, came to Colonel Lenox's place in the dance, when, struck with the incongruity, he took the princess's hand, just as she was about to be turned by Colonel Lenox, and led her to the bottom of the dance. The Duke of York and the Princess Augusta came next, and they turned the colonel without the least particularity or exception. The Duke of Clarence, with the Princess Elizabeth, came next, and his highness followed the example of the Prince of Wales. The dance proceeded, however, and Lenox and his partner danced down. When they came to the prince and princess, his royal highness took his sister, and led her to her chair by the queen. Her majesty, addressing herself to the Prince of Wales, said—" You seem heated, sir, and tired !" "I am heated and tired, madam," said the prince, " not with the dance, but with dancing in such company." " Then, sir," said the queen, " it will be better for me to withdraw, and put an end to the ball !" " It certainly will be so," replied the prince, " for I never will countenance insults given to my family, however they may be treated by others." Accordingly, at the end of the dance, her majesty and the princesses withdrew, and the ball concluded. The Prince of Wales explained to Lady Catherine Barnard the reason of his conduct, and assured her that it gave him much pain that he had been under the necessity of acting in a manner that might subject a lady to a moment's embarrassment.'

A person named Swift wrote a pamphlet on the affair, taking the duke's side of the question. This occasioned another duel, in which Swift was shot in the body by Colonel Lenox. The wound, however, was not mortal, for there is another pamphlet extant, written by Swift on his own duel.

Colonel Lenox immediately after exchanged into the thirty-fifth regiment, then quartered at Edinburgh. On his joining this regiment, the officers gave a grand entertainment, the venerable castle of the Scottish metropolis was brilliantly illuminated, and twenty guineas were given to the men for a merry-making. Political feeling, the paltry conduct of the duke, the bold and straightforward bearing of the colonel, and probably a lurking feeling of Jacobitism—Lenox being a left-handed descendant of the Stuart race—made him the most popular man in Edinburgh at the time. The writer has frequently heard an old lady describe the clapping of hands, and other popular emanations of applause, with which Colonel Lenox was received in the streets of Edinburgh.

MANDRIN.

It is a curious consideration regarding France, that she had a personage equivalent to the Robin Hood of England and the Rob Roy of the Scottish Highlands, after the middle of the eighteenth

century. We must look mainly to bad government and absurd fiscal arrangements for an explanation of this fact. Louis Mandrin had served in the war of 1740, in one of the light corps which made it their business to undertake unusual dangers for the surprise of the enemy. The peace of 1748 left him idle and without resource ; he had no other mode of supporting life than to be continually risking it. In these circumstances, he bethought him of assembling a corps of men like himself, and putting himself at their head ; and began in the interior of France an open war against the farmers and receivers of the royal revenues. He made himself master of Autun, and of some other towns, and pillaged the public treasuries to pay his troops, whom he also employed in forcing the people to purchase contraband merchandise. He beat off many detachments of troops sent against him. The court, which was at Marly, began to be afraid. The royal troops showed a strong reluctance to operate against Mandrin, considering it derogatory to engage in such a war ; and the people began to regard him as their protector against the oppressions of the revenue officers.

At length, a regiment did attack and destroy Mandrin's corps. He escaped into Switzerland, whence for a time he continued to infest the borders of Dauphiné. By the baseness of a mistress, he was at length taken and conducted into France ; his captors unscrupulously breaking the laws of Switzerland to effect their object, as Napoleon afterwards broke those of Baden for the seizure of the Duc d'Enghien. Conducted to Valence, he was there tried, and on his own confession condemned to the wheel. He was executed on the 26th of May 1755.

CORPUS CHRISTI DAY (1864).

This is a festival of the Roman Catholic Church held on the Thursday after Whit Sunday, being designed in honour of the doctrine of transubstantiation. It is a day of great show and rejoicing ; was so in England before the Reformation, as it still is in all Catholic countries. The main feature of the festival is a procession, in which the pyx containing the consecrated bread is carried, both within the church and throughout the adjacent streets, by one who has a canopy held over him. Sundry figures follow, representing favourite saints in a characteristic manner—Ursula with her many maidens, St George killing the dragon, Christopher wading the river with the infant Saviour upon his shoulders, Sebastian stuck full of arrows, Catherine with her wheel ; these again succeeded by priests bearing each a piece of the sacred plate of the church. The streets are decorated with boughs, the pavement strewed with flowers, and a venerative multitude accompany the procession. As the pyx approaches, every one falls prostrate before it. The excitement is usually immense.

After the procession there used to be mystery or miracle plays, a part of the ceremonial which in some districts of this island long survived the Reformation, the Protestant clergy vainly endeavouring to extinguish what was not merely religion, but amusement.

MAY 27.

St Julius, martyr, about 302. St John, pope, martyr, 526. St Bede, confessor, 'father of the Church,' 735.

Born.—Alighieri Dante, poet, 1265, *Florence;* Caspar Scioppius, learned grammarian, Catholic controversialist, 1576, *Neumarck;* Cardinal Louis de Noailles, 1651, *Paris;* Rev. T. D. Fosbroke, antiquarian writer, 1770.

Died.—John Calvin, theologian, 1564, *Geneva;* Gui de Faur, seigneur de Pibrac, reformer of the bar of France, 1584; Vincent Voiture, prince of the belles-lettres of France in his day, 1648; Archibald, Marquis of Argyle, beheaded at *Edinburgh,* 1661; Dominique Bouhours, Jesuit (grammar and critical literature), 1702, *Clermont;* Charles de la Rue, eminent French preacher, one of the fabricators of the 'Delphin Classics,' 1725; Comte de Lœwendhall, marshal of France, 1755; Henry Dundas, first Viscount Melville, statesman, 1811, *Edinburgh;* Noah Webster, author of an English dictionary, 1843, *Newhaven, U.S.*

JOHN CALVIN.

It would be difficult to name a theologian who has exercised a deeper and more tenacious influence on the human mind than John Calvin. To him the Protestantism of France and Switzerland, the Puritanism of England and New England, and, above all, the Presbyterianism of Scotland, owed their life and vigour. Luther has been called the heart of the Reformation, but Calvin its head.

He was the son of a cooper, and was born at Noyon, in Picardy, on the 10th of July 1509. Manifesting in his childhood a pious disposition, he was destined for the priesthood; and, aided by a wealthy family of Noyon, his father sent him to the University of Paris. At the age of twelve he obtained a benefice, and other preferment followed; but as his talents developed, it was thought he would make a better lawyer than divine; and at Paris, Orleans, and Bruges, he studied law under the most celebrated professors. Calvin was in nowise averse to this change in his profession, for he had begun to read the Bible, and to grow dissatisfied with the doctrines of the Catholic Church; but, when at Bruges, he met Wolmar the Reformer, who fully confirmed him in the Protestant faith, and inspired him with a burning desire for its propagation. For this purpose he resolved to leave law and return to divinity. He went to Paris, and whilst there induced the Rector of the University to deliver a discourse on All Saints' Day, in which the tenets of the reformers were boldly set forth. In consequence of the excitement produced, both had to fly for their lives; and Calvin found refuge at Angoulême, where he supported himself by teaching Greek. In this retreat he composed the greater part of *The Institutes of the Christian Religion,* which he published at Basle in 1535. When we consider the excellent Latinity of this work, its severe logic, the range and force of its thought, its fame and effects, it does indeed appear the most wonderful literary achievement by a young man under twenty-six recorded in history. In 1536 he visited Geneva, where Protestantism had the same year been established, and, at the earnest request of Farel and some

leading citizens, he was induced to settle there as preacher. His presence was quickly felt in Geneva. In conjunction with Farel, he drew up a plan for its government, which was passed into law, but which, when carried into execution, was felt so intolerable, that the citizens rebelled, and drove Farel and Calvin out of the town.

Calvin then took up his residence in Strasburg, where he became minister of a French congregation, into which he introduced his own form of church government. Great efforts were meanwhile made in Geneva to bring back its inhabitants to the fold of Rome; but Calvin addressed such able epistles to them that the reactionists made no progress.

In 1541 he was invited back to Geneva, and at once became the virtual ruler of the city. He laid before the council his scheme of government, which they implicitly accepted. The code was as minute as severe, and carried as it were the private regulations of a stern and pious father in his household out into the public sphere of the commonwealth, and annexed thereto all the pains and penalties of the magistrate. It was Calvin's aim to make Geneva a model city, an example and light to the world. His rule was tyrannous; but, if gaiety vanished, and vice hid itself in hypocrisy, at least industry, education, and literature of a certain sort flourished under his sway.

The painful passage in Calvin's career was the martyrdom of Servetus. With Michael Servetus, a physician, he had at one time carried on a theological correspondence, which unfortunately degenerated into acrimony and abuse on both sides; and of Calvin, ever afterwards, Servetus was accustomed to speak with the utmost contempt. The exasperation was mutual, and of the bitterest kind. In 1546 Calvin wrote to Farel, vowing that if ever Servetus came within his grasp he should not escape scathless. Besides, Servetus had written a book on the Trinity, in which he had expressed opinions akin to those of the Unitarians, and which subjected him to the charge of heresy alike by Catholics and Protestants. In the summer of 1553, Servetus was rash enough to enter Geneva on his way to Italy, when he was arrested, thrown into prison, and brought to trial as a heretic—Calvin acting throughout as informer, prosecutor, and judge. He was sentenced to death, and, on the 27th of October, was burned at the stake with more than ordinary cruelty. Dreadful as such a deed now seems to us, it was then a matter of course. All parties in those times considered it the duty of the magistrate to extirpate opinions deemed erroneous. A Protestant led to martyrdom did not dream of pleading for mercy on the ground of freedom of conscience, or of toleration. In his eyes the crime of his persecutors lay in their hatred of the truth as manifested in him. If only his cords were loosed, and he endowed with power, he in like manner would find it his duty to prosecute his adversaries until they consented to confess the truth in unity with him. Yet, after making every allowance for the spirit of his age, it is impossible to escape the painful conclusion that there was as much revenge as mistaken justice in Calvin's treatment of his lone antagonist ; and his sincerest admirers cannot but shudder and avert their gaze, when in imagination they draw near the forlorn Spaniard in his fiery agony.

The labours of Calvin were unceasing and excessive. He preached every day for two weeks of each month ; he gave three lessons in divinity every week ; and assisted at all the deliberations of the consistory and company of pastors. In his study he maintained an active correspondence with theologians and politicians in every part of Europe ; defended the principles of the Reformation in a multitude of treatises ; and expounded and fortified that set of doctrines which bears his name in voluminous commentaries on the Scriptures. In person he was spare and delicate, and he suffered constantly from ill health. His habits were frugal and simple to the last degree. For years he only allowed himself one meagre meal daily. He had a prodigious memory, a keen understanding, and a will of iron. He was a man to fear or to reverence, but not to love. Emaciated to a skeleton, he died on the 27th of May 1564, aged only fifty-five. On his death-bed he took God to witness that he had preached the Gospel purely, and exhorted all to walk worthy of the divine goodness.

PIBRAC.

Pibrac was perhaps the most eminent man at the French bar during the sixteenth century. At the Council of Trent, he sustained with distinguished eloquence the interests of the French crown and the liberties of the Gallican Church. His state services were many, and he added to them the composition of a set of *Moral Quatrains,* which parents for ages after used to make their children learn by heart. He was remarkable for the amiableness of his character ; nevertheless —and it is a humbling proof of the effects of religious bigotry—this eminent and admirable man wrote an apology for the Bartholomew massacre.

BRITISH ANTHROPOPHAGI.

Cannibalism, so ordinary a feature of savage life in many parts of the earth in our day, may for that reason be presumed to have marked the people of the British isles when they were in the same primitive state. The earliest notices that we have upon this subject are certain accusations brought against the Saxon conquerors of England, in the old chronicles called the *Welsh Triads.* In these historical documents it is alleged that Ethelfrith, King of England, encouraged cannibalism at his court ; and that Gwrgi, a truant Welshman there, became so enamoured of human flesh, that he would eat no other. It was his custom to have a male and female Kymry killed for his own eating every day, except Saturday, when he slaughtered two of each, in order to be spared the sin of breaking the Sabbath. A northern chief, named Gwenddoleu, is also stated to have had his treasure guarded by two rapacious birds, for whom he had two Kymry slain daily.

St Jerome, who visited Gaul in his youth, about the year 380, has the following passage in

one of his works :—'Cum ipse adolescentulus in Galliâ viderim Attacottos, gentem Britannicam, humanis vesci carnibus ; et cum per sylvas porcorum greges, et armentorum pecudumque reperiant, pastorum *nates* et feminarum *papillas* solere abscindere ; et has solas ciborum delicias arbitrari.'* That is, he learned that the Attacotti, the people of the country now called Scotland, when hunting in the woods, preferred the shepherd to his flocks, and chose only the most fleshy and delicate parts for eating. This reminds us extremely of the late reports brought home by M. de Chaillu regarding the people of the gorilla country in Western Africa. Gibbon, in adverting to it, makes it the occasion of a compliment to Scotland. ' If,' says he, ' in the neighbourhood of the commercial and literary town of Glasgow, a race of cannibals has already existed, we may contemplate, in the period of the Scottish history, the opposite extremes of savage and civilized life. Such reflections tend to enlarge the circle of our ideas, and to encourage the pleasing hope that New Zealand may produce, in a future age, the Hume of the Southern Hemisphere.'

There is reason to fear that cannibalism was not quite extinct in Scotland even in ages which may be deemed comparatively civilized. Andrew Wyntoun has a grisly passage in his rhyming chronicle regarding a man who lived so brief a while before his own day, that he might easily have heard of him from surviving contemporaries. It was about the year 1339, when a large part of Scotland, even the best and most fertile, had been desolated by the armies of Edward III.

> ' About Perth thare was the countrie
> Sae waste, that wonder wes to see ;
> For intill well-great space thereby,
> Wes nother house left nor herb'ry.
> Of deer thare wes then sic foison [abundance],
> That they wold near come to the town.
> Sae great default was near that stead,
> That mony were in hunger dead.

> ' A carle they said was near thereby,
> That wold set settis [traps] commonly,
> Children and women for to slay,
> And swains that he might over-ta ;
> And ate them all that he get might :
> Chrysten Cleek till name be hight.
> That sa'ry life continued he,
> While waste but folk was the countrie.'†

Lindsay of Pitscottie has a still more dismal story regarding the close of the reign of James II. (about 1460), a time also within the recollection of people living in the epoch of the historian. He says : ' About this time there was ane brigand ta'en, with his haill family, who haunted a place in Angus. This mischievous man had ane execrable fashion, to tak all young men and children he could steal away quietly, or tak away without knowledge, and eat them, and the younger they were, esteemed them the mair tender and delicious. For the whilk cause and damnable abuse, he with his wife and bairns were all burnt, except ane young wench of a year old, wha was saved and brought to Dundee, where she was brought up and fostered ; and when she cam to a woman's years, she was condemned and burnt

* Quoted in Gibbon's *Decline and Fall.*
† Wyntoun's *Chronicle,* ii. 236.

quick for that crime. It is said that when she was coming to the place of execution, there gathered ane huge multitude of people, and specially of women, cursing her that she was so unhappy to commit so damnable deeds. To whom she turned about with an ireful countenance, saying, "Wherefore chide ye with me, as if I had committed ane unworthy act? Give me credence, and trow me, if ye had experience of eating men and women's flesh, ye wold think it so delicious, that ye wold never forbear it again." So, but [without] any sign of repentance, this unhappy traitor died in the sight of the people.'*

MAY 28.

St Caraunus (Cheron), martyr, 5th century. St Germanus, Bishop of Paris, 576.

Born.—James Sforza, the Great, 1639, *Cotignola ;* George I. of England, 1660 ; John Smeaton, engineer, 1724, *Ansthorpe ;* William Pitt, minister of George III., 1759, *Hayes, Kent ;* Thomas Moore, poet, 1780, *Dublin.*

Died.—St Bernard of Savoy, 1008; Thomas Howard, Earl of Suffolk, 1626, *Walden ;* Admiral de Tourville, 1701, *Paris ;* Madame de Montespan, mistress of Louis XIV., 1708 ; Electress Sophia of Hanover, 1714 ; George Earl Marischal, 1778, *Potsdam ;* Bishop Richard Hurd, 1808, *Hartlebury ;* William Eden, Lord Auckland, 1814 ; Sir Humphry Davy, chemist, 1829, *Geneva ;* William Erskine (*Memoirs of Emperor Baber,* &c.), 1852, *Edinburgh.*

THOMAS MOORE.

The public is well aware of Moore's life in outline: that he was the son of a grocer in Aungier Street, in Dublin ; that he migrated at an early period of life to London, and there, and at his rural retreat near Devizes, produced a brilliant succession of poems, marked by a manner entirely his own,—also several prose works, chiefly in biography ; that he was the friend of Byron, Rogers, Scott, and Lord John Russell, and a favourite visitor of Bowood, Holland House, and other aristocratic mansions;—a bright little man, of the most amiable manners and the pleasantest accomplishments, whom everybody liked, whom Ireland viewed with pride, and whom all Britain mourned.

In 1835, Moore visited his native city, and, led by his usual kindly feelings, sought out the house in Aungier Street in which he had been born, and where he spent the first twenty years of his life. The account he gives of this visit in his *Diary* is, to our apprehension, a poem, and one of the finest he ever wrote. 'Drove about a little,' he says, 'in Mrs Meara's car, accompanied by Hume, and put in practice what I had long been contemplating—a visit to No. 12, Aungier Street, the house in which I was born. On accosting the man who stood at the door, and asking whether he was the owner of the house, he looked rather gruffly and suspiciously at me, and answered, "Yes ;" but the moment I mentioned who I was, adding that it was the house I was born in, and that I wished to be permitted to look through the rooms, his countenance brightened up with the most cordial feeling, and seizing me by the hand, he pulled me along to the small room behind the shop (where we used to breakfast in old times), exclaiming to his wife (who was sitting there), with a voice tremulous with feeling, "Here's Sir Thomas Moore, who was born in this house, come to ask us to let him see the rooms ; and it's proud I am to have him under the old roof." He then without delay, and entering at once into my feelings, led me through every part of the house, beginning with the small old yard and its appurtenances, then the little dark kitchen where I used to have my bread and milk in the morning before I went to school ; from thence to the front and back drawing-rooms, the former looking more large and respectable than I could have expected, and the latter, with its little closet, where I remember such gay supper-parties, both room and closet fuller than they could well hold, and Joe Kelly and Wesley Doyle singing away together so sweetly. The bedrooms and garrets were next visited, and the only material alteration I observed in them was the removal of the wooden partition by which a little corner was separated off from the back bedroom (in which the two apprentices slept) to form a bedroom for me. The many thoughts that came rushing upon me in thus visiting, for the first time since our family left it, the house in which I passed the first nineteen or twenty years of my life, may be more easily conceived than told ; and I must say, that if a man had been got up specially to conduct me through such a scene, it could not have been done with more tact, sympathy, and intelligent feeling than it was by this plain, honest grocer ; for, as I remarked to Hume, as we entered the shop, "Only think, a grocer's still !" When we returned to the drawing-room, there was the wife with a decanter of port and glasses on the table, begging us to take some refreshment ; and I with great pleasure drank her and her good husband's health. When I say that the shop is still a grocer's, I must add, for the honour of old times, that it has a good deal gone down in the world since then, and is of a much inferior grade of grocery to that of my poor father—who, by the way, was himself one of nature's gentlemen, having all the repose and good breeding of manner by which the true gentleman in all classes is distinguished. Went, with all my recollections of the old shop about me, to the grand dinner at the Park [the Lord-Lieutenant's palace] ; company forty in number, and the whole force of the kitchen put in requisition. Sat at the head of the table, next to the carving aide-de-camp, and amused myself with reading over the *menu,* and tasting all the things with the most learned names.'

SIR HUMPHRY DAVY.

Dr John Davy, in his interesting *Memoirs of the Life of* [his brother] *Sir Humphry Davy,* relates with much feeling the latter days of the great philosopher. A short while before his death, being at Rome, he mended a little, and as this process went on, ' the sentiment of gratitude to Divine Providence was overflowing, and he was most amiable and affectionate in manner.

* Lindsay's *Chronicles of Scotland.* Edition, 1814 p. 163.

He often inculcated the propriety, in regard to happiness, of the subjugation of self, as the very bane of comfort, and the most active cause of the dereliction of social duties, and the destruction of good and friendly feelings; and he expressed frequently the intention, if his life were spared, of devoting it to purposes of utility (seeming to think lightly of what he had done already), and to the service of his friends, rather than to the pursuits of ambition, pleasure, or happiness, with himself for their main object.'

A BISHOP'S GHOST.

Henry Burgwash, who became Bishop of Lincoln on the 28th of May 1320, is chiefly memorable on account of a curious ghost story recorded of him in connexion with the manor of Fingest, in Bucks. Until the year 1845, Buckinghamshire was in the diocese of Lincoln, and formerly the bishops of that see possessed considerable estates and two places of residence in the county. They had the palace of Wooburn, near Marlow, and a manorial residence at Fingest, a small secluded village near Wycomb. Their manor-house of Fingest, the ruins of which still exist, stood near the church, and was but a plain mansion, of no great size or pretensions. And why those princely prelates, who possessed three or four baronial palaces, and scores of manor-houses superior to this, chose so often to reside here, is unknown. Perhaps it was on account of its sheltered situation, or from its suitableness for meditation, or because the surrounding country was thickly wooded and well stocked with deer; for in the 'merrie days of Old England,' bishops thought no harm in heading a hunting party. Be this as it may, certain it is that many of the early prelates of Lincoln, although their palace of Wooburn was near at hand, often preferred to reside at their humble manor-house of Fingest. One of these was Henry Burgwash, who has left reminiscences of his residence here more amusing to posterity than creditable to himself. 'He was,' says Fuller, 'neither good for church nor state, sovereign nor subjects; but was covetous, ambitious, rebellious, injurious. Yet he was twice lord treasurer, once chancellor, and once sent ambassador to Bavaria. He died A.D. 1340. Such as wish to be merry,' continues Fuller, 'may read the pleasant story of his apparition being condemned after death to be *viridis viridarius*—a green forester.' In his *Church History*, Fuller gives this pleasant story: 'This Burgwash was he who, by mere might, against all right and reason, took in the common land of many poor people (without making the least reparation), therewith to complete his park at Tinghurst (Fingest). These wronged persons, though seeing their own bread, beef, and mutton turned into the bishop's venison, durst not contest with him who was Chancellor of England, though he had neither law nor equity in his proceeding.' He persisted in this cruel act of injustice even to the day of his death; but having brought on himself the hatred and maledictions of the poor, he could not rest quietly in his grave; for his spirit was doomed to wander about that land which he had,

while living, so unjustly appropriated to himself. It so happened, however, as we are gravely informed by his biographer, that on a certain night he appeared to one of his former familiar friends, apparelled like a forester, all in green, with a bow and quiver, and a bugle-horn hanging by his side. To this gentleman he made known his miserable case. He said, that on account of the injuries he had done the poor while living, he was now compelled to be the park-keeper of that place which he had so wrongfully enclosed. He therefore entreated his friend to repair to the canons of Lincoln, and in his name to request them to have the bishop's park reduced to its former extent, and to restore to the poor the land which he had taken from them. His friend duly carried his message to the canons, who, with equal readiness, complied with their dead bishop's ghostly request, and deputed one of their prebendaries, William Bacheler, to see the restoration properly effected. The bishop's park was reduced, and the common restored to its former dimensions; and the ghostly park-keeper was no more seen.

VAUXHALL.

The public garden of London, in the reigns of James I. and Charles I., was a royal one, or what had been so, between Charing Cross and St James's Park. From a playfully contrived water-work, which, on being unguardedly pressed by the foot, sprinkled the bystanders, it was called *Spring Garden*. There was bowling there, promenading, eating and drinking, and, in consequence of the last, occasional quarrelling and fighting; so at last the permission for the public to use Spring Garden was withdrawn. During the Commonwealth, Mulberry Garden, where Buckingham Palace is now situated, was for a time a similar resort. Immediately after the Restoration, a piece of ground in Lambeth, opposite Millbank, was appropriated as a public garden for amusements and recreation; which character it was destined to support for nearly two centuries. From a manor called Fulke's Hall, the residence of Fulke de Breauté, the mercenary follower of King John, came the name so long familiarized to the ears of Londoners—*Vauxhall*.

Pepys, writing on the 28th of May 1667, says—'By water to Fox-hall, and there walked in the Spring Gardens [the name of the old garden had been transferred to this new one]. A great deal of company, and the weather and garden pleasant; and it is very cheap going thither, for a man may spend what he will or nothing, all as one. But to hear the nightingale and the birds, and here fiddles and there a harp, and here a jew's trump and there laughing, and there fine people walking, is mighty divertising.' The repeated references to Vauxhall, in the writings of the comic dramatists of the ensuing age, fully show how well these divertisements continued to be appreciated.

Through a large part of the eighteenth century, Vauxhall was in the management of a man who necessarily on that account became very noted, Jonathan Tyers. On the 29th of May 1786, a jubilee night celebrated the fiftieth anniversary of his management, being after all somewhat within the truth, as in reality he had opened the gardens in 1732. On that occasion, there was an entertainment called a *Ridotto al fresco*, at which two-thirds of the company appeared in masks and dominoes, a hundred soldiers standing on guard at the gates to maintain order.

Tyers went to a great expense in decorating the gardens with paintings by Hogarth, Hayman, and other eminent artists ; and having, by a judicious outlay, succeeded in realizing a large fortune, he retired to a country seat known as Denbighs, in the beautiful valley of the Mole. Here he amused himself by constructing a very

VAUXHALL, 1751.

extraordinary garden, for his own recreation. The peculiarly eccentric tastes—as regards house and garden decorations—of retired caterers for public amusements, such as showmen and exhibitors of various kinds, are pretty well known ; but few ever designed a garden like that of Tyers. One of its ornaments was a representation of the Valley of the Shadow of Death, thus described by Mr Hughson : 'Awful and tremendous the view, on a descent into this gloomy vale ! There was a large alcove, divided into two compartments, in one of which the unbeliever was represented dying in great agony. Near him were his books, which had encouraged him in his libertine course, such as Hobbes, Tindal, &c. In the other was the Christian, represented in a placid and serene state, prepared for the mansions of the blest !' After the death of Jonathan Tyers, his son succeeded to the proprietorship of Vauxhall ; he was the friend of Johnson, and is frequently mentioned by Boswell under the familiar designation of Tom Tyers.

In a *Description of Vauxhall*, many times published during the last century, we read the following account of what was called the Dark Walk : 'It is very agreeable to all whose minds are adapted to contemplation and scenes devoted to solitude, and the votaries that court her shrine ; and it must be confessed that there is

something in the amiable simplicity of unadorned nature, that spreads over the mind a more noble sort of tranquillity, and a greater sensation of pleasure, than can be received from the nicer scenes of art.

" How simple nature's hand, with noble grace,
    Diffuses artless beauties o'er the place."

' This walk in the evening is dark, which renders it more agreeable to those minds who love to enjoy the full scope of imagination, to listen to the orchestra, and view the lamps glittering through the trees.'

This is all very fine and flowery, but the medal has its reverse ; and the newspapers of 1759 speak of the loose persons of both sexes who frequented the Dark Walk, yelling 'in sounds fully as terrific as the imagined horrors of Cavalcanti's bloodhounds;' they further state that ladies were sometimes forcibly driven from their friends into those dark recesses, where dangerous terrors were wantonly inflicted upon them. In 1763, the licensing magistrates bound the proprietors to do away with the dark walks, and to provide a sufficient number of watchmen to keep the peace.

The following extract, from a poem published in 1773, does not speak favourably of the company that used to visit the gardens at that time.

'Such is Vauxhall—
For certain every knave that's willing,
May get admittance for a shilling;
And since Dan Tyers doth none prohibit,
But rather seems to strip each gibbet,
His clean-swept, dirty, boxing place,
There is no wonder that the thief
Comes here to steal a handkerchief;
For had you, Tyers, each jail ransacked,
Or issued an insolvent act,
Inviting debtors, lords, and thieves,
To sup beneath your smoke-dried leaves,—
And then each knave to kindly cram
With fusty chickens, tarts, and ham,—
You had not made such a collection,
For your disgrace and my selection.'

Horace Walpole, writing in 1750, gives a lively account of the frolics of a fashionable party at these gardens in the June of that year. 'I had a card from Lady Caroline Petersham, to go with her to Vauxhall. I went accordingly to her house, and found her and the little Ashe, or the Pollard Ashe, as they call her; they had just finished their last layer of red, and looked as handsome as crimson could make them. . . We marched to our barge, with a boat of French horns attending, and little Ashe singing. We paraded some time up the river, and at last debarked at Vauxhall. . . Here we picked up Lord Granby, arrived very drunk from Jenny's Whim [a tavern]. . . At last we assembled in our booth, Lady Caroline in the front, with the visor of her hat erect, and looking gloriously handsome. She had fetched my brother Orford from the next box, where he was enjoying himself with his *petite partie*, to help us to mince chickens. We minced seven chickens into a china dish, which Lady Caroline stewed over a lamp, with three pats of butter and a flagon of water—stirring, and rattling, and laughing; and we every minute expecting the dish to fly about our ears. She had brought Betty the fruit-girl, with hampers of strawberries and cherries, from Rogers's; and made her wait upon us, and then made her sup by herself at a little table. . . In short, the air of our party was sufficient, as you will easily imagine, to take up the whole attention of the gardens; so much so, that from eleven o'clock to half an hour after one, we had the whole concourse round our booth; at last they came into the little gardens of each booth on the sides of ours, till Harry Vane took up a bumper and drank their healths, and was proceeding to treat them with still greater freedoms. It was three o'clock before we got home.'

Innumerable jokes used to be passed on the smallness of the chickens, and the exceeding thinness of the slices of ham, supplied to the company at Vauxhall. It has been said that the person who cut the meat was so dexterous from long practice, that he could cover the whole eleven acres of the gardens with slices from one ham. However that may be, the writer well remembers the peculiar manner in which the waiters carried the plates, to prevent the thin shavings of ham from being blown away!

The *Connoisseur*, in 1755, gives the following amusing account of a penurious citizen's reflections on a dish of ham at Vauxhall: 'When it was brought, our honest friend twirled the dish

692

about three or four times, and surveyed it with a settled countenance. Then, taking up a slice of the ham on the point of his fork, and dangling it to and fro, he asked the waiter how much there was of it. "A shilling's worth, sir," said the fellow. "Prithee," said the cit, "how much dost think it weighs?" "An ounce, sir." "Ah! a shilling an ounce, that is sixteen shillings per pound; a reasonable profit, truly! Let me see. Suppose, now, the whole ham weighs thirty pounds: at a shilling per ounce, that is sixteen shillings per pound. Why, your master makes exactly twenty-four pounds off every ham; and if he buys them at the best hand, and salts and cures them himself, they don't stand him in ten shillings a-piece!"'

In the *British Magazine* for August 1782, there is a description of what may be termed a royal scene at Vauxhall. It states:

'The Prince of Wales was at Vauxhall, and spent a considerable part of the evening in comfort with a set of gay friends; but when the music was over, being discovered by the company, he was so surrounded, crushed, pursued, and overcome, that he was under the necessity of making a hasty retreat. The ladies followed the prince—the gentlemen pursued the ladies—the curious ran to see what was the matter—the mischievous ran to increase the tumult—and in two minutes the boxes were deserted; the lame were overthrown—the well-dressed were demolished—and for half an hour the whole company were contracted in one narrow channel, and borne along with the rapidity of a torrent, to the infinite danger of powdered locks, painted cheeks, and crazy constitutions.'

Mainly owing to the constant patronage of the Prince of Wales, Vauxhall was a place of fashionable resort all through his time. Nor were the proprietors ungrateful to the prince. In 1791, they built a new gallery in his honour, and decorated it with a transparency of an allegorical and most extraordinary character. It represented the prince in armour, leaning against a horse, which was held by Britannia. Minerva held his helmet, while *Providence was engaged in fixing on his spurs*. Fame, above, blowing a trumpet, and crowning him with laurels!

AN ARTIFICIAL MEMORY.

John Bruen, of Stapleford, in Cheshire, who died in 1625, was a man of considerable fortune, who had received his education at Alban Hall, in the University of Oxford. Though he was of Puritan principles, he was no slave to the narrow bigotry of a sect. Hospitable, generous, and charitable, he was beloved and admired by men of all persuasions. He was conscientiously punctual in all the public and private duties of religion, and divinity was his constant study and delight. He was a great frequenter of the public sermons of his times, called prophecyings; and it was his invariable practice to commit the substance of all that he heard to writing.

The old adage of 'like master, like man,' was fully verified in the instance of Bruen's servant, one Robert Pasfield, who was equally as fond of sermons as his master, but though 'mighty in the Scriptures,' could neither read nor write.

So, for the help of his memory, he invented and framed a girdle of leather, long and large, which went twice about him. This he divided into several parts, allotting each book in the Bible, in its order, to one of these divisions; then, for the chapters, he affixed points or thongs of leather to the several divisions, and made knots by fives and tens thereupon to distinguish the chapters of each book; and by other points he divided the chapters into their particular contents or verses. This he used, instead of pen and ink, to take notes of sermons; and made so good use of it, that when he came home from the conventicle, he could repeat the sermon through all its several heads, and quote the various texts mentioned in it, to his own great comfort, and the benefit of others. This girdle Mr Bruen kept, after Pasfield's decease, in his study, and would often merrily call it the Girdle of Verity.

MAY 29.

St Cyril, martyr (3rd century?). St Conon and his son, martyrs, of Iconia in Asia (about 275). St Maximinus, Bishop of Thiers, 349. Saints Sisinnius, Martyrius, and Alexander, martyrs, in the territory of Trent, 397.

Born.—Charles II. of England, 1630, *London;* Sarah Duchess of Marlborough, 1660; Louis Daubenton, 1716, *Montbard;* Patrick Henry, American patriot and orator, 1736, *Virginia;* Joseph Fouché, police minister of Napoleon I., 1763, *Nantes.*

Died.—Cardinal Beaton, assassinated at St Andrews, 1546; Stephen des Courcelles, learned Protestant divine, 1658, *Amsterdam;* Dr Andrew Ducarel, English antiquary, 1785, *South Lambeth;* Empress Josephine, 1814, *Malmaison;* W. H. Pyne, miscellaneous writer, 1843, *Paddington;* Sir Thomas Dick Lauder, Bart., miscellaneous writer, 1848, *Edinburgh.*

CHARLES II.

It is a great pity that Charles II. was so dissolute, and so reckless of the duties of his high station, for his life was an interesting one in many respects; and, after all, the national joy attending his restoration, and his cheerfulness, wit, and good-nature, give him a rather pleasant association with English history. His parents, Charles I. and Henrietta Maria (daughter of Henry IV. of France), who had been married in 1626, had a child named Charles James born to them in March 1629, but who did not live above a day. Their second infant, who was destined to live and to reign, saw the light on the 29th of May 1630, his birth being distinguished by the appearance, it was said, of a star at mid-day.

It was on his thirtieth birthday, the 29th of May 1660, that the distresses and vicissitudes of his early life were closed by his triumphal entry as king into London. His restoration might properly be dated from the 8th of May, when he was proclaimed as sovereign of the three kingdoms in London: but the day of his entry into the metropolis, being also his birthday, was adopted as the date of that happy event. Never had England known a day of greater happiness. Defend the Commonwealth who may—make a hero of Protector Oliver with

highest eloquence and deftest literary art—the intoxicated delight of the people in getting quit of them, and all connected with them, is their sufficient condemnation. The truth is, it had all along been a government of great difficulty, and a government of difficulty must needs be tyrannical. The old monarchy, ill-conducted as it had been under Charles I., shone white by comparison. It was happiness overmuch for the nation to get back under it, with or without guarantees for its better behaviour in future. An army lately in rebellion joyfully marshalled the king along from Dover to London. Thousands of mounted gentleman joined the escort, 'brandishing their swords, and shouting with inexpressible joy.' Evelyn saw the king arrive, and set down a note of it in his diary. He speaks of the way strewed with flowers; the streets hung with tapestry; the bells madly ringing; the fountains running with wine; the magistrates and the companies all out in their ceremonial dresses—chains of gold, and banners; nobles in cloth of silver and gold; the windows and balconies full of ladies; 'trumpets, music, and myriads of people flocking even so far as from Rochester, so as they were seven hours in passing the city, even from two in the afternoon till nine at night.' 'It was the Lord's doing,' he piously adds; unable to account for so happy a revolution as coming about by the ordinary chain of causes and effects.

It belongs more particularly to the purpose of this work to state, that among the acts passed by parliament immediately after, was one enacting 'That in all succeeding ages the 29th of May be celebrated in every church and chapel in England, and the dominions thereof, by rendering thanks to God for the king's peaceable restoration to actual possession and exercise of his legal authority over his subjects,' &c. The service for the Restoration, like that for the preservation from the Gunpowder Treason, and the death of Charles I., was kept up till the year 1859.

THE ROYAL OAK.

The restoration of the king, after a twelve years' interregnum from the death of his father, naturally brought into public view some of the remarkable events of his intermediate life. None took a more prominent place than what had happened in September 1651, immediately after his Scottish army had been overthrown by Cromwell at Worcester. It was heretofore obscurely, but now became clearly known, that the royal person had for a day been concealed in a bushy oak in a Shropshire forest, while the Commonwealth's troopers were ranging about in search of the fugitives from the late battle. The incident was romantic and striking in itself, and, in proportion to the joy in having the king once more in his legal place, was the interest felt in the tree by which he had been to all appearance providentially preserved. The ROYAL OAK accordingly became one of the familiar domestic ideas of the English people. A spray of oak in the hat was the badge of a loyalist on the recurrence of the Restoration-day. A picture of an oak tree, with a crowned figure sitting amidst the branches, and a few dragoons scouring about the neighbouring ground, was assumed as a sign upon many a tavern in town and country. (Some taverns still bear at least the name—one in Paddington, near London). And 'Oak Apple-day' became a convertible term for the Restoration-day among the rustic population. We thus find it necessary to introduce—first, a brief account of the king's connexion with the oak; and, second, a notice of the popular observance still remembered, if not practised, in memory of its preservation of a king.

The King at Boscobel.

After the defeat of the royal army at Worcester, (September 3, 1651,) the king and his principal officers determined on seeking safety by returning along the west of England to Scotland. As they proceeded, however, the king bethought him that the party was too large to make a safe retreat, and if he could get to London before the news of the battle, he might obtain a passage *incognito* in a vessel for France or Holland. On Kinver Heath they were brought to a stand-still by the failure of their guide to find the way. In the midst of the dismay which prevailed, the Earl of Derby stated to the king that he had lately, when in similar difficulty, been beholden for his life to a place of concealment on the borders of Staffordshire—a place called Boscobel. Another voice, that of Charles Giffard, the proprietor of this very place, broke the silence—'I will undertake to guide his majesty to Boscobel before daybreak.' It was immediately determined that the king, with a very small party of associates, should proceed under Giffard's care to the promised shelter.

By daybreak, Charles had reached White Ladies, a house taking its name from a ruined monastery hard by, and in the possession of Giffard's family, who were all Catholics. Here he was kindly received, put into a peasant's dress, and sent off to the neighbouring house of Boscobel, under the care of a dependent of the family, named Richard Penderel. His friends took leave of him, and pursued their journey to the North.

Boscobel was a small mansion which had been not long before built by Mr Giffard, and called so from a fancy of the builder, as being situated in *Bosco-bello*—Italian for a fair wood. The king knew how suitable it was as a place of concealment, not only from its remote and obscure situation, but because the Catholics always had hiding-holes in their houses for priests. At this time the house was occupied by a family of peasants, named Penderel, whose employment it was to cut and sell the wood, having 'some cows' grass to live upon.' They were simple, upright people, devoted to their master; and, probably from habit as Catholics, accustomed to assist in concealing proscribed persons. Certain it is, the house contains two 'priests' holes,'* one entered by a trap in the floor of a small closet; though it does not appear

* It was during his wanderings in this district that Charles became acquainted with and was aided by Father Huddlestone, who ultimately gave him the last sacrament on his death-bed, after he had solemnly declared

that Charles took any advantage of such a retreat while living at the place.

Charles, in his anxiety to make toward London, determined to set out on foot, 'in a country fellow's habit, with a pair of ordinary grey cloth breeches, a leathern doublet, and green jerkin,' taking no one with him but 'trusty Dick Penderel,' as one of the brethren was called; they had, however, scarcely reached the edge of the wood, when a troop of the rebel soldiery obliged them to lie close all day there, in a drenching rain. During this time the king altered his mind and determined to go towards the Severn, and so to France, from some Welsh seaport. At midnight they started on their journey; but after some hair-breadth escapes, finding the journey difficult and dangerous, they returned to Boscobel. Here they found Colonel William Careless, who had seen the last man killed in the Worcester fight, and whom the king at once took into his confidence. Being Sunday, the king kept in the house, or amused himself by reading in the close arbour in the little garden; and the next day he took the colonel's advice, 'to get up into a great oak, in a pretty plain place, where we might see round about us.' This tree was about a bowshot distance from the house. Charles describes it as 'a great oak, that had been lopped some three or four years before, and being grown out again very bushy and thick, could not be seen through.' There Charles and the colonel stayed the whole day, having taken up with them some bread and cheese and small beer, the colonel having a pillow placed on his knees, that the king might rest his head on it as he sat among the branches. While there, they saw many soldiers beating the woods for persons escaped.

After an uneasy day, the king left the friendly shelter of Boscobel at midnight, for Mr Whitgrave's house at Mosely; the day after, he went to Colonel Lane's, at Bently; from whence, disguised as a serving-man, he rode with Lane's sister toward Bristol, intending to take ship there; but after many misadventures and much uncertain rambling, he at last succeeded in obtaining a vessel at Shoreham, in Sussex, which carried him across to Fécamp, in Normandy.

The appearance of the lonely house in the wood, that gave such important shelter to the king, has been preserved in a contemporary engraving here copied. It was a roomy, half-timbered building, with a central turret of brick-work and timber, forming the entrance stair. A small portion of the wood was cleared around it for a little enclosed garden, having a few flower-beds, in front of the house; and an artificial 'mount,' with a summer-house upon it, reached by a flight of steps. Here Charles sat during the only Sunday he passed at Boscobel. Blount says:—'His majesty spent some part of this Lord's-day in reading, in a pretty arbour in Boscobel garden, which grew upon a mount, and wherein there was a stone table, and seats about it; and commended the place for its retiredness.'

himself a member of the Romish Church. James II., alluding to both events, observed that 'the father had once saved his brother's life, and afterwards saved his soul.'

At the back of this arbour was the gate leading toward the wood where the friendly oak of

shelter stood. Dr Stukely, who visited the place in the early part of the last century, speaks of

BOSCOBEL HOUSE.

the oak, as 'not far from Boscobel House, just by a horse track passing through the wood.' The celebrity of the tree led to its partial destruction; Blount tells us, ' Since his majesty's happy restoration, hundreds of people for many miles round have flocked to see the famous Boscobel, which had once the honour to be the palace of his sacred majesty, but chiefly to behold the Royal Oak, which has been deprived of all its young boughs by the numerous visitors, who keep them in memory of his majesty's happy preservation; insomuch, that Mr Fitzherbert, who was afterwards proprietor, was forced in a due season of the year to crop part of it for its preservation, and put himself to the charge of fencing it about with a high pale, the better to transmit the happy memory of it to posterity.' Stukely, half a century later, says :—' The tree is now enclosed with a brick wall, the inside whereof is covered with laurel. Close by its side grows a young thriving plant from one of its acorns. Over the door of the enclosure, I took this inscription in marble :—

"Felicissimam arborem, quam in asylum potentissimi Regis Caroli II. Deus. O. M., per quem reges regnant, hic crescere voluit, tam in perpetuam rei tantæ memoriam, quam specimen firmæ in reges fidei, muro cinctam posteris commendârunt Basilius et Jana Fitzherbert.

Quercus amica Jovi.'''

The enclosure has long since disappeared; but the inscription is still preserved in the farmhouse at Boscobel. Burgess, in his *Eidodendron*, speaking of this tree, says :—' It succumbed at length to the reiterated attentions of its votaries; and a huge bulk of timber, consisting of many loads, was taken away by handfuls. Several saplings were raised in different parts of the country from its acorns, one of which grew near St James's palace, where Marlborough House now stands; and there was another in the Botanic Gardens, Chelsea; the former has long since been felled,

and of the latter the recollection seems almost to be lost.' On the north side of the Serpentine in Hyde Park, near the powder magazine, flourished two old trees, said to have been planted by Charles II. from acorns of the Boscobel oak. They were both blighted in a severe frost a few years ago; one has been entirely removed, but the stem and a few branches of the other still remain, covered with ivy, and protected by an iron fence. In the Bodleian library is preserved a fragment of the original tree, turned into the form of a salver, or stand for a tankard; the inscription upon it records it as the gift of Mrs Letitia Lane, a member of the family who aided Charles in his escape.

It was the intention of the king to institute a new order, into which those only were to be admitted who were eminently distinguished for their loyalty—they were to be styled ' Knights of the Royal Oak;' but these knights were soon abolished, ' it being wisely judged,' says Noble, in his *Memoirs of the Cromwell Family*, ' that the order was calculated only to keep awake animosities which it was the part of wisdom to lull to sleep.' He adds, that the names of the intended knights are to be seen in the *Baronetage*, published in 5 vols. 8vo, 1741, and that Henry Cromwell, ' first cousin, one remove, to Oliver, Lord Protector,' was among the number. This gentleman was a zealous royalist, instrumental in the restoration of the royal family ; ' and as he knew the name of Cromwell would not be very grateful in the court of Charles the Second, he disused it, and styled himself only plain Henry Williams, Esq., by which name he was set down in the list of such persons as were to be made Knights of the Royal Oak.'* It may be

* Mrs Williams was equally ardent. Noble says, ' her loyalty exceeded all due moderation.' There is a curious MS. volume of religious and loyal rhapsody by her, preserved in the British Museum. Harleian MS. No. 2311.

here remarked that the Cromwell family derived its origin from Wales, and that they bore the name of Williams before they assumed that of Cromwell, on the marriage of Richard Williams with the sister of Cromwell Earl of Essex, prime minister of Henry VIII.; by which he became much enriched, all grants of dissolved religious houses, &c., passing to him by the names of Richard Williams, otherwise Cromwell. He was great-great-grandfather to Oliver, Lord Protector.

At the coronation of Charles II., the first triumphal arch erected in Leadenhall Street, near Lime Street, for the king to pass under on his way from the Tower to Westminster, is described in Ogilby's contemporary account of the ceremony as having in its centre a figure of Charles, royally attired, behind whom, 'on a large table, is deciphered the Royal Oak bearing crowns and sceptres instead of acorns; amongst the leaves, in a label—

"——— Miraturque novas
Frondes et non sua poma."

(——— Leaves unknown
Admiring, and strange apples not her own.)

As designing its reward for the shelter afforded his majesty after the battle of Worcester.' In the Lord Mayor's show of the same year, a pageant was placed near the Nag's Head tavern, in Cheapside, 'like a wood, in the vacant part thereof several persons in the habit of woodmen and wood-nymphs disport themselves, dancing about the Royal Oak;' while the rural god Sylvanus indulged in a long and laudatory speech in honour of the celebrated tree.

Colonel Careless, the companion of Charles in the oak, was especially honoured at the Restora-

tion, by the change of his name to Carlos, at the king's express desire, that it might thus assimilate with his own; and the grant of 'this very honourable coat of arms, which is thus described in the letters patent, "upon an oak *proper*, in a field *or*, a fess *gules*, charged with three royal crowns *of the second*, by the name of Carlos. And for his crest a civic crown, or oak garland, with a sword and sceptre crossed through it saltier-wise."'.

The Penderels were also honoured by court notice and a government pension. 'Trusty Dick' came to London, and died in his majesty's service. He was buried in 1671, under an altar tomb in the churchyard of St Giles's-in-the-Fields, then a suburban parish, and a fitting residence for the honest country woodman. The

tomb still preserves its characteristic features, and an epitaph remarkable for a high-flown confusion of ideas and much grandiloquent verbosity.

The Barber-Surgeons' Company of London possess a curious memorial of the celebrated tree which sheltered Charles at Boscobel. It is a cup

of silver, partially gilt, the stem and body representing an oak tree, from which hang acorns, fashioned as little bells; they ring as the cup passes from hand to hand round the festive board of the Company on great occasions. The cover represents the Royal Crown of England. Though curious in itself as a quaint and characteristic piece of plate, it derives an additional interest from the fact of its having been made by order of Charles the Second, and presented by him to the Company, the Master at that time being Sir Charles Scarborough, who was chief physician to the king.

Oak Apple-Day.

There are still a few dreamy old towns and villages in rural England where almost every ruin that Time has unroofed, and every mouldering wall his silent teeth have gnawed through, are attributed to the cannon of Cromwell and his grim Ironsides; though, in many instances, history has left no record that either the stern Protector or his dreaded troopers were ever near the spot. In many of these old-fashioned and out-of-the-way places, the 29th of May is still celebrated, in memory of King Charles's preservation in the oak of Boscobel, and his Restoration. The Royal Oak is also a common alehouse sign in these localities, on which the Merry Monarch is pictured peeping through the branches at the Roundheads below, looking not unlike some boy caught stealing apples, who dare not descend for fear of the owners of the fruit. Oak Apple-day is the name generally given to this rural holiday, which has taken the place of the old May-day games of our more remote ancestors ; though the Maypoles are still decorated 'and danced around on the 29th of this month, as they were in the more memorable May-days of the olden time. But Oak Apple-day is not the merry old May-day which our forefathers delighted to honour. Sweet May, as they loved to call her, is dead; for although they still decorate the May-pole with flowers, and place a garish figure in the centre of the largest garland, it is but the emblem of a dead king now, instead of the beautiful nymph which our ancestors typified, wreathed with May-buds, and scattering flowers on the earth, and which our grave Milton pictured as the flowery May, that came 'dancing from the East,' and throwing from her green lap

'The yellow cowslip and the pale primrose !'

On the 29th of May—one of the bright holidays of our boyish years—we were up and away at the first peep of dawn to the woods, to gather branches of oak and hawthorn, so that we might bring home the foliage and the May-buds as green and white and fresh as when the boughs were unbroken, and the blossoms ungathered.

Many an old man and woman, awakened out of their sleep as we went sounding our bullock-horns through the streets at that early hour, must have wished our breath as hushed as that of Cromwell or King Charles, as the horrible noise we made rang through their chambers. Some, perhaps, would awaken with a sigh, and, recalling the past, lie half dreaming of the old years that had departed, when they were also young, and rose with the dawn as we did, and went out with merry hearts a-Maying.

We were generally accompanied by a few happy girls—our sisters, or the children of our neighbours—whose mothers had gone out to bring home May-blossoms when they were girls and their husbands boys, as we then were. The girls brought home sprays of hawthorn, sheeted over with moonlight-coloured May-blossoms, which, along with wild and garden flowers, they wove into the garlands they made to hang in the oak branches, across the streets, and on the May-pole; and great rivalry there was as to which girl could make the handsomest May-garland.

If it were a dewy morning, the girls always bathed their faces in May-dew, to make them fair. It was our part to cut down and drag, or carry home huge branches of oak, with which, as Herrick says, we made 'each street a park—green, and trimmed with trees.' Beautiful did the old woods look in the golden dawn, while the dewy mist still hung about the trees, and nothing seemed awake but the early birds in all that silent land of trees. We almost recall the past with regret, as we remember how we stopped the singing of 'those little angels of the trees.' by blowing our unmelodious horns; and marvel that neither Faun nor Dryad arose to drive us from their affrighted haunts. We climbed the huge oaks like the Druids of old, and, although we had no golden pruning-hooks,

we were well supplied with saws, axes, and knives, with which we hacked and hewed at the great branches, until they came down with a loud crash, sometimes before we were aware, when we now and then came down with the boughs we had been bestriding. Very often the branches were so large, we were compelled to make a rude hurdle, on which we dragged them home; a dozen of us hauling with all our strength at the high pile of oak-boughs, careful to keep upon the road-side grass, lest the dust should soil the beautiful foliage. Yet with all our care there was the tramp of the feet of our companions beside us along the dusty highway ; and though the sun soon dried up the dew which had hung on the fresh-gathered leaves, it was no longer the sweet green oak that decorated the woods— no longer the maiden May, with the dew upon her bloom—but a dusty and tattered Doll Tear-sheet, that dragged her bemired green skirt along the street, compared with the vernal boughs and sheeted blossoms we had gathered in the golden dawn. Many a wreck of over-reaching ambition strewed the roadway from the woods, in the shape of huge oaken branches which the spoilers had cast aside, after toiling under the too weighty load until their strength was exhausted.

Publicans, and others who could afford it, would purchase the biggest branches that could be bought of poor countrymen, or others whom they sent out—for there was great rivalry as to who should have the largest bough at his door ; and wherever the monster branch was placed, that we made our head-quarters for the day, and there was heard the loudest sounding of horns. Neither the owners of the woods, gamekeepers, nor woodmen interfered with us, beyond a caution not to touch the young trees ; for lopping a few branches off the large oaks was never considered to do them any harm, nor do we remember that ever a summons was issued for trespassing on the 29th of May. Beautiful did the old towns and villages look, with their long lines of green boughs projecting from every house, while huge gaudy garlands of every colour hung suspended across the middle of the streets, which, as you looked at them in the far distance, seemed to touch one another, like lighted lamps at the bottom of a long road, forming to appearance one continuous streak of fire. Then there were flags hung out here and there, which were used at the club-feasts and Whitsuntide holidays—red, blue, yellow, purple, and white blending harmoniously with the green of the branches and their gilded oak-apples, and the garlands that were formed of every flower in season, and rainbow-coloured ribbons that went streaming out and fluttering in the wind, which set all the banners in motion, and gave a look of life to the quiet streets of these sleepy old towns. But as all is not gold that glitters, so were those gaudy-looking garlands not altogether what they appeared—for ribbons were expensive, and we were poor; so we hoarded up our blue sugar-paper, and saved clean sheets of our pink blotting-paper, with other sheets of varied colour— and these, when made up into bows, and shaped like flowers, and hung too high over head for the cheat to be discovered, might be taken for silk, as the gilded oak-apples might pass for gold; and many a real star or ribbon, which the ambitious wearers had wasted a life to obtain, were never worn nor gazed upon with greater pleasure than that afforded us by the cunning of our own hands. And in these garlands were hung the strings of birds' eggs we had collected from hundreds of nests—some of us contributing above a hundred eggs—which were strung like pearls. Those of the great hawks, carrion crows, rooks, magpies, and such like, in the centre, and dwindling—

'Fine by degrees, and beautifully less,'

to the eggs of the tiny wren, which are not larger than a good-sized pea. No doubt it is as cruel to rob birds'-nests as it is to sack cities; but as generals must have spoil for their soldiers, so we believed we could not have garlands without plundering the homes of our sweet singing-birds, to celebrate the 29th of May. Tired enough at night we were, through having risen so early, and pacing about all day long; and sore and swollen were our lips, through blowing our horns so many hours; and yet these rural holidays bring back pleasant memories—for time might be worse misspent than in thus celebrating the 29th of May.   T. M.

Cavalier Claims.

The dispensers of patronage under the Restoration had no enviable office. The entry of Charles II. into his kingdom was no sooner known, than all who had any claim, however slight, upon royal consideration, hastened to exercise the right of petition. Ignoring the Convention of Breda, by which the king bound himself to respect the *status quo* as far as possible, the nobility and gentry sought to recover their alienated estates, clergymen prayed to be reinstated in the pulpits from which they had been ejected, and old placeholders demanded the removal of those who had pushed them from their official stools. Secretary Nicholas was overwhelmed with claims on account of risks run, sufferings endured, goods supplied, and money advanced on behalf of the good cause; petitions which might have been endorsed, like that of the captain who entreated the wherewithal to supply his wants and pay his debts, 'The king says he cannot grant anything in this kind till his own estates be better settled.'

The *Calendar of State Papers* for the year 1660 is little else than a list of royalist grievances, for the bulk of documents to which it forms an index are cavalier petitions. As might be expected, it is rather monotonous reading; still, some interesting and curious details may be gathered from its pages. The first petition preserved therein is that of twenty officers of the Marquis of Hertford's Sherborne troop, who seek to be made partakers of the universal joy by receiving some provision for the remainder of their days; 'the late king' having promised that they should have the same pay as long as they lived.' The gallant twenty seem to have thought, with Macbeth, that if a thing was to be done, it were well it were done quickly, for their petition is

dated the 29th of May. It is true the numeral is supplied by Mrs Green, but even giving them the benefit of the doubt, it is evident that the appeal must have been presented within three days of Charles II.'s ascension to the throne. If that monarch had endorsed all the promises of his father, he would have made some curious appointments; a quartermaster of artillery actually applies for the office of king's painter, the patron of Vandyke 'having promised him the office on seeing a cannon painted by him when he came with the artillery after the taking of Hawksby House.' Another artillery officer, Colonel Dudley, puts forth somewhat stronger claims for reward, having lost £2000 and an estate of £200 a-year, had his sick wife turned out of doors, his men taken, 'one of them, Major Harcourt, being miserably burned with matches, and himself stripped and carried in scorn to Worcester, which he had fortified as general of artillery, where he was kept under double guard; but escaped, and being pursued, he took to the trees in the daytime, and travelled in the night till he got to London; was retaken, brought before the Committee of Insurrection, sent to the gatehouse, and sentenced to be shot; but escaped with Sir H. Bates and ten others during sermontime; lived three weeks in an enemy's haymow, went on crutches to Bristol, and escaped.' George Paterick asks a place in his majesty's barge, having served the late king sixteen years by sea and land; been often imprisoned, twice tried for his life, and three times banished the river, and forbidden to ply as a waterman. One soldier solicits compensation for fifteen wounds received at Edgehill, and another for his sufferings after Worcester fight, when 'the barbarous soldiers of the grand rebel, Cromwell, hung him on a tree till they thought him dead.' The Cromwellian system of colonization is aptly illustrated by the petition of Lieut.-Col. Hunt, praying his majesty to order the return of thirty soldiers taken prisoners at Salisbury, 'who were sold as slaves in Barbadoes;' and by that of John Fowler, captain of pioneers at Worcester, 'sent by the rebels to the West Indies as a present to the barbarous people there, *which penalty he underwent with satisfaction and content*.' The evil case to which the exiled king had been reduced is exemplified by the complaint of 'his majesty's regiment of guards in Flanders,' that they had not received a penny for six months, and were compelled to leave officers in prison for their debts, before they could march to their winter quarters at Namur, where their credit was so bad, that the officers had to sell their clothes, 'some even to their last shirt,' to procure necessaries.

The brief abstracts of the memorials of less active partisans speak even more eloquently of the misery wrought by civil strife. Thomas Freebody solicits admission among the poor knights of Windsor, having been imprisoned seven times, banished twice, and compelled on three occasions to find sureties for a thousand pounds. James Towers was forced, on account of his loyalty, to throw dice for his life; and, winning the cast, was banished. Thomas Holyoke, a clergyman, saw his aged father forced from his habitation, his mother beaten so that her death was hastened, his servant killed, while he was deprived of property bringing in £300 a-year, and obliged to live on the charity of commiserating friends. Another clergyman recounts how he suffered imprisonment for three years, and was twice corporally punished for preaching against rebellion and using the Common Prayer-book. Sir Edward Pierce, advocate at Doctors' Commons, followed Charles I. to York as judge marshal of the army, which he augmented by a regiment of horse. He lost thereby his property, his profession, and his books; 'was decimated and imprisoned, yet wrote and published at much danger and expense many things very serviceable to king and church.' Abraham Dowcett supplied the late king with pen and ink, at hazard of his life conveyed letters between him and his queen, and afterwards plotted his escape from Carisbrook Castle, for which he was imprisoned and his property sequestrated. The brothers Samburne seem to have earned the commissionership of excise, for which they petition. After being exiled for executing several commissions on behalf of both the king and his father, and spent £25,000 in supplying war material to their armies, they transmitted letters for the members of the royal family, 'when no one else would sail;' and when Charles II. arrived at Rouen, after the battle of Worcester, James Samburne was the only person to whom he made himself known, or whom he would entrust with dispatches to the queen-mother. The Samburnes further assisted Charles by prevailing upon a Mr Scott to advance him 'money for Paris,' and religiously preserved a portion of his majesty's disguise as a precious relic.

Lady petitioners muster strong, and for the most part show good cause why their prayers should be granted. Some of them afford remarkable proof of what women will do and suffer for a cause with which they sympathize. Katherine de Luke asks for the lease of certain waste lands near Yarmouth; she served Charles I. by carrying letters when none else durst run the risk, for which she was sent to Bridewell, and whipped every other day, burnt with lighted matches, and otherwise tortured to make her betray her trust. Her husband died of his wounds, her son was sold to slavery, and she herself obliged to live abroad for sixteen years. Elizabeth Cary, an aged widow, was imprisoned in Windsor Castle, Newgate, Bridewell, the Bishop of London's house, and lastly in the Mews, at the time of the late king's martyrdom, for peculiar service in carrying his majesty's gracious proclamation and declaration from Oxford to London. She had her back broken at Henley-on-Thames, where a gibbet was erected for her execution. This extremity she escaped, and succeeded in finding shelter in her own county. Her loyalty was rewarded by a pension of £40 a-year. Elizabeth Pinckney, who buried her husband after Reading fight, seeks the continuation of an annuity of £20 he had earned by thirty-six years' service. She complains that since 1643 she had waited on all parliaments for justice, 'but they have imprisoned her, beaten her with whips, kicked, pulled, and torn her, till shame was cried upon them.' Ann Dartigueran says her father lost his life in the cause, leaving her nothing but sadness to inherit. Mrs Mary Graves certainly deserved well of the restored monarch; for when he made his last attempt to recover his crown by force, she sent him twelve horses, ten furnished with men and money, and two empty, on one of which the king rode at Worcester, escaping from the field on the other. This service cost the loyal lady her liberty, an estate of £600 a-year, and two thousand pounds' worth of personal property. Nothing daunted, she prevailed upon her husband to let her send provisions from Ireland to Chester in aid of Sir George Booth's rising, for which she was again imprisoned, and her remaining property seized. In a second appeal, Mrs Graves says she sent one Francis Yates to conduct his majesty out of Worcester to Whitehaven, for doing which he was hanged; and she had been obliged to maintain his widow and five children ever since. To this petition is appended a paper, signed by Richard Penderel, certifying that Edward Martin was tenant of White Ladies, where Charles hid himself for a time, disguised in a suit of his host; and further, that Francis Yates's wife was the first person to give the fugitive prince any food after the defeat, which he ate in a wood, upon a blanket. Charles afterwards borrowed ten shillings of Yates himself, 'for a present necessity,' and 'was pleased to take his bill out of his hand and kept it in his own, the better to avoid suspicion;' Yates seeing his charge safe from Boscobel to Mosely, a service which, as is stated above, cost the faithful yeoman his life.

After such stories of suffering and devotion, one has no sympathy to spare for Robert Thomas, whose principal claim upon royal consideration seems to be his having lost his mother, 'who was his majesty's seamstress from his birth;' or for one Maddox, who seeks a re-appointment as tailor to the crown, excusing himself for not waiting upon his customer for twelve years by a vague assertion of being prevented by 'sufferings for his loyalty.' An old man of ninety-five asks to be restored to his post of cormorant-keeper, an office conferred on him by James I.; and another claims favour for 'having served his majesty in his young days as keeper of his batoons, paumes, tennis-shoes, and ankle-socks.' E. Fawcett, too, who taught his majesty to shoot with the long-bow, 'an exercise honoured by kings and maintained by statutes,' solicits and obtains the office of keeper of the long-bows; having in anticipation provided four of the late king's bows, with all necessaries, for the use of his majesty and his brothers, when they shall be inclined to practise the ancient art. Edward Harrison, describing himself as 70 years old, and the father of twenty-one children, encloses a certificate from the Company of Embroiderers, to the effect that he is the ablest workman living. He wishes to be re-appointed embroiderer to the king, having filled that situation under James, and having preserved the king's best cloth of state and his rich carpet embroidered in pearls from being cut in pieces and burnt, and restored them with other goods to his majesty.

While Robert Chamberlain prays for a mark of

favour before going to his grave, being 110 years of age, Walter Braems asks for a collectorship of customs, for ' being fetched out of his sick bed at fourteen years old and carried to Dover Castle, and there honoured by being the youngest prisoner in England for his majesty's service.' John Southcott, with an eye to the future, wants to be made clerk of the green cloth to his majesty's children, ' when he shall have issue ; ' and Squire Beverton, Mayor of Canterbury, is encouraged to beg a receivership because his majesty was pleased to acknowledge his loyalty, on his entry into Canterbury, ' with gracious smiles and expressions.'

To have satisfied the many claims put forward by those who had espoused the royal cause, Charles II. needed to have possessed the wealth of a Lydian monarch and the patronage of an American president. As it was, he was compelled to turn a deaf ear to most suppliants, at the risk of their complaining, as one unsuccessful petitioner does, that ' those who are loyal have little encouragement, being deprived of the benefit of the law ; destitute of all favours, countenances, and respect ; and left as a scorn to those who have basely abused them.'

INEDITED AUTOGRAPHS.
SARAH DUCHESS OF MARLBOROUGH.

Sarah Jennings, the wife of the great general, John Duke of Marlborough, has been painted in terms far too black by Lord Macaulay, a fact easily to be accounted for by her coming into opposition to his lordship's hero, King William.

AUTOGRAPH OF THE DUCHESS OF MARLBOROUGH.

Her worst fault was her imperious temper. It was her destiny to become the intimate friend of King James's second daughter, the Princess Anne, a gentle and timid woman of limited understanding, who, in her public career, felt the necessity of a strong-minded female friend to lean upon. There is something very conciliating in the account her grace gives of the commencement of her friendship with the princess. Anne justly deemed a feeling of equality necessary for friendship. ' She grew uneasy to be treated by me with the form and ceremony due to her rank ; nor could she hear from me the sound of words which implied in them distance and superiority. It was this turn of mind that made her one day propose to me, that whenever I should happen to be absent from her, we might in all our letters write ourselves by feigned names, such as would import nothing of distinction of rank between us. *Morley* and *Freeman* were the names her fancy hit upon ; and she left me to choose by which of them I

would be called. My frank, open temper, naturally led me to pitch upon Freeman, and so the princess took the other ; and from this time Mrs Morley and Mrs Freeman began to converse as equals, made so by affection and friendship.'*

Through the reign of her father, when in difficulties from his wish to make her embrace the Catholic faith—through that of William and Mary, when called upon by those sovereigns, her cousin and sister, to give up her friendship with the duchess, because of the duke having become odious to them—Anne maintained her love for Mrs Freeman ; but when she became queen, a series of unfortunate circumstances led her to withdraw her attachment. The queen now disliked the duke, and another and humbler confidante, Mrs Masham, had engaged her affections. It was in vain that Sarah sought to replace herself on the old footing with Mrs Morley. She had to drink to the dregs the bitter cup of the discarded favourite.† Her narrative of this distressing crisis, and particularly of her last interview with the queen—when with tears, but in vain, she entreated to be told of any fault she had committed—can scarcely be read without a feeling of sympathy. She could not help at last telling the queen that her majesty would yet suffer for such an instance of inhumanity ; to which the only answer was, ' That will be to myself.' And then they parted, to meet no more.

She quotes a letter of her husband on the subject : ' It has always,' he says, ' been my observation in disputes, especially in that of kindness and friendship, that all reproaches, though ever so just, serve to no end but making the breach wider. I cannot help being of opinion, that, however insignificant we are, there is a power above that puts a period to our happiness or unhappiness. If anybody had told me eight years ago, that after such great success, and after you had been a faithful servant twenty-seven years, we should be obliged to seek happiness in a private life, I could not have believed that possible.'

LONG INTERMISSION.

There is a well-known anecdote of a silent man, who, riding over a bridge, turned about and asked his servant if he liked eggs, to which the servant answered, ' Yes ; ' whereupon nothing more passed till next year, when, riding over the same bridge, he turned about to his servant once more, and

---

* *An Account of the Conduct of the Dowager Duchess of Marlborough*, 1742, p. 14.

† Mrs Masham, born Abigail Hill, was full cousin to the Duchess, but originally in penurious circumstances. She had been introduced by Sarah herself to the service in which she was ultimately able to supplant her patroness. These circumstances must have feathered the dart that went to the heart of the proud lady. From the notoriety of Mrs Masham's rise in the position of a waiting-woman, seems to have come the practice of Swift, Fielding, and other wits in using Abigail as a term for a lady's maid.

said, ' How ? ' to which the instant answer was, ' Poached, sir.' Even this sinks, as an example of long intermission of discourse, beside an anecdote of a minister of Campsie, near Glasgow. It is stated that the worthy pastor, whose name was Archibald Denniston, was put out of his charge in 1655, and not replaced till after the Restoration. He had, before leaving his charge, begun a discourse, and finished the first head. At his return in 1661, he took up the second, calmly introducing it with the remark that ' the times were altered, but the doctrines of the gospel were always the same.'*

In the newspapers of July 1862, there appeared a paragraph which throws even the minister of Campsie's interrupted sermon into the shade. It was as follows : ' At the moment of the destruction of Pompeii by an eruption of Mount Vesuvius, A.D. 79, a theatrical representation was being given in the Amphitheatre. A speculator, named Langini, taking advantage of that historical reminiscence, has just constructed a theatre on the ruins of Pompeii ; and the opening of which new theatre he announces in the following terms : —" After a lapse of 1800 years, the theatre of the city will be re-opened with *La Figlia del Reggimento*. I solicit from the nobility and gentry a continuance of the favour constantly bestowed on my predecessor, Marcus Quintus Martius ; and beg to assure them that I shall make every effort to equal the rare qualities he displayed during his management." '

MAY 30.

St Felix, pope and martyr, 274. St Maguil, recluse in Picardy, about 685. St Walstan, farm labourer at Taverham in Norfolk, devoted to God, 1016. St Ferdinand III., first king of Castile and Leon in union, 1252.

Born.—Peter the Great, of Russia, 1672, *Moscow ;* Henry Viscount Sidmouth, statesman, 1757, *Reading ;* John Charles, third Earl Spencer, Chancellor of the Exchequer (1830-4), 1782 ; Samuel Spalding, writer in physiology, theory of morals, and biblical criticism, 1807, *London.*

Died.—King Arthur, 542 ; St Hubert, 727, *Ardennes ;* Jerome of Prague, religious reformer, burnt at *Constance,* 1416 ; Joan d'Arc, burnt at *Rouen,* 1431 ; Charles IX. of France, 1574, *Vincennes ;* Peter Paul Rubens, painter, 1640 ; Charles Montagu, Earl of Halifax, statesman, 1715 ; Alexander Pope, poet, 1744, *Twickenham ;* Elizabeth Elstob, learned in Anglo-Saxon, 1756, *Bulstrode ;* Voltaire, 1778, *Paris.*

KING ARTHUR.

According to British story, at the time when the Saxons were ravaging our island, but had not yet made themselves masters of it, the Britons were ruled by a wise and valiant king, named Uther Pendragon. Among the most distinguished of Uther's nobles was Gorlois Duke of Cornwall, whose wife Igerna was a woman of surpassing beauty. Once, when King Uther was as usual holding his royal feast of Easter, Gorlois attended with his lady ; and the king, who had

not seen her before, immediately fell in love with her, and manifested his passion so openly, that Gorlois took away his wife abruptly, and went home with her to Cornwall without asking for Uther's leave. The latter, in great anger, led an army into Cornwall to punish his offending vassal, who, conscious of his inability to resist the king in the field, shut up his wife in the impregnable castle of Tintagel, while he took shelter in another castle, where he was immediately besieged by the formidable Uther Pendragon. During the siege, Uther, with the assistance of his magician, Merlin, obtained access to the beautiful Igerna in the same manner as Jupiter approached Alcmena, namely, by assuming the form of her husband ; the consequence was the birth of the child who was destined to be the Hercules of the Britons, and who when born was named Arthur. In the sequel, Gorlois was killed, and then Uther married the widow.

Such, according to Geoffrey of Monmouth, and the so-called British historians, was the origin of King Arthur. On the death of Uther, Arthur was unanimously chosen to succeed him, and was crowned at Silchester. No sooner had he ascended the throne than he was called upon to war against the Saxons, who, under a new chief named Colgrin, had united with the Picts and Scots, and made themselves masters of the northern parts of the island. With the assistance of his nephew, Hoel King of Brittany, Arthur overcame the Anglo-Saxons, and made them promise to leave the island. But, instead of going to their own country, they only sailed round the coasts, and landing again at Totness, laid waste the country with fire and sword till they reached the city of Bath, which they besieged. Arthur, leaving his nephew Hoel sick at Alcluyd (Dumbarton), hastened southward to encounter the invaders, and defeated them with great slaughter at a place which is called in the story Mount Badon. Having thus crushed the Saxons, Arthur returned to Alcluyd, and soon reduced the Picts and Scots to such a condition, that they sought shelter in the islands in Loch Lomond, and there made their peace with him. Not content with these successes, Arthur next conquered Ireland, Iceland, Gothland, and the Orcades ; to which he afterwards added Norway and Denmark, placing over them all tributary kings chosen from among his own chieftains. Next he turned his arms against Gaul, which also he subdued, having defeated and slain its governor Flollo in single combat, under the walls of Paris. The conquest of the whole of Gaul occupied nine years, at the end of which Arthur returned to Paris, and there distributed the conquered provinces among his followers.

Arthur was now in the zenith of his power, and on his return to his native land he made a proud display of his greatness, by calling to a great council at Caerleon all these tributary princes, and there in great pomp he was crowned again. Before the festivities were ended, an unexpected occurrence turned the thoughts of the assembled princes to new adventures. Twelve aged men arrived as ambassadors from Lucius Tiberius, the 'procurator' of the republic of

---

* The fact is stated on the credit of tradition in the Statistical Account of the parish, 1795.

Rome, bearing a letter by which King Arthur was summoned in peremptory language to restore to Rome the provinces which he had unjustly usurped on the Continent, and also to pay the tribute which Britain had formerly paid to the Imperial power. A great council was immediately held, and it was resolved at once to retort by demanding tribute of Rome, and to march an army immediately into Italy, to subdue the Imperial city. Arthur next entrusted the government of Britain to his nephew Modred and his queen Guanhumara, and then embarked at Southampton for the Continent. They landed near Mont St Michael, where Arthur slew a Spanish giant, who had carried away Helena, the niece of Hoel of Brittany. The army of the Britons now proceeded on their march, and soon encountered the Romans, who had advanced into Gaul to meet them; but who, after much fighting and great slaughter, were driven out of the country, with the loss of their commander, Lucius Tiberius, who was slain by Arthur's nephew, Walgan, the Gawain of later romance. At the approach of the following spring, King Arthur began his march to Rome, but as he was beginning to pass the Alps he was arrested by disastrous news from Britain.

Modred, who had been left there as regent during the absence of the king, conspired with the queen, whom he married, and usurped the crown; and he had called in a new horde of Saxons to support him in his usurpation. On hearing of these events, Arthur divided his forces into two armies, one of which he left in Gaul, under the command of Hoel of Brittany, while with the other he passed over to Britain, and landed at Rutupiæ, or Richborough, in Kent, where Modred awaited them with a powerful army. Although Arthur lost a great number of his best men, and among the rest his nephew Walgan, Modred was defeated and put to flight, and he was only able to rally his troops when he reached Winchester. When the news of this defeat reached the queen, who was in York, she fled to Caerleon, and took refuge in a nunnery, where she resolved to pass the remainder of her life in penitence. Arthur followed his nephew to Winchester, and there defeated him in a second battle; but Modred escaped again, and made his retreat towards Cornwall. He was overtaken, and finally defeated in a third battle, which was far more obstinate and fatal than those which preceded. Modred was slain, and King Arthur himself was mortally wounded. They carried him to the Isle of Avallon (Glastonbury), to be cured of his wounds; but all the efforts of the physicians were vain, and he died and was buried there, Geoffrey of Monmouth says, in the year 542. Before his death, he resigned the crown to his kinsman Constantine.

Such is an outline of the fabulous history of King Arthur, as it is given by the earliest narrator, Geoffrey of Monmouth, who wrote in the year 1147. The numerous stories of King Arthur, and his knights of the round table, which now swell out the story, are the works of the romance writers of later periods. There was a time when every writer or reader of British history was expected to put entire faith in this narra-

tive; but that faith has gradually diminished, until it has become a matter of serious doubt whether such a personage ever existed. There are few indeed now who take Geoffrey of Monmouth's history for anything but fable. The name of a King Arthur was certainly not known to any chroniclers in this country before the Norman period, and Giraldus Cambrensis, towards the end of the twelfth century, bears testimony to the fact that Geoffrey's stories were not Welsh. From different circumstances connected with their publication, it seems probable that they were derived from Brittany, and one of the opinions regarding them is that Arthur may have been a personage in the mythic history of the Bretons. However, be this as it may, the history of King Arthur has become an important part of our literature; and as it sinks lower in the estimate of the historian, it seems to have become more popular than ever, and to have increased in favour with the poet. In proof of this, we need only point to Tennyson and Bulwer.

JOAN D'ARC.

When Horace Walpole wished to amuse his father by reading a historical work to him, the aged statesman, 'hackneyed in the ways of men,' exclaimed—'Anything but history; that must be false.' Dr Johnson, according to Boswell, held a somewhat similar opinion; and Gibbon, alluding to the fallacies of history, said, 'the spectators of events knew too little, the actors were too deeply interested, to speak the real truth.' The French heroine affords a remarkable instance of historic uncertainty. Historians, one copying the words of another, assert she was burned at Rouen, in 1431; while documentary evidence of the most authentic character, completely negativing the story of her being burned, shews she was alive, and happily married, several years after the period alleged to be that of her execution.

Many of these documents are in the registry of the city of Mentz, and prove she came thither in 1436. The magistrates, to make sure that she was not an impostor, sent for her brothers, Pierre and Jean, who at once recognised her. Several entries in the city records enumerate the presents, with the names of the donors, that were given to her on the occasion of her marriage with the Chevalier d'Armoise, and even the marriage contract between Robert d'Armoise, Knight, and Jeanne d'Arc, la Pucelle d'Orleans, has been discovered.

The archives of the city of Orleans contain important evidence on this subject. In the treasurer's accounts for 1435, there is an entry of eleven francs and eight sous paid to messengers who had brought letters from 'Jeanne, la Pucelle.' Under the date of 1436, there is another entry of twelve livres paid to Jean de Lys, brother of 'Jeanne, la Pucelle,' that he might go and see her. The King of France ennobled Joan's family, giving them the appellation of de Lys, derived from the *fleur de lys*, on account of her services to the state; and the entry in the Orleans records corresponds with and corroborates the one in the registry of Mentz, which states that the magistrates of the latter city sent for her brothers to identify her. These totally independent sources of evidence confirm each other in a still more remarkable manner. In the treasurer's accounts of Orleans for the year 1439, there are entries of various sums expended for wine, banquets, and public rejoicings, on the occasion of Robert d'Armoise and Jeanne, his wife, visiting that city. Also a memorandum that the council, after mature deliberation, had presented to Jeanne d'Armoise the sum of 210 livres, for the services rendered by her during the siege of the said city of Orleans. There are several other documents, of equally unquestionable authority, confirming those already quoted here; and the only answer made to them by persons who insist that Joan was burned is, that they are utterly unexplainable.

It has been urged, however, that Dame d'Armoise was an impostor; but if she were, why did the brothers of the real Joan recognise and identify her? Admitting that they did, for the purpose of profiting by the fraud, how could the citizens of Orleans, who knew her so well, and fought side by side with her during the memorable siege, allow themselves to be so grossly deceived? The idea that Joan was not burned, but another criminal substituted for her, was so prevalent at the period, that there are accounts of several impostors who assumed to be her, and of their detection and punishment; but we never hear of the Dame d'Armoise having been punished.

In fine, there are many more arguments in favour of the opinion that Joan was not burned, which need not be entered into here. The French antiquaries, best qualified to form a correct opinion on the subject, believe that she was not burned, but kept in prison until after the Duke of Bedford's death, in 1435, and then liberated; and so we may leave the question—a very pretty puzzle as it stands.

POPE'S GARDEN.

If we could always discover the personal tastes and pleasurable pursuits of authors, we should find these the best of comments on their literary productions. The outline of our life is generally the work of circumstance, and much of the filling-in is done after an acquired manner; but the fancies a man indulges when he gives the reins to his natural disposition are the clearest index of his mind.

No one will deny to Pope excellence of a certain sort. Though, in his verse, we look in vain for the spontaneous and elegant simplicity of nature, yet, in polish and finish, and artificial skill, he stands unrivalled among English poets. And apropos of this ought to be noted how much time and skill he expended on his garden. Next to his mother and his fame, this he loved best. He altered it and trimmed it like a favourite poem, and was never satisfied he had done enough to adorn it. Himself a sad slip of nature, with a large endowment of sensitiveness and love of admiration, he was never very anxious to appear in public—indeed, had he wished, being such an invalid as he was, it would have been out of his power; so he settled at Twicken-

ham, where Lord Bacon and many other literary celebrities had lived before him, and adorned his moderate acres with the graces of artificial elegance. Here, during many long years, he cherished his good mother—and here, when she died, he built a tomb, and planted mournful cypress; here he penned and planned, with his intimate friends, deep designs to overthrow his enemies, and to astonish the world, or listened to philosophy for the use of his *Essay on Man*, or clipped and filed his elegant lines and sharp-toothed satires.

When we read of Pope's delightful little sanctum, when we hear Walpole describing 'the retiring and again assembling shades, the dusky groves, the larger lawn, and the solemnity of the termination at the cypresses that led up to his mother's tomb,' we almost wonder that so much envy and spite, and filthiness and bitter hatred, could there find a hiding-place. Such hostility did the publication of the *Dunciad*—in which he lashed unmercifully all his literary foes, and many who had given him no cause of offence—bring upon the reckless satirist, that his sanctuary, it is hinted, might for a short time have been considered a prison. He was threatened with a cudgelling, and afraid to venture forth. His old friends and new enemies, Lady Mary Montagu and Lord Hervey, seized upon this opportunity of annoying him, and jointly produced a pamphlet, of which the following was the title: *A Pop upon Pope; or a true and faithful account of a late horrid and barbarous whipping, committed on the body of Sawney Pope, poet, as he was innocently walking in Ham Walks, near the River Thames, meditating verses for the good of the public. Supposed to have been done by two evil-disposed persons, out of spite and revenge for a harmless lampoon which the said poet had writ upon them.* So sensitive was Pope, that believing this fabulous incident would find people to credit it, he inserted in the *Daily Post*, June 14, 1728, a contradiction:—' Whereas there has been a scandalous paper cried aloud about the streets, under the title of a *Pop upon Pope*, insinuating that I was whipped in Ham Walks on Thursday last; this is to give notice, that I did not stir out of my house at Twickenham on that day, and the same is a malicious and ill-grounded report.—A. P.'

That part of Pope's garden which has always excited the greatest curiosity was the grotto and subterraneous passage which he made.* Pope himself describes them thus fully in 1725 :—' I have put my last hand to my works of this kind, in happily finishing the subterraneous way and grotto. I there formed a spring of the clearest water, which falls in a perpetual rill that echoes through the cavern day and night. From the River Thames you see through my arch up a walk of the wilderness to a kind of open temple, wholly

* It has never been properly explained that Pope's villa was a *roadside house*, backed by a lawn verging on the Thames, that the garden was a neighbouring piece of ground on the *opposite* side of the way, and that the grotto and subterranean passage were formed *under the road*, as a means of connecting the aforesaid lawn with the garden —a Cockneyish expedient to mask a vulgarizing circumstance.—*Ed.*

composed of shells in a rustic manner, and from that distance under the temple you look down through a sloping arcade of trees, and see the sails on the river passing suddenly and vanishing, as through a perspective glass. When you shut the doors of this grotto, it becomes on the instant, from a luminous room, a camera obscura ; on the walls of which all objects of the river—hills, woods, and boats—are forming a moving picture in their visible radiations ; and when you have a mind to light it up, it affords you a very different scene. It is finished with shells, interspersed with pieces of looking-glass in angular forms ; and in the ceiling is a star of the same material, at which, when a lamp (of an orbicular figure of thin alabaster) is hung in the middle, a thousand pointed rays glitter, and are reflected over the place.

'There are connected to this grotto by a narrower passage two porches, one towards the river, of smooth stones, full of light, and open ; the other towards the gardens, shadowed with trees, rough with shell, flints, and iron ore. The bottom is paved with simple pebble, as is also the adjoining walk up the wilderness to the temple, in the natural taste agreeing not ill with the little dripping murmur and the aquatic idea of the whole place. It wants nothing to complete it but a good statue with an inscription, like the beautiful antique one which you know I am so fond of :

" Hujus Nympha loci, sacri custodia fontis,
    Dormio, dum blandæ sentio murmur aquæ ;
  Parce meum, quisquis tangis cava murmura, somnum
    Rumpere, si bibas, sive lavare, tace."

" Nymph of the grot, these sacred springs I keep,
  And to the murmur of these waters sleep ;
  Ah ! spare my slumbers, gently tread the cave,
  And drink in silence, or in silence lave."

You'll think I have been very poetical in this description, but it is pretty near the truth. I wish you were here to bear testimony how little it owes to art, either the place itself or the image I give of it.'

It would be easy to draw a parallel between this grotto and the poet's mind, and instructive to compare the false taste, and eloquence, and pettiness of both. But let us rather, at this present time, hear what became of it. Dodsley, in his Cave of Pope, foreshadows its future fate :

" Then some small gem, or moss, or shining ore,
    Departing, each shall pilfer : in fond hope
  To please their friends in every distant shore,
    Boasting a relic from the cave of Pope."

The inevitable destiny came in due time. The poet's garden first disappeared. Horace Walpole writes to Horace Mann in 1760 : 'I must tell you a private woe that has happened to me in my neighbourhood. Sir William Stanhope bought Pope's house and garden. The former was so small and bad, one could not avoid pardoning his hollowing out that fragment of the rock of Parnassus into habitable chambers ; but— would you believe it?—he has cut down the sacred groves themselves. In short, it was a little bit of ground of five acres, enclosed with three lanes, and seeing nothing. Pope had twisted and twirled, and rhymed and harmonized this, till it

appeared two or three sweet little lawns opening and opening beyond one another, and the whole surrounded with thick, impenetrable woods. Sir William, by advice of his son-in-law, Mr Ellis, has hacked and hewed these groves, wriggled a winding gravel walk through them, with an edging of shrubs, in what they call modern taste, and, in short, desired the three lanes to walk in again ; and now is forced to shut them out again by a wall, for there was not a Muse could walk there but she was spied by every country fellow that went by with a pipe in his mouth.'

Pope's house itself was pulled down by Lady Howe (who purchased it in 1807), in order that she might be rid of the endless stream of pilgrims.

THE SHREWSBURY SHOW.

Three remarkable examples of the pageantry of the Middle Ages, in rather distant parts of England, remain at present as the only existing representatives of this particular branch of mediæval manners—the Preston Guild, the festival of the Lady Godiva at Coventry, and the Shrewsbury Show. Attempts have recently been made in each of these cases to revive customs which had already lost much of their ancient character, and which appeared to be becoming obsolete ; but probably with only temporary success. It is not, indeed, easy, through the great changes of society, to make permanent customs which belong exclusively to the past. The municipal system of the Middle Ages, and the local power and influence of the guild, which alone supported these customs, have themselves passed away.

As in other old towns, the guilds or trading corporations of Shrewsbury were numerous, and had no doubt existed from an early period—all these fraternities or companies were in existence long before they were incorporated. The guilds of the town of Shrewsbury presented one peculiarity which, as far as we know, did not exist elsewhere. On the southern side of the town, separated from it by the river, lies a large space of high ground called Kingsland, probably because in early times it belonged to the kings of Mercia. At a rather remote period, the exact date of which appears not to be known, this piece of ground came into the possession of the corporation ; and it has furnished during many ages a delightful promenade to the inhabitants, pleasant by its healthful air and by the beautiful views it presents on all sides. It was on this spot that the Shrewsbury guilds held their great annual festivities, and hither they directed the annual procession which, as in other places, was held about the period of the feast of Corpus Christi. The day of the Shrewsbury Show, which appears from records of the reign of Henry VI. to have then been held 'time out of mind,' is the second Monday after Trinity Sunday. At some period, which also is not very clearly known, portions of land were distributed to the different guilds, who built upon them their halls, or, as they called them, harbours. The word harbour meant properly a place of entertainment, but it is one of the peculiarities of the local dialects on the borders of Wales to neglect the *h*, and these buildings are now always called arbours. Seven of these arbours are, we believe, still left. They are halls built chiefly of wood, each appropriated to a particular guild, and furnished with a large table (or tables) and benches, on which the members of the guild feasted at the annual festival, and probably on other occasions. Other buildings, sometimes of brick, were attached to the hall, for people who had the care of the place, and a court or space of ground round, generally rectangular, was surrounded by a hedge and a ditch, with an entrance gateway more or less ornamented. These halls appear to have been first built after the restoration of Charles II. The first of which there is any account was that of the Tailors, of which there is the following notice in account books of the Tailors' Company for the year 1661.

Pd. for making ye harbour on Kingsland　02 11 10
Pd. for seates...　　...　　...　　...　　00 10 02
Pd. for cutting ye bryars and ditching, and
　spent yt day　...　　...　　...　　00 01 04

Thus the building of the Tailors' arbour cost the sum total of £3, 3s. 4d. It was of wood, and underwent various repairs, and perhaps received additions during the following years; and it is still standing, though in a dilapidated condition. Our cut represents the entrance gateway as it now appears, and the bridge over the ditch

THE TAILORS' ARBOUR.

which surrounds it. The ornamental part above, on which are carved the arms of the Tailors' Company, was erected in 1669, at an expense of £1, 10s., as we learn from the same books.

Our second cut will give a better general notion of the arrangement of these buildings. It is the Shoemakers' arbour, the best preserved and most interesting of them all. The hall of timber is seen within the enclosure; the upper part is open-work, which admits light into the interior.

At the back of it is a small brick house, no doubt more modern than the arbour itself. The gateway, which is much more handsome than usual, and is built of stone, bears the date of 1679, and the initials, H. P. and E. A., of the wardens of the Shoemakers' guild at that time. At the sides of the arms of the company are two now sadly-mutilated statues of the patron saints of the Shoemakers, Crispin and Crispinianus, and on the square tablet below the following rather naïve rhymes, now nearly effaced, were inscribed:

'We are but images of stonne,
　Doe us noe harme, we can doe nonne.'

The Shearmen's Company (or Clothworkers) had a large tree in their enclosure, with seats ingeniously fixed among the branches, to which those who liked mounted to carouse, while the less venturesome members of the fraternity contented themselves with feasting below.

Shrewsbury Show has been in former times looked forward to yearly by the inhabitants in general as a day of great enjoyment, although at present it is only enjoyment to the lower orders. Each company marched in their livery, with a pageant in front, preceded by their minstrels or band of music. The pageants were prepared with great labour and expense, the costume, &c., being carefully preserved from year to year. The choice of the subject for the pageant for each guild seems in some cases to have been rather arbitrary—at least during the period of which we have any account of them; and most of them are doubtless entirely changed from the mediæval pageants. Thus the pageant of the Shearmen represented sometimes King Edward VI., and at others Bishop Blaise. The Shoemakers have always been faithful to their patron saints, Crispin and Crispinianus. The Tailors have had at different times a queen, understood to represent Queen Elizabeth; two knights, carrying drawn swords; or Adam and Eve, the two latter dressed in aprons of leaves sewed together. The last of these only receive any explanation—the Tailors looked upon Adam and Eve as the first who exercised their craft. The Butchers had as their pageant a personage called the Knight of the Cleaver, who carried as his distinguishing badge an axe or cleaver, and was followed by a number of boys decked gaily with ribbons, and brandishing fencing-swords, who were called his Fencers. The Barber-Chirurgeons and Weavers united in one body, and had for their pageant what is described as 'Catherine working a spinning-wheel,' which was no doubt intended to represent St Catherine and her wheel, which was anything but a spinning-wheel. The Bricklayers, Carpenters, and Joiners had adopted for their pageant King Henry VIII.; but some years ago they deserted the bluff king temporarily for a character called 'Jack Bishop.' The Hatters and Cabinetmakers, for some reason unknown, selected as their pageant an Indian chief, who was to ride on horseback brandishing a spear. The Bakers seem to have studied Latin sufficiently deep to have learnt that *sine Cerere friget Venus*, and they adopted the two goddesses Venus and Ceres; sometimes giving one and sometimes the other. The pageant of the Skinners and Glovers was a figure of a stag, accompanied by huntsmen blowing horns. The Smiths had Vulcan, whom they clothed in complete armour, giving him two attendants, armed with blunderbusses, which they occasionally discharged, to the great delight of the mob. The Saddlers have a horse fully caparisoned, and led by a jockey. The united Printers, Painters, and others, have of late years adopted as their pageant Peter Paul Rubens. It was probably this grouping together of the guilds, in order to distinguish the number of pageants, which has caused the arbitrary selection of new subjects. On some of the late occasions, a new personage was placed at the head of the procession to represent King Henry II., because he granted the first charter to the town.

In the forenoon of the day of the show, the performers usually muster in the court of the castle, and then go to assemble in the market-square, there to be marshalled for the procession. On the occasion at which we were present, in the summer of 1860, the number of pageants was reduced to seven. First came the pageant of the Shoemakers—Crispin, in a bright new leathern doublet, and his martial companion, also in a new suit, both on horseback. Next came a pageant of Cupid and a stag, with what may be supposed to have been intended for his mother, Venus, in a handsome car, raised on a platform drawn by four white horses—the pageant of the Tailors, Drapers, and Skinners. The third pageant was the Knight of the Cleaver, who also had a new suit, and who represented on this

THE SHOEMAKERS' ARBOUR.

occasion the Butchers and Tanners. Henry VIII., his personage padded out to very portly dimensions, in very dashing costume, who might almost have been taken by his swagger for the immortal Falstaff, and carrying a short staff or sceptre in his hand, rode next, as the head of the Bricklayers, Carpenters, and Joiners. Then came the Indian chief, the pageant of the Cabinet-makers, Hatters, and others; followed by Vulcan, representing the Smiths, and who, as usual, was equipped in complete armour; and Queen Catherine (?), as the representative of the Flax-dressers and Thread-manufacturers. The showy ranks of the trades of former times had dwindled into small parties of working men,

706

who marched two and two after each pageant, without costume, or only distinguished by a ribbon; each, however, preceded by a rather substantial band; and the fact that all these bands were in immediate hearing of each other, and all playing at the same time, and not together, will give a notion of the uproar which the whole created. The procession started soon after midday, and the confusion was increased by the sudden fall of a shower of rain just at that moment; whereupon Cupid was rendered not a bit more picturesque by having a great-coat thrown over his shoulders, while both he and Venus took shelter under an umbrella. In this manner the procession turned the High Street, and proceeded along Pride Hill and Castle Street round the Castle end of the town—back, and by way of Dogpole and Wylecop, over the English Bridge into the Abbey Foregate. In the course of this perambulation they made many halts, and frequently partook of beer; so that when, after making the circuit of the Abbey Church, they returned over the English Bridge into the town, the procession had lost most of the order which it had observed at starting—whoever represented the guilds had quitted their ranks, and the principal personages were evidently already much the worse for wear. Venus looked sleepy, and Queen Catherine had so far lost all the little dignity she had ever possessed, that she seemed to have a permanent inclination to slip from her horse; while King Henry, look-

ing more arrogant than ever, brandished his sceptre with so little discretion, that an occasional blow on his horse's head caused him every now and then to be nearly ejected from his seat. At the Abbey Foregate the greater part of the crowd deserted, and took the shortest way to Kingsland, while the procession, much more slenderly escorted, returned along the High Street, and proceeded by way of Mardol over the Welsh Bridge, and reached Kingsland through the other suburb of Frankwell.

Our view of the procession, taken from a photograph by a very skilful amateur, made four or five years before the date of the one we have just described, represents it returning disordered and straggling over the English Bridge, and just entering the Wylecop. It will be seen that the

THE PROCESSION.

guildmen who formed anything like procession have disappeared, and that most of the mob has departed to Kingsland. The man on foot with his rod is the Marshal, who marched in advance of the procession. Behind him comes Henry VIII., with an unmistakable air of weariness, and probably of beer. Behind him are Crispin and Crispinianus, on horseback. Then comes Cupid's car, the god of love seated between two dames, an arrangement which we are unable to explain; a little further we see Vulcan in his suit of armour. Even the musicians are here no longer visible.

Formerly, the different guilds, who assembled in considerable numbers, each gave a collation in

their particular arbour; and the mayor and corporation proceeded in ceremony and on horseback from the town to Kingsland, and there visited the different arbours in succession. They were expected to partake in the collation of each, so that the labour in the way of eating was then very considerable. This part of the custom has long been laid aside, and the corporation of Shrewsbury now takes no part personally in the celebration, which is chiefly a speculation among those who profit by it, supported by a few who are zealous for the preservation of old customs. We may form some idea of the style in which the procession was got up in the latter part of the seventeenth century from the items of the expenses of the Tailors' guild in the 'Show' of the year 1687, collected from the records of that guild by Mr Henry Pidgeon, a very intelligent antiquary of Shrewsbury, to whom we owe a short but valuable essay on the guilds of that town, published some years ago in Eddowes's *Shrewsbury Journal*. These expenses are as follows (it must be borne in mind that the pageant of the Tailors' Company was the queen, here represented by the 'gyrle').

	£	s.	d.
1687. Pd. 4 doz. and 9 yards ribbon, at 3s. per doz.	0	14	0
— Drinke att Kingsland ...	0	16	0
— Wine att do.	0	6	0
— Bunns, 8d., bread, 12d., tobacco and pipes, 19d. ...	0	3	3
— Drums and music	1	4	0
— Carrying ye colours	0	1	6
— John Boulton and William Lewis	0	3	0
— The woman for looking after ye drinke, &c.	0	2	0
— Man for do.. ...	0	1	0
— Man att ye gate	0	1	6
— Trumpitter in ye harbor ...	0	3	0
— For ruffles and a shute of knotts	0	6	0
— For making ye peake and altering ye gloves	0	1	6
— For a payre of gloves for ye gyrle and given ye gyrle ...	0	3	6
— For moweing ye harbor, and cutting ye hedge	0	2	6
— Woman for bringing and fetching ye saddle	0	1	0
— The man for fetching ye horse and dressing him ...	0	1	6
— For altering ye mantua	0	1	6
— For levinian to line ye sleaves ...	0	0	10
— Given to Mrs Scott for dressing ye gyrle	0	5	0
— For a band-box	0	0	6

In 1861, a revival of the show was again attempted, and it was believed that it would be rendered more popular by grafting upon it an exhibition of 'Olympic Games,' including the ordinary old English country pastimes, to which a second day was appropriated; but the attempt was not successful. On this occasion, the 'Black Prince' was introduced as a pageant, to represent the Bakers and Cabinetmakers; and a dispute about the payment of his expenses, which was decided in the local court, brought out the following bill of charges, which is quite as quaint as the account of expenses of the Tailors for 1687, given above from the accounts of that guild.

1861. Expenses of one of the stewards of the common brethren of hatters, cabinetmakers, &c., in the procession to Kingsland, at Shrewsbury Show, and to find a band of music, a herald, and a horse properly caparisoned for the pageant.

	£	s.	d.
Earnest money to the prince, who was then in want of it	0	1	0
Band of music, 8 performers	3	0	0
Ale for ditto	0	10	0
Horse for the prince	0	10	0
Herald	0	1	0
The prince's state allowance ...	0	6	6
Flowers, gloves, stockings, and calico for repairing his unmentionables, used on a former occasion	0	5	3

Repairing the turban	0	1	6
Spent in ale for the prince's retinue during the royal progress to Kingsland... ...	0	7	0
Ditto after the return from ditto	0	6	6
Paid for repairing the prince's robes, which were shabby	0	5	0
For flags, banners, &c., to adorn the procession	0	4	0

It remains to be added, that the scene on Kingsland is now only that of a very great fair, with all its ordinary accompaniments of booths for drinking and dancing, shows, &c., to which crowds of visitors are brought by the railways from considerable distances, and which is kept up to a late hour. The ' arbours ' are merely used as places for the sale of refreshments. Towards nine o'clock in the evening the pageants are again arranged in procession to proceed on their return into the town; and as many of the actors as are in a condition to do so take part in them. The arbours and the ground on which they stand were purchased by the corporation from the guild and all cleared away, preparatory to the enclosure of Kingsland, which has now become a favourite site for genteel villa residences.

MAY 31.

St Petronilla, 1st century. Saints Cantius and Cantianus, brothers, and Cantianilla, their sister, martyrs, 304.

Born.—Dr James Currie, miscellaneous writer, 1756, *Kirkpatrick-Fleming, Dumfriesshire ;* Friedrich von Hardenberg, Prussian statesman, 1772 ; Ludwig Tieck, German poet, novelist, and dramatist, 1773.

Died.—Bishop Simon Patrick, 1707, *Ely ;* William Baxter, editor of Latin classics, antiquary, 1723, *buried at Islington ;* Philip, Duke of Wharton, 1731, *Tarragona ;* Frederick William I. of Prussia. 1740 ; Marshal Lannes, (Duc de Montebello), 1809 ; Joseph Grimaldi, comedian, 1837 ; Thomas Chalmers, D.D., 1847 ; Charlotte Brontë, novelist, 1855 ; Daniel Sharpe, F.R.S., geologist, 1856.

PHILIP DUKE OF WHARTON.

Brilliant almost beyond comparison was the prospect with which this erratic nobleman began his earthly career. His family, hereditary lords of Wharton Castle and large estates in Westmoreland, had acquired, by his grandfather's marriage with the heiress of the Goodwins, considerable property, including two other mansions, in the county of Buckingham. His father, Thomas, fifth Lord Wharton, was endowed with uncommon talent, and had greatly distinguished himself at court, in the senate, and in the country. Having proved himself a skilful politician, an able debater, and no less a zealous advocate of the people than supporter of the reigning sovereign, he had considerably advanced his family, both in dignity and influence. In addition to his hereditary title of Baron Wharton, he had been created Viscount Winchenden and Earl of Wharton in 1706; and in 1715, George I. made him Earl of Rathfarnham and Marquis of Catherlough in Ireland, and Marquis of Wharton and Malmesbury in England. He was also entrusted with several posts of honour and emolument.

Thus, possessed of a large income, high in the favour of his sovereign, the envy or admiration of the nobility, and the idol of the people, he lived in princely splendour—chiefly at Wooburn, in Bucks, his favourite country-seat, on which he had expended £100,000 merely in ornamenting and improving it. With the view of qualifying Philip, his only surviving son, for the eminent position he had achieved for him, he had him educated at home under his own supervision. And the boy's early years were as full of promise as the fondest or most ambitious father could desire. Handsome and graceful in person, he was equally remarkable for the vigour and acuteness of his intellect. He learned with great facility ancient and modern languages, and, being naturally eloquent, and trained by his father in the art of oratory, he became a ready and effective speaker. When he was only about nine years old, Addison, who visited his father at Winchenden House, Bucks, was charmed and astonished at 'the little lad's' knowledge and intelligence ; and Young, the author of the *Night Thoughts,* called him 'a truly prodigious genius.' But these flattering promises were soon marred by his early predilection for low and dissolute society ; and his own habits speedily resembled those of his boon companions. His father, alarmed at his perilous situation, endeavoured to rescue him from the slough into which he was sinking ; but his advice and efforts were only met by his son's increased deceit and alienation. When scarcely fifteen years old, he contracted a clandestine marriage with a lady greatly his inferior in family and station. When his father became acquainted with this, his last hope vanished. His ambitious spirit could not bear the blow, and he died within six weeks after the marriage. Hope still lingered with the fonder and deeper affections of his mother. But self-gratification was the ruling passion of her son ; and, reckless of the feelings of others, he rushed deeper and deeper into vice and degradation. His mother's lingering hope was crushed, and she died broken-hearted within twelve months after his father. These self-caused bereavements, enough to have softened the heart of a common murderer, made no salutary impression on him. He rather seemed to hail them as welcome events, which opened for him the way to more licentious indulgence. For he now devoted himself unreservedly to a life of vicious and sottish pleasures ; but, being still a minor, he was in some measure subject to the control of his guardians, who, puzzled what was best to do with such a character, decided on a very hazardous course. They engaged a Frenchman as his tutor or companion, and sent him to travel on the Continent, with a special injunction to remain some considerable time at Geneva, for the reformation of his moral and religious character.

Proceeding first to Holland, he visited Hanover and other German courts, and was everywhere honourably received. Next proceeding to Geneva, he soon became thoroughly disgusted at the manners of the place, and, with contempt both for it and for the tutor who had taken him there, he suddenly quitted both. He left

behind him a bear's cub, with a note to his tutor, stating that, being no longer able to submit to his treatment, he had committed to his care his young bear, which he thought would be a more suitable companion to him than himself— a piece of wit which might easily have been turned against himself. He had proceeded to Lyons, which he reached on the 13th of October 1716, and immediately sent from thence a fine horse as a present to the Pretender, who was then living at Avignon. On receiving this present the Pretender invited him to his court, and, on his arrival there, welcomed him with enthusiasm, and conferred on him the title of Duke of Northumberland. From Lyons he went to Paris, and presented himself to Mary D'Este, widow of the abdicated King James II. Lord Stair, the British ambassador at the French court, endeavoured to reclaim him by acts of courtesy and kindness, accompanied with some wholesome advice. The duke returned his civilities with politeness—his advice with levity. About the close of the year 1716, he returned to England, and soon after passed to Ireland ; where he was allowed, though still a minor, to take his seat in parliament as Marquis of Catherlough. Despite his pledges to the Pretender, he now joined his adversaries, the king and government who debarred him from the throne. So able and important was his support, that the king, hoping to secure him on his side, conferred on him the title of Duke of Wharton. When he returned to England, he took his seat in the house as duke, and almost his first act was to oppose the government from whom he had received his new dignity.

Shortly afterwards he professed to have changed his opinions, and told the ministerial leaders that it was his earnest desire to retrace his steps, and to give the king and his government all the support in his power. He was once more taken into the confidence of ministers. He attended all their private conferences ; he acquainted himself with all their intentions ; ascertained all their weak points ; then, on the first important ministerial measure that occurred, he used all the information thus obtained to oppose the government, and revealed, with unblushing effrontery, the secrets with which they had entrusted him, and summoned all his powers of eloquence to overthrow the ministers into whose confidence he had so dishonourably insinuated himself. He made a most able and effective speech—damaging, indeed, to the ministry, but still more damaging to his own character. His fickle and unprincipled conduct excited the contempt of all parties, each of whom he had in turn courted and betrayed. Lost to honour, overwhelmed with debt, and shunned by all respectable society, he abandoned himself to drunkenness and debauchery. 'He drank immoderately,' says Dr King, 'and was very abusive and sometimes mischievous in his wine ; so that he drew on himself frequent challenges, which he would never answer. On other accounts likewise, his character was become very prostitute.' So that, having lost his honour, he left his country and went to Spain. While at Madrid he was recalled by a writ of Privy Seal, which he treated with contempt, and openly avowed his adherence to the Pretender. By a decree in Chancery his estates were vested in the hands of trustees, who allowed him an income of £1200 a-year. In April 1726, his first wife died, and soon afterwards he professed the Roman Catholic faith, and married one of the maids of honour to the Queen of Spain. This lady, who is said to have been penniless, was the daughter of an Irish colonel in the service of the King of Spain, and appears only to have increased the duke's troubles and inconsistency; for shortly after his marriage he entered the same service, and fought against his own countrymen at the siege of Gibraltar. For this he was censured even by the Pretender, who advised him to return to England; but, contemptuous of advice from every quarter alike, he proceeded to Paris. Sir Edward Keane, who was then at Paris, thus speaks of him: 'The Duke of Wharton has not been sober, or scarce had a pipe out of his mouth, since he left St Ildefonso. . . . . . He declared himself to be the Pretender's prime minister, and Duke of Wharton and Northumberland. "Hitherto," added he, "my master's interest has been managed by the Duke of Perth, and three or four other old women, who meet under the portal of St Germains. He wanted a Whig, and a brisk one, too, to put them in a right train, and I am the man. You may look on me as Sir Philip Wharton, Knight of the Garter, running a race with Sir Robert Walpole, Knight of the Bath—running a course, and he shall be hard pressed, I assure you. He bought my family pictures, but they shall not be long in his possession; that account is still open; neither he nor King George shall be six months at ease, as long as I have the honour to serve in the employment I am now in." He mentioned great things from Muscovy, and talked such nonsense and contradictions, that it is neither worth my while to remember, nor yours to read them. I used him very *cavalièrement*, upon which he was much affronted—sword and pistol next day. But before I slept, a gentleman was sent to desire that everything might be forgotten. What a pleasure must it have been to have killed a prime minister!'*

From Paris the duke went to Rouen, and living there very extravagantly, he was obliged to quit it, leaving behind his horses and equipage. He returned to Paris, and finding his finances utterly exhausted, entered a monastery with the design of spending the remainder of his life in study and seclusion; but left it in two months, and, accompanied by the duchess and a single servant, proceeded to Spain. His erratic career was now near its close. His dissolute life had ruined his constitution, and in 1731 his health began rapidly to fail. He found temporary relief from a mineral water in Catalonia, and shortly afterwards relapsing into his former state of debility, he again set off on horseback to travel to the same springs; but ere he reached them, he fell from his horse in a fainting fit, near a small village, from whence he was carried by some Bernardine monks to a small convent near

* Seward's *Anecdotes*, ii., 294.

710

at hand. Here, after languishing for a few days, he died, at the age of thirty-two, without a friend to soothe his dying moments, without a servant to minister to his bodily sufferings or perform the last offices of nature. On the 1st of June 1731, the day after his decease, he was buried at the convent in as plain and humble manner as the poorest member of the community. Thus, in obscurity, and dependent on the charity of a few poor monks, died Philip Duke of Wharton—the possessor of six peerages, the inheritor of a lordly castle, and two other noble mansions, with ample estates, and endowed with talents that might have raised him to wealth and reputation, had he been born in poverty and obscurity. By his death his family, long the pride of the north, and all his titles, became extinct. The remnant of his estates was sold to pay his debts; and his widow, who survived him many years, lived in great privacy in London, on a small pension from the court of Spain. Not long before he died, he sent to a friend in England a manuscript tragedy on Mary Queen of Scots, and some poems; and finished his letter with these lines from Dryden:

'Be kind to my remains; and oh! defend
Against your judgment your departed friend!
Let not the insulting foe my fame pursue,
But shade those laurels that descend to you.'

Notwithstanding this piteous appeal, Pope has enshrined his character in the following lines:

'Clodio—the scorn and wonder of our days,
Whose ruling passion was the lust of praise;
Born with whate'er could win it from the wise,
Women and fools must like him, or he dies;
Though wondering senates hung on all he spoke,
The club must hail him master of the joke.
Shall parts so various aim at nothing new?
He'll shine a Tully and a Wilmot too.
Thus, with each gift of nature and of art,
And wanting nothing but an honest heart;
Grown all to all, from no one vice exempt,
And most contemptible to shun contempt;
His passion still to covet general praise,
His life to forfeit it a thousand ways:
His constant bounty no one friend has made;
His angel tongue no mortal can persuade;
A fool, with more of wit than half mankind,
Too quick for thought, for action too refined;
A tyrant to the wife his heart approves,
A rebel to the very king he loves;
He dies, sad outcast of each church and state,
And, harder still! flagitious, yet not great.
Ask you, why Clodio broke through every rule?
'Twas all for fear the knaves should call him fool.
*   *   *   *   *
What riches give us, let us first inquire:
Meat, fire, and clothes. What more? Meat, clothes, and fire.
Is this too little? Would you more than live?
Alas! 'tis more than Turner finds they give;
Alas! 'tis more than—all his visions past—
Unhappy Wharton, waking, found at last!'

CHARLOTTE BRONTË.

At the end of 1847, a novel was published which quickly passed from professed readers of fiction into the hands of almost every one who had any interest in English literature. Grave business men, who seldom adventured into lighter reading than the *Times*, found themselves sitting until past midnight entranced in its pages, and feverish with curiosity until they had engrossed the final mystery of its plot. Devoured by excitement, many returned to its pages to note anew its felicities of diction, and the graphic, if sometimes rude force, with which character, scenery, and events were portrayed. That novel was *Jane Eyre*, by Currer Bell. Who was Currer Bell? was the world's question. Was Currer a man or a woman? The truth of the case was so surprising as to be quite out of the range of conjecture. *Jane Eyre*, a work which in parts seemed welded with the strength of a Titan, was the performance of a delicate lady of thirty, who had little experience of the world beyond her father's lonely parsonage of Haworth, set high among the bleak Yorkshire moors. Even her father did not learn the secret of his daughter's authorship until her book was famous. One afternoon she went into his study, and said—

'Papa, I've been writing a book.'
'Have you, my dear?'
'Yes; and I want you to read it.'
'I am afraid it will try my eyes too much.'
'But it is not in manuscript, it is printed.'
'My dear! you've never thought of the expense it will be! It will be almost sure to be a loss, for how can you get a book sold? No one knows you or your name.'
'But, papa, I don't think it will be a loss; no more will you, if you will just let me read you a review or two, and tell you more about it.'

So she sat down and read some of the reviews to her father; and then, giving him a copy of *Jane Eyre*, she left him to read it. When he came in to tea, he said, 'Girls, do you know Charlotte has been writing a book, and it is much better than likely?'

This Charlotte was the daughter of the Rev. Patrick Brontë, a tall and handsome Irishman, from County Down, who in 1812 married Miss Branwell, an elegant little Cornishwoman from Penzance. They had six children, one son and five daughters, who were left motherless by Mrs Brontë's premature death in 1821. Within a few years, two of her girls followed her to the tomb, leaving Charlotte, Emily Jane, Anne, and Patrick Branwell survivors. A stranger group of four old-fashioned children—shy, pale, nervous, tiny, and precocious—was probably never seen. Their father was eccentric and reserved; and, thrown on their own resources for amusement, they read all that fell into their hands. They wrote tales, plays, and poems; edited imaginary newspapers and magazines; and dwelt day by day in a perfect dream world.

These literary tastes formed in childhood strengthened as the sisters grew in years; and amid many and bitter cares, they were not the least among their sources of solace. Their first venture into print was made in 1846. It consisted of a small volume of *Poems*, by Currer, Ellis, and Acton Bell, the initials of each name being alone true. The book excited little attention, and brought them neither money nor fame. They next resolved to try their hands at novels; and Charlotte wrote *The Professor*, Emily *Wuthering Heights*, and Anne *Agnes Grey*.

Emily's and Anne's novels were accepted by publishers; but none would have Charlotte's. Then it was that, undaunted by disappointment and rebuffs, she set to work and produced *Jane Eyre*, which was followed in 1849 by *Shirley*, and in 1852 by *Villette*.

The family affections of the Brontës were of the deepest and tenderest character, and in them it was their sad lot to be wounded again and again. Their brother Branwell, on whom their love and hopes were fixed, fell into vice and dissipation; and, after worse than dying many times, passed to his final rest in September 1848, at the age of thirty. Haworth parsonage was unhealthily situated by the side of the graveyard, and the ungenial climate of the moors but ill accorded with constitutions exotic in their delicacy. Ere three months had elapsed from Branwell's death, Emily Jane glided from earth, in her twenty-ninth year; and within other six months Anne followed, at the age of twenty-seven, leaving poor Charlotte alone with her aged father. It was a joy to all to hear that on the 29th of June 1854 she had become the wife of the Rev. A. Bell Nicholls, who for years had been her father's curate, and had daily seen and silently loved her. The joy however was soon quenched, for on the 31st May 1855 Charlotte also died, before she had attained her fortieth year. Last of all, in 1861 the Brontë family became extinct with the decease of the father, at the advanced age of eighty-four.

CECILY, DUCHESS OF YORK.

Cecily, Duchess of York, who died on the 31st May 1495, was doomed to witness in her own family more appalling calamities than probably are to be found in the history of any other individual.

She was a Lancastrian by birth, her mother being Joan Beaufort, a daughter of John of Gaunt. Her father was that rich and powerful nobleman, Ralph Neville, Earl of Westmoreland. She was the youngest of twenty-one children, and, on her becoming the wife of Richard Plantagenet, Duke of York, her numerous, wealthy, and powerful family exerted all their influence to place her on the throne of England. But, after a series of splendid achievements, almost unparalleled in history, the whole family of the Nevilles were swept away, long before their sister Cecily—who by their conquering swords became the mother of kings—had descended in sorrow to the grave.

To avoid confusion, the sad catalogue of her misfortunes requires to be recorded in chronological order. Her nephew, Humphrey, Earl of Stafford, was killed at the first battle of St Albans, in 1455. Her brother-in-law, Stafford, Duke of Buckingham, was killed at the battle of Northampton, in 1460. Her husband, Richard, Duke of York, was slain in 1460, at the battle of Wakefield, just as the crown of England was almost within his ambitious grasp. Her nephew, Sir Thomas Neville, and her husband's nephew, Sir Edward Bourchier, were killed at the same time and place. Her brother, the Earl of Salisbury, was taken prisoner, and put to death

711

after the battle ; and her son Edmund, Earl of Rutland, a boy but twelve years of age, was captured when flying with his tutor from the fatal field, and cruelly murdered in cold blood by Lord Clifford, ever after surnamed the Butcher. Her nephew, Sir John Neville, was killed at the battle of Towton, in 1461 ; and her nephew, Sir Henry Neville, was made prisoner and put to death at Banbury, in 1469. Two other nephews, Richard Neville, Earl of Warwick, 'the king-maker,' and John Neville, Marquis of Montague, were killed at the battle of Barnet, in 1471. Edward, Prince of Wales, who married her great-niece, was barbarously murdered after the battle of Tewkesbury, in the same year. Her son George, Duke of Clarence, was put to death—drowned in a malmsey butt, as it is said—in the Tower of London, in 1478, his wife Cecily having previously been poisoned. Her son-in-law, Charles the Bold, Duke of Burgundy, was killed at the battle of Nancy, in 1477. Her eldest son, Edward the Fourth, King of England, fell a victim to his passions in the prime of manhood, in 1483. Lord Harrington, the first husband of her niece, Catherine Neville, was killed at Wakefield ; and Catherine's second husband, William Lord Hastings, was beheaded, without even the form of a trial, in 1483. Her great nephew Vere, son of the Earl of Oxford, died a prisoner in the Tower, his father being in exile and his mother in poverty. Her son-in-law, Holland, Duke of Exeter, who married her daughter Anne, lived long in exile, and in such poverty as to be compelled to beg his bread ; and in 1473 his corpse was found stripped naked on the sea-shore, near Dover. Her two grandsons, King Edward V. and Richard Duke of York, were murdered in the Tower in 1483. Her son-in-law, Sir Thomas St Ledger, the second husband of her daughter Anne, was executed at Exeter in 1483 ; and her great-nephew, Henry Stafford, Duke of Buckingham, was beheaded at or about the same time. Her grandson, Edward, Prince of Wales, son of Richard III., through whom she might naturally expect the honour of being the ancestress of a line of English kings, died in 1484, and his mother soon followed him to the tomb. Her youngest son, Richard III., was killed at Bosworth Field, in 1485 ; and her grandson, John de la Pole, Earl of Lincoln, was slain at the battle of Stoke in 1487.

Surviving all those troubles, and all her children, with the sole exception of Margaret, Duchess of Burgundy, she died at a good old age, after seeing three of her descendants kings of England, and her grand-daughter, Elizabeth, queen of Henry VII. By her death, she was saved the additional affliction of the loss of her grand-son, Edward, Earl of Warwick, the last male of the princely house of Plantagenet, who was tyrannically put to death by a cruel and jealous monarch in 1499.

When her husband was killed at the battle of Wakefield, the conquerors cut off his head, and putting a paper crown on it, in derision of his royal claims, placed it over the principal gate of the city of York. But when her son Edward came to the throne, he caused the mangled

remains of his father to be collected, and buried with regal ceremonies in the chancel of the Collegiate Church at Fotheringay, founded and endowed by the piety and liberality of his ancestors. And Cecily, according to directions contained in her will, was buried at Fotheringay, beside the husband whose loss she had mourned for thirty-five long years. It was fated that she was to be denied the last long rest usually allotted to mortals. At the Reforma-

CECILY, DUCHESS OF YORK.

tion, the Collegiate Church of Fotheringay was razed to the ground, and the bodies of Richard and Cecily, Duke and Duchess of York, were exposed to public view. A Mr Creuso, who saw them, says :—'Their bodies appeared very plainly, the Duchess Cecily had about her neck, hanging on a ribbon, a pardon from Rome, which, penned in a fine Roman hand, was as fair and fresh to be seen as if it had been written the day before.' The discovery having been made known to Queen Elizabeth, she ordered the remains to be carefully re-interred, with all decent solemnities.

THE COTSWOLD GAMES.

The range of hills overlooking the fertile and beautiful vale of Evesham is celebrated by Drayton, in his curious topographical poem, the *Poly-Olbion*, as the yearly meeting-place of the country folks around to exhibit the best bred cattle, and pass a day in jovial festivity. He pictures these rustics dancing hand-in-hand to the music of the bagpipe and tabor, around a flag-staff erected on the highest hill—the flag inscribed '*Heigh for Cotswold!*'—while others feasted upon the grass, presided over by the winner of the prize.

'————The Shepherds' King,
Whose flock hath chanced that year the earliest lamb to bring,
In his gay baldrick sits at his low grassy board,
With flawns, lards, clowted cream, and country dainties stored ;

And, whilst the bagpipe plays, each lusty jocund
　　swain
Quaffs sillibubs in cans to all upon the plain,
And to their country girls, whose nosegays they
　　do wear,
Some roundelays do sing; the rest the burthen bear.'

The description pleasantly, but yet painfully,
reminds us of the halcyon period in the history
of England procured by the pacific policy of
Elizabeth and James I., and which apparently
would have been indefinitely prolonged—with a
great progress in wealth and all the arts of
peace—but for the collision between Puritanism
and the will of an injudicious sovereign, which
brought about the civil war. The rural population were, during James's reign, at ease and
happy; and their exuberant good spirits found
vent in festive assemblages, of which this
Cotswold meeting was but an example. But the
spirit of religious austerity was abroad, making
continual encroachments on the genial feelings
of the people; and, rather oddly, it was as a
countercheck to that spirit that the Cotswold
meeting attained its full character as a festive
assemblage.

There lived at that time at Burton-on-the-
Heath, in Warwickshire, one Robert Dover, an
attorney, who entertained rather strong views of
the menacing character of Puritanism. He
deemed it a public enemy, and was eager to put
it down. Seizing upon the idea of the Cotswold
meeting, he resolved to enlarge and systematize
it into a regular gathering of all ranks of people
in the province—with leaping and wrestling, as
before, for the men, and dancing for the maids,
but with the addition of coursing and horse-
racing for the upper classes. With a formal
permission from King James, he made all the
proper arrangements, and established the Cotswold games in a style which secured general
applause, never failing each year to appear upon
the ground himself—well mounted, and accoutred
as what would now be called a master of the
ceremonies. Things went on thus for the best
part of forty years, till (to quote the language of
Anthony Wood), 'the rascally rebellion was
begun by the Presbyterians, which gave a stop
to their proceedings, and spoiled all that was
generous and ingenious elsewhere.' Dover
himself, in milder strains, thus tells his own
story:—

'I've heard our fine refined clergy teach,
　Of the commandments, that it is a breach
　To play at any game for gain or coin;
'Tis theft, they say—men's goods you do purloin;
　For beasts or birds in combat for to fight,
　Oh, 'tis not lawful, but a cruel sight.
　One silly beast another to pursue
'Gainst nature is, and fearful to the view;
　And man with man their activeness to try
　Forbidden is—much harm doth come thereby;
　Had we their faith to credit what they say,
　We must believe all sports are ta'en away;
　Whereby I see, instead of active things,
　What harm the same unto our nation brings;
　The pipe and pot are made the only prize
　Which all our spriteful youth do exercise.

The effect of restrictions upon wholesome out-
of-doors amusements in driving people into sot-
ting public-houses is remarked in our own day,

and it is curious to find Mr Dover pointing out
the same result 250 years ago. His poem occurs
at the close of a rare volume published in 1636,
entirely composed of commendatory verses on
the exploits at Cotswold, and entitled *Annalia
Dubrensia*. Some of the best poets of the day
contributed to the collection, and among them
were Ben Jonson, Michael Drayton, Thomas
Randolph, Thomas Heywood, Owen Feltham,
and Shackerly Marmyon. 'Rare Ben' contributed the most characteristic effusion of the
series, which, curiously enough, he appears to
have overlooked, when collecting such waifs and
strays for the volume he published with the
quaint title of *Underwoods*; neither does it
appear in his *Collection of Epigrams*. He calls
it 'an epigram to my jovial good friend, Mr
Robert Dover, on his great instauration of hunting and dancing at Cotswold.'

'I cannot bring my Muse to drop vies *
　'Twixt Cotswold and the Olympic exercise;
　But I can tell thee, Dover, how thy games
　Renew the glories of our blessed James:
　How they do keep alive his memory
　With the glad country and posterity;
　How they advance true love, and neighbourhood,
　And do both church and commonwealth the good—
　In spite of hypocrites, who are the worst
　Of subjects; let such envy till they burst.'

Drayton is very complimentary to Dover:—

'We'll have thy statue in some rock cut out,
　With brave inscriptions garnished about;
　And under written—"Lo! this is the man
　Dover, that first these noble sports began."
　Lads of the hills and lasses of the vale,
　In many a song and many a merry tale,
　Shall mention thee; and, having leave to play,
　Unto thy name shall make a holiday.
　The Cotswold shepherds, as their flocks they keep,
　To put off lazy drowsiness and sleep,
　Shall sit to tell, and hear thy story told,
　That night shall come ere they their flocks can
　　fold.'

The remaining thirty-one poems, with the exception of that by Randolph, have little claim
to notice, being not unfrequently turgid and
tedious, if not absurdly hyperbolical. They are
chiefly useful for clearly pointing out the nature
of these renowned games, which are also exhibited in a quaint wood-cut frontispiece. In
this, Dover (in accordance with the antique heroic
in art) appears on horseback, in full costume,
three times the size of life; and bearing in his
hand a wand, as ruler of the sports. In the
central summit of the picture is seen a castle,
from which volleys were fired in the course of
the sports, and which was named Dover Castle,
in honour of Master Robert; one of his poetic
friends assuring him—

'———— thy castle shall exceed as far
　The other Dover, as sweet peace doth war!'

This redoubtable castle was a temporary erec-

* This word may be taken in the sense of comparison.
To vie is interpreted by Halliwell as 'to wager or put
down a certain sum upon a hand of cards;' and the word
is still in use as a verb, with the sense of to compete. As
the line halts, however, there is probably a word of one
syllable wanting between 'drop' and 'vies'

tion of woodwork, brought to the spot every year. The sports took place at Whitsuntide, and consisted of horse-racing (for which small honorary prizes were given), hunting, and coursing (the best dog being rewarded with a silver collar), dancing by the maidens, wrestling, leaping, tumbling, cudgel-play, quarter-staff, casting the hammer, &c., by the men.

Tents were erected for the gentry, who came in numbers from all quarters, and here refresh-ments were supplied in abundance; while tables stood in the open air, or cloths were spread on the ground, for the commonalty.

> 'None ever hungry from these games come home,
> Or e'er make plaint of viands or of room;
> He all the rank at night so brave dismisses,
> With ribands of his favour and with blisses.'

Horses and men were abundantly decorated with yellow ribbons (Dover's colour), and he

THE COTSWOLD GAMES.

was duly honoured by all as king of their sports for a series of years. They ceased during the Cromwellian era, but were revived at the Restoration; and the memory of their founder is still preserved in the name Dover's Hill, applied to an eminence of the Cotswold range, about a mile from the village of Campden.

Shakspeare, whose slightest allusion to any subject gives it an undying interest, has immortalized these sports. Justice Shallow, in his enumeration of the four bravest roisterers of his early days, names 'Will Squell, a Cotswold man;' and the mishap of Master Page's fallow greyhound, who was 'out-run on Cotsale,' occupies some share of the dialogue in the opening scene of the *Merry Wives of Windsor*.

JUNE

—— After her came jolly JUNE, arrayed
All in green leaves, as he a player were ;
Yet in his time he wrought as well as played,
That by his plough-irons mote right well appear.
Upon a crab he rode, that did him bear,
With crooked crawling steps, an uncouth pace,
And backward rode, as bargemen wont to fare,
Bending their force contrary to their face ;
Like that ungracious crew which feigns demurest grace.   SPENSER.

(DESCRIPTIVE.)

JUNE has now come, bending beneath her weight of roses, to ornament the halls and bowers which summer has hung with green. For this is the Month of Roses, and their beauty and fragrance conjure up again many in poetical creation which Memory had buried. We think of Herrick's Sappho, and how the roses were always white until they tried to rival her fair complexion, and, blushing for shame because they were vanquished, have ever since remained red ; of Shakspeare's Juliet, musing as she leant over the balcony in the moonlight, and thinking that the rose ' by any other name would smell as sweet.' They carry us back to Chaucer's Emilie, whom we again see pacing the garden in the early morning, her hair blown backward, while, as she gathers roses carefully, she 'thrusts among the thorns her little hand.' We again see Milton's Eve in Eden, standing half-veiled in a cloud of fragrance—'so thick the

715

blushing roses round about her blow.' This is the season to wander into the fields and woods, with a volume of sterling poetry for companionship, and compare the descriptive passages with the objects that lie around. We never enjoy reading portions of Spenser's *Faery Queen* so much as when among the great green trees in summer. We then feel his meaning, where he describes arbours that are not the work of art, ' but by the trees' own inclination made.' We look up at the great network of branches, and think how silently they have been fashioned. Through many a quiet night, and many a golden dawn, and all day long, even when the twilight threw her grey veil over them, the work advanced ; from when the warp was formed of tender sprays and tiny buds, until the woof of leaves was woven with a shuttle of sunshine and showers, which the unseen wind sent in and out through the branches. No human eye could see how the work was done, for the pattern of leaves was woven motionless—here a brown bud came, and there a dot of green was thrown in ; yet no hand was visible during the workmanship, though we know the great Power that stirred in that mysterious loom, and wove the green drapery of summer. Now in the woods, like a fair lady of the olden time peeping through her embowered lattice, the tall woodbine leans out from among the leaves, as if to look at the procession that is ever passing, of golden-belted bees, and gauze-winged dragonflies, birds that dart by as if sent with hasty messages, and butterflies, the gaudy outriders, that make for themselves a pathway between the overhanging blossoms. All these she sees from the green turret in which she is imprisoned, while the bees go sounding their humming horns through every flowery town in the forest. The wild roses, compelled to obey the commands of summer, blush as they expose their beauty by the wayside, and hurry to hide themselves again amid the green when the day is done, seeming as if they tried 'to shut, and become buds again.' Like pillars of fire, the foxgloves blaze through the shadowy green of the underwood, as if to throw a light on the lesser flowers that grow around their feet. Pleasant is it now after a long walk to sit down on the slope of some hill, and gaze over the outstretched landscape, from the valley at our feet to where the river loses itself in the distant sunshine. In all those widely-spread farmhouses and cottages—some so far away that they appear but little larger than mole-hills—the busy stir of every-day life is going on, though neither sound nor motion are audible or visible from this green slope. From those quiet homes move christening, marrying, and burying processions. Thousands who have tilled the earth within the space our eye commands, ' now sleep beneath it.' There is no one living who ever saw yonder aged oak look younger that it does now. The head lies easy which erected that grey old stile, that has stood bleaching so many years in sun and wind, it looks like dried bones; the very step is worn hollow by the feet of those who have passed away for ever. How quiet yonder fields appear through which the brown footpath stretches ;

there those that have gone walked and talked, and played, and made love, and through them led their children by the hand, to gather the wild roses of June, that still flower as they did in those very spots where their grandfathers gathered them, when, a century back, they were children. And yet it may be that these fields, which look so beautiful in our eyes, and awaken such pleasant memories of departed summers, bring back no such remembrances to the unlettered hind ; that he thinks only of the years he has toiled in them, of the hard struggle he has had to get bread for his family, and the aching bones he has gone home with at night. Perhaps, when he walks out with his children, he thinks how badly he was paid for plashing that hedge, or repairing that flowery embankment ; how long it took him to plough or harrow that field; how cold the days were then, and, when his wants were greatest, what little wages he received. The flaunting woodbine may have no charms for his eye, nor the bee humming round the globe of crimson clover ; perhaps he pauses not to listen to the singing of the birds, but, with eyes bent on the ground, he ' homeward plods his weary way.' Cottages buried in woodbine or covered with roses are not the haunts of peace and homes of love which poets so often picture, nor are they the gloomy abodes which some cynical politicians magnify into dens of misery.

How peaceably yonder village at the foot of this hill seems to sleep in the June sunshine, beneath the overshadowing trees, above which the blue smoke ascends, nothing else seeming to stir ! What rich colours some of those thatched roofs present—moss and lichen, and stonecrop which is now one blaze of gold. That whitewashed wall, glimmering through the foliage, just lights up the picture where it wanted opening; even the sunlight, flashed back from the windows, lets in golden gleams through the green. That bit of brown road by the red wall, on one side of which runs the brook, spanned by a rustic bridge, is of itself a picture—with the white cow standing by the gate, where the great elder-tree is now covered with bunches of creamy-coloured bloom. Water is always beautiful in a landscape; it is the glass in which the face of heaven is mirrored, in which the trees and flowers can see themselves, for aught we know, so hidden from us in the secret of their existence and the life they live. Now, one of those out-of-door pictures may be seen which almost every landscape painter has tried to fix on canvas—that of cattle standing in water at noon-day. We always fancy they look best in a large pond overhung with trees, that is placed in a retiring corner of rich pasture lands, with their broad sweeps of grass and wild flowers. In a river or a long stream the water stretches too far away, and mars the snugness of the picture, which ought to be bordered with green, while the herd is of various colours. In a pond surrounded with trees we see the sunlight chequering the still water as it streams through the branches, while a mass of shadow lies under the lower boughs—part of it falling on a portion of the cattle, while the rest stand in a warm, green light ; and should one happen to be red, and dashed with the sunlight that comes in through the leaves, it shows such flecks of ruddy gold as no artist ever yet painted. We see the shadows of the inverted trees thrown deep down, and below a blue, unfathomable depth of sky, which conjures back those ocean chasms that have never yet been sounded.

We now hear that sharp rasping sound in the fields which the mower makes every time he whets his scythe, telling us that he has already cut down myriads of those beautiful wild flowers and feathered grasses which the morning sun shone upon. We enter the field, and pick a few fading flowers out of the great swathes; and, while watching him at his work, see how at one sweep he makes a desert, where a moment before all was brightness and beauty. How one might moralize over this globe of white clover, which a bee was rifling of its sweets just before the scythe swept it down, and dwell upon the homes of ground-building birds and earth-burrowing animals and insects, which the destroyer lays bare. But these thoughts have no place in his mind. He may, while whetting his scythe, wonder how many more times he will have to sharpen it before he cuts his way up to the hedge, where his provision basket, beer bottle, and the clothes he has thrown off, lie in the shade, guarded by his dog—and when there slake his thirst. Many of those grasses which he cuts down so thoughtlessly are as beautiful as the rarest flowers that ever bloomed, though they must be examined minutely for their elegant forms and splendid colours. No plumage that ever nodded over the brow of Beauty, not even that of the rare bird of paradise, can excel the graceful silky sweep of the feather-grass, which ladies used to wear in their head-dresses. The silky bent grass, which the least stir of air sets in motion, is as glossy and beautiful as the richest satin that ever enfolded the elegant form of maidenhood. The quaking or tottering grass is hung with hundreds of beautiful spikelets, which are all shaken by the least movement of an insect's wing; and when in motion, the shifting light that plays upon its many-coloured flowers makes them glitter like jewels. But let the gentlest breeze that ever blew breathe through a bed of this beautiful grass, and you might fancy that thousands of fairy bells were swinging, and that the hair-like stems were the ropes pulled by the greenwood elves, which are thinner than the finest silk. It has many pretty names, such as pearl-grass, silk-grass; while the country children call it Ringing-all-the-bells-in-London, on account of its purple spikelets being ever in motion. Nothing was ever yet woven in loom to which art could give such graceful colouring as is shown in the luminous pink and dazzling sea-green of the soft meadow-grass; the flowers spread over a panicle of velvet bloom, which is so soft and yielding, that the lightest footed insect sinks into its downy carpeting when passing. Many grasses which the mower is now sweeping down would, to the eye of a common observer, appear all alike; though upon close examination they will be found to differ as much as one flower does from another. Amongst these are the fox-tail and other grasses, which have all round heads, and seem at the first glance only to vary in length and thickness; they are also so common, that there is hardly a field without them. We take up a handful of grass from the swathe just cut down, and find dozens of these round-headed flowers in it. One is of a rich golden green, with a covering of bright silvery hairs, so thinly interspersed, that they hide not the golden ground beneath; another is a rich purple tint, that rivals the glowing bloom of the dark-shaded pansy; while, besides colours, the stems will be found to vary, some being pointed and pinched until they resemble the limbs of a daddy-long-legs. This is the scented vernal grass, that gives out the rich aroma we now inhale from the new-mown field. It seldom grows more than a foot high, and has, as you see, a close-set panicle, just like wheat; and in these yellow dots, on the green valves that hold the flowers, the fragrance is supposed to lie which scents the June air for miles round when the grass is cut and dried.

The rough, the smooth, and the annual meadow-grasses are those which everybody knows. But for the rough meadow-grass, we should not obtain so many glimpses of green as are seen in our squares and streets—for it will grow in the smokiest of cities; while to the smooth meadow-grass we are indebted for that first green flush of spring—that spring green which no dyer can imitate, and which first shows through the hoary mantle of winter. The annual meadow-grass grows wherever a pinch of earth can be found for it to root in. It is the children's garden in the damp, sunless back yards of our cities; it springs up between the stones of the pavement, and grows in the crevices of decaying walls. Neither summer suns which scorch, nor biting frosts which blacken, can destroy it; for it seeds eight or nine months of the year, and, do what you will, is sure to come up again. Pull it up you cannot, excepting in wet weather, when all the earth its countless fibres adhere to comes with it; for it finds nourishment in everything it lays hold of, nor has it, like some of the other grasses, to go far into the earth for support.

In the next field we see the haymakers hard at work, turning the grass over, and shaking it up with their forks, or letting it float loose on the wind, to be blown as far as it can go; while the air that passes through it carries the pleasant smell of new-mown hay to the far away fields and villages it sweeps by. How happy haymakers always appear, as if work to them were pleasure; even the little children, while they laugh as they throw hay over one another, are unconciously assisting the labourers, for it cannot be dispersed too much. What a blessing it would be if all labour could be made so pleasant! Some are gathering the hay into windrows, great long unbroken ridges, that extend from one end of the field to the other, and look like motionless waves in the distance, while between them all the space is raked up tidily. Then comes the last process, to roll those long windrows into haycocks, turning the hay on their forks over and over, and clearing the ground at every turn, as boys do the huge snowball, which it takes four or five of them to move—until the haycock is as high as a man's head, and not a vestige of a windrow is left when the work is finished by the rakers. Rolling those huge haycocks together is hard work; and when you see it done, you marvel not at the quantity of beer the men drink, labouring as they do in the hot open sunshine of June. We then see the loaded hay wagons leaving the fields, rocking as they cross the furrows, over which wheels but rarely roll, moving along green lanes and between high hedgerows, which take toll from the wains as they pass, until new hay hangs down from every branch. What labour it would save the birds in building, if hay was led two or three months earlier, for nothing could be more soft and downy for the lining of their nests than many of the feathered heads of those dried grasses. Onward moves the rocking wagon towards the rick-yard, where the gate stands open, and we can see the men on the half-formed stack waiting for the coming load.

When the stack is nearly finished, only a strong man can pitch up a fork full of hay; and it needs some practice to use the long forks which are required when the rick has nearly reached to its fullest height. What a delicious smell of new-mown hay there will be in every room of that old farmhouse for days after the stacks are finished; we almost long to take up our lodging there for a week or two for the sake of the fragrance. And there, in the 'home close,' as it is called, sits the milkmaid on her three-legged stool, which she hides somewhere under the hedge, that she may not have to carry it to and fro every time she goes to milk, talking to her cow while she is milking as if it understood her: for the flies make it restless, and she is fearful that it may kick over the contents of her pail. Now she breaks forth into song—unconscious that she is overheard—the burthen of which is that her lover may be true, ending with a wish that she were a linnet, 'to sing her love to rest,' which he, wearied with his day's labour, will not require, but will begin to snore a minute after his tired head presses the pillow.

But we cannot leave the milkmaid, surrounded with the smell of new-mown hay, without taking a final glance at the grasses; and when we state that there are already upwards of two thousand varieties known and named, and that the discoveries of every year continue to add to the number, it will be seen that the space of a large volume would be required only to enumerate the different classes into which they are divided. The oat-like, the wheat-like, and the water-grasses, of which latter the tall common seed is the chief, are very numerous. It is from grasses that we have obtained the bread we eat, and we have now many varieties in England, growing wild, that yield small grains of excellent corn, and that could, by cultivation, be rendered as valuable as our choicest cereals. It is through being surrounded by the sea, and having so few mountain ranges to shut out the breezes, the sunshine, and the showers, that England is covered with the most beautiful grasses that are to be found in the world. The open sea wooes every wind that blows, and draws all the showers towards our old homesteads, and clothes our island with that delicious green which is the wonder and admiration of foreigners. It also feeds those flocks and herds which are our pride; for nowhere else can be seen such as those pastured on English ground. Our Saxon forefathers had no other name for grass than that we still retain, though they made many pleasant allusions to it in describing the labours of the months—such as grass-month, milk-month, mow-month, hay-month, and after-month, or the month after their hay was harvested. After-month is a word still in use, though now applied to the second crop of grass, which springs up after the hay-field has been cleared. None are fonder than Englishmen of seeing a 'bit of grass' before their doors. Look at the retired old citizen, who spent the best years of his life poring over ledgers in some half-lighted office in the neighbourhood of the Bank, how delighted he is with the little grass-plat which the window of his suburban retreat opens into. What hours he spends over it, patting it down with his spade, smoothing it with his garden-roller; stooping down until his aged back aches, while clipping it with his shears; then standing at a distance to admire it; then calling his dear old wife out to see how green and pretty it looks. It keeps him in health, for in attending to it he finds both amusement and exercise; and perhaps the happiest moments of his life are those passed in watching his grandchildren roll over it, while his married sons and daughters sit smiling by his side. Hundreds of such men, and many such spots, lie scattered beside the roads that run every way through the great metropolitan suburbs; and it is pleasant, when returning from a walk through the dusty roads of June, to peep over the low walls, or through the palisades, and see the happy groups sitting in the cool of evening by the bit of grass before their doors, and which they call 'going out on the lawn.'

(HISTORICAL.)

Ovid, in his *Fasti*, makes Juno claim the honour of giving a name to this month; but there had been ample time before his day for an obscurity to invest the origin of the term, and he lived before it was the custom to investigate such matters critically. Standing as the fourth month in the Roman calendar, it was in reality dedicated *à Junioribus*—that is, to the junior or inferior branch of the original legislature of Rome, as May was *à Majoribus*, or to the superior branch. 'Romulus assigned to this month a complement of thirty days, though in the old Latin or Alban calendar it consisted of twenty-six only. Numa deprived it of one day, which was restored by Julius Cæsar; since which time it has remained undisturbed.'— *Brady*.

CHARACTERISTICS OF JUNE.

Though the summer solstice takes place on the 21st day, June is only the third month of the year in respect of temperature, being preceded in this respect by July and August. The mornings, in the early part of the month especially, are liable to be even frosty, to the extensive damage of the buds of the fruit-trees. Nevertheless, June is the month of greatest summer beauty—the month during which the trees are in their best and freshest garniture. 'The leafy month of June,' Coleridge well calls it, the month when the flowers are at the richest in hue and profusion. In English landscape, the conical clusters of the chesnut buds, and the tassels of the laburnum and lilac, vie above with the variegated show of wild flowers below. Nature is now a pretty maiden of seventeen; she may show maturer charms afterwards, but she can never be again so gaily, so freshly beautiful. Dr Aiken says justly that June is in reality, in this climate, what the poets only dream May to be. The mean temperature of the air was given by an observer in Scotland as 59° Fahrenheit, against 60° for August and 61° for July.

The sun, formally speaking, reaches the most northerly point in the zodiac, and enters the constellation of Cancer, on the 21st of June; but for several days about that time there is no observable difference in his position, or his hours of rising and setting. At Greenwich he is above the horizon from 3.43 morning, to 8.17 evening, thus making a day of 16h. 26m. At Edinburgh, the longest day is about 17½ hours. At that season, in Scotland, there is a glow equal to dawn, in the north, through the whole of the brief night. The present writer was able at Edinburgh to read the title-page of a book, by the light of the northern sky, at midnight of the 14th of June 1849. In Shetland, the light at midnight is like a good twilight, and the text of any ordinary book may then be easily read. It is even alleged that, by the aid of refraction, and in favourable circumstances, the body of the sun has been seen at that season, from the top of a hill in Orkney, though the fact cannot be said to be authenticated.

Marriage Superstitions and Customs.

JUNE was the month which the Romans considered the most propitious season of the year for contracting matrimonial engagements, especially if the day chosen were that of the full moon or the conjunction of the sun and moon; the month of May was especially to be avoided, as under the influence of spirits adverse to happy households. All these pagan superstitions were retained in the Middle Ages, with many others which belonged more particularly to the spirit of Christianity: people then had recourse to all kinds of divination, love philters, magical invocations, prayers, fastings, and other follies, which were modified according to the country and the individual. A girl had only to agitate the water in a bucket of spring-water with her hand, or to throw broken eggs over another person's head, if she wished to see the image of the man she

should marry. A union could never be happy if the bridal party, in going to church, met a monk, a priest, a hare, a dog, cat, lizard, or serpent; while all would go well if it were a wolf, a spider, or a toad. Nor was it an unimportant matter to choose the wedding day carefully; the feast of Saint Joseph was especially to be avoided, and it is supposed, that as this day fell in mid-Lent, it was the reason why all the councils and synods of the church forbade marriage during that season of fasting; indeed, all penitential days and vigils throughout the year were considered unsuitable for these joyous ceremonies. The church blamed those husbands who married early in the morning, in dirty or negligent attire, reserving their better dresses for balls and feasts; and the clergy were forbidden to celebrate the rites after sunset, because the crowd often carried the party by main force to the alehouse, or beat them and hindered their departure from the church until they had paid a ransom. The people always manifested a strong aversion for badly assorted marriages. In such cases, the procession would be accompanied to the altar in the midst of a frightful concert of bells, saucepans, and frying-pans, or this tumult was reserved for the night, when the happy couple were settled in their own house. The church tried in vain to defend widowers and widows who chose to enter the nuptial bonds a second time; a synodal order of the Archbishop of Lyons, in 1577, thus describes the conduct it excommunicated: 'Marching in masks, throwing poisons, horrible and dangerous liquids before the door, sounding tambourines, doing all kinds of dirty things they can think of, until they have drawn from the husband large sums of money by force.'

A considerable sum of money was anciently put into a purse or plate, and presented by the bridegroom to the bride on the wedding-night, as a sort of purchase of her person; a custom common to the Greeks as well as the Romans, and which seems to have prevailed among the Jews and many Eastern nations. It was changed in the Middle Ages, and in the north of Europe, for the *morgengabe*, or morning present; the bride having the privilege, the morning after the wedding-day, of asking for any sum of money or any estate that she pleased, and which could not in honour be refused by her husband. The demand at times became really serious, if the wife were of an avaricious temper. Something of the same kind prevailed in England under the name of the Dow Purse. A trace of this is still kept up in Cumberland where the bridegroom provides himself with gold and crown pieces, and, when the service reaches the point, 'With all my worldly goods I thee endow,' he takes up the money, hands the clergyman his fee, and pours the rest into a handkerchief which is held by the bridesmaid for the bride. When Clovis was married to the Princess Clotilde, he offered, by his proxy, a sou and a denier, which became the marriage offering by law in France; and to this day pieces of money are given to the bride, varying only in value according to the rank of the parties.

How the ring came to be used is not well ascertained, as in former days it did not occupy its present prominent position, but was given with other presents to mark the completion of a contract. Its form is intended as a symbol of eternity, and of the intention of both parties to keep for ever the solemn covenant into which they have entered before God, and of which it is a pledge. When the persons were betrothed as children, among the Anglo-Saxons, the bridegroom gave a pledge, or 'wed' (a term from which we derive the word wedding); part of this wed consisted of a ring, which was placed on the maiden's right hand, and there religiously kept until transferred to the other hand at the second ceremony. Our marriage service is very nearly the same as that used by our forefathers, a few obsolete words only being changed. The bride was taken 'for fairer, for fouler, for better, for worse;' and promised 'to be buxom and bonny' to her future husband. The bridegroom put the ring on each of the bride's left-hand fingers in turn, saying at the first, 'in the name of the Father;' at the second, 'in the name of the Son,' at the third, 'in the name of the Holy Ghost;' and at the fourth, 'Amen.' The father presented his son-in-law with one of his daughter's shoes as a token of the transfer of authority, and the bride was made to feel the change by a blow on her head given with the shoe. The husband was bound by oath to use his wife well, in failure of which she might leave him; yet as a point of honour he was allowed 'to bestow on his wife and apprentices moderate castigation.' An old Welsh law tells us that three blows with a broomstick, on any 'part of the person except the head, is a fair allowance;' and another provides that the stick be not longer than the husband's arm, nor thicker than his middle finger.*

An English wedding, in the time of good Queen Bess, was a joyous public festival; among the higher ranks, the bridegroom presented the company with scarves, gloves, and garters of the favourite colours of the wedding pair; and the ceremony wound up with banquetings, masques, pageants, and epithalamiums. A gay procession formed a part of the humbler marriages; the bride was led to church between two boys wearing bride-laces and rosemary tied about their silken sleeves, and before her was carried a silver cup filled with wine, in which was a large branch of gilded rosemary, hung about with silk ribbons of all colours. Next came the musicians, and then the bridesmaids, some bearing great bridecakes, others garlands of gilded wheat; thus they marched to church amidst the shouts and benedictions of the spectators.

The penny weddings, at which each of the guests gave a contribution for the feast, were reprobated by the straiter-laced sort as leading to disorders and licentiousness; but it was found impossible to suppress them. All that could be done was to place restrictions upon the amount allowed to be given; in Scotland five shillings was the limit.

The customs of marrying and giving in marriage in Sweden, in former years, were of a somewhat barbarous character; it was beneath the dignity of a Scandinavian warrior to court a lady's

favour by gallantry and submission—he waited until she had bestowed her affections on another, and was on her way to the marriage ceremony, when, collecting his faithful followers, who were always ready for the fight, they fell upon the wedding *cortège*, and the stronger carried away the bride. It was much in favour of this practice that marriages were always celebrated at night. A pile of lances is still preserved behind the altar of the ancient church of Husaby, in Gothland, into which were fitted torches, and which were borne before the bridegroom for the double purpose of giving light and protection. It was the province of the groomsmen, or, as they were named, 'best men,' to carry these; and the strongest and stoutest of the bridegroom's friends were chosen for this duty. Three or four days before the marriage, the ceremony of the bride's bath took place, when the lady went in great state to the bath, accompanied by all her friends, married and single; the day closing with a banquet and ball. On the marriage-day the young couple sat on a raised platform, under a canopy of silk; all the wedding presents being arranged on a bench covered with silk, and consisting of plate, jewels, and money. To this day the bridegroom has a great fear of the trolls and sprites which still inhabit Sweden; and, as an antidote against their power, he sews into his clothes various strong smelling herbs, such as garlick, chives, and rosemary. The young women always carry bouquets of these in their hands to the feast, whilst they deck themselves out with loads of jewellery, gold bells, and *grelots* as large as small apples, with chains, belts, and stomachers. No bridegroom could be induced on that day to stand near a closed gate, or where cross roads meet; he says he takes these precautions 'against envy and malice.' On the other hand, if the bride be prudent, she will take care when at the altar to put her right foot before that of the bridegroom, for then she will get the better of her husband during her married life; she will also be studious to get the first sight of him before he can see her, because that will preserve her influence over him. It is customary to fill the bride's pocket with bread, which she gives to the poor she meets on her road to church, a misfortune being averted with every alms bestowed; but the beggar will not eat it, as he thereby brings wretchedness on himself. On their return from church, the bride and bridegroom must visit their cowhouses and stables, that the cattle may thrive and multiply.

In Norway, the marriages of the *bonder* or peasantry are conducted with very gay ceremonies, and in each parish there is a set of ornaments for the temporary use of the bride, including a showy coronal and girdle; so that the poorest woman in the land has the gratification of appearing for one day in her life in a guise which she probably thinks equal to that of a queen. The museum of national antiquities at Copenhagen contains a number of such sets of bridal decorations which were formerly used in Denmark. In the International Exhibition at London, in 1862, the Norwegian court showed the model of a peasant couple, as dressed and decorated for their wedding; and every beholder

* Thrupp.

720

must have been arrested by its homely splendours. Annexed is a cut representing the bride.

NORWEGIAN BRIDE.

In pagan days, when Rolf married King Erik's daughter, the king and queen sat throned in state, whilst courtiers passed in front, offering gifts of oxen, cows, swine, sheep, sucking-pigs, geese, and even cats. A shield, sword, and axe were among the bride's wedding outfit, that she might, if necessary, defend herself from her husband's blows.

In the vast steppes of south-eastern Russia, on the shores of the Caspian and Black Sea, marriage ceremonies recall the patriarchal customs of the earliest stages of society. The evening before the day when the affianced bride is given to her husband, she pays visits to her master and the inhabitants of the village, in the simple dress of a peasant, consisting of a red cloth jacket, descending as low as the knees, a very short white petticoat, fastened at the waist with a red woollen scarf, above which is an embroidered chemise. The legs, which are always bare above the ankle, are sometimes protected by red or yellow morocco boots. The girls of the village who accompany her are, on the contrary, attired in their best, recalling the old paintings of Byzantine art, where the Virgin is adorned with a coronal. They know how to arrange with great art the leaves and scarlet berries of various kinds of trees in their hair, the tresses of which are plaited as a crown, or hang down on the shoulders. A necklace of pearls or coral is wound at least a dozen times round the neck, on which they hang religious medals, with enamel paintings imitating mosaic. At each

house the betrothed throws herself on her knees before the head of it, and kisses his feet as she begs his pardon; the fair penitent is immediately raised and kissed, receiving some small present, whilst she in return gives a small roll of bread, of a symbolic form. On her return home all her beautiful hair is cut off, as henceforth she must wear the *platoke*, or turban, a woollen or linen shawl which is rolled round the head, and is the only distinction between the married and unmarried. It is invariably presented by the husband, as the Indian shawl among ourselves; which, however, we have withdrawn from its original destination, which ought only to be a head-dress. The despoiled bride expresses her regrets with touching grace, in one of their simple songs: 'Oh, my curls, my fair golden hair! Not for one only, not for two years only, have I arranged you—every Saturday you were bathed, every Sunday you were ornamented, and to-day, in a single hour, I must lose you!' The old woman whose duty it is to roll the turban round the brow, wishing her happiness, says, ' I cover your head with the *platoke*, my sister, and I wish you health and happiness. Be pure as water, and fruitful as the earth.' When the marriage is over, the husband takes his wife to the inhabitants of the village, and shows them the change of dress effected the night before.

Among the various tribes of Asia none are so rich or well dressed as the Armenians; to them belongs chiefly the merchandise of precious stones, which they export to Constantinople. The Armenian girl whose marriage is to be described had delicate flowers of celestial blue painted all over her breast and neck, her eyebrows were dyed black, and the tips of her fingers and nails of a bright orange. She wore on each hand valuable rings set with precious stones, and round her neck a string of very fine turquoises; her shirt was of the finest spun silk, her jacket and trousers of cashmere of a bright colour. The priest and his deacon arrived; the latter bringing a bag containing the sacerdotal garments, in which the priest arrayed himself, placing a mitre ornamented with precious stones on his head, and a collar of metal,—on which the twelve apostles were represented in bas-relief,— round his neck. He began by blessing a sort of temporary altar in the middle of the room; the mother of the bride took her by the hand, and leading her forward, she bowed at the feet of her future husband, to show that she acknowledged him as lord and master. The priest, placing their hands in each other, pronounced a prayer, and then drew their heads together until they touched three times, while with his right hand he made a motion as if blessing them; a second time their hands were joined, and the bridegroom was asked, ' Will you be her husband?' ' I will,' he answered, raising at the same time the veil of the bride, in token that she was now his, and letting it fall again. The priest then took two wreaths of flowers, ornamented with a quantity of hanging gold threads, from the hands of the deacon, put them on the heads of the married couple, changed them three times from one head to the other, repeating each time, ' I unite you, and bind you one to another

—live in peace.' Such are the customs in the very land where man was first created; and, among nations who change so little as those in the East, we may fairly believe them to be among the most ancient.

WHIT-SUNDAY WOMAN-SHOW IN RUSSIA.

A custom has long prevailed at St Petersburg which can only be regarded as a relic of a rude state of society; for it is nothing more or less than a show of marriageable women or girls, with a view of obtaining husbands. The women certainly have a choice in the matter, and in this respect they are not brought to market in the same sense as fat cattle or sheep; but still it is only under the influence of a very coarse estimate of the sex that the custom can prevail. The manner of managing the show in past years was as follows. On Whit Sunday afternoon the Summer Garden, a place of popular resort in St Petersburg, was thronged with bachelors and maidens, looking out for wives and husbands respectively. The girls put on their best adornments; and these were sometimes more costly than would seem to be suitable for persons in humble life, were it not that this kind of pride is much cherished among the peasantry in many countries. Bunches of silver tea-spoons, a large silver ladle, or some other household luxury, were in many instances held in the hand, to denote that the maiden could bring something valuable to her husband. The young men, on their part, did not fail to look their best. The maidens were accompanied by their parents, or by some elder member of their family, in order that everything might be conducted in a decorous manner. The bachelors, strolling and sauntering to and fro, would notice the maidens as they passed, and the maidens would blushingly try to look their best. Supposing a young man were favourably impressed with what he saw, he did not immediately address the object of his admiration, but had a little quiet talk with one of the seniors, most probably a woman. He told her his name, residence, and occupation; he gave a brief inventory of his worldly goods, naming the number of roubles (if any) which he had been able to save. On his side he asked questions, one of which was sure to relate to the amount of dowry promised for the maiden. The woman with whom this conversation was held was often no relative to the maiden, but a sort of marriage broker or saleswoman, who conducted these delicate negotiations, either in friendliness or for a fee. If the references on either side were unsatisfactory, the colloquy ended without any bargain being struck; and, even if favourable, nothing was immediately decided. Many admirers for the same girl might probably come forward in this way. In the evening a family conclave was held concerning the chances of each maiden, at which the offer of each bachelor was calmly considered, chiefly in relation to the question of roubles. The test was very little other than that 'the highest bidder shall be the purchaser.' A note was sent to the young man whose offer was deemed most eligible; and it was very rarely that the girl made any objection to the spouse thus selected for her.

The St Petersburg correspondent of one of the London newspapers, who was at the Woman Show on Whit Sunday, 1861, stated that the custom has been gradually declining for many years; that there were very few candidates for matrimony on that occasion; and that the total abandonment of the usage was likely soon to occur, under the influence of opinion more congenial to the tastes of Europeans generally.

CREELING THE BRIDEGROOM.

A curious custom in connexion with marriage prevailed at one time in Scotland, and, from the manner in which it was carried out, was called 'Creeling the Bridegroom.' The mode of procedure in the village of Galashiels was as follows. Early in the day after the marriage, those interested in the proceeding assembled at the house of the newly-wedded couple, bringing with them a 'creel,' or basket, which they filled with stones. The young husband, on being brought to the door, had the creel firmly fixed upon his back, and with it in this position had to run the round of the town, or at least the chief portion of it, followed by a number of men to see that he did not drop his burden; the only condition on which he was allowed to do so being that his wife should come after him, and kiss him. As relief depended altogether upon the wife, it would sometimes happen that the husband did not need to run more than a few yards; but when she was more than ordinarily bashful, or wished to have a little sport at the expense of her lord and master—which it may be supposed would not unfrequently be the case—he had to carry his load a considerable distance. This custom was very strictly enforced; for the person who was last creeled had charge of the ceremony, and he was naturally anxious that no one should escape. The practice, as far as Galashiels was concerned, came to an end with the last century, in the person of one Robert Young, who on the ostensible plea of a 'sore back,' lay a-bed all the day after his marriage, and obstinately refused to get up and be creeled; he had been twice married before, and no doubt felt that he had had enough of creeling.

MARRIAGE LAWS AND CUSTOMS IN THE EAST OF ENGLAND.

There is a saying of Hesiod's (*Works and Days*, l. 700), to the effect that it is better to marry a woman from the neighbourhood, than one from a distance. With this may be compared the Scotch proverb, 'It is better to marry over the midden, than over the moor,' *i.e.* to take for your wife one who lives close by—the other side of the muckheap—than to fetch one from the other side of the moor. I am not aware of the existence of any proverb to this effect in East Anglia; but the usual practice of the working classes is in strict accordance with it. Whole parishes have intermarried to such an extent that almost everybody is related to, or connected with everybody else. One curious result of this is that no one is counted as a 'relation' beyond first cousins, for if 'relationship' went further than that it might almost as well include the whole parish.

A very strong inducement to marry a near neighbour, lies, no doubt, in the great advantage of having a mother, aunt, or sister at hand whose help can be obtained in case of sickness; I have frequently heard complaints of the inconvenience of 'having nobody belonging to them,' made by sick people, whose near relations live at a distance, and who in consequence are obliged to call in paid help when ill.

'Marry in Lent,
And you'll live to repent,'

is a common saying in East Anglia ; and so also is

'To change the name, and not the letter,
Is a change for the worst, and not for the better;'

i.e., it is unlucky for a woman to marry a man whose surname begins with the same letter as her own.

A curious custom with regard to marriages still exists : at any rate, I knew of its being observed a few years ago ; it is that if a younger sister marries before the elder one, the elder must *dance in the hog's trough*. In the case to which I refer, a brother went through the ceremony also, and the dancers performed their part so well, that they danced both the ends off the trough, and the trough itself into two pieces. In the West of England it is a fixed rule that the lady should dance in *green stockings ;* but I am not aware of any peculiar stockings being required on the occasion in East Anglia.

The attendance at the weddings of agricultural labourers is naturally small; but it is very remarkable that neither father nor mother of bride or bridegroom come with them to church. I can hardly recollect more than one instance of any of the parents being present at the ceremony, and then what brought the bridegroom's father was the circumstance of the ring being left behind. The omission had not been discovered by the wedding party, and the father came striding up the church, very red and hot, in time to shove a tiny screw of paper into the bridegroom's hand before the clergyman held out his book for the ring to be laid upon it.

The usual attendants at a labourer's wedding are only three—the official father, the bridesmaid, and the groomsman ; the two latter being, if possible, an engaged couple, who purpose to be the next pair to come up to the altar on a similar errand upon their own account.

The parties very frequently object to sign their names, and try to get off from doing so, even when they can write very fairly, preferring to set their *mark* to the entry in the register : and, unless the clergyman is awake to this disinclination, and presses the point, many good writers will appear in the books as 'marksmen,' a circumstance which much impairs the value of the comparative number of names and marks in the marriage registers as a test of the state of education among the poor.

The bridegroom sometimes considers it his duty to profess that he considers the job a very dear one—not particularly complimentary to the bride,—and once a man took the trouble to pay my fee entirely in threepenny and fourpenny pieces ; which was, I suppose, a very good joke ; not so much so, however, as when a friend of mine had his fee paid in coppers.

Suffolk.   C. W. J.

JUNE 1.

St Justin, the philosopher, 167. St Pamphilius, priest and martyr, 309. St Caprias, abbot, 430. St Wistan, Prince of Mercia, martyr, 849. St Peter of Pisa, founder of the Hermits of St Jerome, 1435.

Born.—Robert Cecil, Earl of Salisbury, minister to Elizabeth and James I., 1560; Nicolas Poussin, painter, 1594, *Andelys in Normandy ;* Secretary John Thurloe, 1616, *Abbots Roding, Essex;* Sir John Dugdale, antiquary, 1628, *Shustoke ;* John Tweddell (Eastern travels), 1769, *Threepwood, near Hexham.*

Died.—Henry Dandolo, doge of Venice, 1205, *bur. in St Sophia, Constantinople ;* Jerome of Prague, religious

reformer, burnt at *Constance,* 1416; Christopher Marlowe, dramatist, 1593 ; James Gillray, caricaturist, 1815, *London ;* Sir David Wilkie, artist, died at sea off *Gibraltar,* 1841 ; Pope Gregory XVI. 1846.

JAMES GILLRAY.

In the churchyard of St James, Piccadilly, there is a flat stone, bearing the following inscription :—

IN MEMORY
OF MR JAMES GILLRAY,
CARICATURIST,
WHO DEPARTED THIS LIFE
1ST JUNE, 1815,
AGED 58 YEARS.

Gillray was the son of a native of Lanarkshire,* a soldier in the British army, who lost an arm at the fatal field of Fontenoy.

Like Hogarth, Gillray commenced his career as a mere letter engraver; but, tiring of this monotonous occupation, he ran away, and joined a company of wandering comedians. After experiencing the well-known hardships of a stroller's life, he returned to London, and became a student of the Royal Academy and an engraver. Admirably as many of his engravings, particularly landscapes, are executed, it is as a caricaturist that he is best known. In this peculiar art he never had even a rival, so much have his works surpassed those of all other practitioners. The happy tact with which he seized upon the points in manners and politics most open to ridicule, was equalled only by the exquisite skill and spirit with which he satirically portrayed them. By continual practice he became so facile, that he used to etch his ideas at once upon the copper, without making a preliminary drawing, his only guides being sketches of the characters he intended to introduce made upon small pieces of card, which he always carried in his pocket, ready to catch a face or form that might be serviceable.

The history of George III. may be said to have been inscribed by the graver of Gillray, and sure never monarch had such an historian. The unroyal familiarity of manner ; awkward, shuffling gait, undignified carriage, and fatuous countenance ; the habit of entering into conversation with persons of low rank ; the volubility with which he poured out his pointless questions, without waiting for any other answer than his own 'hay ? hay ? hay ?' his love of money, his homely savings ; have all been trebly emphasized by the great caricaturist of his reign ; and not less ably because the pencil of the public satirist was pointed by private pique. Gillray had accompanied Loutherbourg into France, to assist him in making sketches for his grand picture of the siege of Valenciennes. On their return, the king, who made pretensions to be a patron of art, desired to look over their sketches, and expressed great admiration of Loutherbourg's, which were plain landscape drawings, sufficiently finished to be intelligible. But when he saw Gillray's rude, though spirited sketches of

* Gillray is a Highland name, meaning Ruddy Lad ; but it is found in the south of Scotland. The writer remembers a family of the name in a county adjacent to Lanarkshire.

French soldiers, he threw them aside with contempt, saying, 'I don't understand caricatures,' an action and observation that the caricaturist never forgot or forgave.

Gillray's character affords a sad example of the reckless imprudence that too frequently accompanies talent and genius. For many years he resided in the house of his publisher, Mrs Humphrey, by whom he was most liberally supplied with every indulgence; during this time he produced nearly all his most celebrated works, which were bought up with unparalleled eagerness, and circulated not only over all England, but most parts of Europe. Though under a positive engagement not to work for any other publisher, yet so great was his insatiable desire for strong liquors, that he often etched plates for unscrupulous persons, cleverly disguising his style and handling. The last of his works is dated 1811. In that year he sank into a state in which imbecility was only enlivened by delirium, and which continued till his death.

The accompanying illustration, not a bad specimen of Gillray's style, is taken from a popular caricature on the peace concluded between Great Britain and France in 1802, entitled *The First Kiss these Ten Years; or, the*

THE FIRST KISS THESE TEN YEARS.

Meeting of Britannia and Citizen François. Britannia appears as a portly lady in full dress, her shield and spear leaning neglected against the wall. The Frenchman expresses his delight at the meeting in warm terms, saying, 'Madame, permittez me to pay my profound esteem to your engaging person; and to seal on your divine lips my everlasting attachment.' The lady, who is blushing deeply, replies—'Monsieur, you are truly a well-bred gentleman! And though you make me blush, yet you kiss so delicately that I

724

cannot refuse you, though I were sure you would deceive me again.' On the wall, just behind these two principal figures, are framed portraits of George the Third and Bonaparte fiercely scowling at each other. This caricature became as popular in France as it was in England. Immense quantities of impressions were sent to, and sold on the Continent, and even the great Napoleon himself expressed the high amusement he derived from it.

THE 'GLORIOUS FIRST OF JUNE.'

We should need to bring back the horrors of the first French Revolution to enable us to understand the wild delight with which Lord Howe's victory, in 1794, was regarded in England. A king, a queen, and a princess guillotined in France, a reign of terror prevailing in that country, and a war threatening half the monarchs in Europe, had impressed the English with an intense desire to thwart the republicans. Our army was badly organized and badly generalled in those days; but the navy was in all its glory. In April 1794, Lord Howe, as Admiral-in-chief of the Channel fleet, went out to look after the French fleet at Brest, and a great French convoy known to be expected from America and the West Indies. He had with him twenty-six sail of the line, and five frigates. For some weeks the fleet was in the Atlantic, baffled by foggy weather in the attempt to discover the enemy; but towards the close of May the two fleets sighted each other, and a great naval battle became imminent. The French admirals had often before avoided when possible a close contest with the English; but on this occasion Admiral Villaret Joyeuse, knowing that a convoy of enormous value was at stake, determined to meet his formidable opponent. The two fleets were about equal in the number of ships; but the French had the advantage in number of guns, weight of metal, and number of men. On the 1st of June, Howe achieved a great victory over Villaret Joyeuse, the details of which are given in all the histories of the period.

The English valued this victory quite as much for the moral effect it wrought in Europe generally, as for the immediate material injury it inflicted on the French. They had long been anxious concerning Lord Howe's movements; and when they learned that he had really captured or destroyed a large part of the French fleet, the joy was great. In those days it took a considerable time to bring any news from the Bay of Biscay to London; insomuch that it was not till the 10th that the admiral's despatches reached the Government. On the evening of that day the Earl of Chatham made known the news at the opera; and the audience, roused with excitement, called loudly for 'God save the king' and 'Rule Britannia,' which was sung by Morichelli, Morelli, and Rovedicco, opera stars of that period. Signora Banti, a greater star than the rest, being seen in one of the boxes, was compelled to go down to the stage, and join her voice to the rest in a second performance of these songs. The Duke of Clarence went and told the news to the manager of Covent Garden

Theatre; Lord Mulgrave and Colonel Phipps did the same at Drury Lane Theatre; Mr Suett and Mr Incledon made the announcement on the stage to the audiences of the two theatres; and then ensued the most lively expressions of delight.

LORD HOWE'S VICTORY OF THE FIRST OF JUNE.

Of course there was much ringing of bells and firing of guns to celebrate the victory; and, in accordance with English custom, there was some breaking of windows during the illumination saturnalia in the evenings. The conduct of Earl Stanhope on this occasion was marked by some of the eccentricity which belonged to his character. He was among those statesmen (and they were not a few) who deprecated any interference with the internal affairs of France; and who, though not approving of regicide and the reign of terror, still saw something to admire in the new-born but misused liberty of that country. The earl, in spite of his own rank, had concurred with the French in regarding an 'Aristocrat' as necessarily an enemy to the well-being of the people. On the 13th, he inserted the following singular advertisement in the newspapers:— 'Whereas a mixed band of ruffians attacked my house in Mansfield Street, in the dead of the night between the 11th and 12th of June instant, and set it on fire at different times: and whereas a gentleman's carriage passed several times to and fro in front of my house, and the aristocrat, or other person, who was in the said carriage, gave money to the people in the street to encourage them: this is to request the friends of liberty and good order to send me any authentic information they can procure respecting the name and place of abode of the said aristocrat, or other person, who was in the carriage above-mentioned, in order that he may be made amenable to the law.' The words 'aristocrat' and 'liberty' were then more terrible than they are now.

St Patrick's Purgatory.

Three legendary stories excited the minds of the people in the middle ages—that of the Wandering Jew, that of Prester John, and that of St Patrick's Purgatory. The two former were insignificant in comparison with the last. It was about the middle of the twelfth century that a Benedictine monk, named Henry of Saltrey, established the wondrous and widespread reputation of an insignificant islet in a dreary lake, among the barren morasses and mountains of Donegal, by giving to the world the Legend of the Knight. This legend, extravagant in our eyes, but in perfect accordance with the ideas of that age, was a sort of composition out of various previous notions, including one which held that the land of departed souls lay in the west.

It represented its hero, Sir Owen, as an Irishman, who with courage and fidelity had served in the wars of King Stephen of England. Returning to Ireland to see his parents, he was seized with sudden remorse for his many sins; for he had lived a life of bloodshed and rapine, and had not scrupled to plunder churches, maltreat nuns, and apply the most sacred things to his own profane use and benefit. In this penitent mood he determined to visit St Patrick's Purgatory, with the view of washing away the guilt of so many misdemeanours.

Respecting the origin of the Purgatory, the legend states that when St Patrick was endeavouring to convert the Irish by telling them of the torments of the infernal regions, the people cried, 'We cannot believe such things, unless we see them.' So, the saint, miraculously causing the earth to open, showed them the flaming entrance of the place of punishment; and the unbelieving heathens were at once converted to the true faith. St Patrick, then placed a gate on the cave, and building an abbey near it, entrusted the key to the prior, so that he had the privilege of admitting pilgrims. The penitent who wished to enter had to pass a probation of fifteen days in prayer and fasting; and, on the sixteenth, having received the sacrament, he was led in solemn procession to the gate. Having entered, the gate was locked by the prior, and not opened till the following day. If the pilgrim were found when the gate was re-opened, he was received with great joy; if not, he was understood to have perished in the Purgatory, and his name was never after mentioned.

The knight, having duly performed the preliminary ceremonies, entered the cave, and travelled till he came to a spacious hall, where he was kindly received by fifteen venerable men, clothed in white garments, who gave him directions for his future guidance. Leaving the old men, and travelling onwards, he was soon attacked by troops of demons, whom he successfully resisted by earnest prayer. Still pushing on, he passed through four 'fields' of punishment, by fire, ice, serpents, &c., that need not be too particularly described. He ascended a lofty mountain, from whence he was blown by a hurricane into a horribly filthy river; and, after many adventures, surrounded by millions of demons, and wretched souls in dreadful tortures, he succeeded in crossing a narrow bridge, and found his troubles over, the malignant demons not daring to follow him farther. Pursuing his journey, he soon arrived at a wall as bright as glass, and entering a golden gate, found himself in the garden of Eden among those happy souls who had expiated their sins, and were now waiting to be received into the celestial Paradise. Here, Owen wished to remain, but was told that he must again return to the world, there to die and leave his corporeal fabric. As he was for ever exempt from the punishment of Purgatory, he was shown a short and pleasant road back to the mouth of the cave; where he was received with great joy by the prior and monks of the abbey.

The legend, in its original Latin prose, soon spread over all Europe, and was repeated by Matthew Paris as a historical and geographical fact. It was also rendered into several metrical versions in the vulgar tongues. It was introduced into an Italian romance of chivalry, Don Quixote's favourite work, entitled *Guerrino il Meschino;* and later still it was dramatised by Calderon, the celebrated Spanish poet. It was introduced even into a Dutch romance, founded on the story of Fortunatus, and in the forms of a chap-book and broadside, is current in Spain and Italy at the present day.

The earliest authentic record of a visit to Lough Derg is in the form of letters testimonial, granted, in 1358, by Edward III. to Ungarus of Rimini and Nicholas of Beccaria, in proof of their having faithfully performed the pilgrimage

to St Patrick's Purgatory. There are some documents of a similar description in the archiepiscopal archives of Armagh; and in 1397 Richard II. granted a safe conduct pass to Raymond, Viscount Perilhos, and Knight of Rhodes, to visit the Purgatory with a retinue of twenty men and thirty horses. Raymond wrote an account of his pilgrimage, which is little more than a paraphrase of the Legend of the Knight, interspersed with personal history and political matters.* There is yet another account of a pilgrimage by one William Staunton in 1409, preserved among the Cottonian MSS. in the British Museum. Staunton's story differs slightly from that of the knight. He was fortunate enough to meet with a countryman in the Purgatory, one St John of Bridlington, who protected him from the demons. He also had a romantic and affecting interview with a pre-deceased sister and her lover there; and was ultimately rescued by a fair woman, who drew him out of the fiery gulf with a rope that he had once charitably given to a beggar.

Later, however, in the fifteenth century, doubts began to be expressed regarding the

truth of the marvellous stories of the Purgatory; and these, with the increasing intelligence of the age, led to its suppression, as thus recorded in the annals of Ulster, under the date 1497: 'The Cave of St. Patrick's Purgatory, in Lough Derg, was destroyed about the festival of St. Patrick this year, by the guardian of Donegal and the representatives of the bishop in the deanery of Lough Erne, by authority of the Pope; the people in general having understood from the history of the knight and other old books that this was not the Purgatory which St Patrick obtained from God, though the people in general were visiting it.'

The learned Jesuit, Bolandus, in the *Acta Sanctorum,* ascribes the suppression of the Purgatory to the inordinate rapacity of its custodians. The story is exceedingly amusing; but want of space compels us to curtail it. A pious Dutch monk, having obtained permission

* The above cut, representing a pilgrim entering St Patrick's Purgatory, was copied by the writer from an illuminated manuscript of the fifteenth century in the Bibliothèque Nationale, Paris, No. 7588, A.F., and published in the *Ulster Journal of Archæology.* A good view of the island is given in Doyle's *Tours in Ulster.*

to visit holy places as a religious mendicant, came to Lough Derg, and solicited admission to the Purgatory. The prior informed him that he could not be admitted without a license from the bishop of the diocese. The monk went to the bishop; but, as he was both poor and poor-like, the prelate's servants uncourteously shut the door in his face. The monk was a man of energy and perseverance; so he waited till he saw the bishop, and then, falling on his knees, solicited the license. 'Certainly,' said the bishop, 'but you must first pay me a sum of money, my usual fee.' The monk replied boldly, to the effect that the free gifts of God should not be sold for money; hinted that such a proceeding would be tainted with the leprosy of simony; and, by dint of sturdy solicitation, succeeded in obtaining the license. The bishop then told him that was not all: he must next obtain permission from Magrath, the hereditary ecclesiastical tenant of the territory in which the Purgatory was situated. The monk went to Magrath, who in turn demanded his fee; but at last, wearied with importunity, and seeing he could not receive what the other had not to give, conceded the required permission. The monk then returned to the prior, fortified with the licenses of the bishop and Magrath, but was most ungraciously received. The prior could in nowise understand how the monk could have the audacity to come there without money, when he knew that the convent was supported solely by the fees of pilgrims. The undaunted Dutchman spoke as boldly to the prior as he had to the bishop; and at last, but with a very bad grace, he was permitted to go through the prescribed ceremonies, and enter the Purgatory. In a high state of religious excitement and expectation, the monk was shut up in the cave; but neither heard nor saw anything during the whole twenty-four hours. Some, probably, would have taken a different view of the matter; but the disappointed and enthusiastic monk, implicitly believing the marvellous legends, considered that the miracle had ceased on account of having been made a source of profit. So going to Rome, the monk represented the whole affair to the sovereign pontiff, and the result was the suppression of the Purgatory, as above related.

The ancient renown of Lough Derg was thus destroyed; but an annual pilgrimage of the lowest classes commenced soon afterwards, and occasioned such scenes of licentious disorder, that in 1623 the Lords Justices commanded that all the buildings on the island should be utterly demolished. Bishop Spottiswood, who superintended this demolition, describes the 'Cave' as 'a poor beggarly hole, made with stones laid together with men's hands, such as husbandmen make to keep hogs from the rain.'

The annual pilgrimage has never been completely abolished, and continues to the present day, commencing on the 1st of June, and lasting to the 15th of August; during which time from about eight to ten thousand persons—all, with a very few exceptions, of the lowest class of society—visit the island. The penitential style is entirely done away with, the word purgatory

is abandoned, and a chapel called 'the prison' serves instead. The pilgrims, now termed 'stationers,' enter 'prison' at seven o'clock in the evening, the men ranging themselves on one side of the edifice, the women on the other. Here they remain without food or sleep for twenty-four hours; but they are allowed to drink water, and under certain restrictions may occasionally pass in and out of the building during that time. The rest of their penance consists in repeating a mechanical routine of prayers, painfully perambulating with bare feet, and crawling on bare knees over certain rocky paths, denominated saints' beds.

The tourist visitor to Lough Derg, during pilgrimage time, will meet with nothing to charm the eye or gratify the mind. The spot, once so celebrated, is as squalid and commonplace as can well be conceived. All romantic ideas will speedily be put to flight by the visitor observing the business word TICKETS, painted up over a hutch, made in railway-office style, in the shed which serves as a ferry-house. Here the pilgrim pays for his passage over to the island—one shilling, or as much more as he pleases, for the first-class, in the stern of the boat; or sixpence for the second-class, in the bow. Arrived on the island he again pays one shilling, or as much more as he can afford (it being well understood that the more he pays the greater spiritual advantages he will gain,) to the prior, for which he receives a ticket entitling him to the privilege of confession. Thus, though pilgrims are expected to disburse according to their means, the poor man need not pay more than eighteen-pence. There are two chapels on the island, one named St Patrick's, is used as the 'prison,' the other, St Mary's, as the confessional. There is also a house for the prior and his four assistant priests, and five lodging-houses for the use of pilgrims. All these are common whitewashed buildings, such as may be seen in any Irish village, without the slightest pretension to even simple neatness; and Mr Otway has not unaptly described them as filthy, dreary, and detestable.

Still, the degrading penance performed at this place is flavoured by a certain spice of romantic interest, arising from the real or mythical dangers the pilgrims are supposed to incur. In 1796 the ferry-boat, when conveying pilgrims to the island, upset, and seventy persons were drowned. Tradition states that a similar accident happened once before that period, and prophecy asserts that the boat 'is to be lost' a third time. Again, it is freely reported, and currently believed, that if any one of the pilgrims should chance to fall asleep when in 'prison,' the great enemy of mankind would be entitled to fly off in the twinkling of an eye with the whole number; a truly horrible event, which it is said has twice occurred already, and, of course, must happen a third time. To prevent such a very undesirable catastrophe, each woman takes a large pin into prison with her, the point of which she freely employs upon the person of any of her neighbours who seem likely to be overcome by sleep. For a like purpose a few long sticks are distributed among the men, to tap the heads of drowsy sinners. And it not unfrequently happens that those who are the least sleepy, and consequently the most busy in tapping their brother pilgrims' heads at the commencement of the twenty-four hours' imprisonment, become sleepy sinners themselves towards the latter part of the time ; and then, as may readily be supposed, the taps are returned with compound interest.

The island is very small, not measuring more than three hundred paces in any direction, and contains about three roods of barren rocky ground. For this small space the Protestant proprietor receives a rental of £300 per annum.

JUNE 2.

Saints Pothinus, Bishop of Lyons, Sanctus, Attalus, Blandina, and the other martyrs of Lyons, 177. St Erasmus, bishop and martyr, 303. Saints Marcellinus and Peter, martyrs, about 304.

Born.—Nicolas le Fevre, 1544, *Paris*
Died.—Thomas, Duke of Norfolk, executed, 1572, *Tower of London ;* James Douglas, Earl of Morton, beheaded at *Edinburgh*, 1581; Sir Edward Leigh, 1671, *Rushall ;* Madeleine de Scuderi, romances, miscellaneous writings, 1701.

THE REGENT MORTON—'HALIFAX LAW.'

After ruling Scotland under favour of Elizabeth for nearly ten years, Morton fell a victim to court faction, which probably could not have availed against him if he had not forfeited public esteem by his greed and cruelty. It must have been a striking sight when that proud, stern, resolute face, which had frowned so many better men down, came to speak from a scaffold, protesting innocence of the crime for which he had been condemned, but owning sins enough to justify

THE MAIDEN.

God for his fate. As is well known, the instrument employed on the occasion was one forming

a sort of prototype of the afterwards more famous guillotine, and named The Maiden, of which a portraiture is here presented, drawn from the original, still preserved in Edinburgh.

Morton is believed to have been the person who introduced The Maiden into Scotland, and he is thought to have taken the idea from a similar instrument which had long graced a mount near Halifax, in Yorkshire, as the appointed means of ready punishment for offences against forest law in that part of England.

Halifax Law.

'There is and hath been of ancient time a law, or rather a custom, at Halifax, that whosoever doth commit any felony, and is taken with the same, or confess the fact upon examination, if it be valued by four constables to amount to the sum of thirteen-pence halfpenny, he is forthwith beheaded upon one of the next market days (which fall usually upon the Tuesdays, Thursdays, and Saturdays), or else upon the same day that he is so convicted, if market be then holden. The engine wherewith the execution is done is a square block of wood, of the length of four feet and a half, which doth ride up and down in a slot, rabet, or regall, between two pieces of timber that are framed and set upright, of five yards in height. In the nether end of the sliding block is an axe, keyed or fastened with an iron into the wood, which, being drawn up to the top of the frame, is there fastened by a wooden pin (with a notch made into the same, after the manner of a Samson's post), unto the middest of which pin also there is a long rope fastened, that cometh down among the people; so that when the offender hath made his confession, and hath laid his neck over the nethermost block, every man then present doth either take hold of the rope (or putteth forth his arm so near to the same as he can get, in token that he is willing to see justice executed), and pulling out the pin in this manner, the head block wherein the axe is fastened doth fall down with such a violence, that if the neck of the transgressor were so big as that of a bull, it should be cut in sunder at a stroke, and roll from the body by an huge distance. If it be so that the offender be apprehended for an ox, sheep, kine, horse, or any such cattle, the self beast or other of the same kind shall have the end of the rope tied somewhere unto them, so that they being driven, do draw out the pin whereby the offender is executed.'—*Holinshed's Chronicle*, ed. 1587.

This sharp practice, in which originated the alliterative line in the Beggars' Litany : 'From Hell, Hull, and Halifax, good Lord deliver us !' seems to date from time immemorial. To make an offender amenable to Halifax Law, it was necessary he should be taken within 'the forest of Hardwick and liberty of Halifax' with the stolen property (of the value of thirteen-pence halfpenny or more) in his hands or on his back, or he could be convicted on his own confession. Upon apprehension the offender was taken before the Lord Bailiff, who immediately issued his summons to the constables of four towns within the district, to choose four 'Frith burghers' from each to act as jurymen. Before this tribunal accuser and accused were confronted, and the stolen article produced for valuation. No oaths were administered; and if the evidence against the prisoner failed to establish the charge, he was set at liberty there and then. If the verdict went against him, he left the court for the block, if it happened to be Saturday (the principal market-day), otherwise he was reserved for that day, being exposed in the stocks on the intervening Tuesdays and Thursdays. If the condemned could contrive to outrun the constable, and get outside the liberty of Halifax, he secured his own; he could not be followed and recaptured, but was liable to lose his head if ever he ventured within the jurisdiction again. One Lacy actually suffered after living peaceably outside the precincts for seven years; and a local proverbial phrase, 'I trow not, quoth Dinnis,' commemorates the escape of a criminal of that name, who being asked by people he met in his flight whether Dinnis was not to be beheaded that day, replied, 'I trow not!' He very wisely never returned to the dangerous neighbourhood. After the sentence had been duly carried out, a coroner's inquest was held at Halifax, when a verdict was given respecting the felony for which the unlucky thief had been executed, to be entered in the records of the Crown Office.

On the 27th and 30th days of April 1650, Abraham Wilkinson, John Wilkinson, and Anthony Mitchell were charged before the sixteen representatives of Halifax, Skircoat, Sowerby, and Warley, with stealing sixteen yards of russet-coloured kersey and two colts; nine yards of cloth and the colts being produced in court. Mitchell and one of the Wilkinsons confessed, and the sentence passed with the following form,—

'THE DETERMINATE SENTENCE. — The prisoners, that is to say, Abraham Wilkinson and Anthony Mitchell, being apprehended within the liberty of Halifax, and brought before us, with nine yards of cloth as aforesaid, and the two colts above mentioned, which cloth is apprized to nine shillings, and the black colt to forty-eight shillings, and the grey colt to three pounds: All which aforesaid being feloniously taken from the above said persons, and found with the said prisoners; by the antient custom and liberty of Halifax, whereof the memory of man is not to the contrary, the said Abraham Wilkinson and Anthony Mitchell are to suffer death, by having their heads severed and cut from their bodies, at Halifax gibbet.'

The two felons were accordingly executed the same day, it being the great market-day, making the twelfth execution recorded from 1623 to 1650. This was destined to be the last; the bailiff was warned that if another such sentence was carried out, he would be called to account for it; and so the custom fell into desuetude, and Halifax Law ceased to be a special terror of thieves and vagabonds.

SCUDERI AND HER ROMANCES.

Fame occurs to authors in various ways. Some are famous in their lifetime and for ever; some are unknown in their lifetime, and become famous after death; some are famous in their lifetime, and are unread after death, but their names are remembered as once famous; and some are famous in their lifetime, but after death are so completely forgotten, that posterity loses even the record of their very names. Mademoiselle de Scuderi is not in the last unfortunate case. She was famous in her own day, she is now seldom read save by the literary antiquary; but it is not forgotten that she was famous. Her name is perpetually quoted, proverbially, as an instance of the evanescence of a great reputation.

Madeleine de Scuderi was born at Havre-de-Grace, in 1607. Her family was noble, but of decayed fortune. Her mother dying while she was a child, she was adopted by an uncle, who, as he could not leave her money, spared neither pains nor expense in giving her a first-rate education. At his death, about her thirty-third year, she went to Paris to find a home with her brother George, a celebrated playwright, patronized by Richelieu, and thought a rival of Corneille. George could not afford to maintain her in idleness, and finding she had a lively wit and a ready pen, he set her to compose romances, which he published as his own. They sold well, and pleased far better than his dramas. George was an eccentric character, and it was said that he used to lock Madeleine up, in order that she might produce a proper quantity of writing daily. Soon the secret oozed out, and she speedily became one of the best known women, not only in Paris, but in Europe. Her publisher, Courbé, grew a rich man by the sale of her works, which were translated into every European language. When princes and ambassadors came to Paris, a visit to Mademoiselle de Scuderi was one of their earliest pleasures. She received a pension from Mazarin, which, at the request of Madame de Maintenon, Louis XIV. augmented to 2,000 livres a year. Philosophers and divines united in her praise. Leibnitz sought the honour of her friendship and correspondence. Her *Discourse on Glory* received the prize of eloquence from the French Academy, in 1671. Her house was the centre of Parisian literary society, and she was the queen of the blue stockings, whom Molière ridiculed in his *Femmes Savantes* and his *Précieuses Ridicules*. No woman, in fact, who has ever written received more honours, more flatteries, and more substantial rewards. Endowed with great goodsense and amiability, she bore her prosperity through a very long life without offence, and without making a personal enemy. She was ugly; she knew it, owned it, and jested over it. It used to be said, that all who were happy enough to be her friends soon forgot her plain face, in the sweetness of her temper and the vivacity of her conversation. One gossip records her strong family pride, and the amusing gravity with which she was in the habit of saying, 'Since the ruin of our family,' as if it had been the overthrow of the Roman empire. She was never married, though she had many admirers; and, after a blameless and happy life, expired at the advanced age of ninety-four, on the 2nd of June 1701.

Mademoiselle de Scuderi was a voluminous

writer. Her romances alone occupy about fifty volumes, of from five to fifteen hundred pages each. Most of them are prodigiously long; *Le Grand Cyrus* and *Clélie* each occupy ten volumes, and took years to appear. They are, moreover, encumbered with episodes, the main story sometimes forming no more than a third of the whole. She laid her scenes nominally in ancient times and the East; but her characters are only French men and women masquerading under Oriental names. She delighted in company, and many wondered when she found leisure to write; but society was her study, and what she heard and saw she, with a romantic gloss, reproduced. She put her friends into her books, and all knew who was who, and detected one another's houses, furniture, and gardens in Nineveh, Rome, and Athens. Even under such cumbrous travestie we might resort to her pages for pictures of French society under *le grand Monarque*, but she made no attempt to depict the realities of life. In high-flying sentimental conversations about love and friendship all her personages pass their days; and their generosity, purity, and courage are only equalled by their uniform good-breeding and faculty for making fine speeches. Long ago has the world lost its taste for writing in that strain, and the de Scuderi romances would only move a modern novel reader to laughter, and then to yawning and sleep.

BAPTISM OF KING ETHELBERT.

Ethelbert was the Saxon king reigning in Kent, when Augustine landed there and introduced Christianity in a formal manner into England. After a while, this monarch joined the Christian church; his baptism, which Arthur Stanley considers as the most important since Constantine, excepting that of Clovis,* took place on the 2nd of June 597. Unfortunately the place is not known; but we know that on the ensuing Christmas-day, as a natural consequence of the example set by the king, ten thousand of the people were baptized in the waters of the Swale, at the mouth of the Medway.

JUNE 3.

St Cecilius, confessor, 211. St Clotildis or Clotilda, Queen of France, 545. St Lifard, abbot, near Orleans, 6th century. St Coemgen or Keivin, bishop and confessor in Ireland, 618. St Genesius, bishop and confessor, about 662.

Born.—Dr John Gregory, miscellaneous writer, 1724, *Aberdeen;* Dr James Hutton, one of the founders of geology, 1726, *Edinburgh;* Robert Tannahill, Scottish poet, 1774, *Paisley;* Sir William C. Ross, artist, 1794, *London*

Died.—Bishop (John) Aylmer, 1594, *Fulham;* William Harvey, discoverer of the circulation of the blood, 1657, *bur. Hempstead, Essex;* Admiral Opdam, blown up at sea, 1665; Dr Edmund Calamy, nonconformist divine, 1732; Jethro Tull, speculative experimenter in agriculture, 1740.

JETHRO TULL.

Jethro Tull was the inventor and indefatigable advocate of 'drill-sowing and frequent hoeing,'

* Stanley's *Historical Memorials of Canterbury*, p. 20.

two of the greatest improvements that have been introduced into the modern system of agriculture. He was educated for the profession of the law, but an acute disease compelled him to relinquish a sedentary life. During his travels in search of health, he directed his attention to the agriculture of the various countries he traversed; and, observing that vines grew and produced well by frequently stirring the soil, without any addition of manure, he rashly concluded that all plants might be cultivated in a similar manner. On his return to England, Tull commenced a life-long series of experiments on his own farm at Shalborne, in Berkshire; and in spite of a most painful disease, and the almost forcible opposition of besotted neighbours and brutally ignorant farm-labourers, he succeeded in gathering remunerative crops from the hungriest and barrenest of soils. His great invention was that of drill-sowing; the saving of seed effected by this practice is incalculable. From the scarcely numerable millions of acres that have been drill-sown since Tull's time, one-third at least of the seed has been saved. Nor is this all; the best informed agriculturists assert that this saving is of less importance than the facility which drill-sowing affords for the destruction of weeds and loosening of the soil by the hoe. It is true, that like many other speculative inventors, Tull arrived at conclusions scarcely justified by the results of his experiments, and principal among these was the erroneous notion that loosening and pulverizing the soil might supersede the use of manure altogether; but he lived long enough to discover his mistake, and he was honest and manly enough to acknowledge it.

Panegyrical inscriptions, graven on ponderous marble and perennial brass, point out the last resting-places of the destroyers of the human race; but, strange to say, no man can tell where the remains of Jethro Tull, the benefactor of his kind, were deposited. Mr Johnson, speaking of Tull, says, 'His grave is undetermined; if he died at Shalborne, there is no trace of his burial in its parish register. The tradition of the neighbourhood is, that he died and was buried in Italy. His deeds, his triumphs, were of the peaceful kind with which the world in general is little enamoured: but their results were momentous to his native land. His drill has saved to it, in seed alone, the food of millions; and his horse-hoe system, by which he attempted to cultivate without manure, taught the farmer that deep ploughing and pulverization of the soil render a much smaller application of fertilizers necessary.'

KING JAMES AND THE TOWER LIONS.

On the 3rd June 1605, King James and his family went to the Tower of London, to see the lions. From the time of Henry III., who placed in the Tower three leopards which had been sent him as a present from the Emperor Frederick, in allusion to the three leopards on the royal shield, there had always been some examples of the larger carnivora kept in this grim old seat of English royalty. It came to be considered as a proper piece of regal magnificence, and the keeper was always a gentleman. In the fourteenth century, to maintain a lion in the Tower cost sixpence a day, while human prisoners were supported for one penny. It cost, in 1532, £6, 13s. 4d. to pay for and bring home a lion. To go and see these Tower lions became an indispensable duty of all country visitors of London, insomuch as to give rise to a proverbial expression, 'the lions' passing as equivalent to all kinds of city wonders which country people go to see. Travelling menageries did not long ago exist, and wild animals were great rarities. In such circumstances, the curiosity felt about the lions in the Tower can be readily appreciated. Even down to the reign of William IV., the collection of these animals was kept up in considerable strength; but at length it was thought best to consign the remnant of the Tower lions to the Zoological Gardens in the Regent's Park, where they have ever since flourished.

The taste of King James was not of the most refined character. It pleased him to have an addition made to the Tower lion-house, with an arrangement of trap-doors, in order that a lion might be occasionally set to combat with dogs, bulls, or bears, for the diversion of the court. The arena was now completed; so the monarch and a great number of courtiers came to see a fight. The designed gallery for their use was not ready; but they found seats on a temporary platform. When the under-keepers on this occasion got a couple of the lions turned out into the place of combat, they acted much like Don Quixote's lions: more amazed and puzzled than anything else, they merely stood looking about them till a couple of pieces of mutton were thrown to them. After a live cock had also been devoured by the savage creatures, a live lamb was let down to them by a rope. 'Being come to the ground, the lamb lay upon his knees, and both the lions stood in their former places, and only beheld the lamb. Presently the lamb rose up and went unto the lions, who very gently looked upon and smelled on him, without any hurt. Then the lamb was very softly drawn up again, in as good plight as he was let down.'

Afterwards, a different lion, a male one, was brought into the arena by himself, and a couple of mastiffs were let in upon him; by which he was fiercely attacked, but with little effect. 'A brended dog took the lion by the face, and turned him upon his back—but the lion spoiled them all; the best dog died the next day.'*

In this and other combats of the same kind, the conduct of the lions was generally conformable to the observations of modern naturalists regarding the character of the so-called king of beasts. The royal family and principal courtiers having come to the Tower on the 23rd June 1609, a bear which had killed a child, a horse, and six strong mastiffs, was let in upon a lion, with only the effect of frightening the creature. 'Then were divers other lions put into that place one after another; but they showed no more sport nor valour than the first, and every of them, so soon as they espied the trap doors open, ran hastily into their dens. Lastly, there were put forth together the two young lusty lions which were bred in that yard, and were now grown great. These at first began to march

* Howes's *Chronicle*.

proudly towards the bear, which the bear perceiving came hastily out of a corner to meet them; but both lion and lioness skipped up and down, and fearfully fled from the bear; and so these, like the former lions, not willing to endure any fight, sought the next way into their den.'

Such were amongst the amusements of the English court 250 years ago.

THE EMPRESS JOSEPHINE AND HER HOROSCOPE.

On the 3rd of June 1814, a distinguished company of mourners assembled in the church of Ruel, in France, the parish in which the palace of Malmaison is situated. There were the Prince of Mecklenburg, General Sacken, several marshals of France, senators, general officers, ecclesiastics, prefects, sub-prefects, maires, and foreigners of note; and there were eight thousand townspeople and peasants from the neighbourhood, come to pay the last tribute of respect to one who, in the closing years of her life, had won their esteem and affection.

It was the funeral of the ex-Empress Josephine, a lady whose sixty years of life had been chequered in a most remarkable way. Josephine appears, as a woman, to have been actuated in some degree by a prediction made concerning her when a girl. Mademoiselle Ducrest, Madame Junot, and others who have written on Josephine's career, mention this prediction. Josephine—or, with her full name, Marie Josephine Rose Tascher de la Pagerie—was the daughter of a French naval officer, and was born in the French colony of Martinique, in 1763. When a sensitive, imaginative girl of about fifteen, her 'fortune was told,' by an old mulatto woman named Euphemie, in words somewhat as follows:—'You will marry a fair man. Your star promises you two alliances. Your first husband will be born in Martinique, but will pass his life in Europe, with girded sword. An unhappy lawsuit will separate you. He will perish in a tragical manner. Your second husband will be a dark man, of European origin and small fortune; but he will fill the world with his glory and fame. You will then become an eminent lady, more than a queen. Then, after having astonished the world, you will die unhappy.'

The writers on whose authority this mystic horoscope is put forward, do not fail to point out how perfectly the events of Josephine's life fit into it. By an arrangement between the two families, Mademoiselle de la Pagerie was married to the Comte de Beauharnois, a fair man, and a native of Martinique. The young people never liked each other; and when they went to Paris, each fell into the evil course of life which was likely to result from such aversion, and to which the state of morals in France lent only too much temptation. In a fit of jealousy, he went to Martinique to rake up evidence concerning his wife's conduct before marriage, and on return raised a suit against her: this was 'the unhappy lawsuit' that 'separated them.' From 1787 till 1790 she lived at Martinique with her two children, Eugene (afterwards one of Napoleon's best generals) and Hortense (afterwards mother of Napoleon III.) On their return to Paris, a reconciliation took place between her and her husband ; and a period of comparative happiness lasted till 1793, when the guillotine put an end to his career. He 'perished in a tragical way.' Madame Beauharnois was imprisoned ; she contrived to send her son and daughter away from home ; but the Terrorists would not consent to let loose one who had been the wife of a count, and who for that reason was one of the aristocracy. While in prison, she showed that she did not forget the old mulatto woman's prediction. She and three other ladies of note being imprisoned in the same cell, they were all alike subject to the brutal language of the gaolers placed over them ; and once, when the others were tearfully lamenting their fate, and anticipating the horrors of the guillotine, Josephine exclaimed—'I shall not die : I shall be queen of France !' The Duchess d'Aiguillon, one of her companions, with a feeble attempt at banter, asked her to 'name her future household ;' to which Josephine at once replied, 'I will make you one of my ladies of honour.' They wept, for they feared she was becoming demented. Robespierre's fall occurred in time to save the life of Josephine. After three years more of successful adventurous life, she was married to the young victorious general, Napoleon Bonaparte : 'a dark man, of European origin and small fortune.' Napoleon proceeded in his wonderful career of conquest, military and political, until at length he became emperor in 1804. Then was Josephine indeed 'an eminent lady, more than a queen ;' and her husband 'filled the world with his glory and fame.' But the wheel of fortune was now turning. Napoleon had no children by Josephine, and he began to fear for the succession to his great empire. His ambition led him to propose marriage to the Archduchess Marie Louise of Austria, after his victorious campaign of 1809 ; he obtained poor Josephine's consent, in a heart-breaking scene, and the church allowed him to annul his first marriage, on grounds which would never have been allowed but for his enormous power. Josephine did 'die unhappy,' as a divorced wife ; and thus fulfilled the last clause of the alleged prediction.

SUPERSTITIONS ABOUT DISEASES.

Perhaps under this head may be classed the notion that a *galvanic ring*, as it is called, worn on the finger, will cure rheumatism. One sometimes sees people with a clumsy-looking silver ring which has a piece of copper let into the inside, and this, though in constant contact throughout, is supposed (aided by the moisture of the hand) to keep up a gentle, but continual galvanic current, and so to alleviate or remove rheumatism.

This notion has an air of science about it which may perhaps redeem it from the character of mere superstition ; but the following case can be put in no such claim. I recollect that when I was a boy a person came to my father (a clergyman), and asked for a 'sacramental shilling,' i. e., one out of the alms collected at the Holy Communion, to be made into a ring, and worn as a cure for epilepsy. He naturally declined to give one for 'superstitious uses,' and no

doubt was thought very cruel by the unfortunate applicant.

Ruptured children are expected to be cured by being passed through a young tree, which has been split for the purpose. After the operation has been performed, the tree is bound up, and, if it grows together again, the child will be cured of its rupture. I have not heard anything about this for many years; perhaps it has fallen into disuse. There is an article on the subject in one of Hone's books, I think, and there the witch elm is specified as the proper tree for the purpose; but, whether from the scarcity of that tree, or from any other cause, I am not aware that it was considered necessary in this locality.

Ague is a disease about which various strange notions are prevalent. One is that it cannot be cured by a regular doctor—it is out of their reach altogether, and can only be touched by some old woman's nostrum. It is frequently treated with spiders and cobwebs. * These, indeed, are said to contain arsenic; and, if so, there may be a touch of truth in the treatment. Fright is also looked upon as a cure for ague. I suppose that, on the principle that *similia similibus curantur*, it is imagined that the shaking induced by the fright will counteract and destroy the shaking of the ague fit. An old woman has told me that she was actually cured in this manner when she was young. She had had ague for a long time, and nothing would cure it. Now it happened that she had a fat pig in the sty, and a fat pig is an important personage in a poor man's establishment. Well aware of the importance of piggy in her eyes, and determined to give her as great a shock as possible, her husband came to her with a very long face as she was tottering down stairs one day, and told her that *the pig was dead.* Horror at this fearful news overcame all other feelings ; she forgot all about her ague, and hurried to the scene of the catastrophe, where she found to her great relief that the pig was alive and well ; but the fright had done its work, and from that day to this (she must be about eighty years old) she has never had a touch of the ague, though she has resided on the same spot.

Equally strange are some of the notions about smallpox. Fried mice are relied on as a specific for it, and I am afraid that it is considered necessary that they should be fried *alive.*

With respect to whooping-cough, again, it is believed that if you ask a person riding on a piebald horse what to do for it, his recommendation will be success-

* Mrs Delany, in a letter dated March 1, 1743-4, gives these two *infallible recipes for ague* :—

1st. Pounded ginger, made into a paste with brandy, spread on sheep's leather, and a plaister of it laid over the navel.

2nd. A spider put into a goose-quill, well sealed and secured, and hung about the child's neck as low as the pit of his stomach. Either of these I am assured will give ease.—*Probatum est.*

Upon this Lady Llanover notes :—' Although the prescription of the spider *in the quill* will probably only create amusement from its apparent absurdity, considered merely as an *old charm,* yet there is no doubt of the medicinal virtue of spiders and their webs, which have been long known to the Celtic inhabitants of Great Britain and Ireland' (See *Notes and Queries,* No. 242, where particulars are given of the efficacy of spiders' webs, rolled up like a pill, and swallowed when the ague fit is coming on). Dr Graham (in his *Domestic Medicine*) prescribed spiders' webs for ague and intermittent fever, and also names powder made of spiders given for the ague; and mentions his knowledge of a spider having been sewn up in a rag and worn as a periapt round the neck to charm away the ague.

ful if attended to. My grandfather at one time used always to ride a piebald horse, and he has frequently been stopped by people asking for a cure for whooping-cough. His invariable answer was, 'Patience and water-gruel;' perhaps, upon the whole, the best advice that could be given.

Earrings are considered to be a cure for sore eyes, and perhaps they may be useful so long as the ear is sore, the ring acting as a mild seton; but their efficacy is believed in even after the ear has healed.

Warts are another thing expected to be cured by charms. A gentleman well known to me, states that, when he was a boy, the landlady of an inn where he happened to be took compassion on his warty hands, and undertook to cure them by rubbing them with bacon. It was necessary, however, that the bacon should be *stolen;* so the good lady *took it secretly* from her own larder, which was supposed to answer the condition sufficiently. If I recollect rightly, the warts remained as bad as ever, which was perhaps due to the bacon not having been *bona fide* stolen.

I do not know whether landladies in general are supposed to have a special faculty against warts; but one, a near neighbour of mine, has the credit of being able to charm them away by counting them. I have been told by boys that she has actually done so for them, and that the warts have disappeared. I have no reason to think that they were telling me a downright lie, but suppose that their imagination must have been strong to overcome even such horny things as warts. A mere coincidence would have been almost more remarkable.

There is a very distressing eruption about the mouth and throat, called the thrush, common among infants and persons in the last extremity of sickness. There is a notion about this disease that a person must have it once in his life, either at his birth or death. Nurses like to see it in babies; they say that it is healthy, and makes them feed more freely; but, if a sick person shows it, he is given over as past recovery, which is really indeed extremely rare in such cases.

I am no doctor, and do not know whether the disease is really the same in both cases, but it appears to be so.   C. W. J.

Suffolk.

The following conversation, which took place in a Dorsetshire village, illustrates the popular nosology and therapeutics of that county :—

'Well, Betty,' said a lady, 'how are you?'

'Pure, thank you ma'am; but I has been rather poorlyish.'

'What has been the matter with you?'

'Why, ma'am, I was troubled with the *rising of the lights;* but I tooked a dose of *shot,* and that has a-keepit them down.'*

As a pendent to this take the following, hitherto unprinted. An old cottager in Morayshire, who had long been bed-rid, was charitably visited by a neighbouring lady, much given to the administration of favourite medicines. One day she left a bolus for him, from which she expected strengthening effects, and she called next day to inquire for her patient, as usual.

'Well, John, you would take the medicine I left with you?'

'Oh, no, ma'am,' replied John; 'it wadna gang east.'

The Scotch, it must be understood, are accustomed to be precise about the 'airts' or cardinal points, and generally direct you to places in that way. This poor old fellow, constantly lying on one side, had come to have a geographical idea of the direction which anything took in passing into his gullet.

* *Notes and Queries,* 2nd ser. vi. 522.

JUNE 4.

St Quirinus, Bishop of Siscia, martyr, 304. St Optatus, Bishop of Milevum, confessor, 4th century. St Breaca, or Breague, virgin, of Ireland. St Nenooc, or Nennoca, virgin, of Britain, 467. St Burian, of Ireland. St Petroc, abbot and confessor, about 564. St Walter, abbot of Fontenelle, or St Vandrilles, 1150. St Walter, abbot in San-Serviliano, 13th century.

Born.—George III., of Great Britain, 1738, *London;* John Scott, Earl of Eldon, Chancellor of England, 1751, *Newcastle;* James Pennethorne, architect, 1801, *Worcester.*

Died.—M. A. Muret (Muretus), commentator on the ancient classics, 1585, *Rome;* Archbishop Juxon, 1663, *St John's, Oxford;* Admiral Sir Charles Wager, 1743; Marshal Davoust, 1823; Marguerite, Countess of Blessington, novelist, &c., 1849, *Paris;* Henry Grattan, statesman, 1820, *London.*

KING GEORGE THE THIRD'S BIRTHDAY.

At page 275 of the volume of the *Gentleman's Magazine* for 1738, under a sub-title, 'Wednesday, 24,' meaning the 24th of May, occurs the following little paragraph: 'This morning, between six and seven, the Princess of Wales was happily delivered of a prince at Norfolk House, St James's Square, the Archbishop of Canterbury being present.' This prince was he who afterwards reigned sixty years over England as George III.

The 4th of June, which was assumed as the prince's birthday on the change of style, must yet for many years be remembered on account of the affectionate and constantly growing interest felt in it during the old king's reign. A royal birthday in the present time, notwithstanding the respect and love cherished for the occupant of the throne, is nothing to what it was

'——When George the Third was king.'

The reverence felt for this sovereign by the generality of his subjects was most remarkable. It was a kind of religion with many of them. He was spoken of as 'the best of characters,' 'the good old king;' no phrase of veneration or love seemed to be thought inapplicable to him. And surely, though he had his faults as a ruler, and they were of a not very innocuous character, it is something, as shewing the power of personal or private goodness and worth, that King George was thus held in general regard.

The esteem for the personal virtues of the king, joined to a feeling of political duty which the circumstances of the country made appear necessary, caused the 4th of June to be observed as a holiday—not a formal and ostensible, but a *sincere* holiday—over the whole empire. Every municipality met with its best citizens to drink the king's health. There were bonfires in many streets. The boys kept up from morning to night an incessant fusillade with their mimic artillery. Rioting often arose from the very joyousness of the occasion. It is a curious proof of the intense feeling connected with the day, that in Edinburgh a *Fourth of June Club* continued for many years after King George's death to meet and dine, and drink to his amiable memory.

The feelings of the people regarding the king were brought to an unusually high pitch in the year 1809, when he entered on the fiftieth year of his reign. Passing over the formal celebrations of the day, let us revive, from a contemporary periodical, a poem written on that occasion, as by Norman Nicholson, a shepherd among the Grampian Hills, who professed to have then just entered upon the fiftieth year of his own professional life. It is entitled,

Jubilee for Jubilee.

Frae the Grampian Hills will the Royal ear hear it,
   And listen to Norman the Shepherd's plain tale !
The north wind is blawing, and gently will bear it,
   Unvarnish'd and honest, o'er hill and o'er dale.
When London it reaches, at court, Sire, receive it,
   Like a tale you may read it, or like a sang sing.
Poor Norman is easy—but you may believe it,
   I'm fifty years shepherd—you're fifty a king !

Your jubilee, then, wi' my ain I will mingle,
   For you and mysel' twa fat lambkins I'll slay ;
Fresh turf I will lay in a heap on my ingle,
   An' wi' my auld neebours I'll rant out the day.
My pipes that I played on lang syne, I will blaw them,
   My chanter I'll teach to lilt over the spring ;
My drones to the tune I will round an' round thraw
     them,
   O' fifty years shepherd, and fifty a king !

The flock o' Great Britain ye've lang weel attended,
   The flock o' Great Britain demanded your care ;
Frae the tod and the wolf they've been snugly defended,
   And led to fresh pasture, fresh water, and air.
My flocks I ha'e led day by day o'er the heather,
   At night they around me ha'e danced in a ring ;
I've been their protector thro' foul and fair weather—
   I'm fifty years shepherd—you're fifty a king !

Their fleeces I've shorn, frae the cauld to protect me,
   Their fleeces they gave, when a burden they grew ;
When escaped frae the sheers, their looks did respect
     me,
   Sae the flock o' Great Britain still looks upon you.
They grudge not their monarch a mite o' their riches,
   Their active industry is ay on the wing ;
Then you and me, Sire, I think are twa matches—
   I'm fifty years shepherd—you're fifty a king !

Me wi' my sheep, Sire, and *you* wi' your subjects,
   On that festive day will baith gladly rejoice ;
Our twa hoary heads will be fou' o' new projects,
   To please our leal vassals that made us their choice.
Wi' sweet rips o' hay I will treat a' my wethers,
   The juice o' the vine to your lords you will bring ;
The respect they ha'e for us is better than brithers'—
   I'm fifty years shepherd—you're fifty a king !

I live in the cottage where Norval was bred in,
   You live in the palace your ancestors reared ;
Nae guest uninvited dare come to your weddin',
   Or ruthless invader pluck us by the beard.
Then thanks to the island we live, whar our
     shipping
   Swim round us abreast, or like geese in a string ;
For safe, I can say, as my brose I am sipping,
   I'm fifty years shepherd— you're fifty a king !

But ah ! Royal George, and ah ! humble Norman,
   Life to us baith draws near to a close ;
The year's far awa that has our natal hour, man,
   The time's at our elbow that brings us repose !
Then e'en let it come, Sire, if conscience acquit us,
   A sigh frae our bosoms Death never shall wring ;
And may the next jub'lee amang angels meet us,—
   To hail the auld shepherd, and worthy auld king !

DAVOUST.—APPARENT INCONSISTENCIES OF HUMAN NATURE.

The name of Davoust is held in greater horror than that of any other of Napoleon's generals, on account of the frightful oppression he exercised upon the citizens of Hamburg, when occupying that city for his master in 1813. His rapacity is described as unbounded. It is at the same time true that he was faithful beyond example to Napoleon through all the proceedings of the two subsequent years ; and after Waterloo, when a Bourbon decree prescribed several of his brother marshals, he wrote to the minister St Cyr, demanding that his name should be substituted for theirs, as they had only acted under his orders as the late war minister—a piece of generosity reminding us of chivalrous times. It is another curious and unexpected trait of Davoust, that he was a bibliophilist, and possessed a fine vellum library.

One is continually surprised by incongruities in human character, although there is perhaps no peculiarity of human nature more conspicuous than what are called its inconsistencies. It would at first sight appear impossible that a noted murderer could be tender-hearted ; yet it is recorded of Eugene Aram, that he had been observed to walk aside to avoid treading on a worm. Archbishop Whately, in his annotations to Bacon, has the following paragraph : 'When Thurtell the murderer was executed, there was a shout of derision raised against the phrenologists for saying that his organ of *benevolence* was large. But they replied that there was also large *destructiveness*, and a moral deficiency, which would account for a man goaded to rage (by being cheated of almost all he had by the man he killed) committing that act. It is a remarkable confirmation of their view, that a gentleman who visited the prison where Thurtell was confined (shortly after the execution), found the jailors, &c., full of pity and affection for him. They said he was a kind, good-hearted fellow, so obliging and friendly, that they had never had a prisoner whom they so much regretted. And such seems to have been his general character, when not influenced at once by the desire of revenge and of gain.'

The gentle benevolence and piety of Izaak Walton shine through all his writings. The amiable sentimentalism of Mackenzie's novels (now unduly neglected) was forty years ago deeply impressed on the public mind. Yet both of these men were keen pursuers of sports which infer the destruction, and, what is worse, the torture of the humbler animals. It is related that Mr Mackenzie's wife, hearing him one day tell how many brace of grouse he had bagged in a late visit to the Highlands, and what a nice set of flies he had bought to take to Gala Water next week, exclaimed, 'Harry, Harry, you keep all your feeling for your books !' The writer knew this fine-toned author when he was eighty-five years of age, and retains a vivid recollection of the hearty, world-like, life-enjoying style of the man, so incongruous with all that one would imagine regarding him who wrote the story of La Roche.

Take in connexion with these remarks what Mr Baker has set forth in his work, styled *The Rifle and the Hound in Ceylon* (1854): 'I would always encourage a love of sport in a lad; guided by its true spirit of fair play, it is a feeling that will make him above doing a mean thing in every station of life, and will give him real feelings of humanity. I have had great experience in the characters of thorough sportsmen, and I can safely say that I never saw one that was not a straightforward, honourable man, who would scorn to take a dirty advantage of man or animal. In fact, all real sportsmen that I have met have been really tender-hearted men; men who shun cruelty to an animal, and who are easily moved by a tale of distress.'

THE FATE OF AMY ROBSART.

On the 4th of June 1550, Lord Robert Dudley, who subsequently was a great figure in English history, under the title of Earl of Leicester, was married to Amy, the daughter of Sir John Robsart, a gentleman of ancient family and large possessions in Cornwall. It was perhaps an imprudent marriage, for the bridegroom was only eighteen; but there was nothing clandestine or secret about it—on the contrary, it took place at the palace of Sheen, in the presence of the young king, Edward VI. The pair lived together ten years, but had no children. As this time elapsed, Dudley rose in the favour of his sovereign Elizabeth—even to such a degree that he might evidently, if unmarried, have aspired to her royal hand.

It is an odd consideration regarding Elizabeth and her high reputation as a sovereign, that one of her most famous ministers, and one who enjoyed her personal favour during a long course of years—whom, indeed, she *loved*, if she ever loved any—was a man proved to have been guilty of nearly every vice, a selfish adventurer, a treacherous hypocrite, and a murderer. We have now to speak of the first of a tolerably long series of wickednesses which have to be charged to the account of Leicester. He was still but Lord Robert Dudley when, in September 1560, he got quit of the wife of his youth, Amy Robsart. We know extremely little of this lady. There is one letter of hers preserved, and it only tells a Mr Flowerden, probably a steward of her husband, to sell the wool of certain sheep 'for six shillings the stone, as you would sell for yourself.' The lady came to her end at Cumnor Hall, a solitary manor-house in Berkshire, not far from Oxford. This house was the residence of a dependent of Dudley, one Anthony Forster, whose epitaph in the neighbouring church still proclaims him as a gentleman of birth and consideration, distinguished by skill in music and a taste for horticulture—a worthy, sagacious, and eloquent man, but whom we may surmise to have nevertheless been not incapable of serving Dudley in some of his worst ends. The immediate instrument, however, appears to have been Sir Richard Varney, another dependent of the aspiring courtier. By this man and his servant, who alone were in the house, the chamber of the unfortunate lady was

THE BEAR AT CUMNOR.

invaded by night, and after strangling her, and damaging her much about the head and neck, they threw her down a stair, to support their tale that she had died by an accidental fall. Dudley paid all proper external respect to her memory, by burying her magnificently in St Mary's Church, Oxford, at an expense of two thousand pounds. He did not, however, escape suspicion. The neighbouring gentry were so fully assured of the evil treatment of the lady, that they sought to get an inquiry made into the circumstances. We also find Burleigh afterwards presenting, among the reasons why it was inexpedient for the queen to marry Leicester, 'that he is infamed by the death of his wife.' Many actions of his subsequent life show how fully he was capable of ordering one woman out of the world to make way for another.

Mickle, a poet of the latter half of the eighteenth century, composed a ballad on the tragic death of Amy Robsart, whom he erroneously thought to have been a countess. Its smooth, euphonious strains gave a charm to a composition which a critical taste would scarcely approve of.

> '———Sore and sad that lady grieved,
>   In Cumnor Hall, so lone and drear ;
> Full many a piercing scream was heard,
>   And many a cry of mortal fear.
> The death-bell thrice was heard to ring,
>   An aërial voice was heard to call ;
> And thrice the raven flapped its wing
>   Around the towers of Cumnor Hall.
>
>   *   *   *
>
> And in that manor now no more
>   Is cheerful feast and sprightly ball :
> For ever since that dreary hour
>   Have spirits haunted Cumnor Hall.
> The village maids, with fearful glance,
>   Avoid the ancient moss-grown wall ;
> Nor ever lead the sprightly dance
>   Among the groves of Cumnor Hall.'

The place, nevertheless, from its natural beauties, its antique church, and the romance connected with the ancient hall, has an attraction for strangers. The BEAR—the inn which forms the opening scene of the romance of *Kenilworth*—a very curious specimen of old homely architecture, still exists at Cumnor, with the Dudley arms (the bear and ragged staff) over the door, strangely realizing to us the dismal connexion of Leicester with the spot.

JUNE 5.

St Dorotheus, of Tyre, martyr, 4th century. St Dorotheus the Theban, abbot, 4th century. Other Saints named Dorotheus. St Illidius, Bishop of Auvergne, confessor, about 385. St Boniface, Archbishop of Mentz, Apostle of Germany, and martyr, 755.

ST BONIFACE, THE APOSTLE OF THE GERMANS.

The true name of this saint was Winfrid, or Winfrith. He was the son of a West-Saxon chieftain, and was born at Crediton, in Devonshire, about the year 680. Having shown from his infancy a remarkable seriousness of character, he was sent, when in his seventh year, to

school in the monastery at Exeter. He made rapid and great proficiency in learning, and, having been ordained to the priesthood about the year 710, he was soon afterwards chosen by the West-Saxon clergy to represent them in an important mission to the Archbishop of Canterbury ; and it was probably in the course of it that he formed the design of seeking to effect the conversion of the heathen Germans who occupied central Europe. Remaining firm in his design, he proceeded to Friesland in 716 ; but, on account of obstacles caused by the unsettled state of the country, he returned home and remained in England until 718, in the autumn of which year he went through France to Rome, where he formed a lasting friendship with the Anglo-Saxon princess-nun Eadburga, better known by her nickname of Bugga. The pope approved of the designs of Winfrid, and, in May 719, he gave him authority to undertake the conversion of the Thuringians. After making some converts in Thuringia, where his success appears to have fallen short of his anticipations, Boniface visited France, and went thence to Utrecht, where his countryman Wilbrord was preaching the gospel with success ; but he soon returned to the first scene of his own labours, where he made many converts among the Saxons and Hessians. In 723, the pope, Gregory II., invited him to Rome, and there signified his approval of his missionary labours by ordaining him a bishop, and formally renewing his commission to convert the Germans. The pope at the same time conferred upon him the name of Boniface, by which he was ever afterwards known. After visiting the court of Charles Martel, Boniface returned into Germany, and there established himself in the character of Bishop of the Hessians.

The favour shown by the pope to Boniface had another object besides the mere desire of converting pagans. The German tribes in the country entrusted to his care had already been partially converted—but it was by Irish monks, the followers of Columbanus and St Gall, who, like most of the Frankish clergy, did not admit in its full extent the authority of the pope, and were in other respects looked upon as unorthodox and schismatical ; and Gregory saw in the great zeal and orthodoxy of Boniface the means of drawing the German Christians from heterodoxy to Rome. Accordingly, we find him in the earlier period of his labours engaged in contentions with the clergy already established in this part of Germany than with the pagans. In the course of these, the pope himself was obliged sometimes to check the zeal of his bishop. Still, in his excursions through the wilds of the Hercynian forest, the great resort of the pagan tribes, Boniface and his companions were often exposed to personal dangers. However, supported by the pope, and aided by the exertions of a crowd of zealous followers, the energetic missionary gradually overcame all obstacles. In his choice of assistants he seemed always to prefer those from his native country, and he was joined by numerous Anglo-Saxon ecclesiastics of both sexes. Among his Anglo-Saxon nuns was St Waltpurgis, so celebrated in German legend. A bold proceeding on the part of the bishop sealed the success of Christianity among the Hessians and Thuringians. One of the great objects of worship of the former was a venerable oak, of vast magnitude, which stood in the forest at Geismar, near Fritzlar, and which was looked upon, according to the Latin narrative, as dedicated to Jupiter, probably to Woden. Boniface resolved to destroy this tree; and the Hessians, in the full belief that their gods would come forward in its defence, seem to have accepted it as a trial of strength between these and what they looked upon merely as the gods of the Christians, so that a crowd of pagans, as well as a large number of the preachers of the gospel, were assembled to witness it. Boniface seized the axe in his own hands, and, after a few strokes, a violent wind which had arisen, and of which he had probably taken advantage to apply his axe to the side on which the wind came, threw the tree down with a tremendous crash, which split the trunk into four pieces. The pagans were struck with equal wonder and terror; and, acknowledging that their gods were conquered, they submitted without further opposition. Boniface caused the tree to be cut up, and built of it a wooden oratory dedicated to St Peter.

In 732, a new pope, Gregory III., ordained Boniface Archbishop of the Germans, and he soon afterwards built two principal churches—that of Fritzlar, dedicated to St Peter; and that of Amanaburg, where he had first established his headquarters, dedicated to St Michael. From this time the number of churches among the German tribes increased rapidly. In 740, he preached with great success among the Bagoarii, or people of Bavaria. He subsequently divided their territory into four dioceses, and ordained four bishops over them. About this time a new field was opening to his zeal. The throne of the Franks was nominally occupied by one of a race of insignificant princes whose name was hardly known out of his palace, while the sceptre was really wielded by Charles Martel; and, as it was in the power of the Church of Rome to confirm the family of the latter in supplanting their feeble rivals, they naturally leaned towards the orthodox party, in opposition to the schismatical spirit of the French clergy. In 741, Charles Martel died, and his sons, Karlomann and Pepin, were equally anxious to conciliate the pope. During the following years several councils were held, under the influence of Boniface, for the purpose of reforming the Frankish Church, while the conversion of the Germans also proceeded with activity. In 744, Boniface founded the celebrated monastery of Fulda, over which he placed one of his disciples, a Bavarian, named Sturm, in one of the wildest parts of the Thuringian forest. In 745, at the end of rather severe proceedings against some of the Saxon ecclesiastics, the archbishopric of Mentz, or Mayence, was created. Next year Karlomann retired to a monastery, and left the entire kingdom of the Franks to his brother Pepin. The design of changing the Frankish dynasty was, during the following year, a subject of anxious consultation between the pope and the bishops; and, the authority of

the pope Zacharias having been obtained, King Childeric, the last of the Merovingian monarchs of the Franks, was deposed and condemned to a monastery, and Pepin received the reward of his zeal in enforcing the unity of the church. In 751, Boniface performed the coronation ceremonies at Soissons which made Pepin king of the Franks. Thus the Roman Catholic Church gradually usurped the right of deposing and creating sovereigns.

Boniface was now aged, and weak in bodily health; yet, so far from faltering in his exertions, he at this moment determined on undertaking the conversion of the Frieslanders, the object with which especially he had started on his missionary labours in his youth. His first expedition, in 754, was very successful; and he built a monastery at a town named Trehet, and ordained a bishop there. He returned thence to Germany, well satisfied with his labours, and next year proceeded again into Friesland, accompanied by a considerable number of priests and other companions, to give permanence to what he had effected in the preceding year. On the 4th of June they encamped for the night on the river Bordau, at a spot where a number of converts were to assemble next day to be baptized; but that day brought the labours of the Anglo-Saxon missionary to an abrupt conclusion. The country was still in a very wild and unsettled state, and many of the tribes lived entirely by plundering one another, and were scattered about in strong parties under their several chieftains. One of these had watched the movements of Boniface and his companions, under the impression that they carried with them great wealth. On the morning of the 5th of June, before the hour appointed for the ceremony of baptism, the pagans made their appearance, approaching in a threatening attitude. Boniface had a few armed attendants, who went forth from his encampment to meet the assailants; but the archbishop called them back, probably because they were evidently too weak to resist; and, exhorting his presbyters and deacons to resign themselves to their inevitable fate, went forth, carrying the relics of saints in his hands. The pagans rushed upon them, and put them all to the sword; and then, separating into two parties (they were probably two tribes who had joined together), they fought for the plunder, until a great number of one party was slain. The victorious party then entered the tents, and were disappointed at finding there nothing to satisfy their cupidity but a few books and relics, which they threw away in contempt. They were afterwards attacked and beaten by the Christians, who recovered the books and relics; and gathering together the bodies and limbs of the martyrs (for the pagans had hacked them to pieces, in the rage caused by their disappointment), carried them first to the church of Trehet, whence they were subsequently removed to Fulda, and they were at a later period transferred with great pomp to Mentz.

Such was the fate of one of the earliest of our English missionaries in his labours in central Europe. In reading his adventures we may almost think that we are following one of his successors in our own day in their perilous wanderings among the savages of Africa, or some other people equally ignorant and uncultivated. Boniface was an extraordinary man in an extraordinary age; and few men, either in that age or any other, have left their impress more strongly marked on the course of European civilization, at a time when learning, amid a world which was beginning to open its eyes to its importance, exercised a sort of magic influence over society. He was a man of great learning as well as a man of energy, yet his literary remains are few, and consist chiefly of a collection of letters, most of them of a private and familiar character, which, rude enough in the style of the Latin in which they are written, form still a pleasing monument of the manners and sentiments of our forefathers in the earlier part of the eighth century. Boniface was an Englishman to the end of his life.

Born.—Socrates, Grecian philosopher (6th Thargelion), B.C. 468; Joseph de Tournefort, botanist, 1656; Dr Adam Smith, political economist, 1723, *Kirkcaldy ;* Ernest Augustus, King of Hanover, 1771.

Died.—Count D'Egmont and Count Horn, beheaded at *Brussels*, 1568 ; John Henry Hottinger, learned orientalist, 1667, *drowned in River Limmat ;* Rev. Dr Henry Sacheverell, 1724; John Paisiello, musical composer, 1816, *Naples ;* Carl Maria Von Weber, musical composer, 1826, *London ;* T. H. Lister, novelist, 1842, *London ;* Jacques Pradier, French sculptor, 1852.

VISITING CARDS OF THE 18TH AND 19TH CENTURIES.

From the lady of fashion—who orders her carriage every afternoon, and takes the round of Belgravia, leaving a card at the door of twenty acquaintances who are all out on the same errand—to the man of business, and even the postman, who presents his card on Christmas-day morning, these little square bits of cardboard have become an established institution of polite society. The last century has, however, left us an example of how to make these trifles matters of taste and art. The good, quiet, moral society of Vienna, Dresden, and Berlin, in which, according to contemporary historians, it was so pleasant to live, piqued itself upon its delicacy of taste ; and instead of our insipid card, with the name and quality of the visitor printed upon it, it distributed real *souvenirs*, charming vignettes, some of which are models of composition and engraving. The greatest artists, Raphael Mengs, Cassanova, Fischer, and Bartsch, did not disdain to please fashionable people by drawing the pretty things which Raphael Morghen engraved. About four or five hundred of these cards have been collected by Mons. Piogey, among which we meet with the greatest names of the empire, and a few Italians and French whom business or chance led to Germany.

The taste for these elegancies was undoubtedly borrowed from Paris ; we find there a whole generation of designers and ornamenters, who

devoted their graving tools entirely to cards and addresses for the fashionable world, theatre and concert tickets, letters announcing marriages, ceremonies, programmes, &c. It was the recreation and most profitable work of Choffart, Moreau, Gravelot, and, above all, St Aubyn—the most indefatigable of all those who tried to amuse an age which only wished to forget itself. But the clouds which rose on the political horizon darkened that of art. *Ennui* glided like the canker-worm into this corrupt society ; then a disgust for these trifles adorned by wit ; after that followed a more serious, grander, more humane pre-occupation; so that, their task ended, their academy closed, and their diplomas laid on their country's altar, these designers without employment resigned their pencils in despair—Moreau becoming professor of the central schools under the Directory, after being the king's designer in 1770.

The other kingdoms of Europe, and Germany in particular, inherited from the French the taste for this amiable superfluity, the ornamenting of

trifles for the higher classes. In that country only could such a collection of cards be made, where every one is so conservative that nothing

is lost; and yet what a curious assemblage of names, with adjuncts which testify to the taste, character, and studies of each! What an assistance to the historian, what a charm for the novelist, the fortuitous *réunion* of all these personages affords; the greater part of whom have left no other remembrance than the card, addressed as much to posterity as to their friends.

There is an interesting one of the Marquis de Galle, minister plenipotentiary to the King of the Two Sicilies, designed and engraved by Raphael Morghen, representing Neptune resting on an urn, looking on the Bay of Naples, which is studded with lateen sails, and Vesuvius in a state of eruption. A naiad is advancing towards him, and between the two lies a monumental stone on which the name is inscribed, shaded by delicate shrubs; at the top a Cupid raises a *fleur-de-lis* resting on an eagle.

There are no less than four cards of Cassanova; the best is an aqua fortis of large size, in which an Austrian soldier is crushing a Turk under his feet; he holds a flag in his left hand, and a sword in his right, whilst in a tempestuous sky an eagle is hovering. The

scene is both grand and poetical. The ass, carrying the flag with the name inscribed, is another; and a man playing a drum, on a fiery charger, forms a third.

Adam Bartsch, the celebrated author of the *Pientre Graveur*, a work published at Vienna in twenty-one volumes, was evidently a great lover of the canine species; here is a spaniel holding the card in his mouth, and there is a second, in which a savage dog has just torn a roll of paper with the date 1795; beneath is written, 'Adam Bartsch has the pleasure of presenting his compliments and good wishes for the new year.'

Fischer of Berne, makes a rebus of

his name, an artist's fancy and monogram of a new kind; namely, two men and a woman drawing out a net.

Raphael Mengs has not disdained drawing the card of the Marquis de Llano—a wreath of roses, bordered with olives. Another is that of the Comte Aloyse d'Harrach, lieutenant-general, of whom Georges Wille, in his interesting memoirs, writes: '12 Feb. 1767.—M. le Comte and Madame la Comtesse d'Harrach, Austrian nobles, came to visit me; they are well known here, and perfectly amiable; the Comtesse draws very beautifully.'

Generally the name of the artist is unknown; for most people bought the subject engraved, and wrote their name on it, thus beginning at the end. Such is one of the Aulic Councillor de Martines, and that of the Comtesse de Sinzendorf. Great amateurs and persons of high rank, such as the Prince d'Auersperg, Count d'Harseg (Envoy Extraordinary of his Imperial Majesty), and the Prince Esterhazy, did not do so; the last mentioned has a beautiful vignette of a Cupid supporting a medallion wreathed with flowers, on which is the name of Francis Esterhazy, one of the illustrious family of diplomatists and statesmen who trace back their title to A.D. 960. This one sat as councillor in the last German Diet of 1804, when the Germanic empire ceased to exist. Some have engraved the bust of their favourite hero beside their name: as the Comte of Wrakslaw has that of the Archduke Charles defending the approach to Vienna, which is recognisable by the spire of its cathedral. We meet with the name of Demidoff, then a simple captain in the service of the Empress of Russia. Two Englishmen also appear in the collection—Lord Lyttelton with his dog, and Mr Stapleton with a medallion portrait; and many others whose names may be found in the *Almanach de Gotha*, but not many in the memory of man. One peculiarity belongs to the cards of English society, that all landscapes are more or less authentic; Bath, the city of English elegance at that period, is a frequent subject. Sometimes it is Milsom Street, with its long perspective of fashionable houses; North Parade, or Queen's Square, where Sheridan might point out his favourite residence, and Beau Brummel recognise himself parading the terrace.

The Italian cards are in a very different style; you see at once the imitation of the antique, and in some cases the Greek and Roman *chefs-d'œuvre* are copied. Bas-reliefs, bronzes, niellos, mosaics, are found on these bits of card, which are changed into objects of great interest. The Comte de Nobili has several different and always tasteful ones; sometimes a sacrifice of sheep or oxen, or the appearance of Psyche before Venus and her son, seated in family conclave.

Le Comte de Nobili

Among other noble strangers, we notice the Marquis de Las-Casas', Ambassador of Spain: the sun, mounted on his car, is leaving the shores of the east. The architect Blondel inscribes

his name above the cornice of a ruined monument; and M. Burdett places his in the centre of the tomb of Metella. Long as we might linger over these relics of the past, we have given sufficient examples to point out the taste of the age, and a fashion which has had its day, and perished.

SACHEVERELL'S RESTING-PLACE.

Of the famous Sacheverell—whose trial in the latter part of Anne's reign almost maddened the people of England—it is curious to learn the *ultimate situation*, from the following paragraph :—

'The skeletons in our crowded London graveyards lie in layers which are quite historical in their significance, and which would be often startling if the circumstances of their juxtaposition could be made known. A cutting from an old London newspaper (title and date uncertain), and which exists in the well-known repertory of Green, of Covent Garden, contains an example of skeleton contact which is unusually curious, if reliable. It is there stated that Dr Sacheverell is buried in St Andrew's, Holborn, and that the notorious Mother Needham of Hogarth is lying above him, and above her again is interred Booth, the actor—a strange stratification of famous or notorious clay.'

JUNE 6.

St Philip the Deacon, 1st century. St Gudwall, Bishop of St Maloi, confessor, end of 6th or beginning of 7th century. St Claude, Archbishop of Besançon, confessor, 696 or 703. St Norbert, Archbishop of Magdeburg, and founder of the Premonstratensian Order, confessor, 1134.

Born.—Diego Velasquez, eminent Spanish artist, 1599, *Seville ;* Pierre Corneille, French dramatist, 1606, *Rouen ;* Jean Baptist Languet, 1675, *Dijon ;* Dr Nathaniel Lardner, theologian, 1684, *Hawkhurst.*

Died.—Ludovico Giovanni Ariosto, eminent Italian poet, 1533, *Ferrara ;* Memnon de Coehorn, eminent engineer, the 'Vauban of Holland,' 1704, *Hague ;* Louise, Duchesse de la Vallière, mistress of Louis XIV., 1710; George, Lord Anson, eminent naval commander, circumnavigator, 1762, *Moor Park ;* Patrick Henry, American patriot and orator, 1799 ; Jeremy Bentham, writer on legal and political reforms, 1832, *London.*

JEREMY BENTHAM.

The son of a prosperous London solicitor, Jeremy Bentham was born on the 15th of February 1748, in Houndsditch —not then the murky and unsavoury neighbourhood that it is now. With a dwarfish body and a precocious mind, the boy was hawked about by his father as an infant prodigy, while his nursery was crowded with masters in French and music, drawing and dancing. Determined to lose no time in making a man of him, the father sent him to Westminster at eight, to Oxford at twelve, and entered him at Lincoln's Inn at sixteen. By these hasty operations the elder Bentham in a great measure frustrated his own plans. The nervous and feeble city child, thrown among rough lads, like

Cowper conceived a horror of society, and sought refuge from the tyranny of his kind in solitary study and meditation. His prospects at the bar were good; but what between conscientious scruples about doing as other lawyers did, and his preference for books over men and money, it at last became plain to his father that legal eminence would never be attained by Jeremy; and, after many struggles, he threw him up as a hopeless creature, leaving him thenceforth to follow his own devices.

The young man had in reality a love for legal studies, but for philosophical ends, and not as a means of livelihood. His favourite authors were Montesquieu, Barrington, Beccaria, and Helvetius. He had been haunted for a long while by the question, What is genius? When reading Helvetius, the etymology of the word suggested to him that it must mean invention. Helvetius also taught him that legislation was the most important of all subjects. Then came the further question, 'Have I a genius for legislation?' which, after a short course of self-examination, he tremblingly decided in the affirmative. From that time forward he devoted himself more and more exclusively to the reform of legislation. In 1769, he encountered in a pamphlet of Dr Priestley's the phrase, 'The greatest happiness of the greatest number,' which he chose for his lode-star, and identified with his name. He described himself at this time as 'seeking and picking his way; getting the better of prejudice and nonsense; making a little bit of discovery here, another there, and putting the little bits together.' In 1776 appeared, anonymously, his first publication, *A Fragment on Government*, which attracted considerable notice, and was attributed to some of the chief men of the day. In lonely lodgings, and oppressed with his father's displeasure, 'Mine,' he writes, 'was a miserable life.' Lord Shelburne, having discovered the author of the *Fragment*, called on Bentham, and invited him to his seat of Bowood. Visit followed visit, until he became almost domesticated in Shelburne's family. There he met congenial society, and 'was raised,' as he relates, 'from the bottomless pit of humiliation, and made to feel that I was something.' Between 1785 and 1787 he made an extensive tour over Europe, and whilst living at Kirchoff, in Southern Russia, at the house of his brother, who was in the service of the Czar, he produced the celebrated *Defence of Usury*, one of the most pleasantly written and conclusively reasoned of his minor works. His father dying, he came into possession of a handsome inheritance, and settled in Queen Square Place, Westminster, once Milton's house, where he abode without change until death, for half a century. His life henceforward was that of a literary recluse, with habits of the most regular and persevering industry. His writings were for years almost completely neglected; and for this the manner was chiefly to blame. It was through the medium of M. Dumont's French translations, and that of the higher class English reviews, that the ideas of Jeremy Bentham reached the public. He only became tolerable, only became intelligible, as Sydney Smith remarked, 'after he had been washed, trimmed, shaved, and forced into

clean linen.' In France he first attained something like popularity. Happening, when in Paris, in 1825, to enter one of the supreme law courts, he was recognised, and the whole body of advocates at once rose to do him reverence, and the judges invited him to sit beside them.

Bentham stirred very little abroad, being content to take exercise in his garden; and it used to be said that he was as surely to be found at home as Robinson Crusoe on his island. Easily found at home, it was easier to procure an interview with the king than with the philosopher. There was never a man so desirous of shunning others, unless some strong sense of duty, or prospect of usefulness, subdued his love of seclusion. Once, when Madame de Staël called on him, expressing an earnest desire for an audience, he sent to tell her that he certainly had nothing to say to her, and he could not see the necessity of an interview for anything she could have to say to him. On another occasion, Mr Edgeworth, in his somewhat pompous manner, called and delivered this message to the servant, 'Tell Mr Bentham that Mr Richard Lovell Edgeworth desires to see him;' to which he returned for answer, 'Tell Mr Richard Lovell Edgeworth that Mr Bentham does not desire to see *him*.'

With the exception of music, his tastes were all of a grave kind. Living in Milton's house, he had a slab put up in his garden, 'Sacred to Milton, prince of poets,' and as a duty once read his works; but he had no enjoyment of poetry, and assured young ladies that it was a sad misapplication of time. Like Franklin in appearance, he made a curious picture: his white hair, long and flowing, his neck bare; in a quaker-cut coat, list shoes, and white worsted stockings drawn over his breeches' knees. In his garden, in this odd guise, he might be seen trotting along on what he called his 'ante-prandial circumgyra-

JEREMY BENTHAM.

tions. In-doors, he dined in his work-room, where the green window-curtains were pinned over with slips of paper, being notes taken at the moment of passing thoughts, to be located and collated at a future time. This strange hermit was not without creatures and creations of his own. There was his stick, Dapple, which he laid on the shoulders of honoured visitors in friendly knighthood on meet occasions. There was his sacred tea-pot, Dickey, regularly set upon a lamp to sing. Last, and not least, were his favourite cats, chief among whom was Langborne. Him, Bentham boasted he had made a man of. First he raised him to the dignity of Sir John; but as he advanced in years he was put into the church, and as the Rev. Dr John Langborne he died.

At the mature age of eighty-five, with unimpaired intellect, with cheerful serenity, Bentham died, on the 6th of June 1832. To his physician and friend, Dr Southwood Smith, he left his body for dissection; and three days after his decease Dr Smith delivered an oration over it at the School of Anatomy, Webb Street, Maze Pond.

It would be difficult to exaggerate the importance of Bentham's labours as a jurist, and of his services as the instructor of statesmen and politicians, who, with more practical faculties, were able to work out the legal reforms he suggested and devised. At first, when he proposed changes in the fabric of English law, he was regarded as a harmless lunatic; as he persisted, he grew into estimation as a dangerous and sacrilegious madman; and for long years he wrote and published without gaining a single influential co-adjutor. Towards the close of his career he became girt about with appreciation and help of the most useful kind. In 1823, the *Westminster Review*, started at his cost and conducted by his disciples, ably represented him in politics and literature. Undoubtedly he suffered from the seclusion in which he lived, and many crotchets he entertained were bred in his ignorance of human nature. A knowledge of men is indispensable for those who would teach or make laws for them; and to know the world, an author must live in it, and observe how many circumstances conspire to defeat the most reasonable expectations and deductions that can be formed on paper. From the same cause Bentham's style suffered. His early writings were terse, clear, and frequently happy in expression; his later were greatly the reverse. By much living and thinking alone he had forgot the familiar language of his kind. Bentham's moral philosophy is constantly attacked as 'cold-blooded, calculating, selfish;' and when we consider his prosaic temper, it is not to be wondered that more ideal spirits should revolt from the prominence he gives to the material over the spiritual interests of life; but of his good-will to mankind, and his earnest wish to promote their happiness, there can be no question; 'he did what he could,' and higher praise than this can be accorded to no one. Universal genius we shall never find in one man; instead, we attain it in pieces. One man can do one thing supremely well, and another another. Bentham did what Wordsworth could not, and Wordsworth what Bentham could not, and each depreciated the other. Let us be more catholic than either, and try to honour the eminent services of both, and

never erect our peculiar likings, necessarily narrow and imperfect, into a standard of universal judgment.

EDWARD III. OF ENGLAND AND PHILIP VI. OF FRANCE—QUARREL ABOUT HOMAGE.

The claim of one sovereign for homage from another, on account of a superiority over certain parts of that other's dominions, was surely not the wisest institution of the Middle Ages. It does not seem to have ever been a clear claim in any case, and as far as it could be substantiated at all, it was liable to be stretched so far as to excite hostile resistance. England was but just emerged from a long war with Scotland, arising from an overstretched claim over its monarch, when its own kings were plunged into one of a century long, in consequence of a similar claim over themselves on the part of the French monarch.

When Philip the Sixth had made good his somewhat questionable pretensions to the French throne, he lost no time in summoning Edward III. of England to come and pay homage as a vassal for Guienne. The latter, who through his mother claimed the whole French empire, refused an audience to the ambassadors, and sent word that the son of a king would not bow before the son of a count. Fresh envoys were despatched, to inform him that his fiefs and revenues would be seized if he persisted in his refusal; and as a war would at that time have been extremely inconvenient, Edward yielded to the advice of his peers, and wrote respectfully to Philip, 'that he had long intended to visit France to acquit himself of his debt; and that, all obstacles being now removed, he should shortly cross over.'

The 6th of June 1329 was the day fixed for the monarchs to meet at the cathedral of Amiens, and the grandeur which Edward displayed in his own dress and that of his followers made it evident that he was more anxious to parade his power and riches than to honour Philip. He wore a robe of Cramoisy velvet spotted with gold leopards, the crown on his head, the sword at his side, and gold spurs; three bishops, four counts, six barons, and forty noble knights were in his train. Philip, on his side, had forgotten nothing to render the ceremony as pompous as possible. He was seated on a superb throne, dressed in a long robe of violet velvet, spotted with gold *fleurs-de-lis;* his diadem set with precious stones, and holding a golden sceptre in his hand. The kings of Navarre, Bohemia, and Majorca stood by his side, with dukes, counts, and church dignitaries in abundance. Edward himself was struck with the magnificence of this numerous and brilliant *entourage;* on his return to England, when his queen questioned him about the king her uncle, he was never weary of speaking 'of the great state and honour in France, to which no other kingdom could be compared.'

As soon as Edward had approached the throne, the high chamberlain commanded him to take off his crown, his sword, and spurs, and to kneel before the king on a cushion that was prepared —a most humiliating ceremony for so proud a spirit; he, however, obeyed, having advanced too far to recede, but all present remarked the indignation depicted on his face, to see himself forced to so lowly an attitude before such illustrious witnesses. The same officer then said, 'Sire, you must, as Count de Guienne, pay liege homage to monseigneur the king, and promise him faith and loyalty.' Here all Edward's pride was awakened, he declared he did not owe liege homage; both sides disputed the question warmly; at length, on his promising to consult his archives as soon as he returned to England, to know exactly to what he was pledged, and to send the declaration, sealed with the great seal, they let him off in these general terms: 'Sire,' said the chamberlain, 'you are the vassal of the King of France for Guienne and its appurtenances, which you hold of him as peer of France, according to the form of peace made between his predecessors and yours, as you and your ancestors have done for the same duchy to former kings.' To which Edward replied, 'Voire,' the old French word for yes. 'If it be so,' replied the Viscount de Melun, 'the king, our sire, receives you under protest.' The French monarch said, 'Voire,' and kissed the King of England on his mouth, holding his hands in his own. Thus ended a ceremony which enraged Edward so much that he swore eternal hatred to the prince who had treated him with so much haughtiness.

On his return to England he was in no haste to make the required search, but the Duke de Bourbon and other nobles were sent to this country to receive a formal and authentic declaration. The French jurisconsults, who accompanied them, spent much time with the English parliament in examining previous acts of homage, and it was proved that the king was liege man in his rank of Duke of Guienne. The necessary papers were sent to Philip, and Edward never rested until he had prepared the army which was to attack France, and begin that fearful war which lasted above a century.

THE MOHOCKS.

On the 6th of June 1712, Sir Mark Cole and three other gentlemen were tried at the Old Bailey for riot, assault, and beating the watch. A paper of the day asserts that these were 'Mohocks,' that they had attacked the watch in Devereux Street, slit two persons' noses, cut a woman in the arm with a penknife so as to disable her for life, rolled a woman in a tub down Snow Hill, misused other women in a barbarous manner by setting them on their heads, and overset several coaches and chairs with short clubs, loaded with lead at both ends, expressly made for the purpose. In their defence, the prisoners denied that they were Mohocks, alleging that they were 'Scourers,' and had gone out, with a magistrate's sanction, to scour the streets, arrest Mohocks and other offenders, and deliver them up to justice. On the night in question they had attacked a notorious gambling-house, and taken thirteen men out of it. While engaged in this meritorious manner, they learned that the Mohocks were in Devereux Street, and on proceeding thither found three men desperately wounded, lying on the ground; they were then attacked by the watch, and felt bound to defend themselves. As an instance of the gross misconduct of the watch, it was further alleged that they, the watch, had on the same night actually presumed to arrest a peer of the realm, Lord Hitchinbroke, and had latterly adopted the practice of going their rounds by night accompanied by savage dogs. The jury, however, in spite of this defence, returned a verdict of 'guilty;' and the judge fined the culprits in the sum of three shillings and fourpence each.

It is scarcely credible that, so late as the last century, a number of young men of rank and fashion, assuming the name of a savage tribe, emulated their barbarous actions by wantonly inflicting the most disgusting cruelties on the peaceable inhabitants, particularly women, of London. And after these **Mohocks**, as they styled themselves, had held the town in terror for two years, after a royal proclamation had offered £100 reward for the apprehension of any one of them, when these four persons were at last brought to justice, the amount of punishment inflicted was merely the paltry fine of 3s. 4d.

Gay thus alludes to the Mohocks, and this very trial, in his *Trivia*:

' Who has not heard the Scourers' midnight fame?
Who has not trembled at the Mohocks' name?
Was there a watchman took his hourly rounds,
Safe from their blows or new-invented wounds?
I pass their desperate deeds and mischief done,
Where from Snow Hill black steepy torrents run;
How matrons, hooped within the hogshead's womb,
Are tumbled furious thence: the rolling tomb
O'er the stones thunders, bounds from side to side—
So Regulus, to save his country, died.'

One of the miscellaneous publications, issued by the circle of wits that revolved round Pope and Swift, is entitled, *An Argument, proving from History, Reason, and Scripture, that the present Race of Mohocks and Hawkubites are the Gog and Magog mentioned in the Revelations; and therefore that this vain and transitory World will shortly be brought to its final Dissolution. Written by a reverend Divine, who took it from the Mouth of the Spirit of a Person who was slain by the Mohocks.*

The 'Spirit' introduces himself by saying, 'I am the porter that was barbarously slain in Fleet Street. By the Mohocks and Hawkubites was I slain, when they laid violent hands upon me. They put their hook into my mouth, they divided my nostrils asunder, they sent me, as they thought, to my long home; but now I am returned again to foretell their destruction.' When the Spirit disappears, the assumed reverend author sings:—

' From Mohock and from Hawkubite,
    Good Lord, deliver me!
Who wander through the streets at night,
    Committing cruelty.
They slash our sons with bloody knives,
    And on our daughters fall;
And if they murder not our wives,
    We have good luck withal.

Coaches and chairs they overturn,
　Nay, carts most easily ,
Therefore from Gog and Magog,
　Good Lord, deliver me !'

WILLIAM HUNNIS.

On the 6th of June 1597, died William Hunnis, chapel-master to Queen Elizabeth, and previously Gentleman of the Chapel under Edward the Sixth. Hunnis was a rhymester—we cannot call him a poet—as well as a musician ; and according to his last will and testament, thus written in metre by himself, he experienced the once pro-verbial poverty of the rhyming race :

' To God my soul I do bequeath, because it is his own,
My body to be laid in grave, where, to my friends best known ;
Executors I will none make, thereby great strife may grow,
Because the goods that I shall leave will not pay all I owe.'

Immediately after the Reformation a very general spirit for versifying the Psalms and other parts of Scripture prevailed in England. Hunnis, not the least idle of those versifiers, published several collections, under quaint titles, now worth far more than their weight in gold to the bibliomaniacs. *Seven Sobs of a Sorrowful Soul for Sin*, comprehending the seven peniten-tial psalms in metre, was dedicated to Frances, Countess of Sussex, the foundress of Sydney-Sussex College at Oxford. Under the happy title of *A Handful of Honeysuckles*, he published *Blessings out of Deuteronomie, Prayers and Meditations*, in metre, with musical notes. His spiritual nosegays were numerous, to say nothing of his *Recreations on Adam's Banishment*, the *Lost Sheep*, and other similar topics ; he turned the whole book of Genesis into rhyme, under the title of *A Hiveful of Honey*.

Christopher Tye, a contemporary of Hunnis, and organist to Queen Elizabeth, rendered the Acts of the Apostles into English verse, and having set them to music, they were sung in the Chapel Royal, but never became popular. The impropriety of the design, as well as the infeli-city of its execution, was perceived even in that undiscerning age. Of the Acts, as versified by Tye, the initial stanzas of the fourteenth chapter may be selected as the least offensive for a speci-men :

' It chanced in Iconium,
　As they oft' times did use,
Together they into did come
　The synagogue of Jews,
Where they did preach, and only seek
　God's grace them to achieve ;
That so they speak, to Jew and Greek,
　That many did believe.'

The early Puritans violently opposed the study of the classics, or the reading of transla-tions from them, asserting that the customary mode of training youths in the Roman poets encourages idolatry and pagan superstition ; their employing themselves so zealously in rendering the Bible into English metre was that it might serve as ' a substitute for the ungodliness of the heathens.' A favourite book for those versifiers was the Song of Solomon, of which many versions were made. One, entitled *Sion's Muse*, is thus alluded to in a satire of Bishop Hall, written in ridicule of the spiritual poetry with which the age was inundated. After mentioning several of these productions, the nervous though inelegant satirist adds :

' Yea, and the prophet of the heavenly lyre,
Great Solomon, sings in the English choir ;
And is become a new found sonnetist,
Singing his love, the holy spouse of Christ :
Like as she were some light-skirts of the rest,
In mightiest inkhornisms he can thither wrest.
Ye Sion Muses shall by my dear will,
For this your zeal and far-admired skill,
Be straight transported from Jerusalem,
Unto the holy house of Bethlehem.'*

Robert Wisdome, archdeacon of Ely, was also one of those versifiers ; but he is chiefly memor-able for a metrical prayer, intended to be sung in churches, against the Pope and Turk, of whom he had conceived most alarming apprehensions. As there is no stanza in this prayer which could be considered unprofane at the present day, it is impossible to quote it. Among other wits, how-ever, the facetious Bishop Corbet has happily ridiculed it. Supposing himself seized with a sudden impulse to hear or to write a puritanical hymn, he invokes the ghost of Wisdome, as the most skilful poet in this mode of composition, to come and assist him. But he advises Wisdome to steal back again to his tomb in Carfax Church, at Oxford, silent and unperceived, for fear of being discovered and intercepted by the terrible Pope or Turk. The epigram is as follows :—

'TO THE GHOST OF ROBERT WISDOME.
' Thou, once a body, now but air,
　Arch-botcher of a psalm or prayer,
　　From Carfax come !
And patch us up a zealous lay,
With an old *ever and for aye*,
　Or *all and some*. †
Or such a spirit lend me,
As may a hymn down send me,
　To purge my brain ;
But, Robert, look behind thee,
Lest Turk or Pope do find thee,
　And go to bed again.'

JUNE 7.

St Paul, Bishop of Constantinople and martyr, 350. St Colman, Bishop of Dromore, confessor, about 610. St Godeschalc, Prince of the Western Vandals, and his companions, martyrs, 1066. St Robert, Abbot of New-minster, 1159. St Meriadec, Bishop of Vannes, con-fessor, 1302.

Born.—John Rennie, engineer, 1761, *Prestonkirk, Haddingtonshire* ; Robert Jenkinson, Earl of Liverpool, prime minister of George IV., 1770 ; Rev. W. D. Cony-beare, geologist, 1787, *London.*

Died.—St Willibald, 790, *Aichstadt* ; Robert Bruce,

_____
* A witty allusion to the *Old Bethlehem Hospital* of London, which was converted into a receptacle for luna-tics, and the name of which, subsequently corrupted into *Bedlam*, has been the origin of bedlamite, and other modern words.

† The words in italics were favourite phrases used by Wisdome in his versifications.

King of Scots 1329, *Cardross Castle, Dumbartonshire*, John Aubrey, antiquary, (*bur.*), 1697 ; Bishop John Sage, religious controversialist, 1711, *Edinburgh ;* William Aikman, Scottish portrait-painter, 1731, *London;* Bishop William Warburton, 1779, *Gloucester ;* Frederick William III., King of Prussia, 1840 ; Sir John Graham Dalyell, Bart., naturalist, antiquary, 1851, *Edinburgh.*

BISHOP WARBURTON.

A much less familiar name to our generation is Warburton than Johnson ; but, had any one in the last century predicted such a freak of fame in the blaze of the Bishop's learning and rhetoric, he would certainly have been listened to with incredulity. Johnson and Warburton were contemporaries ; Warburton by eleven years was Johnson's senior, but their lives flowed together for three score and ten, and five years alone divided the death of the great Bishop from the great Doctor. Strange to say, they only once met, as Boswell records ; namely, at the house of Mrs French, in London, well known for her elegant assemblies and bringing eminent characters together ; and the interview proved mutually agreeable. On one occasion it was told the Doctor that Warburton had said, 'I admire Johnson, but I cannot bear his style ;' to which he replied, 'That is exactly my case as to him.'

William Warburton was born on the 24th December 1698, at Newark, where his father was town-clerk, and died when William was in his eighth year. His mother had him educated for an attorney, and when he was twenty-one he commenced business in Newark. Finding little to do, he threw up law and entered the church, and was fortunate enough to find a patron in Sir Robert Sutton, who, after various favours, presented him to the living of Brant Broughton, in Nottinghamshire. There, in the quiet of the country, he sedulously devoted himself to those literary pursuits, by which he raised himself to fame and fortune. In a visit to London, in 1726, he identified himself with the party which hated Pope, and, considering what followed in after years, was unfortunate enough to write a letter in which he said that Dryden borrowed for want of leisure and Pope for want of genius. Twelve years afterwards, in 1739, the orthodoxy of Pope's *Essay on Man* having been attacked, Warburton published a series of letters in its defence, which led to an introduction and a very intimate friendship between the divine and the poet. When Pope died in 1744, it was found that he had left Warburton half his library and the copyrights of all his works, valued by Johnson at £4000. Pope's attachment to Warburton had driven Bolingbroke from his side, and after his death some sparring ensued between the old friend and the new, in the course of which Bolingbroke addressed Warburton in a pamphlet entitled *A Familiar Epistle to the most Impudent Man Living.* By Pope he was introduced to Ralph Allen, of Prior Park, Bath—Fielding's Squire Allworthy—whose niece he married in 1745, and through her inherited Allen's extensive property.

In the years intervening between these events Warburton had made even greater progress in an ecclesiastical sense. In 1736, he published his celebrated defence of *The Alliance between Church and State*, and, in 1738, the first volume of his great work, *The Divine Legation of Moses demonstrated on the Principles of a Religious Deist, from the Omission of the Doctrine of a Future State of Rewards and Punishments in the Jewish Dispensation.* It had often been brought as a reproach against Moses that his code contained no reference to heaven or hell, and theologians had ineffectually resisted it with a variety of apologies. Warburton, on the other hand, boldly allowing the charge, went on to argue that therein lay an infallible proof of the divine mission of the Hebrew lawgiver, for, unless he had been miraculously assisted, it was impossible that he could have dispensed with the armoury of hopes and terrors supplied by the doctrine of immortality. As might be expected, a violent storm of controversy broke out over this novel and audacious defence. The large and varied stores of learning with which he illustrated the course of his argument won the admiration of readers who cordially disliked his conclusion. In allusion to Warburton's abundant and well applied reading, Johnson observed : 'His table is always full. He brings things from the north, and the south, and from every quarter. In his *Divine Legation* you are always entertained. He carries you round and round, without carrying you forward to the point ; but then you have no wish to be carried forward.' Honours and promotion now flowed on Warburton, culminating, in 1759, in his elevation to the bishopric of Gloucester, which he held for twenty years, until his death in 1779.

A powerful and daring, if not unscrupulous reasoner, Warburton reaped the full measure of his fame in his own generation. A brilliant intellect, whose highest effort was a paradox like the *Divine Legation*, may astonish for a season, but can never command enduring regard. His lack of earnest faith in his opinions inevitably produced in his writings a shallowness of tone, causing the discerning reader to query whether Warburton, had he chosen, might not have pleaded with equal effect on the other side. His antagonists, who were many and respectable, he treated with a supercilious contempt, passable, perhaps, in a *Dunciad*, but inexcusable in a clergyman dealing with clergymen. Warburton had never been trained to bridle his tongue when his anger was roused. What should we now-a-days think of a bishop saying, as he did of Wilkes in the House of Lords, that 'the blackest fiends in hell will not keep company with him when he arrives there ?'

REVOLUTION HOUSE, WHITTINGTON.

On the 7th of June 1688, died Mr John D'Arcy, one of a small group of eminent men who held a meeting at Whittington, near Chesterfield, in Derbyshire, which was believed to be preparatory in an important degree to the Revolution. The house in which the meeting took place, being a tavern under the sign of the Cock and Magpie, continued to be recognised for a century after as the *Revolution House ;* there was even a particular room in it which the people called the *Plotters' Parlour.* If one might believe the traditionary report, it was here, in this Plotters' Parlour, in the Revolution House, on the moor near Chesterfield, that the great change of 1688 was deliberated upon and arranged. For this reason, the esteemed antiquary, Mr Pegge, wrote an account of the house, and had a drawing of it published.

When the story is carefully sifted, we find that a meeting of some importance to the forthcoming Revolution did take place here in the summer of 1688. The Earl of Danby (after the Revolution, Duke of Leeds), who had been minister to Charles II. some years before, but had since suffered a long imprisonment under Whig influence in the Tower, was now anxious to see some steps taken by which the Protestant religion might be saved from King James II. He was disposed for this purpose to associate with his former enemies, the Whigs. It was necessary, in the first place, that he should be reconciled to the leaders of that party. With this view it appears to have been that he, in company with Mr John D'Arcy, held a meeting in the public-house at Whittington with the Duke of Devonshire. The date of the meeting is not known, but it must have been some time before the 7th of June, when, according to any authority we have on the subject, Mr John D'Arcy died. At that time, most certainly, no definite design of bringing in the Prince of Orange had been formed, excepting in one mind, that of Edward Russell; nor was it till after the birth of the Prince of Wales (June 10, 1688), that overtures were made on the subject to various nobles, including Danby and Devonshire. The meeting of these two grandees at Whittington was entirely preliminary—limited to the private explanations by which they were enabled soon after to associate in the enterprise. In a narrative left by Danby himself, it is stated that the Duke of Devonshire *afterwards* came to Sir Henry Goodricke's house in Yorkshire to meet him for a second time, and concert what they should each do when the prince should land. It was there agreed that, on the landing of the Prince of Orange, the duke should take possession of Nottingham, while Danby seized upon York. The paper inviting the prince over, signed by seven persons, Devonshire, Danby, Shrewsbury, Lumley, Compton (Bishop of London), Edward Russell, and Henry Sidney, was sent away to Holland in the hands of Mr Herbert, in an open boat, on the Friday after the acquittal of the seven bishops—an event which took place on the 30th of June.

When it was subsequently known that the Duke of Devonshire and the Earl of Danby were among the chiefs who had brought about the Revolution, the country people about Whittington could not but recall the mysterious private meeting which these two nobles had held in the parlour of the village inn early in the preceding summer; and it was of course very natural for them, imperfectly informed as they were, to suppose that the entire affair of the Revolution had then and there been concerted.

746

Even on the view of a more restricted connexion with the event, the house must be considered as an interesting one, and its portraiture is here accordingly given. The Plotters' Parlour is in the centre of the range of buildings, immediately

REVOLUTION HOUSE.

to the left of a projecting piece of building seen conspicuously in the view.*

There is another house which is supposed to have been connected in a remarkable manner with the Revolution—Lady Place; an Elizabethan mansion situated on a beautiful bend of the Thames, between Maidenhead and Henley. A crypt, of more ancient date than the house, is considered as the place where the secret meetings were held of those who invited over the Prince of Orange, as is expressed on a mural tablet inserted in one of the walls. Here it is first stated that the crypt is part of a Benedictine monastery founded at the time of the Norman Conquest; then the inscription proceeds: ' Be it remembered that in this place, six hundred years afterwards, the Revolution of 1688 was begun. This house was then in the possession of the

VAULTS AT LADY PLACE.

family of Lord Lovelace, by whom private meetings of the nobility were assembled in the

GROUND PLAN.

References.—*a*, the kitchen; *b*, a room called The House; *c*, little parlour; *d*, The Plotters' Parlour; *e*, brew-house; *f*, stables.

vault; and it is said that several consultations for calling in the Prince of Orange were held in this recess; on which account this vault was visited by that powerful prince after he had ascended the throne.'

All such traditionary stories, unsupported by evidence, must of course be treated with some degree of suspicion ; yet it has been thought worth while to give in this paper a print exhibiting the interior of the crypt, with the mural tablet containing the inscription.

In connexion with this period of our history, the reader will readily recall the striking chapter in which Lord Macaulay recites the trial of the bishops, which occurred in the very month here under notice, and, as is well known, operated powerfully in effecting the change of dynasty. The noble historian makes a good point of the zeal of the people of Cornwall in behalf of their fellow-countryman, Trelawny, Bishop of Bristol, who was one of the seven. This dignitary was the son of Sir Jonathan Trelawny, of Trelawny, in Cornwall, baronet, and his successor in the baronetcy. Mr Davies Gilbert, in his *Parochial History of Cornwall*, says that the bishop enjoyed high popularity in his native district, and an intense excitement arose there when his danger was known, insomuch that the prompt acquittal of the bishops alone prevented the people from rising in arms. ' A song,' he adds, ' was made on the occasion, of which all the exact words, except those of what may be called the burden, were lost ; but the whole has recently been restored, modernized, and improved by the Rev. Robert Stephen Hawker, of Whitstone, near Stratton.' The original song ' is said to have resounded in every house, in every highway, and in every street.' The reader will probably be gratified to see the restored ballad, which the kindness of Mr Hawker has enabled us here to reproduce.

' TRELAWNY.

' A good sword and a trusty hand !
    A merry heart and true !
King James's men shall understand
    What Cornish lads can do !

And have they fix'd the where and when ?
    And shall Trelawny die?
Here's twenty thousand Cornish men
    Will know the reason why !

Out spake their captain brave and bold;
    A merry wight was he;
" If London Tower were Michael's Hold,
    We'll set Trelawny free !

We'll cross the Tamar, land to land,
    The Severn is no stay,
With one and all, and hand to hand,
    And who shall bid us nay !

And when we come to London Wall,
    A pleasant sight to view ;
Come forth ! come forth ! ye cowards all,
    Here's men as good as you !

Trelawny he's in keep and hold,
    Trelawny he may die ;
But here's twenty thousand Cornish bold
    Will know the reason why !" '

It is worthy of notice that the opposition which Trelawny had presented to the arbitrary acts of

King James did not prevent his Majesty from afterwards advancing him to the see of Exeter, an event which happened just before the Revolution. By Queen Anne he was afterwards translated to Winchester, in which see he died in 1721.

LONDON, ON THE 7TH OF JUNE 1780,

Was in the almost unchecked possession of a mob composed of the vilest of the populace, in consequence of a singular series of circumstances. A movement for tolerance to the small minority of Catholics—resulting in an act (1778) for the removal of some of their disabilities in England, and the introduction of a bill (1779) for a similar measure applicable to the mere handful of that class of religionists in Scotland—had roused all the intolerant Protestant feeling in the country, and caused shameful riots in Edinburgh. A so-called Protestant Association, headed by a half insane member of the House of Commons—Lord George Gordon, brother of the Duke of Gordon—busied itself in the early part of 1780 to besiege the Houses of Parliament with petitions for the repeal of the one act and the prevention of the other. On the 2nd of June a prodigious Protestant meeting was held in St George's Fields—on a spot since, with curious retribution, occupied by a Catholic cathedral—and a ' monster petition,' as it would now be called, was carried in procession through the principal streets of the city, to be laid before Parliament. Lord George had by this time, by his wild speeches, wrought up his adherents to a pitch bordering on frenzy. In the lobbies of the Houses scenes of violence occurred, resembling very much those which were a few years later exhibited at the doors of the French Convention, but without any serious consequences. The populace, however, had been thoroughly roused, and the destruction of several houses belonging to foreign Catholics was effected that night. Two days after, a Sunday, a Catholic chapel in Moorfields was sacked and burned, while the magistrates and military presented no effective resistance.

The consignment of a few of the rioters next day to Newgate roused the mob to a pitch of violence before unattained, and from that time till Thursday afternoon one destructive riot prevailed. On the first evening, the houses of several eminent men well affected to the Catholics and several Catholic chapels were destroyed. Next day, Tuesday, the 6th, there was scarcely a shop open in London. The streets were filled with an uncontrolled mob. The Houses of Parliament assembled with difficulty, and dispersed in terror. The middle-class inhabitants—a pacific and innocent set of people—went about in consternation, some removing their goods, some carrying away their aged and sick relations. Blue ribbons were generally mounted, to give assurance of sound Protestantism, and it was a prevalent movement to chalk up ' No POPERY,' in large letters on doors.* In the evening, Newgate was attacked and set fire to, and 300

* A foreign Jew in Houndsditch inscribed on his door, ' This house is a sound Protestant.' Grimaldi, an Italian actor newly come to England, with exquisite satire, put on his door, ' No RELIGION.'

prisoners let loose. The house of Lord Mansfield, at the north-east corner of Bloomsbury Square, was gutted and burnt, the justice and his lady barely making their escape by a backdoor. The house and distillery of a Mr Langdale, a Catholic, at the top of Holborn Hill, were destroyed, and there the mob got wildly drunk with spirits, which flowed along the streets like water. While they in many various places were throwing the household furniture of Catholics out upon the street, and setting fire to it in great piles, or attacking and burning the various prisons of the metropolis, there were bands of regular soldiery and militia looking on with arms in their hands, but paralysed from acting for want of authority from the magistrates. Mr Wheatley's famous picture, of which a copy is annexed, gives us a faint idea of the scenes thus presented; but the shouts of the mob, the cries of women, the ring of forehammers breaking open houses, the abandonment of a debased multitude lapping gin from the gutters, the many scenes of particular rapine carried on by thieves and murderers, must be left to the imagination. Thirty-six great conflagrations raged that night in London; only at the Bank was the populace repelled—only on

THE 'NO-POPERY' RIOTS.

Blackfriars Bridge was there any firing on them by the military. Day broke upon the metropolis next day as upon a city suddenly taken possession of by a hostile and barbarous army. It was only then, and by some courage on the part of the king, that steps were taken to meet violence with appropriate measures. The troops were fully empowered to act, and in the course of Thursday they had everywhere beaten and routed the rioters, of whom 210 were killed, and 248 ascertained to be wounded. Of those subsequently tried, 59 were found guilty, and of these the number actually executed was twenty.

The leader of this strange outburst was thrown into the Tower, and tried for high treason; but a jury decided that the case did not warrant such a charge, and he was acquitted. The best condemnation that could be administered to the zealots he had led was the admission generally made of his insanity—followed up by the fact,

some years later, of his wholly abandoning Christianity, and embracing Judaism. It is remarkable that Lord George's family, all through the seventeenth century, were a constant trouble to the state from their tenacity in the Catholic faith, and only in his father's generation had been converted to Protestantism, the agent in the case being a duchess-mother, an Englishwoman, who was rewarded for the act with a pension of £1000 a-year. Through this Duchess of Gordon, however, Lord George was great-grandson of the half-mad Charles Earl of Peterborough, and hence, probably, the maniacal conduct which cost London so much.

THE DUNMOW FLITCH OF BACON.

Far back in the grey dimnesses of the middle ages, while as yet men were making crusades, and the English commons had not a voice in the state, we see a joke arise among the flats of Essex. What makes it the more remarkable is, it arose in connexion with a religious house—the priory of Dunmow—showing that the men who then devoted themselves to prayers could occasionally make play out of the comicalities of human nature. The subject of the jest here was the notable liability of the married state to trivial janglements and difficulties, not by any means detracting from its general approvableness as a mode of life for a pair of mutually suitable persons, but yet something sufficiently tangible and real to vary what might otherwise be a too smooth surface of affairs, and, anyhow, a favourite subject of comment, mirthful and sad, for bystanders, according to the feeling with which they might be inclined to view the misfortunes of their neighbours. How it should have occurred to a set of celibate monks to establish a perennial jest regarding matrimony we need not inquire, for we should get no answer. It only appears that they did so. Taking it upon themselves to assume that perfect harmony between married persons for any considerable length of time was a thing of the greatest rarity—so much so as to be scarce possible—they ordered, and made their order known, that if any pair could, after a twelvemonth of matrimony, come forward and make oath at Dunmow that, during the whole time, they had never had a quarrel, never regretted their marriage, and, if again open to an engagement, would make exactly that they had made, they should be rewarded with a flitch of bacon. It is dubiously said that the order originated with Robert Fitzwalter, a favourite of King John, who revivified the Dunmow priory about the beginning of the thirteenth century; but we do not in truth see him in any way concerned in the matter beyond his being a patron of the priory, and as we find the priors alone acting in it afterwards, it seems a more reasonable belief that the joke from the first was theirs.

And that the joke was not altogether an ill-based one certainly appears on an *e facie* view of the history of the custom, as far as it has been preserved, for between the time of King John and the Reformation—in which upwards of three centuries slid away—there are shown but three instances of an application for the flitch by properly qualified parties. The first was made in 1445 by one Richard Wright, of Badbury, in the county of Norfolk, a labouring man; his claim was allowed, and the flitch rendered to him. The second was made in 1467 by one Stephen Samuel, of Ayston-parva, in Essex, a husbandman. Having made the proper oaths before Roger Bulcott, prior, in presence of the convent and a number of neighbours, he, too, obtained the bacon. The third application on record came from Thomas le Fuller, of Cogshall, in Essex, before John Tils, prior, in the presence of the convent and neighbours. This person also made good his claim, and carried off a gammon of bacon. We cannot, however, suppose that there was no application before 1445. It is more reasonable to surmise that the records of earlier applications have been lost. Of this, indeed, we may be said to have some evidence in the declaration of Chaucer's

Wife of Bath regarding one of her many husbands:—

> 'The bacon was not fet for [t]hem, I trow,
> That some men have in Essex, at Dunmow.'

It seems very probable that the offer held out by the prior of Dunmow was not at all times equally prominent in the attention of the public. Sometimes it would be forgotten, or nearly so, for a generation or two, and then, through some accidental circumstances, it would be revived, and a qualified claimant would come forward. Such a lapse from memory may be presumed to have taken place just before 1445, when a poet, bewailing the corruption of the times, declared that he could

> '——— find no man now that will enquire
> The perfect ways unto Dunmow,
> For they repent them within a year,
> And many within a week, I trow.'

But see the natural consequence of this public notice of the custom. Immediately comes honest Richard Wright, all the way from Norfolk, to show that matrimonial harmony and happiness were not so wholly extinct in the land. He claimed the flitch, 'and had his claim allowed.'

The priory of Dunmow was of course amongst the religious establishments suppressed by the Defender of the Faith. The old religion of the place was gone; but the bacon was saved. To the honour of the secular proprietors be it said, they either held it as a solemn engagement which they had inherited with the land, or they had the sense to appreciate and desire the continuance of the ancient joke. Doubtless, the records of many applications during the sixteenth and seventeenth centuries are lost to us; but at length, in 1701, we are apprized of one which seems to have been conducted and acted upon with all due state and ceremony. The record of it in the court roll of Dunmow is as follows:

'Dunmow, Super Prioratu.　At a Court Baron of the Right Worshipful Sir Thomas May, Knight, there holden upon Friday the 7th day of June, in the 13th year of the reign of our sovereign Lord William III., by the grace of God, &c., and in the year of our Lord 1701, before Thomas Wheeler, Gent., Steward of the said Manor. It is thus enrolled:

Homage.　Elizabeth Beaumont, spinster. Henrietta Beaumont, spinster. Annabella Beaumont, spinster. Jane Beaumont, spinster. Mary Wheeler, spinster.　Jurat.

'Be it remembered, that at this court, in full and open court, it is found and presented by the homage aforesaid, that William Parsley, of Much Easton, in the county of Essex, butcher, and Jane his wife, have been married for the space of three years last past, and upward; and it is likewise found, presented, and adjudged by the homage aforesaid, that the said William Parsley and Jane his wife, by means of their quiet, peaceable, tender, and loving cohabitation for the space of time aforesaid (as appears by the said homage), are fit and qualified persons to be admitted by the court to receive the ancient and accustomed oath, whereby to entitle themselves to have the bacon of Dunmow delivered unto them, according to the custom of the Manor.

'Whereupon, at this court, in full and open court, came the said William Parsley, and Jane his wife, in their proper persons, and humbly prayed they might be admitted to take the oath aforesaid. Whereupon the said Steward with the jury, suitors, and other officers of the court, proceeded with the usual solemnity to the ancient and accustomed place for the administration of the oath, and receiving the gammon aforesaid, (that is to say) the two great stones lying near the church door, within the said Manor, when the said William Parsley and Jane his wife, kneeling down on the said two stones, the said Steward did administer unto them the above-mentioned oath, in these words, or to the effect following, viz.:—

'You do swear by custom of confession,
  That you ne'er made nuptial transgression ;
Nor since you were married man and wife,
  By household brawls or contentious strife,
Or otherwise, in bed or at board,
Offended each other in deed or in word :
Or in a twelvemonth's time and a day,
Repented not in any way ;
Or since the church clerk said Amen,
Wished yourselves unmarried again,
But continue true and in desire
As when you joined hands in holy quire.'

'And immediately thereupon, the said William Parsley and Jane his wife claiming the said gammon of bacon, the court pronounced the sentence for the same, in these words, or to the effect following :—

'Since to these conditions, without any fear,
  Of your own accord you do freely swear,
A whole gammon of bacon you do receive,
And bear it away with love and good leave :
For this is the custom of Dunmow well known ;
Tho' the pleasure be ours, the bacon's your own.'

'And accordingly a gammon of bacon was delivered unto the said William Parsley and Jane his wife, with the usual solemnity.

Examined per THOMAS WHEELER, *Steward.*'*

At the same time Mr Reynolds, Steward to Sir Charles Barrington of Hatfield, Broad Oaks, received a second gammon.

Exactly half a century afterwards, John Shakeshaft, woolcomber, of Weathersfield, Essex, appeared with his wife at the Court Baron, and, after satisfying a jury of six maidens and six bachelors, received the prize, and the lucky pair were duly chaired through the town, attended by the Steward and other officers of the manor, the flitch being carried before them in triumph. The woolcomber showed himself as shrewd a man as he was a good husband, realizing a considerable sum by selling slices of the well-won bacon among the five thousand spectators of the

THE DUNMOW PROCESSION, 1751.

show. A picture of the procession was painted by David Osborne [from an engraving of which our representation of the scene is taken]. The bacon was again presented in 1763 ; but the name of the recipient has escaped record. After this the custom was discountenanced by the lord

of the manor, the swearing stones were removed from the churchyard, and the old oaken chair remained undisturbed in the priory. One John Gilder and his wife claimed the flitch in 1772 ; but when he and his sympathizers arrived at the

   * Lansdowne MS. 846.

priory, they found the gates fast ; the expectant couple were compelled to go away empty-handed, and the Dunmow festival henceforth was consigned to the limbo of extinct customs.

THE DUNMOW CHAIR.

In 1851 the lord of the manor was astonished by a worthy couple named Harrels demanding to be rewarded for their matrimonial felicity—a demand to which he declined to accede. However, the good people were so disappointed, and their neighbours so discontented thereat, that a compromise took place ; the usual ceremony was dispensed with, but the candidates for the flitch received the bacon, after taking the prescribed oath at a rural fête at Easton Park.

In 1855, Mr Harrison Ainsworth determined to revive the old custom ; the lord of the manor refused to allow the ceremony to take place at Little Dunmow, and some of the clergy and gentry strenuously opposed its transference to Great Dunmow. On the 19th of July, however, Mr and Mrs Barlow, of Chipping Ongar, and the Chevalier de Chatelain and his English wife, appeared before a mixed jury of bachelors and spinsters in the town-hall of Dunmow. Mr Ainsworth was judge, Mr Robert Bell counsel for the claimants, Mr Dudley Costello conducting the examination in opposition. After two hours and a half questioning and deliberation, both couples were declared to have fulfilled the necessary conditions, and the court, council, and claimants adjourned to the Windmill Field, where the oath was administered in the presence of fully seven thousand people, and the flitches presented to the deserving quartett.

The whimsical custom of rewarding immaculate couples with a huge piece of bacon is not peculiar to Dunmow. For 100 years the abbots of St Meleine, in Bretagne, bestowed a similar prize for connubial contentment, and a tenure binding the lord of the manor of Whichenoure, in Staffordshire, to deliver a flitch of bacon to any husband ready to swear he had never repented becoming a Benedict, but would, if free again, choose his wife above all other women, dates as far back as the reign of the third Edward, but no actual award of the Whichenoure prize is recorded.

MOUTH MUSIC.

There appeared at the Egyptian Hall, in Piccadilly, on June 7, 1830, one of those queer musicians who get a living by producing music (or what passes as such) in modes quite out of the usual character. This was Michael Boai, the chin performer. Strange as it was, the music had its points of interest in a scientific or acoustic sense. When the cavity of the mouth is lessened by the voluntary action of the muscles, it will resonate higher or more acute tones than when in its more expanded state. The tones themselves may be produced in some other way ; but the audible pitch may be varied in a remarkable degree by variations in the size and form of the interior of the mouth. Every whistling school-boy knows this practically, without thinking about it ; during his whistling the pitch of the note is determined by the shape, not only of the lips, but of the interior of the mouth. Herr Von Joel earned his living for many years by what may perhaps be termed high-class whistling, until the muscles of his mouth refused any longer to adapt themselves to this hard service. Boys sometimes produce a kind of music through the small teeth of a comb covered with tissue-paper, by breathing ; the differences of tone or pitch being produced by varying the shape of the mouth. The Jew's-harp is a really beautiful example of this kind ; the metal spring or vibrator produces only one note ; the variations in the mouth effect all the rest. Herr Eulenstein, an accomplished performer on this instrument, destroyed all his teeth by too long a continuance in this practice. Some men can produce music from a tobacco-pipe, by placing one end between the teeth, varying the cavity of the mouth, and maintaining a series of slight percussions upon the stem. This has even been done with a common walking-stick. Several years ago, there were four performers known as the Bohemian minstrels or brothers, who attracted attention in London by their peculiar music ; three sang in the ordinary way ; the fourth, without articulating any words, brought forth sounds of vast depth and power by a peculiar action of the muscles of the mouth ; and to these sounds were given a character like those of the strings of a contrabasso by the movements of the tongue. Some time afterwards, a party of Tyrolese imitated, or attempted to imitate, the several instruments of an orchestra, by the most extraordinary contortions of mouth and lips, and even by breathing violently through the nose ; the scene was too ridiculous to merit much notice, but it served to illustrate the matter under consideration. Picco, the blind Sardinian shepherd, who produced the most rapid music, with variations of an elaborate kind, on a little whistle only two or three inches long, worked his mouth in a remarkable way, to vary its capacity ; insomuch that the musical instrument was quite as much his own mouth as the whistle. Michael Boai, in his chin performances, depended in like manner on the rapid changes in the shape and size which he gave to the cavity of the mouth. The absurd mode of striking the chin (something like that in which the flint and steel were formerly used in striking a light), caused the lips to clap or slap together, and this produced the sound; but the *pitch* of the sound was made to vary according to the shape of the mouth. The intonation was sufficiently accurate to permit of a guitar and violin accompaniment.

A BEE BATTLE.

On the 7th of June 1827, occurred one of those battles of bees which naturalists have more than once had opportunity of observing. Among the many other remarkable instincts—sentiments, we may almost call them—possessed by these insects, is a sort of sense of property, right of location, or law of *meum* and *tuum*. According to an account in the *Carlisle Patriot*, on the day in question, at the village of Cargo, in Cumberland, a struggle took place between two swarms of bees. A day or two earlier, one of these communities had swarmed in the usual way, and been safely hived. On the day of battle, a swarm of bees from some neighbouring hive was seen to be flying over the garden in which the first-mentioned hive was situated. They instantly darted down upon the hive, and completely covered it; in a little time they began to enter the hive, and poured into it in such numbers that it soon became completely filled. Then commenced a terrible struggle. A loud humming noise was heard, and presently both armies of combatants rushed forth; the besiegers and the besieged did not fight within the beleaguered city, but in the open air. The battle raged with such fury, that the ground beneath was soon covered with the wounded and slain; the wounded crawled about painfully, unable to rise and rejoin their fellow-warriors. Not until one party was vanquished and driven away, did the sanguinary battle end. The victors then resumed possession of the hive. The local narrative does not furnish the means for deciding the question; but it seems most probable that there were some rights of property in the case, and that the interlopers were ejected.

SUPERSTITIONS ABOUT BEES IN SUFFOLK.

It is unlucky that a stray swarm of bees should settle on your premises, unclaimed by their owner.

Going to my father's house one afternoon, I found the household in a state of excitement, as a stray swarm of bees had settled on the pump. A hive had been procured, and the coachman and I hived them securely. After this had been done, I was saying that they might think themselves fortunate in getting a hive of bees so cheap; but I found that this was not agreed to by all, for one man employed about the premises looked very grave, and shook his head. On my asking him what was the matter, he told me in a solemn undertone that he did not mean to say that there was anything in it, but people *did* say that if a stray swarm of bees came to a house, and were not claimed by their owner, there would be a death in the family within the year; and it was evident that he believed in the omen. As it turned out, there was a death in my house, though not in my father's, about seven months afterwards, and I have no doubt but that this was taken as a fulfilment of the portent.

Bees will not thrive if you quarrel about them.

I was congratulating a parishioner on her bees looking so well, and at the same time expressing my surprise that her next-door neighbour's hives, which had formerly been so prosperous, now seemed quite deserted. 'Ah!' she answered 'them bees couldn't du.' 'How was that?' I asked. 'Why,' she said, 'there was words about them, and bees'll niver du if there's words about them.' This was a superstition so favourable to peace and goodwill in families,

that I could not find it in my heart to say a word against it.

It has been shewn in a contemporary publication,* that it is customary in many parts of England, when a death takes place, to go and formally impart the fact to the bees, to ask them to the funeral, and to fix a piece of crape upon their hives; thus treating these insects as beings possessed of something like human intelligence, and therefore entitled to all the respect which one member of a family pays to the rest. Not long before penning these notes, I met with an instance of this feeling about bees. A neighbour of mine had bought a hive of bees at an auction of the goods of a farmer who had recently died. The bees seemed very sickly, and not likely to thrive, when my neighbour's servant bethought him that they had never been put in mourning for their late master; on this he got a piece of crape and tied it to a stick, which he fastened to the hive. After this the bees recovered, and when I saw them they were in a very flourishing state—a result which was unhesitatingly attributed to their having been put into mourning.

C. W. J.

JUNE 8.

St Maximinus, first Archbishop of Aix, confessor, end of 1st or beginning of 2nd century. St Gildard, or Godard, Bishop of Rouen, confessor, 6th century. St Medard, Bishop of Noyon, confessor, 6th century. St Syra, virgin, of Ireland, 7th century. St Clou, or Clodulphus, Bishop of Metz, confessor, 696. St William, Archbishop of York, confessor, 1154.

CANONIZATION OF THE JAPANESE MARTYRS.

The canonization of saints has only been accepted as a dogma of faith by the Church of Rome since the twelfth century, and it was then confined to those who had suffered martyrdom for their religious principles. So rapid, however, was the increase of saints, that it was soon found necessary to place a limit to their admission to the canon: at first bishops were permitted to make them; this privilege was taken away, and the Pope alone had the power; another prudent regulation was that the holy man should have departed this life one hundred years at least before he was canonized, which no doubt prevented many a man, popular in his day, from attaining the honour, when his character was judged by a future generation.

We have in very recent times seen a remarkable example of this ceremony. Pius the Ninth determined to add to the list of saints twenty-three missionaries who had been martyred in Japan during the seventeenth century. Great preparations were made for the event; letters of invitation were written, not only to the Bishops of the Romish church, but also to those of the Eastern churches, and, in spite of the marked repugnance of some of the governments—who feared a political demonstration—the attendance was very large. These ecclesiastics formed the most interesting part of the procession to St Peter's. Wearing the dresses of those early Syrian and Armenian churches which had been founded by the Apostles themselves, and the symbols which created so warm a discussion among the Fathers—the stole, the alb, the mitre with

* *Notes and Queries, passim.*

crosses, Greek and Latin, the forms of which were heretic or orthodox, according to the judgment of the observer. The procession was similar to the one already described under Easter Day; the only difference, perhaps, was that St Peter's was entirely lighted up with wax lights; a mistake, as was generally agreed, there not being sufficient brilliancy to set off the gay colours of the cardinals, the bishops, the bearers of the flabelli, and guarda nobili.

Born.—John Domenic Cassini, astronomer, 1635, *Perinaldo, Nice;* Alexander Cagliostro, remarkable impostor, 1743, *Palermo;* Rev. Thomas Dunham Whitaker, English antiquary, 1759, *Rainham, Norfolk;* Robert Stevenson, engineer, 1772, *Glasgow;* Thomas Rickman, architect, 1776, *Maidenhead.*

Died.—Emperor Nero, 68, *Rome;* Mohammed, founder of the Moslem religion. 632; Louis X. of France, 1316, *Vincennes;* Edward, 'the Black Prince,' 1376, *Westminster;* Sir Thomas Randolph, minister of Elizabeth, 1590; Henry Arnauld, 1692, *Angers;* C. Huygens, Dutch mathematician, 1695, *Hague;* Princess Sophia, of Hanover, 1714, *Hanover;* Shah-Nâdir (Kouli Khan), usurper of the throne of Persia, murdered, 1747; Ambrose Philips, dramatist, miscellaneous writer, 1749; W. Pulteney, Earl of Bath, statesman, 1764: Abbé John Winckelmann, antiquary, 1768, *Trieste;* Gottfried Augustus Bürger, German poet, 1794; Thomas Paine, political writer, 1809, *Baltimore;* Dr Richard Carmichael (writings on medical subjects), 1849, *near Dublin;* Douglas Jerrold, comic writer, 1857, *London.*

CAGLIOSTRO.

'The quack of quacks, the most perfect scoundrel that in these latter ages has marked the world's history,' says Mr Carlyle, 'we have found in the Count Alessandro di Cagliostro, pupil of the Sage Althotas, foster-child of the Scherif of Mecca, probable son of the last King of Trebisond; named also Acharat, and unfortunate child of nature; by profession healer of diseases, abolisher of wrinkles, friend of the poor and impotent, grand master of the Egyptian mason-lodge of high science, spirit-summoner, gold-cook, grand cophta, prophet, priest, and thaumaturgic moralist and swindler; really a liar of the first magnitude, thoroughpaced in all provinces of lying, what one may call the king of liars.'

This desperate character was the son of Pietro Balsamo, a poor shopkeeper of Palermo, and was born in 1743. He was placed in a monastery, and being set to read the *Lives of the Saints* to the monks whilst they ate their meals, he was detected interpolating naughty fictions of his own, and was at once discharged. He then professed to study for a painter, and associating with vicious company, he forged theatre tickets, and then a will, robbed an uncle, cheated a goldsmith under pretence of shewing a hidden treasure, was accused of murder, and at last, Palermo growing too hot for him, he fled, no one knew whither. According to his own account, he went to Alexandria, and there, by changing hemp into silk, made much money; thence to Malta, where he studied chemistry.

His first authentic appearance, however, was at Rome selling pen-drawings, or rather prints touched up with Indian ink, and passed off as such. There he met Lorenza, the daughter of a girdle-maker, a comely young woman, who became his wife, and leaving Rome, the pair made their appearance at Venice, at Marseilles, at Madrid, Cadiz, Lisbon, Brussels, and other places, sometimes under one grand title, and sometimes under another, until, finally, they assumed that of the Count Alessandro and the Countess Seraphina Cagliostro. In a coach-and-four they rolled through Europe, found access to the highest society, and mysteriously dispensed potions, washes, charms, and love philtres. By a wine of Egypt, sold in drops more precious than nectar, they promised restoration to the vigour and beauty of youth to worn-out men and wrinkled women. Seraphina adduced herself as a living evidence of the efficacy of the elixir. Though young and blooming, she averred she was sixty, and had a son a veteran in the Dutch service. All, however, was not prosperity with them. Often they were reduced to miserable straits. Dupes who had their eyes opened were often very troublesome, and in a visit to London the count got for a while into the King's Bench Prison.

London, however, recompensed Alessandro and Seraphina by initiating both into the mysteries of Freemasonry, by which they were enabled to achieve their highest triumphs. From a bookseller the count professed to have purchased for five guineas certain manuscripts belonging to one George Cofton, in which he discovered the original system of Egyptian masonry instituted by Enoch and Elijah. In the process of centuries masonry had wofully declined from its pristine purity and splendour. The masonry of men had sunk into mere buffoonery, and that of women had become almost extinct; and the count proclaimed it as his mission to restore the sacred brotherhood to its ancient glory. Among the old and forgotten arcana were the philosopher's stone, an elixir of immortal youth, and a pentagon which restored its possessor to the primeval innocence forfeited by the fall. The prolonged and intricate series of rites by which these boons were to be attained conveniently deferred experiment and detection. From city to city, from Russia to France, travelled the count as the Grand Cophta, and the countess as the Grand Priestess, of the revived masonic faith. Their reputed success at this distance of time seems almost incredible. In dimly-lighted rooms, mysteriously decorated, the count in broken language, for he was master of none, and in unintelligible jargon, discoursed of the wonders and promises of Egyptian masonry, and led captive as believers people who would have scorned to be thought credulous. His calm, assured, and serious manner seemed to throw a seductive spell over those with whom he came in contact, and he decoyed them into his net even while their judgment protested. The old trade in Egyptian drops, beauty-waters, and secret-favours, under the influence of freemasonry, developed amazingly, and the prices in proportion rose.

Settling in Strasburg, he lived in magnificent state, but at the same time prosecuting assiduous labour in hospitals and the hovels of the poor, with open purse and drug-box containing 'extract of Saturn.' Miraculous cures attested his skill, and wonder grew on wonder. The Prince Cardinal de Rohan expressed a wish to see him, to which he answered:—'If Monseigneur the Cardinal is sick, let him come, and I will cure him; if he is well, he has no need of me, I none of him.' The rebuff effected its purpose to a marvel. It filled the cardinal with keener desire to make his acquaintance. A short interview was granted, from which he retired 'penetrated with a religious awe;' others, long and solitary, followed. 'Your soul,' said the count to the cardinal, 'is worthy of mine; you deserve to be made partaker of all my secrets.' Under such bewitching flatteries, Prince Louis de Rohan yielded himself unreservedly into Cagliostro's power, the richest and choicest of his many conquests.

From Strasburg the cardinal led the count and countess off to Paris, where they plied their arts with more distinguished success than ever, and, for a consideration, produced the apparition of any departed spirit that might be desired. In this blaze of prosperity destruction was near. De Rohan, the dupe in that mysterious and famous business of the Diamond Necklace, which he sold or imagined he sold to Marie Antoinette, was thrown into the Bastile, and with him his friends the Cagliostros. After an imprisonment of nine months, they were released, but ordered to leave France. They went to London, and lived for two years in Sloane Street, Knightsbridge, doing a fair business; selling 'Egyptian pills at 30s. the dram.' In May 1787, they left England, and after wandering over the Continent, driven from place to place by suspicious governments, by some miscalculation they ventured to Rome, and commenced to organize an Egyptian lodge. The Holy Inquisition had long had an eye on their doings, and now within its power, they were seized, at the end of 1789, and consigned to the castle of St Angelo. After a year and a half of tedious trial and examination, his holiness gave judgment, that the manuscript of Egyptian masonry be burnt by the common hangman; that all that intermeddle with such masonry are accursed; that Giuseppe Balsamo, justly forfeited of life for being a Freemason, shall nevertheless in mercy be forgiven, instructed in the duties of penitence, and kept safe henceforth until death in ward of the holy church. Thus ended the career of Cagliostro. In the fortress of St Leo he died, in 1795, at the age of fifty-two. His wife, who was confined in a convent, survived him for several years.

Mr Carlyle, who has written the story of *The Arch Quack* in a most graphic manner, thus describes the impression made on him by his portrait:—

'One of the most authentic documents preserved of Joseph Balsamo is the picture of his visage. An effigy once universally diffused in oil-paint, aqua-tint, marble, stucco, and perhaps gingerbread, decorating millions of apartments. Fittest of visages, worthy to be worn by the quack of quacks! A most portentous face of scoundrelism: a fat, snub, abominable face; dew-lapped, flat-nosed, greasy, full of greediness,

sensuality, ox-like obstinacy; a forehead impudent, refusing to be ashamed; and then two eyes turned up seraphically languishing, as if in divine contemplation and adoration; a touch of quiz, too; on the whole, perhaps the most perfect quack-face produced by the eighteenth century.'

THOMAS DUNHAM WHITAKER.

Sir Henry Spelman, in his work showing (to his own satisfaction) how impossible it was for the appropriators of church lands to thrive upon them, takes as one of his illustrative examples a story connected with the parsonage of Rainham. In the reign of Charles I., Sir Roger Townsend, proposing to rebuild his house at Rainham, conveyed thither a large quantity of stones from the ruins of Croxford Abbey, in the neighbourhood. But these stones, as often as any attempt was made to build them up into an unhallowed edifice, obstinately persisted in falling to the ground. The sacrilegious owner of the estate next tried them in the construction of a bridge; but the well-keyed arch fell as soon as the framework on which it had been constructed was removed. At last, the stones were applied to the rebuilding of a parsonage-house, and, in this semi-ecclesiastical edifice, they quietly rested, till the middle of the last century, when they were once more removed by Lord Townsend, who wished to include the site of the building within the walls of his park. It was in this last parsonage-house that the antiquary Whitaker first saw the light.

Mr Whitaker is celebrated for having founded a new school of topographical literature, or rather, we may say, revived an ancient one, that had been allowed to become extinct. In the days of Leland and Camden, the fathers of this interesting study, an antiquary was not thought the worse for being a man of genius and learning; and consequently we find the ripest scholars of the age employed in archæological pursuits. But in succeeding times, the topographers wofully degenerated, as may be evidenced by the awful array of local histories that load the shelves of our public libraries; as heavy in matter, and dull in manner, as they are ponderous in mere physical gravity: dense folios, containing little more than transcripts of parish registers, title deeds, and monumental inscriptions, and often not having the simple negative merit of being correct copies of the originals.

Mr Whitaker was the first to redeem his favourite study from this state of degradation. In his histories of Whalley, Craven, and Richmondshire, he shewed that a topographical study of antiquities could be united with a keen relish for the beautiful in nature and in art; that the grave meditations of the moralist and the edifying labours of the biographer might be combined with the lofty aspirations of the poet; that the study of British antiquities might not only be facilitated, but enlivened, by bringing to classical information, correct taste, and an acquaintance with the Gothic, Anglo-Saxon, and Celtic languages and dialects, with a habit of detecting the numerous traces that the latter have left in the rude mother-tongue of our rustic population. And thus it is that topographical and antiquarian works are now read with pleasure and avidity by young and old, grave and gay, and not suffered to lie on the dusty back shelf of a library, to be produced only on the transfer of a manor, a dispute on a pedigree, or the sale of an advowson.

A curious speculation in Mr Whitaker's *History of Craven*, as to the probability of Henry Lord Clifford, first Earl of Cumberland, being the hero of the well-known and beautiful ballad, *The Nut-Brown Maid*, is worthy of notice. This young nobleman, under the influence of a miserly father and jealous stepmother, was led by the extravagance of the court into pecuniary embarrassments. The method which he took to supply his necessities was characteristic of his era. Instead of resorting to Jew money-lenders, and bill-discounting attorneys, post-obits, life-insurances, and other means of raising money by anticipation, as he might have done at the present day, he became an outlaw, collected a band of dissolute followers, harassed religious houses, plundered their tenants, and sometimes obliged the inhabitants of whole districts to take refuge in their churches. He reformed, however, in good time, and married Lady Margaret Percy, daughter of the Earl of Northumberland. The ballad was first printed about 1502, and from its containing the word 'spleen,' just previously introduced into the English language by the study of the Greek medical writers, it could not possibly have been written long before it was put to the press. Clifford was a celebrated bow-man, to whom would well apply the words of the ballad—

'Such an archere, as men say ye be ;'

besides, the outlaw particularly describes Westmoreland as his heritage, thus identifying himself with Clifford. So we must either suppose the whole story to be a fiction, or refer it to one of the adventures of the outlaw, who had led that wild life within a very few years of the time when the ballad was written. The great lineage of the 'Maid' well agrees with Lady Percy, and it is probable that the reckless young man may have lurked in the forests of the Percy family, won the lady in a disguise, which he had assured her covered a knight, and the inversion of the rank of the parties in the ballad may be considered as nothing more than a decent veil of poetical fiction thrown over a recent and well-known fact.

TOM PAINE.

If Paine had died before passing the prime of life, his name might have been held in some respect among liberal politicians for the services he rendered to the American colonies in the crisis of their difficulties with the British ministry. What he did on that occasion is pointedly brought out in a work by Elkanah Watson, a New Englander, who gives at the same time a curious account * of the personal appearance of this notable man. It was about the close of the war, when Mr Watson was pursuing commerce at Nantes, that Paine arrived there in the *Alliance* frigate, as secretary of Colonel Laurens, minister-

* *Men and Times of the Revolution,* &c. New York, 1856.

extraordinary from the Congress, and took up his quarters at the boarding-house where the narrator resided. 'I could not,' says Mr Watson, 'repress the deepest emotions of gratitude towards him, as the instrument of Providence in accelerating the declaration of our independence. He certainly was a prominent agent in preparing the public sentiment of America for that glorious event. The idea of independence had not occupied the popular mind, and when guardedly approached on the topic, it shrunk from the conception, as fraught with doubt, with peril, and with suffering. In 1776, I was present, at Providence, Rhode Island, in a social assembly of most of the prominent leaders of the State. I recollect that the subject of independence was cautiously introduced by an ardent Whig, and the thought seemed to excite the abhorrence of the whole circle. A few weeks after, Paine's *Common Sense* appeared, and passed through the continent like an electric spark. It everywhere flashed conviction, and aroused a determined spirit, which resulted in the Declaration of Independence upon the 4th of July ensuing. The name of Paine was precious to every Whig heart, and had resounded throughout Europe. On his arrival being announced, the Mayor, and some of the most distinguished citizens of Nantes, called upon him to render their homage of respect. I often officiated as interpreter, although humbled and mortified at his filthy appearance, and awkward and unseemly address. Besides, as he had been roasted alive on his arrival at L'Orient, for the * * * *, and well basted with brimstone, he was absolutely offensive, and perfumed the whole apartment. He was soon rid of his respectable visitors, who left the room with marks of astonishment and disgust. I took the liberty, on his asking for the loan of a clean shirt, of speaking to him frankly of his dirty appearance and brimstone odour, and prevailed upon him to stew for an hour in a hot bath. This, however, was not done without much entreaty, and I did not succeed until, receiving a file of English newspapers, I promised, after he was in the bath, he should have the reading of them, and not before. He at once consented, and accompanied me to the bath, where I instructed the keeper in French (which Paine did not understand) to gradually increase the heat of the water, until "le Monsieur était bien bouilli." He became so much absorbed in his reading that he was nearly parboiled before leaving the bath, much to his improvement and my satisfaction.'

The idea of Tom Paine 'bien bouilli' is amusing, but some people will think that 'bien rôti' would have been a more appropriate treatment.

JUNE 9.

St Vincent, martyr, 2nd or 3rd century. Saints Primus and Felicianus, martyrs, 286. St Pelagia, virgin and martyr, 311. St Columba, or Columkille, Abbot and Apostle of the Picts, 597. St Richard, Bishop of Andria, confessor, about 8th century.

ST COLUMBA.

A short distance from one of the wildest districts of the western coast of Scotland, opposite the mountains of Mull, only three miles to the south of Staffa, so famous for its stately caverns, lies a little island, which is celebrated as the centre from which the knowledge of the Gospel spread over Scotland, and indeed over all the North, and which, rocky and solitary, and now insignificant as it may be, was a seat of what was felt as marvellous learning in the earliest period of mediæval civilization. Its original name appears to have been Hi or I, which was Latinized into the, perhaps, more poetical form of Iona, but it is now commonly called I-com-kill, or I of Columba of the Cells, from the saint who once possessed it, and from the numerous cells or monastic establishments which he founded.

Columba was an Irish priest and monk of the sixth century, who was earnest in his desire to spread among the ignorant pagans of the North that ascetic form of Christianity which had already taken root in Ireland. According to Bede, from whom we gather nearly all we know of this remarkable man, it was in the year 565 that Columba left his native island to preach to the Picts, the inhabitants of the Scottish Highlands. Encouraged by their chieftain, his mission was attended with success. The chieftain gave him, as a place to establish himself and his companions, the island of I, which Bede describes as in size, 'only of about five families, according to the calculation of the English,' or, as this is explained by the Anglo-Saxon Chronicle, five hides of land. It is now three miles in length, and not quite a mile broad. Here Columba built a church and a monastery, of which he became abbot, and collected round him a body of monks, under a rule which was remarkable chiefly for the strict enforcement of self-denial and asceticism. Their hours each day were divided between prayer, reading or hearing the Scriptures, and the labours required for producing the necessaries of life, chiefly cultivating the land, and fishing. Others were employed in writing copies of the books of the church service, which were wanted for their own use, or for the religious missions sent out amongst the neighbouring barbarians. The art most cultivated among the early Irish monks appears to have been caligraphy, and Columba himself is said to have been a very skilful penman, and, we may no doubt add, illuminator; and copies of the Psalter and Gospel, still preserved in Ireland, are attributed to him. Such of Columba's monks at I as were capable, were employed in instructing others, and this employment seems to have best suited their tastes, and education became the great object to which Columba's successors devoted themselves. For ages youths of noble, and even of royal blood, flocked hither from all parts, not only of Scotland, England, and Ireland, but from Scandinavia, to profit by the teaching of the monks; at the same time, colonies of Columba's monks went forth to establish themselves in various parts of the Scottish Highlands, and the neighbouring islands, in Iceland, and even in Norway. Bede tells us that, about thirty-two years after he settled in I, or Iona, which would carry us, according to his dates, to the year 597, St Columba died and was buried in his island monastery, being then seventy-seven years old. The 9th of June is usually assigned as the day of his death. The reputation of Iona as a seat of learning, and as a place of extraordinary sanctity, continued to increase after the death of the founder of its religious establishment, and his memory was

756

held in the most affectionate love. His disciples, or we may say the monks of his order, who formed the Pictish church, became known by the name of Culdees, a Celtic word meaning simply monks. Their first religious house of any importance on the mainland was Abernethy, the church of which is said to have been built in Columba's lifetime, and which became the principal seat of royalty and episcopacy in the Pictish kingdom. St Andrew's, also, was a foundation of the Culdees, as well as Dunkeld, Dunblane, Brechin, and many other important churches. From the particular position held by Columba towards his disciples in all parts, when Culdee bishoprics were established, all the bishops were considered as placed under the authority of the abbots of Iona, so that these abbots were virtually the Metropolitans of the Scottish church. In the ninth century the Danes, who ravaged with great ferocity the Scottish coasts, repeatedly visited Iona, and so completely destroyed its monks and their monastery, that the island itself disappears from history, until the twelfth century, when, in the reign of William the Lion, it was re-occupied by a convent of Cluniac monks. Long before this the Culdees had lost their character for sanctity and purity of life, and they were now so much degenerated that the Scottish King David I. (who reigned from 1124 to 1153), after an ineffectual attempt to reform them, suppressed the Culdees altogether, and supplied their place with monks and canons of other orders, but chiefly of that of St Augustine.

Born.—Andrew M. Ramsay, author of *Travels of Cyrus*, 1686, *Ayr;* George Stephenson, engineer, 1781, *Wylam, Northumberland;* John Howard Payne, American actor and dramatist, 1792, *New York;* Schamyl, patriotic imaum of Circassia, 1797.

Died.—Jeanne D'Albret, Queen of Navarre, mother of Henry IV., 1572; Secretary Maitland, 1573, *Edinburgh;* William Lilly, astrologer, 1681, *Walton;* Benedict Pictet, learned Protestant divine, 1724, *Geneva;* Dr William Kenrick, 1779; Louis XVII. of France, 1795, *Temple, Paris;* Dr Abraham Rees, encyclopædist, 1825, *Finsbury.*

JOHN HOWARD PAYNE.

Thousands have had their tenderest sympathies awakened by the almost universal song of 'Home, sweet home,' without knowing that its author's name was John Howard Payne, and that it was first sung in a once popular, but now forgotten, melodrama, entitled *Clari; or, the Maid of Milan.* Payne was a native of America, born in 1792. Early turning his attention to the stage, he soon became a popular actor, and writer of dramatic pieces, both in England and his native country. Few persons have been so greatly loved by so large a circle of private friends. Dying at Tunis, where he latterly filled the office of United States consul, he was buried in the Christian cemetery of St George, where a monument was erected over his grave by his 'grateful country,' expressive of his merits as a poet and dramatist, and stating that he died 'after a tedious illness,' on the 1st of April 1852. His remains were removed from Tunis and re-interred at Washington, America, in 1883.

An amusing proof of the singular popularity of Mr Payne's song was afforded, soon after its first appearance, by a Dumbartonshire clergyman of the Established Presbyterian Church. He was preaching upon the domestic affections —he had wrought himself up a good deal— finally, forgetting all the objections of his cloth to stage matters, he recited the whole of the verses of 'Home, sweet home,' to the unutterable astonishment of his congregation.

SCHAMYL, IMAM OF CIRCASSIA.

It was in 1834 that Schamyl succeeded to that leadership among his countrymen in which he has acquired such distinction. Some tragical circumstances occurring about that time served first to impress the Circassians that in their new leader they had found one possessing a charmed life. The prestige which invested him was enhanced by his extremely reserved habits and isolated mode of life. He was consequently enabled to keep in check the best of the Russian generals, and came off conqueror in a hundred fights. His passionate love for his mountain home and freedom, claimed the sympathy of all Europe; such heroism is one of the finest traits in history, though, perhaps, his fall may be necessary for the march of civilization.

The greatest blow he ever received until the last was the capture of his son, nine years of age, by the Russians. Schamyl offered ransom and prisoners in exchange, but in vain. After the lapse of fifteen years, he made an incursion into the Russian territory, and carried off two Georgian princesses, who occupied a high rank at the court, and this time the exchange was accepted; though it was believed that Djammel-Eddin renounced civilization to return to barbarism with deep regret. Three years after he died.

Schamyl was not only a great warrior, but also a great legislator: he worked long hours in his private room surrounded by books and parchments; then he would leave home for a fortnight, and go from camp to camp preaching the Koran to his people, and rousing their love of

SCHAMYL.

independence. On his return, his people rushed to meet him, singing verses from their holy book, and accompanying him home. Scarcely had he dismounted, when his children, to whom he was passionately attached, were in his arms. He had three wives, but never would permit them to be distinguished above the other women of the encampment.

Each day he received the Naïbs who came on business, treating them with hospitality but simplicity. He himself always ate alone and with great sobriety; bread, milk, honey, rice, fruit, and tea composed his meals. He was adored by his people, and from one end of the Caucasus to the other his name was a talisman. His morals were of the utmost purity, and he put to death any offender with the strictest severity.

At the time of Schamyl's capture he was sixty-two years of age, and it is astonishing that at that period his eye should have retained the quickness and penetration of earlier years; incessantly seeking to read the depths of the soul, and to guess the most secret thoughts of those about him. Always distrustful amidst his devoted soldiers, whom he had learnt to fascinate completely, he yet killed any of them whom he doubted, before his suspicions were changed into certainty, and many an innocent life was sacrificed for his repose. After the example of the dervishes, Schamyl dyed his beard with henna; his hands, small and well-shaped, were attended to with the greatest care. His head-dress was formed of a lamb-skin cap, surmounted by voluminous folds of a muslin turban. He wore a tunic, on the front of which was placed a cartouche-box, and for arms he carried a Circassian poniard and a sword; the blades of both were of the most costly description.

When he introduced his military code into the mountains, he instituted an order of chivalry to reward his brave murides, which he called the 'Sign of courage.' It was composed of three degrees; the insignia were of engraved silver: the first, in the form of a crescent, bore for its device a sabre, with the inscription : 'This is the mark of the brave.' Through this they must pass to the second, which was a disk with

the figures cut through, a sabre with the device : 'He who is thinking of the consequences is wanting in courage.' The third and highest

INSIGNIA OF SCHAMYL'S ORDER OF BRAVERY.

was like the second, with a sabre, a pistol, and the Arabic words : 'He who is thinking of the consequences is wanting in bravery. Be devoted, and you shall be saved.'

Schamyl was not prodigal of his rewards, so that his people were very proud of these distinctions, and often sacrificed their lives in the hope of gaining them ; those few that have been brought to Europe have been taken from the breasts of the dead, and are only to be found in the private arsenals of the Russian Emperor.

It was reserved for Prince Bariatinsky to conquer the unconquered chieftain : a cordon was drawn around the mountains, and Schamyl took refuge in his strong aoûl of Gounib, provisioned and fortified for two years, and situated on a plateau in the form of a triangle, with a narrow road up to each corner. The Russians managed to climb up the rocks, and came unexpectedly on the Circassians ; a terrible combat ensued, and Schamyl saw that resistance had become useless. He was much surprised when he found that his life was to be spared, and when he reached St Petersburg, and saw its magnificence, he understood for the first time what a powerful enemy he had had to oppose, and wondered how a prince with such fortresses could attach so much importance to the possession of the rock of Gounib.

Admitted to the highest society, he was dazzled with the costumes and diamonds of the ladies ; 'I was far from expecting,' said he, 'to find Mahomet's paradise on earth.' One evening when he met with the French ambassador, he spoke to him of Abd-el-Kader. Hearing that the Arab chief had struggled as long as himself, but with superior forces, his face lighted up, because he felt he had done more. 'We have had the same fate,' he remarked. 'It is true,' was the answer, 'but he who has once been great will always be great.'

The Emperor Alexander granted him a pension sufficient for the comfortable maintenance of himself and his family, and a residence in a town which the government chose for him.

758

WILLIAM LILLY.

William Lilly was the last of the great English astrologers of the sixteenth and seventeenth centuries. He was born, as he tells us in his autobiography, at Diseworth in Leicestershire, on the 1st of May 1602, and received a tolerably good school education. In 1620, he went to London to seek service, which he obtained in the family of a Leicestershire man in the City, who had realized some property by business, the nature of which seems to be rather uncertain. It was said that he had been a tailor, and hence some of Lilly's enemies in after years reproached the astrologer with having been originally of that calling, though he denies it, and assures us that his duties in this family were of a much more menial character. At length, after the death of his master, Lilly married the young widow, and thus became a moneyed man. He appears to have had what we may perhaps call a taste for astrology, and had apparently picked up acquaintance with many of the pretenders in that science, and towards the year 1632 began to study it earnestly. About the year 1641 he set up as a regular practitioner. The political troubles in which the country was then involved, and the general agitation which resulted from them, opened a great field for those who speculated on popular credulity. They began to foretell and give information and advice upon public events, and were soon employed as instruments and agents by the rival parties. Lilly tells us that he first leaned towards the king's party, but that, having been treated in an insulting manner by the other astrologers who prophesied on that side, he deserted and became a confirmed Roundhead, and, as he says, he afterwards 'prophesied all on their side.' His prophecies, for the publication of which he had established an almanack which bore the title of *Merlinus Anglicus*, were indeed so many political weapons in the hands of the party leaders, and were used with very considerable effect. Butler, who is understood to have intended to picture Lilly under the character of Sidrophel, alludes to the use which was thus made of his prophecies—

'Do not our great reformers use
This Sidrophel to forbode news?
To write of victories next year,
And casties taken, yet i' th' air?
Of battles fought at sea, and ships
Sunk, two years hence? the last eclipse?
A total o'erthrow given the king
In Cornwall, horse and foot, next spring?
And has not he point-blank foretold
Whats'e'er the close committee would?
Made Mars and Saturn for the cause,
The Moon for fundamental laws?
The Ram, the Bull, and Goat, declare
Against the Book of Common Prayer?
The Scorpion take the protestation,
And Bear engage for reformation?
Made all the royal stars recant,
Compound, and take the covenant?'

As Lilly's prophecies greatly encouraged the soldiers, he naturally gained favour with the chiefs of the army, and there is good reason for believing that he was patronized and befriended by Cromwell. The Presbyterians, who looked upon astrology with aversion, and classed it with witchcraft, took advantage of some expressions in his almanacks which seemed to reflect upon the parliament, and sought to bring him under the vengeance of that body, when it was in its greatest power, but he found no less powerful protectors. During the Protectorate, Lilly's position was a flourishing and no doubt a lucrative one, and he appears to have become rich. He bought some of the confiscated estates of royalists. Towards the close of the Protectorate, he prophesied the Restoration, and thus made his peace with the government of Charles II., or more probably he was considered too insignificant an object to provoke the vengeance of the triumphant royalists. He was, however, compelled to surrender the estates he had purchased. Nevertheless, *Merlinus Anglicus*, which had become the most celebrated almanack of the day, was now distinguished for its loyalty. The only instance, however, in which the court seems to have taken any notice of Lilly, arose out of a remarkable prophecy in his almanack for 1666, which seemed to foretell the great fire of London in that year. As the fire was at first ascribed to a plot against the country, Lilly was suspected of knowing something of the conspiracy, and was arrested and closely examined, but his innocence was sufficiently evident. From this time he sank into comparative obscurity, and, probably finding that astrology and almanack-making were no longer profitable, he obtained a licence and began to practise as a physician. He died at an advanced age on the 9th of June 1681. He left an autobiography, addressed to the credulous Elias Ashmole, which is at the same time a curious record of the manners and sentiments of the time, and a remarkable picture of the self-conceit of its author. Lilly's almanack, *Merlinus Anglicus*, continued to be published under his name long after his death; but no new astrologer arose to take the position he had once held, for the flourishing days of astrology were over.

THE PARKS AND THE MALL.—THE BEAUX.

It would be an interesting task to trace the history of London fashionable life through the last two centuries, and even a short sketch of it cannot be otherwise than amusing and instructive. Some might, indeed, consider it a history of frivolous things and frivolous sentiments; but when we look back to the past, setting aside the curiosity always felt in contemplating manners or customs which are new to us, even frivolous things have their meaning in tracing the continual movement of the public mind and intelligence.

Our 'modish' forefathers in London two or three generations ago lived much more out of doors than is the custom with fashionable society now-a-days. Spring Garden, the Mulberry Gardens, the Mall, the Park, were places of constant resort from early in the forenoon till late at night, and in addition to these there were continually masquerades, ridottos, &c., where the company was at least nominally more select. The masquerades, too, differed only from the public walks in the circumstance that in the former people dressed in characters, for it was the custom to wear masks everywhere; and intrigue was carried on and kept up quite as much in the promenade of the Park or the Mall, as in the masquerade itself. In the seventeenth and eighteenth centuries, as in the middle ages, May was the gay month in society, and its gaiety was usually carried through the month following. May and June were the fashionable months of the year. It was with the first of May that the *season* in London was considered as commencing, and on that day, proverbially, the parks and the Mall began to fill. Poor Robin's Almanack for 1698 remarks, at the beginning of May—

'Now at Hide Park, if fair it be,
A show of ladies you may see.'

And the same joking prognosticator, for an earlier date (1669), says of the same month,— 'The first day of this month (if the weather be fair), Jupiter being in his exaltation, prognosticates great resort of people to Hide Park, Spring Garden,' &c.

The style of fashionable life which continued during a great part of the last century took its rise after the Restoration, and appears to have been carried on with greatest freedom from the reign of Charles II. to that of George II. Among the earlier places of fashionable resort was Spring Garden, celebrated in the journal of Pepys, in the time of the former of these monarchs, when it was the favourite place of promenade and intrigue. Arbours, where refreshments might be had, were distributed about the garden; and in Howard's comedy of the *English Mounsieur*, published in 1674, it is spoken of as 'a place will afford the sight of all our English beauties.' This play contains a good picture of the society in Spring Garden at that time; indeed, we shall find nowhere so vivid and striking a picture of fashionable life in England during the period mentioned above, as in the contemporary comedies, which we shall accordingly take as our principal guides in the following remarks.

Spring Garden was gradually abandoned as the fashionable world threw itself more entirely into the parks. Hyde Park had been long frequented, chiefly by carriages and equestrians; but St James's Park was nearer to the town, and with its no less celebrated promenade of the Mall, presented the further advantage of being near to the palace, and it thus became not unfrequently the lounge of the king and of the courtiers. There was great freedom in society at that time; and people who were sufficiently well-dressed accosted each other without hesitation, and without requiring any of the formalities of introduction. Thus the Park was a place of general conversation; persons of either sex 'joked' each other, sometimes rather practically, talked nonsense, (sometimes) sense, employed wit and sarcasm as well as flattery on each other, flirted (though they might be perfect strangers), and intrigued. The promenaders were so much at their ease, that they even sung in the Park. The Park and the Mall were frequented every day, and not only at all hours, but far into the night, though there were certain hours at which they were more crowded with company than at other times. Company was not wanting there even at an early hour in the forenoon. In the comedy of *Feigned Friendship*, two ladies, one disguised as a young man, are introduced in the Mall early, and meet an acquaintance who addresses them—

'*Townley*. G'morrow to your ladyship. You would not lose the fine morning.'

'*Lady G*. But did not expect so good company as Mr Townley.'

'*Townley*. Small want of that, I believe, madam, while this gentleman is with you.'

'*Lady G*. Truly we have pass'd an hour or two very divertingly. The Mall afforded us a large field of satyr, and this spark, I thank him, has managed his province much to my satisfaction. He comes up just to your pitch of malice and wit. I fancy your humours be very suitable. I must have you acquainted.'

One of the fashionable hours in the Park was that between twelve and one, being the hour preceding dinner. The ordinary dinner hour of good society appears to have been two o'clock, although at the beginning of the last century, very fashionable people had already adopted five. In Congreve's *Way of the World*, printed in 1700, a turn in the Park before dinner is spoken of as a common practice:—

'*Mirabell*. Fainall, are you for the Mall?'

'*Fain*. Ay, I'll take a turn before dinner.'

'*Witwood*. Ay, we'll all walk in the park; the ladies talked of being there.'

Seven o'clock in the evening was the next fashionable hour. The late dinner was then over, and 'modish' people again sought the open air. In the contemporary plays, gentlemen are introduced making appointments with the other sex for this hour. Hence the evening promenade was productive of a large amount of scandal. The first scene of the second act of Wilkinson's comedy of *Vice Reclaimed*, printed in 1703, is laid

760

in St James's Park in the morning. Two ladies begin their conversation as follows:—

'*Annabella*. 'Tis an inviting morning, yet little or no company.'

'*Lucia*. So much the better. I love retirement. Besides, this place is grown so scandalous, 'tis forfeiting reputation to be seen in an evening.'

Yet, with the gayer part of fashionable society, the evening appears to have been the favourite time in the Park. It included a good portion of the night. In Durfey's *Marriage Hater Matched*, Lady Hockley says of her dog, 'I carried him to the Park every night with me.' In Shadwell's comedy of *The Humorist*, a wit asks a lady in a tone of surprise, 'O madam, where were you that I missed you last night at the Park?' And in Wycherley's *Gentleman Dancing Master*, Mistress Flirt, making conditions of marriage, insists upon having her coach, adding, 'Nor will I have such pitiful horses as cannot carry me every night to the Park; for I will not miss a night in the Park, I'd have you to know.' There were various spots in or about the Park which obtained a reputation in the annals of gallantry. Barn Elms, near its south-west corner (St James's Park was then much more extensive than at present) was a locality famed for duelling and love-making; and Rosamond's Pond, near it, and surrounded with pleasant trees, was not only a well-known place of meeting for lovers, but had a more melancholy celebrity for the number of disappointed maidens who committed suicide in it. On the site now occupied by Buckingham Palace were the famed Mulberry Gardens, which had usurped the place of Spring Garden, and which, like it, had their shady tortuous walks and their arbours fitted up for refreshments and intrigues. The Mulberry Gardens often furnished scenes to the contemporary stage. They were entered from the Park, and were open till a late hour in the night. People talk of enjoying 'the garden by moonlight;' and some of the female characters in Shadwell's *Humorist* (1671), give us the following description:—

'*Frisk*. O me, madam! why does not your ladyship frequent the Mulberry Garden oftener? I vow we had the pleasantest divertisement there last night.'

'*Strick*. Ay, I was there, madam Frisk, and the garden was very full, madam, of gentlemen and ladies that made love together till twelve o'clock at night, the prettyly'st: I vow 'twould do one's heart good to see them.'

'*Theo*. Why that's a time for cats to make love in, not men and women.'

In the reign of George I., the elegant scenes of the London parks were transferred for a few weeks in autumn to Tunbridge Wells. There, it is stated, '*after prayers*, all the company appear on the walks in the greatest splendour, music playing all the time; and the ladies and gentlemen divert themselves with raffling, hazard, drinking of tea, and walking, till two, when they go to dinner.' There was no ceremony. 'Every gentleman is equally received by the fair sex upon the walks.' 'You engage with the ladies at play without any introduction.' 'At night, on the walks, there is all manner of play till midnight.' The tourist who gives us this account calmly adds: 'I believe there is no place in the world better to begin an intrigue in than this, nor than London to finish it.'*

From an early period in this history of fashionable life, we have illustrations of its external features in contemporary prints; and, farther on, caricatures and satirical prints contribute their aid. We are thus enabled to give a few cuts, representing groups of the elegant loungers of the parks at successive periods. The first, taken from a large contemporary view of a public ceremony, represents a group of fashionables of

the male sex in the reign of William III. The second cut is of a rather later date, and represents a gentleman and lady meeting in the fashionable promenade of perhaps the earlier part of the reign of George I.

While the tone of the comedies and novels of the hundred years succeeding the Restoration leave us in no doubt as to the laxity of fashionable morals, it stands in curious contrast to this fact that the external aspect of the *beau monde* was decidedly formal. The gait of both men and women was artificial; their phrases of compliment wholly wanted natural ease and grace. A gentleman walking with a lady generally carried his hat in his hand or under his arm (the wig being the protection he trusted to for the

* *A Journey through England,* 2 vols. 4th edit. 1724. Vol. i., p. 93.

comfort of his poll). Take, as an indication of this practice, a conversation between Sylvia and Courtley, in Otway's *Soldier's Fortune*, 1681 :—

'*Silv.* In next place, whene'er we meet in the Mall, I desire you to look back at me.'

'*Court.* Which if I chance to do, be sure at next turning to pick up some tawdry fluttering fop or another.'

'*Silv.* That I made acquaintance with all at the musique meeting.

'*Court.* Right, just such another spark to saunter by your side with his hat under his arm.'

Of the freedoms taken on the promenades there is no want of illustrations. In Cibber's *Double Gallant* (1707), the jealous husband, Sir Solomon, says—

'I'll step into the park, and see if I can meet with my hopeful spouse there! I warrant, engaged in some innocent freedom (as she calls it), as walking in a mask, to laugh at the impertinence of fops that don't know her; but 'tis more likely, I'm afraid, a plot to intrigue with those that do.'

Masks were, as already stated, in common use among the lady promenaders, who, under cover of this disguise, assisted by a hood and scarf which helped to conceal their person, were enabled to carry on conversations and to follow adventures on which they would hardly have ventured uncovered. In Dilke's comedy of *The Pretenders* (1698), Sir Bellamore Blunt, who is a stranger to London fashionable society, is astonished at the forward manner of the young Lady Ophelia :—

'*Sir Bell.* Why so? where are you going then ?'

'*Ophelia.* (*aside*) I'll soon try his reality; may you be trusted, sir ?'

'*Sir Bell.* Indeed, I may, madam.'

'*Ophelia.* Then know I'm going to my chamber, to fetch my mask, hood, and scarf, and so jaunt it a little.'

'*Sir Bell.* Jaunt it ! What's the meaning of that ?'

'*Ophelia.* Why, that's to take a hackney coach, scour from playhouse to playhouse, till I meet with some young fellow that has power enough to attack me, stock enough to treat and present me, and folly enough to be laughed at for his pains.'

London society was haunted by two rather considerable classes of what we may perhaps term parasites, the Beaux and the Wits, of which the latter were by far the most respectable, because many of those who pretended to literary talent or taste, and frequented the society of the wits, were men of wealth, or at least easy circumstances. The beaux might also be divided into two classes, those who were beaux by mere vanity and affectation, and those who were adventurers in the world, who appear to have been by far the more numerous class. These lived upon society in every possible manner, and were especially the attendants on the gambling-table. The Park was the resort of the beaux, while the wits frequented the coffee-houses, and both met in the theatres. A beau, or as he was otherwise called, a fop or a spark, affected the most extravagant degree of fashion in his clothing, and he spent much of his time in the hands of his hairdresser and perfumer. He affected also grand and new words, and fine set phrases, in this emulating the character of the wit. He was known by two signs especially, the care bestowed upon his wig, and the skilful manner in which he displayed his snuff-box—for without a snuff-box nobody could be a beau. In Cibber's *Double Gallant* (1707), a lady, speaking of a monkey, says—

'Now, I think he looks very humorous and agreeable; I vow, in a white periwig he might do mischief; could he but talk, and take snuff, there's ne'er a fop in town wou'd go beyond him.'

And in the comedy of *The Relapse* (1708), the counsel given to any one who wants to conciliate a beau is, 'say nothing to him, apply yourself to his favourites, speak to his periwig, his cravat, his feather, his snuff-box.' The beau is represented as aiming by these fopperies at making conquests among the ladies, and so marrying a fortune. 'Every fop,' says one of the personages in the comedy of *The Apparition* (1714), 'every fop with a long wig and a snuff-box thinks he may pretend to an heiress of a thousand pounds a year.' In this character the beau was commonly accused, partly out of vanity and partly to promote his speculations on the sex, of injuring reputations by boasting of favours never

GROUP OF PARK FASHIONABLES, TIME OF GEORGE II.

received, and of forging love-letters addressed to himself, in support of his boasts. In Carlyle's comedy of *The Fortune Hunters* (1689), the leading characters in which are beaux of this description, the beau Shamtown is introduced in bed at five o'clock in the afternoon, soliloquizing over his useless life, confessing to the writing of billets-doux to himself in the names of amorous ladies, and lamenting over his want of success.

'Yet still,' he says, 'I kept my reputation up; wheresoe'er I came, fresh billet-doux on billet-doux were receiv'd; sent by myself, heaven knows, unto myself, on my own charges.' He subsequently produces a letter, written by himself, which he professes to have received from a lady, and which in no equivocal terms offers him an interview. That the practice was a dangerous one, we do not need the tragical case of Don

GROUP OF PARK FASHIONABLES, ABOUT 1780.

Matthias in *Gil Blas* to assure us. Another characteristic of the beau was, that he always carried with him a pocket looking-glass. It must not be forgotten that the beaux and wits together pretended to rule the theatre, and to decide what new pieces should be approved by the public and what rejected. Hence the

dramatic writers of the day, in their prologues and epilogues, often address themselves to these two classes. Thus Farquhar, in the prologue to his comedy of *Sir Harry Wildair*, says of the dramatic writer—

'He gains his ends, if his light fancy takes
　St James's beaux and Covent Garden rakes.'

The popular writers of those days abound in satirical descriptions of the beaux. Thus a poem entitled *Islington Wells*, published in 1691, speaks of a beau ' bedaubed with lace,' and alludes especially to his love of fine language.

' For using vulgar words and phrases,
 Their mouth most inf'nitely debases,
 To say they've melancholy been
 Is barbarous; no, they are *chagrin*.
 To say a lady's looks are well
 Is common ; no, her air is *belle*.
 If any thing offends, the wig
 Is lost, and they're in such fatigue.'

In Delke's comedy of *The Pretender*, already quoted, we have the following description of the beau of 1678—

' *Sir Bellamour Blunt.* What the devil dost mean by that foolish word *beau* ?'

' *Vainthroat.* Why, faith, the title and qualifications of a beau have long been the standing mark for the random shot of all the poets of the age. And to very little purpose. The beaux bravely stand their ground still, egad. The truth on't is, they are a sort of case-hardened animals, as uncapable of scandal as they are insensible of any impression either from satyr or good sense.'

' *Sir Bell.* And prithee how must these case-hardened animals be distinguisht ?'

' *Vain.* Barring reflection, I believe the best way to be acquainted with the whole tribe of 'em, wou'd be to get a general register drawn from all the perfumers' shop books in town. Or, which is more scandalous, to examine the chaulks in all the chairmen's cellars about the Pall Mall ; where each morning the poor fellows sit, looking pensively upon their long scores, shaking their heads, and saying,—Ah ! how many times have we trotted with such a powder'd son of nine fathers from the Chocolate-house to the play, and never yet saw a groat of his money !'

Ten years later, the comedy of *The Relapse* introduced on the stage a picture of the aristocratic beau, in the character of Lord Foppington—a sort of Lord Dundreary of his day—who, rallied on his pretensions by a party of ladies, gives the following account of his mode of life :—

' I rise, madam, about ten o'clock. I don't rise sooner, because 'tis the worst thing in the world for the complection ; not that I pretend to be a beau, but a man must endeavour to look wholesome, lest he make so nauseous a figure in the side-box, the ladies should be compelled to turn their eyes upon the play. So at ten o'clock, I say, I rise. Naw if I find 'tis a good day, I resolve to take a turn in the Park, and see the fine women ; so huddle on my cloaths, and gett dress'd by one. If it be nasty weather, I take a turn in the Chocolate-hause, where, as you walk, madam, you have the prettiest prospect in the world ; you have looking-glasses all round you——But I'm afraid I tire the company.'

' *Berinthia.* Not at all. Pray go on.'

' *Lord Fop.* Why then, ladies, from thence I go to dinner at Lacket's, where you are so nicely and delicately serv'd, that, stap my vitals ! they shall compose you a dish no bigger than a saucer shall come to fifty shillings. Between eating my dinner and washing my mouth, ladies, I spend my time till I go to the play ; where, till nine a clack, I entertain myself with looking upon the company ; and usually dispose of one hour more in leading them aut. So there's twelve of the four and twenty pretty well over. The other twelve, madam, are disposed of in two articles : in the first four I toast myself drunk, and in t'other eight I sleep myself sober again. Thus, ladies, you see my life is an eternal round of delights.'

The ladies afterwards go on to remind him of another characteristic of the true beau—

' *Amanda.* But I thought, my lord, you beaux spent a great deal of your time in intrigues : you have given us no account of 'em yet.'

' *Lord Fop.* Why, madam——as to time for my intrigues, I usually make detachments of it from my other pleasures, according to the exigency. Far your ladyship may please to take notice that those who intrigue with women of quality have rarely occasion for above half an hour at a time. People of that rank being under those decorums, they can seldom give you a longer view than will just serve to shoot 'em flying. So that the course of my other pleasures is not very much interrupted by my amours.'

The last description of the beau we shall quote belongs to a still later date. It is taken from that well-known romance, ' Chrysal,' relating the adventures of a guinea, and published in the year 1760. Chrysal became at one time the property of a town beau, of whose manners and circumstances he gives an amusing description. This beau, having pawned a laced waistcoat for three guineas, ' returned home, and changing his dress, repaired to a coffee-house at the court-end of the town, where he talked over the news of the day,' —' till he carelessly outstayed all his engagements for supper, when a Welsh-rabbit and three-penny-worth of punch made him amends for the want of a dinner, and he went home satisfied.' He made great show of finery and extravagance, but lived in private very parsimoniously, in one room, up three pairs of stairs, fronting a fashionable street, but with a back door into an obscure alley, by which he could enter unseen. He was attended only by his hairdresser, laundress, and tailor, at their appointed times. Here is a journal of one day of his life.

' As he had sat up late, it was near noon when he arose, by which genteel indulgence he saved coals, for his fire was never lighted till after he was up. He then sallied out to breakfast in a tarnished lace frock and his thick-soled shoes, read the papers in the coffee house (*too soon after breakfast to take anything*), and then walked a turn in the Park, till it was time to dress for dinner, when he went home, and finding his stomach out of order, *from his last night's debauch* and his *late breakfasting*, he sent the maid of the house for a bason of pea-soup from the cook's shop *to settle it*, by the time he had taken which, it was too late for him to think of going anywhere to dine, *though he had several appointments with people of the first fashion*. When this frugal meal was over, he set about the real business of the day. He took out and brushed his best cloaths, set his shirt to the fire to air, put on his stockings and shoes, and then sitting down to his toilet, on which his washes, paints, tooth-powders, and lip-salves were all placed in order, had just finished his face, when his hairdresser came, one hour under whose hands compleated him a first-rate beau. When he had contemplated himself for some time with pride of heart, and practised his looks and gestures at the glass, a chair was called, which carried him to a scene of equal magnificence and confusion. From the brilliant appearance of the company, and the ease and self-complacency in all their looks, it should have seemed that there was not one poor or unhappy person among them. But the case of my master had convinced me what little faith is to be given to appearances, as I also found upon a nearer view that many of the gayest there were in no better a condition than he! After some time passed in conversation he sat down to cards.'

The character of the beau degenerated about 1770 into that of the Macaroni, of which we shall give a separate account on another occasion. It reappeared in the Dandy of about 1816, but may be said to have since become utterly extinct. Our third and last cuts are taken from engravings of the time, and represent groups of fashionable promenaders in the reigns of George II. and George III. They were among the last of those who gave celebrity to the Park and the Mall.

JUNE 10.

Saints Getulius and companions, martyrs, 2nd century. St Landry, or Laudericus, Bishop of Paris, confessor, 7th century. St Margaret, Queen of Scotland, 1093. Blessed Henry, or Rigo of Treviso, confessor, 1315.

Born.—James, Prince of Wales, commonly called 'the Pretender,' 1688, *London*; John Dollond, eminent optician, 1706, *Spitalfields*; James Short, maker of reflecting telescopes, 1710, *Edinburgh*.

Died.—Emperor Frederick Barbarossa, 1190, *Cilicia*; Thomas Hearne, antiquary, 1735, *Oxford*; James Smith, promoter of sub-soil ploughing, 1850, *Kinzeancleuch, Ayrshire*.

BIRTH OF JAMES PRINCE OF WALES.

'The 10th [June 1688], being Trinity Sunday, between nine and ten in the morning, fifteen minutes before ten, the queen was delivered of a prince at St James's, by Mrs Wilkins the midwife, to whom the king gave 500 guineas for her paines: 'tis said the queen was very quick, so that few persons were by. As soon as known, the cannon at the Tower were discharged, and at night bonefires and ringing of bells were in several places.'—*Luttrell's Brief Relation of State Affairs.*

It is the fate of many human beings to receive the reverse of a welcome on their introduction into the world; but seldom has an infant been so unwelcome, or to so large a body of people, as this poor little Prince of Wales. To his parents, indeed, his birth was as a miracle calling for devoutest gratitude; but to the great bulk of the English nation it was as the pledge of a continued attempt to re-establish the Church of Rome, and their hearts sunk within them at the news. Their only resource for a while was to support a very ill-founded rumour that the infant was supposititious—introduced in a warming-pan, it was said, into the queen's bedroom, that he might serve to exclude the Protestant princesses, Mary and Anne, from the throne.

How uncertain are all calculations of the results of remarkable events! What seemed likely to confirm the king on his throne, and assist in restoring the Catholic religion, proved

'THE OLD PRETENDER.'

very soon to have quite the contrary effect. It precipitated the Revolution, and before the close of the year, the little babe, which unconsciously was the subject of so much hope and dread, was, on a wet winter night, conveyed mysteriously across the Thames to Lambeth church, thence carried in a hackney coach to a boat, and embarked for France, leaving Protestantism in that safety which it has ever since enjoyed.

Unwelcome at birth, this child came to a manhood only to be marked by the hatred and repugnance of a great nation. He lived for upwards of seventy-seven years as an exiled pretender to the throne of Britain. He participated in two attempts at raising civil war for the recovery of what he considered his rights, but on no occasion showed any vigorous qualities. A modern novelist of the highest reputation, and who is incapable of doing any gross injustice in his dealings with living men, has represented James as in London at the death of Queen Anne, and so lost in a base love affair as to prove incapable of seizing a throne then said to have been open to him. It is highly questionable how far, even in fiction, it is allowable thus to put historical characters in an unworthy light, the alleged facts being wholly baseless. Leaving this aside, it fully appears from the Stuart papers, as far as published, that the so-called Pretender was a man of amiable character and refined sentiments, who conceived that the interests of the British people were identical with his own. He had not the audacious and adventurous nature of his son Charles, but he was equally free from Charles's faults. If he had been placed on the throne, and there had been no religious difficulties in the case, he would probably have made a very respectable ruler. With reference to the son, Charles, it is rather remarkable that, after parting with him, when he was going to France in 1744, to prepare for his Scotch adventure, the father and the son do not appear ever to have met again, though they were both alive for upwards of twenty years after. The 'Old Pretender,' as James at length came to be called, died at the beginning of 1766. To quote the notes of a Scottish adherent lying before us, and it is appropriate to do so, as a pendent to Luttrell's statement of the birth: 'The 1st of January (about a quarter after nine o'clock at night) put a period to all the troubles and disappointments of good old MR JAMES MISFORTUNATE.'

HEARNE, THE ANTIQUARY.

Old Tom Hearne, as he is fondly and familiarly termed by many even at the present day—though in reality he never came to be an old man—was an eminent antiquary, collector, and editor of ancient books and manuscripts. One of his biographers states that even from his earliest youth ' he had a natural and violent propensity for antiquarian pursuits.' His father being parish clerk of Little Waltham, in Berkshire, the infant Hearne, as soon as he knew his letters, began to decipher the ancient inscriptions on the tombstones in the parish churchyard. By the patronage of a Mr Cherry, he received a liberal education, which enabled him to accept the humble, but congenial post of janitor to the Bodleian Library. His industry and acquirements soon raised him to the situation of assistant librarian, and high and valuable preferments were within his reach; but he suddenly relinquished his much-loved office, and all hopes of promotion, through conscientious feelings as a non-juror and a Jacobite. Profoundly learned in books, but with little knowledge of the world and its ways, unpolished in manners and careless in dress, feeling imperatively bound to introduce his extreme religious and political sentiments at every opportunity, Hearne made many enemies, and became the butt and jest of the ignorant and thoughtless, though he enjoyed the approbation, favour, and confidence of some of his eminent contemporaries. Posterity has borne testimony to his unwearied industry and abilities; and it may be said that he united much piety, learning, and talent with the greatest plainness and simplicity of manners. Anxiety to recover ancient manuscripts became in him a kind of religion, and he was accustomed to return thanks in his prayers when he made a discovery of this kind.

Warton, the laureate, informs us of a waggish trick which was once played upon this simple-hearted man. There was an ale-house at Oxford in his time known by the sign of Whittington and his Cat. The kitchen of the house was paved with the bones of sheeps' trotters, curiously disposed in compartments. Thither Hearne was brought one evening, and shown this floor as a veritable tessellated Roman pavement just discovered. The Roman workmanship of the floor was not quite evident to Hearne at the first glance; but being reminded that the Standsfield Roman pavement, on which he had just published a dissertation, was dedicated to Bacchus, he was easily induced, in the antiquarian and classical spirit of the hour, to quaff a copious and unwonted libation of potent ale in honour of the pagan deity. More followed, and then Hearne, becoming convinced of the ancient character of the pavement, went down upon his knees to examine it more closely. The ale had by this time taken possession of his brain, and once down, he proved quite unable to rise again. The wags led the enthusiastic antiquary to his lodgings, and saw him safely put to bed. Hearne died in his fifty-seventh year, and, to the surprise of everybody, was found to possess upwards of a thousand pounds, which was divided among his poor brothers and sisters.

BOARSTALL HOUSE.

This old mansion, memorable as the object of frequent contests in the civil wars, was finally surrendered to the Parliament on the 10th of June 1646. Willis called it ' a noble seat,' and Hearne described it as ' an old house moated round, and every way fit for a strong garrison, with a tower at the north end much like a small castle.' This tower, which is still standing, formed the gate-house. It is a large, square, massive building, with a strong embattled turret at each corner. The entrance was across a drawbridge, and under a massive arch protected by a portcullis and thick ponderous door, strengthened with large studs and plates of iron. The whole mansion, with its exterior fortifications, formed a post of strength and importance. Its importance, however, consisted not so much in its strength as its situation; it stood at the western verge of Buckinghamshire, two miles from Brill, and about half way between Oxford and Aylesbury. Aylesbury was a powerful garrison belonging to the Parliament, and Oxford was the king's chief and strongest hold.

GATEWAY OF BOARSTALL HOUSE. *

and his usual place of residence during the civil wars. While Boarstall, therefore, remained a royal garrison, it was able to harass and plunder the enemy at Aylesbury, and to prevent their making sudden and unexpected incursions on Oxford and its neighbourhood.

At an early period in the civil wars Boarstall House, then belonging to Lady Dynham, widow of Sir John Dynham, was taken possession of by the Royalists, and converted into a garrison; but in 1644, when it was decided to concentrate

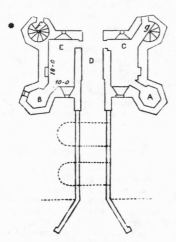

GROUND PLAN.

References.—A and B, turrets at the front angles; *f* and *g*, back turrets, with stairs from the garden; C and E, principal apartments on ground floor; L, passage through the building.

the king's forces, Boarstall, among other of the smaller garrisons, was abandoned. No sooner was this done than the impolicy of the measure became apparent. Parliamentary troops from Aylesbury took possession of it, and by harassing the garrison at Oxford, and by seizing provisions on the way there, soon convinced the Royalists that Boarstall was a military position of importance. It was therefore determined to attempt its recovery, and Colonel Gage undertook the enterprise. With a chosen party of infantry, a troop of horse, and three pieces of cannon, he reached Boarstall before daybreak. After a slight resistance, he gained possession of the church and out-buildings, from whence he battered the house with cannon, and soon forced the garrison to crave a parley. The result was that the house was at once surrendered, with its ammunition and provisions for man and horse; the garrison being allowed to depart only with their arms and horses.* Lady Dynham, being secretly on the side of the parliament, withdrew in disguise.

The house was again garrisoned for the king, under the command of Sir William Campion, who was directed to make it as strong and secure as possible. For this purpose he was ordered 'to pull down the church and other adjacent buildings,' and 'to cut down the trees for the making of pallisadoes, and other necessaries for use and defence.' Sir William Campion certainly did not pull down the church, though he probably demolished part of its tower. The house, as fortified by Campion, was thus described by one of the king's officers: 'There's a pallisado, or rather a stockado, without (outside) the graffe; a deep graffe and wide, full of water; a pallisado above the false bray; another six or seven feet above that, near the top of the curtain.' The parliamentarian garrison at Aylesbury suffering seriously from that at Boarstall, several attempts were made to recover it, but without success. It was attacked by Sir William Walley in 1644; by General Skippon in May 1645; and by Fairfax himself soon afterwards. All were repulsed with considerable loss. The excitement produced in the minds of the people of the district by this warfare is described by Anthony à Wood, then a schoolboy at Thame, as intense. One day a body of parliamentary troopers would rush close past the castle, while the garrison was at dinner expecting no such visit. Another day, as the parliamentary excise committee was sitting with a guard at Thame, Campion, the governor of Boarstall, would rush in with twenty cavaliers, and force them to fly, but not without a short stand at the bridge below Thame Mill, where half a score of the party was killed. On another occasion a large parliamentary party at Thame was attacked and dispersed by the cavaliers from Oxford and Boarstall, who took home twenty-seven officers and 200 soldiers as prisoners, together with between 200 and 300 horses. Some venison pasties prepared at the vicarage for the parliamentary soldiers fell as a prize to the schoolboys in the vicar's care.

In such desultory warfare did the years 1644

* Clarendon's *History of the Rebellion*. vol. ii., p. 494.

and 1645 pass in Buckinghamshire, while the issue of the great quarrel between king and commons was pending. Happy for England that it has to look back upwards of two centuries for such experiences, while, sad to say, in other countries equally civilized, it has been seen that they may still befall!

There was more than terror and excitement among the Bucks peasantry. Labourers were forcibly impressed into the garrisons; farmers' horses and carts were required for service without remuneration;* their crops, cattle, and provender carried off;† gentlemen's houses were plundered of their plate, money, and provisions; hedges were torn up, trees cut down, and the country almost turned into a wilderness. A contemporary publication, referring to Boarstall in 1644, says:—
'The garrison is amongst the pastures in the fat of that fertile country, which, though heretofore esteemed the garden of England, is now much wasted by being burthened with finding provision for two armies.' And Taylor, the 'water-poet,' in his 'Lecture to the People, addressed to the farmers of Bucks and Oxfordshire, says

'You crests are fallen down,
And now your journies to the market town
Are not to sell your pease, your oats, your wheat;
But of nine horses stolen from you to intreat
But one to be restored: and this you do
To a buffed captain, or, perhaps unto
His surly corporal.'

Nor was it only the property of the peaceable that suffered; their personal liberty, and very lives, were insecure. In November 1645, a considerable force from Boarstall and Oxford made a rapid predatory expedition through Buckinghamshire, carrying away with them several of the principal inhabitants, whom they detained till they were ransomed.‡ In 1646, a party of dragoons from Aylesbury carried off Master Tyringham, parson of Tyringham, and his two nephews. They deprived them of their horses, their coats, and their money. 'They commanded Master Tyringham to pull off his cassock, who being not sudden in obeying the command, nor over hasty to untie his girdle to disroabe himself of the distinctive garment of his profession, one of the dragoons, to quicken him, cut him through the hat into the head with a sword, and with another blow cut him over his fingers. Master Tyringham, wondering at so barbarous usage without any provocation, came towards him that had thus wounded him, and desired him to hold his hands, pleading that he was a clergyman, a prisoner, and disarmed.' He was then hurried off to Aylesbury, but before reaching there he was deprived of his hat and cap, his jerkin and boots, and so severely wounded in one of his arms that it was found necessary the next day to amputate it. 'Master Tyringham (though almost three score years old) bore the loss of his arme with incredible resolution and courage.'§

* Letter to Sir W. Campion from Prince Rupert, cited by Lipscomb, vol. i., p. 77.
† Records of Bucks, vol. ii., p. 94—306.
‡ Idem, vol. ii., p. 370.
§ Idem, vol. ii., p. 262.

Thus both parties were addicted to plunder, which is the inevitable consequence of civil war, and wanton cruelty is sure to follow in its train.

In 1646, Sir William Fairfax again attacked Boarstall House, and though its valiant little garrison for some time resolutely resisted, it wisely decided, on account of the king's failing resources, to surrender on terms which were honourable to both parties. The deed of surrender was signed on the 6th of June 1646, but did not take effect till the 10th. On Wednesday, June 10th, says A. Wood, 'the garrison of Boarstall was surrendered for the use of the Parliament. The schoolboys were allowed by their master a free liberty that day, and many of them went thither (four miles distant) about eight or nine of the clock in the morning, to see the form of surrender, the strength of the garrison, and the soldiers of each party. They, and particularly A. Wood, had instructions given them before they went, that not one of them should either taste any liquor or eat any provision in the garrison; and the reason was, for fear the royal party, who were to march out thence, should mix poison among the liquor or provision that they should leave there. But as A. Wood remembered, he could not get into the garrison, but stood, as hundreds did, without the works, where he saw the governor, Sir William Campion, a little man, who upon some occasion lay flat on the ground on his belly, to write a letter, or bill, or the form of a pass, or some such thing.'

Boarstall House, being now entirely relinquished by the Royalists, was taken possession of by its owner, Lady Dynham. In 1651, Sir Thomas Fanshawe, who had been taken prisoner at the battle of Worcester, was brought here by his custodians on their way to London. He was kindly received by Lady Dynham, 'who would have given him,' writes Lady Fanshawe, 'all the money she had in the house; but he returned her thanks, and told her that he had so ill kept his own, that he would not tempt his governor with more; but that if she would give him a shirt or two, and a few handkerchiefs, he would keep them as long as he could for her sake. She fetched him some shifts of her own, and some handkerchiefs, saying, that she was ashamed to give them to him, but having none of her son's shirts at home, she desired him to wear them.'*

The country having become more settled, Lady Dynham repaired her house and the church; but the tower of the latter, which had been demolished, was not restored. In 1668. Anthony Wood again visited Boarstall, and has recorded this curious account of it: 'A. W. went to Borstall, neare Brill, in Bucks, the habitation of the Lady Penelope Dinham, being quite altered since A. W. was there in 1646. For whereas then it was a garrison, with high bulwarks about it, deep trenches, and pallisadoes, now it had pleasant gardens about it, and several sets of trees well growne.
* * * * * *
Between nine and ten of the clock at night, being an hour or two after supper, there was

* Seward's *Anecdotes*, vol. iii., p. 309.

767

seen by them, M. H. and A. W., and those of the family of Borstall, a *Draco volans* fall from the sky. It made the place so light for a time, that a man might see to read. It seemed to A. W. to be as long as All Saints' steeple in Oxon, being long and narrow; and when it came to the lower region, it vanished into sparkles, and, as some say, gave a report. Great raines and inundations followed.'*

Towards the close of the seventeenth century, Sir John Aubrey, Bart., by his marriage with Mary Lewis, the representative of Sir John Dynham, became possessed of Boarstall; and it continued to be the property and residence of his descendants till it was pulled down by Sir John Aubrey, about the year 1783. This Sir John Aubrey married Mary, daughter of Sir James Colebrooke, Bart., by whom he had a son, named after himself, who was born the 6th of December 1771, and came to an early and melancholy death.

When about five years old he was attacked with some slight ailment, for which his nurse had to give him a dose of medicine. After administering the medicine, she prepared for him some gruel, which he refused, saying 'it was nasty.' She put some sugar into it, and thus induced him to swallow it. Within a few hours he was a corpse! She had made the gruel of oatmeal with which arsenic had been mixed to poison rats. Thus died, on the 2nd of January 1777, the heir of Boarstall, and of all his father's possessions—the only child of his parents—the idol of his mother. The poor nurse, it is said, became distracted—the mother never recovered from the effects of the blow. She lingered out a year of grief, and then died at the early age of thirty-two, and, as her affecting memorial states, 'is deposited by the side of her most beloved son.' Sir John Aubrey, having thus lost his wife and child, pulled down the house in which they died, with the exception of the turreted gateway, and removed his residence to Dorton, carrying with him a painted window, and some other relics from the demolished house of Boarstall. He also pulled down the old church, which had been much shattered in the civil war, and in 1818 built an entirely new one on the same spot. He married a second time, but dying in 1826 without issue, he was succeeded by his nephew, Sir Thomas Digby Aubrey, by whose death, in 1856, the male line of this very ancient family became extinct, and Boarstall is now the property of Mrs Charles Spencer Ricketts, of Dorton House.

The gate-house at Boarstall, which still exists in fair preservation, was built in 1312 by John de Hadlo, who then had license from Edward II. 'to make a castle of his manor-house at Borstall.'† Since the civil wars the drawbridge has been removed, and one of two arches, bearing the date of 1735, has been substituted, one side of the moat has been filled in, and some slight alterations made in the building itself, but it has still the appearance of a strong fortress, and is a good specimen of the castellated architecture of the period when it was built.

* *Life of A. Wood*, p. 155-6.
† Dugdale's *Baronage*, vol. ii., p. 61.

Boarstall, according to a very ancient tradition, acquired its name from an interesting incident. It is situated within the limits of the ancient forest of Bernwood, which was very extensive and thickly wooded. This forest, in the neighbourhood of Brill, where Edward the Confessor had a palace, was infested with a ferocious wild boar, which had not only become a terror to the rustics, but a great annoyance to the royal hunting expeditions. At length one Nigel, a huntsman, dug a pit in a certain spot which he had observed the boar to frequent, and placing a sow in the pit, covered it with brushwood. The boar came after the sow, and falling into the pit, was easily killed by Nigel, who carried its head on his sword to the king, who was then residing at Brill. The king knighted him, and amply rewarded him. He gave him and his heirs for ever a hide of arable land, called Derehyde, a wood called Hulewood, with the custody of Bernwood Forest to hold from the king *per unum cornu quod est chartæ predictæ Forestæ*, and by the service of paying ten shillings yearly for the said land, and forty shillings yearly for all profits of the forest, excepting the indictment of herbage and hunting, which were reserved to the king. On the land thus acquired, perhaps on the very spot where he slew the boar. Nigel built a lodge or mansion, which, in commemoration of his achievement, he named Boar-stall. In testimony of this tradition, a field is still called 'Sow Close,' and the chartulary of Boarstall, which is a large folio in vellum, contains a rude delineation of the site of Borstall House and manor, and underneath the portraiture of a huntsman kneeling before the king, and presenting to him a boar's head on the point of a

sword, and the king rewarding him in return with a coat-of-arms. The armorial bearings, which are, arg. a fesse gu. two crescents, and a horn verde, could not, of course, have been conferred by Edward the Confessor, but by some subsequent king. As, however, these arms were borne by Nigel's successors, they must here be regarded as an anachronistical ornament added by the draughtsman. 'The same figure of a boar's head presented to the king was, says Kennett, carved on the head of an old bedstead lately remaining in that strong and ancient house ; and the said arms of Fitz-Nigel are now seen in the windows and in other parts.' The tradition further states that the king (Edward the Confessor) conveyed his grant to Nigel by presenting to him a horn as the charter of his land, and badge of his office as forester. In proof of this, an antique horn, said to be the identical one given to Nigel, has descended with the manor, and is still in the possession of the present proprietor of Dorton House. This horn, which is two feet four inches long, is of a dark brown colour, resembling tortoiseshell. It is tipped at each end with silver gilt, and fitted with a leathern thong to hang round the neck ; to this thong are suspended an old brass ring bearing the rude impression of a horn, a brass plate with a small horn of brass attached to it, and several smaller plates of brass impressed with *fleurs-de-lis*, which, says Kennett, are the arms of the Lizares, who intruded into the estate soon after the reign of William the Conqueror. There was also over one of the doors in the tower a painting or carving upon wood representing the king knighting Nigel. The late Sir Thomas Aubrey carried this to Oving House, his place of residence, and had it renovated, but where it is now is unknown.

JUNE 11.

St Barnabas, the Apostle, 1st century. St Tochumra, Virgin, of Ireland. Another Tochumra, Virgin.

Barnaby's Day.

Before the change of style, the 11th of June was the day of the summer solstice. This was expressed proverbially in England—

'Barnaby bright,
The longest day and the shortest night.'

It appears to have been customary on St Barnaby's day for the priests and clerks in English churches to wear garlands of the rose and the woodroff. A miraculous walnut-tree in the abbey churchyard of Glastonbury was supposed to bud invariably on St Barnaby's day.

Born.—George Wither, poet, 1588, *Bentworth, Hants ;* Sir Kenelm Digby (speculative philosophical works), 1603, *Gothurst.*

Died.—Roger Bacon, 1292, *Oxford ;* Sir Kenelm Digby, 1665 ; Duc de Vendôme, French commander, 1712 ; George I. of England, 1727, *near Osnaburgh, Hanover ;* Dr William Robertson, historian, 1793, *Edinburgh ;* Samuel Ireland, engraver, 1800, *London ;* Dugald Stewart (moral philosophy), 1828, *Edinburgh ;* Rev. Dr Alexander Crombie (educational works), 1842, *London ;* Rev. Professor Baden Powell, 1860, *London.*

ROGER BACON.

English science has a double interest in the name of Bacon, and the older of the two individuals who bore it is certainly not the least illustrious, although we know very little of his personal history. He lived in an age when the world in general cared little about the quiet life of the laborious student. According to the account usually received, Roger Bacon was born near Ilchester, in Somersetshire, in the year 1214. It is said (for there is very little satisfactory authority for all this) that he displayed great eagerness for learning at a very early age, and that he was sent to study at Oxford when still a boy ; yet it appears that there was a Gloucestershire tradition as old as the beginning of the last century, that Roger Bacon was born in the parish of Bisley, in that county, and that he received his first education at a chapel dedicated to St Mary, now called Bury Hill, in the parish of Hampton, in which a chamber was shown called Bacon's Study. After he had made himself master of all that could be learnt at Oxford, Bacon went, as was usual at that time, to the much more important school of scientific labour, the University of Paris, where he is said to have become a doctor in the civil law, and so celebrated by his teaching as to acquire the appellative of the 'Wonderful Doctor.' He there made the acquaintance of Robert Grosteste, who was his friend and patron as long as he lived. He is said to have returned to England in 1240, when, if the date given as that of his birth be correct, he was still only twenty-six years of age, and he then established himself in Oxford. It seems doubtful if it were before or after his return to England that he entered the order of the Franciscans, or Friar Preachers, who were then great cultivators of science, and who are said to have been recommended to him by Grosteste ; but all we know of his life at this period seems to shew that in Oxford he took up his abode in the convent of that order. It is stated that, in the course of twenty years, he spent in his studies and experiments no less than £2000 sterling, which would be equivalent to a very large sum of money in the reckoning of the present day. We receive this statement from Bacon himself, and it is evident that Bacon's family was rich ; yet he remained almost unknown within his convent, and apparently neglected, if not despised by his fellow friars, until he was at length dragged from his obscurity by Pope Clement IV. The facts of the Pope's interference we also obtain from Bacon himself.

It is, moreover, by no means certain that Bacon was all this time in Oxford, but, on the contrary, we have every reason to believe that he passed a part of it in France. After he had spent all his own money in science, he applied to 'his rich brother' in England for assistance ; but his brother, who was a stanch royalist, had been reduced to poverty through his opposition to the liberal party in the baronial wars, and was not able to give him any assistance, and the terms in which Roger Bacon speaks shews that he was at that time residing in France. Bacon had another difficulty to deal with, for he now not only wanted money to pursue his studies, but he was not allowed to make public the discoveries he had made. It was a rule of the Franciscan order that no friar should be permitted the use of writing materials, or enjoy the liberty of publishing, without having first obtained leave from his superiors, and it is probable that he had already excited their watchful jealousy, and they had applied the rule to him with excessive strictness. Bacon's own account gives a curious picture of some of the difficulties which then stood in the way of science—it is addressed to Pope Clement.

'When your holiness wrote to me on the last occasion, the writings you demanded were not yet composed, although you supposed they were. For whilst I was in a different state of life [that is, before he entered the order of the Franciscans], I had written nothing on science; nor in my present condition had I ever been required to do so by my superiors; nay, a strict prohibition had been passed to the contrary, under penalty of forfeiture of the book, and many days' fasting on bread and water, if any work written by me, or belonging to my house, should be communicated to strangers. Nor could I get a fair copy made, except by employing transcribers unconnected with our order; and then they would have copied my works to serve themselves or others, without any regard to my wishes; as authors' works are often pirated by the knavery of the transcribers at Paris. And certainly if it had been in my power to have communicated any discoveries freely, I should have composed many things for my brother the scholar, and for others my most intimate friends. But as I despaired of the means of communicating my thoughts, I forbore to communicate them to writing. . . . . For, although I had at various times put together, in a hasty manner, some few chapters on different subjects, at the entreaty of my friends, there was nothing noteworthy in these writings; . . . they were such as I myself hold in no estimation, as being deficient in continuity and perfection.'

It appears that, before his accession to the papacy, Clement's curiosity had been excited by some accidental information he obtained relating to Bacon's wonderful knowledge and discoveries, and that he had written to ask the philosopher for some of his writings. The above extract is a portion of Bacon's reply to the pope's demand. Clement was an old soldier, and, however arbitrary he may have been in temper, he appears to have cared little for popular prejudices. In 1266, the year after he became pope, he despatched a brief to Bacon, enjoining, notwithstanding the order of any ecclesiastical superior or any rule of his order to the contrary, that he should communicate to him a copy of the important work which had been the subject of their previous correspondence. Bacon was thus fully brought before the world, and under Pope Clement's protection he continued for some years to diffuse his extraordinary knowledge. It was at this time that he produced his three great philosophical and scientific works, the *Opus Majus*, the *Opus Minus*, and the *Opus Tertium*, all three completed within the space of fifteen months.

In the thirteenth century, a man like Bacon was exposed to two very dangerous accusations. People in general, in their ignorant wonder at the extraordinary things he was said to be able to perform, believed him to be a magician, while the bigoted Churchman, alarmed at everything like an expansion of the human intelligence, sought to set him down as a heretic. Bacon incurred both these imputations; but, though the liberal views he expresses in his works, even

on religious questions, could not but be distasteful to the church, yet he was safe during Pope Clement's time. Several short papacies followed, until, in 1277, Pope Nicolas III. ascended the papal throne, a man of a different temper from Clement. At the beginning of his papacy, the general of the Franciscans, who had just been made a cardinal, brought forward an accusation of heresy against Bacon, and, with the pope's approval, caused him to be thrown into prison. When, ten years afterwards, the persecuting general of the Franciscans became pope himself, under the name of Nicolas IV., Bacon still remained a close prisoner, and it was only, we are told, towards the close of Nicolas's life that some of his friends were able to exercise sufficient interest to obtain his freedom. Nicolas IV. died in 1292; and, according to what appear to be the most reliable accounts, Bacon died on St Barnabas's day, the 11th of June 1292, although the real year of his death is by no means satisfactorily ascertained. He is said to have died in the convent of the Franciscans, at Oxford, and to have been buried in their church. Thus, in consequence of the fatal weight of the Roman Catholic Church on the minds of society, this great man had to pass all the earlier part of it in forced obscurity, and after only a few years in the middle, during which he was enabled to give some of his scientific knowledge to the world, he was rewarded for it during the latter part of his life with a prison. The real amount of his discoveries is very imperfectly known; but it is certain that they were far in advance of the age in which he lived, and that there was no branch of science which he had not sounded to its depths. His favourite subjects of study are said to have been mathematics, mechanics, and chemistry. He is said to have invented the camera obscura, the air-pump, and the diving-bell, but, though this statement may admit of some doubt, he was certainly acquainted with the nature and use of optical lenses and with gunpowder, at least with regard to the explosive powers of the latter, for the projectile power of gunpowder appears not to have been known till the following century. A great number of books remain under Bacon's name, but a considerable portion of them are of a spurious character. Tradition still points out in Oxford the building and even the room which is supposed to have been the scene of Roger Bacon's studies.

We may now turn from the real to the legendary character of Roger Bacon. When we consider the circumstances of the age, it is a proof of the extraordinary reverence in which the science of the friar Roger Bacon was held, that he not only became the subject of popular legends, but that in the course of years nearly all the English legends on science and magic became concentrated under the name of Friar Bacon. We have no means of tracing the history of these legends, which are extremely curious, as forming a sort of picture of the efforts, successful for a time, of the scholastic theology to smother the spirit of science. They were collected, still with a strong Romish prejudice, in the sixteenth century, into a popular volume, entitled *The History of Friar Bacon: containing the wonderful things that he did in his life; also the manner of his death; with the lives and deaths of the two conjurers, Bungye and Vandermast,* a work which has been reprinted in Mr Thoms's interesting collection of *Early Prose Romances.* Bungye and Vandermast are comparatively modern creations, introduced partly to work up the legends into a story, and for the same purpose legends are worked into it which have nothing to do with the memory of Roger Bacon. According to this story, 'In most men's opinions he was borne in the west part of England, and was sonne to a wealthy farmer, who put him to the schoole to the parson of the towne where hee was borne; not with intent that hee should turne fryer (as he did), but to get so much understanding, that he might manage the better that wealth hee was to leave him. But young Bacon took his learning so fast, that the priest could not teach him any more, which made him desire his master that he would speake to his father to put him to Oxford, that he might not lose that little learning that hee had gained.' The father made an outward show of receiving the application favourably, but he had no sooner got his son away from the priest, than he deprived him of his books, treated him roughly, and sent him to the plough, telling him that was his business. 'Young Bacon thought this but hard dealing, yet would he not reply, but within sixe or eight dayes he gave his father the slip, and went to a cloyester some twenty miles off, where he was entertained, and so continued his learning, and in small time came to be so famous, that he was sent for to the University of Oxford, where he long time studied, and grew so excellent in the secrets of art and nature, that not England onely, but all Christendome admired him.'

Such was Bacon's youth, according to the legend. His fame soon attracted the notice of the king (what king we are not told), and his wonderful feats of magic at court gained him great reputation, which leads him into all sorts of queer adventures. On one occasion, with an ingenuity worthy of the bar in its best moments, he saves a man from a rash contract with the devil. But one of the most famous exploits connected with the history of the legendary Friar Bacon was the manufacture of the brazen head, famous on account of the misfortune which attended it. It is, in fact, the grand incident in the legend. 'Friar Bacon, reading one day of the many conquests of England, bethought himselfe how he might keepe it hereafter from the like conquests, and so make himselfe famous hereafter to all posterities.' After deep study, he found that the only way to effect this was by making a head of brass, and if he could make this head speak, he would be able to encompass England with an impregnable wall of the same material. Bacon took into his confidence Friar Bungye, and, having made their brazen head, they consulted the demon who was under their power, and were informed by him that, if they subjected the head to a certain process during a month, it would speak in the course of that period, but that he could

not tell them the exact day or hour, and that, if they heard him not before he had done speaking, their labour would be lost. The two friars proceeded as they were directed, and watched incessantly during three weeks, at the end of which time Bacon employed his man Miles, a shrewd fellow, and a bit of a magician himself, as a temporary watch while they snatched a few hours' repose. Accordingly, Bacon and Bungye went to sleep, while Miles watched. Miles had not been long thus employed, when the head, with some preparatory noise, pronounced very deliberately the words, 'Time is.' Miles thought that so unimportant an announcement was not a sufficient reason for waking his master, and took no further notice of it. Half an hour later, the head said in the same manner, 'Time was,' and, after a similar interval, 'Time is past;' but Miles treated it all as a matter of no importance, until, shortly after uttering these last words, the brazen head fell to the ground with a terrible noise, and was broken to pieces. The two friars, thus awakened, found that their design had been entirely ruined, and so, 'the greate worke of these learned fryers was overthrown (to their great griefes) by this simple fellow.'

The next story is curious as presenting a legendary account of two of the great inventions ascribed to Roger Bacon. One day the king of England invaded France with a great army, and when he had besieged a town three months without producing any effect, Friar Bacon went over to assist him. After boasting to the king of many inventions of a description on which people were often speculating in the sixteenth century, Bacon proceeded to work. In the first place, having raised a great mound, 'Fryer Bacon went with the king to the top of it, and did with a perspect shew to him the towne, as plainly as if hee had beene in it.' This is evidently an allusion to the use of the camera obscura. The king, having thus made himself acquainted with the interior of the town, ordered, with Bacon's advice, that the assault should be given next day at noon. When the time approached, 'in the morning Fryer Bacon went up to the mount, and set his glasses and other instruments up . . . . . and, ere nine of the clocke, Fryer Bacon had burnt the state house of the towne, with other houses, only by his mathematicall glasses, which made the whole towne in an uprore, for none did know whence it came; whilest that they were quenching of the same, Fryer Bacon did wave his flagge, upon which signall given, the king set upon the towne, and tooke it with little or no resistence.' This is clearly an allusion to the effects of burning lenses.

Other stories follow of a more trivial character, and not belonging to the story of Friar Bacon. At length, according to this legendary history, after many strange adventures, Bacon became disgusted with 'his wicked life,' burnt all his magical (? scientific) books, and gave himself up entirely to the study of divinity—a very orthodox and Catholic conclusion. He retained, however, sufficient cunning to cheat the fiend, for it is implied that he had sold his soul to the devil, whether he died inside the church or outside, so 'then caused he to be made in the church wall a cell, where he locked himself in, and there remained till his death . . . . . Thus lived he some two yeeres space in that cell, never coming forth : his meat and drink he received in at a window, and at that window he did discourse with those that came to him. His grave he digged with his owne nayles, and was laid there when he dyed. Thus was the life and death of this famous fryer, who lived most part of his life a magician, and dyed a true penitent sinner, and an anchorite.'

A PHILOSOPHER OF THE SEVENTEENTH CENTURY.

Such were the natural gifts of Sir Kenelm Digby, that although, as the son of one of the gunpowder conspirators, he began his career under unfavourable circumstances, he eventually succeeded in winning almost general admiration. He even became a favourite with the king, who had executed his father, and was prejudiced against his name. And if he be estimated by the versatility of his genius, he would not be undeserving of the pinnacle of fame on which his admirers have placed him. There seemed no post in literature, science, politics, or warfare, that he could not undertake with credit. He was a philosopher, a theologian, a linguist, a mathematician, a metaphysician, a politician, a commander by land and by sea, and distinguished himself in each capacity. The estimation in which he was held appears in the following lines written for his epitaph :

' Under this tomb the matchless Digby lies,
  Digby the great, the valiant, and the wise ;
This age's wonder, for his noble parts,
Skilled in six tongues, and learned in all the arts ;
Born on the day he died, the eleventh of June,
And that day bravely fought at Scanderoon ;
It's rare that one and the same day should be
  His day of birth, of death, of victory !'

The name of Sir Kenelm Digby is depreciated in our day by the patronage he bestowed on alchemy and other arts, now generally concluded upon as vain and superstitious. He was understood to possess a means of curing wounds, independent of all traceable physical causes. Mr Howell, the author of *Dendrologie*, having been seriously wounded in the hand while attempting to prevent a couple of friends from fighting, found various surgeons unserviceable for a cure, but at length applied to Sir Kenelm. 'It was my chance,' says the latter, 'to be lodged hard by him ; and four or five days after, as I was making myself ready, he came to my house, and prayed me to view his wounds, "for I understand," said he, "that you have extraordinary remedies on such occasions, and my surgeons apprehend some fear that it may grow to a gangrene, and so the hand must be cut off." In effect, his countenance discovered that he was in much pain, which he said was insupportable, in regard of the extreme inflammation. I told him I would willingly serve him ; but if haply he knew the manner how I would cure him, without touching or seeing him, it may be he would not

expose himself to my manner of curing, because he would think it, peradventure, either ineffectual or superstitious. He replied, "The wonderful things which many have related unto me of your way of medicinement, makes me nothing doubt at all of its efficacy, and all that I have to say unto you is comprehended in the Spanish proverb, *Hagase el milagro y hagalo Mahoma,*—Let the miracle be done, though Mahomet do it." I asked him then for anything that had the blood upon it ; so he presently sent for his garter, wherewith his hand was first bound ; and as I called for a basin of water, as if I would wash my hands, I took a handful of powder of vitriol, which I had in my study, and presently dissolved it. As soon as the bloody garter was brought me, I put it within the basin observing in the interim what Mr Howell did, who stood talking with a gentleman in a corner of my chamber, not regarding at all what I was doing ; but he started suddenly, as if he had found some strange alteration in himself. I asked him what he ailed ? "I know not what ails me ; but I find that I feel no more pain. Methinks that a pleasing kind of freshness, as it were a wet cold napkin, did spread over my hand, which hath taken away the inflammation that tormented me before." I replied, "Since then, that you feel already so good effect of my medicament, I advise you to cast away all your plasters ; only keep the wound clean, and in a moderate temper betwixt heat and cold." This was presently reported to the Duke of Buckingham, and a little after to the king, who were both very curious to know the circumstance of the business, which was, that after dinner I took the garter out of the water, and put it to dry before a great fire. It was scarce dry, but Mr Howell's servant came running, that his master felt as much burning as ever he had done, if not more ; for the heat was such as if his hand were twixt coles of fire.' Sir Kenelm sent the servant back, and told him to return to him unless he found his master eased. The servant went, 'and at the instant,' continues Sir Kenelm, 'I did put again the garter into the water ; thereupon he found his master without any pain at all. To be brief, there was no sense of pain afterwards ; but within five or six days the wounds were cicatrized and entirely healed.' Sir Kenelm represented himself as having learnt this secret from a Carmelite friar who had been taught it in Armenia or Persia.

Amongst the marvels of Sir Kenelm's discoveries in metaphysics and alchemy, we may notice the following as far more amusing than instructive. To remove warts he recommends the hands to be washed in an empty basin into which the moon shines ; and declares that the 'moonshine will have humidity enough to cleanse the hands because of the star from which it is derived.' He tells us of a man, who, having lived from boyhood among wild beasts in a wood, had learnt to 'wind at a great distance by his nose where wholesome fruits or roots did grow,' and could follow persons, whom he knew, by scenting their footsteps like a dog. At a scientific meeting in France he made 'several considerable relations, whereof two·

did ravish the hearers to admiration. The one was of a king's house in England, which, having stood covered with lead for five or six ages, and being sold after that, was found to contain three-fourths of silver in the lead thereof. The other was of a fixed salt, drawn out of a certain potter's earth in France, which salt being for some time exposed to the sunbeams became salt-petre, then vitriol, then lead, then tin, copper, silver, and, at the end of fourteen months, gold; which he experienced himself and another able naturalist besides him.'

Butler, who keenly satirizes the philosophical credulity of his day, thus ridicules a belief in sympathetic powder, and similar nostrums :—

> 'Cure warts and corns with application
> Of medicines to the imagination;
> Fright agues into dogs, and scare
> With rhymes the tooth-ache and catarrh;
> And fire a mine in China here
> With sympathetic gunpowder.'

But every age has its mania in science and philosophy, and though men of talent and research are not always secure against the prevailing delusion, they seldom fail to leave behind them some valuable, though perhaps miniature fruit of their investigations. It was the mania of Sir Kenelm Digby, and the philosophers of his day, — and perhaps it is of our day too, — to expect too much from science. Yet such expectations often stimulate to the discovery of facts, which, by others, were considered impossibilities. Glanvil, whose faith in the powers of witches was as firm as Sir Kenelm Digby's in sympathetic powder, among many ridiculous conjectures of the possible achievements of science, hit on a very remarkable one, which cannot but be striking to us. In a work addressed to the Royal Society just two centuries ago, he says; 'I doubt not but that posterity will find many things that now are but rumours verified into practical realities. It may be, some ages hence, a voyage to the southern unknown tracts, yea, possibly, to the moon, will not be more strange than one to America. To those that come after us, it may be as ordinary to buy a pair of wings to fly into the remotest regions, as now a pair of boots to ride a journey. And to *confer, at the distance of the Indies, by sympathetic conveyances*, may be as usual to future times as to us in literary correspondence.' This last conjecture, the possibility of which has now been realized, doubtless appeared, when hazarded two centuries ago, as visionary and impossible as a flight to the moon. Even Butler, were he living in these days of electric communication, would not have thought it so impossible to fire a mine in China by touching a wire in Britain. Glanvil, with much pertinency, further remarks, 'Antiquity would not have believed the almost incredible force of our cannons, and would as coldly have entertained the wonders of the telescope. In these we all condemn antique incredulity. And it is likely posterity will have as much cause to pity ours. But those who are acquainted with the diligent and ingenious endeavours of true philosophers will despair of nothing.'

GEORGE WITHERS.

'I lived,' says this remarkable man, 'to see eleven signal changes, in which not a few signal transactions providentially occurred : to wit, under the government of Queen Elizabeth, King James, Charles I., the King and Parliament together, the King alone, the Army, Oliver Cromwell, Richard Cromwell, a Council of State, the Parliament again, and the now King Charles II.' Withers was brought up as a rigid Puritan. Imbued with a mania for scribbling, and a thorough detestation of what Mr Carlyle calls shams, he left behind him upwards of a hundred and forty satirical pieces, the greater part in verse. In early life he took service under Charles I., but when the civil war broke out, he sold his estate to raise a troop of horse, which he commanded on the side of the Parliament. He was once taken prisoner by the Royalists, and about to be put to death as a traitor; but Sir John Denham begged his life, saying to the king—'If your Majesty kills Withers, I will then be the worst poet in England.'

As Withers's satires were conscientiously directed against all that he considered wrong, either in his own or the opposite party, he very often was made acquainted with the interior of a prison; but in spite of these drawbacks, he managed to rub through life, favoured in some degree by both sides, as he held office under Charles II. as well as under Cromwell. He died on the 2nd of May 1667, having reached (for a poet) the tolerable age of seventy-nine

SIR JOHN FRANKLIN.

Sir John Franklin sailed, June 1845, in command of an expedition, composed of two vessels, the *Erebus* and *Terror*, for the discovery of the supposed North-west Passage. Several years having elapsed without affording any news of these ships, expedition after expedition was sent out with a view to ascertain their fate, but without any clear intelligence as to the vessels or their commander till 1859, when Captain F. L. M'Clintock, in command of a little vessel which had been fitted out at the expense of Lady Franklin, discovered, at Point Victory, in King William's Island, a record, contained in a canister, to the effect that the *Erebus* and *Terror* had been frozen up in lat. 70·05 N., and long. 98·23 W., from September 1846, and that Sir John Franklin died there on the 11th of June 1847. It further appeared that, at the date of the record, April 25, 1848, the survivors of the expedition, having abandoned their vessels, were about to attempt to escape by land; in which attempt, however, it has been learned by other means every one perished.

Franklin's expedition must be admitted to have been wholly an unfortunate one; but there is, after all, some consolation in looking to the many gallant efforts to succour and retrieve it— in the course of one of which the North-west Passage was actually discovered—and in remembering the constancy of a tender affection, through which, after many failures, the fate of the expedition was finally ascertained.

JUNE 12.

Saints Basilides, Quirinus, or Cyrinus, Nabor, and Nazarius, martyrs. St Onuphrius, hermit. St Ternan, Bishop of the Picts, confessor, 5th century. St Eskill, of Sweden, bishop and martyr, 11th century. St John of Sahagun, confessor, 1479.

Born.—Rev. Charles Kingsley, novelist, 1819 ; Harriet Martineau, novelist, historian, miscellaneous writer, 1802.

Died.—James III. of Scotland, killed near Bannockburn, Stirlingshire, 1488 ; Adrian Turnebus, eminent French scholar, 1565, *Paris ;* James, Duke of Berwick, French commander, 1734, *Philipsburgh ;* William Collins, poet, 1759, *Chichester* ; R. F. P. Brunck, eminent philologist, 1803 ; General Pierre Augereau (Duc de Castiglione), 1816 ; Edward Troughton, astronomical instrument maker, 1835, *London ;* Dr Thomas Arnold, miscellaneous writer, eminent teacher, 1842, *Rugby ;* Rev. John Hodgson, author of *History of Northumberland*, 1845 ; Dr Robert Brown, eminent botanist, 1858.

COLLINS.

The story of the life of Collins is a very sad one : Dr Johnson, in his *Lives of the Poets*, well expresses the unhappy tenor of it. 'Collins,' he says, ' who, while he *studied to live*, felt no evil but poverty, no sooner *lived to study* than his life was assailed by more dreadful calamities, disease and insanity.'

The poet's father, a hatter and influential man in Chichester, procured his son a good education, first at Winchester school, and then at Oxford. Accordingly, Collins promised well : but the seeds of disease, sown already, though yet concealed, silently took root ; and strange vacillation and indecision trailed in the path of a mind otherwise well fitted for accomplishing noble designs. Suddenly and unaccountably throwing up his advantages and position at Oxford, he proceeded to London as a literary adventurer. His was not the strong nature to breast so rough a sea ; and when home-supplies, for some reason, at length failed, he was speedily reduced to poverty. Nevertheless, at the age of twenty-six, an opportune legacy removed for ever this trouble ; and then it seemed he was about to enter upon a brighter existence. Then it was that the most terrible of all personal calamities began to assail him. Every remedy, hopeful or hopeless, was tried. He left off study entirely ; he took to drinking ; he travelled in France ; he resided in an asylum at Chelsea ; he put himself under the care of his sister in his native city. All was in vain ; he died, when not quite forty, regretted and pitied by many kind friends.

As we may naturally suppose, Collins wrote but little. At school he produced his *Oriental Eclogues*, and published them when at college, in 1742, some four or five years afterwards. These poems he grew to despise, and fretted at the public, because it continued to read them. In 1746 he published his *Odes*, when the public again crossed him ; but this time by *not* reading what he had written. He was so annoyed that he burnt all the remaining copies. One lost poem, of some length, entitled an *Ode on the Popular Superstitions of the Highlands of Scotland*, was recovered and published in 1788.

774

Time has avenged the neglect which Collins experienced in his own day. His *Ode on the Passions* is universally admired ; the *Ode to Evening* is a masterpiece ; there are not two more popular stanzas to be found than those which commence ' How sleep the brave ;' nor a sweeter verse in all the language of friendship than that in the dirge for his poet-friend :—

' Remembrance oft shall haunt the shore
    When Thames in summer wreaths is dressed ;
And oft suspend the dashing oar
    To bid his gentle spirit rest.'

ROBERT BROWN.

A kind, modest, great man—so early in the history of science, that he may be called the originator of vegetable physiology ; so late in the actual chronology of the world that he died on the 12th of June 1858 (at, it is true, the advanced age of eighty-five)—has to be described under this homely appellative. His gentle, yet dignified presence in his department of the British Museum will long be a pleasing image in the memory of living men of science. The son of a minister of the depressed episcopal church of Scotland at Montrose, he entered life as an army surgeon, but quickly gravitated to his right place ; first acting as naturalist in an Australian surveying expedition ; afterwards as keeper of the natural history collections of Sir Joseph Banks ; finally, as keeper of the botanical collection in the National Museum. His great work was the Botany of New Holland, published in 1814 ; but he wrote many papers, equally valuable in point of matter, for the Linnæan and Royal Societies. What was a dry assemblage of facts under an utterly wrong classification before his time, became through his labours a clearly apprehensible portion of the great scheme of nature. The microscope was the grand means by which this end was carried out—an instrument little thought of before his day, but which, through his example in botany, was soon after introduced in the examination of the animal kingdom, with the noblest results. Indeed, it may be said that, whereas little more than the externals of plants and animals were formerly cared for, we now have become familiar with their internal constitution, their growth and development, and their several true places in nature, and for this, primarily, we must thank Mr Robert Brown.

Animal-Named Plants.

A great number of plants are recognised, popularly at least, by names involving reference to some animal, or what appears as such. Sometimes this animal element in the name is manifestly appropriate to something in the character of the plant ; but often it is so utterly irrelative to anything in the plant itself, its locality, and uses, that we are forced to look for other reasons for its being applied. According to an ingenious correspondent, it will generally be found that in these latter cases the animal name is a corruption of some early term having a totally different signification.

Our correspondent readily admits that cats love cat-mint, that the bee-orchis and the fly-orchis resemble respectively the bee and the fly, and that the flower of the single columbine is like an assemblage of doves [Lat. *columba*, a dove] ; hence the animal names are here presumably real. He allows that the crane's-bill, the stork's-bill, fox-tail grass, hare's-tail grass, adder's-tongue fern, hare's-ear, lark's-spur, mare's-tail, mouse-tail, and snake's-head, are all appropriate on the plain meaning of the terms. He goes on, however, to cite a more considerable number, regarding which he holds it certain that the appellative is a metamorphose of some word, generally in another language, with no meaning such as the term would suggest to ordinary ears. We let him state his ideas in his own way :—

The name hare-bell is at present assigned to the wild hyacinth (*Scilla Nutans*), but properly belonging to the blue-bell (*Campanula rotundifolia*). Harebell may be traced to the Welsh *awyr-bel*, a balloon ; that is, an inflated ball or distended globe or bell, to which description this flower corresponds ; the name therefore would be more correctly spelled ' Airbell.' Foxglove, embodying the entire sense of the Latin *Digitalis purpurea*, is simply the red-glove, or red-gauntlet, for fox or foxy, as the Latin *fuscus*, and Italian *fosco*, signifies tawny or red, and hence is derived the name of the fox himself. The toad-flax (*Cymbalaria Italica*) is so named from the appearance it presents of a multitudinous mass of threads (flax), matted together in a cluster or branch, for which our old language had the significant term tod, which may be met with in several of our older dictionaries, from tot, or total, a mass or assemblage of things. So the toad-pipe (*Equisetum Arvense*), which consists of a cluster of jointed hair-like tubes, as also the bastard-toad-flax, a plant with many clustering stems, both have the term toad or tod applied to them for the same reason. Louse-wort (*Pedicularis palustris*) appears to be only a corruption of loose-wort, the plant being otherwise called the red-rattle, from its near resemblance to the yellow-rattle (*Rhinanthus*), the seeds of which, being loosely held in a spacious inflated capsule, may be distinctly heard to rattle when the ripe, dry seed-vessel is shaken. Buck-bean (*Menyanthes trifoliata*) is more correctly bog-bean, its habitat being in very wet bog land. Swallow-wort, otherwise celandine (*Chelidonium Majus*), is properly sallow-wort, having received this name from the dark yellow juice which exudes freely from its stems and roots when they are broken. Horse-radish takes its name from its excessive pungency, horse, as thus used, being derived from the old English curs, or Welsh *gwres*, signifying hot or fierce ; and the horse-chestnut, not from any relation to a chestnut horse, but for a like reason, namely, that it is hot or bitter, and therein differs from the sweet or edible chestnut. The horse-mint also is pungent and disagreeable to the taste and to the smell, as compared with the cultivated kinds of mint.

Bear's garlic or the common wild garlic (*Allium ursinum*), may be traced in the Latin specific name, ursinum, and this, although it would at the present time be interpreted as ' pertaining to a bear,' may have had what is termed a barbarous origin, viz., curs-inon or urs-inon, the hot or strong onion. The bear gets his own name, Ursa, from the same original, as describing his savage ferocity. The sow-thistle, which is not indeed a true thistle, has the latter part of its name from the thistle-like appearance of its leaves ; when these are handled, however, they are found to be perfectly inoffensive—they are formidable to the eye only, being too soft to inflict the slightest puncture ; hence sote or sooth-thistle, that is soft thistle. The duck-weed, or ducks-meat, is by no means choice food for ducks, but simply ditchweed. It is that minute, round, leaf-like plant which so densely covers old moats and ponds with a green mantle. Its Latin name, Lemna, confirms this, derived as it is from the Greek Limné, a stagnant pool. The

corruption in this case may have originated in a misconstruction of the Saxon word Dig, which signifies both a ditch and a duck. This is still used in both senses in districts in our own country where a Saxon dialect prevails.

Colts'-foot (*Tussilago farfara*) seems to be either from cough-wood or cold-wood, in accordance with the Latin name, which is derived from Tussis, a cough. We are disposed to regard it as a corruption, and to conclude that it refers to the medicinal use of the plant, because, in our English species at least, we see no resemblance to the foot of a horse, whereas its virtue in the cure of colds, coughs, and hoarseness, has, whether justly or not, been believed in from time immemorial. Pliny tells us that it had been in use from remote times, even at his day, the fume of the burning weed being inhaled through a reed.

Lastly may be instanced the well-known gooseberry, notable for two things of very opposite character—for its fruit and its thorns,—the latter hardly less dreaded than the former is coveted, and in the name given to this tree may be found a combined reference to these two features—its terrors and its attractions. In the Italian, Uva spina, this is very plainly shewn. The old English name carberry, probably has the same meaning ; and the north country name, grozar or groser, as also the French groseille, and the Latin grossularia, scarcely conceal in their slightly inverted form the original gorse, which means prickly. In short, we regard the name gooseberry as simply a modified form of gorseberry. There was a time when goose was both written and pronounced gos, as is shewn by the still current word gosling, a young goose, and gorse (the furze or whin) is familiarly pronounced exactly in the same way ; therefore the transition of gorse to goose will not be wondered at.

ARCHERY IN ENGLAND.

In an epistle to the sheriffs of London, dated 12th June 1349, Edward III. sets forth how ' the people of our realm, as well of good quality as mean, have commonly in their sports before these times exercised their skill of shooting arrows ; whence it is well known that honour and profit have accrued to our whole realm, and to us, by the help of God, no small assistance in our warlike acts.' Now, however, ' the said skill being as it were wholly laid aside,' the king proceeds to command the sheriffs to make public proclamation that ' every one of the said city, strong in body, at leisure times on holidays, use in their recreations bows and arrows, or pellets or bolts, and learn and exercise the art of shooting, forbidding all and singular on our behalf, that they do not after any manner apply themselves to the throwing of stones, wood, or iron, handball, football, bandyball, cambuck, or cockfighting, nor suchlike vain plays, which have no profit in them.'

It is not surprising that the king was thus anxious to keep alive archery, for from the Conquest, when it proved so important at Hastings, it had borne a distinguished part in the national military history. Even in his own time, notwithstanding the king's complaint of its decay, it was (to use modern language) an arm of the greatest potency. Crecy, Poitiers, and Agincourt were, in fact, archers' victories. At Homildon, the men-at-arms merely looked on while the chivalry of Scotland fell before the clothyard shafts. In one skirmish in the French wars, eighty bowmen defeated two hundred French knights ; and in another a hundred and

twenty were disposed of by a sixth of their number. There is a well-known act of the Scottish parliament, in the reign of James I., expressive of the eagerness of the rulers of that nation to bring them up to a par with the English in this respect.

In the reign of Edward IV., it was enacted that every Englishman, whatever his station, the clergy and judges alone excepted, should own a bow his own height, and keep it always ready for use, and also provide for his sons' practising the art from the age of seven. Butts were ordered to be erected in every township, where the inhabitants were to shoot 'up and down,' every Sunday and feast day, under penalty of one halfpenny. In one of his plain-speaking sermons, Latimer censured the degeneration of his time in respect to archery. ' In my time my poor father was as delighted to teach me to shoot as to learn any other thing ; and so, I think, other men did their children ; he taught me how to draw, how to lay my body and my bow, and not to draw with strength of arm as other nations do, but with strength of body. I had my bow bought me according to my age and strength ; as I increased in them, so my bows were made bigger and bigger ; for men shall never shoot well, except they be brought up to it. It is a goodly art, a wholesome kind of exercise, and much commended as physic.' From this time the art began to decline. Henry VII. found it necessary to forbid the use of the cross-bow, which was growing into favour, and threatening to supersede its old conqueror, and his successor fined the possessor of the former weapon ten pounds. Henry VIII. was himself fond of the exercise, and his brother Arthur was famed for his skill, so that archers did not lack encouragement. ' On the May-day then next following, the second year of his reign,' says Holinshed, ' his grace being young, and willing not to be idle, rose in the morning very early, to fetch May, or green boughs ; himself fresh and richly appareled and clothed, all his knights, squires, 776

and gentlemen in white satin, and all his guard and yeomen of the crown in white sarcenet ; and so went every man with his bow and arrows shooting to the wood, and so returning again to the court, every man with a green bough in his cap. Now at his returning, many hearing of his going a Maying, were desirous to see him shoot, for at that time his grace shot as strong and as great a length as any of his guard. There came to his grace a certain man with bow and arrows, and desired his grace to take the muster of him, and to see him shoot ; for at that time his grace was contented. The man put then one foot in his bosom, and so did shoot, and shot a very good shot, and well towards his mark ; whereof not only his grace, but all others greatly marvelled. So the king gave him a reward for his so doing, which person after of the people and of those in the court was called, Foot-in-Bosom.' Henry conferred on Barlow, one of his guard, the jocular title of Duke of Shoreditch, as an acknowledgment of his skill with the bow, a title long afterwards held by the principal marksman of the city. In 1544 the learned Ascham took up his pen in the cause of the bow, and to counsel the gentlemen and yeomen of England not to change it for any other weapon, and bravely does he in his *Toxophilus* defend the ancient arm, and show ' how fit shooting is for all kinds of men ; how honest a pastime for the mind ; how wholesome an exercise for the body ; not vile for great men to use, nor costly for poor men to sustain ; not lurking in holes and corners for ill men at their pleasure to misuse it, but abiding in the open sight and face of the world, for good men if at fault, by their wisdom to correct it.' He attributes the falling-off in the skill of Englishmen to their practising at measured distances, instead of shooting at casual marks, or changing the distance at every shot.

On the 17th of September 1583, there was a grand muster of London archers. Three thousand of them (of whom 942 wore gold chains), attended by bellmen, footmen, and pages, and led by the Duke of Shoreditch, and the Marquises of Clerkenwell, Islington, Shacklewell, Hoxton, and St John's Wood, marched through the city (taking up the city dignitaries on the route) to Hoxton Fields, where a grand shooting match took place, the victors in the contest being carried home by torchlight to a banquet at the Bishop of London's palace.

Charles I., himself skilled in the use of the long bow, appointed two special commissions to enforce the practice of archery ; but with the civil war the art died out ; in that terrible struggle the weapon that had won so many fields took no part, except it might be to a small extent in the guerilla warfare carried on against Cromwell in the Scottish Highlands. Charles II. had his keeper of the bows ; but the office was a sinecure. In 1675, the London bowmen assembled in honour of Mayor Viners of 't'other Bottle' fame, and now and then spasmodic efforts were made to renew the popularity of the sport, but its day had gone, never to return.

In war, hoblers, or mounted archers, were employed to disperse small bodies of troops, and frustrate any attempts of the beaten foe to rally. The regular bowmen were drawn up on a 'hearse,' by which the men were brought as near the enemy as possible, the front of the formation being broad, while its sides tapered gradually to the rear. They were generally protected against the charge of horsemen by a barrier of pikes, or in default

> 'Sharp stakes cut out of hedges
> They pitched on the ground confusedly,
> To keep the horsemen off from breaking in.'

Each archer carried sixteen heavy and eight light shafts. The range of the former was about 240 yards, for Drayton records, as an extraordinary feat, that an English archer at Agincourt

> 'Shooting at a French twelve score away,
> Quite through the body stuck him to a tree.'

The lighter arrows, used to gall the enemy, would of course have a longer range. Neade says an old English bow would carry from 18 to 20 score yards, but this seems rather too liberal an estimate. Shakspeare says : 'A good archer would clap in the clout at twelve score, and carry a forehand shaft a fourteen and a fourteen and a half.' The balladmongers make Robin Hood and Little John shoot a measured mile, and give the father of the Sherwood outlaw credit for having sent an arrow two north country miles and an inch at a shot !

Wych, hazel, ash, and elm were used for ordinary bows, but war-bows were always made of yew. The prices were usually fixed by statute. In Elizabeth's reign they were as follows :—Best foreign yew, 6s. 8d. ; second best, 3s. 4d. ; English yew, and 'livery' bows (of coarsest foreign yew), 2s. Bows were rubbed with wax, resin, and tallow, and covered with waxed cloth, to resist the effects of damp, heat, and frost. Each bow was supplied with three good hempen strings, well whipped with fine thread.

The length of a bow was regulated by the height of the archer, the rule being that it should exceed his stature by the length of his foot. The arrows used at Agincourt were a yard long without the head, but the usual length was from twenty-seven to thirty-three inches. They were made of many woods,— hazel, turkeywood, fustic, alder, beech, blackthorn, elder, sallow ; the best being of birch, oak, ash, service-tree, and hornbeam. The grey goose feather was considered the best for winging them, and the various counties were laid under contribution for a supply of feathers whenever war was impending.

The ancient weapon of England has degenerated into a plaything ; but in the Volunteer movement we have a revival of the spirit which made the long bow so formidable in the 'happy hitting hands' of our ancestors; and we may say of the rifle as Ascham said of the bow, 'Youth should use it for the most honest pastime in peace, that men might handle it as a most sure weapon in war.'

JUNE 13.

St Anthony of Padua, confessor, 1231.   St Damhnade of Ireland, virgin.

ST ANTHONY OF PADUA.

Few of the mediæval saints adopted into the Romish calendar have attained to such lasting celebrity as St Anthony, or Antonio, of Padua. All over Italy his memory is held in the highest veneration ; but at Padua in particular, where his festival is enthusiastically kept, he is spoken of as *Il Santo*, or the saint, as if no other was of any importance. Besides larger memoirs of St Anthony, there are current in the north of Italy small chap-books or tracts describing his character and his miracles. From one of these, purchased in the year 1862 from a stall in Padua, we offer the following as a specimen of the existing folk-lore of Venetian Lombardy. St Anthony was born at Lisbon on the 15th of August 1195. At twenty-five years of age he entered a convent of Franciscans, and as a preaching friar most zealous in checking heresy, he gained great fame in Italy, which became the scene of his labours. In this great work the power of miracle came to his aid. On one occasion, at Rimini, there was a person who held heretical opinions, and in order to convince him of his error, Anthony caused the fishes in the water to lift up their heads and listen to

ST ANTHONY PREACHING TO THE FISHES.

his discourse. This miracle, which of course converted the heretic. is represented in a variety of cheap prints, to be seen on almost every stall in Italy, and is the subject of a wood-cut in the chap-book from which we quote, here faithfully represented. On another occasion, to reclaim a heretic, he caused the man's mule, after three days' abstinence from food, to kneel down and venerate the host, instead of rushing to a bundle of hay that was set before it. This miracle was equally efficacious. Then we are told of St Anthony causing a new-born babe to speak, and tell who was its father; also, of a wonderful miracle he wrought in saving the life of a poor woman's child. The woman had gone to hear St Anthony preach, leaving her child alone in the house, and during her absence it fell into a pot on the fire; but, strangely enough, instead of finding it scalded to death, the mother found it standing up whole in the boiling cauldron. What with zealous labours and fastings, St Anthony cut short his days, and died in the odour of sanctity on the 13th of June 1231. Padua, now claiming him as patron saint and protector, set about erecting a grand temple to his memory. This large and handsome church was completed in 1307. It is a gigantic building, in the pointed Lombardo-Venetian style, with several towers and minarets of an Eastern character. The chief object of attraction in the interior is the chapel specially devoted to Il Santo. It consists of the northern transept, gorgeously decorated with sculptures, bronzes, and gilding. The altar is of white marble, inlaid, resting on the tomb of St Anthony, which is a sarcophagus of verd antique. Around it, in candelabra and in suspended lamps, lights burn night and day; and at nearly all hours a host of devotees may be seen kneeling in front of the shrine, or standing behind with hands devoutly and imploringly touching the sarcophagus, as if trying to draw succour and consolation from the marble of the tomb. The visitor to this splendid shrine is not less struck with the more than usual quantity of votive offerings suspended on the walls and end of the altar. These consist mainly of small framed sketches in oil or water colours, representing some circumstance that calls for particular thankfulness. St Anthony of Padua, as appears from these pictures, is a saint ever ready to rescue persons from destructive accidents, such as the overturning of wagons or carriages, the falling from windows or roofs of houses, the upsetting of boats, and such like; on any of these occurrences a person has only to call vehemently and with faith on St Anthony in order to be rescued. The hundreds of small pictures we speak of represent these appalling scenes, with a figure of St Anthony in the sky interposing to save life and limb. On each are inscribed the letters P. G. R., with the date of the accident;—the letters being an abbreviation of the words *Per Grazzia Ricevuto*—for grace or favour received. On visiting the shrine, we remarked that many are quite recent; one of them depicting an accident by a railway train. The other chief object of interest in the church is a chapel behind the high altar appropriated as a reliquary. Here, within a splendidly decorated cupboard, as it might be called, are treasured up certain relics of the now long deceased saint. The principal relic is the tongue of Il Santo, which is contained within an elegant case of silver gilt, as here represented. This

with other relics is exhibited once a year, at the

TONGUE OF ST ANTHONY IN ITS SHRINE AT PADUA.

great festival on the 13th of June, when Padua holds its grandest holiday.

. It is to be remarked that the article entitled 'St Anthony and the Pigs,' inserted under January 17, ought properly to have been placed here, as the patronship of animals belongs truly to St Anthony of Padua, most probably in consequence of his sermon to the fishes.

Born.—C. J. Agricola, Roman commander, 40, *Frejus, in Provence;* Madame D'Arblay (*née* Frances Burney), English novelist, 1752, *Lyme Regis;* Dr Thomas Young, natural philosopher, 1773, *Melverton, Somersetshire;* Rev. Dr Thomas Arnold, 1795, *Cowes, Isle of Wight.*

Died.—Charles Francis Panard, French dramatist 1765; Simon Andrew Tissot, eminent Swiss physician, 1797, *Lausanne;* Richard Lovell Edgeworth, writer on education, 1817, *Edgeworthstown, Ireland.*

AGRICOLA.

The admirable, honest, and impartial biography of Cnæus Julius Agricola, written by the Roman historian Tacitus, who married his daughter, paints him in all the grave, but attractive colours of a noble Roman; assigning to him a valour and virtue, joined to a prudence and skill, which would not have failed to do honour to the best times of the Republic.

But Agricola is chiefly interesting to us from his connexion with our own country. His first service was in Britain, under Suetonius Paulinus, the Roman general who finally subdued the rebellious Iceni, under Boadicea, their queen, when 80,000 men are said to have fallen. Agricola afterwards, under the wise reign of Vespasian, was made governor of Britain. He succeeded in destroying the strongholds of North Wales and the Isle of Anglesea, which had resisted all previous efforts, and finally reduced the province to peace; after which he shewed himself at once an enlightened and consummate general, by seeking to civilize the people, by encouraging education, by erecting buildings, by making roads, and by availing himself of all those means which benefit a barbarous country, while they effectually subdue it. When he had in this way established the tranquillity of the province, he proceeded to extend it. Crossing the Tweed, he steadily advanced northwards, the enemy retreating before him. He built a line of forts from the Firth of Forth to the Clyde, and sent the fleet to explore the unknown coast, and to act in concert with his land forces, till at length, having hemmed in the natives on every side, he gained the decisive battle of the Mons Grampius, in which Galgacus so bravely resisted him; after this he retired into the original province, and was recalled by Domitian out of jealousy.

Agricola died soon after his return to Rome, in the year 93, in his fifty-fourth year; the circumstances of his death were somewhat peculiar, and Tacitus throws out a hint that he might have been poisoned.

FANATICISM ANALYSED BY ARNOLD.

Arnold regarded fanaticism as a form of selfishness. 'There is an ascending scale,' said he, ' from the grossest personal selfishness, such as that of Cæsar or Napoleon, to party selfishness, such as that of Sylla, or fanatical selfishness, that is the idolatry of an idea or principle, such as that of Robespierre or Dominic, and some of the Covenanters. In all of these, excepting perhaps the first, we feel a sympathy more or less, because there is something of personal self-devotion and sincerity; but fanaticism is idolatry, and it has the moral evil of idolatry in it; that is, a fanatic worships something which is the creature of his own devices, and thus even his self-devotion in support of it is only an apparent self-sacrifice, for it is in fact making the parts of his nature or his mind which he least values offer sacrifice to that which he most values.'

On another occasion he said : ' The life and character of Robespierre has to me a most important lesson; it shows the frightful consequences of making everything give way to a favourite notion. The man was a just man, and humane naturally, but he would narrow everything to meet his own views, and nothing could check him at last. It is a most solemn warning to us, of what fanaticism may lead to in God's world.'[*]

It is a pity that Arnold did not take us on from personal to what may be called class or institutional fanaticism, for it is a principle which may affect any number of men. We should have been glad to see from his pen an analysis of that spirit under which a collective body of men will grasp, deny justice, act falsely

[*] Stanley's *Life of Dr Arnold*, ii. 41.

and cruelly, all for the good of the institution which they represent, while quite incapable of any such procedure on their own several accounts. Here, too, acting for an idea, there is an apparent exemption from selfishness , but an Arnold could have shown how something personal is, after all, generally involved in such kinds of procedure ; the more dangerous, indeed, as well as troublesome, that it can put on so plausible a disguise. There are even such things as fanaticisms upon a national scale, though these are necessarily of rarer occurrence ; and then do we see a whole people propelled on to prodigious exterminating wars, in which they madly ruin, and are ruined, while other nations look on in horror and dismay. In these cases, civilization and religion afford no check or alleviation of the calamity : the one only gives greater means of destruction ; the other, as usual, blesses all banners alike. The sacred name of patriotism serves equally in attack and defence, being only a mask to the selfish feelings actually concerned. All such things are, in fact, IDOLATRIES—the worship of something which is ' the creature of our own devices,' to the entire slighting and putting aside of those principles of justice and kindness towards others which God has established as the only true guides of human conduct.

JUNE 14.

St Basil the Great, Archbishop of Cæsarea, confessor, 379. Saints Rufinus and Valerius, martyrs. St Docmael, or Toël, confessor, 6th century. St Nennus, or Nehemias, abbot, 7th century. St Psalmodius, hermit, 7th century. St Methodius, confessor, Patriarch of Constantinople, 846.

Born.—Thomas Pennant, naturalist, miscellaneous writer, 1723, *Bowring, Flintshire.*

Died.—Father Garasse, French Jesuit controversialist, 1631, *Poitiers ;* Sir Harry Vane, English patriot, beheaded, 1662, *Tower of London ;* Marin Leroi, sieur de Gomberville, author of *Polexandre* and other romances, 1674 ; Dr Ralph Bathurst, 1704, *Oxford ;* Claude Fleury, confessor to Louis XV. (ecclesiastical history), 1723 ; Colin Maclaurin, mathematician, 1746 ; General J. B. Kleber, assassinated, 1800, *Cairo ;* General Louis Dessaix, killed at Marengo, 1800.

THE HASTINGS DIAMOND.

At a levee held on the 14th of June, 1786, a very valuable diamond, of unusual size and brilliancy, was presented to George III., ostensibly as a gift from the Nizam, or native ruler of the Deccan. At the period when this magnificent peace offering was given to the king, the impeachment of Warren Hastings was advancing in Parliament ; and it was very generally said, even publicly in the House of Commons, that this, with several other diamonds, was the purchase-money of Hastings's acquittal. Caricatures on the subject appeared in the windows of the print shops. One represented Hastings wheeling the king to market in a barrow, and saying, ' What a man buys he may sell again.' In another, the king was exhibited in a kneeling posture, with his mouth open, and Hastings throwing diamonds into it. An Italian juggler, then in London, pretending to eat paving-stones, had placarded the walls with bills describing himself as 'The Great Stone-eater'; the caricaturists, improving upon the hint, represented the king in the character of 'The Greatest Stone-eater'; and the following ballad was sung about the streets, to the infinite amusement of the populace.

'A FULL AND TRUE ACCOUNT
OF THE
WONDERFUL DIAMOND PRESENTED TO THE KING'S
MAJESTY,
BY WARREN HASTINGS, ESQ.,
ON WEDNESDAY, THE 14TH OF JUNE, 1786.

' I'll sing you a song of a diamond so fine,
That soon in the crown of our monarch will shine,
Of its size and its value the whole country rings,
By Hastings bestowed on the best of all kings.
             Derry down, &c.

From India this jewel was lately brought o'er,
Though sunk in the sea, it was found on the shore,
And just in the nick to St James's it got,
Carried in a bag by the great Major Scott.
             Derry down, &c.

Lord Sydney stepp'd forth when the tidings were
    known,
It's his office to carry such news to the throne,
Though quite out of breath, to the closet he ran,
And stammered with joy, ere his tale he began.
             Derry down, &c.

Here's a jewel, my liege, there's none such in the
    land,
Major Scott, with three bows put it into my hand ;
And he swore, when he gave it, the wise ones were
    bit,
For it never was shewn to Dundas or to Pitt.
             Derry down, &c.

"For Dundas," cried our sovereign, "unpolished and
    rough,
Give him a Scotch pebble, it's more than enough ;
And jewels to Pitt, Hastings justly refuses,
For he has already more gifts than he uses."
             Derry down, &c.

" But run, Jenkyn, run !" adds the king in delight,
" Bring the queen and the princesses here for a sight ;
They never would pardon the negligence shown,
If we kept from their knowledge so glorious a
    stone."   Derry down, &c.

" But guard the door, Jenkyn, no credit we'll win,
If the prince in a frolic should chance to step in ;
The boy to such secrets of state we'll not call,
Let him wait till he gets our crown, income, and
    all."   Derry down, &c.,

In the princesses run, and surprised cry " O la !
'Tis as big as the egg of a pigeon, papa !"
" And a pigeon of plumage worth plucking is he,"
Replies our good monarch, "who sent it to me."
             Derry down, &c.

Madam Schwellenbergh peeped through the door at
    a chink,
And tipped on the diamond a sly German wink ;
As much as to say, " Can he ever be cruel
To him who has sent us so glorious a jewel ?"
             Derry down, &c.

Now God save the queen, while the people I teach
How the king may grow rich while the commons
    impeach ;
Let nabobs go plunder and rob as they will,
And throw in their diamonds as grist to his mill.
             Derry down, &c.'

MUTINIES OF 1797.

Following hard upon the quasi national insolvency of February 1797—the natural consequence of an unsuccessful war—came a series of seamen's mutinies which threatened to paralyse the best arm remaining to England, and lay her open to the invasion of her enemies.

For some years the seamen of the navy had complained of their treatment, and, as was afterwards generally acknowledged, with just cause. Their pay, and their prospective pensions from Greenwich Hospital, had received no augmentation since the time of Charles II. ; prize money went almost wholly to the officers ; and the captains and lieutenants often displayed much cruelty towards the men. In the month of March, petitions from four ships of war were sent to Lord Howe, who commanded the Channel fleet, intreating his lordship, as 'The Seaman's Friend.' to intercede with the Admiralty for the sailors, as a means of obtaining better treatment for them. The petitions were deemed rather mutinous in tone, but no special notice was taken of them. In April the Government were startled to hear that a mutiny had been planned at Spithead ; the fleet was ordered hastily out to sea, as the most prudent course ; but the seamen took matters at once into their own hands. The officers were deposed and guarded ; delegates from all the ships in the Channel fleet met in the state cabin of the *Queen Charlotte;* and these delegates drew up an oath of fidelity, which all the men accepted. The proceeding was of course unlawful ; but their wrongs were grievous, and their general conduct in other ways was admirable. A humiliating correspondence was opened by the Admiralty ; offers, in a petty, narrow spirit were made ; and these offers were accepted by the mutineers on the 23rd, although not without some distrust. Mutiny broke out again on the 7th of May, because the men found that the royal pardon was not accompanied by an effectual redress of grievances. Again the mutineers displayed surprising dignity and forbearance, deposing their officers, it is true, but maintaining admirable discipline on board the several ships. The Government, now thoroughly alarmed, hastily obtained an act of parliament for increased pay and food, prize-money and pension, to the seamen of the Royal Navy. Mr Pitt displayed extreme mortification when asking the House of Commons to vote £460,000 for this purpose, and urged the members to pass the bill with as few comments as possible. Lord Howe, the best man who could have been selected for the duty, went down to Portsmouth with the act of parliament and the royal pardon in his pocket. On the 15th of May he had the pleasure of seeing the mutineers return to their duty. All was not over, however. The Nore fleet mutinied on the 20th, and called themselves a 'floating republic,' under the presidency of Richard Parker, a sailor of some education and much ambition. This was a mutiny that obtained very little of the public sympathy ; it was not a demand for redress of real grievances, so much as an attempt to republicanize the fleet. The seamen at the Nore shared all the advantages of the new arrangements, and could only make new demands which the Government was quite justified in resisting. King, government, parliament, and people were against these mutineers at the Nore. Batteries, served with red-hot shot, were planted along the Kent and Essex shores to shoot them; and the seamen at Spithead made it known that they had no sympathy with Parker's proceedings. Dissensions then broke out in the several ships of the rebel fleet; many of the seamen hoisted the national flag in honour of the king's birthday on the 4th of June, against the wish of Richard Parker; and this audacious man felt his power gradually slipping through his hands. The ships left the rebel fleet one by one, according as their crews felt the consciousness of being in the wrong. At length, on the 14th, the crisis arrived. Parker exercised his presidency on board the *Sandwich*, 90 guns, from which he had expelled Vice-Admiral Buckner. The crew of that ship, in spite of his remonstrances, carried it under the guns at Sheerness, and delivered him up to a guard of soldiers. All the ships returned to their duty; very few of the men were punished; and soon afterwards a royal pardon was issued. Some of the more active leaders, however, were tried and executed. Parker's trial, on board the *Neptune*, lasted three days; he was cool and collected, and acknowledged the justice of the fatal sentence passed on him. His wife, a woman far superior to the general class of sailors' wives, made a strenuous effort to gain admission to Queen Charlotte, to beg her husband's life, offering a large reward to some of the attendants at the palace if they would further her views. All failed, and Parker was executed.

Circumstances which transpired during the trial brought to light the fact that many men had entered the navy whose antecedents were inconsistent with a sailor's life. Disqualified attorneys, cashiered excisemen, and dismissed clerks, wanting the means of daily support, were enticed by high bounty into the service; while two or three delegates or agitators from political societies, influenced by the excitement of the times, became seamen as a means of revolutionizing or republicanizing the royal fleets. Richard Parker in all probability belonged to one of these two classes, perhaps to both.

JUNE 15.

Saints Vitus, or Guy, Crescentia, and Modestus, martyrs, 4th century. St Vaughe, or Vorech, hermit in Cornwall, 585. St Landelin, Abbot of Crespin, 686. St Bernard of Menthon, confessor, 1008. Blessed Gregory LewiBarbadigo, Cardinal Bishop of Padua, confessor, 1697.

ST VITUS.

This saint has an importance from a purely accidental cause. In the Romish hagiology, we only find that he was a Sicilian boy who was made a Christian by his nurse, and, subsequently fleeing from a pagan father's wrath into Italy, fell a martyr under the sweeping persecution by Diocletian.* Somehow a chapel near Ulm was

* Butler's *Lives of the Saints.*

dedicated to him; and to this chapel came annually some women who laboured under a nervous or hysteric affection impelling them to violent motion. This ailment came to be called St Vitus's Dance, and perhaps the term was gradually extended to other affections involving involuntary muscular motion, of which there seems to be a considerable number. In modern times, in English medical practice, the name of St Vitus's Dance is confined to an ailment which chiefly befalls young persons during the five or six years preceding puberty, and manifests itself in an inability to command the movements of the limbs. As to its cause, whether nervous or intestinal, and equally as to the means of its cure, the greatest dubiety seems to prevail.*

Born.—Edward, 'the Black Prince,' 1330, *Woodstock ;* Thomas Randolph, poet, 1605, *Badby, Northamptonshire ;* Anthony Francis de Fourcroy, eminent French chemist, 1755, *Paris.*

Died.—Wat Tyler, plebeian insurgent, slain in Smithfield, 1381 ; Philip the Good, of Burgundy, 1467, *Bruges ;* René Aubert de Vertot, French historian, 1735, *Paris ;* James Short, maker of reflecting telescopes, 1768 ; Francis Pilatre de Rosier, killed by falling from a balloon, 1785, *near Boulogne ;* Freteau de St Just, guillotined, 1794, *Paris ;* Thomas Campbell, poet, 1844 *Boulogne.*

EDWARD THE BLACK PRINCE.

In the whole range of English history there is no name so completely wrapped up in the idea of English chivalry as that of Edward the Black Prince. Born on the 15th of June 1330, the son of Edward III. and Philippa of Hainault, he was only in his sixteenth year when he accompanied

EDWARD, THE BLACK PRINCE.

his father in the expedition into France which was crowned by the battle of Crecy. On that

* *Cyclopædia of Practical Medicine,* i. 407.

memorable day, Sunday, the 26th of August, the young prince, supported by the Earls of Warwick and Hereford, the gallant John Chandos, and Godfroi d'Harcourt, had the command of the vanguard, or first of the three divisions into which the English army was divided, which in fact bore the brunt of the battle. It was the beginning of an entirely new system of military tactics, and the English men-at-arms on this occasion had dismounted from their horses, and engaged on foot the far more numerous mounted men-at-arms of France, who were led by princes and nobles, always looked upon as the ablest and bravest of the feudal chivalry of France. The English, encouraged by the conduct of their young leader, fought steadily in their ranks, but the struggle seemed so unequal, that the Earls of Northampton and Arundel, who commanded the second, or central division of the English army, hastened to their assistance; yet, though the force of the enemy appeared still so overwhelming, King Edward, who commanded the third division, or rear-guard, continued to stand aloof, and held his division in inaction. He appears to have had the greatest confidence in his son, and he was far better aware of the importance of the change in military tactics which he was inaugurating than any of his contemporaries. The Earls of Northampton and Arundel, however, when they moved up to support the Prince, dispatched a messenger to the king, who was surveying the battle calmly from the mound of a windmill, to ask him for immediate succour. When he had delivered his message, the king asked him, 'Is my son dead? or is he struck to the ground, or so wounded that he cannot help himself?' 'God forbid, Sir,' the messenger replied, 'but he is hard beset, and your aid would be right welcome.' The king replied firmly, 'Return to those who sent you, and tell them from me that they must not send for me to-day as long as my son is alive. Let the boy earn his spurs.* I desire, if it be God's will, that the day be his, and that the honour of it remain to him and to those whom I have appointed to support him.' The king's confidence gave courage to the English soldiers as well as to the English commanders, and led to that great and decisive victory, in which nearly all the great baronage of France perished. Next day, King Edward's heralds reported that there lay on the field of battle, on the side of the French, the bodies of eleven princes, of eighty knights bannerets, or knights who led their own troops into the field under their own banners, of twelve hundred knights, and of about thirty thousand ordinary soldiers. Among the most illustrious of the slain were John of Luxemburg, King of Bohemia, and his son Charles, who had been elected, through the French interest at Rome, King of the Romans, and was a claimant to the empire. It is said that the crest of the King of Bohemia, three ostrich feathers, with the motto *ich dien* (I serve), being presented to the young prince, he adopted it as

* The spurs were the distinguishing characteristic of knighthood, and the young knight sought to shew himself worthy of them, or, in other words, 'to earn them,' by some gallant deed of chivalry.

782

his own, and hence this has ever since been the crest of the princes of Wales.

Edward had been created Duke of Cornwall in the year 1337, which is understood to be the first creation of a dukedom by an English monarch, and since that time the eldest son of the King of England is considered as being born Duke of Cornwall. His father had knighted him when the army landed in Normandy on this expedition, and he is said to have gained the popular title of the Black Prince from the circumstance of his usually wearing black armour.

In the hour of battle, the Black Prince never belied the promises he had given on the field of Crecy. At Calais, he is said by his valour to have saved his father from being taken by the enemy; and he was with him again in the great victory gained over the Spaniards at sea in the year 1350. In the August of 1355, the prince proceeded to Bordeaux to take the command in Gascony, and his destructive excursion through the French provinces in the south brought on, on the 19th of September in the following year, the celebrated battle of Poitiers, which was, if anything, a more extraordinary victory than that of Crecy. It was fought in some respects under circumstances not very dissimilar; though the numbers on each side were much less, for the army of the Black Prince is believed to have been under ten thousand men, while that of the King of France was estimated at about fifty thousand. The prince, believing that his father was advancing into France from Calais, had formed the rash design of marching through the heart of France to join him, and he was not made aware of his mistake until he found himself so completely surprised by the French army in the neighbourhood of Poitiers, that it was impossible to avoid a battle with these unequal numbers. It is right to say that the victory must be attributed quite as much to his own great military talents, and to the steady bravery of his officers and troops, as to the blunders and rashness of the French. The quaint old historian Stowe, in describing the prowess of the Black Prince in this battle, warms up with his subject. 'Then,' says he, 'bestirreth himself the worthy Prince of Wales, cutting and hewing the Frenchmen with a sharpe sword. In the meantime, Captain de la Buche (the Captal de Buch) marches a compane aboute under the hanging of the hill, which he with the Prince a little before forsooke. . . . . . and so sodainly breaking forth unlooked for, and shewing by the enscyne of St George that hee was our friend, the prince with great courage giveth a fresh charge on the French armie, being desirous to breake their rankes before the Captaine aforesayd should set on the side of the battayle. The prince, lustily encountring with his enemies, goeth into the middle of the throng, and where hee seeth most company, there he layeth about him on every side. . . . . . This was the courage of the prince, who at the length thrusteth thorow the throngs of them that guarded the French king; then should you see an ancient (*ensign*) beginne to nod and stumble, the bearers of them to fall downe, the blood of slaves and princes ran mingled together into the waters which were nigh. In like sort the bore of Cornewall rageth, who seeketh to have none other way to the French king's standard then by blood onely ; but when they came there, they met with a company of stout menne to withstand them ; the Englishmen fight, the Frenchmen also lay on, but at length, God having so disposed, the prince presseth forward on his enemies, and like a fierce lion beating downe the proud, hee came to the yielding upp of the French king.' It is hardly necessary to state that the latter, and his youngest son Philippe, a boy of thirteen, who had remained by his side during the whole battle, and was, in fact, the only one of his sons who shewed any courage, were taken, and carried prisoners to Bordeaux. King John of France seemed not greatly to have felt his defeat, and he appeared almost to have forgotten it in his admiration of the knightly courtesy of the Black Prince, who that night served his prisoner at the supper table. The hostilities between England and France were ended for the present by a truce, and the latter country was left to all the consequences of bad government, popular discontent and insurrection, and the ravages and tyranny of the free companies.

The bravery and military talents of the Black Prince seem to have dazzled people's eyes to qualities of a description less to be admired. He appears to have been generous in disposition, and to have been respected and beloved by his friends, and he possessed in a high degree what were then considered noble and courtly feelings ; but he shewed on many occasions an inclination to be arbitrary, and he could often be cruel and ferocious. But these, too, were then considered as qualities of a great soldier. He possessed a restless desire of activity, and at the same time a desire to gain popularity. These qualities, perhaps, made him fitter for the governor of a turbulent province than for a statesman at home. He was therefore entrusted with the government of Gascony, and in 1362 his father conferred upon him the duchy of Aquitain. He subsequently married his cousin Joan, the "fair maid of Kent," by whom he had two sons, Edward, who died in infancy, and Richard, called from the place of his birth, Richard of Bordeaux, who subsequently ascended the throne of England as Richard II.

In the year 1365, Pedro, the cruel King of Castile, was dethroned by his subjects, who chose his bastard brother, Enrique (or Henry), king in his stead, and the Black Prince rejoiced in the prospect of another active campaign, when, in the following year, Pedro sought his assistance to recover his throne. The war which occupied the year 1367 presents no great interest for English readers. Prince Edward was victorious again in the battle of Navaretta, fought on the 5th of April, and Pedro was restored to his throne, but only to disgust his protector by his ingratitude. The prince returned to Bordeaux sick in body, and apparently in mind, and his disease soon assumed the character of dropsy. Charles V., now King of France, had made up his mind to undertake a new war in England, and he began by exciting a spirit of insurrection in the provinces under the government and feudal sovereignty of the Black Prince, in which he was so completely successful, that we cannot suppose that the prince had succeeded in making himself popular among his own subjects. The rapidity with which town after town revolted from him to the French king, at length so roused the prince's anger, that he rose from his bed of sickness at Angoulême, and took the field in person. His valour was rewarded by the capture of Limoges, which had been treacherously surrendered to the French ; but his reputation was stained by the massacre in cold blood, by his imperious orders, of 3000 citizens, and by the destruction of the town. This was the last military action in which he commanded in person. In January 1371, he resigned his government to the Duke of Lancaster, his brother, and returned to England. The history of the remaining years of the life of the Prince of Wales is imperfectly known. He appears to have given great displeasure to his father by opposing the misgovernment of the closing period of his reign, and by espousing the popular cause ; and extravagant hopes appear to have been raised of the reforms which would take place when the prince himself succeeded to the throne. These prospects, however, were destined never to be realized, for the Black Prince died on the 8th of June 1376, nearly a year before the death of his father. He was deeply lamented by the whole nation.

JAMES EARL OF BOTHWELL.

On the 15th of June 1567, a very hot sunny day, two little armies lay facing each other on a piece of gently sloping ground in Haddingtonshire. Along the crest of the rising ground were about two thousand men, many of them mounted, being chiefly the retainers of a powerful noble, James Earl of Bothwell. Beside the leader were one or two females on horseback, not as taking part in the war, but as under protection. The principal lady was Mary queen of Scots, who had lately wedded Bothwell, knowing or unknowing (who can ever tell which?) that he reeked with the blood of her former husband, Darnley. The army grouped on the slope below was composed of troops hastily assembled by a few nobles who professed indignation at this horrible marriage, and anxiety on account of the danger into which it brought the heir of the crown, the son of Mary, an infant of a year old. All through that long summer day there went on conferences for various issues, with a view to avoiding a hostile collision between the armies. And at length, towards evening, the queen consented to pass under the care of the insurgent lords, on a promise of respectful treatment. The blood-stained Bothwell then took leave of her, and withdrew within his own country to the eastward. They had been married but a month—and they never met again. The infatuated queen, refusing to declare against him or give him up, was deposed, while her infant son was crowned as king in her stead. Bothwell, hunted from the land, took to sea; was chased there ; and obtained refuge in Denmark. His bold and unscrupulous mind had speculated with confidence on being at the head of everything in Scotland through the queen's means. But public opinion was too strong for him. The Scotch people had been accustomed to see a good deal of violence practised by their men of affairs, but they could not stand seeing one king killed, and his murderer placed almost in the throne beside his widow.

It is only of late years that we have got any clear account of Bothwell's subsequent history. It appears that Frederick king of Denmark for some time treated him as a refugee of distinction, who might in time be once more a ruler in his own country. By and by, when made aware of how he stood in Scotland, the Danish monarch became cooler, and remanded the exile to the castle of Malmö, in Sweden, which then belonged to Denmark, and where he was treated as a prisoner, but still an honourable one. Frederick was pulled various ways; the Protestant government in Scotland demanding the rendition of Bothwell as a murderer and the associate of a Catholic sovereign,—Mary, and her friend the king of France, claiming his liberation; Bothwell himself offering to assist in getting the Orkneys back to Denmark as the purchase-money of freedom and assistance. Five years passed in fruitless negotiations. The cause of Mary being in 1573 regarded as ruined, Frederick unrelentingly assigned the Scottish noble to a stricter and baser imprisonment, in the castle of Drachsholm in the island of Zealand. Here his seclusion was so great, that a report of his being dead spread abroad without contradiction; and Mary herself, in her English prison, regarded herself as a widow some years before she really was one. It is now ascertained that Bothwell died on the 14th of April 1578, when he must have been about forty-seven or forty-eight years of age, and after he had endured a captivity more or less strict of nearly eleven years. He was buried in the neighbouring church of Faareveile. So ended a dream of ambition which at first must have seemed of fair enough prospects, being not much out of keeping with the spirit of the age, but which had been signally unfortunate in its results, precipitating both of the principal parties into utter ruin, and leaving their names to suspicion and reproach through all ages.

Mr Horace Marryat, travelling in Denmark in 1858, paid a visit to Faareveile church, and there, in a vault, found the coffin of Bothwell, which had originally been deposited in a chapel of the Adeler family, but afterwards placed in the church, that it might be more conveniently open to the visits of strangers. On the lid being raised, the English visitor beheld the figure of a man of about middle height, whose red hair mixed with grey denoted the age of fifty; with 'high cheek bones, remarkably prominent long hooked nose, somewhat depressed towards the end (this may have been the effect of emaciation), wide mouth; hands and feet small, well-shaped, those of a high-bred man.' The whole aspect suggested to Mr Marryat the idea of 'an ugly Scotchman,' though we think it hard to judge of a man's looks after he has been three hundred years in his grave. Mr

Marryat remarks, 'Bothwell's life was a troubled one; but had he selected a site in all Christendom for quiet and repose in death, he could have found none more peaceful, more soft and calm, than the village church of Faareveile.'* It is worthy of remark, that on being first discovered, 'the body was found enveloped in the finest linen, the head reposing on a pillow of satin;' which looks like an evidence that Bothwell was treated with consideration to the last. If it be true, as alleged, that he was for some time chained up in a dungeon—and Mr Marryat tells us he saw, in what is now a wine-cellar, the ring to which he is believed to have been fixed—it may be that the one fact is not irreconcilable with the other, as the consignment to chains in a dungeon might be only a part of the horrible medical treatment for an insane person customary in that age.

A curious relic of Bothwell came before the public in November 1856, in the form of a book from his library. Life is full of surprises. Who could have dreamt that the murderous Scotch earl of the sixteenth century had a library at all? From this volume it fully appeared that he must have possessed one, for it bore his arms stamped on its side; of course, he could not have had a book-stamp unless he had had a plurality of books on which to get it impressed. Another curious and unexpected circumstance was the nature of the book. Had it been one devoted to the arts of the chase, or a copy of *Boccaccio*, one would not have been much surprised: strange to say, it was a philosophical book—*L'Arithmétique et Géométrie de Maistre Etienne de la Roche*,' printed at Paris in 1538. Of the fact of Bothwell's ownership the book left no room for doubt, for not only were the arms impressed, but the inscription, 'JACOBUS HEPBORN, Comes Bothv. D. Hailes Crichtoniæ Liddes. et Magn. Admiral. Scotiæ.' It was supposed that the binding had been executed in France. The volume was purchased by Mr James Gibson Craig, of Edinburgh, for thirteen guineas, and deposited in his beautiful and extensive collection, beside an equally precious volume from the library of Queen Mary.

RISING OF THE NILE.

The great advantages which Egypt derives from the annual inundation of the Nile in saving the country from total barrenness, cause us to feel little wonder at the inhabitants still calling it 'the most holy river;' or that they should believe that it draws its source from paradise. In former days it had its appointed priests, festivals, and sacrifices, and if its rising were delayed for a single day, they took the most beautiful young girl they could find, and dressing her richly, drowned her in the waters, as a victim to turn away the god's anger, and merit his favours. The caliphs abolished this cruel sacrifice, substituting one less barbarous but more ridiculous: they threw into its waters a letter, in which it was commanded to rise if it were the will of God. The inundation usually commences on the 15th of June, the greatest

* *A Residence in Jutland*, &c. 2 vols. 1860, i. 419.

height is at the autumnal equinox, and the waters gradually subside until the following April. The quality of the Nile water for drinking purposes is highly extolled: it is among waters what champagne is among wines, and the priests of Apis would not give it to the sacred bull lest he should become too fat. Benjamin of Tudela describes it as both drink and medicine; and Purchas goes farther: ' Nilus water I thinke to be the profitablest and wholesomest in the world by being both bread and drink.' However long it is kept, it never becomes impure, and it will be remembered that on the late visit of the Pasha of Egypt to this country, he brought jars of the Nile water to use during his absence from home.

JUNE 16.

Saints Ferreolus, or Fargeau, and Ferrutius, martyrs, 211 or 212. Saints Quiricus, or Cyr, and Julitta, martyrs, 304. St Aurelian, Archbishop of Arles, confessor, 552. St John Francis Regis, confessor, 1640.

Born.—Edward I. of England, 1239; Sir John Cheke, learned writer, promoter of the study of polite literature in England, 1514, *Cambridge;* Louis, Duc de Saint-Simon, author of *Memoirs of the Court of France,* 1675, *Paris;* Henrietta Stuart, Duchess of Orleans, 1644, *Exeter.*

Died.—Hugⁱ the Great, father of Hugh Capet, head of the third series of French kings, 956; Sir Richard Fanshawe, accomplished cavalier, ambassador to Spain, 1666, *Madrid;* Sir Tristram Beresford, 1701; John Churchill, Duke of Marlborough, 1722, *Windsor Lodge;* Bishop Joseph Butler, 1752, *Bath;* Jean Baptiste Gresset, French comic poet, 1777, *Amiens.*

SIR TRISTRAM BERESFORD—LEGEND OF THE BLACK RIBBON.

Although Sir Tristram Beresford was the direct ancestor of the Waterford family, and did something for the Protestant cause at the Revolution, he would not have been particularly mentioned in this place but for his connexion with an uncommonly fascinating ghost legend— the foundation of a passage in one of Scott's beautiful ballads:

' For evermore that lady wore
A covering on her wrist.'

The lady to whom Sir Tristram was married, Nicola Sophia Hamilton, daughter of Hugh Lord Glenawley, was educated along with John, second Earl of Tyrone, and, according to the family legend, they were so taught that a belief in a future state was not among their convictions. It was agreed, nevertheless, between the two young people, that in the event of one dying before the other, the deceased should *if possible* return and give certainty to the survivor on that solemn question. In due time they went out on their respective destinations in life; but still an intimacy and occasional visiting were kept up. The Earl died on the 14th of October 1693, in his twenty-ninth year, and it was two or three days after when Lady Beresford attracted her husband's attention at the breakfast-table by a pallid and care-worn look, and her wearing a

black ribbon round her wrist. He inquired the cause of these circumstances; but she declined to give any explanation. She asked, however, very anxiously for the post, as she expected to hear of the death of her friend the Earl of Tyrone. Sir Tristram ridiculed the possibility of her knowing such an event beforehand. ' Nevertheless,' said she, ' my friend died on Tuesday last at four o'clock.' The husband was startled when a letter from Lord Tyrone's steward was soon after handed in, relating how his master had suddenly died at the very time stated by Lady Beresford. ' I can tell you more,' said the lady, ' and it is a piece of intelligence which I know will prove welcome: I shall ere long present you with a son.' This prediction was likewise in due time verified.

During the remaining years of their union the lady continued to wear the black ribbon round her wrist; but her husband died without being made privy to the secret. The widow made an imprudent second marriage with an officer named Gorges, and was very unhappy during her latter years. A month after the birth of a fourth child to Colonel Gorges, the day being her birthday, her friends came to congratulate her, and one of them, a clergyman, told her with a blithe countenance that he had just learned from parochial documents that she was a year younger than she thought—she was only forty-seven. ' Oh, then,' said she, ' you have signed my death-warrant. If I am only forty-seven to-day, I have but a few hours to live, and these I must devote to settling my affairs.' The company having all departed, excepting one intimate female friend, Lady Beresford told that person how it was that she was certain of her approaching death, and at the same time explained the circumstance connected with the sable wristband.

During the night preceding the conversation with her husband Sir Tristram Beresford, she awoke suddenly, and beheld the figure of Lord Tyrone at her bedside. She screamed, and endeavoured, but in vain, to awaken her husband. At length recovering some degree of composure, she asked Lord Tyrone how and why he had come there. He reminded her of their mutual promise, and added, ' I departed this life on Tuesday last at four o'clock. I am permitted to give you assurance of another world. I can also inform you that you will bear a son to Sir Tristram, after whose death you will marry again, and have other children, and will die in the forty-seventh year of your age.' ' And how,' said she, ' shall I be certain that my seeing you now, and hearing such important intelligence, are not mere dreams or illusions?' The spirit waved his hand, and the bed-curtains were instantly raised and drawn through a large iron hoop, by which the tester of the bed was suspended. She remained unsatisfied, for she might, she said, exercising the greater strength which one had in sleep, have raised the curtains herself. He then pencilled his name in her pocket-book. Still she doubted—she might imagine in the morning that she had written the name herself. Then, asking her to hold out her hand, the spirit laid a finger as cold as ice upon her wrist, which was immediately impressed with a black mark, underneath which the flesh appeared to have shrunk. And then he vanished. Soon after completing her recital, and having finally arranged her affairs, the lady calmly expired in the arms of her friend. The ribbon being then removed, the mark was seen for the first time by any eye but her own. It has been stated that the ribbon and also the pocket-book containing the spiritual autograph were, nearly a century after, in the possession of Lady Beresford's grand-daughter, Lady Betty Cobbe, whose husband (son of Cobbe, Archbishop of Dublin) died in his house in Marlborough Buildings, Bath, so recently as 1814. The peerage books inform us that Lady Beresford died on the 23rd February 1713, and was buried in the Earl of Cork's tomb, in St Patrick's Cathedral, Dublin.

The circumstance of the black ribbon, equally picturesque and mysterious, is what has mainly given this family tale the currency which it has in the upper circles of British society. It is, however, remarkable that in this particular it is not without precedent in the annals of demonology. Mrs Grant, in her *Superstitions of the Highlands*, tells a story of a widow in good circumstances who, going home through a wood at dusk, was encountered by the spirit of her deceased husband, who led her carefully along a difficult bridge, but *left a blue mark on her wrist*, which the neighbours had opportunities of seeing during the week that she survived the adventure.

Calmet, in his well-known work, *The Phantom World*, quotes a similar tale as told by the reformer Melancthon, whose word, he says, 'ought not to be doubted.'* According to this narration, an aunt of Melancthon, having lost her husband when she was far advanced in pregnancy, ' saw one day towards evening two persons come into her house; one of them wore the form of her deceased husband, the other that of a tall Franciscan. At first she was frightened, but her husband reassured her, and told her that he had important things to communicate to her; at the same time he begged the Franciscan to pass into the next room, while he imparted his wishes to his wife. Then he begged of her to have some masses said for the relief of his soul, and tried to persuade her to give her hand without fear; as she was unwilling to give it, he assured her she would feel no pain. She gave him her hand, and her hand felt no pain when she withdrew it, but was so blackened that it remained discoloured all her life. After that, the husband called in the Franciscan; they went out and disappeared.'

Richard Baxter relates, as coming under his own observation, a circumstance which involves the same kind of material phenomenon as the story of Lady Beresford. A little after the Restoration, when the parliament was passing acts which pressed sore on the dissenters, a lady of good quality and of that persuasion came to him to relate a strange thing that had befallen her. While praying for the deliverance of the faithful from the evils that seemed impending over them, ' it was suddenly given her, that there should be a speedy deliverance, even in a very

short time. She desired to know which way; and it was by somewhat on the king, which I refused to hear out, whether it was change or death. It being set strongly on her as a revelation, she prayed earnestly that if this were a true divine impulse and revelation, God would certify her by some visible sign; and she ventured to choose the sign herself, and laid her hand on the outside of the upper part of her leg, begging of God that, if it were a true answer, he would make on that place some visible mark. There was presently the mark of black spots, like as if a hand had burnt it, which her sister witnessed she saw presently, there being no such thing before.'*

Dr Henry More heard from one Mrs Dark, of Westminster, that her deceased husband, when young and in good health, ' going out of his house one morning with the intention of returning to dinner, was, as he walked the streets, struck upon the thigh by an invisible hand (for he could see no man near him to strike him). He returned indeed about dinner-time, but could eat nothing; only he complained of the sad accident that befell him, and grew forthwith so mortally sick that he died in three days. After he was dead, there was found upon the place where he was struck the perfect figure of a man's hand, the four fingers, palm, and thumb, black and sunk into the flesh, as if one should clap his hand upon a lump of dough.'†

SIR JOHN SUCKLING.

One of the best specimens of the gay and accomplished courtier of Charles the First's time, ere the evil days of civil war fell upon the land, is afforded to us by the poet, Sir John Suckling. His father having been secretary of state to James I., and comptroller of the household to Charles, Suckling may be said to have been bred at court: yet his education was not neglected, and such was the precocity of his talent and facility in acquiring knowledge, that he was able to speak Latin when only five years of age, and to write it when no more than eight. Ere he had attained the full period of manhood, he had travelled over the greater part of Europe, and been received as a welcome visitor at the principal continental courts. He also served a short but stirring campaign under Gustavus Adolphus, in which he was present at three battles, five sieges, and several lesser engagements.

On his return from travel, Sir John at once took first place among the leaders of wit and fashion; as an old writer observes, ' he was allowed to have the peculiar happiness of making everything he did become him.' When Charles marched against the Scottish Covenanters in 1639, Suckling raised 100 horsemen for the royal service, so very splendidly equipped (the troop cost him the large sum of £12,000), that Charles, not wisely undervaluing his sturdy northern subjects, said that if anything would make the Scotch fight well, it would be the prospect of plunder exhibited by the rich dresses of Suckling's men. This ill-judged expedition produced little result, save a crowd of satirists to ridicule its fruitless

* He quotes Melancthon's Works, fol. 326.

* *Certainty of a World of Spirits*, p. 181.
† *Antidote against Atheism*, p. 166.

display; and, in the only skirmish that occurred, near Dunse, the English cavalry, including Suckling's troop, galloped off the field, pursued by a smaller body of the enemy. A satirical ballad was composed on this affair and Suckling's part in it, to a well-known and very lively old English tune, called *John Dory*, which became exceedingly popular, and was sung and printed with many variations. From its peculiar style and manner, we suspect that the ballad was composed by Suckling as a piece of good-humoured banter against himself, and that subsequently the more spiteful variations were added by others.* A few verses of the original are worth reprinting:

' Sir John he got him an ambling nag,
    To Scotland for to ride-a,
With a hundred horse more, all his own he swore,
    To guard him on every side-a.

No errant knight e'er went to fight
    With half so gay a bravada,
Had you seen but his look, you'd have sworn on a
        book,
    He'd have conquered a whole armada.

The ladies ran all to the windows, to see
    So gallant and warlike a sight-a,
And as he passed by they cried with a sigh,
    Sir John, why will you go fight-a?

None liked him so well as his own colonel,
    Who took him for John de Wert-a;†
But when there were shows of gunning and blows,
    My gallant was nothing so pert-a.

The colonel sent for him back again,
    To quarter him in the van-a,
But Sir John did swear, he would not come there,
    To be killed the very first man-a.'

Suckling's best poem is certainly the celebrated ballad he composed on the marriage of Lord Broghill with Lady Margaret Howard, daughter of the Earl of Suffolk, commencing:—

' I tell thee, Dick, where I have been,
    Where I the rarest things have seen,
        Oh! things beyond compare.
Such sights again cannot be found
    In any place on English ground,
        Be it at wake or fair.'

The description of the bride in this ballad has been universally admired; it must be understood that the person speaking is supposed to be a clownish countryman.

' Her finger was so small, the ring
    Would not stay on, which they did bring,
        It was too wide a peck:
And, to say truth, (for out it must)
    It look't like the great collar (just)
        About our young colt's neck.

Her feet, beneath her petticoat,
    Like little mice stole in and out,

* Perhaps the biographers of Suckling have attached more consequence to his conduct on this occasion than the facts warranted. It has not been remembered that the army brought by King Charles against the Scots in 1639 was wholly without heart in the cause, and indisposed to fight. When such is the humour of a body of soldiery, the commanders are usually left no choice but to make a precipitate retreat.—*Ed.*

† De Wert was a celebrated German general, who had been styled the terror of the French.

As if they feared the light;
But, oh! she dances such a way,
No sun upon an Easter day,
    Is half so fine a sight.

Her cheeks, so rare a white was on,
No daisy makes comparison;
    (Who sees them is undone;)
For streaks of red were mingled there,
Such as are on a Katherine pear,
    The side that's next the sun.

Her lips were red, and one was thin
Compared to that was next her chin;
    Some bee had stung it newly;
But, Dick, her eyes so guard her face,
I durst no more upon them gaze
    Than on the sun in July.'

The grace and elegance of Suckling's ballads and songs were, in his own day, considered inimitable. Phillips says that, 'They have a touch of a gentle spirit, and seem to savour more of the grape than the lamp.'

One trait in Suckling's character must not be passed unnoticed; in language and idea he was one of the purest, if not the very purest poetical writer of his license-loving era. Indeed, his writings are more unexceptionable in expression, more fit to be read and circulated at the present day, than the productions of many of the so-termed Puritans, his contemporaries. Nor were all Suckling's writings mere poetical trifles. He was the author of a prose work, entitled *An Account of Religion by Reason.* Its aim is to answer the objections then made against admitting a belief in the Christian faith as a matter of reason. This is a work of considerable merit, written with great clearness, ingenuity, and force, and in a manner evidently indicating a sincere piety in the author.

In the short parliament of 1640, the gay poet was elected for Bramber in Sussex; but he was not destined to live much longer in his own country. Becoming engaged in a reactionary conspiracy, he was obliged to fly to Paris, where he lived for some time in great penury. There is in the British Museum a copy of a printed brochure, containing a ballad account of his distresses, as from himself, which gives us the one certain date connected with his life, 16th June 1641. It is believed to have been soon after this time that the cavalier bard, in despair of further happiness, put a period to his own life, when he could not have been much more than thirty-two years of age.

BATTLE OF STOKE.

On the 16th of June 1487, the last contest between the rival houses of York and Lancaster—the last great battle on English soil—was fought near Stoke, in Nottinghamshire. The fortunes of the Red Rose prevailed, firmly securing the house of Tudor on the throne of England; but the destruction of life was lamentable, six thousand men being numbered among the slain.

The Earl of Lincoln, Martin Swartz, Lord Thomas Fitzgerald, and Francis Viscount Lovel, commanded the Yorkist party. Henry VII., aided by the choice of the English nobility, defended in person his right to the throne. The battle commenced by the Earl of Lincoln descending to the attack from a hill still called 'The Rampire,' hoping by a furious charge to break the first line of the king's army, and thus throw the main body into confusion. But, after fighting desperately for three hours, during which the German auxiliaries under Swartz exhibited great valour, and the Irish under Fitzgerald, armed only with darts and knives, obstinately maintained their ground, the royal troops prevailed, and the insurgents were routed with immense slaughter.

Lambert Simnel, the puppet set up by the Earl of Lincoln to clear his own way to the crown, was taken prisoner, and by an artful stroke of policy was made turnspit in the king's kitchen. But the dead bodies of the earl and all the other principal leaders, save that of Lord Lovel, were found where they had fallen sword-in-hand on the fatal field. Lord Lovel, as it has been often told, was never seen, living or dead, after the battle. Some assert that he was drowned when endeavouring to escape across the river Trent, the weight of his armour preventing the subsequent discovery of his body. Another report was that he fled to the north, where, under the guise of a peasant, he ended his days in peace. Lord Bacon, in his *History of Henry the Seventh*, says that 'he lived long after in a cave or vault.' And this last account has been partly corroborated in modern times. William Cowper, Esquire, Clerk of the House of Commons, writing from Herlingfordbury Park in 1738, says :—'In 1708, upon occasion of new-laying a chimney at Minster Lovel, there was discovered a large vault or room underground, in which was the entire skeleton of a man, as having been sitting at a table, which was before him, with a book, paper, pen, &c.; in another part of the room lay a cap, all much mouldered and decayed. Which the family and others judged to be this Lord Lovel, whose exit has hitherto been so uncertain.'

JUNE 17.

Saints Nicander and Marcian, martyrs, about 303. St Prior, hermit in Egypt, 4th century. St Avitus, or Avy, abbot, near Orleans, about 530. St Botulph, abbot of Ikanho, 655. St Molingus, or Dairchilla, bishop and confessor in Ireland, 697.

Born.—John Wesley, founder of the sect of Methodists, 1703, *Epworth ;* Andrew Crosse, electrician, 1784 ; Ferdinand Freiligrath, German poet, 1810.

Died.—John Sobieski (John III. of Poland), 1696, *Warsaw ;* Joseph Addison, poet, miscellaneous writer, 1719, *Holland House ;* Louis Hector, Duke de Villars, illustrious French commander, 1734, *Turin ;* Claude-Prosper Joliot de Crebillon, French poet, 1762 ; Selina, Countess of Huntingdon, 1791 ; Lord William Bentinck, statesman, 1839 ; Richard H. Barham, comic poet, 1845, *Amen Corner, London ;* Madame Sontag, vocalist, 1854, *Mexico.*

JOHN WESLEY.

The founder of Methodism was, as is well known, the son of a clergyman of the Established Church, and became such himself, attaining his thirty-fifth year without doing anything remarkable, beyond a missionary excursion to the American Indians. Being in London on the 24th of May 1738, he went, 'very unwillingly' to a meeting in Aldersgate Street where one was reading Luther's preface to the Epistle to the Romans. Listening to the reader, 'at about a quarter before nine o'clock,' light flashed upon his mind, and he was converted. Until that evening, he used to say, that although a teacher of others, he had never known what Christianity really was. Following the example of Whitefield, he commenced preaching in the open air, and his life henceforward was consecrated to religious labours among the people. His early efforts were directed to supplement the services of the Church of England, but gradually he superseded them. He built chapels, organized a ministry and worship, allowed laymen to preach, and at last found himself at the head of a great and independent religious community, which in 1790 numbered 76,000 in Great Britain and 57,000 in America. Wesley died in London on the 2nd of March 1791, in his 88th year, and the 65th of his ministry, and was buried in the yard of the Methodist chapel in the City Road.

It would be difficult to find in the whole circle of biography a man who worked harder and longer than John Wesley. Not an hour did he leave unappropriated. For fifty years he rose at four in the morning, summer and winter, and was accustomed to preach a sermon at five, an exercise he esteemed 'the healthiest in the world.' This early devotion, he said, 'is the glory of the Methodists. Whenever they drop it they will dwindle away to nothing.' Travelling did not suspend his industry. 'Though I am always in haste,' he says of himself, 'I am never in a hurry, because I never undertake any more work than I can go through with perfect calmness of spirit. It is true I travel 4000 or 5000 miles in a year, but I generally travel alone in my carriage, and am as retired ten hours a-day as if I were in a wilderness. On other days, I never spend less than three hours, and frequently ten or twelve, alone.' In this way he found time to read much and to write voluminously. In eating and drinking he was very abstemious. Suppers he abhorred, and sometimes for years he never tasted animal food. Once for three or four years he lived almost exclusively on potatoes. From wine, beer, and spirits he habitually abstained, preferring water. Throughout his long life he enjoyed nearly uninterrupted health. He could sleep at will, and he owns that he never lost a night's sleep from his childhood. His fine health he attributed to his regular habits, his temperance, and to the frequent changes of air he experienced in travelling ; also to his serene temper ; he had a thousand cares resting upon him, but they never worried him. 'I *feel* and *grieve*,' he writes, 'but by the grace of God I fret at nothing.' To the end of his life his complexion was fresh, his walk agile, his eye keen and active. A curious and pleasant picture he left in the memory of many who saw him in the street in his old age, and noted his lithe little figure, his long hair, white and bright as silver, his radiant countenance, his active pace and energetic air. He died painlessly, not of disease, but healthily worn out. Order and method pervaded all his doings. At the middle of 1790 he closed his cash-book with these words written in a tremulous hand:— 'For upwards of seventy-six years I have kept my accounts exactly : I will not attempt it any longer, being satisfied that I save all I can and give all I can ; that is, all I have.' This was strictly true. From his youth up he lived on a trifle yearly, and gave the balance of his income away. When at Oxford he had £30 one year ; he lived on £28, and gave £2 away. Next year having £60, he lived on £28, and gave away £32. The third year he had £90, and the fourth £120, yet he still limited himself to £28, and made alms of the rest. It is said that in the course of his life he gave away not less than £30,000. This great sum was chiefly derived from the sale of his writings. He was his own printer and bookseller, and managed his trade with economy and success.

Marvellous were Wesley's powers as a leader and administrator. Never general drilled a more heterogeneous army, and never was general more reverentially obeyed. He exacted no service which he did not in his own person exceed. Who could work more than he worked? who spare himself less? His example gave life and inspiration to all who came near him. His strong will and his quick, decisive intellect naturally raised him to kingship, and gathered around him willing and joyful subjects. The constructive force and order of his own mind were reflected in the organization of Methodism, and in the increase and permanence of that community we discern the highest testimony to the vigour and sagacity of his character.

His failures usually arose from the misapplication of those qualities by which he triumphed. As instances we may take Kingswood school and his marriage. At Kingswood, near Bristol, he set up a boarding-school for the sons of his preachers, who, being seldom at home, could not supervise the education of their children. Wesley devised the discipline of the school, and ordered that each day should be divided into three parts ; eight hours for sleep, from eight at night to four in the morning, eight hours for study, and eight for meals and—play, no, play John Wesley could see no use for ; amusement was proscribed at Kingswood. The hours not spent in sleep and study were to be used for prayer, self-examination, singing, and working in the garden in fine, and in the house in wet weather. The boys were never to be left alone, but always under the eye of a master who was to keep them busy and from idle talk. There were no holidays, and no vacations allowed, because a week from school might undo the good habits they were forming. It is needless to say that Kingswood school would not work, and gave Wesley endless trouble. He changed masters, and expelled some scholars for 'incorrigible wickedness,' but in vain. The rules were perpetually broken, and he never appears to have had a glimpse of the fact that he was striving after the impossible.

Of the nature of boyhood he had no conception, and why he could not turn out rows of juvenile Wesleys, caring for nothing but work and devotion, was by him set down to any cause but the right one. In his forty-eighth year he married Mrs Vizelle, a widow with four children and a fortune. Her money Wesley would not touch, but had it settled upon her. Some time before he had published *Thoughts on a Single Life*, in which he extolled celibacy, and advised the unmarried, who found it possible, to remain single ; alleging that he was a bachelor because he thought he could be more useful in that state. It was a sad day when he changed his mind, and fell in love with Mrs Vizelle. He stipulated with her that he should not preach one sermon nor travel one mile the less after marriage than before ; 'if I thought I should,' said he, 'well as I love you, I should never see your face more.' With these views, what could a wife be to him but an incumbrance? At first she conformed to his ascetic habits and travelled with him, but soon she grew tired of his rigid and restless life, and of the society of the humble Methodists to whom she was introduced. She began to grumble, but Wesley was far too busy to attend to her wails ; then she grew jealous, opened his letters, followed him from town to town as a spy, and plagued him in every way, openly and secretly, that her malice could contrive. 'By her outrageous jealousy and abominable temper,' says Southey, 'she deserves to be classed in a triad with Xantippe and the wife of Job, as one of the three bad wives.' Wesley, however, was not a man to be henpecked. 'Know me,' said he, in one of his letters to her, 'and know yourself. Suspect me no more, asperse me no more, provoke me no more : do not any longer contend for mastery, for power, money, or praise : be content to be a private insignificant person, known and loved by God and me. . . . . Of what importance is your character to mankind? If you were buried just now, or if you had never lived, what loss would it be to the cause of God?' After having been a thorn in his flesh for twenty years, she left his house, carrying off his journals and papers, which she never returned. He simply states the fact in his diary, saying he knew not what the cause had been, and adds, '*Non eam reliqui, non dimisi, non revocabo*,—I did not forsake her, I did not dismiss her, I will not recall her.' She lived ten years after her flight, and, in 1781, died at Camberwell, where a stone in the churchyard attests that ' she was a woman of exemplary virtue, a tender parent, and a sincere friend,' but it mercifully says nothing of her conjugal life.

AUTOGRAPH OF JOHN WESLEY.

LORD WILLIAM BENTINCK.

The inscription which was placed on a statue of Lord William Bentinck, at Calcutta—the composition of Lord Macaulay—gives a fine picture of an enlightened and disinterested public servant. It states that 'during seven years he ruled India with eminent prudence, integrity, and benevolence,' never forgetting that 'the end of government is the happiness of the governed.' He 'abolished cruel rites;' he 'effaced humiliating distinctions;' he 'gave liberty to the expression of public opinion;' and his 'constant study was to elevate the intellectual and moral character of the nations committed to his charge.' It is interesting to compare such a character as this with the accounts we have of the proconsuls of the Roman world; hardly anything could more expressively mark the progress which humanity has made in the last eighteen hundred years, than that such a man as Lord William Bentinck should have adorned our latter times.

THE BATTLE OF BUNKER HILL.

On a hill eighty-seven feet high, once called Breed's Hill, but now known as Bunker Hill, on the peninsula of Charlestown, north of Boston, Massachusetts, rises a granite obelisk 220 feet in height, built to commemorate the first important battle in the American War of Independence.

Three distinguished generals, Howe, Clinton, and Burgoyne, with 12,000 veteran British troops, and a formidable fleet, occupied Boston. They were besieged by an undisciplined crowd of colonists, without arms, ammunition, supplies, or organization. On the morning of the 17th of June 1775, the British officers in Boston, and on the ships in the harbour, saw to their astonishment a breastwork on Bunker Hill, which had been thrown up in the night, and was every moment growing stronger, so as to threaten their position in a serious manner. This was the work of about fifteen hundred Yankees, under Colonel Prescott.

No time was to be lost. The ships in the harbour and a battery on Copp's Hill opened fire; but those were not the days of Armstrong artillery. General Howe took 3000 infantry, and crossed over to Charlestown in boats to storm the works. It was a fine summer day, and the hills, spires, and roofs of the city were covered with spectators. Soon a fire, bursting from the wooden houses of the village of Charlestown, added to the grandeur of the spectacle.

General Howe was too proud of British valour to turn the works, but, forming his troops in two columns, marched to the assault. The Americans, who had little artillery, and no ammunition to waste, waited in silence until the British were within ten rods, and preparing to charge when a sheet of fire broke out along their breastworks with such deadly aim, that whole ranks were cut down, and those not killed or wounded fled precipitately to the water-side. They were rallied, and advanced a second time with a like result. General Clinton, who had watched the progress of the battle from the heights of Boston, now came with reinforcements;

some gunboats enfiladed the works, and a third attack, aided by a flank diversion, and the fact that the Americans had expended their small store of ammunition, was successful. The rebels were driven from their works at the point of the bayonet. Having no bayonets themselves, they fell sullenly back, fighting with the butts of their muskets. The British loss was about 1000 killed and wounded, out of a force of 3000; that of the Americans, 400 or 500. It was a British victory which gave hope and confidence to the Americans, and has been celebrated by them as one of the most glorious events of their War of Independence.

THE ROXBURGHE CLUB.

This fraternity—the parent of the whole tribe of book-printing clubs which have occupied so broad a space in the literary system of our age—was formed on the 17th of June 1812. The plant shot forth from a hot-bed of bibliomania, which had been created by the sale of the Duke of Roxburghe's library. On that occasion Earl Spencer, the youthful Duke of Devonshire, the Marquis of Blandford, and a whole host of minor men, lovers of old and rare books, were brought together in a state of high excitement, to contend with each other for the rarities exposed under the hammer of Mr Evans, in the Duke of Roxburghe's mansion in St James's Square. On the 16th of June, a number of them had chanced to dine together in the house of Mr Bolland (afterwards Justice Bolland), on Adelphi Terrace. They had to look forward to the exposure on the ensuing day of a most rare and remarkable volume, a folio edition of Boccaccio, printed by Valdarfer of Venice in 1471. They agreed 'to meet again at dinner on the ensuing evening, at the St Alban's tavern, in order to talk over the fight which would by that time have taken place over the body of Valdarfer; and they did so. Earl Spencer, the unsuccessful candidate for the volume (which had sold at £2260), occupied the chair; Dr Dibdin acted as croupier. There were sixteen other gentlemen present, all of them possessors of choice libraries, and all keen appreciators of scarce and curious books. The lively Dibdin* tells us that they drank toasts which were as hieroglyphical characters to the public, but 'all understood and cordially greeted by those who gave and those who received them.' We may presume that the immortal memory of William Caxton was one of the most prominent; that sundry illustrious booksellers, and even notable binders (bibliopegists they called them), were not forgotten. The club was constituted by the persons there assembled; but by the time they had had two annual assemblages, the number was swelled to *thirty-one*, at which it was fixed. It was by an after thought that the club commenced its system of printing and reprinting, each member fixing upon some precious article, of which only as many copies were thrown off as afforded one to each, presented gratuitously. By this happy plan the friendly spirit of the brethren was of course promoted, at the same time that some valuable

* *Reminiscences of a Literary Life*, 2 vols. 1836, i. 374.

examples of ancient literature were rescued from oblivion. In the Scottish imitative societies—the Bannatyne Club, Maitland Club, &c.—the same plan was adopted; while in others of later institution the reprints have been effected by an equal annual subscription.

JUNE 18.

Saints Marcus and Marcellianus, martyrs, 286. St Amand, Bishop of Bordeaux. St Marina, of Bithynia, virgin, 8th century. St Elizabeth, of Sconauge, virgin and abbess, 1165.

Born.—Robert Stewart, Marquis of Londonderry, minister of George IV., 1769, *London;* Karl Wenceslaus Rodecker von Rotteck, historian, 1775, *Frieburg, in Breisgau.*

Died.—Caliph Othman, assassinated at Medina, 655; Bishop Thomas Bilson, 1616; A. Philips, poet, '749, *near Vauxhall, London;* Gerard Van Swieten, eminent physician and teacher of medicine, 1772, *Schoenbrunn, Vienna;* Arthur Murphy, dramatist, 1805, *Knightsbridge;* General Sir Thomas Picton, 1815, *Waterloo;* William Coombe, novelist and comic poet, 1823, *London;* William Cobbett, political writer, 1835; John Roby, author of *Traditions of Lancashire,* drowned at sea off Portpatrick, 1850.

THE BATTLE OF WATERLOO.

When William IV. was lying on his deathbed at Windsor, the firing for the anniversary of Waterloo took place, and on his inquiring and learning the cause, he breathed out faintly, 'It was a great day for England.' We may say it was so, in no spirit of vainglorious boasting on account of a well-won victory, but as viewed in the light of a liberation for England, and the civilized world generally, from the dangerous ambition of an unscrupulous and too powerful adversary.

When Napoleon recovered his throne at Paris, in March 1815, he could only wring from an exhausted and but partially loyal country about two hundred thousand men to oppose to nearly a million of troops which the allied sovereigns were ready to muster against him. His first business was to sustain the attack of the united British and Prussians, posted in the Netherlands, and it was his obvious policy to make an attack on these himself before any others could come up to their assistance. His rapid advance at the beginning of June, before the English and Prussian commanders were aware of his having left Paris; his quick and brilliant assaults on the separate bodies of Prussians and British at Ligny and Quatre Bras on the 16th, were movements marked by all his brilliant military genius. And even when, on the 18th, he commenced the greater battle of Waterloo with both, the advantage still remained to him in the divided positions of his double enemy, giving him the power of bringing his whole host concentratedly upon one of theirs; thus neutralizing to some extent their largely superior forces. And, beyond a doubt, through the superior skill and daring which he thus shewed, as well as the wonderful gallantry of his soldiery, the victory at Waterloo ought to have been his. There was

just one obstacle, and it was decisive—the British infantry stood in their squares immovable upon the plain till the afternoon, when the arrival of the Prussians gave their side the superiority. It is unnecessary to repeat details which have been told in a hundred chronicles. Enough that that evening saw the noble and in large part veteran army of Napoleon retreating and dispersing never to re-assemble, and that within a month his sovereignty in France had definitely closed. A heroic, but essentially rash and ill-omened adventure, had ended in consigning him to those six years of miserable imprisonment which form such an anti-climax to the twenty of conquest and empire that went before.

If we must consider it a discredit to Wellington that he was unaware on the evening of the 15th that action was so near—even attending a ball that evening in Brussels—it was amply redeemed by the marvellous coolness and sagacity with which he made all his subsequent arrangements, and the patience with which he sustained the shock of the enemy, both at Quatre Bras on the 16th, and on the 18th in the more terrible fight of Waterloo. Thrown on that occasion into the central position among the opponents of Bonaparte, he was naturally and justly hailed as the saviour of Europe, though at the same time nothing can be more clear than the important part which the equal force of Prussians bore in meeting the French battalions. Thenceforth the name of Wellington was venerated above that of any living Englishman.

According to Alison, the battle of Waterloo was fought by 80,000 French and 250 guns, against 67,000 English, Hanoverians, Belgians, &c., with 156 guns, to which were subsequently added certain large bodies of Prussians, who came in time to assist in gaining the day. There were strictly but 22,000 British troops on the field, of whom the total number killed was 1417, and wounded 4923. The total loss of the allied forces on that bloody day was 22,378, of whom there were killed 4172. It was considered for that time a very sanguinary conflict, but—

'The glory ends not, and the pain is past.'

BURLESQUE AND SATIRICAL HERALDRY.

Horace Walpole and a select few of his friends once beguiled the tedium of a dull day at Strawberry Hill by concocting a satirical coat-of-arms for a club in St James's Street, which at that time had an unfortunate character for high play as well as deep drinking. The club was known as 'the Old and Young Club,' and met at Arthur's. Lady Hervey gives a clue to the peculiarity of its designation in a letter dated 1756, in which she laments that 'luxury increases, all public places are full, and Arthur's is the resort of old and young, courtiers and anti-courtiers—nay, even of ministers.' The arms were invented in 1756 by Walpole, Williams, George Selwyn, and the Honourable Richard Edgecumbe, and drawn by the latter. This drawing formed lot twelve of the twenty-second day's sale at Strawberry Hill in 1842, and is here engraved, we believe, for the first time.

The arms may be thus described :—On a green field (in allusion to the baize on a card table)

COG IT   CLARET   NUMMI

AMOR

three cards (aces); between, a chevron sable (for a hazard table), two rouleaus of guineas in saltier, and a pair of dice; on a canton, sable, a white election-ball. The crest is an arm issuing from an earl's coronet, and shaking a dice-box. The arms are surrounded by a claret-bottle ticket and its chain; the supporters are an old and a young Knave of Clubs; and the motto, 'Cogit amor nummi,' involves a pun in the first word, the letters being so separated as to allude to the cogging of dice for dishonest play.

Burlesque heraldry very probably had its origin in the mock tournaments, got up in broad caricature by the Hanse Towns of Germany in the sixteenth and seventeenth centuries, when the real tournaments had lost their chivalric charm, and feudalism was fast fading away. The wealthy *bourgeoisie* of the great commercial towns delighted in holding these mock encounters, and parodied in every particular the tourneys and jousts of the old noblesse; dressing their combatants in the most grotesque fashion, with tubs for breastplates and buckets for helmets, and furnishing them with squires who bore their shields with coat-armour of absurd significance. In that curious old poem, *The Tournament of Tottenham*, preserved in *Percy's Reliques*, the plebeians who fight for Tyb the Reve's daughter proclaim their blazonry in accordance with their calling; one bears

     '—— A riddle and a rake,
     Powdered with a burning drake,
     And three cantells of a cake
         In each corner.'

Another combatant declares—

     'In my arms I bear well,
     A dough trough and a peel,
     A saddle without a panel,
         With a fleece of wool.'

Severe satirical allusions to individuals were sometimes indulged in; the most celebrated being the coat-of-arms invented by Roy, and placed in the title-page of his bold and bitter

attack on Wolsey; a satire in which Roy risked his life. It is printed in red and black, and described in caustic verse, of which we quote only as much as will explain it :—

     'Of the proud cardinal this is the shield,
     Borne up between two angels of Satan :
     The six bloody axes in a bare field
     Sheweth the cruelty of the red man.
     The six bulls' heads in a field black
     Betokeneth his sturdy furiousness.
     The bandog in the midst doth express
     The mastiff cur bred in Ipswich town,
     Gnawing with his teeth a king's crown.
     The club signifieth plain his tyranny
     Covered over with a cardinal's hat.'

Walpole, with his antiquarian tastes, must have been fully aware of these old satires; but he

had a nearer and cleverer example in 'The Undertakers' Arms,' designed and published by Hogarth as a satire on medical quacks, whom he considers their best friends, and thus describes the coat : 'The Company of Undertakers beareth, sable, an urinal proper, between twelve quack heads of the second, and twelve cane heads, or, consultant. On a chief, nebuly, ermine, one complete doctor, issuant, checky, sustaining in his right hand a baton of the second. On the dexter and sinister sides, two demi-doctors, issuant of the second, and two cane-heads issuant of the third; the first having one eye couchant, towards the dexter side of the escutcheon; the second faced per pale, proper and gules, guardant. With this motto, *Et plurima mortis imago* (the general image of death).' The humour of this satire is by no means restricted to the whimsical adaptation of heraldic terms to the design, in which there is more than meets the eye, or will be understood without a Parthian glance at the quacks of Hogarth's era, and whom the artist hated with his usual sturdy dislike of humbug. Thus the coarse-faced central figure of the upper triad, arrayed in a harlequin jacket, is intended for one Mrs Mapp, an Amazonian quack-doctress, who gained both fame and money as a bonesetter—her strength of arm being only equalled by her strength of language; there are some records of her sayings extant that are perfectly unquotable in the present day, yet she was called in by eminent physicians, and to the assistance of eminent people. To the right of this Amazon is the famous Chevalier Taylor, the oculist (indicated by the eye in the head of his cane), whose impudence was unparalleled, and whose memoirs, written by himself, if possible outdo even that in effrontery. To the lady's left is Dr Ward, whose pills and nostrums gulled a foolish public to his own emolument. Ward was marked with what old wives call 'a claret stain' on his left cheek; and here heraldry is made of humorous use in depicting his face, per pale, gules.

In 1785 a curious duodecimo volume was published, called *The Heraldry of Nature; or, instructions for the King-at-Arms: comprising the arms, supporting crests and mottoes of the Peers of England. Blazoned from the authority of Truth, and characteristically descriptive of the several qualities that distinguish their possessors.* The author explains his position in a preface, where he states that he has 'rejected the common and patented bearings already painted on the carriages of our nobility, and instituted what he judges a wiser delineation of the honours they deserve.' He flies at the highest game, and begins with King George the Third himself, whose coat he thus describes:—'First, argent, a cradle proper; second, gules, a rod and sceptre, transverse ways; third, azure, five cups and balls proper; fourth, gules, the sun eclipsed proper; fifth, argent, a stag's head between three jockey caps; sixth, or, a house in ruins. Supporters: the dexter, Solomon treading on his crown; the sinister, a jackass proper. Crest: Britannia in despair. Motto: "Neque tangunt levia" (little things don't move me).'

The irregularities of the Prince of Wales are severely alluded to in his shield of arms, but the satire is too broad for modern quotation. The whole of the nobility are similarly provided with coats indicative of their characters. Two are here selected as good specimens of the whole. The first is that of the Duke of Norfolk, whose indolence, habit of late hours, and deep drinking were notorious; at public dinners he would drink himself into a state of insensibility, and then his servants would lift him in a chair to his bedroom, and take that opportunity of washing him;

QUO ME BACCHE RAPIS.

for his repugnance to soap and water was equal to his love of wine. The arms are 'quarterly;

or, three quart bottles, azure; sable, a tent bed argent; azure, three tapers proper; and gules, a broken flagon of the first. Supporters: dexter, a Silenus tottering; sinister, a grape-squeezer; both proper. Crest: a naked arm holding a corkscrew. Motto: "Quo me, Bacche, rapis" (Bacchus, where are you running with me?).'

For Seymour Duke of Somerset a simpler but not more complimentary coat is invented:— 'Vert, a mastiff couchant, spotted proper. Supporters: dexter, a bear muzzled argent; sinister, a savage proper. Crest: a Wiltshire cheese,

STRENVA NOS EXERCET INERTIA.

decayed. Motto: "Strenua nos exercet inertia" (The laziest dog that ever lounged).'

Though most of the nobility are 'tarred with the same brush,' a few receive very complimentary coat-armour. Thus the Duke of Buccleuch bears 'azure a palm-tree, or. Supporters: the dexter, Mercy; the sinister, Fortitude. Crest: the good Samaritan. Motto: "Humani nihil alienum" (I'm a true philanthropist).' The foppish St John has his arms borne by two beaux, a box of lipsalve for a crest, and as a motto 'Felix, qui placuit.'

Hone, whose erudition in parody was sufficient to save him in three separate trials for alleged profanity by the proven plea of past usages, invented for one of his satirical works a clever burlesque of the national arms of England; the shield being emblazoned in a lottery wheel, the animals were represented in the last stage of starvation, and all firmly muzzled. The shield

is supported by a lancer (depicted as a centaur), who keeps the crown in its place with his lance. The other supporter is a lawyer (the Attorney-

General, with an *ex-officio* information in his bag), whose rampant condition is expressed with so much grotesque humour, that we end our selection with a copy of this figure.

THE BRITISH SOLDIER IN TROUSERS.

On the 18th of June 1823, the British infantry soldier first appeared in trousers, in lieu of other nether garments. The changes in military costume had been very gradual, marking the slowness with which novelties are sanctioned at head-quarters. When the regiments of the line first began to be formed, about two centuries ago, the dress of the officers and men partook somewhat of the general character of civil costume in the reign of Charles II. We have now before us a series of coloured engravings, showing the chief changes in uniform from that time to the beginning of the present century. Under the year 1685, the 11th foot are represented in full breeches, coloured stockings, and high shoes. Under date 1688, the 7th and 5th foot appear in green breeches of somewhat less amplitude, white stockings, and high shoes. Under 1692, the 1st royals and the 10th foot are shewn in red breeches and stockings; while another regiment appears in high boots coming up over blue breeches. In 1742, various regiments appear in purple, blue, and red breeches, white leggings or gaiters up to the thigh, and a purple garter under the knee. This dress is shewn very frequently in Hogarth's pictures. In 1759, the foot-soldiers shewn in the 'Death of General Wolfe' have a sort of knee-cap covering the breeches and gaiters. In 1793, the 87th foot are represented in tight green pantaloons and Hessian boots. During the great wars in the early part of the present century, pantaloons were sometimes worn, breeches at others, but gaiters or leggings in almost every instance.

The reform which took place in 1823 was announced in a Horse Guards' order, when the Duke of York was commander-in-chief. The order stated that 'His Majesty has been pleased to approve of the discontinuance of breeches, leggings, and shoes, as part of the clothing of the infantry soldiers; and of blue grey cloth trousers and half-boots being substituted.' After adverting to the deposit of patterns and the issue of supplies, the order makes provision for the very curious anomaly that used to mark the clothing system of the British army. 'In order to indemnify the colonels for the additional expense they will in consequence incur, the waistcoat hitherto provided with the clothing will be considered as an article of necessaries to be provided by the soldier; who, being relieved from the long and short gaiters, and also from the stoppage hitherto made in aid of the extra expense of the trousers (in all cases where such have been allowed to be furnished as part of the clothing of regiments), and being moreover supplied with articles of a description calculated to last longer than the breeches and shoes now used, cannot fail to be benefited by the above arrangement.' Non-professional readers may well be puzzled by the complexity of this announcement. The truth is, that until Lord Herbert of Lea (better known as Mr Sidney Herbert) became Secretary of State for War, a double deception was practised on the rank and file of the British army, little creditable to the nation. The legislature voted annually, for the clothing of the troops, a sum much larger than was actually applied to that purpose; and the same legislature, by a similarly annual vote, gave about a shilling a day to each private soldier as *pay*, the greater part of which was anything but pay to him. In the first place, the colonel of each regiment had an annual allowance for clothing his men, with a well-understood agreement that he

was to be permitted to purchase the clothing at a much lower rate, and put the balance in his own pocket. This balance usually varied from £600 to £1000 per annum, and was one of the prizes that made the 'clothing colonels' of regiments so much envied by their less fortunate brother-officers. In the second place, although the soldiers received their shilling a day, or thereabouts, as pay, so many deductions were made for the minor articles of sustenance and clothing, that only about fourpence remained at the actual disposal of each man. The two anomalies are brought into conjunction in a singular way in the above-quoted order, in reference to the soldier's waistcoat; the colonel was to be relieved from buying that said garment, and the poor soldier was to add the waistcoat to the number of 'necessaries' which he was to provide out of his slender pay. The miseries attendant on the Crimean war, by awaking public attention to the condition of the soldiers, led to the abandonment of the 'clothing colonel' system.

JUNE 19.

Saints Gervasius and Protasius, martyrs, 1st century. St Die or Deodatus, Bishop of Nevers and Abbot of Jointures, 679 or 680. St Boniface, Archbishop of Magdeburg, Apostle of Russia and martyr, 1009. St Juliano Falconieri, virgin, 1340.

The Fête Dieu.

This day is kept by Roman Catholics as one of their highest festivals; it is held as a celebration of the name of God, when the people bring their offerings to him as the King of Heaven. The consecrated host is carried through the open air, the whole population turning out to do honour to it, and kneeling as it passes by.

Such processions as we see in the streets on this day are evidently borrowed from heathen times: the paintings which cover the Egyptian temples shew us how that people worshipped their god Isis in procession; and the chisel of Phidias, on the bas-reliefs of the Parthenon, has preserved the details of the Greek great festival in honour of Minerva, established many hundred years before Christ. First came the old men, bearing branches of the olive tree; then the young men, their heads crowned with flowers, singing hymns; children followed, dressed in their simple tunics or in their natural graces. The young Athenian ladies, who lived an almost cloistral life, came out on this occasion richly dressed, and walked singing to the notes of the flute and the lyre: the elder and more distinguished matrons also formed a part of the procession, dressed in white, and carrying the sacred baskets, covered with veils. After these came the lower orders, bearing seats and parasols, the slaves alone being forbidden to take part in it. The most important object, however, was a ship, which was moved along by hidden machinery, from the mast of which floated the *peplus*, or mantle of Minerva, saffron-coloured, and without sleeves, such as we see on the statues of the goddess; it was embroidered, under the direction of skilled workwomen, by young virgins of the most distinguished families in Athens. The embroideries represented the various warlike episodes in heroic times. The grand object of the procession was to place the *peplus* on Minerva's statue, and to lay offerings of every kind at the foot of her altar.

From these customs the early Christians adopted the practice of accompanying their bishop into the fields, where litanies were read, and the blessing of God implored upon their agricultural produce. Greater ceremonies were afterwards added; such as the carrying of long poles decorated with flowers, boys dressed in sacred vestments, and chanting the ancient church canticles. In the dark ages of superstition we find they advanced still further, and processions en chemise' were much in fashion: it was a mark of penitence which the people carried to its utmost limit during times of public calamity. Such were those in 1315, when a season of cold and rain had desolated the provinces of France: the people for five leagues round St Denis marched in procession—the women barefoot, the men entirely naked—religiously carrying the bodies of French saints and other relics.

St Louis himself, in the year 1270, on the eve of his departure to the last crusade he shared in, and which resulted in his death, went bare-foot from the palace to the cathedral of Notre Dame, followed by the young princes his children, by the Count D'Artois, and a large number of nobles, to implore the help of heaven on his enterprise. Our king, Henry the Eighth, when a child, walked barefoot in procession to the cele-brated shrine of Our Ladye of Walsingham, and presented a rich necklace as his offering. In later days he was only too glad to strip this rich chapel of all its treasures, and dissolve the monastery which had subsisted on the offerings of the pious pilgrims. That such processions became anything but religious, we may easily gather from the sermons that were preached against them: 'Alack! for pity!' says one, 'these solemn and accustomable processions be now grown into a right foul and detestable abuse, so that the most part of men and women do come forth rather to set out and shew themselves, and to pass the time with vain and unprofitable tales and merry fables, than to make general supplications and prayers to God. I will not speak of the rage and furor of these upland-ish processions and gangings about, which be spent in rioting. Furthermore, the banners and badges of the cross be so irre-verently handled and abused, that it is marvel God destroy us not in one day.'

To pass on now to a descrip-tion of the modern procession of the Fête Dieu, such as may be seen in any of the cities of Belgium, or even in more splen-dour in the south of France, Nismes, Avignon, or Marseilles. On rising in the morning, the whole scene is changed as by magic from the night before: the streets are festooned and garlanded with coloured paper, flowers, and evergreens, in every direction. Linen awnings are spread across to give shelter from the darting rays of the sun. The fronts of the houses are concealed by hangings, sometimes tastefully arranged by upholsterers, but more frequently consisting of curtains, coverlids, carpets, and pieces of old tapestry, which produce a very *bizarre* effect. The bells are ringing in every church, and crowds are meeting at the one from which the procession is to start, or arranging themselves in the rows of chairs which are pre-pared in the streets; others are leaning out of the windows, whilst the sellers of cakes and bonbons make a good profit by the disposal of their tempting wares.

But the distant sound of the drum is heard, which announces the approach of the procession: first come some hundreds of men, women, and children belonging to various *confréries*, which answer in some degree to our sick and burial clubs, each preceded by the head man, who is adorned with numerous medals and ribbons. The children are the prettiest part: dressed in pure white muslin, their hair hanging in curls, crowned with flowers, and carrying baskets of flowers ornamented with blue ribbons. Some adopt particular characters; four boys will carry reed pens and large books in which they are diligently writing, thus personating the four evangelists; there are many virgins, one in deep black, with a long crape veil, a large black heart on her bosom, pierced with silver arrows: those boasting of the longest hair are Magdalens. The monks and secular clergy follow the people, interspersed with military bands and other music. Near the end appears, like a white cloud, a choir of girls in long veils, crowns, and tarlatan dresses—satisfying, under a pretext of devotion, the most absorbing passion of women—love of the toilette; then, lastly, comes the canopy and dais under which the

CHILDREN'S ALTAR AT THE FÊTE DIEU.

priest of the highest rank walks, carrying the Holy Sacrament, 'Corpus Christi.' This is the most striking part: silk, gold, velvet, and feathers are used in rich profusion. The splendid dresses of the cardinals or priests who surround it ; the acolytes, in white, throwing up the silver censers, filling the air with a cloud of incense ; the people coming out of the crowd with large baskets of poppies and other flowers to throw before it, and then all falling on their knees as it passes, while the deep voices of the clergy solemnly chant the Litany, form a very picturesque and striking scene. After the principal streets have been visited, all return to the church, which is highly decorated and illuminated: the incense ascends, the organ resounds with the full force of its pipes ; trombones, ophicleides, and drums make the pillars of the nave tremble, and the host is restored to its accustomed ark on the high altar.

As you walk through the streets during the week you will see at every corner, and before many *porte-cochères*, little tables on which poor children spread a napkin and light some tapers, adding one or two plaster figures of the Virgin or saints ; to every passer-by they cry, 'Do not forget the little chapel.' These are a remnant of the chapels which in former days were decorated with great pomp to serve as stations for the procession, where Mass was said in the open air. The religious tolerance which has been proclaimed by the French laws has much lessened the repetition of these ceremonies in Paris since 1830 ; and perhaps the last great display there was when the Comte d'Artois, afterwards Charles the Tenth, walked in the procession to the ancient church of St Germain l'Auxerrois carrying a lighted taper in his hand.

Born.—James VI. of Scotland, I. of Great Britain, 1566, *Edinburgh Castle ;* Blaise Pascal, French religious writer, 1623, *Clermont, in Auvergne ;* Philip van Limborch. Arminian theologian, 1633, *Amsterdam.*

Died.—St Romuald, 1027, *Ancona ;* Piers Gaveston, favourite of Edward II., executed 1312, *Gaversyke ;* Dr William Sherlock, Dean of St Paul's, Master of the Temple, theologian, controversialist, 1707, *Hampstead ;* Nicolas Lemery, one of the fathers of true chemistry, 1715, *Paris ;* John Brown, D.D., Scotch Dissenting divine, author of the *Self-Interpreting Bible,* &c., 1787, *Haddington ;* Sir Joseph Banks, naturalist, 1820, *Spring Grove.*

BIRTH OF JAMES I.

King James—so learned, yet so childish; so grotesque, yet so arbitrary ; so sagacious, yet so weak—'the wisest fool in Christendom,' as Henry IV. termed him—does not personally occupy a high place in the national regards ; but by the accident of birth and the current of events he was certainly a personage of vast importance to these islands. To him, probably, it is owing that there is such a thing as the United Kingdom of Great Britain and Ireland among the states of Europe.

This sovereign, the son of Henry Lord Darnley and Mary Queen of Scots, was born on the 19th of June 1566, in a small room in the ancient palace within Edinburgh Castle. We know how it was—namely, for security—that the queen

selected Edinburgh Castle for her expected accouchement ; but it is impossible to imagine by what principle of selection she chose that this event should take place in a room not above eight feet square. There, however, is the room still shewn, to the wonder of everybody who sees it. The young prince was ushered into the world between nine and ten in the morning, and Sir James Melville instantly mounted horse to convey the news of the birth of an heir-apparent of Scotland, and heir-presumptive of England, to Queen Elizabeth. Darnley came at two in the afternoon to see his royal spouse and his child. 'My lord,' said Mary, 'God has given us a son.' Partially uncovering the infant's face, she added a protest that it was his, and no other man's son. Then, turning to an English gentleman present, she said, 'This is the son who I hope shall first unite the two kingdoms of Scotland and England.' Sir William Stanley said, 'Why, madam, shall he succeed before your majesty and his father?' 'Alas!' answered Mary, 'his father has broken to me ;' alluding to his joining the murderous conspiracy against Rizzio. 'Sweet madam,' said Darnley, 'is this the promise you made that you would forget and forgive all ?' 'I have forgiven all,' said the queen, 'but will never forget. What if Fawdonside's pistol had shot ? [She had felt the cold steel on her bosom.] What would have become of him and me both ?' 'Madam,' said Darnley, 'these things are past.' 'Then,' said the queen, 'let them go.'*

A curious circumstance, recalling one of the superstitions of the age, is related in connexion with Queen Mary's accouchement. The Countess of Athole, who was believed to possess magical gifts, lay in within the castle at the same time as the queen. One Andrew Lundie informed John Knox that, having occasion to be in Edinburgh on business at that time, he went up to the castle to inquire for Lady Reres, the queen's wet-nurse, and found her labouring under a very awkward kind of illness, which she explained as Lady Athole's labour pains thrown upon her by enchantment. She said, 'she was never so troubled with no bairn that ever she bare.'†

The infant king—for he was crowned at

CRADLE OF KING JAMES I. OF ENGLAND.

* This interesting conversation is reported in Lord Herries's *Memoirs.*

† Bannatyne's *Memorials,* p. 228.

thirteen months old—spent his early years in Stirling Castle, under the care of the Countess of Marr, 'as to his mouth,' and that of George Buchanan, as to his education. The descendants of the Countess possessed till a recent period, and perhaps still do so, the heavy wooden cradle in which the first British monarch was rocked. A figure of it is presented on the preceding page.

PASCAL.

A mind of singular strength and keenness, united to a fragile and sensitive body, afflicted with disease and tormented by austerity, constituted Blaise Pascal. As soon as he could talk, he amazed every one by his precocious intelligence. He was an only son, and his father, a learned man, and president of the Court of Aids in Auvergne, proud of his boy, resigned his office, and went to reside in Paris, for the more effectual prosecution of his education. He had been taught something of geometry, for which he shewed a marvellous aptitude; but his instructors, wishing to concentrate his attention on Latin and Greek, removed every book treating of mathematics out of his way. The passion was not thus to be defeated. On day Blaise was caught sitting on the floor making diagrams in charcoal, and on examination it was discovered that he had worked out several problems in Euclid for himself. No check was henceforth placed on his inclination, and he quickly became a first-rate mathematician. At sixteen he produced a treatise on Conic Sections, which was praised by Descartes, and at nineteen he devised an ingenious calculating machine. At twenty-four he experimentally verified Torricelli's conjecture that the atmosphere had weight, and gave the reason of Nature's horror of a vacuum.

There is no telling what might have been the height of his success as a natural philosopher, had he not, when about twenty-five, come under overpowering religious convictions, which led him to abandon science as unworthy of the attention of an immortal creature. The inmates of the convent of Port Royal had received the Augustinian writings of Bishop Jansen with fervent approval, and had brought on themselves the violent enmity of the Jesuits. With the cause of the Port Royalists, or Jansenists, Pascal identified himself with his whole heart, and an effective and terrible ally he proved. In 1656, under the signature of Louis de Montalte, he issued his *Lettres Ecrites à un Provincial par un de ses Amis,* in which he attacked the principles and practices of the Jesuits with a vigour of wit, sarcasm, and eloquence unanswerable. The *Provincial Letters* have long taken their place among the classics of universal literature by common consent.

Jansenism has been defined as Calvinism in doctrine united to the rites and strictest discipline of the Church of Rome; and Pascal's life and teaching illustrate the accuracy of the definition. His opinions were Calvinistic, and his habits those of a Catholic saint of the first order of merit. His health was always wretched; his body was reduced to skin and bone, and from pain he was seldom free. Yet he wore a girdle armed with iron spikes, which he was accustomed to drive in upon his fleshless ribs as often as he felt languid or drowsy. His meals he fixed at a certain weight, and, whatever his appetite, he ate neither more nor less. All seasonings and spices he prohibited, and was never known to say of any dish, ' This is very nice.' Indeed, he strove to be unconscious of the flavour of food, and used to gulp it over to prevent his palate receiving any gratification. For the same reason he dreaded alike to love and to be loved. Toward his sister, who reverenced him as a sacred being, he assumed an artificial harshness of manner—for the express purpose, as he acknowledged, of repelling her sisterly affection. He rebuked a mother who permitted her own children to kiss her, and was annoyed when some one chanced to say that he had just seen a beautiful woman.

He died in 1662, aged thirty-nine, and the examination of his body revealed a fearful spectacle. The stomach and liver were shrivelled up, and the intestines were in a gangrenous state. The brain was of unusual size and density, and, strange to say, there was no trace of sutures in the skull, except the sagittal, which was pressed open by the brain, as if for relief. The frontal suture, instead of the ordinary dovetailing which takes place in childhood, had become filled with a calculus, or non-natural deposit, which could be felt through the scalp, and obtruded on the *dura mater.* Of the coronal suture there was no sign. His brain was thus enclosed in a solid, unyielding case or helmet, with a gap at the sagittal suture. Within the cranium, at the part opposite the ventricles, were two depressions filled with coagulated blood in a corrupt state, and which had produced a gangrenous spot on the *dura mater.* How Pascal, racked with such agonies from within, should have supplemented them by such afflictions from without, is one of those mysteries in which human nature is so prolific. Regarding himself as a Christian and a type of others, well might he say, as he often did, 'illness is the natural state of the Christian.'

In his last years Pascal was engaged on a *Defence of Christianity,* and after his death the fathers of Port Royal published the materials he had accumulated for its construction, as the *Pensées de Pascal.* The manuscripts happily were preserved,—fragmentary, elliptical, enigmatical, interlined, blotted, and sometimes quite illegible though they were. Some years ago, M. Cousin suggested the collation of the printed text with the autograph, when the startling fact came to light that *The Thoughts* the world for generations had been reading as Pascal's, had been garbled in the most distressing manner by the original editors, cut down, extended, and modified according to their own notions and apprehensions of their adversaries. In 1852, a faithful version of *The Thoughts* was published in Paris by M. Ernest Havet, and their revival in their natural state has deepened anew our regret for the sublime genius which perished ere its prime, two hundred years ago.

MAGNA CHARTA.

The 19th of June 1215 remains an ever-memorable day to Englishmen, and to all nations descended from Englishmen, as that on which the

Magna Charta was signed. The mean wickedness and tyranny of King John had raised nearly the whole body of his subjects in rebellion against him, and it at length appeared that he had scarcely any support but that which he derived from a band of foreign mercenaries. Appalled at the position in which he found himself, he agreed to meet the army of the barons under their elected general, Fitz-Walter, on Runnymead, by the Thames, near Windsor, in order to come to a pacification with them. They prepared a charter, assuring the rights and privileges of the various sections of the community, and this he felt himself compelled to sign, though not without a secret resolution to disregard it, if possible, afterwards.

It was a stage, and a great one, in the establishment of English freedom. The barons secured that there should be no liability to irregular taxation, and it was conceded that the freemen, merchants, and villains (bond labourers) should be safe from all but legally imposed penalties. As far as practicable, guarantees were exacted from the king for the fulfilment of the conditions. Viewed in contrast with the general condition of Europe at that time, the making good of such claims for the subjects seems to imply a remarkable peculiarity of character inherent in English society. With such a fact possible in the thirteenth, we are prepared for the greater struggles of the seventeenth century, and for the happy union of law and liberty which now makes England the admiration of continental nations.

JUNE 20.

St Silverius, pope and martyr, 538. St Gobain, priest and martyr, 7th century. St Idaberga, or Edburge, of Mercia, virgin, about 7th century. St Bain, Bishop of Terouanne, or St Omer, about 711.

TRANSLATION OF KING EDWARD.

In the Middle Ages it sometimes happened that, from miracles wrought at the tomb of some holy person, he had a posthumous increase of reputation, making it necessary or proper that his remains should be deposited in some more honourable or convenient place. Then was effected what was called a translation of his body, usually a ceremony of an impressive character, and which it consequently became necessary to celebrate by an anniversary. Thus it happens that some saints enjoy a double distinction in the calendar: one day to commemorate their martyrdom or natural death, another to keep in memory the translation of their bodies.

The unfortunate young Saxon King Edward, a victim to maternal jealousy, has a place in the calendar (March 18), on account of his tragical end. The removal of his body from its original tomb at Wareham, to Salisbury Cathedral, three years after his decease, was commemorated on another day (June 20), being that on which the translation was performed (anno 982). It was probably rather from a feeling for the early and cruel death of this young sovereign, than from any

798

reverence for his assumed sanctity, that *The Translation of King Edward* was allowed to maintain its place in the reformed Church of England calendar.

Born.—Dr George Hickes, Dean of Worcester (nonjurant bishop of Thetford), learned theologian and controversialist, 1642, *Newsham, Yorkshire;* Dr Adam Ferguson, historian, 1723, *Logierait, Perthshire;* Theophilus Lindsey, Unitarian divine, 1723, *Middlewick;* Anna Letitia Aiken (Mrs Barbauld), 1743, *Kibworth.*

Died.—William Cavendish, second Earl of Devonshire, 1628, *Derby;* Henrietta Stuart, Duchess of Orleans, 1670, *St Cloud;* Charles Coffin, French poet, 1749; Charles Frederick Abel, musical composer, 1787; Anna Maria Porter, novelist, 1832; William IV., King of Great Britain, 1837, *Windsor.*

RICHARD BRANDON, AND OTHER FINISHERS OF THE LAW.

On the 20th of June 1649 there died, in his own house at Rosemary Lane, Richard Brandon, the official executioner for the City of London, and the man who, as is generally supposed, decapitated Charles the First. A rare tract, published at the time, entitled *The Confession of the Hangman*, states that Brandon acknowledged he had £30 for his pains, all paid him in half crowns, within an hour after the blow was given; and that he had an orange stuck full of cloves, and a handkerchief out of the king's pocket, so soon as he was carried off from the scaffold, for which orange he was proffered twenty shillings by a gentleman in White Hall, but refused the same, and afterwards sold it for ten shillings in Rosemary Lane. The tract further informs us that the sheriffs of the City 'sent great store of wine for the funeral, and a multitude of people stood waiting to see his corpse carried to the churchyard, some crying out, "Hang him, the rogue! Bury him in a dunghill;" others pressing upon him, saying they would quarter him for executing the king. Insomuch that the churchwardens and masters of the parish were fain to come for the suppression of them, and with great difficulty he was at last carried to Whitechapel churchyard, having a bunch of rosemary at each end of his coffin, on the top thereof, with a rope tied across from one end to the other.' In the Burial Register of Whitechapel there is the following entry under 1649 : ' June 21st, Richard Brandon, a man out of Rosemary Lane. This R. Brandon is supposed to have cut off the head of Charles the First.'*

A broadside, published about the same time, is entitled, *A Dialogue between the Hangman and Death*, from which the following passages may be quoted as specimens of the whole :—

' *Death.*—Lay down thy axe, and cast thy ropes away,
'Tis I command, 'tis thou that must obey :
Thy part is played, and thou goest off the stage,
The bloodiest actor in this present age.
Brandon.—But, Death, thou know'st that I for many years—
As by old Tyburn's records it appears—
Have monthly paid my taxes unto thee,
Tied up in twisted hemp for more security ;
And now, of late, I think thou didst put me to it,

* See p. 129 of the present volume.

When none but Brandon could be found to do it ;
I gave the blow caused thousands' hearts to ache—
Nay, more than that, it made three kingdoms quake.
Yet, in obedience to thy powerful call,
Down went the cedar with some shrubs, and all
To satisfy thy ne'er contented lust ;
Now, for reward, thou tellest me that I must
Lay down my tools, and with thee pack from hence—
Grim sir, you give a fearful recompense.'

The executioner, however, must submit to the
'hangman of creation;' and the author, at the
end of the dialogue, thus gives his epitaph :—

' Who do you think lies buried here ?
One that did help to make hemp dear.
The poorest subject did abhor him,
And yet his king did kneel before him ;
He would his master not betray,
Yet he his master did destroy.
And yet as Judas—in records 'tis found
Judas had thirty pence, he thirty pound.'

Brandon inherited his wretched office from his
father ; the predecessor of the Brandons was one
Derrick, who has given his name to a temporary
kind of crane, used by sailors and builders for
suspending and raising heavy weights. Derrick
served under the Provost Marshal in the expedition against Cadiz, commanded by Robert Earl
of Essex. On this occasion Derrick forfeited
his life for an outrage committed on a woman ;
but Essex pardoned him, probably on account of
his useful character, as he was employed to hang
twenty-three others. Yet, such are the revolutions of fortune, it subsequently became Derrick's
duty to decapitate his preserver Essex. These
particulars we learn from the following verse of
a contemporary ballad, called *Essex's Good Night,*
in which the unfortunate nobleman is represented saying—

' Derrick, thou know'st at Cales I saved
Thy life—lost for a rape there done ;
As thou thyself can testify,
Thine own hand three-and-twenty hung.
But now thou seest myself is come,
By chance into thy hands I light;
Strike out thy blow, that I may know
Thou Essex loved at his good-night.'

Brandon was succeeded by Dunn, who is mentioned in *Hudibras,* and in the following royalist
epigram on the death of Hugh Peters :—

' Behold the last and best edition
Of Hugh, the author of sedition ;
So full of errors, 'twas not fit
To read, till Dunn corrected it ;
But now 'tis perfect—ay, and more,
'Tis better bound than 'twas before.
Now loyalty may gladly sing,
Exit rebellion, in a string ;
And if you say, you say amiss,
Hugh now an Independent is.'

Dunn's successor was John Ketch, 'whose
name,' as the late Lord Macaulay said, ' has
during a century and a half been vulgarly given
to all who have succeeded him [in London] in
his odious office.'

The scaffold has had its code of etiquette.
When the Duke of Hamilton, Earl of Holland,
and Lord Capel were beheaded, they were
brought to the block one by one, according to

their rank—the duke first, earl next, and baron
last. When Capel was going to address the
crowd with his hat on, he was told to take it off,
such being the custom of the scaffold. At a later
period, the Earl of Kilmarnock, waiving his
right with graceful politeness, offered Lord
Balmerino the sad precedence ; but the sheriffs
objected, saying they could not permit the established etiquette to be infringed. With the lower
orders, however, there was less ceremony. When
the noted chimney-sweep, Sam Hall, was riding
up Holborn Hill in a cart, on his last journey, a
highwayman, dressed in the fashion, with an
elegant nosegay in his button-hole, who shared
the vehicle with Sam, cried out, ' Stand off,
fellow !' ' Stand off yourself, Mr Highwayman,'
the sweep indignantly retorted, ' I have quite as
good a right to be here as you have.'

The ghastly implements of the executioner have
been recognised in heraldry. A grandee of Spain
bears in his coat-armour a ladder with a gibbet.
The wheel, block, and axe, the rack, and other
implements of torture are borne by several
German houses of distinction ; and the Scottish
family of Dalziel bear *sable* a hanged man with
his arms extended *argent;* formerly, as the
herald informs us, ' they carried him hanging on
a gallows.'

A LETTER FROM JONATHAN WILD.

In the town-clerk's office of the City of London are
deposited many old manuscripts, highly curious in
their character, in relation both to events of importance and to phases of social life. Within the last few
years many of them have undergone examination and
classification. In 1841 was found among them an
original letter from Jonathan Wild, the noted thief-
taker, asking for remuneration for services he had
rendered to the cause of justice. The letter, which
was written in 1723, ran thus: ' To the Right
Honourable the Lord Mayor and the Court of Aldermen.—The Humble Petition of Jonathan Wild,
Sheweth : That your petitioner has been at great
trouble and charge in apprehending and convicting
divers felons for returning from transportation since
October, 1720 (the names of whom are mentioned in
an account hereto annexed). That your petitioner
has never received any reward or gratuity for such his
service. That he is very desirous to become a freeman of this honourable city, wherefore your petitioner
most humbly prays that your Honours will (in consideration of his said services) be pleased to admit him
into the freedom of this honourable city. And your
petitioner shall ever pray, &c.—JONATHAN WILD.'
There is appended to the petition, ' An account of the
persons apprehended, taken, and convicted for returning from transportation, by Jonathan Wyld
(another form of spelling the name), since October
1720, for which he has received no reward, viz. :
John Filewood, *alias* Violett, William Bard, Charles
Hinchman, Samuel Whittle, Martin Grey, James
Dalton, Robert Godfrey, *alias* Perkins, Old Harry,
alias Harry Williams, Henry Woodford, John Mosse.
Several others have been taken by him, and afterwards sent abroad, viz. : Moll King, John Jones, &c.,
who were notorious street-robbers in the city of
London.' There is a record that Jonathan Wild's
petition was read by the Court of Aldermen, but we
do not find evidence that the coveted freedom of the
city was awarded to him.

JUNE 21.

St Eusebius, Bishop of Samosata, and martyr, 379 or 380. St Aaron, Abbot in Brittany, 6th century. St Meen, Mevenus, or Melanus, Abbot in Brittany, about 617. St Leufredus, or Leufroi, abbot, 738. St Ralph, Archbishop of Bourges, confessor, 866. St Aloysius, or Lewis Gonzaga, confessor, 1591.

Born.—Anthony Collins, author of a *Philosophical Enquiry into Liberty and Necessity*, &c., 1676, *Heston, near Hounslow, Middlesex.*

Died.—Thales, Grecian philosopher, B.C. 546, *Olympia;* Edward III. of England, 1377, *Sheen, Richmond;* John Skelton, poet, 1529; Captain John Smith, colonizer of Virginia, 1631; Sir Inigo Jones, architect, 1651; William Beckford, Lord Mayor of London, 1770; John Armstrong, poet, 1797, *London;* Gilbert, first Earl of Minto, statesman. 1814; Mrs Mary Anne Clarke (*née* Farquhar), 1852.

SKELTON.

Skelton was poet laureate in the reign of Henry the Eighth. He had been at one time Henry's tutor, and was honoured with some appointment at the date of that monarch's accession, as a small token of royal favour. But neither his influence nor his merits seem to have procured him any other advancement in the church than the curacy of Trumpington, a village near Cambridge, and a living in Norfolk. He indulged a vein much too satirical to please those to whom his satire had reference, and probably made himself many enemies. 'A pleasant conceited fellow, and of a very sharp wit; exceeding bold, and could nip to the very quick when he once set hold.'

Skelton lived in the first dawn of that revival in poetry which brightened into a clear noon in the reign of Queen Bess; his verse is the veriest jingle imaginable. The reader will be curious to examine a specimen of the poetry of one whom so great a scholar as Erasmus called 'the glory and light of British literature.' One of the laureate's most fanciful effusions is a poem on a dead sparrow, named Philip, of whom Gib, the cat, had got hold. Perhaps the following is the most presentable extract we can make:

> 'Alas! my heart it stings,
> Remembering pretty things;
> Alas! mine heart it sleeth
> My Philip's doleful death.
> When I remember it,
> How prettily it would sit;
> Many times and oft,
> Upon my finger aloft,
> I played with him, tittle-tattle,
> And fed him with my spattle,
> With his bill between my lips,
> It was my pretty Phips.
> Many a pretty kusse
> Had I off his sweet musse.
> And now the cause is thus,
> That he is slain me fro,
> To my great pain and woe.'

But Skelton's favourite theme was abuses in the church. This is the title of one of his indiscriminate satirical attacks: *Here after foloweth a little boke called Colyn Clout, compiled by Master Skelton, Poet Laureate.* As a clue to

what is coming, the author is pleased to prefix a Latin motto: 'Who will rise up with me against the evil-doers, or who will defend my cause against the workers of iniquity? *No man, Lord.*' Skelton begins at once to cut at what he considers the root of the evil;—to wit, the bishops. He tells us what strange reports of their doings have reached him:

> 'Men say indede
> How they take no hede
> Their sely shepe to fede,
> But plucke away and pul
> The fleces of their wull.'

He hears how

> 'They gaspe and they gape,
> Al to have promocion;'

and then he draws an inference which must have been harrowing to a bishop's conscience:

> 'Whiles the heades doe this,
> The remnaunt is amis
> Of the clergy all,
> Both great and small.'

Skelton is willing to make all possible excuses for their lordships; he allows, indeed, the report of 'the temporality' to be well founded, that

> 'bishoppes disdain
> Sermons for to make,
> Or such labour to take;'

but he says this is not to be ascribed in every case to sloth, for that some of them have actually no alternative:

> 'They have but small art,
> And right sclender cunnyng
> Within their heades wunning.'

Then he proceeds to deal at some length with the minor orders. He dwells on sundry personal vices, to which those more insignificant offenders were commonly addicted, but reserves his severest satire for their vile ignorance. They know nothing, he says: they catch a 'Dominus Vobiscum by the head,' and make it serve all religious ends. And yet such men will presume to the office of teacher:

> 'Take they cures of soules
> And woketh never what they rede,
> Pater noster nor crede;'

and as to their construing:

> 'Construe not worth a whistle
> Nether Gospel nor Pistle.'

We must really join with the poet in his philosophic deduction from this survey:

> 'A priest without a letter,
> Without his virtue be greater,
> Doutlesse were much better
> Upon him for to take
> A mattocke or a rake.'

It was not to be expected that so virulent a truth-teller would escape the net of the wicked. It happened that Skelton—not being allowed, as a priest, to marry—had thought himself justified in evading what he considered an unfair rule by simply overlooking the ceremony. For this ingenious proceeding, Nix, Bishop of Norwich, took occasion to suspend him. But worse was to come. Having presumed to attack Wolsey in the very height of his power, that proud prelate was fain to procure a writ of arrest ; and so honest Skelton had to take sanctuary at Westminster, and remained there till his death.

One of Skelton's poems is a long one in his usual incoherent style, entitled *The Tunning of Eleanour Rumming*, referring to an alewife so called, who dwelt

> 'In a certain stead
> Beside Leatherhead ;'

where he says—

> 'She breweth noppy ale,
> And maketh thereof fast sale
> To travellers, to tinkers,
> To sweaters, to swinkers,
> And all good ale-drinkers.'

She was, he assures us, one of the most frightful of her sex, being

> '———— ugly of cheer,
> Her face all bowsy,
> Wondrously wrinkled ;
> Her een bleared,
> And she gray-haired.
> Her kirtle Bristow-red,
> With cloths upon her head
> That weigh a sow of lead.'

And when the reader surveys the annexed portrait of Eleanour, borrowed from the frontispiece of one of the original editions of the poem, he will probably acknowledge that Skelton did her no injustice.

ELEANOUR RUMMING.

> 'When Skelton wore the laurel crown,
> My ale put all the alewives down.'

Mr Dalloway, one of Skelton's editors, speculates on the possibility of the poet having made acquaintance with the Leatherhead alewife while residing with his royal master at Nonsuch Palace, eight miles off ; and he alleges that the domicile near the bridge still exists. This must be considered as requiring authentication. It appears, however, that there existed about the middle of the last century an alehouse on the road from Cambridge to Hardwicke, which bore a swinging sign, on which there could alone be discerned a couple of handled beer mugs, exactly in the relative situation of the two pots in the hands of Eleanour Rumming, as represented in her portrait. It looks as if it were a copy of that portrait, from which all had been obliterated but the pots ; or, if this surmise could not be received, there must have been some general

characteristic involved in such an arrangement of two ale-pots on a sign or portrait. The gentleman who communicated a sketch of the sign and its couple of pots to the *Gentleman's Magazine* for May 1794, recalled the *Thepas Amphikupellon* of Vulcan, adverted to by Homer, and as to which learned commentators were divided—some asserting it was a cup with two handles, while others believed it to be a cup internally divided. The sign of the *Two-pot House*—for so it was called—had convinced him that 'the Grecian poet designed to introduce neither a bi-ansated nor a bi-cellular pot, but a pot for each hand ; and consequently that a brace of pots, instead of a single one, were the legitimate object of his description.'

HENRY HUDSON, THE NAVIGATOR.

This ill-fated mariner was one of the most remarkable of our great English navigators of the

Elizabethan age, yet his history previous to the year 1607, when he sailed on his first recorded voyage, is entirely unknown. The Dutch appear to have invented, in order to support their claim to New Netherlands, a history of his previous life, according to which he had passed a part of it in the service of Holland; but this is not believed by the best modern writers on the subject. We first find Henry Hudson, in the year just mentioned, a captain in the service of the Muscovy Company, whose trade was carried on principally with the North, and who did not yet despair of increasing it by the discovery of a passage to China by the north-east or by the north-west. Hudson laboured with a rare energy to prove the truth or fallacy of their hopes, and he was at least successful in showing that some of them were delusive; and he would no doubt have done much more, had he not been cut off in the midst of his career. He acted first on a plan which had been proposed by an English navigator, named Robert Thorne, as early as the year 1527—that of sailing right across the north pole; and he left London for this voyage on the 23rd of April 1607. Among his companions was his son, John Hudson, who is described in the log-book as 'a boy,' and who seems to have accompanied his father in all his expeditions. He sailed by way of Greenland towards Spitzbergen, and in his progress met with the now well-known ice-barrier between those localities, and he was the first modern navigator who sailed along it. He eventually reached the coast of Spitzbergen, but after many efforts to overcome the difficulties which presented themselves in his way, he was obliged to abandon the hope of reaching the pole; and, after convincing himself that that route was impracticable, he returned home, and on the 15th of September arrived at Tilbury, in the Thames. On the 22nd of April in the following year (1608) Hudson, still in the employment of the Muscovy Company, sailed from London with the design of ascertaining the possibility of reaching China by the north-east, and, as we may now suppose, was again unsuccessful; he reached Gravesend on his return on the 26th of August. After his return from this voyage, Hudson was invited to Holland by the Dutch East India Company, and it was in their service that he made his third voyage. Sailing from Amsterdam on the 6th of April 1609, with two ships, manned partly by Dutch and partly by English sailors, he on the 5th of May reached the North Cape. It was originally intended to renew the search for a north-east passage, but in consequence of a mutiny amongst his crew when near Nova Zembla, he abandoned this plan, and sailed westward to seek a passage through America in lat. 40°. He had received vague information of the existence of the great inland lakes, and imagined that they might indicate a passage by sea through the mainland of America. It was on this voyage that he discovered the great river which has since borne his name; but his hopes were again disappointed, and he returned to England, and arrived at Dartmouth, in Devonshire, on the 7th of November. Hudson was detained in England by orders of the government, on what grounds is not known, while his

ship returned to Holland. The indefatigable navigator had now formed a design of seeking a passage by what has been named after him, Hudson's Straits; and on the 17th of April 1610 he started from London with this object, in a ship named the *Discovery*. During the period between the middle of July and the first days of August he passed through Hudson's Straits, and on the 4th of the latter month he entered the great bay which, from the name of its discoverer, has ever since been called Hudson's Bay. The months of August, September, and October were spent in exploring the southern coast of this bay, until, at the beginning of November, Hudson took up his winter quarters in what is supposed to have been the south-east corner of James's Bay, and the ship was soon frozen in. Hudson did not leave these winter quarters until the 18th of June following, and his departure was followed by the melancholy events which we have now to relate.

We have no reason for believing that Hudson was a harsh-tempered man; but his crew appears to have been composed partly of men of wild and desperate characters, who could only be kept in order by very severe discipline. Before leaving the Thames, he had felt it necessary to send away a man named Colburne, who appears to have been appointed as his second in command, probably because this man had shewn an inclination to dispute his plans and to disobey his orders; and while wandering about the southern coasts of Hudson's Bay, signs of insubordination had manifested themselves on more than one occasion, and had required all Hudson's energy to suppress them. The master's mate, Robert Juet, and the boatswain seem to have distinguished themselves by their opposition on these occasions; and shortly before they entered winter quarters they were deprived of their offices. But, as we learn from the rather full account left by Abacuk Prickett, one of the survivors of this voyage, the principal leader of the discontented was an individual who had experienced great personal kindnesses from Henry Hudson. This was a young man named Henry Green, of a respectable family of Kent, but who had been abandoned by his relatives for his extravagance and ill-conduct; during Hudson's last residence in London, Green seems to have been literally living on his charity. Finding that this Green could write well, and believing that he would be otherwise useful, Hudson took him out with him on his voyage as a sort of supernumerary, for he was not entered on the books of the company who sent out the ship, and had therefore no wages; but Hudson gave him provisions and lodgings in the ship as his personal attendant. In the beginning of the voyage Green quarrelled with several of the crew, and made himself otherwise disagreeable; but the favour of the captain (or master) saved him from the consequences, and he seems to have gradually gained the respect of the sailors for his reckless bravery. While the ship was locked up in the ice for the winter, the carpenter greatly provoked Hudson by refusing to obey his orders to build a timber hut on shore; and next day, when the carpenter chose to go on shore to shoot wild fowl, as it had been ordered that nobody should go away from the ship alone, Green, who had been industriously exciting the men against their captain, went with him. Hudson, who had perhaps received some intimation of his treacherous behaviour, was angry at his acting in this contemptuous manner, and shewed his displeasure in a way which embittered Green's resentment. Under these circumstances, it was not difficult to excite discontent among the men, for it seems to have been the first time that any of them had passed a winter in the ice, and they were not very patient under its rigour, for some of them were entirely disabled by the frost. One day, at the close of the winter, when the greater part of the crew were to go out a-fishing in the shallop (a large two-masted boat), Green plotted with others to seize the shallop, sail away with it, and leave the captain and a few disabled men in the ship; but this plot was defeated by a different arrangement made accidentally by Hudson. The conspiracy against the latter was now ripe, and Prickett, who was evidently more consenting to it than he is willing to acknowledge, tells us that when night approached, on the eve of the 21st of June, Green and Wilson, the new boatswain, came to him where he lay lame in his cabin, and told him 'that they and the rest and their associates would shift the company and turne the master and all the sicke men into the shallop, and let them shift for themselves.' The conspirators were up all night, while Hudson, apparently quite unconscious of what was going on, had retired to his cabin and bed. Probably he was in the habit of fastening his door; at all events, they waited till he rise in the morning, and as he left his cabin at an early hour, three of the men seized him from behind and pinioned him; and when he asked what they meant, they told him he should know when he was in the shallop. They then took all the sick and lame men out of their beds, and these, with the carpenter and one or two others who at the last remained faithful to their captain—not forgetting the boy John Hudson—were forced into the shallop. Then, as Prickett tells us, 'they stood out of the ice, the shallop being fast to the sterne of the shippe, and so (when they were nigh out, for I cannot say they were cleane out) they cut her head fast from the sterne of our shippe, then out with their topsails, and towards the east they [the mutineers] stood in a cleare sea.' This was the last that was ever seen or heard of Henry Hudson and his companions in misfortune. Most of them cripples, in consequence of the severity of the winter, without provisions, or means of procuring them, they must soon have perished in this inhospitable climate. The fate of the mutineers was not much better. For some time they wandered among coasts with which they were unacquainted, ran short of provisions, and failed in their attempts to gain a sufficient supply by fishing or shooting; and for some time seem to have lived upon little more than 'cockle-grass.' At first they seem to have proceeded without any rule or order; but finally Henry Green was allowed to assume the office of master or captain, and they were not decided as to the country in which they would finally seek a refuge, for they

thought 'that England was no safe place for them, and Henry Greene swore the shippe should not come into any place (but keep the sea still) till he had the king's majestie's hand and seal to shew for his safetie.' What prospect Green had of obtaining a pardon, especially while he kept out at sea, is altogether unknown; but he was not destined to survive long the effects of his treachery. On the 28th of July the mutineers came to the mouth of Hudson's Straits, and landed at the promontory which he had named Digges's Cape, in search of fowl. They there met with some of the natives, who showed so friendly a disposition, that Green—contrary, it seems, to the opinion of his companions—landed next day without arms to hold further intercourse with them. But the Indians, perceiving that they were unarmed, suddenly attacked them, and in the first onset Green was killed, and the others with great difficulty got off their boat and reached the ship, where Green's three companions, who were all distinguished by their activity in the mutiny, died of their wounds. Prickett, sorely wounded, and another man, alone escaped. Thus four of the most able hands were lost, and those who remained were hardly sufficient to conduct the ship. For some time they were driven about almost helpless, but they succeeded in killing a good quantity of fowl, which restored their courage. But when the fowls were eaten, they were again driven to great extremities. 'Now went our candles to wracke, and Bennet, our cooke, made a messe of meate of the bones of the fowle, frying them with candle-grease till they were crispe, and, with vinegar put to them, made a good dish of meate. Our vinegar was shared, and to every man a pound of candles delivered for a weeke, as a great daintie.' At this time Robert Juet, who had encouraged them by the assurance that they would soon be on the coast of Ireland, died of absolute starvation. 'So our men cared not which end went forward, insomuch as our master was driven to looke to their labour as well as his owne; for some of them would sit and see the fore sayle or mayne sayle flie up to the tops, the sheets being either flowne or broken, and would not helpe it themselves nor call to others for helpe, which much grieved the master.' At last they arrived on the Irish coast, but were received with distrust, and with difficulty obtained the means to proceed to Plymouth, from whence they sailed round to the Thames, and so to London. Prickett was a retainer of Sir Dudley Digges, one of the subscribers to the enterprise, through whom probably they hoped to escape punishment; but they are said to have been immediately thrown into prison, though what further proceedings were taken against them is unknown. Next year a captain named Batton was sent out in search of Hudson and his companions, and passed the winter of 1612 in Hudson's Bay, but returned without having obtained any intelligence of them. Thus perished this great but ill-fated navigator. Yet the name of the apparently obscure Englishman, of whose personal history we know so little, has survived not only in one of the most important rivers of the new continent, in the Strait through which he passed, and in the bay in which he wintered and perished, but in the vast extent of territory which lies between this bay and the Pacific Ocean, and which has so long been under the influence of the Hudson's Bay Company; and the results of his voyages have been still more remarkable, for, as it has been well observed, he not only bequeathed to his native country the fur-trade of the territory last mentioned, and the whale-fisheries of Spitzbergen, but he gave to the Dutch that North American colony which, having afterwards fallen into the hands of England, developed itself into the United States.

SEPULCHRAL VAGARIES.

Although it has been the general practice of our country, ever since the Norman era, to bury the dead in churchyards or other regular cemeteries, yet many irregular and peculiar burials have taken place in every generation. A few examples may be useful and interesting. They will serve to illustrate human eccentricity, and go far to account for the frequent discovery of human remains in mysterious or unexpected situations.

Many irregular interments are merely the result of the caprices of the persons there buried. Perhaps there is nothing that more forcibly shews the innate eccentricity of a man than the whims and oddities which he displays about his burial. He will not permit even death to terminate his eccentricity. His very grave is made to commemorate it, for the amusement or pity of future generations. These sepulchral vagaries, however, vary considerably both in character and degree. Some are whimsical and fantastical in the extreme; others, apparently, consist only in shunning the usual and appointed places of interment; while the peculiarity of others appears, not in the place, but in the mode of burial. We will now exemplify these remarks.

From a small Hertfordshire village, named Flaunden, there runs a lonely footpath across the fields to another village. Just at the most dreary part of this road, the stranger is startled by suddenly coming upon a modern-looking altar tomb, standing close by the path. It is built of bricks, is about two feet and a half high, and covered with a large stone slab, bearing this inscription :

' SACRED TO THE MEMORY OF
MR WILLIAM LIBERTY,
OF CHORLEY WOOD, BRICKMAKER,
WHO WAS BY HIS OWN DESIRE BURIED IN A VAULT
IN THIS PART OF HIS ESTATE.
HE DIED 21 APRIL 1777, AGED 53 YEARS.

HERE ALSO LIETH THE BODY OF
MRS ALICE LIBERTY.
WIDOW OF THE ABOVE-NAMED
WILLIAM LIBERTY,
SHE DIED 29 MAY 1809, AGED 82 YEARS.'

There is nothing peculiar about the tomb. It is just such a one as may be seen in any cemetery. But why was it placed here? Was it to commemorate Mr Liberty's independence of sepulchral rites and usages? or to inform posterity that this ground once was his own? or was it to scare the simple rustic as he passes by in the shades of evening? Certain it is that—

' The lated peasant dreads the dell,
For superstition 's wont to tell
Of many a grisly sound and sight,
Scaring its path at dead of night.'

About a mile from Great Missenden, a large Buckinghamshire village, stands a queer-looking building—a sort of dwarf pyramid, which is locally called 'Captain Backhouse's tomb.' It is built of flints, strengthened with bricks; is about eleven feet square at the base; the walls up to about four or five feet are perpendicular; then they taper pyramidically, but instead of terminating in a point, a flat slab-stone about three feet square forms the summit. There is a small Gothic window in the north wall, and another in the south; the western and part of the southern walls are covered with ivy. (See the accompanying illustration.) This singular tomb stands in a thick wood

CAPTAIN BACKHOUSE'S TOMB.

or plantation, on a lofty eminence, about a quarter of a mile from Havenfield Lodge, the house in which Mr Backhouse resided. He had been a major or captain in the East Indian service, but quitting his military life, he purchased this estate, on which he built himself a house of one story, in Eastern fashion, and employed himself in planting and improving his property. He is described as a tall, athletic man, of a stern and eccentric character.

As he advanced in life his eccentricity increased, and one of his eccentric acts was the erection of his own sepulchre within his own grounds, and under his own superintendence. ' I'll have nothing to do,' said he, ' with the church or the churchyard ! Bury me there, in my own wood on the hill, and my sword with me, and I'll defy all the evil spirits in existence to injure me !' He died, at the age of eighty, on the 21st of June 1800, and was buried, or rather deposited, according to his own directions, in the queer sepulchre he himself had erected. His sword was placed in the coffin with him, and the coffin reared upright within a niche or recess in the western wall, which was then built up in front, so that he was in fact *immured*. It is said in the village that he was never married, but had two or three illegitimate sons, one of whom became a Lieutenant-General. This gentleman, returning from India about seven years after his father's death, had his father's body removed to the parish churchyard, placing over his grave a large handsome slab, with a suitable inscription ; and this fact is recorded in the parish register—

' August 8th, 1807.—The remains of Thomas Backhouse, Esq., removed, by a faculty from the Archdeacon of Buckingham, from the mausoleum in Havenfield to the churchyard of Great Missenden, and there interred.'

This removal has given rise to a popular notion in the village that Mr Backhouse was buried on his estate, ' to keep possession of it till his son returned. For, don't you see,' say these village oracles, 'that when his son came back from abroad, and took possession of the property, he had his father's corpse taken from the queer tomb in Havenfield Wood, and decently buried in the churchyard?'

This 'queer tomb' has occasioned some amusing adventures, one of which was the following. As some boys were birds'-nesting in Havenfield Wood, they came up to this tomb, and began to talk about the dead man that was buried there, and that it was still haunted by his ghost; when one boy said to another, 'Jack, I'll lay you a penny you dursn't put your head into that window, and shout out, Old Backhouse!' 'Done!' said Jack. They struck hands, and the wager was laid. Jack boldly threw down his cap, and thrust his head in through the window, and called aloud, 'Old ——' His first word roused an owl within from a comfortable slumber; and she, bewildered with terror, rushed to the same window, her usual place of exit, to escape from this unwonted intrusion. Jack, still more terrified than the owl, gave his head a sudden jerk up, and stuck it fast in the narrow part of the window. Believing the owl to be the dead man's ghost, his terror was beyond conception. He struggled, he kicked, he shrieked vociferously. With this hubbub the owl became more and more terrified. She rushed about within—flapping her wings, hooting, screeching, and every moment threatening frightful onslaughts on poor Jack's head. The rest of the boys, imagining Jack was held fast by some horrid hobgoblin, rushed away in consternation, screaming and bellowing at the full pitch of their voices. Fortunately, their screams drew to them some workmen from a neighbouring field, who, on hearing the cause of the alarm, hastened to poor Jack's assistance. He had liberated himself from his thraldom, but was lying panting and unconscious on the ground. He was carried home, and for some days it was feared his intellect was impaired; but after a few weeks he perfectly recovered, though he never again put his head into Captain Backhouse's tomb, and his adventure has become safely enrolled among the traditions of Missenden.

Sir William Temple, Bart., a distinguished statesman and author, who died at his seat of Moor Park, near Farnham, in 1700, ordered his heart to be enclosed in a silver box, or china basin, and buried under 'a sun-dial in his garden, over against a window from whence he used to contemplate and admire the works of God, after he had retired from worldly business.' Sir James Tillie, knight, who died in 1712, at his seat of Pentilly Castle, in Cornwall, was buried by his own desire under a tower or summer-house which stood in a favourite part of his park, and in which he had passed many joyous hours with his friends. *

A baronet, of some military fame, who died in a mıdland county in 1823, directed in his will that after hɪ death his body should be opened by a medical man, and afterwards covered with a sere-cloth, or other such perishable material, and thus interred, without a coffin, in a particular spot in his park; and that over his grave should be sown a quantity of acorns, from which the most promising plant being selected, it should be there preserved and carefully cultured, 'that after my death my body may not be entirely useless, but may serve to rear a good English oak.' He left a small legacy to his gardener, 'to see that the plant is well watered, and kept free from weeds.' The directions of the testator were fully complied

* The story of his being buried in an arm-chair, with 'a table before him garnished with bottles, glasses, &c.' as stated in Notes and Queries, vol. vi. 448, is without foundation, as proved by his will

with, except that the interment, instead of being in the prescribed spot, took place in the churchyard adjoining the mansion. The oak over the grave is now a fine healthy tree.

Baskerville, the famous printer, who died in 1775, is said to have been buried by his own desire under a windmill near his garden. Samuel Johnson, an eccentric dancing-master in Cheshire, who died in 1773, aged eighty-two, was, by his own request to the owner, buried in a plantation forming part of the pleasure-grounds of the Old Hall at Gawsworth, near Macclesfield; and a stone stating the circumstances still stands over his grave. A farmer named Trigg, of Stevenage, Herts, directed his body to be enclosed in lead, and deposited in the tie-beam of the roof of a building which was once his barn; and where it may still be seen. The coffin enclosing the body of another eccentric character rests on a table in the summer-house belonging to a family residence in Northamptonshire.

Mr Hull, a bencher of the Inner Temple, who died in 1772, was buried beneath Leith Hill Tower, in Surrey, which he had himself erected a few years before his death.

Thomas Hollis, a gentleman of considerable property, resided for some years before his death on his estate at Corscomb, in Dorset. He was very benevolent, an extreme Liberal, and no less eccentric. In his will, which was in other respects remarkable, he ordered his body to be buried ten feet deep in any one of certain fields of his lying near his house; and that the whole field should immediately afterwards be ploughed over, that no trace of his burial-place might remain. It is remarkable that, while giving directions to a workman in one of these very fields, he suddenly fell down, and almost instantly expired, on the 1st of January 1774, in the fifty-fourth year of his age, when he was buried according to his directions. It is the popular opinion that these irregular burials are the result of infidelity. But this opinion must be received with great caution, for in most instances it might be proved to be erroneous. Mr Hollis, for example, was a large benefactor to both Church and Dissent. He attended the public worship of both; nearly rebuilt, at his own cost, the parish church at Corscomb; and the last words he uttered were, 'Lord have mercy upon me! Receive my soul!'*

Instances of persons desiring to be buried in some favourite spot are too numerous to be specified. A few examples only will suffice to illustrate this peculiarity. Mr Booth, of Brush House, Yorkshire, desired to be buried in his shrubbery, because he himself had planted it, and passed some of his happiest hours about it. Doctor Renny, a physician at Newport Pagnel, Bucks, for a similar reason was buried in his garden, on a raised plot of ground, surrounded by a sunk fence. In the same county, near a village named Radnage, Thomas Withers, an opulent German, who died January 1st, 1843, aged sixty-three, was by his own direction buried 'beneath the shade of his own trees, and in his own ground.' But one of the most interesting burials of this description is on the Chiltern Hills, in the same county. It is called The Shepherd's Grave, and though in the parish of Aston Clinton, is yet far away from the village and the habitations of man; it is in a lonely spot on the Chilterns, that remarkable range of hills which crosses Buckinghamshire, and stretches on the one side into Berks, and on the other into Bedfordshire. High on a towering knoll, it commands a fine panoramic view of the whole surrounding country. To this spot, about a century ago, a shepherd named Faithful was wont to lead his flock day by day, to depasture on the heathery turf around. Here, from

* Hutchins's History of Dorset, vol. i. 425.

morning to night, was his usual resting-place. Here he sat to eat his rustic meals. Here he rested to watch his sheep, as, widely spread before and around him, they diligently nibbled the scanty herbage of these chalky downs. Here, without losing sight of his flock, he could survey a vast expanse of earth and heaven—could contemplate the scenes of nature, and admire many a celebrated work of man. Here, as he sat at perfect ease, his eye could travel into six counties—a hundred churches came within the compass of his glance—mansions and cottages, towns and villages in abundance lay beneath his feet. And he was not a man whose mind slept while his eyes beheld the wonders of nature or of art; he became a wise and a learned, though unlettered philosopher.

> 'His head was silvered o'er with age,
> And long experience made him sage;
> In summer's heat and winter's cold
> He fed his flock and penned his fold;
> His wisdom and his honest fame
> Through all the country raised his name.'

The spot which had been from youth to age the scene of his labours, his meditations, and enjoyments, had become so endeared to him, that he wished it to become his last earthly resting-place. 'When my spirit has fled to those glorious scenes above,' said he to his fellow-shepherds, 'then lay my body here.' He died, and there they buried him. And let no one say it was to him unconsecrated ground. It had been hallowed by his strict attention to duties; by meditations which had refined and elevated his mind; by heavenly aspirations, and spiritual communion with Him who is the only true sanctifier of all that is holy. His neighbours cut in the turf over his grave this rude epitaph—

> 'Faithful lived, and Faithful died,
> Faithful lies buried on the hill side;
> The hill so wide the fields surround,
> In the day of judgment he'll be found.'

Up to a recent period the shepherds and rustics of the neighbourhood were accustomed 'to scour' the letters; and as they were very large, and the soil chalky, the words were visible at a great distance. The 'scouring' having been discontinued, the word 'Faithful' alone could be discerned in 1848, but the grave is still held in reverence, and generally approached with solemnity by the rustics of the neighbourhood.

A burial, which turned out to be remarkable in its results, took place on the moors near Hope, in Derbyshire. In the year 1674 a farmer and his female servant, in crossing these moors on their way to Ireland, were lost in the snow, with which they continued covered from January to May. Their bodies on being found were in such an offensive state that the coroner ordered them to be buried on the spot. Twenty-nine years after their burial, for some reason or other now unknown, their graves were opened, and their bodies were found to be in as perfect a state as those of persons just dead. The skin had a fair and natural colour, and the flesh was soft and pliant; and the joints moved freely, without the least stiffness. In 1716, forty-two years after the accident, they were again examined in the presence of the clergyman of Hope, and were found still in the same state of preservation. Even such portions of dress as had been left on them had undergone no very considerable change. Their graves were about three feet deep, and in a moist and mossy soil.[*] The antiseptic qualities of moss are well known.

Many ancient burials were curious, as the following instances exemplify. Geoffrey de Mandeville, Earl of Essex, though the founder of the rich Abbey of Walden, and in other ways a liberal benefactor to the Church, was excommunicated for taking possession of the Abbey of Ramsey and converting it into a fortress, which he did in a case of extremity, to save himself from the sword of his pursuers. While under this sentence of excommunication, he was mortally wounded in the head by an arrow from the bow of a common soldier. 'He made light of the wound,' says an ancient writer, 'but he died of it in a few days, under excommunication. See here the just judgment of God, memorable through all ages! While that abbey was converted into a fortress, blood exuded from the walls of the church and the cloister adjoining, witnessing the Divine indignation, and prognosticating the destruction of the impious. This was seen by many persons, and I observed it with my own eyes.'[*]

Having died while under sentence of excommunication, the earl, notwithstanding his liberal benefactions to the Church, was inadmissible to Christian burial. But just before he breathed his last some Knights-Templars visited him, and finding him very penitent, from a sense of compassion, or of gratitude for bounties received from him, they threw over him 'the habit of their order, marked with a red cross,' and as soon as he expired, 'carried his dead body into their orchard at the Old Temple in London; and coffining it in lead, hanged it on a crooked tree.' Some time afterwards, 'by the industry and expenses' of the Prior of Walden, absolution for the earl was obtained from Pope Alexander III.; and now his dead body, which had been hung like a scarecrow on the branch of a tree, became so precious that the Templars and the Prior of Walden contended for the honour of burying it. The Templars, however, triumphed by burying it privately or secretly in the porch before the west door of the New Temple.[†] 'So that his body,' continues Dugdale, 'was received amongst Christians, and divine offices celebrated for him.'

Howel Sele was buried in the hollow trunk of a tree, which from him received the name of 'Howel's Oak.' Owen Glendour, his cousin, but feudal adversary, having killed him in single combat, Madoc, a friend and companion of Owen, in order to hide the dead body from Howel's vassals who were searching for him, thrust it into a hollow tree. The circumstance is thus given in the popular ballad, in the words of Madoc:—

> 'I marked a broad and blasted oak,
> Scorched by the lightning's livid glare;
> Hollow its stem from branch to root,
> And all its shrivelled arms were bare.
> Be this, I cried, his proper grave
> (The thought in me was deadly sin);
> Aloft we raised the helpless chief,
> And dropped his bleeding corpse within.'

The tree is still pointed out to strangers as 'Howel's Oak,' or, 'The spirit's blasted tree.'

> 'And to this day the peasant still,
> With cautious fear, avoids the ground;
> In each wild branch a spectre sees,
> And trembles at each rising sound.'

We sometimes meet with a peculiar kind of ancient burial, which is chiefly interesting from the amusing legends connected with it. This is where the stone coffin, which contains the remains of the deceased, is placed within an external recess in the wall of a church, or under a low arch passing completely through the wall, so that the coffin, being in the middle of the wall, is seen equally within and without the church. At Brent Pelham, Herts, there is a monument of this

---

[*] See *Wanderings of a Pen and Pencil*, 336.

[*] Henry of Huntingdon's *Chronicle*.
[†] Dugdale's *Baronage*, vol. i. p. 203.

description in the north wall of the nave. It is supposed to commemorate O' Piers Shonkes, lord of a manor in the parish. The local tradition is, that by killing a certain serpent he so exasperated the spiritual dragon, that he declared he would have the body of Shonkes when he died, whether he was buried within or without the church. To avoid such a calamity, Shonkes ordered his body to be placed *in the wall*, so as to be neither inside nor outside the church. This tomb, says Chauncey, had formerly the following inscription over it :—

'Tantum fama manet, Cadmi Sanctiq. Georgi
Posthuma, Tempus edax ossa, sepulchra vorat ;
Hoc tamen in muro tutus, qui perdidit anguem,
Invito, positus, Demonæ Shonkus erat.'

' Nothing of Cadmus nor St George, those names
Of great renown, survives them but their fames ;
Time was so sharp set as to make no bones
Of theirs, nor of their monumental stones.
But Shonkes one serpent kills, t'other defies,
And in this wall as in a fortress lies.'*

In the north wall of the church of Tremeirchion, North Wales, there is a tomb which is said to commemorate a necromancer priest, who died vicar of the parish about 1340. The tradition here is that this priestly wizard made a compact with the ' Prince of Magicians,' that if he would permit him to practise the black art with impunity during his life, he should possess his body at his death, whether he was buried in or out of the church. The wily priest outwitted his subtle master, by ordering his body to be buried neither inside nor outside of the church, but in the middle of its wall.† There are so many similar tombs, with similar legends connected with them, that one cannot but wonder the master of subtilty should have been so often outwitted by the same manœuvre.

The dreadful punishment of immuring persons, or burying them alive in the walls of convents, was undoubtedly sometimes resorted to by monastic communities. Skeletons thus built up in cells or niches have frequently been found in the ruins of monasteries and nunneries. A skeleton thus immured was discovered in the convent of Penwortham, Lancashire ; and Sir Walter Scott, who mentions a similar discovery in the ruins of Coldingham Abbey, thus describes the process of immuring :—' A small niche, sufficient to inclose the body, was made in the massive wall of the convent ; a slender pittance of food and water was deposited in it, and the awful words, VADE IN PACEM, were the signal for immuring the criminal.'

On this awful species of punishment Sir Walter Scott has founded one of the striking episodes in his poem of *Marmion*. We can only give a short extract. Two criminals are to be immured—a beautiful nun who had fled after her lover, and a sordid wretch whom she had employed to poison her rival. They are now in a secret crypt or vault under the convent, awaiting the awful sentence.

' Yet well the luckless wretch might shriek,
Well might her paleness terror speak !
For there were seen, in that dark wall,
Two niches,—narrow, deep, and tall ;
Who enters at such griesly door,
Shall ne'er, I ween, find exit more.
  *   *   *   *   *
And now that blind old abbot rose,
To speak the chapter's doom
On those the wall was to inclose
Alive, within the tomb,

* *History of Herts*, vol. i. 284.
† *Notes and Queries*, vol. ii. 513.

But stopped, because that woeful maid,
Gathering her powers, to speak essayed.'

After revealing the cause of her flight, she is very effectively described as concluding with these prophetic words—

'Yet dread me from my living tomb,
Ye vassal slaves of bloody Rome !
  *   *   *   *   *
Behind a darker hour ascends !
The altars quake, the crosier bends ;
The ire of a despotic king
Rides forth upon destruction's wing.
Then shall these vaults, so strong and deep,
Burst open to the sea-winds' sweep ;
Some traveller then shall find my bones,
Whitening amid disjointed stones,
And, ignorant of priests' cruelty,
Marvel such relics here should be.'

We have also instances on record of persons being buried alive in the earth. Leland, in his account of Brackley, in Northamptonshire, says :— ' In the churcheyarde lyethe an image of a priest revested (divested), the whiche was Vicar of Brakeley, and there buried quike by the tyranny of a Lord of the Towne, for a displeasure that he tooke with hym for an horse taken, as some say, for a mortuarie. But the Lord, as it is there sayde, went to Rome for absolution, and toke greate repentauns.'

In *Notes and Queries*, vol. vi. p. 245, we are informed that, in the parish of Ensbury, Dorset, there is a tradition that on a spot called Patty Barn a man was many years ago buried alive up to the neck, and a guard set over him to prevent his being removed or fed by friends, so that he was left to die in this wretched state from starvation.

Another instance of this kind of burial, with which we will conclude, is connected with a curious family legend. Sir Robert de Shurland, Lord of Shurland, in the Isle of Sheppy, Kent, was attached to a lady who unhappily died unanointed and unaneled, and consequently the priest refused to bury her with the rites of sepulture. Sir Robert, roused to madness by the indignity, ordered his vassals to bury the priest alive. Perhaps he did not expect to be obeyed. But his obsequious vassals instantly executed his command to the letter. Hereupon the impetuous knight, having somewhat cooled, became alarmed ; and fearing the consequences of his sacrilegious murder, mounted his favourite charger, swam across the arm of the sea which separated Sheppy from the main land, galloped to court, and obtained the king's pardon for a crime which he had, he said, unwittingly committed in a fit of grief and indignation. ' He made the church a present, by the way,' to atone for his crime ; but the prior of a neighbouring convent predicted that the gallant steed which had now saved his life would hereafter be the cause of his death. Like a prudent man, he ordered the poor horse to be stabbed, and thrown into the sea with a stone tied round his neck ; and, in self-gratulation, assumed the motto, ' Fato prudentia major' (Prudence is superior to fate). Twenty years afterwards the aged knight was hobbling on the sands, in all the ' dignity of gout,' when he saw a horse's skeleton with a stone fastened round the neck. Giving it a kick, ' Ah !' he exclaimed, ' this must be my poor old horse.' The sharp points of the vertebræ pierced through his velvet shoe, and inflicted a wound in his toe which ended in mortification and death ; thus fulfilling the prediction. The tomb of Sir Robert Shurland is still to be seen in Minster Church, under a Gothic arch in the south wall. The effigy is cross-legged, and on the right side is sculptured a horse's head emerging from the waves of the sea, as if in the act of swimming. The vane of the tower of the church represented in Grose's time a horse's head, and the church was called 'The Horse Church.'[*]

John Wilkinson, the great ironfounder, having made his fortune by the manufacture of iron, determined that his body should be encased by his favourite metal when he died. In his will he directed that he should be buried in his garden, in an iron coffin, with an iron monument over him of twenty tons weight; and he was so buried within thirty yards of his mansion of Castlehead. He had the coffin made long before his death, and used to take pleasure in showing it to his visitors, very much to the horror of many of them. He would also make a present of an iron coffin to any one who might desire to possess one. When he came to be placed in his narrow bed, it was found that the coffin he had provided was too small, so he was temporarily interred until another could be made. When placed in the ground a second time, the coffin was found to be too near the surface; accordingly it was taken up, and an excavation cut in the rock, after which it was buried a third time. On the Castlehead estates being sold in 1828, the family directed the coffin again to be taken up, and removed to the neighbouring chapel-yard of Lindale, where it now lies. A man who assisted at all the four interments was still living at the latter place in 1862.[†]

JUNE 22.

St Alban, protomartyr of Britain, 303. St Paulinus, Bishop of Nola, confessor, 431.

ST ALBAN.

St Alban has the honour of being regarded as the first British martyr. The bloody persecution of Dioclesian, which raged in other parts of the Roman empire with such terrible fury that Dioclesian declared the Christians exterminated, was kept in check in Gaul and Britain by Constantius, who governed those provinces with almost regal authority. But some few are alleged to have suffered, and among these St Alban was first. He sheltered a priest, whose name was Amphibalus, who is said to have converted him; and when he could conceal him no longer, he assisted his escape by changing clothes with him. For this act Alban was brought before the governor, condemned, and beheaded.

The execution took place at Verulam, and in remembrance of the martyr, the name of Verulam was changed to St Alban's. Ingulphus tells us, in his *History of the Abbey of Croyland*, that Offa, king of Mercia, 'founded a monastery of Black Monks at the city of Verulam, in honour of God and of St Alban, the protomartyr of the English,' in the year 793. In time, this became one of the richest and most beautiful abbacies in England, and its superior was in 1154 invested by Pope Adrian IV. with the privilege of taking the first place among the mitred abbots in parliament. Of its original grandeur some idea, though but a faint one, may still be acquired by a survey of the church, which continues to be used as a parochial place of worship.

When we view the ancient and still surviving grandeur of the church of St Alban's and its

[*] See Grose's *Antiquities*, vol. iii. 77.
[†] Smiles's *Lives of the Engineers*, vol. ii. 338, *note*.

appurtenances, it becomes a curious reflection that great doubts now exist whether St Alban himself ever had an existence.

Born.—Robert Nelson (works of divinity), 1656, *London*; Jacques Delille, French poet, 1738, *Aigues-Perse, Auvergne*; Thomas Day, author of *Sandford and Merton*, 1748, *London*.

Died.—Nicolas Machiavel, Florentine statesman, 1527, *Florence*; Bishop John Fisher, beheaded on *Tower Hill*, 1535; Catherine Philips, poetess, 1664, *Fleet Street, London*; Matthew Henry, biblical commentator, 1714; Jean-Pierre de Bougainville, French poet, 1763; R. B. Haydon, artist, 1846, *London*.

BATTLE OF MORAT.

On the 22nd of June 1476, was fought at Morat in Switzerland one of the most sanguinary battles on record. The defeated party was Charles Duke of Burgundy, the last of a series of independent princes, who, with a territory which now forms eastern France, had for four generations maintained themselves in great power and splendour. Philip de Commines tells us of the magnificence of Charles the Bold, Duke of Burgundy, and of the luxurious opulence of his subjects, from personal observation. Up to the year 1475, he was an object of terror to the astute Louis XI., who had reason to dread that, if the duke succeeded in mastering Provence, the kings of France would not be able to hold intercourse with the rest of Europe, except by his permission. Everything seemed in a fair way to make Charles a dangerously powerful sovereign, when an infatuation overtook him, in consequence of a dispute arising from a trivial cause with his poor neighbours the Swiss.

Charles, having taken from them the town of Granson, imprudently advanced to meet them at the bottom of their own mountains, carrying with him all the plate, jewels, and other articles which he generally used at home. Most unexpectedly, a panic seized the mass of his army, and the Swiss gained a victory, attended by little slaughter, but by the seizure of an immense amount of valuables (April 2, 1476). The allies of the duke quickly showed by their coldness how slight a hold he had upon their friendship, and how critical another defeat would be: but he nevertheless persisted in his absurd war, and in less than three months came to another collision with the Swiss, in circumstances fully as unfavourable to himself as before. The two armies, each about 30,000 strong, met in a straitened situation beside the lake of Morat, when once more the forces of the duke were defeated, but this time with immense slaughter. All the Burgundians who stood to fight, or could be overtaken by the cavalry of the enemy, were massacred; so that 'cruel as at Morat' became a proverb. The wretched duke escaped; but the mortification of defeat did not give him wisdom. He persisted in the war for a few months longer, and was slain in a final defeat at Nancy, in Lorraine (January 1477), along with the best of his remaining adherents. The fall of the house of Burgundy was accomplished in less than a year. It naturally excited great wonder and much comment among surrounding states. De Commines could not conceive what should provoke the displeasure of the Almighty against the duke, 'unless it was his self-love and arrogance,'—a sufficient reason for the fall of both princes and people, without the supposition of any miracle, as has been proved in many cases, and will yet be in many others.

DAY, THE DIVER.

On the 22nd of June 1774, a man named John Day lost his life in a manner singularly exhibiting the great ignorance with respect to the simplest physical facts which prevailed at the period. Day, an ignorant but ingenious millwright, fancied that he had invented a plan by which he could remain below water, at any depth, and without any communication with the air, for at least twenty-four hours; returning to the surface whenever he thought proper. As no useful purpose could be promoted by this assumed discovery, Day thought of turning it to account as a means of making money by betting, and accordingly placed himself in communication with one Blake, a well-known sporting character of the period. A contract was soon entered into between Blake and Day, the former engaging to furnish funds for constructing Day's diving machine, and to pay him ten per cent. on the amount of all bets gained by it.

Day's plan, if it had no other merit, had that of simplicity. His machine was merely a watertight box, or compartment, attached to an old vessel by means of screws. After entering the box, and carefully closing the hole of entrance, the vessel was to be sunk, and Day, being provided with a wax taper and a watch, would at the time appointed disengage his box from the vessel by drawing the screws, and thus rise to the surface. Granting that a man could live, let alone a taper burn, without a constant supply of fresh air, nothing could be easier than Day's proposed plan; but, at the present time, it must be a very young and ill-informed child that does not perceive the glaring absurdity of the proposition.

So confident, however, were the partners in this strangest of gambling speculations, that Blake at once commenced accepting bets that he would not, within the space of three months, cause a man to be sunk 100 feet deep under water, without any communication with air, for twelve hours; the man, at the exact termination of that time, rising to the surface of his own accord, and by his own exertions. While Blake was busy making his bets, Day on his part was as actively engaged at Plymouth in constructing his machine. He then seems to have acquired, from the shipwrights he employed, some idea of the difficulty of his undertaking, as far as regards the great pressure of water at a considerable depth. This caused delay, as he was induced to make his diving-box larger and stronger than he at first intended, and the three months elapsed before all was ready. Blake consequently lost his bets; but he paid them cheerfully, hoping for better luck the next time.

Soon afterwards, the machine being finished, Blake went down to Plymouth to superintend the first trial of the affair. A place in Plymouth Sound, twenty-two fathoms (132 feet) in depth, having been selected, the vessel was towed thither; and Day, provided with a bed, a watch, a taper, some biscuits, and a bottle of water, entered the box which was to be his tomb. The box was then tightly closed according to his directions, and the vessel to which it was attached sank to the bottom, from whence neither it nor the unfortunate man ever arose.

Thus a clever, enterprising, but ignorant man perished, through want of a knowledge possessed by almost every child at the present day. Nor was the ingenious country millwright alone ignorant that fresh air is the first necessity of life. A pretentious monthly periodical of the time, *The British Magazine of Arts, Sciences, and Literature*, though it assigns four probable reasons for Day's failure, never alludes to the most patent and prominent one—the want of fresh air.

A BALLOON DUEL.

Perhaps the most remarkable duel ever fought took place in 1808. It was peculiarly French in its tone, and could hardly have occurred under any other than a French state of society. M. de Grandpré and M. le Pique had a quarrel, arising out of jealousy concerning a lady engaged at the Imperial Opera, one Mademoiselle Tirevit. They agreed to fight a duel to settle their respective claims; and in order that the heat of angry passion should not interfere with the polished elegance of the proceeding, they postponed the duel for a month—the lady agreeing to bestow her smiles on the survivor of the two, if the other was killed; or at all events, this was inferred by the two men, if not actually expressed. The duellists were to fight in the air. Two balloons were constructed, precisely alike. On the day denoted, De Grandpré and his second entered the car of one balloon, Le Pique and his second that of the other; it was in the garden of the Tuileries, amid an immense concourse of spectators. The gentlemen were to fire, not at each other, but at each other's balloons, in order to bring them down by the escape of gas; and as pistols might hardly have served for this purpose, each aëronaut took a blunderbuss in his car. At a given signal the ropes that retained the cars were cut, and the balloons ascended. The wind was moderate, and kept the balloons at about their original distance of eighty yards apart. When about half a mile above the surface of the earth, a preconcerted signal for firing was given. M. le Pique fired, but missed. M. de Grandpré fired, and sent a ball through Le Pique's balloon. The balloon collapsed, the car descended with frightful rapidity, and Le Pique and his second were dashed to pieces. De Grandpré continued his ascent triumphantly, and terminated his aërial voyage successfully at a distance of seven leagues from Paris!

JUNE 23.

St Etheldreda, or Audry, virgin and abbess of Ely, 679. St Mary of Oignies, 1213.

Born.—Bishop John Fell, 1625, *Longworth ;* Gottfried Wilhelm Leibnitz, historian, philosopher, 1646, *Leipsic.*

Died. —Caius Flaminius, killed at the battle of Thrasimene, B.C. 217 ; Louis I. of France (Le Débonnaire), 840 ; Mary Tudor, Duchess of Suffolk, 1533 ; Mark Akenside, poet, 1770 ; Catherine Macaulay (Mrs Graham), historian, 1791, *Binfield;* James Mill, author of the *History of India*, &c., 1836, *Kensington;* Lady Hester Stanhope, 1839, *Lebanon;* John Lord Campbell, Lord Chancellor of England, 1861.

MRS MACAULAY.

There was a Macaulay's *History of England* long before Lord Macaulay's was heard of ; and in its day a famous history it was. The first volume appeared in 1763 and the fifth in 1771, and the five quartos sold rapidly, and were replaced by two or three editions in octavo. It was entitled, *The History of England from the Accession of James I. to the Elevation of the House of Hanover*, and the author was Mrs Catharine Macaulay.

The historian was the daughter of John Sawbridge. a gentleman resident at Ollantigh, near Wye, Kent, where she was born in 1733. From her girlhood she was an eager and promiscuous reader, her favourite books being, as she herself tells us, ' the histories which exhibit liberty in its most exalted state in the annals of the Roman and Greek Republics.' 'Liberty,' she says, ' became the object of a secondary worship in my delighted imagination.' She was married when in her twenth-seventh year to Dr George Macaulay, a London physician, and excited by the conflict her enthusiastic republican opinions encountered in society, she set about writing her *History*, in which all characters and events were viewed through democratic spectacles. Female authorship was then more of a singularity than it is now, and her theme and her politics quickly raised her name into notoriety, and she was flattered and abused with equal vehemence. Her adversaries said she was horribly ugly (which she was not), and that in despair of admiration as a woman she was aspiring after glory as a man. Dr Wilson, a son of the Bishop of Sodor and Man, made her the present of a house and library in Bath worth £1,500, and, to the scandal of sober people, placed her statue in the chancel of St Stephen's, Walbrook, London, of which he was rector. One of her heartiest admirers was John Wilkes, and in the popular furor for 'Wilkes and Liberty' her *History* greatly profited. She made a trip to Paris in 1777, and there received most grateful attentions from Franklin, Turgot, Marmontel, and other Liberals. Madame Roland in her *Memoires* says : ' It was my ambition to be for France what Mrs Macaulay was for England.' In a dispute with Mrs Macaulay, Dr Johnson observed, ' You are to recollect, madam, that there is a monarchy in heaven ;' to which she replied, ' If I thought so, sir, I should never wish to go there.' One day at her house he put on a grave face, and said, ' Madam, I am now become a convert to your way of thinking. I am convinced that all mankind are upon an equal footing ; and, to give you an unquestionable proof, madam, that I am in earnest. here is a very sensible, civil, well-behaved fellow-citizen, your footman ; I desire that he may be allowed to sit down and dine with us.' ' I thus,' relates

810

the doctor, ' shewed her the absurdity of the levelling doctrine. She has never liked me since. Your levellers wish to level *down* as far as themselves ; but they cannot bear levelling *up* to themselves.'

Dr Macaulay died in 1778, and shortly after Mrs Macaulay married Mr Graham, a young Scotchman, a brother of the noted quack of the same name. The disparity of their years exposed her to much ridicule, and so offended Dr Wilson, that he removed her statue from St Stephen's, to the great satisfaction of his parishioners, who contemplated raising a motion in the ecclesiastical courts concerning it. She had corresponded for some years with Washington, and in 1785, accompanied by Mr Graham, she made a voyage to America, and spent three weeks in his society at Mount Vernon. On her return, she retired to a country-house in Leicestershire, where she died in 1791, aged 58.

In addition to her *History*, Mrs Macaulay was an active pamphleteer on politics, morals, and metaphysics, and always commanded a fair share of public attention. The *History* is sometimes met with at this day on the second-hand bookstalls, selling at little more than the price of waste paper. It is written in a vivacious style, but embodies no original thought or research, and is neither better nor worse than a series of republican harangues, in which the facts of English history under the Stuarts are wrought up from books which may be found in every gentleman's library.

JAMES MILL.

Though in a high degree romantic and wonderful, about no portion of their history do Englishmen shew less interest than in that which relates their struggles and conquests in India. On scarcely any matter is the attention of the House of Commons yielded less willingly than on Indian affairs. The reasons for this apathy may perhaps be traced to the complete division existing between the Hindoo and Englishman in race, mind, religion, and manners ; and to the multitude of diverse tribes and nations who crowd Hindostan, turning India into a mere geographical expression, and complicating its history in a way to which even German history affords but a faint resemblance. We may imagine how all this might have been changed had the peninsula of Hindostan, like China. been ruled by one emperor, whose power Britain had sapped and overthrown. Instead of this the great drama is diffused in a myriad of episodes, and that unity is lost by which alone popular interest can be enthralled.

Until James Mill published his *History of British India*, in 1818, any one who wished to attain the truth concerning most parts of that history had to seek for it in a chaos of books and documents. It was Mill's merit out of that chaos to evolve order. Many who have opened Mill's history for amusement, have closed it in weariness ; but Mill made no attempt at brilliancy, and was only careful to describe events accurately and clearly. From the first openings of intercourse with India to the establishment of the East India Company, in the reign of Queen

Anne, down to the end of the Mahratta war in 1805, he ran a straight, broad, and firm road through what had before been a jungle of hearsay, and voluminous and confused authorities. Mill was no mere compiler. He was a hard thinker and a philosopher; he thoroughly absorbed his matter, and reproduced it from his brain in a masterly digest, which has won the praise of all whose business it has been to consult him with serious purpose.

James Mill was the son of a shoemaker and small farmer, and was born at Montrose, on the 6th of April 1773. He was a thoughtful lad, and Sir John Stuart, of Fettercairn, unwilling that his talents should be hidden, sent him to Edinburgh University, with the purpose of educating him for a minister in the Scottish Church. Mill, however, had little inclination for the pulpit, and Dugald Stewart's lectures confirmed his taste for literature and philosophy in preference to theology. Long afterwards, in writing to a friend, he said, 'The taste for the studies which have formed my favourite pursuits, and which will be so to the end of my life, I owe to Dugald Stewart.' For some years he acted as a tutor or teacher, and in 1800, when in London, he accepted the editorship of *The Literary Journal*. This paper was a failure, but he soon secured other work, and for twenty years supported himself by writing for magazines and newspapers. Shortly after coming to London he married. In 1806 was born his celebrated son, John Stuart Mill, whose education, as well as that of eight other sons and daughters, he conducted. About 1806 he commenced the *History of British India* in the hours he could rescue from business, and in twelve years completed and gave it to the world in three quarto volumes. In the course of the history, he had meted out censure freely and honestly to the East India Company; but so highly were the directors impressed with the merits of the work, that in the spring of 1819 they appointed Mill to manage their finances, and subsequently their entire correspondence with India. In possession of affluence, Mill's pen was active as ever, his favourite themes being political economy and metaphysics. He was the intimate friend and constant visitor of Jeremy Bentham; their opinions on nearly all things coincided, and by many he was considered Bentham's ablest lieutenant. Mill died at Kensington, of consumption, on the 23rd of June 1836.

THE BOOK-FISH.

On the 23rd of June 1626, a cod-fish was brought to Cambridge market, which, upon being opened, was found to contain a book in its maw or stomach. The book was much soiled, and covered with slime, though it had been wrapped in a piece of sail-cloth. It was a duodecimo work written by one John Frith, comprising several treatises on religious subjects. In a letter now in the British Museum, written by Mr Mead, of Christchurch College, to Sir M. Stuteville, the writer says: 'I saw all with mine own eyes, the fish, the maw, the piece of sail-cloth, the book, and observed all I have written;

only I saw not the opening of the fish, which not many did, being upon the fish-woman's stall in the market, who first cut off his head, to which the maw hanging, and seeming much stuffed with somewhat, it was searched, and all found as aforesaid. He that had had his nose as near as I yester morning, would have been persuaded there was no imposture here without witness. The fish came from Lynn.'

The treatises contained in this book were written by Frith when in prison. Strange to say, he had been long confined in a fish cellar at Oxford, where many of his fellow-prisoners died from the impure exhalations of unsound salt fish. He was removed from thence to the Tower, and in 1533 was burned at the stake for his adherence to the reformed religion. The authorities at Cambridge reprinted the work, which had been completely forgotten, till it turned up in this strange manner. The reprint is entitled *Vox*

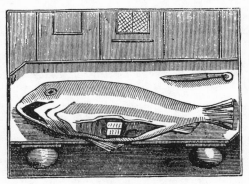

BOOK-FISH.

Piscis, or the Book-Fish, and is adorned with a woodcut representing the stall in Cambridge market, with the fish, book, and knife.

It also contains a few very feeble undergraduate jokes on the occasion; one is quite enough as a specimen of Cambridge wit at the period. 'A young scholar, who had, in a stationer's shop, peeped into the title of the Civil Law, then viewing this unconcocted book in the cod-fish, made a quibble thereupon; saying that it might have been found in the *Code*, but could never have entered into the *Digest*.'

CRESLOW PASTURES. A GHOST STORY.

The ancient manor of Creslow, which lies about half way between Aylesbury and Winslow, was granted by Charles II. to Thomas, first Lord Clifford of Chudleigh, on the 23rd of June 1673, and has continued ever since the property of his successors.

From possessing a fine old manor-house and the remains of an ancient church, as well as from historic associations, Creslow is not undeserving of notice. In the reign of Edward the Confessor, this manor was held by Aluren, a female, from whom it passed at the Conquest to Edward Sarisberi, a Norman lord. 'About the year 1120,' says Browne Willis, 'it was given to the Knights Templars, and on the suppression of that community, it passed to the Knights Hospitallers, from whom, at the dissolution of monasteries, it passed to the Crown. From this time till it passed to Lord Clifford, Creslow Manor was used as feeding ground for cattle for the royal household; and it is remarkable that nearly the whole of this manor, containing more than 850 acres, has been pasture land from the time of the Domesday survey, and the cattle now fed here are among the finest in the kingdom. While Creslow pastures continued in possession of the Crown, they were committed to the custody of a keeper. In 1596, James Quarles, Esq., Chief Clerk of the Royal Kitchen, was keeper of Creslow pastures. He was succeeded by Benett Mayne, a relative of the regicide, who was succeeded in 1634 by the regicide Cornelius Holland. This Cornelius Holland, whose father died insolvent in the Fleet, was 'a poore boy in court waiting on Sir Henry Vane,' by whose interest he was appointed by Charles I. keeper of Creslow pastures. He subsequently deserted the cause of his royal patron, and was rewarded by the Parliament with many lucrative posts. He entered the House of Commons in 1642, and after taking a very prominent part against the king, signed his death-warrant. He became so wealthy that, though he had ten children, he gave a daughter on her marriage £5,000, equal to ten times that sum at the present day. He is traditionally accused of having destroyed or dismantled many of the churches in the neighbourhood of Creslow.

At the Restoration, being absolutely excepted from the royal amnesty, he escaped execution only by flying to Lausanne, where, says Noble, 'he ended his days in universal contempt.'

Creslow, though once a parish with a fair proportion of inhabitants, now contains only the manor-house, and the remains of an ancient church. Originally the church consisted of a chancel, nave, and tower; but the present building, which is used as a coach-house, constituted apparently only the nave. It is forty-four feet long, and twenty-four feet wide, and built of hewn stone, though most other churches in the county are composed of rubble. The south wall, which contains the entrance to the coach-house, has been sadly mutilated. The north wall remains in tolerable preservation, and presents many features of interest. The doorway, which is of the Norman, or very early English period, is decorated with the billet and zigzag ornaments. The present windows, which have evidently superseded others of an earlier date, belong to the decorated style, and consisted each of two trefoil-headed lights divided by a chamfered mullion.

The boundary of the churchyard is not known, but the ground all round the church has been used for sepulture. A stone coffin, which is said to have been taken from the floor of the church, is now used, turned upside down and cracked through the middle, as a paving stone near the west door of the mansion.

From the quantity of human remains found about the church, it is evident that the interments here have been unusually numerous for a village cemetery. But this is accounted for by the fact that the Hospitallers, for their valiant exploits at the siege of Ascalon, were rewarded by Pope Adrian IV. with the privilege of exemption from all public interdicts and excommunications, so that in times of any national interdict, when all other churches were closed, the noble and wealthy would seek, at any cost or inconvenience, interment for their friends where the rites of sepulture could be duly celebrated. Here, then, in this privileged little cemetery, not only were interred many a puissant knight of St John, and their dependents, but some of the proudest and wealthiest barons of the land.

'I do love these ancient ruins;
　We never tread upon them but we set
　Our foot upon some reverend history;
　And questionless here in this open court,
　Which now lies naked to the injuries
　Of stormy weather, some men lie interred
Loved the church so well, and gave so largely to 't,
They thought it should have canopied their bones
Till Doomsday. But all things have an end:
Churches and cities, which have diseases like to
　　men,
Must have like death that we have.'

The mansion, though diminished in size and beauty, is still a spacious and handsome edifice. It is a picturesque and venerable looking build-

CRESLOW CHURCH, NORTH SIDE.

CRESLOW MANOR HOUSE.

ing with numerous gables and ornamental chimneys, some ancient mullioned windows, and a square tower with octagonal turret. The walls of the tower are of stone, six feet thick ; the turret is forty-three feet high, with a newel staircase and loopholes. Some of the more interesting objects within the house are the ground room in the tower, a large chamber called the banqueting room, with vaulted timber roof ; a large oak door with massive hinges, and locks and bolts of a peculiar construction ; and various remains of sculpture and carving in different parts of the house. Two ancient cellars, called ' the crypt' and ' the dungeon,' deserve special attention. The crypt, which is excavated in the solid limestone rock, is entered by a flight of stone steps, and has but one small window to admit light and air. It is about twelve feet square, and its roof, which is a good specimen of light Gothic vaulting, is supported by arches springing from four columns, groined at their intersections, and ornamented with carved flowers and bosses, the central one being about ten feet from the floor. The 'dungeon,' which is near the crypt, is entered by a separate flight of stone steps, and is a plain rectangular building, eighteen feet long, eight and a half wide, and six in height. The roof, which is but slightly vaulted, is formed of exceedingly massive stones. There is no window, or external opening into this cellar, and, for whatever purpose intended, it must have always been a gloomy, darksome vault, of extreme security. It now contains several skulls and other human bones—some of the thigh-bones, measuring more than nineteen inches, must have belonged to persons of gigantic stature. This dungeon had formerly a subterranean communication with the crypt, from which there was a newel staircase to a chamber above, which still retains the Gothic doorway, with hood-moulding resting on two well sculptured human heads, with grotesque faces. This chamber, which is supposed to have been the preceptor's private room, has also a good Gothic window of two lights, with head tracery of the decorated period. This is the haunted chamber. For Creslow, like all old manor-houses, has its ghost story. But the ghost is not a knight-templar or knight of St John, but a lady. Seldom, indeed, has she been seen, but often has she been heard, only too plainly, by those who have ventured to sleep in this room, or enter after midnight. She appears to come from the crypt or dungeon, and always enters this room by the Gothic door. After entering, she is heard to walk about, sometimes in a gentle, stately manner, apparently with a long silk train sweeping the floor—sometimes her motion is quick and hurried, her silk dress rustling violently, as if she were engaged in a desperate struggle. As these mysterious visitations had anything but a somniferous effect on wearied mortals, this chamber, though furnished as a bedroom, was seldom so used, and was never entered by servants without trepidation and awe. Occasionally, however, some one was found bold enough to dare the harmless noises of the mysterious intruder, and many are the stories respecting such adventures. The following will suffice as a specimen, and may be depended on as authentic. About the year 1850, a gentleman who resided some miles distant, rode over to a dinner-party, and as the night became exceedingly dark and rainy, he was urged to stay over the night, if he had no objection to sleep in a haunted chamber. The offer of a bed in such a room, so far from deterring him, induced him at once to accept the invitation. He was a strong-minded man, of a powerful frame, and undaunted courage, and entertained a sovereign contempt for all ghost stories. The room was prepared for him. He would neither have a fire nor a burning candle, but requested a box of lucifers, that he might light a candle if he wished. Arming himself, in jest, with a cutlass and a brace of pistols, he took a serio-comic farewell of the family, and entered his formidable dormitory. Morning came, and ushered in one of those glorious autumnal days which often succeed a night of soaking rain. The sun shone brilliantly on the old manor-house. Every loophole and cranny in the tower was so penetrated by his rays, that the venerable owls, that had long inherited its roof, could scarcely find a dark corner to doze in, after their nocturnal labours. The family and their guests assembled in the breakfast room, and every countenance seemed cheered and brightened by the loveliness of the morning. They drew round the table, when lo ! the host remarked that the tenant of the haunted chamber was absent. A servant was sent to summon him to breakfast, but he soon returned, saying he had knocked loudly at his door but received no answer, and that a jug of hot water left at his door was still standing there unused. On hearing this, two or three gentlemen ran up to his room, and after knocking at his door, and receiving no answer, they opened it, and entered the room. It was empty. The sword and the pistols were lying on a chair near the bed, which had been used, but its occupant was gone. The ghost had put him to flight. Inquiry was made of the servants : they had neither seen nor heard anything of him, but on first coming down in the morning they found an outer door unfastened. As he was a county magistrate, it was now supposed that he was gone to attend the board which met that morning at an early hour. The gentlemen proceeded to the stable, and found his horse was still there. This by no means diminished the mystery. The party sat down to breakfast, not without feelings of perplexity, mingled with no little curiosity. Many strong conjectures were discussed ; and just as a lady suggested dragging the fish-ponds. in walked the knight-errant ! Had the ghost herself appeared at that moment, she could scarcely have caused more consternation. Such was the general eagerness for an account of the knight's adventures, that, before beginning his breakfast, he promised to relate fully and candidly all the particulars of the case. ' Having entered my room,' said he, ' I locked and bolted both doors, carefully examined the whole room. and satisfied myself that there was no living creature in it but myself, nor any entrance but those I had secured. I got into bed, and, with the conviction I should sleep as usual till six in the morning, I was soon lost in a comfortable slumber. Suddenly I was aroused, and on raising my head to listen, I heard a sound certainly resembling the light, soft tread of a lady's footstep, accompanied with the rustling as of a silk gown. I sprang out of bed and lighted a candle. There was nothing to be seen, and nothing now to be heard. I carefully examined the whole room. I looked under the bed, into the fire-place, up the chimney, and at both the doors, which were fastened as I had left them. I looked at my watch, and found it was a few minutes past twelve. As all was now perfectly quiet, I extinguished the candle, and entered my bed, and soon fell asleep. I was again aroused. The noise was now louder than before. It appeared like the violent rustling of a stiff silk dress. I sprang out of bed, darted to the spot where the noise was, and tried to grasp the intruder in my arms. My arms met together, but enclosed nothing. The noise passed to another part of the room, and I followed it, groping near the floor, to prevent anything passing under my arms. It was in vain, I could feel nothing—the noise had passed away through the Gothic door, and all was still as death! I lighted a candle, and examined the Gothic door, and there I saw—the old monks' faces grinning at my perplexity; but the door was shut and fastened, just as I had left it. I again examined the whole room, but could find nothing to account for the noise. I now left the candle burning, though I never sleep comfortably with a light in my room. I got into bed, but felt, it must be acknowledged, not a little perplexed at not being able to detect the cause of the noise, nor to account for its cessation when the candle was lighted. While ruminating on these things, I fell asleep, and began to dream about murders, and secret burials, and all sorts of horrible things; and just as I fancied myself knocked down by a knight-templar I awoke, and found the sun shining so brightly, that I thought a walk would be far more refreshing than another disturbed sleep; so I dressed and went out before the servants were down. Such, then, is a full, true, and particular account of my night's adventure, and, though I cannot account for the noises in the haunted chamber, I am still no believer in ghosts.'

Doubtless there are no ghosts ;
Yet somehow it is better not to move,
Lest cold hands seize upon us from behind.
　　　　　　　　　　　　　　　DOBELL.

THE FIRST ENGLISH REGATTA.

Lady Montagu's description of a regatta, or *fête* held on the water, which she witnessed at Venice, stimulated the English people of fashion to have something of a similar kind on the Thames, and after much preparation and several disappointments, caused by unfavourable weather, the long expected show took place on the 23rd of June 1775. The programme, which was submitted to the public a month before, requested ladies and gentlemen to arrange their own parties, except those who should apply to the managers of the Regatta for seats in the barges lent by the several City Companies for the occasion. The rowers were to be uniformly dressed in accordance with the three marine colours—white, red, and blue. The white division was directed to take position at the two arches on each side of the centre arch of Westminster Bridge. The red division at the four

814

arches next the Surrey shore ; and the blue at the four on the Middlesex side of the river. The company were to embark between five and six o'clock in the evening, and at seven all the boats were to move up the river to Ranelagh in procession. The marshal of the white, in a twelve-oared barge, leading his division; the marshals of the red and blue, with their respective divisions, following at intervals of three minutes between each.

Early in the afternoon, the river, from London Bridge to Millbank, was crowded with pleasure boats, and scaffolds, gaily decorated with flags, were erected wherever a view of the Thames could be obtained. Half-a-guinea was asked for a seat in a coal-barge ; and vessels fitted for the purpose drove a brisk trade in refreshments of various kinds. The avenues to Westminster Bridge were covered with gaming-tables, and constables guarded every passage to the water, taking from half-a-crown to one penny for liberty to pass. Soon after six o'clock, concerts were held under the arches of Westminster Bridge ; and a salute of twenty-one cannons announced the arrival of the Lord Mayor. A race of wager-boats followed, and then the procession moved in a picturesque irregularity to Ranelagh. The ladies were dressed in white, the gentlemen in undress frocks of all colours ; about 200,000 persons were supposed to be on the river at one time.

The company arrived at Ranelagh at nine o'clock, where they joined those who came by land in a new building, called the Temple of Neptune. This was a temporary octagon, lined with stripes of white, red, and blue cloth, and having lustres hanging between each pillar. Supper and dancing followed, and the entertainment did not conclude till the next morning. Many accidents occurred when the boats were returning after the *fête*, and seven persons were unfortunately drowned.

JUNE 24.

Nativity of St John the Baptist. * The Martyrs of Rome under Nero, 1st century. St Bartholomew of Dunelm.

Midsummer Day—the Natibity of St John the Baptist.

Considering the part borne by the Baptist in the transactions on which Christianity is founded, it is not wonderful that the day set apart for the observance of his nativity (June 24) should be, in all ages and most parts of Europe, one of the most popular of religious festivals. It enjoys the greater distinction that it is considered as Midsummer Day, and therefore has inherited a number of observances from heathen times. These are now curiously mixed with those springing from Christian feelings, insomuch that it is not easy to distinguish them from the other. It is only clear, from their superstitious character, that they have been originally pagan. To use the quaint phrase of an old translator of Scaliger, they 'form the footesteps of auncient gentility ;' that is, gentilism or heathenism.

The observances connected with the Nativity of St John commenced on the previous evening, called, as usual, the eve or vigil of the festival, or Midsummer eve. On that evening the people

* The festivals of the Saints are generally celebrated on the anniversary of their death, but an exception to this rule holds in the case of John the Baptist.

were accustomed to go into the woods and break down branches of trees, which they brought to their homes, and planted over their doors, amidst great demonstrations of joy, to make good the Scripture prophecy respecting the Baptist, that many should rejoice in his birth. This custom was universal in England till the recent change in manners. In Oxford there was a specialty in the observance, of a curious nature. Within the first court of Magdalen College, from a stone pulpit at one corner, a sermon was always preached on St John's Day; at the same time the court was embowered with green boughs, ' that the preaching might resemble that of the Baptist in the wilderness.'

Towards night, materials for a fire were collected in a public place and kindled. To this the name of bonfire was given, a term of which the most rational explanation seems to be, that it was composed of contributions collected as *boons*, or gifts of social and charitable feeling. Around this fire the people danced with almost frantic mirth, the men and boys occasionally jumping through it, not to show their agility, but as a compliance with ancient custom. There can be no doubt that this leaping through the fire is one of the most ancient of all known superstitions, and is identical with that followed by Manasseh. We learn that, till a late period, the practice was followed in Ireland on St John's Eve.

It was customary in towns to keep a watch walking about during the Midsummer Night, although no such practice might prevail at the place from motives of precaution. This was done at Nottingham till the reign of Charles I. Every citizen either went himself, or sent a substitute; and an oath for the preservation of peace was duly administered to the company at their first meeting at sunset. They paraded the town in parties during the night, every person wearing a garland of flowers upon his head, additionally embellished in some instances with ribbons and jewels. In London, during the middle ages, this watch, consisting of not less than two thousand men, paraded both on this night and on the eves of St Paul's and St Peter's days. The watchmen were provided with cressets, or torches, carried in barred pots on the tops of long poles, which, added to the bonfires on the streets, must have given the town a striking appearance in an age when there was no regular street-lighting. The great came to give their countenance to this marching watch, and made it quite a pageant. A London poet, looking back from 1616, thus alludes to the scene :—

' The goodly buildings that till then did hide
    Their rich array, open'd their windows wide,
    Where kings, great peers, and many a noble dame,
    Whose bright pearl-glittering robes did mock the
        flame
    Of the night's burning lights, did sit to see
    How every senator in his degree,
    Adorn'd with shining gold and purple weeds,
    And stately mounted on rich-trapped steeds,
    Their guard attending, through the streets did ride,
    Before their foot-bands, graced with glittering pride
   Of rich-gilt arms, whose glory did present
   A sunshine to the eye, as if it meant,

    Among the cresset lights shot up on high,
    To chase dark night for ever from the sky;
    While in the streets the sticklers to and fro,
    To keep decorum, still did come and go,
    Where tables set were plentifully spread,
    And at each door neighbour with neighbour fed.'

King Henry VIII., hearing of the marching watch, came privately, in 1510, to see it; and was so much pleased with what he saw, that he came with Queen Catherine and a noble train to attend openly that of St Peter's Eve, a few nights after. But this king, in the latter part of his reign, thought proper to abolish the ancient custom, probably from a dread of so great a muster of armed citizens.

Some of the superstitious notions connected with St John's Eve are of a highly fanciful nature. The Irish believe that the souls of all people on this night leave their bodies, and wander to the place, by land or sea, where death shall finally separate them from the tenement of clay. It is not improbable that this notion was originally universal, and was the cause of the widespread custom of watching or sitting up awake on St John's night, for we may well believe that there would be a general wish to prevent the soul from going upon that somewhat dismal ramble. In England, and perhaps in other countries also, it was believed that, if any one sat up fasting all night in the church porch, he would see the spirits of those who were to die in the parish during the ensuing twelvemonths come and knock at the church door, in the order and succession in which they were to die. We can easily perceive a possible connexion between this dreary fancy and that of the soul's midnight ramble. The civic vigils just described were no doubt a result, though a more remote one, of the same idea. There is a Low Dutch proverb used by those who have been kept awake all night by troubles of any kind—' We have passed St John Baptist's night.' In a book written in the seventeenth century for the instruction of a young nobleman, the author warns his pupil against certain ' fearful superstitions, as to watch upon St John's evening, and the first Tuesday in the month of March, to conjure the moon, to lie upon your back, having your ears stopped with laurel leaves, and to fall asleep not thinking of God, and such like follies, all forged by the infernal Cyclops and Pluto's servants.' A circumstance mentioned by Grose supports our conjecture—that to sleep on St John's Eve was thought to ensure a wandering of the spirit, while watching was regarded as conferring the power of seeing the vagrant spirits of those who slept. Amongst a company who sat up in a church porch, one fell so deeply asleep that he could not be waked. His companions afterwards averred that, whilst he was in this state, they beheld his spirit go and knock at the church door.

The same notion of a temporary liberation of the soul is perhaps at the bottom of a number of superstitious practices resembling those appropriate to Hallow-eve. It was supposed, for example, that if an unmarried woman, fasting, laid a cloth at midnight with bread and cheese, and sat down as if to eat, leaving the street-door open, the person whom she was to marry would come into the room and drink to her by bowing, after which, setting down the glass, with another bow he would retire. It was customary on this eve to gather certain plants which were supposed to have a supernatural character. The fern is one of those herbs which have their seed on the back of the leaf, so small as to escape the sight. It was concluded, according to the strange irrelative reasoning of former times, that to possess this seed, not easily visible, was a means of rendering one's self invisible. Young men would go out at midnight of St John's Eve, and endeavour to catch some in a plate, but without touching the plant—an attempt rather trying to patience, and which often failed. Our Elizabethan dramatists and poets, including Shakspeare and Jonson, have many allusions to the invisibility-conferring powers of fern seed. The people also gathered on this night the rose, St John's wort, vervain, trefoil, and rue, all of which were thought to have magical properties. They set the orpine in clay upon pieces of slate or potsherd in their houses, calling it a Midsummer Man. As the stalk was found next morning to incline to the right or left, the anxious maiden knew whether her lover would prove true to her or not. Young women likewise sought for what they called pieces of coal, but in reality, certain hard, black, dead roots, often found under the living mugwort, designing to place these under their pillows, that they might dream of their lovers. Some of these foolish fancies are pleasantly strung together in the *Connoisseur*, a periodical paper of the middle of the last century. 'I and my two sisters tried the dumb cake together; you must know two must make it, two bake it, two break it, and the third put it under each of their pillows (but you must not speak a word all the time), and then you will dream of the man you are to have. This we did; and, to be sure, I did nothing all night but dream of Mr Blossom. The same night, exactly at twelve o'clock, I sowed hemp-seed in our backyard, and said to myself—"Hemp-seed I sow, hemp-seed I hoe, and he that is my true love come after me and mow.' Will you believe me? I looked back and saw him as plain as eyes could see him. After that I took a clean shift and wetted it, and turned it wrong side out, and hung it to the fire upon the back of a chair; and very likely my sweetheart would have come and turned it right again (for I heard his step), but I was frightened, and could not help speaking, which broke the charm. I likewise stuck up two Midsummer Men, one for myself and one for him. Now, if his had died away, we should never have come together; but I assure you his bowed and turned to mine. Our maid Betty tells me, if I go backwards, without speaking a word, into the garden upon Midsummer Eve, and gather a rose, and keep it in a clean sheet of paper, without looking at it till Christmas Day, it will be as fresh as in June; and if I then stick it in my bosom, he that is to be my husband will come and take it out.' So also, in a poem entitled the *Cottage Girl*, published in 1786:—

'The moss rose that, at fall of dew,
　Ere eve its duskier curtain drew,

Was freshly gather'd from its stem,
She values as the ruby gem;
And, guarded from the piercing air,
With all an anxious lover's care,
She bids it, for her shepherd's sake,
Await the new-year's frolic wake,
When, faded in its alter'd hue,
She reads—the rustic is untrue!
But if its leaves the crimson paint,
Her sickening hopes no longer faint;
The rose upon her bosom worn,
She meets him at the peep of morn,
And lo! her lips with kisses prest,
He plucks it from her panting breast.'

We may suppose, from the following version of a German poem, entitled *The St John's Wort*, that precisely the same notions prevail amongst the peasant youth of that country:—

'The young maid stole through the cottage door,
And blush'd as she sought the plant of power:
"Thou silver glow-worm, oh, lend me thy light,
I must gather the mystic St John's wort to-night—
The wonderful herb, whose leaf will decide
If the coming year shall make me a bride."
　　　And the glow-worm came
　　　With its silvery flame,
　　　And sparkled and shone
　　　Through the night of St John.
And soon has the young maid her love-knot tied.
　　　With noiseless tread,
　　　To her chamber she sped,
Where the spectral moon her white beams shed:
"Bloom here, bloom here, thou plant of power,
To deck the young bride in her bridal hour!"
But it droop'd its head, that plant of power,
And died the mute death of the voiceless flower;
And a wither'd wreath on the ground it lay,
More meet for a burial than bridal day.
And when a year was past away,
All pale on her bier the young maid lay;
　　　And the glow-worm came
　　　With its silvery flame,
　　　And sparkled and shone
　　　Through the night of St John,
As they closed the cold grave o'er the maid's cold clay.'

Some years ago there was exhibited before the Society of Antiquaries a ring which had been found in a ploughed field near Cawood in Yorkshire, and which appeared, from the style of its inscriptions, to be of the fifteenth century. It bore for a device *two orpine plants* joined by a true love knot, with this motto above, *Ma fiancée velt*, that is, My sweetheart wills, or is desirous. The stalks of the plants were bent towards each other, in token, no doubt, that the parties represented by them were to come together in marriage. The motto under the ring was *Joye l'amour feu*. So universal, in time as in place, are these popular notions.

The observance of St John's Day seems to have been, by a practical bull, confined mainly to the previous evening. On the day itself, we only find that the people kept their doors and beds embowered in the branches set up the night before, upon the understanding that these had a virtue in averting thunder, tempest, and all kinds of noxious physical agencies.

The Eve of St John is a great day among the mason-lodges of Scotland. What happens with them at Melrose may be considered as a fair example of the whole. 'Immediately after the election of office-bearers for the year ensuing, the brethren walk in procession three times round the Cross, and afterwards dine together, under the presidency of the newly-elected Grand Master. About six in the evening, the members again turn out and form into line two abreast, each bearing a lighted flambeau, and decorated with their peculiar emblems and insignia. Headed by the heraldic banners of the lodge, the procession follows the same route, three times round the Cross, and then proceeds to the Abbey. On these occasions, the crowded streets present a scene of the most animated description. The joyous strains of a well-conducted band, the waving torches, and incessant showers of fireworks, make the scene a carnival. But at this time the venerable Abbey is the chief point of attraction and resort, and as the mystic torch-bearers thread their way through its mouldering aisles, and round its massive pillars, the outlines of its gorgeous ruins become singularly illuminated and brought into bold and striking relief. . . . . . The whole extent of the Abbey is with "measured step and slow" gone three times round. But when near the *finale*, the whole masonic body gather to the chancel, and forming one grand semicircle around it, where the heart of King Robert Bruce lies deposited near the high altar, and the band strikes up the patriotic air, "Scots wha ha'e wi' Wallace bled," the effect produced is overpowering. Midst showers of rockets and the glare of blue lights the scene closes, the whole reminding one of some popular saturnalia held in a monkish town during the middle ages.'—*Wade's Hist. Melrose*, 1861, p. 146.

Born.—Theodore Beza, reforming divine, 1519, *Vezelai, in Burgundy*; John Churchill, Duke of Marlborough, 1650, *Ashe, Devonshire*; Dr Alexander Adam, eminent classical teacher, 1741, *Rafford, near Forres*; Deodatus de Dolomieu, mineralogist, 1750, *Grenoble*; Josephine, Empress of the French, 1763, *Martinico*; General Hoche, 1768, *Montreuil*; Rear-Admiral Sir John Ross, Arctic navigator, 1777; Alexander Dumas, French novelist, 1803.

Died.—Vespasian, Emperor of Rome, 79, *Cutilia*; Nicolas Claude Pieresc, 1637, *Aix, Provence*; John Hampden, illustrious patriot, 1643, *Thame*; Bishop Isaac Barrow, 1680, *St Asaph*; Nicolas Harrison, historian, 1720; Dr Thomas Amory, English Presbyterian divine, miscellaneous writer, 1774.

FOUNDATION OF THE ORDER OF THE GARTER.

It is concluded by the best modern authorities that the celebrated Order of the Garter, which European sovereigns are glad to accept from the British monarch, was instituted some time between the 24th of June and the 6th of August 1348. The founder, Edward III., was, as is well known, addicted to the exercises of chivalry, and was frequently holding jousts and tournaments, at some of which he himself did not disdain to wield a spear. Some years before this date, he had gone some way in forming an order of the *Round Table*, in commemoration of the legend of King Arthur, and, in January 1344, he had caused an actual round table of two hundred feet diameter to be constructed in Windsor

Castle, where the knights were entertained at his expense, the effect being that he thus gathered

around him a host of ardent spirits, highly suitable to assist in his contemplated wars against France. Before the date above mentioned, a turn had been given to the views of the king, leading him to adopt a totally different idea for the basis of the order. 'The popular account is, that, during a festival at court, a lady happened to drop her garter, which was taken up by King Edward, who, observing a significant smile among the bystanders, exclaimed, with some displeasure, "Honi soit qui mal y pense"—"Shame to him who thinks ill of it." In the spirit of gallantry, which belonged no less to the age than to his own disposition, conformably with the custom of wearing a lady's favour, and perhaps to prevent any further impertinence, the king is said to have placed the garter round his own knee.'—*Tighe and Davis's Annals of Windsor*.

It is commonly said that the fair owner of the garter was the Countess of Salisbury; but this is a point of as much doubt as delicacy, and there have not been wanting those who consider the whole story fabulous. Scepticism, however, rests mainly on the ridiculous character of the incident above described, a most fallacious basis, we must say in all humility, and rather indeed a support to the popular story, considering how outrageously foolish are many of the authenticated practices of chivalry. It is to be remarked that the tale is far from being modern. It is related by Polydore Virgil so early as the reign of Henry VII.

Although the order is believed to have been not founded before June 24th, 1348, it is certain that the garter itself was become an object of some note at court in the autumn of the preceding year, when at a great tournament held in honour of the king's return from France, 'garters with the motto of the order embroidered thereon, and robes and other habiliments, as well as banners and couches, ornamented with the same ensign, were issued from the great wardrobe at the charge of the sovereign.'* The royal mind was evidently by this time deeply interested in the garter. A surcoat furnished to him in 1348, for a spear play or hastilude at Canterbury, was covered with garters. At the same time, the youthful Prince of Wales presented twenty-four garters to the knights of the society.

* Beltz's *Memorials of the Order of the Garter*, 1841, p. 2.

RELIEF OF SHIPWRECKED MARINERS AT BAMBOROUGH CASTLE.

By his will of this date, in 1720, Lord Crewe, Bishop of Durham, left Bamborough Castle, and extensive manors in its neighbourhood, for various charitable and other purposes, including the improvement of certain church livings. The annual proceeds amounted a few years ago to £8126, 8s. 8d., being much more than was necessary for the purposes originally contemplated. The trustees have accordingly for many years devoted a part of the funds to the support of an establishment in the castle of Bamborough, directed to the benefit of distressed vessels and shipwrecked seamen.

This castle crowns the summit of a basalt rock, a hundred and fifty feet high, starting up from a sandy tract on a dangerous part of the coast of Northumberland. The buildings are most picturesque, and they derive a moral interest from the purpose to which they are devoted. 'The trustees have ready in the castle such implements as are required to give assistance to stranded vessels; a nine-pounder is placed at the bottom of the great tower, which gives signals to ships in distress, and, in case of wreck, announces the same to the custom-house officers and their servants, who hasten to prevent the wreck being plundered. A constant watch is kept at the top of the great tower, whence signals are also made to the fishermen of Holy Island, as soon as any vessel is discovered to be in distress, when the fishermen immediately put

BAMBOROUGH CASTLE.

off to its assistance, and the signals are so regulated as to point out the particular direction in which the vessel lies; and this is partly indicated by flags by day, and rockets at night. Owing to the size and fury of the breakers, it is generally impossible for boats to put off from the main land in a severe storm, but such difficulty occurs but rarely in putting off from Holy Island.

'In addition to these arrangements for mariners in distress, men on horseback constantly patrol the coast, a distance of eight miles, from sunset to sunrise, every stormy night. Whenever a case of shipwreck occurs, it is their duty to forward intelligence to the castle without delay; and, as a further inducement to this,

premiums are often given for the earliest notice of such distress. During the continuance of fogs, which are frequent and sudden, a gun is fired at short intervals. By these means many lives are saved, and an asylum is offered to shipwrecked persons in the castle. The trustees also covenant with the tenants of the estate, that they shall furnish carts, horses, and men, in proportion to their respective farms, to protect and bring away whatever can be saved from the wrecks. There are likewise the necessary tackle and instruments kept for raising vessels which have sunk, and whatever goods may be saved are deposited in the castle. The bodies of those who are lost are decently interred at the expense of this charity—in fact, to sailors on that perilous coast, Bamborough Castle is what the convent of St Bernard is to travellers in the Alps.' *

The Rev. Mr Bowles thus addresses Bamborough Castle with reference to its charitable purpose :—

'Ye holy towers, that shade the wave-worn steep,
  Long may ye rear your aged brows sublime,
Though, hurrying silent by, relentless Time
Assail you, and the winter whirlwinds sweep !
For far from blazing Grandeur's crowded halls,
  Here Charity hath fix'd her chosen seat ;
Oft list'ning tearful when the wild winds beat
With hollow bodings round your ancient walls !
And Pity, at the dark and stormy hour
  Of midnight, when the moon is hid on high,
Keeps her lone watch upon the topmost tower,
  And turns her ear to each expiring cry !
Blest if her aid some fainting wretch might save,
And snatch him, cold and speechless, from the
  wave.'

THE WELL-FLOWERING AT BUXTON.

The example of Tissington has been followed by several of the towns of Derbyshire, and the decoration of their wells has become a most popular amusement. It was about the year 1840 that the Duke of Devonshire, who did so much for the improvement of the fashionable watering-place of Buxton, supplied the town with water at his own expense, and the people, out of gratitude, determined henceforward to decorate the taps with flowers ; this has become such a festival from the crowds arriving for miles round, as well as from Manchester and other towns, that it is the busiest day in the year, and looked forward to with the utmost pleasure by young and old. Vehicles of all kinds, and sadly overloaded, pour in at an early hour ; the streets are filled with admiring groups, and bands of music parade the town. The crescent walks are planted with small firs, and the pinnacles of the bath-house have each a little flag—alternately pink, white, blue, and yellow—the effect of which is extremely good, connected as they are by festoons of laurel. But the grand centres of attraction are the two wells. On an occasion when we visited the place, that

* Edwards's *Remarkable Charities*, p. 87.

ST ANNE'S WELL, BUXTON, DECORATED.

of St Anne's was arched over ; the whole groundwork covered with flowers stuck into plaster, and on a ground of buttercups were inscribed, in red daisies, the words 'Life, Love, Liberty, and Truth.' Ferns and rockwork were gracefully arranged at the foot, and amidst them a swan made of the white rocket, extremely well modelled ; an oak branch supported two pretty white doves, and pillars wreathed with rhododendrons completed the design, which was on the whole very pretty. We can scarcely say so much for the well in the higher town, which was a most ambitious attempt to depict 'Samson slaying the lion,' in ferns, mosses, fir cones, blue bells, buttercups, peonies, and daisies—a structure twenty feet high, the foreground being occupied with miniature fountains, rockwork, and grass. Much pains had been lavished upon it ; but the success was not great.

The morris-dancers form an interesting part of the day's amusements. Formerly they were little girls dressed in white muslin ; but as this was considered objectionable, they have been replaced by young men gaily decorated with ribbons, who come dancing down the hill, and when they reach the pole in the centre of the crescent fasten the long ribbons to it, and in mystic evolutions plait them into a variety of forms, as they execute what is called the Ribbon Dance. In the meantime the children are delighting themselves in the shows, of which there are abundance, the men at the entrance of each clashing their cymbals, and proclaiming the superiority of their own in particular—whether it be a dwarf or a giant, a lion or a serpent ; and the merry-go-rounds and swing-boats find plenty of customers. Altogether, it must be allowed that there is a genial and kindly influence in the well-flowering which we should be sorry to see abolished in these days, when holidays, and the right use of them, is a question occupying so many minds.

The tap-dressing at Wirksworth is too similar to those at Tissington and Buxton to require any further description. This curious little town, surrounded by hills, looks gay indeed every Whitsuntide, which is the season at which the wakes are held and the taps dressed ; the mills around are emptied of their workers, and friends assemble from all the neighbourhood. This custom has been established for more than a hundred years, in gratitude for the supply of water which was procured for the town when the present pipes were laid down.

JUNE 25.

Saints Agoard and Aglibert, martyrs, near Paris, about 400. St Prosper of Aquitain, confessor, 463. St Maximus, Bishop of Turin, confessor, 5th century. St Moloc, bishop and confessor in Scotland, 7th century. St Adelbert of Northumberland, confessor, about 740. St William of Monte-Vergine, 1142.

Born.—John Horne Tooke, political character, author of the *Diversions of Purley*, 1736, *Westminster*.

Died.—John Marston, dramatist, 1634 (?); Roger Gale, learned antiquary, 1744, *Scruton, Yorkshire ;* Lady Miller, 1781 ; Charles Barbaroux, Girondist politician, guillotined, 1793; William Smellie, naturalist, miscellaneous writer, 1795, *Edinburgh ;* Thomas Sandby, R.A., 1798; J. C. L. de Sismondi, historian, 1842, *near Geneva ;* Louis Buonaparte, ex-king of Holland, 1846.

LADY MILLER—BATHEASTON POETICS.

Lady Miller of Batheaston was a literary amateur at a time when few women addressed the public. She was, moreover, a woman of warm emotional nature, of some taste, and even of a certain degree of talent. In company with her husband, Sir John, she made a tour of Italy, and wrote an account of it, which appeared under the modest title of *Letters written during a Tour of Italy by an Englishwoman.* On returning to their home at Batheaston, this amiable pair of enthusiasts brought with them an elegant antique vase, which they deposited on an altar in their saloon. The apartment was formally dedicated to Apollo, Lady Miller taking upon herself the august office of high priestess, the vase itself being considered as the shrine of the deity. A general invitation was then issued to all votaries of fashion and poetry to assemble in the temple twice a week in honour of the son of Latona. As Batheaston was but a suburb of Bath, it may be supposed that the invitation was well responded to ; for, besides the mental gratification about to be described, an excellent collation always concluded the ceremonies.

The worship of Apollo was conducted by each candidate for fame dropping a votive offering, in the form of a short piece of poetry, into the urn, as the whole assemblage marched round it in solemn procession. A lady was deputed to take the pieces one by one out of the urn, and hand them to a gentleman, who read them aloud. The merits of the poems were then considered, and the prizes adjudged, the blushing authors of the four best compositions being presented to the high-priestess, Lady Miller, and by her crowned with myrtles, amidst the plaudits of the company.

The poetry was no doubt very poor, and the whole affair rather namby-pambyish ; but it certainly was much more harmless than many of the fashionable follies of the day. The meetings

820

lasted for several years, till at length they were put an end to by a most unwarrantable breach of good manners and hospitable confidence. Some unknown person disgracefully and maliciously contaminated the sacred urn with licentious and satirical compositions, to the great annoyance of the ladies present, and the chagrin of the host and hostess. The urn was thenceforth closed, and the meetings were discontinued for ever. Of the more legitimate kind of satire on the Batheaston meetings, freely indulged in by the wits of the day, the following is a good specimen :—

Addressed to Lady Miller, on the Urn at Batheaston.

'Miller, the Urn in ancient time, 'tis said,
  Held the collected ashes of the dead :
So thine, the wonder of these modern days,
  Stands open night and day for lifeless lays.
Leave not unfinished, then, the well-formed plan,
  Complete the work thy classic taste began ;
And oh, in future, ere thou dost unurn them,
  Remember first to raise a pile, and burn them.'

JOHN HORNE TOOKE.

This person was looked upon as one of the political pests of his era. A renegade priest, who openly scoffed at his former calling, and who led that kind of life which is called in England 'not respectable,' he could not well be much esteemed as a private citizen, notwithstanding the learning and ingenuity of his own generally admired work, *The Diversions of Purley.* It is, however, rather startling to reflect that all the public questions on which Mr Tooke's opinions were deemed mischievous have since been settled in his favour. His opposition to the American war, for which he was fined and imprisoned, is now fully sanctioned by the general opinion of his countrymen. His advocacy of a reform of the House of Commons—which by the way he stultified sadly by sitting for Old Sarum—must be presumed to have received the stamp of public favour, since the measure was carried only twenty years after his death. He was the first prominent Englishman to proclaim the advantages of free-trade ; was, it might almost be said, the father of the modern doctrine on that subject, and was for this one heresy perhaps more ridiculed and condemned than for any of the rest. And yet we have seen this social heresy established, and that with such triumphantly happy results, that its enemies were in a very few years silenced, and its maxims beginning to be received and acted upon in nearly every civilized country, excepting America, where Mr Tooke would doubtless have expected it to be first taken by the hand. One cannot thus trace the history of Mr Tooke's opinions without feeling how powerfully it speaks as a lesson of toleration.

The equivocal name of Mr Tooke's great work is said to have led to some queer results. The committee of a village library at Canonmills, near Edinburgh, ordered it, on its publication, as an entertaining popular work, and were surprised when they found themselves in possession of a solid quarto full of profound etymological disquisitions.

Mr Tooke is described by Samuel Rogers, who knew him intimately, as a charming companion,

JUNE 26.

Saints John and Paul, martyrs in Rome, about 362. St Vigilius, Bishop of Trent, 400 or 405. St Maxentius, Abbot in Poitou, about 515. St Babolen, Abbot in France, 7th century. The Venerable Raingarda of Auvergne, widow, 1135. St Anthelm, Bishop of Bellay, confessor, 1178.

Born.—Dr Philip Doddridge, eminent English Nonconformist divine, 1702, *London ;* George Morland, artist, 1763, *Haymarket.*

Died.—Julian, emperor, slain *near Samara, upon the Tigris,* 363; Innocent V., pope, 1276; Francisco Pizarro, assassinated at *Lima,* 1541; Archbishop Robert Leighton, 1684. *Warwick Lane, London ;* Ralph Cudworth, English 'latitudinarian' divine, author of the *True Intellectual System of the Universe,* 1688, *Cambridge ;* John Flavel, eminent Nonconformist divine, miscellaneous writer, 1691, *Exeter ;* Alexis Czarowitz of Russia, died under sentence, 1718, *Petersburg ;* Cardinal Julius Alberoni, Spanish minister, 1752, *Placentia ;* Rev. Gilbert White, naturalist, 1793, *Selborne ;* Samuel Crompton, inventor of ' The Mule' (spinning machine), 1827; George IV. of England, 1830, *Windsor ;* William Smyth (historical writings, poetry, &c.), 1849, *Norwich.*

ARCHBISHOP LEIGHTON.

The ordinary biographies of Archbishop Leighton fail to make us acquainted with a strange escapade of his youth—namely, his being temporarily expelled from the University of Edinburgh. The provost of that day, Provost Aikenhead—who *ex officio* was rector of the University—having in some way provoked the wrath of the students, one of them, Mr Robert Leighton, the future archbishop, formed an epigram upon him, turning upon the name Aikenhead (*q.d.*, head of oak), and the pimpled visage borne by the unfortunate official :

' That whilk his name pretends is falsely said,
  To wit, that of ane aik his head is made ;
For if that it had been composed so,
  His fiery nose had flamed it long ago.'

For this the young man was called before the faculty of masters, and solemnly expelled. His guardian, Sir James Steuart, was absent at the time, but on his return was influential enough to get him *reponed.**

Another semi-comic anecdote of the amiable prelate is quite as little known. It chanced to him that he never was married. While he held the see of Dunblane, he was of course a subject of considerable interest to the celibate ladies living in his neighbourhood. One day he received a visit from one who had come to a mature period of life. Her manner was solemn, yet somewhat embarrassed : it was evident from the first that there was something very particular upon her mind. The good bishop spoke with his usual kindness, encouraged her to be communicative, and by and by drew from her that she had had a very strange dream, or rather, as she thought, a revelation from heaven. On further questioning, she confessed that it had been intimated to her that she was to be united in marriage to the

* See *Scottish Pasquils,* 1827 ; Laing's *Fugitive Poetry of the Seventeenth Century ; Notes and Queries.* 1st ser. **xi.** 150.

bishop. One may imagine what a start this would give to a quiet scholar who had long ago married his books, and never thought of any other bride. He recovered, however, and very gently addressing her, said that ' doubtless these intimations were not to be despised. As yet, however, the designs of heaven were but imperfectly explained, as they had been revealed to only one of the parties. He would wait to see if any similar communication should be made to himself, and whenever it happened he would be sure to let her know.' Nothing could be more admirable than this humour but the benevolence shown in so bringing an estimable woman off from a false position.

JUNE 27.

St John of Moutier and Chinon, priest and confessor, 6th century. St Ladislas I., King of Hungary, confessor, 1095.

Born.—Louis XII. (' the Just') of France, 1462, *Blois ;* Charles IX. of France, 1550, *St Germain ;* Charles XII. of Sweden, 1682.

Died.—Jean Rotrou, most eminent French dramatist before Corneille, 1650; Christian Heinecken, prodigy of precocious learning, 1725, *Lübeck ;* Abbé de Chaulieu, French poet, 1740; Nicholas Tindal, historian, 1774 *Greenwich Hospital ;* Dr William Dodd, executed at *Tyburn,* 1777 ; Runjeet Singh, chief of Lahore, 1839, *Lahore ;* John Murray, eminent publisher, 1843, *London.*

CHRISTIAN HEINECKEN.

Christian Heinecken, one of the most remarkable beings recorded in the history of mankind, was born of respectable parentage, at Lubec, in 1721. If he had come into the world during the dim and distant ages of antiquity, we might have set down the whole story as a myth, and thus dismissed it as unworthy of consideration. But the comparatively late period of his birth, and the unimpeachable character of the numerous witnesses that testify to his extraordinary precocity, leave us no alternative from belief and wonder. He spoke, we are told, and spoke sensibly too, within a few hours after his birth ; when ten months old, he could converse on most subjects ; when a year old he was perfect in the Old Testament, and in another short month he mastered the New. When two and a half years old, he could answer any question in ancient or modern history or geography. He next acquired Latin and French, both of which he spoke with great facility at the Court of Denmark, to which he was taken in his fourth year. His feeble constitution prevented him from being weaned until he was five years old, when he died in consequence of this necessary change of diet.

Some German *savans,* and one Frenchman, have written learned disquisitions in the attempt to explain on natural principles this wonderful precocity ; but the result of their lucubrations has only been to prove that it is utterly inexplicable.

THE UNFORTUNATE DR DODD.

The son of a Lincolnshire vicar—educated at Cambridge—possessed of talents and a handsome person—witty and agreeable—Dodd might be said to have a good start in life. With something of the ballast of common sense and a decent degree of probity, he ought to have been a successful man. Wanting these, it is instructive to see what came of him. In 1751, at twenty-two years of age, he is found in London, without a profession or an income, yet indulging in all the enjoyments he had a mind for. When his father heard that he had married a gay, penniless girl, and furnished a house (it was, by the by, in Wardour-street), he came up to town in a state of alarm. What was to be done? The church was, in those days, simply looked on as a profession. The elder Dodd had no scruples any more than his son. It was decreed that William should take orders.

The step was, in a worldly point of view, successful. Dodd had from nature a showy oratorical power, and he cultivated it by the most careful study of the arts of elocution. Accordingly, in a succession of metropolitan cures, he shone out as a popular preacher of the highest attraction. George III. made him his chaplain in ordinary, and he was appointed tutor to the future Earl of Chesterfield. Meanwhile Dr Dodd and his wife lived in extravagant style, and were in perpetual pecuniary straits. They set up a coach, and took a country-house at Ealing. The doctor worked hard for the booksellers, and as he lacked leisure for original thought, he played the plagiary with considerable vigour. He took pupils at high fees, and neglected them. He drew a lottery ticket for £1000, but the money only seduced him into new depths of waste. Had he only possessed an ordinary share of worldly wisdom, riches and advancement in the church would certainly have been his portion; but goaded by his necessities, and impatient for preferment, he was foolish enough, in 1774, to address an anonymous letter to the Lord Chancellor Apsley's wife, offering 3000 guineas if by her assistance Dr Dodd was appointed to St George's, Hanover-square, then vacant. The letter was at once traced to him, complaint was made to the king, and he was dismissed with disgrace from his office of chaplain to his majesty. The newspapers teemed with satire and invective over his simony, and Foote turned the transaction into a farce at the Haymarket. Covered with shame, he retired for a time to the Continent, and on his return resumed preaching in London, and seemed in a fair way to recover his lost popularity, when he committed his last fatal act. Importuned by creditors, he forged a bond on his old pupil, now Lord Chesterfield, for £4200. By a curious train of circumstances the fraud was detected. Dodd was arrested, brought to trial, and sentenced to death. Powerful exertions were made for his pardon. Curiously enough, in 1772, a highwayman who had stopped Dodd's coach and shot at him was captured, and on Dodd's evidence was hanged; whereon he preached and published a sermon, entitled *The Frequency of Capital Punishments inconsistent with Justice, Sound Policy, and Religion.* Petitions with upwards of 20,000 signatures were addressed to the king. A cry was raised for his respite, for the credit of the

clergy; but it was answered that if the honour of the clergy was tarnished, it was by Dodd's crime, and not by his punishment. Dodd appealed to Dr Johnson for his intercession, and Johnson, though he knew little of Dodd, bestirred himself on his behalf with all the energy of his tender heart. He drew up a petition of Dr Dodd to the king, and of Mrs Dodd to the queen; wrote *The Convict's Address to his Unhappy Brethren*, a sermon which Dodd delivered in the chapel of Newgate; also *Dr Dodd's last solemn Declaration*, and various other documents and letters to people in power; all without effect. The king had an inclination to mercy; but the year before Daniel and Robert Perreau, wine-merchants, had been executed for forgery; and he was plainly told, 'If your majesty pardon Dr Dodd, you will have murdered the Perreaus.' The law was therefore allowed to take its course, and on the 27th of June 1777, Dodd was conveyed, along with another malefactor, in an open cart, from Newgate to Tyburn, and there hanged in the presence of an immense crowd. As soon as his body was cut down, it was hurried to the house of Davies, an undertaker, in Goodge-street, Tottenham Court Road, where it was placed in a hot bath, and every exertion made to restore life, but in vain.

JOHN MURRAY.

Within the past century no name has been more frequent on the title-pages of first-rate books than that of John Murray; and few perhaps are aware that one reason of its long continuance arises from the fact that there has been a dynasty of three John Murrays.

The founder of the house was John Mac-Murray, who was born in Edinburgh about 1745, and commenced life in the Marines. In 1768 Lieut. MacMurray growing tired of his profession, bought for £400 the stock and good-will of Paul Sandby, bookseller, 32 Fleet Street, opposite St Dunstan's Church, and close to Falcon Court, the site of the office of Wynkyn de Worde, whose sign was the Falcon. He was anxious to secure his friend Falconer, the author of *The Shipwreck*, as a partner; but Falconer declined, and the following year lost his life in the wreck of the 'Aurora,' off the African coast. Dropping the prefix of Mac, as Scotsmen were not then popular in London, Murray contrived, with much diligence, to improve and extend the business he had purchased. At the end of twenty-five years, in 1793, he died, leaving his trade, under executors, to his son John, at that time a minor of fifteen, having been born in the house over the Fleet Street shop on the 27th November 1778. John II. was educated at the best schools his father could find; among others at the High School of Edinburgh, and at Dr Burney's at Gosport, where he lost an eye by the writing-master's penknife accidentally running into it. For a time young Murray had for a partner Samuel Highley, a long-tried assistant of his father's; but feeling hampered by his associate's slow and cautious ways, he obtained a dissolution of the connexion in 1803—Highley moving off a few doors to carry on bookselling, and leaving Murray to his more hazardous adventures as a publisher. One of his earliest and greatest projects was the *Quarterly Review*. To George Canning, in 1807, he wrote—'There is a work entitled the *Edinburgh Review*, written with such unquestionable talent, that it has already attained an extent of circulation not equalled by any similar publication. The principles of this work are, however, so radically bad, that I have been led to consider the effect which such sentiments, so generally diffused, are likely to produce, and to think that some means equally popular ought to be adopted to counteract their dangerous tendency. . . . . Should you, sir, think the idea worthy of encouragement, I should with equal pride and willingness engage my arduous exertions to promote its success; but as my object is nothing short of producing a work of the greatest talent and importance, I shall entertain it no longer if it be not so fortunate as to obtain the high patronage which I have thus, sir, taken the liberty to solicit. Permit me, sir, to add, that the person who thus addresses you is no adventurer, but a man of some property, inheriting a business that has been established for nearly a century.' Canning was willing, and other helpers were found. On the 1st February 1809 the first number of the *Quarterly Review* appeared, and its success was instant and decisive, the circulation quickly rising to 12,000 copies. The *Review* was the origin of Mr Murray's eminent fortune. It brought around him such a galaxy of genius as no publisher before or since has had at his service. In 1812 he removed from under the shadow of Temple Bar to a western position in Albemarle Street, where his drawing-room became the resort in London of Scott, Byron, Campbell, Heber, D'Israeli, Canning, Hallam, Croker, Barrow, Madame de Staël, Crabbe, Southey, Belzoni, Washington Irving, Lockhart, and many more, remembered and forgotten. Murray's life-long distinction was his masterly enterprise, his fine combination of liberality with prudence, and his consummate literary and commercial tact. His transactions were the admiration and despair of lesser men.

An intimate alliance of business and friendship subsisted for a time between Murray and the Ballantynes and Constable of Edinburgh. Constable gave Scott £1000 for the copyright of *Marmion* before it was written, of which Murray took a fourth; and when Scott was in his difficulties he gracefully made him a present of his share. Murray published *The Tales of my Landlord*, and the secret of the Great Unknown was manifest to him from the beginning. He early foresaw the result of the reckless trading of John Ballantyne, and, after repeated warnings, finally broke off connexion with him. Happy would it have been for Scott had he taken the same course.

Mr Murray made Lord Byron's acquaintance in 1811, and gave him £600 for the first two cantos of *Childe Harold*, while the poet's fame was unestablished, thus shewing in a most happy instance that independent perception of literary talent which may be said to be the highest gift of the great publisher. It is understood that by Mr Murray's aid and advice the poet profited largely. Hearing in 1815 that he was in pecuniary difficulties, Murray sent him a draft for £1500, promising another for the same amount in the course of a few months, and offering to sell his copyrights if necessity required. From first to last he paid Byron £20,000 for his poems. Byron playfully styled him 'the Anak of stationers,' and presented him with a handsome Bible, with the text 'Now Barabbas was a robber,' altered to 'Barabbas was a publisher.' Byron gave Moore his *Autobiography*, and Murray lent Moore £2000 on the security of the manuscript; and when Moore repaid the hard cash in order to destroy the memoir, Murray made up the loss by giving Moore £4000 for his *Life of Byron*.

When Crabbe came to town in the summer of 1817, he was soon a visitor of Murray's, whom he describes as a much younger and more lively man than he had imagined. For his *Poems* Murray offered the amply generous sum of £3000. It will scarcely be believed that Crabbe had friends so insensible to the publisher's liberality, and so inconceivably foolish, as to think this sum too little. Having, by their advice, opened negotiations with another firm, the simple-minded poet was alarmed to find a very much smaller price put upon his verses. In great anxiety, and fearful that he had lost what was to him a fortune, he wrote, saying he was willing to accept his offer. Receiving no answer, he persuaded Rogers and Moore to go to Albemarle Street and diplomatize for him. To his delight, their intervention proved unnecessary. 'Oh, yes,' said Murray, when they had described their errand, 'I have heard from Mr Crabbe, and looked on the matter as quite settled.'

Southey was one of Murray's regular and most industrious workmen. In 1810 he wrote an article on Nelson for the *Quarterly*. Murray offered him £100 to expand it for separate publication, and Southey turned out his perspicuous and famous *Life of Lord Nelson*. At a later date he received a further sum of £200 to revise the work as a volume of the *Family Library*. This is only one out of many instances which might be recorded in illustration of Murray's generosity.

Washington Irving was another of his authors. He gave £200 for the *Sketch Book*, which he increased to £400 when it proved successful. For *Bracebridge Hall* he paid £1000, for the *Chronicles of Granada* £2000, and for the *Life of Columbus* £3000. He wished to secure Irving's services as editor of a monthly magazine at £1000 a year; but the American could not endure the thought of permanent residence out of his own country.

In 1826, seduced by others more sanguine than himself, he started *The Representative*, a daily newspaper, price sevenpence, intended to rival *The Times*. This venture proved a complete failure, and was stopped at the end of six months, with a loss to Mr Murray of £20,000. It was the solitary serious miscalculation of his life, and such a venture has not been repeated by the house of Murray.

On the 27th of June 1843, Mr Murray closed his arduous and honourable career at the age of sixty-five, and was succeeded by his son John

Murray III., who to this day maintains undimmed the glory of his father's house, as publisher of the best books by the best authors.

REVIVALS AFTER SUS. PER COLL.

The efforts made for the restoration of the forfeited life of poor Dodd remind us that re-animation after hanging is far from being an uncommon event.

On the 16th August 1264, Henry III. granted a pardon to a woman named Inetta de Balsham, who, having been condemned to death for harbouring thieves, hung on a gallows from nine o'clock of a Monday to sunrise of Thursday, and yet came off with life, as was testified to the king by sufficient evidence.

Dr Plot, who quotes the original words of the pardon, surmises that it might have been a case like one he had heard of from Mr Obadiah Walker, Master of University College, being that of a Swiss who was hung up thirteen times without effect, life being preserved by the condition of the wind-pipe, which was found to be by disease converted into bone.

Dr Plot relates several cases of the resuscitation of women after hanging, and makes the remark that this revival of life appears to happen most frequently in the female sex. One notable case was that of a poor servant girl named Anne Green, who was condemned to death at Oxford in 1650 for alleged child-murder, although her offence could only be so interpreted by superstition and pedantry. This poor woman, while hanging, had her legs pulled, and her breast knocked by a soldier's musket; she was afterwards trampled on, and the rope was left unslackened around her neck. Yet, when in the hands of the doctors for dissection, she gave symptoms of life, and in fourteen hours was so far well as to be able to speak. Eager inquiries were made as to her sensations from the moment of suspension; but she remembered nothing—she came back to life like one awakening out of a deep sleep. This poor woman obtained a pardon, was afterwards married, and had three children.

A second female malefactor, the servant of a Mrs Cope, at Oxford, was hanged there in 1658, and kept suspended an unusually long time, to make sure of the extinction of life; after which, being cut down, her body was allowed to fall to the ground with a violence which might have been sufficient to kill many unhanged persons. Yet she revived. In this case the authorities insisted on fulfilling their imperfect duty next day.* Plot gives a third case, that of Marjory Mausole, of Arley, in Staffordshire, without informing us of its date or any other circumstances.

On the 2nd of September 1724, a poor woman named Margaret Dickson, married, but separated from her husband, was hanged at Edinburgh for the crime of concealing pregnancy in the case of a dead child. After suspension, the body was inclosed in a coffin at the gallows' foot, and carried off in a cart by her relatives, to be interred in her parish churchyard at Musselburgh, six

* Plot's *Nat. Hist. of Oxfordshire*, chap. 8, § 11—20.

824

miles off. Some surgeon apprentices rudely stopped the cart before it left town, and broke down part of the *cooms*, or sloping roof of the coffin,—thus undesignedly letting in air. The subsequent jolting of the vehicle restored animation before it had got above two miles from the city, and Maggy was carried home a living woman, though faint and hardly conscious. Her neighbours flocked around her in wonder; a minister came to pray over her; and her husband, relenting under a renewed affection, took her home again. She lived for many years after, had several more children creditably born, and used to be pointed out in the streets of Edinburgh, where she cried salt, as *Half-hanget Maggy Dickson.**

The instances of men reviving after hanging are scarcely less numerous than those of females. In 1705, a housebreaker named Smith being hung up at Tyburn, a reprieve came after he had been suspended for a quarter of an hour. He was taken down, bled, and revived. One William Duell, duly hanged in London in 1740, and taken to the Surgeons' Hall to be anatomized, came to life again, and was transported. At Cork a man was hanged in January 1767 for a street robbery, and immediately after carried to a place appointed, where a surgeon made an incision in his windpipe, and in about six hours recovered him. The almost incredible fact is added, that the fellow had the hardihood to attend the theatre the same evening.† William Brodie, executed in Edinburgh, October 1788, for robbing the excise-office, had similar arrangements made for his recovery. It was found, however, that he had had a greater fall than he bargained for with the hangman, and thus the design was frustrated.

On the 3rd of October 1696, a man named Richard Johnson was hanged at Shrewsbury. He had previously, on a hypocritical pretence, obtained a promise from the under-sheriff that his body should be laid in his coffin without being stripped. He hung half an hour, and still showed signs of life, when a man went up to the scaffold to see what was wrong with him. On a hasty examination, it was found that the culprit had wreathed cords round and under his body, connected with a pair of hooks at his neck, by which the usual effect of the rope was prevented, the whole of this apparatus being adroitly concealed under a double shirt and a flowing periwig. On the trick being discovered, he was taken down, and immediately hanged in an effectual manner.‡

It may be remarked, as helping to account for the great number of recoveries from hanging, that in former days a criminal was allowed to slide or slip gently from a ladder, so as to have very little fall; and consequently, as a rule, he suffered only *asphyxia*, and not a breaking of the vertebral column. In the mode followed now-a-days, hanging is a process very effectual for its end, so as to make resuscitation almost impossible.

* The date of this case is usually given wrong. The particulars here stated are authentic.

† *Notes and Queries*, 1st ser. vol. ix. p. 281.

‡ *Gentleman's Magazine*, April 1857.

JUNE 28.

St Irenæus, Bishop of Lyons, martyr, 202. Saints Plutarch, Serenus, Hero, and others, martyrs, beginning of 3rd century. Saints Potamiana or Potamiena, and Basilides, martyrs, 3rd century. St Leo II., pope and confessor, 683.

Born.—Henry VIII. of England, 1491, *Greenwich;* Sir Peter Paul Rubens, artist, 1577, *Cologne;* Jean Jacques Rousseau, 1712, *Geneva;* Charles Mathews, comedian, 1776, *London.*

Died.—Alphonso V. of Arragon, 'the Magnanimous,' 1458; Abraham Ortelius, Dutch geographer, 1598, *Antwerp;* Thomas Creech, translator of Roman poets into English verse, 1701, *Oxford;* Maurice, Duc de Noailles, French commander, 1766; Francis Wheatley, R.A. (picture of the London Riots of 1780,) 1801; Charles Mathews, comedian, 1835, *Plymouth;* James Henry Fitzroy, Lord Raglan, British commander, 1855.

KING HENRY VIII.

Henry's cruelty towards several of his wives, and to the statesmen who thwarted him in his views, has left an indelible impression against him on the minds of the English people. Our age, however, has seen a man of signal ability come forward in his defence, and, it must be confessed, with considerable success.

'If,' says Mr Froude, 'Henry VIII. had died previous to the first agitation of the divorce, his loss would have been deplored as one of the heaviest misfortunes which had ever befallen the country; and he would have left a name which would have taken its place in history by the side of that of the Black Prince or of the conqueror of Agincourt. Left at the most trying age, with his character unformed, with the means at his disposal of gratifying every inclination, and married by his ministers when a boy to an unattractive woman, far his senior, he had lived for thirty-six years almost without blame, and bore through England the reputation of an upright and virtuous king. Nature had been prodigal to him of her rarest gifts. In person he is said to have resembled his grandfather, Edward IV., who was the handsomest man in Europe. His form and bearing were princely; and, amidst the easy freedom of his address, his manner remained majestic. No knight in England could match him in the tournament except the Duke of Suffolk; he drew with ease as strong a bow as was borne by any yeoman of his guard; and these powers were sustained in unfailing vigour by a temperate habit and by constant exercise. Of his intellectual ability we are not left to judge from the suspicious panegyrics of his contemporaries. His state papers and letters may be placed by the side of those of Wolsey or of Cromwell, and they lose nothing in the comparison. Though they are broadly different, the perception is equally clear, the expression equally powerful, and they breathe throughout an irresistible vigour of purpose. In addition to this, he had a fine musical taste, carefully cultivated, and he spoke and wrote in four languages; and his knowledge of a multitude of other subjects, with which his versatile ability made him conversant, would have formed the reputation of any ordinary man. He was

among the best physicians of his age; he was his own engineer, invented improvements in artillery and new constructions in ship-building; and this not with the condescending incapacity of a royal amateur, but with thorough workmanlike understanding. His reading was vast, especially in theology. In all directions of human activity, Henry displayed natural powers of the highest order, at the highest stretch of industrious culture. He was "attentive," as it is called, "to his religious duties," being present at the services in chapel two or three times a day with unfailing regularity, and showing to outward appearance a real sense of religious obligation in the energy and purity of his life. In private, he was good-humoured and good-natured. His letters to his secretaries, though never undignified, are simple, easy, and unrestrained; and the letters written by them to him are similarly plain and businesslike, as if the writers knew that the person whom they were addressing disliked compliments, and chose to be treated as a man. Again, from their correspondence with one another, when they describe interviews with him, we gather the same pleasant impression. He seems to have been always kind, always considerate; inquiring into their private concerns with genuine interest, and winning, as a consequence, their warm and unaffected attachment. As a ruler he had been eminently popular. All his wars had been successful. He had the splendid tastes in which the English people most delighted, and he had substantially acted out his own theory of his duty.'

QUICK WORK IN COAT MAKING.

In 1811, Sir John Throckmorton, a Berkshire baronet, offered to lay a wager of a thousand guineas to the following effect: that at eight o'clock on a particular evening he would sit down to dinner in a well-woven, well-dyed, well-made suit, the wool of which formed the fleece on sheep's backs at five o'clock on that same morning. It is no wonder that, among a class of persons accustomed to betting, such a wager should eagerly be accepted, seeing that the achievement of the challenged result appeared all but impossible. Mr Coxetter, of Greenham Mills, at Newbury, was entrusted with the work.

At five in the morning on the 28th of June he caused two South Down sheep to be shorn. The wool was washed, carded, stubbed, roved, spun, and woven; the cloth was scoured, fulled, tented, raised, sheared, dyed, and dressed; the tailor was at hand, and made up the finished cloth into garments; and at a quarter past six in the evening Sir John Throckmorton sat down to dinner at the head of his guests, in a complete damson-coloured suit that had been thus made—winning the wager, with an hour and three-quarters to spare. Of course every possible preparation was made beforehand; but still the achievement was sufficiently remarkable, and was long talked of with pride among the clothiers.

JUNE 29.

St Peter the Apostle, 68. St Hemma, widow, 1045.

St Peter the Apostle.

The 29th of June is a festival of the Anglican Church in honour of St Peter the Apostle. It is familiarly known that St Peter, the son of Jonas, and brother of Andrew, obtained this name (signifying a rock) from the Saviour, in place of his original one of Simon, on becoming an apostle. He suffered martyrdom by the cross at Rome in the year 68, under the tyrannous rule of Nero. On the strange, obscure history, which exhibits a succession of bishops from Peter, resulting in the religious principality of Rome, it is not necessary here to enter. The veneration, however, felt, even in reformed England, for the alleged founder of the Church of Rome, is shown in the festival still held in commemoration of his martyrdom, and the great number of churches which are from time to time dedicated to him.

St Peter has in England ' 830 churches dedicated in his sole honour, and 30 jointly with St Paul, and 10 in connexion with some other saint, making 1070 in all.'—*Calendar of the Anglican Church.*

It is well known to be customary for the popes on their elevation to change their Christian name. This custom was introduced in 884 by Peter di Porca (Sergius the Second), out of a feeling of humility, deeming that it would be presumptuous to have himself styled Peter the Second. Following in the same line of sentiment, no pope has ever retained or assumed the name of Peter.

Born.—Sir Henry Yelverton, eminent English judge, 1566, *Islington;* Rev. John Williams, 'the apostle of Polynesia,' 1796, *Tottenham.*

Died.—Margaret Beaufort, Countess of Richmond (mother of King Henry VII.), 1509; Pierre de Marca, archbishop of Paris, historian, 1662; Bishop Zachary Pearce, 1774; Francesco Caraccioli, Neapolitan patriot, shot, 1799; Valentine Green, eminent mezzotint engraver, 1813, *London ;* Rev. David Williams, originator of the Royal Literary Fund, 1816; Rev. Edward Smedley, miscellaneous writer, editor of *Encyclopædia Metropolitana,* 1836, *Dulwich ;* Henry Clay, American statesman, 1852, *Washington ;* Elizabeth Barrett Browning, poetess, 1861, *Florence.*

MARGARET BEAUFORT, COUNTESS OF RICHMOND.

Margaret was the daughter and heiress of John Beaufort, Duke of Somerset, grandson of John of Gaunt, Duke of Lancaster. Being very beautiful, as well as the heiress of great possessions, she was at the early age of fifteen years anxiously sought in marriage by two persons of high rank and influence. One was a son of the Duke of Suffolk, then Prime Minister; the other was Edmund, Earl of Richmond, half-brother to the reigning monarch, Henry the Sixth. Wavering between these two proposals, Margaret, in her perplexity, requested advice from an elderly gentlewoman, her confidential friend. The matron recommended her not to consult her own inclinations, but to take an early opportunity of submitting the question to St Nicholas, the patron saint of undecided maidens. She did so, and the saint appeared to her in a vision, dressed in great splendour, and advised her to marry Edmund. Following this advice, she became the mother of Henry Tudor, who afterwards became King Henry VII. Edmund died soon after the birth of his son, and Margaret married twice afterwards : first, Humphrey Stafford, son

826

of the Duke of Buckingham ; and, secondly, Thomas Lord Stanley, subsequently Earl of Derby. We are not told if she consulted St Nicholas in the choice of her second and third husbands.

Margaret founded several colleges, and employed herself in acts of real charity and pure devotion not common at the period. After a useful and exemplary life, she died at the age of sixty-eight years ; having just lived to see her grandson Henry VIII. seated on the throne of England. She is included among the royal authors as a translator of some religious works from the French, one of which, entitled *The Soul's Perfection,* was printed in William Caxton's house by Wynkyn de Worde. At the end of this work are the following verses :—

' This heavenly book, more precious than gold,
  Was late direct,* with great humility,
For godly pleasure therein to behold,
  Unto the right noble Margaret, as ye see,
The King's mother of excellent bounty,
  Harry the Seventh ; that Jesu him preserve,
This mighty Princess hath commanded me
  T' imprint this book, her grace for to deserve.'

THE ROYAL LITERARY FUND AND ITS ORIGIN.

On the 18th of May 1790, a society passing under the name of the Royal Literary Fund was constituted in London. It professes to have in view the relief of literary men of merit from distress, and the succour of such of their surviving relatives as may be in want or difficulty. Persons of rank, dignitaries of the church, and authors in good circumstances, assemble at the dinner,

DAVID WILLIAMS.

patronizing a collection for the fund, which seldom falls short of £800. The society at the close of 1861 possessed a permanent fund of £22,500, and the money distributed that year among deserving objects amounted to £1350. There is clearly here an agency for good—not

* Dedicated. We have modernized the orthography of the lines.

perhaps so ordered as to do the utmost good which it might be made to do (this has been strongly insisted upon in some quarters)—still a very good and serviceable institution, and one which stands in England without any parallel.

This fund has been in operation since a few years before the close of the eighteenth century. It took its origin from an obscure man of letters, named David Williams, who was born at a village near Cardigan, in 1738. The career of Williams was one not calculated to meet the entire approval of the prelates who sometimes preside at the aforesaid annual dinner. He was originally a Unitarian clergyman, at one time settled at Highgate. Afterwards, he set up an even more liberal form of religious worship in Margaret Street, Cavendish Square, where Dr Thomas Somerville, of Jedburgh, one Sunday heard him discourse without a text on the evils of gaming, and remarked the ominous indifference of the congregation.* At one time, during a short snatch of conjugal life, he kept a tolerably successful boarding-school at Chelsea, where, it is related, he had Benjamin Franklin for a guest, at the time when the American philosopher was subjected to the abuse of Wedderburn before the Privy Council. He wrote books on education, on public worship, on political principles, a moral liturgy, and much besides, cherishing high aims for the benefit of his fellow-creatures, while not only little patronized or encouraged by them, but regarded by most as a dangerous enthusiast and innovator. When the French Revolution drew on, Williams was found in Paris, mingling with the Girondists, and helping them to form constitutions. When sanguinary violence supervened, he came home, and calmly entered upon his cherished plans for getting up a fund for the benefit of poor literary men. The difficulties naturally to be encountered in this scheme must have been greatly enhanced in the case of an originator whom all the upper classes of that day must have regarded as himself a social pest—a man to be classed, as Canning actually classed him, with 'creatures villanous and low.' He nevertheless persevered through many years, during which his own means of subsistence were of the most precarious kind; and having in time gathered £6000, succeeded in constituting the society. To the mere church-and-king Tories of that day, the whole of this history must have appeared a bewildering anomaly; but the truth is, that David Williams was a man of the noblest natural impulses, and the mission which he undertook was precisely in accordance with them. Had Canning ever met him, he would have found a man of dignified aspect and elegant manners, instead of the human reptile he had pictured in his imagination. His whole life, unapprovable as it must have appeared to many, had been framed with a view to what was for the good of mankind. The Literary Fund only happens to be the one thing practically good, and therefore practicable, which Williams had to deal with.

This benevolent person died on the 29th June 1816, and was buried in St Anne's Church, Soho.

* *Memoirs of Rev. Thomas Somerville.* 1861.

HENRY CLAY.

After Washington, Jefferson, and Jackson, Henry Clay of Kentucky has been the most popular statesman of America. With an ordinary education, he made his way, first to distinction as a barrister, and next to eminence as a politician, purely by the force of his talents, and particularly that of oratory. His career as a statesman was unfortunately not quite consistent or unsullied, and hence he failed to obtain the highest success. In 1832 he was the candidate of his party for the Presidency, but was defeated by General Jackson, with only influence enough left to quiet for the time the national discordances respecting the tariff and slavery, by what were considered judicious compromises — moderate duties, and a division of the unpeopled territory by a line, separating the free and slave states that should be founded in the future. In 1840 he might have been elected to the Presidency; but his timid party set him aside for General Harrison, who was considered a more available candidate. Later, he had the mortification of giving place to General Scott and General Taylor. In 1844 he was a candidate, but was defeated by Mr Polk, who was elected by the party in favour of the annexation of Texas, and of going to war with England rather than give up the claim to Oregon, or what is now British Columbia, up to the parallel of 54° 40'. The party motto was, 'Fifty-four forty, or fight!' but after the election they accepted a compromise and a lower parallel. Disappointed in his ambition, mortified by the ingratitude of his party, Mr Clay retired from the Senate in 1842, but was induced to return in 1849. His last efforts were in favour of the slavery compromises of 1850; he died in 1852.

Mr Clay was tall, raw-boned, and homely, but his face lighted up with expression, his voice was musical, and his manners extremely fascinating. Few men have had more or warmer personal friends. His oratory possessed a power over his hearers of which the reader of his speeches can form no conception. It was a kind of personal magnetism, going some way to justify those who suspect that there is a mystic influence in high-class oratory. He was loved with enthusiasm. No man in America ever had so great a *personal* influence, while few men of as high a position have left so little behind them to justify contemporary judgments to posterity.

MRS BROWNING.

When in the summer of 1861 the sad news reached England that Mrs Browning was no more, the newspapers confessed with singular accord that the world had lost in her the greatest poetess that had appeared in all its generations.

Elizabeth Barrett, the subject of this supreme eulogy, was the daughter of a gentleman of fortune, and at his country-seat in Herefordshire, among the lovely scenery of the Malvern Hills, she passed her girlhood. At the age of ten she began to attempt writing in prose and verse; and at fifteen her powers as a writer were well known to her friends. She was a diligent student, and was soon able to read

Greek, not as a task, but as a recreation and delight. She began to contribute to the magazines, and a series of essays on the Greek poets proved how deeply she had passed into and absorbed their spirit. In 1833 she published an anonymous translation of the *Prometheus Bound* of Æschylus, which afterwards she superseded by a better version. Her public fame dates, however, from 1838, when she collected her best verses from the periodicals, and published them as *The Seraphim and other Poems*. At this time occurred a tragic accident, which for years threw a black shadow over Miss Barrett's life. A blood-vessel having broke on her lungs, the physicians ordered her to Torquay, where a house was taken for her by the sea-side, at the foot of the cliffs. Under the influence of the mild Devonshire breezes she was rapidly recovering, when, one bright summer morning, her brother and two other young men, his friends, went out in a small boat for a trip of a few hours. Just as they crossed the bar, the vessel capsized, and all on board perished. Even their bodies were never recovered. This sudden and dreadful calamity almost killed Miss Barrett. During a whole year she lay in the house incapable of removal, whilst the sound of the waves rang in her ears as the moans of the dying. Literature was her only solace. Her physician pleaded with her to abandon her studies, and, to quiet his importunities, she had a small edition of Plato bound so as to resemble a novel. When at last removed to London, it was in an invalid carriage, at the slow rate of twenty miles a day. In a commodious and darkened room in her father's house in Wimpole Street she nursed her remnant of life, seeing a few choice friends, reading the best books in many languages, and writing poetry according to her inspiration. Miss Mitford tells us that many a time did she joyfully travel the five-and-forty miles between Reading and London, returning the same evening, without making another call, in order to spend some hours with Miss Barrett. Gradually her health improved, and in 1846 the brightness of her life was restored and perfected in her marriage with Robert Browning. They went to Italy, first to Pisa, and then settled in Florence. Mrs Browning's heart became quickly involved in Italy's struggles for liberty and unity, and various and fervent were the poetical expressions of her hopes and alarms for the result. Her love for Italy became a passion stronger even than natural patriotism. Inexplicably to English readers, she praised and trusted the Emperor of the French as Italy's earnest friend and deliverer; more ardent words of faith in the goodness and wisdom of Louis Napoleon have seldom been heard, than those the English poetess uttered concerning him. Blest in assured fame, in a rising Italy, in a pleasant Florentine home, in a husband equal in heart and intellect, and in a son in the prime of boyhood—a brief illness snapped the thread of her frail life, and she was borne to the tomb, bewailed scarcely less in Tuscany than in England.

Mrs Browning wrote much and rapidly, and her poetry partakes largely of that mystical

obscurity which is the fault of so much of the verse produced in the present age. Indeed, it would be easy to produce many passages from her writings which might be set as puzzles for solution by the ingenious. At the same time there is much in her poetry which, for high imagination, subtlety, and delicacy of thought, force, music, and happy diction, is certainly unsurpassed by anything that ever woman wrote. Mrs Browning has been likened to Shelley, and the resemblances between them are in many respects very remarkable.

Miss Mitford describes Mrs Browning in her early womanhood as 'of a slight, delicate figure, with a shower of dark curls falling on each side of a most expressive face; large, tender eyes, richly fringed by dark eyelashes; a smile like a sunbeam; and such a look of youthfulness, that I had some difficulty in persuading a friend that she was the translatress of *Æschylus* and the authoress of the *Essay on Mind*. She was certainly one of the most interesting persons that I had ever seen.' Allowing for the influences of time and suffering, Mrs Browning remained the same until the end.

JUNE 30.

St Paul the Apostle, 68. St Martial, Bishop of Limoges, 3rd century.

Died.—Bishop Gavin Dunbar, 1547; Cardinal Baronius, eminent ecclesiastical writer, 1607, *Rome*; Alexander Brome, poet, 1666; Archibald Campbell, ninth Earl of Argyle, beheaded, 1685, *Edinburgh*; Sir Thomas Pope Blount, miscellaneous writer, 1697, *Tittenhanger*; Dr Thomas Edwards, learned divine, 1785, *Nuneaton*; Richard Parker, head of the naval mutiny at the Nore, hanged, 1797; Rev. Henry Kett, drowned, 1825; Sultan Mahmoud, of Turkey, 1839; James Silk Buckingham, miscellaneous writer, 1855.

MRS PIOZZI (THRALE).

Many people are remembered for the sake of others; their memory survives to after times because of some with whom they were connected, rather than on account of their own peculiar merits. The world is well contented to feed its curiosity with their sayings and doings, in consideration of the influence which they exercised over, or the acquaintance they had with, some one or other of its favourite heroes.

Mrs Thrale-Piozzi, (*née* Hester Salusbury) enjoys this sort of parasitical celebrity. Not that we wish to insinuate that she had not sufficient merit to deserve to be remembered on her own account. A woman of agreeable manners and lively wit, possessed of great personal attractions, if we may not say beauty, she could make no unskilful use of a ready pen, and enjoyed in her own day a literary notoriety. Yet it is not the leader of fashion, nor the star of society, nor the intelligent writer, that the present generation troubles itself to remember, so much as the sprightly hostess and dear intimate friend of Dr Samuel Johnson.

Henry Thrale, Mrs Thrale's first husband, entertained and commanded the best London society. Engaged in business as a brewer, as his father had been before him, he was, in education, manners, and style of living, a perfect gentleman. Having neglected to avail himself of no advantages which wealth offered, or ambition to rise in the world prompted him to turn to his profit, he contrived to secure his position still more firmly by marrying a lady of good family and fair expectations. There was no passionate attachment in the case; it was a mere matter of business. The lady, indeed, according to her own account, seems scarcely to have been consulted; but, romance set aside, she made a good wife, and he, on the whole, a good husband. Such a wife was a valuable acquisition to Thrale's rising importance; doubtless her wit and spirit were the soul of that motley fashionable group, half literary, half aristocratic, which his wealth and generous hospitality drew together to Streatham.

It must have been at one time no small privilege to be a guest at Mrs Thrale's table. Here was the author of *Rasselas*, 'facile princeps,' a centre of attraction, flattered and fondled, in spite of his uncouthness and occasional rudeness; here was 'little Burney,' Madame D'Arblay, jotting down notes stealthily for the *Diary*; here Garrick thought much of himself, as usual, and listened condescendingly to Goldsmith's 'palaver,' or writhed to hear the plaguy hostess telling how she sat on his knee as a child; here, too, was Bozzy, lively and observing, if not always dignified; here were Reynolds, and Burke, and Langton, and Beauclerk—lords, ladies, and ecclesiastics.

Johnson himself was introduced to the Thrales by Arthur Murphy, on the first reasonable pretext which Murphy could frame, and the result gave satisfaction to all parties. The shock of his appearance did not prove too much for them, for the introducer had taken care to give them due warning. Mr Thrale took to Johnson, and that 'figure large and well formed,' that 'countenance of the cast of an ancient statue,' as Boswell has it, gravely humorous, began to appear weekly at Mr Thrale's table; and when the family removed to Streatham, they persuaded the lexicographer to accompany them, because he was ill, and sadly in want of kind attention. He continued to live with them almost entirely for twenty years, and Mrs Thrale's good care succeeded at length, as she herself informs us, in restoring him to better health and greater tidiness.

Johnson delighted in Mrs Thrale. He scolded her, or petted her, or paid her compliments, or wrote odes to her, or joined with her in her pleasant literary labours, according to the form which his solid respect and fatherly affection assumed at any particular time. She gives us a specimen of his friendly flattery—a translation which he made at the moment from a little Italian poem:

> 'Long may live my lovely Hetty,
> Always young, and always pretty;
> Always pretty, always young,
> Live my lovely Hetty long;
> Always young, and always pretty,
> Long may live my lovely Hetty!'

After Thrale's death, in 1781, Mrs Thrale left Streatham, and Johnson had to leave it also. From this time to 1784, though there is evidence of some little unpleasantness having arisen, we find Johnson keeping up a familiar correspondence with the widow, and occasionally in her company. But on June 30 of that year she put his patience and good sense utterly to flight for a time, by informing him that she designed immediately to unite herself to Mr Piozzi, who had been the music-master of her daughters. He wrote to her in great haste, what she describes afterwards as 'a rough letter,' and certainly it was:

'MADAM,—If I interpret your letter right, you are ignominiously married; if it is yet undone, let us [——] more [——] together. If you have abandoned your children and your religion, God forgive your wickedness; if you have forfeited your fame and your country, may your folly do no further mischief. If the last act is yet to do, I, who have loved you, esteemed you, reverenced you, and [——]; I, who long thought you the first of womankind, entreat that, before your fate is irrevocable, I may once more see you. I was, I once was, Madam,

'Most truly yours,
'July 2, 1784.   'SAM. JOHNSON.
'I will come down if you permit it.'

To this he received a reply:

'July 4, 1784.

SIR,—I have this morning received from you so rough a letter in reply to one which was both tenderly and respectfully written, that I am forced to desire the conclusion of a correspondence which I can bear to continue no longer. The birth of my second husband is not meaner than that of my first; his sentiments are not meaner, his profession is not meaner, and his superiority in what he professes is acknowledged by all mankind. It is want of fortune, then, that is ignominious; the character of the man I have chosen has no other claim to such an epithet. The religion to which he has always been a zealous adherent will, I hope, teach him to forgive insults he has not deserved; mine will, I hope, enable me to bear them at once with dignity and patience. To hear that I have forfeited my fame is indeed the greatest insult I ever yet received. My fame is as unsullied as snow, or I should think it unworthy of him who must henceforth protect it.

'I write by the coach, the more speedily and effectually to prevent your coming hither. Perhaps by my fame (and I hope it is so) you mean only that celebrity which is a consideration of a much lower kind. I care for that only as it may give pleasure to my husband and his friends.

'Farewell, dear sir, and accept my best wishes. You have always commanded my esteem, and long enjoyed the fruits of a friendship never infringed by one harsh expression on my part during twenty years of familiar talk. Never did I oppose your will, or control your wish, nor can your unmerited severity itself lessen my regard; but, till you have changed your opinion of Mr Piozzi, let us converse no more. God bless you.'

Upon receiving this rejoinder, the old man penned a more amiable epistle, not apologizing, yet, as he says, with tears in his eyes; in answer to which, Mrs Piozzi informs us, she wrote him 'a very kind and affectionate farewell,' though she did not see fit to publish it afterwards, as we might have expected. Immediately upon this she went to Italy with her new husband, and Johnson died the same year.

It is painful to contemplate such an end to a friendship of twenty years; but with what we now know of the case through the labours of Mr Hayward,* there is no room for hesitation as to which was in the wrong. There had been no cessation of benefits or of friendly feeling from Mrs Thrale to Johnson up to the moment of his writing her the 'rough' letter. The only prompting cause of that letter was that she, the widow of a brewer in good circumstances, was going to gratify a somewhat romantic attachment which she had formed to a man not in any particular inferior to her first husband, except in worldly means. The outrage was as unreasonable in its foundation as it was gross in its style. True, what is called society took the same unfavourable view of Mrs Thrale's second marriage; but the same society would have continued to smile on Mrs Thrale as the mistress of Mr Piozzi, if the sin could only have been tolerably concealed. Society, which admired wealth in a brewer, could see no merit in an Italian gentleman—for such it appears he was—whom poverty condemned to use an honourable and dignifying knowledge for his bread. Was it for a sage like Johnson to endorse the silly disapprobation of such a tribunal, and to insult a woman who for many years had literally nursed him as a daughter would a father? The only true palliation of his offence is to be found—and let us find it—in his age and infirm health.

THE PILLORY.

An act of the British parliament, dated June 30, 1837, put an end to the use of the pillory in the United Kingdom, a mode of punishment so barbarous, and at the same time so indefinite in its severity, that we can only wonder it should not have been extinguished long before.

The pillory was for many ages common to most European countries. Known in France as

the *pillori* or *carcan*, and in Germany as the *pranger*, it seems to have existed in England before the Conquest in the shape of the stretch-neck, in which the head only of the criminal was confined. By a statute of Edward I. it was enacted that every stretch-neck, or pillory, should be made of convenient strength, so that execution might be done upon offenders without peril to their bodies. It usually consisted of a wooden frame erected on a stool, with holes and folding boards for the admission of the head and hands, as shown in the sketch of Robert Ockam undergoing his punishment for perjury in the reign of Henry VIII. In the companion engraving, taken from a MS. of the thirteenth century, we have an example of a pillory constructed for punishing a number of offenders at the same time, but this form was of rare occurrence.*

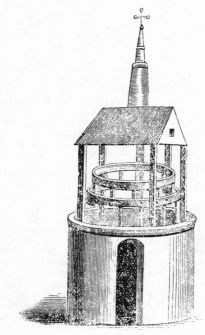

PILLORY FOR A NUMBER OF PERSONS.

Rushworth says this instrument was invented for the special benefit of mountebanks and quacks, 'that having gotten upon banks and forms to abuse the people, were exalted in the same kind;' but it seems to have been freely used for cheats of all descriptions. Fabian records that Robert Basset, mayor of London in 1287, 'did sharpe correction upon bakers for making bread of light weight; he caused divers of them to be put in the pillory, as also one Agnes Daintie, for selling of mingled butter.' We find, too, from the *Liber Albus*, that fraudulent corn, coal, and cattle dealers, cutters of purses, sellers of sham gold rings, keepers of infamous houses, forgers of letters, bonds, and deeds, counterfeiters of papal bulls, users of

* See the second edition of *Autobiography, Letters, &c., of Mrs Piozzi.* By A. Hayward, Esq., Q.C. 2 vols. 1862.

* Douce's *Illustrations of Shakspeare*, ii. 146, 147.

unstamped measures, and forestallers of the markets, incurred the same punishment. One man was pilloried for pretending to be a sheriff's serjeant, and arresting the bakers of Stratford with the view of obtaining a fine from them for some imaginary breach of the city regulations. Another, for pretending to be the summoner of the Archbishop of Canterbury, and summoning the prioress of Clerkenwell. Other offences, visited in the same way, were playing with false dice, begging under false pretences, decoying children for the purpose of begging and practising soothsaying and magic.

Had the heroes of the pillory been only cheats, thieves, scandalmongers, and perjurers, it would rank no higher among instruments of punishment than the stocks and the ducking stool. Thanks to Archbishop Laud and Star Chamber tyrants, it figured so conspicuously in the political and polemical disputes which heralded the downfall of the monarchy, as to justify a writer of our own time in saying, 'Noble hearts had been tried and tempered in it; daily had been elevated in it mental independence, manly self-reliance, robust, athletic endurance. All from within that has undying worth, it had but the more plainly exposed to public gaze from without.'* This rise in dignity dates from 1637, when a decree of the Star Chamber prohibited the printing of any book or pamphlet without a license from the Archbishop of Canterbury, the Bishop of London, or the authorities of the two universities ; and ordered all but 'allowed' printers, who presumed to set up a printing press, to be set in the pillory, and whipped through the City of London. One of the first victims of this ordinance was Leighton (father of the archbishop of that name), who for printing his *Zion's Plea against Prelacy*, was fined £10,000, degraded from the ministry, pilloried, branded, and whipped, besides having an ear cropped, and his nostril slit. Lilburn and Warton were also indicted for unlawfully printing, publishing, and dispersing libellous and seditious works ; and upon refusing to appear to answer the interrogatories of the court, were sentenced to pay £500 each, and to be whipped from the Fleet Prison to the pillory at Westminster ; a sentence which was carried into execution on the 18th of April 1638. The undaunted Lilburn, when elevated in the pillory, distributed copies of the obnoxious publications, and spoke so boldly against the tyranny of his persecutors, that it was thought necessary to gag him. Prynne, after standing several times in the pillory for having by his denunciations of lady actresses libelled Queen Henrietta by anticipation, solaced his hours of imprisonment by writing his *News from Ipswich*, by which he incurred a third exposure and the loss of his remaining ear; this was in 1637. He did not suffer alone, Burton and Dr Bastwick being companions in misfortune with him. The latter's offence consisted in publishing a reply to one Short, directed against the bishops of Rome, and concluding with 'From plague, pestilence, and famine, from bishops, priests, and deacons, good Lord deliver us !' How the two bore their

* Forster's *Essay on Defoe*.

punishment is told in a letter from Garrard to Lord Strafford : 'In the palace-yard two pillories were erected, and there the sentence of the Star Chamber against Burton, Bastwick, and Prynne was executed. They stood two hours in the pillory. The place was full of people, who cried and howled terribly, especially when Burton was cropped. Dr Bastwick was very merry ; his wife, Dr Poe's daughter, got on a stool and kissed him. His ears being cut off, she called for them, put them in a clean handkerchief, and carried them away with her. Bastwick told the people the lords had collar-days at court, but this was his collar-day, rejoicing much in it.'* The sufferers were cheered with the acclamation of the lookers-on, notes were taken of all they said, and manuscript copies distributed through the city.

Half a century later, and the once popular informer, Titus Oates, expiated his betrayal of innocent lives in the pillory. Found guilty of perjury on two separate indictments, the inventor of the Popish Plot was condemned in 1685 to public exposure on three consecutive days. The first day's punishment in Palace Yard nearly cost the criminal his life; but his partisans mustered in such force in the city on the succeeding day that they were able to upset the pillory, and nearly succeeded in rescuing their idol from the hands of the authorities. According to his sentence, Oates was to stand every year of his life in the pillory on five different days : before the gate of Westminster Hall on the 9th of August, at Charing Cross on the 10th, at the Temple on the 11th, at the Royal Exchange on the 2nd of September, and at Tyburn on the 24th of April; but, fortunately for the infamous creature, the Revolution deprived his determined enemies of power, and turned the criminal into a pensioner on Government.

The next famous sufferer at the pillory was a man of very different stamp. In 1703, the Government offered a reward of fifty pounds for the apprehension of a certain spare, brown-complexioned hose-factor, the author of a scandalous and seditious pamphlet, entitled *The Shortest Way with the Dissenters*. Rather than his printer and publisher should suffer in his stead, honest Daniel Defoe gave himself up, and was sentenced to be pilloried three times; and on the 29th of July the daring satirist stood unabashed, but not earless, on the pillory in Cheapside—the punishment being repeated two days afterwards in the Temple, where a sympathising crowd flung garlands, instead of rotten eggs and garbage, at the stout-hearted pamphleteer, drank his health with acclamations, while his noble *Hymn to the Pillory* was passed from hand to hand, and many a voice recited the stinging lines :

'Tell them the men that placed him here
    Are scandals to the times ;
    Are at a loss to find his guilt,
        And can't commit his crimes !'

Even his bitterest foes bear witness to Defoe's triumph. One Tory rhymester exclaims :

'All round him Philistines admiring stand,
    And keep their Dagon safe from Israel's hand ;

* Strafford's *Letters*, ii. 85.

They, dirt themselves, protected him from filth,
And for the faction's money drank his health.'

The subjects of this ignominious punishment did not always escape so lightly; when there was nothing to excite the sympathy of the people in their favour— still more when there was something in their case which the people regarded with antipathy and disgust — they ran great danger of receiving severer punishment than the law intended to inflict. In 1756, two thief-takers, named Egan and Salmon, were exposed in Smithfield for perjury, and were so roughly treated by the drovers, that Salmon was severely bruised, and Egan died of the injuries he received. In 1763, a man was killed in a similar way at Bow, and in 1780 a coachman, named Read, died on the pillory at Southwark before his time of exposure had expired.

The form of judgment expressed that the offender should be set 'in and upon the pillory;' and in 1759, the sheriff of Middlesex was fined £50 and imprisoned for two months, for not confining Dr Shebbeare's neck and arms in the pillory, and for allowing the doctor's servant to supply his master with refreshment, and shelter him with an umbrella. A droll circumstance connected with the punishment may here be introduced. A man being condemned to the pillory in or about Elizabeth's time, the foot-board on which he was placed proved to be rotten, and down it fell, leaving him hanging by the neck in danger of his life. On being liberated he brought an action against the town for the insufficiency of its pillory, and recovered damages.*

We have in our possession a dateless pamphlet (apparently about 1790), entitled *A Warning to the Fair Sex, or the Matrimonial Deceiver, being the History of the noted George*

* *Anecdotes and Traditions,* p. 53.

OATES IN THE PILLORY (FROM A CONTEMPORARY PRINT).

Miller, who was married to upwards of thirty different women, on purpose to plunder them. It gives a detail of the procedure of Mr Miller, which simply consisted in his addressing a love-letter to his intended victim, seeking an interview, and declaring that since he saw her life was insupportable, unless under the hope of obtaining her affections. It seldom took more than a week to secure a new wife for this fellow, and usually in three days more he had bagged all her money and deserted her. Most of the thirty wives were servants with accumulations of wages. George at length was prosecuted by an indignant female, possessed of rather more determination than the rest, and his punishment was—the pillory. The frontispiece represents him in this exalted situation, with a crowd of women of the humbler class — his seraglio, we presume —pelting him with mud, which some are seen raking from the kennel. The helpless, miserable expression of the face projected from a board blackened with dirt, entreating mercy from those who had none to give, might have been an admirable subject for Hogarth.

In 1814, Lord Cochrane, so unjustly convicted as a party to an attempted fraud on the Stock Exchange, was sentenced to the pillory. His parliamentary colleague, Sir Francis Burdett, told the Government that if that portion of the sentence were carried into effect, he would stand in the pillory by Lord Cochrane's side, and they must be responsible for the consequences. The authorities discreetly took the hint, and contented themselves with degrading, fining, and imprisoning the hero.

A pillory is still standing at the back of the market-place of Coleshill, Warwickshire, and another lies with the town engine in an unused chancel of Rye Church, Sussex. The latter is said to have been last used in 1813.